To _____

From _____

Date _____

He said to me, "My grace is sufficient for you,
for my power is made perfect in weakness." Therefore I will
boast all the more gladly about my weaknesses, so that Christ's
power may rest on me. That is why, for Christ's sake, I delight in
weaknesses, in insults, in hardships, in persecutions, in difficulties.
For when I am weak, then I am strong.

2 Corinthians 12:9–10

NEW INTERNATIONAL VERSION

NIV

Celebrate Recovery®

Study Bible

ZONDERVAN®

CONTENTS

OLD TESTAMENT

NEW TESTAMENT

BOOKS OF THE BIBLE
IN ALPHABETICAL ORDER

Books of the New Testament are in *italics*.

FOREWORD

You may think recovery is only for drug addicts and alcoholics — people whose lives seem out of control. But that's just not true. The Bible teaches that all of us have addictions in our lives. Sin is addicting, and the Bible says, "all have sinned." Not one of us is perfect. We've all blown it; we've all made mistakes. We've hurt ourselves, we've hurt other people, and others have hurt us.

Because of sin, each of us needs repentance and recovery in order to live the way God intended. That's why, years ago, we at Saddleback developed a Biblical recovery program based on the Beatitudes of Jesus. We named the program Celebrate Recovery.

The goal of the Celebrate Recovery program is not simply to recover from past sins and hurts. The goal is to become Christlike in our character. To date, over 9,000 hurting people have participated in Celebrate Recovery at Saddleback Church, and have experienced a Biblically balanced approach to repentance and recovery.

So no matter what situation you find yourself in, here's good news: regardless of whether your problem is emotional, financial, relational, spiritual, sexual or whatever, regardless of what you need help with, *God wants to help you.*

In Isaiah 57:18 – 19 God says of his people that he has seen how they acted but he will heal them, he will lead them and help them and will comfort those who mourn. So God knows us. He knows where we came from, where we stand today, and where we're going to be tomorrow. And he says:

- If you've been hurt, "I want to heal you."
- If you're confused, "I want to lead you."
- If you've ever felt you were helpless to change anything, "I want to help you."
- If you've ever felt no one understands your problem, "I want to comfort you."
- If you feel worried or afraid, "I want to offer peace to you."

The reality is that you're not going to get well on your own. Persistent temptations must be team-tackled through community. We need each other. Trying to fix your problems on your own only makes them worse than they were when you started. But there's hope. God is ready and waiting to help you if you let him.

I'm excited that you're beginning the journey to recovery. Your life will change. You'll experience freedom from your sinful hurts, hang-ups and habits as you give up control and allow Jesus to be Lord in every area of your life.

Dr. Rick Warren
Senior Pastor

CELEBRATE RECOVERY: A BRIEF HISTORY

The purpose of Saddleback Church's Celebrate Recovery ministry is to fellowship with others and to celebrate God's healing power in our lives through the program's Eight Recovery Principles. This experience allows those who work through the program to experience profound life change and freedom from their hurts, hang-ups and habits. By working and applying these Biblical principles, we begin to grow spiritually. We become free from our addictive, compulsive and dysfunctional behaviors. This freedom creates peace, serenity, joy and — most importantly — a stronger personal relationship with God and with others. As we progress through the program we discover our personal, loving and forgiving Higher Power — Jesus Christ, the one and only true Higher Power.

Pastor John Baker
Founder, Celebrate Recovery

Hi, I'm John Baker, a believer who struggles with alcohol. I have had the honor to lead a program and movement called Celebrate Recovery. In these next few paragraphs, I'd like to give you a brief history of the origins of this program, on which this Bible is based. In order to do this, I have to start with my own testimony.

As I said above, I am in recovery from abuse of alcohol. This sin-addiction had its roots in my own struggle with self-esteem issues in my earliest years — this despite being a good student and athlete.

But even though I was a popular young man on the high school campus and ball field, I still had this overwhelming sense of inadequacy. Even though I had been raised in a Christian home and had early on felt the call to the ministry, I never felt that I would be good enough to be used in God's service.

As a young man I enrolled in the University of Missouri. It was there that I made a new discovery: Using alcohol gave me the self-confidence I had been lacking. As my college career progressed, my use of alcohol increased. My life was now complete: the party never started until I arrived, and it ended when I left. Alcohol gave me a new sense of power and confidence — one I had been looking for for most of my life.

I met and married my wife Cheryl while we were still in college. She was attracted to my outgoing personality that I had manufactured. As we made a new life together, my use of alcohol continued. It followed me into the Air Force. Into the business world. It worked its way into all aspects of my daily life, became an integral part of who I was and what I did. But I never thought it was a problem — I thought it was a tool that I was using to get me to where I wanted to go.

Through all of these years I looked like the model of a successful man. I had a beautiful wife, two great kids — Laura and John Jr. — and a nice house in the suburbs. I was a leader in my church's youth group. And I was climbing the corporate ladder as well. I was promoted eight times in the first eleven years of my business career. By the age of 30 I had reached all of my life's career and financial goals.

But all the while I kept replaying the words of a song in my mind — "Is That All There Is?"

With all the business success came several relocations, and attending church became less and less important to me as my drinking increased. I knew that if I died I was saved; however, I also was beginning to be uncomfortable with my lifestyle, business practices and priorities. To the outside world everything with our family seemed normal, but in my heart I knew something was very wrong. I had to face a major decision: I could do it my way — continue drinking and living by the world's standards — or surrender and repent and do it God's way.

I wish I could tell you that I saw the light and did it God's way. But the truth is, I chose my way. My drinking increased, and I turned my back completely on God.

I was what is known as a functioning alcoholic. I knew I had a problem, but I had never lost a job or been arrested for drunk driving. Up to this point my secret was still safe. Cheryl was in denial, or so I thought. She never labeled me as an "alcoholic" until one day she noticed my new breakfast drink of choice: beer. Over time tensions rose, and one evening over a seemingly minor argument, she asked me to go to counseling with her or to just leave. Much to her surprise, I left, and our 13 month separation began.

You see, the only things my hurts, hangups and habits cost me were my closest and most important relationships: with my Lord and my family. What I had considered the solution for my life's problem — alcohol — had become the problem of my life. Eventually my drinking cost me all purpose and reason for living. I was dying physically, emotionally, mentally and, most importantly, spiritually.

Finally convinced my life had to change, I began to attend AA meetings without Cheryl's knowledge. On February 14, 1991, she and I met for lunch. At that meal I told her that I had begun to work on my recovery. I made my amends and she forgave me. After that meeting our relationship began to improve. We were still separated, but we began to see each other more often, and my relationship with my kids improved as well.

Cheryl and the kids had begun attending a church that met in a high school gym: A church called Saddleback. One Saturday night I was visiting the kids and they asked me to go to church with them on Sunday morning. Much to their surprise, I said yes. I hadn't been in a church for five years!

That Sunday morning, I heard the music and Pastor Rick Warren's message and I knew I was home. Cheryl and I began in earnest to work on our issues that had torn our relationship apart. Five months later, God opened our hearts and we renewed our marriage vows. As a family, we were baptized and became a part of the church community.

All I can say is that this is evidence of the power and grace of God in my life. It was in the context of this community that I found one of my life's verses — 1 Peter 2:9 – 10.

You know, God never wastes a hurt. All the pain and heartache of my sin — my addiction — finally made sense. However, at my AA meetings I was mocked when I talked about my Higher Power — the only true Higher Power, Jesus Christ. And at church I couldn't find a place where individuals would openly relate to my struggle with alcoholism. The men's small groups I tried just didn't want to go that deep with their issues.

But I knew they were there. In a church of thousands of people, I couldn't be the only one struggling with a hurt, hang-up or addictive habit. I wrote Pastor Rick a concise, 13-page, single-spaced letter outlining the vision that God gave me — the vision of Celebrate Recovery, a Christ-centered recovery program. His response? "Great — do it!" Cheryl and I accepted that challenge, and after much prayer and hard work, the Celebrate Recovery program was born.

Since its founding in 1991, through the grace and oversight of God, the ministry of Celebrate Recovery has expanded. The program has been worked by tens of thousands of individuals in thousands of churches around the world. The Celebrate Recovery team has developed a youth edition of the curriculum. We have launched Celebrate Recovery–Inside, a program that works with prison inmates — a segment of the population where addiction also runs high.

God has blessed this program, and through it has brought profound life-change to thousands of people who have struggled for years with their particular hurts, hang-ups and habits. Make no mistake about it, God is in the business of changing the lives of those who admit their powerlessness to control their hurts, hang-ups and habits and turn their lives and will over to him.

If you want more information on Celebrate Recovery or need to find a group near you contact *www.celebraterecovery.com*.

This Bible has been designed to accompany the Celebrate Recovery curriculum and program in the church setting. But it also has been designed to be used by individuals who are not yet a part of the Celebrate Recovery program.

As you begin or continue your process of working the principles and steps on the road to recovery, may you find blessing, comfort and assurance in the pages of this Bible.

John Baker
June 2007

ABOUT THE *CELEBRATE RECOVERY STUDY BIBLE*

God's Word offers a way out for those of us who struggle with life's circumstances or with addictive, dysfunctional or compulsive behaviors. The *Celebrate Recovery Study Bible* provides special features highlighting aspects of Scripture that speak directly to our need to break free from life's hurts, hang-ups and habits. This makes the *Celebrate Recovery Study Bible* a powerful, positive ally to which you'll turn again and again.

Contrary to a common misperception, God's Good News is positive, not negative. It's all about redemption, not condemnation. This Bible will lift you up and show you how to walk, step by attainable step, on a path of healing and liberty from the hurts, hang-ups and habits that have been holding you back.

The *Celebrate Recovery Study Bible* is based on the eight principles and the underlying twelve Christ-centered recovery steps of the proven Celebrate Recovery program (see pages 15 – 44). While this Bible has been designed as a perfect companion to the program (which is now offered in thousands of churches worldwide), it has also been intentionally designed to help anyone who is struggling with their hurts, hang-ups and habits.

Features

The Eight Principles and Twelve Christ-Centered Steps of the Celebrate Recovery Program

Accustomed to a traditional twelve-step program and hesitant to make a switch? The good news is that the familiar twelve steps remain intact under the Celebrate Recovery model, except that the vague language about a Higher Power gets specific, focusing in on the *one* and *only true* Higher Power, our Lord and Savior Jesus Christ.

Celebrate Recovery is built on the eight proven Biblical principles based on the well-loved Beatitudes from Jesus' famous Sermon on the Mount (see page 15). The Christ-centered twelve steps fit neatly and naturally underneath the umbrella of the eight principles, as outlined on pages 17 – 44. Once you become familiar with this framework, you'll grow to love and appreciate your new perspective on the recovery process.

Book Introductions

Before launching into each of the Bible's books, you will have a bird's-eye view of its theme, author and date. These brief introductions include key verses related to recovery, as well as a brief overview of recovery themes in the book. That's right: All 66 books touch on recovery issues. And each one reflects a God who cares deeply about each person struggling to make sense of a fallen world.

Character Studies

Get to know more than 50 Bible characters, each of whom illustrates a particular recovery issue. You'll be amazed at how these ancient personalities jump into focus when you view them simply as people who were in many ways very much like us.

Recovery Stories

One of the most engaging features of this Bible, these real-life, two-page stories document the backgrounds, struggles and ultimate victories of over 50 men and women whose lives have been permanently changed through working the principles and steps of Celebrate Recovery. Each testimony relates to one of the above character studies. They show that the struggles we face today have been common for thousands of years.

Lesson Studies

Each of the eight principles is tied to one or more key words that serve as memory aids. For example, a key word in Principle One is DENIAL; in Principle Four, CONFESS; and in Principle Eight, GIVE. Each letter in these acrostics begins a sentence or phrase that is discussed at the point of an applicable verse in the Bible. The "path" is clearly marked, making your journey through each principle clear-cut and uncomplicated.

Recovery-Related Scripture Ties

Recovery themes are addressed frequently throughout Scripture. Just look for the line in the margin running alongside the passage, as well as for the number or numbers indicating which principles the verses relate to. The numbered principles can be found on page 15.

Daily Devotionals

The 30 days of devotions are designed to be read and reread for reinforcement and encouragement. Celebrate Recovery is not just a program but a means toward real life change, and the key to recovery is to keep the principles alive. These thirty devotions begin on page 1617. As you read through them, then read them again, they will assist you in reviewing the principles as often as you'd like. "Take a Look" questions at the end of each devotion offer you an opportunity to evaluate your situation each time you return to the devotion and its related principle.

Subject Index

The Subject Index begins on page 1604, and will lead you to key texts on a variety of subjects covered in God's Word. A sampling from the beginning of the list includes *abandonment, abuse, addiction, adultery, alcohol use, ambition, anger* and *anxiety.*

Features Topical Index

This second subject index, beginning on page 1597, refers you to particular features in this Bible that touch on recovery themes. For example, if your concern is anorexia, you'll find the page numbers of all features that touch on this issue.

Character Study and Recovery Stories Index

Would you like to work your way through all of the Biblical character sketches or the recovery stories? Find the details on page 1595.

Wherever people long for a way out … wherever broken hearts need hope … this Bible's features offer help and encouragement through every stage of the recovery process.

Celebrate Recovery is a spiritual maturity program. If everybody daily lived Principles Seven and Eight to the best of their ability, this world would be a much better place to live.

John Baker
Founder and Pastor of Celebrate Recovery
Saddleback Church

The Road to Recovery

Based on the Beatitudes
Pastor Rick Warren

Principle One: Realize I'm not God; I admit that I am powerless to control my tendency to do the wrong thing and that my life is unmanageable (Step One).

> *"Blessed are the poor in spirit." (Matthew 5:3)*

Principle Two: Earnestly believe that God exists, that I matter to him and that he has the power to help me recover (Step Two).

> *"Blessed are those who mourn,*
> *for they will be comforted." (Matthew 5:4)*

Principle Three: Consciously choose to commit all my life and will to Christ's care and control (Step Three).

> *"Blessed are the meek." (Matthew 5:5)*

Principle Four: Openly examine and confess my faults to myself, to God and to someone I trust (Steps Four and Five).

> *"Blessed are the pure in heart." (Matthew 5:8)*

Principle Five: Voluntarily submit to every change God wants to make in my life and humbly ask him to remove my character defects (Steps Six and Seven).

> *"Blessed are those who hunger and thirst*
> *for righteousness." (Matthew 5:6)*

Principle Six: Evaluate all my relationships. Offer forgiveness to those who have hurt me and make amends for harm I've done to others, except when to do so would harm them or others (Steps Eight and Nine).

> *"Blessed are the merciful." (Matthew 5:7)*
> *"Blessed are the peacemakers." (Matthew 5:9)*

Principle Seven: Reserve a daily time with God for self-examination, Bible reading and prayer in order to know God and his will for my life and to gain the power to follow his will (Steps Ten and Eleven).

Principle Eight: Yield myself to God to be used to bring this good news to others, both by my example and by my words (Step Twelve).

> *"Blessed are those who are persecuted*
> *because of righteousness." (Matthew 5:10)*

REALIZE I'M NOT GOD; I ADMIT THAT I AM POWERLESS
TO CONTROL MY TENDENCY TO DO THE WRONG THING
AND THAT MY LIFE IS UNMANAGEABLE.

Blessed are the poor in spirit, for theirs is the kingdom of heaven.

MATTHEW 5:3

Our amazing recovery journey starts with Principle One, where we admit that we are powerless to control our hurts, hang-ups and habits and that our lives have become unmanageable, out of control. But before we begin this exciting journey, we need to ask ourselves the following two questions:

ARE WE WEARING A MASK OF DENIAL?
OVER WHAT DO WE REALLY HAVE CONTROL?

Let's look at the first question: Are we wearing a mask of denial? Before we can make any progress in our recovery, we need to face our denial. As soon as we remove our mask, our recovery begins — or begins again! It doesn't matter whether we're new in recovery or we've been in the process and working the principles and steps for years. Denial can rear its ugly head and return at any time. We may trade addictions or get into a new relationship that's unhealthy for us in a different way than a previous one.

God says in Jeremiah 6:14:

They dress the wound of my people as though it were not serious.
'Peace, peace,' they say, when there is no peace.

Denial is serious. We can't heal our wounds, hurts, hang-ups and habits by pretending they're not there. Following are six negative effects DENIAL has had on our lives:

D isables our feelings — 2 Peter 2:19
E nergy drain — Psalm 146:7 – 8
N egates our growth — Psalm 107:13 – 14
I solates us from God — Genesis 3:7 – 8
A lienates us from other human relationships — Ephesians 4:25
L engthens our pain — Jeremiah 30:17

As soon as we start working on this principle and admit that we're powerless, we begin to change. We see that our old ways of trying to control our hurts, hang-ups and habits didn't work. Our attempts were buried by our denial, and our problems were held close by our false sense of power. This leads us to the second question we need to answer:

Over what do we really have control? In Principle One we recognize our need to admit our powerlessness. Our lust for the power to control is rooted in our weaknesses, not in our strengths. We need to realize our human weaknesses and turn our lives over to God. Jesus knew this would be difficult. How difficult? He said this about a related issue, but it applies here as well: "With man this is impossible, but with God all things are possible" (Matthew 19:26).

The following acrostic demonstrates what happens when we admit we're POWERLESS. We begin to let go of the following "serenity robbers":

P ride — Proverbs 29:23

O nly ifs — Luke 12:2 – 3

W orrying — Matthew 6:34

E scape — Ephesians 5:13 – 14

R esentment — Ephesians 4:26 – 27

L oneliness — Hebrews 13:1 – 2

E mptiness — John 10:10

S elfishness — Luke 17:33

S eparation — Romans 8:38 – 39

The power to change comes only from God's grace. In Principle One we start working and living this program in earnest. When we admit we're powerless, we go on to recognize that we need a power greater than ourselves to restore us. That power is the one and only true Higher Power, Jesus Christ.

Hebrews 12:1 invites us, "Therefore, since we are surrounded by such a great cloud of witnesses, let us throw off everything that hinders and the sin that so easily entangles. And let us run with perseverance the race marked out for us."

This verse spells out two important insights as we begin our recovery journey. First, God has a particular race, a unique plan, for each of us — a plan for good, not a life consumed with dependencies, addictions and obsessions. The second thing is that we need to be willing to get rid of all the unnecessary baggage — our hurts, hang-ups and habits — in our lives that keep us stuck ("let us throw off everything that hinders and the sin that so easily entangles"). Working through the eight principles will allow us to discover God's plan and purpose for our lives. The journey begins by taking the first step.

The first step of the Christ-centered twelve steps relates to Principle One.

STEP ONE: We admitted we were powerless over our addictions and compulsive behaviors, that our lives had become unmanageable.

I know that good itself does not dwell in me, that is, in my sinful nature.
For I have the desire to do what is good, but I cannot carry it out.

ROMANS 7:18

PRINCIPLE ONE PRAYER

Dear God, your Word tells me that I can't heal my hurts, hang-ups and habits just by saying they're not there. Help me! Parts of my life — or all of my life — are out of control. I now know that I can't "fix" myself. It seems that the harder I try to do the right thing, the more I struggle. Lord, I want to step out of my denial into the truth. I pray for you to show me the way. In your Son's name, Amen.

PRINCIPLE ONE LESSONS:

DENIAL: Go to 2 Peter 2:19 (p. 1554).

POWERLESS: Go to Proverbs 29:23 (p. 777).

PRINCIPLE TWO

EARNESTLY BELIEVE THAT GOD EXISTS, THAT I MATTER TO HIM AND THAT HE HAS THE POWER TO HELP ME RECOVER.

Blessed are those who mourn, for they will be comforted.

MATTHEW 5:4

In Principle Two we find the power for our recoveries as we earnestly believe that God exists, that we matter to him and that he has the power to help us recover.

Hebrews 11:6 tells us:

Without faith it is impossible to please God, because anyone who comes to him must believe that he exists and that he rewards those who earnestly seek him.

And Psalm 62:5 invites:

Yes, my soul, find rest in God; my hope comes from him.

In the first principle we admitted that we're powerless. It's through this admission that we're able to *believe* and *receive* God's power to help us recover. We do need to be careful, though, not to cover up the pit of our hurts, hang-ups and habits with layers of denial or to try some quick "fix." Instead, we need to expose our hurts, hang-ups and habits to the light so that through God's power we can truly find healing.

In the second principle we come to believe that God exists, that we're important to him and that we're able to find the one true Higher Power, Jesus Christ. We've come to understand that God wants to fill our lives with his love, joy and presence.

In Luke 15:11 – 32 we find the parable of the lost son. This story about a father's love for his wayward son is really a picture of the love of God the Father for all of us. God's love is looking for us, no matter how lost we may feel. God's searching love can find us, no matter how many times we may have fallen into sin. God's hands of mercy are reaching out to pick us up, to love us and to forgive us.

This is the only place where we'll find hope. For that reason Principle Two is called the hope principle.

This is what the word HOPE means in Principle Two:

H igher Power — Romans 11:36
O penness to change — Ephesians 4:22 – 23
P ower to change — Psalm 25:5
E xpectation to change — Philippians 1:6

The second step of the Christ-centered 12 steps relates to Principle Two.

STEP TWO: We came to believe that a power greater than ourselves could restore us to sanity.

> *It is God who works in you to will and to act*
> *in order to fulfill his good purpose.*

Philippians 2:13

In this principle we come to believe that a power greater than ourselves can help us recover — can restore us to sanity. This isn't to say we're crazy. The word sanity in this context means that, as a result of admitting our powerlessness in Principle One, we can move from chaos into hope in Principle Two. Hope comes when we believe that a power greater than ourselves, our Higher Power, Jesus Christ, can and will restore us. Jesus alone can provide that power, since we on our own are powerless over our hurts, hang-ups and habits. He alone can restore order and meaning to our lives. He alone can restore us to sanity.

A working definition of *insanity* in this context might be doing the same thing over and over again but expecting a different result each time.

Sanity, using this model, may, on the other hand, be defined as "wholeness of mind; making decisions based on the truth."

Jesus is the only Higher Power who offers the truth, as well as the power, the way and the life.

The following are just some of the gifts we receive when we come to believe that our true Higher Power, Jesus Christ, has both the power and the will to restore us to SANITY:

S trength — Psalm 46:1
A cceptance — Romans 15:7
N ew life — 2 Corinthians 1:8 – 9
I ntegrity — 3 John 4
T rust — Proverbs 29:25
Y our Higher Power — Romans 5:8

We can't follow through with anything unless and until we get started. But just how much faith do we need to start working this principle? Jesus provides the answer in Matthew 17:20: "Truly I tell you, if you have faith as small as a mustard seed, you can say to this mountain, 'Move from here to there,' and it will move. Nothing will be impossible for you."

It's reassuring to know that we don't need large doses of faith as we begin the recovery process. We need only a little faith, as small as the tiniest of seeds, to effect change, to begin to move away our mountains of hurts, hang-ups and habits.

Eternal life doesn't begin with death; it begins with faith. Hebrews 11:1 explains what faith is: "Faith is confidence in what we hope for and assurance about what we do not see." We can't find salvation through intellectual understanding, monetary gifts, good works or church attendance. The way—the only way—to find salvation is described in Romans 10:9: "If you declare with your mouth, 'Jesus is Lord,' and believe in your heart that God raised him from the dead, you will be saved."

We'll find our true hope in the only Higher Power, Jesus Christ. As we take this step of hope, his Spirit will come with supernatural power to reside in our hearts. The Holy Spirit will give us the courage to reach out and take hold of Christ's hand, to face the present with confidence and the future with realistic expectancy.

Simply put, life without Christ is a hopeless end; with him life is an endless hope.

PRINCIPLE TWO PRAYER

Dear God, I've tried hard to fix and control my life's hurts, hang-ups and habits. I admit that, by myself, I'm powerless to change. I need to begin to believe and receive your power to help me recover. You loved me enough to send your Son to the cross to die for my sins. Help me to open myself up to the hope I can find only in Jesus. Please help me to start living my life in reliance upon this hope, one day at a time. In Jesus' name I pray, Amen.

PRINCIPLE TWO LESSONS:

HOPE: Go to Romans 11:36 (p. 1407).

SANITY: Go to Psalm 46:1 (p. 664).

CONSCIOUSLY CHOOSE TO COMMIT ALL MY LIFE AND WILL TO CHRIST'S CARE AND CONTROL.

Blessed are the meek, for they will inherit the earth.

MATTHEW 5:5

In Principle Three we make the one-time, permanent decision to turn over our lives to the care of God — the most important decision we'll ever make. Our choice, not chance, determines our destiny. And that decision requires only putting our faith into action.

But what is faith? It isn't a sense, sight or reason. Faith is simply taking God at his word. God's Word tells us in Romans 10:9 that "if you declare with your mouth, 'Jesus is Lord,' and believe in your heart that God raised him from the dead, you will be saved." For some people that seems just too simple. But it isn't. Our salvation depends much more on God's love for us than on our love for him.

How do we TURN over our lives and wills to our Higher Power, Jesus Christ? This principle ends with new life, but we must take three actions before that new life can be ours:

T rust — Romans 10:9
U nderstand — Proverbs 3:5 – 6
R epent — Ezekiel 18:30 – 32
N ew life — 2 Corinthians 5:17

Many people don't understand that putting off the decision to accept Jesus Christ as their Higher Power, as their Lord and Savior, is really deciding not to accept him. Principle Three is like opening the door: All you need is the willingness to make the decision. Christ will do the rest. He calls out to us, "Here I am! I stand at the door and knock. If anyone hears my voice and opens the door, I will come in and eat with that person, and they with me" (Revelation 3:20).

If we're going to successfully work Principle Three, we need to get past our old, familiar, negative barriers of pride, fear, guilt, worry and doubt. But how do we break this cycle? The answer is that we need to be proactive, to take the initiative. In fact, Principle Three is all about action. Listen again to the opening words: "Consciously choose to commit..." Making that choice requires ACTION:

A ccept — Romans 10:9
C ommit — Psalm 143:10
T urn it over — Proverbs 3:6
I t's only the beginning — Philippians 1:6
O ne day at a time — Matthew 6:34
N ext step — 1 Corinthians 15:2–4

Turning over our lives to Christ is a one-time, yet permanent, commitment. Once we accept Christ as Lord of our life, it's a done deal. We can't lose our salvation. It comes with a lifetime (in this case, eternal) guarantee from the Holy Spirit: "You also were included in Christ when you heard the message of truth, the gospel of your salvation. When you believed, you were marked in him with a seal, the promised Holy Spirit" (Ephesians 1:13).

The rest of the principle, though — the part about turning over our wills to Christ — requires a daily recommitment. We can begin by going to our Bible regularly, opening it prayerfully, reading it expectantly and living it joyfully.

The third step of the Christ-centered 12 steps relates to Principle Three.

STEP THREE: We made a decision to turn our lives and our wills over to the care of God.

> *I urge you, brothers and sisters, in view of God's mercy,*
> *to offer your bodies as a living sacrifice, holy and pleasing to God —*
> *this is your true and proper worship.*
>
> ROMANS 12:1

Principle Three states that we choose to commit our lives and wills to Christ's care. In the secular 12 steps, Step Three gets the sequence confused, telling us to "turn our wills and our lives over ..." The fact is that we must first commit and surrender our lives to the one and only true Higher Power, Jesus Christ. Then and only then are we empowered to turn over our wills to him.

Principle Three constitutes the core difference between a secular 12-step program and Celebrate Recovery. True and lasting recovery can be achieved only through a personal, committed relationship with Christ.

In the secular 12 steps, Step Three is: "We made a decision to turn our wills and our lives over to the care of God, as we understand him."

We need a God much, much greater than anything that stems from our own imagination or understanding. We need the one true God, the Almighty, the Creator of the universe. First Corinthians 13:12 tells us, "Now we see only a reflection as in a mirror; then we shall see face to face. Now I know in part; then I shall know fully, even as I am fully known." Someday we'll see Jesus face-to-face. The fog of interpretation will be lifted, and our understanding will be perfected.

Praise God that we don't need a complete understanding of Jesus in order to ask him into our lives as Lord and Savior. Why? Because God does more than lead us day by day and year by year. He directs our way moment by moment, one step after another.

If you haven't asked Jesus Christ to be your Higher Power, the Lord and Savior of your life, what are you waiting for? All it takes is praying this prayer with a sincere heart:

PRINCIPLE THREE PRAYER

Dear God, I've tried — and failed — to do it all by myself in my own power. Today I want to turn my life over to you. I ask you to be my Lord and Savior. You're the one and only Higher Power. I ask you to help me think less about myself and my own will. I want to turn over my will, moment by moment, to you, to continuously seek your direction and wisdom for my life. Please continue to help me overcome my hurts, hang-ups and habits, so that victory over them may help others as they see your power at work in my already changed, and still changing, life. Help me to do your will always. In Jesus' name I pray, Amen.

PRINCIPLE THREE LESSONS:

TURN: Go to Romans 10:9 (p. 1404).

ACTION: Go also to Romans 10:9 (p. 1405).

OPENLY EXAMINE AND CONFESS MY FAULTS TO MYSELF,
TO GOD AND TO SOMEONE I TRUST.

Blessed are the pure in heart, for they will see God.

MATTHEW 5:8

Principle Four begins the process of "coming clean." It's here that we openly examine and confess our faults to ourselves, to God and to another person we trust. We begin to chip away at the "truth decay" of our past. The negative effects of our hurts, hang-ups and habits have built up, like a layer of tartar, over the years and have kept us from really seeing the truth about our past and present situations.

In the first part of this principle, we need to "openly examine" our faults. We need to list, or inventory, all of the significant events — both good and bad — in our lives. We need to be as honest as we can in order to allow God to show us our part in each event and how that has affected both ourselves and others. We need to do a searching and fearless inventory, to step out of our denial, because we can't put our faults behind us until we've faced them. We need to see through our denial of the past into the truth of the present — to identify our true feelings, motives and thoughts.

Our inventory brings us to a black-and-white discovery of who we really are at our core. But if we look only at the bad parts of our past, we distort our inventory and open ourselves up to unnecessary pain. Lamentations 3:40 invites us, "Let us examine our ways and test them, and let us return to the LORD." Notice that the verse doesn't say, "Examine your bad, negative ways." We need to honestly focus on both the positives and the negatives of our past.

We accomplish that by taking a MORAL inventory. That word *moral* scares some people. But at its root, it simply means "honest." To make a MORAL inventory, we need to do the following five things:

M ake time — Job 33:33
O pen ourselves up — Job 7:11
R ely on God — Isaiah 40:29
A nalyze our past honestly — Proverbs 20:27
L ist — Lamentations 3:40

In this principle, we list the people we resent or fear, the specific actions others have taken to hurt us, the ways in which those hurtful actions have affected our lives and the wrongs or injuries we've inflicted on others.

This is done by taking a Spiritual Inventory. Through this process, we examine eight key areas of our lives:

Our relationships with others — Matthew 6:12 – 14
Our priorities in life — Matthew 6:33
Our attitude — Ephesians 4:31
Our integrity — Colossians 3:9
Our mind — Romans 12:2
Our body — 1 Corinthians 6:19 – 20
Our family — Joshua 24:15
Our church — Hebrews 10:25

The fourth step of the Christ-centered 12 steps relates to the first part of Principle Four.

STEP FOUR: We made a searching and fearless moral inventory of ourselves.

Let us examine our ways and test them,
and let us return to the LORD.

LAMENTATIONS 3:40

As soon as we complete our inventories in the first part of Principle Four, we need to confess our faults to ourselves, to God and to someone else we trust. After we share our inventories — the good and bad things of our past and present — we'll find the peace and freedom for which we may have been searching our entire lives. We need to confess our shortcomings, resentments and sins. God wants us to come clean, to admit that wrong is wrong, that we're "guilty as charged." We need to CONFESS the specific sins we've discovered in our inventory:

C onfess our shortcomings, resentments and sins — Proverbs 28:13
O bey God's direction — Romans 14:11 – 12
N o more guilt — Romans 8:1
F ace the truth — John 8:12
E ase the pain — Psalm 32:3 – 5
S top the blame — Matthew 7:3
S tart accepting God's forgiveness — 2 Corinthians 5:19

In confession we agree with God regarding our sins, and our fellowship with him is restored. Principle Four sums up how we go about obeying God's direction in confessing our sins: First, we confessed our sins to God so we could be forgiven. Then we confessed them to another person we trust so we could start the healing process.

The fifth step of the Christ-centered 12 steps relates to this part of Principle Four.

STEP FIVE: We admitted to God, to ourselves and to another human being the exact nature of our wrongs.

> *Therefore confess your sins to each other and pray*
> *for each other so that you may be healed.*
>
> JAMES 5:16

Some people feel that if they ADMIT their sins to another they have everything to lose and nothing to gain. Following is the truth about four things we have to lose and three things we have to gain by sharing our inventories with someone we trust:

We lose:

1. Our sense of isolation. Our feeling of aloneness will begin to vanish.

2. Our unwillingness to forgive. When people accept and forgive us, we start to see that we, in turn, can forgive others.

3. Our inflated, false pride. As we realistically see and accept ourselves, we begin to gain true humility, which involves seeing ourselves as we really are and God as he really is.

4. Our sense of denial. Being truthful with another person begins to tear away at our denial. We begin to feel clean and honest.

We gain:

1. Healing that the Bible promises. Look again at James 5:16. The key word here is "healed." Notice that the verse doesn't say, "Confess your sins to one another and you will be forgiven," although we hope this will be so, at least in terms of the other person. God already forgave us when we confessed our sins to him. Now he promises that we'll begin the healing process when we confess our sins to someone else.

2. Freedom. Our secrets have kept us in chains—bound, frozen, unable to move forward in any of our relationships, either with God or with others. Admitting our sins snaps the chains so God's healing power can be released.

3. Support. When we share our inventory with another person, we gain support. Our partner can help us stay focused and provide valuable feedback.

An important part of Celebrate Recovery is for each of us to have accountability relationships. Don't attempt to work through this fourth principle alone. We need sponsors and/or accountability partners for the following three reasons:

1. Having someone fill this role for us is a key part of our recovery program.

By walking alongside us on the road to recovery, a sponsor and/or an accountability partner keeps us on track as we complete the eight principles.

Proverbs 20:5 says:

> *The purposes of a person's heart are deep waters,*
> *but one who has insight draws them out.*

We need a man or woman who understands both us as an individual and what we're going through in order to help us in our recovery.

2. Having a sponsor and/or an accountability partner is Biblical.

Ecclesiastes 4:9 – 10 tells us:

> *Two are better than one, because they have a good return*
> *for their labor: If either of them falls down, one can help the other up.*
> *But pity anyone who falls and has no one to help them up.*

And Proverbs 27:17 points out that, "as iron sharpens iron, so one person sharpens another." The phrase "one another" is used in the New Testament over 50 times.

3. Having a sponsor and/or an accountability partner is the best guard against relapse.

By providing feedback to keep us on track, a sponsor and/or an accountability partner can see our old dysfunctional, self-defeating patterns beginning to resurface and quickly point them out to us. This person can confront us in a spirit of truth and love without piling on shame or guilt.

Ecclesiastes 7:5 states:

> *It is better to heed the rebuke of a wise person*
> *than to listen to the song of fools.*

The trouble with most of us is that we'd rather be ruined by praise than saved by criticism.

As we complete Principle Four, we need to remember that no matter how bad our past actions may have been, we can hold on to the assurance offered by Romans 8:1: "Therefore, there is now no condemnation for those who are in Christ Jesus."

Principle Four can be summed up in one verse, Isaiah 1:18:

> *"Come now, let us settle the matter," says the* LORD.
> *"Though your sins are like scarlet, they shall be as white as snow;*
> *though they are red as crimson, they shall be like wool."*

PRINCIPLE FOUR PRAYER

Dear God, you know my past; you're familiar with all the good and bad things I've done. In this principle, I ask you to give me the strength and courage to list them so I can "come clean" and face both my past and the truth about my present and future. Please help me reach out to those special persons you've placed along my road to recovery. Thank you for providing them to help me maintain balance as I work on my inventory. In Christ's name I pray, Amen.

Principle Four Lessons:

MORAL: Go to Job 33:33 (p. 621).

SPONSOR: Go to Ecclesiastes 4:9 – 12 (p. 786).

INVENTORY: Go to Ephesians 4:31 (p. 1469).

SPIRITUAL INVENTORY: Go to Matthew 6:12 – 13 (p. 1133).

CONFESS: Go to Proverbs 28:13 (p. 775).

ADMIT: Go to James 5:16 (p. 1543).

PRINCIPLE FIVE

VOLUNTARILY SUBMIT TO EVERY CHANGE GOD WANTS TO MAKE IN MY LIFE AND HUMBLY ASK HIM TO REMOVE MY CHARACTER DEFECTS.

Blessed are those who hunger and thirst for righteousness,
for they will be filled.

MATTHEW 5:6

By the time we get to Principle Five, we've already taken some major steps on the road to recovery. We admitted we had a problem we were powerless within ourselves to overcome. We came to believe that God could and would help us. We sought him and turned our lives and wills over to his care and direction. We took a spiritual inventory and shared it both with God and with another person. That was a lot of work — hard work, great work! Now we're going to ask God to remove our character defects.

Principle Five states that each of us is ready to voluntarily submit to every change God wants to make in our lives.

The sixth and seventh steps of the Christ-centered 12 steps relate to Principle Five.

STEP SIX: We were entirely ready to have God remove all these defects of character.

Humble yourselves before the Lord, and he will lift you up.

JAMES 4:10

STEP SEVEN: We humbly asked him to remove all our shortcomings.

If we confess our sins, he is faithful and just and will forgive us
our sins and purify us from all unrighteousness.

1 JOHN 1:9

Most, if not all, of us would be more than willing to have *certain* character defects go away. The sooner the better, we think. Good riddance! But the truth is that some defects are hard to give up. Like weeds in a garden, they've developed deep roots. We've developed our defects of character, our hang-ups and our destructive habits over periods of five, ten, twenty or more years. In this principle we and God — together — are going after these defects. *All* of them.

What does it mean to be entirely READY?

R elease control — Psalm 143:10

E asy does it — Psalm 37:5 – 6

A ccept the change — 1 Peter 1:13 – 14

D o replace our character defects — Matthew 12:43 – 45

Y ield to the growth — 1 John 3:9

To make these positive changes in our lives, we need to be entirely ready to let God be our life-changer. We're not the how-and-when committee. We're the preparation committee. All we have to be is ready.

Once we start the life-changing journey found in Principle Five, we'll find VICTORY over our character defects. We find that victory by doing the following:

V oluntarily submit — Romans 12:1 – 2

I dentify our character defects — Proverbs 16:9

C hange our mind — 2 Corinthians 5:17

T urn over our character defects to God — James 4:10

O ne day at a time — Matthew 6:34

R ecovery is a process — Philippians 1:6

Y ou must choose to change — James 4:6 – 8

Sometimes we discover in ourselves so many character defects that it's hard to know where to start. We need to go back to the wrongs, shortcomings and sins we identified in our Principle Four inventories. Remember, falling down doesn't make us a failure; staying down does. God doesn't just want us to admit our wrongs; he wants to make us right. He wants to give us "hope and a future" (Jeremiah 29:11). God doesn't just want to forgive us; he wants to change us. We need to ask him first to remove those character defects that are causing us the most pain. Ask him today, and be specific.

At first, our old self-doubts and low self-image may tell us we're not worthy of the growth and progress we're already making in the program. We need to turn off those old, negative thoughts and yield to the growth. It's the Holy Spirit's work within us. Through his transforming power we'll find the victory that keeps us from reverting back to our hang-ups and harmful habits.

Once we ask God to remove our character defects, we begin a journey that will lead us to new freedom from our past. We need to be careful not to look for perfection but instead to rejoice in steady progress. We need to seek, and be satisfied with, steady improvement.

The victory we receive in Principle Five is summed up in Romans 12:2:

> *Do not conform to the pattern of this world, but be transformed*
> *by the renewing of your mind. Then you will be able to test and approve*
> *what God's will is — his good, pleasing and perfect will.*

Principle Five Prayer

Dear God, thank you for taking me this far on my recovery journey. Now I pray for your help in making me entirely ready to change my destructive patterns. Give me the strength to deal with the character defects I've turned over to you. Allow me to accept all the changes you want to make in me. Help me to be the person you want me to be. In your Son's name I pray, Amen.

Principle Five Lessons:

READY: Go to Psalm 143:10 (p. 732).

VICTORY: Go to Romans 12:1 – 2 (p. 1409).

PRINCIPLE SIX

EVALUATE ALL MY RELATIONSHIPS. OFFER FORGIVENESS
TO THOSE WHO HAVE HURT ME AND MAKE AMENDS
FOR HARM I'VE DONE TO OTHERS, EXCEPT WHEN
TO DO SO WOULD HARM THEM OR OTHERS.

Blessed are the merciful, for they will be shown mercy.

MATTHEW 5:7

Blessed are the peacemakers, for they will be called children of God.

MATTHEW 5:9

In the first five principles, we worked on repairing the personal side of our lives by admitting our powerlessness, turning our lives and wills over to God's care, doing our moral inventories, sharing our sins with someone else, admitting our shortcomings and asking God to remove them. Now we're ready to begin some repair work on the relational side of our lives. Making our amends and offering our forgiveness mark the beginning of the end of our isolation from God and others.

Principle Six is all about making amends and offering forgiveness. "Forgive me as I learn to forgive" sums up Principle Six. This is right in line with Jesus' words in the prayer he taught his disciples: "Forgive us our debts, as we also have forgiven our debtors" (Matthew 6:12). But some of us balk at making amends. If God has forgiven me, we think, isn't that enough? Why should I dredge up the past? After all, making amends doesn't sound natural. The answer to that objection is simple: Making amends isn't about our past so much as it is about our future. Before we can enjoy the healthy relationships we desire, we need to clean out the guilt, shame and pain that have caused many of our past relationships to fail.

Luke 6:31 instructs each of us to "do to others as you would have them do to you." This verse reminds us to treat others the way we want to be treated. For some of us, that may be difficult. We've been badly hurt and/or abused. Many of us had nothing to do with the wrongs committed against us.

The first part of Principle Six, "Evaluate all my relationships," deals with our willingness to consider making amends and offering our forgiveness. The second part, "Offer forgiveness to those who have hurt me and make amends for harm I've done to others," calls us to action.

We need to pull out the dead weeds in our past broken relationships so that we can clear a place where new relationships can be successfully planted or old ones nurtured. That's why this principle is so important.

How do we make AMENDS?

A dmit the hurt and the harm — Luke 6:37

M ake a list — Luke 6:31

E ncourage one another — Hebrews 10:24

N ot just for them — Luke 6:35

D o it at the right time — Ecclesiastes 3:1

S tart living the promises of recovery — Joel 2:25

It's so important to make AMENDS because we can become addicted to our bitterness, hatred and revenge, just as we may have become addicted to alcohol, drugs or unhealthy relationships. A life characterized by bitterness, resentment and anger will kill us emotionally and shrivel our souls. Such a life will produce the three Ds:

D epression

D espair

D iscouragement

An unforgiving heart will cause us more pain and destruction than it will ever cause the person who has hurt us.

The inability to accept and offer forgiveness can stall, block or even destroy our recovery. Forgiveness breaks that negative cycle. It doesn't settle all the questions of blame, justice or fairness, but it does allow relationships to heal.

Principle Six addresses three types of forgiveness.

The first and most important kind of forgiveness is extended by God to us. Have we accepted God's forgiveness? Have we accepted Jesus' work on the cross? By his willingness to take our punishment, all our sins were canceled. Our debt was paid in full — a free gift for those who are willing to put their faith in him as the true and only Higher Power, Savior and Lord. Jesus himself exclaimed from the cross, "It is finished" (John 19:30) — possibly the most significant three words ever uttered. No matter how grievously we may have injured others or ourselves, the grace of God is always sufficient. His forgiveness is always complete, with no strings attached.

The second kind of forgiveness is the kind we extend from ourselves to others. This type of forgiveness is a process. We first need to be willing to forgive. But in order to become truly free, we have to let go of the pain of the past harm and abuse caused by others.

The third kind of forgiveness may well be the most difficult for us to extend: We need to forgive ourselves. We may find the grace within ourselves to forgive others, and we may accept God's forgiveness, but we may feel as though the guilt and shame of our own pasts are just too horrendous to forgive. But this is what God wants to do with the darkness of our past:

" 'Come now, let us settle the matter,' says the LORD. 'Though your sins are like scarlet, they shall be as white as snow; though they are red as crimson, they shall be like wool'" (Isaiah 1:18). No matter how unloved or worthless we may feel, God loves us and values us highly. Our feelings about ourselves don't change God's assessment of us and our potential one bit.

As we grow as Christians and move through our recovery process, we want to follow the guidance and direction of Jesus Christ. As we get to know him better, we want to model his teachings and his ways. We want to become more like him. If we're going to implement Principle Six to the best of our ability, we need to learn to model God's grace.

But how do we model his GRACE?

G od's gift — Romans 3:23 – 24
R eceived by our faith — Ephesians 2:8 – 9
A ccepted by God's love — Colossians 3:13
C hrist paid the price — Ephesians 1:7
E verlasting gift — 2 Thessalonians 2:16 – 17

As we learn to model God's grace, we'll be able to complete Principle Six and discover healing in our lost and broken relationships — at least as far as that healing depends upon our action. As Romans 12:18 directs us, "If it is possible, as far as it depends on you, live at peace with everyone."

The eighth and ninth steps of the Christ-centered 12 steps relate to Principle Six.

STEP EIGHT: We made a list of all persons we had harmed and became willing to make amends to them all.

> *Fools mock at making amends for sin, but goodwill*
> *is found among the upright.*
>
> PROVERBS 14:9

STEP NINE: We made direct amends to such people whenever possible, except when to do so would injure them or others.

> *Therefore, if you are offering your gift at the altar and*
> *there remember that your brother or sister has something against you,*
> *leave your gift there in front of the altar. First go and be reconciled*
> *to them; then come and offer your gift.*
>
> MATTHEW 5:23 – 24

Forgiveness is all about letting go. Remember playing tug-of-war as a child? As long as the people on each end of the rope are tugging, you have a war. You let go of your end of the rope when you forgive others. No matter how hard they may tug on their end, if you've released yours, the war is over. But until you release that rope, you're a prisoner of war.

Principle Six Prayer

Dear God, thank you for your love, for the grace you freely offer. Help me model your ways when I make my amends to those I've hurt and offer my forgiveness to those who've injured me. Help me set aside my selfishness and speak the truth in love. Help me focus on my own responsibility in the issue, so my actions won't be conditional. I know I can forgive others because you first forgave me. Thank you for loving me. In Jesus' name I pray, Amen.

Principle Six Lessons:

AMENDS: Go to Luke 6:37 (p. 1241).

FORGIVENESS: Go to Romans 3:22 – 26 (p. 1391).

GRACE: Go to Romans 3:23 – 24 (p. 1392).

PRINCIPLE SEVEN

RESERVE A DAILY TIME WITH GOD FOR
SELF-EXAMINATION, BIBLE READING AND PRAYER
IN ORDER TO KNOW GOD AND HIS WILL FOR MY LIFE AND
TO GAIN THE POWER TO FOLLOW HIS WILL.

Blessed are the pure in heart, for they will see God.

MATTHEW 5:8

When we get to Principle Seven, we've arrived at an important junction. We've already traveled a long way on our road to recovery. Our journey so far has required facing our denial; surrendering our lives to Jesus Christ; taking an honest look at our lives; listing, confessing and sharing our wrongdoings; being humble enough to allow God to make major changes in us; becoming willing to forgive or make amends; offering our forgiveness to those who've hurt us; and making amends for the harm we've caused others.

We've come to understand that we could never have made it this far on our own steam. In fact, the only reason we've reached this point is that we made a decision way back in Principle Three to turn over our lives and wills to God's care.

Jesus explains it this way in John 8:31 – 32: "If you hold to my teaching, you are really my disciples. Then you will know the truth, and the truth will set you free." Then in John 14:6 he defines truth by identifying it with himself: "I am the way and the truth and the life. No one comes to the Father except through me." We've been set free from our habits because of the Truth (Jesus Christ) we've invited into our hearts.

STEP TEN: We continued to take personal inventory and, when we were wrong, promptly admitted it.

We've arrived at the CROSSROADS of our recoveries. This isn't a place to stop and rest on our past accomplishments. We need to thank God for getting us this far on our road to recovery; to praise him for the many victories over our hurts, hang-ups and habits that we've already seen in working the first six principles; and to continue working the last two principles with the same devotion and enthusiasm that got us to this point in our recoveries. First Corinthians 10:12 puts it this way: "If you think you are standing firm, be careful that you don't fall!"

Most recovery material refers to Steps Ten through Twelve (Principles Seven and Eight) as the maintenance steps. It's certainly true that in these principles we'll live out our recoveries for the remainder of our time here on Earth — one day at a time! But we need to do much more than just maintain our recoveries; we need to continue to *grow* them.

In Principle Seven we desire to grow daily in our new relationships with Jesus Christ and others. Instead of attempting to be in control of every situation and every person with whom we come into contact, or instead of spinning out of control ourselves, we're starting to exhibit self-control, living the way God wants us to. Remember that "self under control" is what we're initially seeking but that self under *God's* control is what we're ultimately striving for.

As we begin to work Principle Seven and Step Ten, we'll see that this step involves three key actions:

T ake time to do a daily inventory — Lamentations 3:40
E valuate both the good and the bad — 1 John 1:8 – 10
N eed to admit our wrongs promptly — Matthew 5:23 – 24

One way to keep daily track of our good and bad behaviors is to keep a journal. Our journal isn't a place to jot down the calories we ingested for lunch today or our carpool schedule for school. It's a tool for us to review and record the good and bad things we did today. We can look for negative patterns, issues that we're repeatedly writing down and having to make amends for. We can share these pitfalls with our sponsors or accountability partners and set up an action plan to overcome them with God's help.

Journaling will help us live in daily humility — in reality, not in denial. Through God's guidance we can make choices about the emotions that affect our thinking and actions. When we take this step seriously, we can begin to take positive *action* — instead of getting caught up in a continuous spiral of *reaction*.

In Principle Seven, we actually do three different inventories:

1. *An ongoing inventory.* We can maintain an ongoing inventory throughout the day. The best time to admit we're wrong is at the exact time we're made aware of it. Why wait?

2. *A daily inventory.* At the end of each day we can look back over our daily activities, both the good and the bad, paying special attention to points at which we might have harmed someone else or reacted out of anger or fear. But once again, we need to remember to keep our daily inventory balanced. We should be sure to include the things we did right throughout the day, no matter how easy they may be to overlook or discount.

3. *A periodic inventory.* We should take a periodic inventory every 90 days or so. We may want to get away on a mini-retreat. We should bring our daily journal with us, and pray as we read through the entries for the last 90 days. We should ask God to show us areas in our life in which we can improve during the next 90 days. But we should also remember to identify and celebrate the victories we've already experienced.

Principle Seven is so important. It also includes Step Eleven of the Christ-centered 12 steps.

STEP ELEVEN: We sought through prayer and meditation to improve our conscious contact with God, praying only for knowledge of his will for us and power to carry that out.

Principle Seven is our best defense against reverting back to our old ways. If we work this principle daily, relying on God's power, it will not only help us grow in him but will prevent our RELAPSE:

R eserve a daily quiet time — Mark 14:38

E valuate — Romans 12:3,9 – 10,12,16 – 17

L isten to Jesus — 1 Thessalonians 5:21

A lone with and quiet before God — Psalm 46:10

P lug in to God's power — Philippians 4:6

S low down — Philippians 4:7

E njoy your growth — 1 Thessalonians 5:16 – 18

By this point in our recoveries we've learned that when we start our day working Principle Seven and having a quiet time with God, and when we end it by doing our daily inventory, we have a pretty good day — a reasonably happy day. Not only will this help to prevent relapse, but it will cultivate in us an attitude of gratitude.

To help maintain this grateful attitude, we can focus our gratitude on at least four areas of our lives:

Be thankful to God — Psalm 107:15

Be thankful for others — Colossians 3:15 – 16

Be thankful for our recovery — Hebrews 12:1

Be thankful for our church — Psalm 100:4

PRINCIPLE SEVEN PRAYER

Dear God, help me to set aside the hassles and racket of the world, so I can focus my mind and listen just to you for the next few minutes. Help me to get to know you better. Help me to better understand your plan and purpose for my life. Father, help me to live this day within the boundaries of today, seeking your will and living this one day as you would have me live it.

I pray that others may view me as yours — not just in response to my words but, more important, on account of my actions. Thank you for your love, your grace, your perfect forgiveness. Thank you for all those important individuals you've placed in my life — in my program, in my recovery and within my church family. Your will be done, not mine. In your Son's name I pray, Amen.

Principle Seven Lessons:

CROSSROADS: Go to Lamentations 3:40 (p. 964).

SPIRITUAL INVENTORY: Go to Matthew 22:37 – 40 (p. 1168).

RELAPSE: Go to Mark 14:38 (p. 1216).

GRATITUDE: Go to Psalm 107:15 (p. 710).

PRINCIPLE EIGHT

YIELD MYSELF TO GOD TO BE USED TO BRING
THIS GOOD NEWS TO OTHERS, BOTH BY
MY EXAMPLE AND BY MY WORDS.

Blessed are those who are persecuted because of righteousness,
for theirs is the kingdom of heaven.

MATTHEW 5:10

Major, miraculous progress and growth have occurred in our lives since we started our recovery program, since we began working Principle One. We've stepped out of our denial into God's grace. We've taken an honest spiritual inventory. We've worked on getting right with God, ourselves and others. And we've grown in our relationship with Christ. We've discovered a new way to live life, and we're finding the serenity we've always sought. But the most exciting part is yet to come — in Principle Eight.

Principle Eight is the "giving back" principle. It's about giving back because we want to, not because we have to. We want to share with others who are still trapped in their hurts, hang-ups and habits the freedom and victory God has given us.

What is giving back all about? What does it truly mean to give? First of all, Principle Eight doesn't ask us to give in unhealthy ways, ways that might hurt us or cause us to relapse into our old, codependent behaviors. No, Principle Eight is all about healthy, non-codependent giving of ourselves — giving freely, without the slightest expectation that we will receive anything in return. No one has ever been honored, after all, for what they've received. Honor has always been a reward to those who gave.

Matthew 10:8 sums up the heart of Principle Eight:

Freely you have received; freely give.

In Principle Eight we learn what it truly means to GIVE.

G od, the first Giver — Romans 8:32

I becomes we — Ecclesiastes 4:9 – 10,12

V ictories shared — 2 Corinthians 1:3 – 4

E xample of our actions — 1 John 3:18

Once we understand how to freely give of ourselves in healthy ways, we can start living the eighth principle, and in particular Step Twelve of the Christ-centered 12 steps.

STEP TWELVE: Having had a spiritual experience as the result of these steps, we tried to carry this message to others and practice these principles in all our affairs.

Sometimes we get to Principle Eight and feel as though we really don't have anything to offer someone else. We feel as though we're not worthy of helping another person, that we're not eligible to be used by God in this way. Nothing could be further from the truth.

Here's an example. Take an old, beat-up soda can — dirty, dented, even squashed. A few years ago it would have been thrown into the garbage and deemed useless, of no continuing value. Modern technology has changed that. Today it can be recycled, melted down, purified and made into a new can — shiny and clean — that can be used again.

That's what Principle Eight does. It recycles our pain by allowing God's fire and light to shine on it — to melt down our old hurts, hang-ups and habits so we can be used again in a positive way. Our lives can be recycled to show others how we've worked the principles and steps, with Jesus' healing, and how we've come through the darkness of our pain into Christ's glorious freedom and light.

Society tells us that pain is useless. In fact, some people believe that *people* in pain are useless. At Celebrate Recovery, we know that pain has value, as do the people who experience it. So while the world says no, Principle Eight shouts a resounding YES:

Y ield myself to God — Galatians 6:1 – 2
E xample is important — 1 Timothy 1:5
S erve others as Jesus Christ did — John 13:14 – 15

The road to recovery leads to service. When we reach Principle Eight, the road splits. Some will choose to serve at Celebrate Recovery. Others will prefer to devote their skills to other areas in the church.

We need to share our experiences, victories and hopes with newcomers. We do that as leaders, sponsors and accountability partners. But the church also needs our service. As we lend a hand outside Celebrate Recovery, we can share with others and motivate them to get into recovery when they're ready to face their own hurts, hang-ups and habits.

The world is populated by two kinds of people — givers and takers. The takers eat well, but the givers sleep well. Be a giver. There are many, many areas in which to serve. Make suggestions. Get involved.

Principle Eight comes down to this: Do what you can with what you have, where you are.

Make your life a mission, not an intermission.

Live out Principles Seven and Eight on a daily basis for the remainder of your time on this earth, and your life will be full and rewarding as you follow God's purpose for you.

Every morning, before you get out of bed, pray this prayer:

Principle Eight Prayer

Dear Jesus, as it would please you, bring me someone today whom I can serve. Amen.

Principle Eight Lessons:

GIVE: Go to Romans 8:32 (p. 1402).

YES: Go to Galatians 6:1 – 2 (p. 1459).

The Old Testament

THEME: God desires to relate to his creation on an intimate level.

AUTHOR: Genesis doesn't identify its author, but Scripture and church tradition ascribe authorship to Moses.

DATE OF WRITING: Genesis was probably written between 1446 and 1406 BC.

ENCOURAGEMENT FROM GENESIS: "Do not be afraid ... I am your shield, your very great reward" (Genesis 15:1).

CHALLENGE FROM GENESIS: "If you do what is right, will you not be accepted? But if you do not do what is right, sin is crouching at your door; it desires to have you, but you must rule over it" (Genesis 4:7).

REFLECTION FROM GENESIS: "Is anything too hard for the LORD?" (Genesis 18:14).

Genesis is a book of beginnings that sets the stage for all of history. In Genesis we're invited to witness the creation of the world. We get to see the world that God created and pronounced "good." Adam and Eve were able to speak freely with God, to enjoy an intimate, open, honest relationship with him — until sin entered the picture. The book of Genesis sets the scene for the rest of the Bible, for the ongoing story of a loving God who wants to reinstate a relationship with the creatures he created in his image.

Part of our recovery is our acceptance of this world as it currently is: fallen, broken and sinful. Yet when we put our faith in Christ, things begin to get better. In Genesis we face the realities of this world and the origins of the hardships we endure. Even more importantly, in Genesis we discover God's plan to bring blessing to all humankind through the seed of Abraham.

The Beginning

1 In the beginning God created the heavens and the earth. ²Now the earth was formless and empty, darkness was over the surface of the deep, and the Spirit of God was hovering over the waters.

³And God said, "Let there be light," and there was light. ⁴God saw that the light was good, and he separated the light from the darkness. ⁵God called the light "day," and the darkness he called "night." And there was evening, and there was morning — the first day.

⁶And God said, "Let there be a vault between the waters to separate water from water." ⁷So God made the vault and separated the water under the vault from the water above it. And it was so. ⁸God called the vault "sky." And there was evening, and there was morning — the second day.

⁹And God said, "Let the water under the sky be gathered to one place, and let dry ground appear." And it was so. ¹⁰God called the dry ground "land,"

and the gathered waters he called "seas." And God saw that it was good.

¹¹Then God said, "Let the land produce vegetation: seed-bearing plants and trees on the land that bear fruit with seed in it, according to their various kinds." And it was so. ¹²The land produced vegetation: plants bearing seed according to their kinds and trees bearing fruit with seed in it according to their kinds. And God saw that it was good. ¹³And there was evening, and there was morning—the third day.

¹⁴And God said, "Let there be lights in the vault of the sky to separate the day from the night, and let them serve as signs to mark sacred times, and days and years, ¹⁵and let them be lights in the vault of the sky to give light on the earth." And it was so. ¹⁶God made two great lights—the greater light to govern the day and the lesser light to govern the night. He also made the stars. ¹⁷God set them in the vault of the sky to give light on the earth, ¹⁸to govern the day and the night, and to separate light from darkness. And God saw that it was good. ¹⁹And there was evening, and there was morning—the fourth day.

²⁰And God said, "Let the water teem with living creatures, and let birds fly above the earth across the vault of the sky." ²¹So God created the great creatures of the sea and every living thing with which the water teems and that moves about in it, according to their kinds, and every winged bird according to its kind. And God saw that it was good. ²²God blessed them and said, "Be fruitful and increase in number and fill the water in the seas, and let the birds increase on the earth." ²³And there was evening, and there was morning—the fifth day.

²⁴And God said, "Let the land produce living creatures according to their kinds: the livestock, the creatures that move along the ground, and the wild animals, each according to its kind." And it was so. ²⁵God made the wild animals according to their kinds, the livestock according to their kinds, and all the creatures that move along the ground according to their kinds. And God saw that it was good.

²⁶Then God said, "Let us make mankind in our image, in our likeness, so that they may rule over the fish in the sea and the birds in the sky, over the livestock and all the wild animals,ᵃ and over all the creatures that move along the ground."

²⁷So God created mankind in his own image,
in the image of God he created them;
male and female he created them.

²⁸God blessed them and said to them, "Be fruitful and increase in number; fill the earth and subdue it. Rule over the fish in the sea and the birds in the sky and over every living creature that moves on the ground."

²⁹Then God said, "I give you every seed-bearing plant on the face of the whole earth and every tree that has fruit with seed in it. They will be yours for food. ³⁰And to all the beasts of the earth and all the birds in the sky and all the creatures that move along the ground—everything that has the breath of life in it—I give every green plant for food." And it was so.

³¹God saw all that he had made, and it was very good. And there was evening, and there was morning—the sixth day.

2 Thus the heavens and the earth were completed in all their vast array.

²By the seventh day God had finished

ᵃ *26* Probable reading of the original Hebrew text (see Syriac); Masoretic Text *the earth* the work he had been doing; so on the seventh day he rested from all his work. ³Then God blessed the seventh day and made it holy, because on it he rested from all the work of creating that he had done.

Adam and Eve

⁴This is the account of the heavens and the earth when they were created, when the LORD God made the earth and the heavens.

⁵Now no shrub had yet appeared on the earth*ᵃ* and no plant had yet sprung up, for the LORD God had not sent rain on the earth and there was no one to work the ground, ⁶but streams*ᵇ* came up from the earth and watered the whole surface of the ground. ⁷Then the LORD God formed a man*ᶜ* from the dust of the ground and breathed into his nostrils the breath of life, and the man became a living being.

⁸Now the LORD God had planted a garden in the east, in Eden; and there he put the man he had formed. ⁹The LORD God made all kinds of trees grow out of the ground—trees that were pleasing to the eye and good for food. In the middle of the garden were the tree of life and the tree of the knowledge of good and evil.

¹⁰A river watering the garden flowed from Eden; from there it was separated into four headwaters. ¹¹The name of the first is the Pishon; it winds through the entire land of Havilah, where there is gold. ¹²(The gold of that land is good; aromatic resin*ᵈ* and onyx are also there.) ¹³The name of the second river is the Gihon; it winds through the entire land of Cush.*ᵉ* ¹⁴The name of the third river is the Tigris; it runs along the east side of Ashur. And the fourth river is the Euphrates.

¹⁵The LORD God took the man and put him in the Garden of Eden to work it and take care of it. ¹⁶And the LORD God commanded the man, "You are free to eat from any tree in the garden; ¹⁷but you must not eat from the tree of the knowledge of good and evil, for when you eat from it you will certainly die."

¹⁸The LORD God said, "It is not good for the man to be alone. I will make a helper suitable for him."

¹⁹Now the LORD God had formed out of the ground all the wild animals and all the birds in the sky. He brought them to the man to see what he would name them; and whatever the man called each living creature, that was its name. ²⁰So the man gave names to all the livestock, the birds in the sky and all the wild animals.

But for Adam*ᶠ* no suitable helper was found. ²¹So the LORD God caused the man to fall into a deep sleep; and while he was sleeping, he took one of the man's ribs*ᵍ* and then closed up the place with flesh. ²²Then the LORD God made a woman from the rib*ʰ* he had taken out of the man, and he brought her to the man.

²³The man said,

"This is now bone of my bones
    and flesh of my flesh;
she shall be called 'woman,'
    for she was taken out of man."

²⁴That is why a man leaves his father and mother and is united to his wife, and they become one flesh.

²⁵Adam and his wife were both naked, and they felt no shame.

The Fall

3 Now the serpent was more crafty than any of the wild animals the LORD God had made. He said to the woman, "Did God really say, 'You must not eat from any tree in the garden'?"

²The woman said to the serpent, "We may eat fruit from the trees in the garden, ³but God did say, 'You must not eat fruit from the tree that is in the middle of the

---

ᵃ 5 Or *land*; also in verse 6   *ᵇ 6* Or *mist*   *ᶜ 7* The Hebrew for *man (adam)* sounds like and may be related to the Hebrew for *ground (adamah)*; it is also the name *Adam* (see verse 20).   *ᵈ 12* Or *good; pearls*   *ᵉ 13* Possibly southeast Mesopotamia   *ᶠ 20* Or *the man*   *ᵍ 21* Or *took part of the man's side*   *ʰ 22* Or *part*

My Name Is Eve

GENESIS 3:1-7

Understanding recovery begins with understanding our fundamental problem: Our sin separates us from God and the blessings he wants us to enjoy. Sin's story begins with the temptation of Eve by Satan, in the guise of a serpent. Even under the perfect conditions found in the Garden of Eden, temptation found Eve. The devil's strategy was to lead the first woman to distort the word of God (see Genesis 3:1–3) and to doubt his goodness (see vv. 4–6). Eve twisted God's words by adding to them and thereby misrepresenting his directive (see v. 3). Further, God's goodness was attacked by the serpent's assertion that Eve's sin wouldn't result in death (see v. 4), as well as Satan disparaging God's motives in his directions to Adam and Eve (see v. 5). God, the enemy insinuated, was holding out on the world's first couple. Eve bought into this last lie: "When the woman saw that the fruit of the tree was good for food and pleasing to the eye, and also desirable for gaining wisdom, she took some and ate it" (v. 6). Eve's sin spread almost immediately to the only other person on the planet, her husband. She took some of the fruit to Adam and he also ate.

At this point in the story, we see that some of the serpent's predictions did indeed prove to be true. Satan had informed Eve that "when you eat ... your eyes will be opened" (v. 5) and that these first two humans would have personal experience with both good and evil. The promise of the serpent, though, was that this would make them "like God" (v. 5). The great irony of this deception was that both Adam and Eve were already "like God," having been created in his own image (see 1:26–27). Their eyes were now opened, and they did in fact know both good and evil, but the outcome of this experience was shame (see v. 7).

This is the tragic beginning of sin's deadly, destructive work. Lives continue to be devastated as God's words are distorted and his goodness is doubted. The consequences of sin, as well as God's plans for humanity's recovery, are spelled out already in Adam and Eve's story.

garden, and you must not touch it, or you will die.'"

⁴"You will not certainly die," the serpent said to the woman. ⁵"For God knows that when you eat from it your eyes will be opened, and you will be like God, knowing good and evil."

⁶When the woman saw that the fruit of the tree was good for food and pleasing to the eye, and also desirable for gaining wisdom, she took some and ate it. She also gave some to her husband, who was with her, and he ate it. ⁷Then the eyes of both of them were opened, and they realized they were naked; so they sewed fig leaves together and made coverings for themselves.

⁸Then the man and his wife heard the sound of the LORD God as he was walking in the garden in the cool of the day, and they hid from the LORD God among the trees of the garden. ⁹But the LORD God called to the man, "Where are you?"

¹⁰He answered, "I heard you in the garden, and I was afraid because I was naked; so I hid."

DENIAL LESSON [*Principle One*]

For the previous entry in the DENIAL lesson, go to Psalm 107:13 – 14 (page 708).

For a discussion of Principles One through Eight and a listing of their related lessons, go to pages xvii – xliv.

Then the eyes of both of them were opened, and they realized they were naked; so they sewed fig leaves together and made coverings for themselves. Then the man and his wife heard the sound of the LORD God as he was walking in the garden in the cool of the day, and they hid from the LORD God among the trees of the garden.

GENESIS 3:7 – 8

The power to change comes only through God's grace. Principle One states: "Realize I'm not God. I admit that I'm powerless to control my tendency to do the wrong thing and that my life has become unmanageable." If we admit that we're powerless, we recognize our need for a power greater than ourselves to restore us. That power is our Higher Power, the one and only true Higher Power, Jesus Christ.

In Principle One we discover that we've been in DENIAL of our habits. The next letter in DENIAL is *I*. Denial ISOLATES US FROM GOD. Adam and Eve are an unforgettable example of how secrets and denial separate us from true fellowship with God. After they sinned, the first couple's secret alienated them from God. Genesis 3:7 tells us how they tried to isolate themselves from God because they were naked and felt ashamed. In verse 12 Adam tried to rationalize his sin. First he attempted to transfer the responsibility to God: "The woman you put here with me ..." Then he tried to push the blame onto Eve: " ... she gave me some fruit from the tree, and I ate it."

But God's light shines on the truth, even while our denial keeps us in the darkness of isolation: "If we claim to have fellowship with him yet walk in the darkness, we lie and do not live out the truth. But if we walk in the light, as he is in the light, we have fellowship with one another, and the blood of Jesus, his Son, purifies us from all sin" (1 John 1:6 – 7).

The next letter in DENIAL is *A*. Go to Ephesians 4:25 (page 1467).

My Name Is Regina

I'M A BELIEVER WHO STRUGGLES WITH DRUG AND ALCOHOL ADDICTION AND ANOREXIA

Please read about Eve's deception by the serpent (Satan) in Genesis 3:1 – 7.

During my first eight years of life, my family would have been considered perfect by most observers. As the daughter of a pastor and a stay-at-home mother, I lived in a nearly idyllic setting. But my world was dramatically changed when my mother was diagnosed with cancer. When she came home from the hospital, I was allowed only to gaze at her through her bedroom door. I began to think I had only myself to rely on.

My mom survived, but the remainder of my childhood was characterized by regular moves. I wasn't good at making friends. At summer camp when I was 12 years old, I smoked marijuana for the first time. My monthly habit gradually became daily, after which I discovered other drugs. Like Eve, I falsely viewed these substances as "good ... pleasing ... and also desirable for gaining wisdom" (Genesis 3:6). I felt good when I was high and saw myself as fitting in better, with a heightened openness to new insights and understanding.

The difficulty was that I was a Christian; ironically, as my addiction grew, so did my love for God. I served on leadership teams at church, taught Bible studies and mentored other young women in their walks with the Lord. Yet no matter how deeply I delved into God's Word, the temptations never eased up.

I began a career in veterinary medicine, and one morning I assisted in putting an old, cancer-ridden dog to sleep. Her name was Amazing Grace. Intrigued, I asked the presiding vet how the name had been chosen. The doctor smiled and replied, "I've been repeating the same thing to her owners for years: 'She's a dud. You shouldn't have kept her. The price you'll spend on her won't be worth the time you have with her.' The dog's owners only looked at me and asked, 'What if God had said that about us?' " One more seed of the greatness of God's love was planted that day in my heart.

My pastor began talking about a mission trip, but God made it clear that I couldn't simultaneously be a missionary and a drug addict. I did go to Romania and Hungary, and a passion for reaching the world grew in my heart. Still, temptation was never far away, and within one month of returning home I was back into my addiction. Why, once again, was I using drugs after God had so clearly intervened? I went to my pastor for help. His answer: Pray and read the Bible more. I tried, but I turned back to my habit.

I hit bottom, waking up in an emergency room after my mom used a hammer to break into my bathroom, where she found me unconscious. I lost my job due to the overdose and faced misdemeanor and felony possession charges. Sin's deadly and destructive work had almost taken its ultimate toll. A couple of days later a friend told me about Celebrate Recovery, and I walked into the Chemical Dependency group that Friday evening.

Just weeks after my overdose I departed for Israel. I was afraid I'd be unable to stay sober, but while there I made the best decision of my life—to believe what people had told me about Celebrate Recovery: "If you just start to walk through it, you'll see a miracle at the end."

When I returned home the Lord provided me with a support system. I found a sponsor, formed an accountability team and started working through the principles. I began to understand that my poor self-image was causing me to struggle with anorexia. But as I started to see myself as a child of God, I accepted God's forgiveness for the wreckage I'd caused. I asked for forgiveness and for restored relationships with my family. My mom was again diagnosed with breast cancer, and instead of running away from that relationship, I was able to stand beside her as she endured treatments and surgery.

Serving at Celebrate Recovery for the past few years has changed my life. I've handed out bulletins, led a Step Study, facilitated our Newcomers' group and led our Women's Chemically Addicted group. God didn't forget about my desire to reach the world. I've shared my story of recovery and freedom through Christ all over southern California and in many other states. I've traveled throughout Malaysia and Singapore, speaking to churches and pastors about the program. I spent a summer volunteering in a drug rehab center, leading Step Studies and sponsoring girls. Finally, God called me to El Salvador to take the Celebrate Recovery program into a drug rehab center with approximately 50 ex-gangsters, all male, and I was privileged to lead these men through the very principles that have saved my life.

I've celebrated five years of sobriety, a feat I could never have accomplished without following the Lord's will. As I've walked through job changes, parental illnesses and the deaths of friends, I've learned the truth of Philippians 4:13. I no longer live in bondage to substances, food addictions, negative feelings or the words and opinions of others. I implicitly trust God's Word and never doubt his goodness. I wake up each morning and commit my day to the Lord, knowing that he'll provide precisely the degree of strength I need for that day.

Regina

¹¹And he said, "Who told you that you were naked? Have you eaten from the tree that I commanded you not to eat from?"

¹²The man said, "The woman you put here with me — she gave me some fruit from the tree, and I ate it."

¹³Then the LORD God said to the woman, "What is this you have done?"

The woman said, "The serpent deceived me, and I ate."

¹⁴So the LORD God said to the serpent, "Because you have done this,

> "Cursed are you above all livestock
>   and all wild animals!
> You will crawl on your belly
>   and you will eat dust
>   all the days of your life.
> ¹⁵And I will put enmity
>   between you and the woman,
>   and between your offspring[a] and
>   hers;
> he will crush[b] your head,
>   and you will strike his heel."

¹⁶To the woman he said,

> "I will make your pains in childbearing
>   very severe;
>   with painful labor you will give birth
>   to children.
> Your desire will be for your husband,
>   and he will rule over you."

¹⁷To Adam he said, "Because you listened to your wife and ate fruit from the tree about which I commanded you, 'You must not eat from it,'

> "Cursed is the ground because of you;
>   through painful toil you will eat food
>   from it
>   all the days of your life.
> ¹⁸It will produce thorns and thistles for
>   you,
>   and you will eat the plants of the
>   field.
> ¹⁹By the sweat of your brow
>   you will eat your food

until you return to the ground,
    since from it you were taken;
for dust you are
    and to dust you will return."

²⁰Adam[c] named his wife Eve,[d] because she would become the mother of all the living.

²¹The LORD God made garments of skin for Adam and his wife and clothed them. ²²And the LORD God said, "The man has now become like one of us, knowing good and evil. He must not be allowed to reach out his hand and take also from the tree of life and eat, and live forever." ²³So the LORD God banished him from the Garden of Eden to work the ground from which he had been taken. ²⁴After he drove the man out, he placed on the east side[e] of the Garden of Eden cherubim and a flaming sword flashing back and forth to guard the way to the tree of life.

Cain and Abel

4 Adam[c] made love to his wife Eve, and she became pregnant and gave birth to Cain.[f] She said, "With the help of the LORD I have brought forth[g] a man." ²Later she gave birth to his brother Abel.

Now Abel kept flocks, and Cain worked the soil. ³In the course of time Cain brought some of the fruits of the soil as an offering to the LORD. ⁴And Abel also brought an offering — fat portions from some of the firstborn of his flock. The LORD looked with favor on Abel and his offering, ⁵but on Cain and his offering he did not look with favor. So Cain was very angry, and his face was downcast.

⁶Then the LORD said to Cain, "Why are you angry? Why is your face downcast? ⁷If you do what is right, will you not be accepted? But if you do not do what is right, sin is crouching at your door; it desires to have you, but you must rule over it."

⁸Now Cain said to his brother Abel,

---

a 15 Or *seed*   *b 15* Or *strike*   *c 20,1* Or *The man*   *d 20 Eve* probably means *living.*   *e 24* Or *placed in front*
f 1 Cain sounds like the Hebrew for *brought forth* or *acquired.*   *g 1* Or *have acquired*

MY NAME IS ADAM

GENESIS 3:6–24

Adam's sin is followed immediately by the evidence of his (and Eve's) first experience of shame (see Genesis 3:6–7). Both tried to deal with their sin by their own devices (see v. 7), by camouflaging their wrongdoing to the best of their ability. This reaction could be labeled the world's first religion. Religion, though, is no substitute for the relationship God desires with each of us. Our best efforts leave us helpless, wallowing in our sin and shame. Adam and Eve, hearing God walking in the garden, hid themselves (see v. 8). At this point in Adam's story the road to recovery begins, and that beginning is found in God's redemptive actions:

- God loves us so much that he confronts us even as we try to hide from him (see vv. 9–10). God confronted Adam first (see vv. 9–12) and then Eve (see v. 13).

- God's confrontation is designed to lead us to confess our sin (see vv. 11,13).

- God clearly outlined the consequences of the first sin for the serpent, Satan (see vv. 14–15); for Eve (see v. 16); and for Adam (see vv. 17–19).

- God promised a future Redeemer, who would crush Satan (see v. 15).

- God provided a covering for the sin of the first human couple until their sin could be removed on the basis of Christ's sacrifice (see v. 21; see also Romans 3:21–26).

How did Adam and Eve respond to God's gracious intervention? To avoid responsibility, Adam tried to blame others: "the woman" (v. 12)—and apparently God, since he had created Eve and put her in the garden with Adam. Eve in turn pointed the finger at "the serpent" (v. 13). But excuses don't cancel consequences. Adam and Eve found themselves cast out of the garden, where the curses pronounced by God continue in effect to this day (see vv. 22–24). Genesis 5:3 contains a subtle but tragic hint about our own need for recovery: "When Adam had lived 130 years, he had a son in his own likeness, in his own image." Now, instead of being born in the image and likeness of God, each of us is born in the image and likeness of our fallen, sinful human ancestors, beginning with Adam.

What can we learn about recovery from the story of Adam?

- Consider the reality of the consequences your hurts, hang-ups and habits bring to your own life and to the lives of others.

- Come when God calls to you, even as you're trying to hide your sin and shame.

- Confess your sins when he confronts you by his Holy Spirit, knowing that "if we confess our sins, he is faithful and just and will forgive us our sins and purify us from all unrighteousness" (1 John 1:9).

- Commit yourself to Christ, who will conform you to his image: "We all, who with unveiled faces contemplate the Lord's glory, are being transformed into his image with ever-increasing glory, which comes from the Lord, who is the Spirit" (2 Corinthians 3:18).

- Carry the Good News you've discovered to others, knowing that sin has made the need for recovery universal: "For all have sinned and fall short of the glory of God" (Romans 3:23).

My Name Is Dave

I'M A BELIEVER WHO STRUGGLES WITH ALCOHOL AND DRUG ADDICTION

Please read the story of Adam and Eve's attempt to hide from God in Genesis 3:6 – 11.

I grew up in a loving home, where we learned a little about God and Jesus. I knew that God existed, but not much more than that. Looking back, I realize that my concept of him was woefully inaccurate.

I was introduced to alcohol and drugs shortly after I completed the eighth grade. Once I started using, I quit going to church; like Adam, I hid from God. As my addiction grew, trouble with the law followed close behind. I received my first DWI when I was 16 years old. By the time I turned 25, I had been arrested four times for drunk driving. Additionally, I was arrested several times for drug-related offenses. I was leading a self-centered, selfish life. I wrecked numerous vehicles and ruined the lives of so many people. I had no relationship with God and wasn't looking for one. I utilized drugs, alcohol and material possessions to mask the pain and shame I was feeling inside. When I found myself in deep trouble, I would pray, but I wasn't even sure who I was praying to. I mouthed the words out of desperation, without sincerity.

I was introduced to a secular 12-step program after my second arrest. After attending the program for the court-ordered 12 months, I graduated and went on with my life. It wasn't until my fourth arrest that I finally admitted that my life had become unmanageable. I remember sitting in my jail cell contemplating suicide. I had reached rock bottom and had finally come to realize that "good itself does not dwell in me, that is, in my sinful nature. For I have the desire to do what is good, but I cannot carry it out" (Romans 7:18). I went back to the secular recovery program and began genuinely working through the steps. For the first time in my adult life, I was sober.

Despite my sobriety, I found myself in the midst of a divorce. I couldn't understand it. I had stopped using drugs and alcohol. Wasn't that enough? I was devastated at the thought of being separated from my son. A year later I met someone new. Cathy had been attending church and insisted that I join her if we were going to start a relationship. The first time I went to church with her, I was amazed. There were basketball hoops inside the church. People were singing, smiling and hugging each other. This was so different from the churches I had experienced as a child. I felt the presence of the Lord and realized that God loved me even as I continued to try to hide from him.

Soon Cathy and I began living together, which caused a huge struggle in our lives. I wasn't ready for a personal relationship with the Lord; I was just going to church to be with Cathy. I agreed to attend a Bible study with Christians who were in recovery. I had never felt such freedom. This church and the people in it were genuine. The men's ministry was such an encouragement to me. They lifted me up in prayer every day, and, as a result, I answered when God called, knelt down with my pastor, and accepted Jesus Christ as my Savior and Lord. For years I'd been shackled by my addiction to alcohol and drugs. I don't ever want to forget where I came from or how I arrived—and God doesn't want me to either.

One night I met a man and began sharing my story with him. He began praying with me, and much to my surprise he prayed that I would move out of Cathy's home. Cathy and I weren't married at that point, and I felt convicted. I immediately went home and told Cathy that I was moving out until we got married. God answered prayer, and we were married a short time later. We joined our church and got involved in a small group. It was obvious, though, that God wanted more from us. He moved in our hearts to start a recovery ministry, a place where we could reach others struggling with addictions—where we could share with them the love of Jesus Christ and the 12 steps. As we were searching for a program to utilize in our church, we stumbled upon Celebrate Recovery. In January of 1999 we held our first meeting. It's comforting to realize that, even though the people who attend Celebrate Recovery come from different backgrounds, the answer to all of our hurts, hang-ups and habits is the same: the one and only higher power, Jesus Christ.

Scripture tells us that Adam and Eve "heard the sound of the LORD God as he was walking in the garden in the cool of the day, and they hid from the LORD God among the trees of the garden" (Genesis 3:8). Like Adam, my sin caused me to hide from God, but it was shortly after that point that my road to recovery began.

"Let's go out to the field."*a* While they were in the field, Cain attacked his brother Abel and killed him.

9Then the LORD said to Cain, "Where is your brother Abel?"

"I don't know," he replied. "Am I my brother's keeper?"

10The LORD said, "What have you done? Listen! Your brother's blood cries out to me from the ground. 11Now you are under a curse and driven from the ground, which opened its mouth to receive your brother's blood from your hand. 12When you work the ground, it will no longer yield its crops for you. You will be a restless wanderer on the earth."

13Cain said to the LORD, "My punishment is more than I can bear. 14Today you are driving me from the land, and I will be hidden from your presence; I will be a restless wanderer on the earth, and whoever finds me will kill me."

15But the LORD said to him, "Not so*b*; anyone who kills Cain will suffer vengeance seven times over." Then the LORD put a mark on Cain so that no one who found him would kill him. 16So Cain went out from the LORD's presence and lived in the land of Nod,*c* east of Eden.

17Cain made love to his wife, and she became pregnant and gave birth to Enoch. Cain was then building a city, and he named it after his son Enoch. 18To Enoch was born Irad, and Irad was the father of Mehujael, and Mehujael was the father of Methushael, and Methushael was the father of Lamech.

19Lamech married two women, one named Adah and the other Zillah. 20Adah gave birth to Jabal; he was the father of those who live in tents and raise livestock. 21His brother's name was Jubal; he was the father of all who play stringed instruments and pipes. 22Zillah also had a son, Tubal-Cain, who forged all kinds of tools out of*d* bronze and iron. Tubal-Cain's sister was Naamah.

23Lamech said to his wives,

"Adah and Zillah, listen to me;
    wives of Lamech, hear my words.
I have killed a man for wounding me,
    a young man for injuring me.
24If Cain is avenged seven times,
    then Lamech seventy-seven times."

25Adam made love to his wife again, and she gave birth to a son and named him Seth,*e* saying, "God has granted me another child in place of Abel, since Cain killed him." 26Seth also had a son, and he named him Enosh.

At that time people began to call on*f* the name of the LORD.

From Adam to Noah

5 This is the written account of Adam's family line.

When God created mankind, he made them in the likeness of God. 2He created them male and female and blessed them. And he named them "Mankind"*g* when they were created.

3When Adam had lived 130 years, he had a son in his own likeness, in his own image; and he named him Seth. 4After Seth was born, Adam lived 800 years and had other sons and daughters. 5Altogether, Adam lived a total of 930 years, and then he died.

6When Seth had lived 105 years, he became the father*h* of Enosh. 7After he became the father of Enosh, Seth lived 807 years and had other sons and daughters. 8Altogether, Seth lived a total of 912 years, and then he died.

9When Enosh had lived 90 years, he became the father of Kenan. 10After he became the father of Kenan, Enosh lived 815 years and had other sons and daughters.

---

a 8 Samaritan Pentateuch, Septuagint, Vulgate and Syriac; Masoretic Text does not have *"Let's go out to the field."*
b 15 Septuagint, Vulgate and Syriac; Hebrew *Very well*   *c 16 Nod* means *wandering* (see verses 12 and 14).
d 22 Or *who instructed all who work in*   *e 25 Seth* probably means *granted.*   *f 26* Or *to proclaim*
g 2 Hebrew *adam*   *h 6 Father* may mean *ancestor;* also in verses 7-26.

11 Altogether, Enosh lived a total of 905 years, and then he died.

12 When Kenan had lived 70 years, he became the father of Mahalalel. 13 After he became the father of Mahalalel, Kenan lived 840 years and had other sons and daughters. 14 Altogether, Kenan lived a total of 910 years, and then he died.

15 When Mahalalel had lived 65 years, he became the father of Jared. 16 After he became the father of Jared, Mahalalel lived 830 years and had other sons and daughters. 17 Altogether, Mahalalel lived a total of 895 years, and then he died.

18 When Jared had lived 162 years, he became the father of Enoch. 19 After he became the father of Enoch, Jared lived 800 years and had other sons and daughters. 20 Altogether, Jared lived a total of 962 years, and then he died.

21 When Enoch had lived 65 years, he became the father of Methuselah. 22 After he became the father of Methuselah, Enoch walked faithfully with God 300 years and had other sons and daughters. 23 Altogether, Enoch lived a total of 365 years. 24 Enoch walked faithfully with God; then he was no more, because God took him away.

25 When Methuselah had lived 187 years, he became the father of Lamech. 26 After he became the father of Lamech, Methuselah lived 782 years and had other sons and daughters. 27 Altogether, Methuselah lived a total of 969 years, and then he died.

28 When Lamech had lived 182 years, he had a son. 29 He named him Noah[a] and said, "He will comfort us in the labor and painful toil of our hands caused by the ground the LORD has cursed." 30 After Noah was born, Lamech lived 595 years and had other sons and daughters. 31 Altogether, Lamech lived a total of 777 years, and then he died.

32 After Noah was 500 years old, he became the father of Shem, Ham and Japheth.

Wickedness in the World

6 When human beings began to increase in number on the earth and daughters were born to them, 2 the sons of God saw that the daughters of humans were beautiful, and they married any of them they chose. 3 Then the LORD said, "My Spirit will not contend with[b] humans forever, for they are mortal[c]; their days will be a hundred and twenty years."

4 The Nephilim were on the earth in those days — and also afterward — when the sons of God went to the daughters of humans and had children by them. They were the heroes of old, men of renown.

5 The LORD saw how great the wickedness of the human race had become on the earth, and that every inclination of the thoughts of the human heart was only evil all the time. 6 The LORD regretted that he had made human beings on the earth, and his heart was deeply troubled. 7 So the LORD said, "I will wipe from the face of the earth the human race I have created — and with them the animals, the birds and the creatures that move along the ground — for I regret that I have made them." 8 But Noah found favor in the eyes of the LORD.

Noah and the Flood

9 This is the account of Noah and his family.

Noah was a righteous man, blameless among the people of his time, and he walked faithfully with God. 10 Noah had three sons: Shem, Ham and Japheth.

11 Now the earth was corrupt in God's sight and was full of violence. 12 God saw how corrupt the earth had become, for all the people on earth had corrupted their ways. 13 So God said to Noah, "I am going to put an end to all people, for the earth is filled with violence because of them. I am surely going to destroy both them and the earth. 14 So make yourself an ark of cypress[d] wood; make rooms in it and coat it

---

a 29 *Noah* sounds like the Hebrew for *comfort*.   b 3 Or *My spirit will not remain in*   c 3 Or *corrupt*
d 14 The meaning of the Hebrew for this word is uncertain.

with pitch inside and out. ¹⁵This is how you are to build it: The ark is to be three hundred cubits long, fifty cubits wide and thirty cubits high.ᵃ ¹⁶Make a roof for it, leaving below the roof an opening one cubitᵇ high all around.ᶜ Put a door in the side of the ark and make lower, middle and upper decks. ¹⁷I am going to bring floodwaters on the earth to destroy all life under the heavens, every creature that has the breath of life in it. Everything on earth will perish. ¹⁸But I will establish my covenant with you, and you will enter the ark — you and your sons and your wife and your sons' wives with you. ¹⁹You are to bring into the ark two of all living creatures, male and female, to keep them alive with you. ²⁰Two of every kind of bird, of every kind of animal and of every kind of creature that moves along the ground will come to you to be kept alive. ²¹You are to take every kind of food that is to be eaten and store it away as food for you and for them."

²²Noah did everything just as God commanded him.

7 The LORD then said to Noah, "Go into the ark, you and your whole family, because I have found you righteous in this generation. ²Take with you seven pairs of every kind of clean animal, a male and its mate, and one pair of every kind of unclean animal, a male and its mate, ³and also seven pairs of every kind of bird, male and female, to keep their various kinds alive throughout the earth. ⁴Seven days from now I will send rain on the earth for forty days and forty nights, and I will wipe from the face of the earth every living creature I have made."

⁵And Noah did all that the LORD commanded him.

⁶Noah was six hundred years old when the floodwaters came on the earth. ⁷And Noah and his sons and his wife and his sons' wives entered the ark to escape the waters of the flood. ⁸Pairs of clean and unclean animals, of birds and of all creatures that move along the ground, ⁹male and female, came to Noah and entered the ark, as God had commanded Noah. ¹⁰And after the seven days the floodwaters came on the earth.

¹¹In the six hundredth year of Noah's life, on the seventeenth day of the second month — on that day all the springs of the great deep burst forth, and the floodgates of the heavens were opened. ¹²And rain fell on the earth forty days and forty nights.

¹³On that very day Noah and his sons, Shem, Ham and Japheth, together with his wife and the wives of his three sons, entered the ark. ¹⁴They had with them every wild animal according to its kind, all livestock according to their kinds, every creature that moves along the ground according to its kind and every bird according to its kind, everything with wings. ¹⁵Pairs of all creatures that have the breath of life in them came to Noah and entered the ark. ¹⁶The animals going in were male and female of every living thing, as God had commanded Noah. Then the LORD shut him in.

¹⁷For forty days the flood kept coming on the earth, and as the waters increased they lifted the ark high above the earth. ¹⁸The waters rose and increased greatly on the earth, and the ark floated on the surface of the water. ¹⁹They rose greatly on the earth, and all the high mountains under the entire heavens were covered. ²⁰The waters rose and covered the mountains to a depth of more than fifteen cubits.ᵈ,ᵉ ²¹Every living thing that moved on land perished — birds, livestock, wild animals, all the creatures that swarm over the earth, and all mankind. ²²Everything on dry land that had the breath of life in its nostrils died. ²³Every living thing on the face of the earth was wiped out; people and

---

ᵃ 15 That is, about 450 feet long, 75 feet wide and 45 feet high or about 135 meters long, 23 meters wide and 14 meters high   ᵇ 16 That is, about 18 inches or about 45 centimeters   ᶜ 16 The meaning of the Hebrew for this clause is uncertain.   ᵈ 20 That is, about 23 feet or about 6.8 meters   ᵉ 20 Or *rose more than fifteen cubits, and the mountains were covered* animals and the creatures that move along the ground and the birds were wiped from the earth. Only Noah was left, and those with him in the ark.

²⁴The waters flooded the earth for a hundred and fifty days.

8 But God remembered Noah and all the wild animals and the livestock that were with him in the ark, and he sent a wind over the earth, and the waters receded. ²Now the springs of the deep and the floodgates of the heavens had been closed, and the rain had stopped falling from the sky. ³The water receded steadily from the earth. At the end of the hundred and fifty days the water had gone down, ⁴and on the seventeenth day of the seventh month the ark came to rest on the mountains of Ararat. ⁵The waters continued to recede until the tenth month, and on the first day of the tenth month the tops of the mountains became visible.

⁶After forty days Noah opened a window he had made in the ark ⁷and sent out a raven, and it kept flying back and forth until the water had dried up from the earth. ⁸Then he sent out a dove to see if the water had receded from the surface of the ground. ⁹But the dove could find nowhere to perch because there was water over all the surface of the earth; so it returned to Noah in the ark. He reached out his hand and took the dove and brought it back to himself in the ark. ¹⁰He waited seven more days and again sent out the dove from the ark. ¹¹When the dove returned to him in the evening, there in its beak was a freshly plucked olive leaf! Then Noah knew that the water had receded from the earth. ¹²He waited seven more days and sent the dove out again, but this time it did not return to him.

¹³By the first day of the first month of Noah's six hundred and first year, the water had dried up from the earth. Noah then removed the covering from the ark and saw that the surface of the ground was dry.

¹⁴By the twenty-seventh day of the second month the earth was completely dry.

¹⁵Then God said to Noah, ¹⁶"Come out of the ark, you and your wife and your sons and their wives. ¹⁷Bring out every kind of living creature that is with you—the birds, the animals, and all the creatures that move along the ground—so they can multiply on the earth and be fruitful and increase in number on it."

¹⁸So Noah came out, together with his sons and his wife and his sons' wives. ¹⁹All the animals and all the creatures that move along the ground and all the birds—everything that moves on land—came out of the ark, one kind after another.

²⁰Then Noah built an altar to the LORD and, taking some of all the clean animals and clean birds, he sacrificed burnt offerings on it. ²¹The LORD smelled the pleasing aroma and said in his heart: "Never again will I curse the ground because of humans, even thoughᵃ every inclination of the human heart is evil from childhood. And never again will I destroy all living creatures, as I have done.

²²"As long as the earth endures,
   seedtime and harvest,
   cold and heat,
   summer and winter,
   day and night
   will never cease."

God's Covenant With Noah

9 Then God blessed Noah and his sons, saying to them, "Be fruitful and increase in number and fill the earth. ²The fear and dread of you will fall on all the beasts of the earth, and on all the birds in the sky, on every creature that moves along the ground, and on all the fish in the sea; they are given into your hands. ³Everything that lives and moves about will be food for you. Just as I gave you the green plants, I now give you everything.

⁴"But you must not eat meat that has its lifeblood still in it. ⁵And for your lifeblood

---

ᵃ 21 Or humans, for

I will surely demand an accounting. I will demand an accounting from every animal. And from each human being, too, I will demand an accounting for the life of another human being.

6 "Whoever sheds human blood,
    by humans shall their blood be shed;
for in the image of God
    has God made mankind.

7 As for you, be fruitful and increase in number; multiply on the earth and increase upon it."

8 Then God said to Noah and to his sons with him: 9 "I now establish my covenant with you and with your descendants after you 10 and with every living creature that was with you — the birds, the livestock and all the wild animals, all those that came out of the ark with you — every living creature on earth. 11 I establish my covenant with you: Never again will all life be destroyed by the waters of a flood; never again will there be a flood to destroy the earth."

12 And God said, "This is the sign of the covenant I am making between me and you and every living creature with you, a covenant for all generations to come: 13 I have set my rainbow in the clouds, and it will be the sign of the covenant between me and the earth. 14 Whenever I bring clouds over the earth and the rainbow appears in the clouds, 15 I will remember my covenant between me and you and all living creatures of every kind. Never again will the waters become a flood to destroy all life. 16 Whenever the rainbow appears in the clouds, I will see it and remember the everlasting covenant between God and all living creatures of every kind on the earth."

17 So God said to Noah, "This is the sign of the covenant I have established between me and all life on the earth."

The Sons of Noah

18 The sons of Noah who came out of the ark were Shem, Ham and Japheth. (Ham was the father of Canaan.) 19 These were the three sons of Noah, and from them came the people who were scattered over the whole earth.

20 Noah, a man of the soil, proceeded[a] to plant a vineyard. 21 When he drank some of its wine, he became drunk and lay uncovered inside his tent. 22 Ham, the father of Canaan, saw his father naked and told his two brothers outside. 23 But Shem and Japheth took a garment and laid it across their shoulders; then they walked in backward and covered their father's naked body. Their faces were turned the other way so that they would not see their father naked.

24 When Noah awoke from his wine and found out what his youngest son had done to him, 25 he said,

"Cursed be Canaan!
    The lowest of slaves
    will he be to his brothers."

26 He also said,

"Praise be to the Lord, the God of
        Shem!
    May Canaan be the slave of Shem.
27 May God extend Japheth's[b] territory;
    may Japheth live in the tents of Shem,
    and may Canaan be the slave of
        Japheth."

28 After the flood Noah lived 350 years. 29 Noah lived a total of 950 years, and then he died.

The Table of Nations

10 This is the account of Shem, Ham and Japheth, Noah's sons, who themselves had sons after the flood.

The Japhethites

2 The sons[c] of Japheth:
    Gomer, Magog, Madai, Javan, Tubal, Meshek and Tiras.

---

a 20 Or soil, was the first   b 27 Japheth sounds like the Hebrew for extend.   c 2 Sons may mean descendants or successors or nations; also in verses 3, 4, 6, 7, 20-23, 29 and 31.

³The sons of Gomer:
　Ashkenaz, Riphath and Togarmah.
⁴The sons of Javan:
　Elishah, Tarshish, the Kittites and
　the Rodanites.ᵃ ⁵(From these the
　maritime peoples spread out into
　their territories by their clans with-
　in their nations, each with its own
　language.)

The Hamites

⁶The sons of Ham:
　Cush, Egypt, Put and Canaan.
⁷The sons of Cush:
　Seba, Havilah, Sabtah, Raamah and
　Sabteka.
　The sons of Raamah:
　Sheba and Dedan.

⁸Cush was the fatherᵇ of Nimrod, who became a mighty warrior on the earth. ⁹He was a mighty hunter before the LORD; that is why it is said, "Like Nimrod, a mighty hunter before the LORD." ¹⁰The first centers of his kingdom were Babylon, Uruk, Akkad and Kalneh, inᶜ Shinar.ᵈ ¹¹From that land he went to Assyria, where he built Nineveh, Rehoboth Ir,ᵉ Calah ¹²and Resen, which is between Nineveh and Calah — which is the great city.

¹³Egypt was the father of
　the Ludites, Anamites, Lehabites,
　Naphtuhites, ¹⁴Pathrusites, Kaslu-
　hites (from whom the Philistines
　came) and Caphtorites.
¹⁵Canaan was the father of
　Sidon his firstborn,ᶠ and of the Hit-
　tites, ¹⁶Jebusites, Amorites, Girga-
　shites, ¹⁷Hivites, Arkites, Sinites,
　¹⁸Arvadites, Zemarites and Ha-
　mathites.

Later the Canaanite clans scattered ¹⁹and the borders of Canaan reached from Sidon toward Gerar as far as Gaza, and then toward Sodom, Gomorrah, Admah and Zeboyim, as far as Lasha.

²⁰These are the sons of Ham by their clans and languages, in their territories and nations.

The Semites

²¹Sons were also born to Shem, whose older brother wasᵍ Japheth; Shem was the ancestor of all the sons of Eber.

²²The sons of Shem:
　Elam, Ashur, Arphaxad, Lud and
　Aram.
²³The sons of Aram:
　Uz, Hul, Gether and Meshek.ʰ
²⁴Arphaxad was the father ofⁱ Shelah,
　and Shelah the father of Eber.
²⁵Two sons were born to Eber:
　One was named Peleg,ʲ because in
　his time the earth was divided; his
　brother was named Joktan.
²⁶Joktan was the father of
　Almodad, Sheleph, Hazarmaveth,
　Jerah, ²⁷Hadoram, Uzal, Diklah,
　²⁸Obal, Abimael, Sheba, ²⁹Ophir,
　Havilah and Jobab. All these were
　sons of Joktan.

³⁰The region where they lived stretched from Mesha toward Sephar, in the eastern hill country.

³¹These are the sons of Shem by their clans and languages, in their territories and nations.

³²These are the clans of Noah's sons, according to their lines of descent, within their nations. From these the nations spread out over the earth after the flood.

The Tower of Babel

11 Now the whole world had one language and a common speech. ²As people moved eastward,ᵏ

ᵃ 4 Some manuscripts of the Masoretic Text and Samaritan Pentateuch (see also Septuagint and 1 Chron. 1:7); most manuscripts of the Masoretic Text *Dodanim* ᵇ 8 *Father* may mean *ancestor* or *predecessor* or *founder*; also in verses 13, 15, 24 and 26. ᶜ 10 Or *Uruk and Akkad — all of them in* ᵈ 10 That is, Babylonia ᵉ 11 Or *Nineveh with its city squares* ᶠ 15 Or *of the Sidonians, the foremost* ᵍ 21 Or *Shem, the older brother of* ʰ 23 See Septuagint and 1 Chron. 1:17; Hebrew *Mash.* ⁱ 24 Hebrew; Septuagint *father of Cainan, and Cainan was the father of* ʲ 25 *Peleg* means *division.* ᵏ 2 Or *from the east*; or *in the east* they found a plain in Shinar[a] and settled there.

³They said to each other, "Come, let's make bricks and bake them thoroughly." They used brick instead of stone, and tar for mortar. ⁴Then they said, "Come, let us build ourselves a city, with a tower that reaches to the heavens, so that we may make a name for ourselves; otherwise we will be scattered over the face of the whole earth."

⁵But the LORD came down to see the city and the tower the people were building. ⁶The LORD said, "If as one people speaking the same language they have begun to do this, then nothing they plan to do will be impossible for them. ⁷Come, let us go down and confuse their language so they will not understand each other."

⁸So the LORD scattered them from there over all the earth, and they stopped building the city. ⁹That is why it was called Babel[b] — because there the LORD confused the language of the whole world. From there the LORD scattered them over the face of the whole earth.

From Shem to Abram

¹⁰This is the account of Shem's family line.

Two years after the flood, when Shem was 100 years old, he became the father[c] of Arphaxad. ¹¹And after he became the father of Arphaxad, Shem lived 500 years and had other sons and daughters.

¹²When Arphaxad had lived 35 years, he became the father of Shelah. ¹³And after he became the father of Shelah, Arphaxad lived 403 years and had other sons and daughters.[d]

¹⁴When Shelah had lived 30 years, he became the father of Eber. ¹⁵And after he became the father of Eber, Shelah lived 403 years and had other sons and daughters.

¹⁶When Eber had lived 34 years, he became the father of Peleg. ¹⁷And after he became the father of Peleg, Eber lived 430 years and had other sons and daughters.

¹⁸When Peleg had lived 30 years, he became the father of Reu. ¹⁹And after he became the father of Reu, Peleg lived 209 years and had other sons and daughters.

²⁰When Reu had lived 32 years, he became the father of Serug. ²¹And after he became the father of Serug, Reu lived 207 years and had other sons and daughters.

²²When Serug had lived 30 years, he became the father of Nahor. ²³And after he became the father of Nahor, Serug lived 200 years and had other sons and daughters.

²⁴When Nahor had lived 29 years, he became the father of Terah. ²⁵And after he became the father of Terah, Nahor lived 119 years and had other sons and daughters.

²⁶After Terah had lived 70 years, he became the father of Abram, Nahor and Haran.

Abram's Family

²⁷This is the account of Terah's family line.

Terah became the father of Abram, Nahor and Haran. And Haran became the father of Lot. ²⁸While his father Terah was still alive, Haran died in Ur of the Chaldeans, in the land of his birth. ²⁹Abram and Nahor both married. The name of Abram's wife was Sarai, and the name of Nahor's wife was Milkah; she was the daughter of Haran, the father of both Milkah and Iskah. ³⁰Now Sarai was childless because she was not able to conceive.

³¹Terah took his son Abram, his grandson Lot son of Haran, and his daughter-in-law Sarai, the wife of his son Abram, and together they set out from Ur of the Chaldeans to go to Canaan. But when they came to Harran, they settled there.

---

a 2 That is, Babylonia   *b 9* That is, Babylon; *Babel* sounds like the Hebrew for *confused.*   *c 10 Father* may mean *ancestor;* also in verses 11-25.   *d 12,13* Hebrew; Septuagint (see also Luke 3:35, 36 and note at Gen. 10:24) *35 years, he became the father of Cainan. 13And after he became the father of Cainan, Arphaxad lived 430 years and had other sons and daughters, and then he died. When Cainan had lived 130 years, he became the father of Shelah. And after he became the father of Shelah, Cainan lived 330 years and had other sons and daughters*

32Terah lived 205 years, and he died in Harran.

The Call of Abram

12 The LORD had said to Abram, "Go from your country, your people and your father's household to the land I will show you.

2 "I will make you into a great nation,
    and I will bless you;
I will make your name great,
    and you will be a blessing.*a*
3 I will bless those who bless you,
    and whoever curses you I will curse;
and all peoples on earth
    will be blessed through you."*b*

4So Abram went, as the LORD had told him; and Lot went with him. Abram was seventy-five years old when he set out from Harran. 5He took his wife Sarai, his nephew Lot, all the possessions they had accumulated and the people they had acquired in Harran, and they set out for the land of Canaan, and they arrived there.

6Abram traveled through the land as far as the site of the great tree of Moreh at Shechem. At that time the Canaanites were in the land. 7The LORD appeared to Abram and said, "To your offspring*c* I will give this land." So he built an altar there to the LORD, who had appeared to him.

8From there he went on toward the hills east of Bethel and pitched his tent, with Bethel on the west and Ai on the east. There he built an altar to the LORD and called on the name of the LORD.

9Then Abram set out and continued toward the Negev.

Abram in Egypt

10Now there was a famine in the land, and Abram went down to Egypt to live there for a while because the famine was severe. 11As he was about to enter Egypt, he said to his wife Sarai, "I know what a beautiful woman you are. 12When the Egyptians see you, they will say, 'This is his wife.' Then they will kill me but will let you live. 13Say you are my sister, so that I will be treated well for your sake and my life will be spared because of you."

14When Abram came to Egypt, the Egyptians saw that Sarai was a very beautiful woman. 15And when Pharaoh's officials saw her, they praised her to Pharaoh, and she was taken into his palace. 16He treated Abram well for her sake, and Abram acquired sheep and cattle, male and female donkeys, male and female servants, and camels.

17But the LORD inflicted serious diseases on Pharaoh and his household because of Abram's wife Sarai. 18So Pharaoh summoned Abram. "What have you done to me?" he said. "Why didn't you tell me she was your wife? 19Why did you say, 'She is my sister,' so that I took her to be my wife? Now then, here is your wife. Take her and go!" 20Then Pharaoh gave orders about Abram to his men, and they sent him on his way, with his wife and everything he had.

Abram and Lot Separate

13 So Abram went up from Egypt to the Negev, with his wife and everything he had, and Lot went with him. 2Abram had become very wealthy in livestock and in silver and gold.

3From the Negev he went from place to place until he came to Bethel, to the place between Bethel and Ai where his tent had been earlier 4and where he had first built an altar. There Abram called on the name of the LORD.

5Now Lot, who was moving about with Abram, also had flocks and herds and tents. 6But the land could not support them while they stayed together, for their possessions were so great that they were not able to stay together. 7And quarreling arose between Abram's herders and Lot's. The Canaanites and Perizzites were also living in the land at that time.

---

a 2 Or *be seen as blessed*   *b 3* Or *earth / will use your name in blessings* (see 48:20)   *c 7* Or *seed*

My Name Is Carl

I'M A BELIEVER WHO STRUGGLES WITH FEAR, SEXUAL ADDICTION AND ALCOHOLISM

Please read the story of Abram's fear-based deception of Pharaoh, as well as of God's future blessings, in Genesis 12:10 — 13:2.

I've spent most of my life hampered by feelings of insecurity, worthlessness, panic, anxiety and downright terror.

I was raised in the 1950s by an alcoholic father and a controlling mother. There was no physical abuse, but my parents used rage and fear to intimidate me into submission. When I was six years old, my family was returning home one evening from visiting my grandparents when I offered a stick of gum to one of my siblings. Dad, immediately realizing that I'd stolen the gum from my grandparents, confronted me. I admitted my transgression, fully expecting a spanking when we got home. Instead, Dad pulled over and asked curtly, "Do you know what happens to thieves?" I responded in the negative, and he replied, "They go to prison." He pointed to a dark, scary building we were just passing and informed me that this was the very prison where I'd be staying for the next 20 years. He instructed me to hand over all of my possessions and beg God for his forgiveness. My brother, sisters and I were all screaming in fear. My spirit was broken. After that harrowing experience I gradually learned to anticipate my parents' moods and to feed them the appropriate responses. Instead of becoming resentful, I tried all the harder to please them. I craved love and affection but felt absolutely unworthy.

My experiences were reinforced by my religious upbringing. Salvation, according my parents' theology, was based on an impossible-to-achieve degree of perfection. I truly thought that if I committed a mortal sin and died without confessing it, God would send me to hell for all eternity. I learned to put on a mask of piety, while inside I was consumed by terror and guilt. As my faith was pushed aside by my fears, I was left to my own strategies to establish some semblance of security.

I was married for 19 years before divorcing. My wife and I fought often; after token resistance, my pattern was to feel guilty and give in. We were miserable, but, afraid of losing her, I started going to prostitutes and was eventually found out. After the divorce I decided to live for myself, without regard for anyone else's approval. The illusion of control brought a measure of comfort. I partied for the next four years, but the price tag was steep. I became addicted to prostitution, pornography and alcohol, and began experimenting with drugs. But no matter what I did I couldn't escape the childlike fear that still gripped me. I began working as a bouncer at a local bar, smuggled steroids across the border for my personal use, took karate and got tattooed. Gradually I came to realize, though, that I had simply traded in one form of bondage for another.

At this point God reached out to me. I began attending church and for the first time in my life heard who Jesus really is. I'd been taught that he was a victim; only now did I learn that he'd *chosen* to die, and that he'd done it for me!

It took a DUI to get me into recovery. Pastor Rick Warren began a series of sermons on recovery, and the following Friday the Lord introduced me to Celebrate Recovery. I knew right away that I had found my promised land. No one there enabled, judged or attempted to fix me. Instead, they offered me the one thing I'd always craved: unconditional love. I can relate to Abram and am especially amazed at how graciously, in spite of Abram's failure, God increased his wealth. After Abram was forced out of his denial, he began a journey of recovery.

As time passed, I was blessed with the complete restoration of my relationship with my parents. I shared Christ with my mom, and God gave me the words and the loving heart to meet her where she was. She accepted the Lord, as did my dad shortly thereafter. One month later Dad went home to be with Christ.

Like Abram, I went from being a man of fear to becoming a man of faith. The Lord did for me what I could never have done for myself: He loved me enough to empower me with the gift that was to transform my life. He enabled me to choose not to be held hostage to my feelings, but instead to live by faith, despite my feelings. God regularly helps me combat the old lies through the study of Biblical truth.

Today I'm celebrating 15 years of sobriety. I'm so grateful to the Lord for the principles and steps of Celebrate Recovery, as well as for my accountability partners. His power and unconditional love have endowed me with a passion to be used by him to serve others, which I do especially as a co-leader of the Adult Children of Alcoholics group and as an encourager-coach for the Men's Recovery groups.

As 1 John 4:18 so aptly reminds me, "There is no fear in love. But perfect love drives out fear."

Carl

⑥ ⁸So Abram said to Lot, "Let's not have any quarreling between you and me, or between your herders and mine, for we are close relatives. ⁹Is not the whole land before you? Let's part company. If you go to the left, I'll go to the right; if you go to the right, I'll go to the left."

¹⁰Lot looked around and saw that the whole plain of the Jordan toward Zoar was well watered, like the garden of the Lᴏʀᴅ, like the land of Egypt. (This was before the Lᴏʀᴅ destroyed Sodom and Gomorrah.) ¹¹So Lot chose for himself the whole plain of the Jordan and set out toward the east. The two men parted company: ¹²Abram lived in the land of Canaan, while Lot lived among the cities of the plain and pitched his tents near Sodom. ¹³Now the people of Sodom were wicked and were sinning greatly against the Lᴏʀᴅ.

¹⁴The Lᴏʀᴅ said to Abram after Lot had parted from him, "Look around from where you are, to the north and south, to the east and west. ¹⁵All the land that you see I will give to you and your offspringᵃ forever. ¹⁶I will make your offspring like the dust of the earth, so that if anyone could count the dust, then your offspring could be counted. ¹⁷Go, walk through the length and breadth of the land, for I am giving it to you."

¹⁸So Abram went to live near the great trees of Mamre at Hebron, where he pitched his tents. There he built an altar to the Lᴏʀᴅ.

Abram Rescues Lot

14 At the time when Amraphel was king of Shinar,ᵇ Arioch king of Ellasar, Kedorlaomer king of Elam and Tidal king of Goyim, ²these kings went to war against Bera king of Sodom, Birsha king of Gomorrah, Shinab king of Admah, Shemeber king of Zeboyim, and the king of Bela (that is, Zoar). ³All these latter kings joined forces in the Valley of Siddim (that is, the Dead Sea Valley). ⁴For twelve years they had been subject to Kedorlaomer, but in the thirteenth year they rebelled.

⁵In the fourteenth year, Kedorlaomer and the kings allied with him went out and defeated the Rephaites in Ashteroth Karnaim, the Zuzites in Ham, the Emites in Shaveh Kiriathaim ⁶and the Horites in the hill country of Seir, as far as El Paran near the desert. ⁷Then they turned back and went to En Mishpat (that is, Kadesh), and they conquered the whole territory of the Amalekites, as well as the Amorites who were living in Hazezon Tamar.

⁸Then the king of Sodom, the king of Gomorrah, the king of Admah, the king of Zeboyim and the king of Bela (that is, Zoar) marched out and drew up their battle lines in the Valley of Siddim ⁹against Kedorlaomer king of Elam, Tidal king of Goyim, Amraphel king of Shinar and Arioch king of Ellasar—four kings against five. ¹⁰Now the Valley of Siddim was full of tar pits, and when the kings of Sodom and Gomorrah fled, some of the men fell into them and the rest fled to the hills. ¹¹The four kings seized all the goods of Sodom and Gomorrah and all their food; then they went away. ¹²They also carried off Abram's nephew Lot and his possessions, since he was living in Sodom.

¹³A man who had escaped came and reported this to Abram the Hebrew. Now Abram was living near the great trees of Mamre the Amorite, a brotherᶜ of Eshkol and Aner, all of whom were allied with Abram. ¹⁴When Abram heard that his relative had been taken captive, he called out the 318 trained men born in his household and went in pursuit as far as Dan. ¹⁵During the night Abram divided his men to attack them and he routed them, pursuing them as far as Hobah, north of Damascus. ¹⁶He recovered all the goods and brought back his relative Lot and his possessions, together with the women and the other people.

¹⁷After Abram returned from defeating

ᵃ 15 Or seed; also in verse 16   ᵇ 1 That is, Babylonia; also in verse 9   ᶜ 13 Or a relative; or an ally

MY NAME IS ABRAM

GENESIS 12:10 — 13:18

Abram (whose name was later changed to Abraham) is elsewhere in the Bible identified as "the man of faith" (Galatians 3:9). The first nine verses of Genesis 12 provide powerful validation of Abram's great faith. Despite this, Abram knew fear and anxiety. When faith is shoved aside by fear, we're left to our own strategies for establishing a sense of security. Famine sent Abram on a journey to Egypt. As he approached the land of Pharaoh, he devised a deception that required his wife, Sarai, to lie. Abram was willing to surrender his wife to Pharaoh in a ploy to save his own life.

For a time the illusion of control brought comfort. Abram's scheme seemed to be working. In fact, he grew wealthier on account of Pharaoh's delight in Sarai (see Genesis 12:16). But God, who had great plans for Abram, brought Abram's secrets into the light (see vv. 17 – 18). Pharaoh confronted Abram with the predictable results of his trickery and sent him packing (see vv. 19 – 20). Abram, "the man of faith," was rightly rebuked by a pagan king.

Our fears can crowd out our faith during times of testing. And some people live with a generalized sense of fear all the time. A pervasive cloud of anxiety hovers around them, and their fear is a continuous emotional state, independent of any clear threat. Like Abram, we're tempted to grasp for more and more control over our circumstances. This lust for power often leads people to manipulate those they love, including family members and friends. But controlling behavior leaves no room for faith to operate.

Control over our world is ultimately an illusion. Only God is big enough to manage our circumstances. God loved Abram, and he loves us, too much to let us live lives of delusion. At some point our schemes inevitably fall apart and our secrets are exposed. Abram experienced a painful, public exposure of his lies. Out of this mess came a message: Relinquish the reins to God.

Upon his return to the promised land, Abram faced a pressing, practical problem. He and Lot had grown so wealthy in herds that they could no longer occupy the same area of grazing land (see 13:5 – 7). God had deeded all of Canaan to Abram. But Abram was now ready to trust God completely. Although Abram had every right to determine which area would be apportioned to Lot, he allowed his nephew to choose. Not surprisingly, Lot selected the best for himself.

Faith that is tested and proven provides a fresh perspective on God's goodness. Abram, willing to trust God in this new dilemma, received a fresh revelation: God assured him that all of the promised land remained in his possession (see 13:14 – 17).

Abram's exercise of faith in this situation had its roots in his renewed worship of God (see 13:3 – 4). God, not Abram or even Pharaoh, was in charge in Egypt. Forced out of his denial, Abram began a journey of recovery that took him "from place to place until he came to Bethel" (13:3) — meaning "house of God." Significantly, this was the precise location at which Abram "had first built an altar" (13:4).

Overcoming fear isn't about finding a new faith. Freedom from fear is exercising faith in the same God we've trusted all along but applying it to new situations. Significantly, Abram returned to Bethel and "called on the name of the LORD" (13:4).

Kedorlaomer and the kings allied with him, the king of Sodom came out to meet him in the Valley of Shaveh (that is, the King's Valley).

18 Then Melchizedek king of Salem brought out bread and wine. He was priest of God Most High, 19 and he blessed Abram, saying,

"Blessed be Abram by God Most High,
    Creator of heaven and earth.
20 And praise be to God Most High,
    who delivered your enemies into
        your hand."

Then Abram gave him a tenth of everything.

21 The king of Sodom said to Abram, "Give me the people and keep the goods for yourself."

22 But Abram said to the king of Sodom, "With raised hand I have sworn an oath to the LORD, God Most High, Creator of heaven and earth, 23 that I will accept nothing belonging to you, not even a thread or the strap of a sandal, so that you will never be able to say, 'I made Abram rich.' 24 I will accept nothing but what my men have eaten and the share that belongs to the men who went with me — to Aner, Eshkol and Mamre. Let them have their share."

The LORD's Covenant With Abram

15 After this, the word of the LORD came to Abram in a vision:

"Do not be afraid, Abram.
    I am your shield,*a*
    your very great reward.*b*"

2 But Abram said, "Sovereign LORD, what can you give me since I remain childless and the one who will inherit*c* my estate is Eliezer of Damascus?" 3 And Abram said, "You have given me no children; so a servant in my household will be my heir." 4 Then the word of the LORD came to him: "This man will not be your heir, but a son who is your own flesh and blood will be your heir." 5 He took him outside and said, "Look up at the sky and count the stars — if indeed you can count them." Then he said to him, "So shall your offspring*d* be."

6 Abram believed the LORD, and he credited it to him as righteousness.

7 He also said to him, "I am the LORD, who brought you out of Ur of the Chaldeans to give you this land to take possession of it."

8 But Abram said, "Sovereign LORD, how can I know that I will gain possession of it?"

9 So the LORD said to him, "Bring me a heifer, a goat and a ram, each three years old, along with a dove and a young pigeon."

10 Abram brought all these to him, cut them in two and arranged the halves opposite each other; the birds, however, he did not cut in half. 11 Then birds of prey came down on the carcasses, but Abram drove them away.

12 As the sun was setting, Abram fell into a deep sleep, and a thick and dreadful darkness came over him. 13 Then the LORD said to him, "Know for certain that for four hundred years your descendants will be strangers in a country not their own and that they will be enslaved and mistreated there. 14 But I will punish the nation they serve as slaves, and afterward they will come out with great possessions. 15 You, however, will go to your ancestors in peace and be buried at a good old age. 16 In the fourth generation your descendants will come back here, for the sin of the Amorites has not yet reached its full measure."

17 When the sun had set and darkness had fallen, a smoking firepot with a blazing torch appeared and passed between the pieces. 18 On that day the LORD made a covenant with Abram and said, "To your descendants I give this land, from the Wadi*e* of Egypt to the great river, the Euphrates — 19 the land of the Kenites, Kenizzites, Kadmonites, 20 Hittites, Perizzites, Rephaites,

---

a 1 Or *sovereign*   *b 1* Or *shield; / your reward will be very great*   *c 2* The meaning of the Hebrew for this phrase is uncertain.   *d 5* Or *seed*   *e 18* Or *river*

21Amorites, Canaanites, Girgashites and Jebusites."

Hagar and Ishmael

16 Now Sarai, Abram's wife, had borne him no children. But she had an Egyptian slave named Hagar; 2so she said to Abram, "The LORD has kept me from having children. Go, sleep with my slave; perhaps I can build a family through her."

Abram agreed to what Sarai said. 3So after Abram had been living in Canaan ten years, Sarai his wife took her Egyptian slave Hagar and gave her to her husband to be his wife. 4He slept with Hagar, and she conceived.

When she knew she was pregnant, she began to despise her mistress. 5Then Sarai said to Abram, "You are responsible for the wrong I am suffering. I put my slave in your arms, and now that she knows she is pregnant, she despises me. May the LORD judge between you and me."

6"Your slave is in your hands," Abram said. "Do with her whatever you think best." Then Sarai mistreated Hagar; so she fled from her.

7The angel of the LORD found Hagar near a spring in the desert; it was the spring that is beside the road to Shur. 8And he said, "Hagar, slave of Sarai, where have you come from, and where are you going?"

"I'm running away from my mistress Sarai," she answered.

9Then the angel of the LORD told her, "Go back to your mistress and submit to her." 10The angel added, "I will increase your descendants so much that they will be too numerous to count."

11The angel of the LORD also said to her:

"You are now pregnant
and you will give birth to a son.
You shall name him Ishmael,[a]
for the LORD has heard of your
misery.

12He will be a wild donkey of a man;
his hand will be against everyone
and everyone's hand against him,
and he will live in hostility
toward[b] all his brothers."

13She gave this name to the LORD who spoke to her: "You are the God who sees me," for she said, "I have now seen[c] the One who sees me." 14That is why the well was called Beer Lahai Roi[d]; it is still there, between Kadesh and Bered.

15So Hagar bore Abram a son, and Abram gave the name Ishmael to the son she had borne. 16Abram was eighty-six years old when Hagar bore him Ishmael.

The Covenant of Circumcision

17 When Abram was ninety-nine years old, the LORD appeared to him and said, "I am God Almighty[e]; walk before me faithfully and be blameless. 2Then I will make my covenant between me and you and will greatly increase your numbers."

3Abram fell facedown, and God said to him, 4"As for me, this is my covenant with you: You will be the father of many nations. 5No longer will you be called Abram[f]; your name will be Abraham,[g] for I have made you a father of many nations. 6I will make you very fruitful; I will make nations of you, and kings will come from you. 7I will establish my covenant as an everlasting covenant between me and you and your descendants after you for the generations to come, to be your God and the God of your descendants after you. 8The whole land of Canaan, where you now reside as a foreigner, I will give as an everlasting possession to you and your descendants after you; and I will be their God."

9Then God said to Abraham, "As for you, you must keep my covenant, you and your descendants after you for the generations to come. 10This is my covenant

---

a 11 *Ishmael* means *God hears.*   b 12 Or *live to the east / of*   c 13 Or *seen the back of*   d 14 *Beer Lahai Roi* means *well of the Living One who sees me.*   e 1 Hebrew *El-Shaddai*   f 5 *Abram* means *exalted father.*   g 5 *Abraham* probably means *father of many.*

with you and your descendants after you, the covenant you are to keep: Every male among you shall be circumcised. [11]You are to undergo circumcision, and it will be the sign of the covenant between me and you. [12]For the generations to come every male among you who is eight days old must be circumcised, including those born in your household or bought with money from a foreigner — those who are not your offspring. [13]Whether born in your household or bought with your money, they must be circumcised. My covenant in your flesh is to be an everlasting covenant. [14]Any uncircumcised male, who has not been circumcised in the flesh, will be cut off from his people; he has broken my covenant."

[15]God also said to Abraham, "As for Sarai your wife, you are no longer to call her Sarai; her name will be Sarah. [16]I will bless her and will surely give you a son by her. I will bless her so that she will be the mother of nations; kings of peoples will come from her."

[17]Abraham fell facedown; he laughed and said to himself, "Will a son be born to a man a hundred years old? Will Sarah bear a child at the age of ninety?" [18]And Abraham said to God, "If only Ishmael might live under your blessing!"

[19]Then God said, "Yes, but your wife Sarah will bear you a son, and you will call him Isaac.[a] I will establish my covenant with him as an everlasting covenant for his descendants after him. [20]And as for Ishmael, I have heard you: I will surely bless him; I will make him fruitful and will greatly increase his numbers. He will be the father of twelve rulers, and I will make him into a great nation. [21]But my covenant I will establish with Isaac, whom Sarah will bear to you by this time next year." [22]When he had finished speaking with Abraham, God went up from him.

[23]On that very day Abraham took his son Ishmael and all those born in his household or bought with his money, every male in his household, and circumcised them, as God told him. [24]Abraham was ninety-nine years old when he was circumcised, [25]and his son Ishmael was thirteen; [26]Abraham and his son Ishmael were both circumcised on that very day. [27]And every male in Abraham's household, including those born in his household or bought from a foreigner, was circumcised with him.

The Three Visitors

18 The LORD appeared to Abraham near the great trees of Mamre while he was sitting at the entrance to his tent in the heat of the day. [2]Abraham looked up and saw three men standing nearby. When he saw them, he hurried from the entrance of his tent to meet them and bowed low to the ground.

[3]He said, "If I have found favor in your eyes, my lord,[b] do not pass your servant by. [4]Let a little water be brought, and then you may all wash your feet and rest under this tree. [5]Let me get you something to eat, so you can be refreshed and then go on your way — now that you have come to your servant."

"Very well," they answered, "do as you say."

[6]So Abraham hurried into the tent to Sarah. "Quick," he said, "get three seahs[c] of the finest flour and knead it and bake some bread."

[7]Then he ran to the herd and selected a choice, tender calf and gave it to a servant, who hurried to prepare it. [8]He then brought some curds and milk and the calf that had been prepared, and set these before them. While they ate, he stood near them under a tree.

[9]"Where is your wife Sarah?" they asked him.

"There, in the tent," he said.

[10]Then one of them said, "I will surely return to you about this time next year, and Sarah your wife will have a son."

Now Sarah was listening at the entrance

---

[a] 19 *Isaac* means *he laughs.*   [b] 3 Or *eyes, Lord*   [c] 6 That is, probably about 36 pounds or about 16 kilograms

to the tent, which was behind him. [11]Abraham and Sarah were already very old, and Sarah was past the age of childbearing. [12]So Sarah laughed to herself as she thought, "After I am worn out and my lord is old, will I now have this pleasure?"

[13]Then the Lord said to Abraham, "Why did Sarah laugh and say, 'Will I really have a child, now that I am old?' [14]Is anything too hard for the Lord? I will return to you at the appointed time next year, and Sarah will have a son."

[15]Sarah was afraid, so she lied and said, "I did not laugh."

But he said, "Yes, you did laugh."

Abraham Pleads for Sodom

[16]When the men got up to leave, they looked down toward Sodom, and Abraham walked along with them to see them on their way. [17]Then the Lord said, "Shall I hide from Abraham what I am about to do? [18]Abraham will surely become a great and powerful nation, and all nations on earth will be blessed through him.[a] [19]For I have chosen him, so that he will direct his children and his household after him to keep the way of the Lord by doing what is right and just, so that the Lord will bring about for Abraham what he has promised him."

[20]Then the Lord said, "The outcry against Sodom and Gomorrah is so great and their sin so grievous [21]that I will go down and see if what they have done is as bad as the outcry that has reached me. If not, I will know."

[22]The men turned away and went toward Sodom, but Abraham remained standing before the Lord.[b] [23]Then Abraham approached him and said: "Will you sweep away the righteous with the wicked? [24]What if there are fifty righteous people in the city? Will you really sweep it away and not spare[c] the place for the sake of the fifty righteous people in it? [25]Far be it from you to do such a thing—to kill the righteous with the wicked, treating the righteous and the wicked alike. Far be it from you! Will not the Judge of all the earth do right?"

[26]The Lord said, "If I find fifty righteous people in the city of Sodom, I will spare the whole place for their sake."

[27]Then Abraham spoke up again: "Now that I have been so bold as to speak to the Lord, though I am nothing but dust and ashes, [28]what if the number of the righteous is five less than fifty? Will you destroy the whole city for lack of five people?"

"If I find forty-five there," he said, "I will not destroy it."

[29]Once again he spoke to him, "What if only forty are found there?"

He said, "For the sake of forty, I will not do it."

[30]Then he said, "May the Lord not be angry, but let me speak. What if only thirty can be found there?"

He answered, "I will not do it if I find thirty there."

[31]Abraham said, "Now that I have been so bold as to speak to the Lord, what if only twenty can be found there?"

He said, "For the sake of twenty, I will not destroy it."

[32]Then he said, "May the Lord not be angry, but let me speak just once more. What if only ten can be found there?"

He answered, "For the sake of ten, I will not destroy it."

[33]When the Lord had finished speaking with Abraham, he left, and Abraham returned home.

Sodom and Gomorrah Destroyed

19 The two angels arrived at Sodom in the evening, and Lot was sitting in the gateway of the city. When he saw them, he got up to meet them and bowed down with his face to the ground. [2]"My lords," he said, "please turn aside to your servant's house. You can wash your feet and spend the night and then go on your way early in the morning."

---

[a] 18 Or will use his name in blessings (see 48:20)   [b] 22 Masoretic Text; an ancient Hebrew scribal tradition but the Lord remained standing before Abraham   [c] 24 Or forgive; also in verse 26

"No," they answered, "we will spend the night in the square."

³But he insisted so strongly that they did go with him and entered his house. He prepared a meal for them, baking bread without yeast, and they ate. ⁴Before they had gone to bed, all the men from every part of the city of Sodom—both young and old—surrounded the house. ⁵They called to Lot, "Where are the men who came to you tonight? Bring them out to us so that we can have sex with them."

⁶Lot went outside to meet them and shut the door behind him ⁷and said, "No, my friends. Don't do this wicked thing. ⁸Look, I have two daughters who have never slept with a man. Let me bring them out to you, and you can do what you like with them. But don't do anything to these men, for they have come under the protection of my roof."

⁹"Get out of our way," they replied. "This fellow came here as a foreigner, and now he wants to play the judge! We'll treat you worse than them." They kept bringing pressure on Lot and moved forward to break down the door.

¹⁰But the men inside reached out and pulled Lot back into the house and shut the door. ¹¹Then they struck the men who were at the door of the house, young and old, with blindness so that they could not find the door.

¹²The two men said to Lot, "Do you have anyone else here—sons-in-law, sons or daughters, or anyone else in the city who belongs to you? Get them out of here, ¹³because we are going to destroy this place. The outcry to the LORD against its people is so great that he has sent us to destroy it."

¹⁴So Lot went out and spoke to his sons-in-law, who were pledged to marry*ᵃ* his daughters. He said, "Hurry and get out of this place, because the LORD is about to destroy the city!" But his sons-in-law thought he was joking.

¹⁵With the coming of dawn, the angels urged Lot, saying, "Hurry! Take your wife and your two daughters who are here, or you will be swept away when the city is punished."

¹⁶When he hesitated, the men grasped his hand and the hands of his wife and of his two daughters and led them safely out of the city, for the LORD was merciful to them. ¹⁷As soon as they had brought them out, one of them said, "Flee for your lives! Don't look back, and don't stop anywhere in the plain! Flee to the mountains or you will be swept away!"

¹⁸But Lot said to them, "No, my lords,*ᵇ* please! ¹⁹Your*ᶜ* servant has found favor in your*ᶜ* eyes, and you*ᶜ* have shown great kindness to me in sparing my life. But I can't flee to the mountains; this disaster will overtake me, and I'll die. ²⁰Look, here is a town near enough to run to, and it is small. Let me flee to it—it is very small, isn't it? Then my life will be spared."

²¹He said to him, "Very well, I will grant this request too; I will not overthrow the town you speak of. ²²But flee there quickly, because I cannot do anything until you reach it." (That is why the town was called Zoar.*ᵈ*)

²³By the time Lot reached Zoar, the sun had risen over the land. ²⁴Then the LORD rained down burning sulfur on Sodom and Gomorrah—from the LORD out of the heavens. ²⁵Thus he overthrew those cities and the entire plain, destroying all those living in the cities—and also the vegetation in the land. ²⁶But Lot's wife looked back, and she became a pillar of salt.

²⁷Early the next morning Abraham got up and returned to the place where he had stood before the LORD. ²⁸He looked down toward Sodom and Gomorrah, toward all the land of the plain, and he saw dense smoke rising from the land, like smoke from a furnace.

ᵃ 14 Or *were married to*   *ᵇ* 18 Or *No, Lord*; or *No, my lord*   *ᶜ* 19 The Hebrew is singular.   *ᵈ* 22 *Zoar* means *small.*

29So when God destroyed the cities of the plain, he remembered Abraham, and he brought Lot out of the catastrophe that overthrew the cities where Lot had lived.

Lot and His Daughters

30Lot and his two daughters left Zoar and settled in the mountains, for he was afraid to stay in Zoar. He and his two daughters lived in a cave. 31One day the older daughter said to the younger, "Our father is old, and there is no man around here to give us children — as is the custom all over the earth. 32Let's get our father to drink wine and then sleep with him and preserve our family line through our father."

33That night they got their father to drink wine, and the older daughter went in and slept with him. He was not aware of it when she lay down or when she got up.

34The next day the older daughter said to the younger, "Last night I slept with my father. Let's get him to drink wine again tonight, and you go in and sleep with him so we can preserve our family line through our father." 35So they got their father to drink wine that night also, and the younger daughter went in and slept with him. Again he was not aware of it when she lay down or when she got up.

36So both of Lot's daughters became pregnant by their father. 37The older daughter had a son, and she named him Moab*a*; he is the father of the Moabites of today. 38The younger daughter also had a son, and she named him Ben-Ammi*b*; he is the father of the Ammonites*c* of today.

Abraham and Abimelek

20 Now Abraham moved on from there into the region of the Negev and lived between Kadesh and Shur. For a while he stayed in Gerar, 2and there Abraham said of his wife Sarah, "She is my sister." Then Abimelek king of Gerar sent for Sarah and took her.

3But God came to Abimelek in a dream one night and said to him, "You are as good as dead because of the woman you have taken; she is a married woman."

4Now Abimelek had not gone near her, so he said, "Lord, will you destroy an innocent nation? 5Did he not say to me, 'She is my sister,' and didn't she also say, 'He is my brother'? I have done this with a clear conscience and clean hands."

6Then God said to him in the dream, "Yes, I know you did this with a clear conscience, and so I have kept you from sinning against me. That is why I did not let you touch her. 7Now return the man's wife, for he is a prophet, and he will pray for you and you will live. But if you do not return her, you may be sure that you and all who belong to you will die."

8Early the next morning Abimelek summoned all his officials, and when he told them all that had happened, they were very much afraid. 9Then Abimelek called Abraham in and said, "What have you done to us? How have I wronged you that you have brought such great guilt upon me and my kingdom? You have done things to me that should never be done." 10And Abimelek asked Abraham, "What was your reason for doing this?"

11Abraham replied, "I said to myself, 'There is surely no fear of God in this place, and they will kill me because of my wife.' 12Besides, she really is my sister, the daughter of my father though not of my mother; and she became my wife. 13And when God had me wander from my father's household, I said to her, 'This is how you can show your love to me: Everywhere we go, say of me, "He is my brother."'"

14Then Abimelek brought sheep and cattle and male and female slaves and gave them to Abraham, and he returned Sarah his wife to him. 15And Abimelek said, "My land is before you; live wherever you like."

16To Sarah he said, "I am giving your brother a thousand shekels*d* of silver. This

---

a 37 Moab sounds like the Hebrew for *from father.*   *b 38* Ben-Ammi means *son of my father's people.*
c 38 Hebrew *Bene-Ammon*   *d 16* That is, about 25 pounds or about 12 kilograms

is to cover the offense against you before all who are with you; you are completely vindicated."

¹⁷Then Abraham prayed to God, and God healed Abimelek, his wife and his female slaves so they could have children again, ¹⁸for the LORD had kept all the women in Abimelek's household from conceiving because of Abraham's wife Sarah.

The Birth of Isaac

21 Now the LORD was gracious to Sarah as he had said, and the LORD did for Sarah what he had promised. ²Sarah became pregnant and bore a son to Abraham in his old age, at the very time God had promised him. ³Abraham gave the name Isaacᵃ to the son Sarah bore him. ⁴When his son Isaac was eight days old, Abraham circumcised him, as God commanded him. ⁵Abraham was a hundred years old when his son Isaac was born to him.

⁶Sarah said, "God has brought me laughter, and everyone who hears about this will laugh with me." ⁷And she added, "Who would have said to Abraham that Sarah would nurse children? Yet I have borne him a son in his old age."

Hagar and Ishmael Sent Away

⁸The child grew and was weaned, and on the day Isaac was weaned Abraham held a great feast. ⁹But Sarah saw that the son whom Hagar the Egyptian had borne to Abraham was mocking, ¹⁰and she said to Abraham, "Get rid of that slave woman and her son, for that woman's son will never share in the inheritance with my son Isaac."

¹¹The matter distressed Abraham greatly because it concerned his son. ¹²But God said to him, "Do not be so distressed about the boy and your slave woman. Listen to whatever Sarah tells you, because it is through Isaac that your offspringᵇ will be reckoned. ¹³I will make the son of the

slave into a nation also, because he is your offspring."

¹⁴Early the next morning Abraham took some food and a skin of water and gave them to Hagar. He set them on her shoulders and then sent her off with the boy. She went on her way and wandered in the Desert of Beersheba.

¹⁵When the water in the skin was gone, she put the boy under one of the bushes. ¹⁶Then she went off and sat down about a bowshot away, for she thought, "I cannot watch the boy die." And as she sat there, sheᶜ began to sob.

¹⁷God heard the boy crying, and the angel of God called to Hagar from heaven and said to her, "What is the matter, Hagar? Do not be afraid; God has heard the boy crying as he lies there. ¹⁸Lift the boy up and take him by the hand, for I will make him into a great nation."

¹⁹Then God opened her eyes and she saw a well of water. So she went and filled the skin with water and gave the boy a drink.

²⁰God was with the boy as he grew up. He lived in the desert and became an archer. ²¹While he was living in the Desert of Paran, his mother got a wife for him from Egypt.

The Treaty at Beersheba

²²At that time Abimelek and Phicol the commander of his forces said to Abraham, "God is with you in everything you do. ²³Now swear to me here before God that you will not deal falsely with me or my children or my descendants. Show to me and the country where you now reside as a foreigner the same kindness I have shown to you."

²⁴Abraham said, "I swear it."

²⁵Then Abraham complained to Abimelek about a well of water that Abimelek's servants had seized. ²⁶But Abimelek said, "I don't know who has done this. You did not tell me, and I heard about it only today."

ᵃ 3 *Isaac* means *he laughs.*   ᵇ 12 Or *seed*   ᶜ 16 Hebrew; Septuagint *the child*

27So Abraham brought sheep and cattle and gave them to Abimelek, and the two men made a treaty. 28Abraham set apart seven ewe lambs from the flock, 29and Abimelek asked Abraham, "What is the meaning of these seven ewe lambs you have set apart by themselves?"

30He replied, "Accept these seven lambs from my hand as a witness that I dug this well."

31So that place was called Beersheba,*a* because the two men swore an oath there.

32After the treaty had been made at Beersheba, Abimelek and Phicol the commander of his forces returned to the land of the Philistines. 33Abraham planted a tamarisk tree in Beersheba, and there he called on the name of the LORD, the Eternal God. 34And Abraham stayed in the land of the Philistines for a long time.

Abraham Tested

22 Some time later God tested Abraham. He said to him, "Abraham!"

"Here I am," he replied.

2Then God said, "Take your son, your only son, whom you love — Isaac — and go to the region of Moriah. Sacrifice him there as a burnt offering on a mountain I will show you."

3Early the next morning Abraham got up and loaded his donkey. He took with him two of his servants and his son Isaac. When he had cut enough wood for the burnt offering, he set out for the place God had told him about. 4On the third day Abraham looked up and saw the place in the distance. 5He said to his servants, "Stay here with the donkey while I and the boy go over there. We will worship and then we will come back to you."

6Abraham took the wood for the burnt offering and placed it on his son Isaac, and he himself carried the fire and the knife.

As the two of them went on together, 7Isaac spoke up and said to his father Abraham, "Father?"

"Yes, my son?" Abraham replied.

"The fire and wood are here," Isaac said, "but where is the lamb for the burnt offering?"

8Abraham answered, "God himself will provide the lamb for the burnt offering, my son." And the two of them went on together.

9When they reached the place God had told him about, Abraham built an altar there and arranged the wood on it. He bound his son Isaac and laid him on the altar, on top of the wood. 10Then he reached out his hand and took the knife to slay his son. 11But the angel of the LORD called out to him from heaven, "Abraham! Abraham!"

"Here I am," he replied.

12"Do not lay a hand on the boy," he said. "Do not do anything to him. Now I know that you fear God, because you have not withheld from me your son, your only son."

13Abraham looked up and there in a thicket he saw a ram*b* caught by its horns. He went over and took the ram and sacrificed it as a burnt offering instead of his son. 14So Abraham called that place The LORD Will Provide. And to this day it is said, "On the mountain of the LORD it will be provided."

15The angel of the LORD called to Abraham from heaven a second time 16and said, "I swear by myself, declares the LORD, that because you have done this and have not withheld your son, your only son, 17I will surely bless you and make your descendants as numerous as the stars in the sky and as the sand on the seashore. Your descendants will take possession of the cities of their enemies, 18and through your offspring*c* all nations on earth will be blessed,*d* because you have obeyed me."

---

a 31 Beersheba can mean *well of seven* and *well of the oath.*   *b 13* Many manuscripts of the Masoretic Text, Samaritan Pentateuch, Septuagint and Syriac; most manuscripts of the Masoretic Text *a ram behind him*
c 18 Or *seed*   *d 18* Or *and all nations on earth will use the name of your offspring in blessings* (see 48:20)

19Then Abraham returned to his servants, and they set off together for Beersheba. And Abraham stayed in Beersheba.

Nahor's Sons

20Some time later Abraham was told, "Milkah is also a mother; she has borne sons to your brother Nahor: 21Uz the firstborn, Buz his brother, Kemuel (the father of Aram), 22Kesed, Hazo, Pildash, Jidlaph and Bethuel." 23Bethuel became the father of Rebekah. Milkah bore these eight sons to Abraham's brother Nahor. 24His concubine, whose name was Reumah, also had sons: Tebah, Gaham, Tahash and Maakah.

The Death of Sarah

23 Sarah lived to be a hundred and twenty-seven years old. 2She died at Kiriath Arba (that is, Hebron) in the land of Canaan, and Abraham went to mourn for Sarah and to weep over her.

3Then Abraham rose from beside his dead wife and spoke to the Hittites.*a* He said, 4"I am a foreigner and stranger among you. Sell me some property for a burial site here so I can bury my dead."

5The Hittites replied to Abraham, 6"Sir, listen to us. You are a mighty prince among us. Bury your dead in the choicest of our tombs. None of us will refuse you his tomb for burying your dead."

7Then Abraham rose and bowed down before the people of the land, the Hittites. 8He said to them, "If you are willing to let me bury my dead, then listen to me and intercede with Ephron son of Zohar on my behalf 9so he will sell me the cave of Machpelah, which belongs to him and is at the end of his field. Ask him to sell it to me for the full price as a burial site among you."

10Ephron the Hittite was sitting among his people and he replied to Abraham in the hearing of all the Hittites who had come to the gate of his city. 11"No, my lord," he said. "Listen to me; I give*b* you the field, and I give*b* you the cave that is in it. I give*b* it to you in the presence of my people. Bury your dead."

12Again Abraham bowed down before the people of the land 13and he said to Ephron in their hearing, "Listen to me, if you will. I will pay the price of the field. Accept it from me so I can bury my dead there."

14Ephron answered Abraham, 15"Listen to me, my lord; the land is worth four hundred shekels*c* of silver, but what is that between you and me? Bury your dead."

16Abraham agreed to Ephron's terms and weighed out for him the price he had named in the hearing of the Hittites: four hundred shekels of silver, according to the weight current among the merchants.

17So Ephron's field in Machpelah near Mamre—both the field and the cave in it, and all the trees within the borders of the field—was deeded 18to Abraham as his property in the presence of all the Hittites who had come to the gate of the city. 19Afterward Abraham buried his wife Sarah in the cave in the field of Machpelah near Mamre (which is at Hebron) in the land of Canaan. 20So the field and the cave in it were deeded to Abraham by the Hittites as a burial site.

Isaac and Rebekah

24 Abraham was now very old, and the LORD had blessed him in every way. 2He said to the senior servant in his household, the one in charge of all that he had, "Put your hand under my thigh. 3I want you to swear by the LORD, the God of heaven and the God of earth, that you will not get a wife for my son from the daughters of the Canaanites, among whom I am living, 4but will go to my country and my own relatives and get a wife for my son Isaac."

5The servant asked him, "What if the

---

a 3 Or *the descendants of Heth*; also in verses 5, 7, 10, 16, 18 and 20   *b 11* Or *sell*   *c 15* That is, about 10 pounds or about 4.6 kilograms woman is unwilling to come back with me to this land? Shall I then take your son back to the country you came from?"

6"Make sure that you do not take my son back there," Abraham said. 7"The Lord, the God of heaven, who brought me out of my father's household and my native land and who spoke to me and promised me on oath, saying, 'To your offspring*a* I will give this land'— he will send his angel before you so that you can get a wife for my son from there. 8If the woman is unwilling to come back with you, then you will be released from this oath of mine. Only do not take my son back there." 9So the servant put his hand under the thigh of his master Abraham and swore an oath to him concerning this matter.

10Then the servant left, taking with him ten of his master's camels loaded with all kinds of good things from his master. He set out for Aram Naharaim*b* and made his way to the town of Nahor. 11He had the camels kneel down near the well outside the town; it was toward evening, the time the women go out to draw water.

12Then he prayed, "Lord, God of my master Abraham, make me successful today, and show kindness to my master Abraham. 13See, I am standing beside this spring, and the daughters of the townspeople are coming out to draw water. 14May it be that when I say to a young woman, 'Please let down your jar that I may have a drink,' and she says, 'Drink, and I'll water your camels too'— let her be the one you have chosen for your servant Isaac. By this I will know that you have shown kindness to my master."

15Before he had finished praying, Rebekah came out with her jar on her shoulder. She was the daughter of Bethuel son of Milkah, who was the wife of Abraham's brother Nahor. 16The woman was very beautiful, a virgin; no man had ever slept with her. She went down to the spring, filled her jar and came up again.

17The servant hurried to meet her and said, "Please give me a little water from your jar."

18"Drink, my lord," she said, and quickly lowered the jar to her hands and gave him a drink.

19After she had given him a drink, she said, "I'll draw water for your camels too, until they have had enough to drink." 20So she quickly emptied her jar into the trough, ran back to the well to draw more water, and drew enough for all his camels. 21Without saying a word, the man watched her closely to learn whether or not the Lord had made his journey successful.

22When the camels had finished drinking, the man took out a gold nose ring weighing a beka*c* and two gold bracelets weighing ten shekels.*d* 23Then he asked, "Whose daughter are you? Please tell me, is there room in your father's house for us to spend the night?"

24She answered him, "I am the daughter of Bethuel, the son that Milkah bore to Nahor." 25And she added, "We have plenty of straw and fodder, as well as room for you to spend the night."

26Then the man bowed down and worshiped the Lord, 27saying, "Praise be to the Lord, the God of my master Abraham, who has not abandoned his kindness and faithfulness to my master. As for me, the Lord has led me on the journey to the house of my master's relatives."

28The young woman ran and told her mother's household about these things. 29Now Rebekah had a brother named Laban, and he hurried out to the man at the spring. 30As soon as he had seen the nose ring, and the bracelets on his sister's arms, and had heard Rebekah tell what the man said to her, he went out to the man and found him standing by the camels near the spring. 31"Come, you who are blessed by the Lord," he said. "Why are you standing out here? I have prepared the house and a place for the camels."

---

a 7 Or *seed*   *b 10* That is, Northwest Mesopotamia   *c 22* That is, about 1/5 ounce or about 5.7 grams
d 22 That is, about 4 ounces or about 115 grams

³²So the man went to the house, and the camels were unloaded. Straw and fodder were brought for the camels, and water for him and his men to wash their feet. ³³Then food was set before him, but he said, "I will not eat until I have told you what I have to say."

"Then tell us," Laban said.

³⁴So he said, "I am Abraham's servant. ³⁵The Lord has blessed my master abundantly, and he has become wealthy. He has given him sheep and cattle, silver and gold, male and female servants, and camels and donkeys. ³⁶My master's wife Sarah has borne him a son in her old age, and he has given him everything he owns. ³⁷And my master made me swear an oath, and said, 'You must not get a wife for my son from the daughters of the Canaanites, in whose land I live, ³⁸but go to my father's family and to my own clan, and get a wife for my son.'

³⁹"Then I asked my master, 'What if the woman will not come back with me?'

⁴⁰"He replied, 'The Lord, before whom I have walked faithfully, will send his angel with you and make your journey a success, so that you can get a wife for my son from my own clan and from my father's family. ⁴¹You will be released from my oath if, when you go to my clan, they refuse to give her to you—then you will be released from my oath.'

⁴²"When I came to the spring today, I said, 'Lord, God of my master Abraham, if you will, please grant success to the journey on which I have come. ⁴³See, I am standing beside this spring. If a young woman comes out to draw water and I say to her, "Please let me drink a little water from your jar," ⁴⁴and if she says to me, "Drink, and I'll draw water for your camels too," let her be the one the Lord has chosen for my master's son.'

⁴⁵"Before I finished praying in my heart, Rebekah came out, with her jar on her shoulder. She went down to the spring and drew water, and I said to her, 'Please give me a drink.'

⁴⁶"She quickly lowered her jar from her shoulder and said, 'Drink, and I'll water your camels too.' So I drank, and she watered the camels also.

⁴⁷"I asked her, 'Whose daughter are you?'

"She said, 'The daughter of Bethuel son of Nahor, whom Milkah bore to him.'

"Then I put the ring in her nose and the bracelets on her arms, ⁴⁸and I bowed down and worshiped the Lord. I praised the Lord, the God of my master Abraham, who had led me on the right road to get the granddaughter of my master's brother for his son. ⁴⁹Now if you will show kindness and faithfulness to my master, tell me; and if not, tell me, so I may know which way to turn."

⁵⁰Laban and Bethuel answered, "This is from the Lord; we can say nothing to you one way or the other. ⁵¹Here is Rebekah; take her and go, and let her become the wife of your master's son, as the Lord has directed."

⁵²When Abraham's servant heard what they said, he bowed down to the ground before the Lord. ⁵³Then the servant brought out gold and silver jewelry and articles of clothing and gave them to Rebekah; he also gave costly gifts to her brother and to her mother. ⁵⁴Then he and the men who were with him ate and drank and spent the night there.

When they got up the next morning, he said, "Send me on my way to my master."

⁵⁵But her brother and her mother replied, "Let the young woman remain with us ten days or so; then you*a* may go."

⁵⁶But he said to them, "Do not detain me, now that the Lord has granted success to my journey. Send me on my way so I may go to my master."

⁵⁷Then they said, "Let's call the young woman and ask her about it." ⁵⁸So they called Rebekah and asked her, "Will you go with this man?"

"I will go," she said.

---

a 55 Or *she*

⁵⁹So they sent their sister Rebekah on her way, along with her nurse and Abraham's servant and his men. ⁶⁰And they blessed Rebekah and said to her,

"Our sister, may you increase
  to thousands upon thousands;
may your offspring possess
  the cities of their enemies."

⁶¹Then Rebekah and her attendants got ready and mounted the camels and went back with the man. So the servant took Rebekah and left.

⁶²Now Isaac had come from Beer Lahai Roi, for he was living in the Negev. ⁶³He went out to the field one evening to meditate,ᵃ and as he looked up, he saw camels approaching. ⁶⁴Rebekah also looked up and saw Isaac. She got down from her camel ⁶⁵and asked the servant, "Who is that man in the field coming to meet us?"

"He is my master," the servant answered. So she took her veil and covered herself.

⁶⁶Then the servant told Isaac all he had done. ⁶⁷Isaac brought her into the tent of his mother Sarah, and he married Rebekah. So she became his wife, and he loved her; and Isaac was comforted after his mother's death.

The Death of Abraham

25 Abraham had taken another wife, whose name was Keturah. ²She bore him Zimran, Jokshan, Medan, Midian, Ishbak and Shuah. ³Jokshan was the father of Sheba and Dedan; the descendants of Dedan were the Ashurites, the Letushites and the Leummites. ⁴The sons of Midian were Ephah, Epher, Hanok, Abida and Eldaah. All these were descendants of Keturah.

⁵Abraham left everything he owned to Isaac. ⁶But while he was still living, he gave gifts to the sons of his concubines and sent them away from his son Isaac to the land of the east.

⁷Abraham lived a hundred and seventy-five years. ⁸Then Abraham breathed his last and died at a good old age, an old man and full of years; and he was gathered to his people. ⁹His sons Isaac and Ishmael buried him in the cave of Machpelah near Mamre, in the field of Ephron son of Zohar the Hittite, ¹⁰the field Abraham had bought from the Hittites.ᵇ There Abraham was buried with his wife Sarah. ¹¹After Abraham's death, God blessed his son Isaac, who then lived near Beer Lahai Roi.

Ishmael's Sons

¹²This is the account of the family line of Abraham's son Ishmael, whom Sarah's slave, Hagar the Egyptian, bore to Abraham.

¹³These are the names of the sons of Ishmael, listed in the order of their birth: Nebaioth the firstborn of Ishmael, Kedar, Adbeel, Mibsam, ¹⁴Mishma, Dumah, Massa, ¹⁵Hadad, Tema, Jetur, Naphish and Kedemah. ¹⁶These were the sons of Ishmael, and these are the names of the twelve tribal rulers according to their settlements and camps. ¹⁷Ishmael lived a hundred and thirty-seven years. He breathed his last and died, and he was gathered to his people. ¹⁸His descendants settled in the area from Havilah to Shur, near the eastern border of Egypt, as you go toward Ashur. And they lived in hostility towardᶜ all the tribes related to them.

Jacob and Esau

¹⁹This is the account of the family line of Abraham's son Isaac.

Abraham became the father of Isaac, ²⁰and Isaac was forty years old when he married Rebekah daughter of Bethuel the Aramean from Paddan Aramᵈ and sister of Laban the Aramean.

²¹Isaac prayed to the LORD on behalf of

ᵃ 63 The meaning of the Hebrew for this word is uncertain.   ᵇ 10 Or the descendants of Heth   ᶜ 18 Or lived to the east of   ᵈ 20 That is, Northwest Mesopotamia his wife, because she was childless. The LORD answered his prayer, and his wife Rebekah became pregnant. ²²The babies jostled each other within her, and she said, "Why is this happening to me?" So she went to inquire of the LORD.

²³The LORD said to her,

"Two nations are in your womb,
    and two peoples from within you
        will be separated;
one people will be stronger than the
        other,
    and the older will serve the younger."

²⁴When the time came for her to give birth, there were twin boys in her womb. ²⁵The first to come out was red, and his whole body was like a hairy garment; so they named him Esau.ᵃ ²⁶After this, his brother came out, with his hand grasping Esau's heel; so he was named Jacob.ᵇ Isaac was sixty years old when Rebekah gave birth to them.

²⁷The boys grew up, and Esau became a skillful hunter, a man of the open country, while Jacob was content to stay at home among the tents. ²⁸Isaac, who had a taste for wild game, loved Esau, but Rebekah loved Jacob.

²⁹Once when Jacob was cooking some stew, Esau came in from the open country, famished. ³⁰He said to Jacob, "Quick, let me have some of that red stew! I'm famished!" (That is why he was also called Edom.ᶜ)

³¹Jacob replied, "First sell me your birthright."

³²"Look, I am about to die," Esau said. "What good is the birthright to me?"

³³But Jacob said, "Swear to me first." So he swore an oath to him, selling his birthright to Jacob.

³⁴Then Jacob gave Esau some bread and some lentil stew. He ate and drank, and then got up and left.

So Esau despised his birthright.

Isaac and Abimelek

26 Now there was a famine in the land—besides the previous famine in Abraham's time—and Isaac went to Abimelek king of the Philistines in Gerar. ²The LORD appeared to Isaac and said, "Do not go down to Egypt; live in the land where I tell you to live. ³Stay in this land for a while, and I will be with you and will bless you. For to you and your descendants I will give all these lands and will confirm the oath I swore to your father Abraham. ⁴I will make your descendants as numerous as the stars in the sky and will give them all these lands, and through your offspringᵈ all nations on earth will be blessed,ᵉ ⁵because Abraham obeyed me and did everything I required of him, keeping my commands, my decrees and my instructions." ⁶So Isaac stayed in Gerar.

⁷When the men of that place asked him about his wife, he said, "She is my sister," because he was afraid to say, "She is my wife." He thought, "The men of this place might kill me on account of Rebekah, because she is beautiful."

⁸When Isaac had been there a long time, Abimelek king of the Philistines looked down from a window and saw Isaac caressing his wife Rebekah. ⁹So Abimelek summoned Isaac and said, "She is really your wife! Why did you say, 'She is my sister'?"

Isaac answered him, "Because I thought I might lose my life on account of her."

¹⁰Then Abimelek said, "What is this you have done to us? One of the men might well have slept with your wife, and you would have brought guilt upon us."

¹¹So Abimelek gave orders to all the people: "Anyone who harms this man or his wife shall surely be put to death."

¹²Isaac planted crops in that land and the same year reaped a hundredfold, because the LORD blessed him. ¹³The man

---

ᵃ 25 *Esau* may mean *hairy*.   ᵇ 26 *Jacob* means *he grasps the heel*, a Hebrew idiom for *he deceives*.   ᶜ 30 *Edom* means *red*.   ᵈ 4 Or *seed*   ᵉ 4 Or *and all nations on earth will use the name of your offspring in blessings* (see 48:20)

MY NAME IS JACOB

GENESIS 25–32

Jacob was given a name predictive of his personality—its meaning: trickster. Early in life he set out to live up to his name. He tricked his twin brother Esau out of both his birthright and his blessing (see Genesis 25:27–34; 27:1–29). Esau's anger meant that Jacob had to flee for his life (see 27:41—28:9). Seeking shelter and ultimately a wife from his uncle Laban, the trickster was tricked. Jacob ended up in bondage to Laban, with *two* wives and a family filled with jealousy and resentment (see 29:15—30:24). Once again, Jacob tried to solve his problems through deceit and manipulation (see 30:25–42). And, for a period of time, it seemed to be working (see 30:43).

But soon Laban's sons complained that Jacob had grown rich at their father's expense. Jacob heard about their grumbling and also noted a change in Laban's attitude toward him (see 31:1–2). But fleeing could only mean going home. And going home meant facing Esau.

Jacob became very afraid when he heard that Esau was riding in his direction, accompanied by 400 men. He divided his own people and flocks into two groups, hoping that one of the two would survive Esau's wrath (see 32:1–8). Finally, as a last resort, Jacob turned to God for deliverance. He took his problems to God (see 32:9), he prayed in accordance with God's promises (see 32:9), he took a spiritual inventory (see 32:10), he sought God's strength at his own point of weakness (see 32:11), and he confidently claimed God's promises (see 32:12).

However, Jacob was still a schemer, and he put into motion a plan to bribe Esau (see 32:13–21). But God had a greater plan and Jacob ended up in a wrestling match with God (see 32:22–31). He wrestled all night and held on, even when it hurt (see 32:25), until he had received the Lord's blessing.

So Jacob had been touched powerfully by God, but he still had to face his brother Esau. But Esau ran to meet the one who had robbed him of his birthright and blessing. Rather than acting in vengeance, Esau embraced his brother, and the two of them wept together (see 33:4). The result was a pure product of God's grace. As if that were not enough, God chose Jacob to become the father of a nation destined to bring blessings to all people. His new destiny required a new name—Israel—which means, "he struggles with God."

In recovery, there will be steps along the way that we don't understand, steps that will cause us pain. We might even want to revert to our old patterns of lying and manipulation, of tricking others who are in our lives—even the people we love the most. But as long as we hold on tightly to God, even when it hurts, we can receive the blessings of freedom, reconciliation with God and healing from our hurts, hang-ups and habits.

As we cling desperately to God, there is for us, as there was for Jacob, the promise of a new name: "To the one who is victorious, I will give . . . a white stone with a new name written on it, known only to the one who receives it" (Revelation 2:17).

became rich, and his wealth continued to grow until he became very wealthy. ¹⁴He had so many flocks and herds and servants that the Philistines envied him. ¹⁵So all the wells that his father's servants had dug in the time of his father Abraham, the Philistines stopped up, filling them with earth.

¹⁶Then Abimelek said to Isaac, "Move away from us; you have become too powerful for us."

¹⁷So Isaac moved away from there and encamped in the Valley of Gerar, where he settled. ¹⁸Isaac reopened the wells that had been dug in the time of his father Abraham, which the Philistines had stopped up after Abraham died, and he gave them the same names his father had given them.

¹⁹Isaac's servants dug in the valley and discovered a well of fresh water there. ²⁰But the herders of Gerar quarreled with those of Isaac and said, "The water is ours!" So he named the well Esek,ᵃ because they disputed with him. ²¹Then they dug another well, but they quarreled over that one also; so he named it Sitnah.ᵇ ²²He moved on from there and dug another well, and no one quarreled over it. He named it Rehoboth,ᶜ saying, "Now the Lord has given us room and we will flourish in the land."

²³From there he went up to Beersheba. ²⁴That night the Lord appeared to him and said, "I am the God of your father Abraham. Do not be afraid, for I am with you; I will bless you and will increase the number of your descendants for the sake of my servant Abraham."

²⁵Isaac built an altar there and called on the name of the Lord. There he pitched his tent, and there his servants dug a well.

²⁶Meanwhile, Abimelek had come to him from Gerar, with Ahuzzath his personal adviser and Phicol the commander of his forces. ²⁷Isaac asked them, "Why have you come to me, since you were hostile to me and sent me away?"

²⁸They answered, "We saw clearly that the Lord was with you; so we said, 'There ought to be a sworn agreement between us' — between us and you. Let us make a treaty with you ²⁹that you will do us no harm, just as we did not harm you but always treated you well and sent you away peacefully. And now you are blessed by the Lord."

³⁰Isaac then made a feast for them, and they ate and drank. ³¹Early the next morning the men swore an oath to each other. Then Isaac sent them on their way, and they went away peacefully.

³²That day Isaac's servants came and told him about the well they had dug. They said, "We've found water!" ³³He called it Shibah,ᵈ and to this day the name of the town has been Beersheba.ᵉ

Jacob Takes Esau's Blessing

³⁴When Esau was forty years old, he married Judith daughter of Beeri the Hittite, and also Basemath daughter of Elon the Hittite. ³⁵They were a source of grief to Isaac and Rebekah.

27 When Isaac was old and his eyes were so weak that he could no longer see, he called for Esau his older son and said to him, "My son."

"Here I am," he answered.

²Isaac said, "I am now an old man and don't know the day of my death. ³Now then, get your equipment — your quiver and bow — and go out to the open country to hunt some wild game for me. ⁴Prepare me the kind of tasty food I like and bring it to me to eat, so that I may give you my blessing before I die."

⁵Now Rebekah was listening as Isaac spoke to his son Esau. When Esau left for the open country to hunt game and bring it back, ⁶Rebekah said to her son Jacob, "Look, I overheard your father say to your brother Esau, ⁷'Bring me some game and prepare me some tasty food to eat, so that I

ᵃ 20 *Esek* means *dispute.*   ᵇ 21 *Sitnah* means *opposition.*   ᶜ 22 *Rehoboth* means *room.*   ᵈ 33 *Shibah* can mean *oath* or *seven.*   ᵉ 33 *Beersheba* can mean *well of the oath* and *well of seven.*

may give you my blessing in the presence of the Lord before I die.' ⁸Now, my son, listen carefully and do what I tell you: ⁹Go out to the flock and bring me two choice young goats, so I can prepare some tasty food for your father, just the way he likes it. ¹⁰Then take it to your father to eat, so that he may give you his blessing before he dies."

¹¹Jacob said to Rebekah his mother, "But my brother Esau is a hairy man while I have smooth skin. ¹²What if my father touches me? I would appear to be tricking him and would bring down a curse on myself rather than a blessing."

¹³His mother said to him, "My son, let the curse fall on me. Just do what I say; go and get them for me."

¹⁴So he went and got them and brought them to his mother, and she prepared some tasty food, just the way his father liked it. ¹⁵Then Rebekah took the best clothes of Esau her older son, which she had in the house, and put them on her younger son Jacob. ¹⁶She also covered his hands and the smooth part of his neck with the goatskins. ¹⁷Then she handed to her son Jacob the tasty food and the bread she had made.

¹⁸He went to his father and said, "My father."

"Yes, my son," he answered. "Who is it?"

¹⁹Jacob said to his father, "I am Esau your firstborn. I have done as you told me. Please sit up and eat some of my game, so that you may give me your blessing."

²⁰Isaac asked his son, "How did you find it so quickly, my son?"

"The Lord your God gave me success," he replied.

²¹Then Isaac said to Jacob, "Come near so I can touch you, my son, to know whether you really are my son Esau or not."

²²Jacob went close to his father Isaac, who touched him and said, "The voice is the voice of Jacob, but the hands are the hands of Esau." ²³He did not recognize him, for his hands were hairy like those of his brother Esau; so he proceeded to bless him. ²⁴"Are you really my son Esau?" he asked.

"I am," he replied.

²⁵Then he said, "My son, bring me some of your game to eat, so that I may give you my blessing."

Jacob brought it to him and he ate; and he brought some wine and he drank. ²⁶Then his father Isaac said to him, "Come here, my son, and kiss me."

²⁷So he went to him and kissed him. When Isaac caught the smell of his clothes, he blessed him and said,

"Ah, the smell of my son
    is like the smell of a field
    that the Lord has blessed.
²⁸May God give you heaven's dew
    and earth's richness —
    an abundance of grain and new
        wine.
²⁹May nations serve you
    and peoples bow down to you.
Be lord over your brothers,
    and may the sons of your mother
        bow down to you.
May those who curse you be cursed
    and those who bless you be blessed."

³⁰After Isaac finished blessing him, and Jacob had scarcely left his father's presence, his brother Esau came in from hunting. ³¹He too prepared some tasty food and brought it to his father. Then he said to him, "My father, please sit up and eat some of my game, so that you may give me your blessing."

³²His father Isaac asked him, "Who are you?"

"I am your son," he answered, "your firstborn, Esau."

³³Isaac trembled violently and said, "Who was it, then, that hunted game and brought it to me? I ate it just before you came and I blessed him — and indeed he will be blessed!"

³⁴When Esau heard his father's words, he burst out with a loud and bitter cry and said to his father, "Bless me — me too, my father!"

³⁵But he said, "Your brother came deceitfully and took your blessing."

36Esau said, "Isn't he rightly named Jacob*a*? This is the second time he has taken advantage of me: He took my birthright, and now he's taken my blessing!" Then he asked, "Haven't you reserved any blessing for me?"

37Isaac answered Esau, "I have made him lord over you and have made all his relatives his servants, and I have sustained him with grain and new wine. So what can I possibly do for you, my son?"

38Esau said to his father, "Do you have only one blessing, my father? Bless me too, my father!" Then Esau wept aloud.

39His father Isaac answered him,

"Your dwelling will be
    away from the earth's richness,
    away from the dew of heaven above.
40You will live by the sword
    and you will serve your brother.
But when you grow restless,
    you will throw his yoke
    from off your neck."

41Esau held a grudge against Jacob because of the blessing his father had given him. He said to himself, "The days of mourning for my father are near; then I will kill my brother Jacob."

42When Rebekah was told what her older son Esau had said, she sent for her younger son Jacob and said to him, "Your brother Esau is planning to avenge himself by killing you. **43**Now then, my son, do what I say: Flee at once to my brother Laban in Harran. **44**Stay with him for a while until your brother's fury subsides. **45**When your brother is no longer angry with you and forgets what you did to him, I'll send word for you to come back from there. Why should I lose both of you in one day?"

46Then Rebekah said to Isaac, "I'm disgusted with living because of these Hittite women. If Jacob takes a wife from among the women of this land, from Hittite women like these, my life will not be worth living."

28 So Isaac called for Jacob and blessed him. Then he commanded him: "Do not marry a Canaanite woman. **2**Go at once to Paddan Aram,*b* to the house of your mother's father Bethuel. Take a wife for yourself there, from among the daughters of Laban, your mother's brother. **3**May God Almighty*c* bless you and make you fruitful and increase your numbers until you become a community of peoples. **4**May he give you and your descendants the blessing given to Abraham, so that you may take possession of the land where you now reside as a foreigner, the land God gave to Abraham." **5**Then Isaac sent Jacob on his way, and he went to Paddan Aram, to Laban son of Bethuel the Aramean, the brother of Rebekah, who was the mother of Jacob and Esau.

6Now Esau learned that Isaac had blessed Jacob and had sent him to Paddan Aram to take a wife from there, and that when he blessed him he commanded him, "Do not marry a Canaanite woman," **7**and that Jacob had obeyed his father and mother and had gone to Paddan Aram. **8**Esau then realized how displeasing the Canaanite women were to his father Isaac; **9**so he went to Ishmael and married Mahalath, the sister of Nebaioth and daughter of Ishmael son of Abraham, in addition to the wives he already had.

Jacob's Dream at Bethel

10Jacob left Beersheba and set out for Harran. **11**When he reached a certain place, he stopped for the night because the sun had set. Taking one of the stones there, he put it under his head and lay down to sleep. **12**He had a dream in which he saw a stairway resting on the earth, with its top reaching to heaven, and the angels of God were ascending and descending on it. **13**There above it*d* stood the LORD, and he said: "I am the LORD, the God of your father Abraham and the God of Isaac. I will

---

a 36 Jacob means *he grasps the heel,* a Hebrew idiom for *he takes advantage of* or *he deceives.*   *b 2* That is, Northwest Mesopotamia; also in verses 5, 6 and 7   *c 3* Hebrew *El-Shaddai*   *d 13* Or *There beside him* give you and your descendants the land on which you are lying. ¹⁴Your descendants will be like the dust of the earth, and you will spread out to the west and to the east, to the north and to the south. All peoples on earth will be blessed through you and your offspring.ᵃ ¹⁵I am with you and will watch over you wherever you go, and I will bring you back to this land. I will not leave you until I have done what I have promised you."

¹⁶When Jacob awoke from his sleep, he thought, "Surely the LORD is in this place, and I was not aware of it." ¹⁷He was afraid and said, "How awesome is this place! This is none other than the house of God; this is the gate of heaven."

¹⁸Early the next morning Jacob took the stone he had placed under his head and set it up as a pillar and poured oil on top of it. ¹⁹He called that place Bethel,ᵇ though the city used to be called Luz.

²⁰Then Jacob made a vow, saying, "If God will be with me and will watch over me on this journey I am taking and will give me food to eat and clothes to wear ²¹so that I return safely to my father's household, then the LORDᶜ will be my God ²²andᵈ this stone that I have set up as a pillar will be God's house, and of all that you give me I will give you a tenth."

Jacob Arrives in Paddan Aram

29 Then Jacob continued on his journey and came to the land of the eastern peoples. ²There he saw a well in the open country, with three flocks of sheep lying near it because the flocks were watered from that well. The stone over the mouth of the well was large. ³When all the flocks were gathered there, the shepherds would roll the stone away from the well's mouth and water the sheep. Then they would return the stone to its place over the mouth of the well.

⁴Jacob asked the shepherds, "My brothers, where are you from?"

"We're from Harran," they replied.

⁵He said to them, "Do you know Laban, Nahor's grandson?"

"Yes, we know him," they answered.

⁶Then Jacob asked them, "Is he well?"

"Yes, he is," they said, "and here comes his daughter Rachel with the sheep."

⁷"Look," he said, "the sun is still high; it is not time for the flocks to be gathered. Water the sheep and take them back to pasture."

⁸"We can't," they replied, "until all the flocks are gathered and the stone has been rolled away from the mouth of the well. Then we will water the sheep."

⁹While he was still talking with them, Rachel came with her father's sheep, for she was a shepherd. ¹⁰When Jacob saw Rachel daughter of his uncle Laban, and Laban's sheep, he went over and rolled the stone away from the mouth of the well and watered his uncle's sheep. ¹¹Then Jacob kissed Rachel and began to weep aloud. ¹²He had told Rachel that he was a relative of her father and a son of Rebekah. So she ran and told her father.

¹³As soon as Laban heard the news about Jacob, his sister's son, he hurried to meet him. He embraced him and kissed him and brought him to his home, and there Jacob told him all these things. ¹⁴Then Laban said to him, "You are my own flesh and blood."

Jacob Marries Leah and Rachel

After Jacob had stayed with him for a whole month, ¹⁵Laban said to him, "Just because you are a relative of mine, should you work for me for nothing? Tell me what your wages should be."

¹⁶Now Laban had two daughters; the name of the older was Leah, and the name of the younger was Rachel. ¹⁷Leah had weakᵉ eyes, but Rachel had a lovely figure

---

ᵃ 14 Or *will use your name and the name of your offspring in blessings* (see 48:20)   ᵇ 19 *Bethel* means *house of God.*
ᶜ 20,21 Or *Since God . . . father's household, the LORD*   ᵈ 21,22 Or *household, and the LORD will be my God,* ²²*then*
ᵉ 17 Or *delicate*

and was beautiful. ¹⁸Jacob was in love with Rachel and said, "I'll work for you seven years in return for your younger daughter Rachel."

¹⁹Laban said, "It's better that I give her to you than to some other man. Stay here with me." ²⁰So Jacob served seven years to get Rachel, but they seemed like only a few days to him because of his love for her.

²¹Then Jacob said to Laban, "Give me my wife. My time is completed, and I want to make love to her."

²²So Laban brought together all the people of the place and gave a feast. ²³But when evening came, he took his daughter Leah and brought her to Jacob, and Jacob made love to her. ²⁴And Laban gave his servant Zilpah to his daughter as her attendant.

²⁵When morning came, there was Leah! So Jacob said to Laban, "What is this you have done to me? I served you for Rachel, didn't I? Why have you deceived me?"

²⁶Laban replied, "It is not our custom here to give the younger daughter in marriage before the older one. ²⁷Finish this daughter's bridal week; then we will give you the younger one also, in return for another seven years of work."

²⁸And Jacob did so. He finished the week with Leah, and then Laban gave him his daughter Rachel to be his wife. ²⁹Laban gave his servant Bilhah to his daughter Rachel as her attendant. ³⁰Jacob made love to Rachel also, and his love for Rachel was greater than his love for Leah. And he worked for Laban another seven years.

Jacob's Children

³¹When the LORD saw that Leah was not loved, he enabled her to conceive, but Rachel remained childless. ³²Leah became pregnant and gave birth to a son. She named him Reuben,ᵃ for she said, "It is because the LORD has seen my misery. Surely my husband will love me now."

³³She conceived again, and when she gave birth to a son she said, "Because the LORD heard that I am not loved, he gave me this one too." So she named him Simeon.ᵇ

³⁴Again she conceived, and when she gave birth to a son she said, "Now at last my husband will become attached to me, because I have borne him three sons." So he was named Levi.ᶜ

³⁵She conceived again, and when she gave birth to a son she said, "This time I will praise the LORD." So she named him Judah.ᵈ Then she stopped having children.

30

When Rachel saw that she was not bearing Jacob any children, she became jealous of her sister. So she said to Jacob, "Give me children, or I'll die!"

²Jacob became angry with her and said, "Am I in the place of God, who has kept you from having children?"

³Then she said, "Here is Bilhah, my servant. Sleep with her so that she can bear children for me and I too can build a family through her."

⁴So she gave him her servant Bilhah as a wife. Jacob slept with her, ⁵and she became pregnant and bore him a son. ⁶Then Rachel said, "God has vindicated me; he has listened to my plea and given me a son." Because of this she named him Dan.ᵉ

⁷Rachel's servant Bilhah conceived again and bore Jacob a second son. ⁸Then Rachel said, "I have had a great struggle with my sister, and I have won." So she named him Naphtali.ᶠ

⁹When Leah saw that she had stopped having children, she took her servant Zilpah and gave her to Jacob as a wife. ¹⁰Leah's servant Zilpah bore Jacob a son. ¹¹Then Leah said, "What good fortune!"ᵍ So she named him Gad.ʰ

¹²Leah's servant Zilpah bore Jacob a second son. ¹³Then Leah said, "How happy I

ᵃ 32 *Reuben* sounds like the Hebrew for *he has seen my misery*; the name means *see, a son.*   ᵇ 33 *Simeon* probably means *one who hears.*   ᶜ 34 *Levi* sounds like and may be derived from the Hebrew for *attached.*   ᵈ 35 *Judah* sounds like and may be derived from the Hebrew for *praise.*   ᵉ 6 *Dan* here means *he has vindicated.*   ᶠ 8 *Naphtali* means *my struggle.*   ᵍ 11 Or *"A troop is coming!"*   ʰ 11 *Gad* can mean *good fortune* or *a troop.*

am! The women will call me happy." So she named him Asher.[a]

[14]During wheat harvest, Reuben went out into the fields and found some mandrake plants, which he brought to his mother Leah. Rachel said to Leah, "Please give me some of your son's mandrakes."

[15]But she said to her, "Wasn't it enough that you took away my husband? Will you take my son's mandrakes too?"

"Very well," Rachel said, "he can sleep with you tonight in return for your son's mandrakes."

[16]So when Jacob came in from the fields that evening, Leah went out to meet him. "You must sleep with me," she said. "I have hired you with my son's mandrakes." So he slept with her that night.

[17]God listened to Leah, and she became pregnant and bore Jacob a fifth son. [18]Then Leah said, "God has rewarded me for giving my servant to my husband." So she named him Issachar.[b]

[19]Leah conceived again and bore Jacob a sixth son. [20]Then Leah said, "God has presented me with a precious gift. This time my husband will treat me with honor, because I have borne him six sons." So she named him Zebulun.[c]

[21]Some time later she gave birth to a daughter and named her Dinah.

[22]Then God remembered Rachel; he listened to her and enabled her to conceive. [23]She became pregnant and gave birth to a son and said, "God has taken away my disgrace." [24]She named him Joseph,[d] and said, "May the LORD add to me another son."

Jacob's Flocks Increase

[25]After Rachel gave birth to Joseph, Jacob said to Laban, "Send me on my way so I can go back to my own homeland. [26]Give me my wives and children, for whom I have served you, and I will be on my way. You know how much work I've done for you."

[27]But Laban said to him, "If I have found favor in your eyes, please stay. I have learned by divination that the LORD has blessed me because of you." [28]He added, "Name your wages, and I will pay them."

[29]Jacob said to him, "You know how I have worked for you and how your livestock has fared under my care. [30]The little you had before I came has increased greatly, and the LORD has blessed you wherever I have been. But now, when may I do something for my own household?"

[31]"What shall I give you?" he asked.

"Don't give me anything," Jacob replied. "But if you will do this one thing for me, I will go on tending your flocks and watching over them: [32]Let me go through all your flocks today and remove from them every speckled or spotted sheep, every dark-colored lamb and every spotted or speckled goat. They will be my wages. [33]And my honesty will testify for me in the future, whenever you check on the wages you have paid me. Any goat in my possession that is not speckled or spotted, or any lamb that is not dark-colored, will be considered stolen."

[34]"Agreed," said Laban. "Let it be as you have said." [35]That same day he removed all the male goats that were streaked or spotted, and all the speckled or spotted female goats (all that had white on them) and all the dark-colored lambs, and he placed them in the care of his sons. [36]Then he put a three-day journey between himself and Jacob, while Jacob continued to tend the rest of Laban's flocks.

[37]Jacob, however, took fresh-cut branches from poplar, almond and plane trees and made white stripes on them by peeling the bark and exposing the white inner wood of the branches. [38]Then he placed the peeled branches in all the watering troughs, so that they would be directly in front of the flocks when they came to drink. When the flocks were in heat and came to drink, [39]they mated in front of the

---

[a] 13 Asher means happy.   [b] 18 Issachar sounds like the Hebrew for reward.   [c] 20 Zebulun probably means honor.   [d] 24 Joseph means may he add.

branches. And they bore young that were streaked or speckled or spotted. 40Jacob set apart the young of the flock by themselves, but made the rest face the streaked and dark-colored animals that belonged to Laban. Thus he made separate flocks for himself and did not put them with Laban's animals. 41Whenever the stronger females were in heat, Jacob would place the branches in the troughs in front of the animals so they would mate near the branches, 42but if the animals were weak, he would not place them there. So the weak animals went to Laban and the strong ones to Jacob. 43In this way the man grew exceedingly prosperous and came to own large flocks, and female and male servants, and camels and donkeys.

Jacob Flees From Laban

31 Jacob heard that Laban's sons were saying, "Jacob has taken everything our father owned and has gained all this wealth from what belonged to our father." 2And Jacob noticed that Laban's attitude toward him was not what it had been.

3Then the LORD said to Jacob, "Go back to the land of your fathers and to your relatives, and I will be with you."

4So Jacob sent word to Rachel and Leah to come out to the fields where his flocks were. 5He said to them, "I see that your father's attitude toward me is not what it was before, but the God of my father has been with me. 6You know that I've worked for your father with all my strength, 7yet your father has cheated me by changing my wages ten times. However, God has not allowed him to harm me. 8If he said, 'The speckled ones will be your wages,' then all the flocks gave birth to speckled young; and if he said, 'The streaked ones will be your wages,' then all the flocks bore streaked young. 9So God has taken away your father's livestock and has given them to me.

10"In breeding season I once had a dream in which I looked up and saw that the male goats mating with the flock were streaked, speckled or spotted. 11The angel of God said to me in the dream, 'Jacob.' I answered, 'Here I am.' 12And he said, 'Look up and see that all the male goats mating with the flock are streaked, speckled or spotted, for I have seen all that Laban has been doing to you. 13I am the God of Bethel, where you anointed a pillar and where you made a vow to me. Now leave this land at once and go back to your native land.' "

14Then Rachel and Leah replied, "Do we still have any share in the inheritance of our father's estate? 15Does he not regard us as foreigners? Not only has he sold us, but he has used up what was paid for us. 16Surely all the wealth that God took away from our father belongs to us and our children. So do whatever God has told you."

17Then Jacob put his children and his wives on camels, 18and he drove all his livestock ahead of him, along with all the goods he had accumulated in Paddan Aram,*a* to go to his father Isaac in the land of Canaan.

19When Laban had gone to shear his sheep, Rachel stole her father's household gods. 20Moreover, Jacob deceived Laban the Aramean by not telling him he was running away. 21So he fled with all he had, crossed the Euphrates River, and headed for the hill country of Gilead.

Laban Pursues Jacob

22On the third day Laban was told that Jacob had fled. 23Taking his relatives with him, he pursued Jacob for seven days and caught up with him in the hill country of Gilead. 24Then God came to Laban the Aramean in a dream at night and said to him, "Be careful not to say anything to Jacob, either good or bad."

25Jacob had pitched his tent in the hill country of Gilead when Laban overtook him, and Laban and his relatives camped there too. 26Then Laban said to Jacob,

---

a 18 That is, Northwest Mesopotamia

"What have you done? You've deceived me, and you've carried off my daughters like captives in war. ²⁷Why did you run off secretly and deceive me? Why didn't you tell me, so I could send you away with joy and singing to the music of timbrels and harps? ²⁸You didn't even let me kiss my grandchildren and my daughters goodbye. You have done a foolish thing. ²⁹I have the power to harm you; but last night the God of your father said to me, 'Be careful not to say anything to Jacob, either good or bad.' ³⁰Now you have gone off because you longed to return to your father's household. But why did you steal my gods?"

³¹Jacob answered Laban, "I was afraid, because I thought you would take your daughters away from me by force. ³²But if you find anyone who has your gods, that person shall not live. In the presence of our relatives, see for yourself whether there is anything of yours here with me; and if so, take it." Now Jacob did not know that Rachel had stolen the gods.

³³So Laban went into Jacob's tent and into Leah's tent and into the tent of the two female servants, but he found nothing. After he came out of Leah's tent, he entered Rachel's tent. ³⁴Now Rachel had taken the household gods and put them inside her camel's saddle and was sitting on them. Laban searched through everything in the tent but found nothing.

³⁵Rachel said to her father, "Don't be angry, my lord, that I cannot stand up in your presence; I'm having my period." So he searched but could not find the household gods.

³⁶Jacob was angry and took Laban to task. "What is my crime?" he asked Laban. "How have I wronged you that you hunt me down? ³⁷Now that you have searched through all my goods, what have you found that belongs to your household? Put it here in front of your relatives and mine, and let them judge between the two of us.

³⁸"I have been with you for twenty years now. Your sheep and goats have not miscarried, nor have I eaten rams from your flocks. ³⁹I did not bring you animals torn by wild beasts; I bore the loss myself. And you demanded payment from me for whatever was stolen by day or night. ⁴⁰This was my situation: The heat consumed me in the daytime and the cold at night, and sleep fled from my eyes. ⁴¹It was like this for the twenty years I was in your household. I worked for you fourteen years for your two daughters and six years for your flocks, and you changed my wages ten times. ⁴²If the God of my father, the God of Abraham and the Fear of Isaac, had not been with me, you would surely have sent me away empty-handed. But God has seen my hardship and the toil of my hands, and last night he rebuked you."

⁴³Laban answered Jacob, "The women are my daughters, the children are my children, and the flocks are my flocks. All you see is mine. Yet what can I do today about these daughters of mine, or about the children they have borne? ⁴⁴Come now, let's make a covenant, you and I, and let it serve as a witness between us."

⁴⁵So Jacob took a stone and set it up as a pillar. ⁴⁶He said to his relatives, "Gather some stones." So they took stones and piled them in a heap, and they ate there by the heap. ⁴⁷Laban called it Jegar Sahadutha, and Jacob called it Galeed.ᵃ

⁴⁸Laban said, "This heap is a witness between you and me today." That is why it was called Galeed. ⁴⁹It was also called Mizpah,ᵇ because he said, "May the Lord keep watch between you and me when we are away from each other. ⁵⁰If you mistreat my daughters or if you take any wives besides my daughters, even though no one is with us, remember that God is a witness between you and me."

⁵¹Laban also said to Jacob, "Here is this heap, and here is this pillar I have set up

---

ᵃ 47 The Aramaic *Jegar Sahadutha* and the Hebrew *Galeed* both mean *witness heap.*   ᵇ 49 *Mizpah* means *watchtower.*

between you and me. ⁵²This heap is a witness, and this pillar is a witness, that I will not go past this heap to your side to harm you and that you will not go past this heap and pillar to my side to harm me. ⁵³May the God of Abraham and the God of Nahor, the God of their father, judge between us."

So Jacob took an oath in the name of the Fear of his father Isaac. ⁵⁴He offered a sacrifice there in the hill country and invited his relatives to a meal. After they had eaten, they spent the night there.

⁵⁵Early the next morning Laban kissed his grandchildren and his daughters and blessed them. Then he left and returned home.ᵃ

Jacob Prepares to Meet Esau

32 ᵇ Jacob also went on his way, and the angels of God met him. ²When Jacob saw them, he said, "This is the camp of God!" So he named that place Mahanaim.ᶜ

³Jacob sent messengers ahead of him to his brother Esau in the land of Seir, the country of Edom. ⁴He instructed them: "This is what you are to say to my lord Esau: 'Your servant Jacob says, I have been staying with Laban and have remained there till now. ⁵I have cattle and donkeys, sheep and goats, male and female servants. Now I am sending this message to my lord, that I may find favor in your eyes.'"

⁶When the messengers returned to Jacob, they said, "We went to your brother Esau, and now he is coming to meet you, and four hundred men are with him."

⁷In great fear and distress Jacob divided the people who were with him into two groups,ᵈ and the flocks and herds and camels as well. ⁸He thought, "If Esau comes and attacks one group,ᵉ the groupᵉ that is left may escape."

⁹Then Jacob prayed, "O God of my father Abraham, God of my father Isaac, LORD, you who said to me, 'Go back to your country and your relatives, and I will make you prosper,' ¹⁰I am unworthy of all the kindness and faithfulness you have shown your servant. I had only my staff when I crossed this Jordan, but now I have become two camps. ¹¹Save me, I pray, from the hand of my brother Esau, for I am afraid he will come and attack me, and also the mothers with their children. ¹²But you have said, 'I will surely make you prosper and will make your descendants like the sand of the sea, which cannot be counted.'"

¹³He spent the night there, and from what he had with him he selected a gift for his brother Esau: ¹⁴two hundred female goats and twenty male goats, two hundred ewes and twenty rams, ¹⁵thirty female camels with their young, forty cows and ten bulls, and twenty female donkeys and ten male donkeys. ¹⁶He put them in the care of his servants, each herd by itself, and said to his servants, "Go ahead of me, and keep some space between the herds."

¹⁷He instructed the one in the lead: "When my brother Esau meets you and asks, 'Who do you belong to, and where are you going, and who owns all these animals in front of you?' ¹⁸then you are to say, 'They belong to your servant Jacob. They are a gift sent to my lord Esau, and he is coming behind us.'"

¹⁹He also instructed the second, the third and all the others who followed the herds: "You are to say the same thing to Esau when you meet him. ²⁰And be sure to say, 'Your servant Jacob is coming behind us.'" For he thought, "I will pacify him with these gifts I am sending on ahead; later, when I see him, perhaps he will receive me." ²¹So Jacob's gifts went on ahead of him, but he himself spent the night in the camp.

Jacob Wrestles With God

²²That night Jacob got up and took his two wives, his two female servants and his

---

ᵃ 55 In Hebrew texts this verse (31:55) is numbered 32:1.   ᵇ In Hebrew texts 32:1-32 is numbered 32:2-33.
ᶜ 2 Mahanaim means two camps.   ᵈ 7 Or camps   ᵉ 8 Or camp

eleven sons and crossed the ford of the Jabbok. 23After he had sent them across the stream, he sent over all his possessions. 24So Jacob was left alone, and a man wrestled with him till daybreak. 25When the man saw that he could not overpower him, he touched the socket of Jacob's hip so that his hip was wrenched as he wrestled with the man. 26Then the man said, "Let me go, for it is daybreak."

But Jacob replied, "I will not let you go unless you bless me."

27The man asked him, "What is your name?"

"Jacob," he answered.

28Then the man said, "Your name will no longer be Jacob, but Israel,*a* because you have struggled with God and with humans and have overcome."

29Jacob said, "Please tell me your name."

But he replied, "Why do you ask my name?" Then he blessed him there.

30So Jacob called the place Peniel,*b* saying, "It is because I saw God face to face, and yet my life was spared."

31The sun rose above him as he passed Peniel,*c* and he was limping because of his hip. 32Therefore to this day the Israelites do not eat the tendon attached to the socket of the hip, because the socket of Jacob's hip was touched near the tendon.

Jacob Meets Esau

33 Jacob looked up and there was Esau, coming with his four hundred men; so he divided the children among Leah, Rachel and the two female servants. 2He put the female servants and their children in front, Leah and her children next, and Rachel and Joseph in the rear. 3He himself went on ahead and bowed down to the ground seven times as he approached his brother.

4But Esau ran to meet Jacob and embraced him; he threw his arms around his neck and kissed him. And they wept.

5Then Esau looked up and saw the women and children. "Who are these with you?" he asked.

Jacob answered, "They are the children God has graciously given your servant."

6Then the female servants and their children approached and bowed down. 7Next, Leah and her children came and bowed down. Last of all came Joseph and Rachel, and they too bowed down.

8Esau asked, "What's the meaning of all these flocks and herds I met?"

"To find favor in your eyes, my lord," he said.

9But Esau said, "I already have plenty, my brother. Keep what you have for yourself."

10"No, please!" said Jacob. "If I have found favor in your eyes, accept this gift from me. For to see your face is like seeing the face of God, now that you have received me favorably. 11Please accept the present that was brought to you, for God has been gracious to me and I have all I need." And because Jacob insisted, Esau accepted it.

12Then Esau said, "Let us be on our way; I'll accompany you."

13But Jacob said to him, "My lord knows that the children are tender and that I must care for the ewes and cows that are nursing their young. If they are driven hard just one day, all the animals will die. 14So let my lord go on ahead of his servant, while I move along slowly at the pace of the flocks and herds before me and the pace of the children, until I come to my lord in Seir."

15Esau said, "Then let me leave some of my men with you."

"But why do that?" Jacob asked. "Just let me find favor in the eyes of my lord."

16So that day Esau started on his way back to Seir. 17Jacob, however, went to Sukkoth, where he built a place for himself and made shelters for his livestock. That is why the place is called Sukkoth.*d*

18After Jacob came from Paddan Aram,*e*

---

a 28 Israel *probably means* he struggles with God.   *b 30* Peniel *means* face of God.   *c 31* Hebrew Penuel, a variant of *Peniel*   *d 17* Sukkoth *means* shelters.   *e 18* That is, Northwest Mesopotamia

My Name Is Kenny

I'M A BELIEVER WHO STRUGGLES WITH ALCOHOLISM AND DRUG ADDICTION

Please read about Jacob's preparations to meet Esau, his wrestling with God and the ultimate reunion between the estranged twin brothers in Genesis 32–33.

I grew up with my mother, stepfather and brother. My mother and I were close, but my stepfather ruled with an iron fist, expecting things to be done on command and with complete obedience. From early on I learned to walk on eggshells. I went to public school, excelled at sports and found acceptance.

When I was 15 years old, my mother and stepfather divorced, and I immediately began to rebel. I took a job at a local liquor store as a stock boy, and before long I'd figured out a way to steal 12-packs of beer. Slowly but surely school and sports became less a priority. As my addiction progressed, I began getting in trouble with the law. Before my eighteenth birthday I'd been arrested five times: twice for being drunk and belligerent, twice for DUI and once for assault and battery. That same year I was involved in an affair with a married woman, resulting in her divorce. I dropped out of high school in my senior year to begin my career in construction.

I started using methamphetamine and, for a few years, speed worked for me. But as my addiction progressed, I became isolated and began to lose jobs. To feed my ever-increasing addiction, I resorted to stealing and manipulation. I had become the "trickster." My mother had acquired an expensive stamp collection from my grandfather, and I began to steal from her piece by piece; I finally resorted to pawning off her diamond rings. When she realized what I was doing, she was forced to kick me out.

I was now homeless and jobless. Over the next two years I was arrested twice: for possession and for being under the influence. I received a sentence of 45 days in the county jail. Upon my release, my mom graciously allowed me back home. During this time she began attending Saddleback Church. One Sunday she filled out a visitor card with my name, indicating that I wanted to know Christ. The trickster had been tricked.

Shortly thereafter I received a call from a man involved with the new believer's ministry. Not knowing how else to respond, I cooperated with him. Finally, he asked whether I would be willing to say the sinners' prayer. I shared with him that I wasn't ready and that I was struggling with drugs and alcohol. I didn't want to be a hypocrite. He told me about Celebrate Recovery, and the seed was planted. The next Friday I walked into a Celebrate Recovery meeting for the first time. That evening I met some great guys and accepted the Lord.

I began to work at a friend's family patio store. Unfortunately, I was still a schemer, and, like Jacob, I ended up in a wrestling match with God. I disappeared from church and cut off contact with my accountability partners. Not surprisingly, I relapsed. This most miserable and lonely time of my life came to an end when I was arrested nine months later for the last time.

This time I was sentenced to six months in the county jail. I was court ordered to attend an AIDS awareness class and given an HIV blood test. The instructor advised us that no news from them would be good news. Two weeks later the guards handed me a medical slip labeled "Blood Test" in bold red letters. I realized with a sinking heart that I was HIV positive. I was terrified, feeling, as Jacob did, that 400 potentially menacing men were closing in on me. While sitting in the medical facility with tears streaming down my face, I reflected back on my whole life; all of those years of scheming and striving, and for what? My past had caught up with me. I could no longer run from the consequences of the pain I'd caused everyone, including myself, by my thoughtless choices.

I was finally called in and told that there had been a mistake, a computer error. I wasn't HIV positive after all. I realized that this could all too easily have gone the other way, and I knew at that moment that I had to change everything in my life.

Upon my release, I connected with a sponsor right away and started accepting direction from him. The first night back at Celebrate Recovery I was greeted by Big Al with one of his bear hugs. The unconditional love I felt that night gave me the strength to come back. I found encouragement through my sponsor, the Tuesday night Step Study, the Friday night Open Share groups and the awesome fellowship. God restored my relationship with my mother, father and stepfather and later blessed me with a beautiful, godly wife.

I'm often still afraid but hold on tightly to God even when the process hurts, because that's the path to healing. Through all of this, I've come to know the most compassionate and forgiving Father a man could ever hope for.

In an almost unbelievable, graphic example of God's grace, "Esau ran to meet Jacob and embraced him; he threw his arms around his neck and kissed him. And they wept" (Genesis 33:4).

Kenny

he arrived safely at the city of Shechem in Canaan and camped within sight of the city. ¹⁹For a hundred pieces of silver,ª he bought from the sons of Hamor, the father of Shechem, the plot of ground where he pitched his tent. ²⁰There he set up an altar and called it El Elohe Israel.ᵇ

Dinah and the Shechemites

34 Now Dinah, the daughter Leah had borne to Jacob, went out to visit the women of the land. ²When Shechem son of Hamor the Hivite, the ruler of that area, saw her, he took her and raped her. ³His heart was drawn to Dinah daughter of Jacob; he loved the young woman and spoke tenderly to her. ⁴And Shechem said to his father Hamor, "Get me this girl as my wife."

⁵When Jacob heard that his daughter Dinah had been defiled, his sons were in the fields with his livestock; so he did nothing about it until they came home.

⁶Then Shechem's father Hamor went out to talk with Jacob. ⁷Meanwhile, Jacob's sons had come in from the fields as soon as they heard what had happened. They were shocked and furious, because Shechem had done an outrageous thing inᶜ Israel by sleeping with Jacob's daughter — a thing that should not be done.

⁸But Hamor said to them, "My son Shechem has his heart set on your daughter. Please give her to him as his wife. ⁹Intermarry with us; give us your daughters and take our daughters for yourselves. ¹⁰You can settle among us; the land is open to you. Live in it, tradeᵈ in it, and acquire property in it."

¹¹Then Shechem said to Dinah's father and brothers, "Let me find favor in your eyes, and I will give you whatever you ask. ¹²Make the price for the bride and the gift I am to bring as great as you like, and I'll pay whatever you ask me. Only give me the young woman as my wife."

¹³Because their sister Dinah had been defiled, Jacob's sons replied deceitfully as they spoke to Shechem and his father Hamor. ¹⁴They said to them, "We can't do such a thing; we can't give our sister to a man who is not circumcised. That would be a disgrace to us. ¹⁵We will enter into an agreement with you on one condition only: that you become like us by circumcising all your males. ¹⁶Then we will give you our daughters and take your daughters for ourselves. We'll settle among you and become one people with you. ¹⁷But if you will not agree to be circumcised, we'll take our sister and go."

¹⁸Their proposal seemed good to Hamor and his son Shechem. ¹⁹The young man, who was the most honored of all his father's family, lost no time in doing what they said, because he was delighted with Jacob's daughter. ²⁰So Hamor and his son Shechem went to the gate of their city to speak to the men of their city. ²¹"These men are friendly toward us," they said. "Let them live in our land and trade in it; the land has plenty of room for them. We can marry their daughters and they can marry ours. ²²But the men will agree to live with us as one people only on the condition that our males be circumcised, as they themselves are. ²³Won't their livestock, their property and all their other animals become ours? So let us agree to their terms, and they will settle among us."

²⁴All the men who went out of the city gate agreed with Hamor and his son Shechem, and every male in the city was circumcised.

²⁵Three days later, while all of them were still in pain, two of Jacob's sons, Simeon and Levi, Dinah's brothers, took their swords and attacked the unsuspecting city, killing every male. ²⁶They put Hamor and his son Shechem to the sword and took Dinah from Shechem's house and left. ²⁷The sons of Jacob came upon the dead bodies and looted the city whereᵉ their sister had

---

ª 19 Hebrew *hundred kesitahs*; a kesitah was a unit of money of unknown weight and value.   ᵇ 20 *El Elohe Israel* can mean *El is the God of Israel* or *mighty is the God of Israel*.   ᶜ 7 Or *against*   ᵈ 10 Or *move about freely*; also in verse 21   ᵉ 27 Or *because*

MY NAME IS ESAU

GENESIS 33

Esau's life was marred by family struggle, beginning already when his "younger" twin brother and rival-to-be was born grasping his heel (see Genesis 25:26). Esau is often presented as a fool. He certainly made a snap decision in trading his inheritance for a bowl of stew (see 25:29–34) and later grieved both his parents by marrying two pagan Hittite women (see 26:34–35; 27:46). But Esau was also robbed of the firstborn's blessing by his devious brother, who conspired with his own mother (see 27:1–29). This tragic account reflects a home with a fatal flaw. Each parent had a favorite son, and in both cases their selection was based on personal preferences (see 25:27–28). The lack of mutual love and respect between the parents is especially glaring in Rebekah's deception of her own husband. The theft of his blessing led Esau to swear, "The days of mourning for my father are near; then I will kill my brother Jacob" (27:41). Jacob, at Mom's direction, fled for his life to his uncle in faraway Haran (see 27:42–45).

As Jacob at long last traveled back home from the north, he both plotted and prayed, fearful of facing Esau (see 32:1—33:3). But to Jacob's relief he found a brother who had recovered from his hatred and had set aside his drive to retaliate. Esau hugged and kissed Jacob and wept with him over their separation and reunion (see 33:1–5). Esau had learned to forgive and, in so doing, he recovered a brother and a friend. Although Esau wanted nothing in payment from Jacob, this formerly rash young man now had the grace to accept a gift anyway (see 33:8–12). He was reconciled to Jacob and respected by his brother's family (see 33:6–7).

Hanging on to bitterness, refusing to forgive what is past, can prevent us from enjoying God's provision in the present. Esau had made foolish decisions. But he had also been grievously wronged. Yet somewhere along the way he had found the wisdom and grace to let go of his past. We need to do the same in our recovery. What's done is done. We may have been wronged by members of our own family. But bitterness only prolongs our suffering. An unforgiving spirit builds barriers that isolate us from the love we could otherwise be enjoying. As God's children, each of us is commanded to "be kind and compassionate to one another, forgiving each other, just as in Christ God forgave you" (Ephesians 4:32). God's pardon to us was unconditional, and we too are to forgive without reservation. Setting aside our right to assign blame can bring reconciliation with others and healing to our own hearts.

Esau was willing to take his eyes off Jacob, look around at what God had given him, and announce that he already had plenty (see 33:9). We need to take a cue from Esau: We need to lay aside bitterness and take an unobstructed look at our own blessings.

been defiled. 28They seized their flocks and herds and donkeys and everything else of theirs in the city and out in the fields. 29They carried off all their wealth and all their women and children, taking as plunder everything in the houses.

30Then Jacob said to Simeon and Levi, "You have brought trouble on me by making me obnoxious to the Canaanites and Perizzites, the people living in this land. We are few in number, and if they join forces against me and attack me, I and my household will be destroyed."

31But they replied, "Should he have treated our sister like a prostitute?"

Jacob Returns to Bethel

35 Then God said to Jacob, "Go up to Bethel and settle there, and build an altar there to God, who appeared to you when you were fleeing from your brother Esau."

2So Jacob said to his household and to all who were with him, "Get rid of the foreign gods you have with you, and purify yourselves and change your clothes. 3Then come, let us go up to Bethel, where I will build an altar to God, who answered me in the day of my distress and who has been with me wherever I have gone." 4So they gave Jacob all the foreign gods they had and the rings in their ears, and Jacob buried them under the oak at Shechem. 5Then they set out, and the terror of God fell on the towns all around them so that no one pursued them.

6Jacob and all the people with him came to Luz (that is, Bethel) in the land of Canaan. 7There he built an altar, and he called the place El Bethel,a because it was there that God revealed himself to him when he was fleeing from his brother.

8Now Deborah, Rebekah's nurse, died and was buried under the oak outside Bethel. So it was named Allon Bakuth.b

9After Jacob returned from Paddan Aram,c God appeared to him again and blessed him. 10God said to him, "Your name is Jacob,d but you will no longer be called Jacob; your name will be Israel.e" So he named him Israel.

11And God said to him, "I am God Almightyf; be fruitful and increase in number. A nation and a community of nations will come from you, and kings will be among your descendants. 12The land I gave to Abraham and Isaac I also give to you, and I will give this land to your descendants after you." 13Then God went up from him at the place where he had talked with him.

14Jacob set up a stone pillar at the place where God had talked with him, and he poured out a drink offering on it; he also poured oil on it. 15Jacob called the place where God had talked with him Bethel.g

The Deaths of Rachel and Isaac

16Then they moved on from Bethel. While they were still some distance from Ephrath, Rachel began to give birth and had great difficulty. 17And as she was having great difficulty in childbirth, the midwife said to her, "Don't despair, for you have another son." 18As she breathed her last—for she was dying—she named her son Ben-Oni.h But his father named him Benjamin.i

19So Rachel died and was buried on the way to Ephrath (that is, Bethlehem). 20Over her tomb Jacob set up a pillar, and to this day that pillar marks Rachel's tomb.

21Israel moved on again and pitched his tent beyond Migdal Eder. 22While Israel was living in that region, Reuben went in and slept with his father's concubine Bilhah, and Israel heard of it.

Jacob had twelve sons:
23The sons of Leah:

---

a 7 El Bethel means God of Bethel.   b 8 Allon Bakuth means oak of weeping.   c 9 That is, Northwest Mesopotamia; also in verse 26   d 10 Jacob means he grasps the heel, a Hebrew idiom for he deceives.   e 10 Israel probably means he struggles with God.   f 11 Hebrew El-Shaddai   g 15 Bethel means house of God.   h 18 Ben-Oni means son of my trouble.   i 18 Benjamin means son of my right hand.

Reuben the firstborn of Jacob,
Simeon, Levi, Judah, Issachar and
Zebulun.
24 The sons of Rachel:
Joseph and Benjamin.
25 The sons of Rachel's servant Bilhah:
Dan and Naphtali.
26 The sons of Leah's servant Zilpah:
Gad and Asher.

These were the sons of Jacob, who were born to him in Paddan Aram.

27 Jacob came home to his father Isaac in Mamre, near Kiriath Arba (that is, Hebron), where Abraham and Isaac had stayed. 28 Isaac lived a hundred and eighty years. 29 Then he breathed his last and died and was gathered to his people, old and full of years. And his sons Esau and Jacob buried him.

Esau's Descendants

36 This is the account of the family line of Esau (that is, Edom).

2 Esau took his wives from the women of Canaan: Adah daughter of Elon the Hittite, and Oholibamah daughter of Anah and granddaughter of Zibeon the Hivite — 3 also Basemath daughter of Ishmael and sister of Nebaioth.

4 Adah bore Eliphaz to Esau, Basemath bore Reuel, 5 and Oholibamah bore Jeush, Jalam and Korah. These were the sons of Esau, who were born to him in Canaan.

6 Esau took his wives and sons and daughters and all the members of his household, as well as his livestock and all his other animals and all the goods he had acquired in Canaan, and moved to a land some distance from his brother Jacob. 7 Their possessions were too great for them to remain together; the land where they were staying could not support them both because of their livestock. 8 So Esau (that is, Edom) settled in the hill country of Seir.

9 This is the account of the family line of Esau the father of the Edomites in the hill country of Seir.

10 These are the names of Esau's sons:
Eliphaz, the son of Esau's wife Adah, and Reuel, the son of Esau's wife Basemath.
11 The sons of Eliphaz:
Teman, Omar, Zepho, Gatam and Kenaz.
12 Esau's son Eliphaz also had a concubine named Timna, who bore him Amalek. These were grandsons of Esau's wife Adah.
13 The sons of Reuel:
Nahath, Zerah, Shammah and Mizzah. These were grandsons of Esau's wife Basemath.
14 The sons of Esau's wife Oholibamah daughter of Anah and granddaughter of Zibeon, whom she bore to Esau:
Jeush, Jalam and Korah.

15 These were the chiefs among Esau's descendants:
The sons of Eliphaz the firstborn of Esau:
Chiefs Teman, Omar, Zepho, Kenaz, 16 Korah,*a* Gatam and Amalek. These were the chiefs descended from Eliphaz in Edom; they were grandsons of Adah.
17 The sons of Esau's son Reuel:
Chiefs Nahath, Zerah, Shammah and Mizzah. These were the chiefs descended from Reuel in Edom; they were grandsons of Esau's wife Basemath.
18 The sons of Esau's wife Oholibamah:
Chiefs Jeush, Jalam and Korah. These were the chiefs descended from Esau's wife Oholibamah daughter of Anah.

---

a 16 Masoretic Text; Samaritan Pentateuch (also verse 11 and 1 Chron. 1:36) does not have *Korah*.

My Name Is Bill

I'M A BELIEVER WHO STRUGGLES WITH ADDICTIVE BEHAVIORS AND CODEPENDENCY

Please read in Genesis 33 the account of the harmonious reunion between Esau and his brother, Jacob, who had years earlier so grievously wronged him.

"Can't you do anything right?" "What's wrong with you?" "I wish you'd never been born." The seeds of shame were sown and repeatedly fertilized throughout my youth. My dad was an abusive alcoholic, a man in pain. In his confused evaluation I was bad, unworthy of his love and utterly displeasing to him. When he died I didn't cry—not because I didn't care, but because I'd been taught that a man doesn't cry. I became the man of the house, a surrogate husband for my mom and a surrogate dad for my brother. I began to resent this emotional connection with my mom, and this carried over into my relationships with all other women.

At about this time a confusing thing happened to me: I was sexually abused by a woman in her 30s. My feelings were conflicted, though, because it felt good but I also felt damaged and ashamed. I had no one to turn to, not even God. Growing up, I'd been taught to be afraid of God, knowing that I could never achieve his impossible standards of perfection. Since I'd been made to believe from the outset that I was a mistake, my self-image became performance-based; whatever value I may have had came from *what* I did, not from *who* I was. At times, even today, I still fight that all-too-familiar battle.

I excelled as a student in academics and as an adult in work, all the while seeking drugs, sex and self-made pornographic movies as an escape. One morning I found a note from my wife. She stated simply that she couldn't "do this" anymore and proceeded to leave both me and my son behind. The ordeal crushed my heart. I resented my mom for the emotional abuse and now my wife for abandoning me. I became a man trapped in a catch-22: I hated women but couldn't live without them.

I wandered for many years in an emotional wasteland before finally hitting the wall. I lost my career, my financial well-being and my perceived ability to control my own life. It was then that my story shifted. God allowed Leslie, my wife now of 15 years, to lead me to the Lord.

Through her loving and patient intervention I became a new creation in Christ. But that was only the start of the process, not the end. I was still struggling with the poisonous influence of all the junk I had accumulated in my life. I grappled endlessly with the pervasive question *why*. I wept and cursed at God — and he responded by allowing me to see precisely what I needed, right there in the midst of all my pain. I needed to reduce the size of my rearview mirror. I needed to heal. I needed to understand why I was perpetually abusing the woman I loved more than life itself. I needed to get in touch with my feelings, to deal with the abuse I had endured in an appropriate manner — not in a way that continued to hurt my wife and others. I needed to forgive and to let God take control. I submitted myself to the process of recovery through the Celebrate Recovery program. It was hard, painful work, and at times it still is. But the results over time tell the story: Nothing is beyond repair — *nothing*.

My life had been one of struggle, much like Esau's. I had made foolish decisions and allowed my pain to turn into anger that was directed at others. In Genesis 33 Esau, who had been so wronged, demonstrated without words that he had found forgiveness in his heart and recovery from his hatred (see Genesis 33:1 – 5). Like him, I have truly learned to forgive, neither expecting nor wanting anything in return (see vv. 8 – 12). There's no doubt that I had every "reason" to retaliate, but instead, through the intervention of Celebrate Recovery, I've asked God to forgive my deceitful heart. I've managed with the Holy Spirit's help to let go of my past. I thank God daily for the gift of forgiveness because nothing less could have brought reconciliation into my life and healing to my heart.

Bill

¹⁹These were the sons of Esau (that is, Edom), and these were their chiefs.

²⁰These were the sons of Seir the Horite, who were living in the region:

Lotan, Shobal, Zibeon, Anah, ²¹Dishon, Ezer and Dishan. These sons of Seir in Edom were Horite chiefs.

²²The sons of Lotan:

Hori and Homam.ᵃ Timna was Lotan's sister.

²³The sons of Shobal:

Alvan, Manahath, Ebal, Shepho and Onam.

²⁴The sons of Zibeon:

Aiah and Anah. This is the Anah who discovered the hot springsᵇ in the desert while he was grazing the donkeys of his father Zibeon.

²⁵The children of Anah:

Dishon and Oholibamah daughter of Anah.

²⁶The sons of Dishonᶜ:

Hemdan, Eshban, Ithran and Keran.

²⁷The sons of Ezer:

Bilhan, Zaavan and Akan.

²⁸The sons of Dishan:

Uz and Aran.

²⁹These were the Horite chiefs:

Lotan, Shobal, Zibeon, Anah, ³⁰Dishon, Ezer and Dishan. These were the Horite chiefs, according to their divisions, in the land of Seir.

The Rulers of Edom

³¹These were the kings who reigned in Edom before any Israelite king reigned:

³²Bela son of Beor became king of Edom. His city was named Dinhabah.

³³When Bela died, Jobab son of Zerah from Bozrah succeeded him as king.

³⁴When Jobab died, Husham from the land of the Temanites succeeded him as king.

³⁵When Husham died, Hadad son of Bedad, who defeated Midian in the country of Moab, succeeded him as king. His city was named Avith.

³⁶When Hadad died, Samlah from Masrekah succeeded him as king.

³⁷When Samlah died, Shaul from Rehoboth on the river succeeded him as king.

³⁸When Shaul died, Baal-Hanan son of Akbor succeeded him as king.

³⁹When Baal-Hanan son of Akbor died, Hadadᵈ succeeded him as king. His city was named Pau, and his wife's name was Mehetabel daughter of Matred, the daughter of Me-Zahab.

⁴⁰These were the chiefs descended from Esau, by name, according to their clans and regions:

Timna, Alvah, Jetheth, ⁴¹Oholibamah, Elah, Pinon, ⁴²Kenaz, Teman, Mibzar, ⁴³Magdiel and Iram. These were the chiefs of Edom, according to their settlements in the land they occupied.

This is the family line of Esau, the father of the Edomites.

Joseph's Dreams

37 Jacob lived in the land where his father had stayed, the land of Canaan.

²This is the account of Jacob's family line.

Joseph, a young man of seventeen, was tending the flocks with his brothers, the sons of Bilhah and the sons of Zilpah, his father's wives, and he brought their father a bad report about them.

³Now Israel loved Joseph more than any of his other sons, because he had been born

---

ᵃ 22 Hebrew *Hemam*, a variant of *Homam* (see 1 Chron. 1:39)   ᵇ 24 Vulgate; Syriac *discovered water*; the meaning of the Hebrew for this word is uncertain.   ᶜ 26 Hebrew *Dishan*, a variant of *Dishon*   ᵈ 39 Many manuscripts of the Masoretic Text, Samaritan Pentateuch and Syriac (see also 1 Chron. 1:50); most manuscripts of the Masoretic Text *Hadar* to him in his old age; and he made an ornate*a* robe for him. ⁴When his brothers saw that their father loved him more than any of them, they hated him and could not speak a kind word to him.

⁵Joseph had a dream, and when he told it to his brothers, they hated him all the more. ⁶He said to them, "Listen to this dream I had: ⁷We were binding sheaves of grain out in the field when suddenly my sheaf rose and stood upright, while your sheaves gathered around mine and bowed down to it."

⁸His brothers said to him, "Do you intend to reign over us? Will you actually rule us?" And they hated him all the more because of his dream and what he had said.

⁹Then he had another dream, and he told it to his brothers. "Listen," he said, "I had another dream, and this time the sun and moon and eleven stars were bowing down to me."

¹⁰When he told his father as well as his brothers, his father rebuked him and said, "What is this dream you had? Will your mother and I and your brothers actually come and bow down to the ground before you?" ¹¹His brothers were jealous of him, but his father kept the matter in mind.

Joseph Sold by His Brothers

¹²Now his brothers had gone to graze their father's flocks near Shechem, ¹³and Israel said to Joseph, "As you know, your brothers are grazing the flocks near Shechem. Come, I am going to send you to them."

"Very well," he replied.

¹⁴So he said to him, "Go and see if all is well with your brothers and with the flocks, and bring word back to me." Then he sent him off from the Valley of Hebron.

When Joseph arrived at Shechem, ¹⁵a man found him wandering around in the fields and asked him, "What are you looking for?"

¹⁶He replied, "I'm looking for my brothers. Can you tell me where they are grazing their flocks?"

¹⁷"They have moved on from here," the man answered. "I heard them say, 'Let's go to Dothan.'"

So Joseph went after his brothers and found them near Dothan. ¹⁸But they saw him in the distance, and before he reached them, they plotted to kill him.

¹⁹"Here comes that dreamer!" they said to each other. ²⁰"Come now, let's kill him and throw him into one of these cisterns and say that a ferocious animal devoured him. Then we'll see what comes of his dreams."

²¹When Reuben heard this, he tried to rescue him from their hands. "Let's not take his life," he said. ²²"Don't shed any blood. Throw him into this cistern here in the wilderness, but don't lay a hand on him." Reuben said this to rescue him from them and take him back to his father.

²³So when Joseph came to his brothers, they stripped him of his robe — the ornate robe he was wearing — ²⁴and they took him and threw him into the cistern. The cistern was empty; there was no water in it.

²⁵As they sat down to eat their meal, they looked up and saw a caravan of Ishmaelites coming from Gilead. Their camels were loaded with spices, balm and myrrh, and they were on their way to take them down to Egypt.

²⁶Judah said to his brothers, "What will we gain if we kill our brother and cover up his blood? ²⁷Come, let's sell him to the Ishmaelites and not lay our hands on him; after all, he is our brother, our own flesh and blood." His brothers agreed.

²⁸So when the Midianite merchants came by, his brothers pulled Joseph up out of the cistern and sold him for twenty shekels*b* of silver to the Ishmaelites, who took him to Egypt.

²⁹When Reuben returned to the cistern and saw that Joseph was not there, he tore

---

a 3 The meaning of the Hebrew for this word is uncertain; also in verses 23 and 32.   *b 28* That is, about 8 ounces or about 230 grams his clothes. ³⁰He went back to his brothers and said, "The boy isn't there! Where can I turn now?"

³¹Then they got Joseph's robe, slaughtered a goat and dipped the robe in the blood. ³²They took the ornate robe back to their father and said, "We found this. Examine it to see whether it is your son's robe."

³³He recognized it and said, "It is my son's robe! Some ferocious animal has devoured him. Joseph has surely been torn to pieces."

³⁴Then Jacob tore his clothes, put on sackcloth and mourned for his son many days. ³⁵All his sons and daughters came to comfort him, but he refused to be comforted. "No," he said, "I will continue to mourn until I join my son in the grave." So his father wept for him.

³⁶Meanwhile, the Midianites[a] sold Joseph in Egypt to Potiphar, one of Pharaoh's officials, the captain of the guard.

Judah and Tamar

38 At that time, Judah left his brothers and went down to stay with a man of Adullam named Hirah. ²There Judah met the daughter of a Canaanite man named Shua. He married her and made love to her; ³she became pregnant and gave birth to a son, who was named Er. ⁴She conceived again and gave birth to a son and named him Onan. ⁵She gave birth to still another son and named him Shelah. It was at Kezib that she gave birth to him.

⁶Judah got a wife for Er, his firstborn, and her name was Tamar. ⁷But Er, Judah's firstborn, was wicked in the LORD's sight; so the LORD put him to death. ⁸Then Judah said to Onan, "Sleep with your brother's wife and fulfill your duty to her as a brother-in-law to raise up offspring for your brother." ⁹But Onan knew that the child would not be his; so whenever he slept with his brother's wife, he spilled his semen on the ground to keep from providing offspring for his brother. ¹⁰What he

did was wicked in the LORD's sight; so the LORD put him to death also.

¹¹Judah then said to his daughter-in-law Tamar, "Live as a widow in your father's household until my son Shelah grows up." For he thought, "He may die too, just like his brothers." So Tamar went to live in her father's household.

¹²After a long time Judah's wife, the daughter of Shua, died. When Judah had recovered from his grief, he went up to Timnah, to the men who were shearing his sheep, and his friend Hirah the Adullamite went with him.

¹³When Tamar was told, "Your father-in-law is on his way to Timnah to shear his sheep," ¹⁴she took off her widow's clothes, covered herself with a veil to disguise herself, and then sat down at the entrance to Enaim, which is on the road to Timnah. For she saw that, though Shelah had now grown up, she had not been given to him as his wife.

¹⁵When Judah saw her, he thought she was a prostitute, for she had covered her face. ¹⁶Not realizing that she was his daughter-in-law, he went over to her by the roadside and said, "Come now, let me sleep with you."

"And what will you give me to sleep with you?" she asked.

¹⁷"I'll send you a young goat from my flock," he said.

"Will you give me something as a pledge until you send it?" she asked.

¹⁸He said, "What pledge should I give you?"

"Your seal and its cord, and the staff in your hand," she answered. So he gave them to her and slept with her, and she became pregnant by him. ¹⁹After she left, she took off her veil and put on her widow's clothes again.

²⁰Meanwhile Judah sent the young goat by his friend the Adullamite in order to get his pledge back from the woman, but he did not find her. ²¹He asked the men who lived there, "Where is the shrine prostitute who was beside the road at Enaim?"

---

a 36 Samaritan Pentateuch, Septuagint, Vulgate and Syriac (see also verse 28); Masoretic Text *Medanites*

"There hasn't been any shrine prostitute here," they said.

[22]So he went back to Judah and said, "I didn't find her. Besides, the men who lived there said, 'There hasn't been any shrine prostitute here.'"

[23]Then Judah said, "Let her keep what she has, or we will become a laughingstock. After all, I did send her this young goat, but you didn't find her."

[24]About three months later Judah was told, "Your daughter-in-law Tamar is guilty of prostitution, and as a result she is now pregnant."

Judah said, "Bring her out and have her burned to death!"

[25]As she was being brought out, she sent a message to her father-in-law. "I am pregnant by the man who owns these," she said. And she added, "See if you recognize whose seal and cord and staff these are."

[26]Judah recognized them and said, "She is more righteous than I, since I wouldn't give her to my son Shelah." And he did not sleep with her again.

[27]When the time came for her to give birth, there were twin boys in her womb. [28]As she was giving birth, one of them put out his hand; so the midwife took a scarlet thread and tied it on his wrist and said, "This one came out first." [29]But when he drew back his hand, his brother came out, and she said, "So this is how you have broken out!" And he was named Perez.[a] [30]Then his brother, who had the scarlet thread on his wrist, came out. And he was named Zerah.[b]

Joseph and Potiphar's Wife

39 Now Joseph had been taken down to Egypt. Potiphar, an Egyptian who was one of Pharaoh's officials, the captain of the guard, bought him from the Ishmaelites who had taken him there.

[2]The LORD was with Joseph so that he prospered, and he lived in the house of his Egyptian master. [3]When his master saw that the LORD was with him and that the LORD gave him success in everything he did, [4]Joseph found favor in his eyes and became his attendant. Potiphar put him in charge of his household, and he entrusted to his care everything he owned. [5]From the time he put him in charge of his household and of all that he owned, the LORD blessed the household of the Egyptian because of Joseph. The blessing of the LORD was on everything Potiphar had, both in the house and in the field. [6]So Potiphar left everything he had in Joseph's care; with Joseph in charge, he did not concern himself with anything except the food he ate.

Now Joseph was well-built and handsome, [7]and after a while his master's wife took notice of Joseph and said, "Come to bed with me!"

[8]But he refused. "With me in charge," he told her, "my master does not concern himself with anything in the house; everything he owns he has entrusted to my care. [9]No one is greater in this house than I am. My master has withheld nothing from me except you, because you are his wife. How then could I do such a wicked thing and sin against God?" [10]And though she spoke to Joseph day after day, he refused to go to bed with her or even be with her.

[11]One day he went into the house to attend to his duties, and none of the household servants was inside. [12]She caught him by his cloak and said, "Come to bed with me!" But he left his cloak in her hand and ran out of the house.

[13]When she saw that he had left his cloak in her hand and had run out of the house, [14]she called her household servants. "Look," she said to them, "this Hebrew has been brought to us to make sport of us! He came in here to sleep with me, but I screamed. [15]When he heard me scream for help, he left his cloak beside me and ran out of the house."

[16]She kept his cloak beside her until his

---

[a] 29 *Perez* means *breaking out.*   [b] 30 *Zerah* can mean *scarlet* or *brightness.*

master came home. ¹⁷Then she told him this story: "That Hebrew slave you brought us came to me to make sport of me. ¹⁸But as soon as I screamed for help, he left his cloak beside me and ran out of the house."

¹⁹When his master heard the story his wife told him, saying, "This is how your slave treated me," he burned with anger. ²⁰Joseph's master took him and put him in prison, the place where the king's prisoners were confined.

But while Joseph was there in the prison, ²¹the LORD was with him; he showed him kindness and granted him favor in the eyes of the prison warden. ²²So the warden put Joseph in charge of all those held in the prison, and he was made responsible for all that was done there. ²³The warden paid no attention to anything under Joseph's care, because the LORD was with Joseph and gave him success in whatever he did.

The Cupbearer and the Baker

40 Some time later, the cupbearer and the baker of the king of Egypt offended their master, the king of Egypt. ²Pharaoh was angry with his two officials, the chief cupbearer and the chief baker, ³and put them in custody in the house of the captain of the guard, in the same prison where Joseph was confined. ⁴The captain of the guard assigned them to Joseph, and he attended them.

After they had been in custody for some time, ⁵each of the two men — the cupbearer and the baker of the king of Egypt, who were being held in prison — had a dream the same night, and each dream had a meaning of its own.

⁶When Joseph came to them the next morning, he saw that they were dejected. ⁷So he asked Pharaoh's officials who were in custody with him in his master's house, "Why do you look so sad today?"

⁸"We both had dreams," they answered, "but there is no one to interpret them."

Then Joseph said to them, "Do not interpretations belong to God? Tell me your dreams."

⁹So the chief cupbearer told Joseph his dream. He said to him, "In my dream I saw a vine in front of me, ¹⁰and on the vine were three branches. As soon as it budded, it blossomed, and its clusters ripened into grapes. ¹¹Pharaoh's cup was in my hand, and I took the grapes, squeezed them into Pharaoh's cup and put the cup in his hand."

¹²"This is what it means," Joseph said to him. "The three branches are three days. ¹³Within three days Pharaoh will lift up your head and restore you to your position, and you will put Pharaoh's cup in his hand, just as you used to do when you were his cupbearer. ¹⁴But when all goes well with you, remember me and show me kindness; mention me to Pharaoh and get me out of this prison. ¹⁵I was forcibly carried off from the land of the Hebrews, and even here I have done nothing to deserve being put in a dungeon."

¹⁶When the chief baker saw that Joseph had given a favorable interpretation, he said to Joseph, "I too had a dream: On my head were three baskets of bread.ᵃ ¹⁷In the top basket were all kinds of baked goods for Pharaoh, but the birds were eating them out of the basket on my head."

¹⁸"This is what it means," Joseph said. "The three baskets are three days. ¹⁹Within three days Pharaoh will lift off your head and impale your body on a pole. And the birds will eat away your flesh."

²⁰Now the third day was Pharaoh's birthday, and he gave a feast for all his officials. He lifted up the heads of the chief cupbearer and the chief baker in the presence of his officials: ²¹He restored the chief cupbearer to his position, so that he once again put the cup into Pharaoh's hand — ²²but he impaled the chief baker, just as Joseph had said to them in his interpretation.

²³The chief cupbearer, however, did not remember Joseph; he forgot him.

ᵃ 16 Or *three wicker baskets*

Pharaoh's Dreams

41 When two full years had passed, Pharaoh had a dream: He was standing by the Nile, 2when out of the river there came up seven cows, sleek and fat, and they grazed among the reeds. 3After them, seven other cows, ugly and gaunt, came up out of the Nile and stood beside those on the riverbank. 4And the cows that were ugly and gaunt ate up the seven sleek, fat cows. Then Pharaoh woke up.

5He fell asleep again and had a second dream: Seven heads of grain, healthy and good, were growing on a single stalk. 6After them, seven other heads of grain sprouted—thin and scorched by the east wind. 7The thin heads of grain swallowed up the seven healthy, full heads. Then Pharaoh woke up; it had been a dream.

8In the morning his mind was troubled, so he sent for all the magicians and wise men of Egypt. Pharaoh told them his dreams, but no one could interpret them for him.

9Then the chief cupbearer said to Pharaoh, "Today I am reminded of my shortcomings. 10Pharaoh was once angry with his servants, and he imprisoned me and the chief baker in the house of the captain of the guard. 11Each of us had a dream the same night, and each dream had a meaning of its own. 12Now a young Hebrew was there with us, a servant of the captain of the guard. We told him our dreams, and he interpreted them for us, giving each man the interpretation of his dream. 13And things turned out exactly as he interpreted them to us: I was restored to my position, and the other man was impaled."

14So Pharaoh sent for Joseph, and he was quickly brought from the dungeon. When he had shaved and changed his clothes, he came before Pharaoh.

15Pharaoh said to Joseph, "I had a dream, and no one can interpret it. But I have heard it said of you that when you hear a dream you can interpret it."

16"I cannot do it," Joseph replied to Pharaoh, "but God will give Pharaoh the answer he desires."

17Then Pharaoh said to Joseph, "In my dream I was standing on the bank of the Nile, 18when out of the river there came up seven cows, fat and sleek, and they grazed among the reeds. 19After them, seven other cows came up—scrawny and very ugly and lean. I had never seen such ugly cows in all the land of Egypt. 20The lean, ugly cows ate up the seven fat cows that came up first. 21But even after they ate them, no one could tell that they had done so; they looked just as ugly as before. Then I woke up.

22"In my dream I saw seven heads of grain, full and good, growing on a single stalk. 23After them, seven other heads sprouted—withered and thin and scorched by the east wind. 24The thin heads of grain swallowed up the seven good heads. I told this to the magicians, but none of them could explain it to me."

25Then Joseph said to Pharaoh, "The dreams of Pharaoh are one and the same. God has revealed to Pharaoh what he is about to do. 26The seven good cows are seven years, and the seven good heads of grain are seven years; it is one and the same dream. 27The seven lean, ugly cows that came up afterward are seven years, and so are the seven worthless heads of grain scorched by the east wind: They are seven years of famine.

28"It is just as I said to Pharaoh: God has shown Pharaoh what he is about to do. 29Seven years of great abundance are coming throughout the land of Egypt, 30but seven years of famine will follow them. Then all the abundance in Egypt will be forgotten, and the famine will ravage the land. 31The abundance in the land will not be remembered, because the famine that follows it will be so severe. 32The reason the dream was given to Pharaoh in two forms is that the matter has been firmly decided by God, and God will do it soon.

33"And now let Pharaoh look for a

discerning and wise man and put him in charge of the land of Egypt. 34Let Pharaoh appoint commissioners over the land to take a fifth of the harvest of Egypt during the seven years of abundance. 35They should collect all the food of these good years that are coming and store up the grain under the authority of Pharaoh, to be kept in the cities for food. 36This food should be held in reserve for the country, to be used during the seven years of famine that will come upon Egypt, so that the country may not be ruined by the famine."

37The plan seemed good to Pharaoh and to all his officials. 38So Pharaoh asked them, "Can we find anyone like this man, one in whom is the spirit of God*a*?"

39Then Pharaoh said to Joseph, "Since God has made all this known to you, there is no one so discerning and wise as you. 40You shall be in charge of my palace, and all my people are to submit to your orders. Only with respect to the throne will I be greater than you."

Joseph in Charge of Egypt

41So Pharaoh said to Joseph, "I hereby put you in charge of the whole land of Egypt." 42Then Pharaoh took his signet ring from his finger and put it on Joseph's finger. He dressed him in robes of fine linen and put a gold chain around his neck. 43He had him ride in a chariot as his second-in-command,*b* and people shouted before him, "Make way*c*!" Thus he put him in charge of the whole land of Egypt.

44Then Pharaoh said to Joseph, "I am Pharaoh, but without your word no one will lift hand or foot in all Egypt." 45Pharaoh gave Joseph the name Zaphenath-Paneah and gave him Asenath daughter of Potiphera, priest of On,*d* to be his wife. And Joseph went throughout the land of Egypt.

46Joseph was thirty years old when he entered the service of Pharaoh king of Egypt. And Joseph went out from Pharaoh's presence and traveled throughout Egypt. 47During the seven years of abundance the land produced plentifully. 48Joseph collected all the food produced in those seven years of abundance in Egypt and stored it in the cities. In each city he put the food grown in the fields surrounding it. 49Joseph stored up huge quantities of grain, like the sand of the sea; it was so much that he stopped keeping records because it was beyond measure.

50Before the years of famine came, two sons were born to Joseph by Asenath daughter of Potiphera, priest of On. 51Joseph named his firstborn Manasseh*e* and said, "It is because God has made me forget all my trouble and all my father's household." 52The second son he named Ephraim*f* and said, "It is because God has made me fruitful in the land of my suffering."

53The seven years of abundance in Egypt came to an end, 54and the seven years of famine began, just as Joseph had said. There was famine in all the other lands, but in the whole land of Egypt there was food. 55When all Egypt began to feel the famine, the people cried to Pharaoh for food. Then Pharaoh told all the Egyptians, "Go to Joseph and do what he tells you."

56When the famine had spread over the whole country, Joseph opened all the storehouses and sold grain to the Egyptians, for the famine was severe throughout Egypt. 57And all the world came to Egypt to buy grain from Joseph, because the famine was severe everywhere.

Joseph's Brothers Go to Egypt

42 When Jacob learned that there was grain in Egypt, he said to his sons, "Why do you just keep looking at each other?" 2He continued, "I have heard that there is grain in Egypt. Go down there and buy some for us, so that we may live and not die."

---

a 38 Or *of the gods*   *b 43* Or *in the chariot of his second-in-command;* or *in his second chariot*   *c 43* Or *Bow down*   *d 45* That is, Heliopolis; also in verse 50   *e 51* Manasseh sounds like and may be derived from the Hebrew for *forget.*   *f 52* Ephraim sounds like the Hebrew for *twice fruitful.*

③Then ten of Joseph's brothers went down to buy grain from Egypt. ⁴But Jacob did not send Benjamin, Joseph's brother, with the others, because he was afraid that harm might come to him. ⁵So Israel's sons were among those who went to buy grain, for there was famine in the land of Canaan also.

⁶Now Joseph was the governor of the land, the person who sold grain to all its people. So when Joseph's brothers arrived, they bowed down to him with their faces to the ground. ⁷As soon as Joseph saw his brothers, he recognized them, but he pretended to be a stranger and spoke harshly to them. "Where do you come from?" he asked.

"From the land of Canaan," they replied, "to buy food."

⁸Although Joseph recognized his brothers, they did not recognize him. ⁹Then he remembered his dreams about them and said to them, "You are spies! You have come to see where our land is unprotected."

¹⁰"No, my lord," they answered. "Your servants have come to buy food. ¹¹We are all the sons of one man. Your servants are honest men, not spies."

¹²"No!" he said to them. "You have come to see where our land is unprotected."

¹³But they replied, "Your servants were twelve brothers, the sons of one man, who lives in the land of Canaan. The youngest is now with our father, and one is no more."

¹⁴Joseph said to them, "It is just as I told you: You are spies! ¹⁵And this is how you will be tested: As surely as Pharaoh lives, you will not leave this place unless your youngest brother comes here. ¹⁶Send one of your number to get your brother; the rest of you will be kept in prison, so that your words may be tested to see if you are telling the truth. If you are not, then as surely as Pharaoh lives, you are spies!" ¹⁷And he put them all in custody for three days.

¹⁸On the third day, Joseph said to them, "Do this and you will live, for I fear God: ¹⁹If you are honest men, let one of your brothers stay here in prison, while the rest

of you go and take grain back for your starving households. ²⁰But you must bring your youngest brother to me, so that your words may be verified and that you may not die." This they proceeded to do.

²¹They said to one another, "Surely we are being punished because of our brother. We saw how distressed he was when he pleaded with us for his life, but we would not listen; that's why this distress has come on us."

²²Reuben replied, "Didn't I tell you not to sin against the boy? But you wouldn't listen! Now we must give an accounting for his blood." ²³They did not realize that Joseph could understand them, since he was using an interpreter.

²⁴He turned away from them and began to weep, but then came back and spoke to them again. He had Simeon taken from them and bound before their eyes.

²⁵Joseph gave orders to fill their bags with grain, to put each man's silver back in his sack, and to give them provisions for their journey. After this was done for them, ²⁶they loaded their grain on their donkeys and left.

²⁷At the place where they stopped for the night one of them opened his sack to get feed for his donkey, and he saw his silver in the mouth of his sack. ²⁸"My silver has been returned," he said to his brothers. "Here it is in my sack."

Their hearts sank and they turned to each other trembling and said, "What is this that God has done to us?"

²⁹When they came to their father Jacob in the land of Canaan, they told him all that had happened to them. They said, ³⁰"The man who is lord over the land spoke harshly to us and treated us as though we were spying on the land. ³¹But we said to him, 'We are honest men; we are not spies. ³²We were twelve brothers, sons of one father. One is no more, and the youngest is now with our father in Canaan.'

³³"Then the man who is lord over the land said to us, 'This is how I will know whether you are honest men: Leave one of

your brothers here with me, and take food for your starving households and go. 34But bring your youngest brother to me so I will know that you are not spies but honest men. Then I will give your brother back to you, and you can trade*a* in the land.'"

35As they were emptying their sacks, there in each man's sack was his pouch of silver! When they and their father saw the money pouches, they were frightened. 36Their father Jacob said to them, "You have deprived me of my children. Joseph is no more and Simeon is no more, and now you want to take Benjamin. Everything is against me!"

37Then Reuben said to his father, "You may put both of my sons to death if I do not bring him back to you. Entrust him to my care, and I will bring him back."

38But Jacob said, "My son will not go down there with you; his brother is dead and he is the only one left. If harm comes to him on the journey you are taking, you will bring my gray head down to the grave in sorrow."

The Second Journey to Egypt

43 Now the famine was still severe in the land. 2So when they had eaten all the grain they had brought from Egypt, their father said to them, "Go back and buy us a little more food."

3But Judah said to him, "The man warned us solemnly, 'You will not see my face again unless your brother is with you.' 4If you will send our brother along with us, we will go down and buy food for you. 5But if you will not send him, we will not go down, because the man said to us, 'You will not see my face again unless your brother is with you.'"

6Israel asked, "Why did you bring this trouble on me by telling the man you had another brother?"

7They replied, "The man questioned us closely about ourselves and our family. 'Is your father still living?' he asked us.

'Do you have another brother?' We simply answered his questions. How were we to know he would say, 'Bring your brother down here'?"

8Then Judah said to Israel his father, "Send the boy along with me and we will go at once, so that we and you and our children may live and not die. 9I myself will guarantee his safety; you can hold me personally responsible for him. If I do not bring him back to you and set him here before you, I will bear the blame before you all my life. 10As it is, if we had not delayed, we could have gone and returned twice."

11Then their father Israel said to them, "If it must be, then do this: Put some of the best products of the land in your bags and take them down to the man as a gift—a little balm and a little honey, some spices and myrrh, some pistachio nuts and almonds. 12Take double the amount of silver with you, for you must return the silver that was put back into the mouths of your sacks. Perhaps it was a mistake. 13Take your brother also and go back to the man at once. 14And may God Almighty*b* grant you mercy before the man so that he will let your other brother and Benjamin come back with you. As for me, if I am bereaved, I am bereaved."

15So the men took the gifts and double the amount of silver, and Benjamin also. They hurried down to Egypt and presented themselves to Joseph. 16When Joseph saw Benjamin with them, he said to the steward of his house, "Take these men to my house, slaughter an animal and prepare a meal; they are to eat with me at noon."

17The man did as Joseph told him and took the men to Joseph's house. 18Now the men were frightened when they were taken to his house. They thought, "We were brought here because of the silver that was put back into our sacks the first time. He wants to attack us and overpower us and seize us as slaves and take our donkeys."

19So they went up to Joseph's steward

---

a 34 Or *move about freely*   *b 14* Hebrew *El-Shaddai*

and spoke to him at the entrance to the house. 20"We beg your pardon, our lord," they said, "we came down here the first time to buy food. 21But at the place where we stopped for the night we opened our sacks and each of us found his silver — the exact weight — in the mouth of his sack. So we have brought it back with us. 22We have also brought additional silver with us to buy food. We don't know who put our silver in our sacks."

23"It's all right," he said. "Don't be afraid. Your God, the God of your father, has given you treasure in your sacks; I received your silver." Then he brought Simeon out to them.

24The steward took the men into Joseph's house, gave them water to wash their feet and provided fodder for their donkeys. 25They prepared their gifts for Joseph's arrival at noon, because they had heard that they were to eat there.

26When Joseph came home, they presented to him the gifts they had brought into the house, and they bowed down before him to the ground. 27He asked them how they were, and then he said, "How is your aged father you told me about? Is he still living?"

28They replied, "Your servant our father is still alive and well." And they bowed down, prostrating themselves before him.

29As he looked about and saw his brother Benjamin, his own mother's son, he asked, "Is this your youngest brother, the one you told me about?" And he said, "God be gracious to you, my son." 30Deeply moved at the sight of his brother, Joseph hurried out and looked for a place to weep. He went into his private room and wept there.

31After he had washed his face, he came out and, controlling himself, said, "Serve the food."

32They served him by himself, the brothers by themselves, and the Egyptians who ate with him by themselves, because Egyptians could not eat with Hebrews, for that is detestable to Egyptians. 33The men had been seated before him in the order of their ages, from the firstborn to the youngest; and they looked at each other in astonishment. 34When portions were served to them from Joseph's table, Benjamin's portion was five times as much as anyone else's. So they feasted and drank freely with him.

A Silver Cup in a Sack

44 Now Joseph gave these instructions to the steward of his house: "Fill the men's sacks with as much food as they can carry, and put each man's silver in the mouth of his sack. 2Then put my cup, the silver one, in the mouth of the youngest one's sack, along with the silver for his grain." And he did as Joseph said.

3As morning dawned, the men were sent on their way with their donkeys. 4They had not gone far from the city when Joseph said to his steward, "Go after those men at once, and when you catch up with them, say to them, 'Why have you repaid good with evil? 5Isn't this the cup my master drinks from and also uses for divination? This is a wicked thing you have done.'"

6When he caught up with them, he repeated these words to them. 7But they said to him, "Why does my lord say such things? Far be it from your servants to do anything like that! 8We even brought back to you from the land of Canaan the silver we found inside the mouths of our sacks. So why would we steal silver or gold from your master's house? 9If any of your servants is found to have it, he will die; and the rest of us will become my lord's slaves."

10"Very well, then," he said, "let it be as you say. Whoever is found to have it will become my slave; the rest of you will be free from blame."

11Each of them quickly lowered his sack to the ground and opened it. 12Then the steward proceeded to search, beginning with the oldest and ending with the youngest. And the cup was found in Benjamin's sack. 13At this, they tore their clothes. Then they all loaded their donkeys and returned to the city.

¹⁴Joseph was still in the house when Judah and his brothers came in, and they threw themselves to the ground before him. ¹⁵Joseph said to them, "What is this you have done? Don't you know that a man like me can find things out by divination?"

¹⁶"What can we say to my lord?" Judah replied. "What can we say? How can we prove our innocence? God has uncovered your servants' guilt. We are now my lord's slaves — we ourselves and the one who was found to have the cup."

¹⁷But Joseph said, "Far be it from me to do such a thing! Only the man who was found to have the cup will become my slave. The rest of you, go back to your father in peace."

¹⁸Then Judah went up to him and said: "Pardon your servant, my lord, let me speak a word to my lord. Do not be angry with your servant, though you are equal to Pharaoh himself. ¹⁹My lord asked his servants, 'Do you have a father or a brother?' ²⁰And we answered, 'We have an aged father, and there is a young son born to him in his old age. His brother is dead, and he is the only one of his mother's sons left, and his father loves him.'

²¹"Then you said to your servants, 'Bring him down to me so I can see him for myself.' ²²And we said to my lord, 'The boy cannot leave his father; if he leaves him, his father will die.' ²³But you told your servants, 'Unless your youngest brother comes down with you, you will not see my face again.' ²⁴When we went back to your servant my father, we told him what my lord had said.

²⁵"Then our father said, 'Go back and buy a little more food.' ²⁶But we said, 'We cannot go down. Only if our youngest brother is with us will we go. We cannot see the man's face unless our youngest brother is with us.'

²⁷"Your servant my father said to us, 'You know that my wife bore me two sons. ²⁸One of them went away from me, and I said, "He has surely been torn to pieces." And I have not seen him since. ²⁹If you take this one from me too and harm comes to him, you will bring my gray head down to the grave in misery.'

³⁰"So now, if the boy is not with us when I go back to your servant my father, and if my father, whose life is closely bound up with the boy's life, ³¹sees that the boy isn't there, he will die. Your servants will bring the gray head of our father down to the grave in sorrow. ³²Your servant guaranteed the boy's safety to my father. I said, 'If I do not bring him back to you, I will bear the blame before you, my father, all my life!'

³³"Now then, please let your servant remain here as my lord's slave in place of the boy, and let the boy return with his brothers. ³⁴How can I go back to my father if the boy is not with me? No! Do not let me see the misery that would come on my father."

Joseph Makes Himself Known

45 Then Joseph could no longer control himself before all his attendants, and he cried out, "Have everyone leave my presence!" So there was no one with Joseph when he made himself known to his brothers. ²And he wept so loudly that the Egyptians heard him, and Pharaoh's household heard about it.

³Joseph said to his brothers, "I am Joseph! Is my father still living?" But his brothers were not able to answer him, because they were terrified at his presence.

⁴Then Joseph said to his brothers, "Come close to me." When they had done so, he said, "I am your brother Joseph, the one you sold into Egypt! ⁵And now, do not be distressed and do not be angry with yourselves for selling me here, because it was to save lives that God sent me ahead of you. ⁶For two years now there has been famine in the land, and for the next five years there will be no plowing and reaping. ⁷But God sent me ahead of you to preserve for you a remnant on earth and to save your lives by a great deliverance.ᵃ

ᵃ 7 Or *save you as a great band of survivors*

8"So then, it was not you who sent me here, but God. He made me father to Pharaoh, lord of his entire household and ruler of all Egypt. 9Now hurry back to my father and say to him, 'This is what your son Joseph says: God has made me lord of all Egypt. Come down to me; don't delay. 10You shall live in the region of Goshen and be near me—you, your children and grandchildren, your flocks and herds, and all you have. 11I will provide for you there, because five years of famine are still to come. Otherwise you and your household and all who belong to you will become destitute.'

12"You can see for yourselves, and so can my brother Benjamin, that it is really I who am speaking to you. 13Tell my father about all the honor accorded me in Egypt and about everything you have seen. And bring my father down here quickly."

14Then he threw his arms around his brother Benjamin and wept, and Benjamin embraced him, weeping. 15And he kissed all his brothers and wept over them. Afterward his brothers talked with him.

16When the news reached Pharaoh's palace that Joseph's brothers had come, Pharaoh and all his officials were pleased. 17Pharaoh said to Joseph, "Tell your brothers, 'Do this: Load your animals and return to the land of Canaan, 18and bring your father and your families back to me. I will give you the best of the land of Egypt and you can enjoy the fat of the land.'

19"You are also directed to tell them, 'Do this: Take some carts from Egypt for your children and your wives, and get your father and come. 20Never mind about your belongings, because the best of all Egypt will be yours.'"

21So the sons of Israel did this. Joseph gave them carts, as Pharaoh had commanded, and he also gave them provisions for their journey. 22To each of them he gave new clothing, but to Benjamin he gave three hundred shekels*a* of silver and five sets of clothes. 23And this is what he sent to his father: ten donkeys loaded with the best things of Egypt, and ten female donkeys loaded with grain and bread and other provisions for his journey. 24Then he sent his brothers away, and as they were leaving he said to them, "Don't quarrel on the way!"

25So they went up out of Egypt and came to their father Jacob in the land of Canaan. 26They told him, "Joseph is still alive! In fact, he is ruler of all Egypt." Jacob was stunned; he did not believe them. 27But when they told him everything Joseph had said to them, and when he saw the carts Joseph had sent to carry him back, the spirit of their father Jacob revived. 28And Israel said, "I'm convinced! My son Joseph is still alive. I will go and see him before I die."

Jacob Goes to Egypt

46 So Israel set out with all that was his, and when he reached Beersheba, he offered sacrifices to the God of his father Isaac.

2And God spoke to Israel in a vision at night and said, "Jacob! Jacob!"

"Here I am," he replied.

3"I am God, the God of your father," he said. "Do not be afraid to go down to Egypt, for I will make you into a great nation there. 4I will go down to Egypt with you, and I will surely bring you back again. And Joseph's own hand will close your eyes."

5Then Jacob left Beersheba, and Israel's sons took their father Jacob and their children and their wives in the carts that Pharaoh had sent to transport him. 6So Jacob and all his offspring went to Egypt, taking with them their livestock and the possessions they had acquired in Canaan. 7Jacob brought with him to Egypt his sons and grandsons and his daughters and granddaughters—all his offspring.

8These are the names of the sons of Israel (Jacob and his descendants) who went to Egypt:

---

a 22 That is, about 7 1/2 pounds or about 3.5 kilograms

Reuben the firstborn of Jacob.
9 The sons of Reuben:
Hanok, Pallu, Hezron and Karmi.
10 The sons of Simeon:
Jemuel, Jamin, Ohad, Jakin, Zohar and Shaul the son of a Canaanite woman.
11 The sons of Levi:
Gershon, Kohath and Merari.
12 The sons of Judah:
Er, Onan, Shelah, Perez and Zerah (but Er and Onan had died in the land of Canaan).
The sons of Perez:
Hezron and Hamul.
13 The sons of Issachar:
Tola, Puah,a Jashubb and Shimron.
14 The sons of Zebulun:
Sered, Elon and Jahleel.
15 These were the sons Leah bore to Jacob in Paddan Aram,c besides his daughter Dinah. These sons and daughters of his were thirty-three in all.

16 The sons of Gad:
Zephon,d Haggi, Shuni, Ezbon, Eri, Arodi and Areli.
17 The sons of Asher:
Imnah, Ishvah, Ishvi and Beriah.
Their sister was Serah.
The sons of Beriah:
Heber and Malkiel.
18 These were the children born to Jacob by Zilpah, whom Laban had given to his daughter Leah—sixteen in all.

19 The sons of Jacob's wife Rachel:
Joseph and Benjamin. 20 In Egypt, Manasseh and Ephraim were born to Joseph by Asenath daughter of Potiphera, priest of On.e
21 The sons of Benjamin:
Bela, Beker, Ashbel, Gera, Naaman, Ehi, Rosh, Muppim, Huppim and Ard.

22 These were the sons of Rachel who were born to Jacob—fourteen in all.

23 The son of Dan:
Hushim.
24 The sons of Naphtali:
Jahziel, Guni, Jezer and Shillem.
25 These were the sons born to Jacob by Bilhah, whom Laban had given to his daughter Rachel—seven in all.

26 All those who went to Egypt with Jacob—those who were his direct descendants, not counting his sons' wives—numbered sixty-six persons. 27 With the two sonsf who had been born to Joseph in Egypt, the members of Jacob's family, which went to Egypt, were seventyg in all.

28 Now Jacob sent Judah ahead of him to Joseph to get directions to Goshen. When they arrived in the region of Goshen, 29 Joseph had his chariot made ready and went to Goshen to meet his father Israel. As soon as Joseph appeared before him, he threw his arms around his fatherh and wept for a long time.

30 Israel said to Joseph, "Now I am ready to die, since I have seen for myself that you are still alive."

31 Then Joseph said to his brothers and to his father's household, "I will go up and speak to Pharaoh and will say to him, 'My brothers and my father's household, who were living in the land of Canaan, have come to me. 32 The men are shepherds; they tend livestock, and they have brought along their flocks and herds and everything they own.' 33 When Pharaoh calls you in and asks, 'What is your occupation?' 34 you should answer, 'Your servants have tended livestock from our boyhood on, just as our fathers did.' Then you will be allowed to settle in the region of Goshen, for all shepherds are detestable to the Egyptians."

---

a 13 Samaritan Pentateuch and Syriac (see also 1 Chron. 7:1); Masoretic Text *Puvah*   b 13 Samaritan Pentateuch and some Septuagint manuscripts (see also Num. 26:24 and 1 Chron. 7:1); Masoretic Text *Iob*   c 15 That is, Northwest Mesopotamia   d 16 Samaritan Pentateuch and Septuagint (see also Num. 26:15); Masoretic Text *Ziphion*   e 20 That is, Heliopolis   f 27 Hebrew; Septuagint *the nine children*   g 27 Hebrew (see also Exodus 1:5 and note); Septuagint (see also Acts 7:14) *seventy-five*   h 29 Hebrew *around him*

47

Joseph went and told Pharaoh, "My father and brothers, with their flocks and herds and everything they own, have come from the land of Canaan and are now in Goshen." ²He chose five of his brothers and presented them before Pharaoh.

³Pharaoh asked the brothers, "What is your occupation?"

"Your servants are shepherds," they replied to Pharaoh, "just as our fathers were." ⁴They also said to him, "We have come to live here for a while, because the famine is severe in Canaan and your servants' flocks have no pasture. So now, please let your servants settle in Goshen."

⁵Pharaoh said to Joseph, "Your father and your brothers have come to you, ⁶and the land of Egypt is before you; settle your father and your brothers in the best part of the land. Let them live in Goshen. And if you know of any among them with special ability, put them in charge of my own livestock."

⁷Then Joseph brought his father Jacob in and presented him before Pharaoh. After Jacob blessed*a* Pharaoh, ⁸Pharaoh asked him, "How old are you?"

⁹And Jacob said to Pharaoh, "The years of my pilgrimage are a hundred and thirty. My years have been few and difficult, and they do not equal the years of the pilgrimage of my fathers." ¹⁰Then Jacob blessed*b* Pharaoh and went out from his presence.

¹¹So Joseph settled his father and his brothers in Egypt and gave them property in the best part of the land, the district of Rameses, as Pharaoh directed. ¹²Joseph also provided his father and his brothers and all his father's household with food, according to the number of their children.

Joseph and the Famine

¹³There was no food, however, in the whole region because the famine was severe; both Egypt and Canaan wasted away because of the famine. ¹⁴Joseph collected all the money that was to be found in Egypt and Canaan in payment for the grain they were buying, and he brought it to Pharaoh's palace. ¹⁵When the money of the people of Egypt and Canaan was gone, all Egypt came to Joseph and said, "Give us food. Why should we die before your eyes? Our money is all gone."

¹⁶"Then bring your livestock," said Joseph. "I will sell you food in exchange for your livestock, since your money is gone." ¹⁷So they brought their livestock to Joseph, and he gave them food in exchange for their horses, their sheep and goats, their cattle and donkeys. And he brought them through that year with food in exchange for all their livestock.

¹⁸When that year was over, they came to him the following year and said, "We cannot hide from our lord the fact that since our money is gone and our livestock belongs to you, there is nothing left for our lord except our bodies and our land. ¹⁹Why should we perish before your eyes — we and our land as well? Buy us and our land in exchange for food, and we with our land will be in bondage to Pharaoh. Give us seed so that we may live and not die, and that the land may not become desolate."

²⁰So Joseph bought all the land in Egypt for Pharaoh. The Egyptians, one and all, sold their fields, because the famine was too severe for them. The land became Pharaoh's, ²¹and Joseph reduced the people to servitude,*c* from one end of Egypt to the other. ²²However, he did not buy the land of the priests, because they received a regular allotment from Pharaoh and had food enough from the allotment Pharaoh gave them. That is why they did not sell their land.

²³Joseph said to the people, "Now that I have bought you and your land today for Pharaoh, here is seed for you so you can plant the ground. ²⁴But when the crop

---

a 7 Or *greeted*   *b 10* Or *said farewell to*   *c 21* Samaritan Pentateuch and Septuagint (see also Vulgate); Masoretic Text *and he moved the people into the cities* comes in, give a fifth of it to Pharaoh. The other four-fifths you may keep as seed for the fields and as food for yourselves and your households and your children."

25"You have saved our lives," they said. "May we find favor in the eyes of our lord; we will be in bondage to Pharaoh."

26So Joseph established it as a law concerning land in Egypt — still in force today — that a fifth of the produce belongs to Pharaoh. It was only the land of the priests that did not become Pharaoh's.

27Now the Israelites settled in Egypt in the region of Goshen. They acquired property there and were fruitful and increased greatly in number.

28Jacob lived in Egypt seventeen years, and the years of his life were a hundred and forty-seven. 29When the time drew near for Israel to die, he called for his son Joseph and said to him, "If I have found favor in your eyes, put your hand under my thigh and promise that you will show me kindness and faithfulness. Do not bury me in Egypt, 30but when I rest with my fathers, carry me out of Egypt and bury me where they are buried."

"I will do as you say," he said.

31"Swear to me," he said. Then Joseph swore to him, and Israel worshiped as he leaned on the top of his staff.[a]

Manasseh and Ephraim

48 Some time later Joseph was told, "Your father is ill." So he took his two sons Manasseh and Ephraim along with him. 2When Jacob was told, "Your son Joseph has come to you," Israel rallied his strength and sat up on the bed.

3Jacob said to Joseph, "God Almighty[b] appeared to me at Luz in the land of Canaan, and there he blessed me 4and said to me, 'I am going to make you fruitful and increase your numbers. I will make you a community of peoples, and I will give this land as an everlasting possession to your descendants after you.'

5"Now then, your two sons born to you in Egypt before I came to you here will be reckoned as mine; Ephraim and Manasseh will be mine, just as Reuben and Simeon are mine. 6Any children born to you after them will be yours; in the territory they inherit they will be reckoned under the names of their brothers. 7As I was returning from Paddan,[c] to my sorrow Rachel died in the land of Canaan while we were still on the way, a little distance from Ephrath. So I buried her there beside the road to Ephrath" (that is, Bethlehem).

8When Israel saw the sons of Joseph, he asked, "Who are these?"

9"They are the sons God has given me here," Joseph said to his father.

Then Israel said, "Bring them to me so I may bless them."

10Now Israel's eyes were failing because of old age, and he could hardly see. So Joseph brought his sons close to him, and his father kissed them and embraced them.

11Israel said to Joseph, "I never expected to see your face again, and now God has allowed me to see your children too."

12Then Joseph removed them from Israel's knees and bowed down with his face to the ground. 13And Joseph took both of them, Ephraim on his right toward Israel's left hand and Manasseh on his left toward Israel's right hand, and brought them close to him. 14But Israel reached out his right hand and put it on Ephraim's head, though he was the younger, and crossing his arms, he put his left hand on Manasseh's head, even though Manasseh was the firstborn. 15Then he blessed Joseph and said,

"May the God before whom my fathers
    Abraham and Isaac walked
        faithfully,
the God who has been my shepherd
    all my life to this day,
16the Angel who has delivered me from
        all harm
    — may he bless these boys.

---

a 31 Or *Israel bowed down at the head of his bed*   *b* 3 Hebrew *El-Shaddai*   *c* 7 That is, Northwest Mesopotamia

May they be called by my name
and the names of my fathers
Abraham and Isaac,
and may they increase greatly
on the earth."

17When Joseph saw his father placing his right hand on Ephraim's head he was displeased; so he took hold of his father's hand to move it from Ephraim's head to Manasseh's head. 18Joseph said to him, "No, my father, this one is the firstborn; put your right hand on his head."

19But his father refused and said, "I know, my son, I know. He too will become a people, and he too will become great. Nevertheless, his younger brother will be greater than he, and his descendants will become a group of nations." 20He blessed them that day and said,

"In your*a* name will Israel pronounce
this blessing:
'May God make you like Ephraim
and Manasseh.'"

So he put Ephraim ahead of Manasseh.

21Then Israel said to Joseph, "I am about to die, but God will be with you*b* and take you*b* back to the land of your*b* fathers. 22And to you I give one more ridge of land*c* than to your brothers, the ridge I took from the Amorites with my sword and my bow."

Jacob Blesses His Sons

49 Then Jacob called for his sons and said: "Gather around so I can tell you what will happen to you in days to come.

2"Assemble and listen, sons of Jacob;
listen to your father Israel.

3"Reuben, you are my firstborn,
my might, the first sign of my
strength,
excelling in honor, excelling in power.

4Turbulent as the waters, you will no
longer excel,
for you went up onto your father's
bed,
onto my couch and defiled it.

5"Simeon and Levi are brothers —
their swords*d* are weapons of
violence.
6Let me not enter their council,
let me not join their assembly,
for they have killed men in their
anger
and hamstrung oxen as they
pleased.
7Cursed be their anger, so fierce,
and their fury, so cruel!
I will scatter them in Jacob
and disperse them in Israel.

8"Judah,*e* your brothers will praise you;
your hand will be on the neck of your
enemies;
your father's sons will bow down to
you.
9You are a lion's cub, Judah;
you return from the prey, my son.
Like a lion he crouches and lies down,
like a lioness — who dares to rouse
him?
10The scepter will not depart from Judah,
nor the ruler's staff from between his
feet,*f*
until he to whom it belongs*g* shall come
and the obedience of the nations
shall be his.
11He will tether his donkey to a vine,
his colt to the choicest branch;
he will wash his garments in wine,
his robes in the blood of grapes.
12His eyes will be darker than wine,
his teeth whiter than milk.*h*

13"Zebulun will live by the seashore
and become a haven for ships;
his border will extend toward Sidon.

---

a 20 The Hebrew is singular.   *b 21* The Hebrew is plural.   *c 22* The Hebrew for *ridge of land* is identical with the place name Shechem.   *d 5* The meaning of the Hebrew for this word is uncertain.   *e 8* *Judah* sounds like and may be derived from the Hebrew for *praise*.   *f 10* Or *from his descendants*   *g 10* Or *to whom tribute belongs*; the meaning of the Hebrew for this phrase is uncertain.   *h 12* Or *will be dull from wine, / his teeth white from milk*

14 "Issachar is a rawboned*a* donkey
    lying down among the sheep pens.*b*
15 When he sees how good is his resting
        place
    and how pleasant is his land,
    he will bend his shoulder to the burden
    and submit to forced labor.

16 "Dan*c* will provide justice for his
        people
    as one of the tribes of Israel.
17 Dan will be a snake by the roadside,
        a viper along the path,
    that bites the horse's heels
    so that its rider tumbles backward.

18 "I look for your deliverance, LORD.

19 "Gad*d* will be attacked by a band of
        raiders,
    but he will attack them at their heels.

20 "Asher's food will be rich;
    he will provide delicacies fit for a
        king.

21 "Naphtali is a doe set free
    that bears beautiful fawns.*e*

22 "Joseph is a fruitful vine,
    a fruitful vine near a spring,
    whose branches climb over a wall.*f*
23 With bitterness archers attacked him;
    they shot at him with hostility.
24 But his bow remained steady,
    his strong arms stayed*g* limber,
    because of the hand of the Mighty One
        of Jacob,
    because of the Shepherd, the Rock of
        Israel,
25 because of your father's God, who helps
        you,
    because of the Almighty,*h* who
        blesses you
    with blessings of the skies above,
    blessings of the deep springs below,
    blessings of the breast and womb.

26 Your father's blessings are greater
    than the blessings of the ancient
        mountains,
    than*i* the bounty of the age-old hills.
    Let all these rest on the head of Joseph,
    on the brow of the prince among*j* his
        brothers.

27 "Benjamin is a ravenous wolf;
    in the morning he devours the prey,
    in the evening he divides the plunder."

28 All these are the twelve tribes of Israel,
and this is what their father said to them
when he blessed them, giving each the
blessing appropriate to him.

The Death of Jacob

29 Then he gave them these instructions:
"I am about to be gathered to my people.
Bury me with my fathers in the cave in the
field of Ephron the Hittite, 30 the cave in
the field of Machpelah, near Mamre in Canaan, which Abraham bought along with
the field as a burial place from Ephron the
Hittite. 31 There Abraham and his wife Sarah were buried, there Isaac and his wife
Rebekah were buried, and there I buried
Leah. 32 The field and the cave in it were
bought from the Hittites.*k*"

33 When Jacob had finished giving instructions to his sons, he drew his feet
up into the bed, breathed his last and was
gathered to his people.

50 Joseph threw himself on his
father and wept over him and
kissed him. 2 Then Joseph di-
rected the physicians in his service to em-
balm his father Israel. So the physicians
embalmed him, 3 taking a full forty days,
for that was the time required for embalm-
ing. And the Egyptians mourned for him
seventy days.

4 When the days of mourning had
passed, Joseph said to Pharaoh's court, "If

---

a 14 Or *strong*   *b 14* Or *the campfires;* or *the saddlebags*   *c 16* *Dan* here means *he provides justice.*   *d 19* *Gad*
sounds like the Hebrew for *attack* and also for *band of raiders.*   *e 21* Or *free;* / *he utters beautiful words*   *f 22* Or
Joseph is a wild colt, / *a wild colt near a spring,* / *a wild donkey on a terraced hill*   *g 23,24* Or *archers will attack . . .*
will shoot . . . will remain . . . will stay   *h 25* Hebrew *Shaddai*   *i 26* Or *of my progenitors,* / *as great as*   *j 26* Or
of the one separated from   *k 32* Or *the descendants of Heth*

I have found favor in your eyes, speak to Pharaoh for me. Tell him, 5'My father made me swear an oath and said, "I am about to die; bury me in the tomb I dug for myself in the land of Canaan." Now let me go up and bury my father; then I will return.'"

6Pharaoh said, "Go up and bury your father, as he made you swear to do."

7So Joseph went up to bury his father. All Pharaoh's officials accompanied him — the dignitaries of his court and all the dignitaries of Egypt — 8besides all the members of Joseph's household and his brothers and those belonging to his father's household. Only their children and their flocks and herds were left in Goshen. 9Chariots and horsemen*a* also went up with him. It was a very large company.

10When they reached the threshing floor of Atad, near the Jordan, they lamented loudly and bitterly; and there Joseph observed a seven-day period of mourning for his father. 11When the Canaanites who lived there saw the mourning at the threshing floor of Atad, they said, "The Egyptians are holding a solemn ceremony of mourning." That is why that place near the Jordan is called Abel Mizraim.*b*

12So Jacob's sons did as he had commanded them: 13They carried him to the land of Canaan and buried him in the cave in the field of Machpelah, near Mamre, which Abraham had bought along with the field as a burial place from Ephron the Hittite. 14After burying his father, Joseph returned to Egypt, together with his brothers and all the others who had gone with him to bury his father.

Joseph Reassures His Brothers

15When Joseph's brothers saw that their father was dead, they said, "What if Joseph holds a grudge against us and pays us back for all the wrongs we did to him?" 16So they sent word to Joseph, saying, "Your father left these instructions before he died: 17'This is what you are to say to Joseph: I ask you to forgive your brothers the sins and the wrongs they committed in treating you so badly.' Now please forgive the sins of the servants of the God of your father." When their message came to him, Joseph wept.

18His brothers then came and threw themselves down before him. "We are your slaves," they said.

19But Joseph said to them, "Don't be afraid. Am I in the place of God? 20You intended to harm me, but God intended it for good to accomplish what is now being done, the saving of many lives. 21So then, don't be afraid. I will provide for you and your children." And he reassured them and spoke kindly to them.

The Death of Joseph

22Joseph stayed in Egypt, along with all his father's family. He lived a hundred and ten years 23and saw the third generation of Ephraim's children. Also the children of Makir son of Manasseh were placed at birth on Joseph's knees.*c*

24Then Joseph said to his brothers, "I am about to die. But God will surely come to your aid and take you up out of this land to the land he promised on oath to Abraham, Isaac and Jacob." 25And Joseph made the Israelites swear an oath and said, "God will surely come to your aid, and then you must carry my bones up from this place."

26So Joseph died at the age of a hundred and ten. And after they embalmed him, he was placed in a coffin in Egypt.

---

a 9 Or *charioteers*   *b 11* Abel Mizraim means *mourning of the Egyptians.*   *c 23* That is, were counted as his

Exodus

THEME: God is intimately involved with his people, so much so that he enters history to rescue them.

AUTHOR: Exodus itself, as well as other Scriptures, identifies Moses as the author.

DATE OF WRITING: Exodus was probably written around 1440 BC.

ENCOURAGEMENT FROM EXODUS: "You yourselves have seen what I did to Egypt, and how I carried you on eagles' wings and brought you to myself. Now if you obey me fully and keep my covenant, then out of all nations you will be my treasured possession" (Exodus 19:4–5).

CHALLENGE FROM EXODUS: "Do not be afraid. Stand firm and you will see the deliverance the LORD will bring you today ... The LORD will fight for you; you need only to be still" (Exodus 14:13–14).

REFLECTION FROM EXODUS: "I am the LORD, who heals you" (Exodus 15:26).

At a Glance

Recovery Themes in Exodus

God doesn't want to see his people in slavery to anything or anyone. He didn't want his chosen people, the Israelites, to be enslaved to the Egyptians, nor does he want us to be slaves to our addictions or compulsive behaviors. In the book of Exodus we witness the early stages of God's redemption of his people through his servant Moses. Moses' personal weaknesses showcase for us God's powerful presence in his life and ministry. God called a man who struggled with anger and a poor self-image to become the mediator of his covenant and the first author of Scripture.

In Exodus the nation of Israel first celebrates the Passover. Many centuries later, Jesus celebrated Passover with his disciples before going to the cross to provide our salvation and to free us from our hurts, hang-ups and habits. By joining God in working our recoveries, we find that he always has, and always will, transform weak, broken, ordinary women and men into people who have been redeemed. God wants to, can and will set us free from a life of slavery.

The Israelites Oppressed

1 These are the names of the sons of Israel who went to Egypt with Jacob, each with his family: ²Reuben, Simeon, Levi and Judah; ³Issachar, Zebulun and Benjamin; ⁴Dan and Naphtali; Gad and Asher. ⁵The descendants of Jacob numbered seventy*a* in all; Joseph was already in Egypt.

⁶Now Joseph and all his brothers and all that generation died, ⁷but the Israelites were exceedingly fruitful; they multiplied greatly, increased in numbers and became so numerous that the land was filled with them.

⁸Then a new king, to whom Joseph meant nothing, came to power in Egypt. ⁹"Look," he said to his people, "the Israelites have

---

a 5 Masoretic Text (see also Gen. 46:27); Dead Sea Scrolls and Septuagint (see also Acts 7:14 and note at Gen. 46:27) *seventy-five* become far too numerous for us. ¹⁰Come, we must deal shrewdly with them or they will become even more numerous and, if war breaks out, will join our enemies, fight against us and leave the country."

¹¹So they put slave masters over them to oppress them with forced labor, and they built Pithom and Rameses as store cities for Pharaoh. ¹²But the more they were oppressed, the more they multiplied and spread; so the Egyptians came to dread the Israelites ¹³and worked them ruthlessly. ¹⁴They made their lives bitter with harsh labor in brick and mortar and with all kinds of work in the fields; in all their harsh labor the Egyptians worked them ruthlessly.

¹⁵The king of Egypt said to the Hebrew midwives, whose names were Shiphrah and Puah, ¹⁶"When you are helping the Hebrew women during childbirth on the delivery stool, if you see that the baby is a boy, kill him; but if it is a girl, let her live." ¹⁷The midwives, however, feared God and did not do what the king of Egypt had told them to do; they let the boys live. ¹⁸Then the king of Egypt summoned the midwives and asked them, "Why have you done this? Why have you let the boys live?"

¹⁹The midwives answered Pharaoh, "Hebrew women are not like Egyptian women; they are vigorous and give birth before the midwives arrive."

²⁰So God was kind to the midwives and the people increased and became even more numerous. ²¹And because the midwives feared God, he gave them families of their own.

²²Then Pharaoh gave this order to all his people: "Every Hebrew boy that is born you must throw into the Nile, but let every girl live."

The Birth of Moses

2 Now a man of the tribe of Levi married a Levite woman, ²and she became pregnant and gave birth to a son. When she saw that he was a fine child,

she hid him for three months. ³But when she could hide him no longer, she got a papyrus basket*a* for him and coated it with tar and pitch. Then she placed the child in it and put it among the reeds along the bank of the Nile. ⁴His sister stood at a distance to see what would happen to him.

⁵Then Pharaoh's daughter went down to the Nile to bathe, and her attendants were walking along the riverbank. She saw the basket among the reeds and sent her female slave to get it. ⁶She opened it and saw the baby. He was crying, and she felt sorry for him. "This is one of the Hebrew babies," she said.

⁷Then his sister asked Pharaoh's daughter, "Shall I go and get one of the Hebrew women to nurse the baby for you?"

⁸"Yes, go," she answered. So the girl went and got the baby's mother. ⁹Pharaoh's daughter said to her, "Take this baby and nurse him for me, and I will pay you." So the woman took the baby and nursed him. ¹⁰When the child grew older, she took him to Pharaoh's daughter and he became her son. She named him Moses,*b* saying, "I drew him out of the water."

Moses Flees to Midian

¹¹One day, after Moses had grown up, he went out to where his own people were and watched them at their hard labor. He saw an Egyptian beating a Hebrew, one of his own people. ¹²Looking this way and that and seeing no one, he killed the Egyptian and hid him in the sand. ¹³The next day he went out and saw two Hebrews fighting. He asked the one in the wrong, "Why are you hitting your fellow Hebrew?"

¹⁴The man said, "Who made you ruler and judge over us? Are you thinking of killing me as you killed the Egyptian?" Then Moses was afraid and thought, "What I did must have become known."

¹⁵When Pharaoh heard of this, he tried to kill Moses, but Moses fled from Pharaoh and went to live in Midian, where he sat down by a well. ¹⁶Now a priest of Midian

---

a 3 The Hebrew can also mean *ark*, as in Gen. 6:14.   *b 10* *Moses* sounds like the Hebrew for *draw out.*

My Name Is Tim

I'M A BELIEVER WHO STRUGGLES WITH SEXUAL IDENTITY

Please read the story of Moses' crime and flight in Exodus 2:11 – 15.

Born into the family of a preacher, I grew up believing I was evil for being so horribly different from everyone else in my family. Beatings by my father were a regular occurrence; hardly a day went by when he didn't remind me that I was stupid, worthless and ugly. Mom would never openly admit that he was having affairs; instead, she would attack him verbally and warn him that she'd tell us (the kids) the truth.

Our church had little room for grace; heaven was reserved for those who had earned it. Knowing I was "different" (attracted to men), I would plead with God to change my sexual orientation. As my sexual desires grew stronger, my resolve continued to weaken. I slowly began to retreat into myself. Those few people I did entrust with my secret turned their backs on me, so I began a concerted flight from all personal relationships, most particularly with men.

After my college graduation I moved to California. One night while walking on the beach, I came across a huge rock, which I proceeded to climb in order to "people watch" and reflect upon my life. As the sun sank I remember feeling an unaccustomed sensation — a feeling of hope, of a future filled with promise and possibility. I had stumbled upon a late-night beach hangout for gay men. As I watched, something began to stir in my spirit. I began to wonder whether going down this road with other men might, after all, be worth the risk. I had lived my life loving and following God, and I prayed that he would have enough grace to forgive me. But it was time, I decided, to take the risk and move to a different place in my life. Much as Moses' sin of murder in Exodus 2 led to 40 years of wilderness exile, I began that night a 10-year journey into a man-made hell.

Soon enough I discovered gay chat rooms. For the first time I felt accepted, significant and no longer different. Before long I began to engage in anonymous sexual encounters. At first I experienced excruciating guilt and a determination never to go there again. But, in time, things got easier. My need for affection outweighed my fear of death.

After the Northridge earthquake in 1994, I moved back to my hometown in Arkansas, where I continued to numb myself to the pain of my loneliness through my addiction. An illicit encounter made me feel for a short time that I was the most important person in someone else's life. But there was a pervasive, nagging awareness just below the surface that I was more alone and friendless than ever before.

God's radical tenderness wouldn't tolerate my disobedience and defiance. In his love he stepped back just far enough so that I ached over my senseless separation from him. The loneliness I had experienced atop that rock was nothing compared to the fear and grief of a life without God. My anguish was palpable and my depression bitterly relentless. I wanted out but saw no escape route. I decided as a last-ditch effort to contact a Christian counselor. It was in his office that I learned about Celebrate Recovery.

The only way I've been able to take this path of recovery has been through recognizing that I haven't been walking it alone. Working the 8 principles and the 12 steps has moved me from fear to faith, from hopelessness to dreams of a noble future, from self-reproach and indignity to a life filled with purpose.

In 2005 I attended the Celebrate Recovery summit with my church. One evening we decided to drive to Laguna Beach. The scene began to look vaguely familiar. Yes, there it was: the same rock I'd sat on over ten years earlier. God never ceases to show me signs of his mind-blowing love for me. I ran down the steps, discarded my sandals, climbed the rock and sat down in the exact spot where I'd perched ten years earlier. But this time, despite the physical similarity in the scene, I saw something entirely different: a path that will never lead anywhere other than the place it began — misery. Then and there I thanked God for being faithful to a sinner like me. He has restored me, as he did Moses, to his service. I now serve him gladly as a member of the pastorate.

I can't say that the old feelings are entirely gone, and I know that the danger of relapse can never be erased, even by decades of ministry. But I do know that by the grace of God I can avoid relapse by constantly maintaining my habit of daily, conscious contact with him.

Today I find myself willing to scale every rock in my path, as long as the perspective gives me a clearer view of my Savior, Redeemer and best friend. I've found my authentic "safe place" high atop the true Rock.

Tim

had seven daughters, and they came to draw water and fill the troughs to water their father's flock. ¹⁷Some shepherds came along and drove them away, but Moses got up and came to their rescue and watered their flock.

¹⁸When the girls returned to Reuel their father, he asked them, "Why have you returned so early today?"

¹⁹They answered, "An Egyptian rescued us from the shepherds. He even drew water for us and watered the flock."

²⁰"And where is he?" Reuel asked his daughters. "Why did you leave him? Invite him to have something to eat."

²¹Moses agreed to stay with the man, who gave his daughter Zipporah to Moses in marriage. ²²Zipporah gave birth to a son, and Moses named him Gershom,ᵃ saying, "I have become a foreigner in a foreign land."

²³During that long period, the king of Egypt died. The Israelites groaned in their slavery and cried out, and their cry for help because of their slavery went up to God. ²⁴God heard their groaning and he remembered his covenant with Abraham, with Isaac and with Jacob. ²⁵So God looked on the Israelites and was concerned about them.

Moses and the Burning Bush

3 Now Moses was tending the flock of Jethro his father-in-law, the priest of Midian, and he led the flock to the far side of the wilderness and came to Horeb, the mountain of God. ²There the angel of the LORD appeared to him in flames of fire from within a bush. Moses saw that though the bush was on fire it did not burn up. ³So Moses thought, "I will go over and see this strange sight—why the bush does not burn up."

⁴When the LORD saw that he had gone over to look, God called to him from within the bush, "Moses! Moses!"

And Moses said, "Here I am."

⁵"Do not come any closer," God said. "Take off your sandals, for the place where you are standing is holy ground." ⁶Then he said, "I am the God of your father,ᵇ the God of Abraham, the God of Isaac and the God of Jacob." At this, Moses hid his face, because he was afraid to look at God.

⁷The LORD said, "I have indeed seen the misery of my people in Egypt. I have heard them crying out because of their slave drivers, and I am concerned about their suffering. ⁸So I have come down to rescue them from the hand of the Egyptians and to bring them up out of that land into a good and spacious land, a land flowing with milk and honey—the home of the Canaanites, Hittites, Amorites, Perizzites, Hivites and Jebusites. ⁹And now the cry of the Israelites has reached me, and I have seen the way the Egyptians are oppressing them. ¹⁰So now, go. I am sending you to Pharaoh to bring my people the Israelites out of Egypt."

¹¹But Moses said to God, "Who am I that I should go to Pharaoh and bring the Israelites out of Egypt?"

¹²And God said, "I will be with you. And this will be the sign to you that it is I who have sent you: When you have brought the people out of Egypt, youᶜ will worship God on this mountain."

¹³Moses said to God, "Suppose I go to the Israelites and say to them, 'The God of your fathers has sent me to you,' and they ask me, 'What is his name?' Then what shall I tell them?"

¹⁴God said to Moses, "I AM WHO I AM.ᵈ This is what you are to say to the Israelites: 'I AM has sent me to you.'"

¹⁵God also said to Moses, "Say to the Israelites, 'The LORD,ᵉ the God of your fathers—the God of Abraham, the God of Isaac and the God of Jacob—has sent me to you.'

ᵃ 22 *Gershom* sounds like the Hebrew for *a foreigner there.*   ᵇ 6 Masoretic Text; Samaritan Pentateuch (see Acts 7:32) *fathers*   ᶜ 12 The Hebrew is plural.   ᵈ 14 Or *I WILL BE WHAT I WILL BE*   ᵉ 15 The Hebrew for LORD sounds like and may be related to the Hebrew for *I AM* in verse 14.

"This is my name forever,
 the name you shall call me
 from generation to generation.

16"Go, assemble the elders of Israel and say to them, 'The LORD, the God of your fathers — the God of Abraham, Isaac and Jacob — appeared to me and said: I have watched over you and have seen what has been done to you in Egypt. 17And I have promised to bring you up out of your misery in Egypt into the land of the Canaanites, Hittites, Amorites, Perizzites, Hivites and Jebusites — a land flowing with milk and honey.'

18"The elders of Israel will listen to you. Then you and the elders are to go to the king of Egypt and say to him, 'The LORD, the God of the Hebrews, has met with us. Let us take a three-day journey into the wilderness to offer sacrifices to the LORD our God.' 19But I know that the king of Egypt will not let you go unless a mighty hand compels him. 20So I will stretch out my hand and strike the Egyptians with all the wonders that I will perform among them. After that, he will let you go.

21"And I will make the Egyptians favorably disposed toward this people, so that when you leave you will not go empty-handed. 22Every woman is to ask her neighbor and any woman living in her house for articles of silver and gold and for clothing, which you will put on your sons and daughters. And so you will plunder the Egyptians."

Signs for Moses

4 Moses answered, "What if they do not believe me or listen to me and say, 'The LORD did not appear to you'?"

2Then the LORD said to him, "What is that in your hand?"

"A staff," he replied.

3The LORD said, "Throw it on the ground."

Moses threw it on the ground and it became a snake, and he ran from it. 4Then the LORD said to him, "Reach out your hand and take it by the tail." So Moses reached out and took hold of the snake and it turned back into a staff in his hand. 5"This," said the LORD, "is so that they may believe that the LORD, the God of their fathers — the God of Abraham, the God of Isaac and the God of Jacob — has appeared to you."

6Then the LORD said, "Put your hand inside your cloak." So Moses put his hand into his cloak, and when he took it out, the skin was leprous[a] — it had become as white as snow.

7"Now put it back into your cloak," he said. So Moses put his hand back into his cloak, and when he took it out, it was restored, like the rest of his flesh.

8Then the LORD said, "If they do not believe you or pay attention to the first sign, they may believe the second. 9But if they do not believe these two signs or listen to you, take some water from the Nile and pour it on the dry ground. The water you take from the river will become blood on the ground."

10Moses said to the LORD, "Pardon your servant, Lord. I have never been eloquent, neither in the past nor since you have spoken to your servant. I am slow of speech and tongue."

11The LORD said to him, "Who gave human beings their mouths? Who makes them deaf or mute? Who gives them sight or makes them blind? Is it not I, the LORD? 12Now go; I will help you speak and will teach you what to say."

13But Moses said, "Pardon your servant, Lord. Please send someone else."

14Then the LORD's anger burned against Moses and he said, "What about your brother, Aaron the Levite? I know he can speak well. He is already on his way to meet you, and he will be glad to see you. 15You shall speak to him and put words in his mouth; I will help both of you speak and

---

a 6 The Hebrew word for *leprous* was used for various diseases affecting the skin.

MY NAME IS MOSES

EXODUS 3 – 4

Exodus 3 – 4 records a powerful encounter between Moses and the God of Israel. At first, Moses was convinced that God could no longer use him. He asked the Lord, in a question that revealed both humility and lack of trust, "Who am I that I should go to Pharaoh and bring the Israelites out of Egypt?" (Exodus 3:11). Moses had allowed his past failures and present circumstances to cancel out his hopes for the future.

Perhaps you find that this is your condition right now. If we realize that we're powerless over our tendency to do the wrong thing (Principle One), that's great — as long as we don't stop there. How did the Lord move Moses on to the next step? God did a surprising thing: He refused to answer Moses' question.

What God did do is promise to be with Moses every step of the journey. Then he focused on Moses' future, telling him: "When you have brought the people out of Egypt, you will worship God on this mountain" (v. 12).

Celebrate Recovery is far more than a means to sobriety from our primary addiction. It's a method for accomplishing God's mission for our lives. It's important to begin with the end in view. Our past proves beyond a doubt that we are powerless on our own, but it doesn't limit our future potential in God's program.

Having shifted Moses' perspective toward God's plan, the Lord revealed himself to be the one and only eternal God (see 3:14), reviewed his past faithfulness to the fathers of his people (see v. 15) and reaffirmed his plan to liberate and enrich his people (see vv. 16 – 22).

Nevertheless, Moses was still skeptical. So God continued his call to him by demonstrating his power and sending Aaron to support him and share the journey with him (see 4:1 – 17). Moses trusted God enough to take the next step: that of sharing his experience with Aaron and others (see vv. 27 – 30). The result of Moses' willingness to believe and share with others was, knowing our God, predictable: "They believed. And when they heard that the LORD was concerned about them and had seen their misery, they bowed down and worshiped" (v. 31).

As we meet with others, week by week, on the road to recovery, we'll expand our knowledge of God, identify those God has sent to help us on our journey and convince others that God has seen their wretchedness and is concerned about them too.

will teach you what to do. 16He will speak to the people for you, and it will be as if he were your mouth and as if you were God to him. 17But take this staff in your hand so you can perform the signs with it."

Moses Returns to Egypt

18Then Moses went back to Jethro his father-in-law and said to him, "Let me return to my own people in Egypt to see if any of them are still alive."

Jethro said, "Go, and I wish you well."

19Now the Lord had said to Moses in Midian, "Go back to Egypt, for all those who wanted to kill you are dead." 20So Moses took his wife and sons, put them on a donkey and started back to Egypt. And he took the staff of God in his hand.

21The Lord said to Moses, "When you return to Egypt, see that you perform before Pharaoh all the wonders I have given you the power to do. But I will harden his heart so that he will not let the people go. 22Then say to Pharaoh, 'This is what the Lord says: Israel is my firstborn son, 23and I told you, "Let my son go, so he may worship me." But you refused to let him go; so I will kill your firstborn son.'"

24At a lodging place on the way, the Lord met Moses*a* and was about to kill him. 25But Zipporah took a flint knife, cut off her son's foreskin and touched Moses' feet with it.*b* "Surely you are a bridegroom of blood to me," she said. 26So the Lord let him alone. (At that time she said "bridegroom of blood," referring to circumcision.)

27The Lord said to Aaron, "Go into the wilderness to meet Moses." So he met Moses at the mountain of God and kissed him. 28Then Moses told Aaron everything the Lord had sent him to say, and also about all the signs he had commanded him to perform.

29Moses and Aaron brought together all the elders of the Israelites, 30and Aaron told them everything the Lord had said to Moses. He also performed the signs before the people, 31and they believed. And when they heard that the Lord was concerned about them and had seen their misery, they bowed down and worshiped.

Bricks Without Straw

5 Afterward Moses and Aaron went to Pharaoh and said, "This is what the Lord, the God of Israel, says: 'Let my people go, so that they may hold a festival to me in the wilderness.'"

2Pharaoh said, "Who is the Lord, that I should obey him and let Israel go? I do not know the Lord and I will not let Israel go."

3Then they said, "The God of the Hebrews has met with us. Now let us take a three-day journey into the wilderness to offer sacrifices to the Lord our God, or he may strike us with plagues or with the sword."

4But the king of Egypt said, "Moses and Aaron, why are you taking the people away from their labor? Get back to your work!" 5Then Pharaoh said, "Look, the people of the land are now numerous, and you are stopping them from working."

6That same day Pharaoh gave this order to the slave drivers and overseers in charge of the people: 7"You are no longer to supply the people with straw for making bricks; let them go and gather their own straw. 8But require them to make the same number of bricks as before; don't reduce the quota. They are lazy; that is why they are crying out, 'Let us go and sacrifice to our God.' 9Make the work harder for the people so that they keep working and pay no attention to lies."

10Then the slave drivers and the overseers went out and said to the people, "This is what Pharaoh says: 'I will not give you any more straw. 11Go and get your own straw wherever you can find it, but your work will not be reduced at all.'" 12So the people scattered all over Egypt to gather stubble to use for straw. 13The slave drivers

---

a 24 Hebrew *him*   *b 25* The meaning of the Hebrew for this clause is uncertain.

kept pressing them, saying, "Complete the work required of you for each day, just as when you had straw." 14And Pharaoh's slave drivers beat the Israelite overseers they had appointed, demanding, "Why haven't you met your quota of bricks yesterday or today, as before?"

15Then the Israelite overseers went and appealed to Pharaoh: "Why have you treated your servants this way? 16Your servants are given no straw, yet we are told, 'Make bricks!' Your servants are being beaten, but the fault is with your own people."

17Pharaoh said, "Lazy, that's what you are — lazy! That is why you keep saying, 'Let us go and sacrifice to the LORD.' 18Now get to work. You will not be given any straw, yet you must produce your full quota of bricks."

19The Israelite overseers realized they were in trouble when they were told, "You are not to reduce the number of bricks required of you for each day." 20When they left Pharaoh, they found Moses and Aaron waiting to meet them, 21and they said, "May the LORD look on you and judge you! You have made us obnoxious to Pharaoh and his officials and have put a sword in their hand to kill us."

God Promises Deliverance

22Moses returned to the LORD and said, "Why, Lord, why have you brought trouble on this people? Is this why you sent me? 23Ever since I went to Pharaoh to speak in your name, he has brought trouble on this people, and you have not rescued your people at all."

6 Then the LORD said to Moses, "Now you will see what I will do to Pharaoh: Because of my mighty hand he will let them go; because of my mighty hand he will drive them out of his country."

2God also said to Moses, "I am the LORD. 3I appeared to Abraham, to Isaac and to Jacob as God Almighty,[a] but by my name the LORD[b] I did not make myself fully known to them. 4I also established my covenant with them to give them the land of Canaan, where they resided as foreigners. 5Moreover, I have heard the groaning of the Israelites, whom the Egyptians are enslaving, and I have remembered my covenant.

6"Therefore, say to the Israelites: 'I am the LORD, and I will bring you out from under the yoke of the Egyptians. I will free you from being slaves to them, and I will redeem you with an outstretched arm and with mighty acts of judgment. 7I will take you as my own people, and I will be your God. Then you will know that I am the LORD your God, who brought you out from under the yoke of the Egyptians. 8And I will bring you to the land I swore with uplifted hand to give to Abraham, to Isaac and to Jacob. I will give it to you as a possession. I am the LORD.'"

9Moses reported this to the Israelites, but they did not listen to him because of their discouragement and harsh labor.

10Then the LORD said to Moses, 11"Go, tell Pharaoh king of Egypt to let the Israelites go out of his country."

12But Moses said to the LORD, "If the Israelites will not listen to me, why would Pharaoh listen to me, since I speak with faltering lips[c]?"

Family Record of Moses and Aaron

13Now the LORD spoke to Moses and Aaron about the Israelites and Pharaoh king of Egypt, and he commanded them to bring the Israelites out of Egypt.

14These were the heads of their families[d]:

The sons of Reuben the firstborn son of Israel were Hanok and Pallu, Hezron and Karmi. These were the clans of Reuben.

15The sons of Simeon were Jemuel, Jamin, Ohad, Jakin, Zohar and Shaul

---

a 3 Hebrew El-Shaddai   b 3 See note at 3:15.   c 12 Hebrew I am uncircumcised of lips; also in verse 30
d 14 The Hebrew for families here and in verse 25 refers to units larger than clans.

the son of a Canaanite woman. These were the clans of Simeon.

¹⁶These were the names of the sons of Levi according to their records: Gershon, Kohath and Merari. Levi lived 137 years.

¹⁷The sons of Gershon, by clans, were Libni and Shimei.

¹⁸The sons of Kohath were Amram, Izhar, Hebron and Uzziel. Kohath lived 133 years.

¹⁹The sons of Merari were Mahli and Mushi.

These were the clans of Levi according to their records.

²⁰Amram married his father's sister Jochebed, who bore him Aaron and Moses. Amram lived 137 years.

²¹The sons of Izhar were Korah, Nepheg and Zikri.

²²The sons of Uzziel were Mishael, Elzaphan and Sithri.

²³Aaron married Elisheba, daughter of Amminadab and sister of Nahshon, and she bore him Nadab and Abihu, Eleazar and Ithamar.

²⁴The sons of Korah were Assir, Elkanah and Abiasaph. These were the Korahite clans.

²⁵Eleazar son of Aaron married one of the daughters of Putiel, and she bore him Phinehas.

These were the heads of the Levite families, clan by clan.

²⁶It was this Aaron and Moses to whom the LORD said, "Bring the Israelites out of Egypt by their divisions." ²⁷They were the ones who spoke to Pharaoh king of Egypt about bringing the Israelites out of Egypt — this same Moses and Aaron.

Aaron to Speak for Moses

²⁸Now when the LORD spoke to Moses in Egypt, ²⁹he said to him, "I am the LORD. Tell Pharaoh king of Egypt everything I tell you."

³⁰But Moses said to the LORD, "Since I speak with faltering lips, why would Pharaoh listen to me?"

7 Then the LORD said to Moses, "See, I have made you like God to Pharaoh, and your brother Aaron will be your prophet. ²You are to say everything I command you, and your brother Aaron is to tell Pharaoh to let the Israelites go out of his country. ³But I will harden Pharaoh's heart, and though I multiply my signs and wonders in Egypt, ⁴he will not listen to you. Then I will lay my hand on Egypt and with mighty acts of judgment I will bring out my divisions, my people the Israelites. ⁵And the Egyptians will know that I am the LORD when I stretch out my hand against Egypt and bring the Israelites out of it."

⁶Moses and Aaron did just as the LORD commanded them. ⁷Moses was eighty years old and Aaron eighty-three when they spoke to Pharaoh.

Aaron's Staff Becomes a Snake

⁸The LORD said to Moses and Aaron, ⁹"When Pharaoh says to you, 'Perform a miracle,' then say to Aaron, 'Take your staff and throw it down before Pharaoh,' and it will become a snake."

¹⁰So Moses and Aaron went to Pharaoh and did just as the LORD commanded. Aaron threw his staff down in front of Pharaoh and his officials, and it became a snake. ¹¹Pharaoh then summoned wise men and sorcerers, and the Egyptian magicians also did the same things by their secret arts: ¹²Each one threw down his staff and it became a snake. But Aaron's staff swallowed up their staffs. ¹³Yet Pharaoh's heart became hard and he would not listen to them, just as the LORD had said.

The Plague of Blood

¹⁴Then the LORD said to Moses, "Pharaoh's heart is unyielding; he refuses to let the people go. ¹⁵Go to Pharaoh in the morning as he goes out to the river. Confront him on the bank of the Nile, and take in your hand the staff that was changed into a snake. ¹⁶Then say to him, 'The LORD, the God of the Hebrews, has sent me to say to you: Let my people go, so that they may

worship me in the wilderness. But until now you have not listened. 17This is what the Lord says: By this you will know that I am the Lord: With the staff that is in my hand I will strike the water of the Nile, and it will be changed into blood. 18The fish in the Nile will die, and the river will stink; the Egyptians will not be able to drink its water.'"

19The Lord said to Moses, "Tell Aaron, 'Take your staff and stretch out your hand over the waters of Egypt — over the streams and canals, over the ponds and all the reservoirs — and they will turn to blood.' Blood will be everywhere in Egypt, even in vessels*a* of wood and stone."

20Moses and Aaron did just as the Lord had commanded. He raised his staff in the presence of Pharaoh and his officials and struck the water of the Nile, and all the water was changed into blood. 21The fish in the Nile died, and the river smelled so bad that the Egyptians could not drink its water. Blood was everywhere in Egypt.

22But the Egyptian magicians did the same things by their secret arts, and Pharaoh's heart became hard; he would not listen to Moses and Aaron, just as the Lord had said. 23Instead, he turned and went into his palace, and did not take even this to heart. 24And all the Egyptians dug along the Nile to get drinking water, because they could not drink the water of the river.

The Plague of Frogs

25Seven days passed after the Lord struck the Nile. 8 *b* 1Then the Lord said to Moses, "Go to Pharaoh and say to him, 'This is what the Lord says: Let my people go, so that they may worship me. 2If you refuse to let them go, I will send a plague of frogs on your whole country. 3The Nile will teem with frogs. They will come up into your palace and your bedroom and onto your bed, into the houses of your officials and on your people, and into your ovens and kneading troughs. 4The

frogs will come up on you and your people and all your officials.'"

5Then the Lord said to Moses, "Tell Aaron, 'Stretch out your hand with your staff over the streams and canals and ponds, and make frogs come up on the land of Egypt.'"

6So Aaron stretched out his hand over the waters of Egypt, and the frogs came up and covered the land. 7But the magicians did the same things by their secret arts; they also made frogs come up on the land of Egypt.

8Pharaoh summoned Moses and Aaron and said, "Pray to the Lord to take the frogs away from me and my people, and I will let your people go to offer sacrifices to the Lord."

9Moses said to Pharaoh, "I leave to you the honor of setting the time for me to pray for you and your officials and your people that you and your houses may be rid of the frogs, except for those that remain in the Nile."

10"Tomorrow," Pharaoh said.

Moses replied, "It will be as you say, so that you may know there is no one like the Lord our God. 11The frogs will leave you and your houses, your officials and your people; they will remain only in the Nile."

12After Moses and Aaron left Pharaoh, Moses cried out to the Lord about the frogs he had brought on Pharaoh. 13And the Lord did what Moses asked. The frogs died in the houses, in the courtyards and in the fields. 14They were piled into heaps, and the land reeked of them. 15But when Pharaoh saw that there was relief, he hardened his heart and would not listen to Moses and Aaron, just as the Lord had said.

The Plague of Gnats

16Then the Lord said to Moses, "Tell Aaron, 'Stretch out your staff and strike the dust of the ground,' and throughout the land of Egypt the dust will become gnats." 17They did this, and when Aaron stretched

---

a 19 Or *even on their idols*   *b* In Hebrew texts 8:1-4 is numbered 7:26-29, and 8:5-32 is numbered 8:1-28.

out his hand with the staff and struck the dust of the ground, gnats came on people and animals. All the dust throughout the land of Egypt became gnats. ¹⁸But when the magicians tried to produce gnats by their secret arts, they could not.

Since the gnats were on people and animals everywhere, ¹⁹the magicians said to Pharaoh, "This is the finger of God." But Pharaoh's heart was hard and he would not listen, just as the LORD had said.

The Plague of Flies

²⁰Then the LORD said to Moses, "Get up early in the morning and confront Pharaoh as he goes to the river and say to him, 'This is what the LORD says: Let my people go, so that they may worship me. ²¹If you do not let my people go, I will send swarms of flies on you and your officials, on your people and into your houses. The houses of the Egyptians will be full of flies; even the ground will be covered with them.

²²" 'But on that day I will deal differently with the land of Goshen, where my people live; no swarms of flies will be there, so that you will know that I, the LORD, am in this land. ²³I will make a distinction*a* between my people and your people. This sign will occur tomorrow.' "

²⁴And the LORD did this. Dense swarms of flies poured into Pharaoh's palace and into the houses of his officials; throughout Egypt the land was ruined by the flies.

²⁵Then Pharaoh summoned Moses and Aaron and said, "Go, sacrifice to your God here in the land."

²⁶But Moses said, "That would not be right. The sacrifices we offer the LORD our God would be detestable to the Egyptians. And if we offer sacrifices that are detestable in their eyes, will they not stone us? ²⁷We must take a three-day journey into the wilderness to offer sacrifices to the LORD our God, as he commands us."

²⁸Pharaoh said, "I will let you go to offer sacrifices to the LORD your God in the wilderness, but you must not go very far. Now pray for me."

²⁹Moses answered, "As soon as I leave you, I will pray to the LORD, and tomorrow the flies will leave Pharaoh and his officials and his people. Only let Pharaoh be sure that he does not act deceitfully again by not letting the people go to offer sacrifices to the LORD."

³⁰Then Moses left Pharaoh and prayed to the LORD, ³¹and the LORD did what Moses asked. The flies left Pharaoh and his officials and his people; not a fly remained. ³²But this time also Pharaoh hardened his heart and would not let the people go.

The Plague on Livestock

9 Then the LORD said to Moses, "Go to Pharaoh and say to him, 'This is what the LORD, the God of the Hebrews, says: "Let my people go, so that they may worship me." ²If you refuse to let them go and continue to hold them back, ³the hand of the LORD will bring a terrible plague on your livestock in the field — on your horses, donkeys and camels and on your cattle, sheep and goats. ⁴But the LORD will make a distinction between the livestock of Israel and that of Egypt, so that no animal belonging to the Israelites will die.' "

⁵The LORD set a time and said, "Tomorrow the LORD will do this in the land." ⁶And the next day the LORD did it: All the livestock of the Egyptians died, but not one animal belonging to the Israelites died. ⁷Pharaoh investigated and found that not even one of the animals of the Israelites had died. Yet his heart was unyielding and he would not let the people go.

The Plague of Boils

⁸Then the LORD said to Moses and Aaron, "Take handfuls of soot from a furnace and have Moses toss it into the air in the presence of Pharaoh. ⁹It will become fine dust over the whole land of Egypt, and

---

a 23 Septuagint and Vulgate; Hebrew *will put a deliverance* festering boils will break out on people and animals throughout the land."

¹⁰So they took soot from a furnace and stood before Pharaoh. Moses tossed it into the air, and festering boils broke out on people and animals. ¹¹The magicians could not stand before Moses because of the boils that were on them and on all the Egyptians. ¹²But the LORD hardened Pharaoh's heart and he would not listen to Moses and Aaron, just as the LORD had said to Moses.

The Plague of Hail

¹³Then the LORD said to Moses, "Get up early in the morning, confront Pharaoh and say to him, 'This is what the LORD, the God of the Hebrews, says: Let my people go, so that they may worship me, ¹⁴or this time I will send the full force of my plagues against you and against your officials and your people, so you may know that there is no one like me in all the earth. ¹⁵For by now I could have stretched out my hand and struck you and your people with a plague that would have wiped you off the earth. ¹⁶But I have raised you up[a] for this very purpose, that I might show you my power and that my name might be proclaimed in all the earth. ¹⁷You still set yourself against my people and will not let them go. ¹⁸Therefore, at this time tomorrow I will send the worst hailstorm that has ever fallen on Egypt, from the day it was founded till now. ¹⁹Give an order now to bring your livestock and everything you have in the field to a place of shelter, because the hail will fall on every person and animal that has not been brought in and is still out in the field, and they will die.'"

²⁰Those officials of Pharaoh who feared the word of the LORD hurried to bring their slaves and their livestock inside. ²¹But those who ignored the word of the LORD left their slaves and livestock in the field.

²²Then the LORD said to Moses, "Stretch out your hand toward the sky so that hail will fall all over Egypt — on people and animals and on everything growing in the fields of Egypt." ²³When Moses stretched out his staff toward the sky, the LORD sent thunder and hail, and lightning flashed down to the ground. So the LORD rained hail on the land of Egypt; ²⁴hail fell and lightning flashed back and forth. It was the worst storm in all the land of Egypt since it had become a nation. ²⁵Throughout Egypt hail struck everything in the fields — both people and animals; it beat down everything growing in the fields and stripped every tree. ²⁶The only place it did not hail was the land of Goshen, where the Israelites were.

²⁷Then Pharaoh summoned Moses and Aaron. "This time I have sinned," he said to them. "The LORD is in the right, and I and my people are in the wrong. ²⁸Pray to the LORD, for we have had enough thunder and hail. I will let you go; you don't have to stay any longer."

²⁹Moses replied, "When I have gone out of the city, I will spread out my hands in prayer to the LORD. The thunder will stop and there will be no more hail, so you may know that the earth is the LORD's. ³⁰But I know that you and your officials still do not fear the LORD God."

³¹(The flax and barley were destroyed, since the barley had headed and the flax was in bloom. ³²The wheat and spelt, however, were not destroyed, because they ripen later.)

³³Then Moses left Pharaoh and went out of the city. He spread out his hands toward the LORD; the thunder and hail stopped, and the rain no longer poured down on the land. ³⁴When Pharaoh saw that the rain and hail and thunder had stopped, he sinned again: He and his officials hardened their hearts. ³⁵So Pharaoh's heart was hard and he would not let the Israelites go, just as the LORD had said through Moses.

---

a 16 Or have spared you

The Plague of Locusts

10 Then the LORD said to Moses, "Go to Pharaoh, for I have hardened his heart and the hearts of his officials so that I may perform these signs of mine among them ²that you may tell your children and grandchildren how I dealt harshly with the Egyptians and how I performed my signs among them, and that you may know that I am the LORD."

³So Moses and Aaron went to Pharaoh and said to him, "This is what the LORD, the God of the Hebrews, says: 'How long will you refuse to humble yourself before me? Let my people go, so that they may worship me. ⁴If you refuse to let them go, I will bring locusts into your country tomorrow. ⁵They will cover the face of the ground so that it cannot be seen. They will devour what little you have left after the hail, including every tree that is growing in your fields. ⁶They will fill your houses and those of all your officials and all the Egyptians — something neither your parents nor your ancestors have ever seen from the day they settled in this land till now.'" Then Moses turned and left Pharaoh.

⁷Pharaoh's officials said to him, "How long will this man be a snare to us? Let the people go, so that they may worship the LORD their God. Do you not yet realize that Egypt is ruined?"

⁸Then Moses and Aaron were brought back to Pharaoh. "Go, worship the LORD your God," he said. "But tell me who will be going."

⁹Moses answered, "We will go with our young and our old, with our sons and our daughters, and with our flocks and herds, because we are to celebrate a festival to the LORD."

¹⁰Pharaoh said, "The LORD be with you — if I let you go, along with your women and children! Clearly you are bent on evil.[a] ¹¹No! Have only the men go and worship the LORD, since that's what you have been asking for." Then Moses and Aaron were driven out of Pharaoh's presence.

¹²And the LORD said to Moses, "Stretch out your hand over Egypt so that locusts swarm over the land and devour everything growing in the fields, everything left by the hail."

¹³So Moses stretched out his staff over Egypt, and the LORD made an east wind blow across the land all that day and all that night. By morning the wind had brought the locusts; ¹⁴they invaded all Egypt and settled down in every area of the country in great numbers. Never before had there been such a plague of locusts, nor will there ever be again. ¹⁵They covered all the ground until it was black. They devoured all that was left after the hail — everything growing in the fields and the fruit on the trees. Nothing green remained on tree or plant in all the land of Egypt.

¹⁶Pharaoh quickly summoned Moses and Aaron and said, "I have sinned against the LORD your God and against you. ¹⁷Now forgive my sin once more and pray to the LORD your God to take this deadly plague away from me."

¹⁸Moses then left Pharaoh and prayed to the LORD. ¹⁹And the LORD changed the wind to a very strong west wind, which caught up the locusts and carried them into the Red Sea.[b] Not a locust was left anywhere in Egypt. ²⁰But the LORD hardened Pharaoh's heart, and he would not let the Israelites go.

The Plague of Darkness

²¹Then the LORD said to Moses, "Stretch out your hand toward the sky so that darkness spreads over Egypt — darkness that can be felt." ²²So Moses stretched out his hand toward the sky, and total darkness covered all Egypt for three days. ²³No one could see anyone else or move about for three days. Yet all the Israelites had light in the places where they lived.

²⁴Then Pharaoh summoned Moses and

---

[a] 10 Or *Be careful, trouble is in store for you!*   [b] 19 Or *the Sea of Reeds*

said, "Go, worship the Lord. Even your women and children may go with you; only leave your flocks and herds behind."

25But Moses said, "You must allow us to have sacrifices and burnt offerings to present to the Lord our God. 26Our livestock too must go with us; not a hoof is to be left behind. We have to use some of them in worshiping the Lord our God, and until we get there we will not know what we are to use to worship the Lord."

27But the Lord hardened Pharaoh's heart, and he was not willing to let them go. 28Pharaoh said to Moses, "Get out of my sight! Make sure you do not appear before me again! The day you see my face you will die."

29"Just as you say," Moses replied. "I will never appear before you again."

The Plague on the Firstborn

11 Now the Lord had said to Moses, "I will bring one more plague on Pharaoh and on Egypt. After that, he will let you go from here, and when he does, he will drive you out completely. 2Tell the people that men and women alike are to ask their neighbors for articles of silver and gold." 3(The Lord made the Egyptians favorably disposed toward the people, and Moses himself was highly regarded in Egypt by Pharaoh's officials and by the people.)

4So Moses said, "This is what the Lord says: 'About midnight I will go throughout Egypt. 5Every firstborn son in Egypt will die, from the firstborn son of Pharaoh, who sits on the throne, to the firstborn son of the female slave, who is at her hand mill, and all the firstborn of the cattle as well. 6There will be loud wailing throughout Egypt — worse than there has ever been or ever will be again. 7But among the Israelites not a dog will bark at any person or animal.' Then you will know that the Lord makes a distinction between Egypt and Israel. 8All these of-

ficials of yours will come to me, bowing down before me and saying, 'Go, you and all the people who follow you!' After that I will leave." Then Moses, hot with anger, left Pharaoh.

9The Lord had said to Moses, "Pharaoh will refuse to listen to you — so that my wonders may be multiplied in Egypt." 10Moses and Aaron performed all these wonders before Pharaoh, but the Lord hardened Pharaoh's heart, and he would not let the Israelites go out of his country.

The Passover and the Festival of Unleavened Bread

12 The Lord said to Moses and Aaron in Egypt, 2"This month is to be for you the first month, the first month of your year. 3Tell the whole community of Israel that on the tenth day of this month each man is to take a lamb*a* for his family, one for each household. 4If any household is too small for a whole lamb, they must share one with their nearest neighbor, having taken into account the number of people there are. You are to determine the amount of lamb needed in accordance with what each person will eat. 5The animals you choose must be year-old males without defect, and you may take them from the sheep or the goats. 6Take care of them until the fourteenth day of the month, when all the members of the community of Israel must slaughter them at twilight. 7Then they are to take some of the blood and put it on the sides and tops of the doorframes of the houses where they eat the lambs. 8That same night they are to eat the meat roasted over the fire, along with bitter herbs, and bread made without yeast. 9Do not eat the meat raw or boiled in water, but roast it over a fire — with the head, legs and internal organs. 10Do not leave any of it till morning; if some is left till morning, you must burn it. 11This is how you are to eat it: with your cloak tucked into your belt, your sandals on your feet and your staff in

---

a 3 The Hebrew word can mean *lamb* or *kid*; also in verse 4.

your hand. Eat it in haste; it is the Lord's Passover.

12 "On that same night I will pass through Egypt and strike down every first-born of both people and animals, and I will bring judgment on all the gods of Egypt. I am the Lord. 13 The blood will be a sign for you on the houses where you are, and when I see the blood, I will pass over you. No destructive plague will touch you when I strike Egypt.

14 "This is a day you are to commemorate; for the generations to come you shall celebrate it as a festival to the Lord — a lasting ordinance. 15 For seven days you are to eat bread made without yeast. On the first day remove the yeast from your houses, for whoever eats anything with yeast in it from the first day through the seventh must be cut off from Israel. 16 On the first day hold a sacred assembly, and another one on the seventh day. Do no work at all on these days, except to prepare food for everyone to eat; that is all you may do.

17 "Celebrate the Festival of Unleavened Bread, because it was on this very day that I brought your divisions out of Egypt. Celebrate this day as a lasting ordinance for the generations to come. 18 In the first month you are to eat bread made without yeast, from the evening of the fourteenth day until the evening of the twenty-first day. 19 For seven days no yeast is to be found in your houses. And anyone, whether foreigner or native-born, who eats anything with yeast in it must be cut off from the community of Israel. 20 Eat nothing made with yeast. Wherever you live, you must eat unleavened bread."

21 Then Moses summoned all the elders of Israel and said to them, "Go at once and select the animals for your families and slaughter the Passover lamb. 22 Take a bunch of hyssop, dip it into the blood in the basin and put some of the blood on the top and on both sides of the doorframe. None of you shall go out of the door of your house until morning. 23 When the Lord goes through the land to strike down the Egyptians, he will see the blood on the top and sides of the doorframe and will pass over that doorway, and he will not permit the destroyer to enter your houses and strike you down.

24 "Obey these instructions as a lasting ordinance for you and your descendants. 25 When you enter the land that the Lord will give you as he promised, observe this ceremony. 26 And when your children ask you, 'What does this ceremony mean to you?' 27 then tell them, 'It is the Passover sacrifice to the Lord, who passed over the houses of the Israelites in Egypt and spared our homes when he struck down the Egyptians.'" Then the people bowed down and worshiped. 28 The Israelites did just what the Lord commanded Moses and Aaron.

29 At midnight the Lord struck down all the firstborn in Egypt, from the firstborn of Pharaoh, who sat on the throne, to the firstborn of the prisoner, who was in the dungeon, and the firstborn of all the livestock as well. 30 Pharaoh and all his officials and all the Egyptians got up during the night, and there was loud wailing in Egypt, for there was not a house without someone dead.

The Exodus

31 During the night Pharaoh summoned Moses and Aaron and said, "Up! Leave my people, you and the Israelites! Go, worship the Lord as you have requested. 32 Take your flocks and herds, as you have said, and go. And also bless me."

33 The Egyptians urged the people to hurry and leave the country. "For otherwise," they said, "we will all die!" 34 So the people took their dough before the yeast was added, and carried it on their shoulders in kneading troughs wrapped in clothing. 35 The Israelites did as Moses instructed and asked the Egyptians for articles of silver and gold and for clothing. 36 The Lord had made the Egyptians favorably disposed toward the people, and

they gave them what they asked for; so they plundered the Egyptians.

37 The Israelites journeyed from Rameses to Sukkoth. There were about six hundred thousand men on foot, besides women and children. 38 Many other people went up with them, and also large droves of livestock, both flocks and herds. 39 With the dough the Israelites had brought from Egypt, they baked loaves of unleavened bread. The dough was without yeast because they had been driven out of Egypt and did not have time to prepare food for themselves.

40 Now the length of time the Israelite people lived in Egypt*a* was 430 years. 41 At the end of the 430 years, to the very day, all the Lord's divisions left Egypt. 42 Because the Lord kept vigil that night to bring them out of Egypt, on this night all the Israelites are to keep vigil to honor the Lord for the generations to come.

Passover Restrictions

43 The Lord said to Moses and Aaron, "These are the regulations for the Passover meal:

"No foreigner may eat it. 44 Any slave you have bought may eat it after you have circumcised him, 45 but a temporary resident or a hired worker may not eat it.

46 "It must be eaten inside the house; take none of the meat outside the house. Do not break any of the bones. 47 The whole community of Israel must celebrate it.

48 "A foreigner residing among you who wants to celebrate the Lord's Passover must have all the males in his household circumcised; then he may take part like one born in the land. No uncircumcised male may eat it. 49 The same law applies both to the native-born and to the foreigner residing among you."

50 All the Israelites did just what the Lord had commanded Moses and Aaron. 51 And on that very day the Lord brought the Israelites out of Egypt by their divisions.

Consecration of the Firstborn

13 The Lord said to Moses, 2 "Consecrate to me every firstborn male. The first offspring of every womb among the Israelites belongs to me, whether human or animal."

3 Then Moses said to the people, "Commemorate this day, the day you came out of Egypt, out of the land of slavery, because the Lord brought you out of it with a mighty hand. Eat nothing containing yeast. 4 Today, in the month of Aviv, you are leaving. 5 When the Lord brings you into the land of the Canaanites, Hittites, Amorites, Hivites and Jebusites — the land he swore to your ancestors to give you, a land flowing with milk and honey — you are to observe this ceremony in this month: 6 For seven days eat bread made without yeast and on the seventh day hold a festival to the Lord. 7 Eat unleavened bread during those seven days; nothing with yeast in it is to be seen among you, nor shall any yeast be seen anywhere within your borders. 8 On that day tell your son, 'I do this because of what the Lord did for me when I came out of Egypt.' 9 This observance will be for you like a sign on your hand and a reminder on your forehead that this law of the Lord is to be on your lips. For the Lord brought you out of Egypt with his mighty hand. 10 You must keep this ordinance at the appointed time year after year.

11 "After the Lord brings you into the land of the Canaanites and gives it to you, as he promised on oath to you and your ancestors, 12 you are to give over to the Lord the first offspring of every womb. All the firstborn males of your livestock belong to the Lord. 13 Redeem with a lamb every firstborn donkey, but if you do not redeem it, break its neck. Redeem every firstborn among your sons.

14 "In days to come, when your son asks you, 'What does this mean?' say to him, 'With a mighty hand the Lord brought us out of Egypt, out of the land of slavery.

---

a 40 Masoretic Text; Samaritan Pentateuch and Septuagint *Egypt and Canaan*

15When Pharaoh stubbornly refused to let us go, the Lord killed the firstborn of both people and animals in Egypt. This is why I sacrifice to the Lord the first male offspring of every womb and redeem each of my firstborn sons.' 16And it will be like a sign on your hand and a symbol on your forehead that the Lord brought us out of Egypt with his mighty hand."

Crossing the Sea

17When Pharaoh let the people go, God did not lead them on the road through the Philistine country, though that was shorter. For God said, "If they face war, they might change their minds and return to Egypt." 18So God led the people around by the desert road toward the Red Sea.*a* The Israelites went up out of Egypt ready for battle.

19Moses took the bones of Joseph with him because Joseph had made the Israelites swear an oath. He had said, "God will surely come to your aid, and then you must carry my bones up with you from this place."*b*

20After leaving Sukkoth they camped at Etham on the edge of the desert. 21By day the Lord went ahead of them in a pillar of cloud to guide them on their way and by night in a pillar of fire to give them light, so that they could travel by day or night. 22Neither the pillar of cloud by day nor the pillar of fire by night left its place in front of the people.

14 Then the Lord said to Moses, 2"Tell the Israelites to turn back and encamp near Pi Hahiroth, between Migdol and the sea. They are to encamp by the sea, directly opposite Baal Zephon. 3Pharaoh will think, 'The Israelites are wandering around the land in confusion, hemmed in by the desert.' 4And I will harden Pharaoh's heart, and he will pursue them. But I will gain glory for myself through Pharaoh and all his army, and the Egyptians will know that I am the Lord." So the Israelites did this.

5When the king of Egypt was told that the people had fled, Pharaoh and his officials changed their minds about them and said, "What have we done? We have let the Israelites go and have lost their services!" 6So he had his chariot made ready and took his army with him. 7He took six hundred of the best chariots, along with all the other chariots of Egypt, with officers over all of them. 8The Lord hardened the heart of Pharaoh king of Egypt, so that he pursued the Israelites, who were marching out boldly. 9The Egyptians — all Pharaoh's horses and chariots, horsemen*c* and troops — pursued the Israelites and overtook them as they camped by the sea near Pi Hahiroth, opposite Baal Zephon.

10As Pharaoh approached, the Israelites looked up, and there were the Egyptians, marching after them. They were terrified and cried out to the Lord. 11They said to Moses, "Was it because there were no graves in Egypt that you brought us to the desert to die? What have you done to us by bringing us out of Egypt? 12Didn't we say to you in Egypt, 'Leave us alone; let us serve the Egyptians'? It would have been better for us to serve the Egyptians than to die in the desert!"

13Moses answered the people, "Do not be afraid. Stand firm and you will see the deliverance the Lord will bring you today. The Egyptians you see today you will never see again. 14The Lord will fight for you; you need only to be still."

15Then the Lord said to Moses, "Why are you crying out to me? Tell the Israelites to move on. 16Raise your staff and stretch out your hand over the sea to divide the water so that the Israelites can go through the sea on dry ground. 17I will harden the hearts of the Egyptians so that they will go in after them. And I will gain glory through Pharaoh and all his army, through his chariots and his horsemen. 18The Egyptians will know that I am the Lord when I gain glory through Pharaoh, his chariots and his horsemen."

---

a 18 Or *the Sea of Reeds*   *b 19* See Gen. 50:25.   *c 9* Or *charioteers*; also in verses 17, 18, 23, 26 and 28

19Then the angel of God, who had been traveling in front of Israel's army, withdrew and went behind them. The pillar of cloud also moved from in front and stood behind them, 20coming between the armies of Egypt and Israel. Throughout the night the cloud brought darkness to the one side and light to the other side; so neither went near the other all night long.

21Then Moses stretched out his hand over the sea, and all that night the Lord drove the sea back with a strong east wind and turned it into dry land. The waters were divided, 22and the Israelites went through the sea on dry ground, with a wall of water on their right and on their left.

23The Egyptians pursued them, and all Pharaoh's horses and chariots and horsemen followed them into the sea. 24During the last watch of the night the Lord looked down from the pillar of fire and cloud at the Egyptian army and threw it into confusion. 25He jammed*a* the wheels of their chariots so that they had difficulty driving. And the Egyptians said, "Let's get away from the Israelites! The Lord is fighting for them against Egypt."

26Then the Lord said to Moses, "Stretch out your hand over the sea so that the waters may flow back over the Egyptians and their chariots and horsemen." 27Moses stretched out his hand over the sea, and at daybreak the sea went back to its place. The Egyptians were fleeing toward*b* it, and the Lord swept them into the sea. 28The water flowed back and covered the chariots and horsemen — the entire army of Pharaoh that had followed the Israelites into the sea. Not one of them survived.

29But the Israelites went through the sea on dry ground, with a wall of water on their right and on their left. 30That day the Lord saved Israel from the hands of the Egyptians, and Israel saw the Egyptians lying dead on the shore. 31And when the Israelites saw the mighty hand of the Lord

displayed against the Egyptians, the people feared the Lord and put their trust in him and in Moses his servant.

The Song of Moses and Miriam

15 Then Moses and the Israelites sang this song to the Lord:

"I will sing to the Lord,
 for he is highly exalted.
Both horse and driver
 he has hurled into the sea.

2 "The Lord is my strength and my
   defense*c*;
 he has become my salvation.
He is my God, and I will praise him,
 my father's God, and I will exalt him.
3 The Lord is a warrior;
 the Lord is his name.
4 Pharaoh's chariots and his army
 he has hurled into the sea.
The best of Pharaoh's officers
 are drowned in the Red Sea.*d*
5 The deep waters have covered them;
 they sank to the depths like a stone.
6 Your right hand, Lord,
 was majestic in power.
Your right hand, Lord,
 shattered the enemy.

7 "In the greatness of your majesty
 you threw down those who opposed
   you.
You unleashed your burning anger;
 it consumed them like stubble.
8 By the blast of your nostrils
 the waters piled up.
The surging waters stood up like a wall;
 the deep waters congealed in the
   heart of the sea.
9 The enemy boasted,
 'I will pursue, I will overtake them.
I will divide the spoils;
 I will gorge myself on them.
I will draw my sword
 and my hand will destroy them.'

---

a 25 See Samaritan Pentateuch, Septuagint and Syriac; Masoretic Text *removed*   *b 27* Or *from*   *c 2* Or *song*
d 4 Or *the Sea of Reeds*; also in verse 22

10But you blew with your breath,
  and the sea covered them.
They sank like lead
  in the mighty waters.
11Who among the gods
  is like you, LORD?
Who is like you —
  majestic in holiness,
  awesome in glory,
  working wonders?

12"You stretch out your right hand,
  and the earth swallows your enemies.
13In your unfailing love you will lead
  the people you have redeemed.
In your strength you will guide them
  to your holy dwelling.
14The nations will hear and tremble;
  anguish will grip the people of
    Philistia.
15The chiefs of Edom will be terrified,
  the leaders of Moab will be seized
    with trembling,
the people*a* of Canaan will melt away;
16   terror and dread will fall on them.
By the power of your arm
  they will be as still as a stone —
until your people pass by, LORD,
  until the people you bought*b* pass by.
17You will bring them in and plant them
  on the mountain of your
    inheritance —
the place, LORD, you made for your
    dwelling,
  the sanctuary, Lord, your hands
    established.

18"The LORD reigns
  for ever and ever."

19When Pharaoh's horses, chariots and
horsemen*c* went into the sea, the LORD
brought the waters of the sea back over
them, but the Israelites walked through
the sea on dry ground. 20Then Miriam the
prophet, Aaron's sister, took a timbrel in
her hand, and all the women followed her,
with timbrels and dancing. 21Miriam sang
to them:

"Sing to the LORD,
  for he is highly exalted.
Both horse and driver
  he has hurled into the sea."

The Waters of Marah and Elim

22Then Moses led Israel from the Red
Sea and they went into the Desert of Shur.
For three days they traveled in the desert
without finding water. 23When they came
to Marah, they could not drink its water
because it was bitter. (That is why the place
is called Marah.*d*) 24So the people grumbled against Moses, saying, "What are we
to drink?"

25Then Moses cried out to the LORD, and
the LORD showed him a piece of wood. He
threw it into the water, and the water became fit to drink.

There the LORD issued a ruling and instruction for them and put them to the
test. 26He said, "If you listen carefully to
the LORD your God and do what is right
in his eyes, if you pay attention to his commands and keep all his decrees, I will not
bring on you any of the diseases I brought
on the Egyptians, for I am the LORD, who
heals you."

27Then they came to Elim, where there
were twelve springs and seventy palm trees,
and they camped there near the water.

Manna and Quail

16 The whole Israelite community
set out from Elim and came to
the Desert of Sin, which is between Elim and Sinai, on the fifteenth day
of the second month after they had come
out of Egypt. 2In the desert the whole community grumbled against Moses and Aaron. 3The Israelites said to them, "If only
we had died by the LORD's hand in Egypt!
There we sat around pots of meat and ate all
the food we wanted, but you have brought
us out into this desert to starve this entire
assembly to death."

4Then the LORD said to Moses, "I will

---

a 15 Or *rulers*   *b 16* Or *created*   *c 19* Or *charioteers*   *d 23 Marah* means *bitter.*

rain down bread from heaven for you. The people are to go out each day and gather enough for that day. In this way I will test them and see whether they will follow my instructions. ⁵On the sixth day they are to prepare what they bring in, and that is to be twice as much as they gather on the other days."

⁶So Moses and Aaron said to all the Israelites, "In the evening you will know that it was the LORD who brought you out of Egypt, ⁷and in the morning you will see the glory of the LORD, because he has heard your grumbling against him. Who are we, that you should grumble against us?" ⁸Moses also said, "You will know that it was the LORD when he gives you meat to eat in the evening and all the bread you want in the morning, because he has heard your grumbling against him. Who are we? You are not grumbling against us, but against the LORD."

⁹Then Moses told Aaron, "Say to the entire Israelite community, 'Come before the LORD, for he has heard your grumbling.' "

¹⁰While Aaron was speaking to the whole Israelite community, they looked toward the desert, and there was the glory of the LORD appearing in the cloud.

¹¹The LORD said to Moses, ¹²"I have heard the grumbling of the Israelites. Tell them, 'At twilight you will eat meat, and in the morning you will be filled with bread. Then you will know that I am the LORD your God.' "

¹³That evening quail came and covered the camp, and in the morning there was a layer of dew around the camp. ¹⁴When the dew was gone, thin flakes like frost on the ground appeared on the desert floor. ¹⁵When the Israelites saw it, they said to each other, "What is it?" For they did not know what it was.

Moses said to them, "It is the bread the LORD has given you to eat. ¹⁶This is what the LORD has commanded: 'Everyone is to gather as much as they need. Take an omer*ᵃ* for each person you have in your tent.' "

¹⁷The Israelites did as they were told; some gathered much, some little. ¹⁸And when they measured it by the omer, the one who gathered much did not have too much, and the one who gathered little did not have too little. Everyone had gathered just as much as they needed.

¹⁹Then Moses said to them, "No one is to keep any of it until morning."

²⁰However, some of them paid no attention to Moses; they kept part of it until morning, but it was full of maggots and began to smell. So Moses was angry with them.

²¹Each morning everyone gathered as much as they needed, and when the sun grew hot, it melted away. ²²On the sixth day, they gathered twice as much — two omers*ᵇ* for each person — and the leaders of the community came and reported this to Moses. ²³He said to them, "This is what the LORD commanded: 'Tomorrow is to be a day of sabbath rest, a holy sabbath to the LORD. So bake what you want to bake and boil what you want to boil. Save whatever is left and keep it until morning.' "

²⁴So they saved it until morning, as Moses commanded, and it did not stink or get maggots in it. ²⁵"Eat it today," Moses said, "because today is a sabbath to the LORD. You will not find any of it on the ground today. ²⁶Six days you are to gather it, but on the seventh day, the Sabbath, there will not be any."

²⁷Nevertheless, some of the people went out on the seventh day to gather it, but they found none. ²⁸Then the LORD said to Moses, "How long will you*ᶜ* refuse to keep my commands and my instructions? ²⁹Bear in mind that the LORD has given you the Sabbath; that is why on the sixth day he gives you bread for two days. Everyone is to stay where they are on the seventh day; no one is to go out." ³⁰So the people rested on the seventh day.

ᵃ 16 That is, possibly about 3 pounds or about 1.4 kilograms; also in verses 18, 32, 33 and 36   *ᵇ 22* That is, possibly about 6 pounds or about 2.8 kilograms   *ᶜ 28* The Hebrew is plural.

³¹The people of Israel called the bread manna.ᵃ It was white like coriander seed and tasted like wafers made with honey. ³²Moses said, "This is what the LORD has commanded: 'Take an omer of manna and keep it for the generations to come, so they can see the bread I gave you to eat in the wilderness when I brought you out of Egypt.'"

³³So Moses said to Aaron, "Take a jar and put an omer of manna in it. Then place it before the LORD to be kept for the generations to come."

³⁴As the LORD commanded Moses, Aaron put the manna with the tablets of the covenant law, so that it might be preserved. ³⁵The Israelites ate manna forty years, until they came to a land that was settled; they ate manna until they reached the border of Canaan.

³⁶(An omer is one-tenth of an ephah.)

Water From the Rock

17 The whole Israelite community set out from the Desert of Sin, traveling from place to place as the LORD commanded. They camped at Rephidim, but there was no water for the people to drink. ²So they quarreled with Moses and said, "Give us water to drink."

Moses replied, "Why do you quarrel with me? Why do you put the LORD to the test?"

³But the people were thirsty for water there, and they grumbled against Moses. They said, "Why did you bring us up out of Egypt to make us and our children and livestock die of thirst?"

⁴Then Moses cried out to the LORD, "What am I to do with these people? They are almost ready to stone me."

⁵The LORD answered Moses, "Go out in front of the people. Take with you some of the elders of Israel and take in your hand the staff with which you struck the Nile, and go. ⁶I will stand there before you by the rock at Horeb. Strike the rock, and water will come out of it for the people to drink."

So Moses did this in the sight of the elders of Israel. ⁷And he called the place Massahᵇ and Meribahᶜ because the Israelites quarreled and because they tested the LORD saying, "Is the LORD among us or not?"

The Amalekites Defeated

⁸The Amalekites came and attacked the Israelites at Rephidim. ⁹Moses said to Joshua, "Choose some of our men and go out to fight the Amalekites. Tomorrow I will stand on top of the hill with the staff of God in my hands."

¹⁰So Joshua fought the Amalekites as Moses had ordered, and Moses, Aaron and Hur went to the top of the hill. ¹¹As long as Moses held up his hands, the Israelites were winning, but whenever he lowered his hands, the Amalekites were winning. ¹²When Moses' hands grew tired, they took a stone and put it under him and he sat on it. Aaron and Hur held his hands up — one on one side, one on the other — so that his hands remained steady till sunset. ¹³So Joshua overcame the Amalekite army with the sword.

¹⁴Then the LORD said to Moses, "Write this on a scroll as something to be remembered and make sure that Joshua hears it, because I will completely blot out the name of Amalek from under heaven."

¹⁵Moses built an altar and called it The LORD is my Banner. ¹⁶He said, "Because hands were lifted up againstᵈ the throne of the LORD,ᵉ the LORD will be at war against the Amalekites from generation to generation."

Jethro Visits Moses

18 Now Jethro, the priest of Midian and father-in-law of Moses, heard of everything God had done for Moses and for his people Israel, and how the LORD had brought Israel out of Egypt.

²After Moses had sent away his wife

ᵃ *31 Manna* sounds like the Hebrew for *What is it?* (see verse 15).   ᵇ *7 Massah* means *testing.*   ᶜ *7 Meribah* means *quarreling.*   ᵈ *16 Or to*   ᵉ *16* The meaning of the Hebrew for this clause is uncertain.

Zipporah, his father-in-law Jethro received her [3]and her two sons. One son was named Gershom,[a] for Moses said, "I have become a foreigner in a foreign land"; [4]and the other was named Eliezer,[b] for he said, "My father's God was my helper; he saved me from the sword of Pharaoh."

[5]Jethro, Moses' father-in-law, together with Moses' sons and wife, came to him in the wilderness, where he was camped near the mountain of God. [6]Jethro had sent word to him, "I, your father-in-law Jethro, am coming to you with your wife and her two sons."

[7]So Moses went out to meet his father-in-law and bowed down and kissed him. They greeted each other and then went into the tent. [8]Moses told his father-in-law about everything the LORD had done to Pharaoh and the Egyptians for Israel's sake and about all the hardships they had met along the way and how the LORD had saved them.

[9]Jethro was delighted to hear about all the good things the LORD had done for Israel in rescuing them from the hand of the Egyptians. [10]He said, "Praise be to the LORD, who rescued you from the hand of the Egyptians and of Pharaoh, and who rescued the people from the hand of the Egyptians. [11]Now I know that the LORD is greater than all other gods, for he did this to those who had treated Israel arrogantly." [12]Then Jethro, Moses' father-in-law, brought a burnt offering and other sacrifices to God, and Aaron came with all the elders of Israel to eat a meal with Moses' father-in-law in the presence of God.

[13]The next day Moses took his seat to serve as judge for the people, and they stood around him from morning till evening. [14]When his father-in-law saw all that Moses was doing for the people, he said, "What is this you are doing for the people? Why do you alone sit as judge, while all these people stand around you from morning till evening?"

[15]Moses answered him, "Because the people come to me to seek God's will. [16]Whenever they have a dispute, it is brought to me, and I decide between the parties and inform them of God's decrees and instructions."

[17]Moses' father-in-law replied, "What you are doing is not good. [18]You and these people who come to you will only wear yourselves out. The work is too heavy for you; you cannot handle it alone. [19]Listen now to me and I will give you some advice, and may God be with you. You must be the people's representative before God and bring their disputes to him. [20]Teach them his decrees and instructions, and show them the way they are to live and how they are to behave. [21]But select capable men from all the people — men who fear God, trustworthy men who hate dishonest gain — and appoint them as officials over thousands, hundreds, fifties and tens. [22]Have them serve as judges for the people at all times, but have them bring every difficult case to you; the simple cases they can decide themselves. That will make your load lighter, because they will share it with you. [23]If you do this and God so commands, you will be able to stand the strain, and all these people will go home satisfied."

[24]Moses listened to his father-in-law and did everything he said. [25]He chose capable men from all Israel and made them leaders of the people, officials over thousands, hundreds, fifties and tens. [26]They served as judges for the people at all times. The difficult cases they brought to Moses, but the simple ones they decided themselves.

[27]Then Moses sent his father-in-law on his way, and Jethro returned to his own country.

At Mount Sinai

19 On the first day of the third month after the Israelites left Egypt — on that very day — they came to the Desert of Sinai. [2]After

---

[a] 3 *Gershom* sounds like the Hebrew for *a foreigner there.*   [b] 4 *Eliezer* means *my God is helper.*

they set out from Rephidim, they entered the Desert of Sinai, and Israel camped there in the desert in front of the mountain.

³Then Moses went up to God, and the LORD called to him from the mountain and said, "This is what you are to say to the descendants of Jacob and what you are to tell the people of Israel: ⁴'You yourselves have seen what I did to Egypt, and how I carried you on eagles' wings and brought you to myself. ⁵Now if you obey me fully and keep my covenant, then out of all nations you will be my treasured possession. Although the whole earth is mine, ⁶you*ᵃ* will be for me a kingdom of priests and a holy nation.' These are the words you are to speak to the Israelites."

⁷So Moses went back and summoned the elders of the people and set before them all the words the LORD had commanded him to speak. ⁸The people all responded together, "We will do everything the LORD has said." So Moses brought their answer back to the LORD.

⁹The LORD said to Moses, "I am going to come to you in a dense cloud, so that the people will hear me speaking with you and will always put their trust in you." Then Moses told the LORD what the people had said.

¹⁰And the LORD said to Moses, "Go to the people and consecrate them today and tomorrow. Have them wash their clothes ¹¹and be ready by the third day, because on that day the LORD will come down on Mount Sinai in the sight of all the people. ¹²Put limits for the people around the mountain and tell them, 'Be careful that you do not approach the mountain or touch the foot of it. Whoever touches the mountain is to be put to death. ¹³They are to be stoned or shot with arrows; not a hand is to be laid on them. No person or animal shall be permitted to live.' Only when the ram's horn sounds a long blast may they approach the mountain."

¹⁴After Moses had gone down the mountain to the people, he consecrated them, and they washed their clothes. ¹⁵Then he said to the people, "Prepare yourselves for the third day. Abstain from sexual relations."

¹⁶On the morning of the third day there was thunder and lightning, with a thick cloud over the mountain, and a very loud trumpet blast. Everyone in the camp trembled. ¹⁷Then Moses led the people out of the camp to meet with God, and they stood at the foot of the mountain. ¹⁸Mount Sinai was covered with smoke, because the LORD descended on it in fire. The smoke billowed up from it like smoke from a furnace, and the whole mountainᵇ trembled violently. ¹⁹As the sound of the trumpet grew louder and louder, Moses spoke and the voice of God answered him.ᶜ

²⁰The LORD descended to the top of Mount Sinai and called Moses to the top of the mountain. So Moses went up ²¹and the LORD said to him, "Go down and warn the people so they do not force their way through to see the LORD and many of them perish. ²²Even the priests, who approach the LORD, must consecrate themselves, or the LORD will break out against them."

²³Moses said to the LORD, "The people cannot come up Mount Sinai, because you yourself warned us, 'Put limits around the mountain and set it apart as holy.'"

²⁴The LORD replied, "Go down and bring Aaron up with you. But the priests and the people must not force their way through to come up to the LORD, or he will break out against them."

²⁵So Moses went down to the people and told them.

The Ten Commandments

20

And God spoke all these words:

²"I am the LORD your God, who brought you out of Egypt, out of the land of slavery.

ᵃ 5,6 Or *possession, for the whole earth is mine.* *⁶You* manuscripts and Septuagint *and all the people*   *ᶜ 19* Or *and God answered him with thunder*   *ᵇ 18* Most Hebrew manuscripts; a few Hebrew

³"You shall have no other gods be-fore*a* me.

⁴"You shall not make for yourself an image in the form of anything in heaven above or on the earth beneath or in the waters below. ⁵You shall not bow down to them or worship them; for I, the LORD your God, am a jealous God, punishing the children for the sin of the parents to the third and fourth generation of those who hate me, ⁶but showing love to a thousand generations of those who love me and keep my commandments.

⁷"You shall not misuse the name of the LORD your God, for the LORD will not hold anyone guiltless who misuses his name.

⁸"Remember the Sabbath day by keeping it holy. ⁹Six days you shall labor and do all your work, ¹⁰but the seventh day is a sabbath to the LORD your God. On it you shall not do any work, neither you, nor your son or daughter, nor your male or female servant, nor your animals, nor any foreigner residing in your towns. ¹¹For in six days the LORD made the heavens and the earth, the sea, and all that is in them, but he rested on the seventh day. Therefore the LORD blessed the Sabbath day and made it holy.

¹²"Honor your father and your mother, so that you may live long in the land the LORD your God is giving you.

¹³"You shall not murder.

¹⁴"You shall not commit adultery.

¹⁵"You shall not steal.

¹⁶"You shall not give false testimony against your neighbor.

¹⁷"You shall not covet your neighbor's house. You shall not covet your neighbor's wife, or his male or female servant, his ox or donkey, or anything that belongs to your neighbor."

¹⁸When the people saw the thunder and lightning and heard the trumpet and saw the mountain in smoke, they trembled with fear. They stayed at a distance ¹⁹and said to Moses, "Speak to us yourself and we will listen. But do not have God speak to us or we will die."

²⁰Moses said to the people, "Do not be afraid. God has come to test you, so that the fear of God will be with you to keep you from sinning."

²¹The people remained at a distance, while Moses approached the thick darkness where God was.

Idols and Altars

²²Then the LORD said to Moses, "Tell the Israelites this: 'You have seen for yourselves that I have spoken to you from heaven: ²³Do not make any gods to be alongside me; do not make for yourselves gods of silver or gods of gold.

²⁴"'Make an altar of earth for me and sacrifice on it your burnt offerings and fellowship offerings, your sheep and goats and your cattle. Wherever I cause my name to be honored, I will come to you and bless you. ²⁵If you make an altar of stones for me, do not build it with dressed stones, for you will defile it if you use a tool on it. ²⁶And do not go up to my altar on steps, or your private parts may be exposed.'

21

"These are the laws you are to set before them:

Hebrew Servants

²"If you buy a Hebrew servant, he is to serve you for six years. But in the seventh year, he shall go free, without paying anything. ³If he comes alone, he is to go free alone; but if he has a wife when he comes,

---

a 3 Or *besides*

she is to go with him. ⁴If his master gives him a wife and she bears him sons or daughters, the woman and her children shall belong to her master, and only the man shall go free.

⁵"But if the servant declares, 'I love my master and my wife and children and do not want to go free,' ⁶then his master must take him before the judges.ᵃ He shall take him to the door or the doorpost and pierce his ear with an awl. Then he will be his servant for life.

⁷"If a man sells his daughter as a servant, she is not to go free as male servants do. ⁸If she does not please the master who has selected her for himself,ᵇ he must let her be redeemed. He has no right to sell her to foreigners, because he has broken faith with her. ⁹If he selects her for his son, he must grant her the rights of a daughter. ¹⁰If he marries another woman, he must not deprive the first one of her food, clothing and marital rights. ¹¹If he does not provide her with these three things, she is to go free, without any payment of money.

Personal Injuries

¹²"Anyone who strikes a person with a fatal blow is to be put to death. ¹³However, if it is not done intentionally, but God lets it happen, they are to flee to a place I will designate. ¹⁴But if anyone schemes and kills someone deliberately, that person is to be taken from my altar and put to death.

¹⁵"Anyone who attacksᶜ their father or mother is to be put to death.

¹⁶"Anyone who kidnaps someone is to be put to death, whether the victim has been sold or is still in the kidnapper's possession.

¹⁷"Anyone who curses their father or mother is to be put to death.

¹⁸"If people quarrel and one person hits another with a stone or with their fistᵈ and the victim does not die but is confined to bed, ¹⁹the one who struck the blow will not be held liable if the other can get up and walk around outside with a staff; however, the guilty party must pay the injured person for any loss of time and see that the victim is completely healed.

²⁰"Anyone who beats their male or female slave with a rod must be punished if the slave dies as a direct result, ²¹but they are not to be punished if the slave recovers after a day or two, since the slave is their property.

²²"If people are fighting and hit a pregnant woman and she gives birth prematurelyᵉ but there is no serious injury, the offender must be fined whatever the woman's husband demands and the court allows. ²³But if there is serious injury, you are to take life for life, ²⁴eye for eye, tooth for tooth, hand for hand, foot for foot, ²⁵burn for burn, wound for wound, bruise for bruise.

²⁶"An owner who hits a male or female slave in the eye and destroys it must let the slave go free to compensate for the eye. ²⁷And an owner who knocks out the tooth of a male or female slave must let the slave go free to compensate for the tooth.

²⁸"If a bull gores a man or woman to death, the bull is to be stoned to death, and its meat must not be eaten. But the owner of the bull will not be held responsible. ²⁹If, however, the bull has had the habit of goring and the owner has been warned but has not kept it penned up and it kills a man or woman, the bull is to be stoned and its owner also is to be put to death. ³⁰However, if payment is demanded, the owner may redeem his life by the payment of whatever is demanded. ³¹This law also applies if the bull gores a son or daughter. ³²If the bull gores a male or female slave, the owner must pay thirty shekelsᶠ of silver to the master of the slave, and the bull is to be stoned to death.

³³"If anyone uncovers a pit or digs one and fails to cover it and an ox or a donkey falls into it, ³⁴the one who opened the pit must pay the owner for the loss and take the dead animal in exchange.

ᵃ 6 Or *before God*   ᵇ 8 Or *master so that he does not choose her*   ᶜ 15 Or *kills*   ᵈ 18 Or *with a tool*
ᵉ 22 Or *she has a miscarriage*   ᶠ 32 That is, about 12 ounces or about 345 grams

35"If anyone's bull injures someone else's bull and it dies, the two parties are to sell the live one and divide both the money and the dead animal equally. 36However, if it was known that the bull had the habit of goring, yet the owner did not keep it penned up, the owner must pay, animal for animal, and take the dead animal in exchange.

Protection of Property

22 *a* "Whoever steals an ox or a sheep and slaughters it or sells it must pay back five head of cattle for the ox and four sheep for the sheep.

2"If a thief is caught breaking in at night and is struck a fatal blow, the defender is not guilty of bloodshed; 3but if it happens after sunrise, the defender is guilty of bloodshed.

"Anyone who steals must certainly make restitution, but if they have nothing, they must be sold to pay for their theft. 4If the stolen animal is found alive in their possession — whether ox or donkey or sheep — they must pay back double.

5"If anyone grazes their livestock in a field or vineyard and lets them stray and they graze in someone else's field, the offender must make restitution from the best of their own field or vineyard.

6"If a fire breaks out and spreads into thornbushes so that it burns shocks of grain or standing grain or the whole field, the one who started the fire must make restitution.

7"If anyone gives a neighbor silver or goods for safekeeping and they are stolen from the neighbor's house, the thief, if caught, must pay back double. 8But if the thief is not found, the owner of the house must appear before the judges, and they must*b* determine whether the owner of the house has laid hands on the other person's property. 9In all cases of illegal possession of an ox, a donkey, a sheep, a garment, or any other lost property about which somebody says, 'This is mine,' both parties are to bring their cases before the judges.*c* The one whom the judges declare*d* guilty must pay back double to the other.

10"If anyone gives a donkey, an ox, a sheep or any other animal to their neighbor for safekeeping and it dies or is injured or is taken away while no one is looking, 11the issue between them will be settled by the taking of an oath before the LORD that the neighbor did not lay hands on the other person's property. The owner is to accept this, and no restitution is required. 12But if the animal was stolen from the neighbor, restitution must be made to the owner. 13If it was torn to pieces by a wild animal, the neighbor shall bring in the remains as evidence and shall not be required to pay for the torn animal.

14"If anyone borrows an animal from their neighbor and it is injured or dies while the owner is not present, they must make restitution. 15But if the owner is with the animal, the borrower will not have to pay. If the animal was hired, the money paid for the hire covers the loss.

Social Responsibility

16"If a man seduces a virgin who is not pledged to be married and sleeps with her, he must pay the bride-price, and she shall be his wife. 17If her father absolutely refuses to give her to him, he must still pay the bride-price for virgins.

18"Do not allow a sorceress to live.

19"Anyone who has sexual relations with an animal is to be put to death.

20"Whoever sacrifices to any god other than the LORD must be destroyed.*e*

21"Do not mistreat or oppress a foreigner, for you were foreigners in Egypt.

22"Do not take advantage of the widow or the fatherless. 23If you do and they cry

---

a In Hebrew texts 22:1 is numbered 21:37, and 22:2-31 is numbered 22:1-30.   *b 8* Or *before God, and he will*   *c 9* Or *before God*   *d 9* Or *whom God declares*   *e 20* The Hebrew term refers to the irrevocable giving over of things or persons to the LORD, often by totally destroying them.

out to me, I will certainly hear their cry. [24]My anger will be aroused, and I will kill you with the sword; your wives will become widows and your children fatherless.

[25]"If you lend money to one of my people among you who is needy, do not treat it like a business deal; charge no interest. [26]If you take your neighbor's cloak as a pledge, return it by sunset, [27]because that cloak is the only covering your neighbor has. What else can they sleep in? When they cry out to me, I will hear, for I am compassionate.

[28]"Do not blaspheme God[a] or curse the ruler of your people.

[29]"Do not hold back offerings from your granaries or your vats.[b]

"You must give me the firstborn of your sons. [30]Do the same with your cattle and your sheep. Let them stay with their mothers for seven days, but give them to me on the eighth day.

[31]"You are to be my holy people. So do not eat the meat of an animal torn by wild beasts; throw it to the dogs.

Laws of Justice and Mercy

23 "Do not spread false reports. Do not help a guilty person by being a malicious witness.

[2]"Do not follow the crowd in doing wrong. When you give testimony in a lawsuit, do not pervert justice by siding with the crowd, [3]and do not show favoritism to a poor person in a lawsuit.

[4]"If you come across your enemy's ox or donkey wandering off, be sure to return it. [5]If you see the donkey of someone who hates you fallen down under its load, do not leave it there; be sure you help them with it.

[6]"Do not deny justice to your poor people in their lawsuits. [7]Have nothing to do with a false charge and do not put an innocent or honest person to death, for I will not acquit the guilty.

[8]"Do not accept a bribe, for a bribe blinds those who see and twists the words of the innocent.

[9]"Do not oppress a foreigner; you yourselves know how it feels to be foreigners, because you were foreigners in Egypt.

Sabbath Laws

[10]"For six years you are to sow your fields and harvest the crops, [11]but during the seventh year let the land lie unplowed and unused. Then the poor among your people may get food from it, and the wild animals may eat what is left. Do the same with your vineyard and your olive grove.

[12]"Six days do your work, but on the seventh day do not work, so that your ox and your donkey may rest, and so that the slave born in your household and the foreigner living among you may be refreshed.

[13]"Be careful to do everything I have said to you. Do not invoke the names of other gods; do not let them be heard on your lips.

The Three Annual Festivals

[14]"Three times a year you are to celebrate a festival to me.

[15]"Celebrate the Festival of Unleavened Bread; for seven days eat bread made without yeast, as I commanded you. Do this at the appointed time in the month of Aviv, for in that month you came out of Egypt.

"No one is to appear before me empty-handed.

[16]"Celebrate the Festival of Harvest with the firstfruits of the crops you sow in your field.

"Celebrate the Festival of Ingathering at the end of the year, when you gather in your crops from the field.

[17]"Three times a year all the men are to appear before the Sovereign LORD.

[18]"Do not offer the blood of a sacrifice to me along with anything containing yeast.

"The fat of my festival offerings must not be kept until morning.

[19]"Bring the best of the firstfruits of your soil to the house of the LORD your God.

---

a 28 Or *Do not revile the judges*   *b 29* The meaning of the Hebrew for this phrase is uncertain.

"Do not cook a young goat in its mother's milk.

God's Angel to Prepare the Way

20"See, I am sending an angel ahead of you to guard you along the way and to bring you to the place I have prepared. 21Pay attention to him and listen to what he says. Do not rebel against him; he will not forgive your rebellion, since my Name is in him. 22If you listen carefully to what he says and do all that I say, I will be an enemy to your enemies and will oppose those who oppose you. 23My angel will go ahead of you and bring you into the land of the Amorites, Hittites, Perizzites, Canaanites, Hivites and Jebusites, and I will wipe them out. 24Do not bow down before their gods or worship them or follow their practices. You must demolish them and break their sacred stones to pieces. 25Worship the LORD your God, and his blessing will be on your food and water. I will take away sickness from among you, 26and none will miscarry or be barren in your land. I will give you a full life span.

27"I will send my terror ahead of you and throw into confusion every nation you encounter. I will make all your enemies turn their backs and run. 28I will send the hornet ahead of you to drive the Hivites, Canaanites and Hittites out of your way. 29But I will not drive them out in a single year, because the land would become desolate and the wild animals too numerous for you. 30Little by little I will drive them out before you, until you have increased enough to take possession of the land.

31"I will establish your borders from the Red Sea*a* to the Mediterranean Sea,*b* and from the desert to the Euphrates River. I will give into your hands the people who live in the land, and you will drive them out before you. 32Do not make a covenant with them or with their gods. 33Do not let them live in your land or they will cause you to sin against me, because the worship of their gods will certainly be a snare to you."

The Covenant Confirmed

24 Then the LORD said to Moses, "Come up to the LORD, you and Aaron, Nadab and Abihu, and seventy of the elders of Israel. You are to worship at a distance, 2but Moses alone is to approach the LORD; the others must not come near. And the people may not come up with him."

3When Moses went and told the people all the LORD's words and laws, they responded with one voice, "Everything the LORD has said we will do." 4Moses then wrote down everything the LORD had said.

He got up early the next morning and built an altar at the foot of the mountain and set up twelve stone pillars representing the twelve tribes of Israel. 5Then he sent young Israelite men, and they offered burnt offerings and sacrificed young bulls as fellowship offerings to the LORD. 6Moses took half of the blood and put it in bowls, and the other half he splashed against the altar. 7Then he took the Book of the Covenant and read it to the people. They responded, "We will do everything the LORD has said; we will obey."

8Moses then took the blood, sprinkled it on the people and said, "This is the blood of the covenant that the LORD has made with you in accordance with all these words."

9Moses and Aaron, Nadab and Abihu, and the seventy elders of Israel went up 10and saw the God of Israel. Under his feet was something like a pavement made of lapis lazuli, as bright blue as the sky. 11But God did not raise his hand against these leaders of the Israelites; they saw God, and they ate and drank.

12The LORD said to Moses, "Come up to me on the mountain and stay here, and I will give you the tablets of stone with the law and commandments I have written for their instruction."

13Then Moses set out with Joshua his aide, and Moses went up on the mountain of God. 14He said to the elders, "Wait here

---

a 31 Or *the Sea of Reeds*   *b 31* Hebrew *to the Sea of the Philistines* for us until we come back to you. Aaron and Hur are with you, and anyone involved in a dispute can go to them."

¹⁵When Moses went up on the mountain, the cloud covered it, ¹⁶and the glory of the LORD settled on Mount Sinai. For six days the cloud covered the mountain, and on the seventh day the LORD called to Moses from within the cloud. ¹⁷To the Israelites the glory of the LORD looked like a consuming fire on top of the mountain. ¹⁸Then Moses entered the cloud as he went on up the mountain. And he stayed on the mountain forty days and forty nights.

Offerings for the Tabernacle

25 The LORD said to Moses, ²"Tell the Israelites to bring me an offering. You are to receive the offering for me from everyone whose heart prompts them to give. ³These are the offerings you are to receive from them: gold, silver and bronze; ⁴blue, purple and scarlet yarn and fine linen; goat hair; ⁵ram skins dyed red and another type of durable leather*a*; acacia wood; ⁶olive oil for the light; spices for the anointing oil and for the fragrant incense; ⁷and onyx stones and other gems to be mounted on the ephod and breastpiece.

⁸"Then have them make a sanctuary for me, and I will dwell among them. ⁹Make this tabernacle and all its furnishings exactly like the pattern I will show you.

The Ark

¹⁰"Have them make an ark*b* of acacia wood—two and a half cubits long, a cubit and a half wide, and a cubit and a half high.*c* ¹¹Overlay it with pure gold, both inside and out, and make a gold molding around it. ¹²Cast four gold rings for it and fasten them to its four feet, with two rings on one side and two rings on the other. ¹³Then make poles of acacia wood and overlay them with gold. ¹⁴Insert the poles into the rings on the sides of the ark to carry it. ¹⁵The poles are to remain in the rings of this ark; they are not to be removed. ¹⁶Then put in the ark the tablets of the covenant law, which I will give you.

¹⁷"Make an atonement cover of pure gold—two and a half cubits long and a cubit and a half wide. ¹⁸And make two cherubim out of hammered gold at the ends of the cover. ¹⁹Make one cherub on one end and the second cherub on the other; make the cherubim of one piece with the cover, at the two ends. ²⁰The cherubim are to have their wings spread upward, overshadowing the cover with them. The cherubim are to face each other, looking toward the cover. ²¹Place the cover on top of the ark and put in the ark the tablets of the covenant law that I will give you. ²²There, above the cover between the two cherubim that are over the ark of the covenant law, I will meet with you and give you all my commands for the Israelites.

The Table

²³"Make a table of acacia wood—two cubits long, a cubit wide and a cubit and a half high.*d* ²⁴Overlay it with pure gold and make a gold molding around it. ²⁵Also make around it a rim a handbreadth*e* wide and put a gold molding on the rim. ²⁶Make four gold rings for the table and fasten them to the four corners, where the four legs are. ²⁷The rings are to be close to the rim to hold the poles used in carrying the table. ²⁸Make the poles of acacia wood, overlay them with gold and carry the table with them. ²⁹And make its plates and dishes of pure gold, as well as its pitchers and bowls for the pouring out of offerings. ³⁰Put the bread of the Presence on this table to be before me at all times.

The Lampstand

³¹"Make a lampstand of pure gold. Hammer out its base and shaft, and make

---

a 5 Possibly the hides of large aquatic mammals   *b 10* That is, a chest   *c 10* That is, about 3 3/4 feet long and 2 1/4 feet wide and high or about 1.1 meters long and 68 centimeters wide and high; similarly in verse 17   *d 23* That is, about 3 feet long, 1 1/2 feet wide and 2 1/4 feet high or about 90 centimeters long, 45 centimeters wide and 68 centimeters high   *e 25* That is, about 3 inches or about 7.5 centimeters its flowerlike cups, buds and blossoms of one piece with them. 32Six branches are to extend from the sides of the lampstand—three on one side and three on the other. 33Three cups shaped like almond flowers with buds and blossoms are to be on one branch, three on the next branch, and the same for all six branches extending from the lampstand. 34And on the lampstand there are to be four cups shaped like almond flowers with buds and blossoms. 35One bud shall be under the first pair of branches extending from the lampstand, a second bud under the second pair, and a third bud under the third pair—six branches in all. 36The buds and branches shall all be of one piece with the lampstand, hammered out of pure gold.

37"Then make its seven lamps and set them up on it so that they light the space in front of it. 38Its wick trimmers and trays are to be of pure gold. 39A talent*a* of pure gold is to be used for the lampstand and all these accessories. 40See that you make them according to the pattern shown you on the mountain.

The Tabernacle

26 "Make the tabernacle with ten curtains of finely twisted linen and blue, purple and scarlet yarn, with cherubim woven into them by a skilled worker. 2All the curtains are to be the same size—twenty-eight cubits long and four cubits wide.*b* 3Join five of the curtains together, and do the same with the other five. 4Make loops of blue material along the edge of the end curtain in one set, and do the same with the end curtain in the other set. 5Make fifty loops on one curtain and fifty loops on the end curtain of the other set, with the loops opposite each other. 6Then make fifty gold clasps and use them to fasten the curtains together so that the tabernacle is a unit.

7"Make curtains of goat hair for the tent over the tabernacle—eleven altogether. 8All eleven curtains are to be the same size—thirty cubits long and four cubits wide.*c* 9Join five of the curtains together into one set and the other six into another set. Fold the sixth curtain double at the front of the tent. 10Make fifty loops along the edge of the end curtain in one set and also along the edge of the end curtain in the other set. 11Then make fifty bronze clasps and put them in the loops to fasten the tent together as a unit. 12As for the additional length of the tent curtains, the half curtain that is left over is to hang down at the rear of the tabernacle. 13The tent curtains will be a cubit*d* longer on both sides; what is left will hang over the sides of the tabernacle so as to cover it. 14Make for the tent a covering of ram skins dyed red, and over that a covering of the other durable leather.*e*

15"Make upright frames of acacia wood for the tabernacle. 16Each frame is to be ten cubits long and a cubit and a half wide,*f* 17with two projections set parallel to each other. Make all the frames of the tabernacle in this way. 18Make twenty frames for the south side of the tabernacle 19and make forty silver bases to go under them—two bases for each frame, one under each projection. 20For the other side, the north side of the tabernacle, make twenty frames 21and forty silver bases—two under each frame. 22Make six frames for the far end, that is, the west end of the tabernacle, 23and make two frames for the corners at the far end. 24At these two corners they must be double from the bottom all the way to the top and fitted into a single ring; both shall be like that. 25So there will be eight frames and sixteen silver bases—two under each frame.

26"Also make crossbars of acacia wood: five for the frames on one side of the tabernacle, 27five for those on the other side, and five for the frames on the west, at the far

---

a 39 That is, about 75 pounds or about 34 kilograms   *b 2* That is, about 42 feet long and 6 feet wide or about 13 meters long and 1.8 meters wide   *c 8* That is, about 45 feet long and 6 feet wide or about 13.5 meters long and 1.8 meters wide   *d 13* That is, about 18 inches or about 45 centimeters   *e 14* Possibly the hides of large aquatic mammals (see 25:5)   *f 16* That is, about 15 feet long and 2 1/4 feet wide or about 4.5 meters long and 68 centimeters wide end of the tabernacle. [28]The center crossbar is to extend from end to end at the middle of the frames. [29]Overlay the frames with gold and make gold rings to hold the crossbars. Also overlay the crossbars with gold.

[30]"Set up the tabernacle according to the plan shown you on the mountain.

[31]"Make a curtain of blue, purple and scarlet yarn and finely twisted linen, with cherubim woven into it by a skilled worker. [32]Hang it with gold hooks on four posts of acacia wood overlaid with gold and standing on four silver bases. [33]Hang the curtain from the clasps and place the ark of the covenant law behind the curtain. The curtain will separate the Holy Place from the Most Holy Place. [34]Put the atonement cover on the ark of the covenant law in the Most Holy Place. [35]Place the table outside the curtain on the north side of the tabernacle and put the lampstand opposite it on the south side.

[36]"For the entrance to the tent make a curtain of blue, purple and scarlet yarn and finely twisted linen — the work of an embroiderer. [37]Make gold hooks for this curtain and five posts of acacia wood overlaid with gold. And cast five bronze bases for them.

The Altar of Burnt Offering

27 "Build an altar of acacia wood, three cubits[a] high; it is to be square, five cubits long and five cubits wide.[b] [2]Make a horn at each of the four corners, so that the horns and the altar are of one piece, and overlay the altar with bronze. [3]Make all its utensils of bronze — its pots to remove the ashes, and its shovels, sprinkling bowls, meat forks and firepans. [4]Make a grating for it, a bronze network, and make a bronze ring at each of the four corners of the network. [5]Put it under the ledge of the altar so that

it is halfway up the altar. [6]Make poles of acacia wood for the altar and overlay them with bronze. [7]The poles are to be inserted into the rings so they will be on two sides of the altar when it is carried. [8]Make the altar hollow, out of boards. It is to be made just as you were shown on the mountain.

The Courtyard

[9]"Make a courtyard for the tabernacle. The south side shall be a hundred cubits[c] long and is to have curtains of finely twisted linen, [10]with twenty posts and twenty bronze bases and with silver hooks and bands on the posts. [11]The north side shall also be a hundred cubits long and is to have curtains, with twenty posts and twenty bronze bases and with silver hooks and bands on the posts.

[12]"The west end of the courtyard shall be fifty cubits[d] wide and have curtains, with ten posts and ten bases. [13]On the east end, toward the sunrise, the courtyard shall also be fifty cubits wide. [14]Curtains fifteen cubits[e] long are to be on one side of the entrance, with three posts and three bases, [15]and curtains fifteen cubits long are to be on the other side, with three posts and three bases.

[16]"For the entrance to the courtyard, provide a curtain twenty cubits[f] long, of blue, purple and scarlet yarn and finely twisted linen — the work of an embroiderer — with four posts and four bases. [17]All the posts around the courtyard are to have silver bands and hooks, and bronze bases. [18]The courtyard shall be a hundred cubits long and fifty cubits wide,[g] with curtains of finely twisted linen five cubits[h] high, and with bronze bases. [19]All the other articles used in the service of the tabernacle, whatever their function, including all the tent pegs for it and those for the courtyard, are to be of bronze.

---

[a] 1 That is, about 4 1/2 feet or about 1.4 meters   [b] 1 That is, about 7 1/2 feet or about 2.3 meters long and wide
[c] 9 That is, about 150 feet or about 45 meters; also in verse 11   [d] 12 That is, about 75 feet or about 23 meters; also in verse 13   [e] 14 That is, about 23 feet or about 6.8 meters; also in verse 15   [f] 16 That is, about 30 feet or about 9 meters   [g] 18 That is, about 150 feet long and 75 feet wide or about 45 meters long and 23 meters wide
[h] 18 That is, about 7 1/2 feet or about 2.3 meters

Oil for the Lampstand

20"Command the Israelites to bring you clear oil of pressed olives for the light so that the lamps may be kept burning. 21In the tent of meeting, outside the curtain that shields the ark of the covenant law, Aaron and his sons are to keep the lamps burning before the LORD from evening till morning. This is to be a lasting ordinance among the Israelites for the generations to come.

The Priestly Garments

28 "Have Aaron your brother brought to you from among the Israelites, along with his sons Nadab and Abihu, Eleazar and Ithamar, so they may serve me as priests. 2Make sacred garments for your brother Aaron to give him dignity and honor. 3Tell all the skilled workers to whom I have given wisdom in such matters that they are to make garments for Aaron, for his consecration, so he may serve me as priest. 4These are the garments they are to make: a breastpiece, an ephod, a robe, a woven tunic, a turban and a sash. They are to make these sacred garments for your brother Aaron and his sons, so they may serve me as priests. 5Have them use gold, and blue, purple and scarlet yarn, and fine linen.

The Ephod

6"Make the ephod of gold, and of blue, purple and scarlet yarn, and of finely twisted linen — the work of skilled hands. 7It is to have two shoulder pieces attached to two of its corners, so it can be fastened. 8Its skillfully woven waistband is to be like it — of one piece with the ephod and made with gold, and with blue, purple and scarlet yarn, and with finely twisted linen.

9"Take two onyx stones and engrave on them the names of the sons of Israel 10in the order of their birth — six names on one stone and the remaining six on the other.

11Engrave the names of the sons of Israel on the two stones the way a gem cutter engraves a seal. Then mount the stones in gold filigree settings 12and fasten them on the shoulder pieces of the ephod as memorial stones for the sons of Israel. Aaron is to bear the names on his shoulders as a memorial before the LORD. 13Make gold filigree settings 14and two braided chains of pure gold, like a rope, and attach the chains to the settings.

The Breastpiece

15"Fashion a breastpiece for making decisions — the work of skilled hands. Make it like the ephod: of gold, and of blue, purple and scarlet yarn, and of finely twisted linen. 16It is to be square — a span*a* long and a span wide — and folded double. 17Then mount four rows of precious stones on it. The first row shall be carnelian, chrysolite and beryl; 18the second row shall be turquoise, lapis lazuli and emerald; 19the third row shall be jacinth, agate and amethyst; 20the fourth row shall be topaz, onyx and jasper.*b* Mount them in gold filigree settings. 21There are to be twelve stones, one for each of the names of the sons of Israel, each engraved like a seal with the name of one of the twelve tribes.

22"For the breastpiece make braided chains of pure gold, like a rope. 23Make two gold rings for it and fasten them to two corners of the breastpiece. 24Fasten the two gold chains to the rings at the corners of the breastpiece, 25and the other ends of the chains to the two settings, attaching them to the shoulder pieces of the ephod at the front. 26Make two gold rings and attach them to the other two corners of the breastpiece on the inside edge next to the ephod. 27Make two more gold rings and attach them to the bottom of the shoulder pieces on the front of the ephod, close to the seam just above the waistband of the ephod. 28The rings of the breastpiece are

---

a 16 That is, about 9 inches or about 23 centimeters   *b 20* The precise identification of some of these precious stones is uncertain.

to be tied to the rings of the ephod with blue cord, connecting it to the waistband, so that the breastpiece will not swing out from the ephod.

29"Whenever Aaron enters the Holy Place, he will bear the names of the sons of Israel over his heart on the breastpiece of decision as a continuing memorial before the Lord. 30 Also put the Urim and the Thummim in the breastpiece, so they may be over Aaron's heart whenever he enters the presence of the Lord. Thus Aaron will always bear the means of making decisions for the Israelites over his heart before the Lord.

Other Priestly Garments

31"Make the robe of the ephod entirely of blue cloth, 32 with an opening for the head in its center. There shall be a woven edge like a collar*a* around this opening, so that it will not tear. 33 Make pomegranates of blue, purple and scarlet yarn around the hem of the robe, with gold bells between them. 34 The gold bells and the pomegranates are to alternate around the hem of the robe. 35 Aaron must wear it when he ministers. The sound of the bells will be heard when he enters the Holy Place before the Lord and when he comes out, so that he will not die.

36"Make a plate of pure gold and engrave on it as on a seal: HOLY TO THE LORD. 37 Fasten a blue cord to it to attach it to the turban; it is to be on the front of the turban. 38 It will be on Aaron's forehead, and he will bear the guilt involved in the sacred gifts the Israelites consecrate, whatever their gifts may be. It will be on Aaron's forehead continually so that they will be acceptable to the Lord.

39"Weave the tunic of fine linen and make the turban of fine linen. The sash is to be the work of an embroiderer. 40 Make tunics, sashes and caps for Aaron's sons to give them dignity and honor. 41 After you put these clothes on your brother Aar-

on and his sons, anoint and ordain them. Consecrate them so they may serve me as priests.

42"Make linen undergarments as a covering for the body, reaching from the waist to the thigh. 43 Aaron and his sons must wear them whenever they enter the tent of meeting or approach the altar to minister in the Holy Place, so that they will not incur guilt and die.

"This is to be a lasting ordinance for Aaron and his descendants.

Consecration of the Priests

29 "This is what you are to do to consecrate them, so they may serve me as priests: Take a young bull and two rams without defect. 2 And from the finest wheat flour make round loaves without yeast, thick loaves without yeast and with olive oil mixed in, and thin loaves without yeast and brushed with olive oil. 3 Put them in a basket and present them along with the bull and the two rams. 4 Then bring Aaron and his sons to the entrance to the tent of meeting and wash them with water. 5 Take the garments and dress Aaron with the tunic, the robe of the ephod, the ephod itself and the breastpiece. Fasten the ephod on him by its skillfully woven waistband. 6 Put the turban on his head and attach the sacred emblem to the turban. 7 Take the anointing oil and anoint him by pouring it on his head. 8 Bring his sons and dress them in tunics 9 and fasten caps on them. Then tie sashes on Aaron and his sons.*b* The priesthood is theirs by a lasting ordinance.

"Then you shall ordain Aaron and his sons.

10"Bring the bull to the front of the tent of meeting, and Aaron and his sons shall lay their hands on its head. 11 Slaughter it in the Lord's presence at the entrance to the tent of meeting. 12 Take some of the bull's blood and put it on the horns of the altar with your finger, and pour out the rest of

---

a 32 The meaning of the Hebrew for this word is uncertain.   *b 9* Hebrew; Septuagint *on them* it at the base of the altar. ¹³Then take all the fat on the internal organs, the long lobe of the liver, and both kidneys with the fat on them, and burn them on the altar. ¹⁴But burn the bull's flesh and its hide and its intestines outside the camp. It is a sin offering.ᵃ

¹⁵"Take one of the rams, and Aaron and his sons shall lay their hands on its head. ¹⁶Slaughter it and take the blood and splash it against the sides of the altar. ¹⁷Cut the ram into pieces and wash the internal organs and the legs, putting them with the head and the other pieces. ¹⁸Then burn the entire ram on the altar. It is a burnt offering to the LORD, a pleasing aroma, a food offering presented to the LORD.

¹⁹"Take the other ram, and Aaron and his sons shall lay their hands on its head. ²⁰Slaughter it, take some of its blood and put it on the lobes of the right ears of Aaron and his sons, on the thumbs of their right hands, and on the big toes of their right feet. Then splash blood against the sides of the altar. ²¹And take some blood from the altar and some of the anointing oil and sprinkle it on Aaron and his garments and on his sons and their garments. Then he and his sons and their garments will be consecrated.

²²"Take from this ram the fat, the fat tail, the fat on the internal organs, the long lobe of the liver, both kidneys with the fat on them, and the right thigh. (This is the ram for the ordination.) ²³From the basket of bread made without yeast, which is before the LORD, take one round loaf, one thick loaf with olive oil mixed in, and one thin loaf. ²⁴Put all these in the hands of Aaron and his sons and have them wave them before the LORD as a wave offering. ²⁵Then take them from their hands and burn them on the altar along with the burnt offering for a pleasing aroma to the LORD, a food offering presented to the LORD. ²⁶After you take the breast of the ram for Aaron's ordi-

nation, wave it before the LORD as a wave offering, and it will be your share.

²⁷"Consecrate those parts of the ordination ram that belong to Aaron and his sons: the breast that was waved and the thigh that was presented. ²⁸This is always to be the perpetual share from the Israelites for Aaron and his sons. It is the contribution the Israelites are to make to the LORD from their fellowship offerings.

²⁹"Aaron's sacred garments will belong to his descendants so that they can be anointed and ordained in them. ³⁰The son who succeeds him as priest and comes to the tent of meeting to minister in the Holy Place is to wear them seven days.

³¹"Take the ram for the ordination and cook the meat in a sacred place. ³²At the entrance to the tent of meeting, Aaron and his sons are to eat the meat of the ram and the bread that is in the basket. ³³They are to eat these offerings by which atonement was made for their ordination and consecration. But no one else may eat them, because they are sacred. ³⁴And if any of the meat of the ordination ram or any bread is left over till morning, burn it up. It must not be eaten, because it is sacred.

³⁵"Do for Aaron and his sons everything I have commanded you, taking seven days to ordain them. ³⁶Sacrifice a bull each day as a sin offering to make atonement. Purify the altar by making atonement for it, and anoint it to consecrate it. ³⁷For seven days make atonement for the altar and consecrate it. Then the altar will be most holy, and whatever touches it will be holy.

³⁸"This is what you are to offer on the altar regularly each day: two lambs a year old. ³⁹Offer one in the morning and the other at twilight. ⁴⁰With the first lamb offer a tenth of an ephahᵇ of the finest flour mixed with a quarter of a hinᶜ of oil from pressed olives, and a quarter of a hin of wine as a drink offering. ⁴¹Sacrifice the other lamb at twilight with the same grain

---

ᵃ 14 Or *purification offering*; also in verse 36   ᵇ 40 That is, probably about 3 1/2 pounds or about 1.6 kilograms
ᶜ 40 That is, probably about 1 quart or about 1 liter

offering and its drink offering as in the morning—a pleasing aroma, a food offering presented to the LORD.

42 "For the generations to come this burnt offering is to be made regularly at the entrance to the tent of meeting, before the LORD. There I will meet you and speak to you; 43 there also I will meet with the Israelites, and the place will be consecrated by my glory.

44 "So I will consecrate the tent of meeting and the altar and will consecrate Aaron and his sons to serve me as priests. 45 Then I will dwell among the Israelites and be their God. 46 They will know that I am the LORD their God, who brought them out of Egypt so that I might dwell among them. I am the LORD their God.

The Altar of Incense

30 "Make an altar of acacia wood for burning incense. 2 It is to be square, a cubit long and a cubit wide, and two cubits high*a*— its horns of one piece with it. 3 Overlay the top and all the sides and the horns with pure gold, and make a gold molding around it. 4 Make two gold rings for the altar below the molding—two on each of the opposite sides—to hold the poles used to carry it. 5 Make the poles of acacia wood and overlay them with gold. 6 Put the altar in front of the curtain that shields the ark of the covenant law—before the atonement cover that is over the tablets of the covenant law—where I will meet with you.

7 "Aaron must burn fragrant incense on the altar every morning when he tends the lamps. 8 He must burn incense again when he lights the lamps at twilight so incense will burn regularly before the LORD for the generations to come. 9 Do not offer on this altar any other incense or any burnt offering or grain offering, and do not pour a drink offering on it. 10 Once a year Aaron shall make atonement on its horns. This annual

atonement must be made with the blood of the atoning sin offering*b* for the generations to come. It is most holy to the LORD."

Atonement Money

11 Then the LORD said to Moses, 12 "When you take a census of the Israelites to count them, each one must pay the LORD a ransom for his life at the time he is counted. Then no plague will come on them when you number them. 13 Each one who crosses over to those already counted is to give a half shekel,*c* according to the sanctuary shekel, which weighs twenty gerahs. This half shekel is an offering to the LORD. 14 All who cross over, those twenty years old or more, are to give an offering to the LORD. 15 The rich are not to give more than a half shekel and the poor are not to give less when you make the offering to the LORD to atone for your lives. 16 Receive the atonement money from the Israelites and use it for the service of the tent of meeting. It will be a memorial for the Israelites before the LORD, making atonement for your lives."

Basin for Washing

17 Then the LORD said to Moses, 18 "Make a bronze basin, with its bronze stand, for washing. Place it between the tent of meeting and the altar, and put water in it. 19 Aaron and his sons are to wash their hands and feet with water from it. 20 Whenever they enter the tent of meeting, they shall wash with water so that they will not die. Also, when they approach the altar to minister by presenting a food offering to the LORD, 21 they shall wash their hands and feet so that they will not die. This is to be a lasting ordinance for Aaron and his descendants for the generations to come."

Anointing Oil

22 Then the LORD said to Moses, 23 "Take the following fine spices: 500 shekels*d* of liquid myrrh, half as much (that is, 250

---

a 2 That is, about 1 1/2 feet long and wide and 3 feet high or about 45 centimeters long and wide and 90 centimeters high   *b 10* Or *purification offering*   *c 13* That is, about 1/5 ounce or about 5.8 grams; also in verse 15   *d 23* That is, about 12 1/2 pounds or about 5.8 kilograms; also in verse 24 shekels) of fragrant cinnamon, 250 shekels[a] of fragrant calamus, 24500 shekels of cassia — all according to the sanctuary shekel — and a hin[b] of olive oil. 25Make these into a sacred anointing oil, a fragrant blend, the work of a perfumer. It will be the sacred anointing oil. 26Then use it to anoint the tent of meeting, the ark of the covenant law, 27the table and all its articles, the lampstand and its accessories, the altar of incense, 28the altar of burnt offering and all its utensils, and the basin with its stand. 29You shall consecrate them so they will be most holy, and whatever touches them will be holy.

30"Anoint Aaron and his sons and consecrate them so they may serve me as priests. 31Say to the Israelites, 'This is to be my sacred anointing oil for the generations to come. 32Do not pour it on anyone else's body and do not make any other oil using the same formula. It is sacred, and you are to consider it sacred. 33Whoever makes perfume like it and puts it on anyone other than a priest must be cut off from their people.'"

Incense

34Then the Lord said to Moses, "Take fragrant spices — gum resin, onycha and galbanum — and pure frankincense, all in equal amounts, 35and make a fragrant blend of incense, the work of a perfumer. It is to be salted and pure and sacred. 36Grind some of it to powder and place it in front of the ark of the covenant law in the tent of meeting, where I will meet with you. It shall be most holy to you. 37Do not make any incense with this formula for yourselves; consider it holy to the Lord. 38Whoever makes incense like it to enjoy its fragrance must be cut off from their people."

Bezalel and Oholiab

31 Then the Lord said to Moses, 2"See, I have chosen Bezalel son of Uri, the son of Hur, of the tribe of Judah, 3and I have filled him with the Spirit of God, with wisdom, with understanding, with knowledge and with all kinds of skills — 4to make artistic designs for work in gold, silver and bronze, 5to cut and set stones, to work in wood, and to engage in all kinds of crafts. 6Moreover, I have appointed Oholiab son of Ahisamak, of the tribe of Dan, to help him. Also I have given ability to all the skilled workers to make everything I have commanded you: 7the tent of meeting, the ark of the covenant law with the atonement cover on it, and all the other furnishings of the tent — 8the table and its articles, the pure gold lampstand and all its accessories, the altar of incense, 9the altar of burnt offering and all its utensils, the basin with its stand — 10and also the woven garments, both the sacred garments for Aaron the priest and the garments for his sons when they serve as priests, 11and the anointing oil and fragrant incense for the Holy Place. They are to make them just as I commanded you."

The Sabbath

12Then the Lord said to Moses, 13"Say to the Israelites, 'You must observe my Sabbaths. This will be a sign between me and you for the generations to come, so you may know that I am the Lord, who makes you holy.

14" 'Observe the Sabbath, because it is holy to you. Anyone who desecrates it is to be put to death; those who do any work on that day must be cut off from their people. 15For six days work is to be done, but the seventh day is a day of sabbath rest, holy to the Lord. Whoever does any work on the Sabbath day is to be put to death. 16The Israelites are to observe the Sabbath, celebrating it for the generations to come as a lasting covenant. 17It will be a sign between me and the Israelites forever, for in six days the Lord made the heavens and the earth, and on the seventh day he rested and was refreshed.'"

18When the Lord finished speaking to

---

a 23 That is, about 6 1/4 pounds or about 2.9 kilograms   b 24 That is, probably about 1 gallon or about 3.8 liters

Moses on Mount Sinai, he gave him the two tablets of the covenant law, the tablets of stone inscribed by the finger of God.

The Golden Calf

32 When the people saw that Moses was so long in coming down from the mountain, they gathered around Aaron and said, "Come, make us gods[a] who will go before us. As for this fellow Moses who brought us up out of Egypt, we don't know what has happened to him."

2Aaron answered them, "Take off the gold earrings that your wives, your sons and your daughters are wearing, and bring them to me." 3So all the people took off their earrings and brought them to Aaron. 4He took what they handed him and made it into an idol cast in the shape of a calf, fashioning it with a tool. Then they said, "These are your gods,[b] Israel, who brought you up out of Egypt."

5When Aaron saw this, he built an altar in front of the calf and announced, "Tomorrow there will be a festival to the LORD." 6So the next day the people rose early and sacrificed burnt offerings and presented fellowship offerings. Afterward they sat down to eat and drink and got up to indulge in revelry.

7Then the LORD said to Moses, "Go down, because your people, whom you brought up out of Egypt, have become corrupt. 8They have been quick to turn away from what I commanded them and have made themselves an idol cast in the shape of a calf. They have bowed down to it and sacrificed to it and have said, 'These are your gods, Israel, who brought you up out of Egypt.'

9"I have seen these people," the LORD said to Moses, "and they are a stiff-necked people. 10Now leave me alone so that my anger may burn against them and that I may destroy them. Then I will make you into a great nation."

11But Moses sought the favor of the LORD his God. "LORD," he said, "why should your anger burn against your people, whom you brought out of Egypt with great power and a mighty hand? 12Why should the Egyptians say, 'It was with evil intent that he brought them out, to kill them in the mountains and to wipe them off the face of the earth'? Turn from your fierce anger; relent and do not bring disaster on your people. 13Remember your servants Abraham, Isaac and Israel, to whom you swore by your own self: 'I will make your descendants as numerous as the stars in the sky and I will give your descendants all this land I promised them, and it will be their inheritance forever.'" 14Then the LORD relented and did not bring on his people the disaster he had threatened.

15Moses turned and went down the mountain with the two tablets of the covenant law in his hands. They were inscribed on both sides, front and back. 16The tablets were the work of God; the writing was the writing of God, engraved on the tablets.

17When Joshua heard the noise of the people shouting, he said to Moses, "There is the sound of war in the camp."

18Moses replied:

"It is not the sound of victory,
    it is not the sound of defeat;
    it is the sound of singing that I hear."

19When Moses approached the camp and saw the calf and the dancing, his anger burned and he threw the tablets out of his hands, breaking them to pieces at the foot of the mountain. 20And he took the calf the people had made and burned it in the fire; then he ground it to powder, scattered it on the water and made the Israelites drink it.

21He said to Aaron, "What did these people do to you, that you led them into such great sin?"

22"Do not be angry, my lord," Aaron answered. "You know how prone these people are to evil. 23They said to me, 'Make us

---

[a] 1 Or a god; also in verses 23 and 31   [b] 4 Or This is your god; also in verse 8

gods who will go before us. As for this fellow Moses who brought us up out of Egypt, we don't know what has happened to him.' 24So I told them, 'Whoever has any gold jewelry, take it off.' Then they gave me the gold, and I threw it into the fire, and out came this calf!"

25Moses saw that the people were running wild and that Aaron had let them get out of control and so become a laughingstock to their enemies. 26So he stood at the entrance to the camp and said, "Whoever is for the LORD, come to me." And all the Levites rallied to him.

27Then he said to them, "This is what the LORD, the God of Israel, says: 'Each man strap a sword to his side. Go back and forth through the camp from one end to the other, each killing his brother and friend and neighbor.'" 28The Levites did as Moses commanded, and that day about three thousand of the people died. 29Then Moses said, "You have been set apart to the LORD today, for you were against your own sons and brothers, and he has blessed you this day."

30The next day Moses said to the people, "You have committed a great sin. But now I will go up to the LORD; perhaps I can make atonement for your sin."

31So Moses went back to the LORD and said, "Oh, what a great sin these people have committed! They have made themselves gods of gold. 32But now, please forgive their sin — but if not, then blot me out of the book you have written."

33The LORD replied to Moses, "Whoever has sinned against me I will blot out of my book. 34Now go, lead the people to the place I spoke of, and my angel will go before you. However, when the time comes for me to punish, I will punish them for their sin."

35And the LORD struck the people with a plague because of what they did with the calf Aaron had made.

33 Then the LORD said to Moses, "Leave this place, you and the people you brought up out of Egypt, and go up to the land I promised on oath to Abraham, Isaac and Jacob, saying,

'I will give it to your descendants.' 2I will send an angel before you and drive out the Canaanites, Amorites, Hittites, Perizzites, Hivites and Jebusites. 3Go up to the land flowing with milk and honey. But I will not go with you, because you are a stiff-necked people and I might destroy you on the way."

4When the people heard these distressing words, they began to mourn and no one put on any ornaments. 5For the LORD had said to Moses, "Tell the Israelites, 'You are a stiff-necked people. If I were to go with you even for a moment, I might destroy you. Now take off your ornaments and I will decide what to do with you.'" 6So the Israelites stripped off their ornaments at Mount Horeb.

The Tent of Meeting

7Now Moses used to take a tent and pitch it outside the camp some distance away, calling it the "tent of meeting." Anyone inquiring of the LORD would go to the tent of meeting outside the camp. 8And whenever Moses went out to the tent, all the people rose and stood at the entrances to their tents, watching Moses until he entered the tent. 9As Moses went into the tent, the pillar of cloud would come down and stay at the entrance, while the LORD spoke with Moses. 10Whenever the people saw the pillar of cloud standing at the entrance to the tent, they all stood and worshiped, each at the entrance to their tent. 11The LORD would speak to Moses face to face, as one speaks to a friend. Then Moses would return to the camp, but his young aide Joshua son of Nun did not leave the tent.

Moses and the Glory of the LORD

12Moses said to the LORD, "You have been telling me, 'Lead these people,' but you have not let me know whom you will send with me. You have said, 'I know you by name and you have found favor with me.' 13If you are pleased with me, teach me your ways so I may know you and continue to find favor with you. Remember that this nation is your people."

14The Lord replied, "My Presence will go with you, and I will give you rest."

15Then Moses said to him, "If your Presence does not go with us, do not send us up from here. 16How will anyone know that you are pleased with me and with your people unless you go with us? What else will distinguish me and your people from all the other people on the face of the earth?"

17And the Lord said to Moses, "I will do the very thing you have asked, because I am pleased with you and I know you by name."

18Then Moses said, "Now show me your glory."

19And the Lord said, "I will cause all my goodness to pass in front of you, and I will proclaim my name, the Lord, in your presence. I will have mercy on whom I will have mercy, and I will have compassion on whom I will have compassion. 20But," he said, "you cannot see my face, for no one may see me and live."

21Then the Lord said, "There is a place near me where you may stand on a rock. 22When my glory passes by, I will put you in a cleft in the rock and cover you with my hand until I have passed by. 23Then I will remove my hand and you will see my back; but my face must not be seen."

The New Stone Tablets

34 The Lord said to Moses, "Chisel out two stone tablets like the first ones, and I will write on them the words that were on the first tablets, which you broke. 2Be ready in the morning, and then come up on Mount Sinai. Present yourself to me there on top of the mountain. 3No one is to come with you or be seen anywhere on the mountain; not even the flocks and herds may graze in front of the mountain."

4So Moses chiseled out two stone tablets like the first ones and went up Mount Sinai early in the morning, as the Lord had commanded him; and he carried the two stone tablets in his hands. 5Then the Lord came down in the cloud and stood there with him and proclaimed his name, the Lord. 6And he passed in front of Moses, proclaiming, "The Lord, the Lord, the compassionate and gracious God, slow to anger, abounding in love and faithfulness, 7maintaining love to thousands, and forgiving wickedness, rebellion and sin. Yet he does not leave the guilty unpunished; he punishes the children and their children for the sin of the parents to the third and fourth generation."

8Moses bowed to the ground at once and worshiped. 9"Lord," he said, "if I have found favor in your eyes, then let the Lord go with us. Although this is a stiff-necked people, forgive our wickedness and our sin, and take us as your inheritance."

10Then the Lord said: "I am making a covenant with you. Before all your people I will do wonders never before done in any nation in all the world. The people you live among will see how awesome is the work that I, the Lord, will do for you. 11Obey what I command you today. I will drive out before you the Amorites, Canaanites, Hittites, Perizzites, Hivites and Jebusites. 12Be careful not to make a treaty with those who live in the land where you are going, or they will be a snare among you. 13Break down their altars, smash their sacred stones and cut down their Asherah poles.*a* 14Do not worship any other god, for the Lord, whose name is Jealous, is a jealous God.

15"Be careful not to make a treaty with those who live in the land; for when they prostitute themselves to their gods and sacrifice to them, they will invite you and you will eat their sacrifices. 16And when you choose some of their daughters as wives for your sons and those daughters prostitute themselves to their gods, they will lead your sons to do the same.

17"Do not make any idols.

18"Celebrate the Festival of Unleavened Bread. For seven days eat bread made

---

a 13 That is, wooden symbols of the goddess Asherah

without yeast, as I commanded you. Do this at the appointed time in the month of Aviv, for in that month you came out of Egypt.

19"The first offspring of every womb belongs to me, including all the firstborn males of your livestock, whether from herd or flock. 20Redeem the firstborn donkey with a lamb, but if you do not redeem it, break its neck. Redeem all your firstborn sons.

"No one is to appear before me empty-handed.

21"Six days you shall labor, but on the seventh day you shall rest; even during the plowing season and harvest you must rest.

22"Celebrate the Festival of Weeks with the firstfruits of the wheat harvest, and the Festival of Ingathering at the turn of the year.ª 23Three times a year all your men are to appear before the Sovereign Lord, the God of Israel. 24I will drive out nations before you and enlarge your territory, and no one will covet your land when you go up three times each year to appear before the Lord your God.

25"Do not offer the blood of a sacrifice to me along with anything containing yeast, and do not let any of the sacrifice from the Passover Festival remain until morning.

26"Bring the best of the firstfruits of your soil to the house of the Lord your God.

"Do not cook a young goat in its mother's milk."

27Then the Lord said to Moses, "Write down these words, for in accordance with these words I have made a covenant with you and with Israel." 28Moses was there with the Lord forty days and forty nights without eating bread or drinking water. And he wrote on the tablets the words of the covenant—the Ten Commandments.

The Radiant Face of Moses

29When Moses came down from Mount Sinai with the two tablets of the covenant law in his hands, he was not aware that his face was radiant because he had spoken with the Lord. 30When Aaron and all the Israelites saw Moses, his face was radiant, and they were afraid to come near him. 31But Moses called to them; so Aaron and all the leaders of the community came back to him, and he spoke to them. 32Afterward all the Israelites came near him, and he gave them all the commands the Lord had given him on Mount Sinai.

33When Moses finished speaking to them, he put a veil over his face. 34But whenever he entered the Lord's presence to speak with him, he removed the veil until he came out. And when he came out and told the Israelites what he had been commanded, 35they saw that his face was radiant. Then Moses would put the veil back over his face until he went in to speak with the Lord.

Sabbath Regulations

35 Moses assembled the whole Israelite community and said to them, "These are the things the Lord has commanded you to do: 2For six days, work is to be done, but the seventh day shall be your holy day, a day of sabbath rest to the Lord. Whoever does any work on it is to be put to death. 3Do not light a fire in any of your dwellings on the Sabbath day."

Materials for the Tabernacle

4Moses said to the whole Israelite community, "This is what the Lord has commanded: 5From what you have, take an offering for the Lord. Everyone who is willing is to bring to the Lord an offering of gold, silver and bronze; 6blue, purple and scarlet yarn and fine linen; goat hair; 7ram skins dyed red and another type of durable leatherᵇ; acacia wood; 8olive oil for the light; spices for the anointing oil and for the fragrant incense; 9and onyx stones and other gems to be mounted on the ephod and breastpiece.

10"All who are skilled among you are to

ª 22 That is, in the autumn   ᵇ 7 Possibly the hides of large aquatic mammals; also in verse 23 come and make everything the LORD has commanded: [11]the tabernacle with its tent and its covering, clasps, frames, crossbars, posts and bases; [12]the ark with its poles and the atonement cover and the curtain that shields it; [13]the table with its poles and all its articles and the bread of the Presence; [14]the lampstand that is for light with its accessories, lamps and oil for the light; [15]the altar of incense with its poles, the anointing oil and the fragrant incense; the curtain for the doorway at the entrance to the tabernacle; [16]the altar of burnt offering with its bronze grating, its poles and all its utensils; the bronze basin with its stand; [17]the curtains of the courtyard with its posts and bases, and the curtain for the entrance to the courtyard; [18]the tent pegs for the tabernacle and for the courtyard, and their ropes; [19]the woven garments worn for ministering in the sanctuary—both the sacred garments for Aaron the priest and the garments for his sons when they serve as priests."

[20]Then the whole Israelite community withdrew from Moses' presence, [21]and everyone who was willing and whose heart moved them came and brought an offering to the LORD for the work on the tent of meeting, for all its service, and for the sacred garments. [22]All who were willing, men and women alike, came and brought gold jewelry of all kinds: brooches, earrings, rings and ornaments. They all presented their gold as a wave offering to the LORD. [23]Everyone who had blue, purple or scarlet yarn or fine linen, or goat hair, ram skins dyed red or the other durable leather brought them. [24]Those presenting an offering of silver or bronze brought it as an offering to the LORD, and everyone who had acacia wood for any part of the work brought it. [25]Every skilled woman spun with her hands and brought what she had spun—blue, purple or scarlet yarn or fine linen. [26]And all the women who were willing and had the skill spun the goat hair. [27]The leaders brought onyx stones and other gems to be mounted on the ephod and breastpiece. [28]They also brought spices and olive oil for the light and for the anointing oil and for the fragrant incense. [29]All the Israelite men and women who were willing brought to the LORD freewill offerings for all the work the LORD through Moses had commanded them to do.

Bezalel and Oholiab

[30]Then Moses said to the Israelites, "See, the LORD has chosen Bezalel son of Uri, the son of Hur, of the tribe of Judah, [31]and he has filled him with the Spirit of God, with wisdom, with understanding, with knowledge and with all kinds of skills— [32]to make artistic designs for work in gold, silver and bronze, [33]to cut and set stones, to work in wood and to engage in all kinds of artistic crafts. [34]And he has given both him and Oholiab son of Ahisamak, of the tribe of Dan, the ability to teach others. [35]He has filled them with skill to do all kinds of work as engravers, designers, embroiderers in blue, purple and scarlet yarn and fine linen, and weavers—all of them skilled workers and designers. [1]So Bezalel, Oholiab and every skilled person to whom the LORD has given skill and ability to know how to carry out all the work of constructing the sanctuary are to do the work just as the LORD has commanded."

36

[2]Then Moses summoned Bezalel and Oholiab and every skilled person to whom the LORD had given ability and who was willing to come and do the work. [3]They received from Moses all the offerings the Israelites had brought to carry out the work of constructing the sanctuary. And the people continued to bring freewill offerings morning after morning. [4]So all the skilled workers who were doing all the work on the sanctuary left what they were doing [5]and said to Moses, "The people are bringing more than enough for doing the work the LORD commanded to be done."

[6]Then Moses gave an order and they sent this word throughout the camp: "No man or woman is to make anything else as an offering for the sanctuary." And so

the people were restrained from bringing more, 7because what they already had was more than enough to do all the work.

The Tabernacle

8All those who were skilled among the workers made the tabernacle with ten curtains of finely twisted linen and blue, purple and scarlet yarn, with cherubim woven into them by expert hands. 9All the curtains were the same size — twenty-eight cubits long and four cubits wide.a 10They joined five of the curtains together and did the same with the other five. 11Then they made loops of blue material along the edge of the end curtain in one set, and the same was done with the end curtain in the other set. 12They also made fifty loops on one curtain and fifty loops on the end curtain of the other set, with the loops opposite each other. 13Then they made fifty gold clasps and used them to fasten the two sets of curtains together so that the tabernacle was a unit.

14They made curtains of goat hair for the tent over the tabernacle — eleven altogether. 15All eleven curtains were the same size — thirty cubits long and four cubits wide.b 16They joined five of the curtains into one set and the other six into another set. 17Then they made fifty loops along the edge of the end curtain in one set and also along the edge of the end curtain in the other set. 18They made fifty bronze clasps to fasten the tent together as a unit. 19Then they made for the tent a covering of ram skins dyed red, and over that a covering of the other durable leather.c

20They made upright frames of acacia wood for the tabernacle. 21Each frame was ten cubits long and a cubit and a half wide,d 22with two projections set parallel to each other. They made all the frames of the tabernacle in this way. 23They made twenty frames for the south side of the tabernacle

24and made forty silver bases to go under them — two bases for each frame, one under each projection. 25For the other side, the north side of the tabernacle, they made twenty frames 26and forty silver bases — two under each frame. 27They made six frames for the far end, that is, the west end of the tabernacle, 28and two frames were made for the corners of the tabernacle at the far end. 29At these two corners the frames were double from the bottom all the way to the top and fitted into a single ring; both were made alike. 30So there were eight frames and sixteen silver bases — two under each frame.

31They also made crossbars of acacia wood: five for the frames on one side of the tabernacle, 32five for those on the other side, and five for the frames on the west, at the far end of the tabernacle. 33They made the center crossbar so that it extended from end to end at the middle of the frames. 34They overlaid the frames with gold and made gold rings to hold the crossbars. They also overlaid the crossbars with gold.

35They made the curtain of blue, purple and scarlet yarn and finely twisted linen, with cherubim woven into it by a skilled worker. 36They made four posts of acacia wood for it and overlaid them with gold. They made gold hooks for them and cast their four silver bases. 37For the entrance to the tent they made a curtain of blue, purple and scarlet yarn and finely twisted linen — the work of an embroiderer; 38and they made five posts with hooks for them. They overlaid the tops of the posts and their bands with gold and made their five bases of bronze.

The Ark

37 Bezalel made the ark of acacia wood — two and a half cubits long, a cubit and a half wide, and a cubit and a half high.e 2He overlaid

---

a 9 That is, about 42 feet long and 6 feet wide or about 13 meters long and 1.8 meters wide   b 15 That is, about 45 feet long and 6 feet wide or about 14 meters long and 1.8 meters wide   c 19 Possibly the hides of large aquatic mammals (see 35:7)   d 21 That is, about 15 feet long and 2 1/4 feet wide or about 4.5 meters long and 68 centimeters wide   e 1 That is, about 3 3/4 feet long and 2 1/4 feet wide and high or about 1.1 meters long and 68 centimeters wide and high; similarly in verse 6 it with pure gold, both inside and out, and made a gold molding around it. ³He cast four gold rings for it and fastened them to its four feet, with two rings on one side and two rings on the other. ⁴Then he made poles of acacia wood and overlaid them with gold. ⁵And he inserted the poles into the rings on the sides of the ark to carry it.

⁶He made the atonement cover of pure gold — two and a half cubits long and a cubit and a half wide. ⁷Then he made two cherubim out of hammered gold at the ends of the cover. ⁸He made one cherub on one end and the second cherub on the other; at the two ends he made them of one piece with the cover. ⁹The cherubim had their wings spread upward, overshadowing the cover with them. The cherubim faced each other, looking toward the cover.

The Table

¹⁰They*a* made the table of acacia wood — two cubits long, a cubit wide and a cubit and a half high.*b* ¹¹Then they overlaid it with pure gold and made a gold molding around it. ¹²They also made around it a rim a handbreadth*c* wide and put a gold molding on the rim. ¹³They cast four gold rings for the table and fastened them to the four corners, where the four legs were. ¹⁴The rings were put close to the rim to hold the poles used in carrying the table. ¹⁵The poles for carrying the table were made of acacia wood and were overlaid with gold. ¹⁶And they made from pure gold the articles for the table — its plates and dishes and bowls and its pitchers for the pouring out of drink offerings.

The Lampstand

¹⁷They made the lampstand of pure gold. They hammered out its base and shaft, and made its flowerlike cups, buds and blossoms of one piece with them. ¹⁸Six branch-es extended from the sides of the lampstand — three on one side and three on the other. ¹⁹Three cups shaped like almond flowers with buds and blossoms were on one branch, three on the next branch and the same for all six branches extending from the lampstand. ²⁰And on the lampstand were four cups shaped like almond flowers with buds and blossoms. ²¹One bud was under the first pair of branches extending from the lampstand, a second bud under the second pair, and a third bud under the third pair — six branches in all. ²²The buds and the branches were all of one piece with the lampstand, hammered out of pure gold.

²³They made its seven lamps, as well as its wick trimmers and trays, of pure gold. ²⁴They made the lampstand and all its accessories from one talent*d* of pure gold.

The Altar of Incense

²⁵They made the altar of incense out of acacia wood. It was square, a cubit long and a cubit wide and two cubits high*e* — its horns of one piece with it. ²⁶They overlaid the top and all the sides and the horns with pure gold, and made a gold molding around it. ²⁷They made two gold rings below the molding — two on each of the opposite sides — to hold the poles used to carry it. ²⁸They made the poles of acacia wood and overlaid them with gold.

²⁹They also made the sacred anointing oil and the pure, fragrant incense — the work of a perfumer.

The Altar of Burnt Offering

38 They*f* built the altar of burnt offering of acacia wood, three cubits*g* high; it was square, five cubits long and five cubits wide.*h* ²They made a horn at each of the four corners, so that the horns and the altar were

---

a 10 Or *He*; also in verses 11-29   *b 10* That is, about 3 feet long, 1 1/2 feet wide and 2 1/4 feet high or about 90 centimeters long, 45 centimeters wide and 68 centimeters high   *c 12* That is, about 3 inches or about 7.5 centimeters   *d 24* That is, about 75 pounds or about 34 kilograms   *e 25* That is, about 1 1/2 feet long and wide and 3 feet high or about 45 centimeters long and wide and 90 centimeters high   *f 1* Or *He*; also in verses 2-9   *g 1* That is, about 4 1/2 feet or about 1.4 meters   *h 1* That is, about 7 1/2 feet or about 2.3 meters long and wide of one piece, and they overlaid the altar with bronze. ³They made all its utensils of bronze — its pots, shovels, sprinkling bowls, meat forks and firepans. ⁴They made a grating for the altar, a bronze network, to be under its ledge, halfway up the altar. ⁵They cast bronze rings to hold the poles for the four corners of the bronze grating. ⁶They made the poles of acacia wood and overlaid them with bronze. ⁷They inserted the poles into the rings so they would be on the sides of the altar for carrying it. They made it hollow, out of boards.

The Basin for Washing

⁸They made the bronze basin and its bronze stand from the mirrors of the women who served at the entrance to the tent of meeting.

The Courtyard

⁹Next they made the courtyard. The south side was a hundred cubits*a* long and had curtains of finely twisted linen, ¹⁰with twenty posts and twenty bronze bases, and with silver hooks and bands on the posts. ¹¹The north side was also a hundred cubits long and had twenty posts and twenty bronze bases, with silver hooks and bands on the posts.

¹²The west end was fifty cubits*b* wide and had curtains, with ten posts and ten bases, with silver hooks and bands on the posts. ¹³The east end, toward the sunrise, was also fifty cubits wide. ¹⁴Curtains fifteen cubits*c* long were on one side of the entrance, with three posts and three bases, ¹⁵and curtains fifteen cubits long were on the other side of the entrance to the courtyard, with three posts and three bases. ¹⁶All the curtains around the courtyard were of finely twisted linen. ¹⁷The bases for the posts were bronze. The hooks and bands on the posts were silver, and their tops were

overlaid with silver; so all the posts of the courtyard had silver bands.

¹⁸The curtain for the entrance to the courtyard was made of blue, purple and scarlet yarn and finely twisted linen — the work of an embroiderer. It was twenty cubits*d* long and, like the curtains of the courtyard, five cubits*e* high, ¹⁹with four posts and four bronze bases. Their hooks and bands were silver, and their tops were overlaid with silver. ²⁰All the tent pegs of the tabernacle and of the surrounding courtyard were bronze.

The Materials Used

²¹These are the amounts of the materials used for the tabernacle, the tabernacle of the covenant law, which were recorded at Moses' command by the Levites under the direction of Ithamar son of Aaron, the priest. ²²(Bezalel son of Uri, the son of Hur, of the tribe of Judah, made everything the LORD commanded Moses; ²³with him was Oholiab son of Ahisamak, of the tribe of Dan — an engraver and designer, and an embroiderer in blue, purple and scarlet yarn and fine linen.) ²⁴The total amount of the gold from the wave offering used for all the work on the sanctuary was 29 talents and 730 shekels,*f* according to the sanctuary shekel.

²⁵The silver obtained from those of the community who were counted in the census was 100 talents*g* and 1,775 shekels,*h* according to the sanctuary shekel — ²⁶one beka per person, that is, half a shekel,*i* according to the sanctuary shekel, from everyone who had crossed over to those counted, twenty years old or more, a total of 603,550 men. ²⁷The 100 talents of silver were used to cast the bases for the sanctuary and for the curtain — 100 bases from the 100 talents, one talent for each base. ²⁸They used the 1,775 shekels to make the

---

a 9 That is, about 150 feet or about 45 meters   *b 12* That is, about 75 feet or about 23 meters   *c 14* That is, about 22 feet or about 6.8 meters   *d 18* That is, about 30 feet or about 9 meters   *e 18* That is, about 7 1/2 feet or about 2.3 meters   *f 24* The weight of the gold was a little over a ton or about 1 metric ton.   *g 25* That is, about 3 3/4 tons or about 3.4 metric tons; also in verse 27   *h 25* That is, about 44 pounds or about 20 kilograms; also in verse 28   *i 26* That is, about 1/5 ounce or about 5.7 grams hooks for the posts, to overlay the tops of the posts, and to make their bands.

²⁹The bronze from the wave offering was 70 talents and 2,400 shekels.ᵃ ³⁰They used it to make the bases for the entrance to the tent of meeting, the bronze altar with its bronze grating and all its utensils, ³¹the bases for the surrounding courtyard and those for its entrance and all the tent pegs for the tabernacle and those for the surrounding courtyard.

The Priestly Garments

39 From the blue, purple and scarlet yarn they made woven garments for ministering in the sanctuary. They also made sacred garments for Aaron, as the Lord commanded Moses.

The Ephod

²Theyᵇ made the ephod of gold, and of blue, purple and scarlet yarn, and of finely twisted linen. ³They hammered out thin sheets of gold and cut strands to be worked into the blue, purple and scarlet yarn and fine linen — the work of skilled hands. ⁴They made shoulder pieces for the ephod, which were attached to two of its corners, so it could be fastened. ⁵Its skillfully woven waistband was like it — of one piece with the ephod and made with gold, and with blue, purple and scarlet yarn, and with finely twisted linen, as the Lord commanded Moses.

⁶They mounted the onyx stones in gold filigree settings and engraved them like a seal with the names of the sons of Israel. ⁷Then they fastened them on the shoulder pieces of the ephod as memorial stones for the sons of Israel, as the Lord commanded Moses.

The Breastpiece

⁸They fashioned the breastpiece — the work of a skilled craftsman. They made it like the ephod: of gold, and of blue, purple and scarlet yarn, and of finely twisted linen. ⁹It was square — a spanᶜ long and a span wide — and folded double. ¹⁰Then they mounted four rows of precious stones on it. The first row was carnelian, chrysolite and beryl; ¹¹the second row was turquoise, lapis lazuli and emerald; ¹²the third row was jacinth, agate and amethyst; ¹³the fourth row was topaz, onyx and jasper.ᵈ They were mounted in gold filigree settings. ¹⁴There were twelve stones, one for each of the names of the sons of Israel, each engraved like a seal with the name of one of the twelve tribes.

¹⁵For the breastpiece they made braided chains of pure gold, like a rope. ¹⁶They made two gold filigree settings and two gold rings, and fastened the rings to two of the corners of the breastpiece. ¹⁷They fastened the two gold chains to the rings at the corners of the breastpiece, ¹⁸and the other ends of the chains to the two settings, attaching them to the shoulder pieces of the ephod at the front. ¹⁹They made two gold rings and attached them to the other two corners of the breastpiece on the inside edge next to the ephod. ²⁰Then they made two more gold rings and attached them to the bottom of the shoulder pieces on the front of the ephod, close to the seam just above the waistband of the ephod. ²¹They tied the rings of the breastpiece to the rings of the ephod with blue cord, connecting it to the waistband so that the breastpiece would not swing out from the ephod — as the Lord commanded Moses.

Other Priestly Garments

²²They made the robe of the ephod entirely of blue cloth — the work of a weaver — ²³with an opening in the center of the robe like the opening of a collar,ᵉ and a band around this opening, so that it would not tear. ²⁴They made pomegranates of blue, purple and scarlet yarn and finely twisted linen around the hem of the robe.

ᵃ 29 The weight of the bronze was about 2 1/2 tons or about 2.4 metric tons.   ᵇ 2 Or He; also in verses 7, 8 and 22
ᶜ 9 That is, about 9 inches or about 23 centimeters   ᵈ 13 The precise identification of some of these precious stones is uncertain.   ᵉ 23 The meaning of the Hebrew for this word is uncertain.

25And they made bells of pure gold and attached them around the hem between the pomegranates. 26The bells and pomegranates alternated around the hem of the robe to be worn for ministering, as the Lord commanded Moses.

27For Aaron and his sons, they made tunics of fine linen — the work of a weaver — 28and the turban of fine linen, the linen caps and the undergarments of finely twisted linen. 29The sash was made of finely twisted linen and blue, purple and scarlet yarn — the work of an embroiderer — as the Lord commanded Moses.

30They made the plate, the sacred emblem, out of pure gold and engraved on it, like an inscription on a seal: HOLY TO THE LORD. 31Then they fastened a blue cord to it to attach it to the turban, as the Lord commanded Moses.

Moses Inspects the Tabernacle

32So all the work on the tabernacle, the tent of meeting, was completed. The Israelites did everything just as the Lord commanded Moses. 33Then they brought the tabernacle to Moses: the tent and all its furnishings, its clasps, frames, crossbars, posts and bases; 34the covering of ram skins dyed red and the covering of another durable leather[a] and the shielding curtain; 35the ark of the covenant law with its poles and the atonement cover; 36the table with all its articles and the bread of the Presence; 37the pure gold lampstand with its row of lamps and all its accessories, and the olive oil for the light; 38the gold altar, the anointing oil, the fragrant incense, and the curtain for the entrance to the tent; 39the bronze altar with its bronze grating, its poles and all its utensils; the basin with its stand; 40the curtains of the courtyard with its posts and bases, and the curtain for the entrance to the courtyard; the ropes and tent pegs for the courtyard; all the furnishings for the tabernacle, the tent of meeting; 41and the woven garments worn for ministering in the sanctuary, both the sacred garments for Aaron the priest and the garments for his sons when serving as priests.

42The Israelites had done all the work just as the Lord had commanded Moses. 43Moses inspected the work and saw that they had done it just as the Lord had commanded. So Moses blessed them.

Setting Up the Tabernacle

40 Then the Lord said to Moses: 2"Set up the tabernacle, the tent of meeting, on the first day of the first month. 3Place the ark of the covenant law in it and shield the ark with the curtain. 4Bring in the table and set out what belongs on it. Then bring in the lampstand and set up its lamps. 5Place the gold altar of incense in front of the ark of the covenant law and put the curtain at the entrance to the tabernacle.

6"Place the altar of burnt offering in front of the entrance to the tabernacle, the tent of meeting; 7place the basin between the tent of meeting and the altar and put water in it. 8Set up the courtyard around it and put the curtain at the entrance to the courtyard.

9"Take the anointing oil and anoint the tabernacle and everything in it; consecrate it and all its furnishings, and it will be holy. 10Then anoint the altar of burnt offering and all its utensils; consecrate the altar, and it will be most holy. 11Anoint the basin and its stand and consecrate them.

12"Bring Aaron and his sons to the entrance to the tent of meeting and wash them with water. 13Then dress Aaron in the sacred garments, anoint him and consecrate him so he may serve me as priest. 14Bring his sons and dress them in tunics. 15Anoint them just as you anointed their father, so they may serve me as priests. Their anointing will be to a priesthood that will continue throughout their generations." 16Moses did everything just as the Lord commanded him.

---

[a] 34 Possibly the hides of large aquatic mammals

17So the tabernacle was set up on the first day of the first month in the second year. 18When Moses set up the tabernacle, he put the bases in place, erected the frames, inserted the crossbars and set up the posts. 19Then he spread the tent over the tabernacle and put the covering over the tent, as the Lord commanded him.

20He took the tablets of the covenant law and placed them in the ark, attached the poles to the ark and put the atonement cover over it. 21Then he brought the ark into the tabernacle and hung the shielding curtain and shielded the ark of the covenant law, as the Lord commanded him.

22Moses placed the table in the tent of meeting on the north side of the tabernacle outside the curtain 23and set out the bread on it before the Lord, as the Lord commanded him.

24He placed the lampstand in the tent of meeting opposite the table on the south side of the tabernacle 25and set up the lamps before the Lord, as the Lord commanded him.

26Moses placed the gold altar in the tent of meeting in front of the curtain 27and burned fragrant incense on it, as the Lord commanded him.

28Then he put up the curtain at the entrance to the tabernacle. 29He set the altar of burnt offering near the entrance to the tabernacle, the tent of meeting, and offered on it burnt offerings and grain offerings, as the Lord commanded him.

30He placed the basin between the tent of meeting and the altar and put water in it for washing, 31and Moses and Aaron and his sons used it to wash their hands and feet. 32They washed whenever they entered the tent of meeting or approached the altar, as the Lord commanded Moses.

33Then Moses set up the courtyard around the tabernacle and altar and put up the curtain at the entrance to the courtyard. And so Moses finished the work.

The Glory of the Lord

34Then the cloud covered the tent of meeting, and the glory of the Lord filled the tabernacle. 35Moses could not enter the tent of meeting because the cloud had settled on it, and the glory of the Lord filled the tabernacle.

36In all the travels of the Israelites, whenever the cloud lifted from above the tabernacle, they would set out; 37but if the cloud did not lift, they did not set out — until the day it lifted. 38So the cloud of the Lord was over the tabernacle by day, and fire was in the cloud by night, in the sight of all the Israelites during all their travels.

Leviticus

THEME: God's call to holiness is the overwhelming message of this book.

AUTHOR: Leviticus states that its content was given to Moses by God at Mount Sinai. Other Scripture passages also identify Moses as the author.

DATE OF WRITING: Leviticus was probably written around 1440 BC.

ENCOURAGEMENT FROM LEVITICUS: "I am the Lord your God . . . I broke the bars of your yoke and enabled you to walk with heads held high" (Leviticus 26:13).

CHALLENGE FROM LEVITICUS: "You are to be holy to me because I, the Lord, am holy, and I have set you apart from the nations to be my own" (Leviticus 20:26).

REFLECTION FROM LEVITICUS: "Do not seek revenge or bear a grudge . . . but love your neighbor as yourself" (Leviticus 19:18).

At a Glance

Recovery Themes in Leviticus

Leviticus sets up the details of the covenant between God and his people. God is holy, and his people must be holy as well. In order to enjoy a relationship with him, God's people are to reflect his character. By doing so, they show that they are set apart from the world. They belong to God—for the purpose of serving him.

Leviticus states that atonement, or freedom from sin, is possible only through blood sacrifice. Fellowship with God is maintained by following his laws. Jesus Christ made the ultimate blood sacrifice for us. His life and death fulfilled the law, and we're now free from sin, free to enjoy communion with God through faith in Jesus. Christ-centered recovery is a call to holiness. By following Jesus' example and setting ourselves apart for service, we bring God's purposes alive in a hurting world.

The Burnt Offering

1 The Lord called to Moses and spoke to him from the tent of meeting. He said, 2"Speak to the Israelites and say to them: 'When anyone among you brings an offering to the Lord, bring as your offering an animal from either the herd or the flock.

3"'If the offering is a burnt offering from the herd, you are to offer a male without defect. You must present it at the entrance to the tent of meeting so that it will be acceptable to the Lord. 4You are to lay your hand on the head of the burnt offering, and it will be accepted on your behalf to make atonement for you. 5You are to slaughter the young bull before the Lord, and then Aaron's sons the priests shall bring the blood and splash it against the sides of the altar at the entrance to the tent of meeting. 6You are to skin the burnt offering and cut it into pieces. 7The sons of Aaron the priest are to put fire on the altar and arrange wood on the fire. 8Then Aaron's sons the priests shall arrange the pieces, including the head and the fat, on the wood that is burning on the altar. 9You are to wash the internal organs and the legs with water, and the priest is to burn all of it on the altar. It is a burnt offering, a food offering, an aroma pleasing to the Lord.

10"'If the offering is a burnt offering

from the flock, from either the sheep or the goats, you are to offer a male without defect. [11] You are to slaughter it at the north side of the altar before the LORD, and Aaron's sons the priests shall splash its blood against the sides of the altar. [12] You are to cut it into pieces, and the priest shall arrange them, including the head and the fat, on the wood that is burning on the altar. [13] You are to wash the internal organs and the legs with water, and the priest is to bring all of them and burn them on the altar. It is a burnt offering, a food offering, an aroma pleasing to the LORD.

[14] "If the offering to the LORD is a burnt offering of birds, you are to offer a dove or a young pigeon. [15] The priest shall bring it to the altar, wring off the head and burn it on the altar; its blood shall be drained out on the side of the altar. [16] He is to remove the crop and the feathers[a] and throw them down east of the altar where the ashes are. [17] He shall tear it open by the wings, not dividing it completely, and then the priest shall burn it on the wood that is burning on the altar. It is a burnt offering, a food offering, an aroma pleasing to the LORD.

The Grain Offering

2 " 'When anyone brings a grain offering to the LORD, their offering is to be of the finest flour. They are to pour olive oil on it, put incense on it [2] and take it to Aaron's sons the priests. The priest shall take a handful of the flour and oil, together with all the incense, and burn this as a memorial[b] portion on the altar, a food offering, an aroma pleasing to the LORD. [3] The rest of the grain offering belongs to Aaron and his sons; it is a most holy part of the food offerings presented to the LORD.

[4] " 'If you bring a grain offering baked in an oven, it is to consist of the finest flour: either thick loaves made without yeast and with olive oil mixed in or thin loaves made

without yeast and brushed with olive oil. [5] If your grain offering is prepared on a griddle, it is to be made of the finest flour mixed with oil, and without yeast. [6] Crumble it and pour oil on it; it is a grain offering. [7] If your grain offering is cooked in a pan, it is to be made of the finest flour and some olive oil. [8] Bring the grain offering made of these things to the LORD; present it to the priest, who shall take it to the altar. [9] He shall take out the memorial portion from the grain offering and burn it on the altar as a food offering, an aroma pleasing to the LORD. [10] The rest of the grain offering belongs to Aaron and his sons; it is a most holy part of the food offerings presented to the LORD.

[11] " 'Every grain offering you bring to the LORD must be made without yeast, for you are not to burn any yeast or honey in a food offering presented to the LORD. [12] You may bring them to the LORD as an offering of the firstfruits, but they are not to be offered on the altar as a pleasing aroma. [13] Season all your grain offerings with salt. Do not leave the salt of the covenant of your God out of your grain offerings; add salt to all your offerings.

[14] " 'If you bring a grain offering of firstfruits to the LORD, offer crushed heads of new grain roasted in the fire. [15] Put oil and incense on it; it is a grain offering. [16] The priest shall burn the memorial portion of the crushed grain and the oil, together with all the incense, as a food offering presented to the LORD.

The Fellowship Offering

3 " 'If your offering is a fellowship offering, and you offer an animal from the herd, whether male or female, you are to present before the LORD an animal without defect. [2] You are to lay your hand on the head of your offering and slaughter it at the entrance to the tent of meeting. Then Aaron's sons the priests

---

a 16 Or *crop with its contents*; the meaning of the Hebrew for this word is uncertain.   *b 2* Or *representative*; also in verses 9 and 16 shall splash the blood against the sides of the altar. ³From the fellowship offering you are to bring a food offering to the LORD: the internal organs and all the fat that is connected to them, ⁴both kidneys with the fat on them near the loins, and the long lobe of the liver, which you will remove with the kidneys. ⁵Then Aaron's sons are to burn it on the altar on top of the burnt offering that is lying on the burning wood; it is a food offering, an aroma pleasing to the LORD.

⁶"If you offer an animal from the flock as a fellowship offering to the LORD, you are to offer a male or female without defect. ⁷If you offer a lamb, you are to present it before the LORD, ⁸lay your hand on its head and slaughter it in front of the tent of meeting. Then Aaron's sons shall splash its blood against the sides of the altar. ⁹From the fellowship offering you are to bring a food offering to the LORD: its fat, the entire fat tail cut off close to the backbone, the internal organs and all the fat that is connected to them, ¹⁰both kidneys with the fat on them near the loins, and the long lobe of the liver, which you will remove with the kidneys. ¹¹The priest shall burn them on the altar as a food offering presented to the LORD.

¹²"If your offering is a goat, you are to present it before the LORD, ¹³lay your hand on its head and slaughter it in front of the tent of meeting. Then Aaron's sons shall splash its blood against the sides of the altar. ¹⁴From what you offer you are to present this food offering to the LORD: the internal organs and all the fat that is connected to them, ¹⁵both kidneys with the fat on them near the loins, and the long lobe of the liver, which you will remove with the kidneys. ¹⁶The priest shall burn them on the altar as a food offering, a pleasing aroma. All the fat is the LORD's.

¹⁷"This is a lasting ordinance for the generations to come, wherever you live: You must not eat any fat or any blood.'"

The Sin Offering

4 The LORD said to Moses, ²"Say to the Israelites: 'When anyone sins unintentionally and does what is forbidden in any of the LORD's commands—

³"If the anointed priest sins, bringing guilt on the people, he must bring to the LORD a young bull without defect as a sin offering[a] for the sin he has committed. ⁴He is to present the bull at the entrance to the tent of meeting before the LORD. He is to lay his hand on its head and slaughter it there before the LORD. ⁵Then the anointed priest shall take some of the bull's blood and carry it into the tent of meeting. ⁶He is to dip his finger into the blood and sprinkle some of it seven times before the LORD, in front of the curtain of the sanctuary. ⁷The priest shall then put some of the blood on the horns of the altar of fragrant incense that is before the LORD in the tent of meeting. The rest of the bull's blood he shall pour out at the base of the altar of burnt offering at the entrance to the tent of meeting. ⁸He shall remove all the fat from the bull of the sin offering—all the fat that is connected to the internal organs, ⁹both kidneys with the fat on them near the loins, and the long lobe of the liver, which he will remove with the kidneys— ¹⁰just as the fat is removed from the ox[b] sacrificed as a fellowship offering. Then the priest shall burn them on the altar of burnt offering. ¹¹But the hide of the bull and all its flesh, as well as the head and legs, the internal organs and the intestines— ¹²that is, all the rest of the bull—he must take outside the camp to a place ceremonially clean, where the ashes are thrown, and burn it there in a wood fire on the ash heap.

¹³"If the whole Israelite community sins unintentionally and does what is forbidden in any of the LORD's commands, even though the community is unaware of the

---

a 3 Or *purification offering*; here and throughout this chapter   b 10 The Hebrew word can refer to either male or female.

matter, when they realize their guilt ¹⁴and the sin they committed becomes known, the assembly must bring a young bull as a sin offering and present it before the tent of meeting. ¹⁵The elders of the community are to lay their hands on the bull's head before the Lord, and the bull shall be slaughtered before the Lord. ¹⁶Then the anointed priest is to take some of the bull's blood into the tent of meeting. ¹⁷He shall dip his finger into the blood and sprinkle it before the Lord seven times in front of the curtain. ¹⁸He is to put some of the blood on the horns of the altar that is before the Lord in the tent of meeting. The rest of the blood he shall pour out at the base of the altar of burnt offering at the entrance to the tent of meeting. ¹⁹He shall remove all the fat from it and burn it on the altar, ²⁰and do with this bull just as he did with the bull for the sin offering. In this way the priest will make atonement for the community, and they will be forgiven. ²¹Then he shall take the bull outside the camp and burn it as he burned the first bull. This is the sin offering for the community.

²²"'When a leader sins unintentionally and does what is forbidden in any of the commands of the Lord his God, when he realizes his guilt ²³and the sin he has committed becomes known, he must bring as his offering a male goat without defect. ²⁴He is to lay his hand on the goat's head and slaughter it at the place where the burnt offering is slaughtered before the Lord. It is a sin offering. ²⁵Then the priest shall take some of the blood of the sin offering with his finger and put it on the horns of the altar of burnt offering and pour out the rest of the blood at the base of the altar. ²⁶He shall burn all the fat on the altar as he burned the fat of the fellowship offering. In this way the priest will make atonement for the leader's sin, and he will be forgiven.

²⁷"'If any member of the community sins unintentionally and does what is forbidden in any of the Lord's commands,

when they realize their guilt ²⁸and the sin they have committed becomes known, they must bring as their offering for the sin they committed a female goat without defect. ²⁹They are to lay their hand on the head of the sin offering and slaughter it at the place of the burnt offering. ³⁰Then the priest is to take some of the blood with his finger and put it on the horns of the altar of burnt offering and pour out the rest of the blood at the base of the altar. ³¹They shall remove all the fat, just as the fat is removed from the fellowship offering, and the priest shall burn it on the altar as an aroma pleasing to the Lord. In this way the priest will make atonement for them, and they will be forgiven.

³²"'If someone brings a lamb as their sin offering, they are to bring a female without defect. ³³They are to lay their hand on its head and slaughter it for a sin offering at the place where the burnt offering is slaughtered. ³⁴Then the priest shall take some of the blood of the sin offering with his finger and put it on the horns of the altar of burnt offering and pour out the rest of the blood at the base of the altar. ³⁵They shall remove all the fat, just as the fat is removed from the lamb of the fellowship offering, and the priest shall burn it on the altar on top of the food offerings presented to the Lord. In this way the priest will make atonement for them for the sin they have committed, and they will be forgiven.

5 "'If anyone sins because they do not speak up when they hear a public charge to testify regarding something they have seen or learned about, they will be held responsible.

²"'If anyone becomes aware that they are guilty—if they unwittingly touch anything ceremonially unclean (whether the carcass of an unclean animal, wild or domestic, or of any unclean creature that moves along the ground) and they are unaware that they have become unclean, but then they come to realize their guilt; ³or if they touch human uncleanness (anything that would

make them unclean) even though they are unaware of it, but then they learn of it and realize their guilt; ⁴or if anyone thoughtlessly takes an oath to do anything, whether good or evil (in any matter one might carelessly swear about) even though they are unaware of it, but then they learn of it and realize their guilt— ⁵when anyone becomes aware that they are guilty in any of these matters, they must confess in what way they have sinned. ⁶As a penalty for the sin they have committed, they must bring to the Lord a female lamb or goat from the flock as a sin offeringᵃ; and the priest shall make atonement for them for their sin.

⁷"'Anyone who cannot afford a lamb is to bring two doves or two young pigeons to the Lord as a penalty for their sin—one for a sin offering and the other for a burnt offering. ⁸They are to bring them to the priest, who shall first offer the one for the sin offering. He is to wring its head from its neck, not dividing it completely, ⁹and is to splash some of the blood of the sin offering against the side of the altar; the rest of the blood must be drained out at the base of the altar. It is a sin offering. ¹⁰The priest shall then offer the other as a burnt offering in the prescribed way and make atonement for them for the sin they have committed, and they will be forgiven.

¹¹"'If, however, they cannot afford two doves or two young pigeons, they are to bring as an offering for their sin a tenth of an ephahᵇ of the finest flour for a sin offering. They must not put olive oil or incense on it, because it is a sin offering. ¹²They are to bring it to the priest, who shall take a handful of it as a memorialᶜ portion and burn it on the altar on top of the food offerings presented to the Lord. It is a sin offering. ¹³In this way the priest will make atonement for them for any of these sins they have committed, and they will be forgiven. The rest of the offering will belong to the priest, as in the case of the grain offering.'"

The Guilt Offering

¹⁴The Lord said to Moses: ¹⁵"When anyone is unfaithful to the Lord by sinning unintentionally in regard to any of the Lord's holy things, they are to bring to the Lord as a penalty a ram from the flock, one without defect and of the proper value in silver, according to the sanctuary shekel.ᵈ It is a guilt offering. ¹⁶They must make restitution for what they have failed to do in regard to the holy things, pay an additional penalty of a fifth of its value and give it all to the priest. The priest will make atonement for them with the ram as a guilt offering, and they will be forgiven.

¹⁷"If anyone sins and does what is forbidden in any of the Lord's commands, even though they do not know it, they are guilty and will be held responsible. ¹⁸They are to bring to the priest as a guilt offering a ram from the flock, one without defect and of the proper value. In this way the priest will make atonement for them for the wrong they have committed unintentionally, and they will be forgiven. ¹⁹It is a guilt offering; they have been guilty ofᵉ wrongdoing against the Lord."

6 ᶠ The Lord said to Moses: ²"If anyone sins and is unfaithful to the Lord by deceiving a neighbor about something entrusted to them or left in their care or about something stolen, or if they cheat their neighbor, ³or if they find lost property and lie about it, or if they swear falsely about any such sin that people may commit— ⁴when they sin in any of these ways and realize their guilt, they must return what they have stolen or taken by extortion, or what was entrusted to them, or the lost property they found, ⁵or whatever it was they swore falsely about. They must make restitution in full, add a fifth of the

---

ᵃ 6 Or *purification offering*; here and throughout this chapter   ᵇ 11 That is, probably about 3 1/2 pounds or about 1.6 kilograms   ᶜ 12 Or *representative*   ᵈ 15 That is, about 2/5 ounce or about 12 grams   ᵉ 19 Or *offering; atonement has been made for their*   ᶠ In Hebrew texts 6:1-7 is numbered 5:20-26, and 6:8-30 is numbered 6:1-23.

value to it and give it all to the owner on the day they present their guilt offering. [6]And as a penalty they must bring to the priest, that is, to the LORD, their guilt offering, a ram from the flock, one without defect and of the proper value. [7]In this way the priest will make atonement for them before the LORD, and they will be forgiven for any of the things they did that made them guilty."

The Burnt Offering

[8]The LORD said to Moses: [9]"Give Aaron and his sons this command: 'These are the regulations for the burnt offering: The burnt offering is to remain on the altar hearth throughout the night, till morning, and the fire must be kept burning on the altar. [10]The priest shall then put on his linen clothes, with linen undergarments next to his body, and shall remove the ashes of the burnt offering that the fire has consumed on the altar and place them beside the altar. [11]Then he is to take off these clothes and put on others, and carry the ashes outside the camp to a place that is ceremonially clean. [12]The fire on the altar must be kept burning; it must not go out. Every morning the priest is to add firewood and arrange the burnt offering on the fire and burn the fat of the fellowship offerings on it. [13]The fire must be kept burning on the altar continuously; it must not go out.

The Grain Offering

[14]"'These are the regulations for the grain offering: Aaron's sons are to bring it before the LORD, in front of the altar. [15]The priest is to take a handful of the finest flour and some olive oil, together with all the incense on the grain offering, and burn the memorial[a] portion on the altar as an aroma pleasing to the LORD. [16]Aaron and his sons shall eat the rest of it, but it is to be eaten without yeast in the sanctuary area; they are to eat it in the courtyard of the tent of meeting. [17]It

must not be baked with yeast; I have given it as their share of the food offerings presented to me. Like the sin offering[b] and the guilt offering, it is most holy. [18]Any male descendant of Aaron may eat it. For all generations to come it is his perpetual share of the food offerings presented to the LORD. Whatever touches them will become holy.[c] "

[19]The LORD also said to Moses, [20]"This is the offering Aaron and his sons are to bring to the LORD on the day he[d] is anointed: a tenth of an ephah[e] of the finest flour as a regular grain offering, half of it in the morning and half in the evening. [21]It must be prepared with oil on a griddle; bring it well-mixed and present the grain offering broken[f] in pieces as an aroma pleasing to the LORD. [22]The son who is to succeed him as anointed priest shall prepare it. It is the LORD's perpetual share and is to be burned completely. [23]Every grain offering of a priest shall be burned completely; it must not be eaten."

The Sin Offering

[24]The LORD said to Moses, [25]"Say to Aaron and his sons: 'These are the regulations for the sin offering: The sin offering is to be slaughtered before the LORD in the place the burnt offering is slaughtered; it is most holy. [26]The priest who offers it shall eat it; it is to be eaten in the sanctuary area, in the courtyard of the tent of meeting. [27]Whatever touches any of the flesh will become holy, and if any of the blood is spattered on a garment, you must wash it in the sanctuary area. [28]The clay pot the meat is cooked in must be broken; but if it is cooked in a bronze pot, the pot is to be scoured and rinsed with water. [29]Any male in a priest's family may eat it; it is most holy. [30]But any sin offering whose blood is brought into the tent of meeting to make atonement in the Holy Place must not be eaten; it must be burned up.

---

[a] 15 Or representative   [b] 17 Or purification offering; also in verses 25 and 30   [c] 18 Or Whoever touches them must be holy; similarly in verse 27   [d] 20 Or each   [e] 20 That is, probably about 3 1/2 pounds or about 1.6 kilograms   [f] 21 The meaning of the Hebrew for this word is uncertain.

The Guilt Offering

7 "'These are the regulations for the guilt offering, which is most holy: ²The guilt offering is to be slaughtered in the place where the burnt offering is slaughtered, and its blood is to be splashed against the sides of the altar. ³All its fat shall be offered: the fat tail and the fat that covers the internal organs, ⁴both kidneys with the fat on them near the loins, and the long lobe of the liver, which is to be removed with the kidneys. ⁵The priest shall burn them on the altar as a food offering presented to the LORD. It is a guilt offering. ⁶Any male in a priest's family may eat it, but it must be eaten in the sanctuary area; it is most holy.

⁷"'The same law applies to both the sin offering[a] and the guilt offering: They belong to the priest who makes atonement with them. ⁸The priest who offers a burnt offering for anyone may keep its hide for himself. ⁹Every grain offering baked in an oven or cooked in a pan or on a griddle belongs to the priest who offers it, ¹⁰and every grain offering, whether mixed with olive oil or dry, belongs equally to all the sons of Aaron.

The Fellowship Offering

¹¹"'These are the regulations for the fellowship offering anyone may present to the LORD:

¹²"'If they offer it as an expression of thankfulness, then along with this thank offering they are to offer thick loaves made without yeast and with olive oil mixed in, thin loaves made without yeast and brushed with oil, and thick loaves of the finest flour well-kneaded and with oil mixed in. ¹³Along with their fellowship offering of thanksgiving they are to present an offering with thick loaves of bread made with yeast. ¹⁴They are to bring one of each kind as an offering, a contribution to the LORD; it belongs to the priest who splashes the blood of the fellowship offering against the altar. ¹⁵The meat of their fellowship offering of thanksgiving must be eaten on the day it is offered; they must leave none of it till morning.

¹⁶"'If, however, their offering is the result of a vow or is a freewill offering, the sacrifice shall be eaten on the day they offer it, but anything left over may be eaten on the next day. ¹⁷Any meat of the sacrifice left over till the third day must be burned up. ¹⁸If any meat of the fellowship offering is eaten on the third day, the one who offered it will not be accepted. It will not be reckoned to their credit, for it has become impure; the person who eats any of it will be held responsible.

¹⁹"'Meat that touches anything ceremonially unclean must not be eaten; it must be burned up. As for other meat, anyone ceremonially clean may eat it. ²⁰But if anyone who is unclean eats any meat of the fellowship offering belonging to the LORD, they must be cut off from their people. ²¹Anyone who touches something unclean—whether human uncleanness or an unclean animal or any unclean creature that moves along the ground[b]—and then eats any of the meat of the fellowship offering belonging to the LORD must be cut off from their people.'"

Eating Fat and Blood Forbidden

²²The LORD said to Moses, ²³"Say to the Israelites: 'Do not eat any of the fat of cattle, sheep or goats. ²⁴The fat of an animal found dead or torn by wild animals may be used for any other purpose, but you must not eat it. ²⁵Anyone who eats the fat of an animal from which a food offering may be[c] presented to the LORD must be cut off from their people. ²⁶And wherever you live, you must not eat the blood of any bird or animal. ²⁷Anyone who eats blood must be cut off from their people.'"

The Priests' Share

²⁸The LORD said to Moses, ²⁹"Say to the Israelites: 'Anyone who brings a fellowship

---

[a] 7 Or *purification offering*; also in verse 37   [b] 21 A few Hebrew manuscripts, Samaritan Pentateuch, Syriac and Targum (see 5:2); most Hebrew manuscripts *any unclean, detestable thing*   [c] 25 Or *offering is*

offering to the LORD is to bring part of it as their sacrifice to the LORD. 30With their own hands they are to present the food offering to the LORD; they are to bring the fat, together with the breast, and wave the breast before the LORD as a wave offering. 31The priest shall burn the fat on the altar, but the breast belongs to Aaron and his sons. 32You are to give the right thigh of your fellowship offerings to the priest as a contribution. 33The son of Aaron who offers the blood and the fat of the fellowship offering shall have the right thigh as his share. 34From the fellowship offerings of the Israelites, I have taken the breast that is waved and the thigh that is presented and have given them to Aaron the priest and his sons as their perpetual share from the Israelites.'"

35This is the portion of the food offerings presented to the LORD that were allotted to Aaron and his sons on the day they were presented to serve the LORD as priests. 36On the day they were anointed, the LORD commanded that the Israelites give this to them as their perpetual share for the generations to come.

37These, then, are the regulations for the burnt offering, the grain offering, the sin offering, the guilt offering, the ordination offering and the fellowship offering, 38which the LORD gave Moses at Mount Sinai in the Desert of Sinai on the day he commanded the Israelites to bring their offerings to the LORD.

The Ordination of Aaron and His Sons

8 The LORD said to Moses, 2"Bring Aaron and his sons, their garments, the anointing oil, the bull for the sin offering,*a* the two rams and the basket containing bread made without yeast, 3and gather the entire assembly at the entrance to the tent of meeting." 4Moses did as the LORD commanded him, and the assembly gathered at the entrance to the tent of meeting.

5Moses said to the assembly, "This is what the LORD has commanded to be done." 6Then Moses brought Aaron and his sons forward and washed them with water. 7He put the tunic on Aaron, tied the sash around him, clothed him with the robe and put the ephod on him. He also fastened the ephod with a decorative waistband, which he tied around him. 8He placed the breastpiece on him and put the Urim and Thummim in the breastpiece. 9Then he placed the turban on Aaron's head and set the gold plate, the sacred emblem, on the front of it, as the LORD commanded Moses.

10Then Moses took the anointing oil and anointed the tabernacle and everything in it, and so consecrated them. 11He sprinkled some of the oil on the altar seven times, anointing the altar and all its utensils and the basin with its stand, to consecrate them. 12He poured some of the anointing oil on Aaron's head and anointed him to consecrate him. 13Then he brought Aaron's sons forward, put tunics on them, tied sashes around them and fastened caps on them, as the LORD commanded Moses.

14He then presented the bull for the sin offering, and Aaron and his sons laid their hands on its head. 15Moses slaughtered the bull and took some of the blood, and with his finger he put it on all the horns of the altar to purify the altar. He poured out the rest of the blood at the base of the altar. So he consecrated it to make atonement for it. 16Moses also took all the fat around the internal organs, the long lobe of the liver, and both kidneys and their fat, and burned it on the altar. 17But the bull with its hide and its flesh and its intestines he burned up outside the camp, as the LORD commanded Moses.

18He then presented the ram for the burnt offering, and Aaron and his sons laid their hands on its head. 19Then Moses slaughtered the ram and splashed the blood against the sides of the altar. 20He cut the ram into pieces and burned the head,

---

a 2 Or purification offering; also in verse 14

the pieces and the fat. 21He washed the internal organs and the legs with water and burned the whole ram on the altar. It was a burnt offering, a pleasing aroma, a food offering presented to the LORD, as the LORD commanded Moses.

22He then presented the other ram, the ram for the ordination, and Aaron and his sons laid their hands on its head. 23Moses slaughtered the ram and took some of its blood and put it on the lobe of Aaron's right ear, on the thumb of his right hand and on the big toe of his right foot. 24Moses also brought Aaron's sons forward and put some of the blood on the lobes of their right ears, on the thumbs of their right hands and on the big toes of their right feet. Then he splashed blood against the sides of the altar. 25After that, he took the fat, the fat tail, all the fat around the internal organs, the long lobe of the liver, both kidneys and their fat and the right thigh. 26And from the basket of bread made without yeast, which was before the LORD, he took one thick loaf, one thick loaf with olive oil mixed in, and one thin loaf, and he put these on the fat portions and on the right thigh. 27He put all these in the hands of Aaron and his sons, and they waved them before the LORD as a wave offering. 28Then Moses took them from their hands and burned them on the altar on top of the burnt offering as an ordination offering, a pleasing aroma, a food offering presented to the LORD. 29Moses also took the breast, which was his share of the ordination ram, and waved it before the LORD as a wave offering, as the LORD commanded Moses.

30Then Moses took some of the anointing oil and some of the blood from the altar and sprinkled them on Aaron and his garments and on his sons and their garments. So he consecrated Aaron and his garments and his sons and their garments.

31Moses then said to Aaron and his sons, "Cook the meat at the entrance to the tent of meeting and eat it there with the bread from the basket of ordination offerings, as I was commanded: 'Aaron and his sons are to eat it.' 32Then burn up the rest of the meat and the bread. 33Do not leave the entrance to the tent of meeting for seven days, until the days of your ordination are completed, for your ordination will last seven days. 34What has been done today was commanded by the LORD to make atonement for you. 35You must stay at the entrance to the tent of meeting day and night for seven days and do what the LORD requires, so you will not die; for that is what I have been commanded."

36So Aaron and his sons did everything the LORD commanded through Moses.

The Priests Begin Their Ministry

9 On the eighth day Moses summoned Aaron and his sons and the elders of Israel. 2He said to Aaron, "Take a bull calf for your sin offering*a* and a ram for your burnt offering, both without defect, and present them before the LORD. 3Then say to the Israelites: 'Take a male goat for a sin offering, a calf and a lamb— both a year old and without defect—for a burnt offering, 4and an ox*b* and a ram for a fellowship offering to sacrifice before the LORD, together with a grain offering mixed with olive oil. For today the LORD will appear to you.'"

5They took the things Moses commanded to the front of the tent of meeting, and the entire assembly came near and stood before the LORD. 6Then Moses said, "This is what the LORD has commanded you to do, so that the glory of the LORD may appear to you."

7Moses said to Aaron, "Come to the altar and sacrifice your sin offering and your burnt offering and make atonement for yourself and the people; sacrifice the offering that is for the people and make atonement for them, as the LORD has commanded."

---

a 2 Or *purification offering*; here and throughout this chapter   *b* 4 The Hebrew word can refer to either male or female; also in verses 18 and 19.

⁸So Aaron came to the altar and slaughtered the calf as a sin offering for himself. ⁹His sons brought the blood to him, and he dipped his finger into the blood and put it on the horns of the altar; the rest of the blood he poured out at the base of the altar. ¹⁰On the altar he burned the fat, the kidneys and the long lobe of the liver from the sin offering, as the LORD commanded Moses; ¹¹the flesh and the hide he burned up outside the camp.

¹²Then he slaughtered the burnt offering. His sons handed him the blood, and he splashed it against the sides of the altar. ¹³They handed him the burnt offering piece by piece, including the head, and he burned them on the altar. ¹⁴He washed the internal organs and the legs and burned them on top of the burnt offering on the altar.

¹⁵Aaron then brought the offering that was for the people. He took the goat for the people's sin offering and slaughtered it and offered it for a sin offering as he did with the first one.

¹⁶He brought the burnt offering and offered it in the prescribed way. ¹⁷He also brought the grain offering, took a handful of it and burned it on the altar in addition to the morning's burnt offering.

¹⁸He slaughtered the ox and the ram as the fellowship offering for the people. His sons handed him the blood, and he splashed it against the sides of the altar. ¹⁹But the fat portions of the ox and the ram — the fat tail, the layer of fat, the kidneys and the long lobe of the liver — ²⁰these they laid on the breasts, and then Aaron burned the fat on the altar. ²¹Aaron waved the breasts and the right thigh before the LORD as a wave offering, as Moses commanded.

²²Then Aaron lifted his hands toward the people and blessed them. And having sacrificed the sin offering, the burnt offering and the fellowship offering, he stepped down.

²³Moses and Aaron then went into the tent of meeting. When they came out, they blessed the people; and the glory of the LORD appeared to all the people. ²⁴Fire came out from the presence of the LORD and consumed the burnt offering and the fat portions on the altar. And when all the people saw it, they shouted for joy and fell facedown.

The Death of Nadab and Abihu

10 Aaron's sons Nadab and Abihu took their censers, put fire in them and added incense; and they offered unauthorized fire before the LORD, contrary to his command. ²So fire came out from the presence of the LORD and consumed them, and they died before the LORD. ³Moses then said to Aaron, "This is what the LORD spoke of when he said:

> "'Among those who approach me
>   I will be proved holy;
> in the sight of all the people
>   I will be honored.'"

Aaron remained silent.

⁴Moses summoned Mishael and Elzaphan, sons of Aaron's uncle Uzziel, and said to them, "Come here; carry your cousins outside the camp, away from the front of the sanctuary." ⁵So they came and carried them, still in their tunics, outside the camp, as Moses ordered.

⁶Then Moses said to Aaron and his sons Eleazar and Ithamar, "Do not let your hair become unkempt[a] and do not tear your clothes, or you will die and the LORD will be angry with the whole community. But your relatives, all the Israelites, may mourn for those the LORD has destroyed by fire. ⁷Do not leave the entrance to the tent of meeting or you will die, because the LORD's anointing oil is on you." So they did as Moses said.

⁸Then the LORD said to Aaron, ⁹"You and your sons are not to drink wine or other fermented drink whenever you go into the tent of meeting, or you will die. This

---

ᵃ 6 Or *Do not uncover your heads*

is a lasting ordinance for the generations to come, ¹⁰so that you can distinguish between the holy and the common, between the unclean and the clean, ¹¹and so you can teach the Israelites all the decrees the LORD has given them through Moses."

¹²Moses said to Aaron and his remaining sons, Eleazar and Ithamar, "Take the grain offering left over from the food offerings prepared without yeast and presented to the LORD and eat it beside the altar, for it is most holy. ¹³Eat it in the sanctuary area, because it is your share and your sons' share of the food offerings presented to the LORD; for so I have been commanded. ¹⁴But you and your sons and your daughters may eat the breast that was waved and the thigh that was presented. Eat them in a ceremonially clean place; they have been given to you and your children as your share of the Israelites' fellowship offerings. ¹⁵The thigh that was presented and the breast that was waved must be brought with the fat portions of the food offerings, to be waved before the LORD as a wave offering. This will be the perpetual share for you and your children, as the LORD has commanded."

¹⁶When Moses inquired about the goat of the sin offering*a* and found that it had been burned up, he was angry with Eleazar and Ithamar, Aaron's remaining sons, and asked, ¹⁷"Why didn't you eat the sin offering in the sanctuary area? It is most holy; it was given to you to take away the guilt of the community by making atonement for them before the LORD. ¹⁸Since its blood was not taken into the Holy Place, you should have eaten the goat in the sanctuary area, as I commanded."

¹⁹Aaron replied to Moses, "Today they sacrificed their sin offering and their burnt offering before the LORD, but such things as this have happened to me. Would the LORD have been pleased if I had eaten the sin offering today?" ²⁰When Moses heard this, he was satisfied.

Clean and Unclean Food

11 The LORD said to Moses and Aaron, ²"Say to the Israelites: 'Of all the animals that live on land, these are the ones you may eat: ³You may eat any animal that has a divided hoof and that chews the cud.

⁴"'There are some that only chew the cud or only have a divided hoof, but you must not eat them. The camel, though it chews the cud, does not have a divided hoof; it is ceremonially unclean for you. ⁵The hyrax, though it chews the cud, does not have a divided hoof; it is unclean for you. ⁶The rabbit, though it chews the cud, does not have a divided hoof; it is unclean for you. ⁷And the pig, though it has a divided hoof, does not chew the cud; it is unclean for you. ⁸You must not eat their meat or touch their carcasses; they are unclean for you.

⁹"'Of all the creatures living in the water of the seas and the streams you may eat any that have fins and scales. ¹⁰But all creatures in the seas or streams that do not have fins and scales — whether among all the swarming things or among all the other living creatures in the water — you are to regard as unclean. ¹¹And since you are to regard them as unclean, you must not eat their meat; you must regard their carcasses as unclean. ¹²Anything living in the water that does not have fins and scales is to be regarded as unclean by you.

¹³"'These are the birds you are to regard as unclean and not eat because they are unclean: the eagle,*b* the vulture, the black vulture, ¹⁴the red kite, any kind of black kite, ¹⁵any kind of raven, ¹⁶the horned owl, the screech owl, the gull, any kind of hawk, ¹⁷the little owl, the cormorant, the great owl, ¹⁸the white owl, the desert owl, the osprey, ¹⁹the stork, any kind of heron, the hoopoe and the bat.

²⁰"'All flying insects that walk on all fours are to be regarded as unclean by you. ²¹There are, however, some flying insects

---

a 16 Or *purification offering*; also in verses 17 and 19 and animals in this chapter is uncertain.   *b 13* The precise identification of some of the birds, insects that walk on all fours that you may eat: those that have jointed legs for hopping on the ground. ²²Of these you may eat any kind of locust, katydid, cricket or grasshopper. ²³But all other flying insects that have four legs you are to regard as unclean.

²⁴"'You will make yourselves unclean by these; whoever touches their carcasses will be unclean till evening. ²⁵Whoever picks up one of their carcasses must wash their clothes, and they will be unclean till evening.

²⁶"'Every animal that does not have a divided hoof or that does not chew the cud is unclean for you; whoever touches the carcass of any of them will be unclean. ²⁷Of all the animals that walk on all fours, those that walk on their paws are unclean for you; whoever touches their carcasses will be unclean till evening. ²⁸Anyone who picks up their carcasses must wash their clothes, and they will be unclean till evening. These animals are unclean for you.

²⁹"'Of the animals that move along the ground, these are unclean for you: the weasel, the rat, any kind of great lizard, ³⁰the gecko, the monitor lizard, the wall lizard, the skink and the chameleon. ³¹Of all those that move along the ground, these are unclean for you. Whoever touches them when they are dead will be unclean till evening. ³²When one of them dies and falls on something, that article, whatever its use, will be unclean, whether it is made of wood, cloth, hide or sackcloth. Put it in water; it will be unclean till evening, and then it will be clean. ³³If one of them falls into a clay pot, everything in it will be unclean, and you must break the pot. ³⁴Any food you are allowed to eat that has come into contact with water from any such pot is unclean, and any liquid that is drunk from such a pot is unclean. ³⁵Anything that one of their carcasses falls on becomes unclean; an oven or cooking pot must be broken up. They are unclean, and you are to regard them as unclean. ³⁶A spring, however, or a cistern for collecting water remains clean, but anyone who touches one of these carcasses is unclean. ³⁷If a carcass falls on any seeds that are to be planted, they remain clean. ³⁸But if water has been put on the seed and a carcass falls on it, it is unclean for you.

³⁹"'If an animal that you are allowed to eat dies, anyone who touches its carcass will be unclean till evening. ⁴⁰Anyone who eats some of its carcass must wash their clothes, and they will be unclean till evening. Anyone who picks up the carcass must wash their clothes, and they will be unclean till evening.

⁴¹"'Every creature that moves along the ground is to be regarded as unclean; it is not to be eaten. ⁴²You are not to eat any creature that moves along the ground, whether it moves on its belly or walks on all fours or on many feet; it is unclean. ⁴³Do not defile yourselves by any of these creatures. Do not make yourselves unclean by means of them or be made unclean by them. ⁴⁴I am the LORD your God; consecrate yourselves and be holy, because I am holy. Do not make yourselves unclean by any creature that moves along the ground. ⁴⁵I am the LORD, who brought you up out of Egypt to be your God; therefore be holy, because I am holy.

⁴⁶"'These are the regulations concerning animals, birds, every living thing that moves about in the water and every creature that moves along the ground. ⁴⁷You must distinguish between the unclean and the clean, between living creatures that may be eaten and those that may not be eaten.'"

Purification After Childbirth

12 The LORD said to Moses, ²"Say to the Israelites: 'A woman who becomes pregnant and gives birth to a son will be ceremonially unclean for seven days, just as she is unclean during her monthly period. ³On the eighth day the boy is to be circumcised. ⁴Then the woman must wait thirty-three days to be purified from her bleeding. She must not touch anything sacred or go to the sanctuary until the days of her purification are over. ⁵If she gives birth to a daughter, for two weeks the woman will be unclean, as during her period. Then she must wait sixty-six days to be purified from her bleeding.

⁶"'When the days of her purification for a son or daughter are over, she is to bring to the priest at the entrance to the tent of meeting a year-old lamb for a burnt offering and a young pigeon or a dove for a sin offering.ᵃ ⁷He shall offer them before the LORD to make atonement for her, and then she will be ceremonially clean from her flow of blood.

"'These are the regulations for the woman who gives birth to a boy or a girl. ⁸But if she cannot afford a lamb, she is to bring two doves or two young pigeons, one for a burnt offering and the other for a sin offering. In this way the priest will make atonement for her, and she will be clean.'"

Regulations About Defiling Skin Diseases

13 The LORD said to Moses and Aaron, ²"When anyone has a swelling or a rash or a shiny spot on their skin that may be a defiling skin disease,ᵇ they must be brought to Aaron the priest or to one of his sonsᶜ who is a priest. ³The priest is to examine the sore on the skin, and if the hair in the sore has turned white and the sore appears to be more than skin deep, it is a defiling skin disease. When the priest examines that person, he shall pronounce them ceremonially unclean. ⁴If the shiny spot on the skin is white but does not appear to be more than skin deep and the hair in it has not turned white, the priest is to isolate the affected person for seven days. ⁵On the seventh day the priest is to examine them, and if he sees that the sore is unchanged and has not spread in the skin, he is to isolate them for another seven days. ⁶On the seventh day the priest is to examine them

again, and if the sore has faded and has not spread in the skin, the priest shall pronounce them clean; it is only a rash. They must wash their clothes, and they will be clean. ⁷But if the rash does spread in their skin after they have shown themselves to the priest to be pronounced clean, they must appear before the priest again. ⁸The priest is to examine that person, and if the rash has spread in the skin, he shall pronounce them unclean; it is a defiling skin disease.

⁹"When anyone has a defiling skin disease, they must be brought to the priest. ¹⁰The priest is to examine them, and if there is a white swelling in the skin that has turned the hair white and if there is raw flesh in the swelling, ¹¹it is a chronic skin disease and the priest shall pronounce them unclean. He is not to isolate them, because they are already unclean.

¹²"If the disease breaks out all over their skin and, so far as the priest can see, it covers all the skin of the affected person from head to foot, ¹³the priest is to examine them, and if the disease has covered their whole body, he shall pronounce them clean. Since it has all turned white, they are clean. ¹⁴But whenever raw flesh appears on them, they will be unclean. ¹⁵When the priest sees the raw flesh, he shall pronounce them unclean. The raw flesh is unclean; they have a defiling disease. ¹⁶If the raw flesh changes and turns white, they must go to the priest. ¹⁷The priest is to examine them, and if the sores have turned white, the priest shall pronounce the affected person clean; then they will be clean.

¹⁸"When someone has a boil on their skin and it heals, ¹⁹and in the place where the boil was, a white swelling or reddish-white spot appears, they must present themselves to the priest. ²⁰The priest is to examine it, and if it appears to be more than skin deep and the hair in it has turned

---

ᵃ 6 Or *purification offering*; also in verse 8   ᵇ 2 The Hebrew word for *defiling skin disease*, traditionally translated "leprosy," was used for various diseases affecting the skin; here and throughout verses 3-46.   ᶜ 2 Or *descendants* white, the priest shall pronounce that person unclean. It is a defiling skin disease that has broken out where the boil was. [21]But if, when the priest examines it, there is no white hair in it and it is not more than skin deep and has faded, then the priest is to isolate them for seven days. [22]If it is spreading in the skin, the priest shall pronounce them unclean; it is a defiling disease. [23]But if the spot is unchanged and has not spread, it is only a scar from the boil, and the priest shall pronounce them clean.

[24]"When someone has a burn on their skin and a reddish-white or white spot appears in the raw flesh of the burn, [25]the priest is to examine the spot, and if the hair in it has turned white, and it appears to be more than skin deep, it is a defiling disease that has broken out in the burn. The priest shall pronounce them unclean; it is a defiling skin disease. [26]But if the priest examines it and there is no white hair in the spot and if it is not more than skin deep and has faded, then the priest is to isolate them for seven days. [27]On the seventh day the priest is to examine that person, and if it is spreading in the skin, the priest shall pronounce them unclean; it is a defiling skin disease. [28]If, however, the spot is unchanged and has not spread in the skin but has faded, it is a swelling from the burn, and the priest shall pronounce them clean; it is only a scar from the burn.

[29]"If a man or woman has a sore on their head or chin, [30]the priest is to examine the sore, and if it appears to be more than skin deep and the hair in it is yellow and thin, the priest shall pronounce them unclean; it is a defiling skin disease on the head or chin. [31]But if, when the priest examines the sore, it does not seem to be more than skin deep and there is no black hair in it, then the priest is to isolate the affected person for seven days. [32]On the seventh day the priest is to examine the sore, and if it has not spread and there is no yellow hair in it and it does not appear to be more than

skin deep, [33]then the man or woman must shave themselves, except for the affected area, and the priest is to keep them isolated another seven days. [34]On the seventh day the priest is to examine the sore, and if it has not spread in the skin and appears to be no more than skin deep, the priest shall pronounce them clean. They must wash their clothes, and they will be clean. [35]But if the sore does spread in the skin after they are pronounced clean, [36]the priest is to examine them, and if he finds that the sore has spread in the skin, he does not need to look for yellow hair; they are unclean. [37]If, however, the sore is unchanged so far as the priest can see, and if black hair has grown in it, the affected person is healed. They are clean, and the priest shall pronounce them clean.

[38]"When a man or woman has white spots on the skin, [39]the priest is to examine them, and if the spots are dull white, it is a harmless rash that has broken out on the skin; they are clean.

[40]"A man who has lost his hair and is bald is clean. [41]If he has lost his hair from the front of his scalp and has a bald forehead, he is clean. [42]But if he has a reddish-white sore on his bald head or forehead, it is a defiling disease breaking out on his head or forehead. [43]The priest is to examine him, and if the swollen sore on his head or forehead is reddish-white like a defiling skin disease, [44]the man is diseased and is unclean. The priest shall pronounce him unclean because of the sore on his head.

[45]"Anyone with such a defiling disease must wear torn clothes, let their hair be unkempt,[a] cover the lower part of their face and cry out, 'Unclean! Unclean!' [46]As long as they have the disease they remain unclean. They must live alone; they must live outside the camp.

Regulations About Defiling Molds

[47]"As for any fabric that is spoiled with a defiling mold — any woolen or linen

---

[a] 45 Or clothes, uncover their head

clothing, 48any woven or knitted material of linen or wool, any leather or anything made of leather — 49if the affected area in the fabric, the leather, the woven or knitted material, or any leather article, is greenish or reddish, it is a defiling mold and must be shown to the priest. 50The priest is to examine the affected area and isolate the article for seven days. 51On the seventh day he is to examine it, and if the mold has spread in the fabric, the woven or knitted material, or the leather, whatever its use, it is a persistent defiling mold; the article is unclean. 52He must burn the fabric, the woven or knitted material of wool or linen, or any leather article that has been spoiled; because the defiling mold is persistent, the article must be burned.

53"But if, when the priest examines it, the mold has not spread in the fabric, the woven or knitted material, or the leather article, 54he shall order that the spoiled article be washed. Then he is to isolate it for another seven days. 55After the article has been washed, the priest is to examine it again, and if the mold has not changed its appearance, even though it has not spread, it is unclean. Burn it, no matter which side of the fabric has been spoiled. 56If, when the priest examines it, the mold has faded after the article has been washed, he is to tear the spoiled part out of the fabric, the leather, or the woven or knitted material. 57But if it reappears in the fabric, in the woven or knitted material, or in the leather article, it is a spreading mold; whatever has the mold must be burned. 58Any fabric, woven or knitted material, or any leather article that has been washed and is rid of the mold, must be washed again. Then it will be clean."

59These are the regulations concerning defiling molds in woolen or linen clothing, woven or knitted material, or any leather article, for pronouncing them clean or unclean.

Cleansing From Defiling Skin Diseases

14 The LORD said to Moses, 2"These are the regulations for any diseased person at the time of their ceremonial cleansing, when they are brought to the priest: 3The priest is to go outside the camp and examine them. If they have been healed of their defiling skin disease,*a* 4the priest shall order that two live clean birds and some cedar wood, scarlet yarn and hyssop be brought for the person to be cleansed. 5Then the priest shall order that one of the birds be killed over fresh water in a clay pot. 6He is then to take the live bird and dip it, together with the cedar wood, the scarlet yarn and the hyssop, into the blood of the bird that was killed over the fresh water. 7Seven times he shall sprinkle the one to be cleansed of the defiling disease, and then pronounce them clean. After that, he is to release the live bird in the open fields.

8"The person to be cleansed must wash their clothes, shave off all their hair and bathe with water; then they will be ceremonially clean. After this they may come into the camp, but they must stay outside their tent for seven days. 9On the seventh day they must shave off all their hair; they must shave their head, their beard, their eyebrows and the rest of their hair. They must wash their clothes and bathe themselves with water, and they will be clean.

10"On the eighth day they must bring two male lambs and one ewe lamb a year old, each without defect, along with three-tenths of an ephah*b* of the finest flour mixed with olive oil for a grain offering, and one log*c* of oil. 11The priest who pronounces them clean shall present both the one to be cleansed and their offerings before the LORD at the entrance to the tent of meeting.

12"Then the priest is to take one of the male lambs and offer it as a guilt offering,

---

a 3 The Hebrew word for *defiling skin disease*, traditionally translated "leprosy," was used for various diseases affecting the skin; also in verses 7, 32, 54 and 57.   *b 10* That is, probably about 11 pounds or about 5 kilograms
c 10 That is, about 1/3 quart or about 0.3 liter; also in verses 12, 15, 21 and 24

along with the log of oil; he shall wave them before the LORD as a wave offering. ¹³He is to slaughter the lamb in the sanctuary area where the sin offering*a* and the burnt offering are slaughtered. Like the sin offering, the guilt offering belongs to the priest; it is most holy. ¹⁴The priest is to take some of the blood of the guilt offering and put it on the lobe of the right ear of the one to be cleansed, on the thumb of their right hand and on the big toe of their right foot. ¹⁵The priest shall then take some of the log of oil, pour it in the palm of his own left hand, ¹⁶dip his right forefinger into the oil in his palm, and with his finger sprinkle some of it before the LORD seven times. ¹⁷The priest is to put some of the oil remaining in his palm on the lobe of the right ear of the one to be cleansed, on the thumb of their right hand and on the big toe of their right foot, on top of the blood of the guilt offering. ¹⁸The rest of the oil in his palm the priest shall put on the head of the one to be cleansed and make atonement for them before the LORD.

¹⁹"Then the priest is to sacrifice the sin offering and make atonement for the one to be cleansed from their uncleanness. After that, the priest shall slaughter the burnt offering ²⁰and offer it on the altar, together with the grain offering, and make atonement for them, and they will be clean.

²¹"If, however, they are poor and cannot afford these, they must take one male lamb as a guilt offering to be waved to make atonement for them, together with a tenth of an ephah*b* of the finest flour mixed with olive oil for a grain offering, a log of oil, ²²and two doves or two young pigeons, such as they can afford, one for a sin offering and the other for a burnt offering.

²³"On the eighth day they must bring them for their cleansing to the priest at the entrance to the tent of meeting, before the LORD. ²⁴The priest is to take the lamb for the guilt offering, together with

the log of oil, and wave them before the LORD as a wave offering. ²⁵He shall slaughter the lamb for the guilt offering and take some of its blood and put it on the lobe of the right ear of the one to be cleansed, on the thumb of their right hand and on the big toe of their right foot. ²⁶The priest is to pour some of the oil into the palm of his own left hand, ²⁷and with his right forefinger sprinkle some of the oil from his palm seven times before the LORD. ²⁸Some of the oil in his palm he is to put on the same places he put the blood of the guilt offering — on the lobe of the right ear of the one to be cleansed, on the thumb of their right hand and on the big toe of their right foot. ²⁹The rest of the oil in his palm the priest shall put on the head of the one to be cleansed, to make atonement for them before the LORD. ³⁰Then he shall sacrifice the doves or the young pigeons, such as the person can afford, ³¹one as a sin offering and the other as a burnt offering, together with the grain offering. In this way the priest will make atonement before the LORD on behalf of the one to be cleansed."

³²These are the regulations for anyone who has a defiling skin disease and who cannot afford the regular offerings for their cleansing.

Cleansing From Defiling Molds

³³The LORD said to Moses and Aaron, ³⁴"When you enter the land of Canaan, which I am giving you as your possession, and I put a spreading mold in a house in that land, ³⁵the owner of the house must go and tell the priest, 'I have seen something that looks like a defiling mold in my house.' ³⁶The priest is to order the house to be emptied before he goes in to examine the mold, so that nothing in the house will be pronounced unclean. After this the priest is to go in and inspect the house. ³⁷He is to examine the mold on the walls, and if it has greenish or reddish depressions that

---

a 13 Or *purification offering*; also in verses 19, 22 and 31 kilograms

b 21 That is, probably about 3 1/2 pounds or about 1.6

appear to be deeper than the surface of the wall, 38the priest shall go out the doorway of the house and close it up for seven days. 39On the seventh day the priest shall return to inspect the house. If the mold has spread on the walls, 40he is to order that the contaminated stones be torn out and thrown into an unclean place outside the town. 41He must have all the inside walls of the house scraped and the material that is scraped off dumped into an unclean place outside the town. 42Then they are to take other stones to replace these and take new clay and plaster the house.

43"If the defiling mold reappears in the house after the stones have been torn out and the house scraped and plastered, 44the priest is to go and examine it and, if the mold has spread in the house, it is a persistent defiling mold; the house is unclean. 45It must be torn down — its stones, timbers and all the plaster — and taken out of the town to an unclean place.

46"Anyone who goes into the house while it is closed up will be unclean till evening. 47Anyone who sleeps or eats in the house must wash their clothes.

48"But if the priest comes to examine it and the mold has not spread after the house has been plastered, he shall pronounce the house clean, because the defiling mold is gone. 49To purify the house he is to take two birds and some cedar wood, scarlet yarn and hyssop. 50He shall kill one of the birds over fresh water in a clay pot. 51Then he is to take the cedar wood, the hyssop, the scarlet yarn and the live bird, dip them into the blood of the dead bird and the fresh water, and sprinkle the house seven times. 52He shall purify the house with the bird's blood, the fresh water, the live bird, the cedar wood, the hyssop and the scarlet yarn. 53Then he is to release the live bird in the open fields outside the town. In this way he will make atonement for the house, and it will be clean."

54These are the regulations for any defiling skin disease, for a sore, 55for defiling molds in fabric or in a house, 56and for a swelling, a rash or a shiny spot, 57to determine when something is clean or unclean.

These are the regulations for defiling skin diseases and defiling molds.

Discharges Causing Uncleanness

15 The LORD said to Moses and Aaron, 2"Speak to the Israelites and say to them: 'When any man has an unusual bodily discharge, such a discharge is unclean. 3Whether it continues flowing from his body or is blocked, it will make him unclean. This is how his discharge will bring about uncleanness:

4"'Any bed the man with a discharge lies on will be unclean, and anything he sits on will be unclean. 5Anyone who touches his bed must wash their clothes and bathe with water, and they will be unclean till evening. 6Whoever sits on anything that the man with a discharge sat on must wash their clothes and bathe with water, and they will be unclean till evening.

7"'Whoever touches the man who has a discharge must wash their clothes and bathe with water, and they will be unclean till evening.

8"'If the man with the discharge spits on anyone who is clean, they must wash their clothes and bathe with water, and they will be unclean till evening.

9"'Everything the man sits on when riding will be unclean, 10and whoever touches any of the things that were under him will be unclean till evening; whoever picks up those things must wash their clothes and bathe with water, and they will be unclean till evening.

11"'Anyone the man with a discharge touches without rinsing his hands with water must wash their clothes and bathe with water, and they will be unclean till evening.

12"'A clay pot that the man touches must be broken, and any wooden article is to be rinsed with water.

13"'When a man is cleansed from his discharge, he is to count off seven days for his ceremonial cleansing; he must wash his clothes and bathe himself with fresh water, and he will be clean. [14]On the eighth day he must take two doves or two young pigeons and come before the LORD to the entrance to the tent of meeting and give them to the priest. [15]The priest is to sacrifice them, the one for a sin offering[a] and the other for a burnt offering. In this way he will make atonement before the LORD for the man because of his discharge.

[16]"'When a man has an emission of semen, he must bathe his whole body with water, and he will be unclean till evening. [17]Any clothing or leather that has semen on it must be washed with water, and it will be unclean till evening. [18]When a man has sexual relations with a woman and there is an emission of semen, both of them must bathe with water, and they will be unclean till evening.

[19]"'When a woman has her regular flow of blood, the impurity of her monthly period will last seven days, and anyone who touches her will be unclean till evening.

[20]"'Anything she lies on during her period will be unclean, and anything she sits on will be unclean. [21]Anyone who touches her bed will be unclean; they must wash their clothes and bathe with water, and they will be unclean till evening. [22]Anyone who touches anything she sits on will be unclean; they must wash their clothes and bathe with water, and they will be unclean till evening. [23]Whether it is the bed or anything she was sitting on, when anyone touches it, they will be unclean till evening.

[24]"'If a man has sexual relations with her and her monthly flow touches him, he will be unclean for seven days; any bed he lies on will be unclean.

[25]"'When a woman has a discharge of blood for many days at a time other than her monthly period or has a discharge that continues beyond her period, she will be unclean as long as she has the discharge, just as in the days of her period. [26]Any bed she lies on while her discharge continues will be unclean, as is her bed during her monthly period, and anything she sits on will be unclean, as during her period. [27]Anyone who touches them will be unclean; they must wash their clothes and bathe with water, and they will be unclean till evening.

[28]"'When she is cleansed from her discharge, she must count off seven days, and after that she will be ceremonially clean. [29]On the eighth day she must take two doves or two young pigeons and bring them to the priest at the entrance to the tent of meeting. [30]The priest is to sacrifice one for a sin offering and the other for a burnt offering. In this way he will make atonement for her before the LORD for the uncleanness of her discharge.

[31]"'You must keep the Israelites separate from things that make them unclean, so they will not die in their uncleanness for defiling my dwelling place,[b] which is among them.'"

[32]These are the regulations for a man with a discharge, for anyone made unclean by an emission of semen, [33]for a woman in her monthly period, for a man or a woman with a discharge, and for a man who has sexual relations with a woman who is ceremonially unclean.

The Day of Atonement

16 The LORD spoke to Moses after the death of the two sons of Aaron who died when they approached the LORD. [2]The LORD said to Moses: "Tell your brother Aaron that he is not to come whenever he chooses into the Most Holy Place behind the curtain in front of the atonement cover on the ark, or else he will die. For I will appear in the cloud over the atonement cover.

[3]"This is how Aaron is to enter the Most Holy Place: He must first bring a young bull for a sin offering[c] and a ram for a burnt offering. [4]He is to put on the sacred linen

---

tunic, with linen undergarments next to his body; he is to tie the linen sash around him and put on the linen turban. These are sacred garments; so he must bathe himself with water before he puts them on. ⁵From the Israelite community he is to take two male goats for a sin offering and a ram for a burnt offering.

⁶"Aaron is to offer the bull for his own sin offering to make atonement for himself and his household. ⁷Then he is to take the two goats and present them before the LORD at the entrance to the tent of meeting. ⁸He is to cast lots for the two goats — one lot for the LORD and the other for the scapegoat.ᵃ ⁹Aaron shall bring the goat whose lot falls to the LORD and sacrifice it for a sin offering. ¹⁰But the goat chosen by lot as the scapegoat shall be presented alive before the LORD to be used for making atonement by sending it into the wilderness as a scapegoat.

¹¹"Aaron shall bring the bull for his own sin offering to make atonement for himself and his household, and he is to slaughter the bull for his own sin offering. ¹²He is to take a censer full of burning coals from the altar before the LORD and two handfuls of finely ground fragrant incense and take them behind the curtain. ¹³He is to put the incense on the fire before the LORD, and the smoke of the incense will conceal the atonement cover above the tablets of the covenant law, so that he will not die. ¹⁴He is to take some of the bull's blood and with his finger sprinkle it on the front of the atonement cover; then he shall sprinkle some of it with his finger seven times before the atonement cover.

¹⁵"He shall then slaughter the goat for the sin offering for the people and take its blood behind the curtain and do with it as he did with the bull's blood: He shall sprinkle it on the atonement cover and in front of it. ¹⁶In this way he will make atonement for the Most Holy Place because of the uncleanness and rebellion of the Israelites,

whatever their sins have been. He is to do the same for the tent of meeting, which is among them in the midst of their uncleanness. ¹⁷No one is to be in the tent of meeting from the time Aaron goes in to make atonement in the Most Holy Place until he comes out, having made atonement for himself, his household and the whole community of Israel.

¹⁸"Then he shall come out to the altar that is before the LORD and make atonement for it. He shall take some of the bull's blood and some of the goat's blood and put it on all the horns of the altar. ¹⁹He shall sprinkle some of the blood on it with his finger seven times to cleanse it and to consecrate it from the uncleanness of the Israelites.

²⁰"When Aaron has finished making atonement for the Most Holy Place, the tent of meeting and the altar, he shall bring forward the live goat. ²¹He is to lay both hands on the head of the live goat and confess over it all the wickedness and rebellion of the Israelites — all their sins — and put them on the goat's head. He shall send the goat away into the wilderness in the care of someone appointed for the task. ²²The goat will carry on itself all their sins to a remote place; and the man shall release it in the wilderness.

²³"Then Aaron is to go into the tent of meeting and take off the linen garments he put on before he entered the Most Holy Place, and he is to leave them there. ²⁴He shall bathe himself with water in the sanctuary area and put on his regular garments. Then he shall come out and sacrifice the burnt offering for himself and the burnt offering for the people, to make atonement for himself and for the people. ²⁵He shall also burn the fat of the sin offering on the altar.

²⁶"The man who releases the goat as a scapegoat must wash his clothes and bathe himself with water; afterward he may come into the camp. ²⁷The bull and the goat for

---

ᵃ 8 The meaning of the Hebrew for this word is uncertain; also in verses 10 and 26.

the sin offerings, whose blood was brought into the Most Holy Place to make atonement, must be taken outside the camp; their hides, flesh and intestines are to be burned up. 28The man who burns them must wash his clothes and bathe himself with water; afterward he may come into the camp.

29"This is to be a lasting ordinance for you: On the tenth day of the seventh month you must deny yourselves[a] and not do any work — whether native-born or a foreigner residing among you — 30because on this day atonement will be made for you, to cleanse you. Then, before the LORD, you will be clean from all your sins. 31It is a day of sabbath rest, and you must deny yourselves; it is a lasting ordinance. 32The priest who is anointed and ordained to succeed his father as high priest is to make atonement. He is to put on the sacred linen garments 33and make atonement for the Most Holy Place, for the tent of meeting and the altar, and for the priests and all the members of the community.

34"This is to be a lasting ordinance for you: Atonement is to be made once a year for all the sins of the Israelites.' "

And it was done, as the LORD commanded Moses.

Eating Blood Forbidden

17 The LORD said to Moses, 2"Speak to Aaron and his sons and to all the Israelites and say to them: 'This is what the LORD has commanded: 3Any Israelite who sacrifices an ox,[b] a lamb or a goat in the camp or outside of it 4instead of bringing it to the entrance to the tent of meeting to present it as an offering to the LORD in front of the tabernacle of the LORD — that person shall be considered guilty of bloodshed; they have shed blood and must be cut off from their people. 5This is so the Israelites will bring to the LORD the sacrifices they are now making in the open fields. They must bring them to the priest, that is, to the LORD, at the entrance to the tent of meeting and sacrifice them as fellowship offerings. 6The priest is to splash the blood against the altar of the LORD at the entrance to the tent of meeting and burn the fat as an aroma pleasing to the LORD. 7They must no longer offer any of their sacrifices to the goat idols[c] to whom they prostitute themselves. This is to be a lasting ordinance for them and for the generations to come.'

8"Say to them: 'Any Israelite or any foreigner residing among them who offers a burnt offering or sacrifice 9and does not bring it to the entrance to the tent of meeting to sacrifice it to the LORD must be cut off from the people of Israel.

10"'I will set my face against any Israelite or any foreigner residing among them who eats blood, and I will cut them off from the people. 11For the life of a creature is in the blood, and I have given it to you to make atonement for yourselves on the altar; it is the blood that makes atonement for one's life.[d] 12Therefore I say to the Israelites, "None of you may eat blood, nor may any foreigner residing among you eat blood."

13"'Any Israelite or any foreigner residing among you who hunts any animal or bird that may be eaten must drain out the blood and cover it with earth, 14because the life of every creature is its blood. That is why I have said to the Israelites, "You must not eat the blood of any creature, because the life of every creature is its blood; anyone who eats it must be cut off."

15"'Anyone, whether native-born or foreigner, who eats anything found dead or torn by wild animals must wash their clothes and bathe with water, and they will be ceremonially unclean till evening; then they will be clean. 16But if they do not wash their clothes and bathe themselves, they will be held responsible.' "

---

a 29 Or *must fast*; also in verse 31   *b 3* The Hebrew word can refer to either male or female.   *c 7* Or *the demons*   *d 11* Or *atonement by the life in the blood*

Unlawful Sexual Relations

18 The Lord said to Moses, ²"Speak to the Israelites and say to them: 'I am the Lord your God. ³You must not do as they do in Egypt, where you used to live, and you must not do as they do in the land of Canaan, where I am bringing you. Do not follow their practices. ⁴You must obey my laws and be careful to follow my decrees. I am the Lord your God. ⁵Keep my decrees and laws, for the person who obeys them will live by them. I am the Lord.

⁶"'No one is to approach any close relative to have sexual relations. I am the Lord.

⁷"'Do not dishonor your father by having sexual relations with your mother. She is your mother; do not have relations with her.

⁸"'Do not have sexual relations with your father's wife; that would dishonor your father.

⁹"'Do not have sexual relations with your sister, either your father's daughter or your mother's daughter, whether she was born in the same home or elsewhere.

¹⁰"'Do not have sexual relations with your son's daughter or your daughter's daughter; that would dishonor you.

¹¹"'Do not have sexual relations with the daughter of your father's wife, born to your father; she is your sister.

¹²"'Do not have sexual relations with your father's sister; she is your father's close relative.

¹³"'Do not have sexual relations with your mother's sister, because she is your mother's close relative.

¹⁴"'Do not dishonor your father's brother by approaching his wife to have sexual relations; she is your aunt.

¹⁵"'Do not have sexual relations with your daughter-in-law. She is your son's wife; do not have relations with her.

¹⁶"'Do not have sexual relations with your brother's wife; that would dishonor your brother.

¹⁷"'Do not have sexual relations with both a woman and her daughter. Do not have sexual relations with either her son's daughter or her daughter's daughter; they are her close relatives. That is wickedness.

¹⁸"'Do not take your wife's sister as a rival wife and have sexual relations with her while your wife is living.

¹⁹"'Do not approach a woman to have sexual relations during the uncleanness of her monthly period.

²⁰"'Do not have sexual relations with your neighbor's wife and defile yourself with her.

²¹"'Do not give any of your children to be sacrificed to Molek, for you must not profane the name of your God. I am the Lord.

²²"'Do not have sexual relations with a man as one does with a woman; that is detestable.

²³"'Do not have sexual relations with an animal and defile yourself with it. A woman must not present herself to an animal to have sexual relations with it; that is a perversion.

²⁴"'Do not defile yourselves in any of these ways, because this is how the nations that I am going to drive out before you became defiled. ²⁵Even the land was defiled; so I punished it for its sin, and the land vomited out its inhabitants. ²⁶But you must keep my decrees and my laws. The native-born and the foreigners residing among you must not do any of these detestable things, ²⁷for all these things were done by the people who lived in the land before you, and the land became defiled. ²⁸And if you defile the land, it will vomit you out as it vomited out the nations that were before you.

²⁹"'Everyone who does any of these detestable things—such persons must be cut off from their people. ³⁰Keep my requirements and do not follow any of the detestable customs that were practiced before you came and do not defile yourselves with them. I am the Lord your God.'"

Various Laws

19 The Lord said to Moses, ²"Speak to the entire assembly of Israel and say to them: 'Be holy because I, the Lord your God, am holy.

³"'Each of you must respect your mother and father, and you must observe my Sabbaths. I am the LORD your God.

⁴"'Do not turn to idols or make metal gods for yourselves. I am the LORD your God.

⁵"'When you sacrifice a fellowship offering to the LORD, sacrifice it in such a way that it will be accepted on your behalf. ⁶It shall be eaten on the day you sacrifice it or on the next day; anything left over until the third day must be burned up. ⁷If any of it is eaten on the third day, it is impure and will not be accepted. ⁸Whoever eats it will be held responsible because they have desecrated what is holy to the LORD; they must be cut off from their people.

⁹"'When you reap the harvest of your land, do not reap to the very edges of your field or gather the gleanings of your harvest. ¹⁰Do not go over your vineyard a second time or pick up the grapes that have fallen. Leave them for the poor and the foreigner. I am the LORD your God.

¹¹"'Do not steal.

"'Do not lie.

"'Do not deceive one another.

¹²"'Do not swear falsely by my name and so profane the name of your God. I am the LORD.

¹³"'Do not defraud or rob your neighbor.

"'Do not hold back the wages of a hired worker overnight.

¹⁴"'Do not curse the deaf or put a stumbling block in front of the blind, but fear your God. I am the LORD.

¹⁵"'Do not pervert justice; do not show partiality to the poor or favoritism to the great, but judge your neighbor fairly.

¹⁶"'Do not go about spreading slander among your people.

"'Do not do anything that endangers your neighbor's life. I am the LORD.

¹⁷"'Do not hate a fellow Israelite in your heart. Rebuke your neighbor frankly so you will not share in their guilt.

¹⁸"'Do not seek revenge or bear a grudge against anyone among your people, but love your neighbor as yourself. I am the LORD.

¹⁹"'Keep my decrees.

"'Do not mate different kinds of animals.

"'Do not plant your field with two kinds of seed.

"'Do not wear clothing woven of two kinds of material.

²⁰"'If a man sleeps with a female slave who is promised to another man but who has not been ransomed or given her freedom, there must be due punishment.ᵃ Yet they are not to be put to death, because she had not been freed. ²¹The man, however, must bring a ram to the entrance to the tent of meeting for a guilt offering to the LORD. ²²With the ram of the guilt offering the priest is to make atonement for him before the LORD for the sin he has committed, and his sin will be forgiven.

²³"'When you enter the land and plant any kind of fruit tree, regard its fruit as forbidden.ᵇ For three years you are to consider it forbiddenᵇ; it must not be eaten. ²⁴In the fourth year all its fruit will be holy, an offering of praise to the LORD. ²⁵But in the fifth year you may eat its fruit. In this way your harvest will be increased. I am the LORD your God.

²⁶"'Do not eat any meat with the blood still in it.

"'Do not practice divination or seek omens.

²⁷"'Do not cut the hair at the sides of your head or clip off the edges of your beard.

²⁸"'Do not cut your bodies for the dead or put tattoo marks on yourselves. I am the LORD.

²⁹"'Do not degrade your daughter by making her a prostitute, or the land will turn to prostitution and be filled with wickedness.

³⁰"'Observe my Sabbaths and have reverence for my sanctuary. I am the LORD.

³¹"'Do not turn to mediums or seek out

ᵃ 20 Or be an inquiry   ᵇ 23 Hebrew uncircumcised

spiritists, for you will be defiled by them. I am the LORD your God.

32 " 'Stand up in the presence of the aged, show respect for the elderly and revere your God. I am the LORD.

33 " 'When a foreigner resides among you in your land, do not mistreat them. 34 The foreigner residing among you must be treated as your native-born. Love them as yourself, for you were foreigners in Egypt. I am the LORD your God.

35 " 'Do not use dishonest standards when measuring length, weight or quantity. 36 Use honest scales and honest weights, an honest ephah*a* and an honest hin.*b* I am the LORD your God, who brought you out of Egypt.

37 " 'Keep all my decrees and all my laws and follow them. I am the LORD.' "

Punishments for Sin

20 The LORD said to Moses, 2 "Say to the Israelites: 'Any Israelite or any foreigner residing in Israel who sacrifices any of his children to Molek is to be put to death. The members of the community are to stone him. 3 I myself will set my face against him and will cut him off from his people; for by sacrificing his children to Molek, he has defiled my sanctuary and profaned my holy name. 4 If the members of the community close their eyes when that man sacrifices one of his children to Molek and if they fail to put him to death, 5 I myself will set my face against him and his family and will cut them off from their people together with all who follow him in prostituting themselves to Molek.

6 " 'I will set my face against anyone who turns to mediums and spiritists to prostitute themselves by following them, and I will cut them off from their people.

7 " 'Consecrate yourselves and be holy, because I am the LORD your God. 8 Keep my decrees and follow them. I am the LORD, who makes you holy.

9 " 'Anyone who curses their father or mother is to be put to death. Because they have cursed their father or mother, their blood will be on their own head.

10 " 'If a man commits adultery with another man's wife — with the wife of his neighbor — both the adulterer and the adulteress are to be put to death.

11 " 'If a man has sexual relations with his father's wife, he has dishonored his father. Both the man and the woman are to be put to death; their blood will be on their own heads.

12 " 'If a man has sexual relations with his daughter-in-law, both of them are to be put to death. What they have done is a perversion; their blood will be on their own heads.

13 " 'If a man has sexual relations with a man as one does with a woman, both of them have done what is detestable. They are to be put to death; their blood will be on their own heads.

14 " 'If a man marries both a woman and her mother, it is wicked. Both he and they must be burned in the fire, so that no wickedness will be among you.

15 " 'If a man has sexual relations with an animal, he is to be put to death, and you must kill the animal.

16 " 'If a woman approaches an animal to have sexual relations with it, kill both the woman and the animal. They are to be put to death; their blood will be on their own heads.

17 " 'If a man marries his sister, the daughter of either his father or his mother, and they have sexual relations, it is a disgrace. They are to be publicly removed from their people. He has dishonored his sister and will be held responsible.

18 " 'If a man has sexual relations with a woman during her monthly period, he has exposed the source of her flow, and she has also uncovered it. Both of them are to be cut off from their people.

---

a 36 An ephah was a dry measure having the capacity of about 3/5 of a bushel or about 22 liters.   *b 36* A hin was a liquid measure having the capacity of about 1 gallon or about 3.8 liters.

¹⁹"'Do not have sexual relations with the sister of either your mother or your father, for that would dishonor a close relative; both of you would be held responsible.

²⁰"'If a man has sexual relations with his aunt, he has dishonored his uncle. They will be held responsible; they will die childless.

²¹"'If a man marries his brother's wife, it is an act of impurity; he has dishonored his brother. They will be childless.

²²"'Keep all my decrees and laws and follow them, so that the land where I am bringing you to live may not vomit you out. ²³You must not live according to the customs of the nations I am going to drive out before you. Because they did all these things, I abhorred them. ²⁴But I said to you, "You will possess their land; I will give it to you as an inheritance, a land flowing with milk and honey." I am the Lord your God, who has set you apart from the nations.

²⁵"'You must therefore make a distinction between clean and unclean animals and between unclean and clean birds. Do not defile yourselves by any animal or bird or anything that moves along the ground—those that I have set apart as unclean for you. ²⁶You are to be holy to me because I, the Lord, am holy, and I have set you apart from the nations to be my own.

²⁷"'A man or woman who is a medium or spiritist among you must be put to death. You are to stone them; their blood will be on their own heads.'"

Rules for Priests

21 The Lord said to Moses, "Speak to the priests, the sons of Aaron, and say to them: 'A priest must not make himself ceremonially unclean for any of his people who die, ²except for a close relative, such as his mother or father, his son or daughter, his brother, ³or an unmarried sister who is dependent on him since she has no husband—for her he may make himself unclean. ⁴He must not make himself unclean for people related to him by marriage,ᵃ and so defile himself.

⁵"'Priests must not shave their heads or shave off the edges of their beards or cut their bodies. ⁶They must be holy to their God and must not profane the name of their God. Because they present the food offerings to the Lord, the food of their God, they are to be holy.

⁷"'They must not marry women defiled by prostitution or divorced from their husbands, because priests are holy to their God. ⁸Regard them as holy, because they offer up the food of your God. Consider them holy, because I the Lord am holy—I who make you holy.

⁹"'If a priest's daughter defiles herself by becoming a prostitute, she disgraces her father; she must be burned in the fire.

¹⁰"'The high priest, the one among his brothers who has had the anointing oil poured on his head and who has been ordained to wear the priestly garments, must not let his hair become unkemptᵇ or tear his clothes. ¹¹He must not enter a place where there is a dead body. He must not make himself unclean, even for his father or mother, ¹²nor leave the sanctuary of his God or desecrate it, because he has been dedicated by the anointing oil of his God. I am the Lord.

¹³"'The woman he marries must be a virgin. ¹⁴He must not marry a widow, a divorced woman, or a woman defiled by prostitution, but only a virgin from his own people, ¹⁵so that he will not defile his offspring among his people. I am the Lord, who makes him holy.'"

¹⁶The Lord said to Moses, ¹⁷"Say to Aaron: 'For the generations to come none of your descendants who has a defect may come near to offer the food of his God. ¹⁸No man who has any defect may come near: no man who is blind or lame, disfigured or

---

ᵃ 4 Or *unclean as a leader among his people*   ᵇ 10 Or *not uncover his head* deformed; [19]no man with a crippled foot or hand, [20]or who is a hunchback or a dwarf, or who has any eye defect, or who has festering or running sores or damaged testicles. [21]No descendant of Aaron the priest who has any defect is to come near to present the food offerings to the LORD. He has a defect; he must not come near to offer the food of his God. [22]He may eat the most holy food of his God, as well as the holy food; [23]yet because of his defect, he must not go near the curtain or approach the altar, and so desecrate my sanctuary. I am the LORD, who makes them holy.'"

[24]So Moses told this to Aaron and his sons and to all the Israelites.

22 The LORD said to Moses, [2]"Tell Aaron and his sons to treat with respect the sacred offerings the Israelites consecrate to me, so they will not profane my holy name. I am the LORD.

[3]"Say to them: 'For the generations to come, if any of your descendants is ceremonially unclean and yet comes near the sacred offerings that the Israelites consecrate to the LORD, that person must be cut off from my presence. I am the LORD.

[4]"If a descendant of Aaron has a defiling skin disease[a] or a bodily discharge, he may not eat the sacred offerings until he is cleansed. He will also be unclean if he touches something defiled by a corpse or by anyone who has an emission of semen, [5]or if he touches any crawling thing that makes him unclean, or any person who makes him unclean, whatever the uncleanness may be. [6]The one who touches any such thing will be unclean till evening. He must not eat any of the sacred offerings unless he has bathed himself with water. [7]When the sun goes down, he will be clean, and after that he may eat the sacred offerings, for they are his food. [8]He must not eat anything found dead or torn by wild animals, and so become unclean through it. I am the LORD.

[9]"'The priests are to perform my service in such a way that they do not become guilty and die for treating it with contempt. I am the LORD, who makes them holy.

[10]"'No one outside a priest's family may eat the sacred offering, nor may the guest of a priest or his hired worker eat it. [11]But if a priest buys a slave with money, or if slaves are born in his household, they may eat his food. [12]If a priest's daughter marries anyone other than a priest, she may not eat any of the sacred contributions. [13]But if a priest's daughter becomes a widow or is divorced, yet has no children, and she returns to live in her father's household as in her youth, she may eat her father's food. No unauthorized person, however, may eat it.

[14]"'Anyone who eats a sacred offering by mistake must make restitution to the priest for the offering and add a fifth of the value to it. [15]The priests must not desecrate the sacred offerings the Israelites present to the LORD [16]by allowing them to eat the sacred offerings and so bring upon them guilt requiring payment. I am the LORD, who makes them holy.'"

Unacceptable Sacrifices

[17]The LORD said to Moses, [18]"Speak to Aaron and his sons and to all the Israelites and say to them: 'If any of you — whether an Israelite or a foreigner residing in Israel — presents a gift for a burnt offering to the LORD, either to fulfill a vow or as a freewill offering, [19]you must present a male without defect from the cattle, sheep or goats in order that it may be accepted on your behalf. [20]Do not bring anything with a defect, because it will not be accepted on your behalf. [21]When anyone brings from the herd or flock a fellowship offering to the LORD to fulfill a special vow or as a freewill offering, it must be without defect or blemish to be acceptable. [22]Do not offer to the LORD the blind, the injured or the maimed, or anything with warts or

---

[a] 4 The Hebrew word for *defiling skin disease*, traditionally translated "leprosy," was used for various diseases affecting the skin.

festering or running sores. Do not place any of these on the altar as a food offering presented to the LORD. 23You may, however, present as a freewill offering an ox*a* or a sheep that is deformed or stunted, but it will not be accepted in fulfillment of a vow. 24You must not offer to the LORD an animal whose testicles are bruised, crushed, torn or cut. You must not do this in your own land, 25and you must not accept such animals from the hand of a foreigner and offer them as the food of your God. They will not be accepted on your behalf, because they are deformed and have defects.'"

26The LORD said to Moses, 27"When a calf, a lamb or a goat is born, it is to remain with its mother for seven days. From the eighth day on, it will be acceptable as a food offering presented to the LORD. 28Do not slaughter a cow or a sheep and its young on the same day.

29"When you sacrifice a thank offering to the LORD, sacrifice it in such a way that it will be accepted on your behalf. 30It must be eaten that same day; leave none of it till morning. I am the LORD.

31"Keep my commands and follow them. I am the LORD. 32Do not profane my holy name, for I must be acknowledged as holy by the Israelites. I am the LORD, who made you holy 33and who brought you out of Egypt to be your God. I am the LORD."

The Appointed Festivals

23 The LORD said to Moses, 2"Speak to the Israelites and say to them: 'These are my appointed festivals, the appointed festivals of the LORD, which you are to proclaim as sacred assemblies.

The Sabbath

3" 'There are six days when you may work, but the seventh day is a day of sabbath rest, a day of sacred assembly. You are not to do any work; wherever you live, it is a sabbath to the LORD.

The Passover and the Festival of Unleavened Bread

4" 'These are the LORD's appointed festivals, the sacred assemblies you are to proclaim at their appointed times: 5The LORD's Passover begins at twilight on the fourteenth day of the first month. 6On the fifteenth day of that month the LORD's Festival of Unleavened Bread begins; for seven days you must eat bread made without yeast. 7On the first day hold a sacred assembly and do no regular work. 8For seven days present a food offering to the LORD. And on the seventh day hold a sacred assembly and do no regular work.'"

Offering the Firstfruits

9The LORD said to Moses, 10"Speak to the Israelites and say to them: 'When you enter the land I am going to give you and you reap its harvest, bring to the priest a sheaf of the first grain you harvest. 11He is to wave the sheaf before the LORD so it will be accepted on your behalf; the priest is to wave it on the day after the Sabbath. 12On the day you wave the sheaf, you must sacrifice as a burnt offering to the LORD a lamb a year old without defect, 13together with its grain offering of two-tenths of an ephah*b* of the finest flour mixed with olive oil — a food offering presented to the LORD, a pleasing aroma — and its drink offering of a quarter of a hin*c* of wine. 14You must not eat any bread, or roasted or new grain, until the very day you bring this offering to your God. This is to be a lasting ordinance for the generations to come, wherever you live.

The Festival of Weeks

15" 'From the day after the Sabbath, the day you brought the sheaf of the wave offering, count off seven full weeks. 16Count

---

a 23 The Hebrew word can refer to either male or female.
kilograms; also in verse 17   *c 13* That is, about 1 quart or about 1 liter

b 13 That is, probably about 7 pounds or about 3.2

off fifty days up to the day after the seventh Sabbath, and then present an offering of new grain to the LORD. ¹⁷From wherever you live, bring two loaves made of two-tenths of an ephah of the finest flour, baked with yeast, as a wave offering of firstfruits to the LORD. ¹⁸Present with this bread seven male lambs, each a year old and without defect, one young bull and two rams. They will be a burnt offering to the LORD, together with their grain offerings and drink offerings — a food offering, an aroma pleasing to the LORD. ¹⁹Then sacrifice one male goat for a sin offering*ᵃ* and two lambs, each a year old, for a fellowship offering. ²⁰The priest is to wave the two lambs before the LORD as a wave offering, together with the bread of the firstfruits. They are a sacred offering to the LORD for the priest. ²¹On that same day you are to proclaim a sacred assembly and do no regular work. This is to be a lasting ordinance for the generations to come, wherever you live.

²²"'When you reap the harvest of your land, do not reap to the very edges of your field or gather the gleanings of your harvest. Leave them for the poor and for the foreigner residing among you. I am the LORD your God.'"

The Festival of Trumpets

²³The LORD said to Moses, ²⁴"Say to the Israelites: 'On the first day of the seventh month you are to have a day of sabbath rest, a sacred assembly commemorated with trumpet blasts. ²⁵Do no regular work, but present a food offering to the LORD.'"

The Day of Atonement

²⁶The LORD said to Moses, ²⁷"The tenth day of this seventh month is the Day of Atonement. Hold a sacred assembly and deny yourselves,*ᵇ* and present a food offering to the LORD. ²⁸Do not do any work on that day, because it is the Day of Atonement, when atonement is made for you be-

fore the LORD your God. ²⁹Those who do not deny themselves on that day must be cut off from their people. ³⁰I will destroy from among their people anyone who does any work on that day. ³¹You shall do no work at all. This is to be a lasting ordinance for the generations to come, wherever you live. ³²It is a day of sabbath rest for you, and you must deny yourselves. From the evening of the ninth day of the month until the following evening you are to observe your sabbath."

The Festival of Tabernacles

³³The LORD said to Moses, ³⁴"Say to the Israelites: 'On the fifteenth day of the seventh month the LORD's Festival of Tabernacles begins, and it lasts for seven days. ³⁵The first day is a sacred assembly; do no regular work. ³⁶For seven days present food offerings to the LORD, and on the eighth day hold a sacred assembly and present a food offering to the LORD. It is the closing special assembly; do no regular work.

³⁷("'These are the LORD's appointed festivals, which you are to proclaim as sacred assemblies for bringing food offerings to the LORD — the burnt offerings and grain offerings, sacrifices and drink offerings required for each day. ³⁸These offerings are in addition to those for the LORD's Sabbaths and*ᶜ* in addition to your gifts and whatever you have vowed and all the freewill offerings you give to the LORD.)

³⁹"'So beginning with the fifteenth day of the seventh month, after you have gathered the crops of the land, celebrate the festival to the LORD for seven days; the first day is a day of sabbath rest, and the eighth day also is a day of sabbath rest. ⁴⁰On the first day you are to take branches from luxuriant trees — from palms, willows and other leafy trees — and rejoice before the LORD your God for seven days. ⁴¹Celebrate this as a festival to the LORD for seven days each year. This is to be a lasting ordinance

---

ᵃ 19 Or *purification offering   ᵇ 27* Or *and fast*; similarly in verses 29 and 32   *ᶜ 38* Or *These festivals are in addition to the LORD's Sabbaths, and these offerings are* for the generations to come; celebrate it in the seventh month. 42Live in temporary shelters for seven days: All native-born Israelites are to live in such shelters 43so your descendants will know that I had the Israelites live in temporary shelters when I brought them out of Egypt. I am the LORD your God.'"

44So Moses announced to the Israelites the appointed festivals of the LORD.

Olive Oil and Bread Set Before the LORD

24 The LORD said to Moses, 2"Command the Israelites to bring you clear oil of pressed olives for the light so that the lamps may be kept burning continually. 3Outside the curtain that shields the ark of the covenant law in the tent of meeting, Aaron is to tend the lamps before the LORD from evening till morning, continually. This is to be a lasting ordinance for the generations to come. 4The lamps on the pure gold lampstand before the LORD must be tended continually.

5"Take the finest flour and bake twelve loaves of bread, using two-tenths of an ephah*a* for each loaf. 6Arrange them in two stacks, six in each stack, on the table of pure gold before the LORD. 7By each stack put some pure incense as a memorial*b* portion to represent the bread and to be a food offering presented to the LORD. 8This bread is to be set out before the LORD regularly, Sabbath after Sabbath, on behalf of the Israelites, as a lasting covenant. 9It belongs to Aaron and his sons, who are to eat it in the sanctuary area, because it is a most holy part of their perpetual share of the food offerings presented to the LORD."

A Blasphemer Put to Death

10Now the son of an Israelite mother and an Egyptian father went out among the Israelites, and a fight broke out in the camp between him and an Israelite. 11The son of the Israelite woman blasphemed the Name

with a curse; so they brought him to Moses. (His mother's name was Shelomith, the daughter of Dibri the Danite.) 12They put him in custody until the will of the LORD should be made clear to them.

13Then the LORD said to Moses: 14"Take the blasphemer outside the camp. All those who heard him are to lay their hands on his head, and the entire assembly is to stone him. 15Say to the Israelites: 'Anyone who curses their God will be held responsible; 16anyone who blasphemes the name of the LORD is to be put to death. The entire assembly must stone them. Whether foreigner or native-born, when they blaspheme the Name they are to be put to death.

17"'Anyone who takes the life of a human being is to be put to death. 18Anyone who takes the life of someone's animal must make restitution—life for life. 19Anyone who injures their neighbor is to be injured in the same manner: 20fracture for fracture, eye for eye, tooth for tooth. The one who has inflicted the injury must suffer the same injury. 21Whoever kills an animal must make restitution, but whoever kills a human being is to be put to death. 22You are to have the same law for the foreigner and the native-born. I am the LORD your God.'"

23Then Moses spoke to the Israelites, and they took the blasphemer outside the camp and stoned him. The Israelites did as the LORD commanded Moses.

The Sabbath Year

25 The LORD said to Moses at Mount Sinai, 2"Speak to the Israelites and say to them: 'When you enter the land I am going to give you, the land itself must observe a sabbath to the LORD. 3For six years sow your fields, and for six years prune your vineyards and gather their crops. 4But in the seventh year the land is to have a year of sabbath rest, a sabbath to the LORD. Do not sow your fields or prune your vineyards.

---

a 5 That is, probably about 7 pounds or about 3.2 kilograms   *b 7* Or *representative*

5Do not reap what grows of itself or harvest the grapes of your untended vines. The land is to have a year of rest. 6Whatever the land yields during the sabbath year will be food for you—for yourself, your male and female servants, and the hired worker and temporary resident who live among you, 7as well as for your livestock and the wild animals in your land. Whatever the land produces may be eaten.

The Year of Jubilee

8"'Count off seven sabbath years—seven times seven years—so that the seven sabbath years amount to a period of forty-nine years. 9Then have the trumpet sounded everywhere on the tenth day of the seventh month; on the Day of Atonement sound the trumpet throughout your land. 10Consecrate the fiftieth year and proclaim liberty throughout the land to all its inhabitants. It shall be a jubilee for you; each of you is to return to your family property and to your own clan. 11The fiftieth year shall be a jubilee for you; do not sow and do not reap what grows of itself or harvest the untended vines. 12For it is a jubilee and is to be holy for you; eat only what is taken directly from the fields.

13"'In this Year of Jubilee everyone is to return to their own property.

14"'If you sell land to any of your own people or buy land from them, do not take advantage of each other. 15You are to buy from your own people on the basis of the number of years since the Jubilee. And they are to sell to you on the basis of the number of years left for harvesting crops. 16When the years are many, you are to increase the price, and when the years are few, you are to decrease the price, because what is really being sold to you is the number of crops. 17Do not take advantage of each other, but fear your God. I am the LORD your God.

18"'Follow my decrees and be careful to obey my laws, and you will live safely in the land. 19Then the land will yield its fruit, and you will eat your fill and live there in safety. 20You may ask, "What will we eat in the seventh year if we do not plant or harvest our crops?" 21I will send you such a blessing in the sixth year that the land will yield enough for three years. 22While you plant during the eighth year, you will eat from the old crop and will continue to eat from it until the harvest of the ninth year comes in.

23"'The land must not be sold permanently, because the land is mine and you reside in my land as foreigners and strangers. 24Throughout the land that you hold as a possession, you must provide for the redemption of the land.

25"'If one of your fellow Israelites becomes poor and sells some of their property, their nearest relative is to come and redeem what they have sold. 26If, however, there is no one to redeem it for them but later on they prosper and acquire sufficient means to redeem it themselves, 27they are to determine the value for the years since they sold it and refund the balance to the one to whom they sold it; they can then go back to their own property. 28But if they do not acquire the means to repay, what was sold will remain in the possession of the buyer until the Year of Jubilee. It will be returned in the Jubilee, and they can then go back to their property.

29"'Anyone who sells a house in a walled city retains the right of redemption a full year after its sale. During that time the seller may redeem it. 30If it is not redeemed before a full year has passed, the house in the walled city shall belong permanently to the buyer and the buyer's descendants. It is not to be returned in the Jubilee. 31But houses in villages without walls around them are to be considered as belonging to the open country. They can be redeemed, and they are to be returned in the Jubilee.

32"'The Levites always have the right to redeem their houses in the Levitical towns, which they possess. 33So the property of the Levites is redeemable—that is, a house sold in any town they hold—and is to be returned in the Jubilee, because the houses in the towns of the Levites are their property among the Israelites. ³⁴But the pasture-land belonging to their towns must not be sold; it is their permanent possession.

³⁵"'If any of your fellow Israelites become poor and are unable to support themselves among you, help them as you would a foreigner and stranger, so they can continue to live among you. ³⁶Do not take interest or any profit from them, but fear your God, so that they may continue to live among you. ³⁷You must not lend them money at interest or sell them food at a profit. ³⁸I am the LORD your God, who brought you out of Egypt to give you the land of Canaan and to be your God.

³⁹"'If any of your fellow Israelites become poor and sell themselves to you, do not make them work as slaves. ⁴⁰They are to be treated as hired workers or temporary residents among you; they are to work for you until the Year of Jubilee. ⁴¹Then they and their children are to be released, and they will go back to their own clans and to the property of their ancestors. ⁴²Because the Israelites are my servants, whom I brought out of Egypt, they must not be sold as slaves. ⁴³Do not rule over them ruthlessly, but fear your God.

⁴⁴"'Your male and female slaves are to come from the nations around you; from them you may buy slaves. ⁴⁵You may also buy some of the temporary residents living among you and members of their clans born in your country, and they will become your property. ⁴⁶You can bequeath them to your children as inherited property and can make them slaves for life, but you must not rule over your fellow Israelites ruthlessly.

⁴⁷"'If a foreigner residing among you becomes rich and any of your fellow Israelites become poor and sell themselves to the foreigner or to a member of the foreigner's clan, ⁴⁸they retain the right of redemption after they have sold themselves. One of their relatives may redeem them: ⁴⁹An uncle or a cousin or any blood relative in their clan may redeem them. Or if they prosper, they may redeem themselves. ⁵⁰They and

their buyer are to count the time from the year they sold themselves up to the Year of Jubilee. The price for their release is to be based on the rate paid to a hired worker for that number of years. ⁵¹If many years remain, they must pay for their redemption a larger share of the price paid for them. ⁵²If only a few years remain until the Year of Jubilee, they are to compute that and pay for their redemption accordingly. ⁵³They are to be treated as workers hired from year to year; you must see to it that those to whom they owe service do not rule over them ruthlessly.

⁵⁴"'Even if someone is not redeemed in any of these ways, they and their children are to be released in the Year of Jubilee, ⁵⁵for the Israelites belong to me as servants. They are my servants, whom I brought out of Egypt. I am the LORD your God.

Reward for Obedience

26 "'Do not make idols or set up an image or a sacred stone for yourselves, and do not place a carved stone in your land to bow down before it. I am the LORD your God.

²"'Observe my Sabbaths and have reverence for my sanctuary. I am the LORD.

³"'If you follow my decrees and are careful to obey my commands, ⁴I will send you rain in its season, and the ground will yield its crops and the trees their fruit. ⁵Your threshing will continue until grape harvest and the grape harvest will continue until planting, and you will eat all the food you want and live in safety in your land.

⁶"'I will grant peace in the land, and you will lie down and no one will make you afraid. I will remove wild beasts from the land, and the sword will not pass through your country. ⁷You will pursue your enemies, and they will fall by the sword before you. ⁸Five of you will chase a hundred, and a hundred of you will chase ten thousand, and your enemies will fall by the sword before you.

⁹"'I will look on you with favor and make you fruitful and increase your numbers,

and I will keep my covenant with you. ¹⁰You will still be eating last year's harvest when you will have to move it out to make room for the new. ¹¹I will put my dwelling place*ᵃ* among you, and I will not abhor you. ¹²I will walk among you and be your God, and you will be my people. ¹³I am the LORD your God, who brought you out of Egypt so that you would no longer be slaves to the Egyptians; I broke the bars of your yoke and enabled you to walk with heads held high.

Punishment for Disobedience

¹⁴"'But if you will not listen to me and carry out all these commands, ¹⁵and if you reject my decrees and abhor my laws and fail to carry out all my commands and so violate my covenant, ¹⁶then I will do this to you: I will bring on you sudden terror, wasting diseases and fever that will destroy your sight and sap your strength. You will plant seed in vain, because your enemies will eat it. ¹⁷I will set my face against you so that you will be defeated by your enemies; those who hate you will rule over you, and you will flee even when no one is pursuing you.

¹⁸"'If after all this you will not listen to me, I will punish you for your sins seven times over. ¹⁹I will break down your stubborn pride and make the sky above you like iron and the ground beneath you like bronze. ²⁰Your strength will be spent in vain, because your soil will not yield its crops, nor will the trees of your land yield their fruit.

²¹"'If you remain hostile toward me and refuse to listen to me, I will multiply your afflictions seven times over, as your sins deserve. ²²I will send wild animals against you, and they will rob you of your children, destroy your cattle and make you so few in number that your roads will be deserted.

²³"'If in spite of these things you do not accept my correction but continue to be hostile toward me, ²⁴I myself will be hostile toward you and will afflict you for your sins seven times over. ²⁵And I will bring the sword on you to avenge the breaking of the covenant. When you withdraw into your cities, I will send a plague among you, and you will be given into enemy hands. ²⁶When I cut off your supply of bread, ten women will be able to bake your bread in one oven, and they will dole out the bread by weight. You will eat, but you will not be satisfied.

²⁷"'If in spite of this you still do not listen to me but continue to be hostile toward me, ²⁸then in my anger I will be hostile toward you, and I myself will punish you for your sins seven times over. ²⁹You will eat the flesh of your sons and the flesh of your daughters. ³⁰I will destroy your high places, cut down your incense altars and pile your dead bodies*ᵇ* on the lifeless forms of your idols, and I will abhor you. ³¹I will turn your cities into ruins and lay waste your sanctuaries, and I will take no delight in the pleasing aroma of your offerings. ³²I myself will lay waste the land, so that your enemies who live there will be appalled. ³³I will scatter you among the nations and will draw out my sword and pursue you. Your land will be laid waste, and your cities will lie in ruins. ³⁴Then the land will enjoy its sabbath years all the time that it lies desolate and you are in the country of your enemies; then the land will rest and enjoy its sabbaths. ³⁵All the time that it lies desolate, the land will have the rest it did not have during the sabbaths you lived in it.

³⁶"'As for those of you who are left, I will make their hearts so fearful in the lands of their enemies that the sound of a wind-blown leaf will put them to flight. They will run as though fleeing from the sword, and they will fall, even though no one is pursuing them. ³⁷They will stumble over one another as though fleeing from the sword, even though no one is pursuing them. So you will not be able to stand before your enemies. ³⁸You will perish among the nations; the land of your enemies will devour

---

ᵃ 11 Or *my tabernacle*   *ᵇ 30* Or *your funeral offerings* you. ³⁹Those of you who are left will waste away in the lands of their enemies because of their sins; also because of their ancestors' sins they will waste away.

⁴⁰"But if they will confess their sins and the sins of their ancestors—their unfaithfulness and their hostility toward me, ⁴¹which made me hostile toward them so that I sent them into the land of their enemies—then when their uncircumcised hearts are humbled and they pay for their sin, ⁴²I will remember my covenant with Jacob and my covenant with Isaac and my covenant with Abraham, and I will remember the land. ⁴³For the land will be deserted by them and will enjoy its sabbaths while it lies desolate without them. They will pay for their sins because they rejected my laws and abhorred my decrees. ⁴⁴Yet in spite of this, when they are in the land of their enemies, I will not reject them or abhor them so as to destroy them completely, breaking my covenant with them. I am the LORD their God. ⁴⁵But for their sake I will remember the covenant with their ancestors whom I brought out of Egypt in the sight of the nations to be their God. I am the LORD.'"

⁴⁶These are the decrees, the laws and the regulations that the LORD established at Mount Sinai between himself and the Israelites through Moses.

Redeeming What Is the LORD's

27 The LORD said to Moses, ²"Speak to the Israelites and say to them: 'If anyone makes a special vow to dedicate a person to the LORD by giving the equivalent value, ³set the value of a male between the ages of twenty and sixty at fifty shekels^a of silver, according to the sanctuary shekel^b; ⁴for a female, set her value at thirty shekels^c; ⁵for a person between the ages of five and twen-

ty, set the value of a male at twenty shekels^d and of a female at ten shekels^e; ⁶for a person between one month and five years, set the value of a male at five shekels^f of silver and that of a female at three shekels^g of silver; ⁷for a person sixty years old or more, set the value of a male at fifteen shekels^h and of a female at ten shekels. ⁸If anyone making the vow is too poor to pay the specified amount, the person being dedicated is to be presented to the priest, who will set the value according to what the one making the vow can afford.

⁹"If what they vowed is an animal that is acceptable as an offering to the LORD, such an animal given to the LORD becomes holy. ¹⁰They must not exchange it or substitute a good one for a bad one, or a bad one for a good one; if they should substitute one animal for another, both it and the substitute become holy. ¹¹If what they vowed is a ceremonially unclean animal—one that is not acceptable as an offering to the LORD—the animal must be presented to the priest, ¹²who will judge its quality as good or bad. Whatever value the priest then sets, that is what it will be. ¹³If the owner wishes to redeem the animal, a fifth must be added to its value.

¹⁴"If anyone dedicates their house as something holy to the LORD, the priest will judge its quality as good or bad. Whatever value the priest then sets, so it will remain. ¹⁵If the one who dedicates their house wishes to redeem it, they must add a fifth to its value, and the house will again become theirs.

¹⁶"If anyone dedicates to the LORD part of their family land, its value is to be set according to the amount of seed required for it—fifty shekels of silver to a homer^i of barley seed. ¹⁷If they dedicate a field during the Year of Jubilee, the value that has been set remains. ¹⁸But if they dedicate a field

---

^{a} 3 That is, about 1 1/4 pounds or about 575 grams; also in verse 16 ^{b} 3 That is, about 2/5 ounce or about 12 grams; also in verse 25 ^{c} 4 That is, about 12 ounces or about 345 grams ^{d} 5 That is, about 8 ounces or about 230 grams ^{e} 5 That is, about 4 ounces or about 115 grams; also in verse 7 ^{f} 6 That is, about 2 ounces or about 58 grams ^{g} 6 That is, about 1 1/4 ounces or about 35 grams ^{h} 7 That is, about 6 ounces or about 175 grams ^{i} 16 That is, probably about 300 pounds or about 135 kilograms after the Jubilee, the priest will determine the value according to the number of years that remain until the next Year of Jubilee, and its set value will be reduced. ¹⁹If the one who dedicates the field wishes to redeem it, they must add a fifth to its value, and the field will again become theirs. ²⁰If, however, they do not redeem the field, or if they have sold it to someone else, it can never be redeemed. ²¹When the field is released in the Jubilee, it will become holy, like a field devoted to the LORD; it will become priestly property.

²²"If anyone dedicates to the LORD a field they have bought, which is not part of their family land, ²³the priest will determine its value up to the Year of Jubilee, and the owner must pay its value on that day as something holy to the LORD. ²⁴In the Year of Jubilee the field will revert to the person from whom it was bought, the one whose land it was. ²⁵Every value is to be set according to the sanctuary shekel, twenty gerahs to the shekel.

²⁶"No one, however, may dedicate the firstborn of an animal, since the firstborn already belongs to the LORD; whether an ox*a* or a sheep, it is the LORD's. ²⁷If it is one of the unclean animals, it may be bought back at its set value, adding a fifth of the value to it. If it is not redeemed, it is to be sold at its set value.

²⁸"But nothing that a person owns and devotes*b* to the LORD — whether a human being or an animal or family land — may be sold or redeemed; everything so devoted is most holy to the LORD.

²⁹"No person devoted to destruction*c* may be ransomed; they are to be put to death.

³⁰"A tithe of everything from the land, whether grain from the soil or fruit from the trees, belongs to the LORD; it is holy to the LORD. ³¹Whoever would redeem any of their tithe must add a fifth of the value to it. ³²Every tithe of the herd and flock — every tenth animal that passes under the shepherd's rod — will be holy to the LORD. ³³No one may pick out the good from the bad or make any substitution. If anyone does make a substitution, both the animal and its substitute become holy and cannot be redeemed.'"

³⁴These are the commands the LORD gave Moses at Mount Sinai for the Israelites.

---

a 26 The Hebrew word can refer to either male or female.   *b 28* The Hebrew term refers to the irrevocable giving over of things or persons to the LORD.   *c 29* The Hebrew term refers to the irrevocable giving over of things or persons to the LORD, often by totally destroying them.

Numbers

THEME: Numbers shows God guiding and comforting his people as he offers forgiveness, reconciliation and hope.

AUTHOR: Moses has traditionally been identified as the author. He was commanded by God to keep a detailed record of Israel's history. Although editors may have added information from Israel's later history, it's reasonable to assume that Moses wrote the book's essential content.

DATE OF WRITING: Moses probably wrote Numbers around 1406 BC, just before his death.

ENCOURAGEMENT FROM NUMBERS: "The LORD bless you and keep you; the LORD make his face shine on you and be gracious to you; the LORD turn his face toward you and give you peace" (Numbers 6:24–26).

CHALLENGE FROM NUMBERS: "The LORD said to Moses, 'Say to the Israelites: "Any man or woman who wrongs another in any way and so is unfaithful to the LORD is guilty and must confess the sin they have committed. They must make full restitution for the wrong they have done"'" (Numbers 5:5–7).

REFLECTION FROM NUMBERS: "The LORD is slow to anger, abounding in love and forgiving sin and rebellion" (Numbers 14:18).

The book of Numbers describes Israel's 40 years in the wilderness. The nation has just been rescued from slavery and is on its way to the land God has promised his people. They've seen with their own eyes God's awesome power, and they have a leader in Moses who receives his direction directly from God himself. In spite of all this, they constantly complain. And when they finally catch sight of the promised land, they're too afraid to enter it. God has assured them that he'll go with them, but they let their fears get in the way. Because they're unwilling to trust God, he sentences them to 40 years of wandering in the wilderness.

To gain freedom over our own hurts, hang-ups and habits, we too must overcome our fear of change and put our trust in God's grace. Our fears and doubts may have piled up over a lifetime, but the only way to access the promised freedom from life's pain is to trust God.

Unlike with Israel, God hasn't sentenced any of us to a lifetime away from him. We can choose at any time to enter his presence through prayer and study. And, through Christ we can eventually gain access to the promised land of eternal life. In order to do that we have to leave behind our hurts, hang-ups and habits, as comfortable as they may have become to us. We must leave them in Christ's care, and allow him free rein to transform our character.

The Census

1 The LORD spoke to Moses in the tent of meeting in the Desert of Sinai on the first day of the second month of the second year after the Israelites came out of Egypt. He said: ²"Take a census of the whole Israelite community by their clans and families, listing every man by name, one by one. ³You and Aaron are to count according to their divisions all the men in Israel who are twenty years old or more and able to serve in the army. ⁴One man from each tribe, each of them the head of his family, is to help you. ⁵These are the names of the men who are to assist you:

from Reuben, Elizur son of Shedeur;
⁶from Simeon, Shelumiel son of Zurishaddai;
⁷from Judah, Nahshon son of Amminadab;
⁸from Issachar, Nethanel son of Zuar;
⁹from Zebulun, Eliab son of Helon;
¹⁰from the sons of Joseph:
from Ephraim, Elishama son of Ammihud;
from Manasseh, Gamaliel son of Pedahzur;
¹¹from Benjamin, Abidan son of Gideoni;
¹²from Dan, Ahiezer son of Ammishaddai;
¹³from Asher, Pagiel son of Okran;
¹⁴from Gad, Eliasaph son of Deuel;
¹⁵from Naphtali, Ahira son of Enan."

¹⁶These were the men appointed from the community, the leaders of their ancestral tribes. They were the heads of the clans of Israel.

¹⁷Moses and Aaron took these men whose names had been specified, ¹⁸and they called the whole community together on the first day of the second month. The people registered their ancestry by their clans and families, and the men twenty years old or more were listed by name, one by one, ¹⁹as the LORD commanded Moses.

And so he counted them in the Desert of Sinai:

²⁰From the descendants of Reuben the firstborn son of Israel:
All the men twenty years old or more who were able to serve in the army were listed by name, one by one, according to the records of their clans and families. ²¹The number from the tribe of Reuben was 46,500.

²²From the descendants of Simeon:
All the men twenty years old or more who were able to serve in the army were counted and listed by name, one by one, according to the records of their clans and families. ²³The number from the tribe of Simeon was 59,300.

²⁴From the descendants of Gad:
All the men twenty years old or more who were able to serve in the army were listed by name, according to the records of their clans and families. ²⁵The number from the tribe of Gad was 45,650.

²⁶From the descendants of Judah:
All the men twenty years old or more who were able to serve in the army were listed by name, according to the records of their clans and families. ²⁷The number from the tribe of Judah was 74,600.

²⁸From the descendants of Issachar:
All the men twenty years old or more who were able to serve in the army were listed by name, according to the records of their clans and families. ²⁹The number from the tribe of Issachar was 54,400.

³⁰From the descendants of Zebulun:
All the men twenty years old or more who were able to serve in the army were listed by name, according to the records of their clans and families. ³¹The number from the tribe of Zebulun was 57,400.

32 From the sons of Joseph:

From the descendants of Ephraim:

All the men twenty years old or more who were able to serve in the army were listed by name, according to the records of their clans and families. 33 The number from the tribe of Ephraim was 40,500.

34 From the descendants of Manasseh:

All the men twenty years old or more who were able to serve in the army were listed by name, according to the records of their clans and families. 35 The number from the tribe of Manasseh was 32,200.

36 From the descendants of Benjamin:

All the men twenty years old or more who were able to serve in the army were listed by name, according to the records of their clans and families. 37 The number from the tribe of Benjamin was 35,400.

38 From the descendants of Dan:

All the men twenty years old or more who were able to serve in the army were listed by name, according to the records of their clans and families. 39 The number from the tribe of Dan was 62,700.

40 From the descendants of Asher:

All the men twenty years old or more who were able to serve in the army were listed by name, according to the records of their clans and families. 41 The number from the tribe of Asher was 41,500.

42 From the descendants of Naphtali:

All the men twenty years old or more who were able to serve in the army were listed by name, according to the records of their clans and families. 43 The number from the tribe of Naphtali was 53,400.

44 These were the men counted by Moses and Aaron and the twelve leaders of Israel, each one representing his family. 45 All the Israelites twenty years old or more who were able to serve in Israel's army were counted according to their families. 46 The total number was 603,550.

47 The ancestral tribe of the Levites, however, was not counted along with the others. 48 The LORD had said to Moses: 49 "You must not count the tribe of Levi or include them in the census of the other Israelites. 50 Instead, appoint the Levites to be in charge of the tabernacle of the covenant law — over all its furnishings and everything belonging to it. They are to carry the tabernacle and all its furnishings; they are to take care of it and encamp around it. 51 Whenever the tabernacle is to move, the Levites are to take it down, and whenever the tabernacle is to be set up, the Levites shall do it. Anyone else who approaches it is to be put to death. 52 The Israelites are to set up their tents by divisions, each of them in their own camp under their standard. 53 The Levites, however, are to set up their tents around the tabernacle of the covenant law so that my wrath will not fall on the Israelite community. The Levites are to be responsible for the care of the tabernacle of the covenant law."

54 The Israelites did all this just as the LORD commanded Moses.

The Arrangement of the Tribal Camps

2 The LORD said to Moses and Aaron: 2 "The Israelites are to camp around the tent of meeting some distance from it, each of them under their standard and holding the banners of their family."

3 On the east, toward the sunrise, the divisions of the camp of Judah are to encamp under their standard. The leader of the people of Judah is Nahshon son of Amminadab. 4 His division numbers 74,600.

5 The tribe of Issachar will camp next to them. The leader of the people of Issachar is Nethanel son of Zuar. 6 His division numbers 54,400.

7 The tribe of Zebulun will be next.

The leader of the people of Zebulun is Eliab son of Helon. [8]His division numbers 57,400.

[9]All the men assigned to the camp of Judah, according to their divisions, number 186,400. They will set out first.

[10]On the south will be the divisions of the camp of Reuben under their standard. The leader of the people of Reuben is Elizur son of Shedeur. [11]His division numbers 46,500.

[12]The tribe of Simeon will camp next to them. The leader of the people of Simeon is Shelumiel son of Zurishaddai. [13]His division numbers 59,300.

[14]The tribe of Gad will be next. The leader of the people of Gad is Eliasaph son of Deuel.[a] [15]His division numbers 45,650.

[16]All the men assigned to the camp of Reuben, according to their divisions, number 151,450. They will set out second.

[17]Then the tent of meeting and the camp of the Levites will set out in the middle of the camps. They will set out in the same order as they encamp, each in their own place under their standard.

[18]On the west will be the divisions of the camp of Ephraim under their standard. The leader of the people of Ephraim is Elishama son of Ammihud. [19]His division numbers 40,500.

[20]The tribe of Manasseh will be next to them. The leader of the people of Manasseh is Gamaliel son of Pedahzur. [21]His division numbers 32,200.

[22]The tribe of Benjamin will be next. The leader of the people of Benjamin is Abidan son of Gideoni. [23]His division numbers 35,400.

[24]All the men assigned to the camp of Ephraim, according to their divisions, number 108,100. They will set out third.

[25]On the north will be the divisions of the camp of Dan under their standard. The leader of the people of Dan is Ahiezer son of Ammishaddai. [26]His division numbers 62,700.

[27]The tribe of Asher will camp next to them. The leader of the people of Asher is Pagiel son of Okran. [28]His division numbers 41,500.

[29]The tribe of Naphtali will be next. The leader of the people of Naphtali is Ahira son of Enan. [30]His division numbers 53,400.

[31]All the men assigned to the camp of Dan number 157,600. They will set out last, under their standards.

[32]These are the Israelites, counted according to their families. All the men in the camps, by their divisions, number 603,550. [33]The Levites, however, were not counted along with the other Israelites, as the LORD commanded Moses.

[34]So the Israelites did everything the LORD commanded Moses; that is the way they encamped under their standards, and that is the way they set out, each of them with their clan and family.

The Levites

3 This is the account of the family of Aaron and Moses at the time the LORD spoke to Moses at Mount Sinai.

[2]The names of the sons of Aaron were Nadab the firstborn and Abihu, Eleazar and Ithamar. [3]Those were the names of Aaron's sons, the anointed priests, who were ordained to serve as priests. [4]Nadab and Abihu, however, died before the LORD when they made an offering with unauthorized fire before him in the Desert of Sinai.

---

[a] 14 Many manuscripts of the Masoretic Text, Samaritan Pentateuch and Vulgate (see also 1:14); most manuscripts of the Masoretic Text *Reuel*

They had no sons, so Eleazar and Ithamar served as priests during the lifetime of their father Aaron.

5The LORD said to Moses, 6"Bring the tribe of Levi and present them to Aaron the priest to assist him. 7They are to perform duties for him and for the whole community at the tent of meeting by doing the work of the tabernacle. 8They are to take care of all the furnishings of the tent of meeting, fulfilling the obligations of the Israelites by doing the work of the tabernacle. 9Give the Levites to Aaron and his sons; they are the Israelites who are to be given wholly to him.*a* 10Appoint Aaron and his sons to serve as priests; anyone else who approaches the sanctuary is to be put to death."

11The LORD also said to Moses, 12"I have taken the Levites from among the Israelites in place of the first male offspring of every Israelite woman. The Levites are mine, 13for all the firstborn are mine. When I struck down all the firstborn in Egypt, I set apart for myself every firstborn in Israel, whether human or animal. They are to be mine. I am the LORD."

14The LORD said to Moses in the Desert of Sinai, 15"Count the Levites by their families and clans. Count every male a month old or more." 16So Moses counted them, as he was commanded by the word of the LORD.

17These were the names of the sons of Levi:

Gershon, Kohath and Merari.

18These were the names of the Gershonite clans:

Libni and Shimei.

19The Kohathite clans:

Amram, Izhar, Hebron and Uzziel.

20The Merarite clans:

Mahli and Mushi.

These were the Levite clans, according to their families.

21To Gershon belonged the clans of the Libnites and Shimeites; these were the Gershonite clans. 22The number of all the males a month old or more who were counted was 7,500. 23The Gershonite clans were to camp on the west, behind the tabernacle. 24The leader of the families of the Gershonites was Eliasaph son of Lael. 25At the tent of meeting the Gershonites were responsible for the care of the tabernacle and tent, its coverings, the curtain at the entrance to the tent of meeting, 26the curtains of the courtyard, the curtain at the entrance to the courtyard surrounding the tabernacle and altar, and the ropes — and everything related to their use.

27To Kohath belonged the clans of the Amramites, Izharites, Hebronites and Uzzielites; these were the Kohathite clans. 28The number of all the males a month old or more was 8,600.*b* The Kohathites were responsible for the care of the sanctuary. 29The Kohathite clans were to camp on the south side of the tabernacle. 30The leader of the families of the Kohathite clans was Elizaphan son of Uzziel. 31They were responsible for the care of the ark, the table, the lampstand, the altars, the articles of the sanctuary used in ministering, the curtain, and everything related to their use. 32The chief leader of the Levites was Eleazar son of Aaron, the priest. He was appointed over those who were responsible for the care of the sanctuary.

33To Merari belonged the clans of the Mahlites and the Mushites; these were the Merarite clans. 34The number of all the males a month old or more who were counted was 6,200. 35The leader of the families of the Merarite clans was Zuriel son of Abihail; they were to camp on the north side of the tabernacle. 36The Merarites were appointed to take care of the frames of the tabernacle, its crossbars, posts, bases, all its equipment, and everything related to their use, 37as well as the

---

a 9 Most manuscripts of the Masoretic Text; some manuscripts of the Masoretic Text, Samaritan Pentateuch and Septuagint (see also 8:16) *to me*   *b* 28 Hebrew; some Septuagint manuscripts *8,300* posts of the surrounding courtyard with their bases, tent pegs and ropes.

38Moses and Aaron and his sons were to camp to the east of the tabernacle, toward the sunrise, in front of the tent of meeting. They were responsible for the care of the sanctuary on behalf of the Israelites. Anyone else who approached the sanctuary was to be put to death.

39The total number of Levites counted at the LORD's command by Moses and Aaron according to their clans, including every male a month old or more, was 22,000.

40The LORD said to Moses, "Count all the firstborn Israelite males who are a month old or more and make a list of their names. 41Take the Levites for me in place of all the firstborn of the Israelites, and the livestock of the Levites in place of all the firstborn of the livestock of the Israelites. I am the LORD."

42So Moses counted all the firstborn of the Israelites, as the LORD commanded him. 43The total number of firstborn males a month old or more, listed by name, was 22,273.

44The LORD also said to Moses, 45"Take the Levites in place of all the firstborn of Israel, and the livestock of the Levites in place of their livestock. The Levites are to be mine. I am the LORD. 46To redeem the 273 firstborn Israelites who exceed the number of the Levites, 47collect five shekels*a* for each one, according to the sanctuary shekel, which weighs twenty gerahs. 48Give the money for the redemption of the additional Israelites to Aaron and his sons."

49So Moses collected the redemption money from those who exceeded the number redeemed by the Levites. 50From the firstborn of the Israelites he collected silver weighing 1,365 shekels,*b* according to the sanctuary shekel. 51Moses gave the redemption money to Aaron and his sons, as he was commanded by the word of the LORD.

The Kohathites

4 The LORD said to Moses and Aaron: 2"Take a census of the Kohathite branch of the Levites by their clans and families. 3Count all the men from thirty to fifty years of age who come to serve in the work at the tent of meeting.

4"This is the work of the Kohathites at the tent of meeting: the care of the most holy things. 5When the camp is to move, Aaron and his sons are to go in and take down the shielding curtain and put it over the ark of the covenant law. 6Then they are to cover the curtain with a durable leather,*c* spread a cloth of solid blue over that and put the poles in place.

7"Over the table of the Presence they are to spread a blue cloth and put on it the plates, dishes and bowls, and the jars for drink offerings; the bread that is continually there is to remain on it. 8They are to spread a scarlet cloth over them, cover that with the durable leather and put the poles in place.

9"They are to take a blue cloth and cover the lampstand that is for light, together with its lamps, its wick trimmers and trays, and all its jars for the olive oil used to supply it. 10Then they are to wrap it and all its accessories in a covering of the durable leather and put it on a carrying frame.

11"Over the gold altar they are to spread a blue cloth and cover that with the durable leather and put the poles in place.

12"They are to take all the articles used for ministering in the sanctuary, wrap them in a blue cloth, cover that with the durable leather and put them on a carrying frame.

13"They are to remove the ashes from the bronze altar and spread a purple cloth

---

a 47   That is, about 2 ounces or about 58 grams   *b 50*   That is, about 35 pounds or about 16 kilograms
c 6   Possibly the hides of large aquatic mammals; also in verses 8, 10, 11, 12, 14 and 25

over it. ¹⁴Then they are to place on it all the utensils used for ministering at the altar, including the firepans, meat forks, shovels and sprinkling bowls. Over it they are to spread a covering of the durable leather and put the poles in place.

¹⁵"After Aaron and his sons have finished covering the holy furnishings and all the holy articles, and when the camp is ready to move, only then are the Kohathites to come and do the carrying. But they must not touch the holy things or they will die. The Kohathites are to carry those things that are in the tent of meeting.

¹⁶"Eleazar son of Aaron, the priest, is to have charge of the oil for the light, the fragrant incense, the regular grain offering and the anointing oil. He is to be in charge of the entire tabernacle and everything in it, including its holy furnishings and articles."

¹⁷The Lord said to Moses and Aaron, ¹⁸"See that the Kohathite tribal clans are not destroyed from among the Levites. ¹⁹So that they may live and not die when they come near the most holy things, do this for them: Aaron and his sons are to go into the sanctuary and assign to each man his work and what he is to carry. ²⁰But the Kohathites must not go in to look at the holy things, even for a moment, or they will die."

The Gershonites

²¹The Lord said to Moses, ²²"Take a census also of the Gershonites by their families and clans. ²³Count all the men from thirty to fifty years of age who come to serve in the work at the tent of meeting.

²⁴"This is the service of the Gershonite clans in their carrying and their other work: ²⁵They are to carry the curtains of the tabernacle, that is, the tent of meeting, its covering and its outer covering of durable leather, the curtains for the entrance to the tent of meeting, ²⁶the curtains of the courtyard surrounding the tabernacle and altar, the curtain for the entrance to the courtyard, the ropes and all the equip-

ment used in the service of the tent. The Gershonites are to do all that needs to be done with these things. ²⁷All their service, whether carrying or doing other work, is to be done under the direction of Aaron and his sons. You shall assign to them as their responsibility all they are to carry. ²⁸This is the service of the Gershonite clans at the tent of meeting. Their duties are to be under the direction of Ithamar son of Aaron, the priest.

The Merarites

²⁹"Count the Merarites by their clans and families. ³⁰Count all the men from thirty to fifty years of age who come to serve in the work at the tent of meeting. ³¹As part of all their service at the tent, they are to carry the frames of the tabernacle, its crossbars, posts and bases, ³²as well as the posts of the surrounding courtyard with their bases, tent pegs, ropes, all their equipment and everything related to their use. Assign to each man the specific things he is to carry. ³³This is the service of the Merarite clans as they work at the tent of meeting under the direction of Ithamar son of Aaron, the priest."

The Numbering of the Levite Clans

³⁴Moses, Aaron and the leaders of the community counted the Kohathites by their clans and families. ³⁵All the men from thirty to fifty years of age who came to serve in the work at the tent of meeting, ³⁶counted by clans, were 2,750. ³⁷This was the total of all those in the Kohathite clans who served at the tent of meeting. Moses and Aaron counted them according to the Lord's command through Moses.

³⁸The Gershonites were counted by their clans and families. ³⁹All the men from thirty to fifty years of age who came to serve in the work at the tent of meeting, ⁴⁰counted by their clans and families, were 2,630. ⁴¹This was the total of those in the Gershonite clans who served at the tent of meeting. Moses and Aaron counted them according to the Lord's command.

⁴²The Merarites were counted by their clans and families. ⁴³All the men from thirty to fifty years of age who came to serve in the work at the tent of meeting, ⁴⁴counted by their clans, were 3,200. ⁴⁵This was the total of those in the Merarite clans. Moses and Aaron counted them according to the LORD's command through Moses.

⁴⁶So Moses, Aaron and the leaders of Israel counted all the Levites by their clans and families. ⁴⁷All the men from thirty to fifty years of age who came to do the work of serving and carrying the tent of meeting ⁴⁸numbered 8,580. ⁴⁹At the LORD's command through Moses, each was assigned his work and told what to carry.

Thus they were counted, as the LORD commanded Moses.

The Purity of the Camp

5 The LORD said to Moses, ²"Command the Israelites to send away from the camp anyone who has a defiling skin disease^a or a discharge of any kind, or who is ceremonially unclean because of a dead body. ³Send away male and female alike; send them outside the camp so they will not defile their camp, where I dwell among them." ⁴The Israelites did so; they sent them outside the camp. They did just as the LORD had instructed Moses.

Restitution for Wrongs

⁵The LORD said to Moses, ⁶"Say to the Israelites: 'Any man or woman who wrongs another in any way^b and so is unfaithful to the LORD is guilty ⁷and must confess the sin they have committed. They must make full restitution for the wrong they have done, add a fifth of the value to it and give it all to the person they have wronged. ⁸But if that person has no close relative to whom restitution can be made for the wrong, the restitution belongs to the LORD and must be given to the priest, along with the ram with which atonement is made for the

wrongdoer. ⁹All the sacred contributions the Israelites bring to a priest will belong to him. ¹⁰Sacred things belong to their owners, but what they give to the priest will belong to the priest.' "

The Test for an Unfaithful Wife

¹¹Then the LORD said to Moses, ¹²"Speak to the Israelites and say to them: 'If a man's wife goes astray and is unfaithful to him ¹³so that another man has sexual relations with her, and this is hidden from her husband and her impurity is undetected (since there is no witness against her and she has not been caught in the act), ¹⁴and if feelings of jealousy come over her husband and he suspects his wife and she is impure — or if he is jealous and suspects her even though she is not impure — ¹⁵then he is to take his wife to the priest. He must also take an offering of a tenth of an ephah^c of barley flour on her behalf. He must not pour olive oil on it or put incense on it, because it is a grain offering for jealousy, a reminder-offering to draw attention to wrongdoing.

¹⁶" 'The priest shall bring her and have her stand before the LORD. ¹⁷Then he shall take some holy water in a clay jar and put some dust from the tabernacle floor into the water. ¹⁸After the priest has had the woman stand before the LORD, he shall loosen her hair and place in her hands the reminder-offering, the grain offering for jealousy, while he himself holds the bitter water that brings a curse. ¹⁹Then the priest shall put the woman under oath and say to her, "If no other man has had sexual relations with you and you have not gone astray and become impure while married to your husband, may this bitter water that brings a curse not harm you. ²⁰But if you have gone astray while married to your husband and you have made yourself impure by having sexual relations with a man other than your husband" — ²¹here the priest is to put the woman under this curse — "may the

---

^a 2 The Hebrew word for *defiling skin disease*, traditionally translated "leprosy," was used for various diseases affecting the skin.   ^b 6 Or *woman who commits any wrong common to mankind*   ^c 15 That is, probably about 3 1/2 pounds or about 1.6 kilograms

Lord cause you to become a curse*a* among your people when he makes your womb miscarry and your abdomen swell. 22May this water that brings a curse enter your body so that your abdomen swells or your womb miscarries."

"'Then the woman is to say, "Amen. So be it."

23"'The priest is to write these curses on a scroll and then wash them off into the bitter water. 24He shall make the woman drink the bitter water that brings a curse, and this water that brings a curse and causes bitter suffering will enter her. 25The priest is to take from her hands the grain offering for jealousy, wave it before the Lord and bring it to the altar. 26The priest is then to take a handful of the grain offering as a memorial*b* offering and burn it on the altar; after that, he is to have the woman drink the water. 27If she has made herself impure and been unfaithful to her husband, this will be the result: When she is made to drink the water that brings a curse and causes bitter suffering, it will enter her, her abdomen will swell and her womb will miscarry, and she will become a curse. 28If, however, the woman has not made herself impure, but is clean, she will be cleared of guilt and will be able to have children.

29"'This, then, is the law of jealousy when a woman goes astray and makes herself impure while married to her husband, 30or when feelings of jealousy come over a man because he suspects his wife. The priest is to have her stand before the Lord and is to apply this entire law to her. 31The husband will be innocent of any wrongdoing, but the woman will bear the consequences of her sin.'"

The Nazirite

6 The Lord said to Moses, 2"Speak to the Israelites and say to them: 'If a man or woman wants to make a special vow, a vow of dedication to the Lord

as a Nazirite, 3they must abstain from wine and other fermented drink and must not drink vinegar made from wine or other fermented drink. They must not drink grape juice or eat grapes or raisins. 4As long as they remain under their Nazirite vow, they must not eat anything that comes from the grapevine, not even the seeds or skins.

5"'During the entire period of their Nazirite vow, no razor may be used on their head. They must be holy until the period of their dedication to the Lord is over; they must let their hair grow long.

6"'Throughout the period of their dedication to the Lord, the Nazirite must not go near a dead body. 7Even if their own father or mother or brother or sister dies, they must not make themselves ceremonially unclean on account of them, because the symbol of their dedication to God is on their head. 8Throughout the period of their dedication, they are consecrated to the Lord.

9"'If someone dies suddenly in the Nazirite's presence, thus defiling the hair that symbolizes their dedication, they must shave their head on the seventh day—the day of their cleansing. 10Then on the eighth day they must bring two doves or two young pigeons to the priest at the entrance to the tent of meeting. 11The priest is to offer one as a sin offering*c* and the other as a burnt offering to make atonement for the Nazirite because they sinned by being in the presence of the dead body. That same day they are to consecrate their head again. 12They must rededicate themselves to the Lord for the same period of dedication and must bring a year-old male lamb as a guilt offering. The previous days do not count, because they became defiled during their period of dedication.

13"'Now this is the law of the Nazirite when the period of their dedication is over. They are to be brought to the entrance to the tent of meeting. 14There they are to present their offerings to the Lord: a year-old male

---

a 21 That is, may he cause your name to be used in cursing (see Jer. 29:22); or, may others see that you are cursed; similarly in verse 27.   *b 26* Or *representative*   *c 11* Or *purification offering*; also in verses 14 and 16 lamb without defect for a burnt offering, a year-old ewe lamb without defect for a sin offering, a ram without defect for a fellowship offering, 15together with their grain offerings and drink offerings, and a basket of bread made with the finest flour and without yeast — thick loaves with olive oil mixed in, and thin loaves brushed with olive oil.

16"'The priest is to present all these before the LORD and make the sin offering and the burnt offering. 17He is to present the basket of unleavened bread and is to sacrifice the ram as a fellowship offering to the LORD, together with its grain offering and drink offering.

18"'Then at the entrance to the tent of meeting, the Nazirite must shave off the hair that symbolizes their dedication. They are to take the hair and put it in the fire that is under the sacrifice of the fellowship offering.

19"'After the Nazirite has shaved off the hair that symbolizes their dedication, the priest is to place in their hands a boiled shoulder of the ram, and one thick loaf and one thin loaf from the basket, both made without yeast. 20The priest shall then wave these before the LORD as a wave offering; they are holy and belong to the priest, together with the breast that was waved and the thigh that was presented. After that, the Nazirite may drink wine.

21"'This is the law of the Nazirite who vows offerings to the LORD in accordance with their dedication, in addition to whatever else they can afford. They must fulfill the vows they have made, according to the law of the Nazirite.'"

The Priestly Blessing

22The LORD said to Moses, 23"Tell Aaron and his sons, 'This is how you are to bless the Israelites. Say to them:

24"'"The LORD bless you
    and keep you;
25the LORD make his face shine on you
    and be gracious to you;
26the LORD turn his face toward you
    and give you peace."'

27"So they will put my name on the Israelites, and I will bless them."

Offerings at the Dedication of the Tabernacle

7 When Moses finished setting up the tabernacle, he anointed and consecrated it and all its furnishings. He also anointed and consecrated the altar and all its utensils. 2Then the leaders of Israel, the heads of families who were the tribal leaders in charge of those who were counted, made offerings. 3They brought as their gifts before the LORD six covered carts and twelve oxen — an ox from each leader and a cart from every two. These they presented before the tabernacle.

4The LORD said to Moses, 5"Accept these from them, that they may be used in the work at the tent of meeting. Give them to the Levites as each man's work requires."

6So Moses took the carts and oxen and gave them to the Levites. 7He gave two carts and four oxen to the Gershonites, as their work required, 8and he gave four carts and eight oxen to the Merarites, as their work required. They were all under the direction of Ithamar son of Aaron, the priest. 9But Moses did not give any to the Kohathites, because they were to carry on their shoulders the holy things, for which they were responsible.

10When the altar was anointed, the leaders brought their offerings for its dedication and presented them before the altar. 11For the LORD had said to Moses, "Each day one leader is to bring his offering for the dedication of the altar."

12The one who brought his offering on the first day was Nahshon son of Amminadab of the tribe of Judah.

13His offering was one silver plate weighing a hundred and thirty shekelsa and one silver sprinkling bowl

---

a 13 That is, about 3 1/4 pounds or about 1.5 kilograms; also elsewhere in this chapter weighing seventy shekels,[a] both according to the sanctuary shekel, each filled with the finest flour mixed with olive oil as a grain offering; [14]one gold dish weighing ten shekels,[b] filled with incense; [15]one young bull, one ram and one male lamb a year old for a burnt offering; [16]one male goat for a sin offering[c]; [17]and two oxen, five rams, five male goats and five male lambs a year old to be sacrificed as a fellowship offering. This was the offering of Nahshon son of Amminadab.

[18]On the second day Nethanel son of Zuar, the leader of Issachar, brought his offering.

[19]The offering he brought was one silver plate weighing a hundred and thirty shekels and one silver sprinkling bowl weighing seventy shekels, both according to the sanctuary shekel, each filled with the finest flour mixed with olive oil as a grain offering; [20]one gold dish weighing ten shekels, filled with incense; [21]one young bull, one ram and one male lamb a year old for a burnt offering; [22]one male goat for a sin offering; [23]and two oxen, five rams, five male goats and five male lambs a year old to be sacrificed as a fellowship offering. This was the offering of Nethanel son of Zuar.

[24]On the third day, Eliab son of Helon, the leader of the people of Zebulun, brought his offering.

[25]His offering was one silver plate weighing a hundred and thirty shekels and one silver sprinkling bowl weighing seventy shekels, both according to the sanctuary shekel, each filled with the finest flour mixed with olive oil as a grain offering; [26]one gold dish weighing ten shekels, filled with incense; [27]one young bull, one ram and one male lamb a year old for a burnt offering; [28]one male goat for a sin offering; [29]and two

oxen, five rams, five male goats and five male lambs a year old to be sacrificed as a fellowship offering. This was the offering of Eliab son of Helon.

[30]On the fourth day Elizur son of Shedeur, the leader of the people of Reuben, brought his offering.

[31]His offering was one silver plate weighing a hundred and thirty shekels and one silver sprinkling bowl weighing seventy shekels, both according to the sanctuary shekel, each filled with the finest flour mixed with olive oil as a grain offering; [32]one gold dish weighing ten shekels, filled with incense; [33]one young bull, one ram and one male lamb a year old for a burnt offering; [34]one male goat for a sin offering; [35]and two oxen, five rams, five male goats and five male lambs a year old to be sacrificed as a fellowship offering. This was the offering of Elizur son of Shedeur.

[36]On the fifth day Shelumiel son of Zurishaddai, the leader of the people of Simeon, brought his offering.

[37]His offering was one silver plate weighing a hundred and thirty shekels and one silver sprinkling bowl weighing seventy shekels, both according to the sanctuary shekel, each filled with the finest flour mixed with olive oil as a grain offering; [38]one gold dish weighing ten shekels, filled with incense; [39]one young bull, one ram and one male lamb a year old for a burnt offering; [40]one male goat for a sin offering; [41]and two oxen, five rams, five male goats and five male lambs a year old to be sacrificed as a fellowship offering. This was the offering of Shelumiel son of Zurishaddai.

[42]On the sixth day Eliasaph son of Deuel, the leader of the people of Gad, brought his offering.

---

[a] 13 That is, about 1 3/4 pounds or about 800 grams; also elsewhere in this chapter   [b] 14 That is, about 4 ounces or about 115 grams; also elsewhere in this chapter   [c] 16 Or *purification offering*; also elsewhere in this chapter

43His offering was one silver plate weighing a hundred and thirty shekels and one silver sprinkling bowl weighing seventy shekels, both according to the sanctuary shekel, each filled with the finest flour mixed with olive oil as a grain offering; 44one gold dish weighing ten shekels, filled with incense; 45one young bull, one ram and one male lamb a year old for a burnt offering; 46one male goat for a sin offering; 47and two oxen, five rams, five male goats and five male lambs a year old to be sacrificed as a fellowship offering. This was the offering of Eliasaph son of Deuel.

48On the seventh day Elishama son of Ammihud, the leader of the people of Ephraim, brought his offering.

49His offering was one silver plate weighing a hundred and thirty shekels and one silver sprinkling bowl weighing seventy shekels, both according to the sanctuary shekel, each filled with the finest flour mixed with olive oil as a grain offering; 50one gold dish weighing ten shekels, filled with incense; 51one young bull, one ram and one male lamb a year old for a burnt offering; 52one male goat for a sin offering; 53and two oxen, five rams, five male goats and five male lambs a year old to be sacrificed as a fellowship offering. This was the offering of Elishama son of Ammihud.

54On the eighth day Gamaliel son of Pedahzur, the leader of the people of Manasseh, brought his offering.

55His offering was one silver plate weighing a hundred and thirty shekels and one silver sprinkling bowl weighing seventy shekels, both according to the sanctuary shekel, each filled with the finest flour mixed with olive oil as a grain offering; 56one gold dish weighing ten shekels, filled with incense; 57one young bull, one ram and one male lamb a year old for a burnt

offering; 58one male goat for a sin offering; 59and two oxen, five rams, five male goats and five male lambs a year old to be sacrificed as a fellowship offering. This was the offering of Gamaliel son of Pedahzur.

60On the ninth day Abidan son of Gideoni, the leader of the people of Benjamin, brought his offering.

61His offering was one silver plate weighing a hundred and thirty shekels and one silver sprinkling bowl weighing seventy shekels, both according to the sanctuary shekel, each filled with the finest flour mixed with olive oil as a grain offering; 62one gold dish weighing ten shekels, filled with incense; 63one young bull, one ram and one male lamb a year old for a burnt offering; 64one male goat for a sin offering; 65and two oxen, five rams, five male goats and five male lambs a year old to be sacrificed as a fellowship offering. This was the offering of Abidan son of Gideoni.

66On the tenth day Ahiezer son of Ammishaddai, the leader of the people of Dan, brought his offering.

67His offering was one silver plate weighing a hundred and thirty shekels and one silver sprinkling bowl weighing seventy shekels, both according to the sanctuary shekel, each filled with the finest flour mixed with olive oil as a grain offering; 68one gold dish weighing ten shekels, filled with incense; 69one young bull, one ram and one male lamb a year old for a burnt offering; 70one male goat for a sin offering; 71and two oxen, five rams, five male goats and five male lambs a year old to be sacrificed as a fellowship offering. This was the offering of Ahiezer son of Ammishaddai.

72On the eleventh day Pagiel son of Okran, the leader of the people of Asher, brought his offering.

73His offering was one silver plate weighing a hundred and thirty shekels and one silver sprinkling bowl weighing seventy shekels, both according to the sanctuary shekel, each filled with the finest flour mixed with olive oil as a grain offering; 74one gold dish weighing ten shekels, filled with incense; 75one young bull, one ram and one male lamb a year old for a burnt offering; 76one male goat for a sin offering; 77and two oxen, five rams, five male goats and five male lambs a year old to be sacrificed as a fellowship offering. This was the offering of Pagiel son of Okran.

78On the twelfth day Ahira son of Enan, the leader of the people of Naphtali, brought his offering.

79His offering was one silver plate weighing a hundred and thirty shekels and one silver sprinkling bowl weighing seventy shekels, both according to the sanctuary shekel, each filled with the finest flour mixed with olive oil as a grain offering; 80one gold dish weighing ten shekels, filled with incense; 81one young bull, one ram and one male lamb a year old for a burnt offering; 82one male goat for a sin offering; 83and two oxen, five rams, five male goats and five male lambs a year old to be sacrificed as a fellowship offering. This was the offering of Ahira son of Enan.

84These were the offerings of the Israelite leaders for the dedication of the altar when it was anointed: twelve silver plates, twelve silver sprinkling bowls and twelve gold dishes. 85Each silver plate weighed a hundred and thirty shekels, and each sprinkling bowl seventy shekels. Altogether, the silver dishes weighed two thousand four hundred shekels,*a* according to the sanctuary shekel. 86The twelve gold dishes filled with incense weighed ten shekels each, according to the sanctuary shekel. Altogether, the gold dishes weighed a hundred and twenty shekels.*b* 87The total number of animals for the burnt offering came to twelve young bulls, twelve rams and twelve male lambs a year old, together with their grain offering. Twelve male goats were used for the sin offering. 88The total number of animals for the sacrifice of the fellowship offering came to twenty-four oxen, sixty rams, sixty male goats and sixty male lambs a year old. These were the offerings for the dedication of the altar after it was anointed.

89When Moses entered the tent of meeting to speak with the LORD, he heard the voice speaking to him from between the two cherubim above the atonement cover on the ark of the covenant law. In this way the LORD spoke to him.

Setting Up the Lamps

8 The LORD said to Moses, 2"Speak to Aaron and say to him, 'When you set up the lamps, see that all seven light up the area in front of the lampstand.'"

3Aaron did so; he set up the lamps so that they faced forward on the lampstand, just as the LORD commanded Moses. 4This is how the lampstand was made: It was made of hammered gold—from its base to its blossoms. The lampstand was made exactly like the pattern the LORD had shown Moses.

The Setting Apart of the Levites

5The LORD said to Moses: 6"Take the Levites from among all the Israelites and make them ceremonially clean. 7To purify them, do this: Sprinkle the water of cleansing on them; then have them shave their whole bodies and wash their clothes. And so they will purify themselves. 8Have them take a young bull with its grain offering of the finest flour mixed with olive oil; then you are to take a second young bull for a sin offering.*c* 9Bring the Levites to the front of the tent of

---

a 85 That is, about 60 pounds or about 28 kilograms   *b* 86 That is, about 3 pounds or about 1.4 kilograms
c 8 Or *purification offering*; also in verse 12

meeting and assemble the whole Israelite community. ¹⁰You are to bring the Levites before the LORD, and the Israelites are to lay their hands on them. ¹¹Aaron is to present the Levites before the LORD as a wave offering from the Israelites, so that they may be ready to do the work of the LORD.

¹²"Then the Levites are to lay their hands on the heads of the bulls, using one for a sin offering to the LORD and the other for a burnt offering, to make atonement for the Levites. ¹³Have the Levites stand in front of Aaron and his sons and then present them as a wave offering to the LORD. ¹⁴In this way you are to set the Levites apart from the other Israelites, and the Levites will be mine.

¹⁵"After you have purified the Levites and presented them as a wave offering, they are to come to do their work at the tent of meeting. ¹⁶They are the Israelites who are to be given wholly to me. I have taken them as my own in place of the firstborn, the first male offspring from every Israelite woman. ¹⁷Every firstborn male in Israel, whether human or animal, is mine. When I struck down all the firstborn in Egypt, I set them apart for myself. ¹⁸And I have taken the Levites in place of all the firstborn sons in Israel. ¹⁹From among all the Israelites, I have given the Levites as gifts to Aaron and his sons to do the work at the tent of meeting on behalf of the Israelites and to make atonement for them so that no plague will strike the Israelites when they go near the sanctuary."

²⁰Moses, Aaron and the whole Israelite community did with the Levites just as the LORD commanded Moses. ²¹The Levites purified themselves and washed their clothes. Then Aaron presented them as a wave offering before the LORD and made atonement for them to purify them. ²²After that, the Levites came to do their work at the tent of meeting under the supervision of Aaron and his sons. They did with the Levites just as the LORD commanded Moses.

²³The LORD said to Moses, ²⁴"This applies to the Levites: Men twenty-five years old or more shall come to take part in the work at the tent of meeting, ²⁵but at the age of fifty, they must retire from their regular service and work no longer. ²⁶They may assist their brothers in performing their duties at the tent of meeting, but they themselves must not do the work. This, then, is how you are to assign the responsibilities of the Levites."

The Passover

9 The LORD spoke to Moses in the Desert of Sinai in the first month of the second year after they came out of Egypt. He said, ²"Have the Israelites celebrate the Passover at the appointed time. ³Celebrate it at the appointed time, at twilight on the fourteenth day of this month, in accordance with all its rules and regulations."

⁴So Moses told the Israelites to celebrate the Passover, ⁵and they did so in the Desert of Sinai at twilight on the fourteenth day of the first month. The Israelites did everything just as the LORD commanded Moses.

⁶But some of them could not celebrate the Passover on that day because they were ceremonially unclean on account of a dead body. So they came to Moses and Aaron that same day ⁷and said to Moses, "We have become unclean because of a dead body, but why should we be kept from presenting the LORD's offering with the other Israelites at the appointed time?"

⁸Moses answered them, "Wait until I find out what the LORD commands concerning you."

⁹Then the LORD said to Moses, ¹⁰"Tell the Israelites: 'When any of you or your descendants are unclean because of a dead body or are away on a journey, they are still to celebrate the LORD's Passover, ¹¹but they are to do it on the fourteenth day of the second month at twilight. They are to eat the lamb, together with unleavened bread and bitter herbs. ¹²They must not leave any of it till morning or break any of its bones. When they celebrate the Passover, they must follow all the regulations. ¹³But if anyone who is ceremonially clean and not on a journey fails to celebrate the Passover,

they must be cut off from their people for not presenting the Lord's offering at the appointed time. They will bear the consequences of their sin.

¹⁴"'A foreigner residing among you is also to celebrate the Lord's Passover in accordance with its rules and regulations. You must have the same regulations for both the foreigner and the native-born.'"

The Cloud Above the Tabernacle

¹⁵On the day the tabernacle, the tent of the covenant law, was set up, the cloud covered it. From evening till morning the cloud above the tabernacle looked like fire. ¹⁶That is how it continued to be; the cloud covered it, and at night it looked like fire. ¹⁷Whenever the cloud lifted from above the tent, the Israelites set out; wherever the cloud settled, the Israelites encamped. ¹⁸At the Lord's command the Israelites set out, and at his command they encamped. As long as the cloud stayed over the tabernacle, they remained in camp. ¹⁹When the cloud remained over the tabernacle a long time, the Israelites obeyed the Lord's order and did not set out. ²⁰Sometimes the cloud was over the tabernacle only a few days; at the Lord's command they would encamp, and then at his command they would set out. ²¹Sometimes the cloud stayed only from evening till morning, and when it lifted in the morning, they set out. Whether by day or by night, whenever the cloud lifted, they set out. ²²Whether the cloud stayed over the tabernacle for two days or a month or a year, the Israelites would remain in camp and not set out; but when it lifted, they would set out. ²³At the Lord's command they encamped, and at the Lord's command they set out. They obeyed the Lord's order, in accordance with his command through Moses.

The Silver Trumpets

10 The Lord said to Moses: ²"Make two trumpets of hammered silver, and use them for calling the community together and for having the camps set out. ³When both are sounded, the whole community is to assemble before you at the entrance to the tent of meeting. ⁴If only one is sounded, the leaders — the heads of the clans of Israel — are to assemble before you. ⁵When a trumpet blast is sounded, the tribes camping on the east are to set out. ⁶At the sounding of a second blast, the camps on the south are to set out. The blast will be the signal for setting out. ⁷To gather the assembly, blow the trumpets, but not with the signal for setting out.

⁸"The sons of Aaron, the priests, are to blow the trumpets. This is to be a lasting ordinance for you and the generations to come. ⁹When you go into battle in your own land against an enemy who is oppressing you, sound a blast on the trumpets. Then you will be remembered by the Lord your God and rescued from your enemies. ¹⁰Also at your times of rejoicing — your appointed festivals and New Moon feasts — you are to sound the trumpets over your burnt offerings and fellowship offerings, and they will be a memorial for you before your God. I am the Lord your God."

The Israelites Leave Sinai

¹¹On the twentieth day of the second month of the second year, the cloud lifted from above the tabernacle of the covenant law. ¹²Then the Israelites set out from the Desert of Sinai and traveled from place to place until the cloud came to rest in the Desert of Paran. ¹³They set out, this first time, at the Lord's command through Moses.

¹⁴The divisions of the camp of Judah went first, under their standard. Nahshon son of Amminadab was in command. ¹⁵Nethanel son of Zuar was over the division of the tribe of Issachar, ¹⁶and Eliab son of Helon was over the division of the tribe of Zebulun. ¹⁷Then the tabernacle was taken down, and the Gershonites and Merarites, who carried it, set out.

¹⁸The divisions of the camp of Reuben went next, under their standard. Elizur son of Shedeur was in command. ¹⁹Shelumiel son of Zurishaddai was over the division of

the tribe of Simeon, 20and Eliasaph son of Deuel was over the division of the tribe of Gad. 21Then the Kohathites set out, carrying the holy things. The tabernacle was to be set up before they arrived.

22The divisions of the camp of Ephraim went next, under their standard. Elishama son of Ammihud was in command. 23Gamaliel son of Pedahzur was over the division of the tribe of Manasseh, 24and Abidan son of Gideoni was over the division of the tribe of Benjamin.

25Finally, as the rear guard for all the units, the divisions of the camp of Dan set out under their standard. Ahiezer son of Ammishaddai was in command. 26Pagiel son of Okran was over the division of the tribe of Asher, 27and Ahira son of Enan was over the division of the tribe of Naphtali. 28This was the order of march for the Israelite divisions as they set out.

29Now Moses said to Hobab son of Reuel the Midianite, Moses' father-in-law, "We are setting out for the place about which the LORD said, 'I will give it to you.' Come with us and we will treat you well, for the LORD has promised good things to Israel."

30He answered, "No, I will not go; I am going back to my own land and my own people."

31But Moses said, "Please do not leave us. You know where we should camp in the wilderness, and you can be our eyes. 32If you come with us, we will share with you whatever good things the LORD gives us."

33So they set out from the mountain of the LORD and traveled for three days. The ark of the covenant of the LORD went before them during those three days to find them a place to rest. 34The cloud of the LORD was over them by day when they set out from the camp.

35Whenever the ark set out, Moses said,

"Rise up, LORD!
  May your enemies be scattered;
  may your foes flee before you."

36Whenever it came to rest, he said,

"Return, LORD,
  to the countless thousands of Israel."

Fire From the LORD

11 Now the people complained about their hardships in the hearing of the LORD, and when he heard them his anger was aroused. Then fire from the LORD burned among them and consumed some of the outskirts of the camp. 2When the people cried out to Moses, he prayed to the LORD and the fire died down. 3So that place was called Taberah,a because fire from the LORD had burned among them.

Quail From the LORD

4The rabble with them began to crave other food, and again the Israelites started wailing and said, "If only we had meat to eat! 5We remember the fish we ate in Egypt at no cost — also the cucumbers, melons, leeks, onions and garlic. 6But now we have lost our appetite; we never see anything but this manna!"

7The manna was like coriander seed and looked like resin. 8The people went around gathering it, and then ground it in a hand mill or crushed it in a mortar. They cooked it in a pot or made it into loaves. And it tasted like something made with olive oil. 9When the dew settled on the camp at night, the manna also came down.

10Moses heard the people of every family wailing at the entrance to their tents. The LORD became exceedingly angry, and Moses was troubled. 11He asked the LORD, "Why have you brought this trouble on your servant? What have I done to displease you that you put the burden of all these people on me? 12Did I conceive all these people? Did I give them birth? Why do you tell me to carry them in my arms, as a nurse carries an infant, to the land you promised on oath to their ancestors?

---

a 3 *Taberah* means *burning*.

13Where can I get meat for all these people? They keep wailing to me, 'Give us meat to eat!' 14I cannot carry all these people by myself; the burden is too heavy for me. 15If this is how you are going to treat me, please go ahead and kill me — if I have found favor in your eyes — and do not let me face my own ruin."

16The LORD said to Moses: "Bring me seventy of Israel's elders who are known to you as leaders and officials among the people. Have them come to the tent of meeting, that they may stand there with you. 17I will come down and speak with you there, and I will take some of the power of the Spirit that is on you and put it on them. They will share the burden of the people with you so that you will not have to carry it alone.

18"Tell the people: 'Consecrate yourselves in preparation for tomorrow, when you will eat meat. The LORD heard you when you wailed, "If only we had meat to eat! We were better off in Egypt!" Now the LORD will give you meat, and you will eat it. 19You will not eat it for just one day, or two days, or five, ten or twenty days, 20but for a whole month — until it comes out of your nostrils and you loathe it — because you have rejected the LORD, who is among you, and have wailed before him, saying, "Why did we ever leave Egypt?"'"

21But Moses said, "Here I am among six hundred thousand men on foot, and you say, 'I will give them meat to eat for a whole month!' 22Would they have enough if flocks and herds were slaughtered for them? Would they have enough if all the fish in the sea were caught for them?"

23The LORD answered Moses, "Is the LORD's arm too short? Now you will see whether or not what I say will come true for you."

24So Moses went out and told the people what the LORD had said. He brought together seventy of their elders and had them stand around the tent. 25Then the LORD came down in the cloud and spoke with him, and he took some of the power of the Spirit that was on him and put it on the seventy elders. When the Spirit rested on them, they prophesied — but did not do so again.

26However, two men, whose names were Eldad and Medad, had remained in the camp. They were listed among the elders, but did not go out to the tent. Yet the Spirit also rested on them, and they prophesied in the camp. 27A young man ran and told Moses, "Eldad and Medad are prophesying in the camp."

28Joshua son of Nun, who had been Moses' aide since youth, spoke up and said, "Moses, my lord, stop them!"

29But Moses replied, "Are you jealous for my sake? I wish that all the LORD's people were prophets and that the LORD would put his Spirit on them!" 30Then Moses and the elders of Israel returned to the camp.

31Now a wind went out from the LORD and drove quail in from the sea. It scattered them up to two cubits*a* deep all around the camp, as far as a day's walk in any direction. 32All that day and night and all the next day the people went out and gathered quail. No one gathered less than ten homers.*b* Then they spread them out all around the camp. 33But while the meat was still between their teeth and before it could be consumed, the anger of the LORD burned against the people, and he struck them with a severe plague. 34Therefore the place was named Kibroth Hattaavah,*c* because there they buried the people who had craved other food.

35From Kibroth Hattaavah the people traveled to Hazeroth and stayed there.

Miriam and Aaron Oppose Moses

12 Miriam and Aaron began to talk against Moses because of his Cushite wife, for he had married a Cushite. 2"Has the LORD spoken

---

a 31 That is, about 3 feet or about 90 centimeters   *b 32* That is, possibly about 1 3/4 tons or about 1.6 metric tons
c 34 Kibroth Hattaavah means graves of craving.

only through Moses?" they asked. "Hasn't he also spoken through us?" And the Lord heard this.

³(Now Moses was a very humble man, more humble than anyone else on the face of the earth.)

⁴At once the Lord said to Moses, Aaron and Miriam, "Come out to the tent of meeting, all three of you." So the three of them went out. ⁵Then the Lord came down in a pillar of cloud; he stood at the entrance to the tent and summoned Aaron and Miriam. When the two of them stepped forward, ⁶he said, "Listen to my words:

"When there is a prophet among you,
    I, the Lord, reveal myself to them in
        visions,
    I speak to them in dreams.
⁷But this is not true of my servant
        Moses;
    he is faithful in all my house.
⁸With him I speak face to face,
    clearly and not in riddles;
    he sees the form of the Lord.
Why then were you not afraid
    to speak against my servant Moses?"

⁹The anger of the Lord burned against them, and he left them.

¹⁰When the cloud lifted from above the tent, Miriam's skin was leprous*ᵃ* — it became as white as snow. Aaron turned toward her and saw that she had a defiling skin disease, ¹¹and he said to Moses, "Please, my lord, I ask you not to hold against us the sin we have so foolishly committed. ¹²Do not let her be like a stillborn infant coming from its mother's womb with its flesh half eaten away."

¹³So Moses cried out to the Lord, "Please, God, heal her!"

¹⁴The Lord replied to Moses, "If her father had spit in her face, would she not have been in disgrace for seven days? Confine her outside the camp for seven days; after that she can be brought back." ¹⁵So Miriam was confined outside the camp for sev-

en days, and the people did not move on till she was brought back.

¹⁶After that, the people left Hazeroth and encamped in the Desert of Paran.

Exploring Canaan

13 The Lord said to Moses, ²"Send some men to explore the land of Canaan, which I am giving to the Israelites. From each ancestral tribe send one of its leaders."

³So at the Lord's command Moses sent them out from the Desert of Paran. All of them were leaders of the Israelites. ⁴These are their names:

from the tribe of Reuben, Shammua
    son of Zakkur;
⁵from the tribe of Simeon, Shaphat son
    of Hori;
⁶from the tribe of Judah, Caleb son of
    Jephunneh;
⁷from the tribe of Issachar, Igal son of
    Joseph;
⁸from the tribe of Ephraim, Hoshea
    son of Nun;
⁹from the tribe of Benjamin, Palti son
    of Raphu;
¹⁰from the tribe of Zebulun, Gaddiel
    son of Sodi;
¹¹from the tribe of Manasseh (a tribe of
    Joseph), Gaddi son of Susi;
¹²from the tribe of Dan, Ammiel son of
    Gemalli;
¹³from the tribe of Asher, Sethur son of
    Michael;
¹⁴from the tribe of Naphtali, Nahbi son
    of Vophsi;
¹⁵from the tribe of Gad, Geuel son of
    Maki.

¹⁶These are the names of the men Moses sent to explore the land. (Moses gave Hoshea son of Nun the name Joshua.)

¹⁷When Moses sent them to explore Canaan, he said, "Go up through the Negev and on into the hill country. ¹⁸See what the land is like and whether the people

---

ᵃ 10 The Hebrew for *leprous* was used for various diseases affecting the skin.

who live there are strong or weak, few or many. ¹⁹What kind of land do they live in? Is it good or bad? What kind of towns do they live in? Are they unwalled or fortified? ²⁰How is the soil? Is it fertile or poor? Are there trees in it or not? Do your best to bring back some of the fruit of the land." (It was the season for the first ripe grapes.)

²¹So they went up and explored the land from the Desert of Zin as far as Rehob, toward Lebo Hamath. ²²They went up through the Negev and came to Hebron, where Ahiman, Sheshai and Talmai, the descendants of Anak, lived. (Hebron had been built seven years before Zoan in Egypt.) ²³When they reached the Valley of Eshkol,ᵃ they cut off a branch bearing a single cluster of grapes. Two of them carried it on a pole between them, along with some pomegranates and figs. ²⁴That place was called the Valley of Eshkol because of the cluster of grapes the Israelites cut off there. ²⁵At the end of forty days they returned from exploring the land.

Report on the Exploration

²⁶They came back to Moses and Aaron and the whole Israelite community at Kadesh in the Desert of Paran. There they reported to them and to the whole assembly and showed them the fruit of the land. ²⁷They gave Moses this account: "We went into the land to which you sent us, and it does flow with milk and honey! Here is its fruit. ²⁸But the people who live there are powerful, and the cities are fortified and very large. We even saw descendants of Anak there. ²⁹The Amalekites live in the Negev; the Hittites, Jebusites and Amorites live in the hill country; and the Canaanites live near the sea and along the Jordan."

³⁰Then Caleb silenced the people before Moses and said, "We should go up and take possession of the land, for we can certainly do it."

³¹But the men who had gone up with him said, "We can't attack those people;

they are stronger than we are." ³²And they spread among the Israelites a bad report about the land they had explored. They said, "The land we explored devours those living in it. All the people we saw there are of great size. ³³We saw the Nephilim there (the descendants of Anak come from the Nephilim). We seemed like grasshoppers in our own eyes, and we looked the same to them."

The People Rebel

14 That night all the members of the community raised their voices and wept aloud. ²All the Israelites grumbled against Moses and Aaron, and the whole assembly said to them, "If only we had died in Egypt! Or in this wilderness! ³Why is the LORD bringing us to this land only to let us fall by the sword? Our wives and children will be taken as plunder. Wouldn't it be better for us to go back to Egypt?" ⁴And they said to each other, "We should choose a leader and go back to Egypt."

⁵Then Moses and Aaron fell facedown in front of the whole Israelite assembly gathered there. ⁶Joshua son of Nun and Caleb son of Jephunneh, who were among those who had explored the land, tore their clothes ⁷and said to the entire Israelite assembly, "The land we passed through and explored is exceedingly good. ⁸If the LORD is pleased with us, he will lead us into that land, a land flowing with milk and honey, and will give it to us. ⁹Only do not rebel against the LORD. And do not be afraid of the people of the land, because we will devour them. Their protection is gone, but the LORD is with us. Do not be afraid of them."

¹⁰But the whole assembly talked about stoning them. Then the glory of the LORD appeared at the tent of meeting to all the Israelites. ¹¹The LORD said to Moses, "How long will these people treat me with contempt? How long will they refuse to believe in me, in spite of all the signs I have

---

ᵃ 23 *Eshkol* means *cluster*; also in verse 24.

performed among them? ¹²I will strike them down with a plague and destroy them, but I will make you into a nation greater and stronger than they."

¹³Moses said to the Lord, "Then the Egyptians will hear about it! By your power you brought these people up from among them. ¹⁴And they will tell the inhabitants of this land about it. They have already heard that you, Lord, are with these people and that you, Lord, have been seen face to face, that your cloud stays over them, and that you go before them in a pillar of cloud by day and a pillar of fire by night. ¹⁵If you put all these people to death, leaving none alive, the nations who have heard this report about you will say, ¹⁶'The Lord was not able to bring these people into the land he promised them on oath, so he slaughtered them in the wilderness.'

¹⁷"Now may the Lord's strength be displayed, just as you have declared: ¹⁸'The Lord is slow to anger, abounding in love and forgiving sin and rebellion. Yet he does not leave the guilty unpunished; he punishes the children for the sin of the parents to the third and fourth generation.' ¹⁹In accordance with your great love, forgive the sin of these people, just as you have pardoned them from the time they left Egypt until now."

²⁰The Lord replied, "I have forgiven them, as you asked. ²¹Nevertheless, as surely as I live and as surely as the glory of the Lord fills the whole earth, ²²not one of those who saw my glory and the signs I performed in Egypt and in the wilderness but who disobeyed me and tested me ten times — ²³not one of them will ever see the land I promised on oath to their ancestors. No one who has treated me with contempt will ever see it. ²⁴But because my servant Caleb has a different spirit and follows me wholeheartedly, I will bring him into the land he went to, and his descendants will inherit it. ²⁵Since the Amalekites and the Canaanites are living in the valleys, turn

back tomorrow and set out toward the desert along the route to the Red Sea.ᵃ"

²⁶The Lord said to Moses and Aaron: ²⁷"How long will this wicked community grumble against me? I have heard the complaints of these grumbling Israelites. ²⁸So tell them, 'As surely as I live, declares the Lord, I will do to you the very thing I heard you say: ²⁹In this wilderness your bodies will fall — every one of you twenty years old or more who was counted in the census and who has grumbled against me. ³⁰Not one of you will enter the land I swore with uplifted hand to make your home, except Caleb son of Jephunneh and Joshua son of Nun. ³¹As for your children that you said would be taken as plunder, I will bring them in to enjoy the land you have rejected. ³²But as for you, your bodies will fall in this wilderness. ³³Your children will be shepherds here for forty years, suffering for your unfaithfulness, until the last of your bodies lies in the wilderness. ³⁴For forty years — one year for each of the forty days you explored the land — you will suffer for your sins and know what it is like to have me against you.' ³⁵I, the Lord, have spoken, and I will surely do these things to this whole wicked community, which has banded together against me. They will meet their end in this wilderness; here they will die."

³⁶So the men Moses had sent to explore the land, who returned and made the whole community grumble against him by spreading a bad report about it — ³⁷these men who were responsible for spreading the bad report about the land were struck down and died of a plague before the Lord. ³⁸Of the men who went to explore the land, only Joshua son of Nun and Caleb son of Jephunneh survived.

³⁹When Moses reported this to all the Israelites, they mourned bitterly. ⁴⁰Early the next morning they set out for the highest point in the hill country, saying, "Now we are ready to go up to the land the Lord promised. Surely we have sinned!"

ᵃ 25 Or *the Sea of Reeds*

[41] But Moses said, "Why are you disobeying the LORD's command? This will not succeed! [42] Do not go up, because the LORD is not with you. You will be defeated by your enemies, [43] for the Amalekites and the Canaanites will face you there. Because you have turned away from the LORD, he will not be with you and you will fall by the sword."

[44] Nevertheless, in their presumption they went up toward the highest point in the hill country, though neither Moses nor the ark of the LORD's covenant moved from the camp. [45] Then the Amalekites and the Canaanites who lived in that hill country came down and attacked them and beat them down all the way to Hormah.

Supplementary Offerings

15 The LORD said to Moses, [2] "Speak to the Israelites and say to them: 'After you enter the land I am giving you as a home [3] and you present to the LORD food offerings from the herd or the flock, as an aroma pleasing to the LORD — whether burnt offerings or sacrifices, for special vows or freewill offerings or festival offerings — [4] then the person who brings an offering shall present to the LORD a grain offering of a tenth of an ephah[a] of the finest flour mixed with a quarter of a hin[b] of olive oil. [5] With each lamb for the burnt offering or the sacrifice, prepare a quarter of a hin of wine as a drink offering.

[6] "'With a ram prepare a grain offering of two-tenths of an ephah[c] of the finest flour mixed with a third of a hin[d] of olive oil, [7] and a third of a hin of wine as a drink offering. Offer it as an aroma pleasing to the LORD.

[8] "'When you prepare a young bull as a burnt offering or sacrifice, for a special vow or a fellowship offering to the LORD, [9] bring with the bull a grain offering of three-tenths of an ephah[e] of the finest flour mixed with half a hin[f] of olive oil, [10] and also bring half a hin of wine as a drink offering. This will be a food offering, an aroma pleasing to the LORD. [11] Each bull or ram, each lamb or young goat, is to be prepared in this manner. [12] Do this for each one, for as many as you prepare.

[13] "'Everyone who is native-born must do these things in this way when they present a food offering as an aroma pleasing to the LORD. [14] For the generations to come, whenever a foreigner or anyone else living among you presents a food offering as an aroma pleasing to the LORD, they must do exactly as you do. [15] The community is to have the same rules for you and for the foreigner residing among you; this is a lasting ordinance for the generations to come. You and the foreigner shall be the same before the LORD: [16] The same laws and regulations will apply both to you and to the foreigner residing among you.'"

[17] The LORD said to Moses, [18] "Speak to the Israelites and say to them: 'When you enter the land to which I am taking you [19] and you eat the food of the land, present a portion as an offering to the LORD. [20] Present a loaf from the first of your ground meal and present it as an offering from the threshing floor. [21] Throughout the generations to come you are to give this offering to the LORD from the first of your ground meal.

Offerings for Unintentional Sins

[22] "'Now if you as a community unintentionally fail to keep any of these commands the LORD gave Moses — [23] any of the LORD's commands to you through him, from the day the LORD gave them and continuing through the generations to come — [24] and if this is done unintentionally without the community being aware of it, then the whole community is to offer a young bull for a burnt offering as an aroma

---

[a] 4 That is, probably about 3 1/2 pounds or about 1.6 kilograms   [b] 4 That is, about 1 quart or about 1 liter; also in verse 5   [c] 6 That is, probably about 7 pounds or about 3.2 kilograms   [d] 6 That is, about 1 1/3 quarts or about 1.3 liters; also in verse 7   [e] 9 That is, probably about 11 pounds or about 5 kilograms   [f] 9 That is, about 2 quarts or about 1.9 liters; also in verse 10

pleasing to the LORD, along with its prescribed grain offering and drink offering, and a male goat for a sin offering.*a* 25 The priest is to make atonement for the whole Israelite community, and they will be forgiven, for it was not intentional and they have presented to the LORD for their wrong a food offering and a sin offering. 26 The whole Israelite community and the foreigners residing among them will be forgiven, because all the people were involved in the unintentional wrong.

27 "But if just one person sins unintentionally, that person must bring a year-old female goat for a sin offering. 28 The priest is to make atonement before the LORD for the one who erred by sinning unintentionally, and when atonement has been made, that person will be forgiven. 29 One and the same law applies to everyone who sins unintentionally, whether a native-born Israelite or a foreigner residing among you.

30 "But anyone who sins defiantly, whether native-born or foreigner, blasphemes the LORD and must be cut off from the people of Israel. 31 Because they have despised the LORD's word and broken his commands, they must surely be cut off; their guilt remains on them.'"

The Sabbath-Breaker Put to Death

32 While the Israelites were in the wilderness, a man was found gathering wood on the Sabbath day. 33 Those who found him gathering wood brought him to Moses and Aaron and the whole assembly, 34 and they kept him in custody, because it was not clear what should be done to him. 35 Then the LORD said to Moses, "The man must die. The whole assembly must stone him outside the camp." 36 So the assembly took him outside the camp and stoned him to death, as the LORD commanded Moses.

Tassels on Garments

37 The LORD said to Moses, 38 "Speak to the Israelites and say to them: 'Throughout the generations to come you are to make tassels on the corners of your garments, with a blue cord on each tassel. 39 You will have these tassels to look at and so you will remember all the commands of the LORD, that you may obey them and not prostitute yourselves by chasing after the lusts of your own hearts and eyes. 40 Then you will remember to obey all my commands and will be consecrated to your God. 41 I am the LORD your God, who brought you out of Egypt to be your God. I am the LORD your God.'"

Korah, Dathan and Abiram

16 Korah son of Izhar, the son of Kohath, the son of Levi, and certain Reubenites — Dathan and Abiram, sons of Eliab, and On son of Peleth — became insolent*b* 2 and rose up against Moses. With them were 250 Israelite men, well-known community leaders who had been appointed members of the council. 3 They came as a group to oppose Moses and Aaron and said to them, "You have gone too far! The whole community is holy, every one of them, and the LORD is with them. Why then do you set yourselves above the LORD's assembly?"

4 When Moses heard this, he fell facedown. 5 Then he said to Korah and all his followers: "In the morning the LORD will show who belongs to him and who is holy, and he will have that person come near him. The man he chooses he will cause to come near him. 6 You, Korah, and all your followers are to do this: Take censers 7 and tomorrow put burning coals and incense in them before the LORD. The man the LORD chooses will be the one who is holy. You Levites have gone too far!"

8 Moses also said to Korah, "Now listen, you Levites! 9 Isn't it enough for you that the God of Israel has separated you from the rest of the Israelite community and brought you near himself to do the work at the LORD's tabernacle and to stand before the community and minister to them? 10 He

---

a 24 Or *purification offering*; also in verses 25 and 27   *b* 1 Or *Peleth — took men* has brought you and all your fellow Levites near himself, but now you are trying to get the priesthood too. ¹¹It is against the Lord that you and all your followers have banded together. Who is Aaron that you should grumble against him?"

¹²Then Moses summoned Dathan and Abiram, the sons of Eliab. But they said, "We will not come! ¹³Isn't it enough that you have brought us up out of a land flowing with milk and honey to kill us in the wilderness? And now you also want to lord it over us! ¹⁴Moreover, you haven't brought us into a land flowing with milk and honey or given us an inheritance of fields and vineyards. Do you want to treat these men like slaves*a*? No, we will not come!"

¹⁵Then Moses became very angry and said to the Lord, "Do not accept their offering. I have not taken so much as a donkey from them, nor have I wronged any of them."

¹⁶Moses said to Korah, "You and all your followers are to appear before the Lord tomorrow—you and they and Aaron. ¹⁷Each man is to take his censer and put incense in it—250 censers in all—and present it before the Lord. You and Aaron are to present your censers also." ¹⁸So each of them took his censer, put burning coals and incense in it, and stood with Moses and Aaron at the entrance to the tent of meeting. ¹⁹When Korah had gathered all his followers in opposition to them at the entrance to the tent of meeting, the glory of the Lord appeared to the entire assembly. ²⁰The Lord said to Moses and Aaron, ²¹"Separate yourselves from this assembly so I can put an end to them at once."

²²But Moses and Aaron fell facedown and cried out, "O God, the God who gives breath to all living things, will you be angry with the entire assembly when only one man sins?"

²³Then the Lord said to Moses, ²⁴"Say to the assembly, 'Move away from the tents of Korah, Dathan and Abiram.'"

²⁵Moses got up and went to Dathan and Abiram, and the elders of Israel followed him. ²⁶He warned the assembly, "Move back from the tents of these wicked men! Do not touch anything belonging to them, or you will be swept away because of all their sins." ²⁷So they moved away from the tents of Korah, Dathan and Abiram. Dathan and Abiram had come out and were standing with their wives, children and little ones at the entrances to their tents.

²⁸Then Moses said, "This is how you will know that the Lord has sent me to do all these things and that it was not my idea: ²⁹If these men die a natural death and suffer the fate of all mankind, then the Lord has not sent me. ³⁰But if the Lord brings about something totally new, and the earth opens its mouth and swallows them, with everything that belongs to them, and they go down alive into the realm of the dead, then you will know that these men have treated the Lord with contempt."

³¹As soon as he finished saying all this, the ground under them split apart ³²and the earth opened its mouth and swallowed them and their households, and all those associated with Korah, together with their possessions. ³³They went down alive into the realm of the dead, with everything they owned; the earth closed over them, and they perished and were gone from the community. ³⁴At their cries, all the Israelites around them fled, shouting, "The earth is going to swallow us too!"

³⁵And fire came out from the Lord and consumed the 250 men who were offering the incense.

³⁶The Lord said to Moses, ³⁷"Tell Eleazar son of Aaron, the priest, to remove the censers from the charred remains and scatter the coals some distance away, for the censers are holy— ³⁸the censers of the men who sinned at the cost of their lives. Hammer the censers into sheets to overlay the altar, for they were presented before the

---

a 14 Or *to deceive these men;* Hebrew *Will you gouge out the eyes of these men*

LORD and have become holy. Let them be a sign to the Israelites."

39 So Eleazar the priest collected the bronze censers brought by those who had been burned to death, and he had them hammered out to overlay the altar, 40 as the LORD directed him through Moses. This was to remind the Israelites that no one except a descendant of Aaron should come to burn incense before the LORD, or he would become like Korah and his followers.

41 The next day the whole Israelite community grumbled against Moses and Aaron. "You have killed the LORD's people," they said.

42 But when the assembly gathered in opposition to Moses and Aaron and turned toward the tent of meeting, suddenly the cloud covered it and the glory of the LORD appeared. 43 Then Moses and Aaron went to the front of the tent of meeting, 44 and the LORD said to Moses, 45 "Get away from this assembly so I can put an end to them at once." And they fell facedown.

46 Then Moses said to Aaron, "Take your censer and put incense in it, along with burning coals from the altar, and hurry to the assembly to make atonement for them. Wrath has come out from the LORD; the plague has started." 47 So Aaron did as Moses said, and ran into the midst of the assembly. The plague had already started among the people, but Aaron offered the incense and made atonement for them. 48 He stood between the living and the dead, and the plague stopped. 49 But 14,700 people died from the plague, in addition to those who had died because of Korah. 50 Then Aaron returned to Moses at the entrance to the tent of meeting, for the plague had stopped.a

The Budding of Aaron's Staff

17 b The LORD said to Moses, 2 "Speak to the Israelites and get twelve staffs from them, one from the leader of each of their ancestral tribes. Write the name of each man on his staff. 3 On the staff of Levi write Aaron's name, for there must be one staff for the head of each ancestral tribe. 4 Place them in the tent of meeting in front of the ark of the covenant law, where I meet with you. 5 The staff belonging to the man I choose will sprout, and I will rid myself of this constant grumbling against you by the Israelites."

6 So Moses spoke to the Israelites, and their leaders gave him twelve staffs, one for the leader of each of their ancestral tribes, and Aaron's staff was among them. 7 Moses placed the staffs before the LORD in the tent of the covenant law.

8 The next day Moses entered the tent and saw that Aaron's staff, which represented the tribe of Levi, had not only sprouted but had budded, blossomed and produced almonds. 9 Then Moses brought out all the staffs from the LORD's presence to all the Israelites. They looked at them, and each of the leaders took his own staff.

10 The LORD said to Moses, "Put back Aaron's staff in front of the ark of the covenant law, to be kept as a sign to the rebellious. This will put an end to their grumbling against me, so that they will not die." 11 Moses did just as the LORD commanded him.

12 The Israelites said to Moses, "We will die! We are lost, we are all lost! 13 Anyone who even comes near the tabernacle of the LORD will die. Are we all going to die?"

Duties of Priests and Levites

18 The LORD said to Aaron, "You, your sons and your family are to bear the responsibility for offenses connected with the sanctuary, and you and your sons alone are to bear the responsibility for offenses connected with the priesthood. 2 Bring your fellow Levites from your ancestral tribe to join you and assist you when you and your sons minister before the tent of the covenant law. 3 They are to be responsible to you and are

---

a 50 In Hebrew texts 16:36-50 is numbered 17:1-15.   b In Hebrew texts 17:1-13 is numbered 17:16-28.

to perform all the duties of the tent, but they must not go near the furnishings of the sanctuary or the altar. Otherwise both they and you will die. ⁴They are to join you and be responsible for the care of the tent of meeting — all the work at the tent — and no one else may come near where you are.

⁵"You are to be responsible for the care of the sanctuary and the altar, so that my wrath will not fall on the Israelites again. ⁶I myself have selected your fellow Levites from among the Israelites as a gift to you, dedicated to the LORD to do the work at the tent of meeting. ⁷But only you and your sons may serve as priests in connection with everything at the altar and inside the curtain. I am giving you the service of the priesthood as a gift. Anyone else who comes near the sanctuary is to be put to death."

Offerings for Priests and Levites

⁸Then the LORD said to Aaron, "I myself have put you in charge of the offerings presented to me; all the holy offerings the Israelites give me I give to you and your sons as your portion, your perpetual share. ⁹You are to have the part of the most holy offerings that is kept from the fire. From all the gifts they bring me as most holy offerings, whether grain or sin*a* or guilt offerings, that part belongs to you and your sons. ¹⁰Eat it as something most holy; every male shall eat it. You must regard it as holy.

¹¹"This also is yours: whatever is set aside from the gifts of all the wave offerings of the Israelites. I give this to you and your sons and daughters as your perpetual share. Everyone in your household who is ceremonially clean may eat it.

¹²"I give you all the finest olive oil and all the finest new wine and grain they give the LORD as the firstfruits of their harvest. ¹³All the land's firstfruits that they bring to the LORD will be yours. Everyone in your household who is ceremonially clean may eat it.

¹⁴"Everything in Israel that is devoted*b* to the LORD is yours. ¹⁵The first offspring of every womb, both human and animal, that is offered to the LORD is yours. But you must redeem every firstborn son and every firstborn male of unclean animals. ¹⁶When they are a month old, you must redeem them at the redemption price set at five shekels*c* of silver, according to the sanctuary shekel, which weighs twenty gerahs.

¹⁷"But you must not redeem the firstborn of a cow, a sheep or a goat; they are holy. Splash their blood against the altar and burn their fat as a food offering, an aroma pleasing to the LORD. ¹⁸Their meat is to be yours, just as the breast of the wave offering and the right thigh are yours. ¹⁹Whatever is set aside from the holy offerings the Israelites present to the LORD I give to you and your sons and daughters as your perpetual share. It is an everlasting covenant of salt before the LORD for both you and your offspring."

²⁰The LORD said to Aaron, "You will have no inheritance in their land, nor will you have any share among them; I am your share and your inheritance among the Israelites.

²¹"I give to the Levites all the tithes in Israel as their inheritance in return for the work they do while serving at the tent of meeting. ²²From now on the Israelites must not go near the tent of meeting, or they will bear the consequences of their sin and will die. ²³It is the Levites who are to do the work at the tent of meeting and bear the responsibility for any offenses they commit against it. This is a lasting ordinance for the generations to come. They will receive no inheritance among the Israelites. ²⁴Instead, I give to the Levites as their inheritance the tithes that the Israelites present as an offering to the LORD. That is why I said concerning them: 'They will have no inheritance among the Israelites.'"

²⁵The LORD said to Moses, ²⁶"Speak to

---

a 9 Or *purification*   *b 14* The Hebrew term refers to the irrevocable giving over of things or persons to the LORD.
c 16 That is, about 2 ounces or about 58 grams

the Levites and say to them: 'When you receive from the Israelites the tithe I give you as your inheritance, you must present a tenth of that tithe as the LORD's offering. ²⁷Your offering will be reckoned to you as grain from the threshing floor or juice from the winepress. ²⁸In this way you also will present an offering to the LORD from all the tithes you receive from the Israelites. From these tithes you must give the LORD's portion to Aaron the priest. ²⁹You must present as the LORD's portion the best and holiest part of everything given to you.'

³⁰"Say to the Levites: 'When you present the best part, it will be reckoned to you as the product of the threshing floor or the winepress. ³¹You and your households may eat the rest of it anywhere, for it is your wages for your work at the tent of meeting. ³²By presenting the best part of it you will not be guilty in this matter; then you will not defile the holy offerings of the Israelites, and you will not die.'"

The Water of Cleansing

19 The LORD said to Moses and Aaron: ²"This is a requirement of the law that the LORD has commanded: Tell the Israelites to bring you a red heifer without defect or blemish and that has never been under a yoke. ³Give it to Eleazar the priest; it is to be taken outside the camp and slaughtered in his presence. ⁴Then Eleazar the priest is to take some of its blood on his finger and sprinkle it seven times toward the front of the tent of meeting. ⁵While he watches, the heifer is to be burned—its hide, flesh, blood and intestines. ⁶The priest is to take some cedar wood, hyssop and scarlet wool and throw them onto the burning heifer. ⁷After that, the priest must wash his clothes and bathe himself with water. He may then come into the camp, but he will be ceremonially unclean till evening. ⁸The man who burns it must also wash his clothes and bathe with water, and he too will be unclean till evening.

⁹"A man who is clean shall gather up the ashes of the heifer and put them in a ceremonially clean place outside the camp. They are to be kept by the Israelite community for use in the water of cleansing; it is for purification from sin. ¹⁰The man who gathers up the ashes of the heifer must also wash his clothes, and he too will be unclean till evening. This will be a lasting ordinance both for the Israelites and for the foreigners residing among them.

¹¹"Whoever touches a human corpse will be unclean for seven days. ¹²They must purify themselves with the water on the third day and on the seventh day; then they will be clean. But if they do not purify themselves on the third and seventh days, they will not be clean. ¹³If they fail to purify themselves after touching a human corpse, they defile the LORD's tabernacle. They must be cut off from Israel. Because the water of cleansing has not been sprinkled on them, they are unclean; their uncleanness remains on them.

¹⁴"This is the law that applies when a person dies in a tent: Anyone who enters the tent and anyone who is in it will be unclean for seven days, ¹⁵and every open container without a lid fastened on it will be unclean.

¹⁶"Anyone out in the open who touches someone who has been killed with a sword or someone who has died a natural death, or anyone who touches a human bone or a grave, will be unclean for seven days.

¹⁷"For the unclean person, put some ashes from the burned purification offering into a jar and pour fresh water over them. ¹⁸Then a man who is ceremonially clean is to take some hyssop, dip it in the water and sprinkle the tent and all the furnishings and the people who were there. He must also sprinkle anyone who touched a human bone or a grave or anyone who has been killed or anyone who has died a natural death. ¹⁹The man who is clean is to sprinkle those who are unclean on the third and seventh days, and on the seventh day he is to purify them. Those who are being cleansed must wash their

clothes and bathe with water, and that evening they will be clean. ²⁰But if those who are unclean do not purify themselves, they must be cut off from the community, because they have defiled the sanctuary of the Lᴏʀᴅ. The water of cleansing has not been sprinkled on them, and they are unclean. ²¹This is a lasting ordinance for them.

"The man who sprinkles the water of cleansing must also wash his clothes, and anyone who touches the water of cleansing will be unclean till evening. ²²Anything that an unclean person touches becomes unclean, and anyone who touches it becomes unclean till evening."

Water From the Rock

20 In the first month the whole Israelite community arrived at the Desert of Zin, and they stayed at Kadesh. There Miriam died and was buried.

²Now there was no water for the community, and the people gathered in opposition to Moses and Aaron. ³They quarreled with Moses and said, "If only we had died when our brothers fell dead before the Lᴏʀᴅ! ⁴Why did you bring the Lᴏʀᴅ's community into this wilderness, that we and our livestock should die here? ⁵Why did you bring us up out of Egypt to this terrible place? It has no grain or figs, grapevines or pomegranates. And there is no water to drink!"

⁶Moses and Aaron went from the assembly to the entrance to the tent of meeting and fell facedown, and the glory of the Lᴏʀᴅ appeared to them. ⁷The Lᴏʀᴅ said to Moses, ⁸"Take the staff, and you and your brother Aaron gather the assembly together. Speak to that rock before their eyes and it will pour out its water. You will bring water out of the rock for the community so they and their livestock can drink."

⁹So Moses took the staff from the Lᴏʀᴅ's presence, just as he commanded him. ¹⁰He and Aaron gathered the assembly together in front of the rock and Moses said to them,

"Listen, you rebels, must we bring you water out of this rock?" ¹¹Then Moses raised his arm and struck the rock twice with his staff. Water gushed out, and the community and their livestock drank.

¹²But the Lᴏʀᴅ said to Moses and Aaron, "Because you did not trust in me enough to honor me as holy in the sight of the Israelites, you will not bring this community into the land I give them."

¹³These were the waters of Meribah,ᵃ where the Israelites quarreled with the Lᴏʀᴅ and where he was proved holy among them.

Edom Denies Israel Passage

¹⁴Moses sent messengers from Kadesh to the king of Edom, saying:

"This is what your brother Israel says: You know about all the hardships that have come on us. ¹⁵Our ancestors went down into Egypt, and we lived there many years. The Egyptians mistreated us and our ancestors, ¹⁶but when we cried out to the Lᴏʀᴅ, he heard our cry and sent an angel and brought us out of Egypt.

"Now we are here at Kadesh, a town on the edge of your territory. ¹⁷Please let us pass through your country. We will not go through any field or vineyard, or drink water from any well. We will travel along the King's Highway and not turn to the right or to the left until we have passed through your territory."

¹⁸But Edom answered:

"You may not pass through here; if you try, we will march out and attack you with the sword."

¹⁹The Israelites replied:

"We will go along the main road, and if we or our livestock drink any of your water, we will pay for it. We only

---

ᵃ 13 Meribah means quarreling.

MY NAME IS MOSES

NUMBERS 20

As our time of sobriety grows longer, it can be hard to remember that we're never beyond temptation. Numbers 20 records an instance of relapse by one of God's greatest servants. Moses had an anger problem. He heard the complaints of the people about the lack of water (see Numbers 20:1–5) and appropriately asked God what he should do (see v. 6). The Lord instructed Moses to speak to a rock, promising that water would flow from it so the people could drink (see vv. 7–8).

Sadly, Moses failed to act according to the centuries-later recommendation of Pastor Rick Warren, who counsels each of us to carry out a regular HEART check, asking ourselves daily whether we're

Hurting

Exhausted

Angry

Resentful

Tense

Had Moses done this, he might have avoided a relapse into anger that for him turned out to have life-changing consequences. This wasn't a new experience for Moses. Exodus 2:11–12 records how his impulsive act of rage led to the murder of an Egyptian, which in turn resulted in 40 years of exile from Egypt (see Acts 7:29–30). How did Moses end up spending 40 years in the wilderness of Midian? He sinned and tried to keep his guilt and shame a secret (see Exodus 2:12). We are indeed as sick as our secrets.

After 40 years Moses was restored to God's service. His patience with a nation of complainers was repeated proof of the reality of his recovery experience. But the danger of relapse isn't erased even by decades of ministry. Moses, as we've seen, was directed to simply speak to the rock. Instead he tongue-lashed the stubborn Israelites and struck the rock in his fury (see Numbers 20:10–11).

The consequences were severe, primarily because Moses was a leader. God placed a limitation on his ministry to God's people. After so many years of faithful service, he wouldn't be the one to lead the people into the promised land (see v. 12). Relapse can be avoided if we consistently take a personal inventory and continuously maintain our conscious contact with God (Principle Seven). We'll never outgrow our need to evaluate our spiritual condition or to listen to God carefully every day.

want to pass through on foot — nothing else."

20 Again they answered:

"You may not pass through."

Then Edom came out against them with a large and powerful army. 21 Since Edom refused to let them go through their territory, Israel turned away from them.

The Death of Aaron

22 The whole Israelite community set out from Kadesh and came to Mount Hor. 23 At Mount Hor, near the border of Edom, the LORD said to Moses and Aaron, 24 "Aaron will be gathered to his people. He will not enter the land I give the Israelites, because both of you rebelled against my command at the waters of Meribah. 25 Get Aaron and his son Eleazar and take them up Mount Hor. 26 Remove Aaron's garments and put them on his son Eleazar, for Aaron will be gathered to his people; he will die there."

27 Moses did as the LORD commanded: They went up Mount Hor in the sight of the whole community. 28 Moses removed Aaron's garments and put them on his son Eleazar. And Aaron died there on top of the mountain. Then Moses and Eleazar came down from the mountain, 29 and when the whole community learned that Aaron had died, all the Israelites mourned for him thirty days.

Arad Destroyed

21 When the Canaanite king of Arad, who lived in the Negev, heard that Israel was coming along the road to Atharim, he attacked the Israelites and captured some of them. 2 Then Israel made this vow to the LORD: "If you will deliver these people into our hands, we will totally destroy[a] their cities." 3 The LORD listened to Israel's plea and gave the Canaanites over to them. They com-

pletely destroyed them and their towns; so the place was named Hormah.[b]

The Bronze Snake

4 They traveled from Mount Hor along the route to the Red Sea,[c] to go around Edom. But the people grew impatient on the way; 5 they spoke against God and against Moses, and said, "Why have you brought us up out of Egypt to die in the wilderness? There is no bread! There is no water! And we detest this miserable food!"

6 Then the LORD sent venomous snakes among them; they bit the people and many Israelites died. 7 The people came to Moses and said, "We sinned when we spoke against the LORD and against you. Pray that the LORD will take the snakes away from us." So Moses prayed for the people.

8 The LORD said to Moses, "Make a snake and put it up on a pole; anyone who is bitten can look at it and live." 9 So Moses made a bronze snake and put it up on a pole. Then when anyone was bitten by a snake and looked at the bronze snake, they lived.

The Journey to Moab

10 The Israelites moved on and camped at Oboth. 11 Then they set out from Oboth and camped in Iye Abarim, in the wilderness that faces Moab toward the sunrise. 12 From there they moved on and camped in the Zered Valley. 13 They set out from there and camped alongside the Arnon, which is in the wilderness extending into Amorite territory. The Arnon is the border of Moab, between Moab and the Amorites. 14 That is why the Book of the Wars of the LORD says:

> ". . . Zahab[d] in Suphah and the ravines,
>   the Arnon 15 and[e] the slopes of the
>   ravines
> that lead to the settlement of Ar
>   and lie along the border of Moab."

---

a 2 The Hebrew term refers to the irrevocable giving over of things or persons to the LORD, often by totally destroying them; also in verse 3.   b 3 Hormah means destruction.   c 4 Or the Sea of Reeds   d 14 Septuagint; Hebrew Waheb   e 14,15 Or "I have been given from Suphah and the ravines / of the Arnon 15 to

My Name Is Brad

I'M A BELIEVER WHO STRUGGLES WITH ALCOHOL AND DRUG ADDICTION

Please read Numbers 20:1–3, the story of Moses' failure to follow God's instructions.

I grew up hiding a dark secret — one I kept for 35 years: I was sexually abused as a small child. Basically, I was raised as an only child because my brothers and sisters were married by the time I was born. My family gave me a lot of attention — special attention I didn't receive at school. I resorted to being the "class clown" to make sure I stayed in the limelight.

My brothers were basketball players, setting numerous records in Newton County, Georgia. Everyone expected me to follow in their footsteps, but already by the age of seven I knew I wasn't star material. Still, I went with the program: mini basketball camps, recreation and middle and high school basketball. But my days on the courts were soon replaced with drug addiction.

At the age of ten my friend and I started using his mother's Valium, smoking cigarettes and stealing beer and liquor from his house. My dad was diagnosed with cancer and died the following year, and my drug use increased as a coping mechanism. By the time I was 13, I was using marijuana, and then I became an IV drug user. My family and friends begged me to stop, but to no avail. I was in complete denial, assuring myself that I could stop at any time.

Then, at the age of 17, I was arrested and charged with a DUI and possession with the intent to distribute. I started attending church with a girlfriend, and one night at a youth rally I accepted Jesus as my Savior. I felt a calling to the ministry — something I couldn't understand at all. How could God use me, with my past failures and current lifestyle? The reality was that I still hadn't hit bottom. I didn't get involved in church and refused to be discipled. I was terrified of this "calling" on my life and, after three months, relapsed with a vengeance, becoming addicted to methamphetamines and cocaine. The next 11 years proved to be a roller-coaster ride, with the overall progression being steadily downhill.

When I reached 23, God gave me the most beautiful wife and daughter, Reneé and Hayley. But even they weren't enough to stop me from abusing. I'd spend all our money on drugs and partying. Reneé pleaded with me to get help, and I knew she was right, but I still didn't change. After five years of marriage, Renée had suffered all she could. We separated and were headed for divorce. I did finally hit bottom, after which I experienced a "moment of clarity" that convinced me I had only one viable course of action.

Despite the turmoil of my addictive lifestyle, God never let me forget that I belonged to him and that a price had been paid for me. I found myself at my mother and stepfather's house. There, all three of us got on our knees and prayed. I asked God to forgive me, to take the drugs from me and to give me back my family, along with a new life. I began attending AA meetings, and, after six long months of separation, God put our family back together. We began attending church. Ten years later we transferred our membership and became part of the Eastridge Community Church family.

One Sunday morning our pastor overheard a conversation about starting a small group for those struggling with drug abuse. He approached me about starting a Celebrate Recovery ministry. I was hesitant at first, feeling, like Moses, that God couldn't use me because of my past. In the long run, though, I was open to whatever God wanted. As I began to investigate the program, I started to cry, realizing that this was at long last the outcome of God's calling for me. I began working the Celebrate Recovery Participant Guides, and the most amazing thing happened: I found myself learning to deal with the consequences of my addictions and the obstacles plaguing my walk with Christ. Working through the principles and steps of Celebrate Recovery has helped me in so many ways. I have not only a joy and a peace in my soul but also a divine purpose for my life.

Reneé and I serve together in the Celebrate Recovery ministry. She's my best friend, my companion, my joy, my helpmate and my strength. Together we kicked off Celebrate Recovery in our church. The following year I was brought on staff at Celebrate Recovery to oversee the program — a dream come true!

Celebrate Recovery friends are the real deal! God's Word is true: A real friend does stick "closer than a brother" (Proverbs 18:24). And Romans 8:28 assures us that "in all things God works for the good of those who love him, who have been called according to his purpose."

I can truly say that I'm thankful for all that has happened in my life. Sure, I would change a lot of things if I could, but the reality is that I can't. Yet in spite of the pain, my life has come full circle; God has given me the opportunity to share my experiences, victories and hopes with others through Celebrate Recovery.

Brad

16From there they continued on to Beer, the well where the LORD said to Moses, "Gather the people together and I will give them water."

17Then Israel sang this song:

"Spring up, O well!
    Sing about it,
18about the well that the princes dug,
    that the nobles of the people sank—
    the nobles with scepters and staffs."

Then they went from the wilderness to Mattanah, 19from Mattanah to Nahaliel, from Nahaliel to Bamoth, 20and from Bamoth to the valley in Moab where the top of Pisgah overlooks the wasteland.

Defeat of Sihon and Og

21Israel sent messengers to say to Sihon king of the Amorites:

22"Let us pass through your country. We will not turn aside into any field or vineyard, or drink water from any well. We will travel along the King's Highway until we have passed through your territory."

23But Sihon would not let Israel pass through his territory. He mustered his entire army and marched out into the wilderness against Israel. When he reached Jahaz, he fought with Israel. 24Israel, however, put him to the sword and took over his land from the Arnon to the Jabbok, but only as far as the Ammonites, because their border was fortified. 25Israel captured all the cities of the Amorites and occupied them, including Heshbon and all its surrounding settlements. 26Heshbon was the city of Sihon king of the Amorites, who had fought against the former king of Moab and had taken from him all his land as far as the Arnon.

27That is why the poets say:

"Come to Heshbon and let it be rebuilt;
    let Sihon's city be restored.

28"Fire went out from Heshbon,
    a blaze from the city of Sihon.

It consumed Ar of Moab,
    the citizens of Arnon's heights.
29Woe to you, Moab!
    You are destroyed, people of
        Chemosh!
He has given up his sons as fugitives
    and his daughters as captives
    to Sihon king of the Amorites.

30"But we have overthrown them;
    Heshbon's dominion has been
        destroyed all the way to Dibon.
We have demolished them as far as
        Nophah,
    which extends to Medeba."

31So Israel settled in the land of the Amorites.

32After Moses had sent spies to Jazer, the Israelites captured its surrounding settlements and drove out the Amorites who were there. 33Then they turned and went up along the road toward Bashan, and Og king of Bashan and his whole army marched out to meet them in battle at Edrei.

34The LORD said to Moses, "Do not be afraid of him, for I have delivered him into your hands, along with his whole army and his land. Do to him what you did to Sihon king of the Amorites, who reigned in Heshbon."

35So they struck him down, together with his sons and his whole army, leaving them no survivors. And they took possession of his land.

Balak Summons Balaam

22 Then the Israelites traveled to the plains of Moab and camped along the Jordan across from Jericho.

2Now Balak son of Zippor saw all that Israel had done to the Amorites, 3and Moab was terrified because there were so many people. Indeed, Moab was filled with dread because of the Israelites.

4The Moabites said to the elders of Midian, "This horde is going to lick up everything around us, as an ox licks up the grass of the field."

So Balak son of Zippor, who was king of Moab at that time, [5]sent messengers to summon Balaam son of Beor, who was at Pethor, near the Euphrates River, in his native land. Balak said:

"A people has come out of Egypt; they cover the face of the land and have settled next to me. [6]Now come and put a curse on these people, because they are too powerful for me. Perhaps then I will be able to defeat them and drive them out of the land. For I know that whoever you bless is blessed, and whoever you curse is cursed."

[7]The elders of Moab and Midian left, taking with them the fee for divination. When they came to Balaam, they told him what Balak had said.

[8]"Spend the night here," Balaam said to them, "and I will report back to you with the answer the LORD gives me." So the Moabite officials stayed with him.

[9]God came to Balaam and asked, "Who are these men with you?"

[10]Balaam said to God, "Balak son of Zippor, king of Moab, sent me this message: [11]'A people that has come out of Egypt covers the face of the land. Now come and put a curse on them for me. Perhaps then I will be able to fight them and drive them away.'"

[12]But God said to Balaam, "Do not go with them. You must not put a curse on those people, because they are blessed."

[13]The next morning Balaam got up and said to Balak's officials, "Go back to your own country, for the LORD has refused to let me go with you."

[14]So the Moabite officials returned to Balak and said, "Balaam refused to come with us."

[15]Then Balak sent other officials, more numerous and more distinguished than the first. [16]They came to Balaam and said:

"This is what Balak son of Zippor says: Do not let anything keep you from coming to me, [17]because I will reward you handsomely and do whatever you say. Come and put a curse on these people for me."

[18]But Balaam answered them, "Even if Balak gave me all the silver and gold in his palace, I could not do anything great or small to go beyond the command of the LORD my God. [19]Now spend the night here so that I can find out what else the LORD will tell me."

[20]That night God came to Balaam and said, "Since these men have come to summon you, go with them, but do only what I tell you."

Balaam's Donkey

[21]Balaam got up in the morning, saddled his donkey and went with the Moabite officials. [22]But God was very angry when he went, and the angel of the LORD stood in the road to oppose him. Balaam was riding on his donkey, and his two servants were with him. [23]When the donkey saw the angel of the LORD standing in the road with a drawn sword in his hand, it turned off the road into a field. Balaam beat it to get it back on the road.

[24]Then the angel of the LORD stood in a narrow path through the vineyards, with walls on both sides. [25]When the donkey saw the angel of the LORD, it pressed close to the wall, crushing Balaam's foot against it. So he beat the donkey again.

[26]Then the angel of the LORD moved on ahead and stood in a narrow place where there was no room to turn, either to the right or to the left. [27]When the donkey saw the angel of the LORD, it lay down under Balaam, and he was angry and beat it with his staff. [28]Then the LORD opened the donkey's mouth, and it said to Balaam, "What have I done to you to make you beat me these three times?"

[29]Balaam answered the donkey, "You have made a fool of me! If only I had a sword in my hand, I would kill you right now."

[30]The donkey said to Balaam, "Am I not your own donkey, which you have always

ridden, to this day? Have I been in the habit of doing this to you?"

"No," he said.

[1][2][3] 31Then the LORD opened Balaam's eyes, and he saw the angel of the LORD standing in the road with his sword drawn. So he bowed low and fell facedown.

32The angel of the LORD asked him, "Why have you beaten your donkey these three times? I have come here to oppose you because your path is a reckless one before me.[a] 33The donkey saw me and turned away from me these three times. If it had not turned away, I would certainly have killed you by now, but I would have spared it."

[4][5] 34Balaam said to the angel of the LORD, "I have sinned. I did not realize you were standing in the road to oppose me. Now if you are displeased, I will go back."

35The angel of the LORD said to Balaam, "Go with the men, but speak only what I tell you." So Balaam went with Balak's officials.

36When Balak heard that Balaam was coming, he went out to meet him at the Moabite town on the Arnon border, at the edge of his territory. 37Balak said to Balaam, "Did I not send you an urgent summons? Why didn't you come to me? Am I really not able to reward you?"

38"Well, I have come to you now," Balaam replied. "But I can't say whatever I please. I must speak only what God puts in my mouth."

39Then Balaam went with Balak to Kiriath Huzoth. 40Balak sacrificed cattle and sheep, and gave some to Balaam and the officials who were with him. 41The next morning Balak took Balaam up to Bamoth Baal, and from there he could see the outskirts of the Israelite camp.

Balaam's First Message

23 Balaam said, "Build me seven altars here, and prepare seven bulls and seven rams for me." 2Balak did as Balaam said, and the two of them offered a bull and a ram on each altar.

3Then Balaam said to Balak, "Stay here beside your offering while I go aside. Perhaps the LORD will come to meet with me. Whatever he reveals to me I will tell you." Then he went off to a barren height.

4God met with him, and Balaam said, "I have prepared seven altars, and on each altar I have offered a bull and a ram."

5The LORD put a word in Balaam's mouth and said, "Go back to Balak and give him this word."

6So he went back to him and found him standing beside his offering, with all the Moabite officials. 7Then Balaam spoke his message:

"Balak brought me from Aram,
    the king of Moab from the eastern
        mountains.
'Come,' he said, 'curse Jacob for me;
    come, denounce Israel.'
8How can I curse
    those whom God has not cursed?
How can I denounce
    those whom the LORD has not
        denounced?
9From the rocky peaks I see them,
    from the heights I view them.
I see a people who live apart
    and do not consider themselves one
        of the nations.
10Who can count the dust of Jacob
    or number even a fourth of Israel?
Let me die the death of the righteous,
    and may my final end be like theirs!"

11Balak said to Balaam, "What have you done to me? I brought you to curse my enemies, but you have done nothing but bless them!"

12He answered, "Must I not speak what the LORD puts in my mouth?"

Balaam's Second Message

13Then Balak said to him, "Come with me to another place where you can see them; you will not see them all but only the outskirts of their camp. And from there,

---

a 32 The meaning of the Hebrew for this clause is uncertain.

curse them for me." [14]So he took him to the field of Zophim on the top of Pisgah, and there he built seven altars and offered a bull and a ram on each altar.

[15]Balaam said to Balak, "Stay here beside your offering while I meet with him over there."

[16]The LORD met with Balaam and put a word in his mouth and said, "Go back to Balak and give him this word."

[17]So he went to him and found him standing beside his offering, with the Moabite officials. Balak asked him, "What did the LORD say?"

[18]Then he spoke his message:

"Arise, Balak, and listen;
> hear me, son of Zippor.
[19]God is not human, that he should lie,
> not a human being, that he should
>   change his mind.
Does he speak and then not act?
> Does he promise and not fulfill?
[20]I have received a command to bless;
> he has blessed, and I cannot
>   change it.

[21]"No misfortune is seen in Jacob,
> no misery observed[a] in Israel.
The LORD their God is with them;
> the shout of the King is among
>   them.
[22]God brought them out of Egypt;
> they have the strength of a wild ox.
[23]There is no divination against[b] Jacob,
> no evil omens against[b] Israel.
It will now be said of Jacob
> and of Israel, 'See what God has
>   done!'
[24]The people rise like a lioness;
> they rouse themselves like a lion
that does not rest till it devours its prey
> and drinks the blood of its victims."

[25]Then Balak said to Balaam, "Neither curse them at all nor bless them at all!"

[26]Balaam answered, "Did I not tell you I must do whatever the LORD says?"

Balaam's Third Message

[27]Then Balak said to Balaam, "Come, let me take you to another place. Perhaps it will please God to let you curse them for me from there." [28]And Balak took Balaam to the top of Peor, overlooking the wasteland.

[29]Balaam said, "Build me seven altars here, and prepare seven bulls and seven rams for me." [30]Balak did as Balaam had said, and offered a bull and a ram on each altar.

24 Now when Balaam saw that it pleased the LORD to bless Israel, he did not resort to divination as at other times, but turned his face toward the wilderness. [2]When Balaam looked out and saw Israel encamped tribe by tribe, the Spirit of God came on him [3]and he spoke his message:

"The prophecy of Balaam son of Beor,
> the prophecy of one whose eye sees
>   clearly,
[4]the prophecy of one who hears the
>   words of God,
who sees a vision from the
>   Almighty,[c]
who falls prostrate, and whose eyes
>   are opened:

[5]"How beautiful are your tents, Jacob,
> your dwelling places, Israel!

[6]"Like valleys they spread out,
> like gardens beside a river,
like aloes planted by the LORD,
> like cedars beside the waters.
[7]Water will flow from their buckets;
> their seed will have abundant water.

"Their king will be greater than Agag;
> their kingdom will be exalted.

[8]"God brought them out of Egypt;
> they have the strength of a wild ox.
They devour hostile nations
> and break their bones in pieces;
> with their arrows they pierce them.

---

[a] 21 Or *He has not looked on Jacob's offenses / or on the wrongs found*   [b] 23 Or *in*   [c] 4 Hebrew *Shaddai*; also in verse 16

⁹Like a lion they crouch and lie down,
  like a lioness — who dares to rouse
    them?

"May those who bless you be blessed
  and those who curse you be cursed!"

¹⁰Then Balak's anger burned against Balaam. He struck his hands together and said to him, "I summoned you to curse my enemies, but you have blessed them these three times. ¹¹Now leave at once and go home! I said I would reward you handsomely, but the LORD has kept you from being rewarded."

¹²Balaam answered Balak, "Did I not tell the messengers you sent me, ¹³'Even if Balak gave me all the silver and gold in his palace, I could not do anything of my own accord, good or bad, to go beyond the command of the LORD — and I must say only what the LORD says'? ¹⁴Now I am going back to my people, but come, let me warn you of what this people will do to your people in days to come."

Balaam's Fourth Message

¹⁵Then he spoke his message:

"The prophecy of Balaam son of Beor,
  the prophecy of one whose eye sees
    clearly,
¹⁶the prophecy of one who hears the
    words of God,
  who has knowledge from the Most
    High,
who sees a vision from the Almighty,
  who falls prostrate, and whose eyes
    are opened:

¹⁷"I see him, but not now;
  I behold him, but not near.
A star will come out of Jacob;
  a scepter will rise out of Israel.
He will crush the foreheads of Moab,
  the skulls*a* of*b* all the people of
    Sheth.*c*

¹⁸Edom will be conquered;
  Seir, his enemy, will be conquered,
    but Israel will grow strong.
¹⁹A ruler will come out of Jacob
  and destroy the survivors of the
    city."

Balaam's Fifth Message

²⁰Then Balaam saw Amalek and spoke his message:

"Amalek was first among the nations,
  but their end will be utter
    destruction."

Balaam's Sixth Message

²¹Then he saw the Kenites and spoke his message:

"Your dwelling place is secure,
  your nest is set in a rock;
²²yet you Kenites will be destroyed
  when Ashur takes you captive."

Balaam's Seventh Message

²³Then he spoke his message:

"Alas! Who can live when God does
    this?*d*
²⁴   Ships will come from the shores of
      Cyprus;
  they will subdue Ashur and Eber,
    but they too will come to ruin."

²⁵Then Balaam got up and returned home, and Balak went his own way.

Moab Seduces Israel

25 While Israel was staying in Shittim, the men began to indulge in sexual immorality with Moabite women, ²who invited them to the sacrifices to their gods. The people ate the sacrificial meal and bowed down before these gods. ³So Israel yoked themselves to the Baal of Peor. And the LORD's anger burned against them.

---

a 17 Samaritan Pentateuch (see also Jer. 48:45); the meaning of the word in the Masoretic Text is uncertain.
b 17 Or possibly *Moab, / batter*   *c 17* Or *all the noisy boasters*   *d 23* Masoretic Text; with a different word division of the Hebrew *The people from the islands will gather from the north.*

4The LORD said to Moses, "Take all the leaders of these people, kill them and expose them in broad daylight before the LORD, so that the LORD's fierce anger may turn away from Israel."

5So Moses said to Israel's judges, "Each of you must put to death those of your people who have yoked themselves to the Baal of Peor."

6Then an Israelite man brought into the camp a Midianite woman right before the eyes of Moses and the whole assembly of Israel while they were weeping at the entrance to the tent of meeting. 7When Phinehas son of Eleazar, the son of Aaron, the priest, saw this, he left the assembly, took a spear in his hand 8and followed the Israelite into the tent. He drove the spear into both of them, right through the Israelite man and into the woman's stomach. Then the plague against the Israelites was stopped; 9but those who died in the plague numbered 24,000.

10The LORD said to Moses, 11"Phinehas son of Eleazar, the son of Aaron, the priest, has turned my anger away from the Israelites. Since he was as zealous for my honor among them as I am, I did not put an end to them in my zeal. 12Therefore tell him I am making my covenant of peace with him. 13He and his descendants will have a covenant of a lasting priesthood, because he was zealous for the honor of his God and made atonement for the Israelites."

14The name of the Israelite who was killed with the Midianite woman was Zimri son of Salu, the leader of a Simeonite family. 15And the name of the Midianite woman who was put to death was Kozbi daughter of Zur, a tribal chief of a Midianite family.

16The LORD said to Moses, 17"Treat the Midianites as enemies and kill them. 18They treated you as enemies when they deceived you in the Peor incident involving their sister Kozbi, the daughter of a Midianite leader, the woman who was killed when the plague came as a result of that incident."

The Second Census

26 After the plague the LORD said to Moses and Eleazar son of Aaron, the priest, 2"Take a census of the whole Israelite community by families — all those twenty years old or more who are able to serve in the army of Israel." 3So on the plains of Moab by the Jordan across from Jericho, Moses and Eleazar the priest spoke with them and said, 4"Take a census of the men twenty years old or more, as the LORD commanded Moses."

These were the Israelites who came out of Egypt:

5The descendants of Reuben, the firstborn son of Israel, were:

through Hanok, the Hanokite clan;
through Pallu, the Palluite clan;
6through Hezron, the Hezronite clan;
through Karmi, the Karmite clan.
7These were the clans of Reuben; those numbered were 43,730.

8The son of Pallu was Eliab, 9and the sons of Eliab were Nemuel, Dathan and Abiram. The same Dathan and Abiram were the community officials who rebelled against Moses and Aaron and were among Korah's followers when they rebelled against the LORD. 10The earth opened its mouth and swallowed them along with Korah, whose followers died when the fire devoured the 250 men. And they served as a warning sign. 11The line of Korah, however, did not die out.

12The descendants of Simeon by their clans were:

through Nemuel, the Nemuelite clan;
through Jamin, the Jaminite clan;
through Jakin, the Jakinite clan;
13through Zerah, the Zerahite clan;
through Shaul, the Shaulite clan.
14These were the clans of Simeon; those numbered were 22,200.

15The descendants of Gad by their clans were:

through Zephon, the Zephonite clan;
through Haggi, the Haggite clan;

through Shuni, the Shunite clan;
16 through Ozni, the Oznite clan;
through Eri, the Erite clan;
17 through Arodi,*a* the Arodite clan;
through Areli, the Arelite clan.
18 These were the clans of Gad; those numbered were 40,500.

19 Er and Onan were sons of Judah, but they died in Canaan.
20 The descendants of Judah by their clans were:
through Shelah, the Shelanite clan;
through Perez, the Perezite clan;
through Zerah, the Zerahite clan.
21 The descendants of Perez were:
through Hezron, the Hezronite clan;
through Hamul, the Hamulite clan.
22 These were the clans of Judah; those numbered were 76,500.

23 The descendants of Issachar by their clans were:
through Tola, the Tolaite clan;
through Puah, the Puite*b* clan;
24 through Jashub, the Jashubite clan;
through Shimron, the Shimronite clan.
25 These were the clans of Issachar; those numbered were 64,300.

26 The descendants of Zebulun by their clans were:
through Sered, the Seredite clan;
through Elon, the Elonite clan;
through Jahleel, the Jahleelite clan.
27 These were the clans of Zebulun; those numbered were 60,500.

28 The descendants of Joseph by their clans through Manasseh and Ephraim were:

29 The descendants of Manasseh:
through Makir, the Makirite clan
(Makir was the father of Gilead);
through Gilead, the Gileadite clan.

30 These were the descendants of Gilead:
through Iezer, the Iezerite clan;
through Helek, the Helekite clan;
31 through Asriel, the Asrielite clan;
through Shechem, the Shechemite clan;
32 through Shemida, the Shemidaite clan;
through Hepher, the Hepherite clan.
33 (Zelophehad son of Hepher had no sons; he had only daughters, whose names were Mahlah, Noah, Hoglah, Milkah and Tirzah.)
34 These were the clans of Manasseh; those numbered were 52,700.

35 These were the descendants of Ephraim by their clans:
through Shuthelah, the Shuthelahite clan;
through Beker, the Bekerite clan;
through Tahan, the Tahanite clan.
36 These were the descendants of Shuthelah:
through Eran, the Eranite clan.
37 These were the clans of Ephraim; those numbered were 32,500.

These were the descendants of Joseph by their clans.

38 The descendants of Benjamin by their clans were:
through Bela, the Belaite clan;
through Ashbel, the Ashbelite clan;
through Ahiram, the Ahiramite clan;
39 through Shupham,*c* the Shuphamite clan;
through Hupham, the Huphamite clan.
40 The descendants of Bela through Ard and Naaman were:
through Ard,*d* the Ardite clan;
through Naaman, the Naamite clan.

---

a 17 Samaritan Pentateuch and Syriac (see also Gen. 46:16); Masoretic Text *Arod*   *b 23* Samaritan Pentateuch, Septuagint, Vulgate and Syriac (see also 1 Chron. 7:1); Masoretic Text *through Puvah, the Punite*   *c 39* A few manuscripts of the Masoretic Text, Samaritan Pentateuch, Vulgate and Syriac (see also Septuagint); most manuscripts of the Masoretic Text *Shephupham*   *d 40* Samaritan Pentateuch and Vulgate (see also Septuagint); Masoretic Text does not have *through Ard.*

41 These were the clans of Benjamin; those numbered were 45,600.

42 These were the descendants of Dan by their clans:

through Shuham, the Shuhamite clan.

These were the clans of Dan: 43 All of them were Shuhamite clans; and those numbered were 64,400.

44 The descendants of Asher by their clans were:

through Imnah, the Imnite clan;

through Ishvi, the Ishvite clan;

through Beriah, the Beriite clan;

45 and through the descendants of Beriah:

through Heber, the Heberite clan;

through Malkiel, the Malkielite clan.

46 (Asher had a daughter named Serah.)

47 These were the clans of Asher; those numbered were 53,400.

48 The descendants of Naphtali by their clans were:

through Jahzeel, the Jahzeelite clan;

through Guni, the Gunite clan;

49 through Jezer, the Jezerite clan;

through Shillem, the Shillemite clan.

50 These were the clans of Naphtali; those numbered were 45,400.

51 The total number of the men of Israel was 601,730.

52 The LORD said to Moses, 53 "The land is to be allotted to them as an inheritance based on the number of names. 54 To a larger group give a larger inheritance, and to a smaller group a smaller one; each is to receive its inheritance according to the number of those listed. 55 Be sure that the land is distributed by lot. What each group inherits will be according to the names for its ancestral tribe. 56 Each inheritance is to be distributed by lot among the larger and smaller groups."

57 These were the Levites who were counted by their clans:

through Gershon, the Gershonite clan;

through Kohath, the Kohathite clan;

through Merari, the Merarite clan.

58 These also were Levite clans:

the Libnite clan,

the Hebronite clan,

the Mahlite clan,

the Mushite clan,

the Korahite clan.

(Kohath was the forefather of Amram; 59 the name of Amram's wife was Jochebed, a descendant of Levi, who was born to the Levites[a] in Egypt. To Amram she bore Aaron, Moses and their sister Miriam. 60 Aaron was the father of Nadab and Abihu, Eleazar and Ithamar. 61 But Nadab and Abihu died when they made an offering before the LORD with unauthorized fire.)

62 All the male Levites a month old or more numbered 23,000. They were not counted along with the other Israelites because they received no inheritance among them.

63 These are the ones counted by Moses and Eleazar the priest when they counted the Israelites on the plains of Moab by the Jordan across from Jericho. 64 Not one of them was among those counted by Moses and Aaron the priest when they counted the Israelites in the Desert of Sinai. 65 For the LORD had told those Israelites they would surely die in the wilderness, and not one of them was left except Caleb son of Jephunneh and Joshua son of Nun.

Zelophehad's Daughters

27 The daughters of Zelophehad son of Hepher, the son of Gilead, the son of Makir, the son of Manasseh, belonged to the clans of Manasseh son of Joseph. The names of the daughters were Mahlah, Noah, Hoglah, Milkah

---

a 59 Or Jochebed, a daughter of Levi, who was born to Levi

and Tirzah. They came forward ²and stood before Moses, Eleazar the priest, the leaders and the whole assembly at the entrance to the tent of meeting and said, ³"Our father died in the wilderness. He was not among Korah's followers, who banded together against the Lord, but he died for his own sin and left no sons. ⁴Why should our father's name disappear from his clan because he had no son? Give us property among our father's relatives."

⁵So Moses brought their case before the Lord, ⁶and the Lord said to him, ⁷"What Zelophehad's daughters are saying is right. You must certainly give them property as an inheritance among their father's relatives and give their father's inheritance to them.

⁸"Say to the Israelites, 'If a man dies and leaves no son, give his inheritance to his daughter. ⁹If he has no daughter, give his inheritance to his brothers. ¹⁰If he has no brothers, give his inheritance to his father's brothers. ¹¹If his father had no brothers, give his inheritance to the nearest relative in his clan, that he may possess it. This is to have the force of law for the Israelites, as the Lord commanded Moses.'"

Joshua to Succeed Moses

¹²Then the Lord said to Moses, "Go up this mountain in the Abarim Range and see the land I have given the Israelites. ¹³After you have seen it, you too will be gathered to your people, as your brother Aaron was, ¹⁴for when the community rebelled at the waters in the Desert of Zin, both of you disobeyed my command to honor me as holy before their eyes." (These were the waters of Meribah Kadesh, in the Desert of Zin.)

¹⁵Moses said to the Lord, ¹⁶"May the Lord, the God who gives breath to all living things, appoint someone over this community ¹⁷to go out and come in before them, one who will lead them out and bring them in, so the Lord's people will not be like sheep without a shepherd."

¹⁸So the Lord said to Moses, "Take Joshua son of Nun, a man in whom is the spirit of leadership,ᵃ and lay your hand on him. ¹⁹Have him stand before Eleazar the priest and the entire assembly and commission him in their presence. ²⁰Give him some of your authority so the whole Israelite community will obey him. ²¹He is to stand before Eleazar the priest, who will obtain decisions for him by inquiring of the Urim before the Lord. At his command he and the entire community of the Israelites will go out, and at his command they will come in."

²²Moses did as the Lord commanded him. He took Joshua and had him stand before Eleazar the priest and the whole assembly. ²³Then he laid his hands on him and commissioned him, as the Lord instructed through Moses.

Daily Offerings

28 The Lord said to Moses, ²"Give this command to the Israelites and say to them: 'Make sure that you present to me at the appointed time my food offerings, as an aroma pleasing to me.' ³Say to them: 'This is the food offering you are to present to the Lord: two lambs a year old without defect, as a regular burnt offering each day. ⁴Offer one lamb in the morning and the other at twilight, ⁵together with a grain offering of a tenth of an ephahᵇ of the finest flour mixed with a quarter of a hinᶜ of oil from pressed olives. ⁶This is the regular burnt offering instituted at Mount Sinai as a pleasing aroma, a food offering presented to the Lord. ⁷The accompanying drink offering is to be a quarter of a hin of fermented drink with each lamb. Pour out the drink offering to the Lord at the sanctuary. ⁸Offer the second lamb at twilight, along with the same kind of grain offering and drink offering that you offer in the morning. This is a food offering, an aroma pleasing to the Lord.

ᵃ 18 Or the Spirit   ᵇ 5 That is, probably about 3 1/2 pounds or about 1.6 kilograms; also in verses 13, 21 and 29
ᶜ 5 That is, about 1 quart or about 1 liter; also in verses 7 and 14

Sabbath Offerings

9 "'On the Sabbath day, make an offering of two lambs a year old without defect, together with its drink offering and a grain offering of two-tenths of an ephah*a* of the finest flour mixed with olive oil. 10This is the burnt offering for every Sabbath, in addition to the regular burnt offering and its drink offering.

Monthly Offerings

11 "'On the first of every month, present to the LORD a burnt offering of two young bulls, one ram and seven male lambs a year old, all without defect. 12With each bull there is to be a grain offering of three-tenths of an ephah*b* of the finest flour mixed with oil; with the ram, a grain offering of two-tenths of an ephah of the finest flour mixed with oil; 13and with each lamb, a grain offering of a tenth of an ephah of the finest flour mixed with oil. This is for a burnt offering, a pleasing aroma, a food offering presented to the LORD. 14With each bull there is to be a drink offering of half a hin*c* of wine; with the ram, a third of a hin*d*; and with each lamb, a quarter of a hin. This is the monthly burnt offering to be made at each new moon during the year. 15Besides the regular burnt offering with its drink offering, one male goat is to be presented to the LORD as a sin offering.*e*

The Passover

16 "'On the fourteenth day of the first month the LORD's Passover is to be held. 17On the fifteenth day of this month there is to be a festival; for seven days eat bread made without yeast. 18On the first day hold a sacred assembly and do no regular work. 19Present to the LORD a food offering consisting of a burnt offering of two young bulls, one ram and seven male lambs a year old, all without defect. 20With each bull offer a grain offering of three-tenths of an ephah of the finest flour mixed with oil; with the ram, two-tenths; 21and with each of the seven lambs, one-tenth. 22Include one male goat as a sin offering to make atonement for you. 23Offer these in addition to the regular morning burnt offering. 24In this way present the food offering every day for seven days as an aroma pleasing to the LORD; it is to be offered in addition to the regular burnt offering and its drink offering. 25On the seventh day hold a sacred assembly and do no regular work.

The Festival of Weeks

26 "'On the day of firstfruits, when you present to the LORD an offering of new grain during the Festival of Weeks, hold a sacred assembly and do no regular work. 27Present a burnt offering of two young bulls, one ram and seven male lambs a year old as an aroma pleasing to the LORD. 28With each bull there is to be a grain offering of three-tenths of an ephah of the finest flour mixed with oil; with the ram, two-tenths; 29and with each of the seven lambs, one-tenth. 30Include one male goat to make atonement for you. 31Offer these together with their drink offerings, in addition to the regular burnt offering and its grain offering. Be sure the animals are without defect.

The Festival of Trumpets

29 "'On the first day of the seventh month hold a sacred assembly and do no regular work. It is a day for you to sound the trumpets. 2As an aroma pleasing to the LORD, offer a burnt offering of one young bull, one ram and seven male lambs a year old, all without defect. 3With the bull offer a grain offering of three-tenths of an ephah*f* of the finest flour mixed with olive oil; with the ram, two-tenths*g*; 4and with each

---

a 9 That is, probably about 7 pounds or about 3.2 kilograms; also in verses 12, 20 and 28   *b 12* That is, probably about 11 pounds or about 5 kilograms; also in verses 20 and 28   *c 14* That is, about 2 quarts or about 1.9 liters   *d 14* That is, about 1 1/3 quarts or about 1.3 liters   *e 15* Or *purification offering*; also in verse 22   *f 3* That is, probably about 11 pounds or about 5 kilograms; also in verses 9 and 14   *g 3* That is, probably about 7 pounds or about 3.2 kilograms; also in verses 9 and 14 of the seven lambs, one-tenth.[a] [5]Include one male goat as a sin offering[b] to make atonement for you. [6]These are in addition to the monthly and daily burnt offerings with their grain offerings and drink offerings as specified. They are food offerings presented to the LORD, a pleasing aroma.

The Day of Atonement

[7]"'On the tenth day of this seventh month hold a sacred assembly. You must deny yourselves[c] and do no work. [8]Present as an aroma pleasing to the LORD a burnt offering of one young bull, one ram and seven male lambs a year old, all without defect. [9]With the bull offer a grain offering of three-tenths of an ephah of the finest flour mixed with oil; with the ram, two-tenths; [10]and with each of the seven lambs, one-tenth. [11]Include one male goat as a sin offering, in addition to the sin offering for atonement and the regular burnt offering with its grain offering, and their drink offerings.

The Festival of Tabernacles

[12]"'On the fifteenth day of the seventh month, hold a sacred assembly and do no regular work. Celebrate a festival to the LORD for seven days. [13]Present as an aroma pleasing to the LORD a food offering consisting of a burnt offering of thirteen young bulls, two rams and fourteen male lambs a year old, all without defect. [14]With each of the thirteen bulls offer a grain offering of three-tenths of an ephah of the finest flour mixed with oil; with each of the two rams, two-tenths; [15]and with each of the fourteen lambs, one-tenth. [16]Include one male goat as a sin offering, in addition to the regular burnt offering with its grain offering and drink offering.

[17]"'On the second day offer twelve young bulls, two rams and fourteen male lambs a year old, all without defect. [18]With the bulls, rams and lambs, offer their grain

offerings and drink offerings according to the number specified. [19]Include one male goat as a sin offering, in addition to the regular burnt offering with its grain offering, and their drink offerings.

[20]"'On the third day offer eleven bulls, two rams and fourteen male lambs a year old, all without defect. [21]With the bulls, rams and lambs, offer their grain offerings and drink offerings according to the number specified. [22]Include one male goat as a sin offering, in addition to the regular burnt offering with its grain offering and drink offering.

[23]"'On the fourth day offer ten bulls, two rams and fourteen male lambs a year old, all without defect. [24]With the bulls, rams and lambs, offer their grain offerings and drink offerings according to the number specified. [25]Include one male goat as a sin offering, in addition to the regular burnt offering with its grain offering and drink offering.

[26]"'On the fifth day offer nine bulls, two rams and fourteen male lambs a year old, all without defect. [27]With the bulls, rams and lambs, offer their grain offerings and drink offerings according to the number specified. [28]Include one male goat as a sin offering, in addition to the regular burnt offering with its grain offering and drink offering.

[29]"'On the sixth day offer eight bulls, two rams and fourteen male lambs a year old, all without defect. [30]With the bulls, rams and lambs, offer their grain offerings and drink offerings according to the number specified. [31]Include one male goat as a sin offering, in addition to the regular burnt offering with its grain offering and drink offering.

[32]"'On the seventh day offer seven bulls, two rams and fourteen male lambs a year old, all without defect. [33]With the bulls, rams and lambs, offer their grain offerings and drink offerings according to the

---

[a] 4 That is, probably about 3 1/2 pounds or about 1.6 kilograms; also in verses 10 and 15   [b] 5 Or purification offering; also elsewhere in this chapter   [c] 7 Or must fast

number specified. [34]Include one male goat as a sin offering, in addition to the regular burnt offering with its grain offering and drink offering.

[35]"'On the eighth day hold a closing special assembly and do no regular work. [36]Present as an aroma pleasing to the LORD a food offering consisting of a burnt offering of one bull, one ram and seven male lambs a year old, all without defect. [37]With the bull, the ram and the lambs, offer their grain offerings and drink offerings according to the number specified. [38]Include one male goat as a sin offering, in addition to the regular burnt offering with its grain offering and drink offering.

[39]"'In addition to what you vow and your freewill offerings, offer these to the LORD at your appointed festivals: your burnt offerings, grain offerings, drink offerings and fellowship offerings.'"

[40]Moses told the Israelites all that the LORD commanded him.[a]

Vows

30 [b] Moses said to the heads of the tribes of Israel: "This is what the LORD commands: [2]When a man makes a vow to the LORD or takes an oath to obligate himself by a pledge, he must not break his word but must do everything he said.

[3]"When a young woman still living in her father's household makes a vow to the LORD or obligates herself by a pledge [4]and her father hears about her vow or pledge but says nothing to her, then all her vows and every pledge by which she obligated herself will stand. [5]But if her father forbids her when he hears about it, none of her vows or the pledges by which she obligated herself will stand; the LORD will release her because her father has forbidden her.

[6]"If she marries after she makes a vow or after her lips utter a rash promise by which she obligates herself [7]and her husband hears about it but says nothing to her, then her vows or the pledges by which she obligated herself will stand. [8]But if her husband forbids her when he hears about it, he nullifies the vow that obligates her or the rash promise by which she obligates herself, and the LORD will release her.

[9]"Any vow or obligation taken by a widow or divorced woman will be binding on her.

[10]"If a woman living with her husband makes a vow or obligates herself by a pledge under oath [11]and her husband hears about it but says nothing to her and does not forbid her, then all her vows or the pledges by which she obligated herself will stand. [12]But if her husband nullifies them when he hears about them, then none of the vows or pledges that came from her lips will stand. Her husband has nullified them, and the LORD will release her. [13]Her husband may confirm or nullify any vow she makes or any sworn pledge to deny herself.[c] [14]But if her husband says nothing to her about it from day to day, then he confirms all her vows or the pledges binding on her. He confirms them by saying nothing to her when he hears about them. [15]If, however, he nullifies them some time after he hears about them, then he must bear the consequences of her wrongdoing."

[16]These are the regulations the LORD gave Moses concerning relationships between a man and his wife, and between a father and his young daughter still living at home.

Vengeance on the Midianites

31 The LORD said to Moses, [2]"Take vengeance on the Midianites for the Israelites. After that, you will be gathered to your people."

[3]So Moses said to the people, "Arm some of your men to go to war against the Midianites so that they may carry out the LORD's vengeance on them. [4]Send into

---

[a] 40 In Hebrew texts this verse (29:40) is numbered 30:1.   [b] In Hebrew texts 30:1-16 is numbered 30:2-17.
[c] 13 Or to fast

battle a thousand men from each of the tribes of Israel." ⁵So twelve thousand men armed for battle, a thousand from each tribe, were supplied from the clans of Israel. ⁶Moses sent them into battle, a thousand from each tribe, along with Phinehas son of Eleazar, the priest, who took with him articles from the sanctuary and the trumpets for signaling.

⁷They fought against Midian, as the LORD commanded Moses, and killed every man. ⁸Among their victims were Evi, Rekem, Zur, Hur and Reba — the five kings of Midian. They also killed Balaam son of Beor with the sword. ⁹The Israelites captured the Midianite women and children and took all the Midianite herds, flocks and goods as plunder. ¹⁰They burned all the towns where the Midianites had settled, as well as all their camps. ¹¹They took all the plunder and spoils, including the people and animals, ¹²and brought the captives, spoils and plunder to Moses and Eleazar the priest and the Israelite assembly at their camp on the plains of Moab, by the Jordan across from Jericho.

¹³Moses, Eleazar the priest and all the leaders of the community went to meet them outside the camp. ¹⁴Moses was angry with the officers of the army — the commanders of thousands and commanders of hundreds — who returned from the battle.

¹⁵"Have you allowed all the women to live?" he asked them. ¹⁶"They were the ones who followed Balaam's advice and enticed the Israelites to be unfaithful to the LORD in the Peor incident, so that a plague struck the LORD's people. ¹⁷Now kill all the boys. And kill every woman who has slept with a man, ¹⁸but save for yourselves every girl who has never slept with a man.

¹⁹"Anyone who has killed someone or touched someone who was killed must stay outside the camp seven days. On the third and seventh days you must purify yourselves and your captives. ²⁰Purify every garment as well as everything made of leather, goat hair or wood."

²¹Then Eleazar the priest said to the soldiers who had gone into battle, "This is what is required by the law that the LORD gave Moses: ²²Gold, silver, bronze, iron, tin, lead ²³and anything else that can withstand fire must be put through the fire, and then it will be clean. But it must also be purified with the water of cleansing. And whatever cannot withstand fire must be put through that water. ²⁴On the seventh day wash your clothes and you will be clean. Then you may come into the camp."

Dividing the Spoils

²⁵The LORD said to Moses, ²⁶"You and Eleazar the priest and the family heads of the community are to count all the people and animals that were captured. ²⁷Divide the spoils equally between the soldiers who took part in the battle and the rest of the community. ²⁸From the soldiers who fought in the battle, set apart as tribute for the LORD one out of every five hundred, whether people, cattle, donkeys or sheep. ²⁹Take this tribute from their half share and give it to Eleazar the priest as the LORD's part. ³⁰From the Israelites' half, select one out of every fifty, whether people, cattle, donkeys, sheep or other animals. Give them to the Levites, who are responsible for the care of the LORD's tabernacle." ³¹So Moses and Eleazar the priest did as the LORD commanded Moses.

³²The plunder remaining from the spoils that the soldiers took was 675,000 sheep, ³³72,000 cattle, ³⁴61,000 donkeys ³⁵and 32,000 women who had never slept with a man.

³⁶The half share of those who fought in the battle was:

> 337,500 sheep, ³⁷of which the tribute for the LORD was 675;
>
> ³⁸36,000 cattle, of which the tribute for the LORD was 72;
>
> ³⁹30,500 donkeys, of which the tribute for the LORD was 61;
>
> ⁴⁰16,000 people, of whom the tribute for the LORD was 32.

41Moses gave the tribute to Eleazar the priest as the Lord's part, as the Lord commanded Moses.

42The half belonging to the Israelites, which Moses set apart from that of the fighting men— 43the community's half— was 337,500 sheep, 4436,000 cattle, 4530,500 donkeys 46and 16,000 people. 47From the Israelites' half, Moses selected one out of every fifty people and animals, as the Lord commanded him, and gave them to the Levites, who were responsible for the care of the Lord's tabernacle.

48Then the officers who were over the units of the army— the commanders of thousands and commanders of hundreds— went to Moses 49and said to him, "Your servants have counted the soldiers under our command, and not one is missing. 50So we have brought as an offering to the Lord the gold articles each of us acquired— armlets, bracelets, signet rings, earrings and necklaces— to make atonement for ourselves before the Lord."

51Moses and Eleazar the priest accepted from them the gold—all the crafted articles. 52All the gold from the commanders of thousands and commanders of hundreds that Moses and Eleazar presented as a gift to the Lord weighed 16,750 shekels.*a* 53Each soldier had taken plunder for himself. 54Moses and Eleazar the priest accepted the gold from the commanders of thousands and commanders of hundreds and brought it into the tent of meeting as a memorial for the Israelites before the Lord.

The Transjordan Tribes

32 The Reubenites and Gadites, who had very large herds and flocks, saw that the lands of Jazer and Gilead were suitable for livestock. 2So they came to Moses and Eleazar the priest and to the leaders of the community, and said, 3"Ataroth, Dibon, Jazer, Nimrah, Heshbon, Elealeh, Sebam, Nebo and Beon— 4the land the Lord subdued be-

fore the people of Israel—are suitable for livestock, and your servants have livestock. 5If we have found favor in your eyes," they said, "let this land be given to your servants as our possession. Do not make us cross the Jordan."

6Moses said to the Gadites and Reubenites, "Should your fellow Israelites go to war while you sit here? 7Why do you discourage the Israelites from crossing over into the land the Lord has given them? 8This is what your fathers did when I sent them from Kadesh Barnea to look over the land. 9After they went up to the Valley of Eshkol and viewed the land, they discouraged the Israelites from entering the land the Lord had given them. 10The Lord's anger was aroused that day and he swore this oath: 11'Because they have not followed me wholeheartedly, not one of those who were twenty years old or more when they came up out of Egypt will see the land I promised on oath to Abraham, Isaac and Jacob— 12not one except Caleb son of Jephunneh the Kenizzite and Joshua son of Nun, for they followed the Lord wholeheartedly.' 13The Lord's anger burned against Israel and he made them wander in the wilderness forty years, until the whole generation of those who had done evil in his sight was gone.

14"And here you are, a brood of sinners, standing in the place of your fathers and making the Lord even more angry with Israel. 15If you turn away from following him, he will again leave all this people in the wilderness, and you will be the cause of their destruction."

16Then they came up to him and said, "We would like to build pens here for our livestock and cities for our women and children. 17But we will arm ourselves for battle*b* and go ahead of the Israelites until we have brought them to their place. Meanwhile our women and children will live in fortified cities, for protection from the inhabitants of the land. 18We will not

---

a 52 That is, about 420 pounds or about 190 kilograms   *b 17* Septuagint; Hebrew *will be quick to arm ourselves* return to our homes until each of the Israelites has received their inheritance. 19We will not receive any inheritance with them on the other side of the Jordan, because our inheritance has come to us on the east side of the Jordan."

20Then Moses said to them, "If you will do this — if you will arm yourselves before the LORD for battle 21and if all of you who are armed cross over the Jordan before the LORD until he has driven his enemies out before him — 22then when the land is subdued before the LORD, you may return and be free from your obligation to the LORD and to Israel. And this land will be your possession before the LORD.

23"But if you fail to do this, you will be sinning against the LORD; and you may be sure that your sin will find you out. 24Build cities for your women and children, and pens for your flocks, but do what you have promised."

25The Gadites and Reubenites said to Moses, "We your servants will do as our lord commands. 26Our children and wives, our flocks and herds will remain here in the cities of Gilead. 27But your servants, every man who is armed for battle, will cross over to fight before the LORD, just as our lord says."

28Then Moses gave orders about them to Eleazar the priest and Joshua son of Nun and to the family heads of the Israelite tribes. 29He said to them, "If the Gadites and Reubenites, every man armed for battle, cross over the Jordan with you before the LORD, then when the land is subdued before you, you must give them the land of Gilead as their possession. 30But if they do not cross over with you armed, they must accept their possession with you in Canaan."

31The Gadites and Reubenites answered, "Your servants will do what the LORD has said. 32We will cross over before the LORD into Canaan armed, but the property we inherit will be on this side of the Jordan."

33Then Moses gave to the Gadites, the Reubenites and the half-tribe of Manasseh son of Joseph the kingdom of Sihon king of the Amorites and the kingdom of Og king of Bashan — the whole land with its cities and the territory around them.

34The Gadites built up Dibon, Ataroth, Aroer, 35Atroth Shophan, Jazer, Jogbehah, 36Beth Nimrah and Beth Haran as fortified cities, and built pens for their flocks. 37And the Reubenites rebuilt Heshbon, Elealeh and Kiriathaim, 38as well as Nebo and Baal Meon (these names were changed) and Sibmah. They gave names to the cities they rebuilt.

39The descendants of Makir son of Manasseh went to Gilead, captured it and drove out the Amorites who were there. 40So Moses gave Gilead to the Makirites, the descendants of Manasseh, and they settled there. 41Jair, a descendant of Manasseh, captured their settlements and called them Havvoth Jair.a 42And Nobah captured Kenath and its surrounding settlements and called it Nobah after himself.

Stages in Israel's Journey

33 Here are the stages in the journey of the Israelites when they came out of Egypt by divisions under the leadership of Moses and Aaron. 2At the LORD's command Moses recorded the stages in their journey. This is their journey by stages:

3The Israelites set out from Rameses on the fifteenth day of the first month, the day after the Passover. They marched out defiantly in full view of all the Egyptians, 4who were burying all their firstborn, whom the LORD had struck down among them; for the LORD had brought judgment on their gods.

5The Israelites left Rameses and camped at Sukkoth.

6They left Sukkoth and camped at Etham, on the edge of the desert.

7They left Etham, turned back to Pi

---

a 41 Or them the settlements of Jair

Hahiroth, to the east of Baal Zephon, and camped near Migdol.

⁸They left Pi Hahiroth*ᵃ* and passed through the sea into the desert, and when they had traveled for three days in the Desert of Etham, they camped at Marah.

⁹They left Marah and went to Elim, where there were twelve springs and seventy palm trees, and they camped there.

¹⁰They left Elim and camped by the Red Sea.*ᵇ*

¹¹They left the Red Sea and camped in the Desert of Sin.

¹²They left the Desert of Sin and camped at Dophkah.

¹³They left Dophkah and camped at Alush.

¹⁴They left Alush and camped at Rephidim, where there was no water for the people to drink.

¹⁵They left Rephidim and camped in the Desert of Sinai.

¹⁶They left the Desert of Sinai and camped at Kibroth Hattaavah.

¹⁷They left Kibroth Hattaavah and camped at Hazeroth.

¹⁸They left Hazeroth and camped at Rithmah.

¹⁹They left Rithmah and camped at Rimmon Perez.

²⁰They left Rimmon Perez and camped at Libnah.

²¹They left Libnah and camped at Rissah.

²²They left Rissah and camped at Kehelathah.

²³They left Kehelathah and camped at Mount Shepher.

²⁴They left Mount Shepher and camped at Haradah.

²⁵They left Haradah and camped at Makheloth.

²⁶They left Makheloth and camped at Tahath.

²⁷They left Tahath and camped at Terah.

²⁸They left Terah and camped at Mithkah.

²⁹They left Mithkah and camped at Hashmonah.

³⁰They left Hashmonah and camped at Moseroth.

³¹They left Moseroth and camped at Bene Jaakan.

³²They left Bene Jaakan and camped at Hor Haggidgad.

³³They left Hor Haggidgad and camped at Jotbathah.

³⁴They left Jotbathah and camped at Abronah.

³⁵They left Abronah and camped at Ezion Geber.

³⁶They left Ezion Geber and camped at Kadesh, in the Desert of Zin.

³⁷They left Kadesh and camped at Mount Hor, on the border of Edom. ³⁸At the Lord's command Aaron the priest went up Mount Hor, where he died on the first day of the fifth month of the fortieth year after the Israelites came out of Egypt. ³⁹Aaron was a hundred and twenty-three years old when he died on Mount Hor.

⁴⁰The Canaanite king of Arad, who lived in the Negev of Canaan, heard that the Israelites were coming.

⁴¹They left Mount Hor and camped at Zalmonah.

⁴²They left Zalmonah and camped at Punon.

⁴³They left Punon and camped at Oboth.

⁴⁴They left Oboth and camped at Iye Abarim, on the border of Moab.

⁴⁵They left Iye Abarim and camped at Dibon Gad.

⁴⁶They left Dibon Gad and camped at Almon Diblathaim.

⁴⁷They left Almon Diblathaim and

ᵃ 8 Many manuscripts of the Masoretic Text, Samaritan Pentateuch and Vulgate; most manuscripts of the Masoretic Text *left from before Hahiroth*   *ᵇ 10* Or *the Sea of Reeds*; also in verse 11 camped in the mountains of Abarim, near Nebo.

48They left the mountains of Abarim and camped on the plains of Moab by the Jordan across from Jericho. 49There on the plains of Moab they camped along the Jordan from Beth Jeshimoth to Abel Shittim.

50On the plains of Moab by the Jordan across from Jericho the Lord said to Moses, 51"Speak to the Israelites and say to them: 'When you cross the Jordan into Canaan, 52drive out all the inhabitants of the land before you. Destroy all their carved images and their cast idols, and demolish all their high places. 53Take possession of the land and settle in it, for I have given you the land to possess. 54Distribute the land by lot, according to your clans. To a larger group give a larger inheritance, and to a smaller group a smaller one. Whatever falls to them by lot will be theirs. Distribute it according to your ancestral tribes.

55"But if you do not drive out the inhabitants of the land, those you allow to remain will become barbs in your eyes and thorns in your sides. They will give you trouble in the land where you will live. 56And then I will do to you what I plan to do to them.'"

Boundaries of Canaan

34 The Lord said to Moses, 2"Command the Israelites and say to them: 'When you enter Canaan, the land that will be allotted to you as an inheritance is to have these boundaries:

3"'Your southern side will include some of the Desert of Zin along the border of Edom. Your southern boundary will start in the east from the southern end of the Dead Sea, 4cross south of Scorpion Pass, continue on to Zin and go south of Kadesh Barnea. Then it will go to Hazar Addar and over to Azmon, 5where it will turn, join the Wadi of Egypt and end at the Mediterranean Sea.

6"'Your western boundary will be the coast of the Mediterranean Sea. This will be your boundary on the west.

7"'For your northern boundary, run a line from the Mediterranean Sea to Mount Hor 8and from Mount Hor to Lebo Hamath. Then the boundary will go to Zedad, 9continue to Ziphron and end at Hazar Enan. This will be your boundary on the north.

10"'For your eastern boundary, run a line from Hazar Enan to Shepham. 11The boundary will go down from Shepham to Riblah on the east side of Ain and continue along the slopes east of the Sea of Galilee.ᵃ 12Then the boundary will go down along the Jordan and end at the Dead Sea.

"'This will be your land, with its boundaries on every side.'"

13Moses commanded the Israelites: "Assign this land by lot as an inheritance. The Lord has ordered that it be given to the nine and a half tribes, 14because the families of the tribe of Reuben, the tribe of Gad and the half-tribe of Manasseh have received their inheritance. 15These two and a half tribes have received their inheritance east of the Jordan across from Jericho, toward the sunrise."

16The Lord said to Moses, 17"These are the names of the men who are to assign the land for you as an inheritance: Eleazar the priest and Joshua son of Nun. 18And appoint one leader from each tribe to help assign the land. 19These are their names:

Caleb son of Jephunneh,
　from the tribe of Judah;
20Shemuel son of Ammihud,
　from the tribe of Simeon;
21Elidad son of Kislon,
　from the tribe of Benjamin;
22Bukki son of Jogli,
　the leader from the tribe of Dan;
23Hanniel son of Ephod,
　the leader from the tribe of Manasseh son of Joseph;

ᵃ 11 Hebrew *Kinnereth*

²⁴Kemuel son of Shiphtan,
the leader from the tribe of Ephraim son of Joseph;
²⁵Elizaphan son of Parnak,
the leader from the tribe of Zebulun;
²⁶Paltiel son of Azzan,
the leader from the tribe of Issachar;
²⁷Ahihud son of Shelomi,
the leader from the tribe of Asher;
²⁸Pedahel son of Ammihud,
the leader from the tribe of Naphtali."

²⁹These are the men the LORD commanded to assign the inheritance to the
Israelites in the land of Canaan.

Towns for the Levites

35 On the plains of Moab by the
Jordan across from Jericho, the
LORD said to Moses, ²"Com-
mand the Israelites to give the Levites
towns to live in from the inheritance the
Israelites will possess. And give them pasturelands around the towns. ³Then they
will have towns to live in and pasturelands
for the cattle they own and all their other
animals.

⁴"The pasturelands around the towns
that you give the Levites will extend a
thousand cubits*ᵃ* from the town wall.
⁵Outside the town, measure two thousand
cubits*ᵇ* on the east side, two thousand on
the south side, two thousand on the west
and two thousand on the north, with the
town in the center. They will have this area
as pastureland for the towns.

Cities of Refuge

⁶"Six of the towns you give the Levites
will be cities of refuge, to which a person
who has killed someone may flee. In addition, give them forty-two other towns. ⁷In
all you must give the Levites forty-eight
towns, together with their pasturelands.
⁸The towns you give the Levites from the

land the Israelites possess are to be given
in proportion to the inheritance of each
tribe: Take many towns from a tribe that
has many, but few from one that has few."

⁹Then the LORD said to Moses: ¹⁰"Speak
to the Israelites and say to them: 'When
you cross the Jordan into Canaan, ¹¹select
some towns to be your cities of refuge, to
which a person who has killed someone accidentally may flee. ¹²They will be places
of refuge from the avenger, so that anyone
accused of murder may not die before they
stand trial before the assembly. ¹³These six
towns you give will be your cities of refuge.
¹⁴Give three on this side of the Jordan and
three in Canaan as cities of refuge. ¹⁵These
six towns will be a place of refuge for Israelites and for foreigners residing among
them, so that anyone who has killed another accidentally can flee there.

¹⁶"If anyone strikes someone a fatal
blow with an iron object, that person is
a murderer; the murderer is to be put to
death. ¹⁷Or if anyone is holding a stone and
strikes someone a fatal blow with it, that
person is a murderer; the murderer is to
be put to death. ¹⁸Or if anyone is holding a
wooden object and strikes someone a fatal
blow with it, that person is a murderer; the
murderer is to be put to death. ¹⁹The avenger of blood shall put the murderer to death;
when the avenger comes upon the murderer, the avenger shall put the murderer
to death. ²⁰If anyone with malice aforethought shoves another or throws something at them intentionally so that they die
²¹or if out of enmity one person hits another with their fist so that the other dies, that
person is to be put to death; that person is
a murderer. The avenger of blood shall put
the murderer to death when they meet.

²²"'But if without enmity someone suddenly pushes another or throws something
at them unintentionally ²³or, without seeing them, drops on them a stone heavy
enough to kill them, and they die, then
since that other person was not an enemy

ᵃ 4 That is, about 1,500 feet or about 450 meters   *ᵇ 5* That is, about 3,000 feet or about 900 meters and no harm was intended, [24]the assembly must judge between the accused and the avenger of blood according to these regulations. [25]The assembly must protect the one accused of murder from the avenger of blood and send the accused back to the city of refuge to which they fled. The accused must stay there until the death of the high priest, who was anointed with the holy oil.

[26]"But if the accused ever goes outside the limits of the city of refuge to which they fled [27]and the avenger of blood finds them outside the city, the avenger of blood may kill the accused without being guilty of murder. [28]The accused must stay in the city of refuge until the death of the high priest; only after the death of the high priest may they return to their own property.

[29]"This is to have the force of law for you throughout the generations to come, wherever you live.

[30]"'Anyone who kills a person is to be put to death as a murderer only on the testimony of witnesses. But no one is to be put to death on the testimony of only one witness.

[31]"'Do not accept a ransom for the life of a murderer, who deserves to die. They are to be put to death.

[32]"'Do not accept a ransom for anyone who has fled to a city of refuge and so allow them to go back and live on their own land before the death of the high priest.

[33]"'Do not pollute the land where you are. Bloodshed pollutes the land, and atonement cannot be made for the land on which blood has been shed, except by the blood of the one who shed it. [34]Do not defile the land where you live and where I dwell, for I, the LORD, dwell among the Israelites.'"

Inheritance of Zelophehad's Daughters

36 The family heads of the clan of Gilead son of Makir, the son of Manasseh, who were from the clans of the descendants of Joseph, came and spoke before Moses and the leaders, the heads of the Israelite families. [2]They said, "When the LORD commanded my lord to give the land as an inheritance to the Israelites by lot, he ordered you to give the inheritance of our brother Zelophehad to his daughters. [3]Now suppose they marry men from other Israelite tribes; then their inheritance will be taken from our ancestral inheritance and added to that of the tribe they marry into. And so part of the inheritance allotted to us will be taken away. [4]When the Year of Jubilee for the Israelites comes, their inheritance will be added to that of the tribe into which they marry, and their property will be taken from the tribal inheritance of our ancestors."

[5]Then at the LORD's command Moses gave this order to the Israelites: "What the tribe of the descendants of Joseph is saying is right. [6]This is what the LORD commands for Zelophehad's daughters: They may marry anyone they please as long as they marry within their father's tribal clan. [7]No inheritance in Israel is to pass from one tribe to another, for every Israelite shall keep the tribal inheritance of their ancestors. [8]Every daughter who inherits land in any Israelite tribe must marry someone in her father's tribal clan, so that every Israelite will possess the inheritance of their ancestors. [9]No inheritance may pass from one tribe to another, for each Israelite tribe is to keep the land it inherits."

[10]So Zelophehad's daughters did as the LORD commanded Moses. [11]Zelophehad's daughters — Mahlah, Tirzah, Hoglah, Milkah and Noah — married their cousins on their father's side. [12]They married within the clans of the descendants of Manasseh son of Joseph, and their inheritance remained in their father's tribe and clan.

[13]These are the commands and regulations the LORD gave through Moses to the Israelites on the plains of Moab by the Jordan across from Jericho.

Deuteronomy

THEME: The major theme of Deuteronomy is the covenant (promise-based) relationship between God and his people.

AUTHOR: Deuteronomy identifies Moses as its author, and other Scripture passages agree. Some portions of the book were obviously later additions.

DATE OF WRITING: Deuteronomy was probably written around 1400 BC, just prior to Moses' death.

ENCOURAGEMENT FROM DEUTERONOMY: "The LORD your God carried you, as a father carries his son, all the way you went until you reached this place" (Deuteronomy 1:31).

CHALLENGE FROM DEUTERONOMY: "What does the LORD your God ask of you but to fear the LORD your God, to walk in obedience to him, to love him, to serve the LORD your God with all your heart and with all your soul, and to observe the LORD's commands and decrees that I am giving you today for your own good?" (Deuteronomy 10:12 – 13).

REFLECTION FROM DEUTERONOMY: "For the LORD your God is the one who goes with you to fight for you against your enemies to give you victory" (Deuteronomy 20:4).

In Deuteronomy we listen in as a 120-year-old Moses delivers farewell speeches to the new generation of Israelites as they at last prepare to enter the promised land. Like Leviticus, Deuteronomy focuses on legal codes (the Mosaic Law), but this time the focus is on the people, not the priests. In these speeches, Moses is calling this new generation to remembrance and renewal. He attempts to motivate the people by highlighting God's awesome works on behalf of the nation.

As we grow in our recoveries, we must always remember all that God has done for us. On our own power we've made mistakes and allowed our lives to become unmanageable. In order to stay in God's power, we must continue to focus on his work in our lives. When we focus on his love and power, we see that, not only can our lives be healed, but we can also give back into his service. Just as Moses prepared the Israelites to venture into the promised land by helping them focus on all that God had done, so we also are prepared to go back to a needy world as empowered servants of God.

The Command to Leave Horeb

1 These are the words Moses spoke to all Israel in the wilderness east of the Jordan — that is, in the Arabah — opposite Suph, between Paran and Tophel, Laban, Hazeroth and Dizahab. ²(It takes eleven days to go from Horeb to Kadesh Barnea by the Mount Seir road.)

³In the fortieth year, on the first day of the eleventh month, Moses proclaimed to

the Israelites all that the LORD had commanded him concerning them. ⁴This was after he had defeated Sihon king of the Amorites, who reigned in Heshbon, and at Edrei had defeated Og king of Bashan, who reigned in Ashtaroth.

⁵East of the Jordan in the territory of Moab, Moses began to expound this law, saying:

⁶The LORD our God said to us at Horeb, "You have stayed long enough at this mountain. ⁷Break camp and advance into the hill country of the Amorites; go to all the neighboring peoples in the Arabah, in the mountains, in the western foothills, in the Negev and along the coast, to the land of the Canaanites and to Lebanon, as far as the great river, the Euphrates. ⁸See, I have given you this land. Go in and take possession of the land the LORD swore he would give to your fathers — to Abraham, Isaac and Jacob — and to their descendants after them."

The Appointment of Leaders

⁹At that time I said to you, "You are too heavy a burden for me to carry alone. ¹⁰The LORD your God has increased your numbers so that today you are as numerous as the stars in the sky. ¹¹May the LORD, the God of your ancestors, increase you a thousand times and bless you as he has promised! ¹²But how can I bear your problems and your burdens and your disputes all by myself? ¹³Choose some wise, understanding and respected men from each of your tribes, and I will set them over you."

¹⁴You answered me, "What you propose to do is good."

¹⁵So I took the leading men of your tribes, wise and respected men, and appointed them to have authority over you — as commanders of thousands, of hundreds, of fifties and of tens and as tribal officials. ¹⁶And I charged your judges at that time, "Hear the disputes between your people and judge fairly, whether the case is between two Israelites or between an Israelite and a foreigner residing among you. ¹⁷Do not show partiality in judging; hear both small and great alike. Do not be afraid of anyone, for judgment belongs to God. Bring me any case too hard for you, and I will hear it." ¹⁸And at that time I told you everything you were to do.

Spies Sent Out

¹⁹Then, as the LORD our God commanded us, we set out from Horeb and went toward the hill country of the Amorites through all that vast and dreadful wilderness that you have seen, and so we reached Kadesh Barnea. ²⁰Then I said to you, "You have reached the hill country of the Amorites, which the LORD our God is giving us. ²¹See, the LORD your God has given you the land. Go up and take possession of it as the LORD, the God of your ancestors, told you. Do not be afraid; do not be discouraged."

²²Then all of you came to me and said, "Let us send men ahead to spy out the land for us and bring back a report about the route we are to take and the towns we will come to."

²³The idea seemed good to me; so I selected twelve of you, one man from each tribe. ²⁴They left and went up into the hill country, and came to the Valley of Eshkol and explored it. ²⁵Taking with them some of the fruit of the land, they brought it down to us and reported, "It is a good land that the LORD our God is giving us."

Rebellion Against the LORD

²⁶But you were unwilling to go up; you rebelled against the command of the LORD your God. ²⁷You grumbled in your tents and said, "The LORD hates us; so he brought us out of Egypt to deliver us into the hands of the Amorites to destroy us. ²⁸Where can we go? Our brothers have made our hearts melt in fear. They say, 'The people are stronger and taller than we are; the cities are large, with walls

up to the sky. We even saw the Anakites there.'"

²⁹Then I said to you, "Do not be terrified; do not be afraid of them. ³⁰The Lord your God, who is going before you, will fight for you, as he did for you in Egypt, before your very eyes, ³¹and in the wilderness. There you saw how the Lord your God carried you, as a father carries his son, all the way you went until you reached this place."

³²In spite of this, you did not trust in the Lord your God, ³³who went ahead of you on your journey, in fire by night and in a cloud by day, to search out places for you to camp and to show you the way you should go.

³⁴When the Lord heard what you said, he was angry and solemnly swore: ³⁵"No one from this evil generation shall see the good land I swore to give your ancestors, ³⁶except Caleb son of Jephunneh. He will see it, and I will give him and his descendants the land he set his feet on, because he followed the Lord wholeheartedly."

³⁷Because of you the Lord became angry with me also and said, "You shall not enter it, either. ³⁸But your assistant, Joshua son of Nun, will enter it. Encourage him, because he will lead Israel to inherit it. ³⁹And the little ones that you said would be taken captive, your children who do not yet know good from bad—they will enter the land. I will give it to them and they will take possession of it. ⁴⁰But as for you, turn around and set out toward the desert along the route to the Red Sea.ᵃ"

⁴¹Then you replied, "We have sinned against the Lord. We will go up and fight, as the Lord our God commanded us." So every one of you put on his weapons, thinking it easy to go up into the hill country.

⁴²But the Lord said to me, "Tell them, 'Do not go up and fight, because I will not be with you. You will be defeated by your enemies.'"

⁴³So I told you, but you would not listen. You rebelled against the Lord's command and in your arrogance you marched up into the hill country. ⁴⁴The Amorites who lived in those hills came out against you; they chased you like a swarm of bees and beat you down from Seir all the way to Hormah. ⁴⁵You came back and wept before the Lord, but he paid no attention to your weeping and turned a deaf ear to you. ⁴⁶And so you stayed in Kadesh many days—all the time you spent there.

Wanderings in the Wilderness

2 Then we turned back and set out toward the wilderness along the route to the Red Sea,ᵃ as the Lord had directed me. For a long time we made our way around the hill country of Seir.

²Then the Lord said to me, ³"You have made your way around this hill country long enough; now turn north. ⁴Give the people these orders: 'You are about to pass through the territory of your relatives the descendants of Esau, who live in Seir. They will be afraid of you, but be very careful. ⁵Do not provoke them to war, for I will not give you any of their land, not even enough to put your foot on. I have given Esau the hill country of Seir as his own. ⁶You are to pay them in silver for the food you eat and the water you drink.'"

⁷The Lord your God has blessed you in all the work of your hands. He has watched over your journey through this vast wilderness. These forty years the Lord your God has been with you, and you have not lacked anything.

⁸So we went on past our relatives the descendants of Esau, who live in Seir. We turned from the Arabah road, which comes up from Elath and Ezion Geber, and traveled along the desert road of Moab.

⁹Then the Lord said to me, "Do not harass the Moabites or provoke them to war, for I will not give you any part of their land. I have given Ar to the descendants of Lot as a possession."

ᵃ 40,1 Or the Sea of Reeds

¹⁰(The Emites used to live there — a people strong and numerous, and as tall as the Anakites. ¹¹Like the Anakites, they too were considered Rephaites, but the Moabites called them Emites. ¹²Horites used to live in Seir, but the descendants of Esau drove them out. They destroyed the Horites from before them and settled in their place, just as Israel did in the land the LORD gave them as their possession.)

¹³And the LORD said, "Now get up and cross the Zered Valley." So we crossed the valley.

¹⁴Thirty-eight years passed from the time we left Kadesh Barnea until we crossed the Zered Valley. By then, that entire generation of fighting men had perished from the camp, as the LORD had sworn to them. ¹⁵The LORD's hand was against them until he had completely eliminated them from the camp.

¹⁶Now when the last of these fighting men among the people had died, ¹⁷the LORD said to me, ¹⁸"Today you are to pass by the region of Moab at Ar. ¹⁹When you come to the Ammonites, do not harass them or provoke them to war, for I will not give you possession of any land belonging to the Ammonites. I have given it as a possession to the descendants of Lot."

²⁰(That too was considered a land of the Rephaites, who used to live there; but the Ammonites called them Zamzummites. ²¹They were a people strong and numerous, and as tall as the Anakites. The LORD destroyed them from before the Ammonites, who drove them out and settled in their place. ²²The LORD had done the same for the descendants of Esau, who lived in Seir, when he destroyed the Horites from before them. They drove them out and have lived in their place to this day. ²³And as for the Avvites who lived in villages as far as Gaza, the Caphtorites coming out from Caphtor[a] destroyed them and settled in their place.)

Defeat of Sihon King of Heshbon

²⁴"Set out now and cross the Arnon Gorge. See, I have given into your hand Sihon the Amorite, king of Heshbon, and his country. Begin to take possession of it and engage him in battle. ²⁵This very day I will begin to put the terror and fear of you on all the nations under heaven. They will hear reports of you and will tremble and be in anguish because of you."

²⁶From the Desert of Kedemoth I sent messengers to Sihon king of Heshbon offering peace and saying, ²⁷"Let us pass through your country. We will stay on the main road; we will not turn aside to the right or to the left. ²⁸Sell us food to eat and water to drink for their price in silver. Only let us pass through on foot — ²⁹as the descendants of Esau, who live in Seir, and the Moabites, who live in Ar, did for us — until we cross the Jordan into the land the LORD our God is giving us." ³⁰But Sihon king of Heshbon refused to let us pass through. For the LORD your God had made his spirit stubborn and his heart obstinate in order to give him into your hands, as he has now done.

³¹The LORD said to me, "See, I have begun to deliver Sihon and his country over to you. Now begin to conquer and possess his land."

³²When Sihon and all his army came out to meet us in battle at Jahaz, ³³the LORD our God delivered him over to us and we struck him down, together with his sons and his whole army. ³⁴At that time we took all his towns and completely destroyed[b] them — men, women and children. We left no survivors. ³⁵But the livestock and the plunder from the towns we had captured we carried off for ourselves. ³⁶From Aroer on the rim of the Arnon Gorge, and from the town in the gorge, even as far as Gilead, not one town was too strong for us. The LORD our God gave us all of them. ³⁷But in accordance with the command of the LORD our God, you did not encroach on

---

a 23 That is, Crete   *b 34* The Hebrew term refers to the irrevocable giving over of things or persons to the LORD, often by totally destroying them.

any of the land of the Ammonites, neither the land along the course of the Jabbok nor that around the towns in the hills.

Defeat of Og King of Bashan

3 Next we turned and went up along the road toward Bashan, and Og king of Bashan with his whole army marched out to meet us in battle at Edrei. ²The LORD said to me, "Do not be afraid of him, for I have delivered him into your hands, along with his whole army and his land. Do to him what you did to Sihon king of the Amorites, who reigned in Heshbon."

³So the LORD our God also gave into our hands Og king of Bashan and all his army. We struck them down, leaving no survivors. ⁴At that time we took all his cities. There was not one of the sixty cities that we did not take from them — the whole region of Argob, Og's kingdom in Bashan. ⁵All these cities were fortified with high walls and with gates and bars, and there were also a great many unwalled villages. ⁶We completely destroyed*ᵃ* them, as we had done with Sihon king of Heshbon, destroying*ᵃ* every city — men, women and children. ⁷But all the livestock and the plunder from their cities we carried off for ourselves.

⁸So at that time we took from these two kings of the Amorites the territory east of the Jordan, from the Arnon Gorge as far as Mount Hermon. ⁹(Hermon is called Sirion by the Sidonians; the Amorites call it Senir.) ¹⁰We took all the towns on the plateau, and all Gilead, and all Bashan as far as Salekah and Edrei, towns of Og's kingdom in Bashan. ¹¹(Og king of Bashan was the last of the Rephaites. His bed was decorated with iron and was more than nine cubits long and four cubits wide.*ᵇ* It is still in Rabbah of the Ammonites.)

Division of the Land

¹²Of the land that we took over at that time, I gave the Reubenites and the Gad-ites the territory north of Aroer by the Arnon Gorge, including half the hill country of Gilead, together with its towns. ¹³The rest of Gilead and also all of Bashan, the kingdom of Og, I gave to the half-tribe of Manasseh. (The whole region of Argob in Bashan used to be known as a land of the Rephaites. ¹⁴Jair, a descendant of Manasseh, took the whole region of Argob as far as the border of the Geshurites and the Maakathites; it was named after him, so that to this day Bashan is called Havvoth Jair.*ᶜ*) ¹⁵And I gave Gilead to Makir. ¹⁶But to the Reubenites and the Gadites I gave the territory extending from Gilead down to the Arnon Gorge (the middle of the gorge being the border) and out to the Jabbok River, which is the border of the Ammonites. ¹⁷Its western border was the Jordan in the Arabah, from Kinnereth to the Sea of the Arabah (that is, the Dead Sea), below the slopes of Pisgah.

¹⁸I commanded you at that time: "The LORD your God has given you this land to take possession of it. But all your able-bodied men, armed for battle, must cross over ahead of the other Israelites. ¹⁹However, your wives, your children and your livestock (I know you have much livestock) may stay in the towns I have given you, ²⁰until the LORD gives rest to your fellow Israelites as he has to you, and they too have taken over the land that the LORD your God is giving them across the Jordan. After that, each of you may go back to the possession I have given you."

Moses Forbidden to Cross the Jordan

²¹At that time I commanded Joshua: "You have seen with your own eyes all that the LORD your God has done to these two kings. The LORD will do the same to all the kingdoms over there where you are going. ²²Do not be afraid of them; the LORD your God himself will fight for you."

²³At that time I pleaded with the LORD:

ᵃ 6 The Hebrew term refers to the irrevocable giving over of things or persons to the LORD, often by totally destroying them.   *ᵇ 11* That is, about 14 feet long and 6 feet wide or about 4 meters long and 1.8 meters wide   *ᶜ 14* Or *called the settlements of Jair*

24"Sovereign LORD, you have begun to show to your servant your greatness and your strong hand. For what god is there in heaven or on earth who can do the deeds and mighty works you do? 25Let me go over and see the good land beyond the Jordan—that fine hill country and Lebanon."

26But because of you the LORD was angry with me and would not listen to me. "That is enough," the LORD said. "Do not speak to me anymore about this matter. 27Go up to the top of Pisgah and look west and north and south and east. Look at the land with your own eyes, since you are not going to cross this Jordan. 28But commission Joshua, and encourage and strengthen him, for he will lead this people across and will cause them to inherit the land that you will see." 29So we stayed in the valley near Beth Peor.

Obedience Commanded

4 Now, Israel, hear the decrees and laws I am about to teach you. Follow them so that you may live and may go in and take possession of the land the LORD, the God of your ancestors, is giving you. 2Do not add to what I command you and do not subtract from it, but keep the commands of the LORD your God that I give you.

3You saw with your own eyes what the LORD did at Baal Peor. The LORD your God destroyed from among you everyone who followed the Baal of Peor, 4but all of you who held fast to the LORD your God are still alive today.

5See, I have taught you decrees and laws as the LORD my God commanded me, so that you may follow them in the land you are entering to take possession of it. 6Observe them carefully, for this will show your wisdom and understanding to the nations, who will hear about all these decrees and say, "Surely this great nation is a wise and understanding people." 7What other nation is so great as to have their gods near them the way the LORD our God is near us whenever we pray to him? 8And what other nation is so great as to have such righteous decrees and laws as this body of laws I am setting before you today?

9Only be careful, and watch yourselves closely so that you do not forget the things your eyes have seen or let them fade from your heart as long as you live. Teach them to your children and to their children after them. 10Remember the day you stood before the LORD your God at Horeb, when he said to me, "Assemble the people before me to hear my words so that they may learn to revere me as long as they live in the land and may teach them to their children." 11You came near and stood at the foot of the mountain while it blazed with fire to the very heavens, with black clouds and deep darkness. 12Then the LORD spoke to you out of the fire. You heard the sound of words but saw no form; there was only a voice. 13He declared to you his covenant, the Ten Commandments, which he commanded you to follow and then wrote them on two stone tablets. 14And the LORD directed me at that time to teach you the decrees and laws you are to follow in the land that you are crossing the Jordan to possess.

Idolatry Forbidden

15You saw no form of any kind the day the LORD spoke to you at Horeb out of the fire. Therefore watch yourselves very carefully, 16so that you do not become corrupt and make for yourselves an idol, an image of any shape, whether formed like a man or a woman, 17or like any animal on earth or any bird that flies in the air, 18or like any creature that moves along the ground or any fish in the waters below. 19And when you look up to the sky and see the sun, the moon and the stars—all the heavenly array—do not be enticed into bowing down to them and worshiping things the LORD your God has apportioned to all the nations under heaven. 20But as for you, the LORD took you and brought you out of the iron-smelting furnace, out of Egypt, to be the people of his inheritance, as you now are.

²¹The LORD was angry with me because of you, and he solemnly swore that I would not cross the Jordan and enter the good land the LORD your God is giving you as your inheritance. ²²I will die in this land; I will not cross the Jordan; but you are about to cross over and take possession of that good land. ²³Be careful not to forget the covenant of the LORD your God that he made with you; do not make for yourselves an idol in the form of anything the LORD your God has forbidden. ²⁴For the LORD your God is a consuming fire, a jealous God.

²⁵After you have had children and grandchildren and have lived in the land a long time — if you then become corrupt and make any kind of idol, doing evil in the eyes of the LORD your God and arousing his anger, ²⁶I call the heavens and the earth as witnesses against you this day that you will quickly perish from the land that you are crossing the Jordan to possess. You will not live there long but will certainly be destroyed. ²⁷The LORD will scatter you among the peoples, and only a few of you will survive among the nations to which the LORD will drive you. ²⁸There you will worship man-made gods of wood and stone, which cannot see or hear or eat or smell. ²⁹But if from there you seek the LORD your God, you will find him if you seek him with all your heart and with all your soul. ³⁰When you are in distress and all these things have happened to you, then in later days you will return to the LORD your God and obey him. ³¹For the LORD your God is a merciful God; he will not abandon or destroy you or forget the covenant with your ancestors, which he confirmed to them by oath.

The LORD Is God

³²Ask now about the former days, long before your time, from the day God created human beings on the earth; ask from one end of the heavens to the other. Has anything so great as this ever happened, or has anything like it ever been heard of? ³³Has any other people heard the voice of God*a* speaking out of fire, as you have, and lived? ³⁴Has any god ever tried to take for himself one nation out of another nation, by testings, by signs and wonders, by war, by a mighty hand and an outstretched arm, or by great and awesome deeds, like all the things the LORD your God did for you in Egypt before your very eyes?

³⁵You were shown these things so that you might know that the LORD is God; besides him there is no other. ³⁶From heaven he made you hear his voice to discipline you. On earth he showed you his great fire, and you heard his words from out of the fire. ³⁷Because he loved your ancestors and chose their descendants after them, he brought you out of Egypt by his Presence and his great strength, ³⁸to drive out before you nations greater and stronger than you and to bring you into their land to give it to you for your inheritance, as it is today.

³⁹Acknowledge and take to heart this day that the LORD is God in heaven above and on the earth below. There is no other. ⁴⁰Keep his decrees and commands, which I am giving you today, so that it may go well with you and your children after you and that you may live long in the land the LORD your God gives you for all time.

Cities of Refuge

⁴¹Then Moses set aside three cities east of the Jordan, ⁴²to which anyone who had killed a person could flee if they had unintentionally killed a neighbor without malice aforethought. They could flee into one of these cities and save their life. ⁴³The cities were these: Bezer in the wilderness plateau, for the Reubenites; Ramoth in Gilead, for the Gadites; and Golan in Bashan, for the Manassites.

Introduction to the Law

⁴⁴This is the law Moses set before the Israelites. ⁴⁵These are the stipulations,

---

a 33 Or *of a god*

decrees and laws Moses gave them when they came out of Egypt ⁴⁶and were in the valley near Beth Peor east of the Jordan, in the land of Sihon king of the Amorites, who reigned in Heshbon and was defeated by Moses and the Israelites as they came out of Egypt. ⁴⁷They took possession of his land and the land of Og king of Bashan, the two Amorite kings east of the Jordan. ⁴⁸This land extended from Aroer on the rim of the Arnon Gorge to Mount Sirion*a* (that is, Hermon), ⁴⁹and included all the Arabah east of the Jordan, as far as the Dead Sea,*b* below the slopes of Pisgah.

The Ten Commandments

5 Moses summoned all Israel and said:

Hear, Israel, the decrees and laws I declare in your hearing today. Learn them and be sure to follow them. ²The LORD our God made a covenant with us at Horeb. ³It was not with our ancestors*c* that the LORD made this covenant, but with us, with all of us who are alive here today. ⁴The LORD spoke to you face to face out of the fire on the mountain. ⁵(At that time I stood between the LORD and you to declare to you the word of the LORD, because you were afraid of the fire and did not go up the mountain.) And he said:

⁶"I am the LORD your God, who brought you out of Egypt, out of the land of slavery.

⁷"You shall have no other gods before*d* me.

⁸"You shall not make for yourself an image in the form of anything in heaven above or on the earth beneath or in the waters below. ⁹You shall not bow down to them or worship them; for I, the LORD your God, am a jealous God, punishing the children for the sin of the parents to the third and fourth generation of those who hate me, ¹⁰but showing love to a thousand generations of those who love me and keep my commandments.

¹¹"You shall not misuse the name of the LORD your God, for the LORD will not hold anyone guiltless who misuses his name.

¹²"Observe the Sabbath day by keeping it holy, as the LORD your God has commanded you. ¹³Six days you shall labor and do all your work, ¹⁴but the seventh day is a sabbath to the LORD your God. On it you shall not do any work, neither you, nor your son or daughter, nor your male or female servant, nor your ox, your donkey or any of your animals, nor any foreigner residing in your towns, so that your male and female servants may rest, as you do. ¹⁵Remember that you were slaves in Egypt and that the LORD your God brought you out of there with a mighty hand and an outstretched arm. Therefore the LORD your God has commanded you to observe the Sabbath day.

¹⁶"Honor your father and your mother, as the LORD your God has commanded you, so that you may live long and that it may go well with you in the land the LORD your God is giving you.

¹⁷"You shall not murder.

¹⁸"You shall not commit adultery.

¹⁹"You shall not steal.

²⁰"You shall not give false testimony against your neighbor.

²¹"You shall not covet your neighbor's wife. You shall not set your desire on your neighbor's house or land, his male or female servant,

---

a 48 Syriac (see also 3:9); Hebrew *Siyon*   *b 49* Hebrew *the Sea of the Arabah*   *c 3* Or *not only with our parents*   *d 7* Or *besides* his ox or donkey, or anything that belongs to your neighbor."

²²These are the commandments the Lᴏʀᴅ proclaimed in a loud voice to your whole assembly there on the mountain from out of the fire, the cloud and the deep darkness; and he added nothing more. Then he wrote them on two stone tablets and gave them to me.

²³When you heard the voice out of the darkness, while the mountain was ablaze with fire, all the leaders of your tribes and your elders came to me. ²⁴And you said, "The Lᴏʀᴅ our God has shown us his glory and his majesty, and we have heard his voice from the fire. Today we have seen that a person can live even if God speaks with them. ²⁵But now, why should we die? This great fire will consume us, and we will die if we hear the voice of the Lᴏʀᴅ our God any longer. ²⁶For what mortal has ever heard the voice of the living God speaking out of fire, as we have, and survived? ²⁷Go near and listen to all that the Lᴏʀᴅ our God says. Then tell us whatever the Lᴏʀᴅ our God tells you. We will listen and obey."

²⁸The Lᴏʀᴅ heard you when you spoke to me, and the Lᴏʀᴅ said to me, "I have heard what this people said to you. Everything they said was good. ²⁹Oh, that their hearts would be inclined to fear me and keep all my commands always, so that it might go well with them and their children forever!

³⁰"Go, tell them to return to their tents. ³¹But you stay here with me so that I may give you all the commands, decrees and laws you are to teach them to follow in the land I am giving them to possess."

³²So be careful to do what the Lᴏʀᴅ your God has commanded you; do not turn aside to the right or to the left. ³³Walk in obedience to all that the Lᴏʀᴅ your God has commanded you, so that you may live and prosper and prolong your days in the land that you will possess.

Love the Lᴏʀᴅ Your God

6 These are the commands, decrees and laws the Lᴏʀᴅ your God directed me to teach you to observe in the land that you are crossing the Jordan to possess, ²so that you, your children and their children after them may fear the Lᴏʀᴅ your God as long as you live by keeping all his decrees and commands that I give you, and so that you may enjoy long life. ³Hear, Israel, and be careful to obey so that it may go well with you and that you may increase greatly in a land flowing with milk and honey, just as the Lᴏʀᴅ, the God of your ancestors, promised you.

⁴Hear, O Israel: The Lᴏʀᴅ our God, the Lᴏʀᴅ is one.ᵃ ⁵Love the Lᴏʀᴅ your God with all your heart and with all your soul and with all your strength. ⁶These commandments that I give you today are to be on your hearts. ⁷Impress them on your children. Talk about them when you sit at home and when you walk along the road, when you lie down and when you get up. ⁸Tie them as symbols on your hands and bind them on your foreheads. ⁹Write them on the doorframes of your houses and on your gates.

¹⁰When the Lᴏʀᴅ your God brings you into the land he swore to your fathers, to Abraham, Isaac and Jacob, to give you — a land with large, flourishing cities you did not build, ¹¹houses filled with all kinds of good things you did not provide, wells you did not dig, and vineyards and olive groves you did not plant — then when you eat and are satisfied, ¹²be careful that you do not forget the Lᴏʀᴅ, who brought you out of Egypt, out of the land of slavery.

¹³Fear the Lᴏʀᴅ your God, serve him only and take your oaths in his name. ¹⁴Do not follow other gods, the gods of the peoples around you; ¹⁵for the Lᴏʀᴅ your God, who is among you, is a jealous God and his anger will burn against you, and he will destroy you from the face of the land. ¹⁶Do

---

ᵃ 4 Or The Lᴏʀᴅ our God is one Lᴏʀᴅ; or The Lᴏʀᴅ is our God, the Lᴏʀᴅ is one; or The Lᴏʀᴅ is our God, the Lᴏʀᴅ alone not put the LORD your God to the test as you did at Massah. [17]Be sure to keep the commands of the LORD your God and the stipulations and decrees he has given you. [18]Do what is right and good in the LORD's sight, so that it may go well with you and you may go in and take over the good land the LORD promised on oath to your ancestors, [19]thrusting out all your enemies before you, as the LORD said.

[20]In the future, when your son asks you, "What is the meaning of the stipulations, decrees and laws the LORD our God has commanded you?" [21]tell him: "We were slaves of Pharaoh in Egypt, but the LORD brought us out of Egypt with a mighty hand. [22]Before our eyes the LORD sent signs and wonders — great and terrible — on Egypt and Pharaoh and his whole household. [23]But he brought us out from there to bring us in and give us the land he promised on oath to our ancestors. [24]The LORD commanded us to obey all these decrees and to fear the LORD our God, so that we might always prosper and be kept alive, as is the case today. [25]And if we are careful to obey all this law before the LORD our God, as he has commanded us, that will be our righteousness."

Driving Out the Nations

7 When the LORD your God brings you into the land you are entering to possess and drives out before you many nations — the Hittites, Girgashites, Amorites, Canaanites, Perizzites, Hivites and Jebusites, seven nations larger and stronger than you — [2]and when the LORD your God has delivered them over to you and you have defeated them, then you must destroy them totally.[a] Make no treaty with them, and show them no mercy. [3]Do not intermarry with them. Do not give your daughters to their sons or take their daughters for your sons, [4]for they will turn your children away from following me to serve other gods, and the LORD's anger will burn against you and will quickly destroy you. [5]This is what you are to do to them: Break down their altars, smash their sacred stones, cut down their Asherah poles[b] and burn their idols in the fire. [6]For you are a people holy to the LORD your God. The LORD your God has chosen you out of all the peoples on the face of the earth to be his people, his treasured possession.

[7]The LORD did not set his affection on you and choose you because you were more numerous than other peoples, for you were the fewest of all peoples. [8]But it was because the LORD loved you and kept the oath he swore to your ancestors that he brought you out with a mighty hand and redeemed you from the land of slavery, from the power of Pharaoh king of Egypt. [9]Know therefore that the LORD your God is God; he is the faithful God, keeping his covenant of love to a thousand generations of those who love him and keep his commandments. [10]But

those who hate him he will repay to
  their face by destruction;
he will not be slow to repay to their
  face those who hate him.

[11]Therefore, take care to follow the commands, decrees and laws I give you today.

[12]If you pay attention to these laws and are careful to follow them, then the LORD your God will keep his covenant of love with you, as he swore to your ancestors. [13]He will love you and bless you and increase your numbers. He will bless the fruit of your womb, the crops of your land — your grain, new wine and olive oil — the calves of your herds and the lambs of your flocks in the land he swore to your ancestors to give you. [14]You will be blessed more than any other people; none of your men or women will be childless, nor will any of your livestock be without young. [15]The LORD will keep you free from every dis-

---

[a] 2 The Hebrew term refers to the irrevocable giving over of things or persons to the LORD, often by totally destroying them; also in verse 26.   [b] 5 That is, wooden symbols of the goddess Asherah; here and elsewhere in Deuteronomy

ease. He will not inflict on you the horrible diseases you knew in Egypt, but he will inflict them on all who hate you. [16]You must destroy all the peoples the LORD your God gives over to you. Do not look on them with pity and do not serve their gods, for that will be a snare to you.

[17]You may say to yourselves, "These nations are stronger than we are. How can we drive them out?" [18]But do not be afraid of them; remember well what the LORD your God did to Pharaoh and to all Egypt. [19]You saw with your own eyes the great trials, the signs and wonders, the mighty hand and outstretched arm, with which the LORD your God brought you out. The LORD your God will do the same to all the peoples you now fear. [20]Moreover, the LORD your God will send the hornet among them until even the survivors who hide from you have perished. [21]Do not be terrified by them, for the LORD your God, who is among you, is a great and awesome God. [22]The LORD your God will drive out those nations before you, little by little. You will not be allowed to eliminate them all at once, or the wild animals will multiply around you. [23]But the LORD your God will deliver them over to you, throwing them into great confusion until they are destroyed. [24]He will give their kings into your hand, and you will wipe out their names from under heaven. No one will be able to stand up against you; you will destroy them. [25]The images of their gods you are to burn in the fire. Do not covet the silver and gold on them, and do not take it for yourselves, or you will be ensnared by it, for it is detestable to the LORD your God. [26]Do not bring a detestable thing into your house or you, like it, will be set apart for destruction. Regard it as vile and utterly detest it, for it is set apart for destruction.

Do Not Forget the LORD

8 Be careful to follow every command I am giving you today, so that you may live and increase and may enter and possess the land the LORD promised on oath to your ancestors. [2]Remember how the LORD your God led you all the way in the wilderness these forty years, to humble and test you in order to know what was in your heart, whether or not you would keep his commands. [3]He humbled you, causing you to hunger and then feeding you with manna, which neither you nor your ancestors had known, to teach you that man does not live on bread alone but on every word that comes from the mouth of the LORD. [4]Your clothes did not wear out and your feet did not swell during these forty years. [5]Know then in your heart that as a man disciplines his son, so the LORD your God disciplines you.

[6]Observe the commands of the LORD your God, walking in obedience to him and revering him. [7]For the LORD your God is bringing you into a good land — a land with brooks, streams, and deep springs gushing out into the valleys and hills; [8]a land with wheat and barley, vines and fig trees, pomegranates, olive oil and honey; [9]a land where bread will not be scarce and you will lack nothing; a land where the rocks are iron and you can dig copper out of the hills.

[10]When you have eaten and are satisfied, praise the LORD your God for the good land he has given you. [11]Be careful that you do not forget the LORD your God, failing to observe his commands, his laws and his decrees that I am giving you this day. [12]Otherwise, when you eat and are satisfied, when you build fine houses and settle down, [13]and when your herds and flocks grow large and your silver and gold increase and all you have is multiplied, [14]then your heart will become proud and you will forget the LORD your God, who brought you out of Egypt, out of the land of slavery. [15]He led you through the vast and dreadful wilderness, that thirsty and waterless land, with its venomous snakes and scorpions. He brought you water out of hard rock. [16]He gave you manna to eat in the wilderness, something your ancestors had never known, to humble and test

you so that in the end it might go well with you. [17] You may say to yourself, "My power and the strength of my hands have produced this wealth for me." [18] But remember the LORD your God, for it is he who gives you the ability to produce wealth, and so confirms his covenant, which he swore to your ancestors, as it is today.

[19] If you ever forget the LORD your God and follow other gods and worship and bow down to them, I testify against you today that you will surely be destroyed. [20] Like the nations the LORD destroyed before you, so you will be destroyed for not obeying the LORD your God.

Not Because of Israel's Righteousness

9 Hear, Israel: You are now about to cross the Jordan to go in and dispossess nations greater and stronger than you, with large cities that have walls up to the sky. [2] The people are strong and tall — Anakites! You know about them and have heard it said: "Who can stand up against the Anakites?" [3] But be assured today that the LORD your God is the one who goes across ahead of you like a devouring fire. He will destroy them; he will subdue them before you. And you will drive them out and annihilate them quickly, as the LORD has promised you.

[4] After the LORD your God has driven them out before you, do not say to yourself, "The LORD has brought me here to take possession of this land because of my righteousness." No, it is on account of the wickedness of these nations that the LORD is going to drive them out before you. [5] It is not because of your righteousness or your integrity that you are going in to take possession of their land; but on account of the wickedness of these nations, the LORD your God will drive them out before you, to accomplish what he swore to your fathers, to Abraham, Isaac and Jacob. [6] Understand, then, that it is not because of your righteousness that the LORD your God is giving you this good land to possess, for you are a stiff-necked people.

The Golden Calf

[7] Remember this and never forget how you aroused the anger of the LORD your God in the wilderness. From the day you left Egypt until you arrived here, you have been rebellious against the LORD. [8] At Horeb you aroused the LORD's wrath so that he was angry enough to destroy you. [9] When I went up on the mountain to receive the tablets of stone, the tablets of the covenant that the LORD had made with you, I stayed on the mountain forty days and forty nights; I ate no bread and drank no water. [10] The LORD gave me two stone tablets inscribed by the finger of God. On them were all the commandments the LORD proclaimed to you on the mountain out of the fire, on the day of the assembly.

[11] At the end of the forty days and forty nights, the LORD gave me the two stone tablets, the tablets of the covenant. [12] Then the LORD told me, "Go down from here at once, because your people whom you brought out of Egypt have become corrupt. They have turned away quickly from what I commanded them and have made an idol for themselves."

[13] And the LORD said to me, "I have seen this people, and they are a stiff-necked people indeed! [14] Let me alone, so that I may destroy them and blot out their name from under heaven. And I will make you into a nation stronger and more numerous than they."

[15] So I turned and went down from the mountain while it was ablaze with fire. And the two tablets of the covenant were in my hands. [16] When I looked, I saw that you had sinned against the LORD your God; you had made for yourselves an idol cast in the shape of a calf. You had turned aside quickly from the way that the LORD had commanded you. [17] So I took the two tablets and threw them out of my hands, breaking them to pieces before your eyes.

[18] Then once again I fell prostrate before the LORD for forty days and forty nights; I ate no bread and drank no water, because of all the sin you had committed, doing what

was evil in the LORD's sight and so arousing his anger. ¹⁹I feared the anger and wrath of the LORD, for he was angry enough with you to destroy you. But again the LORD listened to me. ²⁰And the LORD was angry enough with Aaron to destroy him, but at that time I prayed for Aaron too. ²¹Also I took that sinful thing of yours, the calf you had made, and burned it in the fire. Then I crushed it and ground it to powder as fine as dust and threw the dust into a stream that flowed down the mountain.

²²You also made the LORD angry at Taberah, at Massah and at Kibroth Hattaavah.

²³And when the LORD sent you out from Kadesh Barnea, he said, "Go up and take possession of the land I have given you." But you rebelled against the command of the LORD your God. You did not trust him or obey him. ²⁴You have been rebellious against the LORD ever since I have known you.

²⁵I lay prostrate before the LORD those forty days and forty nights because the LORD had said he would destroy you. ²⁶I prayed to the LORD and said, "Sovereign LORD, do not destroy your people, your own inheritance that you redeemed by your great power and brought out of Egypt with a mighty hand. ²⁷Remember your servants Abraham, Isaac and Jacob. Overlook the stubbornness of this people, their wickedness and their sin. ²⁸Otherwise, the country from which you brought us will say, 'Because the LORD was not able to take them into the land he had promised them, and because he hated them, he brought them out to put them to death in the wilderness.' ²⁹But they are your people, your inheritance that you brought out by your great power and your outstretched arm."

Tablets Like the First Ones

10 At that time the LORD said to me, "Chisel out two stone tablets like the first ones and come up to me on the mountain. Also make a wooden ark.ᵃ

²I will write on the tablets the words that were on the first tablets, which you broke. Then you are to put them in the ark."

³So I made the ark out of acacia wood and chiseled out two stone tablets like the first ones, and I went up on the mountain with the two tablets in my hands. ⁴The LORD wrote on these tablets what he had written before, the Ten Commandments he had proclaimed to you on the mountain, out of the fire, on the day of the assembly. And the LORD gave them to me. ⁵Then I came back down the mountain and put the tablets in the ark I had made, as the LORD commanded me, and they are there now.

⁶(The Israelites traveled from the wells of Bene Jaakan to Moserah. There Aaron died and was buried, and Eleazar his son succeeded him as priest. ⁷From there they traveled to Gudgodah and on to Jotbathah, a land with streams of water. ⁸At that time the LORD set apart the tribe of Levi to carry the ark of the covenant of the LORD, to stand before the LORD to minister and to pronounce blessings in his name, as they still do today. ⁹That is why the Levites have no share or inheritance among their fellow Israelites; the LORD is their inheritance, as the LORD your God told them.)

¹⁰Now I had stayed on the mountain forty days and forty nights, as I did the first time, and the LORD listened to me at this time also. It was not his will to destroy you. ¹¹"Go," the LORD said to me, "and lead the people on their way, so that they may enter and possess the land I swore to their ancestors to give them."

Fear the LORD

¹²And now, Israel, what does the LORD your God ask of you but to fear the LORD your God, to walk in obedience to him, to love him, to serve the LORD your God with all your heart and with all your soul, ¹³and to observe the LORD's commands and decrees that I am giving you today for your own good?

ᵃ 1 That is, a chest

¹⁴To the LORD your God belong the heavens, even the highest heavens, the earth and everything in it. ¹⁵Yet the LORD set his affection on your ancestors and loved them, and he chose you, their descendants, above all the nations—as it is today. ¹⁶Circumcise your hearts, therefore, and do not be stiff-necked any longer. ¹⁷For the LORD your God is God of gods and Lord of lords, the great God, mighty and awesome, who shows no partiality and accepts no bribes. ¹⁸He defends the cause of the fatherless and the widow, and loves the foreigner residing among you, giving them food and clothing. ¹⁹And you are to love those who are foreigners, for you yourselves were foreigners in Egypt. ²⁰Fear the LORD your God and serve him. Hold fast to him and take your oaths in his name. ²¹He is the one you praise; he is your God, who performed for you those great and awesome wonders you saw with your own eyes. ²²Your ancestors who went down into Egypt were seventy in all, and now the LORD your God has made you as numerous as the stars in the sky.

Love and Obey the LORD

11 Love the LORD your God and keep his requirements, his decrees, his laws and his commands always. ²Remember today that your children were not the ones who saw and experienced the discipline of the LORD your God: his majesty, his mighty hand, his outstretched arm; ³the signs he performed and the things he did in the heart of Egypt, both to Pharaoh king of Egypt and to his whole country; ⁴what he did to the Egyptian army, to its horses and chariots, how he overwhelmed them with the waters of the Red Sea*a* as they were pursuing you, and how the LORD brought lasting ruin on them. ⁵It was not your children who saw what he did for you in the wilderness until you arrived at this place, ⁶and what he did to Dathan and Abiram, sons of Eliab the Reubenite, when the earth opened its

mouth right in the middle of all Israel and swallowed them up with their households, their tents and every living thing that belonged to them. ⁷But it was your own eyes that saw all these great things the LORD has done.

⁸Observe therefore all the commands I am giving you today, so that you may have the strength to go in and take over the land that you are crossing the Jordan to possess, ⁹and so that you may live long in the land the LORD swore to your ancestors to give to them and their descendants, a land flowing with milk and honey. ¹⁰The land you are entering to take over is not like the land of Egypt, from which you have come, where you planted your seed and irrigated it by foot as in a vegetable garden. ¹¹But the land you are crossing the Jordan to take possession of is a land of mountains and valleys that drinks rain from heaven. ¹²It is a land the LORD your God cares for; the eyes of the LORD your God are continually on it from the beginning of the year to its end.

¹³So if you faithfully obey the commands I am giving you today—to love the LORD your God and to serve him with all your heart and with all your soul— ¹⁴then I will send rain on your land in its season, both autumn and spring rains, so that you may gather in your grain, new wine and olive oil. ¹⁵I will provide grass in the fields for your cattle, and you will eat and be satisfied.

¹⁶Be careful, or you will be enticed to turn away and worship other gods and bow down to them. ¹⁷Then the LORD's anger will burn against you, and he will shut up the heavens so that it will not rain and the ground will yield no produce, and you will soon perish from the good land the LORD is giving you. ¹⁸Fix these words of mine in your hearts and minds; tie them as symbols on your hands and bind them on your foreheads. ¹⁹Teach them to your children, talking about them when you sit at home and when you walk along the road, when you lie down and when you get up. ²⁰Write

---

a 4 Or the Sea of Reeds

them on the doorframes of your houses and on your gates, 21so that your days and the days of your children may be many in the land the LORD swore to give your ancestors, as many as the days that the heavens are above the earth.

22If you carefully observe all these commands I am giving you to follow—to love the LORD your God, to walk in obedience to him and to hold fast to him— 23then the LORD will drive out all these nations before you, and you will dispossess nations larger and stronger than you. 24Every place where you set your foot will be yours: Your territory will extend from the desert to Lebanon, and from the Euphrates River to the Mediterranean Sea. 25No one will be able to stand against you. The LORD your God, as he promised you, will put the terror and fear of you on the whole land, wherever you go.

26See, I am setting before you today a blessing and a curse— 27the blessing if you obey the commands of the LORD your God that I am giving you today; 28the curse if you disobey the commands of the LORD your God and turn from the way that I command you today by following other gods, which you have not known. 29When the LORD your God has brought you into the land you are entering to possess, you are to proclaim on Mount Gerizim the blessings, and on Mount Ebal the curses. 30As you know, these mountains are across the Jordan, westward, toward the setting sun, near the great trees of Moreh, in the territory of those Canaanites living in the Arabah in the vicinity of Gilgal. 31You are about to cross the Jordan to enter and take possession of the land the LORD your God is giving you. When you have taken it over and are living there, 32be sure that you obey all the decrees and laws I am setting before you today.

The One Place of Worship

12 These are the decrees and laws you must be careful to follow in the land that the LORD, the God of your ancestors, has given you to possess—as long as you live in the land. 2Destroy completely all the places on the high mountains, on the hills and under every spreading tree, where the nations you are dispossessing worship their gods. 3Break down their altars, smash their sacred stones and burn their Asherah poles in the fire; cut down the idols of their gods and wipe out their names from those places.

4You must not worship the LORD your God in their way. 5But you are to seek the place the LORD your God will choose from among all your tribes to put his Name there for his dwelling. To that place you must go; 6there bring your burnt offerings and sacrifices, your tithes and special gifts, what you have vowed to give and your freewill offerings, and the firstborn of your herds and flocks. 7There, in the presence of the LORD your God, you and your families shall eat and shall rejoice in everything you have put your hand to, because the LORD your God has blessed you.

8You are not to do as we do here today, everyone doing as they see fit, 9since you have not yet reached the resting place and the inheritance the LORD your God is giving you. 10But you will cross the Jordan and settle in the land the LORD your God is giving you as an inheritance, and he will give you rest from all your enemies around you so that you will live in safety. 11Then to the place the LORD your God will choose as a dwelling for his Name— there you are to bring everything I command you: your burnt offerings and sacrifices, your tithes and special gifts, and all the choice possessions you have vowed to the LORD. 12And there rejoice before the LORD your God— you, your sons and daughters, your male and female servants, and the Levites from your towns who have no allotment or inheritance of their own. 13Be careful not to sacrifice your burnt offerings anywhere you please. 14Offer them only at the place the LORD will choose in one of your tribes, and there observe everything I command you.

15Nevertheless, you may slaughter your animals in any of your towns and eat as much of the meat as you want, as if it were gazelle or deer, according to the blessing the LORD your God gives you. Both the ceremonially unclean and the clean may eat it. 16But you must not eat the blood; pour it out on the ground like water. 17You must not eat in your own towns the tithe of your grain and new wine and olive oil, or the firstborn of your herds and flocks, or whatever you have vowed to give, or your freewill offerings or special gifts. 18Instead, you are to eat them in the presence of the LORD your God at the place the LORD your God will choose — you, your sons and daughters, your male and female servants, and the Levites from your towns — and you are to rejoice before the LORD your God in everything you put your hand to. 19Be careful not to neglect the Levites as long as you live in your land.

20When the LORD your God has enlarged your territory as he promised you, and you crave meat and say, "I would like some meat," then you may eat as much of it as you want. 21If the place where the LORD your God chooses to put his Name is too far away from you, you may slaughter animals from the herds and flocks the LORD has given you, as I have commanded you, and in your own towns you may eat as much of them as you want. 22Eat them as you would gazelle or deer. Both the ceremonially unclean and the clean may eat. 23But be sure you do not eat the blood, because the blood is the life, and you must not eat the life with the meat. 24You must not eat the blood; pour it out on the ground like water. 25Do not eat it, so that it may go well with you and your children after you, because you will be doing what is right in the eyes of the LORD.

26But take your consecrated things and whatever you have vowed to give, and go to the place the LORD will choose. 27Present your burnt offerings on the altar of the LORD your God, both the meat and the blood. The blood of your sacrifices must be poured beside the altar of the LORD your God, but you may eat the meat. 28Be careful to obey all these regulations I am giving you, so that it may always go well with you and your children after you, because you will be doing what is good and right in the eyes of the LORD your God.

29The LORD your God will cut off before you the nations you are about to invade and dispossess. But when you have driven them out and settled in their land, 30and after they have been destroyed before you, be careful not to be ensnared by inquiring about their gods, saying, "How do these nations serve their gods? We will do the same." 31You must not worship the LORD your God in their way, because in worshiping their gods, they do all kinds of detestable things the LORD hates. They even burn their sons and daughters in the fire as sacrifices to their gods.

32See that you do all I command you; do not add to it or take away from it.a

Worshiping Other Gods

13b If a prophet, or one who foretells by dreams, appears among you and announces to you a sign or wonder, 2and if the sign or wonder spoken of takes place, and the prophet says, "Let us follow other gods" (gods you have not known) "and let us worship them," 3you must not listen to the words of that prophet or dreamer. The LORD your God is testing you to find out whether you love him with all your heart and with all your soul. 4It is the LORD your God you must follow, and him you must revere. Keep his commands and obey him; serve him and hold fast to him. 5That prophet or dreamer must be put to death for inciting rebellion against the LORD your God, who brought you out of Egypt and redeemed you from the land of slavery. That prophet or dreamer tried to turn you from the way the LORD your God

---

a 32 In Hebrew texts this verse (12:32) is numbered 13:1.   b In Hebrew texts 13:1-18 is numbered 13:2-19.

commanded you to follow. You must purge the evil from among you.

⁶If your very own brother, or your son or daughter, or the wife you love, or your closest friend secretly entices you, saying, "Let us go and worship other gods" (gods that neither you nor your ancestors have known, ⁷gods of the peoples around you, whether near or far, from one end of the land to the other), ⁸do not yield to them or listen to them. Show them no pity. Do not spare them or shield them. ⁹You must certainly put them to death. Your hand must be the first in putting them to death, and then the hands of all the people. ¹⁰Stone them to death, because they tried to turn you away from the LORD your God, who brought you out of Egypt, out of the land of slavery. ¹¹Then all Israel will hear and be afraid, and no one among you will do such an evil thing again.

¹²If you hear it said about one of the towns the LORD your God is giving you to live in ¹³that troublemakers have arisen among you and have led the people of their town astray, saying, "Let us go and worship other gods" (gods you have not known), ¹⁴then you must inquire, probe and investigate it thoroughly. And if it is true and it has been proved that this detestable thing has been done among you, ¹⁵you must certainly put to the sword all who live in that town. You must destroy it completely,ᵃ both its people and its livestock. ¹⁶You are to gather all the plunder of the town into the middle of the public square and completely burn the town and all its plunder as a whole burnt offering to the LORD your God. That town is to remain a ruin forever, never to be rebuilt, ¹⁷and none of the condemned thingsᵃ are to be found in your hands. Then the LORD will turn from his fierce anger, will show you mercy, and will have compassion on you. He will increase your numbers, as he promised on oath to your ancestors—

¹⁸because you obey the LORD your God by keeping all his commands that I am giving you today and doing what is right in his eyes.

Clean and Unclean Food

14 You are the children of the LORD your God. Do not cut yourselves or shave the front of your heads for the dead, ²for you are a people holy to the LORD your God. Out of all the peoples on the face of the earth, the LORD has chosen you to be his treasured possession.

³Do not eat any detestable thing. ⁴These are the animals you may eat: the ox, the sheep, the goat, ⁵the deer, the gazelle, the roe deer, the wild goat, the ibex, the antelope and the mountain sheep.ᵇ ⁶You may eat any animal that has a divided hoof and that chews the cud. ⁷However, of those that chew the cud or that have a divided hoof you may not eat the camel, the rabbit or the hyrax. Although they chew the cud, they do not have a divided hoof; they are ceremonially unclean for you. ⁸The pig is also unclean; although it has a divided hoof, it does not chew the cud. You are not to eat their meat or touch their carcasses.

⁹Of all the creatures living in the water, you may eat any that has fins and scales. ¹⁰But anything that does not have fins and scales you may not eat; for you it is unclean.

¹¹You may eat any clean bird. ¹²But these you may not eat: the eagle, the vulture, the black vulture, ¹³the red kite, the black kite, any kind of falcon, ¹⁴any kind of raven, ¹⁵the horned owl, the screech owl, the gull, any kind of hawk, ¹⁶the little owl, the great owl, the white owl, ¹⁷the desert owl, the osprey, the cormorant, ¹⁸the stork, any kind of heron, the hoopoe and the bat.

¹⁹All flying insects are unclean to you; do not eat them. ²⁰But any winged creature that is clean you may eat.

²¹Do not eat anything you find already dead. You may give it to the foreigner

---

ᵃ 15,17 The Hebrew term refers to the irrevocable giving over of things or persons to the LORD, often by totally destroying them.   ᵇ 5 The precise identification of some of the birds and animals in this chapter is uncertain.

residing in any of your towns, and they may eat it, or you may sell it to any other foreigner. But you are a people holy to the Lord your God.

Do not cook a young goat in its mother's milk.

Tithes

22Be sure to set aside a tenth of all that your fields produce each year. 23Eat the tithe of your grain, new wine and olive oil, and the firstborn of your herds and flocks in the presence of the Lord your God at the place he will choose as a dwelling for his Name, so that you may learn to revere the Lord your God always. 24But if that place is too distant and you have been blessed by the Lord your God and cannot carry your tithe (because the place where the Lord will choose to put his Name is so far away), 25then exchange your tithe for silver, and take the silver with you and go to the place the Lord your God will choose. 26Use the silver to buy whatever you like: cattle, sheep, wine or other fermented drink, or anything you wish. Then you and your household shall eat there in the presence of the Lord your God and rejoice. 27And do not neglect the Levites living in your towns, for they have no allotment or inheritance of their own.

28At the end of every three years, bring all the tithes of that year's produce and store it in your towns, 29so that the Levites (who have no allotment or inheritance of their own) and the foreigners, the fatherless and the widows who live in your towns may come and eat and be satisfied, and so that the Lord your God may bless you in all the work of your hands.

The Year for Canceling Debts

15 At the end of every seven years you must cancel debts. 2This is how it is to be done: Every creditor shall cancel any loan they have made to a fellow Israelite. They shall not require payment from anyone among their own people, because the Lord's time for cancel-

ing debts has been proclaimed. 3You may require payment from a foreigner, but you must cancel any debt your fellow Israelite owes you. 4However, there need be no poor people among you, for in the land the Lord your God is giving you to possess as your inheritance, he will richly bless you, 5if only you fully obey the Lord your God and are careful to follow all these commands I am giving you today. 6For the Lord your God will bless you as he has promised, and you will lend to many nations but will borrow from none. You will rule over many nations but none will rule over you.

7If anyone is poor among your fellow Israelites in any of the towns of the land the Lord your God is giving you, do not be hardhearted or tightfisted toward them. 8Rather, be openhanded and freely lend them whatever they need. 9Be careful not to harbor this wicked thought: "The seventh year, the year for canceling debts, is near," so that you do not show ill will toward the needy among your fellow Israelites and give them nothing. They may then appeal to the Lord against you, and you will be found guilty of sin. 10Give generously to them and do so without a grudging heart; then because of this the Lord your God will bless you in all your work and in everything you put your hand to. 11There will always be poor people in the land. Therefore I command you to be openhanded toward your fellow Israelites who are poor and needy in your land.

Freeing Servants

12If any of your people — Hebrew men or women — sell themselves to you and serve you six years, in the seventh year you must let them go free. 13And when you release them, do not send them away empty-handed. 14Supply them liberally from your flock, your threshing floor and your winepress. Give to them as the Lord your God has blessed you. 15Remember that you were slaves in Egypt and the Lord your God redeemed you. That is why I give you this command today.

16But if your servant says to you, "I do not want to leave you," because he loves you and your family and is well off with you, 17then take an awl and push it through his earlobe into the door, and he will become your servant for life. Do the same for your female servant.

18Do not consider it a hardship to set your servant free, because their service to you these six years has been worth twice as much as that of a hired hand. And the LORD your God will bless you in everything you do.

The Firstborn Animals

19Set apart for the LORD your God every firstborn male of your herds and flocks. Do not put the firstborn of your cows to work, and do not shear the firstborn of your sheep. 20Each year you and your family are to eat them in the presence of the LORD your God at the place he will choose. 21If an animal has a defect, is lame or blind, or has any serious flaw, you must not sacrifice it to the LORD your God. 22You are to eat it in your own towns. Both the ceremonially unclean and the clean may eat it, as if it were gazelle or deer. 23But you must not eat the blood; pour it out on the ground like water.

The Passover

16 Observe the month of Aviv and celebrate the Passover of the LORD your God, because in the month of Aviv he brought you out of Egypt by night. 2Sacrifice as the Passover to the LORD your God an animal from your flock or herd at the place the LORD will choose as a dwelling for his Name. 3Do not eat it with bread made with yeast, but for seven days eat unleavened bread, the bread of affliction, because you left Egypt in haste — so that all the days of your life you may remember the time of your departure from Egypt. 4Let no yeast be found in your possession in all your land for seven days. Do not let any of the meat you sacrifice on the evening of the first day remain until morning.

5You must not sacrifice the Passover in any town the LORD your God gives you 6except in the place he will choose as a dwelling for his Name. There you must sacrifice the Passover in the evening, when the sun goes down, on the anniversary*a* of your departure from Egypt. 7Roast it and eat it at the place the LORD your God will choose. Then in the morning return to your tents. 8For six days eat unleavened bread and on the seventh day hold an assembly to the LORD your God and do no work.

The Festival of Weeks

9Count off seven weeks from the time you begin to put the sickle to the standing grain. 10Then celebrate the Festival of Weeks to the LORD your God by giving a freewill offering in proportion to the blessings the LORD your God has given you. 11And rejoice before the LORD your God at the place he will choose as a dwelling for his Name — you, your sons and daughters, your male and female servants, the Levites in your towns, and the foreigners, the fatherless and the widows living among you. 12Remember that you were slaves in Egypt, and follow carefully these decrees.

The Festival of Tabernacles

13Celebrate the Festival of Tabernacles for seven days after you have gathered the produce of your threshing floor and your winepress. 14Be joyful at your festival — you, your sons and daughters, your male and female servants, and the Levites, the foreigners, the fatherless and the widows who live in your towns. 15For seven days celebrate the festival to the LORD your God at the place the LORD will choose. For the LORD your God will bless you in all your harvest and in all the work of your hands, and your joy will be complete.

16Three times a year all your men must

---

a 6 Or *down, at the time of day*

appear before the LORD your God at the place he will choose: at the Festival of Unleavened Bread, the Festival of Weeks and the Festival of Tabernacles. No one should appear before the LORD empty-handed: [17]Each of you must bring a gift in proportion to the way the LORD your God has blessed you.

Judges

[18]Appoint judges and officials for each of your tribes in every town the LORD your God is giving you, and they shall judge the people fairly. [19]Do not pervert justice or show partiality. Do not accept a bribe, for a bribe blinds the eyes of the wise and twists the words of the innocent. [20]Follow justice and justice alone, so that you may live and possess the land the LORD your God is giving you.

Worshiping Other Gods

[21]Do not set up any wooden Asherah pole beside the altar you build to the LORD your God, [22]and do not erect a sacred stone, for these the LORD your God hates.

17

Do not sacrifice to the LORD your God an ox or a sheep that has any defect or flaw in it, for that would be detestable to him.

[2]If a man or woman living among you in one of the towns the LORD gives you is found doing evil in the eyes of the LORD your God in violation of his covenant, [3]and contrary to my command has worshiped other gods, bowing down to them or to the sun or the moon or the stars in the sky, [4]and this has been brought to your attention, then you must investigate it thoroughly. If it is true and it has been proved that this detestable thing has been done in Israel, [5]take the man or woman who has done this evil deed to your city gate and stone that person to death. [6]On the testimony of two or three witnesses a person is to be put to death, but no one is to be put to death on the testimony of only one witness. [7]The hands of the witnesses must be the first in putting that person to death, and then the hands of all

the people. You must purge the evil from among you.

Law Courts

[8]If cases come before your courts that are too difficult for you to judge — whether bloodshed, lawsuits or assaults — take them to the place the LORD your God will choose. [9]Go to the Levitical priests and to the judge who is in office at that time. Inquire of them and they will give you the verdict. [10]You must act according to the decisions they give you at the place the LORD will choose. Be careful to do everything they instruct you to do. [11]Act according to whatever they teach you and the decisions they give you. Do not turn aside from what they tell you, to the right or to the left. [12]Anyone who shows contempt for the judge or for the priest who stands ministering there to the LORD your God is to be put to death. You must purge the evil from Israel. [13]All the people will hear and be afraid, and will not be contemptuous again.

The King

[14]When you enter the land the LORD your God is giving you and have taken possession of it and settled in it, and you say, "Let us set a king over us like all the nations around us," [15]be sure to appoint over you a king the LORD your God chooses. He must be from among your fellow Israelites. Do not place a foreigner over you, one who is not an Israelite. [16]The king, moreover, must not acquire great numbers of horses for himself or make the people return to Egypt to get more of them, for the LORD has told you, "You are not to go back that way again." [17]He must not take many wives, or his heart will be led astray. He must not accumulate large amounts of silver and gold.

[18]When he takes the throne of his kingdom, he is to write for himself on a scroll a copy of this law, taken from that of the Levitical priests. [19]It is to be with him, and he is to read it all the days of his life so that he may learn to revere the LORD his God

and follow carefully all the words of this law and these decrees [20]and not consider himself better than his fellow Israelites and turn from the law to the right or to the left. Then he and his descendants will reign a long time over his kingdom in Israel.

Offerings for Priests and Levites

18 The Levitical priests — indeed, the whole tribe of Levi — are to have no allotment or inheritance with Israel. They shall live on the food offerings presented to the LORD, for that is their inheritance. [2]They shall have no inheritance among their fellow Israelites; the LORD is their inheritance, as he promised them.

[3]This is the share due the priests from the people who sacrifice a bull or a sheep: the shoulder, the internal organs and the meat from the head. [4]You are to give them the firstfruits of your grain, new wine and olive oil, and the first wool from the shearing of your sheep, [5]for the LORD your God has chosen them and their descendants out of all your tribes to stand and minister in the LORD's name always.

[6]If a Levite moves from one of your towns anywhere in Israel where he is living, and comes in all earnestness to the place the LORD will choose, [7]he may minister in the name of the LORD his God like all his fellow Levites who serve there in the presence of the LORD. [8]He is to share equally in their benefits, even though he has received money from the sale of family possessions.

Occult Practices

[9]When you enter the land the LORD your God is giving you, do not learn to imitate the detestable ways of the nations there. [10]Let no one be found among you who sacrifices their son or daughter in the fire, who practices divination or sorcery, interprets omens, engages in witchcraft, [11]or casts spells, or who is a medium or spiritist or who consults the dead. [12]Anyone who does these things is detestable to the LORD; because of these same detestable practices the LORD your God will drive out those nations before you. [13]You must be blameless before the LORD your God.

The Prophet

[14]The nations you will dispossess listen to those who practice sorcery or divination. But as for you, the LORD your God has not permitted you to do so. [15]The LORD your God will raise up for you a prophet like me from among you, from your fellow Israelites. You must listen to him. [16]For this is what you asked of the LORD your God at Horeb on the day of the assembly when you said, "Let us not hear the voice of the LORD our God nor see this great fire anymore, or we will die."

[17]The LORD said to me: "What they say is good. [18]I will raise up for them a prophet like you from among their fellow Israelites, and I will put my words in his mouth. He will tell them everything I command him. [19]I myself will call to account anyone who does not listen to my words that the prophet speaks in my name. [20]But a prophet who presumes to speak in my name anything I have not commanded, or a prophet who speaks in the name of other gods, is to be put to death."

[21]You may say to yourselves, "How can we know when a message has not been spoken by the LORD?" [22]If what a prophet proclaims in the name of the LORD does not take place or come true, that is a message the LORD has not spoken. That prophet has spoken presumptuously, so do not be alarmed.

Cities of Refuge

19 When the LORD your God has destroyed the nations whose land he is giving you, and when you have driven them out and settled in their towns and houses, [2]then set aside for yourselves three cities in the land the LORD your God is giving you to possess. [3]Determine the distances involved and divide into three parts the land the LORD your God is giving you as an inheritance, so

that a person who kills someone may flee for refuge to one of these cities.

⁴This is the rule concerning anyone who kills a person and flees there for safety — anyone who kills a neighbor unintentionally, without malice aforethought. ⁵For instance, a man may go into the forest with his neighbor to cut wood, and as he swings his ax to fell a tree, the head may fly off and hit his neighbor and kill him. That man may flee to one of these cities and save his life. ⁶Otherwise, the avenger of blood might pursue him in a rage, overtake him if the distance is too great, and kill him even though he is not deserving of death, since he did it to his neighbor without malice aforethought. ⁷This is why I command you to set aside for yourselves three cities.

⁸If the LORD your God enlarges your territory, as he promised on oath to your ancestors, and gives you the whole land he promised them, ⁹because you carefully follow all these laws I command you today — to love the LORD your God and to walk always in obedience to him — then you are to set aside three more cities. ¹⁰Do this so that innocent blood will not be shed in your land, which the LORD your God is giving you as your inheritance, and so that you will not be guilty of bloodshed.

¹¹But if out of hate someone lies in wait, assaults and kills a neighbor, and then flees to one of these cities, ¹²the killer shall be sent for by the town elders, be brought back from the city, and be handed over to the avenger of blood to die. ¹³Show no pity. You must purge from Israel the guilt of shedding innocent blood, so that it may go well with you.

¹⁴Do not move your neighbor's boundary stone set up by your predecessors in the inheritance you receive in the land the LORD your God is giving you to possess.

Witnesses

¹⁵One witness is not enough to convict anyone accused of any crime or offense they may have committed. A matter must be established by the testimony of two or three witnesses.

¹⁶If a malicious witness takes the stand to accuse someone of a crime, ¹⁷the two people involved in the dispute must stand in the presence of the LORD before the priests and the judges who are in office at the time. ¹⁸The judges must make a thorough investigation, and if the witness proves to be a liar, giving false testimony against a fellow Israelite, ¹⁹then do to the false witness as that witness intended to do to the other party. You must purge the evil from among you. ²⁰The rest of the people will hear of this and be afraid, and never again will such an evil thing be done among you. ²¹Show no pity: life for life, eye for eye, tooth for tooth, hand for hand, foot for foot.

Going to War

20 When you go to war against your enemies and see horses and chariots and an army greater than yours, do not be afraid of them, because the LORD your God, who brought you up out of Egypt, will be with you. ²When you are about to go into battle, the priest shall come forward and address the army. ³He shall say: "Hear, Israel: Today you are going into battle against your enemies. Do not be fainthearted or afraid; do not panic or be terrified by them. ⁴For the LORD your God is the one who goes with you to fight for you against your enemies to give you victory."

⁵The officers shall say to the army: "Has anyone built a new house and not yet begun to live in it? Let him go home, or he may die in battle and someone else may begin to live in it. ⁶Has anyone planted a vineyard and not begun to enjoy it? Let him go home, or he may die in battle and someone else enjoy it. ⁷Has anyone become pledged to a woman and not married her? Let him go home, or he may die in battle and someone else marry her." ⁸Then the officers shall add, "Is anyone afraid or fainthearted? Let him go home so that his fellow

soldiers will not become disheartened too." ⁹When the officers have finished speaking to the army, they shall appoint commanders over it.

¹⁰When you march up to attack a city, make its people an offer of peace. ¹¹If they accept and open their gates, all the people in it shall be subject to forced labor and shall work for you. ¹²If they refuse to make peace and they engage you in battle, lay siege to that city. ¹³When the LORD your God delivers it into your hand, put to the sword all the men in it. ¹⁴As for the women, the children, the livestock and everything else in the city, you may take these as plunder for yourselves. And you may use the plunder the LORD your God gives you from your enemies. ¹⁵This is how you are to treat all the cities that are at a distance from you and do not belong to the nations nearby.

¹⁶However, in the cities of the nations the LORD your God is giving you as an inheritance, do not leave alive anything that breathes. ¹⁷Completely destroy*a* them — the Hittites, Amorites, Canaanites, Perizzites, Hivites and Jebusites — as the LORD your God has commanded you. ¹⁸Otherwise, they will teach you to follow all the detestable things they do in worshiping their gods, and you will sin against the LORD your God.

¹⁹When you lay siege to a city for a long time, fighting against it to capture it, do not destroy its trees by putting an ax to them, because you can eat their fruit. Do not cut them down. Are the trees people, that you should besiege them?*b* ²⁰However, you may cut down trees that you know are not fruit trees and use them to build siege works until the city at war with you falls.

Atonement for an Unsolved Murder

21 If someone is found slain, lying in a field in the land the LORD your God is giving you to possess, and it is not known who the killer was, ²your elders and judges shall go out and measure the distance from the body to the neighboring towns. ³Then the elders of the town nearest the body shall take a heifer that has never been worked and has never worn a yoke ⁴and lead it down to a valley that has not been plowed or planted and where there is a flowing stream. There in the valley they are to break the heifer's neck. ⁵The Levitical priests shall step forward, for the LORD your God has chosen them to minister and to pronounce blessings in the name of the LORD and to decide all cases of dispute and assault. ⁶Then all the elders of the town nearest the body shall wash their hands over the heifer whose neck was broken in the valley, ⁷and they shall declare: "Our hands did not shed this blood, nor did our eyes see it done. ⁸Accept this atonement for your people Israel, whom you have redeemed, LORD, and do not hold your people guilty of the blood of an innocent person." Then the bloodshed will be atoned for, ⁹and you will have purged from yourselves the guilt of shedding innocent blood, since you have done what is right in the eyes of the LORD.

Marrying a Captive Woman

¹⁰When you go to war against your enemies and the LORD your God delivers them into your hands and you take captives, ¹¹if you notice among the captives a beautiful woman and are attracted to her, you may take her as your wife. ¹²Bring her into your home and have her shave her head, trim her nails ¹³and put aside the clothes she was wearing when captured. After she has lived in your house and mourned her father and mother for a full month, then you may go to her and be her husband and she shall be your wife. ¹⁴If you are not pleased with her, let her go wherever she wishes. You must not sell her or treat her as a slave, since you have dishonored her.

---

a 17 The Hebrew term refers to the irrevocable giving over of things or persons to the LORD, often by totally destroying them.　*b 19* Or *down to use in the siege, for the fruit trees are for the benefit of people.*

The Right of the Firstborn

15If a man has two wives, and he loves one but not the other, and both bear him sons but the firstborn is the son of the wife he does not love, 16when he wills his property to his sons, he must not give the rights of the firstborn to the son of the wife he loves in preference to his actual firstborn, the son of the wife he does not love. 17He must acknowledge the son of his unloved wife as the firstborn by giving him a double share of all he has. That son is the first sign of his father's strength. The right of the firstborn belongs to him.

A Rebellious Son

18If someone has a stubborn and rebellious son who does not obey his father and mother and will not listen to them when they discipline him, 19his father and mother shall take hold of him and bring him to the elders at the gate of his town. 20They shall say to the elders, "This son of ours is stubborn and rebellious. He will not obey us. He is a glutton and a drunkard." 21Then all the men of his town are to stone him to death. You must purge the evil from among you. All Israel will hear of it and be afraid.

Various Laws

22If someone guilty of a capital offense is put to death and their body is exposed on a pole, 23you must not leave the body hanging on the pole overnight. Be sure to bury it that same day, because anyone who is hung on a pole is under God's curse. You must not desecrate the land the LORD your God is giving you as an inheritance.

22 If you see your fellow Israelite's ox or sheep straying, do not ignore it but be sure to take it back to its owner. 2If they do not live near you or if you do not know who owns it, take it home with you and keep it until they come looking for it. Then give it back. 3Do the same if you find their donkey or cloak or anything else they have lost. Do not ignore it.

4If you see your fellow Israelite's donkey or ox fallen on the road, do not ignore it. Help the owner get it to its feet.

5A woman must not wear men's clothing, nor a man wear women's clothing, for the LORD your God detests anyone who does this.

6If you come across a bird's nest beside the road, either in a tree or on the ground, and the mother is sitting on the young or on the eggs, do not take the mother with the young. 7You may take the young, but be sure to let the mother go, so that it may go well with you and you may have a long life.

8When you build a new house, make a parapet around your roof so that you may not bring the guilt of bloodshed on your house if someone falls from the roof.

9Do not plant two kinds of seed in your vineyard; if you do, not only the crops you plant but also the fruit of the vineyard will be defiled.[a]

10Do not plow with an ox and a donkey yoked together.

11Do not wear clothes of wool and linen woven together.

12Make tassels on the four corners of the cloak you wear.

Marriage Violations

13If a man takes a wife and, after sleeping with her, dislikes her 14and slanders her and gives her a bad name, saying, "I married this woman, but when I approached her, I did not find proof of her virginity," 15then the young woman's father and mother shall bring to the town elders at the gate proof that she was a virgin. 16Her father will say to the elders, "I gave my daughter in marriage to this man, but he dislikes her. 17Now he has slandered her and said, 'I did not find your daughter to be a virgin.' But here is the proof of my daughter's virginity." Then her parents shall display the cloth before the elders of the town, 18and the

---

a 9 Or be forfeited to the sanctuary

elders shall take the man and punish him. ¹⁹They shall fine him a hundred shekels[a] of silver and give them to the young woman's father, because this man has given an Israelite virgin a bad name. She shall continue to be his wife; he must not divorce her as long as he lives.

²⁰If, however, the charge is true and no proof of the young woman's virginity can be found, ²¹she shall be brought to the door of her father's house and there the men of her town shall stone her to death. She has done an outrageous thing in Israel by being promiscuous while still in her father's house. You must purge the evil from among you.

²²If a man is found sleeping with another man's wife, both the man who slept with her and the woman must die. You must purge the evil from Israel.

²³If a man happens to meet in a town a virgin pledged to be married and he sleeps with her, ²⁴you shall take both of them to the gate of that town and stone them to death — the young woman because she was in a town and did not scream for help, and the man because he violated another man's wife. You must purge the evil from among you.

²⁵But if out in the country a man happens to meet a young woman pledged to be married and rapes her, only the man who has done this shall die. ²⁶Do nothing to the woman; she has committed no sin deserving death. This case is like that of someone who attacks and murders a neighbor, ²⁷for the man found the young woman out in the country, and though the betrothed woman screamed, there was no one to rescue her.

²⁸If a man happens to meet a virgin who is not pledged to be married and rapes her and they are discovered, ²⁹he shall pay her father fifty shekels[b] of silver. He must marry the young woman, for he has violated her. He can never divorce her as long as he lives.

³⁰A man is not to marry his father's wife; he must not dishonor his father's bed.[c]

Exclusion From the Assembly

23[d] No one who has been emasculated by crushing or cutting may enter the assembly of the LORD.

²No one born of a forbidden marriage[e] nor any of their descendants may enter the assembly of the LORD, not even in the tenth generation.

³No Ammonite or Moabite or any of their descendants may enter the assembly of the LORD, not even in the tenth generation. ⁴For they did not come to meet you with bread and water on your way when you came out of Egypt, and they hired Balaam son of Beor from Pethor in Aram Naharaim[f] to pronounce a curse on you. ⁵However, the LORD your God would not listen to Balaam but turned the curse into a blessing for you, because the LORD your God loves you. ⁶Do not seek a treaty of friendship with them as long as you live.

⁷Do not despise an Edomite, for the Edomites are related to you. Do not despise an Egyptian, because you resided as foreigners in their country. ⁸The third generation of children born to them may enter the assembly of the LORD.

Uncleanness in the Camp

⁹When you are encamped against your enemies, keep away from everything impure. ¹⁰If one of your men is unclean because of a nocturnal emission, he is to go outside the camp and stay there. ¹¹But as evening approaches he is to wash himself, and at sunset he may return to the camp.

¹²Designate a place outside the camp where you can go to relieve yourself. ¹³As part of your equipment have something to dig with, and when you relieve yourself, dig a hole and cover up your excrement. ¹⁴For the LORD your God moves about in your

---

a 19 That is, about 2 1/2 pounds or about 1.2 kilograms   b 29 That is, about 1 1/4 pounds or about 575 grams
c 30 In Hebrew texts this verse (22:30) is numbered 23:1.   d In Hebrew texts 23:1-25 is numbered 23:2-26.
e 2 Or one of illegitimate birth   f 4 That is, Northwest Mesopotamia

camp to protect you and to deliver your enemies to you. Your camp must be holy, so that he will not see among you anything indecent and turn away from you.

Miscellaneous Laws

15If a slave has taken refuge with you, do not hand them over to their master. 16Let them live among you wherever they like and in whatever town they choose. Do not oppress them.

17No Israelite man or woman is to become a shrine prostitute. 18You must not bring the earnings of a female prostitute or of a male prostitute*a* into the house of the LORD your God to pay any vow, because the LORD your God detests them both.

19Do not charge a fellow Israelite interest, whether on money or food or anything else that may earn interest. 20You may charge a foreigner interest, but not a fellow Israelite, so that the LORD your God may bless you in everything you put your hand to in the land you are entering to possess.

21If you make a vow to the LORD your God, do not be slow to pay it, for the LORD your God will certainly demand it of you and you will be guilty of sin. 22But if you refrain from making a vow, you will not be guilty. 23Whatever your lips utter you must be sure to do, because you made your vow freely to the LORD your God with your own mouth.

24If you enter your neighbor's vineyard, you may eat all the grapes you want, but do not put any in your basket. 25If you enter your neighbor's grainfield, you may pick kernels with your hands, but you must not put a sickle to their standing grain.

24 If a man marries a woman who becomes displeasing to him because he finds something indecent about her, and he writes her a certificate of divorce, gives it to her and sends her from his house, 2and if after she leaves his house she becomes the wife of another man, 3and her second husband dislikes her and writes her a certificate of divorce, gives it to her and sends her from his house, or if he dies, 4then her first husband, who divorced her, is not allowed to marry her again after she has been defiled. That would be detestable in the eyes of the LORD. Do not bring sin upon the land the LORD your God is giving you as an inheritance.

5If a man has recently married, he must not be sent to war or have any other duty laid on him. For one year he is to be free to stay at home and bring happiness to the wife he has married.

6Do not take a pair of millstones — not even the upper one — as security for a debt, because that would be taking a person's livelihood as security.

7If someone is caught kidnapping a fellow Israelite and treating or selling them as a slave, the kidnapper must die. You must purge the evil from among you.

8In cases of defiling skin diseases,*b* be very careful to do exactly as the Levitical priests instruct you. You must follow carefully what I have commanded them. 9Remember what the LORD your God did to Miriam along the way after you came out of Egypt.

10When you make a loan of any kind to your neighbor, do not go into their house to get what is offered to you as a pledge. 11Stay outside and let the neighbor to whom you are making the loan bring the pledge out to you. 12If the neighbor is poor, do not go to sleep with their pledge in your possession. 13Return their cloak by sunset so that your neighbor may sleep in it. Then they will thank you, and it will be regarded as a righteous act in the sight of the LORD your God.

14Do not take advantage of a hired worker who is poor and needy, whether that worker is a fellow Israelite or a foreigner residing in one of your towns. 15Pay them

---

a 18 Hebrew *of a dog*   *b 8* The Hebrew word for *defiling skin diseases*, traditionally translated "leprosy," was used for various diseases affecting the skin.

their wages each day before sunset, because they are poor and are counting on it. Otherwise they may cry to the LORD against you, and you will be guilty of sin.

¹⁶Parents are not to be put to death for their children, nor children put to death for their parents; each will die for their own sin.

¹⁷Do not deprive the foreigner or the fatherless of justice, or take the cloak of the widow as a pledge. ¹⁸Remember that you were slaves in Egypt and the LORD your God redeemed you from there. That is why I command you to do this.

¹⁹When you are harvesting in your field and you overlook a sheaf, do not go back to get it. Leave it for the foreigner, the fatherless and the widow, so that the LORD your God may bless you in all the work of your hands. ²⁰When you beat the olives from your trees, do not go over the branches a second time. Leave what remains for the foreigner, the fatherless and the widow. ²¹When you harvest the grapes in your vineyard, do not go over the vines again. Leave what remains for the foreigner, the fatherless and the widow. ²²Remember that you were slaves in Egypt. That is why I command you to do this.

25 When people have a dispute, they are to take it to court and the judges will decide the case, acquitting the innocent and condemning the guilty. ²If the guilty person deserves to be beaten, the judge shall make them lie down and have them flogged in his presence with the number of lashes the crime deserves, ³but the judge must not impose more than forty lashes. If the guilty party is flogged more than that, your fellow Israelite will be degraded in your eyes.

⁴Do not muzzle an ox while it is treading out the grain.

⁵If brothers are living together and one of them dies without a son, his widow must not marry outside the family. Her husband's brother shall take her and marry her and fulfill the duty of a brother-in-law to her. ⁶The first son she bears shall carry on the name of the dead brother so that his name will not be blotted out from Israel.

⁷However, if a man does not want to marry his brother's wife, she shall go to the elders at the town gate and say, "My husband's brother refuses to carry on his brother's name in Israel. He will not fulfill the duty of a brother-in-law to me." ⁸Then the elders of his town shall summon him and talk to him. If he persists in saying, "I do not want to marry her," ⁹his brother's widow shall go up to him in the presence of the elders, take off one of his sandals, spit in his face and say, "This is what is done to the man who will not build up his brother's family line." ¹⁰That man's line shall be known in Israel as The Family of the Unsandaled.

¹¹If two men are fighting and the wife of one of them comes to rescue her husband from his assailant, and she reaches out and seizes him by his private parts, ¹²you shall cut off her hand. Show her no pity.

¹³Do not have two differing weights in your bag — one heavy, one light. ¹⁴Do not have two differing measures in your house — one large, one small. ¹⁵You must have accurate and honest weights and measures, so that you may live long in the land the LORD your God is giving you. ¹⁶For the LORD your God detests anyone who does these things, anyone who deals dishonestly.

¹⁷Remember what the Amalekites did to you along the way when you came out of Egypt. ¹⁸When you were weary and worn out, they met you on your journey and attacked all who were lagging behind; they had no fear of God. ¹⁹When the LORD your God gives you rest from all the enemies around you in the land he is giving you to possess as an inheritance, you shall blot out the name of Amalek from under heaven. Do not forget!

Firstfruits and Tithes

26 When you have entered the land the LORD your God is giving you as an inheritance and have taken possession of it and settled

in it, ²take some of the firstfruits of all that you produce from the soil of the land the LORD your God is giving you and put them in a basket. Then go to the place the LORD your God will choose as a dwelling for his Name ³and say to the priest in office at the time, "I declare today to the LORD your God that I have come to the land the LORD swore to our ancestors to give us." ⁴The priest shall take the basket from your hands and set it down in front of the altar of the LORD your God. ⁵Then you shall declare before the LORD your God: "My father was a wandering Aramean, and he went down into Egypt with a few people and lived there and became a great nation, powerful and numerous. ⁶But the Egyptians mistreated us and made us suffer, subjecting us to harsh labor. ⁷Then we cried out to the LORD, the God of our ancestors, and the LORD heard our voice and saw our misery, toil and oppression. ⁸So the LORD brought us out of Egypt with a mighty hand and an outstretched arm, with great terror and with signs and wonders. ⁹He brought us to this place and gave us this land, a land flowing with milk and honey; ¹⁰and now I bring the firstfruits of the soil that you, LORD, have given me." Place the basket before the LORD your God and bow down before him. ¹¹Then you and the Levites and the foreigners residing among you shall rejoice in all the good things the LORD your God has given to you and your household.

¹²When you have finished setting aside a tenth of all your produce in the third year, the year of the tithe, you shall give it to the Levite, the foreigner, the fatherless and the widow, so that they may eat in your towns and be satisfied. ¹³Then say to the LORD your God: "I have removed from my house the sacred portion and have given it to the Levite, the foreigner, the fatherless and the widow, according to all you commanded. I have not turned aside from your commands nor have I forgotten any of them. ¹⁴I have not eaten any of the sacred portion while I was in mourning, nor have I

removed any of it while I was unclean, nor have I offered any of it to the dead. I have obeyed the LORD my God; I have done everything you commanded me. ¹⁵Look down from heaven, your holy dwelling place, and bless your people Israel and the land you have given us as you promised on oath to our ancestors, a land flowing with milk and honey."

Follow the LORD's Commands

¹⁶The LORD your God commands you this day to follow these decrees and laws; carefully observe them with all your heart and with all your soul. ¹⁷You have declared this day that the LORD is your God and that you will walk in obedience to him, that you will keep his decrees, commands and laws — that you will listen to him. ¹⁸And the LORD has declared this day that you are his people, his treasured possession as he promised, and that you are to keep all his commands. ¹⁹He has declared that he will set you in praise, fame and honor high above all the nations he has made and that you will be a people holy to the LORD your God, as he promised.

The Altar on Mount Ebal

27 Moses and the elders of Israel commanded the people: "Keep all these commands that I give you today. ²When you have crossed the Jordan into the land the LORD your God is giving you, set up some large stones and coat them with plaster. ³Write on them all the words of this law when you have crossed over to enter the land the LORD your God is giving you, a land flowing with milk and honey, just as the LORD, the God of your ancestors, promised you. ⁴And when you have crossed the Jordan, set up these stones on Mount Ebal, as I command you today, and coat them with plaster. ⁵Build there an altar to the LORD your God, an altar of stones. Do not use any iron tool on them. ⁶Build the altar of the LORD your God with fieldstones and offer burnt offerings on it to the LORD your God. ⁷Sacrifice fellowship offerings there, eating them and rejoicing in the presence of the LORD your God. [8]And you shall write very clearly all the words of this law on these stones you have set up."

Curses From Mount Ebal

[9]Then Moses and the Levitical priests said to all Israel, "Be silent, Israel, and listen! You have now become the people of the LORD your God. [10]Obey the LORD your God and follow his commands and decrees that I give you today."

[11]On the same day Moses commanded the people:

[12]When you have crossed the Jordan, these tribes shall stand on Mount Gerizim to bless the people: Simeon, Levi, Judah, Issachar, Joseph and Benjamin. [13]And these tribes shall stand on Mount Ebal to pronounce curses: Reuben, Gad, Asher, Zebulun, Dan and Naphtali.

[14]The Levites shall recite to all the people of Israel in a loud voice:

[15]"Cursed is anyone who makes an idol — a thing detestable to the LORD, the work of skilled hands — and sets it up in secret."

Then all the people shall say, "Amen!"

[16]"Cursed is anyone who dishonors their father or mother."

Then all the people shall say, "Amen!"

[17]"Cursed is anyone who moves their neighbor's boundary stone."

Then all the people shall say, "Amen!"

[18]"Cursed is anyone who leads the blind astray on the road."

Then all the people shall say, "Amen!"

[19]"Cursed is anyone who withholds justice from the foreigner, the fatherless or the widow."

Then all the people shall say, "Amen!"

[20]"Cursed is anyone who sleeps with his father's wife, for he dishonors his father's bed."

Then all the people shall say, "Amen!"

[21]"Cursed is anyone who has sexual relations with any animal."

Then all the people shall say, "Amen!"

[22]"Cursed is anyone who sleeps with his sister, the daughter of his father or the daughter of his mother."

Then all the people shall say, "Amen!"

[23]"Cursed is anyone who sleeps with his mother-in-law."

Then all the people shall say, "Amen!"

[24]"Cursed is anyone who kills their neighbor secretly."

Then all the people shall say, "Amen!"

[25]"Cursed is anyone who accepts a bribe to kill an innocent person."

Then all the people shall say, "Amen!"

[26]"Cursed is anyone who does not uphold the words of this law by carrying them out."

Then all the people shall say, "Amen!"

Blessings for Obedience

28 If you fully obey the LORD your God and carefully follow all his commands I give you today, the LORD your God will set you high above all the nations on earth. [2]All these blessings will come on you and accompany you if you obey the LORD your God:

[3]You will be blessed in the city and blessed in the country.

[4]The fruit of your womb will be blessed, and the crops of your land and the young of your livestock — the calves of your herds and the lambs of your flocks.

[5]Your basket and your kneading trough will be blessed.

⁶You will be blessed when you come in and blessed when you go out.

⁷The LORD will grant that the enemies who rise up against you will be defeated before you. They will come at you from one direction but flee from you in seven.

⁸The LORD will send a blessing on your barns and on everything you put your hand to. The LORD your God will bless you in the land he is giving you.

⁹The LORD will establish you as his holy people, as he promised you on oath, if you keep the commands of the LORD your God and walk in obedience to him. ¹⁰Then all the peoples on earth will see that you are called by the name of the LORD, and they will fear you. ¹¹The LORD will grant you abundant prosperity — in the fruit of your womb, the young of your livestock and the crops of your ground — in the land he swore to your ancestors to give you.

¹²The LORD will open the heavens, the storehouse of his bounty, to send rain on your land in season and to bless all the work of your hands. You will lend to many nations but will borrow from none. ¹³The LORD will make you the head, not the tail. If you pay attention to the commands of the LORD your God that I give you this day and carefully follow them, you will always be at the top, never at the bottom. ¹⁴Do not turn aside from any of the commands I give you today, to the right or to the left, following other gods and serving them.

Curses for Disobedience

¹⁵However, if you do not obey the LORD your God and do not carefully follow all his commands and decrees I am giving you today, all these curses will come on you and overtake you:

¹⁶You will be cursed in the city and cursed in the country.

¹⁷Your basket and your kneading trough will be cursed.

¹⁸The fruit of your womb will be cursed, and the crops of your land, and the calves of your herds and the lambs of your flocks.

¹⁹You will be cursed when you come in and cursed when you go out.

²⁰The LORD will send on you curses, confusion and rebuke in everything you put your hand to, until you are destroyed and come to sudden ruin because of the evil you have done in forsaking him.ᵃ ²¹The LORD will plague you with diseases until he has destroyed you from the land you are entering to possess. ²²The LORD will strike you with wasting disease, with fever and inflammation, with scorching heat and drought, with blight and mildew, which will plague you until you perish. ²³The sky over your head will be bronze, the ground beneath you iron. ²⁴The LORD will turn the rain of your country into dust and powder; it will come down from the skies until you are destroyed.

²⁵The LORD will cause you to be defeated before your enemies. You will come at them from one direction but flee from them in seven, and you will become a thing of horror to all the kingdoms on earth. ²⁶Your carcasses will be food for all the birds and the wild animals, and there will be no one to frighten them away. ²⁷The LORD will afflict you with the boils of Egypt and with tumors, festering sores and the itch, from which you cannot be cured. ²⁸The LORD will afflict you with madness, blindness and confusion of mind. ²⁹At midday you will grope about like a blind person in the dark. You will be unsuccessful in everything you do; day after day you will be oppressed and robbed, with no one to rescue you.

³⁰You will be pledged to be married to a woman, but another will take her and rape her. You will build a house, but you will not live in it. You will plant a vineyard, but you will not even begin to enjoy its fruit. ³¹Your ox will be slaughtered before your eyes, but you will eat none of it. Your don-

---

ᵃ 20 Hebrew *me*

key will be forcibly taken from you and will not be returned. Your sheep will be given to your enemies, and no one will rescue them. ³²Your sons and daughters will be given to another nation, and you will wear out your eyes watching for them day after day, powerless to lift a hand. ³³A people that you do not know will eat what your land and labor produce, and you will have nothing but cruel oppression all your days. ³⁴The sights you see will drive you mad. ³⁵The LORD will afflict your knees and legs with painful boils that cannot be cured, spreading from the soles of your feet to the top of your head.

³⁶The LORD will drive you and the king you set over you to a nation unknown to you or your ancestors. There you will worship other gods, gods of wood and stone. ³⁷You will become a thing of horror, a byword and an object of ridicule among all the peoples where the LORD will drive you.

³⁸You will sow much seed in the field but you will harvest little, because locusts will devour it. ³⁹You will plant vineyards and cultivate them but you will not drink the wine or gather the grapes, because worms will eat them. ⁴⁰You will have olive trees throughout your country but you will not use the oil, because the olives will drop off. ⁴¹You will have sons and daughters but you will not keep them, because they will go into captivity. ⁴²Swarms of locusts will take over all your trees and the crops of your land.

⁴³The foreigners who reside among you will rise above you higher and higher, but you will sink lower and lower. ⁴⁴They will lend to you, but you will not lend to them. They will be the head, but you will be the tail.

⁴⁵All these curses will come on you. They will pursue you and overtake you until you are destroyed, because you did not obey the LORD your God and observe the commands and decrees he gave you. ⁴⁶They will be a sign and a wonder to you and your descendants forever. ⁴⁷Because you did not serve the LORD your God joy-

fully and gladly in the time of prosperity, ⁴⁸therefore in hunger and thirst, in nakedness and dire poverty, you will serve the enemies the LORD sends against you. He will put an iron yoke on your neck until he has destroyed you.

⁴⁹The LORD will bring a nation against you from far away, from the ends of the earth, like an eagle swooping down, a nation whose language you will not understand, ⁵⁰a fierce-looking nation without respect for the old or pity for the young. ⁵¹They will devour the young of your livestock and the crops of your land until you are destroyed. They will leave you no grain, new wine or olive oil, nor any calves of your herds or lambs of your flocks until you are ruined. ⁵²They will lay siege to all the cities throughout your land until the high fortified walls in which you trust fall down. They will besiege all the cities throughout the land the LORD your God is giving you.

⁵³Because of the suffering your enemy will inflict on you during the siege, you will eat the fruit of the womb, the flesh of the sons and daughters the LORD your God has given you. ⁵⁴Even the most gentle and sensitive man among you will have no compassion on his own brother or the wife he loves or his surviving children, ⁵⁵and he will not give to one of them any of the flesh of his children that he is eating. It will be all he has left because of the suffering your enemy will inflict on you during the siege of all your cities. ⁵⁶The most gentle and sensitive woman among you — so sensitive and gentle that she would not venture to touch the ground with the sole of her foot — will begrudge the husband she loves and her own son or daughter ⁵⁷the afterbirth from her womb and the children she bears. For in her dire need she intends to eat them secretly because of the suffering your enemy will inflict on you during the siege of your cities.

⁵⁸If you do not carefully follow all the words of this law, which are written in this book, and do not revere this glorious and awesome name — the LORD your God —

59the LORD will send fearful plagues on you and your descendants, harsh and prolonged disasters, and severe and lingering illnesses. 60He will bring on you all the diseases of Egypt that you dreaded, and they will cling to you. 61The LORD will also bring on you every kind of sickness and disaster not recorded in this Book of the Law, until you are destroyed. 62You who were as numerous as the stars in the sky will be left but few in number, because you did not obey the LORD your God. 63Just as it pleased the LORD to make you prosper and increase in number, so it will please him to ruin and destroy you. You will be uprooted from the land you are entering to possess.

64Then the LORD will scatter you among all nations, from one end of the earth to the other. There you will worship other gods — gods of wood and stone, which neither you nor your ancestors have known. 65Among those nations you will find no repose, no resting place for the sole of your foot. There the LORD will give you an anxious mind, eyes weary with longing, and a despairing heart. 66You will live in constant suspense, filled with dread both night and day, never sure of your life. 67In the morning you will say, "If only it were evening!" and in the evening, "If only it were morning!" — because of the terror that will fill your hearts and the sights that your eyes will see. 68The LORD will send you back in ships to Egypt on a journey I said you should never make again. There you will offer yourselves for sale to your enemies as male and female slaves, but no one will buy you.

Renewal of the Covenant

29 *a* These are the terms of the covenant the LORD commanded Moses to make with the Israelites in Moab, in addition to the covenant he had made with them at Horeb.

2Moses summoned all the Israelites and said to them:

Your eyes have seen all that the LORD did in Egypt to Pharaoh, to all his officials and to all his land. 3With your own eyes you saw those great trials, those signs and great wonders. 4But to this day the LORD has not given you a mind that understands or eyes that see or ears that hear. 5Yet the LORD says, "During the forty years that I led you through the wilderness, your clothes did not wear out, nor did the sandals on your feet. 6You ate no bread and drank no wine or other fermented drink. I did this so that you might know that I am the LORD your God."

7When you reached this place, Sihon king of Heshbon and Og king of Bashan came out to fight against us, but we defeated them. 8We took their land and gave it as an inheritance to the Reubenites, the Gadites and the half-tribe of Manasseh.

9Carefully follow the terms of this covenant, so that you may prosper in everything you do. 10All of you are standing today in the presence of the LORD your God — your leaders and chief men, your elders and officials, and all the other men of Israel, 11together with your children and your wives, and the foreigners living in your camps who chop your wood and carry your water. 12You are standing here in order to enter into a covenant with the LORD your God, a covenant the LORD is making with you this day and sealing with an oath, 13to confirm you this day as his people, that he may be your God as he promised you and as he swore to your fathers, Abraham, Isaac and Jacob. 14I am making this covenant, with its oath, not only with you 15who are standing here with us today in the presence of the LORD our God but also with those who are not here today.

16You yourselves know how we lived in Egypt and how we passed through the countries on the way here. 17You saw among them their detestable images and idols of wood and stone, of silver and gold. 18Make sure there is no man or woman, clan or tribe among you today whose heart

---

a In Hebrew texts 29:1 is numbered 28:69, and 29:2-29 is numbered 29:1-28.

turns away from the LORD our God to go and worship the gods of those nations; make sure there is no root among you that produces such bitter poison.

19When such a person hears the words of this oath and they invoke a blessing on themselves, thinking, "I will be safe, even though I persist in going my own way," they will bring disaster on the watered land as well as the dry. 20The LORD will never be willing to forgive them; his wrath and zeal will burn against them. All the curses written in this book will fall on them, and the LORD will blot out their names from under heaven. 21The LORD will single them out from all the tribes of Israel for disaster, according to all the curses of the covenant written in this Book of the Law.

22Your children who follow you in later generations and foreigners who come from distant lands will see the calamities that have fallen on the land and the diseases with which the LORD has afflicted it. 23The whole land will be a burning waste of salt and sulfur — nothing planted, nothing sprouting, no vegetation growing on it. It will be like the destruction of Sodom and Gomorrah, Admah and Zeboyim, which the LORD overthrew in fierce anger. 24All the nations will ask: "Why has the LORD done this to this land? Why this fierce, burning anger?"

25And the answer will be: "It is because this people abandoned the covenant of the LORD, the God of their ancestors, the covenant he made with them when he brought them out of Egypt. 26They went off and worshiped other gods and bowed down to them, gods they did not know, gods he had not given them. 27Therefore the LORD's anger burned against this land, so that he brought on it all the curses written in this book. 28In furious anger and in great wrath the LORD uprooted them from their land and thrust them into another land, as it is now."

29The secret things belong to the LORD our God, but the things revealed belong to us and to our children forever, that we may follow all the words of this law.

Prosperity After Turning to the LORD

30 When all these blessings and curses I have set before you come on you and you take them to heart wherever the LORD your God disperses you among the nations, 2and when you and your children return to the LORD your God and obey him with all your heart and with all your soul according to everything I command you today, 3then the LORD your God will restore your fortunes*a* and have compassion on you and gather you again from all the nations where he scattered you. 4Even if you have been banished to the most distant land under the heavens, from there the LORD your God will gather you and bring you back. 5He will bring you to the land that belonged to your ancestors, and you will take possession of it. He will make you more prosperous and numerous than your ancestors. 6The LORD your God will circumcise your hearts and the hearts of your descendants, so that you may love him with all your heart and with all your soul, and live. 7The LORD your God will put all these curses on your enemies who hate and persecute you. 8You will again obey the LORD and follow all his commands I am giving you today. 9Then the LORD your God will make you most prosperous in all the work of your hands and in the fruit of your womb, the young of your livestock and the crops of your land. The LORD will again delight in you and make you prosperous, just as he delighted in your ancestors, 10if you obey the LORD your God and keep his commands and decrees that are written in this Book of the Law and turn to the LORD your God with all your heart and with all your soul.

The Offer of Life or Death

11Now what I am commanding you today is not too difficult for you or beyond

---

a 3 Or will bring you back from captivity

your reach. ¹²It is not up in heaven, so that you have to ask, "Who will ascend into heaven to get it and proclaim it to us so we may obey it?" ¹³Nor is it beyond the sea, so that you have to ask, "Who will cross the sea to get it and proclaim it to us so we may obey it?" ¹⁴No, the word is very near you; it is in your mouth and in your heart so you may obey it.

¹⁵See, I set before you today life and prosperity, death and destruction. ¹⁶For I command you today to love the LORD your God, to walk in obedience to him, and to keep his commands, decrees and laws; then you will live and increase, and the LORD your God will bless you in the land you are entering to possess.

¹⁷But if your heart turns away and you are not obedient, and if you are drawn away to bow down to other gods and worship them, ¹⁸I declare to you this day that you will certainly be destroyed. You will not live long in the land you are crossing the Jordan to enter and possess.

¹⁹This day I call the heavens and the earth as witnesses against you that I have set before you life and death, blessings and curses. Now choose life, so that you and your children may live ²⁰and that you may love the LORD your God, listen to his voice, and hold fast to him. For the LORD is your life, and he will give you many years in the land he swore to give to your fathers, Abraham, Isaac and Jacob.

Joshua to Succeed Moses

31 Then Moses went out and spoke these words to all Israel: ²"I am now a hundred and twenty years old and I am no longer able to lead you. The LORD has said to me, 'You shall not cross the Jordan.' ³The LORD your God himself will cross over ahead of you. He will destroy these nations before you, and you will take possession of their land. Joshua also will cross over ahead of you, as the LORD said. ⁴And the LORD will do to them what he did to Sihon and Og, the kings of the Amorites, whom he destroyed along with their land. ⁵The LORD will deliver them to you, and you must do to them all that I have commanded you. ⁶Be strong and courageous. Do not be afraid or terrified because of them, for the LORD your God goes with you; he will never leave you nor forsake you."

⁷Then Moses summoned Joshua and said to him in the presence of all Israel, "Be strong and courageous, for you must go with this people into the land that the LORD swore to their ancestors to give them, and you must divide it among them as their inheritance. ⁸The LORD himself goes before you and will be with you; he will never leave you nor forsake you. Do not be afraid; do not be discouraged."

Public Reading of the Law

⁹So Moses wrote down this law and gave it to the Levitical priests, who carried the ark of the covenant of the LORD, and to all the elders of Israel. ¹⁰Then Moses commanded them: "At the end of every seven years, in the year for canceling debts, during the Festival of Tabernacles, ¹¹when all Israel comes to appear before the LORD your God at the place he will choose, you shall read this law before them in their hearing. ¹²Assemble the people — men, women and children, and the foreigners residing in your towns — so they can listen and learn to fear the LORD your God and follow carefully all the words of this law. ¹³Their children, who do not know this law, must hear it and learn to fear the LORD your God as long as you live in the land you are crossing the Jordan to possess."

Israel's Rebellion Predicted

¹⁴The LORD said to Moses, "Now the day of your death is near. Call Joshua and present yourselves at the tent of meeting, where I will commission him." So Moses and Joshua came and presented themselves at the tent of meeting.

¹⁵Then the LORD appeared at the tent in a pillar of cloud, and the cloud stood over the entrance to the tent. ¹⁶And the LORD

said to Moses: "You are going to rest with your ancestors, and these people will soon prostitute themselves to the foreign gods of the land they are entering. They will forsake me and break the covenant I made with them. 17 And in that day I will become angry with them and forsake them; I will hide my face from them, and they will be destroyed. Many disasters and calamities will come on them, and in that day they will ask, 'Have not these disasters come on us because our God is not with us?' 18 And I will certainly hide my face in that day because of all their wickedness in turning to other gods.

19 "Now write down this song and teach it to the Israelites and have them sing it, so that it may be a witness for me against them. 20 When I have brought them into the land flowing with milk and honey, the land I promised on oath to their ancestors, and when they eat their fill and thrive, they will turn to other gods and worship them, rejecting me and breaking my covenant. 21 And when many disasters and calamities come on them, this song will testify against them, because it will not be forgotten by their descendants. I know what they are disposed to do, even before I bring them into the land I promised them on oath." 22 So Moses wrote down this song that day and taught it to the Israelites.

23 The LORD gave this command to Joshua son of Nun: "Be strong and courageous, for you will bring the Israelites into the land I promised them on oath, and I myself will be with you."

24 After Moses finished writing in a book the words of this law from beginning to end, 25 he gave this command to the Levites who carried the ark of the covenant of the LORD: 26 "Take this Book of the Law and place it beside the ark of the covenant of the LORD your God. There it will remain as a witness against you. 27 For I know how rebellious and stiff-necked you are. If you have been rebellious against the LORD while I am still alive and with you, how much more will you rebel after I die! 28 Assemble before me all the elders of your tribes and all your officials, so that I can speak these words in their hearing and call the heavens and the earth to testify against them. 29 For I know that after my death you are sure to become utterly corrupt and to turn from the way I have commanded you. In days to come, disaster will fall on you because you will do evil in the sight of the LORD and arouse his anger by what your hands have made."

The Song of Moses

30 And Moses recited the words of this song from beginning to end in the hearing of the whole assembly of Israel:

32 Listen, you heavens, and I will speak;
　　hear, you earth, the words of
　　　my mouth.
2 Let my teaching fall like rain
　　and my words descend like dew,
　like showers on new grass,
　　like abundant rain on tender plants.

3 I will proclaim the name of the LORD.
　　Oh, praise the greatness of our
　　　God!
4 He is the Rock, his works are perfect,
　　and all his ways are just.
　A faithful God who does no wrong,
　　upright and just is he.

5 They are corrupt and not his children;
　　to their shame they are a warped and
　　　crooked generation.
6 Is this the way you repay the LORD,
　　you foolish and unwise people?
　Is he not your Father, your Creator,*a*
　　who made you and formed you?

7 Remember the days of old;
　　consider the generations long past.
　Ask your father and he will tell you,
　　your elders, and they will explain to
　　　you.

---

a 6 Or *Father, who bought you*

8 When the Most High gave the nations
        their inheritance,
    when he divided all mankind,
he set up boundaries for the peoples
        according to the number of the sons
        of Israel.*a*
9 For the LORD's portion is his people,
    Jacob his allotted inheritance.

10 In a desert land he found him,
    in a barren and howling waste.
He shielded him and cared for him;
    he guarded him as the apple of his
        eye,
11 like an eagle that stirs up its nest
    and hovers over its young,
    that spreads its wings to catch them
    and carries them aloft.
12 The LORD alone led him;
    no foreign god was with him.

13 He made him ride on the heights of the
        land
    and fed him with the fruit of the
        fields.
He nourished him with honey from the
        rock,
    and with oil from the flinty crag,
14 with curds and milk from herd and
        flock
    and with fattened lambs and goats,
with choice rams of Bashan
    and the finest kernels of wheat.
You drank the foaming blood of the
        grape.

15 Jeshurun*b* grew fat and kicked;
    filled with food, they became heavy
        and sleek.
They abandoned the God who made
        them
    and rejected the Rock their Savior.
16 They made him jealous with their
        foreign gods
    and angered him with their
        detestable idols.
17 They sacrificed to false gods, which are
        not God —

gods they had not known,
    gods that recently appeared,
    gods your ancestors did not fear.
18 You deserted the Rock, who fathered
        you;
    you forgot the God who gave you
        birth.

19 The LORD saw this and rejected them
    because he was angered by his sons
        and daughters.
20 "I will hide my face from them," he
        said,
    "and see what their end will be;
for they are a perverse generation,
    children who are unfaithful.
21 They made me jealous by what is no
        god
    and angered me with their worthless
        idols.
I will make them envious by those who
        are not a people;
    I will make them angry by a nation
        that has no understanding.
22 For a fire will be kindled by my wrath,
    one that burns down to the realm of
        the dead below.
It will devour the earth and its harvests
    and set afire the foundations of the
        mountains.

23 "I will heap calamities on them
    and spend my arrows against them.
24 I will send wasting famine against
        them,
    consuming pestilence and deadly
        plague;
I will send against them the fangs of
        wild beasts,
    the venom of vipers that glide in the
        dust.
25 In the street the sword will make them
        childless;
    in their homes terror will reign.
The young men and young women will
        perish,
    the infants and those with gray hair.

---

a 8 Masoretic Text; Dead Sea Scrolls (see also Septuagint) *sons of God*   *b 15* Jeshurun means *the upright one,*
that is, Israel.

26 I said I would scatter them
  and erase their name from human
    memory,
27 but I dreaded the taunt of the enemy,
  lest the adversary misunderstand
  and say, 'Our hand has triumphed;
  the LORD has not done all this.'"

28 They are a nation without sense,
  there is no discernment in them.
29 If only they were wise and would
    understand this
  and discern what their end will be!
30 How could one man chase a thousand,
  or two put ten thousand to flight,
  unless their Rock had sold them,
  unless the LORD had given them up?
31 For their rock is not like our Rock,
  as even our enemies concede.
32 Their vine comes from the vine of Sodom
  and from the fields of Gomorrah.
  Their grapes are filled with poison,
  and their clusters with bitterness.
33 Their wine is the venom of serpents,
  the deadly poison of cobras.

34 "Have I not kept this in reserve
  and sealed it in my vaults?
35 It is mine to avenge; I will repay.
  In due time their foot will slip;
  their day of disaster is near
  and their doom rushes upon them."

36 The LORD will vindicate his people
  and relent concerning his servants
  when he sees their strength is gone
  and no one is left, slave or free.a
37 He will say: "Now where are their gods,
  the rock they took refuge in,
38 the gods who ate the fat of their
    sacrifices
  and drank the wine of their drink
    offerings?
  Let them rise up to help you!
  Let them give you shelter!
39 "See now that I myself am he!
  There is no god besides me.

I put to death and I bring to life,
  I have wounded and I will heal,
  and no one can deliver out of my
    hand.
40 I lift my hand to heaven and solemnly
    swear:
  As surely as I live forever,
41 when I sharpen my flashing sword
  and my hand grasps it in judgment,
  I will take vengeance on my adversaries
  and repay those who hate me.
42 I will make my arrows drunk with
    blood,
  while my sword devours flesh:
  the blood of the slain and the captives,
  the heads of the enemy leaders."

43 Rejoice, you nations, with his people,b,c
  for he will avenge the blood of his
    servants;
  he will take vengeance on his enemies
  and make atonement for his land and
    people.

44 Moses came with Joshuad son of Nun and spoke all the words of this song in the hearing of the people. 45 When Moses finished reciting all these words to all Israel, 46 he said to them, "Take to heart all the words I have solemnly declared to you this day, so that you may command your children to obey carefully all the words of this law. 47 They are not just idle words for you — they are your life. By them you will live long in the land you are crossing the Jordan to possess."

Moses to Die on Mount Nebo

48 On that same day the LORD told Moses, 49 "Go up into the Abarim Range to Mount Nebo in Moab, across from Jericho, and view Canaan, the land I am giving the Israelites as their own possession. 50 There on the mountain that you have climbed you will die and be gathered to your people, just as your brother Aaron died on Mount

---

a 36 Or and they are without a ruler or leader   b 43 Or Make his people rejoice, you nations
c 43 Masoretic Text; Dead Sea Scrolls (see also Septuagint) people, / and let all the angels worship him, /
d 44 Hebrew Hoshea, a variant of Joshua

Hor and was gathered to his people. ⁵¹This is because both of you broke faith with me in the presence of the Israelites at the waters of Meribah Kadesh in the Desert of Zin and because you did not uphold my holiness among the Israelites. ⁵²Therefore, you will see the land only from a distance; you will not enter the land I am giving to the people of Israel."

Moses Blesses the Tribes

33 This is the blessing that Moses the man of God pronounced on the Israelites before his death. ²He said:

"The LORD came from Sinai
    and dawned over them from Seir;
he shone forth from Mount Paran.
He came with*a* myriads of holy ones
    from the south, from his mountain
        slopes.*b*
³ Surely it is you who love the people;
    all the holy ones are in your hand.
At your feet they all bow down,
    and from you receive instruction,
⁴the law that Moses gave us,
    the possession of the assembly of
        Jacob.
⁵ He was king over Jeshurun*c*
    when the leaders of the people
        assembled,
    along with the tribes of Israel.

⁶ "Let Reuben live and not die,
    nor*d* his people be few."

⁷And this he said about Judah:

"Hear, LORD, the cry of Judah;
    bring him to his people.
With his own hands he defends his
    cause.
    Oh, be his help against his foes!"

⁸About Levi he said:

"Your Thummim and Urim belong
    to your faithful servant.

You tested him at Massah;
    you contended with him at the
        waters of Meribah.
⁹ He said of his father and mother,
    'I have no regard for them.'
He did not recognize his brothers
    or acknowledge his own children,
but he watched over your word
    and guarded your covenant.
¹⁰ He teaches your precepts to Jacob
    and your law to Israel.
He offers incense before you
    and whole burnt offerings on your
        altar.
¹¹ Bless all his skills, LORD,
    and be pleased with the work of his
        hands.
Strike down those who rise against him,
    his foes till they rise no more."

¹²About Benjamin he said:

"Let the beloved of the LORD rest secure
    in him,
    for he shields him all day long,
    and the one the LORD loves rests
        between his shoulders."

¹³About Joseph he said:

"May the LORD bless his land
    with the precious dew from heaven
        above
    and with the deep waters that lie
        below;
¹⁴with the best the sun brings forth
    and the finest the moon can yield;
¹⁵with the choicest gifts of the ancient
    mountains
    and the fruitfulness of the everlasting
        hills;
¹⁶with the best gifts of the earth and its
    fullness
    and the favor of him who dwelt in the
        burning bush.
Let all these rest on the head of Joseph,
    on the brow of the prince among*e* his
        brothers.

---

a 2 Or *from*   *b 2* The meaning of the Hebrew for this phrase is uncertain.   *c 5 Jeshurun* means *the upright one,* that is, Israel; also in verse 26.   *d 6* Or *but let*   *e 16* Or *of the one separated from*

17 In majesty he is like a firstborn bull;
    his horns are the horns of a wild ox.
With them he will gore the nations,
    even those at the ends of the earth.
Such are the ten thousands of Ephraim;
    such are the thousands of
        Manasseh."

18 About Zebulun he said:

"Rejoice, Zebulun, in your going out,
    and you, Issachar, in your tents.
19 They will summon peoples to the
        mountain
    and there offer the sacrifices of the
        righteous;
they will feast on the abundance of the
        seas,
    on the treasures hidden in the sand."

20 About Gad he said:

"Blessed is he who enlarges Gad's
        domain!
    Gad lives there like a lion,
        tearing at arm or head.
21 He chose the best land for himself;
    the leader's portion was kept for him.
When the heads of the people
        assembled,
    he carried out the LORD's righteous
        will,
    and his judgments concerning
        Israel."

22 About Dan he said:

"Dan is a lion's cub,
    springing out of Bashan."

23 About Naphtali he said:

"Naphtali is abounding with the favor
        of the LORD
    and is full of his blessing;
    he will inherit southward to the lake."

24 About Asher he said:

"Most blessed of sons is Asher;
    let him be favored by his brothers,
    and let him bathe his feet in oil.

25 The bolts of your gates will be iron and
        bronze,
    and your strength will equal your
        days.

26 "There is no one like the God of
        Jeshurun,
    who rides across the heavens to help
        you
    and on the clouds in his majesty.
27 The eternal God is your refuge,
    and underneath are the everlasting
        arms.
He will drive out your enemies before
        you,
    saying, 'Destroy them!'
28 So Israel will live in safety;
    Jacob will dwell*a* secure
in a land of grain and new wine,
    where the heavens drop dew.
29 Blessed are you, Israel!
    Who is like you,
    a people saved by the LORD?
He is your shield and helper
    and your glorious sword.
Your enemies will cower before you,
    and you will tread on their heights."

The Death of Moses

34 Then Moses climbed Mount Nebo from the plains of Moab to the top of Pisgah, across from Jericho. There the LORD showed him the whole land—from Gilead to Dan, 2 all of Naphtali, the territory of Ephraim and Manasseh, all the land of Judah as far as the Mediterranean Sea, 3 the Negev and the whole region from the Valley of Jericho, the City of Palms, as far as Zoar. 4 Then the LORD said to him, "This is the land I promised on oath to Abraham, Isaac and Jacob when I said, 'I will give it to your descendants.' I have let you see it with your eyes, but you will not cross over into it."

5 And Moses the servant of the LORD died there in Moab, as the LORD had said. 6 He buried him*b* in Moab, in the valley opposite

a 28 Septuagint; Hebrew *Jacob's spring is*   *b 6* Or *He was buried*

Beth Peor, but to this day no one knows where his grave is. 7Moses was a hundred and twenty years old when he died, yet his eyes were not weak nor his strength gone. 8The Israelites grieved for Moses in the plains of Moab thirty days, until the time of weeping and mourning was over.

9Now Joshua son of Nun was filled with the spirit[a] of wisdom because Moses had laid his hands on him. So the Israelites lis-tened to him and did what the LORD had commanded Moses.

10Since then, no prophet has risen in Is-rael like Moses, whom the LORD knew face to face, 11who did all those signs and won-ders the LORD sent him to do in Egypt—to Pharaoh and to all his officials and to his whole land. 12For no one has ever shown the mighty power or performed the awesome deeds that Moses did in the sight of all Israel.

THEME: God is the ultimate promise keeper and the giver of second chances.

AUTHOR: The author of Joshua is unknown; evidence points to Joshua as the author of at least a portion of the book.

DATE OF WRITING: If Joshua wrote this book, it was probably written around 1390 BC, just before his death.

ENCOURAGEMENT FROM JOSHUA: "You know with all your heart and soul that not one of all the good promises the Lord your God gave you has failed" (Joshua 23:14).

CHALLENGE FROM JOSHUA: "Have I not commanded you? Be strong and courageous. Do not be afraid; do not be discouraged, for the Lord your God will be with you wherever you go" (Joshua 1:9).

REFLECTION FROM JOSHUA: "Not one of all the Lord's good promises to Israel failed; every one was fulfilled" (Joshua 21:45).

In Joshua the people of Israel finally enter the promised land, but not without a fight. The book of Joshua details the conquest, allotment and occupation of the land and outlines the strategy Joshua used to capture Canaan. As Israel's designated leader, Joshua broke down the mission into smaller, more achievable segments to win the victory. Yet for all of Israel's planning, the book of Joshua demonstrates the absolute necessity of obedience. It wasn't military strength but God's faithfulness that ultimately gave Israel victory.

Like Joshua, we can't attempt to overcome our hurts, hang-ups and habits without a well thought-out plan. We must enter each battle one step at a time. As we move through the steps and principles, we must remember that the steps have no power in and of themselves. Without Jesus at the center of our recovery, we're lost. But when we stay obedient to God, giving our lives to his care and modeling our behavior after that of his Son, Jesus Christ, we can be assured of victory over our pain. It is essential to apply all of the principles, one at a time, to experience victory after victory.

Joshua Installed as Leader

1 After the death of Moses the servant of the Lord, the Lord said to Joshua son of Nun, Moses' aide: 2"Moses my servant is dead. Now then, you and all these people, get ready to cross the Jordan River into the land I am about to give to them — to the Israelites. 3I will give you every place where you set your foot, as I promised Moses. 4Your territory will extend from the desert to Lebanon, and from the great river, the Euphrates — all the Hittite country — to the Mediterranean Sea in the west. 5No one will be able to stand against you all the days of your life. As I was with Moses, so I will be with you; I will never leave you nor forsake you. 6Be strong and courageous, because you will lead these people to inherit the land I swore to their ancestors to give them.

7"Be strong and very courageous. Be careful to obey all the law my servant Moses gave you; do not turn from it to the right or to the left, that you may be successful wherever you go. 8Keep this Book of the Law always on your lips; meditate on it day and night, so that you may be careful to do everything written in it. Then you will be prosperous and successful. 9Have I not commanded you? Be strong and courageous. Do not be afraid; do not be discouraged, for the LORD your God will be with you wherever you go."

10So Joshua ordered the officers of the people: 11"Go through the camp and tell the people, 'Get your provisions ready. Three days from now you will cross the Jordan here to go in and take possession of the land the LORD your God is giving you for your own.'"

12But to the Reubenites, the Gadites and the half-tribe of Manasseh, Joshua said, 13"Remember the command that Moses the servant of the LORD gave you after he said, 'The LORD your God will give you rest by giving you this land.' 14Your wives, your children and your livestock may stay in the land that Moses gave you east of the Jordan, but all your fighting men, ready for battle, must cross over ahead of your fellow Israelites. You are to help them 15until the LORD gives them rest, as he has done for you, and until they too have taken possession of the land the LORD your God is giving them. After that, you may go back and occupy your own land, which Moses the servant of the LORD gave you east of the Jordan toward the sunrise."

16Then they answered Joshua, "Whatever you have commanded us we will do, and wherever you send us we will go. 17Just as we fully obeyed Moses, so we will obey you. Only may the LORD your God be with you as he was with Moses. 18Whoever rebels against your word and does not obey it, whatever you may command them, will be put to death. Only be strong and courageous!"

Rahab and the Spies

2 Then Joshua son of Nun secretly sent two spies from Shittim. "Go, look over the land," he said, "especially Jericho." So they went and entered the house of a prostitute named Rahab and stayed there.

2The king of Jericho was told, "Look, some of the Israelites have come here tonight to spy out the land." 3So the king of Jericho sent this message to Rahab: "Bring out the men who came to you and entered your house, because they have come to spy out the whole land."

4But the woman had taken the two men and hidden them. She said, "Yes, the men came to me, but I did not know where they had come from. 5At dusk, when it was time to close the city gate, they left. I don't know which way they went. Go after them quickly. You may catch up with them." 6(But she had taken them up to the roof and hidden them under the stalks of flax she had laid out on the roof.) 7So the men set out in pursuit of the spies on the road that leads to the fords of the Jordan, and as soon as the pursuers had gone out, the gate was shut.

8Before the spies lay down for the night, she went up on the roof 9and said to them, "I know that the LORD has given you this land and that a great fear of you has fallen on us, so that all who live in this country are melting in fear because of you. 10We have heard how the LORD dried up the water of the Red Sea[a] for you when you came out of Egypt, and what you did to Sihon and Og, the two kings of the Amorites east of the Jordan, whom you completely destroyed.[b] 11When we heard of it, our hearts melted in fear and everyone's courage failed because

---

a 10 Or *the Sea of Reeds*   *b* 10 The Hebrew term refers to the irrevocable giving over of things or persons to the LORD, often by totally destroying them.

of you, for the LORD your God is God in heaven above and on the earth below.

¹²"Now then, please swear to me by the LORD that you will show kindness to my family, because I have shown kindness to you. Give me a sure sign ¹³that you will spare the lives of my father and mother, my brothers and sisters, and all who belong to them — and that you will save us from death."

¹⁴"Our lives for your lives!" the men assured her. "If you don't tell what we are doing, we will treat you kindly and faithfully when the LORD gives us the land."

¹⁵So she let them down by a rope through the window, for the house she lived in was part of the city wall. ¹⁶She said to them, "Go to the hills so the pursuers will not find you. Hide yourselves there three days until they return, and then go on your way."

¹⁷Now the men had said to her, "This oath you made us swear will not be binding on us ¹⁸unless, when we enter the land, you have tied this scarlet cord in the window through which you let us down, and unless you have brought your father and mother, your brothers and all your family into your house. ¹⁹If any of them go outside your house into the street, their blood will be on their own heads; we will not be responsible. As for those who are in the house with you, their blood will be on our head if a hand is laid on them. ²⁰But if you tell what we are doing, we will be released from the oath you made us swear."

²¹"Agreed," she replied. "Let it be as you say."

So she sent them away, and they departed. And she tied the scarlet cord in the window.

²²When they left, they went into the hills and stayed there three days, until the pursuers had searched all along the road and returned without finding them. ²³Then the two men started back. They went down out of the hills, forded the river and came to Joshua son of Nun and told him everything that had happened to them. ²⁴They said to Joshua, "The LORD has surely given the whole land into our hands; all the people are melting in fear because of us."

Crossing the Jordan

3 Early in the morning Joshua and all the Israelites set out from Shittim and went to the Jordan, where they camped before crossing over. ²After three days the officers went throughout the camp, ³giving orders to the people: "When you see the ark of the covenant of the LORD your God, and the Levitical priests carrying it, you are to move out from your positions and follow it. ⁴Then you will know which way to go, since you have never been this way before. But keep a distance of about two thousand cubits*ᵃ* between you and the ark; do not go near it."

⁵Joshua told the people, "Consecrate yourselves, for tomorrow the LORD will do amazing things among you."

⁶Joshua said to the priests, "Take up the ark of the covenant and pass on ahead of the people." So they took it up and went ahead of them.

⁷And the LORD said to Joshua, "Today I will begin to exalt you in the eyes of all Israel, so they may know that I am with you as I was with Moses. ⁸Tell the priests who carry the ark of the covenant: 'When you reach the edge of the Jordan's waters, go and stand in the river.'"

⁹Joshua said to the Israelites, "Come here and listen to the words of the LORD your God. ¹⁰This is how you will know that the living God is among you and that he will certainly drive out before you the Canaanites, Hittites, Hivites, Perizzites, Girgashites, Amorites and Jebusites. ¹¹See, the ark of the covenant of the Lord of all the earth will go into the Jordan ahead of you. ¹²Now then, choose twelve men from the tribes of Israel, one from each tribe. ¹³And as soon as the priests who carry the ark of the LORD — the Lord of all the earth — set

---

ᵃ *4* That is, about 3,000 feet or about 900 meters

MY NAME IS RAHAB

JOSHUA 2:1–21

Rahab, like the rest of Jericho's inhabitants, was deeply frightened (see Joshua 2:9). As a pagan prostitute in a doomed city, her prospects seemed bleak. Across the Jordan, on the plains of Moab, an invasion force had gathered. Its numbers were beyond counting, but the menacing army wasn't the only cause for fear. Word had spread that the Israelite God had roundly defeated the gods and army of Egypt. If the greatest empire in the world couldn't stop Israel, what hope remained for a Canaanite city like Jericho?

Rahab inhabited a house in the city wall, from which vantage point she prospered in her trade. There were always men hungry for pleasure. Most lived in the city, but the road that passed by Jericho also ensured a steady stream of weary travelers seeking what Rahab could provide.

Two strangers, hoping to escape notice, appeared at her door. What was more common than travelers seeking out a harlot? But the two were spotted and identified as Israelite spies. Rahab saw an opportunity, hid the Israelites and then lied to the king's men, sending them out of the city in pointless pursuit of these enemies of Jericho (see vv. 2–7). Why not? What did she owe the king or anyone else in Jericho? The Israelites would soon overwhelm the city. Besides, something new was growing in her heart — an unaccustomed stirring called hope.

Her hope was based on what she'd learned about the invisible God of Israel. His name — "I AM" — was unlike that of any other god. The gods she knew were little deities who were supposed to control weather, crops or fertility. She could bargain with them, just as she was accustomed to haggling with a man over the price of her services. This "I AM" wasn't in the business of wrangling over terms, so Rahab negotiated instead with the spies in an effort to ensure her family's survival (see vv. 8–16). But in doing so, Rahab gained more than safety: She received a new life. The God of Israel enfolded her into the community of his people. She left a life of shame to ultimately become a wife and a mother. Amazingly, from Rahab would come the line of David and his greatest descendant: the Messiah of Israel and the Savior of humankind (see Matthew 1:5–6).

All of this began with Rahab's faith in a God she had come to know secondhand through nearly unbelievable stories of his great works (see Joshua 2:8–11). Rahab placed her hope in a God greater than those fashioned by human beings. This is the same God who can deliver us. He's great enough to dry up the "seas" to make our way safe (see v. 10); destroy all the obstacles that threaten to destroy us (see v. 10); and demonstrate that he's greater than heaven and earth (see v. 11).

How did Rahab tap into God's might? She formed an accurate understanding of him (see vv. 8–11); trusted those who had experienced God's power and entered his service (see vv.12–14); served him by helping the spies escape (see vv. 15–16); and followed the instructions of those who had already learned God's ways (see vv. 17–21).

Rahab's faith and service not only saved her (see Hebrews 11:31) but gave her a home among God's people (see Joshua 6:22–23). The symbol of salvation for Rahab and her family was the scarlet cord in her window (see 2:18,21). Today we can cling to another "scarlet cord" — the blood of Jesus, which cleanses us and makes us God's prized possessions. We've been "redeemed from the empty way of life" that once enslaved us by "the precious blood of Christ" (1 Peter 1:18–19). Rahab hoped for mere survival but gained salvation on the basis of her faith. Many enter recovery seeking sobriety — and find the Savior.

foot in the Jordan, its waters flowing downstream will be cut off and stand up in a heap."

¹⁴So when the people broke camp to cross the Jordan, the priests carrying the ark of the covenant went ahead of them. ¹⁵Now the Jordan is at flood stage all during harvest. Yet as soon as the priests who carried the ark reached the Jordan and their feet touched the water's edge, ¹⁶the water from upstream stopped flowing. It piled up in a heap a great distance away, at a town called Adam in the vicinity of Zarethan, while the water flowing down to the Sea of the Arabah (that is, the Dead Sea) was completely cut off. So the people crossed over opposite Jericho. ¹⁷The priests who carried the ark of the covenant of the LORD stopped in the middle of the Jordan and stood on dry ground, while all Israel passed by until the whole nation had completed the crossing on dry ground.

4 When the whole nation had finished crossing the Jordan, the LORD said to Joshua, ²"Choose twelve men from among the people, one from each tribe, ³and tell them to take up twelve stones from the middle of the Jordan, from right where the priests are standing, and carry them over with you and put them down at the place where you stay tonight."

⁴So Joshua called together the twelve men he had appointed from the Israelites, one from each tribe, ⁵and said to them, "Go over before the ark of the LORD your God into the middle of the Jordan. Each of you is to take up a stone on his shoulder, according to the number of the tribes of the Israelites, ⁶to serve as a sign among you. In the future, when your children ask you, 'What do these stones mean?' ⁷tell them that the flow of the Jordan was cut off before the ark of the covenant of the LORD. When it crossed the Jordan, the waters of the Jordan were cut off. These stones are to be a memorial to the people of Israel forever."

⁸So the Israelites did as Joshua commanded them. They took twelve stones from the middle of the Jordan, according to the number of the tribes of the Israelites, as the LORD had told Joshua; and they carried them over with them to their camp, where they put them down. ⁹Joshua set up the twelve stones that had been[a] in the middle of the Jordan at the spot where the priests who carried the ark of the covenant had stood. And they are there to this day.

¹⁰Now the priests who carried the ark remained standing in the middle of the Jordan until everything the LORD had commanded Joshua was done by the people, just as Moses had directed Joshua. The people hurried over, ¹¹and as soon as all of them had crossed, the ark of the LORD and the priests came to the other side while the people watched. ¹²The men of Reuben, Gad and the half-tribe of Manasseh crossed over, ready for battle, in front of the Israelites, as Moses had directed them. ¹³About forty thousand armed for battle crossed over before the LORD to the plains of Jericho for war.

¹⁴That day the LORD exalted Joshua in the sight of all Israel; and they stood in awe of him all the days of his life, just as they had stood in awe of Moses.

¹⁵Then the LORD said to Joshua, ¹⁶"Command the priests carrying the ark of the covenant law to come up out of the Jordan."

¹⁷So Joshua commanded the priests, "Come up out of the Jordan."

¹⁸And the priests came up out of the river carrying the ark of the covenant of the LORD. No sooner had they set their feet on the dry ground than the waters of the Jordan returned to their place and ran at flood stage as before.

¹⁹On the tenth day of the first month the people went up from the Jordan and camped at Gilgal on the eastern border of Jericho. ²⁰And Joshua set up at Gilgal the twelve stones they had taken out of the

---

a 9 Or *Joshua also set up twelve stones*

Jordan. 21He said to the Israelites, "In the future when your descendants ask their parents, 'What do these stones mean?' 22tell them, 'Israel crossed the Jordan on dry ground.' 23For the LORD your God dried up the Jordan before you until you had crossed over. The LORD your God did to the Jordan what he had done to the Red Sea*a* when he dried it up before us until we had crossed over. 24He did this so that all the peoples of the earth might know that the hand of the LORD is powerful and so that you might always fear the LORD your God."

5 Now when all the Amorite kings west of the Jordan and all the Canaanite kings along the coast heard how the LORD had dried up the Jordan before the Israelites until they*b* had crossed over, their hearts melted in fear and they no longer had the courage to face the Israelites.

Circumcision and Passover at Gilgal

2At that time the LORD said to Joshua, "Make flint knives and circumcise the Israelites again." 3So Joshua made flint knives and circumcised the Israelites at Gibeath Haaraloth.*c*

4Now this is why he did so: All those who came out of Egypt — all the men of military age — died in the wilderness on the way after leaving Egypt. 5All the people that came out had been circumcised, but all the people born in the wilderness during the journey from Egypt had not. 6The Israelites had moved about in the wilderness forty years until all the men who were of military age when they left Egypt had died, since they had not obeyed the LORD. For the LORD had sworn to them that they would not see the land he had solemnly promised their ancestors to give us, a land flowing with milk and honey. 7So he raised up their sons in their place, and these were the ones Joshua circumcised. They were still uncircumcised because they had not been circumcised on the way. 8And after

the whole nation had been circumcised, they remained where they were in camp until they were healed.

9Then the LORD said to Joshua, "Today I have rolled away the reproach of Egypt from you." So the place has been called Gilgal*d* to this day.

10On the evening of the fourteenth day of the month, while camped at Gilgal on the plains of Jericho, the Israelites celebrated the Passover. 11The day after the Passover, that very day, they ate some of the produce of the land: unleavened bread and roasted grain. 12The manna stopped the day after*e* they ate this food from the land; there was no longer any manna for the Israelites, but that year they ate the produce of Canaan.

The Fall of Jericho

13Now when Joshua was near Jericho, he looked up and saw a man standing in front of him with a drawn sword in his hand. Joshua went up to him and asked, "Are you for us or for our enemies?"

14"Neither," he replied, "but as commander of the army of the LORD I have now come." Then Joshua fell facedown to the ground in reverence, and asked him, "What message does my Lord*f* have for his servant?"

15The commander of the LORD's army replied, "Take off your sandals, for the place where you are standing is holy." And Joshua did so.

6 Now the gates of Jericho were securely barred because of the Israelites. No one went out and no one came in.

2Then the LORD said to Joshua, "See, I have delivered Jericho into your hands, along with its king and its fighting men. 3March around the city once with all the armed men. Do this for six days. 4Have seven priests carry trumpets of rams' horns in front of the ark. On the seventh day, march around the city seven times, with the priests blowing the trumpets. 5When you hear them sound a long blast on the trum-

---

a 23 Or *the Sea of Reeds*   *b 1* Another textual tradition *we*   *c 3* *Gibeath Haaraloth* means *the hill of foreskins.*   *d 9* *Gilgal* sounds like the Hebrew for *roll.*   *e 12* Or *the day*   *f 14* Or *lord* pets, have the whole army give a loud shout; then the wall of the city will collapse and the army will go up, everyone straight in."

⁶So Joshua son of Nun called the priests and said to them, "Take up the ark of the covenant of the LORD and have seven priests carry trumpets in front of it." ⁷And he ordered the army, "Advance! March around the city, with an armed guard going ahead of the ark of the LORD."

⁸When Joshua had spoken to the people, the seven priests carrying the seven trumpets before the LORD went forward, blowing their trumpets, and the ark of the LORD's covenant followed them. ⁹The armed guard marched ahead of the priests who blew the trumpets, and the rear guard followed the ark. All this time the trumpets were sounding. ¹⁰But Joshua had commanded the army, "Do not give a war cry, do not raise your voices, do not say a word until the day I tell you to shout. Then shout!" ¹¹So he had the ark of the LORD carried around the city, circling it once. Then the army returned to camp and spent the night there.

¹²Joshua got up early the next morning and the priests took up the ark of the LORD. ¹³The seven priests carrying the seven trumpets went forward, marching before the ark of the LORD and blowing the trumpets. The armed men went ahead of them and the rear guard followed the ark of the LORD, while the trumpets kept sounding. ¹⁴So on the second day they marched around the city once and returned to the camp. They did this for six days.

¹⁵On the seventh day, they got up at daybreak and marched around the city seven times in the same manner, except that on that day they circled the city seven times. ¹⁶The seventh time around, when the priests sounded the trumpet blast, Joshua commanded the army, "Shout! For the LORD has given you the city! ¹⁷The city and all that is in it are to be devoted*ᵃ* to the LORD. Only Rahab the prostitute and all who are with her in her house shall be spared, because she hid the spies we sent. ¹⁸But keep away from the devoted things, so that you will not bring about your own destruction by taking any of them. Otherwise you will make the camp of Israel liable to destruction and bring trouble on it. ¹⁹All the silver and gold and the articles of bronze and iron are sacred to the LORD and must go into his treasury."

²⁰When the trumpets sounded, the army shouted, and at the sound of the trumpet, when the men gave a loud shout, the wall collapsed; so everyone charged straight in, and they took the city. ²¹They devoted the city to the LORD and destroyed with the sword every living thing in it — men and women, young and old, cattle, sheep and donkeys.

²²Joshua said to the two men who had spied out the land, "Go into the prostitute's house and bring her out and all who belong to her, in accordance with your oath to her." ²³So the young men who had done the spying went in and brought out Rahab, her father and mother, her brothers and sisters and all who belonged to her. They brought out her entire family and put them in a place outside the camp of Israel.

²⁴Then they burned the whole city and everything in it, but they put the silver and gold and the articles of bronze and iron into the treasury of the LORD's house. ²⁵But Joshua spared Rahab the prostitute, with her family and all who belonged to her, because she hid the men Joshua had sent as spies to Jericho — and she lives among the Israelites to this day.

²⁶At that time Joshua pronounced this solemn oath: "Cursed before the LORD is the one who undertakes to rebuild this city, Jericho:

"At the cost of his firstborn son
   he will lay its foundations;
at the cost of his youngest
   he will set up its gates."

ᵃ 17 The Hebrew term refers to the irrevocable giving over of things or persons to the LORD, often by totally destroying them; also in verses 18 and 21.

My Name Is Leticia

I'M A BELIEVER WHO STRUGGLES WITH DRUGS AND WITH SEXUAL AND PHYSICAL ABUSE

Please read in Joshua 2:1 – 21 and 6:12 – 25 the account of the prostitute Rahab, who learned all she could about God and took a risk to follow him.

Born in Mexico and raised in Las Cruces, New Mexico, I labored as a migrant worker to help Dad make ends meet. My prospects were bleak, but I never realized there was anything wrong with my life until I had the opportunity to compare it with someone else's. I wanted to feel the love I witnessed in my friend's family and tried to excel in school to earn it. But my parents were both miserable; Mom drank to "lessen the pain."

While in my teens, I started to drink, party and smoke marijuana. My success in school hadn't gotten me anywhere, so I quit trying, finally running away at 17 and lying about my age so I could work at a neighborhood bar — where I *did* get plenty of attention. I joined the National Guard to get out of Las Cruces, only to find that I was pregnant. I had an abortion, at the same time increasing my use of marijuana and starting to use speed. I met and married a fellow guardsman, and by the age of 27 I was experimenting with cocaine.

I left my husband and met a man named Steven. For almost a year I bought drugs and he sold them from a motel room. After countless beatings, I became pregnant while in my addicted state. I was blessed with a beautiful son, but Steven was arrested, leaving Isaac and me with nothing but a stolen car. I was penniless, desperate and going through withdrawals. During my first attempt at prostitution, I was beaten and raped, but my son was hungry, so I kept trying until I made some money. The shame and guilt were overwhelming, and I escaped those feelings by increasing my drug usage.

Late in 1996 my world came crashing in on me. Because of my possession of a stolen vehicle, the state took Isaac from me. I'll never forget my baby crying and reaching out for me. With my hands cuffed behind me, I couldn't even reach back. Sobbing, I pleaded with the undercover officer to let me hold him. "Not a chance," he replied curtly. "He's a good boy in spite of you." Pain has a way of branding itself on your mind, heart and soul. I'd lost everything that mattered to me, and I asked myself why I wasn't dead.

I was taken to the Bernalillo County Detention Center, where I'd been before. To my shock, one of the guards approached me with a message: "God woke me up this morning at 5:00 to pray for you. I saw you dead in a ditch, and here you are 15 minutes before my shift ends." If I hadn't ridden in with the undercover cop, I wouldn't have been in jail, but would I have been in that ditch?

In April of 1998, two months before my sentencing, I accepted Jesus as my Savior and Lord. God placed obedient women in my cell block to assist me in learning to read the Bible, and we held Bible studies together. Something unfamiliar was beginning to grow in my heart: hope. I was sentenced to nine years (eight after credit for the time I'd served).

I lost my parental rights to Isaac, but my sister eventually adopted him. He was with family, and God had his plan in motion. I arrived at the New Mexico Women's Correctional Facility on August 12, 1998, confident that God would see me through this ordeal.

I attended substance abuse, domestic violence and parenting classes, as well as Alcoholics Anonymous and Narcotics Anonymous. In addition, as I participated in the Celebrate Recovery—Inside program for 20 months, I learned to accept God's love and mercy. I also learned to ask for forgiveness, and to forgive others as well as myself. During my incarceration God used me because I made myself available to him. I was allowed to work closely with volunteers and to counsel and pray with and for the other women. I spent four years in prison.

Since my release, God has continued to bless me beyond belief. I don't take anything for granted anymore. Two of my sisters have become Christians, and Ramona, Isaac's new mom, is one of them. God has blessed me with a wonderful man, Bob, and we were married on September 13, 2003. I now have my son with me one out of every three weeks. Praise God!

I followed in Rahab's footsteps by learning all I could about God, trusting and learning from other Christians and serving him as he calls me. I continue to use the principles I've learned in Celebrate Recovery. I have people in my life to hold me accountable, and I regularly take a personal inventory, reminding myself that bad choices have bad consequences.

God has blessed me with John and Cheryl Baker, my brother and sister in Christ, who continue to believe in me and even blessed me with an opportunity to share my testimony in person with President Bush. He hugged me and kissed my forehead, telling me, "You've done good, girl." He said that to *me*, a forgiven ex-prostitute, ex-dope addict and ex-murderer (my unborn child). As I've told others, "Only meeting Jesus can top that day!"

Leticia

²⁷So the Lord was with Joshua, and his fame spread throughout the land.

Achan's Sin

7 But the Israelites were unfaithful in regard to the devoted things*ᵃ*; Achan son of Karmi, the son of Zimri,*ᵇ* the son of Zerah, of the tribe of Judah, took some of them. So the Lord's anger burned against Israel.

²Now Joshua sent men from Jericho to Ai, which is near Beth Aven to the east of Bethel, and told them, "Go up and spy out the region." So the men went up and spied out Ai.

³When they returned to Joshua, they said, "Not all the army will have to go up against Ai. Send two or three thousand men to take it and do not weary the whole army, for only a few people live there." ⁴So about three thousand went up; but they were routed by the men of Ai, ⁵who killed about thirty-six of them. They chased the Israelites from the city gate as far as the stone quarries and struck them down on the slopes. At this the hearts of the people melted in fear and became like water.

⁶Then Joshua tore his clothes and fell facedown to the ground before the ark of the Lord, remaining there till evening. The elders of Israel did the same, and sprinkled dust on their heads. ⁷And Joshua said, "Alas, Sovereign Lord, why did you ever bring this people across the Jordan to deliver us into the hands of the Amorites to destroy us? If only we had been content to stay on the other side of the Jordan! ⁸Pardon your servant, Lord. What can I say, now that Israel has been routed by its enemies? ⁹The Canaanites and the other people of the country will hear about this and they will surround us and wipe out our name from the earth. What then will you do for your own great name?"

¹⁰The Lord said to Joshua, "Stand up! What are you doing down on your face?

¹¹Israel has sinned; they have violated my covenant, which I commanded them to keep. They have taken some of the devoted things; they have stolen, they have lied, they have put them with their own possessions. ¹²That is why the Israelites cannot stand against their enemies; they turn their backs and run because they have been made liable to destruction. I will not be with you anymore unless you destroy whatever among you is devoted to destruction.

¹³"Go, consecrate the people. Tell them, 'Consecrate yourselves in preparation for tomorrow; for this is what the Lord, the God of Israel, says: There are devoted things among you, Israel. You cannot stand against your enemies until you remove them.

¹⁴"'In the morning, present yourselves tribe by tribe. The tribe the Lord chooses shall come forward clan by clan; the clan the Lord chooses shall come forward family by family; and the family the Lord chooses shall come forward man by man. ¹⁵Whoever is caught with the devoted things shall be destroyed by fire, along with all that belongs to him. He has violated the covenant of the Lord and has done an outrageous thing in Israel!'"

¹⁶Early the next morning Joshua had Israel come forward by tribes, and Judah was chosen. ¹⁷The clans of Judah came forward, and the Zerahites were chosen. He had the clan of the Zerahites come forward by families, and Zimri was chosen. ¹⁸Joshua had his family come forward man by man, and Achan son of Karmi, the son of Zimri, the son of Zerah, of the tribe of Judah, was chosen.

¹⁹Then Joshua said to Achan, "My son, give glory to the Lord, the God of Israel, and honor him. Tell me what you have done; do not hide it from me."

²⁰Achan replied, "It is true! I have sinned against the Lord, the God of Israel. This is what I have done: ²¹When I saw in the

---

ᵃ 1 The Hebrew term refers to the irrevocable giving over of things or persons to the Lord, often by totally destroying them; also in verses 11, 12, 13 and 15.   *ᵇ 1* See Septuagint and 1 Chron. 2:6; Hebrew *Zabdi*; also in verses 17 and 18.

plunder a beautiful robe from Babylonia,ᵃ two hundred shekelsᵇ of silver and a bar of gold weighing fifty shekels,ᶜ I coveted them and took them. They are hidden in the ground inside my tent, with the silver underneath."

²²So Joshua sent messengers, and they ran to the tent, and there it was, hidden in his tent, with the silver underneath. ²³They took the things from the tent, brought them to Joshua and all the Israelites and spread them out before the Lᴏʀᴅ.

²⁴Then Joshua, together with all Israel, took Achan son of Zerah, the silver, the robe, the gold bar, his sons and daughters, his cattle, donkeys and sheep, his tent and all that he had, to the Valley of Achor. ²⁵Joshua said, "Why have you brought this trouble on us? The Lᴏʀᴅ will bring trouble on you today."

Then all Israel stoned him, and after they had stoned the rest, they burned them. ²⁶Over Achan they heaped up a large pile of rocks, which remains to this day. Then the Lᴏʀᴅ turned from his fierce anger. Therefore that place has been called the Valley of Achorᵈ ever since.

Ai Destroyed

8 Then the Lᴏʀᴅ said to Joshua, "Do not be afraid; do not be discouraged. Take the whole army with you, and go up and attack Ai. For I have delivered into your hands the king of Ai, his people, his city and his land. ²You shall do to Ai and its king as you did to Jericho and its king, except that you may carry off their plunder and livestock for yourselves. Set an ambush behind the city."

³So Joshua and the whole army moved out to attack Ai. He chose thirty thousand of his best fighting men and sent them out at night ⁴with these orders: "Listen carefully. You are to set an ambush behind the city. Don't go very far from it. All of you be on the alert. ⁵I and all those with me will advance on the city, and when the men come out against us, as they did before, we will flee from them. ⁶They will pursue us until we have lured them away from the city, for they will say, 'They are running away from us as they did before.' So when we flee from them, ⁷you are to rise up from ambush and take the city. The Lᴏʀᴅ your God will give it into your hand. ⁸When you have taken the city, set it on fire. Do what the Lᴏʀᴅ has commanded. See to it; you have my orders."

⁹Then Joshua sent them off, and they went to the place of ambush and lay in wait between Bethel and Ai, to the west of Ai — but Joshua spent that night with the people.

¹⁰Early the next morning Joshua mustered his army, and he and the leaders of Israel marched before them to Ai. ¹¹The entire force that was with him marched up and approached the city and arrived in front of it. They set up camp north of Ai, with the valley between them and the city. ¹²Joshua had taken about five thousand men and set them in ambush between Bethel and Ai, to the west of the city. ¹³So the soldiers took up their positions — with the main camp to the north of the city and the ambush to the west of it. That night Joshua went into the valley.

¹⁴When the king of Ai saw this, he and all the men of the city hurried out early in the morning to meet Israel in battle at a certain place overlooking the Arabah. But he did not know that an ambush had been set against him behind the city. ¹⁵Joshua and all Israel let themselves be driven back before them, and they fled toward the wilderness. ¹⁶All the men of Ai were called to pursue them, and they pursued Joshua and were lured away from the city. ¹⁷Not a man remained in Ai or Bethel who did not go after Israel. They left the city open and went in pursuit of Israel.

¹⁸Then the Lᴏʀᴅ said to Joshua, "Hold out toward Ai the javelin that is in your

---

ᵃ 21 Hebrew *Shinar*   ᵇ 21 That is, about 5 pounds or about 2.3 kilograms   ᶜ 21 That is, about 1 1/4 pounds or about 575 grams   ᵈ 26 *Achor* means *trouble.*

hand, for into your hand I will deliver the city." So Joshua held out toward the city the javelin that was in his hand. ¹⁹As soon as he did this, the men in the ambush rose quickly from their position and rushed forward. They entered the city and captured it and quickly set it on fire.

²⁰The men of Ai looked back and saw the smoke of the city rising up into the sky, but they had no chance to escape in any direction; the Israelites who had been fleeing toward the wilderness had turned back against their pursuers. ²¹For when Joshua and all Israel saw that the ambush had taken the city and that smoke was going up from it, they turned around and attacked the men of Ai. ²²Those in the ambush also came out of the city against them, so that they were caught in the middle, with Israelites on both sides. Israel cut them down, leaving them neither survivors nor fugitives. ²³But they took the king of Ai alive and brought him to Joshua.

²⁴When Israel had finished killing all the men of Ai in the fields and in the wilderness where they had chased them, and when every one of them had been put to the sword, all the Israelites returned to Ai and killed those who were in it. ²⁵Twelve thousand men and women fell that day—all the people of Ai. ²⁶For Joshua did not draw back the hand that held out his javelin until he had destroyed*a* all who lived in Ai. ²⁷But Israel did carry off for themselves the livestock and plunder of this city, as the LORD had instructed Joshua.

²⁸So Joshua burned Ai*b* and made it a permanent heap of ruins, a desolate place to this day. ²⁹He impaled the body of the king of Ai on a pole and left it there until evening. At sunset, Joshua ordered them to take the body from the pole and throw it down at the entrance of the city gate. And they raised a large pile of rocks over it, which remains to this day.

The Covenant Renewed at Mount Ebal

³⁰Then Joshua built on Mount Ebal an altar to the LORD, the God of Israel, ³¹as Moses the servant of the LORD had commanded the Israelites. He built it according to what is written in the Book of the Law of Moses—an altar of uncut stones, on which no iron tool had been used. On it they offered to the LORD burnt offerings and sacrificed fellowship offerings. ³²There, in the presence of the Israelites, Joshua wrote on stones a copy of the law of Moses. ³³All the Israelites, with their elders, officials and judges, were standing on both sides of the ark of the covenant of the LORD, facing the Levitical priests who carried it. Both the foreigners living among them and the native-born were there. Half of the people stood in front of Mount Gerizim and half of them in front of Mount Ebal, as Moses the servant of the LORD had formerly commanded when he gave instructions to bless the people of Israel.

³⁴Afterward, Joshua read all the words of the law—the blessings and the curses—just as it is written in the Book of the Law. ³⁵There was not a word of all that Moses had commanded that Joshua did not read to the whole assembly of Israel, including the women and children, and the foreigners who lived among them.

The Gibeonite Deception

9 Now when all the kings west of the Jordan heard about these things—the kings in the hill country, in the western foothills, and along the entire coast of the Mediterranean Sea as far as Lebanon (the kings of the Hittites, Amorites, Canaanites, Perizzites, Hivites and Jebusites)— ²they came together to wage war against Joshua and Israel.

³However, when the people of Gibeon heard what Joshua had done to Jericho and Ai, ⁴they resorted to a ruse: They went as a delegation whose donkeys were loaded*c*

---

a 26 The Hebrew term refers to the irrevocable giving over of things or persons to the LORD, often by totally destroying them.   *b 28* Ai means *the ruin.*   *c 4* Most Hebrew manuscripts; some Hebrew manuscripts, Vulgate and Syriac (see also Septuagint) *They prepared provisions and loaded their donkeys* with worn-out sacks and old wineskins, cracked and mended. ⁵They put worn and patched sandals on their feet and wore old clothes. All the bread of their food supply was dry and moldy. ⁶Then they went to Joshua in the camp at Gilgal and said to him and the Israelites, "We have come from a distant country; make a treaty with us."

⁷The Israelites said to the Hivites, "But perhaps you live near us, so how can we make a treaty with you?"

⁸"We are your servants," they said to Joshua.

But Joshua asked, "Who are you and where do you come from?"

⁹They answered: "Your servants have come from a very distant country because of the fame of the LORD your God. For we have heard reports of him: all that he did in Egypt, ¹⁰and all that he did to the two kings of the Amorites east of the Jordan — Sihon king of Heshbon, and Og king of Bashan, who reigned in Ashtaroth. ¹¹And our elders and all those living in our country said to us, 'Take provisions for your journey; go and meet them and say to them, "We are your servants; make a treaty with us."' ¹²This bread of ours was warm when we packed it at home on the day we left to come to you. But now see how dry and moldy it is. ¹³And these wineskins that we filled were new, but see how cracked they are. And our clothes and sandals are worn out by the very long journey."

¹⁴The Israelites sampled their provisions but did not inquire of the LORD. ¹⁵Then Joshua made a treaty of peace with them to let them live, and the leaders of the assembly ratified it by oath.

¹⁶Three days after they made the treaty with the Gibeonites, the Israelites heard that they were neighbors, living near them. ¹⁷So the Israelites set out and on the third day came to their cities: Gibeon, Kephirah, Beeroth and Kiriath Jearim. ¹⁸But the Israelites did not attack them, because the leaders of the assembly had sworn an oath to them by the LORD, the God of Israel.

The whole assembly grumbled against the leaders, ¹⁹but all the leaders answered, "We have given them our oath by the LORD, the God of Israel, and we cannot touch them now. ²⁰This is what we will do to them: We will let them live, so that God's wrath will not fall on us for breaking the oath we swore to them." ²¹They continued, "Let them live, but let them be woodcutters and water carriers in the service of the whole assembly." So the leaders' promise to them was kept.

²²Then Joshua summoned the Gibeonites and said, "Why did you deceive us by saying, 'We live a long way from you,' while actually you live near us? ²³You are now under a curse: You will never be released from service as woodcutters and water carriers for the house of my God."

²⁴They answered Joshua, "Your servants were clearly told how the LORD your God had commanded his servant Moses to give you the whole land and to wipe out all its inhabitants from before you. So we feared for our lives because of you, and that is why we did this. ²⁵We are now in your hands. Do to us whatever seems good and right to you."

²⁶So Joshua saved them from the Israelites, and they did not kill them. ²⁷That day he made the Gibeonites woodcutters and water carriers for the assembly, to provide for the needs of the altar of the LORD at the place the LORD would choose. And that is what they are to this day.

The Sun Stands Still

10 Now Adoni-Zedek king of Jerusalem heard that Joshua had taken Ai and totally destroyed[a] it, doing to Ai and its king as he had done to Jericho and its king, and that the people of Gibeon had made a treaty of peace with Israel and had become their allies. ²He and

---

[a] *1* The Hebrew term refers to the irrevocable giving over of things or persons to the LORD, often by totally destroying them; also in verses 28, 35, 37, 39 and 40.

his people were very much alarmed at this, because Gibeon was an important city, like one of the royal cities; it was larger than Ai, and all its men were good fighters. ³So Adoni-Zedek king of Jerusalem appealed to Hoham king of Hebron, Piram king of Jarmuth, Japhia king of Lachish and Debir king of Eglon. ⁴"Come up and help me attack Gibeon," he said, "because it has made peace with Joshua and the Israelites."

⁵Then the five kings of the Amorites — the kings of Jerusalem, Hebron, Jarmuth, Lachish and Eglon — joined forces. They moved up with all their troops and took up positions against Gibeon and attacked it.

⁶The Gibeonites then sent word to Joshua in the camp at Gilgal: "Do not abandon your servants. Come up to us quickly and save us! Help us, because all the Amorite kings from the hill country have joined forces against us."

⁷So Joshua marched up from Gilgal with his entire army, including all the best fighting men. ⁸The LORD said to Joshua, "Do not be afraid of them; I have given them into your hand. Not one of them will be able to withstand you."

⁹After an all-night march from Gilgal, Joshua took them by surprise. ¹⁰The LORD threw them into confusion before Israel, so Joshua and the Israelites defeated them completely at Gibeon. Israel pursued them along the road going up to Beth Horon and cut them down all the way to Azekah and Makkedah. ¹¹As they fled before Israel on the road down from Beth Horon to Azekah, the LORD hurled large hailstones down on them, and more of them died from the hail than were killed by the swords of the Israelites.

¹²On the day the LORD gave the Amorites over to Israel, Joshua said to the LORD in the presence of Israel:

"Sun, stand still over Gibeon,
　and you, moon, over the Valley of
　　Aijalon."

¹³So the sun stood still,
　and the moon stopped,
　　till the nation avenged itself on*ᵃ* its
　　　enemies,

as it is written in the Book of Jashar.

The sun stopped in the middle of the sky and delayed going down about a full day. ¹⁴There has never been a day like it before or since, a day when the LORD listened to a human being. Surely the LORD was fighting for Israel!

¹⁵Then Joshua returned with all Israel to the camp at Gilgal.

Five Amorite Kings Killed

¹⁶Now the five kings had fled and hidden in the cave at Makkedah. ¹⁷When Joshua was told that the five kings had been found hiding in the cave at Makkedah, ¹⁸he said, "Roll large rocks up to the mouth of the cave, and post some men there to guard it. ¹⁹But don't stop; pursue your enemies! Attack them from the rear and don't let them reach their cities, for the LORD your God has given them into your hand."

²⁰So Joshua and the Israelites defeated them completely, but a few survivors managed to reach their fortified cities. ²¹The whole army then returned safely to Joshua in the camp at Makkedah, and no one uttered a word against the Israelites.

²²Joshua said, "Open the mouth of the cave and bring those five kings out to me." ²³So they brought the five kings out of the cave — the kings of Jerusalem, Hebron, Jarmuth, Lachish and Eglon. ²⁴When they had brought these kings to Joshua, he summoned all the men of Israel and said to the army commanders who had come with him, "Come here and put your feet on the necks of these kings." So they came forward and placed their feet on their necks.

²⁵Joshua said to them, "Do not be afraid; do not be discouraged. Be strong and courageous. This is what the LORD will do to all the enemies you are going to fight." ²⁶Then

---

ᵃ 13 Or *nation triumphed over*

Joshua put the kings to death and exposed their bodies on five poles, and they were left hanging on the poles until evening.

²⁷At sunset Joshua gave the order and they took them down from the poles and threw them into the cave where they had been hiding. At the mouth of the cave they placed large rocks, which are there to this day.

Southern Cities Conquered

²⁸That day Joshua took Makkedah. He put the city and its king to the sword and totally destroyed everyone in it. He left no survivors. And he did to the king of Makkedah as he had done to the king of Jericho.

²⁹Then Joshua and all Israel with him moved on from Makkedah to Libnah and attacked it. ³⁰The LORD also gave that city and its king into Israel's hand. The city and everyone in it Joshua put to the sword. He left no survivors there. And he did to its king as he had done to the king of Jericho.

³¹Then Joshua and all Israel with him moved on from Libnah to Lachish; he took up positions against it and attacked it. ³²The LORD gave Lachish into Israel's hands, and Joshua took it on the second day. The city and everyone in it he put to the sword, just as he had done to Libnah. ³³Meanwhile, Horam king of Gezer had come up to help Lachish, but Joshua defeated him and his army—until no survivors were left.

³⁴Then Joshua and all Israel with him moved on from Lachish to Eglon; they took up positions against it and attacked it. ³⁵They captured it that same day and put it to the sword and totally destroyed everyone in it, just as they had done to Lachish.

³⁶Then Joshua and all Israel with him went up from Eglon to Hebron and attacked it. ³⁷They took the city and put it to the sword, together with its king, its villages and everyone in it. They left no survivors. Just as at Eglon, they totally destroyed it and everyone in it.

³⁸Then Joshua and all Israel with him turned around and attacked Debir. ³⁹They took the city, its king and its villages, and put them to the sword. Everyone in it they totally destroyed. They left no survivors. They did to Debir and its king as they had done to Libnah and its king and to Hebron.

⁴⁰So Joshua subdued the whole region, including the hill country, the Negev, the western foothills and the mountain slopes, together with all their kings. He left no survivors. He totally destroyed all who breathed, just as the LORD, the God of Israel, had commanded. ⁴¹Joshua subdued them from Kadesh Barnea to Gaza and from the whole region of Goshen to Gibeon. ⁴²All these kings and their lands Joshua conquered in one campaign, because the LORD, the God of Israel, fought for Israel.

⁴³Then Joshua returned with all Israel to the camp at Gilgal.

Northern Kings Defeated

11 When Jabin king of Hazor heard of this, he sent word to Jobab king of Madon, to the kings of Shimron and Akshaph, ²and to the northern kings who were in the mountains, in the Arabah south of Kinnereth, in the western foothills and in Naphoth Dor on the west; ³to the Canaanites in the east and west; to the Amorites, Hittites, Perizzites and Jebusites in the hill country; and to the Hivites below Hermon in the region of Mizpah. ⁴They came out with all their troops and a large number of horses and chariots—a huge army, as numerous as the sand on the seashore. ⁵All these kings joined forces and made camp together at the Waters of Merom to fight against Israel.

⁶The LORD said to Joshua, "Do not be afraid of them, because by this time tomorrow I will hand all of them, slain, over to Israel. You are to hamstring their horses and burn their chariots."

⁷So Joshua and his whole army came against them suddenly at the Waters of Merom and attacked them, ⁸and the LORD gave them into the hand of Israel. They defeated them and pursued them all the way to Greater Sidon, to Misrephoth Maim, and

to the Valley of Mizpah on the east, until no survivors were left. 9Joshua did to them as the LORD had directed: He hamstrung their horses and burned their chariots.

10At that time Joshua turned back and captured Hazor and put its king to the sword. (Hazor had been the head of all these kingdoms.) 11Everyone in it they put to the sword. They totally destroyed*a* them, not sparing anyone that breathed, and he burned Hazor itself.

12Joshua took all these royal cities and their kings and put them to the sword. He totally destroyed them, as Moses the servant of the LORD had commanded. 13Yet Israel did not burn any of the cities built on their mounds — except Hazor, which Joshua burned. 14The Israelites carried off for themselves all the plunder and livestock of these cities, but all the people they put to the sword until they completely destroyed them, not sparing anyone that breathed. 15As the LORD commanded his servant Moses, so Moses commanded Joshua, and Joshua did it; he left nothing undone of all that the LORD commanded Moses.

16So Joshua took this entire land: the hill country, all the Negev, the whole region of Goshen, the western foothills, the Arabah and the mountains of Israel with their foothills, 17from Mount Halak, which rises toward Seir, to Baal Gad in the Valley of Lebanon below Mount Hermon. He captured all their kings and put them to death. 18Joshua waged war against all these kings for a long time. 19Except for the Hivites living in Gibeon, not one city made a treaty of peace with the Israelites, who took them all in battle. 20For it was the LORD himself who hardened their hearts to wage war against Israel, so that he might destroy them totally, exterminating them without mercy, as the LORD had commanded Moses.

21At that time Joshua went and destroyed the Anakites from the hill country:

from Hebron, Debir and Anab, from all the hill country of Judah, and from all the hill country of Israel. Joshua totally destroyed them and their towns. 22No Anakites were left in Israelite territory; only in Gaza, Gath and Ashdod did any survive.

23So Joshua took the entire land, just as the LORD had directed Moses, and he gave it as an inheritance to Israel according to their tribal divisions. Then the land had rest from war.

List of Defeated Kings

12 These are the kings of the land whom the Israelites had defeated and whose territory they took over east of the Jordan, from the Arnon Gorge to Mount Hermon, including all the eastern side of the Arabah:

2Sihon king of the Amorites, who reigned in Heshbon.

He ruled from Aroer on the rim of the Arnon Gorge — from the middle of the gorge — to the Jabbok River, which is the border of the Ammonites. This included half of Gilead. 3He also ruled over the eastern Arabah from the Sea of Galilee*b* to the Sea of the Arabah (that is, the Dead Sea), to Beth Jeshimoth, and then southward below the slopes of Pisgah.

4And the territory of Og king of Bashan, one of the last of the Rephaites, who reigned in Ashtaroth and Edrei.

5He ruled over Mount Hermon, Salekah, all of Bashan to the border of the people of Geshur and Maakah, and half of Gilead to the border of Sihon king of Heshbon.

6Moses, the servant of the LORD, and the Israelites conquered them. And Moses the servant of the LORD gave their land to the Reubenites, the Gadites and the half-tribe of Manasseh to be their possession.

---

a 11 The Hebrew term refers to the irrevocable giving over of things or persons to the LORD, often by totally destroying them; also in verses 12, 20 and 21.   *b 3* Hebrew *Kinnereth*

7Here is a list of the kings of the land that Joshua and the Israelites conquered on the west side of the Jordan, from Baal Gad in the Valley of Lebanon to Mount Halak, which rises toward Seir. Joshua gave their lands as an inheritance to the tribes of Israel according to their tribal divisions. 8The lands included the hill country, the western foothills, the Arabah, the mountain slopes, the wilderness and the Negev. These were the lands of the Hittites, Amorites, Canaanites, Perizzites, Hivites and Jebusites. These were the kings:

9the king of Jericho	one
the king of Ai (near Bethel)	one
10the king of Jerusalem	one
the king of Hebron	one
11the king of Jarmuth	one
the king of Lachish	one
12the king of Eglon	one
the king of Gezer	one
13the king of Debir	one
the king of Geder	one
14the king of Hormah	one
the king of Arad	one
15the king of Libnah	one
the king of Adullam	one
16the king of Makkedah	one
the king of Bethel	one
17the king of Tappuah	one
the king of Hepher	one
18the king of Aphek	one
the king of Lasharon	one
19the king of Madon	one
the king of Hazor	one
20the king of Shimron Meron	one
the king of Akshaph	one
21the king of Taanach	one
the king of Megiddo	one
22the king of Kedesh	one
the king of Jokneam in Carmel	one
23the king of Dor (in Naphoth Dor)	one
the king of Goyim in Gilgal	one
24the king of Tirzah	one
thirty-one kings in all.	

Land Still to Be Taken

13 When Joshua had grown old, the LORD said to him, "You are now very old, and there are still very large areas of land to be taken over.

2"This is the land that remains: all the regions of the Philistines and Geshurites, 3from the Shihor River on the east of Egypt to the territory of Ekron on the north, all of it counted as Canaanite though held by the five Philistine rulers in Gaza, Ashdod, Ashkelon, Gath and Ekron; the territory of the Avvites 4on the south; all the land of the Canaanites, from Arah of the Sidonians as far as Aphek and the border of the Amorites; 5the area of Byblos; and all Lebanon to the east, from Baal Gad below Mount Hermon to Lebo Hamath.

6"As for all the inhabitants of the mountain regions from Lebanon to Misrephoth Maim, that is, all the Sidonians, I myself will drive them out before the Israelites. Be sure to allocate this land to Israel for an inheritance, as I have instructed you, 7and divide it as an inheritance among the nine tribes and half of the tribe of Manasseh."

Division of the Land East of the Jordan

8The other half of Manasseh,a the Reubenites and the Gadites had received the inheritance that Moses had given them east of the Jordan, as he, the servant of the LORD, had assigned it to them.

9It extended from Aroer on the rim of the Arnon Gorge, and from the town in the middle of the gorge, and included the whole plateau of Medeba as far as Dibon, 10and all the towns of Sihon king of the Amorites, who ruled in Heshbon, out to the border of the Ammonites. 11It also included Gilead, the territory of the people of Geshur and Maakah, all of Mount

---

a 8 Hebrew With it (that is, with the other half of Manasseh)

Hermon and all Bashan as far as Salekah— [12]that is, the whole kingdom of Og in Bashan, who had reigned in Ashtaroth and Edrei. (He was the last of the Rephaites.) Moses had defeated them and taken over their land. [13]But the Israelites did not drive out the people of Geshur and Maakah, so they continue to live among the Israelites to this day.

[14]But to the tribe of Levi he gave no inheritance, since the food offerings presented to the LORD, the God of Israel, are their inheritance, as he promised them.

[15]This is what Moses had given to the tribe of Reuben, according to its clans:

[16]The territory from Aroer on the rim of the Arnon Gorge, and from the town in the middle of the gorge, and the whole plateau past Medeba [17]to Heshbon and all its towns on the plateau, including Dibon, Bamoth Baal, Beth Baal Meon, [18]Jahaz, Kedemoth, Mephaath, [19]Kiriathaim, Sibmah, Zereth Shahar on the hill in the valley, [20]Beth Peor, the slopes of Pisgah, and Beth Jeshimoth— [21]all the towns on the plateau and the entire realm of Sihon king of the Amorites, who ruled at Heshbon. Moses had defeated him and the Midianite chiefs, Evi, Rekem, Zur, Hur and Reba—princes allied with Sihon—who lived in that country. [22]In addition to those slain in battle, the Israelites had put to the sword Balaam son of Beor, who practiced divination. [23]The boundary of the Reubenites was the bank of the Jordan. These towns and their villages were the inheritance of the Reubenites, according to their clans.

[24]This is what Moses had given to the tribe of Gad, according to its clans:

[25]The territory of Jazer, all the towns

of Gilead and half the Ammonite country as far as Aroer, near Rabbah; [26]and from Heshbon to Ramath Mizpah and Betonim, and from Mahanaim to the territory of Debir; [27]and in the valley, Beth Haram, Beth Nimrah, Sukkoth and Zaphon with the rest of the realm of Sihon king of Heshbon (the east side of the Jordan, the territory up to the end of the Sea of Galilee[a]). [28]These towns and their villages were the inheritance of the Gadites, according to their clans.

[29]This is what Moses had given to the half-tribe of Manasseh, that is, to half the family of the descendants of Manasseh, according to its clans:

[30]The territory extending from Mahanaim and including all of Bashan, the entire realm of Og king of Bashan—all the settlements of Jair in Bashan, sixty towns, [31]half of Gilead, and Ashtaroth and Edrei (the royal cities of Og in Bashan). This was for the descendants of Makir son of Manasseh—for half of the sons of Makir, according to their clans.

[32]This is the inheritance Moses had given when he was in the plains of Moab across the Jordan east of Jericho. [33]But to the tribe of Levi, Moses had given no inheritance; the LORD, the God of Israel, is their inheritance, as he promised them.

Division of the Land West of the Jordan

14 Now these are the areas the Israelites received as an inheritance in the land of Canaan, which Eleazar the priest, Joshua son of Nun and the heads of the tribal clans of Israel allotted to them. [2]Their inheritances were assigned by lot to the nine and a half tribes, as the LORD had commanded through Moses. [3]Moses had granted the two and a half tribes their inheritance east of the Jordan but had not

---

[a] 27 Hebrew *Kinnereth*

granted the Levites an inheritance among the rest, ⁴for Joseph's descendants had become two tribes — Manasseh and Ephraim. The Levites received no share of the land but only towns to live in, with pasturelands for their flocks and herds. ⁵So the Israelites divided the land, just as the LORD had commanded Moses.

Allotment for Caleb

⁶Now the people of Judah approached Joshua at Gilgal, and Caleb son of Jephunneh the Kenizzite said to him, "You know what the LORD said to Moses the man of God at Kadesh Barnea about you and me. ⁷I was forty years old when Moses the servant of the LORD sent me from Kadesh Barnea to explore the land. And I brought him back a report according to my convictions, ⁸but my fellow Israelites who went up with me made the hearts of the people melt in fear. I, however, followed the LORD my God wholeheartedly. ⁹So on that day Moses swore to me, 'The land on which your feet have walked will be your inheritance and that of your children forever, because you have followed the LORD my God wholeheartedly.'^a

¹⁰"Now then, just as the LORD promised, he has kept me alive for forty-five years since the time he said this to Moses, while Israel moved about in the wilderness. So here I am today, eighty-five years old! ¹¹I am still as strong today as the day Moses sent me out; I'm just as vigorous to go out to battle now as I was then. ¹²Now give me this hill country that the LORD promised me that day. You yourself heard then that the Anakites were there and their cities were large and fortified, but, the LORD helping me, I will drive them out just as he said."

¹³Then Joshua blessed Caleb son of Jephunneh and gave him Hebron as his inheritance. ¹⁴So Hebron has belonged to Caleb son of Jephunneh the Kenizzite ever since, because he followed the LORD, the God of Israel, wholeheartedly. ¹⁵(Hebron used to be called Kiriath Arba after Arba, who was the greatest man among the Anakites.)

Then the land had rest from war.

Allotment for Judah

15 The allotment for the tribe of Judah, according to its clans, extended down to the territory of Edom, to the Desert of Zin in the extreme south.

²Their southern boundary started from the bay at the southern end of the Dead Sea, ³crossed south of Scorpion Pass, continued on to Zin and went over to the south of Kadesh Barnea. Then it ran past Hezron up to Addar and curved around to Karka. ⁴It then passed along to Azmon and joined the Wadi of Egypt, ending at the Mediterranean Sea. This is their^b southern boundary.

⁵The eastern boundary is the Dead Sea as far as the mouth of the Jordan.

The northern boundary started from the bay of the sea at the mouth of the Jordan, ⁶went up to Beth Hoglah and continued north of Beth Arabah to the Stone of Bohan son of Reuben. ⁷The boundary then went up to Debir from the Valley of Achor and turned north to Gilgal, which faces the Pass of Adummim south of the gorge. It continued along to the waters of En Shemesh and came out at En Rogel. ⁸Then it ran up the Valley of Ben Hinnom along the southern slope of the Jebusite city (that is, Jerusalem). From there it climbed to the top of the hill west of the Hinnom Valley at the northern end of the Valley of Rephaim. ⁹From the hilltop the boundary headed toward the spring of the waters of Nephtoah, came out at the towns of Mount Ephron and went down toward Baalah (that is, Kiriath

---

^a 9 Deut. 1:36   ^b 4 Septuagint; Hebrew *your*

Jearim). [10]Then it curved westward from Baalah to Mount Seir, ran along the northern slope of Mount Jearim (that is, Kesalon), continued down to Beth Shemesh and crossed to Timnah. [11]It went to the northern slope of Ekron, turned toward Shikkeron, passed along to Mount Baalah and reached Jabneel. The boundary ended at the sea.

[12]The western boundary is the coastline of the Mediterranean Sea.

These are the boundaries around the people of Judah by their clans.

[13]In accordance with the LORD's command to him, Joshua gave to Caleb son of Jephunneh a portion in Judah — Kiriath Arba, that is, Hebron. (Arba was the forefather of Anak.) [14]From Hebron Caleb drove out the three Anakites — Sheshai, Ahiman and Talmai, the sons of Anak. [15]From there he marched against the people living in Debir (formerly called Kiriath Sepher). [16]And Caleb said, "I will give my daughter Aksah in marriage to the man who attacks and captures Kiriath Sepher." [17]Othniel son of Kenaz, Caleb's brother, took it; so Caleb gave his daughter Aksah to him in marriage.

[18]One day when she came to Othniel, she urged him[a] to ask her father for a field. When she got off her donkey, Caleb asked her, "What can I do for you?"

[19]She replied, "Do me a special favor. Since you have given me land in the Negev, give me also springs of water." So Caleb gave her the upper and lower springs.

[20]This is the inheritance of the tribe of Judah, according to its clans:

[21]The southernmost towns of the tribe of Judah in the Negev toward the boundary of Edom were:

Kabzeel, Eder, Jagur, [22]Kinah, Dimonah, Adadah, [23]Kedesh, Hazor, Ithnan, [24]Ziph, Telem, Bealoth, [25]Hazor Hadattah, Kerioth Hezron (that is, Hazor), [26]Amam, Shema, Moladah, [27]Hazar Gaddah, Heshmon, Beth Pelet, [28]Hazar Shual, Beersheba, Biziothiah, [29]Baalah, Iyim, Ezem, [30]Eltolad, Kesil, Hormah, [31]Ziklag, Madmannah, Sansannah, [32]Lebaoth, Shilhim, Ain and Rimmon — a total of twenty-nine towns and their villages.

[33]In the western foothills:

Eshtaol, Zorah, Ashnah, [34]Zanoah, En Gannim, Tappuah, Enam, [35]Jarmuth, Adullam, Sokoh, Azekah, [36]Shaaraim, Adithaim and Gederah (or Gederothaim)[b] — fourteen towns and their villages.

[37]Zenan, Hadashah, Migdal Gad, [38]Dilean, Mizpah, Joktheel, [39]Lachish, Bozkath, Eglon, [40]Kabbon, Lahmas, Kitlish, [41]Gederoth, Beth Dagon, Naamah and Makkedah — sixteen towns and their villages.

[42]Libnah, Ether, Ashan, [43]Iphtah, Ashnah, Nezib, [44]Keilah, Akzib and Mareshah — nine towns and their villages.

[45]Ekron, with its surrounding settlements and villages; [46]west of Ekron, all that were in the vicinity of Ashdod, together with their villages; [47]Ashdod, its surrounding settlements and villages; and Gaza, its settlements and villages, as far as the Wadi of Egypt and the coastline of the Mediterranean Sea.

[48]In the hill country:

Shamir, Jattir, Sokoh, [49]Dannah, Kiriath Sannah (that is, Debir), [50]Anab, Eshtemoh, Anim, [51]Goshen, Holon and Giloh — eleven towns and their villages.

[52]Arab, Dumah, Eshan, [53]Janim, Beth Tappuah, Aphekah, [54]Humtah,

---

a 18 Hebrew and some Septuagint manuscripts; other Septuagint manuscripts (see also note at Judges 1:14) *Othniel, he urged her*   *b 36* Or *Gederah and Gederothaim*

Kiriath Arba (that is, Hebron) and Zior — nine towns and their villages.

55 Maon, Carmel, Ziph, Juttah, 56 Jezreel, Jokdeam, Zanoah, 57 Kain, Gibeah and Timnah — ten towns and their villages.

58 Halhul, Beth Zur, Gedor, 59 Maarath, Beth Anoth and Eltekon — six towns and their villages.[a]

60 Kiriath Baal (that is, Kiriath Jearim) and Rabbah — two towns and their villages.

61 In the wilderness:

Beth Arabah, Middin, Sekakah, 62 Nibshan, the City of Salt and En Gedi — six towns and their villages.

63 Judah could not dislodge the Jebusites, who were living in Jerusalem; to this day the Jebusites live there with the people of Judah.

Allotment for Ephraim and Manasseh

16 The allotment for Joseph began at the Jordan, east of the springs of Jericho, and went up from there through the desert into the hill country of Bethel. 2 It went on from Bethel (that is, Luz),[b] crossed over to the territory of the Arkites in Ataroth, 3 descended westward to the territory of the Japhletites as far as the region of Lower Beth Horon and on to Gezer, ending at the Mediterranean Sea.

4 So Manasseh and Ephraim, the descendants of Joseph, received their inheritance.

5 This was the territory of Ephraim, according to its clans:

The boundary of their inheritance went from Ataroth Addar in the east to Upper Beth Horon 6 and continued to the Mediterranean Sea. From Mikmethath on the north it curved eastward to Taanath Shiloh, passing by it to Janoah on the east. 7 Then it went down from Janoah to Ataroth and Naarah, touched Jericho and came out at the Jordan. 8 From Tappuah the border went west to the Kanah Ravine and ended at the Mediterranean Sea. This was the inheritance of the tribe of the Ephraimites, according to its clans. 9 It also included all the towns and their villages that were set aside for the Ephraimites within the inheritance of the Manassites.

10 They did not dislodge the Canaanites living in Gezer; to this day the Canaanites live among the people of Ephraim but are required to do forced labor.

17 This was the allotment for the tribe of Manasseh as Joseph's firstborn, that is, for Makir, Manasseh's firstborn. Makir was the ancestor of the Gileadites, who had received Gilead and Bashan because the Makirites were great soldiers. 2 So this allotment was for the rest of the people of Manasseh — the clans of Abiezer, Helek, Asriel, Shechem, Hepher and Shemida. These are the other male descendants of Manasseh son of Joseph by their clans.

3 Now Zelophehad son of Hepher, the son of Gilead, the son of Makir, the son of Manasseh, had no sons but only daughters, whose names were Mahlah, Noah, Hoglah, Milkah and Tirzah. 4 They went to Eleazar the priest, Joshua son of Nun, and the leaders and said, "The LORD commanded Moses to give us an inheritance among our relatives." So Joshua gave them an inheritance along with the brothers of their father, according to the LORD's command. 5 Manasseh's share consisted of ten tracts of land besides Gilead and Bashan east of the Jordan, 6 because the daughters of the tribe of Manasseh received an inheritance among the sons. The land of Gilead belonged to the rest of the descendants of Manasseh.

7 The territory of Manasseh extended from Asher to Mikmethath east of

---

a 59 The Septuagint adds another district of eleven towns, including Tekoa and Ephrathah (Bethlehem).
b 2 Septuagint; Hebrew *Bethel to Luz*

Shechem. The boundary ran southward from there to include the people living at En Tappuah. 8(Manasseh had the land of Tappuah, but Tappuah itself, on the boundary of Manasseh, belonged to the Ephraimites.) 9Then the boundary continued south to the Kanah Ravine. There were towns belonging to Ephraim lying among the towns of Manasseh, but the boundary of Manasseh was the northern side of the ravine and ended at the Mediterranean Sea. 10On the south the land belonged to Ephraim, on the north to Manasseh. The territory of Manasseh reached the Mediterranean Sea and bordered Asher on the north and Issachar on the east.

11Within Issachar and Asher, Manasseh also had Beth Shan, Ibleam and the people of Dor, Endor, Taanach and Megiddo, together with their surrounding settlements (the third in the list is Naphoth*a*).

12Yet the Manassites were not able to occupy these towns, for the Canaanites were determined to live in that region. 13However, when the Israelites grew stronger, they subjected the Canaanites to forced labor but did not drive them out completely.

14The people of Joseph said to Joshua, "Why have you given us only one allotment and one portion for an inheritance? We are a numerous people, and the LORD has blessed us abundantly."

15"If you are so numerous," Joshua answered, "and if the hill country of Ephraim is too small for you, go up into the forest and clear land for yourselves there in the land of the Perizzites and Rephaites."

16The people of Joseph replied, "The hill country is not enough for us, and all the Canaanites who live in the plain have chariots fitted with iron, both those in Beth Shan and its settlements and those in the Valley of Jezreel."

17But Joshua said to the tribes of Joseph — to Ephraim and Manasseh — "You are numerous and very powerful. You will have not only one allotment 18but the forested hill country as well. Clear it, and its farthest limits will be yours; though the Canaanites have chariots fitted with iron and though they are strong, you can drive them out."

Division of the Rest of the Land

18 The whole assembly of the Israelites gathered at Shiloh and set up the tent of meeting there. The country was brought under their control, 2but there were still seven Israelite tribes who had not yet received their inheritance.

3So Joshua said to the Israelites: "How long will you wait before you begin to take possession of the land that the LORD, the God of your ancestors, has given you? 4Appoint three men from each tribe. I will send them out to make a survey of the land and to write a description of it, according to the inheritance of each. Then they will return to me. 5You are to divide the land into seven parts. Judah is to remain in its territory on the south and the tribes of Joseph in their territory on the north. 6After you have written descriptions of the seven parts of the land, bring them here to me and I will cast lots for you in the presence of the LORD our God. 7The Levites, however, do not get a portion among you, because the priestly service of the LORD is their inheritance. And Gad, Reuben and the half-tribe of Manasseh have already received their inheritance on the east side of the Jordan. Moses the servant of the LORD gave it to them."

8As the men started on their way to map out the land, Joshua instructed them, "Go and make a survey of the land and write a description of it. Then return to me, and I will cast lots for you here at Shiloh in the presence of the LORD." 9So the men left and went through the land. They wrote its

---

a 11 That is, Naphoth Dor

description on a scroll, town by town, in seven parts, and returned to Joshua in the camp at Shiloh. ¹⁰Joshua then cast lots for them in Shiloh in the presence of the LORD, and there he distributed the land to the Israelites according to their tribal divisions.

Allotment for Benjamin

¹¹The first lot came up for the tribe of Benjamin according to its clans. Their allotted territory lay between the tribes of Judah and Joseph:

¹²On the north side their boundary began at the Jordan, passed the northern slope of Jericho and headed west into the hill country, coming out at the wilderness of Beth Aven. ¹³From there it crossed to the south slope of Luz (that is, Bethel) and went down to Ataroth Addar on the hill south of Lower Beth Horon.

¹⁴From the hill facing Beth Horon on the south the boundary turned south along the western side and came out at Kiriath Baal (that is, Kiriath Jearim), a town of the people of Judah. This was the western side.

¹⁵The southern side began at the outskirts of Kiriath Jearim on the west, and the boundary came out at the spring of the waters of Nephtoah. ¹⁶The boundary went down to the foot of the hill facing the Valley of Ben Hinnom, north of the Valley of Rephaim. It continued down the Hinnom Valley along the southern slope of the Jebusite city and so to En Rogel. ¹⁷It then curved north, went to En Shemesh, continued to Geliloth, which faces the Pass of Adummim, and ran down to the Stone of Bohan son of Reuben. ¹⁸It continued to the northern slope of Beth Arabah*a* and on down into the Arabah. ¹⁹It then went to the northern slope of Beth Hoglah and came out at the northern bay of the Dead Sea, at the mouth of the Jordan in the south. This was the southern boundary.

²⁰The Jordan formed the boundary on the eastern side.

These were the boundaries that marked out the inheritance of the clans of Benjamin on all sides.

²¹The tribe of Benjamin, according to its clans, had the following towns:

Jericho, Beth Hoglah, Emek Keziz, ²²Beth Arabah, Zemaraim, Bethel, ²³Avvim, Parah, Ophrah, ²⁴Kephar Ammoni, Ophni and Geba — twelve towns and their villages.

²⁵Gibeon, Ramah, Beeroth, ²⁶Mizpah, Kephirah, Mozah, ²⁷Rekem, Irpeel, Taralah, ²⁸Zelah, Haeleph, the Jebusite city (that is, Jerusalem), Gibeah and Kiriath — fourteen towns and their villages.

This was the inheritance of Benjamin for its clans.

Allotment for Simeon

19 The second lot came out for the tribe of Simeon according to its clans. Their inheritance lay within the territory of Judah. ²It included:

Beersheba (or Sheba),*b* Moladah, ³Hazar Shual, Balah, Ezem, ⁴Eltolad, Bethul, Hormah, ⁵Ziklag, Beth Markaboth, Hazar Susah, ⁶Beth Lebaoth and Sharuhen — thirteen towns and their villages;

⁷Ain, Rimmon, Ether and Ashan — four towns and their villages — ⁸and all the villages around these towns as far as Baalath Beer (Ramah in the Negev).

This was the inheritance of the tribe of the Simeonites, according to its clans. ⁹The inheritance of the Simeonites was taken from the share of Judah, because Judah's portion was more than they needed. So the Simeonites received their inheritance within the territory of Judah.

---

a 18 Septuagint; Hebrew *slope facing the Arabah*   *b* 2 Or *Beersheba, Sheba*; 1 Chron. 4:28 does not have *Sheba*.

Allotment for Zebulun

[10]The third lot came up for Zebulun according to its clans:

The boundary of their inheritance went as far as Sarid. [11]Going west it ran to Maralah, touched Dabbesheth, and extended to the ravine near Jokneam. [12]It turned east from Sarid toward the sunrise to the territory of Kisloth Tabor and went on to Daberath and up to Japhia. [13]Then it continued eastward to Gath Hepher and Eth Kazin; it came out at Rimmon and turned toward Neah. [14]There the boundary went around on the north to Hannathon and ended at the Valley of Iphtah El. [15]Included were Kattath, Nahalal, Shimron, Idalah and Bethlehem. There were twelve towns and their villages.

[16]These towns and their villages were the inheritance of Zebulun, according to its clans.

Allotment for Issachar

[17]The fourth lot came out for Issachar according to its clans. [18]Their territory included:

Jezreel, Kesulloth, Shunem, [19]Hapharaim, Shion, Anaharath, [20]Rabbith, Kishion, Ebez, [21]Remeth, En Gannim, En Haddah and Beth Pazzez. [22]The boundary touched Tabor, Shahazumah and Beth Shemesh, and ended at the Jordan. There were sixteen towns and their villages.

[23]These towns and their villages were the inheritance of the tribe of Issachar, according to its clans.

Allotment for Asher

[24]The fifth lot came out for the tribe of Asher according to its clans. [25]Their territory included:

Helkath, Hali, Beten, Akshaph, [26]Allammelek, Amad and Mishal.

On the west the boundary touched Carmel and Shihor Libnath. [27]It then turned east toward Beth Dagon, touched Zebulun and the Valley of Iphtah El, and went north to Beth Emek and Neiel, passing Kabul on the left. [28]It went to Abdon,[a] Rehob, Hammon and Kanah, as far as Greater Sidon. [29]The boundary then turned back toward Ramah and went to the fortified city of Tyre, turned toward Hosah and came out at the Mediterranean Sea in the region of Akzib, [30]Ummah, Aphek and Rehob. There were twenty-two towns and their villages.

[31]These towns and their villages were the inheritance of the tribe of Asher, according to its clans.

Allotment for Naphtali

[32]The sixth lot came out for Naphtali according to its clans:

[33]Their boundary went from Heleph and the large tree in Zaanannim, passing Adami Nekeb and Jabneel to Lakkum and ending at the Jordan. [34]The boundary ran west through Aznoth Tabor and came out at Hukkok. It touched Zebulun on the south, Asher on the west and the Jordan[b] on the east. [35]The fortified towns were Ziddim, Zer, Hammath, Rakkath, Kinnereth, [36]Adamah, Ramah, Hazor, [37]Kedesh, Edrei, En Hazor, [38]Iron, Migdal El, Horem, Beth Anath and Beth Shemesh. There were nineteen towns and their villages.

[39]These towns and their villages were the inheritance of the tribe of Naphtali, according to its clans.

Allotment for Dan

[40]The seventh lot came out for the tribe of Dan according to its clans. [41]The territory of their inheritance included:

---

a 28 Some Hebrew manuscripts (see also 21:30); most Hebrew manuscripts *Ebron*   b 34 Septuagint; Hebrew *west, and Judah, the Jordan,*

Zorah, Eshtaol, Ir Shemesh, 42Shaalabbin, Aijalon, Ithlah, 43Elon, Timnah, Ekron, 44Eltekeh, Gibbethon, Baalath, 45Jehud, Bene Berak, Gath Rimmon, 46Me Jarkon and Rakkon, with the area facing Joppa.

47(When the territory of the Danites was lost to them, they went up and attacked Leshem, took it, put it to the sword and occupied it. They settled in Leshem and named it Dan after their ancestor.)

48These towns and their villages were the inheritance of the tribe of Dan, according to its clans.

Allotment for Joshua

49When they had finished dividing the land into its allotted portions, the Israelites gave Joshua son of Nun an inheritance among them, 50as the LORD had commanded. They gave him the town he asked for — Timnath Serah*a* in the hill country of Ephraim. And he built up the town and settled there.

51These are the territories that Eleazar the priest, Joshua son of Nun and the heads of the tribal clans of Israel assigned by lot at Shiloh in the presence of the LORD at the entrance to the tent of meeting. And so they finished dividing the land.

Cities of Refuge

20 Then the LORD said to Joshua: 2"Tell the Israelites to designate the cities of refuge, as I instructed you through Moses, 3so that anyone who kills a person accidentally and unintentionally may flee there and find protection from the avenger of blood. 4When they flee to one of these cities, they are to stand in the entrance of the city gate and state their case before the elders of that city. Then the elders are to admit the fugitive into their city and provide a place to live among them. 5If the avenger of blood comes in pursuit, the elders must not surrender the fugitive, because the fugitive

killed their neighbor unintentionally and without malice aforethought. 6They are to stay in that city until they have stood trial before the assembly and until the death of the high priest who is serving at that time. Then they may go back to their own home in the town from which they fled."

7So they set apart Kedesh in Galilee in the hill country of Naphtali, Shechem in the hill country of Ephraim, and Kiriath Arba (that is, Hebron) in the hill country of Judah. 8East of the Jordan (on the other side from Jericho) they designated Bezer in the wilderness on the plateau in the tribe of Reuben, Ramoth in Gilead in the tribe of Gad, and Golan in Bashan in the tribe of Manasseh. 9Any of the Israelites or any foreigner residing among them who killed someone accidentally could flee to these designated cities and not be killed by the avenger of blood prior to standing trial before the assembly.

Towns for the Levites

21 Now the family heads of the Levites approached Eleazar the priest, Joshua son of Nun, and the heads of the other tribal families of Israel 2at Shiloh in Canaan and said to them, "The LORD commanded through Moses that you give us towns to live in, with pasturelands for our livestock." 3So, as the LORD had commanded, the Israelites gave the Levites the following towns and pasturelands out of their own inheritance:

4The first lot came out for the Kohathites, according to their clans. The Levites who were descendants of Aaron the priest were allotted thirteen towns from the tribes of Judah, Simeon and Benjamin. 5The rest of Kohath's descendants were allotted ten towns from the clans of the tribes of Ephraim, Dan and half of Manasseh.

6The descendants of Gershon were allotted thirteen towns from the clans of the tribes of Issachar, Asher, Naphtali and the half-tribe of Manasseh in Bashan.

---

a 50 Also known as *Timnath Heres* (see Judges 2:9)

⁷The descendants of Merari, according to their clans, received twelve towns from the tribes of Reuben, Gad and Zebulun.

⁸So the Israelites allotted to the Levites these towns and their pasturelands, as the LORD had commanded through Moses.

⁹From the tribes of Judah and Simeon they allotted the following towns by name ¹⁰(these towns were assigned to the descendants of Aaron who were from the Kohathite clans of the Levites, because the first lot fell to them):

¹¹They gave them Kiriath Arba (that is, Hebron), with its surrounding pastureland, in the hill country of Judah. (Arba was the forefather of Anak.) ¹²But the fields and villages around the city they had given to Caleb son of Jephunneh as his possession.

¹³So to the descendants of Aaron the priest they gave Hebron (a city of refuge for one accused of murder), Libnah, ¹⁴Jattir, Eshtemoa, ¹⁵Holon, Debir, ¹⁶Ain, Juttah and Beth Shemesh, together with their pasturelands — nine towns from these two tribes.

¹⁷And from the tribe of Benjamin they gave them Gibeon, Geba, ¹⁸Anathoth and Almon, together with their pasturelands — four towns.

¹⁹The total number of towns for the priests, the descendants of Aaron, came to thirteen, together with their pasturelands.

²⁰The rest of the Kohathite clans of the Levites were allotted towns from the tribe of Ephraim:

²¹In the hill country of Ephraim they were given Shechem (a city of refuge for one accused of murder) and Gezer, ²²Kibzaim and Beth Horon, together with their pasturelands — four towns.

²³Also from the tribe of Dan they received Eltekeh, Gibbethon, ²⁴Aijalon and Gath Rimmon, together with their pasturelands — four towns.

²⁵From half the tribe of Manasseh they received Taanach and Gath Rimmon, together with their pasturelands — two towns.

²⁶All these ten towns and their pasturelands were given to the rest of the Kohathite clans.

²⁷The Levite clans of the Gershonites were given:

from the half-tribe of Manasseh,
Golan in Bashan (a city of refuge for one accused of murder) and Be Eshterah, together with their pasturelands — two towns;

²⁸from the tribe of Issachar,
Kishion, Daberath, ²⁹Jarmuth and En Gannim, together with their pasturelands — four towns;

³⁰from the tribe of Asher,
Mishal, Abdon, ³¹Helkath and Rehob, together with their pasturelands — four towns;

³²from the tribe of Naphtali,
Kedesh in Galilee (a city of refuge for one accused of murder), Hammoth Dor and Kartan, together with their pasturelands — three towns.

³³The total number of towns of the Gershonite clans came to thirteen, together with their pasturelands.

³⁴The Merarite clans (the rest of the Levites) were given:

from the tribe of Zebulun,
Jokneam, Kartah, ³⁵Dimnah and Nahalal, together with their pasturelands — four towns;

³⁶from the tribe of Reuben,
Bezer, Jahaz, ³⁷Kedemoth and Mephaath, together with their pasturelands — four towns;

³⁸from the tribe of Gad,
Ramoth in Gilead (a city of refuge for one accused of murder), Mahanaim, ³⁹Heshbon and Jazer, together with their pasturelands — four towns in all.

⁴⁰The total number of towns allotted to the Merarite clans, who were the rest of the Levites, came to twelve.

41The towns of the Levites in the territory held by the Israelites were forty-eight in all, together with their pasturelands. 42Each of these towns had pasturelands surrounding it; this was true for all these towns.

43So the LORD gave Israel all the land he had sworn to give their ancestors, and they took possession of it and settled there. 44The LORD gave them rest on every side, just as he had sworn to their ancestors. Not one of their enemies withstood them; the LORD gave all their enemies into their hands. 45Not one of all the LORD's good promises to Israel failed; every one was fulfilled.

Eastern Tribes Return Home

22 Then Joshua summoned the Reubenites, the Gadites and the half-tribe of Manasseh 2and said to them, "You have done all that Moses the servant of the LORD commanded, and you have obeyed me in everything I commanded. 3For a long time now — to this very day — you have not deserted your fellow Israelites but have carried out the mission the LORD your God gave you. 4Now that the LORD your God has given them rest as he promised, return to your homes in the land that Moses the servant of the LORD gave you on the other side of the Jordan. 5But be very careful to keep the commandment and the law that Moses the servant of the LORD gave you: to love the LORD your God, to walk in obedience to him, to keep his commands, to hold fast to him and to serve him with all your heart and with all your soul."

6Then Joshua blessed them and sent them away, and they went to their homes. 7(To the half-tribe of Manasseh Moses had given land in Bashan, and to the other half of the tribe Joshua gave land on the west side of the Jordan along with their fellow Israelites.) When Joshua sent them home, he blessed them, 8saying, "Return to your homes with your great wealth — with large herds of livestock, with silver, gold, bronze and iron, and a great quantity of clothing — and divide the plunder from your enemies with your fellow Israelites."

9So the Reubenites, the Gadites and the half-tribe of Manasseh left the Israelites at Shiloh in Canaan to return to Gilead, their own land, which they had acquired in accordance with the command of the LORD through Moses.

10When they came to Geliloth near the Jordan in the land of Canaan, the Reubenites, the Gadites and the half-tribe of Manasseh built an imposing altar there by the Jordan. 11And when the Israelites heard that they had built the altar on the border of Canaan at Geliloth near the Jordan on the Israelite side, 12the whole assembly of Israel gathered at Shiloh to go to war against them.

13So the Israelites sent Phinehas son of Eleazar, the priest, to the land of Gilead — to Reuben, Gad and the half-tribe of Manasseh. 14With him they sent ten of the chief men, one from each of the tribes of Israel, each the head of a family division among the Israelite clans.

15When they went to Gilead — to Reuben, Gad and the half-tribe of Manasseh — they said to them: 16"The whole assembly of the LORD says: 'How could you break faith with the God of Israel like this? How could you turn away from the LORD and build yourselves an altar in rebellion against him now? 17Was not the sin of Peor enough for us? Up to this very day we have not cleansed ourselves from that sin, even though a plague fell on the community of the LORD! 18And are you now turning away from the LORD?

"'If you rebel against the LORD today, tomorrow he will be angry with the whole community of Israel. 19If the land you possess is defiled, come over to the LORD's land, where the LORD's tabernacle stands, and share the land with us. But do not rebel against the LORD or against us by building an altar for yourselves, other than the altar of the LORD our God. 20When Achan son of Zerah was unfaithful in regard to the devoted things,[a] did not wrath come on the whole community of Israel? He was not the only one who died for his sin.'"

21 Then Reuben, Gad and the half-tribe of Manasseh replied to the heads of the clans of Israel: 22 "The Mighty One, God, the LORD! The Mighty One, God, the LORD! He knows! And let Israel know! If this has been in rebellion or disobedience to the LORD, do not spare us this day. 23 If we have built our own altar to turn away from the LORD and to offer burnt offerings and grain offerings, or to sacrifice fellowship offerings on it, may the LORD himself call us to account.

24 "No! We did it for fear that some day your descendants might say to ours, 'What do you have to do with the LORD, the God of Israel? 25 The LORD has made the Jordan a boundary between us and you — you Reubenites and Gadites! You have no share in the LORD.' So your descendants might cause ours to stop fearing the LORD.

26 "That is why we said, 'Let us get ready and build an altar — but not for burnt offerings or sacrifices.' 27 On the contrary, it is to be a witness between us and you and the generations that follow, that we will worship the LORD at his sanctuary with our burnt offerings, sacrifices and fellowship offerings. Then in the future your descendants will not be able to say to ours, 'You have no share in the LORD.'

28 "And we said, 'If they ever say this to us, or to our descendants, we will answer: Look at the replica of the LORD's altar, which our ancestors built, not for burnt offerings and sacrifices, but as a witness between us and you.'

29 "Far be it from us to rebel against the LORD and turn away from him today by building an altar for burnt offerings, grain offerings and sacrifices, other than the altar of the LORD our God that stands before his tabernacle."

30 When Phinehas the priest and the leaders of the community — the heads of the clans of the Israelites — heard what Reuben, Gad and Manasseh had to say, they were pleased. 31 And Phinehas son of Eleazar, the priest, said to Reuben, Gad and Manasseh, "Today we know that the LORD is with us, because you have not been unfaithful to the LORD in this matter. Now you have rescued the Israelites from the LORD's hand."

32 Then Phinehas son of Eleazar, the priest, and the leaders returned to Canaan from their meeting with the Reubenites and Gadites in Gilead and reported to the Israelites. 33 They were glad to hear the report and praised God. And they talked no more about going to war against them to devastate the country where the Reubenites and the Gadites lived.

34 And the Reubenites and the Gadites gave the altar this name: A Witness Between Us — that the LORD is God.

Joshua's Farewell to the Leaders

23 After a long time had passed and the LORD had given Israel rest from all their enemies around them, Joshua, by then a very old man, 2 summoned all Israel — their elders, leaders, judges and officials — and said to them: "I am very old. 3 You yourselves have seen everything the LORD your God has done to all these nations for your sake; it was the LORD your God who fought for you. 4 Remember how I have allotted as an inheritance for your tribes all the land of the nations that remain — the nations I conquered — between the Jordan and the Mediterranean Sea in the west. 5 The LORD your God himself will push them out for your sake. He will drive them out before you, and you will take possession of their land, as the LORD your God promised you.

6 "Be very strong; be careful to obey all that is written in the Book of the Law of Moses, without turning aside to the right or to the left. 7 Do not associate with these

---

[a] 20 The Hebrew term refers to the irrevocable giving over of things or persons to the LORD, often by totally destroying them.

nations that remain among you; do not invoke the names of their gods or swear by them. You must not serve them or bow down to them. 8But you are to hold fast to the Lord your God, as you have until now.

9"The Lord has driven out before you great and powerful nations; to this day no one has been able to withstand you. 10One of you routs a thousand, because the Lord your God fights for you, just as he promised. 11So be very careful to love the Lord your God.

12"But if you turn away and ally yourselves with the survivors of these nations that remain among you and if you intermarry with them and associate with them, 13then you may be sure that the Lord your God will no longer drive out these nations before you. Instead, they will become snares and traps for you, whips on your backs and thorns in your eyes, until you perish from this good land, which the Lord your God has given you.

14"Now I am about to go the way of all the earth. You know with all your heart and soul that not one of all the good promises the Lord your God gave you has failed. Every promise has been fulfilled; not one has failed. 15But just as all the good things the Lord your God has promised you have come to you, so he will bring on you all the evil things he has threatened, until the Lord your God has destroyed you from this good land he has given you. 16If you violate the covenant of the Lord your God, which he commanded you, and go and serve other gods and bow down to them, the Lord's anger will burn against you, and you will quickly perish from the good land he has given you."

The Covenant Renewed at Shechem

24 Then Joshua assembled all the tribes of Israel at Shechem. He summoned the elders, leaders, judges and officials of Israel, and they presented themselves before God.

2Joshua said to all the people, "This is what the Lord, the God of Israel, says: 'Long ago your ancestors, including Terah the father of Abraham and Nahor, lived beyond the Euphrates River and worshiped other gods. 3But I took your father Abraham from the land beyond the Euphrates and led him throughout Canaan and gave him many descendants. I gave him Isaac, 4and to Isaac I gave Jacob and Esau. I assigned the hill country of Seir to Esau, but Jacob and his family went down to Egypt.

5"'Then I sent Moses and Aaron, and I afflicted the Egyptians by what I did there, and I brought you out. 6When I brought your people out of Egypt, you came to the sea, and the Egyptians pursued them with chariots and horsemen*a* as far as the Red Sea.*b* 7But they cried to the Lord for help, and he put darkness between you and the Egyptians; he brought the sea over them and covered them. You saw with your own eyes what I did to the Egyptians. Then you lived in the wilderness for a long time.

8"'I brought you to the land of the Amorites who lived east of the Jordan. They fought against you, but I gave them into your hands. I destroyed them from before you, and you took possession of their land. 9When Balak son of Zippor, the king of Moab, prepared to fight against Israel, he sent for Balaam son of Beor to put a curse on you. 10But I would not listen to Balaam, so he blessed you again and again, and I delivered you out of his hand.

11"'Then you crossed the Jordan and came to Jericho. The citizens of Jericho fought against you, as did also the Amorites, Perizzites, Canaanites, Hittites, Girgashites, Hivites and Jebusites, but I gave them into your hands. 12I sent the hornet ahead of you, which drove them out before you—also the two Amorite kings. You did not do it with your own sword and bow. 13So I gave you a land on which you did not toil and cities you did not build; and you

a 6 Or charioteers   *b 6 Or the Sea of Reeds*

live in them and eat from vineyards and olive groves that you did not plant.'

¹⁴"Now fear the LORD and serve him with all faithfulness. Throw away the gods your ancestors worshiped beyond the Euphrates River and in Egypt, and serve the LORD. ¹⁵But if serving the LORD seems undesirable to you, then choose for yourselves this day whom you will serve, whether the gods your ancestors served beyond the Euphrates, or the gods of the Amorites, in whose land you are living. But as for me and my household, we will serve the LORD."

¹⁶Then the people answered, "Far be it from us to forsake the LORD to serve other gods! ¹⁷It was the LORD our God himself who brought us and our parents up out of Egypt, from that land of slavery, and performed those great signs before our eyes. He protected us on our entire journey and among all the nations through which we traveled. ¹⁸And the LORD drove out before us all the nations, including the Amorites, who lived in the land. We too will serve the LORD, because he is our God."

¹⁹Joshua said to the people, "You are not

SPIRITUAL INVENTORY LESSON [*Principle Four*]

For the previous entry in the SPIRITUAL INVENTORY lesson,
go to 1 Corinthians 6:19–20 (page 1425).

For a discussion of Principles One through Eight and a listing of their related lessons,
go to pages xvii–xliv.

If serving the LORD seems undesirable to you, then choose for yourselves this day whom you will serve ... But as for me and my household, we will serve the LORD.

JOSHUA 24:15

Principle Four begins the process of "coming clean." It's here that we openly examine and confess our faults to ourselves, to God and to someone else we trust. In the first part of Principle Four we openly examine our lives.

As part of completing Principle Four, we do a SPIRITUAL INVENTORY. We look at eight critical areas of our lives. The seventh area is OUR FAMILY. In the Old Testament, Joshua, Israel's leader, made a bold statement regarding his own family: "As for me and my household, we will serve the LORD."

We need to ask ourselves the following questions with regard to our families:

1. Have we mistreated anyone in our family?

2. Against whom in our family do we harbor resentment?

3. To whom do we owe amends?

4. What family secret have we been denying?

God designed families to serve as our safety net from life's storms. To the extent that this depends on us, we need to provide a haven for our family. If that isn't possible and we ourselves don't feel safe there, we should let the church or Celebrate Recovery serve in the role of family for us.

The eighth and final area of our Spiritual Inventory is OUR CHURCH.
Go to Hebrews 10:25 (page 1532).

able to serve the LORD. He is a holy God; he is a jealous God. He will not forgive your rebellion and your sins. ²⁰If you forsake the LORD and serve foreign gods, he will turn and bring disaster on you and make an end of you, after he has been good to you."

²¹But the people said to Joshua, "No! We will serve the LORD."

²²Then Joshua said, "You are witnesses against yourselves that you have chosen to serve the LORD."

"Yes, we are witnesses," they replied.

²³"Now then," said Joshua, "throw away the foreign gods that are among you and yield your hearts to the LORD, the God of Israel."

²⁴And the people said to Joshua, "We will serve the LORD our God and obey him."

²⁵On that day Joshua made a covenant for the people, and there at Shechem he reaffirmed for them decrees and laws. ²⁶And Joshua recorded these things in the Book of the Law of God. Then he took a large stone and set it up there under the oak near the holy place of the LORD.

²⁷"See!" he said to all the people. "This stone will be a witness against us. It has heard all the words the LORD has said to us. It will be a witness against you if you are untrue to your God."

²⁸Then Joshua dismissed the people, each to their own inheritance.

Buried in the Promised Land

²⁹After these things, Joshua son of Nun, the servant of the LORD, died at the age of a hundred and ten. ³⁰And they buried him in the land of his inheritance, at Timnath Serah^a in the hill country of Ephraim, north of Mount Gaash.

³¹Israel served the LORD throughout the lifetime of Joshua and of the elders who outlived him and who had experienced everything the LORD had done for Israel.

³²And Joseph's bones, which the Israelites had brought up from Egypt, were buried at Shechem in the tract of land that Jacob bought for a hundred pieces of silver^b from the sons of Hamor, the father of Shechem. This became the inheritance of Joseph's descendants.

³³And Eleazar son of Aaron died and was buried at Gibeah, which had been allotted to his son Phinehas in the hill country of Ephraim.

---

^a 30 Also known as *Timnath Heres* (see Judges 2:9)   ^b 32 Hebrew *hundred kesitahs*; a kesitah was a unit of money of unknown weight and value.

Judges

THEME: Through the repeated cycle of disobedience, oppression, repentance and deliverance, Judges portrays God as a God of both judgment and forgiveness.

AUTHOR: The author of Judges is unknown. Jewish tradition attributes the book to the prophet Samuel, but it may have been written by one of Samuel's associates or by a compiler during the period after the exile.

DATE OF WRITING: Judges was probably written around 1000 BC, during the time of the monarchy — the later period during which Israel was ruled by kings rather than judges.

ENCOURAGEMENT FROM JUDGES: "The LORD relented because of their groaning under those who oppressed and afflicted them (Judges 2:18).

CHALLENGE FROM JUDGES: "The LORD is with you, mighty warrior . . . Go in the strength you have . . . I will be with you" (Judges 6:12,14,16).

REFLECTION FROM JUDGES: "In those days Israel had no king; everyone did as they saw fit" (Judges 21:25).

Recovery Themes in Judges

In Judges, the people of Israel, now occupying the promised land, begin to compromise their faith and obedience. Even after having experienced God's victory in taking the land, they begin to turn their hearts from him and worship idols. Periodically, when they cry out in repentance to God, he raises up a judge to free them from their oppressors. Yet in a tragically repetitive cycle, as soon as a particular judge dies, the people revert back to their idolatry. The book closes (see Reflection from Judges, above) with a telling commentary on Israel's spiritual state of affairs.

Unfortunately, relapse is a reality for many in recovery. Even after experiencing the once-and-for-all grace of Jesus Christ, we can sometimes get bogged down in the affairs of the world and return to our old addictions or compulsive behaviors. Thankfully, when we return to Jesus with a repentant heart, we are forgiven.

In recovery we must do all we can to avoid relapse, the consequences of which can be disastrous. By keeping our minds centered on Jesus and what he's done for us, we can avoid making decisions that will turn us back to our old ways. The message of Judges, though, is that God is ready to receive back those who repent and turn to him. He wants us to make victory, not defeat, the pattern of our lives.

Israel Fights the Remaining Canaanites

1 After the death of Joshua, the Israelites asked the LORD, "Who of us is to go up first to fight against the Canaanites?"

²The LORD answered, "Judah shall go up; I have given the land into their hands."

³The men of Judah then said to the Simeonites their fellow Israelites, "Come up with us into the territory allotted to us, to

fight against the Canaanites. We in turn will go with you into yours." So the Simeonites went with them.

4When Judah attacked, the LORD gave the Canaanites and Perizzites into their hands, and they struck down ten thousand men at Bezek. 5It was there that they found Adoni-Bezek and fought against him, putting to rout the Canaanites and Perizzites. 6Adoni-Bezek fled, but they chased him and caught him, and cut off his thumbs and big toes.

7Then Adoni-Bezek said, "Seventy kings with their thumbs and big toes cut off have picked up scraps under my table. Now God has paid me back for what I did to them." They brought him to Jerusalem, and he died there.

8The men of Judah attacked Jerusalem also and took it. They put the city to the sword and set it on fire.

9After that, Judah went down to fight against the Canaanites living in the hill country, the Negev and the western foothills. 10They advanced against the Canaanites living in Hebron (formerly called Kiriath Arba) and defeated Sheshai, Ahiman and Talmai. 11From there they advanced against the people living in Debir (formerly called Kiriath Sepher).

12And Caleb said, "I will give my daughter Aksah in marriage to the man who attacks and captures Kiriath Sepher." 13Othniel son of Kenaz, Caleb's younger brother, took it; so Caleb gave his daughter Aksah to him in marriage.

14One day when she came to Othniel, she urged him*a* to ask her father for a field. When she got off her donkey, Caleb asked her, "What can I do for you?"

15She replied, "Do me a special favor. Since you have given me land in the Negev, give me also springs of water." So Caleb gave her the upper and lower springs.

16The descendants of Moses' father-in-law, the Kenite, went up from the City of Palms*b* with the people of Judah to live among the inhabitants of the Desert of Judah in the Negev near Arad.

17Then the men of Judah went with the Simeonites their fellow Israelites and attacked the Canaanites living in Zephath, and they totally destroyed*c* the city. Therefore it was called Hormah.*d* 18Judah also took*e* Gaza, Ashkelon and Ekron — each city with its territory.

19The LORD was with the men of Judah. They took possession of the hill country, but they were unable to drive the people from the plains, because they had chariots fitted with iron. 20As Moses had promised, Hebron was given to Caleb, who drove from it the three sons of Anak. 21The Benjamites, however, did not drive out the Jebusites, who were living in Jerusalem; to this day the Jebusites live there with the Benjamites.

22Now the tribes of Joseph attacked Bethel, and the LORD was with them. 23When they sent men to spy out Bethel (formerly called Luz), 24the spies saw a man coming out of the city and they said to him, "Show us how to get into the city and we will see that you are treated well." 25So he showed them, and they put the city to the sword but spared the man and his whole family. 26He then went to the land of the Hittites, where he built a city and called it Luz, which is its name to this day.

27But Manasseh did not drive out the people of Beth Shan or Taanach or Dor or Ibleam or Megiddo and their surrounding settlements, for the Canaanites were determined to live in that land. 28When Israel became strong, they pressed the Canaanites into forced labor but never drove them out completely. 29Nor did Ephraim drive out the Canaanites living in Gezer, but the Canaanites continued to live there among them. 30Neither did Zebulun drive out the

---

a 14 Hebrew; Septuagint and Vulgate *Othniel, he urged her*   *b 16* That is, Jericho   *c 17* The Hebrew term refers to the irrevocable giving over of things or persons to the LORD, often by totally destroying them.   *d 17* *Hormah* means *destruction.*   *e 18* Hebrew; Septuagint *Judah did not take*

Canaanites living in Kitron or Nahalol, so these Canaanites lived among them, but Zebulun did subject them to forced labor. [31]Nor did Asher drive out those living in Akko or Sidon or Ahlab or Akzib or Helbah or Aphek or Rehob. [32]The Asherites lived among the Canaanite inhabitants of the land because they did not drive them out. [33]Neither did Naphtali drive out those living in Beth Shemesh or Beth Anath; but the Naphtalites too lived among the Canaanite inhabitants of the land, and those living in Beth Shemesh and Beth Anath became forced laborers for them. [34]The Amorites confined the Danites to the hill country, not allowing them to come down into the plain. [35]And the Amorites were determined also to hold out in Mount Heres, Aijalon and Shaalbim, but when the power of the tribes of Joseph increased, they too were pressed into forced labor. [36]The boundary of the Amorites was from Scorpion Pass to Sela and beyond.

The Angel of the LORD at Bokim

2 The angel of the LORD went up from Gilgal to Bokim and said, "I brought you up out of Egypt and led you into the land I swore to give to your ancestors. I said, 'I will never break my covenant with you, [2]and you shall not make a covenant with the people of this land, but you shall break down their altars.' Yet you have disobeyed me. Why have you done this? [3]And I have also said, 'I will not drive them out before you; they will become traps for you, and their gods will become snares to you.'"

[4]When the angel of the LORD had spoken these things to all the Israelites, the people wept aloud, [5]and they called that place Bokim.[a] There they offered sacrifices to the LORD.

Disobedience and Defeat

[6]After Joshua had dismissed the Israelites, they went to take possession of the land, each to their own inheritance. [7]The people served the LORD throughout the lifetime of Joshua and of the elders who outlived him and who had seen all the great things the LORD had done for Israel.

[8]Joshua son of Nun, the servant of the LORD, died at the age of a hundred and ten. [9]And they buried him in the land of his inheritance, at Timnath Heres[b] in the hill country of Ephraim, north of Mount Gaash.

[10]After that whole generation had been gathered to their ancestors, another generation grew up who knew neither the LORD nor what he had done for Israel. [11]Then the Israelites did evil in the eyes of the LORD and served the Baals. [12]They forsook the LORD, the God of their ancestors, who had brought them out of Egypt. They followed and worshiped various gods of the peoples around them. They aroused the LORD's anger [13]because they forsook him and served Baal and the Ashtoreths. [14]In his anger against Israel the LORD gave them into the hands of raiders who plundered them. He sold them into the hands of their enemies all around, whom they were no longer able to resist. [15]Whenever Israel went out to fight, the hand of the LORD was against them to defeat them, just as he had sworn to them. They were in great distress.

[16]Then the LORD raised up judges,[c] who saved them out of the hands of these raiders. [17]Yet they would not listen to their judges but prostituted themselves to other gods and worshiped them. They quickly turned from the ways of their ancestors, who had been obedient to the LORD's commands. [18]Whenever the LORD raised up a judge for them, he was with the judge and saved them out of the hands of their enemies as long as the judge lived; for the LORD relented because of their groaning under those who oppressed and afflicted them. [19]But when the judge died, the people returned to ways even more corrupt than

---

[a] 5 *Bokim* means *weepers.*   [b] 9 Also known as *Timnath Serah* (see Joshua 19:50 and 24:30)   [c] 16 Or *leaders*; similarly in verses 17-19

those of their ancestors, following other gods and serving and worshiping them. They refused to give up their evil practices and stubborn ways.

20Therefore the LORD was very angry with Israel and said, "Because this nation has violated the covenant I ordained for their ancestors and has not listened to me, 21I will no longer drive out before them any of the nations Joshua left when he died. 22I will use them to test Israel and see whether they will keep the way of the LORD and walk in it as their ancestors did." 23The LORD had allowed those nations to remain; he did not drive them out at once by giving them into the hands of Joshua.

3 These are the nations the LORD left to test all those Israelites who had not experienced any of the wars in Canaan 2(he did this only to teach warfare to the descendants of the Israelites who had not had previous battle experience): 3the five rulers of the Philistines, all the Canaanites, the Sidonians, and the Hivites living in the Lebanon mountains from Mount Baal Hermon to Lebo Hamath. 4They were left to test the Israelites to see whether they would obey the LORD's commands, which he had given their ancestors through Moses.

5The Israelites lived among the Canaanites, Hittites, Amorites, Perizzites, Hivites and Jebusites. 6They took their daughters in marriage and gave their own daughters to their sons, and served their gods.

Othniel

7The Israelites did evil in the eyes of the LORD; they forgot the LORD their God and served the Baals and the Asherahs. 8The anger of the LORD burned against Israel so that he sold them into the hands of Cushan-Rishathaim king of Aram Naharaim,a to whom the Israelites were subject for eight years. 9But when they cried out to the LORD, he raised up for them a deliver-

er, Othniel son of Kenaz, Caleb's younger brother, who saved them. 10The Spirit of the LORD came on him, so that he became Israel's judgeb and went to war. The LORD gave Cushan-Rishathaim king of Aram into the hands of Othniel, who overpowered him. 11So the land had peace for forty years, until Othniel son of Kenaz died.

Ehud

12Again the Israelites did evil in the eyes of the LORD, and because they did this evil the LORD gave Eglon king of Moab power over Israel. 13Getting the Ammonites and Amalekites to join him, Eglon came and attacked Israel, and they took possession of the City of Palms.c 14The Israelites were subject to Eglon king of Moab for eighteen years.

15Again the Israelites cried out to the LORD, and he gave them a deliverer — Ehud, a left-handed man, the son of Gera the Benjamite. The Israelites sent him with tribute to Eglon king of Moab. 16Now Ehud had made a double-edged sword about a cubitd long, which he strapped to his right thigh under his clothing. 17He presented the tribute to Eglon king of Moab, who was a very fat man. 18After Ehud had presented the tribute, he sent on their way those who had carried it. 19But on reaching the stone images near Gilgal he himself went back to Eglon and said, "Your Majesty, I have a secret message for you."

The king said to his attendants, "Leave us!" And they all left.

20Ehud then approached him while he was sitting alone in the upper room of his palacee and said, "I have a message from God for you." As the king rose from his seat, 21Ehud reached with his left hand, drew the sword from his right thigh and plunged it into the king's belly. 22Even the handle sank in after the blade, and his bowels discharged. Ehud did not pull the sword out, and the fat closed in over it. 23Then

---

a 8 That is, Northwest Mesopotamia   b 10 Or leader   c 13 That is, Jericho   d 16 That is, about 18 inches or about 45 centimeters   e 20 The meaning of the Hebrew for this word is uncertain; also in verse 24.

Ehud went out to the porch[a]; he shut the doors of the upper room behind him and locked them.

²⁴After he had gone, the servants came and found the doors of the upper room locked. They said, "He must be relieving himself in the inner room of the palace." ²⁵They waited to the point of embarrassment, but when he did not open the doors of the room, they took a key and unlocked them. There they saw their lord fallen to the floor, dead.

²⁶While they waited, Ehud got away. He passed by the stone images and escaped to Seirah. ²⁷When he arrived there, he blew a trumpet in the hill country of Ephraim, and the Israelites went down with him from the hills, with him leading them.

²⁸"Follow me," he ordered, "for the LORD has given Moab, your enemy, into your hands." So they followed him down and took possession of the fords of the Jordan that led to Moab; they allowed no one to cross over. ²⁹At that time they struck down about ten thousand Moabites, all vigorous and strong; not one escaped. ³⁰That day Moab was made subject to Israel, and the land had peace for eighty years.

Shamgar

³¹After Ehud came Shamgar son of Anath, who struck down six hundred Philistines with an oxgoad. He too saved Israel.

Deborah

4 Again the Israelites did evil in the eyes of the LORD, now that Ehud was dead. ²So the LORD sold them into the hands of Jabin king of Canaan, who reigned in Hazor. Sisera, the commander of his army, was based in Harosheth Haggoyim. ³Because he had nine hundred chariots fitted with iron and had cruelly oppressed the Israelites for twenty years, they cried to the LORD for help.

⁴Now Deborah, a prophet, the wife of Lappidoth, was leading[b] Israel at that time. ⁵She held court under the Palm of Deborah between Ramah and Bethel in the hill country of Ephraim, and the Israelites went up to her to have their disputes decided. ⁶She sent for Barak son of Abinoam from Kedesh in Naphtali and said to him, "The LORD, the God of Israel, commands you: 'Go, take with you ten thousand men of Naphtali and Zebulun and lead them up to Mount Tabor. ⁷I will lead Sisera, the commander of Jabin's army, with his chariots and his troops to the Kishon River and give him into your hands.'"

⁸Barak said to her, "If you go with me, I will go; but if you don't go with me, I won't go."

⁹"Certainly I will go with you," said Deborah. "But because of the course you are taking, the honor will not be yours, for the LORD will deliver Sisera into the hands of a woman." So Deborah went with Barak to Kedesh. ¹⁰There Barak summoned Zebulun and Naphtali, and ten thousand men went up under his command. Deborah also went up with him.

¹¹Now Heber the Kenite had left the other Kenites, the descendants of Hobab, Moses' brother-in-law,[c] and pitched his tent by the great tree in Zaanannim near Kedesh.

¹²When they told Sisera that Barak son of Abinoam had gone up to Mount Tabor, ¹³Sisera summoned from Harosheth Haggoyim to the Kishon River all his men and his nine hundred chariots fitted with iron.

¹⁴Then Deborah said to Barak, "Go! This is the day the LORD has given Sisera into your hands. Has not the LORD gone ahead of you?" So Barak went down Mount Tabor, with ten thousand men following him. ¹⁵At Barak's advance, the LORD routed Sisera and all his chariots and army by the sword, and Sisera got down from his chariot and fled on foot.

¹⁶Barak pursued the chariots and army as far as Harosheth Haggoyim, and all Sisera's troops fell by the sword; not a man was

---

[a] 23 The meaning of the Hebrew for this word is uncertain.   [b] 4 Traditionally *judging*   [c] 11 Or *father-in-law*

MY NAME IS DEBORAH

JUDGES 4

Victory isn't achieved in a vacuum. Many forces come together in our fight to be free of our hurts, hang-ups and habits. Deborah was the fourth judge God raised up to deliver his people from their enemies. These judges were primarily dedicated to leading the Israelites in battle against their enemies. Deborah was one of the greatest of the judges in this capacity. But she also "held court under the Palm of Deborah," where many "went up to her to have their disputes decided" (Judges 4:5). This description reminds us more of the mediation role of a modern judge, and it's a vital one when it comes to recovery. Recovery requires that we evaluate all our relationships, offer forgiveness and, where appropriate, make amends (Principle Six; see Matthew 5:7,9).

Ironically, Deborah's peacemaking ability was essential to her success as a warrior. Every real victory in life is a spiritual victory, a triumph given by God. And any war, including a ministry of recovery, needs its leaders. Celebrate Recovery operates in the center of spiritual warfare, often as the last hope for severely wounded warriors. Recovery leaders can't hope to be successful unless they consistently work to heal the hurting relationships in their life and ministry. They need to disengage themselves from conflict, both for their own sakes and as models for others to emulate.

Israel won a decisive battle through God's intervention. Her army was outnumbered and her technology inferior, but God sent a storm to bog down the Canaanite chariots and engineered the death of the Canaanite general, Sisera (see Judges 4:11 – 24; 5:19 – 27). God gave Israel the victory, a triumph that brought peace to God's people for 40 years.

What was God's strategy? He worked through leaders who had abandoned personal, sinful pride (see 4:6 – 10) — a prerequisite for anyone who longs to experience the riches of recovery, but most critically so for leaders. Deborah could have chosen to lead the army herself, but instead she called upon Barak, who suffered from a paralyzing fear due to a lack of trust in God. Note, however, that Barak did not hesitate when Deborah rebuked him, pointing out that if she came along "the honor will not be yours, for the LORD will deliver Sisera into the hands of a woman" (v. 9). In these ancient times it was considered a disgrace for a soldier to die at the hands of a woman, and this would be considered a personal reflection against Barak.

These two individuals were concerned about the desperate condition of the enslaved Israelites and were willing to promote God's glory, not their own. These same two priorities must dominate any successful recovery experience and must be characteristic of leaders in Celebrate Recovery. Pride is the enemy of peace — and only peacemakers can lead in God's battles.

left. ¹⁷Sisera, meanwhile, fled on foot to the tent of Jael, the wife of Heber the Kenite, because there was an alliance between Jabin king of Hazor and the family of Heber the Kenite.

¹⁸Jael went out to meet Sisera and said to him, "Come, my lord, come right in. Don't be afraid." So he entered her tent, and she covered him with a blanket.

¹⁹"I'm thirsty," he said. "Please give me some water." She opened a skin of milk, gave him a drink, and covered him up.

²⁰"Stand in the doorway of the tent," he told her. "If someone comes by and asks you, 'Is anyone in there?' say 'No.'"

²¹But Jael, Heber's wife, picked up a tent peg and a hammer and went quietly to him while he lay fast asleep, exhausted. She drove the peg through his temple into the ground, and he died.

²²Just then Barak came by in pursuit of Sisera, and Jael went out to meet him. "Come," she said, "I will show you the man you're looking for." So he went in with her, and there lay Sisera with the tent peg through his temple — dead.

²³On that day God subdued Jabin king of Canaan before the Israelites. ²⁴And the hand of the Israelites pressed harder and harder against Jabin king of Canaan until they destroyed him.

The Song of Deborah

5 On that day Deborah and Barak son of Abinoam sang this song:

²"When the princes in Israel take the
    lead,
  when the people willingly offer
    themselves —
  praise the LORD!

³"Hear this, you kings! Listen, you
    rulers!
  I, even I, will sing to^a the LORD;
  I will praise the LORD, the God of
    Israel, in song.

⁴"When you, LORD, went out from Seir,
  when you marched from the land of
    Edom,
 the earth shook, the heavens poured,
  the clouds poured down water.
⁵The mountains quaked before the
    LORD, the One of Sinai,
  before the LORD, the God of Israel.

⁶"In the days of Shamgar son of Anath,
  in the days of Jael, the highways were
    abandoned;
  travelers took to winding paths.
⁷Villagers in Israel would not fight;
  they held back until I, Deborah,
    arose,
  until I arose, a mother in Israel.
⁸God chose new leaders
  when war came to the city gates,
 but not a shield or spear was seen
  among forty thousand in Israel.
⁹My heart is with Israel's princes,
  with the willing volunteers among
    the people.
  Praise the LORD!

¹⁰"You who ride on white donkeys,
  sitting on your saddle blankets,
  and you who walk along the road,
 consider ¹¹the voice of the singers^b at
    the watering places.
  They recite the victories of the LORD,
  the victories of his villagers in Israel.

"Then the people of the LORD
  went down to the city gates.
¹²'Wake up, wake up, Deborah!
  Wake up, wake up, break out in song!
 Arise, Barak!
  Take captive your captives, son of
    Abinoam.'

¹³"The remnant of the nobles came down;
  the people of the LORD came down to
    me against the mighty.
¹⁴Some came from Ephraim, whose roots
    were in Amalek;
  Benjamin was with the people who
    followed you.

---

^a 3 Or of   ^b 11 The meaning of the Hebrew for this word is uncertain.

From Makir captains came down,
    from Zebulun those who bear a
        commander's*a* staff.
15 The princes of Issachar were with
    Deborah;
    yes, Issachar was with Barak,
    sent under his command into the
        valley.
In the districts of Reuben
    there was much searching of heart.
16 Why did you stay among the sheep
    pens*b*
    to hear the whistling for the flocks?
In the districts of Reuben
    there was much searching of heart.
17 Gilead stayed beyond the Jordan.
    And Dan, why did he linger by the
        ships?
Asher remained on the coast
    and stayed in his coves.
18 The people of Zebulun risked their very
        lives;
    so did Naphtali on the terraced fields.

19 "Kings came, they fought,
    the kings of Canaan fought.
At Taanach, by the waters of Megiddo,
    they took no plunder of silver.
20 From the heavens the stars fought,
    from their courses they fought
        against Sisera.
21 The river Kishon swept them away,
    the age-old river, the river Kishon.
    March on, my soul; be strong!
22 Then thundered the horses' hooves —
    galloping, galloping go his mighty
        steeds.
23 'Curse Meroz,' said the angel of the
    LORD.
    'Curse its people bitterly,
    because they did not come to help the
        LORD,
    to help the LORD against the mighty.'

24 "Most blessed of women be Jael,
    the wife of Heber the Kenite,
    most blessed of tent-dwelling women.

25 He asked for water, and she gave him
        milk;
    in a bowl fit for nobles she brought
        him curdled milk.
26 Her hand reached for the tent peg,
    her right hand for the workman's
        hammer.
She struck Sisera, she crushed his head,
    she shattered and pierced his temple.
27 At her feet he sank,
    he fell; there he lay.
At her feet he sank, he fell;
    where he sank, there he fell — dead.

28 "Through the window peered Sisera's
        mother;
    behind the lattice she cried out,
'Why is his chariot so long in coming?
    Why is the clatter of his chariots
        delayed?'
29 The wisest of her ladies answer her;
    indeed, she keeps saying to herself,
30 'Are they not finding and dividing the
        spoils:
    a woman or two for each man,
colorful garments as plunder for Sisera,
    colorful garments embroidered,
highly embroidered garments for my
        neck —
    all this as plunder?'

31 "So may all your enemies perish, LORD!
    But may all who love you be like the
        sun
    when it rises in its strength."

Then the land had peace forty years.

Gideon

6 The Israelites did evil in the eyes
of the LORD, and for seven years
he gave them into the hands of the
Midianites. ² Because the power of Midian
was so oppressive, the Israelites prepared
shelters for themselves in mountain clefts,
caves and strongholds. ³ Whenever the Israelites planted their crops, the Midianites, Amalekites and other eastern peoples

---

a 14 The meaning of the Hebrew for this word is uncertain.   *b 16* Or *the campfires*; or *the saddlebags*

My Name Is Norma

I'M A BELIEVER WHO STRUGGLES WITH CODEPENDENCY AND ANGER

Please read the story of Deborah's leadership of God's people in Judges 4.

I was raised in a loving Christian home with godly parents and a lot of love. As the oldest of three, I was quite typical of a child in that position. I considered myself to be like Deborah, Israel's judge and peacemaker, since I worked hard at caring for others. But because I had a habit of pointing out every broken rule, I also felt unappreciated.

Steve and I met just before I graduated from high school. We dated for two years and then married. The first time I ever truly had to give something to God was when we realized in the third month of my pregnancy that our baby wouldn't live. I was shocked and crushed, but my husband immediately reminded me to depend on God and "take things one day at a time."

In the early 1980s financial difficulty brought us to the brink of bankruptcy and the loss of our home, but God intervened, and we slowly began to recover financially. Then we faced a bitter lawsuit, again with the potential of financial ruin, but once again we relied on God. We won the lawsuit and gave God the glory. These markers are important because they were turning points for us — pivotal moments when we turned over our wills to God.

In August, 2001, I attended a Celebrate Recovery meeting at Saddleback Church to check out this Christ-centered ministry. As I learned about recovery, I was forced to admit to myself that there was a part of my heart that was resentful and angry regarding my marriage. Steve and I were different in the ways we communicated, and our conflicts caused us both pain. We had created many unhealthy habits over the years by continuing to repeat the same mistakes over and over again. I had thought — mistakenly, as I would come to learn — that I could live with these bitter feelings because everything else was so good. I'll never forget sitting at the table at home after one meeting and crying as God called me to be a leader, like Deborah. He wanted me to serve in this ministry of recovery, not just for my own benefit but also to help others.

I had spent the majority of our 32 years together using Steve's anger as an excuse for my pain. It was easy to point to him as the culprit, which then let *me* off the hook. I had read

Matthew 7:3 ("Why do you look at the speck of sawdust in your brother's eye and pay no attention to the plank in your own eye?") many times, but each time I had missed its application for me, refusing to see myself as the one in need of change.

The more information I received about Celebrate Recovery, the more aware I became that I needed to step out of denial and confess the hidden hurts and chaos in my own life and marriage. As I worked the principles, God began to show me my hidden motives, my self-righteous attitude and my other character flaws. I was controlling, critical and perfectionistic — the very traits I deplore in others.

I must also admit that I spend a lot of energy trying to make sure other people are happy, often at my own expense — a cycle that continues to build within me a resentment of others. I'm a "people pleaser" who finds it difficult to say no. I've learned through Celebrate Recovery that my desire to please others has kept me from creating healthy relationships, and I'm learning to look to God for affirmation.

Principle Six was the most difficult principle for me, but it was also the one that changed my heart. I remember the night I apologized to Steve from my heart for my arrogance in blaming him totally for the problems in our marriage. I believe now that my anger, resentment and bitterness may have hurt our marriage more than Steve's anger. Step Nine of the Christ-centered 12 steps was a turning point for us. God began to change me, giving me an awesome peace and joy in our marriage. Self-pity began to disappear, and my selfish, negative thoughts surfaced less frequently. God began erasing my past hurts and replacing them with future memories we were creating in the present. The change in Steve is obvious, as I now live with a softer-spoken, humbled husband who is turning over his tendency to harbor anger toward God. In fact, we're both learning to relinquish to God our controlling tendencies. Through the process our marriage has been healed and cleansed, and we're experiencing a new closeness, tenderness and intimacy.

I have come to understand that pain is an unavoidable part of life but that I do have a choice regarding my response to hurts and my tendency to harbor bitterness in my heart. I have found Psalm 32:3 – 5 to be a reflection of my thoughts:

> When I kept silent, my bones wasted away through my groaning all day long. For day and night your hand was heavy on me; my strength was sapped as in the heat of summer. Then I acknowledged my sin to you and did not cover up my iniquity. I said, "I will confess my transgressions to the LORD." And you forgave the guilt of my sin.

invaded the country. ⁴They camped on the land and ruined the crops all the way to Gaza and did not spare a living thing for Israel, neither sheep nor cattle nor donkeys. ⁵They came up with their livestock and their tents like swarms of locusts. It was impossible to count them or their camels; they invaded the land to ravage it. ⁶Midian so impoverished the Israelites that they cried out to the Lord for help.

⁷When the Israelites cried out to the Lord because of Midian, ⁸he sent them a prophet, who said, "This is what the Lord, the God of Israel, says: I brought you up out of Egypt, out of the land of slavery. ⁹I rescued you from the hand of the Egyptians. And I delivered you from the hand of all your oppressors; I drove them out before you and gave you their land. ¹⁰I said to you, 'I am the Lord your God; do not worship the gods of the Amorites, in whose land you live.' But you have not listened to me."

¹¹The angel of the Lord came and sat down under the oak in Ophrah that belonged to Joash the Abiezrite, where his son Gideon was threshing wheat in a winepress to keep it from the Midianites. ¹²When the angel of the Lord appeared to Gideon, he said, "The Lord is with you, mighty warrior."

¹³"Pardon me, my lord," Gideon replied, "but if the Lord is with us, why has all this happened to us? Where are all his wonders that our ancestors told us about when they said, 'Did not the Lord bring us up out of Egypt?' But now the Lord has abandoned us and given us into the hand of Midian."

¹⁴The Lord turned to him and said, "Go in the strength you have and save Israel out of Midian's hand. Am I not sending you?"

¹⁵"Pardon me, my lord," Gideon replied, "but how can I save Israel? My clan is the weakest in Manasseh, and I am the least in my family."

¹⁶The Lord answered, "I will be with you, and you will strike down all the Midianites, leaving none alive."

¹⁷Gideon replied, "If now I have found favor in your eyes, give me a sign that it is really you talking to me. ¹⁸Please do not go away until I come back and bring my offering and set it before you."

And the Lord said, "I will wait until you return."

¹⁹Gideon went inside, prepared a young goat, and from an ephah^a of flour he made bread without yeast. Putting the meat in a basket and its broth in a pot, he brought them out and offered them to him under the oak.

²⁰The angel of God said to him, "Take the meat and the unleavened bread, place them on this rock, and pour out the broth." And Gideon did so. ²¹Then the angel of the Lord touched the meat and the unleavened bread with the tip of the staff that was in his hand. Fire flared from the rock, consuming the meat and the bread. And the angel of the Lord disappeared. ²²When Gideon realized that it was the angel of the Lord, he exclaimed, "Alas, Sovereign Lord! I have seen the angel of the Lord face to face!"

²³But the Lord said to him, "Peace! Do not be afraid. You are not going to die."

²⁴So Gideon built an altar to the Lord there and called it The Lord Is Peace. To this day it stands in Ophrah of the Abiezrites.

²⁵That same night the Lord said to him, "Take the second bull from your father's herd, the one seven years old.^{b} Tear down your father's altar to Baal and cut down the Asherah pole^c beside it. ²⁶Then build a proper kind of^d altar to the Lord your God on the top of this height. Using the wood of the Asherah pole that you cut down, offer the second^e bull as a burnt offering."

²⁷So Gideon took ten of his servants and did as the Lord told him. But because he

---

^{a} 19 That is, probably about 36 pounds or about 16 kilograms ^{b} 25 Or *Take a full-grown, mature bull from your father's herd* ^{c} 25 That is, a wooden symbol of the goddess Asherah; also in verses 26, 28 and 30 ^{d} 26 Or *build with layers of stone an* ^{e} 26 Or *full-grown*; also in verse 28

MY NAME IS GIDEON

Gideon is an unlikely hero. We meet him hiding his harvest from the Midianites (see Judges 6:11). Later he reluctantly carried out the Lord's instructions — in the dark because "he was afraid of his family and the townspeople" (v. 27). God was aware of Gideon's fears and patiently built up his faith. He began by identifying Gideon in terms of his future purpose, not his present reality. The angel addressed Gideon: "The LORD is with you, mighty warrior" (v. 12). In Celebrate Recovery we too are defined by our relationship to God, not by our hurts, hang-ups or habits. To the Lord, the man cowering in the winepress was already a mighty warrior. Gideon's response demonstrates the impact of the lies being spread by his culture: "The LORD has abandoned us and given us into the hand of Midian" (v. 13). God had given the Israelites into the hand of the Midianites, not because he had abandoned them, but because Israel "did evil in the eyes of the LORD" (v. 1).

God turned the tables on the spineless Gideon by identifying him as his own choice to set Israel free. Gideon pointed out to God the weakness of his clan and family. God's response was a simple promise: "I will be with you" (v. 16). It's important for us to recognize our helplessness but even more vital to acknowledge God's power. The issues that enslave us will be defeated by God's divine power as we take our first tentative steps of faith. Gideon's next step was worship (see vv. 17–19). In Celebrate Recovery, every Large Group time and every Step Study begins with worship. We shift our focus from our problems to God's person and power.

As Gideon worshiped, the angel performed a sign, and Gideon's pathological fear (dread) of men was replaced by a healthy fear (reverence) of God. Jolted because he had seen "the angel of the LORD face to face" (v. 22), Gideon was reassured that God's desire for him was peace (see v. 24). This peace isn't about the absence of conflict, but about the presence of the wholeness created by God's company. Knowing God as our peace prepares us for a change.

Change has to include the destruction of our idols. God commanded Gideon to destroy the symbols of worship constructed by his own father. Gideon tried to handle this secretly but was identified as the destroyer of the pagan altar (see vv. 25–29). Addiction to a chemical substance or a people-pleasing pattern like codependency is another form of idolatry. An idol may be described as anything that occupies the place God deserves in our life.

Gideon's obedience in destroying his father's altar prepared him to carry out God's plan. But his faithfulness also brought light to his father's darkened heart. When the locals wanted to kill Gideon, his father, Joash, logically pointed out, "If Baal really is a god, he can defend himself when someone breaks down his altar" (v. 31).

Sadly, even Joash's unexpected and dramatic testimony failed to convince Gideon that God could use him to free Israel. This reluctant inductee requested two more signs, both of which God granted (see vv. 36–40). Gideon's at first grudging but later growing faith prepared him for the seemingly strange steps that would lead to victory over Israel's powerful enemies (see ch. 7). Some of the recovering steps may seem equally odd or unnecessary. But each step is critical if we're determined to trek the proven path to freedom.

If addiction could have brought peace, our pain wouldn't be destroying our career, family and life. If manipulation of others had brought satisfaction, we would already know the joy of real love. If bitterness toward our abuser had changed our past, we wouldn't be struggling with shame today. Gideon put out his fleece to test the validity of the Lord's plans (see 6:36–40) — and God came through. That same God will turn us into his "mighty warriors."

was afraid of his family and the townspeople, he did it at night rather than in the daytime.

28In the morning when the people of the town got up, there was Baal's altar, demolished, with the Asherah pole beside it cut down and the second bull sacrificed on the newly built altar!

29They asked each other, "Who did this?"

When they carefully investigated, they were told, "Gideon son of Joash did it."

30The people of the town demanded of Joash, "Bring out your son. He must die, because he has broken down Baal's altar and cut down the Asherah pole beside it."

31But Joash replied to the hostile crowd around him, "Are you going to plead Baal's cause? Are you trying to save him? Whoever fights for him shall be put to death by morning! If Baal really is a god, he can defend himself when someone breaks down his altar." 32So because Gideon broke down Baal's altar, they gave him the name Jerub-Baal*a* that day, saying, "Let Baal contend with him."

33Now all the Midianites, Amalekites and other eastern peoples joined forces and crossed over the Jordan and camped in the Valley of Jezreel. 34Then the Spirit of the LORD came on Gideon, and he blew a trumpet, summoning the Abiezrites to follow him. 35He sent messengers throughout Manasseh, calling them to arms, and also into Asher, Zebulun and Naphtali, so that they too went up to meet them.

36Gideon said to God, "If you will save Israel by my hand as you have promised— 37look, I will place a wool fleece on the threshing floor. If there is dew only on the fleece and all the ground is dry, then I will know that you will save Israel by my hand, as you said." 38And that is what happened. Gideon rose early the next day; he squeezed the fleece and wrung out the dew—a bowlful of water.

39Then Gideon said to God, "Do not be angry with me. Let me make just one more request. Allow me one more test with the fleece, but this time make the fleece dry and let the ground be covered with dew." 40That night God did so. Only the fleece was dry; all the ground was covered with dew.

Gideon Defeats the Midianites

7 Early in the morning, Jerub-Baal (that is, Gideon) and all his men camped at the spring of Harod. The camp of Midian was north of them in the valley near the hill of Moreh. 2The LORD said to Gideon, "You have too many men. I cannot deliver Midian into their hands, or Israel would boast against me, 'My own strength has saved me.' 3Now announce to the army, 'Anyone who trembles with fear may turn back and leave Mount Gilead.'" So twenty-two thousand men left, while ten thousand remained.

4But the LORD said to Gideon, "There are still too many men. Take them down to the water, and I will thin them out for you there. If I say, 'This one shall go with you,' he shall go; but if I say, 'This one shall not go with you,' he shall not go."

5So Gideon took the men down to the water. There the LORD told him, "Separate those who lap the water with their tongues as a dog laps from those who kneel down to drink." 6Three hundred of them drank from cupped hands, lapping like dogs. All the rest got down on their knees to drink.

7The LORD said to Gideon, "With the three hundred men that lapped I will save you and give the Midianites into your hands. Let all the others go home." 8So Gideon sent the rest of the Israelites home but kept the three hundred, who took over the provisions and trumpets of the others.

Now the camp of Midian lay below him in the valley. 9During that night the LORD said to Gideon, "Get up, go down against the camp, because I am going to give it into your hands. 10If you are afraid to attack, go

---

a 32 Jerub-Baal probably means *let Baal contend.*

down to the camp with your servant Purah
[11]and listen to what they are saying. Afterward, you will be encouraged to attack the
camp." So he and Purah his servant went
down to the outposts of the camp. [12]The
Midianites, the Amalekites and all the other eastern peoples had settled in the valley,
thick as locusts. Their camels could no
more be counted than the sand on the seashore.

[13]Gideon arrived just as a man was telling a friend his dream. "I had a dream," he
was saying. "A round loaf of barley bread
came tumbling into the Midianite camp. It
struck the tent with such force that the tent
overturned and collapsed."

[14]His friend responded, "This can be
nothing other than the sword of Gideon
son of Joash, the Israelite. God has given
the Midianites and the whole camp into his
hands."

[15]When Gideon heard the dream and its
interpretation, he bowed down and worshiped. He returned to the camp of Israel
and called out, "Get up! The LORD has giv-
en the Midianite camp into your hands."
[16]Dividing the three hundred men into
three companies, he placed trumpets and
empty jars in the hands of all of them, with
torches inside.

[17]"Watch me," he told them. "Follow my
lead. When I get to the edge of the camp,
do exactly as I do. [18]When I and all who
are with me blow our trumpets, then from
all around the camp blow yours and shout,
'For the LORD and for Gideon.'"

[19]Gideon and the hundred men with
him reached the edge of the camp at the
beginning of the middle watch, just after
they had changed the guard. They blew
their trumpets and broke the jars that were
in their hands. [20]The three companies blew
the trumpets and smashed the jars. Grasping the torches in their left hands and holding in their right hands the trumpets they
were to blow, they shouted, "A sword for
the LORD and for Gideon!" [21]While each
man held his position around the camp, all
the Midianites ran, crying out as they fled.

[22]When the three hundred trumpets sounded, the LORD caused the men
throughout the camp to turn on each other with their swords. The army fled to Beth
Shittah toward Zererah as far as the border
of Abel Meholah near Tabbath. [23]Israelites
from Naphtali, Asher and all Manasseh
were called out, and they pursued the Midianites. [24]Gideon sent messengers throughout the hill country of Ephraim, saying,
"Come down against the Midianites and
seize the waters of the Jordan ahead of
them as far as Beth Barah."

So all the men of Ephraim were called
out and they seized the waters of the Jordan as far as Beth Barah. [25]They also captured two of the Midianite leaders, Oreb
and Zeeb. They killed Oreb at the rock of
Oreb, and Zeeb at the winepress of Zeeb.
They pursued the Midianites and brought
the heads of Oreb and Zeeb to Gideon, who
was by the Jordan.

Zebah and Zalmunna

8 Now the Ephraimites asked Gideon, "Why have you treated us like
this? Why didn't you call us when
you went to fight Midian?" And they challenged him vigorously.

[2]But he answered them, "What have I
accomplished compared to you? Aren't the
gleanings of Ephraim's grapes better than
the full grape harvest of Abiezer? [3]God
gave Oreb and Zeeb, the Midianite leaders, into your hands. What was I able to
do compared to you?" At this, their resentment against him subsided.

[4]Gideon and his three hundred men, exhausted yet keeping up the pursuit, came
to the Jordan and crossed it. [5]He said to
the men of Sukkoth, "Give my troops some
bread; they are worn out, and I am still
pursuing Zebah and Zalmunna, the kings
of Midian."

[6]But the officials of Sukkoth said, "Do
you already have the hands of Zebah and
Zalmunna in your possession? Why should
we give bread to your troops?"

[7]Then Gideon replied, "Just for that,

My Name Is Jan

I'M A BELIEVER WHO STRUGGLES WITH CODEPENDENCY

Please read about Gideon's reluctant obedience and God's use of this "mighty warrior" in Judges 6 and 7.

As a boy, I never knew where I stood with my dad. At times it seemed that we were fairly close, but then aloofness would come between us. I wanted to please both my parents but never quite felt that I did.

I was an average student, but my mind was prone to wandering. When I was 16 years old, I wanted to quit school. After a teacher got me to agree to do my homework, though, the situation improved. But I was convinced that I could never go further in academia. I stated on graduation night that if I ever got into another classroom, it would be too soon.

I joined the U.S. Air Force, though, only to meet with more classrooms and the expectation to learn. And learn I did. In Spain I found some buddies — Jim Beam, Johnny Walker, his brother Hira, and Bud Weiser — who helped me cope with my homesickness. When I sobered up, I found that I was still lonely. Another friend introduced me to Jesus Christ. That's when I began to experience real change. After one buddy died of alcohol poisoning, I began to hang out exclusively with my Christian brothers and sisters. I told the Lord I wanted to do whatever he had in mind for my life.

I enrolled in the University of Maryland and learned Spanish, managing to get my first year of college under my belt before my discharge. I entered the University of New Mexico, majoring in Spanish and Portuguese, after which I pursued a master of divinity degree in seminary, tackling Greek and Hebrew. I pursued much of my higher education in an effort to please those who cared about me — my parents; my wife, Fern; and my children, Penny, James and Paul.

I pastored several churches and then, to keep food on the table, went to work with the New Mexico Corrections Department. I started as a case manager, in training as a correctional officer. Most of the time I was so naive that I didn't have enough sense to be afraid, even of the inmates. I was selected to be a supervisor, a difficult position for me. How could I, a person who wanted to please everyone, be appreciated while supervising in a prison?

I had to hire, promote, fire and discipline staff members, as well as keep the inmates on track. Sometimes my stomach would churn under the pressure.

I was promoted a number of times: to director of programs, deputy warden, warden of a small institution, associate warden of the main penitentiary and finally to deputy warden of another larger prison. I repressed most of my emotions, afraid that no one would understand.

There were nights when I didn't sleep due to worries about staff problems, especially when I had to promote someone over someone else who I knew wanted the position. I didn't know at that point what *codependent* meant, but I was miserable trying to be the "good guy" who needed to be liked.

Sometimes I would "tough it out" alone, but more often I would ask God for his blessing on something I intended to do, asking for a "sign" that he was okay with it. When I retired, I told God that I wanted to serve a small church — and I even told him where: right where I had grown up. But God had other plans.

I'm so glad that I remained open to my Lord. He arranged to bring people into my life who wanted to start a prison ministry program in the same institution from which I had retired. The deputy secretary had a vision for faith-based living units in New Mexico prisons. She got me involved, and I took her suggestion to some friends who had been involved with the Kairos Prison Ministry. I attended a Purpose Driven Church conference in 1998, and we began in December of that year to use Celebrate Recovery in the second state prison in the nation to initiate a faith-based living component. It was also the first state prison to use Celebrate Recovery.

I have always sold myself short, and it may be that I should, because without my real "Higher Power" I wouldn't be helping to bring Celebrate Recovery into numerous prisons and jails across America and to other nations. I now have the honor of serving as the national director of Celebrate Recovery — Inside. I've learned that God can take someone like me — someone who is afraid to take chances and who prefers to stay in the background; someone like Gideon, who hid his harvest, his talent and his life — and use that reluctant individual for his glory. God assured Gideon, "'I will be with you'" (Judges 6:16). He makes that same promise to all of his children, including me.

Jan

when the LORD has given Zebah and Zalmunna into my hand, I will tear your flesh with desert thorns and briers."

⁸From there he went up to Peniel*a* and made the same request of them, but they answered as the men of Sukkoth had. ⁹So he said to the men of Peniel, "When I return in triumph, I will tear down this tower."

¹⁰Now Zebah and Zalmunna were in Karkor with a force of about fifteen thousand men, all that were left of the armies of the eastern peoples; a hundred and twenty thousand swordsmen had fallen. ¹¹Gideon went up by the route of the nomads east of Nobah and Jogbehah and attacked the unsuspecting army. ¹²Zebah and Zalmunna, the two kings of Midian, fled, but he pursued them and captured them, routing their entire army.

¹³Gideon son of Joash then returned from the battle by the Pass of Heres. ¹⁴He caught a young man of Sukkoth and questioned him, and the young man wrote down for him the names of the seventy-seven officials of Sukkoth, the elders of the town. ¹⁵Then Gideon came and said to the men of Sukkoth, "Here are Zebah and Zalmunna, about whom you taunted me by saying, 'Do you already have the hands of Zebah and Zalmunna in your possession? Why should we give bread to your exhausted men?'" ¹⁶He took the elders of the town and taught the men of Sukkoth a lesson by punishing them with desert thorns and briers. ¹⁷He also pulled down the tower of Peniel and killed the men of the town.

¹⁸Then he asked Zebah and Zalmunna, "What kind of men did you kill at Tabor?"

"Men like you," they answered, "each one with the bearing of a prince."

¹⁹Gideon replied, "Those were my brothers, the sons of my own mother. As surely as the LORD lives, if you had spared their lives, I would not kill you." ²⁰Turning to Jether, his oldest son, he said, "Kill them!"

But Jether did not draw his sword, because he was only a boy and was afraid.

²¹Zebah and Zalmunna said, "Come, do it yourself. 'As is the man, so is his strength.'" So Gideon stepped forward and killed them, and took the ornaments off their camels' necks.

Gideon's Ephod

²²The Israelites said to Gideon, "Rule over us — you, your son and your grandson — because you have saved us from the hand of Midian."

²³But Gideon told them, "I will not rule over you, nor will my son rule over you. The LORD will rule over you." ²⁴And he said, "I do have one request, that each of you give me an earring from your share of the plunder." (It was the custom of the Ishmaelites to wear gold earrings.)

²⁵They answered, "We'll be glad to give them." So they spread out a garment, and each of them threw a ring from his plunder onto it. ²⁶The weight of the gold rings he asked for came to seventeen hundred shekels,*b* not counting the ornaments, the pendants and the purple garments worn by the kings of Midian or the chains that were on their camels' necks. ²⁷Gideon made the gold into an ephod, which he placed in Ophrah, his town. All Israel prostituted themselves by worshiping it there, and it became a snare to Gideon and his family.

Gideon's Death

²⁸Thus Midian was subdued before the Israelites and did not raise its head again. During Gideon's lifetime, the land had peace forty years.

²⁹Jerub-Baal son of Joash went back home to live. ³⁰He had seventy sons of his own, for he had many wives. ³¹His concubine, who lived in Shechem, also bore him a son, whom he named Abimelek. ³²Gideon son of Joash died at a good old age and

---

a 8 Hebrew *Penuel,* a variant of *Peniel;* also in verses 9 and 17   *b 26* That is, about 43 pounds or about 20 kilograms was buried in the tomb of his father Joash in Ophrah of the Abiezrites.

³³No sooner had Gideon died than the Israelites again prostituted themselves to the Baals. They set up Baal-Berith as their god ³⁴and did not remember the LORD their God, who had rescued them from the hands of all their enemies on every side. ³⁵They also failed to show any loyalty to the family of Jerub-Baal (that is, Gideon) in spite of all the good things he had done for them.

Abimelek

9 Abimelek son of Jerub-Baal went to his mother's brothers in Shechem and said to them and to all his mother's clan, ²"Ask all the citizens of Shechem, 'Which is better for you: to have all seventy of Jerub-Baal's sons rule over you, or just one man?' Remember, I am your flesh and blood."

³When the brothers repeated all this to the citizens of Shechem, they were inclined to follow Abimelek, for they said, "He is related to us." ⁴They gave him seventy shekels*a* of silver from the temple of Baal-Berith, and Abimelek used it to hire reckless scoundrels, who became his followers. ⁵He went to his father's home in Ophrah and on one stone murdered his seventy brothers, the sons of Jerub-Baal. But Jotham, the youngest son of Jerub-Baal, escaped by hiding. ⁶Then all the citizens of Shechem and Beth Millo gathered beside the great tree at the pillar in Shechem to crown Abimelek king.

⁷When Jotham was told about this, he climbed up on the top of Mount Gerizim and shouted to them, "Listen to me, citizens of Shechem, so that God may listen to you. ⁸One day the trees went out to anoint a king for themselves. They said to the olive tree, 'Be our king.'

⁹"But the olive tree answered, 'Should I give up my oil, by which both gods and humans are honored, to hold sway over the trees?'

¹⁰"Next, the trees said to the fig tree, 'Come and be our king.'

¹¹"But the fig tree replied, 'Should I give up my fruit, so good and sweet, to hold sway over the trees?'

¹²"Then the trees said to the vine, 'Come and be our king.'

¹³"But the vine answered, 'Should I give up my wine, which cheers both gods and humans, to hold sway over the trees?'

¹⁴"Finally all the trees said to the thornbush, 'Come and be our king.'

¹⁵"The thornbush said to the trees, 'If you really want to anoint me king over you, come and take refuge in my shade; but if not, then let fire come out of the thornbush and consume the cedars of Lebanon!'

¹⁶"Have you acted honorably and in good faith by making Abimelek king? Have you been fair to Jerub-Baal and his family? Have you treated him as he deserves? ¹⁷Remember that my father fought for you and risked his life to rescue you from the hand of Midian. ¹⁸But today you have revolted against my father's family. You have murdered his seventy sons on a single stone and have made Abimelek, the son of his female slave, king over the citizens of Shechem because he is related to you. ¹⁹So have you acted honorably and in good faith toward Jerub-Baal and his family today? If you have, may Abimelek be your joy, and may you be his, too! ²⁰But if you have not, let fire come out from Abimelek and consume you, the citizens of Shechem and Beth Millo, and let fire come out from you, the citizens of Shechem and Beth Millo, and consume Abimelek!"

²¹Then Jotham fled, escaping to Beer, and he lived there because he was afraid of his brother Abimelek.

²²After Abimelek had governed Israel three years, ²³God stirred up animosity between Abimelek and the citizens of Shechem so that they acted treacherously against Abimelek. ²⁴God did this in order that the crime against Jerub-Baal's seventy

---

a 4 That is, about 1 3/4 pounds or about 800 grams

sons, the shedding of their blood, might be avenged on their brother Abimelek and on the citizens of Shechem, who had helped him murder his brothers. 25In opposition to him these citizens of Shechem set men on the hilltops to ambush and rob everyone who passed by, and this was reported to Abimelek.

26Now Gaal son of Ebed moved with his clan into Shechem, and its citizens put their confidence in him. 27After they had gone out into the fields and gathered the grapes and trodden them, they held a festival in the temple of their god. While they were eating and drinking, they cursed Abimelek. 28Then Gaal son of Ebed said, "Who is Abimelek, and why should we Shechemites be subject to him? Isn't he Jerub-Baal's son, and isn't Zebul his deputy? Serve the family of Hamor, Shechem's father! Why should we serve Abimelek? 29If only this people were under my command! Then I would get rid of him. I would say to Abimelek, 'Call out your whole army!' "*a*

30When Zebul the governor of the city heard what Gaal son of Ebed said, he was very angry. 31Under cover he sent messengers to Abimelek, saying, "Gaal son of Ebed and his clan have come to Shechem and are stirring up the city against you. 32Now then, during the night you and your men should come and lie in wait in the fields. 33In the morning at sunrise, advance against the city. When Gaal and his men come out against you, seize the opportunity to attack them."

34So Abimelek and all his troops set out by night and took up concealed positions near Shechem in four companies. 35Now Gaal son of Ebed had gone out and was standing at the entrance of the city gate just as Abimelek and his troops came out from their hiding place.

36When Gaal saw them, he said to Zebul, "Look, people are coming down from the tops of the mountains!"

Zebul replied, "You mistake the shadows of the mountains for men."

37But Gaal spoke up again: "Look, people are coming down from the central hill,*b* and a company is coming from the direction of the diviners' tree."

38Then Zebul said to him, "Where is your big talk now, you who said, 'Who is Abimelek that we should be subject to him?' Aren't these the men you ridiculed? Go out and fight them!"

39So Gaal led out*c* the citizens of Shechem and fought Abimelek. 40Abimelek chased him all the way to the entrance of the gate, and many were killed as they fled. 41Then Abimelek stayed in Arumah, and Zebul drove Gaal and his clan out of Shechem.

42The next day the people of Shechem went out to the fields, and this was reported to Abimelek. 43So he took his men, divided them into three companies and set an ambush in the fields. When he saw the people coming out of the city, he rose to attack them. 44Abimelek and the companies with him rushed forward to a position at the entrance of the city gate. Then two companies attacked those in the fields and struck them down. 45All that day Abimelek pressed his attack against the city until he had captured it and killed its people. Then he destroyed the city and scattered salt over it.

46On hearing this, the citizens in the tower of Shechem went into the stronghold of the temple of El-Berith. 47When Abimelek heard that they had assembled there, 48he and all his men went up Mount Zalmon. He took an ax and cut off some branches, which he lifted to his shoulders. He ordered the men with him, "Quick! Do what you have seen me do!" 49So all the men cut branches and followed Abimelek. They piled them against the stronghold and set it on fire with the people still inside. So all the people in the tower of Shechem, about a thousand men and women, also died.

---

a 29 Septuagint; Hebrew *him.*" *Then he said to Abimelek, "Call out your whole army!"*   *b 37* The Hebrew for this phrase means *the navel of the earth.*   *c 39* Or *Gaal went out in the sight of*

⁵⁰Next Abimelek went to Thebez and besieged it and captured it. ⁵¹Inside the city, however, was a strong tower, to which all the men and women — all the people of the city — had fled. They had locked themselves in and climbed up on the tower roof. ⁵²Abimelek went to the tower and attacked it. But as he approached the entrance to the tower to set it on fire, ⁵³a woman dropped an upper millstone on his head and cracked his skull.

⁵⁴Hurriedly he called to his armor-bearer, "Draw your sword and kill me, so that they can't say, 'A woman killed him.'" So his servant ran him through, and he died. ⁵⁵When the Israelites saw that Abimelek was dead, they went home.

⁵⁶Thus God repaid the wickedness that Abimelek had done to his father by murdering his seventy brothers. ⁵⁷God also made the people of Shechem pay for all their wickedness. The curse of Jotham son of Jerub-Baal came on them.

Tola

10 After the time of Abimelek, a man of Issachar named Tola son of Puah, the son of Dodo, rose to save Israel. He lived in Shamir, in the hill country of Ephraim. ²He led*ᵃ* Israel twenty-three years; then he died, and was buried in Shamir.

Jair

³He was followed by Jair of Gilead, who led Israel twenty-two years. ⁴He had thirty sons, who rode thirty donkeys. They controlled thirty towns in Gilead, which to this day are called Havvoth Jair.*ᵇ* ⁵When Jair died, he was buried in Kamon.

Jephthah

⁶Again the Israelites did evil in the eyes of the LORD. They served the Baals and the Ashtoreths, and the gods of Aram, the gods of Sidon, the gods of Moab, the gods of the Ammonites and the gods of the Philistines. And because the Israelites forsook the LORD and no longer served him, ⁷he became angry with them. He sold them into the hands of the Philistines and the Ammonites, ⁸who that year shattered and crushed them. For eighteen years they oppressed all the Israelites on the east side of the Jordan in Gilead, the land of the Amorites. ⁹The Ammonites also crossed the Jordan to fight against Judah, Benjamin and Ephraim; Israel was in great distress. ¹⁰Then the Israelites cried out to the LORD, "We have sinned against you, forsaking our God and serving the Baals."

¹¹The LORD replied, "When the Egyptians, the Amorites, the Ammonites, the Philistines, ¹²the Sidonians, the Amalekites and the Maonites*ᶜ* oppressed you and you cried to me for help, did I not save you from their hands? ¹³But you have forsaken me and served other gods, so I will no longer save you. ¹⁴Go and cry out to the gods you have chosen. Let them save you when you are in trouble!"

¹⁵But the Israelites said to the LORD, "We have sinned. Do with us whatever you think best, but please rescue us now." ¹⁶Then they got rid of the foreign gods among them and served the LORD. And he could bear Israel's misery no longer.

¹⁷When the Ammonites were called to arms and camped in Gilead, the Israelites assembled and camped at Mizpah. ¹⁸The leaders of the people of Gilead said to each other, "Whoever will take the lead in attacking the Ammonites will be head over all who live in Gilead."

11 Jephthah the Gileadite was a mighty warrior. His father was Gilead; his mother was a prostitute. ²Gilead's wife also bore him sons, and when they were grown up, they drove Jephthah away. "You are not going to get any inheritance in our family," they said, "because you are the son of another woman."

ᵃ 2 Traditionally *judged*; also in verse 3   *ᵇ 4* Or *called the settlements of Jair*   *ᶜ 12* Hebrew; some Septuagint manuscripts *Midianites*

3So Jephthah fled from his brothers and settled in the land of Tob, where a gang of scoundrels gathered around him and followed him.

4Some time later, when the Ammonites were fighting against Israel, 5the elders of Gilead went to get Jephthah from the land of Tob. 6"Come," they said, "be our commander, so we can fight the Ammonites."

7Jephthah said to them, "Didn't you hate me and drive me from my father's house? Why do you come to me now, when you're in trouble?"

8The elders of Gilead said to him, "Nevertheless, we are turning to you now; come with us to fight the Ammonites, and you will be head over all of us who live in Gilead."

9Jephthah answered, "Suppose you take me back to fight the Ammonites and the LORD gives them to me — will I really be your head?"

10The elders of Gilead replied, "The LORD is our witness; we will certainly do as you say." 11So Jephthah went with the elders of Gilead, and the people made him head and commander over them. And he repeated all his words before the LORD in Mizpah.

12Then Jephthah sent messengers to the Ammonite king with the question: "What do you have against me that you have attacked my country?"

13The king of the Ammonites answered Jephthah's messengers, "When Israel came up out of Egypt, they took away my land from the Arnon to the Jabbok, all the way to the Jordan. Now give it back peaceably."

14Jephthah sent back messengers to the Ammonite king, 15saying:

"This is what Jephthah says: Israel did not take the land of Moab or the land of the Ammonites. 16But when they came up out of Egypt, Israel went through the wilderness to the Red Sea*a* and on to Kadesh. 17Then Israel sent messengers to the king of Edom, saying, 'Give us permission to go through your country,' but the king of Edom would not listen. They sent also to the king of Moab, and he refused. So Israel stayed at Kadesh.

18"Next they traveled through the wilderness, skirted the lands of Edom and Moab, passed along the eastern side of the country of Moab, and camped on the other side of the Arnon. They did not enter the territory of Moab, for the Arnon was its border.

19"Then Israel sent messengers to Sihon king of the Amorites, who ruled in Heshbon, and said to him, 'Let us pass through your country to our own place.' 20Sihon, however, did not trust Israel*b* to pass through his territory. He mustered all his troops and encamped at Jahaz and fought with Israel.

21"Then the LORD, the God of Israel, gave Sihon and his whole army into Israel's hands, and they defeated them. Israel took over all the land of the Amorites who lived in that country, 22capturing all of it from the Arnon to the Jabbok and from the desert to the Jordan.

23"Now since the LORD, the God of Israel, has driven the Amorites out before his people Israel, what right have you to take it over? 24Will you not take what your god Chemosh gives you? Likewise, whatever the LORD our God has given us, we will possess. 25Are you any better than Balak son of Zippor, king of Moab? Did he ever quarrel with Israel or fight with them? 26For three hundred years Israel occupied Heshbon, Aroer, the surrounding settlements and all the towns along the Arnon. Why didn't you retake them during that time? 27I have not wronged you, but you are doing me wrong by waging war against

---

a 16 Or *the Sea of Reeds*   *b 20* Or *however, would not make an agreement for Israel* me. Let the LORD, the Judge, decide the dispute this day between the Israelites and the Ammonites.”

28The king of Ammon, however, paid no attention to the message Jephthah sent him.

29Then the Spirit of the LORD came on Jephthah. He crossed Gilead and Manasseh, passed through Mizpah of Gilead, and from there he advanced against the Ammonites. 30And Jephthah made a vow to the LORD: “If you give the Ammonites into my hands, 31whatever comes out of the door of my house to meet me when I return in triumph from the Ammonites will be the LORD's, and I will sacrifice it as a burnt offering.”

32Then Jephthah went over to fight the Ammonites, and the LORD gave them into his hands. 33He devastated twenty towns from Aroer to the vicinity of Minnith, as far as Abel Keramim. Thus Israel subdued Ammon.

34When Jephthah returned to his home in Mizpah, who should come out to meet him but his daughter, dancing to the sound of timbrels! She was an only child. Except for her he had neither son nor daughter. 35When he saw her, he tore his clothes and cried, “Oh no, my daughter! You have brought me down and I am devastated. I have made a vow to the LORD that I cannot break.”

36“My father,” she replied, “you have given your word to the LORD. Do to me just as you promised, now that the LORD has avenged you of your enemies, the Ammonites. 37But grant me this one request,” she said. “Give me two months to roam the hills and weep with my friends, because I will never marry.”

38“You may go,” he said. And he let her go for two months. She and her friends went into the hills and wept because she would never marry. 39After the two months, she returned to her father, and he did to her as he had vowed. And she was a virgin.

From this comes the Israelite tradition 40that each year the young women of Israel go out for four days to commemorate the daughter of Jephthah the Gileadite.

Jephthah and Ephraim

12 The Ephraimite forces were called out, and they crossed over to Zaphon. They said to Jephthah, “Why did you go to fight the Ammonites without calling us to go with you? We're going to burn down your house over your head.”

2Jephthah answered, “I and my people were engaged in a great struggle with the Ammonites, and although I called, you didn't save me out of their hands. 3When I saw that you wouldn't help, I took my life in my hands and crossed over to fight the Ammonites, and the LORD gave me the victory over them. Now why have you come up today to fight me?”

4Jephthah then called together the men of Gilead and fought against Ephraim. The Gileadites struck them down because the Ephraimites had said, “You Gileadites are renegades from Ephraim and Manasseh.” 5The Gileadites captured the fords of the Jordan leading to Ephraim, and whenever a survivor of Ephraim said, “Let me cross over,” the men of Gilead asked him, “Are you an Ephraimite?” If he replied, “No,” 6they said, “All right, say ‘Shibboleth.’” If he said, “Sibboleth,” because he could not pronounce the word correctly, they seized him and killed him at the fords of the Jordan. Forty-two thousand Ephraimites were killed at that time.

7Jephthah led[a] Israel six years. Then Jephthah the Gileadite died and was buried in a town in Gilead.

Ibzan, Elon and Abdon

8After him, Ibzan of Bethlehem led Israel. 9He had thirty sons and thirty daughters. He gave his daughters away in marriage to those outside his clan, and for his

---

a 7 Traditionally judged; also in verses 8-14

sons he brought in thirty young women as wives from outside his clan. Ibzan led Israel seven years. ¹⁰Then Ibzan died and was buried in Bethlehem.

¹¹After him, Elon the Zebulunite led Israel ten years. ¹²Then Elon died and was buried in Aijalon in the land of Zebulun.

¹³After him, Abdon son of Hillel, from Pirathon, led Israel. ¹⁴He had forty sons and thirty grandsons, who rode on seventy donkeys. He led Israel eight years. ¹⁵Then Abdon son of Hillel died and was buried at Pirathon in Ephraim, in the hill country of the Amalekites.

The Birth of Samson

13 Again the Israelites did evil in the eyes of the LORD, so the LORD delivered them into the hands of the Philistines for forty years.

²A certain man of Zorah, named Manoah, from the clan of the Danites, had a wife who was childless, unable to give birth. ³The angel of the LORD appeared to her and said, "You are barren and childless, but you are going to become pregnant and give birth to a son. ⁴Now see to it that you drink no wine or other fermented drink and that you do not eat anything unclean. ⁵You will become pregnant and have a son whose head is never to be touched by a razor because the boy is to be a Nazirite, dedicated to God from the womb. He will take the lead in delivering Israel from the hands of the Philistines."

⁶Then the woman went to her husband and told him, "A man of God came to me. He looked like an angel of God, very awesome. I didn't ask him where he came from, and he didn't tell me his name. ⁷But he said to me, 'You will become pregnant and have a son. Now then, drink no wine or other fermented drink and do not eat anything unclean, because the boy will be a Nazirite of God from the womb until the day of his death.'"

⁸Then Manoah prayed to the LORD: "Pardon your servant, Lord. I beg you to let the man of God you sent to us come again to teach us how to bring up the boy who is to be born."

⁹God heard Manoah, and the angel of God came again to the woman while she was out in the field; but her husband Manoah was not with her. ¹⁰The woman hurried to tell her husband, "He's here! The man who appeared to me the other day!"

¹¹Manoah got up and followed his wife. When he came to the man, he said, "Are you the man who talked to my wife?"

"I am," he said.

¹²So Manoah asked him, "When your words are fulfilled, what is to be the rule that governs the boy's life and work?"

¹³The angel of the LORD answered, "Your wife must do all that I have told her. ¹⁴She must not eat anything that comes from the grapevine, nor drink any wine or other fermented drink nor eat anything unclean. She must do everything I have commanded her."

¹⁵Manoah said to the angel of the LORD, "We would like you to stay until we prepare a young goat for you."

¹⁶The angel of the LORD replied, "Even though you detain me, I will not eat any of your food. But if you prepare a burnt offering, offer it to the LORD." (Manoah did not realize that it was the angel of the LORD.)

¹⁷Then Manoah inquired of the angel of the LORD, "What is your name, so that we may honor you when your word comes true?"

¹⁸He replied, "Why do you ask my name? It is beyond understanding.ᵃ" ¹⁹Then Manoah took a young goat, together with the grain offering, and sacrificed it on a rock to the LORD. And the LORD did an amazing thing while Manoah and his wife watched: ²⁰As the flame blazed up from the altar toward heaven, the angel of the LORD ascended in the flame. Seeing this, Manoah and his wife fell with their faces to the ground. ²¹When the angel of the LORD did not show

---

ᵃ 18 Or *is wonderful*

MY NAME IS SAMSON

JUDGES 13–16

Samson's story presents the irony of a powerful and yet absolutely powerless man. God gave Samson incredible physical strength. But neither physical strength nor strength of will can overcome our sinful addictions. Samson's particular addiction was sexual, and his obsession led him to squander his God-given strength. Addictions are often attempts to meet personal needs through physical pleasures. Each human being comes into this world equipped with a nearly insatiable, lifelong need for love. Only God is big enough to satisfy that demand. In fact, we're created to love, and to be loved, by God. Sex can seem to be a powerful substitute for love. That shouldn't be surprising, since sexual love is designed by God to be enjoyed by a husband and wife with such intensity that their intimacy reflects the love Jesus has for his church (see Ephesians 5:28–32).

What was Samson's overriding failure? He failed to enjoy and share God's love and the love of others. In addition, he didn't care enough about his own people to use his strength to set them free. This strongest of men settled for the substitute and sacrificed his God-given asset.

Samson never fulfilled his purpose in life, even though he frequently demonstrated evidence of his amazing power. Regularly in his story we're told that "the Spirit of the LORD came powerfully upon him" (e.g., see Judges 14:19). If we've worked through the first seven principles on the road to recovery, we've both experienced and displayed God's power. However, if we fail to continuously practice Principle Eight, we're in danger. Recovery includes sharing our experience of change with others. Real recovery will make the needs of others more important to us than our own: "Do nothing out of selfish ambition or vain conceit. Rather, in humility value others above yourselves, not looking to your own interests but each of you to the interests of the others" (Philippians 2:3–4).

Samson, like the rest of the judges God empowered, was born to deliver others from bondage. Instead, Samson squandered his gifts on personal gratification. Sobriety doesn't equal recovery. It's the beginning point of a process that will help us to fulfill God's purposes in our lives. Those purposes include using our pain as a platform for proclaiming God's power to heal broken lives and set captives free.

himself again to Manoah and his wife, Manoah realized that it was the angel of the LORD.

22"We are doomed to die!" he said to his wife. "We have seen God!"

23But his wife answered, "If the LORD had meant to kill us, he would not have accepted a burnt offering and grain offering from our hands, nor shown us all these things or now told us this."

24The woman gave birth to a boy and named him Samson. He grew and the LORD blessed him, 25and the Spirit of the LORD began to stir him while he was in Mahaneh Dan, between Zorah and Eshtaol.

Samson's Marriage

14 Samson went down to Timnah and saw there a young Philistine woman. 2When he returned, he said to his father and mother, "I have seen a Philistine woman in Timnah; now get her for me as my wife."

3His father and mother replied, "Isn't there an acceptable woman among your relatives or among all our people? Must you go to the uncircumcised Philistines to get a wife?"

But Samson said to his father, "Get her for me. She's the right one for me." 4(His parents did not know that this was from the LORD, who was seeking an occasion to confront the Philistines; for at that time they were ruling over Israel.)

5Samson went down to Timnah together with his father and mother. As they approached the vineyards of Timnah, suddenly a young lion came roaring toward him. 6The Spirit of the LORD came powerfully upon him so that he tore the lion apart with his bare hands as he might have torn a young goat. But he told neither his father nor his mother what he had done. 7Then he went down and talked with the woman, and he liked her.

8Some time later, when he went back to marry her, he turned aside to look at the lion's carcass, and in it he saw a swarm of bees and some honey. 9He scooped out the honey with his hands and ate as he went along. When he rejoined his parents, he gave them some, and they too ate it. But he did not tell them that he had taken the honey from the lion's carcass.

10Now his father went down to see the woman. And there Samson held a feast, as was customary for young men. 11When the people saw him, they chose thirty men to be his companions.

12"Let me tell you a riddle," Samson said to them. "If you can give me the answer within the seven days of the feast, I will give you thirty linen garments and thirty sets of clothes. 13If you can't tell me the answer, you must give me thirty linen garments and thirty sets of clothes."

"Tell us your riddle," they said. "Let's hear it."

14He replied,

"Out of the eater, something to eat;
    out of the strong, something
        sweet."

For three days they could not give the answer.

15On the fourtha day, they said to Samson's wife, "Coax your husband into explaining the riddle for us, or we will burn you and your father's household to death. Did you invite us here to steal our property?"

16Then Samson's wife threw herself on him, sobbing, "You hate me! You don't really love me. You've given my people a riddle, but you haven't told me the answer."

"I haven't even explained it to my father or mother," he replied, "so why should I explain it to you?" 17She cried the whole seven days of the feast. So on the seventh day he finally told her, because she continued to press him. She in turn explained the riddle to her people.

18Before sunset on the seventh day the men of the town said to him,

---

a 15 Some Septuagint manuscripts and Syriac; Hebrew *seventh*

"What is sweeter than honey?
   What is stronger than a lion?"

Samson said to them,

"If you had not plowed with my heifer,
   you would not have solved my
      riddle."

¹⁹Then the Spirit of the LORD came powerfully upon him. He went down to Ashkelon, struck down thirty of their men, stripped them of everything and gave their clothes to those who had explained the riddle. Burning with anger, he returned to his father's home. ²⁰And Samson's wife was given to one of his companions who had attended him at the feast.

Samson's Vengeance on the Philistines

15 Later on, at the time of wheat harvest, Samson took a young goat and went to visit his wife. He said, "I'm going to my wife's room." But her father would not let him go in.

²"I was so sure you hated her," he said, "that I gave her to your companion. Isn't her younger sister more attractive? Take her instead."

³Samson said to them, "This time I have a right to get even with the Philistines; I will really harm them." ⁴So he went out and caught three hundred foxes and tied them tail to tail in pairs. He then fastened a torch to every pair of tails, ⁵lit the torches and let the foxes loose in the standing grain of the Philistines. He burned up the shocks and standing grain, together with the vineyards and olive groves.

⁶When the Philistines asked, "Who did this?" they were told, "Samson, the Timnite's son-in-law, because his wife was given to his companion."

So the Philistines went up and burned her and her father to death. ⁷Samson said to them, "Since you've acted like this, I swear that I won't stop until I get my revenge on you." ⁸He attacked them viciously and slaughtered many of them. Then he went down and stayed in a cave in the rock of Etam.

⁹The Philistines went up and camped in Judah, spreading out near Lehi. ¹⁰The people of Judah asked, "Why have you come to fight us?"

"We have come to take Samson prisoner," they answered, "to do to him as he did to us."

¹¹Then three thousand men from Judah went down to the cave in the rock of Etam and said to Samson, "Don't you realize that the Philistines are rulers over us? What have you done to us?"

He answered, "I merely did to them what they did to me."

¹²They said to him, "We've come to tie you up and hand you over to the Philistines."

Samson said, "Swear to me that you won't kill me yourselves."

¹³"Agreed," they answered. "We will only tie you up and hand you over to them. We will not kill you." So they bound him with two new ropes and led him up from the rock. ¹⁴As he approached Lehi, the Philistines came toward him shouting. The Spirit of the LORD came powerfully upon him. The ropes on his arms became like charred flax, and the bindings dropped from his hands. ¹⁵Finding a fresh jawbone of a donkey, he grabbed it and struck down a thousand men.

¹⁶Then Samson said,

"With a donkey's jawbone
   I have made donkeys of them.ᵃ
With a donkey's jawbone
   I have killed a thousand men."

¹⁷When he finished speaking, he threw away the jawbone; and the place was called Ramath Lehi.ᵇ

¹⁸Because he was very thirsty, he cried out to the LORD, "You have given your servant this great victory. Must I now die of

---

ᵃ 16 Or *made a heap or two*; the Hebrew for *donkey* sounds like the Hebrew for *heap*.   ᵇ 17 *Ramath Lehi* means *jawbone hill*.

My Name Is Wayne

I'M A BELIEVER WHO STRUGGLES WITH SEXUAL ADDICTION

Please read the story of Samson and his narcissistic lifestyle in
Judges 14:1 — 16:31.

I grew up functioning as an emotional substitute-husband for my mom. Listening to her
share negatively about my dad caused me to hate him. There was always arguing and yelling, usually ending with Dad angrily retreating to the basement or going out for hours. I
cherished my mom and our close relationship but failed to recognize its toxic nature.

I was a shy child who desperately wanted to be "in" but experienced only isolation. Many
times I found myself the butt of the other kids' bullying. One positive in my life was that
Mom sent me to church school. I accepted Jesus as my Savior when I was 11. This was life
changing, though I still wasn't handling my emotional world well.

During my teenage years I picked up the warped idea that if girls had a sexual interest in
me, it might satisfy my yearning to be liked. I began to fantasize, poring over pornographic
magazines, a habit that eventually led to other inappropriate behaviors. I was caught several
times, and my mom was devastated. I retreated into a lonely, confused world.

I met my wife, Robin, in high school, and we got married during our senior year in college.
Not surprisingly, my mother never seemed happy for me. Robin and I had a baby right
away, and I was overwhelmed with responsibility. Three months before our son was born,
my mom died of cancer. I was so angry. She had abandoned me, and I was left to help my
dad — the parent who had drifted into a strange and secretive world of hoarding and living
like a hermit. I was too ashamed to have my wife and son even meet him, and I struggled
with conflicting emotions of love and hatred. To escape my pain and anger, I acted out
secretly through physical pleasure. My addiction grew in intensity and boldness. Pornography, strip clubs, prostitutes and adultery all crept into my marriage. I was overwhelmed
by guilt and remorse. How could I allow my addiction to become more important than the
people I loved? I begged God to forgive me, but the thoughts, fantasies and acting out
would only return.

I became an "empty suit" at church — leading, praying for others and teaching church school, while inside I was a shell. I felt trapped and even contemplated suicide. But what would everyone think of this "perfect Christian" ending his life this way?

In 1995 I was finally caught in a lie by my wife. Forced to admit my compulsion toward pornography, I agreed to counseling. I slowly and painfully began to face my feelings, my past and my loneliness, and to learn ways to change my behavior. Although some of the fog lifted in my life, months of victory were followed by unrest and acting out. I wasn't tackling the central issue: I lacked the power to change. I needed help beyond the understanding that counseling was providing.

In the fall of 2000, I hit rock bottom. At Saddleback Church I had heard testimonies about the powerful help people had found at Celebrate Recovery. Still, I struggled with a dilemma: If I chose to go, I risked being found out. But I was convinced that I had no other option if I really desired to live the Christian life God wanted me to. It was then that my sexual sobriety began.

Not only is God teaching me through the materials of the ministry, but he's changing me through the relationships I've made there. Like Samson, my life had revolved around self-satisfaction, not people. I failed to care about others, and now God was using others to care about me.

Through Celebrate Recovery God tugged on my heart to work the steps and principles fully — and that included coming clean with my wife and seeking her forgiveness. This step of obedience wasn't easy. What good would it do to dredge up my past, to risk losing her, to crush her spirit? But through the Holy Spirit I found the confidence that God would be there with me. So I sat down with Robin and made the incredibly painful admissions. Months of anger and anguish followed, but her strong faith convicted her that she needed to follow God's example and forgive me.

At first I didn't want to let myself believe that Robin's forgiveness was complete. I kept waiting for the other shoe to drop. But God was working in her life too. She began attending Celebrate Recovery with me, and God has been changing both of us. I had never before realized what closeness there could be in a marriage, especially one that had almost been destroyed by my addiction and sin.

As I continue to work on developing my character in God's way, I'm experiencing so much peace. I have a deep desire to put people, instead of my personal gratification, first in my life. And in some miraculous way God has been seeing fit to use me, to take my hurts and turn them into opportunities to minister to others. Talk about a change of direction!

Wayne

thirst and fall into the hands of the uncircumcised?" [19] Then God opened up the hollow place in Lehi, and water came out of it. When Samson drank, his strength returned and he revived. So the spring was called En Hakkore,[a] and it is still there in Lehi.

[20] Samson led[b] Israel for twenty years in the days of the Philistines.

Samson and Delilah

16 One day Samson went to Gaza, where he saw a prostitute. He went in to spend the night with her. [2] The people of Gaza were told, "Samson is here!" So they surrounded the place and lay in wait for him all night at the city gate. They made no move during the night, saying, "At dawn we'll kill him."

[3] But Samson lay there only until the middle of the night. Then he got up and took hold of the doors of the city gate, together with the two posts, and tore them loose, bar and all. He lifted them to his shoulders and carried them to the top of the hill that faces Hebron.

[4] Some time later, he fell in love with a woman in the Valley of Sorek whose name was Delilah. [5] The rulers of the Philistines went to her and said, "See if you can lure him into showing you the secret of his great strength and how we can overpower him so we may tie him up and subdue him. Each one of us will give you eleven hundred shekels[c] of silver."

[6] So Delilah said to Samson, "Tell me the secret of your great strength and how you can be tied up and subdued."

[7] Samson answered her, "If anyone ties me with seven fresh bowstrings that have not been dried, I'll become as weak as any other man."

[8] Then the rulers of the Philistines brought her seven fresh bowstrings that had not been dried, and she tied him with them. [9] With men hidden in the room, she called to him, "Samson, the Philistines are upon you!" But he snapped the bowstrings as easily as a piece of string snaps when it comes close to a flame. So the secret of his strength was not discovered.

[10] Then Delilah said to Samson, "You have made a fool of me; you lied to me. Come now, tell me how you can be tied."

[11] He said, "If anyone ties me securely with new ropes that have never been used, I'll become as weak as any other man."

[12] So Delilah took new ropes and tied him with them. Then, with men hidden in the room, she called to him, "Samson, the Philistines are upon you!" But he snapped the ropes off his arms as if they were threads.

[13] Delilah then said to Samson, "All this time you have been making a fool of me and lying to me. Tell me how you can be tied."

He replied, "If you weave the seven braids of my head into the fabric on the loom and tighten it with the pin, I'll become as weak as any other man." So while he was sleeping, Delilah took the seven braids of his head, wove them into the fabric [14] and[d] tightened it with the pin.

Again she called to him, "Samson, the Philistines are upon you!" He awoke from his sleep and pulled up the pin and the loom, with the fabric.

[15] Then she said to him, "How can you say, 'I love you,' when you won't confide in me? This is the third time you have made a fool of me and haven't told me the secret of your great strength." [16] With such nagging she prodded him day after day until he was sick to death of it.

[17] So he told her everything. "No razor has ever been used on my head," he said, "because I have been a Nazirite dedicated to God from my mother's womb. If my head were shaved, my strength would leave me, and I would become as weak as any other man."

---

[a] 19 En Hakkore means *caller's spring.*   [b] 20 Traditionally *judged*   [c] 5 That is, about 28 pounds or about 13 kilograms   [d] 13,14 Some Septuagint manuscripts; Hebrew *replied, "I can if you weave the seven braids of my head into the fabric on the loom."* [14] *So she*

MY NAME IS DELILAH

JUDGES 16:4–21

Delilah was a woman devoted to a life of deception. Her greatest "accomplishment" was the destruction of a man who loved her—a man named Samson. Samson was an easy target for a woman's trickery, since women were this strong man's greatest weakness. Delilah's con on Samson was paid for by the Philistine rulers in the staggering amount of "eleven hundred shekels of silver" (about 28 pounds) each (see Judges 16:5).

Isn't it amazing the degree to which living a lie makes us susceptible to the lies of others? Three times Samson misled this wily woman, and each time she complained, "You have made a fool of me" (vv. 10,13,15).

In reality, Delilah needed no help in the area of foolishness. She prostituted herself to land a fortune in silver, a ruse that included lying to a man who was in love with her. With the success of her betrayal of Samson, Delilah disappears from the Biblical account. Her inheritance: The knowledge that the man who loved her was maimed, humiliated and enslaved by her deception and greed. By the time Samson awakened to his blindness to the truth about Delilah, his eyes had been physically gouged out (see v. 21).

How often do deception and addiction go hand in hand? Like Delilah, the addict will weave a skillful web of deception in order to continue feeding his insatiable habit. And, sadly, it's often easiest to go on deceiving those who love us, over and over again. The end product is a life wasted—our own—and all too frequently other lives are devastated—those we love, or at least those who love us.

The only escape from a life of dishonesty is an encounter with the truth—his name is Jesus. He's the one who said, "I am the way and the truth and the life. No one comes to the Father except through me" (John 14:6). If we've wasted our lives in self-deception and in the manipulation and betrayal of those who love us, there's still a way back to God. He can break the pattern of deception in our lives. Recovery forces us to face the truth in order to end the insanity that has taken over our life. David voiced a simple prayer that we may wish to make our own: "Into your hands I commit my spirit; deliver me, LORD, my faithful God" (Psalm 31:5).

18When Delilah saw that he had told her everything, she sent word to the rulers of the Philistines, "Come back once more; he has told me everything." So the rulers of the Philistines returned with the silver in their hands. 19After putting him to sleep on her lap, she called for someone to shave off the seven braids of his hair, and so began to subdue him.*a* And his strength left him.

20Then she called, "Samson, the Philistines are upon you!"

He awoke from his sleep and thought, "I'll go out as before and shake myself free." But he did not know that the LORD had left him.

21Then the Philistines seized him, gouged out his eyes and took him down to Gaza. Binding him with bronze shackles, they set him to grinding grain in the prison. 22But the hair on his head began to grow again after it had been shaved.

The Death of Samson

23Now the rulers of the Philistines assembled to offer a great sacrifice to Dagon their god and to celebrate, saying, "Our god has delivered Samson, our enemy, into our hands."

24When the people saw him, they praised their god, saying,

"Our god has delivered our enemy
    into our hands,
the one who laid waste our land
    and multiplied our slain."

25While they were in high spirits, they shouted, "Bring out Samson to entertain us." So they called Samson out of the prison, and he performed for them.

When they stood him among the pillars, 26Samson said to the servant who held his hand, "Put me where I can feel the pillars that support the temple, so that I may lean against them." 27Now the temple was crowded with men and women; all the rulers of the Philistines were there, and on the roof were about three thousand men and women watching Samson perform. 28Then Samson prayed to the LORD, "Sovereign LORD, remember me. Please, God, strengthen me just once more, and let me with one blow get revenge on the Philistines for my two eyes." 29Then Samson reached toward the two central pillars on which the temple stood. Bracing himself against them, his right hand on the one and his left hand on the other, 30Samson said, "Let me die with the Philistines!" Then he pushed with all his might, and down came the temple on the rulers and all the people in it. Thus he killed many more when he died than while he lived.

31Then his brothers and his father's whole family went down to get him. They brought him back and buried him between Zorah and Eshtaol in the tomb of Manoah his father. He had led*b* Israel twenty years.

Micah's Idols

17 Now a man named Micah from the hill country of Ephraim 2said to his mother, "The eleven hundred shekels*c* of silver that were taken from you and about which I heard you utter a curse — I have that silver with me; I took it."

Then his mother said, "The LORD bless you, my son!"

3When he returned the eleven hundred shekels of silver to his mother, she said, "I solemnly consecrate my silver to the LORD for my son to make an image overlaid with silver. I will give it back to you."

4So after he returned the silver to his mother, she took two hundred shekels*d* of silver and gave them to a silversmith, who used them to make the idol. And it was put in Micah's house.

5Now this man Micah had a shrine, and he made an ephod and some household gods and installed one of his sons as his

---

a 19 Hebrew; some Septuagint manuscripts *and he began to weaken*   *b 31* Traditionally *judged*   *c 2* That is, about 28 pounds or about 13 kilograms   *d 4* That is, about 5 pounds or about 2.3 kilograms priest. 6In those days Israel had no king; everyone did as they saw fit.

7A young Levite from Bethlehem in Judah, who had been living within the clan of Judah, 8left that town in search of some other place to stay. On his way*a* he came to Micah's house in the hill country of Ephraim.

9Micah asked him, "Where are you from?"

"I'm a Levite from Bethlehem in Judah," he said, "and I'm looking for a place to stay."

10Then Micah said to him, "Live with me and be my father and priest, and I'll give you ten shekels*b* of silver a year, your clothes and your food." 11So the Levite agreed to live with him, and the young man became like one of his sons to him. 12Then Micah installed the Levite, and the young man became his priest and lived in his house. 13And Micah said, "Now I know that the LORD will be good to me, since this Levite has become my priest."

The Danites Settle in Laish

18 In those days Israel had no king. And in those days the tribe of the Danites was seeking a place of their own where they might settle, because they had not yet come into an inheritance among the tribes of Israel. 2So the Danites sent five of their leading men from Zorah and Eshtaol to spy out the land and explore it. These men represented all the Danites. They told them, "Go, explore the land."

So they entered the hill country of Ephraim and came to the house of Micah, where they spent the night. 3When they were near Micah's house, they recognized the voice of the young Levite; so they turned in there and asked him, "Who brought you here? What are you doing in this place? Why are you here?"

4He told them what Micah had done for him, and said, "He has hired me and I am his priest."

5Then they said to him, "Please inquire of God to learn whether our journey will be successful."

6The priest answered them, "Go in peace. Your journey has the LORD's approval."

7So the five men left and came to Laish, where they saw that the people were living in safety, like the Sidonians, at peace and secure. And since their land lacked nothing, they were prosperous.*c* Also, they lived a long way from the Sidonians and had no relationship with anyone else.*d*

8When they returned to Zorah and Eshtaol, their fellow Danites asked them, "How did you find things?"

9They answered, "Come on, let's attack them! We have seen the land, and it is very good. Aren't you going to do something? Don't hesitate to go there and take it over. 10When you get there, you will find an unsuspecting people and a spacious land that God has put into your hands, a land that lacks nothing whatever."

11Then six hundred men of the Danites, armed for battle, set out from Zorah and Eshtaol. 12On their way they set up camp near Kiriath Jearim in Judah. This is why the place west of Kiriath Jearim is called Mahaneh Dan*e* to this day. 13From there they went on to the hill country of Ephraim and came to Micah's house.

14Then the five men who had spied out the land of Laish said to their fellow Danites, "Do you know that one of these houses has an ephod, some household gods and an image overlaid with silver? Now you know what to do." 15So they turned in there and went to the house of the young Levite at Micah's place and greeted him. 16The six hundred Danites, armed for battle, stood at the entrance of the gate. 17The five men who had spied out the land went inside and

---

a 8 Or *To carry on his profession*   *b* 10 That is, about 4 ounces or about 115 grams   *c* 7 The meaning of the Hebrew for this clause is uncertain.   *d* 7 Hebrew; some Septuagint manuscripts *with the Arameans*   *e* 12 *Mahaneh Dan* means *Dan's camp*.

My Name Is Marnie

I'M A BELIEVER WHO STRUGGLES WITH SEXUAL ADDICTION AND ANOREXIA

Please read the story of Delilah's deception of Samson in Judges 16:1 – 22.

A broken home, tortuous abuse, poverty, fits of rage, and being torn away from everyone I held dear — all of these together add up to only a fraction of the childhood woes that thrust me into a forbidden lifestyle fueled by fantasy, sex and lust. As a young woman I was on a suicide mission, devoted to a life of deception. My lifestyle had frightening similarities to those of the Biblical women I'd learned to look down on during my childhood religious training: Jezebel, Potiphar's wife and Delilah. Yes, Delilah, that wily woman whose greatest accomplishment in life — and claim to perpetual infamy — was the destruction of the man who loved her most.

Just as he had done to Delilah, the enemy sank his fangs deep into my soul as I convinced myself that my marriage was a mistake. Bitterness, resentment and hatred were starting to paint an ugly picture of our marital relationship, and my visions of a "normal" lifestyle were rapidly falling by the wayside. My husband and I endured months of arguing, and our lives were littered by the debris of broken promises. I felt taken advantage of, disrespected and unappreciated. Robbed of any voice or element of control, and with my dreams swept aside by disillusionment, I found myself emotionally bankrupt. At that point my behavior erupted into uncontrollable fury. My solution: adultery. Just ten months after our wedding, I had an affair.

My insatiable appetite for more of the same manifested itself as I attempted to fill the void within me, only to discover that the beast of my lust was insatiable. My form of self-punishment and control was to starve myself, both spiritually and physically. I was on a quest for the "perfect" figure, no matter what the cost. This lifestyle, coupled with my sexual addiction, left me weak and depleted. I weighed a mere 92 pounds and was rapidly self-destructing.

Desperate to find freedom from my self-imposed web of deception, I picked up the phone and called Saddleback Church. I remember stumbling into my first Celebrate Recovery meeting broken and out of touch with reality. My view of life had become so distorted, and my actions so out of control, that I doubt the enemy himself could have kept up with me. During recovery, though, I began to recall the Christian values I had learned as a child but later buried due to my anger and resentment toward God. He had finally gotten my attention, and I began to relate to Paul's words in Romans 7:15 – 20:

> I do not understand what I do. For what I want to do I do not do, but what I hate I do. And if I do what I do not want to do, I agree that the law is good. As it is, it is no longer I myself who do it, but it is sin living in me. For I know that good itself does not dwell in me, that is, in my sinful nature. For I have the desire to do what is good, but I cannot carry it out. For I do not do the good I want to do, but the evil I do not want to do — this I keep on doing. Now if I do what I do not want to do, it is no longer I who do it, but it is sin living in me that does it.

My pain had finally exceeded my fear. I had reached rock bottom.

I began to recognize that my internal struggle wasn't uncommon, and I came to understand that the pain of my past played a crucial part in my present behavior. I recognized that I was trapped in a cycle of addiction. Most importantly, I realized how far I'd fallen from my early relationship with Christ. As David so poignantly articulated in Psalm 40:12, "Troubles without number surround me; my sins have overtaken me, and I cannot see. They are more than the hairs of my head, and my heart fails within me."

I began to seriously explore the new, uncharted territory of Celebrate Recovery. After working Principle Four ("Openly examine and confess my faults to myself, to God and to someone else I trust"), I found myself on the path of true healing. I clearly heard and accepted God's promise of freedom, and I stopped acting out.

I have reconciled with my husband, and today my relationships are built on honesty and trust. My marriage has been restored, and we've been blessed with a precious gift, a beautiful baby girl. I've learned to embrace my pain and have made the choice to abandon my life of deception and destruction.

As I reflect on my life today, I thank God for his unfailing truth and understanding. He has taken my tragedy and turned it into a testament of my faith. Most of all I thank him that my life, unlike Delilah's, is not being wasted. God has chosen instead to use me in his service.

Marnie

took the idol, the ephod and the household gods while the priest and the six hundred armed men stood at the entrance of the gate.

¹⁸When the five men went into Micah's house and took the idol, the ephod and the household gods, the priest said to them, "What are you doing?"

¹⁹They answered him, "Be quiet! Don't say a word. Come with us, and be our father and priest. Isn't it better that you serve a tribe and clan in Israel as priest rather than just one man's household?" ²⁰The priest was very pleased. He took the ephod, the household gods and the idol and went along with the people. ²¹Putting their little children, their livestock and their possessions in front of them, they turned away and left.

²²When they had gone some distance from Micah's house, the men who lived near Micah were called together and overtook the Danites. ²³As they shouted after them, the Danites turned and said to Micah, "What's the matter with you that you called out your men to fight?"

²⁴He replied, "You took the gods I made, and my priest, and went away. What else do I have? How can you ask, 'What's the matter with you?'"

²⁵The Danites answered, "Don't argue with us, or some of the men may get angry and attack you, and you and your family will lose your lives." ²⁶So the Danites went their way, and Micah, seeing that they were too strong for him, turned around and went back home.

²⁷Then they took what Micah had made, and his priest, and went on to Laish, against a people at peace and secure. They attacked them with the sword and burned down their city. ²⁸There was no one to rescue them because they lived a long way from Sidon and had no relationship with anyone else. The city was in a valley near Beth Rehob.

The Danites rebuilt the city and settled there. ²⁹They named it Dan after their ancestor Dan, who was born to Israel — though the city used to be called Laish. ³⁰There the Danites set up for themselves the idol, and Jonathan son of Gershom, the son of Moses,ᵃ and his sons were priests for the tribe of Dan until the time of the captivity of the land. ³¹They continued to use the idol Micah had made, all the time the house of God was in Shiloh.

A Levite and His Concubine

19 In those days Israel had no king. Now a Levite who lived in a remote area in the hill country of Ephraim took a concubine from Bethlehem in Judah. ²But she was unfaithful to him. She left him and went back to her parents' home in Bethlehem, Judah. After she had been there four months, ³her husband went to her to persuade her to return. He had with him his servant and two donkeys. She took him into her parents' home, and when her father saw him, he gladly welcomed him. ⁴His father-in-law, the woman's father, prevailed on him to stay; so he remained with him three days, eating and drinking, and sleeping there.

⁵On the fourth day they got up early and he prepared to leave, but the woman's father said to his son-in-law, "Refresh yourself with something to eat; then you can go." ⁶So the two of them sat down to eat and drink together. Afterward the woman's father said, "Please stay tonight and enjoy yourself." ⁷And when the man got up to go, his father-in-law persuaded him, so he stayed there that night. ⁸On the morning of the fifth day, when he rose to go, the woman's father said, "Refresh yourself. Wait till afternoon!" So the two of them ate together.

⁹Then when the man, with his concubine and his servant, got up to leave, his father-in-law, the woman's father, said, "Now

---

ᵃ 30 Many Hebrew manuscripts, some Septuagint manuscripts and Vulgate; many other Hebrew manuscripts and some other Septuagint manuscripts *Manasseh* look, it's almost evening. Spend the night here; the day is nearly over. Stay and enjoy yourself. Early tomorrow morning you can get up and be on your way home." ¹⁰But, unwilling to stay another night, the man left and went toward Jebus (that is, Jerusalem), with his two saddled donkeys and his concubine.

¹¹When they were near Jebus and the day was almost gone, the servant said to his master, "Come, let's stop at this city of the Jebusites and spend the night."

¹²His master replied, "No. We won't go into any city whose people are not Israelites. We will go on to Gibeah." ¹³He added, "Come, let's try to reach Gibeah or Ramah and spend the night in one of those places." ¹⁴So they went on, and the sun set as they neared Gibeah in Benjamin. ¹⁵There they stopped to spend the night. They went and sat in the city square, but no one took them in for the night.

¹⁶That evening an old man from the hill country of Ephraim, who was living in Gibeah (the inhabitants of the place were Benjamites), came in from his work in the fields. ¹⁷When he looked and saw the traveler in the city square, the old man asked, "Where are you going? Where did you come from?"

¹⁸He answered, "We are on our way from Bethlehem in Judah to a remote area in the hill country of Ephraim where I live. I have been to Bethlehem in Judah and now I am going to the house of the LORD.ᵃ No one has taken me in for the night. ¹⁹We have both straw and fodder for our donkeys and bread and wine for ourselves your servants — me, the woman and the young man with us. We don't need anything."

²⁰"You are welcome at my house," the old man said. "Let me supply whatever you need. Only don't spend the night in the square." ²¹So he took him into his house and fed his donkeys. After they had washed their feet, they had something to eat and drink.

²²While they were enjoying themselves, some of the wicked men of the city surrounded the house. Pounding on the door, they shouted to the old man who owned the house, "Bring out the man who came to your house so we can have sex with him."

²³The owner of the house went outside and said to them, "No, my friends, don't be so vile. Since this man is my guest, don't do this outrageous thing. ²⁴Look, here is my virgin daughter, and his concubine. I will bring them out to you now, and you can use them and do to them whatever you wish. But as for this man, don't do such an outrageous thing."

²⁵But the men would not listen to him. So the man took his concubine and sent her outside to them, and they raped her and abused her throughout the night, and at dawn they let her go. ²⁶At daybreak the woman went back to the house where her master was staying, fell down at the door and lay there until daylight.

²⁷When her master got up in the morning and opened the door of the house and stepped out to continue on his way, there lay his concubine, fallen in the doorway of the house, with her hands on the threshold. ²⁸He said to her, "Get up; let's go." But there was no answer. Then the man put her on his donkey and set out for home.

²⁹When he reached home, he took a knife and cut up his concubine, limb by limb, into twelve parts and sent them into all the areas of Israel. ³⁰Everyone who saw it was saying to one another, "Such a thing has never been seen or done, not since the day the Israelites came up out of Egypt. Just imagine! We must do something! So speak up!"

The Israelites Punish the Benjamites

20 Then all Israel from Dan to Beersheba and from the land of Gilead came together as one and assembled before the LORD in Mizpah. ²The leaders of all the people of the tribes

---

ᵃ 18 Hebrew, Vulgate, Syriac and Targum; Septuagint *going home* of Israel took their places in the assembly of God's people, four hundred thousand men armed with swords. ³(The Benjamites heard that the Israelites had gone up to Mizpah.) Then the Israelites said, "Tell us how this awful thing happened."

⁴So the Levite, the husband of the murdered woman, said, "I and my concubine came to Gibeah in Benjamin to spend the night. ⁵During the night the men of Gibeah came after me and surrounded the house, intending to kill me. They raped my concubine, and she died. ⁶I took my concubine, cut her into pieces and sent one piece to each region of Israel's inheritance, because they committed this lewd and outrageous act in Israel. ⁷Now, all you Israelites, speak up and tell me what you have decided to do."

⁸All the men rose up together as one, saying, "None of us will go home. No, not one of us will return to his house. ⁹But now this is what we'll do to Gibeah: We'll go up against it in the order decided by casting lots. ¹⁰We'll take ten men out of every hundred from all the tribes of Israel, and a hundred from a thousand, and a thousand from ten thousand, to get provisions for the army. Then, when the army arrives at Gibeah*a* in Benjamin, it can give them what they deserve for this outrageous act done in Israel." ¹¹So all the Israelites got together and united as one against the city.

¹²The tribes of Israel sent messengers throughout the tribe of Benjamin, saying, "What about this awful crime that was committed among you? ¹³Now turn those wicked men of Gibeah over to us so that we may put them to death and purge the evil from Israel."

But the Benjamites would not listen to their fellow Israelites. ¹⁴From their towns they came together at Gibeah to fight against the Israelites. ¹⁵At once the Benjamites mobilized twenty-six thousand swordsmen from their towns, in addition to seven hundred able young men from those living in Gibeah. ¹⁶Among all these soldiers there were seven hundred select troops who were left-handed, each of whom could sling a stone at a hair and not miss.

¹⁷Israel, apart from Benjamin, mustered four hundred thousand swordsmen, all of them fit for battle.

¹⁸The Israelites went up to Bethel*b* and inquired of God. They said, "Who of us is to go up first to fight against the Benjamites?"

The LORD replied, "Judah shall go first."

¹⁹The next morning the Israelites got up and pitched camp near Gibeah. ²⁰The Israelites went out to fight the Benjamites and took up battle positions against them at Gibeah. ²¹The Benjamites came out of Gibeah and cut down twenty-two thousand Israelites on the battlefield that day. ²²But the Israelites encouraged one another and again took up their positions where they had stationed themselves the first day. ²³The Israelites went up and wept before the LORD until evening, and they inquired of the LORD. They said, "Shall we go up again to fight against the Benjamites, our fellow Israelites?"

The LORD answered, "Go up against them."

²⁴Then the Israelites drew near to Benjamin the second day. ²⁵This time, when the Benjamites came out from Gibeah to oppose them, they cut down another eighteen thousand Israelites, all of them armed with swords.

²⁶Then all the Israelites, the whole army, went up to Bethel, and there they sat weeping before the LORD. They fasted that day until evening and presented burnt offerings and fellowship offerings to the LORD. ²⁷And the Israelites inquired of the LORD. (In those days the ark of the covenant of God was there, ²⁸with Phinehas son of Eleazar, the son of Aaron, ministering before

---

a 10 One Hebrew manuscript; most Hebrew manuscripts *Geba*, a variant of *Gibeah*   *b 18* Or *to the house of God*; also in verse 26 it.) They asked, "Shall we go up again to fight against the Benjamites, our fellow Israelites, or not?"

The LORD responded, "Go, for tomorrow I will give them into your hands."

²⁹Then Israel set an ambush around Gibeah. ³⁰They went up against the Benjamites on the third day and took up positions against Gibeah as they had done before. ³¹The Benjamites came out to meet them and were drawn away from the city. They began to inflict casualties on the Israelites as before, so that about thirty men fell in the open field and on the roads — the one leading to Bethel and the other to Gibeah. ³²While the Benjamites were saying, "We are defeating them as before," the Israelites were saying, "Let's retreat and draw them away from the city to the roads."

³³All the men of Israel moved from their places and took up positions at Baal Tamar, and the Israelite ambush charged out of its place on the westᵃ of Gibeah.ᵇ ³⁴Then ten thousand of Israel's able young men made a frontal attack on Gibeah. The fighting was so heavy that the Benjamites did not realize how near disaster was. ³⁵The LORD defeated Benjamin before Israel, and on that day the Israelites struck down 25,100 Benjamites, all armed with swords. ³⁶Then the Benjamites saw that they were beaten.

Now the men of Israel had given way before Benjamin, because they relied on the ambush they had set near Gibeah. ³⁷Those who had been in ambush made a sudden dash into Gibeah, spread out and put the whole city to the sword. ³⁸The Israelites had arranged with the ambush that they should send up a great cloud of smoke from the city, ³⁹and then the Israelites would counterattack.

The Benjamites had begun to inflict casualties on the Israelites (about thirty), and they said, "We are defeating them as in the first battle." ⁴⁰But when the column of smoke began to rise from the city, the Benjamites turned and saw the whole city going up in smoke. ⁴¹Then the Israelites counterattacked, and the Benjamites were terrified, because they realized that disaster had come on them. ⁴²So they fled before the Israelites in the direction of the wilderness, but they could not escape the battle. And the Israelites who came out of the towns cut them down there. ⁴³They surrounded the Benjamites, chased them and easilyᶜ overran them in the vicinity of Gibeah on the east. ⁴⁴Eighteen thousand Benjamites fell, all of them valiant fighters. ⁴⁵As they turned and fled toward the wilderness to the rock of Rimmon, the Israelites cut down five thousand men along the roads. They kept pressing after the Benjamites as far as Gidom and struck down two thousand more.

⁴⁶On that day twenty-five thousand Benjamite swordsmen fell, all of them valiant fighters. ⁴⁷But six hundred of them turned and fled into the wilderness to the rock of Rimmon, where they stayed four months. ⁴⁸The men of Israel went back to Benjamin and put all the towns to the sword, including the animals and everything else they found. All the towns they came across they set on fire.

Wives for the Benjamites

21 The men of Israel had taken an oath at Mizpah: "Not one of us will give his daughter in marriage to a Benjamite."

²The people went to Bethel,ᵈ where they sat before God until evening, raising their voices and weeping bitterly. ³"LORD, God of Israel," they cried, "why has this happened to Israel? Why should one tribe be missing from Israel today?"

⁴Early the next day the people built an altar and presented burnt offerings and fellowship offerings.

ᵃ 33 Some Septuagint manuscripts and Vulgate; the meaning of the Hebrew for this word is uncertain.   ᵇ 33 Hebrew *Geba*, a variant of *Gibeah*   ᶜ 43 The meaning of the Hebrew for this word is uncertain.   ᵈ 2 Or *to the house of God*

⁵Then the Israelites asked, "Who from all the tribes of Israel has failed to assemble before the LORD?" For they had taken a solemn oath that anyone who failed to assemble before the LORD at Mizpah was to be put to death.

⁶Now the Israelites grieved for the tribe of Benjamin, their fellow Israelites. "Today one tribe is cut off from Israel," they said. ⁷"How can we provide wives for those who are left, since we have taken an oath by the LORD not to give them any of our daughters in marriage?" ⁸Then they asked, "Which one of the tribes of Israel failed to assemble before the LORD at Mizpah?" They discovered that no one from Jabesh Gilead had come to the camp for the assembly. ⁹For when they counted the people, they found that none of the people of Jabesh Gilead were there.

¹⁰So the assembly sent twelve thousand fighting men with instructions to go to Jabesh Gilead and put to the sword those living there, including the women and children. ¹¹"This is what you are to do," they said. "Kill every male and every woman who is not a virgin." ¹²They found among the people living in Jabesh Gilead four hundred young women who had never slept with a man, and they took them to the camp at Shiloh in Canaan.

¹³Then the whole assembly sent an offer of peace to the Benjamites at the rock of Rimmon. ¹⁴So the Benjamites returned at that time and were given the women of Jabesh Gilead who had been spared. But there were not enough for all of them.

¹⁵The people grieved for Benjamin, because the LORD had made a gap in the tribes of Israel. ¹⁶And the elders of the assembly said, "With the women of Benjamin destroyed, how shall we provide wives for the men who are left? ¹⁷The Benjamite survivors must have heirs," they said, "so that a tribe of Israel will not be wiped out. ¹⁸We can't give them our daughters as wives, since we Israelites have taken this oath: 'Cursed be anyone who gives a wife to a Benjamite.' ¹⁹But look, there is the annual festival of the LORD in Shiloh, which lies north of Bethel, east of the road that goes from Bethel to Shechem, and south of Lebonah."

²⁰So they instructed the Benjamites, saying, "Go and hide in the vineyards ²¹and watch. When the young women of Shiloh come out to join in the dancing, rush from the vineyards and each of you seize one of them to be your wife. Then return to the land of Benjamin. ²²When their fathers or brothers complain to us, we will say to them, 'Do us the favor of helping them, because we did not get wives for them during the war. You will not be guilty of breaking your oath because you did not give your daughters to them.'"

²³So that is what the Benjamites did. While the young women were dancing, each man caught one and carried her off to be his wife. Then they returned to their inheritance and rebuilt the towns and settled in them.

²⁴At that time the Israelites left that place and went home to their tribes and clans, each to his own inheritance.

²⁵In those days Israel had no king; everyone did as they saw fit.

THEME: Participation in the family of God is based on faith in, and obedience to, God.

AUTHOR: The author of the book of Ruth is unknown. Jewish tradition holds that the prophet Samuel wrote Ruth, but there is little evidence to support this view.

DATE OF WRITING: The events in Ruth probably occurred during the period of the judges (1375 – 1050 BC), but the book was likely written after 1000 BC.

ENCOURAGEMENT FROM RUTH: "May you be richly rewarded by the Lord, the God of Israel, under whose wings you have come to take refuge" (Ruth 2:12).

REFLECTION FROM RUTH: "But Ruth replied, 'Don't urge me to leave you or to turn back from you. Where you go I will go, and where you stay I will stay. Your people will be my people and your God my God. Where you die I will die, and there I will be buried' " (Ruth 1:16 – 17).

Even when things are bad, when it seems as though everyone has turned their backs on God, there are those among us who stay loyal and obedient. This is the story found in the book of Ruth. Naomi's husband and sons have died in a faraway land, leaving her alone with her foreign-born daughter-in-law. She has returned to her childhood home in Bethlehem, ready to restart her life there. Unfortunately, unless someone intervenes, these two widows will live in poverty. A kindly man named Boaz becomes the women's "guardian-redeemer," purchasing back Naomi's ancestral land, marrying Ruth and fathering a son by her. This redemption points to God's saving work in our lives. The New Testament refers to Christ's church as his bride. Only his intervention can redeem and restore us.

Ruth and Naomi were powerless to change their lives. They needed a rescuer who could and would pay the price of redemption. Boaz became that liberator. Christ has done the same for each of us, being both able and willing to pay the ultimate price — his life — to "buy us back" from our broken lives of hurts, hang-ups and habits. Once we are able to admit that we're powerless and come to understand that Christ alone can save us, his redemption becomes available to us. When we put our trust in him, he provides us hope. Jesus seeks us out, anxious to provide the redemption we so desperately need.

Naomi Loses Her Husband and Sons

1 In the days when the judges ruled,[a] there was a famine in the land. So a man from Bethlehem in Judah, together with his wife and two sons, went to live for a while in the country of Moab. ²The man's name was Elimelek, his wife's name was Naomi, and the names of his two sons were Mahlon and Kilion. They were Ephrathites from Bethlehem, Judah. And they went to Moab and lived there.

³Now Elimelek, Naomi's husband, died,

---

a 1 Traditionally *judged*

and she was left with her two sons. ⁴They married Moabite women, one named Orpah and the other Ruth. After they had lived there about ten years, ⁵both Mahlon and Kilion also died, and Naomi was left without her two sons and her husband.

Naomi and Ruth Return to Bethlehem

⁶When Naomi heard in Moab that the LORD had come to the aid of his people by providing food for them, she and her daughters-in-law prepared to return home from there. ⁷With her two daughters-in-law she left the place where she had been living and set out on the road that would take them back to the land of Judah.

⁸Then Naomi said to her two daughters-in-law, "Go back, each of you, to your mother's home. May the LORD show you kindness, as you have shown kindness to your dead husbands and to me. ⁹May the LORD grant that each of you will find rest in the home of another husband."

Then she kissed them goodbye and they wept aloud ¹⁰and said to her, "We will go back with you to your people."

¹¹But Naomi said, "Return home, my daughters. Why would you come with me? Am I going to have any more sons, who could become your husbands? ¹²Return home, my daughters; I am too old to have another husband. Even if I thought there was still hope for me — even if I had a husband tonight and then gave birth to sons — ¹³would you wait until they grew up? Would you remain unmarried for them? No, my daughters. It is more bitter for me than for you, because the LORD's hand has turned against me!"

¹⁴At this they wept aloud again. Then Orpah kissed her mother-in-law goodbye, but Ruth clung to her.

¹⁵"Look," said Naomi, "your sister-in-law is going back to her people and her gods. Go back with her."

¹⁶But Ruth replied, "Don't urge me to leave you or to turn back from you. Where you go I will go, and where you stay I will stay. Your people will be my people and your God my God. ¹⁷Where you die I will die, and there I will be buried. May the LORD deal with me, be it ever so severely, if even death separates you and me." ¹⁸When Naomi realized that Ruth was determined to go with her, she stopped urging her.

¹⁹So the two women went on until they came to Bethlehem. When they arrived in Bethlehem, the whole town was stirred because of them, and the women exclaimed, "Can this be Naomi?"

²⁰"Don't call me Naomi,ᵃ" she told them. "Call me Mara,ᵇ because the Almightyᶜ has made my life very bitter. ²¹I went away full, but the LORD has brought me back empty. Why call me Naomi? The LORD has afflictedᵈ me; the Almighty has brought misfortune upon me."

²²So Naomi returned from Moab accompanied by Ruth the Moabite, her daughter-in-law, arriving in Bethlehem as the barley harvest was beginning.

Ruth Meets Boaz in the Grain Field

2 Now Naomi had a relative on her husband's side, a man of standing from the clan of Elimelek, whose name was Boaz.

²And Ruth the Moabite said to Naomi, "Let me go to the fields and pick up the leftover grain behind anyone in whose eyes I find favor."

Naomi said to her, "Go ahead, my daughter." ³So she went out, entered a field and began to glean behind the harvesters. As it turned out, she was working in a field belonging to Boaz, who was from the clan of Elimelek.

⁴Just then Boaz arrived from Bethlehem and greeted the harvesters, "The LORD be with you!"

"The LORD bless you!" they answered.

⁵Boaz asked the overseer of his harvest-

ᵃ 20 *Naomi* means *pleasant.*   ᵇ 20 *Mara* means *bitter.*   ᶜ 20 Hebrew *Shaddai*; also in verse 21
ᵈ 21 Or *has testified against*

ers, "Who does that young woman belong to?"

6The overseer replied, "She is the Moabite who came back from Moab with Naomi. 7She said, 'Please let me glean and gather among the sheaves behind the harvesters.' She came into the field and has remained here from morning till now, except for a short rest in the shelter."

8So Boaz said to Ruth, "My daughter, listen to me. Don't go and glean in another field and don't go away from here. Stay here with the women who work for me. 9Watch the field where the men are harvesting, and follow along after the women. I have told the men not to lay a hand on you. And whenever you are thirsty, go and get a drink from the water jars the men have filled."

10At this, she bowed down with her face to the ground. She asked him, "Why have I found such favor in your eyes that you notice me—a foreigner?"

11Boaz replied, "I've been told all about what you have done for your mother-in-law since the death of your husband—how you left your father and mother and your homeland and came to live with a people you did not know before. 12May the LORD repay you for what you have done. May you be richly rewarded by the LORD, the God of Israel, under whose wings you have come to take refuge."

13"May I continue to find favor in your eyes, my lord," she said. "You have put me at ease by speaking kindly to your servant—though I do not have the standing of one of your servants."

14At mealtime Boaz said to her, "Come over here. Have some bread and dip it in the wine vinegar."

When she sat down with the harvesters, he offered her some roasted grain. She ate all she wanted and had some left over. 15As she got up to glean, Boaz gave orders to his men, "Let her gather among the sheaves and don't reprimand her. 16Even pull out some stalks for her from the bundles and leave them for her to pick up, and don't rebuke her."

17So Ruth gleaned in the field until evening. Then she threshed the barley she had gathered, and it amounted to about an ephah.a 18She carried it back to town, and her mother-in-law saw how much she had gathered. Ruth also brought out and gave her what she had left over after she had eaten enough.

19Her mother-in-law asked her, "Where did you glean today? Where did you work? Blessed be the man who took notice of you!"

Then Ruth told her mother-in-law about the one at whose place she had been working. "The name of the man I worked with today is Boaz," she said.

20"The LORD bless him!" Naomi said to her daughter-in-law. "He has not stopped showing his kindness to the living and the dead." She added, "That man is our close relative; he is one of our guardian-redeemers.b"

21Then Ruth the Moabite said, "He even said to me, 'Stay with my workers until they finish harvesting all my grain.'"

22Naomi said to Ruth her daughter-in-law, "It will be good for you, my daughter, to go with the women who work for him, because in someone else's field you might be harmed."

23So Ruth stayed close to the women of Boaz to glean until the barley and wheat harvests were finished. And she lived with her mother-in-law.

Ruth and Boaz at the Threshing Floor

3 One day Ruth's mother-in-law Naomi said to her, "My daughter, I must find a homec for you, where you will be well provided for. 2Now Boaz, with

---

a 17 That is, probably about 30 pounds or about 13 kilograms   b 20 The Hebrew word for guardian-redeemer is a legal term for one who has the obligation to redeem a relative in serious difficulty (see Lev. 25:25-55).   c 1 Hebrew find rest (see 1:9) whose women you have worked, is a relative of ours. Tonight he will be winnowing barley on the threshing floor. ³Wash, put on perfume, and get dressed in your best clothes. Then go down to the threshing floor, but don't let him know you are there until he has finished eating and drinking. ⁴When he lies down, note the place where he is lying. Then go and uncover his feet and lie down. He will tell you what to do."

⁵"I will do whatever you say," Ruth answered. ⁶So she went down to the threshing floor and did everything her mother-in-law told her to do.

⁷When Boaz had finished eating and drinking and was in good spirits, he went over to lie down at the far end of the grain pile. Ruth approached quietly, uncovered his feet and lay down. ⁸In the middle of the night something startled the man; he turned—and there was a woman lying at his feet!

⁹"Who are you?" he asked.

"I am your servant Ruth," she said. "Spread the corner of your garment over me, since you are a guardian-redeemer*a* of our family."

¹⁰"The Lord bless you, my daughter," he replied. "This kindness is greater than that which you showed earlier: You have not run after the younger men, whether rich or poor. ¹¹And now, my daughter, don't be afraid. I will do for you all you ask. All the people of my town know that you are a woman of noble character. ¹²Although it is true that I am a guardian-redeemer of our family, there is another who is more closely related than I. ¹³Stay here for the night, and in the morning if he wants to do his duty as your guardian-redeemer, good; let him redeem you. But if he is not willing, as surely as the Lord lives I will do it. Lie here until morning."

¹⁴So she lay at his feet until morning, but got up before anyone could be recognized; and he said, "No one must know that a woman came to the threshing floor."

¹⁵He also said, "Bring me the shawl you are wearing and hold it out." When she did so, he poured into it six measures of barley and placed the bundle on her. Then he*b* went back to town.

¹⁶When Ruth came to her mother-in-law, Naomi asked, "How did it go, my daughter?"

Then she told her everything Boaz had done for her ¹⁷and added, "He gave me these six measures of barley, saying, 'Don't go back to your mother-in-law empty-handed.'"

¹⁸Then Naomi said, "Wait, my daughter, until you find out what happens. For the man will not rest until the matter is settled today."

Boaz Marries Ruth

4 Meanwhile Boaz went up to the town gate and sat down there just as the guardian-redeemer*c* he had mentioned came along. Boaz said, "Come over here, my friend, and sit down." So he went over and sat down.

²Boaz took ten of the elders of the town and said, "Sit here," and they did so. ³Then he said to the guardian-redeemer, "Naomi, who has come back from Moab, is selling the piece of land that belonged to our relative Elimelek. ⁴I thought I should bring the matter to your attention and suggest that you buy it in the presence of these seated here and in the presence of the elders of my people. If you will redeem it, do so. But if you*d* will not, tell me, so I will know. For no one has the right to do it except you, and I am next in line."

"I will redeem it," he said.

⁵Then Boaz said, "On the day you buy the land from Naomi, you also acquire

---

a 9 The Hebrew word for *guardian-redeemer* is a legal term for one who has the obligation to redeem a relative in serious difficulty (see Lev. 25:25-55); also in verses 12 and 13.　*b 15* Most Hebrew manuscripts; many Hebrew manuscripts, Vulgate and Syriac *she*　*c 1* The Hebrew word for *guardian-redeemer* is a legal term for one who has the obligation to redeem a relative in serious difficulty (see Lev. 25:25-55); also in verses 3, 6, 8 and 14.　*d 4* Many Hebrew manuscripts, Septuagint, Vulgate and Syriac; most Hebrew manuscripts *he*

Ruth the Moabite, the[a] dead man's widow, in order to maintain the name of the dead with his property."

⁶At this, the guardian-redeemer said, "Then I cannot redeem it because I might endanger my own estate. You redeem it yourself. I cannot do it."

⁷(Now in earlier times in Israel, for the redemption and transfer of property to become final, one party took off his sandal and gave it to the other. This was the method of legalizing transactions in Israel.)

⁸So the guardian-redeemer said to Boaz, "Buy it yourself." And he removed his sandal.

⁹Then Boaz announced to the elders and all the people, "Today you are witnesses that I have bought from Naomi all the property of Elimelek, Kilion and Mahlon. ¹⁰I have also acquired Ruth the Moabite, Mahlon's widow, as my wife, in order to maintain the name of the dead with his property, so that his name will not disappear from among his family or from his hometown. Today you are witnesses!"

¹¹Then the elders and all the people at the gate said, "We are witnesses. May the LORD make the woman who is coming into your home like Rachel and Leah, who together built up the family of Israel. May you have standing in Ephrathah and be famous in Bethlehem. ¹²Through the offspring the LORD gives you by this young woman, may your family be like that of Perez, whom Tamar bore to Judah."

Naomi Gains a Son

¹³So Boaz took Ruth and she became his wife. When he made love to her, the LORD enabled her to conceive, and she gave birth to a son. ¹⁴The women said to Naomi: "Praise be to the LORD, who this day has not left you without a guardian-redeemer. May he become famous throughout Israel! ¹⁵He will renew your life and sustain you in your old age. For your daughter-in-law, who loves you and who is better to you than seven sons, has given him birth."

¹⁶Then Naomi took the child in her arms and cared for him. ¹⁷The women living there said, "Naomi has a son!" And they named him Obed. He was the father of Jesse, the father of David.

The Genealogy of David

¹⁸This, then, is the family line of Perez:

Perez was the father of Hezron,
¹⁹Hezron the father of Ram,
Ram the father of Amminadab,
²⁰Amminadab the father of Nahshon,
Nahshon the father of Salmon,[b]
²¹Salmon the father of Boaz,
Boaz the father of Obed,
²²Obed the father of Jesse,
and Jesse the father of David.

---

[a] 5 Vulgate and Syriac; Hebrew (see also Septuagint) *Naomi and from Ruth the Moabite, you acquire the*
[b] 20 A few Hebrew manuscripts, some Septuagint manuscripts and Vulgate (see also verse 21 and Septuagint of 1 Chron. 2:11); most Hebrew manuscripts *Salma*

1 Samuel

THEME: First Samuel emphasizes that obedience, not ritual or tradition, pleases God.

AUTHOR: The author of 1 Samuel is unknown. Scripture mentions the records of the prophets Samuel, Nathan and Gad as sources that may have been incorporated into this written history of Israel.

DATE OF WRITING: The two books of Samuel were originally one book that was probably written around 925 BC, shortly after the division of the nation into the northern and southern kingdoms (930 BC).

ENCOURAGEMENT FROM 1 SAMUEL: "The LORD does not look at the things people look at. People look at the outward appearance, but the LORD looks at the heart" (1 Samuel 16:7).

CHALLENGE FROM 1 SAMUEL: "Be sure to fear the LORD and serve him faithfully with all your heart; consider what great things he has done for you" (1 Samuel 12:24).

REFLECTION FROM 1 SAMUEL: "There is no one holy like the LORD; there is no one besides you; there is no Rock like our God" (1 Samuel 2:2).

At the beginning of 1 Samuel, all is not well in Israel. The nation's worship has been corrupted by the influence of evil men. Israel has suffered repeated defeat at the hands of the Philistines, culminating in the loss of the ark of the Lord. As a result, God's glory departs from the tabernacle.

Samuel is both the last of the judges and the first of the prophets. Because of his committed ministry, Israel experiences a remarkable revival. Again, however, the people grow restless, this time demanding a king. God provides them with an earthly king while remaining their one true King. Saul becomes the first Israelite king, but his failure ends his reign. As Saul declines, God begins to raise up a new leader: David. Throughout its pages, 1 Samuel highlights the consequences of sin. In Saul's case, God withdrew his blessing from Saul's life and reign.

Sin still has consequences, both in our lives in general and, more particularly, in our recovery journeys. Although we've been forgiven since putting our faith in Jesus Christ, some of our past sins may continue to carry consequences. Broken relationships, damage to our bodies and minds and painful memories of past failures may still be a part of our reality. Recovery is the path for healing sin's damage so that we can experience the blessings our heavenly Father is anxious to pour into our lives. No matter what we've done in the past, because of God's amazing grace we can be forgiven and restored. Like David, each of us has the potential and opportunity to become a man or woman after God's "own heart" (Acts 13:22).

The Birth of Samuel

1 There was a certain man from Ramathaim, a Zuphite[a] from the hill country of Ephraim, whose name was Elkanah son of Jeroham, the son of Elihu, the son of Tohu, the son of Zuph, an Ephraimite. [2]He had two wives; one was called Hannah and the other Peninnah. Peninnah had children, but Hannah had none.

[3]Year after year this man went up from his town to worship and sacrifice to the LORD Almighty at Shiloh, where Hophni and Phinehas, the two sons of Eli, were priests of the LORD. [4]Whenever the day came for Elkanah to sacrifice, he would give portions of the meat to his wife Peninnah and to all her sons and daughters. [5]But to Hannah he gave a double portion because he loved her, and the LORD had closed her womb. [6]Because the LORD had closed Hannah's womb, her rival kept provoking her in order to irritate her. [7]This went on year after year. Whenever Hannah went up to the house of the LORD, her rival provoked her till she wept and would not eat. [8]Her husband Elkanah would say to her, "Hannah, why are you weeping? Why don't you eat? Why are you downhearted? Don't I mean more to you than ten sons?"

[9]Once when they had finished eating and drinking in Shiloh, Hannah stood up. Now Eli the priest was sitting on his chair by the doorpost of the LORD's house. [10]In her deep anguish Hannah prayed to the LORD, weeping bitterly. [11]And she made a vow, saying, "LORD Almighty, if you will only look on your servant's misery and remember me, and not forget your servant but give her a son, then I will give him to the LORD for all the days of his life, and no razor will ever be used on his head."

[12]As she kept on praying to the LORD, Eli observed her mouth. [13]Hannah was praying in her heart, and her lips were moving but her voice was not heard. Eli thought she was drunk [14]and said to her, "How long are you going to stay drunk? Put away your wine."

[15]"Not so, my lord," Hannah replied, "I am a woman who is deeply troubled. I have not been drinking wine or beer; I was pouring out my soul to the LORD. [16]Do not take your servant for a wicked woman; I have been praying here out of my great anguish and grief."

[17]Eli answered, "Go in peace, and may the God of Israel grant you what you have asked of him."

[18]She said, "May your servant find favor in your eyes." Then she went her way and ate something, and her face was no longer downcast.

[19]Early the next morning they arose and worshiped before the LORD and then went back to their home at Ramah. Elkanah made love to his wife Hannah, and the LORD remembered her. [20]So in the course of time Hannah became pregnant and gave birth to a son. She named him Samuel,[b] saying, "Because I asked the LORD for him."

Hannah Dedicates Samuel

[21]When her husband Elkanah went up with all his family to offer the annual sacrifice to the LORD and to fulfill his vow, [22]Hannah did not go. She said to her husband, "After the boy is weaned, I will take him and present him before the LORD, and he will live there always."[c]

[23]"Do what seems best to you," her husband Elkanah told her. "Stay here until you have weaned him; only may the LORD make good his[d] word." So the woman stayed at home and nursed her son until she had weaned him.

[24]After he was weaned, she took the boy with her, young as he was, along with a three-year-old bull,[e] an ephah[f] of flour and a skin of wine, and brought him to the

---

a 1 See Septuagint and 1 Chron. 6:26-27,33-35; or *from Ramathaim Zuphim.*   *b 20* *Samuel* sounds like the Hebrew for *heard by God.*   *c 22* Masoretic Text; Dead Sea Scrolls *always. I have dedicated him as a Nazirite — all the days of his life."*   *d 23* Masoretic Text; Dead Sea Scrolls, Septuagint and Syriac *your*   *e 24* Dead Sea Scrolls, Septuagint and Syriac; Masoretic Text *with three bulls*   *f 24* That is, probably about 36 pounds or about 16 kilograms

My Name Is Hannah

1 Samuel 1

Hannah's story reveals God's power to bring a child of blessing out of a deeply dysfunctional family. This child, Samuel, became the last and greatest of Israel's judges, the transitional leader between the judges and the kings of Israel. Samuel would anoint David as God's choice of king for Israel. And David, in turn, would receive a covenant promise from God that one of his descendants would rule forever on his throne. This vital chain of events and characters leading to the Messiah begins with a troubled woman's agonizing prayer.

Hannah's husband, Elkanah, was faithful in his annual journeys to offer sacrifices at the tabernacle at Shiloh. Despite his piety, though, his home life was far from ideal. When we observe the effects of polygamy in the Scriptures, we can't help but notice that the result was inevitably conflict. Elkanah's second wife, Peninnah, had given him children, while Hannah, the favored wife, was barren. Still, Elkanah made his greater love for Hannah all too apparent (see 1 Samuel 1:4–5). Peninnah retaliated by mocking Hannah's evident infertility (see vv. 6–7).

To Peninnah's satisfaction, Hannah proved a vulnerable target. She wept and refused to eat, triggering Elkanah's efforts to console her. These dynamics spurred a continuing cycle of verbal abuse and rivalry, repeated year after year during what should have been a joyous time of family worship. Having hit bottom, "in her deep anguish Hannah prayed to the LORD, weeping bitterly" (v. 10). She pleaded with God for a son, pledging to dedicate him to the Lord's service for his entire life (see v. 11). Hannah prayed with such silent intensity, that Eli the high priest rebuked her for what he perceived to be a drunken state (see vv. 12–14). Hannah explained that she wasn't intoxicated but "deeply troubled" (v. 15). Eli, recognizing her sincerity and faith, sent her back to her family with a blessing and a petition on her behalf. Hannah, her depression lifted, returned to her camp and ate (see v. 18).

Notice that Hannah's faith changed her before her visible circumstances changed. God may not change our circumstances, either, until we allow him to change us. There's always a best time to begin recovery: now. After she returned home, Hannah's faith was rewarded with the conception and birth of a son. When the child was weaned, Hannah kept her vow; she gave him back to the Lord for lifelong tabernacle service.

We're all familiar with the adage "Home is where the heart is." That's true, but how often isn't it also the source of our deepest hurt? Hannah lived with perpetual verbal abuse. Infertility in her culture was a source of deep shame — a common emotion of the abused. It isn't surprising that Hannah under those circumstances descended into depression. Nevertheless, she held on to the truth: There is a God who knows us personally and cares deeply for each of us. He knows us and our situation and has the power to change both. Hiding our pain is a popular strategy in our culture. We're encouraged to deny, bury or blame others for it. Hannah, in contrast, poured out her agony before the Lord and before Eli. We too need to lay our anguish and grief at Jesus' feet.

Hannah held back nothing, not even her treasured son. A painful past can fill our hearts with fear concerning the future of our children. We know from experience that this world is a hurtful place, and our own parents may have lived out a deeply flawed pattern of parenthood. When worry about this issue grips our hearts, we must look at Hannah's faith. We must relinquish our pain and anxiety to God, recognizing that his principles of recovery are also the principles that develop great parenting skills. We must model God's truth to our children, and be sure to share with them our story of recovery.

house of the LORD at Shiloh. 25When the bull had been sacrificed, they brought the boy to Eli, 26and she said to him, "Pardon me, my lord. As surely as you live, I am the woman who stood here beside you praying to the LORD. 27I prayed for this child, and the LORD has granted me what I asked of him. 28So now I give him to the LORD. For his whole life he will be given over to the LORD." And he worshiped the LORD there.

Hannah's Prayer

2 Then Hannah prayed and said:

"My heart rejoices in the LORD;
    in the LORD my horn*a* is lifted high.
My mouth boasts over my enemies,
    for I delight in your deliverance.

2 "There is no one holy like the LORD;
    there is no one besides you;
    there is no Rock like our God.

3 "Do not keep talking so proudly
    or let your mouth speak such
        arrogance,
for the LORD is a God who knows,
    and by him deeds are weighed.

4 "The bows of the warriors are broken,
    but those who stumbled are armed
        with strength.
5 Those who were full hire themselves
    out for food,
    but those who were hungry are
        hungry no more.
She who was barren has borne seven
    children,
    but she who has had many sons pines
        away.

6 "The LORD brings death and makes
    alive;
    he brings down to the grave and
        raises up.
7 The LORD sends poverty and wealth;
    he humbles and he exalts.
8 He raises the poor from the dust
    and lifts the needy from the ash heap;

he seats them with princes
    and has them inherit a throne of
        honor.

"For the foundations of the earth are
    the LORD's;
    on them he has set the world.
9 He will guard the feet of his faithful
    servants,
    but the wicked will be silenced in the
        place of darkness.

"It is not by strength that one prevails;
10   those who oppose the LORD will be
        broken.
The Most High will thunder from
    heaven;
    the LORD will judge the ends of the
        earth.

"He will give strength to his king
    and exalt the horn of his anointed."

11 Then Elkanah went home to Ramah, but the boy ministered before the LORD under Eli the priest.

Eli's Wicked Sons

12 Eli's sons were scoundrels; they had no regard for the LORD. 13Now it was the practice of the priests that, whenever any of the people offered a sacrifice, the priest's servant would come with a three-pronged fork in his hand while the meat was being boiled 14and would plunge the fork into the pan or kettle or caldron or pot. Whatever the fork brought up the priest would take for himself. This is how they treated all the Israelites who came to Shiloh. 15But even before the fat was burned, the priest's servant would come and say to the person who was sacrificing, "Give the priest some meat to roast; he won't accept boiled meat from you, but only raw."

16If the person said to him, "Let the fat be burned first, and then take whatever you want," the servant would answer, "No, hand it over now; if you don't, I'll take it by force."

---

a 1 *Horn* here symbolizes strength; also in verse 10.

My Name Is Elaine

I'M A BELIEVER WHO STRUGGLES WITH CODEPENDENCY

Please read the story of Hannah's dedication of her son in
1 Samuel 1:1 — 2:11.

I grew up in a loving home. We took vacations together and kept in close touch with our extended family. Faith and church attendance were important in our lives, and I was involved in church youth groups throughout my young adult life.

I met my husband in the summer of 1966. We started dating in the fall, and he asked me to marry him just before Christmas. I should have known things weren't going to be easy. One clue was Howard's arrival at church on the day of our wedding two minutes before we were to walk down the aisle. Howard wasn't accustomed to family gatherings, but I naively thought I could "fix" him. I also convinced myself that his drinking habit wouldn't be a problem. Nine months and twelve days after our marriage, our son Jim was born, followed two-and-a-half years later by his brother, Troy. At this point I was attending church only a couple of times annually; my life felt complete without it.

My parents and siblings never realized the anguish I was enduring due to Howard's drinking and unfaithfulness. It was easier for me to look the other way and pretend I wasn't hurting. I didn't want to become a statistic and was determined to keep our family together.

I put my hope in Howard's repeated promises to change. Every time I reached my limit and thought I couldn't go on any longer, he'd promise to clean up his life. Things would, in fact, get better for a while, but he would revert back to his old patterns, hurting me again and again. After 28 years I was still holding on to the false hope that I could remedy the situation.

We moved to California in 1982. At that point Howard started using drugs along with alcohol. He hit bottom in 1994, and our sons and I managed to get him into rehab. Afterward I thought everything would be okay. "What else could go wrong?" I asked myself, fully expecting a negative answer. But Howard made an inappropriate comment to our younger son's wife. She was offended, and although Howard tried to apologize, the damage had been done. The incident tore apart our family and caused lasting bitterness. That was the final straw. I was ready to give up on my marriage, convinced that I didn't have it in me to forgive Howard this time.

In the spring of 1995 Jim asked whether we would like to attend his church's Easter service with him and his wife, Gail. We agreed, and that was our first Sunday at Saddleback Church. Howard wanted to return the following weekend, and God began softening both our hearts.

Howard committed his life to Christ, and I recommitted mine. Now, with Jesus Christ included in the equation, I began for the first time to experience real hope. Jim, Gail, Howard and I were baptized together, and Jim and Gail have stayed with us through our tough times. They have three adopted children: Andrew, Carly and Jeff. Our grandchildren have brought so much joy into our lives and are truly gifts from God.

Howard and I began attending Celebrate Recovery, and in the Step Study I started working through the 12 steps. I remember well the first question in Step One: "What areas of your life do you have control over?" I noticed everyone around me writing, and I sat there in panic. I couldn't think of one area over which I had control. That was the first time I admitted that I was powerless, absolutely unable to change on my own. I identified with the Biblical Hannah as I gave my still-estranged son, Troy, over to the Lord.

I was blessed to be able to work through the steps with a special group of ladies with whom I've maintained a close bond. My friend Diane and I have been together every Friday night at Celebrate Recovery for over six years now. And I've seen a miracle happen in my husband. We renewed our wedding vows, and in February of next year we'll celebrate our 40th wedding anniversary.

Although I prayed daily for reconciliation with my son, I hadn't seen Troy in several years and had never met my grandson Jordan. Two years ago I began receiving Mother's Day cards from Troy, and at last he called to talk. He phoned again after their new baby, Jacob, was born, and when I was in the hospital with pneumonia, he called to say that he and the boys were coming out to California for a visit.

One evening I went to Jim's house, and Troy walked into the room with both his sons. This was the beginning of our healing process, and I know God will continue to help us every step of the way. Sometimes I'm asked, "How could you forgive 28 years of shame and grief and pain?" The reality is that it's hard for me *not* to forgive when I know that Jesus sacrificed so much for my forgiveness. We can't change ourselves, or others, by forcing the issue through sheer willpower. Only Jesus Christ, our Higher Power, can facilitate lasting change in our lives.

Elaine

¹⁷This sin of the young men was very great in the LORD's sight, for they[a] were treating the LORD's offering with contempt.

¹⁸But Samuel was ministering before the LORD — a boy wearing a linen ephod. ¹⁹Each year his mother made him a little robe and took it to him when she went up with her husband to offer the annual sacrifice. ²⁰Eli would bless Elkanah and his wife, saying, "May the LORD give you children by this woman to take the place of the one she prayed for and gave to[b] the LORD." Then they would go home. ²¹And the LORD was gracious to Hannah; she gave birth to three sons and two daughters. Meanwhile, the boy Samuel grew up in the presence of the LORD.

²²Now Eli, who was very old, heard about everything his sons were doing to all Israel and how they slept with the women who served at the entrance to the tent of meeting. ²³So he said to them, "Why do you do such things? I hear from all the people about these wicked deeds of yours. ²⁴No, my sons; the report I hear spreading among the LORD's people is not good. ²⁵If one person sins against another, God[c] may mediate for the offender; but if anyone sins against the LORD, who will intercede for them?" His sons, however, did not listen to their father's rebuke, for it was the LORD's will to put them to death.

²⁶And the boy Samuel continued to grow in stature and in favor with the LORD and with people.

Prophecy Against the House of Eli

²⁷Now a man of God came to Eli and said to him, "This is what the LORD says: 'Did I not clearly reveal myself to your ancestor's family when they were in Egypt under Pharaoh? ²⁸I chose your ancestor out of all the tribes of Israel to be my priest, to go up to my altar, to burn incense, and to wear an ephod in my presence. I also gave your ancestor's family all the food offerings presented by the Israelites. ²⁹Why do you[d] scorn my sacrifice and offering that I prescribed for my dwelling? Why do you honor your sons more than me by fattening yourselves on the choice parts of every offering made by my people Israel?'

³⁰"Therefore the LORD, the God of Israel, declares: 'I promised that members of your family would minister before me forever.' But now the LORD declares: 'Far be it from me! Those who honor me I will honor, but those who despise me will be disdained. ³¹The time is coming when I will cut short your strength and the strength of your priestly house, so that no one in it will reach old age, ³²and you will see distress in my dwelling. Although good will be done to Israel, no one in your family line will ever reach old age. ³³Every one of you that I do not cut off from serving at my altar I will spare only to destroy your sight and sap your strength, and all your descendants will die in the prime of life.

³⁴"'And what happens to your two sons, Hophni and Phinehas, will be a sign to you — they will both die on the same day. ³⁵I will raise up for myself a faithful priest, who will do according to what is in my heart and mind. I will firmly establish his priestly house, and they will minister before my anointed one always. ³⁶Then everyone left in your family line will come and bow down before him for a piece of silver and a loaf of bread and plead, "Appoint me to some priestly office so I can have food to eat."'"

The LORD Calls Samuel

3 The boy Samuel ministered before the LORD under Eli. In those days the word of the LORD was rare; there were not many visions.

²One night Eli, whose eyes were becoming so weak that he could barely see, was lying down in his usual place. ³The lamp of God had not yet gone out, and Samuel

---

[a] 17 Dead Sea Scrolls and Septuagint; Masoretic Text *people*   [b] 20 Dead Sea Scrolls; Masoretic Text *and asked from*
[c] 25 Or *the judges*   [d] 29 The Hebrew is plural.

was lying down in the house of the LORD, where the ark of God was. ⁴Then the LORD called Samuel.

Samuel answered, "Here I am." ⁵And he ran to Eli and said, "Here I am; you called me."

But Eli said, "I did not call; go back and lie down." So he went and lay down.

⁶Again the LORD called, "Samuel!" And Samuel got up and went to Eli and said, "Here I am; you called me."

"My son," Eli said, "I did not call; go back and lie down."

⁷Now Samuel did not yet know the LORD: The word of the LORD had not yet been revealed to him.

⁸A third time the LORD called, "Samuel!" And Samuel got up and went to Eli and said, "Here I am; you called me."

Then Eli realized that the LORD was calling the boy. ⁹So Eli told Samuel, "Go and lie down, and if he calls you, say, 'Speak, LORD, for your servant is listening.'" So Samuel went and lay down in his place.

¹⁰The LORD came and stood there, calling as at the other times, "Samuel! Samuel!"

Then Samuel said, "Speak, for your servant is listening."

¹¹And the LORD said to Samuel: "See, I am about to do something in Israel that will make the ears of everyone who hears about it tingle. ¹²At that time I will carry out against Eli everything I spoke against his family—from beginning to end. ¹³For I told him that I would judge his family forever because of the sin he knew about; his sons blasphemed God,ᵃ and he failed to restrain them. ¹⁴Therefore I swore to the house of Eli, 'The guilt of Eli's house will never be atoned for by sacrifice or offering.'"

¹⁵Samuel lay down until morning and then opened the doors of the house of the LORD. He was afraid to tell Eli the vision, ¹⁶but Eli called him and said, "Samuel, my son."

Samuel answered, "Here I am."

¹⁷"What was it he said to you?" Eli asked. "Do not hide it from me. May God deal with you, be it ever so severely, if you hide from me anything he told you." ¹⁸So Samuel told him everything, hiding nothing from him. Then Eli said, "He is the LORD; let him do what is good in his eyes."

¹⁹The LORD was with Samuel as he grew up, and he let none of Samuel's words fall to the ground. ²⁰And all Israel from Dan to Beersheba recognized that Samuel was attested as a prophet of the LORD. ²¹The LORD continued to appear at Shiloh, and there he revealed himself to Samuel through his word.

4

And Samuel's word came to all Israel.

The Philistines Capture the Ark

Now the Israelites went out to fight against the Philistines. The Israelites camped at Ebenezer, and the Philistines at Aphek. ²The Philistines deployed their forces to meet Israel, and as the battle spread, Israel was defeated by the Philistines, who killed about four thousand of them on the battlefield. ³When the soldiers returned to camp, the elders of Israel asked, "Why did the LORD bring defeat on us today before the Philistines? Let us bring the ark of the LORD's covenant from Shiloh, so that he may go with us and save us from the hand of our enemies."

⁴So the people sent men to Shiloh, and they brought back the ark of the covenant of the LORD Almighty, who is enthroned between the cherubim. And Eli's two sons, Hophni and Phinehas, were there with the ark of the covenant of God.

⁵When the ark of the LORD's covenant came into the camp, all Israel raised such a great shout that the ground shook. ⁶Hearing the uproar, the Philistines asked, "What's all this shouting in the Hebrew camp?"

When they learned that the ark of the LORD had come into the camp, ⁷the

---

ᵃ 13 An ancient Hebrew scribal tradition (see also Septuagint); Masoretic Text *sons made themselves contemptible*

Philistines were afraid. "A god has*a* come into the camp," they said. "Oh no! Nothing like this has happened before. 8We're doomed! Who will deliver us from the hand of these mighty gods? They are the gods who struck the Egyptians with all kinds of plagues in the wilderness. 9Be strong, Philistines! Be men, or you will be subject to the Hebrews, as they have been to you. Be men, and fight!"

10So the Philistines fought, and the Israelites were defeated and every man fled to his tent. The slaughter was very great; Israel lost thirty thousand foot soldiers. 11The ark of God was captured, and Eli's two sons, Hophni and Phinehas, died.

Death of Eli

12That same day a Benjamite ran from the battle line and went to Shiloh with his clothes torn and dust on his head. 13When he arrived, there was Eli sitting on his chair by the side of the road, watching, because his heart feared for the ark of God. When the man entered the town and told what had happened, the whole town sent up a cry.

14Eli heard the outcry and asked, "What is the meaning of this uproar?"

The man hurried over to Eli, 15who was ninety-eight years old and whose eyes had failed so that he could not see. 16He told Eli, "I have just come from the battle line; I fled from it this very day."

Eli asked, "What happened, my son?"

17The man who brought the news replied, "Israel fled before the Philistines, and the army has suffered heavy losses. Also your two sons, Hophni and Phinehas, are dead, and the ark of God has been captured."

18When he mentioned the ark of God, Eli fell backward off his chair by the side of the gate. His neck was broken and he died, for he was an old man, and he was heavy. He had led*b* Israel forty years.

19His daughter-in-law, the wife of Phinehas, was pregnant and near the time of delivery. When she heard the news that the ark of God had been captured and that her father-in-law and her husband were dead, she went into labor and gave birth, but was overcome by her labor pains. 20As she was dying, the women attending her said, "Don't despair; you have given birth to a son." But she did not respond or pay any attention.

21She named the boy Ichabod,*c* saying, "The Glory has departed from Israel" — because of the capture of the ark of God and the deaths of her father-in-law and her husband. 22She said, "The Glory has departed from Israel, for the ark of God has been captured."

The Ark in Ashdod and Ekron

5 After the Philistines had captured the ark of God, they took it from Ebenezer to Ashdod. 2Then they carried the ark into Dagon's temple and set it beside Dagon. 3When the people of Ashdod rose early the next day, there was Dagon, fallen on his face on the ground before the ark of the LORD! They took Dagon and put him back in his place. 4But the following morning when they rose, there was Dagon, fallen on his face on the ground before the ark of the LORD! His head and hands had been broken off and were lying on the threshold; only his body remained. 5That is why to this day neither the priests of Dagon nor any others who enter Dagon's temple at Ashdod step on the threshold.

6The LORD's hand was heavy on the people of Ashdod and its vicinity; he brought devastation on them and afflicted them with tumors.*d* 7When the people of Ashdod saw what was happening, they said, "The ark of the god of Israel must not stay here with us, because his hand is heavy on us and on Dagon our god." 8So they called

---

a 7 Or *"Gods have* (see Septuagint)   *b 18* Traditionally *judged*   *c 21* *Ichabod* means *no glory.*   *d 6* Hebrew; Septuagint and Vulgate *tumors. And rats appeared in their land, and there was death and destruction throughout the city* together all the rulers of the Philistines and asked them, "What shall we do with the ark of the god of Israel?"

They answered, "Have the ark of the god of Israel moved to Gath." So they moved the ark of the God of Israel.

⁹But after they had moved it, the Lord's hand was against that city, throwing it into a great panic. He afflicted the people of the city, both young and old, with an outbreak of tumors.ᵃ ¹⁰So they sent the ark of God to Ekron.

As the ark of God was entering Ekron, the people of Ekron cried out, "They have brought the ark of the god of Israel around to us to kill us and our people." ¹¹So they called together all the rulers of the Philistines and said, "Send the ark of the god of Israel away; let it go back to its own place, or itᵇ will kill us and our people." For death had filled the city with panic; God's hand was very heavy on it. ¹²Those who did not die were afflicted with tumors, and the outcry of the city went up to heaven.

The Ark Returned to Israel

6 When the ark of the Lord had been in Philistine territory seven months, ²the Philistines called for the priests and the diviners and said, "What shall we do with the ark of the Lord? Tell us how we should send it back to its place."

³They answered, "If you return the ark of the god of Israel, do not send it back to him without a gift; by all means send a guilt offering to him. Then you will be healed, and you will know why his hand has not been lifted from you."

⁴The Philistines asked, "What guilt offering should we send to him?"

They replied, "Five gold tumors and five gold rats, according to the number of the Philistine rulers, because the same plague has struck both you and your rulers. ⁵Make models of the tumors and of the rats that are destroying the country, and give glory to Israel's god. Perhaps he will lift his hand

from you and your gods and your land. ⁶Why do you harden your hearts as the Egyptians and Pharaoh did? When Israel's god dealt harshly with them, did they not send the Israelites out so they could go on their way?

⁷"Now then, get a new cart ready, with two cows that have calved and have never been yoked. Hitch the cows to the cart, but take their calves away and pen them up. ⁸Take the ark of the Lord and put it on the cart, and in a chest beside it put the gold objects you are sending back to him as a guilt offering. Send it on its way, ⁹but keep watching it. If it goes up to its own territory, toward Beth Shemesh, then the Lord has brought this great disaster on us. But if it does not, then we will know that it was not his hand that struck us but that it happened to us by chance."

¹⁰So they did this. They took two such cows and hitched them to the cart and penned up their calves. ¹¹They placed the ark of the Lord on the cart and along with it the chest containing the gold rats and the models of the tumors. ¹²Then the cows went straight up toward Beth Shemesh, keeping on the road and lowing all the way; they did not turn to the right or to the left. The rulers of the Philistines followed them as far as the border of Beth Shemesh.

¹³Now the people of Beth Shemesh were harvesting their wheat in the valley, and when they looked up and saw the ark, they rejoiced at the sight. ¹⁴The cart came to the field of Joshua of Beth Shemesh, and there it stopped beside a large rock. The people chopped up the wood of the cart and sacrificed the cows as a burnt offering to the Lord. ¹⁵The Levites took down the ark of the Lord, together with the chest containing the gold objects, and placed them on the large rock. On that day the people of Beth Shemesh offered burnt offerings and made sacrifices to the Lord. ¹⁶The five rulers of the Philistines saw all this and then returned that same day to Ekron.

ᵃ 9 Or *with tumors in the groin* (see Septuagint)   ᵇ 11 Or *he*

¹⁷These are the gold tumors the Philistines sent as a guilt offering to the LORD—one each for Ashdod, Gaza, Ashkelon, Gath and Ekron. ¹⁸And the number of the gold rats was according to the number of Philistine towns belonging to the five rulers—the fortified towns with their country villages. The large rock on which the Levites set the ark of the LORD is a witness to this day in the field of Joshua of Beth Shemesh.

¹⁹But God struck down some of the inhabitants of Beth Shemesh, putting seventy*a* of them to death because they looked into the ark of the LORD. The people mourned because of the heavy blow the LORD had dealt them. ²⁰And the people of Beth Shemesh asked, "Who can stand in the presence of the LORD, this holy God? To whom will the ark go up from here?"

²¹Then they sent messengers to the people of Kiriath Jearim, saying, "The Philistines have returned the ark of the LORD. Come down and take it up to your town."

7 ¹So the men of Kiriath Jearim came and took up the ark of the LORD. They brought it to Abinadab's house on the hill and consecrated Eleazar his son to guard the ark of the LORD. ²The ark remained at Kiriath Jearim a long time—twenty years in all.

Samuel Subdues the Philistines at Mizpah

Then all the people of Israel turned back to the LORD. ³So Samuel said to all the Israelites, "If you are returning to the LORD with all your hearts, then rid yourselves of the foreign gods and the Ashtoreths and commit yourselves to the LORD and serve him only, and he will deliver you out of the hand of the Philistines." ⁴So the Israelites put away their Baals and Ashtoreths, and served the LORD only.

⁵Then Samuel said, "Assemble all Israel at Mizpah, and I will intercede with the LORD for you." ⁶When they had assembled at Mizpah, they drew water and poured it out before the LORD. On that day they fasted and there they confessed, "We have sinned against the LORD." Now Samuel was serving as leader*b* of Israel at Mizpah.

⁷When the Philistines heard that Israel had assembled at Mizpah, the rulers of the Philistines came up to attack them. When the Israelites heard of it, they were afraid because of the Philistines. ⁸They said to Samuel, "Do not stop crying out to the LORD our God for us, that he may rescue us from the hand of the Philistines." ⁹Then Samuel took a suckling lamb and sacrificed it as a whole burnt offering to the LORD. He cried out to the LORD on Israel's behalf, and the LORD answered him.

¹⁰While Samuel was sacrificing the burnt offering, the Philistines drew near to engage Israel in battle. But that day the LORD thundered with loud thunder against the Philistines and threw them into such a panic that they were routed before the Israelites. ¹¹The men of Israel rushed out of Mizpah and pursued the Philistines, slaughtering them along the way to a point below Beth Kar.

¹²Then Samuel took a stone and set it up between Mizpah and Shen. He named it Ebenezer,*c* saying, "Thus far the LORD has helped us."

¹³So the Philistines were subdued and they stopped invading Israel's territory. Throughout Samuel's lifetime, the hand of the LORD was against the Philistines. ¹⁴The towns from Ekron to Gath that the Philistines had captured from Israel were restored to Israel, and Israel delivered the neighboring territory from the hands of the Philistines. And there was peace between Israel and the Amorites.

¹⁵Samuel continued as Israel's leader all the days of his life. ¹⁶From year to year he went on a circuit from Bethel to Gilgal to Mizpah, judging Israel in all those places. ¹⁷But he always went back to Ramah, where

---

a 19 A few Hebrew manuscripts; most Hebrew manuscripts and Septuagint *50,070*   *b 6* Traditionally *judge*; also in verse 15   *c 12* *Ebenezer* means *stone of help.*

his home was, and there he also held court for Israel. And he built an altar there to the Lord.

Israel Asks for a King

8 When Samuel grew old, he appointed his sons as Israel's leaders.[a] 2The name of his firstborn was Joel and the name of his second was Abijah, and they served at Beersheba. 3But his sons did not follow his ways. They turned aside after dishonest gain and accepted bribes and perverted justice.

4So all the elders of Israel gathered together and came to Samuel at Ramah. 5They said to him, "You are old, and your sons do not follow your ways; now appoint a king to lead[b] us, such as all the other nations have."

6But when they said, "Give us a king to lead us," this displeased Samuel; so he prayed to the Lord. 7And the Lord told him: "Listen to all that the people are saying to you; it is not you they have rejected, but they have rejected me as their king. 8As they have done from the day I brought them up out of Egypt until this day, forsaking me and serving other gods, so they are doing to you. 9Now listen to them; but warn them solemnly and let them know what the king who will reign over them will claim as his rights."

10Samuel told all the words of the Lord to the people who were asking him for a king. 11He said, "This is what the king who will reign over you will claim as his rights: He will take your sons and make them serve with his chariots and horses, and they will run in front of his chariots. 12Some he will assign to be commanders of thousands and commanders of fifties, and others to plow his ground and reap his harvest, and still others to make weapons of war and equipment for his chariots. 13He will take your daughters to be perfumers and cooks and bakers. 14He will take the best of your fields and vineyards and olive groves and give them to his attendants. 15He will take a tenth

of your grain and of your vintage and give it to his officials and attendants. 16Your male and female servants and the best of your cattle[c] and donkeys he will take for his own use. 17He will take a tenth of your flocks, and you yourselves will become his slaves. 18When that day comes, you will cry out for relief from the king you have chosen, but the Lord will not answer you in that day."

19But the people refused to listen to Samuel. "No!" they said. "We want a king over us. 20Then we will be like all the other nations, with a king to lead us and to go out before us and fight our battles."

21When Samuel heard all that the people said, he repeated it before the Lord. 22The Lord answered, "Listen to them and give them a king."

Then Samuel said to the Israelites, "Everyone go back to your own town."

Samuel Anoints Saul

9 There was a Benjamite, a man of standing, whose name was Kish son of Abiel, the son of Zeror, the son of Bekorath, the son of Aphiah of Benjamin. 2Kish had a son named Saul, as handsome a young man as could be found anywhere in Israel, and he was a head taller than anyone else.

3Now the donkeys belonging to Saul's father Kish were lost, and Kish said to his son Saul, "Take one of the servants with you and go and look for the donkeys." 4So he passed through the hill country of Ephraim and through the area around Shalisha, but they did not find them. They went on into the district of Shaalim, but the donkeys were not there. Then he passed through the territory of Benjamin, but they did not find them.

5When they reached the district of Zuph, Saul said to the servant who was with him, "Come, let's go back, or my father will stop thinking about the donkeys and start worrying about us."

6But the servant replied, "Look, in this

---

[a] 1 Traditionally *judges*   [b] 5 Traditionally *judge*; also in verses 6 and 20   [c] 16 Septuagint; Hebrew *young men*

town there is a man of God; he is highly respected, and everything he says comes true. Let's go there now. Perhaps he will tell us what way to take."

[7]Saul said to his servant, "If we go, what can we give the man? The food in our sacks is gone. We have no gift to take to the man of God. What do we have?"

[8]The servant answered him again. "Look," he said, "I have a quarter of a shekel[a] of silver. I will give it to the man of God so that he will tell us what way to take."

[9](Formerly in Israel, if someone went to inquire of God, they would say, "Come, let us go to the seer," because the prophet of today used to be called a seer.)

[10]"Good," Saul said to his servant. "Come, let's go." So they set out for the town where the man of God was.

[11]As they were going up the hill to the town, they met some young women coming out to draw water, and they asked them, "Is the seer here?"

[12]"He is," they answered. "He's ahead of you. Hurry now; he has just come to our town today, for the people have a sacrifice at the high place. [13]As soon as you enter the town, you will find him before he goes up to the high place to eat. The people will not begin eating until he comes, because he must bless the sacrifice; afterward, those who are invited will eat. Go up now; you should find him about this time."

[14]They went up to the town, and as they were entering it, there was Samuel, coming toward them on his way up to the high place.

[15]Now the day before Saul came, the Lord had revealed this to Samuel: [16]"About this time tomorrow I will send you a man from the land of Benjamin. Anoint him ruler over my people Israel; he will deliver them from the hand of the Philistines. I have looked on my people, for their cry has reached me."

[17]When Samuel caught sight of Saul, the Lord said to him, "This is the man I spoke to you about; he will govern my people."

[18]Saul approached Samuel in the gateway and asked, "Would you please tell me where the seer's house is?"

[19]"I am the seer," Samuel replied. "Go up ahead of me to the high place, for today you are to eat with me, and in the morning I will send you on your way and will tell you all that is in your heart. [20]As for the donkeys you lost three days ago, do not worry about them; they have been found. And to whom is all the desire of Israel turned, if not to you and your whole family line?"

[21]Saul answered, "But am I not a Benjamite, from the smallest tribe of Israel, and is not my clan the least of all the clans of the tribe of Benjamin? Why do you say such a thing to me?"

[22]Then Samuel brought Saul and his servant into the hall and seated them at the head of those who were invited — about thirty in number. [23]Samuel said to the cook, "Bring the piece of meat I gave you, the one I told you to lay aside."

[24]So the cook took up the thigh with what was on it and set it in front of Saul. Samuel said, "Here is what has been kept for you. Eat, because it was set aside for you for this occasion from the time I said, 'I have invited guests.'" And Saul dined with Samuel that day.

[25]After they came down from the high place to the town, Samuel talked with Saul on the roof of his house. [26]They rose about daybreak, and Samuel called to Saul on the roof, "Get ready, and I will send you on your way." When Saul got ready, he and Samuel went outside together. [27]As they were going down to the edge of the town, Samuel said to Saul, "Tell the servant to go on ahead of us" — and the servant did so — "but you stay here for a while, so that I may give you a message from God."

10 Then Samuel took a flask of olive oil and poured it on Saul's head and kissed him, saying, "Has not the Lord anointed you ruler over

---

his inheritance?[a] [2]When you leave me today, you will meet two men near Rachel's tomb, at Zelzah on the border of Benjamin. They will say to you, 'The donkeys you set out to look for have been found. And now your father has stopped thinking about them and is worried about you. He is asking, "What shall I do about my son?"'

[3]"Then you will go on from there until you reach the great tree of Tabor. Three men going up to worship God at Bethel will meet you there. One will be carrying three young goats, another three loaves of bread, and another a skin of wine. [4]They will greet you and offer you two loaves of bread, which you will accept from them.

[5]"After that you will go to Gibeah of God, where there is a Philistine outpost. As you approach the town, you will meet a procession of prophets coming down from the high place with lyres, timbrels, pipes and harps being played before them, and they will be prophesying. [6]The Spirit of the LORD will come powerfully upon you, and you will prophesy with them; and you will be changed into a different person. [7]Once these signs are fulfilled, do whatever your hand finds to do, for God is with you.

[8]"Go down ahead of me to Gilgal. I will surely come down to you to sacrifice burnt offerings and fellowship offerings, but you must wait seven days until I come to you and tell you what you are to do."

Saul Made King

[9]As Saul turned to leave Samuel, God changed Saul's heart, and all these signs were fulfilled that day. [10]When he and his servant arrived at Gibeah, a procession of prophets met him; the Spirit of God came powerfully upon him, and he joined in their prophesying. [11]When all those who had formerly known him saw him prophesying with the prophets, they asked each other, "What is this that has happened to the son of Kish? Is Saul also among the prophets?"

[12]A man who lived there answered, "And who is their father?" So it became a saying: "Is Saul also among the prophets?" [13]After Saul stopped prophesying, he went to the high place.

[14]Now Saul's uncle asked him and his servant, "Where have you been?"

"Looking for the donkeys," he said. "But when we saw they were not to be found, we went to Samuel."

[15]Saul's uncle said, "Tell me what Samuel said to you."

[16]Saul replied, "He assured us that the donkeys had been found." But he did not tell his uncle what Samuel had said about the kingship.

[17]Samuel summoned the people of Israel to the LORD at Mizpah [18]and said to them, "This is what the LORD, the God of Israel, says: 'I brought Israel up out of Egypt, and I delivered you from the power of Egypt and all the kingdoms that oppressed you.' [19]But you have now rejected your God, who saves you out of all your disasters and calamities. And you have said, 'No, appoint a king over us.' So now present yourselves before the LORD by your tribes and clans."

[20]When Samuel had all Israel come forward by tribes, the tribe of Benjamin was taken by lot. [21]Then he brought forward the tribe of Benjamin, clan by clan, and Matri's clan was taken. Finally Saul son of Kish was taken. But when they looked for him, he was not to be found. [22]So they inquired further of the LORD, "Has the man come here yet?"

And the LORD said, "Yes, he has hidden himself among the supplies."

[23]They ran and brought him out, and as he stood among the people he was a head taller than any of the others. [24]Samuel said to all the people, "Do you see the man the LORD has chosen? There is no one like him among all the people."

Then the people shouted, "Long live the king!"

---

[a] 1 Hebrew; Septuagint and Vulgate *over his people Israel? You will reign over the LORD's people and save them from the power of their enemies round about. And this will be a sign to you that the LORD has anointed you ruler over his inheritance:*

25Samuel explained to the people the rights and duties of kingship. He wrote them down on a scroll and deposited it before the Lord. Then Samuel dismissed the people to go to their own homes.

26Saul also went to his home in Gibeah, accompanied by valiant men whose hearts God had touched. 27But some scoundrels said, "How can this fellow save us?" They despised him and brought him no gifts. But Saul kept silent.

Saul Rescues the City of Jabesh

11 Nahash*a* the Ammonite went up and besieged Jabesh Gilead. And all the men of Jabesh said to him, "Make a treaty with us, and we will be subject to you."

2But Nahash the Ammonite replied, "I will make a treaty with you only on the condition that I gouge out the right eye of every one of you and so bring disgrace on all Israel."

3The elders of Jabesh said to him, "Give us seven days so we can send messengers throughout Israel; if no one comes to rescue us, we will surrender to you."

4When the messengers came to Gibeah of Saul and reported these terms to the people, they all wept aloud. 5Just then Saul was returning from the fields, behind his oxen, and he asked, "What is wrong with everyone? Why are they weeping?" Then they repeated to him what the men of Jabesh had said.

6When Saul heard their words, the Spirit of God came powerfully upon him, and he burned with anger. 7He took a pair of oxen, cut them into pieces, and sent the pieces by messengers throughout Israel, proclaiming, "This is what will be done to the oxen of anyone who does not follow Saul and Samuel." Then the terror of the Lord fell on the people, and they came out together

as one. 8When Saul mustered them at Bezek, the men of Israel numbered three hundred thousand and those of Judah thirty thousand.

9They told the messengers who had come, "Say to the men of Jabesh Gilead, 'By the time the sun is hot tomorrow, you will be rescued.'" When the messengers went and reported this to the men of Jabesh, they were elated. 10They said to the Ammonites, "Tomorrow we will surrender to you, and you can do to us whatever you like."

11The next day Saul separated his men into three divisions; during the last watch of the night they broke into the camp of the Ammonites and slaughtered them until the heat of the day. Those who survived were scattered, so that no two of them were left together.

Saul Confirmed as King

12The people then said to Samuel, "Who was it that asked, 'Shall Saul reign over us?' Turn these men over to us so that we may put them to death."

13But Saul said, "No one will be put to death today, for this day the Lord has rescued Israel."

14Then Samuel said to the people, "Come, let us go to Gilgal and there renew the kingship." 15So all the people went to Gilgal and made Saul king in the presence of the Lord. There they sacrificed fellowship offerings before the Lord, and Saul and all the Israelites held a great celebration.

Samuel's Farewell Speech

12 Samuel said to all Israel, "I have listened to everything you said to me and have set a king over you. 2Now you have a king as your leader. As for me, I am old and gray, and my sons are here with you. I have been your

---

a 1 Masoretic Text; Dead Sea Scrolls *gifts. Now Nahash king of the Ammonites oppressed the Gadites and Reubenites severely. He gouged out all their right eyes and struck terror and dread in Israel. Not a man remained among the Israelites beyond the Jordan whose right eye was not gouged out by Nahash king of the Ammonites, except that seven thousand men fled from the Ammonites and entered Jabesh Gilead. About a month later,* 1Nahash leader from my youth until this day. ³Here I stand. Testify against me in the presence of the Lord and his anointed. Whose ox have I taken? Whose donkey have I taken? Whom have I cheated? Whom have I oppressed? From whose hand have I accepted a bribe to make me shut my eyes? If I have done any of these things, I will make it right."

⁴"You have not cheated or oppressed us," they replied. "You have not taken anything from anyone's hand."

⁵Samuel said to them, "The Lord is witness against you, and also his anointed is witness this day, that you have not found anything in my hand."

"He is witness," they said.

⁶Then Samuel said to the people, "It is the Lord who appointed Moses and Aaron and brought your ancestors up out of Egypt. ⁷Now then, stand here, because I am going to confront you with evidence before the Lord as to all the righteous acts performed by the Lord for you and your ancestors.

⁸"After Jacob entered Egypt, they cried to the Lord for help, and the Lord sent Moses and Aaron, who brought your ancestors out of Egypt and settled them in this place.

⁹"But they forgot the Lord their God; so he sold them into the hand of Sisera, the commander of the army of Hazor, and into the hands of the Philistines and the king of Moab, who fought against them. ¹⁰They cried out to the Lord and said, 'We have sinned; we have forsaken the Lord and served the Baals and the Ashtoreths. But now deliver us from the hands of our enemies, and we will serve you.' ¹¹Then the Lord sent Jerub-Baal,ᵃ Barak,ᵇ Jephthah and Samuel,ᶜ and he delivered you from the hands of your enemies all around you, so that you lived in safety.

¹²"But when you saw that Nahash king of the Ammonites was moving against you,

you said to me, 'No, we want a king to rule over us' — even though the Lord your God was your king. ¹³Now here is the king you have chosen, the one you asked for; see, the Lord has set a king over you. ¹⁴If you fear the Lord and serve and obey him and do not rebel against his commands, and if both you and the king who reigns over you follow the Lord your God — good! ¹⁵But if you do not obey the Lord, and if you rebel against his commands, his hand will be against you, as it was against your ancestors.

¹⁶"Now then, stand still and see this great thing the Lord is about to do before your eyes! ¹⁷Is it not wheat harvest now? I will call on the Lord to send thunder and rain. And you will realize what an evil thing you did in the eyes of the Lord when you asked for a king."

¹⁸Then Samuel called on the Lord, and that same day the Lord sent thunder and rain. So all the people stood in awe of the Lord and of Samuel.

¹⁹The people all said to Samuel, "Pray to the Lord your God for your servants so that we will not die, for we have added to all our other sins the evil of asking for a king."

²⁰"Do not be afraid," Samuel replied. "You have done all this evil; yet do not turn away from the Lord, but serve the Lord with all your heart. ²¹Do not turn away after useless idols. They can do you no good, nor can they rescue you, because they are useless. ²²For the sake of his great name the Lord will not reject his people, because the Lord was pleased to make you his own. ²³As for me, far be it from me that I should sin against the Lord by failing to pray for you. And I will teach you the way that is good and right. ²⁴But be sure to fear the Lord and serve him faithfully with all your heart; consider what great things he has done for you. ²⁵Yet if you persist in doing evil, both you and your king will perish."

ᵃ 11 Also called *Gideon*   ᵇ 11 Some Septuagint manuscripts and Syriac; Hebrew *Bedan*   ᶜ 11 Hebrew; some Septuagint manuscripts and Syriac *Samson*

Samuel Rebukes Saul

13

Saul was thirty[a] years old when he became king, and he reigned over Israel forty-[b] two years.

[2]Saul chose three thousand men from Israel; two thousand were with him at Mikmash and in the hill country of Bethel, and a thousand were with Jonathan at Gibeah in Benjamin. The rest of the men he sent back to their homes.

[3]Jonathan attacked the Philistine outpost at Geba, and the Philistines heard about it. Then Saul had the trumpet blown throughout the land and said, "Let the Hebrews hear!" [4]So all Israel heard the news: "Saul has attacked the Philistine outpost, and now Israel has become obnoxious to the Philistines." And the people were summoned to join Saul at Gilgal.

[5]The Philistines assembled to fight Israel, with three thousand[c] chariots, six thousand charioteers, and soldiers as numerous as the sand on the seashore. They went up and camped at Mikmash, east of Beth Aven. [6]When the Israelites saw that their situation was critical and that their army was hard pressed, they hid in caves and thickets, among the rocks, and in pits and cisterns. [7]Some Hebrews even crossed the Jordan to the land of Gad and Gilead.

Saul remained at Gilgal, and all the troops with him were quaking with fear. [8]He waited seven days, the time set by Samuel; but Samuel did not come to Gilgal, and Saul's men began to scatter. [9]So he said, "Bring me the burnt offering and the fellowship offerings." And Saul offered up the burnt offering. [10]Just as he finished making the offering, Samuel arrived, and Saul went out to greet him.

[11]"What have you done?" asked Samuel.

Saul replied, "When I saw that the men were scattering, and that you did not come

at the set time, and that the Philistines were assembling at Mikmash, [12]I thought, 'Now the Philistines will come down against me at Gilgal, and I have not sought the LORD's favor.' So I felt compelled to offer the burnt offering."

[13]"You have done a foolish thing," Samuel said. "You have not kept the command the LORD your God gave you; if you had, he would have established your kingdom over Israel for all time. [14]But now your kingdom will not endure; the LORD has sought out a man after his own heart and appointed him ruler of his people, because you have not kept the LORD's command."

[15]Then Samuel left Gilgal[d] and went up to Gibeah in Benjamin, and Saul counted the men who were with him. They numbered about six hundred.

Israel Without Weapons

[16]Saul and his son Jonathan and the men with them were staying in Gibeah[e] in Benjamin, while the Philistines camped at Mikmash. [17]Raiding parties went out from the Philistine camp in three detachments. One turned toward Ophrah in the vicinity of Shual, [18]another toward Beth Horon, and the third toward the borderland overlooking the Valley of Zeboyim facing the wilderness.

[19]Not a blacksmith could be found in the whole land of Israel, because the Philistines had said, "Otherwise the Hebrews will make swords or spears!" [20]So all Israel went down to the Philistines to have their plow points, mattocks, axes and sickles[f] sharpened. [21]The price was two-thirds of a shekel[g] for sharpening plow points and mattocks, and a third of a shekel[h] for sharpening forks and axes and for repointing goads.

[22]So on the day of the battle not a soldier with Saul and Jonathan had a sword

---

[a] 1 A few late manuscripts of the Septuagint; Hebrew does not have *thirty*.   [b] 1 Probable reading of the original Hebrew text (see Acts 13:21); Masoretic Text does not have *forty-*.   [c] 5 Some Septuagint manuscripts and Syriac; Hebrew *thirty thousand*   [d] 15 Hebrew; Septuagint *Gilgal and went his way; the rest of the people went after Saul to meet the army, and they went out of Gilgal*   [e] 16 Two Hebrew manuscripts; most Hebrew manuscripts *Geba*, a variant of *Gibeah*   [f] 20 Septuagint; Hebrew *plow points*   [g] 21 That is, about 1/4 ounce or about 8 grams   [h] 21 That is, about 1/8 ounce or about 4 grams

or spear in his hand; only Saul and his son Jonathan had them.

Jonathan Attacks the Philistines

14 23Now a detachment of Philistines had gone out to the pass at Mikmash. 1One day Jonathan son of Saul said to his young armorbearer, "Come, let's go over to the Philistine outpost on the other side." But he did not tell his father.

2Saul was staying on the outskirts of Gibeah under a pomegranate tree in Migron. With him were about six hundred men, 3among whom was Ahijah, who was wearing an ephod. He was a son of Ichabod's brother Ahitub son of Phinehas, the son of Eli, the Lord's priest in Shiloh. No one was aware that Jonathan had left.

4On each side of the pass that Jonathan intended to cross to reach the Philistine outpost was a cliff; one was called Bozez and the other Seneh. 5One cliff stood to the north toward Mikmash, the other to the south toward Geba.

6Jonathan said to his young armorbearer, "Come, let's go over to the outpost of those uncircumcised men. Perhaps the Lord will act in our behalf. Nothing can hinder the Lord from saving, whether by many or by few."

7"Do all that you have in mind," his armor-bearer said. "Go ahead; I am with you heart and soul."

8Jonathan said, "Come on, then; we will cross over toward them and let them see us. 9If they say to us, 'Wait there until we come to you,' we will stay where we are and not go up to them. 10But if they say, 'Come up to us,' we will climb up, because that will be our sign that the Lord has given them into our hands."

11So both of them showed themselves to the Philistine outpost. "Look!" said the Philistines. "The Hebrews are crawling out of the holes they were hiding in." 12The men of the outpost shouted to Jonathan and his armor-bearer, "Come up to us and we'll teach you a lesson."

So Jonathan said to his armor-bearer, "Climb up after me; the Lord has given them into the hand of Israel."

13Jonathan climbed up, using his hands and feet, with his armor-bearer right behind him. The Philistines fell before Jonathan, and his armor-bearer followed and killed behind him. 14In that first attack Jonathan and his armor-bearer killed some twenty men in an area of about half an acre.

Israel Routs the Philistines

15Then panic struck the whole army — those in the camp and field, and those in the outposts and raiding parties — and the ground shook. It was a panic sent by God.*a*

16Saul's lookouts at Gibeah in Benjamin saw the army melting away in all directions. 17Then Saul said to the men who were with him, "Muster the forces and see who has left us." When they did, it was Jonathan and his armor-bearer who were not there.

18Saul said to Ahijah, "Bring the ark of God." (At that time it was with the Israelites.)*b* 19While Saul was talking to the priest, the tumult in the Philistine camp increased more and more. So Saul said to the priest, "Withdraw your hand."

20Then Saul and all his men assembled and went to the battle. They found the Philistines in total confusion, striking each other with their swords. 21Those Hebrews who had previously been with the Philistines and had gone up with them to their camp went over to the Israelites who were with Saul and Jonathan. 22When all the Israelites who had hidden in the hill country of Ephraim heard that the Philistines were on the run, they joined the battle in hot pursuit. 23So on that day the Lord saved Israel, and the battle moved on beyond Beth Aven.

---

a 15 Or *a terrible panic*   *b 18* Hebrew; Septuagint *"Bring the ephod." (At that time he wore the ephod before the Israelites.)*

Jonathan Eats Honey

24 Now the Israelites were in distress that day, because Saul had bound the people under an oath, saying, "Cursed be anyone who eats food before evening comes, before I have avenged myself on my enemies!" So none of the troops tasted food.

25 The entire army entered the woods, and there was honey on the ground. 26 When they went into the woods, they saw the honey oozing out; yet no one put his hand to his mouth, because they feared the oath. 27 But Jonathan had not heard that his father had bound the people with the oath, so he reached out the end of the staff that was in his hand and dipped it into the honeycomb. He raised his hand to his mouth, and his eyes brightened.*a* 28 Then one of the soldiers told him, "Your father bound the army under a strict oath, saying, 'Cursed be anyone who eats food today!' That is why the men are faint."

29 Jonathan said, "My father has made trouble for the country. See how my eyes brightened when I tasted a little of this honey. 30 How much better it would have been if the men had eaten today some of the plunder they took from their enemies. Would not the slaughter of the Philistines have been even greater?"

31 That day, after the Israelites had struck down the Philistines from Mikmash to Aijalon, they were exhausted. 32 They pounced on the plunder and, taking sheep, cattle and calves, they butchered them on the ground and ate them, together with the blood. 33 Then someone said to Saul, "Look, the men are sinning against the LORD by eating meat that has blood in it."

"You have broken faith," he said. "Roll a large stone over here at once." 34 Then he said, "Go out among the men and tell them, 'Each of you bring me your cattle and sheep, and slaughter them here and eat them. Do not sin against the LORD by eating meat with blood still in it.'"

So everyone brought his ox that night and slaughtered it there. 35 Then Saul built an altar to the LORD; it was the first time he had done this.

36 Saul said, "Let us go down and pursue the Philistines by night and plunder them till dawn, and let us not leave one of them alive."

"Do whatever seems best to you," they replied.

But the priest said, "Let us inquire of God here."

37 So Saul asked God, "Shall I go down and pursue the Philistines? Will you give them into Israel's hand?" But God did not answer him that day.

38 Saul therefore said, "Come here, all you who are leaders of the army, and let us find out what sin has been committed today. 39 As surely as the LORD who rescues Israel lives, even if the guilt lies with my son Jonathan, he must die." But not one of them said a word.

40 Saul then said to all the Israelites, "You stand over there; I and Jonathan my son will stand over here."

"Do what seems best to you," they replied.

41 Then Saul prayed to the LORD, the God of Israel, "Why have you not answered your servant today? If the fault is in me or my son Jonathan, respond with Urim, but if the men of Israel are at fault,*b* respond with Thummim." Jonathan and Saul were taken by lot, and the men were cleared. 42 Saul said, "Cast the lot between me and Jonathan my son." And Jonathan was taken.

43 Then Saul said to Jonathan, "Tell me what you have done."

So Jonathan told him, "I tasted a little honey with the end of my staff. And now I must die!"

44 Saul said, "May God deal with me, be it ever so severely, if you do not die, Jonathan."

45 But the men said to Saul, "Should Jonathan die — he who has brought about this great deliverance in Israel? Never! As

---

a 27 Or *his strength was renewed*; similarly in verse 29   *b* 41 Septuagint; Hebrew does not have "*Why . . . at fault.*"

surely as the LORD lives, not a hair of his head will fall to the ground, for he did this today with God's help." So the men rescued Jonathan, and he was not put to death.

⁴⁶Then Saul stopped pursuing the Philistines, and they withdrew to their own land.

⁴⁷After Saul had assumed rule over Israel, he fought against their enemies on every side: Moab, the Ammonites, Edom, the kings*a* of Zobah, and the Philistines. Wherever he turned, he inflicted punishment on them.*b* ⁴⁸He fought valiantly and defeated the Amalekites, delivering Israel from the hands of those who had plundered them.

Saul's Family

⁴⁹Saul's sons were Jonathan, Ishvi and Malki-Shua. The name of his older daughter was Merab, and that of the younger was Michal. ⁵⁰His wife's name was Ahinoam daughter of Ahimaaz. The name of the commander of Saul's army was Abner son of Ner, and Ner was Saul's uncle. ⁵¹Saul's father Kish and Abner's father Ner were sons of Abiel.

⁵²All the days of Saul there was bitter war with the Philistines, and whenever Saul saw a mighty or brave man, he took him into his service.

The LORD Rejects Saul as King

15 Samuel said to Saul, "I am the one the LORD sent to anoint you king over his people Israel; so listen now to the message from the LORD. ²This is what the LORD Almighty says: 'I will punish the Amalekites for what they did to Israel when they waylaid them as they came up from Egypt. ³Now go, attack the Amalekites and totally destroy*c* all that belongs to them. Do not spare them; put to death men and women, children and infants, cattle and sheep, camels and donkeys.'"

⁴So Saul summoned the men and mus-tered them at Telaim—two hundred thousand foot soldiers and ten thousand from Judah. ⁵Saul went to the city of Amalek and set an ambush in the ravine. ⁶Then he said to the Kenites, "Go away, leave the Amalekites so that I do not destroy you along with them; for you showed kindness to all the Israelites when they came up out of Egypt." So the Kenites moved away from the Amalekites.

⁷Then Saul attacked the Amalekites all the way from Havilah to Shur, near the eastern border of Egypt. ⁸He took Agag king of the Amalekites alive, and all his people he totally destroyed with the sword. ⁹But Saul and the army spared Agag and the best of the sheep and cattle, the fat calves*d* and lambs—everything that was good. These they were unwilling to destroy completely, but everything that was despised and weak they totally destroyed.

¹⁰Then the word of the LORD came to Samuel: ¹¹"I regret that I have made Saul king, because he has turned away from me and has not carried out my instructions." Samuel was angry, and he cried out to the LORD all that night.

¹²Early in the morning Samuel got up and went to meet Saul, but he was told, "Saul has gone to Carmel. There he has set up a monument in his own honor and has turned and gone on down to Gilgal."

¹³When Samuel reached him, Saul said, "The LORD bless you! I have carried out the LORD's instructions."

¹⁴But Samuel said, "What then is this bleating of sheep in my ears? What is this lowing of cattle that I hear?"

¹⁵Saul answered, "The soldiers brought them from the Amalekites; they spared the best of the sheep and cattle to sacrifice to the LORD your God, but we totally destroyed the rest."

¹⁶"Enough!" Samuel said to Saul. "Let me tell you what the LORD said to me last night."

---

a 47 Masoretic Text; Dead Sea Scrolls and Septuagint *king*   *b 47* Hebrew; Septuagint *he was victorious*   *c 3* The Hebrew term refers to the irrevocable giving over of things or persons to the LORD, often by totally destroying them; also in verses 8, 9, 15, 18, 20 and 21.   *d 9* Or *the grown bulls*; the meaning of the Hebrew for this phrase is uncertain.

"Tell me," Saul replied.

17Samuel said, "Although you were once small in your own eyes, did you not become the head of the tribes of Israel? The LORD anointed you king over Israel. 18And he sent you on a mission, saying, 'Go and completely destroy those wicked people, the Amalekites; wage war against them until you have wiped them out.' 19Why did you not obey the LORD? Why did you pounce on the plunder and do evil in the eyes of the LORD?"

20"But I did obey the LORD," Saul said. "I went on the mission the LORD assigned me. I completely destroyed the Amalekites and brought back Agag their king. 21The soldiers took sheep and cattle from the plunder, the best of what was devoted to God, in order to sacrifice them to the LORD your God at Gilgal."

22But Samuel replied:

"Does the LORD delight in burnt
        offerings and sacrifices
    as much as in obeying the LORD?
To obey is better than sacrifice,
    and to heed is better than the fat of
        rams.
23 For rebellion is like the sin of
        divination,
    and arrogance like the evil of idolatry.
Because you have rejected the word of
        the LORD,
    he has rejected you as king."

24Then Saul said to Samuel, "I have sinned. I violated the LORD's command and your instructions. I was afraid of the men and so I gave in to them. 25Now I beg you, forgive my sin and come back with me, so that I may worship the LORD."

26But Samuel said to him, "I will not go back with you. You have rejected the word of the LORD, and the LORD has rejected you as king over Israel!"

27As Samuel turned to leave, Saul caught hold of the hem of his robe, and it tore. 28Samuel said to him, "The LORD has torn the kingdom of Israel from you today and has given it to one of your neighbors — to one better than you. 29He who is the Glory of Israel does not lie or change his mind; for he is not a human being, that he should change his mind."

30Saul replied, "I have sinned. But please honor me before the elders of my people and before Israel; come back with me, so that I may worship the LORD your God." 31So Samuel went back with Saul, and Saul worshiped the LORD.

32Then Samuel said, "Bring me Agag king of the Amalekites."

Agag came to him in chains.a And he thought, "Surely the bitterness of death is past."

33But Samuel said,

"As your sword has made women
        childless,
    so will your mother be childless
        among women."

And Samuel put Agag to death before the LORD at Gilgal.

34Then Samuel left for Ramah, but Saul went up to his home in Gibeah of Saul. 35Until the day Samuel died, he did not go to see Saul again, though Samuel mourned for him. And the LORD regretted that he had made Saul king over Israel.

Samuel Anoints David

16 The LORD said to Samuel, "How long will you mourn for Saul, since I have rejected him as king over Israel? Fill your horn with oil and be on your way; I am sending you to Jesse of Bethlehem. I have chosen one of his sons to be king."

2But Samuel said, "How can I go? If Saul hears about it, he will kill me."

The LORD said, "Take a heifer with you and say, 'I have come to sacrifice to the LORD.' 3Invite Jesse to the sacrifice, and I will show you what to do. You are to anoint for me the one I indicate."

---

a 32 The meaning of the Hebrew for this phrase is uncertain.

⁴Samuel did what the LORD said. When he arrived at Bethlehem, the elders of the town trembled when they met him. They asked, "Do you come in peace?"

⁵Samuel replied, "Yes, in peace; I have come to sacrifice to the LORD. Consecrate yourselves and come to the sacrifice with me." Then he consecrated Jesse and his sons and invited them to the sacrifice.

⁶When they arrived, Samuel saw Eliab and thought, "Surely the LORD's anointed stands here before the LORD."

⁷But the LORD said to Samuel, "Do not consider his appearance or his height, for I have rejected him. The LORD does not look at the things people look at. People look at the outward appearance, but the LORD looks at the heart."

⁸Then Jesse called Abinadab and had him pass in front of Samuel. But Samuel said, "The LORD has not chosen this one either." ⁹Jesse then had Shammah pass by, but Samuel said, "Nor has the LORD chosen this one." ¹⁰Jesse had seven of his sons pass before Samuel, but Samuel said to him, "The LORD has not chosen these." ¹¹So he asked Jesse, "Are these all the sons you have?"

"There is still the youngest," Jesse answered. "He is tending the sheep."

Samuel said, "Send for him; we will not sit down until he arrives."

¹²So he sent for him and had him brought in. He was glowing with health and had a fine appearance and handsome features.

Then the LORD said, "Rise and anoint him; this is the one."

¹³So Samuel took the horn of oil and anointed him in the presence of his brothers, and from that day on the Spirit of the LORD came powerfully upon David. Samuel then went to Ramah.

David in Saul's Service

¹⁴Now the Spirit of the LORD had departed from Saul, and an evil*ᵃ* spirit from the LORD tormented him.

¹⁵Saul's attendants said to him, "See, an evil spirit from God is tormenting you. ¹⁶Let our lord command his servants here to search for someone who can play the lyre. He will play when the evil spirit from God comes on you, and you will feel better."

¹⁷So Saul said to his attendants, "Find someone who plays well and bring him to me."

¹⁸One of the servants answered, "I have seen a son of Jesse of Bethlehem who knows how to play the lyre. He is a brave man and a warrior. He speaks well and is a fine-looking man. And the LORD is with him."

¹⁹Then Saul sent messengers to Jesse and said, "Send me your son David, who is with the sheep." ²⁰So Jesse took a donkey loaded with bread, a skin of wine and a young goat and sent them with his son David to Saul.

²¹David came to Saul and entered his service. Saul liked him very much, and David became one of his armor-bearers. ²²Then Saul sent word to Jesse, saying, "Allow David to remain in my service, for I am pleased with him."

²³Whenever the spirit from God came on Saul, David would take up his lyre and play. Then relief would come to Saul; he would feel better, and the evil spirit would leave him.

David and Goliath

17 Now the Philistines gathered their forces for war and assembled at Sokoh in Judah. They pitched camp at Ephes Dammim, between Sokoh and Azekah. ²Saul and the Israelites assembled and camped in the Valley of Elah and drew up their battle line to meet the Philistines. ³The Philistines occupied one hill and the Israelites another, with the valley between them.

⁴A champion named Goliath, who was from Gath, came out of the Philistine camp. His height was six cubits and a

---

ᵃ 14 Or *and a harmful*; similarly in verses 15, 16 and 23 span.*a* 5He had a bronze helmet on his head and wore a coat of scale armor of bronze weighing five thousand shekels*b*; 6on his legs he wore bronze greaves, and a bronze javelin was slung on his back. 7His spear shaft was like a weaver's rod, and its iron point weighed six hundred shekels.*c* His shield bearer went ahead of him.

8Goliath stood and shouted to the ranks of Israel, "Why do you come out and line up for battle? Am I not a Philistine, and are you not the servants of Saul? Choose a man and have him come down to me. 9If he is able to fight and kill me, we will become your subjects; but if I overcome him and kill him, you will become our subjects and serve us." 10Then the Philistine said, "This day I defy the armies of Israel! Give me a man and let us fight each other." 11On hearing the Philistine's words, Saul and all the Israelites were dismayed and terrified.

12Now David was the son of an Ephrathite named Jesse, who was from Bethlehem in Judah. Jesse had eight sons, and in Saul's time he was very old. 13Jesse's three oldest sons had followed Saul to the war: The firstborn was Eliab; the second, Abinadab; and the third, Shammah. 14David was the youngest. The three oldest followed Saul, 15but David went back and forth from Saul to tend his father's sheep at Bethlehem.

16For forty days the Philistine came forward every morning and evening and took his stand.

17Now Jesse said to his son David, "Take this ephah*d* of roasted grain and these ten loaves of bread for your brothers and hurry to their camp. 18Take along these ten cheeses to the commander of their unit. See how your brothers are and bring back some assurance*e* from them. 19They are with Saul and all the men of Israel in the Valley of Elah, fighting against the Philistines."

20Early in the morning David left the flock in the care of a shepherd, loaded up and set out, as Jesse had directed. He reached the camp as the army was going out to its battle positions, shouting the war cry. 21Israel and the Philistines were drawing up their lines facing each other. 22David left his things with the keeper of supplies, ran to the battle lines and asked his brothers how they were. 23As he was talking with them, Goliath, the Philistine champion from Gath, stepped out from his lines and shouted his usual defiance, and David heard it. 24Whenever the Israelites saw the man, they all fled from him in great fear.

25Now the Israelites had been saying, "Do you see how this man keeps coming out? He comes out to defy Israel. The king will give great wealth to the man who kills him. He will also give him his daughter in marriage and will exempt his family from taxes in Israel."

26David asked the men standing near him, "What will be done for the man who kills this Philistine and removes this disgrace from Israel? Who is this uncircumcised Philistine that he should defy the armies of the living God?"

27They repeated to him what they had been saying and told him, "This is what will be done for the man who kills him."

28When Eliab, David's oldest brother, heard him speaking with the men, he burned with anger at him and asked, "Why have you come down here? And with whom did you leave those few sheep in the wilderness? I know how conceited you are and how wicked your heart is; you came down only to watch the battle."

29"Now what have I done?" said David. "Can't I even speak?" 30He then turned away to someone else and brought up the same matter, and the men answered him as before. 31What David said was overheard and reported to Saul, and Saul sent for him.

---

a 4 That is, about 9 feet 9 inches or about 3 meters   *b 5* That is, about 125 pounds or about 58 kilograms
c 7 That is, about 15 pounds or about 6.9 kilograms   *d 17* That is, probably about 36 pounds or about 16 kilograms
e 18 Or *some token;* or *some pledge of spoils*

³²David said to Saul, "Let no one lose heart on account of this Philistine; your servant will go and fight him."

³³Saul replied, "You are not able to go out against this Philistine and fight him; you are only a young man, and he has been a warrior from his youth."

³⁴But David said to Saul, "Your servant has been keeping his father's sheep. When a lion or a bear came and carried off a sheep from the flock, ³⁵I went after it, struck it and rescued the sheep from its mouth. When it turned on me, I seized it by its hair, struck it and killed it. ³⁶Your servant has killed both the lion and the bear; this uncircumcised Philistine will be like one of them, because he has defied the armies of the living God. ³⁷The LORD who rescued me from the paw of the lion and the paw of the bear will rescue me from the hand of this Philistine."

Saul said to David, "Go, and the LORD be with you."

³⁸Then Saul dressed David in his own tunic. He put a coat of armor on him and a bronze helmet on his head. ³⁹David fastened on his sword over the tunic and tried walking around, because he was not used to them.

"I cannot go in these," he said to Saul, "because I am not used to them." So he took them off. ⁴⁰Then he took his staff in his hand, chose five smooth stones from the stream, put them in the pouch of his shepherd's bag and, with his sling in his hand, approached the Philistine.

⁴¹Meanwhile, the Philistine, with his shield bearer in front of him, kept coming closer to David. ⁴²He looked David over and saw that he was little more than a boy, glowing with health and handsome, and he despised him. ⁴³He said to David, "Am I a dog, that you come at me with sticks?" And the Philistine cursed David by his gods. ⁴⁴"Come here," he said, "and I'll give your flesh to the birds and the wild animals!"

⁴⁵David said to the Philistine, "You come against me with sword and spear and javelin, but I come against you in the name of the LORD Almighty, the God of the armies of Israel, whom you have defied. ⁴⁶This day the LORD will deliver you into my hands, and I'll strike you down and cut off your head. This very day I will give the carcasses of the Philistine army to the birds and the wild animals, and the whole world will know that there is a God in Israel. ⁴⁷All those gathered here will know that it is not by sword or spear that the LORD saves; for the battle is the LORD's, and he will give all of you into our hands."

⁴⁸As the Philistine moved closer to attack him, David ran quickly toward the battle line to meet him. ⁴⁹Reaching into his bag and taking out a stone, he slung it and struck the Philistine on the forehead. The stone sank into his forehead, and he fell facedown on the ground.

⁵⁰So David triumphed over the Philistine with a sling and a stone; without a sword in his hand he struck down the Philistine and killed him.

⁵¹David ran and stood over him. He took hold of the Philistine's sword and drew it from the sheath. After he killed him, he cut off his head with the sword.

When the Philistines saw that their hero was dead, they turned and ran. ⁵²Then the men of Israel and Judah surged forward with a shout and pursued the Philistines to the entrance of Gath^a and to the gates of Ekron. Their dead were strewn along the Shaaraim road to Gath and Ekron. ⁵³When the Israelites returned from chasing the Philistines, they plundered their camp.

⁵⁴David took the Philistine's head and brought it to Jerusalem; he put the Philistine's weapons in his own tent.

⁵⁵As Saul watched David going out to meet the Philistine, he said to Abner, commander of the army, "Abner, whose son is that young man?"

Abner replied, "As surely as you live, Your Majesty, I don't know."

---

^a 52 Some Septuagint manuscripts; Hebrew *of a valley*

56The king said, "Find out whose son this young man is."

57As soon as David returned from killing the Philistine, Abner took him and brought him before Saul, with David still holding the Philistine's head.

58"Whose son are you, young man?" Saul asked him.

David said, "I am the son of your servant Jesse of Bethlehem."

Saul's Growing Fear of David

18 After David had finished talking with Saul, Jonathan became one in spirit with David, and he loved him as himself. 2From that day Saul kept David with him and did not let him return home to his family. 3And Jonathan made a covenant with David because he loved him as himself. 4Jonathan took off the robe he was wearing and gave it to David, along with his tunic, and even his sword, his bow and his belt.

5Whatever mission Saul sent him on, David was so successful that Saul gave him a high rank in the army. This pleased all the troops, and Saul's officers as well.

6When the men were returning home after David had killed the Philistine, the women came out from all the towns of Israel to meet King Saul with singing and dancing, with joyful songs and with timbrels and lyres. 7As they danced, they sang:

"Saul has slain his thousands,
    and David his tens of thousands."

8Saul was very angry; this refrain displeased him greatly. "They have credited David with tens of thousands," he thought, "but me with only thousands. What more can he get but the kingdom?" 9And from that time on Saul kept a close eye on David.

10The next day an evil*a* spirit from God came forcefully on Saul. He was prophesying in his house, while David was playing the lyre, as he usually did. Saul had a spear in his hand 11and he hurled it, saying to himself, "I'll pin David to the wall." But David eluded him twice.

12Saul was afraid of David, because the LORD was with David but had departed from Saul. 13So he sent David away from him and gave him command over a thousand men, and David led the troops in their campaigns. 14In everything he did he had great success, because the LORD was with him. 15When Saul saw how successful he was, he was afraid of him. 16But all Israel and Judah loved David, because he led them in their campaigns.

17Saul said to David, "Here is my older daughter Merab. I will give her to you in marriage; only serve me bravely and fight the battles of the LORD." For Saul said to himself, "I will not raise a hand against him. Let the Philistines do that!"

18But David said to Saul, "Who am I, and what is my family or my clan in Israel, that I should become the king's son-in-law?" 19So*b* when the time came for Merab, Saul's daughter, to be given to David, she was given in marriage to Adriel of Meholah.

20Now Saul's daughter Michal was in love with David, and when they told Saul about it, he was pleased. 21"I will give her to him," he thought, "so that she may be a snare to him and so that the hand of the Philistines may be against him." So Saul said to David, "Now you have a second opportunity to become my son-in-law."

22Then Saul ordered his attendants: "Speak to David privately and say, 'Look, the king likes you, and his attendants all love you; now become his son-in-law.'"

23They repeated these words to David. But David said, "Do you think it is a small matter to become the king's son-in-law? I'm only a poor man and little known."

24When Saul's servants told him what David had said, 25Saul replied, "Say to David, 'The king wants no other price for the bride than a hundred Philistine foreskins, to take revenge on his enemies.'" Saul's

---

a 10 Or *a harmful*   *b* 19 Or *However,*

plan was to have David fall by the hands of the Philistines.

²⁶When the attendants told David these things, he was pleased to become the king's son-in-law. So before the allotted time elapsed, ²⁷David took his men with him and went out and killed two hundred Philistines and brought back their foreskins. They counted out the full number to the king so that David might become the king's son-in-law. Then Saul gave him his daughter Michal in marriage.

²⁸When Saul realized that the LORD was with David and that his daughter Michal loved David, ²⁹Saul became still more afraid of him, and he remained his enemy the rest of his days.

³⁰The Philistine commanders continued to go out to battle, and as often as they did, David met with more success than the rest of Saul's officers, and his name became well known.

Saul Tries to Kill David

19 Saul told his son Jonathan and all the attendants to kill David. But Jonathan had taken a great liking to David ²and warned him, "My father Saul is looking for a chance to kill you. Be on your guard tomorrow morning; go into hiding and stay there. ³I will go out and stand with my father in the field where you are. I'll speak to him about you and will tell you what I find out."

⁴Jonathan spoke well of David to Saul his father and said to him, "Let not the king do wrong to his servant David; he has not wronged you, and what he has done has benefited you greatly. ⁵He took his life in his hands when he killed the Philistine. The LORD won a great victory for all Israel, and you saw it and were glad. Why then would you do wrong to an innocent man like David by killing him for no reason?"

⁶Saul listened to Jonathan and took this oath: "As surely as the LORD lives, David will not be put to death."

⁷So Jonathan called David and told him the whole conversation. He brought him to Saul, and David was with Saul as before.

⁸Once more war broke out, and David went out and fought the Philistines. He struck them with such force that they fled before him.

⁹But an evil*ᵃ* spirit from the LORD came on Saul as he was sitting in his house with his spear in his hand. While David was playing the lyre, ¹⁰Saul tried to pin him to the wall with his spear, but David eluded him as Saul drove the spear into the wall. That night David made good his escape.

¹¹Saul sent men to David's house to watch it and to kill him in the morning. But Michal, David's wife, warned him, "If you don't run for your life tonight, tomorrow you'll be killed." ¹²So Michal let David down through a window, and he fled and escaped. ¹³Then Michal took an idol and laid it on the bed, covering it with a garment and putting some goats' hair at the head.

¹⁴When Saul sent the men to capture David, Michal said, "He is ill."

¹⁵Then Saul sent the men back to see David and told them, "Bring him up to me in his bed so that I may kill him." ¹⁶But when the men entered, there was the idol in the bed, and at the head was some goats' hair.

¹⁷Saul said to Michal, "Why did you deceive me like this and send my enemy away so that he escaped?"

Michal told him, "He said to me, 'Let me get away. Why should I kill you?'"

¹⁸When David had fled and made his escape, he went to Samuel at Ramah and told him all that Saul had done to him. Then he and Samuel went to Naioth and stayed there. ¹⁹Word came to Saul: "David is in Naioth at Ramah"; ²⁰so he sent men to capture him. But when they saw a group of prophets prophesying, with Samuel standing there as their leader, the Spirit of God came on Saul's men, and they also prophesied. ²¹Saul was told about it, and he sent

---

ᵃ 9 Or *But a harmful*

more men, and they prophesied too. Saul sent men a third time, and they also prophesied. ²²Finally, he himself left for Ramah and went to the great cistern at Seku. And he asked, "Where are Samuel and David?"

"Over in Naioth at Ramah," they said.

²³So Saul went to Naioth at Ramah. But the Spirit of God came even on him, and he walked along prophesying until he came to Naioth. ²⁴He stripped off his garments, and he too prophesied in Samuel's presence. He lay naked all that day and all that night. This is why people say, "Is Saul also among the prophets?"

David and Jonathan

20 Then David fled from Naioth at Ramah and went to Jonathan and asked, "What have I done? What is my crime? How have I wronged your father, that he is trying to kill me?"

²"Never!" Jonathan replied. "You are not going to die! Look, my father doesn't do anything, great or small, without letting me know. Why would he hide this from me? It isn't so!"

³But David took an oath and said, "Your father knows very well that I have found favor in your eyes, and he has said to himself, 'Jonathan must not know this or he will be grieved.' Yet as surely as the Lord lives and as you live, there is only a step between me and death."

⁴Jonathan said to David, "Whatever you want me to do, I'll do for you."

⁵So David said, "Look, tomorrow is the New Moon feast, and I am supposed to dine with the king; but let me go and hide in the field until the evening of the day after tomorrow. ⁶If your father misses me at all, tell him, 'David earnestly asked my permission to hurry to Bethlehem, his hometown, because an annual sacrifice is being made there for his whole clan.' ⁷If he says, 'Very well,' then your servant is safe. But if he loses his temper, you can be sure that he is determined to harm me. ⁸As for you, show kindness to your servant, for you

have brought him into a covenant with you before the Lord. If I am guilty, then kill me yourself! Why hand me over to your father?"

⁹"Never!" Jonathan said. "If I had the least inkling that my father was determined to harm you, wouldn't I tell you?"

¹⁰David asked, "Who will tell me if your father answers you harshly?"

¹¹"Come," Jonathan said, "let's go out into the field." So they went there together.

¹²Then Jonathan said to David, "I swear by the Lord, the God of Israel, that I will surely sound out my father by this time the day after tomorrow! If he is favorably disposed toward you, will I not send you word and let you know? ¹³But if my father intends to harm you, may the Lord deal with Jonathan, be it ever so severely, if I do not let you know and send you away in peace. May the Lord be with you as he has been with my father. ¹⁴But show me unfailing kindness like the Lord's kindness as long as I live, so that I may not be killed, ¹⁵and do not ever cut off your kindness from my family — not even when the Lord has cut off every one of David's enemies from the face of the earth."

¹⁶So Jonathan made a covenant with the house of David, saying, "May the Lord call David's enemies to account." ¹⁷And Jonathan had David reaffirm his oath out of love for him, because he loved him as he loved himself.

¹⁸Then Jonathan said to David, "Tomorrow is the New Moon feast. You will be missed, because your seat will be empty. ¹⁹The day after tomorrow, toward evening, go to the place where you hid when this trouble began, and wait by the stone Ezel. ²⁰I will shoot three arrows to the side of it, as though I were shooting at a target. ²¹Then I will send a boy and say, 'Go, find the arrows.' If I say to him, 'Look, the arrows are on this side of you; bring them here,' then come, because, as surely as the Lord lives, you are safe; there is no danger. ²²But if I say to the boy, 'Look, the arrows are beyond you,' then you must go, because

the Lord has sent you away. [23]And about the matter you and I discussed — remember, the Lord is witness between you and me forever."

[24]So David hid in the field, and when the New Moon feast came, the king sat down to eat. [25]He sat in his customary place by the wall, opposite Jonathan,[a] and Abner sat next to Saul, but David's place was empty. [26]Saul said nothing that day, for he thought, "Something must have happened to David to make him ceremonially unclean — surely he is unclean." [27]But the next day, the second day of the month, David's place was empty again. Then Saul said to his son Jonathan, "Why hasn't the son of Jesse come to the meal, either yesterday or today?"

[28]Jonathan answered, "David earnestly asked me for permission to go to Bethlehem. [29]He said, 'Let me go, because our family is observing a sacrifice in the town and my brother has ordered me to be there. If I have found favor in your eyes, let me get away to see my brothers.' That is why he has not come to the king's table."

[30]Saul's anger flared up at Jonathan and he said to him, "You son of a perverse and rebellious woman! Don't I know that you have sided with the son of Jesse to your own shame and to the shame of the mother who bore you? [31]As long as the son of Jesse lives on this earth, neither you nor your kingdom will be established. Now send someone to bring him to me, for he must die!"

[32]"Why should he be put to death? What has he done?" Jonathan asked his father. [33]But Saul hurled his spear at him to kill him. Then Jonathan knew that his father intended to kill David.

[34]Jonathan got up from the table in fierce anger; on that second day of the feast he did not eat, because he was grieved at his father's shameful treatment of David.

[35]In the morning Jonathan went out to the field for his meeting with David. He had a small boy with him, [36]and he said to the boy, "Run and find the arrows I shoot." As the boy ran, he shot an arrow beyond him. [37]When the boy came to the place where Jonathan's arrow had fallen, Jonathan called out after him, "Isn't the arrow beyond you?" [38]Then he shouted, "Hurry! Go quickly! Don't stop!" The boy picked up the arrow and returned to his master. [39](The boy knew nothing about all this; only Jonathan and David knew.) [40]Then Jonathan gave his weapons to the boy and said, "Go, carry them back to town."

[41]After the boy had gone, David got up from the south side of the stone and bowed down before Jonathan three times, with his face to the ground. Then they kissed each other and wept together — but David wept the most.

[42]Jonathan said to David, "Go in peace, for we have sworn friendship with each other in the name of the Lord, saying, 'The Lord is witness between you and me, and between your descendants and my descendants forever.' " Then David left, and Jonathan went back to the town.[b]

David at Nob

21 [c] David went to Nob, to Ahimelek the priest. Ahimelek trembled when he met him, and asked, "Why are you alone? Why is no one with you?"

[2]David answered Ahimelek the priest, "The king sent me on a mission and said to me, 'No one is to know anything about the mission I am sending you on.' As for my men, I have told them to meet me at a certain place. [3]Now then, what do you have on hand? Give me five loaves of bread, or whatever you can find."

[4]But the priest answered David, "I don't have any ordinary bread on hand; however, there is some consecrated bread here — provided the men have kept themselves from women."

---

[a] 25 Septuagint; Hebrew *wall. Jonathan arose*   [b] 42 In Hebrew texts this sentence (20:42b) is numbered 21:1.
[c] In Hebrew texts 21:1-15 is numbered 21:2-16.

⁵David replied, "Indeed women have been kept from us, as usual whenever*a* I set out. The men's bodies are holy even on missions that are not holy. How much more so today!" ⁶So the priest gave him the consecrated bread, since there was no bread there except the bread of the Presence that had been removed from before the LORD and replaced by hot bread on the day it was taken away.

⁷Now one of Saul's servants was there that day, detained before the LORD; he was Doeg the Edomite, Saul's chief shepherd.

⁸David asked Ahimelek, "Don't you have a spear or a sword here? I haven't brought my sword or any other weapon, because the king's mission was urgent."

⁹The priest replied, "The sword of Goliath the Philistine, whom you killed in the Valley of Elah, is here; it is wrapped in a cloth behind the ephod. If you want it, take it; there is no sword here but that one."

David said, "There is none like it; give it to me."

David at Gath

¹⁰That day David fled from Saul and went to Achish king of Gath. ¹¹But the servants of Achish said to him, "Isn't this David, the king of the land? Isn't he the one they sing about in their dances:

"'Saul has slain his thousands,
and David his tens of thousands'?"

¹²David took these words to heart and was very much afraid of Achish king of Gath. ¹³So he pretended to be insane in their presence; and while he was in their hands he acted like a madman, making marks on the doors of the gate and letting saliva run down his beard.

¹⁴Achish said to his servants, "Look at the man! He is insane! Why bring him to me? ¹⁵Am I so short of madmen that you have to bring this fellow here to carry on like this in front of me? Must this man come into my house?"

David at Adullam and Mizpah

22 David left Gath and escaped to the cave of Adullam. When his brothers and his father's household heard about it, they went down to him there. ²All those who were in distress or in debt or discontented gathered around him, and he became their commander. About four hundred men were with him.

³From there David went to Mizpah in Moab and said to the king of Moab, "Would you let my father and mother come and stay with you until I learn what God will do for me?" ⁴So he left them with the king of Moab, and they stayed with him as long as David was in the stronghold.

⁵But the prophet Gad said to David, "Do not stay in the stronghold. Go into the land of Judah." So David left and went to the forest of Hereth.

Saul Kills the Priests of Nob

⁶Now Saul heard that David and his men had been discovered. And Saul was seated, spear in hand, under the tamarisk tree on the hill at Gibeah, with all his officials standing at his side. ⁷He said to them, "Listen, men of Benjamin! Will the son of Jesse give all of you fields and vineyards? Will he make all of you commanders of thousands and commanders of hundreds? ⁸Is that why you have all conspired against me? No one tells me when my son makes a covenant with the son of Jesse. None of you is concerned about me or tells me that my son has incited my servant to lie in wait for me, as he does today."

⁹But Doeg the Edomite, who was standing with Saul's officials, said, "I saw the son of Jesse come to Ahimelek son of Ahitub at Nob. ¹⁰Ahimelek inquired of the LORD for him; he also gave him provisions and the sword of Goliath the Philistine." ¹¹Then the king sent for the priest Ahimelek son of Ahitub and all the men of his family, who were the priests at Nob, and they all came to the king. ¹²Saul said, "Listen now, son of Ahitub."

---

a 5 Or from us in the past few days since

"Yes, my lord," he answered.

[13]Saul said to him, "Why have you conspired against me, you and the son of Jesse, giving him bread and a sword and inquiring of God for him, so that he has rebelled against me and lies in wait for me, as he does today?"

[14]Ahimelek answered the king, "Who of all your servants is as loyal as David, the king's son-in-law, captain of your bodyguard and highly respected in your household? [15]Was that day the first time I inquired of God for him? Of course not! Let not the king accuse your servant or any of his father's family, for your servant knows nothing at all about this whole affair."

[16]But the king said, "You will surely die, Ahimelek, you and your whole family."

[17]Then the king ordered the guards at his side: "Turn and kill the priests of the LORD, because they too have sided with David. They knew he was fleeing, yet they did not tell me."

But the king's officials were unwilling to raise a hand to strike the priests of the LORD.

[18]The king then ordered Doeg, "You turn and strike down the priests." So Doeg the Edomite turned and struck them down. That day he killed eighty-five men who wore the linen ephod. [19]He also put to the sword Nob, the town of the priests, with its men and women, its children and infants, and its cattle, donkeys and sheep.

[20]But one son of Ahimelek son of Ahitub, named Abiathar, escaped and fled to join David. [21]He told David that Saul had killed the priests of the LORD. [22]Then David said to Abiathar, "That day, when Doeg the Edomite was there, I knew he would be sure to tell Saul. I am responsible for the death of your whole family. [23]Stay with me; don't be afraid. The man who wants to kill you is trying to kill me too. You will be safe with me."

David Saves Keilah

23 When David was told, "Look, the Philistines are fighting against Keilah and are looting the threshing floors," [2]he inquired of the LORD, saying, "Shall I go and attack these Philistines?"

The LORD answered him, "Go, attack the Philistines and save Keilah."

[3]But David's men said to him, "Here in Judah we are afraid. How much more, then, if we go to Keilah against the Philistine forces!"

[4]Once again David inquired of the LORD, and the LORD answered him, "Go down to Keilah, for I am going to give the Philistines into your hand." [5]So David and his men went to Keilah, fought the Philistines and carried off their livestock. He inflicted heavy losses on the Philistines and saved the people of Keilah. [6](Now Abiathar son of Ahimelek had brought the ephod down with him when he fled to David at Keilah.)

Saul Pursues David

[7]Saul was told that David had gone to Keilah, and he said, "God has delivered him into my hands, for David has imprisoned himself by entering a town with gates and bars." [8]And Saul called up all his forces for battle, to go down to Keilah to besiege David and his men.

[9]When David learned that Saul was plotting against him, he said to Abiathar the priest, "Bring the ephod." [10]David said, "LORD, God of Israel, your servant has heard definitely that Saul plans to come to Keilah and destroy the town on account of me. [11]Will the citizens of Keilah surrender me to him? Will Saul come down, as your servant has heard? LORD, God of Israel, tell your servant."

And the LORD said, "He will."

[12]Again David asked, "Will the citizens of Keilah surrender me and my men to Saul?"

And the LORD said, "They will."

[13]So David and his men, about six hundred in number, left Keilah and kept moving from place to place. When Saul was told that David had escaped from Keilah, he did not go there.

[14]David stayed in the wilderness strongholds and in the hills of the Desert of Ziph.

Day after day Saul searched for him, but God did not give David into his hands.

15While David was at Horesh in the Desert of Ziph, he learned that*a* Saul had come out to take his life. 16And Saul's son Jonathan went to David at Horesh and helped him find strength in God. 17"Don't be afraid," he said. "My father Saul will not lay a hand on you. You will be king over Israel, and I will be second to you. Even my father Saul knows this." 18The two of them made a covenant before the LORD. Then Jonathan went home, but David remained at Horesh.

19The Ziphites went up to Saul at Gibeah and said, "Is not David hiding among us in the strongholds at Horesh, on the hill of Hakilah, south of Jeshimon? 20Now, Your Majesty, come down whenever it pleases you to do so, and we will be responsible for giving him into your hands."

21Saul replied, "The LORD bless you for your concern for me. 22Go and get more information. Find out where David usually goes and who has seen him there. They tell me he is very crafty. 23Find out about all the hiding places he uses and come back to me with definite information. Then I will go with you; if he is in the area, I will track him down among all the clans of Judah."

24So they set out and went to Ziph ahead of Saul. Now David and his men were in the Desert of Maon, in the Arabah south of Jeshimon. 25Saul and his men began the search, and when David was told about it, he went down to the rock and stayed in the Desert of Maon. When Saul heard this, he went into the Desert of Maon in pursuit of David.

26Saul was going along one side of the mountain, and David and his men were on the other side, hurrying to get away from Saul. As Saul and his forces were closing in on David and his men to capture them, 27a messenger came to Saul, saying, "Come quickly! The Philistines are raiding the land." 28Then Saul broke off his pursuit of David and went to meet the Philistines. That is why they call this place Sela Hammahlekoth.*b* 29And David went up from there and lived in the strongholds of En Gedi.*c*

David Spares Saul's Life

24*d* After Saul returned from pursuing the Philistines, he was told, "David is in the Desert of En Gedi." 2So Saul took three thousand able young men from all Israel and set out to look for David and his men near the Crags of the Wild Goats.

3He came to the sheep pens along the way; a cave was there, and Saul went in to relieve himself. David and his men were far back in the cave. 4The men said, "This is the day the LORD spoke of when he said*e* to you, 'I will give your enemy into your hands for you to deal with as you wish.'" Then David crept up unnoticed and cut off a corner of Saul's robe.

5Afterward, David was conscience-stricken for having cut off a corner of his robe. 6He said to his men, "The LORD forbid that I should do such a thing to my master, the LORD's anointed, or lay my hand on him; for he is the anointed of the LORD." 7With these words David sharply rebuked his men and did not allow them to attack Saul. And Saul left the cave and went his way.

8Then David went out of the cave and called out to Saul, "My lord the king!" When Saul looked behind him, David bowed down and prostrated himself with his face to the ground. 9He said to Saul, "Why do you listen when men say, 'David is bent on harming you'? 10This day you have seen with your own eyes how the LORD delivered you into my hands in the cave. Some urged me to kill you, but I spared you; I said, 'I will not lay my hand on my lord, because he is the LORD's anoint-

---

a 15 Or *he was afraid because*   *b 28* *Sela Hammahlekoth* means *rock of parting.*   *c 29* In Hebrew texts this verse (23:29) is numbered 24:1.   *d* In Hebrew texts 24:1-22 is numbered 24:2-23.   *e 4* Or *"Today the LORD is saying* ed.' [11]See, my father, look at this piece of your robe in my hand! I cut off the corner of your robe but did not kill you. See that there is nothing in my hand to indicate that I am guilty of wrongdoing or rebellion. I have not wronged you, but you are hunting me down to take my life. [12]May the LORD judge between you and me. And may the LORD avenge the wrongs you have done to me, but my hand will not touch you. [13]As the old saying goes, 'From evildoers come evil deeds,' so my hand will not touch you.

[14]"Against whom has the king of Israel come out? Who are you pursuing? A dead dog? A flea? [15]May the LORD be our judge and decide between us. May he consider my cause and uphold it; may he vindicate me by delivering me from your hand."

[16]When David finished saying this, Saul asked, "Is that your voice, David my son?" And he wept aloud. [17]"You are more righteous than I," he said. "You have treated me well, but I have treated you badly. [18]You have just now told me about the good you did to me; the LORD delivered me into your hands, but you did not kill me. [19]When a man finds his enemy, does he let him get away unharmed? May the LORD reward you well for the way you treated me today. [20]I know that you will surely be king and that the kingdom of Israel will be established in your hands. [21]Now swear to me by the LORD that you will not kill off my descendants or wipe out my name from my father's family."

[22]So David gave his oath to Saul. Then Saul returned home, but David and his men went up to the stronghold.

David, Nabal and Abigail

25 Now Samuel died, and all Israel assembled and mourned for him; and they buried him at his home in Ramah. Then David moved down into the Desert of Paran.[a]

[2]A certain man in Maon, who had property there at Carmel, was very wealthy. He had a thousand goats and three thousand sheep, which he was shearing in Carmel. [3]His name was Nabal and his wife's name was Abigail. She was an intelligent and beautiful woman, but her husband was surly and mean in his dealings—he was a Calebite.

[4]While David was in the wilderness, he heard that Nabal was shearing sheep. [5]So he sent ten young men and said to them, "Go up to Nabal at Carmel and greet him in my name. [6]Say to him: 'Long life to you! Good health to you and your household! And good health to all that is yours!

[7]" 'Now I hear that it is sheep-shearing time. When your shepherds were with us, we did not mistreat them, and the whole time they were at Carmel nothing of theirs was missing. [8]Ask your own servants and they will tell you. Therefore be favorable toward my men, since we come at a festive time. Please give your servants and your son David whatever you can find for them.' "

[9]When David's men arrived, they gave Nabal this message in David's name. Then they waited.

[10]Nabal answered David's servants, "Who is this David? Who is this son of Jesse? Many servants are breaking away from their masters these days. [11]Why should I take my bread and water, and the meat I have slaughtered for my shearers, and give it to men coming from who knows where?"

[12]David's men turned around and went back. When they arrived, they reported every word. [13]David said to his men, "Each of you strap on your sword!" So they did, and David strapped his on as well. About four hundred men went up with David, while two hundred stayed with the supplies.

[14]One of the servants told Abigail, Nabal's wife, "David sent messengers from the wilderness to give our master his greetings, but he hurled insults at them. [15]Yet these men were very good to us. They did not mistreat us, and the whole time we were

---

a 1 Hebrew and some Septuagint manuscripts; other Septuagint manuscripts *Maon*

MY NAME IS ABIGAIL

1 SAMUEL 25

As individuals travel the road to recovery, they frequently need to cope with difficult conditions at home. Abigail lived with a foolish, angry man, and she faced possible destruction at the hands of a shrewd but equally angry man. What do you do when you're surrounded by anger and insanity? Abigail's example provides some direction for such chaotic conditions. Her husband, Nabal, whose name means "fool," displayed behavior that matched that label. David was at the time the fugitive leader of a band of renegades. Nabal's foolishness and David's fury together threatened Abigail and her entire household.

Nabal was "surly and mean in his dealings" (1 Samuel 25:3). In contrast, his wife, Abigail, was "an intelligent and beautiful woman" (v. 3). David and his small but skilled band of mercenaries had been living side-by-side with Nabal's shepherds and flocks. They could have taken whatever they wanted, but instead they were courteous to Nabal's men to the point of protecting Nabal's flocks (see v. 16). In return for this service, David humbly asked Nabal for help in feeding his men. David allowed Nabal to determine the nature and extent of the gift (see vv. 4–8). Unwisely, Nabal not only turned David down flat but also insulted David and his men (see vv. 10–11).

David, infuriated by this ingratitude, rode off with 400 men with the intention of destroying Nabal's household (see vv. 21–22). Nabal's worried servants carried this alarming news to Abigail. How did she respond?

- She confronted the problem by gathering up the resources available to her (see v. 18). Lesson: Don't try to change others; do what you can do. Recovery forces us to focus on the steps we *can* take, not on what is beyond our control.

- She abandoned pride (see vv. 23–25). Scripture repeatedly teaches that "God opposes the proud but shows favor to the humble" (1 Peter 5:5).

- She humbly and kindly shared Biblical truth with David. She pointed out the fact that vengeance belongs to God (see Deuteronomy 32:35).

- She returned to her irrational, surly husband and told him the truth instead of running away (see 1 Samuel 25:36–37).

What were the results of Abigail's faith and perseverance in a hostile home?

- David blessed her for saving him from the results of his own vengeful anger (see vv. 32–34).

- Abigail saved many lives (see v. 35).

- The Lord dealt justly with Nabal (see vv. 37–39).

- The widowed Abigail married the future king of Israel (see vv. 39–42).

Trying to change others and running away from difficult circumstances aren't part of the recovery journey. All that God requires of us is that we take the steps we have within our ability to take. Trusting God and applying his principles will bring blessings we can't anticipate, both to us and to those special people God places in our lives.

out in the fields near them nothing was missing. ¹⁶Night and day they were a wall around us the whole time we were herding our sheep near them. ¹⁷Now think it over and see what you can do, because disaster is hanging over our master and his whole household. He is such a wicked man that no one can talk to him."

¹⁸Abigail acted quickly. She took two hundred loaves of bread, two skins of wine, five dressed sheep, five seahs*ᵃ* of roasted grain, a hundred cakes of raisins and two hundred cakes of pressed figs, and loaded them on donkeys. ¹⁹Then she told her servants, "Go on ahead; I'll follow you." But she did not tell her husband Nabal.

²⁰As she came riding her donkey into a mountain ravine, there were David and his men descending toward her, and she met them. ²¹David had just said, "It's been useless—all my watching over this fellow's property in the wilderness so that nothing of his was missing. He has paid me back evil for good. ²²May God deal with David,*ᵇ* be it ever so severely, if by morning I leave alive one male of all who belong to him!"

²³When Abigail saw David, she quickly got off her donkey and bowed down before David with her face to the ground. ²⁴She fell at his feet and said: "Pardon your servant, my lord, and let me speak to you; hear what your servant has to say. ²⁵Please pay no attention, my lord, to that wicked man Nabal. He is just like his name—his name means Fool, and folly goes with him. And as for me, your servant, I did not see the men my lord sent. ²⁶And now, my lord, as surely as the LORD your God lives and as you live, since the LORD has kept you from bloodshed and from avenging yourself with your own hands, may your enemies and all who are intent on harming my lord be like Nabal. ²⁷And let this gift, which your servant has brought to my lord, be given to the men who follow you.

²⁸"Please forgive your servant's presumption. The LORD your God will certainly make a lasting dynasty for my lord, because you fight the LORD's battles, and no wrongdoing will be found in you as long as you live. ²⁹Even though someone is pursuing you to take your life, the life of my lord will be bound securely in the bundle of the living by the LORD your God, but the lives of your enemies he will hurl away as from the pocket of a sling. ³⁰When the LORD has fulfilled for my lord every good thing he promised concerning him and has appointed him ruler over Israel, ³¹my lord will not have on his conscience the staggering burden of needless bloodshed or of having avenged himself. And when the LORD your God has brought my lord success, remember your servant."

³²David said to Abigail, "Praise be to the LORD, the God of Israel, who has sent you today to meet me. ³³May you be blessed for your good judgment and for keeping me from bloodshed this day and from avenging myself with my own hands. ³⁴Otherwise, as surely as the LORD, the God of Israel, lives, who has kept me from harming you, if you had not come quickly to meet me, not one male belonging to Nabal would have been left alive by daybreak."

³⁵Then David accepted from her hand what she had brought him and said, "Go home in peace. I have heard your words and granted your request."

³⁶When Abigail went to Nabal, he was in the house holding a banquet like that of a king. He was in high spirits and very drunk. So she told him nothing at all until daybreak. ³⁷Then in the morning, when Nabal was sober, his wife told him all these things, and his heart failed him and he became like a stone. ³⁸About ten days later, the LORD struck Nabal and he died.

³⁹When David heard that Nabal was dead, he said, "Praise be to the LORD, who has upheld my cause against Nabal for treating me with contempt. He has kept

---

ᵃ 18 That is, probably about 60 pounds or about 27 kilograms   *ᵇ 22* Some Septuagint manuscripts; Hebrew *with David's enemies*

My Name Is Lisa

I'M A BELIEVER WHO STRUGGLES WITH CODEPENDENCY AND ANGER

Please read the story of Abigail and David in 1 Samuel 25.

I was abandoned by my mother when I was nine years old, only to be reunited with her and sucked back into her treacherous lifestyle a year later. It was then that I fell victim to sexual impropriety involving several of her many boyfriends. In an attempt to escape, I began drinking, doing drugs and behaving promiscuously. I would have done anything to feel loved, and I craved affection.

I got married at 19, and that was the last day I ever saw my mother — not because she didn't approve of my marriage but because she was murdered five days later, stabbed to death in her home in the middle of the night. The killer set fire to her house in an attempt to cover up the murder, and to this day the crime remains unsolved. I have no doubt, though, that her death was the result of one of her violent, codependent relationships.

Like Abigail (see 1 Samuel 25), I was married to an angry and destructive man, a blackout drinker who was totally controlling. He dictated what I was to wear, how I would wear it, whether or not I could work and who I could have as friends. The marriage did, however, produce my greatest treasures: my sons Jason and Eric.

After my inevitable divorce, I became promiscuous, which ultimately resulted in an abortion and in my relinquishing a child for adoption. I got married a second time, not unpredictably to an angry man. He drank, did drugs and verbally and physically abused me. I justified his behaviors and my relationships by comparing them to my childhood experiences. I truly believed that love equaled sex and abuse.

While in the midst of my second divorce, I found my way into Saddleback Church. Also during that time I met a man named Peter. He was cute, sweet and made me laugh. I soon learned that Peter drank, and his walls were covered with pornography. I thought this was normal, so we moved in together. I invited Peter to church, and we attended for a while. But Peter decided we should stop going, and, as a good, codependent girlfriend, I agreed.

Our life together became miserable. I began to resent Peter's addictions to pornography and alcohol and finally found a way to let him know how I felt: I had an affair, wanting to hurt Peter as much as his magazines were hurting me. I tried everything to be whatever Peter wanted in a woman, but deep down I felt degraded and unloved. I told myself that I wasn't pretty enough, thin enough or sexy enough to compete with the women in his videos.

As our relationship fell apart, we remembered Saddleback and once again attended a service together. The pastors were preaching a series of sermons titled "Road to Recovery." We listened to testimonies from individuals whose lives had been transformed by God through Celebrate Recovery.

I began my journey to freedom and healing as I joined Celebrate Recovery and started working the principles. During this time the Spirit of God became incredibly real to me, and God led me to deal with my anger. As I worked Principle Four and Step Four, I grasped for the first time that the sexual and physical abuse of my childhood weren't my fault. Despite the knowledge that I had truly been a victim, I was able at that point to let go of the victim mentality.

I made the decision to forgive and trust again, and I started with Peter. Forgiveness came first. Peter was vulnerable enough to admit everything he had done, no matter how much he knew it would hurt me, and I was able to begin forgiving him.

The more I trusted God, the more I trusted Peter. And the more I trusted God, the more I realized how loved, treasured and valued I was by him — and the more Peter began to truly cherish, love and value me. We were married on December 17, 1994.

Peter and I have continued to grow in intimacy with each other and with God. I finally realized that true joy and peace weren't to be found in sex, drugs, food or men, but only in Jesus Christ. Through my relationship with Jesus, I've been able to forgive those who have abused me, ask forgiveness from those I've hurt and recognize that since Jesus forgave me, I'm free to forgive myself. I can live my life in response to God's grace, not in pursuit of it. I've become a whole person who can love others as I love myself.

I'll be forever grateful for what God has done in my life. I now have boundaries and safe relationships with my brothers and sisters in Christ. It has been the thrill of my life to help other women who are struggling with similar circumstances. Like Abigail, I now share Biblical truth with others (see 1 Samuel 25:23 – 31). I love sharing my story with newcomers in the hope that they'll realize that Celebrate Recovery is a safe place.

Lisa

his servant from doing wrong and has brought Nabal's wrongdoing down on his own head."

Then David sent word to Abigail, asking her to become his wife. ⁴⁰His servants went to Carmel and said to Abigail, "David has sent us to you to take you to become his wife."

⁴¹She bowed down with her face to the ground and said, "I am your servant and am ready to serve you and wash the feet of my lord's servants." ⁴²Abigail quickly got on a donkey and, attended by her five female servants, went with David's messengers and became his wife. ⁴³David had also married Ahinoam of Jezreel, and they both were his wives. ⁴⁴But Saul had given his daughter Michal, David's wife, to Paltielᵃ son of Laish, who was from Gallim.

David Again Spares Saul's Life

26 The Ziphites went to Saul at Gibeah and said, "Is not David hiding on the hill of Hakilah, which faces Jeshimon?"

²So Saul went down to the Desert of Ziph, with his three thousand select Israelite troops, to search there for David. ³Saul made his camp beside the road on the hill of Hakilah facing Jeshimon, but David stayed in the wilderness. When he saw that Saul had followed him there, ⁴he sent out scouts and learned that Saul had definitely arrived.

⁵Then David set out and went to the place where Saul had camped. He saw where Saul and Abner son of Ner, the commander of the army, had lain down. Saul was lying inside the camp, with the army encamped around him.

⁶David then asked Ahimelek the Hittite and Abishai son of Zeruiah, Joab's brother, "Who will go down into the camp with me to Saul?"

"I'll go with you," said Abishai.

⁷So David and Abishai went to the army by night, and there was Saul, lying asleep inside the camp with his spear stuck in the ground near his head. Abner and the soldiers were lying around him.

⁸Abishai said to David, "Today God has delivered your enemy into your hands. Now let me pin him to the ground with one thrust of the spear; I won't strike him twice."

⁹But David said to Abishai, "Don't destroy him! Who can lay a hand on the Lord's anointed and be guiltless? ¹⁰As surely as the Lord lives," he said, "the Lord himself will strike him, or his time will come and he will die, or he will go into battle and perish. ¹¹But the Lord forbid that I should lay a hand on the Lord's anointed. Now get the spear and water jug that are near his head, and let's go."

¹²So David took the spear and water jug near Saul's head, and they left. No one saw or knew about it, nor did anyone wake up. They were all sleeping, because the Lord had put them into a deep sleep.

¹³Then David crossed over to the other side and stood on top of the hill some distance away; there was a wide space between them. ¹⁴He called out to the army and to Abner son of Ner, "Aren't you going to answer me, Abner?"

Abner replied, "Who are you who calls to the king?"

¹⁵David said, "You're a man, aren't you? And who is like you in Israel? Why didn't you guard your lord the king? Someone came to destroy your lord the king. ¹⁶What you have done is not good. As surely as the Lord lives, you and your men must die, because you did not guard your master, the Lord's anointed. Look around you. Where are the king's spear and water jug that were near his head?"

¹⁷Saul recognized David's voice and said, "Is that your voice, David my son?"

David replied, "Yes it is, my lord the king." ¹⁸And he added, "Why is my lord pursuing his servant? What have I done, and what wrong am I guilty of? ¹⁹Now

---

ᵃ 44 Hebrew *Palti*, a variant of *Paltiel*

let my lord the king listen to his servant's words. If the LORD has incited you against me, then may he accept an offering. If, however, people have done it, may they be cursed before the LORD! They have driven me today from my share in the LORD's inheritance and have said, 'Go, serve other gods.' 20Now do not let my blood fall to the ground far from the presence of the LORD. The king of Israel has come out to look for a flea — as one hunts a partridge in the mountains."

21Then Saul said, "I have sinned. Come back, David my son. Because you considered my life precious today, I will not try to harm you again. Surely I have acted like a fool and have been terribly wrong."

22"Here is the king's spear," David answered. "Let one of your young men come over and get it. 23The LORD rewards everyone for their righteousness and faithfulness. The LORD delivered you into my hands today, but I would not lay a hand on the LORD's anointed. 24As surely as I valued your life today, so may the LORD value my life and deliver me from all trouble."

25Then Saul said to David, "May you be blessed, David my son; you will do great things and surely triumph."

So David went on his way, and Saul returned home.

David Among the Philistines

27 But David thought to himself, "One of these days I will be destroyed by the hand of Saul. The best thing I can do is to escape to the land of the Philistines. Then Saul will give up searching for me anywhere in Israel, and I will slip out of his hand."

2So David and the six hundred men with him left and went over to Achish son of Maok king of Gath. 3David and his men settled in Gath with Achish. Each man had his family with him, and David had his two wives: Ahinoam of Jezreel and Abigail of Carmel, the widow of Nabal. 4When Saul was told that David had fled to Gath, he no longer searched for him.

5Then David said to Achish, "If I have found favor in your eyes, let a place be assigned to me in one of the country towns, that I may live there. Why should your servant live in the royal city with you?"

6So on that day Achish gave him Ziklag, and it has belonged to the kings of Judah ever since. 7David lived in Philistine territory a year and four months.

8Now David and his men went up and raided the Geshurites, the Girzites and the Amalekites. (From ancient times these peoples had lived in the land extending to Shur and Egypt.) 9Whenever David attacked an area, he did not leave a man or woman alive, but took sheep and cattle, donkeys and camels, and clothes. Then he returned to Achish.

10When Achish asked, "Where did you go raiding today?" David would say, "Against the Negev of Judah" or "Against the Negev of Jerahmeel" or "Against the Negev of the Kenites." 11He did not leave a man or woman alive to be brought to Gath, for he thought, "They might inform on us and say, 'This is what David did.'" And such was his practice as long as he lived in Philistine territory. 12Achish trusted David and said to himself, "He has become so obnoxious to his people, the Israelites, that he will be my servant for life."

28 In those days the Philistines gathered their forces to fight against Israel. Achish said to David, "You must understand that you and your men will accompany me in the army."

2David said, "Then you will see for yourself what your servant can do."

Achish replied, "Very well, I will make you my bodyguard for life."

Saul and the Medium at Endor

3Now Samuel was dead, and all Israel had mourned for him and buried him in his own town of Ramah. Saul had expelled the mediums and spiritists from the land.

4The Philistines assembled and came and set up camp at Shunem, while Saul gathered all Israel and set up camp at Gilboa. 5When

Saul saw the Philistine army, he was afraid; terror filled his heart. [6]He inquired of the LORD, but the LORD did not answer him by dreams or Urim or prophets. [7]Saul then said to his attendants, "Find me a woman who is a medium, so I may go and inquire of her."

"There is one in Endor," they said.

[8]So Saul disguised himself, putting on other clothes, and at night he and two men went to the woman. "Consult a spirit for me," he said, "and bring up for me the one I name."

[9]But the woman said to him, "Surely you know what Saul has done. He has cut off the mediums and spiritists from the land. Why have you set a trap for my life to bring about my death?"

[10]Saul swore to her by the LORD, "As surely as the LORD lives, you will not be punished for this."

[11]Then the woman asked, "Whom shall I bring up for you?"

"Bring up Samuel," he said.

[12]When the woman saw Samuel, she cried out at the top of her voice and said to Saul, "Why have you deceived me? You are Saul!"

[13]The king said to her, "Don't be afraid. What do you see?"

The woman said, "I see a ghostly figure[a] coming up out of the earth."

[14]"What does he look like?" he asked.

"An old man wearing a robe is coming up," she said.

Then Saul knew it was Samuel, and he bowed down and prostrated himself with his face to the ground.

[15]Samuel said to Saul, "Why have you disturbed me by bringing me up?"

"I am in great distress," Saul said. "The Philistines are fighting against me, and God has departed from me. He no longer answers me, either by prophets or by dreams. So I have called on you to tell me what to do."

[16]Samuel said, "Why do you consult me, now that the LORD has departed from you

and become your enemy? [17]The LORD has done what he predicted through me. The LORD has torn the kingdom out of your hands and given it to one of your neighbors — to David. [18]Because you did not obey the LORD or carry out his fierce wrath against the Amalekites, the LORD has done this to you today. [19]The LORD will deliver both Israel and you into the hands of the Philistines, and tomorrow you and your sons will be with me. The LORD will also give the army of Israel into the hands of the Philistines."

[20]Immediately Saul fell full length on the ground, filled with fear because of Samuel's words. His strength was gone, for he had eaten nothing all that day and all that night.

[21]When the woman came to Saul and saw that he was greatly shaken, she said, "Look, your servant has obeyed you. I took my life in my hands and did what you told me to do. [22]Now please listen to your servant and let me give you some food so you may eat and have the strength to go on your way."

[23]He refused and said, "I will not eat."

But his men joined the woman in urging him, and he listened to them. He got up from the ground and sat on the couch.

[24]The woman had a fattened calf at the house, which she butchered at once. She took some flour, kneaded it and baked bread without yeast. [25]Then she set it before Saul and his men, and they ate. That same night they got up and left.

Achish Sends David Back to Ziklag

29 The Philistines gathered all their forces at Aphek, and Israel camped by the spring in Jezreel. [2]As the Philistine rulers marched with their units of hundreds and thousands, David and his men were marching at the rear with Achish. [3]The commanders of the Philistines asked, "What about these Hebrews?"

Achish replied, "Is this not David, who was an officer of Saul king of Israel? He has already been with me for over a year, and

---

[a] 13 Or *see spirits*; or *see gods*

from the day he left Saul until now, I have found no fault in him."

[4]But the Philistine commanders were angry with Achish and said, "Send the man back, that he may return to the place you assigned him. He must not go with us into battle, or he will turn against us during the fighting. How better could he regain his master's favor than by taking the heads of our own men? [5]Isn't this the David they sang about in their dances:

> "'Saul has slain his thousands,
>   and David his tens of thousands'?"

[6]So Achish called David and said to him, "As surely as the LORD lives, you have been reliable, and I would be pleased to have you serve with me in the army. From the day you came to me until today, I have found no fault in you, but the rulers don't approve of you. [7]Now turn back and go in peace; do nothing to displease the Philistine rulers."

[8]"But what have I done?" asked David. "What have you found against your servant from the day I came to you until now? Why can't I go and fight against the enemies of my lord the king?"

[9]Achish answered, "I know that you have been as pleasing in my eyes as an angel of God; nevertheless, the Philistine commanders have said, 'He must not go up with us into battle.' [10]Now get up early, along with your master's servants who have come with you, and leave in the morning as soon as it is light."

[11]So David and his men got up early in the morning to go back to the land of the Philistines, and the Philistines went up to Jezreel.

David Destroys the Amalekites

30 David and his men reached Ziklag on the third day. Now the Amalekites had raided the Negev and Ziklag. They had attacked Ziklag and burned it, [2]and had taken captive the women and everyone else in it, both young and old. They killed none of them, but carried them off as they went on their way.

[3]When David and his men reached Ziklag, they found it destroyed by fire and their wives and sons and daughters taken captive. [4]So David and his men wept aloud until they had no strength left to weep. [5]David's two wives had been captured — Ahinoam of Jezreel and Abigail, the widow of Nabal of Carmel. [6]David was greatly distressed because the men were talking of stoning him; each one was bitter in spirit because of his sons and daughters. But David found strength in the LORD his God.

[7]Then David said to Abiathar the priest, the son of Ahimelek, "Bring me the ephod." Abiathar brought it to him, [8]and David inquired of the LORD, "Shall I pursue this raiding party? Will I overtake them?"

"Pursue them," he answered. "You will certainly overtake them and succeed in the rescue."

[9]David and the six hundred men with him came to the Besor Valley, where some stayed behind. [10]Two hundred of them were too exhausted to cross the valley, but David and the other four hundred continued the pursuit.

[11]They found an Egyptian in a field and brought him to David. They gave him water to drink and food to eat — [12]part of a cake of pressed figs and two cakes of raisins. He ate and was revived, for he had not eaten any food or drunk any water for three days and three nights.

[13]David asked him, "Who do you belong to? Where do you come from?"

He said, "I am an Egyptian, the slave of an Amalekite. My master abandoned me when I became ill three days ago. [14]We raided the Negev of the Kerethites, some territory belonging to Judah and the Negev of Caleb. And we burned Ziklag."

[15]David asked him, "Can you lead me down to this raiding party?"

He answered, "Swear to me before God that you will not kill me or hand me over to my master, and I will take you down to them."

[16]He led David down, and there they were, scattered over the countryside, eating,

drinking and reveling because of the great amount of plunder they had taken from the land of the Philistines and from Judah. ¹⁷David fought them from dusk until the evening of the next day, and none of them got away, except four hundred young men who rode off on camels and fled. ¹⁸David recovered everything the Amalekites had taken, including his two wives. ¹⁹Nothing was missing: young or old, boy or girl, plunder or anything else they had taken. David brought everything back. ²⁰He took all the flocks and herds, and his men drove them ahead of the other livestock, saying, "This is David's plunder."

²¹Then David came to the two hundred men who had been too exhausted to follow him and who were left behind at the Besor Valley. They came out to meet David and the men with him. As David and his men approached, he asked them how they were. ²²But all the evil men and troublemakers among David's followers said, "Because they did not go out with us, we will not share with them the plunder we recovered. However, each man may take his wife and children and go."

²³David replied, "No, my brothers, you must not do that with what the Lord has given us. He has protected us and delivered into our hands the raiding party that came against us. ²⁴Who will listen to what you say? The share of the man who stayed with the supplies is to be the same as that of him who went down to the battle. All will share alike." ²⁵David made this a statute and ordinance for Israel from that day to this.

²⁶When David reached Ziklag, he sent some of the plunder to the elders of Judah, who were his friends, saying, "Here is a gift for you from the plunder of the Lord's enemies."

²⁷David sent it to those who were in Bethel, Ramoth Negev and Jattir; ²⁸to those in Aroer, Siphmoth, Eshtemoa ²⁹and Rakal; to those in the towns of the Jerahmeelites and the Kenites; ³⁰to those in Hormah, Bor Ashan, Athak ³¹and Hebron; and to

those in all the other places where he and his men had roamed.

Saul Takes His Life

31 Now the Philistines fought against Israel; the Israelites fled before them, and many fell dead on Mount Gilboa. ²The Philistines were in hot pursuit of Saul and his sons, and they killed his sons Jonathan, Abinadab and Malki-Shua. ³The fighting grew fierce around Saul, and when the archers overtook him, they wounded him critically.

⁴Saul said to his armor-bearer, "Draw your sword and run me through, or these uncircumcised fellows will come and run me through and abuse me."

But his armor-bearer was terrified and would not do it; so Saul took his own sword and fell on it. ⁵When the armor-bearer saw that Saul was dead, he too fell on his sword and died with him. ⁶So Saul and his three sons and his armor-bearer and all his men died together that same day.

⁷When the Israelites along the valley and those across the Jordan saw that the Israelite army had fled and that Saul and his sons had died, they abandoned their towns and fled. And the Philistines came and occupied them.

⁸The next day, when the Philistines came to strip the dead, they found Saul and his three sons fallen on Mount Gilboa. ⁹They cut off his head and stripped off his armor, and they sent messengers throughout the land of the Philistines to proclaim the news in the temple of their idols and among their people. ¹⁰They put his armor in the temple of the Ashtoreths and fastened his body to the wall of Beth Shan.

¹¹When the people of Jabesh Gilead heard what the Philistines had done to Saul, ¹²all their valiant men marched through the night to Beth Shan. They took down the bodies of Saul and his sons from the wall of Beth Shan and went to Jabesh, where they burned them. ¹³Then they took their bones and buried them under a tamarisk tree at Jabesh, and they fasted seven days.

THEME: An overriding theme of 2 Samuel is that sin has consequences.

AUTHOR: The author of 2 Samuel is unknown. Scripture mentions the records of the prophets Samuel, Nathan and Gad as sources that may have been incorporated into this written history of Israel.

DATE OF WRITING: The two books of Samuel were originally one book that was probably written around 925 BC, shortly after the division of the nation into the northern and southern kingdoms (930 BC).

ENCOURAGEMENT FROM 2 SAMUEL: "[The LORD] reached down from on high and took hold of me; he drew me out of deep waters . . . He brought me out into a spacious place; he rescued me because he delighted in me" (2 Samuel 22:17,20).

CHALLENGE FROM 2 SAMUEL: "I will not sacrifice to the LORD my God burnt offerings that cost me nothing" (2 Samuel 24:24).

REFLECTION FROM 2 SAMUEL: "So we must die. But that is not what God desires; rather, he devises ways so that a banished person does not remain banished from him" (2 Samuel 14:14).

The theme of 2 Samuel is familiar to Bible readers: Obedience to God brings blessing, while disobedience results in trouble and judgment. The first ten chapters of 2 Samuel describe the rewards of obedience as David's rule is extended first over Judah and then over all of Israel. David's sin of sexual impurity results in adultery, and his subsequent murder of Bathsheba's husband in an effort to hide the truth behind her pregnancy is the turning point of the book. After these actions, David's life story becomes a continuous chronicle of painful consequences. He and Bathsheba, now his wife, lose their infant son, and incest, murder, rebellion and resentment taint his family story in this book.

While 2 Samuel illustrates that sin has direct consequences in life, the book also makes it clear that these do not cancel out God's long-term plan of redemption. In 2 Samuel God makes a covenant with David, announcing that the Messiah will come from his line. Even after David's sin, this covenant is not broken.

As we walk with God down the path of recovery, it's important to realize that, as low as we may have fallen, God isn't finished with us. Sometimes in recovery it's easy to feel as though we've done and seen too much for God to continue to love us. The truth is that he already knows exactly what we've done. He's seen it all — and he still loves us anyway! God has already forgiven us, and as we go through our recovery with Christ in control, we see that we can still fulfill God's purpose for us in this world.

David Hears of Saul's Death

1 After the death of Saul, David returned from striking down the Amalekites and stayed in Ziklag two days. ²On the third day a man arrived from Saul's camp with his clothes torn and dust on his head. When he came to David, he fell to the ground to pay him honor.

³"Where have you come from?" David asked him.

He answered, "I have escaped from the Israelite camp."

⁴"What happened?" David asked. "Tell me."

"The men fled from the battle," he replied. "Many of them fell and died. And Saul and his son Jonathan are dead."

⁵Then David said to the young man who brought him the report, "How do you know that Saul and his son Jonathan are dead?"

⁶"I happened to be on Mount Gilboa," the young man said, "and there was Saul, leaning on his spear, with the chariots and their drivers in hot pursuit. ⁷When he turned around and saw me, he called out to me, and I said, 'What can I do?'

⁸"He asked me, 'Who are you?'

" 'An Amalekite,' I answered.

⁹"Then he said to me, 'Stand here by me and kill me! I'm in the throes of death, but I'm still alive.'

¹⁰"So I stood beside him and killed him, because I knew that after he had fallen he could not survive. And I took the crown that was on his head and the band on his arm and have brought them here to my lord."

¹¹Then David and all the men with him took hold of their clothes and tore them. ¹²They mourned and wept and fasted till evening for Saul and his son Jonathan, and for the army of the LORD and for the nation of Israel, because they had fallen by the sword.

¹³David said to the young man who brought him the report, "Where are you from?"

"I am the son of a foreigner, an Amalekite," he answered.

¹⁴David asked him, "Why weren't you afraid to lift your hand to destroy the LORD's anointed?"

¹⁵Then David called one of his men and said, "Go, strike him down!" So he struck him down, and he died. ¹⁶For David had said to him, "Your blood be on your own head. Your own mouth testified against you when you said, 'I killed the LORD's anointed.' "

David's Lament for Saul and Jonathan

¹⁷David took up this lament concerning Saul and his son Jonathan, ¹⁸and he ordered that the people of Judah be taught this lament of the bow (it is written in the Book of Jashar):

¹⁹"A gazelle*a* lies slain on your heights,
Israel.
   How the mighty have fallen!

²⁰"Tell it not in Gath,
   proclaim it not in the streets of
      Ashkelon,
lest the daughters of the Philistines be
   glad,
   lest the daughters of the
      uncircumcised rejoice.

²¹"Mountains of Gilboa,
   may you have neither dew nor rain,
   may no showers fall on your terraced
      fields.*b*
For there the shield of the mighty was
   despised,
   the shield of Saul—no longer rubbed
      with oil.

²²"From the blood of the slain,
   from the flesh of the mighty,
the bow of Jonathan did not turn back,
   the sword of Saul did not return
      unsatisfied.

²³Saul and Jonathan—
   in life they were loved and admired,
   and in death they were not parted.
They were swifter than eagles,
   they were stronger than lions.

---

a 19 Gazelle here symbolizes a human dignitary.   *b 21* Or / nor fields that yield grain for offerings

²⁴"Daughters of Israel,
>   weep for Saul,
> who clothed you in scarlet and finery,
>   who adorned your garments with
>   ornaments of gold.

²⁵"How the mighty have fallen in battle!
>   Jonathan lies slain on your heights.
²⁶I grieve for you, Jonathan my brother;
>   you were very dear to me.
> Your love for me was wonderful,
>   more wonderful than that of women.

²⁷"How the mighty have fallen!
>   The weapons of war have perished!"

David Anointed King Over Judah

2 In the course of time, David inquired of the Lord. "Shall I go up to one of the towns of Judah?" he asked.

The Lord said, "Go up."

David asked, "Where shall I go?"

"To Hebron," the Lord answered.

²So David went up there with his two wives, Ahinoam of Jezreel and Abigail, the widow of Nabal of Carmel. ³David also took the men who were with him, each with his family, and they settled in Hebron and its towns. ⁴Then the men of Judah came to Hebron, and there they anointed David king over the tribe of Judah.

When David was told that it was the men from Jabesh Gilead who had buried Saul, ⁵he sent messengers to them to say to them, "The Lord bless you for showing this kindness to Saul your master by burying him. ⁶May the Lord now show you kindness and faithfulness, and I too will show you the same favor because you have done this. ⁷Now then, be strong and brave, for Saul your master is dead, and the people of Judah have anointed me king over them."

War Between the Houses of David and Saul

⁸Meanwhile, Abner son of Ner, the commander of Saul's army, had taken Ish-Bosheth son of Saul and brought him over to Mahanaim. ⁹He made him king over Gilead, Ashuri and Jezreel, and also over Ephraim, Benjamin and all Israel.

¹⁰Ish-Bosheth son of Saul was forty years old when he became king over Israel, and he reigned two years. The tribe of Judah, however, remained loyal to David. ¹¹The length of time David was king in Hebron over Judah was seven years and six months.

¹²Abner son of Ner, together with the men of Ish-Bosheth son of Saul, left Mahanaim and went to Gibeon. ¹³Joab son of Zeruiah and David's men went out and met them at the pool of Gibeon. One group sat down on one side of the pool and one group on the other side.

¹⁴Then Abner said to Joab, "Let's have some of the young men get up and fight hand to hand in front of us."

"All right, let them do it," Joab said.

¹⁵So they stood up and were counted off — twelve men for Benjamin and Ish-Bosheth son of Saul, and twelve for David. ¹⁶Then each man grabbed his opponent by the head and thrust his dagger into his opponent's side, and they fell down together. So that place in Gibeon was called Helkath Hazzurim.[a]

¹⁷The battle that day was very fierce, and Abner and the Israelites were defeated by David's men.

¹⁸The three sons of Zeruiah were there: Joab, Abishai and Asahel. Now Asahel was as fleet-footed as a wild gazelle. ¹⁹He chased Abner, turning neither to the right nor to the left as he pursued him. ²⁰Abner looked behind him and asked, "Is that you, Asahel?"

"It is," he answered.

²¹Then Abner said to him, "Turn aside to the right or to the left; take on one of the young men and strip him of his weapons." But Asahel would not stop chasing him.

²²Again Abner warned Asahel, "Stop chasing me! Why should I strike you down? How could I look your brother Joab in the face?"

---

^a 16 *Helkath Hazzurim* means *field of daggers* or *field of hostilities.*

23But Asahel refused to give up the pursuit; so Abner thrust the butt of his spear into Asahel's stomach, and the spear came out through his back. He fell there and died on the spot. And every man stopped when he came to the place where Asahel had fallen and died.

24But Joab and Abishai pursued Abner, and as the sun was setting, they came to the hill of Ammah, near Giah on the way to the wasteland of Gibeon. 25Then the men of Benjamin rallied behind Abner. They formed themselves into a group and took their stand on top of a hill.

26Abner called out to Joab, "Must the sword devour forever? Don't you realize that this will end in bitterness? How long before you order your men to stop pursuing their fellow Israelites?"

27Joab answered, "As surely as God lives, if you had not spoken, the men would have continued pursuing them until morning."

28So Joab blew the trumpet, and all the troops came to a halt; they no longer pursued Israel, nor did they fight anymore.

29All that night Abner and his men marched through the Arabah. They crossed the Jordan, continued through the morning hours*a* and came to Mahanaim.

30Then Joab stopped pursuing Abner and assembled the whole army. Besides Asahel, nineteen of David's men were found missing. 31But David's men had killed three hundred and sixty Benjamites who were with Abner. 32They took Asahel and buried him in his father's tomb at Bethlehem. Then Joab and his men marched all night and arrived at Hebron by daybreak.

3 The war between the house of Saul and the house of David lasted a long time. David grew stronger and stronger, while the house of Saul grew weaker and weaker.

2Sons were born to David in Hebron:

His firstborn was Amnon the son of Ahinoam of Jezreel;

3his second, Kileab the son of Abigail the widow of Nabal of Carmel;

the third, Absalom the son of Maakah daughter of Talmai king of Geshur;

4the fourth, Adonijah the son of Haggith;

the fifth, Shephatiah the son of Abital;

5and the sixth, Ithream the son of David's wife Eglah.

These were born to David in Hebron.

Abner Goes Over to David

6During the war between the house of Saul and the house of David, Abner had been strengthening his own position in the house of Saul. 7Now Saul had had a concubine named Rizpah daughter of Aiah. And Ish-Bosheth said to Abner, "Why did you sleep with my father's concubine?"

8Abner was very angry because of what Ish-Bosheth said. So he answered, "Am I a dog's head — on Judah's side? This very day I am loyal to the house of your father Saul and to his family and friends. I haven't handed you over to David. Yet now you accuse me of an offense involving this woman! 9May God deal with Abner, be it ever so severely, if I do not do for David what the LORD promised him on oath 10and transfer the kingdom from the house of Saul and establish David's throne over Israel and Judah from Dan to Beersheba." 11Ish-Bosheth did not dare to say another word to Abner, because he was afraid of him.

12Then Abner sent messengers on his behalf to say to David, "Whose land is it? Make an agreement with me, and I will help you bring all Israel over to you."

13"Good," said David. "I will make an agreement with you. But I demand one thing of you: Do not come into my presence unless you bring Michal daughter of Saul when you come to see me." 14Then

---

a 29 See Septuagint; the meaning of the Hebrew for this phrase is uncertain.

David sent messengers to Ish-Bosheth son of Saul, demanding, "Give me my wife Michal, whom I betrothed to myself for the price of a hundred Philistine foreskins."

15So Ish-Bosheth gave orders and had her taken away from her husband Paltiel son of Laish. 16Her husband, however, went with her, weeping behind her all the way to Bahurim. Then Abner said to him, "Go back home!" So he went back.

17Abner conferred with the elders of Israel and said, "For some time you have wanted to make David your king. 18Now do it! For the LORD promised David, 'By my servant David I will rescue my people Israel from the hand of the Philistines and from the hand of all their enemies.'"

19Abner also spoke to the Benjamites in person. Then he went to Hebron to tell David everything that Israel and the whole tribe of Benjamin wanted to do. 20When Abner, who had twenty men with him, came to David at Hebron, David prepared a feast for him and his men. 21Then Abner said to David, "Let me go at once and assemble all Israel for my lord the king, so that they may make a covenant with you, and that you may rule over all that your heart desires." So David sent Abner away, and he went in peace.

Joab Murders Abner

22Just then David's men and Joab returned from a raid and brought with them a great deal of plunder. But Abner was no longer with David in Hebron, because David had sent him away, and he had gone in peace. 23When Joab and all the soldiers with him arrived, he was told that Abner son of Ner had come to the king and that the king had sent him away and that he had gone in peace.

24So Joab went to the king and said, "What have you done? Look, Abner came to you. Why did you let him go? Now he is gone! 25You know Abner son of Ner; he came to deceive you and observe your movements and find out everything you are doing."

26Joab then left David and sent messengers after Abner, and they brought him back from the cistern at Sirah. But David did not know it. 27Now when Abner returned to Hebron, Joab took him aside into an inner chamber, as if to speak with him privately. And there, to avenge the blood of his brother Asahel, Joab stabbed him in the stomach, and he died.

28Later, when David heard about this, he said, "I and my kingdom are forever innocent before the LORD concerning the blood of Abner son of Ner. 29May his blood fall on the head of Joab and on his whole family! May Joab's family never be without someone who has a running sore or leprosy*a* or who leans on a crutch or who falls by the sword or who lacks food."

30(Joab and his brother Abishai murdered Abner because he had killed their brother Asahel in the battle at Gibeon.)

31Then David said to Joab and all the people with him, "Tear your clothes and put on sackcloth and walk in mourning in front of Abner." King David himself walked behind the bier. 32They buried Abner in Hebron, and the king wept aloud at Abner's tomb. All the people wept also.

33The king sang this lament for Abner:

"Should Abner have died as the lawless
    die?
34   Your hands were not bound,
      your feet were not fettered.
You fell as one falls before the wicked."

And all the people wept over him again.

35Then they all came and urged David to eat something while it was still day; but David took an oath, saying, "May God deal with me, be it ever so severely, if I taste bread or anything else before the sun sets!"

36All the people took note and were pleased; indeed, everything the king did pleased them. 37So on that day all the people there and all Israel knew that the king

---

a 29 The Hebrew for *leprosy* was used for various diseases affecting the skin.

had no part in the murder of Abner son of Ner.

³⁸Then the king said to his men, "Do you not realize that a commander and a great man has fallen in Israel this day? ³⁹And today, though I am the anointed king, I am weak, and these sons of Zeruiah are too strong for me. May the LORD repay the evildoer according to his evil deeds!"

Ish-Bosheth Murdered

4 When Ish-Bosheth son of Saul heard that Abner had died in Hebron, he lost courage, and all Israel became alarmed. ²Now Saul's son had two men who were leaders of raiding bands. One was named Baanah and the other Rekab; they were sons of Rimmon the Beerothite from the tribe of Benjamin — Beeroth is considered part of Benjamin, ³because the people of Beeroth fled to Gittaim and have resided there as foreigners to this day.

⁴(Jonathan son of Saul had a son who was lame in both feet. He was five years old when the news about Saul and Jonathan came from Jezreel. His nurse picked him up and fled, but as she hurried to leave, he fell and became disabled. His name was Mephibosheth.)

⁵Now Rekab and Baanah, the sons of Rimmon the Beerothite, set out for the house of Ish-Bosheth, and they arrived there in the heat of the day while he was taking his noonday rest. ⁶They went into the inner part of the house as if to get some wheat, and they stabbed him in the stomach. Then Rekab and his brother Baanah slipped away.

⁷They had gone into the house while he was lying on the bed in his bedroom. After they stabbed and killed him, they cut off his head. Taking it with them, they traveled all night by way of the Arabah. ⁸They brought the head of Ish-Bosheth to David at Hebron and said to the king, "Here is the head of Ish-Bosheth son of Saul, your enemy, who tried to kill you. This day the LORD has avenged my lord the king against Saul and his offspring."

⁹David answered Rekab and his brother Baanah, the sons of Rimmon the Beerothite, "As surely as the LORD lives, who has delivered me out of every trouble, ¹⁰when someone told me, 'Saul is dead,' and thought he was bringing good news, I seized him and put him to death in Ziklag. That was the reward I gave him for his news! ¹¹How much more — when wicked men have killed an innocent man in his own house and on his own bed — should I not now demand his blood from your hand and rid the earth of you!"

¹²So David gave an order to his men, and they killed them. They cut off their hands and feet and hung the bodies by the pool in Hebron. But they took the head of Ish-Bosheth and buried it in Abner's tomb at Hebron.

David Becomes King Over Israel

5 All the tribes of Israel came to David at Hebron and said, "We are your own flesh and blood. ²In the past, while Saul was king over us, you were the one who led Israel on their military campaigns. And the LORD said to you, 'You will shepherd my people Israel, and you will become their ruler.'"

³When all the elders of Israel had come to King David at Hebron, the king made a covenant with them at Hebron before the LORD, and they anointed David king over Israel. ⁴David was thirty years old when he became king, and he reigned forty years. ⁵In Hebron he reigned over Judah seven years and six months, and in Jerusalem he reigned over all Israel and Judah thirty-three years.

David Conquers Jerusalem

⁶The king and his men marched to Jerusalem to attack the Jebusites, who lived there. The Jebusites said to David, "You will not get in here; even the blind and the lame can ward you off." They thought, "David cannot get in here." ⁷Nevertheless, David captured the fortress of Zion — which is the City of David.

[8]On that day David had said, "Anyone who conquers the Jebusites will have to use the water shaft to reach those 'lame and blind' who are David's enemies.[a]" That is why they say, "The 'blind and lame' will not enter the palace."

[9]David then took up residence in the fortress and called it the City of David. He built up the area around it, from the terraces[b] inward. [10]And he became more and more powerful, because the LORD God Almighty was with him.

[11]Now Hiram king of Tyre sent envoys to David, along with cedar logs and carpenters and stonemasons, and they built a palace for David. [12]Then David knew that the LORD had established him as king over Israel and had exalted his kingdom for the sake of his people Israel.

[13]After he left Hebron, David took more concubines and wives in Jerusalem, and more sons and daughters were born to him. [14]These are the names of the children born to him there: Shammua, Shobab, Nathan, Solomon, [15]Ibhar, Elishua, Nepheg, Japhia, [16]Elishama, Eliada and Eliphelet.

David Defeats the Philistines

[17]When the Philistines heard that David had been anointed king over Israel, they went up in full force to search for him, but David heard about it and went down to the stronghold. [18]Now the Philistines had come and spread out in the Valley of Rephaim; [19]so David inquired of the LORD, "Shall I go and attack the Philistines? Will you deliver them into my hands?"

The LORD answered him, "Go, for I will surely deliver the Philistines into your hands."

[20]So David went to Baal Perazim, and there he defeated them. He said, "As waters break out, the LORD has broken out against my enemies before me." So that place was called Baal Perazim.[c] [21]The Philistines abandoned their idols there, and David and his men carried them off.

[22]Once more the Philistines came up and spread out in the Valley of Rephaim; [23]so David inquired of the LORD, and he answered, "Do not go straight up, but circle around behind them and attack them in front of the poplar trees. [24]As soon as you hear the sound of marching in the tops of the poplar trees, move quickly, because that will mean the LORD has gone out in front of you to strike the Philistine army." [25]So David did as the LORD commanded him, and he struck down the Philistines all the way from Gibeon[d] to Gezer.

The Ark Brought to Jerusalem

6 David again brought together all the able young men of Israel — thirty thousand. [2]He and all his men went to Baalah[e] in Judah to bring up from there the ark of God, which is called by the Name,[f] the name of the LORD Almighty, who is enthroned between the cherubim on the ark. [3]They set the ark of God on a new cart and brought it from the house of Abinadab, which was on the hill. Uzzah and Ahio, sons of Abinadab, were guiding the new cart [4]with the ark of God on it,[g] and Ahio was walking in front of it. [5]David and all Israel were celebrating with all their might before the LORD, with castanets,[h] harps, lyres, timbrels, sistrums and cymbals.

[6]When they came to the threshing floor of Nakon, Uzzah reached out and took hold of the ark of God, because the oxen stumbled. [7]The LORD's anger burned against Uzzah because of his irreverent act; therefore God struck him down, and he died there beside the ark of God.

[8]Then David was angry because the LORD's wrath had broken out against

---

[a] 8 Or are hated by David   [b] 9 Or the Millo   [c] 20 Baal Perazim means the lord who breaks out.
[d] 25 Septuagint (see also 1 Chron. 14:16); Hebrew Geba   [e] 2 That is, Kiriath Jearim (see 1 Chron. 13:6)
[f] 2 Hebrew; Septuagint and Vulgate do not have the Name.   [g] 3,4 Dead Sea Scrolls and some Septuagint
manuscripts; Masoretic Text cart [4]and they brought it with the ark of God from the house of Abinadab, which was on the hill   [h] 5 Masoretic Text; Dead Sea Scrolls and Septuagint (see also 1 Chron. 13:8) songs

Uzzah, and to this day that place is called Perez Uzzah.ᵃ

⁹David was afraid of the Lord that day and said, "How can the ark of the Lord ever come to me?" ¹⁰He was not willing to take the ark of the Lord to be with him in the City of David. Instead, he took it to the house of Obed-Edom the Gittite. ¹¹The ark of the Lord remained in the house of Obed-Edom the Gittite for three months, and the Lord blessed him and his entire household.

¹²Now King David was told, "The Lord has blessed the household of Obed-Edom and everything he has, because of the ark of God." So David went to bring up the ark of God from the house of Obed-Edom to the City of David with rejoicing. ¹³When those who were carrying the ark of the Lord had taken six steps, he sacrificed a bull and a fattened calf. ¹⁴Wearing a linen ephod, David was dancing before the Lord with all his might, ¹⁵while he and all Israel were bringing up the ark of the Lord with shouts and the sound of trumpets.

¹⁶As the ark of the Lord was entering the City of David, Michal daughter of Saul watched from a window. And when she saw King David leaping and dancing before the Lord, she despised him in her heart.

¹⁷They brought the ark of the Lord and set it in its place inside the tent that David had pitched for it, and David sacrificed burnt offerings and fellowship offerings before the Lord. ¹⁸After he had finished sacrificing the burnt offerings and fellowship offerings, he blessed the people in the name of the Lord Almighty. ¹⁹Then he gave a loaf of bread, a cake of dates and a cake of raisins to each person in the whole crowd of Israelites, both men and women. And all the people went to their homes.

²⁰When David returned home to bless his household, Michal daughter of Saul came out to meet him and said, "How the king of Israel has distinguished himself today, going around half-naked in full view of the slave girls of his servants as any vulgar fellow would!"

²¹David said to Michal, "It was before the Lord, who chose me rather than your father or anyone from his house when he appointed me ruler over the Lord's people Israel—I will celebrate before the Lord. ²²I will become even more undignified than this, and I will be humiliated in my own eyes. But by these slave girls you spoke of, I will be held in honor."

²³And Michal daughter of Saul had no children to the day of her death.

God's Promise to David

7 After the king was settled in his palace and the Lord had given him rest from all his enemies around him, ²he said to Nathan the prophet, "Here I am, living in a house of cedar, while the ark of God remains in a tent."

³Nathan replied to the king, "Whatever you have in mind, go ahead and do it, for the Lord is with you."

⁴But that night the word of the Lord came to Nathan, saying:

⁵"Go and tell my servant David, 'This is what the Lord says: Are you the one to build me a house to dwell in? ⁶I have not dwelt in a house from the day I brought the Israelites up out of Egypt to this day. I have been moving from place to place with a tent as my dwelling. ⁷Wherever I have moved with all the Israelites, did I ever say to any of their rulers whom I commanded to shepherd my people Israel, "Why have you not built me a house of cedar?"'

⁸"Now then, tell my servant David, 'This is what the Lord Almighty says: I took you from the pasture, from tending the flock, and appointed you ruler over my people Israel. ⁹I have been with you wherever you have gone, and I have cut off all your enemies from before you. Now I will

⑦
⑧

ᵃ 8 *Perez Uzzah* means *outbreak against Uzzah.*

make your name great, like the names of the greatest men on earth. [10]And I will provide a place for my people Israel and will plant them so that they can have a home of their own and no longer be disturbed. Wicked people will not oppress them anymore, as they did at the beginning [11]and have done ever since the time I appointed leaders[a] over my people Israel. I will also give you rest from all your enemies.

"'The Lord declares to you that the Lord himself will establish a house for you: [12]When your days are over and you rest with your ancestors, I will raise up your offspring to succeed you, your own flesh and blood, and I will establish his kingdom. [13]He is the one who will build a house for my Name, and I will establish the throne of his kingdom forever. [14]I will be his father, and he will be my son. When he does wrong, I will punish him with a rod wielded by men, with floggings inflicted by human hands. [15]But my love will never be taken away from him, as I took it away from Saul, whom I removed from before you. [16]Your house and your kingdom will endure forever before me[b]; your throne will be established forever.'"

[17]Nathan reported to David all the words of this entire revelation.

David's Prayer

[18]Then King David went in and sat before the Lord, and he said:

"Who am I, Sovereign Lord, and what is my family, that you have brought me this far? [19]And as if this were not enough in your sight, Sovereign Lord, you have also spoken about the future of the house of your servant — and this decree, Sovereign Lord, is for a mere human![c]

[20]"What more can David say to you? For you know your servant, Sovereign Lord. [21]For the sake of your word and according to your will, you have done this great thing and made it known to your servant.

[22]"How great you are, Sovereign Lord! There is no one like you, and there is no God but you, as we have heard with our own ears. [23]And who is like your people Israel — the one nation on earth that God went out to redeem as a people for himself, and to make a name for himself, and to perform great and awesome wonders by driving out nations and their gods from before your people, whom you redeemed from Egypt?[d] [24]You have established your people Israel as your very own forever, and you, Lord, have become their God.

[25]"And now, Lord God, keep forever the promise you have made concerning your servant and his house. Do as you promised, [26]so that your name will be great forever. Then people will say, 'The Lord Almighty is God over Israel!' And the house of your servant David will be established in your sight.

[27]"Lord Almighty, God of Israel, you have revealed this to your servant, saying, 'I will build a house for you.' So your servant has found courage to pray this prayer to you. [28]Sovereign Lord, you are God! Your covenant is trustworthy, and you have promised these good things to your servant. [29]Now be pleased to bless the house of your servant, that it may continue forever in your sight; for you, Sovereign Lord, have spoken, and with your blessing the house of your servant will be blessed forever."

---

a 11 Traditionally *judges*   *b 16* Some Hebrew manuscripts and Septuagint; most Hebrew manuscripts *you*
c 19 Or *for the human race*   *d 23* See Septuagint and 1 Chron. 17:21; Hebrew *wonders for your land and before your people, whom you redeemed from Egypt, from the nations and their gods.*

David's Victories

8 In the course of time, David defeated the Philistines and subdued them, and he took Metheg Ammah from the control of the Philistines.

² David also defeated the Moabites. He made them lie down on the ground and measured them off with a length of cord. Every two lengths of them were put to death, and the third length was allowed to live. So the Moabites became subject to David and brought him tribute.

³ Moreover, David defeated Hadadezer son of Rehob, king of Zobah, when he went to restore his monument at*ᵃ* the Euphrates River. ⁴ David captured a thousand of his chariots, seven thousand charioteers*ᵇ* and twenty thousand foot soldiers. He hamstrung all but a hundred of the chariot horses.

⁵ When the Arameans of Damascus came to help Hadadezer king of Zobah, David struck down twenty-two thousand of them. ⁶ He put garrisons in the Aramean kingdom of Damascus, and the Arameans became subject to him and brought tribute. The LORD gave David victory wherever he went.

⁷ David took the gold shields that belonged to the officers of Hadadezer and brought them to Jerusalem. ⁸ From Tebah*ᶜ* and Berothai, towns that belonged to Hadadezer, King David took a great quantity of bronze.

⁹ When Tou*ᵈ* king of Hamath heard that David had defeated the entire army of Hadadezer, ¹⁰ he sent his son Joram*ᵉ* to King David to greet him and congratulate him on his victory in battle over Hadadezer, who had been at war with Tou. Joram brought with him articles of silver, of gold and of bronze.

¹¹ King David dedicated these articles to the LORD, as he had done with the silver and gold from all the nations he had subdued: ¹² Edom*ᶠ* and Moab, the Ammonites and the Philistines, and Amalek. He also dedicated the plunder taken from Hadadezer son of Rehob, king of Zobah.

¹³ And David became famous after he returned from striking down eighteen thousand Edomites*ᵍ* in the Valley of Salt.

¹⁴ He put garrisons throughout Edom, and all the Edomites became subject to David. The LORD gave David victory wherever he went.

David's Officials

¹⁵ David reigned over all Israel, doing what was just and right for all his people. ¹⁶ Joab son of Zeruiah was over the army; Jehoshaphat son of Ahilud was recorder; ¹⁷ Zadok son of Ahitub and Ahimelek son of Abiathar were priests; Seraiah was secretary; ¹⁸ Benaiah son of Jehoiada was over the Kerethites and Pelethites; and David's sons were priests.*ʰ*

David and Mephibosheth

9 David asked, "Is there anyone still left of the house of Saul to whom I can show kindness for Jonathan's sake?"

² Now there was a servant of Saul's household named Ziba. They summoned him to appear before David, and the king said to him, "Are you Ziba?"

"At your service," he replied.

³ The king asked, "Is there no one still alive from the house of Saul to whom I can show God's kindness?"

Ziba answered the king, "There is still a son of Jonathan; he is lame in both feet."

⁴ "Where is he?" the king asked.

Ziba answered, "He is at the house of Makir son of Ammiel in Lo Debar."

⁵ So King David had him brought from

ᵃ 3 Or *his control along*   *ᵇ 4* Septuagint (see also Dead Sea Scrolls and 1 Chron. 18:4); Masoretic Text *captured seventeen hundred of his charioteers*   *ᶜ 8* See some Septuagint manuscripts (see also 1 Chron. 18:8); Hebrew *Betah*.
ᵈ 9 Hebrew *Toi,* a variant of *Tou;* also in verse 10   *ᵉ 10* A variant of *Hadoram*   *ᶠ 12* Some Hebrew manuscripts, Septuagint and Syriac (see also 1 Chron. 18:11); most Hebrew manuscripts *Aram*   *ᵍ 13* A few Hebrew manuscripts, Septuagint and Syriac (see also 1 Chron. 18:12); most Hebrew manuscripts *Aram* (that is, Arameans)   *ʰ 18* Or *were chief officials* (see Septuagint and Targum; see also 1 Chron. 18:17)

Lo Debar, from the house of Makir son of Ammiel.

⁶When Mephibosheth son of Jonathan, the son of Saul, came to David, he bowed down to pay him honor.

David said, "Mephibosheth!"

"At your service," he replied.

⁷"Don't be afraid," David said to him, "for I will surely show you kindness for the sake of your father Jonathan. I will restore to you all the land that belonged to your grandfather Saul, and you will always eat at my table."

⁸Mephibosheth bowed down and said, "What is your servant, that you should notice a dead dog like me?"

⁹Then the king summoned Ziba, Saul's steward, and said to him, "I have given your master's grandson everything that belonged to Saul and his family. ¹⁰You and your sons and your servants are to farm the land for him and bring in the crops, so that your master's grandson may be provided for. And Mephibosheth, grandson of your master, will always eat at my table." (Now Ziba had fifteen sons and twenty servants.)

¹¹Then Ziba said to the king, "Your servant will do whatever my lord the king commands his servant to do." So Mephibosheth ate at David's*a* table like one of the king's sons.

¹²Mephibosheth had a young son named Mika, and all the members of Ziba's household were servants of Mephibosheth. ¹³And Mephibosheth lived in Jerusalem, because he always ate at the king's table; he was lame in both feet.

David Defeats the Ammonites

10 In the course of time, the king of the Ammonites died, and his son Hanun succeeded him as king. ²David thought, "I will show kindness to Hanun son of Nahash, just as his father showed kindness to me." So David sent a delegation to express his sympathy to Hanun concerning his father.

When David's men came to the land of the Ammonites, ³the Ammonite commanders said to Hanun their lord, "Do you think David is honoring your father by sending envoys to you to express sympathy? Hasn't David sent them to you only to explore the city and spy it out and overthrow it?" ⁴So Hanun seized David's envoys, shaved off half of each man's beard, cut off their garments at the buttocks, and sent them away.

⁵When David was told about this, he sent messengers to meet the men, for they were greatly humiliated. The king said, "Stay at Jericho till your beards have grown, and then come back."

⁶When the Ammonites realized that they had become obnoxious to David, they hired twenty thousand Aramean foot soldiers from Beth Rehob and Zobah, as well as the king of Maakah with a thousand men, and also twelve thousand men from Tob.

⁷On hearing this, David sent Joab out with the entire army of fighting men. ⁸The Ammonites came out and drew up in battle formation at the entrance of their city gate, while the Arameans of Zobah and Rehob and the men of Tob and Maakah were by themselves in the open country.

⁹Joab saw that there were battle lines in front of him and behind him; so he selected some of the best troops in Israel and deployed them against the Arameans. ¹⁰He put the rest of the men under the command of Abishai his brother and deployed them against the Ammonites. ¹¹Joab said, "If the Arameans are too strong for me, then you are to come to my rescue; but if the Ammonites are too strong for you, then I will come to rescue you. ¹²Be strong, and let us fight bravely for our people and the cities of our God. The LORD will do what is good in his sight."

¹³Then Joab and the troops with him advanced to fight the Arameans, and they fled before him. ¹⁴When the Ammonites

---

a 11 Septuagint; Hebrew *my*

realized that the Arameans were fleeing, they fled before Abishai and went inside the city. So Joab returned from fighting the Ammonites and came to Jerusalem.

15 After the Arameans saw that they had been routed by Israel, they regrouped. 16 Hadadezer had Arameans brought from beyond the Euphrates River; they went to Helam, with Shobak the commander of Hadadezer's army leading them.

17 When David was told of this, he gathered all Israel, crossed the Jordan and went to Helam. The Arameans formed their battle lines to meet David and fought against him. 18 But they fled before Israel, and David killed seven hundred of their charioteers and forty thousand of their foot soldiers.[a] He also struck down Shobak the commander of their army, and he died there. 19 When all the kings who were vassals of Hadadezer saw that they had been routed by Israel, they made peace with the Israelites and became subject to them.

So the Arameans were afraid to help the Ammonites anymore.

David and Bathsheba

11 In the spring, at the time when kings go off to war, David sent Joab out with the king's men and the whole Israelite army. They destroyed the Ammonites and besieged Rabbah. But David remained in Jerusalem.

2 One evening David got up from his bed and walked around on the roof of the palace. From the roof he saw a woman bathing. The woman was very beautiful, 3 and David sent someone to find out about her. The man said, "She is Bathsheba, the daughter of Eliam and the wife of Uriah the Hittite." 4 Then David sent messengers to get her. She came to him, and he slept with her. (Now she was purifying herself from her monthly uncleanness.) Then she went back home. 5 The woman conceived and sent word to David, saying, "I am pregnant."

6 So David sent this word to Joab: "Send me Uriah the Hittite." And Joab sent him to David. 7 When Uriah came to him, David asked him how Joab was, how the soldiers were and how the war was going. 8 Then David said to Uriah, "Go down to your house and wash your feet." So Uriah left the palace, and a gift from the king was sent after him. 9 But Uriah slept at the entrance to the palace with all his master's servants and did not go down to his house.

10 David was told, "Uriah did not go home." So he asked Uriah, "Haven't you just come from a military campaign? Why didn't you go home?"

11 Uriah said to David, "The ark and Israel and Judah are staying in tents,[b] and my commander Joab and my lord's men are camped in the open country. How could I go to my house to eat and drink and make love to my wife? As surely as you live, I will not do such a thing!"

12 Then David said to him, "Stay here one more day, and tomorrow I will send you back." So Uriah remained in Jerusalem that day and the next. 13 At David's invitation, he ate and drank with him, and David made him drunk. But in the evening Uriah went out to sleep on his mat among his master's servants; he did not go home.

14 In the morning David wrote a letter to Joab and sent it with Uriah. 15 In it he wrote, "Put Uriah out in front where the fighting is fiercest. Then withdraw from him so he will be struck down and die."

16 So while Joab had the city under siege, he put Uriah at a place where he knew the strongest defenders were. 17 When the men of the city came out and fought against Joab, some of the men in David's army fell; moreover, Uriah the Hittite died.

18 Joab sent David a full account of the battle. 19 He instructed the messenger: "When you have finished giving the king this account of the battle, 20 the king's anger may flare up, and he may ask you, 'Why did you get so close to the city to fight? Didn't

---

a 18 Some Septuagint manuscripts (see also 1 Chron. 19:18); Hebrew horsemen   b 11 Or staying at Sukkoth you know they would shoot arrows from the wall? [21]Who killed Abimelek son of Jerub-Besheth[a]? Didn't a woman drop an upper millstone on him from the wall, so that he died in Thebez? Why did you get so close to the wall?' If he asks you this, then say to him, 'Moreover, your servant Uriah the Hittite is dead.'"

[22]The messenger set out, and when he arrived he told David everything Joab had sent him to say. [23]The messenger said to David, "The men overpowered us and came out against us in the open, but we drove them back to the entrance of the city gate. [24]Then the archers shot arrows at your servants from the wall, and some of the king's men died. Moreover, your servant Uriah the Hittite is dead."

[25]David told the messenger, "Say this to Joab: 'Don't let this upset you; the sword devours one as well as another. Press the attack against the city and destroy it.' Say this to encourage Joab."

[26]When Uriah's wife heard that her husband was dead, she mourned for him. [27]After the time of mourning was over, David had her brought to his house, and she became his wife and bore him a son. But the thing David had done displeased the LORD.

Nathan Rebukes David

12 The LORD sent Nathan to David. When he came to him, he said, "There were two men in a certain town, one rich and the other poor. [2]The rich man had a very large number of sheep and cattle, [3]but the poor man had nothing except one little ewe lamb he had bought. He raised it, and it grew up with him and his children. It shared his food, drank from his cup and even slept in his arms. It was like a daughter to him.

[4]"Now a traveler came to the rich man, but the rich man refrained from taking one of his own sheep or cattle to prepare a meal for the traveler who had come to him. In-

stead, he took the ewe lamb that belonged to the poor man and prepared it for the one who had come to him."

[5]David burned with anger against the man and said to Nathan, "As surely as the LORD lives, the man who did this must die! [6]He must pay for that lamb four times over, because he did such a thing and had no pity."

[7]Then Nathan said to David, "You are the man! This is what the LORD, the God of Israel, says: 'I anointed you king over Israel, and I delivered you from the hand of Saul. [8]I gave your master's house to you, and your master's wives into your arms. I gave you all Israel and Judah. And if all this had been too little, I would have given you even more. [9]Why did you despise the word of the LORD by doing what is evil in his eyes? You struck down Uriah the Hittite with the sword and took his wife to be your own. You killed him with the sword of the Ammonites. [10]Now, therefore, the sword will never depart from your house, because you despised me and took the wife of Uriah the Hittite to be your own.'

[11]"This is what the LORD says: 'Out of your own household I am going to bring calamity on you. Before your very eyes I will take your wives and give them to one who is close to you, and he will sleep with your wives in broad daylight. [12]You did it in secret, but I will do this thing in broad daylight before all Israel.'"

[13]Then David said to Nathan, "I have sinned against the LORD."

Nathan replied, "The LORD has taken away your sin. You are not going to die. [14]But because by doing this you have shown utter contempt for[b] the LORD, the son born to you will die."

[15]After Nathan had gone home, the LORD struck the child that Uriah's wife had borne to David, and he became ill. [16]David pleaded with God for the child. He fasted and spent the nights lying in sackcloth[c] on

---

a 21 Also known as *Jerub-Baal* (that is, Gideon)   *b 14* An ancient Hebrew scribal tradition; Masoretic Text *for the enemies of*   *c 16* Dead Sea Scrolls and Septuagint; Masoretic Text does not have *in sackcloth*.

MY NAME IS DAVID

2 SAMUEL 12

How often does history record the humbling of someone who was both a great warrior and a great king? Not very often. One man, David, fits both of these descriptions. Yet in 2 Samuel 12 we see the conqueror confronted (see 2 Samuel 12:1 – 14) and the king sickened by his own sins (see vv. 15 – 17). David's desperate condition — and that of his innocent newborn son — came as the direct result of the terrible secrets in his life.

David's most shocking transgressions are laid out in 2 Samuel 11 for all to examine, despite his determination to keep his wrongdoings secret. He committed adultery with Bathsheba, the wife of Uriah, after which he lied to Uriah. When Uriah, a loyal soldier and man of integrity, refused to comply with what David intended as a neat cover-up, the king arranged for his death. All of this to keep his own sin under wraps. But, as Jesus himself warns us, "There is nothing concealed that will not be disclosed, or hidden that will not be made known. What you have said in the dark will be heard in the daylight, and what you have whispered in the ear in the inner rooms will be proclaimed from the roofs" (Luke 12:2 – 3).

Often that light comes to us in the form of a friend, a minister, an accountability partner or a sponsor. It might not have appeared that way at first glance, but the reality is that God blessed David with Nathan's confrontation. Nathan had the God-given wisdom of knowing just how to reach into the hidden recesses of David's heart (see 2 Samuel 12:1 – 12).

It's vital for us to build relationships with individuals we can trust. It's important that we get close enough to at least one other person to allow them to really get to know us — warts and all. Why? Because we may need someone who knows how to reach us with the very truth from which we're running. Each of us needs a Nathan in our life.

The result of this confrontation in David's life was threefold:

- Confession and cleansing (see v. 13). What's true for us today was no less true for David: "If we confess our sins, he is faithful and just and will forgive us our sins and purify us from all unrighteousness" (1 John 1:9; see also Psalm 51). God forgives all our sins, but he doesn't promise to deliver us from all of their . . .

- Consequences (see 2 Samuel 12:15 – 19). Yet even as he corrects and chastens us in love, our God offers us his . . .

- Comfort (see vv. 20 – 25). We need to confess our sins to God and to someone else we can trust to hold us accountable in the future.

the ground. ¹⁷The elders of his household stood beside him to get him up from the ground, but he refused, and he would not eat any food with them.

¹⁸On the seventh day the child died. David's attendants were afraid to tell him that the child was dead, for they thought, "While the child was still living, he wouldn't listen to us when we spoke to him. How can we now tell him the child is dead? He may do something desperate."

¹⁹David noticed that his attendants were whispering among themselves, and he realized the child was dead. "Is the child dead?" he asked.

"Yes," they replied, "he is dead."

²⁰Then David got up from the ground. After he had washed, put on lotions and changed his clothes, he went into the house of the Lord and worshiped. Then he went to his own house, and at his request they served him food, and he ate.

²¹His attendants asked him, "Why are you acting this way? While the child was alive, you fasted and wept, but now that the child is dead, you get up and eat!"

²²He answered, "While the child was still alive, I fasted and wept. I thought, 'Who knows? The Lord may be gracious to me and let the child live.' ²³But now that he is dead, why should I go on fasting? Can I bring him back again? I will go to him, but he will not return to me."

²⁴Then David comforted his wife Bathsheba, and he went to her and made love to her. She gave birth to a son, and they named him Solomon. The Lord loved him; ²⁵and because the Lord loved him, he sent word through Nathan the prophet to name him Jedidiah.ᵃ

²⁶Meanwhile Joab fought against Rabbah of the Ammonites and captured the royal citadel. ²⁷Joab then sent messengers to David, saying, "I have fought against Rabbah and taken its water supply. ²⁸Now muster the rest of the troops and besiege the city and capture it. Otherwise I will take the city, and it will be named after me."

²⁹So David mustered the entire army and went to Rabbah, and attacked and captured it. ³⁰David took the crown from their king'sᵇ head, and it was placed on his own head. It weighed a talentᶜ of gold, and it was set with precious stones. David took a great quantity of plunder from the city ³¹and brought out the people who were there, consigning them to labor with saws and with iron picks and axes, and he made them work at brickmaking.ᵈ David did this to all the Ammonite towns. Then he and his entire army returned to Jerusalem.

Amnon and Tamar

13 In the course of time, Amnon son of David fell in love with Tamar, the beautiful sister of Absalom son of David.

²Amnon became so obsessed with his sister Tamar that he made himself ill. She was a virgin, and it seemed impossible for him to do anything to her.

³Now Amnon had an adviser named Jonadab son of Shimeah, David's brother. Jonadab was a very shrewd man. ⁴He asked Amnon, "Why do you, the king's son, look so haggard morning after morning? Won't you tell me?"

Amnon said to him, "I'm in love with Tamar, my brother Absalom's sister."

⁵"Go to bed and pretend to be ill," Jonadab said. "When your father comes to see you, say to him, 'I would like my sister Tamar to come and give me something to eat. Let her prepare the food in my sight so I may watch her and then eat it from her hand.'"

⁶So Amnon lay down and pretended to be ill. When the king came to see him, Amnon said to him, "I would like my sister Tamar to come and make some special bread in my sight, so I may eat from her hand."

⁷David sent word to Tamar at the palace:

ᵃ 25 *Jedidiah* means *loved by the Lord.*   ᵇ 30 Or *from Milkom's* (that is, Molek's)   ᶜ 30 That is, about 75 pounds or about 34 kilograms   ᵈ 31 The meaning of the Hebrew for this clause is uncertain.

My Name Is Dave

I'M A BELIEVER WHO STRUGGLES WITH PORNOGRAPHY AND LUST

Please read the story of Nathan's challenge to David in 2 Samuel 12:1 – 25.

I grew up in a highly dysfunctional family situation in the coastal foothills of western Oregon. Beginning at the age of five, I was sexually molested on a regular basis for two years by an older cousin. By the age of eight, I had discovered that several family members used pornographic materials; their carelessness left a nearly limitless supply at my disposal. I found that pornography was a powerful way to escape, but these images were forever burned into my impressionable young mind.

In college I discovered adult videos. These images were much more explicit — even "better" to my hungry eyes than the motionless pictures in magazines. My addiction had reached a new level. Yet, like David, I was physically and emotionally sickened by the sins and secrets I attempted to conceal in the dark.

I remember longing for connections with women like the ones I saw my college friends enjoying. But inside I felt trapped, alone and often afraid. My addiction was preventing me from enjoying real relationships with others.

While in college I gave my life to Christ, fully expecting that my new relationship with God would eliminate my need for pornography. But to my dismay this deterrent only worked for a few weeks. At the age of 25, I met and married a wonderful woman. I was armed with a new resolve to stop; I finally had a real connection with a woman I loved, and I was thoroughly convinced that I'd have no future need to continue acting out. This time the reprieve lasted for about six months. It was humbling for me to recognize at last that I was powerless to stop. My addiction grew progressively more dangerous and destructive. I had yet to learn the difference between knowing who God is and allowing him to dwell in my life and take charge.

I'm happy to report, though, that I did at this point openly confess my secret sins and check into a treatment facility. It was there that I really began to learn about my addiction, where it came from, what was driving my behaviors and what it was I was really running from.

Armed with new knowledge, I began attending traditional substance abuse meetings. While I did manage to achieve some short-term sobriety, I was still unwilling to let go completely, to surrender my own will to God's. As a consequence, I relapsed a couple of times, with serious consequences. These lapses resulted in the end of my first marriage. It was this reality that finally brought me to the end of myself. I simply couldn't go on in this way and recognized for the very first time that I had no recourse but to rely on the help of God and others. At long last I was able to surrender to God's care.

Just as God sent Nathan to help David, he sent me a recovery buddy who was willing to hold me accountable and whom I could trust with all my secrets. I spent a great deal of time with this godly friend over the next few years. His passion was fly-fishing, and he spent countless hours teaching me this art. We took trips together, and it was there, out in the wild on the rivers and the lakes, that God began to speak to me. Away from the telephone and the stresses of running a business, God spoke to me, and I began to connect with him in a way I'd never been able to do before. Through my real friends in recovery, I began to recognize and accept the grace Jesus had all along been extending to me.

My home church launched a Celebrate Recovery program. From early on this ministry began to change my perspective on recovery, as well as my relationship with Christ. For the very first time, my two worlds came together and meshed perfectly. I knew I was home, and I began to catch the vision that if this ministry could change my life, it could change many other lives as well.

It's been an amazing journey for me just to be a part of Celebrate Recovery. Jesus Christ saved my life, and Celebrate Recovery was the change agent he used to help me find healing. Now I find myself empowered to give back (to others, in Christ's name) the same grace and love God gave me.

Despite his own deep dive into sin, David retained the courage and confidence that God would do great things for him. Similarly, I knew in my heart that all things were possible through Christ's enabling power. Like David, I had been willing to go to almost any length to conceal my sins of lust and desire. In the final analysis, Scripture identifies David, despite his terrible sin, as a man after God's own heart (see 1 Samuel 13:14; Acts 13:22). Through Celebrate Recovery, I've put away the sinful man in me and am striving to become a man who truly seeks after God's heart.

Dave

"Go to the house of your brother Amnon and prepare some food for him." [8]So Tamar went to the house of her brother Amnon, who was lying down. She took some dough, kneaded it, made the bread in his sight and baked it. [9]Then she took the pan and served him the bread, but he refused to eat.

"Send everyone out of here," Amnon said. So everyone left him. [10]Then Amnon said to Tamar, "Bring the food here into my bedroom so I may eat from your hand." And Tamar took the bread she had prepared and brought it to her brother Amnon in his bedroom. [11]But when she took it to him to eat, he grabbed her and said, "Come to bed with me, my sister."

[12]"No, my brother!" she said to him. "Don't force me! Such a thing should not be done in Israel! Don't do this wicked thing. [13]What about me? Where could I get rid of my disgrace? And what about you? You would be like one of the wicked fools in Israel. Please speak to the king; he will not keep me from being married to you." [14]But he refused to listen to her, and since he was stronger than she, he raped her.

[15]Then Amnon hated her with intense hatred. In fact, he hated her more than he had loved her. Amnon said to her, "Get up and get out!"

[16]"No!" she said to him. "Sending me away would be a greater wrong than what you have already done to me."

But he refused to listen to her. [17]He called his personal servant and said, "Get this woman out of my sight and bolt the door after her." [18]So his servant put her out and bolted the door after her. She was wearing an ornate*a* robe, for this was the kind of garment the virgin daughters of the king wore. [19]Tamar put ashes on her head and tore the ornate robe she was wearing. She put her hands on her head and went away, weeping aloud as she went.

[20]Her brother Absalom said to her, "Has that Amnon, your brother, been with you? Be quiet for now, my sister; he is your brother. Don't take this thing to heart." And Tamar lived in her brother Absalom's house, a desolate woman.

[21]When King David heard all this, he was furious. [22]And Absalom never said a word to Amnon, either good or bad; he hated Amnon because he had disgraced his sister Tamar.

Absalom Kills Amnon

[23]Two years later, when Absalom's sheepshearers were at Baal Hazor near the border of Ephraim, he invited all the king's sons to come there. [24]Absalom went to the king and said, "Your servant has had shearers come. Will the king and his attendants please join me?"

[25]"No, my son," the king replied. "All of us should not go; we would only be a burden to you." Although Absalom urged him, he still refused to go but gave him his blessing.

[26]Then Absalom said, "If not, please let my brother Amnon come with us."

The king asked him, "Why should he go with you?" [27]But Absalom urged him, so he sent with him Amnon and the rest of the king's sons.

[28]Absalom ordered his men, "Listen! When Amnon is in high spirits from drinking wine and I say to you, 'Strike Amnon down,' then kill him. Don't be afraid. Haven't I given you this order? Be strong and brave." [29]So Absalom's men did to Amnon what Absalom had ordered. Then all the king's sons got up, mounted their mules and fled.

[30]While they were on their way, the report came to David: "Absalom has struck down all the king's sons; not one of them is left." [31]The king stood up, tore his clothes and lay down on the ground; and all his attendants stood by with their clothes torn.

[32]But Jonadab son of Shimeah, David's brother, said, "My lord should not think that they killed all the princes; only

---

a 18 The meaning of the Hebrew for this word is uncertain; also in verse 19.

MY NAME IS TAMAR

2 SAMUEL 13

David was a giant slayer. One of the best-known stories recorded of David is his victory over Goliath (see 1 Samuel 17). Sadly, the giant David couldn't overcome was his own lust. David was frequently repentant and knew the joy of being forgiven, but forgiveness doesn't automatically cancel the ongoing consequences of our sin. This powerful pattern of lust was passed on to David's oldest son, Amnon, who yearned sexually for his half-sister Tamar. On the advice of a friend, Amnon pursued a plot to manipulate both Tamar and their mutual father, David — by exploiting his family's love and sympathy (see 2 Samuel 13:6–10).

The result was the rape of Tamar by her half-brother Amnon (see vv. 11–14), the horror of which was followed by additional insults from him. After using her to satisfy his lust, he held her in complete contempt. In fact, his hatred of Tamar exceeded the powerful desire he had felt for her before he had raped her. As though the assault had been her fault, Amnon venomously commanded her, "Get up and get out!" (v. 15). Tamar refused to walk away because, having lost her virginity, she no longer could have been offered by the king to a potential husband. In response to her plea to stay, Amnon instructed a servant to throw her out of the house (see vv. 16–18).

Absalom, Tamar's full brother, took her into his own home, probably in hopes of keeping the family scandal a secret (see v. 20). But this did nothing to heal Tamar's hurt. King David learned about what had happened, but, although "he was furious" (v. 21), he failed to take action against Amnon. Apparently David joined Absalom in his compulsion to keep this a family secret. God's law clearly commanded the execution or banishment of anyone guilty of incest (see Leviticus 18:9,11,29), but David failed to carry out his responsibilities as a father and as the king of Israel. As the incident was concealed, the sickness spread throughout the family. Absalom "hated Amnon because he had disgraced his sister Tamar" (2 Samuel 13:22) — so much so that his loathing bore fruit in a successful plot to murder Amnon. This time David, manipulated by Absalom, unwittingly sent Amnon into a trap (see 2 Samuel 13:23–27), just as he had Tamar. Soon David found himself separated from Absalom, who had fled following his murder of Amnon.

Nearly lost in the chaos of this dysfunctional, violent family, stood Tamar — the victim both of Amnon and of the failures and sins of others in her family. Nothing in this text suggests that Tamar did anything to bring this abuse upon herself. The Bible provides no details concerning the balance of Tamar's life. The text reveals only that the abuse inflicted on her by her half-brother left her "a desolate woman" (v. 20). In Tamar's day, as in our own time, the horrors of incest and abuse are often passed along from one generation to the next. The victim is pressured into keeping the secret and suffers her shame in solitude. The pattern of manipulation, violence, pain and bitterness — in the place of love — continues. But this vicious cycle can be broken by God's power.

Celebrate Recovery offers a path of healing to the victims of abuse. Restoration to wholeness is indeed possible through God's power. Shame can be left behind once we come to realize and accept that the abuse wasn't our fault. Forgiving those who have harmed us is possible with God's help. As our memories begin to surface, we can face with confidence the secrets we've so long suppressed. By accepting God's unconditional love, we can learn to love and trust again. Our past misery can become a means of ministry to others as we share with them the message of God's healing power in our life.

Amnon is dead. This has been Absalom's express intention ever since the day Amnon raped his sister Tamar. ³³My lord the king should not be concerned about the report that all the king's sons are dead. Only Amnon is dead."

³⁴Meanwhile, Absalom had fled.

Now the man standing watch looked up and saw many people on the road west of him, coming down the side of the hill. The watchman went and told the king, "I see men in the direction of Horonaim, on the side of the hill."ᵃ

³⁵Jonadab said to the king, "See, the king's sons have come; it has happened just as your servant said."

³⁶As he finished speaking, the king's sons came in, wailing loudly. The king, too, and all his attendants wept very bitterly.

³⁷Absalom fled and went to Talmai son of Ammihud, the king of Geshur. But King David mourned many days for his son.

³⁸After Absalom fled and went to Geshur, he stayed there three years. ³⁹And King David longed to go to Absalom, for he was consoled concerning Amnon's death.

Absalom Returns to Jerusalem

14 Joab son of Zeruiah knew that the king's heart longed for Absalom. ²So Joab sent someone to Tekoa and had a wise woman brought from there. He said to her, "Pretend you are in mourning. Dress in mourning clothes, and don't use any cosmetic lotions. Act like a woman who has spent many days grieving for the dead. ³Then go to the king and speak these words to him." And Joab put the words in her mouth.

⁴When the woman from Tekoa wentᵇ to the king, she fell with her face to the ground to pay him honor, and she said, "Help me, Your Majesty!"

⁵The king asked her, "What is troubling you?"

She said, "I am a widow; my husband is dead. ⁶I your servant had two sons. They got into a fight with each other in the field, and no one was there to separate them. One struck the other and killed him. ⁷Now the whole clan has risen up against your servant; they say, 'Hand over the one who struck his brother down, so that we may put him to death for the life of his brother whom he killed; then we will get rid of the heir as well.' They would put out the only burning coal I have left, leaving my husband neither name nor descendant on the face of the earth."

⁸The king said to the woman, "Go home, and I will issue an order in your behalf."

⁹But the woman from Tekoa said to him, "Let my lord the king pardon me and my family, and let the king and his throne be without guilt."

¹⁰The king replied, "If anyone says anything to you, bring them to me, and they will not bother you again."

¹¹She said, "Then let the king invoke the LORD his God to prevent the avenger of blood from adding to the destruction, so that my son will not be destroyed."

"As surely as the LORD lives," he said, "not one hair of your son's head will fall to the ground."

¹²Then the woman said, "Let your servant speak a word to my lord the king."

"Speak," he replied.

¹³The woman said, "Why then have you devised a thing like this against the people of God? When the king says this, does he not convict himself, for the king has not brought back his banished son? ¹⁴Like water spilled on the ground, which cannot be recovered, so we must die. But that is not what God desires; rather, he devises ways so that a banished person does not remain banished from him.

¹⁵"And now I have come to say this to my lord the king because the people have made me afraid. Your servant thought, 'I will speak to the king; perhaps he will grant his

---

ᵃ 34 Septuagint; Hebrew does not have this sentence.   ᵇ 4 Many Hebrew manuscripts, Septuagint, Vulgate and Syriac; most Hebrew manuscripts *spoke* servant's request. ¹⁶Perhaps the king will agree to deliver his servant from the hand of the man who is trying to cut off both me and my son from God's inheritance.'

¹⁷"And now your servant says, 'May the word of my lord the king secure my inheritance, for my lord the king is like an angel of God in discerning good and evil. May the Lord your God be with you.'"

¹⁸Then the king said to the woman, "Don't keep from me the answer to what I am going to ask you."

"Let my lord the king speak," the woman said.

¹⁹The king asked, "Isn't the hand of Joab with you in all this?"

The woman answered, "As surely as you live, my lord the king, no one can turn to the right or to the left from anything my lord the king says. Yes, it was your servant Joab who instructed me to do this and who put all these words into the mouth of your servant. ²⁰Your servant Joab did this to change the present situation. My lord has wisdom like that of an angel of God—he knows everything that happens in the land."

²¹The king said to Joab, "Very well, I will do it. Go, bring back the young man Absalom."

²²Joab fell with his face to the ground to pay him honor, and he blessed the king. Joab said, "Today your servant knows that he has found favor in your eyes, my lord the king, because the king has granted his servant's request."

²³Then Joab went to Geshur and brought Absalom back to Jerusalem. ²⁴But the king said, "He must go to his own house; he must not see my face." So Absalom went to his own house and did not see the face of the king.

²⁵In all Israel there was not a man so highly praised for his handsome appearance as Absalom. From the top of his head to the sole of his foot there was no blemish in him. ²⁶Whenever he cut the hair of his head—he used to cut his hair once a year because it became too heavy for him—he would weigh it, and its weight was two hundred shekels^a by the royal standard.

²⁷Three sons and a daughter were born to Absalom. His daughter's name was Tamar, and she became a beautiful woman.

²⁸Absalom lived two years in Jerusalem without seeing the king's face. ²⁹Then Absalom sent for Joab in order to send him to the king, but Joab refused to come to him. So he sent a second time, but he refused to come. ³⁰Then he said to his servants, "Look, Joab's field is next to mine, and he has barley there. Go and set it on fire." So Absalom's servants set the field on fire.

³¹Then Joab did go to Absalom's house, and he said to him, "Why have your servants set my field on fire?"

³²Absalom said to Joab, "Look, I sent word to you and said, 'Come here so I can send you to the king to ask, "Why have I come from Geshur? It would be better for me if I were still there!" ' Now then, I want to see the king's face, and if I am guilty of anything, let him put me to death."

³³So Joab went to the king and told him this. Then the king summoned Absalom, and he came in and bowed down with his face to the ground before the king. And the king kissed Absalom.

Absalom's Conspiracy

15 In the course of time, Absalom provided himself with a chariot and horses and with fifty men to run ahead of him. ²He would get up early and stand by the side of the road leading to the city gate. Whenever anyone came with a complaint to be placed before the king for a decision, Absalom would call out to him, "What town are you from?" He would answer, "Your servant is from one of the tribes of Israel." ³Then Absalom would say to him, "Look, your claims are valid and proper, but there is no representative of the king to hear you." ⁴And Absalom would

---

^a 26 That is, about 5 pounds or about 2.3 kilograms

My Name Is Jana

I'M A BELIEVER WHO STRUGGLES WITH SEXUAL AND PHYSICAL ABUSE

Please read the tragic story of David's daughter Tamar in 2 Samuel 13 (the remainder of the book deals with the aftermath of her abuse).

I grew up on a large farm in southeastern Oklahoma with my four siblings. During the busy seasons I worked the farm from sunrise to sunset seven days a week and felt like a slave, trapped and hopeless. While on the outside we presented ourselves as a wholesome, upstanding Christian family, our reality was much different. As a young girl I learned to put on a happy face because appearances were all-important (feelings didn't exist). I longed for someone to perceive the pain I held inside and to rescue me from my own private hell.

My mother was the master of guilt and shame, and my father was a rage-aholic who sexually abused me, torturing me in unimaginable ways and laughing at my terror. Like Tamar, I tried to keep the abuse a family secret, but this only intensified my pain. When I was 12 years old, I threatened to tell someone, and my dad in turn tried to kill me. I often wondered whether the abuse was a form of God's punishment for some small sin I had committed, but I still questioned why he didn't intervene to protect me.

I got pregnant at 16, left home and got married. My family saw me as a disgrace. When I was eight months pregnant, I found myself looking down the barrel of my husband's shotgun for the first time. Another time he hit me and gave me a black eye. Talk about jumping from the frying pan into the fire! When he turned his anger toward my one-year-old daughter, I finally got up the courage to leave him and face my parents' wrath, as well as my own shame and guilt. My marriage soon ended.

I knew there weren't many options for me in terms of moving away from our small town and supporting myself and my daughter. I did attend summer school, though, and earned a college degree in three-and-a-half years. Despite this positive accomplishment, I had, like Tamar, become a desolate woman, and I tried to escape from the reality of my life in any way I could. I looked to male relationships, alcohol, drugs and further education. And I remarried, trying to fill the gaping void in my heart. Not surprisingly, that ill-considered union didn't last either. I desperately wanted to believe that God would help me but didn't feel I could trust him.

Still looking for someone to fulfill that "happily ever after" fantasy, I married for a third time. The two of us faced numerous challenges, and I started to think this marriage was yet another mistake. But I found myself turning more and more to God and finally realized that, no matter what happened with my marriage, I needed to work on myself. Otherwise I would just keep trying to run from myself.

I decided to attend my first Celebrate Recovery meeting. As I worked the program, I grew closer to God. Trust, though, was still a huge issue for me. For me to turn over my life and will to God meant that I had to *really* trust him — a scary proposition for me. But I'm so glad I did! Through God's grace I was able to forgive my parents for their abuse and forgive myself for passing along my dysfunctional behavior to my daughter. I also learned that God can handle my anger. I felt his loving arms around me and heard him explain that he'd been waiting for just that moment. And I knew that he would use my experiences to help others, believing that God never wastes a hurt.

Like Tamar, I was almost lost in the chaos of a dysfunctional, abusive family. And like her, I was in no way responsible for the abuse I had endured. I was pressured to keep the "family secret," but with God's power I've broken the cycle of abuse for my family.

Celebrate Recovery has forged a path of healing for me. I've been restored to wholeness and am no longer a "desolate woman" (2 Samuel 13:20). I firmly believe, in fact, that all of my experiences were part of God's purpose for my life. God will use our greatest hurts to serve him if we'll only let him. In my case, my story of overcoming abuse has given me the opportunity to encourage God's people in Kenya.

God has allowed me to meet with various groups of hurting people in that African country. I've shared God's glory in churches, prisons, schools and orphanages there. In fact, God called me to be the first *mzungu* (white person) ever to visit the Kitale Prison for Women. This prison, as well as many Kenyan churches, is now planning to initiate its own Celebrate Recovery program.

My personal faith in God has grown by leaps and bounds, and I feel at peace now, secure in the knowledge that I'm doing what God wants me to do. Thank you, Celebrate Recovery — and thank you, God!

Jana

add, "If only I were appointed judge in the land! Then everyone who has a complaint or case could come to me and I would see that they receive justice."

5 Also, whenever anyone approached him to bow down before him, Absalom would reach out his hand, take hold of him and kiss him. 6 Absalom behaved in this way toward all the Israelites who came to the king asking for justice, and so he stole the hearts of the people of Israel.

7 At the end of four*a* years, Absalom said to the king, "Let me go to Hebron and fulfill a vow I made to the LORD. 8 While your servant was living at Geshur in Aram, I made this vow: 'If the LORD takes me back to Jerusalem, I will worship the LORD in Hebron.*b*'"

9 The king said to him, "Go in peace." So he went to Hebron.

10 Then Absalom sent secret messengers throughout the tribes of Israel to say, "As soon as you hear the sound of the trumpets, then say, 'Absalom is king in Hebron.'" 11 Two hundred men from Jerusalem had accompanied Absalom. They had been invited as guests and went quite innocently, knowing nothing about the matter. 12 While Absalom was offering sacrifices, he also sent for Ahithophel the Gilonite, David's counselor, to come from Giloh, his hometown. And so the conspiracy gained strength, and Absalom's following kept on increasing.

David Flees

13 A messenger came and told David, "The hearts of the people of Israel are with Absalom."

14 Then David said to all his officials who were with him in Jerusalem, "Come! We must flee, or none of us will escape from Absalom. We must leave immediately, or he will move quickly to overtake us and bring ruin on us and put the city to the sword."

15 The king's officials answered him,

"Your servants are ready to do whatever our lord the king chooses."

16 The king set out, with his entire household following him; but he left ten concubines to take care of the palace. 17 So the king set out, with all the people following him, and they halted at the edge of the city. 18 All his men marched past him, along with all the Kerethites and Pelethites; and all the six hundred Gittites who had accompanied him from Gath marched before the king.

19 The king said to Ittai the Gittite, "Why should you come along with us? Go back and stay with King Absalom. You are a foreigner, an exile from your homeland. 20 You came only yesterday. And today shall I make you wander about with us, when I do not know where I am going? Go back, and take your people with you. May the LORD show you kindness and faithfulness."*c*

21 But Ittai replied to the king, "As surely as the LORD lives, and as my lord the king lives, wherever my lord the king may be, whether it means life or death, there will your servant be."

22 David said to Ittai, "Go ahead, march on." So Ittai the Gittite marched on with all his men and the families that were with him.

23 The whole countryside wept aloud as all the people passed by. The king also crossed the Kidron Valley, and all the people moved on toward the wilderness.

24 Zadok was there, too, and all the Levites who were with him were carrying the ark of the covenant of God. They set down the ark of God, and Abiathar offered sacrifices until all the people had finished leaving the city.

25 Then the king said to Zadok, "Take the ark of God back into the city. If I find favor in the LORD's eyes, he will bring me back and let me see it and his dwelling place again. 26 But if he says, 'I am not pleased with you,' then I am ready; let him do to me whatever seems good to him."

---

a 7 Some Septuagint manuscripts, Syriac and Josephus; Hebrew *forty*   *b 8* Some Septuagint manuscripts; Hebrew does not have *in Hebron.*   *c 20* Septuagint; Hebrew *May kindness and faithfulness be with you*

27The king also said to Zadok the priest, "Do you understand? Go back to the city with my blessing. Take your son Ahimaaz with you, and also Abiathar's son Jonathan. You and Abiathar return with your two sons. 28I will wait at the fords in the wilderness until word comes from you to inform me." 29So Zadok and Abiathar took the ark of God back to Jerusalem and stayed there.

30But David continued up the Mount of Olives, weeping as he went; his head was covered and he was barefoot. All the people with him covered their heads too and were weeping as they went up. 31Now David had been told, "Ahithophel is among the conspirators with Absalom." So David prayed, "Lord, turn Ahithophel's counsel into foolishness."

32When David arrived at the summit, where people used to worship God, Hushai the Arkite was there to meet him, his robe torn and dust on his head. 33David said to him, "If you go with me, you will be a burden to me. 34But if you return to the city and say to Absalom, 'Your Majesty, I will be your servant; I was your father's servant in the past, but now I will be your servant,' then you can help me by frustrating Ahithophel's advice. 35Won't the priests Zadok and Abiathar be there with you? Tell them anything you hear in the king's palace. 36Their two sons, Ahimaaz son of Zadok and Jonathan son of Abiathar, are there with them. Send them to me with anything you hear."

37So Hushai, David's confidant, arrived at Jerusalem as Absalom was entering the city.

David and Ziba

16 When David had gone a short distance beyond the summit, there was Ziba, the steward of Mephibosheth, waiting to meet him. He had a string of donkeys saddled and loaded with two hundred loaves of bread, a hundred cakes of raisins, a hundred cakes of figs and a skin of wine.

2The king asked Ziba, "Why have you brought these?"

Ziba answered, "The donkeys are for the king's household to ride on, the bread and fruit are for the men to eat, and the wine is to refresh those who become exhausted in the wilderness."

3The king then asked, "Where is your master's grandson?"

Ziba said to him, "He is staying in Jerusalem, because he thinks, 'Today the Israelites will restore to me my grandfather's kingdom.'"

4Then the king said to Ziba, "All that belonged to Mephibosheth is now yours."

"I humbly bow," Ziba said. "May I find favor in your eyes, my lord the king."

Shimei Curses David

5As King David approached Bahurim, a man from the same clan as Saul's family came out from there. His name was Shimei son of Gera, and he cursed as he came out. 6He pelted David and all the king's officials with stones, though all the troops and the special guard were on David's right and left. 7As he cursed, Shimei said, "Get out, get out, you murderer, you scoundrel! 8The Lord has repaid you for all the blood you shed in the household of Saul, in whose place you have reigned. The Lord has given the kingdom into the hands of your son Absalom. You have come to ruin because you are a murderer!"

9Then Abishai son of Zeruiah said to the king, "Why should this dead dog curse my lord the king? Let me go over and cut off his head."

10But the king said, "What does this have to do with you, you sons of Zeruiah? If he is cursing because the Lord said to him, 'Curse David,' who can ask, 'Why do you do this?'"

11David then said to Abishai and all his officials, "My son, my own flesh and blood, is trying to kill me. How much more, then, this Benjamite! Leave him alone; let him curse, for the Lord has told him to. 12It may be that the Lord will look upon my misery and restore to me his covenant blessing instead of his curse today."

¹³So David and his men continued along the road while Shimei was going along the hillside opposite him, cursing as he went and throwing stones at him and showering him with dirt. ¹⁴The king and all the people with him arrived at their destination exhausted. And there he refreshed himself.

The Advice of Ahithophel and Hushai

¹⁵Meanwhile, Absalom and all the men of Israel came to Jerusalem, and Ahithophel was with him. ¹⁶Then Hushai the Arkite, David's confidant, went to Absalom and said to him, "Long live the king! Long live the king!"

¹⁷Absalom said to Hushai, "So this is the love you show your friend? If he's your friend, why didn't you go with him?"

¹⁸Hushai said to Absalom, "No, the one chosen by the LORD, by these people, and by all the men of Israel — his I will be, and I will remain with him. ¹⁹Furthermore, whom should I serve? Should I not serve the son? Just as I served your father, so I will serve you."

²⁰Absalom said to Ahithophel, "Give us your advice. What should we do?"

²¹Ahithophel answered, "Sleep with your father's concubines whom he left to take care of the palace. Then all Israel will hear that you have made yourself obnoxious to your father, and the hands of everyone with you will be more resolute." ²²So they pitched a tent for Absalom on the roof, and he slept with his father's concubines in the sight of all Israel.

²³Now in those days the advice Ahithophel gave was like that of one who inquires of God. That was how both David and Absalom regarded all of Ahithophel's advice.

17 Ahithophel said to Absalom, "I would*ᵃ* choose twelve thousand men and set out tonight in pursuit of David. ²I would attack him while he is weary and weak. I would strike him

with terror, and then all the people with him will flee. I would strike down only the king ³and bring all the people back to you. The death of the man you seek will mean the return of all; all the people will be unharmed." ⁴This plan seemed good to Absalom and to all the elders of Israel.

⁵But Absalom said, "Summon also Hushai the Arkite, so we can hear what he has to say as well." ⁶When Hushai came to him, Absalom said, "Ahithophel has given this advice. Should we do what he says? If not, give us your opinion."

⁷Hushai replied to Absalom, "The advice Ahithophel has given is not good this time. ⁸You know your father and his men; they are fighters, and as fierce as a wild bear robbed of her cubs. Besides, your father is an experienced fighter; he will not spend the night with the troops. ⁹Even now, he is hidden in a cave or some other place. If he should attack your troops first,*ᵇ* whoever hears about it will say, 'There has been a slaughter among the troops who follow Absalom.' ¹⁰Then even the bravest soldier, whose heart is like the heart of a lion, will melt with fear, for all Israel knows that your father is a fighter and that those with him are brave.

¹¹"So I advise you: Let all Israel, from Dan to Beersheba — as numerous as the sand on the seashore — be gathered to you, with you yourself leading them into battle. ¹²Then we will attack him wherever he may be found, and we will fall on him as dew settles on the ground. Neither he nor any of his men will be left alive. ¹³If he withdraws into a city, then all Israel will bring ropes to that city, and we will drag it down to the valley until not so much as a pebble is left."

¹⁴Absalom and all the men of Israel said, "The advice of Hushai the Arkite is better than that of Ahithophel." For the LORD had determined to frustrate the good advice of Ahithophel in order to bring disaster on Absalom.

¹⁵Hushai told Zadok and Abiathar, the priests, "Ahithophel has advised Absalom

---

ᵃ 1 Or *Let me*   *ᵇ 9* Or *When some of the men fall at the first attack* and the elders of Israel to do such and such, but I have advised them to do so and so. ¹⁶Now send a message at once and tell David, 'Do not spend the night at the fords in the wilderness; cross over without fail, or the king and all the people with him will be swallowed up.'"

¹⁷Jonathan and Ahimaaz were staying at En Rogel. A female servant was to go and inform them, and they were to go and tell King David, for they could not risk being seen entering the city. ¹⁸But a young man saw them and told Absalom. So the two of them left at once and went to the house of a man in Bahurim. He had a well in his courtyard, and they climbed down into it. ¹⁹His wife took a covering and spread it out over the opening of the well and scattered grain over it. No one knew anything about it.

²⁰When Absalom's men came to the woman at the house, they asked, "Where are Ahimaaz and Jonathan?"

The woman answered them, "They crossed over the brook."ᵃ The men searched but found no one, so they returned to Jerusalem.

²¹After they had gone, the two climbed out of the well and went to inform King David. They said to him, "Set out and cross the river at once; Ahithophel has advised such and such against you." ²²So David and all the people with him set out and crossed the Jordan. By daybreak, no one was left who had not crossed the Jordan.

²³When Ahithophel saw that his advice had not been followed, he saddled his donkey and set out for his house in his hometown. He put his house in order and then hanged himself. So he died and was buried in his father's tomb.

Absalom's Death

²⁴David went to Mahanaim, and Absalom crossed the Jordan with all the men of Israel. ²⁵Absalom had appointed Amasa over the army in place of Joab. Amasa was the son of Jether,ᵇ an Ishmaeliteᶜ who had married Abigail,ᵈ the daughter of Nahash and sister of Zeruiah the mother of Joab. ²⁶The Israelites and Absalom camped in the land of Gilead.

²⁷When David came to Mahanaim, Shobi son of Nahash from Rabbah of the Ammonites, and Makir son of Ammiel from Lo Debar, and Barzillai the Gileadite from Rogelim ²⁸brought bedding and bowls and articles of pottery. They also brought wheat and barley, flour and roasted grain, beans and lentils,ᵉ ²⁹honey and curds, sheep, and cheese from cows' milk for David and his people to eat. For they said, "The people have become exhausted and hungry and thirsty in the wilderness."

18 David mustered the men who were with him and appointed over them commanders of thousands and commanders of hundreds. ²David sent out his troops, a third under the command of Joab, a third under Joab's brother Abishai son of Zeruiah, and a third under Ittai the Gittite. The king told the troops, "I myself will surely march out with you."

³But the men said, "You must not go out; if we are forced to flee, they won't care about us. Even if half of us die, they won't care; but you are worth ten thousand of us.ᶠ It would be better now for you to give us support from the city."

⁴The king answered, "I will do whatever seems best to you."

So the king stood beside the gate while all his men marched out in units of hundreds and of thousands. ⁵The king commanded Joab, Abishai and Ittai, "Be gentle with the young man Absalom for my sake." And all the troops heard the king giving orders concerning Absalom to each of the commanders.

ᵃ 20 Or "They passed by the sheep pen toward the water."   ᵇ 25 Hebrew *Ithra*, a variant of *Jether*   ᶜ 25 Some Septuagint manuscripts (see also 1 Chron. 2:17); Hebrew and other Septuagint manuscripts *Israelite*   ᵈ 25 Hebrew *Abigal*, a variant of *Abigail*   ᵉ 28 Most Septuagint manuscripts and Syriac; Hebrew *lentils, and roasted grain*   ᶠ 3 Two Hebrew manuscripts, some Septuagint manuscripts and Vulgate; most Hebrew manuscripts *care; for now there are ten thousand like us*

6David's army marched out of the city to fight Israel, and the battle took place in the forest of Ephraim. 7There Israel's troops were routed by David's men, and the casualties that day were great — twenty thousand men. 8The battle spread out over the whole countryside, and the forest swallowed up more men that day than the sword.

9Now Absalom happened to meet David's men. He was riding his mule, and as the mule went under the thick branches of a large oak, Absalom's hair got caught in the tree. He was left hanging in midair, while the mule he was riding kept on going. 10When one of the men saw what had happened, he told Joab, "I just saw Absalom hanging in an oak tree."

11Joab said to the man who had told him this, "What! You saw him? Why didn't you strike him to the ground right there? Then I would have had to give you ten shekels[a] of silver and a warrior's belt."

12But the man replied, "Even if a thousand shekels[b] were weighed out into my hands, I would not lay a hand on the king's son. In our hearing the king commanded you and Abishai and Ittai, 'Protect the young man Absalom for my sake.'[c] 13And if I had put my life in jeopardy[d] — and nothing is hidden from the king — you would have kept your distance from me."

14Joab said, "I'm not going to wait like this for you." So he took three javelins in his hand and plunged them into Absalom's heart while Absalom was still alive in the oak tree. 15And ten of Joab's armor-bearers surrounded Absalom, struck him and killed him.

16Then Joab sounded the trumpet, and the troops stopped pursuing Israel, for Joab halted them. 17They took Absalom, threw him into a big pit in the forest and piled up a large heap of rocks over him. Meanwhile, all the Israelites fled to their homes.

18During his lifetime Absalom had taken a pillar and erected it in the King's Valley as a monument to himself, for he thought, "I have no son to carry on the memory of my name." He named the pillar after himself, and it is called Absalom's Monument to this day.

David Mourns

19Now Ahimaaz son of Zadok said, "Let me run and take the news to the king that the LORD has vindicated him by delivering him from the hand of his enemies."

20"You are not the one to take the news today," Joab told him. "You may take the news another time, but you must not do so today, because the king's son is dead."

21Then Joab said to a Cushite, "Go, tell the king what you have seen." The Cushite bowed down before Joab and ran off.

22Ahimaaz son of Zadok again said to Joab, "Come what may, please let me run behind the Cushite."

But Joab replied, "My son, why do you want to go? You don't have any news that will bring you a reward."

23He said, "Come what may, I want to run."

So Joab said, "Run!" Then Ahimaaz ran by way of the plain[e] and outran the Cushite.

24While David was sitting between the inner and outer gates, the watchman went up to the roof of the gateway by the wall. As he looked out, he saw a man running alone. 25The watchman called out to the king and reported it.

The king said, "If he is alone, he must have good news." And the runner came closer and closer.

26Then the watchman saw another runner, and he called down to the gatekeeper, "Look, another man running alone!"

The king said, "He must be bringing good news, too."

---

a 11 That is, about 4 ounces or about 115 grams   *b 12* That is, about 25 pounds or about 12 kilograms   *c 12* A few Hebrew manuscripts, Septuagint, Vulgate and Syriac; most Hebrew manuscripts may be translated *Absalom, whoever you may be.*   *d 13* Or *Otherwise, if I had acted treacherously toward him*   *e 23* That is, the plain of the Jordan

27The watchman said, "It seems to me that the first one runs like Ahimaaz son of Zadok."

"He's a good man," the king said. "He comes with good news."

28Then Ahimaaz called out to the king, "All is well!" He bowed down before the king with his face to the ground and said, "Praise be to the LORD your God! He has delivered up those who lifted their hands against my lord the king."

29The king asked, "Is the young man Absalom safe?"

Ahimaaz answered, "I saw great confusion just as Joab was about to send the king's servant and me, your servant, but I don't know what it was."

30The king said, "Stand aside and wait here." So he stepped aside and stood there.

31Then the Cushite arrived and said, "My lord the king, hear the good news! The LORD has vindicated you today by delivering you from the hand of all who rose up against you."

32The king asked the Cushite, "Is the young man Absalom safe?"

The Cushite replied, "May the enemies of my lord the king and all who rise up to harm you be like that young man."

33The king was shaken. He went up to the room over the gateway and wept. As he went, he said: "O my son Absalom! My son, my son Absalom! If only I had died instead of you — O Absalom, my son, my son!"[a]

19

[b] Joab was told, "The king is weeping and mourning for Absalom." 2And for the whole army the victory that day was turned into mourning, because on that day the troops heard it said, "The king is grieving for his son." 3The men stole into the city that day as men steal in who are ashamed when they flee from battle. 4The king covered his face and cried aloud, "O my son Absalom! O Absalom, my son, my son!"

5Then Joab went into the house to the king and said, "Today you have humiliated all your men, who have just saved your life and the lives of your sons and daughters and the lives of your wives and concubines. 6You love those who hate you and hate those who love you. You have made it clear today that the commanders and their men mean nothing to you. I see that you would be pleased if Absalom were alive today and all of us were dead. 7Now go out and encourage your men. I swear by the LORD that if you don't go out, not a man will be left with you by nightfall. This will be worse for you than all the calamities that have come on you from your youth till now."

8So the king got up and took his seat in the gateway. When the men were told, "The king is sitting in the gateway," they all came before him.

Meanwhile, the Israelites had fled to their homes.

David Returns to Jerusalem

9Throughout the tribes of Israel, all the people were arguing among themselves, saying, "The king delivered us from the hand of our enemies; he is the one who rescued us from the hand of the Philistines. But now he has fled the country to escape from Absalom; 10and Absalom, whom we anointed to rule over us, has died in battle. So why do you say nothing about bringing the king back?"

11King David sent this message to Zadok and Abiathar, the priests: "Ask the elders of Judah, 'Why should you be the last to bring the king back to his palace, since what is being said throughout Israel has reached the king at his quarters? 12You are my relatives, my own flesh and blood. So why should you be the last to bring back the king?' 13And say to Amasa, 'Are you not my own flesh and blood? May God deal with me, be it ever so severely, if you are not the commander of my army for life in place of Joab.'"

14He won over the hearts of the men of

---

a 33 In Hebrew texts this verse (18:33) is numbered 19:1.   *b* In Hebrew texts 19:1-43 is numbered 19:2-44.

Judah so that they were all of one mind. They sent word to the king, "Return, you and all your men." 15Then the king returned and went as far as the Jordan.

Now the men of Judah had come to Gilgal to go out and meet the king and bring him across the Jordan. 16Shimei son of Gera, the Benjamite from Bahurim, hurried down with the men of Judah to meet King David. 17With him were a thousand Benjamites, along with Ziba, the steward of Saul's household, and his fifteen sons and twenty servants. They rushed to the Jordan, where the king was. 18They crossed at the ford to take the king's household over and to do whatever he wished.

When Shimei son of Gera crossed the Jordan, he fell prostrate before the king 19and said to him, "May my lord not hold me guilty. Do not remember how your servant did wrong on the day my lord the king left Jerusalem. May the king put it out of his mind. 20For I your servant know that I have sinned, but today I have come here as the first from the tribes of Joseph to come down and meet my lord the king."

21Then Abishai son of Zeruiah said, "Shouldn't Shimei be put to death for this? He cursed the LORD's anointed."

22David replied, "What does this have to do with you, you sons of Zeruiah? What right do you have to interfere? Should anyone be put to death in Israel today? Don't I know that today I am king over Israel?" 23So the king said to Shimei, "You shall not die." And the king promised him on oath.

24Mephibosheth, Saul's grandson, also went down to meet the king. He had not taken care of his feet or trimmed his mustache or washed his clothes from the day the king left until the day he returned safely. 25When he came from Jerusalem to meet the king, the king asked him, "Why didn't you go with me, Mephibosheth?"

26He said, "My lord the king, since I your servant am lame, I said, 'I will have my donkey saddled and will ride on it, so I can go with the king.' But Ziba my servant betrayed me. 27And he has slandered your servant to my lord the king. My lord the king is like an angel of God; so do whatever you wish. 28All my grandfather's descendants deserved nothing but death from my lord the king, but you gave your servant a place among those who eat at your table. So what right do I have to make any more appeals to the king?"

29The king said to him, "Why say more? I order you and Ziba to divide the land."

30Mephibosheth said to the king, "Let him take everything, now that my lord the king has returned home safely."

31Barzillai the Gileadite also came down from Rogelim to cross the Jordan with the king and to send him on his way from there. 32Now Barzillai was very old, eighty years of age. He had provided for the king during his stay in Mahanaim, for he was a very wealthy man. 33The king said to Barzillai, "Cross over with me and stay with me in Jerusalem, and I will provide for you."

34But Barzillai answered the king, "How many more years will I live, that I should go up to Jerusalem with the king? 35I am now eighty years old. Can I tell the difference between what is enjoyable and what is not? Can your servant taste what he eats and drinks? Can I still hear the voices of male and female singers? Why should your servant be an added burden to my lord the king? 36Your servant will cross over the Jordan with the king for a short distance, but why should the king reward me in this way? 37Let your servant return, that I may die in my own town near the tomb of my father and mother. But here is your servant Kimham. Let him cross over with my lord the king. Do for him whatever you wish."

38The king said, "Kimham shall cross over with me, and I will do for him whatever you wish. And anything you desire from me I will do for you."

39So all the people crossed the Jordan, and then the king crossed over. The king kissed Barzillai and bid him farewell, and Barzillai returned to his home.

40When the king crossed over to Gilgal, Kimham crossed with him. All the troops of Judah and half the troops of Israel had taken the king over.

⁴¹Soon all the men of Israel were coming to the king and saying to him, "Why did our brothers, the men of Judah, steal the king away and bring him and his household across the Jordan, together with all his men?"

⁴²All the men of Judah answered the men of Israel, "We did this because the king is closely related to us. Why are you angry about it? Have we eaten any of the king's provisions? Have we taken anything for ourselves?"

⁴³Then the men of Israel answered the men of Judah, "We have ten shares in the king; so we have a greater claim on David than you have. Why then do you treat us with contempt? Weren't we the first to speak of bringing back our king?"

But the men of Judah pressed their claims even more forcefully than the men of Israel.

Sheba Rebels Against David

20 Now a troublemaker named Sheba son of Bikri, a Benjamite, happened to be there. He sounded the trumpet and shouted,

"We have no share in David,
  no part in Jesse's son!
Every man to his tent, Israel!"

²So all the men of Israel deserted David to follow Sheba son of Bikri. But the men of Judah stayed by their king all the way from the Jordan to Jerusalem.

³When David returned to his palace in Jerusalem, he took the ten concubines he had left to take care of the palace and put them in a house under guard. He provided for them but had no sexual relations with them. They were kept in confinement till the day of their death, living as widows.

⁴Then the king said to Amasa, "Summon the men of Judah to come to me within three days, and be here yourself." ⁵But when Amasa went to summon Judah, he took longer than the time the king had set for him.

⁶David said to Abishai, "Now Sheba son of Bikri will do us more harm than Absalom did. Take your master's men and pursue him, or he will find fortified cities and escape from us."ᵃ ⁷So Joab's men and the Kerethites and Pelethites and all the mighty warriors went out under the command of Abishai. They marched out from Jerusalem to pursue Sheba son of Bikri.

⁸While they were at the great rock in Gibeon, Amasa came to meet them. Joab was wearing his military tunic, and strapped over it at his waist was a belt with a dagger in its sheath. As he stepped forward, it dropped out of its sheath.

⁹Joab said to Amasa, "How are you, my brother?" Then Joab took Amasa by the beard with his right hand to kiss him. ¹⁰Amasa was not on his guard against the dagger in Joab's hand, and Joab plunged it into his belly, and his intestines spilled out on the ground. Without being stabbed again, Amasa died. Then Joab and his brother Abishai pursued Sheba son of Bikri.

¹¹One of Joab's men stood beside Amasa and said, "Whoever favors Joab, and whoever is for David, let him follow Joab!" ¹²Amasa lay wallowing in his blood in the middle of the road, and the man saw that all the troops came to a halt there. When he realized that everyone who came up to Amasa stopped, he dragged him from the road into a field and threw a garment over him. ¹³After Amasa had been removed from the road, everyone went on with Joab to pursue Sheba son of Bikri.

¹⁴Sheba passed through all the tribes of Israel to Abel Beth Maakah and through the entire region of the Bikrites,ᵇ who gathered together and followed him. ¹⁵All the troops with Joab came and besieged Sheba in Abel Beth Maakah. They built a siege ramp up to the city, and it stood against the outer fortifications. While they were

---

ᵃ 6 Or *and do us serious injury*   ᵇ 14 See Septuagint and Vulgate; Hebrew *Berites*.

battering the wall to bring it down, ¹⁶a wise woman called from the city, "Listen! Listen! Tell Joab to come here so I can speak to him." ¹⁷He went toward her, and she asked, "Are you Joab?"

"I am," he answered.

She said, "Listen to what your servant has to say."

"I'm listening," he said.

¹⁸She continued, "Long ago they used to say, 'Get your answer at Abel,' and that settled it. ¹⁹We are the peaceful and faithful in Israel. You are trying to destroy a city that is a mother in Israel. Why do you want to swallow up the LORD's inheritance?"

²⁰"Far be it from me!" Joab replied, "Far be it from me to swallow up or destroy! ²¹That is not the case. A man named Sheba son of Bikri, from the hill country of Ephraim, has lifted up his hand against the king, against David. Hand over this one man, and I'll withdraw from the city."

The woman said to Joab, "His head will be thrown to you from the wall."

²²Then the woman went to all the people with her wise advice, and they cut off the head of Sheba son of Bikri and threw it to Joab. So he sounded the trumpet, and his men dispersed from the city, each returning to his home. And Joab went back to the king in Jerusalem.

David's Officials

²³Joab was over Israel's entire army; Benaiah son of Jehoiada was over the Kerethites and Pelethites; ²⁴Adoniram*ᵃ* was in charge of forced labor; Jehoshaphat son of Ahilud was recorder; ²⁵Sheva was secretary; Zadok and Abiathar were priests; ²⁶and Ira the Jairite*ᵇ* was David's priest.

The Gibeonites Avenged

21 During the reign of David, there was a famine for three successive years; so David sought the face of the LORD. The LORD said, "It is on account of Saul and his blood-stained house; it is because he put the Gibeonites to death."

²The king summoned the Gibeonites and spoke to them. (Now the Gibeonites were not a part of Israel but were survivors of the Amorites; the Israelites had sworn to spare them, but Saul in his zeal for Israel and Judah had tried to annihilate them.) ³David asked the Gibeonites, "What shall I do for you? How shall I make atonement so that you will bless the LORD's inheritance?"

⁴The Gibeonites answered him, "We have no right to demand silver or gold from Saul or his family, nor do we have the right to put anyone in Israel to death."

"What do you want me to do for you?" David asked.

⁵They answered the king, "As for the man who destroyed us and plotted against us so that we have been decimated and have no place anywhere in Israel, ⁶let seven of his male descendants be given to us to be killed and their bodies exposed before the LORD at Gibeah of Saul—the LORD's chosen one."

So the king said, "I will give them to you."

⁷The king spared Mephibosheth son of Jonathan, the son of Saul, because of the oath before the LORD between David and Jonathan son of Saul. ⁸But the king took Armoni and Mephibosheth, the two sons of Aiah's daughter Rizpah, whom she had borne to Saul, together with the five sons of Saul's daughter Merab,*ᶜ* whom she had borne to Adriel son of Barzillai the Meholathite. ⁹He handed them over to the Gibeonites, who killed them and exposed their bodies on a hill before the LORD. All seven of them fell together; they were put to death during the first days of the harvest, just as the barley harvest was beginning.

¹⁰Rizpah daughter of Aiah took sackcloth and spread it out for herself on a rock. From the beginning of the harvest

---

ᵃ 24 Some Septuagint manuscripts (see also 1 Kings 4:6 and 5:14); Hebrew *Adoram*   *ᵇ 26* Hebrew; some Septuagint manuscripts and Syriac (see also 23:38) *Ithrite*   *ᶜ 8* Two Hebrew manuscripts, some Septuagint manuscripts and Syriac (see also 1 Samuel 18:19); most Hebrew and Septuagint manuscripts *Michal* till the rain poured down from the heavens on the bodies, she did not let the birds touch them by day or the wild animals by night. ¹¹When David was told what Aiah's daughter Rizpah, Saul's concubine, had done, ¹²he went and took the bones of Saul and his son Jonathan from the citizens of Jabesh Gilead. (They had stolen their bodies from the public square at Beth Shan, where the Philistines had hung them after they struck Saul down on Gilboa.) ¹³David brought the bones of Saul and his son Jonathan from there, and the bones of those who had been killed and exposed were gathered up.

¹⁴They buried the bones of Saul and his son Jonathan in the tomb of Saul's father Kish, at Zela in Benjamin, and did everything the king commanded. After that, God answered prayer in behalf of the land.

Wars Against the Philistines

¹⁵Once again there was a battle between the Philistines and Israel. David went down with his men to fight against the Philistines, and he became exhausted. ¹⁶And Ishbi-Benob, one of the descendants of Rapha, whose bronze spearhead weighed three hundred shekels*a* and who was armed with a new sword, said he would kill David. ¹⁷But Abishai son of Zeruiah came to David's rescue; he struck the Philistine down and killed him. Then David's men swore to him, saying, "Never again will you go out with us to battle, so that the lamp of Israel will not be extinguished."

¹⁸In the course of time, there was another battle with the Philistines, at Gob. At that time Sibbekai the Hushathite killed Saph, one of the descendants of Rapha.

¹⁹In another battle with the Philistines at Gob, Elhanan son of Jair*b* the Bethlehemite killed the brother of*c* Goliath the Gittite, who had a spear with a shaft like a weaver's rod.

²⁰In still another battle, which took place at Gath, there was a huge man with six fingers on each hand and six toes on each foot — twenty-four in all. He also was descended from Rapha. ²¹When he taunted Israel, Jonathan son of Shimeah, David's brother, killed him.

²²These four were descendants of Rapha in Gath, and they fell at the hands of David and his men.

David's Song of Praise

22 David sang to the LORD the words of this song when the LORD delivered him from the hand of all his enemies and from the hand of Saul. ²He said:

"The LORD is my rock, my fortress and
    my deliverer;
³   my God is my rock, in whom I take
        refuge,
    my shield*d* and the horn*e* of my
        salvation.
He is my stronghold, my refuge and my
        savior —
    from violent people you save me.

⁴"I called to the LORD, who is worthy of
        praise,
    and have been saved from my
        enemies.
⁵The waves of death swirled about me;
    the torrents of destruction
        overwhelmed me.
⁶The cords of the grave coiled around
        me;
    the snares of death confronted me.

⁷"In my distress I called to the LORD;
    I called out to my God.
From his temple he heard my voice;
    my cry came to his ears.
⁸The earth trembled and quaked,
    the foundations of the heavens*f*
        shook;
    they trembled because he was
        angry.

---

a 16 That is, about 7 1/2 pounds or about 3.5 kilograms   *b 19* See 1 Chron. 20:5; Hebrew *Jaare-Oregim.*
c 19 See 1 Chron. 20:5; Hebrew does not have *the brother of.*   *d 3* Or *sovereign*   *e 3* *Horn* here symbolizes
strength.   *f 8* Hebrew; Vulgate and Syriac (see also Psalm 18:7) *mountains*

⁹ Smoke rose from his nostrils;
  consuming fire came from his mouth,
  burning coals blazed out of it.
¹⁰ He parted the heavens and came down;
  dark clouds were under his feet.
¹¹ He mounted the cherubim and flew;
  he soared[a] on the wings of the wind.
¹² He made darkness his canopy around
    him —
  the dark[b] rain clouds of the sky.
¹³ Out of the brightness of his presence
  bolts of lightning blazed forth.
¹⁴ The Lord thundered from heaven;
  the voice of the Most High
    resounded.
¹⁵ He shot his arrows and scattered the
    enemy,
  with great bolts of lightning he
    routed them.
¹⁶ The valleys of the sea were exposed
  and the foundations of the earth laid
    bare
  at the rebuke of the Lord,
    at the blast of breath from his
      nostrils.

¹⁷ "He reached down from on high and
    took hold of me;
  he drew me out of deep waters.
¹⁸ He rescued me from my powerful
    enemy,
  from my foes, who were too strong
    for me.
¹⁹ They confronted me in the day of my
    disaster,
  but the Lord was my support.
²⁰ He brought me out into a spacious
    place;
  he rescued me because he delighted
    in me.

²¹ "The Lord has dealt with me according
    to my righteousness;
  according to the cleanness of my
    hands he has rewarded me.

²² For I have kept the ways of the Lord;
  I am not guilty of turning from my
    God.
²³ All his laws are before me;
  I have not turned away from his
    decrees.
²⁴ I have been blameless before him
  and have kept myself from sin.
²⁵ The Lord has rewarded me according
    to my righteousness,
  according to my cleanness[c] in his
    sight.

²⁶ "To the faithful you show yourself
    faithful,
  to the blameless you show yourself
    blameless,
²⁷ to the pure you show yourself pure,
  but to the devious you show yourself
    shrewd.
²⁸ You save the humble,
  but your eyes are on the haughty to
    bring them low.
²⁹ You, Lord, are my lamp;
  the Lord turns my darkness into
    light.
³⁰ With your help I can advance against a
    troop[d];
  with my God I can scale a wall.

³¹ "As for God, his way is perfect:
  The Lord's word is flawless;
  he shields all who take refuge in him.
³² For who is God besides the Lord?
  And who is the Rock except our God?
³³ It is God who arms me with strength[e]
  and keeps my way secure.
³⁴ He makes my feet like the feet of a deer;
  he causes me to stand on the heights.
³⁵ He trains my hands for battle;
  my arms can bend a bow of bronze.
³⁶ You make your saving help my shield;
  your help has made[f] me great.
³⁷ You provide a broad path for my feet,
  so that my ankles do not give way.

ᵃ 11 Many Hebrew manuscripts (see also Psalm 18:10); most Hebrew manuscripts *appeared*   ᵇ 12 Septuagint (see
also Psalm 18:11); Hebrew *massed*   ᶜ 25 Hebrew; Septuagint and Vulgate (see also Psalm 18:24) *to the cleanness of
my hands*   ᵈ 30 Or *can run through a barricade*   ᵉ 33 Dead Sea Scrolls, some Septuagint manuscripts, Vulgate
and Syriac (see also Psalm 18:32); Masoretic Text *who is my strong refuge*   ᶠ 36 Dead Sea Scrolls; Masoretic Text
shield; / you stoop down to make

38 "I pursued my enemies and crushed
　　them;
　I did not turn back till they were
　　destroyed.
39 I crushed them completely, and they
　　could not rise;
　they fell beneath my feet.
40 You armed me with strength for
　　battle;
　you humbled my adversaries before
　　me.
41 You made my enemies turn their backs
　　in flight,
　and I destroyed my foes.
42 They cried for help, but there was no
　　one to save them —
　to the Lord, but he did not answer.
43 I beat them as fine as the dust of the
　　earth;
　I pounded and trampled them like
　　mud in the streets.

44 "You have delivered me from the
　　attacks of the peoples;
　you have preserved me as the head
　　of nations.
　People I did not know now serve me,
45 　foreigners cower before me;
　as soon as they hear of me, they obey
　　me.
46 They all lose heart;
　they come trembling*a* from their
　　strongholds.

47 "The Lord lives! Praise be to my
　　Rock!
　Exalted be my God, the Rock, my
　　Savior!
48 He is the God who avenges me,
　who puts the nations under me,
49 　who sets me free from my enemies.
　You exalted me above my foes;
　from a violent man you rescued
　　me.
50 Therefore I will praise you, Lord,
　　among the nations;
　I will sing the praises of your
　　name.

51 "He gives his king great victories;
　he shows unfailing kindness to his
　　anointed,
　to David and his descendants
　　forever."

David's Last Words

23 These are the last words of Da-
　vid:

"The inspired utterance of David son of
　Jesse,
　the utterance of the man exalted by
　　the Most High,
　the man anointed by the God of
　　Jacob,
　the hero of Israel's songs:

2 "The Spirit of the Lord spoke through
　　me;
　his word was on my tongue.
3 The God of Israel spoke,
　the Rock of Israel said to me:
'When one rules over people in
　　righteousness,
　when he rules in the fear of God,
4 he is like the light of morning at
　　sunrise
　on a cloudless morning,
　like the brightness after rain
　　that brings grass from the earth.'

5 "If my house were not right with
　　God,
　surely he would not have made with
　　me an everlasting covenant,
　arranged and secured in every part;
　surely he would not bring to fruition
　　my salvation
　and grant me my every desire.
6 But evil men are all to be cast aside like
　　thorns,
　which are not gathered with the
　　hand.
7 Whoever touches thorns
　uses a tool of iron or the shaft of a
　　spear;
　they are burned up where they lie."

---

a 46 Some Septuagint manuscripts and Vulgate (see also Psalm 18:45); Masoretic Text *they arm themselves*

David's Mighty Warriors

[8]These are the names of David's mighty warriors:

Josheb-Basshebeth,[a] a Tahkemonite,[b] was chief of the Three; he raised his spear against eight hundred men, whom he killed[c] in one encounter.

[9]Next to him was Eleazar son of Dodai the Ahohite. As one of the three mighty warriors, he was with David when they taunted the Philistines gathered at Pas Dammim[d] for battle. Then the Israelites retreated, [10]but Eleazar stood his ground and struck down the Philistines till his hand grew tired and froze to the sword. The LORD brought about a great victory that day. The troops returned to Eleazar, but only to strip the dead.

[11]Next to him was Shammah son of Agee the Hararite. When the Philistines banded together at a place where there was a field full of lentils, Israel's troops fled from them. [12]But Shammah took his stand in the middle of the field. He defended it and struck the Philistines down, and the LORD brought about a great victory.

[13]During harvest time, three of the thirty chief warriors came down to David at the cave of Adullam, while a band of Philistines was encamped in the Valley of Rephaim. [14]At that time David was in the stronghold, and the Philistine garrison was at Bethlehem. [15]David longed for water and said, "Oh, that someone would get me a drink of water from the well near the gate of Bethlehem!" [16]So the three mighty warriors broke through the Philistine lines, drew water from the well near the gate of Bethlehem and carried it back to David. But he refused to drink it; instead, he poured it out before the LORD. [17]"Far be it from me, LORD, to do this!" he said. "Is it not the blood of men who went at the risk of their lives?" And David would not drink it.

Such were the exploits of the three mighty warriors.

[18]Abishai the brother of Joab son of Zeruiah was chief of the Three.[e] He raised his spear against three hundred men, whom he killed, and so he became as famous as the Three. [19]Was he not held in greater honor than the Three? He became their commander, even though he was not included among them.

[20]Benaiah son of Jehoiada, a valiant fighter from Kabzeel, performed great exploits. He struck down Moab's two mightiest warriors. He also went down into a pit on a snowy day and killed a lion. [21]And he struck down a huge Egyptian. Although the Egyptian had a spear in his hand, Benaiah went against him with a club. He snatched the spear from the Egyptian's hand and killed him with his own spear. [22]Such were the exploits of Benaiah son of Jehoiada; he too was as famous as the three mighty warriors. [23]He was held in greater honor than any of the Thirty, but he was not included among the Three. And David put him in charge of his bodyguard.

[24]Among the Thirty were:

Asahel the brother of Joab,
Elhanan son of Dodo from Bethlehem,
[25]Shammah the Harodite,
Elika the Harodite,
[26]Helez the Paltite,
Ira son of Ikkesh from Tekoa,
[27]Abiezer from Anathoth,
Sibbekai[f] the Hushathite,
[28]Zalmon the Ahohite,
Maharai the Netophathite,
[29]Heled[g] son of Baanah the Netophathite,

---

[a] 8 Hebrew; some Septuagint manuscripts suggest *Ish-Bosheth,* that is, *Esh-Baal* (see also 1 Chron. 11:11 *Jashobeam*).   [b] 8 Probably a variant of *Hakmonite* (see 1 Chron. 11:11)   [c] 8 Some Septuagint manuscripts (see also 1 Chron. 11:11); Hebrew and other Septuagint manuscripts *Three; it was Adino the Eznite who killed eight hundred men*   [d] 9 See 1 Chron. 11:13; Hebrew *gathered there.*   [e] 18 Most Hebrew manuscripts (see also 1 Chron. 11:20); two Hebrew manuscripts and Syriac *Thirty*   [f] 27 Some Septuagint manuscripts (see also 21:18; 1 Chron. 11:29); Hebrew *Mebunnai*   [g] 29 Some Hebrew manuscripts and Vulgate (see also 1 Chron. 11:30); most Hebrew manuscripts *Heleb*

Ithai son of Ribai from Gibeah in Benjamin,

30 Benaiah the Pirathonite,

Hiddai*a* from the ravines of Gaash,

31 Abi-Albon the Arbathite,

Azmaveth the Barhumite,

32 Eliahba the Shaalbonite,

the sons of Jashen,

Jonathan 33 son of*b* Shammah the Hararite,

Ahiam son of Sharar*c* the Hararite,

34 Eliphelet son of Ahasbai the Maakathite,

Eliam son of Ahithophel the Gilonite,

35 Hezro the Carmelite,

Paarai the Arbite,

36 Igal son of Nathan from Zobah,

the son of Hagri,*d*

37 Zelek the Ammonite,

Naharai the Beerothite, the armorbearer of Joab son of Zeruiah,

38 Ira the Ithrite,

Gareb the Ithrite

39 and Uriah the Hittite.

There were thirty-seven in all.

David Enrolls the Fighting Men

24 Again the anger of the LORD burned against Israel, and he incited David against them, saying, "Go and take a census of Israel and Judah."

2 So the king said to Joab and the army commanders*e* with him, "Go throughout the tribes of Israel from Dan to Beersheba and enroll the fighting men, so that I may know how many there are."

3 But Joab replied to the king, "May the LORD your God multiply the troops a hundred times over, and may the eyes of my lord the king see it. But why does my lord the king want to do such a thing?"

4 The king's word, however, overruled Joab and the army commanders; so they left the presence of the king to enroll the fighting men of Israel.

5 After crossing the Jordan, they camped near Aroer, south of the town in the gorge, and then went through Gad and on to Jazer. 6 They went to Gilead and the region of Tahtim Hodshi, and on to Dan Jaan and around toward Sidon. 7 Then they went toward the fortress of Tyre and all the towns of the Hivites and Canaanites. Finally, they went on to Beersheba in the Negev of Judah.

8 After they had gone through the entire land, they came back to Jerusalem at the end of nine months and twenty days.

9 Joab reported the number of the fighting men to the king: In Israel there were eight hundred thousand able-bodied men who could handle a sword, and in Judah five hundred thousand.

10 David was conscience-stricken after he had counted the fighting men, and he said to the LORD, "I have sinned greatly in what I have done. Now, LORD, I beg you, take away the guilt of your servant. I have done a very foolish thing."

11 Before David got up the next morning, the word of the LORD had come to Gad the prophet, David's seer: 12 "Go and tell David, 'This is what the LORD says: I am giving you three options. Choose one of them for me to carry out against you.'"

13 So Gad went to David and said to him, "Shall there come on you three*f* years of famine in your land? Or three months of fleeing from your enemies while they pursue you? Or three days of plague in your land? Now then, think it over and decide how I should answer the one who sent me."

14 David said to Gad, "I am in deep distress. Let us fall into the hands of the LORD, for his mercy is great; but do not let me fall into human hands."

---

a 30 Hebrew; some Septuagint manuscripts (see also 1 Chron. 11:32) *Hurai*   *b 33* Some Septuagint manuscripts (see also 1 Chron. 11:34); Hebrew does not have *son of.*   *c 33* Hebrew; some Septuagint manuscripts (see also 1 Chron. 11:35) *Sakar*   *d 36* Some Septuagint manuscripts (see also 1 Chron. 11:38); Hebrew *Haggadi*   *e 2* Septuagint (see also verse 4 and 1 Chron. 21:2); Hebrew *Joab the army commander*   *f 13* Septuagint (see also 1 Chron. 21:12); Hebrew *seven*

¹⁵So the LORD sent a plague on Israel from that morning until the end of the time designated, and seventy thousand of the people from Dan to Beersheba died. ¹⁶When the angel stretched out his hand to destroy Jerusalem, the LORD relented concerning the disaster and said to the angel who was afflicting the people, "Enough! Withdraw your hand." The angel of the LORD was then at the threshing floor of Araunah the Jebusite.

¹⁷When David saw the angel who was striking down the people, he said to the LORD, "I have sinned; I, the shepherd,ᵃ have done wrong. These are but sheep. What have they done? Let your hand fall on me and my family."

David Builds an Altar

¹⁸On that day Gad went to David and said to him, "Go up and build an altar to the LORD on the threshing floor of Araunah the Jebusite." ¹⁹So David went up, as the LORD had commanded through Gad. ²⁰When Araunah looked and saw the king and his officials coming toward him, he went out and bowed down before the king with his face to the ground.

²¹Araunah said, "Why has my lord the king come to his servant?"

"To buy your threshing floor," David answered, "so I can build an altar to the LORD, that the plague on the people may be stopped."

²²Araunah said to David, "Let my lord the king take whatever he wishes and offer it up. Here are oxen for the burnt offering, and here are threshing sledges and ox yokes for the wood. ²³Your Majesty, Araunahᵇ gives all this to the king." Araunah also said to him, "May the LORD your God accept you."

²⁴But the king replied to Araunah, "No, I insist on paying you for it. I will not sacrifice to the LORD my God burnt offerings that cost me nothing."

So David bought the threshing floor and the oxen and paid fifty shekelsᶜ of silver for them. ²⁵David built an altar to the LORD there and sacrificed burnt offerings and fellowship offerings. Then the LORD answered his prayer in behalf of the land, and the plague on Israel was stopped.

ᵃ 17 Dead Sea Scrolls and Septuagint; Masoretic Text does not have *the shepherd.*   ᵇ 23 Some Hebrew manuscripts and Septuagint; most Hebrew manuscripts *King Araunah*   ᶜ 24 That is, about 1 1/4 pounds or about 575 grams

1 Kings

THEME: The book's major premise is that obedience brings blessing and disobedience results in judgment.

AUTHOR: First and Second Kings were originally one book, the author of which is unknown. Although Jewish tradition attributes the work to Jeremiah the prophet, few scholars today agree.

DATE OF WRITING: First Kings was probably written between 560 and 550 BC, during the Babylonian exile of the Jews (586–538 BC).

ENCOURAGEMENT FROM 1 KINGS: "Hear the supplication of your servant . . . Hear from heaven, your dwelling place, and when you hear, forgive" (1 Kings 8:30).

CHALLENGE FROM 1 KINGS: "Be strong, act like a man, and observe what the LORD your God requires: Walk in obedience to him, and keep his decrees and commands, his laws and regulations . . . so that you may prosper in all you do and wherever you go" (1 Kings 2:2–3).

REFLECTION FROM 1 KINGS: "Praise be to the LORD . . . Not one word has failed of all the good promises he gave" (1 Kings 8:56).

First and Second Kings tell the history of the monarchy in Israel. First Kings examines two parallel sets of kings and nations (the northern and southern kingdoms) of disobedient people. The first half of 1 Kings covers the reign of Solomon, who carried Israel to the peak of its size and glory. Solomon's accomplishments, including the construction of the temple, brought him worldwide fame. As he aged, however, his zeal for God diminished. The cycle of dysfunction passed down from his father, David, was repeated in the once promising life of his talented son. Solomon became more focused on his earthly kingdom than on his eternal purpose. Through dealings with pagan kings, he ushered idolatry back into Jerusalem and into his own life.

The second half of 1 Kings concerns the divided kingdoms of Israel and Judah, as well as the ministry of the prophet Elijah. God loved his people enough to send a prophet who would challenge their kings. It often takes a person loving enough to confront us about our lives' hurts, hang-ups and habits to help us see our need for help and healing. If we're blessed to have someone in our lives who cares enough to point out areas that need our attention, both before we begin recovery and while we're working out our recoveries, we need to pay close attention to what they have to say. Whether this caring party is a concerned family member or a trusted sponsor or an accountability partner, we need to be sensitive to God's Holy Spirit working through others to lead us back to himself.

Adonijah Sets Himself Up as King

1 When King David was very old, he could not keep warm even when they put covers over him. ²So his attendants said to him, "Let us look for a young virgin to serve the king and take care of him. She can lie beside him so that our lord the king may keep warm."

³Then they searched throughout Israel for a beautiful young woman and found Abishag, a Shunammite, and brought her to the king. ⁴The woman was very beautiful; she took care of the king and waited on him, but the king had no sexual relations with her.

⁵Now Adonijah, whose mother was Haggith, put himself forward and said, "I will be king." So he got chariots and horses*a* ready, with fifty men to run ahead of him. ⁶(His father had never rebuked him by asking, "Why do you behave as you do?" He was also very handsome and was born next after Absalom.)

⁷Adonijah conferred with Joab son of Zeruiah and with Abiathar the priest, and they gave him their support. ⁸But Zadok the priest, Benaiah son of Jehoiada, Nathan the prophet, Shimei and Rei and David's special guard did not join Adonijah.

⁹Adonijah then sacrificed sheep, cattle and fattened calves at the Stone of Zoheleth near En Rogel. He invited all his brothers, the king's sons, and all the royal officials of Judah, ¹⁰but he did not invite Nathan the prophet or Benaiah or the special guard or his brother Solomon.

¹¹Then Nathan asked Bathsheba, Solomon's mother, "Have you not heard that Adonijah, the son of Haggith, has become king, and our lord David knows nothing about it? ¹²Now then, let me advise you how you can save your own life and the life of your son Solomon. ¹³Go in to King David and say to him, 'My lord the king, did you not swear to me your servant: "Surely Solomon your son shall be king after me, and he will sit on my throne"? Why then

has Adonijah become king?' ¹⁴While you are still there talking to the king, I will come in and add my word to what you have said."

¹⁵So Bathsheba went to see the aged king in his room, where Abishag the Shunammite was attending him. ¹⁶Bathsheba bowed down, prostrating herself before the king.

"What is it you want?" the king asked.

¹⁷She said to him, "My lord, you yourself swore to me your servant by the LORD your God: 'Solomon your son shall be king after me, and he will sit on my throne.' ¹⁸But now Adonijah has become king, and you, my lord the king, do not know about it. ¹⁹He has sacrificed great numbers of cattle, fattened calves, and sheep, and has invited all the king's sons, Abiathar the priest and Joab the commander of the army, but he has not invited Solomon your servant. ²⁰My lord the king, the eyes of all Israel are on you, to learn from you who will sit on the throne of my lord the king after him. ²¹Otherwise, as soon as my lord the king is laid to rest with his ancestors, I and my son Solomon will be treated as criminals."

²²While she was still speaking with the king, Nathan the prophet arrived. ²³And the king was told, "Nathan the prophet is here." So he went before the king and bowed with his face to the ground.

²⁴Nathan said, "Have you, my lord the king, declared that Adonijah shall be king after you, and that he will sit on your throne? ²⁵Today he has gone down and sacrificed great numbers of cattle, fattened calves, and sheep. He has invited all the king's sons, the commanders of the army and Abiathar the priest. Right now they are eating and drinking with him and saying, 'Long live King Adonijah!' ²⁶But me your servant, and Zadok the priest, and Benaiah son of Jehoiada, and your servant Solomon he did not invite. ²⁷Is this something my lord the king has done without letting

---

a 5 Or *charioteers*

his servants know who should sit on the throne of my lord the king after him?"

David Makes Solomon King

28Then King David said, "Call in Bathsheba." So she came into the king's presence and stood before him.

29The king then took an oath: "As surely as the Lord lives, who has delivered me out of every trouble, 30I will surely carry out this very day what I swore to you by the Lord, the God of Israel: Solomon your son shall be king after me, and he will sit on my throne in my place."

31Then Bathsheba bowed down with her face to the ground, prostrating herself before the king, and said, "May my lord King David live forever!"

32King David said, "Call in Zadok the priest, Nathan the prophet and Benaiah son of Jehoiada." When they came before the king, 33he said to them: "Take your lord's servants with you and have Solomon my son mount my own mule and take him down to Gihon. 34There have Zadok the priest and Nathan the prophet anoint him king over Israel. Blow the trumpet and shout, 'Long live King Solomon!' 35Then you are to go up with him, and he is to come and sit on my throne and reign in my place. I have appointed him ruler over Israel and Judah."

36Benaiah son of Jehoiada answered the king, "Amen! May the Lord, the God of my lord the king, so declare it. 37As the Lord was with my lord the king, so may he be with Solomon to make his throne even greater than the throne of my lord King David!"

38So Zadok the priest, Nathan the prophet, Benaiah son of Jehoiada, the Kerethites and the Pelethites went down and had Solomon mount King David's mule, and they escorted him to Gihon. 39Zadok the priest took the horn of oil from the sacred tent and anointed Solomon. Then they sounded the trumpet and all the people shouted, "Long live King Solomon!" 40And all the people went up after him, playing pipes and rejoicing greatly, so that the ground shook with the sound.

41Adonijah and all the guests who were with him heard it as they were finishing their feast. On hearing the sound of the trumpet, Joab asked, "What's the meaning of all the noise in the city?"

42Even as he was speaking, Jonathan son of Abiathar the priest arrived. Adonijah said, "Come in. A worthy man like you must be bringing good news."

43"Not at all!" Jonathan answered. "Our lord King David has made Solomon king. 44The king has sent with him Zadok the priest, Nathan the prophet, Benaiah son of Jehoiada, the Kerethites and the Pelethites, and they have put him on the king's mule, 45and Zadok the priest and Nathan the prophet have anointed him king at Gihon. From there they have gone up cheering, and the city resounds with it. That's the noise you hear. 46Moreover, Solomon has taken his seat on the royal throne. 47Also, the royal officials have come to congratulate our lord King David, saying, 'May your God make Solomon's name more famous than yours and his throne greater than yours!' And the king bowed in worship on his bed 48and said, 'Praise be to the Lord, the God of Israel, who has allowed my eyes to see a successor on my throne today.'"

49At this, all Adonijah's guests rose in alarm and dispersed. 50But Adonijah, in fear of Solomon, went and took hold of the horns of the altar. 51Then Solomon was told, "Adonijah is afraid of King Solomon and is clinging to the horns of the altar. He says, 'Let King Solomon swear to me today that he will not put his servant to death with the sword.'"

52Solomon replied, "If he shows himself to be worthy, not a hair of his head will fall to the ground; but if evil is found in him, he will die." 53Then King Solomon sent men, and they brought him down from the altar. And Adonijah came and bowed down to King Solomon, and Solomon said, "Go to your home."

David's Charge to Solomon

2 When the time drew near for David to die, he gave a charge to Solomon his son.

2"I am about to go the way of all the earth," he said. "So be strong, act like a man, 3and observe what the LORD your God requires: Walk in obedience to him, and keep his decrees and commands, his laws and regulations, as written in the Law of Moses. Do this so that you may prosper in all you do and wherever you go 4and that the LORD may keep his promise to me: 'If your descendants watch how they live, and if they walk faithfully before me with all their heart and soul, you will never fail to have a successor on the throne of Israel.'

5"Now you yourself know what Joab son of Zeruiah did to me — what he did to the two commanders of Israel's armies, Abner son of Ner and Amasa son of Jether. He killed them, shedding their blood in peacetime as if in battle, and with that blood he stained the belt around his waist and the sandals on his feet. 6Deal with him according to your wisdom, but do not let his gray head go down to the grave in peace.

7"But show kindness to the sons of Barzillai of Gilead and let them be among those who eat at your table. They stood by me when I fled from your brother Absalom.

8"And remember, you have with you Shimei son of Gera, the Benjamite from Bahurim, who called down bitter curses on me the day I went to Mahanaim. When he came down to meet me at the Jordan, I swore to him by the LORD: 'I will not put you to death by the sword.' 9But now, do not consider him innocent. You are a man of wisdom; you will know what to do to him. Bring his gray head down to the grave in blood."

10Then David rested with his ancestors and was buried in the City of David. 11He had reigned forty years over Israel — seven years in Hebron and thirty-three in Jerusalem. 12So Solomon sat on the throne of his father David, and his rule was firmly established.

Solomon's Throne Established

13Now Adonijah, the son of Haggith, went to Bathsheba, Solomon's mother. Bathsheba asked him, "Do you come peacefully?"

He answered, "Yes, peacefully." 14Then he added, "I have something to say to you."

"You may say it," she replied.

15"As you know," he said, "the kingdom was mine. All Israel looked to me as their king. But things changed, and the kingdom has gone to my brother; for it has come to him from the LORD. 16Now I have one request to make of you. Do not refuse me."

"You may make it," she said.

17So he continued, "Please ask King Solomon — he will not refuse you — to give me Abishag the Shunammite as my wife."

18"Very well," Bathsheba replied, "I will speak to the king for you."

19When Bathsheba went to King Solomon to speak to him for Adonijah, the king stood up to meet her, bowed down to her and sat down on his throne. He had a throne brought for the king's mother, and she sat down at his right hand.

20"I have one small request to make of you," she said. "Do not refuse me."

The king replied, "Make it, my mother; I will not refuse you."

21So she said, "Let Abishag the Shunammite be given in marriage to your brother Adonijah."

22King Solomon answered his mother, "Why do you request Abishag the Shunammite for Adonijah? You might as well request the kingdom for him — after all, he is my older brother — yes, for him and for Abiathar the priest and Joab son of Zeruiah!"

23Then King Solomon swore by the LORD: "May God deal with me, be it ever so severely, if Adonijah does not pay with his life for this request! 24And now, as surely as the LORD lives — he who has established me securely on the throne of my father David and has founded a dynasty for me as he promised — Adonijah shall be put to death today!" 25So King Solomon gave orders to

Benaiah son of Jehoiada, and he struck down Adonijah and he died.

26 To Abiathar the priest the king said, "Go back to your fields in Anathoth. You deserve to die, but I will not put you to death now, because you carried the ark of the Sovereign LORD before my father David and shared all my father's hardships." 27 So Solomon removed Abiathar from the priesthood of the LORD, fulfilling the word the LORD had spoken at Shiloh about the house of Eli.

28 When the news reached Joab, who had conspired with Adonijah though not with Absalom, he fled to the tent of the LORD and took hold of the horns of the altar. 29 King Solomon was told that Joab had fled to the tent of the LORD and was beside the altar. Then Solomon ordered Benaiah son of Jehoiada, "Go, strike him down!"

30 So Benaiah entered the tent of the LORD and said to Joab, "The king says, 'Come out!'"

But he answered, "No, I will die here."

Benaiah reported to the king, "This is how Joab answered me."

31 Then the king commanded Benaiah, "Do as he says. Strike him down and bury him, and so clear me and my whole family of the guilt of the innocent blood that Joab shed. 32 The LORD will repay him for the blood he shed, because without my father David knowing it he attacked two men and killed them with the sword. Both of them—Abner son of Ner, commander of Israel's army, and Amasa son of Jether, commander of Judah's army—were better men and more upright than he. 33 May the guilt of their blood rest on the head of Joab and his descendants forever. But on David and his descendants, his house and his throne, may there be the LORD's peace forever."

34 So Benaiah son of Jehoiada went up and struck down Joab and killed him, and he was buried at his home out in the country. 35 The king put Benaiah son of Jehoiada over the army in Joab's position and replaced Abiathar with Zadok the priest.

36 Then the king sent for Shimei and said to him, "Build yourself a house in Jerusalem and live there, but do not go anywhere else. 37 The day you leave and cross the Kidron Valley, you can be sure you will die; your blood will be on your own head."

38 Shimei answered the king, "What you say is good. Your servant will do as my lord the king has said." And Shimei stayed in Jerusalem for a long time.

39 But three years later, two of Shimei's slaves ran off to Achish son of Maakah, king of Gath, and Shimei was told, "Your slaves are in Gath." 40 At this, he saddled his donkey and went to Achish at Gath in search of his slaves. So Shimei went away and brought the slaves back from Gath.

41 When Solomon was told that Shimei had gone from Jerusalem to Gath and had returned, 42 the king summoned Shimei and said to him, "Did I not make you swear by the LORD and warn you, 'On the day you leave to go anywhere else, you can be sure you will die'? At that time you said to me, 'What you say is good. I will obey.' 43 Why then did you not keep your oath to the LORD and obey the command I gave you?"

44 The king also said to Shimei, "You know in your heart all the wrong you did to my father David. Now the LORD will repay you for your wrongdoing. 45 But King Solomon will be blessed, and David's throne will remain secure before the LORD forever."

46 Then the king gave the order to Benaiah son of Jehoiada, and he went out and struck Shimei down and he died.

The kingdom was now established in Solomon's hands.

Solomon Asks for Wisdom

3 Solomon made an alliance with Pharaoh king of Egypt and married his daughter. He brought her to the City of David until he finished building his palace and the temple of the LORD, and the wall around Jerusalem. 2 The people, however, were still sacrificing at the high places, because a temple had not yet been built for

the Name of the LORD. ³Solomon showed his love for the LORD by walking according to the instructions given him by his father David, except that he offered sacrifices and burned incense on the high places.

⁴The king went to Gibeon to offer sacrifices, for that was the most important high place, and Solomon offered a thousand burnt offerings on that altar. ⁵At Gibeon the LORD appeared to Solomon during the night in a dream, and God said, "Ask for whatever you want me to give you."

⁶Solomon answered, "You have shown great kindness to your servant, my father David, because he was faithful to you and righteous and upright in heart. You have continued this great kindness to him and have given him a son to sit on his throne this very day.

⁷"Now, LORD my God, you have made your servant king in place of my father David. But I am only a little child and do not know how to carry out my duties. ⁸Your servant is here among the people you have chosen, a great people, too numerous to count or number. ⁹So give your servant a discerning heart to govern your people and to distinguish between right and wrong. For who is able to govern this great people of yours?"

¹⁰The Lord was pleased that Solomon had asked for this. ¹¹So God said to him, "Since you have asked for this and not for long life or wealth for yourself, nor have asked for the death of your enemies but for discernment in administering justice, ¹²I will do what you have asked. I will give you a wise and discerning heart, so that there will never have been anyone like you, nor will there ever be. ¹³Moreover, I will give you what you have not asked for — both wealth and honor — so that in your lifetime you will have no equal among kings. ¹⁴And if you walk in obedience to me and keep my decrees and commands as David your father did, I will give you a long life." ¹⁵Then Solomon awoke — and he realized it had been a dream.

He returned to Jerusalem, stood before the ark of the Lord's covenant and sacri-

ficed burnt offerings and fellowship offerings. Then he gave a feast for all his court.

A Wise Ruling

¹⁶Now two prostitutes came to the king and stood before him. ¹⁷One of them said, "Pardon me, my lord. This woman and I live in the same house, and I had a baby while she was there with me. ¹⁸The third day after my child was born, this woman also had a baby. We were alone; there was no one in the house but the two of us.

¹⁹"During the night this woman's son died because she lay on him. ²⁰So she got up in the middle of the night and took my son from my side while I your servant was asleep. She put him by her breast and put her dead son by my breast. ²¹The next morning, I got up to nurse my son — and he was dead! But when I looked at him closely in the morning light, I saw that it wasn't the son I had borne."

²²The other woman said, "No! The living one is my son; the dead one is yours."

But the first one insisted, "No! The dead one is yours; the living one is mine." And so they argued before the king.

²³The king said, "This one says, 'My son is alive and your son is dead,' while that one says, 'No! Your son is dead and mine is alive.'"

²⁴Then the king said, "Bring me a sword." So they brought a sword for the king. ²⁵He then gave an order: "Cut the living child in two and give half to one and half to the other."

²⁶The woman whose son was alive was deeply moved out of love for her son and said to the king, "Please, my lord, give her the living baby! Don't kill him!"

But the other said, "Neither I nor you shall have him. Cut him in two!"

²⁷Then the king gave his ruling: "Give the living baby to the first woman. Do not kill him; she is his mother."

²⁸When all Israel heard the verdict the king had given, they held the king in awe, because they saw that he had wisdom from God to administer justice.

Solomon's Officials and Governors

4 So King Solomon ruled over all Israel. ²And these were his chief officials:

Azariah son of Zadok—the priest;
³Elihoreph and Ahijah, sons of Shisha—secretaries;
Jehoshaphat son of Ahilud—recorder;
⁴Benaiah son of Jehoiada—commander in chief;
Zadok and Abiathar—priests;
⁵Azariah son of Nathan—in charge of the district governors;
Zabud son of Nathan—a priest and adviser to the king;
⁶Ahishar—palace administrator;
Adoniram son of Abda—in charge of forced labor.

⁷Solomon had twelve district governors over all Israel, who supplied provisions for the king and the royal household. Each one had to provide supplies for one month in the year. ⁸These are their names:

Ben-Hur—in the hill country of Ephraim;
⁹Ben-Deker—in Makaz, Shaalbim, Beth Shemesh and Elon Bethhanan;
¹⁰Ben-Hesed—in Arubboth (Sokoh and all the land of Hepher were his);
¹¹Ben-Abinadab—in Naphoth Dor (he was married to Taphath daughter of Solomon);
¹²Baana son of Ahilud—in Taanach and Megiddo, and in all of Beth Shan next to Zarethan below Jezreel, from Beth Shan to Abel Meholah across to Jokmeam;
¹³Ben-Geber—in Ramoth Gilead (the settlements of Jair son of Manasseh in Gilead were his, as well as the region of Argob in Bashan and its sixty large walled cities with bronze gate bars);
¹⁴Ahinadab son of Iddo—in Mahanaim;
¹⁵Ahimaaz—in Naphtali (he had married Basemath daughter of Solomon);
¹⁶Baana son of Hushai—in Asher and in Aloth;
¹⁷Jehoshaphat son of Paruah—in Issachar;
¹⁸Shimei son of Ela—in Benjamin;
¹⁹Geber son of Uri—in Gilead (the country of Sihon king of the Amorites and the country of Og king of Bashan). He was the only governor over the district.

Solomon's Daily Provisions

²⁰The people of Judah and Israel were as numerous as the sand on the seashore; they ate, they drank and they were happy. ²¹And Solomon ruled over all the kingdoms from the Euphrates River to the land of the Philistines, as far as the border of Egypt. These countries brought tribute and were Solomon's subjects all his life.

²²Solomon's daily provisions were thirty cors*a* of the finest flour and sixty cors*b* of meal, ²³ten head of stall-fed cattle, twenty of pasture-fed cattle and a hundred sheep and goats, as well as deer, gazelles, roebucks and choice fowl. ²⁴For he ruled over all the kingdoms west of the Euphrates River, from Tiphsah to Gaza, and had peace on all sides. ²⁵During Solomon's lifetime Judah and Israel, from Dan to Beersheba, lived in safety, everyone under their own vine and under their own fig tree.

²⁶Solomon had four*c* thousand stalls for chariot horses, and twelve thousand horses.*d*

²⁷The district governors, each in his month, supplied provisions for King Solomon and all who came to the king's table. They saw to it that nothing was lacking. ²⁸They also brought to the proper place their quotas of barley and straw for the chariot horses and the other horses.

---

a 22 That is, probably about 5 1/2 tons or about 5 metric tons   *b 22* That is, probably about 11 tons or about 10 metric tons   *c 26* Some Septuagint manuscripts (see also 2 Chron. 9:25); Hebrew *forty*   *d 26* Or *charioteers*

Solomon's Wisdom

29God gave Solomon wisdom and very great insight, and a breadth of understanding as measureless as the sand on the seashore. 30Solomon's wisdom was greater than the wisdom of all the people of the East, and greater than all the wisdom of Egypt. 31He was wiser than anyone else, including Ethan the Ezrahite — wiser than Heman, Kalkol and Darda, the sons of Mahol. And his fame spread to all the surrounding nations. 32He spoke three thousand proverbs and his songs numbered a thousand and five. 33He spoke about plant life, from the cedar of Lebanon to the hyssop that grows out of walls. He also spoke about animals and birds, reptiles and fish. 34From all nations people came to listen to Solomon's wisdom, sent by all the kings of the world, who had heard of his wisdom.a

Preparations for Building the Temple

5 b When Hiram king of Tyre heard that Solomon had been anointed king to succeed his father David, he sent his envoys to Solomon, because he had always been on friendly terms with David. 2Solomon sent back this message to Hiram:

3"You know that because of the wars waged against my father David from all sides, he could not build a temple for the Name of the Lord his God until the Lord put his enemies under his feet. 4But now the Lord my God has given me rest on every side, and there is no adversary or disaster. 5I intend, therefore, to build a temple for the Name of the Lord my God, as the Lord told my father David, when he said, 'Your son whom I will put on the throne in your place will build the temple for my Name.'

6"So give orders that cedars of Lebanon be cut for me. My men will work with yours, and I will pay you for your men whatever wages you set. You know that we have no one so skilled in felling timber as the Sidonians."

7When Hiram heard Solomon's message, he was greatly pleased and said, "Praise be to the Lord today, for he has given David a wise son to rule over this great nation." 8So Hiram sent word to Solomon:

"I have received the message you sent me and will do all you want in providing the cedar and juniper logs. 9My men will haul them down from Lebanon to the Mediterranean Sea, and I will float them as rafts by sea to the place you specify. There I will separate them and you can take them away. And you are to grant my wish by providing food for my royal household."

10In this way Hiram kept Solomon supplied with all the cedar and juniper logs he wanted, 11and Solomon gave Hiram twenty thousand corsc of wheat as food for his household, in addition to twenty thousand bathsd,e of pressed olive oil. Solomon continued to do this for Hiram year after year. 12The Lord gave Solomon wisdom, just as he had promised him. There were peaceful relations between Hiram and Solomon, and the two of them made a treaty.

13King Solomon conscripted laborers from all Israel — thirty thousand men. 14He sent them off to Lebanon in shifts of ten thousand a month, so that they spent one month in Lebanon and two months at home. Adoniram was in charge of the forced labor. 15Solomon had seventy thousand carriers and eighty thousand stonecutters in the hills, 16as well as thirty-three hundredf foremen who supervised the project and directed the workers. 17At the king's command they removed from the

a 34 In Hebrew texts 4:21-34 is numbered 5:1-14.   b In Hebrew texts 5:1-18 is numbered 5:15-32.   c 11 That is, probably about 3,600 tons or about 3,250 metric tons   d 11 Septuagint (see also 2 Chron. 2:10); Hebrew twenty cors   e 11 That is, about 120,000 gallons or about 440,000 liters   f 16 Hebrew; some Septuagint manuscripts (see also 2 Chron. 2:2,18) thirty-six hundred quarry large blocks of high-grade stone to provide a foundation of dressed stone for the temple. 18The craftsmen of Solomon and Hiram and workers from Byblos cut and prepared the timber and stone for the building of the temple.

Solomon Builds the Temple

6 In the four hundred and eightieth[a] year after the Israelites came out of Egypt, in the fourth year of Solomon's reign over Israel, in the month of Ziv, the second month, he began to build the temple of the LORD.

2The temple that King Solomon built for the LORD was sixty cubits long, twenty wide and thirty high.[b] 3The portico at the front of the main hall of the temple extended the width of the temple, that is twenty cubits,[c] and projected ten cubits[d] from the front of the temple. 4He made narrow windows high up in the temple walls. 5Against the walls of the main hall and inner sanctuary he built a structure around the building, in which there were side rooms. 6The lowest floor was five cubits[e] wide, the middle floor six cubits[f] and the third floor seven.[g] He made offset ledges around the outside of the temple so that nothing would be inserted into the temple walls.

7In building the temple, only blocks dressed at the quarry were used, and no hammer, chisel or any other iron tool was heard at the temple site while it was being built.

8The entrance to the lowest[h] floor was on the south side of the temple; a stairway led up to the middle level and from there to the third. 9So he built the temple and completed it, roofing it with beams and cedar planks. 10And he built the side rooms all along the temple. The height of each was five cubits, and they were attached to the temple by beams of cedar.

11The word of the LORD came to Solomon: 12"As for this temple you are building, if you follow my decrees, observe my laws and keep all my commands and obey them, I will fulfill through you the promise I gave to David your father. 13And I will live among the Israelites and will not abandon my people Israel."

14So Solomon built the temple and completed it. 15He lined its interior walls with cedar boards, paneling them from the floor of the temple to the ceiling, and covered the floor of the temple with planks of juniper. 16He partitioned off twenty cubits at the rear of the temple with cedar boards from floor to ceiling to form within the temple an inner sanctuary, the Most Holy Place. 17The main hall in front of this room was forty cubits[i] long. 18The inside of the temple was cedar, carved with gourds and open flowers. Everything was cedar; no stone was to be seen.

19He prepared the inner sanctuary within the temple to set the ark of the covenant of the LORD there. 20The inner sanctuary was twenty cubits long, twenty wide and twenty high. He overlaid the inside with pure gold, and he also overlaid the altar of cedar. 21Solomon covered the inside of the temple with pure gold, and he extended gold chains across the front of the inner sanctuary, which was overlaid with gold. 22So he overlaid the whole interior with gold. He also overlaid with gold the altar that belonged to the inner sanctuary.

23For the inner sanctuary he made a pair of cherubim out of olive wood, each ten cubits high. 24One wing of the first cherub was five cubits long, and the other wing five cubits — ten cubits from wing tip to wing tip. 25The second cherub also measured ten cubits, for the two cherubim were identical in size and shape. 26The height of each cherub was ten cubits. 27He placed

---

a 1 Hebrew; Septuagint four hundred and fortieth   b 2 That is, about 90 feet long, 30 feet wide and 45 feet high or about 27 meters long, 9 meters wide and 14 meters high   c 3 That is, about 30 feet or about 9 meters; also in verses 16 and 20   d 3 That is, about 15 feet or about 4.5 meters; also in verses 23-26   e 6 That is, about 7 1/2 feet or about 2.3 meters; also in verses 10 and 24   f 6 That is, about 9 feet or about 2.7 meters   g 6 That is, about 11 feet or about 3.2 meters   h 8 Septuagint; Hebrew middle   i 17 That is, about 60 feet or about 18 meters the cherubim inside the innermost room of the temple, with their wings spread out. The wing of one cherub touched one wall, while the wing of the other touched the other wall, and their wings touched each other in the middle of the room. 28 He overlaid the cherubim with gold.

29 On the walls all around the temple, in both the inner and outer rooms, he carved cherubim, palm trees and open flowers. 30 He also covered the floors of both the inner and outer rooms of the temple with gold.

31 For the entrance to the inner sanctuary he made doors out of olive wood that were one fifth of the width of the sanctuary. 32 And on the two olive-wood doors he carved cherubim, palm trees and open flowers, and overlaid the cherubim and palm trees with hammered gold. 33 In the same way, for the entrance to the main hall he made doorframes out of olive wood that were one fourth of the width of the hall. 34 He also made two doors out of juniper wood, each having two leaves that turned in sockets. 35 He carved cherubim, palm trees and open flowers on them and overlaid them with gold hammered evenly over the carvings.

36 And he built the inner courtyard of three courses of dressed stone and one course of trimmed cedar beams.

37 The foundation of the temple of the LORD was laid in the fourth year, in the month of Ziv. 38 In the eleventh year in the month of Bul, the eighth month, the temple was finished in all its details according to its specifications. He had spent seven years building it.

Solomon Builds His Palace

7 It took Solomon thirteen years, however, to complete the construction of his palace. 2 He built the Palace of the Forest of Lebanon a hundred cubits long, fifty wide and thirty high,*a* with four rows of cedar columns supporting trimmed cedar beams. 3 It was roofed with cedar above the beams that rested on the columns — forty-five beams, fifteen to a row. 4 Its windows were placed high in sets of three, facing each other. 5 All the doorways had rectangular frames; they were in the front part in sets of three, facing each other.*b*

6 He made a colonnade fifty cubits long and thirty wide.*c* In front of it was a portico, and in front of that were pillars and an overhanging roof.

7 He built the throne hall, the Hall of Justice, where he was to judge, and he covered it with cedar from floor to ceiling.*d* 8 And the palace in which he was to live, set farther back, was similar in design. Solomon also made a palace like this hall for Pharaoh's daughter, whom he had married.

9 All these structures, from the outside to the great courtyard and from foundation to eaves, were made of blocks of high-grade stone cut to size and smoothed on their inner and outer faces. 10 The foundations were laid with large stones of good quality, some measuring ten cubits*e* and some eight.*f* 11 Above were high-grade stones, cut to size, and cedar beams. 12 The great courtyard was surrounded by a wall of three courses of dressed stone and one course of trimmed cedar beams, as was the inner courtyard of the temple of the LORD with its portico.

The Temple's Furnishings

13 King Solomon sent to Tyre and brought Huram,*g* 14 whose mother was a widow from the tribe of Naphtali and whose father was from Tyre and a skilled craftsman in bronze. Huram was filled with wisdom, with understanding and with knowledge

---

a 2 That is, about 150 feet long, 75 feet wide and 45 feet high or about 45 meters long, 23 meters wide and 14 meters high   *b 5* The meaning of the Hebrew for this verse is uncertain.   *c 6* That is, about 75 feet long and 45 feet wide or about 23 meters long and 14 meters wide   *d 7* Vulgate and Syriac; Hebrew *floor*   *e 10* That is, about 15 feet or about 4.5 meters; also in verse 23   *f 10* That is, about 12 feet or about 3.6 meters   *g 13* Hebrew *Hiram,* a variant of *Huram;* also in verses 40 and 45 to do all kinds of bronze work. He came to King Solomon and did all the work assigned to him.

¹⁵He cast two bronze pillars, each eighteen cubits high and twelve cubits in circumference.ᵃ ¹⁶He also made two capitals of cast bronze to set on the tops of the pillars; each capital was five cubitsᵇ high. ¹⁷A network of interwoven chains adorned the capitals on top of the pillars, seven for each capital. ¹⁸He made pomegranates in two rowsᶜ encircling each network to decorate the capitals on top of the pillars.ᵈ He did the same for each capital. ¹⁹The capitals on top of the pillars in the portico were in the shape of lilies, four cubitsᵉ high. ²⁰On the capitals of both pillars, above the bowl-shaped part next to the network, were the two hundred pomegranates in rows all around. ²¹He erected the pillars at the portico of the temple. The pillar to the south he named Jakinᶠ and the one to the north Boaz.ᵍ ²²The capitals on top were in the shape of lilies. And so the work on the pillars was completed.

²³He made the Sea of cast metal, circular in shape, measuring ten cubits from rim to rim and five cubits high. It took a line of thirty cubitsʰ to measure around it. ²⁴Below the rim, gourds encircled it—ten to a cubit. The gourds were cast in two rows in one piece with the Sea.

²⁵The Sea stood on twelve bulls, three facing north, three facing west, three facing south and three facing east. The Sea rested on top of them, and their hindquarters were toward the center. ²⁶It was a handbreadthⁱ in thickness, and its rim was like the rim of a cup, like a lily blossom. It held two thousand baths.ʲ

²⁷He also made ten movable stands of bronze; each was four cubits long, four wide and three high.ᵏ ²⁸This is how the stands were made: They had side panels attached to uprights. ²⁹On the panels between the uprights were lions, bulls and cherubim—and on the uprights as well. Above and below the lions and bulls were wreaths of hammered work. ³⁰Each stand had four bronze wheels with bronze axles, and each had a basin resting on four supports, cast with wreaths on each side. ³¹On the inside of the stand there was an opening that had a circular frame one cubitˡ deep. This opening was round, and with its basework it measured a cubit and a half.ᵐ Around its opening there was engraving. The panels of the stands were square, not round. ³²The four wheels were under the panels, and the axles of the wheels were attached to the stand. The diameter of each wheel was a cubit and a half. ³³The wheels were made like chariot wheels; the axles, rims, spokes and hubs were all of cast metal.

³⁴Each stand had four handles, one on each corner, projecting from the stand. ³⁵At the top of the stand there was a circular band half a cubitⁿ deep. The supports and panels were attached to the top of the stand. ³⁶He engraved cherubim, lions and palm trees on the surfaces of the supports and on the panels, in every available space, with wreaths all around. ³⁷This is the way he made the ten stands. They were all cast in the same molds and were identical in size and shape.

³⁸He then made ten bronze basins, each holding forty bathsᵒ and measuring four cubits across, one basin to go on each of the

---

ᵃ 15 That is, about 27 feet high and 18 feet in circumference or about 8.1 meters high and 5.4 meters in circumference ᵇ 16 That is, about 7 1/2 feet or about 2.3 meters; also in verse 23   ᶜ 18 Two Hebrew manuscripts and Septuagint; most Hebrew manuscripts *made the pillars, and there were two rows*   ᵈ 18 Many Hebrew manuscripts and Syriac; most Hebrew manuscripts *pomegranates*   ᵉ 19 That is, about 6 feet or about 1.8 meters; also in verse 38   ᶠ 21 *Jakin* probably means *he establishes.*   ᵍ 21 *Boaz* probably means *in him is strength.*   ʰ 23 That is, about 45 feet or about 14 meters   ⁱ 26 That is, about 3 inches or about 7.5 centimeters   ʲ 26 That is, about 12,000 gallons or about 44,000 liters; the Septuagint does not have this sentence.   ᵏ 27 That is, about 6 feet long and wide and about 4 1/2 feet high or about 1.8 meters long and wide and 1.4 meters high   ˡ 31 That is, about 18 inches or about 45 centimeters   ᵐ 31 That is, about 2 1/4 feet or about 68 centimeters; also in verse 32   ⁿ 35 That is, about 9 inches or about 23 centimeters   ᵒ 38 That is, about 240 gallons or about 880 liters ten stands. ³⁹He placed five of the stands on the south side of the temple and five on the north. He placed the Sea on the south side, at the southeast corner of the temple. ⁴⁰He also made the pots*ᵃ* and shovels and sprinkling bowls.

So Huram finished all the work he had undertaken for King Solomon in the temple of the Lord:

⁴¹ the two pillars;

the two bowl-shaped capitals on top of the pillars;

the two sets of network decorating the two bowl-shaped capitals on top of the pillars;

⁴² the four hundred pomegranates for the two sets of network (two rows of pomegranates for each network decorating the bowl-shaped capitals on top of the pillars);

⁴³ the ten stands with their ten basins;

⁴⁴ the Sea and the twelve bulls under it;

⁴⁵ the pots, shovels and sprinkling bowls.

All these objects that Huram made for King Solomon for the temple of the Lord were of burnished bronze. ⁴⁶The king had them cast in clay molds in the plain of the Jordan between Sukkoth and Zarethan. ⁴⁷Solomon left all these things unweighed, because there were so many; the weight of the bronze was not determined.

⁴⁸Solomon also made all the furnishings that were in the Lord's temple:

the golden altar;

the golden table on which was the bread of the Presence;

⁴⁹ the lampstands of pure gold (five on the right and five on the left, in front of the inner sanctuary);

the gold floral work and lamps and tongs;

⁵⁰ the pure gold basins, wick trimmers, sprinkling bowls, dishes and censers;

and the gold sockets for the doors of the innermost room, the Most Holy Place, and also for the doors of the main hall of the temple.

⁵¹When all the work King Solomon had done for the temple of the Lord was finished, he brought in the things his father David had dedicated — the silver and gold and the furnishings — and he placed them in the treasuries of the Lord's temple.

The Ark Brought to the Temple

8 Then King Solomon summoned into his presence at Jerusalem the elders of Israel, all the heads of the tribes and the chiefs of the Israelite families, to bring up the ark of the Lord's covenant from Zion, the City of David. ²All the Israelites came together to King Solomon at the time of the festival in the month of Ethanim, the seventh month.

³When all the elders of Israel had arrived, the priests took up the ark, ⁴and they brought up the ark of the Lord and the tent of meeting and all the sacred furnishings in it. The priests and Levites carried them up, ⁵and King Solomon and the entire assembly of Israel that had gathered about him were before the ark, sacrificing so many sheep and cattle that they could not be recorded or counted.

⁶The priests then brought the ark of the Lord's covenant to its place in the inner sanctuary of the temple, the Most Holy Place, and put it beneath the wings of the cherubim. ⁷The cherubim spread their wings over the place of the ark and overshadowed the ark and its carrying poles. ⁸These poles were so long that their ends could be seen from the Holy Place in front of the inner sanctuary, but not from outside the Holy Place; and they are still there today. ⁹There was nothing in the ark except the two stone tablets that Moses had placed in it at Horeb, where the Lord made a cov-

---

ᵃ 40 Many Hebrew manuscripts, Septuagint, Syriac and Vulgate (see also verse 45 and 2 Chron. 4:11); many other Hebrew manuscripts *basins* enant with the Israelites after they came out of Egypt.

¹⁰When the priests withdrew from the Holy Place, the cloud filled the temple of the Lord. ¹¹And the priests could not perform their service because of the cloud, for the glory of the Lord filled his temple.

¹²Then Solomon said, "The Lord has said that he would dwell in a dark cloud; ¹³I have indeed built a magnificent temple for you, a place for you to dwell forever."

¹⁴While the whole assembly of Israel was standing there, the king turned around and blessed them. ¹⁵Then he said:

"Praise be to the Lord, the God of Israel, who with his own hand has fulfilled what he promised with his own mouth to my father David. For he said, ¹⁶'Since the day I brought my people Israel out of Egypt, I have not chosen a city in any tribe of Israel to have a temple built so that my Name might be there, but I have chosen David to rule my people Israel.'

¹⁷"My father David had it in his heart to build a temple for the Name of the Lord, the God of Israel. ¹⁸But the Lord said to my father David, 'You did well to have it in your heart to build a temple for my Name. ¹⁹Nevertheless, you are not the one to build the temple, but your son, your own flesh and blood—he is the one who will build the temple for my Name.'

²⁰"The Lord has kept the promise he made: I have succeeded David my father and now I sit on the throne of Israel, just as the Lord promised, and I have built the temple for the Name of the Lord, the God of Israel. ²¹I have provided a place there for the ark, in which is the covenant of the Lord that he made with our ancestors when he brought them out of Egypt."

Solomon's Prayer of Dedication

²²Then Solomon stood before the altar of the Lord in front of the whole assembly of Israel, spread out his hands toward heaven ²³and said:

"Lord, the God of Israel, there is no God like you in heaven above or on earth below—you who keep your covenant of love with your servants who continue wholeheartedly in your way. ²⁴You have kept your promise to your servant David my father; with your mouth you have promised and with your hand you have fulfilled it—as it is today.

²⁵"Now Lord, the God of Israel, keep for your servant David my father the promises you made to him when you said, 'You shall never fail to have a successor to sit before me on the throne of Israel, if only your descendants are careful in all they do to walk before me faithfully as you have done.' ²⁶And now, God of Israel, let your word that you promised your servant David my father come true.

²⁷"But will God really dwell on earth? The heavens, even the highest heaven, cannot contain you. How much less this temple I have built! ²⁸Yet give attention to your servant's prayer and his plea for mercy, Lord my God. Hear the cry and the prayer that your servant is praying in your presence this day. ²⁹May your eyes be open toward this temple night and day, this place of which you said, 'My Name shall be there,' so that you will hear the prayer your servant prays toward this place. ³⁰Hear the supplication of your servant and of your people Israel when they pray toward this place. Hear from heaven, your dwelling place, and when you hear, forgive.

³¹"When anyone wrongs their neighbor and is required to take an oath and they come and swear the oath before your altar in this temple, ³²then hear from heaven and act. Judge between your servants, condemning the guilty by bringing

down on their heads what they have done, and vindicating the innocent by treating them in accordance with their innocence.

33"When your people Israel have been defeated by an enemy because they have sinned against you, and when they turn back to you and give praise to your name, praying and making supplication to you in this temple, 34then hear from heaven and forgive the sin of your people Israel and bring them back to the land you gave to their ancestors.

35"When the heavens are shut up and there is no rain because your people have sinned against you, and when they pray toward this place and give praise to your name and turn from their sin because you have afflicted them, 36then hear from heaven and forgive the sin of your servants, your people Israel. Teach them the right way to live, and send rain on the land you gave your people for an inheritance.

37"When famine or plague comes to the land, or blight or mildew, locusts or grasshoppers, or when an enemy besieges them in any of their cities, whatever disaster or disease may come, 38and when a prayer or plea is made by anyone among your people Israel—being aware of the afflictions of their own hearts, and spreading out their hands toward this temple— 39then hear from heaven, your dwelling place. Forgive and act; deal with everyone according to all they do, since you know their hearts (for you alone know every human heart), 40so that they will fear you all the time they live in the land you gave our ancestors.

41"As for the foreigner who does not belong to your people Israel but has come from a distant land because of your name— 42for they will hear of your great name and your mighty hand and your outstretched arm— when they come and pray toward this temple, 43then hear from heaven, your dwelling place. Do whatever the foreigner asks of you, so that all the peoples of the earth may know your name and fear you, as do your own people Israel, and may know that this house I have built bears your Name.

44"When your people go to war against their enemies, wherever you send them, and when they pray to the Lord toward the city you have chosen and the temple I have built for your Name, 45then hear from heaven their prayer and their plea, and uphold their cause.

46"When they sin against you—for there is no one who does not sin— and you become angry with them and give them over to their enemies, who take them captive to their own lands, far away or near; 47and if they have a change of heart in the land where they are held captive, and repent and plead with you in the land of their captors and say, 'We have sinned, we have done wrong, we have acted wickedly'; 48and if they turn back to you with all their heart and soul in the land of their enemies who took them captive, and pray to you toward the land you gave their ancestors, toward the city you have chosen and the temple I have built for your Name; 49then from heaven, your dwelling place, hear their prayer and their plea, and uphold their cause. 50And forgive your people, who have sinned against you; forgive all the offenses they have committed against you, and cause their captors to show them mercy; 51for they are your people and your inheritance, whom you brought out of Egypt, out of that iron-smelting furnace.

52"May your eyes be open to your servant's plea and to the plea of your people Israel, and may you listen to them whenever they cry out to you. 53For you singled them out from all the nations of the world to be your own inheritance, just as you declared through your servant Moses when you, Sovereign Lord, brought our ancestors out of Egypt."

54 When Solomon had finished all these prayers and supplications to the Lord, he rose from before the altar of the Lord, where he had been kneeling with his hands spread out toward heaven. 55 He stood and blessed the whole assembly of Israel in a loud voice, saying:

56 "Praise be to the Lord, who has given rest to his people Israel just as he promised. Not one word has failed of all the good promises he gave through his servant Moses. 57 May the Lord our God be with us as he was with our ancestors; may he never leave us nor forsake us. 58 May he turn our hearts to him, to walk in obedience to him and keep the commands, decrees and laws he gave our ancestors. 59 And may these words of mine, which I have prayed before the Lord, be near to the Lord our God day and night, that he may uphold the cause of his servant and the cause of his people Israel according to each day's need, 60 so that all the peoples of the earth may know that the Lord is God and that there is no other. 61 And may your hearts be fully committed to the Lord our God, to live by his decrees and obey his commands, as at this time."

The Dedication of the Temple

62 Then the king and all Israel with him offered sacrifices before the Lord. 63 Solomon offered a sacrifice of fellowship offerings to the Lord: twenty-two thousand cattle and a hundred and twenty thousand sheep and goats. So the king and all the Israelites dedicated the temple of the Lord.

64 On that same day the king consecrated the middle part of the courtyard in front of the temple of the Lord, and there he of-fered burnt offerings, grain offerings and the fat of the fellowship offerings, because the bronze altar that stood before the Lord was too small to hold the burnt offerings, the grain offerings and the fat of the fellowship offerings.

65 So Solomon observed the festival at that time, and all Israel with him — a vast assembly, people from Lebo Hamath to the Wadi of Egypt. They celebrated it before the Lord our God for seven days and seven days more, fourteen days in all. 66 On the following day he sent the people away. They blessed the king and then went home, joyful and glad in heart for all the good things the Lord had done for his servant David and his people Israel.

The Lord Appears to Solomon

9 When Solomon had finished building the temple of the Lord and the royal palace, and had achieved all he had desired to do, 2 the Lord appeared to him a second time, as he had appeared to him at Gibeon. 3 The Lord said to him:

"I have heard the prayer and plea you have made before me; I have consecrated this temple, which you have built, by putting my Name there forever. My eyes and my heart will always be there.

4 "As for you, if you walk before me faithfully with integrity of heart and uprightness, as David your father did, and do all I command and observe my decrees and laws, 5 I will establish your royal throne over Israel forever, as I promised David your father when I said, 'You shall never fail to have a successor on the throne of Israel.'

6 "But if you[a] or your descendants turn away from me and do not observe the commands and decrees I have given you[a] and go off to serve other gods and worship them, 7 then I will cut off Israel from the land I have

---

a 6 The Hebrew is plural.

given them and will reject this temple I have consecrated for my Name. Israel will then become a byword and an object of ridicule among all peoples. ⁸This temple will become a heap of rubble. All*ᵃ* who pass by will be appalled and will scoff and say, 'Why has the LORD done such a thing to this land and to this temple?' ⁹People will answer, 'Because they have forsaken the LORD their God, who brought their ancestors out of Egypt, and have embraced other gods, worshiping and serving them — that is why the LORD brought all this disaster on them.'"

Solomon's Other Activities

¹⁰At the end of twenty years, during which Solomon built these two buildings — the temple of the LORD and the royal palace — ¹¹King Solomon gave twenty towns in Galilee to Hiram king of Tyre, because Hiram had supplied him with all the cedar and juniper and gold he wanted. ¹²But when Hiram went from Tyre to see the towns that Solomon had given him, he was not pleased with them. ¹³"What kind of towns are these you have given me, my brother?" he asked. And he called them the Land of Kabul,*ᵇ* a name they have to this day. ¹⁴Now Hiram had sent to the king 120 talents*ᶜ* of gold.

¹⁵Here is the account of the forced labor King Solomon conscripted to build the LORD's temple, his own palace, the terraces,*ᵈ* the wall of Jerusalem, and Hazor, Megiddo and Gezer. ¹⁶(Pharaoh king of Egypt had attacked and captured Gezer. He had set it on fire. He killed its Canaanite inhabitants and then gave it as a wedding gift to his daughter, Solomon's wife. ¹⁷And Solomon rebuilt Gezer.) He built up Lower Beth Horon, ¹⁸Baalath, and Tadmor*ᵉ* in the desert, within his land, ¹⁹as well as all his store

cities and the towns for his chariots and for his horses*ᶠ* — whatever he desired to build in Jerusalem, in Lebanon and throughout all the territory he ruled.

²⁰There were still people left from the Amorites, Hittites, Perizzites, Hivites and Jebusites (these peoples were not Israelites). ²¹Solomon conscripted the descendants of all these peoples remaining in the land — whom the Israelites could not exterminate*ᵍ* — to serve as slave labor, as it is to this day. ²²But Solomon did not make slaves of any of the Israelites; they were his fighting men, his government officials, his officers, his captains, and the commanders of his chariots and charioteers. ²³They were also the chief officials in charge of Solomon's projects — 550 officials supervising those who did the work.

²⁴After Pharaoh's daughter had come up from the City of David to the palace Solomon had built for her, he constructed the terraces.

²⁵Three times a year Solomon sacrificed burnt offerings and fellowship offerings on the altar he had built for the LORD, burning incense before the LORD along with them, and so fulfilled the temple obligations.

²⁶King Solomon also built ships at Ezion Geber, which is near Elath in Edom, on the shore of the Red Sea.*ʰ* ²⁷And Hiram sent his men — sailors who knew the sea — to serve in the fleet with Solomon's men. ²⁸They sailed to Ophir and brought back 420 talents*ⁱ* of gold, which they delivered to King Solomon.

The Queen of Sheba Visits Solomon

10 When the queen of Sheba heard about the fame of Solomon and his relationship to the LORD, she came to test Solomon with hard questions. ²Arriving at Jerusalem with a very great caravan — with camels carrying

---

ᵃ 8 See some Septuagint manuscripts, Old Latin, Syriac, Arabic and Targum; Hebrew *And though this temple is now imposing, all*   *ᵇ 13* *Kabul* sounds like the Hebrew for *good-for-nothing.*   *ᶜ 14* That is, about 4 1/2 tons or about 4 metric tons   *ᵈ 15* Or *the Millo*; also in verse 24   *ᵉ 18* The Hebrew may also be read *Tamar.*   *ᶠ 19* Or *charioteers*   *ᵍ 21* The Hebrew term refers to the irrevocable giving over of things or persons to the LORD, often by totally destroying them.   *ʰ 26* Or *the Sea of Reeds*   *ⁱ 28* That is, about 16 tons or about 14 metric tons spices, large quantities of gold, and precious stones — she came to Solomon and talked with him about all that she had on her mind. ³Solomon answered all her questions; nothing was too hard for the king to explain to her. ⁴When the queen of Sheba saw all the wisdom of Solomon and the palace he had built, ⁵the food on his table, the seating of his officials, the attending servants in their robes, his cupbearers, and the burnt offerings he made at⁴ the temple of the Lord, she was overwhelmed.

⁶She said to the king, "The report I heard in my own country about your achievements and your wisdom is true. ⁷But I did not believe these things until I came and saw with my own eyes. Indeed, not even half was told me; in wisdom and wealth you have far exceeded the report I heard. ⁸How happy your people must be! How happy your officials, who continually stand before you and hear your wisdom! ⁹Praise be to the Lord your God, who has delighted in you and placed you on the throne of Israel. Because of the Lord's eternal love for Israel, he has made you king to maintain justice and righteousness."

¹⁰And she gave the king 120 talents⁵ of gold, large quantities of spices, and precious stones. Never again were so many spices brought in as those the queen of Sheba gave to King Solomon.

¹¹(Hiram's ships brought gold from Ophir; and from there they brought great cargoes of almugwood⁶ and precious stones. ¹²The king used the almugwood to make supports⁴ for the temple of the Lord and for the royal palace, and to make harps and lyres for the musicians. So much almugwood has never been imported or seen since that day.)

¹³King Solomon gave the queen of Sheba all she desired and asked for, besides what he had given her out of his royal bounty.

Then she left and returned with her retinue to her own country.

Solomon's Splendor

¹⁴The weight of the gold that Solomon received yearly was 666 talents,ᵉ ¹⁵not including the revenues from merchants and traders and from all the Arabian kings and the governors of the territories.

¹⁶King Solomon made two hundred large shields of hammered gold; six hundred shekelsᶠ of gold went into each shield. ¹⁷He also made three hundred small shields of hammered gold, with three minasᵍ of gold in each shield. The king put them in the Palace of the Forest of Lebanon.

¹⁸Then the king made a great throne covered with ivory and overlaid with fine gold. ¹⁹The throne had six steps, and its back had a rounded top. On both sides of the seat were armrests, with a lion standing beside each of them. ²⁰Twelve lions stood on the six steps, one at either end of each step. Nothing like it had ever been made for any other kingdom. ²¹All King Solomon's goblets were gold, and all the household articles in the Palace of the Forest of Lebanon were pure gold. Nothing was made of silver, because silver was considered of little value in Solomon's days. ²²The king had a fleet of trading shipsʰ at sea along with the ships of Hiram. Once every three years it returned, carrying gold, silver and ivory, and apes and baboons.

²³King Solomon was greater in riches and wisdom than all the other kings of the earth. ²⁴The whole world sought audience with Solomon to hear the wisdom God had put in his heart. ²⁵Year after year, everyone who came brought a gift — articles of silver and gold, robes, weapons and spices, and horses and mules.

²⁶Solomon accumulated chariots and horses; he had fourteen hundred chariots

---

a 5 Or *the ascent by which he went up to* a variant of *algumwood*; also in verse 12   *b 10* That is, about 4 1/2 tons or about 4 metric tons   *c 11* Probably a variant of *algumwood*; also in verse 12   *d 12* The meaning of the Hebrew for this word is uncertain.   *e 14* That is, about 25 tons or about 23 metric tons   *f 16* That is, about 15 pounds or about 6.9 kilograms; also in verse 29   *g 17* That is, about 3 3/4 pounds or about 1.7 kilograms; or perhaps reference is to double minas, that is, about 7 1/2 pounds or about 3.5 kilograms.   *h 22* Hebrew *of ships of Tarshish* and twelve thousand horses,*a* which he kept in the chariot cities and also with him in Jerusalem. 27The king made silver as common in Jerusalem as stones, and cedar as plentiful as sycamore-fig trees in the foothills. 28Solomon's horses were imported from Egypt and from Kue*b* — the royal merchants purchased them from Kue at the current price. 29They imported a chariot from Egypt for six hundred shekels of silver, and a horse for a hundred and fifty.*c* They also exported them to all the kings of the Hittites and of the Arameans.

Solomon's Wives

11 King Solomon, however, loved many foreign women besides Pharaoh's daughter — Moabites, Ammonites, Edomites, Sidonians and Hittites. 2They were from nations about which the LORD had told the Israelites, "You must not intermarry with them, because they will surely turn your hearts after their gods." Nevertheless, Solomon held fast to them in love. 3He had seven hundred wives of royal birth and three hundred concubines, and his wives led him astray. 4As Solomon grew old, his wives turned his heart after other gods, and his heart was not fully devoted to the LORD his God, as the heart of David his father had been. 5He followed Ashtoreth the goddess of the Sidonians, and Molek the detestable god of the Ammonites. 6So Solomon did evil in the eyes of the LORD; he did not follow the LORD completely, as David his father had done.

7On a hill east of Jerusalem, Solomon built a high place for Chemosh the detestable god of Moab, and for Molek the detestable god of the Ammonites. 8He did the same for all his foreign wives, who burned incense and offered sacrifices to their gods.

9The LORD became angry with Solomon because his heart had turned away from the LORD, the God of Israel, who had appeared to him twice. 10Although he had forbidden Solomon to follow other gods, Solomon did

not keep the LORD's command. 11So the LORD said to Solomon, "Since this is your attitude and you have not kept my covenant and my decrees, which I commanded you, I will most certainly tear the kingdom away from you and give it to one of your subordinates. 12Nevertheless, for the sake of David your father, I will not do it during your lifetime. I will tear it out of the hand of your son. 13Yet I will not tear the whole kingdom from him, but will give him one tribe for the sake of David my servant and for the sake of Jerusalem, which I have chosen."

Solomon's Adversaries

14Then the LORD raised up against Solomon an adversary, Hadad the Edomite, from the royal line of Edom. 15Earlier when David was fighting with Edom, Joab the commander of the army, who had gone up to bury the dead, had struck down all the men in Edom. 16Joab and all the Israelites stayed there for six months, until they had destroyed all the men in Edom. 17But Hadad, still only a boy, fled to Egypt with some Edomite officials who had served his father. 18They set out from Midian and went to Paran. Then taking people from Paran with them, they went to Egypt, to Pharaoh king of Egypt, who gave Hadad a house and land and provided him with food.

19Pharaoh was so pleased with Hadad that he gave him a sister of his own wife, Queen Tahpenes, in marriage. 20The sister of Tahpenes bore him a son named Genubath, whom Tahpenes brought up in the royal palace. There Genubath lived with Pharaoh's own children.

21While he was in Egypt, Hadad heard that David rested with his ancestors and that Joab the commander of the army was also dead. Then Hadad said to Pharaoh, "Let me go, that I may return to my own country."

22"What have you lacked here that you want to go back to your own country?" Pharaoh asked.

---

a 26 Or *charioteers*   *b 28* Probably *Cilicia*   *c 29* That is, about 3 3/4 pounds or about 1.7 kilograms

"Nothing," Hadad replied, "but do let me go!"

23And God raised up against Solomon another adversary, Rezon son of Eliada, who had fled from his master, Hadadezer king of Zobah. 24When David destroyed Zobah's army, Rezon gathered a band of men around him and became their leader; they went to Damascus, where they settled and took control. 25Rezon was Israel's adversary as long as Solomon lived, adding to the trouble caused by Hadad. So Rezon ruled in Aram and was hostile toward Israel.

Jeroboam Rebels Against Solomon

26Also, Jeroboam son of Nebat rebelled against the king. He was one of Solomon's officials, an Ephraimite from Zeredah, and his mother was a widow named Zeruah.

27Here is the account of how he rebelled against the king: Solomon had built the terraces*a* and had filled in the gap in the wall of the city of David his father. 28Now Jeroboam was a man of standing, and when Solomon saw how well the young man did his work, he put him in charge of the whole labor force of the tribes of Joseph.

29About that time Jeroboam was going out of Jerusalem, and Ahijah the prophet of Shiloh met him on the way, wearing a new cloak. The two of them were alone out in the country, 30and Ahijah took hold of the new cloak he was wearing and tore it into twelve pieces. 31Then he said to Jeroboam, "Take ten pieces for yourself, for this is what the LORD, the God of Israel, says: 'See, I am going to tear the kingdom out of Solomon's hand and give you ten tribes. 32But for the sake of my servant David and the city of Jerusalem, which I have chosen out of all the tribes of Israel, he will have one tribe. 33I will do this because they have*b* forsaken me and worshiped Ashtoreth the goddess of the Sidonians, Chemosh the god of the Moabites, and Molek the god of the Ammonites, and have not walked in obedience to me, nor done what is right in my eyes, nor kept my decrees and laws as David, Solomon's father, did.

34"But I will not take the whole kingdom out of Solomon's hand; I have made him ruler all the days of his life for the sake of David my servant, whom I chose and who obeyed my commands and decrees. 35I will take the kingdom from his son's hands and give you ten tribes. 36I will give one tribe to his son so that David my servant may always have a lamp before me in Jerusalem, the city where I chose to put my Name. 37However, as for you, I will take you, and you will rule over all that your heart desires; you will be king over Israel. 38If you do whatever I command you and walk in obedience to me and do what is right in my eyes by obeying my decrees and commands, as David my servant did, I will be with you. I will build you a dynasty as enduring as the one I built for David and will give Israel to you. 39I will humble David's descendants because of this, but not forever.'"

40Solomon tried to kill Jeroboam, but Jeroboam fled to Egypt, to Shishak the king, and stayed there until Solomon's death.

Solomon's Death

41As for the other events of Solomon's reign—all he did and the wisdom he displayed—are they not written in the book of the annals of Solomon? 42Solomon reigned in Jerusalem over all Israel forty years. 43Then he rested with his ancestors and was buried in the city of David his father. And Rehoboam his son succeeded him as king.

Israel Rebels Against Rehoboam

12 Rehoboam went to Shechem, for all Israel had gone there to make him king. 2When Jeroboam son of Nebat heard this (he was still in Egypt, where he had fled from King Solomon), he returned from*c* Egypt. 3So they sent for

---

a 27 Or *the Millo*   *b 33* Hebrew; Septuagint, Vulgate and Syriac *because he has*   *c 2* Or *he remained in*

Jeroboam, and he and the whole assembly of Israel went to Rehoboam and said to him: ⁴"Your father put a heavy yoke on us, but now lighten the harsh labor and the heavy yoke he put on us, and we will serve you."

⁵Rehoboam answered, "Go away for three days and then come back to me." So the people went away.

⁶Then King Rehoboam consulted the elders who had served his father Solomon during his lifetime. "How would you advise me to answer these people?" he asked.

⁷They replied, "If today you will be a servant to these people and serve them and give them a favorable answer, they will always be your servants."

⁸But Rehoboam rejected the advice the elders gave him and consulted the young men who had grown up with him and were serving him. ⁹He asked them, "What is your advice? How should we answer these people who say to me, 'Lighten the yoke your father put on us'?"

¹⁰The young men who had grown up with him replied, "These people have said to you, 'Your father put a heavy yoke on us, but make our yoke lighter.' Now tell them, 'My little finger is thicker than my father's waist. ¹¹My father laid on you a heavy yoke; I will make it even heavier. My father scourged you with whips; I will scourge you with scorpions.'"

¹²Three days later Jeroboam and all the people returned to Rehoboam, as the king had said, "Come back to me in three days." ¹³The king answered the people harshly. Rejecting the advice given him by the elders, ¹⁴he followed the advice of the young men and said, "My father made your yoke heavy; I will make it even heavier. My father scourged you with whips; I will scourge you with scorpions." ¹⁵So the king did not listen to the people, for this turn of events was from the LORD, to fulfill the word the LORD had spoken to Jeroboam son of Nebat through Ahijah the Shilonite.

¹⁶When all Israel saw that the king refused to listen to them, they answered the king:

"What share do we have in David,
    what part in Jesse's son?
To your tents, Israel!
    Look after your own house, David!"

So the Israelites went home. ¹⁷But as for the Israelites who were living in the towns of Judah, Rehoboam still ruled over them.

¹⁸King Rehoboam sent out Adoniram,ᵃ who was in charge of forced labor, but all Israel stoned him to death. King Rehoboam, however, managed to get into his chariot and escape to Jerusalem. ¹⁹So Israel has been in rebellion against the house of David to this day.

²⁰When all the Israelites heard that Jeroboam had returned, they sent and called him to the assembly and made him king over all Israel. Only the tribe of Judah remained loyal to the house of David.

²¹When Rehoboam arrived in Jerusalem, he mustered all Judah and the tribe of Benjamin — a hundred and eighty thousand able young men — to go to war against Israel and to regain the kingdom for Rehoboam son of Solomon.

²²But this word of God came to Shemaiah the man of God: ²³"Say to Rehoboam son of Solomon king of Judah, to all Judah and Benjamin, and to the rest of the people, ²⁴'This is what the LORD says: Do not go up to fight against your brothers, the Israelites. Go home, every one of you, for this is my doing.'" So they obeyed the word of the LORD and went home again, as the LORD had ordered.

Golden Calves at Bethel and Dan

²⁵Then Jeroboam fortified Shechem in the hill country of Ephraim and lived there. From there he went out and built up Peniel.ᵇ

²⁶Jeroboam thought to himself, "The

ᵃ 18 Some Septuagint manuscripts and Syriac (see also 4:6 and 5:14); Hebrew *Adoram*   ᵇ 25 Hebrew *Penuel*, a variant of *Peniel* kingdom will now likely revert to the house of David. 27If these people go up to offer sacrifices at the temple of the Lord in Jerusalem, they will again give their allegiance to their lord, Rehoboam king of Judah. They will kill me and return to King Rehoboam."

28After seeking advice, the king made two golden calves. He said to the people, "It is too much for you to go up to Jerusalem. Here are your gods, Israel, who brought you up out of Egypt." 29One he set up in Bethel, and the other in Dan. 30And this thing became a sin; the people came to worship the one at Bethel and went as far as Dan to worship the other.*a*

31Jeroboam built shrines on high places and appointed priests from all sorts of people, even though they were not Levites. 32He instituted a festival on the fifteenth day of the eighth month, like the festival held in Judah, and offered sacrifices on the altar. This he did in Bethel, sacrificing to the calves he had made. And at Bethel he also installed priests at the high places he had made. 33On the fifteenth day of the eighth month, a month of his own choosing, he offered sacrifices on the altar he had built at Bethel. So he instituted the festival for the Israelites and went up to the altar to make offerings.

The Man of God From Judah

13 By the word of the Lord a man of God came from Judah to Bethel, as Jeroboam was standing by the altar to make an offering. 2By the word of the Lord he cried out against the altar: "Altar, altar! This is what the Lord says: 'A son named Josiah will be born to the house of David. On you he will sacrifice the priests of the high places who make offerings here, and human bones will be burned on you.'" 3That same day the man of God gave a sign: "This is the sign the Lord has declared: The altar will be split apart and the ashes on it will be poured out."

4When King Jeroboam heard what the man of God cried out against the altar at Bethel, he stretched out his hand from the altar and said, "Seize him!" But the hand he stretched out toward the man shriveled up, so that he could not pull it back. 5Also, the altar was split apart and its ashes poured out according to the sign given by the man of God by the word of the Lord.

6Then the king said to the man of God, "Intercede with the Lord your God and pray for me that my hand may be restored." So the man of God interceded with the Lord, and the king's hand was restored and became as it was before.

7The king said to the man of God, "Come home with me for a meal, and I will give you a gift."

8But the man of God answered the king, "Even if you were to give me half your possessions, I would not go with you, nor would I eat bread or drink water here. 9For I was commanded by the word of the Lord: 'You must not eat bread or drink water or return by the way you came.'" 10So he took another road and did not return by the way he had come to Bethel.

11Now there was a certain old prophet living in Bethel, whose sons came and told him all that the man of God had done there that day. They also told their father what he had said to the king. 12Their father asked them, "Which way did he go?" And his sons showed him which road the man of God from Judah had taken. 13So he said to his sons, "Saddle the donkey for me." And when they had saddled the donkey for him, he mounted it 14and rode after the man of God. He found him sitting under an oak tree and asked, "Are you the man of God who came from Judah?"

"I am," he replied.

15So the prophet said to him, "Come home with me and eat."

16The man of God said, "I cannot turn back and go with you, nor can I eat bread or drink water with you in this place. 17I have

---

a 30 Probable reading of the original Hebrew text; Masoretic Text *people went to the one as far as Dan* been told by the word of the LORD: 'You must not eat bread or drink water there or return by the way you came.'"

¹⁸The old prophet answered, "I too am a prophet, as you are. And an angel said to me by the word of the LORD: 'Bring him back with you to your house so that he may eat bread and drink water.'" (But he was lying to him.) ¹⁹So the man of God returned with him and ate and drank in his house.

²⁰While they were sitting at the table, the word of the LORD came to the old prophet who had brought him back. ²¹He cried out to the man of God who had come from Judah, "This is what the LORD says: 'You have defied the word of the LORD and have not kept the command the LORD your God gave you. ²²You came back and ate bread and drank water in the place where he told you not to eat or drink. Therefore your body will not be buried in the tomb of your ancestors.'"

²³When the man of God had finished eating and drinking, the prophet who had brought him back saddled his donkey for him. ²⁴As he went on his way, a lion met him on the road and killed him, and his body was left lying on the road, with both the donkey and the lion standing beside it. ²⁵Some people who passed by saw the body lying there, with the lion standing beside the body, and they went and reported it in the city where the old prophet lived.

²⁶When the prophet who had brought him back from his journey heard of it, he said, "It is the man of God who defied the word of the LORD. The LORD has given him over to the lion, which has mauled him and killed him, as the word of the LORD had warned him."

²⁷The prophet said to his sons, "Saddle the donkey for me," and they did so. ²⁸Then he went out and found the body lying on the road, with the donkey and the lion standing beside it. The lion had neither eaten the body nor mauled the donkey. ²⁹So the prophet picked up the body of the man of God, laid it on the donkey, and brought it back to his own city to mourn for him and bury him. ³⁰Then he laid the body in his own tomb, and they mourned over him and said, "Alas, my brother!"

³¹After burying him, he said to his sons, "When I die, bury me in the grave where the man of God is buried; lay my bones beside his bones. ³²For the message he declared by the word of the LORD against the altar in Bethel and against all the shrines on the high places in the towns of Samaria will certainly come true."

³³Even after this, Jeroboam did not change his evil ways, but once more appointed priests for the high places from all sorts of people. Anyone who wanted to become a priest he consecrated for the high places. ³⁴This was the sin of the house of Jeroboam that led to its downfall and to its destruction from the face of the earth.

Ahijah's Prophecy Against Jeroboam

14 At that time Abijah son of Jeroboam became ill, ²and Jeroboam said to his wife, "Go, disguise yourself, so you won't be recognized as the wife of Jeroboam. Then go to Shiloh. Ahijah the prophet is there—the one who told me I would be king over this people. ³Take ten loaves of bread with you, some cakes and a jar of honey, and go to him. He will tell you what will happen to the boy." ⁴So Jeroboam's wife did what he said and went to Ahijah's house in Shiloh.

Now Ahijah could not see; his sight was gone because of his age. ⁵But the LORD had told Ahijah, "Jeroboam's wife is coming to ask you about her son, for he is ill, and you are to give her such and such an answer. When she arrives, she will pretend to be someone else."

⁶So when Ahijah heard the sound of her footsteps at the door, he said, "Come in, wife of Jeroboam. Why this pretense? I have been sent to you with bad news. ⁷Go, tell Jeroboam that this is what the LORD, the God of Israel, says: 'I raised you up from among the people and appointed you ruler over my people Israel. ⁸I tore the kingdom away from the house of David and gave it to you, but you have not been like my ser-

vant David, who kept my commands and followed me with all his heart, doing only what was right in my eyes. ⁹You have done more evil than all who lived before you. You have made for yourself other gods, idols made of metal; you have aroused my anger and turned your back on me.

¹⁰"Because of this, I am going to bring disaster on the house of Jeroboam. I will cut off from Jeroboam every last male in Israel—slave or free.ᵃ I will burn up the house of Jeroboam as one burns dung, until it is all gone. ¹¹Dogs will eat those belonging to Jeroboam who die in the city, and the birds will feed on those who die in the country. The LORD has spoken!'

¹²"As for you, go back home. When you set foot in your city, the boy will die. ¹³All Israel will mourn for him and bury him. He is the only one belonging to Jeroboam who will be buried, because he is the only one in the house of Jeroboam in whom the LORD, the God of Israel, has found anything good.

¹⁴"The LORD will raise up for himself a king over Israel who will cut off the family of Jeroboam. Even now this is beginning to happen.ᵇ ¹⁵And the LORD will strike Israel, so that it will be like a reed swaying in the water. He will uproot Israel from this good land that he gave to their ancestors and scatter them beyond the Euphrates River, because they aroused the LORD's anger by making Asherah poles.ᶜ ¹⁶And he will give Israel up because of the sins Jeroboam has committed and has caused Israel to commit."

¹⁷Then Jeroboam's wife got up and left and went to Tirzah. As soon as she stepped over the threshold of the house, the boy died. ¹⁸They buried him, and all Israel mourned for him, as the LORD had said through his servant the prophet Ahijah.

¹⁹The other events of Jeroboam's reign, his wars and how he ruled, are written in the book of the annals of the kings of Israel.

²⁰He reigned for twenty-two years and then rested with his ancestors. And Nadab his son succeeded him as king.

Rehoboam King of Judah

²¹Rehoboam son of Solomon was king in Judah. He was forty-one years old when he became king, and he reigned seventeen years in Jerusalem, the city the LORD had chosen out of all the tribes of Israel in which to put his Name. His mother's name was Naamah; she was an Ammonite.

²²Judah did evil in the eyes of the LORD. By the sins they committed they stirred up his jealous anger more than those who were before them had done. ²³They also set up for themselves high places, sacred stones and Asherah poles on every high hill and under every spreading tree. ²⁴There were even male shrine prostitutes in the land; the people engaged in all the detestable practices of the nations the LORD had driven out before the Israelites.

²⁵In the fifth year of King Rehoboam, Shishak king of Egypt attacked Jerusalem. ²⁶He carried off the treasures of the temple of the LORD and the treasures of the royal palace. He took everything, including all the gold shields Solomon had made. ²⁷So King Rehoboam made bronze shields to replace them and assigned these to the commanders of the guard on duty at the entrance to the royal palace. ²⁸Whenever the king went to the LORD's temple, the guards bore the shields, and afterward they returned them to the guardroom.

²⁹As for the other events of Rehoboam's reign, and all he did, are they not written in the book of the annals of the kings of Judah? ³⁰There was continual warfare between Rehoboam and Jeroboam. ³¹And Rehoboam rested with his ancestors and was buried with them in the City of David. His mother's name was Naamah; she was an Ammonite. And Abijahᵈ his son succeeded him as king.

ᵃ 10 Or Israel—every ruler or leader   ᵇ 14 The meaning of the Hebrew for this sentence is uncertain. ᶜ 15 That is, wooden symbols of the goddess Asherah; here and elsewhere in 1 Kings   ᵈ 31 Some Hebrew manuscripts and Septuagint (see also 2 Chron. 12:16); most Hebrew manuscripts Abijam

Abijah King of Judah

15 In the eighteenth year of the reign of Jeroboam son of Nebat, Abijah[a] became king of Judah, [2]and he reigned in Jerusalem three years. His mother's name was Maakah daughter of Abishalom.[b]

[3]He committed all the sins his father had done before him; his heart was not fully devoted to the LORD his God, as the heart of David his forefather had been. [4]Nevertheless, for David's sake the LORD his God gave him a lamp in Jerusalem by raising up a son to succeed him and by making Jerusalem strong. [5]For David had done what was right in the eyes of the LORD and had not failed to keep any of the LORD's commands all the days of his life—except in the case of Uriah the Hittite.

[6]There was war between Abijah[c] and Jeroboam throughout Abijah's lifetime. [7]As for the other events of Abijah's reign, and all he did, are they not written in the book of the annals of the kings of Judah? There was war between Abijah and Jeroboam. [8]And Abijah rested with his ancestors and was buried in the City of David. And Asa his son succeeded him as king.

Asa King of Judah

[9]In the twentieth year of Jeroboam king of Israel, Asa became king of Judah, [10]and he reigned in Jerusalem forty-one years. His grandmother's name was Maakah daughter of Abishalom.

[11]Asa did what was right in the eyes of the LORD, as his father David had done. [12]He expelled the male shrine prostitutes from the land and got rid of all the idols his ancestors had made. [13]He even deposed his grandmother Maakah from her position as queen mother, because she had made a repulsive image for the worship of Asherah. Asa cut it down and burned it in the Kidron Valley. [14]Although he did not remove the high places, Asa's heart was fully committed to the LORD all his life. [15]He brought into the temple of the LORD the silver and gold and the articles that he and his father had dedicated.

[16]There was war between Asa and Baasha king of Israel throughout their reigns. [17]Baasha king of Israel went up against Judah and fortified Ramah to prevent anyone from leaving or entering the territory of Asa king of Judah.

[18]Asa then took all the silver and gold that was left in the treasuries of the LORD's temple and of his own palace. He entrusted it to his officials and sent them to Ben-Hadad son of Tabrimmon, the son of Hezion, the king of Aram, who was ruling in Damascus. [19]"Let there be a treaty between me and you," he said, "as there was between my father and your father. See, I am sending you a gift of silver and gold. Now break your treaty with Baasha king of Israel so he will withdraw from me."

[20]Ben-Hadad agreed with King Asa and sent the commanders of his forces against the towns of Israel. He conquered Ijon, Dan, Abel Beth Maakah and all Kinnereth in addition to Naphtali. [21]When Baasha heard this, he stopped building Ramah and withdrew to Tirzah. [22]Then King Asa issued an order to all Judah—no one was exempt—and they carried away from Ramah the stones and timber Baasha had been using there. With them King Asa built up Geba in Benjamin, and also Mizpah.

[23]As for all the other events of Asa's reign, all his achievements, all he did and the cities he built, are they not written in the book of the annals of the kings of Judah? In his old age, however, his feet became diseased. [24]Then Asa rested with his ancestors and was buried with them in the city of his father David. And Jehoshaphat his son succeeded him as king.

---

a 1 Some Hebrew manuscripts and Septuagint (see also 2 Chron. 12:16); most Hebrew manuscripts *Abijam*; also in verses 7 and 8   *b 2* A variant of *Absalom*; also in verse 10   *c 6* Some Hebrew manuscripts and Syriac *Abijam* (that is, *Abijah*); most Hebrew manuscripts *Rehoboam*

Nadab King of Israel

²⁵Nadab son of Jeroboam became king of Israel in the second year of Asa king of Judah, and he reigned over Israel two years. ²⁶He did evil in the eyes of the Lord, following the ways of his father and committing the same sin his father had caused Israel to commit.

²⁷Baasha son of Ahijah from the tribe of Issachar plotted against him, and he struck him down at Gibbethon, a Philistine town, while Nadab and all Israel were besieging it. ²⁸Baasha killed Nadab in the third year of Asa king of Judah and succeeded him as king.

²⁹As soon as he began to reign, he killed Jeroboam's whole family. He did not leave Jeroboam anyone that breathed, but destroyed them all, according to the word of the Lord given through his servant Ahijah the Shilonite. ³⁰This happened because of the sins Jeroboam had committed and had caused Israel to commit, and because he aroused the anger of the Lord, the God of Israel.

³¹As for the other events of Nadab's reign, and all he did, are they not written in the book of the annals of the kings of Israel? ³²There was war between Asa and Baasha king of Israel throughout their reigns.

Baasha King of Israel

³³In the third year of Asa king of Judah, Baasha son of Ahijah became king of all Israel in Tirzah, and he reigned twenty-four years. ³⁴He did evil in the eyes of the Lord, following the ways of Jeroboam and committing the same sin Jeroboam had caused Israel to commit.

16 Then the word of the Lord came to Jehu son of Hanani concerning Baasha: ²"I lifted you up from the dust and appointed you ruler over my people Israel, but you followed the ways of Jeroboam and caused my people Israel to sin and to arouse my anger by their sins. ³So I am about to wipe out Baasha and his house, and I will make your house like that of Jeroboam son of Nebat. ⁴Dogs will eat those belonging to Baasha who die in the city, and birds will feed on those who die in the country."

⁵As for the other events of Baasha's reign, what he did and his achievements, are they not written in the book of the annals of the kings of Israel? ⁶Baasha rested with his ancestors and was buried in Tirzah. And Elah his son succeeded him as king.

⁷Moreover, the word of the Lord came through the prophet Jehu son of Hanani to Baasha and his house, because of all the evil he had done in the eyes of the Lord, arousing his anger by the things he did, becoming like the house of Jeroboam — and also because he destroyed it.

Elah King of Israel

⁸In the twenty-sixth year of Asa king of Judah, Elah son of Baasha became king of Israel, and he reigned in Tirzah two years.

⁹Zimri, one of his officials, who had command of half his chariots, plotted against him. Elah was in Tirzah at the time, getting drunk in the home of Arza, the palace administrator at Tirzah. ¹⁰Zimri came in, struck him down and killed him in the twenty-seventh year of Asa king of Judah. Then he succeeded him as king.

¹¹As soon as he began to reign and was seated on the throne, he killed off Baasha's whole family. He did not spare a single male, whether relative or friend. ¹²So Zimri destroyed the whole family of Baasha, in accordance with the word of the Lord spoken against Baasha through the prophet Jehu — ¹³because of all the sins Baasha and his son Elah had committed and had caused Israel to commit, so that they aroused the anger of the Lord, the God of Israel, by their worthless idols.

¹⁴As for the other events of Elah's reign, and all he did, are they not written in the book of the annals of the kings of Israel?

Zimri King of Israel

¹⁵In the twenty-seventh year of Asa king of Judah, Zimri reigned in Tirzah seven days. The army was encamped near

Gibbethon, a Philistine town. ¹⁶When the Israelites in the camp heard that Zimri had plotted against the king and murdered him, they proclaimed Omri, the commander of the army, king over Israel that very day there in the camp. ¹⁷Then Omri and all the Israelites with him withdrew from Gibbethon and laid siege to Tirzah. ¹⁸When Zimri saw that the city was taken, he went into the citadel of the royal palace and set the palace on fire around him. So he died, ¹⁹because of the sins he had committed, doing evil in the eyes of the LORD and following the ways of Jeroboam and committing the same sin Jeroboam had caused Israel to commit.

²⁰As for the other events of Zimri's reign, and the rebellion he carried out, are they not written in the book of the annals of the kings of Israel?

Omri King of Israel

²¹Then the people of Israel were split into two factions; half supported Tibni son of Ginath for king, and the other half supported Omri. ²²But Omri's followers proved stronger than those of Tibni son of Ginath. So Tibni died and Omri became king.

²³In the thirty-first year of Asa king of Judah, Omri became king of Israel, and he reigned twelve years, six of them in Tirzah. ²⁴He bought the hill of Samaria from Shemer for two talents[a] of silver and built a city on the hill, calling it Samaria, after Shemer, the name of the former owner of the hill.

²⁵But Omri did evil in the eyes of the LORD and sinned more than all those before him. ²⁶He followed completely the ways of Jeroboam son of Nebat, committing the same sin Jeroboam had caused Israel to commit, so that they aroused the anger of the LORD, the God of Israel, by their worthless idols.

²⁷As for the other events of Omri's reign, what he did and the things he achieved, are they not written in the book of the annals of the kings of Israel? ²⁸Omri rested with his ancestors and was buried in Samaria. And Ahab his son succeeded him as king.

Ahab Becomes King of Israel

²⁹In the thirty-eighth year of Asa king of Judah, Ahab son of Omri became king of Israel, and he reigned in Samaria over Israel twenty-two years. ³⁰Ahab son of Omri did more evil in the eyes of the LORD than any of those before him. ³¹He not only considered it trivial to commit the sins of Jeroboam son of Nebat, but he also married Jezebel daughter of Ethbaal king of the Sidonians, and began to serve Baal and worship him. ³²He set up an altar for Baal in the temple of Baal that he built in Samaria. ³³Ahab also made an Asherah pole and did more to arouse the anger of the LORD, the God of Israel, than did all the kings of Israel before him.

³⁴In Ahab's time, Hiel of Bethel rebuilt Jericho. He laid its foundations at the cost of his firstborn son Abiram, and he set up its gates at the cost of his youngest son Segub, in accordance with the word of the LORD spoken by Joshua son of Nun.

Elijah Announces a Great Drought

17 Now Elijah the Tishbite, from Tishbe[b] in Gilead, said to Ahab, "As the LORD, the God of Israel, lives, whom I serve, there will be neither dew nor rain in the next few years except at my word."

Elijah Fed by Ravens

²Then the word of the LORD came to Elijah: ³"Leave here, turn eastward and hide in the Kerith Ravine, east of the Jordan. ⁴You will drink from the brook, and I have directed the ravens to supply you with food there."

⁵So he did what the LORD had told him. He went to the Kerith Ravine, east of the Jordan, and stayed there. ⁶The ravens brought him bread and meat in the morn-

---

ing and bread and meat in the evening, and he drank from the brook.

Elijah and the Widow at Zarephath

⁷Some time later the brook dried up because there had been no rain in the land. ⁸Then the word of the Lord came to him: ⁹"Go at once to Zarephath in the region of Sidon and stay there. I have directed a widow there to supply you with food." ¹⁰So he went to Zarephath. When he came to the town gate, a widow was there gathering sticks. He called to her and asked, "Would you bring me a little water in a jar so I may have a drink?" ¹¹As she was going to get it, he called, "And bring me, please, a piece of bread."

¹²"As surely as the Lord your God lives," she replied, "I don't have any bread — only a handful of flour in a jar and a little olive oil in a jug. I am gathering a few sticks to take home and make a meal for myself and my son, that we may eat it — and die."

¹³Elijah said to her, "Don't be afraid. Go home and do as you have said. But first make a small loaf of bread for me from what you have and bring it to me, and then make something for yourself and your son. ¹⁴For this is what the Lord, the God of Israel, says: 'The jar of flour will not be used up and the jug of oil will not run dry until the day the Lord sends rain on the land.'"

¹⁵She went away and did as Elijah had told her. So there was food every day for Elijah and for the woman and her family. ¹⁶For the jar of flour was not used up and the jug of oil did not run dry, in keeping with the word of the Lord spoken by Elijah.

¹⁷Some time later the son of the woman who owned the house became ill. He grew worse and worse, and finally stopped breathing. ¹⁸She said to Elijah, "What do you have against me, man of God? Did you come to remind me of my sin and kill my son?"

¹⁹"Give me your son," Elijah replied. He took him from her arms, carried him to the upper room where he was staying, and laid

him on his bed. ²⁰Then he cried out to the Lord, "Lord my God, have you brought tragedy even on this widow I am staying with, by causing her son to die?" ²¹Then he stretched himself out on the boy three times and cried out to the Lord, "Lord my God, let this boy's life return to him!"

²²The Lord heard Elijah's cry, and the boy's life returned to him, and he lived. ²³Elijah picked up the child and carried him down from the room into the house. He gave him to his mother and said, "Look, your son is alive!"

²⁴Then the woman said to Elijah, "Now I know that you are a man of God and that the word of the Lord from your mouth is the truth."

Elijah and Obadiah

18 After a long time, in the third year, the word of the Lord came to Elijah: "Go and present yourself to Ahab, and I will send rain on the land." ²So Elijah went to present himself to Ahab.

Now the famine was severe in Samaria, ³and Ahab had summoned Obadiah, his palace administrator. (Obadiah was a devout believer in the Lord. ⁴While Jezebel was killing off the Lord's prophets, Obadiah had taken a hundred prophets and hidden them in two caves, fifty in each, and had supplied them with food and water.) ⁵Ahab had said to Obadiah, "Go through the land to all the springs and valleys. Maybe we can find some grass to keep the horses and mules alive so we will not have to kill any of our animals." ⁶So they divided the land they were to cover, Ahab going in one direction and Obadiah in another.

⁷As Obadiah was walking along, Elijah met him. Obadiah recognized him, bowed down to the ground, and said, "Is it really you, my lord Elijah?"

⁸"Yes," he replied. "Go tell your master, 'Elijah is here.'"

⁹"What have I done wrong," asked Obadiah, "that you are handing your servant over to Ahab to be put to death? ¹⁰As surely

as the LORD your God lives, there is not a nation or kingdom where my master has not sent someone to look for you. And whenever a nation or kingdom claimed you were not there, he made them swear they could not find you. ¹¹But now you tell me to go to my master and say, 'Elijah is here.' ¹²I don't know where the Spirit of the LORD may carry you when I leave you. If I go and tell Ahab and he doesn't find you, he will kill me. Yet I your servant have worshiped the LORD since my youth. ¹³Haven't you heard, my lord, what I did while Jezebel was killing the prophets of the LORD? I hid a hundred of the LORD's prophets in two caves, fifty in each, and supplied them with food and water. ¹⁴And now you tell me to go to my master and say, 'Elijah is here.' He will kill me!"

¹⁵Elijah said, "As the LORD Almighty lives, whom I serve, I will surely present myself to Ahab today."

Elijah on Mount Carmel

¹⁶So Obadiah went to meet Ahab and told him, and Ahab went to meet Elijah. ¹⁷When he saw Elijah, he said to him, "Is that you, you troubler of Israel?"

¹⁸"I have not made trouble for Israel," Elijah replied. "But you and your father's family have. You have abandoned the LORD's commands and have followed the Baals. ¹⁹Now summon the people from all over Israel to meet me on Mount Carmel. And bring the four hundred and fifty prophets of Baal and the four hundred prophets of Asherah, who eat at Jezebel's table."

²⁰So Ahab sent word throughout all Israel and assembled the prophets on Mount Carmel. ²¹Elijah went before the people and said, "How long will you waver between two opinions? If the LORD is God, follow him; but if Baal is God, follow him."

But the people said nothing.

²²Then Elijah said to them, "I am the only one of the LORD's prophets left, but Baal has four hundred and fifty prophets. ²³Get two bulls for us. Let Baal's prophets choose one for themselves, and let them cut it into pieces and put it on the wood but not set fire to it. I will prepare the other bull and put it on the wood but not set fire to it. ²⁴Then you call on the name of your god, and I will call on the name of the LORD. The god who answers by fire — he is God."

Then all the people said, "What you say is good."

²⁵Elijah said to the prophets of Baal, "Choose one of the bulls and prepare it first, since there are so many of you. Call on the name of your god, but do not light the fire." ²⁶So they took the bull given them and prepared it.

Then they called on the name of Baal from morning till noon. "Baal, answer us!" they shouted. But there was no response; no one answered. And they danced around the altar they had made.

²⁷At noon Elijah began to taunt them. "Shout louder!" he said. "Surely he is a god! Perhaps he is deep in thought, or busy, or traveling. Maybe he is sleeping and must be awakened." ²⁸So they shouted louder and slashed themselves with swords and spears, as was their custom, until their blood flowed. ²⁹Midday passed, and they continued their frantic prophesying until the time for the evening sacrifice. But there was no response, no one answered, no one paid attention.

³⁰Then Elijah said to all the people, "Come here to me." They came to him, and he repaired the altar of the LORD, which had been torn down. ³¹Elijah took twelve stones, one for each of the tribes descended from Jacob, to whom the word of the LORD had come, saying, "Your name shall be Israel." ³²With the stones he built an altar in the name of the LORD, and he dug a trench around it large enough to hold two seahs*a* of seed. ³³He arranged the wood, cut the bull into pieces and laid it on the wood. Then he said to them, "Fill four large jars

---

a 32 That is, probably about 24 pounds or about 11 kilograms with water and pour it on the offering and on the wood."

³⁴"Do it again," he said, and they did it again.

"Do it a third time," he ordered, and they did it the third time. ³⁵The water ran down around the altar and even filled the trench.

³⁶At the time of sacrifice, the prophet Elijah stepped forward and prayed: "Lᴏʀᴅ, the God of Abraham, Isaac and Israel, let it be known today that you are God in Israel and that I am your servant and have done all these things at your command. ³⁷Answer me, Lᴏʀᴅ, answer me, so these people will know that you, Lᴏʀᴅ, are God, and that you are turning their hearts back again."

³⁸Then the fire of the Lᴏʀᴅ fell and burned up the sacrifice, the wood, the stones and the soil, and also licked up the water in the trench.

³⁹When all the people saw this, they fell prostrate and cried, "The Lᴏʀᴅ — he is God! The Lᴏʀᴅ — he is God!"

⁴⁰Then Elijah commanded them, "Seize the prophets of Baal. Don't let anyone get away!" They seized them, and Elijah had them brought down to the Kishon Valley and slaughtered there.

⁴¹And Elijah said to Ahab, "Go, eat and drink, for there is the sound of a heavy rain." ⁴²So Ahab went off to eat and drink, but Elijah climbed to the top of Carmel, bent down to the ground and put his face between his knees.

⁴³"Go and look toward the sea," he told his servant. And he went up and looked.

"There is nothing there," he said.

Seven times Elijah said, "Go back."

⁴⁴The seventh time the servant reported, "A cloud as small as a man's hand is rising from the sea."

So Elijah said, "Go and tell Ahab, 'Hitch up your chariot and go down before the rain stops you.'"

⁴⁵Meanwhile, the sky grew black with clouds, the wind rose, a heavy rain started

falling and Ahab rode off to Jezreel. ⁴⁶The power of the Lᴏʀᴅ came on Elijah and, tucking his cloak into his belt, he ran ahead of Ahab all the way to Jezreel.

Elijah Flees to Horeb

19 Now Ahab told Jezebel everything Elijah had done and how he had killed all the prophets with the sword. ²So Jezebel sent a messenger to Elijah to say, "May the gods deal with me, be it ever so severely, if by this time tomorrow I do not make your life like that of one of them."

³Elijah was afraidᵃ and ran for his life. When he came to Beersheba in Judah, he left his servant there, ⁴while he himself went a day's journey into the wilderness. He came to a broom bush, sat down under it and prayed that he might die. "I have had enough, Lᴏʀᴅ," he said. "Take my life; I am no better than my ancestors." ⁵Then he lay down under the bush and fell asleep.

All at once an angel touched him and said, "Get up and eat." ⁶He looked around, and there by his head was some bread baked over hot coals, and a jar of water. He ate and drank and then lay down again.

⁷The angel of the Lᴏʀᴅ came back a second time and touched him and said, "Get up and eat, for the journey is too much for you." ⁸So he got up and ate and drank. Strengthened by that food, he traveled forty days and forty nights until he reached Horeb, the mountain of God. ⁹There he went into a cave and spent the night.

The Lᴏʀᴅ Appears to Elijah

And the word of the Lᴏʀᴅ came to him: "What are you doing here, Elijah?"

¹⁰He replied, "I have been very zealous for the Lᴏʀᴅ God Almighty. The Israelites have rejected your covenant, torn down your altars, and put your prophets to death with the sword. I am the only one left, and now they are trying to kill me too."

¹¹The Lᴏʀᴅ said, "Go out and stand on

ᵃ 3 Or *Elijah saw*

MY NAME IS ELIJAH

1 KINGS 19

First Kings 19 contains a story familiar to many. Elijah, having been used by God to demonstrate his power to his people beyond any doubt, having slain a host of pagan priests, and having outrun a chariot (see 1 Kings 18), experienced a panic attack. The burned-out prophet ran from Jezreel in central Israel all the way to Beersheba, the southernmost city of Judah. From there he went into the wilderness, collapsed under a broom bush and asked God to let him die.

Many of us know the disappointment and depression that can follow after we finally "make it to the top." Elijah had accomplished all a prophet could possibly do. But instead of finding satisfaction and safety in the God he knew to be all-powerful, he surrendered to fear (see 1 Kings 19:1–4). Even in this time of weakness, though, God provided food and direction, and Elijah continued his arduous journey for 40 more days, arriving at last at Horeb (Mount Sinai, where Moses had long ago received the Law). Here, though, Elijah continued to wallow in self-pity and depression.

God's question in verse 9 is a good one to consider if you're where Elijah was: "What are you doing here, Elijah?" Elijah's answer, though technically correct—or almost correct—came from his insanity rather than from the reality to be found in God's power and protection. He replied, "I have been very zealous for the LORD God Almighty. The Israelites have rejected your covenant, torn down your altars, and put your prophets to death with the sword. I am the only one left, and now they are trying to kill me too" (v. 10).

God didn't rebuke Elijah for his depression. Instead, he revealed himself to the despondent prophet. As instructed by the Lord, Elijah exited the cave, where he had been holding a one-man pity party, to wait on the mountain for the Lord to pass by (see v. 11). God's power was showcased in a great wind, in an earthquake and finally in a fire. But the Lord wasn't present in any of these spectacular events. At last, following the fire, God spoke to his prophet in a gentle whisper.

There's a vital lesson in Elijah's experience. Recovery isn't a pinnacle to be reached on an occasional mountain-top; it's a God-empowered process. We may have worked the principles. We may even be an Elijah, carrying the message of Christ-centered recovery to others. We may have experienced some great victories recently. Or we may be cowering and crying in the cave like Elijah, overwhelmed by fear or depression. No matter where we find ourselves, we need to turn down the volume of the tumult within and perk up our ears for that soothing whisper. God asks us to seek him daily in prayer and meditation on his Word, so that our fear and sense of failure can be displaced by an informed and growing faith.

the mountain in the presence of the LORD, for the LORD is about to pass by."

Then a great and powerful wind tore the mountains apart and shattered the rocks before the LORD, but the LORD was not in the wind. After the wind there was an earthquake, but the LORD was not in the earthquake. 12After the earthquake came a fire, but the LORD was not in the fire. And after the fire came a gentle whisper. 13When Elijah heard it, he pulled his cloak over his face and went out and stood at the mouth of the cave.

Then a voice said to him, "What are you doing here, Elijah?"

14He replied, "I have been very zealous for the LORD God Almighty. The Israelites have rejected your covenant, torn down your altars, and put your prophets to death with the sword. I am the only one left, and now they are trying to kill me too."

15The LORD said to him, "Go back the way you came, and go to the Desert of Damascus. When you get there, anoint Hazael king over Aram. 16Also, anoint Jehu son of Nimshi king over Israel, and anoint Elisha son of Shaphat from Abel Meholah to succeed you as prophet. 17Jehu will put to death any who escape the sword of Hazael, and Elisha will put to death any who escape the sword of Jehu. 18Yet I reserve seven thousand in Israel—all whose knees have not bowed down to Baal and whose mouths have not kissed him."

The Call of Elisha

19So Elijah went from there and found Elisha son of Shaphat. He was plowing with twelve yoke of oxen, and he himself was driving the twelfth pair. Elijah went up to him and threw his cloak around him. 20Elisha then left his oxen and ran after Elijah. "Let me kiss my father and mother goodbye," he said, "and then I will come with you."

"Go back," Elijah replied. "What have I done to you?"

21So Elisha left him and went back. He took his yoke of oxen and slaughtered them. He burned the plowing equipment to cook the meat and gave it to the people, and they ate. Then he set out to follow Elijah and became his servant.

Ben-Hadad Attacks Samaria

20 Now Ben-Hadad king of Aram mustered his entire army. Accompanied by thirty-two kings with their horses and chariots, he went up and besieged Samaria and attacked it. 2He sent messengers into the city to Ahab king of Israel, saying, "This is what Ben-Hadad says: 3'Your silver and gold are mine, and the best of your wives and children are mine.'"

4The king of Israel answered, "Just as you say, my lord the king. I and all I have are yours."

5The messengers came again and said, "This is what Ben-Hadad says: 'I sent to demand your silver and gold, your wives and your children. 6But about this time tomorrow I am going to send my officials to search your palace and the houses of your officials. They will seize everything you value and carry it away.'"

7The king of Israel summoned all the elders of the land and said to them, "See how this man is looking for trouble! When he sent for my wives and my children, my silver and my gold, I did not refuse him."

8The elders and the people all answered, "Don't listen to him or agree to his demands."

9So he replied to Ben-Hadad's messengers, "Tell my lord the king, 'Your servant will do all you demanded the first time, but this demand I cannot meet.'" They left and took the answer back to Ben-Hadad.

10Then Ben-Hadad sent another message to Ahab: "May the gods deal with me, be it ever so severely, if enough dust remains in Samaria to give each of my men a handful."

11The king of Israel answered, "Tell him: 'One who puts on his armor should not boast like one who takes it off.'"

12Ben-Hadad heard this message while

My Name Is Steve

I'M A BELIEVER WHO STRUGGLES WITH FOOD ADDICTION AND CODEPENDENCY

Please read in 1 Kings 19:1 – 18 the story of Elijah's breakdown and the Lord's gracious restoration of his prophet.

The first five years of my life were an idyllic time filled with Little League, friends, bicycles, ice cream and animal crackers. Then, for whatever reason, my mom and dad started drinking. Dad was a quiet drunk, but Mom was an angry drunk. The days of happy innocence were gone. My brother, Craig, and I would try to stop the abusive yelling, screaming and hitting between my parents. I was usually the one to cry out in desperation, "Please stop!"

To cope with this as a little boy, I used food in an effort to fill the emotional void that constantly nagged at me like an insatiable hunger. During my teen years I strived to gain my parents' attention by lying, manipulating, shoplifting and using vulgarity. I was confused, broken and angry about the insanity alcoholism had brought into my family. Mom's health later deteriorated because of her drinking, and she died of cirrhosis of the liver. She was gone and, shockingly, I was relieved.

Without telling my dad, I enlisted in the U.S. Air Force. God understood my brokenness and, totally without my knowledge, was watching over and relentlessly pursuing me. He sent me several Christian friends and acquaintances who shared the Good News with me. At a church service I accepted Christ in an act of sheer desperation. The change was profound, though, and it was good to feel peace. Still, my compulsive behaviors remained, and I struggled with feelings of rejection and betrayal. Somehow I managed to continue attending church and reading my Bible.

After my discharge I started college and met my wife. Our marriage soon became volatile. At first she was merely verbally and emotionally abusive, but her rages soon turned into physical abuse. I retreated further and further into myself, continuously trying to "fix" her problems and make our marriage happy. Within 18 months we had two babies. I needed to reach out and eventually talked to our pastor about our problems. He counseled me to pray harder and to read my Bible. Nothing changed, and I became confused and angry with God. One day I realized to my shock that the same thing that had happened to my dad had now happened to me. My daughters were going to grow up experiencing the same insane life I had endured as a child. I felt alone and hopeless. One night I found my wife and our older daughter embroiled in a violent argument. This was the act that finally destroyed our little family. Our marriage ended in divorce.

In 1 Kings 19 Elijah, failing to find satisfaction in God, surrendered to his fear and succumbed to self-pity, burnout and depression. And now, without a wife or family to give me significance, I too retreated into my own personal cave of despair. God questioned Elijah, asking pointedly, "What are you doing here, Elijah?" (1 Kings 19:9), and later he addressed his hurting prophet in a gentle whisper (see v. 12). My own gentle whisper came in the form of my new coworker. He invited me to visit his church, where I was introduced to Celebrate Recovery. Nudged by the Holy Spirit, I exited my cave and waited for the Lord to pass by (see v. 13). The following Friday night God tugged on my heart to join Celebrate Recovery. It was at that point that my journey toward recovery began.

Through working the principles I've learned to face myself. I was overwhelmed by the reality of my own compulsive behaviors, by my obsession to "fix" everyone around me. To attempt to tackle all of the problems at once, I realized, would be absolutely futile, a recipe for failure. Celebrate Recovery has taught me that recovery isn't something to be obtained, but it's a goal to strive for, a process. My lifelong search for significance and value has at long last brought me to a place where I've found meaning and personal worth in my relationship with Jesus Christ, my Higher Power. The opportunity to serve others allows me to help them find this same significance for themselves.

I'm by no means perfect, but my life journey continues in the honesty, grace and truth embodied in the Biblically-based principles of Celebrate Recovery. I'm grateful to Jesus Christ because he loves me and believes in me, and because he has saved me from myself and given me healthy self-esteem, love for others and, most of all, eternal life. His grace and truth are truly my refuge.

If we find ourselves cowering and seething in our own personal cares, like Elijah, there is hope. We'll find hope in attending the Celebrate Recovery group in our area, and in connecting on a deeper level with our Higher Power, Jesus Christ. He is ever present, and the Celebrate Recovery group is a safe place in which to find restoration and renewal.

he and the kings were drinking in their tents,[a] and he ordered his men: "Prepare to attack." So they prepared to attack the city.

Ahab Defeats Ben-Hadad

13 Meanwhile a prophet came to Ahab king of Israel and announced, "This is what the LORD says: 'Do you see this vast army? I will give it into your hand today, and then you will know that I am the LORD.'"

14 "But who will do this?" asked Ahab.

The prophet replied, "This is what the LORD says: 'The junior officers under the provincial commanders will do it.'"

"And who will start the battle?" he asked.

The prophet answered, "You will."

15 So Ahab summoned the 232 junior officers under the provincial commanders. Then he assembled the rest of the Israelites, 7,000 in all. 16 They set out at noon while Ben-Hadad and the 32 kings allied with him were in their tents getting drunk. 17 The junior officers under the provincial commanders went out first.

Now Ben-Hadad had dispatched scouts, who reported, "Men are advancing from Samaria."

18 He said, "If they have come out for peace, take them alive; if they have come out for war, take them alive."

19 The junior officers under the provincial commanders marched out of the city with the army behind them 20 and each one struck down his opponent. At that, the Arameans fled, with the Israelites in pursuit. But Ben-Hadad king of Aram escaped on horseback with some of his horsemen. 21 The king of Israel advanced and overpowered the horses and chariots and inflicted heavy losses on the Arameans.

22 Afterward, the prophet came to the king of Israel and said, "Strengthen your position and see what must be done, because next spring the king of Aram will attack you again."

23 Meanwhile, the officials of the king of Aram advised him, "Their gods are gods of the hills. That is why they were too strong for us. But if we fight them on the plains, surely we will be stronger than they. 24 Do this: Remove all the kings from their commands and replace them with other officers. 25 You must also raise an army like the one you lost — horse for horse and chariot for chariot — so we can fight Israel on the plains. Then surely we will be stronger than they." He agreed with them and acted accordingly.

26 The next spring Ben-Hadad mustered the Arameans and went up to Aphek to fight against Israel. 27 When the Israelites were also mustered and given provisions, they marched out to meet them. The Israelites camped opposite them like two small flocks of goats, while the Arameans covered the countryside.

28 The man of God came up and told the king of Israel, "This is what the LORD says: 'Because the Arameans think the LORD is a god of the hills and not a god of the valleys, I will deliver this vast army into your hands, and you will know that I am the LORD.'"

29 For seven days they camped opposite each other, and on the seventh day the battle was joined. The Israelites inflicted a hundred thousand casualties on the Aramean foot soldiers in one day. 30 The rest of them escaped to the city of Aphek, where the wall collapsed on twenty-seven thousand of them. And Ben-Hadad fled to the city and hid in an inner room.

31 His officials said to him, "Look, we have heard that the kings of Israel are merciful. Let us go to the king of Israel with sackcloth around our waists and ropes around our heads. Perhaps he will spare your life."

32 Wearing sackcloth around their waists and ropes around their heads, they went to the king of Israel and said, "Your servant Ben-Hadad says: 'Please let me live.'"

The king answered, "Is he still alive? He is my brother."

---

a 12 Or in Sukkoth; also in verse 16

[33] The men took this as a good sign and were quick to pick up his word. "Yes, your brother Ben-Hadad!" they said.

"Go and get him," the king said. When Ben-Hadad came out, Ahab had him come up into his chariot.

[34] "I will return the cities my father took from your father," Ben-Hadad offered. "You may set up your own market areas in Damascus, as my father did in Samaria."

Ahab said, "On the basis of a treaty I will set you free." So he made a treaty with him, and let him go.

A Prophet Condemns Ahab

[35] By the word of the LORD one of the company of the prophets said to his companion, "Strike me with your weapon," but he refused.

[36] So the prophet said, "Because you have not obeyed the LORD, as soon as you leave me a lion will kill you." And after the man went away, a lion found him and killed him.

[37] The prophet found another man and said, "Strike me, please." So the man struck him and wounded him. [38] Then the prophet went and stood by the road waiting for the king. He disguised himself with his headband down over his eyes. [39] As the king passed by, the prophet called out to him, "Your servant went into the thick of the battle, and someone came to me with a captive and said, 'Guard this man. If he is missing, it will be your life for his life, or you must pay a talent[a] of silver.' [40] While your servant was busy here and there, the man disappeared."

"That is your sentence," the king of Israel said. "You have pronounced it yourself."

[41] Then the prophet quickly removed the headband from his eyes, and the king of Israel recognized him as one of the prophets. [42] He said to the king, "This is what the LORD says: 'You have set free a man I had determined should die.[b] Therefore it

is your life for his life, your people for his people.'" [43] Sullen and angry, the king of Israel went to his palace in Samaria.

Naboth's Vineyard

21 Some time later there was an incident involving a vineyard belonging to Naboth the Jezreelite. The vineyard was in Jezreel, close to the palace of Ahab king of Samaria. [2] Ahab said to Naboth, "Let me have your vineyard to use for a vegetable garden, since it is close to my palace. In exchange I will give you a better vineyard or, if you prefer, I will pay you whatever it is worth."

[3] But Naboth replied, "The LORD forbid that I should give you the inheritance of my ancestors."

[4] So Ahab went home, sullen and angry because Naboth the Jezreelite had said, "I will not give you the inheritance of my ancestors." He lay on his bed sulking and refused to eat.

[5] His wife Jezebel came in and asked him, "Why are you so sullen? Why won't you eat?"

[6] He answered her, "Because I said to Naboth the Jezreelite, 'Sell me your vineyard; or if you prefer, I will give you another vineyard in its place.' But he said, 'I will not give you my vineyard.'"

[7] Jezebel his wife said, "Is this how you act as king over Israel? Get up and eat! Cheer up. I'll get you the vineyard of Naboth the Jezreelite."

[8] So she wrote letters in Ahab's name, placed his seal on them, and sent them to the elders and nobles who lived in Naboth's city with him. [9] In those letters she wrote:

"Proclaim a day of fasting and seat Naboth in a prominent place among the people. [10] But seat two scoundrels opposite him and have them bring charges that he has cursed both God and the king. Then take him out and stone him to death."

---

[a] 39   That is, about 75 pounds or about 34 kilograms   [b] 42   The Hebrew term refers to the irrevocable giving over of things or persons to the LORD, often by totally destroying them.

¹¹So the elders and nobles who lived in Naboth's city did as Jezebel directed in the letters she had written to them. ¹²They proclaimed a fast and seated Naboth in a prominent place among the people. ¹³Then two scoundrels came and sat opposite him and brought charges against Naboth before the people, saying, "Naboth has cursed both God and the king." So they took him outside the city and stoned him to death. ¹⁴Then they sent word to Jezebel: "Naboth has been stoned to death."

¹⁵As soon as Jezebel heard that Naboth had been stoned to death, she said to Ahab, "Get up and take possession of the vineyard of Naboth the Jezreelite that he refused to sell you. He is no longer alive, but dead." ¹⁶When Ahab heard that Naboth was dead, he got up and went down to take possession of Naboth's vineyard.

¹⁷Then the word of the LORD came to Elijah the Tishbite: ¹⁸"Go down to meet Ahab king of Israel, who rules in Samaria. He is now in Naboth's vineyard, where he has gone to take possession of it. ¹⁹Say to him, 'This is what the LORD says: Have you not murdered a man and seized his property?' Then say to him, 'This is what the LORD says: In the place where dogs licked up Naboth's blood, dogs will lick up your blood—yes, yours!' "

²⁰Ahab said to Elijah, "So you have found me, my enemy!"

"I have found you," he answered, "because you have sold yourself to do evil in the eyes of the LORD. ²¹He says, 'I am going to bring disaster on you. I will wipe out your descendants and cut off from Ahab every last male in Israel—slave or free.ᵃ ²²I will make your house like that of Jeroboam son of Nebat and that of Baasha son of Ahijah, because you have aroused my anger and have caused Israel to sin.'

²³"And also concerning Jezebel the LORD says: 'Dogs will devour Jezebel by the wall ofᵇ Jezreel.'

²⁴"Dogs will eat those belonging to Ahab who die in the city, and the birds will feed on those who die in the country."

²⁵(There was never anyone like Ahab, who sold himself to do evil in the eyes of the LORD, urged on by Jezebel his wife. ²⁶He behaved in the vilest manner by going after idols, like the Amorites the LORD drove out before Israel.)

²⁷When Ahab heard these words, he tore his clothes, put on sackcloth and fasted. He lay in sackcloth and went around meekly.

²⁸Then the word of the LORD came to Elijah the Tishbite: ²⁹"Have you noticed how Ahab has humbled himself before me? Because he has humbled himself, I will not bring this disaster in his day, but I will bring it on his house in the days of his son."

Micaiah Prophesies Against Ahab

22 For three years there was no war between Aram and Israel. ²But in the third year Jehoshaphat king of Judah went down to see the king of Israel. ³The king of Israel had said to his officials, "Don't you know that Ramoth Gilead belongs to us and yet we are doing nothing to retake it from the king of Aram?"

⁴So he asked Jehoshaphat, "Will you go with me to fight against Ramoth Gilead?"

Jehoshaphat replied to the king of Israel, "I am as you are, my people as your people, my horses as your horses." ⁵But Jehoshaphat also said to the king of Israel, "First seek the counsel of the LORD."

⁶So the king of Israel brought together the prophets—about four hundred men—and asked them, "Shall I go to war against Ramoth Gilead, or shall I refrain?"

"Go," they answered, "for the Lord will give it into the king's hand."

⁷But Jehoshaphat asked, "Is there no longer a prophet of the LORD here whom we can inquire of?"

⁸The king of Israel answered Jehosha-

ᵃ 21 Or Israel—every ruler or leader   ᵇ 23 Most Hebrew manuscripts; a few Hebrew manuscripts, Vulgate and Syriac (see also 2 Kings 9:26) the plot of ground at phat, "There is still one prophet through whom we can inquire of the LORD, but I hate him because he never prophesies anything good about me, but always bad. He is Micaiah son of Imlah."

"The king should not say such a thing," Jehoshaphat replied.

9So the king of Israel called one of his officials and said, "Bring Micaiah son of Imlah at once."

10Dressed in their royal robes, the king of Israel and Jehoshaphat king of Judah were sitting on their thrones at the threshing floor by the entrance of the gate of Samaria, with all the prophets prophesying before them. 11Now Zedekiah son of Kenaanah had made iron horns and he declared, "This is what the LORD says: 'With these you will gore the Arameans until they are destroyed.'"

12All the other prophets were prophesying the same thing. "Attack Ramoth Gilead and be victorious," they said, "for the LORD will give it into the king's hand."

13The messenger who had gone to summon Micaiah said to him, "Look, the other prophets without exception are predicting success for the king. Let your word agree with theirs, and speak favorably."

14But Micaiah said, "As surely as the LORD lives, I can tell him only what the LORD tells me."

15When he arrived, the king asked him, "Micaiah, shall we go to war against Ramoth Gilead, or not?"

"Attack and be victorious," he answered, "for the LORD will give it into the king's hand."

16The king said to him, "How many times must I make you swear to tell me nothing but the truth in the name of the LORD?"

17Then Micaiah answered, "I saw all Israel scattered on the hills like sheep without a shepherd, and the LORD said, 'These people have no master. Let each one go home in peace.'"

18The king of Israel said to Jehoshaphat, "Didn't I tell you that he never prophesies anything good about me, but only bad?"

19Micaiah continued, "Therefore hear the word of the LORD: I saw the LORD sitting on his throne with all the multitudes of heaven standing around him on his right and on his left. 20And the LORD said, 'Who will entice Ahab into attacking Ramoth Gilead and going to his death there?'

"One suggested this, and another that. 21Finally, a spirit came forward, stood before the LORD and said, 'I will entice him.'

22"'By what means?' the LORD asked.

"'I will go out and be a deceiving spirit in the mouths of all his prophets,' he said.

"'You will succeed in enticing him,' said the LORD. 'Go and do it.'

23"So now the LORD has put a deceiving spirit in the mouths of all these prophets of yours. The LORD has decreed disaster for you."

24Then Zedekiah son of Kenaanah went up and slapped Micaiah in the face. "Which way did the spirit from[a] the LORD go when he went from me to speak to you?" he asked.

25Micaiah replied, "You will find out on the day you go to hide in an inner room."

26The king of Israel then ordered, "Take Micaiah and send him back to Amon the ruler of the city and to Joash the king's son 27and say, 'This is what the king says: Put this fellow in prison and give him nothing but bread and water until I return safely.'"

28Micaiah declared, "If you ever return safely, the LORD has not spoken through me." Then he added, "Mark my words, all you people!"

Ahab Killed at Ramoth Gilead

29So the king of Israel and Jehoshaphat king of Judah went up to Ramoth Gilead. 30The king of Israel said to Jehoshaphat, "I will enter the battle in disguise, but you wear your royal robes." So the king of Israel disguised himself and went into battle.

---

a 24 Or *Spirit of*

³¹Now the king of Aram had ordered his thirty-two chariot commanders, "Do not fight with anyone, small or great, except the king of Israel." ³²When the chariot commanders saw Jehoshaphat, they thought, "Surely this is the king of Israel." So they turned to attack him, but when Jehoshaphat cried out, ³³the chariot commanders saw that he was not the king of Israel and stopped pursuing him.

³⁴But someone drew his bow at random and hit the king of Israel between the sections of his armor. The king told his chariot driver, "Wheel around and get me out of the fighting. I've been wounded." ³⁵All day long the battle raged, and the king was propped up in his chariot facing the Arameans. The blood from his wound ran onto the floor of the chariot, and that evening he died. ³⁶As the sun was setting, a cry spread through the army: "Every man to his town. Every man to his land!"

³⁷So the king died and was brought to Samaria, and they buried him there. ³⁸They washed the chariot at a pool in Samaria (where the prostitutes bathed),ᵃ and the dogs licked up his blood, as the word of the LORD had declared.

³⁹As for the other events of Ahab's reign, including all he did, the palace he built and adorned with ivory, and the cities he fortified, are they not written in the book of the annals of the kings of Israel? ⁴⁰Ahab rested with his ancestors. And Ahaziah his son succeeded him as king.

Jehoshaphat King of Judah

⁴¹Jehoshaphat son of Asa became king of Judah in the fourth year of Ahab king of Israel. ⁴²Jehoshaphat was thirty-five years old when he became king, and he reigned in Jerusalem twenty-five years. His mother's name was Azubah daughter of Shilhi. ⁴³In everything he followed the ways of his father Asa and did not stray from them; he did what was right in the eyes of the LORD. The high places, however, were not removed, and the people continued to offer sacrifices and burn incense there.ᵇ ⁴⁴Jehoshaphat was also at peace with the king of Israel.

⁴⁵As for the other events of Jehoshaphat's reign, the things he achieved and his military exploits, are they not written in the book of the annals of the kings of Judah? ⁴⁶He rid the land of the rest of the male shrine prostitutes who remained there even after the reign of his father Asa. ⁴⁷There was then no king in Edom; a provincial governor ruled.

⁴⁸Now Jehoshaphat built a fleet of trading shipsᶜ to go to Ophir for gold, but they never set sail — they were wrecked at Ezion Geber. ⁴⁹At that time Ahaziah son of Ahab said to Jehoshaphat, "Let my men sail with yours," but Jehoshaphat refused.

⁵⁰Then Jehoshaphat rested with his ancestors and was buried with them in the city of David his father. And Jehoram his son succeeded him as king.

Ahaziah King of Israel

⁵¹Ahaziah son of Ahab became king of Israel in Samaria in the seventeenth year of Jehoshaphat king of Judah, and he reigned over Israel two years. ⁵²He did evil in the eyes of the LORD, because he followed the ways of his father and mother and of Jeroboam son of Nebat, who caused Israel to sin. ⁵³He served and worshiped Baal and aroused the anger of the LORD, the God of Israel, just as his father had done.

ᵃ 38 Or *Samaria and cleaned the weapons*   ᵇ 43 In Hebrew texts this sentence (22:43b) is numbered 22:44, and 22:44-53 is numbered 22:45-54.   ᶜ 48 Hebrew *of ships of Tarshish*

2 Kings

At a Glance

The book of 2 Kings continues the saga of 1 Kings — the tragedy of two nations headed for destruction and captivity. The records of the kings of Israel and Judah are reviewed here. Nineteen kings of Israel expand evil and lead the people into destruction and captivity. In Judah, godly kings occasionally emerge to carry out reforms. In the end, though, sin outweighs righteousness, and Judah too is led off into captivity. The decline and collapse of these two kingdoms occurred because the people failed to heed the warnings of God's messengers. Again, God demonstrates his control of history and his plan for all people.

In spite of the darkness, the book contains points of light. God sends prophets that perform miracles and fulfill past prophecies. Elisha is anointed as Elijah's successor and becomes known as a great miracle worker. The light of the prophets within the dark days of Israel offers us encouragement as we proceed in recovery. No matter how dark our days have been, no matter how deep we've been in darkness, God always sends a light. We've been rescued from overwhelming darkness by the light of Jesus Christ. In our journey we may still encounter days that seem dark, but we need to remember that Jesus is the light, and in him there is no darkness (see John 8:12; 1 John 1:5). Our responsibility is to walk toward his light, even if those around us continue to choose darkness.

Recovery Themes in 2 Kings

The LORD's Judgment on Ahaziah

1 After Ahab's death, Moab rebelled against Israel. ²Now Ahaziah had fallen through the lattice of his upper room in Samaria and injured himself. So he sent messengers, saying to them, "Go and consult Baal-Zebub, the god of Ekron, to see if I will recover from this injury."

³But the angel of the LORD said to Elijah the Tishbite, "Go up and meet the messengers of the king of Samaria and ask them, 'Is it because there is no God in Israel that you are going off to consult Baal-Zebub, the god of Ekron?' ⁴Therefore this is what the LORD says: 'You will not leave the bed you are lying on. You will certainly die!'" So Elijah went.

⁵When the messengers returned to the king, he asked them, "Why have you come back?"

⁶"A man came to meet us," they replied. "And he said to us, 'Go back to the king who sent you and tell him, "This is what the LORD says: Is it because there is no God in Israel that you are sending messengers to consult Baal-Zebub, the god of Ekron? Therefore you will not leave the bed you are lying on. You will certainly die!"'"

⁷The king asked them, "What kind of man was it who came to meet you and told you this?"

⁸They replied, "He had a garment of hair*ᵃ* and had a leather belt around his waist."

The king said, "That was Elijah the Tishbite."

⁹Then he sent to Elijah a captain with his company of fifty men. The captain went up to Elijah, who was sitting on the top of a hill, and said to him, "Man of God, the king says, 'Come down!'"

¹⁰Elijah answered the captain, "If I am a man of God, may fire come down from heaven and consume you and your fifty men!" Then fire fell from heaven and consumed the captain and his men.

¹¹At this the king sent to Elijah another captain with his fifty men. The captain said to him, "Man of God, this is what the king says, 'Come down at once!'"

¹²"If I am a man of God," Elijah replied, "may fire come down from heaven and consume you and your fifty men!" Then the fire of God fell from heaven and consumed him and his fifty men.

¹³So the king sent a third captain with his fifty men. This third captain went up and fell on his knees before Elijah. "Man of God," he begged, "please have respect for my life and the lives of these fifty men, your servants! ¹⁴See, fire has fallen from heaven and consumed the first two captains and all their men. But now have respect for my life!"

¹⁵The angel of the LORD said to Elijah, "Go down with him; do not be afraid of him." So Elijah got up and went down with him to the king.

¹⁶He told the king, "This is what the LORD says: Is it because there is no God in Israel for you to consult that you have sent messengers to consult Baal-Zebub, the god of Ekron? Because you have done this, you will never leave the bed you are lying on. You will certainly die!" ¹⁷So he died, according to the word of the LORD that Elijah had spoken.

Because Ahaziah had no son, Joram*ᵇ* succeeded him as king in the second year of Jehoram son of Jehoshaphat king of Judah. ¹⁸As for all the other events of Ahaziah's reign, and what he did, are they not written in the book of the annals of the kings of Israel?

Elijah Taken Up to Heaven

2 When the LORD was about to take Elijah up to heaven in a whirlwind, Elijah and Elisha were on their way from Gilgal. ²Elijah said to Elisha, "Stay here; the LORD has sent me to Bethel."

But Elisha said, "As surely as the LORD lives and as you live, I will not leave you." So they went down to Bethel.

ᵃ 8 Or *He was a hairy man*   *ᵇ 17* Hebrew *Jehoram,* a variant of *Joram*

³The company of the prophets at Bethel came out to Elisha and asked, "Do you know that the LORD is going to take your master from you today?"

"Yes, I know," Elisha replied, "so be quiet."

⁴Then Elijah said to him, "Stay here, Elisha; the LORD has sent me to Jericho."

And he replied, "As surely as the LORD lives and as you live, I will not leave you." So they went to Jericho.

⁵The company of the prophets at Jericho went up to Elisha and asked him, "Do you know that the LORD is going to take your master from you today?"

"Yes, I know," he replied, "so be quiet."

⁶Then Elijah said to him, "Stay here; the LORD has sent me to the Jordan."

And he replied, "As surely as the LORD lives and as you live, I will not leave you." So the two of them walked on.

⁷Fifty men from the company of the prophets went and stood at a distance, facing the place where Elijah and Elisha had stopped at the Jordan. ⁸Elijah took his cloak, rolled it up and struck the water with it. The water divided to the right and to the left, and the two of them crossed over on dry ground.

⁹When they had crossed, Elijah said to Elisha, "Tell me, what can I do for you before I am taken from you?"

"Let me inherit a double portion of your spirit," Elisha replied.

¹⁰"You have asked a difficult thing," Elijah said, "yet if you see me when I am taken from you, it will be yours—otherwise, it will not."

¹¹As they were walking along and talking together, suddenly a chariot of fire and horses of fire appeared and separated the two of them, and Elijah went up to heaven in a whirlwind. ¹²Elisha saw this and cried out, "My father! My father! The chariots and horsemen of Israel!" And Elisha saw him no more. Then he took hold of his garment and tore it in two.

¹³Elisha then picked up Elijah's cloak that had fallen from him and went back and stood on the bank of the Jordan. ¹⁴He took the cloak that had fallen from Elijah and struck the water with it. "Where now is the LORD, the God of Elijah?" he asked. When he struck the water, it divided to the right and to the left, and he crossed over.

¹⁵The company of the prophets from Jericho, who were watching, said, "The spirit of Elijah is resting on Elisha." And they went to meet him and bowed to the ground before him. ¹⁶"Look," they said, "we your servants have fifty able men. Let them go and look for your master. Perhaps the Spirit of the LORD has picked him up and set him down on some mountain or in some valley."

"No," Elisha replied, "do not send them."

¹⁷But they persisted until he was too embarrassed to refuse. So he said, "Send them." And they sent fifty men, who searched for three days but did not find him. ¹⁸When they returned to Elisha, who was staying in Jericho, he said to them, "Didn't I tell you not to go?"

Healing of the Water

¹⁹The people of the city said to Elisha, "Look, our lord, this town is well situated, as you can see, but the water is bad and the land is unproductive."

²⁰"Bring me a new bowl," he said, "and put salt in it." So they brought it to him.

²¹Then he went out to the spring and threw the salt into it, saying, "This is what the LORD says: 'I have healed this water. Never again will it cause death or make the land unproductive.'" ²²And the water has remained pure to this day, according to the word Elisha had spoken.

Elisha Is Jeered

²³From there Elisha went up to Bethel. As he was walking along the road, some boys came out of the town and jeered at him. "Get out of here, baldy!" they said. "Get out of here, baldy!" ²⁴He turned around, looked at them and called down a curse on them in the name of the LORD. Then two bears came out of the woods and mauled

forty-two of the boys. 25And he went on to Mount Carmel and from there returned to Samaria.

Moab Revolts

3 Joram*a* son of Ahab became king of Israel in Samaria in the eighteenth year of Jehoshaphat king of Judah, and he reigned twelve years. 2He did evil in the eyes of the Lord, but not as his father and mother had done. He got rid of the sacred stone of Baal that his father had made. 3Nevertheless he clung to the sins of Jeroboam son of Nebat, which he had caused Israel to commit; he did not turn away from them.

4Now Mesha king of Moab raised sheep, and he had to pay the king of Israel a tribute of a hundred thousand lambs and the wool of a hundred thousand rams. 5But after Ahab died, the king of Moab rebelled against the king of Israel. 6So at that time King Joram set out from Samaria and mobilized all Israel. 7He also sent this message to Jehoshaphat king of Judah: "The king of Moab has rebelled against me. Will you go with me to fight against Moab?"

"I will go with you," he replied. "I am as you are, my people as your people, my horses as your horses."

8"By what route shall we attack?" he asked.

"Through the Desert of Edom," he answered.

9So the king of Israel set out with the king of Judah and the king of Edom. After a roundabout march of seven days, the army had no more water for themselves or for the animals with them.

10"What!" exclaimed the king of Israel. "Has the Lord called us three kings together only to deliver us into the hands of Moab?"

11But Jehoshaphat asked, "Is there no prophet of the Lord here, through whom we may inquire of the Lord?"

An officer of the king of Israel answered, "Elisha son of Shaphat is here. He used to pour water on the hands of Elijah.*b*"

12Jehoshaphat said, "The word of the Lord is with him." So the king of Israel and Jehoshaphat and the king of Edom went down to him.

13Elisha said to the king of Israel, "Why do you want to involve me? Go to the prophets of your father and the prophets of your mother."

"No," the king of Israel answered, "because it was the Lord who called us three kings together to deliver us into the hands of Moab."

14Elisha said, "As surely as the Lord Almighty lives, whom I serve, if I did not have respect for the presence of Jehoshaphat king of Judah, I would not pay any attention to you. 15But now bring me a harpist."

While the harpist was playing, the hand of the Lord came on Elisha 16and he said, "This is what the Lord says: I will fill this valley with pools of water. 17For this is what the Lord says: You will see neither wind nor rain, yet this valley will be filled with water, and you, your cattle and your other animals will drink. 18This is an easy thing in the eyes of the Lord; he will also deliver Moab into your hands. 19You will overthrow every fortified city and every major town. You will cut down every good tree, stop up all the springs, and ruin every good field with stones."

20The next morning, about the time for offering the sacrifice, there it was — water flowing from the direction of Edom! And the land was filled with water.

21Now all the Moabites had heard that the kings had come to fight against them; so every man, young and old, who could bear arms was called up and stationed on the border. 22When they got up early in the morning, the sun was shining on the water. To the Moabites across the way, the water looked red — like blood. 23"That's blood!" they said. "Those kings must have fought

---

a 1 Hebrew *Jehoram*, a variant of *Joram*; also in verse 6   *b 11* That is, he was Elijah's personal servant.

and slaughtered each other. Now to the plunder, Moab!"

24But when the Moabites came to the camp of Israel, the Israelites rose up and fought them until they fled. And the Israelites invaded the land and slaughtered the Moabites. 25They destroyed the towns, and each man threw a stone on every good field until it was covered. They stopped up all the springs and cut down every good tree. Only Kir Hareseth was left with its stones in place, but men armed with slings surrounded it and attacked it.

26When the king of Moab saw that the battle had gone against him, he took with him seven hundred swordsmen to break through to the king of Edom, but they failed. 27Then he took his firstborn son, who was to succeed him as king, and offered him as a sacrifice on the city wall. The fury against Israel was great; they withdrew and returned to their own land.

The Widow's Olive Oil

4 The wife of a man from the company of the prophets cried out to Elisha, "Your servant my husband is dead, and you know that he revered the LORD. But now his creditor is coming to take my two boys as his slaves."

2Elisha replied to her, "How can I help you? Tell me, what do you have in your house?"

"Your servant has nothing there at all," she said, "except a small jar of olive oil."

3Elisha said, "Go around and ask all your neighbors for empty jars. Don't ask for just a few. 4Then go inside and shut the door behind you and your sons. Pour oil into all the jars, and as each is filled, put it to one side."

5She left him and shut the door behind her and her sons. They brought the jars to her and she kept pouring. 6When all the jars were full, she said to her son, "Bring me another one."

But he replied, "There is not a jar left." Then the oil stopped flowing.

7She went and told the man of God, and he said, "Go, sell the oil and pay your debts. You and your sons can live on what is left."

The Shunammite's Son Restored to Life

8One day Elisha went to Shunem. And a well-to-do woman was there, who urged him to stay for a meal. So whenever he came by, he stopped there to eat. 9She said to her husband, "I know that this man who often comes our way is a holy man of God. 10Let's make a small room on the roof and put in it a bed and a table, a chair and a lamp for him. Then he can stay there whenever he comes to us."

11One day when Elisha came, he went up to his room and lay down there. 12He said to his servant Gehazi, "Call the Shunammite." So he called her, and she stood before him. 13Elisha said to him, "Tell her, 'You have gone to all this trouble for us. Now what can be done for you? Can we speak on your behalf to the king or the commander of the army?'"

She replied, "I have a home among my own people."

14"What can be done for her?" Elisha asked.

Gehazi said, "She has no son, and her husband is old."

15Then Elisha said, "Call her." So he called her, and she stood in the doorway. 16"About this time next year," Elisha said, "you will hold a son in your arms."

"No, my lord!" she objected. "Please, man of God, don't mislead your servant!"

17But the woman became pregnant, and the next year about that same time she gave birth to a son, just as Elisha had told her.

18The child grew, and one day he went out to his father, who was with the reapers. 19He said to his father, "My head! My head!"

His father told a servant, "Carry him to his mother." 20After the servant had lifted him up and carried him to his mother, the boy sat on her lap until noon, and then he died. 21She went up and laid him on the bed of the man of God, then shut the door and went out.

^{22}She called her husband and said, "Please send me one of the servants and a donkey so I can go to the man of God quickly and return."

^{23}"Why go to him today?" he asked. "It's not the New Moon or the Sabbath."

"That's all right," she said.

^{24}She saddled the donkey and said to her servant, "Lead on; don't slow down for me unless I tell you." ^{25}So she set out and came to the man of God at Mount Carmel.

When he saw her in the distance, the man of God said to his servant Gehazi, "Look! There's the Shunammite! ^{26}Run to meet her and ask her, 'Are you all right? Is your husband all right? Is your child all right?'"

"Everything is all right," she said.

^{27}When she reached the man of God at the mountain, she took hold of his feet. Gehazi came over to push her away, but the man of God said, "Leave her alone! She is in bitter distress, but the Lord has hidden it from me and has not told me why."

^{28}"Did I ask you for a son, my lord?" she said. "Didn't I tell you, 'Don't raise my hopes'?"

^{29}Elisha said to Gehazi, "Tuck your cloak into your belt, take my staff in your hand and run. Don't greet anyone you meet, and if anyone greets you, do not answer. Lay my staff on the boy's face."

^{30}But the child's mother said, "As surely as the Lord lives and as you live, I will not leave you." So he got up and followed her.

^{31}Gehazi went on ahead and laid the staff on the boy's face, but there was no sound or response. So Gehazi went back to meet Elisha and told him, "The boy has not awakened."

^{32}When Elisha reached the house, there was the boy lying dead on his couch. ^{33}He went in, shut the door on the two of them and prayed to the Lord. ^{34}Then he got on the bed and lay on the boy, mouth to mouth, eyes to eyes, hands to hands. As he stretched himself out on him, the boy's body grew warm. ^{35}Elisha turned away and walked back and forth in the room and then got on the bed and stretched out

on him once more. The boy sneezed seven times and opened his eyes.

^{36}Elisha summoned Gehazi and said, "Call the Shunammite." And he did. When she came, he said, "Take your son." ^{37}She came in, fell at his feet and bowed to the ground. Then she took her son and went out.

Death in the Pot

^{38}Elisha returned to Gilgal and there was a famine in that region. While the company of the prophets was meeting with him, he said to his servant, "Put on the large pot and cook some stew for these prophets."

^{39}One of them went out into the fields to gather herbs and found a wild vine and picked as many of its gourds as his garment could hold. When he returned, he cut them up into the pot of stew, though no one knew what they were. ^{40}The stew was poured out for the men, but as they began to eat it, they cried out, "Man of God, there is death in the pot!" And they could not eat it.

^{41}Elisha said, "Get some flour." He put it into the pot and said, "Serve it to the people to eat." And there was nothing harmful in the pot.

Feeding of a Hundred

^{42}A man came from Baal Shalishah, bringing the man of God twenty loaves of barley bread baked from the first ripe grain, along with some heads of new grain. "Give it to the people to eat," Elisha said.

^{43}"How can I set this before a hundred men?" his servant asked.

But Elisha answered, "Give it to the people to eat. For this is what the Lord says: 'They will eat and have some left over.'" ^{44}Then he set it before them, and they ate and had some left over, according to the word of the Lord.

Naaman Healed of Leprosy

5 Now Naaman was commander of the army of the king of Aram. He was a great man in the sight of his master and highly regarded, because

through him the Lord had given victory to Aram. He was a valiant soldier, but he had leprosy.[a]

²Now bands of raiders from Aram had gone out and had taken captive a young girl from Israel, and she served Naaman's wife. ³She said to her mistress, "If only my master would see the prophet who is in Samaria! He would cure him of his leprosy."

⁴Naaman went to his master and told him what the girl from Israel had said. ⁵"By all means, go," the king of Aram replied. "I will send a letter to the king of Israel." So Naaman left, taking with him ten talents[b] of silver, six thousand shekels[c] of gold and ten sets of clothing. ⁶The letter that he took to the king of Israel read: "With this letter I am sending my servant Naaman to you so that you may cure him of his leprosy."

⁷As soon as the king of Israel read the letter, he tore his robes and said, "Am I God? Can I kill and bring back to life? Why does this fellow send someone to me to be cured of his leprosy? See how he is trying to pick a quarrel with me!"

⁸When Elisha the man of God heard that the king of Israel had torn his robes, he sent him this message: "Why have you torn your robes? Have the man come to me and he will know that there is a prophet in Israel." ⁹So Naaman went with his horses and chariots and stopped at the door of Elisha's house. ¹⁰Elisha sent a messenger to say to him, "Go, wash yourself seven times in the Jordan, and your flesh will be restored and you will be cleansed."

¹¹But Naaman went away angry and said, "I thought that he would surely come out to me and stand and call on the name of the Lord his God, wave his hand over the spot and cure me of my leprosy. ¹²Are not Abana and Pharpar, the rivers of Damascus, better than all the waters of Israel? Couldn't I wash in them and be cleansed?" So he turned and went off in a rage.

¹³Naaman's servants went to him and said, "My father, if the prophet had told you to do some great thing, would you not have done it? How much more, then, when he tells you, 'Wash and be cleansed'!" ¹⁴So he went down and dipped himself in the Jordan seven times, as the man of God had told him, and his flesh was restored and became clean like that of a young boy.

¹⁵Then Naaman and all his attendants went back to the man of God. He stood before him and said, "Now I know that there is no God in all the world except in Israel. So please accept a gift from your servant."

¹⁶The prophet answered, "As surely as the Lord lives, whom I serve, I will not accept a thing." And even though Naaman urged him, he refused.

¹⁷"If you will not," said Naaman, "please let me, your servant, be given as much earth as a pair of mules can carry, for your servant will never again make burnt offerings and sacrifices to any other god but the Lord. ¹⁸But may the Lord forgive your servant for this one thing: When my master enters the temple of Rimmon to bow down and he is leaning on my arm and I have to bow there also—when I bow down in the temple of Rimmon, may the Lord forgive your servant for this."

¹⁹"Go in peace," Elisha said.

After Naaman had traveled some distance, ²⁰Gehazi, the servant of Elisha the man of God, said to himself, "My master was too easy on Naaman, this Aramean, by not accepting from him what he brought. As surely as the Lord lives, I will run after him and get something from him."

²¹So Gehazi hurried after Naaman. When Naaman saw him running toward him, he got down from the chariot to meet him. "Is everything all right?" he asked.

²²"Everything is all right," Gehazi answered. "My master sent me to say, 'Two young men from the company of the prophets have just come to me from the

---

[a] 1 The Hebrew for *leprosy* was used for various diseases affecting the skin; also in verses 3, 6, 7, 11 and 27.
[b] 5 That is, about 750 pounds or about 340 kilograms   [c] 5 That is, about 150 pounds or about 69 kilograms

hill country of Ephraim. Please give them a talent^a of silver and two sets of clothing.'"

²³"By all means, take two talents," said Naaman. He urged Gehazi to accept them, and then tied up the two talents of silver in two bags, with two sets of clothing. He gave them to two of his servants, and they carried them ahead of Gehazi. ²⁴When Gehazi came to the hill, he took the things from the servants and put them away in the house. He sent the men away and they left.

²⁵When he went in and stood before his master, Elisha asked him, "Where have you been, Gehazi?"

"Your servant didn't go anywhere," Gehazi answered.

²⁶But Elisha said to him, "Was not my spirit with you when the man got down from his chariot to meet you? Is this the time to take money or to accept clothes — or olive groves and vineyards, or flocks and herds, or male and female slaves? ²⁷Naaman's leprosy will cling to you and to your descendants forever." Then Gehazi went from Elisha's presence and his skin was leprous — it had become as white as snow.

An Axhead Floats

6 The company of the prophets said to Elisha, "Look, the place where we meet with you is too small for us. ²Let us go to the Jordan, where each of us can get a pole; and let us build a place there for us to meet."

And he said, "Go."

³Then one of them said, "Won't you please come with your servants?"

"I will," Elisha replied. ⁴And he went with them.

They went to the Jordan and began to cut down trees. ⁵As one of them was cutting down a tree, the iron axhead fell into the water. "Oh no, my lord!" he cried out. "It was borrowed!"

⁶The man of God asked, "Where did it fall?" When he showed him the place, Elisha cut a stick and threw it there, and made the iron float. ⁷"Lift it out," he said. Then the man reached out his hand and took it.

Elisha Traps Blinded Arameans

⁸Now the king of Aram was at war with Israel. After conferring with his officers, he said, "I will set up my camp in such and such a place."

⁹The man of God sent word to the king of Israel: "Beware of passing that place, because the Arameans are going down there." ¹⁰So the king of Israel checked on the place indicated by the man of God. Time and again Elisha warned the king, so that he was on his guard in such places.

¹¹This enraged the king of Aram. He summoned his officers and demanded of them, "Tell me! Which of us is on the side of the king of Israel?"

¹²"None of us, my lord the king," said one of his officers, "but Elisha, the prophet who is in Israel, tells the king of Israel the very words you speak in your bedroom."

¹³"Go, find out where he is," the king ordered, "so I can send men and capture him." The report came back: "He is in Dothan." ¹⁴Then he sent horses and chariots and a strong force there. They went by night and surrounded the city.

¹⁵When the servant of the man of God got up and went out early the next morning, an army with horses and chariots had surrounded the city. "Oh no, my lord! What shall we do?" the servant asked.

¹⁶"Don't be afraid," the prophet answered. "Those who are with us are more than those who are with them."

¹⁷And Elisha prayed, "Open his eyes, LORD, so that he may see." Then the LORD opened the servant's eyes, and he looked and saw the hills full of horses and chariots of fire all around Elisha.

¹⁸As the enemy came down toward him, Elisha prayed to the LORD, "Strike this army with blindness." So he struck them with blindness, as Elisha had asked.

¹⁹Elisha told them, "This is not the road

---

^a 22 That is, about 75 pounds or about 34 kilograms

and this is not the city. Follow me, and I will lead you to the man you are looking for." And he led them to Samaria.

²⁰After they entered the city, Elisha said, "LORD, open the eyes of these men so they can see." Then the LORD opened their eyes and they looked, and there they were, inside Samaria.

²¹When the king of Israel saw them, he asked Elisha, "Shall I kill them, my father? Shall I kill them?"

²²"Do not kill them," he answered. "Would you kill those you have captured with your own sword or bow? Set food and water before them so that they may eat and drink and then go back to their master." ²³So he prepared a great feast for them, and after they had finished eating and drinking, he sent them away, and they returned to their master. So the bands from Aram stopped raiding Israel's territory.

Famine in Besieged Samaria

²⁴Some time later, Ben-Hadad king of Aram mobilized his entire army and marched up and laid siege to Samaria. ²⁵There was a great famine in the city; the siege lasted so long that a donkey's head sold for eighty shekels^a of silver, and a quarter of a cab^b of seed pods^c for five shekels.^{d}

²⁶As the king of Israel was passing by on the wall, a woman cried to him, "Help me, my lord the king!"

²⁷The king replied, "If the LORD does not help you, where can I get help for you? From the threshing floor? From the winepress?" ²⁸Then he asked her, "What's the matter?"

She answered, "This woman said to me, 'Give up your son so we may eat him today, and tomorrow we'll eat my son.' ²⁹So we cooked my son and ate him. The next day I said to her, 'Give up your son so we may eat him,' but she had hidden him."

³⁰When the king heard the woman's words, he tore his robes. As he went along the wall, the people looked, and they saw that, under his robes, he had sackcloth on his body. ³¹He said, "May God deal with me, be it ever so severely, if the head of Elisha son of Shaphat remains on his shoulders today!"

³²Now Elisha was sitting in his house, and the elders were sitting with him. The king sent a messenger ahead, but before he arrived, Elisha said to the elders, "Don't you see how this murderer is sending someone to cut off my head? Look, when the messenger comes, shut the door and hold it shut against him. Is not the sound of his master's footsteps behind him?" ³³While he was still talking to them, the messenger came down to him.

The king said, "This disaster is from the LORD. Why should I wait for the LORD any longer?"

7 Elisha replied, "Hear the word of the LORD. This is what the LORD says: About this time tomorrow, a seah^e of the finest flour will sell for a shekel^f and two seahs^g of barley for a shekel at the gate of Samaria."

²The officer on whose arm the king was leaning said to the man of God, "Look, even if the LORD should open the floodgates of the heavens, could this happen?"

"You will see it with your own eyes," answered Elisha, "but you will not eat any of it!"

The Siege Lifted

³Now there were four men with leprosy^h at the entrance of the city gate. They said to each other, "Why stay here until we die? ⁴If we say, 'We'll go into the city'—the famine is there, and we will die. And if we stay here, we will die. So let's go over to the camp of the Arameans and surrender. If

---

^{a} 25 That is, about 2 pounds or about 920 grams ^{b} 25 That is, probably about 1/4 pound or about 100 grams
^{c} 25 Or of doves' dung ^{d} 25 That is, about 2 ounces or about 58 grams ^{e} 1 That is, probably about 12 pounds
or about 5.5 kilograms of flour; also in verses 16 and 18 ^{f} 1 That is, about 2/5 ounce or about 12 grams; also in
verses 16 and 18 ^{g} 1 That is, probably about 20 pounds or about 9 kilograms of barley; also in verses 16 and 18
^{h} 3 The Hebrew for leprosy was used for various diseases affecting the skin; also in verse 8.

they spare us, we live; if they kill us, then we die."

5 At dusk they got up and went to the camp of the Arameans. When they reached the edge of the camp, no one was there, 6 for the Lord had caused the Arameans to hear the sound of chariots and horses and a great army, so that they said to one another, "Look, the king of Israel has hired the Hittite and Egyptian kings to attack us!" 7 So they got up and fled in the dusk and abandoned their tents and their horses and donkeys. They left the camp as it was and ran for their lives.

8 The men who had leprosy reached the edge of the camp, entered one of the tents and ate and drank. Then they took silver, gold and clothes, and went off and hid them. They returned and entered another tent and took some things from it and hid them also.

9 Then they said to each other, "What we're doing is not right. This is a day of good news and we are keeping it to ourselves. If we wait until daylight, punishment will overtake us. Let's go at once and report this to the royal palace."

10 So they went and called out to the city gatekeepers and told them, "We went into the Aramean camp and no one was there — not a sound of anyone — only tethered horses and donkeys, and the tents left just as they were." 11 The gatekeepers shouted the news, and it was reported within the palace.

12 The king got up in the night and said to his officers, "I will tell you what the Arameans have done to us. They know we are starving; so they have left the camp to hide in the countryside, thinking, 'They will surely come out, and then we will take them alive and get into the city.'"

13 One of his officers answered, "Have some men take five of the horses that are left in the city. Their plight will be like that of all the Israelites left here — yes, they will only be like all these Israelites who are doomed. So let us send them to find out what happened."

14 So they selected two chariots with their horses, and the king sent them after the Aramean army. He commanded the drivers, "Go and find out what has happened." 15 They followed them as far as the Jordan, and they found the whole road strewn with the clothing and equipment the Arameans had thrown away in their headlong flight. So the messengers returned and reported to the king. 16 Then the people went out and plundered the camp of the Arameans. So a seah of the finest flour sold for a shekel, and two seahs of barley sold for a shekel, as the LORD had said.

17 Now the king had put the officer on whose arm he leaned in charge of the gate, and the people trampled him in the gateway, and he died, just as the man of God had foretold when the king came down to his house. 18 It happened as the man of God had said to the king: "About this time tomorrow, a seah of the finest flour will sell for a shekel and two seahs of barley for a shekel at the gate of Samaria."

19 The officer had said to the man of God, "Look, even if the LORD should open the floodgates of the heavens, could this happen?" The man of God had replied, "You will see it with your own eyes, but you will not eat any of it!" 20 And that is exactly what happened to him, for the people trampled him in the gateway, and he died.

The Shunammite's Land Restored

8 Now Elisha had said to the woman whose son he had restored to life, "Go away with your family and stay for a while wherever you can, because the LORD has decreed a famine in the land that will last seven years." 2 The woman proceeded to do as the man of God said. She and her family went away and stayed in the land of the Philistines seven years.

3 At the end of the seven years she came back from the land of the Philistines and went to appeal to the king for her house and land. 4 The king was talking to Gehazi, the servant of the man of God, and had said, "Tell me about all the great things Elisha has done." 5 Just as Gehazi was telling

the king how Elisha had restored the dead to life, the woman whose son Elisha had brought back to life came to appeal to the king for her house and land.

Gehazi said, "This is the woman, my lord the king, and this is her son whom Elisha restored to life." 6The king asked the woman about it, and she told him.

Then he assigned an official to her case and said to him, "Give back everything that belonged to her, including all the income from her land from the day she left the country until now."

Hazael Murders Ben-Hadad

7Elisha went to Damascus, and Ben-Hadad king of Aram was ill. When the king was told, "The man of God has come all the way up here," 8he said to Hazael, "Take a gift with you and go to meet the man of God. Consult the LORD through him; ask him, 'Will I recover from this illness?'"

9Hazael went to meet Elisha, taking with him as a gift forty camel-loads of all the finest wares of Damascus. He went in and stood before him, and said, "Your son Ben-Hadad king of Aram has sent me to ask, 'Will I recover from this illness?'"

10Elisha answered, "Go and say to him, 'You will certainly recover.' Nevertheless,a the LORD has revealed to me that he will in fact die." 11He stared at him with a fixed gaze until Hazael was embarrassed. Then the man of God began to weep.

12"Why is my lord weeping?" asked Hazael.

"Because I know the harm you will do to the Israelites," he answered. "You will set fire to their fortified places, kill their young men with the sword, dash their little children to the ground, and rip open their pregnant women."

13Hazael said, "How could your servant, a mere dog, accomplish such a feat?"

"The LORD has shown me that you will become king of Aram," answered Elisha.

14Then Hazael left Elisha and returned to his master. When Ben-Hadad asked, "What did Elisha say to you?" Hazael replied, "He told me that you would certainly recover." 15But the next day he took a thick cloth, soaked it in water and spread it over the king's face, so that he died. Then Hazael succeeded him as king.

Jehoram King of Judah

16In the fifth year of Joram son of Ahab king of Israel, when Jehoshaphat was king of Judah, Jehoram son of Jehoshaphat began his reign as king of Judah. 17He was thirty-two years old when he became king, and he reigned in Jerusalem eight years. 18He followed the ways of the kings of Israel, as the house of Ahab had done, for he married a daughter of Ahab. He did evil in the eyes of the LORD. 19Nevertheless, for the sake of his servant David, the LORD was not willing to destroy Judah. He had promised to maintain a lamp for David and his descendants forever.

20In the time of Jehoram, Edom rebelled against Judah and set up its own king. 21So Jehoramb went to Zair with all his chariots. The Edomites surrounded him and his chariot commanders, but he rose up and broke through by night; his army, however, fled back home. 22To this day Edom has been in rebellion against Judah. Libnah revolted at the same time.

23As for the other events of Jehoram's reign, and all he did, are they not written in the book of the annals of the kings of Judah? 24Jehoram rested with his ancestors and was buried with them in the City of David. And Ahaziah his son succeeded him as king.

Ahaziah King of Judah

25In the twelfth year of Joram son of Ahab king of Israel, Ahaziah son of Jehoram king of Judah began to reign. 26Ahaziah was twenty-two years old when he

---

a 10 The Hebrew may also be read Go and say, 'You will certainly not recover,' for.   b 21 Hebrew Joram, a variant of Jehoram; also in verses 23 and 24 became king, and he reigned in Jerusalem one year. His mother's name was Athaliah, a granddaughter of Omri king of Israel. ²⁷He followed the ways of the house of Ahab and did evil in the eyes of the LORD, as the house of Ahab had done, for he was related by marriage to Ahab's family.

²⁸Ahaziah went with Joram son of Ahab to war against Hazael king of Aram at Ramoth Gilead. The Arameans wounded Joram; ²⁹so King Joram returned to Jezreel to recover from the wounds the Arameans had inflicted on him at Ramoth*ᵃ* in his battle with Hazael king of Aram.

Then Ahaziah son of Jehoram king of Judah went down to Jezreel to see Joram son of Ahab, because he had been wounded.

Jehu Anointed King of Israel

9 The prophet Elisha summoned a man from the company of the prophets and said to him, "Tuck your cloak into your belt, take this flask of olive oil with you and go to Ramoth Gilead. ²When you get there, look for Jehu son of Jehoshaphat, the son of Nimshi. Go to him, get him away from his companions and take him into an inner room. ³Then take the flask and pour the oil on his head and declare, 'This is what the LORD says: I anoint you king over Israel.' Then open the door and run; don't delay!"

⁴So the young prophet went to Ramoth Gilead. ⁵When he arrived, he found the army officers sitting together. "I have a message for you, commander," he said.

"For which of us?" asked Jehu.

"For you, commander," he replied.

⁶Jehu got up and went into the house. Then the prophet poured the oil on Jehu's head and declared, "This is what the LORD, the God of Israel, says: 'I anoint you king over the LORD's people Israel. ⁷You are to destroy the house of Ahab your master, and I will avenge the blood of my servants the prophets and the blood of all the LORD's servants shed by Jezebel. ⁸The whole house of Ahab will perish. I will cut off from Ahab every last male in Israel — slave or free.*ᵇ* ⁹I will make the house of Ahab like the house of Jeroboam son of Nebat and like the house of Baasha son of Ahijah. ¹⁰As for Jezebel, dogs will devour her on the plot of ground at Jezreel, and no one will bury her.'" Then he opened the door and ran.

¹¹When Jehu went out to his fellow officers, one of them asked him, "Is everything all right? Why did this maniac come to you?"

"You know the man and the sort of things he says," Jehu replied.

¹²"That's not true!" they said. "Tell us."

Jehu said, "Here is what he told me: 'This is what the LORD says: I anoint you king over Israel.'"

¹³They quickly took their cloaks and spread them under him on the bare steps. Then they blew the trumpet and shouted, "Jehu is king!"

Jehu Kills Joram and Ahaziah

¹⁴So Jehu son of Jehoshaphat, the son of Nimshi, conspired against Joram. (Now Joram and all Israel had been defending Ramoth Gilead against Hazael king of Aram, ¹⁵but King Joram*ᶜ* had returned to Jezreel to recover from the wounds the Arameans had inflicted on him in the battle with Hazael king of Aram.) Jehu said, "If you desire to make me king, don't let anyone slip out of the city to go and tell the news in Jezreel." ¹⁶Then he got into his chariot and rode to Jezreel, because Joram was resting there and Ahaziah king of Judah had gone down to see him.

¹⁷When the lookout standing on the tower in Jezreel saw Jehu's troops approaching, he called out, "I see some troops coming."

"Get a horseman," Joram ordered. "Send him to meet them and ask, 'Do you come in peace?'"

ᵃ 29 Hebrew *Ramah,* a variant of *Ramoth*   *ᵇ 8* Or *Israel — every ruler or leader*   *ᶜ 15* Hebrew *Jehoram,* a variant of *Joram;* also in verses 17 and 21-24

18The horseman rode off to meet Jehu and said, "This is what the king says: 'Do you come in peace?'"

"What do you have to do with peace?" Jehu replied. "Fall in behind me."

The lookout reported, "The messenger has reached them, but he isn't coming back."

19So the king sent out a second horseman. When he came to them he said, "This is what the king says: 'Do you come in peace?'"

Jehu replied, "What do you have to do with peace? Fall in behind me."

20The lookout reported, "He has reached them, but he isn't coming back either. The driving is like that of Jehu son of Nimshi—he drives like a maniac."

21"Hitch up my chariot," Joram ordered. And when it was hitched up, Joram king of Israel and Ahaziah king of Judah rode out, each in his own chariot, to meet Jehu. They met him at the plot of ground that had belonged to Naboth the Jezreelite. 22When Joram saw Jehu he asked, "Have you come in peace, Jehu?"

"How can there be peace," Jehu replied, "as long as all the idolatry and witchcraft of your mother Jezebel abound?"

23Joram turned about and fled, calling out to Ahaziah, "Treachery, Ahaziah!"

24Then Jehu drew his bow and shot Joram between the shoulders. The arrow pierced his heart and he slumped down in his chariot. 25Jehu said to Bidkar, his chariot officer, "Pick him up and throw him on the field that belonged to Naboth the Jezreelite. Remember how you and I were riding together in chariots behind Ahab his father when the Lord spoke this prophecy against him: 26'Yesterday I saw the blood of Naboth and the blood of his sons, declares the Lord, and I will surely make you pay for it on this plot of ground, declares the Lord.'a Now then, pick him up and throw him on that plot, in accordance with the word of the Lord."

27When Ahaziah king of Judah saw what had happened, he fled up the road to Beth Haggan.b Jehu chased him, shouting, "Kill him too!" They wounded him in his chariot on the way up to Gur near Ibleam, but he escaped to Megiddo and died there. 28His servants took him by chariot to Jerusalem and buried him with his ancestors in his tomb in the City of David. 29(In the eleventh year of Joram son of Ahab, Ahaziah had become king of Judah.)

Jezebel Killed

30Then Jehu went to Jezreel. When Jezebel heard about it, she put on eye makeup, arranged her hair and looked out of a window. 31As Jehu entered the gate, she asked, "Have you come in peace, you Zimri, you murderer of your master?"c

32He looked up at the window and called out, "Who is on my side? Who?" Two or three eunuchs looked down at him. 33"Throw her down!" Jehu said. So they threw her down, and some of her blood spattered the wall and the horses as they trampled her underfoot.

34Jehu went in and ate and drank. "Take care of that cursed woman," he said, "and bury her, for she was a king's daughter." 35But when they went out to bury her, they found nothing except her skull, her feet and her hands. 36They went back and told Jehu, who said, "This is the word of the Lord that he spoke through his servant Elijah the Tishbite: On the plot of ground at Jezreel dogs will devour Jezebel's flesh.d 37Jezebel's body will be like dung on the ground in the plot at Jezreel, so that no one will be able to say, 'This is Jezebel.'"

Ahab's Family Killed

10 Now there were in Samaria seventy sons of the house of Ahab. So Jehu wrote letters and sent them to Samaria: to the officials of Jezreel,e to the elders and to the guardians of Ahab's

---

a 26 See 1 Kings 21:19.   b 27 Or fled by way of the garden house   c 31 Or "Was there peace for Zimri, who murdered his master?"   d 36 See 1 Kings 21:23.   e 1 Hebrew; some Septuagint manuscripts and Vulgate of the city children. He said, 2"You have your master's sons with you and you have chariots and horses, a fortified city and weapons. Now as soon as this letter reaches you, 3choose the best and most worthy of your master's sons and set him on his father's throne. Then fight for your master's house."

4But they were terrified and said, "If two kings could not resist him, how can we?"

5So the palace administrator, the city governor, the elders and the guardians sent this message to Jehu: "We are your servants and we will do anything you say. We will not appoint anyone as king; you do whatever you think best."

6Then Jehu wrote them a second letter, saying, "If you are on my side and will obey me, take the heads of your master's sons and come to me in Jezreel by this time tomorrow."

Now the royal princes, seventy of them, were with the leading men of the city, who were rearing them. 7When the letter arrived, these men took the princes and slaughtered all seventy of them. They put their heads in baskets and sent them to Jehu in Jezreel. 8When the messenger arrived, he told Jehu, "They have brought the heads of the princes."

Then Jehu ordered, "Put them in two piles at the entrance of the city gate until morning."

9The next morning Jehu went out. He stood before all the people and said, "You are innocent. It was I who conspired against my master and killed him, but who killed all these? 10Know, then, that not a word the LORD has spoken against the house of Ahab will fail. The LORD has done what he announced through his servant Elijah." 11So Jehu killed everyone in Jezreel who remained of the house of Ahab, as well as all his chief men, his close friends and his priests, leaving him no survivor.

12Jehu then set out and went toward Samaria. At Beth Eked of the Shepherds, 13he met some relatives of Ahaziah king of Judah and asked, "Who are you?"

They said, "We are relatives of Ahaziah, and we have come down to greet the families of the king and of the queen mother."

14"Take them alive!" he ordered. So they took them alive and slaughtered them by the well of Beth Eked—forty-two of them. He left no survivor.

15After he left there, he came upon Jehonadab son of Rekab, who was on his way to meet him. Jehu greeted him and said, "Are you in accord with me, as I am with you?"

"I am," Jehonadab answered.

"If so," said Jehu, "give me your hand." So he did, and Jehu helped him up into the chariot. 16Jehu said, "Come with me and see my zeal for the LORD." Then he had him ride along in his chariot.

17When Jehu came to Samaria, he killed all who were left there of Ahab's family; he destroyed them, according to the word of the LORD spoken to Elijah.

Servants of Baal Killed

18Then Jehu brought all the people together and said to them, "Ahab served Baal a little; Jehu will serve him much. 19Now summon all the prophets of Baal, all his servants and all his priests. See that no one is missing, because I am going to hold a great sacrifice for Baal. Anyone who fails to come will no longer live." But Jehu was acting deceptively in order to destroy the servants of Baal.

20Jehu said, "Call an assembly in honor of Baal." So they proclaimed it. 21Then he sent word throughout Israel, and all the servants of Baal came; not one stayed away. They crowded into the temple of Baal until it was full from one end to the other. 22And Jehu said to the keeper of the wardrobe, "Bring robes for all the servants of Baal." So he brought out robes for them.

23Then Jehu and Jehonadab son of Rekab went into the temple of Baal. Jehu said to the servants of Baal, "Look around and see that no one who serves the LORD is here with you—only servants of Baal." 24So they went in to make sacrifices and burnt offerings. Now Jehu had posted eighty men outside with this warning: "If one of you lets any of the men I am placing in your hands escape, it will be your life for his life."

²⁵As soon as Jehu had finished making the burnt offering, he ordered the guards and officers: "Go in and kill them; let no one escape." So they cut them down with the sword. The guards and officers threw the bodies out and then entered the inner shrine of the temple of Baal. ²⁶They brought the sacred stone out of the temple of Baal and burned it. ²⁷They demolished the sacred stone of Baal and tore down the temple of Baal, and people have used it for a latrine to this day.

²⁸So Jehu destroyed Baal worship in Israel. ²⁹However, he did not turn away from the sins of Jeroboam son of Nebat, which he had caused Israel to commit — the worship of the golden calves at Bethel and Dan.

³⁰The LORD said to Jehu, "Because you have done well in accomplishing what is right in my eyes and have done to the house of Ahab all I had in mind to do, your descendants will sit on the throne of Israel to the fourth generation." ³¹Yet Jehu was not careful to keep the law of the LORD, the God of Israel, with all his heart. He did not turn away from the sins of Jeroboam, which he had caused Israel to commit.

³²In those days the LORD began to reduce the size of Israel. Hazael overpowered the Israelites throughout their territory ³³east of the Jordan in all the land of Gilead (the region of Gad, Reuben and Manasseh), from Aroer by the Arnon Gorge through Gilead to Bashan.

³⁴As for the other events of Jehu's reign, all he did, and all his achievements, are they not written in the book of the annals of the kings of Israel?

³⁵Jehu rested with his ancestors and was buried in Samaria. And Jehoahaz his son succeeded him as king. ³⁶The time that Jehu reigned over Israel in Samaria was twenty-eight years.

Athaliah and Joash

11 When Athaliah the mother of Ahaziah saw that her son was dead, she proceeded to destroy the whole royal family. ²But Jehosheba, the daughter of King Jehoram[a] and sister of Ahaziah, took Joash son of Ahaziah and stole him away from among the royal princes, who were about to be murdered. She put him and his nurse in a bedroom to hide him from Athaliah; so he was not killed. ³He remained hidden with his nurse at the temple of the LORD for six years while Athaliah ruled the land.

⁴In the seventh year Jehoiada sent for the commanders of units of a hundred, the Carites and the guards and had them brought to him at the temple of the LORD. He made a covenant with them and put them under oath at the temple of the LORD. Then he showed them the king's son. ⁵He commanded them, saying, "This is what you are to do: You who are in the three companies that are going on duty on the Sabbath — a third of you guarding the royal palace, ⁶a third at the Sur Gate, and a third at the gate behind the guard, who take turns guarding the temple — ⁷and you who are in the other two companies that normally go off Sabbath duty are all to guard the temple for the king. ⁸Station yourselves around the king, each of you with weapon in hand. Anyone who approaches your ranks[b] is to be put to death. Stay close to the king wherever he goes."

⁹The commanders of units of a hundred did just as Jehoiada the priest ordered. Each one took his men — those who were going on duty on the Sabbath and those who were going off duty — and came to Jehoiada the priest. ¹⁰Then he gave the commanders the spears and shields that had belonged to King David and that were in the temple of the LORD. ¹¹The guards, each with weapon in hand, stationed themselves around the king — near the altar and the temple,

---

ᵃ 2 Hebrew *Joram*, a variant of *Jehoram*   ᵇ 8 Or *approaches the precincts* from the south side to the north side of the temple.

¹²Jehoiada brought out the king's son and put the crown on him; he presented him with a copy of the covenant and proclaimed him king. They anointed him, and the people clapped their hands and shouted, "Long live the king!"

¹³When Athaliah heard the noise made by the guards and the people, she went to the people at the temple of the LORD. ¹⁴She looked and there was the king, standing by the pillar, as the custom was. The officers and the trumpeters were beside the king, and all the people of the land were rejoicing and blowing trumpets. Then Athaliah tore her robes and called out, "Treason! Treason!"

¹⁵Jehoiada the priest ordered the commanders of units of a hundred, who were in charge of the troops: "Bring her out between the ranks*a* and put to the sword anyone who follows her." For the priest had said, "She must not be put to death in the temple of the LORD." ¹⁶So they seized her as she reached the place where the horses enter the palace grounds, and there she was put to death.

¹⁷Jehoiada then made a covenant between the LORD and the king and people that they would be the LORD's people. He also made a covenant between the king and the people. ¹⁸All the people of the land went to the temple of Baal and tore it down. They smashed the altars and idols to pieces and killed Mattan the priest of Baal in front of the altars.

Then Jehoiada the priest posted guards at the temple of the LORD. ¹⁹He took with him the commanders of hundreds, the Carites, the guards and all the people of the land, and together they brought the king down from the temple of the LORD and went into the palace, entering by way of the gate of the guards. The king then took his place on the royal throne. ²⁰All the people of the land rejoiced, and the city was calm, because Athaliah had been slain with the sword at the palace.

²¹Joash*b* was seven years old when he began to reign.*c*

Joash Repairs the Temple

12 *d* In the seventh year of Jehu, Joash*e* became king, and he reigned in Jerusalem forty years. His mother's name was Zibiah; she was from Beersheba. ²Joash did what was right in the eyes of the LORD all the years Jehoiada the priest instructed him. ³The high places, however, were not removed; the people continued to offer sacrifices and burn incense there.

⁴Joash said to the priests, "Collect all the money that is brought as sacred offerings to the temple of the LORD — the money collected in the census, the money received from personal vows and the money brought voluntarily to the temple. ⁵Let every priest receive the money from one of the treasurers, then use it to repair whatever damage is found in the temple."

⁶But by the twenty-third year of King Joash the priests still had not repaired the temple. ⁷Therefore King Joash summoned Jehoiada the priest and the other priests and asked them, "Why aren't you repairing the damage done to the temple? Take no more money from your treasurers, but hand it over for repairing the temple." ⁸The priests agreed that they would not collect any more money from the people and that they would not repair the temple themselves.

⁹Jehoiada the priest took a chest and bored a hole in its lid. He placed it beside the altar, on the right side as one enters the temple of the LORD. The priests who guarded the entrance put into the chest all the money that was brought to the temple of the LORD. ¹⁰Whenever they saw that there

---

a 15 Or *out from the precincts*   *b 21* Hebrew *Jehoash,* a variant of *Joash*   *c 21* In Hebrew texts this verse (11:21) is numbered 12:1.   *d* In Hebrew texts 12:1-21 is numbered 12:2-22.   *e 1* Hebrew *Jehoash,* a variant of *Joash*; also in verses 2, 4, 6, 7 and 18 was a large amount of money in the chest, the royal secretary and the high priest came, counted the money that had been brought into the temple of the LORD and put it into bags. ¹¹When the amount had been determined, they gave the money to the men appointed to supervise the work on the temple. With it they paid those who worked on the temple of the LORD — the carpenters and builders, ¹²the masons and stonecutters. They purchased timber and blocks of dressed stone for the repair of the temple of the LORD, and met all the other expenses of restoring the temple.

¹³The money brought into the temple was not spent for making silver basins, wick trimmers, sprinkling bowls, trumpets or any other articles of gold or silver for the temple of the LORD; ¹⁴it was paid to the workers, who used it to repair the temple. ¹⁵They did not require an accounting from those to whom they gave the money to pay the workers, because they acted with complete honesty. ¹⁶The money from the guilt offerings and sin offerings*a* was not brought into the temple of the LORD; it belonged to the priests.

¹⁷About this time Hazael king of Aram went up and attacked Gath and captured it. Then he turned to attack Jerusalem. ¹⁸But Joash king of Judah took all the sacred objects dedicated by his predecessors — Jehoshaphat, Jehoram and Ahaziah, the kings of Judah — and the gifts he himself had dedicated and all the gold found in the treasuries of the temple of the LORD and of the royal palace, and he sent them to Hazael king of Aram, who then withdrew from Jerusalem.

¹⁹As for the other events of the reign of Joash, and all he did, are they not written in the book of the annals of the kings of Judah? ²⁰His officials conspired against him and assassinated him at Beth Millo, on the road down to Silla. ²¹The officials who murdered him were Jozabad son of Shime-

ath and Jehozabad son of Shomer. He died and was buried with his ancestors in the City of David. And Amaziah his son succeeded him as king.

Jehoahaz King of Israel

13 In the twenty-third year of Joash son of Ahaziah king of Judah, Jehoahaz son of Jehu became king of Israel in Samaria, and he reigned seventeen years. ²He did evil in the eyes of the LORD by following the sins of Jeroboam son of Nebat, which he had caused Israel to commit, and he did not turn away from them. ³So the LORD's anger burned against Israel, and for a long time he kept them under the power of Hazael king of Aram and Ben-Hadad his son.

⁴Then Jehoahaz sought the LORD's favor, and the LORD listened to him, for he saw how severely the king of Aram was oppressing Israel. ⁵The LORD provided a deliverer for Israel, and they escaped from the power of Aram. So the Israelites lived in their own homes as they had before. ⁶But they did not turn away from the sins of the house of Jeroboam, which he had caused Israel to commit; they continued in them. Also, the Asherah pole*b* remained standing in Samaria.

⁷Nothing had been left of the army of Jehoahaz except fifty horsemen, ten chariots and ten thousand foot soldiers, for the king of Aram had destroyed the rest and made them like the dust at threshing time.

⁸As for the other events of the reign of Jehoahaz, all he did and his achievements, are they not written in the book of the annals of the kings of Israel? ⁹Jehoahaz rested with his ancestors and was buried in Samaria. And Jehoash*c* his son succeeded him as king.

Jehoash King of Israel

¹⁰In the thirty-seventh year of Joash king of Judah, Jehoash son of Jehoahaz became

---

a 16 Or purification offerings   *b 6 That is, a wooden symbol of the goddess Asherah; here and elsewhere in 2 Kings*
c 9 Hebrew Joash, a variant of Jehoash; also in verses 12-14 and 25

king of Israel in Samaria, and he reigned sixteen years. [11]He did evil in the eyes of the LORD and did not turn away from any of the sins of Jeroboam son of Nebat, which he had caused Israel to commit; he continued in them.

[12]As for the other events of the reign of Jehoash, all he did and his achievements, including his war against Amaziah king of Judah, are they not written in the book of the annals of the kings of Israel? [13]Jehoash rested with his ancestors, and Jeroboam succeeded him on the throne. Jehoash was buried in Samaria with the kings of Israel.

[14]Now Elisha had been suffering from the illness from which he died. Jehoash king of Israel went down to see him and wept over him. "My father! My father!" he cried. "The chariots and horsemen of Israel!"

[15]Elisha said, "Get a bow and some arrows," and he did so. [16]"Take the bow in your hands," he said to the king of Israel. When he had taken it, Elisha put his hands on the king's hands.

[17]"Open the east window," he said, and he opened it. "Shoot!" Elisha said, and he shot. "The LORD's arrow of victory, the arrow of victory over Aram!" Elisha declared. "You will completely destroy the Arameans at Aphek."

[18]Then he said, "Take the arrows," and the king took them. Elisha told him, "Strike the ground." He struck it three times and stopped. [19]The man of God was angry with him and said, "You should have struck the ground five or six times; then you would have defeated Aram and completely destroyed it. But now you will defeat it only three times."

[20]Elisha died and was buried.

Now Moabite raiders used to enter the country every spring. [21]Once while some Israelites were burying a man, suddenly they saw a band of raiders; so they threw the man's body into Elisha's tomb. When the body touched Elisha's bones, the man came to life and stood up on his feet.

[22]Hazael king of Aram oppressed Israel throughout the reign of Jehoahaz. [23]But the LORD was gracious to them and had compassion and showed concern for them because of his covenant with Abraham, Isaac and Jacob. To this day he has been unwilling to destroy them or banish them from his presence.

[24]Hazael king of Aram died, and Ben-Hadad his son succeeded him as king. [25]Then Jehoash son of Jehoahaz recaptured from Ben-Hadad son of Hazael the towns he had taken in battle from his father Jehoahaz. Three times Jehoash defeated him, and so he recovered the Israelite towns.

Amaziah King of Judah

14 In the second year of Jehoash[a] son of Jehoahaz king of Israel, Amaziah son of Joash king of Judah began to reign. [2]He was twenty-five years old when he became king, and he reigned in Jerusalem twenty-nine years. His mother's name was Jehoaddan; she was from Jerusalem. [3]He did what was right in the eyes of the LORD, but not as his father David had done. In everything he followed the example of his father Joash. [4]The high places, however, were not removed; the people continued to offer sacrifices and burn incense there.

[5]After the kingdom was firmly in his grasp, he executed the officials who had murdered his father the king. [6]Yet he did not put the children of the assassins to death, in accordance with what is written in the Book of the Law of Moses where the LORD commanded: "Parents are not to be put to death for their children, nor children put to death for their parents; each will die for their own sin."[b]

[7]He was the one who defeated ten thousand Edomites in the Valley of Salt and captured Sela in battle, calling it Joktheel, the name it has to this day.

[8]Then Amaziah sent messengers to Jehoash son of Jehoahaz, the son of Jehu,

---

[a] 1 Hebrew *Joash*, a variant of *Jehoash*; also in verses 13, 23 and 27   [b] 6 Deut. 24:16

king of Israel, with the challenge: "Come, let us face each other in battle."

⁹But Jehoash king of Israel replied to Amaziah king of Judah: "A thistle in Lebanon sent a message to a cedar in Lebanon, 'Give your daughter to my son in marriage.' Then a wild beast in Lebanon came along and trampled the thistle underfoot. ¹⁰You have indeed defeated Edom and now you are arrogant. Glory in your victory, but stay at home! Why ask for trouble and cause your own downfall and that of Judah also?"

¹¹Amaziah, however, would not listen, so Jehoash king of Israel attacked. He and Amaziah king of Judah faced each other at Beth Shemesh in Judah. ¹²Judah was routed by Israel, and every man fled to his home. ¹³Jehoash king of Israel captured Amaziah king of Judah, the son of Joash, the son of Ahaziah, at Beth Shemesh. Then Jehoash went to Jerusalem and broke down the wall of Jerusalem from the Ephraim Gate to the Corner Gate—a section about four hundred cubits long.ᵃ ¹⁴He took all the gold and silver and all the articles found in the temple of the Lord and in the treasuries of the royal palace. He also took hostages and returned to Samaria.

¹⁵As for the other events of the reign of Jehoash, what he did and his achievements, including his war against Amaziah king of Judah, are they not written in the book of the annals of the kings of Israel? ¹⁶Jehoash rested with his ancestors and was buried in Samaria with the kings of Israel. And Jeroboam his son succeeded him as king.

¹⁷Amaziah son of Joash king of Judah lived for fifteen years after the death of Jehoash son of Jehoahaz king of Israel. ¹⁸As for the other events of Amaziah's reign, are they not written in the book of the annals of the kings of Judah?

¹⁹They conspired against him in Jerusalem, and he fled to Lachish, but they sent men after him to Lachish and killed him there. ²⁰He was brought back by horse and

was buried in Jerusalem with his ancestors, in the City of David.

²¹Then all the people of Judah took Azariah,ᵇ who was sixteen years old, and made him king in place of his father Amaziah. ²²He was the one who rebuilt Elath and restored it to Judah after Amaziah rested with his ancestors.

Jeroboam II King of Israel

²³In the fifteenth year of Amaziah son of Joash king of Judah, Jeroboam son of Jehoash king of Israel became king in Samaria, and he reigned forty-one years. ²⁴He did evil in the eyes of the Lord and did not turn away from any of the sins of Jeroboam son of Nebat, which he had caused Israel to commit. ²⁵He was the one who restored the boundaries of Israel from Lebo Hamath to the Dead Sea,ᶜ in accordance with the word of the Lord, the God of Israel, spoken through his servant Jonah son of Amittai, the prophet from Gath Hepher.

²⁶The Lord had seen how bitterly everyone in Israel, whether slave or free, was suffering;ᵈ there was no one to help them. ²⁷And since the Lord had not said he would blot out the name of Israel from under heaven, he saved them by the hand of Jeroboam son of Jehoash.

²⁸As for the other events of Jeroboam's reign, all he did, and his military achievements, including how he recovered for Israel both Damascus and Hamath, which had belonged to Judah, are they not written in the book of the annals of the kings of Israel? ²⁹Jeroboam rested with his ancestors, the kings of Israel. And Zechariah his son succeeded him as king.

Azariah King of Judah

15 In the twenty-seventh year of Jeroboam king of Israel, Azariahᵉ son of Amaziah king of Judah began to reign. ²He was sixteen years

---

ᵃ *13* That is, about 600 feet or about 180 meters   ᵇ *21* Also called *Uzziah*   ᶜ *25* Hebrew *the Sea of the Arabah*
ᵈ *26* Or *Israel was suffering. They were without a ruler or leader, and*   ᵉ *1* Also called *Uzziah*; also in verses 6, 7, 8, 17, 23 and 27

old when he became king, and he reigned in Jerusalem fifty-two years. His mother's name was Jekoliah; she was from Jerusalem. ³He did what was right in the eyes of the LORD, just as his father Amaziah had done. ⁴The high places, however, were not removed; the people continued to offer sacrifices and burn incense there.

⁵The LORD afflicted the king with leprosy*a* until the day he died, and he lived in a separate house.*b* Jotham the king's son had charge of the palace and governed the people of the land.

⁶As for the other events of Azariah's reign, and all he did, are they not written in the book of the annals of the kings of Judah? ⁷Azariah rested with his ancestors and was buried near them in the City of David. And Jotham his son succeeded him as king.

Zechariah King of Israel

⁸In the thirty-eighth year of Azariah king of Judah, Zechariah son of Jeroboam became king of Israel in Samaria, and he reigned six months. ⁹He did evil in the eyes of the LORD, as his predecessors had done. He did not turn away from the sins of Jeroboam son of Nebat, which he had caused Israel to commit.

¹⁰Shallum son of Jabesh conspired against Zechariah. He attacked him in front of the people,*c* assassinated him and succeeded him as king. ¹¹The other events of Zechariah's reign are written in the book of the annals of the kings of Israel. ¹²So the word of the LORD spoken to Jehu was fulfilled: "Your descendants will sit on the throne of Israel to the fourth generation."*d*

Shallum King of Israel

¹³Shallum son of Jabesh became king in the thirty-ninth year of Uzziah king of Judah, and he reigned in Samaria one month. ¹⁴Then Menahem son of Gadi went from Tirzah up to Samaria. He attacked Shallum son of Jabesh in Samaria, assassinated him and succeeded him as king.

¹⁵The other events of Shallum's reign, and the conspiracy he led, are written in the book of the annals of the kings of Israel.

¹⁶At that time Menahem, starting out from Tirzah, attacked Tiphsah and everyone in the city and its vicinity, because they refused to open their gates. He sacked Tiphsah and ripped open all the pregnant women.

Menahem King of Israel

¹⁷In the thirty-ninth year of Azariah king of Judah, Menahem son of Gadi became king of Israel, and he reigned in Samaria ten years. ¹⁸He did evil in the eyes of the LORD. During his entire reign he did not turn away from the sins of Jeroboam son of Nebat, which he had caused Israel to commit.

¹⁹Then Pul*e* king of Assyria invaded the land, and Menahem gave him a thousand talents*f* of silver to gain his support and strengthen his own hold on the kingdom. ²⁰Menahem exacted this money from Israel. Every wealthy person had to contribute fifty shekels*g* of silver to be given to the king of Assyria. So the king of Assyria withdrew and stayed in the land no longer.

²¹As for the other events of Menahem's reign, and all he did, are they not written in the book of the annals of the kings of Israel? ²²Menahem rested with his ancestors. And Pekahiah his son succeeded him as king.

Pekahiah King of Israel

²³In the fiftieth year of Azariah king of Judah, Pekahiah son of Menahem became king of Israel in Samaria, and he reigned two years. ²⁴Pekahiah did evil in the eyes of the LORD. He did not turn away from

---

a 5 The Hebrew for *leprosy* was used for various diseases affecting the skin.   *b 5* Or *in a house where he was relieved of responsibilities*   *c 10* Hebrew; some Septuagint manuscripts *in Ibleam*   *d 12* 2 Kings 10:30
e 19 Also called *Tiglath-Pileser*   *f 19* That is, about 38 tons or about 34 metric tons   *g 20* That is, about 1 1/4 pounds or about 575 grams

the sins of Jeroboam son of Nebat, which he had caused Israel to commit. ²⁵One of his chief officers, Pekah son of Remaliah, conspired against him. Taking fifty men of Gilead with him, he assassinated Pekahiah, along with Argob and Arieh, in the citadel of the royal palace at Samaria. So Pekah killed Pekahiah and succeeded him as king.

²⁶The other events of Pekahiah's reign, and all he did, are written in the book of the annals of the kings of Israel.

Pekah King of Israel

²⁷In the fifty-second year of Azariah king of Judah, Pekah son of Remaliah became king of Israel in Samaria, and he reigned twenty years. ²⁸He did evil in the eyes of the LORD. He did not turn away from the sins of Jeroboam son of Nebat, which he had caused Israel to commit.

²⁹In the time of Pekah king of Israel, Tiglath-Pileser king of Assyria came and took Ijon, Abel Beth Maakah, Janoah, Kedesh and Hazor. He took Gilead and Galilee, including all the land of Naphtali, and deported the people to Assyria. ³⁰Then Hoshea son of Elah conspired against Pekah son of Remaliah. He attacked and assassinated him, and then succeeded him as king in the twentieth year of Jotham son of Uzziah.

³¹As for the other events of Pekah's reign, and all he did, are they not written in the book of the annals of the kings of Israel?

Jotham King of Judah

³²In the second year of Pekah son of Remaliah king of Israel, Jotham son of Uzziah king of Judah began to reign. ³³He was twenty-five years old when he became king, and he reigned in Jerusalem sixteen years. His mother's name was Jerusha daughter of Zadok. ³⁴He did what was right in the eyes of the LORD, just as his father Uzziah had done. ³⁵The high places, however, were not removed; the people continued to offer sacrifices and burn incense there. Jotham rebuilt the Upper Gate of the temple of the LORD.

³⁶As for the other events of Jotham's reign, and what he did, are they not written in the book of the annals of the kings of Judah? ³⁷(In those days the LORD began to send Rezin king of Aram and Pekah son of Remaliah against Judah.) ³⁸Jotham rested with his ancestors and was buried with them in the City of David, the city of his father. And Ahaz his son succeeded him as king.

Ahaz King of Judah

16 In the seventeenth year of Pekah son of Remaliah, Ahaz son of Jotham king of Judah began to reign. ²Ahaz was twenty years old when he became king, and he reigned in Jerusalem sixteen years. Unlike David his father, he did not do what was right in the eyes of the LORD his God. ³He followed the ways of the kings of Israel and even sacrificed his son in the fire, engaging in the detestable practices of the nations the LORD had driven out before the Israelites. ⁴He offered sacrifices and burned incense at the high places, on the hilltops and under every spreading tree.

⁵Then Rezin king of Aram and Pekah son of Remaliah king of Israel marched up to fight against Jerusalem and besieged Ahaz, but they could not overpower him. ⁶At that time, Rezin king of Aram recovered Elath for Aram by driving out the people of Judah. Edomites then moved into Elath and have lived there to this day.

⁷Ahaz sent messengers to say to Tiglath-Pileser king of Assyria, "I am your servant and vassal. Come up and save me out of the hand of the king of Aram and of the king of Israel, who are attacking me." ⁸And Ahaz took the silver and gold found in the temple of the LORD and in the treasuries of the royal palace and sent it as a gift to the king of Assyria. ⁹The king of Assyria complied by attacking Damascus and capturing it. He deported its inhabitants to Kir and put Rezin to death.

¹⁰Then King Ahaz went to Damascus to meet Tiglath-Pileser king of Assyria. He

saw an altar in Damascus and sent to Uriah the priest a sketch of the altar, with detailed plans for its construction. ¹¹So Uriah the priest built an altar in accordance with all the plans that King Ahaz had sent from Damascus and finished it before King Ahaz returned. ¹²When the king came back from Damascus and saw the altar, he approached it and presented offerings*a* on it. ¹³He offered up his burnt offering and grain offering, poured out his drink offering, and splashed the blood of his fellowship offerings against the altar. ¹⁴As for the bronze altar that stood before the Lord, he brought it from the front of the temple — from between the new altar and the temple of the Lord — and put it on the north side of the new altar.

¹⁵King Ahaz then gave these orders to Uriah the priest: "On the large new altar, offer the morning burnt offering and the evening grain offering, the king's burnt offering and his grain offering, and the burnt offering of all the people of the land, and their grain offering and their drink offering. Splash against this altar the blood of all the burnt offerings and sacrifices. But I will use the bronze altar for seeking guidance." ¹⁶And Uriah the priest did just as King Ahaz had ordered.

¹⁷King Ahaz cut off the side panels and removed the basins from the movable stands. He removed the Sea from the bronze bulls that supported it and set it on a stone base. ¹⁸He took away the Sabbath canopy*b* that had been built at the temple and removed the royal entryway outside the temple of the Lord, in deference to the king of Assyria.

¹⁹As for the other events of the reign of Ahaz, and what he did, are they not written in the book of the annals of the kings of Judah? ²⁰Ahaz rested with his ancestors and was buried with them in the City of David. And Hezekiah his son succeeded him as king.

Hoshea Last King of Israel

17 In the twelfth year of Ahaz king of Judah, Hoshea son of Elah became king of Israel in Samaria, and he reigned nine years. ²He did evil in the eyes of the Lord, but not like the kings of Israel who preceded him.

³Shalmaneser king of Assyria came up to attack Hoshea, who had been Shalmaneser's vassal and had paid him tribute. ⁴But the king of Assyria discovered that Hoshea was a traitor, for he had sent envoys to So*c* king of Egypt, and he no longer paid tribute to the king of Assyria, as he had done year by year. Therefore Shalmaneser seized him and put him in prison. ⁵The king of Assyria invaded the entire land, marched against Samaria and laid siege to it for three years. ⁶In the ninth year of Hoshea, the king of Assyria captured Samaria and deported the Israelites to Assyria. He settled them in Halah, in Gozan on the Habor River and in the towns of the Medes.

Israel Exiled Because of Sin

⁷All this took place because the Israelites had sinned against the Lord their God, who had brought them up out of Egypt from under the power of Pharaoh king of Egypt. They worshiped other gods ⁸and followed the practices of the nations the Lord had driven out before them, as well as the practices that the kings of Israel had introduced. ⁹The Israelites secretly did things against the Lord their God that were not right. From watchtower to fortified city they built themselves high places in all their towns. ¹⁰They set up sacred stones and Asherah poles on every high hill and under every spreading tree. ¹¹At every high place they burned incense, as the nations whom the Lord had driven out before them had done. They did wicked things that aroused the Lord's anger. ¹²They worshiped idols, though the Lord had said, "You shall not do this."*d* ¹³The

---

a 12 Or *and went up*   *b 18* Or *the dais of his throne* (see Septuagint)   *c 4* *So* is probably an abbreviation for *Osorkon.*   *d 12* Exodus 20:4,5

Lord warned Israel and Judah through all his prophets and seers: "Turn from your evil ways. Observe my commands and decrees, in accordance with the entire Law that I commanded your ancestors to obey and that I delivered to you through my servants the prophets."

14But they would not listen and were as stiff-necked as their ancestors, who did not trust in the Lord their God. 15They rejected his decrees and the covenant he had made with their ancestors and the statutes he had warned them to keep. They followed worthless idols and themselves became worthless. They imitated the nations around them although the Lord had ordered them, "Do not do as they do."

16They forsook all the commands of the Lord their God and made for themselves two idols cast in the shape of calves, and an Asherah pole. They bowed down to all the starry hosts, and they worshiped Baal. 17They sacrificed their sons and daughters in the fire. They practiced divination and sought omens and sold themselves to do evil in the eyes of the Lord, arousing his anger.

18So the Lord was very angry with Israel and removed them from his presence. Only the tribe of Judah was left, 19and even Judah did not keep the commands of the Lord their God. They followed the practices Israel had introduced. 20Therefore the Lord rejected all the people of Israel; he afflicted them and gave them into the hands of plunderers, until he thrust them from his presence.

21When he tore Israel away from the house of David, they made Jeroboam son of Nebat their king. Jeroboam enticed Israel away from following the Lord and caused them to commit a great sin. 22The Israelites persisted in all the sins of Jeroboam and did not turn away from them 23until the Lord removed them from his presence, as he had warned through all his servants the prophets. So the people of Israel were taken from their homeland into exile in Assyria, and they are still there.

Samaria Resettled

24The king of Assyria brought people from Babylon, Kuthah, Avva, Hamath and Sepharvaim and settled them in the towns of Samaria to replace the Israelites. They took over Samaria and lived in its towns. 25When they first lived there, they did not worship the Lord; so he sent lions among them and they killed some of the people. 26It was reported to the king of Assyria: "The people you deported and resettled in the towns of Samaria do not know what the god of that country requires. He has sent lions among them, which are killing them off, because the people do not know what he requires."

27Then the king of Assyria gave this order: "Have one of the priests you took captive from Samaria go back to live there and teach the people what the god of the land requires." 28So one of the priests who had been exiled from Samaria came to live in Bethel and taught them how to worship the Lord.

29Nevertheless, each national group made its own gods in the several towns where they settled, and set them up in the shrines the people of Samaria had made at the high places. 30The people from Babylon made Sukkoth Benoth, those from Kuthah made Nergal, and those from Hamath made Ashima; 31the Avvites made Nibhaz and Tartak, and the Sepharvites burned their children in the fire as sacrifices to Adrammelek and Anammelek, the gods of Sepharvaim. 32They worshiped the Lord, but they also appointed all sorts of their own people to officiate for them as priests in the shrines at the high places. 33They worshiped the Lord, but they also served their own gods in accordance with the customs of the nations from which they had been brought.

34To this day they persist in their former practices. They neither worship the Lord nor adhere to the decrees and regulations, the laws and commands that the Lord gave the descendants of Jacob, whom he named Israel. 35When the Lord made a covenant with the Israelites, he commanded them: "Do not worship any other gods or bow down to them, serve them or sacrifice to them. 36But the LORD, who brought you up out of Egypt with mighty power and outstretched arm, is the one you must worship. To him you shall bow down and to him offer sacrifices. 37You must always be careful to keep the decrees and regulations, the laws and commands he wrote for you. Do not worship other gods. 38Do not forget the covenant I have made with you, and do not worship other gods. 39Rather, worship the LORD your God; it is he who will deliver you from the hand of all your enemies."

40They would not listen, however, but persisted in their former practices. 41Even while these people were worshiping the LORD, they were serving their idols. To this day their children and grandchildren continue to do as their ancestors did.

Hezekiah King of Judah

18 In the third year of Hoshea son of Elah king of Israel, Hezekiah son of Ahaz king of Judah began to reign. 2He was twenty-five years old when he became king, and he reigned in Jerusalem twenty-nine years. His mother's name was Abijah*a* daughter of Zechariah. 3He did what was right in the eyes of the LORD, just as his father David had done. 4He removed the high places, smashed the sacred stones and cut down the Asherah poles. He broke into pieces the bronze snake Moses had made, for up to that time the Israelites had been burning incense to it. (It was called Nehushtan.*b*)

5Hezekiah trusted in the LORD, the God of Israel. There was no one like him among all the kings of Judah, either before him or after him. 6He held fast to the LORD and did not stop following him; he kept the commands the LORD had given Moses. 7And the LORD was with him; he was successful in whatever he undertook. He re-

belled against the king of Assyria and did not serve him. 8From watchtower to fortified city, he defeated the Philistines, as far as Gaza and its territory.

9In King Hezekiah's fourth year, which was the seventh year of Hoshea son of Elah king of Israel, Shalmaneser king of Assyria marched against Samaria and laid siege to it. 10At the end of three years the Assyrians took it. So Samaria was captured in Hezekiah's sixth year, which was the ninth year of Hoshea king of Israel. 11The king of Assyria deported Israel to Assyria and settled them in Halah, in Gozan on the Habor River and in towns of the Medes. 12This happened because they had not obeyed the LORD their God, but had violated his covenant—all that Moses the servant of the LORD commanded. They neither listened to the commands nor carried them out.

13In the fourteenth year of King Hezekiah's reign, Sennacherib king of Assyria attacked all the fortified cities of Judah and captured them. 14So Hezekiah king of Judah sent this message to the king of Assyria at Lachish: "I have done wrong. Withdraw from me, and I will pay whatever you demand of me." The king of Assyria exacted from Hezekiah king of Judah three hundred talents*c* of silver and thirty talents*d* of gold. 15So Hezekiah gave him all the silver that was found in the temple of the LORD and in the treasuries of the royal palace.

16At this time Hezekiah king of Judah stripped off the gold with which he had covered the doors and doorposts of the temple of the LORD, and gave it to the king of Assyria.

Sennacherib Threatens Jerusalem

17The king of Assyria sent his supreme commander, his chief officer and his field commander with a large army, from Lachish to King Hezekiah at Jerusalem. They came up to Jerusalem and stopped at the aqueduct of the Upper Pool, on the road to

---

a 2 Hebrew *Abi,* a variant of *Abijah*   *b 4 Nehushtan* sounds like the Hebrew for both *bronze* and *snake.*
c 14 That is, about 11 tons or about 10 metric tons   *d 14* That is, about 1 ton or about 1 metric ton

the Washerman's Field. [18]They called for the king; and Eliakim son of Hilkiah the palace administrator, Shebna the secretary, and Joah son of Asaph the recorder went out to them.

[19]The field commander said to them, "Tell Hezekiah:

"'This is what the great king, the king of Assyria, says: On what are you basing this confidence of yours? [20]You say you have the counsel and the might for war — but you speak only empty words. On whom are you depending, that you rebel against me? [21]Look, I know you are depending on Egypt, that splintered reed of a staff, which pierces the hand of anyone who leans on it! Such is Pharaoh king of Egypt to all who depend on him. [22]But if you say to me, "We are depending on the LORD our God" — isn't he the one whose high places and altars Hezekiah removed, saying to Judah and Jerusalem, "You must worship before this altar in Jerusalem"?

[23]"'Come now, make a bargain with my master, the king of Assyria: I will give you two thousand horses — if you can put riders on them! [24]How can you repulse one officer of the least of my master's officials, even though you are depending on Egypt for chariots and horsemen[a]? [25]Furthermore, have I come to attack and destroy this place without word from the LORD? The LORD himself told me to march against this country and destroy it.'"

[26]Then Eliakim son of Hilkiah, and Shebna and Joah said to the field commander, "Please speak to your servants in Aramaic, since we understand it. Don't speak to us in Hebrew in the hearing of the people on the wall."

[27]But the commander replied, "Was it only to your master and you that my master sent me to say these things, and not to the people sitting on the wall — who, like you, will have to eat their own excrement and drink their own urine?"

[28]Then the commander stood and called out in Hebrew, "Hear the word of the great king, the king of Assyria! [29]This is what the king says: Do not let Hezekiah deceive you. He cannot deliver you from my hand. [30]Do not let Hezekiah persuade you to trust in the LORD when he says, 'The LORD will surely deliver us; this city will not be given into the hand of the king of Assyria.'

[31]"Do not listen to Hezekiah. This is what the king of Assyria says: Make peace with me and come out to me. Then each of you will eat fruit from your own vine and fig tree and drink water from your own cistern, [32]until I come and take you to a land like your own — a land of grain and new wine, a land of bread and vineyards, a land of olive trees and honey. Choose life and not death!

"Do not listen to Hezekiah, for he is misleading you when he says, 'The LORD will deliver us.' [33]Has the god of any nation ever delivered his land from the hand of the king of Assyria? [34]Where are the gods of Hamath and Arpad? Where are the gods of Sepharvaim, Hena and Ivvah? Have they rescued Samaria from my hand? [35]Who of all the gods of these countries has been able to save his land from me? How then can the LORD deliver Jerusalem from my hand?"

[36]But the people remained silent and said nothing in reply, because the king had commanded, "Do not answer him."

[37]Then Eliakim son of Hilkiah the palace administrator, Shebna the secretary, and Joah son of Asaph the recorder went to Hezekiah, with their clothes torn, and told him what the field commander had said.

Jerusalem's Deliverance Foretold

19 When King Hezekiah heard this, he tore his clothes and put on sackcloth and went into the temple of the LORD. [2]He sent Eliakim the

---

a 24 Or *charioteers*

palace administrator, Shebna the secretary and the leading priests, all wearing sackcloth, to the prophet Isaiah son of Amoz. ³They told him, "This is what Hezekiah says: This day is a day of distress and rebuke and disgrace, as when children come to the moment of birth and there is no strength to deliver them. ⁴It may be that the LORD your God will hear all the words of the field commander, whom his master, the king of Assyria, has sent to ridicule the living God, and that he will rebuke him for the words the LORD your God has heard. Therefore pray for the remnant that still survives."

⁵When King Hezekiah's officials came to Isaiah, ⁶Isaiah said to them, "Tell your master, 'This is what the LORD says: Do not be afraid of what you have heard — those words with which the underlings of the king of Assyria have blasphemed me. ⁷Listen! When he hears a certain report, I will make him want to return to his own country, and there I will have him cut down with the sword.'"

⁸When the field commander heard that the king of Assyria had left Lachish, he withdrew and found the king fighting against Libnah.

⁹Now Sennacherib received a report that Tirhakah, the king of Cush,ᵃ was marching out to fight against him. So he again sent messengers to Hezekiah with this word: ¹⁰"Say to Hezekiah king of Judah: Do not let the god you depend on deceive you when he says, 'Jerusalem will not be given into the hands of the king of Assyria.' ¹¹Surely you have heard what the kings of Assyria have done to all the countries, destroying them completely. And will you be delivered? ¹²Did the gods of the nations that were destroyed by my predecessors deliver them — the gods of Gozan, Harran, Rezeph and the people of Eden who were in Tel Assar? ¹³Where is the king of Hamath or the king of Arpad? Where are the kings of Lair, Sepharvaim, Hena and Ivvah?"

Hezekiah's Prayer

¹⁴Hezekiah received the letter from the messengers and read it. Then he went up to the temple of the LORD and spread it out before the LORD. ¹⁵And Hezekiah prayed to the LORD: "LORD, the God of Israel, enthroned between the cherubim, you alone are God over all the kingdoms of the earth. You have made heaven and earth. ¹⁶Give ear, LORD, and hear; open your eyes, LORD, and see; listen to the words Sennacherib has sent to ridicule the living God.

¹⁷"It is true, LORD, that the Assyrian kings have laid waste these nations and their lands. ¹⁸They have thrown their gods into the fire and destroyed them, for they were not gods but only wood and stone, fashioned by human hands. ¹⁹Now, LORD our God, deliver us from his hand, so that all the kingdoms of the earth may know that you alone, LORD, are God."

Isaiah Prophesies Sennacherib's Fall

²⁰Then Isaiah son of Amoz sent a message to Hezekiah: "This is what the LORD, the God of Israel, says: I have heard your prayer concerning Sennacherib king of Assyria. ²¹This is the word that the LORD has spoken against him:

" 'Virgin Daughter Zion
      despises you and mocks you.
  Daughter Jerusalem
      tosses her head as you flee.
²² Who is it you have ridiculed and
          blasphemed?
      Against whom have you raised your
          voice
  and lifted your eyes in pride?
      Against the Holy One of Israel!
²³ By your messengers
      you have ridiculed the Lord.
  And you have said,
      "With my many chariots
  I have ascended the heights of the
          mountains,
      the utmost heights of Lebanon.

ᵃ 9 That is, the upper Nile region

I have cut down its tallest cedars,
  the choicest of its junipers.
I have reached its remotest parts,
  the finest of its forests.
24 I have dug wells in foreign lands
  and drunk the water there.
With the soles of my feet
  I have dried up all the streams of
    Egypt."

25 " 'Have you not heard?
  Long ago I ordained it.
In days of old I planned it;
  now I have brought it to pass,
that you have turned fortified cities
  into piles of stone.
26 Their people, drained of power,
  are dismayed and put to shame.
They are like plants in the field,
  like tender green shoots,
like grass sprouting on the roof,
  scorched before it grows up.

27 " 'But I know where you are
  and when you come and go
  and how you rage against me.
28 Because you rage against me
  and because your insolence has
    reached my ears,
I will put my hook in your nose
  and my bit in your mouth,
and I will make you return
  by the way you came.'

29 "This will be the sign for you, Hezekiah:

"This year you will eat what grows by
    itself,
  and the second year what springs
    from that.
But in the third year sow and reap,
  plant vineyards and eat their fruit.
30 Once more a remnant of the kingdom
    of Judah
  will take root below and bear fruit
    above.
31 For out of Jerusalem will come a
    remnant,
  and out of Mount Zion a band of
    survivors.

"The zeal of the LORD Almighty will accomplish this.

32 "Therefore this is what the LORD says
concerning the king of Assyria:

" 'He will not enter this city
  or shoot an arrow here.
He will not come before it with shield
  or build a siege ramp against it.
33 By the way that he came he will return;
  he will not enter this city,
              declares the LORD.
34 I will defend this city and save it,
  for my sake and for the sake of David
    my servant.' "

35 That night the angel of the LORD
went out and put to death a hundred and
eighty-five thousand in the Assyrian camp.
When the people got up the next morning—there were all the dead bodies! 36 So
Sennacherib king of Assyria broke camp
and withdrew. He returned to Nineveh and
stayed there.

37 One day, while he was worshiping
in the temple of his god Nisrok, his sons
Adrammelek and Sharezer killed him with
the sword, and they escaped to the land of
Ararat. And Esarhaddon his son succeeded
him as king.

Hezekiah's Illness

20 In those days Hezekiah became ill and was at the point
of death. The prophet Isaiah
son of Amoz went to him and said, "This
is what the LORD says: Put your house in
order, because you are going to die; you will
not recover."

2 Hezekiah turned his face to the wall
and prayed to the LORD, 3 "Remember,
LORD, how I have walked before you faithfully and with wholehearted devotion and
have done what is good in your eyes." And
Hezekiah wept bitterly.

4 Before Isaiah had left the middle court,
the word of the LORD came to him: 5 "Go
back and tell Hezekiah, the ruler of my people, 'This is what the LORD, the God of your

father David, says: I have heard your prayer and seen your tears; I will heal you. On the third day from now you will go up to the temple of the LORD. ⁶I will add fifteen years to your life. And I will deliver you and this city from the hand of the king of Assyria. I will defend this city for my sake and for the sake of my servant David.'"

⁷Then Isaiah said, "Prepare a poultice of figs." They did so and applied it to the boil, and he recovered.

⁸Hezekiah had asked Isaiah, "What will be the sign that the LORD will heal me and that I will go up to the temple of the LORD on the third day from now?"

⁹Isaiah answered, "This is the LORD's sign to you that the LORD will do what he has promised: Shall the shadow go forward ten steps, or shall it go back ten steps?"

¹⁰"It is a simple matter for the shadow to go forward ten steps," said Hezekiah. "Rather, have it go back ten steps."

¹¹Then the prophet Isaiah called on the LORD, and the LORD made the shadow go back the ten steps it had gone down on the stairway of Ahaz.

Envoys From Babylon

¹²At that time Marduk-Baladan son of Baladan king of Babylon sent Hezekiah letters and a gift, because he had heard of Hezekiah's illness. ¹³Hezekiah received the envoys and showed them all that was in his storehouses — the silver, the gold, the spices and the fine olive oil — his armory and everything found among his treasures. There was nothing in his palace or in all his kingdom that Hezekiah did not show them.

¹⁴Then Isaiah the prophet went to King Hezekiah and asked, "What did those men say, and where did they come from?"

"From a distant land," Hezekiah replied. "They came from Babylon."

¹⁵The prophet asked, "What did they see in your palace?"

"They saw everything in my palace," Hezekiah said. "There is nothing among my treasures that I did not show them."

¹⁶Then Isaiah said to Hezekiah, "Hear the word of the LORD: ¹⁷The time will surely come when everything in your palace, and all that your predecessors have stored up until this day, will be carried off to Babylon. Nothing will be left, says the LORD. ¹⁸And some of your descendants, your own flesh and blood who will be born to you, will be taken away, and they will become eunuchs in the palace of the king of Babylon."

¹⁹"The word of the LORD you have spoken is good," Hezekiah replied. For he thought, "Will there not be peace and security in my lifetime?"

²⁰As for the other events of Hezekiah's reign, all his achievements and how he made the pool and the tunnel by which he brought water into the city, are they not written in the book of the annals of the kings of Judah? ²¹Hezekiah rested with his ancestors. And Manasseh his son succeeded him as king.

Manasseh King of Judah

21 Manasseh was twelve years old when he became king, and he reigned in Jerusalem fifty-five years. His mother's name was Hephzibah. ²He did evil in the eyes of the LORD, following the detestable practices of the nations the LORD had driven out before the Israelites. ³He rebuilt the high places his father Hezekiah had destroyed; he also erected altars to Baal and made an Asherah pole, as Ahab king of Israel had done. He bowed down to all the starry hosts and worshiped them. ⁴He built altars in the temple of the LORD, of which the LORD had said, "In Jerusalem I will put my Name." ⁵In the two courts of the temple of the LORD, he built altars to all the starry hosts. ⁶He sacrificed his own son in the fire, practiced divination, sought omens, and consulted mediums and spiritists. He did much evil in the eyes of the LORD, arousing his anger.

⁷He took the carved Asherah pole he had made and put it in the temple, of which the LORD had said to David and to his son Solomon, "In this temple and in Jerusalem,

which I have chosen out of all the tribes of Israel, I will put my Name forever. [8]I will not again make the feet of the Israelites wander from the land I gave their ancestors, if only they will be careful to do everything I commanded them and will keep the whole Law that my servant Moses gave them." [9]But the people did not listen. Manasseh led them astray, so that they did more evil than the nations the LORD had destroyed before the Israelites.

[10]The LORD said through his servants the prophets: [11]"Manasseh king of Judah has committed these detestable sins. He has done more evil than the Amorites who preceded him and has led Judah into sin with his idols. [12]Therefore this is what the LORD, the God of Israel, says: I am going to bring such disaster on Jerusalem and Judah that the ears of everyone who hears of it will tingle. [13]I will stretch out over Jerusalem the measuring line used against Samaria and the plumb line used against the house of Ahab. I will wipe out Jerusalem as one wipes a dish, wiping it and turning it upside down. [14]I will forsake the remnant of my inheritance and give them into the hands of enemies. They will be looted and plundered by all their enemies; [15]they have done evil in my eyes and have aroused my anger from the day their ancestors came out of Egypt until this day."

[16]Moreover, Manasseh also shed so much innocent blood that he filled Jerusalem from end to end — besides the sin that he had caused Judah to commit, so that they did evil in the eyes of the LORD.

[17]As for the other events of Manasseh's reign, and all he did, including the sin he committed, are they not written in the book of the annals of the kings of Judah? [18]Manasseh rested with his ancestors and was buried in his palace garden, the garden of Uzza. And Amon his son succeeded him as king.

Amon King of Judah

[19]Amon was twenty-two years old when he became king, and he reigned in Jerusalem two years. His mother's name was Meshullemeth daughter of Haruz; she was from Jotbah. [20]He did evil in the eyes of the LORD, as his father Manasseh had done. [21]He followed completely the ways of his father, worshiping the idols his father had worshiped, and bowing down to them. [22]He forsook the LORD, the God of his ancestors, and did not walk in obedience to him.

[23]Amon's officials conspired against him and assassinated the king in his palace. [24]Then the people of the land killed all who had plotted against King Amon, and they made Josiah his son king in his place.

[25]As for the other events of Amon's reign, and what he did, are they not written in the book of the annals of the kings of Judah? [26]He was buried in his tomb in the garden of Uzza. And Josiah his son succeeded him as king.

The Book of the Law Found

22 Josiah was eight years old when he became king, and he reigned in Jerusalem thirty-one years. His mother's name was Jedidah daughter of Adaiah; she was from Bozkath. [2]He did what was right in the eyes of the LORD and followed completely the ways of his father David, not turning aside to the right or to the left.

[3]In the eighteenth year of his reign, King Josiah sent the secretary, Shaphan son of Azaliah, the son of Meshullam, to the temple of the LORD. He said: [4]"Go up to Hilkiah the high priest and have him get ready the money that has been brought into the temple of the LORD, which the doorkeepers have collected from the people. [5]Have them entrust it to the men appointed to supervise the work on the temple. And have these men pay the workers who repair the temple of the LORD — [6]the carpenters, the builders and the masons. Also have them purchase timber and dressed stone to repair the temple. [7]But they need not account for the money entrusted to them, because they are honest in their dealings."

[8] Hilkiah the high priest said to Shaphan the secretary, "I have found the Book of the Law in the temple of the LORD." He gave it to Shaphan, who read it. [9] Then Shaphan the secretary went to the king and reported to him: "Your officials have paid out the money that was in the temple of the LORD and have entrusted it to the workers and supervisors at the temple." [10] Then Shaphan the secretary informed the king, "Hilkiah the priest has given me a book." And Shaphan read from it in the presence of the king.

[11] When the king heard the words of the Book of the Law, he tore his robes. [12] He gave these orders to Hilkiah the priest, Ahikam son of Shaphan, Akbor son of Micaiah, Shaphan the secretary and Asaiah the king's attendant: [13] "Go and inquire of the LORD for me and for the people and for all Judah about what is written in this book that has been found. Great is the LORD's anger that burns against us because those who have gone before us have not obeyed the words of this book; they have not acted in accordance with all that is written there concerning us."

[14] Hilkiah the priest, Ahikam, Akbor, Shaphan and Asaiah went to speak to the prophet Huldah, who was the wife of Shallum son of Tikvah, the son of Harhas, keeper of the wardrobe. She lived in Jerusalem, in the New Quarter.

[15] She said to them, "This is what the LORD, the God of Israel, says: Tell the man who sent you to me, [16] 'This is what the LORD says: I am going to bring disaster on this place and its people, according to everything written in the book the king of Judah has read. [17] Because they have forsaken me and burned incense to other gods and aroused my anger by all the idols their hands have made,[a] my anger will burn against this place and will not be quenched.' [18] Tell the king of Judah, who sent you to inquire of the LORD, 'This is what the LORD, the God of Israel, says concerning the words you heard: [19] Because your heart was responsive and you humbled yourself before the LORD when you heard what I have spoken against this place and its people — that they would become a curse[b] and be laid waste — and because you tore your robes and wept in my presence, I also have heard you, declares the LORD. [20] Therefore I will gather you to your ancestors, and you will be buried in peace. Your eyes will not see all the disaster I am going to bring on this place.' "

So they took her answer back to the king.

Josiah Renews the Covenant

23 Then the king called together all the elders of Judah and Jerusalem. [2] He went up to the temple of the LORD with the people of Judah, the inhabitants of Jerusalem, the priests and the prophets — all the people from the least to the greatest. He read in their hearing all the words of the Book of the Covenant, which had been found in the temple of the LORD. [3] The king stood by the pillar and renewed the covenant in the presence of the LORD — to follow the LORD and keep his commands, statutes and decrees with all his heart and all his soul, thus confirming the words of the covenant written in this book. Then all the people pledged themselves to the covenant.

[4] The king ordered Hilkiah the high priest, the priests next in rank and the doorkeepers to remove from the temple of the LORD all the articles made for Baal and Asherah and all the starry hosts. He burned them outside Jerusalem in the fields of the Kidron Valley and took the ashes to Bethel. [5] He did away with the idolatrous priests appointed by the kings of Judah to burn incense on the high places of the towns of Judah and on those around Jerusalem — those who burned incense to Baal, to the sun and moon, to the con-

---

[a] 17 Or *by everything they have done*   [b] 19 That is, their names would be used in cursing (see Jer. 29:22); or, others would see that they are cursed.

stellations and to all the starry hosts. [6] He took the Asherah pole from the temple of the LORD to the Kidron Valley outside Jerusalem and burned it there. He ground it to powder and scattered the dust over the graves of the common people. [7] He also tore down the quarters of the male shrine prostitutes that were in the temple of the LORD, the quarters where women did weaving for Asherah.

[8] Josiah brought all the priests from the towns of Judah and desecrated the high places, from Geba to Beersheba, where the priests had burned incense. He broke down the gateway at the entrance of the Gate of Joshua, the city governor, which was on the left of the city gate. [9] Although the priests of the high places did not serve at the altar of the LORD in Jerusalem, they ate unleavened bread with their fellow priests.

[10] He desecrated Topheth, which was in the Valley of Ben Hinnom, so no one could use it to sacrifice their son or daughter in the fire to Molek. [11] He removed from the entrance to the temple of the LORD the horses that the kings of Judah had dedicated to the sun. They were in the court[a] near the room of an official named Nathan-Melek. Josiah then burned the chariots dedicated to the sun.

[12] He pulled down the altars the kings of Judah had erected on the roof near the upper room of Ahaz, and the altars Manasseh had built in the two courts of the temple of the LORD. He removed them from there, smashed them to pieces and threw the rubble into the Kidron Valley. [13] The king also desecrated the high places that were east of Jerusalem on the south of the Hill of Corruption — the ones Solomon king of Israel had built for Ashtoreth the vile goddess of the Sidonians, for Chemosh the vile god of Moab, and for Molek the detestable god of the people of Ammon. [14] Josiah smashed the sacred stones and cut down the Asherah poles and covered the sites with human bones.

[15] Even the altar at Bethel, the high place made by Jeroboam son of Nebat, who had caused Israel to sin — even that altar and high place he demolished. He burned the high place and ground it to powder, and burned the Asherah pole also. [16] Then Josiah looked around, and when he saw the tombs that were there on the hillside, he had the bones removed from them and burned on the altar to defile it, in accordance with the word of the LORD proclaimed by the man of God who foretold these things.

[17] The king asked, "What is that tombstone I see?"

The people of the city said, "It marks the tomb of the man of God who came from Judah and pronounced against the altar of Bethel the very things you have done to it."

[18] "Leave it alone," he said. "Don't let anyone disturb his bones." So they spared his bones and those of the prophet who had come from Samaria.

[19] Just as he had done at Bethel, Josiah removed all the shrines at the high places that the kings of Israel had built in the towns of Samaria and that had aroused the LORD's anger. [20] Josiah slaughtered all the priests of those high places on the altars and burned human bones on them. Then he went back to Jerusalem.

[21] The king gave this order to all the people: "Celebrate the Passover to the LORD your God, as it is written in this Book of the Covenant." [22] Neither in the days of the judges who led Israel nor in the days of the kings of Israel and the kings of Judah had any such Passover been observed. [23] But in the eighteenth year of King Josiah, this Passover was celebrated to the LORD in Jerusalem.

[24] Furthermore, Josiah got rid of the mediums and spiritists, the household gods, the idols and all the other detestable things seen in Judah and Jerusalem. This he did to fulfill the requirements of the law written in the book that Hilkiah the priest had discovered in the temple of the LORD.

---

[a] 11 The meaning of the Hebrew for this word is uncertain.

²⁵Neither before nor after Josiah was there a king like him who turned to the LORD as he did—with all his heart and with all his soul and with all his strength, in accordance with all the Law of Moses.

²⁶Nevertheless, the LORD did not turn away from the heat of his fierce anger, which burned against Judah because of all that Manasseh had done to arouse his anger. ²⁷So the LORD said, "I will remove Judah also from my presence as I removed Israel, and I will reject Jerusalem, the city I chose, and this temple, about which I said, 'My Name shall be there.'^a"

²⁸As for the other events of Josiah's reign, and all he did, are they not written in the book of the annals of the kings of Judah? ²⁹While Josiah was king, Pharaoh Necho king of Egypt went up to the Euphrates River to help the king of Assyria. King Josiah marched out to meet him in battle, but Necho faced him and killed him at Megiddo. ³⁰Josiah's servants brought his body in a chariot from Megiddo to Jerusalem and buried him in his own tomb. And the people of the land took Jehoahaz son of Josiah and anointed him and made him king in place of his father.

Jehoahaz King of Judah

³¹Jehoahaz was twenty-three years old when he became king, and he reigned in Jerusalem three months. His mother's name was Hamutal daughter of Jeremiah; she was from Libnah. ³²He did evil in the eyes of the LORD, just as his predecessors had done. ³³Pharaoh Necho put him in chains at Riblah in the land of Hamath so that he might not reign in Jerusalem, and he imposed on Judah a levy of a hundred talents^b of silver and a talent^c of gold. ³⁴Pharaoh Necho made Eliakim son of Josiah king in place of his father Josiah and changed Eliakim's name to Jehoiakim. But he took Jehoahaz and carried him off to Egypt, and there he died. ³⁵Jehoiakim paid Pharaoh Necho the silver and gold he demanded. In order to do so, he taxed the land and exacted the silver and gold from the people of the land according to their assessments.

Jehoiakim King of Judah

³⁶Jehoiakim was twenty-five years old when he became king, and he reigned in Jerusalem eleven years. His mother's name was Zebidah daughter of Pedaiah; she was from Rumah. ³⁷And he did evil in the eyes of the LORD, just as his predecessors had done.

24 During Jehoiakim's reign, Nebuchadnezzar king of Babylon invaded the land, and Jehoiakim became his vassal for three years. But then he turned against Nebuchadnezzar and rebelled. ²The LORD sent Babylonian,^d Aramean, Moabite and Ammonite raiders against him to destroy Judah, in accordance with the word of the LORD proclaimed by his servants the prophets. ³Surely these things happened to Judah according to the LORD's command, in order to remove them from his presence because of the sins of Manasseh and all he had done, ⁴including the shedding of innocent blood. For he had filled Jerusalem with innocent blood, and the LORD was not willing to forgive.

⁵As for the other events of Jehoiakim's reign, and all he did, are they not written in the book of the annals of the kings of Judah? ⁶Jehoiakim rested with his ancestors. And Jehoiachin his son succeeded him as king.

⁷The king of Egypt did not march out from his own country again, because the king of Babylon had taken all his territory, from the Wadi of Egypt to the Euphrates River.

Jehoiachin King of Judah

⁸Jehoiachin was eighteen years old when he became king, and he reigned in Jerusa-

---

^a 27 1 Kings 8:29   ^b 33 That is, about 3 3/4 tons or about 3.4 metric tons   ^c 33 That is, about 75 pounds or about 34 kilograms   ^d 2 Or *Chaldean*

lem three months. His mother's name was Nehushta daughter of Elnathan; she was from Jerusalem. [9]He did evil in the eyes of the LORD, just as his father had done.

[10]At that time the officers of Nebuchadnezzar king of Babylon advanced on Jerusalem and laid siege to it, [11]and Nebuchadnezzar himself came up to the city while his officers were besieging it. [12]Jehoiachin king of Judah, his mother, his attendants, his nobles and his officials all surrendered to him.

In the eighth year of the reign of the king of Babylon, he took Jehoiachin prisoner. [13]As the LORD had declared, Nebuchadnezzar removed the treasures from the temple of the LORD and from the royal palace, and cut up the gold articles that Solomon king of Israel had made for the temple of the LORD. [14]He carried all Jerusalem into exile: all the officers and fighting men, and all the skilled workers and artisans — a total of ten thousand. Only the poorest people of the land were left.

[15]Nebuchadnezzar took Jehoiachin captive to Babylon. He also took from Jerusalem to Babylon the king's mother, his wives, his officials and the prominent people of the land. [16]The king of Babylon also deported to Babylon the entire force of seven thousand fighting men, strong and fit for war, and a thousand skilled workers and artisans. [17]He made Mattaniah, Jehoiachin's uncle, king in his place and changed his name to Zedekiah.

Zedekiah King of Judah

[18]Zedekiah was twenty-one years old when he became king, and he reigned in Jerusalem eleven years. His mother's name was Hamutal daughter of Jeremiah; she was from Libnah. [19]He did evil in the eyes of the LORD, just as Jehoiakim had done. [20]It was because of the LORD's anger that all this happened to Jerusalem and Judah, and in the end he thrust them from his presence.

The Fall of Jerusalem

Now Zedekiah rebelled against the king of Babylon.

25 So in the ninth year of Zedekiah's reign, on the tenth day of the tenth month, Nebuchadnezzar king of Babylon marched against Jerusalem with his whole army. He encamped outside the city and built siege works all around it. [2]The city was kept under siege until the eleventh year of King Zedekiah.

[3]By the ninth day of the fourth[a] month the famine in the city had become so severe that there was no food for the people to eat. [4]Then the city wall was broken through, and the whole army fled at night through the gate between the two walls near the king's garden, though the Babylonians[b] were surrounding the city. They fled toward the Arabah,[c] [5]but the Babylonian[d] army pursued the king and overtook him in the plains of Jericho. All his soldiers were separated from him and scattered, [6]and he was captured.

He was taken to the king of Babylon at Riblah, where sentence was pronounced on him. [7]They killed the sons of Zedekiah before his eyes. Then they put out his eyes, bound him with bronze shackles and took him to Babylon.

[8]On the seventh day of the fifth month, in the nineteenth year of Nebuchadnezzar king of Babylon, Nebuzaradan commander of the imperial guard, an official of the king of Babylon, came to Jerusalem. [9]He set fire to the temple of the LORD, the royal palace and all the houses of Jerusalem. Every important building he burned down. [10]The whole Babylonian army under the commander of the imperial guard broke down the walls around Jerusalem. [11]Nebuzaradan the commander of the guard carried into exile the people who remained in the city, along with the rest of the populace and those who had deserted to the king of

---

a 3 Probable reading of the original Hebrew text (see Jer. 52:6); Masoretic Text does not have *fourth*.   *b 4* Or *Chaldeans*; also in verses 13, 25 and 26   *c 4* Or *the Jordan Valley*   *d 5* Or *Chaldean*; also in verses 10 and 24

Babylon. ¹²But the commander left behind some of the poorest people of the land to work the vineyards and fields.

¹³The Babylonians broke up the bronze pillars, the movable stands and the bronze Sea that were at the temple of the LORD and they carried the bronze to Babylon. ¹⁴They also took away the pots, shovels, wick trimmers, dishes and all the bronze articles used in the temple service. ¹⁵The commander of the imperial guard took away the censers and sprinkling bowls — all that were made of pure gold or silver.

¹⁶The bronze from the two pillars, the Sea and the movable stands, which Solomon had made for the temple of the LORD, was more than could be weighed. ¹⁷Each pillar was eighteen cubits*ᵃ* high. The bronze capital on top of one pillar was three cubits*ᵇ* high and was decorated with a network and pomegranates of bronze all around. The other pillar, with its network, was similar.

¹⁸The commander of the guard took as prisoners Seraiah the chief priest, Zephaniah the priest next in rank and the three doorkeepers. ¹⁹Of those still in the city, he took the officer in charge of the fighting men, and five royal advisers. He also took the secretary who was chief officer in charge of conscripting the people of the land and sixty of the conscripts who were found in the city. ²⁰Nebuzaradan the commander took them all and brought them to the king of Babylon at Riblah. ²¹There at Riblah, in the land of Hamath, the king had them executed.

So Judah went into captivity, away from her land.

²²Nebuchadnezzar king of Babylon appointed Gedaliah son of Ahikam, the son of Shaphan, to be over the people he had left behind in Judah. ²³When all the army officers and their men heard that the king of Babylon had appointed Gedaliah as governor, they came to Gedaliah at Mizpah — Ishmael son of Nethaniah, Johanan son of Kareah, Seraiah son of Tanhumeth the Netophathite, Jaazaniah the son of the Maakathite, and their men. ²⁴Gedaliah took an oath to reassure them and their men. "Do not be afraid of the Babylonian officials," he said. "Settle down in the land and serve the king of Babylon, and it will go well with you."

²⁵In the seventh month, however, Ishmael son of Nethaniah, the son of Elishama, who was of royal blood, came with ten men and assassinated Gedaliah and also the men of Judah and the Babylonians who were with him at Mizpah. ²⁶At this, all the people from the least to the greatest, together with the army officers, fled to Egypt for fear of the Babylonians.

Jehoiachin Released

²⁷In the thirty-seventh year of the exile of Jehoiachin king of Judah, in the year Awel-Marduk became king of Babylon, he released Jehoiachin king of Judah from prison. He did this on the twenty-seventh day of the twelfth month. ²⁸He spoke kindly to him and gave him a seat of honor higher than those of the other kings who were with him in Babylon. ²⁹So Jehoiachin put aside his prison clothes and for the rest of his life ate regularly at the king's table. ³⁰Day by day the king gave Jehoiachin a regular allowance as long as he lived.

ᵃ 17 That is, about 27 feet or about 8.1 meters   *ᵇ 17* That is, about 4 1/2 feet or about 1.4 meters

1 Chronicles

THEME: Chronicles is primarily concerned with the Davidic dynasty. God promised David that someday one of his descendants would rule an everlasting kingdom, and Chronicles demonstrates God's continuing faithfulness to that promise.

AUTHOR: According to Jewish tradition, Ezra wrote the Chronicles, but his authorship has been questioned. Many modern scholars simply refer to the author as "the Chronicler."

DATE OF WRITING: Although a specific date of composition cannot be determined, Chronicles was probably written between 450 and 400 BC.

ENCOURAGEMENT FROM 1 CHRONICLES: "The LORD searches every heart and understands every desire and every thought. If you seek him, he will be found by you" (1 Chronicles 28:9).

CHALLENGE FROM 1 CHRONICLES: "Look to the LORD and his strength; seek his face always" (1 Chronicles 16:11).

REFLECTION FROM 1 CHRONICLES: "I am in deep distress. Let me fall into the hands of the LORD, for his mercy is very great; but do not let me fall into human hands" (1 Chronicles 21:13).

First and Second Chronicles highlight God's work among his people through David's line. These two books cover the same time period as 2 Samuel through 2 Kings but from a different perspective. The Chronicles showcase God's faithfulness to his people, the power of his word and the importance of worship in the lives of his people. The primary focus of 1 and 2 Chronicles is the temple, which symbolizes God's presence among his people and reminds them that they are his. The entire book of 1 Chronicles is devoted to the life of David.

First Chronicles reminds us that God is faithful. God has made us many promises throughout his Word, and he will fulfill every one. This book also shows us how worship is central in our lives and recoveries. Worship lifts us above our day-to-day problems, helping us to clearly see that God is great and in control. Worship also helps us remember that God is able to help us in our recoveries. The act of praising him reminds us that God has freed us from our hurts, hang-ups and habits and that he has not left us alone. In recovery, even when things are hard, we need to remember to spend time with God, reading his Word and praying.

Historical Records From Adam to Abraham

To Noah's Sons

1 Adam, Seth, Enosh, ²Kenan, Mahalalel, Jared, ³Enoch, Methuselah, Lamech, Noah.

⁴The sons of Noah:ᵃ
Shem, Ham and Japheth.

The Japhethites

⁵The sonsᵇ of Japheth:
Gomer, Magog, Madai, Javan, Tubal, Meshek and Tiras.
⁶The sons of Gomer:
Ashkenaz, Riphathᶜ and Togarmah.
⁷The sons of Javan:
Elishah, Tarshish, the Kittites and the Rodanites.

The Hamites

⁸The sons of Ham:
Cush, Egypt, Put and Canaan.
⁹The sons of Cush:
Seba, Havilah, Sabta, Raamah and Sabteka.
The sons of Raamah:
Sheba and Dedan.
¹⁰Cush was the fatherᵈ of
Nimrod, who became a mighty warrior on earth.
¹¹Egypt was the father of
the Ludites, Anamites, Lehabites, Naphtuhites, ¹²Pathrusites, Kasluhites (from whom the Philistines came) and Caphtorites.
¹³Canaan was the father of
Sidon his firstborn,ᵉ and of the Hittites, ¹⁴Jebusites, Amorites, Girgashites, ¹⁵Hivites, Arkites, Sinites, ¹⁶Arvadites, Zemarites and Hamathites.

The Semites

¹⁷The sons of Shem:
Elam, Ashur, Arphaxad, Lud and Aram.
The sons of Aram:ᶠ
Uz, Hul, Gether and Meshek.
¹⁸Arphaxad was the father of Shelah, and Shelah the father of Eber.
¹⁹Two sons were born to Eber:
One was named Peleg,ᵍ because in his time the earth was divided; his brother was named Joktan.
²⁰Joktan was the father of
Almodad, Sheleph, Hazarmaveth, Jerah, ²¹Hadoram, Uzal, Diklah, ²²Obal,ʰ Abimael, Sheba, ²³Ophir, Havilah and Jobab. All these were sons of Joktan.

²⁴Shem, Arphaxad,ⁱ Shelah,
²⁵Eber, Peleg, Reu,
²⁶Serug, Nahor, Terah
²⁷and Abram (that is, Abraham).

The Family of Abraham

²⁸The sons of Abraham:
Isaac and Ishmael.

Descendants of Hagar

²⁹These were their descendants:
Nebaioth the firstborn of Ishmael, Kedar, Adbeel, Mibsam, ³⁰Mishma, Dumah, Massa, Hadad, Tema, ³¹Jetur, Naphish and Kedemah. These were the sons of Ishmael.

Descendants of Keturah

³²The sons born to Keturah, Abraham's concubine:
Zimran, Jokshan, Medan, Midian, Ishbak and Shuah.
The sons of Jokshan:
Sheba and Dedan.

ᵃ 4 Septuagint; Hebrew does not have this line.   ᵇ 5 Sons may mean descendants or successors or nations; also in verses 6-9, 17 and 23.   ᶜ 6 Many Hebrew manuscripts and Vulgate (see also Septuagint and Gen. 10:3); most Hebrew manuscripts Diphath   ᵈ 10 Father may mean ancestor or predecessor or founder; also in verses 11, 13, 18 and 20.   ᵉ 13 Or of the Sidonians, the foremost   ᶠ 17 One Hebrew manuscript and some Septuagint manuscripts (see also Gen. 10:23); most Hebrew manuscripts do not have this line.   ᵍ 19 Peleg means division.   ʰ 22 Some Hebrew manuscripts and Syriac (see also Gen. 10:28); most Hebrew manuscripts Ebal   ⁱ 24 Hebrew; some Septuagint manuscripts Arphaxad, Cainan (see also note at Gen. 11:10)

33 The sons of Midian:

Ephah, Epher, Hanok, Abida and Eldaah.

All these were descendants of Keturah.

Descendants of Sarah

34 Abraham was the father of Isaac.

The sons of Isaac:

Esau and Israel.

Esau's Sons

35 The sons of Esau:

Eliphaz, Reuel, Jeush, Jalam and Korah.

36 The sons of Eliphaz:

Teman, Omar, Zepho,*a* Gatam and Kenaz;

by Timna: Amalek.*b*

37 The sons of Reuel:

Nahath, Zerah, Shammah and Mizzah.

The People of Seir in Edom

38 The sons of Seir:

Lotan, Shobal, Zibeon, Anah, Dishon, Ezer and Dishan.

39 The sons of Lotan:

Hori and Homam. Timna was Lotan's sister.

40 The sons of Shobal:

Alvan,*c* Manahath, Ebal, Shepho and Onam.

The sons of Zibeon:

Aiah and Anah.

41 The son of Anah:

Dishon.

The sons of Dishon:

Hemdan,*d* Eshban, Ithran and Keran.

42 The sons of Ezer:

Bilhan, Zaavan and Akan.*e*

The sons of Dishan*f*:

Uz and Aran.

The Rulers of Edom

43 These were the kings who reigned in Edom before any Israelite king reigned:

Bela son of Beor, whose city was named Dinhabah.

44 When Bela died, Jobab son of Zerah from Bozrah succeeded him as king.

45 When Jobab died, Husham from the land of the Temanites succeeded him as king.

46 When Husham died, Hadad son of Bedad, who defeated Midian in the country of Moab, succeeded him as king. His city was named Avith.

47 When Hadad died, Samlah from Masrekah succeeded him as king.

48 When Samlah died, Shaul from Rehoboth on the river*g* succeeded him as king.

49 When Shaul died, Baal-Hanan son of Akbor succeeded him as king.

50 When Baal-Hanan died, Hadad succeeded him as king. His city was named Pau,*h* and his wife's name was Mehetabel daughter of Matred, the daughter of Me-Zahab. 51 Hadad also died.

The chiefs of Edom were:

Timna, Alvah, Jetheth, 52 Oholibamah, Elah, Pinon, 53 Kenaz, Teman, Mibzar, 54 Magdiel and Iram. These were the chiefs of Edom.

Israel's Sons

2 These were the sons of Israel: Reuben, Simeon, Levi, Judah, Issachar, Zebulun, 2 Dan, Joseph, Benjamin, Naphtali, Gad and Asher.

---

a 36 Many Hebrew manuscripts, some Septuagint manuscripts and Syriac (see also Gen. 36:11); most Hebrew manuscripts *Zephi*   *b 36* Some Septuagint manuscripts (see also Gen. 36:12); Hebrew *Gatam, Kenaz, Timna and Amalek*   *c 40* Many Hebrew manuscripts and some Septuagint manuscripts (see also Gen. 36:23); most Hebrew manuscripts *Alian*   *d 41* Many Hebrew manuscripts and some Septuagint manuscripts (see also Gen. 36:26); most Hebrew manuscripts *Hamran*   *e 42* Many Hebrew and Septuagint manuscripts (see also Gen. 36:27); most Hebrew manuscripts *Zaavan, Jaakan*   *f 42* See Gen. 36:28; Hebrew *Dishon,* a variant of *Dishan*   *g 48* Possibly the Euphrates   *h 50* Many Hebrew manuscripts, some Septuagint manuscripts, Vulgate and Syriac (see also Gen. 36:39); most Hebrew manuscripts *Pai*

Judah

To Hezron's Sons

³The sons of Judah:

Er, Onan and Shelah. These three were born to him by a Canaanite woman, the daughter of Shua. Er, Judah's firstborn, was wicked in the LORD's sight; so the LORD put him to death. ⁴Judah's daughter-in-law Tamar bore Perez and Zerah to Judah. He had five sons in all.

⁵The sons of Perez:

Hezron and Hamul.

⁶The sons of Zerah:

Zimri, Ethan, Heman, Kalkol and Darda*ᵃ* — five in all.

⁷The son of Karmi:

Achar,*ᵇ* who brought trouble on Israel by violating the ban on taking devoted things.*ᶜ*

⁸The son of Ethan:

Azariah.

⁹The sons born to Hezron were:

Jerahmeel, Ram and Caleb.*ᵈ*

From Ram Son of Hezron

¹⁰Ram was the father of Amminadab, and Amminadab the father of Nahshon, the leader of the people of Judah. ¹¹Nahshon was the father of Salmon,*ᵉ* Salmon the father of Boaz, ¹²Boaz the father of Obed and Obed the father of Jesse.

¹³Jesse was the father of Eliab his firstborn; the second son was Abinadab, the third Shimea, ¹⁴the fourth Nethanel, the fifth Raddai, ¹⁵the sixth Ozem and the seventh David. ¹⁶Their sisters were Zeruiah and Abigail. Zeruiah's three sons were Abishai, Joab and Asahel. ¹⁷Abigail was the mother of Amasa, whose father was Jether the Ishmaelite.

Caleb Son of Hezron

¹⁸Caleb son of Hezron had children by his wife Azubah (and by Jerioth). These were her sons: Jesher, Shobab and Ardon. ¹⁹When Azubah died, Caleb married Ephrath, who bore him Hur. ²⁰Hur was the father of Uri, and Uri the father of Bezalel.

²¹Later, Hezron, when he was sixty years old, married the daughter of Makir the father of Gilead. He made love to her, and she bore him Segub. ²²Segub was the father of Jair, who controlled twenty-three towns in Gilead. ²³(But Geshur and Aram captured Havvoth Jair,*ᶠ* as well as Kenath with its surrounding settlements — sixty towns.) All these were descendants of Makir the father of Gilead.

²⁴After Hezron died in Caleb Ephrathah, Abijah the wife of Hezron bore him Ashhur the father*ᵍ* of Tekoa.

Jerahmeel Son of Hezron

²⁵The sons of Jerahmeel the firstborn of Hezron:

Ram his firstborn, Bunah, Oren, Ozem and*ʰ* Ahijah. ²⁶Jerahmeel had another wife, whose name was Atarah; she was the mother of Onam.

²⁷The sons of Ram the firstborn of Jerahmeel:

Maaz, Jamin and Eker.

²⁸The sons of Onam:

Shammai and Jada.

The sons of Shammai:

Nadab and Abishur.

²⁹Abishur's wife was named Abihail, who bore him Ahban and Molid.

ᵃ 6 Many Hebrew manuscripts, some Septuagint manuscripts and Syriac (see also 1 Kings 4:31); most Hebrew manuscripts *Dara*   *ᵇ 7 Achar* means *trouble; Achar* is called *Achan* in Joshua.   *ᶜ 7* The Hebrew term refers to the irrevocable giving over of things or persons to the LORD, often by totally destroying them.   *ᵈ 9* Hebrew *Kelubai,* a variant of *Caleb*   *ᵉ 11* Septuagint (see also Ruth 4:21); Hebrew *Salma*   *ᶠ 23* Or *captured the settlements of Jair*   *ᵍ 24 Father* may mean *civic leader* or *military leader;* also in verses 42, 45, 49-52 and possibly elsewhere.   *ʰ 25* Or *Oren and Ozem, by*

30 The sons of Nadab:

Seled and Appaim. Seled died without children.

31 The son of Appaim:

Ishi, who was the father of Sheshan. Sheshan was the father of Ahlai.

32 The sons of Jada, Shammai's brother:

Jether and Jonathan. Jether died without children.

33 The sons of Jonathan:

Peleth and Zaza.

These were the descendants of Jerahmeel.

34 Sheshan had no sons — only daughters.

He had an Egyptian servant named Jarha. 35 Sheshan gave his daughter in marriage to his servant Jarha, and she bore him Attai.

36 Attai was the father of Nathan,

Nathan the father of Zabad,

37 Zabad the father of Ephlal,

Ephlal the father of Obed,

38 Obed the father of Jehu,

Jehu the father of Azariah,

39 Azariah the father of Helez,

Helez the father of Eleasah,

40 Eleasah the father of Sismai,

Sismai the father of Shallum,

41 Shallum the father of Jekamiah,

and Jekamiah the father of Elishama.

The Clans of Caleb

42 The sons of Caleb the brother of Jerahmeel:

Mesha his firstborn, who was the father of Ziph, and his son Mareshah,*a* who was the father of Hebron.

43 The sons of Hebron:

Korah, Tappuah, Rekem and Shema. 44 Shema was the father of Raham, and Raham the father of Jorkeam. Rekem was the father of Shammai. 45 The son of Shammai was Maon, and Maon was the father of Beth Zur.

46 Caleb's concubine Ephah was the mother of Haran, Moza and Gazez. Haran was the father of Gazez.

47 The sons of Jahdai:

Regem, Jotham, Geshan, Pelet, Ephah and Shaaph.

48 Caleb's concubine Maakah was the mother of Sheber and Tirhanah. 49 She also gave birth to Shaaph the father of Madmannah and to Sheva the father of Makbenah and Gibea. Caleb's daughter was Aksah. 50 These were the descendants of Caleb.

The sons of Hur the firstborn of Ephrathah:

Shobal the father of Kiriath Jearim, 51 Salma the father of Bethlehem, and Hareph the father of Beth Gader.

52 The descendants of Shobal the father of Kiriath Jearim were:

Haroeh, half the Manahathites, 53 and the clans of Kiriath Jearim: the Ithrites, Puthites, Shumathites and Mishraites. From these descended the Zorathites and Eshtaolites.

54 The descendants of Salma:

Bethlehem, the Netophathites, Atroth Beth Joab, half the Manahathites, the Zorites, 55 and the clans of scribes*b* who lived at Jabez: the Tirathites, Shimeathites and Sucathites. These are the Kenites who came from Hammath, the father of the Rekabites.*c*

The Sons of David

3 These were the sons of David born to him in Hebron:

The firstborn was Amnon the son of Ahinoam of Jezreel;

the second, Daniel the son of Abigail of Carmel;

---

a 42 The meaning of the Hebrew for this phrase is uncertain.   *b 55* Or *of the Sopherites*   *c 55* Or *father of Beth Rekab*

² the third, Absalom the son of Maakah daughter of Talmai king of Geshur;
the fourth, Adonijah the son of
Haggith;
³ the fifth, Shephatiah the son of
Abital;
and the sixth, Ithream, by his wife
Eglah.
⁴ These six were born to David in
Hebron, where he reigned seven
years and six months.

David reigned in Jerusalem thirty-three
years, ⁵ and these were the children born to
him there:

Shammua,ᵃ Shobab, Nathan and
Solomon. These four were by Bath-
shebaᵇ daughter of Ammiel. ⁶ There
were also Ibhar, Elishua,ᶜ Eliphelet,
⁷ Nogah, Nepheg, Japhia, ⁸ Elishama, Eliada and Eliphelet — nine in
all. ⁹ All these were the sons of David, besides his sons by his concubines. And Tamar was their sister.

The Kings of Judah

¹⁰ Solomon's son was Rehoboam,
Abijah his son,
Asa his son,
Jehoshaphat his son,
¹¹ Jehoramᵈ his son,
Ahaziah his son,
Joash his son,
¹² Amaziah his son,
Azariah his son,
Jotham his son,
¹³ Ahaz his son,
Hezekiah his son,
Manasseh his son,
¹⁴ Amon his son,
Josiah his son.
¹⁵ The sons of Josiah:
Johanan the firstborn,
Jehoiakim the second son,
Zedekiah the third,

Shallum the fourth.
¹⁶ The successors of Jehoiakim:
Jehoiachinᵉ his son,
and Zedekiah.

The Royal Line After the Exile

¹⁷ The descendants of Jehoiachin the
captive:
Shealtiel his son, ¹⁸ Malkiram, Pedaiah, Shenazzar, Jekamiah, Hosh-
ama and Nedabiah.
¹⁹ The sons of Pedaiah:
Zerubbabel and Shimei.
The sons of Zerubbabel:
Meshullam and Hananiah.
Shelomith was their sister.
²⁰ There were also five others:
Hashubah, Ohel, Berekiah, Hasadi-
ah and Jushab-Hesed.
²¹ The descendants of Hananiah:
Pelatiah and Jeshaiah, and the sons
of Rephaiah, of Arnan, of Obadiah
and of Shekaniah.
²² The descendants of Shekaniah:
Shemaiah and his sons:
Hattush, Igal, Bariah, Neariah and
Shaphat — six in all.
²³ The sons of Neariah:
Elioenai, Hizkiah and Azrikam —
three in all.
²⁴ The sons of Elioenai:
Hodaviah, Eliashib, Pelaiah, Akkub, Johanan, Delaiah and Ana-
ni — seven in all.

Other Clans of Judah

4 The descendants of Judah:
Perez, Hezron, Karmi, Hur and
Shobal.
² Reaiah son of Shobal was the father
of Jahath, and Jahath the father of
Ahumai and Lahad. These were the
clans of the Zorathites.
³ These were the sonsᶠ of Etam:
Jezreel, Ishma and Idbash. Their

ᵃ 5 Hebrew *Shimea*, a variant of *Shammua*   ᵇ 5 One Hebrew manuscript and Vulgate (see also Septuagint and 2 Samuel 11:3); most Hebrew manuscripts *Bathshua*   ᶜ 6 Two Hebrew manuscripts (see also 2 Samuel 5:15 and 1 Chron. 14:5); most Hebrew manuscripts *Elishama*   ᵈ 11 Hebrew *Joram*, a variant of *Jehoram*   ᵉ 16 Hebrew *Jeconiah*, a variant of *Jehoiachin*; also in verse 17   ᶠ 3 Some Septuagint manuscripts (see also Vulgate); Hebrew *father* sister was named Hazzelelponi. ⁴Penuel was the father of Gedor, and Ezer the father of Hushah.

These were the descendants of Hur, the firstborn of Ephrathah and father*ᵃ* of Bethlehem.

⁵Ashhur the father of Tekoa had two wives, Helah and Naarah.

⁶Naarah bore him Ahuzzam, Hepher, Temeni and Haahashtari. These were the descendants of Naarah.

⁷The sons of Helah:

Zereth, Zohar, Ethnan, ⁸and Koz, who was the father of Anub and Hazzobebah and of the clans of Aharhel son of Harum.

⁹Jabez was more honorable than his brothers. His mother had named him Jabez,*ᵇ* saying, "I gave birth to him in pain." ¹⁰Jabez cried out to the God of Israel, "Oh, that you would bless me and enlarge my territory! Let your hand be with me, and keep me from harm so that I will be free from pain." And God granted his request.

¹¹Kelub, Shuhah's brother, was the father of Mehir, who was the father of Eshton. ¹²Eshton was the father of Beth Rapha, Paseah and Tehinnah the father of Ir Nahash.*ᶜ* These were the men of Rekah.

¹³The sons of Kenaz:

Othniel and Seraiah.

The sons of Othniel:

Hathath and Meonothai.*ᵈ* ¹⁴Meonothai was the father of Ophrah.

Seraiah was the father of Joab,

the father of Ge Harashim.*ᵉ* It was called this because its people were skilled workers.

¹⁵The sons of Caleb son of Jephunneh:

Iru, Elah and Naam.

The son of Elah:

Kenaz.

¹⁶The sons of Jehallelel:

Ziph, Ziphah, Tiria and Asarel.

¹⁷The sons of Ezrah:

Jether, Mered, Epher and Jalon. One of Mered's wives gave birth to Miriam, Shammai and Ishbah the father of Eshtemoa. ¹⁸(His wife from the tribe of Judah gave birth to Jered the father of Gedor, Heber the father of Soko, and Jekuthiel the father of Zanoah.) These were the children of Pharaoh's daughter Bithiah, whom Mered had married.

¹⁹The sons of Hodiah's wife, the sister of Naham:

the father of Keilah the Garmite, and Eshtemoa the Maakathite.

²⁰The sons of Shimon:

Amnon, Rinnah, Ben-Hanan and Tilon.

The descendants of Ishi:

Zoheth and Ben-Zoheth.

²¹The sons of Shelah son of Judah:

Er the father of Lekah, Laadah the father of Mareshah and the clans of the linen workers at Beth Ashbea, ²²Jokim, the men of Kozeba, and Joash and Saraph, who ruled in Moab and Jashubi Lehem. (These records are from ancient times.) ²³They were the potters who lived at Netaim and Gederah; they stayed there and worked for the king.

Simeon

²⁴The descendants of Simeon:

Nemuel, Jamin, Jarib, Zerah and Shaul;

²⁵Shallum was Shaul's son, Mibsam his son and Mishma his son.

²⁶The descendants of Mishma:

Hammuel his son, Zakkur his son and Shimei his son.

²⁷Shimei had sixteen sons and six daughters, but his brothers did not have many children; so their entire clan did not become as numerous as the people of Judah. ²⁸They lived in Beersheba, Moladah, Hazar Shual,

---

ᵃ 4 Father *may mean* civic leader *or* military leader; *also in verses 12, 14, 17, 18 and possibly elsewhere.*   *ᵇ 9* Jabez *sounds like the Hebrew for* pain.   *ᶜ 12 Or* of the city of Nahash   *ᵈ 13 Some Septuagint manuscripts and Vulgate; Hebrew does not have* and Meonothai.   *ᵉ 14* Ge Harashim *means* valley of skilled workers.

29Bilhah, Ezem, Tolad, 30Bethuel, Hormah, Ziklag, 31Beth Markaboth, Hazar Susim, Beth Biri and Shaaraim. These were their towns until the reign of David. 32Their surrounding villages were Etam, Ain, Rimmon, Token and Ashan—five towns— 33and all the villages around these towns as far as Baalath.a These were their settlements. And they kept a genealogical record.

34Meshobab, Jamlech, Joshah son of Amaziah, 35Joel, Jehu son of Joshibiah, the son of Seraiah, the son of Asiel, 36also Elioenai, Jaakobah, Jeshohaiah, Asaiah, Adiel, Jesimiel, Benaiah, 37and Ziza son of Shiphi, the son of Allon, the son of Jedaiah, the son of Shimri, the son of Shemaiah.

38The men listed above by name were leaders of their clans. Their families increased greatly, 39and they went to the outskirts of Gedor to the east of the valley in search of pasture for their flocks. 40They found rich, good pasture, and the land was spacious, peaceful and quiet. Some Hamites had lived there formerly.

41The men whose names were listed came in the days of Hezekiah king of Judah. They attacked the Hamites in their dwellings and also the Meunites who were there and completely destroyedb them, as is evident to this day. Then they settled in their place, because there was pasture for their flocks. 42And five hundred of these Simeonites, led by Pelatiah, Neariah, Rephaiah and Uzziel, the sons of Ishi, invaded the hill country of Seir. 43They killed the remaining Amalekites who had escaped, and they have lived there to this day.

Reuben

5 The sons of Reuben the firstborn of Israel (he was the firstborn, but when he defiled his father's marriage bed, his rights as firstborn were given to the sons of Joseph son of Israel; so he could not be listed in the genealogical record in accordance with his birthright, 2and though Judah was the strongest of his brothers and a ruler came from him, the rights of the firstborn belonged to Joseph)— 3the sons of Reuben the firstborn of Israel:

Hanok, Pallu, Hezron and Karmi.
4The descendants of Joel:
Shemaiah his son, Gog his son, Shimei his son, 5Micah his son, Reaiah his son, Baal his son, 6and Beerah his son, whom Tiglath-Pileserc king of Assyria took into exile. Beerah was a leader of the Reubenites.
7Their relatives by clans, listed according to their genealogical records:
Jeiel the chief, Zechariah, 8and Bela son of Azaz, the son of Shema, the son of Joel. They settled in the area from Aroer to Nebo and Baal Meon. 9To the east they occupied the land up to the edge of the desert that extends to the Euphrates River, because their livestock had increased in Gilead.
10During Saul's reign they waged war against the Hagrites, who were defeated at their hands; they occupied the dwellings of the Hagrites throughout the entire region east of Gilead.

Gad

11The Gadites lived next to them in Bashan, as far as Salekah:
12Joel was the chief, Shapham the second, then Janai and Shaphat, in Bashan.
13Their relatives, by families, were:
Michael, Meshullam, Sheba, Jorai, Jakan, Zia and Eber—seven in all.
14These were the sons of Abihail son of Huri, the son of Jaroah, the son

---

a 33 Some Septuagint manuscripts (see also Joshua 19:8); Hebrew Baal   b 41 The Hebrew term refers to the irrevocable giving over of things or persons to the LORD, often by totally destroying them.   c 6 Hebrew Tilgath-Pilneser, a variant of Tiglath-Pileser; also in verse 26 of Gilead, the son of Michael, the son of Jeshishai, the son of Jahdo, the son of Buz.

15 Ahi son of Abdiel, the son of Guni, was head of their family.

16 The Gadites lived in Gilead, in Bashan and its outlying villages, and on all the pasturelands of Sharon as far as they extended.

17 All these were entered in the genealogical records during the reigns of Jotham king of Judah and Jeroboam king of Israel.

18 The Reubenites, the Gadites and the half-tribe of Manasseh had 44,760 men ready for military service — able-bodied men who could handle shield and sword, who could use a bow, and who were trained for battle. 19 They waged war against the Hagrites, Jetur, Naphish and Nodab. 20 They were helped in fighting them, and God delivered the Hagrites and all their allies into their hands, because they cried out to him during the battle. He answered their prayers, because they trusted in him. 21 They seized the livestock of the Hagrites — fifty thousand camels, two hundred fifty thousand sheep and two thousand donkeys. They also took one hundred thousand people captive, 22 and many others fell slain, because the battle was God's. And they occupied the land until the exile.

The Half-Tribe of Manasseh

23 The people of the half-tribe of Manasseh were numerous; they settled in the land from Bashan to Baal Hermon, that is, to Senir (Mount Hermon).

24 These were the heads of their families: Epher, Ishi, Eliel, Azriel, Jeremiah, Hodaviah and Jahdiel. They were brave warriors, famous men, and heads of their families. 25 But they were unfaithful to the God of their ancestors and prostituted themselves to the gods of the peoples of the land, whom God had destroyed before them. 26 So the God of Israel stirred up the spirit

of Pul king of Assyria (that is, Tiglath-Pileser king of Assyria), who took the Reubenites, the Gadites and the half-tribe of Manasseh into exile. He took them to Halah, Habor, Hara and the river of Gozan, where they are to this day.

Levi

6 *a* The sons of Levi:
Gershon, Kohath and Merari.
2 The sons of Kohath:
Amram, Izhar, Hebron and Uzziel.
3 The children of Amram:
Aaron, Moses and Miriam.
The sons of Aaron:
Nadab, Abihu, Eleazar and Ithamar.
4 Eleazar was the father of Phinehas,
Phinehas the father of Abishua,
5 Abishua the father of Bukki,
Bukki the father of Uzzi,
6 Uzzi the father of Zerahiah,
Zerahiah the father of Meraioth,
7 Meraioth the father of Amariah,
Amariah the father of Ahitub,
8 Ahitub the father of Zadok,
Zadok the father of Ahimaaz,
9 Ahimaaz the father of Azariah,
Azariah the father of Johanan,
10 Johanan the father of Azariah (it was he who served as priest in the temple Solomon built in Jerusalem),
11 Azariah the father of Amariah,
Amariah the father of Ahitub,
12 Ahitub the father of Zadok,
Zadok the father of Shallum,
13 Shallum the father of Hilkiah,
Hilkiah the father of Azariah,
14 Azariah the father of Seraiah,
and Seraiah the father of Jozadak. *b*
15 Jozadak was deported when the LORD sent Judah and Jerusalem into exile by the hand of Nebuchadnezzar.

16 The sons of Levi:
Gershon, *c* Kohath and Merari.

---

a In Hebrew texts 6:1-15 is numbered 5:27-41, and 6:16-81 is numbered 6:1-66.   *b 14* Hebrew *Jehozadak*, a variant of *Jozadak*; also in verse 15   *c 16* Hebrew *Gershom*, a variant of *Gershon*; also in verses 17, 20, 43, 62 and 71

17 These are the names of the sons of
Gershon:
   Libni and Shimei.
18 The sons of Kohath:
   Amram, Izhar, Hebron and Uzziel.
19 The sons of Merari:
   Mahli and Mushi.
These are the clans of the Levites list-
ed according to their fathers:
20 Of Gershon:
   Libni his son, Jahath his son,
   Zimmah his son, 21 Joah his son,
   Iddo his son, Zerah his son
   and Jeatherai his son.
22 The descendants of Kohath:
   Amminadab his son, Korah his son,
   Assir his son, 23 Elkanah his son,
   Ebiasaph his son, Assir his son,
24 Tahath his son, Uriel his son,
   Uzziah his son and Shaul his son.
25 The descendants of Elkanah:
   Amasai, Ahimoth,
26 Elkanah his son,a Zophai his son,
   Nahath his son, 27 Eliab his son,
   Jeroham his son, Elkanah his son
   and Samuel his son.b
28 The sons of Samuel:
   Joelc the firstborn
   and Abijah the second son.
29 The descendants of Merari:
   Mahli, Libni his son,
   Shimei his son, Uzzah his son,
30 Shimea his son, Haggiah his son
   and Asaiah his son.

The Temple Musicians

31 These are the men David put in charge
of the music in the house of the LORD after
the ark came to rest there. 32 They ministered with music before the tabernacle, the
tent of meeting, until Solomon built the
temple of the LORD in Jerusalem. They performed their duties according to the regulations laid down for them.

33 Here are the men who served, together
with their sons:
From the Kohathites:
   Heman, the musician,
   the son of Joel, the son of Samuel,
34 the son of Elkanah, the son of Jeroham,
   the son of Eliel, the son of Toah,
35 the son of Zuph, the son of Elkanah,
   the son of Mahath, the son of
Amasai,
36 the son of Elkanah, the son of Joel,
   the son of Azariah, the son of Zephaniah,
37 the son of Tahath, the son of Assir,
   the son of Ebiasaph, the son of Korah,
38 the son of Izhar, the son of Kohath,
   the son of Levi, the son of Israel;
39 and Heman's associate Asaph, who
   served at his right hand:
   Asaph son of Berekiah, the son of
Shimea,
40 the son of Michael, the son of Baa-
seiah,d
   the son of Malkijah, 41 the son of
Ethni,
   the son of Zerah, the son of Adaiah,
42 the son of Ethan, the son of Zimmah,
   the son of Shimei, 43 the son of Jahath,
   the son of Gershon, the son of Levi;
44 and from their associates, the Merarites, at his left hand:
   Ethan son of Kishi, the son of Abdi,
   the son of Malluk, 45 the son of
Hashabiah,
   the son of Amaziah, the son of Hilkiah,
46 the son of Amzi, the son of Bani,
   the son of Shemer, 47 the son of
Mahli,

---

a 26 Some Hebrew manuscripts, Septuagint and Syriac; most Hebrew manuscripts *Ahimoth* 26*and Elkanah. The sons
of Elkanah:*   b 27 Some Septuagint manuscripts (see also 1 Samuel 1:19,20 and 1 Chron. 6:33,34); Hebrew does not
have *and Samuel his son.*   c 28 Some Septuagint manuscripts and Syriac (see also 1 Samuel 8:2 and 1 Chron. 6:33);
Hebrew does not have *Joel.*   d 40 Most Hebrew manuscripts; some Hebrew manuscripts, one Septuagint
manuscript and Syriac *Maaseiah*

the son of Mushi, the son of Merari, the son of Levi.

48 Their fellow Levites were assigned to all the other duties of the tabernacle, the house of God. 49 But Aaron and his descendants were the ones who presented offerings on the altar of burnt offering and on the altar of incense in connection with all that was done in the Most Holy Place, making atonement for Israel, in accordance with all that Moses the servant of God had commanded.

50 These were the descendants of Aaron:
Eleazar his son, Phinehas his son,
Abishua his son, 51 Bukki his son,
Uzzi his son, Zerahiah his son,
52 Meraioth his son, Amariah his son,
Ahitub his son, 53 Zadok his son
and Ahimaaz his son.

54 These were the locations of their settlements allotted as their territory (they were assigned to the descendants of Aaron who were from the Kohathite clan, because the first lot was for them):

55 They were given Hebron in Judah with its surrounding pasturelands. 56 But the fields and villages around the city were given to Caleb son of Jephunneh.

57 So the descendants of Aaron were given Hebron (a city of refuge), and Libnah,*a* Jattir, Eshtemoa, 58 Hilen, Debir, 59 Ashan, Juttah*b* and Beth Shemesh, together with their pasturelands. 60 And from the tribe of Benjamin they were given Gibeon,*c* Geba, Alemeth and Anathoth, together with their pasturelands.

The total number of towns distributed among the Kohathite clans came to thirteen.

61 The rest of Kohath's descendants were allotted ten towns from the clans of half the tribe of Manasseh.

62 The descendants of Gershon, clan by clan, were allotted thirteen towns from the tribes of Issachar, Asher and Naphtali, and from the part of the tribe of Manasseh that is in Bashan.

63 The descendants of Merari, clan by clan, were allotted twelve towns from the tribes of Reuben, Gad and Zebulun.

64 So the Israelites gave the Levites these towns and their pasturelands. 65 From the tribes of Judah, Simeon and Benjamin they allotted the previously named towns.

66 Some of the Kohathite clans were given as their territory towns from the tribe of Ephraim.

67 In the hill country of Ephraim they were given Shechem (a city of refuge), and Gezer,*d* 68 Jokmeam, Beth Horon, 69 Aijalon and Gath Rimmon, together with their pasturelands.

70 And from half the tribe of Manasseh the Israelites gave Aner and Bileam, together with their pasturelands, to the rest of the Kohathite clans.

71 The Gershonites received the following:
From the clan of the half-tribe of Manasseh
they received Golan in Bashan and also Ashtaroth, together with their pasturelands;
72 from the tribe of Issachar
they received Kedesh, Daberath, 73 Ramoth and Anem, together with their pasturelands;
74 from the tribe of Asher
they received Mashal, Abdon, 75 Hukok and Rehob, together with their pasturelands;
76 and from the tribe of Naphtali
they received Kedesh in Galilee, Hammon and Kiriathaim, together with their pasturelands.

77 The Merarites (the rest of the Levites) received the following:

---

a 57 See Joshua 21:13; Hebrew *given the cities of refuge: Hebron, Libnah.*   *b 59* Syriac (see also Septuagint and Joshua 21:16); Hebrew does not have *Juttah.*   *c 60* See Joshua 21:17; Hebrew does not have *Gibeon.*
d 67 See Joshua 21:21; Hebrew *given the cities of refuge: Shechem, Gezer.*

From the tribe of Zebulun
they received Jokneam, Kartah,[a]
Rimmono and Tabor, together with
their pasturelands;
78 from the tribe of Reuben across the
Jordan east of Jericho
they received Bezer in the wilderness, Jahzah, 79Kedemoth and
Mephaath, together with their pasturelands;
80 and from the tribe of Gad
they received Ramoth in Gilead,
Mahanaim, 81Heshbon and Jazer,
together with their pasturelands.

Issachar

7 The sons of Issachar:
Tola, Puah, Jashub and Shimron—four in all.
2 The sons of Tola:
Uzzi, Rephaiah, Jeriel, Jahmai, Ib-
sam and Samuel—heads of their
families. During the reign of David, the descendants of Tola listed
as fighting men in their genealogy
numbered 22,600.
3 The son of Uzzi:
Izrahiah.
The sons of Izrahiah:
Michael, Obadiah, Joel and Ishiah.
All five of them were chiefs. 4Ac-
cording to their family genealogy,
they had 36,000 men ready for battle, for they had many wives and
children.
5 The relatives who were fighting men
belonging to all the clans of Issachar, as listed in their genealogy,
were 87,000 in all.

Benjamin

6 Three sons of Benjamin:
Bela, Beker and Jediael.
7 The sons of Bela:
Ezbon, Uzzi, Uzziel, Jerimoth and
Iri, heads of families—five in all.

Their genealogical record listed
22,034 fighting men.
8 The sons of Beker:
Zemirah, Joash, Eliezer, Elioenai,
Omri, Jeremoth, Abijah, Anathoth
and Alemeth. All these were the
sons of Beker. 9Their genealogical
record listed the heads of families
and 20,200 fighting men.
10 The son of Jediael:
Bilhan.
The sons of Bilhan:
Jeush, Benjamin, Ehud, Kenaanah, Zethan, Tarshish and Ahisha-
har. 11All these sons of Jediael were
heads of families. There were 17,200
fighting men ready to go out to war.
12 The Shuppites and Huppites were
the descendants of Ir, and the Hu-
shites[b] the descendants of Aher.

Naphtali

13 The sons of Naphtali:
Jahziel, Guni, Jezer and Shillem[c]—
the descendants of Bilhah.

Manasseh

14 The descendants of Manasseh:
Asriel was his descendant through
his Aramean concubine. She gave
birth to Makir the father of Gilead.
15Makir took a wife from among the
Huppites and Shuppites. His sister's
name was Maakah.
Another descendant was named
Zelophehad, who had only daughters.
16Makir's wife Maakah gave birth
to a son and named him Peresh. His
brother was named Sheresh, and his
sons were Ulam and Rakem.
17 The son of Ulam:
Bedan.
These were the sons of Gilead son of
Makir, the son of Manasseh. 18His
sister Hammoleketh gave birth to
Ishhod, Abiezer and Mahlah.

---

a 77 See Septuagint and Joshua 21:34; Hebrew does not have Jokneam, Kartah.   b 12 Or Ir. The sons of Dan:
Hushim, (see Gen. 46:23); Hebrew does not have The sons of Dan.   c 13 Some Hebrew and Septuagint manuscripts
(see also Gen. 46:24 and Num. 26:49); most Hebrew manuscripts Shallum

¹⁹ The sons of Shemida were:

Ahian, Shechem, Likhi and Aniam.

Ephraim

²⁰ The descendants of Ephraim:

Shuthelah, Bered his son,

Tahath his son, Eleadah his son,

Tahath his son, ²¹ Zabad his son

and Shuthelah his son.

Ezer and Elead were killed by the native-born men of Gath, when they went down to seize their livestock. ²² Their father Ephraim mourned for them many days, and his relatives came to comfort him. ²³ Then he made love to his wife again, and she became pregnant and gave birth to a son. He named him Beriah,ᵃ because there had been misfortune in his family. ²⁴ His daughter was Sheerah, who built Lower and Upper Beth Horon as well as Uzzen Sheerah.

²⁵ Rephah was his son, Resheph his son,ᵇ

Telah his son, Tahan his son,

²⁶ Ladan his son, Ammihud his son,

Elishama his son, ²⁷ Nun his son

and Joshua his son.

²⁸ Their lands and settlements included Bethel and its surrounding villages, Naaran to the east, Gezer and its villages to the west, and Shechem and its villages all the way to Ayyah and its villages. ²⁹ Along the borders of Manasseh were Beth Shan, Taanach, Megiddo and Dor, together with their villages. The descendants of Joseph son of Israel lived in these towns.

Asher

³⁰ The sons of Asher:

Imnah, Ishvah, Ishvi and Beriah.

Their sister was Serah.

³¹ The sons of Beriah:

Heber and Malkiel, who was the father of Birzaith.

³² Heber was the father of Japhlet, Shomer and Hotham and of their sister Shua.

³³ The sons of Japhlet:

Pasak, Bimhal and Ashvath.

These were Japhlet's sons.

³⁴ The sons of Shomer:

Ahi, Rohgah,ᶜ Hubbah and Aram.

³⁵ The sons of his brother Helem:

Zophah, Imna, Shelesh and Amal.

³⁶ The sons of Zophah:

Suah, Harnepher, Shual, Beri, Imrah, ³⁷ Bezer, Hod, Shamma, Shilshah, Ithranᵈ and Beera.

³⁸ The sons of Jether:

Jephunneh, Pispah and Ara.

³⁹ The sons of Ulla:

Arah, Hanniel and Rizia.

⁴⁰ All these were descendants of Asher — heads of families, choice men, brave warriors and outstanding leaders. The number of men ready for battle, as listed in their genealogy, was 26,000.

The Genealogy of Saul the Benjamite

8 Benjamin was the father of Bela his firstborn,

Ashbel the second son, Aharah the third,

² Nohah the fourth and Rapha the fifth.

³ The sons of Bela were:

Addar, Gera, Abihud,ᵉ ⁴ Abishua, Naaman, Ahoah, ⁵ Gera, Shephuphan and Huram.

⁶ These were the descendants of Ehud, who were heads of families of those living in Geba and were deported to Manahath:

⁷ Naaman, Ahijah, and Gera, who deported them and who was the father of Uzza and Ahihud.

⁸ Sons were born to Shaharaim in Moab after he had divorced his wives Hushim and Baara. ⁹ By his wife Hodesh he had Jobab, Zibia, Mesha, Malkam, ¹⁰ Jeuz, Sakia and Mirmah. These were his sons, heads of families. ¹¹ By Hushim he had Abitub and Elpaal.

ᵃ 23 *Beriah* sounds like the Hebrew for *misfortune.*   ᵇ 25 Some Septuagint manuscripts; Hebrew does not have *his son.*   ᶜ 34 Or *of his brother Shomer: Rohgah*   ᵈ 37 Possibly a variant of *Jether*   ᵉ 3 Or *Gera the father of Ehud*

12 The sons of Elpaal:

Eber, Misham, Shemed (who built Ono and Lod with its surrounding villages), 13 and Beriah and Shema, who were heads of families of those living in Aijalon and who drove out the inhabitants of Gath.

14 Ahio, Shashak, Jeremoth, 15 Zebadiah, Arad, Eder, 16 Michael, Ishpah and Joha were the sons of Beriah.

17 Zebadiah, Meshullam, Hizki, Heber, 18 Ishmerai, Izliah and Jobab were the sons of Elpaal.

19 Jakim, Zikri, Zabdi, 20 Elienai, Zillethai, Eliel, 21 Adaiah, Beraiah and Shimrath were the sons of Shimei.

22 Ishpan, Eber, Eliel, 23 Abdon, Zikri, Hanan, 24 Hananiah, Elam, Anthothijah, 25 Iphdeiah and Penuel were the sons of Shashak.

26 Shamsherai, Shehariah, Athaliah, 27 Jaareshiah, Elijah and Zikri were the sons of Jeroham.

28 All these were heads of families, chiefs as listed in their genealogy, and they lived in Jerusalem.

29 Jeiel*a* the father*b* of Gibeon lived in Gibeon.

His wife's name was Maakah, 30 and his firstborn son was Abdon, followed by Zur, Kish, Baal, Ner,*c* Nadab, 31 Gedor, Ahio, Zeker 32 and Mikloth, who was the father of Shimeah. They too lived near their relatives in Jerusalem.

33 Ner was the father of Kish, Kish the father of Saul, and Saul the father of Jonathan, Malki-Shua, Abinadab and Esh-Baal.*d*

34 The son of Jonathan:

Merib-Baal,*e* who was the father of Micah.

35 The sons of Micah:

Pithon, Melek, Tarea and Ahaz.

36 Ahaz was the father of Jehoaddah, Jehoaddah was the father of Alemeth, Azmaveth and Zimri, and Zimri was the father of Moza. 37 Moza was the father of Binea; Raphah was his son, Eleasah his son and Azel his son.

38 Azel had six sons, and these were their names:

Azrikam, Bokeru, Ishmael, Sheariah, Obadiah and Hanan. All these were the sons of Azel.

39 The sons of his brother Eshek:

Ulam his firstborn, Jeush the second son and Eliphelet the third. 40 The sons of Ulam were brave warriors who could handle the bow. They had many sons and grandsons — 150 in all.

All these were the descendants of Benjamin.

9 All Israel was listed in the genealogies recorded in the book of the kings of Israel and Judah. They were taken captive to Babylon because of their unfaithfulness.

The People in Jerusalem

2 Now the first to resettle on their own property in their own towns were some Israelites, priests, Levites and temple servants.

3 Those from Judah, from Benjamin, and from Ephraim and Manasseh who lived in Jerusalem were:

4 Uthai son of Ammihud, the son of Omri, the son of Imri, the son of Bani, a descendant of Perez son of Judah.

5 Of the Shelanites*f*:

Asaiah the firstborn and his sons.

6 Of the Zerahites:

Jeuel.

The people from Judah numbered 690.

7 Of the Benjamites:

---

a 29 Some Septuagint manuscripts (see also 9:35); Hebrew does not have *Jeiel*.   *b 29 Father* may mean *civic leader* or *military leader*.   *c 30* Some Septuagint manuscripts (see also 9:36); Hebrew does not have *Ner*.   *d 33* Also known as *Ish-Bosheth*   *e 34* Also known as *Mephibosheth*   *f 5* See Num. 26:20; Hebrew *Shilonites*.

Sallu son of Meshullam, the son of Hodaviah, the son of Hassenuah;

8 Ibneiah son of Jeroham; Elah son of Uzzi, the son of Mikri; and Meshullam son of Shephatiah, the son of Reuel, the son of Ibnijah.

9 The people from Benjamin, as listed in their genealogy, numbered 956. All these men were heads of their families.

10 Of the priests:

Jedaiah; Jehoiarib; Jakin;

11 Azariah son of Hilkiah, the son of Meshullam, the son of Zadok, the son of Meraioth, the son of Ahitub, the official in charge of the house of God;

12 Adaiah son of Jeroham, the son of Pashhur, the son of Malkijah; and Maasai son of Adiel, the son of Jahzerah, the son of Meshullam, the son of Meshillemith, the son of Immer.

13 The priests, who were heads of families, numbered 1,760. They were able men, responsible for ministering in the house of God.

14 Of the Levites:

Shemaiah son of Hasshub, the son of Azrikam, the son of Hashabiah, a Merarite; 15 Bakbakkar, Heresh, Galal and Mattaniah son of Mika, the son of Zikri, the son of Asaph; 16 Obadiah son of Shemaiah, the son of Galal, the son of Jeduthun; and Berekiah son of Asa, the son of Elkanah, who lived in the villages of the Netophathites.

17 The gatekeepers:

Shallum, Akkub, Talmon, Ahiman and their fellow Levites, Shallum their chief 18 being stationed at the King's Gate on the east, up to the present time. These were the gatekeepers belonging to the camp of the Levites. 19 Shallum son of Kore, the son of Ebiasaph, the son of Korah, and his fellow gatekeepers from his family (the Korahites) were responsible for guarding the thresholds of the tent just as their ancestors had been responsible for guarding the entrance to the dwelling of the LORD. 20 In earlier times Phinehas son of Eleazar was the official in charge of the gatekeepers, and the LORD was with him. 21 Zechariah son of Meshelemiah was the gatekeeper at the entrance to the tent of meeting.

22 Altogether, those chosen to be gatekeepers at the thresholds numbered 212. They were registered by genealogy in their villages. The gatekeepers had been assigned to their positions of trust by David and Samuel the seer. 23 They and their descendants were in charge of guarding the gates of the house of the LORD — the house called the tent of meeting. 24 The gatekeepers were on the four sides: east, west, north and south. 25 Their fellow Levites in their villages had to come from time to time and share their duties for seven-day periods. 26 But the four principal gatekeepers, who were Levites, were entrusted with the responsibility for the rooms and treasuries in the house of God. 27 They would spend the night stationed around the house of God, because they had to guard it; and they had charge of the key for opening it each morning.

28 Some of them were in charge of the articles used in the temple service; they counted them when they were brought in and when they were taken out. 29 Others were assigned to take care of the furnishings and all the other articles of the sanctuary, as well as the special flour and wine, and the olive oil, incense and spices. 30 But some of the priests took care of mixing the spices. 31 A Levite named Mattithiah, the firstborn son of Shallum the Korahite, was entrusted with the responsibility for baking the offering bread. 32 Some of the Kohathites, their fellow Levites, were in charge of preparing for every Sabbath the bread set out on the table.

33 Those who were musicians, heads of Levite families, stayed in the rooms of the temple and were exempt from other duties

because they were responsible for the work day and night.

³⁴All these were heads of Levite families, chiefs as listed in their genealogy, and they lived in Jerusalem.

The Genealogy of Saul

³⁵Jeiel the father^a of Gibeon lived in Gibeon.

His wife's name was Maakah, ³⁶and his firstborn son was Abdon, followed by Zur, Kish, Baal, Ner, Nadab, ³⁷Gedor, Ahio, Zechariah and Mikloth. ³⁸Mikloth was the father of Shimeam. They too lived near their relatives in Jerusalem.

³⁹Ner was the father of Kish, Kish the father of Saul, and Saul the father of Jonathan, Malki-Shua, Abinadab and Esh-Baal.^b

⁴⁰The son of Jonathan:
Merib-Baal,^c who was the father of Micah.

⁴¹The sons of Micah:
Pithon, Melek, Tahrea and Ahaz.^d

⁴²Ahaz was the father of Jadah, Jadah^e was the father of Alemeth, Azmaveth and Zimri, and Zimri was the father of Moza. ⁴³Moza was the father of Binea; Rephaiah was his son, Eleasah his son and Azel his son.

⁴⁴Azel had six sons, and these were their names:
Azrikam, Bokeru, Ishmael, Sheariah, Obadiah and Hanan. These were the sons of Azel.

Saul Takes His Life

10 Now the Philistines fought against Israel; the Israelites fled before them, and many fell dead on Mount Gilboa. ²The Philistines were in hot pursuit of Saul and his sons, and they killed his sons Jonathan, Abinadab and Malki-Shua. ³The fighting grew fierce around Saul, and when the archers overtook him, they wounded him.

⁴Saul said to his armor-bearer, "Draw your sword and run me through, or these uncircumcised fellows will come and abuse me."

But his armor-bearer was terrified and would not do it; so Saul took his own sword and fell on it. ⁵When the armor-bearer saw that Saul was dead, he too fell on his sword and died. ⁶So Saul and his three sons died, and all his house died together.

⁷When all the Israelites in the valley saw that the army had fled and that Saul and his sons had died, they abandoned their towns and fled. And the Philistines came and occupied them.

⁸The next day, when the Philistines came to strip the dead, they found Saul and his sons fallen on Mount Gilboa. ⁹They stripped him and took his head and his armor, and sent messengers throughout the land of the Philistines to proclaim the news among their idols and their people. ¹⁰They put his armor in the temple of their gods and hung up his head in the temple of Dagon.

¹¹When all the inhabitants of Jabesh Gilead heard what the Philistines had done to Saul, ¹²all their valiant men went and took the bodies of Saul and his sons and brought them to Jabesh. Then they buried their bones under the great tree in Jabesh, and they fasted seven days.

¹³Saul died because he was unfaithful to the LORD; he did not keep the word of the LORD and even consulted a medium for guidance, ¹⁴and did not inquire of the LORD. So the LORD put him to death and turned the kingdom over to David son of Jesse.

David Becomes King Over Israel

11 All Israel came together to David at Hebron and said, "We are your own flesh and blood. ²In the past, even while Saul was king, you were the one who led Israel on their mili-

---

^a 35 *Father* may mean *civic leader* or *military leader.*   ^b 39 Also known as *Ish-Bosheth*   ^c 40 Also known as *Mephibosheth*   ^d 41 Vulgate and Syriac (see also Septuagint and 8:35); Hebrew does not have *and Ahaz.*
^e 42 Some Hebrew manuscripts and Septuagint (see also 8:36); most Hebrew manuscripts *Jarah, Jarah*

tary campaigns. And the Lord your God said to you, 'You will shepherd my people Israel, and you will become their ruler.'"

³When all the elders of Israel had come to King David at Hebron, he made a covenant with them at Hebron before the Lord, and they anointed David king over Israel, as the Lord had promised through Samuel.

David Conquers Jerusalem

⁴David and all the Israelites marched to Jerusalem (that is, Jebus). The Jebusites who lived there ⁵said to David, "You will not get in here." Nevertheless, David captured the fortress of Zion — which is the City of David.

⁶David had said, "Whoever leads the attack on the Jebusites will become commander-in-chief." Joab son of Zeruiah went up first, and so he received the command.

⁷David then took up residence in the fortress, and so it was called the City of David. ⁸He built up the city around it, from the terraces*a* to the surrounding wall, while Joab restored the rest of the city. ⁹And David became more and more powerful, because the Lord Almighty was with him.

David's Mighty Warriors

¹⁰These were the chiefs of David's mighty warriors — they, together with all Israel, gave his kingship strong support to extend it over the whole land, as the Lord had promised — ¹¹this is the list of David's mighty warriors:

Jashobeam,*b* a Hakmonite, was chief of the officers*c*; he raised his spear against three hundred men, whom he killed in one encounter.

¹²Next to him was Eleazar son of Dodai the Ahohite, one of the three mighty warriors. ¹³He was with David at Pas Dammim when the Philistines gathered there for battle. At a place where there was a field full of barley, the troops fled from the Philistines. ¹⁴But they took their stand in the middle of the field. They defended it and struck the Philistines down, and the Lord brought about a great victory.

¹⁵Three of the thirty chiefs came down to David to the rock at the cave of Adullam, while a band of Philistines was encamped in the Valley of Rephaim. ¹⁶At that time David was in the stronghold, and the Philistine garrison was at Bethlehem. ¹⁷David longed for water and said, "Oh, that someone would get me a drink of water from the well near the gate of Bethlehem!" ¹⁸So the Three broke through the Philistine lines, drew water from the well near the gate of Bethlehem and carried it back to David. But he refused to drink it; instead, he poured it out to the Lord. ¹⁹"God forbid that I should do this!" he said. "Should I drink the blood of these men who went at the risk of their lives?" Because they risked their lives to bring it back, David would not drink it.

Such were the exploits of the three mighty warriors.

²⁰Abishai the brother of Joab was chief of the Three. He raised his spear against three hundred men, whom he killed, and so he became as famous as the Three. ²¹He was doubly honored above the Three and became their commander, even though he was not included among them.

²²Benaiah son of Jehoiada, a valiant fighter from Kabzeel, performed great exploits. He struck down Moab's two mightiest warriors. He also went down into a pit on a snowy day and killed a lion. ²³And he struck down an Egyptian who was five cubits*d* tall. Although the Egyptian had a spear like a weaver's rod in his hand, Benaiah went against him with a club. He snatched the spear from the Egyptian's hand and killed him with his own spear. ²⁴Such were the exploits of Benaiah son of Jehoiada; he too was as famous as the three

---

a 8 Or *the Millo*   *b 11* Possibly a variant of *Jashob-Baal* (see also 2 Samuel 23:8)   *c 11* Or *Thirty*; some Septuagint manuscripts *Three*   *d 23* That is, about 7 feet 6 inches or about 2.3 meters mighty warriors. ²⁵He was held in greater honor than any of the Thirty, but he was not included among the Three. And David put him in charge of his bodyguard.

²⁶The mighty warriors were:
Asahel the brother of Joab,
Elhanan son of Dodo from Bethlehem,
²⁷Shammoth the Harorite,
Helez the Pelonite,
²⁸Ira son of Ikkesh from Tekoa,
Abiezer from Anathoth,
²⁹Sibbekai the Hushathite,
Ilai the Ahohite,
³⁰Maharai the Netophathite,
Heled son of Baanah the Netopha-
thite,
³¹Ithai son of Ribai from Gibeah in
Benjamin,
Benaiah the Pirathonite,
³²Hurai from the ravines of Gaash,
Abiel the Arbathite,
³³Azmaveth the Baharumite,
Eliahba the Shaalbonite,
³⁴the sons of Hashem the Gizonite,
Jonathan son of Shagee the Hararite,
³⁵Ahiam son of Sakar the Hararite,
Eliphal son of Ur,
³⁶Hepher the Mekerathite,
Ahijah the Pelonite,
³⁷Hezro the Carmelite,
Naarai son of Ezbai,
³⁸Joel the brother of Nathan,
Mibhar son of Hagri,
³⁹Zelek the Ammonite,
Naharai the Berothite, the armor-
bearer of Joab son of Zeruiah,
⁴⁰Ira the Ithrite,
Gareb the Ithrite,
⁴¹Uriah the Hittite,
Zabad son of Ahlai,
⁴²Adina son of Shiza the Reubenite,
who was chief of the Reubenites,
and the thirty with him,
⁴³Hanan son of Maakah,
Joshaphat the Mithnite,
⁴⁴Uzzia the Ashterathite,
Shama and Jeiel the sons of Hotham the Aroerite,
⁴⁵Jediael son of Shimri,
his brother Joha the Tizite,
⁴⁶Eliel the Mahavite,
Jeribai and Joshaviah the sons of
Elnaam,
Ithmah the Moabite,
⁴⁷Eliel, Obed and Jaasiel the Mezoba-
ite.

Warriors Join David

12 These were the men who came to David at Ziklag, while he was banished from the presence of Saul son of Kish (they were among the warriors who helped him in battle; ²they were armed with bows and were able to shoot arrows or to sling stones right-handed or left-handed; they were relatives of Saul from the tribe of Benjamin):

³Ahiezer their chief and Joash the sons of Shemaah the Gibeathite; Jeziel and Pelet the sons of Azmaveth; Berakah, Jehu the Anathothite, ⁴and Ishmaiah the Gibeonite, a mighty warrior among the Thirty, who was a leader of the Thirty; Jeremiah, Jahaziel, Johanan, Jozabad the Gederathite,ᵃ ⁵Eluzai, Jerimoth, Bealiah, Shemariah and Shephatiah the Haruphite; ⁶Elkanah, Ishiah, Azarel, Joezer and Jashobeam the Korahites; ⁷and Joelah and Zebadiah the sons of Jeroham from Gedor.

⁸Some Gadites defected to David at his stronghold in the wilderness. They were brave warriors, ready for battle and able to handle the shield and spear. Their faces were the faces of lions, and they were as swift as gazelles in the mountains.
⁹Ezer was the chief,
Obadiah the second in command, Eliab the third,

ᵃ 4 In Hebrew texts the second half of this verse (*Jeremiah . . . Gederathite*) is numbered 12:5, and 12:5-40 is numbered 12:6-41.

¹⁰Mishmannah the fourth, Jeremiah the fifth,

¹¹Attai the sixth, Eliel the seventh,

¹²Johanan the eighth, Elzabad the ninth,

¹³Jeremiah the tenth and Makbannai the eleventh.

¹⁴These Gadites were army commanders; the least was a match for a hundred, and the greatest for a thousand. ¹⁵It was they who crossed the Jordan in the first month when it was overflowing all its banks, and they put to flight everyone living in the valleys, to the east and to the west.

¹⁶Other Benjamites and some men from Judah also came to David in his stronghold. ¹⁷David went out to meet them and said to them, "If you have come to me in peace to help me, I am ready for you to join me. But if you have come to betray me to my enemies when my hands are free from violence, may the God of our ancestors see it and judge you."

¹⁸Then the Spirit came on Amasai, chief of the Thirty, and he said:

"We are yours, David!
  We are with you, son of Jesse!
Success, success to you,
  and success to those who help you,
    for your God will help you."

So David received them and made them leaders of his raiding bands.

¹⁹Some of the tribe of Manasseh defected to David when he went with the Philistines to fight against Saul. (He and his men did not help the Philistines because, after consultation, their rulers sent him away. They said, "It will cost us our heads if he deserts to his master Saul.") ²⁰When David went to Ziklag, these were the men of Manasseh who defected to him: Adnah, Jozabad, Jediael, Michael, Jozabad, Elihu and Zillethai, leaders of units of a thousand in Manasseh. ²¹They helped David against raiding bands, for all of them were brave warriors, and they were commanders in his army. ²²Day after day men came to help David, until he had a great army, like the army of God.[a]

Others Join David at Hebron

²³These are the numbers of the men armed for battle who came to David at Hebron to turn Saul's kingdom over to him, as the Lord had said:

²⁴from Judah, carrying shield and spear — 6,800 armed for battle;

²⁵from Simeon, warriors ready for battle — 7,100;

²⁶from Levi — 4,600, ²⁷including Jehoiada, leader of the family of Aaron, with 3,700 men, ²⁸and Zadok, a brave young warrior, with 22 officers from his family;

²⁹from Benjamin, Saul's tribe — 3,000, most of whom had remained loyal to Saul's house until then;

³⁰from Ephraim, brave warriors, famous in their own clans — 20,800;

³¹from half the tribe of Manasseh, designated by name to come and make David king — 18,000;

³²from Issachar, men who understood the times and knew what Israel should do — 200 chiefs, with all their relatives under their command;

³³from Zebulun, experienced soldiers prepared for battle with every type of weapon, to help David with undivided loyalty — 50,000;

³⁴from Naphtali — 1,000 officers, together with 37,000 men carrying shields and spears;

³⁵from Dan, ready for battle — 28,600;

³⁶from Asher, experienced soldiers prepared for battle — 40,000;

³⁷and from east of the Jordan, from Reuben, Gad and the half-tribe of Manasseh, armed with every type of weapon — 120,000.

³⁸All these were fighting men who volunteered to serve in the ranks. They came

---

to Hebron fully determined to make David king over all Israel. All the rest of the Israelites were also of one mind to make David king. ³⁹The men spent three days there with David, eating and drinking, for their families had supplied provisions for them. ⁴⁰Also, their neighbors from as far away as Issachar, Zebulun and Naphtali came bringing food on donkeys, camels, mules and oxen. There were plentiful supplies of flour, fig cakes, raisin cakes, wine, olive oil, cattle and sheep, for there was joy in Israel.

Bringing Back the Ark

13 David conferred with each of his officers, the commanders of thousands and commanders of hundreds. ²He then said to the whole assembly of Israel, "If it seems good to you and if it is the will of the Lord our God, let us send word far and wide to the rest of our people throughout the territories of Israel, and also to the priests and Levites who are with them in their towns and pasturelands, to come and join us. ³Let us bring the ark of our God back to us, for we did not inquire of[a] it[b] during the reign of Saul." ⁴The whole assembly agreed to do this, because it seemed right to all the people.

⁵So David assembled all Israel, from the Shihor River in Egypt to Lebo Hamath, to bring the ark of God from Kiriath Jearim. ⁶David and all Israel went to Baalah of Judah (Kiriath Jearim) to bring up from there the ark of God the Lord, who is enthroned between the cherubim — the ark that is called by the Name.

⁷They moved the ark of God from Abinadab's house on a new cart, with Uzzah and Ahio guiding it. ⁸David and all the Israelites were celebrating with all their might before God, with songs and with harps, lyres, timbrels, cymbals and trumpets.

⁹When they came to the threshing floor of Kidon, Uzzah reached out his hand to steady the ark, because the oxen stumbled. ¹⁰The Lord's anger burned against Uzzah, and he struck him down because he had put his hand on the ark. So he died there before God.

¹¹Then David was angry because the Lord's wrath had broken out against Uzzah, and to this day that place is called Perez Uzzah.[c]

¹²David was afraid of God that day and asked, "How can I ever bring the ark of God to me?" ¹³He did not take the ark to be with him in the City of David. Instead, he took it to the house of Obed-Edom the Gittite. ¹⁴The ark of God remained with the family of Obed-Edom in his house for three months, and the Lord blessed his household and everything he had.

David's House and Family

14 Now Hiram king of Tyre sent messengers to David, along with cedar logs, stonemasons and carpenters to build a palace for him. ²And David knew that the Lord had established him as king over Israel and that his kingdom had been highly exalted for the sake of his people Israel.

³In Jerusalem David took more wives and became the father of more sons and daughters. ⁴These are the names of the children born to him there: Shammua, Shobab, Nathan, Solomon, ⁵Ibhar, Elishua, Elpelet, ⁶Nogah, Nepheg, Japhia, ⁷Elishama, Beeliada[d] and Eliphelet.

David Defeats the Philistines

⁸When the Philistines heard that David had been anointed king over all Israel, they went up in full force to search for him, but David heard about it and went out to meet them. ⁹Now the Philistines had come and raided the Valley of Rephaim; ¹⁰so David inquired of God: "Shall I go and attack the Philistines? Will you deliver them into my hands?"

The Lord answered him, "Go, I will deliver them into your hands."

¹¹So David and his men went up to Baal

ᵃ 3 Or *we neglected*   ᵇ 3 Or *him*   ᶜ 11 *Perez Uzzah* means *outbreak against Uzzah*.   ᵈ 7 A variant of *Eliada*

Perazim, and there he defeated them. He said, "As waters break out, God has broken out against my enemies by my hand." So that place was called Baal Perazim.*a* 12The Philistines had abandoned their gods there, and David gave orders to burn them in the fire.

13Once more the Philistines raided the valley; 14so David inquired of God again, and God answered him, "Do not go directly after them, but circle around them and attack them in front of the poplar trees. 15As soon as you hear the sound of marching in the tops of the poplar trees, move out to battle, because that will mean God has gone out in front of you to strike the Philistine army." 16So David did as God commanded him, and they struck down the Philistine army, all the way from Gibeon to Gezer.

17So David's fame spread throughout every land, and the LORD made all the nations fear him.

The Ark Brought to Jerusalem

15 After David had constructed buildings for himself in the City of David, he prepared a place for the ark of God and pitched a tent for it. 2Then David said, "No one but the Levites may carry the ark of God, because the LORD chose them to carry the ark of the LORD and to minister before him forever."

3David assembled all Israel in Jerusalem to bring up the ark of the LORD to the place he had prepared for it. 4He called together the descendants of Aaron and the Levites:

5From the descendants of Kohath,
Uriel the leader and 120 relatives;
6from the descendants of Merari,
Asaiah the leader and 220 relatives;
7from the descendants of Gershon,*b*
Joel the leader and 130 relatives;
8from the descendants of Elizaphan,

Shemaiah the leader and 200 relatives;
9from the descendants of Hebron,
Eliel the leader and 80 relatives;
10from the descendants of Uzziel,
Amminadab the leader and 112 relatives.

11Then David summoned Zadok and Abiathar the priests, and Uriel, Asaiah, Joel, Shemaiah, Eliel and Amminadab the Levites. 12He said to them, "You are the heads of the Levitical families; you and your fellow Levites are to consecrate yourselves and bring up the ark of the LORD, the God of Israel, to the place I have prepared for it. 13It was because you, the Levites, did not bring it up the first time that the LORD our God broke out in anger against us. We did not inquire of him about how to do it in the prescribed way." 14So the priests and Levites consecrated themselves in order to bring up the ark of the LORD, the God of Israel. 15And the Levites carried the ark of God with the poles on their shoulders, as Moses had commanded in accordance with the word of the LORD.

16David told the leaders of the Levites to appoint their fellow Levites as musicians to make a joyful sound with musical instruments: lyres, harps and cymbals.

17So the Levites appointed Heman son of Joel; from his relatives, Asaph son of Berekiah; and from their relatives the Merarites, Ethan son of Kushaiah; 18and with them their relatives next in rank: Zechariah,*c* Jaaziel, Shemiramoth, Jehiel, Unni, Eliab, Benaiah, Maaseiah, Mattithiah, Eliphelehu, Mikneiah, Obed-Edom and Jeiel,*d* the gatekeepers.

19The musicians Heman, Asaph and Ethan were to sound the bronze cymbals; 20Zechariah, Jaaziel,*e* Shemiramoth, Jehiel, Unni, Eliab, Maaseiah and Benaiah were to play the lyres according to *alamoth,f* 21and Mattithiah, Eliphelehu, Mikneiah,

---

a 11 *Baal Perazim* means *the lord who breaks out.*   *b* 7 Hebrew *Gershom,* a variant of *Gershon*   *c* 18 Three Hebrew manuscripts and most Septuagint manuscripts (see also verse 20 and 16:5); most Hebrew manuscripts *Zechariah son and* or *Zechariah, Ben and*   *d* 18 Hebrew; Septuagint (see also verse 21) *Jeiel and Azaziah*   *e* 20 See verse 18; Hebrew *Aziel,* a variant of *Jaaziel.*   *f* 20 Probably a musical term

Obed-Edom, Jeiel and Azaziah were to play the harps, directing according to *sheminith*.[a] [22]Kenaniah the head Levite was in charge of the singing; that was his responsibility because he was skillful at it.

[23]Berekiah and Elkanah were to be doorkeepers for the ark. [24]Shebaniah, Joshaphat, Nethanel, Amasai, Zechariah, Benaiah and Eliezer the priests were to blow trumpets before the ark of God. Obed-Edom and Jehiah were also to be doorkeepers for the ark.

[25]So David and the elders of Israel and the commanders of units of a thousand went to bring up the ark of the covenant of the LORD from the house of Obed-Edom, with rejoicing. [26]Because God had helped the Levites who were carrying the ark of the covenant of the LORD, seven bulls and seven rams were sacrificed. [27]Now David was clothed in a robe of fine linen, as were all the Levites who were carrying the ark, and as were the musicians, and Kenaniah, who was in charge of the singing of the choirs. David also wore a linen ephod. [28]So all Israel brought up the ark of the covenant of the LORD with shouts, with the sounding of rams' horns and trumpets, and of cymbals, and the playing of lyres and harps.

[29]As the ark of the covenant of the LORD was entering the City of David, Michal daughter of Saul watched from a window. And when she saw King David dancing and celebrating, she despised him in her heart.

Ministering Before the Ark

16 They brought the ark of God and set it inside the tent that David had pitched for it, and they presented burnt offerings and fellowship offerings before God. [2]After David had finished sacrificing the burnt offerings and fellowship offerings, he blessed the people in the name of the LORD. [3]Then he gave a loaf of bread, a cake of dates and a cake of raisins to each Israelite man and woman.

[4]He appointed some of the Levites to minister before the ark of the LORD, to extol,[b] thank, and praise the LORD, the God of Israel: [5]Asaph was the chief, and next to him in rank were Zechariah, then Jaaziel,[c] Shemiramoth, Jehiel, Mattithiah, Eliab, Benaiah, Obed-Edom and Jeiel. They were to play the lyres and harps, Asaph was to sound the cymbals, [6]and Benaiah and Jahaziel the priests were to blow the trumpets regularly before the ark of the covenant of God.

[7]That day David first appointed Asaph and his associates to give praise to the LORD in this manner:

[8]Give praise to the LORD, proclaim his
    name;
  make known among the nations
    what he has done.
[9]Sing to him, sing praise to him;
  tell of all his wonderful acts.
[10]Glory in his holy name;
  let the hearts of those who seek the
    LORD rejoice.
[11]Look to the LORD and his strength;
  seek his face always.

[12]Remember the wonders he has done,
  his miracles, and the judgments he
    pronounced,
[13]you his servants, the descendants of
    Israel,
  his chosen ones, the children of
    Jacob.
[14]He is the LORD our God;
  his judgments are in all the earth.

[15]He remembers[d] his covenant forever,
  the promise he made, for a thousand
    generations,
[16]the covenant he made with Abraham,
  the oath he swore to Isaac.
[17]He confirmed it to Jacob as a decree,
  to Israel as an everlasting covenant:
[18]"To you I will give the land of Canaan
  as the portion you will inherit."

---

a 21 Probably a musical term   *b 4* Or *petition*; or *invoke*   *c 5* See 15:18,20; Hebrew *Jeiel*, possibly another name for *Jaaziel*.   *d 15* Some Septuagint manuscripts (see also Psalm 105:8); Hebrew *Remember*

¹⁹ When they were but few in number,
  few indeed, and strangers in it,
²⁰ they*^a* wandered from nation to nation,
  from one kingdom to another.
²¹ He allowed no one to oppress them;
  for their sake he rebuked kings:
²² "Do not touch my anointed ones;
  do my prophets no harm."

²³ Sing to the LORD, all the earth;
  proclaim his salvation day after day.
²⁴ Declare his glory among the nations,
  his marvelous deeds among all
    peoples.

²⁵ For great is the LORD and most worthy
    of praise;
  he is to be feared above all gods.
²⁶ For all the gods of the nations are idols,
  but the LORD made the heavens.
²⁷ Splendor and majesty are before him;
  strength and joy are in his dwelling
    place.

²⁸ Ascribe to the LORD, all you families of
    nations,
  ascribe to the LORD glory and
    strength.
²⁹ Ascribe to the LORD the glory due his
    name;
  bring an offering and come before
    him.
Worship the LORD in the splendor of
  his*^b* holiness.
³⁰ Tremble before him, all the earth!
  The world is firmly established; it
    cannot be moved.

³¹ Let the heavens rejoice, let the earth be
    glad;
  let them say among the nations, "The
    LORD reigns!"
³² Let the sea resound, and all that is in it;
  let the fields be jubilant, and
    everything in them!
³³ Let the trees of the forest sing,
  let them sing for joy before the LORD,
  for he comes to judge the earth.

³⁴ Give thanks to the LORD, for he is good;
  his love endures forever.
³⁵ Cry out, "Save us, God our Savior;
  gather us and deliver us from the
    nations,
  that we may give thanks to your holy
    name,
  and glory in your praise."
³⁶ Praise be to the LORD, the God of Israel,
  from everlasting to everlasting.

Then all the people said "Amen" and
"Praise the LORD."

³⁷ David left Asaph and his associates before the ark of the covenant of the LORD to minister there regularly, according to each day's requirements. ³⁸ He also left Obed-Edom and his sixty-eight associates to minister with them. Obed-Edom son of Jeduthun, and also Hosah, were gatekeepers.

³⁹ David left Zadok the priest and his fellow priests before the tabernacle of the LORD at the high place in Gibeon ⁴⁰ to present burnt offerings to the LORD on the altar of burnt offering regularly, morning and evening, in accordance with everything written in the Law of the LORD, which he had given Israel. ⁴¹ With them were Heman and Jeduthun and the rest of those chosen and designated by name to give thanks to the LORD, "for his love endures forever." ⁴² Heman and Jeduthun were responsible for the sounding of the trumpets and cymbals and for the playing of the other instruments for sacred song. The sons of Jeduthun were stationed at the gate.

⁴³ Then all the people left, each for their own home, and David returned home to bless his family.

God's Promise to David

17 After David was settled in his palace, he said to Nathan the prophet, "Here I am, living in a house of cedar, while the ark of the covenant of the LORD is under a tent."

---

a 18-20 One Hebrew manuscript, Septuagint and Vulgate (see also Psalm 105:12); most Hebrew manuscripts *inherit*, / ¹⁹ *though you are but few in number, / few indeed, and strangers in it.*" / ²⁰ *They*   *b* 29 Or LORD *with the splendor of*

²Nathan replied to David, "Whatever you have in mind, do it, for God is with you."

³But that night the word of God came to Nathan, saying:

⁴"Go and tell my servant David, 'This is what the Lord says: You are not the one to build me a house to dwell in. ⁵I have not dwelt in a house from the day I brought Israel up out of Egypt to this day. I have moved from one tent site to another, from one dwelling place to another. ⁶Wherever I have moved with all the Israelites, did I ever say to any of their leaders*a* whom I commanded to shepherd my people, "Why have you not built me a house of cedar?"'

⁷"Now then, tell my servant David, 'This is what the Lord Almighty says: I took you from the pasture, from tending the flock, and appointed you ruler over my people Israel. ⁸I have been with you wherever you have gone, and I have cut off all your enemies from before you. Now I will make your name like the names of the greatest men on earth. ⁹And I will provide a place for my people Israel and will plant them so that they can have a home of their own and no longer be disturbed. Wicked people will not oppress them anymore, as they did at the beginning ¹⁰and have done ever since the time I appointed leaders over my people Israel. I will also subdue all your enemies.

"'I declare to you that the Lord will build a house for you: ¹¹When your days are over and you go to be with your ancestors, I will raise up your offspring to succeed you, one of your own sons, and I will establish his kingdom. ¹²He is the one who will build a house for me, and I will establish his throne forever. ¹³I will be his father, and he will be my son. I will never take my love away from him, as I took it away from your predecessor. ¹⁴I will set him over my house and my kingdom forever; his throne will be established forever.'"

¹⁵Nathan reported to David all the words of this entire revelation.

David's Prayer

¹⁶Then King David went in and sat before the Lord, and he said:

"Who am I, Lord God, and what is my family, that you have brought me this far? ¹⁷And as if this were not enough in your sight, my God, you have spoken about the future of the house of your servant. You, Lord God, have looked on me as though I were the most exalted of men.

¹⁸"What more can David say to you for honoring your servant? For you know your servant, ¹⁹Lord. For the sake of your servant and according to your will, you have done this great thing and made known all these great promises.

²⁰"There is no one like you, Lord, and there is no God but you, as we have heard with our own ears. ²¹And who is like your people Israel — the one nation on earth whose God went out to redeem a people for himself, and to make a name for yourself, and to perform great and awesome wonders by driving out nations from before your people, whom you redeemed from Egypt? ²²You made your people Israel your very own forever, and you, Lord, have become their God.

²³"And now, Lord, let the promise you have made concerning your servant and his house be established forever. Do as you promised, ²⁴so that it will be established and that your name will be great forever. Then peo-

---

a 6 Traditionally *judges*; also in verse 10

ple will say, 'The Lord Almighty, the God over Israel, is Israel's God!' And the house of your servant David will be established before you.

²⁵"You, my God, have revealed to your servant that you will build a house for him. So your servant has found courage to pray to you. ²⁶You, Lord, are God! You have promised these good things to your servant. ²⁷Now you have been pleased to bless the house of your servant, that it may continue forever in your sight; for you, Lord, have blessed it, and it will be blessed forever."

David's Victories

18 In the course of time, David defeated the Philistines and subdued them, and he took Gath and its surrounding villages from the control of the Philistines.

²David also defeated the Moabites, and they became subject to him and brought him tribute.

³Moreover, David defeated Hadadezer king of Zobah, in the vicinity of Hamath, when he went to set up his monument at*ᵃ* the Euphrates River. ⁴David captured a thousand of his chariots, seven thousand charioteers and twenty thousand foot soldiers. He hamstrung all but a hundred of the chariot horses.

⁵When the Arameans of Damascus came to help Hadadezer king of Zobah, David struck down twenty-two thousand of them. ⁶He put garrisons in the Aramean kingdom of Damascus, and the Arameans became subject to him and brought him tribute. The Lord gave David victory wherever he went.

⁷David took the gold shields carried by the officers of Hadadezer and brought them to Jerusalem. ⁸From Tebahᵇ and Kun, towns that belonged to Hadadezer, David took a great quantity of bronze, which Sol-

omon used to make the bronze Sea, the pillars and various bronze articles.

⁹When Tou king of Hamath heard that David had defeated the entire army of Hadadezer king of Zobah, ¹⁰he sent his son Hadoram to King David to greet him and congratulate him on his victory in battle over Hadadezer, who had been at war with Tou. Hadoram brought all kinds of articles of gold, of silver and of bronze.

¹¹King David dedicated these articles to the Lord, as he had done with the silver and gold he had taken from all these nations: Edom and Moab, the Ammonites and the Philistines, and Amalek.

¹²Abishai son of Zeruiah struck down eighteen thousand Edomites in the Valley of Salt. ¹³He put garrisons in Edom, and all the Edomites became subject to David. The Lord gave David victory wherever he went.

David's Officials

¹⁴David reigned over all Israel, doing what was just and right for all his people. ¹⁵Joab son of Zeruiah was over the army; Jehoshaphat son of Ahilud was recorder; ¹⁶Zadok son of Ahitub and Ahimelekᶜ son of Abiathar were priests; Shavsha was secretary; ¹⁷Benaiah son of Jehoiada was over the Kerethites and Pelethites; and David's sons were chief officials at the king's side.

David Defeats the Ammonites

19 In the course of time, Nahash king of the Ammonites died, and his son succeeded him as king. ²David thought, "I will show kindness to Hanun son of Nahash, because his father showed kindness to me." So David sent a delegation to express his sympathy to Hanun concerning his father.

When David's envoys came to Hanun in the land of the Ammonites to express sympathy to him, ³the Ammonite commanders said to Hanun, "Do you think David is

---

ᵃ 3 Or *to restore his control over*   *ᵇ 8* Hebrew *Tibhath,* a variant of *Tebah*   *ᶜ 16* Some Hebrew manuscripts, Vulgate and Syriac (see also 2 Samuel 8:17); most Hebrew manuscripts *Abimelek* honoring your father by sending envoys to you to express sympathy? Haven't his envoys come to you only to explore and spy out the country and overthrow it?" ⁴So Hanun seized David's envoys, shaved them, cut off their garments at the buttocks, and sent them away.

⁵When someone came and told David about the men, he sent messengers to meet them, for they were greatly humiliated. The king said, "Stay at Jericho till your beards have grown, and then come back."

⁶When the Ammonites realized that they had become obnoxious to David, Hanun and the Ammonites sent a thousand talents*a* of silver to hire chariots and charioteers from Aram Naharaim,*b* Aram Maakah and Zobah. ⁷They hired thirty-two thousand chariots and charioteers, as well as the king of Maakah with his troops, who came and camped near Medeba, while the Ammonites were mustered from their towns and moved out for battle.

⁸On hearing this, David sent Joab out with the entire army of fighting men. ⁹The Ammonites came out and drew up in battle formation at the entrance to their city, while the kings who had come were by themselves in the open country.

¹⁰Joab saw that there were battle lines in front of him and behind him; so he selected some of the best troops in Israel and deployed them against the Arameans. ¹¹He put the rest of the men under the command of Abishai his brother, and they were deployed against the Ammonites. ¹²Joab said, "If the Arameans are too strong for me, then you are to rescue me; but if the Ammonites are too strong for you, then I will rescue you. ¹³Be strong, and let us fight bravely for our people and the cities of our God. The LORD will do what is good in his sight."

¹⁴Then Joab and the troops with him advanced to fight the Arameans, and they fled before him. ¹⁵When the Ammonites realized that the Arameans were fleeing, they too fled before his brother Abishai and went inside the city. So Joab went back to Jerusalem.

¹⁶After the Arameans saw that they had been routed by Israel, they sent messengers and had Arameans brought from beyond the Euphrates River, with Shophak the commander of Hadadezer's army leading them.

¹⁷When David was told of this, he gathered all Israel and crossed the Jordan; he advanced against them and formed his battle lines opposite them. David formed his lines to meet the Arameans in battle, and they fought against him. ¹⁸But they fled before Israel, and David killed seven thousand of their charioteers and forty thousand of their foot soldiers. He also killed Shophak the commander of their army.

¹⁹When the vassals of Hadadezer saw that they had been routed by Israel, they made peace with David and became subject to him.

So the Arameans were not willing to help the Ammonites anymore.

The Capture of Rabbah

20 In the spring, at the time when kings go off to war, Joab led out the armed forces. He laid waste the land of the Ammonites and went to Rabbah and besieged it, but David remained in Jerusalem. Joab attacked Rabbah and left it in ruins. ²David took the crown from the head of their king*c* — its weight was found to be a talent*d* of gold, and it was set with precious stones — and it was placed on David's head. He took a great quantity of plunder from the city ³and brought out the people who were there, consigning them to labor with saws and with iron picks and axes. David did this to all the Ammonite towns. Then David and his entire army returned to Jerusalem.

---

a 6 That is, about 38 tons or about 34 metric tons   *b 6* That is, Northwest Mesopotamia   *c 2* Or *of Milkom,* that is, Molek   *d 2* That is, about 75 pounds or about 34 kilograms

War With the Philistines

⁴In the course of time, war broke out with the Philistines, at Gezer. At that time Sibbekai the Hushathite killed Sippai, one of the descendants of the Rephaites, and the Philistines were subjugated.

⁵In another battle with the Philistines, Elhanan son of Jair killed Lahmi the brother of Goliath the Gittite, who had a spear with a shaft like a weaver's rod.

⁶In still another battle, which took place at Gath, there was a huge man with six fingers on each hand and six toes on each foot—twenty-four in all. He also was descended from Rapha. ⁷When he taunted Israel, Jonathan son of Shimea, David's brother, killed him.

⁸These were descendants of Rapha in Gath, and they fell at the hands of David and his men.

David Counts the Fighting Men

21 Satan rose up against Israel and incited David to take a census of Israel. ²So David said to Joab and the commanders of the troops, "Go and count the Israelites from Beersheba to Dan. Then report back to me so that I may know how many there are."

³But Joab replied, "May the LORD multiply his troops a hundred times over. My lord the king, are they not all my lord's subjects? Why does my lord want to do this? Why should he bring guilt on Israel?"

⁴The king's word, however, overruled Joab; so Joab left and went throughout Israel and then came back to Jerusalem. ⁵Joab reported the number of the fighting men to David: In all Israel there were one million one hundred thousand men who could handle a sword, including four hundred and seventy thousand in Judah.

⁶But Joab did not include Levi and Benjamin in the numbering, because the king's command was repulsive to him. ⁷This command was also evil in the sight of God; so he punished Israel.

⁸Then David said to God, "I have sinned greatly by doing this. Now, I beg you, take away the guilt of your servant. I have done a very foolish thing."

⁹The LORD said to Gad, David's seer, ¹⁰"Go and tell David, 'This is what the LORD says: I am giving you three options. Choose one of them for me to carry out against you.'"

¹¹So Gad went to David and said to him, "This is what the LORD says: 'Take your choice: ¹²three years of famine, three months of being swept away*a* before your enemies, with their swords overtaking you, or three days of the sword of the LORD—days of plague in the land, with the angel of the LORD ravaging every part of Israel.' Now then, decide how I should answer the one who sent me."

¹³David said to Gad, "I am in deep distress. Let me fall into the hands of the LORD, for his mercy is very great; but do not let me fall into human hands."

¹⁴So the LORD sent a plague on Israel, and seventy thousand men of Israel fell dead. ¹⁵And God sent an angel to destroy Jerusalem. But as the angel was doing so, the LORD saw it and relented concerning the disaster and said to the angel who was destroying the people, "Enough! Withdraw your hand." The angel of the LORD was then standing at the threshing floor of Araunah*b* the Jebusite.

¹⁶David looked up and saw the angel of the LORD standing between heaven and earth, with a drawn sword in his hand extended over Jerusalem. Then David and the elders, clothed in sackcloth, fell facedown.

¹⁷David said to God, "Was it not I who ordered the fighting men to be counted? I, the shepherd,*c* have sinned and done wrong. These are but sheep. What have they done? LORD my God, let your hand

---

a 12 Hebrew; Septuagint and Vulgate (see also 2 Samuel 24:13) *of fleeing*   *b 15* Hebrew *Ornan,* a variant of *Araunah;* also in verses 18-28   *c 17* Probable reading of the original Hebrew text (see 2 Samuel 24:17 and note); Masoretic Text does not have *the shepherd.*

fall on me and my family, but do not let this plague remain on your people."

David Builds an Altar

[18]Then the angel of the LORD ordered Gad to tell David to go up and build an altar to the LORD on the threshing floor of Araunah the Jebusite. [19]So David went up in obedience to the word that Gad had spoken in the name of the LORD.

[20]While Araunah was threshing wheat, he turned and saw the angel; his four sons who were with him hid themselves. [21]Then David approached, and when Araunah looked and saw him, he left the threshing floor and bowed down before David with his face to the ground.

[22]David said to him, "Let me have the site of your threshing floor so I can build an altar to the LORD, that the plague on the people may be stopped. Sell it to me at the full price."

[23]Araunah said to David, "Take it! Let my lord the king do whatever pleases him. Look, I will give the oxen for the burnt offerings, the threshing sledges for the wood, and the wheat for the grain offering. I will give all this."

[24]But King David replied to Araunah, "No, I insist on paying the full price. I will not take for the LORD what is yours, or sacrifice a burnt offering that costs me nothing."

[25]So David paid Araunah six hundred shekels[a] of gold for the site. [26]David built an altar to the LORD there and sacrificed burnt offerings and fellowship offerings. He called on the LORD, and the LORD answered him with fire from heaven on the altar of burnt offering.

[27]Then the LORD spoke to the angel, and he put his sword back into its sheath. [28]At that time, when David saw that the LORD had answered him on the threshing floor of Araunah the Jebusite, he offered sacrifices there. [29]The tabernacle of the LORD, which Moses had made in the wilderness, and the altar of burnt offering were at that time on the high place at Gibeon. [30]But David could not go before it to inquire of God, because he was afraid of the sword of the angel of the LORD.

22

Then David said, "The house of the LORD God is to be here, and also the altar of burnt offering for Israel."

Preparations for the Temple

[2]So David gave orders to assemble the foreigners residing in Israel, and from among them he appointed stonecutters to prepare dressed stone for building the house of God. [3]He provided a large amount of iron to make nails for the doors of the gateways and for the fittings, and more bronze than could be weighed. [4]He also provided more cedar logs than could be counted, for the Sidonians and Tyrians had brought large numbers of them to David.

[5]David said, "My son Solomon is young and inexperienced, and the house to be built for the LORD should be of great magnificence and fame and splendor in the sight of all the nations. Therefore I will make preparations for it." So David made extensive preparations before his death.

[6]Then he called for his son Solomon and charged him to build a house for the LORD, the God of Israel. [7]David said to Solomon: "My son, I had it in my heart to build a house for the Name of the LORD my God. [8]But this word of the LORD came to me: 'You have shed much blood and have fought many wars. You are not to build a house for my Name, because you have shed much blood on the earth in my sight. [9]But you will have a son who will be a man of peace and rest, and I will give him rest from all his enemies on every side. His name will be Solomon,[b] and I will grant Israel peace and quiet during his reign. [10]He is the one who will build a house for my Name. He

---

[a] 25 That is, about 15 pounds or about 6.9 kilograms Hebrew for *peace.*   [b] 9 *Solomon* sounds like and may be derived from the

will be my son, and I will be his father. And I will establish the throne of his kingdom over Israel forever.'

¹¹"Now, my son, the LORD be with you, and may you have success and build the house of the LORD your God, as he said you would. ¹²May the LORD give you discretion and understanding when he puts you in command over Israel, so that you may keep the law of the LORD your God. ¹³Then you will have success if you are careful to observe the decrees and laws that the LORD gave Moses for Israel. Be strong and courageous. Do not be afraid or discouraged.

¹⁴"I have taken great pains to provide for the temple of the LORD a hundred thousand talents*a* of gold, a million talents*b* of silver, quantities of bronze and iron too great to be weighed, and wood and stone. And you may add to them. ¹⁵You have many workers: stonecutters, masons and carpenters, as well as those skilled in every kind of work ¹⁶in gold and silver, bronze and iron — craftsmen beyond number. Now begin the work, and the LORD be with you."

¹⁷Then David ordered all the leaders of Israel to help his son Solomon. ¹⁸He said to them, "Is not the LORD your God with you? And has he not granted you rest on every side? For he has given the inhabitants of the land into my hands, and the land is subject to the LORD and to his people. ¹⁹Now devote your heart and soul to seeking the LORD your God. Begin to build the sanctuary of the LORD God, so that you may bring the ark of the covenant of the LORD and the sacred articles belonging to God into the temple that will be built for the Name of the LORD."

The Levites

23 When David was old and full of years, he made his son Solomon king over Israel.

²He also gathered together all the leaders of Israel, as well as the priests and Levites. ³The Levites thirty years old or more were counted, and the total number of men was thirty-eight thousand. ⁴David said, "Of these, twenty-four thousand are to be in charge of the work of the temple of the LORD and six thousand are to be officials and judges. ⁵Four thousand are to be gatekeepers and four thousand are to praise the LORD with the musical instruments I have provided for that purpose."

⁶David separated the Levites into divisions corresponding to the sons of Levi: Gershon, Kohath and Merari.

Gershonites

⁷Belonging to the Gershonites:
    Ladan and Shimei.
⁸The sons of Ladan:
    Jehiel the first, Zetham and Joel —
    three in all.
⁹The sons of Shimei:
    Shelomoth, Haziel and Haran —
    three in all.
    These were the heads of the families of Ladan.
¹⁰And the sons of Shimei:
    Jahath, Ziza,*c* Jeush and Beriah.
    These were the sons of Shimei —
    four in all.
¹¹Jahath was the first and Ziza the second, but Jeush and Beriah did not have many sons; so they were counted as one family with one assignment.

Kohathites

¹²The sons of Kohath:
    Amram, Izhar, Hebron and Uzziel — four in all.
¹³The sons of Amram:
    Aaron and Moses.
    Aaron was set apart, he and his descendants forever, to consecrate the most holy things, to offer sacrifices before the LORD, to minister before

---

a 14 That is, about 3,750 tons or about 3,400 metric tons   *b 14* That is, about 37,500 tons or about 34,000 metric tons   *c 10* One Hebrew manuscript, Septuagint and Vulgate (see also verse 11); most Hebrew manuscripts *Zina* him and to pronounce blessings in his name forever. ¹⁴The sons of Moses the man of God were counted as part of the tribe of Levi.

¹⁵The sons of Moses:
Gershom and Eliezer.

¹⁶The descendants of Gershom:
Shubael was the first.

¹⁷The descendants of Eliezer:
Rehabiah was the first.

Eliezer had no other sons, but the sons of Rehabiah were very numerous.

¹⁸The sons of Izhar:
Shelomith was the first.

¹⁹The sons of Hebron:
Jeriah the first, Amariah the second, Jahaziel the third and Jekameam the fourth.

²⁰The sons of Uzziel:
Micah the first and Ishiah the second.

Merarites

²¹The sons of Merari:
Mahli and Mushi.
The sons of Mahli:
Eleazar and Kish.
²²Eleazar died without having sons: he had only daughters. Their cousins, the sons of Kish, married them.

²³The sons of Mushi:
Mahli, Eder and Jerimoth — three in all.

²⁴These were the descendants of Levi by their families — the heads of families as they were registered under their names and counted individually, that is, the workers twenty years old or more who served in the temple of the Lord. ²⁵For David had said, "Since the Lord, the God of Israel, has granted rest to his people and has come to dwell in Jerusalem forever, ²⁶the Levites no longer need to carry the tabernacle or any of the articles used in its service." ²⁷According to the last instructions of David, the Levites were counted from those twenty years old or more.

²⁸The duty of the Levites was to help Aaron's descendants in the service of the temple of the Lord: to be in charge of the courtyards, the side rooms, the purification of all sacred things and the performance of other duties at the house of God. ²⁹They were in charge of the bread set out on the table, the special flour for the grain offerings, the thin loaves made without yeast, the baking and the mixing, and all measurements of quantity and size. ³⁰They were also to stand every morning to thank and praise the Lord. They were to do the same in the evening ³¹and whenever burnt offerings were presented to the Lord on the Sabbaths, at the New Moon feasts and at the appointed festivals. They were to serve before the Lord regularly in the proper number and in the way prescribed for them.

³²And so the Levites carried out their responsibilities for the tent of meeting, for the Holy Place and, under their relatives the descendants of Aaron, for the service of the temple of the Lord.

The Divisions of Priests

24 These were the divisions of the descendants of Aaron:

The sons of Aaron were Nadab, Abihu, Eleazar and Ithamar. ²But Nadab and Abihu died before their father did, and they had no sons; so Eleazar and Ithamar served as the priests. ³With the help of Zadok a descendant of Eleazar and Ahimelek a descendant of Ithamar, David separated them into divisions for their appointed order of ministering. ⁴A larger number of leaders were found among Eleazar's descendants than among Ithamar's, and they were divided accordingly: sixteen heads of families from Eleazar's descendants and eight heads of families from Ithamar's descendants. ⁵They divided them impartially by casting lots, for there were officials of the sanctuary and officials of God among the descendants of both Eleazar and Ithamar.

⁶The scribe Shemaiah son of Nethanel,

a Levite, recorded their names in the presence of the king and of the officials: Zadok the priest, Ahimelek son of Abiathar and the heads of families of the priests and of the Levites — one family being taken from Eleazar and then one from Ithamar.

7 The first lot fell to Jehoiarib,
　the second to Jedaiah,
8 the third to Harim,
　the fourth to Seorim,
9 the fifth to Malkijah,
　the sixth to Mijamin,
10 the seventh to Hakkoz,
　the eighth to Abijah,
11 the ninth to Jeshua,
　the tenth to Shekaniah,
12 the eleventh to Eliashib,
　the twelfth to Jakim,
13 the thirteenth to Huppah,
　the fourteenth to Jeshebeab,
14 the fifteenth to Bilgah,
　the sixteenth to Immer,
15 the seventeenth to Hezir,
　the eighteenth to Happizzez,
16 the nineteenth to Pethahiah,
　the twentieth to Jehezkel,
17 the twenty-first to Jakin,
　the twenty-second to Gamul,
18 the twenty-third to Delaiah
　and the twenty-fourth to Maaziah.

19 This was their appointed order of ministering when they entered the temple of the Lord, according to the regulations prescribed for them by their ancestor Aaron, as the Lord, the God of Israel, had commanded him.

The Rest of the Levites

20 As for the rest of the descendants of Levi:
　from the sons of Amram: Shubael;
　　from the sons of Shubael: Jehdeiah.
21 As for Rehabiah, from his sons:
　　Ishiah was the first.
22 From the Izharites: Shelomoth;

from the sons of Shelomoth: Jahath.
23 The sons of Hebron: Jeriah the first,[a] Amariah the second, Jahaziel the third and Jekameam the fourth.
24 The son of Uzziel: Micah;
　from the sons of Micah: Shamir.
25 The brother of Micah: Ishiah;
　from the sons of Ishiah: Zechariah.
26 The sons of Merari: Mahli and Mushi. The son of Jaaziah: Beno.
27 The sons of Merari:
　from Jaaziah: Beno, Shoham, Zakkur and Ibri.
28 From Mahli: Eleazar, who had no sons.
29 From Kish: the son of Kish: Jerahmeel.
30 And the sons of Mushi: Mahli, Eder and Jerimoth.

These were the Levites, according to their families. 31 They also cast lots, just as their relatives the descendants of Aaron did, in the presence of King David and of Zadok, Ahimelek, and the heads of families of the priests and of the Levites. The families of the oldest brother were treated the same as those of the youngest.

The Musicians

25 David, together with the commanders of the army, set apart some of the sons of Asaph, Heman and Jeduthun for the ministry of prophesying, accompanied by harps, lyres and cymbals. Here is the list of the men who performed this service:

2 From the sons of Asaph:
　Zakkur, Joseph, Nethaniah and Asarelah. The sons of Asaph were under the supervision of Asaph, who prophesied under the king's supervision.
3 As for Jeduthun, from his sons:
　Gedaliah, Zeri, Jeshaiah, Shimei,[b]

---

a 23 Two Hebrew manuscripts and some Septuagint manuscripts (see also 23:19); most Hebrew manuscripts *The sons of Jeriah:*　b 3 One Hebrew manuscript and some Septuagint manuscripts (see also verse 17); most Hebrew manuscripts do not have *Shimei.*

Hashabiah and Mattithiah, six in all, under the supervision of their father Jeduthun, who prophesied, using the harp in thanking and praising the Lord.

4 As for Heman, from his sons:

Bukkiah, Mattaniah, Uzziel, Shubael and Jerimoth; Hananiah, Hanani, Eliathah, Giddalti and Romamti-Ezer; Joshbekashah, Mallothi, Hothir and Mahazioth. 5 (All these were sons of Heman the king's seer. They were given him through the promises of God to exalt him. God gave Heman fourteen sons and three daughters.)

6 All these men were under the supervision of their father for the music of the temple of the Lord, with cymbals, lyres and harps, for the ministry at the house of God. Asaph, Jeduthun and Heman were under the supervision of the king. 7 Along with their relatives — all of them trained and skilled in music for the Lord — they numbered 288. 8 Young and old alike, teacher as well as student, cast lots for their duties.

9 The first lot, which was for Asaph,
    fell to Joseph,
    his sons and relatives*a*   12*b*
the second to Gedaliah,
    him and his relatives and
    sons   12
10 the third to Zakkur,
    his sons and relatives   12
11 the fourth to Izri,*c*
    his sons and relatives   12
12 the fifth to Nethaniah,
    his sons and relatives   12
13 the sixth to Bukkiah,
    his sons and relatives   12
14 the seventh to Jesarelah,*d*
    his sons and relatives   12
15 the eighth to Jeshaiah,
    his sons and relatives   12
16 the ninth to Mattaniah,
    his sons and relatives   12

17 the tenth to Shimei,
    his sons and relatives   12
18 the eleventh to Azarel,*e*
    his sons and relatives   12
19 the twelfth to Hashabiah,
    his sons and relatives   12
20 the thirteenth to Shubael,
    his sons and relatives   12
21 the fourteenth to Mattithiah,
    his sons and relatives   12
22 the fifteenth to Jerimoth,
    his sons and relatives   12
23 the sixteenth to Hananiah,
    his sons and relatives   12
24 the seventeenth to Joshbekashah,
    his sons and relatives   12
25 the eighteenth to Hanani,
    his sons and relatives   12
26 the nineteenth to Mallothi,
    his sons and relatives   12
27 the twentieth to Eliathah,
    his sons and relatives   12
28 the twenty-first to Hothir,
    his sons and relatives   12
29 the twenty-second to Giddalti,
    his sons and relatives   12
30 the twenty-third to Mahazioth,
    his sons and relatives   12
31 the twenty-fourth to Romamti-
    Ezer,
    his sons and relatives   12.

The Gatekeepers

26 The divisions of the gatekeepers:

From the Korahites: Meshelemiah son of Kore, one of the sons of Asaph. 2 Meshelemiah had sons:

Zechariah the firstborn,
Jediael the second,
Zebadiah the third,
Jathniel the fourth,
3 Elam the fifth,
Jehohanan the sixth
and Eliehoenai the seventh.

---

a 9 See Septuagint; Hebrew does not have *his sons and relatives. twelve.*   *c 11* A variant of *Zeri*   *d 14* A variant of *Asarelah*   *b 9* See the total in verse 7; Hebrew does not have   *e 18* A variant of *Uzziel*

⁴Obed-Edom also had sons:
  Shemaiah the firstborn,
  Jehozabad the second,
  Joah the third,
  Sakar the fourth,
  Nethanel the fifth,
  ⁵Ammiel the sixth,
  Issachar the seventh
  and Peullethai the eighth.
  (For God had blessed Obed-Edom.)

⁶Obed-Edom's son Shemaiah also had sons, who were leaders in their father's family because they were very capable men. ⁷The sons of Shemaiah: Othni, Rephael, Obed and Elzabad; his relatives Elihu and Semakiah were also able men. ⁸All these were descendants of Obed-Edom; they and their sons and their relatives were capable men with the strength to do the work — descendants of Obed-Edom, 62 in all.

⁹Meshelemiah had sons and relatives, who were able men — 18 in all.

¹⁰Hosah the Merarite had sons: Shimri the first (although he was not the firstborn, his father had appointed him the first), ¹¹Hilkiah the second, Tabaliah the third and Zechariah the fourth. The sons and relatives of Hosah were 13 in all.

¹²These divisions of the gatekeepers, through their leaders, had duties for ministering in the temple of the LORD, just as their relatives had. ¹³Lots were cast for each gate, according to their families, young and old alike.

¹⁴The lot for the East Gate fell to Shelemiah.ᵃ Then lots were cast for his son Zechariah, a wise counselor, and the lot for the North Gate fell to him. ¹⁵The lot for the South Gate fell to Obed-Edom, and the lot for the storehouse fell to his sons. ¹⁶The lots for the West Gate and the Shalleketh Gate on the upper road fell to Shuppim and Hosah.

Guard was alongside of guard: ¹⁷There were six Levites a day on the east, four a day on the north, four a day on the south and two at a time at the storehouse. ¹⁸As for the courtᵇ to the west, there were four at the road and two at the courtᵇ itself.

¹⁹These were the divisions of the gatekeepers who were descendants of Korah and Merari.

The Treasurers and Other Officials

²⁰Their fellow Levites wereᶜ in charge of the treasuries of the house of God and the treasuries for the dedicated things.

²¹The descendants of Ladan, who were Gershonites through Ladan and who were heads of families belonging to Ladan the Gershonite, were Jehieli, ²²the sons of Jehieli, Zetham and his brother Joel. They were in charge of the treasuries of the temple of the LORD.

²³From the Amramites, the Izharites, the Hebronites and the Uzzielites:

²⁴Shubael, a descendant of Gershom son of Moses, was the official in charge of the treasuries. ²⁵His relatives through Eliezer: Rehabiah his son, Jeshaiah his son, Joram his son, Zikri his son and Shelomith his son. ²⁶Shelomith and his relatives were in charge of all the treasuries for the things dedicated by King David, by the heads of families who were the commanders of thousands and commanders of hundreds, and by the other army commanders. ²⁷Some of the plunder taken in battle they dedicated for the repair of the temple of the LORD. ²⁸And everything dedicated by Samuel the seer and by Saul son of Kish, Abner son of Ner and Joab son of Zeruiah, and all the other

---

ᵃ 14 A variant of *Meshelemiah*   ᵇ 18 The meaning of the Hebrew for this word is uncertain.   ᶜ 20 Septuagint; Hebrew *As for the Levites, Ahijah was* dedicated things were in the care of Shelomith and his relatives.

29 From the Izharites: Kenaniah and his sons were assigned duties away from the temple, as officials and judges over Israel.

30 From the Hebronites: Hashabiah and his relatives — seventeen hundred able men — were responsible in Israel west of the Jordan for all the work of the LORD and for the king's service. 31 As for the Hebronites, Jeriah was their chief according to the genealogical records of their families. In the fortieth year of David's reign a search was made in the records, and capable men among the Hebronites were found at Jazer in Gilead. 32 Jeriah had twenty-seven hundred relatives, who were able men and heads of families, and King David put them in charge of the Reubenites, the Gadites and the half-tribe of Manasseh for every matter pertaining to God and for the affairs of the king.

Army Divisions

27 This is the list of the Israelites — heads of families, commanders of thousands and commanders of hundreds, and their officers, who served the king in all that concerned the army divisions that were on duty month by month throughout the year. Each division consisted of 24,000 men.

2 In charge of the first division, for the first month, was Jashobeam son of Zabdiel. There were 24,000 men in his division. 3 He was a descendant of Perez and chief of all the army officers for the first month.

4 In charge of the division for the second month was Dodai the Ahohite; Mikloth was the leader of his division. There were 24,000 men in his division.

5 The third army commander, for the third month, was Benaiah son of Je-

hoiada the priest. He was chief and there were 24,000 men in his division. 6 This was the Benaiah who was a mighty warrior among the Thirty and was over the Thirty. His son Ammizabad was in charge of his division.

7 The fourth, for the fourth month, was Asahel the brother of Joab; his son Zebadiah was his successor. There were 24,000 men in his division.

8 The fifth, for the fifth month, was the commander Shamhuth the Izrahite. There were 24,000 men in his division.

9 The sixth, for the sixth month, was Ira the son of Ikkesh the Tekoite. There were 24,000 men in his division.

10 The seventh, for the seventh month, was Helez the Pelonite, an Ephraimite. There were 24,000 men in his division.

11 The eighth, for the eighth month, was Sibbekai the Hushathite, a Zerahite. There were 24,000 men in his division.

12 The ninth, for the ninth month, was Abiezer the Anathothite, a Benjamite. There were 24,000 men in his division.

13 The tenth, for the tenth month, was Maharai the Netophathite, a Zerahite. There were 24,000 men in his division.

14 The eleventh, for the eleventh month, was Benaiah the Pirathonite, an Ephraimite. There were 24,000 men in his division.

15 The twelfth, for the twelfth month, was Heldai the Netophathite, from the family of Othniel. There were 24,000 men in his division.

Leaders of the Tribes

16 The leaders of the tribes of Israel:

over the Reubenites: Eliezer son of Zikri;

over the Simeonites: Shephatiah son of Maakah;

17over Levi: Hashabiah son of Kemuel;
  over Aaron: Zadok;
18over Judah: Elihu, a brother of David;
  over Issachar: Omri son of Michael;
19over Zebulun: Ishmaiah son of Oba-
    diah;
  over Naphtali: Jerimoth son of Azriel;
20over the Ephraimites: Hoshea son of
    Azaziah;
  over half the tribe of Manasseh: Joel
    son of Pedaiah;
21over the half-tribe of Manasseh in
    Gilead: Iddo son of Zechariah;
  over Benjamin: Jaasiel son of Abner;
22over Dan: Azarel son of Jeroham.
These were the leaders of the tribes of
Israel.

23David did not take the number of the
men twenty years old or less, because the
Lord had promised to make Israel as numerous as the stars in the sky. 24Joab son
of Zeruiah began to count the men but did
not finish. God's wrath came on Israel on
account of this numbering, and the number was not entered in the book*a* of the annals of King David.

The King's Overseers

25Azmaveth son of Adiel was in charge
of the royal storehouses.

Jonathan son of Uzziah was in charge of
the storehouses in the outlying districts, in
the towns, the villages and the watchtowers.

26Ezri son of Kelub was in charge of the
workers who farmed the land.

27Shimei the Ramathite was in charge of
the vineyards.

Zabdi the Shiphmite was in charge of the
produce of the vineyards for the wine vats.

28Baal-Hanan the Gederite was in
charge of the olive and sycamore-fig trees
in the western foothills.

Joash was in charge of the supplies of olive oil.

29Shitrai the Sharonite was in charge of
the herds grazing in Sharon.

Shaphat son of Adlai was in charge of the
herds in the valleys.

30Obil the Ishmaelite was in charge of
the camels.

Jehdeiah the Meronothite was in charge
of the donkeys.

31Jaziz the Hagrite was in charge of the
flocks.

All these were the officials in charge of
King David's property.

32Jonathan, David's uncle, was a counselor, a man of insight and a scribe. Jehiel son of Hakmoni took care of the king's
sons.

33Ahithophel was the king's counselor.

Hushai the Arkite was the king's confidant. 34Ahithophel was succeeded by Jehoiada son of Benaiah and by Abiathar.

Joab was the commander of the royal
army.

David's Plans for the Temple

28 David summoned all the officials of Israel to assemble at Jerusalem: the officers over the
tribes, the commanders of the divisions in
the service of the king, the commanders of
thousands and commanders of hundreds,
and the officials in charge of all the property and livestock belonging to the king and
his sons, together with the palace officials,
the warriors and all the brave fighting men.

2King David rose to his feet and said:
"Listen to me, my fellow Israelites, my people. I had it in my heart to build a house as
a place of rest for the ark of the covenant
of the Lord, for the footstool of our God,
and I made plans to build it. 3But God said
to me, 'You are not to build a house for my
Name, because you are a warrior and have
shed blood.'

4"Yet the Lord, the God of Israel, chose
me from my whole family to be king over
Israel forever. He chose Judah as leader,
and from the tribe of Judah he chose my
family, and from my father's sons he was

---

a 24 Septuagint; Hebrew *number*

pleased to make me king over all Israel. [5]Of all my sons — and the Lord has given me many — he has chosen my son Solomon to sit on the throne of the kingdom of the Lord over Israel. [6]He said to me: 'Solomon your son is the one who will build my house and my courts, for I have chosen him to be my son, and I will be his father. [7]I will establish his kingdom forever if he is unswerving in carrying out my commands and laws, as is being done at this time.'

[8]"So now I charge you in the sight of all Israel and of the assembly of the Lord, and in the hearing of our God: Be careful to follow all the commands of the Lord your God, that you may possess this good land and pass it on as an inheritance to your descendants forever.

[9]"And you, my son Solomon, acknowledge the God of your father, and serve him with wholehearted devotion and with a willing mind, for the Lord searches every heart and understands every desire and every thought. If you seek him, he will be found by you; but if you forsake him, he will reject you forever. [10]Consider now, for the Lord has chosen you to build a house as the sanctuary. Be strong and do the work."

[11]Then David gave his son Solomon the plans for the portico of the temple, its buildings, its storerooms, its upper parts, its inner rooms and the place of atonement. [12]He gave him the plans of all that the Spirit had put in his mind for the courts of the temple of the Lord and all the surrounding rooms, for the treasuries of the temple of God and for the treasuries for the dedicated things. [13]He gave him instructions for the divisions of the priests and Levites, and for all the work of serving in the temple of the Lord, as well as for all the articles to be used in its service. [14]He designated the weight of gold for all the gold articles to be used in various kinds of service, and the weight of silver for all the silver articles to be used in various kinds of service: [15]the weight of gold for the gold lampstands and

their lamps, with the weight for each lampstand and its lamps; and the weight of silver for each silver lampstand and its lamps, according to the use of each lampstand; [16]the weight of gold for each table for consecrated bread; the weight of silver for the silver tables; [17]the weight of pure gold for the forks, sprinkling bowls and pitchers; the weight of gold for each gold dish; the weight of silver for each silver dish; [18]and the weight of the refined gold for the altar of incense. He also gave him the plan for the chariot, that is, the cherubim of gold that spread their wings and overshadow the ark of the covenant of the Lord.

[19]"All this," David said, "I have in writing as a result of the Lord's hand on me, and he enabled me to understand all the details of the plan."

[20]David also said to Solomon his son, "Be strong and courageous, and do the work. Do not be afraid or discouraged, for the Lord God, my God, is with you. He will not fail you or forsake you until all the work for the service of the temple of the Lord is finished. [21]The divisions of the priests and Levites are ready for all the work on the temple of God, and every willing person skilled in any craft will help you in all the work. The officials and all the people will obey your every command."

Gifts for Building the Temple

29 Then King David said to the whole assembly: "My son Solomon, the one whom God has chosen, is young and inexperienced. The task is great, because this palatial structure is not for man but for the Lord God. [2]With all my resources I have provided for the temple of my God — gold for the gold work, silver for the silver, bronze for the bronze, iron for the iron and wood for the wood, as well as onyx for the settings, turquoise,[a] stones of various colors, and all kinds of fine stone and marble — all of these in large quantities. [3]Besides, in my

---

a 2   The meaning of the Hebrew for this word is uncertain.

devotion to the temple of my God I now give my personal treasures of gold and silver for the temple of my God, over and above everything I have provided for this holy temple: ⁴three thousand talents*ᵃ* of gold (gold of Ophir) and seven thousand talents*ᵇ* of refined silver, for the overlaying of the walls of the buildings, ⁵for the gold work and the silver work, and for all the work to be done by the craftsmen. Now, who is willing to consecrate themselves to the LORD today?"

⁶Then the leaders of families, the officers of the tribes of Israel, the commanders of thousands and commanders of hundreds, and the officials in charge of the king's work gave willingly. ⁷They gave toward the work on the temple of God five thousand talents*ᶜ* and ten thousand darics*ᵈ* of gold, ten thousand talents*ᵉ* of silver, eighteen thousand talents*ᶠ* of bronze and a hundred thousand talents*ᵍ* of iron. ⁸Anyone who had precious stones gave them to the treasury of the temple of the LORD in the custody of Jehiel the Gershonite. ⁹The people rejoiced at the willing response of their leaders, for they had given freely and wholeheartedly to the LORD. David the king also rejoiced greatly.

David's Prayer

¹⁰David praised the LORD in the presence of the whole assembly, saying,

"Praise be to you, LORD,
  the God of our father Israel,
  from everlasting to everlasting.
¹¹Yours, LORD, is the greatness and the
    power
  and the glory and the majesty and
    the splendor,
  for everything in heaven and earth is
    yours.
Yours, LORD, is the kingdom;
  you are exalted as head over all.

¹²Wealth and honor come from you;
  you are the ruler of all things.
In your hands are strength and power
  to exalt and give strength to all.
¹³Now, our God, we give you thanks,
  and praise your glorious name.

¹⁴"But who am I, and who are my people, that we should be able to give as generously as this? Everything comes from you, and we have given you only what comes from your hand. ¹⁵We are foreigners and strangers in your sight, as were all our ancestors. Our days on earth are like a shadow, without hope. ¹⁶LORD our God, all this abundance that we have provided for building you a temple for your Holy Name comes from your hand, and all of it belongs to you. ¹⁷I know, my God, that you test the heart and are pleased with integrity. All these things I have given willingly and with honest intent. And now I have seen with joy how willingly your people who are here have given to you. ¹⁸LORD, the God of our fathers Abraham, Isaac and Israel, keep these desires and thoughts in the hearts of your people forever, and keep their hearts loyal to you. ¹⁹And give my son Solomon the wholehearted devotion to keep your commands, statutes and decrees and to do everything to build the palatial structure for which I have provided."

²⁰Then David said to the whole assembly, "Praise the LORD your God." So they all praised the LORD, the God of their fathers; they bowed down, prostrating themselves before the LORD and the king.

Solomon Acknowledged as King

²¹The next day they made sacrifices to the LORD and presented burnt offerings to him: a thousand bulls, a thousand rams and a thousand male lambs, together with their drink offerings, and other sacrifices in abundance for all Israel. ²²They ate and

---

ᵃ 4 That is, about 110 tons or about 100 metric tons   *ᵇ 4* That is, about 260 tons or about 235 metric tons   *ᶜ 7* That is, about 190 tons or about 170 metric tons   *ᵈ 7* That is, about 185 pounds or about 84 kilograms   *ᵉ 7* That is, about 380 tons or about 340 metric tons   *ᶠ 7* That is, about 675 tons or about 610 metric tons   *ᵍ 7* That is, about 3,800 tons or about 3,400 metric tons drank with great joy in the presence of the LORD that day.

Then they acknowledged Solomon son of David as king a second time, anointing him before the LORD to be ruler and Zadok to be priest. 23So Solomon sat on the throne of the LORD as king in place of his father David. He prospered and all Israel obeyed him. 24All the officers and warriors, as well as all of King David's sons, pledged their submission to King Solomon.

25The LORD highly exalted Solomon in the sight of all Israel and bestowed on him royal splendor such as no king over Israel ever had before.

The Death of David

26David son of Jesse was king over all Israel. 27He ruled over Israel forty years — seven in Hebron and thirty-three in Jerusalem. 28He died at a good old age, having enjoyed long life, wealth and honor. His son Solomon succeeded him as king.

29As for the events of King David's reign, from beginning to end, they are written in the records of Samuel the seer, the records of Nathan the prophet and the records of Gad the seer, 30together with the details of his reign and power, and the circumstances that surrounded him and Israel and the kingdoms of all the other lands.

2 Chronicles

THEME: Second Chronicles emphasizes that God's blessings result from obedience but that his judgment follows disobedience. If his people would humbly repent, God promised to restore them.

AUTHOR: According to Jewish tradition, Ezra wrote the Chronicles, but his authorship has been questioned. Many modern scholars simply refer to the author as "the Chronicler."

DATE OF WRITING: Although a specific date of composition can't be determined, Chronicles was probably written between 450 and 400 BC

ENCOURAGEMENT FROM 2 CHRONICLES: "LORD, there is no one like you to help the powerless against the mighty. Help us, LORD our God, for we rely on you" (2 Chronicles 14:11).

CHALLENGE FROM 2 CHRONICLES: "Do not be afraid or discouraged because of the king of Assyria and the vast army with him, for there is a greater power with us than with him. With him is only the arm of flesh, but with us is the LORD our God to help us and to fight our battles" (2 Chronicles 32:7 – 8).

REFLECTION FROM 2 CHRONICLES: "[Ahaziah] followed the ways of the house of Ahab, for his mother encouraged him to act wickedly. He did evil in the eyes of the LORD, as the house of Ahab had done, for after his father's death they became his advisers, to his undoing" (2 Chronicles 22:3 – 4).

Second Chronicles begins with Solomon's reign, with special emphasis on the building and dedication of the temple. Disobedience to the law is presented in this book as the problem underlying the Babylonian captivity. This book focuses on such events as Solomon's prayer for wisdom, the dedication of the temple, the visit from the queen of Sheba and a prediction of the length of the Babylonian captivity. The book ends with the Hebrews gaining permission to return to Judah and rebuild the temple. God's abiding faithfulness, even to a rebellious nation, is clearly conveyed in 2 Chronicles.

What a relief to know that God remains faithful to us even when we're rebellious. Many of us have done damage to our own lives and to the lives of others by going our own way. We've decided that we can control our lives better than God can. Even after we've begun our recovery process, we can sometimes take back the reins of our lives and try to do things on our own. The nations of Israel and Judah experienced God's grace firsthand and still had a hard time following him. The same is true for us. God has rescued us from a life of hurts, hang-ups and habits, and yet we find it hard to live the life he designed for us. In times like these, we can find in the history outlined in 2 Chronicles a powerful reminder that God is faithful and can help us return to his ways.

Solomon Asks for Wisdom

1 Solomon son of David established himself firmly over his kingdom, for the LORD his God was with him and made him exceedingly great.

²Then Solomon spoke to all Israel—to the commanders of thousands and commanders of hundreds, to the judges and to all the leaders in Israel, the heads of families— ³and Solomon and the whole assembly went to the high place at Gibeon, for God's tent of meeting was there, which Moses the LORD's servant had made in the wilderness. ⁴Now David had brought up the ark of God from Kiriath Jearim to the place he had prepared for it, because he had pitched a tent for it in Jerusalem. ⁵But the bronze altar that Bezalel son of Uri, the son of Hur, had made was in Gibeon in front of the tabernacle of the LORD; so Solomon and the assembly inquired of him there. ⁶Solomon went up to the bronze altar before the LORD in the tent of meeting and offered a thousand burnt offerings on it.

⁷That night God appeared to Solomon and said to him, "Ask for whatever you want me to give you."

⁸Solomon answered God, "You have shown great kindness to David my father and have made me king in his place. ⁹Now, LORD God, let your promise to my father David be confirmed, for you have made me king over a people who are as numerous as the dust of the earth. ¹⁰Give me wisdom and knowledge, that I may lead this people, for who is able to govern this great people of yours?"

¹¹God said to Solomon, "Since this is your heart's desire and you have not asked for wealth, possessions or honor, nor for the death of your enemies, and since you have not asked for a long life but for wisdom and knowledge to govern my people over whom I have made you king, ¹²therefore wisdom and knowledge will be given

you. And I will also give you wealth, possessions and honor, such as no king who was before you ever had and none after you will have."

¹³Then Solomon went to Jerusalem from the high place at Gibeon, from before the tent of meeting. And he reigned over Israel.

¹⁴Solomon accumulated chariots and horses; he had fourteen hundred chariots and twelve thousand horses,ᵃ which he kept in the chariot cities and also with him in Jerusalem. ¹⁵The king made silver and gold as common in Jerusalem as stones, and cedar as plentiful as sycamore-fig trees in the foothills. ¹⁶Solomon's horses were imported from Egypt and from Kueᵇ— the royal merchants purchased them from Kue at the current price. ¹⁷They imported a chariot from Egypt for six hundred shekelsᶜ of silver, and a horse for a hundred and fifty.ᵈ They also exported them to all the kings of the Hittites and of the Arameans.

Preparations for Building the Temple

2 ᵉ Solomon gave orders to build a temple for the Name of the LORD and a royal palace for himself. ²He conscripted 70,000 men as carriers and 80,000 as stonecutters in the hills and 3,600 as foremen over them.

³Solomon sent this message to Hiramᶠ king of Tyre:

"Send me cedar logs as you did for my father David when you sent him cedar to build a palace to live in. ⁴Now I am about to build a temple for the Name of the LORD my God and to dedicate it to him for burning fragrant incense before him, for setting out the consecrated bread regularly, and for making burnt offerings every morning and evening and on the Sabbaths, at the New Moons and at the appointed festivals of the LORD our God. This is a lasting ordinance for Israel.

ᵃ 14 Or *charioteers*   ᵇ 16 Probably Cilicia   ᶜ 17 That is, about 15 pounds or about 6.9 kilograms   ᵈ 17 That is, about 3 3/4 pounds or about 1.7 kilograms   ᵉ In Hebrew texts 2:1 is numbered 1:18, and 2:2-18 is numbered 2:1-17.   ᶠ 3 Hebrew *Huram*, a variant of *Hiram*; also in verses 11 and 12

⁵"The temple I am going to build will be great, because our God is greater than all other gods. ⁶But who is able to build a temple for him, since the heavens, even the highest heavens, cannot contain him? Who then am I to build a temple for him, except as a place to burn sacrifices before him?

⁷"Send me, therefore, a man skilled to work in gold and silver, bronze and iron, and in purple, crimson and blue yarn, and experienced in the art of engraving, to work in Judah and Jerusalem with my skilled workers, whom my father David provided.

⁸"Send me also cedar, juniper and algum*ᵃ* logs from Lebanon, for I know that your servants are skilled in cutting timber there. My servants will work with yours ⁹to provide me with plenty of lumber, because the temple I build must be large and magnificent. ¹⁰I will give your servants, the woodsmen who cut the timber, twenty thousand cors*ᵇ* of ground wheat, twenty thousand cors*ᶜ* of barley, twenty thousand baths*ᵈ* of wine and twenty thousand baths of olive oil."

¹¹Hiram king of Tyre replied by letter to Solomon:

"Because the LORD loves his people, he has made you their king."

¹²And Hiram added:

"Praise be to the LORD, the God of Israel, who made heaven and earth! He has given King David a wise son, endowed with intelligence and discernment, who will build a temple for the LORD and a palace for himself.

¹³"I am sending you Huram-Abi, a man of great skill, ¹⁴whose mother was from Dan and whose father was from Tyre. He is trained to work in gold and silver, bronze and iron, stone and wood, and with purple and blue and crimson yarn and fine linen. He is experienced in all kinds of engraving and can execute any design given to him. He will work with your skilled workers and with those of my lord, David your father.

¹⁵"Now let my lord send his servants the wheat and barley and the olive oil and wine he promised, ¹⁶and we will cut all the logs from Lebanon that you need and will float them as rafts by sea down to Joppa. You can then take them up to Jerusalem."

¹⁷Solomon took a census of all the foreigners residing in Israel, after the census his father David had taken; and they were found to be 153,600. ¹⁸He assigned 70,000 of them to be carriers and 80,000 to be stonecutters in the hills, with 3,600 foremen over them to keep the people working.

Solomon Builds the Temple

3 Then Solomon began to build the temple of the LORD in Jerusalem on Mount Moriah, where the LORD had appeared to his father David. It was on the threshing floor of Araunah*ᵉ* the Jebusite, the place provided by David. ²He began building on the second day of the second month in the fourth year of his reign.

³The foundation Solomon laid for building the temple of God was sixty cubits long and twenty cubits wide*ᶠ* (using the cubit of the old standard). ⁴The portico at the front of the temple was twenty cubits*ᵍ* long across the width of the building and twenty*ʰ* cubits high.

He overlaid the inside with pure gold. ⁵He paneled the main hall with juniper and covered it with fine gold and decorated it

---

ᵃ 8 Probably a variant of *almug*   *ᵇ 10* That is, probably about 3,600 tons or about 3,200 metric tons of wheat
ᶜ 10 That is, probably about 3,000 tons or about 2,700 metric tons of barley   *ᵈ 10* That is, about 120,000 gallons or
about 440,000 liters   *ᵉ 1* Hebrew *Ornan*, a variant of *Araunah*   *ᶠ 3* That is, about 90 feet long and 30 feet wide or
about 27 meters long and 9 meters wide   *ᵍ 4* That is, about 30 feet or about 9 meters; also in verses 8, 11 and 13
ʰ 4 Some Septuagint and Syriac manuscripts; Hebrew *and a hundred and twenty*

with palm tree and chain designs. ⁶He adorned the temple with precious stones. And the gold he used was gold of Parvaim. ⁷He overlaid the ceiling beams, doorframes, walls and doors of the temple with gold, and he carved cherubim on the walls.

⁸He built the Most Holy Place, its length corresponding to the width of the temple — twenty cubits long and twenty cubits wide. He overlaid the inside with six hundred talents*a* of fine gold. ⁹The gold nails weighed fifty shekels.*b* He also overlaid the upper parts with gold.

¹⁰For the Most Holy Place he made a pair of sculptured cherubim and overlaid them with gold. ¹¹The total wingspan of the cherubim was twenty cubits. One wing of the first cherub was five cubits*c* long and touched the temple wall, while its other wing, also five cubits long, touched the wing of the other cherub. ¹²Similarly one wing of the second cherub was five cubits long and touched the other temple wall, and its other wing, also five cubits long, touched the wing of the first cherub. ¹³The wings of these cherubim extended twenty cubits. They stood on their feet, facing the main hall.*d*

¹⁴He made the curtain of blue, purple and crimson yarn and fine linen, with cherubim worked into it.

¹⁵For the front of the temple he made two pillars, which together were thirty-five cubits*e* long, each with a capital five cubits high. ¹⁶He made interwoven chains*f* and put them on top of the pillars. He also made a hundred pomegranates and attached them to the chains. ¹⁷He erected the pillars in the front of the temple, one to the south and one to the north. The one to the south he named Jakin*g* and the one to the north Boaz.*h*

The Temple's Furnishings

4 He made a bronze altar twenty cubits long, twenty cubits wide and ten cubits high.*i* ²He made the Sea of cast metal, circular in shape, measuring ten cubits from rim to rim and five cubits*j* high. It took a line of thirty cubits*k* to measure around it. ³Below the rim, figures of bulls encircled it — ten to a cubit.*l* The bulls were cast in two rows in one piece with the Sea.

⁴The Sea stood on twelve bulls, three facing north, three facing west, three facing south and three facing east. The Sea rested on top of them, and their hindquarters were toward the center. ⁵It was a handbreadth*m* in thickness, and its rim was like the rim of a cup, like a lily blossom. It held three thousand baths.*n*

⁶He then made ten basins for washing and placed five on the south side and five on the north. In them the things to be used for the burnt offerings were rinsed, but the Sea was to be used by the priests for washing.

⁷He made ten gold lampstands according to the specifications for them and placed them in the temple, five on the south side and five on the north.

⁸He made ten tables and placed them in the temple, five on the south side and five on the north. He also made a hundred gold sprinkling bowls.

⁹He made the courtyard of the priests, and the large court and the doors for the court, and overlaid the doors with bronze. ¹⁰He placed the Sea on the south side, at the southeast corner.

¹¹And Huram also made the pots and shovels and sprinkling bowls.

So Huram finished the work he had un-

---

a 8 That is, about 23 tons or about 21 metric tons   *b* 9 That is, about 1 1/4 pounds or about 575 grams   *c* 11 That is, about 7 1/2 feet or about 2.3 meters; also in verse 15   *d* 13 Or *facing inward*   *e* 15 That is, about 53 feet or about 16 meters   *f* 16 Or possibly *made chains in the inner sanctuary*; the meaning of the Hebrew for this phrase is uncertain.   *g* 17 *Jakin* probably means *he establishes.*   *h* 17 *Boaz* probably means *in him is strength.*   *i* 1 That is, about 30 feet long and wide and 15 feet high or about 9 meters long and wide and 4.5 meters high   *j* 2 That is, about 7 1/2 feet or about 2.3 meters   *k* 2 That is, about 45 feet or about 14 meters   *l* 3 That is, about 18 inches or about 45 centimeters   *m* 5 That is, about 3 inches or about 7.5 centimeters   *n* 5 That is, about 18,000 gallons or about 66,000 liters dertaken for King Solomon in the temple of God:

¹² the two pillars;

the two bowl-shaped capitals on top of the pillars;

the two sets of network decorating the two bowl-shaped capitals on top of the pillars;

¹³ the four hundred pomegranates for the two sets of network (two rows of pomegranates for each network, decorating the bowl-shaped capitals on top of the pillars);

¹⁴ the stands with their basins;

¹⁵ the Sea and the twelve bulls under it;

¹⁶ the pots, shovels, meat forks and all related articles.

All the objects that Huram-Abi made for King Solomon for the temple of the Lord were of polished bronze. ¹⁷The king had them cast in clay molds in the plain of the Jordan between Sukkoth and Zarethan.^a ¹⁸All these things that Solomon made amounted to so much that the weight of the bronze could not be calculated.

¹⁹Solomon also made all the furnishings that were in God's temple:

the golden altar;

the tables on which was the bread of the Presence;

²⁰ the lampstands of pure gold with their lamps, to burn in front of the inner sanctuary as prescribed;

²¹ the gold floral work and lamps and tongs (they were solid gold);

²² the pure gold wick trimmers, sprinkling bowls, dishes and censers; and the gold doors of the temple: the inner doors to the Most Holy Place and the doors of the main hall.

5 When all the work Solomon had done for the temple of the Lord was finished, he brought in the things his father David had dedicated—the sil-

ver and gold and all the furnishings—and he placed them in the treasuries of God's temple.

The Ark Brought to the Temple

²Then Solomon summoned to Jerusalem the elders of Israel, all the heads of the tribes and the chiefs of the Israelite families, to bring up the ark of the Lord's covenant from Zion, the City of David. ³And all the Israelites came together to the king at the time of the festival in the seventh month.

⁴When all the elders of Israel had arrived, the Levites took up the ark, ⁵and they brought up the ark and the tent of meeting and all the sacred furnishings in it. The Levitical priests carried them up; ⁶and King Solomon and the entire assembly of Israel that had gathered about him were before the ark, sacrificing so many sheep and cattle that they could not be recorded or counted.

⁷The priests then brought the ark of the Lord's covenant to its place in the inner sanctuary of the temple, the Most Holy Place, and put it beneath the wings of the cherubim. ⁸The cherubim spread their wings over the place of the ark and covered the ark and its carrying poles. ⁹These poles were so long that their ends, extending from the ark, could be seen from in front of the inner sanctuary, but not from outside the Holy Place; and they are still there today. ¹⁰There was nothing in the ark except the two tablets that Moses had placed in it at Horeb, where the Lord made a covenant with the Israelites after they came out of Egypt.

¹¹The priests then withdrew from the Holy Place. All the priests who were there had consecrated themselves, regardless of their divisions. ¹²All the Levites who were musicians—Asaph, Heman, Jeduthun and their sons and relatives—stood on the east side of the altar, dressed in fine linen and playing cymbals, harps and lyres. They

---

^a 17 Hebrew *Zeredatha*, a variant of *Zarethan*

were accompanied by 120 priests sounding trumpets. 13The trumpeters and musicians joined in unison to give praise and thanks to the Lord. Accompanied by trumpets, cymbals and other instruments, the singers raised their voices in praise to the Lord and sang:

> "He is good;
>   his love endures forever."

Then the temple of the Lord was filled with the cloud, 14and the priests could not perform their service because of the cloud, for the glory of the Lord filled the temple of God.

6 Then Solomon said, "The Lord has said that he would dwell in a dark cloud; 2I have built a magnificent temple for you, a place for you to dwell forever."

3While the whole assembly of Israel was standing there, the king turned around and blessed them. 4Then he said:

> "Praise be to the Lord, the God of Israel, who with his hands has fulfilled what he promised with his mouth to my father David. For he said, 5'Since the day I brought my people out of Egypt, I have not chosen a city in any tribe of Israel to have a temple built so that my Name might be there, nor have I chosen anyone to be ruler over my people Israel. 6But now I have chosen Jerusalem for my Name to be there, and I have chosen David to rule my people Israel.'
>
> 7"My father David had it in his heart to build a temple for the Name of the Lord, the God of Israel. 8But the Lord said to my father David, 'You did well to have it in your heart to build a temple for my Name. 9Nevertheless, you are not the one to build the temple, but your son, your own flesh and blood—he is the one who will build the temple for my Name.'

10"The Lord has kept the promise he made. I have succeeded David my father and now I sit on the throne of Israel, just as the Lord promised, and I have built the temple for the Name of the Lord, the God of Israel. 11There I have placed the ark, in which is the covenant of the Lord that he made with the people of Israel."

Solomon's Prayer of Dedication

12Then Solomon stood before the altar of the Lord in front of the whole assembly of Israel and spread out his hands. 13Now he had made a bronze platform, five cubits long, five cubits wide and three cubits high,*a* and had placed it in the center of the outer court. He stood on the platform and then knelt down before the whole assembly of Israel and spread out his hands toward heaven. 14He said:

> "Lord, the God of Israel, there is no God like you in heaven or on earth—you who keep your covenant of love with your servants who continue wholeheartedly in your way. 15You have kept your promise to your servant David my father; with your mouth you have promised and with your hand you have fulfilled it—as it is today.
>
> 16"Now, Lord, the God of Israel, keep for your servant David my father the promises you made to him when you said, 'You shall never fail to have a successor to sit before me on the throne of Israel, if only your descendants are careful in all they do to walk before me according to my law, as you have done.' 17And now, Lord, the God of Israel, let your word that you promised your servant David come true.
>
> 18"But will God really dwell on earth with humans? The heavens, even the highest heavens, cannot con-

---

a 13 That is, about 7 1/2 feet long and wide and 4 1/2 feet high or about 2.3 meters long and wide and 1.4 meters high tain you. How much less this temple I have built! [19]Yet, Lord my God, give attention to your servant's prayer and his plea for mercy. Hear the cry and the prayer that your servant is praying in your presence. [20]May your eyes be open toward this temple day and night, this place of which you said you would put your Name there. May you hear the prayer your servant prays toward this place. [21]Hear the supplications of your servant and of your people Israel when they pray toward this place. Hear from heaven, your dwelling place; and when you hear, forgive.

[22]"When anyone wrongs their neighbor and is required to take an oath and they come and swear the oath before your altar in this temple, [23]then hear from heaven and act. Judge between your servants, condemning the guilty and bringing down on their heads what they have done, and vindicating the innocent by treating them in accordance with their innocence.

[24]"When your people Israel have been defeated by an enemy because they have sinned against you and when they turn back and give praise to your name, praying and making supplication before you in this temple, [25]then hear from heaven and forgive the sin of your people Israel and bring them back to the land you gave to them and their ancestors.

[26]"When the heavens are shut up and there is no rain because your people have sinned against you, and when they pray toward this place and give praise to your name and turn from their sin because you have afflicted them, [27]then hear from heaven and forgive the sin of your servants, your people Israel. Teach them the right way to live, and send rain on the land you gave your people for an inheritance.

[28]"When famine or plague comes to the land, or blight or mildew, locusts or grasshoppers, or when enemies besiege them in any of their cities, whatever disaster or disease may come, [29]and when a prayer or plea is made by anyone among your people Israel—being aware of their afflictions and pains, and spreading out their hands toward this temple—[30]then hear from heaven, your dwelling place. Forgive, and deal with everyone according to all they do, since you know their hearts (for you alone know the human heart), [31]so that they will fear you and walk in obedience to you all the time they live in the land you gave our ancestors.

[32]"As for the foreigner who does not belong to your people Israel but has come from a distant land because of your great name and your mighty hand and your outstretched arm—when they come and pray toward this temple, [33]then hear from heaven, your dwelling place. Do whatever the foreigner asks of you, so that all the peoples of the earth may know your name and fear you, as do your own people Israel, and may know that this house I have built bears your Name.

[34]"When your people go to war against their enemies, wherever you send them, and when they pray to you toward this city you have chosen and the temple I have built for your Name, [35]then hear from heaven their prayer and their plea, and uphold their cause.

[36]"When they sin against you—for there is no one who does not sin—and you become angry with them and give them over to the enemy, who takes them captive to a land far away or near; [37]and if they have a change of heart in the land where they are held captive, and repent and plead with you in the land of their captivity and say, 'We have sinned, we have done wrong and acted wickedly'; [38]and if they turn back to you with all their

heart and soul in the land of their captivity where they were taken, and pray toward the land you gave their ancestors, toward the city you have chosen and toward the temple I have built for your Name; ³⁹then from heaven, your dwelling place, hear their prayer and their pleas, and uphold their cause. And forgive your people, who have sinned against you.

⁴⁰"Now, my God, may your eyes be open and your ears attentive to the prayers offered in this place.

⁴¹"Now arise, LORD God, and come
    to your resting place,
    you and the ark of your might.
May your priests, LORD God, be
    clothed with salvation,
    may your faithful people rejoice
    in your goodness.
⁴²LORD God, do not reject your
    anointed one.
    Remember the great love
    promised to David your
    servant."

The Dedication of the Temple

7 When Solomon finished praying, fire came down from heaven and consumed the burnt offering and the sacrifices, and the glory of the LORD filled the temple. ²The priests could not enter the temple of the LORD because the glory of the LORD filled it. ³When all the Israelites saw the fire coming down and the glory of the LORD above the temple, they knelt on the pavement with their faces to the ground, and they worshiped and gave thanks to the LORD, saying,

"He is good;
    his love endures forever."

⁴Then the king and all the people offered sacrifices before the LORD. ⁵And King Solomon offered a sacrifice of twenty-two thousand head of cattle and a hundred and twenty thousand sheep and goats. So the king and all the people dedicated the temple of God. ⁶The priests took their positions, as did the Levites with the LORD's musical instruments, which King David had made for praising the LORD and which were used when he gave thanks, saying, "His love endures forever." Opposite the Levites, the priests blew their trumpets, and all the Israelites were standing.

⁷Solomon consecrated the middle part of the courtyard in front of the temple of the LORD, and there he offered burnt offerings and the fat of the fellowship offerings, because the bronze altar he had made could not hold the burnt offerings, the grain offerings and the fat portions.

⁸So Solomon observed the festival at that time for seven days, and all Israel with him — a vast assembly, people from Lebo Hamath to the Wadi of Egypt. ⁹On the eighth day they held an assembly, for they had celebrated the dedication of the altar for seven days and the festival for seven days more. ¹⁰On the twenty-third day of the seventh month he sent the people to their homes, joyful and glad in heart for the good things the LORD had done for David and Solomon and for his people Israel.

The LORD Appears to Solomon

¹¹When Solomon had finished the temple of the LORD and the royal palace, and had succeeded in carrying out all he had in mind to do in the temple of the LORD and in his own palace, ¹²the LORD appeared to him at night and said:

"I have heard your prayer and have chosen this place for myself as a temple for sacrifices.

¹³"When I shut up the heavens so that there is no rain, or command locusts to devour the land or send a plague among my people, ¹⁴if my people, who are called by my name, will humble themselves and pray and seek my face and turn from their wicked ways, then I will hear from heaven, and I will forgive their sin and will heal their land. ¹⁵Now my eyes will be open

and my ears attentive to the prayers offered in this place. [16]I have chosen and consecrated this temple so that my Name may be there forever. My eyes and my heart will always be there.

[17]"As for you, if you walk before me faithfully as David your father did, and do all I command, and observe my decrees and laws, [18]I will establish your royal throne, as I covenanted with David your father when I said, 'You shall never fail to have a successor to rule over Israel.'

[19]"But if you[a] turn away and forsake the decrees and commands I have given you[a] and go off to serve other gods and worship them, [20]then I will uproot Israel from my land, which I have given them, and will reject this temple I have consecrated for my Name. I will make it a byword and an object of ridicule among all peoples. [21]This temple will become a heap of rubble. All[b] who pass by will be appalled and say, 'Why has the Lord done such a thing to this land and to this temple?' [22]People will answer, 'Because they have forsaken the Lord, the God of their ancestors, who brought them out of Egypt, and have embraced other gods, worshiping and serving them—that is why he brought all this disaster on them.'"

Solomon's Other Activities

8 At the end of twenty years, during which Solomon built the temple of the Lord and his own palace, [2]Solomon rebuilt the villages that Hiram[c] had given him, and settled Israelites in them. [3]Solomon then went to Hamath Zobah and captured it. [4]He also built up Tadmor in the desert and all the store cities he had built in Hamath. [5]He rebuilt Upper Beth Horon and Lower Beth Horon as fortified cities, with walls and with gates and bars,

[6]as well as Baalath and all his store cities, and all the cities for his chariots and for his horses[d]—whatever he desired to build in Jerusalem, in Lebanon and throughout all the territory he ruled.

[7]There were still people left from the Hittites, Amorites, Perizzites, Hivites and Jebusites (these people were not Israelites). [8]Solomon conscripted the descendants of all these people remaining in the land—whom the Israelites had not destroyed—to serve as slave labor, as it is to this day. [9]But Solomon did not make slaves of the Israelites for his work; they were his fighting men, commanders of his captains, and commanders of his chariots and charioteers. [10]They were also King Solomon's chief officials—two hundred and fifty officials supervising the men.

[11]Solomon brought Pharaoh's daughter up from the City of David to the palace he had built for her, for he said, "My wife must not live in the palace of David king of Israel, because the places the ark of the Lord has entered are holy."

[12]On the altar of the Lord that he had built in front of the portico, Solomon sacrificed burnt offerings to the Lord, [13]according to the daily requirement for offerings commanded by Moses for the Sabbaths, the New Moons and the three annual festivals—the Festival of Unleavened Bread, the Festival of Weeks and the Festival of Tabernacles. [14]In keeping with the ordinance of his father David, he appointed the divisions of the priests for their duties, and the Levites to lead the praise and to assist the priests according to each day's requirement. He also appointed the gatekeepers by divisions for the various gates, because this was what David the man of God had ordered. [15]They did not deviate from the king's commands to the priests or to the Levites in any matter, including that of the treasuries.

---

a 19 The Hebrew is plural.   *b 21* See some Septuagint manuscripts, Old Latin, Syriac, Arabic and Targum; Hebrew *And though this temple is now so imposing, all*   *c 2* Hebrew *Huram,* a variant of *Hiram;* also in verse 18   *d 6* Or *charioteers*

16All Solomon's work was carried out, from the day the foundation of the temple of the Lord was laid until its completion. So the temple of the Lord was finished.

17Then Solomon went to Ezion Geber and Elath on the coast of Edom. 18And Hiram sent him ships commanded by his own men, sailors who knew the sea. These, with Solomon's men, sailed to Ophir and brought back four hundred and fifty talents[a] of gold, which they delivered to King Solomon.

The Queen of Sheba Visits Solomon

9 When the queen of Sheba heard of Solomon's fame, she came to Jerusalem to test him with hard questions. Arriving with a very great caravan — with camels carrying spices, large quantities of gold, and precious stones — she came to Solomon and talked with him about all she had on her mind. 2Solomon answered all her questions; nothing was too hard for him to explain to her. 3When the queen of Sheba saw the wisdom of Solomon, as well as the palace he had built, 4the food on his table, the seating of his officials, the attending servants in their robes, the cupbearers in their robes and the burnt offerings he made at[b] the temple of the Lord, she was overwhelmed.

5She said to the king, "The report I heard in my own country about your achievements and your wisdom is true. 6But I did not believe what they said until I came and saw with my own eyes. Indeed, not even half the greatness of your wisdom was told me; you have far exceeded the report I heard. 7How happy your people must be! How happy your officials, who continually stand before you and hear your wisdom! 8Praise be to the Lord your God, who has delighted in you and placed you on his throne as king to rule for the Lord your God. Because of the love of your God for Israel and his desire to uphold them forever,

he has made you king over them, to maintain justice and righteousness."

9Then she gave the king 120 talents[c] of gold, large quantities of spices, and precious stones. There had never been such spices as those the queen of Sheba gave to King Solomon.

10(The servants of Hiram and the servants of Solomon brought gold from Ophir; they also brought algumwood[d] and precious stones. 11The king used the algumwood to make steps for the temple of the Lord and for the royal palace, and to make harps and lyres for the musicians. Nothing like them had ever been seen in Judah.)

12King Solomon gave the queen of Sheba all she desired and asked for; he gave her more than she had brought to him. Then she left and returned with her retinue to her own country.

Solomon's Splendor

13The weight of the gold that Solomon received yearly was 666 talents,[e] 14not including the revenues brought in by merchants and traders. Also all the kings of Arabia and the governors of the territories brought gold and silver to Solomon.

15King Solomon made two hundred large shields of hammered gold; six hundred shekels[f] of hammered gold went into each shield. 16He also made three hundred small shields of hammered gold, with three hundred shekels[g] of gold in each shield. The king put them in the Palace of the Forest of Lebanon.

17Then the king made a great throne covered with ivory and overlaid with pure gold. 18The throne had six steps, and a footstool of gold was attached to it. On both sides of the seat were armrests, with a lion standing beside each of them. 19Twelve lions stood on the six steps, one at either end of each step. Nothing like it had ever been made for any other kingdom. 20All

---

a 18 That is, about 17 tons or about 15 metric tons   b 4 Or and the ascent by which he went up to   c 9 That is, about 4 1/2 tons or about 4 metric tons   d 10 Probably a variant of almugwood   e 13 That is, about 25 tons or about 23 metric tons   f 15 That is, about 15 pounds or about 6.9 kilograms   g 16 That is, about 7 1/2 pounds or about 3.5 kilograms

King Solomon's goblets were gold, and all the household articles in the Palace of the Forest of Lebanon were pure gold. Nothing was made of silver, because silver was considered of little value in Solomon's day. ²¹The king had a fleet of trading ships*ᵃ* manned by Hiram's*ᵇ* servants. Once every three years it returned, carrying gold, silver and ivory, and apes and baboons.

²²King Solomon was greater in riches and wisdom than all the other kings of the earth. ²³All the kings of the earth sought audience with Solomon to hear the wisdom God had put in his heart. ²⁴Year after year, everyone who came brought a gift — articles of silver and gold, and robes, weapons and spices, and horses and mules.

²⁵Solomon had four thousand stalls for horses and chariots, and twelve thousand horses,*ᶜ* which he kept in the chariot cities and also with him in Jerusalem. ²⁶He ruled over all the kings from the Euphrates River to the land of the Philistines, as far as the border of Egypt. ²⁷The king made silver as common in Jerusalem as stones, and cedar as plentiful as sycamore-fig trees in the foothills. ²⁸Solomon's horses were imported from Egypt and from all other countries.

Solomon's Death

²⁹As for the other events of Solomon's reign, from beginning to end, are they not written in the records of Nathan the prophet, in the prophecy of Ahijah the Shilonite and in the visions of Iddo the seer concerning Jeroboam son of Nebat? ³⁰Solomon reigned in Jerusalem over all Israel forty years. ³¹Then he rested with his ancestors and was buried in the city of David his father. And Rehoboam his son succeeded him as king.

Israel Rebels Against Rehoboam

10 Rehoboam went to Shechem, for all Israel had gone there to make him king. ²When Jeroboam son of Nebat heard this (he was in Egypt, where he had fled from King Solomon), he returned from Egypt. ³So they sent for Jeroboam, and he and all Israel went to Rehoboam and said to him: ⁴"Your father put a heavy yoke on us, but now lighten the harsh labor and the heavy yoke he put on us, and we will serve you."

⁵Rehoboam answered, "Come back to me in three days." So the people went away.

⁶Then King Rehoboam consulted the elders who had served his father Solomon during his lifetime. "How would you advise me to answer these people?" he asked.

⁷They replied, "If you will be kind to these people and please them and give them a favorable answer, they will always be your servants."

⁸But Rehoboam rejected the advice the elders gave him and consulted the young men who had grown up with him and were serving him. ⁹He asked them, "What is your advice? How should we answer these people who say to me, 'Lighten the yoke your father put on us'?"

¹⁰The young men who had grown up with him replied, "The people have said to you, 'Your father put a heavy yoke on us, but make our yoke lighter.' Now tell them, 'My little finger is thicker than my father's waist. ¹¹My father laid on you a heavy yoke; I will make it even heavier. My father scourged you with whips; I will scourge you with scorpions.'"

¹²Three days later Jeroboam and all the people returned to Rehoboam, as the king had said, "Come back to me in three days." ¹³The king answered them harshly. Rejecting the advice of the elders, ¹⁴he followed the advice of the young men and said, "My father made your yoke heavy; I will make it even heavier. My father scourged you with whips; I will scourge you with scorpions." ¹⁵So the king did not listen to the people, for this turn of events was from God, to fulfill the word the LORD had spoken to Jeroboam son of Nebat through Ahijah the Shilonite.

ᵃ 21 Hebrew *of ships that could go to Tarshish*   *ᵇ 21* Hebrew *Huram,* a variant of *Hiram*   *ᶜ 25* Or *charioteers*

¹⁶When all Israel saw that the king refused to listen to them, they answered the king:

"What share do we have in David,
    what part in Jesse's son?
To your tents, Israel!
    Look after your own house, David!"

So all the Israelites went home. ¹⁷But as for the Israelites who were living in the towns of Judah, Rehoboam still ruled over them.

¹⁸King Rehoboam sent out Adoniram,ᵃ who was in charge of forced labor, but the Israelites stoned him to death. King Rehoboam, however, managed to get into his chariot and escape to Jerusalem. ¹⁹So Israel has been in rebellion against the house of David to this day.

11 When Rehoboam arrived in Jerusalem, he mustered Judah and Benjamin — a hundred and eighty thousand able young men — to go to war against Israel and to regain the kingdom for Rehoboam.

²But this word of the Lord came to Shemaiah the man of God: ³"Say to Rehoboam son of Solomon king of Judah and to all Israel in Judah and Benjamin, ⁴'This is what the Lord says: Do not go up to fight against your fellow Israelites. Go home, every one of you, for this is my doing.'" So they obeyed the words of the Lord and turned back from marching against Jeroboam.

Rehoboam Fortifies Judah

⁵Rehoboam lived in Jerusalem and built up towns for defense in Judah: ⁶Bethlehem, Etam, Tekoa, ⁷Beth Zur, Soko, Adullam, ⁸Gath, Mareshah, Ziph, ⁹Adoraim, Lachish, Azekah, ¹⁰Zorah, Aijalon and Hebron. These were fortified cities in Judah and Benjamin. ¹¹He strengthened their defenses and put commanders in them, with supplies of food, olive oil and wine. ¹²He put shields and spears in all the cities, and made them very strong. So Judah and Benjamin were his.

¹³The priests and Levites from all their districts throughout Israel sided with him. ¹⁴The Levites even abandoned their pasturelands and property and came to Judah and Jerusalem, because Jeroboam and his sons had rejected them as priests of the Lord ¹⁵when he appointed his own priests for the high places and for the goat and calf idols he had made. ¹⁶Those from every tribe of Israel who set their hearts on seeking the Lord, the God of Israel, followed the Levites to Jerusalem to offer sacrifices to the Lord, the God of their ancestors. ¹⁷They strengthened the kingdom of Judah and supported Rehoboam son of Solomon three years, following the ways of David and Solomon during this time.

Rehoboam's Family

¹⁸Rehoboam married Mahalath, who was the daughter of David's son Jerimoth and of Abihail, the daughter of Jesse's son Eliab. ¹⁹She bore him sons: Jeush, Shemariah and Zaham. ²⁰Then he married Maakah daughter of Absalom, who bore him Abijah, Attai, Ziza and Shelomith. ²¹Rehoboam loved Maakah daughter of Absalom more than any of his other wives and concubines. In all, he had eighteen wives and sixty concubines, twenty-eight sons and sixty daughters.

²²Rehoboam appointed Abijah son of Maakah as crown prince among his brothers, in order to make him king. ²³He acted wisely, dispersing some of his sons throughout the districts of Judah and Benjamin, and to all the fortified cities. He gave them abundant provisions and took many wives for them.

Shishak Attacks Jerusalem

12 After Rehoboam's position as king was established and he had become strong, he and all Israelᵇ with him abandoned the law of the Lord. ²Because they had been unfaithful to the Lord, Shishak king of Egypt at-

---

ᵃ 18 Hebrew *Hadoram,* a variant of *Adoniram*   ᵇ 1 That is, Judah, as frequently in 2 Chronicles tacked Jerusalem in the fifth year of King Rehoboam. [3]With twelve hundred chariots and sixty thousand horsemen and the innumerable troops of Libyans, Sukkites and Cushites[a] that came with him from Egypt, [4]he captured the fortified cities of Judah and came as far as Jerusalem.

[5]Then the prophet Shemaiah came to Rehoboam and to the leaders of Judah who had assembled in Jerusalem for fear of Shishak, and he said to them, "This is what the LORD says, 'You have abandoned me; therefore, I now abandon you to Shishak.'"

[6]The leaders of Israel and the king humbled themselves and said, "The LORD is just."

[7]When the LORD saw that they humbled themselves, this word of the LORD came to Shemaiah: "Since they have humbled themselves, I will not destroy them but will soon give them deliverance. My wrath will not be poured out on Jerusalem through Shishak. [8]They will, however, become subject to him, so that they may learn the difference between serving me and serving the kings of other lands."

[9]When Shishak king of Egypt attacked Jerusalem, he carried off the treasures of the temple of the LORD and the treasures of the royal palace. He took everything, including the gold shields Solomon had made. [10]So King Rehoboam made bronze shields to replace them and assigned these to the commanders of the guard on duty at the entrance to the royal palace. [11]Whenever the king went to the LORD's temple, the guards went with him, bearing the shields, and afterward they returned them to the guardroom.

[12]Because Rehoboam humbled himself, the LORD's anger turned from him, and he was not totally destroyed. Indeed, there was some good in Judah.

[13]King Rehoboam established himself firmly in Jerusalem and continued as king. He was forty-one years old when he became king, and he reigned seventeen years in Jerusalem, the city the LORD had chosen out of all the tribes of Israel in which to put his Name. His mother's name was Naamah; she was an Ammonite. [14]He did evil because he had not set his heart on seeking the LORD.

[15]As for the events of Rehoboam's reign, from beginning to end, are they not written in the records of Shemaiah the prophet and of Iddo the seer that deal with genealogies? There was continual warfare between Rehoboam and Jeroboam. [16]Rehoboam rested with his ancestors and was buried in the City of David. And Abijah his son succeeded him as king.

Abijah King of Judah

13 In the eighteenth year of the reign of Jeroboam, Abijah became king of Judah, [2]and he reigned in Jerusalem three years. His mother's name was Maakah,[b] a daughter[c] of Uriel of Gibeah.

There was war between Abijah and Jeroboam. [3]Abijah went into battle with an army of four hundred thousand able fighting men, and Jeroboam drew up a battle line against him with eight hundred thousand able troops.

[4]Abijah stood on Mount Zemaraim, in the hill country of Ephraim, and said, "Jeroboam and all Israel, listen to me! [5]Don't you know that the LORD, the God of Israel, has given the kingship of Israel to David and his descendants forever by a covenant of salt? [6]Yet Jeroboam son of Nebat, an official of Solomon son of David, rebelled against his master. [7]Some worthless scoundrels gathered around him and opposed Rehoboam son of Solomon when he was young and indecisive and not strong enough to resist them.

[8]"And now you plan to resist the kingdom of the LORD, which is in the hands of David's descendants. You are indeed a vast army and have with you the golden calves that

---

[a] 3 That is, people from the upper Nile region   [b] 2 Most Septuagint manuscripts and Syriac (see also 11:20 and 1 Kings 15:2); Hebrew *Micaiah*   [c] 2 Or *granddaughter*

Jeroboam made to be your gods. ⁹But didn't you drive out the priests of the LORD, the sons of Aaron, and the Levites, and make priests of your own as the peoples of other lands do? Whoever comes to consecrate himself with a young bull and seven rams may become a priest of what are not gods.

¹⁰"As for us, the LORD is our God, and we have not forsaken him. The priests who serve the LORD are sons of Aaron, and the Levites assist them. ¹¹Every morning and evening they present burnt offerings and fragrant incense to the LORD. They set out the bread on the ceremonially clean table and light the lamps on the gold lampstand every evening. We are observing the requirements of the LORD our God. But you have forsaken him. ¹²God is with us; he is our leader. His priests with their trumpets will sound the battle cry against you. People of Israel, do not fight against the LORD, the God of your ancestors, for you will not succeed."

¹³Now Jeroboam had sent troops around to the rear, so that while he was in front of Judah the ambush was behind them. ¹⁴Judah turned and saw that they were being attacked at both front and rear. Then they cried out to the LORD. The priests blew their trumpets ¹⁵and the men of Judah raised the battle cry. At the sound of their battle cry, God routed Jeroboam and all Israel before Abijah and Judah. ¹⁶The Israelites fled before Judah, and God delivered them into their hands. ¹⁷Abijah and his troops inflicted heavy losses on them, so that there were five hundred thousand casualties among Israel's able men. ¹⁸The Israelites were subdued on that occasion, and the people of Judah were victorious because they relied on the LORD, the God of their ancestors.

¹⁹Abijah pursued Jeroboam and took from him the towns of Bethel, Jeshanah and Ephron, with their surrounding villages. ²⁰Jeroboam did not regain power during the time of Abijah. And the LORD struck him down and he died.

²¹But Abijah grew in strength. He married fourteen wives and had twenty-two sons and sixteen daughters.

²²The other events of Abijah's reign, what he did and what he said, are written in the annotations of the prophet Iddo.

14 ᵃ And Abijah rested with his ancestors and was buried in the City of David. Asa his son succeeded him as king, and in his days the country was at peace for ten years.

Asa King of Judah

²Asa did what was good and right in the eyes of the LORD his God. ³He removed the foreign altars and the high places, smashed the sacred stones and cut down the Asherah poles.ᵇ ⁴He commanded Judah to seek the LORD, the God of their ancestors, and to obey his laws and commands. ⁵He removed the high places and incense altars in every town in Judah, and the kingdom was at peace under him. ⁶He built up the fortified cities of Judah, since the land was at peace. No one was at war with him during those years, for the LORD gave him rest.

⁷"Let us build up these towns," he said to Judah, "and put walls around them, with towers, gates and bars. The land is still ours, because we have sought the LORD our God; we sought him and he has given us rest on every side." So they built and prospered.

⁸Asa had an army of three hundred thousand men from Judah, equipped with large shields and with spears, and two hundred and eighty thousand from Benjamin, armed with small shields and with bows. All these were brave fighting men.

⁹Zerah the Cushite marched out against them with an army of thousands upon thousands and three hundred chariots, and came as far as Mareshah. ¹⁰Asa went out to meet him, and they took up battle positions in the Valley of Zephathah near Mareshah.

ᵃ In Hebrew texts 14:1 is numbered 13:23, and 14:2-15 is numbered 14:1-14.   ᵇ 3 That is, wooden symbols of the goddess Asherah; here and elsewhere in 2 Chronicles

¹¹Then Asa called to the Lord his God and said, "Lord, there is no one like you to help the powerless against the mighty. Help us, Lord our God, for we rely on you, and in your name we have come against this vast army. Lord, you are our God; do not let mere mortals prevail against you."

¹²The Lord struck down the Cushites before Asa and Judah. The Cushites fled, ¹³and Asa and his army pursued them as far as Gerar. Such a great number of Cushites fell that they could not recover; they were crushed before the Lord and his forces. The men of Judah carried off a large amount of plunder. ¹⁴They destroyed all the villages around Gerar, for the terror of the Lord had fallen on them. They looted all these villages, since there was much plunder there. ¹⁵They also attacked the camps of the herders and carried off droves of sheep and goats and camels. Then they returned to Jerusalem.

Asa's Reform

15 The Spirit of God came on Azariah son of Oded. ²He went out to meet Asa and said to him, "Listen to me, Asa and all Judah and Benjamin. The Lord is with you when you are with him. If you seek him, he will be found by you, but if you forsake him, he will forsake you. ³For a long time Israel was without the true God, without a priest to teach and without the law. ⁴But in their distress they turned to the Lord, the God of Israel, and sought him, and he was found by them. ⁵In those days it was not safe to travel about, for all the inhabitants of the lands were in great turmoil. ⁶One nation was being crushed by another and one city by another, because God was troubling them with every kind of distress. ⁷But as for you, be strong and do not give up, for your work will be rewarded."

⁸When Asa heard these words and the prophecy of Azariah son of *ᵃ* Oded the prophet, he took courage. He removed the detestable idols from the whole land of Judah and Benjamin and from the towns he had captured in the hills of Ephraim. He repaired the altar of the Lord that was in front of the portico of the Lord's temple.

⁹Then he assembled all Judah and Benjamin and the people from Ephraim, Manasseh and Simeon who had settled among them, for large numbers had come over to him from Israel when they saw that the Lord his God was with him.

¹⁰They assembled at Jerusalem in the third month of the fifteenth year of Asa's reign. ¹¹At that time they sacrificed to the Lord seven hundred head of cattle and seven thousand sheep and goats from the plunder they had brought back. ¹²They entered into a covenant to seek the Lord, the God of their ancestors, with all their heart and soul. ¹³All who would not seek the Lord, the God of Israel, were to be put to death, whether small or great, man or woman. ¹⁴They took an oath to the Lord with loud acclamation, with shouting and with trumpets and horns. ¹⁵All Judah rejoiced about the oath because they had sworn it wholeheartedly. They sought God eagerly, and he was found by them. So the Lord gave them rest on every side.

¹⁶King Asa also deposed his grandmother Maakah from her position as queen mother, because she had made a repulsive image for the worship of Asherah. Asa cut it down, broke it up and burned it in the Kidron Valley. ¹⁷Although he did not remove the high places from Israel, Asa's heart was fully committed to the Lord all his life. ¹⁸He brought into the temple of God the silver and gold and the articles that he and his father had dedicated.

¹⁹There was no more war until the thirty-fifth year of Asa's reign.

Asa's Last Years

16 In the thirty-sixth year of Asa's reign Baasha king of Israel went up against Judah and fortified Ramah to prevent anyone from leaving or entering the territory of Asa king of Judah.

ᵃ 8 Vulgate and Syriac (see also Septuagint and verse 1); Hebrew does not have *Azariah son of.*

²Asa then took the silver and gold out of the treasuries of the Lord's temple and of his own palace and sent it to Ben-Hadad king of Aram, who was ruling in Damascus. ³"Let there be a treaty between me and you," he said, "as there was between my father and your father. See, I am sending you silver and gold. Now break your treaty with Baasha king of Israel so he will withdraw from me."

⁴Ben-Hadad agreed with King Asa and sent the commanders of his forces against the towns of Israel. They conquered Ijon, Dan, Abel Maim*ᵃ* and all the store cities of Naphtali. ⁵When Baasha heard this, he stopped building Ramah and abandoned his work. ⁶Then King Asa brought all the men of Judah, and they carried away from Ramah the stones and timber Baasha had been using. With them he built up Geba and Mizpah.

⁷At that time Hanani the seer came to Asa king of Judah and said to him: "Because you relied on the king of Aram and not on the Lord your God, the army of the king of Aram has escaped from your hand. ⁸Were not the Cushites*ᵇ* and Libyans a mighty army with great numbers of chariots and horsemen*ᶜ*? Yet when you relied on the Lord, he delivered them into your hand. ⁹For the eyes of the Lord range throughout the earth to strengthen those whose hearts are fully committed to him. You have done a foolish thing, and from now on you will be at war."

¹⁰Asa was angry with the seer because of this; he was so enraged that he put him in prison. At the same time Asa brutally oppressed some of the people.

¹¹The events of Asa's reign, from beginning to end, are written in the book of the kings of Judah and Israel. ¹²In the thirty-ninth year of his reign Asa was afflicted with a disease in his feet. Though his disease was severe, even in his illness he did not seek help from the Lord, but only from the physicians. ¹³Then in the forty-first year

of his reign Asa died and rested with his ancestors. ¹⁴They buried him in the tomb that he had cut out for himself in the City of David. They laid him on a bier covered with spices and various blended perfumes, and they made a huge fire in his honor.

Jehoshaphat King of Judah

17 Jehoshaphat his son succeeded him as king and strengthened himself against Israel. ²He stationed troops in all the fortified cities of Judah and put garrisons in Judah and in the towns of Ephraim that his father Asa had captured.

³The Lord was with Jehoshaphat because he followed the ways of his father David before him. He did not consult the Baals ⁴but sought the God of his father and followed his commands rather than the practices of Israel. ⁵The Lord established the kingdom under his control; and all Judah brought gifts to Jehoshaphat, so that he had great wealth and honor. ⁶His heart was devoted to the ways of the Lord; furthermore, he removed the high places and the Asherah poles from Judah.

⁷In the third year of his reign he sent his officials Ben-Hail, Obadiah, Zechariah, Nethanel and Micaiah to teach in the towns of Judah. ⁸With them were certain Levites — Shemaiah, Nethaniah, Zebadiah, Asahel, Shemiramoth, Jehonathan, Adonijah, Tobijah and Tob-Adonijah — and the priests Elishama and Jehoram. ⁹They taught throughout Judah, taking with them the Book of the Law of the Lord; they went around to all the towns of Judah and taught the people.

¹⁰The fear of the Lord fell on all the kingdoms of the lands surrounding Judah, so that they did not go to war against Jehoshaphat. ¹¹Some Philistines brought Jehoshaphat gifts and silver as tribute, and the Arabs brought him flocks: seven thousand seven hundred rams and seven thousand seven hundred goats.

ᵃ 4 Also known as *Abel Beth Maakah*   *ᵇ 8* That is, people from the upper Nile region   *ᶜ 8* Or *charioteers*

¹²Jehoshaphat became more and more powerful; he built forts and store cities in Judah ¹³and had large supplies in the towns of Judah. He also kept experienced fighting men in Jerusalem. ¹⁴Their enrollment by families was as follows:

From Judah, commanders of units of 1,000:
Adnah the commander, with 300,000 fighting men;
¹⁵next, Jehohanan the commander, with 280,000;
¹⁶next, Amasiah son of Zikri, who volunteered himself for the service of the LORD, with 200,000.
¹⁷From Benjamin:
Eliada, a valiant soldier, with 200,000 men armed with bows and shields;
¹⁸next, Jehozabad, with 180,000 men armed for battle.

¹⁹These were the men who served the king, besides those he stationed in the fortified cities throughout Judah.

Micaiah Prophesies Against Ahab

18 Now Jehoshaphat had great wealth and honor, and he allied himself with Ahab by marriage. ²Some years later he went down to see Ahab in Samaria. Ahab slaughtered many sheep and cattle for him and the people with him and urged him to attack Ramoth Gilead. ³Ahab king of Israel asked Jehoshaphat king of Judah, "Will you go with me against Ramoth Gilead?"

Jehoshaphat replied, "I am as you are, and my people as your people; we will join you in the war." ⁴But Jehoshaphat also said to the king of Israel, "First seek the counsel of the LORD."

⁵So the king of Israel brought together the prophets — four hundred men — and asked them, "Shall we go to war against Ramoth Gilead, or shall I not?"

"Go," they answered, "for God will give it into the king's hand."

⁶But Jehoshaphat asked, "Is there no lon-ger a prophet of the LORD here whom we can inquire of?"

⁷The king of Israel answered Jehoshaphat, "There is still one prophet through whom we can inquire of the LORD, but I hate him because he never prophesies anything good about me, but always bad. He is Micaiah son of Imlah."

"The king should not say such a thing," Jehoshaphat replied.

⁸So the king of Israel called one of his officials and said, "Bring Micaiah son of Imlah at once."

⁹Dressed in their royal robes, the king of Israel and Jehoshaphat king of Judah were sitting on their thrones at the threshing floor by the entrance of the gate of Samaria, with all the prophets prophesying before them. ¹⁰Now Zedekiah son of Kenaanah had made iron horns, and he declared, "This is what the LORD says: 'With these you will gore the Arameans until they are destroyed.'"

¹¹All the other prophets were prophesying the same thing. "Attack Ramoth Gilead and be victorious," they said, "for the LORD will give it into the king's hand."

¹²The messenger who had gone to summon Micaiah said to him, "Look, the other prophets without exception are predicting success for the king. Let your word agree with theirs, and speak favorably."

¹³But Micaiah said, "As surely as the LORD lives, I can tell him only what my God says."

¹⁴When he arrived, the king asked him, "Micaiah, shall we go to war against Ramoth Gilead, or shall I not?"

"Attack and be victorious," he answered, "for they will be given into your hand."

¹⁵The king said to him, "How many times must I make you swear to tell me nothing but the truth in the name of the LORD?"

¹⁶Then Micaiah answered, "I saw all Israel scattered on the hills like sheep without a shepherd, and the LORD said, 'These people have no master. Let each one go home in peace.'"

¹⁷The king of Israel said to Jehoshaphat, "Didn't I tell you that he never prophesies anything good about me, but only bad?"

¹⁸Micaiah continued, "Therefore hear the word of the Lord: I saw the Lord sitting on his throne with all the multitudes of heaven standing on his right and on his left. ¹⁹And the Lord said, 'Who will entice Ahab king of Israel into attacking Ramoth Gilead and going to his death there?'

"One suggested this, and another that. ²⁰Finally, a spirit came forward, stood before the Lord and said, 'I will entice him.'

"'By what means?' the Lord asked.

²¹"'I will go and be a deceiving spirit in the mouths of all his prophets,' he said.

"'You will succeed in enticing him,' said the Lord. 'Go and do it.'

²²"So now the Lord has put a deceiving spirit in the mouths of these prophets of yours. The Lord has decreed disaster for you."

²³Then Zedekiah son of Kenaanah went up and slapped Micaiah in the face. "Which way did the spirit from*ᵃ* the Lord go when he went from me to speak to you?" he asked.

²⁴Micaiah replied, "You will find out on the day you go to hide in an inner room."

²⁵The king of Israel then ordered, "Take Micaiah and send him back to Amon the ruler of the city and to Joash the king's son, ²⁶and say, 'This is what the king says: Put this fellow in prison and give him nothing but bread and water until I return safely.'"

²⁷Micaiah declared, "If you ever return safely, the Lord has not spoken through me." Then he added, "Mark my words, all you people!"

Ahab Killed at Ramoth Gilead

²⁸So the king of Israel and Jehoshaphat king of Judah went up to Ramoth Gilead. ²⁹The king of Israel said to Jehoshaphat, "I will enter the battle in disguise, but you wear your royal robes." So the king of Israel disguised himself and went into battle.

³⁰Now the king of Aram had ordered his chariot commanders, "Do not fight with anyone, small or great, except the king of Israel." ³¹When the chariot commanders saw Jehoshaphat, they thought, "This is the king of Israel." So they turned to attack him, but Jehoshaphat cried out, and the Lord helped him. God drew them away from him, ³²for when the chariot commanders saw that he was not the king of Israel, they stopped pursuing him.

³³But someone drew his bow at random and hit the king of Israel between the breastplate and the scale armor. The king told the chariot driver, "Wheel around and get me out of the fighting. I've been wounded." ³⁴All day long the battle raged, and the king of Israel propped himself up in his chariot facing the Arameans until evening. Then at sunset he died.

19 When Jehoshaphat king of Judah returned safely to his palace in Jerusalem, ²Jehu the seer, the son of Hanani, went out to meet him and said to the king, "Should you help the wicked and love*ᵇ* those who hate the Lord? Because of this, the wrath of the Lord is on you. ³There is, however, some good in you, for you have rid the land of the Asherah poles and have set your heart on seeking God."

Jehoshaphat Appoints Judges

⁴Jehoshaphat lived in Jerusalem, and he went out again among the people from Beersheba to the hill country of Ephraim and turned them back to the Lord, the God of their ancestors. ⁵He appointed judges in the land, in each of the fortified cities of Judah. ⁶He told them, "Consider carefully what you do, because you are not judging for mere mortals but for the Lord, who is with you whenever you give a verdict. ⁷Now let the fear of the Lord be on you. Judge carefully, for with the Lord our God there is no injustice or partiality or bribery."

⁸In Jerusalem also, Jehoshaphat appoint-

ᵃ 23 Or *Spirit of*   *ᵇ 2* Or *and make alliances with*

ed some of the Levites, priests and heads of Israelite families to administer the law of the LORD and to settle disputes. And they lived in Jerusalem. ⁹He gave them these orders: "You must serve faithfully and wholeheartedly in the fear of the LORD. ¹⁰In every case that comes before you from your people who live in the cities — whether bloodshed or other concerns of the law, commands, decrees or regulations — you are to warn them not to sin against the LORD; otherwise his wrath will come on you and your people. Do this, and you will not sin.

¹¹"Amariah the chief priest will be over you in any matter concerning the LORD, and Zebadiah son of Ishmael, the leader of the tribe of Judah, will be over you in any matter concerning the king, and the Levites will serve as officials before you. Act with courage, and may the LORD be with those who do well."

Jehoshaphat Defeats Moab and Ammon

20 After this, the Moabites and Ammonites with some of the Meunites*a* came to wage war against Jehoshaphat.

²Some people came and told Jehoshaphat, "A vast army is coming against you from Edom,*b* from the other side of the Dead Sea. It is already in Hazezon Tamar" (that is, En Gedi). ³Alarmed, Jehoshaphat resolved to inquire of the LORD, and he proclaimed a fast for all Judah. ⁴The people of Judah came together to seek help from the LORD; indeed, they came from every town in Judah to seek him.

⁵Then Jehoshaphat stood up in the assembly of Judah and Jerusalem at the temple of the LORD in the front of the new courtyard ⁶and said:

"LORD, the God of our ancestors, are you not the God who is in heaven? You rule over all the kingdoms of the nations. Power and might are in your hand, and no one can withstand you.

⁷Our God, did you not drive out the inhabitants of this land before your people Israel and give it forever to the descendants of Abraham your friend? ⁸They have lived in it and have built in it a sanctuary for your Name, saying, ⁹'If calamity comes upon us, whether the sword of judgment, or plague or famine, we will stand in your presence before this temple that bears your Name and will cry out to you in our distress, and you will hear us and save us.'

¹⁰"But now here are men from Ammon, Moab and Mount Seir, whose territory you would not allow Israel to invade when they came from Egypt; so they turned away from them and did not destroy them. ¹¹See how they are repaying us by coming to drive us out of the possession you gave us as an inheritance. ¹²Our God, will you not judge them? For we have no power to face this vast army that is attacking us. We do not know what to do, but our eyes are on you."

¹³All the men of Judah, with their wives and children and little ones, stood there before the LORD.

¹⁴Then the Spirit of the LORD came on Jahaziel son of Zechariah, the son of Benaiah, the son of Jeiel, the son of Mattaniah, a Levite and descendant of Asaph, as he stood in the assembly.

¹⁵He said: "Listen, King Jehoshaphat and all who live in Judah and Jerusalem! This is what the LORD says to you: 'Do not be afraid or discouraged because of this vast army. For the battle is not yours, but God's. ¹⁶Tomorrow march down against them. They will be climbing up by the Pass of Ziz, and you will find them at the end of the gorge in the Desert of Jeruel. ¹⁷You will not have to fight this battle. Take up your positions; stand firm and see the deliverance the LORD will give you, Judah and Jerusalem. Do not be afraid; do not be

---

a 1 Some Septuagint manuscripts; Hebrew *Ammonites* Septuagint and Vulgate *Aram*   *b 2* One Hebrew manuscript; most Hebrew manuscripts, discouraged. Go out to face them tomorrow, and the LORD will be with you.'"

[18]Jehoshaphat bowed down with his face to the ground, and all the people of Judah and Jerusalem fell down in worship before the LORD. [19]Then some Levites from the Kohathites and Korahites stood up and praised the LORD, the God of Israel, with a very loud voice.

[20]Early in the morning they left for the Desert of Tekoa. As they set out, Jehoshaphat stood and said, "Listen to me, Judah and people of Jerusalem! Have faith in the LORD your God and you will be upheld; have faith in his prophets and you will be successful." [21]After consulting the people, Jehoshaphat appointed men to sing to the LORD and to praise him for the splendor of his[a] holiness as they went out at the head of the army, saying:

"Give thanks to the LORD,
    for his love endures forever."

[22]As they began to sing and praise, the LORD set ambushes against the men of Ammon and Moab and Mount Seir who were invading Judah, and they were defeated. [23]The Ammonites and Moabites rose up against the men from Mount Seir to destroy and annihilate them. After they finished slaughtering the men from Seir, they helped to destroy one another.

[24]When the men of Judah came to the place that overlooks the desert and looked toward the vast army, they saw only dead bodies lying on the ground; no one had escaped. [25]So Jehoshaphat and his men went to carry off their plunder, and they found among them a great amount of equipment and clothing[b] and also articles of value — more than they could take away. There was so much plunder that it took three days to collect it. [26]On the fourth day they assembled in the Valley of Berakah, where they praised the LORD. This is why it is called the Valley of Berakah[c] to this day.

[27]Then, led by Jehoshaphat, all the men of Judah and Jerusalem returned joyfully to Jerusalem, for the LORD had given them cause to rejoice over their enemies. [28]They entered Jerusalem and went to the temple of the LORD with harps and lyres and trumpets.

[29]The fear of God came on all the surrounding kingdoms when they heard how the LORD had fought against the enemies of Israel. [30]And the kingdom of Jehoshaphat was at peace, for his God had given him rest on every side.

The End of Jehoshaphat's Reign

[31]So Jehoshaphat reigned over Judah. He was thirty-five years old when he became king of Judah, and he reigned in Jerusalem twenty-five years. His mother's name was Azubah daughter of Shilhi. [32]He followed the ways of his father Asa and did not stray from them; he did what was right in the eyes of the LORD. [33]The high places, however, were not removed, and the people still had not set their hearts on the God of their ancestors.

[34]The other events of Jehoshaphat's reign, from beginning to end, are written in the annals of Jehu son of Hanani, which are recorded in the book of the kings of Israel.

[35]Later, Jehoshaphat king of Judah made an alliance with Ahaziah king of Israel, whose ways were wicked. [36]He agreed with him to construct a fleet of trading ships.[d] After these were built at Ezion Geber, [37]Eliezer son of Dodavahu of Mareshah prophesied against Jehoshaphat, saying, "Because you have made an alliance with Ahaziah, the LORD will destroy what you have made." The ships were wrecked and were not able to set sail to trade.[e]

21

Then Jehoshaphat rested with his ancestors and was buried with them in the City of David. And Jehoram his son succeeded him

---

[a] 21 Or *him with the splendor of*   [b] 25 Some Hebrew manuscripts and Vulgate; most Hebrew manuscripts *corpses*
[c] 26 *Berakah* means *praise*.   [d] 36 Hebrew *of ships that could go to Tarshish*   [e] 37 Hebrew *sail for Tarshish*

as king. ²Jehoram's brothers, the sons of Jehoshaphat, were Azariah, Jehiel, Zechariah, Azariahu, Michael and Shephatiah. All these were sons of Jehoshaphat king of Israel.*a* ³Their father had given them many gifts of silver and gold and articles of value, as well as fortified cities in Judah, but he had given the kingdom to Jehoram because he was his firstborn son.

Jehoram King of Judah

⁴When Jehoram established himself firmly over his father's kingdom, he put all his brothers to the sword along with some of the officials of Israel. ⁵Jehoram was thirty-two years old when he became king, and he reigned in Jerusalem eight years. ⁶He followed the ways of the kings of Israel, as the house of Ahab had done, for he married a daughter of Ahab. He did evil in the eyes of the LORD. ⁷Nevertheless, because of the covenant the LORD had made with David, the LORD was not willing to destroy the house of David. He had promised to maintain a lamp for him and his descendants forever.

⁸In the time of Jehoram, Edom rebelled against Judah and set up its own king. ⁹So Jehoram went there with his officers and all his chariots. The Edomites surrounded him and his chariot commanders, but he rose up and broke through by night. ¹⁰To this day Edom has been in rebellion against Judah.

Libnah revolted at the same time, because Jehoram had forsaken the LORD, the God of his ancestors. ¹¹He had also built high places on the hills of Judah and had caused the people of Jerusalem to prostitute themselves and had led Judah astray.

¹²Jehoram received a letter from Elijah the prophet, which said:

"This is what the LORD, the God of your father David, says: 'You have not followed the ways of your father Jehoshaphat or of Asa king of Judah.

¹³But you have followed the ways of the kings of Israel, and you have led Judah and the people of Jerusalem to prostitute themselves, just as the house of Ahab did. You have also murdered your own brothers, members of your own family, men who were better than you. ¹⁴So now the LORD is about to strike your people, your sons, your wives and everything that is yours, with a heavy blow. ¹⁵You yourself will be very ill with a lingering disease of the bowels, until the disease causes your bowels to come out.'"

¹⁶The LORD aroused against Jehoram the hostility of the Philistines and of the Arabs who lived near the Cushites. ¹⁷They attacked Judah, invaded it and carried off all the goods found in the king's palace, together with his sons and wives. Not a son was left to him except Ahaziah,*b* the youngest.

¹⁸After all this, the LORD afflicted Jehoram with an incurable disease of the bowels. ¹⁹In the course of time, at the end of the second year, his bowels came out because of the disease, and he died in great pain. His people made no funeral fire in his honor, as they had for his predecessors.

²⁰Jehoram was thirty-two years old when he became king, and he reigned in Jerusalem eight years. He passed away, to no one's regret, and was buried in the City of David, but not in the tombs of the kings.

Ahaziah King of Judah

22 The people of Jerusalem made Ahaziah, Jehoram's youngest son, king in his place, since the raiders, who came with the Arabs into the camp, had killed all the older sons. So Ahaziah son of Jehoram king of Judah began to reign.

²Ahaziah was twenty-two*c* years old when he became king, and he reigned in

---

a 2 That is, Judah, as frequently in 2 Chronicles   *b 17* Hebrew *Jehoahaz,* a variant of *Ahaziah*   *c 2* Some Septuagint manuscripts and Syriac (see also 2 Kings 8:26); Hebrew *forty-two*

Jerusalem one year. His mother's name was Athaliah, a granddaughter of Omri.

[4] [5] ³He too followed the ways of the house of Ahab, for his mother encouraged him to act wickedly. ⁴He did evil in the eyes of the Lord, as the house of Ahab had done, for after his father's death they became his advisers, to his undoing. ⁵He also followed their counsel when he went with Joram[a] son of Ahab king of Israel to wage war against Hazael king of Aram at Ramoth Gilead. The Arameans wounded Joram; ⁶so he returned to Jezreel to recover from the wounds they had inflicted on him at Ramoth[b] in his battle with Hazael king of Aram.

Then Ahaziah[c] son of Jehoram king of Judah went down to Jezreel to see Joram son of Ahab because he had been wounded.

⁷Through Ahaziah's visit to Joram, God brought about Ahaziah's downfall. When Ahaziah arrived, he went out with Joram to meet Jehu son of Nimshi, whom the Lord had anointed to destroy the house of Ahab. ⁸While Jehu was executing judgment on the house of Ahab, he found the officials of Judah and the sons of Ahaziah's relatives, who had been attending Ahaziah, and he killed them. ⁹He then went in search of Ahaziah, and his men captured him while he was hiding in Samaria. He was brought to Jehu and put to death. They buried him, for they said, "He was a son of Jehoshaphat, who sought the Lord with all his heart." So there was no one in the house of Ahaziah powerful enough to retain the kingdom.

Athaliah and Joash

¹⁰When Athaliah the mother of Ahaziah saw that her son was dead, she proceeded to destroy the whole royal family of the house of Judah. ¹¹But Jehosheba,[d] the daughter of King Jehoram, took Joash son of Ahaziah and stole him away from among the royal princes who were about to be murdered and put him and his nurse in a bedroom. Because Jehosheba,[d] the daughter of King Jehoram and wife of the priest Jehoiada, was Ahaziah's sister, she hid the child from Athaliah so she could not kill him. ¹²He remained hidden with them at the temple of God for six years while Athaliah ruled the land.

23 In the seventh year Jehoiada showed his strength. He made a covenant with the commanders of units of a hundred: Azariah son of Jeroham, Ishmael son of Jehohanan, Azariah son of Obed, Maaseiah son of Adaiah, and Elishaphat son of Zikri. ²They went throughout Judah and gathered the Levites and the heads of Israelite families from all the towns. When they came to Jerusalem, ³the whole assembly made a covenant with the king at the temple of God.

Jehoiada said to them, "The king's son shall reign, as the Lord promised concerning the descendants of David. ⁴Now this is what you are to do: A third of you priests and Levites who are going on duty on the Sabbath are to keep watch at the doors, ⁵a third of you at the royal palace and a third at the Foundation Gate, and all the others are to be in the courtyards of the temple of the Lord. ⁶No one is to enter the temple of the Lord except the priests and Levites on duty; they may enter because they are consecrated, but all the others are to observe the Lord's command not to enter.[e] ⁷The Levites are to station themselves around the king, each with weapon in hand. Anyone who enters the temple is to be put to death. Stay close to the king wherever he goes."

⁸The Levites and all the men of Judah did just as Jehoiada the priest ordered. Each one took his men — those who were going on duty on the Sabbath and those who were going off duty — for Jehoiada the priest had

---

[a] 5 Hebrew *Jehoram*, a variant of *Joram*; also in verses 6 and 7   [b] 6 Hebrew *Ramah*, a variant of *Ramoth*
[c] 6 Some Hebrew manuscripts, Septuagint, Vulgate and Syriac (see also 2 Kings 8:29); most Hebrew manuscripts *Azariah*   [d] 11 Hebrew *Jehoshabeath*, a variant of *Jehosheba*   [e] 6 Or *are to stand guard where the Lord has assigned them*

not released any of the divisions. ⁹Then he gave the commanders of units of a hundred the spears and the large and small shields that had belonged to King David and that were in the temple of God. ¹⁰He stationed all the men, each with his weapon in his hand, around the king — near the altar and the temple, from the south side to the north side of the temple.

¹¹Jehoiada and his sons brought out the king's son and put the crown on him; they presented him with a copy of the covenant and proclaimed him king. They anointed him and shouted, "Long live the king!"

¹²When Athaliah heard the noise of the people running and cheering the king, she went to them at the temple of the LORD. ¹³She looked, and there was the king, standing by his pillar at the entrance. The officers and the trumpeters were beside the king, and all the people of the land were rejoicing and blowing trumpets, and musicians with their instruments were leading the praises. Then Athaliah tore her robes and shouted, "Treason! Treason!"

¹⁴Jehoiada the priest sent out the commanders of units of a hundred, who were in charge of the troops, and said to them: "Bring her out between the ranks[a] and put to the sword anyone who follows her." For the priest had said, "Do not put her to death at the temple of the LORD." ¹⁵So they seized her as she reached the entrance of the Horse Gate on the palace grounds, and there they put her to death.

¹⁶Jehoiada then made a covenant that he, the people and the king[b] would be the LORD's people. ¹⁷All the people went to the temple of Baal and tore it down. They smashed the altars and idols and killed Mattan the priest of Baal in front of the altars.

¹⁸Then Jehoiada placed the oversight of the temple of the LORD in the hands of the Levitical priests, to whom David had made assignments in the temple, to present the burnt offerings of the LORD as written in the Law of Moses, with rejoicing and singing, as David had ordered. ¹⁹He also stationed gatekeepers at the gates of the LORD's temple so that no one who was in any way unclean might enter.

²⁰He took with him the commanders of hundreds, the nobles, the rulers of the people and all the people of the land and brought the king down from the temple of the LORD. They went into the palace through the Upper Gate and seated the king on the royal throne. ²¹All the people of the land rejoiced, and the city was calm, because Athaliah had been slain with the sword.

Joash Repairs the Temple

24 Joash was seven years old when he became king, and he reigned in Jerusalem forty years. His mother's name was Zibiah; she was from Beersheba. ²Joash did what was right in the eyes of the LORD all the years of Jehoiada the priest. ³Jehoiada chose two wives for him, and he had sons and daughters.

⁴Some time later Joash decided to restore the temple of the LORD. ⁵He called together the priests and Levites and said to them, "Go to the towns of Judah and collect the money due annually from all Israel, to repair the temple of your God. Do it now." But the Levites did not act at once.

⁶Therefore the king summoned Jehoiada the chief priest and said to him, "Why haven't you required the Levites to bring in from Judah and Jerusalem the tax imposed by Moses the servant of the LORD and by the assembly of Israel for the tent of the covenant law?"

⁷Now the sons of that wicked woman Athaliah had broken into the temple of God and had used even its sacred objects for the Baals.

⁸At the king's command, a chest was

---

made and placed outside, at the gate of the temple of the Lord. [9]A proclamation was then issued in Judah and Jerusalem that they should bring to the Lord the tax that Moses the servant of God had required of Israel in the wilderness. [10]All the officials and all the people brought their contributions gladly, dropping them into the chest until it was full. [11]Whenever the chest was brought in by the Levites to the king's officials and they saw that there was a large amount of money, the royal secretary and the officer of the chief priest would come and empty the chest and carry it back to its place. They did this regularly and collected a great amount of money. [12]The king and Jehoiada gave it to those who carried out the work required for the temple of the Lord. They hired masons and carpenters to restore the Lord's temple, and also workers in iron and bronze to repair the temple.

[13]The men in charge of the work were diligent, and the repairs progressed under them. They rebuilt the temple of God according to its original design and reinforced it. [14]When they had finished, they brought the rest of the money to the king and Jehoiada, and with it were made articles for the Lord's temple: articles for the service and for the burnt offerings, and also dishes and other objects of gold and silver. As long as Jehoiada lived, burnt offerings were presented continually in the temple of the Lord.

[15]Now Jehoiada was old and full of years, and he died at the age of a hundred and thirty. [16]He was buried with the kings in the City of David, because of the good he had done in Israel for God and his temple.

The Wickedness of Joash

[17]After the death of Jehoiada, the officials of Judah came and paid homage to the king, and he listened to them. [18]They abandoned the temple of the Lord, the God of their ancestors, and worshiped Asherah poles and idols. Because of their guilt, God's anger came on Judah and Jerusalem. [19]Although the Lord sent prophets to the people to bring them back to him, and though they testified against them, they would not listen.

[20]Then the Spirit of God came on Zechariah son of Jehoiada the priest. He stood before the people and said, "This is what God says: 'Why do you disobey the Lord's commands? You will not prosper. Because you have forsaken the Lord, he has forsaken you.'"

[21]But they plotted against him, and by order of the king they stoned him to death in the courtyard of the Lord's temple. [22]King Joash did not remember the kindness Zechariah's father Jehoiada had shown him but killed his son, who said as he lay dying, "May the Lord see this and call you to account."

[23]At the turn of the year,[a] the army of Aram marched against Joash; it invaded Judah and Jerusalem and killed all the leaders of the people. They sent all the plunder to their king in Damascus. [24]Although the Aramean army had come with only a few men, the Lord delivered into their hands a much larger army. Because Judah had forsaken the Lord, the God of their ancestors, judgment was executed on Joash. [25]When the Arameans withdrew, they left Joash severely wounded. His officials conspired against him for murdering the son of Jehoiada the priest, and they killed him in his bed. So he died and was buried in the City of David, but not in the tombs of the kings.

[26]Those who conspired against him were Zabad,[b] son of Shimeath an Ammonite woman, and Jehozabad, son of Shimrith[c] a Moabite woman. [27]The account of his sons, the many prophecies about him, and the record of the restoration of the temple of God are written in the annotations on the book of the kings. And Amaziah his son succeeded him as king.

---

a 23 Probably in the spring   *b 26* A variant of *Jozabad*   *c 26* A variant of *Shomer*

Amaziah King of Judah

25 Amaziah was twenty-five years old when he became king, and he reigned in Jerusalem twenty-nine years. His mother's name was Jehoaddan; she was from Jerusalem. ²He did what was right in the eyes of the LORD, but not wholeheartedly. ³After the kingdom was firmly in his control, he executed the officials who had murdered his father the king. ⁴Yet he did not put their children to death, but acted in accordance with what is written in the Law, in the Book of Moses, where the LORD commanded: "Parents shall not be put to death for their children, nor children be put to death for their parents; each will die for their own sin."ᵃ

⁵Amaziah called the people of Judah together and assigned them according to their families to commanders of thousands and commanders of hundreds for all Judah and Benjamin. He then mustered those twenty years old or more and found that there were three hundred thousand men fit for military service, able to handle the spear and shield. ⁶He also hired a hundred thousand fighting men from Israel for a hundred talentsᵇ of silver.

⁷But a man of God came to him and said, "Your Majesty, these troops from Israel must not march with you, for the LORD is not with Israel — not with any of the people of Ephraim. ⁸Even if you go and fight courageously in battle, God will overthrow you before the enemy, for God has the power to help or to overthrow."

⁹Amaziah asked the man of God, "But what about the hundred talents I paid for these Israelite troops?"

The man of God replied, "The LORD can give you much more than that."

¹⁰So Amaziah dismissed the troops who had come to him from Ephraim and sent them home. They were furious with Judah and left for home in a great rage.

¹¹Amaziah then marshaled his strength and led his army to the Valley of Salt, where he killed ten thousand men of Seir. ¹²The army of Judah also captured ten thousand men alive, took them to the top of a cliff and threw them down so that all were dashed to pieces.

¹³Meanwhile the troops that Amaziah had sent back and had not allowed to take part in the war raided towns belonging to Judah from Samaria to Beth Horon. They killed three thousand people and carried off great quantities of plunder.

¹⁴When Amaziah returned from slaughtering the Edomites, he brought back the gods of the people of Seir. He set them up as his own gods, bowed down to them and burned sacrifices to them. ¹⁵The anger of the LORD burned against Amaziah, and he sent a prophet to him, who said, "Why do you consult this people's gods, which could not save their own people from your hand?"

¹⁶While he was still speaking, the king said to him, "Have we appointed you an adviser to the king? Stop! Why be struck down?"

So the prophet stopped but said, "I know that God has determined to destroy you, because you have done this and have not listened to my counsel."

¹⁷After Amaziah king of Judah consulted his advisers, he sent this challenge to Jehoashᶜ son of Jehoahaz, the son of Jehu, king of Israel: "Come, let us face each other in battle."

¹⁸But Jehoash king of Israel replied to Amaziah king of Judah: "A thistle in Lebanon sent a message to a cedar in Lebanon, 'Give your daughter to my son in marriage.' Then a wild beast in Lebanon came along and trampled the thistle underfoot. ¹⁹You say to yourself that you have defeated Edom, and now you are arrogant and proud. But stay at home! Why ask for trouble and cause your own downfall and that of Judah also?"

ᵃ 4 Deut. 24:16   ᵇ 6 That is, about 3 3/4 tons or about 3.4 metric tons; also in verse 9   ᶜ 17 Hebrew Joash, a variant of Jehoash; also in verses 18, 21, 23 and 25

20 Amaziah, however, would not listen, for God so worked that he might deliver them into the hands of Jehoash, because they sought the gods of Edom. 21 So Jehoash king of Israel attacked. He and Amaziah king of Judah faced each other at Beth Shemesh in Judah. 22 Judah was routed by Israel, and every man fled to his home. 23 Jehoash king of Israel captured Amaziah king of Judah, the son of Joash, the son of Ahaziah,[a] at Beth Shemesh. Then Jehoash brought him to Jerusalem and broke down the wall of Jerusalem from the Ephraim Gate to the Corner Gate — a section about four hundred cubits[b] long. 24 He took all the gold and silver and all the articles found in the temple of God that had been in the care of Obed-Edom, together with the palace treasures and the hostages, and returned to Samaria.

25 Amaziah son of Joash king of Judah lived for fifteen years after the death of Jehoash son of Jehoahaz king of Israel. 26 As for the other events of Amaziah's reign, from beginning to end, are they not written in the book of the kings of Judah and Israel? 27 From the time that Amaziah turned away from following the LORD, they conspired against him in Jerusalem and he fled to Lachish, but they sent men after him to Lachish and killed him there. 28 He was brought back by horse and was buried with his ancestors in the City of Judah.[c]

Uzziah King of Judah

26 Then all the people of Judah took Uzziah,[d] who was sixteen years old, and made him king in place of his father Amaziah. 2 He was the one who rebuilt Elath and restored it to Judah after Amaziah rested with his ancestors.

3 Uzziah was sixteen years old when he became king, and he reigned in Jerusalem fifty-two years. His mother's name was Jekoliah; she was from Jerusalem. 4 He did what was right in the eyes of the LORD, just as his father Amaziah had done. 5 He sought God during the days of Zechariah, who instructed him in the fear[e] of God. As long as he sought the LORD, God gave him success.

6 He went to war against the Philistines and broke down the walls of Gath, Jabneh and Ashdod. He then rebuilt towns near Ashdod and elsewhere among the Philistines. 7 God helped him against the Philistines and against the Arabs who lived in Gur Baal and against the Meunites. 8 The Ammonites brought tribute to Uzziah, and his fame spread as far as the border of Egypt, because he had become very powerful.

9 Uzziah built towers in Jerusalem at the Corner Gate, at the Valley Gate and at the angle of the wall, and he fortified them. 10 He also built towers in the wilderness and dug many cisterns, because he had much livestock in the foothills and in the plain. He had people working his fields and vineyards in the hills and in the fertile lands, for he loved the soil.

11 Uzziah had a well-trained army, ready to go out by divisions according to their numbers as mustered by Jeiel the secretary and Maaseiah the officer under the direction of Hananiah, one of the royal officials. 12 The total number of family leaders over the fighting men was 2,600. 13 Under their command was an army of 307,500 men trained for war, a powerful force to support the king against his enemies. 14 Uzziah provided shields, spears, helmets, coats of armor, bows and slingstones for the entire army. 15 In Jerusalem he made devices invented for use on the towers and on the corner defenses so that soldiers could shoot arrows and hurl large stones from the walls. His fame spread far and wide, for he was greatly helped until he became powerful.

---

a 23 Hebrew Jehoahaz, a variant of Ahaziah   b 23 That is, about 600 feet or about 180 meters   c 28 Most Hebrew manuscripts; some Hebrew manuscripts, Septuagint, Vulgate and Syriac (see also 2 Kings 14:20) David   d 1 Also called Azariah   e 5 Many Hebrew manuscripts, Septuagint and Syriac; other Hebrew manuscripts vision

[16]But after Uzziah became powerful, his pride led to his downfall. He was unfaithful to the LORD his God, and entered the temple of the LORD to burn incense on the altar of incense. [17]Azariah the priest with eighty other courageous priests of the LORD followed him in. [18]They confronted King Uzziah and said, "It is not right for you, Uzziah, to burn incense to the LORD. That is for the priests, the descendants of Aaron, who have been consecrated to burn incense. Leave the sanctuary, for you have been unfaithful; and you will not be honored by the LORD God."

[19]Uzziah, who had a censer in his hand ready to burn incense, became angry. While he was raging at the priests in their presence before the incense altar in the LORD's temple, leprosy[a] broke out on his forehead. [20]When Azariah the chief priest and all the other priests looked at him, they saw that he had leprosy on his forehead, so they hurried him out. Indeed, he himself was eager to leave, because the LORD had afflicted him.

[21]King Uzziah had leprosy until the day he died. He lived in a separate house[b] — leprous, and banned from the temple of the LORD. Jotham his son had charge of the palace and governed the people of the land.

[22]The other events of Uzziah's reign, from beginning to end, are recorded by the prophet Isaiah son of Amoz. [23]Uzziah rested with his ancestors and was buried near them in a cemetery that belonged to the kings, for people said, "He had leprosy." And Jotham his son succeeded him as king.

Jotham King of Judah

27 Jotham was twenty-five years old when he became king, and he reigned in Jerusalem sixteen years. His mother's name was Jerusha daughter of Zadok. [2]He did what was right in the eyes of the LORD, just as his father Uzziah had done, but unlike him he did not enter the temple of the LORD. The people, however, continued their corrupt practices. [3]Jotham rebuilt the Upper Gate of the temple of the LORD and did extensive work on the wall at the hill of Ophel. [4]He built towns in the hill country of Judah and forts and towers in the wooded areas.

[5]Jotham waged war against the king of the Ammonites and conquered them. That year the Ammonites paid him a hundred talents[c] of silver, ten thousand cors[d] of wheat and ten thousand cors[e] of barley. The Ammonites brought him the same amount also in the second and third years.

[6]Jotham grew powerful because he walked steadfastly before the LORD his God.

[7]The other events in Jotham's reign, including all his wars and the other things he did, are written in the book of the kings of Israel and Judah. [8]He was twenty-five years old when he became king, and he reigned in Jerusalem sixteen years. [9]Jotham rested with his ancestors and was buried in the City of David. And Ahaz his son succeeded him as king.

Ahaz King of Judah

28 Ahaz was twenty years old when he became king, and he reigned in Jerusalem sixteen years. Unlike David his father, he did not do what was right in the eyes of the LORD. [2]He followed the ways of the kings of Israel and also made idols for worshiping the Baals. [3]He burned sacrifices in the Valley of Ben Hinnom and sacrificed his children in the fire, engaging in the detestable practices of the nations the LORD had driven out before the Israelites. [4]He offered sacrifices and burned incense at the high places, on the hilltops and under every spreading tree.

[5]Therefore the LORD his God delivered him into the hands of the king of

---

[a] 19 The Hebrew for *leprosy* was used for various diseases affecting the skin; also in verses 20, 21 and 23.   [b] 21 Or *in a house where he was relieved of responsibilities*   [c] 5 That is, about 3 3/4 tons or about 3.4 metric tons   [d] 5 That is, probably about 1,800 tons or about 1,600 metric tons of wheat   [e] 5 That is, probably about 1,500 tons or about 1,350 metric tons of barley

Aram. The Arameans defeated him and took many of his people as prisoners and brought them to Damascus.

He was also given into the hands of the king of Israel, who inflicted heavy casualties on him. [6]In one day Pekah son of Remaliah killed a hundred and twenty thousand soldiers in Judah—because Judah had forsaken the LORD, the God of their ancestors. [7]Zikri, an Ephraimite warrior, killed Maaseiah the king's son, Azrikam the officer in charge of the palace, and Elkanah, second to the king. [8]The men of Israel took captive from their fellow Israelites who were from Judah two hundred thousand wives, sons and daughters. They also took a great deal of plunder, which they carried back to Samaria.

[9]But a prophet of the LORD named Oded was there, and he went out to meet the army when it returned to Samaria. He said to them, "Because the LORD, the God of your ancestors, was angry with Judah, he gave them into your hand. But you have slaughtered them in a rage that reaches to heaven. [10]And now you intend to make the men and women of Judah and Jerusalem your slaves. But aren't you also guilty of sins against the LORD your God? [11]Now listen to me! Send back your fellow Israelites you have taken as prisoners, for the LORD's fierce anger rests on you."

[12]Then some of the leaders in Ephraim—Azariah son of Jehohanan, Berekiah son of Meshillemoth, Jehizkiah son of Shallum, and Amasa son of Hadlai—confronted those who were arriving from the war. [13]"You must not bring those prisoners here," they said, "or we will be guilty before the LORD. Do you intend to add to our sin and guilt? For our guilt is already great, and his fierce anger rests on Israel."

[14]So the soldiers gave up the prisoners and plunder in the presence of the officials and all the assembly. [15]The men designated by name took the prisoners, and from the plunder they clothed all who were naked. They provided them with clothes and sandals, food and drink, and healing balm. All those who were weak they put on donkeys. So they took them back to their fellow Israelites at Jericho, the City of Palms, and returned to Samaria.

[16]At that time King Ahaz sent to the kings[a] of Assyria for help. [17]The Edomites had again come and attacked Judah and carried away prisoners, [18]while the Philistines had raided towns in the foothills and in the Negev of Judah. They captured and occupied Beth Shemesh, Aijalon and Gederoth, as well as Soko, Timnah and Gimzo, with their surrounding villages. [19]The LORD had humbled Judah because of Ahaz king of Israel,[b] for he had promoted wickedness in Judah and had been most unfaithful to the LORD. [20]Tiglath-Pileser[c] king of Assyria came to him, but he gave him trouble instead of help. [21]Ahaz took some of the things from the temple of the LORD and from the royal palace and from the officials and presented them to the king of Assyria, but that did not help him.

[22]In his time of trouble King Ahaz became even more unfaithful to the LORD. [23]He offered sacrifices to the gods of Damascus, who had defeated him; for he thought, "Since the gods of the kings of Aram have helped them, I will sacrifice to them so they will help me." But they were his downfall and the downfall of all Israel.

[24]Ahaz gathered together the furnishings from the temple of God and cut them in pieces. He shut the doors of the LORD's temple and set up altars at every street corner in Jerusalem. [25]In every town in Judah he built high places to burn sacrifices to other gods and aroused the anger of the LORD, the God of his ancestors.

[26]The other events of his reign and all his ways, from beginning to end, are written in the book of the kings of Judah and Israel. [27]Ahaz rested with his ancestors and

---

[a] 16 Most Hebrew manuscripts; one Hebrew manuscript, Septuagint and Vulgate (see also 2 Kings 16:7) *king*
[b] 19 That is, Judah, as frequently in 2 Chronicles   [c] 20 Hebrew *Tilgath-Pileser,* a variant of *Tiglath-Pileser*

was buried in the city of Jerusalem, but he was not placed in the tombs of the kings of Israel. And Hezekiah his son succeeded him as king.

Hezekiah Purifies the Temple

29 Hezekiah was twenty-five years old when he became king, and he reigned in Jerusalem twenty-nine years. His mother's name was Abijah daughter of Zechariah. ²He did what was right in the eyes of the LORD, just as his father David had done.

³In the first month of the first year of his reign, he opened the doors of the temple of the LORD and repaired them. ⁴He brought in the priests and the Levites, assembled them in the square on the east side ⁵and said: "Listen to me, Levites! Consecrate yourselves now and consecrate the temple of the LORD, the God of your ancestors. Remove all defilement from the sanctuary. ⁶Our parents were unfaithful; they did evil in the eyes of the LORD our God and forsook him. They turned their faces away from the LORD's dwelling place and turned their backs on him. ⁷They also shut the doors of the portico and put out the lamps. They did not burn incense or present any burnt offerings at the sanctuary to the God of Israel. ⁸Therefore, the anger of the LORD has fallen on Judah and Jerusalem; he has made them an object of dread and horror and scorn, as you can see with your own eyes. ⁹This is why our fathers have fallen by the sword and why our sons and daughters and our wives are in captivity. ¹⁰Now I intend to make a covenant with the LORD, the God of Israel, so that his fierce anger will turn away from us. ¹¹My sons, do not be negligent now, for the LORD has chosen you to stand before him and serve him, to minister before him and to burn incense."

¹²Then these Levites set to work:

from the Kohathites,
    Mahath son of Amasai and Joel son of Azariah;

from the Merarites,
    Kish son of Abdi and Azariah son of Jehallelel;
from the Gershonites,
    Joah son of Zimmah and Eden son of Joah;
¹³from the descendants of Elizaphan,
    Shimri and Jeiel;
from the descendants of Asaph,
    Zechariah and Mattaniah;
¹⁴from the descendants of Heman,
    Jehiel and Shimei;
from the descendants of Jeduthun,
    Shemaiah and Uzziel.

¹⁵When they had assembled their fellow Levites and consecrated themselves, they went in to purify the temple of the LORD, as the king had ordered, following the word of the LORD. ¹⁶The priests went into the sanctuary of the LORD to purify it. They brought out to the courtyard of the LORD's temple everything unclean that they found in the temple of the LORD. The Levites took it and carried it out to the Kidron Valley. ¹⁷They began the consecration on the first day of the first month, and by the eighth day of the month they reached the portico of the LORD. For eight more days they consecrated the temple of the LORD itself, finishing on the sixteenth day of the first month.

¹⁸Then they went in to King Hezekiah and reported: "We have purified the entire temple of the LORD, the altar of burnt offering with all its utensils, and the table for setting out the consecrated bread, with all its articles. ¹⁹We have prepared and consecrated all the articles that King Ahaz removed in his unfaithfulness while he was king. They are now in front of the LORD's altar."

²⁰Early the next morning King Hezekiah gathered the city officials together and went up to the temple of the LORD. ²¹They brought seven bulls, seven rams, seven male lambs and seven male goats as a sin offering[a] for the kingdom, for the sanctuary

---

[a] 21 Or *purification offering*; also in verses 23 and 24

and for Judah. The king commanded the priests, the descendants of Aaron, to offer these on the altar of the Lord. 22So they slaughtered the bulls, and the priests took the blood and splashed it against the altar; next they slaughtered the rams and splashed their blood against the altar; then they slaughtered the lambs and splashed their blood against the altar. 23The goats for the sin offering were brought before the king and the assembly, and they laid their hands on them. 24The priests then slaughtered the goats and presented their blood on the altar for a sin offering to atone for all Israel, because the king had ordered the burnt offering and the sin offering for all Israel.

25He stationed the Levites in the temple of the Lord with cymbals, harps and lyres in the way prescribed by David and Gad the king's seer and Nathan the prophet; this was commanded by the Lord through his prophets. 26So the Levites stood ready with David's instruments, and the priests with their trumpets.

27Hezekiah gave the order to sacrifice the burnt offering on the altar. As the offering began, singing to the Lord began also, accompanied by trumpets and the instruments of David king of Israel. 28The whole assembly bowed in worship, while the musicians played and the trumpets sounded. All this continued until the sacrifice of the burnt offering was completed.

29When the offerings were finished, the king and everyone present with him knelt down and worshiped. 30King Hezekiah and his officials ordered the Levites to praise the Lord with the words of David and of Asaph the seer. So they sang praises with gladness and bowed down and worshiped.

31Then Hezekiah said, "You have now dedicated yourselves to the Lord. Come and bring sacrifices and thank offerings to the temple of the Lord." So the assembly brought sacrifices and thank offerings, and all whose hearts were willing brought burnt offerings.

32The number of burnt offerings the assembly brought was seventy bulls, a hundred rams and two hundred male lambs— all of them for burnt offerings to the Lord. 33The animals consecrated as sacrifices amounted to six hundred bulls and three thousand sheep and goats. 34The priests, however, were too few to skin all the burnt offerings; so their relatives the Levites helped them until the task was finished and until other priests had been consecrated, for the Levites had been more conscientious in consecrating themselves than the priests had been. 35There were burnt offerings in abundance, together with the fat of the fellowship offerings and the drink offerings that accompanied the burnt offerings.

So the service of the temple of the Lord was reestablished. 36Hezekiah and all the people rejoiced at what God had brought about for his people, because it was done so quickly.

Hezekiah Celebrates the Passover

30 Hezekiah sent word to all Israel and Judah and also wrote letters to Ephraim and Manasseh, inviting them to come to the temple of the Lord in Jerusalem and celebrate the Passover to the Lord, the God of Israel. 2The king and his officials and the whole assembly in Jerusalem decided to celebrate the Passover in the second month. 3They had not been able to celebrate it at the regular time because not enough priests had consecrated themselves and the people had not assembled in Jerusalem. 4The plan seemed right both to the king and to the whole assembly. 5They decided to send a proclamation throughout Israel, from Beersheba to Dan, calling the people to come to Jerusalem and celebrate the Passover to the Lord, the God of Israel. It had not been celebrated in large numbers according to what was written.

6At the king's command, couriers went throughout Israel and Judah with letters from the king and from his officials, which read:

"People of Israel, return to the LORD, the God of Abraham, Isaac and Israel, that he may return to you who are left, who have escaped from the hand of the kings of Assyria. ⁷Do not be like your parents and your fellow Israelites, who were unfaithful to the LORD, the God of their ancestors, so that he made them an object of horror, as you see. ⁸Do not be stiff-necked, as your ancestors were; submit to the LORD. Come to his sanctuary, which he has consecrated forever. Serve the LORD your God, so that his fierce anger will turn away from you. ⁹If you return to the LORD, then your fellow Israelites and your children will be shown compassion by their captors and will return to this land, for the LORD your God is gracious and compassionate. He will not turn his face from you if you return to him."

¹⁰The couriers went from town to town in Ephraim and Manasseh, as far as Zebulun, but people scorned and ridiculed them. ¹¹Nevertheless, some from Asher, Manasseh and Zebulun humbled themselves and went to Jerusalem. ¹²Also in Judah the hand of God was on the people to give them unity of mind to carry out what the king and his officials had ordered, following the word of the LORD.

¹³A very large crowd of people assembled in Jerusalem to celebrate the Festival of Unleavened Bread in the second month. ¹⁴They removed the altars in Jerusalem and cleared away the incense altars and threw them into the Kidron Valley.

¹⁵They slaughtered the Passover lamb on the fourteenth day of the second month. The priests and the Levites were ashamed and consecrated themselves and brought burnt offerings to the temple of the LORD. ¹⁶Then they took up their regular positions as prescribed in the Law of Moses the man of God. The priests splashed against the altar the blood handed to them by the Levites. ¹⁷Since many in the crowd had not consecrated themselves, the Levites had to kill the Passover lambs for all those who were not ceremonially clean and could not consecrate their lambs[a] to the LORD. ¹⁸Although most of the many people who came from Ephraim, Manasseh, Issachar and Zebulun had not purified themselves, yet they ate the Passover, contrary to what was written. But Hezekiah prayed for them, saying, "May the LORD, who is good, pardon everyone ¹⁹who sets their heart on seeking God — the LORD, the God of their ancestors — even if they are not clean according to the rules of the sanctuary." ²⁰And the LORD heard Hezekiah and healed the people.

²¹The Israelites who were present in Jerusalem celebrated the Festival of Unleavened Bread for seven days with great rejoicing, while the Levites and priests praised the LORD every day with resounding instruments dedicated to the LORD.[b]

²²Hezekiah spoke encouragingly to all the Levites, who showed good understanding of the service of the LORD. For the seven days they ate their assigned portion and offered fellowship offerings and praised[c] the LORD, the God of their ancestors.

²³The whole assembly then agreed to celebrate the festival seven more days; so for another seven days they celebrated joyfully. ²⁴Hezekiah king of Judah provided a thousand bulls and seven thousand sheep and goats for the assembly, and the officials provided them with a thousand bulls and ten thousand sheep and goats. A great number of priests consecrated themselves. ²⁵The entire assembly of Judah rejoiced, along with the priests and Levites and all who had assembled from Israel, including the foreigners who had come from Israel and also those who resided in Judah. ²⁶There was great joy in Jerusalem, for since the days of Solomon son of David

---

a 17 Or *consecrate themselves*   *b 21* Or *priests sang to the LORD every day, accompanied by the LORD's instruments of praise*   *c 22* Or *and confessed their sins to* king of Israel there had been nothing like this in Jerusalem. ²⁷The priests and the Levites stood to bless the people, and God heard them, for their prayer reached heaven, his holy dwelling place.

31 When all this had ended, the Israelites who were there went out to the towns of Judah, smashed the sacred stones and cut down the Asherah poles. They destroyed the high places and the altars throughout Judah and Benjamin and in Ephraim and Manasseh. After they had destroyed all of them, the Israelites returned to their own towns and to their own property.

Contributions for Worship

²Hezekiah assigned the priests and Levites to divisions — each of them according to their duties as priests or Levites — to offer burnt offerings and fellowship offerings, to minister, to give thanks and to sing praises at the gates of the Lord's dwelling. ³The king contributed from his own possessions for the morning and evening burnt offerings and for the burnt offerings on the Sabbaths, at the New Moons and at the appointed festivals as written in the Law of the Lord. ⁴He ordered the people living in Jerusalem to give the portion due the priests and Levites so they could devote themselves to the Law of the Lord. ⁵As soon as the order went out, the Israelites generously gave the firstfruits of their grain, new wine, olive oil and honey and all that the fields produced. They brought a great amount, a tithe of everything. ⁶The people of Israel and Judah who lived in the towns of Judah also brought a tithe of their herds and flocks and a tithe of the holy things dedicated to the Lord their God, and they piled them in heaps. ⁷They began doing this in the third month and finished in the seventh month. ⁸When Hezekiah and his officials came and saw the heaps, they praised the Lord and blessed his people Israel.

⁹Hezekiah asked the priests and Levites about the heaps; ¹⁰and Azariah the chief priest, from the family of Zadok, answered, "Since the people began to bring their contributions to the temple of the Lord, we have had enough to eat and plenty to spare, because the Lord has blessed his people, and this great amount is left over."

¹¹Hezekiah gave orders to prepare storerooms in the temple of the Lord, and this was done. ¹²Then they faithfully brought in the contributions, tithes and dedicated gifts. Konaniah, a Levite, was the overseer in charge of these things, and his brother Shimei was next in rank. ¹³Jehiel, Azaziah, Nahath, Asahel, Jerimoth, Jozabad, Eliel, Ismakiah, Mahath and Benaiah were assistants of Konaniah and Shimei his brother. All these served by appointment of King Hezekiah and Azariah the official in charge of the temple of God.

¹⁴Kore son of Imnah the Levite, keeper of the East Gate, was in charge of the freewill offerings given to God, distributing the contributions made to the Lord and also the consecrated gifts. ¹⁵Eden, Miniamin, Jeshua, Shemaiah, Amariah and Shekaniah assisted him faithfully in the towns of the priests, distributing to their fellow priests according to their divisions, old and young alike.

¹⁶In addition, they distributed to the males three years old or more whose names were in the genealogical records — all who would enter the temple of the Lord to perform the daily duties of their various tasks, according to their responsibilities and their divisions. ¹⁷And they distributed to the priests enrolled by their families in the genealogical records and likewise to the Levites twenty years old or more, according to their responsibilities and their divisions. ¹⁸They included all the little ones, the wives, and the sons and daughters of the whole community listed in these genealogical records. For they were faithful in consecrating themselves.

¹⁹As for the priests, the descendants of Aaron, who lived on the farmlands around their towns or in any other towns, men were designated by name to distribute por-

tions to every male among them and to all who were recorded in the genealogies of the Levites.

20This is what Hezekiah did throughout Judah, doing what was good and right and faithful before the LORD his God. 21In everything that he undertook in the service of God's temple and in obedience to the law and the commands, he sought his God and worked wholeheartedly. And so he prospered.

Sennacherib Threatens Jerusalem

32 After all that Hezekiah had so faithfully done, Sennacherib king of Assyria came and invaded Judah. He laid siege to the fortified cities, thinking to conquer them for himself. 2When Hezekiah saw that Sennacherib had come and that he intended to wage war against Jerusalem, 3he consulted with his officials and military staff about blocking off the water from the springs outside the city, and they helped him. 4They gathered a large group of people who blocked all the springs and the stream that flowed through the land. "Why should the kings*a* of Assyria come and find plenty of water?" they said. 5Then he worked hard repairing all the broken sections of the wall and building towers on it. He built another wall outside that one and reinforced the terraces*b* of the City of David. He also made large numbers of weapons and shields.

6He appointed military officers over the people and assembled them before him in the square at the city gate and encouraged them with these words: 7"Be strong and courageous. Do not be afraid or discouraged because of the king of Assyria and the vast army with him, for there is a greater power with us than with him. 8With him is only the arm of flesh, but with us is the LORD our God to help us and to fight our battles." And the people gained confidence from what Hezekiah the king of Judah said.

9Later, when Sennacherib king of Assyria and all his forces were laying siege to Lachish, he sent his officers to Jerusalem with this message for Hezekiah king of Judah and for all the people of Judah who were there:

10"This is what Sennacherib king of Assyria says: On what are you basing your confidence, that you remain in Jerusalem under siege? 11When Hezekiah says, 'The LORD our God will save us from the hand of the king of Assyria,' he is misleading you, to let you die of hunger and thirst. 12Did not Hezekiah himself remove this god's high places and altars, saying to Judah and Jerusalem, 'You must worship before one altar and burn sacrifices on it'?

13"Do you not know what I and my predecessors have done to all the peoples of the other lands? Were the gods of those nations ever able to deliver their land from my hand? 14Who of all the gods of these nations that my predecessors destroyed has been able to save his people from me? How then can your god deliver you from my hand? 15Now do not let Hezekiah deceive you and mislead you like this. Do not believe him, for no god of any nation or kingdom has been able to deliver his people from my hand or the hand of my predecessors. How much less will your god deliver you from my hand!"

16Sennacherib's officers spoke further against the LORD God and against his servant Hezekiah. 17The king also wrote letters ridiculing the LORD, the God of Israel, and saying this against him: "Just as the gods of the peoples of the other lands did not rescue their people from my hand, so the god of Hezekiah will not rescue his people from my hand." 18Then they called out in Hebrew to the people of Jerusalem who were on the wall, to terrify them and

---

a 4 Hebrew; Septuagint and Syriac *king*   *b 5* Or *the Millo* make them afraid in order to capture the city. [19]They spoke about the God of Jerusalem as they did about the gods of the other peoples of the world — the work of human hands.

[20]King Hezekiah and the prophet Isaiah son of Amoz cried out in prayer to heaven about this. [21]And the Lord sent an angel, who annihilated all the fighting men and the commanders and officers in the camp of the Assyrian king. So he withdrew to his own land in disgrace. And when he went into the temple of his god, some of his sons, his own flesh and blood, cut him down with the sword.

[22]So the Lord saved Hezekiah and the people of Jerusalem from the hand of Sennacherib king of Assyria and from the hand of all others. He took care of them[a] on every side. [23]Many brought offerings to Jerusalem for the Lord and valuable gifts for Hezekiah king of Judah. From then on he was highly regarded by all the nations.

Hezekiah's Pride, Success and Death

[24]In those days Hezekiah became ill and was at the point of death. He prayed to the Lord, who answered him and gave him a miraculous sign. [25]But Hezekiah's heart was proud and he did not respond to the kindness shown him; therefore the Lord's wrath was on him and on Judah and Jerusalem. [26]Then Hezekiah repented of the pride of his heart, as did the people of Jerusalem; therefore the Lord's wrath did not come on them during the days of Hezekiah.

[27]Hezekiah had very great wealth and honor, and he made treasuries for his silver and gold and for his precious stones, spices, shields and all kinds of valuables. [28]He also made buildings to store the harvest of grain, new wine and olive oil; and he made stalls for various kinds of cattle, and pens for the flocks. [29]He built villages and acquired great numbers of flocks and herds, for God had given him very great riches.

[30]It was Hezekiah who blocked the upper outlet of the Gihon spring and channeled the water down to the west side of the City of David. He succeeded in everything he undertook. [31]But when envoys were sent by the rulers of Babylon to ask him about the miraculous sign that had occurred in the land, God left him to test him and to know everything that was in his heart.

[32]The other events of Hezekiah's reign and his acts of devotion are written in the vision of the prophet Isaiah son of Amoz in the book of the kings of Judah and Israel. [33]Hezekiah rested with his ancestors and was buried on the hill where the tombs of David's descendants are. All Judah and the people of Jerusalem honored him when he died. And Manasseh his son succeeded him as king.

Manasseh King of Judah

33 Manasseh was twelve years old when he became king, and he reigned in Jerusalem fifty-five years. [2]He did evil in the eyes of the Lord, following the detestable practices of the nations the Lord had driven out before the Israelites. [3]He rebuilt the high places his father Hezekiah had demolished; he also erected altars to the Baals and made Asherah poles. He bowed down to all the starry hosts and worshiped them. [4]He built altars in the temple of the Lord, of which the Lord had said, "My Name will remain in Jerusalem forever." [5]In both courts of the temple of the Lord, he built altars to all the starry hosts. [6]He sacrificed his children in the fire in the Valley of Ben Hinnom, practiced divination and witchcraft, sought omens, and consulted mediums and spiritists. He did much evil in the eyes of the Lord, arousing his anger.

[7]He took the image he had made and put it in God's temple, of which God had said to David and to his son Solomon, "In this temple and in Jerusalem, which I have chosen out of all the tribes of Israel, I will put

---

a 22 Hebrew; Septuagint and Vulgate *He gave them rest*

my Name forever. [8]I will not again make the feet of the Israelites leave the land I assigned to your ancestors, if only they will be careful to do everything I commanded them concerning all the laws, decrees and regulations given through Moses." [9]But Manasseh led Judah and the people of Jerusalem astray, so that they did more evil than the nations the LORD had destroyed before the Israelites.

[10]The LORD spoke to Manasseh and his people, but they paid no attention. [11]So the LORD brought against them the army commanders of the king of Assyria, who took Manasseh prisoner, put a hook in his nose, bound him with bronze shackles and took him to Babylon. [12]In his distress he sought the favor of the LORD his God and humbled himself greatly before the God of his ancestors. [13]And when he prayed to him, the LORD was moved by his entreaty and listened to his plea; so he brought him back to Jerusalem and to his kingdom. Then Manasseh knew that the LORD is God.

[14]Afterward he rebuilt the outer wall of the City of David, west of the Gihon spring in the valley, as far as the entrance of the Fish Gate and encircling the hill of Ophel; he also made it much higher. He stationed military commanders in all the fortified cities in Judah.

[15]He got rid of the foreign gods and removed the image from the temple of the LORD, as well as all the altars he had built on the temple hill and in Jerusalem; and he threw them out of the city. [16]Then he restored the altar of the LORD and sacrificed fellowship offerings and thank offerings on it, and told Judah to serve the LORD, the God of Israel. [17]The people, however, continued to sacrifice at the high places, but only to the LORD their God.

[18]The other events of Manasseh's reign, including his prayer to his God and the words the seers spoke to him in the name of the LORD, the God of Israel, are written in the annals of the kings of Israel.[a] [19]His prayer and how God was moved by his entreaty, as well as all his sins and unfaithfulness, and the sites where he built high places and set up Asherah poles and idols before he humbled himself — all these are written in the records of the seers.[b] [20]Manasseh rested with his ancestors and was buried in his palace. And Amon his son succeeded him as king.

Amon King of Judah

[21]Amon was twenty-two years old when he became king, and he reigned in Jerusalem two years. [22]He did evil in the eyes of the LORD, as his father Manasseh had done. Amon worshiped and offered sacrifices to all the idols Manasseh had made. [23]But unlike his father Manasseh, he did not humble himself before the LORD; Amon increased his guilt.

[24]Amon's officials conspired against him and assassinated him in his palace. [25]Then the people of the land killed all who had plotted against King Amon, and they made Josiah his son king in his place.

Josiah's Reforms

34 Josiah was eight years old when he became king, and he reigned in Jerusalem thirty-one years. [2]He did what was right in the eyes of the LORD and followed the ways of his father David, not turning aside to the right or to the left.

[3]In the eighth year of his reign, while he was still young, he began to seek the God of his father David. In his twelfth year he began to purge Judah and Jerusalem of high places, Asherah poles and idols. [4]Under his direction the altars of the Baals were torn down; he cut to pieces the incense altars that were above them, and smashed the Asherah poles and the idols. These he broke to pieces and scattered over the graves of those who had sacrificed to them.

---

[a] 18 That is, Judah, as frequently in 2 Chronicles   [b] 19 One Hebrew manuscript and Septuagint; most Hebrew manuscripts *of Hozai*

5He burned the bones of the priests on their altars, and so he purged Judah and Jerusalem. 6In the towns of Manasseh, Ephraim and Simeon, as far as Naphtali, and in the ruins around them, 7he tore down the altars and the Asherah poles and crushed the idols to powder and cut to pieces all the incense altars throughout Israel. Then he went back to Jerusalem.

8In the eighteenth year of Josiah's reign, to purify the land and the temple, he sent Shaphan son of Azaliah and Maaseiah the ruler of the city, with Joah son of Joahaz, the recorder, to repair the temple of the LORD his God.

9They went to Hilkiah the high priest and gave him the money that had been brought into the temple of God, which the Levites who were the gatekeepers had collected from the people of Manasseh, Ephraim and the entire remnant of Israel and from all the people of Judah and Benjamin and the inhabitants of Jerusalem. 10Then they entrusted it to the men appointed to supervise the work on the LORD's temple. These men paid the workers who repaired and restored the temple. 11They also gave money to the carpenters and builders to purchase dressed stone, and timber for joists and beams for the buildings that the kings of Judah had allowed to fall into ruin.

12The workers labored faithfully. Over them to direct them were Jahath and Obadiah, Levites descended from Merari, and Zechariah and Meshullam, descended from Kohath. The Levites—all who were skilled in playing musical instruments—13had charge of the laborers and supervised all the workers from job to job. Some of the Levites were secretaries, scribes and gatekeepers.

The Book of the Law Found

14While they were bringing out the money that had been taken into the temple of the LORD, Hilkiah the priest found the Book of the Law of the LORD that had been given through Moses. 15Hilkiah said to Shaphan the secretary, "I have found the Book of the Law in the temple of the LORD." He gave it to Shaphan.

16Then Shaphan took the book to the king and reported to him: "Your officials are doing everything that has been committed to them. 17They have paid out the money that was in the temple of the LORD and have entrusted it to the supervisors and workers." 18Then Shaphan the secretary informed the king, "Hilkiah the priest has given me a book." And Shaphan read from it in the presence of the king.

19When the king heard the words of the Law, he tore his robes. 20He gave these orders to Hilkiah, Ahikam son of Shaphan, Abdon son of Micah,[a] Shaphan the secretary and Asaiah the king's attendant: 21"Go and inquire of the LORD for me and for the remnant in Israel and Judah about what is written in this book that has been found. Great is the LORD's anger that is poured out on us because those who have gone before us have not kept the word of the LORD; they have not acted in accordance with all that is written in this book."

22Hilkiah and those the king had sent with him[b] went to speak to the prophet Huldah, who was the wife of Shallum son of Tokhath,[c] the son of Hasrah,[d] keeper of the wardrobe. She lived in Jerusalem, in the New Quarter.

23She said to them, "This is what the LORD, the God of Israel, says: Tell the man who sent you to me, 24'This is what the LORD says: I am going to bring disaster on this place and its people—all the curses written in the book that has been read in the presence of the king of Judah. 25Because they have forsaken me and burned incense to other gods and aroused my anger by all that their hands have made,[e] my

---

[a] 20 Also called *Akbor son of Micaiah*   [b] 22 One Hebrew manuscript, Vulgate and Syriac; most Hebrew manuscripts do not have *had sent with him*.   [c] 22 Also called *Tikvah*   [d] 22 Also called *Harhas*   [e] 25 Or *by everything they have done*

anger will be poured out on this place and will not be quenched.' ²⁶Tell the king of Judah, who sent you to inquire of the LORD, 'This is what the LORD, the God of Israel, says concerning the words you heard: ²⁷Because your heart was responsive and you humbled yourself before God when you heard what he spoke against this place and its people, and because you humbled yourself before me and tore your robes and wept in my presence, I have heard you, declares the LORD. ²⁸Now I will gather you to your ancestors, and you will be buried in peace. Your eyes will not see all the disaster I am going to bring on this place and on those who live here.'"

So they took her answer back to the king.

²⁹Then the king called together all the elders of Judah and Jerusalem. ³⁰He went up to the temple of the LORD with the people of Judah, the inhabitants of Jerusalem, the priests and the Levites — all the people from the least to the greatest. He read in their hearing all the words of the Book of the Covenant, which had been found in the temple of the LORD. ³¹The king stood by his pillar and renewed the covenant in the presence of the LORD — to follow the LORD and keep his commands, statutes and decrees with all his heart and all his soul, and to obey the words of the covenant written in this book.

³²Then he had everyone in Jerusalem and Benjamin pledge themselves to it; the people of Jerusalem did this in accordance with the covenant of God, the God of their ancestors.

³³Josiah removed all the detestable idols from all the territory belonging to the Israelites, and he had all who were present in Israel serve the LORD their God. As long as he lived, they did not fail to follow the LORD, the God of their ancestors.

Josiah Celebrates the Passover

35 Josiah celebrated the Passover to the LORD in Jerusalem, and the Passover lamb was slaughtered on the fourteenth day of the first month. ²He appointed the priests to their duties and encouraged them in the service of the LORD's temple. ³He said to the Levites, who instructed all Israel and who had been consecrated to the LORD: "Put the sacred ark in the temple that Solomon son of David king of Israel built. It is not to be carried about on your shoulders. Now serve the LORD your God and his people Israel. ⁴Prepare yourselves by families in your divisions, according to the instructions written by David king of Israel and by his son Solomon.

⁵"Stand in the holy place with a group of Levites for each subdivision of the families of your fellow Israelites, the lay people. ⁶Slaughter the Passover lambs, consecrate yourselves and prepare the lambs for your fellow Israelites, doing what the LORD commanded through Moses."

⁷Josiah provided for all the lay people who were there a total of thirty thousand lambs and goats for the Passover offerings, and also three thousand cattle — all from the king's own possessions.

⁸His officials also contributed voluntarily to the people and the priests and Levites. Hilkiah, Zechariah and Jehiel, the officials in charge of God's temple, gave the priests twenty-six hundred Passover offerings and three hundred cattle. ⁹Also Konaniah along with Shemaiah and Nethanel, his brothers, and Hashabiah, Jeiel and Jozabad, the leaders of the Levites, provided five thousand Passover offerings and five hundred head of cattle for the Levites.

¹⁰The service was arranged and the priests stood in their places with the Levites in their divisions as the king had ordered. ¹¹The Passover lambs were slaughtered, and the priests splashed against the altar the blood handed to them, while the Levites skinned the animals. ¹²They set aside the burnt offerings to give them to the subdivisions of the families of the people to offer to the LORD, as it is written in the Book of Moses. They did the same with the cattle. ¹³They roasted the Passover animals over the fire as prescribed, and

boiled the holy offerings in pots, caldrons and pans and served them quickly to all the people. 14After this, they made preparations for themselves and for the priests, because the priests, the descendants of Aaron, were sacrificing the burnt offerings and the fat portions until nightfall. So the Levites made preparations for themselves and for the Aaronic priests.

15The musicians, the descendants of Asaph, were in the places prescribed by David, Asaph, Heman and Jeduthun the king's seer. The gatekeepers at each gate did not need to leave their posts, because their fellow Levites made the preparations for them.

16So at that time the entire service of the LORD was carried out for the celebration of the Passover and the offering of burnt offerings on the altar of the LORD, as King Josiah had ordered. 17The Israelites who were present celebrated the Passover at that time and observed the Festival of Unleavened Bread for seven days. 18The Passover had not been observed like this in Israel since the days of the prophet Samuel; and none of the kings of Israel had ever celebrated such a Passover as did Josiah, with the priests, the Levites and all Judah and Israel who were there with the people of Jerusalem. 19This Passover was celebrated in the eighteenth year of Josiah's reign.

The Death of Josiah

20After all this, when Josiah had set the temple in order, Necho king of Egypt went up to fight at Carchemish on the Euphrates, and Josiah marched out to meet him in battle. 21But Necho sent messengers to him, saying, "What quarrel is there, king of Judah, between you and me? It is not you I am attacking at this time, but the house with which I am at war. God has told me to hurry; so stop opposing God, who is with me, or he will destroy you."

22Josiah, however, would not turn away from him, but disguised himself to engage him in battle. He would not listen to what Necho had said at God's command but went to fight him on the plain of Megiddo.

23Archers shot King Josiah, and he told his officers, "Take me away; I am badly wounded." 24So they took him out of his chariot, put him in his other chariot and brought him to Jerusalem, where he died. He was buried in the tombs of his ancestors, and all Judah and Jerusalem mourned for him.

25Jeremiah composed laments for Josiah, and to this day all the male and female singers commemorate Josiah in the laments. These became a tradition in Israel and are written in the Laments.

26The other events of Josiah's reign and his acts of devotion in accordance with what is written in the Law of the LORD — 27all the events, from beginning to end, are written in the book of the kings of Israel

36

and Judah. 1And the people of the land took Jehoahaz son of Josiah and made him king in Jerusalem in place of his father.

Jehoahaz King of Judah

2Jehoahaz*a* was twenty-three years old when he became king, and he reigned in Jerusalem three months. 3The king of Egypt dethroned him in Jerusalem and imposed on Judah a levy of a hundred talents*b* of silver and a talent*c* of gold. 4The king of Egypt made Eliakim, a brother of Jehoahaz, king over Judah and Jerusalem and changed Eliakim's name to Jehoiakim. But Necho took Eliakim's brother Jehoahaz and carried him off to Egypt.

Jehoiakim King of Judah

5Jehoiakim was twenty-five years old when he became king, and he reigned in Jerusalem eleven years. He did evil in the eyes of the LORD his God. 6Nebuchadnezzar king of Babylon attacked him and

---

a 2 Hebrew *Joahaz,* a variant of *Jehoahaz;* also in verse 4   *b 3* That is, about 3 3/4 tons or about 3.4 metric tons
c 3 That is, about 75 pounds or about 34 kilograms

bound him with bronze shackles to take him to Babylon. [7]Nebuchadnezzar also took to Babylon articles from the temple of the LORD and put them in his temple[a] there.

[8]The other events of Jehoiakim's reign, the detestable things he did and all that was found against him, are written in the book of the kings of Israel and Judah. And Jehoiachin his son succeeded him as king.

Jehoiachin King of Judah

[9]Jehoiachin was eighteen[b] years old when he became king, and he reigned in Jerusalem three months and ten days. He did evil in the eyes of the LORD. [10]In the spring, King Nebuchadnezzar sent for him and brought him to Babylon, together with articles of value from the temple of the LORD, and he made Jehoiachin's uncle,[c] Zedekiah, king over Judah and Jerusalem.

Zedekiah King of Judah

[11]Zedekiah was twenty-one years old when he became king, and he reigned in Jerusalem eleven years. [12]He did evil in the eyes of the LORD his God and did not humble himself before Jeremiah the prophet, who spoke the word of the LORD. [13]He also rebelled against King Nebuchadnezzar, who had made him take an oath in God's name. He became stiff-necked and hardened his heart and would not turn to the LORD, the God of Israel. [14]Furthermore, all the leaders of the priests and the people became more and more unfaithful, following all the detestable practices of the nations and defiling the temple of the LORD, which he had consecrated in Jerusalem.

The Fall of Jerusalem

[15]The LORD, the God of their ancestors, sent word to them through his messengers again and again, because he had pity on his people and on his dwelling place. [16]But they mocked God's messengers, despised his words and scoffed at his prophets until the wrath of the LORD was aroused against his people and there was no remedy. [17]He brought up against them the king of the Babylonians,[d] who killed their young men with the sword in the sanctuary, and did not spare young men or young women, the elderly or the infirm. God gave them all into the hands of Nebuchadnezzar. [18]He carried to Babylon all the articles from the temple of God, both large and small, and the treasures of the LORD's temple and the treasures of the king and his officials. [19]They set fire to God's temple and broke down the wall of Jerusalem; they burned all the palaces and destroyed everything of value there.

[20]He carried into exile to Babylon the remnant, who escaped from the sword, and they became servants to him and his successors until the kingdom of Persia came to power. [21]The land enjoyed its sabbath rests; all the time of its desolation it rested, until the seventy years were completed in fulfillment of the word of the LORD spoken by Jeremiah.

[22]In the first year of Cyrus king of Persia, in order to fulfill the word of the LORD spoken by Jeremiah, the LORD moved the heart of Cyrus king of Persia to make a proclamation throughout his realm and also to put it in writing:

[23]"This is what Cyrus king of Persia says:

"'The LORD, the God of heaven, has given me all the kingdoms of the earth and he has appointed me to build a temple for him at Jerusalem in Judah. Any of his people among you may go up, and may the LORD their God be with them.'"

---

[a] 7 Or *palace*   [b] 9 One Hebrew manuscript, some Septuagint manuscripts and Syriac (see also 2 Kings 24:8); most Hebrew manuscripts *eight*   [c] 10 Hebrew *brother*, that is, relative (see 2 Kings 24:17)   [d] 17 Or *Chaldeans*

Ezra

THEME: Ezra demonstrates that God is sovereign over all peoples and rulers. He controls history and orchestrates events for his purposes.

AUTHOR: Ezra and Nehemiah were originally one book. Ezra has traditionally been considered the primary author of Ezra–Nehemiah, but his authorship is uncertain.

DATE OF WRITING: Ezra was probably written around 440 BC, during the period of restoration in and around Jerusalem after the exiles had returned from Babylon.

ENCOURAGEMENT FROM EZRA: "What has happened to us is a result of our evil deeds and our great guilt, and yet, our God, you have punished us less than our sins deserved" (Ezra 9:13).

REFLECTION FROM EZRA: "[The LORD] is good; his love . . . endures forever" (Ezra 3:11).

At a Glance

Recovery Themes in Ezra

The book of Ezra describes the return of a handful ("remnant") of Hebrews from Babylon to Jerusalem. Ezra was a direct descendant of the first Israelite high priest, Aaron. The rebuilding of the temple is the subject of the first half of the book; the second half deals with the reformation of God's people. God's faithfulness is first seen in his protection of his people while under the rule of a powerful pagan empire. God also provides strong leaders to administer the return and the reconstruction process.

Ezra records the recovery experienced by those returning from Babylon. Restoration of the temple required first that the people of Israel return to their faith. The identity of the nation of Israel was that they were God's people. Our own identity in recovery is in Jesus Christ. A successful recovery process hinges on our placing our faith in Christ. Once we've done this we're called God's children. Then our identity is in Christ, not in our old hurts, hang-ups and habits. Just as God provided for Israel in the book of Ezra, so he will also supply whatever we need today.

Cyrus Helps the Exiles to Return

1 In the first year of Cyrus king of Persia, in order to fulfill the word of the LORD spoken by Jeremiah, the LORD moved the heart of Cyrus king of Persia to make a proclamation throughout his realm and also to put it in writing:

²"This is what Cyrus king of Persia says:

"'The LORD, the God of heaven, has given me all the kingdoms of the earth and he has appointed me to build a temple for him at Jerusalem in Judah. ³Any of his people among you may go up to Jerusalem in Judah and build the temple of the LORD, the God of Israel, the God who is in Jerusalem, and may their God be with them. ⁴And in any locality where survivors may now be living, the people are to provide them with silver and gold, with goods and livestock, and with freewill offerings for the temple of God in Jerusalem.'"

5Then the family heads of Judah and Benjamin, and the priests and Levites — everyone whose heart God had moved — prepared to go up and build the house of the LORD in Jerusalem. 6All their neighbors assisted them with articles of silver and gold, with goods and livestock, and with valuable gifts, in addition to all the freewill offerings.

7Moreover, King Cyrus brought out the articles belonging to the temple of the LORD, which Nebuchadnezzar had carried away from Jerusalem and had placed in the temple of his god.*a* 8Cyrus king of Persia had them brought by Mithredath the treasurer, who counted them out to Sheshbazzar the prince of Judah.

9This was the inventory:

gold dishes	30
silver dishes	1,000
silver pans*b*	29
10gold bowls	30
matching silver bowls	410
other articles	1,000

11In all, there were 5,400 articles of gold and of silver. Sheshbazzar brought all these along with the exiles when they came up from Babylon to Jerusalem.

The List of the Exiles Who Returned

2 Now these are the people of the province who came up from the captivity of the exiles, whom Nebuchadnezzar king of Babylon had taken captive to Babylon (they returned to Jerusalem and Judah, each to their own town, 2in company with Zerubbabel, Joshua, Nehemiah, Seraiah, Reelaiah, Mordecai, Bilshan, Mispar, Bigvai, Rehum and Baanah):

The list of the men of the people of Israel:

3the descendants of Parosh	2,172
4of Shephatiah	372
5of Arah	775
6of Pahath-Moab (through the line of Jeshua and Joab)	2,812
7of Elam	1,254
8of Zattu	945
9of Zakkai	760
10of Bani	642
11of Bebai	623
12of Azgad	1,222
13of Adonikam	666
14of Bigvai	2,056
15of Adin	454
16of Ater (through Hezekiah)	98
17of Bezai	323
18of Jorah	112
19of Hashum	223
20of Gibbar	95
21the men of Bethlehem	123
22of Netophah	56
23of Anathoth	128
24of Azmaveth	42
25of Kiriath Jearim,*c* Kephirah and Beeroth	743
26of Ramah and Geba	621
27of Mikmash	122
28of Bethel and Ai	223
29of Nebo	52
30of Magbish	156
31of the other Elam	1,254
32of Harim	320
33of Lod, Hadid and Ono	725
34of Jericho	345
35of Senaah	3,630

36The priests:

the descendants of Jedaiah (through the family of Jeshua)	973
37of Immer	1,052
38of Pashhur	1,247
39of Harim	1,017

---

a 7 Or *gods*   *b* 9 The meaning of the Hebrew for this word is uncertain.   *c* 25 See Septuagint (see also Neh. 7:29); Hebrew *Kiriath Arim*.

40The Levites:

the descendants of Jeshua
and Kadmiel (of the line of
Hodaviah)   74

41The musicians:

the descendants of Asaph   128

42The gatekeepers of the temple:

the descendants of
Shallum, Ater, Talmon,
Akkub, Hatita and Shobai   139

43The temple servants:

the descendants of
Ziha, Hasupha, Tabbaoth,
44Keros, Siaha, Padon,
45Lebanah, Hagabah, Akkub,
46Hagab, Shalmai, Hanan,
47Giddel, Gahar, Reaiah,
48Rezin, Nekoda, Gazzam,
49Uzza, Paseah, Besai,
50Asnah, Meunim, Nephusim,
51Bakbuk, Hakupha, Harhur,
52Bazluth, Mehida, Harsha,
53Barkos, Sisera, Temah,
54Neziah and Hatipha

55The descendants of the servants of
Solomon:

the descendants of
Sotai, Hassophereth, Peruda,
56Jaala, Darkon, Giddel,
57Shephatiah, Hattil,
Pokereth-Hazzebaim and Ami

58The temple servants and the
descendants of the servants
of Solomon   392

59The following came up from the
towns of Tel Melah, Tel Harsha, Kerub, Addon and Immer, but they
could not show that their families
were descended from Israel:

60The descendants of
Delaiah, Tobiah and
Nekoda   652

61And from among the priests:

The descendants of
Hobaiah, Hakkoz and Barzillai
(a man who had married
a daughter of Barzillai the
Gileadite and was called by that
name).

62These searched for their family records, but they could not find
them and so were excluded from the
priesthood as unclean. 63The governor ordered them not to eat any of
the most sacred food until there was a
priest ministering with the Urim and
Thummim.

64The whole company numbered
42,360, 65besides their 7,337 male and
female slaves; and they also had 200
male and female singers. 66They had
736 horses, 245 mules, 67435 camels
and 6,720 donkeys.

68When they arrived at the house of the
LORD in Jerusalem, some of the heads of
the families gave freewill offerings toward
the rebuilding of the house of God on its
site. 69According to their ability they gave
to the treasury for this work 61,000 darics*a* of gold, 5,000 minas*b* of silver and 100
priestly garments.

70The priests, the Levites, the musicians,
the gatekeepers and the temple servants
settled in their own towns, along with
some of the other people, and the rest of
the Israelites settled in their towns.

Rebuilding the Altar

3 When the seventh month came and
the Israelites had settled in their
towns, the people assembled together as one in Jerusalem. 2Then Joshua
son of Jozadak and his fellow priests and
Zerubbabel son of Shealtiel and his associates began to build the altar of the God
of Israel to sacrifice burnt offerings on it,
in accordance with what is written in the
Law of Moses the man of God. 3Despite

---

a 69 That is, about 1,100 pounds or about 500 kilograms   *b* 69 That is, about 3 tons or about 2.8 metric tons their fear of the peoples around them, they built the altar on its foundation and sacrificed burnt offerings on it to the LORD, both the morning and evening sacrifices. 4Then in accordance with what is written, they celebrated the Festival of Tabernacles with the required number of burnt offerings prescribed for each day. 5After that, they presented the regular burnt offerings, the New Moon sacrifices and the sacrifices for all the appointed sacred festivals of the LORD, as well as those brought as freewill offerings to the LORD. 6On the first day of the seventh month they began to offer burnt offerings to the LORD, though the foundation of the LORD's temple had not yet been laid.

Rebuilding the Temple

7Then they gave money to the masons and carpenters, and gave food and drink and olive oil to the people of Sidon and Tyre, so that they would bring cedar logs by sea from Lebanon to Joppa, as authorized by Cyrus king of Persia.

8In the second month of the second year after their arrival at the house of God in Jerusalem, Zerubbabel son of Shealtiel, Joshua son of Jozadak and the rest of the people (the priests and the Levites and all who had returned from the captivity to Jerusalem) began the work. They appointed Levites twenty years old and older to supervise the building of the house of the LORD. 9Joshua and his sons and brothers and Kadmiel and his sons (descendants of Hodaviah*a*) and the sons of Henadad and their sons and brothers—all Levites—joined together in supervising those working on the house of God.

10When the builders laid the foundation of the temple of the LORD, the priests in their vestments and with trumpets, and the Levites (the sons of Asaph) with cymbals, took their places to praise the LORD, as prescribed by David king of Israel. 11With praise and thanksgiving they sang to the LORD:

"He is good;
    his love toward Israel endures
        forever."

And all the people gave a great shout of praise to the LORD, because the foundation of the house of the LORD was laid. 12But many of the older priests and Levites and family heads, who had seen the former temple, wept aloud when they saw the foundation of this temple being laid, while many others shouted for joy. 13No one could distinguish the sound of the shouts of joy from the sound of weeping, because the people made so much noise. And the sound was heard far away.

Opposition to the Rebuilding

4 When the enemies of Judah and Benjamin heard that the exiles were building a temple for the LORD, the God of Israel, 2they came to Zerubbabel and to the heads of the families and said, "Let us help you build because, like you, we seek your God and have been sacrificing to him since the time of Esarhaddon king of Assyria, who brought us here."

3But Zerubbabel, Joshua and the rest of the heads of the families of Israel answered, "You have no part with us in building a temple to our God. We alone will build it for the LORD, the God of Israel, as King Cyrus, the king of Persia, commanded us."

4Then the peoples around them set out to discourage the people of Judah and make them afraid to go on building.*b* 5They bribed officials to work against them and frustrate their plans during the entire reign of Cyrus king of Persia and down to the reign of Darius king of Persia.

Later Opposition Under Xerxes and Artaxerxes

6At the beginning of the reign of Xerxes,*c* they lodged an accusation against the people of Judah and Jerusalem.

7And in the days of Artaxerxes king of

---

a 9 Hebrew *Yehudah,* a variant of *Hodaviah*   *b 4* Or *and troubled them as they built*   *c 6* Hebrew *Ahasuerus*

Persia, Bishlam, Mithredath, Tabeel and the rest of his associates wrote a letter to Artaxerxes. The letter was written in Aramaic script and in the Aramaic language.[a,b]

[8]Rehum the commanding officer and Shimshai the secretary wrote a letter against Jerusalem to Artaxerxes the king as follows:

[9]Rehum the commanding officer and Shimshai the secretary, together with the rest of their associates — the judges, officials and administrators over the people from Persia, Uruk and Babylon, the Elamites of Susa, [10]and the other people whom the great and honorable Ashurbanipal deported and settled in the city of Samaria and elsewhere in Trans-Euphrates.

[11](This is a copy of the letter they sent him.)

To King Artaxerxes,

From your servants in Trans-Euphrates:

[12]The king should know that the people who came up to us from you have gone to Jerusalem and are rebuilding that rebellious and wicked city. They are restoring the walls and repairing the foundations.

[13]Furthermore, the king should know that if this city is built and its walls are restored, no more taxes, tribute or duty will be paid, and eventually the royal revenues will suffer.[c]

[14]Now since we are under obligation to the palace and it is not proper for us to see the king dishonored, we are sending this message to inform the king, [15]so that a search may be made in the archives of your predecessors. In these records you will find that this city is a rebellious city, troublesome to kings and provinces, a place with a long history of sedition. That is why this city was destroyed. [16]We inform the king that if this city is built and its walls are restored, you will be left with nothing in Trans-Euphrates.

[17]The king sent this reply:

To Rehum the commanding officer, Shimshai the secretary and the rest of their associates living in Samaria and elsewhere in Trans-Euphrates:

Greetings.

[18]The letter you sent us has been read and translated in my presence. [19]I issued an order and a search was made, and it was found that this city has a long history of revolt against kings and has been a place of rebellion and sedition. [20]Jerusalem has had powerful kings ruling over the whole of Trans-Euphrates, and taxes, tribute and duty were paid to them. [21]Now issue an order to these men to stop work, so that this city will not be rebuilt until I so order. [22]Be careful not to neglect this matter. Why let this threat grow, to the detriment of the royal interests?

[23]As soon as the copy of the letter of King Artaxerxes was read to Rehum and Shimshai the secretary and their associates, they went immediately to the Jews in Jerusalem and compelled them by force to stop.

[24]Thus the work on the house of God in Jerusalem came to a standstill until the second year of the reign of Darius king of Persia.

Tattenai's Letter to Darius

5 Now Haggai the prophet and Zechariah the prophet, a descendant of Iddo, prophesied to the Jews in Judah and Jerusalem in the name of the God of Israel, who was over them. [2]Then Zerubbabel son of Shealtiel and Joshua son

---

[a] 7 Or *written in Aramaic and translated*   [b] 7 The text of 4:8 – 6:18 is in Aramaic.   [c] 13 The meaning of the Aramaic for this clause is uncertain.

of Jozadak set to work to rebuild the house of God in Jerusalem. And the prophets of God were with them, supporting them.

³At that time Tattenai, governor of Trans-Euphrates, and Shethar-Bozenai and their associates went to them and asked, "Who authorized you to rebuild this temple and to finish it?" ⁴They*a* also asked, "What are the names of those who are constructing this building?" ⁵But the eye of their God was watching over the elders of the Jews, and they were not stopped until a report could go to Darius and his written reply be received.

⁶This is a copy of the letter that Tattenai, governor of Trans-Euphrates, and Shethar-Bozenai and their associates, the officials of Trans-Euphrates, sent to King Darius. ⁷The report they sent him read as follows:

To King Darius:

Cordial greetings.

⁸The king should know that we went to the district of Judah, to the temple of the great God. The people are building it with large stones and placing the timbers in the walls. The work is being carried on with diligence and is making rapid progress under their direction.

⁹We questioned the elders and asked them, "Who authorized you to rebuild this temple and to finish it?" ¹⁰We also asked them their names, so that we could write down the names of their leaders for your information.

¹¹This is the answer they gave us:

"We are the servants of the God of heaven and earth, and we are rebuilding the temple that was built many years ago, one that a great king of Israel built and finished. ¹²But because our ancestors angered the God of heaven, he gave them into the hands of Nebuchadnezzar the Chaldean, king of Babylon, who destroyed this temple and deported the people to Babylon.

¹³"However, in the first year of Cyrus king of Babylon, King Cyrus issued a decree to rebuild this house of God. ¹⁴He even removed from the temple*b* of Babylon the gold and silver articles of the house of God, which Nebuchadnezzar had taken from the temple in Jerusalem and brought to the temple*b* in Babylon. Then King Cyrus gave them to a man named Sheshbazzar, whom he had appointed governor, ¹⁵and he told him, 'Take these articles and go and deposit them in the temple in Jerusalem. And rebuild the house of God on its site.'

¹⁶"So this Sheshbazzar came and laid the foundations of the house of God in Jerusalem. From that day to the present it has been under construction but is not yet finished."

¹⁷Now if it pleases the king, let a search be made in the royal archives of Babylon to see if King Cyrus did in fact issue a decree to rebuild this house of God in Jerusalem. Then let the king send us his decision in this matter.

The Decree of Darius

6 King Darius then issued an order, and they searched in the archives stored in the treasury at Babylon. ²A scroll was found in the citadel of Ecbatana in the province of Media, and this was written on it:

Memorandum:

³In the first year of King Cyrus, the king issued a decree concerning the temple of God in Jerusalem:

Let the temple be rebuilt as a place to present sacrifices, and let its foundations be laid. It is to be sixty cubits*c* high and sixty cubits wide, ⁴with three

---

a 4 See Septuagint; Aramaic *We.*   *b 14* Or *palace*   *c 3* That is, about 90 feet or about 27 meters courses of large stones and one of timbers. The costs are to be paid by the royal treasury. 5Also, the gold and silver articles of the house of God, which Nebuchadnezzar took from the temple in Jerusalem and brought to Babylon, are to be returned to their places in the temple in Jerusalem; they are to be deposited in the house of God.

6Now then, Tattenai, governor of Trans-Euphrates, and Shethar-Bozenai and you other officials of that province, stay away from there. 7Do not interfere with the work on this temple of God. Let the governor of the Jews and the Jewish elders rebuild this house of God on its site.

8Moreover, I hereby decree what you are to do for these elders of the Jews in the construction of this house of God:

Their expenses are to be fully paid out of the royal treasury, from the revenues of Trans-Euphrates, so that the work will not stop. 9Whatever is needed — young bulls, rams, male lambs for burnt offerings to the God of heaven, and wheat, salt, wine and olive oil, as requested by the priests in Jerusalem — must be given them daily without fail, 10so that they may offer sacrifices pleasing to the God of heaven and pray for the well-being of the king and his sons.

11Furthermore, I decree that if anyone defies this edict, a beam is to be pulled from their house and they are to be impaled on it. And for this crime their house is to be made a pile of rubble. 12May God, who has caused his Name to dwell there, overthrow any king or people who lifts a hand to change this decree or to destroy this temple in Jerusalem.

I Darius have decreed it. Let it be carried out with diligence.

Completion and Dedication of the Temple

13Then, because of the decree King Darius had sent, Tattenai, governor of Trans-Euphrates, and Shethar-Bozenai and their associates carried it out with diligence. 14So the elders of the Jews continued to build and prosper under the preaching of Haggai the prophet and Zechariah, a descendant of Iddo. They finished building the temple according to the command of the God of Israel and the decrees of Cyrus, Darius and Artaxerxes, kings of Persia. 15The temple was completed on the third day of the month Adar, in the sixth year of the reign of King Darius.

16Then the people of Israel — the priests, the Levites and the rest of the exiles — celebrated the dedication of the house of God with joy. 17For the dedication of this house of God they offered a hundred bulls, two hundred rams, four hundred male lambs and, as a sin offering[a] for all Israel, twelve male goats, one for each of the tribes of Israel. 18And they installed the priests in their divisions and the Levites in their groups for the service of God at Jerusalem, according to what is written in the Book of Moses.

The Passover

19On the fourteenth day of the first month, the exiles celebrated the Passover. 20The priests and Levites had purified themselves and were all ceremonially clean. The Levites slaughtered the Passover lamb for all the exiles, for their relatives the priests and for themselves. 21So the Israelites who had returned from the exile ate it, together with all who had separated themselves from the unclean practices of their Gentile neighbors in order to seek the LORD, the God of Israel. 22For seven days they celebrated with joy the Festival of Unleavened Bread, because the LORD had filled them with joy by changing the attitude of the king of Assyria so that he assisted them in the work on the house of God, the God of Israel.

---

a 17 Or *purification offering*

Ezra Comes to Jerusalem

7 After these things, during the reign of Artaxerxes king of Persia, Ezra son of Seraiah, the son of Azariah, the son of Hilkiah, ²the son of Shallum, the son of Zadok, the son of Ahitub, ³the son of Amariah, the son of Azariah, the son of Meraioth, ⁴the son of Zerahiah, the son of Uzzi, the son of Bukki, ⁵the son of Abishua, the son of Phinehas, the son of Eleazar, the son of Aaron the chief priest— ⁶this Ezra came up from Babylon. He was a teacher well versed in the Law of Moses, which the LORD, the God of Israel, had given. The king had granted him everything he asked, for the hand of the LORD his God was on him. ⁷Some of the Israelites, including priests, Levites, musicians, gatekeepers and temple servants, also came up to Jerusalem in the seventh year of King Artaxerxes.

⁸Ezra arrived in Jerusalem in the fifth month of the seventh year of the king. ⁹He had begun his journey from Babylon on the first day of the first month, and he arrived in Jerusalem on the first day of the fifth month, for the gracious hand of his God was on him. ¹⁰For Ezra had devoted himself to the study and observance of the Law of the LORD, and to teaching its decrees and laws in Israel.

King Artaxerxes' Letter to Ezra

¹¹This is a copy of the letter King Artaxerxes had given to Ezra the priest, a teacher of the Law, a man learned in matters concerning the commands and decrees of the LORD for Israel:

¹²Artaxerxes, king of kings,

To Ezra the priest, teacher of the Law of the God of heaven:

Greetings.

¹³Now I decree that any of the Israelites in my kingdom, including priests and Levites, who volunteer to go to Jerusalem with you, may go. ¹⁴You are sent by the king and his seven advisers to inquire about Judah and Jerusalem with regard to the Law of your God, which is in your hand. ¹⁵Moreover, you are to take with you the silver and gold that the king and his advisers have freely given to the God of Israel, whose dwelling is in Jerusalem, ¹⁶together with all the silver and gold you may obtain from the province of Babylon, as well as the freewill offerings of the people and priests for the temple of their God in Jerusalem. ¹⁷With this money be sure to buy bulls, rams and male lambs, together with their grain offerings and drink offerings, and sacrifice them on the altar of the temple of your God in Jerusalem.

¹⁸You and your fellow Israelites may then do whatever seems best with the rest of the silver and gold, in accordance with the will of your God. ¹⁹Deliver to the God of Jerusalem all the articles entrusted to you for worship in the temple of your God. ²⁰And anything else needed for the temple of your God that you are responsible to supply, you may provide from the royal treasury.

²¹Now I, King Artaxerxes, decree that all the treasurers of Trans-Euphrates are to provide with diligence whatever Ezra the priest, the teacher of the Law of the God of heaven, may ask of you— ²²up to a hundred talents*ᵃ* of silver, a hundred cors*ᵇ* of wheat, a hundred baths*ᶜ* of wine, a hundred baths*ᶜ* of olive oil, and salt without limit. ²³Whatever the God of heaven has prescribed, let it be done with diligence for the temple of the God of heaven. Why should his wrath fall on the realm of the king and of his sons? ²⁴You are also to know that you

---

ᵃ 22 That is, about 3 3/4 tons or about 3.4 metric tons   *ᵇ 22* That is, probably about 18 tons or about 16 metric tons
ᶜ 22 That is, about 600 gallons or about 2,200 liters

have no authority to impose taxes, tribute or duty on any of the priests, Levites, musicians, gatekeepers, temple servants or other workers at this house of God.

25 And you, Ezra, in accordance with the wisdom of your God, which you possess, appoint magistrates and judges to administer justice to all the people of Trans-Euphrates — all who know the laws of your God. And you are to teach any who do not know them. 26 Whoever does not obey the law of your God and the law of the king must surely be punished by death, banishment, confiscation of property, or imprisonment.[a]

27 Praise be to the LORD, the God of our ancestors, who has put it into the king's heart to bring honor to the house of the LORD in Jerusalem in this way 28 and who has extended his good favor to me before the king and his advisers and all the king's powerful officials. Because the hand of the LORD my God was on me, I took courage and gathered leaders from Israel to go up with me.

List of the Family Heads Returning With Ezra

8 These are the family heads and those registered with them who came up with me from Babylon during the reign of King Artaxerxes:

2 of the descendants of Phinehas, Gershom;
of the descendants of Ithamar, Daniel;
of the descendants of David, Hattush 3 of the descendants of Shekaniah;

of the descendants of Parosh, Zechariah, and with him were registered 150 men;
4 of the descendants of Pahath-Moab, Eliehoenai son of Zerahiah, and with him 200 men;

5 of the descendants of Zattu,[b] Shekaniah son of Jahaziel, and with him 300 men;
6 of the descendants of Adin, Ebed son of Jonathan, and with him 50 men;
7 of the descendants of Elam, Jeshaiah son of Athaliah, and with him 70 men;
8 of the descendants of Shephatiah, Zebadiah son of Michael, and with him 80 men;
9 of the descendants of Joab, Obadiah son of Jehiel, and with him 218 men;
10 of the descendants of Bani,[c] Shelomith son of Josiphiah, and with him 160 men;
11 of the descendants of Bebai, Zechariah son of Bebai, and with him 28 men;
12 of the descendants of Azgad, Johanan son of Hakkatan, and with him 110 men;
13 of the descendants of Adonikam, the last ones, whose names were Eliphelet, Jeuel and Shemaiah, and with them 60 men;
14 of the descendants of Bigvai, Uthai and Zakkur, and with them 70 men.

The Return to Jerusalem

15 I assembled them at the canal that flows toward Ahava, and we camped there three days. When I checked among the people and the priests, I found no Levites there. 16 So I summoned Eliezer, Ariel, Shemaiah, Elnathan, Jarib, Elnathan, Nathan, Zechariah and Meshullam, who were leaders, and Joiarib and Elnathan, who were men of learning, 17 and I ordered them to go to Iddo, the leader in Kasiphia. I told them what to say to Iddo and his fellow Levites, the temple servants in Kasiphia, so that they might bring attendants to us for the house of our God. 18 Because the gracious

---

a 26 The text of 7:12-26 is in Aramaic.   b 5 Some Septuagint manuscripts (also 1 Esdras 8:32); Hebrew does not have Zattu.   c 10 Some Septuagint manuscripts (also 1 Esdras 8:36); Hebrew does not have Bani.

hand of our God was on us, they brought us Sherebiah, a capable man, from the descendants of Mahli son of Levi, the son of Israel, and Sherebiah's sons and brothers, 18 in all; ¹⁹and Hashabiah, together with Jeshaiah from the descendants of Merari, and his brothers and nephews, 20 in all. ²⁰They also brought 220 of the temple servants—a body that David and the officials had established to assist the Levites. All were registered by name.

²¹There, by the Ahava Canal, I proclaimed a fast, so that we might humble ourselves before our God and ask him for a safe journey for us and our children, with all our possessions. ²²I was ashamed to ask the king for soldiers and horsemen to protect us from enemies on the road, because we had told the king, "The gracious hand of our God is on everyone who looks to him, but his great anger is against all who forsake him." ²³So we fasted and petitioned our God about this, and he answered our prayer.

²⁴Then I set apart twelve of the leading priests, namely, Sherebiah, Hashabiah and ten of their brothers, ²⁵and I weighed out to them the offering of silver and gold and the articles that the king, his advisers, his officials and all Israel present there had donated for the house of our God. ²⁶I weighed out to them 650 talents*a* of silver, silver articles weighing 100 talents,*b* 100 talents*b* of gold, ²⁷20 bowls of gold valued at 1,000 darics,*c* and two fine articles of polished bronze, as precious as gold.

²⁸I said to them, "You as well as these articles are consecrated to the LORD. The silver and gold are a freewill offering to the LORD, the God of your ancestors. ²⁹Guard them carefully until you weigh them out in the chambers of the house of the LORD in Jerusalem before the leading priests and the Levites and the family heads of Israel." ³⁰Then the priests and Levites received the silver and gold and sacred articles that had

been weighed out to be taken to the house of our God in Jerusalem.

³¹On the twelfth day of the first month we set out from the Ahava Canal to go to Jerusalem. The hand of our God was on us, and he protected us from enemies and bandits along the way. ³²So we arrived in Jerusalem, where we rested three days.

³³On the fourth day, in the house of our God, we weighed out the silver and gold and the sacred articles into the hands of Meremoth son of Uriah, the priest. Eleazar son of Phinehas was with him, and so were the Levites Jozabad son of Jeshua and Noadiah son of Binnui. ³⁴Everything was accounted for by number and weight, and the entire weight was recorded at that time.

³⁵Then the exiles who had returned from captivity sacrificed burnt offerings to the God of Israel: twelve bulls for all Israel, ninety-six rams, seventy-seven male lambs and, as a sin offering,*d* twelve male goats. All this was a burnt offering to the LORD. ³⁶They also delivered the king's orders to the royal satraps and to the governors of Trans-Euphrates, who then gave assistance to the people and to the house of God.

Ezra's Prayer About Intermarriage

9 After these things had been done, the leaders came to me and said, "The people of Israel, including the priests and the Levites, have not kept themselves separate from the neighboring peoples with their detestable practices, like those of the Canaanites, Hittites, Perizzites, Jebusites, Ammonites, Moabites, Egyptians and Amorites. ²They have taken some of their daughters as wives for themselves and their sons, and have mingled the holy race with the peoples around them. And the leaders and officials have led the way in this unfaithfulness."

³When I heard this, I tore my tunic and cloak, pulled hair from my head and beard and sat down appalled. ⁴Then everyone

---

a 26 That is, about 24 tons or about 22 metric tons   *b 26* That is, about 3 3/4 tons or about 3.4 metric tons
c 27 That is, about 19 pounds or about 8.4 kilograms   *d 35* Or *purification offering*

who trembled at the words of the God of Israel gathered around me because of this unfaithfulness of the exiles. And I sat there appalled until the evening sacrifice.

⁵Then, at the evening sacrifice, I rose from my self-abasement, with my tunic and cloak torn, and fell on my knees with my hands spread out to the Lord my God ⁶and prayed:

"I am too ashamed and disgraced, my God, to lift up my face to you, because our sins are higher than our heads and our guilt has reached to the heavens. ⁷From the days of our ancestors until now, our guilt has been great. Because of our sins, we and our kings and our priests have been subjected to the sword and captivity, to pillage and humiliation at the hand of foreign kings, as it is today.

⁸"But now, for a brief moment, the Lord our God has been gracious in leaving us a remnant and giving us a firm place*a* in his sanctuary, and so our God gives light to our eyes and a little relief in our bondage. ⁹Though we are slaves, our God has not forsaken us in our bondage. He has shown us kindness in the sight of the kings of Persia: He has granted us new life to rebuild the house of our God and repair its ruins, and he has given us a wall of protection in Judah and Jerusalem.

¹⁰"But now, our God, what can we say after this? For we have forsaken the commands ¹¹you gave through your servants the prophets when you said: 'The land you are entering to possess is a land polluted by the corruption of its peoples. By their detestable practices they have filled it with their impurity from one end to the other. ¹²Therefore, do not give your daughters in marriage to their sons or take their daughters for your sons.

Do not seek a treaty of friendship with them at any time, that you may be strong and eat the good things of the land and leave it to your children as an everlasting inheritance.'

¹³"What has happened to us is a result of our evil deeds and our great guilt, and yet, our God, you have punished us less than our sins deserved and have given us a remnant like this. ¹⁴Shall we then break your commands again and intermarry with the peoples who commit such detestable practices? Would you not be angry enough with us to destroy us, leaving us no remnant or survivor? ¹⁵Lord, the God of Israel, you are righteous! We are left this day as a remnant. Here we are before you in our guilt, though because of it not one of us can stand in your presence."

The People's Confession of Sin

10 While Ezra was praying and confessing, weeping and throwing himself down before the house of God, a large crowd of Israelites — men, women and children — gathered around him. They too wept bitterly. ²Then Shekaniah son of Jehiel, one of the descendants of Elam, said to Ezra, "We have been unfaithful to our God by marrying foreign women from the peoples around us. But in spite of this, there is still hope for Israel. ³Now let us make a covenant before our God to send away all these women and their children, in accordance with the counsel of my lord and of those who fear the commands of our God. Let it be done according to the Law. ⁴Rise up; this matter is in your hands. We will support you, so take courage and do it."

⁵So Ezra rose up and put the leading priests and Levites and all Israel under oath to do what had been suggested. And they took the oath. ⁶Then Ezra withdrew from before the house of God and went to the

---

a 8 Or *a foothold*

room of Jehohanan son of Eliashib. While he was there, he ate no food and drank no water, because he continued to mourn over the unfaithfulness of the exiles.

⁷A proclamation was then issued throughout Judah and Jerusalem for all the exiles to assemble in Jerusalem. ⁸Anyone who failed to appear within three days would forfeit all his property, in accordance with the decision of the officials and elders, and would himself be expelled from the assembly of the exiles.

⁹Within the three days, all the men of Judah and Benjamin had gathered in Jerusalem. And on the twentieth day of the ninth month, all the people were sitting in the square before the house of God, greatly distressed by the occasion and because of the rain. ¹⁰Then Ezra the priest stood up and said to them, "You have been unfaithful; you have married foreign women, adding to Israel's guilt. ¹¹Now honor*a* the LORD, the God of your ancestors, and do his will. Separate yourselves from the peoples around you and from your foreign wives."

¹²The whole assembly responded with a loud voice: "You are right! We must do as you say. ¹³But there are many people here and it is the rainy season; so we cannot stand outside. Besides, this matter cannot be taken care of in a day or two, because we have sinned greatly in this thing. ¹⁴Let our officials act for the whole assembly. Then let everyone in our towns who has married a foreign woman come at a set time, along with the elders and judges of each town, until the fierce anger of our God in this matter is turned away from us." ¹⁵Only Jonathan son of Asahel and Jahzeiah son of Tikvah, supported by Meshullam and Shabbethai the Levite, opposed this.

¹⁶So the exiles did as was proposed. Ezra the priest selected men who were family heads, one from each family division, and all of them designated by name. On the first day of the tenth month they sat down to investigate the cases, ¹⁷and by the first day of the first month they finished dealing with all the men who had married foreign women.

Those Guilty of Intermarriage

¹⁸Among the descendants of the priests, the following had married foreign women:

From the descendants of Joshua son of Jozadak, and his brothers: Maaseiah, Eliezer, Jarib and Gedaliah. ¹⁹(They all gave their hands in pledge to put away their wives, and for their guilt they each presented a ram from the flock as a guilt offering.)

²⁰From the descendants of Immer: Hanani and Zebadiah.

²¹From the descendants of Harim: Maaseiah, Elijah, Shemaiah, Jehiel and Uzziah.

²²From the descendants of Pashhur: Elioenai, Maaseiah, Ishmael, Nethanel, Jozabad and Elasah.

²³Among the Levites:

Jozabad, Shimei, Kelaiah (that is, Kelita), Pethahiah, Judah and Eliezer.

²⁴From the musicians: Eliashib.

From the gatekeepers: Shallum, Telem and Uri.

²⁵And among the other Israelites:

From the descendants of Parosh: Ramiah, Izziah, Malkijah, Mijamin, Eleazar, Malkijah and Benaiah.

²⁶From the descendants of Elam: Mattaniah, Zechariah, Jehiel, Abdi, Jeremoth and Elijah.

²⁷From the descendants of Zattu: Elioenai, Eliashib, Mattaniah, Jeremoth, Zabad and Aziza.

---

a 11 Or Now make confession to

28 From the descendants of Bebai:
Jehohanan, Hananiah, Zabbai and
Athlai.
29 From the descendants of Bani:
Meshullam, Malluk, Adaiah, Jashub, Sheal and Jeremoth.
30 From the descendants of Pahath-Moab:
Adna, Kelal, Benaiah, Maaseiah,
Mattaniah, Bezalel, Binnui and
Manasseh.
31 From the descendants of Harim:
Eliezer, Ishijah, Malkijah, Shemaiah, Shimeon, 32 Benjamin, Malluk
and Shemariah.
33 From the descendants of Hashum:
Mattenai, Mattattah, Zabad, Eliphelet, Jeremai, Manasseh and Shimei.

34 From the descendants of Bani:
Maadai, Amram, Uel, 35 Benaiah,
Bedeiah, Keluhi, 36 Vaniah, Meremoth, Eliashib, 37 Mattaniah, Mattenai and Jaasu.
38 From the descendants of Binnui:a
Shimei, 39 Shelemiah, Nathan, Adaiah, 40 Maknadebai, Shashai, Sharai,
41 Azarel, Shelemiah, Shemariah,
42 Shallum, Amariah and Joseph.
43 From the descendants of Nebo:
Jeiel, Mattithiah, Zabad, Zebina,
Jaddai, Joel and Benaiah.

44 All these had married foreign women,
and some of them had children by these
wives.b

---

a 37,38 See Septuagint (also 1 Esdras 9:34); Hebrew *Jaasu* 38 *and Bani and Binnui,*   b 44 Or *and they sent them away with their children*

Nehemiah

THEME: The primary message of Nehemiah is that commitment to God requires more than words; it necessitates action.

AUTHOR: Ezra and Nehemiah were originally one book. Ezra has traditionally been considered the primary author of Ezra–Nehemiah, but his authorship is uncertain. If Ezra was the author of Nehemiah, he apparently was quoting directly from the writings of Nehemiah, because the content is described as "the words of Nehemiah" (Nehemiah 1:1), and the book is written in the first person.

DATE OF WRITING: Nehemiah was probably written around 440 BC, during the period of restoration in and around Jerusalem after the exiles had returned from Babylon.

CHALLENGE FROM NEHEMIAH: "Don't be afraid of them. Remember the Lord, who is great and awesome" (Nehemiah 4:14).

ENCOURAGEMENT FROM NEHEMIAH: "Now therefore, our God . . . in all that has happened to us, you remained righteous; you have acted faithfully, while we acted wickedly" (Nehemiah 9:32 – 33).

REFLECTION FROM NEHEMIAH: "All the surrounding nations were afraid and lost their self-confidence, because they realized that this work had been done with the help of our God" (Nehemiah 6:16).

The book of Nehemiah provides a record of the rebuilding of Jerusalem's walls. Upon his return to Jerusalem, Nehemiah challenged his countrymen to reconstruct the city's broken-down walls. The task of reforming God's people would take a longer time, however — consuming years of Nehemiah's leadership. God's covenant with his people is a crucial theme in Nehemiah. The book describes a renewal ceremony in which the people commit themselves to separate from the godless local women some of them have married, in obedience to God's commandments. In the face of overwhelming difficulties and opposition, God's power is evident in the successful restoration of Jerusalem's ruined walls. Amazingly, this challenging task is completed in only 52 days. Even Nehemiah's enemies concede that this feat has been accomplished by God's power.

The book of Nehemiah provides us with numerous practical principles to apply to our recovery. It's important to remember that, like the eight principles of Celebrate Recovery, these ideals can be applied only through faith in Jesus Christ. God alone was able to accomplish the task of restoring not just the physical walls of Jerusalem but also the spiritual healing of his people. Similarly, only God can perform the miracles that take place in recovery.

Nehemiah's Prayer

1 The words of Nehemiah son of Hakaliah:

In the month of Kislev in the twentieth year, while I was in the citadel of Susa, ²Hanani, one of my brothers, came from Judah with some other men, and I questioned them about the Jewish remnant that had survived the exile, and also about Jerusalem.

³They said to me, "Those who survived the exile and are back in the province are in great trouble and disgrace. The wall of Jerusalem is broken down, and its gates have been burned with fire."

⁴When I heard these things, I sat down and wept. For some days I mourned and fasted and prayed before the God of heaven. ⁵Then I said:

"LORD, the God of heaven, the great and awesome God, who keeps his covenant of love with those who love him and keep his commandments, ⁶let your ear be attentive and your eyes open to hear the prayer your servant is praying before you day and night for your servants, the people of Israel. I confess the sins we Israelites, including myself and my father's family, have committed against you. ⁷We have acted very wickedly toward you. We have not obeyed the commands, decrees and laws you gave your servant Moses.

⁸"Remember the instruction you gave your servant Moses, saying, 'If you are unfaithful, I will scatter you among the nations, ⁹but if you return to me and obey my commands, then even if your exiled people are at the farthest horizon, I will gather them from there and bring them to the place I have chosen as a dwelling for my Name.'

¹⁰"They are your servants and your people, whom you redeemed by your great strength and your mighty hand. ¹¹Lord, let your ear be attentive to the prayer of this your servant and to the prayer of your servants who delight in revering your name. Give your servant success today by granting him favor in the presence of this man."

I was cupbearer to the king.

Artaxerxes Sends Nehemiah to Jerusalem

2 In the month of Nisan in the twentieth year of King Artaxerxes, when wine was brought for him, I took the wine and gave it to the king. I had not been sad in his presence before, ²so the king asked me, "Why does your face look so sad when you are not ill? This can be nothing but sadness of heart."

I was very much afraid, ³but I said to the king, "May the king live forever! Why should my face not look sad when the city where my ancestors are buried lies in ruins, and its gates have been destroyed by fire?"

⁴The king said to me, "What is it you want?"

Then I prayed to the God of heaven, ⁵and I answered the king, "If it pleases the king and if your servant has found favor in his sight, let him send me to the city in Judah where my ancestors are buried so that I can rebuild it."

⁶Then the king, with the queen sitting beside him, asked me, "How long will your journey take, and when will you get back?" It pleased the king to send me; so I set a time.

⁷I also said to him, "If it pleases the king, may I have letters to the governors of Trans-Euphrates, so that they will provide me safe-conduct until I arrive in Judah? ⁸And may I have a letter to Asaph, keeper of the royal park, so he will give me timber to make beams for the gates of the citadel by the temple and for the city wall and for the residence I will occupy?" And because the gracious hand of my God was on me, the king granted my requests. ⁹So I went to the governors of Trans-Euphrates and gave them the king's letters. The king had also sent army officers and cavalry with me.

¹⁰When Sanballat the Horonite and Tobiah the Ammonite official heard about this, they were very much disturbed that someone had come to promote the welfare of the Israelites.

Nehemiah Inspects Jerusalem's Walls

¹¹I went to Jerusalem, and after staying there three days ¹²I set out during the night with a few others. I had not told anyone what my God had put in my heart to do for Jerusalem. There were no mounts with me except the one I was riding on.

¹³By night I went out through the Valley Gate toward the Jackal[a] Well and the Dung Gate, examining the walls of Jerusalem, which had been broken down, and its gates, which had been destroyed by fire. ¹⁴Then I moved on toward the Fountain Gate and the King's Pool, but there was not enough room for my mount to get through; ¹⁵so I went up the valley by night, examining the wall. Finally, I turned back and reentered through the Valley Gate. ¹⁶The officials did not know where I had gone or what I was doing, because as yet I had said nothing to the Jews or the priests or nobles or officials or any others who would be doing the work.

¹⁷Then I said to them, "You see the trouble we are in: Jerusalem lies in ruins, and its gates have been burned with fire. Come, let us rebuild the wall of Jerusalem, and we will no longer be in disgrace." ¹⁸I also told them about the gracious hand of my God on me and what the king had said to me.

They replied, "Let us start rebuilding." So they began this good work.

¹⁹But when Sanballat the Horonite, Tobiah the Ammonite official and Geshem the Arab heard about it, they mocked and ridiculed us. "What is this you are doing?" they asked. "Are you rebelling against the king?"

²⁰I answered them by saying, "The God of heaven will give us success. We his servants will start rebuilding, but as for you, you have no share in Jerusalem or any claim or historic right to it."

Builders of the Wall

3 Eliashib the high priest and his fellow priests went to work and rebuilt the Sheep Gate. They dedicated it and set its doors in place, building as far as the Tower of the Hundred, which they dedicated, and as far as the Tower of Hananel. ²The men of Jericho built the adjoining section, and Zakkur son of Imri built next to them.

³The Fish Gate was rebuilt by the sons of Hassenaah. They laid its beams and put its doors and bolts and bars in place. ⁴Meremoth son of Uriah, the son of Hakkoz, repaired the next section. Next to him Meshullam son of Berekiah, the son of Meshezabel, made repairs, and next to him Zadok son of Baana also made repairs. ⁵The next section was repaired by the men of Tekoa, but their nobles would not put their shoulders to the work under their supervisors.[b]

⁶The Jeshanah[c] Gate was repaired by Joiada son of Paseah and Meshullam son of Besodeiah. They laid its beams and put its doors with their bolts and bars in place. ⁷Next to them, repairs were made by men from Gibeon and Mizpah — Melatiah of Gibeon and Jadon of Meronoth — places under the authority of the governor of Trans-Euphrates. ⁸Uzziel son of Harhaiah, one of the goldsmiths, repaired the next section; and Hananiah, one of the perfume-makers, made repairs next to that. They restored Jerusalem as far as the Broad Wall. ⁹Rephaiah son of Hur, ruler of a half-district of Jerusalem, repaired the next section. ¹⁰Adjoining this, Jedaiah son of Harumaph made repairs opposite his house, and Hattush son of Hashabneiah made repairs next to him. ¹¹Malkijah son of Harim and Hasshub son of Pahath-Moab repaired another section and the Tower of the Ovens.

ᵃ 13 Or Serpent or Fig   ᵇ 5 Or their Lord or the governor   ᶜ 6 Or Old

¹²Shallum son of Hallohesh, ruler of a half-district of Jerusalem, repaired the next section with the help of his daughters.

¹³The Valley Gate was repaired by Hanun and the residents of Zanoah. They rebuilt it and put its doors with their bolts and bars in place. They also repaired a thousand cubits*a* of the wall as far as the Dung Gate.

¹⁴The Dung Gate was repaired by Malkijah son of Rekab, ruler of the district of Beth Hakkerem. He rebuilt it and put its doors with their bolts and bars in place.

¹⁵The Fountain Gate was repaired by Shallun son of Kol-Hozeh, ruler of the district of Mizpah. He rebuilt it, roofing it over and putting its doors and bolts and bars in place. He also repaired the wall of the Pool of Siloam,*b* by the King's Garden, as far as the steps going down from the City of David. ¹⁶Beyond him, Nehemiah son of Azbuk, ruler of a half-district of Beth Zur, made repairs up to a point opposite the tombs*c* of David, as far as the artificial pool and the House of the Heroes.

¹⁷Next to him, the repairs were made by the Levites under Rehum son of Bani. Beside him, Hashabiah, ruler of half the district of Keilah, carried out repairs for his district. ¹⁸Next to him, the repairs were made by their fellow Levites under Binnui*d* son of Henadad, ruler of the other half-district of Keilah. ¹⁹Next to him, Ezer son of Jeshua, ruler of Mizpah, repaired another section, from a point facing the ascent to the armory as far as the angle of the wall. ²⁰Next to him, Baruch son of Zabbai zealously repaired another section, from the angle to the entrance of the house of Eliashib the high priest. ²¹Next to him, Meremoth son of Uriah, the son of Hakkoz, repaired another section, from the entrance of Eliashib's house to the end of it.

²²The repairs next to him were made by the priests from the surrounding region. ²³Beyond them, Benjamin and Hasshub made repairs in front of their house; and next to them, Azariah son of Maaseiah, the son of Ananiah, made repairs beside his house. ²⁴Next to him, Binnui son of Henadad repaired another section, from Azariah's house to the angle and the corner, ²⁵and Palal son of Uzai worked opposite the angle and the tower projecting from the upper palace near the court of the guard. Next to him, Pedaiah son of Parosh ²⁶and the temple servants living on the hill of Ophel made repairs up to a point opposite the Water Gate toward the east and the projecting tower. ²⁷Next to them, the men of Tekoa repaired another section, from the great projecting tower to the wall of Ophel.

²⁸Above the Horse Gate, the priests made repairs, each in front of his own house. ²⁹Next to them, Zadok son of Immer made repairs opposite his house. Next to him, Shemaiah son of Shekaniah, the guard at the East Gate, made repairs. ³⁰Next to him, Hananiah son of Shelemiah, and Hanun, the sixth son of Zalaph, repaired another section. Next to them, Meshullam son of Berekiah made repairs opposite his living quarters. ³¹Next to him, Malkijah, one of the goldsmiths, made repairs as far as the house of the temple servants and the merchants, opposite the Inspection Gate, and as far as the room above the corner; ³²and between the room above the corner and the Sheep Gate the goldsmiths and merchants made repairs.

Opposition to the Rebuilding

4*e* When Sanballat heard that we were rebuilding the wall, he became angry and was greatly incensed. He ridiculed the Jews, ²and in the presence of his associates and the army of Samaria, he

---

a 13 That is, about 1,500 feet or about 450 meters   *b 15* Hebrew *Shelah,* a variant of *Shiloah,* that is, Siloam
c 16 Hebrew; Septuagint, some Vulgate manuscripts and Syriac *tomb*   *d 18* Two Hebrew manuscripts and Syriac
(see also Septuagint and verse 24); most Hebrew manuscripts *Bavvai*   *e* In Hebrew texts 4:1-6 is numbered 3:33-38,
and 4:7-23 is numbered 4:1-17.

said, "What are those feeble Jews doing? Will they restore their wall? Will they offer sacrifices? Will they finish in a day? Can they bring the stones back to life from those heaps of rubble—burned as they are?"

3Tobiah the Ammonite, who was at his side, said, "What they are building—even a fox climbing up on it would break down their wall of stones!"

4Hear us, our God, for we are despised. Turn their insults back on their own heads. Give them over as plunder in a land of captivity. 5Do not cover up their guilt or blot out their sins from your sight, for they have thrown insults in the face of*a* the builders.

6So we rebuilt the wall till all of it reached half its height, for the people worked with all their heart.

7But when Sanballat, Tobiah, the Arabs, the Ammonites and the people of Ashdod heard that the repairs to Jerusalem's walls had gone ahead and that the gaps were being closed, they were very angry. 8They all plotted together to come and fight against Jerusalem and stir up trouble against it. 9But we prayed to our God and posted a guard day and night to meet this threat.

10Meanwhile, the people in Judah said, "The strength of the laborers is giving out, and there is so much rubble that we cannot rebuild the wall."

11Also our enemies said, "Before they know it or see us, we will be right there among them and will kill them and put an end to the work."

12Then the Jews who lived near them came and told us ten times over, "Wherever you turn, they will attack us."

13Therefore I stationed some of the people behind the lowest points of the wall at the exposed places, posting them by families, with their swords, spears and bows. 14After I looked things over, I stood up and said to the nobles, the officials and the rest of the people, "Don't be afraid of them. Remember the Lord, who is great and awe-

some, and fight for your families, your sons and your daughters, your wives and your homes."

15When our enemies heard that we were aware of their plot and that God had frustrated it, we all returned to the wall, each to our own work.

16From that day on, half of my men did the work, while the other half were equipped with spears, shields, bows and armor. The officers posted themselves behind all the people of Judah 17who were building the wall. Those who carried materials did their work with one hand and held a weapon in the other, 18and each of the builders wore his sword at his side as he worked. But the man who sounded the trumpet stayed with me.

19Then I said to the nobles, the officials and the rest of the people, "The work is extensive and spread out, and we are widely separated from each other along the wall. 20Wherever you hear the sound of the trumpet, join us there. Our God will fight for us!"

21So we continued the work with half the men holding spears, from the first light of dawn till the stars came out. 22At that time I also said to the people, "Have every man and his helper stay inside Jerusalem at night, so they can serve us as guards by night and as workers by day." 23Neither I nor my brothers nor my men nor the guards with me took off our clothes; each had his weapon, even when he went for water.*b*

Nehemiah Helps the Poor

5 Now the men and their wives raised a great outcry against their fellow Jews. 2Some were saying, "We and our sons and daughters are numerous; in order for us to eat and stay alive, we must get grain."

3Others were saying, "We are mortgaging our fields, our vineyards and our homes to get grain during the famine."

---

a 5 Or *have aroused your anger before*   *b* 23 The meaning of the Hebrew for this clause is uncertain.

4Still others were saying, "We have had to borrow money to pay the king's tax on our fields and vineyards. 5Although we are of the same flesh and blood as our fellow Jews and though our children are as good as theirs, yet we have to subject our sons and daughters to slavery. Some of our daughters have already been enslaved, but we are powerless, because our fields and our vineyards belong to others."

6When I heard their outcry and these charges, I was very angry. 7I pondered them in my mind and then accused the nobles and officials. I told them, "You are charging your own people interest!" So I called together a large meeting to deal with them 8and said: "As far as possible, we have bought back our fellow Jews who were sold to the Gentiles. Now you are selling your own people, only for them to be sold back to us!" They kept quiet, because they could find nothing to say.

9So I continued, "What you are doing is not right. Shouldn't you walk in the fear of our God to avoid the reproach of our Gentile enemies? 10I and my brothers and my men are also lending the people money and grain. But let us stop charging interest! 11Give back to them immediately their fields, vineyards, olive groves and houses, and also the interest you are charging them — one percent of the money, grain, new wine and olive oil."

12"We will give it back," they said. "And we will not demand anything more from them. We will do as you say."

Then I summoned the priests and made the nobles and officials take an oath to do what they had promised. 13I also shook out the folds of my robe and said, "In this way may God shake out of their house and possessions anyone who does not keep this promise. So may such a person be shaken out and emptied!"

At this the whole assembly said, "Amen," and praised the LORD. And the people did as they had promised.

14Moreover, from the twentieth year of King Artaxerxes, when I was appointed to be their governor in the land of Judah, until his thirty-second year — twelve years — neither I nor my brothers ate the food allotted to the governor. 15But the earlier governors — those preceding me — placed a heavy burden on the people and took forty shekels[a] of silver from them in addition to food and wine. Their assistants also lorded it over the people. But out of reverence for God I did not act like that. 16Instead, I devoted myself to the work on this wall. All my men were assembled there for the work; we[b] did not acquire any land.

17Furthermore, a hundred and fifty Jews and officials ate at my table, as well as those who came to us from the surrounding nations. 18Each day one ox, six choice sheep and some poultry were prepared for me, and every ten days an abundant supply of wine of all kinds. In spite of all this, I never demanded the food allotted to the governor, because the demands were heavy on these people.

19Remember me with favor, my God, for all I have done for these people.

Further Opposition to the Rebuilding

6 When word came to Sanballat, Tobiah, Geshem the Arab and the rest of our enemies that I had rebuilt the wall and not a gap was left in it — though up to that time I had not set the doors in the gates — 2Sanballat and Geshem sent me this message: "Come, let us meet together in one of the villages[c] on the plain of Ono."

But they were scheming to harm me; 3so I sent messengers to them with this reply: "I am carrying on a great project and cannot go down. Why should the work stop while I leave it and go down to you?" 4Four times they sent me the same message, and each time I gave them the same answer.

5Then, the fifth time, Sanballat sent his aide to me with the same message, and in

---

a 15 That is, about 1 pound or about 460 grams   b 16 Most Hebrew manuscripts; some Hebrew manuscripts, Septuagint, Vulgate and Syriac I   c 2 Or in Kephirim his hand was an unsealed letter ⁶in which was written:

"It is reported among the nations—and Geshem*a* says it is true—that you and the Jews are plotting to revolt, and therefore you are building the wall. Moreover, according to these reports you are about to become their king ⁷and have even appointed prophets to make this proclamation about you in Jerusalem: 'There is a king in Judah!' Now this report will get back to the king; so come, let us meet together."

⁸I sent him this reply: "Nothing like what you are saying is happening; you are just making it up out of your head."

⁹They were all trying to frighten us, thinking, "Their hands will get too weak for the work, and it will not be completed." But I prayed, "Now strengthen my hands."

¹⁰One day I went to the house of Shemaiah son of Delaiah, the son of Mehetabel, who was shut in at his home. He said, "Let us meet in the house of God, inside the temple, and let us close the temple doors, because men are coming to kill you—by night they are coming to kill you."

¹¹But I said, "Should a man like me run away? Or should someone like me go into the temple to save his life? I will not go!" ¹²I realized that God had not sent him, but that he had prophesied against me because Tobiah and Sanballat had hired him. ¹³He had been hired to intimidate me so that I would commit a sin by doing this, and then they would give me a bad name to discredit me.

¹⁴Remember Tobiah and Sanballat, my God, because of what they have done; remember also the prophet Noadiah and how she and the rest of the prophets have been trying to intimidate me. ¹⁵So the wall was completed on the twenty-fifth of Elul, in fifty-two days.

Opposition to the Completed Wall

¹⁶When all our enemies heard about this, all the surrounding nations were afraid and lost their self-confidence, because they realized that this work had been done with the help of our God.

¹⁷Also, in those days the nobles of Judah were sending many letters to Tobiah, and replies from Tobiah kept coming to them. ¹⁸For many in Judah were under oath to him, since he was son-in-law to Shekaniah son of Arah, and his son Jehohanan had married the daughter of Meshullam son of Berekiah. ¹⁹Moreover, they kept reporting to me his good deeds and then telling him what I said. And Tobiah sent letters to intimidate me.

7 After the wall had been rebuilt and I had set the doors in place, the gatekeepers, the musicians and the Levites were appointed. ²I put in charge of Jerusalem my brother Hanani, along with Hananiah the commander of the citadel, because he was a man of integrity and feared God more than most people do. ³I said to them, "The gates of Jerusalem are not to be opened until the sun is hot. While the gatekeepers are still on duty, have them shut the doors and bar them. Also appoint residents of Jerusalem as guards, some at their posts and some near their own houses."

The List of the Exiles Who Returned

⁴Now the city was large and spacious, but there were few people in it, and the houses had not yet been rebuilt. ⁵So my God put it into my heart to assemble the nobles, the officials and the common people for registration by families. I found the genealogical record of those who had been the first to return. This is what I found written there:

⁶These are the people of the province who came up from the captivity of the exiles whom Nebuchadnezzar king of Babylon had taken captive (they returned to Jerusalem and

---

a 6 Hebrew *Gashmu*, a variant of *Geshem*

Judah, each to his own town, ⁷in company with Zerubbabel, Joshua, Nehemiah, Azariah, Raamiah, Nahamani, Mordecai, Bilshan, Mispereth, Bigvai, Nehum and Baanah):

The list of the men of Israel:

⁸the descendants of Parosh	2,172
⁹of Shephatiah	372
¹⁰of Arah	652
¹¹of Pahath-Moab (through the line of Jeshua and Joab)	2,818
¹²of Elam	1,254
¹³of Zattu	845
¹⁴of Zakkai	760
¹⁵of Binnui	648
¹⁶of Bebai	628
¹⁷of Azgad	2,322
¹⁸of Adonikam	667
¹⁹of Bigvai	2,067
²⁰of Adin	655
²¹of Ater (through Hezekiah)	98
²²of Hashum	328
²³of Bezai	324
²⁴of Hariph	112
²⁵of Gibeon	95
²⁶the men of Bethlehem and Netophah	188
²⁷of Anathoth	128
²⁸of Beth Azmaveth	42
²⁹of Kiriath Jearim, Kephirah and Beeroth	743
³⁰of Ramah and Geba	621
³¹of Mikmash	122
³²of Bethel and Ai	123
³³of the other Nebo	52
³⁴of the other Elam	1,254
³⁵of Harim	320
³⁶of Jericho	345
³⁷of Lod, Hadid and Ono	721
³⁸of Senaah	3,930

³⁹The priests:

the descendants of Jedaiah (through the family of Jeshua)	973
⁴⁰of Immer	1,052
⁴¹of Pashhur	1,247
⁴²of Harim	1,017

⁴³The Levites:

the descendants of Jeshua (through Kadmiel through the line of Hodaviah)	74

⁴⁴The musicians:

the descendants of Asaph	148

⁴⁵The gatekeepers:

the descendants of Shallum, Ater, Talmon, Akkub, Hatita and Shobai	138

⁴⁶The temple servants:

the descendants of
Ziha, Hasupha, Tabbaoth,
⁴⁷Keros, Sia, Padon,
⁴⁸Lebana, Hagaba, Shalmai,
⁴⁹Hanan, Giddel, Gahar,
⁵⁰Reaiah, Rezin, Nekoda,
⁵¹Gazzam, Uzza, Paseah,
⁵²Besai, Meunim, Nephusim,
⁵³Bakbuk, Hakupha, Harhur,
⁵⁴Bazluth, Mehida, Harsha,
⁵⁵Barkos, Sisera, Temah,
⁵⁶Neziah and Hatipha

⁵⁷The descendants of the servants of Solomon:

the descendants of
Sotai, Sophereth, Perida,
⁵⁸Jaala, Darkon, Giddel,
⁵⁹Shephatiah, Hattil,
Pokereth-Hazzebaim and Amon

⁶⁰The temple servants and the descendants of the servants of Solomon	392

⁶¹The following came up from the towns of Tel Melah, Tel Harsha, Kerub, Addon and Immer, but they could not show that their families were descended from Israel:

⁶²the descendants of Delaiah, Tobiah and Nekoda	642

⁶³And from among the priests:

the descendants of
Hobaiah, Hakkoz and Barzillai (a
man who had married a daughter
of Barzillai the Gileadite and was
called by that name).

⁶⁴These searched for their family records, but they could not find them and so were excluded from the priesthood as unclean. ⁶⁵The governor, therefore, ordered them not to eat any of the most sacred food until there should be a priest ministering with the Urim and Thummim.

⁶⁶The whole company numbered 42,360, ⁶⁷besides their 7,337 male and female slaves; and they also had 245 male and female singers. ⁶⁸There were 736 horses, 245 mules,ᵃ ⁶⁹435 camels and 6,720 donkeys.

⁷⁰Some of the heads of the families contributed to the work. The governor gave to the treasury 1,000 daricsᵇ of gold, 50 bowls and 530 garments for priests. ⁷¹Some of the heads of the families gave to the treasury for the work 20,000 daricsᶜ of gold and 2,200 minasᵈ of silver. ⁷²The total given by the rest of the people was 20,000 darics of gold, 2,000 minasᵉ of silver and 67 garments for priests.

⁷³The priests, the Levites, the gatekeepers, the musicians and the temple servants, along with certain of the people and the rest of the Israelites, settled in their own towns.

Ezra Reads the Law

8 When the seventh month came and the Israelites had settled in their towns, ¹all the people came together as one in the square before the Water Gate. They told Ezra the teacher of the Law to bring out the Book of the Law of Moses, which the LORD had commanded for Israel.

²So on the first day of the seventh month Ezra the priest brought the Law before the assembly, which was made up of men and women and all who were able to understand. ³He read it aloud from daybreak till noon as he faced the square before the Water Gate in the presence of the men, women and others who could understand. And all the people listened attentively to the Book of the Law.

⁴Ezra the teacher of the Law stood on a high wooden platform built for the occasion. Beside him on his right stood Mattithiah, Shema, Anaiah, Uriah, Hilkiah and Maaseiah; and on his left were Pedaiah, Mishael, Malkijah, Hashum, Hashbaddanah, Zechariah and Meshullam.

⁵Ezra opened the book. All the people could see him because he was standing above them; and as he opened it, the people all stood up. ⁶Ezra praised the LORD, the great God; and all the people lifted their hands and responded, "Amen! Amen!" Then they bowed down and worshiped the LORD with their faces to the ground.

⁷The Levites—Jeshua, Bani, Sherebiah, Jamin, Akkub, Shabbethai, Hodiah, Maaseiah, Kelita, Azariah, Jozabad, Hanan and Pelaiah—instructed the people in the Law while the people were standing there. ⁸They read from the Book of the Law of God, making it clearᶠ and giving the meaning so that the people understood what was being read.

⁹Then Nehemiah the governor, Ezra the priest and teacher of the Law, and the Levites who were instructing the people said to them all, "This day is holy to the LORD your God. Do not mourn or weep." For all the people had been weeping as they listened to the words of the Law.

¹⁰Nehemiah said, "Go and enjoy choice food and sweet drinks, and send some to those who have nothing prepared. This day

---

ᵃ 68 Some Hebrew manuscripts (see also Ezra 2:66); most Hebrew manuscripts do not have this verse.   ᵇ 70 That is, about 19 pounds or about 8.4 kilograms   ᶜ 71 That is, about 375 pounds or about 170 kilograms; also in verse 72   ᵈ 71 That is, about 1 1/3 tons or about 1.2 metric tons   ᵉ 72 That is, about 1 1/4 tons or about 1.1 metric tons   ᶠ 8 Or God, translating it is holy to our Lord. Do not grieve, for the joy of the LORD is your strength."

11The Levites calmed all the people, saying, "Be still, for this is a holy day. Do not grieve."

12Then all the people went away to eat and drink, to send portions of food and to celebrate with great joy, because they now understood the words that had been made known to them.

13On the second day of the month, the heads of all the families, along with the priests and the Levites, gathered around Ezra the teacher to give attention to the words of the Law. 14They found written in the Law, which the LORD had commanded through Moses, that the Israelites were to live in temporary shelters during the festival of the seventh month 15and that they should proclaim this word and spread it throughout their towns and in Jerusalem: "Go out into the hill country and bring back branches from olive and wild olive trees, and from myrtles, palms and shade trees, to make temporary shelters" — as it is written.*a*

16So the people went out and brought back branches and built themselves temporary shelters on their own roofs, in their courtyards, in the courts of the house of God and in the square by the Water Gate and the one by the Gate of Ephraim. 17The whole company that had returned from exile built temporary shelters and lived in them. From the days of Joshua son of Nun until that day, the Israelites had not celebrated it like this. And their joy was very great.

18Day after day, from the first day to the last, Ezra read from the Book of the Law of God. They celebrated the festival for seven days, and on the eighth day, in accordance with the regulation, there was an assembly.

The Israelites Confess Their Sins

9 On the twenty-fourth day of the same month, the Israelites gathered together, fasting and wearing sackcloth and putting dust on their heads.

2Those of Israelite descent had separated themselves from all foreigners. They stood in their places and confessed their sins and the sins of their ancestors. 3They stood where they were and read from the Book of the Law of the LORD their God for a quarter of the day, and spent another quarter in confession and in worshiping the LORD their God. 4Standing on the stairs of the Levites were Jeshua, Bani, Kadmiel, Shebaniah, Bunni, Sherebiah, Bani and Kenani. They cried out with loud voices to the LORD their God. 5And the Levites — Jeshua, Kadmiel, Bani, Hashabneiah, Sherebiah, Hodiah, Shebaniah and Pethahiah — said: "Stand up and praise the LORD your God, who is from everlasting to everlasting.*b*"

"Blessed be your glorious name, and may it be exalted above all blessing and praise. 6You alone are the LORD. You made the heavens, even the highest heavens, and all their starry host, the earth and all that is on it, the seas and all that is in them. You give life to everything, and the multitudes of heaven worship you.

7"You are the LORD God, who chose Abram and brought him out of Ur of the Chaldeans and named him Abraham. 8You found his heart faithful to you, and you made a covenant with him to give to his descendants the land of the Canaanites, Hittites, Amorites, Perizzites, Jebusites and Girgashites. You have kept your promise because you are righteous.

9"You saw the suffering of our ancestors in Egypt; you heard their cry at the Red Sea.*c* 10You sent signs and wonders against Pharaoh, against all his officials and all the people of his land, for you knew how arrogantly the Egyptians treated them. You made a name for yourself, which remains to this day. 11You divided the sea before

---

a 15 See Lev. 23:37-40.   *b 5* Or *God for ever and ever*   *c 9* Or the *Sea of Reeds* them, so that they passed through it on dry ground, but you hurled their pursuers into the depths, like a stone into mighty waters. ¹²By day you led them with a pillar of cloud, and by night with a pillar of fire to give them light on the way they were to take.

¹³"You came down on Mount Sinai; you spoke to them from heaven. You gave them regulations and laws that are just and right, and decrees and commands that are good. ¹⁴You made known to them your holy Sabbath and gave them commands, decrees and laws through your servant Moses. ¹⁵In their hunger you gave them bread from heaven and in their thirst you brought them water from the rock; you told them to go in and take possession of the land you had sworn with uplifted hand to give them.

¹⁶"But they, our ancestors, became arrogant and stiff-necked, and they did not obey your commands. ¹⁷They refused to listen and failed to remember the miracles you performed among them. They became stiff-necked and in their rebellion appointed a leader in order to return to their slavery. But you are a forgiving God, gracious and compassionate, slow to anger and abounding in love. Therefore you did not desert them, ¹⁸even when they cast for themselves an image of a calf and said, 'This is your god, who brought you up out of Egypt,' or when they committed awful blasphemies.

¹⁹"Because of your great compassion you did not abandon them in the wilderness. By day the pillar of cloud did not fail to guide them on their path, nor the pillar of fire by night to shine on the way they were to take. ²⁰You gave your good Spirit to instruct them. You did not withhold your manna from their mouths, and

you gave them water for their thirst. ²¹For forty years you sustained them in the wilderness; they lacked nothing, their clothes did not wear out nor did their feet become swollen.

²²"You gave them kingdoms and nations, allotting to them even the remotest frontiers. They took over the country of Sihon*ᵃ* king of Heshbon and the country of Og king of Bashan. ²³You made their children as numerous as the stars in the sky, and you brought them into the land that you told their parents to enter and possess. ²⁴Their children went in and took possession of the land. You subdued before them the Canaanites, who lived in the land; you gave the Canaanites into their hands, along with their kings and the peoples of the land, to deal with them as they pleased. ²⁵They captured fortified cities and fertile land; they took possession of houses filled with all kinds of good things, wells already dug, vineyards, olive groves and fruit trees in abundance. They ate to the full and were well-nourished; they reveled in your great goodness.

²⁶"But they were disobedient and rebelled against you; they turned their backs on your law. They killed your prophets, who had warned them in order to turn them back to you; they committed awful blasphemies. ²⁷So you delivered them into the hands of their enemies, who oppressed them. But when they were oppressed they cried out to you. From heaven you heard them, and in your great compassion you gave them deliverers, who rescued them from the hand of their enemies.

²⁸"But as soon as they were at rest, they again did what was evil in your sight. Then you abandoned them to the hand of their enemies so that

---

ᵃ 22 One Hebrew manuscript and Septuagint; most Hebrew manuscripts *Sihon, that is, the country of the* they ruled over them. And when they cried out to you again, you heard from heaven, and in your compassion you delivered them time after time.

29 "You warned them in order to turn them back to your law, but they became arrogant and disobeyed your commands. They sinned against your ordinances, of which you said, 'The person who obeys them will live by them.' Stubbornly they turned their backs on you, became stiff-necked and refused to listen. 30 For many years you were patient with them. By your Spirit you warned them through your prophets. Yet they paid no attention, so you gave them into the hands of the neighboring peoples. 31 But in your great mercy you did not put an end to them or abandon them, for you are a gracious and merciful God.

32 "Now therefore, our God, the great God, mighty and awesome, who keeps his covenant of love, do not let all this hardship seem trifling in your eyes — the hardship that has come on us, on our kings and leaders, on our priests and prophets, on our ancestors and all your people, from the days of the kings of Assyria until today. 33 In all that has happened to us, you have remained righteous; you have acted faithfully, while we acted wickedly. 34 Our kings, our leaders, our priests and our ancestors did not follow your law; they did not pay attention to your commands or the statutes you warned them to keep. 35 Even while they were in their kingdom, enjoying your great goodness to them in the spacious and fertile land you gave them, they did not serve you or turn from their evil ways.

36 "But see, we are slaves today, slaves in the land you gave our ancestors so they could eat its fruit and the other good things it produces. 37 Be-cause of our sins, its abundant harvest goes to the kings you have placed over us. They rule over our bodies and our cattle as they please. We are in great distress.

The Agreement of the People

38 "In view of all this, we are making a binding agreement, putting it in writing, and our leaders, our Levites and our priests are affixing their seals to it."[a]

10

[b] Those who sealed it were:

Nehemiah the governor, the son of Hakaliah.

Zedekiah, 2 Seraiah, Azariah, Jeremiah,
3 Pashhur, Amariah, Malkijah,
4 Hattush, Shebaniah, Malluk,
5 Harim, Meremoth, Obadiah,
6 Daniel, Ginnethon, Baruch,
7 Meshullam, Abijah, Mijamin,
8 Maaziah, Bilgai and Shemaiah.

These were the priests.

9 The Levites:

Jeshua son of Azaniah, Binnui of the sons of Henadad, Kadmiel,
10 and their associates: Shebaniah, Hodiah, Kelita, Pelaiah, Hanan,
11 Mika, Rehob, Hashabiah,
12 Zakkur, Sherebiah, Shebaniah,
13 Hodiah, Bani and Beninu.

14 The leaders of the people:

Parosh, Pahath-Moab, Elam, Zattu, Bani,
15 Bunni, Azgad, Bebai,
16 Adonijah, Bigvai, Adin,
17 Ater, Hezekiah, Azzur,
18 Hodiah, Hashum, Bezai,
19 Hariph, Anathoth, Nebai,
20 Magpiash, Meshullam, Hezir,
21 Meshezabel, Zadok, Jaddua,
22 Pelatiah, Hanan, Anaiah,
23 Hoshea, Hananiah, Hasshub,

---

a 38 In Hebrew texts this verse (9:38) is numbered 10:1.   b In Hebrew texts 10:1-39 is numbered 10:2-40.

24 Hallohesh, Pilha, Shobek,
25 Rehum, Hashabnah, Maaseiah,
26 Ahiah, Hanan, Anan,
27 Malluk, Harim and Baanah.

28 "The rest of the people — priests, Levites, gatekeepers, musicians, temple servants and all who separated themselves from the neighboring peoples for the sake of the Law of God, together with their wives and all their sons and daughters who are able to understand — 29 all these now join their fellow Israelites the nobles, and bind themselves with a curse and an oath to follow the Law of God given through Moses the servant of God and to obey carefully all the commands, regulations and decrees of the LORD our Lord.

30 "We promise not to give our daughters in marriage to the peoples around us or take their daughters for our sons.

31 "When the neighboring peoples bring merchandise or grain to sell on the Sabbath, we will not buy from them on the Sabbath or on any holy day. Every seventh year we will forgo working the land and will cancel all debts.

32 "We assume the responsibility for carrying out the commands to give a third of a shekel*a* each year for the service of the house of our God: 33 for the bread set out on the table; for the regular grain offerings and burnt offerings; for the offerings on the Sabbaths, at the New Moon feasts and at the appointed festivals; for the holy offerings; for sin offerings*b* to make atonement for Israel; and for all the duties of the house of our God.

34 "We — the priests, the Levites and the people — have cast lots to determine when each of our families is to bring to the house of our God at set times each year a contribution of wood to burn on the altar of the LORD our God, as it is written in the Law.

35 "We also assume responsibility for bringing to the house of the LORD each year the firstfruits of our crops and of every fruit tree.

36 "As it is also written in the Law, we will bring the firstborn of our sons and of our cattle, of our herds and of our flocks to the house of our God, to the priests ministering there.

37 "Moreover, we will bring to the storerooms of the house of our God, to the priests, the first of our ground meal, of our grain offerings, of the fruit of all our trees and of our new wine and olive oil. And we will bring a tithe of our crops to the Levites, for it is the Levites who collect the tithes in all the towns where we work. 38 A priest descended from Aaron is to accompany the Levites when they receive the tithes, and the Levites are to bring a tenth of the tithes up to the house of our God, to the storerooms of the treasury. 39 The people of Israel, including the Levites, are to bring their contributions of grain, new wine and olive oil to the storerooms, where the articles for the sanctuary and for the ministering priests, the gatekeepers and the musicians are also kept.

"We will not neglect the house of our God."

The New Residents of Jerusalem

11 Now the leaders of the people settled in Jerusalem. The rest of the people cast lots to bring one out of every ten of them to live in Jerusalem, the holy city, while the remaining nine were to stay in their own towns. 2 The people commended all who volunteered to live in Jerusalem.

3 These are the provincial leaders who settled in Jerusalem (now some Israelites,

---

a 32 That is, about 1/8 ounce or about 4 grams   *b 33* Or *purification offerings* priests, Levites, temple servants and descendants of Solomon's servants lived in the towns of Judah, each on their own property in the various towns, 4while other people from both Judah and Benjamin lived in Jerusalem):

From the descendants of Judah:

Athaiah son of Uzziah, the son of Zechariah, the son of Amariah, the son of Shephatiah, the son of Mahalalel, a descendant of Perez; 5and Maaseiah son of Baruch, the son of Kol-Hozeh, the son of Hazaiah, the son of Adaiah, the son of Joiarib, the son of Zechariah, a descendant of Shelah. 6The descendants of Perez who lived in Jerusalem totaled 468 men of standing.

7From the descendants of Benjamin:

Sallu son of Meshullam, the son of Joed, the son of Pedaiah, the son of Kolaiah, the son of Maaseiah, the son of Ithiel, the son of Jeshaiah, 8and his followers, Gabbai and Sallai — 928 men. 9Joel son of Zikri was their chief officer, and Judah son of Hassenuah was over the New Quarter of the city.

10From the priests:

Jedaiah; the son of Joiarib; Jakin; 11Seraiah son of Hilkiah, the son of Meshullam, the son of Zadok, the son of Meraioth, the son of Ahitub, the official in charge of the house of God, 12and their associates, who carried on work for the temple — 822 men; Adaiah son of Jeroham, the son of Pelaliah, the son of Amzi, the son of Zechariah, the son of Pashhur, the son of Malkijah, 13and his associates, who were heads of families — 242 men; Amashsai son of Azarel, the son of Ahzai, the son of Meshillemoth, the son of Immer, 14and hisa associates, who were men of standing — 128.

Their chief officer was Zabdiel son of Haggedolim.

15From the Levites:

Shemaiah son of Hasshub, the son of Azrikam, the son of Hashabiah, the son of Bunni; 16Shabbethai and Jozabad, two of the heads of the Levites, who had charge of the outside work of the house of God; 17Mattaniah son of Mika, the son of Zabdi, the son of Asaph, the director who led in thanksgiving and prayer; Bakbukiah, second among his associates; and Abda son of Shammua, the son of Galal, the son of Jeduthun. 18The Levites in the holy city totaled 284.

19The gatekeepers:

Akkub, Talmon and their associates, who kept watch at the gates — 172 men.

20The rest of the Israelites, with the priests and Levites, were in all the towns of Judah, each on their ancestral property.

21The temple servants lived on the hill of Ophel, and Ziha and Gishpa were in charge of them.

22The chief officer of the Levites in Jerusalem was Uzzi son of Bani, the son of Hashabiah, the son of Mattaniah, the son of Mika. Uzzi was one of Asaph's descendants, who were the musicians responsible for the service of the house of God. 23The musicians were under the king's orders, which regulated their daily activity.

24Pethahiah son of Meshezabel, one of the descendants of Zerah son of Judah, was the king's agent in all affairs relating to the people.

25As for the villages with their fields, some of the people of Judah lived in Kiriath Arba and its surrounding settlements, in Dibon and its settlements, in Jekabzeel and its villages, 26in Jeshua, in Moladah, in Beth Pelet, 27in Hazar Shual, in Beersheba and its settlements, 28in Ziklag, in Meko-

---

a 14 Most Septuagint manuscripts; Hebrew *their*

nah and its settlements, ²⁹in En Rimmon, in Zorah, in Jarmuth, ³⁰Zanoah, Adullam and their villages, in Lachish and its fields, and in Azekah and its settlements. So they were living all the way from Beersheba to the Valley of Hinnom.

³¹The descendants of the Benjamites from Geba lived in Mikmash, Aija, Bethel and its settlements, ³²in Anathoth, Nob and Ananiah, ³³in Hazor, Ramah and Gittaim, ³⁴in Hadid, Zeboim and Neballat, ³⁵in Lod and Ono, and in Ge Harashim.

³⁶Some of the divisions of the Levites of Judah settled in Benjamin.

Priests and Levites

12 These were the priests and Levites who returned with Zerubbabel son of Shealtiel and with Joshua:

Seraiah, Jeremiah, Ezra,
²Amariah, Malluk, Hattush,
³Shekaniah, Rehum, Meremoth,
⁴Iddo, Ginnethon,^a Abijah,
⁵Mijamin,^b Moadiah, Bilgah,
⁶Shemaiah, Joiarib, Jedaiah,
⁷Sallu, Amok, Hilkiah and Jedaiah.
These were the leaders of the priests and their associates in the days of Joshua.

⁸The Levites were Jeshua, Binnui, Kadmiel, Sherebiah, Judah, and also Mattaniah, who, together with his associates, was in charge of the songs of thanksgiving. ⁹Bakbukiah and Unni, their associates, stood opposite them in the services.

¹⁰Joshua was the father of Joiakim, Joiakim the father of Eliashib, Eliashib the father of Joiada, ¹¹Joiada the father of Jonathan, and Jonathan the father of Jaddua.

¹²In the days of Joiakim, these were the heads of the priestly families:
of Seraiah's family, Meraiah;
of Jeremiah's, Hananiah;
¹³of Ezra's, Meshullam;
of Amariah's, Jehohanan;

¹⁴of Malluk's, Jonathan;
of Shekaniah's,^c Joseph;
¹⁵of Harim's, Adna;
of Meremoth's,^d Helkai;
¹⁶of Iddo's, Zechariah;
of Ginnethon's, Meshullam;
¹⁷of Abijah's, Zikri;
of Miniamin's and of Moadiah's, Piltai;
¹⁸of Bilgah's, Shammua;
of Shemaiah's, Jehonathan;
¹⁹of Joiarib's, Mattenai;
of Jedaiah's, Uzzi;
²⁰of Sallu's, Kallai;
of Amok's, Eber;
²¹of Hilkiah's, Hashabiah;
of Jedaiah's, Nethanel.

²²The family heads of the Levites in the days of Eliashib, Joiada, Johanan and Jaddua, as well as those of the priests, were recorded in the reign of Darius the Persian. ²³The family heads among the descendants of Levi up to the time of Johanan son of Eliashib were recorded in the book of the annals. ²⁴And the leaders of the Levites were Hashabiah, Sherebiah, Jeshua son of Kadmiel, and their associates, who stood opposite them to give praise and thanksgiving, one section responding to the other, as prescribed by David the man of God.

²⁵Mattaniah, Bakbukiah, Obadiah, Meshullam, Talmon and Akkub were gatekeepers who guarded the storerooms at the gates. ²⁶They served in the days of Joiakim son of Joshua, the son of Jozadak, and in the days of Nehemiah the governor and of Ezra the priest, the teacher of the Law.

Dedication of the Wall of Jerusalem

²⁷At the dedication of the wall of Jerusalem, the Levites were sought out from where they lived and were brought to Jerusalem to celebrate joyfully the dedication with songs of thanksgiving and with the music of cymbals, harps and lyres. ²⁸The

---

^a 4 Many Hebrew manuscripts and Vulgate (see also verse 16); most Hebrew manuscripts *Ginnethoi*   ^b 5 A variant of *Miniamin*   ^c 14 Very many Hebrew manuscripts, some Septuagint manuscripts and Syriac (see also verse 3); most Hebrew manuscripts *Shebaniah's*   ^d 15 Some Septuagint manuscripts (see also verse 3); Hebrew *Meraioth's*

musicians also were brought together from the region around Jerusalem — from the villages of the Netophathites, 29from Beth Gilgal, and from the area of Geba and Azmaveth, for the musicians had built villages for themselves around Jerusalem. 30When the priests and Levites had purified themselves ceremonially, they purified the people, the gates and the wall.

31I had the leaders of Judah go up on top ofª the wall. I also assigned two large choirs to give thanks. One was to proceed on top ofᵇ the wall to the right, toward the Dung Gate. 32Hoshaiah and half the leaders of Judah followed them, 33along with Azariah, Ezra, Meshullam, 34Judah, Benjamin, Shemaiah, Jeremiah, 35as well as some priests with trumpets, and also Zechariah son of Jonathan, the son of Shemaiah, the son of Mattaniah, the son of Micaiah, the son of Zakkur, the son of Asaph, 36and his associates — Shemaiah, Azarel, Milalai, Gilalai, Maai, Nethanel, Judah and Hanani — with musical instruments prescribed by David the man of God. Ezra the teacher of the Law led the procession. 37At the Fountain Gate they continued directly up the steps of the City of David on the ascent to the wall and passed above the site of David's palace to the Water Gate on the east.

38The second choir proceeded in the opposite direction. I followed them on top ofᶜ the wall, together with half the people — past the Tower of the Ovens to the Broad Wall, 39over the Gate of Ephraim, the Jeshanahᵈ Gate, the Fish Gate, the Tower of Hananel and the Tower of the Hundred, as far as the Sheep Gate. At the Gate of the Guard they stopped.

40The two choirs that gave thanks then took their places in the house of God; so did I, together with half the officials, 41as well as the priests — Eliakim, Maaseiah, Miniamin, Micaiah, Elioenai, Zechariah and Hananiah with their trumpets — 42and also Maaseiah, Shemaiah, Eleazar, Uzzi, Jehohanan, Malkijah, Elam and Ezer.

The choirs sang under the direction of Jezrahiah. 43And on that day they offered great sacrifices, rejoicing because God had given them great joy. The women and children also rejoiced. The sound of rejoicing in Jerusalem could be heard far away.

44At that time men were appointed to be in charge of the storerooms for the contributions, firstfruits and tithes. From the fields around the towns they were to bring into the storerooms the portions required by the Law for the priests and the Levites, for Judah was pleased with the ministering priests and Levites. 45They performed the service of their God and the service of purification, as did also the musicians and gatekeepers, according to the commands of David and his son Solomon. 46For long ago, in the days of David and Asaph, there had been directors for the musicians and for the songs of praise and thanksgiving to God. 47So in the days of Zerubbabel and of Nehemiah, all Israel contributed the daily portions for the musicians and the gatekeepers. They also set aside the portion for the other Levites, and the Levites set aside the portion for the descendants of Aaron.

Nehemiah's Final Reforms

13 On that day the Book of Moses was read aloud in the hearing of the people and there it was found written that no Ammonite or Moabite should ever be admitted into the assembly of God, 2because they had not met the Israelites with food and water but had hired Balaam to call a curse down on them. (Our God, however, turned the curse into a blessing.) 3When the people heard this law, they excluded from Israel all who were of foreign descent.

4Before this, Eliashib the priest had been put in charge of the storerooms of the house of our God. He was closely associated with Tobiah, 5and he had provided him with a large room formerly used to store

---

ª 31 Or go alongside   ᵇ 31 Or proceed alongside   ᶜ 38 Or them alongside   ᵈ 39 Or Old the grain offerings and incense and temple articles, and also the tithes of grain, new wine and olive oil prescribed for the Levites, musicians and gatekeepers, as well as the contributions for the priests.

6But while all this was going on, I was not in Jerusalem, for in the thirty-second year of Artaxerxes king of Babylon I had returned to the king. Some time later I asked his permission 7and came back to Jerusalem. Here I learned about the evil thing Eliashib had done in providing Tobiah a room in the courts of the house of God. 8I was greatly displeased and threw all Tobiah's household goods out of the room. 9I gave orders to purify the rooms, and then I put back into them the equipment of the house of God, with the grain offerings and the incense.

10I also learned that the portions assigned to the Levites had not been given to them, and that all the Levites and musicians responsible for the service had gone back to their own fields. 11So I rebuked the officials and asked them, "Why is the house of God neglected?" Then I called them together and stationed them at their posts.

12All Judah brought the tithes of grain, new wine and olive oil into the storerooms. 13I put Shelemiah the priest, Zadok the scribe, and a Levite named Pedaiah in charge of the storerooms and made Hanan son of Zakkur, the son of Mattaniah, their assistant, because they were considered trustworthy. They were made responsible for distributing the supplies to their fellow Levites.

14Remember me for this, my God, and do not blot out what I have so faithfully done for the house of my God and its services.

15In those days I saw people in Judah treading winepresses on the Sabbath and bringing in grain and loading it on donkeys, together with wine, grapes, figs and all other kinds of loads. And they were bringing all this into Jerusalem on the Sabbath. Therefore I warned them against

selling food on that day. 16People from Tyre who lived in Jerusalem were bringing in fish and all kinds of merchandise and selling them in Jerusalem on the Sabbath to the people of Judah. 17I rebuked the nobles of Judah and said to them, "What is this wicked thing you are doing — desecrating the Sabbath day? 18Didn't your ancestors do the same things, so that our God brought all this calamity on us and on this city? Now you are stirring up more wrath against Israel by desecrating the Sabbath."

19When evening shadows fell on the gates of Jerusalem before the Sabbath, I ordered the doors to be shut and not opened until the Sabbath was over. I stationed some of my own men at the gates so that no load could be brought in on the Sabbath day. 20Once or twice the merchants and sellers of all kinds of goods spent the night outside Jerusalem. 21But I warned them and said, "Why do you spend the night by the wall? If you do this again, I will arrest you." From that time on they no longer came on the Sabbath. 22Then I commanded the Levites to purify themselves and go and guard the gates in order to keep the Sabbath day holy.

Remember me for this also, my God, and show mercy to me according to your great love.

23Moreover, in those days I saw men of Judah who had married women from Ashdod, Ammon and Moab. 24Half of their children spoke the language of Ashdod or the language of one of the other peoples, and did not know how to speak the language of Judah. 25I rebuked them and called curses down on them. I beat some of the men and pulled out their hair. I made them take an oath in God's name and said: "You are not to give your daughters in marriage to their sons, nor are you to take their daughters in marriage for your sons or for yourselves. 26Was it not because of marriages like these that Solomon king of Israel sinned? Among the many nations there was no king like him. He was loved by his

God, and God made him king over all Israel, but even he was led into sin by foreign women. ²⁷Must we hear now that you too are doing all this terrible wickedness and are being unfaithful to our God by marrying foreign women?"

²⁸One of the sons of Joiada son of Eliashib the high priest was son-in-law to Sanballat the Horonite. And I drove him away from me.

²⁹Remember them, my God, because they defiled the priestly office and the covenant of the priesthood and of the Levites.

³⁰So I purified the priests and the Levites of everything foreign, and assigned them duties, each to his own task. ³¹I also made provision for contributions of wood at designated times, and for the firstfruits.

Remember me with favor, my God.

Esther

THEME: The book of Esther demonstrates that God is in control of history and that he is the hero who saves and protects his own, often using ordinary people and events.

AUTHOR: The author of Esther is unknown, but the writer was certainly a Jew and, given the description of Persian life, probably lived in Persia during this period (Esther became queen in 479 BC).

DATE OF WRITING: Esther was probably written between 460 and 350 BC.

ENCOURAGEMENT FROM ESTHER: "Their sorrow was turned into joy and their mourning into a day of celebration" (Esther 9:22).

REFLECTION FROM ESTHER: "Who knows but that you have come to your royal position for such a time as this?" (Esther 4:14).

The book of Esther demonstrates God's protection of his people even while they're in exile far from home. God's providence and protection are abundantly evident throughout Esther, even though his name is never mentioned in the book. A plot to destroy the Jews is foiled by Esther's courage and by the wise counsel of her cousin Mordecai. Esther provides the only Biblical portrait of the Jews who elected to remain in exile rather than return to Israel. By God's grace, those who were intended by a vindictive adversary to be victims were transformed into victors.

The book of Esther demonstrates unmistakably that God is in control of history. He intervenes in the affairs of nations and in the individual lives of those who trust him. While God disciplines his children, he never abandons them. God uses the pain produced by our own sins and the hurts inflicted on us by others to bring us back into his loving care. Christ-centered recovery offers the power to turn victims into victors. Recovery—true victory—is available through God's power and the principles he provides.

At a Glance

Recovery Themes in Esther

Queen Vashti Deposed

1 This is what happened during the time of Xerxes,[a] the Xerxes who ruled over 127 provinces stretching from India to Cush[b]: ²At that time King Xerxes reigned from his royal throne in the citadel of Susa, ³and in the third year of his reign he gave a banquet for all his nobles and officials. The military leaders of Persia and Media, the princes, and the nobles of the provinces were present.

⁴For a full 180 days he displayed the vast wealth of his kingdom and the splendor and glory of his majesty. ⁵When these days were over, the king gave a banquet, lasting seven days, in the enclosed garden of the king's palace, for all the people from the least to the greatest who were in the citadel

---

a 1 Hebrew *Ahasuerus;* here and throughout Esther   *b 1* That is, the upper Nile region of Susa. 6The garden had hangings of white and blue linen, fastened with cords of white linen and purple material to silver rings on marble pillars. There were couches of gold and silver on a mosaic pavement of porphyry, marble, mother-of-pearl and other costly stones. 7Wine was served in goblets of gold, each one different from the other, and the royal wine was abundant, in keeping with the king's liberality. 8By the king's command each guest was allowed to drink with no restrictions, for the king instructed all the wine stewards to serve each man what he wished.

9Queen Vashti also gave a banquet for the women in the royal palace of King Xerxes.

10On the seventh day, when King Xerxes was in high spirits from wine, he commanded the seven eunuchs who served him — Mehuman, Biztha, Harbona, Bigtha, Abagtha, Zethar and Karkas — 11to bring before him Queen Vashti, wearing her royal crown, in order to display her beauty to the people and nobles, for she was lovely to look at. 12But when the attendants delivered the king's command, Queen Vashti refused to come. Then the king became furious and burned with anger.

13Since it was customary for the king to consult experts in matters of law and justice, he spoke with the wise men who understood the times 14and were closest to the king — Karshena, Shethar, Admatha, Tarshish, Meres, Marsena and Memukan, the seven nobles of Persia and Media who had special access to the king and were highest in the kingdom.

15"According to law, what must be done to Queen Vashti?" he asked. "She has not obeyed the command of King Xerxes that the eunuchs have taken to her."

16Then Memukan replied in the presence of the king and the nobles, "Queen Vashti has done wrong, not only against the king but also against all the nobles and the peoples of all the provinces of King Xerxes. 17For the queen's conduct will become known to all the women, and so they will despise their husbands and say, 'King Xerxes commanded Queen Vashti to be brought before him, but she would not come.' 18This very day the Persian and Median women of the nobility who have heard about the queen's conduct will respond to all the king's nobles in the same way. There will be no end of disrespect and discord.

19"Therefore, if it pleases the king, let him issue a royal decree and let it be written in the laws of Persia and Media, which cannot be repealed, that Vashti is never again to enter the presence of King Xerxes. Also let the king give her royal position to someone else who is better than she. 20Then when the king's edict is proclaimed throughout all his vast realm, all the women will respect their husbands, from the least to the greatest."

21The king and his nobles were pleased with this advice, so the king did as Memukan proposed. 22He sent dispatches to all parts of the kingdom, to each province in its own script and to each people in their own language, proclaiming that every man should be ruler over his own household, using his native tongue.

Esther Made Queen

2 Later when King Xerxes' fury had subsided, he remembered Vashti and what she had done and what he had decreed about her. 2Then the king's personal attendants proposed, "Let a search be made for beautiful young virgins for the king. 3Let the king appoint commissioners in every province of his realm to bring all these beautiful young women into the harem at the citadel of Susa. Let them be placed under the care of Hegai, the king's eunuch, who is in charge of the women; and let beauty treatments be given to them. 4Then let the young woman who pleases the king be queen instead of Vashti." This advice appealed to the king, and he followed it.

5Now there was in the citadel of Susa a Jew of the tribe of Benjamin, named Mordecai son of Jair, the son of Shimei, the son of Kish, [6]who had been carried into exile from Jerusalem by Nebuchadnezzar king of Babylon, among those taken captive with Jehoiachin[a] king of Judah. [7]Mordecai had a cousin named Hadassah, whom he had brought up because she had neither father nor mother. This young woman, who was also known as Esther, had a lovely figure and was beautiful. Mordecai had taken her as his own daughter when her father and mother died.

[8]When the king's order and edict had been proclaimed, many young women were brought to the citadel of Susa and put under the care of Hegai. Esther also was taken to the king's palace and entrusted to Hegai, who had charge of the harem. [9]She pleased him and won his favor. Immediately he provided her with her beauty treatments and special food. He assigned to her seven female attendants selected from the king's palace and moved her and her attendants into the best place in the harem.

[10]Esther had not revealed her nationality and family background, because Mordecai had forbidden her to do so. [11]Every day he walked back and forth near the courtyard of the harem to find out how Esther was and what was happening to her.

[12]Before a young woman's turn came to go in to King Xerxes, she had to complete twelve months of beauty treatments prescribed for the women, six months with oil of myrrh and six with perfumes and cosmetics. [13]And this is how she would go to the king: Anything she wanted was given her to take with her from the harem to the king's palace. [14]In the evening she would go there and in the morning return to another part of the harem to the care of Shaashgaz, the king's eunuch who was in charge of the concubines. She would not return to the king unless he was pleased with her and summoned her by name.

[15]When the turn came for Esther (the young woman Mordecai had adopted, the daughter of his uncle Abihail) to go to the king, she asked for nothing other than what Hegai, the king's eunuch who was in charge of the harem, suggested. And Esther won the favor of everyone who saw her. [16]She was taken to King Xerxes in the royal residence in the tenth month, the month of Tebeth, in the seventh year of his reign.

[17]Now the king was attracted to Esther more than to any of the other women, and she won his favor and approval more than any of the other virgins. So he set a royal crown on her head and made her queen instead of Vashti. [18]And the king gave a great banquet, Esther's banquet, for all his nobles and officials. He proclaimed a holiday throughout the provinces and distributed gifts with royal liberality.

Mordecai Uncovers a Conspiracy

[19]When the virgins were assembled a second time, Mordecai was sitting at the king's gate. [20]But Esther had kept secret her family background and nationality just as Mordecai had told her to do, for she continued to follow Mordecai's instructions as she had done when he was bringing her up.

[21]During the time Mordecai was sitting at the king's gate, Bigthana[b] and Teresh, two of the king's officers who guarded the doorway, became angry and conspired to assassinate King Xerxes. [22]But Mordecai found out about the plot and told Queen Esther, who in turn reported it to the king, giving credit to Mordecai. [23]And when the report was investigated and found to be true, the two officials were impaled on poles. All this was recorded in the book of the annals in the presence of the king.

Haman's Plot to Destroy the Jews

3 After these events, King Xerxes honored Haman son of Hammedatha, the Agagite, elevating him and giving him a seat of honor higher than that of all the other nobles. [2]All the royal officials at the king's gate knelt down and paid honor to Haman, for the king had commanded

---

[a] 6 Hebrew *Jeconiah*, a variant of *Jehoiachin*   [b] 21 Hebrew *Bigthan*, a variant of *Bigthana*

My Name Is Karrie

I'M A BELIEVER WHO STRUGGLES WITH AN EATING DISORDER

Please read Esther 2 and 4 to get the basic story of Esther. This ten-chapter book is well worth reading in its entirety.

I'm a believer who struggles with the aftereffects of physical, emotional and sexual abuse, as well as with an eating disorder. I witnessed dysfunction from an early age, as my father abused alcohol, indulged in several extramarital affairs and was emotionally unavailable. My relationship with him revolved around listening to his sexual and degrading jokes, inappropriate details about his love life and comments about my own developing body. Over a period of 22 years I grew up around other men who also physically, emotionally and sexually abused me. I vowed never to allow myself to be vulnerable again and began to see myself as a body without a soul. My experience confirmed in my mind that self-worth and love were byproducts of physical perfection.

In college, I decided to take my life's direction into my own hands. I married but later realized that my mate was also an abusive alcoholic. After two years, a broken nose, bruises inside and out, an escalating eating disorder and utter despair, I heard the Lord prod me, "Karrie, you don't have to live this way any longer; let me help you." God did intervene — by bringing me to Celebrate Recovery. That very night my life changed. I felt God's Spirit, broke down and cried harder than I ever had before. At that very moment I gave over my life and will to him, and I literally felt him lift from my shoulders my burdens and guilt. My vow never to be vulnerable again slowly began to crack. The Lord started to heal and free me. Now that my trust was solely in God, my husband turned his back on me and our marriage ended.

As I started to work my program, I learned to face my past and to become truly free of the hold it had on me. For many years fear had driven me to stuff my memories deep inside. But God held me close, gently leading me step by step and connecting me with my support team. I realized that I no longer had to face my fears alone. Along with confronting the events of my past, I took a good, hard look at myself: How had I hurt others? I learned that the past abuse wasn't my fault, but as an adult I still had to ask, "How did I respond to that abuse?" I finally recognized the sin of my eating disorder. I was weighing myself daily and measuring my success by how far my fingers could overlap my wrist. I thought I had to be as thin as possible to earn the love of others. I realized that, although I'd forgiven those in my past and was able to accept Jesus' forgiveness, I'd forgotten to forgive myself. Now God required me to take action to mend the destruction caused by my own choices. I sought out my family and friends to ask their forgiveness for the harm I'd caused through my eating addiction and for the anger I'd expressed as a result of my inability to deal with my pain. These were truly the "freedom steps" in my healing.

Many relationships from my past have been restored. Several years into my recovery, God called me to my dad's side as he awaited life-threatening surgery. I'd forgiven him but was fearful because this wasn't yet a safe relationship for me. Still, I knew deep down that I was supposed to go. The night before his surgery, the Lord gave me the courage to ask my dad about his relationship with God. I soon found myself at his knees, leading him through a prayer asking Jesus into his life. I saw a broken, forgiven man that day and learned that no matter how great the offense or abuse, along the path to healing lies forgiveness.

Additionally, God has given me a new husband, a godly man named Bob, who loves me with all his heart. God has also given me a new soul to love: my son, Jackson. Through recovery I've learned that the vow to which I once committed is no longer necessary. Little by little God has taught me to trust others. Like Esther, I've given up living a life based on physical perfection. Instead, I find my purpose in ministering in Celebrate Recovery, using my past experiences to glorify God and serving him on behalf of others. I can't imagine being in a better position for service. I see Christ changing lives right before my eyes, and I've become a new person inside.

Many years ago I faced a decision: I could return to my old ways or, for the first time in my life, I could trust and risk. That day I recall telling Jesus that even though I couldn't see or touch him, I believed in him and would follow him. Through his Word he began speaking to me, through other believers I began to touch him, and through my witness of changed lives around me I began to see him. By allowing Jesus to love you through others, in time you too will see his amazing face.

this concerning him. But Mordecai would not kneel down or pay him honor.

³Then the royal officials at the king's gate asked Mordecai, "Why do you disobey the king's command?" ⁴Day after day they spoke to him but he refused to comply. Therefore they told Haman about it to see whether Mordecai's behavior would be tolerated, for he had told them he was a Jew.

⁵When Haman saw that Mordecai would not kneel down or pay him honor, he was enraged. ⁶Yet having learned who Mordecai's people were, he scorned the idea of killing only Mordecai. Instead Haman looked for a way to destroy all Mordecai's people, the Jews, throughout the whole kingdom of Xerxes.

⁷In the twelfth year of King Xerxes, in the first month, the month of Nisan, the *pur* (that is, the lot) was cast in the presence of Haman to select a day and month. And the lot fell on*ᵃ* the twelfth month, the month of Adar.

⁸Then Haman said to King Xerxes, "There is a certain people dispersed among the peoples in all the provinces of your kingdom who keep themselves separate. Their customs are different from those of all other people, and they do not obey the king's laws; it is not in the king's best interest to tolerate them. ⁹If it pleases the king, let a decree be issued to destroy them, and I will give ten thousand talents*ᵇ* of silver to the king's administrators for the royal treasury."

¹⁰So the king took his signet ring from his finger and gave it to Haman son of Hammedatha, the Agagite, the enemy of the Jews. ¹¹"Keep the money," the king said to Haman, "and do with the people as you please."

¹²Then on the thirteenth day of the first month the royal secretaries were summoned. They wrote out in the script of each province and in the language of each people all Haman's orders to the king's satraps, the governors of the various provinces and the nobles of the various peoples. These were written in the name of King Xerxes himself and sealed with his own ring. ¹³Dispatches were sent by couriers to all the king's provinces with the order to destroy, kill and annihilate all the Jews — young and old, women and children — on a single day, the thirteenth day of the twelfth month, the month of Adar, and to plunder their goods. ¹⁴A copy of the text of the edict was to be issued as law in every province and made known to the people of every nationality so they would be ready for that day.

¹⁵The couriers went out, spurred on by the king's command, and the edict was issued in the citadel of Susa. The king and Haman sat down to drink, but the city of Susa was bewildered.

Mordecai Persuades Esther to Help

4 When Mordecai learned of all that had been done, he tore his clothes, put on sackcloth and ashes, and went out into the city, wailing loudly and bitterly. ²But he went only as far as the king's gate, because no one clothed in sackcloth was allowed to enter it. ³In every province to which the edict and order of the king came, there was great mourning among the Jews, with fasting, weeping and wailing. Many lay in sackcloth and ashes.

⁴When Esther's eunuchs and female attendants came and told her about Mordecai, she was in great distress. She sent clothes for him to put on instead of his sackcloth, but he would not accept them. ⁵Then Esther summoned Hathak, one of the king's eunuchs assigned to attend her, and ordered him to find out what was troubling Mordecai and why.

⁶So Hathak went out to Mordecai in the open square of the city in front of the king's gate. ⁷Mordecai told him everything that had happened to him, including the exact amount of money Haman had promised to pay into the royal treasury for the destruction of the Jews. ⁸He also gave him a copy

---

ᵃ 7 Septuagint; Hebrew does not have *And the lot fell on.*   *ᵇ 9* That is, about 375 tons or about 340 metric tons of the text of the edict for their annihilation, which had been published in Susa, to show to Esther and explain it to her, and he told him to instruct her to go into the king's presence to beg for mercy and plead with him for her people.

⁹Hathak went back and reported to Esther what Mordecai had said. ¹⁰Then she instructed him to say to Mordecai, ¹¹"All the king's officials and the people of the royal provinces know that for any man or woman who approaches the king in the inner court without being summoned the king has but one law: that they be put to death unless the king extends the gold scepter to them and spares their lives. But thirty days have passed since I was called to go to the king."

¹²When Esther's words were reported to Mordecai, ¹³he sent back this answer: "Do not think that because you are in the king's house you alone of all the Jews will escape. ¹⁴For if you remain silent at this time, relief and deliverance for the Jews will arise from another place, but you and your father's family will perish. And who knows but that you have come to your royal position for such a time as this?"

¹⁵Then Esther sent this reply to Mordecai: ¹⁶"Go, gather together all the Jews who are in Susa, and fast for me. Do not eat or drink for three days, night or day. I and my attendants will fast as you do. When this is done, I will go to the king, even though it is against the law. And if I perish, I perish."

¹⁷So Mordecai went away and carried out all of Esther's instructions.

Esther's Request to the King

5 On the third day Esther put on her royal robes and stood in the inner court of the palace, in front of the king's hall. The king was sitting on his royal throne in the hall, facing the entrance. ²When he saw Queen Esther standing in the court, he was pleased with her and held out to her the gold scepter that was in his

hand. So Esther approached and touched the tip of the scepter.

³Then the king asked, "What is it, Queen Esther? What is your request? Even up to half the kingdom, it will be given you."

⁴"If it pleases the king," replied Esther, "let the king, together with Haman, come today to a banquet I have prepared for him."

⁵"Bring Haman at once," the king said, "so that we may do what Esther asks."

So the king and Haman went to the banquet Esther had prepared. ⁶As they were drinking wine, the king again asked Esther, "Now what is your petition? It will be given you. And what is your request? Even up to half the kingdom, it will be granted."

⁷Esther replied, "My petition and my request is this: ⁸If the king regards me with favor and if it pleases the king to grant my petition and fulfill my request, let the king and Haman come tomorrow to the banquet I will prepare for them. Then I will answer the king's question."

Haman's Rage Against Mordecai

⁹Haman went out that day happy and in high spirits. But when he saw Mordecai at the king's gate and observed that he neither rose nor showed fear in his presence, he was filled with rage against Mordecai. ¹⁰Nevertheless, Haman restrained himself and went home.

Calling together his friends and Zeresh, his wife, ¹¹Haman boasted to them about his vast wealth, his many sons, and all the ways the king had honored him and how he had elevated him above the other nobles and officials. ¹²"And that's not all," Haman added. "I'm the only person Queen Esther invited to accompany the king to the banquet she gave. And she has invited me along with the king tomorrow. ¹³But all this gives me no satisfaction as long as I see that Jew Mordecai sitting at the king's gate."

¹⁴His wife Zeresh and all his friends said to him, "Have a pole set up, reaching to a height of fifty cubits,ᵃ and ask the king in

---

ᵃ 14 That is, about 75 feet or about 23 meters

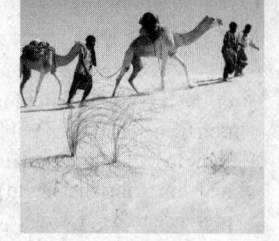

My Name Is Esther

ESTHER 4

As we travel the road to recovery, fear may slow us down. It's not that we expected the trip to be easy. But some elements can be intimidating, like listing and then sharing all the ugliness in our life with another human being. Esther experienced the degree to which fear can make us falter.

Her people, exiled Jews then scattered across the Persian Empire, faced extermination because of the vicious plot of Haman (see Esther 3). Esther, in her role as queen, was their only hope. Mordecai had become his cousin's guardian after the young Esther's parents had died. He now sent a message and documents to Esther detailing the vile scheme and asking her to go to the king and beg for mercy. This was risky business. Esther's predecessor had angered the king and lost her position. To appear before him without a summons could result in execution (see Esther 4:11). Esther understandably balked at what she had to do. She was afraid.

Mordecai responded to her hesitation by pointing out that her refusal would mean her own death, as well as the deaths of her father's family, and that her position may well have been given to her in light of the crisis her people now faced (see v. 14).

Esther, to her credit, responded to the reasoning of a man she trusted, fasted to gain spiritual strength and insight, sought the support of others in her preparations, made a commitment, accepted the potential price (death) she might have to pay (see vv. 15 – 16) and developed a plan (see Esther 5 – 7).

God graciously protected Esther. When she entered the king's chamber, he granted her an audience and listened to her petition. Carefully and methodically Esther moved through her meticulously developed plan.

The product of her faith and hard work was her own survival and that of her people. When fear causes us to falter in our recovery, we must seek help. We must go to our accountability partner, sponsor, recovery leader, pastor or Christian counselor. We don't have to face our fears alone if we take the risk. Our recovery and the well-being of our families require action. However hard the next step might be, turning back now will have tragic consequences both for us and for those we love.

the morning to have Mordecai impaled on it. Then go with the king to the banquet and enjoy yourself." This suggestion delighted Haman, and he had the pole set up.

Mordecai Honored

6 That night the king could not sleep; so he ordered the book of the chronicles, the record of his reign, to be brought in and read to him. ²It was found recorded there that Mordecai had exposed Bigthana and Teresh, two of the king's officers who guarded the doorway, who had conspired to assassinate King Xerxes.

³"What honor and recognition has Mordecai received for this?" the king asked.

"Nothing has been done for him," his attendants answered.

⁴The king said, "Who is in the court?" Now Haman had just entered the outer court of the palace to speak to the king about impaling Mordecai on the pole he had set up for him.

⁵His attendants answered, "Haman is standing in the court."

"Bring him in," the king ordered.

⁶When Haman entered, the king asked him, "What should be done for the man the king delights to honor?"

Now Haman thought to himself, "Who is there that the king would rather honor than me?" ⁷So he answered the king, "For the man the king delights to honor, ⁸have them bring a royal robe the king has worn and a horse the king has ridden, one with a royal crest placed on its head. ⁹Then let the robe and horse be entrusted to one of the king's most noble princes. Let them robe the man the king delights to honor, and lead him on the horse through the city streets, proclaiming before him, 'This is what is done for the man the king delights to honor!'"

¹⁰"Go at once," the king commanded Haman. "Get the robe and the horse and do just as you have suggested for Mordecai the Jew, who sits at the king's gate. Do not neglect anything you have recommended."

¹¹So Haman got the robe and the horse. He robed Mordecai, and led him on horseback through the city streets, proclaiming before him, "This is what is done for the man the king delights to honor!"

¹²Afterward Mordecai returned to the king's gate. But Haman rushed home, with his head covered in grief, ¹³and told Zeresh his wife and all his friends everything that had happened to him.

His advisers and his wife Zeresh said to him, "Since Mordecai, before whom your downfall has started, is of Jewish origin, you cannot stand against him — you will surely come to ruin!" ¹⁴While they were still talking with him, the king's eunuchs arrived and hurried Haman away to the banquet Esther had prepared.

Haman Impaled

7 So the king and Haman went to Queen Esther's banquet, ²and as they were drinking wine on the second day, the king again asked, "Queen Esther, what is your petition? It will be given you. What is your request? Even up to half the kingdom, it will be granted."

³Then Queen Esther answered, "If I have found favor with you, Your Majesty, and if it pleases you, grant me my life — this is my petition. And spare my people — this is my request. ⁴For I and my people have been sold to be destroyed, killed and annihilated. If we had merely been sold as male and female slaves, I would have kept quiet, because no such distress would justify disturbing the king.ᵃ"

⁵King Xerxes asked Queen Esther, "Who is he? Where is he — the man who has dared to do such a thing?"

⁶Esther said, "An adversary and enemy! This vile Haman!"

Then Haman was terrified before the king and queen. ⁷The king got up in a rage, left his wine and went out into the palace

---

ᵃ 4 Or *quiet, but the compensation our adversary offers cannot be compared with the loss the king would suffer* garden. But Haman, realizing that the king had already decided his fate, stayed behind to beg Queen Esther for his life.

⁸Just as the king returned from the palace garden to the banquet hall, Haman was falling on the couch where Esther was reclining.

The king exclaimed, "Will he even molest the queen while she is with me in the house?"

As soon as the word left the king's mouth, they covered Haman's face. ⁹Then Harbona, one of the eunuchs attending the king, said, "A pole reaching to a height of fifty cubits*ᵃ* stands by Haman's house. He had it set up for Mordecai, who spoke up to help the king."

The king said, "Impale him on it!" ¹⁰So they impaled Haman on the pole he had set up for Mordecai. Then the king's fury subsided.

The King's Edict in Behalf of the Jews

8 That same day King Xerxes gave Queen Esther the estate of Haman, the enemy of the Jews. And Mordecai came into the presence of the king, for Esther had told how he was related to her. ²The king took off his signet ring, which he had reclaimed from Haman, and presented it to Mordecai. And Esther appointed him over Haman's estate.

³Esther again pleaded with the king, falling at his feet and weeping. She begged him to put an end to the evil plan of Haman the Agagite, which he had devised against the Jews. ⁴Then the king extended the gold scepter to Esther and she arose and stood before him.

⁵"If it pleases the king," she said, "and if he regards me with favor and thinks it the right thing to do, and if he is pleased with me, let an order be written overruling the dispatches that Haman son of Hammedatha, the Agagite, devised and wrote to destroy the Jews in all the king's provinces.

⁶For how can I bear to see disaster fall on my people? How can I bear to see the destruction of my family?"

⁷King Xerxes replied to Queen Esther and to Mordecai the Jew, "Because Haman attacked the Jews, I have given his estate to Esther, and they have impaled him on the pole he set up. ⁸Now write another decree in the king's name in behalf of the Jews as seems best to you, and seal it with the king's signet ring—for no document written in the king's name and sealed with his ring can be revoked."

⁹At once the royal secretaries were summoned—on the twenty-third day of the third month, the month of Sivan. They wrote out all Mordecai's orders to the Jews, and to the satraps, governors and nobles of the 127 provinces stretching from India to Cush.*ᵇ* These orders were written in the script of each province and the language of each people and also to the Jews in their own script and language. ¹⁰Mordecai wrote in the name of King Xerxes, sealed the dispatches with the king's signet ring, and sent them by mounted couriers, who rode fast horses especially bred for the king.

¹¹The king's edict granted the Jews in every city the right to assemble and protect themselves; to destroy, kill and annihilate the armed men of any nationality or province who might attack them and their women and children,*ᶜ* and to plunder the property of their enemies. ¹²The day appointed for the Jews to do this in all the provinces of King Xerxes was the thirteenth day of the twelfth month, the month of Adar. ¹³A copy of the text of the edict was to be issued as law in every province and made known to the people of every nationality so that the Jews would be ready on that day to avenge themselves on their enemies.

¹⁴The couriers, riding the royal horses, went out, spurred on by the king's com-

---

ᵃ 9 That is, about 75 feet or about 23 meters   *ᵇ 9* That is, the upper Nile region   *ᶜ 11* Or *province, together with their women and children, who might attack them;*

mand, and the edict was issued in the citadel of Susa.

The Triumph of the Jews

15When Mordecai left the king's presence, he was wearing royal garments of blue and white, a large crown of gold and a purple robe of fine linen. And the city of Susa held a joyous celebration. 16For the Jews it was a time of happiness and joy, gladness and honor. 17In every province and in every city to which the edict of the king came, there was joy and gladness among the Jews, with feasting and celebrating. And many people of other nationalities became Jews because fear of the Jews had seized them.

9 On the thirteenth day of the twelfth month, the month of Adar, the edict commanded by the king was to be carried out. On this day the enemies of the Jews had hoped to overpower them, but now the tables were turned and the Jews got the upper hand over those who hated them. 2The Jews assembled in their cities in all the provinces of King Xerxes to attack those determined to destroy them. No one could stand against them, because the people of all the other nationalities were afraid of them. 3And all the nobles of the provinces, the satraps, the governors and the king's administrators helped the Jews, because fear of Mordecai had seized them. 4Mordecai was prominent in the palace; his reputation spread throughout the provinces, and he became more and more powerful.

5The Jews struck down all their enemies with the sword, killing and destroying them, and they did what they pleased to those who hated them. 6In the citadel of Susa, the Jews killed and destroyed five hundred men. 7They also killed Parshandatha, Dalphon, Aspatha, 8Poratha, Adalia, Aridatha, 9Parmashta, Arisai, Aridai and Vaizatha, 10the ten sons of Haman son of Hammedatha, the enemy of the Jews. But they did not lay their hands on the plunder.

11The number of those killed in the citadel of Susa was reported to the king that same day. 12The king said to Queen Esther, "The Jews have killed and destroyed five hundred men and the ten sons of Haman in the citadel of Susa. What have they done in the rest of the king's provinces? Now what is your petition? It will be given you. What is your request? It will also be granted."

13"If it pleases the king," Esther answered, "give the Jews in Susa permission to carry out this day's edict tomorrow also, and let Haman's ten sons be impaled on poles."

14So the king commanded that this be done. An edict was issued in Susa, and they impaled the ten sons of Haman. 15The Jews in Susa came together on the fourteenth day of the month of Adar, and they put to death in Susa three hundred men, but they did not lay their hands on the plunder.

16Meanwhile, the remainder of the Jews who were in the king's provinces also assembled to protect themselves and get relief from their enemies. They killed seventy-five thousand of them but did not lay their hands on the plunder. 17This happened on the thirteenth day of the month of Adar, and on the fourteenth they rested and made it a day of feasting and joy.

18The Jews in Susa, however, had assembled on the thirteenth and fourteenth, and then on the fifteenth they rested and made it a day of feasting and joy. 19That is why rural Jews — those living in villages — observe the fourteenth of the month of Adar as a day of joy and feasting, a day for giving presents to each other.

Purim Established

20Mordecai recorded these events, and he sent letters to all the Jews throughout the provinces of King Xerxes, near and far, 21to have them celebrate annually the fourteenth and fifteenth days of the month of Adar 22as the time when the Jews got relief from their enemies, and as the month when their sorrow was turned into joy and their mourning into a day of celebration. He wrote them to observe the days as days of feasting and joy and giving presents of food to one another and gifts to the poor.

²³So the Jews agreed to continue the celebration they had begun, doing what Mordecai had written to them. ²⁴For Haman son of Hammedatha, the Agagite, the enemy of all the Jews, had plotted against the Jews to destroy them and had cast the *pur* (that is, the lot) for their ruin and destruction. ²⁵But when the plot came to the king's attention,[a] he issued written orders that the evil scheme Haman had devised against the Jews should come back onto his own head, and that he and his sons should be impaled on poles. ²⁶(Therefore these days were called Purim, from the word *pur.*) Because of everything written in this letter and because of what they had seen and what had happened to them, ²⁷the Jews took it on themselves to establish the custom that they and their descendants and all who join them should without fail observe these two days every year, in the way prescribed and at the time appointed. ²⁸These days should be remembered and observed in every generation by every family, and in every province and in every city. And these days of Purim should never fail to be celebrated by the Jews — nor should the memory of these days die out among their descendants.

²⁹So Queen Esther, daughter of Abihail, along with Mordecai the Jew, wrote with full authority to confirm this second letter concerning Purim. ³⁰And Mordecai sent letters to all the Jews in the 127 provinces of Xerxes' kingdom — words of goodwill and assurance — ³¹to establish these days of Purim at their designated times, as Mordecai the Jew and Queen Esther had decreed for them, and as they had established for themselves and their descendants in regard to their times of fasting and lamentation. ³²Esther's decree confirmed these regulations about Purim, and it was written down in the records.

The Greatness of Mordecai

10 King Xerxes imposed tribute throughout the empire, to its distant shores. ²And all his acts of power and might, together with a full account of the greatness of Mordecai, whom the king had promoted, are they not written in the book of the annals of the kings of Media and Persia? ³Mordecai the Jew was second in rank to King Xerxes, preeminent among the Jews, and held in high esteem by his many fellow Jews, because he worked for the good of his people and spoke up for the welfare of all the Jews.

---

a 25 Or *when Esther came before the king*

THEME: We might never understand our suffering while on Earth, and God might never explain himself. Yet he does offer us himself — his presence, comfort and love.

AUTHOR: The author of Job is unknown, but this individual was obviously a well-educated, profound thinker familiar with foreign cultures.

DATE OF WRITING: Although the events of Job most likely took place during the second millennium BC, the story was probably recorded much later, perhaps sometime between the reign of Solomon (970 BC) and the exile to Babylon (586 BC).

ENCOURAGEMENT FROM JOB: "I know that my redeemer lives, and that in the end he will stand on the earth. And after my skin has been destroyed, yet in my flesh I will see God; I myself will see him with my own eyes — I, and not another. How my heart yearns within me!" (Job 19:25 – 27).

CHALLENGE FROM JOB: "Blessed is the one whom God corrects; so do not despise the discipline of the Almighty. For he wounds, but he also binds up; he injures, but his hands also heal" (Job 5:17 – 18).

REFLECTION FROM JOB: "My intercessor is my friend as my eyes pour out tears to God" (Job 16:20).

Job is a book that deals with deep suffering. The reader — but not Job or his friends — gets the inside story in chapter 1: God allows Satan to test Job. This book raises, but doesn't directly answer, the ageless question, "Why do the righteous suffer?" or, in more familiar terms, "Why do bad things happen to good people?" Job's suffering, though, isn't the overall theme of the book. The real focus is on what Job learns from his suffering: that God is sovereign over all creation. Job learns to trust in God's goodness and power, even through the worst of times, by enlarging his concept of God. This godly sufferer acknowledges a redeemer and cries out for a mediator. The problems and questions raised by the book are ultimately answered in Jesus Christ, who identifies with our sufferings.

Recovery can be a painful process of self-evaluation and change. One significant step in this process is to take a moral inventory of ourselves. This unflinching look into our pasts can bring to the surface all kinds of bitter memories — of pain that has been inflicted on us and pain we've caused others. We may not be able to make amends or offer forgiveness face-to-face, either because the person is no longer alive or because we simply cannot locate them. The key for us is the same as it was for Job: We need to enlarge our view of God, while continuing to confess our wrongs and believe in his goodness. We're to continue worshiping him daily — because he's worthy, no matter what our present circumstances. God was right there with Job, and he's just as certainly at our side.

Prologue

1 In the land of Uz there lived a man whose name was Job. This man was blameless and upright; he feared God and shunned evil. ²He had seven sons and three daughters, ³and he owned seven thousand sheep, three thousand camels, five hundred yoke of oxen and five hundred donkeys, and had a large number of servants. He was the greatest man among all the people of the East.

⁴His sons used to hold feasts in their homes on their birthdays, and they would invite their three sisters to eat and drink with them. ⁵When a period of feasting had run its course, Job would make arrangements for them to be purified. Early in the morning he would sacrifice a burnt offering for each of them, thinking, "Perhaps my children have sinned and cursed God in their hearts." This was Job's regular custom.

⁶One day the angels*ᵃ* came to present themselves before the Lord, and Satan*ᵇ* also came with them. ⁷The Lord said to Satan, "Where have you come from?"

Satan answered the Lord, "From roaming throughout the earth, going back and forth on it."

⁸Then the Lord said to Satan, "Have you considered my servant Job? There is no one on earth like him; he is blameless and upright, a man who fears God and shuns evil."

⁹"Does Job fear God for nothing?" Satan replied. ¹⁰"Have you not put a hedge around him and his household and everything he has? You have blessed the work of his hands, so that his flocks and herds are spread throughout the land. ¹¹But now stretch out your hand and strike everything he has, and he will surely curse you to your face."

¹²The Lord said to Satan, "Very well, then, everything he has is in your power, but on the man himself do not lay a finger."

Then Satan went out from the presence of the Lord.

¹³One day when Job's sons and daughters were feasting and drinking wine at the oldest brother's house, ¹⁴a messenger came to Job and said, "The oxen were plowing and the donkeys were grazing nearby, ¹⁵and the Sabeans attacked and made off with them. They put the servants to the sword, and I am the only one who has escaped to tell you!"

¹⁶While he was still speaking, another messenger came and said, "The fire of God fell from the heavens and burned up the sheep and the servants, and I am the only one who has escaped to tell you!"

¹⁷While he was still speaking, another messenger came and said, "The Chaldeans formed three raiding parties and swept down on your camels and made off with them. They put the servants to the sword, and I am the only one who has escaped to tell you!"

¹⁸While he was still speaking, yet another messenger came and said, "Your sons and daughters were feasting and drinking wine at the oldest brother's house, ¹⁹when suddenly a mighty wind swept in from the desert and struck the four corners of the house. It collapsed on them and they are dead, and I am the only one who has escaped to tell you!"

²⁰At this, Job got up and tore his robe and shaved his head. Then he fell to the ground in worship ²¹and said:

> "Naked I came from my mother's womb,
>   and naked I will depart.*ᶜ*
> The Lord gave and the Lord has taken
>   away;
>   may the name of the Lord be
>   praised."

²²In all this, Job did not sin by charging God with wrongdoing.

2 On another day the angels*ᵃ* came to present themselves before the Lord, and Satan also came with them to present himself before him. ²And

---

ᵃ 6,1 Hebrew *the sons of God*   *ᵇ 6* Hebrew *satan* means *adversary*.   *ᶜ 21* Or *will return there*

MY NAME IS JOB

BOOK OF JOB

Job is probably the best example of recovery from hurt to be found in Scripture. His incredible story rebuts the lie that there's always a direct correlation in this life between godly conduct and health, safety and prosperity. Chapters 1 and 2 clue in the reader to the reasons behind Job's sufferings, information not shared with Job himself. Job had but one tool with which to make sense of his ever more painful circumstances: his faith.

Chapters 3 through 37 record the counsel of the sufferer's three friends — or so-called friends, depending on how far we're willing to expand our definition of friendship. These self-righteous know-it-alls insisted that Job must have done something terribly wrong that would explain his suffering. A fourth man, Elihu, who suggested that suffering can purify even the righteous man, came closer to the truth — but his was also an inadequate explanation.

Job reveals a deep knowledge of God through his responses to his ordeal and to the endless debates. In the midst of his suffering he criticized God for treating him unjustly (see Job 9:28 – 35), while at the same time acknowledging a redeemer (see 19:25 – 27) and crying out for a mediator (see 9:33; 33:23). Finally the sufferer, in desperation, demanded an explanation from God himself (see 31:35). But despite Satan's influence (see 1:11; 2:5), Job stopped short of cursing God (see 2:9 – 10). After Elihu's closing remarks, God spoke directly to Job (see chs. 38 – 42), his hurting servant, when he was under no obligation to do so. Instead, God took an opposite tack: "I will question you, and you shall answer me" (38:3). Job replied simply, "I am unworthy — how can I reply to you?" (40:4). God continued his correction of Job, leading to the injured man's sincere repentance (see 42:1 – 6). The Lord rebuked Job's three critics for their mistreatment of his faithful servant and informed them that their own forgiveness rested with Job's prayers on their behalf (see 42:7 – 9). At the end of the book God restored Job (see 42:10,16 – 17).

If we've suffered unjustly, we can identify with Job's heartbreak. Satan and his supporters still afflict the innocent. Abuse — especially the sexual, physical and verbal abuse of women and children — is epidemic in America, as well as elsewhere in the world. Too often abusive behavior repeats itself through multiple generations of a family. Like Job, we may question God's reasons for allowing such suffering. But unlike Job, we who hold the completed Bible in our hands know the true nature of humanity and of this fallen world. Through Christ's atoning death, God proved his perfect love and justice beyond all doubt.

As victims, we need to guard against allowing "friends" or critics to control our understanding of our painful past or present. Instead, like Job, we must be open to experiencing more of God's greatness and goodness. God loved Job enough to confront Job's presumption in accusing God of injustice and demanding answers from him. Job, equipped with an enlarged view of God, acknowledged simply, "I am unworthy" (40:4).

Job never fell into the trap of believing that he deserved all the suffering he was experiencing, and God approved of Job's rebuttal of the principle that all suffering results from an individual's own sin (see 42:7). Still, Job's repentance led to his restoration and to multiplied blessings. Job became a blessing, both to his former critics and to his own family. If we've been abused, we must acknowledge that it wasn't our fault. At the same time, we must refuse to blame God for what happened, allowing him instead to reveal himself more fully to us. We must acknowledge that we have no right to question or criticize him. We must also remember to repent of our sins, pray for those who have wronged us, and enjoy God's work of restoration and blessing.

the LORD said to Satan, "Where have you come from?"

Satan answered the LORD, "From roaming throughout the earth, going back and forth on it."

³Then the LORD said to Satan, "Have you considered my servant Job? There is no one on earth like him; he is blameless and upright, a man who fears God and shuns evil. And he still maintains his integrity, though you incited me against him to ruin him without any reason."

⁴"Skin for skin!" Satan replied. "A man will give all he has for his own life. ⁵But now stretch out your hand and strike his flesh and bones, and he will surely curse you to your face."

⁶The LORD said to Satan, "Very well, then, he is in your hands; but you must spare his life."

⁷So Satan went out from the presence of the LORD and afflicted Job with painful sores from the soles of his feet to the crown of his head. ⁸Then Job took a piece of broken pottery and scraped himself with it as he sat among the ashes.

⁹His wife said to him, "Are you still maintaining your integrity? Curse God and die!"

¹⁰He replied, "You are talking like a foolish*a* woman. Shall we accept good from God, and not trouble?"

In all this, Job did not sin in what he said.

¹¹When Job's three friends, Eliphaz the Temanite, Bildad the Shuhite and Zophar the Naamathite, heard about all the troubles that had come upon him, they set out from their homes and met together by agreement to go and sympathize with him and comfort him. ¹²When they saw him from a distance, they could hardly recognize him; they began to weep aloud, and they tore their robes and sprinkled dust on their heads. ¹³Then they sat on the ground with him for seven days and seven nights. No one said a word to him, because they saw how great his suffering was.

Job Speaks

3 After this, Job opened his mouth and cursed the day of his birth. ²He said:

³ "May the day of my birth perish,
    and the night that said, 'A boy is
        conceived!'
⁴ That day — may it turn to darkness;
    may God above not care about it;
    may no light shine on it.
⁵ May gloom and utter darkness claim it
        once more;
    may a cloud settle over it;
    may blackness overwhelm it.
⁶ That night — may thick darkness
        seize it;
    may it not be included among the
        days of the year
    nor be entered in any of the
        months.
⁷ May that night be barren;
    may no shout of joy be heard in it.
⁸ May those who curse days*b* curse that
        day,
    those who are ready to rouse
        Leviathan.
⁹ May its morning stars become dark;
    may it wait for daylight in vain
    and not see the first rays of dawn,
¹⁰ for it did not shut the doors of the
        womb on me
    to hide trouble from my eyes.

¹¹ "Why did I not perish at birth,
    and die as I came from the womb?
¹² Why were there knees to receive me
    and breasts that I might be nursed?
¹³ For now I would be lying down in
        peace;
    I would be asleep and at rest
¹⁴ with kings and rulers of the earth,
    who built for themselves places now
        lying in ruins,
¹⁵ with princes who had gold,
    who filled their houses with silver.
¹⁶ Or why was I not hidden away in the
        ground like a stillborn child,

---

a 10 The Hebrew word rendered *foolish* denotes moral deficiency.   *b 8* Or *curse the sea*

like an infant who never saw the light
of day?
17 There the wicked cease from turmoil,
and there the weary are at rest.
18 Captives also enjoy their ease;
they no longer hear the slave driver's
shout.
19 The small and the great are there,
and the slaves are freed from their
owners.

20 "Why is light given to those in misery,
and life to the bitter of soul,
21 to those who long for death that does
not come,
who search for it more than for
hidden treasure,
22 who are filled with gladness
and rejoice when they reach the grave?
23 Why is life given to a man
whose way is hidden,
whom God has hedged in?
24 For sighing has become my daily food;
my groans pour out like water.
25 What I feared has come upon me;
what I dreaded has happened to me.
26 I have no peace, no quietness;
I have no rest, but only turmoil."

Eliphaz

4 Then Eliphaz the Temanite replied:

2 "If someone ventures a word with you,
will you be impatient?
But who can keep from speaking?
3 Think how you have instructed many,
how you have strengthened feeble
hands.
4 Your words have supported those who
stumbled;
you have strengthened faltering
knees.
5 But now trouble comes to you, and you
are discouraged;
it strikes you, and you are dismayed.
6 Should not your piety be your
confidence
and your blameless ways your hope?

7 "Consider now: Who, being innocent,
has ever perished?
Where were the upright ever
destroyed?
8 As I have observed, those who plow evil
and those who sow trouble reap it.
9 At the breath of God they perish;
at the blast of his anger they are no
more.
10 The lions may roar and growl,
yet the teeth of the great lions are
broken.
11 The lion perishes for lack of prey,
and the cubs of the lioness are
scattered.

12 "A word was secretly brought to me,
my ears caught a whisper of it.
13 Amid disquieting dreams in the night,
when deep sleep falls on people,
14 fear and trembling seized me
and made all my bones shake.
15 A spirit glided past my face,
and the hair on my body stood on
end.
16 It stopped,
but I could not tell what it was.
A form stood before my eyes,
and I heard a hushed voice:
17 'Can a mortal be more righteous than
God?
Can even a strong man be more pure
than his Maker?
18 If God places no trust in his servants,
if he charges his angels with error,
19 how much more those who live in
houses of clay,
whose foundations are in the dust,
who are crushed more readily than a
moth!
20 Between dawn and dusk they are
broken to pieces;
unnoticed, they perish forever.
21 Are not the cords of their tent pulled up,
so that they die without wisdom?'

5 "Call if you will, but who will
answer you?
To which of the holy ones will you
turn?

²Resentment kills a fool,
    and envy slays the simple.
³I myself have seen a fool taking root,
    but suddenly his house was cursed.
⁴His children are far from safety,
    crushed in court without a defender.
⁵The hungry consume his harvest,
    taking it even from among thorns,
    and the thirsty pant after his wealth.
⁶For hardship does not spring from the
        soil,
    nor does trouble sprout from the
        ground.
⁷Yet man is born to trouble
    as surely as sparks fly upward.

⁸"But if I were you, I would appeal to
        God;
    I would lay my cause before him.
⁹He performs wonders that cannot be
        fathomed,
    miracles that cannot be counted.
¹⁰He provides rain for the earth;
    he sends water on the countryside.
¹¹The lowly he sets on high,
    and those who mourn are lifted to
        safety.
¹²He thwarts the plans of the crafty,
    so that their hands achieve no
        success.
¹³He catches the wise in their craftiness,
    and the schemes of the wily are swept
        away.
¹⁴Darkness comes upon them in the
        daytime;
    at noon they grope as in the night.
¹⁵He saves the needy from the sword in
        their mouth;
    he saves them from the clutches of
        the powerful.
¹⁶So the poor have hope,
    and injustice shuts its mouth.

¹⁷"Blessed is the one whom God corrects;
    so do not despise the discipline of the
        Almighty.ᵃ
¹⁸For he wounds, but he also binds up;
    he injures, but his hands also heal.

¹⁹From six calamities he will rescue you;
    in seven no harm will touch you.
²⁰In famine he will deliver you from
        death,
    and in battle from the stroke of the
        sword.
²¹You will be protected from the lash of
        the tongue,
    and need not fear when destruction
        comes.
²²You will laugh at destruction and famine,
    and need not fear the wild animals.
²³For you will have a covenant with the
        stones of the field,
    and the wild animals will be at peace
        with you.
²⁴You will know that your tent is secure;
    you will take stock of your property
        and find nothing missing.
²⁵You will know that your children will
        be many,
    and your descendants like the grass
        of the earth.
²⁶You will come to the grave in full vigor,
    like sheaves gathered in season.

²⁷"We have examined this, and it is true.
    So hear it and apply it to yourself."

Job

6 Then Job replied:

²"If only my anguish could be
        weighed
    and all my misery be placed on the
        scales!
³It would surely outweigh the sand of the
        seas—
    no wonder my words have been
        impetuous.
⁴The arrows of the Almighty are in me,
    my spirit drinks in their poison;
    God's terrors are marshaled against
        me.
⁵Does a wild donkey bray when it has
        grass,
    or an ox bellow when it has fodder?

ᵃ 17 Hebrew *Shaddai*; here and throughout Job

6 Is tasteless food eaten without salt,
    or is there flavor in the sap of the
        mallow*a*?
7 I refuse to touch it;
    such food makes me ill.

8 "Oh, that I might have my request,
    that God would grant what I hope for,
9 that God would be willing to crush me,
    to let loose his hand and cut off my
        life!
10 Then I would still have this
        consolation —
    my joy in unrelenting pain —
    that I had not denied the words of the
        Holy One.

11 "What strength do I have, that I should
        still hope?
    What prospects, that I should be
        patient?
12 Do I have the strength of stone?
    Is my flesh bronze?
13 Do I have any power to help myself,
    now that success has been driven
        from me?

14 "Anyone who withholds kindness from
        a friend
    forsakes the fear of the Almighty.
15 But my brothers are as undependable as
        intermittent streams,
    as the streams that overflow
16 when darkened by thawing ice
    and swollen with melting snow,
17 but that stop flowing in the dry season,
    and in the heat vanish from their
        channels.
18 Caravans turn aside from their routes;
    they go off into the wasteland and
        perish.
19 The caravans of Tema look for water,
    the traveling merchants of Sheba
        look in hope.
20 They are distressed, because they had
        been confident;
    they arrive there, only to be
        disappointed.

21 Now you too have proved to be of no
        help;
    you see something dreadful and are
        afraid.
22 Have I ever said, 'Give something on
        my behalf,
    pay a ransom for me from your
        wealth,
23 deliver me from the hand of the enemy,
    rescue me from the clutches of the
        ruthless'?

24 "Teach me, and I will be quiet;
    show me where I have been wrong.
25 How painful are honest words!
    But what do your arguments prove?
26 Do you mean to correct what I say,
    and treat my desperate words as wind?
27 You would even cast lots for the
        fatherless
    and barter away your friend.

28 "But now be so kind as to look at me.
    Would I lie to your face?
29 Relent, do not be unjust;
    reconsider, for my integrity is at
        stake.*b*
30 Is there any wickedness on my lips?
    Can my mouth not discern malice?

7 "Do not mortals have hard service
        on earth?
    Are not their days like those of
        hired laborers?
2 Like a slave longing for the evening
        shadows,
    or a hired laborer waiting to be paid,
3 so I have been allotted months of
        futility,
    and nights of misery have been
        assigned to me.
4 When I lie down I think, 'How long
        before I get up?'
    The night drags on, and I toss and
        turn until dawn.
5 My body is clothed with worms and
        scabs,
    my skin is broken and festering.

---

a 6 The meaning of the Hebrew for this phrase is uncertain.   *b 29* Or *my righteousness still stands*

6 "My days are swifter than a weaver's
   shuttle,
   and they come to an end without
      hope.
7 Remember, O God, that my life is but a
   breath;
   my eyes will never see happiness
      again.
8 The eye that now sees me will see me no
   longer;
   you will look for me, but I will be no
      more.
9 As a cloud vanishes and is gone,
   so one who goes down to the grave
      does not return.
10 He will never come to his house again;
   his place will know him no more.

❶
❷
❸

11 "Therefore I will not keep silent;
   I will speak out in the anguish of my
      spirit,
   I will complain in the bitterness of
      my soul.
12 Am I the sea, or the monster of the
   deep,
   that you put me under guard?
13 When I think my bed will comfort me
   and my couch will ease my
      complaint,
14 even then you frighten me with
   dreams
   and terrify me with visions,
15 so that I prefer strangling and death,
   rather than this body of mine.
16 I despise my life; I would not live
   forever.
   Let me alone; my days have no
      meaning.

17 "What is mankind that you make so
   much of them,
   that you give them so much
      attention,
18 that you examine them every morning
   and test them every moment?
19 Will you never look away from me,
   or let me alone even for an instant?

20 If I have sinned, what have I done to
   you,
   you who see everything we do?
   Why have you made me your target?
   Have I become a burden to you?[a]
21 Why do you not pardon my offenses
   and forgive my sins?
   For I will soon lie down in the dust;
   you will search for me, but I will be
      no more."

❹
❺

Bildad

8 Then Bildad the Shuhite replied:

2 "How long will you say such
   things?
   Your words are a blustering wind.
3 Does God pervert justice?
   Does the Almighty pervert what is
      right?
4 When your children sinned against
   him,
   he gave them over to the penalty of
      their sin.
5 But if you will seek God earnestly
   and plead with the Almighty,
6 if you are pure and upright,
   even now he will rouse himself on
      your behalf
   and restore you to your prosperous
      state.
7 Your beginnings will seem humble,
   so prosperous will your future be.

8 "Ask the former generation
   and find out what their ancestors
      learned,
9 for we were born only yesterday and
   know nothing,
   and our days on earth are but a
      shadow.
10 Will they not instruct you and tell you?
   Will they not bring forth words from
      their understanding?
11 Can papyrus grow tall where there is no
   marsh?
   Can reeds thrive without water?

---

a 20 A few manuscripts of the Masoretic Text, an ancient Hebrew scribal tradition and Septuagint; most manuscripts of the Masoretic Text *I have become a burden to myself.*

12 While still growing and uncut,
  they wither more quickly than grass.
13 Such is the destiny of all who forget
  God;
  so perishes the hope of the godless.

14 What they trust in is fragile*a*;
  what they rely on is a spider's web.
15 They lean on the web, but it gives
  way;
  they cling to it, but it does not hold.

---

a 14 The meaning of the Hebrew for this word is uncertain.

MORAL LESSON [*Principle Four*]

For the previous entry in the MORAL lesson, go to Job 33:33 (page 621).

For a discussion of Principles One through Eight and a listing of their related lessons,
go to pages xvii – xliv.

I will not keep silent; I will speak out in the anguish of my spirit,
I will complain in the bitterness of my soul.

JOB 7:11

Principle Four begins our process of "coming clean." It's here that we openly examine and confess our faults to ourselves, to God and to someone else we trust. In the first part of Principle Four we openly examine our lives. We take a MORAL inventory.

The next letter in MORAL is O, which stands for OPEN OURSELVES UP. Remember how, as a child, you would visit the doctor and he'd say "Open wide!" in that funny, sing-song voice? We need to open wide our hearts and minds to release the feelings the pain of our past has blocked or caused us to deny. Denial may have protected us from our negative feelings and repressed our pain for a while, but as the years have slipped by, it has also blocked and prevented our recovery from our hurts, hang-ups and habits. We need to "open wide" to see the real truth.

Once we've seen the truth, we need to express it. In Job 7:11 we find that Job was ready to be honest and open. Perhaps the following questions will help to wake up our feelings and get us started on our inventories. We need to ask ourselves, "What do we feel guilty about?" The first issue that comes to our mind is the one we need to address first in our inventory. Remember the words of Romans 8:1: "There is now no condemnation for those who are in Christ Jesus."

The next question we need to ask is, "What or who do we resent?" Resentment results from burying our hurts. If resentments are suppressed and left to fester, they cause anger, frustration and depression. What we don't talk out creatively, we act out destructively.

Another big question we need to openly ask as part of this principle is, "What are our fears?" Fear prevents us from expressing ourselves honestly and taking a truthful moral inventory. Joshua 1:9 asks, "Have I not commanded you? Be strong and courageous. Do not be afraid; do not be discouraged, for the LORD your God will be with you wherever you go."

These questions are only the beginning of our inventory, and we need to consciously remind ourselves not to become discouraged as we undertake this painful task. Remember: The truth doesn't change; only our feelings do.

The next letter in MORAL is *R*. Go to Isaiah 40:29 (page 850).

¹⁶They are like a well-watered plant in the
        sunshine,
    spreading its shoots over the garden;
¹⁷it entwines its roots around a pile of
        rocks
    and looks for a place among the
        stones.
¹⁸But when it is torn from its spot,
    that place disowns it and says, 'I
        never saw you.'
¹⁹Surely its life withers away,
    and*a* from the soil other plants grow.

²⁰"Surely God does not reject one who is
        blameless
    or strengthen the hands of evildoers.
²¹He will yet fill your mouth with
        laughter
    and your lips with shouts of joy.
²²Your enemies will be clothed in shame,
    and the tents of the wicked will be no
        more."

Job

9

    Then Job replied:

²"Indeed, I know that this is true.
    But how can mere mortals prove
        their innocence before God?
³Though they wished to dispute with
        him,
    they could not answer him one time
        out of a thousand.
⁴His wisdom is profound, his power is
        vast.
    Who has resisted him and come out
        unscathed?
⁵He moves mountains without their
        knowing it
    and overturns them in his anger.
⁶He shakes the earth from its place
    and makes its pillars tremble.
⁷He speaks to the sun and it does not
        shine;
    he seals off the light of the stars.
⁸He alone stretches out the heavens
    and treads on the waves of the sea.

⁹He is the Maker of the Bear*b* and Orion,
    the Pleiades and the constellations of
        the south.
¹⁰He performs wonders that cannot be
        fathomed,
    miracles that cannot be counted.
¹¹When he passes me, I cannot see him;
    when he goes by, I cannot perceive
        him.
¹²If he snatches away, who can stop him?
    Who can say to him, 'What are you
        doing?'
¹³God does not restrain his anger;
    even the cohorts of Rahab cowered at
        his feet.

¹⁴"How then can I dispute with him?
    How can I find words to argue with
        him?
¹⁵Though I were innocent, I could not
        answer him;
    I could only plead with my Judge for
        mercy.
¹⁶Even if I summoned him and he
        responded,
    I do not believe he would give me a
        hearing.
¹⁷He would crush me with a storm
    and multiply my wounds for no
        reason.
¹⁸He would not let me catch my breath
    but would overwhelm me with
        misery.
¹⁹If it is a matter of strength, he is
        mighty!
    And if it is a matter of justice, who
        can challenge him*c*?
²⁰Even if I were innocent, my mouth
        would condemn me;
    if I were blameless, it would
        pronounce me guilty.

²¹"Although I am blameless,
    I have no concern for myself;
    I despise my own life.
²²It is all the same; that is why I say,
    'He destroys both the blameless and
        the wicked.'

---

a 19 Or *Surely all the joy it has / is that*   *b* 9 Or *of Leo*   *c* 19 See Septuagint; Hebrew *me.*

²³ When a scourge brings sudden death,
  he mocks the despair of the innocent.
²⁴ When a land falls into the hands of the
      wicked,
  he blindfolds its judges.
  If it is not he, then who is it?

²⁵ "My days are swifter than a runner;
  they fly away without a glimpse of
      joy.
²⁶ They skim past like boats of papyrus,
  like eagles swooping down on their
      prey.
²⁷ If I say, 'I will forget my complaint,
  I will change my expression, and
      smile,'
²⁸ I still dread all my sufferings,
  for I know you will not hold me
      innocent.
²⁹ Since I am already found guilty,
  why should I struggle in vain?
³⁰ Even if I washed myself with soap
  and my hands with cleansing
      powder,
³¹ you would plunge me into a slime pit
  so that even my clothes would detest
      me.

³² "He is not a mere mortal like me that I
      might answer him,
  that we might confront each other in
      court.
³³ If only there were someone to mediate
      between us,
  someone to bring us together,
³⁴ someone to remove God's rod from me,
  so that his terror would frighten me
      no more.
³⁵ Then I would speak up without fear of
      him,
  but as it now stands with me, I
      cannot.

10 "I loathe my very life;
      therefore I will give free rein to
      my complaint
  and speak out in the bitterness of my
      soul.

² I say to God: Do not declare me guilty,
  but tell me what charges you have
      against me.
³ Does it please you to oppress me,
  to spurn the work of your hands,
  while you smile on the plans of the
      wicked?
⁴ Do you have eyes of flesh?
  Do you see as a mortal sees?
⁵ Are your days like those of a mortal
  or your years like those of a strong
      man,
⁶ that you must search out my faults
  and probe after my sin —
⁷ though you know that I am not guilty
  and that no one can rescue me from
      your hand?

⁸ "Your hands shaped me and made me.
  Will you now turn and destroy me?
⁹ Remember that you molded me like
      clay.
  Will you now turn me to dust again?
¹⁰ Did you not pour me out like milk
  and curdle me like cheese,
¹¹ clothe me with skin and flesh
  and knit me together with bones and
      sinews?
¹² You gave me life and showed me
      kindness,
  and in your providence watched over
      my spirit.

¹³ "But this is what you concealed in your
      heart,
  and I know that this was in your mind:
¹⁴ If I sinned, you would be watching me
  and would not let my offense go
      unpunished.
¹⁵ If I am guilty — woe to me!
  Even if I am innocent, I cannot lift
      my head,
  for I am full of shame
  and drowned in*a* my affliction.
¹⁶ If I hold my head high, you stalk me
      like a lion
  and again display your awesome
      power against me.

---

a 15 Or *and aware of*

¹⁷You bring new witnesses against me
    and increase your anger toward me;
    your forces come against me wave
        upon wave.

¹⁸"Why then did you bring me out of the
        womb?
    I wish I had died before any eye saw
        me.
¹⁹If only I had never come into being,
    or had been carried straight from the
        womb to the grave!
²⁰Are not my few days almost over?
    Turn away from me so I can have a
        moment's joy
²¹before I go to the place of no return,
    to the land of gloom and utter
        darkness,
²²to the land of deepest night,
    of utter darkness and disorder,
    where even the light is like darkness."

Zophar

11

Then Zophar the Naamathite
replied:

²"Are all these words to go unanswered?
    Is this talker to be vindicated?
³Will your idle talk reduce others to
        silence?
    Will no one rebuke you when you
        mock?
⁴You say to God, 'My beliefs are flawless
    and I am pure in your sight.'
⁵Oh, how I wish that God would speak,
    that he would open his lips against
        you
⁶and disclose to you the secrets of
        wisdom,
    for true wisdom has two sides.
    Know this: God has even forgotten
        some of your sin.

⁷"Can you fathom the mysteries of God?
    Can you probe the limits of the
        Almighty?
⁸They are higher than the heavens
        above—what can you do?

They are deeper than the depths
    below—what can you know?
⁹Their measure is longer than the earth
    and wider than the sea.

¹⁰"If he comes along and confines you in
        prison
    and convenes a court, who can
        oppose him?
¹¹Surely he recognizes deceivers;
    and when he sees evil, does he not
        take note?
¹²But the witless can no more become
        wise
    than a wild donkey's colt can be born
        human.ᵃ

¹³"Yet if you devote your heart to him
    and stretch out your hands to him,
¹⁴if you put away the sin that is in your
        hand
    and allow no evil to dwell in your
        tent,
¹⁵then, free of fault, you will lift up your
        face;
    you will stand firm and without fear.
¹⁶You will surely forget your trouble,
    recalling it only as waters gone by.
¹⁷Life will be brighter than noonday,
    and darkness will become like
        morning.
¹⁸You will be secure, because there is
        hope;
    you will look about you and take
        your rest in safety.
¹⁹You will lie down, with no one to make
        you afraid,
    and many will court your favor.
²⁰But the eyes of the wicked will fail,
    and escape will elude them;
    their hope will become a dying gasp."

Job

12

Then Job replied:

²"Doubtless you are the only
people who matter,
    and wisdom will die with you!

ᵃ 12 Or wild donkey can be born tame

3 But I have a mind as well as you;
    I am not inferior to you.
    Who does not know all these things?

4 "I have become a laughingstock to my
        friends,
    though I called on God and he
        answered —
    a mere laughingstock, though
        righteous and blameless!
5 Those who are at ease have contempt
        for misfortune
    as the fate of those whose feet are
        slipping.
6 The tents of marauders are undisturbed,
    and those who provoke God are
        secure —
    those God has in his hand.*a*

7 "But ask the animals, and they will
        teach you,
    or the birds in the sky, and they will
        tell you;
8 or speak to the earth, and it will teach
        you,
    or let the fish in the sea inform you.
9 Which of all these does not know
    that the hand of the Lord has done
        this?
10 In his hand is the life of every creature
    and the breath of all mankind.
11 Does not the ear test words
    as the tongue tastes food?
12 Is not wisdom found among the aged?
    Does not long life bring
        understanding?

13 "To God belong wisdom and power;
    counsel and understanding are his.
14 What he tears down cannot be rebuilt;
    those he imprisons cannot be
        released.
15 If he holds back the waters, there is
        drought;
    if he lets them loose, they devastate
        the land.
16 To him belong strength and insight;
    both deceived and deceiver are his.

17 He leads rulers away stripped
    and makes fools of judges.
18 He takes off the shackles put on by kings
    and ties a loincloth*b* around their
        waist.
19 He leads priests away stripped
    and overthrows officials long
        established.
20 He silences the lips of trusted advisers
    and takes away the discernment of
        elders.
21 He pours contempt on nobles
    and disarms the mighty.
22 He reveals the deep things of darkness
    and brings utter darkness into the
        light.
23 He makes nations great, and destroys
        them;
    he enlarges nations, and disperses
        them.
24 He deprives the leaders of the earth of
        their reason;
    he makes them wander in a trackless
        waste.
25 They grope in darkness with no light;
    he makes them stagger like
        drunkards.

13

"My eyes have seen all this,
    my ears have heard and
    understood it.
2 What you know, I also know;
    I am not inferior to you.
3 But I desire to speak to the Almighty
    and to argue my case with God.
4 You, however, smear me with lies;
    you are worthless physicians, all of
        you!
5 If only you would be altogether silent!
    For you, that would be wisdom.
6 Hear now my argument;
    listen to the pleas of my lips.
7 Will you speak wickedly on God's
        behalf?
    Will you speak deceitfully for him?
8 Will you show him partiality?
    Will you argue the case for God?

---

a 6 Or *those whose god is in their own hand*   *b* 18 Or *shackles of kings / and ties a belt*

9 Would it turn out well if he examined
you?
    Could you deceive him as you might
    deceive a mortal?
10 He would surely call you to account
    if you secretly showed partiality.
11 Would not his splendor terrify you?
    Would not the dread of him fall on
    you?
12 Your maxims are proverbs of ashes;
    your defenses are defenses of clay.

13 "Keep silent and let me speak;
    then let come to me what may.
14 Why do I put myself in jeopardy
    and take my life in my hands?
15 Though he slay me, yet will I hope in him;
    I will surely[a] defend my ways to his
    face.
16 Indeed, this will turn out for my
    deliverance,
    for no godless person would dare
    come before him!
17 Listen carefully to what I say;
    let my words ring in your ears.
18 Now that I have prepared my case,
    I know I will be vindicated.
19 Can anyone bring charges against me?
    If so, I will be silent and die.

20 "Only grant me these two things, God,
    and then I will not hide from you:
21 Withdraw your hand far from me,
    and stop frightening me with your
    terrors.
22 Then summon me and I will answer,
    or let me speak, and you reply to me.
23 How many wrongs and sins have I
    committed?
    Show me my offense and my sin.
24 Why do you hide your face
    and consider me your enemy?
25 Will you torment a windblown leaf?
    Will you chase after dry chaff?
26 For you write down bitter things
    against me
    and make me reap the sins of my
    youth.

27 You fasten my feet in shackles;
    you keep close watch on all my
    paths
    by putting marks on the soles of my
    feet.

28 "So man wastes away like something
    rotten,
    like a garment eaten by moths.

14 "Mortals, born of woman,
    are of few days and full of
    trouble.
2 They spring up like flowers and wither
    away;
    like fleeting shadows, they do not
    endure.
3 Do you fix your eye on them?
    Will you bring them[b] before you for
    judgment?
4 Who can bring what is pure from the
    impure?
    No one!
5 A person's days are determined;
    you have decreed the number of his
    months
    and have set limits he cannot exceed.
6 So look away from him and let him
    alone,
    till he has put in his time like a hired
    laborer.

7 "At least there is hope for a tree:
    If it is cut down, it will sprout again,
    and its new shoots will not fail.
8 Its roots may grow old in the ground
    and its stump die in the soil,
9 yet at the scent of water it will bud
    and put forth shoots like a plant.
10 But a man dies and is laid low;
    he breathes his last and is no more.
11 As the water of a lake dries up
    or a riverbed becomes parched and
    dry,
12 so he lies down and does not rise;
    till the heavens are no more, people
    will not awake
    or be roused from their sleep.

---

a 15 Or He will surely slay me; I have no hope — / yet I will   b 3 Septuagint, Vulgate and Syriac; Hebrew me

13 "If only you would hide me in the grave
    and conceal me till your anger has
        passed!
  If only you would set me a time
    and then remember me!
14 If someone dies, will they live again?
    All the days of my hard service
    I will wait for my renewal*a* to come.
15 You will call and I will answer you;
    you will long for the creature your
        hands have made.
16 Surely then you will count my steps
    but not keep track of my sin.
17 My offenses will be sealed up in a bag;
    you will cover over my sin.

18 "But as a mountain erodes and crumbles
    and as a rock is moved from its place,
19 as water wears away stones
    and torrents wash away the soil,
    so you destroy a person's hope.
20 You overpower them once for all, and
        they are gone;
    you change their countenance and
        send them away.
21 If their children are honored, they do
        not know it;
    if their offspring are brought low,
        they do not see it.
22 They feel but the pain of their own
        bodies
    and mourn only for themselves."

Eliphaz

15

Then Eliphaz the Temanite replied:

2 "Would a wise person answer with
        empty notions
    or fill their belly with the hot east
        wind?
3 Would they argue with useless words,
    with speeches that have no value?
4 But you even undermine piety
    and hinder devotion to God.
5 Your sin prompts your mouth;
    you adopt the tongue of the crafty.

6 Your own mouth condemns you, not
        mine;
    your own lips testify against you.

7 "Are you the first man ever born?
    Were you brought forth before the
        hills?
8 Do you listen in on God's council?
    Do you have a monopoly on wisdom?
9 What do you know that we do not
        know?
    What insights do you have that we do
        not have?
10 The gray-haired and the aged are on
        our side,
    men even older than your father.
11 Are God's consolations not enough for
        you,
    words spoken gently to you?
12 Why has your heart carried you away,
    and why do your eyes flash,
13 so that you vent your rage against God
    and pour out such words from your
        mouth?

14 "What are mortals, that they could be
        pure,
    or those born of woman, that they
        could be righteous?
15 If God places no trust in his holy ones,
    if even the heavens are not pure in
        his eyes,
16 how much less mortals, who are vile
        and corrupt,
    who drink up evil like water!

17 "Listen to me and I will explain to you;
    let me tell you what I have seen,
18 what the wise have declared,
    hiding nothing received from their
        ancestors
19 (to whom alone the land was given
    when no foreigners moved among
        them):
20 All his days the wicked man suffers
        torment,
    the ruthless man through all the
        years stored up for him.

---

a 14 Or *release*

21 Terrifying sounds fill his ears;
  when all seems well, marauders
    attack him.
22 He despairs of escaping the realm of
    darkness;
  he is marked for the sword.
23 He wanders about for food like a
    vulture;
  he knows the day of darkness is at
    hand.
24 Distress and anguish fill him with
    terror;
  troubles overwhelm him, like a king
    poised to attack,
25 because he shakes his fist at God
  and vaunts himself against the
    Almighty,
26 defiantly charging against him
  with a thick, strong shield.

27 "Though his face is covered with fat
  and his waist bulges with flesh,
28 he will inhabit ruined towns
  and houses where no one lives,
  houses crumbling to rubble.
29 He will no longer be rich and his wealth
    will not endure,
  nor will his possessions spread over
    the land.
30 He will not escape the darkness;
  a flame will wither his shoots,
  and the breath of God's mouth will
    carry him away.
31 Let him not deceive himself by trusting
    what is worthless,
  for he will get nothing in return.
32 Before his time he will wither,
  and his branches will not flourish.
33 He will be like a vine stripped of its
    unripe grapes,
  like an olive tree shedding its
    blossoms.
34 For the company of the godless will be
    barren,
  and fire will consume the tents of
    those who love bribes.
35 They conceive trouble and give birth to
    evil;
  their womb fashions deceit."

Job

16

Then Job replied:

2 "I have heard many things like
    these;
  you are miserable comforters, all of
    you!
3 Will your long-winded speeches never
    end?
  What ails you that you keep on
    arguing?
4 I also could speak like you,
  if you were in my place;
  I could make fine speeches against you
  and shake my head at you.
5 But my mouth would encourage you;
  comfort from my lips would bring
    you relief.

6 "Yet if I speak, my pain is not relieved;
  and if I refrain, it does not go away.
7 Surely, God, you have worn me out;
  you have devastated my entire
    household.
8 You have shriveled me up — and it has
    become a witness;
  my gauntness rises up and testifies
    against me.
9 God assails me and tears me in his
    anger
  and gnashes his teeth at me;
  my opponent fastens on me his
    piercing eyes.
10 People open their mouths to jeer at me;
  they strike my cheek in scorn
  and unite together against me.
11 God has turned me over to the ungodly
  and thrown me into the clutches of
    the wicked.
12 All was well with me, but he shattered
    me;
  he seized me by the neck and crushed
    me.
  He has made me his target;
13   his archers surround me.
  Without pity, he pierces my kidneys
  and spills my gall on the ground.
14 Again and again he bursts upon me;
  he rushes at me like a warrior.

¹⁵"I have sewed sackcloth over my skin
  and buried my brow in the dust.
¹⁶My face is red with weeping,
  dark shadows ring my eyes;
¹⁷yet my hands have been free of violence
  and my prayer is pure.

¹⁸"Earth, do not cover my blood;
  may my cry never be laid to rest!
¹⁹Even now my witness is in heaven;
  my advocate is on high.
²⁰My intercessor is my friend^a
  as my eyes pour out tears to God;
²¹on behalf of a man he pleads with God
  as one pleads for a friend.

²²"Only a few years will pass
  before I take the path of no return.

17

¹My spirit is broken,
  my days are cut short,
  the grave awaits me.
²Surely mockers surround me;
  my eyes must dwell on their
  hostility.

³"Give me, O God, the pledge you
  demand.
  Who else will put up security
  for me?
⁴You have closed their minds to
  understanding;
  therefore you will not let them
  triumph.
⁵If anyone denounces their friends for
  reward,
  the eyes of their children will fail.

⁶"God has made me a byword to
  everyone,
  a man in whose face people spit.
⁷My eyes have grown dim with grief;
  my whole frame is but a shadow.
⁸The upright are appalled at this;
  the innocent are aroused against the
  ungodly.
⁹Nevertheless, the righteous will hold to
  their ways,
  and those with clean hands will grow
  stronger.

¹⁰"But come on, all of you, try again!
  I will not find a wise man among you.
¹¹My days have passed, my plans are
  shattered.
  Yet the desires of my heart
¹²turn night into day;
  in the face of the darkness light is
  near.
¹³If the only home I hope for is the grave,
  if I spread out my bed in the realm of
  darkness,
¹⁴if I say to corruption, 'You are my
  father,'
  and to the worm, 'My mother' or 'My
  sister,'
¹⁵where then is my hope—
  who can see any hope for me?
¹⁶Will it go down to the gates of death?
  Will we descend together into the
  dust?"

Bildad

18

Then Bildad the Shuhite replied:

²"When will you end these speeches?
  Be sensible, and then we can talk.
³Why are we regarded as cattle
  and considered stupid in your sight?
⁴You who tear yourself to pieces in your
  anger,
  is the earth to be abandoned for your
  sake?
  Or must the rocks be moved from
  their place?

⁵"The lamp of a wicked man is snuffed
  out;
  the flame of his fire stops burning.
⁶The light in his tent becomes dark;
  the lamp beside him goes out.
⁷The vigor of his step is weakened;
  his own schemes throw him down.
⁸His feet thrust him into a net;
  he wanders into its mesh.
⁹A trap seizes him by the heel;
  a snare holds him fast.

---

^a 20 Or *My friends treat me with scorn*

¹⁰ A noose is hidden for him on the
      ground;
   a trap lies in his path.
¹¹ Terrors startle him on every side
   and dog his every step.
¹² Calamity is hungry for him;
   disaster is ready for him when he
      falls.
¹³ It eats away parts of his skin;
   death's firstborn devours his limbs.
¹⁴ He is torn from the security of his tent
   and marched off to the king of
      terrors.
¹⁵ Fire resides*ᵃ* in his tent;
   burning sulfur is scattered over his
      dwelling.
¹⁶ His roots dry up below
   and his branches wither above.
¹⁷ The memory of him perishes from the
      earth;
   he has no name in the land.
¹⁸ He is driven from light into the realm
      of darkness
   and is banished from the world.
¹⁹ He has no offspring or descendants
      among his people,
   no survivor where once he lived.
²⁰ People of the west are appalled at his
      fate;
   those of the east are seized with
      horror.
²¹ Surely such is the dwelling of an evil
      man;
   such is the place of one who does not
      know God."

Job

19

Then Job replied:
² "How long will you torment
      me
   and crush me with words?
³ Ten times now you have reproached
      me;
   shamelessly you attack me.
⁴ If it is true that I have gone astray,
   my error remains my concern alone.

⁵ If indeed you would exalt yourselves
      above me
   and use my humiliation against me,
⁶ then know that God has wronged me
   and drawn his net around me.

⁷ "Though I cry, 'Violence!' I get no
      response;
   though I call for help, there is no
      justice.
⁸ He has blocked my way so I cannot
      pass;
   he has shrouded my paths in
      darkness.
⁹ He has stripped me of my honor
   and removed the crown from my
      head.
¹⁰ He tears me down on every side till I
      am gone;
   he uproots my hope like a tree.
¹¹ His anger burns against me;
   he counts me among his enemies.
¹² His troops advance in force;
   they build a siege ramp against me
   and encamp around my tent.

¹³ "He has alienated my family from me;
   my acquaintances are completely
      estranged from me.
¹⁴ My relatives have gone away;
   my closest friends have forgotten
      me.
¹⁵ My guests and my female servants
      count me a foreigner;
   they look on me as on a stranger.
¹⁶ I summon my servant, but he does not
      answer,
   though I beg him with my own
      mouth.
¹⁷ My breath is offensive to my wife;
   I am loathsome to my own family.
¹⁸ Even the little boys scorn me;
   when I appear, they ridicule me.
¹⁹ All my intimate friends detest me;
   those I love have turned against me.
²⁰ I am nothing but skin and bones;
   I have escaped only by the skin of my
      teeth.*ᵇ*

ᵃ 15 Or *Nothing he had remains*   *ᵇ 20* Or *only by my gums*

21 "Have pity on me, my friends, have pity,
   for the hand of God has struck me.
22 Why do you pursue me as God does?
   Will you never get enough of my flesh?

23 "Oh, that my words were recorded,
   that they were written on a scroll,
24 that they were inscribed with an iron
   tool on^a lead,
   or engraved in rock forever!
25 I know that my redeemer^b lives,
   and that in the end he will stand on
   the earth.^{c}
26 And after my skin has been destroyed,
   yet^d in^e my flesh I will see God;
27 I myself will see him
   with my own eyes — I, and not
   another.
   How my heart yearns within me!

28 "If you say, 'How we will hound him,
   since the root of the trouble lies in
   him,'^{f}
29 you should fear the sword yourselves;
   for wrath will bring punishment by
   the sword,
   and then you will know that there is
   judgment.^{g}

Zophar

20 Then Zophar the Naamathite
   replied:

2 "My troubled thoughts prompt me to
   answer
   because I am greatly disturbed.
3 I hear a rebuke that dishonors me,
   and my understanding inspires me to
   reply.

4 "Surely you know how it has been from
   of old,
   ever since mankind^h was placed on
   the earth,
5 that the mirth of the wicked is brief,
   the joy of the godless lasts but a
   moment.

6 Though the pride of the godless person
   reaches to the heavens
   and his head touches the clouds,
7 he will perish forever, like his own dung;
   those who have seen him will say,
   'Where is he?'
8 Like a dream he flies away, no more to
   be found,
   banished like a vision of the night.
9 The eye that saw him will not see him
   again;
   his place will look on him no more.
10 His children must make amends to the
   poor;
   his own hands must give back his
   wealth.
11 The youthful vigor that fills his bones
   will lie with him in the dust.

12 "Though evil is sweet in his mouth
   and he hides it under his tongue,
13 though he cannot bear to let it go
   and lets it linger in his mouth,
14 yet his food will turn sour in his
   stomach;
   it will become the venom of serpents
   within him.
15 He will spit out the riches he swallowed;
   God will make his stomach vomit
   them up.
16 He will suck the poison of serpents;
   the fangs of an adder will kill him.
17 He will not enjoy the streams,
   the rivers flowing with honey and
   cream.
18 What he toiled for he must give back
   uneaten;
   he will not enjoy the profit from his
   trading.
19 For he has oppressed the poor and left
   them destitute;
   he has seized houses he did not build.

20 "Surely he will have no respite from his
   craving;
   he cannot save himself by his treasure.

---

^{a} 24 Or and ^{b} 25 Or vindicator ^{c} 25 Or on my grave ^{d} 26 Or And after I awake, / though this body has
been destroyed, / then ^{e} 26 Or destroyed, / apart from ^{f} 28 Many Hebrew manuscripts, Septuagint and
Vulgate; most Hebrew manuscripts me ^{g} 29 Or sword, / that you may come to know the Almighty ^{h} 4 Or Adam

21 Nothing is left for him to devour;
　　his prosperity will not endure.
22 In the midst of his plenty, distress will
　　　overtake him;
　　the full force of misery will come
　　　upon him.
23 When he has filled his belly,
　　God will vent his burning anger
　　　against him
　　and rain down his blows on him.
24 Though he flees from an iron weapon,
　　a bronze-tipped arrow pierces him.
25 He pulls it out of his back,
　　the gleaming point out of his liver.
　　Terrors will come over him;
26 　total darkness lies in wait for his
　　　treasures.
　　A fire unfanned will consume him
　　　and devour what is left in his tent.
27 The heavens will expose his guilt;
　　the earth will rise up against him.
28 A flood will carry off his house,
　　rushing waters*a* on the day of God's
　　　wrath.
29 Such is the fate God allots the wicked,
　　the heritage appointed for them by
　　　God."

Job

21

Then Job replied:

2 "Listen carefully to my words;
　　let this be the consolation you give
　　me.
3 Bear with me while I speak,
　　and after I have spoken, mock on.

4 "Is my complaint directed to a human
　　being?
　　Why should I not be impatient?
5 Look at me and be appalled;
　　clap your hand over your mouth.
6 When I think about this, I am terrified;
　　trembling seizes my body.
7 Why do the wicked live on,
　　growing old and increasing in
　　　power?

8 They see their children established
　　around them,
　　their offspring before their eyes.
9 Their homes are safe and free from fear;
　　the rod of God is not on them.
10 Their bulls never fail to breed;
　　their cows calve and do not miscarry.
11 They send forth their children as a flock;
　　their little ones dance about.
12 They sing to the music of timbrel and
　　lyre;
　　they make merry to the sound of the
　　　pipe.
13 They spend their years in prosperity
　　and go down to the grave in peace.*b*
14 Yet they say to God, 'Leave us alone!
　　We have no desire to know your ways.
15 Who is the Almighty, that we should
　　serve him?
　　What would we gain by praying to
　　　him?'
16 But their prosperity is not in their own
　　hands,
　　so I stand aloof from the plans of the
　　　wicked.

17 "Yet how often is the lamp of the
　　wicked snuffed out?
　　How often does calamity come upon
　　them,
　　the fate God allots in his anger?
18 How often are they like straw before the
　　wind,
　　like chaff swept away by a gale?
19 It is said, 'God stores up the
　　punishment of the wicked for
　　their children.'
　　Let him repay the wicked, so that
　　they themselves will experience
　　it!
20 Let their own eyes see their destruction;
　　let them drink the cup of the wrath
　　of the Almighty.
21 For what do they care about the
　　families they leave behind
　　when their allotted months come to
　　an end?

---

a 28 Or *The possessions in his house will be carried off, / washed away*　　*b* 13 Or *in an instant*

22 "Can anyone teach knowledge to God,
  since he judges even the highest?
23 One person dies in full vigor,
  completely secure and at ease,
24 well nourished in body,*a*
  bones rich with marrow.
25 Another dies in bitterness of soul,
  never having enjoyed anything good.
26 Side by side they lie in the dust,
  and worms cover them both.

27 "I know full well what you are thinking,
  the schemes by which you would
  wrong me.
28 You say, 'Where now is the house of the
  great,
  the tents where the wicked lived?'
29 Have you never questioned those who
  travel?
  Have you paid no regard to their
  accounts —
30 that the wicked are spared from the day
  of calamity,
  that they are delivered from*b* the day
  of wrath?
31 Who denounces their conduct to their
  face?
  Who repays them for what they have
  done?
32 They are carried to the grave,
  and watch is kept over their tombs.
33 The soil in the valley is sweet to them;
  everyone follows after them,
  and a countless throng goes*c* before
  them.

34 "So how can you console me with your
  nonsense?
  Nothing is left of your answers but
  falsehood!"

Eliphaz

22 Then Eliphaz the Temanite replied:

2 "Can a man be of benefit to God?
  Can even a wise person benefit him?

3 What pleasure would it give the
  Almighty if you were righteous?
  What would he gain if your ways
  were blameless?

4 "Is it for your piety that he rebukes
  you
  and brings charges against you?
5 Is not your wickedness great?
  Are not your sins endless?
6 You demanded security from your
  relatives for no reason;
  you stripped people of their clothing,
  leaving them naked.
7 You gave no water to the weary
  and you withheld food from the
  hungry,
8 though you were a powerful man,
  owning land —
  an honored man, living on it.
9 And you sent widows away empty-
  handed
  and broke the strength of the
  fatherless.
10 That is why snares are all around you,
  why sudden peril terrifies you,
11 why it is so dark you cannot see,
  and why a flood of water covers you.

12 "Is not God in the heights of heaven?
  And see how lofty are the highest
  stars!
13 Yet you say, 'What does God know?
  Does he judge through such
  darkness?
14 Thick clouds veil him, so he does not
  see us
  as he goes about in the vaulted
  heavens.'
15 Will you keep to the old path
  that the wicked have trod?
16 They were carried off before their
  time,
  their foundations washed away by a
  flood.
17 They said to God, 'Leave us alone!
  What can the Almighty do to us?'

---

a 24 The meaning of the Hebrew for this word is uncertain.   *b 30* Or *wicked are reserved for the day of calamity, / that they are brought forth to*   *c 33* Or *them, / as a countless throng went*

18 Yet it was he who filled their houses
        with good things,
    so I stand aloof from the plans of the
        wicked.
19 The righteous see their ruin and rejoice;
    the innocent mock them, saying,
20 'Surely our foes are destroyed,
    and fire devours their wealth.'

21 "Submit to God and be at peace with
        him;
    in this way prosperity will come to
        you.
22 Accept instruction from his mouth
    and lay up his words in your heart.
23 If you return to the Almighty, you will
        be restored:
    If you remove wickedness far from
        your tent
24 and assign your nuggets to the dust,
    your gold of Ophir to the rocks in the
        ravines,
25 then the Almighty will be your gold,
    the choicest silver for you.
26 Surely then you will find delight in the
        Almighty
    and will lift up your face to God.
27 You will pray to him, and he will hear
        you,
    and you will fulfill your vows.
28 What you decide on will be done,
    and light will shine on your ways.
29 When people are brought low and you
        say, 'Lift them up!'
    then he will save the downcast.
30 He will deliver even one who is not
        innocent,
    who will be delivered through the
        cleanness of your hands."

Job

23

Then Job replied:

2 "Even today my complaint
    is bitter;
his hand*a* is heavy in spite of*b* my
    groaning.

3 If only I knew where to find him;
    if only I could go to his dwelling!
4 I would state my case before him
    and fill my mouth with arguments.
5 I would find out what he would answer
        me,
    and consider what he would say to
        me.
6 Would he vigorously oppose me?
    No, he would not press charges
        against me.
7 There the upright can establish their
        innocence before him,
    and there I would be delivered
        forever from my judge.

8 "But if I go to the east, he is not there;
    if I go to the west, I do not find him.
9 When he is at work in the north, I do
        not see him;
    when he turns to the south, I catch
        no glimpse of him.
10 But he knows the way that I take;
    when he has tested me, I will come
        forth as gold.
11 My feet have closely followed his
        steps;
    I have kept to his way without
        turning aside.
12 I have not departed from the
        commands of his lips;
    I have treasured the words of his
        mouth more than my daily
        bread.

13 "But he stands alone, and who can
        oppose him?
    He does whatever he pleases.
14 He carries out his decree against me,
    and many such plans he still has in
        store.
15 That is why I am terrified before him;
    when I think of all this, I fear him.
16 God has made my heart faint;
    the Almighty has terrified me.
17 Yet I am not silenced by the darkness,
    by the thick darkness that covers my
        face.

---

a 2 Septuagint and Syriac; Hebrew / *the hand on me*   *b 2* Or *heavy on me in*

24

"Why does the Almighty not
set times for judgment?
Why must those who know
him look in vain for such days?
2 There are those who move boundary
stones;
they pasture flocks they have stolen.
3 They drive away the orphan's donkey
and take the widow's ox in pledge.
4 They thrust the needy from the path
and force all the poor of the land into
hiding.
5 Like wild donkeys in the desert,
the poor go about their labor of
foraging food;
the wasteland provides food for their
children.
6 They gather fodder in the fields
and glean in the vineyards of the
wicked.
7 Lacking clothes, they spend the night
naked;
they have nothing to cover
themselves in the cold.
8 They are drenched by mountain rains
and hug the rocks for lack of shelter.
9 The fatherless child is snatched from
the breast;
the infant of the poor is seized for a
debt.
10 Lacking clothes, they go about naked;
they carry the sheaves, but still go
hungry.
11 They crush olives among the terraces*a*;
they tread the winepresses, yet suffer
thirst.
12 The groans of the dying rise from the
city,
and the souls of the wounded cry out
for help.
But God charges no one with
wrongdoing.

13 "There are those who rebel against the
light,
who do not know its ways
or stay in its paths.
14 When daylight is gone, the murderer
rises up,
kills the poor and needy,
and in the night steals forth like a
thief.
15 The eye of the adulterer watches for dusk;
he thinks, 'No eye will see me,'
and he keeps his face concealed.
16 In the dark, thieves break into houses,
but by day they shut themselves in;
they want nothing to do with the
light.
17 For all of them, midnight is their
morning;
they make friends with the terrors of
darkness.

18 "Yet they are foam on the surface of the
water;
their portion of the land is cursed,
so that no one goes to the vineyards.
19 As heat and drought snatch away the
melted snow,
so the grave snatches away those who
have sinned.
20 The womb forgets them,
the worm feasts on them;
the wicked are no longer remembered
but are broken like a tree.
21 They prey on the barren and childless
woman,
and to the widow they show no
kindness.
22 But God drags away the mighty by his
power;
though they become established,
they have no assurance of life.
23 He may let them rest in a feeling of
security,
but his eyes are on their ways.
24 For a little while they are exalted, and
then they are gone;
they are brought low and gathered up
like all others;
they are cut off like heads of grain.

25 "If this is not so, who can prove me false
and reduce my words to nothing?"

---

a 11 The meaning of the Hebrew for this word is uncertain.

Bildad

25

Then Bildad the Shuhite replied:

2 "Dominion and awe belong to God;
  he establishes order in the heights of
    heaven.
3 Can his forces be numbered?
  On whom does his light not rise?
4 How then can a mortal be righteous
    before God?
  How can one born of woman be pure?
5 If even the moon is not bright
  and the stars are not pure in his eyes,
6 how much less a mortal, who is but a
    maggot —
  a human being, who is only a worm!"

Job

26

Then Job replied:

2 "How you have helped the
    powerless!
  How you have saved the arm that is
    feeble!
3 What advice you have offered to one
    without wisdom!
  And what great insight you have
    displayed!
4 Who has helped you utter these words?
  And whose spirit spoke from your
    mouth?

5 "The dead are in deep anguish,
  those beneath the waters and all that
    live in them.
6 The realm of the dead is naked before
    God;
  Destruction[a] lies uncovered.
7 He spreads out the northern skies over
    empty space;
  he suspends the earth over nothing.
8 He wraps up the waters in his clouds,
  yet the clouds do not burst under
    their weight.
9 He covers the face of the full moon,
  spreading his clouds over it.

10 He marks out the horizon on the face of
    the waters
  for a boundary between light and
    darkness.
11 The pillars of the heavens quake,
  aghast at his rebuke.
12 By his power he churned up the sea;
  by his wisdom he cut Rahab to
    pieces.
13 By his breath the skies became fair;
  his hand pierced the gliding serpent.
14 And these are but the outer fringe of his
    works;
  how faint the whisper we hear of
    him!
  Who then can understand the
    thunder of his power?"

Job's Final Word to His Friends

27

And Job continued his discourse:

2 "As surely as God lives, who has denied
    me justice,
  the Almighty, who has made my life
    bitter,
3 as long as I have life within me,
  the breath of God in my nostrils,
4 my lips will not say anything wicked,
  and my tongue will not utter lies.
5 I will never admit you are in the right;
  till I die, I will not deny my
    integrity.
6 I will maintain my innocence and never
    let go of it;
  my conscience will not reproach me
    as long as I live.

7 "May my enemy be like the wicked,
  my adversary like the unjust!
8 For what hope have the godless when
    they are cut off,
  when God takes away their life?
9 Does God listen to their cry
  when distress comes upon them?
10 Will they find delight in the Almighty?
  Will they call on God at all times?

---

a 6 Hebrew *Abaddon*

¹¹ "I will teach you about the power of
     God;
     the ways of the Almighty I will not
     conceal.
¹² You have all seen this yourselves.
     Why then this meaningless talk?

¹³ "Here is the fate God allots to the
     wicked,
     the heritage a ruthless man receives
     from the Almighty:
¹⁴ However many his children, their fate is
     the sword;
     his offspring will never have enough
     to eat.
¹⁵ The plague will bury those who survive
     him,
     and their widows will not weep for
     them.
¹⁶ Though he heaps up silver like dust
     and clothes like piles of clay,
¹⁷ what he lays up the righteous will wear,
     and the innocent will divide his
     silver.
¹⁸ The house he builds is like a moth's
     cocoon,
     like a hut made by a watchman.
¹⁹ He lies down wealthy, but will do so no
     more;
     when he opens his eyes, all is gone.
²⁰ Terrors overtake him like a flood;
     a tempest snatches him away in the
     night.
²¹ The east wind carries him off, and he is
     gone;
     it sweeps him out of his place.
²² It hurls itself against him without mercy
     as he flees headlong from its power.
²³ It claps its hands in derision
     and hisses him out of his place."

Interlude: Where Wisdom Is Found

28 There is a mine for silver
     and a place where gold is
     refined.
² Iron is taken from the earth,
     and copper is smelted from ore.

³ Mortals put an end to the darkness;
     they search out the farthest recesses
     for ore in the blackest darkness.
⁴ Far from human dwellings they cut a
     shaft,
     in places untouched by human feet;
     far from other people they dangle
     and sway.
⁵ The earth, from which food comes,
     is transformed below as by fire;
⁶ lapis lazuli comes from its rocks,
     and its dust contains nuggets of
     gold.
⁷ No bird of prey knows that hidden
     path,
     no falcon's eye has seen it.
⁸ Proud beasts do not set foot on it,
     and no lion prowls there.
⁹ People assault the flinty rock with their
     hands
     and lay bare the roots of the
     mountains.
¹⁰ They tunnel through the rock;
     their eyes see all its treasures.
¹¹ They search[a] the sources of the rivers
     and bring hidden things to light.

¹² But where can wisdom be found?
     Where does understanding dwell?
¹³ No mortal comprehends its worth;
     it cannot be found in the land of the
     living.
¹⁴ The deep says, "It is not in me";
     the sea says, "It is not with me."
¹⁵ It cannot be bought with the finest
     gold,
     nor can its price be weighed out in
     silver.
¹⁶ It cannot be bought with the gold of
     Ophir,
     with precious onyx or lapis lazuli.
¹⁷ Neither gold nor crystal can compare
     with it,
     nor can it be had for jewels of gold.
¹⁸ Coral and jasper are not worthy of
     mention;
     the price of wisdom is beyond rubies.

---

a 11 Septuagint, Aquila and Vulgate; Hebrew *They dam up*

¹⁹ The topaz of Cush cannot compare
        with it;
    it cannot be bought with pure gold.

²⁰ Where then does wisdom come from?
    Where does understanding dwell?
²¹ It is hidden from the eyes of every
        living thing,
    concealed even from the birds in the
        sky.
²² Destruction*ᵃ* and Death say,
    "Only a rumor of it has reached our
        ears."
²³ God understands the way to it
    and he alone knows where it dwells,
²⁴ for he views the ends of the earth
    and sees everything under the
        heavens.
²⁵ When he established the force of the
        wind
    and measured out the waters,
²⁶ when he made a decree for the rain
    and a path for the thunderstorm,
²⁷ then he looked at wisdom and
        appraised it;
    he confirmed it and tested it.
²⁸ And he said to the human race,
    "The fear of the Lord — that is
        wisdom,
    and to shun evil is understanding."

Job's Final Defense

29

Job continued his discourse:

² "How I long for the months
        gone by,
    for the days when God watched over
        me,
³ when his lamp shone on my head
    and by his light I walked through
        darkness!
⁴ Oh, for the days when I was in my
        prime,
    when God's intimate friendship
        blessed my house,
⁵ when the Almighty was still with me
    and my children were around me,

⁶ when my path was drenched with
        cream
    and the rock poured out for me
        streams of olive oil.

⁷ "When I went to the gate of the city
    and took my seat in the public
        square,
⁸ the young men saw me and stepped
        aside
    and the old men rose to their feet;
⁹ the chief men refrained from speaking
    and covered their mouths with their
        hands;
¹⁰ the voices of the nobles were hushed,
    and their tongues stuck to the roof of
        their mouths.
¹¹ Whoever heard me spoke well of me,
    and those who saw me commended
        me,
¹² because I rescued the poor who cried
        for help,
    and the fatherless who had none to
        assist them.
¹³ The one who was dying blessed me;
    I made the widow's heart sing.
¹⁴ I put on righteousness as my clothing;
    justice was my robe and my turban.
¹⁵ I was eyes to the blind
    and feet to the lame.
¹⁶ I was a father to the needy;
    I took up the case of the stranger.
¹⁷ I broke the fangs of the wicked
    and snatched the victims from their
        teeth.

¹⁸ "I thought, 'I will die in my own house,
    my days as numerous as the grains of
        sand.
¹⁹ My roots will reach to the water,
    and the dew will lie all night on my
        branches.
²⁰ My glory will not fade;
    the bow will be ever new in my
        hand.'

²¹ "People listened to me expectantly,
    waiting in silence for my counsel.

ᵃ 22 Hebrew *Abaddon*

²²After I had spoken, they spoke no more;
    my words fell gently on their ears.
²³They waited for me as for showers
    and drank in my words as the spring
        rain.
²⁴When I smiled at them, they scarcely
        believed it;
    the light of my face was precious to
        them.ᵃ
²⁵I chose the way for them and sat as their
        chief;
    I dwelt as a king among his troops;
    I was like one who comforts
        mourners.

30

"But now they mock me,
    men younger than I,
    whose fathers I would have
        disdained
to put with my sheep dogs.
²Of what use was the strength of their
        hands to me,
    since their vigor had gone from them?
³Haggard from want and hunger,
    they roamedᵇ the parched land
    in desolate wastelands at night.
⁴In the brush they gathered salt herbs,
    and their foodᶜ was the root of the
        broom bush.
⁵They were banished from human
        society,
    shouted at as if they were thieves.
⁶They were forced to live in the dry
        stream beds,
    among the rocks and in holes in the
        ground.
⁷They brayed among the bushes
    and huddled in the undergrowth.
⁸A base and nameless brood,
    they were driven out of the land.

⁹"And now those young men mock me
        in song;
    I have become a byword among them.
¹⁰They detest me and keep their distance;
    they do not hesitate to spit in my
        face.

¹¹Now that God has unstrung my bow
        and afflicted me,
    they throw off restraint in my
        presence.
¹²On my right the tribeᵈ attacks;
    they lay snares for my feet,
    they build their siege ramps
        against me.
¹³They break up my road;
    they succeed in destroying me.
    'No one can help him,' they say.
¹⁴They advance as through a gaping
        breach;
    amid the ruins they come rolling in.
¹⁵Terrors overwhelm me;
    my dignity is driven away as by the
        wind,
    my safety vanishes like a cloud.

¹⁶"And now my life ebbs away;
    days of suffering grip me.
¹⁷Night pierces my bones;
    my gnawing pains never rest.
¹⁸In his great power God becomes like
        clothing to meᵉ;
    he binds me like the neck of my
        garment.
¹⁹He throws me into the mud,
    and I am reduced to dust and ashes.

²⁰"I cry out to you, God, but you do not
        answer;
    I stand up, but you merely look
        at me.
²¹You turn on me ruthlessly;
    with the might of your hand you
        attack me.
²²You snatch me up and drive me before
        the wind;
    you toss me about in the storm.
²³I know you will bring me down to
        death,
    to the place appointed for all the
        living.

²⁴"Surely no one lays a hand on a broken
        man
    when he cries for help in his distress.

ᵃ 24 The meaning of the Hebrew for this clause is uncertain.   ᵇ 3 Or gnawed   ᶜ 4 Or fuel   ᵈ 12 The meaning
of the Hebrew for this word is uncertain.   ᵉ 18 Hebrew; Septuagint power he grasps my clothing

²⁵ Have I not wept for those in trouble?
　　Has not my soul grieved for the poor?
²⁶ Yet when I hoped for good, evil came;
　　when I looked for light, then came
　　　darkness.
²⁷ The churning inside me never stops;
　　days of suffering confront me.
²⁸ I go about blackened, but not by the
　　　sun;
　　I stand up in the assembly and cry
　　　for help.
²⁹ I have become a brother of jackals,
　　a companion of owls.
³⁰ My skin grows black and peels;
　　my body burns with fever.
³¹ My lyre is tuned to mourning,
　　and my pipe to the sound of wailing.

31

¹ "I made a covenant with my
　　eyes
　　not to look lustfully at a young
　　woman.
² For what is our lot from God above,
　　our heritage from the Almighty on
　　　high?
³ Is it not ruin for the wicked,
　　disaster for those who do wrong?
⁴ Does he not see my ways
　　and count my every step?

⁵ "If I have walked with falsehood
　　or my foot has hurried after deceit —
⁶ let God weigh me in honest scales
　　and he will know that I am
　　　blameless —
⁷ if my steps have turned from the path,
　　if my heart has been led by my eyes,
　　or if my hands have been defiled,
⁸ then may others eat what I have sown,
　　and may my crops be uprooted.

⁹ "If my heart has been enticed by a
　　woman,
　　or if I have lurked at my neighbor's
　　　door,
¹⁰ then may my wife grind another man's
　　grain,
　　and may other men sleep with her.

¹¹ For that would have been wicked,
　　a sin to be judged.
¹² It is a fire that burns to Destruction[a];
　　it would have uprooted my harvest.

¹³ "If I have denied justice to any of my
　　servants,
　　whether male or female,
　　when they had a grievance against
　　　me,
¹⁴ what will I do when God confronts me?
　　What will I answer when called to
　　　account?
¹⁵ Did not he who made me in the womb
　　make them?
　　Did not the same one form us both
　　　within our mothers?

¹⁶ "If I have denied the desires of the poor
　　or let the eyes of the widow grow
　　　weary,
¹⁷ if I have kept my bread to myself,
　　not sharing it with the fatherless —
¹⁸ but from my youth I reared them as a
　　father would,
　　and from my birth I guided the
　　　widow —
¹⁹ if I have seen anyone perishing for lack
　　of clothing,
　　or the needy without garments,
²⁰ and their hearts did not bless me
　　for warming them with the fleece
　　　from my sheep,
²¹ if I have raised my hand against the
　　fatherless,
　　knowing that I had influence in
　　　court,
²² then let my arm fall from the shoulder,
　　let it be broken off at the joint.
²³ For I dreaded destruction from God,
　　and for fear of his splendor I could
　　　not do such things.

²⁴ "If I have put my trust in gold
　　or said to pure gold, 'You are my
　　　security,'
²⁵ if I have rejoiced over my great wealth,
　　the fortune my hands had gained,

---

²⁶if I have regarded the sun in its radiance
    or the moon moving in splendor,
²⁷so that my heart was secretly enticed
    and my hand offered them a kiss of
        homage,
²⁸then these also would be sins to be
        judged,
    for I would have been unfaithful to
        God on high.

²⁹"If I have rejoiced at my enemy's
        misfortune
    or gloated over the trouble that came
        to him —
³⁰I have not allowed my mouth to sin
    by invoking a curse against their
        life —
³¹if those of my household have never
        said,
    'Who has not been filled with Job's
        meat?' —
³²but no stranger had to spend the night
        in the street,
    for my door was always open to the
        traveler —
³³if I have concealed my sin as people do,*ᵃ*
    by hiding my guilt in my heart
³⁴because I so feared the crowd
    and so dreaded the contempt of the
        clans
    that I kept silent and would not go
        outside —
³⁵("Oh, that I had someone to hear me!
    I sign now my defense — let the
        Almighty answer me;
    let my accuser put his indictment in
        writing.
³⁶Surely I would wear it on my shoulder,
    I would put it on like a crown.
³⁷I would give him an account of my
        every step;
    I would present it to him as to a
        ruler.) —

³⁸"if my land cries out against me
    and all its furrows are wet with
        tears,
³⁹if I have devoured its yield without
        payment
    or broken the spirit of its tenants,
⁴⁰then let briers come up instead of wheat
    and stinkweed instead of barley."

The words of Job are ended.

Elihu

32 So these three men stopped answering Job, because he was righteous in his own eyes. ²But Elihu son of Barakel the Buzite, of the family of Ram, became very angry with Job for justifying himself rather than God. ³He was also angry with the three friends, because they had found no way to refute Job, and yet had condemned him.*ᵇ* ⁴Now Elihu had waited before speaking to Job because they were older than he. ⁵But when he saw that the three men had nothing more to say, his anger was aroused.

⁶So Elihu son of Barakel the Buzite said:

"I am young in years,
    and you are old;
that is why I was fearful,
    not daring to tell you what I know.
⁷I thought, 'Age should speak;
    advanced years should teach
        wisdom.'
⁸But it is the spirit*ᶜ* in a person,
    the breath of the Almighty, that gives
        them understanding.
⁹It is not only the old*ᵈ* who are wise,
    not only the aged who understand
        what is right.

¹⁰"Therefore I say: Listen to me;
    I too will tell you what I know.
¹¹I waited while you spoke,
    I listened to your reasoning;
while you were searching for words,
¹²   I gave you my full attention.
But not one of you has proved Job
        wrong;
    none of you has answered his
        arguments.

ᵃ 33 Or *as Adam did*   *ᵇ 3* Masoretic Text; an ancient Hebrew scribal tradition *Job, and so had condemned God*
ᶜ 8 Or *Spirit*; also in verse 18   *ᵈ 9* Or *many*; or *great*

¹³ Do not say, 'We have found wisdom;
　　let God, not a man, refute him.'
¹⁴ But Job has not marshaled his words
　　　　against me,
　　and I will not answer him with your
　　　　arguments.

¹⁵ "They are dismayed and have no more
　　　　to say;
　　words have failed them.
¹⁶ Must I wait, now that they are silent,
　　now that they stand there with no
　　　　reply?
¹⁷ I too will have my say;
　　I too will tell what I know.
¹⁸ For I am full of words,
　　and the spirit within me compels me;
¹⁹ inside I am like bottled-up wine,
　　like new wineskins ready to burst.
²⁰ I must speak and find relief;
　　I must open my lips and reply.
²¹ I will show no partiality,
　　nor will I flatter anyone;
²² for if I were skilled in flattery,
　　my Maker would soon take me away.

33

"But now, Job, listen to my
words;
pay attention to everything I
say.
² I am about to open my mouth;
　　my words are on the tip of my
　　　　tongue.
³ My words come from an upright heart;
　　my lips sincerely speak what I know.
⁴ The Spirit of God has made me;
　　the breath of the Almighty gives me
　　　　life.
⁵ Answer me then, if you can;
　　stand up and argue your case before
　　　　me.
⁶ I am the same as you in God's sight;
　　I too am a piece of clay.
⁷ No fear of me should alarm you,
　　nor should my hand be heavy on you.

⁸ "But you have said in my hearing —
　　I heard the very words —

⁹ 'I am pure, I have done no wrong;
　　I am clean and free from sin.
¹⁰ Yet God has found fault with me;
　　he considers me his enemy.
¹¹ He fastens my feet in shackles;
　　he keeps close watch on all my
　　　　paths.'

¹² "But I tell you, in this you are not right,
　　for God is greater than any mortal.
¹³ Why do you complain to him
　　that he responds to no one's words*a*?
¹⁴ For God does speak — now one way,
　　　　now another —
　　though no one perceives it.
¹⁵ In a dream, in a vision of the night,
　　when deep sleep falls on people
　　as they slumber in their beds,
¹⁶ he may speak in their ears
　　and terrify them with warnings,
¹⁷ to turn them from wrongdoing
　　and keep them from pride,
¹⁸ to preserve them from the pit,
　　their lives from perishing by the
　　　　sword.*b*
¹⁹ "Or someone may be chastened on a
　　　　bed of pain
　　with constant distress in their
　　　　bones,
²⁰ so that their body finds food repulsive
　　and their soul loathes the choicest
　　　　meal.
²¹ Their flesh wastes away to nothing,
　　and their bones, once hidden, now
　　　　stick out.
²² They draw near to the pit,
　　and their life to the messengers of
　　　　death.*c*
²³ Yet if there is an angel at their side,
　　a messenger, one out of a thousand,
　　sent to tell them how to be upright,
²⁴ and he is gracious to that person and
　　　　says to God,
　　'Spare them from going down to the
　　　　pit;
　　I have found a ransom for them —

---

a 13 Or *that he does not answer for any of his actions*　　*b* 18 Or *from crossing the river*　　*c* 22 Or *to the place of the dead*

25 let their flesh be renewed like a child's;
  let them be restored as in the days of
    their youth' —
26 then that person can pray to God and
    find favor with him,
  they will see God's face and shout for
    joy;
  he will restore them to full well-being.
27 And they will go to others and say,
  'I have sinned, I have perverted what
    is right,
  but I did not get what I deserved.
28 God has delivered me from going down
    to the pit,
  and I shall live to enjoy the light of
    life.'
29 "God does all these things to a
    person —
  twice, even three times —

30 to turn them back from the pit,
  that the light of life may shine on them.
31 "Pay attention, Job, and listen to me;
  be silent, and I will speak.
32 If you have anything to say, answer me;
  speak up, for I want to vindicate you.
33 But if not, then listen to me;
  be silent, and I will teach you wisdom."

34

Then Elihu said:

2 "Hear my words, you wise
    men;
  listen to me, you men of learning.
3 For the ear tests words
  as the tongue tastes food.
4 Let us discern for ourselves what is
    right;
  let us learn together what is good.

MORAL LESSON [*Principle Four*]

This is the first page of the MORAL lesson.

For a discussion of Principles One through Eight and a listing of their related lessons,
go to pages xvii – xliv.

Listen to me; be silent, and I will teach you wisdom.

JOB 33:33

Principle Four begins our process of "coming clean." It's here that we openly examine and confess our faults to ourselves, to God and to someone else we trust. In the first part of Principle Four we openly examine our life. We take a MORAL inventory.

That word *moral* scares some people. Really, it simply means "honest." In this principle we need to list, or inventory, all the significant events — both good and bad — in our lives. We need to be as truthful as we can be in order to allow God to show us our part in each event and how that has affected both ourselves and others. We chip away at the decay of the past that has, like layers of tartar, built up over the years and kept us from really seeing the truth about our past and present situations.

There are five things we need to do to take a MORAL inventory. The first letter in MORAL is M, which stands for MAKE TIME. Schedule an appointment with yourself — and with God. Set aside a day or a weekend to get alone with your Lord. God tells us in Job 33:33 that he'll provide us with the wisdom and clarity we need to complete our inventories.

The next letter in MORAL is *O*. Go to Job 7:11 (page 599).

5 "Job says, 'I am innocent,
   but God denies me justice.
6 Although I am right,
   I am considered a liar;
 although I am guiltless,
   his arrow inflicts an incurable
      wound.'
7 Is there anyone like Job,
   who drinks scorn like water?
8 He keeps company with evildoers;
   he associates with the wicked.
9 For he says, 'There is no profit
   in trying to please God.'

10 "So listen to me, you men of
      understanding.
   Far be it from God to do evil,
   from the Almighty to do wrong.
11 He repays everyone for what they have
      done;
   he brings on them what their
      conduct deserves.
12 It is unthinkable that God would do
      wrong,
   that the Almighty would pervert
      justice.
13 Who appointed him over the earth?
   Who put him in charge of the whole
      world?
14 If it were his intention
   and he withdrew his spirit*a* and
      breath,
15 all humanity would perish together
   and mankind would return to the
      dust.

16 "If you have understanding, hear this;
   listen to what I say.
17 Can someone who hates justice govern?
   Will you condemn the just and
      mighty One?
18 Is he not the One who says to kings,
   'You are worthless,'
   and to nobles, 'You are wicked,'
19 who shows no partiality to princes
   and does not favor the rich over the
      poor,
   for they are all the work of his hands?

20 They die in an instant, in the middle of
      the night;
   the people are shaken and they pass
      away;
   the mighty are removed without
      human hand.

21 "His eyes are on the ways of mortals;
   he sees their every step.
22 There is no deep shadow, no utter
      darkness,
   where evildoers can hide.
23 God has no need to examine people
      further,
   that they should come before him for
      judgment.
24 Without inquiry he shatters the mighty
   and sets up others in their place.
25 Because he takes note of their deeds,
   he overthrows them in the night and
      they are crushed.
26 He punishes them for their wickedness
   where everyone can see them,
27 because they turned from following
      him
   and had no regard for any of his
      ways.
28 They caused the cry of the poor to come
      before him,
   so that he heard the cry of the needy.
29 But if he remains silent, who can
      condemn him?
   If he hides his face, who can see him?
 Yet he is over individual and nation
      alike,
30   to keep the godless from ruling,
   from laying snares for the people.

31 "Suppose someone says to God,
   'I am guilty but will offend no more.
32 Teach me what I cannot see;
   if I have done wrong, I will not do so
      again.'
33 Should God then reward you on your
      terms,
   when you refuse to repent?
 You must decide, not I;
   so tell me what you know.

---

a 14 Or *Spirit*

34 "Men of understanding declare,
  wise men who hear me say to me,
35 'Job speaks without knowledge;
  his words lack insight.'
36 Oh, that Job might be tested to the
    utmost
  for answering like a wicked man!
37 To his sin he adds rebellion;
  scornfully he claps his hands among
    us
  and multiplies his words against
    God."

35

Then Elihu said:

2 "Do you think this is just?
  You say, 'I am in the right, not God.'
3 Yet you ask him, 'What profit is it to me,*a*
  and what do I gain by not sinning?'

4 "I would like to reply to you
  and to your friends with you.
5 Look up at the heavens and see;
  gaze at the clouds so high above you.
6 If you sin, how does that affect him?
  If your sins are many, what does that
    do to him?
7 If you are righteous, what do you give
    to him,
  or what does he receive from your
    hand?
8 Your wickedness only affects humans
    like yourself,
  and your righteousness only other
    people.

9 "People cry out under a load of
    oppression;
  they plead for relief from the arm of
    the powerful.
10 But no one says, 'Where is God my
    Maker,
  who gives songs in the night,
11 who teaches us more than he teaches*b*
    the beasts of the earth
  and makes us wiser than*c* the birds in
    the sky?'

12 He does not answer when people cry
    out
  because of the arrogance of the
    wicked.
13 Indeed, God does not listen to their
    empty plea;
  the Almighty pays no attention to it.
14 How much less, then, will he listen
  when you say that you do not see him,
  that your case is before him
  and you must wait for him,
15 and further, that his anger never
    punishes
  and he does not take the least notice
    of wickedness.*d*
16 So Job opens his mouth with empty
    talk;
  without knowledge he multiplies
    words."

36

Elihu continued:

2 "Bear with me a little longer
  and I will show you
  that there is more to be said in God's
    behalf.
3 I get my knowledge from afar;
  I will ascribe justice to my Maker.
4 Be assured that my words are not false;
  one who has perfect knowledge is
    with you.

5 "God is mighty, but despises no one;
  he is mighty, and firm in his purpose.
6 He does not keep the wicked alive
  but gives the afflicted their rights.
7 He does not take his eyes off the
    righteous;
  he enthrones them with kings
  and exalts them forever.
8 But if people are bound in chains,
  held fast by cords of affliction,
9 he tells them what they have done —
  that they have sinned arrogantly.
10 He makes them listen to correction
  and commands them to repent of
    their evil.

---

a 3 Or *you*   *b* 10,11 Or *night,* / *11who teaches us by*   *c* 11 Or *us wise by*   *d* 15 Symmachus, Theodotion and Vulgate; the meaning of the Hebrew for this word is uncertain.

11 If they obey and serve him,
     they will spend the rest of their days
          in prosperity
     and their years in contentment.
12 But if they do not listen,
     they will perish by the sword^a
     and die without knowledge.

13 "The godless in heart harbor
          resentment;
     even when he fetters them, they do
          not cry for help.
14 They die in their youth,
     among male prostitutes of the
          shrines.
15 But those who suffer he delivers in their
          suffering;
     he speaks to them in their affliction.

16 "He is wooing you from the jaws of
          distress
     to a spacious place free from
          restriction,
     to the comfort of your table laden
          with choice food.
17 But now you are laden with the
          judgment due the wicked;
     judgment and justice have taken hold
          of you.
18 Be careful that no one entices you by
          riches;
     do not let a large bribe turn you
          aside.
19 Would your wealth or even all your
          mighty efforts
     sustain you so you would not be in
          distress?
20 Do not long for the night,
     to drag people away from their
          homes.^b
21 Beware of turning to evil,
     which you seem to prefer to
          affliction.

22 "God is exalted in his power.
     Who is a teacher like him?
23 Who has prescribed his ways for him,
     or said to him, 'You have done wrong'?

24 Remember to extol his work,
     which people have praised in song.
25 All humanity has seen it;
     mortals gaze on it from afar.
26 How great is God—beyond our
          understanding!
     The number of his years is past
          finding out.

27 "He draws up the drops of water,
     which distill as rain to the streams^c;
28 the clouds pour down their moisture
     and abundant showers fall on
          mankind.
29 Who can understand how he spreads
          out the clouds,
     how he thunders from his pavilion?
30 See how he scatters his lightning about
          him,
     bathing the depths of the sea.
31 This is the way he governs^d the nations
     and provides food in abundance.
32 He fills his hands with lightning
     and commands it to strike its mark.
33 His thunder announces the coming
          storm;
     even the cattle make known its
          approach.^e

37 "At this my heart pounds
          and leaps from its place.
     2 Listen! Listen to the roar of
     his voice,
     to the rumbling that comes from his
          mouth.
3 He unleashes his lightning beneath the
          whole heaven
     and sends it to the ends of the earth.
4 After that comes the sound of his
          roar;
     he thunders with his majestic voice.
     When his voice resounds,
          he holds nothing back.
5 God's voice thunders in marvelous
          ways;
     he does great things beyond our
          understanding.

---

^a 12 Or will cross the river   ^b 20 The meaning of the Hebrew for verses 18-20 is uncertain.   ^c 27 Or distill from
the mist as rain   ^d 31 Or nourishes   ^e 33 Or announces his coming — / the One zealous against evil

⁶He says to the snow, 'Fall on the earth,'
    and to the rain shower, 'Be a mighty
        downpour.'
⁷So that everyone he has made may
        know his work,
    he stops all people from their labor.ᵃ
⁸The animals take cover;
    they remain in their dens.
⁹The tempest comes out from its chamber,
    the cold from the driving winds.
¹⁰The breath of God produces ice,
    and the broad waters become frozen.
¹¹He loads the clouds with moisture;
    he scatters his lightning through
        them.
¹²At his direction they swirl around
    over the face of the whole earth
    to do whatever he commands them.
¹³He brings the clouds to punish people,
    or to water his earth and show his
        love.

¹⁴"Listen to this, Job;
    stop and consider God's wonders.
¹⁵Do you know how God controls the
        clouds
    and makes his lightning flash?
¹⁶Do you know how the clouds hang
        poised,
    those wonders of him who has
        perfect knowledge?
¹⁷You who swelter in your clothes
    when the land lies hushed under the
        south wind,
¹⁸can you join him in spreading out the
        skies,
    hard as a mirror of cast bronze?

¹⁹"Tell us what we should say to him;
    we cannot draw up our case because
        of our darkness.
²⁰Should he be told that I want to speak?
    Would anyone ask to be swallowed
        up?
²¹Now no one can look at the sun,
    bright as it is in the skies
    after the wind has swept them clean.

²²Out of the north he comes in golden
        splendor;
    God comes in awesome majesty.
²³The Almighty is beyond our reach and
        exalted in power;
    in his justice and great righteousness,
        he does not oppress.
²⁴Therefore, people revere him,
    for does he not have regard for all the
        wise in heart?ᵇ"

The Lord Speaks

38 Then the Lord spoke to Job
    out of the storm. He said:

²"Who is this that obscures my plans
    with words without knowledge?
³Brace yourself like a man;
    I will question you,
    and you shall answer me.

⁴"Where were you when I laid the earth's
        foundation?
    Tell me, if you understand.
⁵Who marked off its dimensions? Surely
        you know!
    Who stretched a measuring line
        across it?
⁶On what were its footings set,
    or who laid its cornerstone —
⁷while the morning stars sang together
    and all the angelsᶜ shouted for joy?

⁸"Who shut up the sea behind doors
    when it burst forth from the womb,
⁹when I made the clouds its garment
    and wrapped it in thick darkness,
¹⁰when I fixed limits for it
    and set its doors and bars in place,
¹¹when I said, 'This far you may come
        and no farther;
    here is where your proud waves halt'?

¹²"Have you ever given orders to the
        morning,
    or shown the dawn its place,
¹³that it might take the earth by the edges
    and shake the wicked out of it?

ᵃ 7 Or *work, / he fills all people with fear by his power*
wise.   ᶜ 7 Hebrew *the sons of God*   ᵇ 24 Or *for he does not have regard for any who think they are*

My Name Is Jim

I'M A BELIEVER WHO STRUGGLES WITH FOOD ADDICTION

Please read the beginning of God's lengthy response to Job's questions, complaints and accusations in Job 38.

At seven I accepted Jesus into my heart. In fact, some of my most precious childhood memories revolve around church. The truth is that church was my refuge.

Before I was born, my mom left my abusive and alcoholic dad. Then, when I was only five, my half-brother left for the military. Later on, a move to California tore me from my best friend.

I began to suspect something was wrong with me. Why else would everyone I cared about choose to abandon me? Every significant event in my life was associated with food, and I began to isolate myself, seeking comfort-food in an effort to feel full and satisfied. Convinced that I was worthless, I found it difficult to trust God or anyone else. I graduated from high school weighing 250 pounds and then married a woman who turned out to be verbally abusive. She taunted me with derisive names like "fat boy," "tubby," "porky" and "the pig I sleep with." During our loveless marriage, I put on 170 additional pounds.

My life was characterized by depression, denial and loneliness, even though I regularly attended and still served faithfully in the church. I continued to steadily gain weight until I weighed in at 800 pounds. Friends at church loved and worried about me, but my fear of rejection and criticism made it difficult to reach out to them. I masked my agony with humor, longing for healing but feeling desperately unworthy.

Eventually I had to quit my job because my severely infected legs had swelled up to the point that I could no longer wear pants. My body was breaking down. I had severe sleep apnea and couldn't sleep lying down. Time and again my roommates would check on me during the night because I had stopped breathing.

Then, at 850 pounds, I called the paramedics to take me to the hospital. They made me walk down the stairs to the ambulance and cautioned me not to fall because they wouldn't risk trying to catch me. After a three-day hospital stay, I was told that nothing could be done for me, and I was for all intents and purposes sent home to die. The head of the ambulance crew, though, advised my mom that with her permission they could take me to another hospital.

Once in the ER, I fell asleep. The doctor, assuming I was in a diabetic coma, attempted futilely to awaken me. He ordered a tracheotomy so I could breathe. A three-hour operation turned into a ten-hour surgery, and the doctor thought at one point that I had died on the table. After several weeks in the hospital, I developed severe complications, including kidney, liver and heart failure. I was on dialysis for one week and in a coma for a second. I also endured the embarrassment of needing an entire shift of nurses and doctors to roll me from one side to the other to change my dressings for a bed sore. My pastor visited daily, always reading Jeremiah 29:11. In my extreme need I cried out to God, criticizing, debating and demanding an explanation for my pain, anger, confusion and resentment. How had my life come to this?

A turning point came when I began to improve. Finally the hospital transferred me to another facility, where I spent six months in intensive rehab. I began to stand up a few times each day, eventually graduating to a platform walker, a regular walker and finally to a cane. I was released shortly after my 36th birthday, weighing a mere 297 pounds. What was God's plan for me now? Surely there had to be one if he hadn't seen fit to take me yet. By this point I wanted to live and believed this was my open door.

I wound up at Saddleback Church's Celebrate Recovery program, where I became part of a Step Study group. In this Christ-centered recovery group, I began a journey of healing and understanding. It was only in this context that I really heard the words God had spoken to his suffering servant Job: "I will question you, and you shall answer me" (Job 38:3).

I recognized that I had been looking for human healing from the wounds of abandonment, rejection, depression and verbal abuse, but that these were wounds no human relationship could heal. I had finally come to the end of myself, and only then was I able to apply Principle Three: "Consciously choose to commit all of my life and will to Christ's care and control." I was at long last dead to myself — but ready to be reborn in him.

My restoration process started with new friends and a new church family. My accountability partners and sponsor have given me the unconditional love and support I've always longed for. I've had the privilege of serving as co-leader in the Men's Food Addiction Group and the Codependency Group, and of manning the Celebrate Recovery information table. I'm currently co-leading my third Step Study group and can testify of God's healing power, grace and mercy in my life.

Jim

14 The earth takes shape like clay under a
        seal;
    its features stand out like those of a
        garment.
15 The wicked are denied their light,
    and their upraised arm is broken.

16 "Have you journeyed to the springs of
        the sea
    or walked in the recesses of the
        deep?
17 Have the gates of death been shown to
        you?
    Have you seen the gates of the
        deepest darkness?
18 Have you comprehended the vast
        expanses of the earth?
    Tell me, if you know all this.

19 "What is the way to the abode of
        light?
    And where does darkness reside?
20 Can you take them to their places?
    Do you know the paths to their
        dwellings?
21 Surely you know, for you were already
        born!
    You have lived so many years!

22 "Have you entered the storehouses of
        the snow
    or seen the storehouses of the hail,
23 which I reserve for times of trouble,
    for days of war and battle?
24 What is the way to the place where the
        lightning is dispersed,
    or the place where the east winds are
        scattered over the earth?
25 Who cuts a channel for the torrents of
        rain,
    and a path for the thunderstorm,
26 to water a land where no one lives,
    an uninhabited desert,
27 to satisfy a desolate wasteland
    and make it sprout with grass?
28 Does the rain have a father?
    Who fathers the drops of dew?

29 From whose womb comes the ice?
    Who gives birth to the frost from the
        heavens
30 when the waters become hard as stone,
    when the surface of the deep is
        frozen?

31 "Can you bind the chains^a of the
        Pleiades?
    Can you loosen Orion's belt?
32 Can you bring forth the constellations
        in their seasons^b
    or lead out the Bear^c with its cubs?
33 Do you know the laws of the heavens?
    Can you set up God's^d dominion
        over the earth?

34 "Can you raise your voice to the clouds
    and cover yourself with a flood of
        water?
35 Do you send the lightning bolts on their
        way?
    Do they report to you, 'Here we are'?
36 Who gives the ibis wisdom^e
    or gives the rooster understanding?^{f}
37 Who has the wisdom to count the
        clouds?
    Who can tip over the water jars of
        the heavens
38 when the dust becomes hard
    and the clods of earth stick together?

39 "Do you hunt the prey for the lioness
    and satisfy the hunger of the lions
40 when they crouch in their dens
    or lie in wait in a thicket?
41 Who provides food for the raven
    when its young cry out to God
    and wander about for lack of food?

39

"Do you know when the
mountain goats give birth?
Do you watch when the doe
bears her fawn?
2 Do you count the months till they bear?
    Do you know the time they give
        birth?

---

^{a} 31 Septuagint; Hebrew *beauty* ^{b} 32 Or *the morning star in its season* ^{c} 32 Or *out Leo* ^{d} 33 Or *their*
^{e} 36 That is, wisdom about the flooding of the Nile ^{f} 36 That is, understanding of when to crow; the meaning of
the Hebrew for this verse is uncertain.

³They crouch down and bring forth
their young;
their labor pains are ended.
⁴Their young thrive and grow strong in
the wilds;
they leave and do not return.

⁵"Who let the wild donkey go free?
Who untied its ropes?
⁶I gave it the wasteland as its home,
the salt flats as its habitat.
⁷It laughs at the commotion in the
town;
it does not hear a driver's shout.
⁸It ranges the hills for its pasture
and searches for any green thing.

⁹"Will the wild ox consent to serve you?
Will it stay by your manger at
night?
¹⁰Can you hold it to the furrow with a
harness?
Will it till the valleys behind you?
¹¹Will you rely on it for its great strength?
Will you leave your heavy work to it?
¹²Can you trust it to haul in your grain
and bring it to your threshing floor?

¹³"The wings of the ostrich flap joyfully,
though they cannot compare
with the wings and feathers of the
stork.
¹⁴She lays her eggs on the ground
and lets them warm in the sand,
¹⁵unmindful that a foot may crush
them,
that some wild animal may trample
them.
¹⁶She treats her young harshly, as if they
were not hers;
she cares not that her labor was in
vain,
¹⁷for God did not endow her with
wisdom
or give her a share of good sense.
¹⁸Yet when she spreads her feathers to run,
she laughs at horse and rider.

¹⁹"Do you give the horse its strength
or clothe its neck with a flowing
mane?

²⁰Do you make it leap like a locust,
striking terror with its proud
snorting?
²¹It paws fiercely, rejoicing in its strength,
and charges into the fray.
²²It laughs at fear, afraid of nothing;
it does not shy away from the sword.
²³The quiver rattles against its side,
along with the flashing spear and
lance.
²⁴In frenzied excitement it eats up the
ground;
it cannot stand still when the
trumpet sounds.
²⁵At the blast of the trumpet it snorts,
'Aha!'
It catches the scent of battle from afar,
the shout of commanders and the
battle cry.

²⁶"Does the hawk take flight by your
wisdom
and spread its wings toward the
south?
²⁷Does the eagle soar at your command
and build its nest on high?
²⁸It dwells on a cliff and stays there at
night;
a rocky crag is its stronghold.
²⁹From there it looks for food;
its eyes detect it from afar.
³⁰Its young ones feast on blood,
and where the slain are, there it is."

40

The LORD said to Job:

²"Will the one who contends
with the Almighty correct him?
Let him who accuses God answer
him!"

³Then Job answered the LORD:

⁴"I am unworthy—how can I reply to
you?
I put my hand over my mouth.
⁵I spoke once, but I have no answer—
twice, but I will say no more."

⁶Then the LORD spoke to Job out of the
storm:

⁷"Brace yourself like a man;
   I will question you,
   and you shall answer me.

⁸"Would you discredit my justice?
   Would you condemn me to justify
      yourself?
⁹Do you have an arm like God's,
   and can your voice thunder like his?
¹⁰Then adorn yourself with glory and
      splendor,
   and clothe yourself in honor and
      majesty.
¹¹Unleash the fury of your wrath,
   look at all who are proud and bring
      them low,
¹²look at all who are proud and humble
      them,
   crush the wicked where they stand.
¹³Bury them all in the dust together;
   shroud their faces in the grave.
¹⁴Then I myself will admit to you
   that your own right hand can save
      you.

¹⁵"Look at Behemoth,
   which I made along with you
   and which feeds on grass like an ox.
¹⁶What strength it has in its loins,
   what power in the muscles of its
      belly!
¹⁷Its tail sways like a cedar;
   the sinews of its thighs are close-knit.
¹⁸Its bones are tubes of bronze,
   its limbs like rods of iron.
¹⁹It ranks first among the works of God,
   yet its Maker can approach it with
      his sword.
²⁰The hills bring it their produce,
   and all the wild animals play
      nearby.
²¹Under the lotus plants it lies,
   hidden among the reeds in the
      marsh.
²²The lotuses conceal it in their shadow;
   the poplars by the stream
      surround it.

²³A raging river does not alarm it;
   it is secure, though the Jordan should
      surge against its mouth.
²⁴Can anyone capture it by the eyes,
   or trap it and pierce its nose?

41

ᵃ "Can you pull in Leviathan
   with a fishhook
   or tie down its tongue with a
      rope?
²Can you put a cord through its nose
   or pierce its jaw with a hook?
³Will it keep begging you for mercy?
   Will it speak to you with gentle
      words?
⁴Will it make an agreement with you
   for you to take it as your slave for life?
⁵Can you make a pet of it like a bird
   or put it on a leash for the young
      women in your house?
⁶Will traders barter for it?
   Will they divide it up among the
      merchants?
⁷Can you fill its hide with harpoons
   or its head with fishing spears?
⁸If you lay a hand on it,
   you will remember the struggle and
      never do it again!
⁹Any hope of subduing it is false;
   the mere sight of it is overpowering.
¹⁰No one is fierce enough to rouse it.
   Who then is able to stand against me?
¹¹Who has a claim against me that I must
      pay?
   Everything under heaven belongs
      to me.

¹²"I will not fail to speak of Leviathan's
      limbs,
   its strength and its graceful form.
¹³Who can strip off its outer coat?
   Who can penetrate its double coat of
      armorᵇ?
¹⁴Who dares open the doors of its mouth,
   ringed about with fearsome teeth?
¹⁵Its back hasᶜ rows of shields
   tightly sealed together;

ᵃ In Hebrew texts 41:1-8 is numbered 40:25-32, and 41:9-34 is numbered 41:1-26.   ᵇ 13 Septuagint; Hebrew *double bridle*   ᶜ 15 Or *Its pride is its*

¹⁶each is so close to the next
    that no air can pass between.
¹⁷They are joined fast to one another;
    they cling together and cannot be
      parted.
¹⁸Its snorting throws out flashes of
    light;
    its eyes are like the rays of dawn.
¹⁹Flames stream from its mouth;
    sparks of fire shoot out.
²⁰Smoke pours from its nostrils
    as from a boiling pot over burning
      reeds.
²¹Its breath sets coals ablaze,
    and flames dart from its mouth.
²²Strength resides in its neck;
    dismay goes before it.
²³The folds of its flesh are tightly joined;
    they are firm and immovable.
²⁴Its chest is hard as rock,
    hard as a lower millstone.
²⁵When it rises up, the mighty are
    terrified;
    they retreat before its thrashing.
²⁶The sword that reaches it has no effect,
    nor does the spear or the dart or the
      javelin.
²⁷Iron it treats like straw
    and bronze like rotten wood.
²⁸Arrows do not make it flee;
    slingstones are like chaff to it.
²⁹A club seems to it but a piece of straw;
    it laughs at the rattling of the lance.
³⁰Its undersides are jagged potsherds,
    leaving a trail in the mud like a
      threshing sledge.
³¹It makes the depths churn like a boiling
    caldron
    and stirs up the sea like a pot of
      ointment.
³²It leaves a glistening wake behind it;
    one would think the deep had white
      hair.
³³Nothing on earth is its equal —
    a creature without fear.
³⁴It looks down on all that are haughty;
    it is king over all that are proud."

Job

42

Then Job replied to the LORD:

²"I know that you can do all
    things;
    no purpose of yours can be thwarted.
³You asked, 'Who is this that obscures
    my plans without knowledge?'
    Surely I spoke of things I did not
    understand,
    things too wonderful for me to know.

⁴"You said, 'Listen now, and I will speak;
    I will question you,
    and you shall answer me.'
⁵My ears had heard of you
    but now my eyes have seen you.
⁶Therefore I despise myself
    and repent in dust and ashes."

Epilogue

⁷After the LORD had said these things to Job, he said to Eliphaz the Temanite, "I am angry with you and your two friends, because you have not spoken the truth about me, as my servant Job has. ⁸So now take seven bulls and seven rams and go to my servant Job and sacrifice a burnt offering for yourselves. My servant Job will pray for you, and I will accept his prayer and not deal with you according to your folly. You have not spoken the truth about me, as my servant Job has." ⁹So Eliphaz the Temanite, Bildad the Shuhite and Zophar the Naamathite did what the LORD told them; and the LORD accepted Job's prayer.

¹⁰After Job had prayed for his friends, the LORD restored his fortunes and gave him twice as much as he had before. ¹¹All his brothers and sisters and everyone who had known him before came and ate with him in his house. They comforted and consoled him over all the trouble the LORD had brought on him, and each one gave him a piece of silver^a and a gold ring.

¹²The LORD blessed the latter part of Job's life more than the former part. He

---

^a 11 Hebrew him a kesitah; a kesitah was a unit of money of unknown weight and value.

had fourteen thousand sheep, six thousand camels, a thousand yoke of oxen and a thousand donkeys. ¹³And he also had seven sons and three daughters. ¹⁴The first daughter he named Jemimah, the second Keziah and the third Keren-Happuch. ¹⁵Nowhere in all the land were there found women as beautiful as Job's daughters, and their father granted them an inheritance along with their brothers.

¹⁶After this, Job lived a hundred and forty years; he saw his children and their children to the fourth generation. ¹⁷And so Job died, an old man and full of years.

THEME: Psalms is a compilation of 150 poems that model a personal relationship with God. Because the book covers nearly every area of life and doctrine, its themes and teachings are numerous and varied.

AUTHOR: Psalms is a collection of poems and songs written by David, Asaph, the sons of Korah, Solomon, Moses, Ethan the Ezrahite and various other unknown authors.

DATE OF WRITING: The Psalms were written over a period of almost 1,000 years, dating from about the time of Moses (approximately 1400 BC) to the time of the Babylonian captivity (586 BC) and beyond.

ENCOURAGEMENT FROM THE PSALMS: "If you, LORD, kept a record of sins, Lord, who could stand? But with you there is forgiveness, so that we can, with reverence, serve you" (Psalm 130:3 – 4).

CHALLENGE FROM THE PSALMS: "Tremble and do not sin; when you are on your beds, search your hearts and be silent" (Psalm 4:4).

REFLECTION FROM THE PSALMS: "Who can discern their own errors? Forgive my hidden faults. Keep your servant also from willful sins; may they not rule over me" (Psalm 19:12 – 13).

The book of Psalms explores human experiences and emotions in highly personal and practical ways. Spanning a large portion of Israel's early history, the Psalms address such timeless issues as guilt, fear, forgiveness, anger, joy, war, peace, worship, judgment, praise, grief and prophecy about Christ. Psalms includes many of the songs that comprised ancient Israel's hymnal.

All these years later, isn't it amazing how the Psalms still relate to us today? We all experience the issues expressed in these poems. Each of us goes through seasons of grief and joy, war and peace, uncertainty and hope in God. We can see our own situations and feelings mirrored in the Psalms; we can identify with the authors as they struggled or rejoiced. Reading a psalm aloud to God can serve as a powerful prayer. We can find hope in the Psalms when we realize that people have been struggling in the same ways for generations. Our struggles, our sins, even our hurts, hang-ups and habits — aren't unique. We can cry out to God as many of the psalmists did and find hope. By reading and reflecting on the Psalms, we find the peace and hope that only God can provide.

Recovery Themes in Psalms

BOOK I

Psalms 1 – 41

Psalm 1

¹ Blessed is the one
who does not walk in step with the
wicked
or stand in the way that sinners take
or sit in the company of mockers,
² but whose delight is in the law of the
Lord,
and who meditates on his law day
and night.
³ That person is like a tree planted by
streams of water,
which yields its fruit in season
and whose leaf does not wither —
whatever they do prospers.

⁴ Not so the wicked!
They are like chaff
that the wind blows away.
⁵ Therefore the wicked will not stand in
the judgment,
nor sinners in the assembly of the
righteous.

⁶ For the Lord watches over the way of
the righteous,
but the way of the wicked leads to
destruction.

Psalm 2

¹ Why do the nations conspire*a*
and the peoples plot in vain?
² The kings of the earth rise up
and the rulers band together
against the Lord and against his
anointed, saying,
³ "Let us break their chains
and throw off their shackles."

⁴ The One enthroned in heaven laughs;
the Lord scoffs at them.
⁵ He rebukes them in his anger
and terrifies them in his wrath, saying,

⁶ "I have installed my king
on Zion, my holy mountain."

⁷ I will proclaim the Lord's decree:

He said to me, "You are my son;
today I have become your father.
⁸ Ask me,
and I will make the nations your
inheritance,
the ends of the earth your possession.
⁹ You will break them with a rod of iron*b*;
you will dash them to pieces like
pottery."

¹⁰ Therefore, you kings, be wise;
be warned, you rulers of the earth.
¹¹ Serve the Lord with fear
and celebrate his rule with trembling.
¹² Kiss his son, or he will be angry
and your way will lead to your
destruction,
for his wrath can flare up in a moment.
Blessed are all who take refuge in him.

Psalm 3*c*

A psalm of David. When he fled
from his son Absalom.

¹ Lord, how many are my foes!
How many rise up against me!
² Many are saying of me,
"God will not deliver him."*d*

³ But you, Lord, are a shield around me,
my glory, the One who lifts my head
high.
⁴ I call out to the Lord,
and he answers me from his holy
mountain.

⁵ I lie down and sleep;
I wake again, because the Lord
sustains me.
⁶ I will not fear though tens of thousands
assail me on every side.

⁷ Arise, Lord!
Deliver me, my God!

---

a 1 Hebrew; Septuagint *rage* texts 3:1-8 is numbered 3:2-9.   *b 9* Or *will rule them with an iron scepter* (see Septuagint and Syriac)   *c* In Hebrew   *d 2* The Hebrew has *Selah* (a word of uncertain meaning) here and at the end of verses 4 and 8.

Strike all my enemies on the jaw;
  break the teeth of the wicked.

⁸ From the Lord comes deliverance.
  May your blessing be on your people.

Psalm 4ᵃ

For the director of music. With stringed
instruments. A psalm of David.

¹ Answer me when I call to you,
  my righteous God.
Give me relief from my distress;
  have mercy on me and hear my prayer.

² How long will you people turn my glory
    into shame?
  How long will you love delusions and
    seek false godsᵇ?ᶜ
³ Know that the Lord has set apart his
    faithful servant for himself;
  the Lord hears when I call to him.

⁴ Tremble andᵈ do not sin;
  when you are on your beds,
  search your hearts and be silent.
⁵ Offer the sacrifices of the righteous
  and trust in the Lord.

⁶ Many, Lord, are asking, "Who will
    bring us prosperity?"
  Let the light of your face shine on us.
⁷ Fill my heart with joy
  when their grain and new wine
    abound.

⁸ In peace I will lie down and sleep,
  for you alone, Lord,
  make me dwell in safety.

Psalm 5ᵉ

For the director of music. For pipes.
A psalm of David.

¹ Listen to my words, Lord,
  consider my lament.
² Hear my cry for help,
  my King and my God,
  for to you I pray.

³ In the morning, Lord, you hear my
    voice;
  in the morning I lay my requests
    before you
  and wait expectantly.
⁴ For you are not a God who is pleased
    with wickedness;
  with you, evil people are not welcome.
⁵ The arrogant cannot stand
  in your presence.
You hate all who do wrong;
⁶   you destroy those who tell lies.
The bloodthirsty and deceitful
  you, Lord, detest.
⁷ But I, by your great love,
  can come into your house;
in reverence I bow down
  toward your holy temple.

⁸ Lead me, Lord, in your righteousness
    because of my enemies —
  make your way straight before me.
⁹ Not a word from their mouth can be
    trusted;
  their heart is filled with malice.
Their throat is an open grave;
  with their tongues they tell lies.
¹⁰ Declare them guilty, O God!
  Let their intrigues be their downfall.
Banish them for their many sins,
  for they have rebelled against you.
¹¹ But let all who take refuge in you be glad;
  let them ever sing for joy.
Spread your protection over them,
  that those who love your name may
    rejoice in you.

¹² Surely, Lord, you bless the righteous;
  you surround them with your favor
    as with a shield.

Psalm 6ᶠ

For the director of music. With stringed
instruments. According to *sheminith*.ᵍ
A psalm of David.

¹ Lord, do not rebuke me in your anger
  or discipline me in your wrath.

ᵃ In Hebrew texts 4:1-8 is numbered 4:2-9.   ᵇ 2 Or *seek lies*   ᶜ 2 The Hebrew has *Selah* (a word of uncertain
meaning) here and at the end of verse 4.   ᵈ 4 Or *In your anger* (see Septuagint)   ᵉ In Hebrew texts 5:1-12 is
numbered 5:2-13.   ᶠ In Hebrew texts 6:1-10 is numbered 6:2-11.   ᵍ Title: Probably a musical term

2 Have mercy on me, LORD, for I am
    faint;
  heal me, LORD, for my bones are in
    agony.
3 My soul is in deep anguish.
  How long, LORD, how long?

4 Turn, LORD, and deliver me;
  save me because of your unfailing
    love.
5 Among the dead no one proclaims your
    name.
  Who praises you from the grave?

6 I am worn out from my groaning.

  All night long I flood my bed with
    weeping
  and drench my couch with tears.
7 My eyes grow weak with sorrow;
  they fail because of all my foes.

8 Away from me, all you who do evil,
  for the LORD has heard my
    weeping.
9 The LORD has heard my cry for
    mercy;
  the LORD accepts my prayer.
10 All my enemies will be overwhelmed
    with shame and anguish;
  they will turn back and suddenly be
    put to shame.

Psalm 7[a]

A *shiggaion*[b] of David, which he sang to the LORD
concerning Cush, a Benjamite.

1 LORD my God, I take refuge in you;
  save and deliver me from all who
    pursue me,
2 or they will tear me apart like a lion
  and rip me to pieces with no one to
    rescue me.

3 LORD my God, if I have done this
  and there is guilt on my hands —
4 if I have repaid my ally with evil
  or without cause have robbed my
    foe —

5 then let my enemy pursue and overtake
    me;
  let him trample my life to the ground
  and make me sleep in the dust.[c]

6 Arise, LORD, in your anger;
  rise up against the rage of my
    enemies.
  Awake, my God; decree justice.
7 Let the assembled peoples gather
    around you,
  while you sit enthroned over them on
    high.
8   Let the LORD judge the peoples.
  Vindicate me, LORD, according to my
    righteousness,
  according to my integrity, O Most
    High.
9 Bring to an end the violence of the
    wicked
  and make the righteous secure —
  you, the righteous God
  who probes minds and hearts.

10 My shield[d] is God Most High,
  who saves the upright in heart.
11 God is a righteous judge,
  a God who displays his wrath every
    day.
12 If he does not relent,
  he[e] will sharpen his sword;
  he will bend and string his bow.
13 He has prepared his deadly weapons;
  he makes ready his flaming arrows.

14 Whoever is pregnant with evil
  conceives trouble and gives birth to
    disillusionment.
15 Whoever digs a hole and scoops it out
  falls into the pit they have made.
16 The trouble they cause recoils on them;
  their violence comes down on their
    own heads.

17 I will give thanks to the LORD because
  of his righteousness;
  I will sing the praises of the name of
  the LORD Most High.

---

a In Hebrew texts 7:1-17 is numbered 7:2-18.   *b* Title: Probably a literary or musical term   *c* 5 The Hebrew has
Selah (a word of uncertain meaning) here.   *d* 10 Or *sovereign*   *e* 12 Or *If anyone does not repent, / God*

Psalm 8 *a*

For the director of music. According to *gittith.*[b]
A psalm of David.

[1] LORD, our Lord,
how majestic is your name in all the
earth!

You have set your glory
in the heavens.
[2] Through the praise of children and
infants
you have established a stronghold
against your enemies,
to silence the foe and the avenger.

[3] When I consider your heavens,
the work of your fingers,
the moon and the stars,
which you have set in place,
[4] what is mankind that you are mindful
of them,
human beings that you care for them?[c]

[5] You have made them[d] a little lower than
the angels[e]
and crowned them[d] with glory and
honor.
[6] You made them rulers over the works of
your hands;
you put everything under their[f] feet:
[7] all flocks and herds,
and the animals of the wild,
[8] the birds in the sky,
and the fish in the sea,
all that swim the paths of the seas.

[9] LORD, our Lord,
how majestic is your name in all the
earth!

Psalm 9 *g,h*

For the director of music. To the tune of
"The Death of the Son." A psalm of David.

[1] I will give thanks to you, LORD, with all
my heart;
I will tell of all your wonderful deeds.

[2] I will be glad and rejoice in you;
I will sing the praises of your name,
O Most High.

[3] My enemies turn back;
they stumble and perish before you.
[4] For you have upheld my right and my
cause,
sitting enthroned as the righteous
judge.
[5] You have rebuked the nations and
destroyed the wicked;
you have blotted out their name for
ever and ever.
[6] Endless ruin has overtaken my
enemies,
you have uprooted their cities;
even the memory of them has
perished.

[7] The LORD reigns forever;
he has established his throne for
judgment.
[8] He rules the world in righteousness
and judges the peoples with equity.
[9] The LORD is a refuge for the oppressed,
a stronghold in times of trouble.
[10] Those who know your name trust in you,
for you, LORD, have never forsaken
those who seek you.

[11] Sing the praises of the LORD, enthroned
in Zion;
proclaim among the nations what he
has done.
[12] For he who avenges blood remembers;
he does not ignore the cries of the
afflicted.

[13] LORD, see how my enemies persecute
me!
Have mercy and lift me up from the
gates of death,
[14] that I may declare your praises
in the gates of Daughter Zion,
and there rejoice in your salvation.

---

a In Hebrew texts 8:1-9 is numbered 8:2-10.   *b* Title: Probably a musical term   *c 4 Or what is a human being that
you are mindful of him, / a son of man that you care for him?*   *d 5 Or him*   *e 5 Or than God*   *f 6 Or made him
ruler . . . ; / . . . his*   *g* Psalms 9 and 10 may originally have been a single acrostic poem in which alternating lines
began with the successive letters of the Hebrew alphabet. In the Septuagint they constitute one psalm.   *h* In Hebrew
texts 9:1-20 is numbered 9:2-21.

¹⁵The nations have fallen into the pit they
have dug;
their feet are caught in the net they
have hidden.
¹⁶The LORD is known by his acts of justice;
the wicked are ensnared by the work
of their hands.^a
¹⁷The wicked go down to the realm of the
dead,
all the nations that forget God.
¹⁸But God will never forget the needy;
the hope of the afflicted will never
perish.

¹⁹Arise, LORD, do not let mortals
triumph;
let the nations be judged in your
presence.
²⁰Strike them with terror, LORD;
let the nations know they are only
mortal.

Psalm 10^b

¹Why, LORD, do you stand far off?
Why do you hide yourself in times of
trouble?

²In his arrogance the wicked man hunts
down the weak,
who are caught in the schemes he
devises.
³He boasts about the cravings of his heart;
he blesses the greedy and reviles the
LORD.
⁴In his pride the wicked man does not
seek him;
in all his thoughts there is no room
for God.
⁵His ways are always prosperous;
your laws are rejected by^c him;
he sneers at all his enemies.
⁶He says to himself, "Nothing will ever
shake me."
He swears, "No one will ever do me
harm."

⁷His mouth is full of lies and threats;
trouble and evil are under his
tongue.
⁸He lies in wait near the villages;
from ambush he murders the
innocent.
His eyes watch in secret for his victims;
⁹   like a lion in cover he lies in wait.
He lies in wait to catch the helpless;
he catches the helpless and drags
them off in his net.
¹⁰His victims are crushed, they collapse;
they fall under his strength.
¹¹He says to himself, "God will never
notice;
he covers his face and never sees."

¹²Arise, LORD! Lift up your hand, O God.
Do not forget the helpless.
¹³Why does the wicked man revile God?
Why does he say to himself,
"He won't call me to account"?

¹⁴But you, God, see the trouble of the
afflicted;
you consider their grief and take it in
hand.
The victims commit themselves to
you;
you are the helper of the fatherless.
¹⁵Break the arm of the wicked man;
call the evildoer to account for his
wickedness
that would not otherwise be found
out.

¹⁶The LORD is King for ever and ever;
the nations will perish from his
land.
¹⁷You, LORD, hear the desire of the
afflicted;
you encourage them, and you listen
to their cry,
¹⁸defending the fatherless and the
oppressed,
so that mere earthly mortals
will never again strike terror.

---

^a 16   The Hebrew has *Higgaion* and *Selah* (words of uncertain meaning) here; *Selah* occurs also at the end of verse 20.
^b Psalms 9 and 10 may originally have been a single acrostic poem in which alternating lines began with the successive letters of the Hebrew alphabet. In the Septuagint they constitute one psalm.   ^c 5   See Septuagint; Hebrew / *they are haughty, and your laws are far from*

Psalm 11

For the director of music. Of David.

¹ In the LORD I take refuge.
   How then can you say to me:
   "Flee like a bird to your mountain.
² For look, the wicked bend their bows;
   they set their arrows against the strings
to shoot from the shadows
   at the upright in heart.
³ When the foundations are being
      destroyed,
   what can the righteous do?"

⁴ The LORD is in his holy temple;
   the LORD is on his heavenly throne.
He observes everyone on earth;
   his eyes examine them.
⁵ The LORD examines the righteous,
   but the wicked, those who love
      violence,
   he hates with a passion.
⁶ On the wicked he will rain
   fiery coals and burning sulfur;
   a scorching wind will be their lot.

⁷ For the LORD is righteous,
   he loves justice;
   the upright will see his face.

Psalm 12ᵃ

For the director of music. According to *sheminith.*ᵇ
A psalm of David.

¹ Help, LORD, for no one is faithful
      anymore;
   those who are loyal have vanished
      from the human race.
² Everyone lies to their neighbor;
   they flatter with their lips
   but harbor deception in their hearts.

³ May the LORD silence all flattering lips
   and every boastful tongue —
⁴ those who say,
   "By our tongues we will prevail;
   our own lips will defend us — who is
      lord over us?"

⁵ "Because the poor are plundered and
      the needy groan,
   I will now arise," says the LORD.
   "I will protect them from those who
      malign them."
⁶ And the words of the LORD are
      flawless,
   like silver purified in a crucible,
   like goldᶜ refined seven times.

⁷ You, LORD, will keep the needy safe
   and will protect us forever from the
      wicked,
⁸ who freely strut about
   when what is vile is honored by the
      human race.

Psalm 13ᵈ

For the director of music. A psalm of David.

¹ How long, LORD? Will you forget me
      forever?
   How long will you hide your face
      from me?
² How long must I wrestle with my
      thoughts
   and day after day have sorrow in my
      heart?
   How long will my enemy triumph
      over me?

³ Look on me and answer, LORD my God.
   Give light to my eyes, or I will sleep
      in death,
⁴ and my enemy will say, "I have
      overcome him,"
   and my foes will rejoice when I fall.

⁵ But I trust in your unfailing love;
   my heart rejoices in your salvation.
⁶ I will sing the LORD's praise,
   for he has been good to me.

Psalm 14

For the director of music. Of David.

¹ The foolᵉ says in his heart,
   "There is no God."

ᵃ In Hebrew texts 12:1-8 is numbered 12:2-9.   ᵇ Title: Probably a musical term   ᶜ 6 Probable reading of the
original Hebrew text; Masoretic Text *earth*   ᵈ In Hebrew texts 13:1-6 is numbered 13:2-6.   ᵉ 1 The Hebrew
words rendered *fool* in Psalms denote one who is morally deficient.

They are corrupt, their deeds are vile;
  there is no one who does good.

2 The Lord looks down from heaven
    on all mankind
  to see if there are any who
      understand,
    any who seek God.
3 All have turned away, all have become
      corrupt;
    there is no one who does good,
    not even one.

4 Do all these evildoers know nothing?

  They devour my people as though
      eating bread;
    they never call on the Lord.
5 But there they are, overwhelmed with
      dread,
    for God is present in the company of
      the righteous.
6 You evildoers frustrate the plans of the
      poor,
    but the Lord is their refuge.

7 Oh, that salvation for Israel would
      come out of Zion!
  When the Lord restores his
      people,
    let Jacob rejoice and Israel be glad!

Psalm 15

A psalm of David.

1 Lord, who may dwell in your sacred
      tent?
  Who may live on your holy
      mountain?

2 The one whose walk is blameless,
    who does what is righteous,
    who speaks the truth from their
      heart;
3 whose tongue utters no slander,
    who does no wrong to a neighbor,
    and casts no slur on others;
4 who despises a vile person
    but honors those who fear the
      Lord;

who keeps an oath even when it hurts,
    and does not change their mind;
5 who lends money to the poor without
      interest;
  who does not accept a bribe against
      the innocent.

Whoever does these things
  will never be shaken.

Psalm 16

A miktam[a] of David.

1 Keep me safe, my God,
    for in you I take refuge.

2 I say to the Lord, "You are my Lord;
    apart from you I have no good
      thing."
3 I say of the holy people who are in the
      land,
    "They are the noble ones in whom is
      all my delight."
4 Those who run after other gods will
      suffer more and more.
  I will not pour out libations of blood
      to such gods
    or take up their names on my lips.

5 Lord, you alone are my portion and my
      cup;
    you make my lot secure.
6 The boundary lines have fallen for me
      in pleasant places;
    surely I have a delightful inheritance.
7 I will praise the Lord, who counsels
      me;
    even at night my heart instructs me.
8 I keep my eyes always on the Lord.
    With him at my right hand, I will not
      be shaken.

9 Therefore my heart is glad and my
      tongue rejoices;
    my body also will rest secure,
10 because you will not abandon me to the
      realm of the dead,
    nor will you let your faithful[b] one see
      decay.

---

a Title: Probably a literary or musical term   b 10 Or holy

¹¹ You make known to me the path of life;
    you will fill me with joy in your
        presence,
    with eternal pleasures at your right
        hand.

Psalm 17

A prayer of David.

¹ Hear me, LORD, my plea is just;
    listen to my cry.
  Hear my prayer —
    it does not rise from deceitful lips.
² Let my vindication come from you;
    may your eyes see what is right.

³ Though you probe my heart,
    though you examine me at night and
        test me,
    you will find that I have planned no
        evil;
    my mouth has not transgressed.
⁴ Though people tried to bribe me,
    I have kept myself from the ways of
        the violent
    through what your lips have
        commanded.
⁵ My steps have held to your paths;
    my feet have not stumbled.

⁶ I call on you, my God, for you will
        answer me;
    turn your ear to me and hear my
        prayer.
⁷ Show me the wonders of your great
        love,
    you who save by your right hand
    those who take refuge in you from
        their foes.
⁸ Keep me as the apple of your eye;
    hide me in the shadow of your wings
⁹ from the wicked who are out to destroy
        me,
    from my mortal enemies who
        surround me.
¹⁰ They close up their callous hearts,
    and their mouths speak with
        arrogance.

¹¹ They have tracked me down, they now
        surround me,
    with eyes alert, to throw me to the
        ground.
¹² They are like a lion hungry for prey,
    like a fierce lion crouching in
        cover.

¹³ Rise up, LORD, confront them, bring
        them down;
    with your sword rescue me from the
        wicked.
¹⁴ By your hand save me from such
        people, LORD,
    from those of this world whose
        reward is in this life.
  May what you have stored up for the
        wicked fill their bellies;
    may their children gorge themselves
        on it,
    and may there be leftovers for their
        little ones.

¹⁵ As for me, I will be vindicated and will
        see your face;
    when I awake, I will be satisfied with
        seeing your likeness.

Psalm 18ᵃ

For the director of music. Of David the servant of
the LORD. He sang to the LORD the words of this
song when the LORD delivered him from the hand of
all his enemies and from the hand of Saul. He said:

¹ I love you, LORD, my strength.

² The LORD is my rock, my fortress and
        my deliverer;
    my God is my rock, in whom I take
        refuge,
    my shieldᵇ and the hornᶜ of my
        salvation, my stronghold.

³ I called to the LORD, who is worthy of
        praise,
    and I have been saved from my
        enemies.
⁴ The cords of death entangled me;
    the torrents of destruction
        overwhelmed me.

ᵃ In Hebrew texts 18:1-50 is numbered 18:2-51.   ᵇ 2 Or sovereign   ᶜ 2 Horn here symbolizes strength.

⁵The cords of the grave coiled around
    me;
  the snares of death confronted me.

⁶In my distress I called to the LORD;
  I cried to my God for help.
From his temple he heard my voice;
  my cry came before him, into his ears.
⁷The earth trembled and quaked,
  and the foundations of the
    mountains shook;
  they trembled because he was angry.
⁸Smoke rose from his nostrils;
  consuming fire came from his mouth,
  burning coals blazed out of it.
⁹He parted the heavens and came down;
  dark clouds were under his feet.
¹⁰He mounted the cherubim and flew;
  he soared on the wings of the wind.
¹¹He made darkness his covering, his
    canopy around him —
  the dark rain clouds of the sky.
¹²Out of the brightness of his presence
    clouds advanced,
  with hailstones and bolts of
    lightning.
¹³The LORD thundered from heaven;
  the voice of the Most High
    resounded.ᵃ
¹⁴He shot his arrows and scattered the
    enemy,
  with great bolts of lightning he
    routed them.
¹⁵The valleys of the sea were exposed
  and the foundations of the earth laid
    bare
  at your rebuke, LORD,
  at the blast of breath from your
    nostrils.

¹⁶He reached down from on high and
    took hold of me;
  he drew me out of deep waters.
¹⁷He rescued me from my powerful
    enemy,
  from my foes, who were too strong
    for me.

¹⁸They confronted me in the day of my
    disaster,
  but the LORD was my support.
¹⁹He brought me out into a spacious
    place;
  he rescued me because he delighted
    in me.

²⁰The LORD has dealt with me according
    to my righteousness;
  according to the cleanness of my
    hands he has rewarded me.
²¹For I have kept the ways of the LORD;
  I am not guilty of turning from my
    God.
²²All his laws are before me;
  I have not turned away from his
    decrees.
²³I have been blameless before him
  and have kept myself from sin.
²⁴The LORD has rewarded me according
    to my righteousness,
  according to the cleanness of my
    hands in his sight.

²⁵To the faithful you show yourself
    faithful,
  to the blameless you show yourself
    blameless,
²⁶to the pure you show yourself pure,
  but to the devious you show yourself
    shrewd.
²⁷You save the humble
  but bring low those whose eyes are
    haughty.
²⁸You, LORD, keep my lamp burning;
  my God turns my darkness into
    light.
²⁹With your help I can advance against a
    troopᵇ;
  with my God I can scale a wall.

³⁰As for God, his way is perfect:
  The LORD's word is flawless;
  he shields all who take refuge in him.
³¹For who is God besides the LORD?
  And who is the Rock except our
    God?

ᵃ *13* Some Hebrew manuscripts and Septuagint (see also 2 Samuel 22:14); most Hebrew manuscripts *resounded, /
amid hailstones and bolts of lightning*   ᵇ *29* Or *can run through a barricade*

32 It is God who arms me with strength
   and keeps my way secure.
33 He makes my feet like the feet of a
   deer;
   he causes me to stand on the heights.
34 He trains my hands for battle;
   my arms can bend a bow of bronze.
35 You make your saving help my shield,
   and your right hand sustains me;
   your help has made me great.
36 You provide a broad path for my feet,
   so that my ankles do not give way.

37 I pursued my enemies and overtook
   them;
   I did not turn back till they were
   destroyed.
38 I crushed them so that they could not
   rise;
   they fell beneath my feet.
39 You armed me with strength for battle;
   you humbled my adversaries before
   me.
40 You made my enemies turn their backs
   in flight,
   and I destroyed my foes.
41 They cried for help, but there was no
   one to save them —
   to the Lord, but he did not answer.
42 I beat them as fine as windblown dust;
   I trampled them*a* like mud in the
   streets.
43 You have delivered me from the attacks
   of the people;
   you have made me the head of
   nations.
   People I did not know now serve me,
44   foreigners cower before me;
   as soon as they hear of me, they obey
   me.
45 They all lose heart;
   they come trembling from their
   strongholds.

46 The Lord lives! Praise be to my Rock!
   Exalted be God my Savior!

47 He is the God who avenges me,
   who subdues nations under me,
48   who saves me from my enemies.
   You exalted me above my foes;
   from a violent man you rescued me.
49 Therefore I will praise you, Lord,
   among the nations;
   I will sing the praises of your name.

50 He gives his king great victories;
   he shows unfailing love to his
   anointed,
   to David and to his descendants
   forever.

Psalm 19*b*

For the director of music. A psalm of David.

1 The heavens declare the glory of God;
   the skies proclaim the work of his
   hands.
2 Day after day they pour forth speech;
   night after night they reveal
   knowledge.
3 They have no speech, they use no
   words;
   no sound is heard from them.
4 Yet their voice*c* goes out into all the
   earth,
   their words to the ends of the world.
   In the heavens God has pitched a tent
   for the sun.
5   It is like a bridegroom coming out of
   his chamber,
   like a champion rejoicing to run his
   course.
6 It rises at one end of the heavens
   and makes its circuit to the other;
   nothing is deprived of its warmth.

7 The law of the Lord is perfect,
   refreshing the soul.
   The statutes of the Lord are
   trustworthy,
   making wise the simple.
8 The precepts of the Lord are right,
   giving joy to the heart.

---

a 42 Many Hebrew manuscripts, Septuagint, Syriac and Targum (see also 2 Samuel 22:43); Masoretic Text *I poured
them out*   *b* In Hebrew texts 19:1-14 is numbered 19:2-15.   *c 4* Septuagint, Jerome and Syriac; Hebrew
measuring line

The commands of the LORD are
      radiant,
   giving light to the eyes.
9 The fear of the LORD is pure,
   enduring forever.
The decrees of the LORD are firm,
   and all of them are righteous.

10 They are more precious than gold,
   than much pure gold;
they are sweeter than honey,
   than honey from the honeycomb.
11 By them your servant is warned;
   in keeping them there is great
      reward.
12 But who can discern their own errors?
   Forgive my hidden faults.
13 Keep your servant also from willful
      sins;
   may they not rule over me.
Then I will be blameless,
   innocent of great transgression.

14 May these words of my mouth and this
      meditation of my heart
   be pleasing in your sight,
   LORD, my Rock and my Redeemer.

Psalm 20*a*

For the director of music. A psalm of David.

1 May the LORD answer you when you
      are in distress;
   may the name of the God of Jacob
      protect you.
2 May he send you help from the
      sanctuary
   and grant you support from Zion.
3 May he remember all your sacrifices
   and accept your burnt offerings.*b*
4 May he give you the desire of your
      heart
   and make all your plans succeed.
5 May we shout for joy over your victory
   and lift up our banners in the name
      of our God.

May the LORD grant all your requests.

6 Now this I know:
   The LORD gives victory to his
      anointed.
He answers him from his heavenly
      sanctuary
   with the victorious power of his right
      hand.
7 Some trust in chariots and some in
      horses,
   but we trust in the name of the LORD
      our God.
8 They are brought to their knees and
      fall,
   but we rise up and stand firm.
9 LORD, give victory to the king!
   Answer us when we call!

Psalm 21*c*

For the director of music. A psalm of David.

1 The king rejoices in your strength,
      LORD.
   How great is his joy in the victories
      you give!

2 You have granted him his heart's desire
   and have not withheld the request of
      his lips.*b*
3 You came to greet him with rich
      blessings
   and placed a crown of pure gold on
      his head.
4 He asked you for life, and you gave it to
      him—
   length of days, for ever and ever.
5 Through the victories you gave, his
      glory is great;
   you have bestowed on him splendor
      and majesty.
6 Surely you have granted him unending
      blessings
   and made him glad with the joy of
      your presence.
7 For the king trusts in the LORD;
   through the unfailing love of the
      Most High
   he will not be shaken.

---

a In Hebrew texts 20:1-9 is numbered 20:2-10.   *b 3,2* The Hebrew has *Selah* (a word of uncertain meaning) here.
c In Hebrew texts 21:1-13 is numbered 21:2-14.

8 Your hand will lay hold on all your
　　enemies;
　your right hand will seize your foes.
9 When you appear for battle,
　you will burn them up as in a blazing
　　furnace.
The LORD will swallow them up in his
　　wrath,
　and his fire will consume them.
10 You will destroy their descendants from
　　the earth,
　their posterity from mankind.
11 Though they plot evil against you
　and devise wicked schemes, they
　　cannot succeed.
12 You will make them turn their backs
　when you aim at them with drawn
　　bow.

13 Be exalted in your strength, LORD;
　we will sing and praise your might.

Psalm 22[a]

For the director of music. To the tune of
"The Doe of the Morning." A psalm of David.

1 My God, my God, why have you
　　forsaken me?
　Why are you so far from saving me,
　so far from my cries of anguish?
2 My God, I cry out by day, but you do
　　not answer,
　by night, but I find no rest.[b]

3 Yet you are enthroned as the Holy One;
　you are the one Israel praises.[c]
4 In you our ancestors put their trust;
　they trusted and you delivered them.
5 To you they cried out and were saved;
　in you they trusted and were not put
　　to shame.

6 But I am a worm and not a man,
　scorned by everyone, despised by the
　　people.
7 All who see me mock me;
　they hurl insults, shaking their heads.

8 "He trusts in the LORD," they say,
　"let the LORD rescue him.
Let him deliver him,
　since he delights in him."

9 Yet you brought me out of the womb;
　you made me trust in you, even at my
　　mother's breast.
10 From birth I was cast on you;
　from my mother's womb you have
　　been my God.

11 Do not be far from me,
　for trouble is near
　and there is no one to help.

12 Many bulls surround me;
　strong bulls of Bashan encircle me.
13 Roaring lions that tear their prey
　open their mouths wide against me.
14 I am poured out like water,
　and all my bones are out of joint.
My heart has turned to wax;
　it has melted within me.
15 My mouth[d] is dried up like a
　　potsherd,
　and my tongue sticks to the roof of
　　my mouth;
　you lay me in the dust of death.

16 Dogs surround me,
　a pack of villains encircles me;
　they pierce[e] my hands and my feet.
17 All my bones are on display;
　people stare and gloat over me.
18 They divide my clothes among them
　and cast lots for my garment.

19 But you, LORD, do not be far from me.
　You are my strength; come quickly to
　　help me.
20 Deliver me from the sword,
　my precious life from the power of
　　the dogs.
21 Rescue me from the mouth of the lions;
　save me from the horns of the wild
　　oxen.

---

[a] In Hebrew texts 22:1-31 is numbered 22:2-32.　　[b] 2 Or night, and am not silent　　[c] 3 Or Yet you are holy, /
enthroned on the praises of Israel　　[d] 15 Probable reading of the original Hebrew text; Masoretic Text strength
[e] 16 Dead Sea Scrolls and some manuscripts of the Masoretic Text, Septuagint and Syriac; most manuscripts of the
Masoretic Text me, / like a lion

²²I will declare your name to my people;
in the assembly I will praise you.
²³You who fear the Lord, praise him!
All you descendants of Jacob, honor
him!
Revere him, all you descendants of
Israel!
²⁴For he has not despised or scorned
the suffering of the afflicted one;
he has not hidden his face from him
but has listened to his cry for help.

²⁵From you comes the theme of my praise
in the great assembly;
before those who fear you*a* I will
fulfill my vows.
²⁶The poor will eat and be satisfied;
those who seek the Lord will praise
him —
may your hearts live forever!

²⁷All the ends of the earth
will remember and turn to the Lord,
and all the families of the nations
will bow down before him,
²⁸for dominion belongs to the Lord
and he rules over the nations.

²⁹All the rich of the earth will feast and
worship;
all who go down to the dust will
kneel before him —
those who cannot keep themselves
alive.
³⁰Posterity will serve him;
future generations will be told about
the Lord.
³¹They will proclaim his righteousness,
declaring to a people yet unborn:
He has done it!

Psalm 23

A psalm of David.

¹The Lord is my shepherd, I lack nothing.
²   He makes me lie down in green
pastures,

he leads me beside quiet waters,
³   he refreshes my soul.
He guides me along the right paths
for his name's sake.
⁴Even though I walk
through the darkest valley,*b*
I will fear no evil,
for you are with me;
your rod and your staff,
they comfort me.

⁵You prepare a table before me
in the presence of my enemies.
You anoint my head with oil;
my cup overflows.
⁶Surely your goodness and love will
follow me
all the days of my life,
and I will dwell in the house of the Lord
forever.

Psalm 24

Of David. A psalm.

¹The earth is the Lord's, and everything
in it,
the world, and all who live in it;
²for he founded it on the seas
and established it on the waters.

³Who may ascend the mountain of the
Lord?
Who may stand in his holy place?
⁴The one who has clean hands and a
pure heart,
who does not trust in an idol
or swear by a false god.*c*

⁵They will receive blessing from the Lord
and vindication from God their
Savior.
⁶Such is the generation of those who
seek him,
who seek your face, God of Jacob.*d,e*

⁷Lift up your heads, you gates;
be lifted up, you ancient doors,
that the King of glory may come in.

---

a 25 Hebrew *him*   *b 4* Or *the valley of the shadow of death*   *c 4* Or *swear falsely*   *d 6* Two Hebrew
manuscripts and Syriac (see also Septuagint); most Hebrew manuscripts *face, Jacob*   *e 6* The Hebrew has *Selah*
(a word of uncertain meaning) here and at the end of verse 10.

⓵
⓶
⓷

8 Who is this King of glory?
  The Lord strong and mighty,
  the Lord mighty in battle.
9 Lift up your heads, you gates;
  lift them up, you ancient doors,
  that the King of glory may come in.
10 Who is he, this King of glory?
  The Lord Almighty —
  he is the King of glory.

Psalm 25[a]

Of David.

⓵
⓶
⓷

1 In you, Lord my God,
  I put my trust.

2 I trust in you;
  do not let me be put to shame,
  nor let my enemies triumph over me.
3 No one who hopes in you
  will ever be put to shame,
  but shame will come on those
  who are treacherous without cause.

⓻
⓼

4 Show me your ways, Lord,
  teach me your paths.
5 Guide me in your truth and teach me,
  for you are God my Savior,
  and my hope is in you all day long.

⓸
⓹

6 Remember, Lord, your great mercy
    and love,
  for they are from of old.
7 Do not remember the sins of my youth
  and my rebellious ways;
  according to your love remember me,
  for you, Lord, are good.

8 Good and upright is the Lord;
  therefore he instructs sinners in his
    ways.
9 He guides the humble in what is right
  and teaches them his way.
10 All the ways of the Lord are loving
    and faithful
  toward those who keep the demands
    of his covenant.
11 For the sake of your name, Lord,
  forgive my iniquity, though it is great.

12 Who, then, are those who fear the
    Lord?
  He will instruct them in the ways
    they should choose.[b]
13 They will spend their days in
    prosperity,
  and their descendants will inherit
    the land.
14 The Lord confides in those who fear
    him;
  he makes his covenant known to
    them.

⓵
⓶
⓷

15 My eyes are ever on the Lord,
  for only he will release my feet from
    the snare.

16 Turn to me and be gracious to me,
  for I am lonely and afflicted.
17 Relieve the troubles of my heart
  and free me from my anguish.

⓸
⓹

18 Look on my affliction and my distress
  and take away all my sins.
19 See how numerous are my enemies
  and how fiercely they hate me!

20 Guard my life and rescue me;
  do not let me be put to shame,
  for I take refuge in you.
21 May integrity and uprightness protect
    me,
  because my hope, Lord,[c] is in you.

22 Deliver Israel, O God,
  from all their troubles!

Psalm 26

Of David.

1 Vindicate me, Lord,
  for I have led a blameless life;
  I have trusted in the Lord
  and have not faltered.
2 Test me, Lord, and try me,
  examine my heart and my mind;
3 for I have always been mindful of your
    unfailing love
  and have lived in reliance on your
    faithfulness.

⓻
⓼

---

[a] This psalm is an acrostic poem, the verses of which begin with the successive letters of the Hebrew alphabet.
[b] 12 Or *ways he chooses*   [c] 21 Septuagint; Hebrew does not have *Lord*.

⁴I do not sit with the deceitful,
 nor do I associate with hypocrites.
⁵I abhor the assembly of evildoers
 and refuse to sit with the wicked.
⁶I wash my hands in innocence,
 and go about your altar, LORD,
⁷proclaiming aloud your praise
 and telling of all your wonderful
   deeds.

⁸LORD, I love the house where you live,
 the place where your glory dwells.
⁹Do not take away my soul along with
   sinners,
 my life with those who are
   bloodthirsty,
¹⁰in whose hands are wicked schemes,
 whose right hands are full of
   bribes.

HOPE LESSON [*Principle Two*]

For the previous entry in the HOPE lesson, go to Ephesians 4:22–23 (page 1466).

For a discussion of Principles One through Eight and a listing of their related lessons,
go to pages xvii–xliv.

*Guide me in your truth and teach me, for you are God my Savior,
and my hope is in you all day long.*

PSALM 25:5

In Principle Two we earnestly believe that God exists, that we matter to him and that he has the power to help us recover. It's in this principle that we find the HOPE we need to start our recovery journey.

The next letter in HOPE is *P*, which stands for POWER TO CHANGE. In the past, we may have wanted to change but been unable to do so. We couldn't free ourselves from our hurts, hang-ups or habits. In Principle Two we understand that God's power can change us and our situation. Philippians 4:13 confirms this: "I can do all this through him who gives me strength."

Power to change comes from God's grace. Hope draws its power from a deep trust in God, like that about which the psalmist wrote in Psalm 25:5.

In Principle Two we begin to understand that God's power can change both ourselves and our situation. And once we tap into that power, right actions — Christ-like actions — will follow naturally as by-products of working the principles and following the one and only Higher Power, Jesus Christ.

We begin to understand that God wants to fill our lives with his love, joy and presence. This is impossible without faith. Hebrews 11:6 spells this out clearly: "Without faith it is impossible to please God, because anyone who comes to him must believe that he exists and that he rewards those who earnestly seek him."

Many people today believe their doubts and doubt their beliefs. Has anyone ever seen an idea? Seen love? Seen faith? The reality is, though, that we can see the results of an idea. We can see the *acts* of faith and love, but the real things — the lasting things — in the world are invisible, spiritual realities.

The last letter in HOPE is *E*. Go to Philippians 1:6 (page 1477).

11 I lead a blameless life;
  deliver me and be merciful to me.

12 My feet stand on level ground;
  in the great congregation I will praise
    the LORD.

Psalm 27

Of David.

1 The LORD is my light and my
    salvation—
  whom shall I fear?
  The LORD is the stronghold of my
    life—
  of whom shall I be afraid?

2 When the wicked advance against me
    to devour*a* me,
  it is my enemies and my foes
    who will stumble and fall.
3 Though an army besiege me,
    my heart will not fear;
  though war break out against me,
    even then I will be confident.

4 One thing I ask from the LORD,
    this only do I seek:
  that I may dwell in the house of the
    LORD
  all the days of my life,
  to gaze on the beauty of the LORD
    and to seek him in his temple.
5 For in the day of trouble
    he will keep me safe in his dwelling;
  he will hide me in the shelter of his
    sacred tent
    and set me high upon a rock.

6 Then my head will be exalted
    above the enemies who surround me;
  at his sacred tent I will sacrifice with
    shouts of joy;
  I will sing and make music to the
    LORD.

7 Hear my voice when I call, LORD;
  be merciful to me and answer me.
8 My heart says of you, "Seek his face!"
  Your face, LORD, I will seek.

9 Do not hide your face from me,
  do not turn your servant away in
    anger;
  you have been my helper.
  Do not reject me or forsake me,
    God my Savior.
10 Though my father and mother forsake
    me,
  the LORD will receive me.
11 Teach me your way, LORD;
  lead me in a straight path
    because of my oppressors.
12 Do not turn me over to the desire of my
    foes,
  for false witnesses rise up against me,
    spouting malicious accusations.

13 I remain confident of this:
  I will see the goodness of the LORD
    in the land of the living.
14 Wait for the LORD;
  be strong and take heart
    and wait for the LORD.

Psalm 28

Of David.

1 To you, LORD, I call;
  you are my Rock,
  do not turn a deaf ear to me.
  For if you remain silent,
    I will be like those who go down to
      the pit.
2 Hear my cry for mercy
    as I call to you for help,
  as I lift up my hands
    toward your Most Holy Place.

3 Do not drag me away with the wicked,
    with those who do evil,
  who speak cordially with their neighbors
    but harbor malice in their hearts.
4 Repay them for their deeds
    and for their evil work;
  repay them for what their hands have
    done
    and bring back on them what they
      deserve.

a 2 Or slander

5 Because they have no regard for the
        deeds of the LORD
    and what his hands have done,
  he will tear them down
    and never build them up again.

6 Praise be to the LORD,
    for he has heard my cry for mercy.
7 The LORD is my strength and my
        shield;
    my heart trusts in him, and he helps
        me.
  My heart leaps for joy,
    and with my song I praise him.

8 The LORD is the strength of his people,
    a fortress of salvation for his
        anointed one.
9 Save your people and bless your
        inheritance;
    be their shepherd and carry them
        forever.

Psalm 29

A psalm of David.

1 Ascribe to the LORD, you heavenly
        beings,
    ascribe to the LORD glory and
        strength.
2 Ascribe to the LORD the glory due his
        name;
    worship the LORD in the splendor of
        his*a* holiness.

3 The voice of the LORD is over the waters;
    the God of glory thunders,
    the LORD thunders over the mighty
        waters.
4 The voice of the LORD is powerful;
    the voice of the LORD is majestic.
5 The voice of the LORD breaks the cedars;
    the LORD breaks in pieces the cedars
        of Lebanon.
6 He makes Lebanon leap like a calf,
    Sirion*b* like a young wild ox.
7 The voice of the LORD strikes
    with flashes of lightning.

8 The voice of the LORD shakes the
        desert;
    the LORD shakes the Desert of
        Kadesh.
9 The voice of the LORD twists the oaks*c*
    and strips the forests bare.
  And in his temple all cry, "Glory!"

10 The LORD sits enthroned over the
        flood;
    the LORD is enthroned as King
        forever.
11 The LORD gives strength to his people;
    the LORD blesses his people with
        peace.

Psalm 30*d*

A psalm. A song. For the dedication of the temple.*e*
Of David.

1 I will exalt you, LORD,
    for you lifted me out of the depths
    and did not let my enemies gloat over
        me.
2 LORD my God, I called to you for help,
    and you healed me.
3 You, LORD, brought me up from the
        realm of the dead;
    you spared me from going down to
        the pit.

4 Sing the praises of the LORD, you his
        faithful people;
    praise his holy name.
5 For his anger lasts only a moment,
    but his favor lasts a lifetime;
  weeping may stay for the night,
    but rejoicing comes in the morning.

6 When I felt secure, I said,
    "I will never be shaken."
7 LORD, when you favored me,
    you made my royal mountain*f* stand
        firm;
  but when you hid your face,
    I was dismayed.

8 To you, LORD, I called;
    to the Lord I cried for mercy:

---

a 2 Or *LORD with the splendor of*   *b 6* That is, Mount Hermon   *c 9* Or *LORD makes the deer give birth*   *d* In
Hebrew texts 30:1-12 is numbered 30:2-13.   *e* Title: Or *palace*   *f 7* That is, Mount Zion

9 "What is gained if I am silenced,
    if I go down to the pit?
Will the dust praise you?
    Will it proclaim your faithfulness?
10 Hear, LORD, and be merciful to me;
    LORD, be my help."

11 You turned my wailing into dancing;
    you removed my sackcloth and
        clothed me with joy,
12 that my heart may sing your praises
    and not be silent.
    LORD my God, I will praise you
        forever.

Psalm 31[a]

For the director of music. A psalm of David.

1 In you, LORD, I have taken refuge;
    let me never be put to shame;
    deliver me in your righteousness.
2 Turn your ear to me,
    come quickly to my rescue;
  be my rock of refuge,
    a strong fortress to save me.
3 Since you are my rock and my fortress,
    for the sake of your name lead and
        guide me.
4 Keep me free from the trap that is set
        for me,
    for you are my refuge.
5 Into your hands I commit my spirit;
    deliver me, LORD, my faithful God.

6 I hate those who cling to worthless idols;
    as for me, I trust in the LORD.
7 I will be glad and rejoice in your love,
    for you saw my affliction
    and knew the anguish of my soul.
8 You have not given me into the hands of
        the enemy
    but have set my feet in a spacious place.

9 Be merciful to me, LORD, for I am in
        distress;
    my eyes grow weak with sorrow,
    my soul and body with grief.
10 My life is consumed by anguish
    and my years by groaning;

my strength fails because of my
        affliction,[b]
    and my bones grow weak.
11 Because of all my enemies,
    I am the utter contempt of my
        neighbors
and an object of dread to my closest
        friends—
    those who see me on the street flee
        from me.
12 I am forgotten as though I were dead;
    I have become like broken pottery.
13 For I hear many whispering,
    "Terror on every side!"
They conspire against me
    and plot to take my life.

14 But I trust in you, LORD;
    I say, "You are my God."
15 My times are in your hands;
    deliver me from the hands of my
        enemies,
    from those who pursue me.
16 Let your face shine on your servant;
    save me in your unfailing love.
17 Let me not be put to shame, LORD,
    for I have cried out to you;
but let the wicked be put to shame
    and be silent in the realm of the dead.
18 Let their lying lips be silenced,
    for with pride and contempt
    they speak arrogantly against the
        righteous.

19 How abundant are the good things
    that you have stored up for those who
        fear you,
that you bestow in the sight of all,
    on those who take refuge in you.
20 In the shelter of your presence you hide
        them
    from all human intrigues;
you keep them safe in your dwelling
    from accusing tongues.

21 Praise be to the LORD,
    for he showed me the wonders of his
        love
    when I was in a city under siege.

---

a In Hebrew texts 31:1-24 is numbered 31:2-25.   b 10 Or guilt

22 In my alarm I said,
  "I am cut off from your sight!"
Yet you heard my cry for mercy
  when I called to you for help.

23 Love the LORD, all his faithful
    people!
  The LORD preserves those who are
    true to him,
  but the proud he pays back in full.
24 Be strong and take heart,
  all you who hope in the LORD.

Psalm 32

Of David. A *maskil.*[a]

1 Blessed is the one
  whose transgressions are forgiven,
  whose sins are covered.

2 Blessed is the one
  whose sin the LORD does not count
    against them
  and in whose spirit is no deceit.

3 When I kept silent,
  my bones wasted away
  through my groaning all day long.
4 For day and night
  your hand was heavy on me;
  my strength was sapped
  as in the heat of summer.[b]

5 Then I acknowledged my sin to you
  and did not cover up my iniquity.
I said, "I will confess
  my transgressions to the LORD."
And you forgave
  the guilt of my sin.

---

[a] Title: Probably a literary or musical term   [b] 4 The Hebrew has *Selah* (a word of uncertain meaning) here and at the end of verses 5 and 7.

CONFESS LESSON [*Principle Four*]

For the previous entry in the CONFESS lesson, go to John 8:12 (page 1305).

For a discussion of Principles One through Eight and a listing of their related lessons,
go to pages xvii – xliv.

When I kept silent, my bones wasted away through my groaning
all day long. For day and night your hand was heavy on me; my strength
was sapped as in the heat of summer. Then I acknowledged my sin to you
and did not cover up my iniquity. I said, "I will confess my transgressions
to the LORD." And you forgave the guilt of my sin.

PSALM 32:3–5

Principle Four begins the process of "coming clean." In the second part of Principle Four, we confess our faults to ourselves, to God and to someone else we trust.

The *E* in CONFESS stands for EASE THE PAIN. A person who speaks the truth is always at ease. The next positive change that confession brings is precisely this: It relieves our pain. We're only as sick as our secrets. When we share our deepest secrets, we begin to divide the pain and the shame. A healthy self-worth begins to develop — one that's no longer based on the world's standards but on the truth of Jesus Christ. Pain is inevitable for all of us, but misery is optional.

The next letter in CONFESS is the first *S.* Go to Matthew 7:3 (page 1138).

⁶ Therefore let all the faithful pray to you
　　while you may be found;
　surely the rising of the mighty waters
　　will not reach them.
⁷ You are my hiding place;
　　you will protect me from trouble
　　and surround me with songs of
　　　deliverance.

⑦
⑧
⁸ I will instruct you and teach you in the
　　way you should go;
　I will counsel you with my loving eye
　　on you.
⁹ Do not be like the horse or the mule,
　　which have no understanding
　but must be controlled by bit and
　　bridle
　or they will not come to you.
¹⁰ Many are the woes of the wicked,
　　but the Lord's unfailing love
　　surrounds the one who trusts in him.

⑦
⑧
¹¹ Rejoice in the Lord and be glad, you
　　righteous;
　　sing, all you who are upright in
　　　heart!

Psalm 33

¹ Sing joyfully to the Lord, you righteous;
　　it is fitting for the upright to praise
　　　him.
² Praise the Lord with the harp;
　　make music to him on the ten-
　　　stringed lyre.
³ Sing to him a new song;
　　play skillfully, and shout for joy.

⁴ For the word of the Lord is right and
　　true;
　he is faithful in all he does.
⁵ The Lord loves righteousness and
　　justice;
　the earth is full of his unfailing love.

⁶ By the word of the Lord the heavens
　　were made,
　　their starry host by the breath of his
　　　mouth.

⁷ He gathers the waters of the sea into
　　jars[a];
　　he puts the deep into storehouses.
⁸ Let all the earth fear the Lord;
　　let all the people of the world revere
　　　him.
⁹ For he spoke, and it came to be;
　　he commanded, and it stood firm.

¹⁰ The Lord foils the plans of the nations;
　　he thwarts the purposes of the
　　　peoples.
¹¹ But the plans of the Lord stand firm
　　forever,
　　the purposes of his heart through all
　　　generations.

¹² Blessed is the nation whose God is the
　　Lord,
　　the people he chose for his
　　　inheritance.
¹³ From heaven the Lord looks down
　　and sees all mankind;
¹⁴ from his dwelling place he watches
　　all who live on earth—
¹⁵ he who forms the hearts of all,
　　who considers everything they do.

¹⁶ No king is saved by the size of his
　　army;
　　no warrior escapes by his great
　　　strength.
¹⁷ A horse is a vain hope for deliverance;
　　despite all its great strength it cannot
　　　save.
¹⁸ But the eyes of the Lord are on those
　　who fear him,
　　on those whose hope is in his
　　　unfailing love,
¹⁹ to deliver them from death
　　and keep them alive in famine.

❶
❷
❸
²⁰ We wait in hope for the Lord;
　　he is our help and our shield.
²¹ In him our hearts rejoice,
　　for we trust in his holy name.
²² May your unfailing love be with us,
　　Lord,
　　even as we put our hope in you.

---

a 7 Or *sea as into a heap*

Psalm 34[a,b]

Of David. When he pretended to be insane before
Abimelek, who drove him away, and he left.

1 I will extol the LORD at all times;
  his praise will always be on my
    lips.
2 I will glory in the LORD;
  let the afflicted hear and rejoice.
3 Glorify the LORD with me;
  let us exalt his name together.

4 I sought the LORD, and he answered
    me;
  he delivered me from all my fears.
5 Those who look to him are radiant;
  their faces are never covered with
    shame.
6 This poor man called, and the LORD
    heard him;
  he saved him out of all his troubles.
7 The angel of the LORD encamps around
    those who fear him,
  and he delivers them.

8 Taste and see that the LORD is good;
  blessed is the one who takes refuge in
    him.
9 Fear the LORD, you his holy people,
  for those who fear him lack
    nothing.
10 The lions may grow weak and
    hungry,
  but those who seek the LORD lack no
    good thing.
11 Come, my children, listen to me;
  I will teach you the fear of the
    LORD.
12 Whoever of you loves life
  and desires to see many good days,
13 keep your tongue from evil
  and your lips from telling lies.
14 Turn from evil and do good;
  seek peace and pursue it.

15 The eyes of the LORD are on the
    righteous,
  and his ears are attentive to their cry;

16 but the face of the LORD is against those
    who do evil,
  to blot out their name from the earth.

17 The righteous cry out, and the LORD
    hears them;
  he delivers them from all their
    troubles.
18 The LORD is close to the brokenhearted
  and saves those who are crushed in
    spirit.

19 The righteous person may have many
    troubles,
  but the LORD delivers him from them
    all;
20 he protects all his bones,
  not one of them will be broken.

21 Evil will slay the wicked;
  the foes of the righteous will be
    condemned.
22 The LORD will rescue his servants;
  no one who takes refuge in him will
    be condemned.

Psalm 35

Of David.

1 Contend, LORD, with those who
    contend with me;
  fight against those who fight against
    me.
2 Take up shield and armor;
  arise and come to my aid.
3 Brandish spear and javelin[c]
  against those who pursue me.
Say to me,
  "I am your salvation."

4 May those who seek my life
  be disgraced and put to shame;
may those who plot my ruin
  be turned back in dismay.
5 May they be like chaff before the
    wind,
  with the angel of the LORD driving
    them away;

---

a This psalm is an acrostic poem, the verses of which begin with the successive letters of the Hebrew alphabet.   b In
Hebrew texts 34:1-22 is numbered 34:2-23.   c 3 Or and block the way

⁶ may their path be dark and slippery,
   with the angel of the LORD pursuing
   them.

⁷ Since they hid their net for me without
   cause
   and without cause dug a pit for me,
⁸ may ruin overtake them by surprise —
   may the net they hid entangle them,
   may they fall into the pit, to their ruin.
⁹ Then my soul will rejoice in the LORD
   and delight in his salvation.
¹⁰ My whole being will exclaim,
   "Who is like you, LORD?
   You rescue the poor from those too
     strong for them,
   the poor and needy from those who
     rob them."

¹¹ Ruthless witnesses come forward;
   they question me on things I know
     nothing about.
¹² They repay me evil for good
   and leave me like one bereaved.
¹³ Yet when they were ill, I put on
     sackcloth
   and humbled myself with fasting.
   When my prayers returned to me
     unanswered,
¹⁴   I went about mourning
   as though for my friend or brother.
   I bowed my head in grief
   as though weeping for my mother.
¹⁵ But when I stumbled, they gathered in
     glee;
   assailants gathered against me
     without my knowledge.
   They slandered me without ceasing.
¹⁶ Like the ungodly they maliciously
     mocked;[a]
   they gnashed their teeth at me.

¹⁷ How long, Lord, will you look on?
   Rescue me from their ravages,
   my precious life from these lions.
¹⁸ I will give you thanks in the great
     assembly;
   among the throngs I will praise you.

¹⁹ Do not let those gloat over me
   who are my enemies without cause;
   do not let those who hate me without
     reason
   maliciously wink the eye.
²⁰ They do not speak peaceably,
   but devise false accusations
   against those who live quietly in the
     land.
²¹ They sneer at me and say, "Aha! Aha!
   With our own eyes we have seen it."

²² LORD, you have seen this; do not be
     silent.
   Do not be far from me, Lord.
²³ Awake, and rise to my defense!
   Contend for me, my God and Lord.
²⁴ Vindicate me in your righteousness,
     LORD my God;
   do not let them gloat over me.
²⁵ Do not let them think, "Aha, just what
     we wanted!"
   or say, "We have swallowed him up."

²⁶ May all who gloat over my distress
   be put to shame and confusion;
   may all who exalt themselves over me
   be clothed with shame and disgrace.
²⁷ May those who delight in my vindication
   shout for joy and gladness;
   may they always say, "The LORD be
     exalted,
   who delights in the well-being of his
     servant."

²⁸ My tongue will proclaim your
     righteousness,
   your praises all day long.

Psalm 36[b]

For the director of music. Of David the
servant of the LORD.

¹ I have a message from God in my heart
concerning the sinfulness of the
     wicked:[c]
There is no fear of God
   before their eyes.

---

a 16 Septuagint; Hebrew may mean *Like an ungodly circle of mockers,*   *b* In Hebrew texts 36:1-12 is numbered 36:2-13.   *c 1* Or *A message from God: The transgression of the wicked / resides in their hearts.*

2 In their own eyes they flatter
    themselves
    too much to detect or hate their sin.
3 The words of their mouths are wicked
    and deceitful;
    they fail to act wisely or do good.
4 Even on their beds they plot evil;
    they commit themselves to a sinful
    course
    and do not reject what is wrong.

5 Your love, LORD, reaches to the
    heavens,
    your faithfulness to the skies.
6 Your righteousness is like the highest
    mountains,
    your justice like the great deep.
    You, LORD, preserve both people and
    animals.
7 How priceless is your unfailing love,
    O God!
    People take refuge in the shadow of
    your wings.
8 They feast on the abundance of your
    house;
    you give them drink from your river
    of delights.
9 For with you is the fountain of life;
    in your light we see light.

10 Continue your love to those who know
    you,
    your righteousness to the upright in
    heart.
11 May the foot of the proud not come
    against me,
    nor the hand of the wicked drive me
    away.
12 See how the evildoers lie fallen —
    thrown down, not able to rise!

Psalm 37[a]

Of David.

1 Do not fret because of those who are
    evil
    or be envious of those who do
    wrong;

2 for like the grass they will soon wither,
    like green plants they will soon die
    away.
3 Trust in the LORD and do good;
    dwell in the land and enjoy safe
    pasture.
4 Take delight in the LORD,
    and he will give you the desires of
    your heart.

5 Commit your way to the LORD;
    trust in him and he will do this:
6 He will make your righteous reward
    shine like the dawn,
    your vindication like the noonday
    sun.

7 Be still before the LORD
    and wait patiently for him;
    do not fret when people succeed in their
    ways,
    when they carry out their wicked
    schemes.

8 Refrain from anger and turn from
    wrath;
    do not fret — it leads only to evil.
9 For those who are evil will be
    destroyed,
    but those who hope in the LORD will
    inherit the land.

10 A little while, and the wicked will be no
    more;
    though you look for them, they will
    not be found.
11 But the meek will inherit the land
    and enjoy peace and prosperity.

12 The wicked plot against the righteous
    and gnash their teeth at them;
13 but the Lord laughs at the wicked,
    for he knows their day is coming.

14 The wicked draw the sword
    and bend the bow
    to bring down the poor and needy,
    to slay those whose ways are
    upright.

a This psalm is an acrostic poem, the stanzas of which begin with the successive letters of the Hebrew alphabet.

15 But their swords will pierce their own
        hearts,
    and their bows will be broken.

16 Better the little that the righteous have
        than the wealth of many wicked;
17 for the power of the wicked will be
        broken,
    but the Lord upholds the righteous.

18 The blameless spend their days under
        the Lord's care,
    and their inheritance will endure
        forever.
19 In times of disaster they will not wither;
    in days of famine they will enjoy
        plenty.

20 But the wicked will perish:
    Though the Lord's enemies are like
        the flowers of the field,
    they will be consumed, they will go
        up in smoke.

21 The wicked borrow and do not repay,
    but the righteous give generously;
22 those the Lord blesses will inherit the
        land,
    but those he curses will be destroyed.

23 The Lord makes firm the steps
    of the one who delights in him;
24 though he may stumble, he will not fall,
    for the Lord upholds him with his
        hand.

READY LESSON [*Principle Five*]

For the previous entry in the READY lesson, go to Psalm 143:10 (page 732).

For a discussion of Principles One through Eight and a listing of their related lessons,
go to pages xvii – xliv.

Commit your way to the Lord; trust in him and he will do this:
He will make your righteous reward shine like the dawn,
your vindication like the noonday sun.

Psalm 37:5–6

In Principle Five we need to be READY to voluntarily submit to every change God wants to make in our lives and humbly ask him to remove our character defects.

The *E* in READY stands for EASY DOES IT. These principles and steps aren't quick fixes. We need to allow time for God to work in our lives. This principle goes further than just helping us to stop doing wrong. It helps us to start living life God's way.

Our sins are the symptom of our character defects. They're like weeds in a garden. They'll keep reappearing unless they're pulled out by the roots, the underlying defects of character that have caused the particular sin. For example, an alcoholic's major sin is abusing and being addicted to alcohol. This is a sin addiction. It's the act, the sin. The underlying defect of character may be the lack of any positive self-image. So, when alcoholics who fit this description work Principle Five, they go after the actual defect — the lack of a positive self-image — that caused them to sin in the first place by abusing alcohol.

It takes time, but God is ready and willing to help. He promises this in Psalm 37:5–6.

The next letter in READY is *A*. Go to 1 Peter 1:13–14 (page 1547).

²⁵ I was young and now I am old,
yet I have never seen the righteous
forsaken
or their children begging bread.
²⁶ They are always generous and lend
freely;
their children will be a blessing.ᵃ

²⁷ Turn from evil and do good;
then you will dwell in the land
forever.
²⁸ For the LORD loves the just
and will not forsake his faithful ones.

Wrongdoers will be completely
destroyedᵇ;
the offspring of the wicked will
perish.
²⁹ The righteous will inherit the land
and dwell in it forever.

³⁰ The mouths of the righteous utter
wisdom,
and their tongues speak what is just.
³¹ The law of their God is in their hearts;
their feet do not slip.

³² The wicked lie in wait for the
righteous,
intent on putting them to death;
³³ but the LORD will not leave them in the
power of the wicked
or let them be condemned when
brought to trial.

³⁴ Hope in the LORD
and keep his way.
He will exalt you to inherit the land;
when the wicked are destroyed, you
will see it.

³⁵ I have seen a wicked and ruthless man
flourishing like a luxuriant native
tree,
³⁶ but he soon passed away and was no
more;
though I looked for him, he could
not be found.

³⁷ Consider the blameless, observe the
upright;
a future awaits those who seek peace.ᶜ
³⁸ But all sinners will be destroyed;
there will be no futureᵈ for the
wicked.

³⁹ The salvation of the righteous comes
from the LORD;
he is their stronghold in time of
trouble.
⁴⁰ The LORD helps them and delivers
them;
he delivers them from the wicked
and saves them,
because they take refuge in him.

Psalm 38ᵉ

A psalm of David. A petition.

¹ LORD, do not rebuke me in your anger
or discipline me in your wrath.
² Your arrows have pierced me,
and your hand has come down on
me.
³ Because of your wrath there is no
health in my body;
there is no soundness in my bones
because of my sin.
⁴ My guilt has overwhelmed me
like a burden too heavy to bear.

⁵ My wounds fester and are loathsome
because of my sinful folly.
⁶ I am bowed down and brought very
low;
all day long I go about mourning.
⁷ My back is filled with searing pain;
there is no health in my body.
⁸ I am feeble and utterly crushed;
I groan in anguish of heart.

⁹ All my longings lie open before you,
Lord;
my sighing is not hidden from you.
¹⁰ My heart pounds, my strength fails me;
even the light has gone from my eyes.

ᵃ 26 Or *freely; / the names of their children will be used in blessings* (see Gen. 48:20); or *freely; / others will see that their children are blessed*   ᵇ 28 See Septuagint; Hebrew *They will be protected forever*   ᶜ 37 Or *upright; / those who seek peace will have posterity*   ᵈ 38 Or *posterity*   ᵉ In Hebrew texts 38:1-22 is numbered 38:2-23.

11 My friends and companions avoid me
        because of my wounds;
    my neighbors stay far away.
12 Those who want to kill me set their
        traps,
    those who would harm me talk of my
        ruin;
    all day long they scheme and lie.

13 I am like the deaf, who cannot hear,
    like the mute, who cannot speak;
14 I have become like one who does not
        hear,
    whose mouth can offer no reply.
15 LORD, I wait for you;
    you will answer, Lord my God.
16 For I said, "Do not let them gloat
    or exalt themselves over me when my
        feet slip."

17 For I am about to fall,
    and my pain is ever with me.
18 I confess my iniquity;
    I am troubled by my sin.
19 Many have become my enemies
        without cause[a];
    those who hate me without reason
        are numerous.
20 Those who repay my good with evil
    lodge accusations against me,
    though I seek only to do what is
        good.

21 LORD, do not forsake me;
    do not be far from me, my God.
22 Come quickly to help me,
    my Lord and my Savior.

Psalm 39[b]

For the director of music. For Jeduthun.
A psalm of David.

1 I said, "I will watch my ways
    and keep my tongue from sin;
    I will put a muzzle on my mouth
        while in the presence of the wicked."
2 So I remained utterly silent,
    not even saying anything good.

But my anguish increased;
3   my heart grew hot within me.
    While I meditated, the fire burned;
        then I spoke with my tongue:

4 "Show me, LORD, my life's end
    and the number of my days;
    let me know how fleeting my life is.
5 You have made my days a mere
        handbreadth;
    the span of my years is as nothing
        before you.
Everyone is but a breath,
    even those who seem secure.[c]

6 "Surely everyone goes around like a
        mere phantom;
    in vain they rush about, heaping up
        wealth
    without knowing whose it will
        finally be.

7 "But now, Lord, what do I look for?
    My hope is in you.
8 Save me from all my transgressions;
    do not make me the scorn of fools.
9 I was silent; I would not open my
        mouth,
    for you are the one who has done
        this.
10 Remove your scourge from me;
    I am overcome by the blow of your
        hand.
11 When you rebuke and discipline
        anyone for their sin,
    you consume their wealth like a
        moth —
    surely everyone is but a breath.

12 "Hear my prayer, LORD,
    listen to my cry for help;
    do not be deaf to my weeping.
I dwell with you as a foreigner,
    a stranger, as all my ancestors
        were.
13 Look away from me, that I may enjoy
        life again
    before I depart and am no more."

---

a 19 One Dead Sea Scrolls manuscript; Masoretic Text *my vigorous enemies*   *b* In Hebrew texts 39:1-13 is numbered
39:2-14.   *c 5* The Hebrew has *Selah* (a word of uncertain meaning) here and at the end of verse 11.

Psalm 40[a]

For the director of music. Of David. A psalm.

1 I waited patiently for the LORD;
    he turned to me and heard my cry.
2 He lifted me out of the slimy pit,
    out of the mud and mire;
he set my feet on a rock
    and gave me a firm place to stand.
3 He put a new song in my mouth,
    a hymn of praise to our God.
Many will see and fear the LORD
    and put their trust in him.

4 Blessed is the one
    who trusts in the LORD,
who does not look to the proud,
    to those who turn aside to false
        gods.[b]
5 Many, LORD my God,
    are the wonders you have done,
    the things you planned for us.
None can compare with you;
    were I to speak and tell of your deeds,
    they would be too many to declare.

6 Sacrifice and offering you did not
        desire—
    but my ears you have opened[c]—
    burnt offerings and sin offerings[d]
    you did not require.
7 Then I said, "Here I am, I have come—
    it is written about me in the scroll.[e]
8 I desire to do your will, my God;
    your law is within my heart."

9 I proclaim your saving acts in the great
        assembly;
    I do not seal my lips, LORD,
    as you know.
10 I do not hide your righteousness in my
        heart;
    I speak of your faithfulness and your
        saving help.
I do not conceal your love and your
        faithfulness
    from the great assembly.

11 Do not withhold your mercy from me,
    LORD;
    may your love and faithfulness
    always protect me.
12 For troubles without number surround
    me;
    my sins have overtaken me, and I
    cannot see.
They are more than the hairs of my head,
    and my heart fails within me.
13 Be pleased to save me, LORD;
    come quickly, LORD, to help me.

14 May all who want to take my life
    be put to shame and confusion;
may all who desire my ruin
    be turned back in disgrace.
15 May those who say to me, "Aha! Aha!"
    be appalled at their own shame.
16 But may all who seek you
    rejoice and be glad in you;
may those who long for your saving
        help always say,
    "The LORD is great!"

17 But as for me, I am poor and needy;
    may the Lord think of me.
You are my help and my deliverer;
    you are my God, do not delay.

Psalm 41[f]

For the director of music. A psalm of David.

1 Blessed are those who have regard for
    the weak;
    the LORD delivers them in times of
    trouble.
2 The LORD protects and preserves
    them—
    they are counted among the blessed
    in the land—
he does not give them over to the
    desire of their foes.
3 The LORD sustains them on their
    sickbed
    and restores them from their bed of
    illness.

---

a In Hebrew texts 40:1-17 is numbered 40:2-18.   b 4 Or to lies
body you have prepared for me   d 6 Or purification offerings   e 7 Or come / with the scroll written for me   f In
Hebrew texts 41:1-13 is numbered 41:2-14.   c 6 Hebrew; some Septuagint manuscripts but a

⁴ I said, "Have mercy on me, LORD;
    heal me, for I have sinned against
        you."
⁵ My enemies say of me in malice,
    "When will he die and his name
        perish?"
⁶ When one of them comes to see me,
    he speaks falsely, while his heart
        gathers slander;
    then he goes out and spreads it
        around.

⁷ All my enemies whisper together
        against me;
    they imagine the worst for me,
        saying,
⁸ "A vile disease has afflicted him;
    he will never get up from the place
        where he lies."
⁹ Even my close friend,
        someone I trusted,
    one who shared my bread,
        has turned*ᵃ* against me.

¹⁰ But may you have mercy on me,
        LORD;
    raise me up, that I may repay them.
¹¹ I know that you are pleased with me,
    for my enemy does not triumph over
        me.
¹² Because of my integrity you uphold me
    and set me in your presence forever.

¹³ Praise be to the LORD, the God of Israel,
    from everlasting to everlasting.
        Amen and Amen.

BOOK II

Psalms 42 – 72

Psalm 42*ᵇ,ᶜ*

For the director of music. A *maskil*ᵈ
of the Sons of Korah.

¹ As the deer pants for streams of water,
    so my soul pants for you, my God.

² My soul thirsts for God, for the living
        God.
    When can I go and meet with God?
³ My tears have been my food
        day and night,
    while people say to me all day long,
        "Where is your God?"
⁴ These things I remember
    as I pour out my soul:
    how I used to go to the house of God
        under the protection of the Mighty
            One*ᵉ*
    with shouts of joy and praise
        among the festive throng.

⁵ Why, my soul, are you downcast?
    Why so disturbed within me?
    Put your hope in God,
        for I will yet praise him,
        my Savior and my God.

⁶ My soul is downcast within me;
    therefore I will remember you
    from the land of the Jordan,
        the heights of Hermon — from
            Mount Mizar.
⁷ Deep calls to deep
    in the roar of your waterfalls;
    all your waves and breakers
        have swept over me.

⁸ By day the LORD directs his love,
    at night his song is with me —
        a prayer to the God of my life.

⁹ I say to God my Rock,
    "Why have you forgotten me?
    Why must I go about mourning,
        oppressed by the enemy?"
¹⁰ My bones suffer mortal agony
    as my foes taunt me,
    saying to me all day long,
        "Where is your God?"

¹¹ Why, my soul, are you downcast?
    Why so disturbed within me?
    Put your hope in God,
        for I will yet praise him,
        my Savior and my God.

ᵃ 9 Hebrew *has lifted up his heel*   *ᵇ* In many Hebrew manuscripts Psalms 42 and 43 constitute one psalm.   *ᶜ* In Hebrew texts 42:1-11 is numbered 42:2-12.   *ᵈ* Title: Probably a literary or musical term   *ᵉ 4* See Septuagint and Syriac; the meaning of the Hebrew for this line is uncertain.

Psalm 43[a]

1 Vindicate me, my God,
    and plead my cause
    against an unfaithful nation.
  Rescue me from those who are
    deceitful and wicked.
2 You are God my stronghold.
    Why have you rejected me?
  Why must I go about mourning,
    oppressed by the enemy?
3 Send me your light and your faithful
    care,
    let them lead me;
  let them bring me to your holy
    mountain,
    to the place where you dwell.
4 Then I will go to the altar of God,
    to God, my joy and my delight.
  I will praise you with the lyre,
    O God, my God.

5 Why, my soul, are you downcast?
    Why so disturbed within me?
  Put your hope in God,
    for I will yet praise him,
    my Savior and my God.

Psalm 44[b]

For the director of music. Of the Sons of Korah.
A maskil.[c]

1 We have heard it with our ears, O God;
    our ancestors have told us
  what you did in their days,
    in days long ago.
2 With your hand you drove out the
    nations
    and planted our ancestors;
  you crushed the peoples
    and made our ancestors flourish.
3 It was not by their sword that they won
    the land,
    nor did their arm bring them victory;
  it was your right hand, your arm,
    and the light of your face, for you
    loved them.

4 You are my King and my God,
    who decrees[d] victories for Jacob.
5 Through you we push back our
    enemies;
    through your name we trample our
    foes.
6 I put no trust in my bow,
    my sword does not bring me victory;
7 but you give us victory over our
    enemies,
    you put our adversaries to shame.
8 In God we make our boast all day long,
    and we will praise your name
    forever.[e]

9 But now you have rejected and humbled
    us;
    you no longer go out with our
    armies.
10 You made us retreat before the enemy,
    and our adversaries have plundered
    us.
11 You gave us up to be devoured like
    sheep
    and have scattered us among the
    nations.
12 You sold your people for a pittance,
    gaining nothing from their sale.

13 You have made us a reproach to our
    neighbors,
    the scorn and derision of those
    around us.
14 You have made us a byword among the
    nations;
    the peoples shake their heads at us.
15 I live in disgrace all day long,
    and my face is covered with shame
16 at the taunts of those who reproach and
    revile me,
    because of the enemy, who is bent on
    revenge.

17 All this came upon us,
    though we had not forgotten you;
    we had not been false to your
    covenant.

---

a In many Hebrew manuscripts Psalms 42 and 43 constitute one psalm.   b In Hebrew texts 44:1-26 is numbered
44:2-27.   c Title: Probably a literary or musical term   d 4 Septuagint, Aquila and Syriac; Hebrew King, O God; /
command   e 8 The Hebrew has Selah (a word of uncertain meaning) here.

¹⁸ Our hearts had not turned back;
    our feet had not strayed from your
        path.
¹⁹ But you crushed us and made us a
        haunt for jackals;
    you covered us over with deep
        darkness.

²⁰ If we had forgotten the name of our
        God
    or spread out our hands to a foreign
        god,
²¹ would not God have discovered it,
    since he knows the secrets of the
        heart?
²² Yet for your sake we face death all day
        long;
    we are considered as sheep to be
        slaughtered.

²³ Awake, Lord! Why do you sleep?
    Rouse yourself! Do not reject us
        forever.
²⁴ Why do you hide your face
    and forget our misery and
        oppression?

²⁵ We are brought down to the dust;
    our bodies cling to the ground.
²⁶ Rise up and help us;
    rescue us because of your unfailing
        love.

Psalm 45ᵃ

For the director of music. To the tune of "Lilies." Of
the Sons of Korah. A *maskil.ᵇ* A wedding song.

¹ My heart is stirred by a noble theme
    as I recite my verses for the king;
    my tongue is the pen of a skillful
        writer.

² You are the most excellent of men
    and your lips have been anointed
        with grace,
    since God has blessed you forever.

³ Gird your sword on your side, you
        mighty one;

clothe yourself with splendor and
        majesty.
⁴ In your majesty ride forth victoriously
    in the cause of truth, humility and
        justice;
    let your right hand achieve awesome
        deeds.
⁵ Let your sharp arrows pierce the hearts
        of the king's enemies;
    let the nations fall beneath your feet.
⁶ Your throne, O God,ᶜ will last for ever
        and ever;
    a scepter of justice will be the scepter
        of your kingdom.
⁷ You love righteousness and hate
        wickedness;
    therefore God, your God, has set you
        above your companions
    by anointing you with the oil of joy.
⁸ All your robes are fragrant with myrrh
        and aloes and cassia;
    from palaces adorned with ivory
    the music of the strings makes you
        glad.
⁹ Daughters of kings are among your
        honored women;
    at your right hand is the royal bride
        in gold of Ophir.

¹⁰ Listen, daughter, and pay careful
        attention:
    Forget your people and your father's
        house.
¹¹ Let the king be enthralled by your
        beauty;
    honor him, for he is your lord.
¹² The city of Tyre will come with a
        gift,ᵈ
    people of wealth will seek your
        favor.
¹³ All glorious is the princess within her
        chamber;
    her gown is interwoven with gold.
¹⁴ In embroidered garments she is led to
        the king;
    her virgin companions follow her—
        those brought to be with her.

ᵃ In Hebrew texts 45:1-17 is numbered 45:2-18.   ᵇ Title: Probably a literary or musical term   ᶜ 6 Here the king is
addressed as God's representative.   ᵈ 12 Or *A Tyrian robe is among the gifts*

¹⁵Led in with joy and gladness,
they enter the palace of the king.

¹⁶Your sons will take the place of your
fathers;
you will make them princes
throughout the land.

¹⁷I will perpetuate your memory through
all generations;
therefore the nations will praise you
for ever and ever.

Psalm 46^a

For the director of music. Of the Sons of Korah.
According to *alamoth.*^b A song.

¹God is our refuge and strength,
an ever-present help in trouble.
²Therefore we will not fear, though the
earth give way
and the mountains fall into the heart
of the sea,

³though its waters roar and foam
and the mountains quake with their
surging.^c

⁴There is a river whose streams make
glad the city of God,
the holy place where the Most High
dwells.
⁵God is within her, she will not fall;
God will help her at break of day.
⁶Nations are in uproar, kingdoms fall;
he lifts his voice, the earth melts.

⁷The Lord Almighty is with us;
the God of Jacob is our fortress.

⁸Come and see what the Lord has done,
the desolations he has brought on the
earth.
⁹He makes wars cease
to the ends of the earth.
He breaks the bow and shatters the spear;
he burns the shields^d with fire.

---

^a In Hebrew texts 46:1-11 is numbered 46:2-12.   ^b Title: Probably a musical term   ^c 3 The Hebrew has *Selah* (a word of uncertain meaning) here and at the end of verses 7 and 11.   ^d 9 Or *chariots*

SANITY LESSON [*Principle Two*]

This is the first page of the SANITY lesson.

**For a discussion of Principles One through Eight and a listing of their related lessons,
go to pages xvii – xliv.**

God is our refuge and strength, an ever-present help in trouble.

PSALM 46:1

In Principle Two we earnestly believe that God exists, that we matter to him and that he has the power to help us recover. It's in this principle that we find the SANITY to begin to stop making the same poor choices again and again.

The first letter in SANITY is *S*, which stands for STRENGTH. When we accept Jesus as our Higher Power, we receive strength to face the fears that, in the past, have caused us to fight, flee or freeze. In Psalm 73:26 the psalmist affirms a wonderful truth: "My flesh and my heart may fail, but God is the strength of my heart and my portion forever." Relying on our own power is precisely what got us where we are in the first place. We believed that we didn't need God's help, that we were quite capable in our own strength to make the grade. It's almost as though we were disconnected from our true power source, God.

The next letter in SANITY is A. Go to Romans 15:7 (page 1416).

¹⁰He says, "Be still, and know that I am
     God;
   I will be exalted among the
        nations,
   I will be exalted in the earth."

¹¹The LORD Almighty is with us;
   the God of Jacob is our fortress.

Psalm 47ᵃ

For the director of music. Of the Sons of Korah.
A psalm.

¹Clap your hands, all you nations;
   shout to God with cries of joy.

²For the LORD Most High is awesome,
   the great King over all the earth.
³He subdued nations under us,
   peoples under our feet.
⁴He chose our inheritance for us,
   the pride of Jacob, whom he loved.ᵇ

⁵God has ascended amid shouts of joy,
   the LORD amid the sounding of
        trumpets.
⁶Sing praises to God, sing praises;
   sing praises to our King, sing
        praises.
⁷For God is the King of all the earth;
   sing to him a psalm of praise.

⁸God reigns over the nations;
   God is seated on his holy throne.
⁹The nobles of the nations assemble
   as the people of the God of
        Abraham,
   for the kingsᶜ of the earth belong to
        God;
   he is greatly exalted.

Psalm 48ᵈ

A song. A psalm of the Sons of Korah.

¹Great is the LORD, and most worthy of
     praise,
   in the city of our God, his holy
        mountain.

²Beautiful in its loftiness,
   the joy of the whole earth,
   like the heights of Zaphonᵉ is Mount
        Zion,
   the city of the Great King.
³God is in her citadels;
   he has shown himself to be her
        fortress.

⁴When the kings joined forces,
   when they advanced together,
⁵they saw her and were astounded;
   they fled in terror.
⁶Trembling seized them there,
   pain like that of a woman in labor.
⁷You destroyed them like ships of
        Tarshish
   shattered by an east wind.

⁸As we have heard,
   so we have seen
in the city of the LORD Almighty,
   in the city of our God:
   God makes her secure
        forever.ᵇ

⁹Within your temple, O God,
   we meditate on your unfailing
        love.
¹⁰Like your name, O God,
   your praise reaches to the ends of the
        earth;
   your right hand is filled with
        righteousness.
¹¹Mount Zion rejoices,
   the villages of Judah are glad
   because of your judgments.

¹²Walk about Zion, go around her,
   count her towers,
¹³consider well her ramparts,
   view her citadels,
that you may tell of them
   to the next generation.

¹⁴For this God is our God for ever and
        ever;
   he will be our guide even to the end.

ᵃ In Hebrew texts 47:1-9 is numbered 47:2-10.   ᵇ 4,8 The Hebrew has *Selah* (a word of uncertain meaning) here.
ᶜ 9 Or *shields*   ᵈ In Hebrew texts 48:1-14 is numbered 48:2-15.   ᵉ 2 *Zaphon* was the most sacred mountain
of the Canaanites.

RELAPSE LESSON [*Principle Seven*]

For the previous entry in the RELAPSE lesson, go to 1 Thessalonians 5:21 (page 1495).

For a discussion of Principles One through Eight and a listing of their related lessons, go to pages xvii – xliv.

> *Be still, and know that I am God; I will be exalted*
> *among the nations, I will be exalted in the earth.*

PSALM 46:10

In Principle Seven we reserve a daily quiet time with God for self-examination, Bible reading and prayer in order to get to know God and his will for our lives and to gain the power to follow his will. As we work this principle, we begin the journey of applying and living what we've discovered in the first six principles. We live daily in humility — as well as in reality, not in denial. We've done our best to amend our past. Through God's guidance we can now make choices about the emotions that will affect our ongoing thinking and actions. We can start to take *action* — positive action — instead of operating in a mode of continual *reaction*.

The second part of this principle — the call to reserve a daily quiet time with God for Bible reading and prayer in order to get to know him and his will for our lives and to gain the power to follow his will — also relates to Step Eleven of the Christ-centered 12 steps.

Step Eleven: We've sought through prayer and meditation to improve our conscious contact with God, praying for knowledge of his will for us, as well as for the power to carry out that will.

The *A* in RELAPSE stands for ALONE WITH AND QUIET BEFORE GOD. Step Eleven uses the word *meditation*, a term that makes some of us feel uncomfortable. A good working definition of *meditation*, though, is precisely what we're after here: conscious contact with God. An important aspect of meditation is slowing down long enough to hear God. With practice we'll begin to realize the value of spending time alone with God. Even Jesus spent intimate time with his Father. We need to set up and keep a daily appointment for a one-on-one with God. We need to learn to listen carefully and try to discern God's gentle request for us to "be still, and know that I am God."

The enemy will use whatever ploys he can to disrupt our quiet time with God. He'll allow us to fill our schedules with so many good things that we burn out or decide that we just don't have the time to keep our appointment with God. Satan loves it when he can keep us from growing and working on the most important relationship in our lives: our bond with Jesus.

Psalm 1:1 – 3 affirms: "Blessed is the one who does not walk in the step with the wicked or stand in the way that sinners take or sit in the company of mockers, but whose delight is in the law of the LORD, and who meditates on his law day and night. That person is like a tree planted by streams of water, which yields its fruit in season and whose leaf does not wither — whatever they do prospers."

The next letter in RELAPSE is *P*. Go to Philippians 4:6 (page 1482).

Psalm 49[a]

For the director of music. Of the Sons of Korah.
A psalm.

[1] Hear this, all you peoples;
    listen, all who live in this world,
[2] both low and high,
    rich and poor alike:
[3] My mouth will speak words of
        wisdom;
    the meditation of my heart will give
        you understanding.
[4] I will turn my ear to a proverb;
    with the harp I will expound my
        riddle:

[5] Why should I fear when evil days
        come,
    when wicked deceivers surround
        me —
[6] those who trust in their wealth
    and boast of their great riches?
[7] No one can redeem the life of another
    or give to God a ransom for them —
[8] the ransom for a life is costly,
    no payment is ever enough —
[9] so that they should live on forever
    and not see decay.
[10] For all can see that the wise die,
    that the foolish and the senseless also
        perish,
    leaving their wealth to others.
[11] Their tombs will remain their houses[b]
        forever,
    their dwellings for endless
        generations,
    though they had[c] named lands after
        themselves.

[12] People, despite their wealth, do not
        endure;
    they are like the beasts that perish.

[13] This is the fate of those who trust in
        themselves,
    and of their followers, who approve
        their sayings.[d]

[14] They are like sheep and are destined to
        die;
    death will be their shepherd
    (but the upright will prevail over
        them in the morning).
    Their forms will decay in the grave,
    far from their princely mansions.
[15] But God will redeem me from the
        realm of the dead;
    he will surely take me to himself.
[16] Do not be overawed when others grow
        rich,
    when the splendor of their houses
        increases;
[17] for they will take nothing with them
        when they die,
    their splendor will not descend with
        them.
[18] Though while they live they count
        themselves blessed —
    and people praise you when you
        prosper —
[19] they will join those who have gone
        before them,
    who will never again see the light of
        life.

[20] People who have wealth but lack
        understanding
    are like the beasts that perish.

Psalm 50

A psalm of Asaph.

[1] The Mighty One, God, the LORD,
    speaks and summons the earth
    from the rising of the sun to where it
        sets.
[2] From Zion, perfect in beauty,
    God shines forth.
[3] Our God comes
    and will not be silent;
    a fire devours before him,
    and around him a tempest rages.
[4] He summons the heavens above,
    and the earth, that he may judge his
        people:

---

[a] In Hebrew texts 49:1-20 is numbered 49:2-21.   [b] 11 Septuagint and Syriac; Hebrew *In their thoughts their houses will remain*   [c] 11 Or *generations, / for they have*   [d] 13 The Hebrew has *Selah* (a word of uncertain meaning) here and at the end of verse 15.

5 "Gather to me this consecrated people,
  who made a covenant with me by
    sacrifice."
6 And the heavens proclaim his
    righteousness,
  for he is a God of justice.*a,b*

7 "Listen, my people, and I will speak;
  I will testify against you, Israel:
  I am God, your God.
8 I bring no charges against you
      concerning your sacrifices
  or concerning your burnt offerings,
    which are ever before me.
9 I have no need of a bull from your stall
  or of goats from your pens,
10 for every animal of the forest is mine,
  and the cattle on a thousand hills.
11 I know every bird in the mountains,
  and the insects in the fields are mine.
12 If I were hungry I would not tell you,
  for the world is mine, and all that is
    in it.
13 Do I eat the flesh of bulls
  or drink the blood of goats?

14 "Sacrifice thank offerings to God,
  fulfill your vows to the Most High,
15 and call on me in the day of trouble;
  I will deliver you, and you will honor
    me."

16 But to the wicked person, God says:

  "What right have you to recite my laws
  or take my covenant on your lips?
17 You hate my instruction
  and cast my words behind you.
18 When you see a thief, you join with him;
  you throw in your lot with adulterers.
19 You use your mouth for evil
  and harness your tongue to deceit.
20 You sit and testify against your brother
  and slander your own mother's son.
21 When you did these things and I kept
    silent,
  you thought I was exactly*c* like you.

But I now arraign you
  and set my accusations before you.

22 "Consider this, you who forget God,
  or I will tear you to pieces, with no
    one to rescue you:
23 Those who sacrifice thank offerings
    honor me,
  and to the blameless*d* I will show my
    salvation."

Psalm 51*e*

For the director of music. A psalm of David. When
the prophet Nathan came to him after David had
committed adultery with Bathsheba.

1 Have mercy on me, O God,
  according to your unfailing love;
  according to your great compassion
    blot out my transgressions.
2 Wash away all my iniquity
  and cleanse me from my sin.

3 For I know my transgressions,
  and my sin is always before me.
4 Against you, you only, have I sinned
  and done what is evil in your
    sight;
  so you are right in your verdict
  and justified when you judge.
5 Surely I was sinful at birth,
  sinful from the time my mother
    conceived me.
6 Yet you desired faithfulness even in the
    womb;
  you taught me wisdom in that secret
    place.

7 Cleanse me with hyssop, and I will be
    clean;
  wash me, and I will be whiter than
    snow.
8 Let me hear joy and gladness;
  let the bones you have crushed
    rejoice.
9 Hide your face from my sins
  and blot out all my iniquity.

---

a 6 With a different word division of the Hebrew; Masoretic Text *for God himself is judge*   *b* 6 The Hebrew has
Selah (a word of uncertain meaning) here.   *c* 21 Or *thought the 'I AM' was*   *d* 23 Probable reading of the original
Hebrew text; the meaning of the Masoretic Text for this phrase is uncertain.   *e* In Hebrew texts 51:1-19 is numbered
51:3-21.

¹⁰Create in me a pure heart, O God,
and renew a steadfast spirit within
me.
¹¹Do not cast me from your presence
or take your Holy Spirit from me.
¹²Restore to me the joy of your salvation
and grant me a willing spirit, to
sustain me.

¹³Then I will teach transgressors your
ways,
so that sinners will turn back to you.
¹⁴Deliver me from the guilt of bloodshed,
O God,
you who are God my Savior,
and my tongue will sing of your
righteousness.
¹⁵Open my lips, Lord,
and my mouth will declare your
praise.
¹⁶You do not delight in sacrifice, or I
would bring it;
you do not take pleasure in burnt
offerings.
¹⁷My sacrifice, O God, is*a* a broken
spirit;
a broken and contrite heart
you, God, will not despise.

¹⁸May it please you to prosper Zion,
to build up the walls of Jerusalem.
¹⁹Then you will delight in the sacrifices
of the righteous,
in burnt offerings offered whole;
then bulls will be offered on your
altar.

Psalm 52*b*

For the director of music. A *maskilc* of David. When
Doeg the Edomite had gone to Saul and told him:
"David has gone to the house of Ahimelek."

¹Why do you boast of evil, you mighty
hero?
Why do you boast all day long,
you who are a disgrace in the eyes of
God?

²You who practice deceit,
your tongue plots destruction;
it is like a sharpened razor.
³You love evil rather than good,
falsehood rather than speaking the
truth.*d*
⁴You love every harmful word,
you deceitful tongue!

⁵Surely God will bring you down to
everlasting ruin:
He will snatch you up and pluck you
from your tent;
he will uproot you from the land of
the living.
⁶The righteous will see and fear;
they will laugh at you, saying,
⁷"Here now is the man
who did not make God his
stronghold
but trusted in his great wealth
and grew strong by destroying others!"

⁸But I am like an olive tree
flourishing in the house of God;
I trust in God's unfailing love
for ever and ever.
⁹For what you have done I will always
praise you
in the presence of your faithful
people.
And I will hope in your name,
for your name is good.

Psalm 53*e*

For the director of music. According to *mahalath.f*
A *maskilc* of David.

¹The fool says in his heart,
"There is no God."
They are corrupt, and their ways are vile;
there is no one who does good.

²God looks down from heaven
on all mankind
to see if there are any who understand,
any who seek God.

---

a 17 Or *The sacrifices of God are*   *b* In Hebrew texts 52:1-9 is numbered 52:3-11.   *c* Title: Probably a literary or
musical term   *d 3* The Hebrew has *Selah* (a word of uncertain meaning) here and at the end of verse 5.   *e* In
Hebrew texts 53:1-6 is numbered 53:2-7.   *f* Title: Probably a musical term

3 Everyone has turned away, all have
    become corrupt;
  there is no one who does good,
    not even one.

4 Do all these evildoers know nothing?

  They devour my people as though
    eating bread;
  they never call on God.
5 But there they are, overwhelmed with
    dread,
  where there was nothing to dread.
  God scattered the bones of those who
    attacked you;
  you put them to shame, for God
    despised them.

6 Oh, that salvation for Israel would come
    out of Zion!
  When God restores his people,
    let Jacob rejoice and Israel be glad!

Psalm 54[a]

For the director of music. With stringed
instruments. A *maskil*[b] of David. When the Ziphites
had gone to Saul and said, "Is not David hiding
among us?"

1 Save me, O God, by your name;
  vindicate me by your might.
2 Hear my prayer, O God;
  listen to the words of my mouth.

3 Arrogant foes are attacking me;
  ruthless people are trying to kill me —
    people without regard for God.[c]

4 Surely God is my help;
  the Lord is the one who sustains me.

5 Let evil recoil on those who slander me;
  in your faithfulness destroy them.

6 I will sacrifice a freewill offering to you;
  I will praise your name, LORD, for it
    is good.
7 You have delivered me from all my
    troubles,
  and my eyes have looked in triumph
    on my foes.

Psalm 55[d]

For the director of music. With stringed
instruments. A *maskil*[b] of David.

1 Listen to my prayer, O God,
  do not ignore my plea;
2   hear me and answer me.
  My thoughts trouble me and I am
    distraught
3   because of what my enemy is saying,
    because of the threats of the wicked;
  for they bring down suffering on me
    and assail me in their anger.

4 My heart is in anguish within me;
  the terrors of death have fallen on
    me.
5 Fear and trembling have beset me;
  horror has overwhelmed me.
6 I said, "Oh, that I had the wings of a
    dove!
  I would fly away and be at rest.
7 I would flee far away
    and stay in the desert;[e]
8 I would hurry to my place of shelter,
    far from the tempest and storm."

9 Lord, confuse the wicked, confound
    their words,
  for I see violence and strife in the
    city.
10 Day and night they prowl about on its
    walls;
  malice and abuse are within it.
11 Destructive forces are at work in the
    city;
  threats and lies never leave its streets.

12 If an enemy were insulting me,
    I could endure it;
  if a foe were rising against me,
    I could hide.
13 But it is you, a man like myself,
  my companion, my close friend,
14 with whom I once enjoyed sweet
    fellowship
  at the house of God,

---

a In Hebrew texts 54:1-7 is numbered 54:3-9.   *b* Title: Probably a literary or musical term   *c* 3 The Hebrew has
Selah (a word of uncertain meaning) here.   *d* In Hebrew texts 55:1-23 is numbered 55:2-24.   *e* 7 The Hebrew has
Selah (a word of uncertain meaning) here and in the middle of verse 19.

as we walked about
  among the worshipers.

15 Let death take my enemies by surprise;
  let them go down alive to the realm
      of the dead,
  for evil finds lodging among them.

16 As for me, I call to God,
  and the LORD saves me.
17 Evening, morning and noon
  I cry out in distress,
  and he hears my voice.
18 He rescues me unharmed
  from the battle waged against me,
  even though many oppose me.
19 God, who is enthroned from of old,
  who does not change —
he will hear them and humble them,
  because they have no fear of God.

20 My companion attacks his friends;
  he violates his covenant.
21 His talk is smooth as butter,
  yet war is in his heart;
his words are more soothing than oil,
  yet they are drawn swords.

22 Cast your cares on the LORD
  and he will sustain you;
he will never let
  the righteous be shaken.
23 But you, God, will bring down the
      wicked
  into the pit of decay;
the bloodthirsty and deceitful
  will not live out half their days.

But as for me, I trust in you.

2 My adversaries pursue me all day long;
  in their pride many are attacking me.
3 When I am afraid, I put my trust in
      you.
4   In God, whose word I praise —
  in God I trust and am not afraid.
  What can mere mortals do to me?

5 All day long they twist my words;
  all their schemes are for my ruin.
6 They conspire, they lurk,
  they watch my steps,
  hoping to take my life.
7 Because of their wickedness do not^c let
      them escape;
  in your anger, God, bring the nations
      down.

8 Record my misery;
  list my tears on your scroll^d —
  are they not in your record?
9 Then my enemies will turn back
  when I call for help.
  By this I will know that God is for
      me.

10 In God, whose word I praise,
  in the LORD, whose word I praise —
11 in God I trust and am not afraid.
  What can man do to me?

12 I am under vows to you, my God;
  I will present my thank offerings to
      you.
13 For you have delivered me from death
  and my feet from stumbling,
  that I may walk before God
  in the light of life.

Psalm 56^a

For the director of music. To the tune of "A Dove
on Distant Oaks." Of David. A *miktam.*^{b} When the
Philistines had seized him in Gath.

1 Be merciful to me, my God,
  for my enemies are in hot pursuit;
  all day long they press their attack.

Psalm 57^e

For the director of music. To the tune of "Do Not
Destroy." Of David. A *miktam.*^{b} When he had fled
from Saul into the cave.

1 Have mercy on me, my God, have
      mercy on me,
  for in you I take refuge.

---

^{a} In Hebrew texts 56:1-13 is numbered 56:2-14. ^{b} Title: Probably a literary or musical term ^{c} 7 Probable reading
of the original Hebrew text; Masoretic Text does not have *do not.* ^{d} 8 Or *misery; / put my tears in your wineskin*
^{e} In Hebrew texts 57:1-11 is numbered 57:2-12.

I will take refuge in the shadow of your
  wings
    until the disaster has passed.

²I cry out to God Most High,
  to God, who vindicates me.
³He sends from heaven and saves me,
  rebuking those who hotly pursue
    me—ᵃ
  God sends forth his love and his
    faithfulness.

⁴I am in the midst of lions;
  I am forced to dwell among ravenous
    beasts—
  men whose teeth are spears and arrows,
    whose tongues are sharp swords.

⁵Be exalted, O God, above the heavens;
  let your glory be over all the earth.

⁶They spread a net for my feet—
  I was bowed down in distress.
  They dug a pit in my path—
    but they have fallen into it themselves.

⁷My heart, O God, is steadfast,
  my heart is steadfast;
  I will sing and make music.
⁸Awake, my soul!
  Awake, harp and lyre!
  I will awaken the dawn.

⁹I will praise you, Lord, among the
    nations;
  I will sing of you among the peoples.
¹⁰For great is your love, reaching to the
    heavens;
  your faithfulness reaches to the skies.

¹¹Be exalted, O God, above the heavens;
  let your glory be over all the earth.

Psalm 58ᵇ

For the director of music. To the tune of "Do Not
  Destroy." Of David. A *miktam.*ᶜ

¹Do you rulers indeed speak justly?
  Do you judge people with equity?

²No, in your heart you devise injustice,
  and your hands mete out violence on
    the earth.
³Even from birth the wicked go astray;
  from the womb they are wayward,
    spreading lies.
⁴Their venom is like the venom of a
    snake,
  like that of a cobra that has stopped
    its ears,
⁵that will not heed the tune of the
    charmer,
  however skillful the enchanter may be.

⁶Break the teeth in their mouths, O God;
  LORD, tear out the fangs of those lions!
⁷Let them vanish like water that flows
    away;
  when they draw the bow, let their
    arrows fall short.
⁸May they be like a slug that melts away
    as it moves along,
  like a stillborn child that never sees
    the sun.

⁹Before your pots can feel the heat of the
    thorns—
  whether they are green or dry—the
    wicked will be swept away.ᵈ
¹⁰The righteous will be glad when they
    are avenged,
  when they dip their feet in the blood
    of the wicked.
¹¹Then people will say,
  "Surely the righteous still are
    rewarded;
  surely there is a God who judges the
    earth."

Psalm 59ᵉ

For the director of music. To the tune of "Do Not
Destroy." Of David. A *miktam.*ᶜ When Saul had sent
men to watch David's house in order to kill him.

¹Deliver me from my enemies, O God;
  be my fortress against those who are
    attacking me.

ᵃ 3 The Hebrew has *Selah* (a word of uncertain meaning) here and at the end of verse 6.   ᵇ In Hebrew texts 58:1-11
is numbered 58:2-12.   ᶜ Title: Probably a literary or musical term   ᵈ 9 The meaning of the Hebrew for this
verse is uncertain.   ᵉ In Hebrew texts 59:1-17 is numbered 59:2-18.

2 Deliver me from evildoers
  and save me from those who are after
    my blood.

3 See how they lie in wait for me!
  Fierce men conspire against me
  for no offense or sin of mine, LORD.
4 I have done no wrong, yet they are
    ready to attack me.
  Arise to help me; look on my plight!
5 You, LORD God Almighty,
  you who are the God of Israel,
  rouse yourself to punish all the
    nations;
  show no mercy to wicked traitors.*a*

6 They return at evening,
  snarling like dogs,
  and prowl about the city.
7 See what they spew from their
    mouths —
  the words from their lips are sharp as
    swords,
  and they think, "Who can hear us?"
8 But you laugh at them, LORD;
  you scoff at all those nations.

9 You are my strength, I watch for you;
  you, God, are my fortress,
10   my God on whom I can rely.

  God will go before me
  and will let me gloat over those who
    slander me.
11 But do not kill them, Lord our shield,*b*
  or my people will forget.
  In your might uproot them
  and bring them down.
12 For the sins of their mouths,
  for the words of their lips,
  let them be caught in their pride.
  For the curses and lies they utter,
13   consume them in your wrath,
  consume them till they are no more.
  Then it will be known to the ends of the
    earth
  that God rules over Jacob.

14 They return at evening,
  snarling like dogs,
  and prowl about the city.
15 They wander about for food
  and howl if not satisfied.
16 But I will sing of your strength,
  in the morning I will sing of your
    love;
  for you are my fortress,
  my refuge in times of trouble.

17 You are my strength, I sing praise to you;
  you, God, are my fortress,
  my God on whom I can rely.

Psalm 60*c*

For the director of music. To the tune of "The Lily of
the Covenant." A *miktam*d of David. For teaching.
When he fought Aram Naharaim*e* and Aram
Zobah,*f* and when Joab returned and struck down
twelve thousand Edomites in the Valley of Salt.

1 You have rejected us, God, and burst
    upon us;
  you have been angry — now restore us!
2 You have shaken the land and torn it
    open;
  mend its fractures, for it is quaking.
3 You have shown your people desperate
    times;
  you have given us wine that makes us
    stagger.
4 But for those who fear you, you have
    raised a banner
  to be unfurled against the bow.*g*

5 Save us and help us with your right
    hand,
  that those you love may be delivered.
6 God has spoken from his sanctuary:
  "In triumph I will parcel out
    Shechem
  and measure off the Valley of
    Sukkoth.
7 Gilead is mine, and Manasseh is mine;
  Ephraim is my helmet,
  Judah is my scepter.

---

a 5 The Hebrew has *Selah* (a word of uncertain meaning) here and at the end of verse 13.   *b 11* Or *sovereign*
c In Hebrew texts 60:1-12 is numbered 60:3-14.   *d* Title: Probably a literary or musical term   *e* Title: That is,
Arameans of Northwest Mesopotamia   *f* Title: That is, Arameans of central Syria   *g 4* The Hebrew has *Selah*
(a word of uncertain meaning) here.

8 Moab is my washbasin,
   on Edom I toss my sandal;
   over Philistia I shout in triumph."

9 Who will bring me to the fortified
      city?
   Who will lead me to Edom?
10 Is it not you, God, you who have now
      rejected us
   and no longer go out with our
      armies?
11 Give us aid against the enemy,
   for human help is worthless.
12 With God we will gain the victory,
   and he will trample down our
      enemies.

Psalm 61[a]

For the director of music. With stringed
instruments. Of David.

1 Hear my cry, O God;
   listen to my prayer.

2 From the ends of the earth I call to you,
   I call as my heart grows faint;
   lead me to the rock that is higher
      than I.
3 For you have been my refuge,
   a strong tower against the foe.

4 I long to dwell in your tent forever
   and take refuge in the shelter of your
      wings.[b]
5 For you, God, have heard my vows;
   you have given me the heritage of
      those who fear your name.

6 Increase the days of the king's life,
   his years for many generations.
7 May he be enthroned in God's presence
      forever;
   appoint your love and faithfulness to
      protect him.

8 Then I will ever sing in praise of your
      name
   and fulfill my vows day after day.

Psalm 62[c]

For the director of music. For Jeduthun.
A psalm of David.

1 Truly my soul finds rest in God;
   my salvation comes from him.
2 Truly he is my rock and my salvation;
   he is my fortress, I will never be
      shaken.

3 How long will you assault me?
   Would all of you throw me down —
   this leaning wall, this tottering fence?
4 Surely they intend to topple me
   from my lofty place;
   they take delight in lies.
 With their mouths they bless,
   but in their hearts they curse.[d]

5 Yes, my soul, find rest in God;
   my hope comes from him.
6 Truly he is my rock and my salvation;
   he is my fortress, I will not be
      shaken.
7 My salvation and my honor depend on
      God[e];
   he is my mighty rock, my refuge.
8 Trust in him at all times, you people;
   pour out your hearts to him,
   for God is our refuge.

9 Surely the lowborn are but a breath,
   the highborn are but a lie.
 If weighed on a balance, they are
      nothing;
   together they are only a breath.
10 Do not trust in extortion
   or put vain hope in stolen goods;
   though your riches increase,
   do not set your heart on them.

11 One thing God has spoken,
   two things I have heard:
 "Power belongs to you, God,
12   and with you, Lord, is unfailing
      love";
   and, "You reward everyone
      according to what they have done."

---

a In Hebrew texts 61:1-8 is numbered 61:2-9.   *b 4* The Hebrew has *Selah* (a word of uncertain meaning) here.
c In Hebrew texts 62:1-12 is numbered 62:2-13.   *d 4* The Hebrew has *Selah* (a word of uncertain meaning) here and
at the end of verse 8.   *e 7* Or / *God Most High is my salvation and my honor*

Psalm 63[a]

A psalm of David. When he was in
the Desert of Judah.

[1] You, God, are my God,
  earnestly I seek you;
I thirst for you,
  my whole being longs for you,
in a dry and parched land
  where there is no water.

[2] I have seen you in the sanctuary
  and beheld your power and your glory.
[3] Because your love is better than life,
  my lips will glorify you.
[4] I will praise you as long as I live,
  and in your name I will lift up my hands.
[5] I will be fully satisfied as with the
    richest of foods;
  with singing lips my mouth will
    praise you.

[6] On my bed I remember you;
  I think of you through the watches of
    the night.
[7] Because you are my help,
  I sing in the shadow of your wings.
[8] I cling to you;
  your right hand upholds me.

[9] Those who want to kill me will be
    destroyed;
  they will go down to the depths of
    the earth.
[10] They will be given over to the sword
  and become food for jackals.

[11] But the king will rejoice in God;
  all who swear by God will glory in him,
  while the mouths of liars will be
    silenced.

Psalm 64[b]

For the director of music. A psalm of David.

[1] Hear me, my God, as I voice my
    complaint;
  protect my life from the threat of the
    enemy.

[2] Hide me from the conspiracy of the
    wicked,
  from the plots of evildoers.
[3] They sharpen their tongues like swords
  and aim cruel words like deadly
    arrows.
[4] They shoot from ambush at the
    innocent;
  they shoot suddenly, without fear.

[5] They encourage each other in evil
    plans,
  they talk about hiding their snares;
  they say, "Who will see it[c]?"
[6] They plot injustice and say,
  "We have devised a perfect plan!"
  Surely the human mind and heart
    are cunning.

[7] But God will shoot them with his
    arrows;
  they will suddenly be struck down.
[8] He will turn their own tongues against
    them
  and bring them to ruin;
  all who see them will shake their
    heads in scorn.
[9] All people will fear;
  they will proclaim the works of God
  and ponder what he has done.

[10] The righteous will rejoice in the LORD
  and take refuge in him;
  all the upright in heart will glory in
    him!

Psalm 65[d]

For the director of music. A psalm of David. A song.

[1] Praise awaits[e] you, our God, in Zion;
  to you our vows will be fulfilled.
[2] You who answer prayer,
  to you all people will come.
[3] When we were overwhelmed by sins,
  you forgave[f] our transgressions.
[4] Blessed are those you choose
  and bring near to live in your courts!

---

[a] In Hebrew texts 63:1-11 is numbered 63:2-12.   [b] In Hebrew texts 64:1-10 is numbered 64:2-11.   [c] 5 Or us
[d] In Hebrew texts 65:1-13 is numbered 65:2-14.   [e] 1 Or befits; the meaning of the Hebrew for this word is uncertain.
[f] 3 Or made atonement for

We are filled with the good things of
　　your house,
　　of your holy temple.

5 You answer us with awesome and
　　righteous deeds,
　　God our Savior,
the hope of all the ends of the earth
　　and of the farthest seas,
6 who formed the mountains by your
　　power,
　　having armed yourself with strength,
7 who stilled the roaring of the seas,
　　the roaring of their waves,
　　and the turmoil of the nations.
8 The whole earth is filled with awe at
　　your wonders;
　　where morning dawns, where
　　evening fades,
　　you call forth songs of joy.

9 You care for the land and water it;
　　you enrich it abundantly.
The streams of God are filled with water
　　to provide the people with grain,
　　for so you have ordained it.ᵃ
10 You drench its furrows and level its
　　ridges;
　　you soften it with showers and bless
　　its crops.
11 You crown the year with your bounty,
　　and your carts overflow with
　　abundance.
12 The grasslands of the wilderness
　　overflow;
　　the hills are clothed with gladness.
13 The meadows are covered with flocks
　　and the valleys are mantled with
　　grain;
　　they shout for joy and sing.

Psalm 66

For the director of music. A song. A psalm.

1 Shout for joy to God, all the earth!
2 　Sing the glory of his name;
　　make his praise glorious.

3 Say to God, "How awesome are your
　　deeds!
　　So great is your power
　　that your enemies cringe before you.
4 All the earth bows down to you;
　　they sing praise to you,
　　they sing the praises of your name."ᵇ

5 Come and see what God has done,
　　his awesome deeds for mankind!
6 He turned the sea into dry land,
　　they passed through the waters on
　　foot—
　　come, let us rejoice in him.
7 He rules forever by his power,
　　his eyes watch the nations—
　　let not the rebellious rise up against
　　him.

8 Praise our God, all peoples,
　　let the sound of his praise be heard;
9 he has preserved our lives
　　and kept our feet from slipping.
10 For you, God, tested us;
　　you refined us like silver.
11 You brought us into prison
　　and laid burdens on our backs.
12 You let people ride over our heads;
　　we went through fire and water,
　　but you brought us to a place of
　　abundance.

13 I will come to your temple with burnt
　　offerings
　　and fulfill my vows to you—
14 vows my lips promised and my mouth
　　spoke
　　when I was in trouble.
15 I will sacrifice fat animals to you
　　and an offering of rams;
　　I will offer bulls and goats.

16 Come and hear, all you who fear God;
　　let me tell you what he has done for me.
17 I cried out to him with my mouth;
　　his praise was on my tongue.
18 If I had cherished sin in my heart,
　　the Lord would not have listened;

ᵃ 9 Or *for that is how you prepare the land*　　ᵇ 4 The Hebrew has *Selah* (a word of uncertain meaning) here and at the end of verses 7 and 15.

19but God has surely listened
and has heard my prayer.
20Praise be to God,
who has not rejected my prayer
or withheld his love from me!

Psalm 67[a]

For the director of music. With stringed
instruments. A psalm. A song.

1May God be gracious to us and
bless us
and make his face shine on us — [b]
2so that your ways may be known on
earth,
your salvation among all nations.

3May the peoples praise you, God;
may all the peoples praise you.
4May the nations be glad and sing for
joy,
for you rule the peoples with equity
and guide the nations of the earth.
5May the peoples praise you, God;
may all the peoples praise you.

6The land yields its harvest;
God, our God, blesses us.
7May God bless us still,
so that all the ends of the earth will
fear him.

Psalm 68[c]

For the director of music. Of David. A psalm.
A song.

1May God arise, may his enemies be
scattered;
may his foes flee before him.
2May you blow them away like
smoke —
as wax melts before the fire,
may the wicked perish before God.
3But may the righteous be glad
and rejoice before God;
may they be happy and joyful.

4Sing to God, sing in praise of his name,
extol him who rides on the clouds[d];
rejoice before him — his name is the
LORD.
5A father to the fatherless, a defender of
widows,
is God in his holy dwelling.
6God sets the lonely in families,[e]
he leads out the prisoners with
singing;
but the rebellious live in a sun-
scorched land.

7When you, God, went out before your
people,
when you marched through the
wilderness,[f]
8the earth shook, the heavens poured
down rain,
before God, the One of Sinai,
before God, the God of Israel.
9You gave abundant showers, O God;
you refreshed your weary inheritance.
10Your people settled in it,
and from your bounty, God, you
provided for the poor.

11The Lord announces the word,
and the women who proclaim it are a
mighty throng:
12"Kings and armies flee in haste;
the women at home divide the
plunder.
13Even while you sleep among the sheep
pens,[g]
the wings of my dove are sheathed
with silver,
its feathers with shining gold."
14When the Almighty[h] scattered the
kings in the land,
it was like snow fallen on Mount
Zalmon.

15Mount Bashan, majestic mountain,
Mount Bashan, rugged mountain,

---

a In Hebrew texts 67:1-7 is numbered 67:2-8.   b 1 The Hebrew has *Selah* (a word of uncertain meaning) here and at
the end of verse 4.   c In Hebrew texts 68:1-35 is numbered 68:2-36.   d 4 Or *name, / prepare the way for him who
rides through the deserts*   e 6 Or *the desolate in a homeland*   f 7 The Hebrew has *Selah* (a word of uncertain
meaning) here and at the end of verses 19 and 32.   g 13 Or *the campfires; or the saddlebags*   h 14 Hebrew
Shaddai

16 why gaze in envy, you rugged mountain,
  at the mountain where God chooses
    to reign,
  where the LORD himself will dwell
    forever?
17 The chariots of God are tens of
    thousands
  and thousands of thousands;
  the Lord has come from Sinai into
    his sanctuary.*a*
18 When you ascended on high,
  you took many captives;
  you received gifts from people,
  even from*b* the rebellious —
  that you,*c* LORD God, might dwell
    there.

19 Praise be to the Lord, to God our Savior,
  who daily bears our burdens.
20 Our God is a God who saves;
  from the Sovereign LORD comes
    escape from death.
21 Surely God will crush the heads of his
    enemies,
  the hairy crowns of those who go on
    in their sins.
22 The Lord says, "I will bring them from
    Bashan;
  I will bring them from the depths of
    the sea,
23 that your feet may wade in the blood of
    your foes,
  while the tongues of your dogs have
    their share."

24 Your procession, God, has come into
    view,
  the procession of my God and King
    into the sanctuary.
25 In front are the singers, after them the
    musicians;
  with them are the young women
    playing the timbrels.
26 Praise God in the great congregation;
  praise the LORD in the assembly of
    Israel.

27 There is the little tribe of Benjamin,
    leading them,
  there the great throng of Judah's
    princes,
  and there the princes of Zebulun and
    of Naphtali.

28 Summon your power, God*d*;
  show us your strength, our God, as
    you have done before.
29 Because of your temple at Jerusalem
  kings will bring you gifts.
30 Rebuke the beast among the reeds,
  the herd of bulls among the calves of
    the nations.
  Humbled, may the beast bring bars of
    silver.
  Scatter the nations who delight in
    war.
31 Envoys will come from Egypt;
  Cush*e* will submit herself to God.

32 Sing to God, you kingdoms of the
    earth,
  sing praise to the Lord,
33 to him who rides across the highest
    heavens, the ancient heavens,
  who thunders with mighty voice.
34 Proclaim the power of God,
  whose majesty is over Israel,
  whose power is in the heavens.
35 You, God, are awesome in your
    sanctuary;
  the God of Israel gives power and
    strength to his people.

  Praise be to God!

Psalm 69*f*

For the director of music. To the tune of "Lilies."
Of David.

1 Save me, O God,
  for the waters have come up to my
    neck.
2 I sink in the miry depths,
  where there is no foothold.

---

a 17 Probable reading of the original Hebrew text; Masoretic Text *Lord is among them at Sinai in holiness*   *b* 18 Or
gifts for people, / even   *c* 18 Or *they*   *d* 28 Many Hebrew manuscripts, Septuagint and Syriac; most Hebrew
manuscripts *Your God has summoned power for you*   *e* 31 That is, the upper Nile region   *f* In Hebrew texts
69:1-36 is numbered 69:2-37.

I have come into the deep waters;
the floods engulf me.
³ I am worn out calling for help;
my throat is parched.
My eyes fail,
looking for my God.
⁴ Those who hate me without reason
outnumber the hairs of my head;
many are my enemies without cause,
those who seek to destroy me.
I am forced to restore
what I did not steal.

⁵ You, God, know my folly;
my guilt is not hidden from you.

⁶ Lord, the LORD Almighty,
may those who hope in you
not be disgraced because of me;
God of Israel,
may those who seek you
not be put to shame because of me.
⁷ For I endure scorn for your sake,
and shame covers my face.
⁸ I am a foreigner to my own family,
a stranger to my own mother's
children;
⁹ for zeal for your house consumes me,
and the insults of those who insult
you fall on me.
¹⁰ When I weep and fast,
I must endure scorn;
¹¹ when I put on sackcloth,
people make sport of me.
¹² Those who sit at the gate mock me,
and I am the song of the drunkards.

¹³ But I pray to you, LORD,
in the time of your favor;
in your great love, O God,
answer me with your sure salvation.
¹⁴ Rescue me from the mire,
do not let me sink;
deliver me from those who hate me,
from the deep waters.
¹⁵ Do not let the floodwaters engulf me
or the depths swallow me up
or the pit close its mouth over me.

¹⁶ Answer me, LORD, out of the goodness
of your love;
in your great mercy turn to me.
¹⁷ Do not hide your face from your servant;
answer me quickly, for I am in trouble.
¹⁸ Come near and rescue me;
deliver me because of my foes.

¹⁹ You know how I am scorned, disgraced
and shamed;
all my enemies are before you.
²⁰ Scorn has broken my heart
and has left me helpless;
I looked for sympathy, but there was
none,
for comforters, but I found none.
²¹ They put gall in my food
and gave me vinegar for my thirst.

²² May the table set before them become a
snare;
may it become retribution andᵃ a trap.
²³ May their eyes be darkened so they
cannot see,
and their backs be bent forever.
²⁴ Pour out your wrath on them;
let your fierce anger overtake them.
²⁵ May their place be deserted;
let there be no one to dwell in their
tents.
²⁶ For they persecute those you wound
and talk about the pain of those you
hurt.
²⁷ Charge them with crime upon crime;
do not let them share in your
salvation.
²⁸ May they be blotted out of the book of
life
and not be listed with the righteous.

²⁹ But as for me, afflicted and in pain—
may your salvation, God, protect me.

³⁰ I will praise God's name in song
and glorify him with thanksgiving.
³¹ This will please the LORD more than an
ox,
more than a bull with its horns and
hooves.

ᵃ 22 Or snare / and their fellowship become

32 The poor will see and be glad —
  you who seek God, may your hearts
    live!
33 The LORD hears the needy
  and does not despise his captive people.

34 Let heaven and earth praise him,
  the seas and all that move in them,
35 for God will save Zion
  and rebuild the cities of Judah.
  Then people will settle there and
    possess it;
36   the children of his servants will
    inherit it,
  and those who love his name will
    dwell there.

Psalm 70[a]

For the director of music. Of David. A petition.

1 Hasten, O God, to save me;
  come quickly, LORD, to help me.

2 May those who want to take my life
  be put to shame and confusion;
  may all who desire my ruin
  be turned back in disgrace.
3 May those who say to me, "Aha! Aha!"
  turn back because of their shame.
4 But may all who seek you
  rejoice and be glad in you;
  may those who long for your saving
    help always say,
  "The LORD is great!"

5 But as for me, I am poor and needy;
  come quickly to me, O God.
  You are my help and my deliverer;
  LORD, do not delay.

Psalm 71

1 In you, LORD, I have taken refuge;
  let me never be put to shame.
2 In your righteousness, rescue me and
    deliver me;
  turn your ear to me and save me.
3 Be my rock of refuge,
  to which I can always go;

give the command to save me,
  for you are my rock and my fortress.
4 Deliver me, my God, from the hand of
    the wicked,
  from the grasp of those who are evil
    and cruel.

5 For you have been my hope, Sovereign
    LORD,
  my confidence since my youth.
6 From birth I have relied on you;
  you brought me forth from my
    mother's womb.
  I will ever praise you.
7 I have become a sign to many;
  you are my strong refuge.
8 My mouth is filled with your praise,
  declaring your splendor all day long.

9 Do not cast me away when I am old;
  do not forsake me when my strength
    is gone.
10 For my enemies speak against me;
  those who wait to kill me conspire
    together.
11 They say, "God has forsaken him;
  pursue him and seize him,
  for no one will rescue him."
12 Do not be far from me, my God;
  come quickly, God, to help me.
13 May my accusers perish in shame;
  may those who want to harm me
  be covered with scorn and disgrace.

14 As for me, I will always have hope;
  I will praise you more and more.

15 My mouth will tell of your righteous
    deeds,
  of your saving acts all day long —
  though I know not how to relate
    them all.
16 I will come and proclaim your mighty
    acts, Sovereign LORD;
  I will proclaim your righteous deeds,
    yours alone.
17 Since my youth, God, you have taught me,
  and to this day I declare your
    marvelous deeds.

---

a In Hebrew texts 70:1-5 is numbered 70:2-6.

¹⁸Even when I am old and gray,
  do not forsake me, my God,
till I declare your power to the next
    generation,
  your mighty acts to all who are to come.

¹⁹Your righteousness, God, reaches to the
    heavens,
  you who have done great things.
  Who is like you, God?
²⁰Though you have made me see troubles,
    many and bitter,
  you will restore my life again;
from the depths of the earth
  you will again bring me up.
²¹You will increase my honor
  and comfort me once more.

²²I will praise you with the harp
  for your faithfulness, my God;
I will sing praise to you with the lyre,
  Holy One of Israel.
²³My lips will shout for joy
  when I sing praise to you —
  I whom you have delivered.
²⁴My tongue will tell of your righteous acts
    all day long,
  for those who wanted to harm me
    have been put to shame and
      confusion.

Psalm 72

Of Solomon.

¹Endow the king with your justice,
    O God,
  the royal son with your righteousness.
²May he judge your people in
    righteousness,
  your afflicted ones with justice.

³May the mountains bring prosperity to
    the people,
  the hills the fruit of righteousness.
⁴May he defend the afflicted among the
    people
  and save the children of the needy;
  may he crush the oppressor.

⁵May he endure^a as long as the sun,
  as long as the moon, through all
    generations.
⁶May he be like rain falling on a mown
    field,
  like showers watering the earth.
⁷In his days may the righteous flourish
  and prosperity abound till the moon
    is no more.

⁸May he rule from sea to sea
  and from the River^b to the ends of
    the earth.
⁹May the desert tribes bow before him
  and his enemies lick the dust.
¹⁰May the kings of Tarshish and of
    distant shores
  bring tribute to him.
  May the kings of Sheba and Seba
  present him gifts.
¹¹May all kings bow down to him
  and all nations serve him.

¹²For he will deliver the needy who cry
    out,
  the afflicted who have no one to help.
¹³He will take pity on the weak and the
    needy
  and save the needy from death.
¹⁴He will rescue them from oppression
    and violence,
  for precious is their blood in his
    sight.

¹⁵Long may he live!
  May gold from Sheba be given him.
  May people ever pray for him
  and bless him all day long.
¹⁶May grain abound throughout the land;
  on the tops of the hills may it sway.
  May the crops flourish like Lebanon
  and thrive^c like the grass of the field.
¹⁷May his name endure forever;
  may it continue as long as the sun.

Then all nations will be blessed through
    him,^d
  and they will call him blessed.

---

^a 5 Septuagint; Hebrew *You will be feared*   ^b 8 That is, the Euphrates   ^c 16 Probable reading of the original
Hebrew text; Masoretic Text *Lebanon, / from the city*   ^d 17 Or *will use his name in blessings* (see Gen. 48:20)

¹⁸ Praise be to the LORD God, the God of
Israel,
     who alone does marvelous deeds.
¹⁹ Praise be to his glorious name forever;
     may the whole earth be filled with
his glory.
         Amen and Amen.

²⁰ This concludes the prayers of David son
of Jesse.

BOOK III

Psalms 73 – 89

Psalm 73

A psalm of Asaph.

¹ Surely God is good to Israel,
     to those who are pure in heart.

² But as for me, my feet had almost slipped;
     I had nearly lost my foothold.
³ For I envied the arrogant
     when I saw the prosperity of the
wicked.

⁴ They have no struggles;
     their bodies are healthy and strong.^a
⁵ They are free from common human
burdens;
     they are not plagued by human ills.
⁶ Therefore pride is their necklace;
     they clothe themselves with violence.
⁷ From their callous hearts comes
iniquity^b;
     their evil imaginations have no
limits.
⁸ They scoff, and speak with malice;
     with arrogance they threaten
oppression.
⁹ Their mouths lay claim to heaven,
     and their tongues take possession of
the earth.
¹⁰ Therefore their people turn to them
     and drink up waters in abundance.^c

¹¹ They say, "How would God know?
     Does the Most High know
anything?"

¹² This is what the wicked are like —
     always free of care, they go on
amassing wealth.

¹³ Surely in vain I have kept my heart pure
     and have washed my hands in
innocence.
¹⁴ All day long I have been afflicted,
     and every morning brings new
punishments.

¹⁵ If I had spoken out like that,
     I would have betrayed your children.
¹⁶ When I tried to understand all this,
     it troubled me deeply
¹⁷ till I entered the sanctuary of God;
     then I understood their final destiny.

¹⁸ Surely you place them on slippery
ground;
     you cast them down to ruin.
¹⁹ How suddenly are they destroyed,
     completely swept away by terrors!
²⁰ They are like a dream when one
awakes;
     when you arise, Lord,
     you will despise them as fantasies.

²¹ When my heart was grieved
     and my spirit embittered,
²² I was senseless and ignorant;
     I was a brute beast before you.

²³ Yet I am always with you;
     you hold me by my right hand.
²⁴ You guide me with your counsel,
     and afterward you will take me into
glory.
²⁵ Whom have I in heaven but you?
     And earth has nothing I desire
besides you.
²⁶ My flesh and my heart may fail,
     but God is the strength of my heart
     and my portion forever.

---

^a 4 With a different word division of the Hebrew; Masoretic Text *struggles at their death; / their bodies are healthy*
^b 7 Syriac (see also Septuagint); Hebrew *Their eyes bulge with fat*   ^c 10 The meaning of the Hebrew for this verse is uncertain.

27 Those who are far from you will perish;
　　you destroy all who are unfaithful to
　　you.
28 But as for me, it is good to be near God.
　　I have made the Sovereign LORD my
　　refuge;
　　I will tell of all your deeds.

Psalm 74

A maskil[a] of Asaph.

1 O God, why have you rejected us
　　forever?
　　Why does your anger smolder against
　　the sheep of your pasture?
2 Remember the nation you purchased
　　long ago,
　　the people of your inheritance,
　　　whom you redeemed —
　　Mount Zion, where you dwelt.
3 Turn your steps toward these
　　everlasting ruins,
　　all this destruction the enemy has
　　brought on the sanctuary.

4 Your foes roared in the place where you
　　met with us;
　　they set up their standards as signs.
5 They behaved like men wielding axes
　　to cut through a thicket of trees.
6 They smashed all the carved paneling
　　with their axes and hatchets.
7 They burned your sanctuary to the
　　ground;
　　they defiled the dwelling place of
　　your Name.
8 They said in their hearts, "We will
　　crush them completely!"
　　They burned every place where God
　　was worshiped in the land.

9 We are given no signs from God;
　　no prophets are left,
　　and none of us knows how long this
　　will be.
10 How long will the enemy mock you, God?
　　Will the foe revile your name
　　forever?

11 Why do you hold back your hand, your
　　right hand?
　　Take it from the folds of your
　　garment and destroy them!

12 But God is my King from long ago;
　　he brings salvation on the earth.

13 It was you who split open the sea by
　　your power;
　　you broke the heads of the monster
　　in the waters.
14 It was you who crushed the heads of
　　Leviathan
　　and gave it as food to the creatures of
　　the desert.
15 It was you who opened up springs and
　　streams;
　　you dried up the ever-flowing rivers.
16 The day is yours, and yours also the
　　night;
　　you established the sun and moon.
17 It was you who set all the boundaries of
　　the earth;
　　you made both summer and winter.

18 Remember how the enemy has mocked
　　you, LORD,
　　how foolish people have reviled your
　　name.
19 Do not hand over the life of your dove
　　to wild beasts;
　　do not forget the lives of your
　　afflicted people forever.
20 Have regard for your covenant,
　　because haunts of violence fill the
　　dark places of the land.
21 Do not let the oppressed retreat in
　　disgrace;
　　may the poor and needy praise your
　　name.
22 Rise up, O God, and defend your cause;
　　remember how fools mock you all
　　day long.
23 Do not ignore the clamor of your
　　adversaries,
　　the uproar of your enemies, which
　　rises continually.

---

a Title: Probably a literary or musical term

Psalm 75[a]

For the director of music. To the tune of "Do Not
Destroy." A psalm of Asaph. A song.

[7]
[8]

[1] We praise you, God,
    we praise you, for your Name is near;
    people tell of your wonderful deeds.

[2] You say, "I choose the appointed time;
    it is I who judge with equity.
[3] When the earth and all its people quake,
    it is I who hold its pillars firm.[b]
[4] To the arrogant I say, 'Boast no more,'
    and to the wicked, 'Do not lift up
        your horns.[c]
[5] Do not lift your horns against heaven;
    do not speak so defiantly.' "

[1]
[2]
[3]

[6] No one from the east or the west
    or from the desert can exalt
        themselves.
[7] It is God who judges:
    He brings one down, he exalts
        another.
[8] In the hand of the LORD is a cup
    full of foaming wine mixed with
        spices;
    he pours it out, and all the wicked of
        the earth
    drink it down to its very dregs.

[9] As for me, I will declare this forever;
    I will sing praise to the God of Jacob,
[10] who says, "I will cut off the horns of all
        the wicked,
    but the horns of the righteous will be
        lifted up."

Psalm 76[d]

For the director of music. With stringed
instruments. A psalm of Asaph. A song.

[1] God is renowned in Judah;
    in Israel his name is great.
[2] His tent is in Salem,
    his dwelling place in Zion.

[3] There he broke the flashing arrows,
    the shields and the swords, the
        weapons of war.[e]
[4] You are radiant with light,
    more majestic than mountains rich
        with game.
[5] The valiant lie plundered,
    they sleep their last sleep;
    not one of the warriors
        can lift his hands.
[6] At your rebuke, God of Jacob,
    both horse and chariot lie still.

[7] It is you alone who are to be feared.
    Who can stand before you when you
        are angry?
[8] From heaven you pronounced
        judgment,
    and the land feared and was quiet —
[9] when you, God, rose up to judge,
    to save all the afflicted of the land.
[10] Surely your wrath against mankind
        brings you praise,
    and the survivors of your wrath are
        restrained.[f]

[11] Make vows to the LORD your God and
        fulfill them;
    let all the neighboring lands
    bring gifts to the One to be feared.
[12] He breaks the spirit of rulers;
    he is feared by the kings of the
        earth.

Psalm 77[g]

For the director of music. For Jeduthun.
Of Asaph. A psalm.

[1] I cried out to God for help;
    I cried out to God to hear me.
[2] When I was in distress, I sought the
        Lord;
    at night I stretched out untiring
        hands,
    and I would not be comforted.

[1]
[2]
[3]

---

[a] In Hebrew texts 75:1-10 is numbered 75:2-11.   [b] 3 The Hebrew has *Selah* (a word of uncertain meaning) here.
[c] 4 *Horns* here symbolize strength; also in verses 5 and 10.   [d] In Hebrew texts 76:1-12 is numbered 76:2-13.
[e] 3 The Hebrew has *Selah* (a word of uncertain meaning) here and at the end of verse 9.   [f] 10 Or *Surely the wrath of
mankind brings you praise, / and with the remainder of wrath you arm yourself*   [g] In Hebrew texts 77:1-20 is
numbered 77:2-21.

³I remembered you, God, and I groaned;
  I meditated, and my spirit grew faint.ᵃ
⁴You kept my eyes from closing;
  I was too troubled to speak.
⁵I thought about the former days,
  the years of long ago;
⁶I remembered my songs in the night.
  My heart meditated and my spirit
    asked:

⁷"Will the Lord reject forever?
  Will he never show his favor again?
⁸Has his unfailing love vanished forever?
  Has his promise failed for all time?
⁹Has God forgotten to be merciful?
  Has he in anger withheld his
    compassion?"

¹⁰Then I thought, "To this I will appeal:
  the years when the Most High
    stretched out his right hand.
¹¹I will remember the deeds of the Lord;
  yes, I will remember your miracles of
    long ago.
¹²I will consider all your works
  and meditate on all your mighty
    deeds."

¹³Your ways, God, are holy.
  What god is as great as our God?
¹⁴You are the God who performs
    miracles;
  you display your power among the
    peoples.
¹⁵With your mighty arm you redeemed
    your people,
  the descendants of Jacob and Joseph.

¹⁶The waters saw you, God,
  the waters saw you and writhed;
  the very depths were convulsed.
¹⁷The clouds poured down water,
  the heavens resounded with thunder;
  your arrows flashed back and forth.
¹⁸Your thunder was heard in the
    whirlwind,
  your lightning lit up the world;
  the earth trembled and quaked.

¹⁹Your path led through the sea,
  your way through the mighty waters,
  though your footprints were not
    seen.

²⁰You led your people like a flock
  by the hand of Moses and Aaron.

Psalm 78

A *maskil*ᵇ of Asaph.

¹My people, hear my teaching;
  listen to the words of my mouth.
²I will open my mouth with a parable;
  I will utter hidden things, things
    from of old—
³things we have heard and known,
  things our ancestors have told us.
⁴We will not hide them from their
    descendants;
  we will tell the next generation
  the praiseworthy deeds of the Lord,
    his power, and the wonders he has
    done.
⁵He decreed statutes for Jacob
  and established the law in Israel,
  which he commanded our ancestors
    to teach their children,
⁶so the next generation would know them,
  even the children yet to be born,
  and they in turn would tell their
    children.
⁷Then they would put their trust in God
  and would not forget his deeds
  but would keep his commands.
⁸They would not be like their
    ancestors—
  a stubborn and rebellious generation,
  whose hearts were not loyal to God,
    whose spirits were not faithful to
    him.

⁹The men of Ephraim, though armed
    with bows,
  turned back on the day of battle;
¹⁰they did not keep God's covenant
  and refused to live by his law.

---

11 They forgot what he had done,
   the wonders he had shown them.
12 He did miracles in the sight of their
      ancestors
   in the land of Egypt, in the region of
      Zoan.
13 He divided the sea and led them
      through;
   he made the water stand up like a wall.
14 He guided them with the cloud by day
   and with light from the fire all night.
15 He split the rocks in the wilderness
   and gave them water as abundant as
      the seas;
16 he brought streams out of a rocky crag
   and made water flow down like
      rivers.

17 But they continued to sin against him,
   rebelling in the wilderness against
      the Most High.
18 They willfully put God to the test
   by demanding the food they craved.
19 They spoke against God;
   they said, "Can God really
   spread a table in the wilderness?
20 True, he struck the rock,
   and water gushed out,
   streams flowed abundantly,
   but can he also give us bread?
   Can he supply meat for his people?"
21 When the Lord heard them, he was
      furious;
   his fire broke out against Jacob,
   and his wrath rose against Israel,
22 for they did not believe in God
   or trust in his deliverance.
23 Yet he gave a command to the skies above
   and opened the doors of the heavens;
24 he rained down manna for the people
      to eat,
   he gave them the grain of heaven.
25 Human beings ate the bread of angels;
   he sent them all the food they could
      eat.
26 He let loose the east wind from the
      heavens
   and by his power made the south
      wind blow.

27 He rained meat down on them like
      dust,
   birds like sand on the seashore.
28 He made them come down inside their
      camp,
   all around their tents.
29 They ate till they were gorged —
   he had given them what they craved.
30 But before they turned from what they
      craved,
   even while the food was still in their
      mouths,
31 God's anger rose against them;
   he put to death the sturdiest among
      them,
   cutting down the young men of
      Israel.

32 In spite of all this, they kept on
      sinning;
   in spite of his wonders, they did not
      believe.
33 So he ended their days in futility
   and their years in terror.
34 Whenever God slew them, they would
      seek him;
   they eagerly turned to him again.
35 They remembered that God was their
      Rock,
   that God Most High was their
      Redeemer.
36 But then they would flatter him with
      their mouths,
   lying to him with their tongues;
37 their hearts were not loyal to him,
   they were not faithful to his
      covenant.
38 Yet he was merciful;
   he forgave their iniquities
   and did not destroy them.
   Time after time he restrained his anger
   and did not stir up his full wrath.
39 He remembered that they were but
      flesh,
   a passing breeze that does not
      return.
40 How often they rebelled against him in
      the wilderness
   and grieved him in the wasteland!

⁴¹ Again and again they put God to the
   test;
   they vexed the Holy One of Israel.
⁴² They did not remember his power —
   the day he redeemed them from the
   oppressor,
⁴³ the day he displayed his signs in
   Egypt,
   his wonders in the region of Zoan.
⁴⁴ He turned their river into blood;
   they could not drink from their
   streams.
⁴⁵ He sent swarms of flies that devoured
   them,
   and frogs that devastated them.
⁴⁶ He gave their crops to the grasshopper,
   their produce to the locust.
⁴⁷ He destroyed their vines with hail
   and their sycamore-figs with sleet.
⁴⁸ He gave over their cattle to the hail,
   their livestock to bolts of lightning.
⁴⁹ He unleashed against them his hot
   anger,
   his wrath, indignation and
   hostility —
   a band of destroying angels.
⁵⁰ He prepared a path for his anger;
   he did not spare them from death
   but gave them over to the plague.
⁵¹ He struck down all the firstborn of
   Egypt,
   the firstfruits of manhood in the
   tents of Ham.
⁵² But he brought his people out like a
   flock;
   he led them like sheep through the
   wilderness.
⁵³ He guided them safely, so they were
   unafraid;
   but the sea engulfed their enemies.
⁵⁴ And so he brought them to the border
   of his holy land,
   to the hill country his right hand had
   taken.
⁵⁵ He drove out nations before them
   and allotted their lands to them as an
   inheritance;
   he settled the tribes of Israel in their
   homes.

⁵⁶ But they put God to the test
   and rebelled against the Most High;
   they did not keep his statutes.
⁵⁷ Like their ancestors they were disloyal
   and faithless,
   as unreliable as a faulty bow.
⁵⁸ They angered him with their high
   places;
   they aroused his jealousy with their
   idols.
⁵⁹ When God heard them, he was furious;
   he rejected Israel completely.
⁶⁰ He abandoned the tabernacle of Shiloh,
   the tent he had set up among
   humans.
⁶¹ He sent the ark of his might into
   captivity,
   his splendor into the hands of the
   enemy.
⁶² He gave his people over to the sword;
   he was furious with his inheritance.
⁶³ Fire consumed their young men,
   and their young women had no
   wedding songs;
⁶⁴ their priests were put to the sword,
   and their widows could not weep.

⁶⁵ Then the Lord awoke as from sleep,
   as a warrior wakes from the stupor of
   wine.
⁶⁶ He beat back his enemies;
   he put them to everlasting shame.
⁶⁷ Then he rejected the tents of Joseph,
   he did not choose the tribe of
   Ephraim;
⁶⁸ but he chose the tribe of Judah,
   Mount Zion, which he loved.
⁶⁹ He built his sanctuary like the heights,
   like the earth that he established
   forever.
⁷⁰ He chose David his servant
   and took him from the sheep pens;
⁷¹ from tending the sheep he brought him
   to be the shepherd of his people
   Jacob,
   of Israel his inheritance.
⁷² And David shepherded them with
   integrity of heart;
   with skillful hands he led them.

Psalm 79

A psalm of Asaph.

¹O God, the nations have invaded your
  inheritance;
  they have defiled your holy temple,
  they have reduced Jerusalem to
    rubble.
²They have left the dead bodies of your
    servants
  as food for the birds of the sky,
  the flesh of your own people for the
    animals of the wild.
³They have poured out blood like water
  all around Jerusalem,
  and there is no one to bury the dead.
⁴We are objects of contempt to our
    neighbors,
  of scorn and derision to those
    around us.

⁵How long, LORD? Will you be angry
    forever?
  How long will your jealousy burn
    like fire?
⁶Pour out your wrath on the nations
  that do not acknowledge you,
  on the kingdoms
  that do not call on your name;
⁷for they have devoured Jacob
  and devastated his homeland.

⁸Do not hold against us the sins of past
    generations;
  may your mercy come quickly to
    meet us,
  for we are in desperate need.
⁹Help us, God our Savior,
  for the glory of your name;
  deliver us and forgive our sins
  for your name's sake.
¹⁰Why should the nations say,
  "Where is their God?"

  Before our eyes, make known among
    the nations
  that you avenge the outpoured blood
    of your servants.

¹¹May the groans of the prisoners come
    before you;
  with your strong arm preserve those
    condemned to die.
¹²Pay back into the laps of our neighbors
    seven times
  the contempt they have hurled at
    you, Lord.
¹³Then we your people, the sheep of your
    pasture,
  will praise you forever;
  from generation to generation
  we will proclaim your praise.

Psalm 80ᵃ

*For the director of music. To the tune of "The Lilies
of the Covenant." Of Asaph. A psalm.*

¹Hear us, Shepherd of Israel,
  you who lead Joseph like a flock.
  You who sit enthroned between the
    cherubim,
  shine forth ²before Ephraim,
    Benjamin and Manasseh.
  Awaken your might;
  come and save us.

³Restore us, O God;
  make your face shine on us,
  that we may be saved.

⁴How long, LORD God Almighty,
  will your anger smolder
  against the prayers of your people?
⁵You have fed them with the bread of
    tears;
  you have made them drink tears by
    the bowlful.
⁶You have made us an object of derisionᵇ
  to our neighbors,
  and our enemies mock us.

⁷Restore us, God Almighty;
  make your face shine on us,
  that we may be saved.

⁸You transplanted a vine from Egypt;
  you drove out the nations and
    planted it.

ᵃ In Hebrew texts 80:1-19 is numbered 80:2-20.   ᵇ 6 Probable reading of the original Hebrew text; Masoretic Text
contention

⁹ You cleared the ground for it,
　　and it took root and filled the land.
¹⁰ The mountains were covered with its
　　　shade,
　　the mighty cedars with its branches.
¹¹ Its branches reached as far as the Sea,ᵃ
　　its shoots as far as the River.ᵇ

¹² Why have you broken down its walls
　　so that all who pass by pick its
　　　grapes?
¹³ Boars from the forest ravage it,
　　and insects from the fields feed
　　　on it.
¹⁴ Return to us, God Almighty!
　　Look down from heaven and see!
　Watch over this vine,
¹⁵ 　the root your right hand has
　　　planted,
　　the sonᶜ you have raised up for
　　　yourself.

¹⁶ Your vine is cut down, it is burned with
　　fire;
　　at your rebuke your people perish.
¹⁷ Let your hand rest on the man at your
　　right hand,
　　the son of man you have raised up for
　　　yourself.
¹⁸ Then we will not turn away from you;
　　revive us, and we will call on your
　　　name.

¹⁹ Restore us, LORD God Almighty;
　　make your face shine on us,
　　that we may be saved.

Psalm 81ᵈ

For the director of music. According to *gittith*.ᵉ
Of Asaph.

¹ Sing for joy to God our strength;
　　shout aloud to the God of Jacob!
² Begin the music, strike the timbrel,
　　play the melodious harp and lyre.

³ Sound the ram's horn at the New Moon,
　　and when the moon is full, on the
　　　day of our festival;

⁴ this is a decree for Israel,
　　an ordinance of the God of Jacob.
⁵ When God went out against Egypt,
　　he established it as a statute for
　　　Joseph.

I heard an unknown voice say:

⁶ "I removed the burden from their
　　　shoulders;
　　their hands were set free from the
　　　basket.
⁷ In your distress you called and I
　　rescued you,
　　I answered you out of a
　　　thundercloud;
　　I tested you at the waters of
　　　Meribah.ᶠ
⁸ Hear me, my people, and I will warn
　　you—
　　if you would only listen to me, Israel!
⁹ You shall have no foreign god among
　　you;
　　you shall not worship any god other
　　　than me.
¹⁰ I am the LORD your God,
　　who brought you up out of Egypt.
　Open wide your mouth and I will fill it.

¹¹ "But my people would not listen to me;
　　Israel would not submit to me.
¹² So I gave them over to their stubborn
　　hearts
　　to follow their own devices.

¹³ "If my people would only listen to me,
　　if Israel would only follow my ways,
¹⁴ how quickly I would subdue their
　　enemies
　　and turn my hand against their foes!
¹⁵ Those who hate the LORD would cringe
　　before him,
　　and their punishment would last
　　　forever.
¹⁶ But you would be fed with the finest of
　　wheat;
　　with honey from the rock I would
　　　satisfy you."

ᵃ *11* Probably the Mediterranean　　ᵇ *11* That is, the Euphrates　　ᶜ *15* Or *branch*　　ᵈ In Hebrew texts 81:1-16 is
numbered 81:2-17.　　ᵉ Title: Probably a musical term　　ᶠ *7* The Hebrew has *Selah* (a word of uncertain meaning) here.

Psalm 82

A psalm of Asaph.

1 God presides in the great assembly;
   he renders judgment among the
      "gods":

2 "How long will you[a] defend the unjust
   and show partiality to the wicked?[b]
3 Defend the weak and the fatherless;
   uphold the cause of the poor and the
      oppressed.
4 Rescue the weak and the needy;
   deliver them from the hand of the
      wicked.

5 "The 'gods' know nothing, they
      understand nothing.
   They walk about in darkness;
   all the foundations of the earth are
      shaken.

6 "I said, 'You are "gods";
   you are all sons of the Most High.'
7 But you will die like mere mortals;
   you will fall like every other ruler."

8 Rise up, O God, judge the earth,
   for all the nations are your
      inheritance.

Psalm 83[c]

A song. A psalm of Asaph.

1 O God, do not remain silent;
   do not turn a deaf ear,
   do not stand aloof, O God.
2 See how your enemies growl,
   how your foes rear their heads.
3 With cunning they conspire against
      your people;
   they plot against those you cherish.
4 "Come," they say, "let us destroy them
      as a nation,
   so that Israel's name is remembered
      no more."

5 With one mind they plot together;
   they form an alliance against you —

6 the tents of Edom and the Ishmaelites,
   of Moab and the Hagrites,
7 Byblos, Ammon and Amalek,
   Philistia, with the people of Tyre.
8 Even Assyria has joined them
   to reinforce Lot's descendants.[b]

9 Do to them as you did to Midian,
   as you did to Sisera and Jabin at the
      river Kishon,
10 who perished at Endor
   and became like dung on the ground.
11 Make their nobles like Oreb and Zeeb,
   all their princes like Zebah and
      Zalmunna,
12 who said, "Let us take possession
   of the pasturelands of God."

13 Make them like tumbleweed, my God,
   like chaff before the wind.
14 As fire consumes the forest
   or a flame sets the mountains ablaze,
15 so pursue them with your tempest
   and terrify them with your storm.
16 Cover their faces with shame, LORD,
   so that they will seek your name.

17 May they ever be ashamed and
      dismayed;
   may they perish in disgrace.
18 Let them know that you, whose name is
      the LORD —
   that you alone are the Most High
      over all the earth.

Psalm 84[d]

For the director of music. According to *gittith.*[e] Of
the Sons of Korah. A psalm.

1 How lovely is your dwelling place,
   LORD Almighty!
2 My soul yearns, even faints,
   for the courts of the LORD;
   my heart and my flesh cry out
   for the living God.
3 Even the sparrow has found a home,
   and the swallow a nest for herself,
   where she may have her young —

---

a 2 The Hebrew is plural.   *b* 2,8 The Hebrew has *Selah* (a word of uncertain meaning) here.   *c* In Hebrew texts
83:1-18 is numbered 83:2-19.   *d* In Hebrew texts 84:1-12 is numbered 84:2-13.   *e* Title: Probably a musical term

a place near your altar,
  LORD Almighty, my King and my
    God.
4 Blessed are those who dwell in your
    house;
  they are ever praising you.*a*

5 Blessed are those whose strength is in
    you,
  whose hearts are set on pilgrimage.
6 As they pass through the Valley of
    Baka,
  they make it a place of springs;
  the autumn rains also cover it with
    pools.*b*
7 They go from strength to strength,
  till each appears before God in Zion.

8 Hear my prayer, LORD God Almighty;
  listen to me, God of Jacob.
9 Look on our shield,*c* O God;
  look with favor on your anointed
    one.

10 Better is one day in your courts
  than a thousand elsewhere;
  I would rather be a doorkeeper in the
    house of my God
  than dwell in the tents of the wicked.
11 For the LORD God is a sun and shield;
  the LORD bestows favor and honor;
  no good thing does he withhold
  from those whose walk is blameless.

12 LORD Almighty,
  blessed is the one who trusts in you.

Psalm 85*d*

For the director of music. Of the Sons of Korah.
A psalm.

1 You, LORD, showed favor to your land;
  you restored the fortunes of Jacob.
2 You forgave the iniquity of your
    people
  and covered all their sins.*e*
3 You set aside all your wrath
  and turned from your fierce anger.

4 Restore us again, God our Savior,
  and put away your displeasure
    toward us.
5 Will you be angry with us forever?
  Will you prolong your anger through
    all generations?
6 Will you not revive us again,
  that your people may rejoice in you?
7 Show us your unfailing love, LORD,
  and grant us your salvation.

8 I will listen to what God the LORD says;
  he promises peace to his people, his
    faithful servants —
  but let them not turn to folly.
9 Surely his salvation is near those who
    fear him,
  that his glory may dwell in our land.

10 Love and faithfulness meet together;
  righteousness and peace kiss each
    other.
11 Faithfulness springs forth from the
    earth,
  and righteousness looks down from
    heaven.
12 The LORD will indeed give what is good,
  and our land will yield its harvest.
13 Righteousness goes before him
  and prepares the way for his steps.

Psalm 86

A prayer of David.

1 Hear me, LORD, and answer me,
  for I am poor and needy.
2 Guard my life, for I am faithful to you;
  save your servant who trusts in you.
  You are my God; 3 have mercy on me,
    Lord,
  for I call to you all day long.
4 Bring joy to your servant, Lord,
  for I put my trust in you.

5 You, Lord, are forgiving and good,
  abounding in love to all who call to
    you.

---

a 4 The Hebrew has *Selah* (a word of uncertain meaning) here and at the end of verse 8.   *b 6* Or *blessings*   *c 9* Or *sovereign*   *d* In Hebrew texts 85:1-13 is numbered 85:2-14.   *e 2* The Hebrew has *Selah* (a word of uncertain meaning) here.

⁶Hear my prayer, LORD;
  listen to my cry for mercy.
⁷When I am in distress, I call to you,
  because you answer me.

⁸Among the gods there is none like you,
    Lord;
  no deeds can compare with yours.
⁹All the nations you have made
  will come and worship before you,
    Lord;
  they will bring glory to your name.
¹⁰For you are great and do marvelous
    deeds;
  you alone are God.

¹¹Teach me your way, LORD,
  that I may rely on your faithfulness;
give me an undivided heart,
  that I may fear your name.
¹²I will praise you, Lord my God, with all
    my heart;
  I will glorify your name forever.
¹³For great is your love toward me;
  you have delivered me from the depths,
    from the realm of the dead.

¹⁴Arrogant foes are attacking me, O God;
  ruthless people are trying to kill
    me—
  they have no regard for you.
¹⁵But you, Lord, are a compassionate and
    gracious God,
  slow to anger, abounding in love and
    faithfulness.
¹⁶Turn to me and have mercy on me;
  show your strength in behalf of your
    servant;
save me, because I serve you
  just as my mother did.
¹⁷Give me a sign of your goodness,
  that my enemies may see it and be
    put to shame,
  for you, LORD, have helped me and
    comforted me.

Psalm 87

Of the Sons of Korah. A psalm. A song.

¹He has founded his city on the holy
    mountain.
²The LORD loves the gates of Zion
  more than all the other dwellings of
    Jacob.

³Glorious things are said of you,
  city of God:ᵃ
⁴"I will record Rahabᵇ and Babylon
  among those who acknowledge
    me—
  Philistia too, and Tyre, along with
    Cushᶜ—
  and will say, 'This one was born in
    Zion.'"ᵈ
⁵Indeed, of Zion it will be said,
  "This one and that one were born in
    her,
  and the Most High himself will
    establish her."
⁶The LORD will write in the register of
    the peoples:
  "This one was born in Zion."

⁷As they make music they will sing,
  "All my fountains are in you."

Psalm 88ᵉ

A song. A psalm of the Sons of Korah. For the
director of music. According to *mahalath leannoth.*ᶠ
A *maskil*ᵍ of Heman the Ezrahite.

¹LORD, you are the God who
    saves me;
  day and night I cry out to you.
²May my prayer come before you;
  turn your ear to my cry.

³I am overwhelmed with troubles
  and my life draws near to death.
⁴I am counted among those who go
    down to the pit;
  I am like one without strength.

ᵃ 3 The Hebrew has *Selah* (a word of uncertain meaning) here and at the end of verse 6.   ᵇ 4 A poetic name for
Egypt   ᶜ 4 That is, the upper Nile region   ᵈ 4 Or *"I will record concerning those who acknowledge me: / 'This one
was born in Zion.' / Hear this, Rahab and Babylon, / and you too, Philistia, Tyre and Cush."*   ᵉ In Hebrew texts
88:1-18 is numbered 88:2-19.   ᶠ Title: Possibly a tune, "The Suffering of Affliction"   ᵍ Title: Probably a literary
or musical term

⁵I am set apart with the dead,
    like the slain who lie in the grave,
  whom you remember no more,
    who are cut off from your care.

⁶You have put me in the lowest pit,
    in the darkest depths.
⁷Your wrath lies heavily on me;
    you have overwhelmed me with all
      your waves.ᵃ
⁸You have taken from me my closest
      friends
    and have made me repulsive to
      them.
  I am confined and cannot escape;
⁹   my eyes are dim with grief.

  I call to you, LORD, every day;
    I spread out my hands to you.
¹⁰Do you show your wonders to the dead?
    Do their spirits rise up and praise
      you?
¹¹Is your love declared in the grave,
    your faithfulness in Destructionᵇ?
¹²Are your wonders known in the place
      of darkness,
    or your righteous deeds in the land of
      oblivion?

¹³But I cry to you for help, LORD;
    in the morning my prayer comes
      before you.
¹⁴Why, LORD, do you reject me
    and hide your face from me?

¹⁵From my youth I have suffered and
      been close to death;
    I have borne your terrors and am in
      despair.
¹⁶Your wrath has swept over me;
    your terrors have destroyed me.
¹⁷All day long they surround me like a
      flood;
    they have completely engulfed me.
¹⁸You have taken from me friend and
      neighbor—
    darkness is my closest friend.

Psalm 89ᶜ

A *maskil*ᵈ of Ethan the Ezrahite.

¹I will sing of the LORD's great love
      forever;
    with my mouth I will make your
      faithfulness known
    through all generations.
²I will declare that your love stands firm
      forever,
    that you have established your
      faithfulness in heaven itself.
³You said, "I have made a covenant with
      my chosen one,
    I have sworn to David my servant,
⁴'I will establish your line forever
    and make your throne firm through
      all generations.'"ᵉ

⁵The heavens praise your wonders, LORD,
    your faithfulness too, in the assembly
      of the holy ones.
⁶For who in the skies above can compare
      with the LORD?
    Who is like the LORD among the
      heavenly beings?
⁷In the council of the holy ones God is
      greatly feared;
    he is more awesome than all who
      surround him.
⁸Who is like you, LORD God Almighty?
    You, LORD, are mighty, and your
      faithfulness surrounds you.

⁹You rule over the surging sea;
    when its waves mount up, you still
      them.
¹⁰You crushed Rahab like one of the slain;
    with your strong arm you scattered
      your enemies.
¹¹The heavens are yours, and yours also
      the earth;
    you founded the world and all that is
      in it.
¹²You created the north and the south;
    Tabor and Hermon sing for joy at
      your name.

ᵃ 7 The Hebrew has *Selah* (a word of uncertain meaning) here and at the end of verse 10.   ᵇ 11 Hebrew *Abaddon*
ᶜ In Hebrew texts 89:1-52 is numbered 89:2-53.   ᵈ Title: Probably a literary or musical term   ᵉ 4 The Hebrew has
Selah (a word of uncertain meaning) here and at the end of verses 37, 45 and 48.

13 Your arm is endowed with power;
    your hand is strong, your right hand
        exalted.
14 Righteousness and justice are the
        foundation of your throne;
    love and faithfulness go before you.
15 Blessed are those who have learned to
        acclaim you,
    who walk in the light of your
        presence, LORD.
16 They rejoice in your name all day
        long;
    they celebrate your righteousness.
17 For you are their glory and strength,
    and by your favor you exalt our
        horn.*a*
18 Indeed, our shield*b* belongs to the
        LORD,
    our king to the Holy One of Israel.

19 Once you spoke in a vision,
    to your faithful people you said:
"I have bestowed strength on a warrior;
    I have raised up a young man from
        among the people.
20 I have found David my servant;
    with my sacred oil I have anointed
        him.
21 My hand will sustain him;
    surely my arm will strengthen him.
22 The enemy will not get the better of
        him;
    the wicked will not oppress him.
23 I will crush his foes before him
    and strike down his adversaries.
24 My faithful love will be with him,
    and through my name his horn*c* will
        be exalted.
25 I will set his hand over the sea,
    his right hand over the rivers.
26 He will call out to me, 'You are my
        Father,
    my God, the Rock my Savior.'
27 And I will appoint him to be my
        firstborn,
    the most exalted of the kings of the
        earth.

28 I will maintain my love to him forever,
    and my covenant with him will never
        fail.
29 I will establish his line forever,
    his throne as long as the heavens
        endure.

30 "If his sons forsake my law
    and do not follow my statutes,
31 if they violate my decrees
    and fail to keep my commands,
32 I will punish their sin with the rod,
    their iniquity with flogging;
33 but I will not take my love from him,
    nor will I ever betray my faithfulness.
34 I will not violate my covenant
    or alter what my lips have uttered.
35 Once for all, I have sworn by my
        holiness—
    and I will not lie to David—
36 that his line will continue forever
    and his throne endure before me like
        the sun;
37 it will be established forever like the
        moon,
    the faithful witness in the sky."

38 But you have rejected, you have
        spurned,
    you have been very angry with your
        anointed one.
39 You have renounced the covenant with
        your servant
    and have defiled his crown in the
        dust.
40 You have broken through all his walls
    and reduced his strongholds to ruins.
41 All who pass by have plundered him;
    he has become the scorn of his
        neighbors.
42 You have exalted the right hand of his
        foes;
    you have made all his enemies
        rejoice.
43 Indeed, you have turned back the edge
        of his sword
    and have not supported him in
        battle.

---

a 17 Horn here symbolizes strong one.   *b 18* Or *sovereign*   *c 24* Horn here symbolizes strength.

⁴⁴ You have put an end to his splendor
  and cast his throne to the ground.
⁴⁵ You have cut short the days of his
    youth;
  you have covered him with a mantle
    of shame.

⁴⁶ How long, Lord? Will you hide
    yourself forever?
  How long will your wrath burn like
    fire?
⁴⁷ Remember how fleeting is my life.
  For what futility you have created all
    humanity!

❶
❷
❸

⁴⁸ Who can live and not see death,
  or who can escape the power of the
    grave?
⁴⁹ Lord, where is your former great love,
  which in your faithfulness you swore
    to David?
⁵⁰ Remember, Lord, how your servant
    has*a* been mocked,
  how I bear in my heart the taunts of
    all the nations,
⁵¹ the taunts with which your enemies,
    Lord, have mocked,
  with which they have mocked every
    step of your anointed one.

⁵² Praise be to the Lord forever!
  Amen and Amen.

BOOK IV

Psalms 90 – 106

Psalm 90

A prayer of Moses the man of God.

¹ Lord, you have been our dwelling place
  throughout all generations.
² Before the mountains were born
  or you brought forth the whole world,
  from everlasting to everlasting you
    are God.

³ You turn people back to dust,
  saying, "Return to dust, you mortals."

⁴ A thousand years in your sight
  are like a day that has just gone by,
  or like a watch in the night.
⁵ Yet you sweep people away in the sleep
    of death —
  they are like the new grass of the
    morning:
⁶ In the morning it springs up new,
  but by evening it is dry and withered.

⁷ We are consumed by your anger
  and terrified by your indignation.
⁸ You have set our iniquities before you,
  our secret sins in the light of your
    presence.

❹
❺

⁹ All our days pass away under your wrath;
  we finish our years with a moan.
¹⁰ Our days may come to seventy years,
  or eighty, if our strength endures;
  yet the best of them are but trouble and
    sorrow,
  for they quickly pass, and we fly away.
¹¹ If only we knew the power of your
    anger!
  Your wrath is as great as the fear that
    is your due.
¹² Teach us to number our days,
  that we may gain a heart of wisdom.

❼
❽

¹³ Relent, Lord! How long will it be?
  Have compassion on your servants.
¹⁴ Satisfy us in the morning with your
    unfailing love,
  that we may sing for joy and be glad
    all our days.
¹⁵ Make us glad for as many days as you
    have afflicted us,
  for as many years as we have seen
    trouble.
¹⁶ May your deeds be shown to your
    servants,
  your splendor to their children.

¹⁷ May the favor*b* of the Lord our God rest
    on us;
  establish the work of our hands for
    us —
  yes, establish the work of our hands.

---

a 50 Or *your servants have*   *b 17* Or *beauty*

Psalm 91

¹ Whoever dwells in the shelter of the
Most High
will rest in the shadow of the
Almighty.ᵃ
² I will say of the LORD, "He is my refuge
and my fortress,
my God, in whom I trust."

³ Surely he will save you
from the fowler's snare
and from the deadly pestilence.
⁴ He will cover you with his feathers,
and under his wings you will find
refuge;
his faithfulness will be your shield
and rampart.
⁵ You will not fear the terror of night,
nor the arrow that flies by day,
⁶ nor the pestilence that stalks in the
darkness,
nor the plague that destroys at midday.
⁷ A thousand may fall at your side,
ten thousand at your right hand,
but it will not come near you.
⁸ You will only observe with your eyes
and see the punishment of the wicked.

⁹ If you say, "The LORD is my refuge,"
and you make the Most High your
dwelling,
¹⁰ no harm will overtake you,
no disaster will come near your tent.
¹¹ For he will command his angels
concerning you
to guard you in all your ways;
¹² they will lift you up in their hands,
so that you will not strike your foot
against a stone.
¹³ You will tread on the lion and the cobra;
you will trample the great lion and
the serpent.

¹⁴ "Because heᵇ loves me," says the LORD,
"I will rescue him;
I will protect him, for he
acknowledges my name.

¹⁵ He will call on me, and I will answer
him;
I will be with him in trouble,
I will deliver him and honor him.
¹⁶ With long life I will satisfy him
and show him my salvation."

Psalm 92ᶜ

A psalm. A song. For the Sabbath day.

¹ It is good to praise the LORD
and make music to your name,
O Most High,
² proclaiming your love in the morning
and your faithfulness at night,
³ to the music of the ten-stringed lyre
and the melody of the harp.

⁴ For you make me glad by your deeds,
LORD;
I sing for joy at what your hands
have done.
⁵ How great are your works, LORD,
how profound your thoughts!
⁶ Senseless people do not know,
fools do not understand,
⁷ that though the wicked spring up like
grass
and all evildoers flourish,
they will be destroyed forever.

⁸ But you, LORD, are forever exalted.

⁹ For surely your enemies, LORD,
surely your enemies will perish;
all evildoers will be scattered.
¹⁰ You have exalted my hornᵈ like that
of a wild ox;
fine oils have been poured on me.
¹¹ My eyes have seen the defeat of my
adversaries;
my ears have heard the rout of my
wicked foes.

¹² The righteous will flourish like a palm
tree,
they will grow like a cedar of
Lebanon;

ᵃ 1 Hebrew *Shaddai*   ᵇ 14 That is, probably the king   ᶜ In Hebrew texts 92:1-15 is numbered 92:2-16.
ᵈ 10 *Horn* here symbolizes strength.

13 planted in the house of the LORD,
    they will flourish in the courts of our
      God.
14 They will still bear fruit in old age,
    they will stay fresh and green,
15 proclaiming, "The LORD is upright;
    he is my Rock, and there is no
      wickedness in him."

Psalm 93

1 The LORD reigns, he is robed in majesty;
    the LORD is robed in majesty and
      armed with strength;
    indeed, the world is established, firm
      and secure.
2 Your throne was established long ago;
    you are from all eternity.

3 The seas have lifted up, LORD,
    the seas have lifted up their voice;
    the seas have lifted up their
      pounding waves.
4 Mightier than the thunder of the great
      waters,
    mightier than the breakers of the
      sea—
    the LORD on high is mighty.

5 Your statutes, LORD, stand firm;
    holiness adorns your house
    for endless days.

Psalm 94

1 The LORD is a God who avenges.
    O God who avenges, shine forth.
2 Rise up, Judge of the earth;
    pay back to the proud what they
      deserve.
3 How long, LORD, will the wicked,
    how long will the wicked be jubilant?

4 They pour out arrogant words;
    all the evildoers are full of boasting.
5 They crush your people, LORD;
    they oppress your inheritance.
6 They slay the widow and the foreigner;
    they murder the fatherless.
7 They say, "The LORD does not see;
    the God of Jacob takes no notice."

8 Take notice, you senseless ones among
      the people;
    you fools, when will you become
      wise?
9 Does he who fashioned the ear not
      hear?
    Does he who formed the eye not see?
10 Does he who disciplines nations not
      punish?
    Does he who teaches mankind lack
      knowledge?
11 The LORD knows all human plans;
    he knows that they are futile.

12 Blessed is the one you discipline,
    LORD,
    the one you teach from your law;
13 you grant them relief from days of
      trouble,
    till a pit is dug for the wicked.
14 For the LORD will not reject his people;
    he will never forsake his inheritance.
15 Judgment will again be founded on
      righteousness,
    and all the upright in heart will
      follow it.

16 Who will rise up for me against the
      wicked?
    Who will take a stand for me against
      evildoers?
17 Unless the LORD had given me help,
    I would soon have dwelt in the
      silence of death.
18 When I said, "My foot is slipping,"
    your unfailing love, LORD, supported
      me.
19 When anxiety was great within me,
    your consolation brought me joy.

20 Can a corrupt throne be allied with
      you—
    a throne that brings on misery by its
      decrees?
21 The wicked band together against the
      righteous
    and condemn the innocent to death.
22 But the LORD has become my fortress,
    and my God the rock in whom I take
      refuge.

²³He will repay them for their sins
  and destroy them for their
    wickedness;
  the LORD our God will destroy
    them.

Psalm 95

¹Come, let us sing for joy to the LORD;
  let us shout aloud to the Rock of our
    salvation.
²Let us come before him with
    thanksgiving
  and extol him with music and
    song.

³For the LORD is the great God,
  the great King above all gods.
⁴In his hand are the depths of the
    earth,
  and the mountain peaks belong to
    him.
⁵The sea is his, for he made it,
  and his hands formed the dry land.

⁶Come, let us bow down in worship,
  let us kneel before the LORD our
    Maker;
⁷for he is our God
  and we are the people of his
    pasture,
  the flock under his care.

Today, if only you would hear his
    voice,
⁸"Do not harden your hearts as you did
    at Meribah,ᵃ
  as you did that day at Massahᵇ in the
    wilderness,
⁹where your ancestors tested me;
  they tried me, though they had seen
    what I did.
¹⁰For forty years I was angry with that
    generation;
  I said, 'They are a people whose
    hearts go astray,
  and they have not known my ways.'
¹¹So I declared on oath in my anger,
  'They shall never enter my rest.'"

Psalm 96

¹Sing to the LORD a new song;
  sing to the LORD, all the earth.
²Sing to the LORD, praise his name;
  proclaim his salvation day after day.
³Declare his glory among the nations,
  his marvelous deeds among all
    peoples.

⁴For great is the LORD and most worthy
    of praise;
  he is to be feared above all gods.
⁵For all the gods of the nations are idols,
  but the LORD made the heavens.
⁶Splendor and majesty are before him;
  strength and glory are in his
    sanctuary.

⁷Ascribe to the LORD, all you families of
    nations,
  ascribe to the LORD glory and
    strength.
⁸Ascribe to the LORD the glory due his
    name;
  bring an offering and come into his
    courts.
⁹Worship the LORD in the splendor of
    hisᶜ holiness;
  tremble before him, all the earth.
¹⁰Say among the nations, "The LORD
    reigns."
  The world is firmly established, it
    cannot be moved;
  he will judge the peoples with equity.

¹¹Let the heavens rejoice, let the earth be
    glad;
  let the sea resound, and all that is
    in it.
¹²Let the fields be jubilant, and
    everything in them;
  let all the trees of the forest sing for
    joy.
¹³Let all creation rejoice before the LORD,
    for he comes,
  he comes to judge the earth.
  He will judge the world in righteousness
  and the peoples in his faithfulness.

ᵃ 8 *Meribah* means *quarreling.*   ᵇ 8 *Massah* means *testing.*   ᶜ 9 Or LORD *with the splendor of*

Psalm 97

1 The LORD reigns, let the earth be glad;
    let the distant shores rejoice.
2 Clouds and thick darkness surround
        him;
    righteousness and justice are the
        foundation of his throne.
3 Fire goes before him
    and consumes his foes on every
        side.
4 His lightning lights up the world;
    the earth sees and trembles.
5 The mountains melt like wax before the
        LORD,
    before the Lord of all the earth.
6 The heavens proclaim his
        righteousness,
    and all peoples see his glory.

7 All who worship images are put to
        shame,
    those who boast in idols —
    worship him, all you gods!

8 Zion hears and rejoices
    and the villages of Judah are glad
    because of your judgments, LORD.
9 For you, LORD, are the Most High over
        all the earth;
    you are exalted far above all gods.
10 Let those who love the LORD hate evil,
    for he guards the lives of his faithful
        ones
    and delivers them from the hand of
        the wicked.
11 Light shines*a* on the righteous
    and joy on the upright in heart.
12 Rejoice in the LORD, you who are
        righteous,
    and praise his holy name.

Psalm 98

A psalm.

1 Sing to the LORD a new song,
    for he has done marvelous things;
    his right hand and his holy arm
        have worked salvation for him.

2 The LORD has made his salvation
        known
    and revealed his righteousness to the
        nations.
3 He has remembered his love
    and his faithfulness to Israel;
    all the ends of the earth have seen
        the salvation of our God.

4 Shout for joy to the LORD, all the
        earth,
    burst into jubilant song with music;
5 make music to the LORD with the harp,
    with the harp and the sound of
        singing,
6 with trumpets and the blast of the ram's
        horn —
    shout for joy before the LORD, the
        King.

7 Let the sea resound, and everything
        in it,
    the world, and all who live in it.
8 Let the rivers clap their hands,
    let the mountains sing together for
        joy;
9 let them sing before the LORD,
    for he comes to judge the earth.
He will judge the world in
        righteousness
    and the peoples with equity.

Psalm 99

1 The LORD reigns,
    let the nations tremble;
he sits enthroned between the
        cherubim,
    let the earth shake.
2 Great is the LORD in Zion;
    he is exalted over all the nations.
3 Let them praise your great and
        awesome name —
    he is holy.

4 The King is mighty, he loves justice —
    you have established equity;
    in Jacob you have done
        what is just and right.

---

a 11 One Hebrew manuscript and ancient versions (see also 112:4); most Hebrew manuscripts *Light is sown*

5 Exalt the LORD our God
and worship at his footstool;
he is holy.

6 Moses and Aaron were among his priests,
Samuel was among those who called
on his name;
they called on the LORD
and he answered them.
7 He spoke to them from the pillar of cloud;
they kept his statutes and the decrees
he gave them.

8 LORD our God,
you answered them;
you were to Israel a forgiving God,
though you punished their
misdeeds.*a*
9 Exalt the LORD our God
and worship at his holy mountain,
for the LORD our God is holy.

Psalm 100

A psalm. For giving grateful praise.

1 Shout for joy to the LORD, all the earth.
2   Worship the LORD with gladness;
come before him with joyful songs.
3 Know that the LORD is God.
It is he who made us, and we are his*b*;
we are his people, the sheep of his
pasture.

4 Enter his gates with thanksgiving
and his courts with praise;
give thanks to him and praise his name.
5 For the LORD is good and his love
endures forever;
his faithfulness continues through
all generations.

Psalm 101

Of David. A psalm.

1 I will sing of your love and justice;
to you, LORD, I will sing praise.
2 I will be careful to lead a blameless life —
when will you come to me?

I will conduct the affairs of my house
with a blameless heart.
3 I will not look with approval
on anything that is vile.

I hate what faithless people do;
I will have no part in it.
4 The perverse of heart shall be far from me;
I will have nothing to do with what is
evil.

5 Whoever slanders their neighbor in
secret,
I will put to silence;
whoever has haughty eyes and a proud
heart,
I will not tolerate.

6 My eyes will be on the faithful in the
land,
that they may dwell with me;
the one whose walk is blameless
will minister to me.

7 No one who practices deceit
will dwell in my house;
no one who speaks falsely
will stand in my presence.

8 Every morning I will put to silence
all the wicked in the land;
I will cut off every evildoer
from the city of the LORD.

Psalm 102*c*

A prayer of an afflicted person who has grown weak
and pours out a lament before the LORD.

1 Hear my prayer, LORD;
let my cry for help come to you.
2 Do not hide your face from me
when I am in distress.
Turn your ear to me;
when I call, answer me quickly.

3 For my days vanish like smoke;
my bones burn like glowing embers.
4 My heart is blighted and withered like
grass;
I forget to eat my food.

---

a 8 Or *God, / an avenger of the wrongs done to them*   *b 3* Or *and not we ourselves*   *c* In Hebrew texts 102:1-28 is
numbered 102:2-29.

⁵In my distress I groan aloud
  and am reduced to skin and bones.
⁶I am like a desert owl,
  like an owl among the ruins.
⁷I lie awake; I have become
  like a bird alone on a roof.
⁸All day long my enemies taunt me;
  those who rail against me use my
    name as a curse.
⁹For I eat ashes as my food
  and mingle my drink with tears
¹⁰because of your great wrath,
  for you have taken me up and thrown
    me aside.
¹¹My days are like the evening shadow;
  I wither away like grass.

¹²But you, LORD, sit enthroned forever;
  your renown endures through all
    generations.
¹³You will arise and have compassion on
    Zion,
  for it is time to show favor to her;
  the appointed time has come.
¹⁴For her stones are dear to your
    servants;
  her very dust moves them to pity.
¹⁵The nations will fear the name of the
    LORD,
  all the kings of the earth will revere
    your glory.
¹⁶For the LORD will rebuild Zion
  and appear in his glory.

GRATITUDE LESSON [*Principle Seven*]

For the previous entry in the GRATITUDE lesson, go to Hebrews 12:1 (page 1534).

For a discussion of Principles One through Eight and a listing of their related lessons,
go to pages xvii – xliv.

Enter his gates with thanksgiving and his courts with praise;
give thanks to him and praise his name.

PSALM 100:4

In Principle Seven we reserve a daily quiet time with God for self-examination, Bible reading and prayer in order to get to know God and his will for our lives and to gain the power to follow his will. Once we've been working this principle for a while, we'll understand that we have much for which to be thankful: We're growing closer to our Higher Power, the one and only true Higher Power, Jesus Christ. Our relationships are being restored. We're experiencing peace and freedom from our hurts, hang-ups and habits. We've found a new purpose for our lives. It's important for us to maintain an "attitude of GRATITUDE" for all the positive changes that have occurred and are still occurring in our lives.

We can all be thankful for at least four key areas of our lives. The last one is our church. Hebrews 10:25 supports us in this: "[Let us] not give up meeting together, as some are in the habit of doing, but [encourage] one another — and all the more as you see the Day approaching." We need to be deeply appreciative of the role of Christ's bride (the church) in our lives, as Psalm 100:4 reminds us. It's there, in the circle of our own chosen place of Christian fellowship, that we can find a safe environment that offers encouragement, love and acceptance.

For what two aspects of your church or church family are you particularly thankful?

This is the final page of the GRATITUDE lesson.

17 He will respond to the prayer of the
destitute;
he will not despise their plea.

18 Let this be written for a future generation,
that a people not yet created may
praise the LORD:
19 "The LORD looked down from his
sanctuary on high,
from heaven he viewed the earth,
20 to hear the groans of the prisoners
and release those condemned to
death."
21 So the name of the LORD will be
declared in Zion
and his praise in Jerusalem
22 when the peoples and the kingdoms
assemble to worship the LORD.

23 In the course of my life[a] he broke my
strength;
he cut short my days.
24 So I said:
"Do not take me away, my God, in the
midst of my days;
your years go on through all
generations.
25 In the beginning you laid the
foundations of the earth,
and the heavens are the work of your
hands.
26 They will perish, but you remain;
they will all wear out like a garment.
Like clothing you will change them
and they will be discarded.
27 But you remain the same,
and your years will never end.
28 The children of your servants will live
in your presence;
their descendants will be established
before you."

Psalm 103

Of David.

1 Praise the LORD, my soul;
all my inmost being, praise his holy
name.

2 Praise the LORD, my soul,
and forget not all his benefits —
3 who forgives all your sins
and heals all your diseases,
4 who redeems your life from the pit
and crowns you with love and
compassion,
5 who satisfies your desires with good
things
so that your youth is renewed like the
eagle's.

6 The LORD works righteousness
and justice for all the oppressed.

7 He made known his ways to Moses,
his deeds to the people of Israel:
8 The LORD is compassionate and
gracious,
slow to anger, abounding in love.
9 He will not always accuse,
nor will he harbor his anger forever;
10 he does not treat us as our sins deserve
or repay us according to our
iniquities.
11 For as high as the heavens are above the
earth,
so great is his love for those who fear
him;
12 as far as the east is from the west,
so far has he removed our
transgressions from us.

13 As a father has compassion on his
children,
so the LORD has compassion on those
who fear him;
14 for he knows how we are formed,
he remembers that we are dust.
15 The life of mortals is like grass,
they flourish like a flower of the field;
16 the wind blows over it and it is gone,
and its place remembers it no more.
17 But from everlasting to everlasting
the LORD's love is with those who
fear him,
and his righteousness with their
children's children —

---

a 23 Or By his power

18 with those who keep his covenant
and remember to obey his precepts.

19 The LORD has established his throne in
heaven,
and his kingdom rules over all.

20 Praise the LORD, you his angels,
you mighty ones who do his bidding,
who obey his word.
21 Praise the LORD, all his heavenly hosts,
you his servants who do his will.
22 Praise the LORD, all his works
everywhere in his dominion.

Praise the LORD, my soul.

Psalm 104

1 Praise the LORD, my soul.

LORD my God, you are very great;
you are clothed with splendor and
majesty.

2 The LORD wraps himself in light as
with a garment;
he stretches out the heavens like a
tent
3 and lays the beams of his upper
chambers on their waters.
He makes the clouds his chariot
and rides on the wings of the wind.
4 He makes winds his messengers,*a*
flames of fire his servants.

5 He set the earth on its foundations;
it can never be moved.
6 You covered it with the watery depths
as with a garment;
the waters stood above the
mountains.
7 But at your rebuke the waters fled,
at the sound of your thunder they
took to flight;
8 they flowed over the mountains,
they went down into the valleys,
to the place you assigned for them.
9 You set a boundary they cannot cross;
never again will they cover the earth.

10 He makes springs pour water into the
ravines;
it flows between the mountains.
11 They give water to all the beasts of the
field;
the wild donkeys quench their thirst.
12 The birds of the sky nest by the waters;
they sing among the branches.
13 He waters the mountains from his
upper chambers;
the land is satisfied by the fruit of his
work.
14 He makes grass grow for the cattle,
and plants for people to cultivate —
bringing forth food from the earth:
15 wine that gladdens human hearts,
oil to make their faces shine,
and bread that sustains their hearts.
16 The trees of the LORD are well watered,
the cedars of Lebanon that he
planted.
17 There the birds make their nests;
the stork has its home in the
junipers.
18 The high mountains belong to the wild
goats;
the crags are a refuge for the hyrax.

19 He made the moon to mark the
seasons,
and the sun knows when to go down.
20 You bring darkness, it becomes night,
and all the beasts of the forest prowl.
21 The lions roar for their prey
and seek their food from God.
22 The sun rises, and they steal away;
they return and lie down in their
dens.
23 Then people go out to their work,
to their labor until evening.

24 How many are your works, LORD!
In wisdom you made them all;
the earth is full of your creatures.
25 There is the sea, vast and spacious,
teeming with creatures beyond
number —
living things both large and small.

---

a 4 Or *angels*

26 There the ships go to and fro,
and Leviathan, which you formed to
frolic there.

27 All creatures look to you
to give them their food at the proper
time.
28 When you give it to them,
they gather it up;
when you open your hand,
they are satisfied with good things.
29 When you hide your face,
they are terrified;
when you take away their breath,
they die and return to the dust.
30 When you send your Spirit,
they are created,
and you renew the face of the ground.

31 May the glory of the LORD endure
forever;
may the LORD rejoice in his works —
32 he who looks at the earth, and it
trembles,
who touches the mountains, and
they smoke.

33 I will sing to the LORD all my life;
I will sing praise to my God as long
as I live.
34 May my meditation be pleasing to him,
as I rejoice in the LORD.
35 But may sinners vanish from the earth
and the wicked be no more.

Praise the LORD, my soul.

Praise the LORD.*a*

Psalm 105

1 Give praise to the LORD, proclaim his
name;
make known among the nations
what he has done.
2 Sing to him, sing praise to him;
tell of all his wonderful acts.
3 Glory in his holy name;
let the hearts of those who seek the
LORD rejoice.

4 Look to the LORD and his strength;
seek his face always.

5 Remember the wonders he has done,
his miracles, and the judgments he
pronounced,
6 you his servants, the descendants of
Abraham,
his chosen ones, the children of
Jacob.
7 He is the LORD our God;
his judgments are in all the earth.

8 He remembers his covenant forever,
the promise he made, for a thousand
generations,
9 the covenant he made with Abraham,
the oath he swore to Isaac.
10 He confirmed it to Jacob as a decree,
to Israel as an everlasting covenant:
11 "To you I will give the land of
Canaan
as the portion you will inherit."

12 When they were but few in number,
few indeed, and strangers in it,
13 they wandered from nation to nation,
from one kingdom to another.
14 He allowed no one to oppress them;
for their sake he rebuked kings:
15 "Do not touch my anointed ones;
do my prophets no harm."

16 He called down famine on the land
and destroyed all their supplies of
food;
17 and he sent a man before them —
Joseph, sold as a slave.
18 They bruised his feet with shackles,
his neck was put in irons,
19 till what he foretold came to pass,
till the word of the LORD proved him
true.
20 The king sent and released him,
the ruler of peoples set him free.
21 He made him master of his household,
ruler over all he possessed,
22 to instruct his princes as he pleased
and teach his elders wisdom.

---

a 35 Hebrew *Hallelu Yah*; in the Septuagint this line stands at the beginning of Psalm 105.

23 Then Israel entered Egypt;
   Jacob resided as a foreigner in the
     land of Ham.
24 The Lord made his people very
     fruitful;
   he made them too numerous for
     their foes,
25 whose hearts he turned to hate his
     people,
   to conspire against his servants.
26 He sent Moses his servant,
   and Aaron, whom he had chosen.
27 They performed his signs among them,
   his wonders in the land of Ham.
28 He sent darkness and made the land
     dark —
   for had they not rebelled against his
     words?
29 He turned their waters into blood,
   causing their fish to die.
30 Their land teemed with frogs,
   which went up into the bedrooms of
     their rulers.
31 He spoke, and there came swarms of
     flies,
   and gnats throughout their country.
32 He turned their rain into hail,
   with lightning throughout their
     land;
33 he struck down their vines and fig trees
   and shattered the trees of their
     country.
34 He spoke, and the locusts came,
   grasshoppers without number;
35 they ate up every green thing in their
     land,
   ate up the produce of their soil.
36 Then he struck down all the firstborn
     in their land,
   the firstfruits of all their manhood.
37 He brought out Israel, laden with silver
     and gold,
   and from among their tribes no one
     faltered.
38 Egypt was glad when they left,
   because dread of Israel had fallen on
     them.

39 He spread out a cloud as a covering,
   and a fire to give light at night.
40 They asked, and he brought them
     quail;
   he fed them well with the bread of
     heaven.
41 He opened the rock, and water gushed
     out;
   it flowed like a river in the desert.

42 For he remembered his holy promise
   given to his servant Abraham.
43 He brought out his people with
     rejoicing,
   his chosen ones with shouts of joy;
44 he gave them the lands of the nations,
   and they fell heir to what others had
     toiled for —
45 that they might keep his precepts
   and observe his laws.

Praise the Lord.*a*

Psalm 106

1 Praise the Lord.*b*

Give thanks to the Lord, for he is good;
   his love endures forever.

2 Who can proclaim the mighty acts of
     the Lord
   or fully declare his praise?
3 Blessed are those who act justly,
   who always do what is right.

4 Remember me, Lord, when you show
     favor to your people,
   come to my aid when you save them,
5 that I may enjoy the prosperity of your
     chosen ones,
   that I may share in the joy of your
     nation
   and join your inheritance in giving
     praise.

6 We have sinned, even as our ancestors
     did;
   we have done wrong and acted
     wickedly.

---

a 45 Hebrew *Hallelu Yah*   *b 1* Hebrew *Hallelu Yah*; also in verse 48

7 When our ancestors were in Egypt,
    they gave no thought to your
        miracles;
    they did not remember your many
        kindnesses,
    and they rebelled by the sea, the Red
        Sea.^a
8 Yet he saved them for his name's sake,
    to make his mighty power known.
9 He rebuked the Red Sea, and it dried
        up;
    he led them through the depths as
        through a desert.
10 He saved them from the hand of the
        foe;
    from the hand of the enemy he
        redeemed them.
11 The waters covered their adversaries;
    not one of them survived.
12 Then they believed his promises
    and sang his praise.

13 But they soon forgot what he had done
    and did not wait for his plan to
        unfold.
14 In the desert they gave in to their
        craving;
    in the wilderness they put God to the
        test.
15 So he gave them what they asked for,
    but sent a wasting disease among
        them.

16 In the camp they grew envious of
        Moses
    and of Aaron, who was consecrated
        to the LORD.
17 The earth opened up and swallowed
        Dathan;
    it buried the company of Abiram.
18 Fire blazed among their followers;
    a flame consumed the wicked.
19 At Horeb they made a calf
    and worshiped an idol cast from
        metal.
20 They exchanged their glorious God
    for an image of a bull, which eats
        grass.

21 They forgot the God who saved them,
    who had done great things in
        Egypt,
22 miracles in the land of Ham
    and awesome deeds by the Red Sea.
23 So he said he would destroy them —
    had not Moses, his chosen one,
    stood in the breach before him
    to keep his wrath from destroying
        them.

24 Then they despised the pleasant land;
    they did not believe his promise.
25 They grumbled in their tents
    and did not obey the LORD.
26 So he swore to them with uplifted hand
    that he would make them fall in the
        wilderness,
27 make their descendants fall among the
        nations
    and scatter them throughout the
        lands.

28 They yoked themselves to the Baal of
        Peor
    and ate sacrifices offered to lifeless
        gods;
29 they aroused the LORD's anger by their
        wicked deeds,
    and a plague broke out among
        them.
30 But Phinehas stood up and intervened,
    and the plague was checked.
31 This was credited to him as
        righteousness
    for endless generations to come.
32 By the waters of Meribah they angered
        the LORD,
    and trouble came to Moses because
        of them;
33 for they rebelled against the Spirit of
        God,
    and rash words came from Moses'
        lips.^b

34 They did not destroy the peoples
    as the LORD had commanded
        them,

---

^a 7 Or *the Sea of Reeds*; also in verses 9 and 22   ^b 33 Or *against his spirit, / and rash words came from his lips*

³⁵ but they mingled with the nations
⠀⠀and adopted their customs.
³⁶ They worshiped their idols,
⠀⠀which became a snare to them.
³⁷ They sacrificed their sons
⠀⠀and their daughters to false gods.
³⁸ They shed innocent blood,
⠀⠀the blood of their sons and
⠀⠀⠀⠀daughters,
⠀⠀whom they sacrificed to the idols of
⠀⠀⠀⠀Canaan,
⠀⠀and the land was desecrated by their
⠀⠀⠀⠀blood.
³⁹ They defiled themselves by what they
⠀⠀did;
⠀⠀by their deeds they prostituted
⠀⠀⠀⠀themselves.

⁴⁰ Therefore the Lord was angry with his
⠀⠀people
⠀⠀and abhorred his inheritance.
⁴¹ He gave them into the hands of the
⠀⠀nations,
⠀⠀and their foes ruled over them.
⁴² Their enemies oppressed them
⠀⠀and subjected them to their power.
⁴³ Many times he delivered them,
⠀⠀but they were bent on rebellion
⠀⠀and they wasted away in their sin.

⁴⁴ Yet he took note of their distress
⠀⠀when he heard their cry;
⁴⁵ for their sake he remembered his
⠀⠀covenant
⠀⠀and out of his great love he relented.
⁴⁶ He caused all who held them captive
⠀⠀to show them mercy.

⁴⁷ Save us, Lord our God,
⠀⠀and gather us from the nations,
⠀⠀that we may give thanks to your holy
⠀⠀⠀⠀name
⠀⠀and glory in your praise.

⁴⁸ Praise be to the Lord, the God of Israel,
⠀⠀from everlasting to everlasting.

Let all the people say, "Amen!"

Praise the Lord.

BOOK V

Psalms 107 – 150

Psalm 107

¹ Give thanks to the Lord, for he is good;
⠀⠀his love endures forever.

² Let the redeemed of the Lord tell their
⠀⠀story—
⠀⠀those he redeemed from the hand of
⠀⠀⠀⠀the foe,
³ those he gathered from the lands,
⠀⠀from east and west, from north and
⠀⠀⠀⠀south.ᵃ

⁴ Some wandered in desert wastelands,
⠀⠀finding no way to a city where they
⠀⠀⠀⠀could settle.
⁵ They were hungry and thirsty,
⠀⠀and their lives ebbed away.
⁶ Then they cried out to the Lord in
⠀⠀their trouble,
⠀⠀and he delivered them from their
⠀⠀⠀⠀distress.
⁷ He led them by a straight way
⠀⠀to a city where they could settle.
⁸ Let them give thanks to the Lord for
⠀⠀his unfailing love
⠀⠀and his wonderful deeds for
⠀⠀⠀⠀mankind,
⁹ for he satisfies the thirsty
⠀⠀and fills the hungry with good
⠀⠀⠀⠀things.

¹⁰ Some sat in darkness, in utter darkness,
⠀⠀prisoners suffering in iron chains,
¹¹ because they rebelled against God's
⠀⠀commands
⠀⠀and despised the plans of the Most
⠀⠀⠀⠀High.
¹² So he subjected them to bitter labor;
⠀⠀they stumbled, and there was no one
⠀⠀⠀⠀to help.
¹³ Then they cried to the Lord in their
⠀⠀trouble,
⠀⠀and he saved them from their
⠀⠀⠀⠀distress.

ᵃ 3 Hebrew *north and the sea*

14 He brought them out of darkness, the
        utter darkness,
    and broke away their chains.
15 Let them give thanks to the LORD for
        his unfailing love
    and his wonderful deeds for
        mankind,
16 for he breaks down gates of bronze
    and cuts through bars of iron.

17 Some became fools through their
        rebellious ways
    and suffered affliction because of
        their iniquities.
18 They loathed all food
    and drew near the gates of death.
19 Then they cried to the LORD in their
        trouble,
    and he saved them from their distress.

20 He sent out his word and healed
        them;
    he rescued them from the grave.
21 Let them give thanks to the LORD for
        his unfailing love
    and his wonderful deeds for
        mankind.
22 Let them sacrifice thank offerings
    and tell of his works with songs of
        joy.

23 Some went out on the sea in ships;
    they were merchants on the mighty
        waters.
24 They saw the works of the LORD,
    his wonderful deeds in the deep.
25 For he spoke and stirred up a
        tempest
    that lifted high the waves.

DENIAL LESSON [*Principle One*]

For the previous entry in the DENIAL lesson, go to Psalm 146:7 – 8 (page 734).

For a discussion of Principles One through Eight and a listing of their related lessons,
go to pages xvii – xliv.

They cried to the LORD in their trouble, and he saved them
from their distress. He brought them out of darkness,
the utter darkness, and broke away their chains.

PSALM 107:13 – 14

The power to change comes only through God's grace. Principle One states: "Realize I'm not God. I admit that I'm powerless to control my tendency to do the wrong thing and that my life has become unmanageable." If we admit that we're powerless, we recognize our need for a power greater than ourselves to restore us. That power is our Higher Power, the one and only true Higher Power, Jesus Christ.

In Principle One we discover that we've been in DENIAL of our hurts, hang-ups and habits. The next letter in DENIAL is *N*, reminding us that our denial NEGATES OUR GROWTH. We're as sick as our secrets. We can't begin to grow in recovery till we're ready to step out of the darkness of our denial into the blinding brightness of the truth. God is waiting to take our hand and lead us out — though he'll never pull us out against our will. As we travel the road of our recovery, we'll come to understand that God never wastes a hurt. And he's not about to waste the darkness we've been groping our way through. He can't use it, though, until we take that first step.

The next letter in DENIAL is *I*. Go to Genesis 3:7 – 8 (page 5).

26 They mounted up to the heavens and
went down to the depths;
in their peril their courage melted
away.
27 They reeled and staggered like drunkards;
they were at their wits' end.
28 Then they cried out to the LORD in
their trouble,
and he brought them out of their
distress.
29 He stilled the storm to a whisper;
the waves of the sea*a* were hushed.

30 They were glad when it grew calm,
and he guided them to their desired
haven.
31 Let them give thanks to the LORD for
his unfailing love
and his wonderful deeds for mankind.
32 Let them exalt him in the assembly of
the people
and praise him in the council of the
elders.
33 He turned rivers into a desert,
flowing springs into thirsty ground,

a 29 Dead Sea Scrolls; Masoretic Text / *their waves*

ADMIT LESSON [*Principle Four*]

For the previous entry in the ADMIT lesson, go to James 5:16 (page 1543).

For a discussion of Principles One through Eight and a listing of their related lessons,
go to pages xvii – xliv.

They cried to the LORD in their trouble, and he saved them
from their distress. He brought them out of darkness,
the utter darkness, and broke away their chains.

PSALM 107:13–14

Principle Four begins the process of "coming clean." In the second part of Principle Four, we confess our faults to ourselves, to God and to someone else we trust.

When we ADMIT our faults to another person, we receive three great benefits. The second benefit we receive from sharing our Principle Four inventories is *freedom*. Our secrets have kept us in chains — bound, frozen, unable to move forward in any of our relationships with God or others. Admitting our sins snaps the chains so God's healing power can be released.

We need to be sure to share all our sins, because unconfessed sin will fester and keep us bound to our past. In Psalm 32:3 – 4 David recounts what happened to him when he tried to conceal his sins: "When I kept silent, my bones wasted away through my groaning all day long. For day and night your hand was heavy on me; my strength was sapped as in the heat of summer."

The third benefit of sharing our Principle Four inventories with someone we trust is support. That person can keep us focused and provide invaluable feedback. When our old "friend" Denial resurfaces, and we hear Satan's litany of excuses — "It's really not all that bad"; "They deserved it"; "It really wasn't your fault" — our support person can be there to challenge us with the truth. But most of all, we need another person simply to listen to us and hear what we have to say. We need to keep in mind that "openness is to wholeness as secrets are to sickness."

This is the final page of the ADMIT lesson.

34 and fruitful land into a salt waste,
  because of the wickedness of those
    who lived there.
35 He turned the desert into pools of water
  and the parched ground into flowing
    springs;
36 there he brought the hungry to live,
  and they founded a city where they
    could settle.
37 They sowed fields and planted
    vineyards
  that yielded a fruitful harvest;
38 he blessed them, and their numbers
    greatly increased,
  and he did not let their herds
    diminish.

39 Then their numbers decreased, and
    they were humbled
  by oppression, calamity and sorrow;
40 he who pours contempt on nobles
  made them wander in a trackless
    waste.
41 But he lifted the needy out of their
    affliction
  and increased their families like
    flocks.
42 The upright see and rejoice,
  but all the wicked shut their mouths.
43 Let the one who is wise heed these
    things
  and ponder the loving deeds of the
    LORD.

GRATITUDE LESSON [Principle Seven]

This is the first page of the GRATITUDE lesson.

For a discussion of Principles One through Eight and a listing of their related lessons,
go to pages xvii – xliv.

*Let them give thanks to the LORD for his unfailing love
and his wonderful deeds for mankind.*

PSALM 107:15

In Principle Seven we reserve a daily quiet time with God for self-examination, Bible reading and prayer in order to get to know God and his will for our lives and to gain the power to follow his will. Once we've been working this principle for a while, we'll understand that we have much for which to be thankful: We're growing closer to our Higher Power, the one and only true Higher Power, Jesus Christ. Our relationships are being restored. We're experiencing peace and freedom from our hurts, hang-ups and habits. We've found a new purpose for our lives. It's important for us to maintain an "attitude of GRATITUDE" for all the positive changes that have occurred and are still occurring in our lives.

We can all be thankful for at least four key areas of our lives. First and most important, we can be thankful to God for all he's done for us. We need to offer daily prayers of gratitude to our Creator. Psalm 107:15 encourages us to give thanks to God for his unconditional love for us. We need to identify at least two areas of life in which we can see God's work and for which we want to express heartfelt thanks. Or we can reflect on what God has done for us in the last year or so. We shouldn't forget to include what God has done for us this week and even today.

The next area for which we can be thankful is other people God has placed in our lives.
Go to Colossians 3:15 – 16 (page 1489).

Psalm 108[a]

A song. A psalm of David.

1 My heart, O God, is steadfast;
   I will sing and make music with all
      my soul.
2 Awake, harp and lyre!
   I will awaken the dawn.
3 I will praise you, LORD, among the
      nations;
   I will sing of you among the peoples.
4 For great is your love, higher than the
      heavens;
   your faithfulness reaches to the skies.
5 Be exalted, O God, above the heavens;
   let your glory be over all the earth.

6 Save us and help us with your right
      hand,
   that those you love may be delivered.
7 God has spoken from his sanctuary:
   "In triumph I will parcel out
      Shechem
   and measure off the Valley of
      Sukkoth.
8 Gilead is mine, Manasseh is mine;
   Ephraim is my helmet,
   Judah is my scepter.
9 Moab is my washbasin,
   on Edom I toss my sandal;
   over Philistia I shout in triumph."

10 Who will bring me to the fortified city?
   Who will lead me to Edom?
11 Is it not you, God, you who have
      rejected us
   and no longer go out with our armies?
12 Give us aid against the enemy,
   for human help is worthless.
13 With God we will gain the victory,
   and he will trample down our
      enemies.

Psalm 109

For the director of music. Of David. A psalm.

1 My God, whom I praise,
   do not remain silent,
2 for people who are wicked and deceitful
   have opened their mouths against me;
   they have spoken against me with
      lying tongues.
3 With words of hatred they surround me;
   they attack me without cause.
4 In return for my friendship they accuse
      me,
   but I am a man of prayer.
5 They repay me evil for good,
   and hatred for my friendship.

6 Appoint someone evil to oppose my
      enemy;
   let an accuser stand at his right hand.
7 When he is tried, let him be found
      guilty,
   and may his prayers condemn him.
8 May his days be few;
   may another take his place of
      leadership.
9 May his children be fatherless
   and his wife a widow.
10 May his children be wandering beggars;
   may they be driven[b] from their
      ruined homes.
11 May a creditor seize all he has;
   may strangers plunder the fruits of
      his labor.
12 May no one extend kindness to him
   or take pity on his fatherless
      children.
13 May his descendants be cut off,
   their names blotted out from the
      next generation.
14 May the iniquity of his fathers be
      remembered before the LORD;
   may the sin of his mother never be
      blotted out.
15 May their sins always remain before the
      LORD,
   that he may blot out their name from
      the earth.

16 For he never thought of doing a
      kindness,
   but hounded to death the poor
   and the needy and the brokenhearted.

---

a In Hebrew texts 108:1-13 is numbered 108:2-14.   b 10 Septuagint; Hebrew sought

17 He loved to pronounce a curse —
   may it come back on him.
   He found no pleasure in blessing —
   may it be far from him.
18 He wore cursing as his garment;
   it entered into his body like water,
   into his bones like oil.
19 May it be like a cloak wrapped about
   him,
   like a belt tied forever around him.
20 May this be the LORD's payment to my
   accusers,
   to those who speak evil of me.

21 But you, Sovereign LORD,
   help me for your name's sake;
   out of the goodness of your love,
   deliver me.
22 For I am poor and needy,
   and my heart is wounded within me.
23 I fade away like an evening shadow;
   I am shaken off like a locust.
24 My knees give way from fasting;
   my body is thin and gaunt.
25 I am an object of scorn to my
   accusers;
   when they see me, they shake their
   heads.
26 Help me, LORD my God;
   save me according to your unfailing
   love.
27 Let them know that it is your hand,
   that you, LORD, have done it.
28 While they curse, may you bless;
   may those who attack me be put to
   shame,
   but may your servant rejoice.
29 May my accusers be clothed with
   disgrace
   and wrapped in shame as in a
   cloak.

30 With my mouth I will greatly extol the
   LORD;
   in the great throng of worshipers I
   will praise him.

31 For he stands at the right hand of the
   needy,
   to save their lives from those who
   would condemn them.

Psalm 110

Of David. A psalm.

1 The LORD says to my lord:[a]

"Sit at my right hand
   until I make your enemies
   a footstool for your feet."

2 The LORD will extend your mighty
   scepter from Zion, saying,
   "Rule in the midst of your enemies!"
3 Your troops will be willing
   on your day of battle.
Arrayed in holy splendor,
   your young men will come to you
   like dew from the morning's womb.[b]

4 The LORD has sworn
   and will not change his mind:
"You are a priest forever,
   in the order of Melchizedek."

5 The Lord is at your right hand[c];
   he will crush kings on the day of his
   wrath.
6 He will judge the nations, heaping up
   the dead
   and crushing the rulers of the whole
   earth.
7 He will drink from a brook along the
   way,[d]
   and so he will lift his head high.

Psalm 111[e]

1 Praise the LORD.[f]

I will extol the LORD with all my heart
   in the council of the upright and in
   the assembly.

2 Great are the works of the LORD;
   they are pondered by all who delight
   in them.

---

[a] 1 Or Lord   [b] 3 The meaning of the Hebrew for this sentence is uncertain.   [c] 5 Or My lord is at your right
hand, LORD   [d] 7 The meaning of the Hebrew for this clause is uncertain.   [e] This psalm is an acrostic poem, the
lines of which begin with the successive letters of the Hebrew alphabet.   [f] 1 Hebrew Hallelu Yah

3 Glorious and majestic are his deeds,
    and his righteousness endures
        forever.
4 He has caused his wonders to be
    remembered;
    the LORD is gracious and
        compassionate.
5 He provides food for those who fear
    him;
    he remembers his covenant forever.

6 He has shown his people the power of
    his works,
    giving them the lands of other nations.
7 The works of his hands are faithful and
    just;
    all his precepts are trustworthy.
8 They are established for ever and ever,
    enacted in faithfulness and
        uprightness.
9 He provided redemption for his people;
    he ordained his covenant forever —
    holy and awesome is his name.

10 The fear of the LORD is the beginning of
    wisdom;
    all who follow his precepts have good
        understanding.
    To him belongs eternal praise.

Psalm 112[a]

1 Praise the LORD.[b]

Blessed are those who fear the LORD,
    who find great delight in his
        commands.

2 Their children will be mighty in the
    land;
    the generation of the upright will be
        blessed.
3 Wealth and riches are in their houses,
    and their righteousness endures
        forever.
4 Even in darkness light dawns for the
    upright,
    for those who are gracious and
        compassionate and righteous.

5 Good will come to those who are
    generous and lend freely,
    who conduct their affairs with
        justice.
6 Surely the righteous will never be
    shaken;
    they will be remembered forever.
7 They will have no fear of bad news;
    their hearts are steadfast, trusting in
        the LORD.
8 Their hearts are secure, they will have
    no fear;
    in the end they will look in triumph
        on their foes.
9 They have freely scattered their gifts to
    the poor,
    their righteousness endures forever;
    their horn[c] will be lifted high in
        honor.

10 The wicked will see and be vexed,
    they will gnash their teeth and waste
        away;
    the longings of the wicked will come
        to nothing.

Psalm 113

1 Praise the LORD.[d]

Praise the LORD, you his servants;
    praise the name of the LORD.
2 Let the name of the LORD be praised,
    both now and forevermore.
3 From the rising of the sun to the place
    where it sets,
    the name of the LORD is to be praised.

4 The LORD is exalted over all the
    nations,
    his glory above the heavens.
5 Who is like the LORD our God,
    the One who sits enthroned on high,
6 who stoops down to look
    on the heavens and the earth?

7 He raises the poor from the dust
    and lifts the needy from the ash heap;

---

a This psalm is an acrostic poem, the lines of which begin with the successive letters of the Hebrew alphabet.
    b 1 Hebrew Hallelu Yah   c 9 Horn here symbolizes dignity.   d 1 Hebrew Hallelu Yah; also in verse 9

⓵
⓶
⓷

8 he seats them with princes,
  with the princes of his people.
9 He settles the childless woman in her
  home
  as a happy mother of children.

Praise the LORD.

Psalm 114

1 When Israel came out of Egypt,
  Jacob from a people of foreign
  tongue,
2 Judah became God's sanctuary,
  Israel his dominion.

3 The sea looked and fled,
  the Jordan turned back;
4 the mountains leaped like rams,
  the hills like lambs.

5 Why was it, sea, that you fled?
  Why, Jordan, did you turn back?
6 Why, mountains, did you leap like
  rams,
  you hills, like lambs?

7 Tremble, earth, at the presence of the
  Lord,
  at the presence of the God of Jacob,
8 who turned the rock into a pool,
  the hard rock into springs of water.

Psalm 115

⓵
⓶
⓷

1 Not to us, LORD, not to us
  but to your name be the glory,
  because of your love and faithfulness.

2 Why do the nations say,
  "Where is their God?"
3 Our God is in heaven;
  he does whatever pleases him.
4 But their idols are silver and gold,
  made by human hands.
5 They have mouths, but cannot speak,
  eyes, but cannot see.
6 They have ears, but cannot hear,
  noses, but cannot smell.
7 They have hands, but cannot feel,
  feet, but cannot walk,

nor can they utter a sound with their
  throats.
8 Those who make them will be like
  them,
  and so will all who trust in them.

9 All you Israelites, trust in the LORD —
  he is their help and shield.
10 House of Aaron, trust in the LORD —
  he is their help and shield.
11 You who fear him, trust in the LORD —
  he is their help and shield.

⓻
⓼

12 The LORD remembers us and will
  bless us:
  He will bless his people Israel,
  he will bless the house of Aaron,
13 he will bless those who fear the LORD —
  small and great alike.

14 May the LORD cause you to flourish,
  both you and your children.
15 May you be blessed by the LORD,
  the Maker of heaven and earth.

16 The highest heavens belong to the LORD,
  but the earth he has given to
  mankind.
17 It is not the dead who praise the LORD,
  those who go down to the place of
  silence;
18 it is we who extol the LORD,
  both now and forevermore.

Praise the LORD.ᵃ

Psalm 116

⓻
⓼

1 I love the LORD, for he heard my voice;
  he heard my cry for mercy.
2 Because he turned his ear to me,
  I will call on him as long as I live.

3 The cords of death entangled me,
  the anguish of the grave came over
  me;
  I was overcome by distress and
  sorrow.
4 Then I called on the name of the LORD:
  "LORD, save me!"

ᵃ 18 Hebrew *Hallelu Yah*

⁵The Lord is gracious and righteous;
　　our God is full of compassion.
⁶The Lord protects the unwary;
　　when I was brought low, he saved me.

⁷Return to your rest, my soul,
　　for the Lord has been good to you.

⁸For you, Lord, have delivered me from
　　　death,
　　my eyes from tears,
　　my feet from stumbling,
⁹that I may walk before the Lord
　　in the land of the living.

¹⁰I trusted in the Lord when I said,
　　"I am greatly afflicted";
¹¹in my alarm I said,
　　"Everyone is a liar."

¹²What shall I return to the Lord
　　for all his goodness to me?

¹³I will lift up the cup of salvation
　　and call on the name of the Lord.
¹⁴I will fulfill my vows to the Lord
　　in the presence of all his people.

¹⁵Precious in the sight of the Lord
　　is the death of his faithful servants.
¹⁶Truly I am your servant, Lord;
　　I serve you just as my mother did;
　　you have freed me from my chains.

¹⁷I will sacrifice a thank offering to you
　　and call on the name of the Lord.
¹⁸I will fulfill my vows to the Lord
　　in the presence of all his people,
¹⁹in the courts of the house of the Lord —
　　in your midst, Jerusalem.

　　Praise the Lord.[a]

Psalm 117

¹Praise the Lord, all you nations;
　　extol him, all you peoples.
²For great is his love toward us,
　　and the faithfulness of the Lord
　　　endures forever.

　　Praise the Lord.[a]

Psalm 118

¹Give thanks to the Lord, for he is good;
　　his love endures forever.

²Let Israel say:
　　"His love endures forever."
³Let the house of Aaron say:
　　"His love endures forever."
⁴Let those who fear the Lord say:
　　"His love endures forever."

⁵When hard pressed, I cried to the
　　　Lord;
　　he brought me into a spacious place.
⁶The Lord is with me; I will not be
　　　afraid.
　　What can mere mortals do to me?
⁷The Lord is with me; he is my helper.
　　I look in triumph on my enemies.

⁸It is better to take refuge in the Lord
　　than to trust in humans.
⁹It is better to take refuge in the Lord
　　than to trust in princes.
¹⁰All the nations surrounded me,
　　but in the name of the Lord I cut
　　　them down.
¹¹They surrounded me on every side,
　　but in the name of the Lord I cut
　　　them down.
¹²They swarmed around me like bees,
　　but they were consumed as quickly as
　　　burning thorns;
　　in the name of the Lord I cut them
　　　down.
¹³I was pushed back and about to fall,
　　but the Lord helped me.
¹⁴The Lord is my strength and my
　　　defense[b];
　　he has become my salvation.

¹⁵Shouts of joy and victory
　　resound in the tents of the righteous:
　　"The Lord's right hand has done
　　　mighty things!
¹⁶　The Lord's right hand is lifted high;
　　the Lord's right hand has done
　　　mighty things!"

---

a 19,2 Hebrew *Hallelu Yah*   b 14 Or *song*

17 I will not die but live,
and will proclaim what the LORD has
done.
18 The LORD has chastened me severely,
but he has not given me over to death.
19 Open for me the gates of the righteous;
I will enter and give thanks to the
LORD.
20 This is the gate of the LORD
through which the righteous may
enter.
21 I will give you thanks, for you answered
me;
you have become my salvation.

22 The stone the builders rejected
has become the cornerstone;
23 the LORD has done this,
and it is marvelous in our eyes.
24 The LORD has done it this very day;
let us rejoice today and be glad.

25 LORD, save us!
LORD, grant us success!

26 Blessed is he who comes in the name of
the LORD.
From the house of the LORD we bless
you.*a*
27 The LORD is God,
and he has made his light shine on us.
With boughs in hand, join in the festal
procession
up*b* to the horns of the altar.

28 You are my God, and I will praise you;
you are my God, and I will exalt you.

29 Give thanks to the LORD, for he is good;
his love endures forever.

Psalm 119*c*

א Aleph

1 Blessed are those whose ways are
blameless,
who walk according to the law of the
LORD.

2 Blessed are those who keep his statutes
and seek him with all their heart —
3 they do no wrong
but follow his ways.
4 You have laid down precepts
that are to be fully obeyed.
5 Oh, that my ways were steadfast
in obeying your decrees!
6 Then I would not be put to shame
when I consider all your commands.
7 I will praise you with an upright heart
as I learn your righteous laws.
8 I will obey your decrees;
do not utterly forsake me.

ב Beth

9 How can a young person stay on the
path of purity?
By living according to your word.
10 I seek you with all my heart;
do not let me stray from your
commands.
11 I have hidden your word in my heart
that I might not sin against you.
12 Praise be to you, LORD;
teach me your decrees.
13 With my lips I recount
all the laws that come from your
mouth.
14 I rejoice in following your statutes
as one rejoices in great riches.
15 I meditate on your precepts
and consider your ways.
16 I delight in your decrees;
I will not neglect your word.

ג Gimel

17 Be good to your servant while I live,
that I may obey your word.
18 Open my eyes that I may see
wonderful things in your law.
19 I am a stranger on earth;
do not hide your commands from
me.

---

a 26 The Hebrew is plural.   *b* 27 Or *Bind the festal sacrifice with ropes / and take it*   *c* This psalm is an acrostic
poem, the stanzas of which begin with successive letters of the Hebrew alphabet; moreover, the verses of each stanza
begin with the same letter of the Hebrew alphabet.

20 My soul is consumed with longing
   for your laws at all times.
21 You rebuke the arrogant, who are
      accursed,
   those who stray from your
      commands.
22 Remove from me their scorn and
      contempt,
   for I keep your statutes.
23 Though rulers sit together and slander
      me,
   your servant will meditate on your
      decrees.
24 Your statutes are my delight;
   they are my counselors.

ד Daleth

25 I am laid low in the dust;
   preserve my life according to your
      word.
26 I gave an account of my ways and you
      answered me;
   teach me your decrees.
27 Cause me to understand the way of
      your precepts,
   that I may meditate on your
      wonderful deeds.
28 My soul is weary with sorrow;
   strengthen me according to your
      word.
29 Keep me from deceitful ways;
   be gracious to me and teach me your
      law.
30 I have chosen the way of faithfulness;
   I have set my heart on your laws.
31 I hold fast to your statutes, LORD;
   do not let me be put to shame.
32 I run in the path of your commands,
   for you have broadened my
      understanding.

ה He

33 Teach me, LORD, the way of your
      decrees,
   that I may follow it to the end.*a*

34 Give me understanding, so that I may
      keep your law
   and obey it with all my heart.
35 Direct me in the path of your commands,
   for there I find delight.
36 Turn my heart toward your statutes
   and not toward selfish gain.
37 Turn my eyes away from worthless
      things;
   preserve my life according to your
      word.*b*
38 Fulfill your promise to your servant,
   so that you may be feared.
39 Take away the disgrace I dread,
   for your laws are good.
40 How I long for your precepts!
   In your righteousness preserve my
      life.

ו Waw

41 May your unfailing love come to me,
      LORD,
   your salvation, according to your
      promise;
42 then I can answer anyone who taunts
      me,
   for I trust in your word.
43 Never take your word of truth from my
      mouth,
   for I have put my hope in your laws.
44 I will always obey your law,
   for ever and ever.
45 I will walk about in freedom,
   for I have sought out your precepts.
46 I will speak of your statutes before kings
   and will not be put to shame,
47 for I delight in your commands
   because I love them.
48 I reach out for your commands, which I
      love,
   that I may meditate on your decrees.

ז Zayin

49 Remember your word to your servant,
   for you have given me hope.

---

a 33 Or *follow it for its reward*   *b 37* Two manuscripts of the Masoretic Text and Dead Sea Scrolls; most manuscripts of the Masoretic Text *life in your way*

⁵⁰My comfort in my suffering is this:
  Your promise preserves my life.
⁵¹The arrogant mock me unmercifully,
  but I do not turn from your law.
⁵²I remember, LORD, your ancient laws,
  and I find comfort in them.
⁵³Indignation grips me because of the
  wicked,
  who have forsaken your law.
⁵⁴Your decrees are the theme of my song
  wherever I lodge.
⁵⁵In the night, LORD, I remember your
  name,
  that I may keep your law.
⁵⁶This has been my practice:
  I obey your precepts.

ח Heth

⁵⁷You are my portion, LORD;
  I have promised to obey your words.
⁵⁸I have sought your face with all my
  heart;
  be gracious to me according to your
  promise.
⁵⁹I have considered my ways
  and have turned my steps to your
  statutes.
⁶⁰I will hasten and not delay
  to obey your commands.
⁶¹Though the wicked bind me with ropes,
  I will not forget your law.
⁶²At midnight I rise to give you thanks
  for your righteous laws.
⁶³I am a friend to all who fear you,
  to all who follow your precepts.
⁶⁴The earth is filled with your love, LORD;
  teach me your decrees.

ט Teth

⁶⁵Do good to your servant
  according to your word, LORD.
⁶⁶Teach me knowledge and good
  judgment,
  for I trust your commands.
⁶⁷Before I was afflicted I went astray,
  but now I obey your word.
⁶⁸You are good, and what you do is good;
  teach me your decrees.

⁶⁹Though the arrogant have smeared me
  with lies,
  I keep your precepts with all my
  heart.
⁷⁰Their hearts are callous and unfeeling,
  but I delight in your law.
⁷¹It was good for me to be afflicted
  so that I might learn your decrees.
⁷²The law from your mouth is more
  precious to me
  than thousands of pieces of silver
  and gold.

י Yodh

⁷³Your hands made me and formed me;
  give me understanding to learn your
  commands.
⁷⁴May those who fear you rejoice when
  they see me,
  for I have put my hope in your word.
⁷⁵I know, LORD, that your laws are
  righteous,
  and that in faithfulness you have
  afflicted me.
⁷⁶May your unfailing love be my comfort,
  according to your promise to your
  servant.
⁷⁷Let your compassion come to me that I
  may live,
  for your law is my delight.
⁷⁸May the arrogant be put to shame for
  wronging me without cause;
  but I will meditate on your precepts.
⁷⁹May those who fear you turn to me,
  those who understand your statutes.
⁸⁰May I wholeheartedly follow your
  decrees,
  that I may not be put to shame.

כ Kaph

⁸¹My soul faints with longing for your
  salvation,
  but I have put my hope in your word.
⁸²My eyes fail, looking for your promise;
  I say, "When will you comfort me?"
⁸³Though I am like a wineskin in the
  smoke,
  I do not forget your decrees.

84 How long must your servant wait?
     When will you punish my
          persecutors?
85 The arrogant dig pits to trap me,
     contrary to your law.
86 All your commands are trustworthy;
     help me, for I am being persecuted
          without cause.
87 They almost wiped me from the earth,
     but I have not forsaken your
          precepts.
88 In your unfailing love preserve my life,
     that I may obey the statutes of your
          mouth.

ל Lamedh

89 Your word, LORD, is eternal;
     it stands firm in the heavens.
90 Your faithfulness continues through all
          generations;
     you established the earth, and it
          endures.
91 Your laws endure to this day,
     for all things serve you.
92 If your law had not been my delight,
     I would have perished in my
          affliction.
93 I will never forget your precepts,
     for by them you have preserved my
          life.
94 Save me, for I am yours;
     I have sought out your precepts.
95 The wicked are waiting to destroy me,
     but I will ponder your statutes.
96 To all perfection I see a limit,
     but your commands are boundless.

מ Mem

97 Oh, how I love your law!
     I meditate on it all day long.
98 Your commands are always with me
     and make me wiser than my
          enemies.
99 I have more insight than all my
          teachers,
     for I meditate on your statutes.

100 I have more understanding than the
          elders,
     for I obey your precepts.
101 I have kept my feet from every evil path
     so that I might obey your word.
102 I have not departed from your laws,
     for you yourself have taught me.
103 How sweet are your words to my taste,
     sweeter than honey to my mouth!
104 I gain understanding from your
          precepts;
     therefore I hate every wrong path.

נ Nun

105 Your word is a lamp for my feet,
     a light on my path.
106 I have taken an oath and confirmed it,
     that I will follow your righteous laws.
107 I have suffered much;
     preserve my life, LORD, according to
          your word.
108 Accept, LORD, the willing praise of my
          mouth,
     and teach me your laws.
109 Though I constantly take my life in my
          hands,
     I will not forget your law.
110 The wicked have set a snare for me,
     but I have not strayed from your
          precepts.
111 Your statutes are my heritage forever;
     they are the joy of my heart.
112 My heart is set on keeping your decrees
     to the very end.ᵃ

ס Samekh

113 I hate double-minded people,
     but I love your law.
114 You are my refuge and my shield;
     I have put my hope in your word.
115 Away from me, you evildoers,
     that I may keep the commands of my
          God!
116 Sustain me, my God, according to your
          promise, and I will live;
     do not let my hopes be dashed.

ᵃ 112 Or decrees / for their enduring reward

117 Uphold me, and I will be delivered;
      I will always have regard for your
      decrees.
118 You reject all who stray from your
      decrees,
      for their delusions come to nothing.
119 All the wicked of the earth you discard
      like dross;
      therefore I love your statutes.
120 My flesh trembles in fear of you;
      I stand in awe of your laws.

ע Ayin

121 I have done what is righteous and just;
      do not leave me to my oppressors.
122 Ensure your servant's well-being;
      do not let the arrogant oppress me.
123 My eyes fail, looking for your salvation,
      looking for your righteous promise.
124 Deal with your servant according to
      your love
      and teach me your decrees.
125 I am your servant; give me discernment
      that I may understand your statutes.
126 It is time for you to act, LORD;
      your law is being broken.
127 Because I love your commands
      more than gold, more than pure gold,
128 and because I consider all your precepts
      right,
      I hate every wrong path.

פ Pe

129 Your statutes are wonderful;
      therefore I obey them.
130 The unfolding of your words gives
      light;
      it gives understanding to the simple.
131 I open my mouth and pant,
      longing for your commands.
132 Turn to me and have mercy on me,
      as you always do to those who love
      your name.
133 Direct my footsteps according to your
      word;
      let no sin rule over me.
134 Redeem me from human oppression,
      that I may obey your precepts.

135 Make your face shine on your servant
      and teach me your decrees.
136 Streams of tears flow from my eyes,
      for your law is not obeyed.

צ Tsadhe

137 You are righteous, LORD,
      and your laws are right.
138 The statutes you have laid down are
      righteous;
      they are fully trustworthy.
139 My zeal wears me out,
      for my enemies ignore your words.
140 Your promises have been thoroughly
      tested,
      and your servant loves them.
141 Though I am lowly and despised,
      I do not forget your precepts.
142 Your righteousness is everlasting
      and your law is true.
143 Trouble and distress have come
      upon me,
      but your commands give me delight.
144 Your statutes are always righteous;
      give me understanding that I may
      live.

ק Qoph

145 I call with all my heart; answer me,
      LORD,
      and I will obey your decrees.
146 I call out to you; save me
      and I will keep your statutes.
147 I rise before dawn and cry for help;
      I have put my hope in your word.
148 My eyes stay open through the watches
      of the night,
      that I may meditate on your
      promises.
149 Hear my voice in accordance with your
      love;
      preserve my life, LORD, according to
      your laws.
150 Those who devise wicked schemes are
      near,
      but they are far from your law.
151 Yet you are near, LORD,
      and all your commands are true.

152 Long ago I learned from your statutes
that you established them to last
forever.

ר Resh

153 Look on my suffering and deliver me,
for I have not forgotten your law.
154 Defend my cause and redeem me;
preserve my life according to your
promise.
155 Salvation is far from the wicked,
for they do not seek out your
decrees.
156 Your compassion, Lord, is great;
preserve my life according to your
laws.
157 Many are the foes who persecute me,
but I have not turned from your
statutes.
158 I look on the faithless with loathing,
for they do not obey your word.
159 See how I love your precepts;
preserve my life, Lord, in
accordance with your love.
160 All your words are true;
all your righteous laws are eternal.

שׁ Sin and Shin

161 Rulers persecute me without cause,
but my heart trembles at your
word.
162 I rejoice in your promise
like one who finds great spoil.
163 I hate and detest falsehood
but I love your law.
164 Seven times a day I praise you
for your righteous laws.
165 Great peace have those who love your
law,
and nothing can make them
stumble.
166 I wait for your salvation, Lord,
and I follow your commands.
167 I obey your statutes,
for I love them greatly.
168 I obey your precepts and your
statutes,
for all my ways are known to you.

ת Taw

169 May my cry come before you, Lord;
give me understanding according to
your word.
170 May my supplication come before you;
deliver me according to your
promise.
171 May my lips overflow with praise,
for you teach me your decrees.
172 May my tongue sing of your word,
for all your commands are righteous.
173 May your hand be ready to help me,
for I have chosen your precepts.
174 I long for your salvation, Lord,
and your law gives me delight.
175 Let me live that I may praise you,
and may your laws sustain me.
176 I have strayed like a lost sheep.
Seek your servant,
for I have not forgotten your
commands.

Psalm 120

A song of ascents.

1 I call on the Lord in my distress,
and he answers me.
2 Save me, Lord,
from lying lips
and from deceitful tongues.

3 What will he do to you,
and what more besides,
you deceitful tongue?
4 He will punish you with a warrior's
sharp arrows,
with burning coals of the broom bush.

5 Woe to me that I dwell in Meshek,
that I live among the tents of Kedar!
6 Too long have I lived
among those who hate peace.
7 I am for peace;
but when I speak, they are for war.

Psalm 121

A song of ascents.

1 I lift up my eyes to the mountains —
where does my help come from?

2 My help comes from the Lord,
　　the Maker of heaven and earth.

3 He will not let your foot slip —
　　he who watches over you will not
　　　slumber;
4 indeed, he who watches over Israel
　　will neither slumber nor sleep.

5 The Lord watches over you —
　　the Lord is your shade at your right
　　　hand;
6 the sun will not harm you by day,
　　nor the moon by night.

7 The Lord will keep you from all
　　harm —
　　he will watch over your life;
8 the Lord will watch over your coming
　　and going
　　both now and forevermore.

Psalm 122

A song of ascents. Of David.

1 I rejoiced with those who said to me,
　　"Let us go to the house of the
　　　Lord."
2 Our feet are standing
　　in your gates, Jerusalem.

3 Jerusalem is built like a city
　　that is closely compacted together.
4 That is where the tribes go up —
　　the tribes of the Lord —
　to praise the name of the Lord
　　according to the statute given to
　　　Israel.
5 There stand the thrones for judgment,
　　the thrones of the house of David.

6 Pray for the peace of Jerusalem:
　　"May those who love you be
　　　secure.
7 May there be peace within your walls
　　and security within your citadels."
8 For the sake of my family and friends,
　　I will say, "Peace be within you."
9 For the sake of the house of the Lord
　　our God,
　　I will seek your prosperity.

Psalm 123

A song of ascents.

1 I lift up my eyes to you,
　　to you who sit enthroned in heaven.
2 As the eyes of slaves look to the hand of
　　their master,
　　as the eyes of a female slave look to
　　　the hand of her mistress,
　so our eyes look to the Lord our God,
　　till he shows us his mercy.

3 Have mercy on us, Lord, have mercy
　　on us,
　　for we have endured no end of
　　　contempt.
4 We have endured no end
　　of ridicule from the arrogant,
　　of contempt from the proud.

Psalm 124

A song of ascents. Of David.

1 If the Lord had not been on our side —
　　let Israel say —
2 if the Lord had not been on our side
　　when people attacked us,
3 they would have swallowed us alive
　　when their anger flared against us;
4 the flood would have engulfed us,
　　the torrent would have swept over us,
5 the raging waters
　　would have swept us away.

6 Praise be to the Lord,
　　who has not let us be torn by their
　　　teeth.
7 We have escaped like a bird
　　from the fowler's snare;
　the snare has been broken,
　　and we have escaped.
8 Our help is in the name of the Lord,
　　the Maker of heaven and earth.

Psalm 125

A song of ascents.

1 Those who trust in the Lord are like
　　Mount Zion,
　　which cannot be shaken but endures
　　　forever.

2 As the mountains surround Jerusalem,
so the LORD surrounds his people
both now and forevermore.

3 The scepter of the wicked will not
remain
over the land allotted to the
righteous,
for then the righteous might use
their hands to do evil.

4 LORD, do good to those who are good,
to those who are upright in heart.
5 But those who turn to crooked ways
the LORD will banish with the
evildoers.

Peace be on Israel.

Psalm 126

A song of ascents.

1 When the LORD restored the fortunes
of[a] Zion,
we were like those who dreamed.[b]
2 Our mouths were filled with laughter,
our tongues with songs of joy.
Then it was said among the nations,
"The LORD has done great things for
them."
3 The LORD has done great things for us,
and we are filled with joy.

4 Restore our fortunes,[c] LORD,
like streams in the Negev.
5 Those who sow with tears
will reap with songs of joy.
6 Those who go out weeping,
carrying seed to sow,
will return with songs of joy,
carrying sheaves with them.

Psalm 127

A song of ascents. Of Solomon.

1 Unless the LORD builds the house,
the builders labor in vain.
Unless the LORD watches over the city,
the guards stand watch in vain.

2 In vain you rise early
and stay up late,
toiling for food to eat —
for he grants sleep to[d] those he loves.

3 Children are a heritage from the LORD,
offspring a reward from him.
4 Like arrows in the hands of a warrior
are children born in one's youth.
5 Blessed is the man
whose quiver is full of them.
They will not be put to shame
when they contend with their
opponents in court.

Psalm 128

A song of ascents.

1 Blessed are all who fear the LORD,
who walk in obedience to him.
2 You will eat the fruit of your labor;
blessings and prosperity will be
yours.
3 Your wife will be like a fruitful vine
within your house;
your children will be like olive shoots
around your table.
4 Yes, this will be the blessing
for the man who fears the LORD.

5 May the LORD bless you from Zion;
may you see the prosperity of
Jerusalem
all the days of your life.
6 May you live to see your children's
children —
peace be on Israel.

Psalm 129

A song of ascents.

1 "They have greatly oppressed me from
my youth,"
let Israel say;
2 "they have greatly oppressed me from
my youth,
but they have not gained the victory
over me.

---

[a] 1 Or LORD brought back the captives to   [b] 1 Or those restored to health   [c] 4 Or Bring back our captives
[d] 2 Or eat — / for while they sleep he provides for

³ Plowmen have plowed my back
    and made their furrows long.
⁴ But the LORD is righteous;
    he has cut me free from the cords of
        the wicked."

⁵ May all who hate Zion
    be turned back in shame.
⁶ May they be like grass on the roof,
    which withers before it can grow;
⁷ a reaper cannot fill his hands with it,
    nor one who gathers fill his arms.
⁸ May those who pass by not say to them,
    "The blessing of the LORD be on you;
    we bless you in the name of the LORD."

Psalm 130

A song of ascents.

¹ Out of the depths I cry to you, LORD;
²   Lord, hear my voice.
    Let your ears be attentive
        to my cry for mercy.

³ If you, LORD, kept a record of sins,
    Lord, who could stand?
⁴ But with you there is forgiveness,
    so that we can, with reverence, serve
        you.

⁵ I wait for the LORD, my whole being waits,
    and in his word I put my hope.
⁶ I wait for the Lord
    more than watchmen wait for the
        morning,
    more than watchmen wait for the
        morning.

⁷ Israel, put your hope in the LORD,
    for with the LORD is unfailing love
    and with him is full redemption.
⁸ He himself will redeem Israel
    from all their sins.

Psalm 131

A song of ascents. Of David.

¹ My heart is not proud, LORD,
    my eyes are not haughty;

I do not concern myself with great
        matters
    or things too wonderful for me.
² But I have calmed and quieted myself,
    I am like a weaned child with its
        mother;
    like a weaned child I am content.

³ Israel, put your hope in the LORD
    both now and forevermore.

Psalm 132

A song of ascents.

¹ LORD, remember David
    and all his self-denial.

² He swore an oath to the LORD,
    he made a vow to the Mighty One of
        Jacob:
³ "I will not enter my house
    or go to my bed,
⁴ I will allow no sleep to my eyes
    or slumber to my eyelids,
⁵ till I find a place for the LORD,
    a dwelling for the Mighty One of
        Jacob."

⁶ We heard it in Ephrathah,
    we came upon it in the fields of Jaar:ᵃ
⁷ "Let us go to his dwelling place,
    let us worship at his footstool, saying,
⁸ 'Arise, LORD, and come to your resting
        place,
    you and the ark of your might.
⁹ May your priests be clothed with your
        righteousness;
    may your faithful people sing for
        joy.'"

¹⁰ For the sake of your servant David,
    do not reject your anointed one.

¹¹ The LORD swore an oath to David,
    a sure oath he will not revoke:
"One of your own descendants
    I will place on your throne.
¹² If your sons keep my covenant
    and the statutes I teach them,

ᵃ 6 Or *heard of it in Ephrathah, / we found it in the fields of Jearim.* (See 1 Chron. 13:5,6) (And no quotation marks around verses 7-9)

then their sons will sit
   on your throne for ever and ever."

13 For the LORD has chosen Zion,
   he has desired it for his dwelling,
      saying,
14 "This is my resting place for ever and
      ever;
   here I will sit enthroned, for I have
      desired it.
15 I will bless her with abundant
      provisions;
   her poor I will satisfy with food.
16 I will clothe her priests with salvation,
   and her faithful people will ever sing
      for joy.
17 "Here I will make a horn*a* grow for
      David
   and set up a lamp for my anointed
      one.
18 I will clothe his enemies with shame,
   but his head will be adorned with a
      radiant crown."

Psalm 133

A song of ascents. Of David.

1 How good and pleasant it is
   when God's people live together in
      unity!

2 It is like precious oil poured on the head,
   running down on the beard,
  running down on Aaron's beard,
     down on the collar of his robe.
3 It is as if the dew of Hermon
   were falling on Mount Zion.
  For there the LORD bestows his
     blessing,
   even life forevermore.

Psalm 134

A song of ascents.

1 Praise the LORD, all you servants of the
     LORD
  who minister by night in the house of
     the LORD.

2 Lift up your hands in the sanctuary
   and praise the LORD.

3 May the LORD bless you from Zion,
   he who is the Maker of heaven and
     earth.

Psalm 135

1 Praise the LORD.*b*

 Praise the name of the LORD;
   praise him, you servants of the LORD,
2 you who minister in the house of the
     LORD,
   in the courts of the house of our God.

3 Praise the LORD, for the LORD is good;
   sing praise to his name, for that is
     pleasant.
4 For the LORD has chosen Jacob to be his
     own,
   Israel to be his treasured possession.

5 I know that the LORD is great,
   that our Lord is greater than all
     gods.
6 The LORD does whatever pleases him,
   in the heavens and on the earth,
   in the seas and all their depths.
7 He makes clouds rise from the ends of
     the earth;
   he sends lightning with the rain
   and brings out the wind from his
     storehouses.

8 He struck down the firstborn of
     Egypt,
   the firstborn of people and animals.
9 He sent his signs and wonders into your
     midst, Egypt,
   against Pharaoh and all his servants.
10 He struck down many nations
   and killed mighty kings —
11 Sihon king of the Amorites,
   Og king of Bashan,
   and all the kings of Canaan —
12 and he gave their land as an
     inheritance,
   an inheritance to his people Israel.

---

a 17 Horn here symbolizes strong one, that is, king.   *b 1* Hebrew *Hallelu Yah*; also in verses 3 and 21

13 Your name, LORD, endures forever,
  your renown, LORD, through all
    generations.
14 For the LORD will vindicate his people
  and have compassion on his servants.

15 The idols of the nations are silver and
    gold,
  made by human hands.
16 They have mouths, but cannot speak,
  eyes, but cannot see.
17 They have ears, but cannot hear,
  nor is there breath in their mouths.
18 Those who make them will be like
    them,
  and so will all who trust in them.

19 All you Israelites, praise the LORD;
  house of Aaron, praise the LORD;
20 house of Levi, praise the LORD;
  you who fear him, praise the LORD.
21 Praise be to the LORD from Zion,
  to him who dwells in Jerusalem.

Praise the LORD.

Psalm 136

1 Give thanks to the LORD, for he is good.
  His love endures forever.
2 Give thanks to the God of gods.
  His love endures forever.
3 Give thanks to the Lord of lords:
  His love endures forever.

4 to him who alone does great wonders,
  His love endures forever.
5 who by his understanding made the
    heavens,
  His love endures forever.
6 who spread out the earth upon the
    waters,
  His love endures forever.
7 who made the great lights —
  His love endures forever.
8 the sun to govern the day,
  His love endures forever.
9 the moon and stars to govern the night;
  His love endures forever.

10 to him who struck down the firstborn
    of Egypt
  His love endures forever.
11 and brought Israel out from among them
  His love endures forever.
12 with a mighty hand and outstretched
    arm;
  His love endures forever.
13 to him who divided the Red Sea[a]
    asunder
  His love endures forever.
14 and brought Israel through the midst
    of it,
  His love endures forever.
15 but swept Pharaoh and his army into
    the Red Sea;
  His love endures forever.

16 to him who led his people through the
    wilderness;
  His love endures forever.

17 to him who struck down great kings,
  His love endures forever.
18 and killed mighty kings —
  His love endures forever.
19 Sihon king of the Amorites
  His love endures forever.
20 and Og king of Bashan —
  His love endures forever.
21 and gave their land as an inheritance,
  His love endures forever.
22 an inheritance to his servant Israel.
  His love endures forever.

23 He remembered us in our low estate
  His love endures forever.
24 and freed us from our enemies.
  His love endures forever.
25 He gives food to every creature.
  His love endures forever.

26 Give thanks to the God of heaven.
  His love endures forever.

Psalm 137

1 By the rivers of Babylon we sat and wept
  when we remembered Zion.

---

a 13 Or *the Sea of Reeds*; also in verse 15

2 There on the poplars
  we hung our harps,
3 for there our captors asked us for songs,
  our tormentors demanded songs of
    joy;
  they said, "Sing us one of the songs of
    Zion!"

4 How can we sing the songs of the
    LORD
  while in a foreign land?
5 If I forget you, Jerusalem,
  may my right hand forget its skill.
6 May my tongue cling to the roof of my
    mouth
  if I do not remember you,
  if I do not consider Jerusalem
    my highest joy.

7 Remember, LORD, what the Edomites
    did
  on the day Jerusalem fell.
  "Tear it down," they cried,
    "tear it down to its foundations!"
8 Daughter Babylon, doomed to
    destruction,
  happy is the one who repays you
    according to what you have done to
    us.
9 Happy is the one who seizes your
    infants
  and dashes them against the rocks.

Psalm 138

Of David.

1 I will praise you, LORD, with all my
    heart;
  before the "gods" I will sing your
    praise.
2 I will bow down toward your holy
    temple
  and will praise your name
    for your unfailing love and your
    faithfulness,
  for you have so exalted your solemn
    decree
    that it surpasses your fame.
3 When I called, you answered me;
  you greatly emboldened me.

4 May all the kings of the earth praise
    you, LORD,
  when they hear what you have
    decreed.
5 May they sing of the ways of the LORD,
  for the glory of the LORD is great.

6 Though the LORD is exalted, he looks
    kindly on the lowly;
  though lofty, he sees them from afar.
7 Though I walk in the midst of trouble,
  you preserve my life.
  You stretch out your hand against the
    anger of my foes;
  with your right hand you save me.
8 The LORD will vindicate me;
  your love, LORD, endures forever —
  do not abandon the works of your
    hands.

Psalm 139

For the director of music. Of David. A psalm.

1 You have searched me, LORD,
  and you know me.
2 You know when I sit and when I rise;
  you perceive my thoughts from afar.
3 You discern my going out and my lying
    down;
  you are familiar with all my ways.
4 Before a word is on my tongue
  you, LORD, know it completely.
5 You hem me in behind and before,
  and you lay your hand upon me.
6 Such knowledge is too wonderful for me,
  too lofty for me to attain.

7 Where can I go from your Spirit?
  Where can I flee from your presence?
8 If I go up to the heavens, you are there;
  if I make my bed in the depths, you
    are there.
9 If I rise on the wings of the dawn,
  if I settle on the far side of the sea,
10 even there your hand will guide me,
  your right hand will hold me fast.
11 If I say, "Surely the darkness will hide
    me
  and the light become night around
    me,"

¹² even the darkness will not be dark to
you;
the night will shine like the day,
for darkness is as light to you.

¹³ For you created my inmost being;
you knit me together in my mother's
womb.
¹⁴ I praise you because I am fearfully and
wonderfully made;
your works are wonderful,
I know that full well.
¹⁵ My frame was not hidden from you
when I was made in the secret
place,
when I was woven together in the
depths of the earth.
¹⁶ Your eyes saw my unformed body;
all the days ordained for me were
written in your book
before one of them came to be.
¹⁷ How precious to me are your thoughts,ᵃ
God!
How vast is the sum of them!
¹⁸ Were I to count them,
they would outnumber the grains of
sand—
when I awake, I am still with you.

¹⁹ If only you, God, would slay the
wicked!
Away from me, you who are
bloodthirsty!
²⁰ They speak of you with evil intent;
your adversaries misuse your
name.
²¹ Do I not hate those who hate you,
LORD,
and abhor those who are in rebellion
against you?
²² I have nothing but hatred for them;
I count them my enemies.
²³ Search me, God, and know my heart;
test me and know my anxious
thoughts.
²⁴ See if there is any offensive way in me,
and lead me in the way everlasting.

Psalm 140ᵇ

For the director of music. A psalm of David.

¹ Rescue me, LORD, from evildoers;
protect me from the violent,
² who devise evil plans in their hearts
and stir up war every day.
³ They make their tongues as sharp as a
serpent's;
the poison of vipers is on their lips.ᶜ

⁴ Keep me safe, LORD, from the hands of
the wicked;
protect me from the violent,
who devise ways to trip my feet.
⁵ The arrogant have hidden a snare for me;
they have spread out the cords of
their net
and have set traps for me along my
path.

⁶ I say to the LORD, "You are my God."
Hear, LORD, my cry for mercy.
⁷ Sovereign LORD, my strong deliverer,
you shield my head in the day of
battle.
⁸ Do not grant the wicked their desires,
LORD;
do not let their plans succeed.

⁹ Those who surround me proudly rear
their heads;
may the mischief of their lips engulf
them.
¹⁰ May burning coals fall on them;
may they be thrown into the fire,
into miry pits, never to rise.
¹¹ May slanderers not be established in the
land;
may disaster hunt down the violent.

¹² I know that the LORD secures justice for
the poor
and upholds the cause of the needy.
¹³ Surely the righteous will praise your
name,
and the upright will live in your
presence.

ᵃ 17 Or *How amazing are your thoughts concerning me*   ᵇ In Hebrew texts 140:1-13 is numbered 140:2-14.
ᶜ 3 The Hebrew has *Selah* (a word of uncertain meaning) here and at the end of verses 5 and 8.

Psalm 141

A psalm of David.

¹ I call to you, LORD, come quickly to
  me;
　hear me when I call to you.
² May my prayer be set before you like
  incense;
　may the lifting up of my hands be
　like the evening sacrifice.

³ Set a guard over my mouth, LORD;
　keep watch over the door of my lips.

⁴ Do not let my heart be drawn to what is
  evil
　so that I take part in wicked deeds
  along with those who are evildoers;
　do not let me eat their delicacies.

⁵ Let a righteous man strike me — that is
  a kindness;
　let him rebuke me — that is oil on my
　head.
  My head will not refuse it,
　for my prayer will still be against the
　deeds of evildoers.

INVENTORY LESSON [*Principle Four*]

For the previous entry in the INVENTORY lesson, go to Ezekiel 34:16 (page 1007).

For a discussion of Principles One through Eight and a listing of their related lessons,
go to pages xvii – xliv.

*Search me, God, and know my heart; test me and know
my anxious thoughts. See if there is any offensive way in me,
and lead me in the way everlasting.*

PSALM 139:23 – 24

Principle Four begins the process of "coming clean." It's here that we openly examine and confess our faults to ourselves, to God and to someone else we trust. In the first part of Principle Four we openly examine our lives. As we get ready to write out our inventories in Principle Four, we divide them into five specific sections.

The fifth and last area we write about is labeled MY PART. Lamentations 3:40 invites, "Let us examine our ways and test them, and let us return to the LORD." Notice that the verse doesn't say, "Let us examine *their* ways." We dealt with that issue already in the first four sections of our inventories. Now we need to honestly determine the part of any resentments (or any other sin or injury) that we're responsible for. We need to ask God to show us our part in a broken or damaged marriage or other relationship, whether this involves a distant child or parent or even a lost job. In addition, in this section we'll list all the people we've hurt, as well as how we've injured them.

As the psalmist entreated God in Psalm 139:24, we need God's help to show us whatever is evil in ourselves. This will help us to identify where we've missed the mark in our relationships.

Please note: If you've been in an abusive relationship, especially as a small child, you can find great freedom in this part of the inventory. You will come to recognize that you had NO part, NO responsibility for the cause of the resentment. By simply writing the words NONE or NOT GUILTY in this section, you can begin to find freedom from the misplaced shame and guilt you've carried around for far too long.

This is the final page of the INVENTORY lesson.

⁶Their rulers will be thrown down from
    the cliffs,
    and the wicked will learn that my
        words were well spoken.
⁷They will say, "As one plows and breaks
    up the earth,
    so our bones have been scattered at
        the mouth of the grave."

⁸But my eyes are fixed on you, Sovereign
    LORD;
    in you I take refuge—do not give me
        over to death.
⁹Keep me safe from the traps set by
    evildoers,
    from the snares they have laid for me.
¹⁰Let the wicked fall into their own nets,
    while I pass by in safety.

Psalm 142ᵃ

A *maskil*ᵇ of David. When he was in the cave.
A prayer.

¹I cry aloud to the LORD;
    I lift up my voice to the LORD for
        mercy.
²I pour out before him my complaint;
    before him I tell my trouble.

³When my spirit grows faint within me,
    it is you who watch over my way.
In the path where I walk
    people have hidden a snare for me.
⁴Look and see, there is no one at my
    right hand;
    no one is concerned for me.
I have no refuge;
    no one cares for my life.

⁵I cry to you, LORD;
    I say, "You are my refuge,
    my portion in the land of the living."

⁶Listen to my cry,
    for I am in desperate need;
rescue me from those who pursue me,
    for they are too strong for me.
⁷Set me free from my prison,
    that I may praise your name.

Then the righteous will gather about me
    because of your goodness to me.

Psalm 143

A psalm of David.

¹LORD, hear my prayer,
    listen to my cry for mercy;
in your faithfulness and righteousness
    come to my relief.
²Do not bring your servant into
    judgment,
    for no one living is righteous before
        you.

³The enemy pursues me,
    he crushes me to the ground;
he makes me dwell in the darkness
    like those long dead.
⁴So my spirit grows faint within me;
    my heart within me is dismayed.
⁵I remember the days of long ago;
    I meditate on all your works
    and consider what your hands have
        done.
⁶I spread out my hands to you;
    I thirst for you like a parched land.ᶜ

⁷Answer me quickly, LORD;
    my spirit fails.
Do not hide your face from me
    or I will be like those who go down to
        the pit.
⁸Let the morning bring me word of your
    unfailing love,
    for I have put my trust in you.
Show me the way I should go,
    for to you I entrust my life.
⁹Rescue me from my enemies, LORD,
    for I hide myself in you.
¹⁰Teach me to do your will,
    for you are my God;
may your good Spirit
    lead me on level ground.

¹¹For your name's sake, LORD, preserve
    my life;
    in your righteousness, bring me out
        of trouble.

ᵃ In Hebrew texts 142:1-7 is numbered 142:2-8.   ᵇ Title: Probably a literary or musical term   ᶜ 6 The Hebrew has
Selah (a word of uncertain meaning) here.

12 In your unfailing love, silence my
    enemies;
  destroy all my foes,
  for I am your servant.

Psalm 144

Of David.

1 Praise be to the LORD my Rock,
  who trains my hands for war,
  my fingers for battle.
2 He is my loving God and my fortress,
  my stronghold and my deliverer,
  my shield, in whom I take refuge,
  who subdues peoples*a* under me.

3 LORD, what are human beings that you
    care for them,
  mere mortals that you think of them?
4 They are like a breath;
  their days are like a fleeting shadow.

5 Part your heavens, LORD, and come
    down;
  touch the mountains, so that they
    smoke.
6 Send forth lightning and scatter the
    enemy;
  shoot your arrows and rout them.
7 Reach down your hand from on high;
  deliver me and rescue me
from the mighty waters,
  from the hands of foreigners
8 whose mouths are full of lies,
  whose right hands are deceitful.

9 I will sing a new song to you, my
    God;
  on the ten-stringed lyre I will make
    music to you,
10 to the One who gives victory to kings,
  who delivers his servant David.

---

a 2 Many manuscripts of the Masoretic Text, Dead Sea Scrolls, Aquila, Jerome and Syriac; most manuscripts of the Masoretic Text *subdues my people*

ACTION LESSON [*Principle Three*]

For the previous entry in the ACTION lesson, go to Romans 10:9 (page 1405).

For a discussion of Principles One through Eight and a listing of their related lessons,
go to pages xvii – xliv.

*Teach me to do your will, for you are my God;
may your good Spirit lead me on level ground.*

PSALM 143:10

In Principle Three we consciously choose to commit all our lives and will to Christ's care and control. We make the decision to TURN over all our lives and will to our Higher Power, Jesus Christ. In order to turn over our lives to Christ's care and control, we need to take ACTION.

The *C* in ACTION reminds us to COMMIT, to start asking for and following Christ's will for our lives. Most of us have tried to run our lives on our own power and will, and we've found this approach to be less than successful. In Principle Three we learn that we need to change our definition of *willpower*. Willpower becomes our willingness to accept God's power and will to guide our lives. We come to see that there's no room in our hearts for God if we're already full of ourselves. We need to pray the prayer the psalmist prayed in Psalm 143:10.

The next letter in ACTION is *T*. Go to Proverbs 3:6 (page 744).

From the deadly sword ¹¹deliver me;
   rescue me from the hands of foreigners
whose mouths are full of lies,
   whose right hands are deceitful.

¹² Then our sons in their youth
   will be like well-nurtured plants,
and our daughters will be like pillars
   carved to adorn a palace.
¹³ Our barns will be filled
   with every kind of provision.
Our sheep will increase by thousands,
   by tens of thousands in our fields;
¹⁴   our oxen will draw heavy loads.*a*
There will be no breaching of walls,
   no going into captivity,
   no cry of distress in our streets.
¹⁵ Blessed is the people of whom this is true;
   blessed is the people whose God is
      the Lord.

Psalm 145*b*

A psalm of praise. Of David.

¹ I will exalt you, my God the King;
   I will praise your name for ever and
      ever.
² Every day I will praise you
   and extol your name for ever and
      ever.

³ Great is the Lord and most worthy of
      praise;
   his greatness no one can fathom.
⁴ One generation commends your works
      to another;
   they tell of your mighty acts.
⁵ They speak of the glorious splendor of
      your majesty—
   and I will meditate on your
      wonderful works.*c*

---

a 14 Or *our chieftains will be firmly established*   *b* This psalm is an acrostic poem, the verses of which (including verse 13b) begin with the successive letters of the Hebrew alphabet.   *c* 5 Dead Sea Scrolls and Syriac (see also Septuagint); Masoretic Text *On the glorious splendor of your majesty / and on your wonderful works I will meditate*

Ready Lesson [*Principle Five*]

This is the first page of the READY lesson.

For a discussion of Principles One through Eight and a listing of their related lessons,
go to pages xvii–xliv.

Teach me to do your will, for you are my God;
may your good Spirit lead me on level ground.

Psalm 143:10

In Principle Five we need to be READY to voluntarily submit to every change God wants to make in our lives and humbly ask him to remove our character defects.

The *R* in READY stands for RELEASE CONTROL. God is courteous and patient in his dealings with us. Think back to Principle Three, and notice that he didn't impose his will on us. Instead, he waited for us to invite him in. Now in Principle Five we need to be willing to let God enter every area of our lives. He won't come in and clean up an area unless we're willing to ask him to do so. It has been said that "willingness is the key that goes into the lock and opens the door that allows God to begin to remove our character defects." Simply put, the *R*—RELEASE CONTROL—means "let go and let God."

The next letter in READY is *E*. Go to Psalm 37:5–6 (page 657).

⁶They tell of the power of your awesome
  works—
    and I will proclaim your great deeds.
⁷They celebrate your abundant goodness
    and joyfully sing of your
      righteousness.

⁸The LORD is gracious and
    compassionate,
      slow to anger and rich in love.

⁹The LORD is good to all;
    he has compassion on all he has
      made.
¹⁰All your works praise you, LORD;
    your faithful people extol you.
¹¹They tell of the glory of your kingdom
    and speak of your might,
¹²so that all people may know of your
    mighty acts
      and the glorious splendor of your
        kingdom.
¹³Your kingdom is an everlasting
    kingdom,
      and your dominion endures through
        all generations.

The LORD is trustworthy in all he
    promises
      and faithful in all he does.ᵃ
¹⁴The LORD upholds all who fall
    and lifts up all who are bowed
      down.
¹⁵The eyes of all look to you,
    and you give them their food at the
      proper time.
¹⁶You open your hand
    and satisfy the desires of every living
      thing.

¹⁷The LORD is righteous in all his ways
    and faithful in all he does.
¹⁸The LORD is near to all who call on
    him,
      to all who call on him in truth.
¹⁹He fulfills the desires of those who fear
    him;
      he hears their cry and saves them.

²⁰The LORD watches over all who love
    him,
      but all the wicked he will destroy.

²¹My mouth will speak in praise of the
    LORD.
      Let every creature praise his holy
        name
          for ever and ever.

Psalm 146

¹Praise the LORD.ᵇ

Praise the LORD, my soul.

²I will praise the LORD all my life;
    I will sing praise to my God as long
      as I live.
³Do not put your trust in princes,
    in human beings, who cannot save.
⁴When their spirit departs, they return
    to the ground;
      on that very day their plans come to
        nothing.
⁵Blessed are those whose help is the God
    of Jacob,
      whose hope is in the LORD their God.

⁶He is the Maker of heaven and earth,
    the sea, and everything in them—
      he remains faithful forever.
⁷He upholds the cause of the oppressed
    and gives food to the hungry.
  The LORD sets prisoners free,
⁸   the LORD gives sight to the blind,
  the LORD lifts up those who are bowed
      down,
        the LORD loves the righteous.
⁹The LORD watches over the foreigner
    and sustains the fatherless and the
      widow,
        but he frustrates the ways of the
          wicked.

¹⁰The LORD reigns forever,
    your God, O Zion, for all
      generations.

Praise the LORD.

ᵃ 13 One manuscript of the Masoretic Text, Dead Sea Scrolls and Syriac (see also Septuagint); most manuscripts of the
Masoretic Text do not have the last two lines of verse 13.   ᵇ 1 Hebrew *Hallelu Yah*; also in verse 10

Psalm 147

[1] Praise the LORD.[a]

How good it is to sing praises to our
    God,
  how pleasant and fitting to praise him!

[2] The LORD builds up Jerusalem;
  he gathers the exiles of Israel.

[3] He heals the brokenhearted
  and binds up their wounds.
[4] He determines the number of the
    stars
  and calls them each by name.
[5] Great is our Lord and mighty in
    power;
  his understanding has no limit.

---

[a] 1 Hebrew *Hallelu Yah*; also in verse 20

DENIAL LESSON [*Principle One*]

For the previous entry in the DENIAL lesson, go to 2 Peter 2:19 (page 1554).

For a discussion of Principles One through Eight and a listing of their related lessons,
go to pages xvii – xliv.

He upholds the cause of the oppressed and gives food to the hungry.
The LORD sets prisoners free, the LORD gives sight to the blind, the LORD lifts up
those who are bowed down, the LORD loves the righteous.

PSALM 146:7–8

The power to change comes only through God's grace. Principle One states: "Realize I'm not God. I admit that I'm powerless to control my tendency to do the wrong thing and that my life has become unmanageable." If we admit that we're powerless, we recognize our need for a power greater than ourselves to restore us. That power is our Higher Power, the one and only true Higher Power, Jesus Christ.

In Principle One we discover that we've been in DENIAL of our hurts, hang-ups and habits. The next letter in DENIAL is *E*, which stands for ENERGY DRAIN. A major side effect of denial is anxiety. Anxiety causes us to waste precious energy dealing with past hurts and failures, as well as with fear of the future. As we go through the principles, we'll learn that positive change can occur only in the present. Worrying about the past and dreading the future both limit our ability to live happy and productive lives and to enjoy God's plans for us in the present.

We can easily allow our past failures, as well as our fears and worries about the future, to paralyze us. The truth is that the only lasting way to break free from the tyranny of our fears and worries is to hand them over to God. If we want to be free from our hurts, hang-ups and habits, we need to deal with our past failures, resentments, hurts, shame and guilt once and for all. We need to claim the good sense of God's instruction to his people in Isaiah 43:18: "Forget the former things; do not dwell on the past." That doesn't mean we're supposed to ignore the past. Instead, we need to learn from the past, offer forgiveness, make amends and then toss out yesterday's leftover garbage. Only then can we experience release from our guilt, grudges and grief.

In Philippians 3:13–14 the apostle Paul challenges us to follow his example: "Forgetting what is behind and straining toward what is ahead, I press on toward the goal to win the prize for which

⁶ The LORD sustains the humble
    but casts the wicked to the ground.

⁷ Sing to the LORD with grateful
        praise;
    make music to our God on the
        harp.

⁸ He covers the sky with clouds;
    he supplies the earth with rain
    and makes grass grow on the hills.

⁹ He provides food for the cattle
    and for the young ravens when they
        call.

¹⁰ His pleasure is not in the strength of the
        horse,
    nor his delight in the legs of the warrior;
¹¹ the LORD delights in those who fear him,
    who put their hope in his unfailing
        love.

God has called me heavenward in Christ Jesus." Paul had a lot to regret. He had even participated in the murder of Stephen, the first Christian martyr. But because he was able to accept God's complete forgiveness, Paul found the strength to start over. Jesus went to the cross so that all our sins could be forgiven. Christ knows every good and bad thing we've ever done, as well as everything we've ever experienced. And in spite of it all, he loves us so much that he wants to give us a second chance. That second chance begins for us as we work the first principle.

Hebrews 13:6 tells us that we can "say with confidence, 'The LORD is my helper; I will not be afraid. What can mere mortals do to me?'" We may worry about our future and be afraid to change. We all worry about those areas in life over which we lack personal control or the power to change. That's why, as we begin our recovery, we need to store the Serenity Prayer in our heart.

We may have been stuck in our hurt, hang-up or harmful habit for so long that it has become part of how we perceive our identity — part of who we feel we are. We may be thinking, "What will happen if I really give recovery a chance? Will I change? If I give up my old hurts, hang-ups and habits, what will be left of me? What will I become? Who will I be?" We may have been abusing alcohol, prescription drugs or food. We're afraid of what we may do without our substance of choice. We may have been enabling someone else in a dysfunctional relationship for years. Perhaps we wonder, "What if I change and my alcoholic husband gets mad at me?" The truth, though, is that we can face the possibility of change without doubt or fear because as we grow in our recovery, we discover with increasing confidence that the Lord is indeed our helper.

First John 4:18 offers us encouragement: "There is no fear in love. But perfect love drives out fear, because fear has to do with punishment. The one who fears is not made perfect in love." Even if our past has been extremely painful, we may resist change and the freedom that can be found in starting to work through Principle One. Because of our fear of the unknown or our lack of motivation caused by despair or our overwhelming feelings of guilt or worthlessness, we close our minds to the possibility of positive change.

If we would just transfer the energy required to maintain our denial into learning God's truth, a healthy love for others and for ourselves would begin to emerge. As we depend more and more on our Higher Power, Jesus Christ, we'll begin ever more clearly to see the light of truth and reality. That's why we need to claim Psalm 146:7 – 8.

The next letter in DENIAL is N. Go to Psalm 107:13 – 14 (page 708).

¹²Extol the LORD, Jerusalem;
  praise your God, Zion.

¹³He strengthens the bars of your gates
  and blesses your people within you.
¹⁴He grants peace to your borders
  and satisfies you with the finest of
    wheat.

¹⁵He sends his command to the earth;
  his word runs swiftly.
¹⁶He spreads the snow like wool
  and scatters the frost like ashes.
¹⁷He hurls down his hail like pebbles.
  Who can withstand his icy blast?
¹⁸He sends his word and melts them;
  he stirs up his breezes, and the waters
    flow.

¹⁹He has revealed his word to Jacob,
  his laws and decrees to Israel.
²⁰He has done this for no other nation;
  they do not know his laws.ᵃ

  Praise the LORD.

Psalm 148

¹Praise the LORD.ᵇ

  Praise the LORD from the heavens;
    praise him in the heights above.
²Praise him, all his angels;
  praise him, all his heavenly hosts.
³Praise him, sun and moon;
  praise him, all you shining stars.
⁴Praise him, you highest heavens
  and you waters above the skies.

⁵Let them praise the name of the LORD,
  for at his command they were
    created,
⁶and he established them for ever and
    ever—
  he issued a decree that will never
    pass away.

⁷Praise the LORD from the earth,
  you great sea creatures and all ocean
    depths,

⁸lightning and hail, snow and clouds,
  stormy winds that do his bidding,
⁹you mountains and all hills,
  fruit trees and all cedars,
¹⁰wild animals and all cattle,
  small creatures and flying birds,
¹¹kings of the earth and all nations,
  you princes and all rulers on earth,
¹²young men and women,
  old men and children.

¹³Let them praise the name of the LORD,
  for his name alone is exalted;
  his splendor is above the earth and
    the heavens.
¹⁴And he has raised up for his people a
    horn,ᶜ
  the praise of all his faithful servants,
  of Israel, the people close to his heart.

  Praise the LORD.

Psalm 149

¹Praise the LORD.ᵈ

  Sing to the LORD a new song,
    his praise in the assembly of his
      faithful people.

²Let Israel rejoice in their Maker;
  let the people of Zion be glad in their
    King.
³Let them praise his name with dancing
  and make music to him with timbrel
    and harp.
⁴For the LORD takes delight in his
    people;
  he crowns the humble with victory.
⁵Let his faithful people rejoice in this
    honor
  and sing for joy on their beds.

⁶May the praise of God be in their
    mouths
  and a double-edged sword in their
    hands,
⁷to inflict vengeance on the nations
  and punishment on the peoples,

ᵃ 20 Masoretic Text; Dead Sea Scrolls and Septuagint *nation; / he has not made his laws known to them*   ᵇ 1 Hebrew *Hallelu Yah;* also in verse 14   ᶜ 14 *Horn* here symbolizes strength.   ᵈ 1 Hebrew *Hallelu Yah;* also in verse 9

⁸ to bind their kings with fetters,
    their nobles with shackles of
       iron,
⁹ to carry out the sentence written
      against them —
    this is the glory of all his faithful
      people.

Praise the Lord.

Psalm 150

¹ Praise the Lord.^a

Praise God in his sanctuary;
    praise him in his mighty heavens.

² Praise him for his acts of power;
    praise him for his surpassing
      greatness.
³ Praise him with the sounding of the
      trumpet,
    praise him with the harp and lyre,
⁴ praise him with timbrel and dancing,
    praise him with the strings and pipe,
⁵ praise him with the clash of cymbals,
    praise him with resounding cymbals.

⁶ Let everything that has breath praise
    the Lord.

Praise the Lord.

Proverbs

THEME: There is no real wisdom apart from God. To "fear" God (hold him in reverence) is to embark on the path of wisdom (see Proverbs 1:7).

AUTHOR: Solomon wrote most of the sayings that comprise the book of Proverbs, but other authors include Agur and King Lemuel. The scribes of King Hezekiah copied additional proverbs of Solomon to form chapters 25 – 29.

DATE OF WRITING: Solomon's proverbs were written between 970 and 930 BC. Hezekiah's scribes compiled the additional proverbs of Solomon between 729 and 686 BC. Nothing is known of Agur or King Lemuel, so the dates of composition of their proverbs are unknown.

ENCOURAGEMENT FROM PROVERBS: "Whoever conceals their sins does not prosper, but the one who confesses and renounces them finds mercy" (Proverbs 28:13).

CHALLENGE FROM PROVERBS: "Trust in the LORD with all your heart and lean not on your own understanding; in all your ways submit to him, and he will make your paths straight" (Proverbs 3:5 – 6).

REFLECTION FROM PROVERBS: "Fools mock at making amends for sin, but goodwill is found among the upright" (Proverbs 14:9).

At a Glance

Recovery Themes in Proverbs

The book of Proverbs provides principles concerning the problems we face in everyday life. The wide range of issues addressed in Proverbs includes standards for relating wisely and effectively to God, parents, children, our neighbors and coworkers and our government. Solomon, the principal author, used a variety of ways to convey moral wisdom, discipline and understanding. Proverbs makes clear that the foundation of all true wisdom is the fear of the Lord, a reverence in his presence based on an appreciation of his awesome person.

Many of our hurts, hang-ups and habits were developed early in life, in the privacy of our homes, and many proverbs are presented in the context of home and family. Although the majority of our issues may indeed stem from childhood, our greatest problem, according to Proverbs, is our own foolishness. Wisdom is God's way; foolishness is our way. Foolishness isn't a lack of intelligence but rather a desire to maintain the myth of self-sufficiency. It's the assumption that we can do things better than God can, or, worse yet, that we can live as though he doesn't exist or matter. When we decide to give our lives and wills to God and to live his way, we find that we acquire wisdom even as we experience healing.

Purpose and Theme

1 The proverbs of Solomon son of David, king of Israel:

2 for gaining wisdom and instruction;
    for understanding words of insight;
3 for receiving instruction in prudent
     behavior,
    doing what is right and just and fair;
4 for giving prudence to those who are
     simple,*a*
    knowledge and discretion to the
     young—
5 let the wise listen and add to their
     learning,
    and let the discerning get guidance—
6 for understanding proverbs and
     parables,
    the sayings and riddles of the wise.*b*

7 The fear of the LORD is the beginning of
     knowledge,
    but fools*c* despise wisdom and
     instruction.

Prologue: Exhortations to Embrace Wisdom

Warning Against the Invitation of Sinful Men

8 Listen, my son, to your father's
     instruction
    and do not forsake your mother's
     teaching.
9 They are a garland to grace your head
    and a chain to adorn your neck.

10 My son, if sinful men entice you,
    do not give in to them.
11 If they say, "Come along with us;
     let's lie in wait for innocent blood,
     let's ambush some harmless soul;
12 let's swallow them alive, like the grave,
     and whole, like those who go down
      to the pit;

13 we will get all sorts of valuable things
    and fill our houses with plunder;
14 cast lots with us;
    we will all share the loot"—
15 my son, do not go along with them,
    do not set foot on their paths;
16 for their feet rush into evil,
    they are swift to shed blood.
17 How useless to spread a net
    where every bird can see it!
18 These men lie in wait for their own
     blood;
    they ambush only themselves!
19 Such are the paths of all who go after
     ill-gotten gain;
    it takes away the life of those who
     get it.

Wisdom's Rebuke

20 Out in the open wisdom calls aloud,
    she raises her voice in the public
     square;
21 on top of the wall*d* she cries out,
    at the city gate she makes her
     speech:

22 "How long will you who are simple love
     your simple ways?
    How long will mockers delight in
     mockery
    and fools hate knowledge?
23 Repent at my rebuke!
    Then I will pour out my thoughts to
     you,
    I will make known to you my
     teachings.
24 But since you refuse to listen when I call
    and no one pays attention when I
     stretch out my hand,
25 since you disregard all my advice
    and do not accept my rebuke,
26 I in turn will laugh when disaster
     strikes you;
    I will mock when calamity overtakes
     you—

---

a 4 The Hebrew word rendered *simple* in Proverbs denotes a person who is gullible, without moral direction and inclined to evil.   *b 6* Or *understanding a proverb, namely, a parable, / and the sayings of the wise, their riddles*
c 7 The Hebrew words rendered *fool* in Proverbs, and often elsewhere in the Old Testament, denote a person who is morally deficient.   *d 21* Septuagint; Hebrew / *at noisy street corners*

My Name Is Bob

I'M A BELIEVER WHO STRUGGLES WITH ALCOHOLISM

The book of Proverbs contains numerous verses about "the drunkard," two of which are quoted in the following testimony.

Growing up as a "service brat," I lived in different areas of the country — from Brooklyn, New York, to Pearl Harbor, Hawaii. Over the years I attended 17 different schools. My dad was often overseas, and my job as the oldest of four was to be the man of the house. The "people pleaser" in me was more than ready to accept pats on the head for being a "good boy."

My aspiration as I entered college was to play football, but after heat stroke and a concussion, my football career ended before it began. I started carousing with drinkers. My daily round of activities included attending class, studying, working, partying and sleeping a little. I met a girl, got married and managed to complete my degree, do my practice teaching, and teach for a year before the marriage fell apart.

I remarried, and together we started attending Saddleback Church, where I was baptized and became involved with the children's ministry. I wish I could close the book right there with a blithe "We lived happily ever after"; but that's not how it played out. I had no conflict resolution skills and didn't know how to deal with hurt and disappointment. What I did know was how to build walls and dull my feelings with drinking. I hid bottles in the garage and garden for late-night consumption. My wife and I were, by that point, occupying the same house but living separate lives. Eventually this marriage also ended. I was completely broken, living by the credo of Proverbs 23:35: "When will I wake up so I can find another drink?"

Then one day I experienced Principles One and Two in an unforgettable way: I caused an accident due to my first blackout. This was also my first arrest for DUI. It was dusk, and I do remember the squealing of tires and the powerful impact. At first I saw no other vehicles, but then I glanced over an embankment and saw a small car lying on its roof. All the windows were shattered, and I heard someone moaning. I felt revulsion, sorrow, grief, panic, helplessness and utter disbelief. At that moment I realized that I was powerless over alcohol and that my life had become unmanageable.

En route to jail, the officer remarked to his trainee, "The older woman didn't make it." My heart sank. How could I? Why didn't God just take me and spare them? I truly was a drunkard. "In the end [wine] bites like a snake and poisons like a viper" (Proverbs 23:32).

The next morning, after being bailed out of jail, I called Saddleback Church to find out about Celebrate Recovery. I decided to join the Friday night large group and the Monday night Step Study group. Experiencing a glimmer of hope, I prayed, "Lord, keep my heart on the right path; help me face up to my responsibilities and restore me."

One evening on my way to my Step Study group, Principle Three clicked in my mind. I had never reached out to God for help or surrendered my life to Christ. I had the concept in my head but hadn't transferred it to my heart. Picturing Jesus on the seat next to me, I reached over and said, "Here, Lord. These are my burdens, the consequences of my past. It's all yours because I can't do this on my own." What a relief. I was finally able to experience the serenity that everyone in recovery was always talking about. Sweet surrender!

When it came time for my court appearance — the first of many over a 12-month period — I felt serenity wash over me. I was 50 years old, twice divorced and living with my dad. I was no longer concerned about what would happen to me, how long my sentence would be or where I'd serve my time. I accepted the idea that God would use me wherever I was and for however long I would be there. My driver's license was revoked, and I began the humbling journey of asking others for rides. I finally stood before the judge, pled guilty and was sentenced to time in the county jail.

Today the consequences of my choices have been turned around through the opportunity of serving my Higher Power, Jesus Christ. Principle Eight has been so important to my recovery, and I've been able to participate in several ways. I lead Kids' Rock every Friday night while the adults enjoy Solid Rock Café. I also help with the Celebrate Recovery information table. Other brothers in the program and I have started Celebrate Recovery at the Orange County Rescue Mission. We also bring residents to Saddleback Church on Friday evenings so they can experience Celebrate Recovery. I facilitate men's Step Study groups and sponsor others.

My path has led me through overwhelming pain — through a dark forest filled with despair, sorrow, guilt, regret and remorse. I can't change my past, but I can change my path by remaining sober and working with others. My prayer is that I can help prevent someone else from choosing the path I did.

²⁷ when calamity overtakes you like a
storm,
when disaster sweeps over you like a
whirlwind,
when distress and trouble overwhelm
you.

²⁸ "Then they will call to me but I will not
answer;
they will look for me but will not find
me,
²⁹ since they hated knowledge
and did not choose to fear the
LORD.
³⁰ Since they would not accept my advice
and spurned my rebuke,
³¹ they will eat the fruit of their ways
and be filled with the fruit of their
schemes.
³² For the waywardness of the simple will
kill them,
and the complacency of fools will
destroy them;
³³ but whoever listens to me will live in
safety
and be at ease, without fear of harm."

Moral Benefits of Wisdom

2 My son, if you accept my words
and store up my commands within
you,
² turning your ear to wisdom
and applying your heart to
understanding —
³ indeed, if you call out for insight
and cry aloud for understanding,
⁴ and if you look for it as for silver
and search for it as for hidden
treasure,
⁵ then you will understand the fear of the
LORD
and find the knowledge of God.
⁶ For the LORD gives wisdom;
from his mouth come knowledge and
understanding.
⁷ He holds success in store for the
upright,

he is a shield to those whose walk is
blameless,
⁸ for he guards the course of the just
and protects the way of his faithful
ones.

⁹ Then you will understand what is right
and just
and fair — every good path.
¹⁰ For wisdom will enter your heart,
and knowledge will be pleasant to
your soul.
¹¹ Discretion will protect you,
and understanding will guard you.

¹² Wisdom will save you from the ways of
wicked men,
from men whose words are perverse,
¹³ who have left the straight paths
to walk in dark ways,
¹⁴ who delight in doing wrong
and rejoice in the perverseness of
evil,
¹⁵ whose paths are crooked
and who are devious in their ways.

¹⁶ Wisdom will save you also from the
adulterous woman,
from the wayward woman with her
seductive words,
¹⁷ who has left the partner of her youth
and ignored the covenant she made
before God.ᵃ
¹⁸ Surely her house leads down to death
and her paths to the spirits of the
dead.
¹⁹ None who go to her return
or attain the paths of life.

²⁰ Thus you will walk in the ways of the
good
and keep to the paths of the
righteous.
²¹ For the upright will live in the land,
and the blameless will remain in it;
²² but the wicked will be cut off from the
land,
and the unfaithful will be torn
from it.

ᵃ 17 Or covenant of her God

Wisdom Bestows Well-Being

3 My son, do not forget my teaching,
but keep my commands in your
heart,
2 for they will prolong your life many
years
and bring you peace and prosperity.

3 Let love and faithfulness never leave you;
bind them around your neck,
write them on the tablet of your heart.

4 Then you will win favor and a good
name
in the sight of God and man.

5 Trust in the LORD with all your heart
and lean not on your own
understanding;
6 in all your ways submit to him,
and he will make your paths straight.*a*

7 Do not be wise in your own eyes;
fear the LORD and shun evil.

a 6 Or *will direct your paths*

TURN LESSON [*Principle Three*]

For the previous entry in the TURN lesson, go to Romans 10:9 (page 1404).

For a discussion of Principles One through Eight and a listing of their related lessons,
go to pages xvii – xliv.

*Trust in the LORD with all your heart and lean not on your own understanding;
in all your ways submit to him, and he will make your paths straight.*

PROVERBS 3:5 – 6

In Principle Three we consciously choose to commit all our lives and will to Christ's care and control. We make the decision to TURN over every aspect of our lives and will to our Higher Power, Jesus Christ. This principle ends with us having a new life, but first we need to trust, understand and repent.

The second letter in TURN, *U*, stands for UNDERSTAND. Relying solely on our own understanding got most of us into recovery in the first place. After we make the decision to ask Jesus into our lives, we need to begin to seek his will for our lives in all our decisions. We need to get to know him and learn what he wants for us. That's the message of Proverbs 3:5 – 6.

Our understanding is earthbound, finite, human to the core. We operate in a dimension totally unlike that of our Lord, who knows no limitations. We see only the here and now, and our interpretations are often flawed. God, on the other hand, sees and fully understands the forever behind and beyond the present. First Corinthians 13:12 puts it this way: "Now we see only a reflection as in a mirror; then we shall see face to face. Now I know in part; then I shall know fully, even as I am fully known." Someday we'll see Jesus face-to-face. The fog obscuring so much of our big-picture interpretation will be lifted, and our understanding will be perfected.

Praise God that we don't need a flawless understanding of him right now in order for us to ask Jesus into our lives as our Savior and Lord. Why? Because God does more than simply lead us year by year or even day by day. God directs our path with each step.

The next letter in TURN is R. Go to Ezekiel 18:30 – 32 (page 986).

8 This will bring health to your body
  and nourishment to your bones.

9 Honor the LORD with your wealth,
  with the firstfruits of all your crops;
10 then your barns will be filled to
  overflowing,
  and your vats will brim over with
  new wine.

11 My son, do not despise the LORD's
  discipline,
  and do not resent his rebuke,
12 because the LORD disciplines those he
  loves,
  as a father the son he delights in.*a*

13 Blessed are those who find wisdom,
  those who gain understanding,

14 for she is more profitable than silver
  and yields better returns than gold.
15 She is more precious than rubies;
  nothing you desire can compare with
  her.
16 Long life is in her right hand;
  in her left hand are riches and honor.
17 Her ways are pleasant ways,
  and all her paths are peace.
18 She is a tree of life to those who take
  hold of her;
  those who hold her fast will be
  blessed.

19 By wisdom the LORD laid the earth's
  foundations,
  by understanding he set the heavens
  in place;

---

a 12 Hebrew; Septuagint *loves, / and he chastens everyone he accepts as his child*

ACTION LESSON [*Principle Three*]

For the previous entry in the ACTION lesson, go to Psalm 143:10 (page 731).

For a discussion of Principles One through Eight and a listing of their related lessons,
go to pages xvii – xliv.

In all your ways submit to him, and he will make your paths straight.

PROVERBS 3:6

In Principle Three we consciously choose to commit all our lives and will to Christ's care and control. We make the decision to TURN every aspect of our lives and will over to our Higher Power, Jesus Christ. In order to turn our lives over to Christ's care and control, we need to take ACTION.

The letter *T* in ACTION stands for TURN IT OVER. In other words, "let go and let God." That's a popular recovery phase we've heard again and again. Notice that it doesn't tell us to let go of anything in particular, to turn over certain specific aspects of our lives — even the big things — to God. Proverbs 3:6 uses the word "all," not "some"; this verse tells us to let go of *everything*. Jesus Christ doesn't just want a relationship with part of us. He desires to be intimate with us at every level.

What burdens are we lugging around that we need to turn over to Jesus? He invites, "Come to me, all you who are weary and burdened, and I will give you rest. Take my yoke upon you and learn from me, for I am gentle and humble in heart, and you will find rest for your souls. For my yoke is easy and my burden is light" (Matthew 11:28 – 30).

The next letter in ACTION is *I*. Go to Philippians 1:6 (page 1478).

²⁰ by his knowledge the watery depths
were divided,
and the clouds let drop the dew.

²¹ My son, do not let wisdom and
understanding out of your sight,
preserve sound judgment and
discretion;
²² they will be life for you,
an ornament to grace your neck.
²³ Then you will go on your way in safety,
and your foot will not stumble.
²⁴ When you lie down, you will not be
afraid;
when you lie down, your sleep will be
sweet.
²⁵ Have no fear of sudden disaster
or of the ruin that overtakes the
wicked,
²⁶ for the LORD will be at your side
and will keep your foot from being
snared.

²⁷ Do not withhold good from those to
whom it is due,
when it is in your power to act.
²⁸ Do not say to your neighbor,
"Come back tomorrow and I'll give it
to you" —
when you already have it with you.
²⁹ Do not plot harm against your
neighbor,
who lives trustfully near you.
³⁰ Do not accuse anyone for no reason —
when they have done you no harm.

³¹ Do not envy the violent
or choose any of their ways.

³² For the LORD detests the perverse
but takes the upright into his
confidence.
³³ The LORD's curse is on the house of the
wicked,
but he blesses the home of the
righteous.
³⁴ He mocks proud mockers
but shows favor to the humble and
oppressed.

³⁵ The wise inherit honor,
but fools get only shame.

Get Wisdom at Any Cost

4 Listen, my sons, to a father's
instruction;
pay attention and gain
understanding.
² I give you sound learning,
so do not forsake my teaching.
³ For I too was a son to my father,
still tender, and cherished by my
mother.
⁴ Then he taught me, and he said to me,
"Take hold of my words with all your
heart;
keep my commands, and you will
live.
⁵ Get wisdom, get understanding;
do not forget my words or turn away
from them.
⁶ Do not forsake wisdom, and she will
protect you;
love her, and she will watch over you.
⁷ The beginning of wisdom is this: Get^a
wisdom.
Though it cost all you have,^b get
understanding.
⁸ Cherish her, and she will exalt you;
embrace her, and she will honor you.
⁹ She will give you a garland to grace
your head
and present you with a glorious
crown."

¹⁰ Listen, my son, accept what I say,
and the years of your life will be many.
¹¹ I instruct you in the way of wisdom
and lead you along straight paths.
¹² When you walk, your steps will not be
hampered;
when you run, you will not stumble.
¹³ Hold on to instruction, do not let it go;
guard it well, for it is your life.
¹⁴ Do not set foot on the path of the
wicked
or walk in the way of evildoers.

---

^a 7 Or *Wisdom is supreme; therefore get*   ^b 7 Or *wisdom. / Whatever else you get*

¹⁵ Avoid it, do not travel on it;
   turn from it and go on your way.
¹⁶ For they cannot rest until they do evil;
   they are robbed of sleep till they
      make someone stumble.
¹⁷ They eat the bread of wickedness
   and drink the wine of violence.

¹⁸ The path of the righteous is like the
      morning sun,
   shining ever brighter till the full light
      of day.
¹⁹ But the way of the wicked is like deep
      darkness;
   they do not know what makes them
      stumble.

²⁰ My son, pay attention to what I say;
   turn your ear to my words.
²¹ Do not let them out of your sight,
   keep them within your heart;
²² for they are life to those who find them
   and health to one's whole body.
²³ Above all else, guard your heart,
   for everything you do flows from it.
²⁴ Keep your mouth free of perversity;
   keep corrupt talk far from your lips.
²⁵ Let your eyes look straight ahead;
   fix your gaze directly before you.
²⁶ Give careful thought to the*ᵃ* paths for
      your feet
   and be steadfast in all your ways.
²⁷ Do not turn to the right or the left;
   keep your foot from evil.

Warning Against Adultery

5 My son, pay attention to my
      wisdom,
   turn your ear to my words of
      insight,
² that you may maintain discretion
   and your lips may preserve
      knowledge.
³ For the lips of the adulterous woman
      drip honey,
   and her speech is smoother than oil;
⁴ but in the end she is bitter as gall,
   sharp as a double-edged sword.

⁵ Her feet go down to death;
   her steps lead straight to the grave.
⁶ She gives no thought to the way of life;
   her paths wander aimlessly, but she
      does not know it.

⁷ Now then, my sons, listen to me;
   do not turn aside from what I say.
⁸ Keep to a path far from her,
   do not go near the door of her
      house,
⁹ lest you lose your honor to others
   and your dignity*ᵇ* to one who is
      cruel,
¹⁰ lest strangers feast on your wealth
   and your toil enrich the house of
      another.
¹¹ At the end of your life you will groan,
   when your flesh and body are spent.
¹² You will say, "How I hated discipline!
   How my heart spurned correction!
¹³ I would not obey my teachers
   or turn my ear to my instructors.
¹⁴ And I was soon in serious trouble
   in the assembly of God's people."

¹⁵ Drink water from your own cistern,
   running water from your own well.
¹⁶ Should your springs overflow in the
      streets,
   your streams of water in the public
      squares?
¹⁷ Let them be yours alone,
   never to be shared with strangers.
¹⁸ May your fountain be blessed,
   and may you rejoice in the wife of
      your youth.
¹⁹ A loving doe, a graceful deer —
   may her breasts satisfy you always,
   may you ever be intoxicated with her
      love.
²⁰ Why, my son, be intoxicated with
      another man's wife?
   Why embrace the bosom of a
      wayward woman?

²¹ For your ways are in full view of the
      LORD,
   and he examines all your paths.

ᵃ 26 Or *Make level*   *ᵇ 9* Or *years*

²²The evil deeds of the wicked ensnare
them;
the cords of their sins hold them
fast.
²³For lack of discipline they will die,
led astray by their own great folly.

Warnings Against Folly

6 My son, if you have put up security
for your neighbor,
if you have shaken hands in pledge
for a stranger,
²you have been trapped by what you
said,
ensnared by the words of your
mouth.
³So do this, my son, to free yourself,
since you have fallen into your
neighbor's hands:
Go — to the point of exhaustion — ᵃ
and give your neighbor no rest!
⁴Allow no sleep to your eyes,
no slumber to your eyelids.
⁵Free yourself, like a gazelle from the
hand of the hunter,
like a bird from the snare of the
fowler.

⁶Go to the ant, you sluggard;
consider its ways and be wise!
⁷It has no commander,
no overseer or ruler,
⁸yet it stores its provisions in summer
and gathers its food at harvest.

⁹How long will you lie there, you
sluggard?
When will you get up from your
sleep?
¹⁰A little sleep, a little slumber,
a little folding of the hands to
rest —
¹¹and poverty will come on you like a
thief
and scarcity like an armed man.

¹²A troublemaker and a villain,
who goes about with a corrupt
mouth,

¹³who winks maliciously with his eye,
signals with his feet
and motions with his fingers,
¹⁴who plots evil with deceit in his
heart —
he always stirs up conflict.
¹⁵Therefore disaster will overtake him in
an instant;
he will suddenly be destroyed —
without remedy.

¹⁶There are six things the LORD hates,
seven that are detestable to him:
¹⁷   haughty eyes,
a lying tongue,
hands that shed innocent blood,
¹⁸   a heart that devises wicked
schemes,
feet that are quick to rush into
evil,
¹⁹   a false witness who pours out
lies
and a person who stirs up conflict
in the community.

Warning Against Adultery

²⁰My son, keep your father's command
and do not forsake your mother's
teaching.
²¹Bind them always on your heart;
fasten them around your neck.
²²When you walk, they will guide you;
when you sleep, they will watch over
you;
when you awake, they will speak to
you.
²³For this command is a lamp,
this teaching is a light,
and correction and instruction
are the way to life,
²⁴keeping you from your neighbor's
wife,
from the smooth talk of a wayward
woman.

²⁵Do not lust in your heart after her
beauty
or let her captivate you with her eyes.

ᵃ 3 Or *Go and humble yourself,*

26 For a prostitute can be had for a loaf of
     bread,
   but another man's wife preys on your
     very life.
27 Can a man scoop fire into his lap
   without his clothes being burned?
28 Can a man walk on hot coals
   without his feet being scorched?
29 So is he who sleeps with another man's
     wife;
   no one who touches her will go
     unpunished.

30 People do not despise a thief if he steals
   to satisfy his hunger when he is
     starving.
31 Yet if he is caught, he must pay sevenfold,
   though it costs him all the wealth of
     his house.
32 But a man who commits adultery has
     no sense;
   whoever does so destroys himself.
33 Blows and disgrace are his lot,
   and his shame will never be wiped
     away.

34 For jealousy arouses a husband's fury,
   and he will show no mercy when he
     takes revenge.
35 He will not accept any compensation;
   he will refuse a bribe, however great
     it is.

Warning Against the Adulterous Woman

7 My son, keep my words
   and store up my commands within
     you.
2 Keep my commands and you will live;
   guard my teachings as the apple of
     your eye.
3 Bind them on your fingers;
   write them on the tablet of your heart.
4 Say to wisdom, "You are my sister,"
   and to insight, "You are my relative."
5 They will keep you from the adulterous
     woman,
   from the wayward woman with her
     seductive words.

6 At the window of my house
   I looked down through the lattice.
7 I saw among the simple,
   I noticed among the young men,
   a youth who had no sense.
8 He was going down the street near her
     corner,
   walking along in the direction of her
     house
9 at twilight, as the day was fading,
   as the dark of night set in.

10 Then out came a woman to meet him,
   dressed like a prostitute and with
     crafty intent.
11 (She is unruly and defiant,
   her feet never stay at home;
12 now in the street, now in the squares,
   at every corner she lurks.)
13 She took hold of him and kissed him
   and with a brazen face she said:

14 "Today I fulfilled my vows,
   and I have food from my fellowship
     offering at home.
15 So I came out to meet you;
   I looked for you and have found you!
16 I have covered my bed
   with colored linens from Egypt.
17 I have perfumed my bed
   with myrrh, aloes and cinnamon.
18 Come, let's drink deeply of love till
     morning;
   let's enjoy ourselves with love!
19 My husband is not at home;
   he has gone on a long journey.
20 He took his purse filled with money
   and will not be home till full moon."

21 With persuasive words she led him
     astray;
   she seduced him with her smooth
     talk.
22 All at once he followed her
   like an ox going to the slaughter,
   like a deer[a] stepping into a noose[b]
23   till an arrow pierces his liver,
   like a bird darting into a snare,
   little knowing it will cost him his life.

---

[a] 22 Syriac (see also Septuagint); Hebrew *fool*   [b] 22 The meaning of the Hebrew for this line is uncertain.

24 Now then, my sons, listen to me;
	pay attention to what I say.
25 Do not let your heart turn to her ways
	or stray into her paths.
26 Many are the victims she has brought
		down;
	her slain are a mighty throng.
27 Her house is a highway to the grave,
	leading down to the chambers of
		death.

Wisdom's Call

8 Does not wisdom call out?
	Does not understanding raise her
		voice?
2 At the highest point along the way,
	where the paths meet, she takes her
		stand;
3 beside the gate leading into the city,
	at the entrance, she cries aloud:
4 "To you, O people, I call out;
	I raise my voice to all mankind.
5 You who are simple, gain prudence;
	you who are foolish, set your hearts
		on it.*a*
6 Listen, for I have trustworthy things to
		say;
	I open my lips to speak what is right.
7 My mouth speaks what is true,
	for my lips detest wickedness.
8 All the words of my mouth are just;
	none of them is crooked or perverse.
9 To the discerning all of them are right;
	they are upright to those who have
		found knowledge.
10 Choose my instruction instead of
		silver,
	knowledge rather than choice gold,
11 for wisdom is more precious than
		rubies,
	and nothing you desire can compare
		with her.

12 "I, wisdom, dwell together with
		prudence;
	I possess knowledge and discretion.

13 To fear the Lord is to hate evil;
	I hate pride and arrogance,
	evil behavior and perverse speech.
14 Counsel and sound judgment are
		mine;
	I have insight, I have power.
15 By me kings reign
	and rulers issue decrees that are
		just;
16 by me princes govern,
	and nobles — all who rule on
		earth.*b*
17 I love those who love me,
	and those who seek me find me.
18 With me are riches and honor,
	enduring wealth and prosperity.
19 My fruit is better than fine gold;
	what I yield surpasses choice silver.
20 I walk in the way of righteousness,
	along the paths of justice,
21 bestowing a rich inheritance on those
		who love me
	and making their treasuries full.

22 "The Lord brought me forth as the first
		of his works,*c,d*
	before his deeds of old;
23 I was formed long ages ago,
	at the very beginning, when the
		world came to be.
24 When there were no watery depths, I
		was given birth,
	when there were no springs
		overflowing with water;
25 before the mountains were settled in
		place,
	before the hills, I was given birth,
26 before he made the world or its fields
	or any of the dust of the earth.
27 I was there when he set the heavens in
		place,
	when he marked out the horizon on
		the face of the deep,
28 when he established the clouds above
	and fixed securely the fountains of
		the deep,

---

a 5 Septuagint; Hebrew *foolish, instruct your minds*   *b 16* Some Hebrew manuscripts and Septuagint; other
Hebrew manuscripts *all righteous rulers*   *c 22* Or *way*; or *dominion*   *d 22* Or *The Lord possessed me at the
beginning of his work*; or *The Lord brought me forth at the beginning of his work*

²⁹ when he gave the sea its boundary
　　so the waters would not overstep his
　　　command,
　and when he marked out the
　　　foundations of the earth.
³⁰　Then I was constantly*ᵃ* at his side.
　I was filled with delight day after day,
　　rejoicing always in his presence,
³¹ rejoicing in his whole world
　　and delighting in mankind.

³² "Now then, my children, listen to me;
　　blessed are those who keep my ways.
³³ Listen to my instruction and be wise;
　　do not disregard it.
³⁴ Blessed are those who listen to me,
　　watching daily at my doors,
　　waiting at my doorway.
³⁵ For those who find me find life
　　and receive favor from the LORD.
³⁶ But those who fail to find me harm
　　　themselves;
　　all who hate me love death."

Invitations of Wisdom and Folly

9 Wisdom has built her house;
　　she has set up*ᵇ* its seven pillars.
² She has prepared her meat and
　　　mixed her wine;
　she has also set her table.
³ She has sent out her servants, and she calls
　　from the highest point of the city,
⁴　"Let all who are simple come to my
　　　house!"
　To those who have no sense she says,
⁵　"Come, eat my food
　　and drink the wine I have mixed.
⁶ Leave your simple ways and you will live;
　　walk in the way of insight."

⁷ Whoever corrects a mocker invites
　　　insults;
　　whoever rebukes the wicked incurs
　　　abuse.
⁸ Do not rebuke mockers or they will
　　　hate you;
　　rebuke the wise and they will love you.

⁹ Instruct the wise and they will be wiser
　　　still;
　　teach the righteous and they will add
　　　to their learning.

¹⁰ The fear of the LORD is the beginning of
　　　wisdom,
　　and knowledge of the Holy One is
　　　understanding.
¹¹ For through wisdom*ᶜ* your days will be
　　　many,
　　and years will be added to your life.
¹² If you are wise, your wisdom will
　　　reward you;
　　if you are a mocker, you alone will
　　　suffer.

¹³ Folly is an unruly woman;
　　she is simple and knows nothing.
¹⁴ She sits at the door of her house,
　　on a seat at the highest point of the city,
¹⁵ calling out to those who pass by,
　　who go straight on their way,
¹⁶　"Let all who are simple come to my
　　　house!"
　To those who have no sense she says,
¹⁷　"Stolen water is sweet;
　　food eaten in secret is delicious!"
¹⁸ But little do they know that the dead
　　　are there,
　　that her guests are deep in the realm
　　　of the dead.

Proverbs of Solomon

10 The proverbs of Solomon:

A wise son brings joy to his
　　　father,
　　but a foolish son brings grief to his
　　　mother.

² Ill-gotten treasures have no lasting value,
　　but righteousness delivers from death.
³ The LORD does not let the righteous go
　　　hungry,
　　but he thwarts the craving of the
　　　wicked.

ᵃ 30 Or *was the artisan;* or *was a little child*　　*ᵇ 1* Septuagint, Syriac and Targum; Hebrew *has hewn out*
ᶜ 11 Septuagint, Syriac and Targum; Hebrew *me*

⁴Lazy hands make for poverty,
    but diligent hands bring wealth.

⁵He who gathers crops in summer is a
        prudent son,
    but he who sleeps during harvest is a
        disgraceful son.

⁶Blessings crown the head of the
        righteous,
    but violence overwhelms the mouth
        of the wicked.ᵃ

⁷The name of the righteous is used in
        blessings,ᵇ
    but the name of the wicked will rot.

⁸The wise in heart accept commands,
    but a chattering fool comes to ruin.

⁹Whoever walks in integrity walks
        securely,
    but whoever takes crooked paths will
        be found out.

¹⁰Whoever winks maliciously causes
        grief,
    and a chattering fool comes to ruin.

¹¹The mouth of the righteous is a
        fountain of life,
    but the mouth of the wicked conceals
        violence.

¹²Hatred stirs up conflict,
    but love covers over all wrongs.

¹³Wisdom is found on the lips of the
        discerning,
    but a rod is for the back of one who
        has no sense.

¹⁴The wise store up knowledge,
    but the mouth of a fool invites
        ruin.

¹⁵The wealth of the rich is their fortified
        city,
    but poverty is the ruin of the poor.

¹⁶The wages of the righteous is life,
    but the earnings of the wicked are sin
        and death.

¹⁷Whoever heeds discipline shows the
        way to life,
    but whoever ignores correction leads
        others astray.

¹⁸Whoever conceals hatred with lying
        lips
    and spreads slander is a fool.

¹⁹Sin is not ended by multiplying words,
    but the prudent hold their tongues.

²⁰The tongue of the righteous is choice
        silver,
    but the heart of the wicked is of little
        value.

²¹The lips of the righteous nourish many,
    but fools die for lack of sense.

²²The blessing of the LORD brings wealth,
    without painful toil for it.

²³A fool finds pleasure in wicked
        schemes,
    but a person of understanding
        delights in wisdom.

²⁴What the wicked dread will overtake
        them;
    what the righteous desire will be
        granted.

²⁵When the storm has swept by, the
        wicked are gone,
    but the righteous stand firm forever.

²⁶As vinegar to the teeth and smoke to
        the eyes,
    so are sluggards to those who send
        them.

²⁷The fear of the LORD adds length to life,
    but the years of the wicked are cut
        short.

²⁸The prospect of the righteous is joy,
    but the hopes of the wicked come to
        nothing.

²⁹The way of the LORD is a refuge for the
        blameless,
    but it is the ruin of those who do evil.

ᵃ 6 Or righteous, / but the mouth of the wicked conceals violence   ᵇ 7 See Gen. 48:20.

30 The righteous will never be uprooted,
   but the wicked will not remain in the
      land.

31 From the mouth of the righteous comes
   the fruit of wisdom,
   but a perverse tongue will be silenced.

32 The lips of the righteous know what
      finds favor,
   but the mouth of the wicked only
      what is perverse.

11

The LORD detests dishonest
   scales,
   but accurate weights find favor
      with him.

2 When pride comes, then comes
      disgrace,
   but with humility comes wisdom.

3 The integrity of the upright guides
      them,
   but the unfaithful are destroyed by
      their duplicity.

4 Wealth is worthless in the day of wrath,
   but righteousness delivers from death.

5 The righteousness of the blameless
      makes their paths straight,
   but the wicked are brought down by
      their own wickedness.

6 The righteousness of the upright
      delivers them,
   but the unfaithful are trapped by evil
      desires.

7 Hopes placed in mortals die with them;
   all the promise of[a] their power comes
      to nothing.

8 The righteous person is rescued from
      trouble,
   and it falls on the wicked instead.

9 With their mouths the godless destroy
      their neighbors,
   but through knowledge the righteous
      escape.

10 When the righteous prosper, the city
      rejoices;
   when the wicked perish, there are
      shouts of joy.

11 Through the blessing of the upright a
      city is exalted,
   but by the mouth of the wicked it is
      destroyed.

12 Whoever derides their neighbor has no
      sense,
   but the one who has understanding
      holds their tongue.

13 A gossip betrays a confidence,
   but a trustworthy person keeps a
      secret.

14 For lack of guidance a nation falls,
   but victory is won through many
      advisers.

15 Whoever puts up security for a stranger
      will surely suffer,
   but whoever refuses to shake hands
      in pledge is safe.

16 A kindhearted woman gains honor,
   but ruthless men gain only wealth.

17 Those who are kind benefit themselves,
   but the cruel bring ruin on
      themselves.

18 A wicked person earns deceptive
      wages,
   but the one who sows righteousness
      reaps a sure reward.

19 Truly the righteous attain life,
   but whoever pursues evil finds death.

20 The LORD detests those whose hearts
      are perverse,
   but he delights in those whose ways
      are blameless.

21 Be sure of this: The wicked will not go
      unpunished,
   but those who are righteous will go
      free.

---

a 7 Two Hebrew manuscripts; most Hebrew manuscripts, Vulgate, Syriac and Targum *When the wicked die, their hope perishes; / all they expected from*

²² Like a gold ring in a pig's snout
    is a beautiful woman who shows no
       discretion.

²³ The desire of the righteous ends only in
       good,
    but the hope of the wicked only in
       wrath.

²⁴ One person gives freely, yet gains even
       more;
    another withholds unduly, but comes
       to poverty.

²⁵ A generous person will prosper;
    whoever refreshes others will be
       refreshed.

²⁶ People curse the one who hoards grain,
    but they pray God's blessing on the
       one who is willing to sell.

²⁷ Whoever seeks good finds favor,
    but evil comes to one who searches
       for it.

²⁸ Those who trust in their riches will
       fall,
    but the righteous will thrive like a
       green leaf.

²⁹ Whoever brings ruin on their family
       will inherit only wind,
    and the fool will be servant to the
       wise.

³⁰ The fruit of the righteous is a tree of
       life,
    and the one who is wise saves lives.

³¹ If the righteous receive their due on
       earth,
    how much more the ungodly and the
       sinner!

12

    Whoever loves discipline loves
       knowledge,
    but whoever hates correction
       is stupid.

² Good people obtain favor from the
       LORD,
    but he condemns those who devise
       wicked schemes.

³ No one can be established through
       wickedness,
    but the righteous cannot be uprooted.

⁴ A wife of noble character is her
       husband's crown,
    but a disgraceful wife is like decay in
       his bones.

⁵ The plans of the righteous are just,
    but the advice of the wicked is
       deceitful.

⁶ The words of the wicked lie in wait for
       blood,
    but the speech of the upright rescues
       them.

⁷ The wicked are overthrown and are no
       more,
    but the house of the righteous stands
       firm.

⁸ A person is praised according to their
       prudence,
    and one with a warped mind is
       despised.

⁹ Better to be a nobody and yet have a
       servant
    than pretend to be somebody and
       have no food.

¹⁰ The righteous care for the needs of their
       animals,
    but the kindest acts of the wicked are
       cruel.

¹¹ Those who work their land will have
       abundant food,
    but those who chase fantasies have
       no sense.

¹² The wicked desire the stronghold of
       evildoers,
    but the root of the righteous endures.

¹³ Evildoers are trapped by their sinful talk,
    and so the innocent escape trouble.

¹⁴ From the fruit of their lips people are
       filled with good things,
    and the work of their hands brings
       them reward.

15 The way of fools seems right to them,
  but the wise listen to advice.

16 Fools show their annoyance at once,
  but the prudent overlook an insult.

17 An honest witness tells the truth,
  but a false witness tells lies.

18 The words of the reckless pierce like
    swords,
  but the tongue of the wise brings
    healing.

19 Truthful lips endure forever,
  but a lying tongue lasts only a
    moment.

20 Deceit is in the hearts of those who plot
    evil,
  but those who promote peace have
    joy.

21 No harm overtakes the righteous,
  but the wicked have their fill of
    trouble.

22 The LORD detests lying lips,
  but he delights in people who are
    trustworthy.

23 The prudent keep their knowledge to
    themselves,
  but a fool's heart blurts out folly.

24 Diligent hands will rule,
  but laziness ends in forced labor.

25 Anxiety weighs down the heart,
  but a kind word cheers it up.

26 The righteous choose their friends
    carefully,
  but the way of the wicked leads them
    astray.

27 The lazy do not roast*a* any game,
  but the diligent feed on the riches of
    the hunt.

28 In the way of righteousness there is
    life;
  along that path is immortality.

13

A wise son heeds his father's
  instruction,
  but a mocker does not respond
    to rebukes.

2 From the fruit of their lips people enjoy
    good things,
  but the unfaithful have an appetite
    for violence.

3 Those who guard their lips preserve
    their lives,
  but those who speak rashly will come
    to ruin.

4 A sluggard's appetite is never filled,
  but the desires of the diligent are
    fully satisfied.

5 The righteous hate what is false,
  but the wicked make themselves a
    stench
  and bring shame on themselves.

6 Righteousness guards the person of
    integrity,
  but wickedness overthrows the sinner.

7 One person pretends to be rich, yet has
    nothing;
  another pretends to be poor, yet has
    great wealth.

8 A person's riches may ransom their life,
  but the poor cannot respond to
    threatening rebukes.

9 The light of the righteous shines
    brightly,
  but the lamp of the wicked is snuffed
    out.

10 Where there is strife, there is pride,
  but wisdom is found in those who
    take advice.

11 Dishonest money dwindles away,
  but whoever gathers money little by
    little makes it grow.

12 Hope deferred makes the heart sick,
  but a longing fulfilled is a tree of life.

---

a 27 The meaning of the Hebrew for this word is uncertain.

13 Whoever scorns instruction will pay
for it,
  but whoever respects a command is
  rewarded.

14 The teaching of the wise is a fountain of
life,
  turning a person from the snares of
  death.

15 Good judgment wins favor,
  but the way of the unfaithful leads to
  their destruction.*a*

16 All who are prudent act with*b*
knowledge,
  but fools expose their folly.

17 A wicked messenger falls into trouble,
  but a trustworthy envoy brings
  healing.

18 Whoever disregards discipline comes to
poverty and shame,
  but whoever heeds correction is
  honored.

19 A longing fulfilled is sweet to the
soul,
  but fools detest turning from evil.

20 Walk with the wise and become wise,
  for a companion of fools suffers
  harm.

21 Trouble pursues the sinner,
  but the righteous are rewarded with
  good things.

22 A good person leaves an inheritance for
their children's children,
  but a sinner's wealth is stored up for
  the righteous.

23 An unplowed field produces food for
the poor,
  but injustice sweeps it away.

24 Whoever spares the rod hates their
children,
  but the one who loves their children
  is careful to discipline them.

25 The righteous eat to their hearts'
content,
  but the stomach of the wicked goes
  hungry.

14 The wise woman builds her
house,
  but with her own hands the
  foolish one tears hers down.

2 Whoever fears the LORD walks
uprightly,
  but those who despise him are
  devious in their ways.

3 A fool's mouth lashes out with pride,
  but the lips of the wise protect them.

4 Where there are no oxen, the manger is
empty,
  but from the strength of an ox come
  abundant harvests.

5 An honest witness does not deceive,
  but a false witness pours out lies.

6 The mocker seeks wisdom and finds
none,
  but knowledge comes easily to the
  discerning.

7 Stay away from a fool,
  for you will not find knowledge on
  their lips.

8 The wisdom of the prudent is to give
thought to their ways,
  but the folly of fools is deception.

9 Fools mock at making amends for sin,
  but goodwill is found among the
  upright.

10 Each heart knows its own bitterness,
  and no one else can share its joy.

11 The house of the wicked will be
destroyed,
  but the tent of the upright will flourish.

12 There is a way that appears to be right,
  but in the end it leads to death.

---

a 15 Septuagint and Syriac; the meaning of the Hebrew for this phrase is uncertain.   *b 16* Or *prudent protect themselves through*

¹³Even in laughter the heart may ache,
    and rejoicing may end in grief.

¹⁴The faithless will be fully repaid for
        their ways,
    and the good rewarded for theirs.

¹⁵The simple believe anything,
    but the prudent give thought to their
        steps.

¹⁶The wise fear the LORD and shun evil,
    but a fool is hotheaded and yet feels
        secure.

¹⁷A quick-tempered person does foolish
        things,
    and the one who devises evil schemes
        is hated.

¹⁸The simple inherit folly,
    but the prudent are crowned with
        knowledge.

¹⁹Evildoers will bow down in the
        presence of the good,
    and the wicked at the gates of the
        righteous.

²⁰The poor are shunned even by their
        neighbors,
    but the rich have many friends.

²¹It is a sin to despise one's neighbor,
    but blessed is the one who is kind to
        the needy.

²²Do not those who plot evil go astray?
    But those who plan what is good
        find*ᵃ* love and faithfulness.

²³All hard work brings a profit,
    but mere talk leads only to poverty.

²⁴The wealth of the wise is their crown,
    but the folly of fools yields folly.

²⁵A truthful witness saves lives,
    but a false witness is deceitful.

²⁶Whoever fears the LORD has a secure
        fortress,
    and for their children it will be a
        refuge.

²⁷The fear of the LORD is a fountain of
        life,
    turning a person from the snares of
        death.

²⁸A large population is a king's glory,
    but without subjects a prince is ruined.

²⁹Whoever is patient has great
        understanding,
    but one who is quick-tempered
        displays folly.

³⁰A heart at peace gives life to the body,
    but envy rots the bones.

³¹Whoever oppresses the poor shows
        contempt for their Maker,
    but whoever is kind to the needy
        honors God.

³²When calamity comes, the wicked are
        brought down,
    but even in death the righteous seek
        refuge in God.

³³Wisdom reposes in the heart of the
        discerning
    and even among fools she lets herself
        be known.*ᵇ*

³⁴Righteousness exalts a nation,
    but sin condemns any people.

³⁵A king delights in a wise servant,
    but a shameful servant arouses his
        fury.

15 A gentle answer turns away
        wrath,
    but a harsh word stirs up anger.

²The tongue of the wise adorns
        knowledge,
    but the mouth of the fool gushes folly.

³The eyes of the LORD are everywhere,
    keeping watch on the wicked and the
        good.

⁴The soothing tongue is a tree of life,
    but a perverse tongue crushes the
        spirit.

ᵃ 22 Or *show*   ᵇ 33 Hebrew; Septuagint and Syriac *discerning / but in the heart of fools she is not known*

⁵A fool spurns a parent's discipline,
  but whoever heeds correction shows
    prudence.

⁶The house of the righteous contains
    great treasure,
  but the income of the wicked brings
    ruin.

⁷The lips of the wise spread knowledge,
  but the hearts of fools are not upright.

⁸The Lord detests the sacrifice of the
    wicked,
  but the prayer of the upright pleases
    him.

⁹The Lord detests the way of the wicked,
  but he loves those who pursue
    righteousness.

¹⁰Stern discipline awaits anyone who
    leaves the path;
  the one who hates correction will die.

¹¹Death and Destruction*a* lie open before
    the Lord—
  how much more do human hearts!

¹²Mockers resent correction,
  so they avoid the wise.

¹³A happy heart makes the face cheerful,
  but heartache crushes the spirit.

¹⁴The discerning heart seeks knowledge,
  but the mouth of a fool feeds on folly.

¹⁵All the days of the oppressed are
    wretched,
  but the cheerful heart has a continual
    feast.

¹⁶Better a little with the fear of the Lord
  than great wealth with turmoil.

¹⁷Better a small serving of vegetables
    with love
  than a fattened calf with hatred.

¹⁸A hot-tempered person stirs up conflict,
  but the one who is patient calms a
    quarrel.

¹⁹The way of the sluggard is blocked with
    thorns,
  but the path of the upright is a
    highway.

²⁰A wise son brings joy to his father,
  but a foolish man despises his
    mother.

²¹Folly brings joy to one who has no sense,
  but whoever has understanding
    keeps a straight course.

²²Plans fail for lack of counsel,
  but with many advisers they succeed.

²³A person finds joy in giving an apt
    reply—
  and how good is a timely word!

²⁴The path of life leads upward for the
    prudent
  to keep them from going down to the
    realm of the dead.

²⁵The Lord tears down the house of the
    proud,
  but he sets the widow's boundary
    stones in place.

²⁶The Lord detests the thoughts of the
    wicked,
  but gracious words are pure in his
    sight.

²⁷The greedy bring ruin to their
    households,
  but the one who hates bribes will live.

²⁸The heart of the righteous weighs its
    answers,
  but the mouth of the wicked gushes
    evil.

²⁹The Lord is far from the wicked,
  but he hears the prayer of the
    righteous.

³⁰Light in a messenger's eyes brings joy to
    the heart,
  and good news gives health to the
    bones.

---

a 11 Hebrew *Abaddon*

31 Whoever heeds life-giving correction
  will be at home among the wise.

32 Those who disregard discipline despise
  themselves,
  but the one who heeds correction
  gains understanding.

33 Wisdom's instruction is to fear the
  LORD,
  and humility comes before honor.

16 To humans belong the plans of
  the heart,
  but from the LORD comes the
  proper answer of the tongue.

2 All a person's ways seem pure to them,
  but motives are weighed by the LORD.

3 Commit to the LORD whatever you do,
  and he will establish your plans.

4 The LORD works out everything to its
  proper end—
  even the wicked for a day of disaster.

5 The LORD detests all the proud of
  heart.
  Be sure of this: They will not go
  unpunished.

6 Through love and faithfulness sin is
  atoned for;
  through the fear of the LORD evil is
  avoided.

7 When the LORD takes pleasure in
  anyone's way,
  he causes their enemies to make
  peace with them.

8 Better a little with righteousness
  than much gain with injustice.

9 In their hearts humans plan their
  course,
  but the LORD establishes their
  steps.

10 The lips of a king speak as an oracle,
  and his mouth does not betray
  justice.

VICTORY LESSON [*Principle Five*]

For the previous entry in the VICTORY lesson, go to Romans 12:1–2 (page 1409).

For a discussion of Principles One through Eight and a listing of their related lessons,
go to pages xvii–xliv.

In their hearts humans plan their course, but the LORD establishes their steps.

PROVERBS 16:9

In Principle Five, as we voluntarily submit to every change God wants to make in our lives and humbly ask him to remove our character defects, we'll find VICTORY in our recovery.

The *I* in VICTORY stands for IDENTIFY OUR CHARACTER DEFECTS. We need to decide which character defects we want to work on first. We need to go back to the wrongs, shortcomings and sins we discovered in our inventories. God doesn't just want to admit our wrongs; he wants to make us right. He wants to give us "hope and a future" (Jeremiah 29:11). God doesn't just want to forgive us; he wants to change us. We need to ask God first to remove those character defects that are causing us the most pain. We need to be specific. He'll help us determine the steps we need to take from that point on.

The next letter in VICTORY is C. Go to 2 Corinthians 5:17 (page 1443).

¹¹Honest scales and balances belong to
the LORD;
all the weights in the bag are of his
making.

¹²Kings detest wrongdoing,
for a throne is established through
righteousness.

¹³Kings take pleasure in honest lips;
they value the one who speaks what
is right.

¹⁴A king's wrath is a messenger of death,
but the wise will appease it.

¹⁵When a king's face brightens, it means
life;
his favor is like a rain cloud in spring.

¹⁶How much better to get wisdom than
gold,
to get insight rather than silver!

¹⁷The highway of the upright avoids evil;
those who guard their ways preserve
their lives.

¹⁸Pride goes before destruction,
a haughty spirit before a fall.

¹⁹Better to be lowly in spirit along with
the oppressed
than to share plunder with the
proud.

²⁰Whoever gives heed to instruction
prospers,^a
and blessed is the one who trusts in
the LORD.

²¹The wise in heart are called discerning,
and gracious words promote
instruction.^b

²²Prudence is a fountain of life to the
prudent,
but folly brings punishment to fools.

²³The hearts of the wise make their
mouths prudent,
and their lips promote instruction.^c

²⁴Gracious words are a honeycomb,
sweet to the soul and healing to the
bones.

²⁵There is a way that appears to be right,
but in the end it leads to death.

²⁶The appetite of laborers works for
them;
their hunger drives them on.

²⁷A scoundrel plots evil,
and on their lips it is like a scorching
fire.

²⁸A perverse person stirs up conflict,
and a gossip separates close friends.

²⁹A violent person entices their neighbor
and leads them down a path that is
not good.

³⁰Whoever winks with their eye is
plotting perversity;
whoever purses their lips is bent on
evil.

³¹Gray hair is a crown of splendor;
it is attained in the way of
righteousness.

³²Better a patient person than a warrior,
one with self-control than one who
takes a city.

³³The lot is cast into the lap,
but its every decision is from the
LORD.

17

Better a dry crust with peace
and quiet
than a house full of feasting,
with strife.

²A prudent servant will rule over a
disgraceful son
and will share the inheritance as one
of the family.

³The crucible for silver and the furnace
for gold,
but the LORD tests the heart.

---

^a 20 Or *whoever speaks prudently finds what is good
/ and make their lips persuasive*   ^b 21 Or *words make a person persuasive*   ^c 23 Or *prudent*

4 A wicked person listens to deceitful
    lips;
  a liar pays attention to a destructive
    tongue.

5 Whoever mocks the poor shows
    contempt for their Maker;
  whoever gloats over disaster will not
    go unpunished.

6 Children's children are a crown to the
    aged,
  and parents are the pride of their
    children.

7 Eloquent lips are unsuited to a godless
    fool —
  how much worse lying lips to a
    ruler!

8 A bribe is seen as a charm by the one
    who gives it;
  they think success will come at every
    turn.

9 Whoever would foster love covers over
    an offense,
  but whoever repeats the matter
    separates close friends.

10 A rebuke impresses a discerning
    person
  more than a hundred lashes a fool.

11 Evildoers foster rebellion against
    God;
  the messenger of death will be sent
    against them.

12 Better to meet a bear robbed of her
    cubs
  than a fool bent on folly.

13 Evil will never leave the house
  of one who pays back evil for good.

14 Starting a quarrel is like breaching a
    dam;
  so drop the matter before a dispute
    breaks out.

15 Acquitting the guilty and condemning
    the innocent —
  the Lord detests them both.

16 Why should fools have money in hand
    to buy wisdom,
  when they are not able to understand
    it?

17 A friend loves at all times,
  and a brother is born for a time of
    adversity.

18 One who has no sense shakes hands in
    pledge
  and puts up security for a neighbor.

19 Whoever loves a quarrel loves sin;
  whoever builds a high gate invites
    destruction.

20 One whose heart is corrupt does not
    prosper;
  one whose tongue is perverse falls
    into trouble.

21 To have a fool for a child brings grief;
  there is no joy for the parent of a
    godless fool.

22 A cheerful heart is good medicine,
  but a crushed spirit dries up the bones.

23 The wicked accept bribes in secret
  to pervert the course of justice.

24 A discerning person keeps wisdom in
    view,
  but a fool's eyes wander to the ends
    of the earth.

25 A foolish son brings grief to his father
  and bitterness to the mother who
    bore him.

26 If imposing a fine on the innocent is
    not good,
  surely to flog honest officials is not
    right.

27 The one who has knowledge uses words
    with restraint,
  and whoever has understanding is
    even-tempered.

28 Even fools are thought wise if they keep
    silent,
  and discerning if they hold their
    tongues.

18

An unfriendly person pursues
selfish ends
   and against all sound judgment
   starts quarrels.

2 Fools find no pleasure in
   understanding
   but delight in airing their own
   opinions.

3 When wickedness comes, so does
   contempt,
   and with shame comes reproach.

4 The words of the mouth are deep
   waters,
   but the fountain of wisdom is a
   rushing stream.

5 It is not good to be partial to the wicked
   and so deprive the innocent of
   justice.

6 The lips of fools bring them strife,
   and their mouths invite a beating.

7 The mouths of fools are their undoing,
   and their lips are a snare to their very
   lives.

8 The words of a gossip are like choice
   morsels;
   they go down to the inmost parts.

9 One who is slack in his work
   is brother to one who destroys.

10 The name of the LORD is a fortified
   tower;
   the righteous run to it and are safe.

11 The wealth of the rich is their fortified
   city;
   they imagine it a wall too high to
   scale.

12 Before a downfall the heart is haughty,
   but humility comes before honor.

13 To answer before listening —
   that is folly and shame.

14 The human spirit can endure in
   sickness,
   but a crushed spirit who can bear?

15 The heart of the discerning acquires
   knowledge,
   for the ears of the wise seek it out.

16 A gift opens the way
   and ushers the giver into the
   presence of the great.

17 In a lawsuit the first to speak seems
   right,
   until someone comes forward and
   cross-examines.

18 Casting the lot settles disputes
   and keeps strong opponents apart.

19 A brother wronged is more unyielding
   than a fortified city;
   disputes are like the barred gates of a
   citadel.

20 From the fruit of their mouth a person's
   stomach is filled;
   with the harvest of their lips they are
   satisfied.

21 The tongue has the power of life and
   death,
   and those who love it will eat its
   fruit.

22 He who finds a wife finds what is good
   and receives favor from the LORD.

23 The poor plead for mercy,
   but the rich answer harshly.

24 One who has unreliable friends soon
   comes to ruin,
   but there is a friend who sticks closer
   than a brother.

19

Better the poor whose walk is
blameless
   than a fool whose lips are
   perverse.

2 Desire without knowledge is not
   good —
   how much more will hasty feet miss
   the way!

3 A person's own folly leads to their ruin,
   yet their heart rages against the
   LORD.

4 Wealth attracts many friends,
  but even the closest friend of the
    poor person deserts them.

5 A false witness will not go unpunished,
  and whoever pours out lies will not
    go free.

6 Many curry favor with a ruler,
  and everyone is the friend of one who
    gives gifts.

7 The poor are shunned by all their
    relatives —
  how much more do their friends
    avoid them!
Though the poor pursue them with
    pleading,
  they are nowhere to be found.*a*

8 The one who gets wisdom loves life;
  the one who cherishes understanding
    will soon prosper.

9 A false witness will not go unpunished,
  and whoever pours out lies will
    perish.

10 It is not fitting for a fool to live in
    luxury —
  how much worse for a slave to rule
    over princes!

11 A person's wisdom yields patience;
  it is to one's glory to overlook an
    offense.

12 A king's rage is like the roar of a lion,
  but his favor is like dew on the
    grass.

13 A foolish child is a father's ruin,
  and a quarrelsome wife is like
    the constant dripping of a leaky
    roof.

14 Houses and wealth are inherited from
    parents,
  but a prudent wife is from the LORD.

15 Laziness brings on deep sleep,
  and the shiftless go hungry.

16 Whoever keeps commandments keeps
    their life,
  but whoever shows contempt for
    their ways will die.

17 Whoever is kind to the poor lends to
    the LORD,
  and he will reward them for what
    they have done.

18 Discipline your children, for in that
    there is hope;
  do not be a willing party to their
    death.

19 A hot-tempered person must pay the
    penalty;
  rescue them, and you will have to do
    it again.

20 Listen to advice and accept discipline,
  and at the end you will be counted
    among the wise.

21 Many are the plans in a person's heart,
  but it is the LORD's purpose that
    prevails.

22 What a person desires is unfailing
    love*b*;
  better to be poor than a liar.

23 The fear of the LORD leads to life;
  then one rests content, untouched by
    trouble.

24 A sluggard buries his hand in the dish;
  he will not even bring it back to his
    mouth!

25 Flog a mocker, and the simple will learn
    prudence;
  rebuke the discerning, and they will
    gain knowledge.

26 Whoever robs their father and drives
    out their mother
  is a child who brings shame and
    disgrace.

27 Stop listening to instruction, my son,
  and you will stray from the words of
    knowledge.

---

a 7 The meaning of the Hebrew for this sentence is uncertain.   *b 22* Or *Greed is a person's shame*

28 A corrupt witness mocks at justice,
and the mouth of the wicked gulps
down evil.

29 Penalties are prepared for mockers,
and beatings for the backs of fools.

20 Wine is a mocker and beer a
brawler;
whoever is led astray by them
is not wise.

2 A king's wrath strikes terror like the
roar of a lion;
those who anger him forfeit their
lives.

3 It is to one's honor to avoid strife,
but every fool is quick to quarrel.

4 Sluggards do not plow in season;
so at harvest time they look but find
nothing.

5 The purposes of a person's heart are
deep waters,
but one who has insight draws them
out.

6 Many claim to have unfailing love,
but a faithful person who can find?

7 The righteous lead blameless lives;
blessed are their children after
them.

8 When a king sits on his throne to
judge,
he winnows out all evil with his eyes.

9 Who can say, "I have kept my heart
pure;
I am clean and without sin"?

10 Differing weights and differing
measures—
the LORD detests them both.

11 Even small children are known by their
actions,
so is their conduct really pure and
upright?

12 Ears that hear and eyes that see—
the LORD has made them both.

13 Do not love sleep or you will grow poor;
stay awake and you will have food to
spare.

14 "It's no good, it's no good!" says the
buyer—
then goes off and boasts about the
purchase.

15 Gold there is, and rubies in abundance,
but lips that speak knowledge are a
rare jewel.

16 Take the garment of one who puts up
security for a stranger;
hold it in pledge if it is done for an
outsider.

17 Food gained by fraud tastes sweet,
but one ends up with a mouth full of
gravel.

18 Plans are established by seeking
advice;
so if you wage war, obtain guidance.

19 A gossip betrays a confidence;
so avoid anyone who talks too much.

20 If someone curses their father or
mother,
their lamp will be snuffed out in
pitch darkness.

21 An inheritance claimed too soon
will not be blessed at the end.

22 Do not say, "I'll pay you back for this
wrong!"
Wait for the LORD, and he will
avenge you.

23 The LORD detests differing weights,
and dishonest scales do not please
him.

24 A person's steps are directed by the
LORD.
How then can anyone understand
their own way?

25 It is a trap to dedicate something
rashly
and only later to consider one's
vows.

26 A wise king winnows out the wicked;
    he drives the threshing wheel over
        them.

27 The human spirit is*a* the lamp of the
        LORD
    that sheds light on one's inmost
        being.

28 Love and faithfulness keep a king safe;
    through love his throne is made
        secure.

29 The glory of young men is their strength,
    gray hair the splendor of the old.

30 Blows and wounds scrub away evil,
    and beatings purge the inmost being.

a 27 Or *A person's words are*

SPONSOR LESSON [*Principle Four*]

This is the first page of the SPONSOR lesson.

For a discussion of Principles One through Eight and a listing of their related lessons,
go to pages xvii – xliv.

> *The purposes of a person's heart are deep waters,*
> *but one who has insight draws them out.*

PROVERBS 20:5

Principle Four begins the process of "coming clean." It's here that we openly examine and confess our faults to ourselves, to God and to someone else we trust. In order to work this principle, we need to have an accountability relationship established.

There are three reasons we need a sponsor and/or an accountability partner. The first reason is: *Having someone fill this role for us is a key part of our recovery program.* Celebrate Recovery identifies the following four key elements to success. If we include each of these four elements in our program, we'll be well on our way to our solution — well on our way to finding wholeness:

- To the best of our ability, maintain an honest view of reality as we work each principle. The best way to ensure this is to have a sponsor and/or an accountability partner and to develop a strong support team.

- Make recovery group meetings a priority in our schedules. Knowing that a sponsor and/or an accountability partner will be there to greet us or notice if we're absent is an added incentive to attend.

- Maintain our spiritual program with Jesus Christ, through prayer, meditation and studying his Word. Our sponsor and/or accountability partner can encourage us in this critical area.

- Get involved in service, which includes serving as a sponsor or an accountability partner for someone else who is working through the recovery program.

As Proverbs 20:5 makes clear, we need a man or a woman who understands us as individuals and knows what we're going through in order to help us in our recovery.

For the second reason we need a sponsor and/or an accountability partner,
go to Ecclesiastes 4:9 – 12 (page 786).

21

In the Lord's hand the king's heart is a stream of water that he channels toward all who please him.

2 A person may think their own ways are right,
  but the Lord weighs the heart.

3 To do what is right and just
  is more acceptable to the Lord than sacrifice.

4 Haughty eyes and a proud heart —
  the unplowed field of the wicked —
  produce sin.

5 The plans of the diligent lead to profit
  as surely as haste leads to poverty.

6 A fortune made by a lying tongue
  is a fleeting vapor and a deadly snare.*a*

7 The violence of the wicked will drag them away,
  for they refuse to do what is right.

8 The way of the guilty is devious,
  but the conduct of the innocent is upright.

9 Better to live on a corner of the roof
  than share a house with a quarrelsome wife.

10 The wicked crave evil;
   their neighbors get no mercy from them.

11 When a mocker is punished, the simple gain wisdom;
   by paying attention to the wise they get knowledge.

12 The Righteous One*b* takes note of the house of the wicked
   and brings the wicked to ruin.

---

a 6 Some Hebrew manuscripts, Septuagint and Vulgate; most Hebrew manuscripts *vapor for those who seek death*
b 12 Or *The righteous person*

MORAL LESSON [*Principle Four*]

For the previous entry in the MORAL lesson, go to Isaiah 40:29 (page 850).

For a discussion of Principles One through Eight and a listing of their related lessons, go to pages xvii – xliv.

The human spirit is the lamp of the Lord that sheds light on one's inmost being.

PROVERBS 20:27

Principle Four begins our process of "coming clean." It's here that we openly examine and confess our faults to ourselves, to God and to someone else we trust. In the first part of Principle Four we openly examine our lives. We take a MORAL inventory.

The *A* in MORAL stands for ANALYZE OUR PAST HONESTLY. To do a searching and fearless inventory, we need to step out of our denial; we can't put our faults behind us until we've faced them. We have to look beyond and through our denial of the past into the truth of the present — into our true feelings, motives and thoughts. Proverbs 20:27 tells us that we can't hide from God or from ourselves. We need to allow the "lamp of the Lord" to shine on our lives to help reveal the truth to us.

The last letter in MORAL is *L*. Go to Lamentations 3:40 (page 963).

13 Whoever shuts their ears to the cry of
    the poor
  will also cry out and not be answered.

14 A gift given in secret soothes anger,
  and a bribe concealed in the cloak
    pacifies great wrath.

15 When justice is done, it brings joy to
    the righteous
  but terror to evildoers.

16 Whoever strays from the path of
    prudence
  comes to rest in the company of the
    dead.

17 Whoever loves pleasure will become
    poor;
  whoever loves wine and olive oil will
    never be rich.

18 The wicked become a ransom for the
    righteous,
  and the unfaithful for the upright.

19 Better to live in a desert
  than with a quarrelsome and
    nagging wife.

20 The wise store up choice food and olive
    oil,
  but fools gulp theirs down.

21 Whoever pursues righteousness and love
  finds life, prosperity*a* and honor.

22 One who is wise can go up against the
    city of the mighty
  and pull down the stronghold in
    which they trust.

23 Those who guard their mouths and
    their tongues
  keep themselves from calamity.

24 The proud and arrogant person —
    "Mocker" is his name —
  behaves with insolent fury.

25 The craving of a sluggard will be the
    death of him,
  because his hands refuse to work.

26 All day long he craves for more,
  but the righteous give without sparing.

27 The sacrifice of the wicked is
    detestable —
  how much more so when brought
    with evil intent!

28 A false witness will perish,
  but a careful listener will testify
    successfully.

29 The wicked put up a bold front,
  but the upright give thought to their
    ways.

30 There is no wisdom, no insight, no plan
  that can succeed against the LORD.

31 The horse is made ready for the day of
    battle,
  but victory rests with the LORD.

22 A good name is more
desirable than great riches;
to be esteemed is better than
silver or gold.

2 Rich and poor have this in common:
  The LORD is the Maker of them all.

3 The prudent see danger and take
    refuge,
  but the simple keep going and pay
    the penalty.

4 Humility is the fear of the LORD;
  its wages are riches and honor and
    life.

5 In the paths of the wicked are snares
    and pitfalls,
  but those who would preserve their
    life stay far from them.

6 Start children off on the way they
    should go,
  and even when they are old they will
    not turn from it.

7 The rich rule over the poor,
  and the borrower is slave to the
    lender.

---

a 21 Or *righteousness*

⁸Whoever sows injustice reaps calamity,
   and the rod they wield in fury will be
      broken.

⁹The generous will themselves be blessed,
   for they share their food with the
      poor.

¹⁰Drive out the mocker, and out goes
      strife;
   quarrels and insults are ended.

¹¹One who loves a pure heart and who
      speaks with grace
   will have the king for a friend.

¹²The eyes of the Lord keep watch over
      knowledge,
   but he frustrates the words of the
      unfaithful.

¹³The sluggard says, "There's a lion
      outside!
   I'll be killed in the public square!"

¹⁴The mouth of an adulterous woman is a
      deep pit;
   a man who is under the Lord's wrath
      falls into it.

¹⁵Folly is bound up in the heart of a child,
   but the rod of discipline will drive it
      far away.

¹⁶One who oppresses the poor to increase
      his wealth
   and one who gives gifts to the rich —
      both come to poverty.

Thirty Sayings of the Wise

Saying 1

¹⁷Pay attention and turn your ear to the
      sayings of the wise;
   apply your heart to what I teach,
¹⁸for it is pleasing when you keep them in
      your heart
   and have all of them ready on your
      lips.
¹⁹So that your trust may be in the Lord,
   I teach you today, even you.

²⁰Have I not written thirty sayings for
      you,
   sayings of counsel and knowledge,
²¹teaching you to be honest and to speak
      the truth,
   so that you bring back truthful reports
      to those you serve?

Saying 2

²²Do not exploit the poor because they
      are poor
   and do not crush the needy in court,
²³for the Lord will take up their case
   and will exact life for life.

Saying 3

²⁴Do not make friends with a hot-
      tempered person,
   do not associate with one easily
      angered,
²⁵or you may learn their ways
   and get yourself ensnared.

Saying 4

²⁶Do not be one who shakes hands in
      pledge
   or puts up security for debts;
²⁷if you lack the means to pay,
   your very bed will be snatched from
      under you.

Saying 5

²⁸Do not move an ancient boundary stone
   set up by your ancestors.

Saying 6

²⁹Do you see someone skilled in their work?
   They will serve before kings;
   they will not serve before officials of
      low rank.

Saying 7

23 When you sit to dine with a
      ruler,
   note well whatᵃ is before you,
²and put a knife to your throat
   if you are given to gluttony.

ᵃ 1 Or *who*

³ Do not crave his delicacies,
for that food is deceptive.

Saying 8

⁴ Do not wear yourself out to get rich;
do not trust your own cleverness.
⁵ Cast but a glance at riches, and they are
gone,
for they will surely sprout wings
and fly off to the sky like an eagle.

Saying 9

⁶ Do not eat the food of a begrudging
host,
do not crave his delicacies;
⁷ for he is the kind of person
who is always thinking about the
cost.ᵃ
"Eat and drink," he says to you,
but his heart is not with you.
⁸ You will vomit up the little you have
eaten
and will have wasted your
compliments.

Saying 10

⁹ Do not speak to fools,
for they will scorn your prudent
words.

Saying 11

¹⁰ Do not move an ancient boundary
stone
or encroach on the fields of the
fatherless,
¹¹ for their Defender is strong;
he will take up their case against you.

Saying 12

¹² Apply your heart to instruction
and your ears to words of knowledge.

Saying 13

¹³ Do not withhold discipline from a
child;
if you punish them with the rod, they
will not die.

¹⁴ Punish them with the rod
and save them from death.

Saying 14

¹⁵ My son, if your heart is wise,
then my heart will be glad indeed;
¹⁶ my inmost being will rejoice
when your lips speak what is right.

Saying 15

¹⁷ Do not let your heart envy sinners,
but always be zealous for the fear of
the LORD.
¹⁸ There is surely a future hope for you,
and your hope will not be cut off.

Saying 16

¹⁹ Listen, my son, and be wise,
and set your heart on the right path:
²⁰ Do not join those who drink too much
wine
or gorge themselves on meat,
²¹ for drunkards and gluttons become poor,
and drowsiness clothes them in rags.

Saying 17

²² Listen to your father, who gave you life,
and do not despise your mother
when she is old.
²³ Buy the truth and do not sell it —
wisdom, instruction and insight as
well.
²⁴ The father of a righteous child has great
joy;
a man who fathers a wise son rejoices
in him.
²⁵ May your father and mother rejoice;
may she who gave you birth be joyful!

Saying 18

²⁶ My son, give me your heart
and let your eyes delight in my ways,
²⁷ for an adulterous woman is a deep pit,
and a wayward wife is a narrow well.
²⁸ Like a bandit she lies in wait
and multiplies the unfaithful among
men.

ᵃ 7 Or *for as he thinks within himself, / so he is*; or *for as he puts on a feast, / so he is*

Saying 19

29 Who has woe? Who has sorrow?
  Who has strife? Who has
    complaints?
  Who has needless bruises? Who has
    bloodshot eyes?
30 Those who linger over wine,
  who go to sample bowls of mixed
    wine.
31 Do not gaze at wine when it is red,
  when it sparkles in the cup,
  when it goes down smoothly!
32 In the end it bites like a snake
  and poisons like a viper.
33 Your eyes will see strange sights,
  and your mind will imagine
    confusing things.
34 You will be like one sleeping on the
    high seas,
  lying on top of the rigging.
35 "They hit me," you will say, "but I'm not
    hurt!
  They beat me, but I don't feel it!
  When will I wake up
  so I can find another drink?"

Saying 20

24 Do not envy the wicked,
  do not desire their company;
  2 for their hearts plot violence,
  and their lips talk about making
    trouble.

Saying 21

3 By wisdom a house is built,
  and through understanding it is
    established;
4 through knowledge its rooms are
    filled
  with rare and beautiful treasures.

Saying 22

5 The wise prevail through great power,
  and those who have knowledge
    muster their strength.
6 Surely you need guidance to wage
    war,
  and victory is won through many
    advisers.

Saying 23

7 Wisdom is too high for fools;
  in the assembly at the gate they must
    not open their mouths.

Saying 24

8 Whoever plots evil
  will be known as a schemer.
9 The schemes of folly are sin,
  and people detest a mocker.

Saying 25

10 If you falter in a time of trouble,
  how small is your strength!
11 Rescue those being led away to death;
  hold back those staggering toward
    slaughter.
12 If you say, "But we knew nothing about
    this,"
  does not he who weighs the heart
    perceive it?
  Does not he who guards your life
    know it?
  Will he not repay everyone according
    to what they have done?

Saying 26

13 Eat honey, my son, for it is good;
  honey from the comb is sweet to your
    taste.
14 Know also that wisdom is like honey
    for you:
  If you find it, there is a future hope
    for you,
  and your hope will not be cut off.

Saying 27

15 Do not lurk like a thief near the house
    of the righteous,
  do not plunder their dwelling place;
16 for though the righteous fall seven
    times, they rise again,
  but the wicked stumble when
    calamity strikes.

Saying 28

17 Do not gloat when your enemy falls;
  when they stumble, do not let your
    heart rejoice,

My Name Is
The Drunkard

PROVERBS 23:19–21, 29–35

If alcohol has been our primary addiction, we may have the sensation that Solomon was reading our mail—or our mind—when he wrote Proverbs 23:29–35. In verse 31 he vividly describes the appeal of wine, but he has learned that "in the end it bites like a snake and poisons like a viper" (Proverbs 23:32). This wise man spells out some of the consequences of being bitten by this particular snake (see vv. 29–30, 33–35). Finally, he expresses the daily dilemma of the alcoholic: "When will I wake up so I can find another drink?" (v. 35).

How can the drunkard be delivered? The answer isn't found in becoming an expert on alcoholism. It involves far more than acknowledging that we struggle with an alcohol addiction. Hope for deliverance is found in verse 19: "Set your heart on the right path." If we're willing to change pathways, there's hope for freedom from any addictive habit that binds us. This isn't a veiled self-help program, because the key is on *who* keeps our heart. Christ alone has the power to keep us on the path we're too weak to stick to on our own. Verses 19–21 outline some sobriety essentials:

- "Be wise" (v. 19). In the Old Testament, wisdom is the possession of one who places his or her faith in the God of Israel.

- "Set your heart on the right path" (v. 19). Sticking to the one correct path is the only way to stay off any number of hazardous highways. Jesus proclaimed, "I am the way and the truth and the life. No one comes to the Father except through me" (John 14:6). He and he alone is the way we need to go, the truth we need to know and the life we need to live.

- "Do not join those who drink too much wine or gorge themselves on meat" (v. 20). Recovery requires a change in companions. God's method of healing includes commitment to community. We're called to leave our drinking buddies behind and join those who are willing to travel "the right path" with us.

- Never forget the consequences of the wrong path and the wrong companions: "For drunkards and gluttons become poor, and drowsiness clothes them in rags" (v. 21).

Ultimately, our recovery is a personal choice of who or what will control us. Ephesians contains a command and a contrast: "Do not get drunk on wine, which leads to debauchery. Instead, be filled with the Spirit" (Ephesians 5:18). The command is to be filled up with the Holy Spirit—not with wine. The contrast is between a life wasted on wickedness and one lived in the company of those who are high on the joys of worshiping Jesus in a loving community: "[Speak] to one another with psalms, hymns, and songs from the Spirit. Sing and make music from your heart to the Lord, always giving thanks to God the Father for everything, in the name of our Lord Jesus Christ" (vv. 19–20). We can't change our past, but we can change our path by surrendering our life entirely to the care of Jesus Christ, the one true Higher Power.

¹⁸ or the LORD will see and disapprove
   and turn his wrath away from them.

Saying 29

¹⁹ Do not fret because of evildoers
   or be envious of the wicked,
²⁰ for the evildoer has no future hope,
   and the lamp of the wicked will be
      snuffed out.

Saying 30

²¹ Fear the LORD and the king, my son,
   and do not join with rebellious
      officials,
²² for those two will send sudden
      destruction on them,
   and who knows what calamities they
      can bring?

Further Sayings of the Wise

²³ These also are sayings of the wise:

To show partiality in judging is not
   good:
²⁴ Whoever says to the guilty, "You are
      innocent,"
   will be cursed by peoples and
      denounced by nations.
²⁵ But it will go well with those who
      convict the guilty,
   and rich blessing will come on them.

²⁶ An honest answer
   is like a kiss on the lips.

²⁷ Put your outdoor work in order
   and get your fields ready;
   after that, build your house.

²⁸ Do not testify against your neighbor
      without cause—
   would you use your lips to mislead?
²⁹ Do not say, "I'll do to them as they have
      done to me;
   I'll pay them back for what they did."

³⁰ I went past the field of a sluggard,
   past the vineyard of someone who
      has no sense;
³¹ thorns had come up everywhere,
   the ground was covered with
      weeds,
   and the stone wall was in ruins.
³² I applied my heart to what I observed
   and learned a lesson from what I
      saw:
³³ A little sleep, a little slumber,
   a little folding of the hands to
      rest—
³⁴ and poverty will come on you like a
      thief
   and scarcity like an armed man.

More Proverbs of Solomon

25 These are more proverbs of
Solomon, compiled by the men
of Hezekiah king of Judah:

² It is the glory of God to conceal a
      matter;
   to search out a matter is the glory of
      kings.
³ As the heavens are high and the earth is
      deep,
   so the hearts of kings are
      unsearchable.

⁴ Remove the dross from the silver,
   and a silversmith can produce a
      vessel;
⁵ remove wicked officials from the king's
      presence,
   and his throne will be established
      through righteousness.

⁶ Do not exalt yourself in the king's
      presence,
   and do not claim a place among his
      great men;
⁷ it is better for him to say to you, "Come
      up here,"
   than for him to humiliate you before
      his nobles.

What you have seen with your eyes
⁸   do not bringᵃ hastily to court,
for what will you do in the end
   if your neighbor puts you to shame?

ᵃ 7,8 Or *nobles / on whom you had set your eyes.* / ⁸*Do not go*

⁹ If you take your neighbor to court,
    do not betray another's confidence,
¹⁰ or the one who hears it may shame you
    and the charge against you will
        stand.

¹¹ Like apples*a* of gold in settings of silver
    is a ruling rightly given.
¹² Like an earring of gold or an ornament
        of fine gold
    is the rebuke of a wise judge to a
        listening ear.

¹³ Like a snow-cooled drink at harvest time
    is a trustworthy messenger to the one
        who sends him;
    he refreshes the spirit of his master.
¹⁴ Like clouds and wind without rain
    is one who boasts of gifts never given.

¹⁵ Through patience a ruler can be
        persuaded,
    and a gentle tongue can break a bone.

¹⁶ If you find honey, eat just enough —
    too much of it, and you will vomit.
¹⁷ Seldom set foot in your neighbor's
        house —
    too much of you, and they will hate
        you.

¹⁸ Like a club or a sword or a sharp arrow
    is one who gives false testimony
        against a neighbor.
¹⁹ Like a broken tooth or a lame foot
    is reliance on the unfaithful in a time
        of trouble.
²⁰ Like one who takes away a garment on a
        cold day,
    or like vinegar poured on a wound,
    is one who sings songs to a heavy
        heart.

²¹ If your enemy is hungry, give him food
        to eat;
    if he is thirsty, give him water to
        drink.
²² In doing this, you will heap burning
        coals on his head,
    and the LORD will reward you.

²³ Like a north wind that brings
        unexpected rain
    is a sly tongue — which provokes a
        horrified look.

²⁴ Better to live on a corner of the roof
    than share a house with a
        quarrelsome wife.

²⁵ Like cold water to a weary soul
    is good news from a distant land.
²⁶ Like a muddied spring or a polluted
        well
    are the righteous who give way to the
        wicked.

²⁷ It is not good to eat too much honey,
    nor is it honorable to search out
        matters that are too deep.

²⁸ Like a city whose walls are broken
        through
    is a person who lacks self-control.

26 Like snow in summer or rain
        in harvest,
        honor is not fitting for a fool.
² Like a fluttering sparrow or a darting
        swallow,
    an undeserved curse does not come
        to rest.
³ A whip for the horse, a bridle for the
        donkey,
    and a rod for the backs of fools!
⁴ Do not answer a fool according to his
        folly,
    or you yourself will be just like him.
⁵ Answer a fool according to his folly,
    or he will be wise in his own eyes.
⁶ Sending a message by the hands of a
        fool
    is like cutting off one's feet or
        drinking poison.
⁷ Like the useless legs of one who is
        lame
    is a proverb in the mouth of a fool.
⁸ Like tying a stone in a sling
    is the giving of honor to a fool.
⁹ Like a thornbush in a drunkard's hand
    is a proverb in the mouth of a fool.

---

a 11 Or possibly *apricots*

¹⁰ Like an archer who wounds at random
is one who hires a fool or any
passer-by.

¹¹ As a dog returns to its vomit,
so fools repeat their folly.

¹² Do you see a person wise in their own
eyes?
There is more hope for a fool than for
them.

¹³ A sluggard says, "There's a lion in the
road,
a fierce lion roaming the streets!"

¹⁴ As a door turns on its hinges,
so a sluggard turns on his bed.

¹⁵ A sluggard buries his hand in the dish;
he is too lazy to bring it back to his
mouth.

¹⁶ A sluggard is wiser in his own eyes
than seven people who answer
discreetly.

¹⁷ Like one who grabs a stray dog by the
ears
is someone who rushes into a quarrel
not their own.

¹⁸ Like a maniac shooting
flaming arrows of death

¹⁹ is one who deceives their neighbor
and says, "I was only joking!"

²⁰ Without wood a fire goes out;
without a gossip a quarrel dies
down.

²¹ As charcoal to embers and as wood to
fire,
so is a quarrelsome person for
kindling strife.

²² The words of a gossip are like choice
morsels;
they go down to the inmost parts.

²³ Like a coating of silver dross on
earthenware
are fervent*ᵃ* lips with an evil heart.

²⁴ Enemies disguise themselves with their
lips,
but in their hearts they harbor deceit.

²⁵ Though their speech is charming, do
not believe them,
for seven abominations fill their
hearts.

²⁶ Their malice may be concealed by
deception,
but their wickedness will be exposed
in the assembly.

²⁷ Whoever digs a pit will fall into it;
if someone rolls a stone, it will roll
back on them.

²⁸ A lying tongue hates those it hurts,
and a flattering mouth works ruin.

27 Do not boast about tomorrow,
for you do not know what a
day may bring.

² Let someone else praise you, and not
your own mouth;
an outsider, and not your own lips.

³ Stone is heavy and sand a burden,
but a fool's provocation is heavier
than both.

⁴ Anger is cruel and fury overwhelming,
but who can stand before jealousy?

⁵ Better is open rebuke
than hidden love.

⁶ Wounds from a friend can be trusted,
but an enemy multiplies kisses.

⁷ One who is full loathes honey from the
comb,
but to the hungry even what is bitter
tastes sweet.

⁸ Like a bird that flees its nest
is anyone who flees from home.

⁹ Perfume and incense bring joy to the
heart,
and the pleasantness of a friend
springs from their heartfelt advice.

¹⁰ Do not forsake your friend or a friend
of your family,
and do not go to your relative's house
when disaster strikes you —

ᵃ 23 Hebrew; Septuagint *smooth*

better a neighbor nearby than a
   relative far away.

11 Be wise, my son, and bring joy to my
      heart;
   then I can answer anyone who treats
      me with contempt.

12 The prudent see danger and take
      refuge,
   but the simple keep going and pay
      the penalty.

13 Take the garment of one who puts up
      security for a stranger;
   hold it in pledge if it is done for an
      outsider.

14 If anyone loudly blesses their neighbor
      early in the morning,
   it will be taken as a curse.

15 A quarrelsome wife is like the dripping
      of a leaky roof in a rainstorm;
16 restraining her is like restraining the
      wind
   or grasping oil with the hand.

17 As iron sharpens iron,
   so one person sharpens another.

18 The one who guards a fig tree will eat
      its fruit,
   and whoever protects their master
      will be honored.

19 As water reflects the face,
   so one's life reflects the heart.*a*

20 Death and Destruction*b* are never
      satisfied,
   and neither are human eyes.

21 The crucible for silver and the furnace
      for gold,
   but people are tested by their praise.

22 Though you grind a fool in a mortar,
      grinding them like grain with a
      pestle,
   you will not remove their folly from
      them.

23 Be sure you know the condition of your
      flocks,
   give careful attention to your herds;
24 for riches do not endure forever,
   and a crown is not secure for all
      generations.
25 When the hay is removed and new
      growth appears
   and the grass from the hills is
      gathered in,
26 the lambs will provide you with
      clothing,
   and the goats with the price of a field.
27 You will have plenty of goats' milk to
      feed your family
   and to nourish your female servants.

28 The wicked flee though no
      one pursues,
   but the righteous are as bold
      as a lion.

2 When a country is rebellious, it has
      many rulers,
   but a ruler with discernment and
      knowledge maintains order.

3 A ruler*c* who oppresses the poor
   is like a driving rain that leaves no
      crops.

4 Those who forsake instruction praise
      the wicked,
   but those who heed it resist them.

5 Evildoers do not understand what is
      right,
   but those who seek the LORD
      understand it fully.

6 Better the poor whose walk is blameless
   than the rich whose ways are perverse.

7 A discerning son heeds instruction,
   but a companion of gluttons
      disgraces his father.

8 Whoever increases wealth by taking
      interest or profit from the poor
   amasses it for another, who will be
      kind to the poor.

---

a 19 Or *so others reflect your heart back to you*   *b 20* Hebrew *Abaddon*   *c 3* Or *A poor person*

⁹ If anyone turns a deaf ear to my
  instruction,
  even their prayers are detestable.

¹⁰ Whoever leads the upright along an evil
  path
  will fall into their own trap,
  but the blameless will receive a good
  inheritance.

¹¹ The rich are wise in their own eyes;
  one who is poor and discerning sees
  how deluded they are.

¹² When the righteous triumph, there is
  great elation;
  but when the wicked rise to power,
  people go into hiding.

¹³ Whoever conceals their sins does not
  prosper,
  but the one who confesses and
  renounces them finds mercy.

¹⁴ Blessed is the one who always trembles
  before God,
  but whoever hardens their heart falls
  into trouble.

¹⁵ Like a roaring lion or a charging bear
  is a wicked ruler over a helpless
  people.

¹⁶ A tyrannical ruler practices
  extortion,
  but one who hates ill-gotten gain will
  enjoy a long reign.

¹⁷ Anyone tormented by the guilt of
  murder
  will seek refuge in the grave;
  let no one hold them back.

¹⁸ The one whose walk is blameless is kept
  safe,
  but the one whose ways are perverse
  will fall into the pit.^a

---

a 18 Syriac (see Septuagint); Hebrew *into one*

CONFESS LESSON [*Principle Four*]

This is the first page of the CONFESS lesson.

**For a discussion of Principles One through Eight and a listing of their related lessons,
go to pages xvii – xliv.**

*Whoever conceals their sins does not prosper, but the one
who confesses and renounces them finds mercy.*

PROVERBS 28:13

Principle Four begins the process of "coming clean." In the second part of Principle Four, we confess our faults to ourselves, to God and to someone else we trust.

The *C* in CONFESS stands for CONFESS YOUR SHORTCOMINGS, RESENTMENTS AND SINS. God wants us to come clean, to admit that wrong is wrong, that we're "guilty as charged." Confession means that we agree with God regarding our sins. We need to own up to the sins we discovered in our Principle Four inventories. Confession is necessary for restoring our fellowship with God. Our sins have erected a barrier between us and him. After we share our inventories, we'll find the peace and freedom for which we've been searching most of our lives.

The next letter in CONFESS is O. Go to Romans 14:11 – 12 (page 1414).

¹⁹ Those who work their land will have
abundant food,
but those who chase fantasies will
have their fill of poverty.

²⁰ A faithful person will be richly
blessed,
but one eager to get rich will not go
unpunished.

²¹ To show partiality is not good —
yet a person will do wrong for a piece
of bread.

²² The stingy are eager to get rich
and are unaware that poverty awaits
them.

²³ Whoever rebukes a person will in the
end gain favor
rather than one who has a flattering
tongue.

²⁴ Whoever robs their father or
mother
and says, "It's not wrong,"
is partner to one who destroys.

²⁵ The greedy stir up conflict,
but those who trust in the LORD will
prosper.

²⁶ Those who trust in themselves are
fools,
but those who walk in wisdom are
kept safe.

²⁷ Those who give to the poor will lack
nothing,
but those who close their eyes to
them receive many curses.

²⁸ When the wicked rise to power, people
go into hiding;
but when the wicked perish, the
righteous thrive.

29
Whoever remains stiff-
necked after many rebukes
will suddenly be destroyed —
without remedy.

² When the righteous thrive, the people
rejoice;
when the wicked rule, the people
groan.

³ A man who loves wisdom brings joy to
his father,
but a companion of prostitutes
squanders his wealth.

⁴ By justice a king gives a country
stability,
but those who are greedy for*a* bribes
tear it down.

⁵ Those who flatter their neighbors
are spreading nets for their feet.

⁶ Evildoers are snared by their own sin,
but the righteous shout for joy and
are glad.

⁷ The righteous care about justice for the
poor,
but the wicked have no such
concern.

⁸ Mockers stir up a city,
but the wise turn away anger.

⁹ If a wise person goes to court with a
fool,
the fool rages and scoffs, and there is
no peace.

¹⁰ The bloodthirsty hate a person of
integrity
and seek to kill the upright.

¹¹ Fools give full vent to their rage,
but the wise bring calm in the end.

¹² If a ruler listens to lies,
all his officials become wicked.

¹³ The poor and the oppressor have this in
common:
The LORD gives sight to the eyes of
both.

¹⁴ If a king judges the poor with fairness,
his throne will be established
forever.

---

a 4 Or *who give*

15 A rod and a reprimand impart wisdom,
  but a child left undisciplined
    disgraces its mother.

16 When the wicked thrive, so does sin,
  but the righteous will see their
    downfall.

17 Discipline your children, and they will
    give you peace;
  they will bring you the delights you
    desire.

18 Where there is no revelation, people
    cast off restraint;
  but blessed is the one who heeds
    wisdom's instruction.

19 Servants cannot be corrected by mere
    words;
  though they understand, they will
    not respond.

20 Do you see someone who speaks in
    haste?

There is more hope for a fool than for
    them.

21 A servant pampered from youth
  will turn out to be insolent.

22 An angry person stirs up conflict,
  and a hot-tempered person commits
    many sins.

23 Pride brings a person low,
  but the lowly in spirit gain honor.

24 The accomplices of thieves are their
    own enemies;
  they are put under oath and dare not
    testify.

25 Fear of man will prove to be a snare,
  but whoever trusts in the LORD is
    kept safe.

26 Many seek an audience with a ruler,
  but it is from the LORD that one gets
    justice.

POWERLESS LESSON [*Principle One*]

This is the first page of the POWERLESS lesson.

For a discussion of Principles One through Eight and a listing of their related lessons,
go to pages xvii – xliv.

Pride brings a person low, but the lowly in spirit gain honor.

Proverbs 29:23

The power to change comes only through God's grace. Principle One states: "Realize I'm not God. I admit that I'm powerless to control my tendency to do the wrong thing and that my life has become unmanageable." If we admit that we're powerless, we recognize our need for a power greater than ourselves to restore us. That power is our Higher Power, the one and only true Higher Power, Jesus Christ.

In Principle One we discover that we're POWERLESS to control our own lives and that our lives have become unmanageable. As we work this principle we find that we can be freed of nine "serenity robbers." The first letter in POWERLESS is *P*, which stands for PRIDE. We start to see that we no longer have to be trapped by our pride. Ignorance + power + pride = a deadly mixture. Our false pride undermines our faith and cuts us off from God and others. When we welcome God's presence, we leave no room for pride because he makes us aware of our true selves.

The next letter in POWERLESS is *O*. Go to Luke 12:2 – 3 (page 1264).

27 The righteous detest the dishonest;
    the wicked detest the upright.

Sayings of Agur

30 The sayings of Agur son of Ja-
keh — an inspired utterance.

This man's utterance to Ithiel:

"I am weary, God,
    but I can prevail.*a*
2 Surely I am only a brute, not a man;
    I do not have human understanding.
3 I have not learned wisdom,
    nor have I attained to the knowledge
      of the Holy One.
4 Who has gone up to heaven and come
    down?
    Whose hands have gathered up the
      wind?

Who has wrapped up the waters in a
    cloak?
Who has established all the ends of
    the earth?
What is his name, and what is the name
    of his son?
    Surely you know!

5 "Every word of God is flawless;
    he is a shield to those who take refuge
      in him.
6 Do not add to his words,
    or he will rebuke you and prove you a
      liar.

7 "Two things I ask of you, LORD;
    do not refuse me before I die:
8 Keep falsehood and lies far from me;
    give me neither poverty nor riches,
    but give me only my daily bread.

---

a 1 With a different word division of the Hebrew; Masoretic Text *utterance to Ithiel, / to Ithiel and Ukal:*

SANITY LESSON [*Principle Two*]

For the previous entry in the SANITY lesson, go to 3 John 4 (page 1565).

For a discussion of Principles One through Eight and a listing of their related lessons,
go to pages xvii – xliv.

Fear of man will prove to be a snare, but whoever trusts in the LORD is kept safe.

PROVERBS 29:25

In Principle Two we earnestly believe that God exists, that we matter to him and that he has the power to help us recover. It's in this principle that we find the SANITY to begin to stop making the same poor choices again and again.

The *T* in SANITY stands for TRUST. As we work Principle Two, we begin to trust in our relationship with our Higher Power, Jesus Christ, as well as our relationships with others. We begin to make real friends in our recovery, in our groups and in our church. These relationships are of a totally different quality than our past associations with acquaintances and fair-weather friends whom we knew while we were active in our addictions and compulsions. In recovery we find brothers and sisters in Christ, people who are willing to walk beside us on our journey through the principles — friends we can trust, with whom we can share and whose encouragement helps us mutually grow in Christ.

The last letter in SANITY is *Y*. Go to Romans 5:8 (page 1395).

❶
❷
❸

⁹ Otherwise, I may have too much and
    disown you
    and say, 'Who is the LORD?'
Or I may become poor and steal,
    and so dishonor the name of my God.

¹⁰ "Do not slander a servant to their master,
    or they will curse you, and you will
    pay for it.

¹¹ "There are those who curse their fathers
    and do not bless their mothers;
¹² those who are pure in their own eyes
    and yet are not cleansed of their filth;
¹³ those whose eyes are ever so haughty,
    whose glances are so disdainful;
¹⁴ those whose teeth are swords
    and whose jaws are set with knives
to devour the poor from the earth
    and the needy from among mankind.

¹⁵ "The leech has two daughters.
    'Give! Give!' they cry.

"There are three things that are never
    satisfied,
    four that never say, 'Enough!':
¹⁶ the grave, the barren womb,
    land, which is never satisfied with
    water,
    and fire, which never says, 'Enough!'

¹⁷ "The eye that mocks a father,
    that scorns an aged mother,
will be pecked out by the ravens of the
    valley,
    will be eaten by the vultures.

¹⁸ "There are three things that are too
    amazing for me,
    four that I do not understand:
¹⁹ the way of an eagle in the sky,
    the way of a snake on a rock,
the way of a ship on the high seas,
    and the way of a man with a young
    woman.

²⁰ "This is the way of an adulterous
    woman:
    She eats and wipes her mouth
    and says, 'I've done nothing wrong.'

²¹ "Under three things the earth trembles,
    under four it cannot bear up:
²² a servant who becomes king,
    a godless fool who gets plenty to eat,
²³ a contemptible woman who gets
    married,
    and a servant who displaces her
    mistress.

²⁴ "Four things on earth are small,
    yet they are extremely wise:
²⁵ Ants are creatures of little strength,
    yet they store up their food in the
    summer;
²⁶ hyraxes are creatures of little power,
    yet they make their home in the crags;
²⁷ locusts have no king,
    yet they advance together in ranks;
²⁸ a lizard can be caught with the hand,
    yet it is found in kings' palaces.

²⁹ "There are three things that are stately
    in their stride,
    four that move with stately bearing:
³⁰ a lion, mighty among beasts,
    who retreats before nothing;
³¹ a strutting rooster, a he-goat,
    and a king secure against revolt.ᵃ

³² "If you play the fool and exalt yourself,
    or if you plan evil,
    clap your hand over your mouth!
³³ For as churning cream produces butter,
    and as twisting the nose produces
    blood,
    so stirring up anger produces strife."

Sayings of King Lemuel

31 The sayings of King Lemuel—
an inspired utterance his mother taught him.

² Listen, my son! Listen, son of my
    womb!
    Listen, my son, the answer to my
    prayers!
³ Do not spend your strengthᵇ on
    women,
    your vigor on those who ruin kings.

ᵃ 31 The meaning of the Hebrew for this phrase is uncertain.   ᵇ 3 Or *wealth*

⁴It is not for kings, Lemuel —
  it is not for kings to drink wine,
  not for rulers to crave beer,
⁵lest they drink and forget what has been
    decreed,
  and deprive all the oppressed of their
    rights.
⁶Let beer be for those who are perishing,
  wine for those who are in anguish!
⁷Let them drink and forget their poverty
  and remember their misery no more.

⁸Speak up for those who cannot speak
    for themselves,
  for the rights of all who are destitute.
⁹Speak up and judge fairly;
  defend the rights of the poor and
    needy.

Epilogue: The Wife of Noble Character

¹⁰ᵃA wife of noble character who can find?
  She is worth far more than rubies.
¹¹Her husband has full confidence in her
  and lacks nothing of value.
¹²She brings him good, not harm,
  all the days of her life.
¹³She selects wool and flax
  and works with eager hands.
¹⁴She is like the merchant ships,
  bringing her food from afar.
¹⁵She gets up while it is still night;
  she provides food for her family
  and portions for her female servants.
¹⁶She considers a field and buys it;
  out of her earnings she plants a
    vineyard.
¹⁷She sets about her work vigorously;
  her arms are strong for her tasks.
¹⁸She sees that her trading is profitable,
  and her lamp does not go out at
    night.

¹⁹In her hand she holds the distaff
  and grasps the spindle with her
    fingers.
²⁰She opens her arms to the poor
  and extends her hands to the needy.
²¹When it snows, she has no fear for her
    household;
  for all of them are clothed in
    scarlet.
²²She makes coverings for her bed;
  she is clothed in fine linen and
    purple.
²³Her husband is respected at the city
    gate,
  where he takes his seat among the
    elders of the land.
²⁴She makes linen garments and sells
    them,
  and supplies the merchants with
    sashes.
²⁵She is clothed with strength and
    dignity;
  she can laugh at the days to come.
²⁶She speaks with wisdom,
  and faithful instruction is on her
    tongue.
²⁷She watches over the affairs of her
    household
  and does not eat the bread of
    idleness.
²⁸Her children arise and call her blessed;
  her husband also, and he praises her:
²⁹"Many women do noble things,
  but you surpass them all."
³⁰Charm is deceptive, and beauty is
    fleeting;
  but a woman who fears the LORD is
    to be praised.
³¹Honor her for all that her hands have
    done,
  and let her works bring her praise at
    the city gate.

ᵃ 10 Verses 10-31 are an acrostic poem, the verses of which begin with the successive letters of the Hebrew alphabet.

Ecclesiastes

THEME: Life is meaningless without God. Because humans can't fathom God's purposes or understand his ways, submission to him is the best course of action, especially in view of God's final judgment of "every hidden thing" (Ecclesiastes 12:14).

AUTHOR: Though the author refers to himself only as "the Teacher," Solomon has traditionally been credited with the writing of Ecclesiastes. Some suggest that a wise man collected these perspectives as a tool for his son's instruction, while others propose Ezra as a possible author.

DATE OF WRITING: If Solomon was the author of Ecclesiastes, the book may have been written during his period of apostasy (see 1 Kings 11) or shortly afterward (approximately 935 BC). Those who suggest Ezra as the author place its composition during the period of the Babylonian exile or the return to the land (approximately 450 BC).

ENCOURAGEMENT FROM ECCLESIASTES: "Banish anxiety from your heart and cast off the troubles of your body" (Ecclesiastes 11:10).

CHALLENGE FROM ECCLESIASTES: "Remember your Creator in the days of your youth, before the days of trouble come and the years approach when you will say, 'I find no pleasure in them' " (Ecclesiastes 12:1).

REFLECTION FROM ECCLESIASTES: "God will bring every deed into judgment, including every hidden thing, whether it is good or evil" (Ecclesiastes 12:14).

The book of Ecclesiastes records an intense search for meaning and satisfaction, especially in view of the injustice and apparent futility of life. Ecclesiastes recognizes that much of what happens in life is outside our control. This book presents a necessary perspective: Much of what happens in life is beyond our understanding and defies quick, easy solutions.

In Ecclesiastes, as in Celebrate Recovery, this means that our wisest course of action is to be forward looking. We need to start right where we are, learn to fear God and rest in the knowledge that everything we do for him has eternal significance. Recovery doesn't require that we completely understand all the issues. It simply requires the faith needed to take one step at a time in the application of Biblical principles to our lives. These steps are a means to prepare us to serve God, not a humanly devised path to self-improvement. When we choose to give back to God in selfless service, our lives are no longer meaningless. We continue to heal as we point more and more people to Christ.

Everything Is Meaningless

1 The words of the Teacher,*a* son of David, king in Jerusalem:

2 "Meaningless! Meaningless!"
   says the Teacher.
  "Utterly meaningless!
   Everything is meaningless."

3 What do people gain from all their
      labors
   at which they toil under the sun?
4 Generations come and generations go,
   but the earth remains forever.
5 The sun rises and the sun sets,
   and hurries back to where it rises.
6 The wind blows to the south
   and turns to the north;
 round and round it goes,
   ever returning on its course.
7 All streams flow into the sea,
   yet the sea is never full.
 To the place the streams come from,
   there they return again.
8 All things are wearisome,
   more than one can say.
 The eye never has enough of seeing,
   nor the ear its fill of hearing.
9 What has been will be again,
   what has been done will be done
      again;
   there is nothing new under the sun.
10 Is there anything of which one can say,
   "Look! This is something new"?
 It was here already, long ago;
   it was here before our time.
11 No one remembers the former
      generations,
   and even those yet to come
 will not be remembered
   by those who follow them.

Wisdom Is Meaningless

12 I, the Teacher, was king over Israel in Jerusalem. 13 I applied my mind to study and to explore by wisdom all that is done under the heavens. What a heavy burden God has laid on mankind! 14 I have seen all the things that are done under the sun; all of them are meaningless, a chasing after the wind.

15 What is crooked cannot be
      straightened;
   what is lacking cannot be counted.

16 I said to myself, "Look, I have increased in wisdom more than anyone who has ruled over Jerusalem before me; I have experienced much of wisdom and knowledge." 17 Then I applied myself to the understanding of wisdom, and also of madness and folly, but I learned that this, too, is a chasing after the wind.

18 For with much wisdom comes much
      sorrow;
   the more knowledge, the more grief.

Pleasures Are Meaningless

2 I said to myself, "Come now, I will test you with pleasure to find out what is good." But that also proved to be meaningless. 2 "Laughter," I said, "is madness. And what does pleasure accomplish?" 3 I tried cheering myself with wine, and embracing folly — my mind still guiding me with wisdom. I wanted to see what was good for people to do under the heavens during the few days of their lives.

4 I undertook great projects: I built houses for myself and planted vineyards. 5 I made gardens and parks and planted all kinds of fruit trees in them. 6 I made reservoirs to water groves of flourishing trees. 7 I bought male and female slaves and had other slaves who were born in my house. I also owned more herds and flocks than anyone in Jerusalem before me. 8 I amassed silver and gold for myself, and the treasure of kings and provinces. I acquired male and female singers, and a harem*b* as well — the delights of a man's heart. 9 I became greater by far than anyone in Jerusalem before me. In all this my wisdom stayed with me.

---

a 1 Or *the leader of the assembly*; also in verses 2 and 12 uncertain.   *b* 8 The meaning of the Hebrew for this phrase is

¹⁰I denied myself nothing my eyes
 desired;
 I refused my heart no pleasure.
My heart took delight in all my labor,
 and this was the reward for all my toil.
¹¹Yet when I surveyed all that my hands
 had done
 and what I had toiled to achieve,
everything was meaningless, a chasing
 after the wind;
 nothing was gained under the sun.

Wisdom and Folly Are Meaningless

¹²Then I turned my thoughts to consider
 wisdom,
 and also madness and folly.
What more can the king's successor do
 than what has already been done?
¹³I saw that wisdom is better than folly,
 just as light is better than darkness.
¹⁴The wise have eyes in their heads,
 while the fool walks in the darkness;
but I came to realize
 that the same fate overtakes them
 both.

¹⁵Then I said to myself,

"The fate of the fool will overtake me
 also.
 What then do I gain by being wise?"
I said to myself,
 "This too is meaningless."
¹⁶For the wise, like the fool, will not be
 long remembered;
 the days have already come when
 both have been forgotten.
Like the fool, the wise too must die!

Toil Is Meaningless

¹⁷So I hated life, because the work that
is done under the sun was grievous to me.
All of it is meaningless, a chasing after the
wind. ¹⁸I hated all the things I had toiled for
under the sun, because I must leave them
to the one who comes after me. ¹⁹And who
knows whether that person will be wise or
foolish? Yet they will have control over all
the fruit of my toil into which I have poured
my effort and skill under the sun. This too

is meaningless. ²⁰So my heart began to despair over all my toilsome labor under the
sun. ²¹For a person may labor with wisdom, knowledge and skill, and then they
must leave all they own to another who has
not toiled for it. This too is meaningless
and a great misfortune. ²²What do people
get for all the toil and anxious striving with
which they labor under the sun? ²³All their
days their work is grief and pain; even at
night their minds do not rest. This too is
meaningless.

²⁴A person can do nothing better than
to eat and drink and find satisfaction in
their own toil. This too, I see, is from the
hand of God, ²⁵for without him, who can
eat or find enjoyment? ²⁶To the person who
pleases him, God gives wisdom, knowledge
and happiness, but to the sinner he gives
the task of gathering and storing up wealth
to hand it over to the one who pleases God.
This too is meaningless, a chasing after the
wind.

A Time for Everything

3 There is a time for everything,
 and a season for every activity
  under the heavens:

² a time to be born and a time to die,
 a time to plant and a time to uproot,
³ a time to kill and a time to heal,
 a time to tear down and a time to
  build,
⁴ a time to weep and a time to laugh,
 a time to mourn and a time to dance,
⁵ a time to scatter stones and a time to
  gather them,
 a time to embrace and a time to
  refrain from embracing,
⁶ a time to search and a time to
  give up,
 a time to keep and a time to throw
  away,
⁷ a time to tear and a time to mend,
 a time to be silent and a time to
  speak,
⁸ a time to love and a time to hate,
 a time for war and a time for peace.

⁹What do workers gain from their toil? ¹⁰I have seen the burden God has laid on the human race. ¹¹He has made everything beautiful in its time. He has also set eternity in the human heart; yet*a* no one can fathom what God has done from beginning to end. ¹²I know that there is nothing better for people than to be happy and to do good while they live. ¹³That each of them may eat and drink, and find satisfaction in all their toil — this is the gift of God. ¹⁴I know that everything God does will endure forever; nothing can be added to it and nothing taken from it. God does it so that people will fear him.

¹⁵Whatever is has already been,
    and what will be has been before;
    and God will call the past to account.*b*

¹⁶And I saw something else under the sun:

In the place of judgment — wickedness
        was there,
    in the place of justice — wickedness
        was there.

¹⁷I said to myself,

"God will bring into judgment
    both the righteous and the wicked,
for there will be a time for every
        activity,
    a time to judge every deed."

¹⁸I also said to myself, "As for humans, God tests them so that they may see that they are like the animals. ¹⁹Surely the fate of human beings is like that of the animals; the same fate awaits them both: As one dies, so dies the other. All have the same breath*c*; humans have no advantage over animals. Everything is meaningless. ²⁰All go to the same place; all come from dust,

---

a 11 Or *also placed ignorance in the human heart, so that*   *b* 15 Or *God calls back the past*   *c* 19 Or *spirit*

AMENDS LESSON [*Principle Six*]

For the previous entry in the AMENDS lesson, go to Luke 6:35 (page 1240).

For a discussion of Principles One through Eight and a listing of their related lessons,
go to pages xvii – xliv.

There is a time for everything, and a season for every activity under the heavens.

ECCLESIASTES 3:1

Principle Six calls for us to evaluate all our relationships and to offer forgiveness to those who have hurt us and make amends for harm we've done to others, except when doing so would injure them or others. We need to be willing to admit our part in our relationships that have been broken or damaged. We begin by making AMENDS for the harm we've caused others.

The *D* in AMENDS cautions us to DO IT AT THE RIGHT TIME. This principle not only requires courage, good judgment and willingness, but a careful sense of timing.

Ecclesiastes 3:1 tells us that there's a time to *let* things happen and a time to make them happen. There's a right time and a wrong time to offer forgiveness or to make amends. Before making amends, we need to pray, asking Jesus Christ for his guidance, his direction and his perfect timing.

The last letter in AMENDS is S. Go to Joel 2:25 (page 1063).

and to dust all return. 21Who knows if the human spirit rises upward and if the spirit of the animal goes down into the earth?"

22So I saw that there is nothing better for a person than to enjoy their work, because that is their lot. For who can bring them to see what will happen after them?

Oppression, Toil, Friendlessness

4 Again I looked and saw all the oppression that was taking place under the sun:

I saw the tears of the oppressed —
  and they have no comforter;
power was on the side of their
      oppressors —
  and they have no comforter.
2And I declared that the dead,
    who had already died,
are happier than the living,
    who are still alive.
3But better than both
    is the one who has never been born,
who has not seen the evil
    that is done under the sun.

4And I saw that all toil and all achievement spring from one person's envy of another. This too is meaningless, a chasing after the wind.

5Fools fold their hands
    and ruin themselves.
6Better one handful with tranquillity
    than two handfuls with toil
    and chasing after the wind.

7Again I saw something meaningless under the sun:

8There was a man all alone;
    he had neither son nor brother.
There was no end to his toil,
    yet his eyes were not content with his
      wealth.
"For whom am I toiling," he asked,
    "and why am I depriving myself of
      enjoyment?"

This too is meaningless —
    a miserable business!

9Two are better than one,
    because they have a good return for
      their labor:
10If either of them falls down,
    one can help the other up.
But pity anyone who falls
    and has no one to help them up.
11Also, if two lie down together, they will
      keep warm.
    But how can one keep warm alone?
12Though one may be overpowered,
    two can defend themselves.
A cord of three strands is not quickly
    broken.

Advancement Is Meaningless

13Better a poor but wise youth than an old but foolish king who no longer knows how to heed a warning. 14The youth may have come from prison to the kingship, or he may have been born in poverty within his kingdom. 15I saw that all who lived and walked under the sun followed the youth, the king's successor. 16There was no end to all the people who were before them. But those who came later were not pleased with the successor. This too is meaningless, a chasing after the wind.

Fulfill Your Vow to God

5 a Guard your steps when you go to the house of God. Go near to listen rather than to offer the sacrifice of fools, who do not know that they do wrong.

2Do not be quick with your mouth,
    do not be hasty in your heart
    to utter anything before God.
God is in heaven
    and you are on earth,
    so let your words be few.
3A dream comes when there are many
      cares,
    and many words mark the speech of
      a fool.

---

a In Hebrew texts 5:1 is numbered 4:17, and 5:2-20 is numbered 5:1-19.

4When you make a vow to God, do not delay to fulfill it. He has no pleasure in fools; fulfill your vow. 5It is better not to make a vow than to make one and not fulfill it. 6Do not let your mouth lead you into sin. And do not protest to the temple messenger, "My vow was a mistake." Why should God be angry at what you say and destroy the work of your hands? 7Much dreaming and many words are meaningless. Therefore fear God.

Riches Are Meaningless

8If you see the poor oppressed in a district, and justice and rights denied, do not be surprised at such things; for one official is eyed by a higher one, and over them both are others higher still. 9The increase from the land is taken by all; the king himself profits from the fields.

10Whoever loves money never has
    enough;
  whoever loves wealth is never
    satisfied with their income.
  This too is meaningless.

11As goods increase,
  so do those who consume them.
And what benefit are they to the owners
  except to feast their eyes on them?

SPONSOR LESSON [*Principle Four*]

For the previous entry in the SPONSOR lesson, go to Proverbs 20:5 (page 764).

For a discussion of Principles One through Eight and a listing of their related lessons,
go to pages xvii – xliv.

*Two are better than one, because they have a good return
for their labor: If either of them falls down, one can
help the other up. But pity anyone who falls and has
no one to help them up ... Though one may be overpowered,
two can defend themselves. A cord of three
strands is not quickly broken.*

ECCLESIASTES 4:9 – 10, 12

Principle Four begins the process of "coming clean." It's here that we openly examine and confess our faults to ourselves, to God and to someone else we trust. In order to work this principle, we need to have an accountability relationship established.

There are three reasons why we need a sponsor and/or an accountability partner. The second reason is: *Having someone fill this critical role for us is Biblical.* Ecclesiastes 4:9 – 10, 12 tells us that we're better together. We need others in our recovery to come alongside us and hold us accountable. That way, if we fall down, someone will be there to help us up. We need someone else of the same sex as ourselves whom we can trust to keep us balanced during this process. We need encouragement from someone else who will support our progress.

Proverbs 27:17 points out that "as iron sharpens iron, so one person sharpens another." The phrase "one another" is used in the New Testament over 50 times.

For the third reason why we need a sponsor and/or an accountability partner,
go to Ecclesiastes 7:5 (page 789).

GIVE LESSON [*Principle Eight*]

For the previous entry in the GIVE lesson, go to Romans 8:32 (page 1402).

For a discussion of Principles One through Eight and a listing of their related lessons, go to pages xvii – xliv.

> Two are better than one, because they have a good return
> for their labor: If either of them falls down, one can
> help the other up. But pity anyone who falls and has
> no one to help them up … Though one may be overpowered,
> two can defend themselves. A cord of three
> strands is not quickly broken.
>
> ECCLESIASTES 4:9 – 10, 12

Major, miraculous progress and growth have occurred in our lives since we started our recovery program, way back when we began working Principle One. We've stepped out of our denial into God's grace. We've taken an honest, spiritual inventory. We've worked on getting right with God, ourselves and others, and we've grown in our relationship with Christ. We've discovered a new way to live life, and we're finding the serenity we've always been seeking. But the most exciting part is yet to come — Principle Eight: "Yield myself to God to be used by him to bring this good news to others, both through my example and through my words."

Principle Eight is the "giving back" principle. Matthew 10:8 offers a reminder and an instruction: "Freely you have received; freely give." The *I* in GIVE reminds us that when we give, I BECOMES WE. Notice that none of the Christ-centered 12 steps begin with the word *I*. Already in Step One, the very first word is *We*. In fact, the word *we* appears in the 12 steps no fewer than 14 times. The word *I* never appears even once in any of these steps. The road to recovery isn't meant to be traveled alone. This isn't a program to be worked in isolation.

> Jesus replied: "Love the Lord your God with all your heart
> and with all your soul and with all your mind."
> This is the first and greatest commandment. And the second is like it:
> "Love your neighbor as yourself." All the Law and the
> Prophets hang on these two commandments.
>
> MATTHEW 22:37 – 40

When we've reached this principle in our recovery and someone asks us to be their sponsor or accountability partner, we need to agree. The rewards are great, and serving on someone else's behalf in either of these roles is a wonderful way to carry on the message.

The above verses from Ecclesiastes 4 make the concept "we're better together" crystal clear.

The next letter in GIVE is *V*. Go to 2 Corinthians 1:3 – 4 (page 1438).

¹²The sleep of a laborer is sweet,
  whether they eat little or much,
but as for the rich, their abundance
    permits them no sleep.

¹³I have seen a grievous evil under the
sun:

  wealth hoarded to the harm of its
      owners,
¹⁴   or wealth lost through some
        misfortune,
  so that when they have children
      there is nothing left for them to
        inherit.
¹⁵Everyone comes naked from their
        mother's womb,
    and as everyone comes, so they
        depart.
  They take nothing from their toil
      that they can carry in their hands.

¹⁶This too is a grievous evil:

  As everyone comes, so they depart,
      and what do they gain,
    since they toil for the wind?
¹⁷All their days they eat in darkness,
    with great frustration, affliction and
        anger.

¹⁸This is what I have observed to be
good: that it is appropriate for a person
to eat, to drink and to find satisfaction in
their toilsome labor under the sun during
the few days of life God has given them—
for this is their lot. ¹⁹Moreover, when God
gives someone wealth and possessions, and
the ability to enjoy them, to accept their lot
and be happy in their toil—this is a gift of
God. ²⁰They seldom reflect on the days of
their life, because God keeps them occupied with gladness of heart.

6 I have seen another evil under
the sun, and it weighs heavily on
mankind: ²God gives some people
wealth, possessions and honor, so that they
lack nothing their hearts desire, but God
does not grant them the ability to enjoy
them, and strangers enjoy them instead.
This is meaningless, a grievous evil.

³A man may have a hundred children
and live many years; yet no matter how
long he lives, if he cannot enjoy his prosperity and does not receive proper burial,
I say that a stillborn child is better off than
he. ⁴It comes without meaning, it departs
in darkness, and in darkness its name is
shrouded. ⁵Though it never saw the sun or
knew anything, it has more rest than does
that man— ⁶even if he lives a thousand
years twice over but fails to enjoy his prosperity. Do not all go to the same place?

⁷Everyone's toil is for their mouth,
    yet their appetite is never satisfied.
⁸What advantage have the wise over
        fools?
  What do the poor gain
    by knowing how to conduct
        themselves before others?
⁹Better what the eye sees
    than the roving of the appetite.
  This too is meaningless,
      a chasing after the wind.
¹⁰Whatever exists has already been
        named,
    and what humanity is has been
        known;
  no one can contend
      with someone who is stronger.
¹¹The more the words,
      the less the meaning,
    and how does that profit anyone?

¹²For who knows what is good for a person in life, during the few and meaningless
days they pass through like a shadow? Who
can tell them what will happen under the
sun after they are gone?

Wisdom

7 A good name is better than fine
        perfume,
    and the day of death better than the
        day of birth.
²It is better to go to a house of mourning
    than to go to a house of feasting,
  for death is the destiny of everyone;
    the living should take this to heart.

3 Frustration is better than laughter,
  because a sad face is good for the
    heart.
4 The heart of the wise is in the house of
    mourning,
  but the heart of fools is in the house
    of pleasure.
5 It is better to heed the rebuke of a wise
    person
  than to listen to the song of fools.
6 Like the crackling of thorns under the
    pot,
  so is the laughter of fools.
  This too is meaningless.

7 Extortion turns a wise person into a
    fool,
  and a bribe corrupts the heart.

8 The end of a matter is better than its
    beginning,
  and patience is better than pride.

9 Do not be quickly provoked in your
    spirit,
  for anger resides in the lap of fools.

10 Do not say, "Why were the old days
    better than these?"
  For it is not wise to ask such
    questions.

11 Wisdom, like an inheritance, is a good
    thing
  and benefits those who see the sun.
12 Wisdom is a shelter
    as money is a shelter,
  but the advantage of knowledge is this:
    Wisdom preserves those who have it.

13 Consider what God has done:

  Who can straighten
    what he has made crooked?
14 When times are good, be happy;
  but when times are bad, consider this:

① ② ③

SPONSOR LESSON [*Principle Four*]

For the previous entry in the SPONSOR lesson, go to Ecclesiastes 4:9 – 12 (page 786).

For a discussion of Principles One through Eight and a listing of their related lessons, go to pages xvii – xliv.

It is better to heed the rebuke of a wise person than to listen to the song of fools.

ECCLESIASTES 7:5

Principle Four begins the process of "coming clean." It's here that we openly examine and confess our faults to ourselves, to God and to someone else we trust. In order to work this principle, we need to have an accountability relationship established.

There are three reasons why we need a sponsor and/or an accountability partner. The third reason is: *Having someone to fill this role for us is our best safeguard against relapse.* By providing feedback to keep us on track, a sponsor and/or an accountability partner can see our old dysfunctional, self-defeating patterns beginning to resurface and quickly point them out to us. Our sponsor and/or accountability partner can confront us with truth and love without covering us with shame or guilt.

Ecclesiastes 7:5 tells us that it's better to receive criticism from a wise person than praise from a fool. We need to guard our hearts from falling into the trap of being ruined by praise rather than being saved by constructive criticism.

This is the final page of the SPONSOR lesson.

God has made the one
    as well as the other.
Therefore, no one can discover
    anything about their future.

¹⁵In this meaningless life of mine I have
seen both of these:

the righteous perishing in their
        righteousness,
    and the wicked living long in their
        wickedness.
¹⁶Do not be overrighteous,
    neither be overwise—
    why destroy yourself?
¹⁷Do not be overwicked,
    and do not be a fool—
    why die before your time?
¹⁸It is good to grasp the one
    and not let go of the other.
    Whoever fears God will avoid all
        extremes.ᵃ

¹⁹Wisdom makes one wise person more
        powerful
    than ten rulers in a city.

²⁰Indeed, there is no one on earth who is
        righteous,
    no one who does what is right and
        never sins.

²¹Do not pay attention to every word
        people say,
    or you may hear your servant cursing
        you—
²²for you know in your heart
    that many times you yourself have
        cursed others.

²³All this I tested by wisdom and I said,

"I am determined to be wise"—
    but this was beyond me.
²⁴Whatever exists is far off and most
        profound—
    who can discover it?
²⁵So I turned my mind to understand,
    to investigate and to search out
        wisdom and the scheme of things

and to understand the stupidity of
        wickedness
    and the madness of folly.

²⁶I find more bitter than death
    the woman who is a snare,
whose heart is a trap
    and whose hands are chains.
The man who pleases God will escape
        her,
    but the sinner she will ensnare.

²⁷"Look," says the Teacher,ᵇ "this is what
I have discovered:

"Adding one thing to another to
        discover the scheme of
        things—
²⁸   while I was still searching
    but not finding—
I found one upright man among a
        thousand,
    but not one upright woman among
        them all.
²⁹This only have I found:
    God created mankind upright,
    but they have gone in search of many
        schemes."

8   Who is like the wise?
    Who knows the explanation of
        things?
A person's wisdom brightens their
        face
    and changes its hard appearance.

Obey the King

²Obey the king's command, I say, because you took an oath before God. ³Do
not be in a hurry to leave the king's presence. Do not stand up for a bad cause,
for he will do whatever he pleases. ⁴Since
a king's word is supreme, who can say to
him, "What are you doing?"

⁵Whoever obeys his command will
        come to no harm,
    and the wise heart will know the
        proper time and procedure.

ᵃ 18 Or will follow them both   ᵇ 27 Or the leader of the assembly

⁶For there is a proper time and
    procedure for every matter,
  though a person may be weighed
    down by misery.

⁷Since no one knows the future,
  who can tell someone else what is to
    come?
⁸As no one has power over the wind to
    contain it,
  so*ᵃ* no one has power over the time of
    their death.
As no one is discharged in time of war,
  so wickedness will not release those
    who practice it.

⁹All this I saw, as I applied my mind to everything done under the sun. There is a time when a man lords it over others to his own*ᵇ* hurt. ¹⁰Then too, I saw the wicked buried—those who used to come and go from the holy place and receive praise*ᶜ* in the city where they did this. This too is meaningless.

¹¹When the sentence for a crime is not quickly carried out, people's hearts are filled with schemes to do wrong. ¹²Although a wicked person who commits a hundred crimes may live a long time, I know that it will go better with those who fear God, who are reverent before him. ¹³Yet because the wicked do not fear God, it will not go well with them, and their days will not lengthen like a shadow.

¹⁴There is something else meaningless that occurs on earth: the righteous who get what the wicked deserve, and the wicked who get what the righteous deserve. This too, I say, is meaningless. ¹⁵So I commend the enjoyment of life, because there is nothing better for a person under the sun than to eat and drink and be glad. Then joy will accompany them in their toil all the days of the life God has given them under the sun.

¹⁶When I applied my mind to know wisdom and to observe the labor that is done

on earth—people getting no sleep day or night—¹⁷then I saw all that God has done. No one can comprehend what goes on under the sun. Despite all their efforts to search it out, no one can discover its meaning. Even if the wise claim they know, they cannot really comprehend it.

A Common Destiny for All

9 So I reflected on all this and concluded that the righteous and the wise and what they do are in God's hands, but no one knows whether love or hate awaits them. ²All share a common destiny—the righteous and the wicked, the good and the bad,*ᵈ* the clean and the unclean, those who offer sacrifices and those who do not.

As it is with the good,
  so with the sinful;
as it is with those who take oaths,
  so with those who are afraid to take
    them.

³This is the evil in everything that happens under the sun: The same destiny overtakes all. The hearts of people, moreover, are full of evil and there is madness in their hearts while they live, and afterward they join the dead. ⁴Anyone who is among the living has hope*ᵉ*—even a live dog is better off than a dead lion!

⁵For the living know that they will die,
  but the dead know nothing;
they have no further reward,
  and even their name is forgotten.
⁶Their love, their hate
  and their jealousy have long since
    vanished;
never again will they have a part
  in anything that happens under the
    sun.

⁷Go, eat your food with gladness, and drink your wine with a joyful heart, for

---

ᵃ 8 Or *over the human spirit to retain it, / and so*   *ᵇ 9* Or *to their*   *ᶜ 10* Some Hebrew manuscripts and Septuagint (Aquila); most Hebrew manuscripts *and are forgotten*   *ᵈ 2* Septuagint (Aquila), Vulgate and Syriac; Hebrew does not have *and the bad.*   *ᵉ 4* Or *What then is to be chosen? With all who live, there is hope*

God has already approved what you do. [8]Always be clothed in white, and always anoint your head with oil. [9]Enjoy life with your wife, whom you love, all the days of this meaningless life that God has given you under the sun — all your meaningless days. For this is your lot in life and in your toilsome labor under the sun. [10]Whatever your hand finds to do, do it with all your might, for in the realm of the dead, where you are going, there is neither working nor planning nor knowledge nor wisdom.

[11]I have seen something else under the sun:

> The race is not to the swift
>   or the battle to the strong,
> nor does food come to the wise
>   or wealth to the brilliant
>   or favor to the learned;
> but time and chance happen to them
>   all.

[12]Moreover, no one knows when their hour will come:

> As fish are caught in a cruel net,
>   or birds are taken in a snare,
> so people are trapped by evil times
>   that fall unexpectedly upon them.

Wisdom Better Than Folly

[13]I also saw under the sun this example of wisdom that greatly impressed me: [14]There was once a small city with only a few people in it. And a powerful king came against it, surrounded it and built huge siege works against it. [15]Now there lived in that city a man poor but wise, and he saved the city by his wisdom. But nobody remembered that poor man. [16]So I said, "Wisdom is better than strength." But the poor man's wisdom is despised, and his words are no longer heeded.

> [17]The quiet words of the wise are more to
>   be heeded
>   than the shouts of a ruler of fools.
> [18]Wisdom is better than weapons of war,
>   but one sinner destroys much good.

10

> As dead flies give perfume a
>   bad smell,
>   so a little folly outweighs
>   wisdom and honor.
> [2]The heart of the wise inclines to the
>   right,
>   but the heart of the fool to the left.
> [3]Even as fools walk along the road,
>   they lack sense
>   and show everyone how stupid they
>   are.
> [4]If a ruler's anger rises against you,
>   do not leave your post;
>   calmness can lay great offenses to
>   rest.

> [5]There is an evil I have seen under the sun,
>   the sort of error that arises from a
>   ruler:
> [6]Fools are put in many high positions,
>   while the rich occupy the low ones.
> [7]I have seen slaves on horseback,
>   while princes go on foot like slaves.

> [8]Whoever digs a pit may fall into it;
>   whoever breaks through a wall may
>   be bitten by a snake.
> [9]Whoever quarries stones may be
>   injured by them;
>   whoever splits logs may be
>   endangered by them.

> [10]If the ax is dull
>   and its edge unsharpened,
> more strength is needed,
>   but skill will bring success.

> [11]If a snake bites before it is charmed,
>   the charmer receives no fee.

> [12]Words from the mouth of the wise are
>   gracious,
>   but fools are consumed by their own
>   lips.
> [13]At the beginning their words are folly;
>   at the end they are wicked
>   madness —
> [14]   and fools multiply words.

> No one knows what is coming —
>   who can tell someone else what will
>   happen after them?

¹⁵ The toil of fools wearies them;
　　they do not know the way to town.

¹⁶ Woe to the land whose king was a
　　　servant*a*
　　and whose princes feast in the
　　　morning.
¹⁷ Blessed is the land whose king is of
　　　noble birth
　　and whose princes eat at a proper
　　　time —
　　for strength and not for drunkenness.

¹⁸ Through laziness, the rafters sag;
　　because of idle hands, the house leaks.

¹⁹ A feast is made for laughter,
　　wine makes life merry,
　　and money is the answer for
　　　everything.

²⁰ Do not revile the king even in your
　　　thoughts,
　　or curse the rich in your bedroom,
　　because a bird in the sky may carry
　　　your words,
　　and a bird on the wing may report
　　　what you say.

Invest in Many Ventures

11 Ship your grain across the sea;
　　after many days you may
　　receive a return.
² Invest in seven ventures, yes, in eight;
　　you do not know what disaster may
　　　come upon the land.

³ If clouds are full of water,
　　they pour rain on the earth.
　　Whether a tree falls to the south or to
　　　the north,
　　in the place where it falls, there it will
　　　lie.
⁴ Whoever watches the wind will not plant;
　　whoever looks at the clouds will not
　　　reap.

⁵ As you do not know the path of the wind,
　　or how the body is formed*b* in a
　　　mother's womb,

so you cannot understand the work of
　　　God,
　　the Maker of all things.

⁶ Sow your seed in the morning,
　　and at evening let your hands not be
　　　idle,
　　for you do not know which will
　　　succeed,
　　whether this or that,
　　or whether both will do equally well.

Remember Your Creator While Young

⁷ Light is sweet,
　　and it pleases the eyes to see the sun.
⁸ However many years anyone may live,
　　let them enjoy them all.
　　But let them remember the days of
　　　darkness,
　　for there will be many.
　　Everything to come is meaningless.

⁹ You who are young, be happy while you
　　　are young,
　　and let your heart give you joy in the
　　　days of your youth.
　　Follow the ways of your heart
　　and whatever your eyes see,
　　but know that for all these things
　　　God will bring you into judgment.
¹⁰ So then, banish anxiety from your
　　　heart
　　and cast off the troubles of your
　　　body,
　　for youth and vigor are meaningless.

12 Remember your Creator
　　in the days of your youth,
　　before the days of trouble come
　　and the years approach when you
　　　will say,
　　"I find no pleasure in them" —
² before the sun and the light
　　and the moon and the stars grow
　　　dark,
　　and the clouds return after the rain;
³ when the keepers of the house tremble,
　　and the strong men stoop,

---

a 16 Or *king is a child*　　*b 5* Or *know how life* (or *the spirit*) / *enters the body being formed*

when the grinders cease because they
    are few,
  and those looking through the
    windows grow dim;
[4] when the doors to the street are closed
  and the sound of grinding fades;
when people rise up at the sound of birds,
  but all their songs grow faint;
[5] when people are afraid of heights
  and of dangers in the streets;
when the almond tree blossoms
  and the grasshopper drags itself
    along
  and desire no longer is stirred.
Then people go to their eternal home
  and mourners go about the streets.

[6] Remember him — before the silver cord
    is severed,
  and the golden bowl is broken;
before the pitcher is shattered at the
    spring,
  and the wheel broken at the well,
[7] and the dust returns to the ground it
    came from,
  and the spirit returns to God who
    gave it.

[8] "Meaningless! Meaningless!" says the
  Teacher.[a]
  "Everything is meaningless!"

The Conclusion of the Matter

[9] Not only was the Teacher wise, but he also imparted knowledge to the people. He pondered and searched out and set in order many proverbs. [10] The Teacher searched to find just the right words, and what he wrote was upright and true.

[11] The words of the wise are like goads, their collected sayings like firmly embedded nails — given by one shepherd.[b] [12] Be warned, my son, of anything in addition to them.

Of making many books there is no end, and much study wearies the body.

[13] Now all has been heard;
  here is the conclusion of the matter:
Fear God and keep his commandments,
  for this is the duty of all mankind.
[14] For God will bring every deed into
    judgment,
  including every hidden thing,
  whether it is good or evil.

---

[a] 8 Or *the leader of the assembly*; also in verses 9 and 10   [b] 11 Or *Shepherd*

Song of Songs

THEME: Joy is a dominant note of the Song of Songs, but the reader is also warned that love is a powerful emotion that may bring disappointment.

AUTHOR: Solomon has traditionally been named the author of Song of Songs, primarily based on the phrase "Solomon's Song of Songs" (Song of Songs 1:1), but his authorship isn't certain. Some have suggested that the Song of Songs is a collection of love poems written by various authors but compiled by a single editor.

DATE OF WRITING: Evidence suggests a date of composition during the tenth century BC, which would place the writing during or slightly after Solomon's reign (970 – 930 BC).

ENCOURAGEMENT FROM SONG OF SONGS: "See! The winter is past; the rains are over and gone" (Song of Songs 2:11).

CHALLENGE FROM SONG OF SONGS: "Do not arouse or awaken love until it so desires" (Song of Songs 2:7).

REFLECTION FROM SONG OF SONGS: "Many waters cannot quench love; rivers cannot sweep it away" (Song of Songs 8:7).

The Song of Songs is a love song describing the romance and wedding of a shepherdess and her beloved, as well as the joys and pains of marital love. The Song has been interpreted over generations in many different ways. At the very least, it describes ideal physical love within marriage, although it's clear that the poem also aptly describes the love between Christ and his bride, the church.

For many of us, love has had conditions. We've been loved by a parent or spouse and been warned, "I'll love you *if* . . ." God doesn't put such conditions on his love. He loves us because we're his children, regardless of our past or present. In reading Song of Songs, we see that the growing physical and spiritual intimacy is designed to point toward Christ's love for his church. When we understand just how deeply Jesus loves us, we recognize that our undeniable response is to return that love. In recovery we're given the tools to experience an intimate, unqualified love relationship with our Lord and Savior.

1

Solomon's Song of Songs.

She[a]

2 Let him kiss me with the kisses of his
mouth —
for your love is more delightful than
wine.
3 Pleasing is the fragrance of your
perfumes;
your name is like perfume poured out.
No wonder the young women love
you!
4 Take me away with you — let us hurry!
Let the king bring me into his
chambers.

Friends

We rejoice and delight in you[b];
we will praise your love more than
wine.

She

How right they are to adore you!

5 Dark am I, yet lovely,
daughters of Jerusalem,
dark like the tents of Kedar,
like the tent curtains of Solomon.[c]
6 Do not stare at me because I am dark,
because I am darkened by the sun.
My mother's sons were angry with me
and made me take care of the
vineyards;
my own vineyard I had to neglect.
7 Tell me, you whom I love,
where you graze your flock
and where you rest your sheep at
midday.
Why should I be like a veiled woman
beside the flocks of your friends?

Friends

8 If you do not know, most beautiful of
women,
follow the tracks of the sheep

and graze your young goats
by the tents of the shepherds.

He

9 I liken you, my darling, to a mare
among Pharaoh's chariot horses.
10 Your cheeks are beautiful with earrings,
your neck with strings of jewels.
11 We will make you earrings of gold,
studded with silver.

She

12 While the king was at his table,
my perfume spread its fragrance.
13 My beloved is to me a sachet of myrrh
resting between my breasts.
14 My beloved is to me a cluster of henna
blossoms
from the vineyards of En Gedi.

He

15 How beautiful you are, my darling!
Oh, how beautiful!
Your eyes are doves.

She

16 How handsome you are, my beloved!
Oh, how charming!
And our bed is verdant.

He

17 The beams of our house are cedars;
our rafters are firs.

She[d]

2

I am a rose[e] of Sharon,
a lily of the valleys.

He

2 Like a lily among thorns
is my darling among the young women.

She

3 Like an apple[f] tree among the trees of
the forest
is my beloved among the young men.

---

a The main male and female speakers (identified primarily on the basis of the gender of the relevant Hebrew forms)
are indicated by the captions *He* and *She* respectively. The words of others are marked *Friends*. In some instances the
divisions and their captions are debatable.   *b 4* The Hebrew is masculine singular.   *c 5* Or *Salma*   *d* Or *He*
e 1 Probably a member of the crocus family   *f 3* Or possibly *apricot*; here and elsewhere in Song of Songs

I delight to sit in his shade,
and his fruit is sweet to my taste.
4 Let him lead me to the banquet hall,
and let his banner over me be love.
5 Strengthen me with raisins,
refresh me with apples,
for I am faint with love.
6 His left arm is under my head,
and his right arm embraces me.
7 Daughters of Jerusalem, I charge you
by the gazelles and by the does of the
field:
Do not arouse or awaken love
until it so desires.

8 Listen! My beloved!
Look! Here he comes,
leaping across the mountains,
bounding over the hills.
9 My beloved is like a gazelle or a young
stag.
Look! There he stands behind our wall,
gazing through the windows,
peering through the lattice.
10 My beloved spoke and said to me,
"Arise, my darling,
my beautiful one, come with me.
11 See! The winter is past;
the rains are over and gone.
12 Flowers appear on the earth;
the season of singing has come,
the cooing of doves
is heard in our land.
13 The fig tree forms its early fruit;
the blossoming vines spread their
fragrance.
Arise, come, my darling;
my beautiful one, come with me."

He

14 My dove in the clefts of the rock,
in the hiding places on the
mountainside,
show me your face,
let me hear your voice;
for your voice is sweet,
and your face is lovely.

15 Catch for us the foxes,
the little foxes
that ruin the vineyards,
our vineyards that are in bloom.

She

16 My beloved is mine and I am his;
he browses among the lilies.
17 Until the day breaks
and the shadows flee,
turn, my beloved,
and be like a gazelle
or like a young stag
on the rugged hills.*a*

3 All night long on my bed
I looked for the one my heart loves;
I looked for him but did not find
him.
2 I will get up now and go about the city,
through its streets and squares;
I will search for the one my heart loves.
So I looked for him but did not find
him.
3 The watchmen found me
as they made their rounds in the city.
"Have you seen the one my heart
loves?"
4 Scarcely had I passed them
when I found the one my heart
loves.
I held him and would not let him go
till I had brought him to my mother's
house,
to the room of the one who conceived
me.
5 Daughters of Jerusalem, I charge you
by the gazelles and by the does of the
field:
Do not arouse or awaken love
until it so desires.

6 Who is this coming up from the
wilderness
like a column of smoke,
perfumed with myrrh and incense
made from all the spices of the
merchant?

---

a 17 Or *the hills of Bether*

7 Look! It is Solomon's carriage,
    escorted by sixty warriors,
    the noblest of Israel,
8 all of them wearing the sword,
    all experienced in battle,
  each with his sword at his side,
    prepared for the terrors of the night.
9 King Solomon made for himself the
    carriage;
    he made it of wood from Lebanon.
10 Its posts he made of silver,
    its base of gold.
  Its seat was upholstered with purple,
    its interior inlaid with love.
  Daughters of Jerusalem, 11 come out,
    and look, you daughters of Zion.
  Look*a* on King Solomon wearing a
    crown,
    the crown with which his mother
    crowned him
  on the day of his wedding,
    the day his heart rejoiced.

He

4

  How beautiful you are, my darling!
    Oh, how beautiful!
    Your eyes behind your veil are
    doves.
  Your hair is like a flock of goats
    descending from the hills of Gilead.
2 Your teeth are like a flock of sheep just
    shorn,
    coming up from the washing.
  Each has its twin;
    not one of them is alone.
3 Your lips are like a scarlet ribbon;
    your mouth is lovely.
  Your temples behind your veil
    are like the halves of a pomegranate.
4 Your neck is like the tower of David,
    built with courses of stone*b*;
  on it hang a thousand shields,
    all of them shields of warriors.
5 Your breasts are like two fawns,
    like twin fawns of a gazelle
    that browse among the lilies.

6 Until the day breaks
    and the shadows flee,
  I will go to the mountain of myrrh
    and to the hill of incense.
7 You are altogether beautiful, my
    darling;
    there is no flaw in you.

8 Come with me from Lebanon, my
    bride,
    come with me from Lebanon.
  Descend from the crest of Amana,
    from the top of Senir, the summit of
    Hermon,
  from the lions' dens
    and the mountain haunts of
    leopards.
9 You have stolen my heart, my sister, my
    bride;
    you have stolen my heart
  with one glance of your eyes,
    with one jewel of your necklace.
10 How delightful is your love, my sister,
    my bride!
    How much more pleasing is your love
    than wine,
  and the fragrance of your perfume
    more than any spice!
11 Your lips drop sweetness as the
    honeycomb, my bride;
    milk and honey are under your
    tongue.
  The fragrance of your garments
    is like the fragrance of Lebanon.
12 You are a garden locked up, my sister,
    my bride;
    you are a spring enclosed, a sealed
    fountain.
13 Your plants are an orchard of
    pomegranates
    with choice fruits,
    with henna and nard,
14   nard and saffron,
    calamus and cinnamon,
    with every kind of incense tree,
    with myrrh and aloes
    and all the finest spices.

---

a 10,11 Or *interior lovingly inlaid / by the daughters of Jerusalem. / 11Come out, you daughters of Zion, / and look*
b 4 The meaning of the Hebrew for this phrase is uncertain.

¹⁵You are*a* a garden fountain,
  a well of flowing water
  streaming down from Lebanon.

She

¹⁶Awake, north wind,
  and come, south wind!
Blow on my garden,
  that its fragrance may spread
    everywhere.
Let my beloved come into his garden
  and taste its choice fruits.

He

5 I have come into my garden, my
    sister, my bride;
  I have gathered my myrrh with my
    spice.
I have eaten my honeycomb and my
    honey;
  I have drunk my wine and my milk.

Friends

Eat, friends, and drink;
  drink your fill of love.

She

²I slept but my heart was awake.
  Listen! My beloved is knocking:
"Open to me, my sister, my darling,
  my dove, my flawless one.
My head is drenched with dew,
  my hair with the dampness of the
    night."
³I have taken off my robe —
  must I put it on again?
I have washed my feet —
  must I soil them again?
⁴My beloved thrust his hand through
    the latch-opening;
  my heart began to pound for him.
⁵I arose to open for my beloved,
  and my hands dripped with myrrh,
my fingers with flowing myrrh,
  on the handles of the bolt.
⁶I opened for my beloved,
  but my beloved had left; he was gone.
  My heart sank at his departure.*b*

I looked for him but did not find him.
  I called him but he did not answer.
⁷The watchmen found me
  as they made their rounds in the city.
They beat me, they bruised me;
  they took away my cloak,
  those watchmen of the walls!
⁸Daughters of Jerusalem, I charge
    you —
  if you find my beloved,
what will you tell him?
  Tell him I am faint with love.

Friends

⁹How is your beloved better than
    others,
  most beautiful of women?
How is your beloved better than
    others,
  that you so charge us?

She

¹⁰My beloved is radiant and ruddy,
  outstanding among ten thousand.
¹¹His head is purest gold;
  his hair is wavy
  and black as a raven.
¹²His eyes are like doves
  by the water streams,
washed in milk,
  mounted like jewels.
¹³His cheeks are like beds of spice
  yielding perfume.
His lips are like lilies
  dripping with myrrh.
¹⁴His arms are rods of gold
  set with topaz.
His body is like polished ivory
  decorated with lapis lazuli.
¹⁵His legs are pillars of marble
  set on bases of pure gold.
His appearance is like Lebanon,
  choice as its cedars.
¹⁶His mouth is sweetness itself;
  he is altogether lovely.
This is my beloved, this is my friend,
  daughters of Jerusalem.

---

a 15 Or *I am* (spoken by *She*)   *b* 6 Or *heart had gone out to him when he spoke*

Friends

6 Where has your beloved gone,
   most beautiful of women?
   Which way did your beloved turn,
   that we may look for him with you?

She

2 My beloved has gone down to his
      garden,
   to the beds of spices,
   to browse in the gardens
   and to gather lilies.
3 I am my beloved's and my beloved is
      mine;
   he browses among the lilies.

He

4 You are as beautiful as Tirzah, my
      darling,
   as lovely as Jerusalem,
   as majestic as troops with banners.
5 Turn your eyes from me;
      they overwhelm me.
   Your hair is like a flock of goats
      descending from Gilead.
6 Your teeth are like a flock of sheep
      coming up from the washing.
   Each has its twin,
      not one of them is missing.
7 Your temples behind your veil
   are like the halves of a pomegranate.
8 Sixty queens there may be,
   and eighty concubines,
   and virgins beyond number;
9 but my dove, my perfect one, is unique,
   the only daughter of her mother,
   the favorite of the one who bore her.
   The young women saw her and called
      her blessed;
   the queens and concubines praised
      her.

Friends

10 Who is this that appears like the dawn,
   fair as the moon, bright as the sun,
   majestic as the stars in procession?

He

11 I went down to the grove of nut trees
   to look at the new growth in the
      valley,
   to see if the vines had budded
   or the pomegranates were in bloom.
12 Before I realized it,
   my desire set me among the royal
      chariots of my people.*a*

Friends

13 Come back, come back, O Shulammite;
   come back, come back, that we may
      gaze on you!

He

   Why would you gaze on the
      Shulammite
   as on the dance of Mahanaim?*b*

7 *c* How beautiful your sandaled feet,
      O prince's daughter!
   Your graceful legs are like jewels,
   the work of an artist's hands.
2 Your navel is a rounded goblet
   that never lacks blended wine.
   Your waist is a mound of wheat
      encircled by lilies.
3 Your breasts are like two fawns,
   like twin fawns of a gazelle.
4 Your neck is like an ivory tower.
   Your eyes are the pools of Heshbon
      by the gate of Bath Rabbim.
   Your nose is like the tower of
      Lebanon
   looking toward Damascus.
5 Your head crowns you like Mount
      Carmel.
   Your hair is like royal tapestry;
   the king is held captive by its
      tresses.
6 How beautiful you are and how
      pleasing,
   my love, with your delights!
7 Your stature is like that of the palm,
   and your breasts like clusters of
      fruit.

---

a 12 Or *among the chariots of Amminadab;* or *among the chariots of the people of the prince*   *b 13* In Hebrew texts this verse (6:13) is numbered 7:1.   *c* In Hebrew texts 7:1-13 is numbered 7:2-14.

8 I said, "I will climb the palm tree;
 I will take hold of its fruit."
May your breasts be like clusters of
 grapes on the vine,
 the fragrance of your breath like
 apples,
9 and your mouth like the best wine.

She

May the wine go straight to my
 beloved,
 flowing gently over lips and teeth.*a*
10 I belong to my beloved,
 and his desire is for me.
11 Come, my beloved, let us go to the
 countryside,
 let us spend the night in the
 villages.*b*
12 Let us go early to the vineyards
 to see if the vines have budded,
 if their blossoms have opened,
 and if the pomegranates are in
 bloom—
 there I will give you my love.
13 The mandrakes send out their
 fragrance,
 and at our door is every delicacy,
both new and old,
 that I have stored up for you, my
 beloved.

8 If only you were to me like a
 brother,
 who was nursed at my mother's
 breasts!
Then, if I found you outside,
 I would kiss you,
 and no one would despise me.
2 I would lead you
 and bring you to my mother's
 house—
 she who has taught me.
I would give you spiced wine to
 drink,
 the nectar of my pomegranates.
3 His left arm is under my head
 and his right arm embraces me.

4 Daughters of Jerusalem, I charge
 you:
 Do not arouse or awaken love
 until it so desires.

Friends

5 Who is this coming up from the
 wilderness
 leaning on her beloved?

She

Under the apple tree I roused you;
 there your mother conceived you,
 there she who was in labor gave you
 birth.
6 Place me like a seal over your heart,
 like a seal on your arm;
for love is as strong as death,
 its jealousy*c* unyielding as the
 grave.
It burns like blazing fire,
 like a mighty flame.*d*
7 Many waters cannot quench love;
 rivers cannot sweep it away.
If one were to give
 all the wealth of one's house for
 love,
 it*e* would be utterly scorned.

Friends

8 We have a little sister,
 and her breasts are not yet grown.
What shall we do for our sister
 on the day she is spoken for?
9 If she is a wall,
 we will build towers of silver on
 her.
If she is a door,
 we will enclose her with panels of
 cedar.

She

10 I am a wall,
 and my breasts are like towers.
Thus I have become in his eyes
 like one bringing contentment.

---

a 9 Septuagint, Aquila, Vulgate and Syriac; Hebrew *lips of sleepers*   *b 11* Or *the henna bushes*   *c 6* Or *ardor*
d 6 Or *fire, / like the very flame of the* LORD   *e 7* Or *he*

11 Solomon had a vineyard in Baal Hamon;
    he let out his vineyard to tenants.
  Each was to bring for its fruit
    a thousand shekels *a* of silver.
12 But my own vineyard is mine to
      give;
    the thousand shekels are for you,
      Solomon,
    and two hundred *b* are for those who
      tend its fruit.

He

13 You who dwell in the gardens
    with friends in attendance,
    let me hear your voice!

She

14 Come away, my beloved,
    and be like a gazelle
  or like a young stag
    on the spice-laden mountains.

---

a 11 That is, about 25 pounds or about 12 kilograms; also in verse 12   *b 12* That is, about 5 pounds or about 2.3 kilograms

Isaiah

THEME: Isaiah describes God's judgment of sin, as well as God's forgiveness, comfort and hope. Other than Psalms, Isaiah contains the most Messianic prophecies of any Old Testament book.

AUTHOR: The prophet Isaiah is identified as the book's author, and other Scripture passages agree.

DATE OF WRITING: The book of Isaiah was probably written between 700 and 680 BC.

ENCOURAGEMENT FROM ISAIAH: "A bruised reed [the LORD] will not break, and a smoldering wick he will not snuff out" (Isaiah 42:3).

CHALLENGE FROM ISAIAH: "Even youths grow tired and weary, and young men stumble and fall; but those who hope in the LORD will renew their strength. They will soar on wings like eagles; they will run and not grow weary, they will walk and not be faint" (Isaiah 40:30 – 31).

REFLECTION FROM ISAIAH: "Woe to those who go to great depths to hide their plans from the LORD, who do their work in darkness and think, 'Who sees us? Who will know?'" (Isaiah 29:15).

Isaiah is a majestic, powerful book that presents the grand themes of God's justice and redemption. This literary masterpiece reaches a pinnacle in its profound prophecies of the coming Messiah and his kingdom. The first 39 chapters describe God's judgment on Judah and the surrounding nations, while the remaining 27 envision the restoration of Israel and the marvelous transformation of the earth still to come in the future Messianic age.

Isaiah's message is given to Israel during its period of greatest prosperity since the time of David and Solomon. As is so often the case today, this time of wealth and success was accompanied by immorality, out-of-control behavior, a neglect of God's word, putting others ahead of God, greed and an endless variety of other sins. Isaiah confronted these issues head-on by emphasizing salvation through faith, God's holiness, the consequences of sin and God's promises.

In today's world, where things again seem to be spinning out of control, Isaiah is a great place to find hope for the future. The prophet assures us that while we may not know what the future holds, we know the One who holds that future. The hope of change for Israel is the same hope we embrace today: Jesus Christ, the one and only Messiah — the same Savior Isaiah was pointing to. If we begin our recovery process with the hope that we can change, a hope that's focused in the person of Jesus Christ, we will find healing.

1

The vision concerning Judah and Jerusalem that Isaiah son of Amoz saw during the reigns of Uzziah, Jotham, Ahaz and Hezekiah, kings of Judah.

A Rebellious Nation

2 Hear me, you heavens! Listen, earth!
    For the LORD has spoken:
"I reared children and brought them
        up,
    but they have rebelled against me.
3 The ox knows its master,
    the donkey its owner's manger,
but Israel does not know,
    my people do not understand."

4 Woe to the sinful nation,
    a people whose guilt is great,
a brood of evildoers,
    children given to corruption!
They have forsaken the LORD;
    they have spurned the Holy One of
        Israel
    and turned their backs on him.

5 Why should you be beaten anymore?
    Why do you persist in rebellion?
Your whole head is injured,
    your whole heart afflicted.
6 From the sole of your foot to the top of
        your head
    there is no soundness—
only wounds and welts
    and open sores,
not cleansed or bandaged
    or soothed with olive oil.

7 Your country is desolate,
    your cities burned with fire;
your fields are being stripped by
        foreigners
    right before you,
    laid waste as when overthrown by
        strangers.
8 Daughter Zion is left
    like a shelter in a vineyard,
like a hut in a cucumber field,
    like a city under siege.

9 Unless the LORD Almighty
    had left us some survivors,
we would have become like Sodom,
    we would have been like Gomorrah.

10 Hear the word of the LORD,
    you rulers of Sodom;
listen to the instruction of our God,
    you people of Gomorrah!
11 "The multitude of your sacrifices—
    what are they to me?" says the LORD.
"I have more than enough of burnt
        offerings,
    of rams and the fat of fattened
        animals;
I have no pleasure
    in the blood of bulls and lambs and
        goats.
12 When you come to appear before me,
    who has asked this of you,
    this trampling of my courts?
13 Stop bringing meaningless offerings!
    Your incense is detestable to me.
New Moons, Sabbaths and
        convocations—
    I cannot bear your worthless
        assemblies.
14 Your New Moon feasts and your
        appointed festivals
    I hate with all my being.
They have become a burden to me;
    I am weary of bearing them.
15 When you spread out your hands in
        prayer,
    I hide my eyes from you;
even when you offer many prayers,
    I am not listening.

Your hands are full of blood!

16 Wash and make yourselves clean.
    Take your evil deeds out of my
        sight;
    stop doing wrong.
17 Learn to do right; seek justice.
    Defend the oppressed.*a*
Take up the cause of the fatherless;
    plead the case of the widow.

---

a 17 Or *justice. / Correct the oppressor*

¹⁸ "Come now, let us settle the matter,"
       says the LORD.
   "Though your sins are like scarlet,
       they shall be as white as snow;
   though they are red as crimson,
       they shall be like wool.
¹⁹ If you are willing and obedient,
       you will eat the good things of the
           land;
²⁰ but if you resist and rebel,
       you will be devoured by the sword."
               For the mouth of the LORD
                   has spoken.

²¹ See how the faithful city
       has become a prostitute!
   She once was full of justice;
       righteousness used to dwell in her —
           but now murderers!
²² Your silver has become dross,
       your choice wine is diluted with water.
²³ Your rulers are rebels,
       partners with thieves;
   they all love bribes
       and chase after gifts.
   They do not defend the cause of the
           fatherless;
       the widow's case does not come
           before them.

²⁴ Therefore the Lord, the LORD
           Almighty,
       the Mighty One of Israel, declares:
   "Ah! I will vent my wrath on my foes
       and avenge myself on my enemies.
²⁵ I will turn my hand against you;ᵃ
       I will thoroughly purge away your
           dross
       and remove all your impurities.
²⁶ I will restore your leaders as in days of
           old,
       your rulers as at the beginning.
   Afterward you will be called
       the City of Righteousness,
       the Faithful City."

²⁷ Zion will be delivered with justice,
       her penitent ones with righteousness.

²⁸ But rebels and sinners will both be
           broken,
       and those who forsake the LORD will
           perish.

²⁹ "You will be ashamed because of the
           sacred oaks
       in which you have delighted;
   you will be disgraced because of the
           gardens
       that you have chosen.
³⁰ You will be like an oak with fading
           leaves,
       like a garden without water.
³¹ The mighty man will become tinder
       and his work a spark;
   both will burn together,
       with no one to quench the fire."

The Mountain of the LORD

2 This is what Isaiah son of Amoz saw
   concerning Judah and Jerusalem:

² In the last days

   the mountain of the LORD's temple will
           be established
       as the highest of the mountains;
   it will be exalted above the hills,
       and all nations will stream to it.

³ Many peoples will come and say,

   "Come, let us go up to the mountain of
           the LORD,
       to the temple of the God of Jacob.
   He will teach us his ways,
       so that we may walk in his paths."
   The law will go out from Zion,
       the word of the LORD from Jerusalem.
⁴ He will judge between the nations
       and will settle disputes for many
           peoples.
   They will beat their swords into
           plowshares
       and their spears into pruning hooks.
   Nation will not take up sword against
           nation,
       nor will they train for war anymore.

ᵃ 25 That is, against Jerusalem

FORGIVENESS LESSON [*Principle Six*]

For the previous entry in the FORGIVENESS lesson, go to Romans 12:17–18 (page 1412).

For a discussion of Principles One through Eight and a listing of their related lessons, go to pages xvii–xliv.

"Come now, let us settle the matter," says the Lord.
"Though your sins are like scarlet, they shall be as white as snow;
though they are red as crimson, they shall be like wool. If you are willing
and obedient, you will eat the good things of the land."

ISAIAH 1:18–19

Principle Six calls for us to evaluate all our relationships and to offer forgiveness to those who have hurt us and make amends for harm we've done to others, except when doing so would injure them or others. We need to be willing to admit our part in our relationships that have been broken or damaged.

In order to be completely free from resentment, anger, fear, guilt and shame, we need to give and accept forgiveness in all areas of our lives. If we don't, our recovery will be stalled and remain incomplete.

We need to accept God's forgiveness by accepting Jesus' sacrifice for us on the cross, and we need to forgive and ask forgiveness of others. The last kind of forgiveness is perhaps the most difficult for us to extend: We need to forgive ourselves. We may feel such guilt and shame from our past that we think our sins are just too horrendous to be forgivable. But in Isaiah 1:18–19 we're told what God wants to do with the darkness of our past. No matter how unloved or worthless we may feel, God still loves us and highly values us. Our feelings about ourselves don't change God's assessment of us or our potential one bit.

If God himself can forgive us, how can we withhold forgiveness from ourselves? In Matthew 22:36–40 Jesus was asked, "'Teacher, which is the greatest commandment in the Law?' Jesus replied: '"Love the Lord your God with all your heart and with all your soul and with all your mind." This is the first and greatest commandment. And the second is like it: "Love your neighbor as yourself." All the Law and the Prophets hang on these two commandments.'"

How can we love or forgive our neighbors if we can't extend the same love and forgiveness to ourselves? If we haven't forgiven ourselves, our forgiveness of others may be superficial, incomplete or wrongly motivated.

Self-forgiveness isn't a matter of assigning the blame to someone else and thereby letting ourselves off the hook. It's not a license for irresponsibility. It's simply an acknowledgment that, while we recognize our human weaknesses, we've reached the stage in our recovery at which we're able to offer ourselves greater respect.

This is the final page of the FORGIVENESS lesson.

⑦
⑧

⁵Come, descendants of Jacob,
  let us walk in the light of the Lord.

The Day of the Lord

⁶You, Lord, have abandoned your people,
  the descendants of Jacob.
They are full of superstitions from the
  East;
    they practice divination like the
      Philistines
    and embrace pagan customs.
⁷Their land is full of silver and gold;
  there is no end to their treasures.
Their land is full of horses;
  there is no end to their chariots.
⁸Their land is full of idols;
  they bow down to the work of their
    hands,
  to what their fingers have made.
⁹So people will be brought low
  and everyone humbled—
    do not forgive them.ᵃ

¹⁰Go into the rocks, hide in the ground
  from the fearful presence of the Lord
  and the splendor of his majesty!
¹¹The eyes of the arrogant will be
    humbled
  and human pride brought low;
  the Lord alone will be exalted in that
    day.

¹²The Lord Almighty has a day in store
  for all the proud and lofty,
  for all that is exalted
    (and they will be humbled),
¹³for all the cedars of Lebanon, tall and
    lofty,
  and all the oaks of Bashan,
¹⁴for all the towering mountains
  and all the high hills,
¹⁵for every lofty tower
  and every fortified wall,
¹⁶for every trading shipᵇ
  and every stately vessel.
¹⁷The arrogance of man will be brought
    low
  and human pride humbled;

the Lord alone will be exalted in that
  day,
¹⁸ and the idols will totally disappear.

¹⁹People will flee to caves in the rocks
  and to holes in the ground
from the fearful presence of the Lord
  and the splendor of his majesty,
  when he rises to shake the earth.
²⁰In that day people will throw away
  to the moles and bats
their idols of silver and idols of gold,
  which they made to worship.
²¹They will flee to caverns in the rocks
  and to the overhanging crags
from the fearful presence of the Lord
  and the splendor of his majesty,
  when he rises to shake the earth.

²²Stop trusting in mere humans,
  who have but a breath in their
    nostrils.
  Why hold them in esteem?

❶
❷
❸

Judgment on Jerusalem and Judah

3 See now, the Lord,
  the Lord Almighty,
  is about to take from Jerusalem and
    Judah
  both supply and support:
  all supplies of food and all supplies of
    water,
² the hero and the warrior,
  the judge and the prophet,
  the diviner and the elder,
³the captain of fifty and the man of rank,
  the counselor, skilled craftsman and
    clever enchanter.

⁴"I will make mere youths their officials;
  children will rule over them."

⁵People will oppress each other—
  man against man, neighbor against
    neighbor.
The young will rise up against the old,
  the nobody against the honored.

❻

⁶A man will seize one of his brothers
  in his father's house, and say,

"You have a cloak, you be our leader;
    take charge of this heap of ruins!"
7 But in that day he will cry out,
    "I have no remedy.
I have no food or clothing in my
        house;
    do not make me the leader of the
        people."

8 Jerusalem staggers,
    Judah is falling;
their words and deeds are against the
    LORD,
    defying his glorious presence.
9 The look on their faces testifies against
        them;
    they parade their sin like Sodom;
    they do not hide it.
Woe to them!
    They have brought disaster upon
        themselves.

10 Tell the righteous it will be well with
        them,
    for they will enjoy the fruit of their
        deeds.
11 Woe to the wicked!
    Disaster is upon them!
They will be paid back
    for what their hands have done.

12 Youths oppress my people,
    women rule over them.
My people, your guides lead you
        astray;
    they turn you from the path.

13 The LORD takes his place in court;
    he rises to judge the people.
14 The LORD enters into judgment
        against the elders and leaders of his
        people:
    "It is you who have ruined my
        vineyard;
    the plunder from the poor is in your
        houses.
15 What do you mean by crushing my
        people
    and grinding the faces of the poor?"
        declares the Lord,
        the LORD Almighty.

16 The LORD says,
    "The women of Zion are haughty,
walking along with outstretched necks,
    flirting with their eyes,
strutting along with swaying hips,
    with ornaments jingling on their
        ankles.
17 Therefore the Lord will bring sores on
        the heads of the women of Zion;
    the LORD will make their scalps
        bald."

18 In that day the Lord will snatch away
their finery: the bangles and headbands
and crescent necklaces, 19 the earrings and
bracelets and veils, 20 the headdresses and
anklets and sashes, the perfume bottles
and charms, 21 the signet rings and nose
rings, 22 the fine robes and the capes and
cloaks, the purses 23 and mirrors, and the
linen garments and tiaras and shawls.

24 Instead of fragrance there will be a
        stench;
    instead of a sash, a rope;
instead of well-dressed hair, baldness;
    instead of fine clothing, sackcloth;
    instead of beauty, branding.
25 Your men will fall by the sword,
    your warriors in battle.
26 The gates of Zion will lament and
        mourn;
    destitute, she will sit on the ground.

4 1 In that day seven women
will take hold of one man
and say, "We will eat our own food
and provide our own clothes;
only let us be called by your name.
    Take away our disgrace!"

The Branch of the LORD

2 In that day the Branch of the LORD will
be beautiful and glorious, and the fruit of
the land will be the pride and glory of the
survivors in Israel. 3 Those who are left in
Zion, who remain in Jerusalem, will be
called holy, all who are recorded among the
living in Jerusalem. 4 The Lord will wash
away the filth of the women of Zion; he
will cleanse the bloodstains from Jerusa-

lem by a spirit[a] of judgment and a spirit[a] of fire. [5]Then the LORD will create over all of Mount Zion and over those who assemble there a cloud of smoke by day and a glow of flaming fire by night; over everything the glory[b] will be a canopy. [6]It will be a shelter and shade from the heat of the day, and a refuge and hiding place from the storm and rain.

The Song of the Vineyard

5 I will sing for the one I love
a song about his vineyard:
My loved one had a vineyard
on a fertile hillside.
[2]He dug it up and cleared it of stones
and planted it with the choicest
vines.
He built a watchtower in it
and cut out a winepress as well.
Then he looked for a crop of good
grapes,
but it yielded only bad fruit.

[3]"Now you dwellers in Jerusalem and
people of Judah,
judge between me and my vineyard.
[4]What more could have been done for
my vineyard
than I have done for it?
When I looked for good grapes,
why did it yield only bad?
[5]Now I will tell you
what I am going to do to my
vineyard:
I will take away its hedge,
and it will be destroyed;
I will break down its wall,
and it will be trampled.
[6]I will make it a wasteland,
neither pruned nor cultivated,
and briers and thorns will grow there.
I will command the clouds
not to rain on it."

[7]The vineyard of the LORD Almighty
is the nation of Israel,
and the people of Judah
are the vines he delighted in.
And he looked for justice, but saw
bloodshed;
for righteousness, but heard cries of
distress.

Woes and Judgments

[8]Woe to you who add house to house
and join field to field
till no space is left
and you live alone in the land.

[9]The LORD Almighty has declared in my hearing:

"Surely the great houses will become
desolate,
the fine mansions left without
occupants.
[10]A ten-acre vineyard will produce only a
bath[c] of wine;
a homer[d] of seed will yield only an
ephah[e] of grain."

[11]Woe to those who rise early in the
morning
to run after their drinks,
who stay up late at night
till they are inflamed with wine.
[12]They have harps and lyres at their
banquets,
pipes and timbrels and wine,
but they have no regard for the deeds of
the LORD,
no respect for the work of his
hands.
[13]Therefore my people will go into exile
for lack of understanding;
those of high rank will die of hunger
and the common people will be
parched with thirst.
[14]Therefore Death expands its jaws,
opening wide its mouth;
into it will descend their nobles and
masses
with all their brawlers and
revelers.

---

[a] 4 Or the Spirit   [b] 5 Or over all the glory there   [c] 10 That is, about 6 gallons or about 22 liters   [d] 10 That is, probably about 360 pounds or about 160 kilograms   [e] 10 That is, probably about 36 pounds or about 16 kilograms

15 So people will be brought low
   and everyone humbled,
      the eyes of the arrogant humbled.
16 But the LORD Almighty will be exalted
      by his justice,
   and the holy God will be proved holy
      by his righteous acts.
17 Then sheep will graze as in their own
      pasture;
   lambs will feed*a* among the ruins of
      the rich.

18 Woe to those who draw sin along with
      cords of deceit,
   and wickedness as with cart ropes,
19 to those who say, "Let God hurry;
   let him hasten his work
      so we may see it.
   The plan of the Holy One of Israel —
      let it approach, let it come into view,
      so we may know it."

20 Woe to those who call evil good
      and good evil,
   who put darkness for light
      and light for darkness,
   who put bitter for sweet
      and sweet for bitter.

21 Woe to those who are wise in their own
      eyes
   and clever in their own sight.

22 Woe to those who are heroes at
      drinking wine
   and champions at mixing drinks,
23 who acquit the guilty for a bribe,
   but deny justice to the innocent.
24 Therefore, as tongues of fire lick up
      straw
   and as dry grass sinks down in the
      flames,
   so their roots will decay
      and their flowers blow away like
      dust;
   for they have rejected the law of the
      LORD Almighty
   and spurned the word of the Holy
      One of Israel.

25 Therefore the LORD's anger burns
      against his people;
   his hand is raised and he strikes
      them down.
   The mountains shake,
      and the dead bodies are like refuse in
      the streets.

   Yet for all this, his anger is not turned
      away,
   his hand is still upraised.

26 He lifts up a banner for the distant
      nations,
   he whistles for those at the ends of
      the earth.
   Here they come,
      swiftly and speedily!
27 Not one of them grows tired or
      stumbles,
   not one slumbers or sleeps;
   not a belt is loosened at the waist,
      not a sandal strap is broken.
28 Their arrows are sharp,
      all their bows are strung;
   their horses' hooves seem like flint,
      their chariot wheels like a whirlwind.
29 Their roar is like that of the lion,
      they roar like young lions;
   they growl as they seize their prey
      and carry it off with no one to rescue.
30 In that day they will roar over it
      like the roaring of the sea.
   And if one looks at the land,
      there is only darkness and distress;
      even the sun will be darkened by
      clouds.

Isaiah's Commission

6 In the year that King Uzziah died,
   I saw the Lord, high and exalted,
   seated on a throne; and the train of
his robe filled the temple. 2 Above him were
seraphim, each with six wings: With two
wings they covered their faces, with two
they covered their feet, and with two they
were flying. 3 And they were calling to one
another:

---

a 17 Septuagint; Hebrew / *strangers will eat*

MY NAME IS ISAIAH

ISAIAH 6

There are two types of people in the world: those in denial and those living in the truth. Denial is the failure to recognize our predicament. The universal need for recovery goes back to Genesis 3 and humankind's fall into sin. If God isn't in control of our life, the unavoidable truth is that our life is out of control. Denial, then, is more than a warped view of oneself; it's a distorted view of God. Seeing God clearly will wipe away our illusions of self-sufficiency. That was Isaiah's experience on the occasion of his calling and commission.

We may be able to look back and recall clearly the day our sobriety began. Hopefully we can also recollect the day of our conversion. Isaiah remembered vividly the day he came face-to-face with the Lord. Isaiah saw God as the ruler of the universe, seated on his throne, "high and exalted" (Isaiah 6:1); the object of ceaseless angelic worship and praise (see vv. 2–3); infinitely holy (see v. 3); and the One who fills the earth with his glory (see v. 1–3).

The voices of the angels shook the temple and filled it with smoke (see v. 4). Both the smoke and Isaiah's terror (see v. 5) recall the horror of the Israelites when they experienced a close encounter with God at the foot of Mount Sinai (see Exodus 19:18–19; 20:18–19). Terror overcame Isaiah because the infinite holiness of God made his own inherent sinfulness painfully evident. Isaiah, seeing God clearly, couldn't help but confront the glaring contrast of his own sinfulness and that of his people.

The prophet responded as we all must respond if we're to experience recovery. He confessed, "I am a man of unclean lips, and I live among a people of unclean lips" (Isaiah 6:5). Isaiah expected the inevitability of death because "my eyes have seen the King, the LORD Almighty" (Isaiah 6:5). God had much earlier informed his servant Moses, "You cannot see my face, for no one may see me and live" (Exodus 33:20). But Isaiah didn't die. Instead, cleansing touched God's chosen prophet at the very source of his shame and guilt. One of the seraphs touched his "unclean lips" (Isaiah 6:5) with a burning coal from the altar (see v. 6). Fire in the Scriptures represents God's judgment and the refining process that burns away what doesn't belong in our life, leaving us purified and ready to enter God's presence (see 1 Corinthians 3:12–15). God didn't change the rule for Isaiah but provided forgiveness: "Your guilt is taken away and your sin atoned for" (Isaiah 6:7).

God wants to touch and heal us at the point of our own deepest guilt and shame. To experience the healing he wants us to enjoy, it's essential that we openly examine and confess our faults — something we can accomplish by taking a personal moral inventory (Principle Four/Step Four). And God wants to take away our fear through our faith in his forgiveness. His cleansing touch may well be the greatest source of joy we'll experience in our recovery. As in the case of Isaiah, God will apply his healing touch to our specific needs. As great as his gift of forgiveness is, though, it won't be the end of our recovery. God called out for a representative to carry his message (see vv. 8–13), and before he even knew the content of that message Isaiah responded, "Here am I. Send me!" (v. 8). Because Isaiah had experienced God's power and grace in his life, he didn't hesitate to carry God's message to others. Forgiveness frees us to carry out God's will, not our own. We must yield ourselves to God to be used powerfully to bring his Good News to others (Principle Eight).

"Holy, holy, holy is the LORD Almighty;
　　the whole earth is full of his glory."

4 At the sound of their voices the doorposts and thresholds shook and the temple was filled with smoke.

5 "Woe to me!" I cried. "I am ruined! For I am a man of unclean lips, and I live among a people of unclean lips, and my eyes have seen the King, the LORD Almighty." 6 Then one of the seraphim flew to me with a live coal in his hand, which he had taken with tongs from the altar. 7 With it he touched my mouth and said, "See, this has touched your lips; your guilt is taken away and your sin atoned for."

8 Then I heard the voice of the Lord saying, "Whom shall I send? And who will go for us?"

And I said, "Here am I. Send me!"

9 He said, "Go and tell this people:

"'Be ever hearing, but never
　　understanding;
be ever seeing, but never perceiving.'
10 Make the heart of this people
　　calloused;
　　make their ears dull
　　and close their eyes.*a*
Otherwise they might see with their
　　eyes,
　　hear with their ears,
　　understand with their hearts,
and turn and be healed."

11 Then I said, "For how long, Lord?"
And he answered:

"Until the cities lie ruined
　　and without inhabitant,
until the houses are left deserted
　　and the fields ruined and ravaged,
12 until the LORD has sent everyone far
　　away
　　and the land is utterly forsaken.
13 And though a tenth remains in the
　　land,
　　it will again be laid waste.

But as the terebinth and oak
　　leave stumps when they are cut down,
so the holy seed will be the stump in
　　the land."

The Sign of Immanuel

7 When Ahaz son of Jotham, the son of Uzziah, was king of Judah, King Rezin of Aram and Pekah son of Remaliah king of Israel marched up to fight against Jerusalem, but they could not overpower it.

2 Now the house of David was told, "Aram has allied itself with*b* Ephraim"; so the hearts of Ahaz and his people were shaken, as the trees of the forest are shaken by the wind.

3 Then the LORD said to Isaiah, "Go out, you and your son Shear-Jashub,*c* to meet Ahaz at the end of the aqueduct of the Upper Pool, on the road to the Launderer's Field. 4 Say to him, 'Be careful, keep calm and don't be afraid. Do not lose heart because of these two smoldering stubs of firewood — because of the fierce anger of Rezin and Aram and of the son of Remaliah. 5 Aram, Ephraim and Remaliah's son have plotted your ruin, saying, 6 "Let us invade Judah; let us tear it apart and divide it among ourselves, and make the son of Tabeel king over it." 7 Yet this is what the Sovereign LORD says:

"'It will not take place,
　　it will not happen,
8 for the head of Aram is Damascus,
　　and the head of Damascus is only
　　　　Rezin.
Within sixty-five years
　　Ephraim will be too shattered to be a
　　　　people.
9 The head of Ephraim is Samaria,
　　and the head of Samaria is only
　　　　Remaliah's son.
If you do not stand firm in your faith,
　　you will not stand at all.'"

---

a 9,10 Hebrew; Septuagint 'You will be ever hearing, but never understanding; / you will be ever seeing, but never perceiving.' / 10 This people's heart has become calloused; / they hardly hear with their ears, / and they have closed their eyes　*b 2 Or has set up camp in*　*c 3 Shear-Jashub means a remnant will return.*

10Again the LORD spoke to Ahaz, 11"Ask the LORD your God for a sign, whether in the deepest depths or in the highest heights."

12But Ahaz said, "I will not ask; I will not put the LORD to the test."

13Then Isaiah said, "Hear now, you house of David! Is it not enough to try the patience of humans? Will you try the patience of my God also? 14Therefore the Lord himself will give you*a* a sign: The virgin*b* will conceive and give birth to a son, and*c* will call him Immanuel.*d* 15He will be eating curds and honey when he knows enough to reject the wrong and choose the right, 16for before the boy knows enough to reject the wrong and choose the right, the land of the two kings you dread will be laid waste. 17The LORD will bring on you and on your people and on the house of your father a time unlike any since Ephraim broke away from Judah—he will bring the king of Assyria."

Assyria, the LORD's Instrument

18In that day the LORD will whistle for flies from the Nile delta in Egypt and for bees from the land of Assyria. 19They will all come and settle in the steep ravines and in the crevices in the rocks, on all the thornbushes and at all the water holes. 20In that day the Lord will use a razor hired from beyond the Euphrates River—the king of Assyria—to shave your head and private parts, and to cut off your beard also. 21In that day, a person will keep alive a young cow and two goats. 22And because of the abundance of the milk they give, there will be curds to eat. All who remain in the land will eat curds and honey. 23In that day, in every place where there were a thousand vines worth a thousand silver shekels,*e* there will be only briers and thorns. 24Hunters will go there with bow and arrow, for the land will be covered with briers and thorns. 25As for all the hills once cultivated by the hoe, you will no longer go there for fear of the briers and thorns; they will become places where cattle are turned loose and where sheep run.

Isaiah and His Children as Signs

8 The LORD said to me, "Take a large scroll and write on it with an ordinary pen: Maher-Shalal-Hash-Baz."*f* 2So I called in Uriah the priest and Zechariah son of Jeberekiah as reliable witnesses for me. 3Then I made love to the prophetess, and she conceived and gave birth to a son. And the LORD said to me, "Name him Maher-Shalal-Hash-Baz. 4For before the boy knows how to say 'My father' or 'My mother,' the wealth of Damascus and the plunder of Samaria will be carried off by the king of Assyria."

5The LORD spoke to me again:

6"Because this people has rejected
	the gently flowing waters of Shiloah
and rejoices over Rezin
	and the son of Remaliah,
7therefore the Lord is about to bring
		against them
	the mighty floodwaters of the
		Euphrates—
	the king of Assyria with all his pomp.
It will overflow all its channels,
	run over all its banks
8and sweep on into Judah, swirling
		over it,
	passing through it and reaching up
		to the neck.
Its outspread wings will cover the
		breadth of your land,
	Immanuel*d*!"

9Raise the war cry,*g* you nations, and be
		shattered!
	Listen, all you distant lands.
Prepare for battle, and be shattered!
Prepare for battle, and be shattered!

---

a 14 The Hebrew is plural.   *b* 14 Or *young woman*   *c* 14 Masoretic Text; Dead Sea Scrolls *son, and he* or *son, and they*   *d* 14,8 *Immanuel* means *God with us.*   *e* 23 That is, about 25 pounds or about 12 kilograms
f 1 *Maher-Shalal-Hash-Baz* means *quick to the plunder, swift to the spoil*; also in verse 3.   *g* 9 Or *Do your worst*

My Name Is Jay

I'M A BELIEVER WHO STRUGGLES WITH CHEMICAL DEPENDENCY AND ANGER

Please read about the prophet Isaiah's commission from God in Isaiah 6.

I was born in Chicago, the oldest of four children and a shy kid. One of my earliest memories is of feeling inferior to my younger brother. Attention was hard to come by unless I was acting out.

When I was five years old, my parents were having a party, and I got into an argument with my dad, telling him that I was going to run away. His nonchalant response was, "Go ahead"—so I did. I made it all the way to the end of the block before turning around. My dad, I was later to learn, followed me to make sure I didn't get too far, but I was still devastated by his response. I was a loner for most of my first six years of school, always feeling that the other kids were somehow better than I was. I was picked on a lot and became increasingly withdrawn and angry. The hole inside me was steadily growing.

At the age of 11, I entered the public school for the first time (financial issues at that point prevented my continued enrollment in a private, Christian school). Three months into the school year I attended a school dance, where I was introduced to marijuana. I got high and loved it—enough to become a daily user. When I was high I felt as though I were in a dream. The kids from that night at the dance became my family, my brothers. We were inseparable for the next several years. The marijuana made me feel good but also unleashed the anger I had so carefully buried. Until this point in my life, I had succeeded in hiding my emotions, but I now fought with my parents both verbally and physically nearly every day.

When I was 14 years old, my parents divorced. My dad had been cheating on my mom, and his drinking problem had escalated. He blamed the divorce on my brother and me. I once again felt betrayed and alone, and I turned to my friends and to harder drugs.

At 16 I discovered cocaine. This was definitely the drug for me. I felt invincible, confident, funny, the life of the party. Within a year I had become a daily user with a $200-per-day habit. I stole, cheated, dealt and did whatever it took for me to stay high. After three years of daily use, my lifestyle became one of paranoia and isolation. I had previously gone to parties and hung out with friends, but the sin addiction had become everything; I wasn't interested in *anything* anymore. By this point alcohol was as much a part of my routine as cocaine was.

At 18 I got my first DUI; my second came at 19 and my third at 20. The day after my third DUI, I contemplated whether I wanted to drink or kill myself. I was truly at my bottom. For the first time in my life, I got down on my knees and asked God to help me — not to fix my tickets or get me out of my mess, but to mend my brokenness. I finished that prayer and called my cousin, who drove for two hours to my house that night and brought me to an AA meeting the next day. By the grace of God, I've been sober ever since.

For a while sobriety was enough for me. I attended meetings regularly and made new friends, and the desire to drink was fading daily. As I worked on my issues, though, I was confronted, like Isaiah (see Isaiah 6:6 – 8), with my own sinfulness. That old hole inside of me was still growing. I couldn't understand why, after eight years of sobriety, I felt more worthless than ever. Thoughts of suicide started to fill my head again. I was terrified.

At that point I decided to accept Jesus as my Savior. I had been going to churches for years but had never felt worthy to accept the gift of Jesus Christ. The truth is that I'll never *be* worthy of the love God offers. Like Isaiah, "I am a man of unclean lips" (Isaiah 6:5). But my unworthiness is exactly what God's grace is all about; grace comes to me purely as a gift. God reminded me of how his cleansing had touched Isaiah at the source of his shame and guilt. And God did the same for me. That gaping, hungry hole inside me was finally filled.

Now, at 38 years old, I've lost 14 loved ones to their addictions via accidents, overdoses and suicides. God has walked me through some of the most painful times I could ever have imagined. But my relationships are based on the love of Jesus Christ, my Higher Power, not on my addictions. My wife and I serve together in leadership roles at Celebrate Recovery, and we cherish our beautiful baby daughter.

I've seen more lives changed by God's grace than I can count, and I want to continue to serve him in any way he chooses. I no longer fear what lies ahead. With Isaiah, I can enthusiastically respond to God, "Here am I. Send me!" (Isaiah 6:8).

Jay

¹⁰ Devise your strategy, but it will be
        thwarted;
    propose your plan, but it will not
        stand,
    for God is with us.ᵃ

¹¹This is what the LORD says to me with
his strong hand upon me, warning me not
to follow the way of this people:

¹² "Do not call conspiracy
        everything this people calls a
            conspiracy;
    do not fear what they fear,
        and do not dread it.
¹³ The LORD Almighty is the one you are
        to regard as holy,
    he is the one you are to fear,
    he is the one you are to dread.
¹⁴ He will be a holy place;
    for both Israel and Judah he will be
    a stone that causes people to stumble
        and a rock that makes them fall.
    And for the people of Jerusalem he will be
        a trap and a snare.
¹⁵ Many of them will stumble;
    they will fall and be broken,
    they will be snared and captured."

¹⁶ Bind up this testimony of warning
    and seal up God's instruction among
        my disciples.
¹⁷ I will wait for the LORD,
    who is hiding his face from the
        descendants of Jacob.
    I will put my trust in him.

¹⁸ Here am I, and the children the LORD
has given me. We are signs and symbols in
Israel from the LORD Almighty, who dwells
on Mount Zion.

The Darkness Turns to Light

¹⁹When someone tells you to consult
mediums and spiritists, who whisper and
mutter, should not a people inquire of their
God? Why consult the dead on behalf of
the living? ²⁰Consult God's instruction and
the testimony of warning. If anyone does

not speak according to this word, they have
no light of dawn. ²¹Distressed and hungry,
they will roam through the land; when
they are famished, they will become enraged and, looking upward, will curse their
king and their God. ²²Then they will look
toward the earth and see only distress and
darkness and fearful gloom, and they will
be thrust into utter darkness.

9 ᵇ Nevertheless, there will be no more
    gloom for those who were in dis-
    tress. In the past he humbled the
land of Zebulun and the land of Naphtali,
but in the future he will honor Galilee of
the nations, by the Way of the Sea, beyond
the Jordan —

² The people walking in darkness
        have seen a great light;
    on those living in the land of deep
        darkness
    a light has dawned.
³ You have enlarged the nation
        and increased their joy;
    they rejoice before you
        as people rejoice at the harvest,
    as warriors rejoice
        when dividing the plunder.
⁴ For as in the day of Midian's defeat,
        you have shattered
    the yoke that burdens them,
        the bar across their shoulders,
        the rod of their oppressor.
⁵ Every warrior's boot used in battle
        and every garment rolled in blood
    will be destined for burning,
        will be fuel for the fire.
⁶ For to us a child is born,
        to us a son is given,
        and the government will be on his
            shoulders.
    And he will be called
        Wonderful Counselor, Mighty God,
        Everlasting Father, Prince of Peace.
⁷ Of the greatness of his government and
            peace
        there will be no end.

ᵃ 10 Hebrew *Immanuel*   ᵇ In Hebrew texts 9:1 is numbered 8:23, and 9:2-21 is numbered 9:1-20.

He will reign on David's throne
  and over his kingdom,
establishing and upholding it
  with justice and righteousness
  from that time on and forever.
The zeal of the Lord Almighty
  will accomplish this.

The Lord's Anger Against Israel

8 The Lord has sent a message against
  Jacob;
  it will fall on Israel.
9 All the people will know it —
  Ephraim and the inhabitants of
    Samaria —
who say with pride
  and arrogance of heart,
10 "The bricks have fallen down,
  but we will rebuild with dressed stone;
the fig trees have been felled,
  but we will replace them with
    cedars."
11 But the Lord has strengthened Rezin's
  foes against them
  and has spurred their enemies on.
12 Arameans from the east and Philistines
    from the west
  have devoured Israel with open mouth.

Yet for all this, his anger is not turned
    away,
  his hand is still upraised.

13 But the people have not returned to him
    who struck them,
  nor have they sought the Lord
    Almighty.
14 So the Lord will cut off from Israel
    both head and tail,
  both palm branch and reed in a
    single day;
15 the elders and dignitaries are the head,
  the prophets who teach lies are the
    tail.
16 Those who guide this people mislead
    them,
  and those who are guided are led
    astray.

17 Therefore the Lord will take no
    pleasure in the young men,
  nor will he pity the fatherless and
    widows,
for everyone is ungodly and wicked,
  every mouth speaks folly.

Yet for all this, his anger is not turned
    away,
  his hand is still upraised.

18 Surely wickedness burns like a fire;
  it consumes briers and thorns,
it sets the forest thickets ablaze,
  so that it rolls upward in a column of
    smoke.
19 By the wrath of the Lord Almighty
  the land will be scorched
and the people will be fuel for the fire;
  they will not spare one another.
20 On the right they will devour,
  but still be hungry;
on the left they will eat,
  but not be satisfied.
Each will feed on the flesh of their own
    offspring[a]:
21 Manasseh will feed on Ephraim, and
      Ephraim on Manasseh;
    together they will turn against Judah.

Yet for all this, his anger is not turned
    away,
  his hand is still upraised.

10

Woe to those who make unjust
    laws,
  to those who issue oppressive
    decrees,
2 to deprive the poor of their rights
  and withhold justice from the
    oppressed of my people,
making widows their prey
  and robbing the fatherless.
3 What will you do on the day of
    reckoning,
  when disaster comes from afar?
To whom will you run for help?
  Where will you leave your riches?

---

a 20 Or *arm*

⁴Nothing will remain but to cringe
  among the captives
or fall among the slain.

Yet for all this, his anger is not turned
  away,
  his hand is still upraised.

God's Judgment on Assyria

⁵"Woe to the Assyrian, the rod of my
  anger,
  in whose hand is the club of my wrath!
⁶I send him against a godless nation,
  I dispatch him against a people who
  anger me,
  to seize loot and snatch plunder,
  and to trample them down like mud
  in the streets.
⁷But this is not what he intends,
  this is not what he has in mind;
  his purpose is to destroy,
  to put an end to many nations.
⁸'Are not my commanders all kings?' he
  says.
⁹ 'Has not Kalno fared like
  Carchemish?
Is not Hamath like Arpad,
  and Samaria like Damascus?
¹⁰As my hand seized the kingdoms of the
  idols,
  kingdoms whose images excelled
  those of Jerusalem and
  Samaria—
¹¹shall I not deal with Jerusalem and her
  images
  as I dealt with Samaria and her
  idols?'"

¹²When the Lord has finished all his
work against Mount Zion and Jerusalem,
he will say, "I will punish the king of Assyria for the willful pride of his heart and
the haughty look in his eyes. ¹³For he says:

"'By the strength of my hand I have
  done this,
  and by my wisdom, because I have
  understanding.

I removed the boundaries of nations,
  I plundered their treasures;
  like a mighty one I subdued*ᵃ* their
  kings.
¹⁴As one reaches into a nest,
  so my hand reached for the wealth of
  the nations;
  as people gather abandoned eggs,
  so I gathered all the countries;
  not one flapped a wing,
  or opened its mouth to chirp.'"

¹⁵Does the ax raise itself above the person
  who swings it,
  or the saw boast against the one who
  uses it?
As if a rod were to wield the person who
  lifts it up,
  or a club brandish the one who is not
  wood!
¹⁶Therefore, the Lord, the LORD Almighty,
  will send a wasting disease upon his
  sturdy warriors;
under his pomp a fire will be kindled
  like a blazing flame.
¹⁷The Light of Israel will become a fire,
  their Holy One a flame;
  in a single day it will burn and consume
  his thorns and his briers.
¹⁸The splendor of his forests and fertile
  fields
  it will completely destroy,
  as when a sick person wastes away.
¹⁹And the remaining trees of his forests
  will be so few
  that a child could write them down.

The Remnant of Israel

²⁰In that day the remnant of Israel,
  the survivors of Jacob,
  will no longer rely on him
  who struck them down
  but will truly rely on the LORD,
  the Holy One of Israel.
²¹A remnant will return,*ᵇ* a remnant of
  Jacob
  will return to the Mighty God.

ᵃ 13 Or *treasures; / I subdued the mighty,*   *ᵇ 21* Hebrew *shear-jashub* (see 7:3 and note); also in verse 22

²²Though your people be like the sand by
        the sea, Israel,
    only a remnant will return.
    Destruction has been decreed,
        overwhelming and righteous.
²³The Lord, the LORD Almighty, will
        carry out
    the destruction decreed upon the
        whole land.

²⁴Therefore this is what the Lord, the
LORD Almighty, says:

    "My people who live in Zion,
        do not be afraid of the Assyrians,
    who beat you with a rod
        and lift up a club against you, as
            Egypt did.
²⁵Very soon my anger against you will
        end
    and my wrath will be directed to
        their destruction."

²⁶The LORD Almighty will lash them
        with a whip,
    as when he struck down Midian at
        the rock of Oreb;
    and he will raise his staff over the waters,
        as he did in Egypt.
²⁷In that day their burden will be lifted
        from your shoulders,
    their yoke from your neck;
    the yoke will be broken
        because you have grown so fat.ᵃ

²⁸They enter Aiath;
        they pass through Migron;
    they store supplies at Mikmash.
²⁹They go over the pass, and say,
    "We will camp overnight at Geba."
    Ramah trembles;
        Gibeah of Saul flees.
³⁰Cry out, Daughter Gallim!
    Listen, Laishah!
    Poor Anathoth!
³¹Madmenah is in flight;
        the people of Gebim take cover.
³²This day they will halt at Nob;
        they will shake their fist

at the mount of Daughter Zion,
    at the hill of Jerusalem.
³³See, the Lord, the LORD Almighty,
    will lop off the boughs with great
        power.
The lofty trees will be felled,
    the tall ones will be brought low.
³⁴He will cut down the forest thickets
        with an ax;
    Lebanon will fall before the Mighty
        One.

The Branch From Jesse

11

A shoot will come up from the
    stump of Jesse;
    from his roots a Branch will
    bear fruit.
²The Spirit of the LORD will rest on him—
    the Spirit of wisdom and of
        understanding,
    the Spirit of counsel and of might,
    the Spirit of the knowledge and fear
        of the LORD—
³and he will delight in the fear of the
    LORD.

He will not judge by what he sees with
        his eyes,
    or decide by what he hears with his
        ears;
⁴but with righteousness he will judge the
        needy,
    with justice he will give decisions for
        the poor of the earth.
He will strike the earth with the rod of
        his mouth;
    with the breath of his lips he will slay
        the wicked.
⁵Righteousness will be his belt
    and faithfulness the sash around his
        waist.

⁶The wolf will live with the lamb,
    the leopard will lie down with the goat,
    the calf and the lion and the yearlingᵇ
        together;
    and a little child will lead them.

ᵃ 27 Hebrew; Septuagint *broken / from your shoulders*   ᵇ 6 Hebrew; Septuagint *lion will feed*

⁷The cow will feed with the bear,
  their young will lie down together,
  and the lion will eat straw like
    the ox.
⁸The infant will play near the cobra's
    den,
  and the young child will put its hand
    into the viper's nest.
⁹They will neither harm nor destroy
    on all my holy mountain,
  for the earth will be filled with the
    knowledge of the Lᴏʀᴅ
    as the waters cover the sea.

¹⁰In that day the Root of Jesse will stand as a banner for the peoples; the nations will rally to him, and his resting place will be glorious. ¹¹In that day the Lord will reach out his hand a second time to reclaim the surviving remnant of his people from Assyria, from Lower Egypt, from Upper Egypt, from Cush,ᵃ from Elam, from Babylonia,ᵇ from Hamath and from the islands of the Mediterranean.

¹²He will raise a banner for the nations
    and gather the exiles of Israel;
  he will assemble the scattered people of
    Judah
    from the four quarters of the earth.
¹³Ephraim's jealousy will vanish,
    and Judah's enemiesᶜ will be
    destroyed;
  Ephraim will not be jealous of Judah,
    nor Judah hostile toward
    Ephraim.
¹⁴They will swoop down on the slopes of
    Philistia to the west;
  together they will plunder the people
    to the east.
  They will subdue Edom and Moab,
    and the Ammonites will be subject to
    them.
¹⁵The Lᴏʀᴅ will dry up
    the gulf of the Egyptian sea;
  with a scorching wind he will sweep his
    hand
    over the Euphrates River.

He will break it up into seven streams
  so that anyone can cross over in
    sandals.
¹⁶There will be a highway for the
    remnant of his people
  that is left from Assyria,
as there was for Israel
  when they came up from Egypt.

Songs of Praise

12 In that day you will say:

  "I will praise you, Lᴏʀᴅ.
  Although you were angry with me,
your anger has turned away
  and you have comforted me.
²Surely God is my salvation;
  I will trust and not be afraid.
The Lᴏʀᴅ, the Lᴏʀᴅ himself, is my
    strength and my defenseᵈ;
  he has become my salvation."
³With joy you will draw water
  from the wells of salvation.

⁴In that day you will say:

"Give praise to the Lᴏʀᴅ, proclaim his
    name;
  make known among the nations
    what he has done,
  and proclaim that his name is
    exalted.
⁵Sing to the Lᴏʀᴅ, for he has done
    glorious things;
  let this be known to all the world.
⁶Shout aloud and sing for joy, people of
    Zion,
  for great is the Holy One of Israel
    among you."

A Prophecy Against Babylon

13 A prophecy against Babylon
    that Isaiah son of Amoz saw:

²Raise a banner on a bare hilltop,
  shout to them;
beckon to them
  to enter the gates of the nobles.

ᵃ 11 That is, the upper Nile region   ᵇ 11 Hebrew *Shinar*   ᶜ 13 Or *hostility*   ᵈ 2 Or *song*

³I have commanded those I prepared for
    battle;
  I have summoned my warriors to
    carry out my wrath —
  those who rejoice in my triumph.

⁴Listen, a noise on the mountains,
  like that of a great multitude!
Listen, an uproar among the kingdoms,
  like nations massing together!
The LORD Almighty is mustering
  an army for war.
⁵They come from faraway lands,
  from the ends of the heavens —
the LORD and the weapons of his wrath —
  to destroy the whole country.

⁶Wail, for the day of the LORD is near;
  it will come like destruction from the
    Almighty.ᵃ
⁷Because of this, all hands will go limp,
  every heart will melt with fear.
⁸Terror will seize them,
  pain and anguish will grip them;
  they will writhe like a woman in
    labor.
They will look aghast at each other,
  their faces aflame.

⁹See, the day of the LORD is coming
  —a cruel day, with wrath and fierce
    anger—
to make the land desolate
  and destroy the sinners within it.
¹⁰The stars of heaven and their
    constellations
  will not show their light.
The rising sun will be darkened
  and the moon will not give its light.
¹¹I will punish the world for its evil,
  the wicked for their sins.
I will put an end to the arrogance of the
    haughty
  and will humble the pride of the
    ruthless.
¹²I will make people scarcer than pure
    gold,
  more rare than the gold of Ophir.

¹³Therefore I will make the heavens
    tremble;
  and the earth will shake from its
    place
at the wrath of the LORD Almighty,
  in the day of his burning anger.

¹⁴Like a hunted gazelle,
  like sheep without a shepherd,
they will all return to their own people,
  they will flee to their native land.
¹⁵Whoever is captured will be thrust
    through;
  all who are caught will fall by the
    sword.
¹⁶Their infants will be dashed to pieces
    before their eyes;
  their houses will be looted and their
    wives violated.

¹⁷See, I will stir up against them the
    Medes,
  who do not care for silver
  and have no delight in gold.
¹⁸Their bows will strike down the young
    men;
  they will have no mercy on infants,
  nor will they look with compassion
    on children.
¹⁹Babylon, the jewel of kingdoms,
  the pride and glory of the
    Babylonians,ᵇ
will be overthrown by God
  like Sodom and Gomorrah.
²⁰She will never be inhabited
  or lived in through all generations;
there no nomads will pitch their tents,
  there no shepherds will rest their
    flocks.
²¹But desert creatures will lie there,
  jackals will fill her houses;
there the owls will dwell,
  and there the wild goats will leap
    about.
²²Hyenas will inhabit her strongholds,
  jackals her luxurious palaces.
Her time is at hand,
  and her days will not be prolonged.

ᵃ 6 Hebrew *Shaddai*   ᵇ 19 Or *Chaldeans*

14

The Lord will have
compassion on Jacob;
once again he will choose Israel
and will settle them in their own
land.
Foreigners will join them
and unite with the descendants of
Jacob.
2 Nations will take them
and bring them to their own place.
And Israel will take possession of the
nations
and make them male and female
servants in the Lord's land.
They will make captives of their captors
and rule over their oppressors.

3 On the day the Lord gives you relief
from your suffering and turmoil and from
the harsh labor forced on you, 4 you will take
up this taunt against the king of Babylon:

How the oppressor has come to an end!
How his fury*a* has ended!
5 The Lord has broken the rod of the
wicked,
the scepter of the rulers,
6 which in anger struck down peoples
with unceasing blows,
and in fury subdued nations
with relentless aggression.
7 All the lands are at rest and at peace;
they break into singing.
8 Even the junipers and the cedars of
Lebanon
gloat over you and say,
"Now that you have been laid low,
no one comes to cut us down."

9 The realm of the dead below is all astir
to meet you at your coming;
it rouses the spirits of the departed to
greet you —
all those who were leaders in the
world;
it makes them rise from their thrones —
all those who were kings over the
nations.

10 They will all respond,
they will say to you,
"You also have become weak, as we are;
you have become like us."
11 All your pomp has been brought down
to the grave,
along with the noise of your harps;
maggots are spread out beneath you
and worms cover you.

12 How you have fallen from heaven,
morning star, son of the dawn!
You have been cast down to the earth,
you who once laid low the nations!
13 You said in your heart,
"I will ascend to the heavens;
I will raise my throne
above the stars of God;
I will sit enthroned on the mount of
assembly,
on the utmost heights of Mount
Zaphon.*b*
14 I will ascend above the tops of the
clouds;
I will make myself like the Most
High."
15 But you are brought down to the realm
of the dead,
to the depths of the pit.

16 Those who see you stare at you,
they ponder your fate:
"Is this the man who shook the earth
and made kingdoms tremble,
17 the man who made the world a
wilderness,
who overthrew its cities
and would not let his captives go
home?"

18 All the kings of the nations lie in state,
each in his own tomb.
19 But you are cast out of your tomb
like a rejected branch;
you are covered with the slain,
with those pierced by the sword,
those who descend to the stones of
the pit.

---

a 4 Dead Sea Scrolls, Septuagint and Syriac; the meaning of the word in the Masoretic Text is uncertain.   *b 13* Or
of the north; Zaphon was the most sacred mountain of the Canaanites.

Like a corpse trampled underfoot,
20   you will not join them in burial,
for you have destroyed your land
    and killed your people.

Let the offspring of the wicked
    never be mentioned again.
21 Prepare a place to slaughter his children
    for the sins of their ancestors;
they are not to rise to inherit the land
    and cover the earth with their cities.

22 "I will rise up against them,"
    declares the LORD Almighty.
"I will wipe out Babylon's name and
        survivors,
    her offspring and descendants,"
            declares the LORD.
23 "I will turn her into a place for owls
    and into swampland;
I will sweep her with the broom of
        destruction,"
    declares the LORD Almighty.

24 The LORD Almighty has sworn,

"Surely, as I have planned, so it will be,
    and as I have purposed, so it will
        happen.
25 I will crush the Assyrian in my land;
    on my mountains I will trample him
        down.
His yoke will be taken from my people,
    and his burden removed from their
        shoulders."

26 This is the plan determined for the
        whole world;
    this is the hand stretched out over all
        nations.
27 For the LORD Almighty has purposed,
    and who can thwart him?
His hand is stretched out, and who
    can turn it back?

A Prophecy Against the Philistines

28 This prophecy came in the year King
Ahaz died:

29 Do not rejoice, all you Philistines,
    that the rod that struck you is broken;

from the root of that snake will spring
        up a viper,
    its fruit will be a darting, venomous
        serpent.
30 The poorest of the poor will find
        pasture,
    and the needy will lie down in safety.
But your root I will destroy by famine;
    it will slay your survivors.

31 Wail, you gate! Howl, you city!
    Melt away, all you Philistines!
A cloud of smoke comes from the
        north,
    and there is not a straggler in its
        ranks.
32 What answer shall be given
    to the envoys of that nation?
"The LORD has established Zion,
    and in her his afflicted people will
        find refuge."

A Prophecy Against Moab

15

A prophecy against Moab:

Ar in Moab is ruined,
destroyed in a night!
Kir in Moab is ruined,
    destroyed in a night!
2 Dibon goes up to its temple,
    to its high places to weep;
    Moab wails over Nebo and Medeba.
Every head is shaved
    and every beard cut off.
3 In the streets they wear sackcloth;
    on the roofs and in the public squares
they all wail,
    prostrate with weeping.
4 Heshbon and Elealeh cry out,
    their voices are heard all the way to
        Jahaz.
Therefore the armed men of Moab cry
        out,
    and their hearts are faint.

5 My heart cries out over Moab;
    her fugitives flee as far as Zoar,
    as far as Eglath Shelishiyah.
They go up the hill to Luhith,
    weeping as they go;

on the road to Horonaim
  they lament their destruction.
⁶The waters of Nimrim are dried up
  and the grass is withered;
the vegetation is gone
  and nothing green is left.
⁷So the wealth they have acquired and
    stored up
  they carry away over the Ravine of
    the Poplars.
⁸Their outcry echoes along the border of
    Moab;
  their wailing reaches as far as
    Eglaim,
  their lamentation as far as Beer Elim.
⁹The waters of Dimon[a] are full of blood,
  but I will bring still more upon
    Dimon[a] —
a lion upon the fugitives of Moab
  and upon those who remain in the
    land.

16

Send lambs as tribute
  to the ruler of the land,
  from Sela, across the desert,
to the mount of Daughter Zion.
²Like fluttering birds
  pushed from the nest,
so are the women of Moab
  at the fords of the Arnon.

³"Make up your mind," Moab says.
  "Render a decision.
Make your shadow like night —
  at high noon.
Hide the fugitives,
  do not betray the refugees.
⁴Let the Moabite fugitives stay with you;
  be their shelter from the destroyer."

The oppressor will come to an end,
  and destruction will cease;
  the aggressor will vanish from the
    land.
⁵In love a throne will be established;
  in faithfulness a man will sit on it —
  one from the house[b] of David —

one who in judging seeks justice
  and speeds the cause of
    righteousness.

⁶We have heard of Moab's pride —
  how great is her arrogance! —
of her conceit, her pride and her
    insolence;
  but her boasts are empty.
⁷Therefore the Moabites wail,
  they wail together for Moab.
Lament and grieve
  for the raisin cakes of Kir Hareseth.
⁸The fields of Heshbon wither,
  the vines of Sibmah also.
The rulers of the nations
  have trampled down the choicest
    vines,
which once reached Jazer
  and spread toward the desert.
Their shoots spread out
  and went as far as the sea.[c]
⁹So I weep, as Jazer weeps,
  for the vines of Sibmah.
Heshbon and Elealeh,
  I drench you with tears!
The shouts of joy over your ripened
    fruit
  and over your harvests have been
    stilled.
¹⁰Joy and gladness are taken away from
    the orchards;
  no one sings or shouts in the
    vineyards;
no one treads out wine at the presses,
  for I have put an end to the shouting.
¹¹My heart laments for Moab like a harp,
  my inmost being for Kir Hareseth.
¹²When Moab appears at her high place,
  she only wears herself out;
when she goes to her shrine to pray,
  it is to no avail.

¹³This is the word the LORD has already
spoken concerning Moab. ¹⁴But now the
LORD says: "Within three years, as a servant bound by contract would count them,

---

[a] 9 *Dimon*, a wordplay on *Dibon* (see verse 2), sounds like the Hebrew for *blood*.   [b] 5 Hebrew *tent*   [c] 8 Probably the Dead Sea

Moab's splendor and all her many people will be despised, and her survivors will be very few and feeble."

A Prophecy Against Damascus

17 A prophecy against Damascus:

"See, Damascus will no longer
be a city
but will become a heap of ruins.
² The cities of Aroer will be deserted
and left to flocks, which will lie down,
with no one to make them afraid.
³ The fortified city will disappear from
Ephraim,
and royal power from Damascus;
the remnant of Aram will be
like the glory of the Israelites,"
declares the LORD Almighty.

⁴ "In that day the glory of Jacob will fade;
the fat of his body will waste away.
⁵ It will be as when reapers harvest the
standing grain,
gathering the grain in their arms —
as when someone gleans heads of grain
in the Valley of Rephaim.
⁶ Yet some gleanings will remain,
as when an olive tree is beaten,
leaving two or three olives on the
topmost branches,
four or five on the fruitful boughs,"
declares the LORD, the God
of Israel.

⁷ In that day people will look to their
Maker
and turn their eyes to the Holy One
of Israel.
⁸ They will not look to the altars,
the work of their hands,
and they will have no regard for the
Asherah poles*a*
and the incense altars their fingers
have made.

⁹ In that day their strong cities, which
they left because of the Israelites, will be

like places abandoned to thickets and undergrowth. And all will be desolation.

¹⁰ You have forgotten God your Savior;
you have not remembered the Rock,
your fortress.
Therefore, though you set out the finest
plants
and plant imported vines,
¹¹ though on the day you set them out,
you make them grow,
and on the morning when you plant
them, you bring them to bud,
yet the harvest will be as nothing
in the day of disease and incurable
pain.

¹² Woe to the many nations that rage —
they rage like the raging sea!
Woe to the peoples who roar —
they roar like the roaring of great
waters!
¹³ Although the peoples roar like the roar
of surging waters,
when he rebukes them they flee far
away,
driven before the wind like chaff on the
hills,
like tumbleweed before a gale.
¹⁴ In the evening, sudden terror!
Before the morning, they are gone!
This is the portion of those who loot us,
the lot of those who plunder us.

A Prophecy Against Cush

18 Woe to the land of whirring
wings*b*
along the rivers of Cush,*c*
² which sends envoys by sea
in papyrus boats over the water.

Go, swift messengers,
to a people tall and smooth-skinned,
to a people feared far and wide,
an aggressive nation of strange speech,
whose land is divided by rivers.

³ All you people of the world,
you who live on the earth,

---

a 8 That is, wooden symbols of the goddess Asherah   *b 1* Or *of locusts*   *c 1* That is, the upper Nile region

when a banner is raised on the mountains,
    you will see it,
and when a trumpet sounds,
    you will hear it.
⁴ This is what the LORD says to me:
    "I will remain quiet and will look on
        from my dwelling place,
like shimmering heat in the sunshine,
    like a cloud of dew in the heat of
        harvest."
⁵ For, before the harvest, when the
        blossom is gone
    and the flower becomes a ripening
        grape,
he will cut off the shoots with pruning
        knives,
    and cut down and take away the
        spreading branches.
⁶ They will all be left to the mountain
        birds of prey
    and to the wild animals;
the birds will feed on them all summer,
    the wild animals all winter.

⁷ At that time gifts will be brought to the
LORD Almighty

from a people tall and smooth-skinned,
    from a people feared far and wide,
an aggressive nation of strange speech,
    whose land is divided by rivers —

the gifts will be brought to Mount Zion, the
place of the Name of the LORD Almighty.

A Prophecy Against Egypt

19 A prophecy against Egypt:

See, the LORD rides on a swift
    cloud
and is coming to Egypt.
The idols of Egypt tremble before him,
    and the hearts of the Egyptians melt
        with fear.

² "I will stir up Egyptian against
        Egyptian —
    brother will fight against brother,
    neighbor against neighbor,
    city against city,
    kingdom against kingdom.

³ The Egyptians will lose heart,
    and I will bring their plans to
        nothing;
they will consult the idols and the
        spirits of the dead,
    the mediums and the spiritists.
⁴ I will hand the Egyptians over
    to the power of a cruel master,
and a fierce king will rule over them,"
    declares the Lord, the LORD
        Almighty.

⁵ The waters of the river will dry up,
    and the riverbed will be parched and
        dry.
⁶ The canals will stink;
    the streams of Egypt will dwindle
        and dry up.
The reeds and rushes will wither,
⁷   also the plants along the Nile,
    at the mouth of the river.
Every sown field along the Nile
    will become parched, will blow away
        and be no more.
⁸ The fishermen will groan and lament,
    all who cast hooks into the Nile;
those who throw nets on the water
    will pine away.
⁹ Those who work with combed flax will
        despair,
    the weavers of fine linen will lose
        hope.
¹⁰ The workers in cloth will be dejected,
    and all the wage earners will be sick
        at heart.

¹¹ The officials of Zoan are nothing but
        fools;
    the wise counselors of Pharaoh give
        senseless advice.
How can you say to Pharaoh,
    "I am one of the wise men,
    a disciple of the ancient kings"?

¹² Where are your wise men now?
    Let them show you and make known
what the LORD Almighty
    has planned against Egypt.
¹³ The officials of Zoan have become fools,
    the leaders of Memphis are deceived;

the cornerstones of her peoples
have led Egypt astray.
14 The LORD has poured into them
a spirit of dizziness;
they make Egypt stagger in all that she
does,
as a drunkard staggers around in his
vomit.
15 There is nothing Egypt can do —
head or tail, palm branch or reed.

16 In that day the Egyptians will become weaklings. They will shudder with fear at the uplifted hand that the LORD Almighty raises against them. 17 And the land of Judah will bring terror to the Egyptians; everyone to whom Judah is mentioned will be terrified, because of what the LORD Almighty is planning against them.

18 In that day five cities in Egypt will speak the language of Canaan and swear allegiance to the LORD Almighty. One of them will be called the City of the Sun.[a]

19 In that day there will be an altar to the LORD in the heart of Egypt, and a monument to the LORD at its border. 20 It will be a sign and witness to the LORD Almighty in the land of Egypt. When they cry out to the LORD because of their oppressors, he will send them a savior and defender, and he will rescue them. 21 So the LORD will make himself known to the Egyptians, and in that day they will acknowledge the LORD. They will worship with sacrifices and grain offerings; they will make vows to the LORD and keep them. 22 The LORD will strike Egypt with a plague; he will strike them and heal them. They will turn to the LORD, and he will respond to their pleas and heal them.

23 In that day there will be a highway from Egypt to Assyria. The Assyrians will go to Egypt and the Egyptians to Assyria. The Egyptians and Assyrians will worship together. 24 In that day Israel will be the third, along with Egypt and Assyria,

a blessing[b] on the earth. 25 The LORD Almighty will bless them, saying, "Blessed be Egypt my people, Assyria my handiwork, and Israel my inheritance."

A Prophecy Against Egypt and Cush

20 In the year that the supreme commander, sent by Sargon king of Assyria, came to Ashdod and attacked and captured it — 2 at that time the LORD spoke through Isaiah son of Amoz. He said to him, "Take off the sackcloth from your body and the sandals from your feet." And he did so, going around stripped and barefoot.

3 Then the LORD said, "Just as my servant Isaiah has gone stripped and barefoot for three years, as a sign and portent against Egypt and Cush,[c] 4 so the king of Assyria will lead away stripped and barefoot the Egyptian captives and Cushite exiles, young and old, with buttocks bared — to Egypt's shame. 5 Those who trusted in Cush and boasted in Egypt will be dismayed and put to shame. 6 In that day the people who live on this coast will say, 'See what has happened to those we relied on, those we fled to for help and deliverance from the king of Assyria! How then can we escape?'"

A Prophecy Against Babylon

21 A prophecy against the Desert by the Sea:

Like whirlwinds sweeping through the
southland,
an invader comes from the desert,
from a land of terror.

2 A dire vision has been shown to me:
The traitor betrays, the looter takes
loot.
Elam, attack! Media, lay siege!
I will bring to an end all the groaning
she caused.

---

a 18 Some manuscripts of the Masoretic Text, Dead Sea Scrolls, Symmachus and Vulgate; most manuscripts of the Masoretic Text *City of Destruction*   b 24 Or *Assyria, whose names will be used in blessings* (see Gen. 48:20); or *Assyria, who will be seen by others as blessed*   c 3 That is, the upper Nile region; also in verse 5

³At this my body is racked with pain,
　　pangs seize me, like those of a
　　　woman in labor;
I am staggered by what I hear,
　　I am bewildered by what I see.
⁴My heart falters,
　　fear makes me tremble;
the twilight I longed for
　　has become a horror to me.

⁵They set the tables,
　　they spread the rugs,
　　they eat, they drink!
Get up, you officers,
　　oil the shields!

⁶This is what the Lord says to me:

"Go, post a lookout
　　and have him report what he sees.
⁷When he sees chariots
　　with teams of horses,
riders on donkeys
　　or riders on camels,
let him be alert,
　　fully alert."

⁸And the lookout*a* shouted,

"Day after day, my lord, I stand on the
　　watchtower;
every night I stay at my post.
⁹Look, here comes a man in a chariot
　　with a team of horses.
And he gives back the answer:
　　'Babylon has fallen, has fallen!
All the images of its gods
　　lie shattered on the ground!'"

¹⁰My people who are crushed on the
　　threshing floor,
I tell you what I have heard
from the LORD Almighty,
　　from the God of Israel.

A Prophecy Against Edom

¹¹A prophecy against Dumah*b*:

Someone calls to me from Seir,
　　"Watchman, what is left of the night?
　　Watchman, what is left of the night?"

¹²The watchman replies,
　　"Morning is coming, but also the
　　　night.
If you would ask, then ask;
　　and come back yet again."

A Prophecy Against Arabia

¹³A prophecy against Arabia:

You caravans of Dedanites,
　　who camp in the thickets of Arabia,
¹⁴　bring water for the thirsty;
you who live in Tema,
　　bring food for the fugitives.
¹⁵They flee from the sword,
　　from the drawn sword,
from the bent bow
　　and from the heat of battle.

¹⁶This is what the Lord says to me: "Within one year, as a servant bound by contract would count it, all the splendor of Kedar will come to an end. ¹⁷The survivors of the archers, the warriors of Kedar, will be few." The LORD, the God of Israel, has spoken.

A Prophecy About Jerusalem

22 A prophecy against the Valley of Vision:

What troubles you now,
　　that you have all gone up on the roofs,
²you town so full of commotion,
　　you city of tumult and revelry?
Your slain were not killed by the sword,
　　nor did they die in battle.
³All your leaders have fled together;
　　they have been captured without
　　　using the bow.
All you who were caught were taken
　　prisoner together,
　　having fled while the enemy was still
　　　far away.
⁴Therefore I said, "Turn away from me;
　　let me weep bitterly.
Do not try to console me
　　over the destruction of my people."

---

a 8 Dead Sea Scrolls and Syriac; Masoretic Text *A lion*　　*b 11* Dumah, a wordplay on *Edom*, means *silence* or *stillness.*

5 The Lord, the LORD Almighty, has a
    day
    of tumult and trampling and terror
    in the Valley of Vision,
  a day of battering down walls
    and of crying out to the mountains.
6 Elam takes up the quiver,
    with her charioteers and horses;
  Kir uncovers the shield.
7 Your choicest valleys are full of
    chariots,
    and horsemen are posted at the city
    gates.

8 The Lord stripped away the defenses of
    Judah,
    and you looked in that day
    to the weapons in the Palace of the
    Forest.
9 You saw that the walls of the City of
    David
    were broken through in many
    places;
  you stored up water
    in the Lower Pool.
10 You counted the buildings in Jerusalem
    and tore down houses to strengthen
    the wall.
11 You built a reservoir between the two
    walls
    for the water of the Old Pool,
  but you did not look to the One who
    made it,
    or have regard for the One who
    planned it long ago.

12 The Lord, the LORD Almighty,
    called you on that day
  to weep and to wail,
    to tear out your hair and put on
    sackcloth.
13 But see, there is joy and revelry,
    slaughtering of cattle and killing of
    sheep,
    eating of meat and drinking of
    wine!
  "Let us eat and drink," you say,
    "for tomorrow we die!"

14 The LORD Almighty has revealed this
in my hearing: "Till your dying day this sin
will not be atoned for," says the Lord, the
LORD Almighty.

15 This is what the Lord, the LORD Almighty, says:

  "Go, say to this steward,
    to Shebna the palace administrator:
16 What are you doing here and who gave
    you permission
    to cut out a grave for yourself here,
  hewing your grave on the height
    and chiseling your resting place in
    the rock?

17 "Beware, the LORD is about to take firm
    hold of you
    and hurl you away, you mighty man.
18 He will roll you up tightly like a ball
    and throw you into a large country.
  There you will die
    and there the chariots you were so
    proud of
  will become a disgrace to your
    master's house.
19 I will depose you from your office,
    and you will be ousted from your
    position.

20 "In that day I will summon my servant, Eliakim son of Hilkiah. 21 I will clothe
him with your robe and fasten your sash
around him and hand your authority over
to him. He will be a father to those who
live in Jerusalem and to the people of Judah. 22 I will place on his shoulder the key
to the house of David; what he opens no
one can shut, and what he shuts no one can
open. 23 I will drive him like a peg into a
firm place; he will become a seat^a of honor
for the house of his father. 24 All the glory
of his family will hang on him: its offspring
and offshoots — all its lesser vessels, from
the bowls to all the jars.

25 "In that day," declares the LORD Almighty, "the peg driven into the firm place

---

a 23 Or throne

will give way; it will be sheared off and will fall, and the load hanging on it will be cut down." The LORD has spoken.

A Prophecy Against Tyre

23 A prophecy against Tyre:

Wail, you ships of Tarshish!
For Tyre is destroyed
and left without house or harbor.
From the land of Cyprus
word has come to them.

2 Be silent, you people of the island
and you merchants of Sidon,
whom the seafarers have enriched.
3 On the great waters
came the grain of the Shihor;
the harvest of the Nile*a* was the revenue
of Tyre,
and she became the marketplace of
the nations.

4 Be ashamed, Sidon, and you fortress of
the sea,
for the sea has spoken:
"I have neither been in labor nor given
birth;
I have neither reared sons nor
brought up daughters."
5 When word comes to Egypt,
they will be in anguish at the report
from Tyre.

6 Cross over to Tarshish;
wail, you people of the island.
7 Is this your city of revelry,
the old, old city,
whose feet have taken her
to settle in far-off lands?
8 Who planned this against Tyre,
the bestower of crowns,
whose merchants are princes,
whose traders are renowned in the
earth?
9 The LORD Almighty planned it,
to bring down her pride in all her
splendor

and to humble all who are renowned
on the earth.

10 Till*b* your land as they do along the
Nile,
Daughter Tarshish,
for you no longer have a harbor.
11 The LORD has stretched out his hand
over the sea
and made its kingdoms tremble.
He has given an order concerning
Phoenicia
that her fortresses be destroyed.
12 He said, "No more of your reveling,
Virgin Daughter Sidon, now
crushed!

"Up, cross over to Cyprus;
even there you will find no rest."
13 Look at the land of the Babylonians,*c*
this people that is now of no
account!
The Assyrians have made it
a place for desert creatures;
they raised up their siege towers,
they stripped its fortresses bare
and turned it into a ruin.

14 Wail, you ships of Tarshish;
your fortress is destroyed!

15 At that time Tyre will be forgotten for seventy years, the span of a king's life. But at the end of these seventy years, it will happen to Tyre as in the song of the prostitute:

16 "Take up a harp, walk through the city,
you forgotten prostitute;
play the harp well, sing many a song,
so that you will be remembered."

17 At the end of seventy years, the LORD will deal with Tyre. She will return to her lucrative prostitution and will ply her trade with all the kingdoms on the face of the earth. 18 Yet her profit and her earnings will be set apart for the LORD; they will not be stored up or hoarded. Her profits will go to

---

a 2,3 Masoretic Text; Dead Sea Scrolls *Sidon, / who cross over the sea; / your envoys* 3*are on the great waters. / The grain of the Shihor, / the harvest of the Nile,*   *b 10* Dead Sea Scrolls and some Septuagint manuscripts; Masoretic Text *Go through*   *c 13* Or *Chaldeans* those who live before the LORD, for abundant food and fine clothes.

The LORD's Devastation of the Earth

24 See, the LORD is going to lay waste the earth
and devastate it;
he will ruin its face
and scatter its inhabitants —
2 it will be the same
for priest as for people,
for the master as for his servant,
for the mistress as for her servant,
for seller as for buyer,
for borrower as for lender,
for debtor as for creditor.
3 The earth will be completely laid waste
and totally plundered.

The LORD has spoken
this word.

4 The earth dries up and withers,
the world languishes and withers,
the heavens languish with the earth.
5 The earth is defiled by its people;
they have disobeyed the laws,
violated the statutes
and broken the everlasting covenant.
6 Therefore a curse consumes the earth;
its people must bear their guilt.
Therefore earth's inhabitants are
burned up,
and very few are left.
7 The new wine dries up and the vine
withers;
all the merrymakers groan.
8 The joyful timbrels are stilled,
the noise of the revelers has stopped,
the joyful harp is silent.
9 No longer do they drink wine with a
song;
the beer is bitter to its drinkers.
10 The ruined city lies desolate;
the entrance to every house is
barred.
11 In the streets they cry out for wine;
all joy turns to gloom,
all joyful sounds are banished from
the earth.

12 The city is left in ruins,
its gate is battered to pieces.
13 So will it be on the earth
and among the nations,
as when an olive tree is beaten,
or as when gleanings are left after the
grape harvest.

14 They raise their voices, they shout for
joy;
from the west they acclaim the
LORD's majesty.
15 Therefore in the east give glory to the
LORD;
exalt the name of the LORD, the God
of Israel,
in the islands of the sea.
16 From the ends of the earth we hear
singing:
"Glory to the Righteous One."

But I said, "I waste away, I waste away!
Woe to me!
The treacherous betray!
With treachery the treacherous
betray!"
17 Terror and pit and snare await you,
people of the earth.
18 Whoever flees at the sound of terror
will fall into a pit;
whoever climbs out of the pit
will be caught in a snare.

The floodgates of the heavens are
opened,
the foundations of the earth shake.
19 The earth is broken up,
the earth is split asunder,
the earth is violently shaken.
20 The earth reels like a drunkard,
it sways like a hut in the wind;
so heavy upon it is the guilt of its
rebellion
that it falls — never to rise again.

21 In that day the LORD will punish
the powers in the heavens above
and the kings on the earth below.
22 They will be herded together
like prisoners bound in a
dungeon;

they will be shut up in prison
    and be punished[a] after many days.
²³ The moon will be dismayed,
    the sun ashamed;
for the Lord Almighty will reign
    on Mount Zion and in Jerusalem,
    and before its elders — with great
       glory.

Praise to the Lord

25
Lord, you are my God;
    I will exalt you and praise
    your name,
for in perfect faithfulness
    you have done wonderful things,
    things planned long ago.
² You have made the city a heap of
      rubble,
    the fortified town a ruin,
the foreigners' stronghold a city no more;
    it will never be rebuilt.
³ Therefore strong peoples will honor
      you;
    cities of ruthless nations will revere
      you.
⁴ You have been a refuge for the poor,
    a refuge for the needy in their
      distress,
a shelter from the storm
    and a shade from the heat.
For the breath of the ruthless
    is like a storm driving against a wall
⁵   and like the heat of the desert.
You silence the uproar of foreigners;
    as heat is reduced by the shadow of a
      cloud,
    so the song of the ruthless is stilled.

⁶ On this mountain the Lord Almighty
      will prepare
    a feast of rich food for all peoples,
a banquet of aged wine —
    the best of meats and the finest of
      wines.
⁷ On this mountain he will destroy
    the shroud that enfolds all peoples,
the sheet that covers all nations;
⁸   he will swallow up death forever.

The Sovereign Lord will wipe away the
      tears
    from all faces;
he will remove his people's disgrace
    from all the earth.
            The Lord has spoken.

⁹ In that day they will say,

"Surely this is our God;
    we trusted in him, and he saved us.
This is the Lord, we trusted in him;
    let us rejoice and be glad in his
      salvation."

¹⁰ The hand of the Lord will rest on this
      mountain;
    but Moab will be trampled in their
      land
    as straw is trampled down in the
      manure.
¹¹ They will stretch out their hands in it,
    as swimmers stretch out their hands
      to swim.
God will bring down their pride
    despite the cleverness[b] of their
      hands.
¹² He will bring down your high fortified
      walls
    and lay them low;
he will bring them down to the ground,
    to the very dust.

A Song of Praise

26
In that day this song will be
sung in the land of Judah:

We have a strong city;
    God makes salvation
    its walls and ramparts.
² Open the gates
    that the righteous nation may enter,
    the nation that keeps faith.
³ You will keep in perfect peace
    those whose minds are steadfast,
    because they trust in you.
⁴ Trust in the Lord forever,
    for the Lord, the Lord himself, is
      the Rock eternal.

---

a 22 Or *released*   *b 11* The meaning of the Hebrew for this word is uncertain.

⁵He humbles those who dwell on high,
  he lays the lofty city low;
he levels it to the ground
  and casts it down to the dust.
⁶Feet trample it down—
  the feet of the oppressed,
  the footsteps of the poor.

⁷The path of the righteous is level;
  you, the Upright One, make the way
    of the righteous smooth.
⁸Yes, LORD, walking in the way of your
    laws,ᵃ
  we wait for you;
your name and renown
  are the desire of our hearts.
⁹My soul yearns for you in the night;
  in the morning my spirit longs for you.
When your judgments come upon the
    earth,
  the people of the world learn
    righteousness.
¹⁰But when grace is shown to the wicked,
  they do not learn righteousness;
even in a land of uprightness they go on
    doing evil
  and do not regard the majesty of the
    LORD.
¹¹LORD, your hand is lifted high,
  but they do not see it.
Let them see your zeal for your people
    and be put to shame;
  let the fire reserved for your enemies
    consume them.

¹²LORD, you establish peace for us;
  all that we have accomplished you
    have done for us.
¹³LORD our God, other lords besides you
    have ruled over us,
  but your name alone do we honor.
¹⁴They are now dead, they live no more;
  their spirits do not rise.
You punished them and brought them
    to ruin;
  you wiped out all memory of them.
¹⁵You have enlarged the nation, LORD;
  you have enlarged the nation.

You have gained glory for yourself;
  you have extended all the borders of
    the land.

¹⁶LORD, they came to you in their
    distress;
  when you disciplined them,
  they could barely whisper a prayer.ᵇ
¹⁷As a pregnant woman about to give
    birth
  writhes and cries out in her pain,
  so were we in your presence, LORD.
¹⁸We were with child, we writhed in
    labor,
  but we gave birth to wind.
We have not brought salvation to the
    earth,
  and the people of the world have not
    come to life.

¹⁹But your dead will live, LORD;
  their bodies will rise—
let those who dwell in the dust
  wake up and shout for joy—
your dew is like the dew of the
    morning;
  the earth will give birth to her dead.

²⁰Go, my people, enter your rooms
  and shut the doors behind you;
hide yourselves for a little while
  until his wrath has passed by.
²¹See, the LORD is coming out of his
    dwelling
  to punish the people of the earth for
    their sins.
The earth will disclose the blood shed
    on it;
  the earth will conceal its slain no
    longer.

Deliverance of Israel

27 In that day,
    the LORD will punish with his
      sword—
  his fierce, great and powerful
    sword—

ᵃ 8 Or *judgments*   ᵇ 16 The meaning of the Hebrew for this clause is uncertain.

Leviathan the gliding serpent,
  Leviathan the coiling serpent;
he will slay the monster of the sea.

2In that day —

"Sing about a fruitful vineyard:
3 I, the LORD, watch over it;
  I water it continually.
I guard it day and night
  so that no one may harm it.
4 I am not angry.
If only there were briers and thorns
    confronting me!
  I would march against them in battle;
  I would set them all on fire.
5Or else let them come to me for refuge;
  let them make peace with me,
  yes, let them make peace with me."

6In days to come Jacob will take root,
  Israel will bud and blossom
  and fill all the world with fruit.

7Has the LORD struck her
  as he struck down those who struck
    her?
Has she been killed
  as those were killed who killed her?
8By warfare*a* and exile you contend with
    her —
  with his fierce blast he drives her out,
  as on a day the east wind blows.
9By this, then, will Jacob's guilt be
    atoned for,
  and this will be the full fruit of the
    removal of his sin:
When he makes all the altar stones
  to be like limestone crushed to
    pieces,
  no Asherah poles*b* or incense altars
  will be left standing.
10The fortified city stands desolate,
  an abandoned settlement, forsaken
    like the wilderness;
  there the calves graze,
    there they lie down;
  they strip its branches bare.

11When its twigs are dry, they are broken
    off
  and women come and make fires
    with them.
For this is a people without
    understanding;
  so their Maker has no compassion on
    them,
  and their Creator shows them no
    favor.

12In that day the LORD will thresh from
the flowing Euphrates to the Wadi of
Egypt, and you, Israel, will be gathered up
one by one. 13And in that day a great trumpet will sound. Those who were perishing
in Assyria and those who were exiled in
Egypt will come and worship the LORD on
the holy mountain in Jerusalem.

Woe to the Leaders of Ephraim and Judah

28 Woe to that wreath, the pride
  of Ephraim's drunkards,
  to the fading flower, his
  glorious beauty,
set on the head of a fertile valley —
  to that city, the pride of those laid
    low by wine!
2See, the Lord has one who is powerful
    and strong.
  Like a hailstorm and a destructive
    wind,
  like a driving rain and a flooding
    downpour,
  he will throw it forcefully to the
    ground.
3That wreath, the pride of Ephraim's
    drunkards,
  will be trampled underfoot.
4That fading flower, his glorious
    beauty,
  set on the head of a fertile valley,
will be like figs ripe before harvest —
  as soon as people see them and take
    them in hand,
  they swallow them.

---

a 8 See Septuagint; the meaning of the Hebrew for this word is uncertain.   *b 9* That is, wooden symbols of the goddess Asherah

⁵In that day the Lord Almighty
  will be a glorious crown,
a beautiful wreath
  for the remnant of his people.
⁶He will be a spirit of justice
  to the one who sits in judgment,
a source of strength
  to those who turn back the battle at
    the gate.

⁷And these also stagger from wine
  and reel from beer:
Priests and prophets stagger from beer
  and are befuddled with wine;
they reel from beer,
  they stagger when seeing visions,
  they stumble when rendering
    decisions.
⁸All the tables are covered with vomit
  and there is not a spot without filth.

⁹"Who is it he is trying to teach?
  To whom is he explaining his
    message?
To children weaned from their milk,
  to those just taken from the breast?
¹⁰For it is:
  Do this, do that,
  a rule for this, a rule for that*ᵃ*;
  a little here, a little there."

¹¹Very well then, with foreign lips and
    strange tongues
  God will speak to this people,
¹²to whom he said,
  "This is the resting place, let the
    weary rest";
and, "This is the place of repose" —
  but they would not listen.
¹³So then, the word of the Lord to them
    will become:
  Do this, do that,
  a rule for this, a rule for that;
  a little here, a little there —
so that as they go they will fall
    backward;
  they will be injured and snared and
    captured.

¹⁴Therefore hear the word of the Lord,
    you scoffers
  who rule this people in Jerusalem.
¹⁵You boast, "We have entered into a
    covenant with death,
  with the realm of the dead we have
    made an agreement.
When an overwhelming scourge
    sweeps by,
  it cannot touch us,
for we have made a lie our refuge
  and falsehood*ᵇ* our hiding place."

¹⁶So this is what the Sovereign Lord says:

"See, I lay a stone in Zion, a tested
    stone,
  a precious cornerstone for a sure
    foundation;
the one who relies on it
  will never be stricken with panic.
¹⁷I will make justice the measuring line
  and righteousness the plumb line;
hail will sweep away your refuge, the lie,
  and water will overflow your hiding
    place.
¹⁸Your covenant with death will be
    annulled;
  your agreement with the realm of the
    dead will not stand.
When the overwhelming scourge
    sweeps by,
  you will be beaten down by it.
¹⁹As often as it comes it will carry you
    away;
  morning after morning, by day and
    by night,
  it will sweep through."

The understanding of this message
  will bring sheer terror.
²⁰The bed is too short to stretch out on,
  the blanket too narrow to wrap
    around you.
²¹The Lord will rise up as he did at
    Mount Perazim,
  he will rouse himself as in the Valley
    of Gibeon —

---

to do his work, his strange work,
  and perform his task, his alien task.
22 Now stop your mocking,
  or your chains will become heavier;
  the Lord, the Lord Almighty, has
    told me
  of the destruction decreed against
    the whole land.

23 Listen and hear my voice;
  pay attention and hear what I say.
24 When a farmer plows for planting, does
    he plow continually?
  Does he keep on breaking up and
    working the soil?
25 When he has leveled the surface,
  does he not sow caraway and scatter
    cumin?
  Does he not plant wheat in its place,[a]
    barley in its plot,[a]
  and spelt in its field?
26 His God instructs him
  and teaches him the right way.

27 Caraway is not threshed with a
    sledge,
  nor is the wheel of a cart rolled over
    cumin;
  caraway is beaten out with a rod,
    and cumin with a stick.
28 Grain must be ground to make bread;
  so one does not go on threshing it
    forever.
  The wheels of a threshing cart may be
    rolled over it,
  but one does not use horses to grind
    grain.
29 All this also comes from the Lord
    Almighty,
  whose plan is wonderful,
  whose wisdom is magnificent.

Woe to David's City

29
Woe to you, Ariel, Ariel,
  the city where David settled!
  Add year to year
  and let your cycle of festivals go on.

2 Yet I will besiege Ariel;
  she will mourn and lament,
  she will be to me like an altar
    hearth.[b]
3 I will encamp against you on all sides;
  I will encircle you with towers
  and set up my siege works against
    you.
4 Brought low, you will speak from the
    ground;
  your speech will mumble out of the
    dust.
  Your voice will come ghostlike from the
    earth;
  out of the dust your speech will
    whisper.

5 But your many enemies will become
    like fine dust,
  the ruthless hordes like blown
    chaff.
  Suddenly, in an instant,
6   the Lord Almighty will come
  with thunder and earthquake and great
    noise,
  with windstorm and tempest and
    flames of a devouring fire.
7 Then the hordes of all the nations that
    fight against Ariel,
  that attack her and her fortress and
    besiege her,
  will be as it is with a dream,
  with a vision in the night—
8 as when a hungry person dreams of
    eating,
  but awakens hungry still;
  as when a thirsty person dreams of
    drinking,
  but awakens faint and thirsty still.
  So will it be with the hordes of all the
    nations
  that fight against Mount Zion.

9 Be stunned and amazed,
  blind yourselves and be sightless;
  be drunk, but not from wine,
  stagger, but not from beer.

---

a 25 The meaning of the Hebrew for this word is uncertain.
Hebrew for *Ariel*.   b 2 The Hebrew for *altar hearth* sounds like the

¹⁰The LORD has brought over you a deep
sleep:
>   He has sealed your eyes (the
>   prophets);
>   he has covered your heads (the seers).

¹¹For you this whole vision is nothing but words sealed in a scroll. And if you give the scroll to someone who can read, and say, "Read this, please," they will answer, "I can't; it is sealed." ¹²Or if you give the scroll to someone who cannot read, and say, "Read this, please," they will answer, "I don't know how to read."

¹³The Lord says:

> "These people come near to me with
>   their mouth
>   and honor me with their lips,
>   but their hearts are far from me.
> Their worship of me
>   is based on merely human rules they
>   have been taught.ᵃ

¹⁴Therefore once more I will astound
>   these people
>   with wonder upon wonder;
> the wisdom of the wise will perish,
>   the intelligence of the intelligent will
>   vanish."
¹⁵Woe to those who go to great depths
>   to hide their plans from the LORD,
> who do their work in darkness and
>   think,
>   "Who sees us? Who will know?"
¹⁶You turn things upside down,
>   as if the potter were thought to be
>   like the clay!
> Shall what is formed say to the one who
>   formed it,
>   "You did not make me"?
> Can the pot say to the potter,
>   "You know nothing"?

¹⁷In a very short time, will not Lebanon
>   be turned into a fertile field
>   and the fertile field seem like a forest?
¹⁸In that day the deaf will hear the words
>   of the scroll,

and out of gloom and darkness
>   the eyes of the blind will see.
¹⁹Once more the humble will rejoice in
>   the LORD;
>   the needy will rejoice in the Holy
>   One of Israel.
²⁰The ruthless will vanish,
>   the mockers will disappear,
>   and all who have an eye for evil will
>   be cut down—
²¹those who with a word make someone
>   out to be guilty,
>   who ensnare the defender in court
>   and with false testimony deprive the
>   innocent of justice.

²²Therefore this is what the LORD, who redeemed Abraham, says to the descendants of Jacob:

> "No longer will Jacob be ashamed;
>   no longer will their faces grow pale.
²³When they see among them their
>   children,
>   the work of my hands,
> they will keep my name holy;
>   they will acknowledge the holiness of
>   the Holy One of Jacob,
>   and will stand in awe of the God of
>   Israel.
²⁴Those who are wayward in spirit will
>   gain understanding;
>   those who complain will accept
>   instruction."

Woe to the Obstinate Nation

30 "Woe to the obstinate
children,"
>   declares the LORD,
> "to those who carry out plans that are
>   not mine,
>   forming an alliance, but not by my
>   Spirit,
>   heaping sin upon sin;
²who go down to Egypt
>   without consulting me;
> who look for help to Pharaoh's protection,
>   to Egypt's shade for refuge.

ᵃ 13 Hebrew; Septuagint *They worship me in vain; / their teachings are merely human rules*

3 But Pharaoh's protection will be to your
     shame,
   Egypt's shade will bring you
     disgrace.
4 Though they have officials in Zoan
   and their envoys have arrived in
     Hanes,
5 everyone will be put to shame
   because of a people useless to them,
 who bring neither help nor advantage,
   but only shame and disgrace."

6 A prophecy concerning the animals of
the Negev:

 Through a land of hardship and
     distress,
   of lions and lionesses,
   of adders and darting snakes,
 the envoys carry their riches on
     donkeys' backs,
   their treasures on the humps of
     camels,
 to that unprofitable nation,
7   to Egypt, whose help is utterly
       useless.
 Therefore I call her
   Rahab the Do-Nothing.

8 Go now, write it on a tablet for them,
   inscribe it on a scroll,
 that for the days to come
   it may be an everlasting witness.
9 For these are rebellious people,
   deceitful children,
   children unwilling to listen to the
     LORD's instruction.
10 They say to the seers,
   "See no more visions!"
 and to the prophets,
   "Give us no more visions of what is
     right!
 Tell us pleasant things,
   prophesy illusions.
11 Leave this way,
   get off this path,
 and stop confronting us
   with the Holy One of Israel!"

12 Therefore this is what the Holy One of
Israel says:

 "Because you have rejected this
     message,
   relied on oppression
   and depended on deceit,
13 this sin will become for you
   like a high wall, cracked and bulging,
   that collapses suddenly, in an instant.
14 It will break in pieces like pottery,
   shattered so mercilessly
 that among its pieces not a fragment
     will be found
   for taking coals from a hearth
   or scooping water out of a cistern."

15 This is what the Sovereign LORD, the
Holy One of Israel, says:

 "In repentance and rest is your
     salvation,
   in quietness and trust is your
     strength,
   but you would have none of it.
16 You said, 'No, we will flee on horses.'
   Therefore you will flee!
 You said, 'We will ride off on swift
     horses.'
   Therefore your pursuers will be
     swift!
17 A thousand will flee
   at the threat of one;
 at the threat of five
   you will all flee away,
 till you are left
   like a flagstaff on a mountaintop,
   like a banner on a hill."

18 Yet the LORD longs to be gracious to
     you;
   therefore he will rise up to show you
     compassion.
 For the LORD is a God of justice.
   Blessed are all who wait for him!

19 People of Zion, who live in Jerusalem,
you will weep no more. How gracious he
will be when you cry for help! As soon as he
hears, he will answer you. 20 Although the
Lord gives you the bread of adversity and
the water of affliction, your teachers will
be hidden no more; with your own eyes
you will see them. 21 Whether you turn to

the right or to the left, your ears will hear a voice behind you, saying, "This is the way; walk in it." 22Then you will desecrate your idols overlaid with silver and your images covered with gold; you will throw them away like a menstrual cloth and say to them, "Away with you!"

23He will also send you rain for the seed you sow in the ground, and the food that comes from the land will be rich and plentiful. In that day your cattle will graze in broad meadows. 24The oxen and donkeys that work the soil will eat fodder and mash, spread out with fork and shovel. 25In the day of great slaughter, when the towers fall, streams of water will flow on every high mountain and every lofty hill. 26The moon will shine like the sun, and the sunlight will be seven times brighter, like the light of seven full days, when the LORD binds up the bruises of his people and heals the wounds he inflicted.

27See, the Name of the LORD comes from
    afar,
    with burning anger and dense clouds
        of smoke;
his lips are full of wrath,
    and his tongue is a consuming fire.
28His breath is like a rushing torrent,
    rising up to the neck.
He shakes the nations in the sieve of
    destruction;
    he places in the jaws of the peoples
    a bit that leads them astray.
29And you will sing
    as on the night you celebrate a holy
        festival;
your hearts will rejoice
    as when people playing pipes go up
to the mountain of the LORD,
    to the Rock of Israel.
30The LORD will cause people to hear his
        majestic voice
    and will make them see his arm
        coming down
with raging anger and consuming fire,
    with cloudburst, thunderstorm and
        hail.

31The voice of the LORD will shatter
        Assyria;
    with his rod he will strike them
        down.
32Every stroke the LORD lays on them
    with his punishing club
will be to the music of timbrels and
        harps,
    as he fights them in battle with the
        blows of his arm.
33Topheth has long been prepared;
    it has been made ready for the king.
Its fire pit has been made deep and
        wide,
    with an abundance of fire and wood;
the breath of the LORD,
    like a stream of burning sulfur,
    sets it ablaze.

Woe to Those Who Rely on Egypt

31 Woe to those who go down to
        Egypt for help,
    who rely on horses,
who trust in the multitude of their
        chariots
    and in the great strength of their
        horsemen,
but do not look to the Holy One of
        Israel,
    or seek help from the LORD.
2Yet he too is wise and can bring
        disaster;
    he does not take back his words.
He will rise up against that wicked
        nation,
    against those who help evildoers.
3But the Egyptians are mere mortals and
        not God;
    their horses are flesh and not spirit.
When the LORD stretches out his hand,
    those who help will stumble,
    those who are helped will fall;
    all will perish together.

4This is what the LORD says to me:

"As a lion growls,
    a great lion over its prey —
and though a whole band of shepherds
    is called together against it,

it is not frightened by their shouts
  or disturbed by their clamor —
so the Lord Almighty will come down
  to do battle on Mount Zion and on
    its heights.
5 Like birds hovering overhead,
  the Lord Almighty will shield
    Jerusalem;
he will shield it and deliver it,
  he will 'pass over' it and will rescue it."

6 Return, you Israelites, to the One you
have so greatly revolted against. 7 For in
that day every one of you will reject the
idols of silver and gold your sinful hands
have made.

8 "Assyria will fall by no human sword;
  a sword, not of mortals, will devour
    them.
They will flee before the sword
  and their young men will be put to
    forced labor.
9 Their stronghold will fall because of
    terror;
  at the sight of the battle standard
    their commanders will panic,"
declares the Lord,
  whose fire is in Zion,
  whose furnace is in Jerusalem.

The Kingdom of Righteousness

32 See, a king will reign in
  righteousness
  and rulers will rule with justice.
2 Each one will be like a shelter from the
    wind
  and a refuge from the storm,
like streams of water in the desert
  and the shadow of a great rock in a
    thirsty land.
3 Then the eyes of those who see will no
    longer be closed,
  and the ears of those who hear will
    listen.
4 The fearful heart will know and
    understand,
  and the stammering tongue will be
    fluent and clear.

5 No longer will the fool be called noble
  nor the scoundrel be highly respected.
6 For fools speak folly,
  their hearts are bent on evil:
They practice ungodliness
  and spread error concerning the
    Lord;
the hungry they leave empty
  and from the thirsty they withhold
    water.
7 Scoundrels use wicked methods,
  they make up evil schemes
to destroy the poor with lies,
  even when the plea of the needy is
    just.
8 But the noble make noble plans,
  and by noble deeds they stand.

The Women of Jerusalem

9 You women who are so complacent,
  rise up and listen to me;
you daughters who feel secure,
  hear what I have to say!
10 In little more than a year
  you who feel secure will tremble;
the grape harvest will fail,
  and the harvest of fruit will not come.
11 Tremble, you complacent women;
  shudder, you daughters who feel
    secure!
Strip off your fine clothes
  and wrap yourselves in rags.
12 Beat your breasts for the pleasant fields,
  for the fruitful vines
13 and for the land of my people,
  a land overgrown with thorns and
    briers —
yes, mourn for all houses of merriment
  and for this city of revelry.
14 The fortress will be abandoned,
  the noisy city deserted;
citadel and watchtower will become a
    wasteland forever,
  the delight of donkeys, a pasture for
    flocks,
15 till the Spirit is poured on us from on
    high,
  and the desert becomes a fertile field,
  and the fertile field seems like a forest.

16 The Lord's justice will dwell in the
	desert,
	his righteousness live in the fertile
		field.
17 The fruit of that righteousness will be
		peace;
	its effect will be quietness and
		confidence forever.
18 My people will live in peaceful dwelling
		places,
	in secure homes,
	in undisturbed places of rest.
19 Though hail flattens the forest
	and the city is leveled completely,
20 how blessed you will be,
	sowing your seed by every stream,
	and letting your cattle and donkeys
		range free.

Distress and Help

33 Woe to you, destroyer,
	you who have not been
		destroyed!
Woe to you, betrayer,
	you who have not been betrayed!
When you stop destroying,
	you will be destroyed;
when you stop betraying,
	you will be betrayed.

2 Lord, be gracious to us;
	we long for you.
Be our strength every morning,
	our salvation in time of distress.
3 At the uproar of your army, the peoples
		flee;
	when you rise up, the nations scatter.
4 Your plunder, O nations, is harvested as
		by young locusts;
	like a swarm of locusts people
		pounce on it.

5 The Lord is exalted, for he dwells on
		high;
	he will fill Zion with his justice and
		righteousness.
6 He will be the sure foundation for your
		times,

a rich store of salvation and wisdom
		and knowledge;
	the fear of the Lord is the key to this
		treasure.ᵃ

7 Look, their brave men cry aloud in the
		streets;
	the envoys of peace weep bitterly.
8 The highways are deserted,
	no travelers are on the roads.
The treaty is broken,
	its witnessesᵇ are despised,
	no one is respected.
9 The land dries up and wastes away,
	Lebanon is ashamed and withers;
Sharon is like the Arabah,
	and Bashan and Carmel drop their
		leaves.

10 "Now will I arise," says the Lord.
	"Now will I be exalted;
	now will I be lifted up.
11 You conceive chaff,
	you give birth to straw;
	your breath is a fire that consumes you.
12 The peoples will be burned to ashes;
	like cut thornbushes they will be set
		ablaze."

13 You who are far away, hear what I have
		done;
	you who are near, acknowledge my
		power!
14 The sinners in Zion are terrified;
	trembling grips the godless:
"Who of us can dwell with the
		consuming fire?
	Who of us can dwell with everlasting
		burning?"
15 Those who walk righteously
	and speak what is right,
who reject gain from extortion
	and keep their hands from accepting
		bribes,
who stop their ears against plots of
		murder
	and shut their eyes against
		contemplating evil—

ᵃ 6 Or *is a treasure from him*   ᵇ 8 Dead Sea Scrolls; Masoretic Text / *the cities*

16 they are the ones who will dwell on the
    heights,
    whose refuge will be the mountain
        fortress.
Their bread will be supplied,
    and water will not fail them.

17 Your eyes will see the king in his beauty
    and view a land that stretches afar.
18 In your thoughts you will ponder the
        former terror:
    "Where is that chief officer?
Where is the one who took the revenue?
Where is the officer in charge of the
        towers?"
19 You will see those arrogant people no
        more,
    people whose speech is obscure,
    whose language is strange and
        incomprehensible.

20 Look on Zion, the city of our festivals;
    your eyes will see Jerusalem,
    a peaceful abode, a tent that will not
        be moved;
its stakes will never be pulled up,
    nor any of its ropes broken.
21 There the LORD will be our Mighty One.
    It will be like a place of broad rivers
        and streams.
No galley with oars will ride them,
    no mighty ship will sail them.
22 For the LORD is our judge,
    the LORD is our lawgiver,
    the LORD is our king;
    it is he who will save us.

23 Your rigging hangs loose:
    The mast is not held secure,
    the sail is not spread.
Then an abundance of spoils will be
        divided
    and even the lame will carry off
        plunder.
24 No one living in Zion will say, "I am
        ill";
    and the sins of those who dwell there
        will be forgiven.

Judgment Against the Nations

34 Come near, you nations, and
    listen;
    pay attention, you peoples!
Let the earth hear, and all that is in it,
    the world, and all that comes out
        of it!
2 The LORD is angry with all nations;
    his wrath is on all their armies.
He will totally destroy[a] them,
    he will give them over to slaughter.
3 Their slain will be thrown out,
    their dead bodies will stink;
    the mountains will be soaked with
        their blood.
4 All the stars in the sky will be dissolved
    and the heavens rolled up like a
        scroll;
all the starry host will fall
    like withered leaves from the vine,
    like shriveled figs from the fig tree.

5 My sword has drunk its fill in the
        heavens;
    see, it descends in judgment on
        Edom,
    the people I have totally destroyed.
6 The sword of the LORD is bathed in
        blood,
    it is covered with fat—
the blood of lambs and goats,
    fat from the kidneys of rams.
For the LORD has a sacrifice in Bozrah
    and a great slaughter in the land of
        Edom.
7 And the wild oxen will fall with them,
    the bull calves and the great bulls.
Their land will be drenched with blood,
    and the dust will be soaked with fat.

8 For the LORD has a day of vengeance,
    a year of retribution, to uphold Zion's
        cause.
9 Edom's streams will be turned into
        pitch,
    her dust into burning sulfur;
    her land will become blazing pitch!

---

a 2 The Hebrew term refers to the irrevocable giving over of things or persons to the LORD, often by totally destroying
them; also in verse 5.

¹⁰It will not be quenched night or day;
  its smoke will rise forever.
From generation to generation it will lie
    desolate;
  no one will ever pass through it
    again.
¹¹The desert owl[a] and screech owl[a] will
    possess it;
  the great owl[a] and the raven will nest
    there.
God will stretch out over Edom
  the measuring line of chaos
  and the plumb line of desolation.
¹²Her nobles will have nothing there to be
    called a kingdom,
  all her princes will vanish away.
¹³Thorns will overrun her citadels,
  nettles and brambles her
    strongholds.
She will become a haunt for jackals,
  a home for owls.
¹⁴Desert creatures will meet with hyenas,
  and wild goats will bleat to each
    other;
there the night creatures will also lie
    down
  and find for themselves places of rest.
¹⁵The owl will nest there and lay eggs,
  she will hatch them, and care for her
    young
  under the shadow of her wings;
there also the falcons will gather,
  each with its mate.

¹⁶Look in the scroll of the LORD and
read:

None of these will be missing,
  not one will lack her mate.
For it is his mouth that has given the
    order,
  and his Spirit will gather them
    together.
¹⁷He allots their portions;
  his hand distributes them by measure.
They will possess it forever
  and dwell there from generation to
    generation.

Joy of the Redeemed

35 The desert and the parched
    land will be glad;
  the wilderness will rejoice and
    blossom.
Like the crocus, ²it will burst into
    bloom;
  it will rejoice greatly and shout for
    joy.
The glory of Lebanon will be given to it,
  the splendor of Carmel and Sharon;
they will see the glory of the LORD,
  the splendor of our God.

³Strengthen the feeble hands,
  steady the knees that give way;
⁴say to those with fearful hearts,
  "Be strong, do not fear;
your God will come,
  he will come with vengeance;
with divine retribution
  he will come to save you."

⁵Then will the eyes of the blind be
    opened
  and the ears of the deaf unstopped.
⁶Then will the lame leap like a deer,
  and the mute tongue shout for joy.
Water will gush forth in the wilderness
  and streams in the desert.
⁷The burning sand will become a pool,
  the thirsty ground bubbling springs.
In the haunts where jackals once lay,
  grass and reeds and papyrus will
    grow.

⁸And a highway will be there;
  it will be called the Way of Holiness;
  it will be for those who walk on that
    Way.
The unclean will not journey on it;
  wicked fools will not go about on it.
⁹No lion will be there,
  nor any ravenous beast;
  they will not be found there.
But only the redeemed will walk there,
¹⁰ and those the LORD has rescued will
    return.

---

[a] 11 The precise identification of these birds is uncertain.

They will enter Zion with singing;
    everlasting joy will crown their
      heads.
Gladness and joy will overtake them,
    and sorrow and sighing will flee
      away.

Sennacherib Threatens Jerusalem

36 In the fourteenth year of King Hezekiah's reign, Sennacherib king of Assyria attacked all the fortified cities of Judah and captured them. ²Then the king of Assyria sent his field commander with a large army from Lachish to King Hezekiah at Jerusalem. When the commander stopped at the aqueduct of the Upper Pool, on the road to the Launderer's Field, ³Eliakim son of Hilkiah the palace administrator, Shebna the secretary, and Joah son of Asaph the recorder went out to him.

⁴The field commander said to them, "Tell Hezekiah:

"'This is what the great king, the king of Assyria, says: On what are you basing this confidence of yours? ⁵You say you have counsel and might for war — but you speak only empty words. On whom are you depending, that you rebel against me? ⁶Look, I know you are depending on Egypt, that splintered reed of a staff, which pierces the hand of anyone who leans on it! Such is Pharaoh king of Egypt to all who depend on him. ⁷But if you say to me, "We are depending on the Lord our God" — isn't he the one whose high places and altars Hezekiah removed, saying to Judah and Jerusalem, "You must worship before this altar"?

⁸"'Come now, make a bargain with my master, the king of Assyria: I will give you two thousand horses — if you can put riders on them! ⁹How then can you repulse one officer of the least of my master's officials, even though you are depending on Egypt for chariots and horsemen*a*? ¹⁰Furthermore, have I come to attack and destroy this land without the Lord? The Lord himself told me to march against this country and destroy it.'"

¹¹Then Eliakim, Shebna and Joah said to the field commander, "Please speak to your servants in Aramaic, since we understand it. Don't speak to us in Hebrew in the hearing of the people on the wall."

¹²But the commander replied, "Was it only to your master and you that my master sent me to say these things, and not to the people sitting on the wall — who, like you, will have to eat their own excrement and drink their own urine?"

¹³Then the commander stood and called out in Hebrew, "Hear the words of the great king, the king of Assyria! ¹⁴This is what the king says: Do not let Hezekiah deceive you. He cannot deliver you! ¹⁵Do not let Hezekiah persuade you to trust in the Lord when he says, 'The Lord will surely deliver us; this city will not be given into the hand of the king of Assyria.'

¹⁶"Do not listen to Hezekiah. This is what the king of Assyria says: Make peace with me and come out to me. Then each of you will eat fruit from your own vine and fig tree and drink water from your own cistern, ¹⁷until I come and take you to a land like your own — a land of grain and new wine, a land of bread and vineyards.

¹⁸"Do not let Hezekiah mislead you when he says, 'The Lord will deliver us.' Have the gods of any nations ever delivered their lands from the hand of the king of Assyria? ¹⁹Where are the gods of Hamath and Arpad? Where are the gods of Sepharvaim? Have they rescued Samaria from my hand? ²⁰Who of all the gods of these countries have been able to save their lands from me? How then can the Lord deliver Jerusalem from my hand?"

---

a 9 Or *charioteers*

21But the people remained silent and said nothing in reply, because the king had commanded, "Do not answer him."

22Then Eliakim son of Hilkiah the palace administrator, Shebna the secretary and Joah son of Asaph the recorder went to Hezekiah, with their clothes torn, and told him what the field commander had said.

Jerusalem's Deliverance Foretold

37 When King Hezekiah heard this, he tore his clothes and put on sackcloth and went into the temple of the LORD. 2He sent Eliakim the palace administrator, Shebna the secretary, and the leading priests, all wearing sackcloth, to the prophet Isaiah son of Amoz. 3They told him, "This is what Hezekiah says: This day is a day of distress and rebuke and disgrace, as when children come to the moment of birth and there is no strength to deliver them. 4It may be that the LORD your God will hear the words of the field commander, whom his master, the king of Assyria, has sent to ridicule the living God, and that he will rebuke him for the words the LORD your God has heard. Therefore pray for the remnant that still survives."

5When King Hezekiah's officials came to Isaiah, 6Isaiah said to them, "Tell your master, 'This is what the LORD says: Do not be afraid of what you have heard — those words with which the underlings of the king of Assyria have blasphemed me. 7Listen! When he hears a certain report, I will make him want to return to his own country, and there I will have him cut down with the sword.'"

8When the field commander heard that the king of Assyria had left Lachish, he withdrew and found the king fighting against Libnah.

9Now Sennacherib received a report that Tirhakah, the king of Cush,a was marching out to fight against him. When he heard it, he sent messengers to Hezekiah with this word: 10"Say to Hezekiah king of Judah: Do not let the god you depend on deceive you when he says, 'Jerusalem will not be given into the hands of the king of Assyria.' 11Surely you have heard what the kings of Assyria have done to all the countries, destroying them completely. And will you be delivered? 12Did the gods of the nations that were destroyed by my predecessors deliver them — the gods of Gozan, Harran, Rezeph and the people of Eden who were in Tel Assar? 13Where is the king of Hamath or the king of Arpad? Where are the kings of Lair, Sepharvaim, Hena and Ivvah?"

Hezekiah's Prayer

14Hezekiah received the letter from the messengers and read it. Then he went up to the temple of the LORD and spread it out before the LORD. 15And Hezekiah prayed to the LORD: 16"LORD Almighty, the God of Israel, enthroned between the cherubim, you alone are God over all the kingdoms of the earth. You have made heaven and earth. 17Give ear, LORD, and hear; open your eyes, LORD, and see; listen to all the words Sennacherib has sent to ridicule the living God.

18"It is true, LORD, that the Assyrian kings have laid waste all these peoples and their lands. 19They have thrown their gods into the fire and destroyed them, for they were not gods but only wood and stone, fashioned by human hands. 20Now, LORD our God, deliver us from his hand, so that all the kingdoms of the earth may know that you, LORD, are the only God.b"

Sennacherib's Fall

21Then Isaiah son of Amoz sent a message to Hezekiah: "This is what the LORD, the God of Israel, says: Because you have prayed to me concerning Sennacherib king of Assyria, 22this is the word the LORD has spoken against him:

---

a 9 That is, the upper Nile region   b 20 Dead Sea Scrolls (see also 2 Kings 19:19); Masoretic Text *you alone are the LORD*

"Virgin Daughter Zion
   despises and mocks you.
Daughter Jerusalem
   tosses her head as you flee.
²³ Who is it you have ridiculed and
      blasphemed?
   Against whom have you raised your
      voice
   and lifted your eyes in pride?
   Against the Holy One of Israel!
²⁴ By your messengers
   you have ridiculed the Lord.
And you have said,
   'With my many chariots
I have ascended the heights of the
   mountains,
   the utmost heights of Lebanon.
I have cut down its tallest cedars,
   the choicest of its junipers.
I have reached its remotest heights,
   the finest of its forests.
²⁵ I have dug wells in foreign lands*a*
   and drunk the water there.
With the soles of my feet
   I have dried up all the streams of
      Egypt.'

²⁶ "Have you not heard?
   Long ago I ordained it.
In days of old I planned it;
   now I have brought it to pass,
that you have turned fortified cities
   into piles of stone.
²⁷ Their people, drained of power,
   are dismayed and put to shame.
They are like plants in the field,
   like tender green shoots,
like grass sprouting on the roof,
   scorched*b* before it grows up.

²⁸ "But I know where you are
   and when you come and go
   and how you rage against me.
²⁹ Because you rage against me
   and because your insolence has
      reached my ears,

I will put my hook in your nose
   and my bit in your mouth,
and I will make you return
   by the way you came.

³⁰ "This will be the sign for you, Hezekiah:

"This year you will eat what grows by
   itself,
   and the second year what springs
      from that.
But in the third year sow and reap,
   plant vineyards and eat their fruit.
³¹ Once more a remnant of the kingdom
      of Judah
   will take root below and bear fruit
      above.
³² For out of Jerusalem will come a
      remnant,
   and out of Mount Zion a band of
      survivors.
The zeal of the Lord Almighty
   will accomplish this.

³³ "Therefore this is what the Lord says
concerning the king of Assyria:

"He will not enter this city
   or shoot an arrow here.
He will not come before it with shield
   or build a siege ramp against it.
³⁴ By the way that he came he will
      return;
   he will not enter this city,"
                    declares the Lord.
³⁵ "I will defend this city and save it,
   for my sake and for the sake of David
      my servant!"

³⁶ Then the angel of the Lord went out
and put to death a hundred and eighty-five
thousand in the Assyrian camp. When the
people got up the next morning — there
were all the dead bodies! ³⁷ So Sennacherib
king of Assyria broke camp and withdrew.
He returned to Nineveh and stayed there.

³⁸ One day, while he was worshiping
in the temple of his god Nisrok, his sons

---

a 25 Dead Sea Scrolls (see also 2 Kings 19:24); Masoretic Text does not have *in foreign lands*.   *b 27* Some
manuscripts of the Masoretic Text, Dead Sea Scrolls and some Septuagint manuscripts (see also 2 Kings 19:26);
most manuscripts of the Masoretic Text *roof / and terraced fields*

Adrammelek and Sharezer killed him with the sword, and they escaped to the land of Ararat. And Esarhaddon his son succeeded him as king.

Hezekiah's Illness

38 In those days Hezekiah became ill and was at the point of death. The prophet Isaiah son of Amoz went to him and said, "This is what the LORD says: Put your house in order, because you are going to die; you will not recover."

2 Hezekiah turned his face to the wall and prayed to the LORD, 3 "Remember, LORD, how I have walked before you faithfully and with wholehearted devotion and have done what is good in your eyes." And Hezekiah wept bitterly.

4 Then the word of the LORD came to Isaiah: 5 "Go and tell Hezekiah, 'This is what the LORD, the God of your father David, says: I have heard your prayer and seen your tears; I will add fifteen years to your life. 6 And I will deliver you and this city from the hand of the king of Assyria. I will defend this city.

7 "This is the LORD's sign to you that the LORD will do what he has promised: 8 I will make the shadow cast by the sun go back the ten steps it has gone down on the stairway of Ahaz.'" So the sunlight went back the ten steps it had gone down.

9 A writing of Hezekiah king of Judah after his illness and recovery:

10 I said, "In the prime of my life
    must I go through the gates of death
    and be robbed of the rest of my
        years?"
11 I said, "I will not again see the LORD
        himself
    in the land of the living;
    no longer will I look on my fellow man,
    or be with those who now dwell in
        this world.
12 Like a shepherd's tent my house
    has been pulled down and taken
        from me.

Like a weaver I have rolled up my life,
    and he has cut me off from the loom;
    day and night you made an end of me.
13 I waited patiently till dawn,
    but like a lion he broke all my bones;
    day and night you made an end of
        me.
14 I cried like a swift or thrush,
    I moaned like a mourning dove.
My eyes grew weak as I looked to the
        heavens.
    I am being threatened; Lord, come to
        my aid!"

15 But what can I say?
    He has spoken to me, and he himself
        has done this.
    I will walk humbly all my years
    because of this anguish of my soul.
16 Lord, by such things people live;
    and my spirit finds life in them too.
    You restored me to health
    and let me live.
17 Surely it was for my benefit
    that I suffered such anguish.
    In your love you kept me
    from the pit of destruction;
    you have put all my sins
    behind your back.
18 For the grave cannot praise you,
    death cannot sing your praise;
    those who go down to the pit
    cannot hope for your faithfulness.
19 The living, the living — they praise you,
    as I am doing today;
    parents tell their children
    about your faithfulness.

20 The LORD will save me,
    and we will sing with stringed
        instruments
    all the days of our lives
    in the temple of the LORD.

21 Isaiah had said, "Prepare a poultice of figs and apply it to the boil, and he will recover."

22 Hezekiah had asked, "What will be the sign that I will go up to the temple of the LORD?"

Envoys From Babylon

39 At that time Marduk-Baladan son of Baladan king of Babylon sent Hezekiah letters and a gift, because he had heard of his illness and recovery. ²Hezekiah received the envoys gladly and showed them what was in his storehouses — the silver, the gold, the spices, the fine olive oil — his entire armory and everything found among his treasures. There was nothing in his palace or in all his kingdom that Hezekiah did not show them.

³Then Isaiah the prophet went to King Hezekiah and asked, "What did those men say, and where did they come from?"

"From a distant land," Hezekiah replied. "They came to me from Babylon."

⁴The prophet asked, "What did they see in your palace?"

"They saw everything in my palace," Hezekiah said. "There is nothing among my treasures that I did not show them."

⁵Then Isaiah said to Hezekiah, "Hear the word of the LORD Almighty: ⁶The time will surely come when everything in your palace, and all that your predecessors have stored up until this day, will be carried off to Babylon. Nothing will be left, says the LORD. ⁷And some of your descendants, your own flesh and blood who will be born to you, will be taken away, and they will become eunuchs in the palace of the king of Babylon."

⁸"The word of the LORD you have spoken is good," Hezekiah replied. For he thought, "There will be peace and security in my lifetime."

Comfort for God's People

40 Comfort, comfort my people, says your God. ²Speak tenderly to Jerusalem, and proclaim to her that her hard service has been completed, that her sin has been paid for, that she has received from the LORD's hand double for all her sins.

³A voice of one calling:
"In the wilderness prepare
the way for the LORD*ᵃ*;
make straight in the desert
a highway for our God.*ᵇ*
⁴Every valley shall be raised up,
every mountain and hill made low;
the rough ground shall become level,
the rugged places a plain.
⁵And the glory of the LORD will be
revealed,
and all people will see it together.
For the mouth of the LORD
has spoken."

⁶A voice says, "Cry out."
And I said, "What shall I cry?"

"All people are like grass,
and all their faithfulness is like the
flowers of the field.
⁷The grass withers and the flowers fall,
because the breath of the LORD blows
on them.
Surely the people are grass.
⁸The grass withers and the flowers fall,
but the word of our God endures
forever."

⁹You who bring good news to Zion,
go up on a high mountain.
You who bring good news to
Jerusalem,*ᶜ*
lift up your voice with a shout,
lift it up, do not be afraid;
say to the towns of Judah,
"Here is your God!"
¹⁰See, the Sovereign LORD comes with
power,
and he rules with a mighty arm.
See, his reward is with him,
and his recompense accompanies
him.

ᵃ 3 Or *A voice of one calling in the wilderness: / "Prepare the way for the LORD*   *ᵇ 3* Hebrew; Septuagint *make straight the paths of our God*   *ᶜ 9* Or *Zion, bringer of good news, / go up on a high mountain. / Jerusalem, bringer of good news*

11 He tends his flock like a shepherd:
   He gathers the lambs in his arms
and carries them close to his heart;
   he gently leads those that have
     young.

12 Who has measured the waters in the
     hollow of his hand,
   or with the breadth of his hand
     marked off the heavens?
Who has held the dust of the earth in a
     basket,
   or weighed the mountains on the
     scales
   and the hills in a balance?
13 Who can fathom the Spirit*a* of the
     LORD,
   or instruct the LORD as his
     counselor?
14 Whom did the LORD consult to
     enlighten him,
   and who taught him the right way?
Who was it that taught him knowledge,
   or showed him the path of
     understanding?

15 Surely the nations are like a drop in a
     bucket;
   they are regarded as dust on the
     scales;
   he weighs the islands as though they
     were fine dust.
16 Lebanon is not sufficient for altar fires,
   nor its animals enough for burnt
     offerings.
17 Before him all the nations are as
     nothing;
   they are regarded by him as
     worthless
   and less than nothing.
18 With whom, then, will you compare
     God?
   To what image will you liken him?
19 As for an idol, a metalworker casts it,
   and a goldsmith overlays it with
     gold
   and fashions silver chains for it.

20 A person too poor to present such an
     offering
   selects wood that will not rot;
   they look for a skilled worker
   to set up an idol that will not topple.

21 Do you not know?
   Have you not heard?
Has it not been told you from the
     beginning?
   Have you not understood since the
     earth was founded?
22 He sits enthroned above the circle of the
     earth,
   and its people are like grasshoppers.
He stretches out the heavens like a
     canopy,
   and spreads them out like a tent to
     live in.
23 He brings princes to naught
   and reduces the rulers of this world
     to nothing.
24 No sooner are they planted,
   no sooner are they sown,
   no sooner do they take root in the
     ground,
than he blows on them and they
     wither,
   and a whirlwind sweeps them away
     like chaff.

25 "To whom will you compare me?
   Or who is my equal?" says the Holy
     One.
26 Lift up your eyes and look to the
     heavens:
   Who created all these?
He who brings out the starry host one
     by one
   and calls forth each of them by name.
Because of his great power and mighty
     strength,
   not one of them is missing.

27 Why do you complain, Jacob?
   Why do you say, Israel,
"My way is hidden from the LORD;
   my cause is disregarded by my God"?

---

a 13 Or *mind*

28 Do you not know?
   Have you not heard?
The LORD is the everlasting God,
   the Creator of the ends of the earth.
He will not grow tired or weary,
   and his understanding no one can
      fathom.
29 He gives strength to the weary
   and increases the power of the weak.
30 Even youths grow tired and weary,
   and young men stumble and fall;
31 but those who hope in the LORD
   will renew their strength.
They will soar on wings like eagles;
   they will run and not grow weary,
   they will walk and not be faint.

The Helper of Israel

41

"Be silent before me, you
   islands!
   Let the nations renew their
      strength!
Let them come forward and speak;
   let us meet together at the place of
      judgment.

2 "Who has stirred up one from the east,
   calling him in righteousness to his
      service*a*?
He hands nations over to him
   and subdues kings before him.
He turns them to dust with his sword,
   to windblown chaff with his bow.

a 2 Or *east, / whom victory meets at every step*

MORAL LESSON [*Principle Four*]

For the previous entry in the MORAL lesson, go to Job 7:11 (page 599).

For a discussion of Principles One through Eight and a listing of their related lessons,
go to pages xvii – xliv.

He gives strength to the weary and increases the power of the weak.

ISAIAH 40:29

Principle Four begins our process of "coming clean." It's here that we openly examine and confess our faults to ourselves, to God and to someone else we trust. In the first part of Principle Four we openly examine our lives. We take a MORAL inventory.

The *R* in MORAL stands for RELY ON GOD. We need to rely on Jesus to give us the courage and strength this principle requires. Here's a suggestion: When our knees are knocking, it might help to kneel on them. Isaiah 40:29 reminds us that God provides us with his strength when ours won't see us through. We can complete our inventories with God's help. The principles and steps are presented in a certain order for good reason. In this case, we need to complete Principle Three — turning over our lives and our will to God — *before* we can successfully work Principle Four.

Once we know the love and strength of the one and only Higher Power, Jesus Christ, there's no longer any need to fear this principle. Memorize Psalm 31:23 – 24: "Love the LORD, all his faithful people! The LORD preserves those who are true to him, but the proud he pays back in full. Be strong and take heart, all you who hope in the LORD." And remember: Courage isn't the absence of fear but the conquering of it.

The next letter in MORAL is *A*. Go to Proverbs 20:27 (page 765).

³ He pursues them and moves on
unscathed,
    by a path his feet have not traveled
before.
⁴ Who has done this and carried it
through,
    calling forth the generations from
the beginning?
I, the Lord — with the first of them
    and with the last — I am he."

⁵ The islands have seen it and fear;
    the ends of the earth tremble.
They approach and come forward;
⁶   they help each other
    and say to their companions, "Be
strong!"
⁷ The metalworker encourages the
goldsmith,
    and the one who smooths with the
hammer
    spurs on the one who strikes the
anvil.
One says of the welding, "It is good."
    The other nails down the idol so it
    will not topple.

⁸ "But you, Israel, my servant,
    Jacob, whom I have chosen,
    you descendants of Abraham my
friend,
⁹ I took you from the ends of the earth,
    from its farthest corners I called you.
I said, 'You are my servant';
    I have chosen you and have not
    rejected you.
¹⁰ So do not fear, for I am with you;
    do not be dismayed, for I am your
God.
I will strengthen you and help you;
    I will uphold you with my righteous
    right hand.

¹¹ "All who rage against you
    will surely be ashamed and
disgraced;
those who oppose you
    will be as nothing and perish.
¹² Though you search for your enemies,
    you will not find them.

Those who wage war against you
    will be as nothing at all.
¹³ For I am the Lord your God
    who takes hold of your right hand
and says to you, Do not fear;
    I will help you.
¹⁴ Do not be afraid, you worm Jacob,
    little Israel, do not fear,
for I myself will help you," declares the
Lord,
    your Redeemer, the Holy One of
Israel.
¹⁵ "See, I will make you into a threshing
sledge,
    new and sharp, with many teeth.
You will thresh the mountains and
crush them,
    and reduce the hills to chaff.
¹⁶ You will winnow them, the wind will
    pick them up,
    and a gale will blow them away.
But you will rejoice in the Lord
    and glory in the Holy One of Israel.

¹⁷ "The poor and needy search for water,
    but there is none;
    their tongues are parched with thirst.
But I the Lord will answer them;
    I, the God of Israel, will not forsake
    them.
¹⁸ I will make rivers flow on barren
heights,
    and springs within the valleys.
I will turn the desert into pools of
water,
    and the parched ground into springs.
¹⁹ I will put in the desert
    the cedar and the acacia, the myrtle
    and the olive.
I will set junipers in the wasteland,
    the fir and the cypress together,
²⁰ so that people may see and know,
    may consider and understand,
that the hand of the Lord has done this,
    that the Holy One of Israel has
    created it.

²¹ "Present your case," says the Lord.
    "Set forth your arguments," says
    Jacob's King.

22 "Tell us, you idols,
    what is going to happen.
Tell us what the former things were,
    so that we may consider them
    and know their final outcome.
Or declare to us the things to come,
23   tell us what the future holds,
    so we may know that you are gods.
Do something, whether good or bad,
    so that we will be dismayed and filled
        with fear.
24 But you are less than nothing
    and your works are utterly worthless;
    whoever chooses you is detestable.

25 "I have stirred up one from the north,
    and he comes —
    one from the rising sun who calls on
        my name.

He treads on rulers as if they were
        mortar,
    as if he were a potter treading the clay.
26 Who told of this from the beginning, so
        we could know,
    or beforehand, so we could say, 'He
        was right'?
No one told of this,
    no one foretold it,
    no one heard any words from you.
27 I was the first to tell Zion, 'Look, here
        they are!'
    I gave to Jerusalem a messenger of
        good news.
28 I look but there is no one —
    no one among the gods to give
        counsel,
    no one to give answer when I ask them.

INVENTORY LESSON [*Principle Four*]

For the previous entry in the INVENTORY lesson, go to Ephesians 4:31 (page 1469).

For a discussion of Principles One through Eight and a listing of their related lessons,
go to pages xvii – xliv.

*Do not fear, for I am with you; do not be dismayed, for I am your God. I will
strengthen you and help you; I will uphold you with my righteous right hand.*

ISAIAH 41:10

Principle Four begins the process of "coming clean." It's here that we openly examine and confess
our faults to ourselves, to God and to someone else we trust. In the first part of Principle Four
we openly examine our lives. As we get ready to write out our inventories in Principle Four, we
divide them into five specific sections.

The second area about which we write is labeled THE CAUSE. It's a fact that "hurt people hurt
people." In this section we're going to list specific actions someone else has taken to hurt us. What
did the person do to cause us resentment and/or fear? One example might be the alcoholic father
who was emotionally unavailable to you as you were growing up. Another might be the parent
who attempted to control and dominate your life.

This reflective look can be extremely painful; that's why having a sponsor and/or an accountability partner is essential. These people will be there to walk with you through your anguish. Of
course, Jesus will be with you too. God promises that in Isaiah 41:10.

In the third and fourth sections we address areas labeled THE EFFECT and THE DAMAGE.
Go to Ezekiel 34:16 (page 1007).

²⁹See, they are all false!
Their deeds amount to nothing;
their images are but wind and
confusion.

The Servant of the LORD

42 "Here is my servant, whom I
uphold,
my chosen one in whom I
delight;
I will put my Spirit on him,
and he will bring justice to the
nations.
²He will not shout or cry out,
or raise his voice in the streets.
³A bruised reed he will not break,
and a smoldering wick he will not
snuff out.
In faithfulness he will bring forth
justice;
⁴ he will not falter or be discouraged
till he establishes justice on earth.
In his teaching the islands will put
their hope."

⁵This is what God the LORD says —
the Creator of the heavens, who
stretches them out,
who spreads out the earth with all
that springs from it,
who gives breath to its people,
and life to those who walk on it:
⁶"I, the LORD, have called you in
righteousness;
I will take hold of your hand.
I will keep you and will make you
to be a covenant for the people
and a light for the Gentiles,
⁷to open eyes that are blind,
to free captives from prison
and to release from the dungeon
those who sit in darkness.

⁸"I am the LORD; that is my name!
I will not yield my glory to another
or my praise to idols.
⁹See, the former things have taken place,
and new things I declare;
before they spring into being
I announce them to you."

Song of Praise to the LORD

¹⁰Sing to the LORD a new song,
his praise from the ends of the earth,
you who go down to the sea, and all
that is in it,
you islands, and all who live in them.
¹¹Let the wilderness and its towns raise
their voices;
let the settlements where Kedar lives
rejoice.
Let the people of Sela sing for joy;
let them shout from the
mountaintops.
¹²Let them give glory to the LORD
and proclaim his praise in the islands.
¹³The LORD will march out like a
champion,
like a warrior he will stir up his zeal;
with a shout he will raise the battle cry
and will triumph over his enemies.

¹⁴"For a long time I have kept silent,
I have been quiet and held myself
back.
But now, like a woman in childbirth,
I cry out, I gasp and pant.
¹⁵I will lay waste the mountains and hills
and dry up all their vegetation;
I will turn rivers into islands
and dry up the pools.
¹⁶I will lead the blind by ways they have
not known,
along unfamiliar paths I will guide
them;
I will turn the darkness into light before
them
and make the rough places smooth.
These are the things I will do;
I will not forsake them.
¹⁷But those who trust in idols,
who say to images, 'You are our
gods,'
will be turned back in utter shame.

Israel Blind and Deaf

¹⁸"Hear, you deaf;
look, you blind, and see!
¹⁹Who is blind but my servant,
and deaf like the messenger I send?

Who is blind like the one in covenant
with me,
blind like the servant of the LORD?
20 You have seen many things, but you pay
no attention;
your ears are open, but you do not
listen."
21 It pleased the LORD
for the sake of his righteousness
to make his law great and glorious.
22 But this is a people plundered and
looted,
all of them trapped in pits
or hidden away in prisons.
They have become plunder,
with no one to rescue them;
they have been made loot,
with no one to say, "Send them back."

23 Which of you will listen to this
or pay close attention in time to
come?
24 Who handed Jacob over to become loot,
and Israel to the plunderers?
Was it not the LORD,
against whom we have sinned?
For they would not follow his ways;
they did not obey his law.
25 So he poured out on them his burning
anger,
the violence of war.
It enveloped them in flames, yet they
did not understand;
it consumed them, but they did not
take it to heart.

Israel's Only Savior

43 But now, this is what the
LORD says —
he who created you, Jacob,
he who formed you, Israel:
"Do not fear, for I have redeemed you;
I have summoned you by name; you
are mine.
2 When you pass through the waters,
I will be with you;
and when you pass through the rivers,
they will not sweep over you.

When you walk through the fire,
you will not be burned;
the flames will not set you ablaze.
3 For I am the LORD your God,
the Holy One of Israel, your Savior;
I give Egypt for your ransom,
Cush[a] and Seba in your stead.
4 Since you are precious and honored in
my sight,
and because I love you,
I will give people in exchange for you,
nations in exchange for your life.
5 Do not be afraid, for I am with you;
I will bring your children from the
east
and gather you from the west.
6 I will say to the north, 'Give them up!'
and to the south, 'Do not hold them
back.'
Bring my sons from afar
and my daughters from the ends of
the earth —
7 everyone who is called by my name,
whom I created for my glory,
whom I formed and made."

8 Lead out those who have eyes but are
blind,
who have ears but are deaf.
9 All the nations gather together
and the peoples assemble.
Which of their gods foretold this
and proclaimed to us the former
things?
Let them bring in their witnesses to
prove they were right,
so that others may hear and say, "It is
true."
10 "You are my witnesses," declares the
LORD,
"and my servant whom I have
chosen,
so that you may know and believe me
and understand that I am he.
Before me no god was formed,
nor will there be one after me.
11 I, even I, am the LORD,
and apart from me there is no savior.

---

a 3 That is, the upper Nile region

¹²I have revealed and saved and
      proclaimed—
    I, and not some foreign god among
      you.
You are my witnesses," declares the
    LORD, "that I am God.
¹³   Yes, and from ancient days I am he.
No one can deliver out of my hand.
    When I act, who can reverse it?"

God's Mercy and Israel's Unfaithfulness

¹⁴This is what the LORD says—
    your Redeemer, the Holy One of
      Israel:
"For your sake I will send to Babylon
    and bring down as fugitives all the
      Babylonians,ᵃ
    in the ships in which they took pride.
¹⁵I am the LORD, your Holy One,
    Israel's Creator, your King."

¹⁶This is what the LORD says—
    he who made a way through the sea,
    a path through the mighty waters,
¹⁷who drew out the chariots and horses,
    the army and reinforcements
      together,
and they lay there, never to rise again,
    extinguished, snuffed out like a wick:
¹⁸"Forget the former things;
    do not dwell on the past.
¹⁹See, I am doing a new thing!
    Now it springs up; do you not
      perceive it?
I am making a way in the wilderness
    and streams in the wasteland.
²⁰The wild animals honor me,
    the jackals and the owls,
because I provide water in the wilderness
    and streams in the wasteland,
to give drink to my people, my chosen,
²¹   the people I formed for myself
    that they may proclaim my praise.

²²"Yet you have not called on me, Jacob,
    you have not wearied yourselves forᵇ
      me, Israel.

²³You have not brought me sheep for
      burnt offerings,
    nor honored me with your sacrifices.
I have not burdened you with grain
      offerings
    nor wearied you with demands for
      incense.
²⁴You have not bought any fragrant
      calamus for me,
    or lavished on me the fat of your
      sacrifices.
But you have burdened me with your
      sins
    and wearied me with your offenses.

²⁵"I, even I, am he who blots out
    your transgressions, for my own
      sake,
    and remembers your sins no more.
²⁶Review the past for me,
    let us argue the matter together;
    state the case for your innocence.
²⁷Your first father sinned;
    those I sent to teach you rebelled
      against me.
²⁸So I disgraced the dignitaries of your
      temple;
    I consigned Jacob to destructionᶜ
    and Israel to scorn.

Israel the Chosen

44 "But now listen, Jacob, my
      servant,
    Israel, whom I have chosen.
²This is what the LORD says—
    he who made you, who formed you
      in the womb,
    and who will help you:
Do not be afraid, Jacob, my servant,
    Jeshurun,ᵈ whom I have chosen.
³For I will pour water on the thirsty
      land,
    and streams on the dry ground;
I will pour out my Spirit on your
      offspring,
    and my blessing on your descendants.

ᵃ 14 Or *Chaldeans*   ᵇ 22 Or *Jacob; / surely you have grown weary of*   ᶜ 28 The Hebrew term refers to the irrevocable giving over of things or persons to the LORD, often by totally destroying them.   ᵈ 2 *Jeshurun* means *the upright one*, that is, Israel.

4 They will spring up like grass in a
        meadow,
    like poplar trees by flowing streams.
5 Some will say, 'I belong to the LORD';
        others will call themselves by the
        name of Jacob;
    still others will write on their hand,
        'The LORD's,'
    and will take the name Israel.

The LORD, Not Idols

6 "This is what the LORD says —
    Israel's King and Redeemer, the
        LORD Almighty:
    I am the first and I am the last;
        apart from me there is no God.
7 Who then is like me? Let him
        proclaim it.
    Let him declare and lay out
        before me
    what has happened since I established
        my ancient people,
    and what is yet to come —
        yes, let them foretell what will come.
8 Do not tremble, do not be afraid.
    Did I not proclaim this and foretell it
        long ago?
    You are my witnesses. Is there any God
        besides me?
    No, there is no other Rock; I know
        not one."

9 All who make idols are nothing,
    and the things they treasure are
        worthless.
    Those who would speak up for them are
        blind;
    they are ignorant, to their own
        shame.
10 Who shapes a god and casts an idol,
    which can profit nothing?
11 People who do that will be put to
        shame;
    such craftsmen are only human
        beings.
    Let them all come together and take
        their stand;
    they will be brought down to terror
        and shame.

12 The blacksmith takes a tool
    and works with it in the coals;
    he shapes an idol with hammers,
    he forges it with the might of his
        arm.
    He gets hungry and loses his strength;
        he drinks no water and grows faint.
13 The carpenter measures with a line
    and makes an outline with a marker;
    he roughs it out with chisels
    and marks it with compasses.
    He shapes it in human form,
        human form in all its glory,
    that it may dwell in a shrine.
14 He cut down cedars,
    or perhaps took a cypress or oak.
    He let it grow among the trees of the
        forest,
    or planted a pine, and the rain made
        it grow.
15 It is used as fuel for burning;
    some of it he takes and warms
        himself,
    he kindles a fire and bakes bread.
    But he also fashions a god and
        worships it;
    he makes an idol and bows down
        to it.
16 Half of the wood he burns in the fire;
    over it he prepares his meal,
    he roasts his meat and eats his fill.
    He also warms himself and says,
        "Ah! I am warm; I see the fire."
17 From the rest he makes a god, his idol;
    he bows down to it and worships.
    He prays to it and says,
        "Save me! You are my god!"
18 They know nothing, they understand
        nothing;
    their eyes are plastered over so they
        cannot see,
    and their minds closed so they
        cannot understand.
19 No one stops to think,
    no one has the knowledge or
        understanding to say,
    "Half of it I used for fuel;
    I even baked bread over its coals,
    I roasted meat and I ate.

Shall I make a detestable thing from
   what is left?
Shall I bow down to a block of wood?"
20 Such a person feeds on ashes; a deluded
   heart misleads him;
   he cannot save himself, or say,
   "Is not this thing in my right hand a
      lie?"

21 "Remember these things, Jacob,
   for you, Israel, are my servant.
I have made you, you are my servant;
   Israel, I will not forget you.
22 I have swept away your offenses like a
      cloud,
   your sins like the morning mist.
Return to me,
   for I have redeemed you."

23 Sing for joy, you heavens, for the LORD
      has done this;
   shout aloud, you earth beneath.
Burst into song, you mountains,
   you forests and all your trees,
for the LORD has redeemed Jacob,
   he displays his glory in Israel.

Jerusalem to Be Inhabited

24 "This is what the LORD says —
   your Redeemer, who formed you in
      the womb:

I am the LORD,
   the Maker of all things,
   who stretches out the heavens,
   who spreads out the earth by myself,
25 who foils the signs of false prophets
   and makes fools of diviners,
who overthrows the learning of the wise
   and turns it into nonsense,
26 who carries out the words of his servants
   and fulfills the predictions of his
      messengers,

who says of Jerusalem, 'It shall be
      inhabited,'
   of the towns of Judah, 'They shall be
      rebuilt,'
   and of their ruins, 'I will restore them,'

27 who says to the watery deep, 'Be dry,
   and I will dry up your streams,'
28 who says of Cyrus, 'He is my shepherd
   and will accomplish all that I please;
   he will say of Jerusalem, "Let it be rebuilt,"
   and of the temple, "Let its
      foundations be laid."'

45

"This is what the LORD says
   to his anointed,
   to Cyrus, whose right hand I
take hold of
to subdue nations before him
   and to strip kings of their armor,
to open doors before him
   so that gates will not be shut:
2 I will go before you
   and will level the mountains[a];
I will break down gates of bronze
   and cut through bars of iron.
3 I will give you hidden treasures,
   riches stored in secret places,
so that you may know that I am the LORD,
   the God of Israel, who summons you
      by name.
4 For the sake of Jacob my servant,
   of Israel my chosen,
I summon you by name
   and bestow on you a title of honor,
   though you do not acknowledge me.
5 I am the LORD, and there is no other;
   apart from me there is no God.
I will strengthen you,
   though you have not acknowledged
      me,
6 so that from the rising of the sun
   to the place of its setting
people may know there is none besides
      me.
   I am the LORD, and there is no other.
7 I form the light and create darkness,
   I bring prosperity and create disaster;
   I, the LORD, do all these things.

8 "You heavens above, rain down my
      righteousness;
   let the clouds shower it down.

---

a 2 Dead Sea Scrolls and Septuagint; the meaning of the word in the Masoretic Text is uncertain.

Let the earth open wide,
   let salvation spring up,
let righteousness flourish with it;
   I, the Lord, have created it.

⁹ "Woe to those who quarrel with their
     Maker,
   those who are nothing but potsherds
     among the potsherds on the ground.
Does the clay say to the potter,
   'What are you making?'
Does your work say,
   'The potter has no hands'?
¹⁰ Woe to the one who says to a father,
   'What have you begotten?'
or to a mother,
   'What have you brought to birth?'

¹¹ "This is what the Lord says —
   the Holy One of Israel, and its Maker:
Concerning things to come,
   do you question me about my
     children,
   or give me orders about the work of
     my hands?
¹² It is I who made the earth
   and created mankind on it.
My own hands stretched out the
     heavens;
   I marshaled their starry hosts.
¹³ I will raise up Cyrus*a* in my
     righteousness:
   I will make all his ways straight.
He will rebuild my city
   and set my exiles free,
but not for a price or reward,
   says the Lord Almighty."

¹⁴ This is what the Lord says:

"The products of Egypt and the
     merchandise of Cush,*b*
   and those tall Sabeans —
they will come over to you
   and will be yours;
they will trudge behind you,
   coming over to you in chains.
They will bow down before you
   and plead with you, saying,

'Surely God is with you, and there is no
     other;
   there is no other god.'"

¹⁵ Truly you are a God who has been
     hiding himself,
   the God and Savior of Israel.
¹⁶ All the makers of idols will be put to
     shame and disgraced;
   they will go off into disgrace
     together.
¹⁷ But Israel will be saved by the Lord
   with an everlasting salvation;
you will never be put to shame or
     disgraced,
   to ages everlasting.

¹⁸ For this is what the Lord says —
he who created the heavens,
   he is God;
he who fashioned and made the earth,
   he founded it;
he did not create it to be empty,
   but formed it to be inhabited —
he says:
"I am the Lord,
   and there is no other.
¹⁹ I have not spoken in secret,
   from somewhere in a land of
     darkness;
I have not said to Jacob's descendants,
   'Seek me in vain.'
I, the Lord, speak the truth;
   I declare what is right.

²⁰ "Gather together and come;
   assemble, you fugitives from the
     nations.
Ignorant are those who carry about
     idols of wood,
   who pray to gods that cannot save.
²¹ Declare what is to be, present it —
   let them take counsel together.
Who foretold this long ago,
   who declared it from the distant
     past?
Was it not I, the Lord?
   And there is no God apart from me,

---

a 13 Hebrew *him*   *b 14* That is, the upper Nile region

a righteous God and a Savior;
  there is none but me.
22 "Turn to me and be saved,
  all you ends of the earth;
  for I am God, and there is no other.
23 By myself I have sworn,
  my mouth has uttered in all integrity
  a word that will not be revoked:
Before me every knee will bow;
  by me every tongue will swear.
24 They will say of me, 'In the Lord alone
  are deliverance and strength.'"
All who have raged against him
  will come to him and be put to shame.
25 But all the descendants of Israel
  will find deliverance in the Lord
  and will make their boast in him.

Gods of Babylon

46 Bel bows down, Nebo stoops
  low;
  their idols are borne by beasts
  of burden.*a*
The images that are carried about are
  burdensome,
  a burden for the weary.
2 They stoop and bow down together;
  unable to rescue the burden,
  they themselves go off into captivity.

3 "Listen to me, you descendants of Jacob,
  all the remnant of the people of
  Israel,
you whom I have upheld since your
  birth,
  and have carried since you were born.
4 Even to your old age and gray hairs
  I am he, I am he who will sustain
  you.
I have made you and I will carry you;
  I will sustain you and I will rescue
  you.

5 "With whom will you compare me or
  count me equal?
  To whom will you liken me that we
  may be compared?

6 Some pour out gold from their bags
  and weigh out silver on the scales;
they hire a goldsmith to make it into a
  god,
  and they bow down and worship it.
7 They lift it to their shoulders and
  carry it;
  they set it up in its place, and there it
  stands.
  From that spot it cannot move.
Even though someone cries out to it, it
  cannot answer;
  it cannot save them from their
  troubles.

8 "Remember this, keep it in mind,
  take it to heart, you rebels.
9 Remember the former things, those of
  long ago;
  I am God, and there is no other;
  I am God, and there is none like me.
10 I make known the end from the
  beginning,
  from ancient times, what is still to
  come.
  I say, 'My purpose will stand,
  and I will do all that I please.'
11 From the east I summon a bird of prey;
  from a far-off land, a man to fulfill
  my purpose.
What I have said, that I will bring about;
  what I have planned, that I will do.
12 Listen to me, you stubborn-hearted,
  you who are now far from my
  righteousness.
13 I am bringing my righteousness near,
  it is not far away;
  and my salvation will not be delayed.
I will grant salvation to Zion,
  my splendor to Israel.

The Fall of Babylon

47 "Go down, sit in the dust,
  Virgin Daughter Babylon;
  sit on the ground without a
  throne,
  queen city of the Babylonians.*b*

---

a 1 Or *are but beasts and cattle*   *b* 1 Or *Chaldeans*; also in verse 5

No more will you be called
    tender or delicate.
2 Take millstones and grind flour;
    take off your veil.
Lift up your skirts, bare your legs,
    and wade through the streams.
3 Your nakedness will be exposed
    and your shame uncovered.
I will take vengeance;
    I will spare no one."

4 Our Redeemer — the Lord Almighty is
    his name —
    is the Holy One of Israel.

5 "Sit in silence, go into darkness,
    queen city of the Babylonians;
no more will you be called
    queen of kingdoms.
6 I was angry with my people
    and desecrated my inheritance;
I gave them into your hand,
    and you showed them no mercy.
Even on the aged
    you laid a very heavy yoke.
7 You said, 'I am forever —
    the eternal queen!'
But you did not consider these things
    or reflect on what might happen.

8 "Now then, listen, you lover of
    pleasure,
    lounging in your security
and saying to yourself,
    'I am, and there is none besides me.
I will never be a widow
    or suffer the loss of children.'
9 Both of these will overtake you
    in a moment, on a single day:
    loss of children and widowhood.
They will come upon you in full
    measure,
    in spite of your many sorceries
    and all your potent spells.
10 You have trusted in your wickedness
    and have said, 'No one sees me.'
Your wisdom and knowledge mislead
    you
when you say to yourself,
    'I am, and there is none besides me.'

11 Disaster will come upon you,
    and you will not know how to
    conjure it away.
A calamity will fall upon you
    that you cannot ward off with a
    ransom;
a catastrophe you cannot foresee
    will suddenly come upon you.

12 "Keep on, then, with your magic spells
    and with your many sorceries,
    which you have labored at since
    childhood.
Perhaps you will succeed,
    perhaps you will cause terror.
13 All the counsel you have received has
    only worn you out!
Let your astrologers come forward,
those stargazers who make predictions
    month by month,
    let them save you from what is
    coming upon you.
14 Surely they are like stubble;
    the fire will burn them up.
They cannot even save themselves
    from the power of the flame.
These are not coals for warmth;
    this is not a fire to sit by.
15 That is all they are to you —
    these you have dealt with
    and labored with since childhood.
All of them go on in their error;
    there is not one that can save you.

Stubborn Israel

48 "Listen to this, you
    descendants of Jacob,
    you who are called by the
    name of Israel
and come from the line of Judah,
you who take oaths in the name of the
    Lord
    and invoke the God of Israel —
    but not in truth or righteousness —
2 you who call yourselves citizens of the
    holy city
and claim to rely on the God of
    Israel —
    the Lord Almighty is his name:

³I foretold the former things long ago,
  my mouth announced them and I
    made them known;
  then suddenly I acted, and they came
    to pass.
⁴For I knew how stubborn you were;
  your neck muscles were iron,
  your forehead was bronze.
⁵Therefore I told you these things long
    ago;
  before they happened I announced
    them to you
  so that you could not say,
    'My images brought them about;
  my wooden image and metal god
    ordained them.'
⁶You have heard these things; look at
    them all.
  Will you not admit them?

  "From now on I will tell you of new
    things,
  of hidden things unknown to you.
⁷They are created now, and not long ago;
  you have not heard of them before
    today.
  So you cannot say,
    'Yes, I knew of them.'
⁸You have neither heard nor understood;
  from of old your ears have not been
    open.
  Well do I know how treacherous you
    are;
  you were called a rebel from birth.
⁹For my own name's sake I delay my
    wrath;
  for the sake of my praise I hold it
    back from you,
  so as not to destroy you completely.
¹⁰See, I have refined you, though not as
    silver;
  I have tested you in the furnace of
    affliction.
¹¹For my own sake, for my own sake, I do
    this.
  How can I let myself be defamed?
  I will not yield my glory to another.

Israel Freed

¹²"Listen to me, Jacob,
  Israel, whom I have called:
I am he;
  I am the first and I am the last.
¹³My own hand laid the foundations of
    the earth,
  and my right hand spread out the
    heavens;
when I summon them,
  they all stand up together.

¹⁴"Come together, all of you, and listen:
  Which of the idols has foretold these
    things?
The Lord's chosen ally
  will carry out his purpose against
    Babylon;
  his arm will be against the
    Babylonians.ᵃ
¹⁵I, even I, have spoken;
  yes, I have called him.
I will bring him,
  and he will succeed in his mission.

¹⁶"Come near me and listen to this:

"From the first announcement I have
    not spoken in secret;
  at the time it happens, I am there."

And now the Sovereign Lord has sent
    me,
  endowed with his Spirit.

¹⁷This is what the Lord says—
  your Redeemer, the Holy One of
    Israel:
"I am the Lord your God,
  who teaches you what is best for
    you,
  who directs you in the way you
    should go.
¹⁸If only you had paid attention to my
    commands,
  your peace would have been like a
    river,
  your well-being like the waves of the
    sea.

ᵃ 14 Or *Chaldeans*; also in verse 20

¹⁹ Your descendants would have been like
the sand,
your children like its numberless
grains;
their name would never be blotted out
nor destroyed from before me."

²⁰ Leave Babylon,
flee from the Babylonians!
Announce this with shouts of joy
and proclaim it.
Send it out to the ends of the earth;
say, "The LORD has redeemed his
servant Jacob."
²¹ They did not thirst when he led them
through the deserts;
he made water flow for them from
the rock;
he split the rock
and water gushed out.

²² "There is no peace," says the LORD, "for
the wicked."

The Servant of the LORD

49 Listen to me, you islands;
hear this, you distant nations:
Before I was born the LORD
called me;
from my mother's womb he has
spoken my name.
² He made my mouth like a sharpened
sword,
in the shadow of his hand he hid me;
he made me into a polished arrow
and concealed me in his quiver.
³ He said to me, "You are my servant,
Israel, in whom I will display my
splendor."
⁴ But I said, "I have labored in vain;
I have spent my strength for nothing
at all.
Yet what is due me is in the LORD's hand,
and my reward is with my God."

⁵ And now the LORD says—
he who formed me in the womb to be
his servant

to bring Jacob back to him
and gather Israel to himself,
for I am*a* honored in the eyes of the
LORD
and my God has been my strength—
⁶ he says:
"It is too small a thing for you to be my
servant
to restore the tribes of Jacob
and bring back those of Israel I have
kept.
I will also make you a light for the
Gentiles,
that my salvation may reach to the
ends of the earth."

⁷ This is what the LORD says—
the Redeemer and Holy One of
Israel—
to him who was despised and abhorred
by the nation,
to the servant of rulers:
"Kings will see you and stand up,
princes will see and bow down,
because of the LORD, who is faithful,
the Holy One of Israel, who has
chosen you."

Restoration of Israel

⁸ This is what the LORD says:

"In the time of my favor I will answer
you,
and in the day of salvation I will help
you;
I will keep you and will make you
to be a covenant for the people,
to restore the land
and to reassign its desolate
inheritances,
⁹ to say to the captives, 'Come out,'
and to those in darkness, 'Be free!'

"They will feed beside the roads
and find pasture on every barren hill.
¹⁰ They will neither hunger nor thirst,
nor will the desert heat or the sun
beat down on them.

---

a 5 Or him, / but Israel would not be gathered; / yet I will be

He who has compassion on them will
  guide them
  and lead them beside springs of water.
¹¹ I will turn all my mountains into roads,
  and my highways will be raised up.
¹² See, they will come from afar —
  some from the north, some from the
    west,
  some from the region of Aswan.ᵃ"

¹³ Shout for joy, you heavens;
  rejoice, you earth;
  burst into song, you mountains!
For the LORD comforts his people
  and will have compassion on his
    afflicted ones.

¹⁴ But Zion said, "The LORD has forsaken
    me,
  the Lord has forgotten me."

¹⁵ "Can a mother forget the baby at her
    breast
  and have no compassion on the child
    she has borne?
Though she may forget,
  I will not forget you!
¹⁶ See, I have engraved you on the palms
    of my hands;
  your walls are ever before me.
¹⁷ Your children hasten back,
  and those who laid you waste depart
    from you.
¹⁸ Lift up your eyes and look around;
  all your children gather and come to
    you.
As surely as I live," declares the LORD,
  "you will wear them all as
    ornaments;
  you will put them on, like a bride.

¹⁹ "Though you were ruined and made
    desolate
  and your land laid waste,
now you will be too small for your
    people,
  and those who devoured you will be
    far away.

²⁰ The children born during your
    bereavement
  will yet say in your hearing,
'This place is too small for us;
  give us more space to live in.'
²¹ Then you will say in your heart,
  'Who bore me these?
I was bereaved and barren;
  I was exiled and rejected.
Who brought these up?
I was left all alone,
  but these — where have they come
    from?' "

²² This is what the Sovereign LORD says:

"See, I will beckon to the nations,
  I will lift up my banner to the
    peoples;
they will bring your sons in their arms
  and carry your daughters on their
    hips.
²³ Kings will be your foster fathers,
  and their queens your nursing
    mothers.
They will bow down before you with
    their faces to the ground;
  they will lick the dust at your feet.
Then you will know that I am the LORD;
  those who hope in me will not be
    disappointed."

²⁴ Can plunder be taken from warriors,
  or captives be rescued from the
    fierceᵇ?

²⁵ But this is what the LORD says:

"Yes, captives will be taken from
    warriors,
  and plunder retrieved from the
    fierce;
I will contend with those who contend
    with you,
  and your children I will save.
²⁶ I will make your oppressors eat their
    own flesh;
  they will be drunk on their own
    blood, as with wine.

ᵃ 12 Dead Sea Scrolls; Masoretic Text *Sinim*   ᵇ 24 Dead Sea Scrolls, Vulgate and Syriac (see also Septuagint and
verse 25); Masoretic Text *righteous*

Then all mankind will know
  that I, the LORD, am your Savior,
  your Redeemer, the Mighty One of
    Jacob."

Israel's Sin and the Servant's Obedience

50 This is what the LORD says:

"Where is your mother's
    certificate of divorce
  with which I sent her away?
Or to which of my creditors
    did I sell you?
Because of your sins you were sold;
  because of your transgressions your
    mother was sent away.
2 When I came, why was there no one?
  When I called, why was there no one
    to answer?
Was my arm too short to deliver you?
  Do I lack the strength to rescue you?
By a mere rebuke I dry up the sea,
  I turn rivers into a desert;
their fish rot for lack of water
  and die of thirst.
3 I clothe the heavens with darkness
  and make sackcloth its covering."

4 The Sovereign LORD has given me a
    well-instructed tongue,
  to know the word that sustains the
    weary.
He wakens me morning by morning,
  wakens my ear to listen like one
    being instructed.
5 The Sovereign LORD has opened my
    ears;
  I have not been rebellious,
  I have not turned away.
6 I offered my back to those who beat me,
  my cheeks to those who pulled out
    my beard;
I did not hide my face
  from mocking and spitting.
7 Because the Sovereign LORD helps me,
  I will not be disgraced.
Therefore have I set my face like flint,
  and I know I will not be put to
    shame.

8 He who vindicates me is near.
  Who then will bring charges against
    me?
  Let us face each other!
Who is my accuser?
  Let him confront me!
9 It is the Sovereign LORD who helps me.
  Who will condemn me?
They will all wear out like a garment;
  the moths will eat them up.

10 Who among you fears the LORD
  and obeys the word of his servant?
Let the one who walks in the dark,
  who has no light,
trust in the name of the LORD
  and rely on their God.
11 But now, all you who light fires
  and provide yourselves with flaming
    torches,
go, walk in the light of your fires
  and of the torches you have set
    ablaze.
This is what you shall receive from my
    hand:
  You will lie down in torment.

Everlasting Salvation for Zion

51 "Listen to me, you who pursue
    righteousness
  and who seek the LORD:
Look to the rock from which you were
    cut
  and to the quarry from which you
    were hewn;
2 look to Abraham, your father,
  and to Sarah, who gave you birth.
When I called him he was only one man,
  and I blessed him and made him
    many.
3 The LORD will surely comfort Zion
  and will look with compassion on all
    her ruins;
he will make her deserts like Eden,
  her wastelands like the garden of the
    LORD.
Joy and gladness will be found in her,
  thanksgiving and the sound of
    singing.

4 "Listen to me, my people;
    hear me, my nation:
Instruction will go out from me;
    my justice will become a light to the
        nations.
5 My righteousness draws near speedily,
    my salvation is on the way,
    and my arm will bring justice to the
        nations.
The islands will look to me
    and wait in hope for my arm.
6 Lift up your eyes to the heavens,
    look at the earth beneath;
the heavens will vanish like smoke,
    the earth will wear out like a garment
    and its inhabitants die like flies.
But my salvation will last forever,
    my righteousness will never fail.

7 "Hear me, you who know what is right,
    you people who have taken my
        instruction to heart:
Do not fear the reproach of mere
        mortals
    or be terrified by their insults.
8 For the moth will eat them up like a
        garment;
    the worm will devour them like
        wool.
But my righteousness will last forever,
    my salvation through all
        generations."

9 Awake, awake, arm of the Lord,
    clothe yourself with strength!
Awake, as in days gone by,
    as in generations of old.
Was it not you who cut Rahab to pieces,
    who pierced that monster through?
10 Was it not you who dried up the sea,
    the waters of the great deep,
who made a road in the depths of the
        sea
    so that the redeemed might cross
        over?
11 Those the Lord has rescued will
        return.
    They will enter Zion with singing;
    everlasting joy will crown their
        heads.

Gladness and joy will overtake them,
    and sorrow and sighing will flee
        away.

12 "I, even I, am he who comforts you.
    Who are you that you fear mere
        mortals,
    human beings who are but grass,
13 that you forget the Lord your Maker,
    who stretches out the heavens
    and who lays the foundations of the
        earth,
that you live in constant terror every
        day
    because of the wrath of the
        oppressor,
    who is bent on destruction?
For where is the wrath of the oppressor?
14   The cowering prisoners will soon be
        set free;
they will not die in their dungeon,
    nor will they lack bread.
15 For I am the Lord your God,
    who stirs up the sea so that its waves
        roar —
    the Lord Almighty is his name.
16 I have put my words in your mouth
    and covered you with the shadow of
        my hand —
I who set the heavens in place,
    who laid the foundations of the
        earth,
    and who say to Zion, 'You are my
        people.'"

The Cup of the Lord's Wrath

17 Awake, awake!
    Rise up, Jerusalem,
you who have drunk from the hand of
        the Lord
    the cup of his wrath,
you who have drained to its dregs
    the goblet that makes people
        stagger.
18 Among all the children she bore
    there was none to guide her;
among all the children she reared
    there was none to take her by the
        hand.

19 These double calamities have come
        upon you —
    who can comfort you? —
ruin and destruction, famine and
        sword —
    who can*a* console you?
20 Your children have fainted;
        they lie at every street corner,
        like antelope caught in a net.
    They are filled with the wrath of the
        LORD,
        with the rebuke of your God.

21 Therefore hear this, you afflicted one,
        made drunk, but not with wine.
22 This is what your Sovereign LORD says,
        your God, who defends his people:
    "See, I have taken out of your hand
        the cup that made you stagger;
    from that cup, the goblet of my wrath,
        you will never drink again.
23 I will put it into the hands of your
        tormentors,
    who said to you,
        'Fall prostrate that we may walk on
        you.'
    And you made your back like the
        ground,
        like a street to be walked on."

52 Awake, awake, Zion,
        clothe yourself with strength!
        Put on your garments of
        splendor,
    Jerusalem, the holy city.
    The uncircumcised and defiled
        will not enter you again.
2 Shake off your dust;
        rise up, sit enthroned, Jerusalem.
    Free yourself from the chains on your
        neck,
        Daughter Zion, now a captive.

3 For this is what the LORD says:

    "You were sold for nothing,
        and without money you will be
        redeemed."

4 For this is what the Sovereign LORD
says:

    "At first my people went down to Egypt
        to live;
        lately, Assyria has oppressed them.

5 "And now what do I have here?" declares the LORD.

    "For my people have been taken away
        for nothing,
        and those who rule them mock,*b*"
            declares the LORD.
    "And all day long
        my name is constantly blasphemed.
6 Therefore my people will know my
        name;
    therefore in that day they will know
    that it is I who foretold it.
        Yes, it is I."

7 How beautiful on the mountains
    are the feet of those who bring good
        news,
who proclaim peace,
    who bring good tidings,
    who proclaim salvation,
who say to Zion,
    "Your God reigns!"
8 Listen! Your watchmen lift up their
        voices;
    together they shout for joy.
When the LORD returns to Zion,
    they will see it with their own eyes.
9 Burst into songs of joy together,
    you ruins of Jerusalem,
for the LORD has comforted his people,
    he has redeemed Jerusalem.
10 The LORD will lay bare his holy arm
    in the sight of all the nations,
and all the ends of the earth will see
    the salvation of our God.

11 Depart, depart, go out from there!
    Touch no unclean thing!
Come out from it and be pure,
    you who carry the articles of the
        LORD's house.

7
8

---

a 19 Dead Sea Scrolls, Septuagint, Vulgate and Syriac; Masoretic Text / *how can I*   *b* 5 Dead Sea Scrolls and
Vulgate; Masoretic Text *wail*

12 But you will not leave in haste
    or go in flight;
for the Lord will go before you,
    the God of Israel will be your rear
        guard.

The Suffering and Glory of the Servant

13 See, my servant will act wisely[a];
    he will be raised and lifted up and
        highly exalted.
14 Just as there were many who were
        appalled at him[b] —
    his appearance was so disfigured
        beyond that of any human being
    and his form marred beyond human
        likeness —
15 so he will sprinkle many nations,[c]
    and kings will shut their mouths
        because of him.
For what they were not told, they will
        see,
    and what they have not heard, they
        will understand.

53

Who has believed our message
and to whom has the arm of
the Lord been revealed?
2 He grew up before him like a tender
        shoot,
    and like a root out of dry ground.
He had no beauty or majesty to attract
        us to him,
    nothing in his appearance that we
        should desire him.
3 He was despised and rejected by
        mankind,
    a man of suffering, and familiar with
        pain.
Like one from whom people hide their
        faces
    he was despised, and we held him in
        low esteem.

4 Surely he took up our pain
    and bore our suffering,
yet we considered him punished by
        God,
    stricken by him, and afflicted.
5 But he was pierced for our
        transgressions,
    he was crushed for our iniquities;
the punishment that brought us peace
        was on him,
    and by his wounds we are healed.
6 We all, like sheep, have gone astray,
    each of us has turned to our own
        way;
and the Lord has laid on him
    the iniquity of us all.

7 He was oppressed and afflicted,
    yet he did not open his mouth;
he was led like a lamb to the slaughter,
    and as a sheep before its shearers is
        silent,
    so he did not open his mouth.
8 By oppression[d] and judgment he was
        taken away.
    Yet who of his generation protested?
For he was cut off from the land of the
        living;
    for the transgression of my people he
        was punished.[e]
9 He was assigned a grave with the
        wicked,
    and with the rich in his death,
though he had done no violence,
    nor was any deceit in his mouth.

10 Yet it was the Lord's will to crush him
        and cause him to suffer,
    and though the Lord makes[f] his life
        an offering for sin,
he will see his offspring and prolong his
        days,
    and the will of the Lord will prosper
        in his hand.
11 After he has suffered,
    he will see the light of life[g] and be
        satisfied[h];

---

a 13 Or will prosper   b 14 Hebrew you   c 15 Or so will many nations be amazed at him (see also Septuagint)
d 8 Or From arrest   e 8 Or generation considered / that he was cut off from the land of the living, / that he was
punished for the transgression of my people?   f 10 Hebrew though you make   g 11 Dead Sea Scrolls (see also
Septuagint); Masoretic Text does not have the light of life.   h 11 Or (with Masoretic Text) 11He will see the fruit of his
suffering / and will be satisfied

MY NAME IS
THE STRAY SHEEP

ISAIAH 53:6

Every human being can relate to this Bible character. In fact, each of us *is* this character. Every one of us has gone our own way. Specific sins are offshoots of the overriding sin of forging our own path through life. The Hebrew word translated "way" comes from a verb that means "to tread" or "to walk." This "way" is a road, a path created by the trampling of many feet. This road is described in Proverbs 14:12: "There is a way that appears to be right, but in the end it leads to death." Death is the destination of any way that isn't God's way. But we can make the move to God's road from wherever we've started out. We can travel in a new direction in life because God has laid all our sins on Jesus. Christ carried those sins to the cross, where he died in our place. There is a way, a road to recovery, and each of us is invited to travel it.

This route to God passes through Jesus Christ (see John 14:6), and walking on it reverses the damage done from going our own way:

Therefore, brothers and sisters, since we have confidence to enter the Most Holy Place by the blood of Jesus, by a new and living way opened for us through the curtain, that is, his body, and since we have a great priest over the house of God, let us draw near to God with a sincere heart and with the full assurance that faith brings, having our hearts sprinkled to cleanse us from a guilty conscience and having our bodies washed with pure water (see Hebrews 10:19–22).

The first Christians were called those "who belonged to the Way" (Acts 9:2). These early believers didn't find that way on their own, and neither will we. A sheep is too dim-witted to find the right path on its own and too weak-willed to follow it even if it did. We all need help from the Good Shepherd, Jesus Christ (see John 10:11,14), and all we have to do is respond to his voice:

My sheep listen to my voice; I know them, and they follow me. I give them eternal life, and they shall never perish; no one will snatch them out of my hand. My Father, who has given them to me, is greater than all; no one can snatch them out of my Father's hand. I and the Father are one. (John 10:27–30)

Eliminating a particular habit or hang-up isn't recovery. Recovery is a 180-degree reversal of the direction of our life. Recovery is all about following Jesus—about treading in the footsteps of the Good Shepherd.

by his knowledge[a] my righteous servant
　　will justify many,
　and he will bear their iniquities.
[12] Therefore I will give him a portion
　　among the great,[b]
　and he will divide the spoils with the
　　strong,[c]
because he poured out his life unto
　　death,
　and was numbered with the
　　transgressors.
For he bore the sin of many,
　and made intercession for the
　　transgressors.

The Future Glory of Zion

54 "Sing, barren woman,
　　you who never bore a child;
　　burst into song, shout for joy,
you who were never in labor;
because more are the children of the
　　desolate woman
　than of her who has a husband,"
　　　　　　　says the LORD.
[2] "Enlarge the place of your tent,
　stretch your tent curtains wide,
　　do not hold back;
　lengthen your cords,
　　strengthen your stakes.
[3] For you will spread out to the right and
　　to the left;
　your descendants will dispossess
　　nations
　and settle in their desolate cities.

[4] "Do not be afraid; you will not be put to
　　shame.
　Do not fear disgrace; you will not be
　　humiliated.
You will forget the shame of your youth
　and remember no more the reproach
　　of your widowhood.
[5] For your Maker is your husband—
　the LORD Almighty is his name—
　the Holy One of Israel is your
　　Redeemer;
　he is called the God of all the earth.

[6] The LORD will call you back
　as if you were a wife deserted and
　　distressed in spirit—
a wife who married young,
　only to be rejected," says your God.
[7] "For a brief moment I abandoned you,
　but with deep compassion I will
　　bring you back.
[8] In a surge of anger
　I hid my face from you for a moment,
but with everlasting kindness
　I will have compassion on you,"
　　says the LORD your Redeemer.

[9] "To me this is like the days of Noah,
　when I swore that the waters of Noah
　　would never again cover the
　　earth.
So now I have sworn not to be angry
　　with you,
　never to rebuke you again.
[10] Though the mountains be shaken
　and the hills be removed,
yet my unfailing love for you will not be
　　shaken
　nor my covenant of peace be
　　removed,"
　says the LORD, who has compassion
　　on you.

[11] "Afflicted city, lashed by storms and not
　　comforted,
　I will rebuild you with stones of
　　turquoise,[d]
　your foundations with lapis lazuli.
[12] I will make your battlements of rubies,
　your gates of sparkling jewels,
　and all your walls of precious stones.
[13] All your children will be taught by the
　　LORD,
　and great will be their peace.
[14] In righteousness you will be
　　established:
Tyranny will be far from you;
　you will have nothing to fear.
Terror will be far removed;
　it will not come near you.

---

[a] 11 Or *by knowledge of him*　[b] 12 Or *many*　[c] 12 Or *numerous*　[d] 11 The meaning of the Hebrew for this word is uncertain.

My Name Is Hillary

I'M A BELIEVER WHO STRUGGLES WITH ADDICTIVE AND COMPULSIVE BEHAVIORS

Please read Isaiah's statement about lost sheep in Isaiah 53:6.

My struggles began when I was a young girl. I felt cultural pressures from society, my family and my peers — pressures that shaped my belief system with regard to who I was and how I should look. As a way of coping, I developed an eating disorder and began experimenting with alcohol. These were the first big secrets in my life. As I grew older the eating disorder became difficult to hide, and I began to replace that no-longer-effective coping mechanism with drugs, alcohol and sex. I used these substances and compulsive behaviors as a way to mask my pain, boredom and frustration. My addictions left me unable to experience or even recognize healthy emotions, such as joy, peace and contentment. The consequences of my choices caused me unanticipated physical and emotional damage and necessitated more secrets — feelings and events I could never have imagined sharing with another human being. I would have continued on this dangerous path for the rest of my life had not God intervened.

Eight years ago I lost my mother to breast cancer. Up to that point I had convinced myself that I'd mastered the art of denial; I fully believed until the very end that Mom would beat the disease. She had been the rock in my life, and I was totally unprepared to lose her. Ironically, the last week of her life marked the beginning of a new life for me. I knew I could no longer ignore the spiritual void within me. If something didn't change, I realized, the baggage I was carrying would suck me under and drown me.

My journey toward God began at First Christian Church in Sandpoint, Idaho. It was difficult at first. I was grieving the loss of my mother and didn't know anyone else there. The worship music made me cry. Even though I lacked Biblical knowledge, I was fully aware that the life I'd been living was inappropriate. I began to study the Bible, in the process learning who Jesus was and what he stood for. But the most powerful lessons came not from Scripture but from the people around me who were living out that Word. My newfound relationship with Christ couldn't last, I knew, if I continued to drag around my enormous truckload of baggage: my daily struggle with my addictions; my battles with food, intimacy and anger; and the overwhelming amount of pride required by my elaborate cover-up.

When I was in church or around my new Christian friends, I would present the side of myself that was healthy and moving forward. But in the rest of my life, I continued to struggle. I wasn't trying to be phony but honestly assumed that the Christian life didn't incorporate any of my addictions or struggles. In order to be a "good" Christian, I had to perpetuate a certain idea about my life, even if it didn't include the whole truth about me. The truth has a way of striking deep, though, and I finally came to recognize that the only real Truth is found in God's Word. But at that point I just couldn't completely surrender to it.

God knew exactly what I needed. It wasn't long before he placed his hand on my shoulder and led me like a lost sheep to himself. He did this by guiding my steps to Celebrate Recovery. I was surprised to find myself in a setting where I could expose the tender, vulnerable parts of myself and still find love and acceptance. Through Celebrate Recovery I discovered grace, and as a result, the love of Jesus has become tangible and real in my life. I was surrounded by men and women who loved the Lord yet were willing to admit that they still struggled. Through their willingness to be open, I learned more about myself. More important, though, I learned about faith.

I'm so grateful for the people who surround me in Celebrate Recovery, who love me in spite of myself and who lift me up and hold me accountable. I'm no longer afraid to feel the pain, hurt and disappointments in my life because I know that eventually these very feelings and emotions will allow me to experience deep contentment and joy. I now know what it's like to have meaningful, heartfelt connections with other people. It has been one of the greatest joys in my life to serve in this ministry and to watch what God is doing in the lives of others.

I wouldn't trade the journey that has brought me here for any other experience. I continue to work the program and to trust in the wisdom of the process. I understand that if I keep on placing my faith in the power of the Holy Spirit, I'll continue to find the peace I've always longed for.

"We all, like sheep, have gone astray, each of us has turned to our own way" (Isaiah 53:6). I'm no exception, and I now understand Jesus' words in John 10:27: "My sheep listen to my voice; I know them, and they follow me."

¹⁵ If anyone does attack you, it will not be
my doing;
whoever attacks you will surrender
to you.

¹⁶ "See, it is I who created the blacksmith
who fans the coals into flame
and forges a weapon fit for its work.
And it is I who have created the
destroyer to wreak havoc;
¹⁷ no weapon forged against you will
prevail,
and you will refute every tongue that
accuses you.
This is the heritage of the servants of
the LORD,
and this is their vindication from
me,"
declares the LORD.

Invitation to the Thirsty

55 "Come, all you who are
thirsty,
come to the waters;
and you who have no money,
come, buy and eat!
Come, buy wine and milk
without money and without cost.
² Why spend money on what is not
bread,
and your labor on what does not
satisfy?
Listen, listen to me, and eat what is
good,
and you will delight in the richest of
fare.
³ Give ear and come to me;
listen, that you may live.
I will make an everlasting covenant
with you,
my faithful love promised to David.
⁴ See, I have made him a witness to the
peoples,
a ruler and commander of the
peoples.
⁵ Surely you will summon nations you
know not,
and nations you do not know will
come running to you,

because of the LORD your God,
the Holy One of Israel,
for he has endowed you with
splendor."

⁶ Seek the LORD while he may be found;
call on him while he is near.
⁷ Let the wicked forsake their ways
and the unrighteous their thoughts.
Let them turn to the LORD, and he will
have mercy on them,
and to our God, for he will freely
pardon.

⁸ "For my thoughts are not your
thoughts,
neither are your ways my ways,"
declares the LORD.
⁹ "As the heavens are higher than the
earth,
so are my ways higher than your
ways
and my thoughts than your
thoughts.
¹⁰ As the rain and the snow
come down from heaven,
and do not return to it
without watering the earth
and making it bud and flourish,
so that it yields seed for the sower
and bread for the eater,
¹¹ so is my word that goes out from my
mouth:
It will not return to me empty,
but will accomplish what I desire
and achieve the purpose for which I
sent it.
¹² You will go out in joy
and be led forth in peace;
the mountains and hills
will burst into song before you,
and all the trees of the field
will clap their hands.
¹³ Instead of the thornbush will grow the
juniper,
and instead of briers the myrtle will
grow.
This will be for the LORD's renown,
for an everlasting sign,
that will endure forever."

Salvation for Others

56

This is what the LORD says:

"Maintain justice
and do what is right,
for my salvation is close at hand
and my righteousness will soon be
revealed.
² Blessed is the one who does this—
the person who holds it fast,
who keeps the Sabbath without
desecrating it,
and keeps their hands from doing
any evil."

³ Let no foreigner who is bound to the
LORD say,
"The LORD will surely exclude me
from his people."
And let no eunuch complain,
"I am only a dry tree."

⁴ For this is what the LORD says:

"To the eunuchs who keep my
Sabbaths,
who choose what pleases me
and hold fast to my covenant—
⁵ to them I will give within my temple
and its walls
a memorial and a name
better than sons and daughters;
I will give them an everlasting name
that will endure forever.
⁶ And foreigners who bind themselves to
the LORD
to minister to him,
to love the name of the LORD,
and to be his servants,
all who keep the Sabbath without
desecrating it
and who hold fast to my
covenant—
⁷ these I will bring to my holy mountain
and give them joy in my house of
prayer.
Their burnt offerings and sacrifices
will be accepted on my altar;
for my house will be called
a house of prayer for all nations."

⁸ The Sovereign LORD declares—
he who gathers the exiles of Israel:
"I will gather still others to them
besides those already gathered."

God's Accusation Against the Wicked

⁹ Come, all you beasts of the field,
come and devour, all you beasts of
the forest!
¹⁰ Israel's watchmen are blind,
they all lack knowledge;
they are all mute dogs,
they cannot bark;
they lie around and dream,
they love to sleep.
¹¹ They are dogs with mighty appetites;
they never have enough.
They are shepherds who lack
understanding;
they all turn to their own way,
they seek their own gain.
¹² "Come," each one cries, "let me get wine!
Let us drink our fill of beer!
And tomorrow will be like today,
or even far better."

57

The righteous perish,
and no one takes it to heart;
the devout are taken away,
and no one understands
that the righteous are taken away
to be spared from evil.
² Those who walk uprightly
enter into peace;
they find rest as they lie in death.

³ "But you—come here, you children of a
sorceress,
you offspring of adulterers and
prostitutes!
⁴ Who are you mocking?
At whom do you sneer
and stick out your tongue?
Are you not a brood of rebels,
the offspring of liars?
⁵ You burn with lust among the oaks
and under every spreading tree;
you sacrifice your children in the ravines
and under the overhanging crags.

⁶The idols among the smooth stones of
    the ravines are your portion;
indeed, they are your lot.
Yes, to them you have poured out drink
    offerings
    and offered grain offerings.
In view of all this, should I relent?
⁷You have made your bed on a high and
    lofty hill;
there you went up to offer your
    sacrifices.
⁸Behind your doors and your doorposts
    you have put your pagan symbols.
Forsaking me, you uncovered your bed,
    you climbed into it and opened it
    wide;
you made a pact with those whose beds
    you love,
    and you looked with lust on their
    naked bodies.
⁹You went to Molek*a* with olive oil
    and increased your perfumes.
You sent your ambassadors*b* far away;
    you descended to the very realm of
    the dead!
¹⁰You wearied yourself by such going
    about,
    but you would not say, 'It is hopeless.'
You found renewal of your strength,
    and so you did not faint.

¹¹"Whom have you so dreaded and feared
    that you have not been true to me,
and have neither remembered me
    nor taken this to heart?
Is it not because I have long been silent
    that you do not fear me?
¹²I will expose your righteousness and
    your works,
    and they will not benefit you.
¹³When you cry out for help,
    let your collection of idols save you!
The wind will carry all of them off,
    a mere breath will blow them away.
But whoever takes refuge in me
    will inherit the land
    and possess my holy mountain."

Comfort for the Contrite

¹⁴And it will be said:

"Build up, build up, prepare the road!
    Remove the obstacles out of the way
    of my people."
¹⁵For this is what the high and exalted
    One says —
he who lives forever, whose name is
    holy:
"I live in a high and holy place,
    but also with the one who is contrite
    and lowly in spirit,
to revive the spirit of the lowly
    and to revive the heart of the
    contrite.
¹⁶I will not accuse them forever,
    nor will I always be angry,
for then they would faint away because
    of me —
    the very people I have created.
¹⁷I was enraged by their sinful greed;
    I punished them, and hid my face in
    anger,
    yet they kept on in their willful ways.
¹⁸I have seen their ways, but I will heal
    them;
    I will guide them and restore comfort
    to Israel's mourners,
¹⁹   creating praise on their lips.
Peace, peace, to those far and near,"
    says the LORD. "And I will heal
    them."
²⁰But the wicked are like the tossing sea,
    which cannot rest,
    whose waves cast up mire and mud.
²¹"There is no peace," says my God, "for
    the wicked."

True Fasting

58 "Shout it aloud, do not hold
    back.
    Raise your voice like a
    trumpet.
Declare to my people their rebellion
    and to the descendants of Jacob their
    sins.

---

a 9 Or *to the king*   *b* 9 Or *idols*

²For day after day they seek me out;
    they seem eager to know my ways,
as if they were a nation that does what is
        right
    and has not forsaken the commands
        of its God.
They ask me for just decisions
    and seem eager for God to come near
        them.
³'Why have we fasted,' they say,
    'and you have not seen it?
Why have we humbled ourselves,
    and you have not noticed?'

"Yet on the day of your fasting, you do
        as you please
    and exploit all your workers.
⁴Your fasting ends in quarreling and
        strife,
    and in striking each other with
        wicked fists.
You cannot fast as you do today
    and expect your voice to be heard on
        high.
⁵Is this the kind of fast I have chosen,
    only a day for people to humble
        themselves?
Is it only for bowing one's head like a
        reed
    and for lying in sackcloth and
        ashes?
Is that what you call a fast,
    a day acceptable to the LORD?

⁶"Is not this the kind of fasting I have
        chosen:
to loose the chains of injustice
    and untie the cords of the yoke,
to set the oppressed free
    and break every yoke?
⁷Is it not to share your food with the
        hungry
    and to provide the poor wanderer
        with shelter —
when you see the naked, to clothe
        them,
    and not to turn away from your own
        flesh and blood?

⁸Then your light will break forth like the
        dawn,
    and your healing will quickly
        appear;
then your righteousnessᵃ will go before
        you,
    and the glory of the LORD will be
        your rear guard.
⁹Then you will call, and the LORD will
        answer;
    you will cry for help, and he will say:
        Here am I.

"If you do away with the yoke of
        oppression,
    with the pointing finger and
        malicious talk,
¹⁰and if you spend yourselves in behalf of
        the hungry
    and satisfy the needs of the
        oppressed,
then your light will rise in the darkness,
    and your night will become like the
        noonday.
¹¹The LORD will guide you always;
    he will satisfy your needs in a sun-
        scorched land
    and will strengthen your frame.
You will be like a well-watered garden,
    like a spring whose waters never fail.
¹²Your people will rebuild the ancient
        ruins
    and will raise up the age-old
        foundations;
you will be called Repairer of Broken
        Walls,
    Restorer of Streets with Dwellings.

¹³"If you keep your feet from breaking
        the Sabbath
    and from doing as you please on my
        holy day,
if you call the Sabbath a delight
    and the LORD's holy day honorable,
and if you honor it by not going your
        own way
    and not doing as you please or
        speaking idle words,

ᵃ 8 Or *your righteous One*

¹⁴ then you will find your joy in the LORD,
     and I will cause you to ride in
         triumph on the heights of the
         land
     and to feast on the inheritance of
         your father Jacob."
               For the mouth of the LORD
                   has spoken.

Sin, Confession and Redemption

59 Surely the arm of the LORD is
     not too short to save,
     nor his ear too dull to hear.
² But your iniquities have separated
     you from your God;
   your sins have hidden his face from you,
     so that he will not hear.
³ For your hands are stained with blood,
     your fingers with guilt.
Your lips have spoken falsely,
     and your tongue mutters wicked
         things.
⁴ No one calls for justice;
     no one pleads a case with integrity.
They rely on empty arguments, they
         utter lies;
     they conceive trouble and give birth
         to evil.
⁵ They hatch the eggs of vipers
     and spin a spider's web.
Whoever eats their eggs will die,
     and when one is broken, an adder is
         hatched.
⁶ Their cobwebs are useless for clothing;
     they cannot cover themselves with
         what they make.
Their deeds are evil deeds,
     and acts of violence are in their hands.
⁷ Their feet rush into sin;
     they are swift to shed innocent
         blood.
They pursue evil schemes;
     acts of violence mark their ways.
⁸ The way of peace they do not know;
     there is no justice in their paths.
They have turned them into crooked
         roads;
     no one who walks along them will
         know peace.

⁹ So justice is far from us,
     and righteousness does not reach us.
We look for light, but all is darkness;
     for brightness, but we walk in deep
         shadows.
¹⁰ Like the blind we grope along the wall,
     feeling our way like people without
         eyes.
At midday we stumble as if it were
         twilight;
     among the strong, we are like the
         dead.
¹¹ We all growl like bears;
     we moan mournfully like doves.
We look for justice, but find none;
     for deliverance, but it is far away.

¹² For our offenses are many in your
         sight,
     and our sins testify against us.
Our offenses are ever with us,
     and we acknowledge our iniquities:
¹³ rebellion and treachery against the
         LORD,
     turning our backs on our God,
inciting revolt and oppression,
     uttering lies our hearts have
         conceived.
¹⁴ So justice is driven back,
     and righteousness stands at a
         distance;
truth has stumbled in the streets,
     honesty cannot enter.
¹⁵ Truth is nowhere to be found,
     and whoever shuns evil becomes a
         prey.

The LORD looked and was displeased
     that there was no justice.
¹⁶ He saw that there was no one,
     he was appalled that there was no
         one to intervene;
so his own arm achieved salvation for
         him,
     and his own righteousness sustained
         him.
¹⁷ He put on righteousness as his
         breastplate,
     and the helmet of salvation on his
         head;

he put on the garments of vengeance
    and wrapped himself in zeal as in a
        cloak.
18 According to what they have done,
    so will he repay
wrath to his enemies
    and retribution to his foes;
    he will repay the islands their due.
19 From the west, people will fear the
        name of the LORD,
    and from the rising of the sun, they
        will revere his glory.
For he will come like a pent-up flood
    that the breath of the LORD drives
        along.*a*

20 "The Redeemer will come to Zion,
    to those in Jacob who repent of their
        sins,"
                declares the LORD.

21 "As for me, this is my covenant with
them," says the LORD. "My Spirit, who is
on you, will not depart from you, and my
words that I have put in your mouth will
always be on your lips, on the lips of your
children and on the lips of their descendants — from this time on and forever,"
says the LORD.

The Glory of Zion

60 "Arise, shine, for your light
      has come,
      and the glory of the LORD
      rises upon you.
2 See, darkness covers the earth
    and thick darkness is over the peoples,
but the LORD rises upon you
    and his glory appears over you.
3 Nations will come to your light,
    and kings to the brightness of your
        dawn.

4 "Lift up your eyes and look about you:
    All assemble and come to you;
your sons come from afar,
    and your daughters are carried on
        the hip.

5 Then you will look and be radiant,
    your heart will throb and swell with
        joy;
the wealth on the seas will be brought
        to you,
    to you the riches of the nations will
        come.
6 Herds of camels will cover your land,
    young camels of Midian and Ephah.
And all from Sheba will come,
    bearing gold and incense
    and proclaiming the praise of the
        LORD.
7 All Kedar's flocks will be gathered to
        you,
    the rams of Nebaioth will serve you;
they will be accepted as offerings on my
        altar,
    and I will adorn my glorious temple.

8 "Who are these that fly along like clouds,
    like doves to their nests?
9 Surely the islands look to me;
    in the lead are the ships of Tarshish,*b*
bringing your children from afar,
    with their silver and gold,
to the honor of the LORD your God,
    the Holy One of Israel,
    for he has endowed you with splendor.

10 "Foreigners will rebuild your walls,
    and their kings will serve you.
Though in anger I struck you,
    in favor I will show you compassion.
11 Your gates will always stand open,
    they will never be shut, day or night,
so that people may bring you the wealth
        of the nations —
    their kings led in triumphal
        procession.
12 For the nation or kingdom that will not
        serve you will perish;
    it will be utterly ruined.

13 "The glory of Lebanon will come to
        you,
    the juniper, the fir and the cypress
        together,

---

a 19 Or *When enemies come in like a flood, / the Spirit of the LORD will put them to flight*   *b* 9 Or *the trading ships*

to adorn my sanctuary;
    and I will glorify the place for my
        feet.
14 The children of your oppressors will
        come bowing before you;
    all who despise you will bow down at
        your feet
    and will call you the City of the Lord,
        Zion of the Holy One of Israel.

15 "Although you have been forsaken and
        hated,
    with no one traveling through,
    I will make you the everlasting pride
        and the joy of all generations.
16 You will drink the milk of nations
        and be nursed at royal breasts.
    Then you will know that I, the Lord,
        am your Savior,
        your Redeemer, the Mighty One of
            Jacob.
17 Instead of bronze I will bring you gold,
        and silver in place of iron.
    Instead of wood I will bring you bronze,
        and iron in place of stones.
    I will make peace your governor
        and well-being your ruler.
18 No longer will violence be heard in
        your land,
        nor ruin or destruction within your
            borders,
    but you will call your walls Salvation
        and your gates Praise.
19 The sun will no more be your light by
        day,
        nor will the brightness of the moon
            shine on you,
    for the Lord will be your everlasting
        light,
        and your God will be your glory.
20 Your sun will never set again,
        and your moon will wane no more;
    the Lord will be your everlasting light,
        and your days of sorrow will end.
21 Then all your people will be righteous
        and they will possess the land
            forever.

They are the shoot I have planted,
    the work of my hands,
    for the display of my splendor.
22 The least of you will become a
        thousand,
    the smallest a mighty nation.
    I am the Lord;
        in its time I will do this swiftly."

The Year of the Lord's Favor

61 The Spirit of the Sovereign
        Lord is on me,
        because the Lord has
        anointed me
    to proclaim good news to the poor.
    He has sent me to bind up the
        brokenhearted,
        to proclaim freedom for the captives
        and release from darkness for the
            prisoners,[a]
2 to proclaim the year of the Lord's favor
        and the day of vengeance of our God,
    to comfort all who mourn,
3   and provide for those who grieve in
            Zion —
    to bestow on them a crown of beauty
        instead of ashes,
    the oil of joy
        instead of mourning,
    and a garment of praise
        instead of a spirit of despair.
    They will be called oaks of righteousness,
        a planting of the Lord
        for the display of his splendor.

4 They will rebuild the ancient ruins
        and restore the places long
            devastated;
    they will renew the ruined cities
        that have been devastated for
            generations.
5 Strangers will shepherd your flocks;
        foreigners will work your fields and
            vineyards.
6 And you will be called priests of the
        Lord,
    you will be named ministers of our
        God.

---

a 1 Hebrew; Septuagint *the blind*

You will feed on the wealth of nations,
and in their riches you will boast.

⁷Instead of your shame
you will receive a double portion,
and instead of disgrace
you will rejoice in your inheritance.
And so you will inherit a double
portion in your land,
and everlasting joy will be yours.

⁸"For I, the Lord, love justice;
I hate robbery and wrongdoing.
In my faithfulness I will reward my
people
and make an everlasting covenant
with them.
⁹Their descendants will be known
among the nations
and their offspring among the
peoples.
All who see them will acknowledge
that they are a people the Lord has
blessed."

¹⁰I delight greatly in the Lord;
my soul rejoices in my God.
For he has clothed me with garments of
salvation
and arrayed me in a robe of his
righteousness,
as a bridegroom adorns his head like a
priest,
and as a bride adorns herself with her
jewels.
¹¹For as the soil makes the sprout come up
and a garden causes seeds to grow,
so the Sovereign Lord will make
righteousness
and praise spring up before all nations.

Zion's New Name

62 For Zion's sake I will not keep
silent,
for Jerusalem's sake I will not
remain quiet,
till her vindication shines out like the
dawn,
her salvation like a blazing torch.

²The nations will see your vindication,
and all kings your glory;
you will be called by a new name
that the mouth of the Lord will
bestow.
³You will be a crown of splendor in the
Lord's hand,
a royal diadem in the hand of your
God.
⁴No longer will they call you Deserted,
or name your land Desolate.
But you will be called Hephzibah,ᵃ
and your land Beulahᵇ;
for the Lord will take delight in you,
and your land will be married.
⁵As a young man marries a young
woman,
so will your Builder marry you;
as a bridegroom rejoices over his bride,
so will your God rejoice over you.

⁶I have posted watchmen on your walls,
Jerusalem;
they will never be silent day or night.
You who call on the Lord,
give yourselves no rest,
⁷and give him no rest till he establishes
Jerusalem
and makes her the praise of the
earth.

⁸The Lord has sworn by his right hand
and by his mighty arm:
"Never again will I give your grain
as food for your enemies,
and never again will foreigners drink
the new wine
for which you have toiled;
⁹but those who harvest it will eat it
and praise the Lord,
and those who gather the grapes will
drink it
in the courts of my sanctuary."

¹⁰Pass through, pass through the gates!
Prepare the way for the people.
Build up, build up the highway!
Remove the stones.
Raise a banner for the nations.

ᵃ 4 *Hephzibah* means *my delight is in her.*   ᵇ 4 *Beulah* means *married.*

11 The LORD has made proclamation
    to the ends of the earth:
"Say to Daughter Zion,
    'See, your Savior comes!
See, his reward is with him,
    and his recompense accompanies
        him.'"
12 They will be called the Holy People,
    the Redeemed of the LORD;
and you will be called Sought After,
    the City No Longer Deserted.

God's Day of Vengeance and Redemption

63 Who is this coming from
    Edom,
        from Bozrah, with his
    garments stained crimson?
Who is this, robed in splendor,
    striding forward in the greatness of
        his strength?

"It is I, proclaiming victory,
    mighty to save."

2 Why are your garments red,
    like those of one treading the
        winepress?

3 "I have trodden the winepress alone;
    from the nations no one was
        with me.
I trampled them in my anger
    and trod them down in my wrath;
their blood spattered my garments,
    and I stained all my clothing.
4 It was for me the day of vengeance;
    the year for me to redeem had
        come.
5 I looked, but there was no one to help,
    I was appalled that no one gave
        support;
so my own arm achieved salvation
    for me,
    and my own wrath sustained me.
6 I trampled the nations in my anger;
    in my wrath I made them drunk
    and poured their blood on the
        ground."

Praise and Prayer

7 I will tell of the kindnesses of the LORD,
    the deeds for which he is to be
        praised,
    according to all the LORD has done
        for us —
yes, the many good things
    he has done for Israel,
    according to his compassion and
        many kindnesses.
8 He said, "Surely they are my people,
    children who will be true to me";
    and so he became their Savior.
9 In all their distress he too was
        distressed,
    and the angel of his presence saved
        them.a
In his love and mercy he redeemed them;
    he lifted them up and carried them
    all the days of old.
10 Yet they rebelled
    and grieved his Holy Spirit.
So he turned and became their enemy
    and he himself fought against them.

11 Then his people recalledb the days of
        old,
    the days of Moses and his people —
where is he who brought them through
        the sea,
    with the shepherd of his flock?
Where is he who set
    his Holy Spirit among them,
12 who sent his glorious arm of power
    to be at Moses' right hand,
who divided the waters before them,
    to gain for himself everlasting
        renown,
13 who led them through the depths?
Like a horse in open country,
    they did not stumble;
14 like cattle that go down to the plain,
    they were given rest by the Spirit of
        the LORD.
This is how you guided your people
    to make for yourself a glorious name.

---

a 9 Or Savior 9 in their distress. / It was no envoy or angel / but his own presence that saved them   b 11 Or But may he
recall

¹⁵Look down from heaven and see,
  from your lofty throne, holy and
    glorious.
  Where are your zeal and your might?
    Your tenderness and compassion are
      withheld from us.
¹⁶But you are our Father,
    though Abraham does not know us
      or Israel acknowledge us;
  you, Lord, are our Father,
    our Redeemer from of old is your
      name.
¹⁷Why, Lord, do you make us wander
    from your ways
  and harden our hearts so we do not
    revere you?
  Return for the sake of your servants,
    the tribes that are your inheritance.
¹⁸For a little while your people possessed
    your holy place,
  but now our enemies have trampled
    down your sanctuary.
¹⁹We are yours from of old;
  but you have not ruled over them,
    they have not been called*a* by your
      name.

64

b Oh, that you would rend the
  heavens and come down,
  that the mountains would
    tremble before you!
²As when fire sets twigs ablaze
  and causes water to boil,
  come down to make your name known
    to your enemies
  and cause the nations to quake before
    you!
³For when you did awesome things that
    we did not expect,
  you came down, and the mountains
    trembled before you.
⁴Since ancient times no one has heard,
  no ear has perceived,
  no eye has seen any God besides you,
    who acts on behalf of those who wait
      for him.

⁵You come to the help of those who
    gladly do right,
  who remember your ways.
  But when we continued to sin against
    them,
  you were angry.
  How then can we be saved?
⁶All of us have become like one who is
    unclean,
  and all our righteous acts are like
    filthy rags;
  we all shrivel up like a leaf,
    and like the wind our sins sweep us
      away.
⁷No one calls on your name
  or strives to lay hold of you;
  for you have hidden your face from us
    and have given us over to*c* our
      sins.

⁸Yet you, Lord, are our Father.
  We are the clay, you are the potter;
    we are all the work of your hand.
⁹Do not be angry beyond measure,
    Lord;
  do not remember our sins forever.
  Oh, look on us, we pray,
    for we are all your people.
¹⁰Your sacred cities have become a
    wasteland;
  even Zion is a wasteland, Jerusalem a
    desolation.
¹¹Our holy and glorious temple, where
    our ancestors praised you,
  has been burned with fire,
    and all that we treasured lies in
      ruins.
¹²After all this, Lord, will you hold
    yourself back?
  Will you keep silent and punish us
    beyond measure?

Judgment and Salvation

65

"I revealed myself to those
  who did not ask for me;
  I was found by those who did
    not seek me.

---

a 19 Or *We are like those you have never ruled, / like those never called*
and 64:2-12 is numbered 64:1-11.   *c 7* Septuagint, Syriac and Targum; Hebrew *have made us melt because of*   *b* In Hebrew texts 64:1 is numbered 63:19b,

To a nation that did not call on my name,
    I said, 'Here am I, here am I.'
2 All day long I have held out my hands
    to an obstinate people,
who walk in ways not good,
    pursuing their own imaginations —
3 a people who continually provoke me
    to my very face,
offering sacrifices in gardens
    and burning incense on altars of
        brick;
4 who sit among the graves
    and spend their nights keeping secret
        vigil;
who eat the flesh of pigs,
    and whose pots hold broth of impure
        meat;
5 who say, 'Keep away; don't come near me,
    for I am too sacred for you!'
Such people are smoke in my nostrils,
    a fire that keeps burning all day.

6 "See, it stands written before me:
    I will not keep silent but will pay
        back in full;
    I will pay it back into their laps —
7 both your sins and the sins of your
        ancestors,"
    says the LORD.
"Because they burned sacrifices on the
        mountains
    and defied me on the hills,
I will measure into their laps
    the full payment for their former
        deeds."

8 This is what the LORD says:

"As when juice is still found in a cluster
        of grapes
    and people say, 'Don't destroy it,
        there is still a blessing in it,'
so will I do in behalf of my servants;
    I will not destroy them all.
9 I will bring forth descendants from
        Jacob,
    and from Judah those who will
        possess my mountains;
my chosen people will inherit them,
    and there will my servants live.

10 Sharon will become a pasture for
        flocks,
    and the Valley of Achor a resting
        place for herds,
    for my people who seek me.

11 "But as for you who forsake the LORD
    and forget my holy mountain,
who spread a table for Fortune
    and fill bowls of mixed wine for
        Destiny,
12 I will destine you for the sword,
    and all of you will fall in the
        slaughter;
for I called but you did not answer,
    I spoke but you did not listen.
You did evil in my sight
    and chose what displeases me."

13 Therefore this is what the Sovereign
LORD says:

"My servants will eat,
    but you will go hungry;
my servants will drink,
    but you will go thirsty;
my servants will rejoice,
    but you will be put to shame.
14 My servants will sing
    out of the joy of their hearts,
but you will cry out
    from anguish of heart
    and wail in brokenness of spirit.
15 You will leave your name
    for my chosen ones to use in their
        curses;
    the Sovereign LORD will put you to
        death,
    but to his servants he will give
        another name.
16 Whoever invokes a blessing in the land
    will do so by the one true God;
whoever takes an oath in the land
    will swear by the one true God.
For the past troubles will be forgotten
    and hidden from my eyes.

New Heavens and a New Earth

17 "See, I will create
    new heavens and a new earth.

The former things will not be
    remembered,
  nor will they come to mind.
18 But be glad and rejoice forever
    in what I will create,
  for I will create Jerusalem to be a delight
    and its people a joy.
19 I will rejoice over Jerusalem
    and take delight in my people;
  the sound of weeping and of crying
    will be heard in it no more.

20 "Never again will there be in it
    an infant who lives but a few days,
    or an old man who does not live out
    his years;
  the one who dies at a hundred
    will be thought a mere child;
  the one who fails to reach*a* hundred
    will be considered accursed.
21 They will build houses and dwell in
    them;
  they will plant vineyards and eat
    their fruit.
22 No longer will they build houses and
    others live in them,
  or plant and others eat.
  For as the days of a tree,
    so will be the days of my people;
  my chosen ones will long enjoy
    the work of their hands.
23 They will not labor in vain,
    nor will they bear children doomed
    to misfortune;
  for they will be a people blessed by the
    Lord,
  they and their descendants with them.
24 Before they call I will answer;
    while they are still speaking I will
    hear.
25 The wolf and the lamb will feed
    together,
  and the lion will eat straw like the ox,
  and dust will be the serpent's food.
  They will neither harm nor destroy
    on all my holy mountain,"
        says the Lord.

Judgment and Hope

66 This is what the Lord says:

  "Heaven is my throne,
    and the earth is my footstool.
  Where is the house you will build for me?
    Where will my resting place be?
2 Has not my hand made all these things,
    and so they came into being?"
        declares the Lord.

  "These are the ones I look on with
    favor:
    those who are humble and contrite in
    spirit,
    and who tremble at my word.
3 But whoever sacrifices a bull
    is like one who kills a person,
  and whoever offers a lamb
    is like one who breaks a dog's neck;
  whoever makes a grain offering
    is like one who presents pig's blood,
  and whoever burns memorial incense
    is like one who worships an idol.
  They have chosen their own ways,
    and they delight in their
    abominations;
4 so I also will choose harsh treatment for
    them
    and will bring on them what they
    dread.
  For when I called, no one answered,
    when I spoke, no one listened.
  They did evil in my sight
    and chose what displeases me."

5 Hear the word of the Lord,
    you who tremble at his word:
  "Your own people who hate you,
    and exclude you because of my name,
    have said,
  'Let the Lord be glorified,
    that we may see your joy!'
    Yet they will be put to shame.
6 Hear that uproar from the city,
    hear that noise from the temple!
  It is the sound of the Lord
    repaying his enemies all they deserve.

---

a 20 Or *the sinner who reaches*

7 "Before she goes into labor,
    she gives birth;
before the pains come upon her,
    she delivers a son.
8 Who has ever heard of such things?
    Who has ever seen things like this?
Can a country be born in a day
    or a nation be brought forth in a
        moment?
Yet no sooner is Zion in labor
    than she gives birth to her children.
9 Do I bring to the moment of birth
    and not give delivery?" says the LORD.
    "Do I close up the womb
        when I bring to delivery?" says your
        God.
10 "Rejoice with Jerusalem and be glad for
    her,
    all you who love her;
rejoice greatly with her,
    all you who mourn over her.
11 For you will nurse and be satisfied
    at her comforting breasts;
you will drink deeply
    and delight in her overflowing
        abundance."

12 For this is what the LORD says:

"I will extend peace to her like a river,
    and the wealth of nations like a
        flooding stream;
you will nurse and be carried on her arm
    and dandled on her knees.
13 As a mother comforts her child,
    so will I comfort you;
and you will be comforted over
    Jerusalem."

14 When you see this, your heart will rejoice
    and you will flourish like grass;
the hand of the LORD will be made
    known to his servants,
    but his fury will be shown to his foes.
15 See, the LORD is coming with fire,
    and his chariots are like a whirlwind;
he will bring down his anger with fury,
    and his rebuke with flames of fire.

16 For with fire and with his sword
    the LORD will execute judgment on
        all people,
    and many will be those slain by the
        LORD.

17 "Those who consecrate and purify
themselves to go into the gardens, following
one who is among those who eat the flesh of
pigs, rats and other unclean things — they
will meet their end together with the one
they follow," declares the LORD.

18 "And I, because of what they have
planned and done, am about to come[a] and
gather the people of all nations and languages, and they will come and see my
glory.

19 "I will set a sign among them, and I
will send some of those who survive to the
nations — to Tarshish, to the Libyans[b] and
Lydians (famous as archers), to Tubal and
Greece, and to the distant islands that have
not heard of my fame or seen my glory.
They will proclaim my glory among the nations. 20 And they will bring all your people,
from all the nations, to my holy mountain
in Jerusalem as an offering to the LORD —
on horses, in chariots and wagons, and on
mules and camels," says the LORD. "They
will bring them, as the Israelites bring their
grain offerings, to the temple of the LORD
in ceremonially clean vessels. 21 And I will
select some of them also to be priests and
Levites," says the LORD.

22 "As the new heavens and the new
earth that I make will endure before me,"
declares the LORD, "so will your name
and descendants endure. 23 From one New
Moon to another and from one Sabbath to
another, all mankind will come and bow
down before me," says the LORD. 24 "And
they will go out and look on the dead bodies of those who rebelled against me; the
worms that eat them will not die, the fire
that burns them will not be quenched, and
they will be loathsome to all mankind."

---

a 18 The meaning of the Hebrew for this clause is uncertain.   b 19 Some Septuagint manuscripts Put (Libyans);
Hebrew Pul

Jeremiah

THEME: Jeremiah reminds us that faith demands action. Covenant living requires a faithful response to God in the form of proper worship and of helping, not exploiting, the weak and vulnerable.

AUTHOR: The book itself states that its contents are "the words of Jeremiah son of Hilkiah" (Jeremiah 1:1). The prophet Jeremiah dictated most of his prophecies to his secretary, Baruch, who wrote them down word for word. Chapter 52 may have been added by a later editor.

DATE OF WRITING: Jeremiah wrote these words over the course of his ministry (626 – 585 BC). Chapter 52 was added sometime after King Jehoiachin's release from captivity (approximately 560 BC).

ENCOURAGEMENT FROM JEREMIAH: " 'I know the plans I have for you,' declares the LORD, 'plans to prosper you and not to harm you, plans to give you hope and a future' " (Jeremiah 29:11).

CHALLENGE FROM JEREMIAH: " 'You will seek me and find me when you seek me with all your heart. I will be found by you,' declares the LORD" (Jeremiah 29:13 – 14).

REFLECTION FROM JEREMIAH: "LORD, I know that people's lives are not their own; it is not for them to direct their steps. Discipline me, LORD, but only in due measure — not in your anger, or you will reduce me to nothing" (Jeremiah 10:23 – 24).

The prophet Jeremiah's heart was broken for his people. Assigned with the task of warning the stubborn people of Judah of the destruction to come, he was despised and persecuted by his intended audience. Jeremiah wept for his people as he compassionately shared his harsh prophecies. He used sermons and signs to warn that repentance was the only way to escape disaster. The people's harsh response to Jeremiah provides a picture of intense denial. Because they'd failed so miserably in upholding their part of the Mosaic covenant (Law), the promise of a new covenant is made in Jeremiah. This new covenant, the one under which we're privileged to live today, is based on individual heart change through trusting in Christ.

Jeremiah's prophecy clearly shows that our hearts can become hardened to the Word of God. We can turn our minds away from it and continue to go our own way. This path leads to death and destruction: destruction of our relationships, of our emotions, of our walk with God, of all we hold dear. If we opt to listen to Jeremiah's warning and turn our hearts and minds back to God, if we choose to walk in his way, we'll experience life everlasting. Unlike Jeremiah's original audience, we don't have to wait to partake of the new covenant in Christ Jesus. We can come to him with repentance for our old way of life and find healing and hope by allowing him to change our hearts.

1

The words of Jeremiah son of Hilkiah, one of the priests at Anathoth in the territory of Benjamin. ²The word of the LORD came to him in the thirteenth year of the reign of Josiah son of Amon king of Judah, ³and through the reign of Jehoiakim son of Josiah king of Judah, down to the fifth month of the eleventh year of Zedekiah son of Josiah king of Judah, when the people of Jerusalem went into exile.

The Call of Jeremiah

⁴The word of the LORD came to me, saying,

⁵ "Before I formed you in the womb I
knew*a* you,
before you were born I set you apart;
I appointed you as a prophet to the
nations."

⁶"Alas, Sovereign LORD," I said, "I do not know how to speak; I am too young."

⁷But the LORD said to me, "Do not say, 'I am too young.' You must go to everyone I send you to and say whatever I command you. ⁸Do not be afraid of them, for I am with you and will rescue you," declares the LORD.

⁹Then the LORD reached out his hand and touched my mouth and said to me, "I have put my words in your mouth. ¹⁰See, today I appoint you over nations and kingdoms to uproot and tear down, to destroy and overthrow, to build and to plant."

¹¹The word of the LORD came to me: "What do you see, Jeremiah?"

"I see the branch of an almond tree," I replied.

¹²The LORD said to me, "You have seen correctly, for I am watching*b* to see that my word is fulfilled."

¹³The word of the LORD came to me again: "What do you see?"

"I see a pot that is boiling," I answered. "It is tilting toward us from the north."

¹⁴The LORD said to me, "From the north disaster will be poured out on all who live in the land. ¹⁵I am about to summon all the peoples of the northern kingdoms," declares the LORD.

"Their kings will come and set up their
thrones
in the entrance of the gates of
Jerusalem;
they will come against all her
surrounding walls
and against all the towns of Judah.
¹⁶I will pronounce my judgments on my
people
because of their wickedness in
forsaking me,
in burning incense to other gods
and in worshiping what their hands
have made.

¹⁷"Get yourself ready! Stand up and say to them whatever I command you. Do not be terrified by them, or I will terrify you before them. ¹⁸Today I have made you a fortified city, an iron pillar and a bronze wall to stand against the whole land — against the kings of Judah, its officials, its priests and the people of the land. ¹⁹They will fight against you but will not overcome you, for I am with you and will rescue you," declares the LORD.

Israel Forsakes God

2

The word of the LORD came to me: ²"Go and proclaim in the hearing of Jerusalem:

"This is what the LORD says:

"'I remember the devotion of your
youth,
how as a bride you loved me
and followed me through the
wilderness,
through a land not sown.
³Israel was holy to the LORD,
the firstfruits of his harvest;
all who devoured her were held guilty,
and disaster overtook them,'"
declares the LORD.

---

a 5 Or *chose*   *b* 12 The Hebrew for *watching* sounds like the Hebrew for *almond tree*.

⁴Hear the word of the LORD, you
    descendants of Jacob,
  all you clans of Israel.

⁵This is what the LORD says:

"What fault did your ancestors find in
    me,
  that they strayed so far from me?
They followed worthless idols
  and became worthless themselves.
⁶They did not ask, 'Where is the LORD,
  who brought us up out of Egypt
and led us through the barren wilderness,
  through a land of deserts and ravines,
a land of drought and utter darkness,
  a land where no one travels and no
    one lives?'
⁷I brought you into a fertile land
  to eat its fruit and rich produce.
But you came and defiled my land
  and made my inheritance detestable.
⁸The priests did not ask,
  'Where is the LORD?'
Those who deal with the law did not
    know me;
  the leaders rebelled against me.
The prophets prophesied by Baal,
  following worthless idols.

⁹"Therefore I bring charges against you
    again,"
                declares the LORD.
  "And I will bring charges against
    your children's children.
¹⁰Cross over to the coasts of Cyprus and
    look,
  send to Kedar*a* and observe closely;
  see if there has ever been anything
    like this:
¹¹Has a nation ever changed its gods?
  (Yet they are not gods at all.)
But my people have exchanged their
    glorious God
  for worthless idols.
¹²Be appalled at this, you heavens,
  and shudder with great horror,"
                declares the LORD.

¹³"My people have committed two sins:
They have forsaken me,
  the spring of living water,
and have dug their own cisterns,
  broken cisterns that cannot hold
    water.
¹⁴Is Israel a servant, a slave by birth?
  Why then has he become plunder?
¹⁵Lions have roared;
  they have growled at him.
They have laid waste his land;
  his towns are burned and deserted.
¹⁶Also, the men of Memphis and
    Tahpanhes
  have cracked your skull.
¹⁷Have you not brought this on yourselves
  by forsaking the LORD your God
  when he led you in the way?
¹⁸Now why go to Egypt
  to drink water from the Nile*b*?
And why go to Assyria
  to drink water from the Euphrates?
¹⁹Your wickedness will punish you;
  your backsliding will rebuke you.
Consider then and realize
  how evil and bitter it is for you
when you forsake the LORD your God
  and have no awe of me,"
              declares the Lord,
              the LORD Almighty.

²⁰"Long ago you broke off your yoke
  and tore off your bonds;
  you said, 'I will not serve you!'
Indeed, on every high hill
  and under every spreading tree
  you lay down as a prostitute.
²¹I had planted you like a choice vine
  of sound and reliable stock.
How then did you turn against me
  into a corrupt, wild vine?
²²Although you wash yourself with soap
  and use an abundance of cleansing
    powder,
  the stain of your guilt is still before
    me,"
            declares the Sovereign LORD.

---

a 10 In the Syro-Arabian desert   *b 18* Hebrew *Shihor*; that is, a branch of the Nile

23 "How can you say, 'I am not defiled;
    I have not run after the Baals'?
  See how you behaved in the valley;
    consider what you have done.
  You are a swift she-camel
    running here and there,
24 a wild donkey accustomed to the
    desert,
    sniffing the wind in her craving —
    in her heat who can restrain her?
  Any males that pursue her need not tire
    themselves;
    at mating time they will find her.
25 Do not run until your feet are bare
    and your throat is dry.
  But you said, 'It's no use!
    I love foreign gods,
    and I must go after them.'

26 "As a thief is disgraced when he is
    caught,
    so the people of Israel are
      disgraced —
  they, their kings and their officials,
    their priests and their prophets.
27 They say to wood, 'You are my father,'
    and to stone, 'You gave me birth.'
  They have turned their backs to me
    and not their faces;
  yet when they are in trouble, they say,
    'Come and save us!'
28 Where then are the gods you made for
    yourselves?
    Let them come if they can save you
    when you are in trouble!
  For you, Judah, have as many gods
    as you have towns.

29 "Why do you bring charges against me?
    You have all rebelled against me,"
                    declares the LORD.
30 "In vain I punished your people;
    they did not respond to correction.
  Your sword has devoured your prophets
    like a ravenous lion.

31 "You of this generation, consider the
  word of the LORD:

  "Have I been a desert to Israel
    or a land of great darkness?

  Why do my people say, 'We are free to
    roam;
    we will come to you no more'?
32 Does a young woman forget her
    jewelry,
    a bride her wedding ornaments?
  Yet my people have forgotten me,
    days without number.
33 How skilled you are at pursuing love!
    Even the worst of women can learn
    from your ways.
34 On your clothes is found
    the lifeblood of the innocent poor,
    though you did not catch them
    breaking in.
  Yet in spite of all this
35   you say, 'I am innocent;
    he is not angry with me.'
  But I will pass judgment on you
    because you say, 'I have not sinned.'
36 Why do you go about so much,
    changing your ways?
  You will be disappointed by Egypt
    as you were by Assyria.
37 You will also leave that place
    with your hands on your head,
  for the LORD has rejected those you
    trust;
    you will not be helped by them.

3 "If a man divorces his wife
    and she leaves him and marries
    another man,
  should he return to her again?
    Would not the land be completely
    defiled?
  But you have lived as a prostitute with
    many lovers —
    would you now return to me?"
                    declares the LORD.
2 "Look up to the barren heights and see.
    Is there any place where you have not
    been ravished?
  By the roadside you sat waiting for
    lovers,
    sat like a nomad in the desert.
  You have defiled the land
    with your prostitution and
    wickedness.

³Therefore the showers have been
      withheld,
   and no spring rains have fallen.
   Yet you have the brazen look of a
      prostitute;
   you refuse to blush with shame.
⁴Have you not just called to me:
   'My Father, my friend from my
      youth,
⁵will you always be angry?
   Will your wrath continue forever?'
   This is how you talk,
      but you do all the evil you can."

Unfaithful Israel

⁶During the reign of King Josiah, the
LORD said to me, "Have you seen what
faithless Israel has done? She has gone up
on every high hill and under every spreading tree and has committed adultery there.
⁷I thought that after she had done all this
she would return to me but she did not, and
her unfaithful sister Judah saw it. ⁸I gave
faithless Israel her certificate of divorce
and sent her away because of all her adulteries. Yet I saw that her unfaithful sister
Judah had no fear; she also went out and
committed adultery. ⁹Because Israel's immorality mattered so little to her, she defiled the land and committed adultery with
stone and wood. ¹⁰In spite of all this, her
unfaithful sister Judah did not return to me
with all her heart, but only in pretense," declares the LORD.

¹¹The LORD said to me, "Faithless Israel is more righteous than unfaithful Judah.
¹²Go, proclaim this message toward the
north:

   "'Return, faithless Israel,' declares the
      LORD,
   'I will frown on you no longer,
   for I am faithful,' declares the LORD,
   'I will not be angry forever.
¹³Only acknowledge your guilt—
   you have rebelled against the LORD
      your God,
   you have scattered your favors to
      foreign gods

under every spreading tree,
   and have not obeyed me,'"
                  declares the LORD.

¹⁴"Return, faithless people," declares
the LORD, "for I am your husband. I will
choose you—one from a town and two
from a clan—and bring you to Zion.
¹⁵Then I will give you shepherds after my
own heart, who will lead you with knowledge and understanding. ¹⁶In those days,
when your numbers have increased greatly in the land," declares the LORD, "people
will no longer say, 'The ark of the covenant
of the LORD.' It will never enter their minds
or be remembered; it will not be missed,
nor will another one be made. ¹⁷At that
time they will call Jerusalem The Throne
of the LORD, and all nations will gather in
Jerusalem to honor the name of the LORD.
No longer will they follow the stubbornness of their evil hearts. ¹⁸In those days
the people of Judah will join the people of
Israel, and together they will come from a
northern land to the land I gave your ancestors as an inheritance.

¹⁹"I myself said,

   "'How gladly would I treat you like my
      children
   and give you a pleasant land,
   the most beautiful inheritance of any
      nation.'
   I thought you would call me 'Father'
   and not turn away from following me.
²⁰But like a woman unfaithful to her
      husband,
   so you, Israel, have been unfaithful
      to me,"
                  declares the LORD.

²¹A cry is heard on the barren heights,
   the weeping and pleading of the
      people of Israel,
   because they have perverted their
      ways
   and have forgotten the LORD their
      God.

²²"Return, faithless people;
   I will cure you of backsliding."

"Yes, we will come to you,
for you are the LORD our God.
23 Surely the idolatrous commotion on the hills
and mountains is a deception;
surely in the LORD our God
is the salvation of Israel.
24 From our youth shameful gods have consumed
the fruits of our ancestors' labor—
their flocks and herds,
their sons and daughters.
25 Let us lie down in our shame,
and let our disgrace cover us.
We have sinned against the LORD our God,
both we and our ancestors;
from our youth till this day
we have not obeyed the LORD our God."

4 "If you, Israel, will return,
then return to me,"
declares the LORD.
"If you put your detestable idols out of my sight
and no longer go astray,
2 and if in a truthful, just and righteous way
you swear, 'As surely as the LORD lives,'
then the nations will invoke blessings by him
and in him they will boast."

3 This is what the LORD says to the people of Judah and to Jerusalem:

"Break up your unplowed ground
and do not sow among thorns.
4 Circumcise yourselves to the LORD,
circumcise your hearts,
you people of Judah and inhabitants of Jerusalem,
or my wrath will flare up and burn like fire
because of the evil you have done—
burn with no one to quench it.

Disaster From the North

5 "Announce in Judah and proclaim in Jerusalem and say:
'Sound the trumpet throughout the land!'
Cry aloud and say:
'Gather together!
Let us flee to the fortified cities!'
6 Raise the signal to go to Zion!
Flee for safety without delay!
For I am bringing disaster from the north,
even terrible destruction."

7 A lion has come out of his lair;
a destroyer of nations has set out.
He has left his place
to lay waste your land.
Your towns will lie in ruins
without inhabitant.
8 So put on sackcloth,
lament and wail,
for the fierce anger of the LORD
has not turned away from us.

9 "In that day," declares the LORD,
"the king and the officials will lose heart,
the priests will be horrified,
and the prophets will be appalled."

10 Then I said, "Alas, Sovereign LORD! How completely you have deceived this people and Jerusalem by saying, 'You will have peace,' when the sword is at our throats!"

11 At that time this people and Jerusalem will be told, "A scorching wind from the barren heights in the desert blows toward my people, but not to winnow or cleanse; 12 a wind too strong for that comes from me. Now I pronounce my judgments against them."

13 Look! He advances like the clouds,
his chariots come like a whirlwind,
his horses are swifter than eagles.
Woe to us! We are ruined!
14 Jerusalem, wash the evil from your heart and be saved.
How long will you harbor wicked thoughts?

¹⁵ A voice is announcing from Dan,
  proclaiming disaster from the hills of
    Ephraim.
¹⁶ "Tell this to the nations,
  proclaim concerning Jerusalem:
 'A besieging army is coming from a
    distant land,
  raising a war cry against the cities of
    Judah.
¹⁷ They surround her like men guarding a
    field,
  because she has rebelled against me,'"
                        declares the Lord.

¹⁸ "Your own conduct and actions
  have brought this on you.
This is your punishment.
  How bitter it is!
  How it pierces to the heart!"

¹⁹ Oh, my anguish, my anguish!
  I writhe in pain.
Oh, the agony of my heart!
  My heart pounds within me,
  I cannot keep silent.
For I have heard the sound of the
    trumpet;
  I have heard the battle cry.
²⁰ Disaster follows disaster;
  the whole land lies in ruins.
In an instant my tents are destroyed,
  my shelter in a moment.
²¹ How long must I see the battle standard
  and hear the sound of the trumpet?

²² "My people are fools;
  they do not know me.
They are senseless children;
  they have no understanding.
They are skilled in doing evil;
  they know not how to do good."

²³ I looked at the earth,
  and it was formless and empty;
and at the heavens,
  and their light was gone.
²⁴ I looked at the mountains,
  and they were quaking;
all the hills were swaying.
²⁵ I looked, and there were no people;
  every bird in the sky had flown away.

²⁶ I looked, and the fruitful land was a
    desert;
  all its towns lay in ruins
before the Lord, before his fierce
    anger.

²⁷ This is what the Lord says:

"The whole land will be ruined,
  though I will not destroy it
    completely.
²⁸ Therefore the earth will mourn
  and the heavens above grow dark,
because I have spoken and will not
    relent,
  I have decided and will not turn back."

²⁹ At the sound of horsemen and archers
  every town takes to flight.
Some go into the thickets;
  some climb up among the rocks.
All the towns are deserted;
  no one lives in them.

³⁰ What are you doing, you devastated
    one?
  Why dress yourself in scarlet
  and put on jewels of gold?
Why highlight your eyes with makeup?
  You adorn yourself in vain.
Your lovers despise you;
  they want to kill you.

³¹ I hear a cry as of a woman in labor,
  a groan as of one bearing her first
    child —
the cry of Daughter Zion gasping for
    breath,
  stretching out her hands and saying,
"Alas! I am fainting;
  my life is given over to murderers."

Not One Is Upright

5 "Go up and down the streets of
    Jerusalem,
  look around and consider,
  search through her squares.
If you can find but one person
  who deals honestly and seeks the
    truth,
  I will forgive this city.

2 Although they say, 'As surely as the
    LORD lives,'
    still they are swearing falsely."

3 LORD, do not your eyes look for truth?
    You struck them, but they felt no
        pain;
    you crushed them, but they refused
        correction.
They made their faces harder than
        stone
    and refused to repent.
4 I thought, "These are only the poor;
    they are foolish,
for they do not know the way of the
    LORD,
    the requirements of their God.
5 So I will go to the leaders
    and speak to them;
surely they know the way of the LORD,
    the requirements of their God."
But with one accord they too had
        broken off the yoke
    and torn off the bonds.
6 Therefore a lion from the forest will
        attack them,
    a wolf from the desert will ravage
        them,
a leopard will lie in wait near their
        towns
    to tear to pieces any who venture
        out,
for their rebellion is great
    and their backslidings many.

7 "Why should I forgive you?
    Your children have forsaken me
    and sworn by gods that are not
        gods.
I supplied all their needs,
    yet they committed adultery
    and thronged to the houses of
        prostitutes.
8 They are well-fed, lusty stallions,
    each neighing for another man's
        wife.
9 Should I not punish them for this?"
    declares the LORD.
    "Should I not avenge myself
    on such a nation as this?

10 "Go through her vineyards and ravage
        them,
    but do not destroy them completely.
Strip off her branches,
    for these people do not belong to the
        LORD.
11 The people of Israel and the people of
        Judah
    have been utterly unfaithful to me,"
                    declares the LORD.

12 They have lied about the LORD;
    they said, "He will do nothing!
No harm will come to us;
    we will never see sword or famine.
13 The prophets are but wind
    and the word is not in them;
    so let what they say be done to them."

14 Therefore this is what the LORD God
Almighty says:

"Because the people have spoken these
        words,
    I will make my words in your mouth
        a fire
    and these people the wood it
        consumes.
15 People of Israel," declares the LORD,
    "I am bringing a distant nation
        against you —
an ancient and enduring nation,
    a people whose language you do not
        know,
    whose speech you do not understand.
16 Their quivers are like an open grave;
    all of them are mighty warriors.
17 They will devour your harvests and
        food,
    devour your sons and daughters;
they will devour your flocks and herds,
    devour your vines and fig trees.
With the sword they will destroy
    the fortified cities in which you trust.

18 "Yet even in those days," declares the
LORD, "I will not destroy you completely.
19 And when the people ask, 'Why has the
LORD our God done all this to us?' you will
tell them, 'As you have forsaken me and
served foreign gods in your own land, so

now you will serve foreigners in a land not
your own.'

20 "Announce this to the descendants of
Jacob
and proclaim it in Judah:
21 Hear this, you foolish and senseless
people,
who have eyes but do not see,
who have ears but do not hear:
22 Should you not fear me?" declares the
Lord.
"Should you not tremble in my
presence?
I made the sand a boundary for the sea,
an everlasting barrier it cannot cross.
The waves may roll, but they cannot
prevail;
they may roar, but they cannot
cross it.
23 But these people have stubborn and
rebellious hearts;
they have turned aside and gone
away.
24 They do not say to themselves,
'Let us fear the Lord our God,
who gives autumn and spring rains in
season,
who assures us of the regular weeks
of harvest.'
25 Your wrongdoings have kept these away;
your sins have deprived you of good.

26 "Among my people are the wicked
who lie in wait like men who snare
birds
and like those who set traps to catch
people.
27 Like cages full of birds,
their houses are full of deceit;
they have become rich and powerful
28   and have grown fat and sleek.
Their evil deeds have no limit;
they do not seek justice.
They do not promote the case of the
fatherless;
they do not defend the just cause of
the poor.
29 Should I not punish them for this?"
declares the Lord.

"Should I not avenge myself
on such a nation as this?

30 "A horrible and shocking thing
has happened in the land:
31 The prophets prophesy lies,
the priests rule by their own
authority,
and my people love it this way.
But what will you do in the end?

Jerusalem Under Siege

6 "Flee for safety, people of
Benjamin!
Flee from Jerusalem!
Sound the trumpet in Tekoa!
Raise the signal over Beth
Hakkerem!
For disaster looms out of the north,
even terrible destruction.
2 I will destroy Daughter Zion,
so beautiful and delicate.
3 Shepherds with their flocks will come
against her;
they will pitch their tents around
her,
each tending his own portion."

4 "Prepare for battle against her!
Arise, let us attack at noon!
But, alas, the daylight is fading,
and the shadows of evening grow
long.
5 So arise, let us attack at night
and destroy her fortresses!"

6 This is what the Lord Almighty says:

"Cut down the trees
and build siege ramps against
Jerusalem.
This city must be punished;
it is filled with oppression.
7 As a well pours out its water,
so she pours out her wickedness.
Violence and destruction resound in
her;
her sickness and wounds are ever
before me.
8 Take warning, Jerusalem,
or I will turn away from you

and make your land desolate
   so no one can live in it."

⁹This is what the LORD Almighty says:

"Let them glean the remnant of Israel
   as thoroughly as a vine;
pass your hand over the branches again,
   like one gathering grapes."

¹⁰To whom can I speak and give warning?
   Who will listen to me?
Their ears are closed*
   so they cannot hear.
The word of the LORD is offensive to them;
   they find no pleasure in it.
¹¹But I am full of the wrath of the LORD,
   and I cannot hold it in.

"Pour it out on the children in the street
   and on the young men gathered
      together;
both husband and wife will be caught
   in it,
   and the old, those weighed down
      with years.
¹²Their houses will be turned over to
   others,
   together with their fields and their
      wives,
when I stretch out my hand
   against those who live in the land,"
               declares the LORD.
¹³"From the least to the greatest,
   all are greedy for gain;
prophets and priests alike,
   all practice deceit.
¹⁴They dress the wound of my people
   as though it were not serious.
'Peace, peace,' they say,
   when there is no peace.
¹⁵Are they ashamed of their detestable
   conduct?
   No, they have no shame at all;
   they do not even know how to blush.
So they will fall among the fallen;
   they will be brought down when I
      punish them,"
              says the LORD.

¹⁶This is what the LORD says:

"Stand at the crossroads and look;
   ask for the ancient paths,
ask where the good way is, and walk
   in it,
   and you will find rest for your souls.
   But you said, 'We will not walk in it.'
¹⁷I appointed watchmen over you and
   said,
   'Listen to the sound of the trumpet!'
   But you said, 'We will not listen.'
¹⁸Therefore hear, you nations;
   you who are witnesses,
   observe what will happen to them.
¹⁹Hear, you earth:
   I am bringing disaster on this people,
   the fruit of their schemes,
because they have not listened to my
   words
   and have rejected my law.
²⁰What do I care about incense from
      Sheba
   or sweet calamus from a distant
      land?
Your burnt offerings are not acceptable;
   your sacrifices do not please me."

²¹Therefore this is what the LORD says:

"I will put obstacles before this people.
   Parents and children alike will
      stumble over them;
   neighbors and friends will perish."

²²This is what the LORD says:

"Look, an army is coming
   from the land of the north;
a great nation is being stirred up
   from the ends of the earth.
²³They are armed with bow and spear;
   they are cruel and show no mercy.
They sound like the roaring sea
   as they ride on their horses;
they come like men in battle formation
   to attack you, Daughter Zion."

²⁴We have heard reports about them,
   and our hands hang limp.

---

a 10 Hebrew *uncircumcised*

Anguish has gripped us,
　　pain like that of a woman in labor.
²⁵ Do not go out to the fields
　　or walk on the roads,
　for the enemy has a sword,
　　and there is terror on every side.
²⁶ Put on sackcloth, my people,
　　and roll in ashes;
　mourn with bitter wailing
　　as for an only son,
　for suddenly the destroyer
　　will come upon us.

²⁷ "I have made you a tester of metals
　　and my people the ore,
　that you may observe
　　and test their ways.
²⁸ They are all hardened rebels,
　　going about to slander.
　They are bronze and iron;
　　they all act corruptly.
²⁹ The bellows blow fiercely
　　to burn away the lead with fire,
　but the refining goes on in vain;
　　the wicked are not purged out.
³⁰ They are called rejected silver,
　　because the LORD has rejected them."

False Religion Worthless

7 This is the word that came to Jeremiah from the LORD: ²"Stand at the gate of the LORD's house and there proclaim this message:

"'Hear the word of the LORD, all you people of Judah who come through these gates to worship the LORD. ³This is what the LORD Almighty, the God of Israel, says: Reform your ways and your actions, and I will let you live in this place. ⁴Do not trust in deceptive words and say, "This is the temple of the LORD, the temple of the LORD, the temple of the LORD!" ⁵If you really change your ways and your actions and deal with each other justly, ⁶if you do not oppress the foreigner, the fatherless or the widow and do not shed innocent blood in this place, and if you do not follow other gods to your

own harm, ⁷then I will let you live in this place, in the land I gave your ancestors for ever and ever. ⁸But look, you are trusting in deceptive words that are worthless.

⁹ "'Will you steal and murder, commit adultery and perjury,ᵃ burn incense to Baal and follow other gods you have not known, ¹⁰and then come and stand before me in this house, which bears my Name, and say, "We are safe" — safe to do all these detestable things? ¹¹Has this house, which bears my Name, become a den of robbers to you? But I have been watching! declares the LORD.

¹² "'Go now to the place in Shiloh where I first made a dwelling for my Name, and see what I did to it because of the wickedness of my people Israel. ¹³While you were doing all these things, declares the LORD, I spoke to you again and again, but you did not listen; I called you, but you did not answer. ¹⁴Therefore, what I did to Shiloh I will now do to the house that bears my Name, the temple you trust in, the place I gave to you and your ancestors. ¹⁵I will thrust you from my presence, just as I did all your fellow Israelites, the people of Ephraim.'

¹⁶ "So do not pray for this people nor offer any plea or petition for them; do not plead with me, for I will not listen to you. ¹⁷Do you not see what they are doing in the towns of Judah and in the streets of Jerusalem? ¹⁸The children gather wood, the fathers light the fire, and the women knead the dough and make cakes to offer to the Queen of Heaven. They pour out drink offerings to other gods to arouse my anger. ¹⁹But am I the one they are provoking? declares the LORD. Are they not rather harming themselves, to their own shame?

²⁰ "'Therefore this is what the Sovereign LORD says: My anger and my wrath will be poured out on this place — on man and beast, on the trees of the field and on the crops of your land — and it will burn and not be quenched.

²¹ "'This is what the LORD Almighty, the

ᵃ 9 Or *and swear by false gods*

God of Israel, says: Go ahead, add your burnt offerings to your other sacrifices and eat the meat yourselves! 22For when I brought your ancestors out of Egypt and spoke to them, I did not just give them commands about burnt offerings and sacrifices, 23but I gave them this command: Obey me, and I will be your God and you will be my people. Walk in obedience to all I command you, that it may go well with you. 24But they did not listen or pay attention; instead, they followed the stubborn inclinations of their evil hearts. They went backward and not forward. 25From the time your ancestors left Egypt until now, day after day, again and again I sent you my servants the prophets. 26But they did not listen to me or pay attention. They were stiff-necked and did more evil than their ancestors.'

27"When you tell them all this, they will not listen to you; when you call to them, they will not answer. 28Therefore say to them, 'This is the nation that has not obeyed the LORD its God or responded to correction. Truth has perished; it has vanished from their lips.

29"'Cut off your hair and throw it away; take up a lament on the barren heights, for the LORD has rejected and abandoned this generation that is under his wrath.

The Valley of Slaughter

30"'The people of Judah have done evil in my eyes, declares the LORD. They have set up their detestable idols in the house that bears my Name and have defiled it. 31They have built the high places of Topheth in the Valley of Ben Hinnom to burn their sons and daughters in the fire — something I did not command, nor did it enter my mind. 32So beware, the days are coming, declares the LORD, when people will no longer call it Topheth or the Valley of Ben Hinnom, but the Valley of Slaughter, for they will bury the dead in Topheth until there is no more room. 33Then the carcasses of this people will become food for the birds and the wild animals, and there will be no one to fright-

en them away. 34I will bring an end to the sounds of joy and gladness and to the voices of bride and bridegroom in the towns of Judah and the streets of Jerusalem, for the land will become desolate.

8 "'At that time, declares the LORD, the bones of the kings and officials of Judah, the bones of the priests and prophets, and the bones of the people of Jerusalem will be removed from their graves. 2They will be exposed to the sun and the moon and all the stars of the heavens, which they have loved and served and which they have followed and consulted and worshiped. They will not be gathered up or buried, but will be like dung lying on the ground. 3Wherever I banish them, all the survivors of this evil nation will prefer death to life, declares the LORD Almighty.'

Sin and Punishment

4"Say to them, 'This is what the LORD says:

"'When people fall down, do they not
        get up?
    When someone turns away, do they
        not return?
5Why then have these people turned
        away?
    Why does Jerusalem always turn
        away?
They cling to deceit;
    they refuse to return.
6I have listened attentively,
    but they do not say what is right.
None of them repent of their
        wickedness,
    saying, "What have I done?"
Each pursues their own course
    like a horse charging into battle.
7Even the stork in the sky
    knows her appointed seasons,
and the dove, the swift and the thrush
    observe the time of their migration.
But my people do not know
    the requirements of the LORD.

8"'How can you say, "We are wise,
    for we have the law of the LORD,"

when actually the lying pen of the
　　scribes
　　has handled it falsely?
⁹ The wise will be put to shame;
　　they will be dismayed and trapped.
Since they have rejected the word of the
　　LORD,
　　what kind of wisdom do they have?
¹⁰ Therefore I will give their wives to
　　other men
　　and their fields to new owners.
From the least to the greatest,
　　all are greedy for gain;
prophets and priests alike,
　　all practice deceit.
¹¹ They dress the wound of my people
　　as though it were not serious.
"Peace, peace," they say,
　　when there is no peace.
¹² Are they ashamed of their detestable
　　conduct?
　　No, they have no shame at all;
　　they do not even know how to blush.
So they will fall among the fallen;
　　they will be brought down when they
　　are punished,
　　　　　　　　　says the LORD.

¹³ "'I will take away their harvest,
　　　　　　　　declares the LORD.
　　There will be no grapes on the vine.
There will be no figs on the tree,
　　and their leaves will wither.
What I have given them
　　will be taken from them.ᵃ'"

¹⁴ Why are we sitting here?
　　Gather together!
Let us flee to the fortified cities
　　and perish there!
For the LORD our God has doomed us
　　to perish
　　and given us poisoned water to
　　drink,
　　because we have sinned against him.
¹⁵ We hoped for peace
　　but no good has come,

for a time of healing
　　but there is only terror.
¹⁶ The snorting of the enemy's horses
　　is heard from Dan;
at the neighing of their stallions
　　the whole land trembles.
They have come to devour
　　the land and everything in it,
　　the city and all who live there.

¹⁷ "See, I will send venomous snakes
　　　　among you,
　　vipers that cannot be charmed,
　　and they will bite you,"
　　　　　　　　declares the LORD.

¹⁸ You who are my Comforterᵇ in sorrow,
　　my heart is faint within me.
¹⁹ Listen to the cry of my people
　　from a land far away:
"Is the LORD not in Zion?
　　Is her King no longer there?"

"Why have they aroused my anger with
　　their images,
　　with their worthless foreign idols?"

²⁰ "The harvest is past,
　　the summer has ended,
　　and we are not saved."

²¹ Since my people are crushed, I am
　　crushed;
　　I mourn, and horror grips me.
²² Is there no balm in Gilead?
　　Is there no physician there?
Why then is there no healing
　　for the wound of my people?

9 ᶜ ¹ Oh, that my head were a spring of
　　water
　　and my eyes a fountain of tears!
I would weep day and night
　　for the slain of my people.
² Oh, that I had in the desert
　　a lodging place for travelers,
so that I might leave my people
　　and go away from them;
for they are all adulterers,
　　a crowd of unfaithful people.

ᵃ 13 The meaning of the Hebrew for this sentence is uncertain.　　ᵇ 18 The meaning of the Hebrew for this word is uncertain.　　ᶜ In Hebrew texts 9:1 is numbered 8:23, and 9:2-26 is numbered 9:1-25.

3 "They make ready their tongue
    like a bow, to shoot lies;
it is not by truth
    that they triumph*a* in the land.
They go from one sin to another;
    they do not acknowledge me,"
                declares the Lord.
4 "Beware of your friends;
    do not trust anyone in your clan.
For every one of them is a deceiver,*b*
    and every friend a slanderer.
5 Friend deceives friend,
    and no one speaks the truth.
They have taught their tongues to lie;
    they weary themselves with sinning.
6 You*c* live in the midst of deception;
    in their deceit they refuse to
        acknowledge me,"
                declares the Lord.

7 Therefore this is what the Lord Almighty says:

"See, I will refine and test them,
    for what else can I do
    because of the sin of my people?
8 Their tongue is a deadly arrow;
    it speaks deceitfully.
With their mouths they all speak
        cordially to their neighbors,
    but in their hearts they set traps for
        them.
9 Should I not punish them for this?"
        declares the Lord.
"Should I not avenge myself
    on such a nation as this?"

10 I will weep and wail for the mountains
    and take up a lament concerning the
        wilderness grasslands.
They are desolate and untraveled,
    and the lowing of cattle is not
        heard.
The birds have all fled
    and the animals are gone.

11 "I will make Jerusalem a heap of ruins,
    a haunt of jackals;

and I will lay waste the towns of Judah
    so no one can live there."

12 Who is wise enough to understand this? Who has been instructed by the Lord and can explain it? Why has the land been ruined and laid waste like a desert that no one can cross?

13 The Lord said, "It is because they have forsaken my law, which I set before them; they have not obeyed me or followed my law. 14 Instead, they have followed the stubbornness of their hearts; they have followed the Baals, as their ancestors taught them." 15 Therefore this is what the Lord Almighty, the God of Israel, says: "See, I will make this people eat bitter food and drink poisoned water. 16 I will scatter them among nations that neither they nor their ancestors have known, and I will pursue them with the sword until I have made an end of them."

17 This is what the Lord Almighty says:

"Consider now! Call for the wailing
        women to come;
    send for the most skillful of them.
18 Let them come quickly
    and wail over us
till our eyes overflow with tears
    and water streams from our eyelids.
19 The sound of wailing is heard from
        Zion:
    'How ruined we are!
    How great is our shame!
We must leave our land
    because our houses are in ruins.'"

20 Now, you women, hear the word of the
        Lord;
    open your ears to the words of his
        mouth.
Teach your daughters how to wail;
    teach one another a lament.
21 Death has climbed in through our
        windows
    and has entered our fortresses;

---

a 3 Or *lies; / they are not valiant for truth*   *b* 4 Or *a deceiving Jacob*   *c* 6 That is, Jeremiah (the Hebrew is singular)

it has removed the children from the
    streets
    and the young men from the public
        squares.

22Say, "This is what the LORD declares:

"'Dead bodies will lie
    like dung on the open field,
like cut grain behind the reaper,
    with no one to gather them.'"

23This is what the LORD says:

"Let not the wise boast of their wisdom
    or the strong boast of their strength
    or the rich boast of their riches,
24but let the one who boasts boast about
        this:
    that they have the understanding to
        know me,
    that I am the LORD, who exercises
        kindness,
    justice and righteousness on earth,
    for in these I delight,"
                    declares the LORD.

25"The days are coming," declares the
LORD, "when I will punish all who are circumcised only in the flesh— 26Egypt, Judah, Edom, Ammon, Moab and all who
live in the wilderness in distant places.*a* For
all these nations are really uncircumcised,
and even the whole house of Israel is uncircumcised in heart."

God and Idols

10 Hear what the LORD says to you,
people of Israel. 2This is what
the LORD says:

"Do not learn the ways of the nations
    or be terrified by signs in the
        heavens,
    though the nations are terrified by
        them.
3For the practices of the peoples are
        worthless;
    they cut a tree out of the forest,

and a craftsman shapes it with his
    chisel.
4They adorn it with silver and gold;
    they fasten it with hammer and nails
    so it will not totter.
5Like a scarecrow in a cucumber field,
    their idols cannot speak;
they must be carried
    because they cannot walk.
Do not fear them;
    they can do no harm
    nor can they do any good."

6No one is like you, LORD;
    you are great,
    and your name is mighty in power.
7Who should not fear you,
    King of the nations?
    This is your due.
Among all the wise leaders of the
        nations
    and in all their kingdoms,
    there is no one like you.

8They are all senseless and foolish;
    they are taught by worthless wooden
        idols.
9Hammered silver is brought from
        Tarshish
    and gold from Uphaz.
What the craftsman and goldsmith
        have made
    is then dressed in blue and purple—
    all made by skilled workers.
10But the LORD is the true God;
    he is the living God, the eternal King.
When he is angry, the earth trembles;
    the nations cannot endure his wrath.

11"Tell them this: 'These gods, who did
not make the heavens and the earth, will
perish from the earth and from under the
heavens.'"*b*

12But God made the earth by his power;
    he founded the world by his wisdom
    and stretched out the heavens by his
        understanding.

---

a 26 Or *wilderness and who clip the hair by their foreheads*   *b 11* The text of this verse is in Aramaic.

13 When he thunders, the waters in the
    heavens roar;
  he makes clouds rise from the ends
    of the earth.
  He sends lightning with the rain
    and brings out the wind from his
    storehouses.

14 Everyone is senseless and without
    knowledge;
  every goldsmith is shamed by his
    idols.
  The images he makes are a fraud;
    they have no breath in them.
15 They are worthless, the objects of
    mockery;
  when their judgment comes, they
    will perish.
16 He who is the Portion of Jacob is not
    like these,
  for he is the Maker of all things,
  including Israel, the people of his
    inheritance —
    the LORD Almighty is his name.

Coming Destruction

17 Gather up your belongings to leave the
    land,
  you who live under siege.
18 For this is what the LORD says:
  "At this time I will hurl out
    those who live in this land;
  I will bring distress on them
    so that they may be captured."

19 Woe to me because of my injury!
    My wound is incurable!
  Yet I said to myself,
    "This is my sickness, and I must
      endure it."
20 My tent is destroyed;
    all its ropes are snapped.
  My children are gone from me and are
    no more;
  no one is left now to pitch my tent
    or to set up my shelter.
21 The shepherds are senseless
    and do not inquire of the LORD;
  so they do not prosper
    and all their flock is scattered.

22 Listen! The report is coming —
  a great commotion from the land of
    the north!
  It will make the towns of Judah
    desolate,
  a haunt of jackals.

Jeremiah's Prayer

23 LORD, I know that people's lives are not
    their own;
  it is not for them to direct their steps.
24 Discipline me, LORD, but only in due
      measure —
  not in your anger,
    or you will reduce me to nothing.
25 Pour out your wrath on the nations
    that do not acknowledge you,
  on the peoples who do not call on
    your name.
  For they have devoured Jacob;
    they have devoured him completely
    and destroyed his homeland.

The Covenant Is Broken

11 This is the word that came to
Jeremiah from the LORD: 2"Listen to the terms of this covenant
and tell them to the people of Judah and
to those who live in Jerusalem. 3Tell them
that this is what the LORD, the God of Israel, says: 'Cursed is the one who does not
obey the terms of this covenant — 4the
terms I commanded your ancestors when
I brought them out of Egypt, out of the
iron-smelting furnace.' I said, 'Obey me
and do everything I command you, and
you will be my people, and I will be your
God. 5Then I will fulfill the oath I swore to
your ancestors, to give them a land flowing
with milk and honey' — the land you possess today."

I answered, "Amen, LORD."

6The LORD said to me, "Proclaim all
these words in the towns of Judah and
in the streets of Jerusalem: 'Listen to the
terms of this covenant and follow them.
7From the time I brought your ancestors
up from Egypt until today, I warned them
again and again, saying, "Obey me." 8But

they did not listen or pay attention; instead, they followed the stubbornness of their evil hearts. So I brought on them all the curses of the covenant I had commanded them to follow but that they did not keep.'"

⁹Then the Lord said to me, "There is a conspiracy among the people of Judah and those who live in Jerusalem. ¹⁰They have returned to the sins of their ancestors, who refused to listen to my words. They have followed other gods to serve them. Both Israel and Judah have broken the covenant I made with their ancestors. ¹¹Therefore this is what the Lord says: 'I will bring on them a disaster they cannot escape. Although they cry out to me, I will not listen to them. ¹²The towns of Judah and the people of Jerusalem will go and cry out to the gods to whom they burn incense, but they will not help them at all when disaster strikes. ¹³You, Judah, have as many gods as you have towns; and the altars you have set up to burn incense to that shameful god Baal are as many as the streets of Jerusalem.'

¹⁴"Do not pray for this people or offer any plea or petition for them, because I will not listen when they call to me in the time of their distress.

¹⁵ "What is my beloved doing in my
    temple
        as she, with many others, works out
        her evil schemes?
    Can consecrated meat avert your
        punishment?
    When you engage in your wickedness,
        then you rejoice.ᵃ"

¹⁶The Lord called you a thriving olive
    tree
        with fruit beautiful in form.
    But with the roar of a mighty storm
        he will set it on fire,
        and its branches will be broken.

¹⁷The Lord Almighty, who planted you, has decreed disaster for you, because the people of both Israel and Judah have done evil and aroused my anger by burning incense to Baal.

Plot Against Jeremiah

¹⁸Because the Lord revealed their plot to me, I knew it, for at that time he showed me what they were doing. ¹⁹I had been like a gentle lamb led to the slaughter; I did not realize that they had plotted against me, saying,

"Let us destroy the tree and its fruit;
    let us cut him off from the land of the
        living,
    that his name be remembered no
        more."
²⁰But you, Lord Almighty, who judge
        righteously
    and test the heart and mind,
    let me see your vengeance on them,
        for to you I have committed my
        cause.

²¹Therefore this is what the Lord says about the people of Anathoth who are threatening to kill you, saying, "Do not prophesy in the name of the Lord or you will die by our hands" — ²²therefore this is what the Lord Almighty says: "I will punish them. Their young men will die by the sword, their sons and daughters by famine. ²³Not even a remnant will be left to them, because I will bring disaster on the people of Anathoth in the year of their punishment."

Jeremiah's Complaint

12 You are always righteous,
        Lord,
        when I bring a case before you.
    Yet I would speak with you about your
        justice:
    Why does the way of the wicked
        prosper?
    Why do all the faithless live at ease?
²You have planted them, and they have
        taken root;
    they grow and bear fruit.

ᵃ 15 Or *Could consecrated meat avert your punishment? / Then you would rejoice*

You are always on their lips
   but far from their hearts.
3 Yet you know me, Lord;
   you see me and test my thoughts
      about you.
Drag them off like sheep to be
      butchered!
   Set them apart for the day of
      slaughter!
4 How long will the land lie parched
   and the grass in every field be
      withered?
Because those who live in it are
      wicked,
   the animals and birds have perished.
Moreover, the people are saying,
   "He will not see what happens to us."

God's Answer

5 "If you have raced with men on foot
   and they have worn you out,
   how can you compete with horses?
If you stumble*a* in safe country,
   how will you manage in the thickets
      by*b* the Jordan?
6 Your relatives, members of your own
      family—
   even they have betrayed you;
   they have raised a loud cry against
      you.
Do not trust them,
   though they speak well of you.

7 "I will forsake my house,
   abandon my inheritance;
I will give the one I love
   into the hands of her enemies.
8 My inheritance has become to me
   like a lion in the forest.
She roars at me;
   therefore I hate her.
9 Has not my inheritance become to me
   like a speckled bird of prey
   that other birds of prey surround and
      attack?
Go and gather all the wild beasts;
   bring them to devour.

10 Many shepherds will ruin my vineyard
   and trample down my field;
they will turn my pleasant field
   into a desolate wasteland.
11 It will be made a wasteland,
   parched and desolate before me;
the whole land will be laid waste
   because there is no one who cares.
12 Over all the barren heights in the desert
   destroyers will swarm,
for the sword of the Lord will devour
   from one end of the land to the other;
   no one will be safe.
13 They will sow wheat but reap thorns;
   they will wear themselves out but
      gain nothing.
They will bear the shame of their harvest
   because of the Lord's fierce anger."

14 This is what the Lord says: "As for all my wicked neighbors who seize the inheritance I gave my people Israel, I will uproot them from their lands and I will uproot the people of Judah from among them. 15 But after I uproot them, I will again have compassion and will bring each of them back to their own inheritance and their own country. 16 And if they learn well the ways of my people and swear by my name, saying, 'As surely as the Lord lives'—even as they once taught my people to swear by Baal—then they will be established among my people. 17 But if any nation does not listen, I will completely uproot and destroy it," declares the Lord.

A Linen Belt

13 This is what the Lord said to me: "Go and buy a linen belt and put it around your waist, but do not let it touch water." 2 So I bought a belt, as the Lord directed, and put it around my waist.

3 Then the word of the Lord came to me a second time: 4 "Take the belt you bought and are wearing around your waist, and go now to Perath*c* and hide it there in a crev-

---

a 5 Or *you feel secure only*   *b 5* Or *the flooding of*   *c 4* Or possibly *to the Euphrates*; similarly in verses 5-7 ice in the rocks." ⁵So I went and hid it at Perath, as the LORD told me.

⁶Many days later the LORD said to me, "Go now to Perath and get the belt I told you to hide there." ⁷So I went to Perath and dug up the belt and took it from the place where I had hidden it, but now it was ruined and completely useless.

⁸Then the word of the LORD came to me: ⁹"This is what the LORD says: 'In the same way I will ruin the pride of Judah and the great pride of Jerusalem. ¹⁰These wicked people, who refuse to listen to my words, who follow the stubbornness of their hearts and go after other gods to serve and worship them, will be like this belt — completely useless! ¹¹For as a belt is bound around the waist, so I bound all the people of Israel and all the people of Judah to me,' declares the LORD, 'to be my people for my renown and praise and honor. But they have not listened.'

Wineskins

¹²"Say to them: 'This is what the LORD, the God of Israel, says: Every wineskin should be filled with wine.' And if they say to you, 'Don't we know that every wineskin should be filled with wine?' ¹³then tell them, 'This is what the LORD says: I am going to fill with drunkenness all who live in this land, including the kings who sit on David's throne, the priests, the prophets and all those living in Jerusalem. ¹⁴I will smash them one against the other, parents and children alike, declares the LORD. I will allow no pity or mercy or compassion to keep me from destroying them.' "

Threat of Captivity

¹⁵Hear and pay attention,
  do not be arrogant,
    for the LORD has spoken.
¹⁶Give glory to the LORD your God
  before he brings the darkness,
  before your feet stumble
    on the darkening hills.

You hope for light,
  but he will turn it to utter darkness
    and change it to deep gloom.
¹⁷If you do not listen,
  I will weep in secret
  because of your pride;
my eyes will weep bitterly,
  overflowing with tears,
  because the LORD's flock will be
    taken captive.

¹⁸Say to the king and to the queen mother,
  "Come down from your thrones,
for your glorious crowns
  will fall from your heads."
¹⁹The cities in the Negev will be shut up,
  and there will be no one to open
    them.
All Judah will be carried into exile,
  carried completely away.

²⁰Look up and see
  those who are coming from the
    north.
Where is the flock that was entrusted to
    you,
  the sheep of which you boasted?
²¹What will you say when the LORD sets
    over you
  those you cultivated as your special
    allies?
Will not pain grip you
  like that of a woman in labor?
²²And if you ask yourself,
  "Why has this happened to me?" —
it is because of your many sins
  that your skirts have been torn off
  and your body mistreated.
²³Can an Ethiopian[a] change his skin
  or a leopard its spots?
Neither can you do good
  who are accustomed to doing evil.

²⁴"I will scatter you like chaff
  driven by the desert wind.
²⁵This is your lot,
  the portion I have decreed for you,"
    declares the LORD,

---

a 23 Hebrew *Cushite* (probably a person from the upper Nile region)

"because you have forgotten me
and trusted in false gods.
26 I will pull up your skirts over your
face
that your shame may be seen —
27 your adulteries and lustful neighings,
your shameless prostitution!
I have seen your detestable acts
on the hills and in the fields.
Woe to you, Jerusalem!
How long will you be unclean?"

Drought, Famine, Sword

14 This is the word of the Lord that came to Jeremiah concerning the drought:

2 "Judah mourns,
her cities languish;
they wail for the land,
and a cry goes up from Jerusalem.
3 The nobles send their servants for
water;
they go to the cisterns
but find no water.
They return with their jars unfilled;
dismayed and despairing,
they cover their heads.
4 The ground is cracked
because there is no rain in the land;
the farmers are dismayed
and cover their heads.
5 Even the doe in the field
deserts her newborn fawn
because there is no grass.
6 Wild donkeys stand on the barren
heights
and pant like jackals;
their eyes fail
for lack of food."

7 Although our sins testify against us,
do something, Lord, for the sake of
your name.
For we have often rebelled;
we have sinned against you.
8 You who are the hope of Israel,
its Savior in times of distress,

why are you like a stranger in the land,
like a traveler who stays only a night?
9 Why are you like a man taken by
surprise,
like a warrior powerless to save?
You are among us, Lord,
and we bear your name;
do not forsake us!

10 This is what the Lord says about this
people:

"They greatly love to wander;
they do not restrain their feet.
So the Lord does not accept them;
he will now remember their
wickedness
and punish them for their sins."

11 Then the Lord said to me, "Do not
pray for the well-being of this people. 12 Although they fast, I will not listen to their
cry; though they offer burnt offerings and
grain offerings, I will not accept them. Instead, I will destroy them with the sword,
famine and plague."

13 But I said, "Alas, Sovereign Lord! The
prophets keep telling them, 'You will not
see the sword or suffer famine. Indeed, I
will give you lasting peace in this place.'"

14 Then the Lord said to me, "The
prophets are prophesying lies in my name.
I have not sent them or appointed them or
spoken to them. They are prophesying to
you false visions, divinations, idolatries*a*
and the delusions of their own minds.
15 Therefore this is what the Lord says
about the prophets who are prophesying
in my name: I did not send them, yet they
are saying, 'No sword or famine will touch
this land.' Those same prophets will perish by sword and famine. 16 And the people
they are prophesying to will be thrown out
into the streets of Jerusalem because of the
famine and sword. There will be no one to
bury them, their wives, their sons and their
daughters. I will pour out on them the calamity they deserve.

---

a 14 Or *visions, worthless divinations*

¹⁷"Speak this word to them:

"'Let my eyes overflow with tears
    night and day without ceasing;
for the Virgin Daughter, my people,
    has suffered a grievous wound,
    a crushing blow.
¹⁸If I go into the country,
    I see those slain by the sword;
if I go into the city,
    I see the ravages of famine.
Both prophet and priest
    have gone to a land they know not.'"

¹⁹Have you rejected Judah completely?
    Do you despise Zion?
Why have you afflicted us
    so that we cannot be healed?
We hoped for peace
    but no good has come,
for a time of healing
    but there is only terror.
²⁰We acknowledge our wickedness, LORD,
    and the guilt of our ancestors;
    we have indeed sinned against you.
²¹For the sake of your name do not
        despise us;
    do not dishonor your glorious
        throne.
Remember your covenant with us
    and do not break it.
²²Do any of the worthless idols of the
        nations bring rain?
    Do the skies themselves send down
        showers?
No, it is you, LORD our God.
    Therefore our hope is in you,
    for you are the one who does all this.

15 Then the LORD said to me: "Even if Moses and Samuel were to stand before me, my heart would not go out to this people. Send them away from my presence! Let them go! ²And if they ask you, 'Where shall we go?' tell them, 'This is what the LORD says:

"'Those destined for death, to death;
those for the sword, to the sword;
those for starvation, to starvation;
those for captivity, to captivity.'

³"I will send four kinds of destroyers against them," declares the LORD, "the sword to kill and the dogs to drag away and the birds and the wild animals to devour and destroy. ⁴I will make them abhorrent to all the kingdoms of the earth because of what Manasseh son of Hezekiah king of Judah did in Jerusalem.

⁵"Who will have pity on you, Jerusalem?
    Who will mourn for you?
    Who will stop to ask how you are?
⁶You have rejected me," declares the
        LORD.
    "You keep on backsliding.
So I will reach out and destroy you;
    I am tired of holding back.
⁷I will winnow them with a winnowing
        fork
    at the city gates of the land.
I will bring bereavement and
        destruction on my people,
    for they have not changed their
        ways.
⁸I will make their widows more
        numerous
    than the sand of the sea.
At midday I will bring a destroyer
    against the mothers of their young
        men;
suddenly I will bring down on them
    anguish and terror.
⁹The mother of seven will grow faint
    and breathe her last.
Her sun will set while it is still day;
    she will be disgraced and humiliated.
I will put the survivors to the sword
    before their enemies,"
                            declares the LORD.

¹⁰Alas, my mother, that you gave me
        birth,
    a man with whom the whole land
        strives and contends!
I have neither lent nor borrowed,
    yet everyone curses me.

¹¹The LORD said,

"Surely I will deliver you for a good
        purpose;

surely I will make your enemies
     plead with you
in times of disaster and times of
     distress.

12 "Can a man break iron—
     iron from the north—or bronze?

13 "Your wealth and your treasures
     I will give as plunder, without
         charge,
because of all your sins
     throughout your country.
14 I will enslave you to your enemies
     in*a* a land you do not know,
for my anger will kindle a fire
     that will burn against you."

15 LORD, you understand;
     remember me and care for me.
     Avenge me on my persecutors.
You are long-suffering—do not take
     me away;
     think of how I suffer reproach for
         your sake.
16 When your words came, I ate them;
     they were my joy and my heart's
         delight,
for I bear your name,
     LORD God Almighty.
17 I never sat in the company of revelers,
     never made merry with them;
I sat alone because your hand was on
     me
     and you had filled me with
         indignation.
18 Why is my pain unending
     and my wound grievous and
         incurable?
You are to me like a deceptive brook,
     like a spring that fails.

19 Therefore this is what the LORD says:

"If you repent, I will restore you
     that you may serve me;
if you utter worthy, not worthless,
         words,
     you will be my spokesman.

Let this people turn to you,
     but you must not turn to them.
20 I will make you a wall to this people,
     a fortified wall of bronze;
they will fight against you
     but will not overcome you,
for I am with you
     to rescue and save you,"
                   declares the LORD.
21 "I will save you from the hands of the
     wicked
     and deliver you from the grasp of the
         cruel."

Day of Disaster

16 Then the word of the LORD came to me: 2 "You must not marry and have sons or daughters in this place." 3 For this is what the LORD says about the sons and daughters born in this land and about the women who are their mothers and the men who are their fathers: 4 "They will die of deadly diseases. They will not be mourned or buried but will be like dung lying on the ground. They will perish by sword and famine, and their dead bodies will become food for the birds and the wild animals."

5 For this is what the LORD says: "Do not enter a house where there is a funeral meal; do not go to mourn or show sympathy, because I have withdrawn my blessing, my love and my pity from this people," declares the LORD. 6 "Both high and low will die in this land. They will not be buried or mourned, and no one will cut themselves or shave their head for the dead. 7 No one will offer food to comfort those who mourn for the dead—not even for a father or a mother—nor will anyone give them a drink to console them.

8 "And do not enter a house where there is feasting and sit down to eat and drink. 9 For this is what the LORD Almighty, the God of Israel, says: Before your eyes and in your days I will bring an end to the sounds

---

a 14 Some Hebrew manuscripts, Septuagint and Syriac (see also 17:4); most Hebrew manuscripts *I will cause your enemies to bring you / into* of joy and gladness and to the voices of bride and bridegroom in this place.

10"When you tell these people all this and they ask you, 'Why has the LORD decreed such a great disaster against us? What wrong have we done? What sin have we committed against the LORD our God?' 11then say to them, 'It is because your ancestors forsook me,' declares the LORD, 'and followed other gods and served and worshiped them. They forsook me and did not keep my law. 12But you have behaved more wickedly than your ancestors. See how all of you are following the stubbornness of your evil hearts instead of obeying me. 13So I will throw you out of this land into a land neither you nor your ancestors have known, and there you will serve other gods day and night, for I will show you no favor.'

14"However, the days are coming," declares the LORD, "when it will no longer be said, 'As surely as the LORD lives, who brought the Israelites up out of Egypt,' 15but it will be said, 'As surely as the LORD lives, who brought the Israelites up out of the land of the north and out of all the countries where he had banished them.' For I will restore them to the land I gave their ancestors.

16"But now I will send for many fishermen," declares the LORD, "and they will catch them. After that I will send for many hunters, and they will hunt them down on every mountain and hill and from the crevices of the rocks. 17My eyes are on all their ways; they are not hidden from me, nor is their sin concealed from my eyes. 18I will repay them double for their wickedness and their sin, because they have defiled my land with the lifeless forms of their vile images and have filled my inheritance with their detestable idols."

19LORD, my strength and my fortress,
    my refuge in time of distress,
    to you the nations will come
        from the ends of the earth and say,

"Our ancestors possessed nothing but
        false gods,
    worthless idols that did them no
        good.
20Do people make their own gods?
    Yes, but they are not gods!"

21 "Therefore I will teach them—
    this time I will teach them
    my power and might.
Then they will know
    that my name is the LORD.

17

"Judah's sin is engraved with
    an iron tool,
    inscribed with a flint point,
on the tablets of their hearts
    and on the horns of their altars.
2Even their children remember
    their altars and Asherah poles[a]
beside the spreading trees
    and on the high hills.
3My mountain in the land
    and your[b] wealth and all your
        treasures
I will give away as plunder,
    together with your high places,
    because of sin throughout your
        country.
4Through your own fault you will lose
    the inheritance I gave you.
I will enslave you to your enemies
    in a land you do not know,
for you have kindled my anger,
    and it will burn forever."

5This is what the LORD says:

"Cursed is the one who trusts in man,
    who draws strength from mere flesh
    and whose heart turns away from the
        LORD.
6That person will be like a bush in the
        wastelands;
    they will not see prosperity when it
        comes.
They will dwell in the parched places of
        the desert,
    in a salt land where no one lives.

---

a 2 That is, wooden symbols of the goddess Asherah   b 2,3 Or hills / 3and the mountains of the land. / Your

7"But blessed is the one who trusts in the
    LORD,
    whose confidence is in him.
8 They will be like a tree planted by the
        water
    that sends out its roots by the stream.
    It does not fear when heat comes;
        its leaves are always green.
    It has no worries in a year of drought
        and never fails to bear fruit."

9 The heart is deceitful above all things
        and beyond cure.
    Who can understand it?

10 "I the LORD search the heart
        and examine the mind,
    to reward each person according to
        their conduct,
        according to what their deeds
            deserve."

11 Like a partridge that hatches eggs it did
        not lay
    are those who gain riches by unjust
        means.
    When their lives are half gone, their
        riches will desert them,
    and in the end they will prove to be
        fools.

12 A glorious throne, exalted from the
        beginning,
    is the place of our sanctuary.
13 LORD, you are the hope of Israel;
    all who forsake you will be put to
        shame.
    Those who turn away from you will be
        written in the dust
    because they have forsaken the
        LORD,
    the spring of living water.

14 Heal me, LORD, and I will be healed;
    save me and I will be saved,
    for you are the one I praise.
15 They keep saying to me,
    "Where is the word of the LORD?
    Let it now be fulfilled!"

16 I have not run away from being your
        shepherd;
    you know I have not desired the day
        of despair.
    What passes my lips is open before
        you.
17 Do not be a terror to me;
    you are my refuge in the day of
        disaster.
18 Let my persecutors be put to shame,
    but keep me from shame;
    let them be terrified,
    but keep me from terror.
    Bring on them the day of disaster;
    destroy them with double
        destruction.

Keeping the Sabbath Day Holy

19 This is what the LORD said to me:
"Go and stand at the Gate of the People,[a]
through which the kings of Judah go in and
out; stand also at all the other gates of Jerusalem. 20 Say to them, 'Hear the word of
the LORD, you kings of Judah and all people of Judah and everyone living in Jerusalem who come through these gates. 21 This
is what the LORD says: Be careful not to
carry a load on the Sabbath day or bring
it through the gates of Jerusalem. 22 Do not
bring a load out of your houses or do any
work on the Sabbath, but keep the Sabbath
day holy, as I commanded your ancestors.
23 Yet they did not listen or pay attention;
they were stiff-necked and would not listen or respond to discipline. 24 But if you are
careful to obey me, declares the LORD, and
bring no load through the gates of this city
on the Sabbath, but keep the Sabbath day
holy by not doing any work on it, 25 then
kings who sit on David's throne will come
through the gates of this city with their officials. They and their officials will come
riding in chariots and on horses, accompanied by the men of Judah and those living
in Jerusalem, and this city will be inhabited
forever. 26 People will come from the towns
of Judah and the villages around Jerusa-

---

a 19 Or *Army*

lem, from the territory of Benjamin and the western foothills, from the hill country and the Negev, bringing burnt offerings and sacrifices, grain offerings and incense, and bringing thank offerings to the house of the LORD. 27But if you do not obey me to keep the Sabbath day holy by not carrying any load as you come through the gates of Jerusalem on the Sabbath day, then I will kindle an unquenchable fire in the gates of Jerusalem that will consume her fortresses.'"

At the Potter's House

18 This is the word that came to Jeremiah from the LORD: 2"Go down to the potter's house, and there I will give you my message." 3So I went down to the potter's house, and I saw him working at the wheel. 4But the pot he was shaping from the clay was marred in his hands; so the potter formed it into another pot, shaping it as seemed best to him.

5Then the word of the LORD came to me. 6He said, "Can I not do with you, Israel, as this potter does?" declares the LORD. "Like clay in the hand of the potter, so are you in my hand, Israel. 7If at any time I announce that a nation or kingdom is to be uprooted, torn down and destroyed, 8and if that nation I warned repents of its evil, then I will relent and not inflict on it the disaster I had planned. 9And if at another time I announce that a nation or kingdom is to be built up and planted, 10and if it does evil in my sight and does not obey me, then I will reconsider the good I had intended to do for it.

11"Now therefore say to the people of Judah and those living in Jerusalem, 'This is what the LORD says: Look! I am preparing a disaster for you and devising a plan against you. So turn from your evil ways, each one of you, and reform your ways and your actions.' 12But they will reply, 'It's no use. We will continue with our own plans; we will all follow the stubbornness of our evil hearts.'"

13Therefore this is what the LORD says:

"Inquire among the nations:
    Who has ever heard anything like
        this?
A most horrible thing has been done
    by Virgin Israel.
14Does the snow of Lebanon
    ever vanish from its rocky slopes?
Do its cool waters from distant sources
    ever stop flowing?*a*
15Yet my people have forgotten me;
    they burn incense to worthless idols,
which made them stumble in their ways,
    in the ancient paths.
They made them walk in byways,
    on roads not built up.
16Their land will be an object of horror
    and of lasting scorn;
all who pass by will be appalled
    and will shake their heads.
17Like a wind from the east,
    I will scatter them before their
        enemies;
I will show them my back and not my
        face
    in the day of their disaster."

18They said, "Come, let's make plans against Jeremiah; for the teaching of the law by the priest will not cease, nor will counsel from the wise, nor the word from the prophets. So come, let's attack him with our tongues and pay no attention to anything he says."

19Listen to me, LORD;
    hear what my accusers are saying!
20Should good be repaid with evil?
    Yet they have dug a pit for me.
Remember that I stood before you
    and spoke in their behalf
    to turn your wrath away from them.
21So give their children over to famine;
    hand them over to the power of the
        sword.
Let their wives be made childless and
        widows;

---

a 14 The meaning of the Hebrew for this sentence is uncertain.

let their men be put to death,
their young men slain by the sword
in battle.
22 Let a cry be heard from their houses
when you suddenly bring invaders
against them,
for they have dug a pit to capture me
and have hidden snares for my feet.
23 But you, Lord, know
all their plots to kill me.
Do not forgive their crimes
or blot out their sins from your sight.
Let them be overthrown before you;
deal with them in the time of your
anger.

19 This is what the Lord says: "Go and buy a clay jar from a potter. Take along some of the elders of the people and of the priests 2and go out to the Valley of Ben Hinnom, near the entrance of the Potsherd Gate. There proclaim the words I tell you, 3and say, 'Hear the word of the Lord, you kings of Judah and people of Jerusalem. This is what the Lord Almighty, the God of Israel, says: Listen! I am going to bring a disaster on this place that will make the ears of everyone who hears of it tingle. 4For they have forsaken me and made this a place of foreign gods; they have burned incense in it to gods that neither they nor their ancestors nor the kings of Judah ever knew, and they have filled this place with the blood of the innocent. 5They have built the high places of Baal to burn their children in the fire as offerings to Baal — something I did not command or mention, nor did it enter my mind. 6So beware, the days are coming, declares the Lord, when people will no longer call this place Topheth or the Valley of Ben Hinnom, but the Valley of Slaughter.

7 "'In this place I will ruin*a* the plans of Judah and Jerusalem. I will make them fall by the sword before their enemies, at the hands of those who want to kill them, and I will give their carcasses as food to the birds

and the wild animals. 8I will devastate this city and make it an object of horror and scorn; all who pass by will be appalled and will scoff because of all its wounds. 9I will make them eat the flesh of their sons and daughters, and they will eat one another's flesh because their enemies will press the siege so hard against them to destroy them.'

10 "Then break the jar while those who go with you are watching, 11and say to them, 'This is what the Lord Almighty says: I will smash this nation and this city just as this potter's jar is smashed and cannot be repaired. They will bury the dead in Topheth until there is no more room. 12This is what I will do to this place and to those who live here, declares the Lord. I will make this city like Topheth. 13The houses in Jerusalem and those of the kings of Judah will be defiled like this place, Topheth — all the houses where they burned incense on the roofs to all the starry hosts and poured out drink offerings to other gods.'"

14 Jeremiah then returned from Topheth, where the Lord had sent him to prophesy, and stood in the court of the Lord's temple and said to all the people, 15"This is what the Lord Almighty, the God of Israel, says: 'Listen! I am going to bring on this city and all the villages around it every disaster I pronounced against them, because they were stiff-necked and would not listen to my words.'"

Jeremiah and Pashhur

20 When the priest Pashhur son of Immer, the official in charge of the temple of the Lord, heard Jeremiah prophesying these things, 2he had Jeremiah the prophet beaten and put in the stocks at the Upper Gate of Benjamin at the Lord's temple. 3The next day, when Pashhur released him from the stocks, Jeremiah said to him, "The Lord's name for you is not Pashhur, but Terror on Every Side. 4For this is what the Lord says: 'I will make you a terror to your-

---

a 7 The Hebrew for *ruin* sounds like the Hebrew for *jar* (see verses 1 and 10).

self and to all your friends; with your own eyes you will see them fall by the sword of their enemies. I will give all Judah into the hands of the king of Babylon, who will carry them away to Babylon or put them to the sword. ⁵I will deliver all the wealth of this city into the hands of their enemies — all its products, all its valuables and all the treasures of the kings of Judah. They will take it away as plunder and carry it off to Babylon. ⁶And you, Pashhur, and all who live in your house will go into exile to Babylon. There you will die and be buried, you and all your friends to whom you have prophesied lies.'"

Jeremiah's Complaint

⁷You deceived*ᵃ* me, LORD, and I was
    deceived*ᵃ*;
  you overpowered me and prevailed.
I am ridiculed all day long;
  everyone mocks me.
⁸Whenever I speak, I cry out
  proclaiming violence and
    destruction.
So the word of the LORD has brought
  me
  insult and reproach all day long.
⁹But if I say, "I will not mention his word
  or speak anymore in his name,"
his word is in my heart like a fire,
  a fire shut up in my bones.
I am weary of holding it in;
  indeed, I cannot.
¹⁰I hear many whispering,
  "Terror on every side!
  Denounce him! Let's denounce him!"
All my friends
  are waiting for me to slip, saying,
"Perhaps he will be deceived;
  then we will prevail over him
  and take our revenge on him."

¹¹But the LORD is with me like a mighty
  warrior;
so my persecutors will stumble and
  not prevail.

They will fail and be thoroughly
  disgraced;
  their dishonor will never be
    forgotten.
¹²LORD Almighty, you who examine the
  righteous
  and probe the heart and mind,
let me see your vengeance on them,
  for to you I have committed my
    cause.

¹³Sing to the LORD!
  Give praise to the LORD!
He rescues the life of the needy
  from the hands of the wicked.

¹⁴Cursed be the day I was born!
  May the day my mother bore me not
    be blessed!
¹⁵Cursed be the man who brought my
  father the news,
  who made him very glad, saying,
"A child is born to you — a son!"
¹⁶May that man be like the towns
  the LORD overthrew without pity.
May he hear wailing in the morning,
  a battle cry at noon.
¹⁷For he did not kill me in the womb,
  with my mother as my grave,
  her womb enlarged forever.
¹⁸Why did I ever come out of the womb
  to see trouble and sorrow
  and to end my days in shame?

God Rejects Zedekiah's Request

21 The word came to Jeremiah from the LORD when King Zedekiah sent to him Pashhur son of Malkijah and the priest Zephaniah son of Maaseiah. They said: ²"Inquire now of the LORD for us because Nebuchadnezzar*ᵇ* king of Babylon is attacking us. Perhaps the LORD will perform wonders for us as in times past so that he will withdraw from us."

³But Jeremiah answered them, "Tell Zedekiah, ⁴'This is what the LORD, the God

---

ᵃ 7 Or *persuaded*   *ᵇ 2* Hebrew *Nebuchadrezzar*, of which *Nebuchadnezzar* is a variant; here and often in Jeremiah and Ezekiel of Israel, says: I am about to turn against you the weapons of war that are in your hands, which you are using to fight the king of Babylon and the Babylonians*a* who are outside the wall besieging you. And I will gather them inside this city. ⁵I myself will fight against you with an outstretched hand and a mighty arm in furious anger and in great wrath. ⁶I will strike down those who live in this city — both man and beast — and they will die of a terrible plague. ⁷After that, declares the LORD, I will give Zedekiah king of Judah, his officials and the people in this city who survive the plague, sword and famine, into the hands of Nebuchadnezzar king of Babylon and to their enemies who want to kill them. He will put them to the sword; he will show them no mercy or pity or compassion.'

⁸"Furthermore, tell the people, 'This is what the LORD says: See, I am setting before you the way of life and the way of death. ⁹Whoever stays in this city will die by the sword, famine or plague. But whoever goes out and surrenders to the Babylonians who are besieging you will live; they will escape with their lives. ¹⁰I have determined to do this city harm and not good, declares the LORD. It will be given into the hands of the king of Babylon, and he will destroy it with fire.'

¹¹"Moreover, say to the royal house of Judah, 'Hear the word of the LORD. ¹²This is what the LORD says to you, house of David:

"'Administer justice every morning;
    rescue from the hand of the
        oppressor
    the one who has been robbed,
or my wrath will break out and burn
        like fire
    because of the evil you have done —
    burn with no one to quench it.
¹³I am against you, Jerusalem,
    you who live above this valley
    on the rocky plateau, declares the
        LORD —

you who say, "Who can come against us?
    Who can enter our refuge?"
¹⁴I will punish you as your deeds deserve,
    declares the LORD.
I will kindle a fire in your forests
    that will consume everything around
        you.'"

Judgment Against Wicked Kings

22 This is what the LORD says: "Go down to the palace of the king of Judah and proclaim this message there: ²'Hear the word of the LORD to you, king of Judah, you who sit on David's throne — you, your officials and your people who come through these gates. ³This is what the LORD says: Do what is just and right. Rescue from the hand of the oppressor the one who has been robbed. Do no wrong or violence to the foreigner, the fatherless or the widow, and do not shed innocent blood in this place. ⁴For if you are careful to carry out these commands, then kings who sit on David's throne will come through the gates of this palace, riding in chariots and on horses, accompanied by their officials and their people. ⁵But if you do not obey these commands, declares the LORD, I swear by myself that this palace will become a ruin.'"

⁶For this is what the LORD says about the palace of the king of Judah:

"Though you are like Gilead to me,
    like the summit of Lebanon,
I will surely make you like a wasteland,
    like towns not inhabited.
⁷I will send destroyers against you,
    each man with his weapons,
and they will cut up your fine cedar
        beams
    and throw them into the fire.

⁸"People from many nations will pass by this city and will ask one another, 'Why has the LORD done such a thing to this great city?' ⁹And the answer will be: 'Because they have forsaken the covenant of the

---

a 4 Or Chaldeans; also in verse 9

LORD their God and have worshiped and served other gods.'"

¹⁰Do not weep for the dead king or
        mourn his loss;
    rather, weep bitterly for him who is
            exiled,
    because he will never return
        nor see his native land again.

¹¹For this is what the LORD says about Shallum*a* son of Josiah, who succeeded his father as king of Judah but has gone from this place: "He will never return. ¹²He will die in the place where they have led him captive; he will not see this land again."

¹³"Woe to him who builds his palace by
            unrighteousness,
    his upper rooms by injustice,
    making his own people work for
            nothing,
        not paying them for their labor.
¹⁴He says, 'I will build myself a great
            palace
    with spacious upper rooms.'
    So he makes large windows in it,
        panels it with cedar
        and decorates it in red.

¹⁵"Does it make you a king
        to have more and more cedar?
    Did not your father have food and
            drink?
    He did what was right and just,
        so all went well with him.
¹⁶He defended the cause of the poor and
            needy,
        and so all went well.
    Is that not what it means to know me?"
        declares the LORD.
¹⁷"But your eyes and your heart
        are set only on dishonest gain,
    on shedding innocent blood
        and on oppression and extortion."

¹⁸Therefore this is what the LORD says about Jehoiakim son of Josiah king of Judah:

"They will not mourn for him:
    'Alas, my brother! Alas, my sister!'
They will not mourn for him:
    'Alas, my master! Alas, his splendor!'
¹⁹He will have the burial of a donkey—
    dragged away and thrown
    outside the gates of Jerusalem."

²⁰"Go up to Lebanon and cry out,
    let your voice be heard in Bashan,
cry out from Abarim,
    for all your allies are crushed.
²¹I warned you when you felt secure,
    but you said, 'I will not listen!'
This has been your way from your
            youth;
    you have not obeyed me.
²²The wind will drive all your shepherds
            away,
    and your allies will go into exile.
Then you will be ashamed and
            disgraced
    because of all your wickedness.
²³You who live in 'Lebanon,'*b*
    who are nestled in cedar buildings,
how you will groan when pangs come
            upon you,
    pain like that of a woman in labor!

²⁴"As surely as I live," declares the LORD, "even if you, Jehoiachin*c* son of Jehoiakim king of Judah, were a signet ring on my right hand, I would still pull you off. ²⁵I will deliver you into the hands of those who want to kill you, those you fear—Nebuchadnezzar king of Babylon and the Babylonians.*d* ²⁶I will hurl you and the mother who gave you birth into another country, where neither of you was born, and there you both will die. ²⁷You will never come back to the land you long to return to."

²⁸Is this man Jehoiachin a despised,
            broken pot,
    an object no one wants?
Why will he and his children be hurled
            out,
    cast into a land they do not know?

---

a 11 Also called *Jehoahaz*   *b 23* That is, the palace in Jerusalem (see 1 Kings 7:2)   *c 24* Hebrew *Koniah*, a variant of *Jehoiachin*; also in verse 28   *d 25* Or *Chaldeans*

²⁹O land, land, land,
hear the word of the LORD!
³⁰This is what the LORD says:

"Record this man as if childless,
a man who will not prosper in his
lifetime,
for none of his offspring will prosper,
none will sit on the throne of David
or rule anymore in Judah."

The Righteous Branch

23 "Woe to the shepherds who are destroying and scattering the sheep of my pasture!" declares the LORD. ²Therefore this is what the LORD, the God of Israel, says to the shepherds who tend my people: "Because you have scattered my flock and driven them away and have not bestowed care on them, I will bestow punishment on you for the evil you have done," declares the LORD. ³"I myself will gather the remnant of my flock out of all the countries where I have driven them and will bring them back to their pasture, where they will be fruitful and increase in number. ⁴I will place shepherds over them who will tend them, and they will no longer be afraid or terrified, nor will any be missing," declares the LORD.

⁵"The days are coming," declares the LORD,
"when I will raise up for David[a] a
righteous Branch,
a King who will reign wisely
and do what is just and right in the
land.
⁶In his days Judah will be saved
and Israel will live in safety.
This is the name by which he will be
called:
The LORD Our Righteous Savior.

⁷"So then, the days are coming," declares the LORD, "when people will no longer say, 'As surely as the LORD lives, who brought the Israelites up out of Egypt,' ⁸but they will say, 'As surely as the LORD lives, who brought the descendants of Israel up out of the land of the north and out of all the countries where he had banished them.' Then they will live in their own land."

Lying Prophets

⁹Concerning the prophets:

My heart is broken within me;
all my bones tremble.
I am like a drunken man,
like a strong man overcome by wine,
because of the LORD
and his holy words.
¹⁰The land is full of adulterers;
because of the curse[b] the land lies
parched
and the pastures in the wilderness
are withered.
The prophets follow an evil course
and use their power unjustly.

¹¹"Both prophet and priest are godless;
even in my temple I find their
wickedness,"
declares the LORD.
¹²"Therefore their path will become
slippery;
they will be banished to darkness
and there they will fall.
I will bring disaster on them
in the year they are punished,"
declares the LORD.

¹³"Among the prophets of Samaria
I saw this repulsive thing:
They prophesied by Baal
and led my people Israel astray.
¹⁴And among the prophets of Jerusalem
I have seen something horrible:
They commit adultery and live a lie.
They strengthen the hands of evildoers,
so that not one of them turns from
their wickedness.
They are all like Sodom to me;
the people of Jerusalem are like
Gomorrah."

¹⁵Therefore this is what the LORD Almighty says concerning the prophets:

---

a 5 Or *up from David's line*   *b 10* Or *because of these things*

"I will make them eat bitter food
and drink poisoned water,
because from the prophets of Jerusalem
ungodliness has spread throughout
the land."

16This is what the LORD Almighty says:

"Do not listen to what the prophets are
prophesying to you;
they fill you with false hopes.
They speak visions from their own
minds,
not from the mouth of the LORD.
17They keep saying to those who
despise me,
'The LORD says: You will have peace.'
And to all who follow the stubbornness
of their hearts
they say, 'No harm will come to you.'
18But which of them has stood in the
council of the LORD
to see or to hear his word?
Who has listened and heard his
word?
19See, the storm of the LORD
will burst out in wrath,
a whirlwind swirling down
on the heads of the wicked.
20The anger of the LORD will not turn
back
until he fully accomplishes
the purposes of his heart.
In days to come
you will understand it clearly.
21I did not send these prophets,
yet they have run with their
message;
I did not speak to them,
yet they have prophesied.
22But if they had stood in my council,
they would have proclaimed my
words to my people
and would have turned them from their
evil ways
and from their evil deeds.

23"Am I only a God nearby,"
declares the LORD,
"and not a God far away?

24Who can hide in secret places
so that I cannot see them?"
declares the LORD.
"Do not I fill heaven and earth?"
declares the LORD.

25"I have heard what the prophets say
who prophesy lies in my name. They say,
'I had a dream! I had a dream!' 26How long
will this continue in the hearts of these
lying prophets, who prophesy the delusions of their own minds? 27They think the
dreams they tell one another will make my
people forget my name, just as their ancestors forgot my name through Baal worship.
28Let the prophet who has a dream recount
the dream, but let the one who has my word
speak it faithfully. For what has straw to do
with grain?" declares the LORD. 29"Is not
my word like fire," declares the LORD, "and
like a hammer that breaks a rock in pieces?

30"Therefore," declares the LORD, "I
am against the prophets who steal from
one another words supposedly from me.
31Yes," declares the LORD, "I am against
the prophets who wag their own tongues
and yet declare, 'The LORD declares.' 32In-
deed, I am against those who prophesy
false dreams," declares the LORD. "They
tell them and lead my people astray with
their reckless lies, yet I did not send or appoint them. They do not benefit these people in the least," declares the LORD.

False Prophecy

33"When these people, or a prophet or a
priest, ask you, 'What is the message from
the LORD?' say to them, 'What message? I
will forsake you, declares the LORD.' 34If a
prophet or a priest or anyone else claims,
'This is a message from the LORD,' I will
punish them and their household. 35This
is what each of you keeps saying to your
friends and other Israelites: 'What is the
LORD's answer?' or 'What has the LORD
spoken?' 36But you must not mention 'a
message from the LORD' again, because
each one's word becomes their own message. So you distort the words of the living

God, the LORD Almighty, our God. ³⁷This is what you keep saying to a prophet: 'What is the LORD's answer to you?' or 'What has the LORD spoken?' ³⁸Although you claim, 'This is a message from the LORD,' this is what the LORD says: You used the words, 'This is a message from the LORD,' even though I told you that you must not claim, 'This is a message from the LORD.' ³⁹Therefore, I will surely forget you and cast you out of my presence along with the city I gave to you and your ancestors. ⁴⁰I will bring on you everlasting disgrace — everlasting shame that will not be forgotten."

Two Baskets of Figs

24 After Jehoiachin*ᵃ* son of Jehoiakim king of Judah and the officials, the skilled workers and the artisans of Judah were carried into exile from Jerusalem to Babylon by Nebuchadnezzar king of Babylon, the LORD showed me two baskets of figs placed in front of the temple of the LORD. ²One basket had very good figs, like those that ripen early; the other basket had very bad figs, so bad they could not be eaten.

³Then the LORD asked me, "What do you see, Jeremiah?"

"Figs," I answered. "The good ones are very good, but the bad ones are so bad they cannot be eaten."

⁴Then the word of the LORD came to me: ⁵"This is what the LORD, the God of Israel, says: 'Like these good figs, I regard as good the exiles from Judah, whom I sent away from this place to the land of the Babylonians.*ᵇ* ⁶My eyes will watch over them for their good, and I will bring them back to this land. I will build them up and not tear them down; I will plant them and not uproot them. ⁷I will give them a heart to know me, that I am the LORD. They will be my people, and I will be their God, for they will return to me with all their heart.

⁸"'But like the bad figs, which are so bad they cannot be eaten,' says the LORD, 'so will I deal with Zedekiah king of Judah, his officials and the survivors from Jerusalem, whether they remain in this land or live in Egypt. ⁹I will make them abhorrent and an offense to all the kingdoms of the earth, a reproach and a byword, a curse*ᶜ* and an object of ridicule, wherever I banish them. ¹⁰I will send the sword, famine and plague against them until they are destroyed from the land I gave to them and their ancestors.'"

Seventy Years of Captivity

25 The word came to Jeremiah concerning all the people of Judah in the fourth year of Jehoiakim son of Josiah king of Judah, which was the first year of Nebuchadnezzar king of Babylon. ²So Jeremiah the prophet said to all the people of Judah and to all those living in Jerusalem: ³For twenty-three years — from the thirteenth year of Josiah son of Amon king of Judah until this very day — the word of the LORD has come to me and I have spoken to you again and again, but you have not listened.

⁴And though the LORD has sent all his servants the prophets to you again and again, you have not listened or paid any attention. ⁵They said, "Turn now, each of you, from your evil ways and your evil practices, and you can stay in the land the LORD gave to you and your ancestors for ever and ever. ⁶Do not follow other gods to serve and worship them; do not arouse my anger with what your hands have made. Then I will not harm you."

⁷"But you did not listen to me," declares the LORD, "and you have aroused my anger with what your hands have made, and you have brought harm to yourselves."

⁸Therefore the LORD Almighty says this: "Because you have not listened to my words, ⁹I will summon all the peoples of the north and my servant Nebuchadnezzar king of Babylon," declares the LORD, "and I

ᵃ 1 Hebrew *Jeconiah,* a variant of *Jehoiachin*   *ᵇ* 5 Or *Chaldeans*   *ᶜ* 9 That is, their names will be used in cursing (see 29:22); or, others will see that they are cursed.

will bring them against this land and its inhabitants and against all the surrounding nations. I will completely destroy[a] them and make them an object of horror and scorn, and an everlasting ruin. [10]I will banish from them the sounds of joy and gladness, the voices of bride and bridegroom, the sound of millstones and the light of the lamp. [11]This whole country will become a desolate wasteland, and these nations will serve the king of Babylon seventy years.

[12]"But when the seventy years are fulfilled, I will punish the king of Babylon and his nation, the land of the Babylonians,[b] for their guilt," declares the LORD, "and will make it desolate forever. [13]I will bring on that land all the things I have spoken against it, all that are written in this book and prophesied by Jeremiah against all the nations. [14]They themselves will be enslaved by many nations and great kings; I will repay them according to their deeds and the work of their hands."

The Cup of God's Wrath

[15]This is what the LORD, the God of Israel, said to me: "Take from my hand this cup filled with the wine of my wrath and make all the nations to whom I send you drink it. [16]When they drink it, they will stagger and go mad because of the sword I will send among them."

[17]So I took the cup from the LORD's hand and made all the nations to whom he sent me drink it: [18]Jerusalem and the towns of Judah, its kings and officials, to make them a ruin and an object of horror and scorn, a curse[c]—as they are today; [19]Pharaoh king of Egypt, his attendants, his officials and all his people, [20]and all the foreign people there; all the kings of Uz; all the kings of the Philistines (those of Ashkelon, Gaza, Ekron, and the people left at Ashdod); [21]Edom, Moab and Ammon; [22]all the kings of Tyre and Sidon; the kings of the coast-lands across the sea; [23]Dedan, Tema, Buz and all who are in distant places[d]; [24]all the kings of Arabia and all the kings of the foreign people who live in the wilderness; [25]all the kings of Zimri, Elam and Media; [26]and all the kings of the north, near and far, one after the other—all the kingdoms on the face of the earth. And after all of them, the king of Sheshak[e] will drink it too.

[27]"Then tell them, 'This is what the LORD Almighty, the God of Israel, says: Drink, get drunk and vomit, and fall to rise no more because of the sword I will send among you.' [28]But if they refuse to take the cup from your hand and drink, tell them, 'This is what the LORD Almighty says: You must drink it! [29]See, I am beginning to bring disaster on the city that bears my Name, and will you indeed go unpunished? You will not go unpunished, for I am calling down a sword on all who live on the earth, declares the LORD Almighty.'

[30]"Now prophesy all these words against them and say to them:

" 'The LORD will roar from on high;
    he will thunder from his holy
        dwelling
    and roar mightily against his land.
He will shout like those who tread the
        grapes,
    shout against all who live on the
        earth.
[31]The tumult will resound to the ends of
        the earth,
    for the LORD will bring charges
        against the nations;
he will bring judgment on all mankind
    and put the wicked to the sword,' "
                    declares the LORD.

[32]This is what the LORD Almighty says:

"Look! Disaster is spreading
    from nation to nation;
a mighty storm is rising
    from the ends of the earth."

---

[a] 9 The Hebrew term refers to the irrevocable giving over of things or persons to the LORD, often by totally destroying them.   [b] 12 Or *Chaldeans*   [c] 18 That is, their names to be used in cursing (see 29:22); or, to be seen by others as cursed   [d] 23 Or *who clip the hair by their foreheads*   [e] 26 *Sheshak* is a cryptogram for Babylon.

33At that time those slain by the LORD will be everywhere — from one end of the earth to the other. They will not be mourned or gathered up or buried, but will be like dung lying on the ground.

34Weep and wail, you shepherds;
    roll in the dust, you leaders of the
        flock.
For your time to be slaughtered has
        come;
    you will fall like the best of the rams.*a*
35The shepherds will have nowhere to flee,
    the leaders of the flock no place to
        escape.
36Hear the cry of the shepherds,
    the wailing of the leaders of the flock,
        for the LORD is destroying their
            pasture.
37The peaceful meadows will be laid waste
    because of the fierce anger of the
        LORD.
38Like a lion he will leave his lair,
    and their land will become desolate
because of the sword*b* of the oppressor
    and because of the LORD's fierce
        anger.

Jeremiah Threatened With Death

26 Early in the reign of Jehoiakim son of Josiah king of Judah, this word came from the LORD: 2"This is what the LORD says: Stand in the courtyard of the LORD's house and speak to all the people of the towns of Judah who come to worship in the house of the LORD. Tell them everything I command you; do not omit a word. 3Perhaps they will listen and each will turn from their evil ways. Then I will relent and not inflict on them the disaster I was planning because of the evil they have done. 4Say to them, 'This is what the LORD says: If you do not listen to me and follow my law, which I have set before you, 5and if you do not listen to the words of my servants the prophets, whom I have sent to you again and again (though you have not listened), 6then I will make this house like Shiloh and this city a curse*c* among all the nations of the earth.'"

7The priests, the prophets and all the people heard Jeremiah speak these words in the house of the LORD. 8But as soon as Jeremiah finished telling all the people everything the LORD had commanded him to say, the priests, the prophets and all the people seized him and said, "You must die! 9Why do you prophesy in the LORD's name that this house will be like Shiloh and this city will be desolate and deserted?" And all the people crowded around Jeremiah in the house of the LORD.

10When the officials of Judah heard about these things, they went up from the royal palace to the house of the LORD and took their places at the entrance of the New Gate of the LORD's house. 11Then the priests and the prophets said to the officials and all the people, "This man should be sentenced to death because he has prophesied against this city. You have heard it with your own ears!"

12Then Jeremiah said to all the officials and all the people: "The LORD sent me to prophesy against this house and this city all the things you have heard. 13Now reform your ways and your actions and obey the LORD your God. Then the LORD will relent and not bring the disaster he has pronounced against you. 14As for me, I am in your hands; do with me whatever you think is good and right. 15Be assured, however, that if you put me to death, you will bring the guilt of innocent blood on yourselves and on this city and on those who live in it, for in truth the LORD has sent me to you to speak all these words in your hearing."

16Then the officials and all the people said to the priests and the prophets, "This man should not be sentenced to death! He has spoken to us in the name of the LORD our God."

---

a 34 Septuagint; Hebrew *fall and be shattered like fine pottery* (see also 46:16 and 50:16); most Hebrew manuscripts *anger* or, others will see that it is cursed.   *b 38* Some Hebrew manuscripts and Septuagint   *c 6* That is, its name will be used in cursing (see 29:22);

¹⁷Some of the elders of the land stepped forward and said to the entire assembly of people, ¹⁸"Micah of Moresheth prophesied in the days of Hezekiah king of Judah. He told all the people of Judah, 'This is what the LORD Almighty says:

> "'Zion will be plowed like a field,
> Jerusalem will become a heap of
>   rubble,
> the temple hill a mound overgrown
>   with thickets.'ᵃ

¹⁹"Did Hezekiah king of Judah or anyone else in Judah put him to death? Did not Hezekiah fear the LORD and seek his favor? And did not the LORD relent, so that he did not bring the disaster he pronounced against them? We are about to bring a terrible disaster on ourselves!"

²⁰(Now Uriah son of Shemaiah from Kiriath Jearim was another man who prophesied in the name of the LORD; he prophesied the same things against this city and this land as Jeremiah did. ²¹When King Jehoiakim and all his officers and officials heard his words, the king was determined to put him to death. But Uriah heard of it and fled in fear to Egypt. ²²King Jehoiakim, however, sent Elnathan son of Akbor to Egypt, along with some other men. ²³They brought Uriah out of Egypt and took him to King Jehoiakim, who had him struck down with a sword and his body thrown into the burial place of the common people.)

²⁴Furthermore, Ahikam son of Shaphan supported Jeremiah, and so he was not handed over to the people to be put to death.

Judah to Serve Nebuchadnezzar

27 Early in the reign of Zedekiahᵇ son of Josiah king of Judah, this word came to Jeremiah from the LORD: ²This is what the LORD said to me: "Make a yoke out of straps and crossbars and put it on your neck. ³Then send word to the kings of Edom, Moab, Ammon, Tyre and Sidon through the envoys who have come to Jerusalem to Zedekiah king of Judah. ⁴Give them a message for their masters and say, 'This is what the LORD Almighty, the God of Israel, says: "Tell this to your masters: ⁵With my great power and outstretched arm I made the earth and its people and the animals that are on it, and I give it to anyone I please. ⁶Now I will give all your countries into the hands of my servant Nebuchadnezzar king of Babylon; I will make even the wild animals subject to him. ⁷All nations will serve him and his son and his grandson until the time for his land comes; then many nations and great kings will subjugate him.

⁸"'"If, however, any nation or kingdom will not serve Nebuchadnezzar king of Babylon or bow its neck under his yoke, I will punish that nation with the sword, famine and plague, declares the LORD, until I destroy it by his hand. ⁹So do not listen to your prophets, your diviners, your interpreters of dreams, your mediums or your sorcerers who tell you, 'You will not serve the king of Babylon.' ¹⁰They prophesy lies to you that will only serve to remove you far from your lands; I will banish you and you will perish. ¹¹But if any nation will bow its neck under the yoke of the king of Babylon and serve him, I will let that nation remain in its own land to till it and to live there, declares the LORD."'"

¹²I gave the same message to Zedekiah king of Judah. I said, "Bow your neck under the yoke of the king of Babylon; serve him and his people, and you will live. ¹³Why will you and your people die by the sword, famine and plague with which the LORD has threatened any nation that will not serve the king of Babylon? ¹⁴Do not listen to the words of the prophets who say to you, 'You will not serve the king of Babylon,' for they are prophesying lies to

---

ᵃ 18 Micah 3:12   ᵇ 1 A few Hebrew manuscripts and Syriac (see also 27:3,12 and 28:1); most Hebrew manuscripts *Jehoiakim* (Most Septuagint manuscripts do not have this verse.)

you. [15]'I have not sent them,' declares the LORD. 'They are prophesying lies in my name. Therefore, I will banish you and you will perish, both you and the prophets who prophesy to you.'"

[16]Then I said to the priests and all these people, "This is what the LORD says: Do not listen to the prophets who say, 'Very soon now the articles from the LORD's house will be brought back from Babylon.' They are prophesying lies to you. [17]Do not listen to them. Serve the king of Babylon, and you will live. Why should this city become a ruin? [18]If they are prophets and have the word of the LORD, let them plead with the LORD Almighty that the articles remaining in the house of the LORD and in the palace of the king of Judah and in Jerusalem not be taken to Babylon. [19]For this is what the LORD Almighty says about the pillars, the bronze Sea, the movable stands and the other articles that are left in this city, [20]which Nebuchadnezzar king of Babylon did not take away when he carried Jehoiachin[a] son of Jehoiakim king of Judah into exile from Jerusalem to Babylon, along with all the nobles of Judah and Jerusalem— [21]yes, this is what the LORD Almighty, the God of Israel, says about the things that are left in the house of the LORD and in the palace of the king of Judah and in Jerusalem: [22]'They will be taken to Babylon and there they will remain until the day I come for them,' declares the LORD. 'Then I will bring them back and restore them to this place.'"

The False Prophet Hananiah

28 In the fifth month of that same year, the fourth year, early in the reign of Zedekiah king of Judah, the prophet Hananiah son of Azzur, who was from Gibeon, said to me in the house of the LORD in the presence of the priests and all the people: [2]"This is what the LORD Almighty, the God of Israel, says: 'I will break the yoke of the king of Babylon. [3]Within two years I will bring back to this place all the articles of the LORD's house that Nebuchadnezzar king of Babylon removed from here and took to Babylon. [4]I will also bring back to this place Jehoiachin[a] son of Jehoiakim king of Judah and all the other exiles from Judah who went to Babylon,' declares the LORD, 'for I will break the yoke of the king of Babylon.'"

[5]Then the prophet Jeremiah replied to the prophet Hananiah before the priests and all the people who were standing in the house of the LORD. [6]He said, "Amen! May the LORD do so! May the LORD fulfill the words you have prophesied by bringing the articles of the LORD's house and all the exiles back to this place from Babylon. [7]Nevertheless, listen to what I have to say in your hearing and in the hearing of all the people: [8]From early times the prophets who preceded you and me have prophesied war, disaster and plague against many countries and great kingdoms. [9]But the prophet who prophesies peace will be recognized as one truly sent by the LORD only if his prediction comes true."

[10]Then the prophet Hananiah took the yoke off the neck of the prophet Jeremiah and broke it, [11]and he said before all the people, "This is what the LORD says: 'In the same way I will break the yoke of Nebuchadnezzar king of Babylon off the neck of all the nations within two years.'" At this, the prophet Jeremiah went on his way.

[12]After the prophet Hananiah had broken the yoke off the neck of the prophet Jeremiah, the word of the LORD came to Jeremiah: [13]"Go and tell Hananiah, 'This is what the LORD says: You have broken a wooden yoke, but in its place you will get a yoke of iron. [14]This is what the LORD Almighty, the God of Israel, says: I will put an iron yoke on the necks of all these nations to make them serve Nebuchadnezzar king of Babylon, and they will serve him. I will even give him control over the wild animals.'"

---

[a] *20,4* Hebrew *Jeconiah*, a variant of *Jehoiachin*

¹⁵Then the prophet Jeremiah said to Hananiah the prophet, "Listen, Hananiah! The LORD has not sent you, yet you have persuaded this nation to trust in lies. ¹⁶Therefore this is what the LORD says: 'I am about to remove you from the face of the earth. This very year you are going to die, because you have preached rebellion against the LORD.'"

¹⁷In the seventh month of that same year, Hananiah the prophet died.

A Letter to the Exiles

29 This is the text of the letter that the prophet Jeremiah sent from Jerusalem to the surviving elders among the exiles and to the priests, the prophets and all the other people Nebuchadnezzar had carried into exile from Jerusalem to Babylon. ²(This was after King Jehoiachin^a and the queen mother, the court officials and the leaders of Judah and Jerusalem, the skilled workers and the artisans had gone into exile from Jerusalem.) ³He entrusted the letter to Elasah son of Shaphan and to Gemariah son of Hilkiah, whom Zedekiah king of Judah sent to King Nebuchadnezzar in Babylon. It said:

⁴This is what the LORD Almighty, the God of Israel, says to all those I carried into exile from Jerusalem to Babylon: ⁵"Build houses and settle down; plant gardens and eat what they produce. ⁶Marry and have sons and daughters; find wives for your sons and give your daughters in marriage, so that they too may have sons and daughters. Increase in number there; do not decrease. ⁷Also, seek the peace and prosperity of the city to which I have carried you into exile. Pray to the LORD for it, because if it prospers, you too will prosper." ⁸Yes, this is what the LORD Almighty, the God of Israel, says: "Do not let the prophets and diviners among you deceive you. Do not listen to the dreams you encourage them to have. ⁹They are prophesying lies to you in my name. I have not sent them," declares the LORD.

¹⁰This is what the LORD says: "When seventy years are completed for Babylon, I will come to you and fulfill my good promise to bring you back to this place. ¹¹For I know the plans I have for you," declares the LORD, "plans to prosper you and not to harm you, plans to give you hope and a future. ¹²Then you will call on me and come and pray to me, and I will listen to you. ¹³You will seek me and find me when you seek me with all your heart. ¹⁴I will be found by you," declares the LORD, "and will bring you back from captivity.^b I will gather you from all the nations and places where I have banished you," declares the LORD, "and will bring you back to the place from which I carried you into exile."

¹⁵You may say, "The LORD has raised up prophets for us in Babylon," ¹⁶but this is what the LORD says about the king who sits on David's throne and all the people who remain in this city, your fellow citizens who did not go with you into exile — ¹⁷yes, this is what the LORD Almighty says: "I will send the sword, famine and plague against them and I will make them like figs that are so bad they cannot be eaten. ¹⁸I will pursue them with the sword, famine and plague and will make them abhorrent to all the kingdoms of the earth, a curse^c and an object of horror, of scorn and reproach, among all the nations where I drive them. ¹⁹For they have not listened to my words," declares the LORD, "words that I sent to them again and again by my servants the prophets. And you

---

^a 2 Hebrew *Jeconiah*, a variant of *Jehoiachin*   ^b 14 Or *will restore your fortunes*   ^c 18 That is, their names will be used in cursing (see verse 22); or, others will see that they are cursed.

exiles have not listened either," declares the LORD.

²⁰Therefore, hear the word of the LORD, all you exiles whom I have sent away from Jerusalem to Babylon. ²¹This is what the LORD Almighty, the God of Israel, says about Ahab son of Kolaiah and Zedekiah son of Maaseiah, who are prophesying lies to you in my name: "I will deliver them into the hands of Nebuchadnezzar king of Babylon, and he will put them to death before your very eyes. ²²Because of them, all the exiles from Judah who are in Babylon will use this curse: 'May the LORD treat you like Zedekiah and Ahab, whom the king of Babylon burned in the fire.' ²³For they have done outrageous things in Israel; they have committed adultery with their neighbors' wives, and in my name they have uttered lies — which I did not authorize. I know it and am a witness to it," declares the LORD.

Message to Shemaiah

²⁴Tell Shemaiah the Nehelamite, ²⁵"This is what the LORD Almighty, the God of Israel, says: You sent letters in your own name to all the people in Jerusalem, to the priest Zephaniah son of Maaseiah, and to all the other priests. You said to Zephaniah, ²⁶'The LORD has appointed you priest in place of Jehoiada to be in charge of the house of the LORD; you should put any maniac who acts like a prophet into the stocks and neck-irons. ²⁷So why have you not reprimanded Jeremiah from Anathoth, who poses as a prophet among you? ²⁸He has sent this message to us in Babylon: It will be a long time. Therefore build houses and settle down; plant gardens and eat what they produce.'"

²⁹Zephaniah the priest, however, read the letter to Jeremiah the prophet. ³⁰Then the word of the LORD came to Jeremiah: ³¹"Send this message to all the exiles: 'This is what the LORD says about Shemaiah the

Nehelamite: Because Shemaiah has prophesied to you, even though I did not send him, and has persuaded you to trust in lies, ³²this is what the LORD says: I will surely punish Shemaiah the Nehelamite and his descendants. He will have no one left among this people, nor will he see the good things I will do for my people, declares the LORD, because he has preached rebellion against me.'"

Restoration of Israel

30 This is the word that came to Jeremiah from the LORD: ²"This is what the LORD, the God of Israel, says: 'Write in a book all the words I have spoken to you. ³The days are coming,' declares the LORD, 'when I will bring my people Israel and Judah back from captivity*a* and restore them to the land I gave their ancestors to possess,' says the LORD."

⁴These are the words the LORD spoke concerning Israel and Judah: ⁵"This is what the LORD says:

"'Cries of fear are heard —
    terror, not peace.
⁶ Ask and see:
    Can a man bear children?
Then why do I see every strong man
    with his hands on his stomach like a
        woman in labor,
    every face turned deathly pale?
⁷ How awful that day will be!
    No other will be like it.
It will be a time of trouble for Jacob,
    but he will be saved out of it.

⁸ "'In that day,' declares the LORD
        Almighty,
    'I will break the yoke off their necks
and will tear off their bonds;
    no longer will foreigners enslave them.
⁹ Instead, they will serve the LORD their
        God
    and David their king,
    whom I will raise up for them.

❶
❷
❸

---

a 3 Or *will restore the fortunes of my people Israel and Judah*

10 "'So do not be afraid, Jacob my servant;
    do not be dismayed, Israel,'
                    declares the LORD.
  'I will surely save you out of a distant
      place,
    your descendants from the land of
      their exile.
  Jacob will again have peace and
      security,
    and no one will make him afraid.
11 I am with you and will save you,'
    declares the LORD.
  'Though I completely destroy all the
      nations
    among which I scatter you,
    I will not completely destroy you.
  I will discipline you but only in due
      measure;
    I will not let you go entirely
      unpunished.'

12 "This is what the LORD says:

  "'Your wound is incurable,
    your injury beyond healing.
13 There is no one to plead your cause,
    no remedy for your sore,
    no healing for you.
14 All your allies have forgotten you;
    they care nothing for you.
  I have struck you as an enemy would
    and punished you as would the cruel,
  because your guilt is so great
    and your sins so many.
15 Why do you cry out over your wound,
    your pain that has no cure?
  Because of your great guilt and many
      sins
    I have done these things to you.

16 "'But all who devour you will be
      devoured;
    all your enemies will go into exile.
  Those who plunder you will be
      plundered;
    all who make spoil of you I will
      despoil.
17 But I will restore you to health
    and heal your wounds,'
                    declares the LORD,

'because you are called an outcast,
    Zion for whom no one cares.'

18 "This is what the LORD says:

  "'I will restore the fortunes of Jacob's
      tents
    and have compassion on his
      dwellings;
  the city will be rebuilt on her ruins,
    and the palace will stand in its
      proper place.
19 From them will come songs of
      thanksgiving
    and the sound of rejoicing.
  I will add to their numbers,
    and they will not be decreased;
  I will bring them honor,
    and they will not be disdained.
20 Their children will be as in days of old,
    and their community will be
      established before me;
    I will punish all who oppress them.
21 Their leader will be one of their own;
    their ruler will arise from among
      them.
  I will bring him near and he will come
      close to me—
    for who is he who will devote himself
      to be close to me?'
                    declares the LORD.
22 "'So you will be my people,
    and I will be your God.'"

23 See, the storm of the LORD
    will burst out in wrath,
  a driving wind swirling down
    on the heads of the wicked.
24 The fierce anger of the LORD will not
      turn back
    until he fully accomplishes
    the purposes of his heart.
  In days to come
    you will understand this.

31

"At that time," declares the LORD, "I will be the God of all the families of Israel, and they will be my people."

2 This is what the LORD says:

"The people who survive the sword
     will find favor in the wilderness;
I will come to give rest to Israel."

³The Lord appeared to us in the past,ᵃ
saying:

"I have loved you with an everlasting
     love;
I have drawn you with unfailing
     kindness.
⁴I will build you up again,
     and you, Virgin Israel, will be rebuilt.

Again you will take up your timbrels
     and go out to dance with the
       joyful.
⁵Again you will plant vineyards
     on the hills of Samaria;
the farmers will plant them
     and enjoy their fruit.
⁶There will be a day when watchmen cry
     out
on the hills of Ephraim,
'Come, let us go up to Zion,
     to the Lord our God.'"

ᵃ 3 Or *Lord has appeared to us from afar*

DENIAL LESSON [*Principle One*]

For the previous entry in the DENIAL lesson, go to Ephesians 4:25 (page 1467).

For a discussion of Principles One through Eight and a listing of their related lessons,
go to pages xvii – xliv.

"I will restore you to health and heal your wounds," declares the Lord,
"because you are called an outcast, Zion for whom no one cares."

JEREMIAH 30:17

The power to change comes only through God's grace. Principle One states: "Realize I'm not God. I admit that I'm powerless to control my tendency to do the wrong thing and that my life has become unmanageable." If we admit that we're powerless, we recognize our need for a power greater than ourselves to restore us. That power is our Higher Power, the one and only true Higher Power, Jesus Christ.

In Principle One we discover that we've been in DENIAL of our hurts, hang-ups and habits. The last letter in DENIAL is *L*, which reminds us that remaining in denial only LENGTHENS OUR PAIN. We want to cling to the false belief that denial protects us from pain, but the reality is that it allows our wounds to fester and grow, multiplying the hurt by piling on unbearable layers of guilt and shame. Denial only extends our hurts and multiplies our problems. Truth, like surgery, may hurt for a while, but in the long run it cures. God promises to restore our health and heal our wounds.

We're ready to complete Principle One when our pain becomes greater than our fear. When David's pain finally surpassed his fear, he was able to face his denial and feel the reality of that pain: "Have mercy on me, Lord, for I am faint; heal me, Lord, for my bones are in agony. My soul is in deep anguish. How long, Lord, how long?" (Psalm 6:2 – 3).

In the same way, if we want to be rid of our pain, we need to face it and work through the hurt in the early stages of our recovery.

This is the final page of the DENIAL lesson.

7This is what the LORD says:

"Sing with joy for Jacob;
    shout for the foremost of the nations.
Make your praises heard, and say,
    'LORD, save your people,
    the remnant of Israel.'
8See, I will bring them from the land of
        the north
    and gather them from the ends of the
        earth.
Among them will be the blind and the
        lame,
    expectant mothers and women in
        labor;
    a great throng will return.
9They will come with weeping;
    they will pray as I bring them back.
I will lead them beside streams of water
    on a level path where they will not
        stumble,
because I am Israel's father,
    and Ephraim is my firstborn son.

10"Hear the word of the LORD, you
        nations;
    proclaim it in distant coastlands:
'He who scattered Israel will gather
        them
    and will watch over his flock like a
        shepherd.'
11For the LORD will deliver Jacob
    and redeem them from the hand of
        those stronger than they.
12They will come and shout for joy on the
        heights of Zion;
    they will rejoice in the bounty of the
        LORD —
    the grain, the new wine and the olive
        oil,
    the young of the flocks and herds.
They will be like a well-watered garden,
    and they will sorrow no more.
13Then young women will dance and be
        glad,
    young men and old as well.
I will turn their mourning into
        gladness;
    I will give them comfort and joy
        instead of sorrow.

14I will satisfy the priests with abundance,
    and my people will be filled with my
        bounty,"
                declares the LORD.

15This is what the LORD says:

"A voice is heard in Ramah,
    mourning and great weeping,
Rachel weeping for her children
    and refusing to be comforted,
    because they are no more."

16This is what the LORD says:

"Restrain your voice from weeping
    and your eyes from tears,
for your work will be rewarded,"
                declares the LORD.
    "They will return from the land of
        the enemy.
17So there is hope for your descendants,"
                declares the LORD.
    "Your children will return to their
        own land.

18"I have surely heard Ephraim's
        moaning:
    'You disciplined me like an unruly
        calf,
    and I have been disciplined.
Restore me, and I will return,
    because you are the LORD my God.
19After I strayed,
    I repented;
after I came to understand,
    I beat my breast.
I was ashamed and humiliated
    because I bore the disgrace of my
        youth.'
20Is not Ephraim my dear son,
    the child in whom I delight?
Though I often speak against him,
    I still remember him.
Therefore my heart yearns for him;
    I have great compassion for him,"
                declares the LORD.

21"Set up road signs;
    put up guideposts.
Take note of the highway,
    the road that you take.

Return, Virgin Israel,
  return to your towns.
22 How long will you wander,
  unfaithful Daughter Israel?
The Lord will create a new thing on
    earth —
  the woman will return to*a* the man."

23This is what the Lord Almighty, the
God of Israel, says: "When I bring them
back from captivity,*b* the people in the land
of Judah and in its towns will once again
use these words: 'The Lord bless you, you
prosperous city, you sacred mountain.'
24People will live together in Judah and all
its towns — farmers and those who move
about with their flocks. 25I will refresh the
weary and satisfy the faint."

26At this I awoke and looked around. My
sleep had been pleasant to me.

27"The days are coming," declares the
Lord, "when I will plant the kingdoms
of Israel and Judah with the offspring of
people and of animals. 28Just as I watched
over them to uproot and tear down, and to
overthrow, destroy and bring disaster, so I
will watch over them to build and to plant,"
declares the Lord. 29"In those days people
will no longer say,

'The parents have eaten sour grapes,
    and the children's teeth are set on edge.'

30Instead, everyone will die for their own
sin; whoever eats sour grapes — their own
teeth will be set on edge.

31 "The days are coming," declares the Lord,
  "when I will make a new covenant
  with the people of Israel
    and with the people of Judah.
32 It will not be like the covenant
  I made with their ancestors
  when I took them by the hand
    to lead them out of Egypt,
  because they broke my covenant,
    though I was a husband to*c* them,*d*"
              declares the Lord.

33 "This is the covenant I will make with
      the people of Israel
  after that time," declares the Lord.
  "I will put my law in their minds
    and write it on their hearts.
  I will be their God,
    and they will be my people.
34 No longer will they teach their
      neighbor,
  or say to one another, 'Know the
      Lord,'
  because they will all know me,
    from the least of them to the
        greatest,"
              declares the Lord.
  "For I will forgive their wickedness
    and will remember their sins no
        more."

35 This is what the Lord says,

he who appoints the sun
    to shine by day,
who decrees the moon and stars
    to shine by night,
who stirs up the sea
    so that its waves roar —
  the Lord Almighty is his name:
36 "Only if these decrees vanish from my
      sight,"
  declares the Lord,
"will Israel ever cease
    being a nation before me."

37 This is what the Lord says:

"Only if the heavens above can be
      measured
  and the foundations of the earth
      below be searched out
will I reject all the descendants of Israel
  because of all they have done,"
              declares the Lord.

38 "The days are coming," declares the
Lord, "when this city will be rebuilt for
me from the Tower of Hananel to the Corner Gate. 39The measuring line will stretch
from there straight to the hill of Gareb

---

a 22 Or *will protect*   *b* 23 Or *I restore their fortunes*   *c* 32 Hebrew; Septuagint and Syriac / *and I turned away*
from   *d* 32 Or *was their master*

and then turn to Goah. ⁴⁰The whole valley where dead bodies and ashes are thrown, and all the terraces out to the Kidron Valley on the east as far as the corner of the Horse Gate, will be holy to the LORD. The city will never again be uprooted or demolished."

Jeremiah Buys a Field

32 This is the word that came to Jeremiah from the LORD in the tenth year of Zedekiah king of Judah, which was the eighteenth year of Nebuchadnezzar. ²The army of the king of Babylon was then besieging Jerusalem, and Jeremiah the prophet was confined in the courtyard of the guard in the royal palace of Judah.

³Now Zedekiah king of Judah had imprisoned him there, saying, "Why do you prophesy as you do? You say, 'This is what the LORD says: I am about to give this city into the hands of the king of Babylon, and he will capture it. ⁴Zedekiah king of Judah will not escape the Babylonians*a* but will certainly be given into the hands of the king of Babylon, and will speak with him face to face and see him with his own eyes. ⁵He will take Zedekiah to Babylon, where he will remain until I deal with him, declares the LORD. If you fight against the Babylonians, you will not succeed.'"

⁶Jeremiah said, "The word of the LORD came to me: ⁷Hanamel son of Shallum your uncle is going to come to you and say, 'Buy my field at Anathoth, because as nearest relative it is your right and duty to buy it.'

⁸"Then, just as the LORD had said, my cousin Hanamel came to me in the courtyard of the guard and said, 'Buy my field at Anathoth in the territory of Benjamin. Since it is your right to redeem it and possess it, buy it for yourself.'

"I knew that this was the word of the LORD; ⁹so I bought the field at Anathoth from my cousin Hanamel and weighed out for him seventeen shekels*b* of silver.

¹⁰I signed and sealed the deed, had it witnessed, and weighed out the silver on the scales. ¹¹I took the deed of purchase — the sealed copy containing the terms and conditions, as well as the unsealed copy — ¹²and I gave this deed to Baruch son of Neriah, the son of Mahseiah, in the presence of my cousin Hanamel and of the witnesses who had signed the deed and of all the Jews sitting in the courtyard of the guard.

¹³"In their presence I gave Baruch these instructions: ¹⁴'This is what the LORD Almighty, the God of Israel, says: Take these documents, both the sealed and unsealed copies of the deed of purchase, and put them in a clay jar so they will last a long time. ¹⁵For this is what the LORD Almighty, the God of Israel, says: Houses, fields and vineyards will again be bought in this land.'

¹⁶"After I had given the deed of purchase to Baruch son of Neriah, I prayed to the LORD:

¹⁷"Ah, Sovereign LORD, you have made the heavens and the earth by your great power and outstretched arm. Nothing is too hard for you. ¹⁸You show love to thousands but bring the punishment for the parents' sins into the laps of their children after them. Great and mighty God, whose name is the LORD Almighty, ¹⁹great are your purposes and mighty are your deeds. Your eyes are open to the ways of all mankind; you reward each person according to their conduct and as their deeds deserve. ²⁰You performed signs and wonders in Egypt and have continued them to this day, in Israel and among all mankind, and have gained the renown that is still yours. ²¹You brought your people Israel out of Egypt with signs and wonders, by a mighty hand and an outstretched arm and with great terror. ²²You gave them this land you had sworn to give their ancestors, a land flowing with milk

---

a 4 Or *Chaldeans*; also in verses 5, 24, 25, 28, 29 and 43   *b* 9 That is, about 7 ounces or about 200 grams and honey. 23They came in and took possession of it, but they did not obey you or follow your law; they did not do what you commanded them to do. So you brought all this disaster on them.

24"See how the siege ramps are built up to take the city. Because of the sword, famine and plague, the city will be given into the hands of the Babylonians who are attacking it. What you said has happened, as you now see. 25And though the city will be given into the hands of the Babylonians, you, Sovereign LORD, say to me, 'Buy the field with silver and have the transaction witnessed.'"

26Then the word of the LORD came to Jeremiah: 27"I am the LORD, the God of all mankind. Is anything too hard for me? 28Therefore this is what the LORD says: I am about to give this city into the hands of the Babylonians and to Nebuchadnezzar king of Babylon, who will capture it. 29The Babylonians who are attacking this city will come in and set it on fire; they will burn it down, along with the houses where the people aroused my anger by burning incense on the roofs to Baal and by pouring out drink offerings to other gods.

30"The people of Israel and Judah have done nothing but evil in my sight from their youth; indeed, the people of Israel have done nothing but arouse my anger with what their hands have made, declares the LORD. 31From the day it was built until now, this city has so aroused my anger and wrath that I must remove it from my sight. 32The people of Israel and Judah have provoked me by all the evil they have done — they, their kings and officials, their priests and prophets, the people of Judah and those living in Jerusalem. 33They turned their backs to me and not their faces; though I taught them again and again, they would not listen or respond to discipline. 34They set up their vile images in the house that bears my Name and defiled it. 35They built high places for Baal in the Valley of Ben Hinnom to sacrifice their sons and daughters to Molek, though I never commanded — nor did it enter my mind — that they should do such a detestable thing and so make Judah sin.

36"You are saying about this city, 'By the sword, famine and plague it will be given into the hands of the king of Babylon'; but this is what the LORD, the God of Israel, says: 37I will surely gather them from all the lands where I banish them in my furious anger and great wrath; I will bring them back to this place and let them live in safety. 38They will be my people, and I will be their God. 39I will give them singleness of heart and action, so that they will always fear me and that all will then go well for them and for their children after them. 40I will make an everlasting covenant with them: I will never stop doing good to them, and I will inspire them to fear me, so that they will never turn away from me. 41I will rejoice in doing them good and will assuredly plant them in this land with all my heart and soul.

42"This is what the LORD says: As I have brought all this great calamity on this people, so I will give them all the prosperity I have promised them. 43Once more fields will be bought in this land of which you say, 'It is a desolate waste, without people or animals, for it has been given into the hands of the Babylonians.' 44Fields will be bought for silver, and deeds will be signed, sealed and witnessed in the territory of Benjamin, in the villages around Jerusalem, in the towns of Judah and in the towns of the hill country, of the western foothills and of the Negev, because I will restore their fortunes,*a* declares the LORD."

Promise of Restoration

33 While Jeremiah was still confined in the courtyard of the guard, the word of the LORD

---

a 44 Or *will bring them back from captivity*

came to him a second time: [2]"This is what the LORD says, he who made the earth, the LORD who formed it and established it—the LORD is his name: [3]'Call to me and I will answer you and tell you great and unsearchable things you do not know.' [4]For this is what the LORD, the God of Israel, says about the houses in this city and the royal palaces of Judah that have been torn down to be used against the siege ramps and the sword [5]in the fight with the Babylonians[a]: 'They will be filled with the dead bodies of the people I will slay in my anger and wrath. I will hide my face from this city because of all its wickedness.

[6]"'Nevertheless, I will bring health and healing to it; I will heal my people and will let them enjoy abundant peace and security. [7]I will bring Judah and Israel back from captivity[b] and will rebuild them as they were before. [8]I will cleanse them from all the sin they have committed against me and will forgive all their sins of rebellion against me. [9]Then this city will bring me renown, joy, praise and honor before all nations on earth that hear of all the good things I do for it; and they will be in awe and will tremble at the abundant prosperity and peace I provide for it.'

[10]"This is what the LORD says: 'You say about this place, "It is a desolate waste, without people or animals." Yet in the towns of Judah and the streets of Jerusalem that are deserted, inhabited by neither people nor animals, there will be heard once more [11]the sounds of joy and gladness, the voices of bride and bridegroom, and the voices of those who bring thank offerings to the house of the LORD, saying,

"Give thanks to the LORD Almighty,
　for the LORD is good;
　his love endures forever."

For I will restore the fortunes of the land as they were before,' says the LORD.

[12]"This is what the LORD Almighty says: 'In this place, desolate and without people or animals—in all its towns there will again be pastures for shepherds to rest their flocks. [13]In the towns of the hill country, of the western foothills and of the Negev, in the territory of Benjamin, in the villages around Jerusalem and in the towns of Judah, flocks will again pass under the hand of the one who counts them,' says the LORD.

[14]"'The days are coming,' declares the LORD, 'when I will fulfill the good promise I made to the people of Israel and Judah.

[15]"'In those days and at that time
　I will make a righteous Branch
　　sprout from David's line;
　he will do what is just and right in
　　the land.
[16]In those days Judah will be saved
　and Jerusalem will live in safety.
This is the name by which it[c] will be
　　called:
　The LORD Our Righteous Savior.'

[17]For this is what the LORD says: 'David will never fail to have a man to sit on the throne of Israel, [18]nor will the Levitical priests ever fail to have a man to stand before me continually to offer burnt offerings, to burn grain offerings and to present sacrifices.'"

[19]The word of the LORD came to Jeremiah: [20]"This is what the LORD says: 'If you can break my covenant with the day and my covenant with the night, so that day and night no longer come at their appointed time, [21]then my covenant with David my servant—and my covenant with the Levites who are priests ministering before me—can be broken and David will no longer have a descendant to reign on his throne. [22]I will make the descendants of David my servant and the Levites who minister before me as countless as the stars in the sky and as measureless as the sand on the seashore.'"

[23]The word of the LORD came to Jeremiah: [24]"Have you not noticed that these

---

[a] 5 Or *Chaldeans*　　[b] 7 Or *will restore the fortunes of Judah and Israel*　　[c] 16 Or *he*

people are saying, 'The LORD has rejected the two kingdoms*a* he chose'? So they despise my people and no longer regard them as a nation. 25This is what the LORD says: 'If I have not made my covenant with day and night and established the laws of heaven and earth, 26then I will reject the descendants of Jacob and David my servant and will not choose one of his sons to rule over the descendants of Abraham, Isaac and Jacob. For I will restore their fortunes*b* and have compassion on them.'"

Warning to Zedekiah

34 While Nebuchadnezzar king of Babylon and all his army and all the kingdoms and peoples in the empire he ruled were fighting against Jerusalem and all its surrounding towns, this word came to Jeremiah from the LORD: 2"This is what the LORD, the God of Israel, says: Go to Zedekiah king of Judah and tell him, 'This is what the LORD says: I am about to give this city into the hands of the king of Babylon, and he will burn it down. 3You will not escape from his grasp but will surely be captured and given into his hands. You will see the king of Babylon with your own eyes, and he will speak with you face to face. And you will go to Babylon.

4"'Yet hear the LORD's promise to you, Zedekiah king of Judah. This is what the LORD says concerning you: You will not die by the sword; 5you will die peacefully. As people made a funeral fire in honor of your predecessors, the kings who ruled before you, so they will make a fire in your honor and lament, "Alas, master!" I myself make this promise, declares the LORD.'"

6Then Jeremiah the prophet told all this to Zedekiah king of Judah, in Jerusalem, 7while the army of the king of Babylon was fighting against Jerusalem and the other cities of Judah that were still holding out — Lachish and Azekah. These were the only fortified cities left in Judah.

Freedom for Slaves

8The word came to Jeremiah from the LORD after King Zedekiah had made a covenant with all the people in Jerusalem to proclaim freedom for the slaves. 9Everyone was to free their Hebrew slaves, both male and female; no one was to hold a fellow Hebrew in bondage. 10So all the officials and people who entered into this covenant agreed that they would free their male and female slaves and no longer hold them in bondage. They agreed, and set them free. 11But afterward they changed their minds and took back the slaves they had freed and enslaved them again.

12Then the word of the LORD came to Jeremiah: 13"This is what the LORD, the God of Israel, says: I made a covenant with your ancestors when I brought them out of Egypt, out of the land of slavery. I said, 14'Every seventh year each of you must free any fellow Hebrews who have sold themselves to you. After they have served you six years, you must let them go free.'*c* Your ancestors, however, did not listen to me or pay attention to me. 15Recently you repented and did what is right in my sight: Each of you proclaimed freedom to your own people. You even made a covenant before me in the house that bears my Name. 16But now you have turned around and profaned my name; each of you has taken back the male and female slaves you had set free to go where they wished. You have forced them to become your slaves again.

17"Therefore this is what the LORD says: You have not obeyed me; you have not proclaimed freedom to your own people. So I now proclaim 'freedom' for you, declares the LORD — 'freedom' to fall by the sword, plague and famine. I will make you abhorrent to all the kingdoms of the earth. 18Those who have violated my covenant and have not fulfilled the terms of the covenant they made before me, I will treat like the calf they cut in two and then walked between its pieces. 19The leaders of Ju-

---

a 24 Or *families*   *b* 26 Or *will bring them back from captivity*   *c* 14 Deut. 15:12

dah and Jerusalem, the court officials, the priests and all the people of the land who walked between the pieces of the calf, 20I will deliver into the hands of their enemies who want to kill them. Their dead bodies will become food for the birds and the wild animals.

21"I will deliver Zedekiah king of Judah and his officials into the hands of their enemies who want to kill them, to the army of the king of Babylon, which has withdrawn from you. 22I am going to give the order, declares the LORD, and I will bring them back to this city. They will fight against it, take it and burn it down. And I will lay waste the towns of Judah so no one can live there."

The Rekabites

35 This is the word that came to Jeremiah from the LORD during the reign of Jehoiakim son of Josiah king of Judah: 2"Go to the Rekabite family and invite them to come to one of the side rooms of the house of the LORD and give them wine to drink."

3So I went to get Jaazaniah son of Jeremiah, the son of Habazziniah, and his brothers and all his sons — the whole family of the Rekabites. 4I brought them into the house of the LORD, into the room of the sons of Hanan son of Igdaliah the man of God. It was next to the room of the officials, which was over that of Maaseiah son of Shallum the doorkeeper. 5Then I set bowls full of wine and some cups before the Rekabites and said to them, "Drink some wine."

6But they replied, "We do not drink wine, because our forefather Jehonadab*a* son of Rekab gave us this command: 'Neither you nor your descendants must ever drink wine. 7Also you must never build houses, sow seed or plant vineyards; you must never have any of these things, but must always live in tents. Then you will live a long time in the land where you are

nomads.' 8We have obeyed everything our forefather Jehonadab son of Rekab commanded us. Neither we nor our wives nor our sons and daughters have ever drunk wine 9or built houses to live in or had vineyards, fields or crops. 10We have lived in tents and have fully obeyed everything our forefather Jehonadab commanded us. 11But when Nebuchadnezzar king of Babylon invaded this land, we said, 'Come, we must go to Jerusalem to escape the Babylonian*b* and Aramean armies.' So we have remained in Jerusalem."

12Then the word of the LORD came to Jeremiah, saying: 13"This is what the LORD Almighty, the God of Israel, says: Go and tell the people of Judah and those living in Jerusalem, 'Will you not learn a lesson and obey my words?' declares the LORD. 14'Jehonadab son of Rekab ordered his descendants not to drink wine and this command has been kept. To this day they do not drink wine, because they obey their forefather's command. But I have spoken to you again and again, yet you have not obeyed me. 15Again and again I sent all my servants the prophets to you. They said, "Each of you must turn from your wicked ways and reform your actions; do not follow other gods to serve them. Then you will live in the land I have given to you and your ancestors." But you have not paid attention or listened to me. 16The descendants of Jehonadab son of Rekab have carried out the command their forefather gave them, but these people have not obeyed me.'

17"Therefore this is what the LORD God Almighty, the God of Israel, says: 'Listen! I am going to bring on Judah and on everyone living in Jerusalem every disaster I pronounced against them. I spoke to them, but they did not listen; I called to them, but they did not answer.'"

18Then Jeremiah said to the family of the Rekabites, "This is what the LORD Almighty, the God of Israel, says: 'You have obeyed the command of your forefather

---

a 6 Hebrew *Jonadab*, a variant of *Jehonadab*; here and often in this chapter   *b 11* Or *Chaldean*

Jehonadab and have followed all his instructions and have done everything he ordered.' ¹⁹Therefore this is what the LORD Almighty, the God of Israel, says: 'Jehonadab son of Rekab will never fail to have a descendant to serve me.'"

Jehoiakim Burns Jeremiah's Scroll

36 In the fourth year of Jehoiakim son of Josiah king of Judah, this word came to Jeremiah from the LORD: ²"Take a scroll and write on it all the words I have spoken to you concerning Israel, Judah and all the other nations from the time I began speaking to you in the reign of Josiah till now. ³Perhaps when the people of Judah hear about every disaster I plan to inflict on them, they will each turn from their wicked ways; then I will forgive their wickedness and their sin."

⁴So Jeremiah called Baruch son of Neriah, and while Jeremiah dictated all the words the LORD had spoken to him, Baruch wrote them on the scroll. ⁵Then Jeremiah told Baruch, "I am restricted; I am not allowed to go to the LORD's temple. ⁶So you go to the house of the LORD on a day of fasting and read to the people from the scroll the words of the LORD that you wrote as I dictated. Read them to all the people of Judah who come in from their towns. ⁷Perhaps they will bring their petition before the LORD and will each turn from their wicked ways, for the anger and wrath pronounced against this people by the LORD are great."

⁸Baruch son of Neriah did everything Jeremiah the prophet told him to do; at the LORD's temple he read the words of the LORD from the scroll. ⁹In the ninth month of the fifth year of Jehoiakim son of Josiah king of Judah, a time of fasting before the LORD was proclaimed for all the people in Jerusalem and those who had come from the towns of Judah. ¹⁰From the room of Gemariah son of Shaphan the secretary, which was in the upper courtyard at the entrance of the New Gate of the temple, Baruch read to all the people at the LORD's temple the words of Jeremiah from the scroll.

¹¹When Micaiah son of Gemariah, the son of Shaphan, heard all the words of the LORD from the scroll, ¹²he went down to the secretary's room in the royal palace, where all the officials were sitting: Elishama the secretary, Delaiah son of Shemaiah, Elnathan son of Akbor, Gemariah son of Shaphan, Zedekiah son of Hananiah, and all the other officials. ¹³After Micaiah told them everything he had heard Baruch read to the people from the scroll, ¹⁴all the officials sent Jehudi son of Nethaniah, the son of Shelemiah, the son of Cushi, to say to Baruch, "Bring the scroll from which you have read to the people and come." So Baruch son of Neriah went to them with the scroll in his hand. ¹⁵They said to him, "Sit down, please, and read it to us."

So Baruch read it to them. ¹⁶When they heard all these words, they looked at each other in fear and said to Baruch, "We must report all these words to the king." ¹⁷Then they asked Baruch, "Tell us, how did you come to write all this? Did Jeremiah dictate it?"

¹⁸"Yes," Baruch replied, "he dictated all these words to me, and I wrote them in ink on the scroll."

¹⁹Then the officials said to Baruch, "You and Jeremiah, go and hide. Don't let anyone know where you are."

²⁰After they put the scroll in the room of Elishama the secretary, they went to the king in the courtyard and reported everything to him. ²¹The king sent Jehudi to get the scroll, and Jehudi brought it from the room of Elishama the secretary and read it to the king and all the officials standing beside him. ²²It was the ninth month and the king was sitting in the winter apartment, with a fire burning in the firepot in front of him. ²³Whenever Jehudi had read three or four columns of the scroll, the king cut them off with a scribe's knife and threw them into the firepot, until the entire scroll was burned in the fire. ²⁴The king and all his attendants who heard all these words

showed no fear, nor did they tear their clothes. ²⁵Even though Elnathan, Delaiah and Gemariah urged the king not to burn the scroll, he would not listen to them. ²⁶Instead, the king commanded Jerahmeel, a son of the king, Seraiah son of Azriel and Shelemiah son of Abdeel to arrest Baruch the scribe and Jeremiah the prophet. But the Lord had hidden them.

²⁷After the king burned the scroll containing the words that Baruch had written at Jeremiah's dictation, the word of the Lord came to Jeremiah: ²⁸"Take another scroll and write on it all the words that were on the first scroll, which Jehoiakim king of Judah burned up. ²⁹Also tell Jehoiakim king of Judah, 'This is what the Lord says: You burned that scroll and said, "Why did you write on it that the king of Babylon would certainly come and destroy this land and wipe from it both man and beast?" ³⁰Therefore this is what the Lord says about Jehoiakim king of Judah: He will have no one to sit on the throne of David; his body will be thrown out and exposed to the heat by day and the frost by night. ³¹I will punish him and his children and his attendants for their wickedness; I will bring on them and those living in Jerusalem and the people of Judah every disaster I pronounced against them, because they have not listened.'"

³²So Jeremiah took another scroll and gave it to the scribe Baruch son of Neriah, and as Jeremiah dictated, Baruch wrote on it all the words of the scroll that Jehoiakim king of Judah had burned in the fire. And many similar words were added to them.

Jeremiah in Prison

37 Zedekiah son of Josiah was made king of Judah by Nebuchadnezzar king of Babylon; he reigned in place of Jehoiachin*ᵃ* son of Jehoiakim. ²Neither he nor his attendants nor the people of the land paid any atten-

tion to the words the Lord had spoken through Jeremiah the prophet.

³King Zedekiah, however, sent Jehukal son of Shelemiah with the priest Zephaniah son of Maaseiah to Jeremiah the prophet with this message: "Please pray to the Lord our God for us."

⁴Now Jeremiah was free to come and go among the people, for he had not yet been put in prison. ⁵Pharaoh's army had marched out of Egypt, and when the Babylonians*ᵇ* who were besieging Jerusalem heard the report about them, they withdrew from Jerusalem.

⁶Then the word of the Lord came to Jeremiah the prophet: ⁷"This is what the Lord, the God of Israel, says: Tell the king of Judah, who sent you to inquire of me, 'Pharaoh's army, which has marched out to support you, will go back to its own land, to Egypt. ⁸Then the Babylonians will return and attack this city; they will capture it and burn it down.'

⁹"This is what the Lord says: Do not deceive yourselves, thinking, 'The Babylonians will surely leave us.' They will not! ¹⁰Even if you were to defeat the entire Babylonian*ᶜ* army that is attacking you and only wounded men were left in their tents, they would come out and burn this city down."

¹¹After the Babylonian army had withdrawn from Jerusalem because of Pharaoh's army, ¹²Jeremiah started to leave the city to go to the territory of Benjamin to get his share of the property among the people there. ¹³But when he reached the Benjamin Gate, the captain of the guard, whose name was Irijah son of Shelemiah, the son of Hananiah, arrested him and said, "You are deserting to the Babylonians!"

¹⁴"That's not true!" Jeremiah said. "I am not deserting to the Babylonians." But Irijah would not listen to him; instead, he arrested Jeremiah and brought him to the officials. ¹⁵They were angry with Jeremiah

---

ᵃ 1 Hebrew *Koniah*, a variant of *Jehoiachin*   *ᵇ 5* Or *Chaldeans*; also in verses 8, 9, 13 and 14   *ᶜ 10* Or *Chaldean*; also in verse 11 and had him beaten and imprisoned in the house of Jonathan the secretary, which they had made into a prison.

¹⁶Jeremiah was put into a vaulted cell in a dungeon, where he remained a long time. ¹⁷Then King Zedekiah sent for him and had him brought to the palace, where he asked him privately, "Is there any word from the LORD?"

"Yes," Jeremiah replied, "you will be delivered into the hands of the king of Babylon."

¹⁸Then Jeremiah said to King Zedekiah, "What crime have I committed against you or your attendants or this people, that you have put me in prison? ¹⁹Where are your prophets who prophesied to you, 'The king of Babylon will not attack you or this land'? ²⁰But now, my lord the king, please listen. Let me bring my petition before you: Do not send me back to the house of Jonathan the secretary, or I will die there."

²¹King Zedekiah then gave orders for Jeremiah to be placed in the courtyard of the guard and given a loaf of bread from the street of the bakers each day until all the bread in the city was gone. So Jeremiah remained in the courtyard of the guard.

Jeremiah Thrown Into a Cistern

38 Shephatiah son of Mattan, Gedaliah son of Pashhur, Jehukal[a] son of Shelemiah, and Pashhur son of Malkijah heard what Jeremiah was telling all the people when he said, ²"This is what the LORD says: 'Whoever stays in this city will die by the sword, famine or plague, but whoever goes over to the Babylonians[b] will live. They will escape with their lives; they will live.' ³And this is what the LORD says: 'This city will certainly be given into the hands of the army of the king of Babylon, who will capture it.'"

⁴Then the officials said to the king, "This man should be put to death. He is discouraging the soldiers who are left in this city,

as well as all the people, by the things he is saying to them. This man is not seeking the good of these people but their ruin."

⁵"He is in your hands," King Zedekiah answered. "The king can do nothing to oppose you."

⁶So they took Jeremiah and put him into the cistern of Malkijah, the king's son, which was in the courtyard of the guard. They lowered Jeremiah by ropes into the cistern; it had no water in it, only mud, and Jeremiah sank down into the mud.

⁷But Ebed-Melek, a Cushite,[c] an official[d] in the royal palace, heard that they had put Jeremiah into the cistern. While the king was sitting in the Benjamin Gate, ⁸Ebed-Melek went out of the palace and said to him, ⁹"My lord the king, these men have acted wickedly in all they have done to Jeremiah the prophet. They have thrown him into a cistern, where he will starve to death when there is no longer any bread in the city."

¹⁰Then the king commanded Ebed-Melek the Cushite, "Take thirty men from here with you and lift Jeremiah the prophet out of the cistern before he dies."

¹¹So Ebed-Melek took the men with him and went to a room under the treasury in the palace. He took some old rags and worn-out clothes from there and let them down with ropes to Jeremiah in the cistern. ¹²Ebed-Melek the Cushite said to Jeremiah, "Put these old rags and worn-out clothes under your arms to pad the ropes." Jeremiah did so, ¹³and they pulled him up with the ropes and lifted him out of the cistern. And Jeremiah remained in the courtyard of the guard.

Zedekiah Questions Jeremiah Again

¹⁴Then King Zedekiah sent for Jeremiah the prophet and had him brought to the third entrance to the temple of the LORD. "I am going to ask you something," the king said to Jeremiah. "Do not hide anything from me."

---

a 1 Hebrew *Jukal,* a variant of *Jehukal*   *b 2* Or *Chaldeans*; also in verses 18, 19 and 23   *c 7* Probably from the upper Nile region   *d 7* Or *a eunuch*

¹⁵Jeremiah said to Zedekiah, "If I give you an answer, will you not kill me? Even if I did give you counsel, you would not listen to me."

¹⁶But King Zedekiah swore this oath secretly to Jeremiah: "As surely as the LORD lives, who has given us breath, I will neither kill you nor hand you over to those who want to kill you."

¹⁷Then Jeremiah said to Zedekiah, "This is what the LORD God Almighty, the God of Israel, says: 'If you surrender to the officers of the king of Babylon, your life will be spared and this city will not be burned down; you and your family will live. ¹⁸But if you will not surrender to the officers of the king of Babylon, this city will be given into the hands of the Babylonians and they will burn it down; you yourself will not escape from them.'"

¹⁹King Zedekiah said to Jeremiah, "I am afraid of the Jews who have gone over to the Babylonians, for the Babylonians may hand me over to them and they will mistreat me."

²⁰"They will not hand you over," Jeremiah replied. "Obey the LORD by doing what I tell you. Then it will go well with you, and your life will be spared. ²¹But if you refuse to surrender, this is what the LORD has revealed to me: ²²All the women left in the palace of the king of Judah will be brought out to the officials of the king of Babylon. Those women will say to you:

"'They misled you and overcame you—
    those trusted friends of yours.
Your feet are sunk in the mud;
    your friends have deserted you.'

²³"All your wives and children will be brought out to the Babylonians. You yourself will not escape from their hands but will be captured by the king of Babylon; and this city willᵃ be burned down."

²⁴Then Zedekiah said to Jeremiah, "Do not let anyone know about this conversation, or you may die. ²⁵If the officials hear that I talked with you, and they come to you and say, 'Tell us what you said to the king and what the king said to you; do not hide it from us or we will kill you,' ²⁶then tell them, 'I was pleading with the king not to send me back to Jonathan's house to die there.'"

²⁷All the officials did come to Jeremiah and question him, and he told them everything the king had ordered him to say. So they said no more to him, for no one had heard his conversation with the king.

²⁸And Jeremiah remained in the courtyard of the guard until the day Jerusalem was captured.

The Fall of Jerusalem

39 This is how Jerusalem was taken: ¹In the ninth year of Zedekiah king of Judah, in the tenth month, Nebuchadnezzar king of Babylon marched against Jerusalem with his whole army and laid siege to it. ²And on the ninth day of the fourth month of Zedekiah's eleventh year, the city wall was broken through. ³Then all the officials of the king of Babylon came and took seats in the Middle Gate: Nergal-Sharezer of Samgar, Nebo-Sarsekim a chief officer, Nergal-Sharezer a high official and all the other officials of the king of Babylon. ⁴When Zedekiah king of Judah and all the soldiers saw them, they fled; they left the city at night by way of the king's garden, through the gate between the two walls, and headed toward the Arabah.ᵇ

⁵But the Babylonianᶜ army pursued them and overtook Zedekiah in the plains of Jericho. They captured him and took him to Nebuchadnezzar king of Babylon at Riblah in the land of Hamath, where he pronounced sentence on him. ⁶There at Riblah the king of Babylon slaughtered the sons of Zedekiah before his eyes and also killed all the nobles of Judah. ⁷Then he put out Zedekiah's eyes and bound him with bronze shackles to take him to Babylon.

⁸The Babylonians*a* set fire to the royal palace and the houses of the people and broke down the walls of Jerusalem. ⁹Nebuzaradan commander of the imperial guard carried into exile to Babylon the people who remained in the city, along with those who had gone over to him, and the rest of the people. ¹⁰But Nebuzaradan the commander of the guard left behind in the land of Judah some of the poor people, who owned nothing; and at that time he gave them vineyards and fields.

¹¹Now Nebuchadnezzar king of Babylon had given these orders about Jeremiah through Nebuzaradan commander of the imperial guard: ¹²"Take him and look after him; don't harm him but do for him whatever he asks." ¹³So Nebuzaradan the commander of the guard, Nebushazban a chief officer, Nergal-Sharezer a high official and all the other officers of the king of Babylon ¹⁴sent and had Jeremiah taken out of the courtyard of the guard. They turned him over to Gedaliah son of Ahikam, the son of Shaphan, to take him back to his home. So he remained among his own people.

¹⁵While Jeremiah had been confined in the courtyard of the guard, the word of the LORD came to him: ¹⁶"Go and tell Ebed-Melek the Cushite, 'This is what the LORD Almighty, the God of Israel, says: I am about to fulfill my words against this city — words concerning disaster, not prosperity. At that time they will be fulfilled before your eyes. ¹⁷But I will rescue you on that day, declares the LORD; you will not be given into the hands of those you fear. ¹⁸I will save you; you will not fall by the sword but will escape with your life, because you trust in me, declares the LORD.'"

Jeremiah Freed

40 The word came to Jeremiah from the LORD after Nebuzaradan commander of the imperial guard had released him at Ra-

mah. He had found Jeremiah bound in chains among all the captives from Jerusalem and Judah who were being carried into exile to Babylon. ²When the commander of the guard found Jeremiah, he said to him, "The LORD your God decreed this disaster for this place. ³And now the LORD has brought it about; he has done just as he said he would. All this happened because you people sinned against the LORD and did not obey him. ⁴But today I am freeing you from the chains on your wrists. Come with me to Babylon, if you like, and I will look after you; but if you do not want to, then don't come. Look, the whole country lies before you; go wherever you please." ⁵However, before Jeremiah turned to go,*b* Nebuzaradan added, "Go back to Gedaliah son of Ahikam, the son of Shaphan, whom the king of Babylon has appointed over the towns of Judah, and live with him among the people, or go anywhere else you please."

Then the commander gave him provisions and a present and let him go. ⁶So Jeremiah went to Gedaliah son of Ahikam at Mizpah and stayed with him among the people who were left behind in the land.

Gedaliah Assassinated

⁷When all the army officers and their men who were still in the open country heard that the king of Babylon had appointed Gedaliah son of Ahikam as governor over the land and had put him in charge of the men, women and children who were the poorest in the land and who had not been carried into exile to Babylon, ⁸they came to Gedaliah at Mizpah — Ishmael son of Nethaniah, Johanan and Jonathan the sons of Kareah, Seraiah son of Tanhumeth, the sons of Ephai the Netophathite, and Jaazaniah*c* the son of the Maakathite, and their men. ⁹Gedaliah son of Ahikam, the son of Shaphan, took an oath to reassure them and their men. "Do not be afraid to serve the Babylonians,*d*" he said.

---

a 8 Or *Chaldeans*   *b* 5 Or *Jeremiah answered*   *c* 8 Hebrew *Jezaniah*, a variant of *Jaazaniah*   *d* 9 Or *Chaldeans*; also in verse 10

"Settle down in the land and serve the king of Babylon, and it will go well with you. ¹⁰I myself will stay at Mizpah to represent you before the Babylonians who come to us, but you are to harvest the wine, summer fruit and olive oil, and put them in your storage jars, and live in the towns you have taken over."

¹¹When all the Jews in Moab, Ammon, Edom and all the other countries heard that the king of Babylon had left a remnant in Judah and had appointed Gedaliah son of Ahikam, the son of Shaphan, as governor over them, ¹²they all came back to the land of Judah, to Gedaliah at Mizpah, from all the countries where they had been scattered. And they harvested an abundance of wine and summer fruit.

¹³Johanan son of Kareah and all the army officers still in the open country came to Gedaliah at Mizpah ¹⁴and said to him, "Don't you know that Baalis king of the Ammonites has sent Ishmael son of Nethaniah to take your life?" But Gedaliah son of Ahikam did not believe them.

¹⁵Then Johanan son of Kareah said privately to Gedaliah in Mizpah, "Let me go and kill Ishmael son of Nethaniah, and no one will know it. Why should he take your life and cause all the Jews who are gathered around you to be scattered and the remnant of Judah to perish?"

¹⁶But Gedaliah son of Ahikam said to Johanan son of Kareah, "Don't do such a thing! What you are saying about Ishmael is not true."

41

In the seventh month Ishmael son of Nethaniah, the son of Elishama, who was of royal blood and had been one of the king's officers, came with ten men to Gedaliah son of Ahikam at Mizpah. While they were eating together there, ²Ishmael son of Nethaniah and the ten men who were with him got up and struck down Gedaliah son of Ahikam, the son of Shaphan, with the sword, killing the one whom the king of Babylon had appointed as governor over the land. ³Ishmael also killed all the men of Judah who were with Gedaliah at Mizpah, as well as the Babylonian^a soldiers who were there.

⁴The day after Gedaliah's assassination, before anyone knew about it, ⁵eighty men who had shaved off their beards, torn their clothes and cut themselves came from Shechem, Shiloh and Samaria, bringing grain offerings and incense with them to the house of the LORD. ⁶Ishmael son of Nethaniah went out from Mizpah to meet them, weeping as he went. When he met them, he said, "Come to Gedaliah son of Ahikam." ⁷When they went into the city, Ishmael son of Nethaniah and the men who were with him slaughtered them and threw them into a cistern. ⁸But ten of them said to Ishmael, "Don't kill us! We have wheat and barley, olive oil and honey, hidden in a field." So he let them alone and did not kill them with the others. ⁹Now the cistern where he threw all the bodies of the men he had killed along with Gedaliah was the one King Asa had made as part of his defense against Baasha king of Israel. Ishmael son of Nethaniah filled it with the dead.

¹⁰Ishmael made captives of all the rest of the people who were in Mizpah — the king's daughters along with all the others who were left there, over whom Nebuzaradan commander of the imperial guard had appointed Gedaliah son of Ahikam. Ishmael son of Nethaniah took them captive and set out to cross over to the Ammonites.

¹¹When Johanan son of Kareah and all the army officers who were with him heard about all the crimes Ishmael son of Nethaniah had committed, ¹²they took all their men and went to fight Ishmael son of Nethaniah. They caught up with him near the great pool in Gibeon. ¹³When all the people Ishmael had with him saw Johanan son of Kareah and the army officers who were with him, they were glad. ¹⁴All the people Ishmael had taken captive at Mizpah turned and went over to Johanan son

---

^a 3 Or *Chaldean*

of Kareah. ¹⁵But Ishmael son of Nethaniah and eight of his men escaped from Johanan and fled to the Ammonites.

Flight to Egypt

¹⁶Then Johanan son of Kareah and all the army officers who were with him led away all the people of Mizpah who had survived, whom Johanan had recovered from Ishmael son of Nethaniah after Ishmael had assassinated Gedaliah son of Ahikam — the soldiers, women, children and court officials he had recovered from Gibeon. ¹⁷And they went on, stopping at Geruth Kimham near Bethlehem on their way to Egypt ¹⁸to escape the Babylonians.ᵃ They were afraid of them because Ishmael son of Nethaniah had killed Gedaliah son of Ahikam, whom the king of Babylon had appointed as governor over the land.

42

Then all the army officers, including Johanan son of Kareah and Jezaniahᵇ son of Hoshaiah, and all the people from the least to the greatest approached ²Jeremiah the prophet and said to him, "Please hear our petition and pray to the LORD your God for this entire remnant. For as you now see, though we were once many, now only a few are left. ³Pray that the LORD your God will tell us where we should go and what we should do."

⁴"I have heard you," replied Jeremiah the prophet. "I will certainly pray to the LORD your God as you have requested; I will tell you everything the LORD says and will keep nothing back from you."

⁵Then they said to Jeremiah, "May the LORD be a true and faithful witness against us if we do not act in accordance with everything the LORD your God sends you to tell us. ⁶Whether it is favorable or unfavorable, we will obey the LORD our God, to whom we are sending you, so that it will go well with us, for we will obey the LORD our God."

⁷Ten days later the word of the LORD came to Jeremiah. ⁸So he called together Johanan son of Kareah and all the army officers who were with him and all the people from the least to the greatest. ⁹He said to them, "This is what the LORD, the God of Israel, to whom you sent me to present your petition, says: ¹⁰'If you stay in this land, I will build you up and not tear you down; I will plant you and not uproot you, for I have relented concerning the disaster I have inflicted on you. ¹¹Do not be afraid of the king of Babylon, whom you now fear. Do not be afraid of him, declares the LORD, for I am with you and will save you and deliver you from his hands. ¹²I will show you compassion so that he will have compassion on you and restore you to your land.'

¹³"However, if you say, 'We will not stay in this land,' and so disobey the LORD your God, ¹⁴and if you say, 'No, we will go and live in Egypt, where we will not see war or hear the trumpet or be hungry for bread,' ¹⁵then hear the word of the LORD, you remnant of Judah. This is what the LORD Almighty, the God of Israel, says: 'If you are determined to go to Egypt and you do go to settle there, ¹⁶then the sword you fear will overtake you there, and the famine you dread will follow you into Egypt, and there you will die. ¹⁷Indeed, all who are determined to go to Egypt to settle there will die by the sword, famine and plague; not one of them will survive or escape the disaster I will bring on them.' ¹⁸This is what the LORD Almighty, the God of Israel, says: 'As my anger and wrath have been poured out on those who lived in Jerusalem, so will my wrath be poured out on you when you go to Egypt. You will be a curseᶜ and an object of horror, a curseᶜ and an object of reproach; you will never see this place again.'

¹⁹"Remnant of Judah, the LORD has told you, 'Do not go to Egypt.' Be sure of this: I warn you today ²⁰that you made a fatal mistake when you sent me to the LORD

ᵃ 18 Or *Chaldeans*   ᵇ 1 Hebrew; Septuagint (see also 43:2) *Azariah*   ᶜ 18 That is, your name will be used in cursing (see 29:22); or, others will see that you are cursed.

your God and said, 'Pray to the Lord our God for us; tell us everything he says and we will do it.' ²¹I have told you today, but you still have not obeyed the Lord your God in all he sent me to tell you. ²²So now, be sure of this: You will die by the sword, famine and plague in the place where you want to go to settle."

43 When Jeremiah had finished telling the people all the words of the Lord their God — everything the Lord had sent him to tell them — ²Azariah son of Hoshaiah and Johanan son of Kareah and all the arrogant men said to Jeremiah, "You are lying! The Lord our God has not sent you to say, 'You must not go to Egypt to settle there.' ³But Baruch son of Neriah is inciting you against us to hand us over to the Babylonians,ᵃ so they may kill us or carry us into exile to Babylon."

⁴So Johanan son of Kareah and all the army officers and all the people disobeyed the Lord's command to stay in the land of Judah. ⁵Instead, Johanan son of Kareah and all the army officers led away all the remnant of Judah who had come back to live in the land of Judah from all the nations where they had been scattered. ⁶They also led away all those whom Nebuzaradan commander of the imperial guard had left with Gedaliah son of Ahikam, the son of Shaphan — the men, the women, the children and the king's daughters. And they took Jeremiah the prophet and Baruch son of Neriah along with them. ⁷So they entered Egypt in disobedience to the Lord and went as far as Tahpanhes.

⁸In Tahpanhes the word of the Lord came to Jeremiah: ⁹"While the Jews are watching, take some large stones with you and bury them in clay in the brick pavement at the entrance to Pharaoh's palace in Tahpanhes. ¹⁰Then say to them, 'This is what the Lord Almighty, the God of Israel, says: I will send for my servant Nebuchadnezzar king of Babylon, and I will set his

throne over these stones I have buried here; he will spread his royal canopy above them. ¹¹He will come and attack Egypt, bringing death to those destined for death, captivity to those destined for captivity, and the sword to those destined for the sword. ¹²He will set fire to the temples of the gods of Egypt; he will burn their temples and take their gods captive. As a shepherd picks his garment clean of lice, so he will pick Egypt clean and depart. ¹³There in the temple of the sunᵇ in Egypt he will demolish the sacred pillars and will burn down the temples of the gods of Egypt.'"

Disaster Because of Idolatry

44 This word came to Jeremiah concerning all the Jews living in Lower Egypt — in Migdol, Tahpanhes and Memphis — and in Upper Egypt: ²"This is what the Lord Almighty, the God of Israel, says: You saw the great disaster I brought on Jerusalem and on all the towns of Judah. Today they lie deserted and in ruins ³because of the evil they have done. They aroused my anger by burning incense to and worshiping other gods that neither they nor you nor your ancestors ever knew. ⁴Again and again I sent my servants the prophets, who said, 'Do not do this detestable thing that I hate!' ⁵But they did not listen or pay attention; they did not turn from their wickedness or stop burning incense to other gods. ⁶Therefore, my fierce anger was poured out; it raged against the towns of Judah and the streets of Jerusalem and made them the desolate ruins they are today.

⁷"Now this is what the Lord God Almighty, the God of Israel, says: Why bring such great disaster on yourselves by cutting off from Judah the men and women, the children and infants, and so leave yourselves without a remnant? ⁸Why arouse my anger with what your hands have made, burning incense to other gods in Egypt, where you have come to live? You will

destroy yourselves and make yourselves a curse*a* and an object of reproach among all the nations on earth. 9Have you forgotten the wickedness committed by your ancestors and by the kings and queens of Judah and the wickedness committed by you and your wives in the land of Judah and the streets of Jerusalem? 10To this day they have not humbled themselves or shown reverence, nor have they followed my law and the decrees I set before you and your ancestors.

11"Therefore this is what the LORD Almighty, the God of Israel, says: I am determined to bring disaster on you and to destroy all Judah. 12I will take away the remnant of Judah who were determined to go to Egypt to settle there. They will all perish in Egypt; they will fall by the sword or die from famine. From the least to the greatest, they will die by sword or famine. They will become a curse and an object of horror, a curse and an object of reproach. 13I will punish those who live in Egypt with the sword, famine and plague, as I punished Jerusalem. 14None of the remnant of Judah who have gone to live in Egypt will escape or survive to return to the land of Judah, to which they long to return and live; none will return except a few fugitives."

15Then all the men who knew that their wives were burning incense to other gods, along with all the women who were present — a large assembly — and all the people living in Lower and Upper Egypt, said to Jeremiah, 16"We will not listen to the message you have spoken to us in the name of the LORD! 17We will certainly do everything we said we would: We will burn incense to the Queen of Heaven and will pour out drink offerings to her just as we and our ancestors, our kings and our officials did in the towns of Judah and in the streets of Jerusalem. At that time we had plenty of food and were well off and suffered no harm. 18But ever since we stopped burning incense to the Queen of Heaven and pouring out drink offerings to her, we have had nothing and have been perishing by sword and famine."

19The women added, "When we burned incense to the Queen of Heaven and poured out drink offerings to her, did not our husbands know that we were making cakes impressed with her image and pouring out drink offerings to her?"

20Then Jeremiah said to all the people, both men and women, who were answering him, 21"Did not the LORD remember and call to mind the incense burned in the towns of Judah and the streets of Jerusalem by you and your ancestors, your kings and your officials and the people of the land? 22When the LORD could no longer endure your wicked actions and the detestable things you did, your land became a curse and a desolate waste without inhabitants, as it is today. 23Because you have burned incense and have sinned against the LORD and have not obeyed him or followed his law or his decrees or his stipulations, this disaster has come upon you, as you now see."

24Then Jeremiah said to all the people, including the women, "Hear the word of the LORD, all you people of Judah in Egypt. 25This is what the LORD Almighty, the God of Israel, says: You and your wives have done what you said you would do when you promised, 'We will certainly carry out the vows we made to burn incense and pour out drink offerings to the Queen of Heaven.'

"Go ahead then, do what you promised! Keep your vows! 26But hear the word of the LORD, all you Jews living in Egypt: 'I swear by my great name,' says the LORD, 'that no one from Judah living anywhere in Egypt will ever again invoke my name or swear, "As surely as the Sovereign LORD lives." 27For I am watching over them for harm, not for good; the Jews in Egypt will perish

---

a 8 That is, your name will be used in cursing (see 29:22); or, others will see that you are cursed; also in verse 12; similarly in verse 22.

by sword and famine until they are all destroyed. ²⁸Those who escape the sword and return to the land of Judah from Egypt will be very few. Then the whole remnant of Judah who came to live in Egypt will know whose word will stand — mine or theirs.

²⁹"'This will be the sign to you that I will punish you in this place,' declares the LORD, 'so that you will know that my threats of harm against you will surely stand.' ³⁰This is what the LORD says: 'I am going to deliver Pharaoh Hophra king of Egypt into the hands of his enemies who want to kill him, just as I gave Zedekiah king of Judah into the hands of Nebuchadnezzar king of Babylon, the enemy who wanted to kill him.'"

A Message to Baruch

45 When Baruch son of Neriah wrote on a scroll the words Jeremiah the prophet dictated in the fourth year of Jehoiakim son of Josiah king of Judah, Jeremiah said this to Baruch: ²"This is what the LORD, the God of Israel, says to you, Baruch: ³You said, 'Woe to me! The LORD has added sorrow to my pain; I am worn out with groaning and find no rest.' ⁴But the LORD has told me to say to you, 'This is what the LORD says: I will overthrow what I have built and uproot what I have planted, throughout the earth. ⁵Should you then seek great things for yourself? Do not seek them. For I will bring disaster on all people, declares the LORD, but wherever you go I will let you escape with your life.'"

A Message About Egypt

46 This is the word of the LORD that came to Jeremiah the prophet concerning the nations:

²Concerning Egypt:

This is the message against the army of Pharaoh Necho king of Egypt, which was defeated at Carchemish on the Euphrates River by Nebuchadnezzar king of Babylon in the fourth year of Jehoiakim son of Josiah king of Judah:

³"Prepare your shields, both large and
  small,
  and march out for battle!
⁴Harness the horses,
  mount the steeds!
Take your positions
  with helmets on!
Polish your spears,
  put on your armor!
⁵What do I see?
  They are terrified,
they are retreating,
  their warriors are defeated.
They flee in haste
  without looking back,
  and there is terror on every side,"
          declares the LORD.
⁶"The swift cannot flee
  nor the strong escape.
In the north by the River Euphrates
  they stumble and fall.

⁷"Who is this that rises like the Nile,
  like rivers of surging waters?
⁸Egypt rises like the Nile,
  like rivers of surging waters.
She says, 'I will rise and cover the earth;
  I will destroy cities and their people.'
⁹Charge, you horses!
  Drive furiously, you charioteers!
March on, you warriors — men of Cush^a
  and Put who carry shields,
  men of Lydia who draw the bow.
¹⁰But that day belongs to the Lord, the
  LORD Almighty —
  a day of vengeance, for vengeance on
    his foes.
The sword will devour till it is satisfied,
  till it has quenched its thirst with
    blood.
For the Lord, the LORD Almighty, will
  offer sacrifice
  in the land of the north by the River
    Euphrates.

---

^a 9 That is, the upper Nile region

11 "Go up to Gilead and get balm,
       Virgin Daughter Egypt.
But you try many medicines in vain;
       there is no healing for you.
12 The nations will hear of your shame;
       your cries will fill the earth.
One warrior will stumble over another;
       both will fall down together."

13 This is the message the LORD spoke to Jeremiah the prophet about the coming of Nebuchadnezzar king of Babylon to attack Egypt:

14 "Announce this in Egypt, and proclaim
       it in Migdol;
      proclaim it also in Memphis and
       Tahpanhes:
'Take your positions and get ready,
       for the sword devours those around
       you.'
15 Why will your warriors be laid low?
       They cannot stand, for the LORD will
       push them down.
16 They will stumble repeatedly;
       they will fall over each other.
They will say, 'Get up, let us go back
       to our own people and our native
       lands,
      away from the sword of the
       oppressor.'
17 There they will exclaim,
       'Pharaoh king of Egypt is only a loud
       noise;
      he has missed his opportunity.'

18 "As surely as I live," declares the King,
       whose name is the LORD Almighty,
   "one will come who is like Tabor among
       the mountains,
      like Carmel by the sea.
19 Pack your belongings for exile,
       you who live in Egypt,
for Memphis will be laid waste
       and lie in ruins without inhabitant.

20 "Egypt is a beautiful heifer,
       but a gadfly is coming
       against her from the north.
21 The mercenaries in her ranks
       are like fattened calves.

They too will turn and flee together,
       they will not stand their ground,
for the day of disaster is coming upon
       them,
      the time for them to be punished.
22 Egypt will hiss like a fleeing serpent
       as the enemy advances in force;
they will come against her with axes,
       like men who cut down trees.
23 They will chop down her forest,"
                   declares the LORD,
      "dense though it be.
They are more numerous than locusts,
       they cannot be counted.
24 Daughter Egypt will be put to shame,
       given into the hands of the people of
       the north."

25 The LORD Almighty, the God of Israel, says: "I am about to bring punishment on Amon god of Thebes, on Pharaoh, on Egypt and her gods and her kings, and on those who rely on Pharaoh. 26 I will give them into the hands of those who want to kill them — Nebuchadnezzar king of Babylon and his officers. Later, however, Egypt will be inhabited as in times past," declares the LORD.

27 "Do not be afraid, Jacob my servant;
       do not be dismayed, Israel.
I will surely save you out of a distant
       place,
      your descendants from the land of
       their exile.
Jacob will again have peace and
       security,
      and no one will make him afraid.
28 Do not be afraid, Jacob my servant,
       for I am with you," declares the
       LORD.
"Though I completely destroy all the
       nations
      among which I scatter you,
I will not completely destroy you.
I will discipline you but only in due
       measure;
      I will not let you go entirely
       unpunished."

❶
❷
❸

A Message About the Philistines

47 This is the word of the LORD that came to Jeremiah the prophet concerning the Philistines before Pharaoh attacked Gaza:

² This is what the LORD says:

"See how the waters are rising in the
        north;
    they will become an overflowing
        torrent.
They will overflow the land and
        everything in it,
    the towns and those who live in
        them.
The people will cry out;
    all who dwell in the land will wail
³ at the sound of the hooves of galloping
        steeds,
    at the noise of enemy chariots
    and the rumble of their wheels.
Parents will not turn to help their
        children;
    their hands will hang limp.
⁴ For the day has come
    to destroy all the Philistines
and to remove all survivors
    who could help Tyre and Sidon.
The LORD is about to destroy the
        Philistines,
    the remnant from the coasts of
        Caphtor.ᵃ
⁵ Gaza will shave her head in
        mourning;
    Ashkelon will be silenced.
You remnant on the plain,
    how long will you cut yourselves?

⁶ "'Alas, sword of the LORD,
    how long till you rest?
Return to your sheath;
    cease and be still.'
⁷ But how can it rest
    when the LORD has commanded it,
when he has ordered it
    to attack Ashkelon and the coast?"

A Message About Moab

48 Concerning Moab:

This is what the LORD Almighty, the God of Israel, says:

"Woe to Nebo, for it will be ruined.
    Kiriathaim will be disgraced and
        captured;
    the strongholdᵇ will be disgraced and
        shattered.
² Moab will be praised no more;
    in Heshbonᶜ people will plot her
        downfall:
    'Come, let us put an end to that
        nation.'
You, the people of Madmen,ᵈ will also
        be silenced;
    the sword will pursue you.
³ Cries of anguish arise from Horonaim,
    cries of great havoc and destruction.
⁴ Moab will be broken;
    her little ones will cry out.ᵉ
⁵ They go up the hill to Luhith,
    weeping bitterly as they go;
on the road down to Horonaim
    anguished cries over the destruction
        are heard.
⁶ Flee! Run for your lives;
    become like a bushᶠ in the desert.
⁷ Since you trust in your deeds and
        riches,
    you too will be taken captive,
and Chemosh will go into exile,
    together with his priests and
        officials.
⁸ The destroyer will come against every
        town,
    and not a town will escape.
The valley will be ruined
    and the plateau destroyed,
    because the LORD has spoken.
⁹ Put salt on Moab,
    for she will be laid wasteᵍ;
her towns will become desolate,
    with no one to live in them.

ᵃ 4 That is, Crete   ᵇ 1 Or captured; / Misgab   ᶜ 2 The Hebrew for Heshbon sounds like the Hebrew for plot.
ᵈ 2 The name of the Moabite town Madmen sounds like the Hebrew for be silenced.   ᵉ 4 Hebrew; Septuagint
/ proclaim it to Zoar   ᶠ 6 Or like Aroer   ᵍ 9 Or Give wings to Moab, / for she will fly away

¹⁰ "A curse on anyone who is lax in doing
  the LORD's work!
A curse on anyone who keeps their
  sword from bloodshed!

¹¹ "Moab has been at rest from youth,
  like wine left on its dregs,
not poured from one jar to another —
  she has not gone into exile.
So she tastes as she did,
  and her aroma is unchanged.
¹² But days are coming,"
  declares the LORD,
"when I will send men who pour from
  pitchers,
and they will pour her out;
they will empty her pitchers
  and smash her jars.
¹³ Then Moab will be ashamed of Chemosh,
  as Israel was ashamed
  when they trusted in Bethel.

¹⁴ "How can you say, 'We are warriors,
  men valiant in battle'?
¹⁵ Moab will be destroyed and her towns
  invaded;
her finest young men will go down in
  the slaughter,"
  declares the King, whose name is the
  LORD Almighty.
¹⁶ "The fall of Moab is at hand;
  her calamity will come quickly.
¹⁷ Mourn for her, all who live around her,
  all who know her fame;
say, 'How broken is the mighty scepter,
  how broken the glorious staff!'

¹⁸ "Come down from your glory
  and sit on the parched ground,
  you inhabitants of Daughter Dibon,
for the one who destroys Moab
  will come up against you
  and ruin your fortified cities.
¹⁹ Stand by the road and watch,
  you who live in Aroer.
Ask the man fleeing and the woman
  escaping,
  ask them, 'What has happened?'

²⁰ Moab is disgraced, for she is shattered.
  Wail and cry out!
Announce by the Arnon
  that Moab is destroyed.
²¹ Judgment has come to the plateau —
  to Holon, Jahzah and Mephaath,
²²   to Dibon, Nebo and Beth
     Diblathaim,
²³   to Kiriathaim, Beth Gamul and Beth
     Meon,
²⁴   to Kerioth and Bozrah —
  to all the towns of Moab, far and
  near.
²⁵ Moab's horn*a* is cut off;
  her arm is broken,"
                    declares the LORD.

²⁶ "Make her drunk,
  for she has defied the LORD.
Let Moab wallow in her vomit;
  let her be an object of ridicule.
²⁷ Was not Israel the object of your
  ridicule?
Was she caught among thieves,
that you shake your head in scorn
  whenever you speak of her?
²⁸ Abandon your towns and dwell among
  the rocks,
  you who live in Moab.
Be like a dove that makes its nest
  at the mouth of a cave.

²⁹ "We have heard of Moab's pride —
  how great is her arrogance! —
of her insolence, her pride, her conceit
  and the haughtiness of her heart.
³⁰ I know her insolence but it is futile,"
                    declares the LORD,
  "and her boasts accomplish nothing.
³¹ Therefore I wail over Moab,
  for all Moab I cry out,
  I moan for the people of Kir
  Hareseth.
³² I weep for you, as Jazer weeps,
  you vines of Sibmah.
Your branches spread as far as the sea*b*;
  they reached as far as*c* Jazer.

---

a 25 *Horn* here symbolizes strength.   *b 32* Probably the Dead Sea   *c 32* Two Hebrew manuscripts and
Septuagint; most Hebrew manuscripts *as far as the Sea of*

The destroyer has fallen
  on your ripened fruit and grapes.
³³Joy and gladness are gone
  from the orchards and fields of Moab.
I have stopped the flow of wine from
    the presses;
  no one treads them with shouts of
    joy.
Although there are shouts,
  they are not shouts of joy.

³⁴"The sound of their cry rises
  from Heshbon to Elealeh and Jahaz,
from Zoar as far as Horonaim and
    Eglath Shelishiyah,
  for even the waters of Nimrim are
    dried up.
³⁵In Moab I will put an end
  to those who make offerings on the
    high places
  and burn incense to their gods,"
          declares the LORD.
³⁶"So my heart laments for Moab like the
    music of a pipe;
  it laments like a pipe for the people of
    Kir Hareseth.
  The wealth they acquired is gone.
³⁷Every head is shaved
  and every beard cut off;
every hand is slashed
  and every waist is covered with
    sackcloth.
³⁸On all the roofs in Moab
  and in the public squares
there is nothing but mourning,
  for I have broken Moab
  like a jar that no one wants,"
          declares the LORD.
³⁹"How shattered she is! How they wail!
  How Moab turns her back in shame!
Moab has become an object of ridicule,
  an object of horror to all those
    around her."

⁴⁰This is what the LORD says:

"Look! An eagle is swooping down,
  spreading its wings over Moab.

⁴¹Kerioth^a will be captured
  and the strongholds taken.
In that day the hearts of Moab's
    warriors
  will be like the heart of a woman in
    labor.
⁴²Moab will be destroyed as a nation
  because she defied the LORD.
⁴³Terror and pit and snare await you,
  you people of Moab,"
          declares the LORD.
⁴⁴"Whoever flees from the terror
  will fall into a pit,
whoever climbs out of the pit
  will be caught in a snare;
for I will bring on Moab
  the year of her punishment,"
          declares the LORD.

⁴⁵"In the shadow of Heshbon
  the fugitives stand helpless,
for a fire has gone out from Heshbon,
  a blaze from the midst of Sihon;
it burns the foreheads of Moab,
  the skulls of the noisy boasters.
⁴⁶Woe to you, Moab!
  The people of Chemosh are
    destroyed;
your sons are taken into exile
  and your daughters into captivity.

⁴⁷"Yet I will restore the fortunes of Moab
  in days to come,"
          declares the LORD.

Here ends the judgment on Moab.

A Message About Ammon

49

Concerning the Ammonites:

This is what the LORD says:

"Has Israel no sons?
  Has Israel no heir?
Why then has Molek^b taken possession
    of Gad?
  Why do his people live in its towns?
²But the days are coming,"
  declares the LORD,

---

^a 41 Or *The cities*   ^b 1 Or *their king*; also in verse 3

"when I will sound the battle cry
　　against Rabbah of the Ammonites;
it will become a mound of ruins,
　　and its surrounding villages will be
　　　　set on fire.
Then Israel will drive out
　　those who drove her out,"
　　　　　　　　says the LORD.
3 "Wail, Heshbon, for Ai is destroyed!
　　Cry out, you inhabitants of Rabbah!
Put on sackcloth and mourn;
　　rush here and there inside the walls,
for Molek will go into exile,
　　together with his priests and officials.
4 Why do you boast of your valleys,
　　boast of your valleys so fruitful?
Unfaithful Daughter Ammon,
　　you trust in your riches and say,
　　'Who will attack me?'
5 I will bring terror on you
　　from all those around you,"
　　　　　　　declares the Lord,
　　　　　　　the LORD Almighty.
"Every one of you will be driven away,
　　and no one will gather the fugitives.

6 "Yet afterward, I will restore the
　　fortunes of the Ammonites,"
　　　　　　　declares the LORD.

A Message About Edom

7 Concerning Edom:

This is what the LORD Almighty says:

"Is there no longer wisdom in Teman?
　　Has counsel perished from the
　　　　prudent?
　　Has their wisdom decayed?
8 Turn and flee, hide in deep caves,
　　you who live in Dedan,
for I will bring disaster on Esau
　　at the time when I punish him.
9 If grape pickers came to you,
　　would they not leave a few grapes?
If thieves came during the night,
　　would they not steal only as much as
　　　　they wanted?

10 But I will strip Esau bare;
　　I will uncover his hiding places,
　　so that he cannot conceal himself.
His armed men are destroyed,
　　also his allies and neighbors,
　　so there is no one to say,
11 'Leave your fatherless children; I will
　　　　keep them alive.
　　Your widows too can depend on me.' "

12 This is what the LORD says: "If those
who do not deserve to drink the cup must
drink it, why should you go unpunished?
You will not go unpunished, but must
drink it. 13 I swear by myself," declares the
LORD, "that Bozrah will become a ruin and
a curse,[a] an object of horror and reproach;
and all its towns will be in ruins forever."

14 I have heard a message from the LORD;
　　an envoy was sent to the nations to
　　　　say,
"Assemble yourselves to attack it!
　　Rise up for battle!"

15 "Now I will make you small among the
　　　　nations,
　　despised by mankind.
16 The terror you inspire
　　and the pride of your heart have
　　　　deceived you,
you who live in the clefts of the rocks,
　　who occupy the heights of the hill.
Though you build your nest as high as
　　　　the eagle's,
　　from there I will bring you down,"
　　　　　　　declares the LORD.
17 "Edom will become an object of
　　　　horror;
　　all who pass by will be appalled and
　　　　will scoff
　　because of all its wounds.
18 As Sodom and Gomorrah were
　　　　overthrown,
　　along with their neighboring towns,"
　　　　　　　　　　says the LORD,
"so no one will live there;
　　no people will dwell in it.

---

a 13 That is, its name will be used in cursing (see 29:22); or, others will see that it is cursed.

19 "Like a lion coming up from Jordan's
thickets
to a rich pastureland,
I will chase Edom from its land in an
instant.
Who is the chosen one I will appoint
for this?
Who is like me and who can challenge
me?
And what shepherd can stand against
me?"

20 Therefore, hear what the LORD has
planned against Edom,
what he has purposed against those
who live in Teman:
The young of the flock will be dragged
away;
their pasture will be appalled at their
fate.
21 At the sound of their fall the earth will
tremble;
their cry will resound to the Red
Sea.*a*
22 Look! An eagle will soar and swoop
down,
spreading its wings over Bozrah.
In that day the hearts of Edom's
warriors
will be like the heart of a woman in
labor.

A Message About Damascus

23 Concerning Damascus:

"Hamath and Arpad are dismayed,
for they have heard bad news.
They are disheartened,
troubled like*b* the restless sea.
24 Damascus has become feeble,
she has turned to flee
and panic has gripped her;
anguish and pain have seized her,
pain like that of a woman in
labor.
25 Why has the city of renown not been
abandoned,
the town in which I delight?

26 Surely, her young men will fall in the
streets;
all her soldiers will be silenced in
that day,"
declares the LORD Almighty.
27 "I will set fire to the walls of Damascus;
it will consume the fortresses of Ben-
Hadad."

A Message About Kedar and Hazor

28 Concerning Kedar and the kingdoms
of Hazor, which Nebuchadnezzar king of
Babylon attacked:

This is what the LORD says:

"Arise, and attack Kedar
and destroy the people of the East.
29 Their tents and their flocks will be
taken;
their shelters will be carried off
with all their goods and camels.
People will shout to them,
'Terror on every side!'

30 "Flee quickly away!
Stay in deep caves, you who live in
Hazor,"
declares the LORD.
"Nebuchadnezzar king of Babylon has
plotted against you;
he has devised a plan against you.

31 "Arise and attack a nation at ease,
which lives in confidence,"
declares the LORD,
"a nation that has neither gates nor
bars;
its people live far from danger.
32 Their camels will become plunder,
and their large herds will be spoils of
war.
I will scatter to the winds those who are
in distant places*c*
and will bring disaster on them from
every side,"
declares the LORD.
33 "Hazor will become a haunt of jackals,
a desolate place forever.

---

a 21 Or *the Sea of Reeds*   *b 23* Hebrew *on* or *by*   *c 32* Or *who clip the hair by their foreheads*

No one will live there;
> no people will dwell in it."

A Message About Elam

34This is the word of the Lord that came to Jeremiah the prophet concerning Elam, early in the reign of Zedekiah king of Judah:

35This is what the Lord Almighty says:

"See, I will break the bow of Elam,
> the mainstay of their might.
36I will bring against Elam the four winds
> from the four quarters of heaven;
I will scatter them to the four winds,
> and there will not be a nation
> where Elam's exiles do not go.
37I will shatter Elam before their foes,
> before those who want to kill them;
I will bring disaster on them,
> even my fierce anger,"
> > declares the Lord.
"I will pursue them with the sword
> until I have made an end of them.
38I will set my throne in Elam
> and destroy her king and officials,"
> > declares the Lord.

39"Yet I will restore the fortunes of Elam
> in days to come,"
> > declares the Lord.

A Message About Babylon

50
This is the word the Lord spoke through Jeremiah the prophet concerning Babylon and the land of the Babylonians*a*:

2"Announce and proclaim among the nations,
> lift up a banner and proclaim it;
> keep nothing back, but say,
'Babylon will be captured;
> Bel will be put to shame,
> Marduk filled with terror.
Her images will be put to shame
> and her idols filled with terror.'

3A nation from the north will attack her
> and lay waste her land.
No one will live in it;
> both people and animals will flee away.

4"In those days, at that time,"
> declares the Lord,
"the people of Israel and the people of Judah together
> will go in tears to seek the Lord their God.
5They will ask the way to Zion
> and turn their faces toward it.
They will come and bind themselves to the Lord
> in an everlasting covenant
> that will not be forgotten.

6"My people have been lost sheep;
> their shepherds have led them astray
> and caused them to roam on the mountains.
They wandered over mountain and hill
> and forgot their own resting place.
7Whoever found them devoured them;
> their enemies said, 'We are not guilty,
for they sinned against the Lord, their verdant pasture,
> the Lord, the hope of their ancestors.'

8"Flee out of Babylon;
> leave the land of the Babylonians,
> and be like the goats that lead the flock.
9For I will stir up and bring against Babylon
> an alliance of great nations from the land of the north.
They will take up their positions against her,
> and from the north she will be captured.
Their arrows will be like skilled warriors
> who do not return empty-handed.

---

a 1 Or *Chaldeans*; also in verses 8, 25, 35 and 45

¹⁰So Babylonia*ᵃ* will be plundered;
    all who plunder her will have their
        fill,"
                      declares the Lord.

¹¹"Because you rejoice and are glad,
    you who pillage my inheritance,
    because you frolic like a heifer
        threshing grain
    and neigh like stallions,
¹²your mother will be greatly ashamed;
    she who gave you birth will be
        disgraced.
    She will be the least of the nations —
    a wilderness, a dry land, a desert.
¹³Because of the Lord's anger she will not
        be inhabited
    but will be completely desolate.
    All who pass Babylon will be appalled;
    they will scoff because of all her
        wounds.

¹⁴"Take up your positions around
        Babylon,
    all you who draw the bow.
    Shoot at her! Spare no arrows,
    for she has sinned against the Lord.
¹⁵Shout against her on every side!
    She surrenders, her towers fall,
    her walls are torn down.
    Since this is the vengeance of the Lord,
    take vengeance on her;
    do to her as she has done to others.
¹⁶Cut off from Babylon the sower,
    and the reaper with his sickle at
        harvest.
    Because of the sword of the oppressor
    let everyone return to their own
        people,
    let everyone flee to their own land.

¹⁷"Israel is a scattered flock
    that lions have chased away.
    The first to devour them
    was the king of Assyria;
    the last to crush their bones
    was Nebuchadnezzar king of
        Babylon."

¹⁸Therefore this is what the Lord Almighty, the God of Israel, says:

    "I will punish the king of Babylon and
        his land
    as I punished the king of Assyria.
¹⁹But I will bring Israel back to their own
        pasture,
    and they will graze on Carmel and
        Bashan;
    their appetite will be satisfied
    on the hills of Ephraim and Gilead.
²⁰In those days, at that time,"
    declares the Lord,
    "search will be made for Israel's guilt,
    but there will be none,
    and for the sins of Judah,
    but none will be found,
    for I will forgive the remnant I spare.

²¹"Attack the land of Merathaim
    and those who live in Pekod.
    Pursue, kill and completely destroy*ᵇ*
        them,"
                    declares the Lord.
    "Do everything I have commanded
        you.
²²The noise of battle is in the land,
    the noise of great destruction!
²³How broken and shattered
    is the hammer of the whole earth!
    How desolate is Babylon
    among the nations!
²⁴I set a trap for you, Babylon,
    and you were caught before you
        knew it;
    you were found and captured
    because you opposed the Lord.
²⁵The Lord has opened his arsenal
    and brought out the weapons of his
        wrath,
    for the Sovereign Lord Almighty has
        work to do
    in the land of the Babylonians.
²⁶Come against her from afar.
    Break open her granaries;
    pile her up like heaps of grain.

ᵃ 10 Or *Chaldea*   *ᵇ 21* The Hebrew term refers to the irrevocable giving over of things or persons to the Lord, often by totally destroying them; also in verse 26.

Completely destroy her
and leave her no remnant.
27 Kill all her young bulls;
let them go down to the slaughter!
Woe to them! For their day has come,
the time for them to be punished.
28 Listen to the fugitives and refugees
from Babylon
declaring in Zion
how the LORD our God has taken
vengeance,
vengeance for his temple.

29 "Summon archers against Babylon,
all those who draw the bow.
Encamp all around her;
let no one escape.
Repay her for her deeds;
do to her as she has done.
For she has defied the LORD,
the Holy One of Israel.
30 Therefore, her young men will fall in
the streets;
all her soldiers will be silenced in
that day,"
declares the LORD.
31 "See, I am against you, you arrogant one,"
declares the Lord, the LORD
Almighty,
"for your day has come,
the time for you to be punished.
32 The arrogant one will stumble and fall
and no one will help her up;
I will kindle a fire in her towns
that will consume all who are around
her."

33 This is what the LORD Almighty says:

"The people of Israel are oppressed,
and the people of Judah as well.
All their captors hold them fast,
refusing to let them go.
34 Yet their Redeemer is strong;
the LORD Almighty is his name.
He will vigorously defend their cause
so that he may bring rest to their land,
but unrest to those who live in Babylon.

35 "A sword against the Babylonians!"
declares the LORD —
"against those who live in Babylon
and against her officials and wise
men!
36 A sword against her false prophets!
They will become fools.
A sword against her warriors!
They will be filled with terror.
37 A sword against her horses and
chariots
and all the foreigners in her ranks!
They will become weaklings.
A sword against her treasures!
They will be plundered.
38 A drought on*a* her waters!
They will dry up.
For it is a land of idols,
idols that will go mad with terror.

39 "So desert creatures and hyenas will
live there,
and there the owl will dwell.
It will never again be inhabited
or lived in from generation to
generation.
40 As I overthrew Sodom and Gomorrah
along with their neighboring towns,"
declares the LORD,
"so no one will live there;
no people will dwell in it.

41 "Look! An army is coming from the
north;
a great nation and many kings
are being stirred up from the ends of
the earth.
42 They are armed with bows and spears;
they are cruel and without mercy.
They sound like the roaring sea
as they ride on their horses;
they come like men in battle formation
to attack you, Daughter Babylon.
43 The king of Babylon has heard reports
about them,
and his hands hang limp.
Anguish has gripped him,
pain like that of a woman in labor.

a 38 Or *A sword against*

⁴⁴Like a lion coming up from Jordan's
thickets
to a rich pastureland,
I will chase Babylon from its land in an
instant.
Who is the chosen one I will appoint
for this?
Who is like me and who can challenge
me?
And what shepherd can stand against
me?"

⁴⁵Therefore, hear what the LORD has
planned against Babylon,
what he has purposed against the
land of the Babylonians:
The young of the flock will be dragged
away;
their pasture will be appalled at their
fate.
⁴⁶At the sound of Babylon's capture the
earth will tremble;
its cry will resound among the nations.

51

This is what the LORD says:

"See, I will stir up the spirit of
a destroyer
against Babylon and the people of
Leb Kamai.ᵃ
²I will send foreigners to Babylon
to winnow her and to devastate her
land;
they will oppose her on every side
in the day of her disaster.
³Let not the archer string his bow,
nor let him put on his armor.
Do not spare her young men;
completely destroyᵇ her army.
⁴They will fall down slain in Babylon,ᶜ
fatally wounded in her streets.
⁵For Israel and Judah have not been
forsaken
by their God, the LORD Almighty,
though their landᵈ is full of guilt
before the Holy One of Israel.

⁶"Flee from Babylon!
Run for your lives!
Do not be destroyed because of her
sins.
It is time for the LORD's vengeance;
he will repay her what she deserves.
⁷Babylon was a gold cup in the LORD's
hand;
she made the whole earth drunk.
The nations drank her wine;
therefore they have now gone mad.
⁸Babylon will suddenly fall and be
broken.
Wail over her!
Get balm for her pain;
perhaps she can be healed.

⁹"We would have healed Babylon,
but she cannot be healed;
let us leave her and each go to our own
land,
for her judgment reaches to the
skies,
it rises as high as the heavens.'

¹⁰"The LORD has vindicated us;
come, let us tell in Zion
what the LORD our God has done.'

¹¹"Sharpen the arrows,
take up the shields!
The LORD has stirred up the kings of
the Medes,
because his purpose is to destroy
Babylon.
The LORD will take vengeance,
vengeance for his temple.
¹²Lift up a banner against the walls of
Babylon!
Reinforce the guard,
station the watchmen,
prepare an ambush!
The LORD will carry out his purpose,
his decree against the people of
Babylon.
¹³You who live by many waters
and are rich in treasures,

ᵃ 1 Leb Kamai is a cryptogram for Chaldea, that is, Babylonia.   ᵇ 3 The Hebrew term refers to the irrevocable
giving over of things or persons to the LORD, often by totally destroying them.   ᶜ 4 Or Chaldea   ᵈ 5 Or
Almighty, / and the land of the Babylonians

your end has come,
 the time for you to be destroyed.
¹⁴The Lord Almighty has sworn by
 himself:
 I will surely fill you with troops, as
 with a swarm of locusts,
 and they will shout in triumph over
 you.

¹⁵"He made the earth by his power;
 he founded the world by his wisdom
 and stretched out the heavens by his
 understanding.
¹⁶When he thunders, the waters in the
 heavens roar;
 he makes clouds rise from the ends
 of the earth.
 He sends lightning with the rain
 and brings out the wind from his
 storehouses.

¹⁷"Everyone is senseless and without
 knowledge;
 every goldsmith is shamed by his
 idols.
 The images he makes are a fraud;
 they have no breath in them.
¹⁸They are worthless, the objects of
 mockery;
 when their judgment comes, they
 will perish.
¹⁹He who is the Portion of Jacob is not
 like these,
 for he is the Maker of all things,
 including the people of his
 inheritance —
 the Lord Almighty is his name.

²⁰"You are my war club,
 my weapon for battle —
 with you I shatter nations,
 with you I destroy kingdoms,
²¹with you I shatter horse and rider,
 with you I shatter chariot and driver,
²²with you I shatter man and woman,
 with you I shatter old man and youth,
 with you I shatter young man and
 young woman,

²³with you I shatter shepherd and flock,
 with you I shatter farmer and oxen,
 with you I shatter governors and
 officials.

²⁴"Before your eyes I will repay Babylon
and all who live in Babylonia*a* for all the
wrong they have done in Zion," declares
the Lord.

²⁵"I am against you, you destroying
 mountain,
 you who destroy the whole earth,"
 declares the Lord.
 "I will stretch out my hand against you,
 roll you off the cliffs,
 and make you a burned-out
 mountain.
²⁶No rock will be taken from you for a
 cornerstone,
 nor any stone for a foundation,
 for you will be desolate forever,"
 declares the Lord.

²⁷"Lift up a banner in the land!
 Blow the trumpet among the nations!
 Prepare the nations for battle against
 her;
 summon against her these kingdoms:
 Ararat, Minni and Ashkenaz.
 Appoint a commander against her;
 send up horses like a swarm of
 locusts.
²⁸Prepare the nations for battle against
 her —
 the kings of the Medes,
 their governors and all their officials,
 and all the countries they rule.
²⁹The land trembles and writhes,
 for the Lord's purposes against
 Babylon stand —
 to lay waste the land of Babylon
 so that no one will live there.
³⁰Babylon's warriors have stopped
 fighting;
 they remain in their strongholds.
 Their strength is exhausted;
 they have become weaklings.

---

a 24 Or *Chaldea*; also in verse 35

Her dwellings are set on fire;
the bars of her gates are broken.
³¹ One courier follows another
and messenger follows messenger
to announce to the king of Babylon
that his entire city is captured,
³² the river crossings seized,
the marshes set on fire,
and the soldiers terrified."

³³ This is what the LORD Almighty, the God of Israel, says:

"Daughter Babylon is like a threshing
floor
at the time it is trampled;
the time to harvest her will soon
come."

³⁴ "Nebuchadnezzar king of Babylon has
devoured us,
he has thrown us into confusion,
he has made us an empty jar.
Like a serpent he has swallowed us
and filled his stomach with our
delicacies,
and then has spewed us out.
³⁵ May the violence done to our flesh*a* be
on Babylon,"
say the inhabitants of Zion.
"May our blood be on those who live in
Babylonia,"
says Jerusalem.

³⁶ Therefore this is what the LORD says:

"See, I will defend your cause
and avenge you;
I will dry up her sea
and make her springs dry.
³⁷ Babylon will be a heap of ruins,
a haunt of jackals,
an object of horror and scorn,
a place where no one lives.
³⁸ Her people all roar like young lions,
they growl like lion cubs.
³⁹ But while they are aroused,
I will set out a feast for them
and make them drunk,

so that they shout with laughter —
then sleep forever and not awake,"
declares the LORD.
⁴⁰ "I will bring them down
like lambs to the slaughter,
like rams and goats.

⁴¹ "How Sheshak*b* will be captured,
the boast of the whole earth
seized!
How desolate Babylon will be
among the nations!
⁴² The sea will rise over Babylon;
its roaring waves will cover her.
⁴³ Her towns will be desolate,
a dry and desert land,
a land where no one lives,
through which no one travels.
⁴⁴ I will punish Bel in Babylon
and make him spew out what he has
swallowed.
The nations will no longer stream to
him.
And the wall of Babylon will fall.

⁴⁵ "Come out of her, my people!
Run for your lives!
Run from the fierce anger of the
LORD.
⁴⁶ Do not lose heart or be afraid
when rumors are heard in the
land;
one rumor comes this year, another the
next,
rumors of violence in the land
and of ruler against ruler.
⁴⁷ For the time will surely come
when I will punish the idols of
Babylon;
her whole land will be disgraced
and her slain will all lie fallen within
her.
⁴⁸ Then heaven and earth and all that is in
them
will shout for joy over Babylon,
for out of the north
destroyers will attack her,"
declares the LORD.

---

a 35 Or *done to us and to our children*   *b 41* Sheshak is a cryptogram for Babylon.

49 "Babylon must fall because of Israel's
      slain,
    just as the slain in all the earth
    have fallen because of Babylon.
50 You who have escaped the sword,
      leave and do not linger!
    Remember the Lord in a distant land,
    and call to mind Jerusalem."

51 "We are disgraced,
      for we have been insulted
    and shame covers our faces,
    because foreigners have entered
      the holy places of the Lord's
      house."

52 "But days are coming," declares the
      Lord,
    "when I will punish her idols,
    and throughout her land
      the wounded will groan.
53 Even if Babylon ascends to the heavens
    and fortifies her lofty stronghold,
    I will send destroyers against her,"
                    declares the Lord.

54 "The sound of a cry comes from
      Babylon,
    the sound of great destruction
      from the land of the Babylonians.[a]
55 The Lord will destroy Babylon;
      he will silence her noisy din.
    Waves of enemies will rage like great
      waters;
    the roar of their voices will resound.
56 A destroyer will come against
      Babylon;
    her warriors will be captured,
    and their bows will be broken.
    For the Lord is a God of retribution;
      he will repay in full.
57 I will make her officials and wise men
      drunk,
    her governors, officers and warriors
      as well;
    they will sleep forever and not awake,"
      declares the King, whose name is the
      Lord Almighty.

58 This is what the Lord Almighty says:

    "Babylon's thick wall will be leveled
      and her high gates set on fire;
    the peoples exhaust themselves for
      nothing,
    the nations' labor is only fuel for the
      flames."

59 This is the message Jeremiah the prophet gave to the staff officer Seraiah son of Neriah, the son of Mahseiah, when he went to Babylon with Zedekiah king of Judah in the fourth year of his reign. 60 Jeremiah had written on a scroll about all the disasters that would come upon Babylon — all that had been recorded concerning Babylon. 61 He said to Seraiah, "When you get to Babylon, see that you read all these words aloud. 62 Then say, 'Lord, you have said you will destroy this place, so that neither people nor animals will live in it; it will be desolate forever.' 63 When you finish reading this scroll, tie a stone to it and throw it into the Euphrates. 64 Then say, 'So will Babylon sink to rise no more because of the disaster I will bring on her. And her people will fall.'"

The words of Jeremiah end here.

The Fall of Jerusalem

52 Zedekiah was twenty-one years old when he became king, and he reigned in Jerusalem eleven years. His mother's name was Hamutal daughter of Jeremiah; she was from Libnah. 2 He did evil in the eyes of the Lord, just as Jehoiakim had done. 3 It was because of the Lord's anger that all this happened to Jerusalem and Judah, and in the end he thrust them from his presence.

Now Zedekiah rebelled against the king of Babylon.

4 So in the ninth year of Zedekiah's reign, on the tenth day of the tenth month, Nebuchadnezzar king of Babylon marched against Jerusalem with his whole army.

---

[a] 54 Or Chaldeans

They encamped outside the city and built siege works all around it. ⁵The city was kept under siege until the eleventh year of King Zedekiah.

⁶By the ninth day of the fourth month the famine in the city had become so severe that there was no food for the people to eat. ⁷Then the city wall was broken through, and the whole army fled. They left the city at night through the gate between the two walls near the king's garden, though the Babylonians*a* were surrounding the city. They fled toward the Arabah,*b* ⁸but the Babylonian*c* army pursued King Zedekiah and overtook him in the plains of Jericho. All his soldiers were separated from him and scattered, ⁹and he was captured.

He was taken to the king of Babylon at Riblah in the land of Hamath, where he pronounced sentence on him. ¹⁰There at Riblah the king of Babylon killed the sons of Zedekiah before his eyes; he also killed all the officials of Judah. ¹¹Then he put out Zedekiah's eyes, bound him with bronze shackles and took him to Babylon, where he put him in prison till the day of his death.

¹²On the tenth day of the fifth month, in the nineteenth year of Nebuchadnezzar king of Babylon, Nebuzaradan commander of the imperial guard, who served the king of Babylon, came to Jerusalem. ¹³He set fire to the temple of the LORD, the royal palace and all the houses of Jerusalem. Every important building he burned down. ¹⁴The whole Babylonian army, under the commander of the imperial guard, broke down all the walls around Jerusalem. ¹⁵Nebuzaradan the commander of the guard carried into exile some of the poorest people and those who remained in the city, along with the rest of the craftsmen*d* and those who had deserted to the king of Babylon. ¹⁶But Nebuzaradan left behind the rest of the poorest people of the land to work the vineyards and fields.

¹⁷The Babylonians broke up the bronze pillars, the movable stands and the bronze Sea that were at the temple of the LORD and they carried all the bronze to Babylon. ¹⁸They also took away the pots, shovels, wick trimmers, sprinkling bowls, dishes and all the bronze articles used in the temple service. ¹⁹The commander of the imperial guard took away the basins, censers, sprinkling bowls, pots, lampstands, dishes and bowls used for drink offerings — all that were made of pure gold or silver.

²⁰The bronze from the two pillars, the Sea and the twelve bronze bulls under it, and the movable stands, which King Solomon had made for the temple of the LORD, was more than could be weighed. ²¹Each pillar was eighteen cubits high and twelve cubits in circumference*e*; each was four fingers thick, and hollow. ²²The bronze capital on top of one pillar was five cubits*f* high and was decorated with a network and pomegranates of bronze all around. The other pillar, with its pomegranates, was similar. ²³There were ninety-six pomegranates on the sides; the total number of pomegranates above the surrounding network was a hundred.

²⁴The commander of the guard took as prisoners Seraiah the chief priest, Zephaniah the priest next in rank and the three doorkeepers. ²⁵Of those still in the city, he took the officer in charge of the fighting men, and seven royal advisers. He also took the secretary who was chief officer in charge of conscripting the people of the land, sixty of whom were found in the city. ²⁶Nebuzaradan the commander took them all and brought them to the king of Babylon at Riblah. ²⁷There at Riblah, in the land of Hamath, the king had them executed.

So Judah went into captivity, away from her land. ²⁸This is the number of the people Nebuchadnezzar carried into exile:

---

a 7 Or *Chaldeans*; also in verse 17   *b 7* Or *the Jordan Valley*   *c 8* Or *Chaldean*; also in verse 14   *d 15* Or *the populace*   *e 21* That is, about 27 feet high and 18 feet in circumference or about 8.1 meters high and 5.4 meters in circumference   *f 22* That is, about 7 1/2 feet or about 2.3 meters

in the seventh year, 3,023 Jews;
[29] in Nebuchadnezzar's eighteenth year,
832 people from Jerusalem;
[30] in his twenty-third year,
745 Jews taken into exile by Nebuzaradan the commander of the
imperial guard.
There were 4,600 people in all.

Jehoiachin Released

[31] In the thirty-seventh year of the exile of Jehoiachin king of Judah, in the year
Awel-Marduk became king of Babylon, on
the twenty-fifth day of the twelfth month,
he released Jehoiachin king of Judah and
freed him from prison. [32] He spoke kindly
to him and gave him a seat of honor higher than those of the other kings who were
with him in Babylon. [33] So Jehoiachin put
aside his prison clothes and for the rest
of his life ate regularly at the king's table.
[34] Day by day the king of Babylon gave Jehoiachin a regular allowance as long as he
lived, till the day of his death.

Lamentations

THEME: God is just, but he is also a God of hope, love, compassion, faithfulness and salvation, one who doesn't abandon those who turn to him for help.

AUTHOR: The book has been attributed to the prophet Jeremiah from as early as the third century BC, but its authorship is uncertain. Some scholars believe it was compiled from various sources rather than written by a single author.

DATE OF WRITING: Lamentations was written after the fall of Jerusalem to the Babylonians (586 BC) but before the temple was rebuilt (approximately 516 BC).

ENCOURAGEMENT FROM LAMENTATIONS: "Because of the LORD's great love we are not consumed, for his compassions never fail. They are new every morning; great is your faithfulness" (Lamentations 3:22 – 23).

CHALLENGE FROM LAMENTATIONS: "Though he brings grief, he will show compassion, so great is his unfailing love" (Lamentations 3:32).

REFLECTION FROM LAMENTATIONS: "The LORD is good to those whose hope is in him, to the one who seeks him" (Lamentations 3:25).

Lamentations describes Jerusalem's funeral. Because the Judahites have refused to listen to Jeremiah and the other prophets and have not repented, the city has been reduced to rubble by the Babylonians. This poetic book expresses the deep emotions felt by one who had witnessed the slaughter and enslavement of his people. Their sin had indeed brought dire consequences. Although Jerusalem would be partially restored — only to be repeatedly shattered again in the centuries to follow — ultimate restoration (still in the future) will come when Israel repents and confesses Jesus Christ as her long-awaited Messiah.

In our own lives we must recognize the damaging effects that sin has had on us. We find freedom and forgiveness when we pray in repentance; we must not allow ourselves to believe the lie that sin doesn't devastate our lives. In Jesus Christ, we're free *from* sin, not free *to* sin. Lamentations presents a picture of what a life of non-repentance can look like and encourages us to bring all our sins before the Lord, who alone can restore us to sanity and to a life of purpose.

1 *a* How deserted lies the city,
　　once so full of people!
　How like a widow is she,
　　who once was great among the nations!
　She who was queen among the provinces
　　has now become a slave.

2 Bitterly she weeps at night,
　　tears are on her cheeks.
　Among all her lovers
　　there is no one to comfort her.
　All her friends have betrayed her;
　　they have become her enemies.

---

a This chapter is an acrostic poem, the verses of which begin with the successive letters of the Hebrew alphabet.

³ After affliction and harsh labor,
   Judah has gone into exile.
She dwells among the nations;
   she finds no resting place.
All who pursue her have overtaken her
   in the midst of her distress.

⁴ The roads to Zion mourn,
   for no one comes to her appointed
      festivals.
All her gateways are desolate,
   her priests groan,
her young women grieve,
   and she is in bitter anguish.

⁵ Her foes have become her masters;
   her enemies are at ease.
The LORD has brought her grief
   because of her many sins.
Her children have gone into exile,
   captive before the foe.

⁶ All the splendor has departed
   from Daughter Zion.
Her princes are like deer
   that find no pasture;
in weakness they have fled
   before the pursuer.

⁷ In the days of her affliction and
      wandering
   Jerusalem remembers all the
      treasures
   that were hers in days of old.
When her people fell into enemy
      hands,
   there was no one to help her.
Her enemies looked at her
   and laughed at her destruction.

⁸ Jerusalem has sinned greatly
   and so has become unclean.
All who honored her despise her,
   for they have all seen her naked;
she herself groans
   and turns away.

⁹ Her filthiness clung to her skirts;
   she did not consider her future.

Her fall was astounding;
   there was none to comfort her.
"Look, LORD, on my affliction,
   for the enemy has triumphed."

¹⁰ The enemy laid hands
   on all her treasures;
she saw pagan nations
   enter her sanctuary—
those you had forbidden
   to enter your assembly.

¹¹ All her people groan
   as they search for bread;
they barter their treasures for food
   to keep themselves alive.
"Look, LORD, and consider,
   for I am despised."

¹² "Is it nothing to you, all you who pass
      by?
   Look around and see.
Is any suffering like my suffering
   that was inflicted on me,
that the LORD brought on me
   in the day of his fierce anger?

¹³ "From on high he sent fire,
   sent it down into my bones.
He spread a net for my feet
   and turned me back.
He made me desolate,
   faint all the day long.

¹⁴ "My sins have been bound into a yoke*;
   by his hands they were woven
      together.
They have been hung on my neck,
   and the Lord has sapped my
      strength.
He has given me into the hands
   of those I cannot withstand.

¹⁵ "The Lord has rejected
   all the warriors in my midst;
he has summoned an army against me
   to* crush my young men.
In his winepress the Lord has trampled
   Virgin Daughter Judah.

---

a 14 Most Hebrew manuscripts; many Hebrew manuscripts and Septuagint *He kept watch over my sins*   *b 15* Or
has set a time for me / when he will

16 "This is why I weep
  and my eyes overflow with tears.
No one is near to comfort me,
  no one to restore my spirit.
My children are destitute
  because the enemy has prevailed."

17 Zion stretches out her hands,
  but there is no one to comfort her.
The LORD has decreed for Jacob
  that his neighbors become his foes;
Jerusalem has become
  an unclean thing among them.

18 "The LORD is righteous,
  yet I rebelled against his command.
Listen, all you peoples;
  look on my suffering.
My young men and young women
  have gone into exile.

19 "I called to my allies
  but they betrayed me.
My priests and my elders
  perished in the city
while they searched for food
  to keep themselves alive.

20 "See, LORD, how distressed I am!
  I am in torment within,
and in my heart I am disturbed,
  for I have been most rebellious.
Outside, the sword bereaves;
  inside, there is only death.

21 "People have heard my groaning,
  but there is no one to comfort me.
All my enemies have heard of my
    distress;
  they rejoice at what you have done.
May you bring the day you have
    announced
  so they may become like me.

22 "Let all their wickedness come before you;
    deal with them
  as you have dealt with me
    because of all my sins.

My groans are many
  and my heart is faint."

2 *a* How the Lord has covered
      Daughter Zion
    with the cloud of his anger *b*!
He has hurled down the splendor of
    Israel
  from heaven to earth;
he has not remembered his footstool
  in the day of his anger.

2 Without pity the Lord has swallowed
    up
  all the dwellings of Jacob;
in his wrath he has torn down
  the strongholds of Daughter Judah.
He has brought her kingdom and its
    princes
  down to the ground in dishonor.

3 In fierce anger he has cut off
  every horn *c,d* of Israel.
He has withdrawn his right hand
  at the approach of the enemy.
He has burned in Jacob like a flaming
    fire
  that consumes everything around it.

4 Like an enemy he has strung his bow;
  his right hand is ready.
Like a foe he has slain
  all who were pleasing to the eye;
he has poured out his wrath like fire
  on the tent of Daughter Zion.

5 The Lord is like an enemy;
  he has swallowed up Israel.
He has swallowed up all her palaces
  and destroyed her strongholds.
He has multiplied mourning and
    lamentation
  for Daughter Judah.

6 He has laid waste his dwelling like a
    garden;
  he has destroyed his place of
    meeting.

---

a This chapter is an acrostic poem, the verses of which begin with the successive letters of the Hebrew alphabet.
b 1 Or *How the Lord in his anger / has treated Daughter Zion with contempt*   *c* 3 Or *off / all the strength*; or *every king*   *d* 3 *Horn* here symbolizes strength.

The LORD has made Zion forget
    her appointed festivals and her
        Sabbaths;
in his fierce anger he has spurned
    both king and priest.

7 The Lord has rejected his altar
    and abandoned his sanctuary.
He has given the walls of her palaces
    into the hands of the enemy;
they have raised a shout in the house of
        the LORD
    as on the day of an appointed festival.

8 The LORD determined to tear down
    the wall around Daughter Zion.
He stretched out a measuring line
    and did not withhold his hand from
        destroying.
He made ramparts and walls lament;
    together they wasted away.

9 Her gates have sunk into the ground;
    their bars he has broken and
        destroyed.
Her king and her princes are exiled
        among the nations,
    the law is no more,
and her prophets no longer find
    visions from the LORD.

10 The elders of Daughter Zion
    sit on the ground in silence;
they have sprinkled dust on their heads
    and put on sackcloth.
The young women of Jerusalem
    have bowed their heads to the
        ground.

11 My eyes fail from weeping,
    I am in torment within;
my heart is poured out on the ground
    because my people are destroyed,
    because children and infants faint
    in the streets of the city.

12 They say to their mothers,
    "Where is bread and wine?"
as they faint like the wounded
    in the streets of the city,
as their lives ebb away
    in their mothers' arms.

13 What can I say for you?
    With what can I compare you,
        Daughter Jerusalem?
To what can I liken you,
    that I may comfort you,
        Virgin Daughter Zion?
Your wound is as deep as the sea.
    Who can heal you?

14 The visions of your prophets
    were false and worthless;
they did not expose your sin
    to ward off your captivity.
The prophecies they gave you
    were false and misleading.

15 All who pass your way
    clap their hands at you;
they scoff and shake their heads
    at Daughter Jerusalem:
"Is this the city that was called
    the perfection of beauty,
    the joy of the whole earth?"

16 All your enemies open their mouths
    wide against you;
they scoff and gnash their teeth
    and say, "We have swallowed
        her up.
This is the day we have waited for;
    we have lived to see it."

17 The LORD has done what he planned;
    he has fulfilled his word,
    which he decreed long ago.
He has overthrown you without pity,
    he has let the enemy gloat over you,
    he has exalted the horn*a* of your
        foes.

18 The hearts of the people
    cry out to the Lord.
You walls of Daughter Zion,
    let your tears flow like a river
    day and night;
give yourself no relief,
    your eyes no rest.

a 17 *Horn* here symbolizes strength.

¹⁹ Arise, cry out in the night,
    as the watches of the night begin;
pour out your heart like water
    in the presence of the Lord.
Lift up your hands to him
    for the lives of your children,
who faint from hunger
    at every street corner.

²⁰ "Look, Lord, and consider:
    Whom have you ever treated like this?
Should women eat their offspring,
    the children they have cared for?
Should priest and prophet be killed
    in the sanctuary of the Lord?

²¹ "Young and old lie together
    in the dust of the streets;
my young men and young women
    have fallen by the sword.
You have slain them in the day of your
        anger;
    you have slaughtered them without
        pity.

²² "As you summon to a feast day,
    so you summoned against me terrors
        on every side.
In the day of the Lord's anger
    no one escaped or survived;
those I cared for and reared
    my enemy has destroyed."

3 ᵃ I am the man who has seen
        affliction
    by the rod of the Lord's wrath.
² He has driven me away and made me
        walk
    in darkness rather than light;
³ indeed, he has turned his hand against
        me
    again and again, all day long.

⁴ He has made my skin and my flesh
        grow old
    and has broken my bones.
⁵ He has besieged me and surrounded me
    with bitterness and hardship.

⁶ He has made me dwell in darkness
    like those long dead.

⁷ He has walled me in so I cannot escape;
    he has weighed me down with
        chains.
⁸ Even when I call out or cry for help,
    he shuts out my prayer.
⁹ He has barred my way with blocks of
        stone;
    he has made my paths crooked.

¹⁰ Like a bear lying in wait,
    like a lion in hiding,
¹¹ he dragged me from the path and
        mangled me
    and left me without help.
¹² He drew his bow
    and made me the target for his arrows.

¹³ He pierced my heart
    with arrows from his quiver.
¹⁴ I became the laughingstock of all my
        people;
    they mock me in song all day long.
¹⁵ He has filled me with bitter herbs
    and given me gall to drink.

¹⁶ He has broken my teeth with gravel;
    he has trampled me in the dust.
¹⁷ I have been deprived of peace;
    I have forgotten what prosperity is.
¹⁸ So I say, "My splendor is gone
    and all that I had hoped from the
        Lord."

¹⁹ I remember my affliction and my
        wandering,
    the bitterness and the gall.
²⁰ I well remember them,
    and my soul is downcast within me.
²¹ Yet this I call to mind
    and therefore I have hope:

²² Because of the Lord's great love we are
        not consumed,
    for his compassions never fail.
²³ They are new every morning;
    great is your faithfulness.

ᵃ This chapter is an acrostic poem; the verses of each stanza begin with the successive letters of the Hebrew alphabet, and the verses within each stanza begin with the same letter.

²⁴I say to myself, "The LORD is my
portion;
therefore I will wait for him."

²⁵The LORD is good to those whose hope
is in him,
to the one who seeks him;
²⁶it is good to wait quietly
for the salvation of the LORD.
²⁷It is good for a man to bear the yoke
while he is young.

²⁸Let him sit alone in silence,
for the LORD has laid it on him.
²⁹Let him bury his face in the dust —
there may yet be hope.
³⁰Let him offer his cheek to one who
would strike him,
and let him be filled with disgrace.

³¹For no one is cast off
by the Lord forever.
³²Though he brings grief, he will show
compassion,
so great is his unfailing love.
³³For he does not willingly bring
affliction
or grief to anyone.

³⁴To crush underfoot
all prisoners in the land,
³⁵to deny people their rights
before the Most High,
³⁶to deprive them of justice —
would not the Lord see such things?

³⁷Who can speak and have it happen
if the Lord has not decreed it?
³⁸Is it not from the mouth of the Most
High
that both calamities and good things
come?
³⁹Why should the living complain
when punished for their sins?

⁴⁰Let us examine our ways and test
them,
and let us return to the LORD.
⁴¹Let us lift up our hearts and our hands
to God in heaven, and say:
⁴²"We have sinned and rebelled
and you have not forgiven.

⁴³"You have covered yourself with anger
and pursued us;
you have slain without pity.
⁴⁴You have covered yourself with a cloud
so that no prayer can get through.
⁴⁵You have made us scum and refuse
among the nations.

⁴⁶"All our enemies have opened their
mouths
wide against us.
⁴⁷We have suffered terror and pitfalls,
ruin and destruction."
⁴⁸Streams of tears flow from my eyes
because my people are destroyed.

⁴⁹My eyes will flow unceasingly,
without relief,
⁵⁰until the LORD looks down
from heaven and sees.
⁵¹What I see brings grief to my soul
because of all the women of my city.

⁵²Those who were my enemies without
cause
hunted me like a bird.
⁵³They tried to end my life in a pit
and threw stones at me;
⁵⁴the waters closed over my head,
and I thought I was about to perish.

⁵⁵I called on your name, LORD,
from the depths of the pit.
⁵⁶You heard my plea: "Do not close your
ears
to my cry for relief."
⁵⁷You came near when I called you,
and you said, "Do not fear."

⁵⁸You, Lord, took up my case;
you redeemed my life.
⁵⁹LORD, you have seen the wrong done
to me.
Uphold my cause!
⁶⁰You have seen the depth of their
vengeance,
all their plots against me.

⁶¹LORD, you have heard their insults,
all their plots against me —
⁶²what my enemies whisper and mutter
against me all day long.

63 Look at them! Sitting or standing,
   they mock me in their songs.

64 Pay them back what they deserve,
   LORD,
   for what their hands have done.
65 Put a veil over their hearts,
   and may your curse be on them!
66 Pursue them in anger and destroy
   them
   from under the heavens of the LORD.

4 *a* How the gold has lost its luster,
   the fine gold become dull!
   The sacred gems are scattered
   at every street corner.

2 How the precious children of Zion,
   once worth their weight in gold,
   are now considered as pots of clay,
   the work of a potter's hands!

3 Even jackals offer their breasts
   to nurse their young,
   but my people have become heartless
   like ostriches in the desert.

4 Because of thirst the infant's tongue
   sticks to the roof of its mouth;
   the children beg for bread,
   but no one gives it to them.

5 Those who once ate delicacies
   are destitute in the streets.

---

a This chapter is an acrostic poem, the verses of which begin with the successive letters of the Hebrew alphabet.

MORAL LESSON [*Principle Four*]

For the previous entry in the MORAL lesson, go to Proverbs 20:27 (page 765).

For a discussion of Principles One through Eight and a listing of their related lessons,
go to pages xvii – xliv.

Let us examine our ways and test them,
and let us return to the LORD.

LAMENTATIONS 3:40

Principle Four begins our process of "coming clean." It's here that we openly examine and confess our faults to ourselves, to God and to someone else we trust. In the first part of Principle Four we openly examine our lives. We take a MORAL inventory.

The last letter in MORAL, *L*, stands for LIST. Our inventory is basically a written list of the events of our past and present — both the good and the bad. An appropriate balance is important as we assess our situation. Seeing an honest evaluation of our past and present in print brings us face-to-face with the reality of our character defects. Our inventories become a black-and-white discovery of who we truly are at our core. But if we look only at the negative parts of our past, we'll distort our inventories and open ourselves up to unnecessary pain. Notice that Lamentations 3:40 doesn't say, "Examine your bad, negative ways." We need to honestly focus on both the negative and the positive actions of our past and present.

An important word of caution: Don't begin this principle without a sponsor or an accountability partner. We need someone of the same sex as ourselves whom we trust to keep us balanced during this process. We need encouragement from someone else who is willing to support our progress. That's what Celebrate Recovery is all about.

This is the final page of the MORAL lesson.

This is the first page of the CROSSROADS lesson.

For a discussion of Principles One through Eight and a listing of their related lessons,
go to pages xvii–xliv.

*Let us examine our ways and test them,
and let us return to the LORD.*

LAMENTATIONS 3:40

In Principle Seven we reserve a daily quiet time with God for self-examination, Bible reading and prayer in order to get to know God and his will for our lives and to gain the power to follow his will. We're at the CROSSROADS of our recovery. We need to thank God for getting us this far on our road to recovery, to praise him for the many victories we've already experienced over our hurts, hang-ups and habits. But we also need to continue working the last two principles with the same devotion and enthusiasm that got us to this point in our recovery. In the first part of Principle Seven we reserve a daily quiet time with God for self-examination. This relates to Step Ten of the Christ-centered 12 steps.

Step Ten: We continued to take personal inventory and, when we were wrong, promptly admitted it.

This step is made up of three key actions. The first is the letter *T* of Step TEN: TAKE TIME TO DO A DAILY INVENTORY. To inventory something is simply to list it and count it. Businesses take inventories all the time. In our recovery process, taking an inventory provides us with quiet time to tally and consider the good and bad things we've done during a particular day. Lamentations 3:40 exhorts us to "examine our ways and test them, and … return to the LORD."

We need to ask ourselves these questions:

- What good did we do today?

- In what areas did we blow it?

- Did we do or say anything that hurt someone else today?

- Do we owe anyone amends for something we did or said?

- What did we learn from our actions today?

We need to develop the habit of doing this on a daily basis. This forces us to take the time to reflect on our day, to check whether we've harmed someone else, acted or reacted out of fear or selfishness or, on the plus side, gone out of our way to show someone kindness.

By the time we get to Principle Seven, we're starting to do a lot of things right. But if we're not careful, we can slowly slip back into our old hurts, hang-ups and habits. For this reason we need to take regular, ongoing inventories.

The next necessary action is represented by the letter *E* of Step TEN.
Go to 1 John 1:8–10 (page 1557).

Those brought up in royal purple
  now lie on ash heaps.

6 The punishment of my people
  is greater than that of Sodom,
which was overthrown in a moment
  without a hand turned to help her.

7 Their princes were brighter than snow
  and whiter than milk,
their bodies more ruddy than rubies,
  their appearance like lapis lazuli.

8 But now they are blacker than soot;
  they are not recognized in the
    streets.
Their skin has shriveled on their bones;
  it has become as dry as a stick.

9 Those killed by the sword are better off
  than those who die of famine;
racked with hunger, they waste away
  for lack of food from the field.

10 With their own hands compassionate
    women
  have cooked their own children,
who became their food
  when my people were destroyed.

11 The LORD has given full vent to his
    wrath;
  he has poured out his fierce anger.
He kindled a fire in Zion
  that consumed her foundations.

12 The kings of the earth did not believe,
  nor did any of the peoples of the
    world,
that enemies and foes could enter
  the gates of Jerusalem.

13 But it happened because of the sins of
    her prophets
  and the iniquities of her priests,
who shed within her
  the blood of the righteous.

14 Now they grope through the streets
  as if they were blind.
They are so defiled with blood
  that no one dares to touch their
    garments.

15 "Go away! You are unclean!" people cry
  to them.
  "Away! Away! Don't touch us!"
When they flee and wander about,
  people among the nations say,
  "They can stay here no longer."

16 The LORD himself has scattered them;
  he no longer watches over them.
The priests are shown no honor,
  the elders no favor.

17 Moreover, our eyes failed,
  looking in vain for help;
from our towers we watched
  for a nation that could not save us.

18 People stalked us at every step,
  so we could not walk in our streets.
Our end was near, our days were
    numbered,
  for our end had come.

19 Our pursuers were swifter
  than eagles in the sky;
they chased us over the mountains
  and lay in wait for us in the desert.

20 The LORD's anointed, our very life
    breath,
  was caught in their traps.
We thought that under his shadow
  we would live among the nations.

21 Rejoice and be glad, Daughter Edom,
  you who live in the land of Uz.
But to you also the cup will be passed;
  you will be drunk and stripped naked.

22 Your punishment will end, Daughter
    Zion;
  he will not prolong your exile.
But he will punish your sin, Daughter
    Edom,
  and expose your wickedness.

5 Remember, LORD, what has
    happened to us;
  look, and see our disgrace.
2 Our inheritance has been turned over
  to strangers,
  our homes to foreigners.

3 We have become fatherless,
our mothers are widows.
4 We must buy the water we drink;
our wood can be had only at a price.
5 Those who pursue us are at our heels;
we are weary and find no rest.
6 We submitted to Egypt and Assyria
to get enough bread.
7 Our ancestors sinned and are no more,
and we bear their punishment.
8 Slaves rule over us,
and there is no one to free us from
their hands.
9 We get our bread at the risk of our lives
because of the sword in the desert.
10 Our skin is hot as an oven,
feverish from hunger.
11 Women have been violated in Zion,
and virgins in the towns of Judah.
12 Princes have been hung up by their
hands;
elders are shown no respect.
13 Young men toil at the millstones;
boys stagger under loads of wood.

14 The elders are gone from the city gate;
the young men have stopped their
music.
15 Joy is gone from our hearts;
our dancing has turned to mourning.
16 The crown has fallen from our head.
Woe to us, for we have sinned!
17 Because of this our hearts are faint,
because of these things our eyes grow
dim
18 for Mount Zion, which lies desolate,
with jackals prowling over it.

19 You, LORD, reign forever;
your throne endures from generation
to generation.
20 Why do you always forget us?
Why do you forsake us so long?
21 Restore us to yourself, LORD, that we
may return;
renew our days as of old
22 unless you have utterly rejected us
and are angry with us beyond
measure.

Ezekiel

THEME: God is sovereign over all creation, including the course of history. He is absolutely free either to judge or to be gracious and merciful.

AUTHOR: The book identifies its author as Ezekiel, a priest exiled to Babylon by Nebuchadnezzar in 597 BC, before the fall of Jerusalem in 586 BC.

DATE OF WRITING: Ezekiel probably wrote this book over the course of his ministry, between 593 and 571 BC.

ENCOURAGEMENT FROM EZEKIEL: "I will give you a new heart and put a new spirit in you; I will remove from you your heart of stone and give you a heart of flesh" (Ezekiel 36:26).

CHALLENGE FROM EZEKIEL: "Why will you die, people of Israel? For I take no pleasure in the death of anyone, declares the Sovereign LORD. Repent and live!" (Ezekiel 18:31 – 32).

REFLECTION FROM EZEKIEL: "I [the LORD] take no pleasure in the death of the wicked, but rather that they turn from their ways and live. Turn! Turn from your evil ways!" (Ezekiel 33:11).

At a Glance

Ezekiel, an exile taken to Babylon from Judah, used prophecies, parables, signs and symbols to deliver God's message to his fellow exiles. The prophet promised that judgment would be followed by God's future glory. Unfortunately for the people of Jerusalem, that time had not yet come. Jerusalem and the temple would first have to be destroyed.

Although the judgment of God had to come to an unrepentant Judah, God's desire to restore the nation is shown clearly in Ezekiel. That same power is available to us in recovery. God is willing and able to heal our lives. Like that of Israel, our restoration can be accomplished only by the Spirit of God. As the nation was promised a glorious return, so we've been promised that God will restore us to health through his Son.

Recovery Themes in Ezekiel

Ezekiel's Inaugural Vision

1 In my thirtieth year, in the fourth month on the fifth day, while I was among the exiles by the Kebar River, the heavens were opened and I saw visions of God.

²On the fifth of the month — it was the fifth year of the exile of King Jehoiachin — ³the word of the LORD came to Ezekiel the priest, the son of Buzi, by the Kebar River in the land of the Babylonians.*ᵃ* There the hand of the LORD was on him.

⁴I looked, and I saw a windstorm coming out of the north — an immense cloud with flashing lightning and surrounded by brilliant light. The center of the fire looked like glowing metal, ⁵and in the fire was what looked like four living creatures.

ᵃ 3 Or *Chaldeans*

In appearance their form was human, [6]but each of them had four faces and four wings. [7]Their legs were straight; their feet were like those of a calf and gleamed like burnished bronze. [8]Under their wings on their four sides they had human hands. All four of them had faces and wings, [9]and the wings of one touched the wings of another. Each one went straight ahead; they did not turn as they moved.

[10]Their faces looked like this: Each of the four had the face of a human being, and on the right side each had the face of a lion, and on the left the face of an ox; each also had the face of an eagle. [11]Such were their faces. They each had two wings spreading out upward, each wing touching that of the creature on either side; and each had two other wings covering its body. [12]Each one went straight ahead. Wherever the spirit would go, they would go, without turning as they went. [13]The appearance of the living creatures was like burning coals of fire or like torches. Fire moved back and forth among the creatures; it was bright, and lightning flashed out of it. [14]The creatures sped back and forth like flashes of lightning.

[15]As I looked at the living creatures, I saw a wheel on the ground beside each creature with its four faces. [16]This was the appearance and structure of the wheels: They sparkled like topaz, and all four looked alike. Each appeared to be made like a wheel intersecting a wheel. [17]As they moved, they would go in any one of the four directions the creatures faced; the wheels did not change direction as the creatures went. [18]Their rims were high and awesome, and all four rims were full of eyes all around.

[19]When the living creatures moved, the wheels beside them moved; and when the living creatures rose from the ground, the wheels also rose. [20]Wherever the spirit would go, they would go, and the wheels would rise along with them, because the spirit of the living creatures was in the wheels. [21]When the creatures moved, they also moved; when the creatures stood still, they also stood still; and when the creatures rose from the ground, the wheels rose along with them, because the spirit of the living creatures was in the wheels.

[22]Spread out above the heads of the living creatures was what looked something like a vault, sparkling like crystal, and awesome. [23]Under the vault their wings were stretched out one toward the other, and each had two wings covering its body. [24]When the creatures moved, I heard the sound of their wings, like the roar of rushing waters, like the voice of the Almighty,[a] like the tumult of an army. When they stood still, they lowered their wings.

[25]Then there came a voice from above the vault over their heads as they stood with lowered wings. [26]Above the vault over their heads was what looked like a throne of lapis lazuli, and high above on the throne was a figure like that of a man. [27]I saw that from what appeared to be his waist up he looked like glowing metal, as if full of fire, and that from there down he looked like fire; and brilliant light surrounded him. [28]Like the appearance of a rainbow in the clouds on a rainy day, so was the radiance around him.

This was the appearance of the likeness of the glory of the LORD. When I saw it, I fell facedown, and I heard the voice of one speaking.

Ezekiel's Call to Be a Prophet

2 He said to me, "Son of man,[b] stand up on your feet and I will speak to you." [2]As he spoke, the Spirit came into me and raised me to my feet, and I heard him speaking to me.

[3]He said: "Son of man, I am sending you to the Israelites, to a rebellious nation that has rebelled against me; they and their ancestors have been in revolt against

---

[a] 24 Hebrew *Shaddai*   [b] 1 The Hebrew phrase *ben adam* means *human being.* The phrase *son of man* is retained as a form of address here and throughout Ezekiel because of its possible association with "Son of Man" in the New Testament.

me to this very day. ⁴The people to whom I am sending you are obstinate and stubborn. Say to them, 'This is what the Sovereign LORD says.' ⁵And whether they listen or fail to listen—for they are a rebellious people—they will know that a prophet has been among them. ⁶And you, son of man, do not be afraid of them or their words. Do not be afraid, though briers and thorns are all around you and you live among scorpions. Do not be afraid of what they say or be terrified by them, though they are a rebellious people. ⁷You must speak my words to them, whether they listen or fail to listen, for they are rebellious. ⁸But you, son of man, listen to what I say to you. Do not rebel like that rebellious people; open your mouth and eat what I give you."

⁹Then I looked, and I saw a hand stretched out to me. In it was a scroll, ¹⁰which he unrolled before me. On both sides of it were written words of lament and mourning and woe.

3 And he said to me, "Son of man, eat what is before you, eat this scroll; then go and speak to the people of Israel." ²So I opened my mouth, and he gave me the scroll to eat.

³Then he said to me, "Son of man, eat this scroll I am giving you and fill your stomach with it." So I ate it, and it tasted as sweet as honey in my mouth.

⁴He then said to me: "Son of man, go now to the people of Israel and speak my words to them. ⁵You are not being sent to a people of obscure speech and strange language, but to the people of Israel— ⁶not to many peoples of obscure speech and strange language, whose words you cannot understand. Surely if I had sent you to them, they would have listened to you. ⁷But the people of Israel are not willing to listen to you because they are not willing to listen to me, for all the Israelites are hardened and obstinate. ⁸But I will make you as unyielding and hardened as they are. ⁹I will

make your forehead like the hardest stone, harder than flint. Do not be afraid of them or terrified by them, though they are a rebellious people."

¹⁰And he said to me, "Son of man, listen carefully and take to heart all the words I speak to you. ¹¹Go now to your people in exile and speak to them. Say to them, 'This is what the Sovereign LORD says,' whether they listen or fail to listen."

¹²Then the Spirit lifted me up, and I heard behind me a loud rumbling sound as the glory of the LORD rose from the place where it was standing.ᵃ ¹³It was the sound of the wings of the living creatures brushing against each other and the sound of the wheels beside them, a loud rumbling sound. ¹⁴The Spirit then lifted me up and took me away, and I went in bitterness and in the anger of my spirit, with the strong hand of the LORD on me. ¹⁵I came to the exiles who lived at Tel Aviv near the Kebar River. And there, where they were living, I sat among them for seven days—deeply distressed.

Ezekiel's Task as Watchman

¹⁶At the end of seven days the word of the LORD came to me: ¹⁷"Son of man, I have made you a watchman for the people of Israel; so hear the word I speak and give them warning from me. ¹⁸When I say to a wicked person, 'You will surely die,' and you do not warn them or speak out to dissuade them from their evil ways in order to save their life, that wicked person will die forᵇ their sin, and I will hold you accountable for their blood. ¹⁹But if you do warn the wicked person and they do not turn from their wickedness or from their evil ways, they will die for their sin; but you will have saved yourself.

²⁰"Again, when a righteous person turns from their righteousness and does evil, and I put a stumbling block before them, they will die. Since you did not warn them, they

---

ᵃ 12 Probable reading of the original Hebrew text; Masoretic Text *sound—may the glory of the LORD be praised from his place*   ᵇ 18 Or *in*; also in verses 19 and 20 will die for their sin. The righteous things that person did will not be remembered, and I will hold you accountable for their blood. ²¹But if you do warn the righteous person not to sin and they do not sin, they will surely live because they took warning, and you will have saved yourself."

²²The hand of the LORD was on me there, and he said to me, "Get up and go out to the plain, and there I will speak to you." ²³So I got up and went out to the plain. And the glory of the LORD was standing there, like the glory I had seen by the Kebar River, and I fell facedown.

²⁴Then the Spirit came into me and raised me to my feet. He spoke to me and said: "Go, shut yourself inside your house. ²⁵And you, son of man, they will tie with ropes; you will be bound so that you cannot go out among the people. ²⁶I will make your tongue stick to the roof of your mouth so that you will be silent and unable to rebuke them, for they are a rebellious people. ²⁷But when I speak to you, I will open your mouth and you shall say to them, 'This is what the Sovereign LORD says.' Whoever will listen let them listen, and whoever will refuse let them refuse; for they are a rebellious people.

Siege of Jerusalem Symbolized

4 "Now, son of man, take a block of clay, put it in front of you and draw the city of Jerusalem on it. ²Then lay siege to it: Erect siege works against it, build a ramp up to it, set up camps against it and put battering rams around it. ³Then take an iron pan, place it as an iron wall between you and the city and turn your face toward it. It will be under siege, and you shall besiege it. This will be a sign to the people of Israel.

⁴"Then lie on your left side and put the sin of the people of Israel upon yourself.*ᵃ* You are to bear their sin for the number of days you lie on your side. ⁵I have assigned you the same number of days as the years of

their sin. So for 390 days you will bear the sin of the people of Israel.

⁶"After you have finished this, lie down again, this time on your right side, and bear the sin of the people of Judah. I have assigned you 40 days, a day for each year. ⁷Turn your face toward the siege of Jerusalem and with bared arm prophesy against her. ⁸I will tie you up with ropes so that you cannot turn from one side to the other until you have finished the days of your siege.

⁹"Take wheat and barley, beans and lentils, millet and spelt; put them in a storage jar and use them to make bread for yourself. You are to eat it during the 390 days you lie on your side. ¹⁰Weigh out twenty shekels*ᵇ* of food to eat each day and eat it at set times. ¹¹Also measure out a sixth of a hin*ᶜ* of water and drink it at set times. ¹²Eat the food as you would a loaf of barley bread; bake it in the sight of the people, using human excrement for fuel." ¹³The LORD said, "In this way the people of Israel will eat defiled food among the nations where I will drive them."

¹⁴Then I said, "Not so, Sovereign LORD! I have never defiled myself. From my youth until now I have never eaten anything found dead or torn by wild animals. No impure meat has ever entered my mouth."

¹⁵"Very well," he said, "I will let you bake your bread over cow dung instead of human excrement."

¹⁶He then said to me: "Son of man, I am about to cut off the food supply in Jerusalem. The people will eat rationed food in anxiety and drink rationed water in despair, ¹⁷for food and water will be scarce. They will be appalled at the sight of each other and will waste away because of*ᵈ* their sin.

God's Razor of Judgment

5 "Now, son of man, take a sharp sword and use it as a barber's razor to shave your head and your beard. Then take a set of scales and divide up the

---

ᵃ 4 Or *upon your side*   *ᵇ 10* That is, about 8 ounces or about 230 grams   *ᶜ 11* That is, about 2/3 quart or about 0.6 liter   *ᵈ 17* Or *away in* hair. ²When the days of your siege come to an end, burn a third of the hair inside the city. Take a third and strike it with the sword all around the city. And scatter a third to the wind. For I will pursue them with drawn sword. ³But take a few hairs and tuck them away in the folds of your garment. ⁴Again, take a few of these and throw them into the fire and burn them up. A fire will spread from there to all Israel.

⁵"This is what the Sovereign Lord says: This is Jerusalem, which I have set in the center of the nations, with countries all around her. ⁶Yet in her wickedness she has rebelled against my laws and decrees more than the nations and countries around her. She has rejected my laws and has not followed my decrees.

⁷"Therefore this is what the Sovereign Lord says: You have been more unruly than the nations around you and have not followed my decrees or kept my laws. You have not even*a* conformed to the standards of the nations around you.

⁸"Therefore this is what the Sovereign Lord says: I myself am against you, Jerusalem, and I will inflict punishment on you in the sight of the nations. ⁹Because of all your detestable idols, I will do to you what I have never done before and will never do again. ¹⁰Therefore in your midst parents will eat their children, and children will eat their parents. I will inflict punishment on you and will scatter all your survivors to the winds. ¹¹Therefore as surely as I live, declares the Sovereign Lord, because you have defiled my sanctuary with all your vile images and detestable practices, I myself will shave you; I will not look on you with pity or spare you. ¹²A third of your people will die of the plague or perish by famine inside you; a third will fall by the sword outside your walls; and a third I will scatter to the winds and pursue with drawn sword.

¹³"Then my anger will cease and my wrath against them will subside, and I will be avenged. And when I have spent my wrath on them, they will know that I the Lord have spoken in my zeal.

¹⁴"I will make you a ruin and a reproach among the nations around you, in the sight of all who pass by. ¹⁵You will be a reproach and a taunt, a warning and an object of horror to the nations around you when I inflict punishment on you in anger and in wrath and with stinging rebuke. I the Lord have spoken. ¹⁶When I shoot at you with my deadly and destructive arrows of famine, I will shoot to destroy you. I will bring more and more famine upon you and cut off your supply of food. ¹⁷I will send famine and wild beasts against you, and they will leave you childless. Plague and bloodshed will sweep through you, and I will bring the sword against you. I the Lord have spoken."

Doom for the Mountains of Israel

6 The word of the Lord came to me: ²"Son of man, set your face against the mountains of Israel; prophesy against them ³and say: 'You mountains of Israel, hear the word of the Sovereign Lord. This is what the Sovereign Lord says to the mountains and hills, to the ravines and valleys: I am about to bring a sword against you, and I will destroy your high places. ⁴Your altars will be demolished and your incense altars will be smashed; and I will slay your people in front of your idols. ⁵I will lay the dead bodies of the Israelites in front of their idols, and I will scatter your bones around your altars. ⁶Wherever you live, the towns will be laid waste and the high places demolished, so that your altars will be laid waste and devastated, your idols smashed and ruined, your incense altars broken down, and what you have made wiped out. ⁷Your people will fall slain among you, and you will know that I am the Lord.

⁸"'But I will spare some, for some of you will escape the sword when you are scattered

---

a 7 Most Hebrew manuscripts; some Hebrew manuscripts and Syriac *You have* among the lands and nations. ⁹Then in the nations where they have been carried captive, those who escape will remember me — how I have been grieved by their adulterous hearts, which have turned away from me, and by their eyes, which have lusted after their idols. They will loathe themselves for the evil they have done and for all their detestable practices. ¹⁰And they will know that I am the Lord; I did not threaten in vain to bring this calamity on them.

¹¹"This is what the Sovereign Lord says: Strike your hands together and stamp your feet and cry out "Alas!" because of all the wicked and detestable practices of the people of Israel, for they will fall by the sword, famine and plague. ¹²One who is far away will die of the plague, and one who is near will fall by the sword, and anyone who survives and is spared will die of famine. So will I pour out my wrath on them. ¹³And they will know that I am the Lord, when their people lie slain among their idols around their altars, on every high hill and on all the mountaintops, under every spreading tree and every leafy oak — places where they offered fragrant incense to all their idols. ¹⁴And I will stretch out my hand against them and make the land a desolate waste from the desert to Diblah[a] — wherever they live. Then they will know that I am the Lord.'"

The End Has Come

7 The word of the Lord came to me: ²"Son of man, this is what the Sovereign Lord says to the land of Israel:

"The end! The end has come
    upon the four corners of the land!
³The end is now upon you,
    and I will unleash my anger against
        you.
I will judge you according to your
        conduct
    and repay you for all your detestable
        practices.

⁴I will not look on you with pity;
    I will not spare you.
I will surely repay you for your conduct
    and for the detestable practices
        among you.

"'Then you will know that I am the Lord.'

⁵"This is what the Sovereign Lord says:

"'Disaster! Unheard-of[b] disaster!
    See, it comes!
⁶The end has come!
    The end has come!
It has roused itself against you.
    See, it comes!
⁷Doom has come upon you,
    upon you who dwell in the land.
The time has come! The day is near!
    There is panic, not joy, on the
        mountains.
⁸I am about to pour out my wrath on you
    and spend my anger against you.
I will judge you according to your
        conduct
    and repay you for all your detestable
        practices.
⁹I will not look on you with pity;
    I will not spare you.
I will repay you for your conduct
    and for the detestable practices
        among you.

"'Then you will know that it is I the Lord
who strikes you.

¹⁰"'See, the day!
    See, it comes!
Doom has burst forth,
    the rod has budded,
    arrogance has blossomed!
¹¹Violence has arisen,[c]
    a rod to punish the wicked.
None of the people will be left,
    none of that crowd —
none of their wealth,
    nothing of value.
¹²The time has come!
    The day has arrived!

---

[a] 14 Most Hebrew manuscripts; a few Hebrew manuscripts *Riblah*   [b] 5 Most Hebrew manuscripts; some Hebrew manuscripts and Syriac *Disaster after*   [c] 11 Or *The violent one has become*

Let not the buyer rejoice
  nor the seller grieve,
  for my wrath is on the whole crowd.
13 The seller will not recover
  the property that was sold —
  as long as both buyer and seller live.
For the vision concerning the whole
    crowd
  will not be reversed.
Because of their sins, not one of them
  will preserve their life.

14 "'They have blown the trumpet,
  they have made all things ready,
  but no one will go into battle,
  for my wrath is on the whole crowd.
15 Outside is the sword;
  inside are plague and famine.
Those in the country
  will die by the sword;
those in the city
  will be devoured by famine and
    plague.
16 The fugitives who escape
  will flee to the mountains.
Like doves of the valleys,
  they will all moan,
  each for their own sins.
17 Every hand will go limp;
  every leg will be wet with urine.
18 They will put on sackcloth
  and be clothed with terror.
Every face will be covered with shame,
  and every head will be shaved.

19 "'They will throw their silver into the
    streets,
  and their gold will be treated as a
    thing unclean.
Their silver and gold
  will not be able to deliver them
  in the day of the LORD's wrath.
It will not satisfy their hunger
  or fill their stomachs,
  for it has caused them to stumble
    into sin.
20 They took pride in their beautiful
    jewelry
  and used it to make their detestable
    idols.

They made it into vile images;
  therefore I will make it a thing
    unclean for them.
21 I will give their wealth as plunder to
    foreigners
  and as loot to the wicked of the earth,
  who will defile it.
22 I will turn my face away from the
    people,
  and robbers will desecrate the place I
    treasure.
They will enter it
  and will defile it.

23 "'Prepare chains!
  For the land is full of bloodshed,
  and the city is full of violence.
24 I will bring the most wicked of nations
  to take possession of their houses.
I will put an end to the pride of the
    mighty,
  and their sanctuaries will be
    desecrated.
25 When terror comes,
  they will seek peace in vain.
26 Calamity upon calamity will come,
  and rumor upon rumor.
They will go searching for a vision from
    the prophet,
  priestly instruction in the law will
    cease,
  the counsel of the elders will come to
    an end.
27 The king will mourn,
  the prince will be clothed with
    despair,
  and the hands of the people of the
    land will tremble.
I will deal with them according to their
    conduct,
  and by their own standards I will
    judge them.

"'Then they will know that I am the LORD.'"

Idolatry in the Temple

8 In the sixth year, in the sixth month
on the fifth day, while I was sitting in my house and the elders of
Judah were sitting before me, the hand of

the Sovereign LORD came on me there. ²I looked, and I saw a figure like that of a man.*ᵃ* From what appeared to be his waist down he was like fire, and from there up his appearance was as bright as glowing metal. ³He stretched out what looked like a hand and took me by the hair of my head. The Spirit lifted me up between earth and heaven and in visions of God he took me to Jerusalem, to the entrance of the north gate of the inner court, where the idol that provokes to jealousy stood. ⁴And there before me was the glory of the God of Israel, as in the vision I had seen in the plain.

⁵Then he said to me, "Son of man, look toward the north." So I looked, and in the entrance north of the gate of the altar I saw this idol of jealousy.

⁶And he said to me, "Son of man, do you see what they are doing — the utterly detestable things the Israelites are doing here, things that will drive me far from my sanctuary? But you will see things that are even more detestable."

⁷Then he brought me to the entrance to the court. I looked, and I saw a hole in the wall. ⁸He said to me, "Son of man, now dig into the wall." So I dug into the wall and saw a doorway there.

⁹And he said to me, "Go in and see the wicked and detestable things they are doing here." ¹⁰So I went in and looked, and I saw portrayed all over the walls all kinds of crawling things and unclean animals and all the idols of Israel. ¹¹In front of them stood seventy elders of Israel, and Jaazaniah son of Shaphan was standing among them. Each had a censer in his hand, and a fragrant cloud of incense was rising.

¹²He said to me, "Son of man, have you seen what the elders of Israel are doing in the darkness, each at the shrine of his own idol? They say, 'The LORD does not see us; the LORD has forsaken the land.'" ¹³Again, he said, "You will see them doing things that are even more detestable."

¹⁴Then he brought me to the entrance of the north gate of the house of the LORD, and I saw women sitting there, mourning the god Tammuz. ¹⁵He said to me, "Do you see this, son of man? You will see things that are even more detestable than this."

¹⁶He then brought me into the inner court of the house of the LORD, and there at the entrance to the temple, between the portico and the altar, were about twenty-five men. With their backs toward the temple of the LORD and their faces toward the east, they were bowing down to the sun in the east.

¹⁷He said to me, "Have you seen this, son of man? Is it a trivial matter for the people of Judah to do the detestable things they are doing here? Must they also fill the land with violence and continually arouse my anger? Look at them putting the branch to their nose! ¹⁸Therefore I will deal with them in anger; I will not look on them with pity or spare them. Although they shout in my ears, I will not listen to them."

Judgment on the Idolaters

9 Then I heard him call out in a loud voice, "Bring near those who are appointed to execute judgment on the city, each with a weapon in his hand." ²And I saw six men coming from the direction of the upper gate, which faces north, each with a deadly weapon in his hand. With them was a man clothed in linen who had a writing kit at his side. They came in and stood beside the bronze altar.

³Now the glory of the God of Israel went up from above the cherubim, where it had been, and moved to the threshold of the temple. Then the LORD called to the man clothed in linen who had the writing kit at his side ⁴and said to him, "Go throughout the city of Jerusalem and put a mark on the foreheads of those who grieve and lament over all the detestable things that are done in it."

⁵As I listened, he said to the others, "Follow him through the city and kill, without

---

ᵃ 2 Or saw a fiery figure

showing pity or compassion. ⁶Slaughter the old men, the young men and women, the mothers and children, but do not touch anyone who has the mark. Begin at my sanctuary." So they began with the old men who were in front of the temple.

⁷Then he said to them, "Defile the temple and fill the courts with the slain. Go!" So they went out and began killing throughout the city. ⁸While they were killing and I was left alone, I fell facedown, crying out, "Alas, Sovereign Lord! Are you going to destroy the entire remnant of Israel in this outpouring of your wrath on Jerusalem?"

⁹He answered me, "The sin of the people of Israel and Judah is exceedingly great; the land is full of bloodshed and the city is full of injustice. They say, 'The Lord has forsaken the land; the Lord does not see.' ¹⁰So I will not look on them with pity or spare them, but I will bring down on their own heads what they have done."

¹¹Then the man in linen with the writing kit at his side brought back word, saying, "I have done as you commanded."

God's Glory Departs From the Temple

10 I looked, and I saw the likeness of a throne of lapis lazuli above the vault that was over the heads of the cherubim. ²The Lord said to the man clothed in linen, "Go in among the wheels beneath the cherubim. Fill your hands with burning coals from among the cherubim and scatter them over the city." And as I watched, he went in.

³Now the cherubim were standing on the south side of the temple when the man went in, and a cloud filled the inner court. ⁴Then the glory of the Lord rose from above the cherubim and moved to the threshold of the temple. The cloud filled the temple, and the court was full of the radiance of the glory of the Lord. ⁵The sound of the wings of the cherubim could be heard as far away as the outer court, like the voice of God Almighty*a* when he speaks.

⁶When the Lord commanded the man in linen, "Take fire from among the wheels, from among the cherubim," the man went in and stood beside a wheel. ⁷Then one of the cherubim reached out his hand to the fire that was among them. He took up some of it and put it into the hands of the man in linen, who took it and went out. ⁸(Under the wings of the cherubim could be seen what looked like human hands.)

⁹I looked, and I saw beside the cherubim four wheels, one beside each of the cherubim; the wheels sparkled like topaz. ¹⁰As for their appearance, the four of them looked alike; each was like a wheel intersecting a wheel. ¹¹As they moved, they would go in any one of the four directions the cherubim faced; the wheels did not turn about*b* as the cherubim went. The cherubim went in whatever direction the head faced, without turning as they went. ¹²Their entire bodies, including their backs, their hands and their wings, were completely full of eyes, as were their four wheels. ¹³I heard the wheels being called "the whirling wheels." ¹⁴Each of the cherubim had four faces: One face was that of a cherub, the second the face of a human being, the third the face of a lion, and the fourth the face of an eagle.

¹⁵Then the cherubim rose upward. These were the living creatures I had seen by the Kebar River. ¹⁶When the cherubim moved, the wheels beside them moved; and when the cherubim spread their wings to rise from the ground, the wheels did not leave their side. ¹⁷When the cherubim stood still, they also stood still; and when the cherubim rose, they rose with them, because the spirit of the living creatures was in them.

¹⁸Then the glory of the Lord departed from over the threshold of the temple and stopped above the cherubim. ¹⁹While I watched, the cherubim spread their wings and rose from the ground, and as they went, the wheels went with them. They stopped at the entrance of the east gate of

---

a 5 Hebrew *El-Shaddai*   *b 11* Or *aside*

the Lord's house, and the glory of the God of Israel was above them.

²⁰These were the living creatures I had seen beneath the God of Israel by the Kebar River, and I realized that they were cherubim. ²¹Each had four faces and four wings, and under their wings was what looked like human hands. ²²Their faces had the same appearance as those I had seen by the Kebar River. Each one went straight ahead.

God's Sure Judgment on Jerusalem

11 Then the Spirit lifted me up and brought me to the gate of the house of the Lord that faces east. There at the entrance of the gate were twenty-five men, and I saw among them Jaazaniah son of Azzur and Pelatiah son of Benaiah, leaders of the people. ²The Lord said to me, "Son of man, these are the men who are plotting evil and giving wicked advice in this city. ³They say, 'Haven't our houses been recently rebuilt? This city is a pot, and we are the meat in it.' ⁴Therefore prophesy against them; prophesy, son of man."

⁵Then the Spirit of the Lord came on me, and he told me to say: "This is what the Lord says: That is what you are saying, you leaders in Israel, but I know what is going through your mind. ⁶You have killed many people in this city and filled its streets with the dead.

⁷"Therefore this is what the Sovereign Lord says: The bodies you have thrown there are the meat and this city is the pot, but I will drive you out of it. ⁸You fear the sword, and the sword is what I will bring against you, declares the Sovereign Lord. ⁹I will drive you out of the city and deliver you into the hands of foreigners and inflict punishment on you. ¹⁰You will fall by the sword, and I will execute judgment on you at the borders of Israel. Then you will know that I am the Lord. ¹¹This city will not be a pot for you, nor will you be the meat in it; I will execute judgment on you at the borders of Israel. ¹²And you will

know that I am the Lord, for you have not followed my decrees or kept my laws but have conformed to the standards of the nations around you."

¹³Now as I was prophesying, Pelatiah son of Benaiah died. Then I fell facedown and cried out in a loud voice, "Alas, Sovereign Lord! Will you completely destroy the remnant of Israel?"

The Promise of Israel's Return

¹⁴The word of the Lord came to me: ¹⁵"Son of man, the people of Jerusalem have said of your fellow exiles and all the other Israelites, 'They are far away from the Lord; this land was given to us as our possession.'

¹⁶"Therefore say: 'This is what the Sovereign Lord says: Although I sent them far away among the nations and scattered them among the countries, yet for a little while I have been a sanctuary for them in the countries where they have gone.'

¹⁷"Therefore say: 'This is what the Sovereign Lord says: I will gather you from the nations and bring you back from the countries where you have been scattered, and I will give you back the land of Israel again.'

¹⁸"They will return to it and remove all its vile images and detestable idols. ¹⁹I will give them an undivided heart and put a new spirit in them; I will remove from them their heart of stone and give them a heart of flesh. ²⁰Then they will follow my decrees and be careful to keep my laws. They will be my people, and I will be their God. ²¹But as for those whose hearts are devoted to their vile images and detestable idols, I will bring down on their own heads what they have done, declares the Sovereign Lord."

²²Then the cherubim, with the wheels beside them, spread their wings, and the glory of the God of Israel was above them. ²³The glory of the Lord went up from within the city and stopped above the mountain east of it. ²⁴The Spirit lifted me up and brought me to the exiles in Babylonia*ᵃ* in the vision given by the Spirit of God.

ᵃ 24 Or *Chaldea*

Then the vision I had seen went up from me, 25and I told the exiles everything the LORD had shown me.

The Exile Symbolized

12 The word of the LORD came to me: 2"Son of man, you are living among a rebellious people. They have eyes to see but do not see and ears to hear but do not hear, for they are a rebellious people.

3"Therefore, son of man, pack your belongings for exile and in the daytime, as they watch, set out and go from where you are to another place. Perhaps they will understand, though they are a rebellious people. 4During the daytime, while they watch, bring out your belongings packed for exile. Then in the evening, while they are watching, go out like those who go into exile. 5While they watch, dig through the wall and take your belongings out through it. 6Put them on your shoulder as they are watching and carry them out at dusk. Cover your face so that you cannot see the land, for I have made you a sign to the Israelites."

7So I did as I was commanded. During the day I brought out my things packed for exile. Then in the evening I dug through the wall with my hands. I took my belongings out at dusk, carrying them on my shoulders while they watched.

8In the morning the word of the LORD came to me: 9"Son of man, did not the Israelites, that rebellious people, ask you, 'What are you doing?'

10"Say to them, 'This is what the Sovereign LORD says: This prophecy concerns the prince in Jerusalem and all the Israelites who are there.' 11Say to them, 'I am a sign to you.'

"As I have done, so it will be done to them. They will go into exile as captives.

12"The prince among them will put his things on his shoulder at dusk and leave, and a hole will be dug in the wall for him to go through. He will cover his face so that he cannot see the land. 13I will spread my net for him, and he will be caught in my snare; I will bring him to Babylonia, the land of the Chaldeans, but he will not see it, and there he will die. 14I will scatter to the winds all those around him — his staff and all his troops — and I will pursue them with drawn sword.

15"They will know that I am the LORD, when I disperse them among the nations and scatter them through the countries. 16But I will spare a few of them from the sword, famine and plague, so that in the nations where they go they may acknowledge all their detestable practices. Then they will know that I am the LORD."

17The word of the LORD came to me: 18"Son of man, tremble as you eat your food, and shudder in fear as you drink your water. 19Say to the people of the land: 'This is what the Sovereign LORD says about those living in Jerusalem and in the land of Israel: They will eat their food in anxiety and drink their water in despair, for their land will be stripped of everything in it because of the violence of all who live there. 20The inhabited towns will be laid waste and the land will be desolate. Then you will know that I am the LORD.'"

There Will Be No Delay

21The word of the LORD came to me: 22"Son of man, what is this proverb you have in the land of Israel: 'The days go by and every vision comes to nothing'? 23Say to them, 'This is what the Sovereign LORD says: I am going to put an end to this proverb, and they will no longer quote it in Israel.' Say to them, 'The days are near when every vision will be fulfilled. 24For there will be no more false visions or flattering divinations among the people of Israel. 25But I the LORD will speak what I will, and it shall be fulfilled without delay. For in your days, you rebellious people, I will fulfill whatever I say, declares the Sovereign LORD.'"

26The word of the LORD came to me: 27"Son of man, the Israelites are saying, 'The vision he sees is for many years from now, and he prophesies about the distant future.'

²⁸"Therefore say to them, 'This is what the Sovereign LORD says: None of my words will be delayed any longer; whatever I say will be fulfilled, declares the Sovereign LORD.'"

False Prophets Condemned

13 The word of the LORD came to me: ²"Son of man, prophesy against the prophets of Israel who are now prophesying. Say to those who prophesy out of their own imagination: 'Hear the word of the LORD! ³This is what the Sovereign LORD says: Woe to the foolish*a* prophets who follow their own spirit and have seen nothing! ⁴Your prophets, Israel, are like jackals among ruins. ⁵You have not gone up to the breaches in the wall to repair it for the people of Israel so that it will stand firm in the battle on the day of the LORD. ⁶Their visions are false and their divinations a lie. Even though the LORD has not sent them, they say, "The LORD declares," and expect him to fulfill their words. ⁷Have you not seen false visions and uttered lying divinations when you say, "The LORD declares," though I have not spoken?

⁸"'Therefore this is what the Sovereign LORD says: Because of your false words and lying visions, I am against you, declares the Sovereign LORD. ⁹My hand will be against the prophets who see false visions and utter lying divinations. They will not belong to the council of my people or be listed in the records of Israel, nor will they enter the land of Israel. Then you will know that I am the Sovereign LORD.

¹⁰"'Because they lead my people astray, saying, "Peace," when there is no peace, and because, when a flimsy wall is built, they cover it with whitewash, ¹¹therefore tell those who cover it with whitewash that it is going to fall. Rain will come in torrents, and I will send hailstones hurtling down, and violent winds will burst forth. ¹²When the wall collapses, will people not ask you, "Where is the whitewash you covered it with?"

¹³"'Therefore this is what the Sovereign LORD says: In my wrath I will unleash a violent wind, and in my anger hailstones and torrents of rain will fall with destructive fury. ¹⁴I will tear down the wall you have covered with whitewash and will level it to the ground so that its foundation will be laid bare. When it*b* falls, you will be destroyed in it; and you will know that I am the LORD. ¹⁵So I will pour out my wrath against the wall and against those who covered it with whitewash. I will say to you, "The wall is gone and so are those who whitewashed it, ¹⁶those prophets of Israel who prophesied to Jerusalem and saw visions of peace for her when there was no peace, declares the Sovereign LORD."'

¹⁷"Now, son of man, set your face against the daughters of your people who prophesy out of their own imagination. Prophesy against them ¹⁸and say, 'This is what the Sovereign LORD says: Woe to the women who sew magic charms on all their wrists and make veils of various lengths for their heads in order to ensnare people. Will you ensnare the lives of my people but preserve your own? ¹⁹You have profaned me among my people for a few handfuls of barley and scraps of bread. By lying to my people, who listen to lies, you have killed those who should not have died and have spared those who should not live.

²⁰"'Therefore this is what the Sovereign LORD says: I am against your magic charms with which you ensnare people like birds and I will tear them from your arms; I will set free the people that you ensnare like birds. ²¹I will tear off your veils and save my people from your hands, and they will no longer fall prey to your power. Then you will know that I am the LORD. ²²Because you disheartened the righteous with your lies, when I had brought them no grief, and because you encouraged the wicked not to turn from their evil ways and so save their

---

a 3 Or wicked *b 14 Or the city*

lives, 23therefore you will no longer see false visions or practice divination. I will save my people from your hands. And then you will know that I am the LORD.'"

Idolaters Condemned

14 Some of the elders of Israel came to me and sat down in front of me. 2Then the word of the LORD came to me: 3"Son of man, these men have set up idols in their hearts and put wicked stumbling blocks before their faces. Should I let them inquire of me at all? 4Therefore speak to them and tell them, 'This is what the Sovereign LORD says: When any of the Israelites set up idols in their hearts and put a wicked stumbling block before their faces and then go to a prophet, I the LORD will answer them myself in keeping with their great idolatry. 5I will do this to recapture the hearts of the people of Israel, who have all deserted me for their idols.'

6"Therefore say to the people of Israel, 'This is what the Sovereign LORD says: Repent! Turn from your idols and renounce all your detestable practices!

7"'When any of the Israelites or any foreigner residing in Israel separate themselves from me and set up idols in their hearts and put a wicked stumbling block before their faces and then go to a prophet to inquire of me, I the LORD will answer them myself. 8I will set my face against them and make them an example and a byword. I will remove them from my people. Then you will know that I am the LORD.

9"'And if the prophet is enticed to utter a prophecy, I the LORD have enticed that prophet, and I will stretch out my hand against him and destroy him from among my people Israel. 10They will bear their guilt — the prophet will be as guilty as the one who consults him. 11Then the people of Israel will no longer stray from me, nor will they defile themselves anymore with all their sins. They will be my people, and I will be their God, declares the Sovereign LORD.'"

Jerusalem's Judgment Inescapable

12The word of the LORD came to me: 13"Son of man, if a country sins against me by being unfaithful and I stretch out my hand against it to cut off its food supply and send famine upon it and kill its people and their animals, 14even if these three men — Noah, Daniel[a] and Job — were in it, they could save only themselves by their righteousness, declares the Sovereign LORD.

15"Or if I send wild beasts through that country and they leave it childless and it becomes desolate so that no one can pass through it because of the beasts, 16as surely as I live, declares the Sovereign LORD, even if these three men were in it, they could not save their own sons or daughters. They alone would be saved, but the land would be desolate.

17"Or if I bring a sword against that country and say, 'Let the sword pass throughout the land,' and I kill its people and their animals, 18as surely as I live, declares the Sovereign LORD, even if these three men were in it, they could not save their own sons or daughters. They alone would be saved.

19"Or if I send a plague into that land and pour out my wrath on it through bloodshed, killing its people and their animals, 20as surely as I live, declares the Sovereign LORD, even if Noah, Daniel and Job were in it, they could save neither son nor daughter. They would save only themselves by their righteousness.

21"For this is what the Sovereign LORD says: How much worse will it be when I send against Jerusalem my four dreadful judgments — sword and famine and wild beasts and plague — to kill its men and their animals! 22Yet there will be some survivors — sons and daughters who will be brought out of it. They will come to you, and when you see their conduct and their actions, you will be consoled regarding the disaster I have brought on Jerusalem — every disaster I have brought on it. 23You will be consoled when you see their conduct

---

a 14 Or *Danel,* a man of renown in ancient literature; also in verse 20 and their actions, for you will know that I have done nothing in it without cause, declares the Sovereign Lord."

Jerusalem as a Useless Vine

15 The word of the Lord came to me: ²"Son of man, how is the wood of a vine different from that of a branch from any of the trees in the forest? ³Is wood ever taken from it to make anything useful? Do they make pegs from it to hang things on? ⁴And after it is thrown on the fire as fuel and the fire burns both ends and chars the middle, is it then useful for anything? ⁵If it was not useful for anything when it was whole, how much less can it be made into something useful when the fire has burned it and it is charred?

⁶"Therefore this is what the Sovereign Lord says: As I have given the wood of the vine among the trees of the forest as fuel for the fire, so will I treat the people living in Jerusalem. ⁷I will set my face against them. Although they have come out of the fire, the fire will yet consume them. And when I set my face against them, you will know that I am the Lord. ⁸I will make the land desolate because they have been unfaithful, declares the Sovereign Lord."

Jerusalem as an Adulterous Wife

16 The word of the Lord came to me: ²"Son of man, confront Jerusalem with her detestable practices ³and say, 'This is what the Sovereign Lord says to Jerusalem: Your ancestry and birth were in the land of the Canaanites; your father was an Amorite and your mother a Hittite. ⁴On the day you were born your cord was not cut, nor were you washed with water to make you clean, nor were you rubbed with salt or wrapped in cloths. ⁵No one looked on you with pity or had compassion enough to do any of these things for you. Rather, you were thrown out into the open field, for on the day you were born you were despised.

⁶"'Then I passed by and saw you kicking about in your blood, and as you lay there in your blood I said to you, "Live!"ᵃ ⁷I made you grow like a plant of the field. You grew and developed and entered puberty. Your breasts had formed and your hair had grown, yet you were stark naked.

⁸"'Later I passed by, and when I looked at you and saw that you were old enough for love, I spread the corner of my garment over you and covered your naked body. I gave you my solemn oath and entered into a covenant with you, declares the Sovereign Lord, and you became mine.

⁹"'I bathed you with water and washed the blood from you and put ointments on you. ¹⁰I clothed you with an embroidered dress and put sandals of fine leather on you. I dressed you in fine linen and covered you with costly garments. ¹¹I adorned you with jewelry: I put bracelets on your arms and a necklace around your neck, ¹²and I put a ring on your nose, earrings on your ears and a beautiful crown on your head. ¹³So you were adorned with gold and silver; your clothes were of fine linen and costly fabric and embroidered cloth. Your food was honey, olive oil and the finest flour. You became very beautiful and rose to be a queen. ¹⁴And your fame spread among the nations on account of your beauty, because the splendor I had given you made your beauty perfect, declares the Sovereign Lord.

¹⁵"'But you trusted in your beauty and used your fame to become a prostitute. You lavished your favors on anyone who passed by and your beauty became his. ¹⁶You took some of your garments to make gaudy high places, where you carried on your prostitution. You went to him, and he possessed your beauty.ᵇ ¹⁷You also took the fine jewelry I gave you, the jewelry made of my gold and silver, and you made for yourself male idols and engaged in prostitution with them. ¹⁸And you took your embroidered clothes to put on them, and you offered

---

ᵃ 6 A few Hebrew manuscripts, Septuagint and Syriac; most Hebrew manuscripts repeat *and as you lay there in your blood I said to you, "Live!"*   ᵇ 16 The meaning of the Hebrew for this sentence is uncertain.

my oil and incense before them. ¹⁹Also the food I provided for you — the flour, olive oil and honey I gave you to eat — you offered as fragrant incense before them. That is what happened, declares the Sovereign LORD.

²⁰"'And you took your sons and daughters whom you bore to me and sacrificed them as food to the idols. Was your prostitution not enough? ²¹You slaughtered my children and sacrificed them to the idols. ²²In all your detestable practices and your prostitution you did not remember the days of your youth, when you were naked and bare, kicking about in your blood.

²³"'Woe! Woe to you, declares the Sovereign LORD. In addition to all your other wickedness, ²⁴you built a mound for yourself and made a lofty shrine in every public square. ²⁵At every street corner you built your lofty shrines and degraded your beauty, spreading your legs with increasing promiscuity to anyone who passed by. ²⁶You engaged in prostitution with the Egyptians, your neighbors with large genitals, and aroused my anger with your increasing promiscuity. ²⁷So I stretched out my hand against you and reduced your territory; I gave you over to the greed of your enemies, the daughters of the Philistines, who were shocked by your lewd conduct. ²⁸You engaged in prostitution with the Assyrians too, because you were insatiable; and even after that, you still were not satisfied. ²⁹Then you increased your promiscuity to include Babylonia,ᵃ a land of merchants, but even with this you were not satisfied.

³⁰"'I am filled with fury against you,ᵇ declares the Sovereign LORD, when you do all these things, acting like a brazen prostitute! ³¹When you built your mounds at every street corner and made your lofty shrines in every public square, you were unlike a prostitute, because you scorned payment.

³²"'You adulterous wife! You prefer strangers to your own husband! ³³All prostitutes receive gifts, but you give gifts to all your lovers, bribing them to come to you from everywhere for your illicit favors. ³⁴So in your prostitution you are the opposite of others; no one runs after you for your favors. You are the very opposite, for you give payment and none is given to you.

³⁵"'Therefore, you prostitute, hear the word of the LORD! ³⁶This is what the Sovereign LORD says: Because you poured out your lust and exposed your naked body in your promiscuity with your lovers, and because of all your detestable idols, and because you gave them your children's blood, ³⁷therefore I am going to gather all your lovers, with whom you found pleasure, those you loved as well as those you hated. I will gather them against you from all around and will strip you in front of them, and they will see you stark naked. ³⁸I will sentence you to the punishment of women who commit adultery and who shed blood; I will bring on you the blood vengeance of my wrath and jealous anger. ³⁹Then I will deliver you into the hands of your lovers, and they will tear down your mounds and destroy your lofty shrines. They will strip you of your clothes and take your fine jewelry and leave you stark naked. ⁴⁰They will bring a mob against you, who will stone you and hack you to pieces with their swords. ⁴¹They will burn down your houses and inflict punishment on you in the sight of many women. I will put a stop to your prostitution, and you will no longer pay your lovers. ⁴²Then my wrath against you will subside and my jealous anger will turn away from you; I will be calm and no longer angry.

⁴³"'Because you did not remember the days of your youth but enraged me with all these things, I will surely bring down on your head what you have done, declares the Sovereign LORD. Did you not add lewdness to all your other detestable practices?

⁴⁴"'Everyone who quotes proverbs will quote this proverb about you: "Like mother,

---

ᵃ 29 Or Chaldea   ᵇ 30 Or How feverish is your heart,

like daughter." 45You are a true daughter of your mother, who despised her husband and her children; and you are a true sister of your sisters, who despised their husbands and their children. Your mother was a Hittite and your father an Amorite. 46Your older sister was Samaria, who lived to the north of you with her daughters; and your younger sister, who lived to the south of you with her daughters, was Sodom. 47You not only followed their ways and copied their detestable practices, but in all your ways you soon became more depraved than they. 48As surely as I live, declares the Sovereign LORD, your sister Sodom and her daughters never did what you and your daughters have done.

49"'Now this was the sin of your sister Sodom: She and her daughters were arrogant, overfed and unconcerned; they did not help the poor and needy. 50They were haughty and did detestable things before me. Therefore I did away with them as you have seen. 51Samaria did not commit half the sins you did. You have done more detestable things than they, and have made your sisters seem righteous by all these things you have done. 52Bear your disgrace, for you have furnished some justification for your sisters. Because your sins were more vile than theirs, they appear more righteous than you. So then, be ashamed and bear your disgrace, for you have made your sisters appear righteous.

53"'However, I will restore the fortunes of Sodom and her daughters and of Samaria and her daughters, and your fortunes along with them, 54so that you may bear your disgrace and be ashamed of all you have done in giving them comfort. 55And your sisters, Sodom with her daughters and Samaria with her daughters, will return to what they were before; and you and your daughters will return to what you were before. 56You would not even mention your sister Sodom in the day of your pride, 57before your wickedness was uncovered. Even so, you are now scorned by the daughters of Edom[a] and all her neighbors and the daughters of the Philistines — all those around you who despise you. 58You will bear the consequences of your lewdness and your detestable practices, declares the LORD.

59"'This is what the Sovereign LORD says: I will deal with you as you deserve, because you have despised my oath by breaking the covenant. 60Yet I will remember the covenant I made with you in the days of your youth, and I will establish an everlasting covenant with you. 61Then you will remember your ways and be ashamed when you receive your sisters, both those who are older than you and those who are younger. I will give them to you as daughters, but not on the basis of my covenant with you. 62So I will establish my covenant with you, and you will know that I am the LORD. 63Then, when I make atonement for you for all you have done, you will remember and be ashamed and never again open your mouth because of your humiliation, declares the Sovereign LORD.'"

Two Eagles and a Vine

17 The word of the LORD came to me: 2"Son of man, set forth an allegory and tell it to the Israelites as a parable. 3Say to them, 'This is what the Sovereign LORD says: A great eagle with powerful wings, long feathers and full plumage of varied colors came to Lebanon. Taking hold of the top of a cedar, 4he broke off its topmost shoot and carried it away to a land of merchants, where he planted it in a city of traders.

5"'He took one of the seedlings of the land and put it in fertile soil. He planted it like a willow by abundant water, 6and it sprouted and became a low, spreading vine. Its branches turned toward him, but its roots remained under it. So it became a vine and produced branches and put out leafy boughs.

7"'But there was another great eagle with

---

a 57 Many Hebrew manuscripts and Syriac; most Hebrew manuscripts, Septuagint and Vulgate *Aram* powerful wings and full plumage. The vine now sent out its roots toward him from the plot where it was planted and stretched out its branches to him for water. ⁸It had been planted in good soil by abundant water so that it would produce branches, bear fruit and become a splendid vine.'

⁹"Say to them, 'This is what the Sovereign Lord says: Will it thrive? Will it not be uprooted and stripped of its fruit so that it withers? All its new growth will wither. It will not take a strong arm or many people to pull it up by the roots. ¹⁰It has been planted, but will it thrive? Will it not wither completely when the east wind strikes it — wither away in the plot where it grew?'"

¹¹Then the word of the Lord came to me: ¹²"Say to this rebellious people, 'Do you not know what these things mean?' Say to them: 'The king of Babylon went to Jerusalem and carried off her king and her nobles, bringing them back with him to Babylon. ¹³Then he took a member of the royal family and made a treaty with him, putting him under oath. He also carried away the leading men of the land, ¹⁴so that the kingdom would be brought low, unable to rise again, surviving only by keeping his treaty. ¹⁵But the king rebelled against him by sending his envoys to Egypt to get horses and a large army. Will he succeed? Will he who does such things escape? Will he break the treaty and yet escape?

¹⁶"'As surely as I live, declares the Sovereign Lord, he shall die in Babylon, in the land of the king who put him on the throne, whose oath he despised and whose treaty he broke. ¹⁷Pharaoh with his mighty army and great horde will be of no help to him in war, when ramps are built and siege works erected to destroy many lives. ¹⁸He despised the oath by breaking the covenant. Because he had given his hand in pledge and yet did all these things, he shall not escape.

¹⁹"'Therefore this is what the Sovereign Lord says: As surely as I live, I will repay him for despising my oath and breaking my covenant. ²⁰I will spread my net for him, and he will be caught in my snare. I will bring him to Babylon and execute judgment on him there because he was unfaithful to me. ²¹All his choice troops will fall by the sword, and the survivors will be scattered to the winds. Then you will know that I the Lord have spoken.

²²"This is what the Sovereign Lord says: I myself will take a shoot from the very top of a cedar and plant it; I will break off a tender sprig from its topmost shoots and plant it on a high and lofty mountain. ²³On the mountain heights of Israel I will plant it; it will produce branches and bear fruit and become a splendid cedar. Birds of every kind will nest in it; they will find shelter in the shade of its branches. ²⁴All the trees of the forest will know that I the Lord bring down the tall tree and make the low tree grow tall. I dry up the green tree and make the dry tree flourish.

"'I the Lord have spoken, and I will do it.'"

The One Who Sins Will Die

18 The word of the Lord came to me: ²"What do you people mean by quoting this proverb about the land of Israel:

"'The parents eat sour grapes,
    and the children's teeth are set on
        edge'?

³"As surely as I live, declares the Sovereign Lord, you will no longer quote this proverb in Israel. ⁴For everyone belongs to me, the parent as well as the child — both alike belong to me. The one who sins is the one who will die.

⁵"Suppose there is a righteous man
    who does what is just and right.
⁶He does not eat at the mountain shrines
    or look to the idols of Israel.
He does not defile his neighbor's wife
    or have sexual relations with a
        woman during her period.
⁷He does not oppress anyone,
    but returns what he took in pledge
        for a loan.

He does not commit robbery
    but gives his food to the hungry
    and provides clothing for the naked.
8 He does not lend to them at interest
    or take a profit from them.
He withholds his hand from doing
      wrong
    and judges fairly between two
      parties.
9 He follows my decrees
    and faithfully keeps my laws.
That man is righteous;
    he will surely live,
          declares the Sovereign Lord.

10 "Suppose he has a violent son, who sheds blood or does any of these other things[a] 11 (though the father has done none of them):

"He eats at the mountain shrines.
He defiles his neighbor's wife.
12 He oppresses the poor and needy.
He commits robbery.
He does not return what he took in
    pledge.
He looks to the idols.
He does detestable things.
13 He lends at interest and takes a profit.

Will such a man live? He will not! Because he has done all these detestable things, he is to be put to death; his blood will be on his own head.

14 "But suppose this son has a son who sees all the sins his father commits, and though he sees them, he does not do such things:

15 "He does not eat at the mountain
      shrines
    or look to the idols of Israel.
He does not defile his neighbor's wife.
16 He does not oppress anyone
    or require a pledge for a loan.
He does not commit robbery
    but gives his food to the hungry
    and provides clothing for the
      naked.

17 He withholds his hand from
      mistreating the poor
    and takes no interest or profit from
      them.
He keeps my laws and follows my decrees.

He will not die for his father's sin; he will surely live. 18 But his father will die for his own sin, because he practiced extortion, robbed his brother and did what was wrong among his people.

19 "Yet you ask, 'Why does the son not share the guilt of his father?' Since the son has done what is just and right and has been careful to keep all my decrees, he will surely live. 20 The one who sins is the one who will die. The child will not share the guilt of the parent, nor will the parent share the guilt of the child. The righteousness of the righteous will be credited to them, and the wickedness of the wicked will be charged against them.

21 "But if a wicked person turns away from all the sins they have committed and keeps all my decrees and does what is just and right, that person will surely live; they will not die. 22 None of the offenses they have committed will be remembered against them. Because of the righteous things they have done, they will live. 23 Do I take any pleasure in the death of the wicked? declares the Sovereign Lord. Rather, am I not pleased when they turn from their ways and live?

24 "But if a righteous person turns from their righteousness and commits sin and does the same detestable things the wicked person does, will they live? None of the righteous things that person has done will be remembered. Because of the unfaithfulness they are guilty of and because of the sins they have committed, they will die.

25 "Yet you say, 'The way of the Lord is not just.' Hear, you Israelites: Is my way unjust? Is it not your ways that are unjust? 26 If a righteous person turns from their righteousness and commits sin, they will die

---

a 10 Or things to a brother

for it; because of the sin they have committed they will die. ²⁷But if a wicked person turns away from the wickedness they have committed and does what is just and right, they will save their life. ²⁸Because they consider all the offenses they have committed and turn away from them, that person will surely live; they will not die. ²⁹Yet the Israelites say, 'The way of the Lord is not just.' Are my ways unjust, people of Israel? Is it not your ways that are unjust?

³⁰"Therefore, you Israelites, I will judge each of you according to your own ways, declares the Sovereign LORD. Repent! Turn away from all your offenses; then sin will not be your downfall. ³¹Rid yourselves of all the offenses you have committed, and get a new heart and a new spirit. Why will you die, people of Israel? ³²For I take no pleasure in the death of anyone, declares the Sovereign LORD. Repent and live!

A Lament Over Israel's Princes

19 "Take up a lament concerning the princes of Israel ²and say:

"'What a lioness was your mother
    among the lions!
She lay down among them
    and reared her cubs.
³ She brought up one of her cubs,
    and he became a strong lion.
He learned to tear the prey
    and he became a man-eater.
⁴ The nations heard about him,
    and he was trapped in their pit.
They led him with hooks
    to the land of Egypt.

⁵ "'When she saw her hope unfulfilled,
    her expectation gone,
she took another of her cubs
    and made him a strong lion.
⁶ He prowled among the lions,
    for he was now a strong lion.
He learned to tear the prey
    and he became a man-eater.

⁷ He broke down*a* their strongholds
    and devastated their towns.
The land and all who were in it
    were terrified by his roaring.
⁸ Then the nations came against him,
    those from regions round about.
They spread their net for him,
    and he was trapped in their pit.
⁹ With hooks they pulled him into a cage
    and brought him to the king of
        Babylon.
They put him in prison,
    so his roar was heard no longer
    on the mountains of Israel.

¹⁰ "'Your mother was like a vine in your
        vineyard*b*
    planted by the water;
it was fruitful and full of branches
    because of abundant water.
¹¹ Its branches were strong,
    fit for a ruler's scepter.
It towered high
    above the thick foliage,
conspicuous for its height
    and for its many branches.
¹² But it was uprooted in fury
    and thrown to the ground.
The east wind made it shrivel,
    it was stripped of its fruit;
its strong branches withered
    and fire consumed them.
¹³ Now it is planted in the desert,
    in a dry and thirsty land.
¹⁴ Fire spread from one of its main*c*
        branches
    and consumed its fruit.
No strong branch is left on it
    fit for a ruler's scepter.'

"This is a lament and is to be used as a lament."

Rebellious Israel Purged

20 In the seventh year, in the fifth month on the tenth day, some of the elders of Israel came to

---

a 7 Targum (see Septuagint); Hebrew *He knew blood*   *b 10* Two Hebrew manuscripts; most Hebrew manuscripts *your*   *c 14* Or *from under its*

Turn Lesson [*Principle Three*]

For the previous entry in the TURN lesson, go to Proverbs 3:5 – 6 (page 743).

For a discussion of Principles One through Eight and a listing of their related lessons, go to pages xvii – xliv.

> *Therefore, you Israelites, I will judge each of you according*
> *to your own ways, declares the Sovereign LORD. Repent!*
> *Turn away from all your offenses; then sin will not be*
> *your downfall. Rid yourselves of all the offenses you have committed,*
> *and get a new heart and a new spirit. Why will you die,*
> *people of Israel? For I take no pleasure in the death of anyone,*
> *declares the Sovereign LORD. Repent and live!"*

EZEKIEL 18:30–32

In Principle Three we consciously choose to commit all our lives and will to Christ's care and control. We make the decision to TURN over every aspect of our lives and will to our Higher Power, Jesus Christ. This principle ends with us having a new life, but first we need to trust, understand and repent.

The third letter in TURN, *R*, stands for REPENT. Some people approach repentance by thanking the Lord that they aren't as bad as their neighbors. (In Luke 18:9 – 14 Jesus tells his disciples a story about someone like this.) But that's not true repentance. Repentance is a turn in the road; it allows us to enjoy the freedom of our loving relationship with God. True repentance affects our whole person and changes our entire view of life. Repentance is all about seeing our lives from God's point of view instead of from our own.

To truly repent we need to do two things. We need to turn away from our sins, and we need to turn toward God. The Bible has a lot to say about repentance. Some examples:

> *"The time has come," [Jesus] said.*
> *"The kingdom of God has come near.*
> *Repent and believe the good news!"*

MARK 1:15

> *Do not conform to the pattern of this world,*
> *but be transformed by the renewing of your mind. Then you*
> *will be able to test and approve what God's will is —*
> *his good, pleasing and perfect will.*

ROMANS 12:2

Repentance isn't self-loathing; it's God-loving. God isn't looking forward to punishing us. He's standing beside us with open arms, eagerly waiting for us to turn in his direction.

The last letter in TURN is *N*. Go to 2 Corinthians 5:17 (page 1442).

inquire of the LORD, and they sat down in front of me.

²Then the word of the LORD came to me: ³"Son of man, speak to the elders of Israel and say to them, 'This is what the Sovereign LORD says: Have you come to inquire of me? As surely as I live, I will not let you inquire of me, declares the Sovereign LORD.'

⁴"Will you judge them? Will you judge them, son of man? Then confront them with the detestable practices of their ancestors ⁵and say to them: 'This is what the Sovereign LORD says: On the day I chose Israel, I swore with uplifted hand to the descendants of Jacob and revealed myself to them in Egypt. With uplifted hand I said to them, "I am the LORD your God." ⁶On that day I swore to them that I would bring them out of Egypt into a land I had searched out for them, a land flowing with milk and honey, the most beautiful of all lands. ⁷And I said to them, "Each of you, get rid of the vile images you have set your eyes on, and do not defile yourselves with the idols of Egypt. I am the LORD your God."

⁸" 'But they rebelled against me and would not listen to me; they did not get rid of the vile images they had set their eyes on, nor did they forsake the idols of Egypt. So I said I would pour out my wrath on them and spend my anger against them in Egypt. ⁹But for the sake of my name, I brought them out of Egypt. I did it to keep my name from being profaned in the eyes of the nations among whom they lived and in whose sight I had revealed myself to the Israelites. ¹⁰Therefore I led them out of Egypt and brought them into the wilderness. ¹¹I gave them my decrees and made known to them my laws, by which the person who obeys them will live. ¹²Also I gave them my Sabbaths as a sign between us, so they would know that I the LORD made them holy.

¹³" 'Yet the people of Israel rebelled against me in the wilderness. They did not follow my decrees but rejected my laws — by which the person who obeys them will live — and they utterly desecrated my Sab-

baths. So I said I would pour out my wrath on them and destroy them in the wilderness. ¹⁴But for the sake of my name I did what would keep it from being profaned in the eyes of the nations in whose sight I had brought them out. ¹⁵Also with uplifted hand I swore to them in the wilderness that I would not bring them into the land I had given them — a land flowing with milk and honey, the most beautiful of all lands — ¹⁶because they rejected my laws and did not follow my decrees and desecrated my Sabbaths. For their hearts were devoted to their idols. ¹⁷Yet I looked on them with pity and did not destroy them or put an end to them in the wilderness. ¹⁸I said to their children in the wilderness, "Do not follow the statutes of your parents or keep their laws or defile yourselves with their idols. ¹⁹I am the LORD your God; follow my decrees and be careful to keep my laws. ²⁰Keep my Sabbaths holy, that they may be a sign between us. Then you will know that I am the LORD your God."

²¹" 'But the children rebelled against me: They did not follow my decrees, they were not careful to keep my laws, of which I said, "The person who obeys them will live by them," and they desecrated my Sabbaths. So I said I would pour out my wrath on them and spend my anger against them in the wilderness. ²²But I withheld my hand, and for the sake of my name I did what would keep it from being profaned in the eyes of the nations in whose sight I had brought them out. ²³Also with uplifted hand I swore to them in the wilderness that I would disperse them among the nations and scatter them through the countries, ²⁴because they had not obeyed my laws but had rejected my decrees and desecrated my Sabbaths, and their eyes lusted after their parents' idols. ²⁵So I gave them other statutes that were not good and laws through which they could not live; ²⁶I defiled them through their gifts — the sacrifice of every firstborn — that I might fill them with horror so they would know that I am the LORD.'

²⁷"Therefore, son of man, speak to the people of Israel and say to them, 'This is what the Sovereign LORD says: In this also your ancestors blasphemed me by being unfaithful to me: ²⁸When I brought them into the land I had sworn to give them and they saw any high hill or any leafy tree, there they offered their sacrifices, made offerings that aroused my anger, presented their fragrant incense and poured out their drink offerings. ²⁹Then I said to them: What is this high place you go to?'" (It is called Bamah^a to this day.)

Rebellious Israel Renewed

³⁰"Therefore say to the Israelites: 'This is what the Sovereign LORD says: Will you defile yourselves the way your ancestors did and lust after their vile images? ³¹When you offer your gifts — the sacrifice of your children in the fire — you continue to defile yourselves with all your idols to this day. Am I to let you inquire of me, you Israelites? As surely as I live, declares the Sovereign LORD, I will not let you inquire of me.

³²"'You say, "We want to be like the nations, like the peoples of the world, who serve wood and stone." But what you have in mind will never happen. ³³As surely as I live, declares the Sovereign LORD, I will reign over you with a mighty hand and an outstretched arm and with outpoured wrath. ³⁴I will bring you from the nations and gather you from the countries where you have been scattered — with a mighty hand and an outstretched arm and with outpoured wrath. ³⁵I will bring you into the wilderness of the nations and there, face to face, I will execute judgment upon you. ³⁶As I judged your ancestors in the wilderness of the land of Egypt, so I will judge you, declares the Sovereign LORD. ³⁷I will take note of you as you pass under my rod, and I will bring you into the bond of the covenant. ³⁸I will purge you of those who revolt and rebel against me. Although I will bring them out of the land where they

are living, yet they will not enter the land of Israel. Then you will know that I am the LORD.

³⁹"'As for you, people of Israel, this is what the Sovereign LORD says: Go and serve your idols, every one of you! But afterward you will surely listen to me and no longer profane my holy name with your gifts and idols. ⁴⁰For on my holy mountain, the high mountain of Israel, declares the Sovereign LORD, there in the land all the people of Israel will serve me, and there I will accept them. There I will require your offerings and your choice gifts,^b along with all your holy sacrifices. ⁴¹I will accept you as fragrant incense when I bring you out from the nations and gather you from the countries where you have been scattered, and I will be proved holy through you in the sight of the nations. ⁴²Then you will know that I am the LORD, when I bring you into the land of Israel, the land I had sworn with uplifted hand to give to your ancestors. ⁴³There you will remember your conduct and all the actions by which you have defiled yourselves, and you will loathe yourselves for all the evil you have done. ⁴⁴You will know that I am the LORD, when I deal with you for my name's sake and not according to your evil ways and your corrupt practices, you people of Israel, declares the Sovereign LORD.'"

Prophecy Against the South

⁴⁵The word of the LORD came to me: ⁴⁶"Son of man, set your face toward the south; preach against the south and prophesy against the forest of the southland. ⁴⁷Say to the southern forest: 'Hear the word of the LORD. This is what the Sovereign LORD says: I am about to set fire to you, and it will consume all your trees, both green and dry. The blazing flame will not be quenched, and every face from south to north will be scorched by it. ⁴⁸Everyone will see that I the LORD have kindled it; it will not be quenched.'"

---

^a 29 Bamah means high place.   ^b 40 Or and the gifts of your firstfruits

⁴⁹Then I said, "Sovereign LORD, they are saying of me, 'Isn't he just telling parables?'"ᵃ

Babylon as God's Sword of Judgment

21 ᵇ The word of the LORD came to me: ²"Son of man, set your face against Jerusalem and preach against the sanctuary. Prophesy against the land of Israel ³and say to her: 'This is what the LORD says: I am against you. I will draw my sword from its sheath and cut off from you both the righteous and the wicked. ⁴Because I am going to cut off the righteous and the wicked, my sword will be unsheathed against everyone from south to north. ⁵Then all people will know that I the LORD have drawn my sword from its sheath; it will not return again.'

⁶"Therefore groan, son of man! Groan before them with broken heart and bitter grief. ⁷And when they ask you, 'Why are you groaning?' you shall say, 'Because of the news that is coming. Every heart will melt with fear and every hand go limp; every spirit will become faint and every leg will be wet with urine.' It is coming! It will surely take place, declares the Sovereign LORD."

⁸The word of the LORD came to me: ⁹"Son of man, prophesy and say, 'This is what the Lord says:

"'A sword, a sword,
    sharpened and polished —
¹⁰sharpened for the slaughter,
    polished to flash like lightning!

"'Shall we rejoice in the scepter of my royal son? The sword despises every such stick.

¹¹"'The sword is appointed to be
        polished,
    to be grasped with the hand;
it is sharpened and polished,
    made ready for the hand of the
        slayer.

¹²Cry out and wail, son of man,
    for it is against my people;
    it is against all the princes of Israel.
They are thrown to the sword
    along with my people.
Therefore beat your breast.

¹³"'Testing will surely come. And what if even the scepter, which the sword despises, does not continue? declares the Sovereign LORD.'

¹⁴"So then, son of man, prophesy
    and strike your hands together.
Let the sword strike twice,
    even three times.
It is a sword for slaughter —
    a sword for great slaughter,
    closing in on them from every side.
¹⁵So that hearts may melt with fear
    and the fallen be many,
I have stationed the sword for slaughterᶜ
    at all their gates.
Look! It is forged to strike like
        lightning,
    it is grasped for slaughter.
¹⁶Slash to the right, you sword,
    then to the left,
    wherever your blade is turned.
¹⁷I too will strike my hands together,
    and my wrath will subside.
I the LORD have spoken."

¹⁸The word of the LORD came to me: ¹⁹"Son of man, mark out two roads for the sword of the king of Babylon to take, both starting from the same country. Make a signpost where the road branches off to the city. ²⁰Mark out one road for the sword to come against Rabbah of the Ammonites and another against Judah and fortified Jerusalem. ²¹For the king of Babylon will stop at the fork in the road, at the junction of the two roads, to seek an omen: He will cast lots with arrows, he will consult his idols, he will examine the liver. ²²Into his right hand will come the lot for Jerusalem, where he is to set up battering rams,

---

ᵃ 49 In Hebrew texts 20:45-49 is numbered 21:1-5.   ᵇ In Hebrew texts 21:1-32 is numbered 21:6-37.
ᶜ 15 Septuagint; the meaning of the Hebrew for this word is uncertain.

to give the command to slaughter, to sound the battle cry, to set battering rams against the gates, to build a ramp and to erect siege works. 23It will seem like a false omen to those who have sworn allegiance to him, but he will remind them of their guilt and take them captive.

24"Therefore this is what the Sovereign LORD says: 'Because you people have brought to mind your guilt by your open rebellion, revealing your sins in all that you do — because you have done this, you will be taken captive.

25"'You profane and wicked prince of Israel, whose day has come, whose time of punishment has reached its climax, 26this is what the Sovereign LORD says: Take off the turban, remove the crown. It will not be as it was: The lowly will be exalted and the exalted will be brought low. 27A ruin! A ruin! I will make it a ruin! The crown will not be restored until he to whom it rightfully belongs shall come; to him I will give it.'

28"And you, son of man, prophesy and say, 'This is what the Sovereign LORD says about the Ammonites and their insults:

"'A sword, a sword,
    drawn for the slaughter,
polished to consume
    and to flash like lightning!
29Despite false visions concerning you
    and lying divinations about you,
it will be laid on the necks
    of the wicked who are to be slain,
whose day has come,
    whose time of punishment has
        reached its climax.

30"'Let the sword return to its sheath.
    In the place where you were created,
in the land of your ancestry,
    I will judge you.
31I will pour out my wrath on you
    and breathe out my fiery anger
        against you;
I will deliver you into the hands of
        brutal men,
    men skilled in destruction.

32You will be fuel for the fire,
    your blood will be shed in your land,
you will be remembered no more;
    for I the LORD have spoken.'"

Judgment on Jerusalem's Sins

22 The word of the LORD came to me:

2"Son of man, will you judge her? Will you judge this city of bloodshed? Then confront her with all her detestable practices 3and say: 'This is what the Sovereign LORD says: You city that brings on herself doom by shedding blood in her midst and defiles herself by making idols, 4you have become guilty because of the blood you have shed and have become defiled by the idols you have made. You have brought your days to a close, and the end of your years has come. Therefore I will make you an object of scorn to the nations and a laughingstock to all the countries. 5Those who are near and those who are far away will mock you, you infamous city, full of turmoil.

6"'See how each of the princes of Israel who are in you uses his power to shed blood. 7In you they have treated father and mother with contempt; in you they have oppressed the foreigner and mistreated the fatherless and the widow. 8You have despised my holy things and desecrated my Sabbaths. 9In you are slanderers who are bent on shedding blood; in you are those who eat at the mountain shrines and commit lewd acts. 10In you are those who dishonor their father's bed; in you are those who violate women during their period, when they are ceremonially unclean. 11In you one man commits a detestable offense with his neighbor's wife, another shamefully defiles his daughter-in-law, and another violates his sister, his own father's daughter. 12In you are people who accept bribes to shed blood; you take interest and make a profit from the poor. You extort unjust gain from your neighbors. And you have forgotten me, declares the Sovereign LORD.

13"'I will surely strike my hands together at the unjust gain you have made and at the blood you have shed in your midst. 14Will your courage endure or your hands be strong in the day I deal with you? I the LORD have spoken, and I will do it. 15I will disperse you among the nations and scatter you through the countries; and I will put an end to your uncleanness. 16When you have been defiled*a* in the eyes of the nations, you will know that I am the LORD.'"

17Then the word of the LORD came to me: 18"Son of man, the people of Israel have become dross to me; all of them are the copper, tin, iron and lead left inside a furnace. They are but the dross of silver. 19Therefore this is what the Sovereign LORD says: 'Because you have all become dross, I will gather you into Jerusalem. 20As silver, copper, iron, lead and tin are gathered into a furnace to be melted with a fiery blast, so will I gather you in my anger and my wrath and put you inside the city and melt you. 21I will gather you and I will blow on you with my fiery wrath, and you will be melted inside her. 22As silver is melted in a furnace, so you will be melted inside her, and you will know that I the LORD have poured out my wrath on you.'"

23Again the word of the LORD came to me: 24"Son of man, say to the land, 'You are a land that has not been cleansed or rained on in the day of wrath.' 25There is a conspiracy of her princes*b* within her like a roaring lion tearing its prey; they devour people, take treasures and precious things and make many widows within her. 26Her priests do violence to my law and profane my holy things; they do not distinguish between the holy and the common; they teach that there is no difference between the unclean and the clean; and they shut their eyes to the keeping of my Sabbaths, so that I am profaned among them. 27Her officials within her are like wolves tearing their prey; they shed blood and kill people to make unjust gain. 28Her prophets whitewash these deeds for them by false visions and lying divinations. They say, 'This is what the Sovereign LORD says'—when the LORD has not spoken. 29The people of the land practice extortion and commit robbery; they oppress the poor and needy and mistreat the foreigner, denying them justice.

30"I looked for someone among them who would build up the wall and stand before me in the gap on behalf of the land so I would not have to destroy it, but I found no one. 31So I will pour out my wrath on them and consume them with my fiery anger, bringing down on their own heads all they have done, declares the Sovereign LORD."

Two Adulterous Sisters

23 The word of the LORD came to me: 2"Son of man, there were two women, daughters of the same mother. 3They became prostitutes in Egypt, engaging in prostitution from their youth. In that land their breasts were fondled and their virgin bosoms caressed. 4The older was named Oholah, and her sister was Oholibah. They were mine and gave birth to sons and daughters. Oholah is Samaria, and Oholibah is Jerusalem.

5"Oholah engaged in prostitution while she was still mine; and she lusted after her lovers, the Assyrians—warriors 6clothed in blue, governors and commanders, all of them handsome young men, and mounted horsemen. 7She gave herself as a prostitute to all the elite of the Assyrians and defiled herself with all the idols of everyone she lusted after. 8She did not give up the prostitution she began in Egypt, when during her youth men slept with her, caressed her virgin bosom and poured out their lust on her.

9"Therefore I delivered her into the hands of her lovers, the Assyrians, for whom she lusted. 10They stripped her naked, took away her sons and daughters and killed her with the sword. She became a byword among women, and punishment was inflicted on her.

---

a 16 Or *When I have allotted you your inheritance*   *b 25* Septuagint; Hebrew *prophets*

11"Her sister Oholibah saw this, yet in her lust and prostitution she was more depraved than her sister. 12She too lusted after the Assyrians—governors and commanders, warriors in full dress, mounted horsemen, all handsome young men. 13I saw that she too defiled herself; both of them went the same way.

14"But she carried her prostitution still further. She saw men portrayed on a wall, figures of Chaldeans*a* portrayed in red, 15with belts around their waists and flowing turbans on their heads; all of them looked like Babylonian chariot officers, natives of Chaldea.*b* 16As soon as she saw them, she lusted after them and sent messengers to them in Chaldea. 17Then the Babylonians came to her, to the bed of love, and in their lust they defiled her. After she had been defiled by them, she turned away from them in disgust. 18When she carried on her prostitution openly and exposed her naked body, I turned away from her in disgust, just as I had turned away from her sister. 19Yet she became more and more promiscuous as she recalled the days of her youth, when she was a prostitute in Egypt. 20There she lusted after her lovers, whose genitals were like those of donkeys and whose emission was like that of horses. 21So you longed for the lewdness of your youth, when in Egypt your bosom was caressed and your young breasts fondled.*c*

22"Therefore, Oholibah, this is what the Sovereign LORD says: I will stir up your lovers against you, those you turned away from in disgust, and I will bring them against you from every side— 23the Babylonians and all the Chaldeans, the men of Pekod and Shoa and Koa, and all the Assyrians with them, handsome young men, all of them governors and commanders, chariot officers and men of high rank, all mounted on horses. 24They will come against you with weapons,*d* chariots and wagons and with a throng of people; they will take up positions against you on every side with large and small shields and with helmets. I will turn you over to them for punishment, and they will punish you according to their standards. 25I will direct my jealous anger against you, and they will deal with you in fury. They will cut off your noses and your ears, and those of you who are left will fall by the sword. They will take away your sons and daughters, and those of you who are left will be consumed by fire. 26They will also strip you of your clothes and take your fine jewelry. 27So I will put a stop to the lewdness and prostitution you began in Egypt. You will not look on these things with longing or remember Egypt anymore.

28"For this is what the Sovereign LORD says: I am about to deliver you into the hands of those you hate, to those you turned away from in disgust. 29They will deal with you in hatred and take away everything you have worked for. They will leave you stark naked, and the shame of your prostitution will be exposed. Your lewdness and promiscuity 30have brought this on you, because you lusted after the nations and defiled yourself with their idols. 31You have gone the way of your sister; so I will put her cup into your hand.

32"This is what the Sovereign LORD says:

"You will drink your sister's cup,
    a cup large and deep;
it will bring scorn and derision,
    for it holds so much.
33You will be filled with drunkenness
        and sorrow,
    the cup of ruin and desolation,
    the cup of your sister Samaria.
34You will drink it and drain it dry
    and chew on its pieces—
    and you will tear your breasts.

I have spoken, declares the Sovereign LORD.

35"Therefore this is what the Sovereign LORD says: Since you have forgotten me

---

a 14 Or *Babylonians*   *b 15* Or *Babylonia*; also in verse 16   *c 21* Syriac (see also verse 3); Hebrew *caressed because of your young breasts*   *d 24* The meaning of the Hebrew for this word is uncertain.

and turned your back on me, you must bear the consequences of your lewdness and prostitution."

36 The Lord said to me: "Son of man, will you judge Oholah and Oholibah? Then confront them with their detestable practices, 37 for they have committed adultery and blood is on their hands. They committed adultery with their idols; they even sacrificed their children, whom they bore to me, as food for them. 38 They have also done this to me: At that same time they defiled my sanctuary and desecrated my Sabbaths. 39 On the very day they sacrificed their children to their idols, they entered my sanctuary and desecrated it. That is what they did in my house.

40 "They even sent messengers for men who came from far away, and when they arrived you bathed yourself for them, applied eye makeup and put on your jewelry. 41 You sat on an elegant couch, with a table spread before it on which you had placed the incense and olive oil that belonged to me.

42 "The noise of a carefree crowd was around her; drunkards were brought from the desert along with men from the rabble, and they put bracelets on the wrists of the woman and her sister and beautiful crowns on their heads. 43 Then I said about the one worn out by adultery, 'Now let them use her as a prostitute, for that is all she is.' 44 And they slept with her. As men sleep with a prostitute, so they slept with those lewd women, Oholah and Oholibah. 45 But righteous judges will sentence them to the punishment of women who commit adultery and shed blood, because they are adulterous and blood is on their hands.

46 "This is what the Sovereign Lord says: Bring a mob against them and give them over to terror and plunder. 47 The mob will stone them and cut them down with their swords; they will kill their sons and daughters and burn down their houses.

48 "So I will put an end to lewdness in the land, that all women may take warning and not imitate you. 49 You will suffer the penalty for your lewdness and bear the consequences of your sins of idolatry. Then you will know that I am the Sovereign Lord."

Jerusalem as a Cooking Pot

24 In the ninth year, in the tenth month on the tenth day, the word of the Lord came to me: 2 "Son of man, record this date, this very date, because the king of Babylon has laid siege to Jerusalem this very day. 3 Tell this rebellious people a parable and say to them: 'This is what the Sovereign Lord says:

"'Put on the cooking pot; put it on
    and pour water into it.
4 Put into it the pieces of meat,
    all the choice pieces — the leg and the
        shoulder.
Fill it with the best of these bones;
5   take the pick of the flock.
Pile wood beneath it for the bones;
    bring it to a boil
    and cook the bones in it.

6 "'For this is what the Sovereign Lord says:

"'Woe to the city of bloodshed,
    to the pot now encrusted,
    whose deposit will not go away!
Take the meat out piece by piece
    in whatever order it comes.

7 "'For the blood she shed is in her midst:
    She poured it on the bare rock;
she did not pour it on the ground,
    where the dust would cover it.
8 To stir up wrath and take revenge
    I put her blood on the bare rock,
    so that it would not be covered.

9 "'Therefore this is what the Sovereign Lord says:

"'Woe to the city of bloodshed!
    I, too, will pile the wood high.
10 So heap on the wood
    and kindle the fire.
Cook the meat well,
    mixing in the spices;
    and let the bones be charred.

¹¹ Then set the empty pot on the coals
    till it becomes hot and its copper
      glows,
so that its impurities may be melted
    and its deposit burned away.
¹² It has frustrated all efforts;
    its heavy deposit has not been
      removed,
    not even by fire.

¹³ "'Now your impurity is lewdness. Because I tried to cleanse you but you would not be cleansed from your impurity, you will not be clean again until my wrath against you has subsided.

¹⁴ "'I the Lord have spoken. The time has come for me to act. I will not hold back; I will not have pity, nor will I relent. You will be judged according to your conduct and your actions, declares the Sovereign Lord.'"

Ezekiel's Wife Dies

¹⁵ The word of the Lord came to me: ¹⁶ "Son of man, with one blow I am about to take away from you the delight of your eyes. Yet do not lament or weep or shed any tears. ¹⁷ Groan quietly; do not mourn for the dead. Keep your turban fastened and your sandals on your feet; do not cover your mustache and beard or eat the customary food of mourners."

¹⁸ So I spoke to the people in the morning, and in the evening my wife died. The next morning I did as I had been commanded.

¹⁹ Then the people asked me, "Won't you tell us what these things have to do with us? Why are you acting like this?"

²⁰ So I said to them, "The word of the Lord came to me: ²¹ Say to the people of Israel, 'This is what the Sovereign Lord says: I am about to desecrate my sanctuary — the stronghold in which you take pride, the delight of your eyes, the object of your affection. The sons and daughters you left behind will fall by the sword. ²² And you

will do as I have done. You will not cover your mustache and beard or eat the customary food of mourners. ²³ You will keep your turbans on your heads and your sandals on your feet. You will not mourn or weep but will waste away because of^a your sins and groan among yourselves. ²⁴ Ezekiel will be a sign to you; you will do just as he has done. When this happens, you will know that I am the Sovereign Lord.'

²⁵ "And you, son of man, on the day I take away their stronghold, their joy and glory, the delight of their eyes, their heart's desire, and their sons and daughters as well — ²⁶ on that day a fugitive will come to tell you the news. ²⁷ At that time your mouth will be opened; you will speak with him and will no longer be silent. So you will be a sign to them, and they will know that I am the Lord."

A Prophecy Against Ammon

25

The word of the Lord came to me: ² "Son of man, set your face against the Ammonites and prophesy against them. ³ Say to them, 'Hear the word of the Sovereign Lord. This is what the Sovereign Lord says: Because you said "Aha!" over my sanctuary when it was desecrated and over the land of Israel when it was laid waste and over the people of Judah when they went into exile, ⁴ therefore I am going to give you to the people of the East as a possession. They will set up their camps and pitch their tents among you; they will eat your fruit and drink your milk. ⁵ I will turn Rabbah into a pasture for camels and Ammon into a resting place for sheep. Then you will know that I am the Lord. ⁶ For this is what the Sovereign Lord says: Because you have clapped your hands and stamped your feet, rejoicing with all the malice of your heart against the land of Israel, ⁷ therefore I will stretch out my hand against you and give you as plunder to the nations. I will wipe you out from among the nations and exterminate you from the

---

^a 23 Or *away in*

countries. I will destroy you, and you will know that I am the Lord.'"

A Prophecy Against Moab

8"This is what the Sovereign Lord says: 'Because Moab and Seir said, "Look, Judah has become like all the other nations," 9therefore I will expose the flank of Moab, beginning at its frontier towns—Beth Jeshimoth, Baal Meon and Kiriathaim—the glory of that land. 10I will give Moab along with the Ammonites to the people of the East as a possession, so that the Ammonites will not be remembered among the nations; 11and I will inflict punishment on Moab. Then they will know that I am the Lord.'"

A Prophecy Against Edom

12"This is what the Sovereign Lord says: 'Because Edom took revenge on Judah and became very guilty by doing so, 13therefore this is what the Sovereign Lord says: I will stretch out my hand against Edom and kill both man and beast. I will lay it waste, and from Teman to Dedan they will fall by the sword. 14I will take vengeance on Edom by the hand of my people Israel, and they will deal with Edom in accordance with my anger and my wrath; they will know my vengeance, declares the Sovereign Lord.'"

A Prophecy Against Philistia

15"This is what the Sovereign Lord says: 'Because the Philistines acted in vengeance and took revenge with malice in their hearts, and with ancient hostility sought to destroy Judah, 16therefore this is what the Sovereign Lord says: I am about to stretch out my hand against the Philistines, and I will wipe out the Kerethites and destroy those remaining along the coast. 17I will carry out great vengeance on them and punish them in my wrath. Then they will know that I am the Lord, when I take vengeance on them.'"

A Prophecy Against Tyre

26 In the eleventh month of the twelfth*a* year, on the first day of the month, the word of the Lord came to me: 2"Son of man, because Tyre has said of Jerusalem, 'Aha! The gate to the nations is broken, and its doors have swung open to me; now that she lies in ruins I will prosper,' 3therefore this is what the Sovereign Lord says: I am against you, Tyre, and I will bring many nations against you, like the sea casting up its waves. 4They will destroy the walls of Tyre and pull down her towers; I will scrape away her rubble and make her a bare rock. 5Out in the sea she will become a place to spread fishnets, for I have spoken, declares the Sovereign Lord. She will become plunder for the nations, 6and her settlements on the mainland will be ravaged by the sword. Then they will know that I am the Lord.

7"For this is what the Sovereign Lord says: From the north I am going to bring against Tyre Nebuchadnezzar*b* king of Babylon, king of kings, with horses and chariots, with horsemen and a great army. 8He will ravage your settlements on the mainland with the sword; he will set up siege works against you, build a ramp up to your walls and raise his shields against you. 9He will direct the blows of his battering rams against your walls and demolish your towers with his weapons. 10His horses will be so many that they will cover you with dust. Your walls will tremble at the noise of the warhorses, wagons and chariots when he enters your gates as men enter a city whose walls have been broken through. 11The hooves of his horses will trample all your streets; he will kill your people with the sword, and your strong pillars will fall to the ground. 12They will plunder your wealth and loot your merchandise; they will break down your walls and demolish your fine houses and

---

a 1 Probable reading of the original Hebrew text; Masoretic Text does not have *month of the twelfth.*   *b 7* Hebrew *Nebuchadrezzar,* of which *Nebuchadnezzar* is a variant; here and often in Ezekiel and Jeremiah throw your stones, timber and rubble into the sea. ¹³I will put an end to your noisy songs, and the music of your harps will be heard no more. ¹⁴I will make you a bare rock, and you will become a place to spread fishnets. You will never be rebuilt, for I the LORD have spoken, declares the Sovereign LORD.

¹⁵"This is what the Sovereign LORD says to Tyre: Will not the coastlands tremble at the sound of your fall, when the wounded groan and the slaughter takes place in you? ¹⁶Then all the princes of the coast will step down from their thrones and lay aside their robes and take off their embroidered garments. Clothed with terror, they will sit on the ground, trembling every moment, appalled at you. ¹⁷Then they will take up a lament concerning you and say to you:

> "'How you are destroyed, city of renown,
>   peopled by men of the sea!
> You were a power on the seas,
>   you and your citizens;
> you put your terror
>   on all who lived there.
> ¹⁸Now the coastlands tremble
>   on the day of your fall;
> the islands in the sea
>   are terrified at your collapse.'

¹⁹"This is what the Sovereign LORD says: When I make you a desolate city, like cities no longer inhabited, and when I bring the ocean depths over you and its vast waters cover you, ²⁰then I will bring you down with those who go down to the pit, to the people of long ago. I will make you dwell in the earth below, as in ancient ruins, with those who go down to the pit, and you will not return or take your place*a* in the land of the living. ²¹I will bring you to a horrible end and you will be no more. You will be sought, but you will never again be found, declares the Sovereign LORD."

A Lament Over Tyre

27 The word of the LORD came to me: ²"Son of man, take up a lament concerning Tyre. ³Say to Tyre, situated at the gateway to the sea, merchant of peoples on many coasts, 'This is what the Sovereign LORD says:

> "'You say, Tyre,
>   "I am perfect in beauty."
> ⁴Your domain was on the high seas;
>   your builders brought your beauty to
>   perfection.
> ⁵They made all your timbers
>   of juniper from Senir*b*;
> they took a cedar from Lebanon
>   to make a mast for you.
> ⁶Of oaks from Bashan
>   they made your oars;
> of cypress wood*c* from the coasts of
>   Cyprus
> they made your deck, adorned with
>   ivory.
> ⁷Fine embroidered linen from Egypt was
>   your sail
>   and served as your banner;
> your awnings were of blue and purple
>   from the coasts of Elishah.
> ⁸Men of Sidon and Arvad were your
>   oarsmen;
>   your skilled men, Tyre, were aboard
>   as your sailors.
> ⁹Veteran craftsmen of Byblos were on
>   board
>   as shipwrights to caulk your seams.
> All the ships of the sea and their sailors
>   came alongside to trade for your wares.

> ¹⁰"'Men of Persia, Lydia and Put
>   served as soldiers in your army.
> They hung their shields and helmets on
>   your walls,
>   bringing you splendor.
> ¹¹Men of Arvad and Helek
>   guarded your walls on every side;
> men of Gammad
>   were in your towers.

---

a 20 Septuagint; Hebrew *return, and I will give glory*   *b* 5 That is, Mount Hermon   *c* 6 Targum; the Masoretic Text has a different division of the consonants.

They hung their shields around your
walls;
    they brought your beauty to
      perfection.

12 "'Tarshish did business with you because of your great wealth of goods; they
exchanged silver, iron, tin and lead for your
merchandise.

13 "'Greece, Tubal and Meshek did business with you; they traded human beings
and articles of bronze for your wares.

14 "'Men of Beth Togarmah exchanged
chariot horses, cavalry horses and mules
for your merchandise.

15 "'The men of Rhodes[a] traded with
you, and many coastlands were your customers; they paid you with ivory tusks and
ebony.

16 "'Aram[b] did business with you because of your many products; they exchanged turquoise, purple fabric, embroidered work, fine linen, coral and rubies for
your merchandise.

17 "'Judah and Israel traded with you;
they exchanged wheat from Minnith and
confections,[c] honey, olive oil and balm for
your wares.

18 "'Damascus did business with you
because of your many products and great
wealth of goods. They offered wine from
Helbon, wool from Zahar 19and casks of
wine from Izal in exchange for your wares:
wrought iron, cassia and calamus.

20 "'Dedan traded in saddle blankets
with you.

21 "'Arabia and all the princes of Kedar
were your customers; they did business
with you in lambs, rams and goats.

22 "'The merchants of Sheba and Raamah traded with you; for your merchandise they exchanged the finest of all kinds
of spices and precious stones, and gold.

23 "'Harran, Kanneh and Eden and merchants of Sheba, Ashur and Kilmad traded with you. 24In your marketplace they
traded with you beautiful garments, blue

fabric, embroidered work and multicol-
ored rugs with cords twisted and tightly
knotted.

25 "'The ships of Tarshish serve
    as carriers for your wares.
You are filled with heavy cargo
    as you sail the sea.
26 Your oarsmen take you
    out to the high seas.
But the east wind will break you to
    pieces
    far out at sea.
27 Your wealth, merchandise and wares,
    your mariners, sailors and
      shipwrights,
your merchants and all your soldiers,
    and everyone else on board
will sink into the heart of the sea
    on the day of your shipwreck.
28 The shorelands will quake
    when your sailors cry out.
29 All who handle the oars
    will abandon their ships;
the mariners and all the sailors
    will stand on the shore.
30 They will raise their voice
    and cry bitterly over you;
they will sprinkle dust on their heads
    and roll in ashes.
31 They will shave their heads because of
    you
    and will put on sackcloth.
They will weep over you with anguish
    of soul
    and with bitter mourning.
32 As they wail and mourn over you,
    they will take up a lament
      concerning you:
"Who was ever silenced like Tyre,
    surrounded by the sea?"
33 When your merchandise went out on
    the seas,
    you satisfied many nations;
with your great wealth and your
    wares
    you enriched the kings of the earth.

---

³⁴ Now you are shattered by the sea
    in the depths of the waters;
your wares and all your company
    have gone down with you.
³⁵ All who live in the coastlands
    are appalled at you;
their kings shudder with horror
    and their faces are distorted with fear.
³⁶ The merchants among the nations scoff
       at you;
    you have come to a horrible end
    and will be no more.'"

A Prophecy Against the King of Tyre

28 The word of the Lord came to me: ² "Son of man, say to the ruler of Tyre, 'This is what the Sovereign Lord says:

"'In the pride of your heart
    you say, "I am a god;
I sit on the throne of a god
    in the heart of the seas."
But you are a mere mortal and not a god,
    though you think you are as wise as a
       god.
³ Are you wiser than Daniel[a]?
    Is no secret hidden from you?
⁴ By your wisdom and understanding
    you have gained wealth for yourself
and amassed gold and silver
    in your treasuries.
⁵ By your great skill in trading
    you have increased your wealth,
and because of your wealth
    your heart has grown proud.

⁶ "'Therefore this is what the Sovereign Lord says:

"'Because you think you are wise,
    as wise as a god,
⁷ I am going to bring foreigners against
       you,
    the most ruthless of nations;
they will draw their swords against
       your beauty and wisdom
    and pierce your shining splendor.

⁸ They will bring you down to the pit,
    and you will die a violent death
    in the heart of the seas.
⁹ Will you then say, "I am a god,"
    in the presence of those who kill you?
You will be but a mortal, not a god,
    in the hands of those who slay you.
¹⁰ You will die the death of the
       uncircumcised
    at the hands of foreigners.

I have spoken, declares the Sovereign Lord.'"

¹¹ The word of the Lord came to me: ¹² "Son of man, take up a lament concerning the king of Tyre and say to him: 'This is what the Sovereign Lord says:

"'You were the seal of perfection,
    full of wisdom and perfect in beauty.
¹³ You were in Eden,
    the garden of God;
every precious stone adorned you:
    carnelian, chrysolite and emerald,
    topaz, onyx and jasper,
    lapis lazuli, turquoise and beryl.[b]
Your settings and mountings[c] were
       made of gold;
    on the day you were created they
       were prepared.
¹⁴ You were anointed as a guardian
       cherub,
    for so I ordained you.
You were on the holy mount of God;
    you walked among the fiery stones.
¹⁵ You were blameless in your ways
    from the day you were created
    till wickedness was found in you.
¹⁶ Through your widespread trade
    you were filled with violence,
    and you sinned.
So I drove you in disgrace from the
       mount of God,
    and I expelled you, guardian cherub,
    from among the fiery stones.
¹⁷ Your heart became proud
    on account of your beauty,

---

a 3 Or *Danel*, a man of renown in ancient literature   *b 13* The precise identification of some of these precious stones is uncertain.   *c 13* The meaning of the Hebrew for this phrase is uncertain.

and you corrupted your wisdom
    because of your splendor.
So I threw you to the earth;
    I made a spectacle of you before
        kings.
18 By your many sins and dishonest trade
    you have desecrated your
        sanctuaries.
So I made a fire come out from you,
    and it consumed you,
and I reduced you to ashes on the
        ground
    in the sight of all who were watching.
19 All the nations who knew you
    are appalled at you;
you have come to a horrible end
    and will be no more.'"

A Prophecy Against Sidon

20 The word of the LORD came to me:
21 "Son of man, set your face against Sidon;
prophesy against her 22 and say: 'This is
what the Sovereign LORD says:

"'I am against you, Sidon,
    and among you I will display my
        glory.
You will know that I am the LORD,
    when I inflict punishment on you
    and within you am proved to be holy.
23 I will send a plague upon you
    and make blood flow in your streets.
The slain will fall within you,
    with the sword against you on every
        side.
Then you will know that I am the
        LORD.

24 "'No longer will the people of Israel
have malicious neighbors who are painful briers and sharp thorns. Then they will
know that I am the Sovereign LORD.

25 "'This is what the Sovereign LORD says:
When I gather the people of Israel from the
nations where they have been scattered, I
will be proved holy through them in the
sight of the nations. Then they will live in
their own land, which I gave to my servant
Jacob. 26 They will live there in safety and
will build houses and plant vineyards; they
will live in safety when I inflict punishment on all their neighbors who maligned
them. Then they will know that I am the
LORD their God.'"

A Prophecy Against Egypt
Judgment on Pharaoh

29 In the tenth year, in the tenth
month on the twelfth day, the
word of the LORD came to me:
2 "Son of man, set your face against Pharaoh king of Egypt and prophesy against
him and against all Egypt. 3 Speak to him
and say: 'This is what the Sovereign LORD
says:

"'I am against you, Pharaoh king of
    Egypt,
you great monster lying among your
        streams.
You say, "The Nile belongs to me;
    I made it for myself."
4 But I will put hooks in your jaws
    and make the fish of your streams
        stick to your scales.
I will pull you out from among your
        streams,
    with all the fish sticking to your
        scales.
5 I will leave you in the desert,
    you and all the fish of your streams.
You will fall on the open field
    and not be gathered or picked up.
I will give you as food
    to the beasts of the earth and the
        birds of the sky.

6 Then all who live in Egypt will know that
I am the LORD.

"'You have been a staff of reed for the
people of Israel. 7 When they grasped
you with their hands, you splintered and
you tore open their shoulders; when they
leaned on you, you broke and their backs
were wrenched.ᵃ

ᵃ 7 Syriac (see also Septuagint and Vulgate); Hebrew *and you caused their backs to stand*

8"'Therefore this is what the Sovereign LORD says: I will bring a sword against you and kill both man and beast. 9Egypt will become a desolate wasteland. Then they will know that I am the LORD.

"'Because you said, "The Nile is mine; I made it," 10therefore I am against you and against your streams, and I will make the land of Egypt a ruin and a desolate waste from Migdol to Aswan, as far as the border of Cush.a 11The foot of neither man nor beast will pass through it; no one will live there for forty years. 12I will make the land of Egypt desolate among devastated lands, and her cities will lie desolate forty years among ruined cities. And I will disperse the Egyptians among the nations and scatter them through the countries.

13"'Yet this is what the Sovereign LORD says: At the end of forty years I will gather the Egyptians from the nations where they were scattered. 14I will bring them back from captivity and return them to Upper Egypt, the land of their ancestry. There they will be a lowly kingdom. 15It will be the lowliest of kingdoms and will never again exalt itself above the other nations. I will make it so weak that it will never again rule over the nations. 16Egypt will no longer be a source of confidence for the people of Israel but will be a reminder of their sin in turning to her for help. Then they will know that I am the Sovereign LORD.'"

Nebuchadnezzar's Reward

17In the twenty-seventh year, in the first month on the first day, the word of the LORD came to me: 18"Son of man, Nebuchadnezzar king of Babylon drove his army in a hard campaign against Tyre; every head was rubbed bare and every shoulder made raw. Yet he and his army got no reward from the campaign he led against Tyre. 19Therefore this is what the Sovereign LORD says: I am going to give Egypt to Nebuchadnezzar king of Babylon, and he will carry off its wealth. He will loot and plunder the land as pay for his army. 20I have given him Egypt as a reward for his efforts because he and his army did it for me, declares the Sovereign LORD. 21On that day I will make a hornb grow for the Israelites, and I will open your mouth among them. Then they will know that I am the LORD."

A Lament Over Egypt

30 The word of the LORD came to me: 2"Son of man, prophesy and say: 'This is what the Sovereign LORD says:

"'Wail and say,
    "Alas for that day!"
3 For the day is near,
    the day of the LORD is near—
a day of clouds,
    a time of doom for the nations.
4 A sword will come against Egypt,
    and anguish will come upon Cush.c
When the slain fall in Egypt,
    her wealth will be carried away
    and her foundations torn down.

5Cush and Libya, Lydia and all Arabia, Kub and the people of the covenant land will fall by the sword along with Egypt.

6"'This is what the LORD says:

"'The allies of Egypt will fall
    and her proud strength will fail.
From Migdol to Aswan
    they will fall by the sword within her,
        declares the Sovereign LORD.
7"'They will be desolate
    among desolate lands,
and their cities will lie
    among ruined cities.
8 Then they will know that I am the LORD,
    when I set fire to Egypt
    and all her helpers are crushed.

9"'On that day messengers will go out from me in ships to frighten Cush out of

---

a 10 That is, the upper Nile region   b 21 Horn here symbolizes strength.   c 4 That is, the upper Nile region; also in verses 5 and 9 her complacency. Anguish will take hold of them on the day of Egypt's doom, for it is sure to come.

¹⁰ "This is what the Sovereign LORD says:

"'I will put an end to the hordes of Egypt
    by the hand of Nebuchadnezzar king
        of Babylon.
¹¹ He and his army — the most ruthless of
        nations —
    will be brought in to destroy the land.
    They will draw their swords against
        Egypt
    and fill the land with the slain.
¹² I will dry up the waters of the Nile
    and sell the land to an evil nation;
    by the hand of foreigners
        I will lay waste the land and
            everything in it.

I the LORD have spoken.

¹³ "This is what the Sovereign LORD says:

"'I will destroy the idols
    and put an end to the images in
        Memphis.
No longer will there be a prince in
        Egypt,
    and I will spread fear throughout the
        land.
¹⁴ I will lay waste Upper Egypt,
    set fire to Zoan
    and inflict punishment on Thebes.
¹⁵ I will pour out my wrath on Pelusium,
    the stronghold of Egypt,
    and wipe out the hordes of Thebes.
¹⁶ I will set fire to Egypt;
    Pelusium will writhe in agony.
    Thebes will be taken by storm;
    Memphis will be in constant distress.
¹⁷ The young men of Heliopolis and
        Bubastis
    will fall by the sword,
    and the cities themselves will go into
        captivity.
¹⁸ Dark will be the day at Tahpanhes
    when I break the yoke of Egypt;

there her proud strength will come to
        an end.
She will be covered with clouds,
    and her villages will go into captivity.
¹⁹ So I will inflict punishment on Egypt,
    and they will know that I am the
        LORD.'"

Pharaoh's Arms Are Broken

²⁰ In the eleventh year, in the first month on the seventh day, the word of the LORD came to me: ²¹ "Son of man, I have broken the arm of Pharaoh king of Egypt. It has not been bound up to be healed or put in a splint so that it may become strong enough to hold a sword. ²² Therefore this is what the Sovereign LORD says: I am against Pharaoh king of Egypt. I will break both his arms, the good arm as well as the broken one, and make the sword fall from his hand. ²³ I will disperse the Egyptians among the nations and scatter them through the countries. ²⁴ I will strengthen the arms of the king of Babylon and put my sword in his hand, but I will break the arms of Pharaoh, and he will groan before him like a mortally wounded man. ²⁵ I will strengthen the arms of the king of Babylon, but the arms of Pharaoh will fall limp. Then they will know that I am the LORD, when I put my sword into the hand of the king of Babylon and he brandishes it against Egypt. ²⁶ I will disperse the Egyptians among the nations and scatter them through the countries. Then they will know that I am the LORD."

Pharaoh as a Felled Cedar of Lebanon

31 In the eleventh year, in the third month on the first day, the word of the LORD came to me: ² "Son of man, say to Pharaoh king of Egypt and to his hordes:

"'Who can be compared with you in
        majesty?
³ Consider Assyria, once a cedar in
        Lebanon,
    with beautiful branches
        overshadowing the forest;

it towered on high,
　　its top above the thick foliage.
4 The waters nourished it,
　　deep springs made it grow tall;
their streams flowed
　　all around its base
and sent their channels
　　to all the trees of the field.
5 So it towered higher
　　than all the trees of the field;
its boughs increased
　　and its branches grew long,
　　spreading because of abundant
　　　　waters.
6 All the birds of the sky
　　nested in its boughs,
all the animals of the wild
　　gave birth under its branches;
all the great nations
　　lived in its shade.
7 It was majestic in beauty,
　　with its spreading boughs,
for its roots went down
　　to abundant waters.
8 The cedars in the garden of God
　　could not rival it,
　　nor could the junipers
　　　　equal its boughs,
nor could the plane trees
　　compare with its branches —
no tree in the garden of God
　　could match its beauty.
9 I made it beautiful
　　with abundant branches,
the envy of all the trees of Eden
　　in the garden of God.

10 "'Therefore this is what the Sovereign Lord says: Because the great cedar towered over the thick foliage, and because it was proud of its height, 11 I gave it into the hands of the ruler of the nations, for him to deal with according to its wickedness. I cast it aside, 12 and the most ruthless of foreign nations cut it down and left it. Its boughs fell on the mountains and in all the valleys; its branches lay broken in all the ravines of the land. All the nations of the earth came out from under its shade and left it. 13 All the birds settled on the fallen tree, and all the wild animals lived among its branches. 14 Therefore no other trees by the waters are ever to tower proudly on high, lifting their tops above the thick foliage. No other trees so well-watered are ever to reach such a height; they are all destined for death, for the earth below, among mortals who go down to the realm of the dead.

15 "'This is what the Sovereign Lord says: On the day it was brought down to the realm of the dead I covered the deep springs with mourning for it; I held back its streams, and its abundant waters were restrained. Because of it I clothed Lebanon with gloom, and all the trees of the field withered away. 16 I made the nations tremble at the sound of its fall when I brought it down to the realm of the dead to be with those who go down to the pit. Then all the trees of Eden, the choicest and best of Lebanon, the well-watered trees, were consoled in the earth below. 17 They too, like the great cedar, had gone down to the realm of the dead, to those killed by the sword, along with the armed men who lived in its shade among the nations.

18 "'Which of the trees of Eden can be compared with you in splendor and majesty? Yet you, too, will be brought down with the trees of Eden to the earth below; you will lie among the uncircumcised, with those killed by the sword.

"'This is Pharaoh and all his hordes, declares the Sovereign Lord.'"

A Lament Over Pharaoh

32 In the twelfth year, in the twelfth month on the first day, the word of the Lord came to me: 2 "Son of man, take up a lament concerning Pharaoh king of Egypt and say to him:

"'You are like a lion among the nations;
　　you are like a monster in the seas
thrashing about in your streams,
　　churning the water with your feet
　　and muddying the streams.

3 " 'This is what the Sovereign LORD says:

" 'With a great throng of people
    I will cast my net over you,
    and they will haul you up in my net.
4 I will throw you on the land
    and hurl you on the open field.
I will let all the birds of the sky settle on
        you
    and all the animals of the wild gorge
        themselves on you.
5 I will spread your flesh on the
        mountains
    and fill the valleys with your remains.
6 I will drench the land with your
        flowing blood
    all the way to the mountains,
    and the ravines will be filled with
        your flesh.
7 When I snuff you out, I will cover the
        heavens
    and darken their stars;
I will cover the sun with a cloud,
    and the moon will not give its light.
8 All the shining lights in the heavens
    I will darken over you;
I will bring darkness over your land,
        declares the Sovereign LORD.
9 I will trouble the hearts of many
        peoples
    when I bring about your destruction
        among the nations,
    among*a* lands you have not known.
10 I will cause many peoples to be appalled
        at you,
    and their kings will shudder with
        horror because of you
    when I brandish my sword before
        them.
On the day of your downfall
    each of them will tremble
    every moment for his life.

11 " 'For this is what the Sovereign LORD
says:

" 'The sword of the king of Babylon
    will come against you.

12 I will cause your hordes to fall
    by the swords of mighty men —
    the most ruthless of all nations.
They will shatter the pride of Egypt,
    and all her hordes will be
        overthrown.
13 I will destroy all her cattle
    from beside abundant waters
no longer to be stirred by the foot of
        man
    or muddied by the hooves of cattle.
14 Then I will let her waters settle
    and make her streams flow like oil,
        declares the Sovereign LORD.
15 When I make Egypt desolate
    and strip the land of everything
        in it,
    when I strike down all who live there,
    then they will know that I am the
        LORD.'

16 "This is the lament they will chant
for her. The daughters of the nations will
chant it; for Egypt and all her hordes they
will chant it, declares the Sovereign LORD."

Egypt's Descent Into the Realm of the Dead

17 In the twelfth year, on the fifteenth day
of the month, the word of the LORD came
to me: 18 "Son of man, wail for the hordes
of Egypt and consign to the earth below
both her and the daughters of mighty nations, along with those who go down to the
pit. 19 Say to them, 'Are you more favored
than others? Go down and be laid among
the uncircumcised.' 20 They will fall among
those killed by the sword. The sword is
drawn; let her be dragged off with all her
hordes. 21 From within the realm of the
dead the mighty leaders will say of Egypt
and her allies, 'They have come down and
they lie with the uncircumcised, with those
killed by the sword.'
22 "Assyria is there with her whole army;
she is surrounded by the graves of all her
slain, all who have fallen by the sword.
23 Their graves are in the depths of the pit

---

a 9 Hebrew; Septuagint *bring you into captivity among the nations, / to* and her army lies around her grave. All who had spread terror in the land of the living are slain, fallen by the sword.

24 "Elam is there, with all her hordes around her grave. All of them are slain, fallen by the sword. All who had spread terror in the land of the living went down uncircumcised to the earth below. They bear their shame with those who go down to the pit. 25 A bed is made for her among the slain, with all her hordes around her grave. All of them are uncircumcised, killed by the sword. Because their terror had spread in the land of the living, they bear their shame with those who go down to the pit; they are laid among the slain.

26 "Meshek and Tubal are there, with all their hordes around their graves. All of them are uncircumcised, killed by the sword because they spread their terror in the land of the living. 27 But they do not lie with the fallen warriors of old,*a* who went down to the realm of the dead with their weapons of war — their swords placed under their heads and their shields*b* resting on their bones — though these warriors also had terrorized the land of the living.

28 "You too, Pharaoh, will be broken and will lie among the uncircumcised, with those killed by the sword.

29 "Edom is there, her kings and all her princes; despite their power, they are laid with those killed by the sword. They lie with the uncircumcised, with those who go down to the pit.

30 "All the princes of the north and all the Sidonians are there; they went down with the slain in disgrace despite the terror caused by their power. They lie uncircumcised with those killed by the sword and bear their shame with those who go down to the pit.

31 "Pharaoh — he and all his army — will see them and he will be consoled for all his hordes that were killed by the sword, declares the Sovereign LORD. 32 Although I

had him spread terror in the land of the living, Pharaoh and all his hordes will be laid among the uncircumcised, with those killed by the sword, declares the Sovereign LORD."

Renewal of Ezekiel's Call as Watchman

33 The word of the LORD came to me: 2 "Son of man, speak to your people and say to them: 'When I bring the sword against a land, and the people of the land choose one of their men and make him their watchman, 3 and he sees the sword coming against the land and blows the trumpet to warn the people, 4 then if anyone hears the trumpet but does not heed the warning and the sword comes and takes their life, their blood will be on their own head. 5 Since they heard the sound of the trumpet but did not heed the warning, their blood will be on their own head. If they had heeded the warning, they would have saved themselves. 6 But if the watchman sees the sword coming and does not blow the trumpet to warn the people and the sword comes and takes someone's life, that person's life will be taken because of their sin, but I will hold the watchman accountable for their blood.'

7 "Son of man, I have made you a watchman for the people of Israel; so hear the word I speak and give them warning from me. 8 When I say to the wicked, 'You wicked person, you will surely die,' and you do not speak out to dissuade them from their ways, that wicked person will die for*c* their sin, and I will hold you accountable for their blood. 9 But if you do warn the wicked person to turn from their ways and they do not do so, they will die for their sin, though you yourself will be saved.

10 "Son of man, say to the Israelites, 'This is what you are saying: "Our offenses and sins weigh us down, and we are wasting away because of*d* them. How then can we

---

a 27 Septuagint; Hebrew *warriors who were uncircumcised*
Masoretic Text *punishment*   *c 8* Or *in*; also in verse 9   *b 27* Probable reading of the original Hebrew text;
d 10 Or *away in*

live?"' ¹¹Say to them, 'As surely as I live, declares the Sovereign Lᴏʀᴅ, I take no pleasure in the death of the wicked, but rather that they turn from their ways and live. Turn! Turn from your evil ways! Why will you die, people of Israel?'

¹²"Therefore, son of man, say to your people, 'If someone who is righteous disobeys, that person's former righteousness will count for nothing. And if someone who is wicked repents, that person's former wickedness will not bring condemnation. The righteous person who sins will not be allowed to live even though they were formerly righteous.' ¹³If I tell a righteous person that they will surely live, but then they trust in their righteousness and do evil, none of the righteous things that person has done will be remembered; they will die for the evil they have done. ¹⁴And if I say to a wicked person, 'You will surely die,' but they then turn away from their sin and do what is just and right — ¹⁵if they give back what they took in pledge for a loan, return what they have stolen, follow the decrees that give life, and do no evil — that person will surely live; they will not die. ¹⁶None of the sins that person has committed will be remembered against them. They have done what is just and right; they will surely live.

¹⁷"Yet your people say, 'The way of the Lord is not just.' But it is their way that is not just. ¹⁸If a righteous person turns from their righteousness and does evil, they will die for it. ¹⁹And if a wicked person turns away from their wickedness and does what is just and right, they will live by doing so. ²⁰Yet you Israelites say, 'The way of the Lord is not just.' But I will judge each of you according to your own ways."

Jerusalem's Fall Explained

²¹In the twelfth year of our exile, in the tenth month on the fifth day, a man who had escaped from Jerusalem came to me and said, "The city has fallen!" ²²Now the evening before the man arrived, the hand of the Lᴏʀᴅ was on me, and he opened my mouth before the man came to me in the morning. So my mouth was opened and I was no longer silent.

²³Then the word of the Lᴏʀᴅ came to me: ²⁴"Son of man, the people living in those ruins in the land of Israel are saying, 'Abraham was only one man, yet he possessed the land. But we are many; surely the land has been given to us as our possession.' ²⁵Therefore say to them, 'This is what the Sovereign Lᴏʀᴅ says: Since you eat meat with the blood still in it and look to your idols and shed blood, should you then possess the land? ²⁶You rely on your sword, you do detestable things, and each of you defiles his neighbor's wife. Should you then possess the land?'

²⁷"Say this to them: 'This is what the Sovereign Lᴏʀᴅ says: As surely as I live, those who are left in the ruins will fall by the sword, those out in the country I will give to the wild animals to be devoured, and those in strongholds and caves will die of a plague. ²⁸I will make the land a desolate waste, and her proud strength will come to an end, and the mountains of Israel will become desolate so that no one will cross them. ²⁹Then they will know that I am the Lᴏʀᴅ, when I have made the land a desolate waste because of all the detestable things they have done.'

³⁰"As for you, son of man, your people are talking together about you by the walls and at the doors of the houses, saying to each other, 'Come and hear the message that has come from the Lᴏʀᴅ.' ³¹My people come to you, as they usually do, and sit before you to hear your words, but they do not put them into practice. Their mouths speak of love, but their hearts are greedy for unjust gain. ³²Indeed, to them you are nothing more than one who sings love songs with a beautiful voice and plays an instrument well, for they hear your words but do not put them into practice.

³³"When all this comes true — and it surely will — then they will know that a prophet has been among them."

The Lord Will Be Israel's Shepherd

34 The word of the Lord came to me: [2]"Son of man, prophesy against the shepherds of Israel; prophesy and say to them: 'This is what the Sovereign Lord says: Woe to you shepherds of Israel who only take care of yourselves! Should not shepherds take care of the flock? [3]You eat the curds, clothe yourselves with the wool and slaughter the choice animals, but you do not take care of the flock. [4]You have not strengthened the weak or healed the sick or bound up the injured. You have not brought back the strays or searched for the lost. You have ruled them harshly and brutally. [5]So they were scattered because there was no shepherd, and when they were scattered they became food for all the wild animals. [6]My sheep wandered over all the mountains and on every high hill. They were scattered over the whole earth, and no one searched or looked for them.

[7]"'Therefore, you shepherds, hear the word of the Lord: [8]As surely as I live, declares the Sovereign Lord, because my flock lacks a shepherd and so has been plundered and has become food for all the wild animals, and because my shepherds did not search for my flock but cared for themselves rather than for my flock, [9]therefore, you shepherds, hear the word of the Lord: [10]This is what the Sovereign Lord says: I am against the shepherds and will hold them accountable for my flock. I will remove them from tending the flock so that the shepherds can no longer feed themselves. I will rescue my flock from their mouths, and it will no longer be food for them.

[11]"'For this is what the Sovereign Lord says: I myself will search for my sheep and look after them. [12]As a shepherd looks after his scattered flock when he is with them, so will I look after my sheep. I will rescue them from all the places where they were scattered on a day of clouds and darkness. [13]I will bring them out from the nations and gather them from the countries, and I will bring them into their own land. I will pasture them on the mountains of Israel, in the ravines and in all the settlements in the land. [14]I will tend them in a good pasture, and the mountain heights of Israel will be their grazing land. There they will lie down in good grazing land, and there they will feed in a rich pasture on the mountains of Israel. [15]I myself will tend my sheep and have them lie down, declares the Sovereign Lord. [16]I will search for the lost and bring back the strays. I will bind up the injured and strengthen the weak, but the sleek and the strong I will destroy. I will shepherd the flock with justice.

[17]"'As for you, my flock, this is what the Sovereign Lord says: I will judge between one sheep and another, and between rams and goats. [18]Is it not enough for you to feed on the good pasture? Must you also trample the rest of your pasture with your feet? Is it not enough for you to drink clear water? Must you also muddy the rest with your feet? [19]Must my flock feed on what you have trampled and drink what you have muddied with your feet?

[20]"'Therefore this is what the Sovereign Lord says to them: See, I myself will judge between the fat sheep and the lean sheep. [21]Because you shove with flank and shoulder, butting all the weak sheep with your horns until you have driven them away, [22]I will save my flock, and they will no longer be plundered. I will judge between one sheep and another. [23]I will place over them one shepherd, my servant David, and he will tend them; he will tend them and be their shepherd. [24]I the Lord will be their God, and my servant David will be prince among them. I the Lord have spoken.

[25]"'I will make a covenant of peace with them and rid the land of savage beasts so that they may live in the wilderness and sleep in the forests in safety. [26]I will make them and the places surrounding my hill a blessing.[a]

---

a 26   Or *I will cause them and the places surrounding my hill to be named in blessings* (see Gen. 48:20); or *I will cause them and the places surrounding my hill to be seen as blessed*

I will send down showers in season; there will be showers of blessing. 27The trees will yield their fruit and the ground will yield its crops; the people will be secure in their land. They will know that I am the LORD, when I break the bars of their yoke and rescue them from the hands of those who enslaved them. 28They will no longer be plundered by the nations, nor will wild animals devour them. They will live in safety, and no one will make them afraid. 29I will provide for them a land renowned for its crops, and they will no longer be victims of famine in the land or bear the scorn of the nations. 30Then they will know that I, the LORD their God,

am with them and that they, the Israelites, are my people, declares the Sovereign LORD. 31You are my sheep, the sheep of my pasture, and I am your God, declares the Sovereign LORD.'"

A Prophecy Against Edom

35 The word of the LORD came to me: 2"Son of man, set your face against Mount Seir; prophesy against it 3and say: 'This is what the Sovereign LORD says: I am against you, Mount Seir, and I will stretch out my hand against you and make you a desolate waste. 4I will turn your towns into ruins and you will be

---

INVENTORY LESSON [*Principle Four*]

For the previous entry in the INVENTORY lesson, go to Isaiah 41:10 (page 852).

For a discussion of Principles One through Eight and a listing of their related lessons, go to pages xvii – xliv.

I will search for the lost and bring back the strays. I will bind up the injured and strengthen the weak, but the sleek and the strong I will destroy. I will shepherd the flock with justice.

EZEKIEL 34:16

Principle Four begins the process of "coming clean." It's here that we openly examine and confess our faults to ourselves, to God and to someone else we trust. In the first part of Principle Four we openly examine our lives. As we get ready to write out our inventories in Principle Four, we divide them into five specific sections.

The third and fourth sections we write about are labeled THE EFFECT and THE DAMAGE. In these sections we record how someone else's specific, hurtful action has affected, and still affects, our lives.

In addition, we inventory which of our basic instincts were damaged or injured.

- *Social:* Have we suffered from broken relationships, slander or gossip?

- *Security:* Has our physical safety been threatened? Have we faced financial loss?

- *Sexual:* Have we been a victim in abusive sexual relationships? Has intimacy or trust been damaged or broken in this way?

No matter how we've been hurt, no matter how lost we may feel, God wants to comfort and restore us. Memorize Ezekiel 34:16.

In the fifth section we address MY PART. Go to Psalm 139:23 – 24 (page 729).

desolate. Then you will know that I am the Lord.

5 "'Because you harbored an ancient hostility and delivered the Israelites over to the sword at the time of their calamity, the time their punishment reached its climax, 6therefore as surely as I live, declares the Sovereign Lord, I will give you over to bloodshed and it will pursue you. Since you did not hate bloodshed, bloodshed will pursue you. 7I will make Mount Seir a desolate waste and cut off from it all who come and go. 8I will fill your mountains with the slain; those killed by the sword will fall on your hills and in your valleys and in all your ravines. 9I will make you desolate forever; your towns will not be inhabited. Then you will know that I am the Lord.

10 "'Because you have said, "These two nations and countries will be ours and we will take possession of them," even though I the Lord was there, 11therefore as surely as I live, declares the Sovereign Lord, I will treat you in accordance with the anger and jealousy you showed in your hatred of them and I will make myself known among them when I judge you. 12Then you will know that I the Lord have heard all the contemptible things you have said against the mountains of Israel. You said, "They have been laid waste and have been given over to us to devour." 13You boasted against me and spoke against me without restraint, and I heard it. 14This is what the Sovereign Lord says: While the whole earth rejoices, I will make you desolate. 15Because you rejoiced when the inheritance of Israel became desolate, that is how I will treat you. You will be desolate, Mount Seir, you and all of Edom. Then they will know that I am the Lord.'"

Hope for the Mountains of Israel

36 "Son of man, prophesy to the mountains of Israel and say, 'Mountains of Israel, hear the word of the Lord. 2This is what the Sovereign Lord says: The enemy said of you, "Aha! The ancient heights have become our possession."' 3Therefore prophesy and say, 'This is what the Sovereign Lord says: Because they ravaged and crushed you from every side so that you became the possession of the rest of the nations and the object of people's malicious talk and slander, 4therefore, mountains of Israel, hear the word of the Sovereign Lord: This is what the Sovereign Lord says to the mountains and hills, to the ravines and valleys, to the desolate ruins and the deserted towns that have been plundered and ridiculed by the rest of the nations around you— 5this is what the Sovereign Lord says: In my burning zeal I have spoken against the rest of the nations, and against all Edom, for with glee and with malice in their hearts they made my land their own possession so that they might plunder its pastureland.' 6Therefore prophesy concerning the land of Israel and say to the mountains and hills, to the ravines and valleys: 'This is what the Sovereign Lord says: I speak in my jealous wrath because you have suffered the scorn of the nations. 7Therefore this is what the Sovereign Lord says: I swear with uplifted hand that the nations around you will also suffer scorn.

8 "'But you, mountains of Israel, will produce branches and fruit for my people Israel, for they will soon come home. 9I am concerned for you and will look on you with favor; you will be plowed and sown, 10and I will cause many people to live on you—yes, all of Israel. The towns will be inhabited and the ruins rebuilt. 11I will increase the number of people and animals living on you, and they will be fruitful and become numerous. I will settle people on you as in the past and will make you prosper more than before. Then you will know that I am the Lord. 12I will cause people, my people Israel, to live on you. They will possess you, and you will be their inheritance; you will never again deprive them of their children.

13 "'This is what the Sovereign Lord says: Because some say to you, "You devour people and deprive your nation of its

children," [14]therefore you will no longer devour people or make your nation childless, declares the Sovereign LORD. [15]No longer will I make you hear the taunts of the nations, and no longer will you suffer the scorn of the peoples or cause your nation to fall, declares the Sovereign LORD.'"

Israel's Restoration Assured

[16]Again the word of the LORD came to me: [17]"Son of man, when the people of Israel were living in their own land, they defiled it by their conduct and their actions. Their conduct was like a woman's monthly uncleanness in my sight. [18]So I poured out my wrath on them because they had shed blood in the land and because they had defiled it with their idols. [19]I dispersed them among the nations, and they were scattered through the countries; I judged them according to their conduct and their actions. [20]And wherever they went among the nations they profaned my holy name, for it was said of them, 'These are the LORD's people, and yet they had to leave his land.' [21]I had concern for my holy name, which the people of Israel profaned among the nations where they had gone.

[22]"Therefore say to the Israelites, 'This is what the Sovereign LORD says: It is not for your sake, people of Israel, that I am going to do these things, but for the sake of my holy name, which you have profaned among the nations where you have gone. [23]I will show the holiness of my great name, which has been profaned among the nations, the name you have profaned among them. Then the nations will know that I am the LORD, declares the Sovereign LORD, when I am proved holy through you before their eyes.

[24]"'For I will take you out of the nations; I will gather you from all the countries and bring you back into your own land. [25]I will sprinkle clean water on you, and you will be clean; I will cleanse you from all your impurities and from all your idols. [26]I will give you a new heart and put a new spirit in you; I will remove from you your heart of stone and give you a heart of flesh. [27]And I will put my Spirit in you and move you to follow my decrees and be careful to keep my laws. [28]Then you will live in the land I gave your ancestors; you will be my people, and I will be your God. [29]I will save you from all your uncleanness. I will call for the grain and make it plentiful and will not bring famine upon you. [30]I will increase the fruit of the trees and the crops of the field, so that you will no longer suffer disgrace among the nations because of famine. [31]Then you will remember your evil ways and wicked deeds, and you will loathe yourselves for your sins and detestable practices. [32]I want you to know that I am not doing this for your sake, declares the Sovereign LORD. Be ashamed and disgraced for your conduct, people of Israel!

[33]"'This is what the Sovereign LORD says: On the day I cleanse you from all your sins, I will resettle your towns, and the ruins will be rebuilt. [34]The desolate land will be cultivated instead of lying desolate in the sight of all who pass through it. [35]They will say, "This land that was laid waste has become like the garden of Eden; the cities that were lying in ruins, desolate and destroyed, are now fortified and inhabited." [36]Then the nations around you that remain will know that I the LORD have rebuilt what was destroyed and have replanted what was desolate. I the LORD have spoken, and I will do it.'

[37]"This is what the Sovereign LORD says: Once again I will yield to Israel's plea and do this for them: I will make their people as numerous as sheep, [38]as numerous as the flocks for offerings at Jerusalem during her appointed festivals. So will the ruined cities be filled with flocks of people. Then they will know that I am the LORD."

The Valley of Dry Bones

37 The hand of the LORD was on me, and he brought me out by the Spirit of the LORD and set me in the middle of a valley; it was full of bones. [2]He led me back and forth among them, and I saw a great many bones on the floor of the valley, bones that were very dry. ³He asked me, "Son of man, can these bones live?"

I said, "Sovereign Lord, you alone know."

⁴Then he said to me, "Prophesy to these bones and say to them, 'Dry bones, hear the word of the Lord! ⁵This is what the Sovereign Lord says to these bones: I will make breath*ᵃ* enter you, and you will come to life. ⁶I will attach tendons to you and make flesh come upon you and cover you with skin; I will put breath in you, and you will come to life. Then you will know that I am the Lord.'"

⁷So I prophesied as I was commanded. And as I was prophesying, there was a noise, a rattling sound, and the bones came together, bone to bone. ⁸I looked, and tendons and flesh appeared on them and skin covered them, but there was no breath in them.

⁹Then he said to me, "Prophesy to the breath; prophesy, son of man, and say to it, 'This is what the Sovereign Lord says: Come, breath, from the four winds and breathe into these slain, that they may live.'" ¹⁰So I prophesied as he commanded me, and breath entered them; they came to life and stood up on their feet — a vast army.

¹¹Then he said to me: "Son of man, these bones are the people of Israel. They say, 'Our bones are dried up and our hope is gone; we are cut off.' ¹²Therefore prophesy and say to them: 'This is what the Sovereign Lord says: My people, I am going to open your graves and bring you up from them; I will bring you back to the land of Israel. ¹³Then you, my people, will know that I am the Lord, when I open your graves and bring you up from them. ¹⁴I will put my Spirit in you and you will live, and I will settle you in your own land. Then you will know that I the Lord have spoken, and I have done it, declares the Lord.'"

One Nation Under One King

¹⁵The word of the Lord came to me: ¹⁶"Son of man, take a stick of wood and write on it, 'Belonging to Judah and the Israelites associated with him.' Then take another stick of wood, and write on it, 'Belonging to Joseph (that is, to Ephraim) and all the Israelites associated with him.' ¹⁷Join them together into one stick so that they will become one in your hand.

¹⁸"When your people ask you, 'Won't you tell us what you mean by this?' ¹⁹say to them, 'This is what the Sovereign Lord says: I am going to take the stick of Joseph — which is in Ephraim's hand — and of the Israelite tribes associated with him, and join it to Judah's stick. I will make them into a single stick of wood, and they will become one in my hand.' ²⁰Hold before their eyes the sticks you have written on ²¹and say to them, 'This is what the Sovereign Lord says: I will take the Israelites out of the nations where they have gone. I will gather them from all around and bring them back into their own land. ²²I will make them one nation in the land, on the mountains of Israel. There will be one king over all of them and they will never again be two nations or be divided into two kingdoms. ²³They will no longer defile themselves with their idols and vile images or with any of their offenses, for I will save them from all their sinful backsliding,*ᵇ* and I will cleanse them. They will be my people, and I will be their God.

²⁴"'My servant David will be king over them, and they will all have one shepherd. They will follow my laws and be careful to keep my decrees. ²⁵They will live in the land I gave to my servant Jacob, the land where your ancestors lived. They and their children and their children's children will live there forever, and David my servant will be their prince forever. ²⁶I will make a covenant of peace with them; it will be an everlasting covenant. I will establish

---

ᵃ 5 The Hebrew for this word can also mean *wind* or *spirit* (see verses 6-14).   *ᵇ 23* Many Hebrew manuscripts (see also Septuagint); most Hebrew manuscripts *all their dwelling places where they sinned* them and increase their numbers, and I will put my sanctuary among them forever. [27]My dwelling place will be with them; I will be their God, and they will be my people. [28]Then the nations will know that I the LORD make Israel holy, when my sanctuary is among them forever.'"

The LORD's Great Victory Over the Nations

38 The word of the LORD came to me: [2]"Son of man, set your face against Gog, of the land of Magog, the chief prince of[a] Meshek and Tubal; prophesy against him [3]and say: 'This is what the Sovereign LORD says: I am against you, Gog, chief prince of[b] Meshek and Tubal. [4]I will turn you around, put hooks in your jaws and bring you out with your whole army—your horses, your horsemen fully armed, and a great horde with large and small shields, all of them brandishing their swords. [5]Persia, Cush[c] and Put will be with them, all with shields and helmets, [6]also Gomer with all its troops, and Beth Togarmah from the far north with all its troops—the many nations with you.

[7]"'Get ready; be prepared, you and all the hordes gathered about you, and take command of them. [8]After many days you will be called to arms. In future years you will invade a land that has recovered from war, whose people were gathered from many nations to the mountains of Israel, which had long been desolate. They had been brought out from the nations, and now all of them live in safety. [9]You and all your troops and the many nations with you will go up, advancing like a storm; you will be like a cloud covering the land.

[10]"'This is what the Sovereign LORD says: On that day thoughts will come into your mind and you will devise an evil scheme. [11]You will say, "I will invade a land of unwalled villages; I will attack a peaceful and unsuspecting people—all of them

living without walls and without gates and bars. [12]I will plunder and loot and turn my hand against the resettled ruins and the people gathered from the nations, rich in livestock and goods, living at the center of the land.[d]" [13]Sheba and Dedan and the merchants of Tarshish and all her villages[e] will say to you, "Have you come to plunder? Have you gathered your hordes to loot, to carry off silver and gold, to take away livestock and goods and to seize much plunder?"'

[14]"Therefore, son of man, prophesy and say to Gog: 'This is what the Sovereign LORD says: In that day, when my people Israel are living in safety, will you not take notice of it? [15]You will come from your place in the far north, you and many nations with you, all of them riding on horses, a great horde, a mighty army. [16]You will advance against my people Israel like a cloud that covers the land. In days to come, Gog, I will bring you against my land, so that the nations may know me when I am proved holy through you before their eyes.

[17]"'This is what the Sovereign LORD says: You are the one I spoke of in former days by my servants the prophets of Israel. At that time they prophesied for years that I would bring you against them. [18]This is what will happen in that day: When Gog attacks the land of Israel, my hot anger will be aroused, declares the Sovereign LORD. [19]In my zeal and fiery wrath I declare that at that time there shall be a great earthquake in the land of Israel. [20]The fish in the sea, the birds in the sky, the beasts of the field, every creature that moves along the ground, and all the people on the face of the earth will tremble at my presence. The mountains will be overturned, the cliffs will crumble and every wall will fall to the ground. [21]I will summon a sword against Gog on all my mountains, declares the Sovereign LORD. Every man's sword will be against his brother. [22]I will execute

---

a 2 Or *the prince of Rosh,*   *b 3* Or *Gog, prince of Rosh,*   *c 5* That is, the upper Nile region   *d 12* The Hebrew for this phrase means *the navel of the earth.*   *e 13* Or *her strong lions* judgment on him with plague and bloodshed; I will pour down torrents of rain, hailstones and burning sulfur on him and on his troops and on the many nations with him. ²³And so I will show my greatness and my holiness, and I will make myself known in the sight of many nations. Then they will know that I am the LORD.'

39 "Son of man, prophesy against Gog and say: 'This is what the Sovereign LORD says: I am against you, Gog, chief prince of*ª* Meshek and Tubal. ²I will turn you around and drag you along. I will bring you from the far north and send you against the mountains of Israel. ³Then I will strike your bow from your left hand and make your arrows drop from your right hand. ⁴On the mountains of Israel you will fall, you and all your troops and the nations with you. I will give you as food to all kinds of carrion birds and to the wild animals. ⁵You will fall in the open field, for I have spoken, declares the Sovereign LORD. ⁶I will send fire on Magog and on those who live in safety in the coastlands, and they will know that I am the LORD.

⁷"'I will make known my holy name among my people Israel. I will no longer let my holy name be profaned, and the nations will know that I the LORD am the Holy One in Israel. ⁸It is coming! It will surely take place, declares the Sovereign LORD. This is the day I have spoken of.

⁹"'Then those who live in the towns of Israel will go out and use the weapons for fuel and burn them up — the small and large shields, the bows and arrows, the war clubs and spears. For seven years they will use them for fuel. ¹⁰They will not need to gather wood from the fields or cut it from the forests, because they will use the weapons for fuel. And they will plunder those who plundered them and loot those who looted them, declares the Sovereign LORD.

¹¹"'On that day I will give Gog a burial place in Israel, in the valley of those who travel east of the Sea. It will block the way of travelers, because Gog and all his hordes will be buried there. So it will be called the Valley of Hamon Gog.*ᵇ*

¹²"'For seven months the Israelites will be burying them in order to cleanse the land. ¹³All the people of the land will bury them, and the day I display my glory will be a memorable day for them, declares the Sovereign LORD. ¹⁴People will be continually employed in cleansing the land. They will spread out across the land and, along with others, they will bury any bodies that are lying on the ground.

"'After the seven months they will carry out a more detailed search. ¹⁵As they go through the land, anyone who sees a human bone will leave a marker beside it until the gravediggers bury it in the Valley of Hamon Gog, ¹⁶near a town called Hamonah.*ᶜ* And so they will cleanse the land.'

¹⁷"Son of man, this is what the Sovereign LORD says: Call out to every kind of bird and all the wild animals: 'Assemble and come together from all around to the sacrifice I am preparing for you, the great sacrifice on the mountains of Israel. There you will eat flesh and drink blood. ¹⁸You will eat the flesh of mighty men and drink the blood of the princes of the earth as if they were rams and lambs, goats and bulls — all of them fattened animals from Bashan. ¹⁹At the sacrifice I am preparing for you, you will eat fat till you are glutted and drink blood till you are drunk. ²⁰At my table you will eat your fill of horses and riders, mighty men and soldiers of every kind,' declares the Sovereign LORD.

²¹"I will display my glory among the nations, and all the nations will see the punishment I inflict and the hand I lay on them. ²²From that day forward the people of Israel will know that I am the LORD their God. ²³And the nations will know that the people of Israel went into exile for their sin,

---

because they were unfaithful to me. So I hid my face from them and handed them over to their enemies, and they all fell by the sword. 24I dealt with them according to their uncleanness and their offenses, and I hid my face from them.

25"Therefore this is what the Sovereign LORD says: I will now restore the fortunes of Jacob[a] and will have compassion on all the people of Israel, and I will be zealous for my holy name. 26They will forget their shame and all the unfaithfulness they showed toward me when they lived in safety in their land with no one to make them afraid. 27When I have brought them back from the nations and have gathered them from the countries of their enemies, I will be proved holy through them in the sight of many nations. 28Then they will know that I am the LORD their God, for though I sent them into exile among the nations, I will gather them to their own land, not leaving any behind. 29I will no longer hide my face from them, for I will pour out my Spirit on the people of Israel, declares the Sovereign LORD."

The Temple Area Restored

40 In the twenty-fifth year of our exile, at the beginning of the year, on the tenth of the month, in the fourteenth year after the fall of the city—on that very day the hand of the LORD was on me and he took me there. 2In visions of God he took me to the land of Israel and set me on a very high mountain, on whose south side were some buildings that looked like a city. 3He took me there, and I saw a man whose appearance was like bronze; he was standing in the gateway with a linen cord and a measuring rod in his hand. 4The man said to me, "Son of man, look carefully and listen closely and pay attention to everything I am going to show you, for that is why you have been brought here. Tell the people of Israel everything you see."

The East Gate to the Outer Court

5I saw a wall completely surrounding the temple area. The length of the measuring rod in the man's hand was six long cubits,[b] each of which was a cubit and a handbreadth. He measured the wall; it was one measuring rod thick and one rod high.

6Then he went to the east gate. He climbed its steps and measured the threshold of the gate; it was one rod deep. 7The alcoves for the guards were one rod long and one rod wide, and the projecting walls between the alcoves were five cubits[c] thick. And the threshold of the gate next to the portico facing the temple was one rod deep.

8Then he measured the portico of the gateway; 9it[d] was eight cubits[e] deep and its jambs were two cubits[f] thick. The portico of the gateway faced the temple.

10Inside the east gate were three alcoves on each side; the three had the same measurements, and the faces of the projecting walls on each side had the same measurements. 11Then he measured the width of the entrance of the gateway; it was ten cubits and its length was thirteen cubits.[g] 12In front of each alcove was a wall one cubit high, and the alcoves were six cubits square. 13Then he measured the gateway from the top of the rear wall of one alcove to the top of the opposite one; the distance was twenty-five cubits[h] from one parapet opening to the opposite one. 14He measured along the faces of the projecting walls all around the inside of the gateway—sixty cubits.[i] The measurement was up to the portico[j] facing

---

[a] 25 Or *now bring Jacob back from captivity*   [b] 5 That is, about 11 feet or about 3.2 meters; also in verse 12. The long cubit of about 21 inches or about 53 centimeters is the basic unit of measurement of length throughout chapters 40–48.   [c] 7 That is, about 8 3/4 feet or about 2.7 meters; also in verse 48   [d] 8,9 Many Hebrew manuscripts, Septuagint, Vulgate and Syriac; most Hebrew manuscripts *gateway facing the temple; it was one rod deep. 9Then he measured the portico of the gateway; it*   [e] 9 That is, about 14 feet or about 4.2 meters   [f] 9 That is, about 3 1/2 feet or about 1 meter   [g] 11 That is, about 18 feet wide and 23 feet long or about 5.3 meters wide and 6.9 meters long   [h] 13 That is, about 44 feet or about 13 meters; also in verses 21, 25, 29, 30, 33 and 36   [i] 14 That is, about 105 feet or about 32 meters   [j] 14 Septuagint; Hebrew *projecting wall*

the courtyard.*a* 15The distance from the entrance of the gateway to the far end of its portico was fifty cubits.*b* 16The alcoves and the projecting walls inside the gateway were surmounted by narrow parapet openings all around, as was the portico; the openings all around faced inward. The faces of the projecting walls were decorated with palm trees.

The Outer Court

17Then he brought me into the outer court. There I saw some rooms and a pavement that had been constructed all around the court; there were thirty rooms along the pavement. 18It abutted the sides of the gateways and was as wide as they were long; this was the lower pavement. 19Then he measured the distance from the inside of the lower gateway to the outside of the inner court; it was a hundred cubits*c* on the east side as well as on the north.

The North Gate

20Then he measured the length and width of the north gate, leading into the outer court. 21Its alcoves — three on each side — its projecting walls and its portico had the same measurements as those of the first gateway. It was fifty cubits long and twenty-five cubits wide. 22Its openings, its portico and its palm tree decorations had the same measurements as those of the gate facing east. Seven steps led up to it, with its portico opposite them. 23There was a gate to the inner court facing the north gate, just as there was on the east. He measured from one gate to the opposite one; it was a hundred cubits.

The South Gate

24Then he led me to the south side and I saw the south gate. He measured its jambs and its portico, and they had the same measurements as the others. 25The gateway and its portico had narrow openings all around, like the openings of the others. It was fifty cubits long and twenty-five cu-

bits wide. 26Seven steps led up to it, with its portico opposite them; it had palm tree decorations on the faces of the projecting walls on each side. 27The inner court also had a gate facing south, and he measured from this gate to the outer gate on the south side; it was a hundred cubits.

The Gates to the Inner Court

28Then he brought me into the inner court through the south gate, and he measured the south gate; it had the same measurements as the others. 29Its alcoves, its projecting walls and its portico had the same measurements as the others. The gateway and its portico had openings all around. It was fifty cubits long and twenty-five cubits wide. 30(The porticoes of the gateways around the inner court were twenty-five cubits wide and five cubits deep.) 31Its portico faced the outer court; palm trees decorated its jambs, and eight steps led up to it.

32Then he brought me to the inner court on the east side, and he measured the gateway; it had the same measurements as the others. 33Its alcoves, its projecting walls and its portico had the same measurements as the others. The gateway and its portico had openings all around. It was fifty cubits long and twenty-five cubits wide. 34Its portico faced the outer court; palm trees decorated the jambs on either side, and eight steps led up to it.

35Then he brought me to the north gate and measured it. It had the same measurements as the others, 36as did its alcoves, its projecting walls and its portico, and it had openings all around. It was fifty cubits long and twenty-five cubits wide. 37Its portico*d* faced the outer court; palm trees decorated the jambs on either side, and eight steps led up to it.

The Rooms for Preparing Sacrifices

38A room with a doorway was by the portico in each of the inner gateways, where the

---

a 14 The meaning of the Hebrew for this verse is uncertain.   *b 15* That is, about 88 feet or about 27 meters; also in verses 21, 25, 29, 33 and 36   *c 19* That is, about 175 feet or about 53 meters; also in verses 23, 27 and 47   *d 37* Septuagint (see also verses 31 and 34); Hebrew *jambs* burnt offerings were washed. ³⁹In the portico of the gateway were two tables on each side, on which the burnt offerings, sin offerings*a* and guilt offerings were slaughtered. ⁴⁰By the outside wall of the portico of the gateway, near the steps at the entrance of the north gateway were two tables, and on the other side of the steps were two tables. ⁴¹So there were four tables on one side of the gateway and four on the other — eight tables in all — on which the sacrifices were slaughtered. ⁴²There were also four tables of dressed stone for the burnt offerings, each a cubit and a half long, a cubit and a half wide and a cubit high.*b* On them were placed the utensils for slaughtering the burnt offerings and the other sacrifices. ⁴³And double-pronged hooks, each a handbreadth*c* long, were attached to the wall all around. The tables were for the flesh of the offerings.

The Rooms for the Priests

⁴⁴Outside the inner gate, within the inner court, were two rooms, one*d* at the side of the north gate and facing south, and another at the side of the south*e* gate and facing north. ⁴⁵He said to me, "The room facing south is for the priests who guard the temple, ⁴⁶and the room facing north is for the priests who guard the altar. These are the sons of Zadok, who are the only Levites who may draw near to the LORD to minister before him."

⁴⁷Then he measured the court: It was square — a hundred cubits long and a hundred cubits wide. And the altar was in front of the temple.

The New Temple

⁴⁸He brought me to the portico of the temple and measured the jambs of the portico; they were five cubits wide on either side. The width of the entrance was fourteen cubits*f* and its projecting walls were*g* three cubits*h* wide on either side. ⁴⁹The portico was twenty cubits*i* wide, and twelve*j* cubits*k* from front to back. It was reached by a flight of stairs,*l* and there were pillars on each side of the jambs.

41 Then the man brought me to the main hall and measured the jambs; the width of the jambs was six cubits*m* on each side.*n* ²The entrance was ten cubits*o* wide, and the projecting walls on each side of it were five cubits*p* wide. He also measured the main hall; it was forty cubits long and twenty cubits wide.*q*

³Then he went into the inner sanctuary and measured the jambs of the entrance; each was two cubits*r* wide. The entrance was six cubits wide, and the projecting walls on each side of it were seven cubits*s* wide. ⁴And he measured the length of the inner sanctuary; it was twenty cubits, and its width was twenty cubits across the end of the main hall. He said to me, "This is the Most Holy Place."

⁵Then he measured the wall of the temple; it was six cubits thick, and each side room around the temple was four cubits*t* wide. ⁶The side rooms were on three levels, one above another, thirty on each level. There were ledges all around the wall of the temple to serve as supports for the side rooms, so that the supports were not inserted into the wall of the temple. ⁷The side rooms all around the temple were wider at each successive level. The structure surrounding the temple was built in ascending stages, so that the rooms widened as one

---

a 39 Or *purification offerings*   *b 42* That is, about 2 2/3 feet long and wide and 21 inches high or about 80 centimeters long and wide and 53 centimeters high   *c 43* That is, about 3 1/2 inches or about 9 centimeters   *d 44* Septuagint; Hebrew *were rooms for singers, which were*   *e 44* Septuagint; Hebrew *east*   *f 48* That is, about 25 feet or about 7.4 meters   *g 48* Septuagint; Hebrew *entrance was*   *h 48* That is, about 5 1/4 feet or about 1.6 meters   *i 49* That is, about 35 feet or about 11 meters   *j 49* Septuagint; Hebrew *eleven*   *k 49* That is, about 21 feet or about 6.4 meters   *l 49* Hebrew; Septuagint *Ten steps led up to it*   *m 1* That is, about 11 feet or about 3.2 meters; also in verses 3, 5 and 8   *n 1* One Hebrew manuscript and Septuagint; most Hebrew manuscripts *side, the width of the tent*   *o 2* That is, about 18 feet or about 5.3 meters   *p 2* That is, about 8 3/4 feet or about 2.7 meters; also in verses 9, 11 and 12   *q 2* That is, about 70 feet long and 35 feet wide or about 21 meters long and 11 meters wide   *r 3* That is, about 3 1/2 feet or about 1.1 meters; also in verse 22   *s 3* That is, about 12 feet or about 3.7 meters   *t 5* That is, about 7 feet or about 2.1 meters went upward. A stairway went up from the lowest floor to the top floor through the middle floor.

⁸I saw that the temple had a raised base all around it, forming the foundation of the side rooms. It was the length of the rod, six long cubits. ⁹The outer wall of the side rooms was five cubits thick. The open area between the side rooms of the temple ¹⁰and the priests' rooms was twenty cubits wide all around the temple. ¹¹There were entrances to the side rooms from the open area, one on the north and another on the south; and the base adjoining the open area was five cubits wide all around.

¹²The building facing the temple courtyard on the west side was seventy cubits*a* wide. The wall of the building was five cubits thick all around, and its length was ninety cubits.*b*

¹³Then he measured the temple; it was a hundred cubits*c* long, and the temple courtyard and the building with its walls were also a hundred cubits long. ¹⁴The width of the temple courtyard on the east, including the front of the temple, was a hundred cubits.

¹⁵Then he measured the length of the building facing the courtyard at the rear of the temple, including its galleries on each side; it was a hundred cubits.

The main hall, the inner sanctuary and the portico facing the court, ¹⁶as well as the thresholds and the narrow windows and galleries around the three of them — everything beyond and including the threshold was covered with wood. The floor, the wall up to the windows, and the windows were covered. ¹⁷In the space above the outside of the entrance to the inner sanctuary and on the walls at regular intervals all around the inner and outer sanctuary ¹⁸were carved cherubim and palm trees. Palm trees alternated with cherubim. Each cherub had two

faces: ¹⁹the face of a human being toward the palm tree on one side and the face of a lion toward the palm tree on the other. They were carved all around the whole temple. ²⁰From the floor to the area above the entrance, cherubim and palm trees were carved on the wall of the main hall.

²¹The main hall had a rectangular doorframe, and the one at the front of the Most Holy Place was similar. ²²There was a wooden altar three cubits*d* high and two cubits square*e*; its corners, its base*f* and its sides were of wood. The man said to me, "This is the table that is before the LORD." ²³Both the main hall and the Most Holy Place had double doors. ²⁴Each door had two leaves — two hinged leaves for each door. ²⁵And on the doors of the main hall were carved cherubim and palm trees like those carved on the walls, and there was a wooden overhang on the front of the portico. ²⁶On the sidewalls of the portico were narrow windows with palm trees carved on each side. The side rooms of the temple also had overhangs.

The Rooms for the Priests

42 Then the man led me northward into the outer court and brought me to the rooms opposite the temple courtyard and opposite the outer wall on the north side. ²The building whose door faced north was a hundred cubits long and fifty cubits wide.*g* ³Both in the section twenty cubits*h* from the inner court and in the section opposite the pavement of the outer court, gallery faced gallery at the three levels. ⁴In front of the rooms was an inner passageway ten cubits wide and a hundred cubits*i* long.*j* Their doors were on the north. ⁵Now the upper rooms were narrower, for the galleries took more space from them than from the rooms on the lower and middle floors of the building. ⁶The

---

a 12 That is, about 123 feet or about 37 meters   *b 12* That is, about 158 feet or about 48 meters   *c 13* That is, about 175 feet or about 53 meters; also in verses 14 and 15   *d 22* That is, about 5 1/4 feet or about 1.5 meters   *e 22* Septuagint; Hebrew *long*   *f 22* Septuagint; Hebrew *length*   *g 2* That is, about 175 feet long and 88 feet wide or about 53 meters long and 27 meters wide   *h 3* That is, about 35 feet or about 11 meters   *i 4* Septuagint and Syriac; Hebrew *and one cubit*   *j 4* That is, about 18 feet wide and 175 feet long or about 5.3 meters wide and 53 meters long rooms on the top floor had no pillars, as the courts had; so they were smaller in floor space than those on the lower and middle floors. 7There was an outer wall parallel to the rooms and the outer court; it extended in front of the rooms for fifty cubits. 8While the row of rooms on the side next to the outer court was fifty cubits long, the row on the side nearest the sanctuary was a hundred cubits long. 9The lower rooms had an entrance on the east side as one enters them from the outer court.

10On the south side*a* along the length of the wall of the outer court, adjoining the temple courtyard and opposite the outer wall, were rooms 11with a passageway in front of them. These were like the rooms on the north; they had the same length and width, with similar exits and dimensions. Similar to the doorways on the north 12were the doorways of the rooms on the south. There was a doorway at the beginning of the passageway that was parallel to the corresponding wall extending eastward, by which one enters the rooms.

13Then he said to me, "The north and south rooms facing the temple courtyard are the priests' rooms, where the priests who approach the LORD will eat the most holy offerings. There they will put the most holy offerings — the grain offerings, the sin offerings*b* and the guilt offerings — for the place is holy. 14Once the priests enter the holy precincts, they are not to go into the outer court until they leave behind the garments in which they minister, for these are holy. They are to put on other clothes before they go near the places that are for the people."

15When he had finished measuring what was inside the temple area, he led me out by the east gate and measured the area all around: 16He measured the east side with the measuring rod; it was five hundred cubits.*c,d* 17He measured the north side; it

was five hundred cubits*e* by the measuring rod. 18He measured the south side; it was five hundred cubits by the measuring rod. 19Then he turned to the west side and measured; it was five hundred cubits by the measuring rod. 20So he measured the area on all four sides. It had a wall around it, five hundred cubits long and five hundred cubits wide, to separate the holy from the common.

God's Glory Returns to the Temple

43 Then the man brought me to the gate facing east, 2and I saw the glory of the God of Israel coming from the east. His voice was like the roar of rushing waters, and the land was radiant with his glory. 3The vision I saw was like the vision I had seen when he*f* came to destroy the city and like the visions I had seen by the Kebar River, and I fell facedown. 4The glory of the LORD entered the temple through the gate facing east. 5Then the Spirit lifted me up and brought me into the inner court, and the glory of the LORD filled the temple.

6While the man was standing beside me, I heard someone speaking to me from inside the temple. 7He said: "Son of man, this is the place of my throne and the place for the soles of my feet. This is where I will live among the Israelites forever. The people of Israel will never again defile my holy name — neither they nor their kings — by their prostitution and the funeral offerings*g* for their kings at their death.*h* 8When they placed their threshold next to my threshold and their doorposts beside my doorposts, with only a wall between me and them, they defiled my holy name by their detestable practices. So I destroyed them in my anger. 9Now let them put away from me their prostitution and the funeral offerings for their kings, and I will live among them forever.

---

a 10 Septuagint; Hebrew *Eastward*   *b 13* Or *purification offerings*   *c 16* See Septuagint of verse 17; Hebrew *rods*; also in verses 18 and 19.   *d 16* Five hundred cubits equal about 875 feet or about 265 meters; also in verses 17, 18 and 19.   *e 17* Septuagint; Hebrew *rods*   *f 3* Some Hebrew manuscripts and Vulgate; most Hebrew manuscripts *I* *g 7* Or *the memorial monuments*; also in verse 9   *h 7* Or *their high places*

¹⁰"Son of man, describe the temple to the people of Israel, that they may be ashamed of their sins. Let them consider its perfection, ¹¹and if they are ashamed of all they have done, make known to them the design of the temple — its arrangement, its exits and entrances — its whole design and all its regulations[a] and laws. Write these down before them so that they may be faithful to its design and follow all its regulations.

¹²"This is the law of the temple: All the surrounding area on top of the mountain will be most holy. Such is the law of the temple.

The Great Altar Restored

¹³"These are the measurements of the altar in long cubits,[b] that cubit being a cubit and a handbreadth: Its gutter is a cubit deep and a cubit wide, with a rim of one span[c] around the edge. And this is the height of the altar: ¹⁴From the gutter on the ground up to the lower ledge that goes around the altar it is two cubits high, and the ledge is a cubit wide.[d] From this lower ledge to the upper ledge that goes around the altar it is four cubits high, and that ledge is also a cubit wide.[e] ¹⁵Above that, the altar hearth is four cubits high, and four horns project upward from the hearth. ¹⁶The altar hearth is square, twelve cubits[f] long and twelve cubits wide. ¹⁷The upper ledge also is square, fourteen cubits[g] long and fourteen cubits wide. All around the altar is a gutter of one cubit with a rim of half a cubit.[h] The steps of the altar face east."

¹⁸Then he said to me, "Son of man, this is what the Sovereign LORD says: These will be the regulations for sacrificing burnt offerings and splashing blood against the altar when it is built: ¹⁹You are to give a young bull as a sin offering[i] to the Levitical priests of the family of Zadok, who come near to minister before me, declares the Sovereign LORD. ²⁰You are to take some of its blood and put it on the four horns of the altar and on the four corners of the upper ledge and all around the rim, and so purify the altar and make atonement for it. ²¹You are to take the bull for the sin offering and burn it in the designated part of the temple area outside the sanctuary.

²²"On the second day you are to offer a male goat without defect for a sin offering, and the altar is to be purified as it was purified with the bull. ²³When you have finished purifying it, you are to offer a young bull and a ram from the flock, both without defect. ²⁴You are to offer them before the LORD, and the priests are to sprinkle salt on them and sacrifice them as a burnt offering to the LORD.

²⁵"For seven days you are to provide a male goat daily for a sin offering; you are also to provide a young bull and a ram from the flock, both without defect. ²⁶For seven days they are to make atonement for the altar and cleanse it; thus they will dedicate it. ²⁷At the end of these days, from the eighth day on, the priests are to present your burnt offerings and fellowship offerings on the altar. Then I will accept you, declares the Sovereign LORD."

The Priesthood Restored

44 Then the man brought me back to the outer gate of the sanctuary, the one facing east, and it was shut. ²The LORD said to me, "This gate is to remain shut. It must not be opened; no one may enter through it. It is to remain shut because the LORD, the God of Israel, has entered through it. ³The prince himself is the only one who may sit

---

[a] 11 Some Hebrew manuscripts and Septuagint; most Hebrew manuscripts *regulations and its whole design*
[b] 13 That is, about 21 inches or about 53 centimeters; also in verses 14 and 17. The long cubit is the basic unit for linear measurement throughout Ezekiel 40–48.   [c] 13 That is, about 11 inches or about 27 centimeters   [d] 14 That is, about 3 1/2 feet high and 1 3/4 feet wide or about 105 centimeters high and 53 centimeters wide   [e] 14 That is, about 7 feet high and 1 3/4 feet wide or about 2.1 meters high and 53 centimeters wide   [f] 16 That is, about 21 feet or about 6.4 meters   [g] 17 That is, about 25 feet or about 7.4 meters   [h] 17 That is, about 11 inches or about 27 centimeters   [i] 19 Or *purification offering*; also in verses 21, 22 and 25

inside the gateway to eat in the presence of the LORD. He is to enter by way of the portico of the gateway and go out the same way."

4Then the man brought me by way of the north gate to the front of the temple. I looked and saw the glory of the LORD filling the temple of the LORD, and I fell facedown.

5The LORD said to me, "Son of man, look carefully, listen closely and give attention to everything I tell you concerning all the regulations and instructions regarding the temple of the LORD. Give attention to the entrance to the temple and all the exits of the sanctuary. 6Say to rebellious Israel, 'This is what the Sovereign LORD says: Enough of your detestable practices, people of Israel! 7In addition to all your other detestable practices, you brought foreigners uncircumcised in heart and flesh into my sanctuary, desecrating my temple while you offered me food, fat and blood, and you broke my covenant. 8Instead of carrying out your duty in regard to my holy things, you put others in charge of my sanctuary. 9This is what the Sovereign LORD says: No foreigner uncircumcised in heart and flesh is to enter my sanctuary, not even the foreigners who live among the Israelites.

10" 'The Levites who went far from me when Israel went astray and who wandered from me after their idols must bear the consequences of their sin. 11They may serve in my sanctuary, having charge of the gates of the temple and serving in it; they may slaughter the burnt offerings and sacrifices for the people and stand before the people and serve them. 12But because they served them in the presence of their idols and made the people of Israel fall into sin, therefore I have sworn with uplifted hand that they must bear the consequences of their sin, declares the Sovereign LORD. 13They are not to come near to serve me as priests or come near any of my holy things or my most holy offerings; they must bear the shame of their detestable practices. 14And I will appoint them to guard the temple for all the work that is to be done in it.

15" 'But the Levitical priests, who are descendants of Zadok and who guarded my sanctuary when the Israelites went astray from me, are to come near to minister before me; they are to stand before me to offer sacrifices of fat and blood, declares the Sovereign LORD. 16They alone are to enter my sanctuary; they alone are to come near my table to minister before me and serve me as guards.

17" 'When they enter the gates of the inner court, they are to wear linen clothes; they must not wear any woolen garment while ministering at the gates of the inner court or inside the temple. 18They are to wear linen turbans on their heads and linen undergarments around their waists. They must not wear anything that makes them perspire. 19When they go out into the outer court where the people are, they are to take off the clothes they have been ministering in and are to leave them in the sacred rooms, and put on other clothes, so that the people are not consecrated through contact with their garments.

20" 'They must not shave their heads or let their hair grow long, but they are to keep the hair of their heads trimmed. 21No priest is to drink wine when he enters the inner court. 22They must not marry widows or divorced women; they may marry only virgins of Israelite descent or widows of priests. 23They are to teach my people the difference between the holy and the common and show them how to distinguish between the unclean and the clean.

24" 'In any dispute, the priests are to serve as judges and decide it according to my ordinances. They are to keep my laws and my decrees for all my appointed festivals, and they are to keep my Sabbaths holy.

25" 'A priest must not defile himself by going near a dead person; however, if the dead person was his father or mother, son or daughter, brother or unmarried sister, then he may defile himself. 26After he is cleansed, he must wait seven days. 27On the day he goes into the inner court of the sanctuary to minister in the sanctuary, he is to offer a sin offering[a] for himself, declares the Sovereign LORD.

28 "'I am to be the only inheritance the priests have. You are to give them no possession in Israel; I will be their possession. 29 They will eat the grain offerings, the sin offerings and the guilt offerings; and everything in Israel devoted[b] to the LORD will belong to them. 30 The best of all the firstfruits and of all your special gifts will belong to the priests. You are to give them the first portion of your ground meal so that a blessing may rest on your household. 31 The priests must not eat anything, whether bird or animal, found dead or torn by wild animals.

Israel Fully Restored

45 "'When you allot the land as an inheritance, you are to present to the LORD a portion of the land as a sacred district, 25,000 cubits[c] long and 20,000[d] cubits[e] wide; the entire area will be holy. 2 Of this, a section 500 cubits[f] square is to be for the sanctuary, with 50 cubits[g] around it for open land. 3 In the sacred district, measure off a section 25,000 cubits long and 10,000 cubits[h] wide. In it will be the sanctuary, the Most Holy Place. 4 It will be the sacred portion of the land for the priests, who minister in the sanctuary and who draw near to minister before the LORD. It will be a place for their houses as well as a holy place for the sanctuary. 5 An area 25,000 cubits long and 10,000 cubits wide will belong to the Levites, who serve in the temple, as their possession for towns to live in.[i]

6 "'You are to give the city as its property an area 5,000 cubits[j] wide and 25,000 cu-

bits long, adjoining the sacred portion; it will belong to all Israel.

7 "'The prince will have the land bordering each side of the area formed by the sacred district and the property of the city. It will extend westward from the west side and eastward from the east side, running lengthwise from the western to the eastern border parallel to one of the tribal portions. 8 This land will be his possession in Israel. And my princes will no longer oppress my people but will allow the people of Israel to possess the land according to their tribes.

9 "'This is what the Sovereign LORD says: You have gone far enough, princes of Israel! Give up your violence and oppression and do what is just and right. Stop dispossessing my people, declares the Sovereign LORD. 10 You are to use accurate scales, an accurate ephah[k] and an accurate bath.[l] 11 The ephah and the bath are to be the same size, the bath containing a tenth of a homer and the ephah a tenth of a homer; the homer is to be the standard measure for both. 12 The shekel[m] is to consist of twenty gerahs. Twenty shekels plus twenty-five shekels plus fifteen shekels equal one mina.[n]

13 "'This is the special gift you are to offer: a sixth of an ephah[o] from each homer of wheat and a sixth of an ephah[p] from each homer of barley. 14 The prescribed portion of olive oil, measured by the bath, is a tenth of a bath[q] from each cor (which consists of ten baths or one homer, for ten baths are equivalent to a homer). 15 Also one sheep is to be taken from every flock of two hundred from the well-watered pastures of Israel. These will be used for the grain offerings, burnt offerings and fellowship offerings to make atonement for the

---

[a] 27 Or *purification offering*; also in verse 29   [b] 29 The Hebrew term refers to the irrevocable giving over of things or persons to the LORD.   [c] 1 That is, about 8 miles or about 13 kilometers; also in verses 3, 5 and 6   [d] 1 Septuagint (see also verses 3 and 5 and 48:9); Hebrew *10,000*   [e] 1 That is, about 6 1/2 miles or about 11 kilometers   [f] 2 That is, about 875 feet or about 265 meters   [g] 2 That is, about 88 feet or about 27 meters   [h] 3 That is, about 3 1/3 miles or about 5.3 kilometers; also in verse 5   [i] 5 Septuagint; Hebrew *temple; they will have as their possession 20 rooms*   [j] 6 That is, about 1 2/3 miles or about 2.7 kilometers   [k] 10 An ephah was a dry measure having the capacity of about 3/5 bushel or about 22 liters.   [l] 10 A bath was a liquid measure equaling about 6 gallons or about 22 liters.   [m] 12 A shekel weighed about 2/5 ounce or about 12 grams.   [n] 12 That is, 60 shekels; the common mina was 50 shekels. Sixty shekels were about 1 1/2 pounds or about 690 grams.   [o] 13 That is, probably about 6 pounds or about 2.7 kilograms   [p] 13 That is, probably about 5 pounds or about 2.3 kilograms   [q] 14 That is, about 2 1/2 quarts or about 2.2 liters

people, declares the Sovereign LORD. ¹⁶All the people of the land will be required to give this special offering to the prince in Israel. ¹⁷It will be the duty of the prince to provide the burnt offerings, grain offerings and drink offerings at the festivals, the New Moons and the Sabbaths — at all the appointed festivals of Israel. He will provide the sin offerings,ᵃ grain offerings, burnt offerings and fellowship offerings to make atonement for the Israelites.

¹⁸" 'This is what the Sovereign LORD says: In the first month on the first day you are to take a young bull without defect and purify the sanctuary. ¹⁹The priest is to take some of the blood of the sin offering and put it on the doorposts of the temple, on the four corners of the upper ledge of the altar and on the gateposts of the inner court. ²⁰You are to do the same on the seventh day of the month for anyone who sins unintentionally or through ignorance; so you are to make atonement for the temple.

²¹" 'In the first month on the fourteenth day you are to observe the Passover, a festival lasting seven days, during which you shall eat bread made without yeast. ²²On that day the prince is to provide a bull as a sin offering for himself and for all the people of the land. ²³Every day during the seven days of the festival he is to provide seven bulls and seven rams without defect as a burnt offering to the LORD, and a male goat for a sin offering. ²⁴He is to provide as a grain offering an ephah for each bull and an ephah for each ram, along with a hinᵇ of olive oil for each ephah.

²⁵" 'During the seven days of the festival, which begins in the seventh month on the fifteenth day, he is to make the same provision for sin offerings, burnt offerings, grain offerings and oil.

46 " 'This is what the Sovereign LORD says: The gate of the inner court facing east is to be shut on the six working days, but on the Sabbath day and on the day of the New Moon it is to be opened. ²The prince is to enter from the outside through the portico of the gateway and stand by the gatepost. The priests are to sacrifice his burnt offering and his fellowship offerings. He is to bow down in worship at the threshold of the gateway and then go out, but the gate will not be shut until evening. ³On the Sabbaths and New Moons the people of the land are to worship in the presence of the LORD at the entrance of that gateway. ⁴The burnt offering the prince brings to the LORD on the Sabbath day is to be six male lambs and a ram, all without defect. ⁵The grain offering given with the ram is to be an ephah,ᶜ and the grain offering with the lambs is to be as much as he pleases, along with a hinᵈ of olive oil for each ephah. ⁶On the day of the New Moon he is to offer a young bull, six lambs and a ram, all without defect. ⁷He is to provide as a grain offering one ephah with the bull, one ephah with the ram, and with the lambs as much as he wants to give, along with a hin of oil for each ephah. ⁸When the prince enters, he is to go in through the portico of the gateway, and he is to come out the same way.

⁹" 'When the people of the land come before the LORD at the appointed festivals, whoever enters by the north gate to worship is to go out the south gate; and whoever enters by the south gate is to go out the north gate. No one is to return through the gate by which they entered, but each is to go out the opposite gate. ¹⁰The prince is to be among them, going in when they go in and going out when they go out. ¹¹At the feasts and the appointed festivals, the grain offering is to be an ephah with a bull, an ephah with a ram, and with the lambs as much as he pleases, along with a hin of oil for each ephah.

¹²" 'When the prince provides a freewill offering to the LORD — whether a burnt

---

ᵃ 17 Or purification offerings; also in verses 19, 22, 23 and 25   ᵇ 24 That is, about 1 gallon or about 3.8 liters
ᶜ 5 That is, probably about 35 pounds or about 16 kilograms; also in verses 7 and 11   ᵈ 5 That is, about 1 gallon or about 3.8 liters; also in verses 7 and 11

offering or fellowship offerings — the gate facing east is to be opened for him. He shall offer his burnt offering or his fellowship offerings as he does on the Sabbath day. Then he shall go out, and after he has gone out, the gate will be shut.

13 "'Every day you are to provide a year-old lamb without defect for a burnt offering to the LORD; morning by morning you shall provide it. 14 You are also to provide with it morning by morning a grain offering, consisting of a sixth of an ephah*a* with a third of a hin*b* of oil to moisten the flour. The presenting of this grain offering to the LORD is a lasting ordinance. 15 So the lamb and the grain offering and the oil shall be provided morning by morning for a regular burnt offering.

16 "'This is what the Sovereign LORD says: If the prince makes a gift from his inheritance to one of his sons, it will also belong to his descendants; it is to be their property by inheritance. 17 If, however, he makes a gift from his inheritance to one of his servants, the servant may keep it until the year of freedom; then it will revert to the prince. His inheritance belongs to his sons only; it is theirs. 18 The prince must not take any of the inheritance of the people, driving them off their property. He is to give his sons their inheritance out of his own property, so that not one of my people will be separated from their property.'"

19 Then the man brought me through the entrance at the side of the gate to the sacred rooms facing north, which belonged to the priests, and showed me a place at the western end. 20 He said to me, "This is the place where the priests are to cook the guilt offering and the sin offering*c* and bake the grain offering, to avoid bringing them into the outer court and consecrating the people."

21 He then brought me to the outer court and led me around to its four corners, and I saw in each corner another court. 22 In the four corners of the outer court were enclosed*d* courts, forty cubits long and thirty cubits wide;*e* each of the courts in the four corners was the same size. 23 Around the inside of each of the four courts was a ledge of stone, with places for fire built all around under the ledge. 24 He said to me, "These are the kitchens where those who minister at the temple are to cook the sacrifices of the people."

The River From the Temple

47 The man brought me back to the entrance to the temple, and I saw water coming out from under the threshold of the temple toward the east (for the temple faced east). The water was coming down from under the south side of the temple, south of the altar. 2 He then brought me out through the north gate and led me around the outside to the outer gate facing east, and the water was trickling from the south side.

3 As the man went eastward with a measuring line in his hand, he measured off a thousand cubits*f* and then led me through water that was ankle-deep. 4 He measured off another thousand cubits and led me through water that was knee-deep. He measured off another thousand and led me through water that was up to the waist. 5 He measured off another thousand, but now it was a river that I could not cross, because the water had risen and was deep enough to swim in — a river that no one could cross. 6 He asked me, "Son of man, do you see this?"

Then he led me back to the bank of the river. 7 When I arrived there, I saw a great number of trees on each side of the river. 8 He said to me, "This water flows toward the eastern region and goes down into the Arabah,*g* where it enters the Dead Sea. When it empties into the sea, the salty wa-

---

a 14 That is, probably about 6 pounds or about 2.7 kilograms   *b 14* That is, about 1 1/2 quarts or about 1.3 liters   *c 20* Or *purification offering*   *d 22* The meaning of the Hebrew for this word is uncertain.   *e 22* That is, about 70 feet long and 53 feet wide or about 21 meters long and 16 meters wide   *f 3* That is, about 1,700 feet or about 530 meters   *g 8* Or *the Jordan Valley* ter there becomes fresh. ⁹Swarms of living creatures will live wherever the river flows. There will be large numbers of fish, because this water flows there and makes the salt water fresh; so where the river flows everything will live. ¹⁰Fishermen will stand along the shore; from En Gedi to En Eglaim there will be places for spreading nets. The fish will be of many kinds — like the fish of the Mediterranean Sea. ¹¹But the swamps and marshes will not become fresh; they will be left for salt. ¹²Fruit trees of all kinds will grow on both banks of the river. Their leaves will not wither, nor will their fruit fail. Every month they will bear fruit, because the water from the sanctuary flows to them. Their fruit will serve for food and their leaves for healing."

The Boundaries of the Land

¹³This is what the Sovereign Lord says: "These are the boundaries of the land that you will divide among the twelve tribes of Israel as their inheritance, with two portions for Joseph. ¹⁴You are to divide it equally among them. Because I swore with uplifted hand to give it to your ancestors, this land will become your inheritance.

¹⁵"This is to be the boundary of the land:

"On the north side it will run from the Mediterranean Sea by the Hethlon road past Lebo Hamath to Zedad, ¹⁶Berothahᵃ and Sibraim (which lies on the border between Damascus and Hamath), as far as Hazer Hattikon, which is on the border of Hauran. ¹⁷The boundary will extend from the sea to Hazar Enan,ᵇ along the northern border of Damascus, with the border of Hamath to the north. This will be the northern boundary. ¹⁸"On the east side the boundary will run between Hauran and Damascus, along the Jordan between Gilead and the land of Israel, to the Dead Sea and

as far as Tamar.ᶜ This will be the eastern boundary.

¹⁹"On the south side it will run from Tamar as far as the waters of Meribah Kadesh, then along the Wadi of Egypt to the Mediterranean Sea. This will be the southern boundary.

²⁰"On the west side, the Mediterranean Sea will be the boundary to a point opposite Lebo Hamath. This will be the western boundary.

²¹"You are to distribute this land among yourselves according to the tribes of Israel. ²²You are to allot it as an inheritance for yourselves and for the foreigners residing among you and who have children. You are to consider them as native-born Israelites; along with you they are to be allotted an inheritance among the tribes of Israel. ²³In whatever tribe a foreigner resides, there you are to give them their inheritance," declares the Sovereign Lord.

The Division of the Land

48 "These are the tribes, listed by name: At the northern frontier, Dan will have one portion; it will follow the Hethlon road to Lebo Hamath; Hazar Enan and the northern border of Damascus next to Hamath will be part of its border from the east side to the west side.

²"Asher will have one portion; it will border the territory of Dan from east to west.

³"Naphtali will have one portion; it will border the territory of Asher from east to west.

⁴"Manasseh will have one portion; it will border the territory of Naphtali from east to west.

⁵"Ephraim will have one portion; it will border the territory of Manasseh from east to west.

⁶"Reuben will have one portion; it will border the territory of Ephraim from east to west.

ᵃ 15,16 See Septuagint and 48:1; Hebrew *road to go into Zedad,* ¹⁶*Hamath, Berothah.*   ᵇ 17 Hebrew *Enon,* a variant of *Enan*   ᶜ 18 See Syriac; Hebrew *Israel. You will measure to the Dead Sea.*

⁷"Judah will have one portion; it will border the territory of Reuben from east to west.

⁸"Bordering the territory of Judah from east to west will be the portion you are to present as a special gift. It will be 25,000 cubits*a* wide, and its length from east to west will equal one of the tribal portions; the sanctuary will be in the center of it.

⁹"The special portion you are to offer to the LORD will be 25,000 cubits long and 10,000 cubits*b* wide. ¹⁰This will be the sacred portion for the priests. It will be 25,000 cubits long on the north side, 10,000 cubits wide on the west side, 10,000 cubits wide on the east side and 25,000 cubits long on the south side. In the center of it will be the sanctuary of the LORD. ¹¹This will be for the consecrated priests, the Zadokites, who were faithful in serving me and did not go astray as the Levites did when the Israelites went astray. ¹²It will be a special gift to them from the sacred portion of the land, a most holy portion, bordering the territory of the Levites.

¹³"Alongside the territory of the priests, the Levites will have an allotment 25,000 cubits long and 10,000 cubits wide. Its total length will be 25,000 cubits and its width 10,000 cubits. ¹⁴They must not sell or exchange any of it. This is the best of the land and must not pass into other hands, because it is holy to the LORD.

¹⁵"The remaining area, 5,000 cubits*c* wide and 25,000 cubits long, will be for the common use of the city, for houses and for pastureland. The city will be in the center of it ¹⁶and will have these measurements: the north side 4,500 cubits,*d* the south side 4,500 cubits, the east side 4,500 cubits, and the west side 4,500 cubits. ¹⁷The pastureland for the city will be 250 cubits*e* on the north, 250 cubits on the south, 250 cubits on the east, and 250 cubits on the west. ¹⁸What remains of the area, bordering on

the sacred portion and running the length of it, will be 10,000 cubits on the east side and 10,000 cubits on the west side. Its produce will supply food for the workers of the city. ¹⁹The workers from the city who farm it will come from all the tribes of Israel. ²⁰The entire portion will be a square, 25,000 cubits on each side. As a special gift you will set aside the sacred portion, along with the property of the city.

²¹"What remains on both sides of the area formed by the sacred portion and the property of the city will belong to the prince. It will extend eastward from the 25,000 cubits of the sacred portion to the eastern border, and westward from the 25,000 cubits to the western border. Both these areas running the length of the tribal portions will belong to the prince, and the sacred portion with the temple sanctuary will be in the center of them. ²²So the property of the Levites and the property of the city will lie in the center of the area that belongs to the prince. The area belonging to the prince will lie between the border of Judah and the border of Benjamin.

²³"As for the rest of the tribes: Benjamin will have one portion; it will extend from the east side to the west side.

²⁴"Simeon will have one portion; it will border the territory of Benjamin from east to west.

²⁵"Issachar will have one portion; it will border the territory of Simeon from east to west.

²⁶"Zebulun will have one portion; it will border the territory of Issachar from east to west.

²⁷"Gad will have one portion; it will border the territory of Zebulun from east to west.

²⁸"The southern boundary of Gad will run south from Tamar to the waters of Meribah Kadesh, then along the Wadi of Egypt to the Mediterranean Sea.

---

a 8 That is, about 8 miles or about 13 kilometers; also in verses 9, 10, 13, 15, 20 and 21   *b 9* That is, about 3 1/3 miles or about 5.3 kilometers; also in verses 10, 13 and 18   *c 15* That is, about 1 2/3 miles or about 2.7 kilometers   *d 16* That is, about 1 1/2 miles or about 2.4 kilometers; also in verses 30, 32, 33 and 34   *e 17* That is, about 440 feet or about 135 meters

29"This is the land you are to allot as an inheritance to the tribes of Israel, and these will be their portions," declares the Sovereign LORD.

The Gates of the New City

30"These will be the exits of the city: Beginning on the north side, which is 4,500 cubits long, 31the gates of the city will be named after the tribes of Israel. The three gates on the north side will be the gate of Reuben, the gate of Judah and the gate of Levi.

32"On the east side, which is 4,500 cubits long, will be three gates: the gate of Joseph, the gate of Benjamin and the gate of Dan.

33"On the south side, which measures 4,500 cubits, will be three gates: the gate of Simeon, the gate of Issachar and the gate of Zebulun.

34"On the west side, which is 4,500 cubits long, will be three gates: the gate of Gad, the gate of Asher and the gate of Naphtali.

35"The distance all around will be 18,000 cubits.*a*

"And the name of the city from that time on will be:

THE LORD IS THERE."

---

a 35 That is, about 6 miles or about 9.5 kilometers

Daniel

THEME: Daniel's visions give a divine perspective on reality that differs from what is visible: God will ultimately win the victory, so we can live our lives with the expectation of final triumph.

AUTHOR: The book identifies its author as Daniel, and Jesus attributed authorship to Daniel as well. Daniel was among the first Jews carried off to Babylon in 605 BC (captives were taken in three stages, in 605, 597 and 586 BC).

DATE OF WRITING: Daniel was probably written between 536 and 530 BC, shortly after Cyrus captured Babylon in 539 BC.

ENCOURAGEMENT FROM DANIEL: "As soon as you began to pray, a word went out" (Daniel 9:23).

CHALLENGE FROM DANIEL: "Praise and exalt and glorify the King of heaven, because everything he does is right and all his ways are just. And those who walk in pride he is able to humble" (Daniel 4:37).

REFLECTION FROM DANIEL: "We do not make requests of you because we are righteous, but because of your great mercy. Lord, listen! Lord, forgive! Lord, hear and act! For your sake, my God, do not delay, because your city and your people bear your Name" (Daniel 9:18 – 19).

The book of Daniel bridges the gap between Israel's historical books and the New Testament. Certain events of the 70-year Babylonian captivity that are recorded in Daniel are found nowhere else in Scripture. The dreams and visions recorded in the book of Daniel present God's complete control over world history. But the book develops another theme, the need to live a godly life. Daniel led a disciplined life, rejecting any compromise to his faith or lifestyle. Because of Daniel's unwavering commitment, God displayed his power on Daniel's behalf.

Still today, the book of Daniel reminds us that God is in control — not just over history, not just over peoples of the easily forgotten past, but over our own individual futures. Daniel describes the healing and restoration that were in store for Israel, and God desires that we experience this healing as well. Because we've gone our own way in the past, it has become necessary for God to discipline us. But his correction is his way of reaching out to us as a loving Father, his means of reminding us that we're his — and, as his children, we're to live the way he prescribes for us in Scripture.

Discipline is a gift from God that prepares us for his service. Like Daniel, we must resist compromise in our recovery journeys. We're always to remember that Jesus Christ is our one and only true Higher Power, our single source of true healing. When we stand firm in this truth, God pours out his power on us, just as he did on Daniel. And, like Daniel, each of us can count on his promises.

Daniel's Training in Babylon

1 In the third year of the reign of Jehoiakim king of Judah, Nebuchadnezzar king of Babylon came to Jerusalem and besieged it. ²And the Lord delivered Jehoiakim king of Judah into his hand, along with some of the articles from the temple of God. These he carried off to the temple of his god in Babylonia*a* and put in the treasure house of his god.

³Then the king ordered Ashpenaz, chief of his court officials, to bring into the king's service some of the Israelites from the royal family and the nobility— ⁴young men without any physical defect, handsome, showing aptitude for every kind of learning, well informed, quick to understand, and qualified to serve in the king's palace. He was to teach them the language and literature of the Babylonians.*b* ⁵The king assigned them a daily amount of food and wine from the king's table. They were to be trained for three years, and after that they were to enter the king's service.

⁶Among those who were chosen were some from Judah: Daniel, Hananiah, Mishael and Azariah. ⁷The chief official gave them new names: to Daniel, the name Belteshazzar; to Hananiah, Shadrach; to Mishael, Meshach; and to Azariah, Abednego.

⁸But Daniel resolved not to defile himself with the royal food and wine, and he asked the chief official for permission not to defile himself this way. ⁹Now God had caused the official to show favor and compassion to Daniel, ¹⁰but the official told Daniel, "I am afraid of my lord the king, who has assigned your*c* food and drink. Why should he see you looking worse than the other young men your age? The king would then have my head because of you."

¹¹Daniel then said to the guard whom the chief official had appointed over Daniel, Hananiah, Mishael and Azariah, ¹²"Please test your servants for ten days:

Give us nothing but vegetables to eat and water to drink. ¹³Then compare our appearance with that of the young men who eat the royal food, and treat your servants in accordance with what you see." ¹⁴So he agreed to this and tested them for ten days.

¹⁵At the end of the ten days they looked healthier and better nourished than any of the young men who ate the royal food. ¹⁶So the guard took away their choice food and the wine they were to drink and gave them vegetables instead.

¹⁷To these four young men God gave knowledge and understanding of all kinds of literature and learning. And Daniel could understand visions and dreams of all kinds.

¹⁸At the end of the time set by the king to bring them into his service, the chief official presented them to Nebuchadnezzar. ¹⁹The king talked with them, and he found none equal to Daniel, Hananiah, Mishael and Azariah; so they entered the king's service. ²⁰In every matter of wisdom and understanding about which the king questioned them, he found them ten times better than all the magicians and enchanters in his whole kingdom.

²¹And Daniel remained there until the first year of King Cyrus.

Nebuchadnezzar's Dream

2 In the second year of his reign, Nebuchadnezzar had dreams; his mind was troubled and he could not sleep. ²So the king summoned the magicians, enchanters, sorcerers and astrologers*d* to tell him what he had dreamed. When they came in and stood before the king, ³he said to them, "I have had a dream that troubles me and I want to know what it means.*e*"

⁴Then the astrologers answered the king,*f* "May the king live forever! Tell your servants the dream, and we will interpret it."

⁵The king replied to the astrologers, "This

---

a 2 Hebrew *Shinar*   *b 4* Or *Chaldeans*   *c 10* The Hebrew for *your* and *you* in this verse is plural.   *d 2* Or *Chaldeans*; also in verses 4, 5 and 10   *e 3* Or *was*   *f 4* At this point the Hebrew text has *in Aramaic,* indicating that the text from here through the end of chapter 7 is in Aramaic.

MY NAME IS DANIEL

DANIEL 1

Scripture indicates that Daniel, himself a man of impeccable character, was a victim of the sins of others. The southern kingdom of Judah had witnessed God's judgment upon the northern kingdom of Israel, and the Judahites had been repeatedly called to repentance by God's prophets. But the majority had surrendered to idolatry and the depravity that went with it. As always, a righteous remnant suffered along with the guilty when the Babylonians established their domination over Judah. The most promising young men from leading families were sent as captives to Babylon. Among them was Daniel.

Daniel had every human excuse to be bitter against his own people and even against God. As a young man, isolated from his family, he faced temptations that are difficult for us to imagine. He found himself alone in a decadent city, facing a Babylonian blueprint for his future: a pagan education and lifestyle with an implied promise of loyal government service. No one would have blamed Daniel for compromising. He was, after all, at the mercy of the Babylonian king and his officials, destined to be trained to serve the king. Why not conform to their demands? The fact is that Daniel opted not to. His name means "God is My Judge," and Daniel lived up to this high standard, resolving "not to defile himself" (Daniel 1:8).

Daniel's exemplary behavior provides a pattern for any of us who find ourselves the victims of others' sins. It would be easy for us to surrender to bitterness. We might be tempted to believe that God doesn't care. But Daniel refused to give in to sullen hostility. Instead, he took a stand for living according to God's principles. This first chapter of Daniel records God's faithfulness in protecting Daniel and his courageous friends who had chosen the same path. The balance of this book records Daniel's continuing refusal to abandon God through compromise. As his circumstances became more threatening, Daniel was consistently protected and elevated to positions of honor among the king's advisers.

In Daniel 6, we read about an attempt to eliminate God's protection over this now-aging man of faith. Through flattery, Daniel's enemies tricked the king into decreeing that only he was to be worshiped for 30 days. Daniel, continuing his lifelong habit of resistance to compromise, maintained his discipleship by worshiping God openly at three set times each day. This noncompliance with the king's rash demand ultimately placed God's man in a den of ravenous lions. But God protected Daniel, and a relieved King Darius issued a public decree that all his subjects "fear and reverence the God of Daniel" (v. 26). The disciplines of recovery, including our daily time with God, aren't intended for our benefit alone. Each of us, no less than Daniel, can function as a message to the masses of God's power to heal the hurting. We, like Daniel, can be transformed from victims to victors through Jesus Christ—the one true Higher Power.

is what I have firmly decided: If you do not tell me what my dream was and interpret it, I will have you cut into pieces and your houses turned into piles of rubble. 6But if you tell me the dream and explain it, you will receive from me gifts and rewards and great honor. So tell me the dream and interpret it for me."

7Once more they replied, "Let the king tell his servants the dream, and we will interpret it."

8Then the king answered, "I am certain that you are trying to gain time, because you realize that this is what I have firmly decided: 9If you do not tell me the dream, there is only one penalty for you. You have conspired to tell me misleading and wicked things, hoping the situation will change. So then, tell me the dream, and I will know that you can interpret it for me."

10The astrologers answered the king, "There is no one on earth who can do what the king asks! No king, however great and mighty, has ever asked such a thing of any magician or enchanter or astrologer. 11What the king asks is too difficult. No one can reveal it to the king except the gods, and they do not live among humans."

12This made the king so angry and furious that he ordered the execution of all the wise men of Babylon. 13So the decree was issued to put the wise men to death, and men were sent to look for Daniel and his friends to put them to death.

14When Arioch, the commander of the king's guard, had gone out to put to death the wise men of Babylon, Daniel spoke to him with wisdom and tact. 15He asked the king's officer, "Why did the king issue such a harsh decree?" Arioch then explained the matter to Daniel. 16At this, Daniel went in to the king and asked for time, so that he might interpret the dream for him.

17Then Daniel returned to his house and explained the matter to his friends Hananiah, Mishael and Azariah. 18He urged them to plead for mercy from the God of heaven concerning this mystery, so that he and his friends might not be executed with the rest of the wise men of Babylon.

19During the night the mystery was revealed to Daniel in a vision. Then Daniel praised the God of heaven 20and said:

"Praise be to the name of God for ever
        and ever;
    wisdom and power are his.
21 He changes times and seasons;
    he deposes kings and raises up
        others.
He gives wisdom to the wise
    and knowledge to the discerning.
22 He reveals deep and hidden
        things;
    he knows what lies in darkness,
    and light dwells with him.
23 I thank and praise you, God of my
        ancestors:
    You have given me wisdom and
        power,
you have made known to me what we
        asked of you,
    you have made known to us the
        dream of the king."

Daniel Interprets the Dream

24Then Daniel went to Arioch, whom the king had appointed to execute the wise men of Babylon, and said to him, "Do not execute the wise men of Babylon. Take me to the king, and I will interpret his dream for him."

25Arioch took Daniel to the king at once and said, "I have found a man among the exiles from Judah who can tell the king what his dream means."

26The king asked Daniel (also called Belteshazzar), "Are you able to tell me what I saw in my dream and interpret it?"

27Daniel replied, "No wise man, enchanter, magician or diviner can explain to the king the mystery he has asked about, 28but there is a God in heaven who reveals mysteries. He has shown King Nebuchadnezzar what will happen in days to come. Your dream and the visions that passed through your mind as you were lying in bed are these:

29"As Your Majesty was lying there, your

mind turned to things to come, and the revealer of mysteries showed you what is going to happen. ³⁰As for me, this mystery has been revealed to me, not because I have greater wisdom than anyone else alive, but so that Your Majesty may know the interpretation and that you may understand what went through your mind.

³¹"Your Majesty looked, and there before you stood a large statue — an enormous, dazzling statue, awesome in appearance. ³²The head of the statue was made of pure gold, its chest and arms of silver, its belly and thighs of bronze, ³³its legs of iron, its feet partly of iron and partly of baked clay. ³⁴While you were watching, a rock was cut out, but not by human hands. It struck the statue on its feet of iron and clay and smashed them. ³⁵Then the iron, the clay, the bronze, the silver and the gold were all broken to pieces and became like chaff on a threshing floor in the summer. The wind swept them away without leaving a trace. But the rock that struck the statue became a huge mountain and filled the whole earth.

³⁶"This was the dream, and now we will interpret it to the king. ³⁷Your Majesty, you are the king of kings. The God of heaven has given you dominion and power and might and glory; ³⁸in your hands he has placed all mankind and the beasts of the field and the birds in the sky. Wherever they live, he has made you ruler over them all. You are that head of gold.

³⁹"After you, another kingdom will arise, inferior to yours. Next, a third kingdom, one of bronze, will rule over the whole earth. ⁴⁰Finally, there will be a fourth kingdom, strong as iron — for iron breaks and smashes everything — and as iron breaks things to pieces, so it will crush and break all the others. ⁴¹Just as you saw that the feet and toes were partly of baked clay and partly of iron, so this will be a divided kingdom; yet it will have some of the strength of iron in it, even as you saw iron

mixed with clay. ⁴²As the toes were partly iron and partly clay, so this kingdom will be partly strong and partly brittle. ⁴³And just as you saw the iron mixed with baked clay, so the people will be a mixture and will not remain united, any more than iron mixes with clay.

⁴⁴"In the time of those kings, the God of heaven will set up a kingdom that will never be destroyed, nor will it be left to another people. It will crush all those kingdoms and bring them to an end, but it will itself endure forever. ⁴⁵This is the meaning of the vision of the rock cut out of a mountain, but not by human hands — a rock that broke the iron, the bronze, the clay, the silver and the gold to pieces.

"The great God has shown the king what will take place in the future. The dream is true and its interpretation is trustworthy."

⁴⁶Then King Nebuchadnezzar fell prostrate before Daniel and paid him honor and ordered that an offering and incense be presented to him. ⁴⁷The king said to Daniel, "Surely your God is the God of gods and the Lord of kings and a revealer of mysteries, for you were able to reveal this mystery."

⁴⁸Then the king placed Daniel in a high position and lavished many gifts on him. He made him ruler over the entire province of Babylon and placed him in charge of all its wise men. ⁴⁹Moreover, at Daniel's request the king appointed Shadrach, Meshach and Abednego administrators over the province of Babylon, while Daniel himself remained at the royal court.

The Image of Gold and the Blazing Furnace

3 King Nebuchadnezzar made an image of gold, sixty cubits high and six cubits wide,ᵃ and set it up on the plain of Dura in the province of Babylon. ²He then summoned the satraps, prefects, governors, advisers, treasurers, judges, magistrates and all the other provincial

---

ᵃ 1 That is, about 90 feet high and 9 feet wide or about 27 meters high and 2.7 meters wide officials to come to the dedication of the image he had set up. ³So the satraps, prefects, governors, advisers, treasurers, judges, magistrates and all the other provincial officials assembled for the dedication of the image that King Nebuchadnezzar had set up, and they stood before it.

⁴Then the herald loudly proclaimed, "Nations and peoples of every language, this is what you are commanded to do: ⁵As soon as you hear the sound of the horn, flute, zither, lyre, harp, pipe and all kinds of music, you must fall down and worship the image of gold that King Nebuchadnezzar has set up. ⁶Whoever does not fall down and worship will immediately be thrown into a blazing furnace."

⁷Therefore, as soon as they heard the sound of the horn, flute, zither, lyre, harp and all kinds of music, all the nations and peoples of every language fell down and worshiped the image of gold that King Nebuchadnezzar had set up.

⁸At this time some astrologers*a* came forward and denounced the Jews. ⁹They said to King Nebuchadnezzar, "May the king live forever! ¹⁰Your Majesty has issued a decree that everyone who hears the sound of the horn, flute, zither, lyre, harp, pipe and all kinds of music must fall down and worship the image of gold, ¹¹and that whoever does not fall down and worship will be thrown into a blazing furnace. ¹²But there are some Jews whom you have set over the affairs of the province of Babylon — Shadrach, Meshach and Abednego — who pay no attention to you, Your Majesty. They neither serve your gods nor worship the image of gold you have set up."

¹³Furious with rage, Nebuchadnezzar summoned Shadrach, Meshach and Abednego. So these men were brought before the king, ¹⁴and Nebuchadnezzar said to them, "Is it true, Shadrach, Meshach and Abednego, that you do not serve my gods or worship the image of gold I have set up? ¹⁵Now when you hear the sound of the horn, flute, zither, lyre, harp, pipe and all kinds of music, if you are ready to fall down and worship the image I made, very good. But if you do not worship it, you will be thrown immediately into a blazing furnace. Then what god will be able to rescue you from my hand?"

¹⁶Shadrach, Meshach and Abednego replied to him, "King Nebuchadnezzar, we do not need to defend ourselves before you in this matter. ¹⁷If we are thrown into the blazing furnace, the God we serve is able to deliver us from it, and he will deliver us*b* from Your Majesty's hand. ¹⁸But even if he does not, we want you to know, Your Majesty, that we will not serve your gods or worship the image of gold you have set up."

¹⁹Then Nebuchadnezzar was furious with Shadrach, Meshach and Abednego, and his attitude toward them changed. He ordered the furnace heated seven times hotter than usual ²⁰and commanded some of the strongest soldiers in his army to tie up Shadrach, Meshach and Abednego and throw them into the blazing furnace. ²¹So these men, wearing their robes, trousers, turbans and other clothes, were bound and thrown into the blazing furnace. ²²The king's command was so urgent and the furnace so hot that the flames of the fire killed the soldiers who took up Shadrach, Meshach and Abednego, ²³and these three men, firmly tied, fell into the blazing furnace.

²⁴Then King Nebuchadnezzar leaped to his feet in amazement and asked his advisers, "Weren't there three men that we tied up and threw into the fire?"

They replied, "Certainly, Your Majesty."

²⁵He said, "Look! I see four men walking around in the fire, unbound and unharmed, and the fourth looks like a son of the gods."

²⁶Nebuchadnezzar then approached the opening of the blazing furnace and

---

a 8 Or *Chaldeans*   *b 17* Or *If the God we serve is able to deliver us, then he will deliver us from the blazing furnace and*

My Name Is Roger

I'm a believer who struggles with sexual abuse and finances

Please read about young Daniel's integrity in Daniel 1. Other examples of Daniel's courage and resolve may be found in 2:24 – 49 and in chapter 6.

I was born to an unwed mother who worked multiple jobs to provide for her little boy. When I was four years old, she would drop me off at a babysitter's early in the afternoon and come back late at night. One of the sitter's brothers had recently gotten out of jail. At night he would pick out one of the kids to share some "special" playtime with. He taught us things no child should ever learn. I wondered how my mom could leave me like this and questioned whether she knew what was happening. I concluded that she must not care, that I was worth nothing to her.

When I was in the fourth grade, I met my father and began spending time with him. He picked me up every couple of weeks, spent money on toys and then dropped me off with a friend. He played in a band and regularly forgot about me while he played cards. I thought, "Hey, I'm not worth anything to him either, but at least I got some cool toys out of the deal." One weekend he forgot to feed me. When I told my mom, she blew up and I didn't see my dad again for a long time.

After high school I joined the U.S. Marine Corps. I wanted to serve my country but also hoped I would live out some of my childhood fantasies from the Dungeons and Dragons video I had played by the hour. In the game I'd been rewarded for evil. Ironically, I also fantasized that I would die and end the pain of my existence.

I saw many different parts of the world while in the military. I didn't have to worry about food or lodging, and, on top of that, I got paid. The money always seemed to burn a hole in my pocket, though.

While on deployment in the Persian Gulf I came to accept Jesus as my Savior and Lord. Through my small groups and Bible studies, I felt for the first time that someone actually cared for me. Unfortunately, when I got home I didn't connect to a church family. Without that support I became depressed. Unlike Daniel, I began to compromise God's will for good stewardship. I started to neglect the simple things — like paying bills on time, taxes and credit cards. When my first enlistment was up, I chose to reenlist.

When I was released in 1995, I experienced one of the most profound shocks of my life: I had to pay for my housing, my food and everything else I needed. I went from one financial crisis to the next, realizing that something was wrong in my life but assuring myself that I would eventually find a fix.

I attended Saddleback Church and knew immediately that I had found my church home. The teaching, the music and everything else felt right; I belonged. I participated in the classes and was happy. But my resolve was weak, and my attendance slipped.

I met the love of my life and moved in with her, again compromising God's will. Eventually we were engaged, but my lying, as well as the ugly details of my financial past, came to light. I remember my fiancée telling me that, although she did love me, I wasn't marriage-worthy. At that point I was $61,000 dollars in debt and sleeping in the back of my car. Hitting bottom brought me back to my church home.

On my first weekend back, Pastor Rick was talking about the debt trap. God had me right where he wanted me. Pastor Rick informed us about a group that would be dealing with financial recovery. Figuring that I had nothing to lose, I went that Friday night to Celebrate Recovery. I knew after the first meeting that things were going to change. From that point on I put God first and made the program a priority. The people in my group and those I met during the fellowship times were all real. I remember that the first time I shared I expected somebody to ask me to leave because I was so messed up. Instead, I felt love and support from everyone in the room.

As I worked the principles, I felt more peace after each step. Principle Four was the most meaningful for me. When I took my inventory and shared it with my sponsor, I was met with the love of Jesus. When I gave my all to God, I felt so liberated. I started making financial amends and have at long last begun to find contentment.

The Biblical Daniel has become my role model. Before recovery, I was unable to summon anywhere near the kind of strength that Daniel exemplified. Today, though, rather than choosing to live in bitterness on the basis of the sins committed against me during my boyhood, I'm able to stand and to live according to God's principles. I've moved from being a victim to becoming a victor through Jesus Christ, my one and only true Higher Power.

Roger

shouted, "Shadrach, Meshach and Abednego, servants of the Most High God, come out! Come here!"

So Shadrach, Meshach and Abednego came out of the fire, 27and the satraps, prefects, governors and royal advisers crowded around them. They saw that the fire had not harmed their bodies, nor was a hair of their heads singed; their robes were not scorched, and there was no smell of fire on them.

28Then Nebuchadnezzar said, "Praise be to the God of Shadrach, Meshach and Abednego, who has sent his angel and rescued his servants! They trusted in him and defied the king's command and were willing to give up their lives rather than serve or worship any god except their own God. 29Therefore I decree that the people of any nation or language who say anything against the God of Shadrach, Meshach and Abednego be cut into pieces and their houses be turned into piles of rubble, for no other god can save in this way."

30Then the king promoted Shadrach, Meshach and Abednego in the province of Babylon.

Nebuchadnezzar's Dream of a Tree

4 *a* King Nebuchadnezzar,

To the nations and peoples of every language, who live in all the earth:

May you prosper greatly!

2It is my pleasure to tell you about the miraculous signs and wonders that the Most High God has performed for me.

3How great are his signs,
    how mighty his wonders!
His kingdom is an eternal
    kingdom;
his dominion endures from
    generation to generation.

4I, Nebuchadnezzar, was at home in my palace, contented and prosperous. 5I had a dream that made me afraid. As I was lying in bed, the images and visions that passed through my mind terrified me. 6So I commanded that all the wise men of Babylon be brought before me to interpret the dream for me. 7When the magicians, enchanters, astrologers*b* and diviners came, I told them the dream, but they could not interpret it for me. 8Finally, Daniel came into my presence and I told him the dream. (He is called Belteshazzar, after the name of my god, and the spirit of the holy gods is in him.)

9I said, "Belteshazzar, chief of the magicians, I know that the spirit of the holy gods is in you, and no mystery is too difficult for you. Here is my dream; interpret it for me. 10These are the visions I saw while lying in bed: I looked, and there before me stood a tree in the middle of the land. Its height was enormous. 11The tree grew large and strong and its top touched the sky; it was visible to the ends of the earth. 12Its leaves were beautiful, its fruit abundant, and on it was food for all. Under it the wild animals found shelter, and the birds lived in its branches; from it every creature was fed.

13"In the visions I saw while lying in bed, I looked, and there before me was a holy one, a messenger,*c* coming down from heaven. 14He called in a loud voice: 'Cut down the tree and trim off its branches; strip off its leaves and scatter its fruit. Let the animals flee from under it and the birds from its branches. 15But let the stump and its roots, bound with iron and bronze, remain in the ground, in the grass of the field.

---

a In Aramaic texts 4:1-3 is numbered 3:31-33, and 4:4-37 is numbered 4:1-34.   *b 7* Or *Chaldeans*   *c 13* Or *watchman*; also in verses 17 and 23

"'Let him be drenched with the dew of heaven, and let him live with the animals among the plants of the earth. ¹⁶Let his mind be changed from that of a man and let him be given the mind of an animal, till seven times[a] pass by for him.

¹⁷"'The decision is announced by messengers, the holy ones declare the verdict, so that the living may know that the Most High is sovereign over all kingdoms on earth and gives them to anyone he wishes and sets over them the lowliest of people.'

¹⁸"This is the dream that I, King Nebuchadnezzar, had. Now, Belteshazzar, tell me what it means, for none of the wise men in my kingdom can interpret it for me. But you can, because the spirit of the holy gods is in you."

Daniel Interprets the Dream

¹⁹Then Daniel (also called Belteshazzar) was greatly perplexed for a time, and his thoughts terrified him. So the king said, "Belteshazzar, do not let the dream or its meaning alarm you."

Belteshazzar answered, "My lord, if only the dream applied to your enemies and its meaning to your adversaries! ²⁰The tree you saw, which grew large and strong, with its top touching the sky, visible to the whole earth, ²¹with beautiful leaves and abundant fruit, providing food for all, giving shelter to the wild animals, and having nesting places in its branches for the birds — ²²Your Majesty, you are that tree! You have become great and strong; your greatness has grown until it reaches the sky, and your dominion extends to distant parts of the earth.

²³"Your Majesty saw a holy one, a messenger, coming down from heaven and saying, 'Cut down the tree and destroy it, but leave the stump, bound

with iron and bronze, in the grass of the field, while its roots remain in the ground. Let him be drenched with the dew of heaven; let him live with the wild animals, until seven times pass by for him.'

²⁴"This is the interpretation, Your Majesty, and this is the decree the Most High has issued against my lord the king: ²⁵You will be driven away from people and will live with the wild animals; you will eat grass like the ox and be drenched with the dew of heaven. Seven times will pass by for you until you acknowledge that the Most High is sovereign over all kingdoms on earth and gives them to anyone he wishes. ²⁶The command to leave the stump of the tree with its roots means that your kingdom will be restored to you when you acknowledge that Heaven rules. ²⁷Therefore, Your Majesty, be pleased to accept my advice: Renounce your sins by doing what is right, and your wickedness by being kind to the oppressed. It may be that then your prosperity will continue."

The Dream Is Fulfilled

²⁸All this happened to King Nebuchadnezzar. ²⁹Twelve months later, as the king was walking on the roof of the royal palace of Babylon, ³⁰he said, "Is not this the great Babylon I have built as the royal residence, by my mighty power and for the glory of my majesty?"

³¹Even as the words were on his lips, a voice came from heaven, "This is what is decreed for you, King Nebuchadnezzar: Your royal authority has been taken from you. ³²You will be driven away from people and will live with the wild animals; you will eat grass like the ox. Seven times will pass by for you until you acknowledge that the Most High is

---

a 16 Or *years*; also in verses 23, 25 and 32

sovereign over all kingdoms on earth and gives them to anyone he wishes."

33Immediately what had been said about Nebuchadnezzar was fulfilled. He was driven away from people and ate grass like the ox. His body was drenched with the dew of heaven until his hair grew like the feathers of an eagle and his nails like the claws of a bird.

34At the end of that time, I, Nebuchadnezzar, raised my eyes toward heaven, and my sanity was restored. Then I praised the Most High; I honored and glorified him who lives forever.

His dominion is an eternal dominion;
   his kingdom endures from
      generation to generation.
35 All the peoples of the earth
   are regarded as nothing.
He does as he pleases
   with the powers of heaven
   and the peoples of the earth.
No one can hold back his hand
   or say to him: "What have you
      done?"

36At the same time that my sanity was restored, my honor and splendor were returned to me for the glory of my kingdom. My advisers and nobles sought me out, and I was restored to my throne and became even greater than before. 37Now I, Nebuchadnezzar, praise and exalt and glorify the King of heaven, because everything he does is right and all his ways are just. And those who walk in pride he is able to humble.

The Writing on the Wall

5 King Belshazzar gave a great banquet for a thousand of his nobles and drank wine with them. 2While Belshazzar was drinking his wine, he gave orders to bring in the gold and silver goblets that Nebuchadnezzar his father[a] had taken from the temple in Jerusalem, so that the king and his nobles, his wives and his concubines might drink from them. 3So they brought in the gold goblets that had been taken from the temple of God in Jerusalem, and the king and his nobles, his wives and his concubines drank from them. 4As they drank the wine, they praised the gods of gold and silver, of bronze, iron, wood and stone.

5Suddenly the fingers of a human hand appeared and wrote on the plaster of the wall, near the lampstand in the royal palace. The king watched the hand as it wrote. 6His face turned pale and he was so frightened that his legs became weak and his knees were knocking.

7The king summoned the enchanters, astrologers[b] and diviners. Then he said to these wise men of Babylon, "Whoever reads this writing and tells me what it means will be clothed in purple and have a gold chain placed around his neck, and he will be made the third highest ruler in the kingdom."

8Then all the king's wise men came in, but they could not read the writing or tell the king what it meant. 9So King Belshazzar became even more terrified and his face grew more pale. His nobles were baffled.

10The queen,[c] hearing the voices of the king and his nobles, came into the banquet hall. "May the king live forever!" she said. "Don't be alarmed! Don't look so pale! 11There is a man in your kingdom who has the spirit of the holy gods in him. In the time of your father he was found to have insight and intelligence and wisdom like that of the gods. Your father, King Nebuchadnezzar, appointed him chief of the magicians, enchanters, astrologers and diviners. 12He did this because Daniel, whom the king called Belteshazzar, was found to have a keen mind and knowledge and un-

---

a 2 Or *ancestor*; or *predecessor*; also in verses 11, 13 and 18 *mother*   b 7 Or *Chaldeans*; also in verse 11   c 10 Or *queen* derstanding, and also the ability to interpret dreams, explain riddles and solve difficult problems. Call for Daniel, and he will tell you what the writing means."

13 So Daniel was brought before the king, and the king said to him, "Are you Daniel, one of the exiles my father the king brought from Judah? 14 I have heard that the spirit of the gods is in you and that you have insight, intelligence and outstanding wisdom. 15 The wise men and enchanters were brought before me to read this writing and tell me what it means, but they could not explain it. 16 Now I have heard that you are able to give interpretations and to solve difficult problems. If you can read this writing and tell me what it means, you will be clothed in purple and have a gold chain placed around your neck, and you will be made the third highest ruler in the kingdom."

17 Then Daniel answered the king, "You may keep your gifts for yourself and give your rewards to someone else. Nevertheless, I will read the writing for the king and tell him what it means.

18 "Your Majesty, the Most High God gave your father Nebuchadnezzar sovereignty and greatness and glory and splendor. 19 Because of the high position he gave him, all the nations and peoples of every language dreaded and feared him. Those the king wanted to put to death, he put to death; those he wanted to spare, he spared; those he wanted to promote, he promoted; and those he wanted to humble, he humbled. 20 But when his heart became arrogant and hardened with pride, he was deposed from his royal throne and stripped of his glory. 21 He was driven away from people and given the mind of an animal; he lived with the wild donkeys and ate grass like the ox; and his body was drenched with the dew of heaven, until he acknowledged that the Most High God is sovereign over all kingdoms on earth and sets over them anyone he wishes.

22 "But you, Belshazzar, his son,*a* have not humbled yourself, though you knew all this. 23 Instead, you have set yourself up against the Lord of heaven. You had the goblets from his temple brought to you, and you and your nobles, your wives and your concubines drank wine from them. You praised the gods of silver and gold, of bronze, iron, wood and stone, which cannot see or hear or understand. But you did not honor the God who holds in his hand your life and all your ways. 24 Therefore he sent the hand that wrote the inscription.

25 "This is the inscription that was written:

MENE, MENE, TEKEL, PARSIN

26 "Here is what these words mean:

*Mene*b: God has numbered the days of your reign and brought it to an end.
27 *Tekel*c: You have been weighed on the scales and found wanting.
28 *Peres*d: Your kingdom is divided and given to the Medes and Persians."

29 Then at Belshazzar's command, Daniel was clothed in purple, a gold chain was placed around his neck, and he was proclaimed the third highest ruler in the kingdom.

30 That very night Belshazzar, king of the Babylonians,*e* was slain, 31 and Darius the Mede took over the kingdom, at the age of sixty-two.*f*

Daniel in the Den of Lions

6 *g* It pleased Darius to appoint 120 satraps to rule throughout the kingdom, 2 with three administrators over them, one of whom was Daniel. The

---

a 22 Or *descendant;* or *successor*   *b 26 Mene* can mean *numbered* or *mina* (a unit of money).   *c 27 Tekel* can mean *weighed* or *shekel.*   *d 28 Peres* (the singular of *Parsin*) can mean *divided* or *Persia* or *a half mina* or *a half shekel.*   *e 30* Or *Chaldeans*   *f 31* In Aramaic texts this verse (5:31) is numbered 6:1.   *g* In Aramaic texts 6:1-28 is numbered 6:2-29.

satraps were made accountable to them so that the king might not suffer loss. ³Now Daniel so distinguished himself among the administrators and the satraps by his exceptional qualities that the king planned to set him over the whole kingdom. ⁴At this, the administrators and the satraps tried to find grounds for charges against Daniel in his conduct of government affairs, but they were unable to do so. They could find no corruption in him, because he was trustworthy and neither corrupt nor negligent. ⁵Finally these men said, "We will never find any basis for charges against this man Daniel unless it has something to do with the law of his God."

⁶So these administrators and satraps went as a group to the king and said: "May King Darius live forever! ⁷The royal administrators, prefects, satraps, advisers and governors have all agreed that the king should issue an edict and enforce the decree that anyone who prays to any god or human being during the next thirty days, except to you, Your Majesty, shall be thrown into the lions' den. ⁸Now, Your Majesty, issue the decree and put it in writing so that it cannot be altered — in accordance with the law of the Medes and Persians, which cannot be repealed." ⁹So King Darius put the decree in writing.

¹⁰Now when Daniel learned that the decree had been published, he went home to his upstairs room where the windows opened toward Jerusalem. Three times a day he got down on his knees and prayed, giving thanks to his God, just as he had done before. ¹¹Then these men went as a group and found Daniel praying and asking God for help. ¹²So they went to the king and spoke to him about his royal decree: "Did you not publish a decree that during the next thirty days anyone who prays to any god or human being except to you, Your Majesty, would be thrown into the lions' den?"

The king answered, "The decree stands — in accordance with the law of the Medes and Persians, which cannot be repealed."

¹³Then they said to the king, "Daniel, who is one of the exiles from Judah, pays no attention to you, Your Majesty, or to the decree you put in writing. He still prays three times a day." ¹⁴When the king heard this, he was greatly distressed; he was determined to rescue Daniel and made every effort until sundown to save him.

¹⁵Then the men went as a group to King Darius and said to him, "Remember, Your Majesty, that according to the law of the Medes and Persians no decree or edict that the king issues can be changed."

¹⁶So the king gave the order, and they brought Daniel and threw him into the lions' den. The king said to Daniel, "May your God, whom you serve continually, rescue you!"

¹⁷A stone was brought and placed over the mouth of the den, and the king sealed it with his own signet ring and with the rings of his nobles, so that Daniel's situation might not be changed. ¹⁸Then the king returned to his palace and spent the night without eating and without any entertainment being brought to him. And he could not sleep.

¹⁹At the first light of dawn, the king got up and hurried to the lions' den. ²⁰When he came near the den, he called to Daniel in an anguished voice, "Daniel, servant of the living God, has your God, whom you serve continually, been able to rescue you from the lions?"

²¹Daniel answered, "May the king live forever! ²²My God sent his angel, and he shut the mouths of the lions. They have not hurt me, because I was found innocent in his sight. Nor have I ever done any wrong before you, Your Majesty."

²³The king was overjoyed and gave orders to lift Daniel out of the den. And when Daniel was lifted from the den, no wound was found on him, because he had trusted in his God.

²⁴At the king's command, the men who had falsely accused Daniel were brought in and thrown into the lions' den, along with their wives and children. And before they

reached the floor of the den, the lions overpowered them and crushed all their bones.

²⁵Then King Darius wrote to all the nations and peoples of every language in all the earth:

"May you prosper greatly!

²⁶"I issue a decree that in every part of my kingdom people must fear and reverence the God of Daniel.

"For he is the living God
　and he endures forever;
his kingdom will not be destroyed,
　his dominion will never end.
²⁷He rescues and he saves;
　he performs signs and wonders
　in the heavens and on the earth.
He has rescued Daniel
　from the power of the lions."

²⁸So Daniel prospered during the reign of Darius and the reign of Cyrus[a] the Persian.

Daniel's Dream of Four Beasts

7 In the first year of Belshazzar king of Babylon, Daniel had a dream, and visions passed through his mind as he was lying in bed. He wrote down the substance of his dream.

²Daniel said: "In my vision at night I looked, and there before me were the four winds of heaven churning up the great sea. ³Four great beasts, each different from the others, came up out of the sea.

⁴"The first was like a lion, and it had the wings of an eagle. I watched until its wings were torn off and it was lifted from the ground so that it stood on two feet like a human being, and the mind of a human was given to it.

⁵"And there before me was a second beast, which looked like a bear. It was raised up on one of its sides, and it had three ribs in its mouth between its teeth. It was told, 'Get up and eat your fill of flesh!'

⁶"After that, I looked, and there before me was another beast, one that looked like a leopard. And on its back it had four wings like those of a bird. This beast had four heads, and it was given authority to rule.

⁷"After that, in my vision at night I looked, and there before me was a fourth beast — terrifying and frightening and very powerful. It had large iron teeth; it crushed and devoured its victims and trampled underfoot whatever was left. It was different from all the former beasts, and it had ten horns.

⁸"While I was thinking about the horns, there before me was another horn, a little one, which came up among them; and three of the first horns were uprooted before it. This horn had eyes like the eyes of a human being and a mouth that spoke boastfully.

⁹"As I looked,

"thrones were set in place,
　and the Ancient of Days took his seat.
His clothing was as white as snow;
　the hair of his head was white like
　　wool.
His throne was flaming with fire,
　and its wheels were all ablaze.
¹⁰A river of fire was flowing,
　coming out from before him.
Thousands upon thousands attended
　him;
　ten thousand times ten thousand
　　stood before him.
The court was seated,
　and the books were opened.

¹¹"Then I continued to watch because of the boastful words the horn was speaking. I kept looking until the beast was slain and its body destroyed and thrown into the blazing fire. ¹²(The other beasts had been stripped of their authority, but were allowed to live for a period of time.)

¹³"In my vision at night I looked, and there before me was one like a son of man,[b]

a 28 Or Darius, that is, the reign of Cyrus　b 13 The Aramaic phrase bar enash means human being. The phrase son of man is retained here because of its use in the New Testament as a title of Jesus, probably based largely on this verse.

coming with the clouds of heaven. He approached the Ancient of Days and was led into his presence. ¹⁴He was given authority, glory and sovereign power; all nations and peoples of every language worshiped him. His dominion is an everlasting dominion that will not pass away, and his kingdom is one that will never be destroyed.

The Interpretation of the Dream

¹⁵"I, Daniel, was troubled in spirit, and the visions that passed through my mind disturbed me. ¹⁶I approached one of those standing there and asked him the meaning of all this.

"So he told me and gave me the interpretation of these things: ¹⁷'The four great beasts are four kings that will rise from the earth. ¹⁸But the holy people of the Most High will receive the kingdom and will possess it forever — yes, for ever and ever.'

¹⁹"Then I wanted to know the meaning of the fourth beast, which was different from all the others and most terrifying, with its iron teeth and bronze claws — the beast that crushed and devoured its victims and trampled underfoot whatever was left. ²⁰I also wanted to know about the ten horns on its head and about the other horn that came up, before which three of them fell — the horn that looked more imposing than the others and that had eyes and a mouth that spoke boastfully. ²¹As I watched, this horn was waging war against the holy people and defeating them, ²²until the Ancient of Days came and pronounced judgment in favor of the holy people of the Most High, and the time came when they possessed the kingdom.

²³"He gave me this explanation: 'The fourth beast is a fourth kingdom that will appear on earth. It will be different from all the other kingdoms and will devour the whole earth, trampling it down and crushing it. ²⁴The ten horns are ten kings who will come from this kingdom. After them another king will arise, different from the

earlier ones; he will subdue three kings. ²⁵He will speak against the Most High and oppress his holy people and try to change the set times and the laws. The holy people will be delivered into his hands for a time, times and half a time.ᵃ

²⁶"'But the court will sit, and his power will be taken away and completely destroyed forever. ²⁷Then the sovereignty, power and greatness of all the kingdoms under heaven will be handed over to the holy people of the Most High. His kingdom will be an everlasting kingdom, and all rulers will worship and obey him.'

²⁸"This is the end of the matter. I, Daniel, was deeply troubled by my thoughts, and my face turned pale, but I kept the matter to myself."

Daniel's Vision of a Ram and a Goat

8 In the third year of King Belshazzar's reign, I, Daniel, had a vision, after the one that had already appeared to me. ²In my vision I saw myself in the citadel of Susa in the province of Elam; in the vision I was beside the Ulai Canal. ³I looked up, and there before me was a ram with two horns, standing beside the canal, and the horns were long. One of the horns was longer than the other but grew up later. ⁴I watched the ram as it charged toward the west and the north and the south. No animal could stand against it, and none could rescue from its power. It did as it pleased and became great.

⁵As I was thinking about this, suddenly a goat with a prominent horn between its eyes came from the west, crossing the whole earth without touching the ground. ⁶It came toward the two-horned ram I had seen standing beside the canal and charged at it in great rage. ⁷I saw it attack the ram furiously, striking the ram and shattering its two horns. The ram was powerless to stand against it; the goat knocked it to the ground and trampled on it, and none could rescue the ram from its power. ⁸The goat

---

ᵃ 25 Or for a year, two years and half a year

became very great, but at the height of its power the large horn was broken off, and in its place four prominent horns grew up toward the four winds of heaven.

⁹Out of one of them came another horn, which started small but grew in power to the south and to the east and toward the Beautiful Land. ¹⁰It grew until it reached the host of the heavens, and it threw some of the starry host down to the earth and trampled on them. ¹¹It set itself up to be as great as the commander of the army of the Lord; it took away the daily sacrifice from the Lord, and his sanctuary was thrown down. ¹²Because of rebellion, the Lord's people*a* and the daily sacrifice were given over to it. It prospered in everything it did, and truth was thrown to the ground.

¹³Then I heard a holy one speaking, and another holy one said to him, "How long will it take for the vision to be fulfilled — the vision concerning the daily sacrifice, the rebellion that causes desolation, the surrender of the sanctuary and the trampling underfoot of the Lord's people?"

¹⁴He said to me, "It will take 2,300 evenings and mornings; then the sanctuary will be reconsecrated."

The Interpretation of the Vision

¹⁵While I, Daniel, was watching the vision and trying to understand it, there before me stood one who looked like a man. ¹⁶And I heard a man's voice from the Ulai calling, "Gabriel, tell this man the meaning of the vision."

¹⁷As he came near the place where I was standing, I was terrified and fell prostrate. "Son of man,"*b* he said to me, "understand that the vision concerns the time of the end."

¹⁸While he was speaking to me, I was in a deep sleep, with my face to the ground. Then he touched me and raised me to my feet.

¹⁹He said: "I am going to tell you what will happen later in the time of wrath, because the vision concerns the appointed time of the end.*c* ²⁰The two-horned ram that you saw represents the kings of Media and Persia. ²¹The shaggy goat is the king of Greece, and the large horn between its eyes is the first king. ²²The four horns that replaced the one that was broken off represent four kingdoms that will emerge from his nation but will not have the same power.

²³"In the latter part of their reign, when rebels have become completely wicked, a fierce-looking king, a master of intrigue, will arise. ²⁴He will become very strong, but not by his own power. He will cause astounding devastation and will succeed in whatever he does. He will destroy those who are mighty, the holy people. ²⁵He will cause deceit to prosper, and he will consider himself superior. When they feel secure, he will destroy many and take his stand against the Prince of princes. Yet he will be destroyed, but not by human power.

²⁶"The vision of the evenings and mornings that has been given you is true, but seal up the vision, for it concerns the distant future."

²⁷I, Daniel, was worn out. I lay exhausted for several days. Then I got up and went about the king's business. I was appalled by the vision; it was beyond understanding.

Daniel's Prayer

9 In the first year of Darius son of Xerxes*d* (a Mede by descent), who was made ruler over the Babylonian*e* kingdom — ²in the first year of his reign, I, Daniel, understood from the Scriptures, according to the word of the Lord given to Jeremiah the prophet, that the desolation of Jerusalem would last seventy years. ³So I turned to the Lord God and pleaded with him in prayer and petition, in fasting, and in sackcloth and ashes.

---

a 12 Or *rebellion, the armies*   *b 17* The Hebrew phrase *ben adam* means *human being.* The phrase *son of man* is retained as a form of address here because of its possible association with "Son of Man" in the New Testament.
c 19 Or *because the end will be at the appointed time*   *d 1* Hebrew *Ahasuerus*   *e 1* Or *Chaldean*

4I prayed to the LORD my God and confessed:

"Lord, the great and awesome God, who keeps his covenant of love with those who love him and keep his commandments, 5we have sinned and done wrong. We have been wicked and have rebelled; we have turned away from your commands and laws. 6We have not listened to your servants the prophets, who spoke in your name to our kings, our princes and our ancestors, and to all the people of the land.

7"Lord, you are righteous, but this day we are covered with shame — the people of Judah and the inhabitants of Jerusalem and all Israel, both near and far, in all the countries where you have scattered us because of our unfaithfulness to you. 8We and our kings, our princes and our ancestors are covered with shame, LORD, because we have sinned against you. 9The Lord our God is merciful and forgiving, even though we have rebelled against him; 10we have not obeyed the LORD our God or kept the laws he gave us through his servants the prophets. 11All Israel has transgressed your law and turned away, refusing to obey you.

"Therefore the curses and sworn judgments written in the Law of Moses, the servant of God, have been poured out on us, because we have sinned against you. 12You have fulfilled the words spoken against us and against our rulers by bringing on us great disaster. Under the whole heaven nothing has ever been done like what has been done to Jerusalem. 13Just as it is written in the Law of Moses, all this disaster has come on us, yet we have not sought the favor of the LORD our God by turning from our sins and giving attention to your truth. 14The LORD did not hesitate to bring the disaster on us, for the LORD our God is righteous in everything he does; yet we have not obeyed him.

15"Now, Lord our God, who brought your people out of Egypt with a mighty hand and who made for yourself a name that endures to this day, we have sinned, we have done wrong. 16Lord, in keeping with all your righteous acts, turn away your anger and your wrath from Jerusalem, your city, your holy hill. Our sins and the iniquities of our ancestors have made Jerusalem and your people an object of scorn to all those around us.

17"Now, our God, hear the prayers and petitions of your servant. For your sake, Lord, look with favor on your desolate sanctuary. 18Give ear, our God, and hear; open your eyes and see the desolation of the city that bears your Name. We do not make requests of you because we are righteous, but because of your great mercy. 19Lord, listen! Lord, forgive! Lord, hear and act! For your sake, my God, do not delay, because your city and your people bear your Name."

The Seventy "Sevens"

20While I was speaking and praying, confessing my sin and the sin of my people Israel and making my request to the LORD my God for his holy hill — 21while I was still in prayer, Gabriel, the man I had seen in the earlier vision, came to me in swift flight about the time of the evening sacrifice. 22He instructed me and said to me, "Daniel, I have now come to give you insight and understanding. 23As soon as you began to pray, a word went out, which I have come to tell you, for you are highly esteemed. Therefore, consider the word and understand the vision:

24"Seventy 'sevens'a are decreed for your people and your holy city to finishb trans-

---

a 24 Or 'weeks'; also in verses 25 and 26   b 24 Or restrain gression, to put an end to sin, to atone for wickedness, to bring in everlasting righteousness, to seal up vision and prophecy and to anoint the Most Holy Place.[a]

25"Know and understand this: From the time the word goes out to restore and rebuild Jerusalem until the Anointed One,[b] the ruler, comes, there will be seven 'sevens,' and sixty-two 'sevens.' It will be rebuilt with streets and a trench, but in times of trouble. 26After the sixty-two 'sevens,' the Anointed One will be put to death and will have nothing.[c] The people of the ruler who will come will destroy the city and the sanctuary. The end will come like a flood: War will continue until the end, and desolations have been decreed. 27He will confirm a covenant with many for one 'seven.'[d] In the middle of the 'seven'[d] he will put an end to sacrifice and offering. And at the temple[e] he will set up an abomination that causes desolation, until the end that is decreed is poured out on him.[f]"[g]

Daniel's Vision of a Man

10 In the third year of Cyrus king of Persia, a revelation was given to Daniel (who was called Belteshazzar). Its message was true and it concerned a great war.[h] The understanding of the message came to him in a vision.

2At that time I, Daniel, mourned for three weeks. 3I ate no choice food; no meat or wine touched my lips; and I used no lotions at all until the three weeks were over.

4On the twenty-fourth day of the first month, as I was standing on the bank of the great river, the Tigris, 5I looked up and there before me was a man dressed in linen, with a belt of fine gold from Uphaz around his waist. 6His body was like topaz, his face like lightning, his eyes like flaming torches, his arms and legs like the gleam of bur-

nished bronze, and his voice like the sound of a multitude.

7I, Daniel, was the only one who saw the vision; those who were with me did not see it, but such terror overwhelmed them that they fled and hid themselves. 8So I was left alone, gazing at this great vision; I had no strength left, my face turned deathly pale and I was helpless. 9Then I heard him speaking, and as I listened to him, I fell into a deep sleep, my face to the ground.

10A hand touched me and set me trembling on my hands and knees. 11He said, "Daniel, you who are highly esteemed, consider carefully the words I am about to speak to you, and stand up, for I have now been sent to you." And when he said this to me, I stood up trembling.

12Then he continued, "Do not be afraid, Daniel. Since the first day that you set your mind to gain understanding and to humble yourself before your God, your words were heard, and I have come in response to them. 13But the prince of the Persian kingdom resisted me twenty-one days. Then Michael, one of the chief princes, came to help me, because I was detained there with the king of Persia. 14Now I have come to explain to you what will happen to your people in the future, for the vision concerns a time yet to come."

15While he was saying this to me, I bowed with my face toward the ground and was speechless. 16Then one who looked like a man[i] touched my lips, and I opened my mouth and began to speak. I said to the one standing before me, "I am overcome with anguish because of the vision, my lord, and I feel very weak. 17How can I, your servant, talk with you, my lord? My strength is gone and I can hardly breathe."

18Again the one who looked like a man touched me and gave me strength. 19"Do not be afraid, you who are highly

---

[a] 24 Or *the most holy One*   [b] 25 Or *an anointed one*; also in verse 26   [c] 26 Or *death and will have no one*; or *death, but not for himself*   [d] 27 Or *'week'*   [e] 27 Septuagint and Theodotion; Hebrew *wing*   [f] 27 Or *it*
[g] 27 Or *And one who causes desolation will come upon the wing of the abominable temple, until the end that is decreed is poured out on the desolated city*   [h] 1 Or *true and burdensome*   [i] 16 Most manuscripts of the Masoretic Text; one manuscript of the Masoretic Text, Dead Sea Scrolls and Septuagint *Then something that looked like a human hand*

esteemed," he said. "Peace! Be strong now; be strong."

When he spoke to me, I was strengthened and said, "Speak, my lord, since you have given me strength."

20So he said, "Do you know why I have come to you? Soon I will return to fight against the prince of Persia, and when I go, the prince of Greece will come; 21but first I will tell you what is written in the Book of Truth. (No one supports me against them except Michael, your prince. 1And in the first year of Darius the Mede, I took my stand to support and protect him.)

The Kings of the South and the North

2"Now then, I tell you the truth: Three more kings will arise in Persia, and then a fourth, who will be far richer than all the others. When he has gained power by his wealth, he will stir up everyone against the kingdom of Greece. 3Then a mighty king will arise, who will rule with great power and do as he pleases. 4After he has arisen, his empire will be broken up and parceled out toward the four winds of heaven. It will not go to his descendants, nor will it have the power he exercised, because his empire will be uprooted and given to others.

5"The king of the South will become strong, but one of his commanders will become even stronger than he and will rule his own kingdom with great power. 6After some years, they will become allies. The daughter of the king of the South will go to the king of the North to make an alliance, but she will not retain her power, and he and his power*a* will not last. In those days she will be betrayed, together with her royal escort and her father*b* and the one who supported her.

7"One from her family line will arise to take her place. He will attack the forces of the king of the North and enter his fortress; he will fight against them and be victorious. 8He will also seize their gods, their metal images and their valuable articles of silver and gold and carry them off to Egypt. For some years he will leave the king of the North alone. 9Then the king of the North will invade the realm of the king of the South but will retreat to his own country. 10His sons will prepare for war and assemble a great army, which will sweep on like an irresistible flood and carry the battle as far as his fortress.

11"Then the king of the South will march out in a rage and fight against the king of the North, who will raise a large army, but it will be defeated. 12When the army is carried off, the king of the South will be filled with pride and will slaughter many thousands, yet he will not remain triumphant. 13For the king of the North will muster another army, larger than the first; and after several years, he will advance with a huge army fully equipped.

14"In those times many will rise against the king of the South. Those who are violent among your own people will rebel in fulfillment of the vision, but without success. 15Then the king of the North will come and build up siege ramps and will capture a fortified city. The forces of the South will be powerless to resist; even their best troops will not have the strength to stand. 16The invader will do as he pleases; no one will be able to stand against him. He will establish himself in the Beautiful Land and will have the power to destroy it. 17He will determine to come with the might of his entire kingdom and will make an alliance with the king of the South. And he will give him a daughter in marriage in order to overthrow the kingdom, but his plans*c* will not succeed or help him. 18Then he will turn his attention to the coastlands and will take many of them, but a commander will put an end to his insolence and will turn his insolence back on him. 19After this, he will turn back toward the fortresses of his own country but will stumble and fall, to be seen no more.

---

a 6 Or *offspring*   *b* 6 Or *child* (see Vulgate and Syriac)   *c* 17 Or *but she*

20"His successor will send out a tax collector to maintain the royal splendor. In a few years, however, he will be destroyed, yet not in anger or in battle.

21"He will be succeeded by a contemptible person who has not been given the honor of royalty. He will invade the kingdom when its people feel secure, and he will seize it through intrigue. 22Then an overwhelming army will be swept away before him; both it and a prince of the covenant will be destroyed. 23After coming to an agreement with him, he will act deceitfully, and with only a few people he will rise to power. 24When the richest provinces feel secure, he will invade them and will achieve what neither his fathers nor his forefathers did. He will distribute plunder, loot and wealth among his followers. He will plot the overthrow of fortresses — but only for a time.

25"With a large army he will stir up his strength and courage against the king of the South. The king of the South will wage war with a large and very powerful army, but he will not be able to stand because of the plots devised against him. 26Those who eat from the king's provisions will try to destroy him; his army will be swept away, and many will fall in battle. 27The two kings, with their hearts bent on evil, will sit at the same table and lie to each other, but to no avail, because an end will still come at the appointed time. 28The king of the North will return to his own country with great wealth, but his heart will be set against the holy covenant. He will take action against it and then return to his own country.

29"At the appointed time he will invade the South again, but this time the outcome will be different from what it was before. 30Ships of the western coastlands will oppose him, and he will lose heart. Then he will turn back and vent his fury against the holy covenant. He will return and show favor to those who forsake the holy covenant.

31"His armed forces will rise up to desecrate the temple fortress and will abolish the daily sacrifice. Then they will set up the abomination that causes desolation. 32With flattery he will corrupt those who have violated the covenant, but the people who know their God will firmly resist him.

33"Those who are wise will instruct many, though for a time they will fall by the sword or be burned or captured or plundered. 34When they fall, they will receive a little help, and many who are not sincere will join them. 35Some of the wise will stumble, so that they may be refined, purified and made spotless until the time of the end, for it will still come at the appointed time.

The King Who Exalts Himself

36"The king will do as he pleases. He will exalt and magnify himself above every god and will say unheard-of things against the God of gods. He will be successful until the time of wrath is completed, for what has been determined must take place. 37He will show no regard for the gods of his ancestors or for the one desired by women, nor will he regard any god, but will exalt himself above them all. 38Instead of them, he will honor a god of fortresses; a god unknown to his ancestors he will honor with gold and silver, with precious stones and costly gifts. 39He will attack the mightiest fortresses with the help of a foreign god and will greatly honor those who acknowledge him. He will make them rulers over many people and will distribute the land at a price.ᵃ

40"At the time of the end the king of the South will engage him in battle, and the king of the North will storm out against him with chariots and cavalry and a great fleet of ships. He will invade many countries and sweep through them like a flood. 41He will also invade the Beautiful Land. Many countries will fall, but Edom, Moab and the leaders of Ammon will be delivered from his hand. 42He will extend his power over many countries; Egypt will not

---

ᵃ 39 Or *land for a reward*

escape. [43]He will gain control of the treasures of gold and silver and all the riches of Egypt, with the Libyans and Cushites[a] in submission. [44]But reports from the east and the north will alarm him, and he will set out in a great rage to destroy and annihilate many. [45]He will pitch his royal tents between the seas at[b] the beautiful holy mountain. Yet he will come to his end, and no one will help him.

The End Times

12

[1]"At that time Michael, the great prince who protects your people, will arise. There will be a time of distress such as has not happened from the beginning of nations until then. But at that time your people — everyone whose name is found written in the book — will be delivered. [2]Multitudes who sleep in the dust of the earth will awake: some to everlasting life, others to shame and everlasting contempt. [3]Those who are wise[c] will shine like the brightness of the heavens, and those who lead many to righteousness, like the stars for ever and ever. [4]But you, Daniel, roll up and seal the words of the scroll until the time of the end. Many will go here and there to increase knowledge."

[5]Then I, Daniel, looked, and there before me stood two others, one on this bank of the river and one on the opposite bank. [6]One of them said to the man clothed in linen, who was above the waters of the river, "How long will it be before these astonishing things are fulfilled?"

[7]The man clothed in linen, who was above the waters of the river, lifted his right hand and his left hand toward heaven, and I heard him swear by him who lives forever, saying, "It will be for a time, times and half a time.[d] When the power of the holy people has been finally broken, all these things will be completed."

[8]I heard, but I did not understand. So I asked, "My lord, what will the outcome of all this be?"

[9]He replied, "Go your way, Daniel, because the words are rolled up and sealed until the time of the end. [10]Many will be purified, made spotless and refined, but the wicked will continue to be wicked. None of the wicked will understand, but those who are wise will understand.

[11]"From the time that the daily sacrifice is abolished and the abomination that causes desolation is set up, there will be 1,290 days. [12]Blessed is the one who waits for and reaches the end of the 1,335 days.

[13]"As for you, go your way till the end. You will rest, and then at the end of the days you will rise to receive your allotted inheritance."

---

[a] 43 That is, people from the upper Nile region   [b] 45 Or *the sea and*   [c] 3 Or *who impart wisdom*   [d] 7 Or *a year, two years and half a year*

Hosea

THEME: God's covenantal relationship with his people is likened to the intimacy experienced in marriage, reinforcing the theme of God's passionate love for his people.

AUTHOR: The book identifies its contents as "the word of the LORD that came to Hosea son of Beeri" (Hosea 1:1). Hosea was a prophet to the northern kingdom of Israel between 753 and 715 BC, the period during which the capital city of Samaria fell to the Assyrians (722 BC).

DATE OF WRITING: Hosea was probably written about 715 BC.

ENCOURAGEMENT FROM HOSEA: "How can I give you up, Ephraim? How can I hand you over, Israel? . . . My heart is changed within me; all my compassion is aroused. I will not carry out my fierce anger . . . I will not come against their cities" (Hosea 11:8 – 9).

CHALLENGE FROM HOSEA: "The ways of the LORD are right; the righteous walk in them, but the rebellious stumble in them" (Hosea 14:9).

REFLECTION FROM HOSEA: "For I desire mercy, not sacrifice, and acknowledgment of God rather than burnt offerings" (Hosea 6:6).

The book of Hosea is the tragic story of a one-sided love. The prophet's wife, Gomer, has been unfaithful. This painful reality has given Hosea unique insight into God's grief over Israel's unfaithfulness. Just as Gomer has sought out relationships with other men, so also has Israel sought out other gods. But God's faithful love won't permit him to easily divorce his people. Although Hosea calls for repentance, the prophet doesn't expect a positive response. Still, Hosea's unlikely reconciliation with his wife illustrates Israel's future restoration.

Not all of our relationships are healthy, and many are far from ideal. Most of us have been deeply hurt and possibly mistreated by those we love. The offending individual may have been a parent, spouse, family member, friend, coworker or child. God understands our pain; in fact, he feels it himself when those he loves turn their backs on him. Not only does God empathize with our pain, but he's also able to heal it. God is reaching out to us even now with his kind and patient love. He wants to guide us down the road to recovery with his loving kindness.

1

The word of the LORD that came to Hosea son of Beeri during the reigns of Uzziah, Jotham, Ahaz and Hezekiah, kings of Judah, and during the reign of Jeroboam son of Jehoash[a] king of Israel:

Hosea's Wife and Children

²When the LORD began to speak through Hosea, the LORD said to him, "Go, marry a promiscuous woman and have children with her, for like an adulterous wife

a 1 Hebrew Joash, a variant of Jehoash

this land is guilty of unfaithfulness to the LORD." ³So he married Gomer daughter of Diblaim, and she conceived and bore him a son.

⁴Then the LORD said to Hosea, "Call him Jezreel, because I will soon punish the house of Jehu for the massacre at Jezreel, and I will put an end to the kingdom of Israel. ⁵In that day I will break Israel's bow in the Valley of Jezreel."

⁶Gomer conceived again and gave birth to a daughter. Then the LORD said to Hosea, "Call her Lo-Ruhamah (which means "not loved"), for I will no longer show love to Israel, that I should at all forgive them. ⁷Yet I will show love to Judah; and I will save them — not by bow, sword or battle, or by horses and horsemen, but I, the LORD their God, will save them."

⁸After she had weaned Lo-Ruhamah, Gomer had another son. ⁹Then the LORD said, "Call him Lo-Ammi (which means "not my people"), for you are not my people, and I am not your God.ᵃ

¹⁰"Yet the Israelites will be like the sand on the seashore, which cannot be measured or counted. In the place where it was said to them, 'You are not my people,' they will be called 'children of the living God.' ¹¹The people of Judah and the people of Israel will come together; they will appoint one leader and will come up out of the land, for great will be the day of Jezreel.ᵇ

2ᶜ "Say of your brothers, 'My people,' and of your sisters, 'My loved one.'

Israel Punished and Restored

²"Rebuke your mother, rebuke her,
    for she is not my wife,
    and I am not her husband.
Let her remove the adulterous look
    from her face
    and the unfaithfulness from between
      her breasts.
³Otherwise I will strip her naked
    and make her as bare as on the day
      she was born;

I will make her like a desert,
    turn her into a parched land,
    and slay her with thirst.
⁴I will not show my love to her children,
    because they are the children of
      adultery.
⁵Their mother has been unfaithful
    and has conceived them in disgrace.
She said, 'I will go after my lovers,
    who give me my food and my water,
    my wool and my linen, my olive oil
      and my drink.'
⁶Therefore I will block her path with
      thornbushes;
    I will wall her in so that she cannot
      find her way.
⁷She will chase after her lovers but not
      catch them;
    she will look for them but not find
      them.
Then she will say,
    'I will go back to my husband as at
      first,
    for then I was better off than now.'
⁸She has not acknowledged that I was
      the one
    who gave her the grain, the new wine
      and oil,
    who lavished on her the silver and
      gold —
    which they used for Baal.

⁹"Therefore I will take away my grain
      when it ripens,
    and my new wine when it is ready.
I will take back my wool and my linen,
    intended to cover her naked body.
¹⁰So now I will expose her lewdness
    before the eyes of her lovers;
    no one will take her out of my
      hands.
¹¹I will stop all her celebrations:
    her yearly festivals, her New Moons,
    her Sabbath days — all her appointed
      festivals.
¹²I will ruin her vines and her fig trees,
    which she said were her pay from her
      lovers;

ᵃ 9 Or your I AM   ᵇ 11 In Hebrew texts 1:10,11 is numbered 2:1,2.   ᶜ In Hebrew texts 2:1-23 is numbered 2:3-25.

I will make them a thicket,
and wild animals will devour them.
13 I will punish her for the days
she burned incense to the Baals;
she decked herself with rings and
jewelry,
and went after her lovers,
but me she forgot,"
declares the LORD.

14 "Therefore I am now going to allure her;
I will lead her into the wilderness
and speak tenderly to her.
15 There I will give her back her vineyards,
and will make the Valley of Achor*a* a
door of hope.
There she will respond*b* as in the days
of her youth,
as in the day she came up out of Egypt.

16 "In that day," declares the LORD,
"you will call me 'my husband';
you will no longer call me 'my
master.'*c*
17 I will remove the names of the Baals
from her lips;
no longer will their names be
invoked.
18 In that day I will make a covenant for
them
with the beasts of the field, the birds
in the sky
and the creatures that move along
the ground.
Bow and sword and battle
I will abolish from the land,
so that all may lie down in safety.
19 I will betroth you to me forever;
I will betroth you in*d* righteousness
and justice,
in*d* love and compassion.
20 I will betroth you in*d* faithfulness,
and you will acknowledge the LORD.

21 "In that day I will respond,"
declares the LORD —

"I will respond to the skies,
and they will respond to the earth;
22 and the earth will respond to the grain,
the new wine and the olive oil,
and they will respond to Jezreel.*e*
23 I will plant her for myself in the land;
I will show my love to the one I called
'Not my loved one.'*f*
I will say to those called 'Not my
people,*g* 'You are my people';
and they will say, 'You are my God.'"

Hosea's Reconciliation With His Wife

3 The LORD said to me, "Go, show
your love to your wife again, though
she is loved by another man and is
an adulteress. Love her as the LORD loves
the Israelites, though they turn to other
gods and love the sacred raisin cakes."

2 So I bought her for fifteen shekels*h* of
silver and about a homer and a lethek*i* of
barley. 3 Then I told her, "You are to live with
me many days; you must not be a prostitute
or be intimate with any man, and I will behave the same way toward you."

4 For the Israelites will live many days
without king or prince, without sacrifice or
sacred stones, without ephod or household
gods. 5 Afterward the Israelites will return
and seek the LORD their God and David
their king. They will come trembling to the
LORD and to his blessings in the last days.

The Charge Against Israel

4 Hear the word of the LORD, you
Israelites,
because the LORD has a charge to
bring
against you who live in the land:
"There is no faithfulness, no love,
no acknowledgment of God in the
land.
2 There is only cursing,*j* lying and
murder,
stealing and adultery;

---

a 15 Achor means *trouble.*   *b 15* Or *sing*   *c 16* Hebrew *baal*   *d 19,20* Or *with*   *e 22 Jezreel* means *God
plants.*   *f 23* Hebrew *Lo-Ruhamah* (see 1:6)   *g 23* Hebrew *Lo-Ammi* (see 1:9)   *h 2* That is, about 6 ounces or
about 170 grams   *i 2* A homer and a lethek possibly weighed about 430 pounds or about 195 kilograms.
j 2 That is, to pronounce a curse on

they break all bounds,
and bloodshed follows bloodshed.
3 Because of this the land dries up,
and all who live in it waste away;
the beasts of the field, the birds in the
sky
and the fish in the sea are swept away.

4 "But let no one bring a charge,
let no one accuse another,
for your people are like those
who bring charges against a priest.
5 You stumble day and night,
and the prophets stumble with you.
So I will destroy your mother —
6   my people are destroyed from lack of
knowledge.

"Because you have rejected knowledge,
I also reject you as my priests;
because you have ignored the law of
your God,
I also will ignore your children.
7 The more priests there were,
the more they sinned against me;
they exchanged their glorious God*a*
for something disgraceful.
8 They feed on the sins of my people
and relish their wickedness.
9 And it will be: Like people, like priests.
I will punish both of them for their
ways
and repay them for their deeds.

10 "They will eat but not have enough;
they will engage in prostitution but
not flourish,
because they have deserted the LORD
to give themselves 11 to prostitution;
old wine and new wine
take away their understanding.
12 My people consult a wooden idol,
and a diviner's rod speaks to them.
A spirit of prostitution leads them
astray;
they are unfaithful to their God.
13 They sacrifice on the mountaintops
and burn offerings on the hills,

under oak, poplar and terebinth,
where the shade is pleasant.
Therefore your daughters turn to
prostitution
and your daughters-in-law to
adultery.

14 "I will not punish your daughters
when they turn to prostitution,
nor your daughters-in-law
when they commit adultery,
because the men themselves consort
with harlots
and sacrifice with shrine
prostitutes —
a people without understanding will
come to ruin!

15 "Though you, Israel, commit adultery,
do not let Judah become guilty.

"Do not go to Gilgal;
do not go up to Beth Aven.*b*
And do not swear, 'As surely as the
LORD lives!'
16 The Israelites are stubborn,
like a stubborn heifer.
How then can the LORD pasture them
like lambs in a meadow?
17 Ephraim is joined to idols;
leave him alone!
18 Even when their drinks are gone,
they continue their prostitution;
their rulers dearly love shameful
ways.
19 A whirlwind will sweep them away,
and their sacrifices will bring them
shame.

Judgment Against Israel

5 "Hear this, you priests!
Pay attention, you Israelites!
Listen, royal house!
This judgment is against you:
You have been a snare at Mizpah,
a net spread out on Tabor.
2 The rebels are knee-deep in slaughter.
I will discipline all of them.

---

a 7 Syriac (see also an ancient Hebrew scribal tradition); Masoretic Text *me; / I will exchange their glory*   *b 15 Beth Aven* means *house of wickedness* (a derogatory name for Bethel, which means *house of God*).

³ I know all about Ephraim;
  Israel is not hidden from me.
Ephraim, you have now turned to
      prostitution;
  Israel is corrupt.

⁴ "Their deeds do not permit them
    to return to their God.
A spirit of prostitution is in their heart;
  they do not acknowledge the LORD.
⁵ Israel's arrogance testifies against them;
  the Israelites, even Ephraim, stumble
    in their sin;
  Judah also stumbles with them.
⁶ When they go with their flocks and
      herds
    to seek the LORD,
they will not find him;
  he has withdrawn himself from
      them.
⁷ They are unfaithful to the LORD;
  they give birth to illegitimate
    children.
When they celebrate their New Moon
      feasts,
  he will devourᵃ their fields.

⁸ "Sound the trumpet in Gibeah,
    the horn in Ramah.
Raise the battle cry in Beth Avenᵇ;
    lead on, Benjamin.
⁹ Ephraim will be laid waste
    on the day of reckoning.
Among the tribes of Israel
    I proclaim what is certain.
¹⁰ Judah's leaders are like those
    who move boundary stones.
I will pour out my wrath on them
    like a flood of water.
¹¹ Ephraim is oppressed,
    trampled in judgment,
    intent on pursuing idols.ᶜ
¹² I am like a moth to Ephraim,
    like rot to the people of Judah.

¹³ "When Ephraim saw his sickness,
    and Judah his sores,

then Ephraim turned to Assyria,
    and sent to the great king for help.
But he is not able to cure you,
    not able to heal your sores.
¹⁴ For I will be like a lion to Ephraim,
    like a great lion to Judah.
I will tear them to pieces and go away;
    I will carry them off, with no one to
      rescue them.
¹⁵ Then I will return to my lair
    until they have borne their guilt
    and seek my face—
in their misery
    they will earnestly seek me."

Israel Unrepentant

6 "Come, let us return to the LORD.
    He has torn us to pieces
    but he will heal us;
he has injured us
    but he will bind up our wounds.
² After two days he will revive us;
    on the third day he will restore us,
    that we may live in his presence.
³ Let us acknowledge the LORD;
    let us press on to acknowledge him.
As surely as the sun rises,
    he will appear;
he will come to us like the winter
      rains,
    like the spring rains that water the
      earth."

⁴ "What can I do with you, Ephraim?
    What can I do with you, Judah?
Your love is like the morning mist,
    like the early dew that disappears.
⁵ Therefore I cut you in pieces with my
      prophets,
    I killed you with the words of my
      mouth—
    then my judgments go forth like the
      sun.ᵈ
⁶ For I desire mercy, not sacrifice,
    and acknowledgment of God rather
      than burnt offerings.

ᵃ 7 Or *Now their New Moon feasts / will devour them and*   ᵇ 8 *Beth Aven* means *house of wickedness* (a derogatory
name for Bethel, which means *house of God*).   ᶜ 11 The meaning of the Hebrew for this word is uncertain.
ᵈ 5 The meaning of the Hebrew for this line is uncertain.

⁷As at Adam,ᵃ they have broken the
    covenant;
  they were unfaithful to me there.
⁸Gilead is a city of evildoers,
  stained with footprints of blood.
⁹As marauders lie in ambush for a
    victim,
  so do bands of priests;
they murder on the road to Shechem,
  carrying out their wicked schemes.
¹⁰I have seen a horrible thing in Israel:
  There Ephraim is given to
    prostitution,
  Israel is defiled.

¹¹"Also for you, Judah,
  a harvest is appointed.

"Whenever I would restore the fortunes
  of my people,
7 ¹whenever I would heal Israel,
  the sins of Ephraim are exposed
  and the crimes of Samaria revealed.
They practice deceit,
  thieves break into houses,
  bandits rob in the streets;
²but they do not realize
  that I remember all their evil deeds.
Their sins engulf them;
  they are always before me.

³"They delight the king with their
    wickedness,
  the princes with their lies.
⁴They are all adulterers,
  burning like an oven
whose fire the baker need not stir
  from the kneading of the dough till it
    rises.
⁵On the day of the festival of our king
  the princes become inflamed with
    wine,
  and he joins hands with the mockers.
⁶Their hearts are like an oven;
  they approach him with intrigue.
Their passion smolders all night;
  in the morning it blazes like a
    flaming fire.

⁷All of them are hot as an oven;
  they devour their rulers.
All their kings fall,
  and none of them calls on me.

⁸"Ephraim mixes with the nations;
  Ephraim is a flat loaf not turned
    over.
⁹Foreigners sap his strength,
  but he does not realize it.
His hair is sprinkled with gray,
  but he does not notice.
¹⁰Israel's arrogance testifies against him,
  but despite all this
he does not return to the LORD his God
  or search for him.

¹¹"Ephraim is like a dove,
  easily deceived and senseless —
now calling to Egypt,
  now turning to Assyria.
¹²When they go, I will throw my net over
    them;
  I will pull them down like the birds
    in the sky.
When I hear them flocking together,
  I will catch them.
¹³Woe to them,
  because they have strayed from me!
Destruction to them,
  because they have rebelled against me!
I long to redeem them
  but they speak about me falsely.
¹⁴They do not cry out to me from their
    hearts
  but wail on their beds.
They slash themselves,ᵇ appealing to
    their gods
  for grain and new wine,
  but they turn away from me.
¹⁵I trained them and strengthened their
    arms,
  but they plot evil against me.
¹⁶They do not turn to the Most High;
  they are like a faulty bow.
Their leaders will fall by the sword
  because of their insolent words.

ᵃ 7 Or *Like Adam*; or *Like human beings*   ᵇ 14 Some Hebrew manuscripts and Septuagint; most Hebrew
manuscripts *They gather together*

For this they will be ridiculed
  in the land of Egypt.

Israel to Reap the Whirlwind

8 "Put the trumpet to your lips!
    An eagle is over the house of the
      LORD
  because the people have broken my
      covenant
    and rebelled against my law.
2 Israel cries out to me,
    'Our God, we acknowledge you!'
3 But Israel has rejected what is good;
    an enemy will pursue him.
4 They set up kings without my consent;
    they choose princes without my
      approval.
  With their silver and gold
    they make idols for themselves
    to their own destruction.
5 Samaria, throw out your calf-idol!
    My anger burns against them.
  How long will they be incapable of
      purity?
6   They are from Israel!
  This calf—a metalworker has made it;
    it is not God.
  It will be broken in pieces,
    that calf of Samaria.

7 "They sow the wind
    and reap the whirlwind.
  The stalk has no head;
    it will produce no flour.
  Were it to yield grain,
    foreigners would swallow it up.
8 Israel is swallowed up;
    now she is among the nations
    like something no one wants.
9 For they have gone up to Assyria
    like a wild donkey wandering
      alone.
  Ephraim has sold herself to lovers.
10 Although they have sold themselves
      among the nations,
    I will now gather them together.
  They will begin to waste away
    under the oppression of the mighty
      king.

11 "Though Ephraim built many altars for
      sin offerings,
    these have become altars for sinning.
12 I wrote for them the many things of my
      law,
    but they regarded them as something
      foreign.
13 Though they offer sacrifices as gifts to
      me,
    and though they eat the meat,
    the LORD is not pleased with them.
  Now he will remember their
      wickedness
    and punish their sins:
    They will return to Egypt.
14 Israel has forgotten their Maker
    and built palaces;
  Judah has fortified many towns.
  But I will send fire on their cities
    that will consume their fortresses."

Punishment for Israel

9 Do not rejoice, Israel;
    do not be jubilant like the other
      nations.
  For you have been unfaithful to your
      God;
    you love the wages of a prostitute
    at every threshing floor.
2 Threshing floors and winepresses will
      not feed the people;
    the new wine will fail them.
3 They will not remain in the LORD's
      land;
    Ephraim will return to Egypt
    and eat unclean food in Assyria.
4 They will not pour out wine offerings
      to the LORD,
    nor will their sacrifices please him.
  Such sacrifices will be to them like the
      bread of mourners;
    all who eat them will be unclean.
  This food will be for themselves;
    it will not come into the temple of the
      LORD.

5 What will you do on the day of your
      appointed festivals,
    on the feast days of the LORD?

⁶ Even if they escape from destruction,
    Egypt will gather them,
    and Memphis will bury them.
Their treasures of silver will be taken
    over by briers,
    and thorns will overrun their tents.
⁷ The days of punishment are coming,
    the days of reckoning are at hand.
    Let Israel know this.
Because your sins are so many
    and your hostility so great,
the prophet is considered a fool,
    the inspired person a maniac.
⁸ The prophet, along with my God,
    is the watchman over Ephraim,ᵃ
yet snares await him on all his paths,
    and hostility in the house of his God.
⁹ They have sunk deep into corruption,
    as in the days of Gibeah.
God will remember their wickedness
    and punish them for their sins.

¹⁰ "When I found Israel,
    it was like finding grapes in the
        desert;
when I saw your ancestors,
    it was like seeing the early fruit on
        the fig tree.
But when they came to Baal Peor,
    they consecrated themselves to that
        shameful idol
    and became as vile as the thing they
        loved.
¹¹ Ephraim's glory will fly away like a
    bird —
    no birth, no pregnancy, no conception.
¹² Even if they rear children,
    I will bereave them of every one.
Woe to them
    when I turn away from them!
¹³ I have seen Ephraim, like Tyre,
    planted in a pleasant place.
But Ephraim will bring out
    their children to the slayer."

¹⁴ Give them, LORD —
    what will you give them?
Give them wombs that miscarry
    and breasts that are dry.

¹⁵ "Because of all their wickedness in Gilgal,
    I hated them there.
Because of their sinful deeds,
    I will drive them out of my house.
I will no longer love them;
    all their leaders are rebellious.
¹⁶ Ephraim is blighted,
    their root is withered,
    they yield no fruit.
Even if they bear children,
    I will slay their cherished offspring."

¹⁷ My God will reject them
    because they have not obeyed him;
    they will be wanderers among the
        nations.

10

Israel was a spreading vine;
    he brought forth fruit for
        himself.
As his fruit increased,
    he built more altars;
as his land prospered,
    he adorned his sacred stones.
² Their heart is deceitful,
    and now they must bear their guilt.
The LORD will demolish their altars
    and destroy their sacred stones.

³ Then they will say, "We have no king
    because we did not revere the LORD.
But even if we had a king,
    what could he do for us?"
⁴ They make many promises,
    take false oaths
    and make agreements;
therefore lawsuits spring up
    like poisonous weeds in a plowed field.
⁵ The people who live in Samaria fear
    for the calf-idol of Beth Aven.ᵇ
Its people will mourn over it,
    and so will its idolatrous priests,
those who had rejoiced over its splendor,
    because it is taken from them into
        exile.

ᵃ 8 Or *The prophet is the watchman over Ephraim, / the people of my God*   ᵇ 5 *Beth Aven* means *house of wickedness*
(a derogatory name for Bethel, which means *house of God*).

⁶It will be carried to Assyria
    as tribute for the great king.
Ephraim will be disgraced;
    Israel will be ashamed of its foreign
        alliances.
⁷Samaria's king will be destroyed,
    swept away like a twig on the surface
        of the waters.
⁸The high places of wickedness*a* will be
        destroyed—
    it is the sin of Israel.
Thorns and thistles will grow up
    and cover their altars.
Then they will say to the mountains,
    "Cover us!"
    and to the hills, "Fall on us!"

⁹"Since the days of Gibeah, you have
        sinned, Israel,
    and there you have remained.*b*
Will not war again overtake
    the evildoers in Gibeah?
¹⁰When I please, I will punish them;
    nations will be gathered against
        them
    to put them in bonds for their double
        sin.
¹¹Ephraim is a trained heifer
    that loves to thresh;
so I will put a yoke
    on her fair neck.
I will drive Ephraim,
    Judah must plow,
    and Jacob must break up the ground.
¹²Sow righteousness for yourselves,
    reap the fruit of unfailing love,
and break up your unplowed ground;
    for it is time to seek the LORD,
until he comes
    and showers his righteousness on
        you.
¹³But you have planted wickedness,
    you have reaped evil,
    you have eaten the fruit of deception.
Because you have depended on your
        own strength
    and on your many warriors,

¹⁴the roar of battle will rise against your
        people,
    so that all your fortresses will be
        devastated—
as Shalman devastated Beth Arbel on
        the day of battle,
    when mothers were dashed to the
        ground with their children.
¹⁵So will it happen to you, Bethel,
    because your wickedness is great.
When that day dawns,
    the king of Israel will be completely
        destroyed.

God's Love for Israel

11 "When Israel was a child, I
        loved him,
    and out of Egypt I called my son.
²But the more they were called,
    the more they went away from me.*c*
They sacrificed to the Baals
    and they burned incense to images.
³It was I who taught Ephraim to walk,
    taking them by the arms;
but they did not realize
    it was I who healed them.
⁴I led them with cords of human
        kindness,
    with ties of love.
To them I was like one who lifts
    a little child to the cheek,
    and I bent down to feed them.

⁵"Will they not return to Egypt
    and will not Assyria rule over them
    because they refuse to repent?
⁶A sword will flash in their cities;
    it will devour their false prophets
    and put an end to their plans.
⁷My people are determined to turn from
        me.
    Even though they call me God Most
        High,
    I will by no means exalt them.

⁸"How can I give you up, Ephraim?
    How can I hand you over, Israel?

---

a 8 Hebrew *aven,* a reference to Beth Aven (a derogatory name for Bethel); see verse 5.   *b 9* Or *there a stand was taken*   *c 2* Septuagint; Hebrew *them*

How can I treat you like Admah?
How can I make you like Zeboyim?
My heart is changed within me;
all my compassion is aroused.
⁹ I will not carry out my fierce anger,
nor will I devastate Ephraim again.
For I am God, and not a man —
the Holy One among you.
I will not come against their cities.
¹⁰ They will follow the Lord;
he will roar like a lion.
When he roars,
his children will come trembling
from the west.
¹¹ They will come from Egypt,
trembling like sparrows,
from Assyria, fluttering like doves.
I will settle them in their homes,"
declares the Lord.

Israel's Sin

¹² Ephraim has surrounded me with lies,
Israel with deceit.
And Judah is unruly against God,
even against the faithful Holy One.*ᵃ*

12

ᵇ ¹ Ephraim feeds on the wind;
he pursues the east wind all
day
and multiplies lies and violence.
He makes a treaty with Assyria
and sends olive oil to Egypt.
² The Lord has a charge to bring against
Judah;
he will punish Jacob*ᶜ* according to
his ways
and repay him according to his
deeds.
³ In the womb he grasped his brother's
heel;
as a man he struggled with God.
⁴ He struggled with the angel and
overcame him;
he wept and begged for his favor.
He found him at Bethel
and talked with him there —

⁵ the Lord God Almighty,
the Lord is his name!
⁶ But you must return to your God;
maintain love and justice,
and wait for your God always.

⁷ The merchant uses dishonest scales
and loves to defraud.
⁸ Ephraim boasts,
"I am very rich; I have become
wealthy.
With all my wealth they will not find
in me
any iniquity or sin."

⁹ "I have been the Lord your God
ever since you came out of Egypt;
I will make you live in tents again,
as in the days of your appointed
festivals.
¹⁰ I spoke to the prophets,
gave them many visions
and told parables through them."

¹¹ Is Gilead wicked?
Its people are worthless!
Do they sacrifice bulls in Gilgal?
Their altars will be like piles of stones
on a plowed field.
¹² Jacob fled to the country of Aram*ᵈ*;
Israel served to get a wife,
and to pay for her he tended sheep.
¹³ The Lord used a prophet to bring Israel
up from Egypt,
by a prophet he cared for him.
¹⁴ But Ephraim has aroused his bitter
anger;
his Lord will leave on him the guilt of
his bloodshed
and will repay him for his contempt.

The Lord's Anger Against Israel

13

When Ephraim spoke, people
trembled;
he was exalted in Israel.
But he became guilty of Baal worship
and died.

ᵃ 12 In Hebrew texts this verse (11:12) is numbered 12:1.   *ᵇ* In Hebrew texts 12:1-14 is numbered 12:2-15.
ᶜ 2 Jacob means *he grasps the heel,* a Hebrew idiom for *he takes advantage of* or *he deceives.*   *ᵈ 12* That is,
Northwest Mesopotamia

²Now they sin more and more;
   they make idols for themselves from
      their silver,
  cleverly fashioned images,
   all of them the work of craftsmen.
  It is said of these people,
   "They offer human sacrifices!
   They kiss*ᵃ* calf-idols!"
³Therefore they will be like the morning
      mist,
  like the early dew that disappears,
  like chaff swirling from a threshing
      floor,
  like smoke escaping through a
      window.

⁴"But I have been the LORD your God
   ever since you came out of Egypt.
  You shall acknowledge no God but me,
   no Savior except me.
⁵I cared for you in the wilderness,
  in the land of burning heat.
⁶When I fed them, they were satisfied;
   when they were satisfied, they
      became proud;
   then they forgot me.
⁷So I will be like a lion to them,
   like a leopard I will lurk by the path.
⁸Like a bear robbed of her cubs,
   I will attack them and rip them
      open;
  like a lion I will devour them —
   a wild animal will tear them apart.

⁹"You are destroyed, Israel,
   because you are against me, against
      your helper.
¹⁰Where is your king, that he may save
      you?
  Where are your rulers in all your
      towns,
  of whom you said,
   'Give me a king and princes'?
¹¹So in my anger I gave you a king,
   and in my wrath I took him away.
¹²The guilt of Ephraim is stored up,
   his sins are kept on record.

¹³Pains as of a woman in childbirth come
      to him,
  but he is a child without wisdom;
  when the time arrives,
   he doesn't have the sense to come out
      of the womb.

¹⁴"I will deliver this people from the
      power of the grave;
  I will redeem them from death.
  Where, O death, are your plagues?
   Where, O grave, is your destruction?

  "I will have no compassion,
¹⁵ even though he thrives among his
      brothers.
  An east wind from the LORD will
      come,
   blowing in from the desert;
  his spring will fail
   and his well dry up.
  His storehouse will be plundered
   of all its treasures.
¹⁶The people of Samaria must bear their
      guilt,
  because they have rebelled against
      their God.
  They will fall by the sword;
   their little ones will be dashed to the
      ground,
   their pregnant women ripped
      open."*ᵇ*

Repentance to Bring Blessing

14 *ᶜ* Return, Israel, to the LORD your
      God.
    Your sins have been your
      downfall!
²Take words with you
  and return to the LORD.
  Say to him:
   "Forgive all our sins
  and receive us graciously,
   that we may offer the fruit of our
      lips.*ᵈ*
³Assyria cannot save us;
  we will not mount warhorses.

ᵃ 2 Or *"Men who sacrifice / kiss*   *ᵇ 16* In Hebrew texts this verse (13:16) is numbered 14:1.   *ᶜ* In Hebrew texts 14:1-9 is numbered 14:2-10.   *ᵈ 2* Or *offer our lips as sacrifices of bulls*

We will never again say 'Our gods'
  to what our own hands have made,
  for in you the fatherless find
    compassion."

4 "I will heal their waywardness
  and love them freely,
  for my anger has turned away from
    them.
5 I will be like the dew to Israel;
  he will blossom like a lily.
Like a cedar of Lebanon
  he will send down his roots;
6   his young shoots will grow.
His splendor will be like an olive
    tree,
  his fragrance like a cedar of
    Lebanon.

7 People will dwell again in his shade;
  they will flourish like the grain,
they will blossom like the vine —
  Israel's fame will be like the wine of
    Lebanon.
8 Ephraim, what more have I*a* to do with
    idols?
  I will answer him and care for him.
I am like a flourishing juniper;
  your fruitfulness comes from me."

9 Who is wise? Let them realize these
    things.
  Who is discerning? Let them
    understand.
The ways of the LORD are right;
  the righteous walk in them,
  but the rebellious stumble in them.

---

a 8 Or Hebrew; Septuagint *What more has Ephraim*

THEME: God requires heartfelt repentance, in response to which he forgives and restores.

AUTHOR: The prophet Joel is the book's author.

DATE OF WRITING: The time of writing is unknown. Dates as early as 835 BC and as late as 400 BC have been suggested.

CHALLENGE FROM JOEL: " 'Even now,' " declares the LORD, " 'return to me with all your heart, with fasting and weeping and mourning.' Rend your heart and not your garments. Return to the LORD your God, for he is gracious and compassionate, slow to anger and abounding in love" (Joel 2:12 – 13).

ENCOURAGEMENT FROM JOEL: "The LORD will be a refuge for his people" (Joel 3:16).

REFLECTION FROM JOEL: "I will repay you for the years the locusts have eaten ... You will have plenty to eat, until you are full, and you will praise the name of the LORD your God, who has worked wonders for you; never again will my people be shamed. Then you will know ... that I am the LORD your God, and that there is no other" (Joel 2:25 – 27).

Disaster visits Judah with the arrival of a great cloud of locusts. Within hours, the fields are stripped bare. Joel uses this event to illustrate God's message. The plague of locusts foreshadows the pivotal "day of the LORD" to come in the future. This brief book describes both desolation and deliverance.

We've all felt at one time or another as though our lives have been devastated. Maybe the locusts in our lives have come in the form of an abusive relationship. Or they could represent wasted years with an out-of-control lifestyle. Whatever the situation, God is ready to restore the years we've lived in desolation. Today can be the day of the Lord in our lives, if only we'll reach out to God and receive his freely offered gift of grace.

1

The word of the LORD that came to Joel son of Pethuel.

An Invasion of Locusts

² Hear this, you elders;
    listen, all who live in the land.
Has anything like this ever happened in
        your days
    or in the days of your ancestors?

³ Tell it to your children,
    and let your children tell it to their
        children,
    and their children to the next
        generation.
⁴ What the locust swarm has left
    the great locusts have eaten;
what the great locusts have left
    the young locusts have eaten;

what the young locusts have left
  other locusts[a] have eaten.

5 Wake up, you drunkards, and weep!
  Wail, all you drinkers of wine;
wail because of the new wine,
  for it has been snatched from your
    lips.
6 A nation has invaded my land,
  a mighty army without number;
it has the teeth of a lion,
  the fangs of a lioness.
7 It has laid waste my vines
  and ruined my fig trees.
It has stripped off their bark
  and thrown it away,
    leaving their branches white.

8 Mourn like a virgin in sackcloth
  grieving for the betrothed of her
    youth.
9 Grain offerings and drink offerings
  are cut off from the house of the LORD.
The priests are in mourning,
  those who minister before the LORD.
10 The fields are ruined,
  the ground is dried up;
the grain is destroyed,
  the new wine is dried up,
  the olive oil fails.

11 Despair, you farmers,
  wail, you vine growers;
grieve for the wheat and the barley,
  because the harvest of the field is
    destroyed.
12 The vine is dried up
  and the fig tree is withered;
the pomegranate, the palm and the
    apple[b] tree —
  all the trees of the field — are dried up.
Surely the people's joy
  is withered away.

A Call to Lamentation

13 Put on sackcloth, you priests, and mourn;
  wail, you who minister before the
    altar.
Come, spend the night in sackcloth,
  you who minister before my God;
for the grain offerings and drink
    offerings
  are withheld from the house of your
    God.
14 Declare a holy fast;
  call a sacred assembly.
Summon the elders
  and all who live in the land
to the house of the LORD your God,
  and cry out to the LORD.

15 Alas for that day!
  For the day of the LORD is near;
  it will come like destruction from the
    Almighty.[c]

16 Has not the food been cut off
  before our very eyes —
joy and gladness
  from the house of our God?
17 The seeds are shriveled
  beneath the clods.[d]
The storehouses are in ruins,
  the granaries have been broken down,
  for the grain has dried up.
18 How the cattle moan!
  The herds mill about
because they have no pasture;
  even the flocks of sheep are suffering.

19 To you, LORD, I call,
  for fire has devoured the pastures in
    the wilderness
and flames have burned up all the
    trees of the field.
20 Even the wild animals pant for you;
  the streams of water have dried up
and fire has devoured the pastures in
    the wilderness.

An Army of Locusts

2 Blow the trumpet in Zion;
  sound the alarm on my holy hill.

Let all who live in the land tremble,
  for the day of the LORD is coming.

---

a 4 The precise meaning of the four Hebrew words used here for locusts is uncertain.   b 12 Or possibly *apricot*
c 15 Hebrew *Shaddai*   d 17 The meaning of the Hebrew for this word is uncertain.

It is close at hand —
2   a day of darkness and gloom,
    a day of clouds and blackness.
Like dawn spreading across the
        mountains
    a large and mighty army comes,
such as never was in ancient times
    nor ever will be in ages to come.

3 Before them fire devours,
    behind them a flame blazes.
Before them the land is like the garden
        of Eden,
    behind them, a desert waste —
    nothing escapes them.
4 They have the appearance of horses;
    they gallop along like cavalry.
5 With a noise like that of chariots
    they leap over the mountaintops,
like a crackling fire consuming stubble,
    like a mighty army drawn up for
        battle.

6 At the sight of them, nations are in
        anguish;
    every face turns pale.
7 They charge like warriors;
    they scale walls like soldiers.
They all march in line,
    not swerving from their course.
8 They do not jostle each other;
    each marches straight ahead.
They plunge through defenses
    without breaking ranks.
9 They rush upon the city;
    they run along the wall.
They climb into the houses;
    like thieves they enter through the
        windows.

10 Before them the earth shakes,
    the heavens tremble,
the sun and moon are darkened,
    and the stars no longer shine.
11 The LORD thunders
    at the head of his army;
his forces are beyond number,
    and mighty is the army that obeys
        his command.

The day of the LORD is great;
    it is dreadful.
    Who can endure it?

Rend Your Heart

12 "Even now," declares the LORD,
    "return to me with all your heart,
    with fasting and weeping and
        mourning."

13 Rend your heart
    and not your garments.
Return to the LORD your God,
    for he is gracious and compassionate,
slow to anger and abounding in love,
    and he relents from sending
        calamity.
14 Who knows? He may turn and relent
    and leave behind a blessing —
grain offerings and drink offerings
    for the LORD your God.

15 Blow the trumpet in Zion,
    declare a holy fast,
    call a sacred assembly.
16 Gather the people,
    consecrate the assembly;
bring together the elders,
    gather the children,
    those nursing at the breast.
Let the bridegroom leave his room
    and the bride her chamber.
17 Let the priests, who minister before the
        LORD,
    weep between the portico and the
        altar.
Let them say, "Spare your people, LORD.
    Do not make your inheritance an
        object of scorn,
    a byword among the nations.
Why should they say among the peoples,
    'Where is their God?'"

The LORD's Answer

18 Then the LORD was jealous for his land
    and took pity on his people.

19 The LORD replied[a] to them:

"I am sending you grain, new wine and
     olive oil,
     enough to satisfy you fully;
never again will I make you
     an object of scorn to the nations.

20 "I will drive the northern horde far
     from you,
     pushing it into a parched and barren
     land;
its eastern ranks will drown in the
     Dead Sea
     and its western ranks in the
     . Mediterranean Sea.
And its stench will go up;
     its smell will rise."

Surely he has done great things!
21   Do not be afraid, land of Judah;
     be glad and rejoice.
Surely the Lord has done great
     things!
22   Do not be afraid, you wild animals,
     for the pastures in the wilderness are
     becoming green.
The trees are bearing their fruit;
     the fig tree and the vine yield their
     riches.
23 Be glad, people of Zion,
     rejoice in the Lord your God,
for he has given you the autumn rains
     because he is faithful.
He sends you abundant showers,
     both autumn and spring rains, as
     before.
24 The threshing floors will be filled with
     grain;
     the vats will overflow with new wine
     and oil.

25 "I will repay you for the years the
     locusts have eaten —
     the great locust and the young
     locust,
     the other locusts and the locust
     swarm[a] —
my great army that I sent among you.

26 You will have plenty to eat, until you
     are full,
     and you will praise the name of the
     Lord your God,
who has worked wonders for you;
     never again will my people be shamed.
27 Then you will know that I am in Israel,
     that I am the Lord your God,
     and that there is no other;
never again will my people be shamed.

The Day of the Lord

28 "And afterward,
     I will pour out my Spirit on all
     people.
Your sons and daughters will prophesy,
     your old men will dream dreams,
     your young men will see visions.
29 Even on my servants, both men and
     women,
     I will pour out my Spirit in those
     days.
30 I will show wonders in the heavens
     and on the earth,
     blood and fire and billows of smoke.
31 The sun will be turned to darkness
     and the moon to blood
     before the coming of the great and
     dreadful day of the Lord.
32 And everyone who calls
     on the name of the Lord will be
     saved;
for on Mount Zion and in Jerusalem
     there will be deliverance,
     as the Lord has said,
even among the survivors
     whom the Lord calls.[b]

The Nations Judged

3 [c] "In those days and at that time,
     when I restore the fortunes of Judah
     and Jerusalem,
2 I will gather all nations
     and bring them down to the Valley of
     Jehoshaphat.[d]

---

a 25 The precise meaning of the four Hebrew words used here for locusts is uncertain.   b 32 In Hebrew texts
2:28-32 is numbered 3:1-5.   c In Hebrew texts 3:1-21 is numbered 4:1-21.   d 2 Jehoshaphat means the Lord
judges; also in verse 12.

There I will put them on trial
  for what they did to my inheritance,
    my people Israel,
because they scattered my people
      among the nations
  and divided up my land.
³They cast lots for my people
  and traded boys for prostitutes;
    they sold girls for wine to drink.

⁴"Now what have you against me, Tyre and Sidon and all you regions of Philistia? Are you repaying me for something I have done? If you are paying me back, I will swiftly and speedily return on your own heads what you have done. ⁵For you took my silver and my gold and carried off my finest treasures to your temples.*ᵃ* ⁶You sold the people of Judah and Jerusalem to the Greeks, that you might send them far from their homeland.

⁷"See, I am going to rouse them out of the places to which you sold them, and I will return on your own heads what you have done. ⁸I will sell your sons and daughters to the people of Judah, and they will sell them to the Sabeans, a nation far away." The LORD has spoken.

⁹Proclaim this among the nations:
    Prepare for war!
  Rouse the warriors!
    Let all the fighting men draw near
      and attack.

ᵃ 5 Or *palaces*

AMENDS LESSON [*Principle Six*]

For the previous entry in the AMENDS lesson, go to Ecclesiastes 3:1 (page 784).

For a discussion of Principles One through Eight and a listing of their related lessons, go to pages xvii – xliv.

I will repay you for the years the locusts have eaten.

JOEL 2:25

Principle Six calls for us to evaluate all our relationships and to offer forgiveness to those who have hurt us and make amends for harm we've done to others, except when doing so would injure them or others. We need to be willing to admit our part in those relationships that have been broken or damaged. We begin by making AMENDS for the harm we've caused others.

The last letter in AMENDS is S, which stands for START LIVING THE PROMISES OF RECOVERY. Principle Six ends with a caution: " … except when doing so would injure them or others." Philippians 2:3 – 4 cautions: "In humility value others above yourselves, not looking to your own interests but each of you to the interests of the others." We can't wait until we feel like making amends or offering forgiveness; no, living this principle takes an act of the will — or perhaps a crisis of the will. Making amends is an act of obedience to Scripture — and an action that's essential for our personal survival.

As we complete this principle, we'll discover God's gift of true freedom from our past. We'll begin to find the peace and serenity we've long been seeking. We'll become ready to embrace God's purpose for our lives. We need to claim God's promise found in Joel 2:25.

This is the final page of the AMENDS lesson.

¹⁰ Beat your plowshares into swords
    and your pruning hooks into spears.
Let the weakling say,
    "I am strong!"
¹¹ Come quickly, all you nations from
        every side,
    and assemble there.

Bring down your warriors, LORD!

¹² "Let the nations be roused;
    let them advance into the Valley of
        Jehoshaphat,
    for there I will sit
    to judge all the nations on every side.
¹³ Swing the sickle,
    for the harvest is ripe.
Come, trample the grapes,
    for the winepress is full
    and the vats overflow —
so great is their wickedness!"

¹⁴ Multitudes, multitudes
    in the valley of decision!
For the day of the LORD is near
    in the valley of decision.
¹⁵ The sun and moon will be darkened,
    and the stars no longer shine.
¹⁶ The LORD will roar from Zion
    and thunder from Jerusalem;
    the earth and the heavens will
        tremble.

But the LORD will be a refuge for his
        people,
    a stronghold for the people of Israel.

Blessings for God's People

¹⁷ "Then you will know that I, the LORD
        your God,
    dwell in Zion, my holy hill.
Jerusalem will be holy;
    never again will foreigners invade her.

¹⁸ "In that day the mountains will drip
        new wine,
    and the hills will flow with milk;
    all the ravines of Judah will run with
        water.
A fountain will flow out of the LORD's
        house
    and will water the valley of acacias.^a
¹⁹ But Egypt will be desolate,
    Edom a desert waste,
because of violence done to the people
        of Judah,
    in whose land they shed innocent
        blood.
²⁰ Judah will be inhabited forever
    and Jerusalem through all generations.
²¹ Shall I leave their innocent blood
        unavenged?
    No, I will not."

        The LORD dwells in Zion!

---

^a 18 Or *Valley of Shittim*

THEME: True faith is expressed through actions, particularly those that concern social justice.

AUTHOR: Amos, a shepherd of Tekoa (a village about ten miles south of Jerusalem), wrote this book. He was called by God to leave Judah and go to the northern kingdom of Israel to prophesy a message of judgment.

DATE OF WRITING: The book of Amos was written between 760 and 750 BC.

ENCOURAGEMENT FROM AMOS: "Seek good, not evil, that you may live. Then the LORD God Almighty will be with you" (Amos 5:14).

CHALLENGE FROM AMOS: "Hate evil, love good; maintain justice in the courts" (Amos 5:15).

REFLECTION FROM AMOS: "Let justice roll on like a river, righteousness like a never-failing stream!" (Amos 5:24).

The book of Amos addresses the excessive pursuit of luxury, self-indulgence and oppression of the poor that have characterized the period of prosperity Israel has been experiencing. This prophecy is a message of judgment against Judah, Israel and other nations. Amos celebrates the righteousness and judgment of God but also emphasizes God's requirement that his people demonstrate those same characteristics. The way in which individuals of any era treat others reveals much about their relationship with God.

As in the days of Amos, we live in a time of selfish indifference to the hard times others may be going through. We don't have to think too long to recall a time when we've put our personal needs above the needs of others. As we progress in our recovery, it's necessary to take a long, hard look at how we treat others. As an important part of Principle Four, when we take our honest spiritual inventory we need to evaluate how we've treated others in our relationships. We need to look at our part in both the painful and the healthy relationships in which we've been involved. We may find character traits in ourselves that are out of line with what God expects of us. When these are revealed to us, we need to take the necessary steps to change them and love others in the way God calls us.

1 The words of Amos, one of the shepherds of Tekoa — the vision he saw concerning Israel two years before the earthquake, when Uzziah was king of Judah and Jeroboam son of Jehoash[a] was king of Israel.

²He said:

"The LORD roars from Zion
    and thunders from Jerusalem;
the pastures of the shepherds dry up,
    and the top of Carmel withers."

---

[a] 1 Hebrew *Joash*, a variant of *Jehoash*

Judgment on Israel's Neighbors

3This is what the LORD says:

"For three sins of Damascus,
    even for four, I will not relent.
Because she threshed Gilead
    with sledges having iron teeth,
4I will send fire on the house of Hazael
    that will consume the fortresses of
        Ben-Hadad.
5I will break down the gate of Damascus;
    I will destroy the king who is in*a* the
        Valley of Aven*b*
and the one who holds the scepter in
    Beth Eden.
    The people of Aram will go into exile
        to Kir,"
                        says the LORD.

6This is what the LORD says:

"For three sins of Gaza,
    even for four, I will not relent.
Because she took captive whole
    communities
    and sold them to Edom,
7I will send fire on the walls of Gaza
    that will consume her fortresses.
8I will destroy the king*c* of Ashdod
    and the one who holds the scepter in
        Ashkelon.
I will turn my hand against Ekron,
    till the last of the Philistines are
        dead,"
                says the Sovereign LORD.

9This is what the LORD says:

"For three sins of Tyre,
    even for four, I will not relent.
Because she sold whole communities of
    captives to Edom,
    disregarding a treaty of brotherhood,
10I will send fire on the walls of Tyre
    that will consume her fortresses."

11This is what the LORD says:

"For three sins of Edom,
    even for four, I will not relent.

Because he pursued his brother with a
    sword
    and slaughtered the women of the
        land,
because his anger raged continually
    and his fury flamed unchecked,
12I will send fire on Teman
    that will consume the fortresses of
        Bozrah."

13This is what the LORD says:

"For three sins of Ammon,
    even for four, I will not relent.
Because he ripped open the pregnant
    women of Gilead
    in order to extend his borders,
14I will set fire to the walls of Rabbah
    that will consume her fortresses
amid war cries on the day of battle,
    amid violent winds on a stormy
        day.
15Her king*d* will go into exile,
    he and his officials together,"
                        says the LORD.

2 This is what the LORD says:

"For three sins of Moab,
    even for four, I will not relent.
Because he burned to ashes
    the bones of Edom's king,
2I will send fire on Moab
    that will consume the fortresses of
        Kerioth.*e*
Moab will go down in great tumult
    amid war cries and the blast of the
        trumpet.
3I will destroy her ruler
    and kill all her officials with him,"
                        says the LORD.

4This is what the LORD says:

"For three sins of Judah,
    even for four, I will not relent.
Because they have rejected the law of
    the LORD
    and have not kept his decrees,

---

a 5 Or *the inhabitants of*   *b* 5 *Aven* means *wickedness.*   *c* 8 Or *inhabitants*   *d* 15 Or / *Molek*   *e* 2 Or *of*
her cities

because they have been led astray by
false gods,*a*
the gods*b* their ancestors followed,
⁵ I will send fire on Judah
that will consume the fortresses of
Jerusalem."

Judgment on Israel

⁶ This is what the LORD says:

"For three sins of Israel,
even for four, I will not relent.
They sell the innocent for silver,
and the needy for a pair of sandals.
⁷ They trample on the heads of the poor
as on the dust of the ground
and deny justice to the oppressed.
Father and son use the same girl
and so profane my holy name.
⁸ They lie down beside every altar
on garments taken in pledge.
In the house of their god
they drink wine taken as fines.

⁹ "Yet I destroyed the Amorites before
them,
though they were tall as the cedars
and strong as the oaks.
I destroyed their fruit above
and their roots below.
¹⁰ I brought you up out of Egypt
and led you forty years in the
wilderness
to give you the land of the Amorites.

¹¹ "I also raised up prophets from among
your children
and Nazirites from among your
youths.
Is this not true, people of Israel?"
declares the LORD.
¹² "But you made the Nazirites drink
wine
and commanded the prophets not to
prophesy.
¹³ "Now then, I will crush you
as a cart crushes when loaded with
grain.

¹⁴ The swift will not escape,
the strong will not muster their
strength,
and the warrior will not save his life.
¹⁵ The archer will not stand his ground,
the fleet-footed soldier will not get
away,
and the horseman will not save his
life.
¹⁶ Even the bravest warriors
will flee naked on that day,"
declares the LORD.

Witnesses Summoned Against Israel

3 Hear this word, people of Israel, the
word the LORD has spoken against
you — against the whole family I
brought up out of Egypt:

² "You only have I chosen
of all the families of the earth;
therefore I will punish you
for all your sins."

³ Do two walk together
unless they have agreed to do so?
⁴ Does a lion roar in the thicket
when it has no prey?
Does it growl in its den
when it has caught nothing?
⁵ Does a bird swoop down to a trap on
the ground
when no bait is there?
Does a trap spring up from the ground
if it has not caught anything?
⁶ When a trumpet sounds in a city,
do not the people tremble?
When disaster comes to a city,
has not the LORD caused it?

⁷ Surely the Sovereign LORD does
nothing
without revealing his plan
to his servants the prophets.

⁸ The lion has roared —
who will not fear?
The Sovereign LORD has spoken —
who can but prophesy?

---

a 4 Or *by lies*   *b* 4 Or *lies*

⁹Proclaim to the fortresses of Ashdod
  and to the fortresses of Egypt:
"Assemble yourselves on the mountains
    of Samaria;
  see the great unrest within her
  and the oppression among her
    people."

¹⁰"They do not know how to do right,"
    declares the LORD,
  "who store up in their fortresses
  what they have plundered and
    looted."

¹¹Therefore this is what the Sovereign
LORD says:

"An enemy will overrun your land,
  pull down your strongholds
  and plunder your fortresses."

¹²This is what the LORD says:

"As a shepherd rescues from the lion's
    mouth
  only two leg bones or a piece of an
    ear,
so will the Israelites living in Samaria
    be rescued,
  with only the head of a bed
  and a piece of fabric*ᵃ* from a couch.*ᵇ*"

¹³"Hear this and testify against the descendants of Jacob," declares the Lord, the
LORD God Almighty.

¹⁴"On the day I punish Israel for her
    sins,
  I will destroy the altars of Bethel;
the horns of the altar will be cut off
  and fall to the ground.
¹⁵I will tear down the winter house
  along with the summer house;
the houses adorned with ivory will be
    destroyed
  and the mansions will be
    demolished,"
              declares the LORD.

Israel Has Not Returned to God

4 Hear this word, you cows of
    Bashan on Mount Samaria,
  you women who oppress the poor
    and crush the needy
  and say to your husbands, "Bring us
    some drinks!"

²The Sovereign LORD has sworn by his
    holiness:
  "The time will surely come
when you will be taken away with hooks,
  the last of you with fishhooks.*ᶜ*
³You will each go straight out
  through breaches in the wall,
  and you will be cast out toward
    Harmon,*ᵈ*"
              declares the LORD.

⁴"Go to Bethel and sin;
  go to Gilgal and sin yet more.
Bring your sacrifices every morning,
  your tithes every three years.*ᵉ*
⁵Burn leavened bread as a thank offering
  and brag about your freewill
    offerings—
boast about them, you Israelites,
  for this is what you love to do,"
              declares the Sovereign LORD.

⁶"I gave you empty stomachs in every city
  and lack of bread in every town,
  yet you have not returned to me,"
              declares the LORD.

⁷"I also withheld rain from you
  when the harvest was still three
    months away.
I sent rain on one town,
  but withheld it from another.
One field had rain;
  another had none and dried up.
⁸People staggered from town to town for
    water
  but did not get enough to drink,
  yet you have not returned to me,"
              declares the LORD.

ᵃ 12 The meaning of the Hebrew for this phrase is uncertain.   *ᵇ 12* Or *Israelites be rescued, / those who sit in
Samaria / on the edge of their beds / and in Damascus on their couches.*   *ᶜ 2* Or *away in baskets, / the last of you in
fish baskets*   *ᵈ 3* Masoretic Text; with a different word division of the Hebrew (see Septuagint) *out, you mountain of
oppression*   *ᵉ 4* Or *days*

9 "Many times I struck your gardens and
    vineyards,
    destroying them with blight and
        mildew.
Locusts devoured your fig and olive
    trees,
    yet you have not returned to me,"
            declares the LORD.

10 "I sent plagues among you
    as I did to Egypt.
I killed your young men with the
    sword,
    along with your captured horses.
I filled your nostrils with the stench of
    your camps,
    yet you have not returned to me,"
            declares the LORD.

11 "I overthrew some of you
    as I overthrew Sodom and
        Gomorrah.
You were like a burning stick snatched
    from the fire,
    yet you have not returned to me,"
            declares the LORD.

12 "Therefore this is what I will do to you,
    Israel,
    and because I will do this to you,
        Israel,
    prepare to meet your God."

13 He who forms the mountains,
    who creates the wind,
    and who reveals his thoughts to
        mankind,
who turns dawn to darkness,
    and treads on the heights of the
        earth—
    the LORD God Almighty is his
        name.

A Lament and Call to Repentance

5 Hear this word, Israel, this lament I
    take up concerning you:

2 "Fallen is Virgin Israel,
    never to rise again,

deserted in her own land,
    with no one to lift her up."

3 This is what the Sovereign LORD says to
Israel:

"Your city that marches out a thousand
    strong
    will have only a hundred left;
your town that marches out a hundred
    strong
    will have only ten left."

4 This is what the LORD says to Israel:

"Seek me and live;
5   do not seek Bethel,
do not go to Gilgal,
    do not journey to Beersheba.
For Gilgal will surely go into exile,
    and Bethel will be reduced to
        nothing.ᵃ"
6 Seek the LORD and live,
    or he will sweep through the tribes of
        Joseph like a fire;
it will devour them,
    and Bethel will have no one to
        quench it.

7 There are those who turn justice into
        bitterness
    and cast righteousness to the ground.

8 He who made the Pleiades and Orion,
    who turns midnight into dawn
    and darkens day into night,
who calls for the waters of the sea
    and pours them out over the face of
        the land—
    the LORD is his name.
9 With a blinding flash he destroys the
        stronghold
    and brings the fortified city to ruin.

10 There are those who hate the one who
        upholds justice in court
    and detest the one who tells the
        truth.

11 You levy a straw tax on the poor
    and impose a tax on their grain.

ᵃ 5 Hebrew aven, a reference to Beth Aven (a derogatory name for Bethel); see Hosea 4:15.

Therefore, though you have built stone
    mansions,
        you will not live in them;
though you have planted lush
    vineyards,
        you will not drink their wine.
12 For I know how many are your
        offenses
    and how great your sins.

There are those who oppress the
        innocent and take bribes
    and deprive the poor of justice in the
        courts.
13 Therefore the prudent keep quiet in
        such times,
    for the times are evil.

14 Seek good, not evil,
        that you may live.
    Then the Lord God Almighty will be
        with you,
        just as you say he is.
15 Hate evil, love good;
        maintain justice in the courts.
    Perhaps the Lord God Almighty will
        have mercy
        on the remnant of Joseph.

16 Therefore this is what the Lord, the
    Lord God Almighty, says:

"There will be wailing in all the streets
        and cries of anguish in every public
        square.
    The farmers will be summoned to weep
        and the mourners to wail.
17 There will be wailing in all the
        vineyards,
    for I will pass through your midst,"
                    says the Lord.

The Day of the Lord

18 Woe to you who long
        for the day of the Lord!
    Why do you long for the day of the
        Lord?
    That day will be darkness, not light.

19 It will be as though a man fled from a
        lion
        only to meet a bear,
    as though he entered his house
        and rested his hand on the wall
        only to have a snake bite him.
20 Will not the day of the Lord be
        darkness, not light —
    pitch-dark, without a ray of
        brightness?

21 "I hate, I despise your religious festivals;
        your assemblies are a stench to me.
22 Even though you bring me burnt
        offerings and grain offerings,
    I will not accept them.
    Though you bring choice fellowship
        offerings,
    I will have no regard for them.
23 Away with the noise of your songs!
    I will not listen to the music of your
        harps.
24 But let justice roll on like a river,
    righteousness like a never-failing
        stream!

25 "Did you bring me sacrifices and
        offerings
    forty years in the wilderness, people
        of Israel?
26 You have lifted up the shrine of your
        king,
    the pedestal of your idols,
    the star of your god[a] —
    which you made for yourselves.
27 Therefore I will send you into exile
        beyond Damascus,"
    says the Lord, whose name is God
        Almighty.

Woe to the Complacent

6 Woe to you who are complacent in
        Zion,
    and to you who feel secure on
        Mount Samaria,
    you notable men of the foremost nation,
        to whom the people of Israel come!

---

a 26 Or *lifted up Sakkuth your king / and Kaiwan your idols, / your star-gods*; Septuagint *lifted up the shrine of Molek / and the star of your god Rephan, / their idols*

² Go to Kalneh and look at it;
    go from there to great Hamath,
    and then go down to Gath in
        Philistia.
Are they better off than your two
        kingdoms?
    Is their land larger than yours?
³ You put off the day of disaster
    and bring near a reign of terror.
⁴ You lie on beds adorned with ivory
    and lounge on your couches.
You dine on choice lambs
    and fattened calves.
⁵ You strum away on your harps like
        David
    and improvise on musical
        instruments.
⁶ You drink wine by the bowlful
    and use the finest lotions,
    but you do not grieve over the ruin of
        Joseph.
⁷ Therefore you will be among the first to
        go into exile;
    your feasting and lounging will end.

The Lord Abhors the Pride of Israel

⁸ The Sovereign Lord has sworn by himself — the Lord God Almighty declares:

"I abhor the pride of Jacob
    and detest his fortresses;
I will deliver up the city
    and everything in it."

⁹ If ten people are left in one house, they
too will die. ¹⁰ And if the relative who comes
to carry the bodies out of the house to burn
them*ᵃ* asks anyone who might be hiding
there, "Is anyone else with you?" and he says,
"No," then he will go on to say, "Hush! We
must not mention the name of the Lord."

¹¹ For the Lord has given the command,
    and he will smash the great house
        into pieces
    and the small house into bits.

¹² Do horses run on the rocky crags?
    Does one plow the sea*ᵇ* with oxen?
But you have turned justice into
        poison
    and the fruit of righteousness into
        bitterness —
¹³ you who rejoice in the conquest of Lo
        Debar*ᶜ*
    and say, "Did we not take Karnaim*ᵈ*
        by our own strength?"

¹⁴ For the Lord God Almighty declares,
    "I will stir up a nation against you,
        Israel,
    that will oppress you all the way
    from Lebo Hamath to the valley of
        the Arabah."

Locusts, Fire and a Plumb Line

7 This is what the Sovereign Lord
showed me: He was preparing
swarms of locusts after the king's
share had been harvested and just as the
late crops were coming up. ² When they had
stripped the land clean, I cried out, "Sovereign Lord, forgive! How can Jacob survive? He is so small!"

³ So the Lord relented.

"This will not happen," the Lord said.

⁴ This is what the Sovereign Lord
showed me: The Sovereign Lord was calling for judgment by fire; it dried up the
great deep and devoured the land. ⁵ Then I
cried out, "Sovereign Lord, I beg you, stop!
How can Jacob survive? He is so small!"

⁶ So the Lord relented.

"This will not happen either," the Sovereign Lord said.

⁷ This is what he showed me: The Lord
was standing by a wall that had been built
true to plumb,*ᵉ* with a plumb line*ᶠ* in his
hand. ⁸ And the Lord asked me, "What do
you see, Amos?"

"A plumb line," I replied.

Then the Lord said, "Look, I am setting

ᵃ 10 Or *to make a funeral fire in honor of the dead*   *ᵇ 12* With a different word division of the Hebrew; Masoretic
Text *plow there*   *ᶜ 13* *Lo Debar* means *nothing.*   *ᵈ 13* *Karnaim* means *horns; horn* here symbolizes strength.
ᵉ 7 The meaning of the Hebrew for this phrase is uncertain.   *ᶠ 7* The meaning of the Hebrew for this phrase is
uncertain; also in verse 8.

a plumb line among my people Israel; I will spare them no longer.

9 "The high places of Isaac will be destroyed
and the sanctuaries of Israel will be ruined;
with my sword I will rise against the house of Jeroboam."

Amos and Amaziah

10 Then Amaziah the priest of Bethel sent a message to Jeroboam king of Israel: "Amos is raising a conspiracy against you in the very heart of Israel. The land cannot bear all his words. 11 For this is what Amos is saying:

"'Jeroboam will die by the sword,
and Israel will surely go into exile,
away from their native land.'"

12 Then Amaziah said to Amos, "Get out, you seer! Go back to the land of Judah. Earn your bread there and do your prophesying there. 13 Don't prophesy anymore at Bethel, because this is the king's sanctuary and the temple of the kingdom."

14 Amos answered Amaziah, "I was neither a prophet nor the son of a prophet, but I was a shepherd, and I also took care of sycamore-fig trees. 15 But the LORD took me from tending the flock and said to me, 'Go, prophesy to my people Israel.' 16 Now then, hear the word of the LORD. You say,

"'Do not prophesy against Israel,
and stop preaching against the descendants of Isaac.'

17 "Therefore this is what the LORD says:

"'Your wife will become a prostitute in the city,
and your sons and daughters will fall by the sword.
Your land will be measured and divided up,
and you yourself will die in a pagan*a* country.

And Israel will surely go into exile,
away from their native land.'"

A Basket of Ripe Fruit

8 This is what the Sovereign LORD showed me: a basket of ripe fruit. 2 "What do you see, Amos?" he asked.

"A basket of ripe fruit," I answered.

Then the LORD said to me, "The time is ripe for my people Israel; I will spare them no longer.

3 "In that day," declares the Sovereign LORD, "the songs in the temple will turn to wailing.*b* Many, many bodies — flung everywhere! Silence!"

4 Hear this, you who trample the needy
and do away with the poor of the land,

5 saying,

"When will the New Moon be over
that we may sell grain,
and the Sabbath be ended
that we may market wheat?" —
skimping on the measure,
boosting the price
and cheating with dishonest scales,
6 buying the poor with silver
and the needy for a pair of sandals,
selling even the sweepings with the wheat.

7 The LORD has sworn by himself, the Pride of Jacob: "I will never forget anything they have done.

8 "Will not the land tremble for this,
and all who live in it mourn?
The whole land will rise like the Nile;
it will be stirred up and then sink
like the river of Egypt.

9 "In that day," declares the Sovereign LORD,

"I will make the sun go down at noon
and darken the earth in broad daylight.

---

a 17 Hebrew *an unclean*   *b 3* Or *"the temple singers will wail*

¹⁰ I will turn your religious festivals into
      mourning
   and all your singing into weeping.
I will make all of you wear sackcloth
   and shave your heads.
I will make that time like mourning for
      an only son
   and the end of it like a bitter day.

¹¹ "The days are coming," declares the
      Sovereign LORD,
   "when I will send a famine through
      the land —
not a famine of food or a thirst for water,
   but a famine of hearing the words of
      the LORD.
¹² People will stagger from sea to sea
   and wander from north to east,
searching for the word of the LORD,
   but they will not find it.

¹³ "In that day

"the lovely young women and strong
      young men
   will faint because of thirst.
¹⁴ Those who swear by the sin of Samaria —
   who say, 'As surely as your god lives,
      Dan,'
   or, 'As surely as the god*a* of Beersheba
      lives' —
   they will fall, never to rise again."

Israel to Be Destroyed

9 I saw the Lord standing by the altar,
and he said:

"Strike the tops of the pillars
   so that the thresholds shake.
Bring them down on the heads of all
      the people;
   those who are left I will kill with the
      sword.
Not one will get away,
   none will escape.
² Though they dig down to the depths
      below,
   from there my hand will take them.

Though they climb up to the heavens
      above,
   from there I will bring them down.
³ Though they hide themselves on the
      top of Carmel,
   there I will hunt them down and
      seize them.
Though they hide from my eyes at the
      bottom of the sea,
   there I will command the serpent to
      bite them.
⁴ Though they are driven into exile by
      their enemies,
   there I will command the sword to
      slay them.

"I will keep my eye on them
   for harm and not for good."

⁵ The Lord, the LORD Almighty —
he touches the earth and it melts,
   and all who live in it mourn;
the whole land rises like the Nile,
   then sinks like the river of Egypt;
⁶ he builds his lofty palace*b* in the heavens
   and sets its foundation*c* on the earth;
he calls for the waters of the sea
   and pours them out over the face of
      the land —
   the LORD is his name.

⁷ "Are not you Israelites
   the same to me as the Cushites*d*?"
                     declares the LORD.
"Did I not bring Israel up from Egypt,
   the Philistines from Caphtor*e*
   and the Arameans from Kir?

⁸ "Surely the eyes of the Sovereign LORD
   are on the sinful kingdom.
I will destroy it
   from the face of the earth.
Yet I will not totally destroy
   the descendants of Jacob,"
                     declares the LORD.
⁹ "For I will give the command,
   and I will shake the people of Israel
      among all the nations

---

a 14 Hebrew *the way*   *b 6* The meaning of the Hebrew for this phrase is uncertain.   *c 6* The meaning of the
Hebrew for this word is uncertain.   *d 7* That is, people from the upper Nile region   *e 7* That is, Crete

as grain is shaken in a sieve,
and not a pebble will reach the
ground.
10 All the sinners among my people
will die by the sword,
all those who say,
'Disaster will not overtake or meet
us.'

Israel's Restoration

11 "In that day

"I will restore David's fallen shelter —
I will repair its broken walls
and restore its ruins —
and will rebuild it as it used to be,
12 so that they may possess the remnant of
Edom
and all the nations that bear my
name,*a*"
declares the LORD,
who will do these things.

13 "The days are coming," declares the
LORD,

"when the reaper will be overtaken by
the plowman
and the planter by the one treading
grapes.
New wine will drip from the mountains
and flow from all the hills,
14   and I will bring my people Israel
back from exile.*b*

"They will rebuild the ruined cities and
live in them.
They will plant vineyards and drink
their wine;
they will make gardens and eat their
fruit.
15 I will plant Israel in their own land,
never again to be uprooted
from the land I have given them,"
says the LORD your God.

---

a 12 Hebrew; Septuagint *so that the remnant of people / and all the nations that bear my name may seek me*   *b 14* Or
will restore the fortunes of my people Israel

Obadiah

THEME: The book of Obadiah assures God's people that God will punish those who abuse them.

AUTHOR: The author of the book is Obadiah, an otherwise unknown prophet whose name means "servant of the LORD."

DATE OF WRITING: The date of composition of this short book has long been debated. Some connect it with the invasion of Judah by the Philistines and Arabs (850–840 BC). Others relate the events to the fall of Jerusalem to the Babylonians in 586 BC (a more likely scenario).

ENCOURAGEMENT FROM OBADIAH: "On Mount Zion will be deliverance; it will be holy" (Obadiah 17).

CHALLENGE FROM OBADIAH: "You should not gloat over your brother in the day of his misfortune" (Obadiah 12).

REFLECTION FROM OBADIAH: "The kingdom will be the LORD's" (Obadiah 21).

At a Glance

At only 21 verses, Obadiah is the shortest Old Testament book. It deals with the bitter rivalry between Edom, the descendants of Esau, and Israel, the descendants of Jacob, Esau's twin brother (see Genesis 25:19—36:43). Obadiah covers two subjects: Edom's destruction and Israel's restoration. Israel has been deeply damaged by the Edomites, but God assures his people that he will exact vengeance on Edom and reverse the damage.

Our recovery process can easily be sidetracked by bitterness. Many of us find it hard to focus on our own issues because we've been so deeply hurt by those around us. When we become bitter and hold on to old resentments, we find it hard to move beyond them, to progress any further on our path to recovery. When we refuse forgiveness to those who've hurt us, we only prolong our own pain. The people against whom we hold grudges may not even realize that they've hurt us. We need to lean on God and trust that he'll make all things right, according to his will.

Recovery Themes in Obadiah

Obadiah's Vision

¹The vision of Obadiah.

This is what the Sovereign LORD says about Edom—

We have heard a message from the LORD:
    An envoy was sent to the nations to say,
"Rise, let us go against her for battle"—

²"See, I will make you small among the
        nations;
    you will be utterly despised.
³The pride of your heart has deceived you,
    you who live in the clefts of the rocks*a*
    and make your home on the heights,
you who say to yourself,
    'Who can bring me down to the
        ground?'

a 3 Or of Sela

4 Though you soar like the eagle
   and make your nest among the stars,
   from there I will bring you down,"
                          declares the LORD.
5 "If thieves came to you,
   if robbers in the night —
 oh, what a disaster awaits you! —
   would they not steal only as much as
      they wanted?
 If grape pickers came to you,
   would they not leave a few grapes?
6 But how Esau will be ransacked,
   his hidden treasures pillaged!
7 All your allies will force you to the
      border;
   your friends will deceive and
      overpower you;
 those who eat your bread will set a trap
   for you,[a]
 but you will not detect it.

8 "In that day," declares the LORD,
   "will I not destroy the wise men of
      Edom,
   those of understanding in the
      mountains of Esau?
9 Your warriors, Teman, will be terrified,
   and everyone in Esau's mountains
   will be cut down in the slaughter.
10 Because of the violence against your
      brother Jacob,
   you will be covered with shame;
   you will be destroyed forever.
11 On the day you stood aloof
   while strangers carried off his wealth
 and foreigners entered his gates
   and cast lots for Jerusalem,
   you were like one of them.
12 You should not gloat over your brother
   in the day of his misfortune,
 nor rejoice over the people of Judah
   in the day of their destruction,
 nor boast so much
   in the day of their trouble.
13 You should not march through the
      gates of my people
   in the day of their disaster,

nor gloat over them in their calamity
   in the day of their disaster,
 nor seize their wealth
   in the day of their disaster.
14 You should not wait at the crossroads
   to cut down their fugitives,
 nor hand over their survivors
   in the day of their trouble.

15 "The day of the LORD is near
   for all nations.
 As you have done, it will be done to you;
   your deeds will return upon your
      own head.
16 Just as you drank on my holy hill,
   so all the nations will drink
      continually;
 they will drink and drink
   and be as if they had never been.
17 But on Mount Zion will be deliverance;
   it will be holy,
   and Jacob will possess his inheritance.
18 Jacob will be a fire
   and Joseph a flame;
 Esau will be stubble,
   and they will set him on fire and
      destroy him.
 There will be no survivors
   from Esau."
                  The LORD has spoken.

19 People from the Negev will occupy
   the mountains of Esau,
 and people from the foothills will possess
   the land of the Philistines.
 They will occupy the fields of Ephraim
   and Samaria,
   and Benjamin will possess Gilead.
20 This company of Israelite exiles who
      are in Canaan
   will possess the land as far as
      Zarephath;
 the exiles from Jerusalem who are in
      Sepharad
   will possess the towns of the Negev.
21 Deliverers will go up on[b] Mount Zion
   to govern the mountains of Esau.
 And the kingdom will be the LORD's.

---

[a] 7 The meaning of the Hebrew for this clause is uncertain.   [b] 21 Or from

Jonah

THEME: God is the God of all peoples; he is concerned about every nation and individual and will bring his all-encompassing plan for human history to completion.

AUTHOR: The book doesn't identify its author, but tradition has ascribed it to the prophet Jonah. It may be best understood as Jonah's autobiographical account of actual historical events.

DATE OF WRITING: The book was probably written between 785 and 750 BC

ENCOURAGEMENT FROM JONAH: "In my distress I called to the Lord, and he answered me. From deep in the realm of the dead I called for help, and you listened to my cry" (Jonah 2:1 – 2).

CHALLENGE FROM JONAH: "Let everyone call urgently on God. Let them give up their evil ways and their violence" (Jonah 3:8).

REFLECTION FROM JONAH: "When God saw what they did and how they turned from their evil ways, he relented and did not bring on them the destruction he had threatened" (Jonah 3:10).

Jonah fought the assignment God had given him. In fact, he fought so hard that he had to be swallowed by a fish and finally spit out on the shore before he would agree to carry out his mission. Some skeptics want to reject this story as an allegory or a parable. But Scripture presents the account as historical and applies Jonah's three-day imprisonment in the belly of the fish to Jesus' three days in the tomb prior to his resurrection. In commanding Jonah to preach to those in the wicked Assyrian capital of Nineveh, God demonstrated his love for the Gentiles (non-Jewish people) along with his absolute power over nature and over those he calls into his service.

In reading Jonah, we can't help but see how we've resisted the changes God wants for our lives. For example, God wants us to be healthy. He wants, with our cooperation, to heal our hurts, hang-ups and habits. He knows, though, that sometimes we need a little incentive to move in the direction of change. If we refuse to follow his instructions for our lives, he's more than able to provide the incentive to get our attention. This process can be painful. But by choosing to follow his ways instead of our own, we allow him to do extraordinary things in, with and through our lives. Christ-centered recovery produces a willingness to change, to align ourselves with God's will, and an eagerness to go out and share his message of forgiveness and grace with other hurting people.

Jonah Flees From the LORD

1 The word of the LORD came to Jonah son of Amittai: ²"Go to the great city of Nineveh and preach against it, because its wickedness has come up before me."

³But Jonah ran away from the LORD and headed for Tarshish. He went down to Joppa, where he found a ship bound for that port. After paying the fare, he went aboard and sailed for Tarshish to flee from the LORD.

⁴Then the LORD sent a great wind on the sea, and such a violent storm arose that the ship threatened to break up. ⁵All the sailors were afraid and each cried out to his own god. And they threw the cargo into the sea to lighten the ship.

But Jonah had gone below deck, where he lay down and fell into a deep sleep. ⁶The captain went to him and said, "How can you sleep? Get up and call on your god! Maybe he will take notice of us so that we will not perish."

⁷Then the sailors said to each other, "Come, let us cast lots to find out who is responsible for this calamity." They cast lots and the lot fell on Jonah. ⁸So they asked him, "Tell us, who is responsible for making all this trouble for us? What kind of work do you do? Where do you come from? What is your country? From what people are you?"

⁹He answered, "I am a Hebrew and I worship the LORD, the God of heaven, who made the sea and the dry land."

¹⁰This terrified them and they asked, "What have you done?" (They knew he was running away from the LORD, because he had already told them so.)

¹¹The sea was getting rougher and rougher. So they asked him, "What should we do to you to make the sea calm down for us?"

¹²"Pick me up and throw me into the sea," he replied, "and it will become calm. I know that it is my fault that this great storm has come upon you."

¹³Instead, the men did their best to row back to land. But they could not, for the sea grew even wilder than before. ¹⁴Then they cried out to the LORD, "Please, LORD, do not let us die for taking this man's life. Do not hold us accountable for killing an innocent man, for you, LORD, have done as you pleased." ¹⁵Then they took Jonah and threw him overboard, and the raging sea grew calm. ¹⁶At this the men greatly feared the LORD, and they offered a sacrifice to the LORD and made vows to him.

Jonah's Prayer

¹⁷Now the LORD provided a huge fish to swallow Jonah, and Jonah was in the belly of

2 *ᵃ* the fish three days and three nights. ¹From inside the fish Jonah prayed to the LORD his God. ²He said:

"In my distress I called to the LORD,
    and he answered me.
From deep in the realm of the dead I
        called for help,
    and you listened to my cry.
³ You hurled me into the depths,
    into the very heart of the seas,
        and the currents swirled about me;
    all your waves and breakers
        swept over me.
⁴ I said, 'I have been banished
        from your sight;
    yet I will look again
        toward your holy temple.'
⁵ The engulfing waters threatened me,*ᵇ*
    the deep surrounded me;
        seaweed was wrapped around my
            head.
⁶ To the roots of the mountains I sank
        down;
    the earth beneath barred me in
        forever.
But you, LORD my God,
    brought my life up from the pit.

⁷ "When my life was ebbing away,
    I remembered you, LORD,
and my prayer rose to you,
    to your holy temple.

ᵃ In Hebrew texts 2:1 is numbered 1:17, and 2:1-10 is numbered 2:2-11.   *ᵇ 5* Or *waters were at my throat*

MY NAME IS JONAH

Jonah's journey of recovery could be called "stormy." Sadly, he is remembered best as the prophet who ran away from God. His flight was fueled by his bitterness against the Assyrians, who were threatening to overwhelm Israel in the eighth century BC.

Commanded by God to infiltrate the enemy's capital city and warn Nineveh's residents of God's impending judgment, Jonah set his face in the opposite direction (see Jonah 1:1 – 3). His bungled attempt to flee was obviously futile; he knew God as the Creator and controller of all (see 1:9). But bitterness blinds those who feed on it (see Hebrews 12:15), and Jonah's anger crowded out his love for, and obedience to, the Lord.

Not surprisingly, God's love and purpose pursued his delinquent prophet. God is a perfect Father who chastens his children (see Hebrews 12:5 – 12). Tumultuous waves threatened the ship and the safety of all on board. The anger we have toward those we label our enemies more often brings harm to innocent people around us than to our opponents. To his credit, Jonah confessed both his own guilt and the greatness of his God (see Jonah 1:8 – 10).

Jonah's admission and the intensity of the storm convinced the crew to throw him overboard. The calm that ensued presented such a startling contrast that these pagan sailors were led to worship Jonah's God (see Jonah 1:16). Even truth proclaimed in the confession of an angry servant can be used by God. But God wasn't finished with Jonah. He arranged for a fish to swallow the drowning prophet, who survived in its belly for three days and nights. There in the darkness Jonah repented and the Lord miraculously returned him to dry land (see 2:10). As a humbled Jonah preached in wicked Nineveh, its king, nobles and inhabitants repented, and God withheld his threatened destruction (see ch. 3).

We would expect a preacher whose message brought an entire city to its knees to be overjoyed. Instead, Jonah became outraged and depressed. Depression is anger turned inward (see Jonah 4:1 – 9). Ironically, God's patience with Jonah himself confirmed the prophet's description of God (see 4:2). But God's final words to Jonah went much further, affirming his great love for the whole of lost humanity (see 4:10 – 11).

The story cuts off with a question. But there are vital lessons in the account God did see fit to provide. Jonah confessed his faults to himself, God and others (Principle Four). Nevertheless, he wasn't willing to allow God to remove his character defects (Principle Five). God addressed Jonah's bitterness directly, twice asking point-blank: "Is it right for you to be angry?" (4:4,9).

Jonah fumed when God didn't destroy the city. But when the Lord caused a vine to grow suddenly to provide shade for Jonah, the prophet was happy. Then, when the vine withered, he reverted to anger. Ultimately, Jonah wasn't enraged at his enemies or at the loss of the vine; he was angry with God. Presuming to judge God's fairness blocked Jonah's joy over God's forgiveness and grace. His attitude left Jonah unable to honestly answer God's question as to the legitimacy of, and basis for, his anger.

God's answer, of course, is no — we have no legitimate right to be angry. Recovery is more than freedom from our hurts, hang-ups and habits. Recovery is becoming living proof that we're God's children.

My Name Is David

I'M A BELIEVER WHO STRUGGLES WITH ALCOHOLISM

Please read Jonah 1–3.

I started drinking when I was 12 and immediately liked the way it made me feel. I wasn't comfortable with who I was and often felt as though I didn't measure up in the world around me. Alcohol made me feel like I fit in.

Since childhood my biggest desire had been to be an actor. I did manage to break into the industry and filmed 32 shows of a popular children's program. But even though my ego was inflated, I found that alcohol and drugs fit hand in glove with this new lifestyle.

By the age of 19, I was already in the middle stages of alcoholism. Some disturbing blackouts motivated me to seek help through recovery programs. I liked what I saw, but my drinking didn't yet motivate me to surrender my addiction or myself to God. In retrospect, I can see that God had been moving in my life; I just hadn't recognized it. I did, however, decide to accept Jesus Christ as my Savior.

I did well with my new spiritual foundation for several months, but I wasn't ready to let go of my drinking. In fact, a short time later I drifted away from God and drank more than ever. I had lost the ability to choose not to drink, and I felt utterly defeated as a Christian. I decided that I would play no more games and went on to drink solidly over the next five years. During this period I met and married my wife, Debbie.

Finally, in 1994, after numerous attempts at sobriety, my addiction landed me in prison, where I served four-and-a-half years of a ten-year sentence. At the beginning of my prison term I left my wife, who was eight months pregnant, alone with three small children. After all those years of dodging bullets, I had finally taken a direct hit. And I paid real consequences for my actions.

Of all the Biblical characters, I can identify most with Jonah. He ran hard from God, refusing to go to Nineveh and do God's will. Likewise, I fled in the opposite direction when God called, thinking for years that I couldn't be happy doing what he intended me to do for his glory (see Jonah 1:1–3).

My prison time was for me the equivalent of Jonah's "incarceration" in the belly of the great fish (see 2:2–9). When all hope was lost and Jonah thought there was no way out, God restored him to do his work. God humbled me as well, so that I could, with his help, humble myself in repentance and gratitude (see 2:8 – 10). I had the knowledge of recovery and of God's Word, yet I had never before put either into practice. God taught me what it means to live by faith, one day at a time. Once I stopped resisting his direction for my life, I too was able to fulfill his heart's desire — now mine as well — by ministering to others.

I gave my addiction over to God, and he has allowed my wife and me to minister, through Celebrate Recovery, to others who suffer from the same hurts, hang-ups and habits that had plagued our lives. We now have the privilege of watching God work the same miracles in the lives of others.

David

8 "Those who cling to worthless idols
　　turn away from God's love for them.
9 But I, with shouts of grateful praise,
　　will sacrifice to you.
What I have vowed I will make good.
　I will say, 'Salvation comes from the
　　Lord.'"

10 And the Lord commanded the fish,
and it vomited Jonah onto dry land.

Jonah Goes to Nineveh

3 Then the word of the Lord came
to Jonah a second time: 2 "Go to the
great city of Nineveh and proclaim
to it the message I give you."

3 Jonah obeyed the word of the Lord
and went to Nineveh. Now Nineveh was
a very large city; it took three days to go
through it. 4 Jonah began by going a day's
journey into the city, proclaiming, "Forty more days and Nineveh will be overthrown." 5 The Ninevites believed God. A
fast was proclaimed, and all of them, from
the greatest to the least, put on sackcloth.

6 When Jonah's warning reached the king
of Nineveh, he rose from his throne, took
off his royal robes, covered himself with
sackcloth and sat down in the dust. 7 This
is the proclamation he issued in Nineveh:

"By the decree of the king and his nobles:

Do not let people or animals, herds
or flocks, taste anything; do not let
them eat or drink. 8 But let people and
animals be covered with sackcloth.
Let everyone call urgently on God.
Let them give up their evil ways and
their violence. 9 Who knows? God
may yet relent and with compassion
turn from his fierce anger so that we
will not perish."

10 When God saw what they did and how
they turned from their evil ways, he relented and did not bring on them the destruction he had threatened.

Jonah's Anger at the Lord's Compassion

4 But to Jonah this seemed very
wrong, and he became angry. 2 He
prayed to the Lord, "Isn't this what
I said, Lord, when I was still at home?
That is what I tried to forestall by fleeing
to Tarshish. I knew that you are a gracious
and compassionate God, slow to anger and
abounding in love, a God who relents from
sending calamity. 3 Now, Lord, take away
my life, for it is better for me to die than
to live."

4 But the Lord replied, "Is it right for you
to be angry?"

5 Jonah had gone out and sat down at a
place east of the city. There he made himself a shelter, sat in its shade and waited to
see what would happen to the city. 6 Then
the Lord God provided a leafy plant[a] and
made it grow up over Jonah to give shade
for his head to ease his discomfort, and Jonah was very happy about the plant. 7 But at
dawn the next day God provided a worm,
which chewed the plant so that it withered. 8 When the sun rose, God provided
a scorching east wind, and the sun blazed
on Jonah's head so that he grew faint. He
wanted to die, and said, "It would be better
for me to die than to live."

9 But God said to Jonah, "Is it right for
you to be angry about the plant?"

"It is," he said. "And I'm so angry I wish
I were dead."

10 But the Lord said, "You have been
concerned about this plant, though you
did not tend it or make it grow. It sprang
up overnight and died overnight. 11 And
should I not have concern for the great city
of Nineveh, in which there are more than
a hundred and twenty thousand people
who cannot tell their right hand from their
left — and also many animals?"

---

a 6 The precise identification of this plant is uncertain; also in verses 7, 9 and 10.

Micah

THEME: God has compassion on those who repent.

AUTHOR: The prophet Micah wrote this book. A contemporary of Isaiah, he ministered to the people of Judah between 742 and 687 BC.

DATE OF WRITING: The book of Micah was probably written between 740 and 710 BC.

ENCOURAGEMENT FROM MICAH: "Who is a God like you, who pardons sin . . . ? You do not stay angry forever but delight to show mercy. You will again have compassion on us; you will tread our sins underfoot and hurl all our iniquities into the depths of the sea" (Micah 7:18 – 19).

CHALLENGE FROM MICAH: "He has showed you, O mortal, what is good. And what does the LORD require of you? To act justly and to love mercy and to walk humbly with your God" (Micah 6:8).

REFLECTION FROM MICAH: "All the nations may walk in the name of their gods, but we will walk in the name of the LORD our God for ever and ever" (Micah 4:5).

Burdened by his countrymen's abuse of the poor, Micah rebukes anyone who has been using social status or political power for personal gain. The first third of this prophecy exposes the sins of God's people, the middle portion describes God's approaching punishment and the final section provides the hope of restoration following the period of discipline. Restoration, Micah makes clear, will come through a Messiah to be born in Bethlehem (see Micah 5:2).

In Micah and in various other locations throughout the Bible, a believer's life is described in terms of a walk. For that reason we often talk about the progress of recovery as a "road to recovery." When we realize we're out of step with God, we come to understand that without his intervention we are lost. When we turn to the Lord and commit to walking in his ways, we discover that the promise Micah made to his people has indeed been fulfilled in Christ — for us personally. All we need is enough faith to take that first step and then to follow it up, one step at a time.

1 The word of the LORD that came to Micah of Moresheth during the reigns of Jotham, Ahaz and Hezekiah, kings of Judah — the vision he saw concerning Samaria and Jerusalem.

2 Hear, you peoples, all of you,
  listen, earth and all who live in it,
that the Sovereign LORD may bear
    witness against you,
  the Lord from his holy temple.

Judgment Against Samaria and Jerusalem

3 Look! The LORD is coming from his
    dwelling place;

he comes down and treads on the
    heights of the earth.
4 The mountains melt beneath him
    and the valleys split apart,
like wax before the fire,
    like water rushing down a slope.
5 All this is because of Jacob's
    transgression,
    because of the sins of the people of
    Israel.
What is Jacob's transgression?
    Is it not Samaria?
What is Judah's high place?
    Is it not Jerusalem?

6 "Therefore I will make Samaria a heap
    of rubble,
a place for planting vineyards.
I will pour her stones into the valley
    and lay bare her foundations.
7 All her idols will be broken to pieces;
    all her temple gifts will be burned
    with fire;
    I will destroy all her images.
Since she gathered her gifts from the
    wages of prostitutes,
    as the wages of prostitutes they will
    again be used."

Weeping and Mourning

8 Because of this I will weep and wail;
    I will go about barefoot and naked.
I will howl like a jackal
    and moan like an owl.
9 For Samaria's plague is incurable;
    it has spread to Judah.
It has reached the very gate of my people,
    even to Jerusalem itself.
10 Tell it not in Gath[a];
    weep not at all.
In Beth Ophrah[b]
    roll in the dust.
11 Pass by naked and in shame,
    you who live in Shaphir.[c]
Those who live in Zaanan[d]
    will not come out.

Beth Ezel is in mourning;
    it no longer protects you.
12 Those who live in Maroth[e] writhe in
    pain,
    waiting for relief,
because disaster has come from the
    LORD,
    even to the gate of Jerusalem.
13 You who live in Lachish,
    harness fast horses to the chariot.
You are where the sin of Daughter Zion
    began,
    for the transgressions of Israel were
    found in you.
14 Therefore you will give parting gifts
    to Moresheth Gath.
The town of Akzib[f] will prove deceptive
    to the kings of Israel.
15 I will bring a conqueror against you
    who live in Mareshah.[g]
The nobles of Israel
    will flee to Adullam.
16 Shave your head in mourning
    for the children in whom you delight;
make yourself as bald as the vulture,
    for they will go from you into exile.

Human Plans and God's Plans

2 Woe to those who plan iniquity,
    to those who plot evil on their
    beds!
At morning's light they carry it out
    because it is in their power to do it.
2 They covet fields and seize them,
    and houses, and take them.
They defraud people of their homes,
    they rob them of their inheritance.

3 Therefore, the LORD says:

"I am planning disaster against this
    people,
    from which you cannot save
    yourselves.
You will no longer walk proudly,
    for it will be a time of calamity.

---

a 10 Gath sounds like the Hebrew for *tell.*   *b 10 Beth Ophrah* means *house of dust.*   *c 11 Shaphir* means
pleasant.   *d 11 Zaanan* sounds like the Hebrew for *come out.*   *e 12 Maroth* sounds like the Hebrew for *bitter.*
f 14 Akzib means *deception.*   *g 15 Mareshah* sounds like the Hebrew for *conqueror.*

⁴In that day people will ridicule you;
    they will taunt you with this
        mournful song:
'We are utterly ruined;
    my people's possession is divided up.
He takes it from me!
    He assigns our fields to traitors.'"

⁵Therefore you will have no one in the
        assembly of the LORD
    to divide the land by lot.

False Prophets

⁶"Do not prophesy," their prophets say.
    "Do not prophesy about these
        things;
    disgrace will not overtake us."
⁷You descendants of Jacob, should it be
        said,
    "Does the LORD become*ª* impatient?
    Does he do such things?"

"Do not my words do good
    to the one whose ways are upright?
⁸Lately my people have risen up
    like an enemy.
You strip off the rich robe
    from those who pass by without a
        care,
    like men returning from battle.
⁹You drive the women of my people
    from their pleasant homes.
You take away my blessing
    from their children forever.
¹⁰Get up, go away!
    For this is not your resting place,
because it is defiled,
    it is ruined, beyond all remedy.
¹¹If a liar and deceiver comes and says,
    'I will prophesy for you plenty of
        wine and beer,'
    that would be just the prophet for
        this people!

Deliverance Promised

¹²"I will surely gather all of you, Jacob;
    I will surely bring together the
        remnant of Israel.

I will bring them together like sheep in
        a pen,
    like a flock in its pasture;
    the place will throng with people.
¹³The One who breaks open the way will
        go up before them;
    they will break through the gate and
        go out.
Their King will pass through before
        them,
    the LORD at their head."

Leaders and Prophets Rebuked

3 Then I said,

    "Listen, you leaders of Jacob,
    you rulers of Israel.
Should you not embrace justice,
²   you who hate good and love evil;
who tear the skin from my people
    and the flesh from their bones;
³who eat my people's flesh,
    strip off their skin
    and break their bones in pieces;
who chop them up like meat for the pan,
    like flesh for the pot?"

⁴Then they will cry out to the LORD,
    but he will not answer them.
At that time he will hide his face from
        them
    because of the evil they have done.

⁵This is what the LORD says:

"As for the prophets
    who lead my people astray,
they proclaim 'peace'
    if they have something to eat,
but prepare to wage war against anyone
    who refuses to feed them.
⁶Therefore night will come over you,
        without visions,
    and darkness, without divination.
The sun will set for the prophets,
    and the day will go dark for them.
⁷The seers will be ashamed
    and the diviners disgraced.

ª 7 Or *Is the Spirit of the LORD*

They will all cover their faces
　　because there is no answer from
　　　God."
⁸ But as for me, I am filled with power,
　　with the Spirit of the LORD,
　　and with justice and might,
　to declare to Jacob his transgression,
　　to Israel his sin.

⁹ Hear this, you leaders of Jacob,
　　you rulers of Israel,
　who despise justice
　　and distort all that is right;
¹⁰ who build Zion with bloodshed,
　　and Jerusalem with wickedness.
¹¹ Her leaders judge for a bribe,
　　her priests teach for a price,
　and her prophets tell fortunes for
　　　money.
　Yet they look for the LORD's support
　　and say,
　　"Is not the LORD among us?
　　No disaster will come upon us."
¹² Therefore because of you,
　　Zion will be plowed like a field,
　Jerusalem will become a heap of
　　　rubble,
　　the temple hill a mound overgrown
　　　with thickets.

The Mountain of the LORD

4 In the last days
　　the mountain of the LORD's temple
　　　will be established
　as the highest of the mountains;
　it will be exalted above the hills,
　　and peoples will stream to it.

² Many nations will come and say,

　"Come, let us go up to the mountain of
　　the LORD,
　　to the temple of the God of Jacob.
　He will teach us his ways,
　　so that we may walk in his paths."
　The law will go out from Zion,
　　the word of the LORD from
　　　Jerusalem.

³ He will judge between many peoples
　　and will settle disputes for strong
　　　nations far and wide.
　They will beat their swords into
　　　plowshares
　　and their spears into pruning hooks.
　Nation will not take up sword against
　　　nation,
　　nor will they train for war anymore.
⁴ Everyone will sit under their own vine
　　and under their own fig tree,
　and no one will make them afraid,
　　for the LORD Almighty has spoken.
⁵ All the nations may walk
　　in the name of their gods,
　but we will walk in the name of the
　　　LORD
　　our God for ever and ever.

The LORD's Plan

⁶ "In that day," declares the LORD,

　"I will gather the lame;
　　I will assemble the exiles
　　and those I have brought to grief.
⁷ I will make the lame my remnant,
　　those driven away a strong nation.
　The LORD will rule over them in Mount
　　　Zion
　　from that day and forever.
⁸ As for you, watchtower of the flock,
　　stronghold*a* of Daughter Zion,
　the former dominion will be restored to
　　　you;
　　kingship will come to Daughter
　　　Jerusalem."

⁹ Why do you now cry aloud —
　　have you no king*b*?
　Has your ruler*c* perished,
　　that pain seizes you like that of a
　　　woman in labor?
¹⁰ Writhe in agony, Daughter Zion,
　　like a woman in labor,
　for now you must leave the city
　　to camp in the open field.
　You will go to Babylon;
　　there you will be rescued.

---

a 8 Or *hill*　　*b 9* Or *King*　　*c 9* Or *Ruler*

There the LORD will redeem you
   out of the hand of your enemies.

11 But now many nations
   are gathered against you.
They say, "Let her be defiled,
   let our eyes gloat over Zion!"
12 But they do not know
   the thoughts of the LORD;
they do not understand his plan,
   that he has gathered them like
     sheaves to the threshing
     floor.
13 "Rise and thresh, Daughter Zion,
   for I will give you horns of iron;
I will give you hooves of bronze,
   and you will break to pieces many
     nations."
You will devote their ill-gotten gains to
   the LORD,
   their wealth to the Lord of all the
     earth.

A Promised Ruler From Bethlehem

5 *a* Marshal your troops now, city of
   troops,
   for a siege is laid against us.
They will strike Israel's ruler
   on the cheek with a rod.

2 "But you, Bethlehem Ephrathah,
   though you are small among the
     clans*b* of Judah,
out of you will come for me
   one who will be ruler over Israel,
whose origins are from of old,
   from ancient times."

3 Therefore Israel will be abandoned
   until the time when she who is in
     labor bears a son,
and the rest of his brothers return
   to join the Israelites.

4 He will stand and shepherd his flock
   in the strength of the LORD,
   in the majesty of the name of the
     LORD his God.

And they will live securely, for then his
   greatness
   will reach to the ends of the earth.

5 And he will be our peace
   when the Assyrians invade our land
   and march through our fortresses.
We will raise against them seven
     shepherds,
   even eight commanders,
6 who will rule*c* the land of Assyria with
     the sword,
   the land of Nimrod with drawn
     sword.*d*
He will deliver us from the Assyrians
   when they invade our land
   and march across our borders.

7 The remnant of Jacob will be
   in the midst of many peoples
like dew from the LORD,
   like showers on the grass,
which do not wait for anyone
   or depend on man.
8 The remnant of Jacob will be among
     the nations,
   in the midst of many peoples,
like a lion among the beasts of the forest,
   like a young lion among flocks of
     sheep,
which mauls and mangles as it goes,
   and no one can rescue.
9 Your hand will be lifted up in triumph
   over your enemies,
   and all your foes will be destroyed.

10 "In that day," declares the LORD,

"I will destroy your horses from among
   you
   and demolish your chariots.
11 I will destroy the cities of your land
   and tear down all your strongholds.
12 I will destroy your witchcraft
   and you will no longer cast spells.
13 I will destroy your idols
   and your sacred stones from among
     you;

---

a In Hebrew texts 5:1 is numbered 4:14, and 5:2-15 is numbered 5:1-14.   *b 2* Or *rulers*   *c 6* Or *crush*   *d 6* Or *Nimrod in its gates*

you will no longer bow down
    to the work of your hands.
¹⁴I will uproot from among you your
    Asherah poles[a]
    when I demolish your cities.
¹⁵I will take vengeance in anger and wrath
    on the nations that have not obeyed
      me."

The LORD's Case Against Israel

6 Listen to what the LORD says:

"Stand up, plead my case before the
    mountains;
    let the hills hear what you have to say.

²"Hear, you mountains, the LORD's
    accusation;
    listen, you everlasting foundations of
      the earth.
For the LORD has a case against his
    people;
    he is lodging a charge against Israel.

³"My people, what have I done to you?
    How have I burdened you? Answer
      me.
⁴I brought you up out of Egypt
    and redeemed you from the land of
      slavery.
I sent Moses to lead you,
    also Aaron and Miriam.
⁵My people, remember
    what Balak king of Moab plotted
    and what Balaam son of Beor
      answered.
Remember your journey from Shittim
    to Gilgal,
    that you may know the righteous acts
      of the LORD."

⁶With what shall I come before the LORD
    and bow down before the exalted God?
Shall I come before him with burnt
    offerings,
    with calves a year old?

⁷Will the LORD be pleased with
    thousands of rams,
    with ten thousand rivers of olive oil?
Shall I offer my firstborn for my
    transgression,
    the fruit of my body for the sin of my
      soul?
⁸He has shown you, O mortal, what is
    good.
And what does the LORD require of
    you?
To act justly and to love mercy
    and to walk humbly[b] with your God.

Israel's Guilt and Punishment

⁹Listen! The LORD is calling to the
    city—
    and to fear your name is wisdom—
    "Heed the rod and the One who
      appointed it.[c]
¹⁰Am I still to forget your ill-gotten
    treasures, you wicked house,
    and the short ephah,[d] which is
      accursed?
¹¹Shall I acquit someone with dishonest
    scales,
    with a bag of false weights?
¹²Your rich people are violent;
    your inhabitants are liars
    and their tongues speak deceitfully.
¹³Therefore, I have begun to destroy you,
    to ruin[e] you because of your sins.
¹⁴You will eat but not be satisfied;
    your stomach will still be empty.[f]
You will store up but save nothing,
    because what you save[g] I will give to
      the sword.
¹⁵You will plant but not harvest;
    you will press olives but not use the
      oil,
    you will crush grapes but not drink
      the wine.
¹⁶You have observed the statutes of Omri
    and all the practices of Ahab's house;
    you have followed their traditions.

---

a 14 That is, wooden symbols of the goddess Asherah   *b 8* Or *prudently*   *c 9* The meaning of the Hebrew for
this line is uncertain.   *d 10* An ephah was a dry measure.   *e 13* Or *Therefore, I will make you ill and destroy you;*
/ I will ruin   *f 14* The meaning of the Hebrew for this word is uncertain.   *g 14* Or *You will press toward birth but
not give birth, / and what you bring to birth*

Therefore I will give you over to ruin
and your people to derision;
you will bear the scorn of the
nations.ᵃ"

Israel's Misery

7 What misery is mine!
I am like one who gathers summer
fruit
at the gleaning of the vineyard;
there is no cluster of grapes to eat,
none of the early figs that I crave.
² The faithful have been swept from the
land;
not one upright person remains.
Everyone lies in wait to shed blood;
they hunt each other with nets.
³ Both hands are skilled in doing evil;
the ruler demands gifts,
the judge accepts bribes,
the powerful dictate what they
desire—
they all conspire together.
⁴ The best of them is like a brier,
the most upright worse than a thorn
hedge.
The day God visits you has come,
the day your watchmen sound the
alarm.
Now is the time of your confusion.
⁵ Do not trust a neighbor;
put no confidence in a friend.
Even with the woman who lies in your
embrace
guard the words of your lips.
⁶ For a son dishonors his father,
a daughter rises up against her
mother,
a daughter-in-law against her mother-
in-law—
a man's enemies are the members of
his own household.
⁷ But as for me, I watch in hope for the
LORD,
I wait for God my Savior;
my God will hear me.

Israel Will Rise

⁸ Do not gloat over me, my enemy!
Though I have fallen, I will rise.
Though I sit in darkness,
the LORD will be my light.
⁹ Because I have sinned against him,
I will bear the LORD's wrath,
until he pleads my case
and upholds my cause.
He will bring me out into the light;
I will see his righteousness.
¹⁰ Then my enemy will see it
and will be covered with shame,
she who said to me,
"Where is the LORD your God?"
My eyes will see her downfall;
even now she will be trampled
underfoot
like mire in the streets.

¹¹ The day for building your walls will come,
the day for extending your boundaries.
¹² In that day people will come to you
from Assyria and the cities of Egypt,
even from Egypt to the Euphrates
and from sea to sea
and from mountain to mountain.
¹³ The earth will become desolate because
of its inhabitants,
as the result of their deeds.

Prayer and Praise

¹⁴ Shepherd your people with your staff,
the flock of your inheritance,
which lives by itself in a forest,
in fertile pasturelands.ᵇ
Let them feed in Bashan and Gilead
as in days long ago.

¹⁵ "As in the days when you came out of
Egypt,
I will show them my wonders."

¹⁶ Nations will see and be ashamed,
deprived of all their power.
They will put their hands over their
mouths
and their ears will become deaf.

ᵃ 16 Septuagint; Hebrew *scorn due my people*   ᵇ 14 Or *in the middle of Carmel*

¹⁷They will lick dust like a snake,
  like creatures that crawl on the ground.
They will come trembling out of their
    dens;
  they will turn in fear to the LORD our
    God
  and will be afraid of you.
¹⁸Who is a God like you,
  who pardons sin and forgives the
    transgression
  of the remnant of his inheritance?

You do not stay angry forever
  but delight to show mercy.
¹⁹You will again have compassion on us;
  you will tread our sins underfoot
  and hurl all our iniquities into the
    depths of the sea.
²⁰You will be faithful to Jacob,
  and show love to Abraham,
as you pledged on oath to our
    ancestors
  in days long ago.

Nahum

THEME: God cares for his people and will punish those who abuse them. He'll protect them, free them from oppression and restore them.

AUTHOR: The prophet Nahum wrote this book.

DATE OF WRITING: The book of Nahum was written between 663 and 609 BC.

ENCOURAGEMENT FROM NAHUM: "I [the LORD] will break [the] yoke from your neck and tear your shackles away" (Nahum 1:13).

CHALLENGE FROM NAHUM: "Fulfill your vows" (Nahum 1:15).

REFLECTION FROM NAHUM: "The LORD is good, a refuge in times of trouble. He cares for those who trust in him" (Nahum 1:7).

In contrast to the book of Jonah, which records Nineveh's (temporary) repentance, Nahum proclaims the doom that will befall that city. The Ninevites have returned to their violence, idolatry and arrogance, and God has decided to use Babylon to erase the Assyrian city from history. Judah has suffered untold atrocities at the hands of the Ninevites, so the prediction of their doom provides God's people with comfort. God is going to protect his children.

Nahum teaches us two lessons about recovery. First, each of us has been given the chance to turn over our life to God and walk in his ways. By doing this, we not only get to avoid being destroyed by our sins, but we also get to experience a true and abundant life. Second, God is in control. When we see people who've hurt us, it can be hard for us to understand why they haven't yet experienced any noticeable negative consequences for their actions. Nahum reminds us to stay focused on our part of the recovery process, allowing God to handle these other situations. We're his children, and he has assured us of his protection. God pledges to heal the wounds inflicted on us both by our own sins and by the sins of others.

1

A prophecy concerning Nineveh. The book of the vision of Nahum the Elkoshite.

The LORD's Anger Against Nineveh

² The LORD is a jealous and avenging God;
 the LORD takes vengeance and is
  filled with wrath.
The LORD takes vengeance on his foes
 and vents his wrath against his
  enemies.
³ The LORD is slow to anger but great in
  power;

the LORD will not leave the guilty
  unpunished.
His way is in the whirlwind and the
  storm,
 and clouds are the dust of his feet.
⁴ He rebukes the sea and dries it up;
 he makes all the rivers run dry.
Bashan and Carmel wither
 and the blossoms of Lebanon fade.
⁵ The mountains quake before him
 and the hills melt away.
The earth trembles at his presence,
 the world and all who live in it.

6 Who can withstand his indignation?
  Who can endure his fierce anger?
His wrath is poured out like fire;
  the rocks are shattered before him.

7 The LORD is good,
  a refuge in times of trouble.
He cares for those who trust in him,
8   but with an overwhelming flood
he will make an end of Nineveh;
  he will pursue his foes into the realm
    of darkness.

9 Whatever they plot against the LORD
  he will bring*a* to an end;
  trouble will not come a second time.
10 They will be entangled among thorns
  and drunk from their wine;
  they will be consumed like dry
    stubble.*b*
11 From you, Nineveh, has one come forth
  who plots evil against the LORD
  and devises wicked plans.

12 This is what the LORD says:

"Although they have allies and are
    numerous,
  they will be destroyed and pass away.
Although I have afflicted you, Judah,
  I will afflict you no more.
13 Now I will break their yoke from your
    neck
  and tear your shackles away."

14 The LORD has given a command
    concerning you, Nineveh:
"You will have no descendants to
    bear your name.
I will destroy the images and idols
  that are in the temple of your gods.
I will prepare your grave,
  for you are vile."

15 Look, there on the mountains,
  the feet of one who brings good
    news,
  who proclaims peace!

Celebrate your festivals, Judah,
  and fulfill your vows.
No more will the wicked invade you;
  they will be completely destroyed.*c*

Nineveh to Fall

2 *d* An attacker advances against you,
    Nineveh.
  Guard the fortress,
watch the road,
brace yourselves,
marshal all your strength!

2 The LORD will restore the splendor of
    Jacob
  like the splendor of Israel,
though destroyers have laid them waste
  and have ruined their vines.

3 The shields of the soldiers are red;
  the warriors are clad in scarlet.
The metal on the chariots flashes
  on the day they are made ready;
  the spears of juniper are
    brandished.*e*
4 The chariots storm through the
    streets,
  rushing back and forth through the
    squares.
They look like flaming torches;
  they dart about like lightning.

5 Nineveh summons her picked troops,
  yet they stumble on their way.
They dash to the city wall;
  the protective shield is put in place.
6 The river gates are thrown open
  and the palace collapses.
7 It is decreed*f* that Nineveh
  be exiled and carried away.
Her female slaves moan like doves
  and beat on their breasts.
8 Nineveh is like a pool
  whose water is draining away.
"Stop! Stop!" they cry,
  but no one turns back.

---

a 9 Or *What do you foes plot against the LORD? / He will bring it*   *b 10* The meaning of the Hebrew for this verse is
uncertain.   *c 15* In Hebrew texts this verse (1:15) is numbered 2:1.   *d* In Hebrew texts 2:1-13 is numbered 2:2-14.
e 3 Hebrew; Septuagint and Syriac *ready; / the horsemen rush to and fro.*   *f 7* The meaning of the Hebrew for this
word is uncertain.

⁹ Plunder the silver!
   Plunder the gold!
The supply is endless,
   the wealth from all its treasures!
¹⁰ She is pillaged, plundered, stripped!
   Hearts melt, knees give way,
   bodies tremble, every face grows
      pale.

¹¹ Where now is the lions' den,
   the place where they fed their
      young,
where the lion and lioness went,
   and the cubs, with nothing to fear?
¹² The lion killed enough for his cubs
   and strangled the prey for his mate,
filling his lairs with the kill
   and his dens with the prey.

¹³ "I am against you,"
   declares the LORD Almighty.
"I will burn up your chariots in smoke,
   and the sword will devour your
      young lions.
   I will leave you no prey on the earth.
The voices of your messengers
   will no longer be heard."

Woe to Nineveh

3 Woe to the city of blood,
   full of lies,
   full of plunder,
   never without victims!
² The crack of whips,
   the clatter of wheels,
galloping horses
   and jolting chariots!
³ Charging cavalry,
   flashing swords
   and glittering spears!
Many casualties,
   piles of dead,
bodies without number,
   people stumbling over the
      corpses —
⁴ all because of the wanton lust of a
      prostitute,
   alluring, the mistress of sorceries,

who enslaved nations by her
   prostitution
and peoples by her witchcraft.
⁵ "I am against you," declares the LORD
      Almighty.
"I will lift your skirts over your face.
I will show the nations your nakedness
   and the kingdoms your shame.
⁶ I will pelt you with filth,
   I will treat you with contempt
   and make you a spectacle.
⁷ All who see you will flee from you and
      say,
   'Nineveh is in ruins — who will
      mourn for her?'
Where can I find anyone to comfort
      you?"

⁸ Are you better than Thebes,
   situated on the Nile,
   with water around her?
The river was her defense,
   the waters her wall.
⁹ Cush*a* and Egypt were her boundless
      strength;
   Put and Libya were among her allies.
¹⁰ Yet she was taken captive
   and went into exile.
Her infants were dashed to pieces
   at every street corner.
Lots were cast for her nobles,
   and all her great men were put in
      chains.
¹¹ You too will become drunk;
   you will go into hiding
   and seek refuge from the enemy.
¹² All your fortresses are like fig trees
   with their first ripe fruit;
when they are shaken,
   the figs fall into the mouth of the
      eater.
¹³ Look at your troops —
   they are all weaklings.
The gates of your land
   are wide open to your enemies;
   fire has consumed the bars of your
      gates.

---

a 9 That is, the upper Nile region

14 Draw water for the siege,
        strengthen your defenses!
    Work the clay,
        tread the mortar,
        repair the brickwork!
15 There the fire will consume you;
        the sword will cut you down —
        they will devour you like a swarm of
            locusts.
    Multiply like grasshoppers,
        multiply like locusts!
16 You have increased the number of your
            merchants
        till they are more numerous than the
            stars in the sky,
    but like locusts they strip the land
        and then fly away.

17 Your guards are like locusts,
        your officials like swarms of locusts
        that settle in the walls on a cold day —
    but when the sun appears they fly away,
        and no one knows where.
18 King of Assyria, your shepherds*a*
            slumber;
        your nobles lie down to rest.
    Your people are scattered on the
            mountains
        with no one to gather them.
19 Nothing can heal you;
        your wound is fatal.
    All who hear the news about you
        clap their hands at your fall,
    for who has not felt
        your endless cruelty?

---

a 18 That is, rulers

Habakkuk

THEME: The current situation isn't the true and ultimate state of things. We may have to wait for vindication, but it certainly will come.

AUTHOR: The prophet Habakkuk, a contemporary of Jeremiah, wrote this book.

DATE OF WRITING: The book of Habakkuk was probably written between 610 and 605 BC.

ENCOURAGEMENT FROM HABAKKUK: "For the earth will be filled with the knowledge of the glory of the LORD as the waters cover the sea" (Habakkuk 2:14).

CHALLENGE FROM HABAKKUK: "The righteous person will live by his faithfulness" (Habakkuk 2:4).

REFLECTION FROM HABAKKUK: "LORD, I have heard of your fame; I stand in awe of your deeds, LORD. Repeat them in our day, in our time make them known; in wrath remember mercy" (Habakkuk 3:2).

The people of Judah, confronted by prophet after prophet to change their ways, stubbornly refused time after time. The prophet Habakkuk wanted to know how long this cycle would last and when God would bring his judgment to bear. While most prophets warned about judgment, Habakkuk pleaded for it. The book of Habakkuk records the prophet's struggle with faith, ultimately resulting in his confession of the kind of faith that survives difficult circumstances. Habakkuk maintains that God is in control and that he has the freedom to accomplish his purposes in his own way.

Recovery is a journey of both despair and victory. The process can be hard. When we find ourselves face-to-face with our lifelong hurts, hang-ups and habits, the situation can seem bleak. This is the reality of recovery. But the hard times seem small compared to the victory we achieve through Christ if we stay on the path. When we see the changes, both big and small, that Christ is making in us, and when we realize that we no longer need to rely on our old, sinful ways, we see the hope that recovery offers.

1

The prophecy that Habakkuk the prophet received.

Habakkuk's Complaint

2 How long, LORD, must I call for help,
    but you do not listen?
Or cry out to you, "Violence!"
    but you do not save?
3 Why do you make me look at injustice?
    Why do you tolerate wrongdoing?
Destruction and violence are before me;
    there is strife, and conflict abounds.
4 Therefore the law is paralyzed,
    and justice never prevails.
The wicked hem in the righteous,
    so that justice is perverted.

The LORD's Answer

5 "Look at the nations and watch —
    and be utterly amazed.

For I am going to do something in your
    days
        that you would not believe,
        even if you were told.
6 I am raising up the Babylonians,[a]
        that ruthless and impetuous people,
    who sweep across the whole earth
        to seize dwellings not their own.
7 They are a feared and dreaded people;
        they are a law to themselves
        and promote their own honor.
8 Their horses are swifter than leopards,
        fiercer than wolves at dusk.
    Their cavalry gallops headlong;
        their horsemen come from afar.
    They fly like an eagle swooping to
        devour;
9   they all come intent on violence.
    Their hordes[b] advance like a desert
        wind
        and gather prisoners like sand.
10 They mock kings
        and scoff at rulers.
    They laugh at all fortified cities;
        by building earthen ramps they
            capture them.
11 Then they sweep past like the wind and
        go on —
        guilty people, whose own strength is
            their god."

Habakkuk's Second Complaint

12 LORD, are you not from everlasting?
        My God, my Holy One, you[c] will
            never die.
    You, LORD, have appointed them to
        execute judgment;
        you, my Rock, have ordained them to
            punish.
13 Your eyes are too pure to look on evil;
        you cannot tolerate wrongdoing.
    Why then do you tolerate the
        treacherous?
        Why are you silent while the wicked
            swallow up those more righteous
                than themselves?

14 You have made people like the fish in
        the sea,
        like the sea creatures that have no
            ruler.
15 The wicked foe pulls all of them up
        with hooks,
    he catches them in his net,
        he gathers them up in his dragnet;
    and so he rejoices and is glad.
16 Therefore he sacrifices to his net
        and burns incense to his dragnet,
    for by his net he lives in luxury
        and enjoys the choicest food.
17 Is he to keep on emptying his net,
        destroying nations without mercy?

2 I will stand at my watch
    and station myself on the ramparts;
    I will look to see what he will say
        to me,
    and what answer I am to give to this
        complaint.[d]

The LORD's Answer

2 Then the LORD replied:

"Write down the revelation
    and make it plain on tablets
    so that a herald[e] may run with it.
3 For the revelation awaits an appointed
        time;
    it speaks of the end
        and will not prove false.
    Though it linger, wait for it;
        it[f] will certainly come
        and will not delay.

4 "See, the enemy is puffed up;
        his desires are not upright —
    but the righteous person will live by
        his faithfulness[g] —
5 indeed, wine betrays him;
        he is arrogant and never at rest.
    Because he is as greedy as the grave
        and like death is never satisfied,
    he gathers to himself all the nations
        and takes captive all the peoples.

---

a 6 Or Chaldeans   b 9 The meaning of the Hebrew for this word is uncertain.   c 12 An ancient Hebrew scribal
tradition; Masoretic Text we   d 1 Or and what to answer when I am rebuked   e 2 Or so that whoever reads it
f 3 Or Though he linger, wait for him; / he   g 4 Or faith

6 "Will not all of them taunt him with ridicule and scorn, saying,

" 'Woe to him who piles up stolen goods
    and makes himself wealthy by
        extortion!
    How long must this go on?'
7 Will not your creditors suddenly arise?
    Will they not wake up and make you
        tremble?
    Then you will become their prey.
8 Because you have plundered many
        nations,
    the peoples who are left will plunder
        you.
For you have shed human blood;
    you have destroyed lands and cities
        and everyone in them.

9 "Woe to him who builds his house by
        unjust gain,
    setting his nest on high
    to escape the clutches of ruin!
10 You have plotted the ruin of many
        peoples,
    shaming your own house and
        forfeiting your life.
11 The stones of the wall will cry out,
    and the beams of the woodwork will
        echo it.

12 "Woe to him who builds a city with
        bloodshed
    and establishes a town by injustice!
13 Has not the LORD Almighty
        determined
    that the people's labor is only fuel for
        the fire,
    that the nations exhaust themselves
        for nothing?
14 For the earth will be filled with the
        knowledge of the glory of the
        LORD
    as the waters cover the sea.

15 "Woe to him who gives drink to his
        neighbors,

pouring it from the wineskin till they
    are drunk,
so that he can gaze on their naked
    bodies!
16 You will be filled with shame instead of
    glory.
Now it is your turn! Drink and let
    your nakedness be exposed[a]!
The cup from the LORD's right hand is
    coming around to you,
    and disgrace will cover your glory.
17 The violence you have done to Lebanon
        will overwhelm you,
    and your destruction of animals will
        terrify you.
For you have shed human blood;
    you have destroyed lands and cities
        and everyone in them.

18 "Of what value is an idol carved by a
        craftsman?
    Or an image that teaches lies?
For the one who makes it trusts in his
        own creation;
    he makes idols that cannot speak.
19 Woe to him who says to wood, 'Come
        to life!'
    Or to lifeless stone, 'Wake up!'
Can it give guidance?
    It is covered with gold and silver;
        there is no breath in it."

20 The LORD is in his holy temple;
    let all the earth be silent before him.

Habakkuk's Prayer

3 A prayer of Habakkuk the prophet.
On *shigionoth*.[b]

2 LORD, I have heard of your fame;
    I stand in awe of your deeds, LORD.
Repeat them in our day,
    in our time make them known;
    in wrath remember mercy.

3 God came from Teman,
    the Holy One from Mount Paran.[c]

---

a 16 Masoretic Text; Dead Sea Scrolls, Aquila, Vulgate and Syriac (see also Septuagint) *and stagger*   *b 1* Probably a literary or musical term   *c 3* The Hebrew has *Selah* (a word of uncertain meaning) here and at the middle of verse 9 and at the end of verse 13.

His glory covered the heavens
and his praise filled the earth.
⁴His splendor was like the sunrise;
rays flashed from his hand,
where his power was hidden.
⁵Plague went before him;
pestilence followed his steps.
⁶He stood, and shook the earth;
he looked, and made the nations
tremble.
The ancient mountains crumbled
and the age-old hills collapsed —
but he marches on forever.
⁷I saw the tents of Cushan in distress,
the dwellings of Midian in anguish.

⁸Were you angry with the rivers, LORD?
Was your wrath against the streams?
Did you rage against the sea
when you rode your horses
and your chariots to victory?
⁹You uncovered your bow,
you called for many arrows.
You split the earth with rivers;
10   the mountains saw you and writhed.
Torrents of water swept by;
the deep roared
and lifted its waves on high.

¹¹Sun and moon stood still in the heavens
at the glint of your flying arrows,
at the lightning of your flashing
spear.
¹²In wrath you strode through the earth
and in anger you threshed the
nations.

¹³You came out to deliver your people,
to save your anointed one.
You crushed the leader of the land of
wickedness,
you stripped him from head to foot.
¹⁴With his own spear you pierced his head
when his warriors stormed out to
scatter us,
gloating as though about to devour
the wretched who were in hiding.
¹⁵You trampled the sea with your horses,
churning the great waters.

¹⁶I heard and my heart pounded,
my lips quivered at the sound;
decay crept into my bones,
and my legs trembled.
Yet I will wait patiently for the day of
calamity
to come on the nation invading us.
¹⁷Though the fig tree does not bud
and there are no grapes on the vines,
though the olive crop fails
and the fields produce no food,
though there are no sheep in the pen
and no cattle in the stalls,
¹⁸yet I will rejoice in the LORD,
I will be joyful in God my Savior.

¹⁹The Sovereign LORD is my strength;
he makes my feet like the feet of a
deer,
he enables me to tread on the heights.

For the director of music. On my
stringed instruments.

Zephaniah

THEME: Mixing the worship of God with idolatry brings destruction, but seeking God in humility brings salvation.

AUTHOR: The prophet Zephaniah, a contemporary of Nahum and Jeremiah, wrote this book.

DATE OF WRITING: The book was probably written between 635 and 630 BC.

ENCOURAGEMENT FROM ZEPHANIAH: "The LORD your God is with you, the Mighty Warrior who saves. He will take great delight in you; in his love he will no longer rebuke you, but will rejoice over you with singing" (Zephaniah 3:17).

CHALLENGE FROM ZEPHANIAH: "Seek the LORD, all you humble of the land, you who do what he commands. Seek righteousness, seek humility" (Zephaniah 2:3).

REFLECTION FROM ZEPHANIAH: "At that time I will gather you; at that time I will bring you home" (Zephaniah 3:20).

The by-now-familiar message that the day of judgment is coming is repeated once again in Zephaniah. God loves his children — far too much to fail to discipline them. Zephaniah warns that destruction and darkness are coming to Judah, but he also promises that blessings will follow with the appearance of the Messiah.

Many of us came to recovery precisely because our pain had become too great for us to handle on our own. It seemed as though God had left us alone, that he'd abandoned us in our pain. Nothing could be further from the truth. God allows us to experience pain when we've sinned. He loves us too much to let us get by with our sins. We must first recognize that we're out of control, that our lives have become unmanageable. When we realize how much we need God, only then can we turn over our lives to him and experience the healing he alone has to offer.

We often point out in Celebrate Recovery that God never wastes a hurt, and in recovery we see that we're able to serve most meaningfully through, and even because of, our most painful experiences. God will not only heal our wounds, he'll prepare us to help others deal with *their* pain. Recovery involves coming out of darkness and destruction and going on, through Christ's grace, to live a life that gives back.

---

1 The word of the LORD that came to Zephaniah son of Cushi, the son of Gedaliah, the son of Amariah, the son of Hezekiah, during the reign of Josiah son of Amon king of Judah:

Judgment on the Whole Earth in the Day of the LORD

2 "I will sweep away everything
   from the face of the earth,"
                declares the LORD.

3 "I will sweep away both man and beast;
    I will sweep away the birds in the sky
    and the fish in the sea —
    and the idols that cause the wicked to
        stumble."[a]

    "When I destroy all mankind
        on the face of the earth,"
                        declares the LORD,
4 "I will stretch out my hand against
        Judah
    and against all who live in Jerusalem.
I will destroy every remnant of Baal
        worship in this place,
    the very names of the idolatrous
        priests —
5 those who bow down on the roofs
    to worship the starry host,
    those who bow down and swear by the
        LORD
    and who also swear by Molek,[b]
6 those who turn back from following the
        LORD
    and neither seek the LORD nor
        inquire of him."

7 Be silent before the Sovereign LORD,
    for the day of the LORD is near.
The LORD has prepared a sacrifice;
    he has consecrated those he has
        invited.

8 "On the day of the LORD's sacrifice
    I will punish the officials
    and the king's sons
and all those clad
    in foreign clothes.
9 On that day I will punish
    all who avoid stepping on the
        threshold,[c]
    who fill the temple of their gods
    with violence and deceit.

10 "On that day,"
        declares the LORD,
    "a cry will go up from the Fish Gate,
        wailing from the New Quarter,
        and a loud crash from the hills.

11 Wail, you who live in the market
        district[d];
    all your merchants will be wiped out,
    all who trade with[e] silver will be
        destroyed.
12 At that time I will search Jerusalem
        with lamps
    and punish those who are
        complacent,
    who are like wine left on its dregs,
    who think, 'The LORD will do nothing,
        either good or bad.'
13 Their wealth will be plundered,
    their houses demolished.
Though they build houses,
    they will not live in them;
though they plant vineyards,
    they will not drink the wine."

14 The great day of the LORD is near —
    near and coming quickly.
The cry on the day of the LORD is bitter;
    the Mighty Warrior shouts his battle
        cry.
15 That day will be a day of wrath —
    a day of distress and anguish,
    a day of trouble and ruin,
    a day of darkness and gloom,
    a day of clouds and blackness —
16 a day of trumpet and battle cry
against the fortified cities
    and against the corner towers.

17 "I will bring such distress on all people
    that they will grope about like those
        who are blind,
    because they have sinned against the
        LORD.
Their blood will be poured out like dust
    and their entrails like dung.
18 Neither their silver nor their gold
    will be able to save them
    on the day of the LORD's wrath."

In the fire of his jealousy
    the whole earth will be consumed,
for he will make a sudden end
    of all who live on the earth.

---

a 3 The meaning of the Hebrew for this line is uncertain.   b 5 Hebrew *Malkam*   c 9 See 1 Samuel 5:5.
d 11 Or *the Mortar*   e 11 Or *in*

Judah and Jerusalem Judged Along With the Nations

Judah Summoned to Repent

2 Gather together, gather yourselves together,
  you shameful nation,
2 before the decree takes effect
  and that day passes like windblown chaff,
  before the LORD's fierce anger
    comes upon you,
  before the day of the LORD's wrath
    comes upon you.
3 Seek the LORD, all you humble of the land,
  you who do what he commands.
  Seek righteousness, seek humility;
  perhaps you will be sheltered
    on the day of the LORD's anger.

Philistia

4 Gaza will be abandoned
  and Ashkelon left in ruins.
  At midday Ashdod will be emptied
    and Ekron uprooted.
5 Woe to you who live by the sea,
  you Kerethite people;
  the word of the LORD is against you,
    Canaan, land of the Philistines.
  He says, "I will destroy you,
    and none will be left."
6 The land by the sea will become pastures
  having wells for shepherds
    and pens for flocks.
7 That land will belong
  to the remnant of the people of Judah;
  there they will find pasture.
  In the evening they will lie down
    in the houses of Ashkelon.
  The LORD their God will care for them;
  he will restore their fortunes.[a]

Moab and Ammon

8 "I have heard the insults of Moab
  and the taunts of the Ammonites,
who insulted my people
  and made threats against their land.
9 Therefore, as surely as I live,"
  declares the LORD Almighty,
  the God of Israel,
"surely Moab will become like Sodom,
  the Ammonites like Gomorrah —
a place of weeds and salt pits,
  a wasteland forever.
The remnant of my people will plunder them;
  the survivors of my nation will
    inherit their land."

10 This is what they will get in return for their pride,
  for insulting and mocking
    the people of the LORD Almighty.
11 The LORD will be awesome to them
  when he destroys all the gods of the earth.
Distant nations will bow down to him,
  all of them in their own lands.

Cush

12 "You Cushites,[b] too,
  will be slain by my sword."

Assyria

13 He will stretch out his hand against the north
  and destroy Assyria,
  leaving Nineveh utterly desolate
    and dry as the desert.
14 Flocks and herds will lie down there,
  creatures of every kind.
  The desert owl and the screech owl
    will roost on her columns.
  Their hooting will echo through the windows,
    rubble will fill the doorways,
    the beams of cedar will be exposed.
15 This is the city of revelry
  that lived in safety.
She said to herself,
  "I am the one! And there is none besides me."

---

a 7 Or *will bring back their captives*   b 12 That is, people from the upper Nile region

What a ruin she has become,
a lair for wild beasts!
All who pass by her scoff
and shake their fists.

Jerusalem

3 Woe to the city of oppressors,
rebellious and defiled!
2 She obeys no one,
she accepts no correction.
She does not trust in the LORD,
she does not draw near to her God.
3 Her officials within her
are roaring lions;
her rulers are evening wolves,
who leave nothing for the morning.
4 Her prophets are unprincipled;
they are treacherous people.
Her priests profane the sanctuary
and do violence to the law.
5 The LORD within her is righteous;
he does no wrong.
Morning by morning he dispenses his
justice,
and every new day he does not fail,
yet the unrighteous know no shame.

Jerusalem Remains Unrepentant

6 "I have destroyed nations;
their strongholds are demolished.
I have left their streets deserted,
with no one passing through.
Their cities are laid waste;
they are deserted and empty.
7 Of Jerusalem I thought,
'Surely you will fear me
and accept correction!'
Then her place of refuge[a] would not be
destroyed,
nor all my punishments come upon[b]
her.
But they were still eager
to act corruptly in all they did.
8 Therefore wait for me,"
declares the LORD,
"for the day I will stand up to testify.[c]

I have decided to assemble the nations,
to gather the kingdoms
and to pour out my wrath on them—
all my fierce anger.
The whole world will be consumed
by the fire of my jealous anger.

Restoration of Israel's Remnant

9 "Then I will purify the lips of the
peoples,
that all of them may call on the name
of the LORD
and serve him shoulder to shoulder.
10 From beyond the rivers of Cush[d]
my worshipers, my scattered people,
will bring me offerings.
11 On that day you, Jerusalem, will not be
put to shame
for all the wrongs you have done
to me,
because I will remove from you
your arrogant boasters.
Never again will you be haughty
on my holy hill.
12 But I will leave within you
the meek and humble.
The remnant of Israel
will trust in the name of the LORD.
13 They will do no wrong;
they will tell no lies.
A deceitful tongue
will not be found in their mouths.
They will eat and lie down
and no one will make them afraid."

14 Sing, Daughter Zion;
shout aloud, Israel!
Be glad and rejoice with all your heart,
Daughter Jerusalem!
15 The LORD has taken away your
punishment,
he has turned back your enemy.
The LORD, the King of Israel, is with
you;
never again will you fear any harm.
16 On that day
they will say to Jerusalem,

---

a 7 Or *her sanctuary*   b 7 Or *all those I appointed over*   c 8 Septuagint and Syriac; Hebrew *will rise up to plunder*
d 10 That is, the upper Nile region

"Do not fear, Zion;
  do not let your hands hang limp.
17 The Lord your God is with you,
    the Mighty Warrior who saves.
  He will take great delight in you;
    in his love he will no longer rebuke
        you,
    but will rejoice over you with
        singing."

18 "I will remove from you
    all who mourn over the loss of your
        appointed festivals,
    which is a burden and reproach for
        you.

19 At that time I will deal
    with all who oppressed you.
  I will rescue the lame;
    I will gather the exiles.
  I will give them praise and honor
    in every land where they have
        suffered shame.
20 At that time I will gather you;
    at that time I will bring you home.
  I will give you honor and praise
    among all the peoples of the earth
  when I restore your fortunes*a*
    before your very eyes,"
                                    says the Lord.

Haggai

THEME: When people disobey God, there are consequences. But when they follow him, he provides the enthusiasm, strength and resources they need to do his will.

AUTHOR: The book was written by the prophet Haggai, who worked with Zechariah to encourage the returning exiles to complete the rebuilding of the temple in Jerusalem.

DATE OF WRITING: Haggai's messages were given during a four-month period in 520 BC.

ENCOURAGEMENT FROM HAGGAI: " 'I am with you,' declares the LORD" (Haggai 1:13).

CHALLENGE FROM HAGGAI: "This is what the LORD Almighty says: 'Give careful thought to your ways. You have planted much, but harvested little. You eat, but never have enough. You drink, but never have your fill. You put on clothes, but are not warm. You earn wages, only to put them in a purse with holes in it' " (Haggai 1:5 – 6).

REFLECTION FROM HAGGAI: "Now give careful thought to this from this day on — consider how things were before . . . Give careful thought: . . . Until now, the vine and the fig tree, the pomegranate and the olive tree have not borne fruit. From this day on I will bless you" (Haggai 2:15,18 – 19).

At a Glance

Recovery Themes in Haggai

Haggai's message is simple: God's people must change their priorities and rebuild the temple before they can once again enjoy his blessing. Haggai affirms that his message has a divine origin. Over 25 times he points out that his words have come from the Lord. Haggai teaches that God's blessings flow as we follow his ways in our lives.

God has blessed us all in so many ways. Forgiveness of sin and eternal life are gifts we receive only through faith. God wants us to get our priorities straight. He has placed before each of us all the steps we need to take and the decisions we need to make that will lead us into a richer relationship with him. Whether that means accepting Jesus as our Savior and Lord for the first time, or, once we've done that, making amends and/or offering forgiveness, God is waiting to bless us. To enjoy all of the blessings he has given and still wants to give us, we need to apply his principles to every area of our lives.

A Call to Build the House of the LORD

1 In the second year of King Darius, on the first day of the sixth month, the word of the LORD came through the prophet Haggai to Zerubbabel son of Shealtiel, governor of Judah, and to Joshua son of Jozadak,[a] the high priest:

²This is what the LORD Almighty says: "These people say, 'The time has not yet come to rebuild the LORD's house.' "

---

[a] 1 Hebrew *Jehozadak*, a variant of *Jozadak*; also in verses 12 and 14

³Then the word of the LORD came through the prophet Haggai: ⁴"Is it a time for you yourselves to be living in your paneled houses, while this house remains a ruin?"

⁵Now this is what the LORD Almighty says: "Give careful thought to your ways. ⁶You have planted much, but harvested little. You eat, but never have enough. You drink, but never have your fill. You put on clothes, but are not warm. You earn wages, only to put them in a purse with holes in it."

⁷This is what the LORD Almighty says: "Give careful thought to your ways. ⁸Go up into the mountains and bring down timber and build my house, so that I may take pleasure in it and be honored," says the LORD. ⁹"You expected much, but see, it turned out to be little. What you brought home, I blew away. Why?" declares the LORD Almighty. "Because of my house, which remains a ruin, while each of you is busy with your own house. ¹⁰Therefore, because of you the heavens have withheld their dew and the earth its crops. ¹¹I called for a drought on the fields and the mountains, on the grain, the new wine, the olive oil and everything else the ground produces, on people and livestock, and on all the labor of your hands."

¹²Then Zerubbabel son of Shealtiel, Joshua son of Jozadak, the high priest, and the whole remnant of the people obeyed the voice of the LORD their God and the message of the prophet Haggai, because the LORD their God had sent him. And the people feared the LORD.

¹³Then Haggai, the LORD's messenger, gave this message of the LORD to the people: "I am with you," declares the LORD. ¹⁴So the LORD stirred up the spirit of Zerubbabel son of Shealtiel, governor of Judah, and the spirit of Joshua son of Jozadak, the high priest, and the spirit of the whole remnant of the people. They came and began to work on the house of the LORD Almighty, their God, ¹⁵on the twenty-fourth day of the sixth month.

The Promised Glory of the New House

2 In the second year of King Darius, ¹on the twenty-first day of the seventh month, the word of the LORD came through the prophet Haggai: ²"Speak to Zerubbabel son of Shealtiel, governor of Judah, to Joshua son of Jozadak,ᵃ the high priest, and to the remnant of the people. Ask them, ³'Who of you is left who saw this house in its former glory? How does it look to you now? Does it not seem to you like nothing? ⁴But now be strong, Zerubbabel,' declares the LORD. 'Be strong, Joshua son of Jozadak, the high priest. Be strong, all you people of the land,' declares the LORD, 'and work. For I am with you,' declares the LORD Almighty. ⁵'This is what I covenanted with you when you came out of Egypt. And my Spirit remains among you. Do not fear.'

⁶"This is what the LORD Almighty says: 'In a little while I will once more shake the heavens and the earth, the sea and the dry land. ⁷I will shake all nations, and what is desired by all nations will come, and I will fill this house with glory,' says the LORD Almighty. ⁸'The silver is mine and the gold is mine,' declares the LORD Almighty. ⁹'The glory of this present house will be greater than the glory of the former house,' says the LORD Almighty. 'And in this place I will grant peace,' declares the LORD Almighty."

Blessings for a Defiled People

¹⁰On the twenty-fourth day of the ninth month, in the second year of Darius, the word of the LORD came to the prophet Haggai: ¹¹"This is what the LORD Almighty says: 'Ask the priests what the law says: ¹²If someone carries consecrated meat in the fold of their garment, and that fold touches some bread or stew, some wine, olive oil or other food, does it become consecrated?'"

The priests answered, "No."

ᵃ 2 Hebrew *Jehozadak*, a variant of *Jozadak*; also in verse 4

¹³Then Haggai said, "If a person defiled by contact with a dead body touches one of these things, does it become defiled?"

"Yes," the priests replied, "it becomes defiled."

¹⁴Then Haggai said, "'So it is with this people and this nation in my sight,' declares the LORD. 'Whatever they do and whatever they offer there is defiled.

¹⁵"'Now give careful thought to this from this day on[a] — consider how things were before one stone was laid on another in the LORD's temple. ¹⁶When anyone came to a heap of twenty measures, there were only ten. When anyone went to a wine vat to draw fifty measures, there were only twenty. ¹⁷I struck all the work of your hands with blight, mildew and hail, yet you did not return to me,' declares the LORD. ¹⁸'From this day on, from this twenty-fourth day of the ninth month, give careful thought to the day when the foundation of the LORD's temple was laid. Give careful thought: ¹⁹Is there yet any seed left in the barn? Until now, the vine and the fig tree, the pomegranate and the olive tree have not borne fruit.

"'From this day on I will bless you.'"

Zerubbabel the LORD's Signet Ring

²⁰The word of the LORD came to Haggai a second time on the twenty-fourth day of the month: ²¹"Tell Zerubbabel governor of Judah that I am going to shake the heavens and the earth. ²²I will overturn royal thrones and shatter the power of the foreign kingdoms. I will overthrow chariots and their drivers; horses and their riders will fall, each by the sword of his brother.

²³"'On that day,' declares the LORD Almighty, 'I will take you, my servant Zerubbabel son of Shealtiel,' declares the LORD, 'and I will make you like my signet ring, for I have chosen you,' declares the LORD Almighty."

Zechariah

THEME: Zechariah's vision of a coming king and an ultimate, divine victory over evil points not only to Christ's earthly ministry but also to his ultimate return as described in the book of Revelation.

AUTHOR: The book identifies its author as "Zechariah son of Berekiah, the son of Iddo" (Zechariah 1:1). Zechariah, a contemporary of Haggai, was both a priest and a prophet.

DATE OF WRITING: Zechariah was probably written in 520 BC.

ENCOURAGEMENT FROM ZECHARIAH: "They will pass through the sea of trouble . . . I will strengthen them in the LORD and in his name they will live securely" (Zechariah 10:11 – 12).

CHALLENGE FROM ZECHARIAH: "This is what the LORD Almighty said: 'Administer true justice; show mercy and compassion to one another . . . Do not plot evil against each other' " (Zechariah 7:9 – 10).

REFLECTION FROM ZECHARIAH: " 'Not by might nor by power, but by my Spirit,' says the LORD Almighty" (Zechariah 4:6).

For over 12 years the temple sat half-completed. God has called Zechariah to motivate his people to finish the job. The prophet could have used strong words of rebuke, but instead he points out the positive purpose of completing the reconstruction project: The glory of the Messiah will one day inhabit the temple. The book of Zechariah also contains sweeping visions of the events leading up to the Messiah's second coming.

Jesus fulfilled Zechariah's prophecy during his time on Earth, as recorded in the Gospels. The promise of God's glory filling the temple gives each of us the highest possible motivation for recovery. God wants to fill us, his "temples," with the glory of the Messiah, Jesus Christ. No matter what we've done or how unworthy we may feel, God wants to rebuild us so that his glory can be seen and expressed in us.

A Call to Return to the LORD

1 In the eighth month of the second year of Darius, the word of the LORD came to the prophet Zechariah son of Berekiah, the son of Iddo:

² "The LORD was very angry with your ancestors. ³Therefore tell the people: This is what the LORD Almighty says: 'Return to me,' declares the LORD Almighty, 'and I will return to you,' says the LORD Almighty.

⁴Do not be like your ancestors, to whom the earlier prophets proclaimed: This is what the LORD Almighty says: 'Turn from your evil ways and your evil practices.' But they would not listen or pay attention to me, declares the LORD. ⁵Where are your ancestors now? And the prophets, do they live forever? ⁶But did not my words and my decrees, which I commanded my servants the prophets, overtake your ancestors?

"Then they repented and said, 'The LORD Almighty has done to us what our ways and practices deserve, just as he determined to do.'"

The Man Among the Myrtle Trees

7On the twenty-fourth day of the eleventh month, the month of Shebat, in the second year of Darius, the word of the LORD came to the prophet Zechariah son of Berekiah, the son of Iddo.

8During the night I had a vision, and there before me was a man mounted on a red horse. He was standing among the myrtle trees in a ravine. Behind him were red, brown and white horses.

9I asked, "What are these, my lord?"

The angel who was talking with me answered, "I will show you what they are."

10Then the man standing among the myrtle trees explained, "They are the ones the LORD has sent to go throughout the earth."

11And they reported to the angel of the LORD who was standing among the myrtle trees, "We have gone throughout the earth and found the whole world at rest and in peace."

12Then the angel of the LORD said, "LORD Almighty, how long will you withhold mercy from Jerusalem and from the towns of Judah, which you have been angry with these seventy years?" 13So the LORD spoke kind and comforting words to the angel who talked with me.

14Then the angel who was speaking to me said, "Proclaim this word: This is what the LORD Almighty says: 'I am very jealous for Jerusalem and Zion, 15and I am very angry with the nations that feel secure. I was only a little angry, but they went too far with the punishment.'

16"Therefore this is what the LORD says: 'I will return to Jerusalem with mercy, and there my house will be rebuilt. And the measuring line will be stretched out over Jerusalem,' declares the LORD Almighty.

17"Proclaim further: This is what the LORD Almighty says: 'My towns will again overflow with prosperity, and the LORD will again comfort Zion and choose Jerusalem.'"

Four Horns and Four Craftsmen

18Then I looked up, and there before me were four horns. 19I asked the angel who was speaking to me, "What are these?"

He answered me, "These are the horns that scattered Judah, Israel and Jerusalem."

20Then the LORD showed me four craftsmen. 21I asked, "What are these coming to do?"

He answered, "These are the horns that scattered Judah so that no one could raise their head, but the craftsmen have come to terrify them and throw down these horns of the nations who lifted up their horns against the land of Judah to scatter its people."[a]

A Man With a Measuring Line

2[b] Then I looked up, and there before me was a man with a measuring line in his hand. 2I asked, "Where are you going?"

He answered me, "To measure Jerusalem, to find out how wide and how long it is."

3While the angel who was speaking to me was leaving, another angel came to meet him 4and said to him: "Run, tell that young man, 'Jerusalem will be a city without walls because of the great number of people and animals in it. 5And I myself will be a wall of fire around it,' declares the LORD, 'and I will be its glory within.'

6"Come! Come! Flee from the land of the north," declares the LORD, "for I have scattered you to the four winds of heaven," declares the LORD.

7"Come, Zion! Escape, you who live in Daughter Babylon!" 8For this is what the LORD Almighty says: "After the Glorious One has sent me against the nations that have plundered you—for whoever touch-

---

a 21 In Hebrew texts 1:18-21 is numbered 2:1-4.   b In Hebrew texts 2:1-13 is numbered 2:5-17.

es you touches the apple of his eye— ⁹I will surely raise my hand against them so that their slaves will plunder them.*a* Then you will know that the LORD Almighty has sent me.

¹⁰"Shout and be glad, Daughter Zion. For I am coming, and I will live among you," declares the LORD. ¹¹"Many nations will be joined with the LORD in that day and will become my people. I will live among you and you will know that the LORD Almighty has sent me to you. ¹²The LORD will inherit Judah as his portion in the holy land and will again choose Jerusalem. ¹³Be still before the LORD, all mankind, because he has roused himself from his holy dwelling."

Clean Garments for the High Priest

3 Then he showed me Joshua the high priest standing before the angel of the LORD, and Satan*b* standing at his right side to accuse him. ²The LORD said to Satan, "The LORD rebuke you, Satan! The LORD, who has chosen Jerusalem, rebuke you! Is not this man a burning stick snatched from the fire?"

³Now Joshua was dressed in filthy clothes as he stood before the angel. ⁴The angel said to those who were standing before him, "Take off his filthy clothes."

Then he said to Joshua, "See, I have taken away your sin, and I will put fine garments on you."

⁵Then I said, "Put a clean turban on his head." So they put a clean turban on his head and clothed him, while the angel of the LORD stood by.

⁶The angel of the LORD gave this charge to Joshua: ⁷"This is what the LORD Almighty says: 'If you will walk in obedience to me and keep my requirements, then you will govern my house and have charge of my courts, and I will give you a place among these standing here.

⁸"'Listen, High Priest Joshua, you and your associates seated before you, who are men symbolic of things to come: I am going to bring my servant, the Branch. ⁹See, the stone I have set in front of Joshua! There are seven eyes*c* on that one stone, and I will engrave an inscription on it,' says the LORD Almighty, 'and I will remove the sin of this land in a single day.

¹⁰"'In that day each of you will invite your neighbor to sit under your vine and fig tree,' declares the LORD Almighty."

The Gold Lampstand and the Two Olive Trees

4 Then the angel who talked with me returned and woke me up, like someone awakened from sleep. ²He asked me, "What do you see?"

I answered, "I see a solid gold lampstand with a bowl at the top and seven lamps on it, with seven channels to the lamps. ³Also there are two olive trees by it, one on the right of the bowl and the other on its left."

⁴I asked the angel who talked with me, "What are these, my lord?"

⁵He answered, "Do you not know what these are?"

"No, my lord," I replied.

⁶So he said to me, "This is the word of the LORD to Zerubbabel: 'Not by might nor by power, but by my Spirit,' says the LORD Almighty.

⁷"What are you, mighty mountain? Before Zerubbabel you will become level ground. Then he will bring out the capstone to shouts of 'God bless it! God bless it!'"

⁸Then the word of the LORD came to me: ⁹"The hands of Zerubbabel have laid the foundation of this temple; his hands will also complete it. Then you will know that the LORD Almighty has sent me to you.

¹⁰"Who dares despise the day of small things, since the seven eyes of the LORD that range throughout the earth will rejoice when they see the chosen capstone*d* in the hand of Zerubbabel?"

---

a 8,9 Or *says after . . . eye:* ⁹*"I . . . plunder them."*   *b 1* Hebrew *satan* means *adversary.*   *c 9* Or *facets*   *d 10* Or *the plumb line*

¹¹Then I asked the angel, "What are these two olive trees on the right and the left of the lampstand?"

¹²Again I asked him, "What are these two olive branches beside the two gold pipes that pour out golden oil?"

¹³He replied, "Do you not know what these are?"

"No, my lord," I said.

¹⁴So he said, "These are the two who are anointed to*ᵃ* serve the Lord of all the earth."

The Flying Scroll

5 I looked again, and there before me was a flying scroll.
²He asked me, "What do you see?"

I answered, "I see a flying scroll, twenty cubits long and ten cubits wide.*ᵇ*"

³And he said to me, "This is the curse that is going out over the whole land; for according to what it says on one side, every thief will be banished, and according to what it says on the other, everyone who swears falsely will be banished. ⁴The LORD Almighty declares, 'I will send it out, and it will enter the house of the thief and the house of anyone who swears falsely by my name. It will remain in that house and destroy it completely, both its timbers and its stones.'"

The Woman in a Basket

⁵Then the angel who was speaking to me came forward and said to me, "Look up and see what is appearing."

⁶I asked, "What is it?"

He replied, "It is a basket." And he added, "This is the iniquity*ᶜ* of the people throughout the land."

⁷Then the cover of lead was raised, and there in the basket sat a woman! ⁸He said, "This is wickedness," and he pushed her back into the basket and pushed its lead cover down on it.

⁹Then I looked up — and there before me were two women, with the wind in their wings! They had wings like those of a stork, and they lifted up the basket between heaven and earth.

¹⁰"Where are they taking the basket?" I asked the angel who was speaking to me.

¹¹He replied, "To the country of Babylonia*ᵈ* to build a house for it. When the house is ready, the basket will be set there in its place."

Four Chariots

6 I looked up again, and there before me were four chariots coming out from between two mountains — mountains of bronze. ²The first chariot had red horses, the second black, ³the third white, and the fourth dappled — all of them powerful. ⁴I asked the angel who was speaking to me, "What are these, my lord?"

⁵The angel answered me, "These are the four spirits*ᵉ* of heaven, going out from standing in the presence of the Lord of the whole world. ⁶The one with the black horses is going toward the north country, the one with the white horses toward the west,*ᶠ* and the one with the dappled horses toward the south."

⁷When the powerful horses went out, they were straining to go throughout the earth. And he said, "Go throughout the earth!" So they went throughout the earth.

⁸Then he called to me, "Look, those going toward the north country have given my Spirit*ᵍ* rest in the land of the north."

A Crown for Joshua

⁹The word of the LORD came to me: ¹⁰"Take silver and gold from the exiles Heldai, Tobijah and Jedaiah, who have arrived from Babylon. Go the same day to the house of Josiah son of Zephaniah. ¹¹Take the silver and gold and make a crown, and set it on the head of the high priest, Joshua son of Jozadak.*ʰ* ¹²Tell him

---

ᵃ 14 Or *two who bring oil and*   *ᵇ* 2 That is, about 30 feet long and 15 feet wide or about 9 meters long and 4.5 meters wide   *ᶜ* 6 Or *appearance*   *ᵈ* 11 Hebrew *Shinar*   *ᵉ* 5 Or *winds*   *ᶠ* 6 Or *horses after them*   *ᵍ* 8 Or *spirit*   *ʰ* 11 Hebrew *Jehozadak*, a variant of *Jozadak* this is what the LORD Almighty says: 'Here is the man whose name is the Branch, and he will branch out from his place and build the temple of the LORD. ¹³It is he who will build the temple of the LORD, and he will be clothed with majesty and will sit and rule on his throne. And he*a* will be a priest on his throne. And there will be harmony between the two.' ¹⁴The crown will be given to Heldai,*b* Tobijah, Jedaiah and Hen*c* son of Zephaniah as a memorial in the temple of the LORD. ¹⁵Those who are far away will come and help to build the temple of the LORD, and you will know that the LORD Almighty has sent me to you. This will happen if you diligently obey the LORD your God."

Justice and Mercy, Not Fasting

7 In the fourth year of King Darius, the word of the LORD came to Zechariah on the fourth day of the ninth month, the month of Kislev. ²The people of Bethel had sent Sharezer and Regem-Melek, together with their men, to entreat the LORD ³by asking the priests of the house of the LORD Almighty and the prophets, "Should I mourn and fast in the fifth month, as I have done for so many years?"

⁴Then the word of the LORD Almighty came to me: ⁵"Ask all the people of the land and the priests, 'When you fasted and mourned in the fifth and seventh months for the past seventy years, was it really for me that you fasted? ⁶And when you were eating and drinking, were you not just feasting for yourselves? ⁷Are these not the words the LORD proclaimed through the earlier prophets when Jerusalem and its surrounding towns were at rest and prosperous, and the Negev and the western foothills were settled?' "

⁸And the word of the LORD came again to Zechariah: ⁹"This is what the LORD Almighty said: 'Administer true justice; show mercy and compassion to one another. ¹⁰Do not oppress the widow or the father-

less, the foreigner or the poor. Do not plot evil against each other.'

¹¹"But they refused to pay attention; stubbornly they turned their backs and covered their ears. ¹²They made their hearts as hard as flint and would not listen to the law or to the words that the LORD Almighty had sent by his Spirit through the earlier prophets. So the LORD Almighty was very angry.

¹³" 'When I called, they did not listen; so when they called, I would not listen,' says the LORD Almighty. ¹⁴'I scattered them with a whirlwind among all the nations, where they were strangers. The land they left behind them was so desolate that no one traveled through it. This is how they made the pleasant land desolate.' "

The LORD Promises to Bless Jerusalem

8 The word of the LORD Almighty came to me.

²This is what the LORD Almighty says: "I am very jealous for Zion; I am burning with jealousy for her."

³This is what the LORD says: "I will return to Zion and dwell in Jerusalem. Then Jerusalem will be called the Faithful City, and the mountain of the LORD Almighty will be called the Holy Mountain."

⁴This is what the LORD Almighty says: "Once again men and women of ripe old age will sit in the streets of Jerusalem, each of them with cane in hand because of their age. ⁵The city streets will be filled with boys and girls playing there."

⁶This is what the LORD Almighty says: "It may seem marvelous to the remnant of this people at that time, but will it seem marvelous to me?" declares the LORD Almighty.

⁷This is what the LORD Almighty says: "I will save my people from the countries of the east and the west. ⁸I will bring them back to live in Jerusalem; they will be my people, and I will be faithful and righteous to them as their God."

---

a 13 Or *there*   *b 14* Syriac; Hebrew *Helem*   *c 14* Or *and the gracious one, the*

⁹This is what the Lord Almighty says: "Now hear these words, 'Let your hands be strong so that the temple may be built.' This is also what the prophets said who were present when the foundation was laid for the house of the Lord Almighty. ¹⁰Before that time there were no wages for people or hire for animals. No one could go about their business safely because of their enemies, since I had turned everyone against their neighbor. ¹¹But now I will not deal with the remnant of this people as I did in the past," declares the Lord Almighty.

¹²"The seed will grow well, the vine will yield its fruit, the ground will produce its crops, and the heavens will drop their dew. I will give all these things as an inheritance to the remnant of this people. ¹³Just as you, Judah and Israel, have been a curse*a* among the nations, so I will save you, and you will be a blessing.*b* Do not be afraid, but let your hands be strong."

¹⁴This is what the Lord Almighty says: "Just as I had determined to bring disaster on you and showed no pity when your ancestors angered me," says the Lord Almighty, ¹⁵"so now I have determined to do good again to Jerusalem and Judah. Do not be afraid. ¹⁶These are the things you are to do: Speak the truth to each other, and render true and sound judgment in your courts; ¹⁷do not plot evil against each other, and do not love to swear falsely. I hate all this," declares the Lord.

¹⁸The word of the Lord Almighty came to me. ¹⁹This is what the Lord Almighty says: "The fasts of the fourth, fifth, seventh and tenth months will become joyful and glad occasions and happy festivals for Judah. Therefore love truth and peace."

²⁰This is what the Lord Almighty says: "Many peoples and the inhabitants of many cities will yet come, ²¹and the inhabitants of one city will go to another and say, 'Let us go at once to entreat the Lord and seek the Lord Almighty. I myself am going.' ²²And many peoples and powerful nations will come to Jerusalem to seek the Lord Almighty and to entreat him."

²³This is what the Lord Almighty says: "In those days ten people from all languages and nations will take firm hold of one Jew by the hem of his robe and say, 'Let us go with you, because we have heard that God is with you.'"

Judgment on Israel's Enemies

9 A prophecy:

The word of the Lord is against the
    land of Hadrak
and will come to rest on Damascus—
for the eyes of all people and all the
    tribes of Israel
are on the Lord— *c*
²and on Hamath too, which borders on it,
    and on Tyre and Sidon, though they
    are very skillful.
³Tyre has built herself a stronghold;
    she has heaped up silver like dust,
    and gold like the dirt of the streets.
⁴But the Lord will take away her
    possessions
    and destroy her power on the sea,
    and she will be consumed by fire.
⁵Ashkelon will see it and fear;
    Gaza will writhe in agony,
    and Ekron too, for her hope will
    wither.
Gaza will lose her king
    and Ashkelon will be deserted.
⁶A mongrel people will occupy Ashdod,
    and I will put an end to the pride of
    the Philistines.
⁷I will take the blood from their mouths,
    the forbidden food from between
    their teeth.
Those who are left will belong to our
    God
    and become a clan in Judah,
    and Ekron will be like the Jebusites.

---

a 13 That is, your name has been used in cursing (see Jer. 29:22); or, you have been regarded as under a curse.
b 13 Or *and your name will be used in blessings* (see Gen. 48:20); or *and you will be seen as blessed*   *c 1* Or *Damascus. / For the eye of the Lord is on all people, / as well as on the tribes of Israel,*

8 But I will encamp at my temple
   to guard it against marauding forces.
Never again will an oppressor overrun
   my people,
   for now I am keeping watch.

The Coming of Zion's King

9 Rejoice greatly, Daughter Zion!
   Shout, Daughter Jerusalem!
See, your king comes to you,
   righteous and victorious,
lowly and riding on a donkey,
   on a colt, the foal of a donkey.
10 I will take away the chariots from
      Ephraim
   and the warhorses from Jerusalem,
   and the battle bow will be broken.
He will proclaim peace to the nations.
   His rule will extend from sea to sea
   and from the River*a* to the ends of
      the earth.
11 As for you, because of the blood of my
      covenant with you,
   I will free your prisoners from the
      waterless pit.
12 Return to your fortress, you prisoners
      of hope;
   even now I announce that I will
      restore twice as much to you.
13 I will bend Judah as I bend my bow
   and fill it with Ephraim.
I will rouse your sons, Zion,
   against your sons, Greece,
   and make you like a warrior's
      sword.

The Lord Will Appear

14 Then the Lord will appear over them;
   his arrow will flash like lightning.
The Sovereign Lord will sound the
      trumpet;
   he will march in the storms of the
      south,
15   and the Lord Almighty will shield
      them.
They will destroy
   and overcome with slingstones.

They will drink and roar as with wine;
   they will be full like a bowl
   used for sprinkling*b* the corners of
      the altar.
16 The Lord their God will save his
      people on that day
   as a shepherd saves his flock.
They will sparkle in his land
   like jewels in a crown.
17 How attractive and beautiful they
      will be!
   Grain will make the young men
      thrive,
   and new wine the young women.

The Lord Will Care for Judah

10 Ask the Lord for rain in the
      springtime;
   it is the Lord who sends the
      thunderstorms.
He gives showers of rain to all people,
   and plants of the field to everyone.
2 The idols speak deceitfully,
   diviners see visions that lie;
they tell dreams that are false,
   they give comfort in vain.
Therefore the people wander like sheep
   oppressed for lack of a shepherd.

3 "My anger burns against the shepherds,
   and I will punish the leaders;
for the Lord Almighty will care
   for his flock, the people of Judah,
   and make them like a proud horse in
      battle.
4 From Judah will come the cornerstone,
   from him the tent peg,
from him the battle bow,
   from him every ruler.
5 Together they*c* will be like warriors in
      battle
   trampling their enemy into the mud
      of the streets.
They will fight because the Lord is
      with them,
   and they will put the enemy
      horsemen to shame.

---

a 10 That is, the Euphrates   *b 15* Or *bowl,* / *like*   *c 4,5* Or *ruler, all of them together.* / *5They*

6 "I will strengthen Judah
  and save the tribes of Joseph.
I will restore them
  because I have compassion on them.
They will be as though
  I had not rejected them,
for I am the LORD their God
  and I will answer them.
7 The Ephraimites will become like
    warriors,
  and their hearts will be glad as with
    wine.
Their children will see it and be
    joyful;
  their hearts will rejoice in the LORD.
8 I will signal for them
    and gather them in.
Surely I will redeem them;
  they will be as numerous as before.
9 Though I scatter them among the
    peoples,
  yet in distant lands they will
    remember me.
They and their children will survive,
  and they will return.
10 I will bring them back from Egypt
    and gather them from Assyria.
I will bring them to Gilead and
    Lebanon,
  and there will not be room enough
    for them.
11 They will pass through the sea of
    trouble;
  the surging sea will be subdued
    and all the depths of the Nile will
    dry up.
Assyria's pride will be brought down
  and Egypt's scepter will pass away.
12 I will strengthen them in the LORD
  and in his name they will live
    securely,"
              declares the LORD.

11 Open your doors, Lebanon,
   so that fire may devour your
   cedars!
2 Wail, you juniper, for the cedar has
    fallen;
  the stately trees are ruined!

Wail, oaks of Bashan;
  the dense forest has been cut down!
3 Listen to the wail of the shepherds;
  their rich pastures are destroyed!
Listen to the roar of the lions;
  the lush thicket of the Jordan is
    ruined!

Two Shepherds

4 This is what the LORD my God says:
"Shepherd the flock marked for slaughter.
5 Their buyers slaughter them and go unpunished. Those who sell them say, 'Praise the LORD, I am rich!' Their own shepherds do not spare them. 6 For I will no longer have pity on the people of the land," declares the LORD. "I will give everyone into the hands of their neighbors and their king. They will devastate the land, and I will not rescue anyone from their hands."

7 So I shepherded the flock marked for slaughter, particularly the oppressed of the flock. Then I took two staffs and called one Favor and the other Union, and I shepherded the flock. 8 In one month I got rid of the three shepherds.

The flock detested me, and I grew weary of them 9 and said, "I will not be your shepherd. Let the dying die, and the perishing perish. Let those who are left eat one another's flesh."

10 Then I took my staff called Favor and broke it, revoking the covenant I had made with all the nations. 11 It was revoked on that day, and so the oppressed of the flock who were watching me knew it was the word of the LORD.

12 I told them, "If you think it best, give me my pay; but if not, keep it." So they paid me thirty pieces of silver.

13 And the LORD said to me, "Throw it to the potter" — the handsome price at which they valued me! So I took the thirty pieces of silver and threw them to the potter at the house of the LORD.

14 Then I broke my second staff called Union, breaking the family bond between Judah and Israel.

15 Then the LORD said to me, "Take again

the equipment of a foolish shepherd. ¹⁶For I am going to raise up a shepherd over the land who will not care for the lost, or seek the young, or heal the injured, or feed the healthy, but will eat the meat of the choice sheep, tearing off their hooves.

¹⁷"Woe to the worthless shepherd,
    who deserts the flock!
May the sword strike his arm and his
    right eye!
May his arm be completely withered,
    his right eye totally blinded!"

Jerusalem's Enemies to Be Destroyed

12 A prophecy: The word of the LORD concerning Israel.

The LORD, who stretches out the heavens, who lays the foundation of the earth, and who forms the human spirit within a person, declares: ²"I am going to make Jerusalem a cup that sends all the surrounding peoples reeling. Judah will be besieged as well as Jerusalem. ³On that day, when all the nations of the earth are gathered against her, I will make Jerusalem an immovable rock for all the nations. All who try to move it will injure themselves. ⁴On that day I will strike every horse with panic and its rider with madness," declares the LORD. "I will keep a watchful eye over Judah, but I will blind all the horses of the nations. ⁵Then the clans of Judah will say in their hearts, 'The people of Jerusalem are strong, because the LORD Almighty is their God.'

⁶"On that day I will make the clans of Judah like a firepot in a woodpile, like a flaming torch among sheaves. They will consume all the surrounding peoples right and left, but Jerusalem will remain intact in her place.

⁷"The LORD will save the dwellings of Judah first, so that the honor of the house of David and of Jerusalem's inhabitants may not be greater than that of Judah. ⁸On that day the LORD will shield those who live in Jerusalem, so that the feeblest among them will be like David, and the house of David will be like God, like the angel of the LORD going before them. ⁹On that day I will set out to destroy all the nations that attack Jerusalem.

Mourning for the One They Pierced

¹⁰"And I will pour out on the house of David and the inhabitants of Jerusalem a spirit[a] of grace and supplication. They will look on[b] me, the one they have pierced, and they will mourn for him as one mourns for an only child, and grieve bitterly for him as one grieves for a firstborn son. ¹¹On that day the weeping in Jerusalem will be as great as the weeping of Hadad Rimmon in the plain of Megiddo. ¹²The land will mourn, each clan by itself, with their wives by themselves: the clan of the house of David and their wives, the clan of the house of Nathan and their wives, ¹³the clan of the house of Levi and their wives, the clan of Shimei and their wives, ¹⁴and all the rest of the clans and their wives.

Cleansing From Sin

13 "On that day a fountain will be opened to the house of David and the inhabitants of Jerusalem, to cleanse them from sin and impurity.

²"On that day, I will banish the names of the idols from the land, and they will be remembered no more," declares the LORD Almighty. "I will remove both the prophets and the spirit of impurity from the land. ³And if anyone still prophesies, their father and mother, to whom they were born, will say to them, 'You must die, because you have told lies in the LORD's name.' Then their own parents will stab the one who prophesies.

⁴"On that day every prophet will be ashamed of their prophetic vision. They will not put on a prophet's garment of hair in order to deceive. ⁵Each will say, 'I am not

a 10 Or the Spirit   b 10 Or to

a prophet. I am a farmer; the land has been my livelihood since my youth.*a'* 6If someone asks, 'What are these wounds on your body*b*?' they will answer, 'The wounds I was given at the house of my friends.'

The Shepherd Struck, the Sheep Scattered

7"Awake, sword, against my shepherd,
    against the man who is close to me!"
    declares the LORD Almighty.
"Strike the shepherd,
    and the sheep will be scattered,
    and I will turn my hand against the
        little ones.
8In the whole land," declares the LORD,
    "two-thirds will be struck down and
        perish;
    yet one-third will be left in it.
9This third I will put into the fire;
    I will refine them like silver
    and test them like gold.
They will call on my name
    and I will answer them;
I will say, 'They are my people,'
    and they will say, 'The LORD is our
        God.'"

The LORD Comes and Reigns

14 A day of the LORD is coming, Jerusalem, when your possessions will be plundered and divided up within your very walls. 2I will gather all the nations to Jerusalem to fight against it; the city will be captured, the houses ransacked, and the women raped. Half of the city will go into exile, but the rest of the people will not be taken from the city. 3Then the LORD will go out and fight against those nations, as he fights on a day of battle. 4On that day his feet will stand on the Mount of Olives, east of Jerusalem, and the Mount of Olives will be split in two from east to west, forming a great valley, with half of the mountain moving north and half moving south.

5You will flee by my mountain valley, for it will extend to Azel. You will flee as you fled from the earthquake*c* in the days of Uzziah king of Judah. Then the LORD my God will come, and all the holy ones with him.

6On that day there will be neither sunlight nor cold, frosty darkness. 7It will be a unique day — a day known only to the LORD — with no distinction between day and night. When evening comes, there will be light.

8On that day living water will flow out from Jerusalem, half of it east to the Dead Sea and half of it west to the Mediterranean Sea, in summer and in winter.

9The LORD will be king over the whole earth. On that day there will be one LORD, and his name the only name.

10The whole land, from Geba to Rimmon, south of Jerusalem, will become like the Arabah. But Jerusalem will be raised up high from the Benjamin Gate to the site of the First Gate, to the Corner Gate, and from the Tower of Hananel to the royal winepresses, and will remain in its place. 11It will be inhabited; never again will it be destroyed. Jerusalem will be secure.

12This is the plague with which the LORD will strike all the nations that fought against Jerusalem: Their flesh will rot while they are still standing on their feet, their eyes will rot in their sockets, and their tongues will rot in their mouths. 13On that day people will be stricken by the LORD with great panic. They will seize each other by the hand and attack one another. 14Judah too will fight at Jerusalem. The wealth of all the surrounding nations will be collected — great quantities of gold and silver and clothing. 15A similar plague will strike the horses and mules, the camels and donkeys, and all the animals in those camps.

16Then the survivors from all the nations that have attacked Jerusalem will go

---

a 5 Or *farmer; a man sold me in my youth*   *b* 6 Or *wounds between your hands*   *c* 5 Or 5*My mountain valley will be blocked and will extend to Azel. It will be blocked as it was blocked because of the earthquake* up year after year to worship the King, the LORD Almighty, and to celebrate the Festival of Tabernacles. [17]If any of the peoples of the earth do not go up to Jerusalem to worship the King, the LORD Almighty, they will have no rain. [18]If the Egyptian people do not go up and take part, they will have no rain. The LORD[a] will bring on them the plague he inflicts on the nations that do not go up to celebrate the Festival of Tabernacles. [19]This will be the punishment of Egypt and the punishment of all the nations that do not go up to celebrate the Festival of Tabernacles.

[20]On that day HOLY TO THE LORD will be inscribed on the bells of the horses, and the cooking pots in the LORD's house will be like the sacred bowls in front of the altar. [21]Every pot in Jerusalem and Judah will be holy to the LORD Almighty, and all who come to sacrifice will take some of the pots and cook in them. And on that day there will no longer be a Canaanite[b] in the house of the LORD Almighty.

---

[a] 18 Or part, then the LORD   [b] 21 Or merchant

Malachi

THEME: The book of Malachi demonstrates that God demands our best — both in our service and in our lives. What we give and how we live reflect the degree of our love for, and commitment to, him.

AUTHOR: The authorship of Malachi is debated. It's uncertain whether Malachi is the author's name or whether it was used as a title; prophets were called messengers of the Lord, and the term "Malachi" means "my messenger."

DATE OF WRITING: The book of Malachi was probably written about 430 BC.

ENCOURAGEMENT FROM MALACHI: " 'On the day when I act,' says the LORD Almighty, 'they will be my treasured possession. I will spare them, just as a father has compassion and spares his son who serves him' " (Malachi 3:17).

CHALLENGE FROM MALACHI: " 'I the LORD do not change. So you, the descendants of Jacob, are not destroyed. Ever since the time of your ancestors you have turned away from my decrees and have not kept them. Return to me, and I will return to you,' says the LORD Almighty" (Malachi 3:6 – 7).

REFLECTION FROM MALACHI: " 'My name will be great among the nations, from where the sun rises to where it sets. In every place incense and pure offerings will be brought to me, because my name will be great among the nations,' says the LORD Almighty" (Malachi 1:11).

Malachi addresses his message of judgment to a people plagued by corrupt priests, evil practices and a false sense of security. This prophet probes deeply into the problems of hypocrisy, infidelity, mixed marriages, divorce, false worship and arrogance. Judah's people are disillusioned, wondering whether God's Messianic promises will ever be fulfilled. Held captive by doubt rather than characterized by faith, they express their negative outlook by participating in empty ritual, cheating on tithes and offerings and expressing indifference to moral and ceremonial law. Malachi confronts these problems and calls the people to fresh commitment and obedience.

In Malachi, it becomes clear that the sins of the nation will require the Lord's intervention. Only the coming Messiah can purify his people and the temple, as well as remove the threat of continued contamination. In recovery, we find that we too struggle with sins that have contaminated our lives and can be removed only when Jesus comes into our hearts. Only his Spirit can protect us from falling back into our old hurts, hang-ups and habits. Recovery is all about letting Jesus clean us out and make us whole and healthy. Once that happens, our goal is to live out the reality of Christ so that others can recognize his presence in our lives.

1

A prophecy: The word of the LORD to Israel through Malachi.*a*

Israel Doubts God's Love

²"I have loved you," says the LORD.

"But you ask, 'How have you loved us?'

"Was not Esau Jacob's brother?" declares the LORD. "Yet I have loved Jacob, ³but Esau I have hated, and I have turned his hill country into a wasteland and left his inheritance to the desert jackals."

⁴Edom may say, "Though we have been crushed, we will rebuild the ruins."

But this is what the LORD Almighty says: "They may build, but I will demolish. They will be called the Wicked Land, a people always under the wrath of the LORD. ⁵You will see it with your own eyes and say, 'Great is the LORD — even beyond the borders of Israel!'

Breaking Covenant Through Blemished Sacrifices

⁶"A son honors his father, and a slave his master. If I am a father, where is the honor due me? If I am a master, where is the respect due me?" says the LORD Almighty.

"It is you priests who show contempt for my name.

"But you ask, 'How have we shown contempt for your name?'

⁷"By offering defiled food on my altar.

"But you ask, 'How have we defiled you?'

"By saying that the LORD's table is contemptible. ⁸When you offer blind animals for sacrifice, is that not wrong? When you sacrifice lame or diseased animals, is that not wrong? Try offering them to your governor! Would he be pleased with you? Would he accept you?" says the LORD Almighty.

⁹"Now plead with God to be gracious to us. With such offerings from your hands, will he accept you?" — says the LORD Almighty.

¹⁰"Oh, that one of you would shut the temple doors, so that you would not light useless fires on my altar! I am not pleased with you," says the LORD Almighty, "and I will accept no offering from your hands. ¹¹My name will be great among the nations, from where the sun rises to where it sets. In every place incense and pure offerings will be brought to me, because my name will be great among the nations," says the LORD Almighty.

¹²"But you profane it by saying, 'The Lord's table is defiled,' and, 'Its food is contemptible.' ¹³And you say, 'What a burden!' and you sniff at it contemptuously," says the LORD Almighty.

"When you bring injured, lame or diseased animals and offer them as sacrifices, should I accept them from your hands?" says the LORD. ¹⁴"Cursed is the cheat who has an acceptable male in his flock and vows to give it, but then sacrifices a blemished animal to the Lord. For I am a great king," says the LORD Almighty, "and my name is to be feared among the nations.

Additional Warning to the Priests

2

"And now, you priests, this warning is for you. ²If you do not listen, and if you do not resolve to honor my name," says the LORD Almighty, "I will send a curse on you, and I will curse your blessings. Yes, I have already cursed them, because you have not resolved to honor me.

³"Because of you I will rebuke your descendants*b*; I will smear on your faces the dung from your festival sacrifices, and you will be carried off with it. ⁴And you will know that I have sent you this warning so that my covenant with Levi may continue," says the LORD Almighty. ⁵"My covenant was with him, a covenant of life and peace, and I gave them to him; this called for reverence and he revered me and stood in awe of my name. ⁶True instruction was in his mouth and nothing false was found on his lips. He walked with me in peace and uprightness, and turned many from sin.

⁷"For the lips of a priest ought to preserve

---

a 1 Malachi *means* my messenger. *b 3* Or *will blight your grain* knowledge, because he is the messenger of the LORD Almighty and people seek instruction from his mouth. [8]But you have turned from the way and by your teaching have caused many to stumble; you have violated the covenant with Levi," says the LORD Almighty. [9]"So I have caused you to be despised and humiliated before all the people, because you have not followed my ways but have shown partiality in matters of the law."

Breaking Covenant Through Divorce

[10]Do we not all have one Father[a]? Did not one God create us? Why do we profane the covenant of our ancestors by being unfaithful to one another?

[11]Judah has been unfaithful. A detestable thing has been committed in Israel and in Jerusalem: Judah has desecrated the sanctuary the LORD loves by marrying women who worship a foreign god. [12]As for the man who does this, whoever he may be, may the LORD remove him from the tents of Jacob[b]—even though he brings an offering to the LORD Almighty.

[13]Another thing you do: You flood the LORD's altar with tears. You weep and wail because he no longer looks with favor on your offerings or accepts them with pleasure from your hands. [14]You ask, "Why?" It is because the LORD is the witness between you and the wife of your youth. You have been unfaithful to her, though she is your partner, the wife of your marriage covenant.

[15]Has not the one God made you? You belong to him in body and spirit. And what does the one God seek? Godly offspring.[c] So be on your guard, and do not be unfaithful to the wife of your youth.

[16]"The man who hates and divorces his wife," says the LORD, the God of Israel, "does violence to the one he should protect,"[d] says the LORD Almighty.

So be on your guard, and do not be unfaithful.

Breaking Covenant Through Injustice

[17]You have wearied the LORD with your words.

"How have we wearied him?" you ask.

By saying, "All who do evil are good in the eyes of the LORD, and he is pleased with them" or "Where is the God of justice?"

3 "I will send my messenger, who will prepare the way before me. Then suddenly the Lord you are seeking will come to his temple; the messenger of the covenant, whom you desire, will come," says the LORD Almighty.

[2]But who can endure the day of his coming? Who can stand when he appears? For he will be like a refiner's fire or a launderer's soap. [3]He will sit as a refiner and purifier of silver; he will purify the Levites and refine them like gold and silver. Then the LORD will have men who will bring offerings in righteousness, [4]and the offerings of Judah and Jerusalem will be acceptable to the LORD, as in days gone by, as in former years.

[5]"So I will come to put you on trial. I will be quick to testify against sorcerers, adulterers and perjurers, against those who defraud laborers of their wages, who oppress the widows and the fatherless, and deprive the foreigners among you of justice, but do not fear me," says the LORD Almighty.

Breaking Covenant by Withholding Tithes

[6]"I the LORD do not change. So you, the descendants of Jacob, are not destroyed. [7]Ever since the time of your ancestors you have turned away from my decrees and have not kept them. Return to me, and I will return to you," says the LORD Almighty.

"But you ask, 'How are we to return?'

---

[a] 10 Or *father*   [b] 12 Or *12May the LORD remove from the tents of Jacob anyone who gives testimony in behalf of the man who does this*   [c] 15 The meaning of the Hebrew for the first part of this verse is uncertain.   [d] 16 Or *"I hate divorce," says the LORD, the God of Israel, "because the man who divorces his wife covers his garment with violence,"*

8"Will a mere mortal rob God? Yet you rob me.

"But you ask, 'How are we robbing you?'

"In tithes and offerings. 9You are under a curse — your whole nation — because you are robbing me. 10Bring the whole tithe into the storehouse, that there may be food in my house. Test me in this," says the LORD Almighty, "and see if I will not throw open the floodgates of heaven and pour out so much blessing that there will not be room enough to store it. 11I will prevent pests from devouring your crops, and the vines in your fields will not drop their fruit before it is ripe," says the LORD Almighty. 12"Then all the nations will call you blessed, for yours will be a delightful land," says the LORD Almighty.

Israel Speaks Arrogantly Against God

13"You have spoken arrogantly against me," says the LORD.

"Yet you ask, 'What have we said against you?'

14"You have said, 'It is futile to serve God. What do we gain by carrying out his requirements and going about like mourners before the LORD Almighty? 15But now we call the arrogant blessed. Certainly evildoers prosper, and even when they put God to the test, they get away with it.'"

The Faithful Remnant

16Then those who feared the LORD talked with each other, and the LORD listened and heard. A scroll of remembrance was written in his presence concerning those who feared the LORD and honored his name.

17"On the day when I act," says the LORD Almighty, "they will be my treasured possession. I will spare them, just as a father has compassion and spares his son who serves him. 18And you will again see the distinction between the righteous and the wicked, between those who serve God and those who do not.

Judgment and Covenant Renewal

4 a "Surely the day is coming; it will burn like a furnace. All the arrogant and every evildoer will be stubble, and the day that is coming will set them on fire," says the LORD Almighty. "Not a root or a branch will be left to them. 2But for you who revere my name, the sun of righteousness will rise with healing in its rays. And you will go out and frolic like well-fed calves. 3Then you will trample on the wicked; they will be ashes under the soles of your feet on the day when I act," says the LORD Almighty.

4"Remember the law of my servant Moses, the decrees and laws I gave him at Horeb for all Israel.

5"See, I will send the prophet Elijah to you before that great and dreadful day of the LORD comes. 6He will turn the hearts of the parents to their children, and the hearts of the children to their parents; or else I will come and strike the land with total destruction."

---

a In Hebrew texts 4:1-6 is numbered 3:19-24.

The New Testament

Matthew

THEME: Mercy and justice are to be paramount virtues in a Christian's life. Mercy dictates love for fellow human beings and directly affects a believer's relationship to God.

AUTHOR: The author of this Gospel was probably Matthew (Levi), the man who left his tax office to follow Jesus (see character study on page 1140).

DATE OF WRITING: Matthew was probably written between AD 70 and 80.

ENCOURAGEMENT FROM MATTHEW: "Are not two sparrows sold for a penny? Yet not one of them will fall to the ground outside your Father's care. And even the very hairs of your head are all numbered. So don't be afraid; you are worth more than many sparrows" (Matthew 10:29 – 31).

CHALLENGE FROM MATTHEW: "Watch and pray so that you will not fall into temptation. The spirit is willing, but the flesh is weak" (Matthew 26:41).

REFLECTION FROM MATTHEW: "Then Peter came to Jesus and asked, 'Lord, how many times shall I forgive my brother or sister who sins against me? Up to seven times?' Jesus answered, 'I tell you, not seven times, but seventy-seven times'" (Matthew 18:21 – 22).

Jesus Christ is the one and only Higher Power. He alone is able to save us from our sins and provide the way of access into heaven. In order to find true healing from our hurts, hang-ups and habits, we must turn our lives and wills over to his care. But most of us are not willing to trust our lives and future to someone we've never met. That's exactly what makes the Gospel of Matthew so amazing. Our Savior isn't hiding behind some mysterious religious haze. Instead, we are able to meet Jesus in an intimate way for the first time.

In this book we witness Jesus' unflinching confrontation with Satan, learning from our Lord's handling of temptation how we can face down our own enticements to fall back under the spell of whatever has allured us from the way of truth. We get to see him healing the sick, and we are allowed access into his darkest hours and his most glorious moments.

In Matthew Jesus delivers his most famous sermon, the Sermon on the Mount. This sermon is the foundation for the eight principles of Celebrate Recovery. Jesus cares deeply about our hurts, hang-ups and habits and wants us to find victory over them by trusting in him. The book of Matthew begins to give us a picture of what kind of a Savior Jesus is and what he can do for us today.

The Genealogy of Jesus the Messiah

1 This is the genealogy[a] of Jesus the Messiah[b] the son of David, the son of Abraham:

2 Abraham was the father of Isaac,
Isaac the father of Jacob,
Jacob the father of Judah and his brothers,
3 Judah the father of Perez and Zerah, whose mother was Tamar,
Perez the father of Hezron,
Hezron the father of Ram,
4 Ram the father of Amminadab,
Amminadab the father of Nahshon,
Nahshon the father of Salmon,
5 Salmon the father of Boaz, whose mother was Rahab,
Boaz the father of Obed, whose mother was Ruth,
Obed the father of Jesse,
6 and Jesse the father of King David.

David was the father of Solomon, whose mother had been Uriah's wife,
7 Solomon the father of Rehoboam,
Rehoboam the father of Abijah,
Abijah the father of Asa,
8 Asa the father of Jehoshaphat,
Jehoshaphat the father of Jehoram,
Jehoram the father of Uzziah,
9 Uzziah the father of Jotham,
Jotham the father of Ahaz,
Ahaz the father of Hezekiah,
10 Hezekiah the father of Manasseh,
Manasseh the father of Amon,
Amon the father of Josiah,
11 and Josiah the father of Jeconiah[c] and his brothers at the time of the exile to Babylon.

12 After the exile to Babylon:
Jeconiah was the father of Shealtiel,
Shealtiel the father of Zerubbabel,
13 Zerubbabel the father of Abihud,
Abihud the father of Eliakim,
Eliakim the father of Azor,
14 Azor the father of Zadok,
Zadok the father of Akim,
Akim the father of Elihud,
15 Elihud the father of Eleazar,
Eleazar the father of Matthan,
Matthan the father of Jacob,
16 and Jacob the father of Joseph, the husband of Mary, and Mary was the mother of Jesus who is called the Messiah.

17 Thus there were fourteen generations in all from Abraham to David, fourteen from David to the exile to Babylon, and fourteen from the exile to the Messiah.

Joseph Accepts Jesus as His Son

18 This is how the birth of Jesus the Messiah came about[d]: His mother Mary was pledged to be married to Joseph, but before they came together, she was found to be pregnant through the Holy Spirit. 19 Because Joseph her husband was faithful to the law, and yet[e] did not want to expose her to public disgrace, he had in mind to divorce her quietly.

20 But after he had considered this, an angel of the Lord appeared to him in a dream and said, "Joseph son of David, do not be afraid to take Mary home as your wife, because what is conceived in her is from the Holy Spirit. 21 She will give birth to a son, and you are to give him the name Jesus,[f] because he will save his people from their sins."

22 All this took place to fulfill what the Lord had said through the prophet: 23 "The virgin will conceive and give birth to a son, and they will call him Immanuel"[g] (which means "God with us").

24 When Joseph woke up, he did what the angel of the Lord had commanded him and

---

a 1 Or *is an account of the origin*   *b 1* Or *Jesus Christ. Messiah* (Hebrew) and *Christ* (Greek) both mean *Anointed One*; also in verse 18.   *c 11* That is, Jehoiachin; also in verse 12   *d 18* Or *The origin of Jesus the Messiah was like this*   *e 19* Or *was a righteous man and*   *f 21* *Jesus* is the Greek form of *Joshua*, which means *the LORD saves.*   *g 23* Isaiah 7:14

took Mary home as his wife. 25But he did not consummate their marriage until she gave birth to a son. And he gave him the name Jesus.

The Magi Visit the Messiah

2 After Jesus was born in Bethlehem in Judea, during the time of King Herod, Magi*a* from the east came to Jerusalem 2and asked, "Where is the one who has been born king of the Jews? We saw his star when it rose and have come to worship him."

3When King Herod heard this he was disturbed, and all Jerusalem with him. 4When he had called together all the people's chief priests and teachers of the law, he asked them where the Messiah was to be born. 5"In Bethlehem in Judea," they replied, "for this is what the prophet has written:

6" 'But you, Bethlehem, in the land of
Judah,
are by no means least among the
rulers of Judah;
for out of you will come a ruler
who will shepherd my people
Israel.'*b*"

7Then Herod called the Magi secretly and found out from them the exact time the star had appeared. 8He sent them to Bethlehem and said, "Go and search carefully for the child. As soon as you find him, report to me, so that I too may go and worship him."

9After they had heard the king, they went on their way, and the star they had seen when it rose went ahead of them until it stopped over the place where the child was. 10When they saw the star, they were overjoyed. 11On coming to the house, they saw the child with his mother Mary, and they bowed down and worshiped him. Then they opened their treasures and presented him with gifts of gold, frankincense and myrrh. 12And having been warned in

a dream not to go back to Herod, they returned to their country by another route.

The Escape to Egypt

13When they had gone, an angel of the Lord appeared to Joseph in a dream. "Get up," he said, "take the child and his mother and escape to Egypt. Stay there until I tell you, for Herod is going to search for the child to kill him."

14So he got up, took the child and his mother during the night and left for Egypt, 15where he stayed until the death of Herod. And so was fulfilled what the Lord had said through the prophet: "Out of Egypt I called my son."*c*

16When Herod realized that he had been outwitted by the Magi, he was furious, and he gave orders to kill all the boys in Bethlehem and its vicinity who were two years old and under, in accordance with the time he had learned from the Magi. 17Then what was said through the prophet Jeremiah was fulfilled:

18"A voice is heard in Ramah,
weeping and great mourning,
Rachel weeping for her children
and refusing to be comforted,
because they are no more."*d*

The Return to Nazareth

19After Herod died, an angel of the Lord appeared in a dream to Joseph in Egypt 20and said, "Get up, take the child and his mother and go to the land of Israel, for those who were trying to take the child's life are dead."

21So he got up, took the child and his mother and went to the land of Israel. 22But when he heard that Archelaus was reigning in Judea in place of his father Herod, he was afraid to go there. Having been warned in a dream, he withdrew to the district of Galilee, 23and he went and lived in a town called Nazareth. So was fulfilled what was said through the prophets, that he would be called a Nazarene.

---

a 1 Traditionally *wise men*   *b 6* Micah 5:2,4   *c 15* Hosea 11:1   *d 18* Jer. 31:15

John the Baptist Prepares the Way

3 In those days John the Baptist came, preaching in the wilderness of Judea ²and saying, "Repent, for the kingdom of heaven has come near." ³This is he who was spoken of through the prophet Isaiah:

> "A voice of one calling in the wilderness,
> 'Prepare the way for the Lord,
>   make straight paths for him.'"ᵃ

⁴John's clothes were made of camel's hair, and he had a leather belt around his waist. His food was locusts and wild honey. ⁵People went out to him from Jerusalem and all Judea and the whole region of the Jordan. ⁶Confessing their sins, they were baptized by him in the Jordan River.

⁷But when he saw many of the Pharisees and Sadducees coming to where he was baptizing, he said to them: "You brood of vipers! Who warned you to flee from the coming wrath? ⁸Produce fruit in keeping with repentance. ⁹And do not think you can say to yourselves, 'We have Abraham as our father.' I tell you that out of these stones God can raise up children for Abraham. ¹⁰The ax is already at the root of the trees, and every tree that does not produce good fruit will be cut down and thrown into the fire.

¹¹"I baptize you withᵇ water for repentance. But after me comes one who is more powerful than I, whose sandals I am not worthy to carry. He will baptize you withᵇ the Holy Spirit and fire. ¹²His winnowing fork is in his hand, and he will clear his threshing floor, gathering his wheat into the barn and burning up the chaff with unquenchable fire."

The Baptism of Jesus

¹³Then Jesus came from Galilee to the Jordan to be baptized by John. ¹⁴But John tried to deter him, saying, "I need to be baptized by you, and do you come to me?"

¹⁵Jesus replied, "Let it be so now; it is proper for us to do this to fulfill all righteousness." Then John consented.

¹⁶As soon as Jesus was baptized, he went up out of the water. At that moment heaven was opened, and he saw the Spirit of God descending like a dove and alighting on him. ¹⁷And a voice from heaven said, "This is my Son, whom I love; with him I am well pleased."

Jesus Is Tested in the Wilderness

4 Then Jesus was led by the Spirit into the wilderness to be temptedᶜ by the devil. ²After fasting forty days and forty nights, he was hungry. ³The tempter came to him and said, "If you are the Son of God, tell these stones to become bread."

⁴Jesus answered, "It is written: 'Man shall not live on bread alone, but on every word that comes from the mouth of God.'ᵈ"

⁵Then the devil took him to the holy city and had him stand on the highest point of the temple. ⁶"If you are the Son of God," he said, "throw yourself down. For it is written:

> "'He will command his angels
>   concerning you,
>   and they will lift you up in their
>   hands,
>   so that you will not strike your foot
>   against a stone.'ᵉ"

⁷Jesus answered him, "It is also written: 'Do not put the Lord your God to the test.'ᶠ"

⁸Again, the devil took him to a very high mountain and showed him all the kingdoms of the world and their splendor. ⁹"All this I will give you," he said, "if you will bow down and worship me."

¹⁰Jesus said to him, "Away from me, Satan! For it is written: 'Worship the Lord your God, and serve him only.'ᵍ"

¹¹Then the devil left him, and angels came and attended him.

ᵃ 3 Isaiah 40:3   ᵇ 11 Or in   ᶜ 1 The Greek for tempted can also mean tested.   ᵈ 4 Deut. 8:3
ᵉ 6 Psalm 91:11,12   ᶠ 7 Deut. 6:16   ᵍ 10 Deut. 6:13

Jesus Begins to Preach

¹²When Jesus heard that John had been put in prison, he withdrew to Galilee. ¹³Leaving Nazareth, he went and lived in Capernaum, which was by the lake in the area of Zebulun and Naphtali— ¹⁴to fulfill what was said through the prophet Isaiah:

¹⁵ "Land of Zebulun and land of Naphtali,
    the Way of the Sea, beyond the
        Jordan,
    Galilee of the Gentiles—
¹⁶ the people living in darkness
        have seen a great light;
    on those living in the land of the
            shadow of death
        a light has dawned."ᵃ

¹⁷From that time on Jesus began to preach, "Repent, for the kingdom of heaven has come near."

Jesus Calls His First Disciples

¹⁸As Jesus was walking beside the Sea of Galilee, he saw two brothers, Simon called Peter and his brother Andrew. They were casting a net into the lake, for they were fishermen. ¹⁹"Come, follow me," Jesus said, "and I will send you out to fish for people." ²⁰At once they left their nets and followed him.

²¹Going on from there, he saw two other brothers, James son of Zebedee and his brother John. They were in a boat with their father Zebedee, preparing their nets. Jesus called them, ²²and immediately they left the boat and their father and followed him.

Jesus Heals the Sick

²³Jesus went throughout Galilee, teaching in their synagogues, proclaiming the good news of the kingdom, and healing every disease and sickness among the people. ²⁴News about him spread all over Syria, and people brought to him all who were ill with various diseases, those suffering severe pain, the demon-possessed, those having seizures, and the paralyzed; and he healed them. ²⁵Large crowds from Galilee, the Decapolis,ᵇ Jerusalem, Judea and the region across the Jordan followed him.

Introduction to the Sermon on the Mount

5 Now when Jesus saw the crowds, he went up on a mountainside and sat down. His disciples came to him, ²and he began to teach them.

The Beatitudes

He said:

³ "Blessed are the poor in spirit,
        for theirs is the kingdom of heaven.
⁴ Blessed are those who mourn,
        for they will be comforted.
⁵ Blessed are the meek,
        for they will inherit the earth.
⁶ Blessed are those who hunger and thirst
            for righteousness,
        for they will be filled.
⁷ Blessed are the merciful,
        for they will be shown mercy.
⁸ Blessed are the pure in heart,
        for they will see God.
⁹ Blessed are the peacemakers,
        for they will be called children of
            God.
¹⁰ Blessed are those who are persecuted
            because of righteousness,
        for theirs is the kingdom of heaven.

¹¹ "Blessed are you when people insult you, persecute you and falsely say all kinds of evil against you because of me. ¹²Rejoice and be glad, because great is your reward in heaven, for in the same way they persecuted the prophets who were before you.

Salt and Light

¹³ "You are the salt of the earth. But if the salt loses its saltiness, how can it be made salty again? It is no longer good for anything, except to be thrown out and trampled underfoot.

¹⁴ "You are the light of the world. A town

ᵃ 16 Isaiah 9:1,2   ᵇ 25 That is, the Ten Cities

built on a hill cannot be hidden. ¹⁵Neither do people light a lamp and put it under a bowl. Instead they put it on its stand, and it gives light to everyone in the house. ¹⁶In the same way, let your light shine before others, that they may see your good deeds and glorify your Father in heaven.

The Fulfillment of the Law

¹⁷"Do not think that I have come to abolish the Law or the Prophets; I have not come to abolish them but to fulfill them. ¹⁸For truly I tell you, until heaven and earth disappear, not the smallest letter, not the least stroke of a pen, will by any means disappear from the Law until everything is accomplished. ¹⁹Therefore anyone who sets aside one of the least of these commands and teaches others accordingly will be called least in the kingdom of heaven, but whoever practices and teaches these commands will be called great in the kingdom of heaven. ²⁰For I tell you that unless your righteousness surpasses that of the Pharisees and the teachers of the law, you will certainly not enter the kingdom of heaven.

Murder

²¹"You have heard that it was said to the people long ago, 'You shall not murder,ᵃ and anyone who murders will be subject to judgment.' ²²But I tell you that anyone who is angry with a brother or sisterᵇ,ᶜ will be subject to judgment. Again, anyone who says to a brother or sister, 'Raca,'ᵈ is answerable to the court. And anyone who says, 'You fool!' will be in danger of the fire of hell.

²³"Therefore, if you are offering your gift at the altar and there remember that your brother or sister has something against you, ²⁴leave your gift there in front of the altar. First go and be reconciled to them; then come and offer your gift.

²⁵"Settle matters quickly with your adversary who is taking you to court. Do it while you are still together on the way, or your adversary may hand you over to the judge, and the judge may hand you over to the officer, and you may be thrown into prison. ²⁶Truly I tell you, you will not get out until you have paid the last penny.

Adultery

²⁷"You have heard that it was said, 'You shall not commit adultery.'ᵉ ²⁸But I tell you that anyone who looks at a woman lustfully has already committed adultery with her in his heart. ²⁹If your right eye causes you to stumble, gouge it out and throw it away. It is better for you to lose one part of your body than for your whole body to be thrown into hell. ³⁰And if your right hand causes you to stumble, cut it off and throw it away. It is better for you to lose one part of your body than for your whole body to go into hell.

Divorce

³¹"It has been said, 'Anyone who divorces his wife must give her a certificate of divorce.'ᶠ ³²But I tell you that anyone who divorces his wife, except for sexual immorality, makes her the victim of adultery, and anyone who marries a divorced woman commits adultery.

Oaths

³³"Again, you have heard that it was said to the people long ago, 'Do not break your oath, but fulfill to the Lord the vows you have made.' ³⁴But I tell you, do not swear an oath at all: either by heaven, for it is God's throne; ³⁵or by the earth, for it is his footstool; or by Jerusalem, for it is the city of the Great King. ³⁶And do not swear by your head, for you cannot make even one hair white or black. ³⁷All you need to say is simply 'Yes' or 'No'; anything beyond this comes from the evil one.ᵍ

Eye for Eye

³⁸"You have heard that it was said, 'Eye for eye, and tooth for tooth.'ʰ ³⁹But I tell

---

ᵃ 21 Exodus 20:13   ᵇ 22 The Greek word for *brother or sister* (*adelphos*) refers here to a fellow disciple, whether man or woman; also in verse 23.   ᶜ 22 Some manuscripts *brother or sister without cause*   ᵈ 22 An Aramaic term of contempt   ᵉ 27 Exodus 20:14   ᶠ 31 Deut. 24:1   ᵍ 37 Or *from evil*   ʰ 38 Exodus 21:24; Lev. 24:20; Deut. 19:21

CROSSROADS LESSON [*Principle Seven*]

For the previous entry in the CROSSROADS lesson, go to 1 John 1:8 – 10 (page 1557).

For a discussion of Principles One through Eight and a listing of their related lessons, go to pages xvii – xliv.

If you are offering your gift at the altar and there remember
that your brother or sister has something against you,
leave your gift there in front of the altar. First go and be reconciled
to them; then come and offer your gift.

MATTHEW 5:23–24

In Principle Seven we reserve a daily quiet time with God for self-examination, Bible reading and prayer in order to get to know God and his will for our lives and to gain the power to follow his will. We're at the CROSSROADS of our recovery. We need to thank God for getting us this far on our road to recovery, to praise him for the many victories we've already experienced over our hurts, hang-ups and habits. But we also need to continue working the last two principles with the same devotion and enthusiasm that got us to this point in our recovery. In the first part of Principle Seven we reserve a daily quiet time with God for self-examination. This relates to Step Ten of the Christ-centered 12 steps.

Step Ten: We continued to take personal inventory and, when we were wrong, promptly admitted it.

This principle is made up of three key actions. The third action is represented by the letter *N* of Step TEN: NEED TO ADMIT OUR WRONGS PROMPTLY. John 3:21 declares, "Whoever lives by the truth comes into the light, so that it may be seen plainly that what they have done has been in the sight of God." This principle brings us, on a daily basis, into the light. Once we see that light, we have a choice: We can ignore it or we can act on it. If we act on it on a daily basis, we're working Principle Seven. We need to admit our wrongs and make amends promptly.

As soon as we realize that we've blown it, we need to promptly admit it. That's precisely what Jesus is telling us to do in Matthew 5:23 – 24.

One way to easily keep track of our day, focusing on our good and bad behaviors, is to keep a journal. Our journal isn't a place to jot down the calories we've ingested for lunch today or our carpool schedule for school. It's a tool for us to review and record the good and the bad things we've done today.

We should look for negative patterns and issues that we're continually writing down and having to make amends for — again and again. We then need to share them with our sponsor or accountability partner, and set up an action plan so that we can overcome them with God's help. We should start each day's entry with one thing from our experiences of the day for which we're thankful. That will get us writing.

This is the final page of the CROSSROADS lesson.

you, do not resist an evil person. If anyone slaps you on the right cheek, turn to them the other cheek also. 40 And if anyone wants to sue you and take your shirt, hand over your coat as well. 41 If anyone forces you to go one mile, go with them two miles. 42 Give to the one who asks you, and do not turn away from the one who wants to borrow from you.

Love for Enemies

43 "You have heard that it was said, 'Love your neighbor*a* and hate your enemy.' 44 But I tell you, love your enemies and pray for those who persecute you, 45 that you may be children of your Father in heaven. He causes his sun to rise on the evil and the good, and sends rain on the righteous and the unrighteous. 46 If you love those who love you, what reward will you get? Are not even the tax collectors doing that? 47 And if you greet only your own people, what are you doing more than others? Do not even pagans do that? 48 Be perfect, therefore, as your heavenly Father is perfect.

Giving to the Needy

6 "Be careful not to practice your righteousness in front of others to be seen by them. If you do, you will have no reward from your Father in heaven.

2 "So when you give to the needy, do not announce it with trumpets, as the hypocrites do in the synagogues and on the streets, to be honored by others. Truly I tell you, they have received their reward in full. 3 But when you give to the needy, do not let your left hand know what your right hand is doing, 4 so that your giving may be in secret. Then your Father, who sees what is done in secret, will reward you.

Prayer

5 "And when you pray, do not be like the hypocrites, for they love to pray standing in the synagogues and on the street corners to be seen by others. Truly I tell you, they have received their reward in full. 6 But when you pray, go into your room, close the door and pray to your Father, who is unseen. Then your Father, who sees what is done in secret, will reward you. 7 And when you pray, do not keep on babbling like pagans, for they think they will be heard because of their many words. 8 Do not be like them, for your Father knows what you need before you ask him.

9 "This, then, is how you should pray:

"'Our Father in heaven,
    hallowed be your name,
10 your kingdom come,
    your will be done,
        on earth as it is in heaven.
11 Give us today our daily bread.
12 And forgive us our debts,
    as we also have forgiven our debtors.
13 And lead us not into temptation,*b*
    but deliver us from the evil one.*c*'

14 For if you forgive other people when they sin against you, your heavenly Father will also forgive you. 15 But if you do not forgive others their sins, your Father will not forgive your sins.

Fasting

16 "When you fast, do not look somber as the hypocrites do, for they disfigure their faces to show others they are fasting. Truly I tell you, they have received their reward in full. 17 But when you fast, put oil on your head and wash your face, 18 so that it will not be obvious to others that you are fasting, but only to your Father, who is unseen; and your Father, who sees what is done in secret, will reward you.

Treasures in Heaven

19 "Do not store up for yourselves treasures on earth, where moths and vermin destroy, and where thieves break in and steal. 20 But store up for yourselves trea-

---

a 43 Lev. 19:18   *b* 13 The Greek for *temptation* can also mean *testing.*   *c* 13 Or *from evil*; some late manuscripts one, / for yours is the kingdom and the power and the glory forever. Amen.

sures in heaven, where moths and vermin do not destroy, and where thieves do not break in and steal. 21For where your treasure is, there your heart will be also.

22"The eye is the lamp of the body. If your eyes are healthy,*a* your whole body will be full of light. 23But if your eyes are unhealthy,*b* your whole body will be full of darkness. If then the light within you is darkness, how great is that darkness!

24"No one can serve two masters. Either you will hate the one and love the other, or you will be devoted to the one and despise the other. You cannot serve both God and money.

Do Not Worry

25"Therefore I tell you, do not worry about your life, what you will eat or drink; or about your body, what you will wear. Is

---

a 22 The Greek for *healthy* here implies *generous.*   *b 23* The Greek for *unhealthy* here implies *stingy.*

SPIRITUAL INVENTORY LESSON [*Principle Four*]

This is the first page of the SPIRITUAL INVENTORY lesson.

For a discussion of Principles One through Eight and a listing of their related lessons,
go to pages xvii – xliv.

Forgive us our debts, as we also have forgiven our debtors.
And lead us not into temptation, but deliver us from the evil one.

MATTHEW 6:12–13

Principle Four begins the process of "coming clean." It's here that we openly examine and confess our faults to ourselves, to God and to someone else we trust. In the first part of Principle Four we openly examine our lives.

As part of completing Principle Four we do a SPIRITUAL INVENTORY. We look at eight critical areas of our lives. The first is our RELATIONSHIPS WITH OTHERS. We pray, as Jesus taught us in the Lord's Prayer (see Matthew 6:9 – 13), about our need to forgive those who have hurt us, just as we've been forgiven by the Lord. In order to offer forgiveness, we need to evaluate both our past and our present relationships with others.

We need to ask ourselves the following questions regarding our relationships with others:

1. Who has hurt us?

2. Against whom have we been holding a grudge?

3. Against whom are we still seeking revenge?

4. Are we jealous of someone? Who and why?

5. Have we tried to justify our bad attitude by pinning the blame on someone else?

6. Whom have we hurt?

7. Of whom have we been critical or gossiped about?

The second area of our Spiritual Inventory is OUR PRIORITIES IN LIFE.
Go to Matthew 6:33 (page 1134).

not life more than food, and the body more than clothes? 26Look at the birds of the air; they do not sow or reap or store away in barns, and yet your heavenly Father feeds them. Are you not much more valuable than they? 27Can any one of you by worrying add a single hour to your life*a*?

28"And why do you worry about clothes? See how the flowers of the field grow. They do not labor or spin. 29Yet I tell you that not even Solomon in all his splendor was dressed like one of these. 30If that is how God clothes the grass of the field, which is here today and tomorrow is thrown into the fire, will he not much more clothe you — you of little faith? 31So do not worry, saying, 'What shall we eat?' or 'What shall we drink?' or 'What shall we wear?' 32For

---

a 27 Or single cubit to your height

SPIRITUAL INVENTORY LESSON [*Principle Four*]

For the previous entry in the SPIRITUAL INVENTORY lesson, go to Matthew 6:12 – 13 (page 1133).

For a discussion of Principles One through Eight and a listing of their related lessons, go to pages xvii – xliv.

> *Seek first [God's] kingdom and his righteousness,*
> *and all these things will be given to you as well.*
>
> MATTHEW 6:33

Principle Four begins the process of "coming clean." It's here that we openly examine and confess our faults to ourselves, to God and to someone else we trust. In the first part of Principle Four we openly examine our lives.

As part of completing Principle Four we do a SPIRITUAL INVENTORY. We look at eight critical areas of our lives. The second area is OUR PRIORITIES IN LIFE. A guiding principle of human behavior is that we, as human beings, do whatever is important to us. Others can identify our priorities by our actions, not necessarily by our words. In Matthew 6:33 Jesus tells us what will happen if we make him our number-one priority: "All these [other necessary] things will be given to you as well."

We need to ask ourselves the following questions regarding our priorities in life:

1. After making the decision to turn over our lives and our will to God, in what areas of life are we still not putting God first? What closet are we refusing to let him enter and clean out?

2. What in our past is interfering with our willingness or ability to do God's will? Our ambition? Is our life driven by a desire to serve God or is it driven by envy or a desire for life's pleasures?

3. What have been our priorities in our job? Our friendships? Our personal goals?

4. Whom have our priorities affected?

5. What has been good about our priorities?

6. What has been wrong with them?

The third area of our Spiritual Inventory is OUR ATTITUDE. Go to Ephesians 4:31 (page 1470).

the pagans run after all these things, and your heavenly Father knows that you need them. ³³But seek first his kingdom and his righteousness, and all these things will be given to you as well. ³⁴Therefore do not worry about tomorrow, for tomorrow will worry about itself. Each day has enough trouble of its own.

Judging Others

7 "Do not judge, or you too will be judged. ²For in the same way you judge others, you will be judged, and with the measure you use, it will be measured to you.

³"Why do you look at the speck of sawdust in your brother's eye and pay no attention to the plank in your own eye? ⁴How can you say to your brother, 'Let me take the speck out of your eye,' when all the time there is a plank in your own eye? ⁵You hypocrite, first take the plank out of your own eye, and then you will see clearly to remove the speck from your brother's eye.

⁶"Do not give dogs what is sacred; do not throw your pearls to pigs. If you do, they may trample them under their feet, and turn and tear you to pieces.

Ask, Seek, Knock

⁷"Ask and it will be given to you; seek and you will find; knock and the door will be opened to you. ⁸For everyone who asks receives; the one who seeks finds; and to the one who knocks, the door will be opened.

⁹"Which of you, if your son asks for

POWERLESS LESSON [*Principle One*]

For the previous entry in the POWERLESS lesson, go to Luke 12:2 – 3 (page 1264).

For a discussion of Principles One through Eight and a listing of their related lessons, go to pages xvii – xliv.

Do not worry about tomorrow, for tomorrow will worry about itself. Each day has enough trouble of its own.

MATTHEW 6:34

The power to change comes only through God's grace. Principle One states: "Realize I'm not God. I admit that I'm powerless to control my tendency to do the wrong thing and that my life has become unmanageable." If we admit that we're powerless, we recognize our need for a power greater than ourselves to restore us. That power is our Higher Power, the one and only true Higher Power, Jesus Christ.

In Principle One we discover that we're POWERLESS to control our own lives and that our lives have become unmanageable. The *W* in POWERLESS stands for WORRYING. All worrying is a form of failing to trust God. Instead of fretting about things we can't possibly control, we need to focus on what God can do. It's a good idea to keep a copy of the Serenity Prayer in our pocket and in our heart as a continual reminder: "God, grant me the serenity to accept the things I cannot change, the courage to change the things I can, and the wisdom to know the difference."

By working this program and completing the principles, we can find that trust in — that relationship with — the one and only Higher Power, Jesus Christ. As we grow closer to him, we'll find that our anxiety begins to fade away.

The next letter in POWERLESS is *E*. Go to Ephesians 5:13 – 14 (page 1474).

bread, will give him a stone? ¹⁰Or if he asks for a fish, will give him a snake? ¹¹If you, then, though you are evil, know how to give good gifts to your children, how much more will your Father in heaven give good gifts to those who ask him! ¹²So in everything, do to others what you would have them do to you, for this sums up the Law and the Prophets.

The Narrow and Wide Gates

¹³"Enter through the narrow gate. For wide is the gate and broad is the road that leads to destruction, and many enter through it. ¹⁴But small is the gate and narrow the road that leads to life, and only a few find it.

True and False Prophets

¹⁵"Watch out for false prophets. They come to you in sheep's clothing, but inwardly they are ferocious wolves. ¹⁶By their fruit you will recognize them. Do people pick grapes from thornbushes, or figs from thistles? ¹⁷Likewise, every good tree bears good fruit, but a bad tree bears bad fruit.

ACTION LESSON [Principle Three]

For the previous entry in the ACTION lesson, go to Philippians 1:6 (page 1478).

For a discussion of Principles One through Eight and a listing of their related lessons, go to pages xvii–xliv.

Do not worry about tomorrow, for tomorrow will worry about itself.
Each day has enough trouble of its own.

MATTHEW 6:34

In Principle Three we consciously choose to commit all our lives and will to Christ's care and control. We make the decision to TURN every aspect of our lives and will over to our Higher Power, Jesus Christ. In order to turn our lives over to Christ's care and control, we need to take ACTION.

The letter O in ACTION stands for ONE DAY AT A TIME. Our recovery happens just that way. If we remain stuck in yesterday or constantly worry about tomorrow, we'll waste the precious time God is giving us in the present. And it's only in the present that change and growth can occur. We can't change yesterday and we can only pray about tomorrow. In Matthew 6:34 Jesus gives us instructions for living in 24-hour segments.

Every one of us would like to go back and change something — or a lot of things — we did in the past. If we only had the chance, we would do so many things differently. We would choose to spare our family the pain our sin addictions and compulsive behaviors have caused. But we can't change even one thing that's already happened.

On the other side of the coin, we can't live somewhere way off in the future, always worrying about whether this or that is going to happen. We need to pray about tomorrow and then leave the particulars up to God. But we can live in today. And we can, with Christ's guidance and direction, make a difference in the way we live out each one of the todays God gives us. We can make a difference — one day at a time.

The last letter in ACTION is N. Go to 1 Corinthians 15:2–4 (page 1435).

18A good tree cannot bear bad fruit, and a bad tree cannot bear good fruit. 19Every tree that does not bear good fruit is cut down and thrown into the fire. 20Thus, by their fruit you will recognize them.

True and False Disciples

21"Not everyone who says to me, 'Lord, Lord,' will enter the kingdom of heaven, but only the one who does the will of my Father who is in heaven. 22Many will say to me on that day, 'Lord, Lord, did we not prophesy in your name and in your name drive out demons and in your name perform many miracles?' 23Then I will tell them plainly, 'I never knew you. Away from me, you evildoers!'

The Wise and Foolish Builders

24"Therefore everyone who hears these words of mine and puts them into practice is like a wise man who built his house on the rock. 25The rain came down, the streams rose, and the winds blew and beat against that house; yet it did not fall, because it had its foundation on the rock. 26But everyone who hears these words of mine and does not put them into practice

---

VICTORY LESSON [*Principle Five*]

For the previous entry in the VICTORY lesson, go to James 4:10 (page 1542).

For a discussion of Principles One through Eight and a listing of their related lessons,
go to pages xvii – xliv.

Do not worry about tomorrow, for tomorrow will worry about itself.
Each day has enough trouble of its own.

MATTHEW 6:34

In Principle Five, as we voluntarily submit to every change God wants to make in our lives and humbly ask him to remove our character defects, we'll find VICTORY in our recovery.

The next letter in VICTORY is *O*, which stands for ONE DAY AT A TIME. Our character defects didn't develop overnight, so we shouldn't expect them to instantly disappear. Recovery happens one day at a time. Our lifelong hurts, hang-ups and habits need to be worked on in 24-hour increments. There's an old maxim: "Life by the yard is hard; life by the inch is a cinch." Jesus is saying the same thing in Matthew 6:34. He's telling us to live in day-tight compartments.

In Exodus 3:14 "God said to Moses, 'I AM WHO I AM. This is what you are to say to the Israelites: "I AM has sent me to you."'" God is the God of our past, present and future. But the positive changes found in working Principle Five can only be made in the present. We can't change one thing we've done or one thing that's happened to us in our past. We can't always be consumed with worrying about what's going to happen to us in the future either. But with God's help we can steadily work on making the changes we so intensely desire in the present — today, tomorrow and the next day — one day at a time.

Remember, when we get weary or discouraged, Christ is always with us. In Matthew 11:28 he offers us comfort and encouragement: "Come to me, all you who are weary and burdened, and I will give you rest."

The next letter in VICTORY is *R*. Go to Philippians 1:6 (page 1479).

is like a foolish man who built his house on sand. ²⁷The rain came down, the streams rose, and the winds blew and beat against that house, and it fell with a great crash."

²⁸When Jesus had finished saying these things, the crowds were amazed at his teaching, ²⁹because he taught as one who had authority, and not as their teachers of the law.

Jesus Heals a Man With Leprosy

8 When Jesus came down from the mountainside, large crowds followed him. ²A man with leprosy*a* came and knelt before him and said, "Lord, if you are willing, you can make me clean."

³Jesus reached out his hand and touched the man. "I am willing," he said. "Be clean!" Immediately he was cleansed of his leprosy. ⁴Then Jesus said to him, "See that you don't tell anyone. But go, show yourself to the priest and offer the gift Moses commanded, as a testimony to them."

The Faith of the Centurion

⁵When Jesus had entered Capernaum, a centurion came to him, asking for help. ⁶"Lord," he said, "my servant lies at home paralyzed, suffering terribly."

⁷Jesus said to him, "Shall I come and heal him?"

⁸The centurion replied, "Lord, I do not deserve to have you come under my roof. But just say the word, and my servant will be healed. ⁹For I myself am a man under authority, with soldiers under me. I tell this one, 'Go,' and he goes; and that one, 'Come,' and he comes. I say to my servant, 'Do this,' and he does it."

¹⁰When Jesus heard this, he was amazed and said to those following him, "Truly I tell you, I have not found anyone in Isra-

---

a 2 The Greek word traditionally translated *leprosy* was used for various diseases affecting the skin.

CONFESS LESSON [*Principle Four*]

For the previous entry in the CONFESS lesson, go to Psalm 32:3 – 5 (page 652).

For a discussion of Principles One through Eight and a listing of their related lessons, go to pages xvii – xliv.

Why do you look at the speck of sawdust in your brother's eye and pay no attention to the plank in your own eye?

MATTHEW 7:3

Principle Four begins the process of "coming clean." In the second part of Principle Four, we confess our faults to ourselves, to God and to someone else we trust.

The first *S* in CONFESS stands for STOP THE BLAME. That's the third positive change that results from confessing our faults. It's been said that people who can smile when something goes wrong have probably just thought of somebody to blame it on. But the truth is that we can't find peace and serenity if we continue to blame ourselves or others. Our secrets have isolated us from each other long enough. They've prevented intimacy in all of our important relationships. When we confess, we accept the blame for the wrongs we've committed and are freed to move ahead in our recovery.

The last letter in CONFESS is the second S. Go to 2 Corinthians 5:19 (page 1445).

el with such great faith. ¹¹I say to you that many will come from the east and the west, and will take their places at the feast with Abraham, Isaac and Jacob in the kingdom of heaven. ¹²But the subjects of the kingdom will be thrown outside, into the darkness, where there will be weeping and gnashing of teeth."

¹³Then Jesus said to the centurion, "Go! Let it be done just as you believed it would." And his servant was healed at that moment.

Jesus Heals Many

¹⁴When Jesus came into Peter's house, he saw Peter's mother-in-law lying in bed with a fever. ¹⁵He touched her hand and the fever left her, and she got up and began to wait on him.

¹⁶When evening came, many who were demon-possessed were brought to him, and he drove out the spirits with a word and healed all the sick. ¹⁷This was to fulfill what was spoken through the prophet Isaiah:

> "He took up our infirmities
>   and bore our diseases."ᵃ

The Cost of Following Jesus

¹⁸When Jesus saw the crowd around him, he gave orders to cross to the other side of the lake. ¹⁹Then a teacher of the law came to him and said, "Teacher, I will follow you wherever you go."

²⁰Jesus replied, "Foxes have dens and birds have nests, but the Son of Man has no place to lay his head."

²¹Another disciple said to him, "Lord, first let me go and bury my father."

²²But Jesus told him, "Follow me, and let the dead bury their own dead."

Jesus Calms the Storm

²³Then he got into the boat and his disciples followed him. ²⁴Suddenly a furious storm came up on the lake, so that the waves swept over the boat. But Jesus was sleeping. ²⁵The disciples went and woke him, saying, "Lord, save us! We're going to drown!"

²⁶He replied, "You of little faith, why are you so afraid?" Then he got up and rebuked the winds and the waves, and it was completely calm.

²⁷The men were amazed and asked, "What kind of man is this? Even the winds and the waves obey him!"

Jesus Restores Two Demon-Possessed Men

²⁸When he arrived at the other side in the region of the Gadarenes,ᵇ two demon-possessed men coming from the tombs met him. They were so violent that no one could pass that way. ²⁹"What do you want with us, Son of God?" they shouted. "Have you come here to torture us before the appointed time?"

³⁰Some distance from them a large herd of pigs was feeding. ³¹The demons begged Jesus, "If you drive us out, send us into the herd of pigs."

³²He said to them, "Go!" So they came out and went into the pigs, and the whole herd rushed down the steep bank into the lake and died in the water. ³³Those tending the pigs ran off, went into the town and reported all this, including what had happened to the demon-possessed men. ³⁴Then the whole town went out to meet Jesus. And when they saw him, they pleaded with him to leave their region.

Jesus Forgives and Heals a Paralyzed Man

9 Jesus stepped into a boat, crossed over and came to his own town. ²Some men brought to him a paralyzed man, lying on a mat. When Jesus saw their faith, he said to the man, "Take heart, son; your sins are forgiven."

³At this, some of the teachers of the law said to themselves, "This fellow is blaspheming!"

⁴Knowing their thoughts, Jesus said,

ᵃ 17 Isaiah 53:4 (see Septuagint)   ᵇ 28 Some manuscripts *Gergesenes*; other manuscripts *Gerasenes*

MY NAME IS MATTHEW

MATTHEW 9:9–13

Matthew held a lucrative post in Capernaum. He collected taxes on a major trade route that passed by the city. His profession put him in a category with "sinners" (Matthew 9:10–11), according to the religious leaders and most of the people. Tax collectors supported the Roman Empire, represented by the hated Herodian rulers who served as puppet kings in service to Rome. Matthew's profit came from coercing as much as possible from the populace, backed by the power of Roman soldiers. The people seldom saw the Roman rulers or the Herods, but they saw Matthew every day as a symbol of oppression. No wonder the tax collector was in the same category as a thief or prostitute in the minds of the people.

Ironically, although the people saw Matthew as a curse upon God's people, his name in Hebrew means "gift of Yahweh." Jesus saw through to Matthew's potential, rightly identifying him as one who could become a gift to his own people. In the same way, our Savior sees each of us as a treasure, even when others can see only our failings. Jesus not only "saw a man named Matthew" (9:9), but he called the sinner to follow him. Incredibly, Matthew immediately left his tax collector's booth to follow Jesus (see v. 9).

Matthew's recovery involved several essential actions. First, he made a break with his past. Matthew was seated, comfortable in his love of money. But at the invitation from the Messiah, he "got up" (v. 9) and left behind the tools of his sinful trade. Second, Matthew "followed" (v. 9) Jesus. Recovery is a forward process, both in outlook and in motion. Third, Matthew reached out to others who needed to meet Jesus (see v. 10). He began with other outcasts like himself. While he had left his own past behind, he never forgot how desperate he had been for the call of Christ (Principle Eight).

Matthew invited Jesus into his home for dinner and then summoned all the "ugly people" to join in his celebration of God's love. He immediately recognized the importance of sharing what he had found in Christ. In recovery, the "I" must become "we." We can't travel the road to recovery alone. The pronoun *I* never appears in the twelve steps. It's absolutely essential that we work together, never in isolation. Recovery will bring a change in our companions in two ways. We'll exchange our regular associates from those in denial to those who are walking with us on the road to recovery. But, hopefully, some of our old cronies will change too as we provide them with an example of Christ's life-changing power.

Jesus loved the crowd that filled Matthew's house and caused the pious to protest. In fact, when Jesus overheard the criticism of the Pharisees (see v. 11), he declared, "It is not the healthy who need a doctor, but the sick" (v. 12). Jesus was referring to sin-sickness, not to physical ailments.

Jesus went on to share a lesson from the Old Testament with the Pharisees, who considered themselves to be the chosen instructors in God's law. He reminded them that rituals and sacrifices mean little to God in the absence of mercy (see v. 13, which includes a quote from Hosea 6:6). Celebrate Recovery is a reminder to today's churches that Jesus is at home only in places where sinners are sought out and made to feel welcome.

"Why do you entertain evil thoughts in your hearts? [5]Which is easier: to say, 'Your sins are forgiven,' or to say, 'Get up and walk'? [6]But I want you to know that the Son of Man has authority on earth to forgive sins." So he said to the paralyzed man, "Get up, take your mat and go home." [7]Then the man got up and went home. [8]When the crowd saw this, they were filled with awe; and they praised God, who had given such authority to man.

The Calling of Matthew

[9]As Jesus went on from there, he saw a man named Matthew sitting at the tax collector's booth. "Follow me," he told him, and Matthew got up and followed him.

[10]While Jesus was having dinner at Matthew's house, many tax collectors and sinners came and ate with him and his disciples. [11]When the Pharisees saw this, they asked his disciples, "Why does your teacher eat with tax collectors and sinners?"

[12]On hearing this, Jesus said, "It is not the healthy who need a doctor, but the sick. [13]But go and learn what this means: 'I desire mercy, not sacrifice.'[a] For I have not come to call the righteous, but sinners."

Jesus Questioned About Fasting

[14]Then John's disciples came and asked him, "How is it that we and the Pharisees fast often, but your disciples do not fast?"

[15]Jesus answered, "How can the guests of the bridegroom mourn while he is with them? The time will come when the bridegroom will be taken from them; then they will fast.

[16]"No one sews a patch of unshrunk cloth on an old garment, for the patch will pull away from the garment, making the tear worse. [17]Neither do people pour new wine into old wineskins. If they do, the skins will burst; the wine will run out and the wineskins will be ruined. No, they pour new wine into new wineskins, and both are preserved."

Jesus Raises a Dead Girl and Heals a Sick Woman

[18]While he was saying this, a synagogue leader came and knelt before him and said, "My daughter has just died. But come and put your hand on her, and she will live." [19]Jesus got up and went with him, and so did his disciples.

[20]Just then a woman who had been subject to bleeding for twelve years came up behind him and touched the edge of his cloak. [21]She said to herself, "If I only touch his cloak, I will be healed."

[22]Jesus turned and saw her. "Take heart, daughter," he said, "your faith has healed you." And the woman was healed at that moment.

[23]When Jesus entered the synagogue leader's house and saw the noisy crowd and people playing pipes, [24]he said, "Go away. The girl is not dead but asleep." But they laughed at him. [25]After the crowd had been put outside, he went in and took the girl by the hand, and she got up. [26]News of this spread through all that region.

Jesus Heals the Blind and the Mute

[27]As Jesus went on from there, two blind men followed him, calling out, "Have mercy on us, Son of David!"

[28]When he had gone indoors, the blind men came to him, and he asked them, "Do you believe that I am able to do this?"

"Yes, Lord," they replied.

[29]Then he touched their eyes and said, "According to your faith let it be done to you"; [30]and their sight was restored. Jesus warned them sternly, "See that no one knows about this." [31]But they went out and spread the news about him all over that region.

[32]While they were going out, a man who was demon-possessed and could not talk was brought to Jesus. [33]And when the demon was driven out, the man who had been mute spoke. The crowd was amazed and said, "Nothing like this has ever been seen in Israel."

a 13 Hosea 6:6

My Name Is John

I'M A BELIEVER WHO STRUGGLES WITH ALCOHOL

Please read the story of Matthew's calling in Matthew 9:9 – 13.

I was raised in a good, Christian home and trained from an early age to be a servant of God. But after graduating from seminary with a master's degree in divinity, I walked away from my faith to pursue all that the world had to offer. I was a high tech sales rep in the mainframe computer industry, where the corporate motto was "Whatever it takes!" I became ruthless in the pursuit of winning and beating the competition.

I can truly identify with Matthew. My narcissistic craving for sex, drugs and the rock-and-roll lifestyle that justified everything with the Wall Street mentality ("greed is good") knew no limits. It should come as no great surprise that I lost my way in a sea of self-indulgence and ultimately became a blackout drinker. After achieving financial success and earning all the accolades I had come to believe would make a difference, I was on the verge of losing everything that mattered to me: my wife, my little girl and my career. I had already lost any hope that I would ever find that illusive sense of fulfillment. I figured that it just wasn't meant for people like me.

But God had other plans. In 1996 my family and I started attending Saddleback Church in Lake Forest, California, and there I heard the simple message that I did indeed matter to God. One Sunday a man told his story in church to illustrate that God is a God of second chances. He called himself a "functional alcoholic." Those two words hit me like a ton of bricks because that's what I had become, a functional alcoholic who got up every morning to go to work, promising myself on a stack of Bibles that I'd never drink again. Yet once I got home, I'd start the process all over again until I blacked out. My little, five-foot-one wife had to put me to bed.

On June 11, 1996, I came to Celebrate Recovery because I had no place else to go. I was done. I was sick and tired of being sick and tired, and I was ready to accept whatever help somebody had to offer. Three weeks later my relationship with my Lord and Savior was restored. I found my life verse: "Be still, and know that I am God" (Psalm 46:10). It was as though Jesus was saying, "Relax; I'm God and you're not. Trust me to take care of the things you can't. I'll show you how to live as one who is 'gentle and humble in heart'" (Matthew 11:29).

Jesus has been healing my sin addiction ever since that time. As I listen to his call to deny my agenda in favor of his plans for my life (see Mark 8:34), I find myself with a purpose for living and, finally, with a sense of fulfillment in doing what God had been calling me to do for so long. I guess it's possible to read this and doubt that a tangible miracle has taken place in my life. Some may suspect that I'm exaggerating the extent of the miracle, that I wasn't really that bad off. I don't want anyone to conclude that I had anything to do with this life change, so let me share a portion of my psychological profile taken shortly after I came into recovery:

Most people with this profile are hostile, resentful, irritable and angry. This person is despondent, argumentative, narcissistic, obnoxious and guilt ridden. A history of social maladjustment can be expected. Excessive demands may be made on others for attention and sympathy while demands by others are resented. The prognosis for whether or not therapy will be effective? POOR!

That's who I am by nature. Nevertheless, I'm happy, surrounded by friends who will be there whenever I need them, and ready to serve my Lord no matter what he asks of me. My prayer and hope is that, by reading my story, others will find the same power and hope I found when Jesus tapped me on the shoulder and urged, "Come back! I came for people like you, people who've lost their way trying to do it on their own, people who are ready to depend on me for the healing and hope they've always longed for. I'll set you free and take you on a journey that will fill your life with a sense of purpose and peace beyond anything you could ever have imagined." As he did with Matthew, Jesus simply beckoned to me: "Follow me" (Matthew 9:9). All we have to do is respond.

John

³⁴But the Pharisees said, "It is by the prince of demons that he drives out demons."

The Workers Are Few

³⁵Jesus went through all the towns and villages, teaching in their synagogues, proclaiming the good news of the kingdom and healing every disease and sickness. ³⁶When he saw the crowds, he had compassion on them, because they were harassed and helpless, like sheep without a shepherd. ³⁷Then he said to his disciples, "The harvest is plentiful but the workers are few. ³⁸Ask the Lord of the harvest, therefore, to send out workers into his harvest field."

Jesus Sends Out the Twelve

10 Jesus called his twelve disciples to him and gave them authority to drive out impure spirits and to heal every disease and sickness.

²These are the names of the twelve apostles: first, Simon (who is called Peter) and his brother Andrew; James son of Zebedee, and his brother John; ³Philip and Bartholomew; Thomas and Matthew the tax collector; James son of Alphaeus, and Thaddaeus; ⁴Simon the Zealot and Judas Iscariot, who betrayed him.

⁵These twelve Jesus sent out with the following instructions: "Do not go among the Gentiles or enter any town of the Samaritans. ⁶Go rather to the lost sheep of Israel. ⁷As you go, proclaim this message: 'The kingdom of heaven has come near.' ⁸Heal the sick, raise the dead, cleanse those who have leprosy,ᵃ drive out demons. Freely you have received; freely give.

⁹"Do not get any gold or silver or copper to take with you in your belts— ¹⁰no bag for the journey or extra shirt or sandals or a staff, for the worker is worth his keep. ¹¹Whatever town or village you enter, search there for some worthy person and stay at their house until you leave. ¹²As you enter the home, give it your greeting. ¹³If the home is deserving, let your peace rest on it; if it is not, let your peace return to you. ¹⁴If anyone will not welcome you or listen to your words, leave that home or town and shake the dust off your feet. ¹⁵Truly I tell you, it will be more bearable for Sodom and Gomorrah on the day of judgment than for that town.

¹⁶"I am sending you out like sheep among wolves. Therefore be as shrewd as snakes and as innocent as doves. ¹⁷Be on your guard; you will be handed over to the local councils and be flogged in the synagogues. ¹⁸On my account you will be brought before governors and kings as witnesses to them and to the Gentiles. ¹⁹But when they arrest you, do not worry about what to say or how to say it. At that time you will be given what to say, ²⁰for it will not be you speaking, but the Spirit of your Father speaking through you.

²¹"Brother will betray brother to death, and a father his child; children will rebel against their parents and have them put to death. ²²You will be hated by everyone because of me, but the one who stands firm to the end will be saved. ²³When you are persecuted in one place, flee to another. Truly I tell you, you will not finish going through the towns of Israel before the Son of Man comes.

²⁴"The student is not above the teacher, nor a servant above his master. ²⁵It is enough for students to be like their teachers, and servants like their masters. If the head of the house has been called Beelzebul, how much more the members of his household!

²⁶"So do not be afraid of them, for there is nothing concealed that will not be disclosed, or hidden that will not be made known. ²⁷What I tell you in the dark, speak in the daylight; what is whispered in your ear, proclaim from the roofs. ²⁸Do not be afraid of those who kill the body but cannot kill the soul. Rather, be afraid of the One who can destroy both soul and body in hell. ²⁹Are not two sparrows sold for a penny? Yet not one of them will fall to the

---

ᵃ 8 The Greek word traditionally translated *leprosy* was used for various diseases affecting the skin.

ground outside your Father's care.*a* 30 And even the very hairs of your head are all numbered. 31 So don't be afraid; you are worth more than many sparrows.

32 "Whoever acknowledges me before others, I will also acknowledge before my Father in heaven. 33 But whoever disowns me before others, I will disown before my Father in heaven.

34 "Do not suppose that I have come to bring peace to the earth. I did not come to bring peace, but a sword. 35 For I have come to turn

> " 'a man against his father,
>   a daughter against her mother,
>   a daughter-in-law against her mother-
>   in-law —
> 36   a man's enemies will be the members
>   of his own household.'*b*

37 "Anyone who loves their father or mother more than me is not worthy of me; anyone who loves their son or daughter more than me is not worthy of me. 38 Whoever does not take up their cross and follow me is not worthy of me. 39 Whoever finds their life will lose it, and whoever loses their life for my sake will find it.

40 "Anyone who welcomes you welcomes me, and anyone who welcomes me welcomes the one who sent me. 41 Whoever welcomes a prophet as a prophet will receive a prophet's reward, and whoever welcomes a righteous person as a righteous person will receive a righteous person's reward. 42 And if anyone gives even a cup of cold water to one of these little ones who is my disciple, truly I tell you, that person will certainly not lose their reward."

Jesus and John the Baptist

11 After Jesus had finished instructing his twelve disciples, he went on from there to teach and preach in the towns of Galilee.*c*

2 When John, who was in prison, heard about the deeds of the Messiah, he sent his disciples 3 to ask him, "Are you the one who is to come, or should we expect someone else?"

4 Jesus replied, "Go back and report to John what you hear and see: 5 The blind receive sight, the lame walk, those who have leprosy*d* are cleansed, the deaf hear, the dead are raised, and the good news is proclaimed to the poor. 6 Blessed is anyone who does not stumble on account of me."

7 As John's disciples were leaving, Jesus began to speak to the crowd about John: "What did you go out into the wilderness to see? A reed swayed by the wind? 8 If not, what did you go out to see? A man dressed in fine clothes? No, those who wear fine clothes are in kings' palaces. 9 Then what did you go out to see? A prophet? Yes, I tell you, and more than a prophet. 10 This is the one about whom it is written:

> " 'I will send my messenger ahead of
>   you,
>   who will prepare your way before
>   you.'*e*

11 Truly I tell you, among those born of women there has not risen anyone greater than John the Baptist; yet whoever is least in the kingdom of heaven is greater than he. 12 From the days of John the Baptist until now, the kingdom of heaven has been subjected to violence,*f* and violent people have been raiding it. 13 For all the Prophets and the Law prophesied until John. 14 And if you are willing to accept it, he is the Elijah who was to come. 15 Whoever has ears, let them hear.

16 "To what can I compare this generation? They are like children sitting in the marketplaces and calling out to others:

> 17 " 'We played the pipe for you,
>   and you did not dance;

---

a 29 Or *will*; or *knowledge*   *b 36* Micah 7:6   *c 1* Greek *in their towns*   *d 5* The Greek word traditionally translated *leprosy* was used for various diseases affecting the skin.   *e 10* Mal. 3:1   *f 12* Or *been forcefully advancing*

MY NAME IS
JOHN THE BAPTIST

MATTHEW 11:1–15

John the Baptist was a bold preacher who confronted his generation with a plainspoken call to repentance. Jesus confirmed John as a prophet and "more than a prophet" (Matthew 11:9) — John was the predicted messenger who prepared the way for the Christ. Jesus made the amazing statement, in fact, that no one had ever been born who was greater than John (see vv. 9–11). Yet John had a bout with doubt. He recognized Jesus as the Messiah, the long-awaited King of Israel, the Lamb of God. John had even heard the voice of God proclaiming that Jesus was his Son (see 3:17). Why, then, was the Messiah's messenger sitting in the dungeon of a king who had blatantly broken God's laws and who served the hated Romans? John had doubts that were fueled by big questions.

Doubt can divert us from the road to recovery. But doubt doesn't need to spell defeat. Doubt doesn't undo what God has already done in our life. But we need to do what John did with his qualms and questions: Take them to Jesus. He'll respond to us as he did to John. He'll send us messengers proclaiming his words and deeds (see 11:4). Our knowledge of what he has done in the past will confirm for us his healing, life-changing power (see v. 5). He'll commend us and our service to him (see vv. 7–15).

As great as Jesus proclaimed John to be, our Lord attached a puzzling addendum to his statement in verse 11: "Whoever is least in the kingdom of heaven is greater than [John]." John, remarkable as he was, during his own lifetime never got to enjoy the promised benefits of the kingdom. John lived and died under the law, the old Mosaic covenant. But we, as new covenant believers, enjoy many kingdom blessings John never experienced. One of the greatest of these is our unlimited, continuous access to God. With Jesus as our high priest, we can "approach God's throne of grace with confidence, so that we may receive mercy and find grace to help us in our time of need" (Hebrews 4:16). We need to reserve some time alone with God every day (Principle Seven).

When we have a bout with doubt, we can realize that we're going through a time of need. Unlike John, we don't have to send messengers to Jesus. We can take our doubts, questions, sins, needs and desires directly to him. When we do, we need to be ready for his messengers: our sponsor, accountability partner, pastor, friend or counselor. Thousands have already experienced God's life-changing power through Celebrate Recovery. Seek them out and listen to their stories. Even John needed testimonies from others to encourage him in his faith. That's why almost half of the Large Group meetings in Celebrate Recovery focus on a recovery testimony. Jesus wants you to succeed and desires to applaud you for your service, just as he did John.

we sang a dirge,
and you did not mourn.'

18For John came neither eating nor drinking, and they say, 'He has a demon.' 19The Son of Man came eating and drinking, and they say, 'Here is a glutton and a drunkard, a friend of tax collectors and sinners.' But wisdom is proved right by her deeds."

Woe on Unrepentant Towns

20Then Jesus began to denounce the towns in which most of his miracles had been performed, because they did not repent. 21"Woe to you, Chorazin! Woe to you, Bethsaida! For if the miracles that were performed in you had been performed in Tyre and Sidon, they would have repented long ago in sackcloth and ashes. 22But I tell you, it will be more bearable for Tyre and Sidon on the day of judgment than for you. 23And you, Capernaum, will you be lifted to the heavens? No, you will go down to Hades.*a* For if the miracles that were performed in you had been performed in Sodom, it would have remained to this day. 24But I tell you that it will be more bearable for Sodom on the day of judgment than for you."

The Father Revealed in the Son

25At that time Jesus said, "I praise you, Father, Lord of heaven and earth, because you have hidden these things from the wise and learned, and revealed them to little children. 26Yes, Father, for this is what you were pleased to do.

27"All things have been committed to me by my Father. No one knows the Son except the Father, and no one knows the Father except the Son and those to whom the Son chooses to reveal him.

28"Come to me, all you who are weary and burdened, and I will give you rest. 29Take my yoke upon you and learn from me, for I am gentle and humble in heart, and you will find rest for your souls. 30For my yoke is easy and my burden is light."

Jesus Is Lord of the Sabbath

12 At that time Jesus went through the grainfields on the Sabbath. His disciples were hungry and began to pick some heads of grain and eat them. 2When the Pharisees saw this, they said to him, "Look! Your disciples are doing what is unlawful on the Sabbath."

3He answered, "Haven't you read what David did when he and his companions were hungry? 4He entered the house of God, and he and his companions ate the consecrated bread—which was not lawful for them to do, but only for the priests. 5Or haven't you read in the Law that the priests on Sabbath duty in the temple desecrate the Sabbath and yet are innocent? 6I tell you that something greater than the temple is here. 7If you had known what these words mean, 'I desire mercy, not sacrifice,'*b* you would not have condemned the innocent. 8For the Son of Man is Lord of the Sabbath."

9Going on from that place, he went into their synagogue, 10and a man with a shriveled hand was there. Looking for a reason to bring charges against Jesus, they asked him, "Is it lawful to heal on the Sabbath?"

11He said to them, "If any of you has a sheep and it falls into a pit on the Sabbath, will you not take hold of it and lift it out? 12How much more valuable is a person than a sheep! Therefore it is lawful to do good on the Sabbath."

13Then he said to the man, "Stretch out your hand." So he stretched it out and it was completely restored, just as sound as the other. 14But the Pharisees went out and plotted how they might kill Jesus.

God's Chosen Servant

15Aware of this, Jesus withdrew from that place. A large crowd followed him, and he healed all who were ill. 16He warned them not to tell others about him. 17This was to fulfill what was spoken through the prophet Isaiah:

---

a 23 That is, the realm of the dead   *b 7* Hosea 6:6

My Name Is John

I'M A BELIEVER WHO STRUGGLES WITH ABANDONMENT, ALCOHOLISM AND SEXUAL ADDICTION

Please read the story in Matthew 11:2–6 of John the Baptist's struggles with doubt during his imprisonment.

Mine was a life of opposites. Abandoned and put up for adoption at the age of three, I grew up in an abusive environment where I learned to fight for survival. During my childhood I was sexually molested by a scoutmaster and deacon. As a result, I detested the church and distrusted authority figures. I had no skills for resolving anger or dealing with confusing situations.

On the other hand, school was easy for me. I could recall the material without studying. However, since I didn't know how to properly employ my intelligence, I was more disruptive than cooperative. I made friends easily. I wasn't so much drawn into the "bad crowd" as much as I developed my own wrong crowd, into which I actively recruited others.

From my first taste of hard liquor, alcohol became my friend, a painkiller to which I would return over and over again for years. My relationships were developed from pornographic models as I acted out the scripts. I thought that steeping myself in pornography was my right, as well as the manly thing to do. I certainly wanted to be a man at all costs. Whiskey fueled the desire, pornography shaped the scenario and I spiraled out of control.

Twenty years later, I found myself alone in a church pew in Memphis, Tennessee. Like John the Baptist, I recognized Jesus as the Messiah, but I was sitting, utterly dejected, in my own dungeon, battling serious doubts. I brought them to God and, just as Jesus had done for the despondent and doubting John, he graciously responded. Almost a year later, just before my 39th birthday, I accepted Christ as my Savior. Initially that decision only increased my struggles because my conscience was now actively engaged and telling me my lifestyle had to change.

Subsequently I introduced my sons and several others to Jesus. At the same time, though, I continued to struggle with my addictions. I became a deacon and an adult church school teacher, speaking in churches all over the state. I also joined a southern gospel music group that performed all over Virginia and North Carolina. All the while, I was still struggling with infidelity, pornography and drinking. I was leading two completely separate lives and couldn't seem to stop.

On September 11, 2001, I got tied up on the phone and missed my 8:30 a.m. shuttle to the Pentagon. The events of that day assured me that God was giving me another chance. This time I was ready to do anything to change. God sent me my "messenger" (Matthew 11:10) in the form of my sister, a believer, a recovering alcoholic and a mental health worker for the state of Alabama. She convinced me that joining a recovery program was the only way I could hope to stay sober. I retired from the Pentagon, went to Alabama and started working the steps. I soon learned that the 12 Christ-centered steps of recovery are the mechanics needed for living a Christian life one day at a time. I released my resentments and made my amends — and discovered that a passion for the future was replacing the pain of my past. Now I wanted to give away this peace and joy to everyone around me.

I met Vicki, a lady from Canada. Our relationship started differently than any other I had experienced. Rigorously honest with one another from the beginning, we worked my program and attended meetings together. Several months later we realized we were in love, and for the first time in my life I understood what that really meant. A year later we were married. During a time of prayer and fasting, I realized that God was calling me to help others who were struggling. He gave specific directions, and we followed up by selling our house, relinquishing our possessions in North Carolina, leaving our family and friends and moving across the country to San Diego in answer to God's command. What I didn't know was that our new church had a Celebrate Recovery group, the ministry into which God had been directing me.

Our family members thought we were crazy, and some still do. However, I'm convinced that this is precisely where God wants me to be. God has opened many doors since our decision to follow his direction and call. I currently lead a small group in Celebrate Recovery, sponsor several others who are struggling, and attend Southern California Seminary as a MACP student, training to become a licensed counselor. I've been in recovery since 2001, but on some days I still struggle with the temptations of alcohol and pornography. However, through God's help and the principles and steps of Celebrate Recovery, I've been able to remain clean and sober throughout this entire period. God's work in my life has showcased the reality of his healing, life-changing power (see Matthew 11:5).

John

18 "Here is my servant whom I have chosen,
    the one I love, in whom I delight;
I will put my Spirit on him,
    and he will proclaim justice to the
        nations.
19 He will not quarrel or cry out;
    no one will hear his voice in the streets.
20 A bruised reed he will not break,
    and a smoldering wick he will not
        snuff out,
till he has brought justice through to
        victory.
21   In his name the nations will put their
        hope."*a*

Jesus and Beelzebul

22 Then they brought him a demon-possessed man who was blind and mute, and Jesus healed him, so that he could both talk and see. 23 All the people were astonished and said, "Could this be the Son of David?"

24 But when the Pharisees heard this, they said, "It is only by Beelzebul, the prince of demons, that this fellow drives out demons."

25 Jesus knew their thoughts and said to them, "Every kingdom divided against itself will be ruined, and every city or household divided against itself will not stand. 26 If Satan drives out Satan, he is divided against himself. How then can his kingdom stand? 27 And if I drive out demons by Beelzebul, by whom do your people drive them out? So then, they will be your judges. 28 But if it is by the Spirit of God that I drive out demons, then the kingdom of God has come upon you.

29 "Or again, how can anyone enter a strong man's house and carry off his possessions unless he first ties up the strong man? Then he can plunder his house.

30 "Whoever is not with me is against me, and whoever does not gather with me scatters. 31 And so I tell you, every kind of sin and slander can be forgiven, but blasphemy against the Spirit will not be forgiven. 32 Anyone who speaks a word against the

Son of Man will be forgiven, but anyone who speaks against the Holy Spirit will not be forgiven, either in this age or in the age to come.

33 "Make a tree good and its fruit will be good, or make a tree bad and its fruit will be bad, for a tree is recognized by its fruit. 34 You brood of vipers, how can you who are evil say anything good? For the mouth speaks what the heart is full of. 35 A good man brings good things out of the good stored up in him, and an evil man brings evil things out of the evil stored up in him. 36 But I tell you that everyone will have to give account on the day of judgment for every empty word they have spoken. 37 For by your words you will be acquitted, and by your words you will be condemned."

The Sign of Jonah

38 Then some of the Pharisees and teachers of the law said to him, "Teacher, we want to see a sign from you."

39 He answered, "A wicked and adulterous generation asks for a sign! But none will be given it except the sign of the prophet Jonah. 40 For as Jonah was three days and three nights in the belly of a huge fish, so the Son of Man will be three days and three nights in the heart of the earth. 41 The men of Nineveh will stand up at the judgment with this generation and condemn it; for they repented at the preaching of Jonah, and now something greater than Jonah is here. 42 The Queen of the South will rise at the judgment with this generation and condemn it; for she came from the ends of the earth to listen to Solomon's wisdom, and now something greater than Solomon is here.

43 "When an impure spirit comes out of a person, it goes through arid places seeking rest and does not find it. 44 Then it says, 'I will return to the house I left.' When it arrives, it finds the house unoccupied, swept clean and put in order. 45 Then it goes and takes with it seven other spirits more wicked than itself, and they go in and live there. And the final condition of that person is

---

a 21 Isaiah 42:1-4

worse than the first. That is how it will be with this wicked generation."

Jesus' Mother and Brothers

46While Jesus was still talking to the crowd, his mother and brothers stood outside, wanting to speak to him. 47Someone told him, "Your mother and brothers are standing outside, wanting to speak to you."

48He replied to him, "Who is my mother, and who are my brothers?" 49Pointing to his disciples, he said, "Here are my mother and my brothers. 50For whoever does the will of my Father in heaven is my brother and sister and mother."

The Parable of the Sower

13 That same day Jesus went out of the house and sat by the lake. 2Such large crowds gathered around him that he got into a boat and sat in it, while all the people stood on the shore.

READY LESSON [*Principle Five*]

For the previous entry in the READY lesson, go to 1 Peter 1:13–14 (page 1547).

For a discussion of Principles One through Eight and a listing of their related lessons, go to pages xvii–xliv.

When an impure spirit comes out of a person, it goes through arid places seeking rest and does not find it. Then it says, "I will return to the house I left." When it arrives, it finds the house unoccupied, swept clean and put in order. Then it goes and takes with it seven other spirits more wicked than itself, and they go in and live there. And the final condition of that person is worse than the first. That is how it will be with this wicked generation.

MATTHEW 12:43–45

In Principle Five we need to be READY to voluntarily submit to every change God wants to make in our lives and humbly ask him to remove our character defects.

The *D* in READY represents an extremely important step; it stands for DO REPLACE YOUR CHARACTER DEFECTS. We've spent a lot of time in the company of our old hang-ups, hurts and habits. When God removes one of these, we need to replace it with something positive, such as recovery meetings, church activities, service and/or volunteering. If we don't, we open ourselves up to the possibility that a character defect will return.

A codependent's major defect of character may be fear of abandonment. People who fall into this category have probably wasted a lot of time in unhealthy relationships in an unsuccessful attempt to fill a void in their life. When they start working the eight principles, and particularly when they stop spending their time in negative relationships, they find themselves with a lot of time on their hands. They need to fill that void by doing positive things that will build up their self-image rather than tear it down. In addition to working their program and attending meeting after meeting, they need to fellowship and serve with "healthy" people. They need to volunteer. In short, we need to replace our character defects with something positive. There are many opportunities to serve, both in our recovery ministry and in our church.

The last letter in READY is *Y*. Go to 1 John 3:9 (page 1559).

³Then he told them many things in parables, saying: "A farmer went out to sow his seed. ⁴As he was scattering the seed, some fell along the path, and the birds came and ate it up. ⁵Some fell on rocky places, where it did not have much soil. It sprang up quickly, because the soil was shallow. ⁶But when the sun came up, the plants were scorched, and they withered because they had no root. ⁷Other seed fell among thorns, which grew up and choked the plants. ⁸Still other seed fell on good soil, where it produced a crop — a hundred, sixty or thirty times what was sown. ⁹Whoever has ears, let them hear."

¹⁰The disciples came to him and asked, "Why do you speak to the people in parables?"

¹¹He replied, "Because the knowledge of the secrets of the kingdom of heaven has been given to you, but not to them. ¹²Whoever has will be given more, and they will have an abundance. Whoever does not have, even what they have will be taken from them. ¹³This is why I speak to them in parables:

"Though seeing, they do not see;
    though hearing, they do not hear or
        understand.

¹⁴In them is fulfilled the prophecy of Isaiah:

"'You will be ever hearing but never
        understanding;
    you will be ever seeing but never
        perceiving.
¹⁵For this people's heart has become
        calloused;
    they hardly hear with their ears,
    and they have closed their eyes.
Otherwise they might see with their
        eyes,
    hear with their ears,
    understand with their hearts
and turn, and I would heal them.'ᵃ

¹⁶But blessed are your eyes because they see, and your ears because they hear. ¹⁷For truly I tell you, many prophets and righteous people longed to see what you see but did not see it, and to hear what you hear but did not hear it.

¹⁸"Listen then to what the parable of the sower means: ¹⁹When anyone hears the message about the kingdom and does not understand it, the evil one comes and snatches away what was sown in their heart. This is the seed sown along the path. ²⁰The seed falling on rocky ground refers to someone who hears the word and at once receives it with joy. ²¹But since they have no root, they last only a short time. When trouble or persecution comes because of the word, they quickly fall away. ²²The seed falling among the thorns refers to someone who hears the word, but the worries of this life and the deceitfulness of wealth choke the word, making it unfruitful. ²³But the seed falling on good soil refers to someone who hears the word and understands it. This is the one who produces a crop, yielding a hundred, sixty or thirty times what was sown."

The Parable of the Weeds

²⁴Jesus told them another parable: "The kingdom of heaven is like a man who sowed good seed in his field. ²⁵But while everyone was sleeping, his enemy came and sowed weeds among the wheat, and went away. ²⁶When the wheat sprouted and formed heads, then the weeds also appeared.

²⁷"The owner's servants came to him and said, 'Sir, didn't you sow good seed in your field? Where then did the weeds come from?'

²⁸"'An enemy did this,' he replied.

"The servants asked him, 'Do you want us to go and pull them up?'

²⁹"'No,' he answered, 'because while you are pulling the weeds, you may uproot the wheat with them. ³⁰Let both grow together until the harvest. At that time I will tell the harvesters: First collect the weeds and tie them in bundles to be burned; then gather the wheat and bring it into my barn.'"

ᵃ 15 Isaiah 6:9,10 (see Septuagint)

The Parables of the Mustard Seed and the Yeast

31 He told them another parable: "The kingdom of heaven is like a mustard seed, which a man took and planted in his field. 32 Though it is the smallest of all seeds, yet when it grows, it is the largest of garden plants and becomes a tree, so that the birds come and perch in its branches."

33 He told them still another parable: "The kingdom of heaven is like yeast that a woman took and mixed into about sixty pounds[a] of flour until it worked all through the dough."

34 Jesus spoke all these things to the crowd in parables; he did not say anything to them without using a parable. 35 So was fulfilled what was spoken through the prophet:

"I will open my mouth in parables,
I will utter things hidden since the
creation of the world."[b]

The Parable of the Weeds Explained

36 Then he left the crowd and went into the house. His disciples came to him and said, "Explain to us the parable of the weeds in the field."

37 He answered, "The one who sowed the good seed is the Son of Man. 38 The field is the world, and the good seed stands for the people of the kingdom. The weeds are the people of the evil one, 39 and the enemy who sows them is the devil. The harvest is the end of the age, and the harvesters are angels.

40 "As the weeds are pulled up and burned in the fire, so it will be at the end of the age. 41 The Son of Man will send out his angels, and they will weed out of his kingdom everything that causes sin and all who do evil. 42 They will throw them into the blazing furnace, where there will be weeping and gnashing of teeth. 43 Then the righteous will shine like the sun in the kingdom of their Father. Whoever has ears, let them hear.

The Parables of the Hidden Treasure and the Pearl

44 "The kingdom of heaven is like treasure hidden in a field. When a man found it, he hid it again, and then in his joy went and sold all he had and bought that field.

45 "Again, the kingdom of heaven is like a merchant looking for fine pearls. 46 When he found one of great value, he went away and sold everything he had and bought it.

The Parable of the Net

47 "Once again, the kingdom of heaven is like a net that was let down into the lake and caught all kinds of fish. 48 When it was full, the fishermen pulled it up on the shore. Then they sat down and collected the good fish in baskets, but threw the bad away. 49 This is how it will be at the end of the age. The angels will come and separate the wicked from the righteous 50 and throw them into the blazing furnace, where there will be weeping and gnashing of teeth.

51 "Have you understood all these things?" Jesus asked.

"Yes," they replied.

52 He said to them, "Therefore every teacher of the law who has become a disciple in the kingdom of heaven is like the owner of a house who brings out of his storeroom new treasures as well as old."

A Prophet Without Honor

53 When Jesus had finished these parables, he moved on from there. 54 Coming to his hometown, he began teaching the people in their synagogue, and they were amazed. "Where did this man get this wisdom and these miraculous powers?" they asked. 55 "Isn't this the carpenter's son? Isn't his mother's name Mary, and aren't his brothers James, Joseph, Simon and Judas? 56 Aren't all his sisters with us? Where then did this man get all these things?" 57 And they took offense at him.

But Jesus said to them, "A prophet is not

---

a 33 Or about 27 kilograms   *b 35* Psalm 78:2

without honor except in his own town and in his own home."

58And he did not do many miracles there because of their lack of faith.

John the Baptist Beheaded

14 At that time Herod the tetrarch heard the reports about Jesus, 2and he said to his attendants, "This is John the Baptist; he has risen from the dead! That is why miraculous powers are at work in him."

3Now Herod had arrested John and bound him and put him in prison because of Herodias, his brother Philip's wife, 4for John had been saying to him: "It is not lawful for you to have her." 5Herod wanted to kill John, but he was afraid of the people, because they considered John a prophet.

6On Herod's birthday the daughter of Herodias danced for the guests and pleased Herod so much 7that he promised with an oath to give her whatever she asked. 8Prompted by her mother, she said, "Give me here on a platter the head of John the Baptist." 9The king was distressed, but because of his oaths and his dinner guests, he ordered that her request be granted 10and had John beheaded in the prison. 11His head was brought in on a platter and given to the girl, who carried it to her mother. 12John's disciples came and took his body and buried it. Then they went and told Jesus.

Jesus Feeds the Five Thousand

13When Jesus heard what had happened, he withdrew by boat privately to a solitary place. Hearing of this, the crowds followed him on foot from the towns. 14When Jesus landed and saw a large crowd, he had compassion on them and healed their sick.

15As evening approached, the disciples came to him and said, "This is a remote place, and it's already getting late. Send the crowds away, so they can go to the villages and buy themselves some food."

16Jesus replied, "They do not need to go away. You give them something to eat."

17"We have here only five loaves of bread and two fish," they answered.

18"Bring them here to me," he said. 19And he directed the people to sit down on the grass. Taking the five loaves and the two fish and looking up to heaven, he gave thanks and broke the loaves. Then he gave them to the disciples, and the disciples gave them to the people. 20They all ate and were satisfied, and the disciples picked up twelve basketfuls of broken pieces that were left over. 21The number of those who ate was about five thousand men, besides women and children.

Jesus Walks on the Water

22Immediately Jesus made the disciples get into the boat and go on ahead of him to the other side, while he dismissed the crowd. 23After he had dismissed them, he went up on a mountainside by himself to pray. Later that night, he was there alone, 24and the boat was already a considerable distance from land, buffeted by the waves because the wind was against it.

25Shortly before dawn Jesus went out to them, walking on the lake. 26When the disciples saw him walking on the lake, they were terrified. "It's a ghost," they said, and cried out in fear.

27But Jesus immediately said to them: "Take courage! It is I. Don't be afraid."

28"Lord, if it's you," Peter replied, "tell me to come to you on the water."

29"Come," he said.

Then Peter got down out of the boat, walked on the water and came toward Jesus. 30But when he saw the wind, he was afraid and, beginning to sink, cried out, "Lord, save me!"

31Immediately Jesus reached out his hand and caught him. "You of little faith," he said, "why did you doubt?"

32And when they climbed into the boat, the wind died down. 33Then those who were in the boat worshiped him, saying, "Truly you are the Son of God."

34When they had crossed over, they landed at Gennesaret. 35And when the men of that place recognized Jesus, they sent word to all the surrounding country. People brought all their sick to him [36]and begged him to let the sick just touch the edge of his cloak, and all who touched it were healed.

That Which Defiles

15 Then some Pharisees and teachers of the law came to Jesus from Jerusalem and asked, [2]"Why do your disciples break the tradition of the elders? They don't wash their hands before they eat!"

[3]Jesus replied, "And why do you break the command of God for the sake of your tradition? [4]For God said, 'Honor your father and mother'[a] and 'Anyone who curses their father or mother is to be put to death.'[b] [5]But you say that if anyone declares that what might have been used to help their father or mother is 'devoted to God,' [6]they are not to 'honor their father or mother' with it. Thus you nullify the word of God for the sake of your tradition. [7]You hypocrites! Isaiah was right when he prophesied about you:

[8] "'These people honor me with their lips,
  but their hearts are far from me.
[9]They worship me in vain;
  their teachings are merely human rules.'[c]"

[10]Jesus called the crowd to him and said, "Listen and understand. [11]What goes into someone's mouth does not defile them, but what comes out of their mouth, that is what defiles them."

[12]Then the disciples came to him and asked, "Do you know that the Pharisees were offended when they heard this?"

[13]He replied, "Every plant that my heavenly Father has not planted will be pulled up by the roots. [14]Leave them; they are blind guides.[d] If the blind lead the blind, both will fall into a pit."

[15]Peter said, "Explain the parable to us."

[16]"Are you still so dull?" Jesus asked them. [17]"Don't you see that whatever enters the mouth goes into the stomach and then out of the body? [18]But the things that come out of a person's mouth come from the heart, and these defile them. [19]For out of the heart come evil thoughts—murder, adultery, sexual immorality, theft, false testimony, slander. [20]These are what defile a person; but eating with unwashed hands does not defile them."

The Faith of a Canaanite Woman

[21]Leaving that place, Jesus withdrew to the region of Tyre and Sidon. [22]A Canaanite woman from that vicinity came to him, crying out, "Lord, Son of David, have mercy on me! My daughter is demon-possessed and suffering terribly."

[23]Jesus did not answer a word. So his disciples came to him and urged him, "Send her away, for she keeps crying out after us."

[24]He answered, "I was sent only to the lost sheep of Israel."

[25]The woman came and knelt before him. "Lord, help me!" she said.

[26]He replied, "It is not right to take the children's bread and toss it to the dogs."

[27]"Yes it is, Lord," she said. "Even the dogs eat the crumbs that fall from their master's table."

[28]Then Jesus said to her, "Woman, you have great faith! Your request is granted." And her daughter was healed at that moment.

Jesus Feeds the Four Thousand

[29]Jesus left there and went along the Sea of Galilee. Then he went up on a mountainside and sat down. [30]Great crowds came to him, bringing the lame, the blind, the crippled, the mute and many others, and laid them at his feet; and he healed them. [31]The people were amazed when they saw the mute speaking, the crippled made well, the lame walking and the blind seeing. And they praised the God of Israel.

---

[a] 4 Exodus 20:12; Deut. 5:16   [b] 4 Exodus 21:17; Lev. 20:9   [c] 9 Isaiah 29:13   [d] 14 Some manuscripts *blind guides of the blind*

³²Jesus called his disciples to him and said, "I have compassion for these people; they have already been with me three days and have nothing to eat. I do not want to send them away hungry, or they may collapse on the way."

³³His disciples answered, "Where could we get enough bread in this remote place to feed such a crowd?"

³⁴"How many loaves do you have?" Jesus asked.

"Seven," they replied, "and a few small fish."

³⁵He told the crowd to sit down on the ground. ³⁶Then he took the seven loaves and the fish, and when he had given thanks, he broke them and gave them to the disciples, and they in turn to the people. ³⁷They all ate and were satisfied. Afterward the disciples picked up seven basketfuls of broken pieces that were left over. ³⁸The number of those who ate was four thousand men, besides women and children. ³⁹After Jesus had sent the crowd away, he got into the boat and went to the vicinity of Magadan.

The Demand for a Sign

16 The Pharisees and Sadducees came to Jesus and tested him by asking him to show them a sign from heaven.

²He replied, "When evening comes, you say, 'It will be fair weather, for the sky is red,' ³and in the morning, 'Today it will be stormy, for the sky is red and overcast.' You know how to interpret the appearance of the sky, but you cannot interpret the signs of the times.ᵃ ⁴A wicked and adulterous generation looks for a sign, but none will be given it except the sign of Jonah." Jesus then left them and went away.

The Yeast of the Pharisees and Sadducees

⁵When they went across the lake, the disciples forgot to take bread. ⁶"Be care-ful," Jesus said to them. "Be on your guard against the yeast of the Pharisees and Sadducees."

⁷They discussed this among themselves and said, "It is because we didn't bring any bread."

⁸Aware of their discussion, Jesus asked, "You of little faith, why are you talking among yourselves about having no bread? ⁹Do you still not understand? Don't you remember the five loaves for the five thousand, and how many basketfuls you gathered? ¹⁰Or the seven loaves for the four thousand, and how many basketfuls you gathered? ¹¹How is it you don't understand that I was not talking to you about bread? But be on your guard against the yeast of the Pharisees and Sadducees." ¹²Then they understood that he was not telling them to guard against the yeast used in bread, but against the teaching of the Pharisees and Sadducees.

Peter Declares That Jesus Is the Messiah

¹³When Jesus came to the region of Caesarea Philippi, he asked his disciples, "Who do people say the Son of Man is?"

¹⁴They replied, "Some say John the Baptist; others say Elijah; and still others, Jeremiah or one of the prophets."

¹⁵"But what about you?" he asked. "Who do you say I am?"

¹⁶Simon Peter answered, "You are the Messiah, the Son of the living God."

¹⁷Jesus replied, "Blessed are you, Simon son of Jonah, for this was not revealed to you by flesh and blood, but by my Father in heaven. ¹⁸And I tell you that you are Peter,ᵇ and on this rock I will build my church, and the gates of Hadesᶜ will not overcome it. ¹⁹I will give you the keys of the kingdom of heaven; whatever you bind on earth will beᵈ bound in heaven, and whatever you loose on earth will beᵈ loosed in heaven." ²⁰Then he ordered his disciples not to tell anyone that he was the Messiah.

ᵃ 2,3 Some early manuscripts do not have *When evening comes . . . of the times.*   ᵇ 18 The Greek word for *Peter* means *rock.*   ᶜ 18 That is, the realm of the dead   ᵈ 19 Or *will have been*

Jesus Predicts His Death

21From that time on Jesus began to explain to his disciples that he must go to Jerusalem and suffer many things at the hands of the elders, the chief priests and the teachers of the law, and that he must be killed and on the third day be raised to life.

22Peter took him aside and began to rebuke him. "Never, Lord!" he said. "This shall never happen to you!"

23Jesus turned and said to Peter, "Get behind me, Satan! You are a stumbling block to me; you do not have in mind the concerns of God, but merely human concerns."

24Then Jesus said to his disciples, "Whoever wants to be my disciple must deny themselves and take up their cross and follow me. 25For whoever wants to save their life*a* will lose it, but whoever loses their life for me will find it. 26What good will it be for someone to gain the whole world, yet forfeit their soul? Or what can anyone give in exchange for their soul? 27For the Son of Man is going to come in his Father's glory with his angels, and then he will reward each person according to what they have done.

28"Truly I tell you, some who are standing here will not taste death before they see the Son of Man coming in his kingdom."

The Transfiguration

17 After six days Jesus took with him Peter, James and John the brother of James, and led them up a high mountain by themselves. 2There he was transfigured before them. His face shone like the sun, and his clothes became as white as the light. 3Just then there appeared before them Moses and Elijah, talking with Jesus.

4Peter said to Jesus, "Lord, it is good for us to be here. If you wish, I will put up three shelters — one for you, one for Moses and one for Elijah."

5While he was still speaking, a bright cloud covered them, and a voice from the cloud said, "This is my Son, whom I love; with him I am well pleased. Listen to him!"

6When the disciples heard this, they fell facedown to the ground, terrified. 7But Jesus came and touched them. "Get up," he said. "Don't be afraid." 8When they looked up, they saw no one except Jesus.

9As they were coming down the mountain, Jesus instructed them, "Don't tell anyone what you have seen, until the Son of Man has been raised from the dead."

10The disciples asked him, "Why then do the teachers of the law say that Elijah must come first?"

11Jesus replied, "To be sure, Elijah comes and will restore all things. 12But I tell you, Elijah has already come, and they did not recognize him, but have done to him everything they wished. In the same way the Son of Man is going to suffer at their hands." 13Then the disciples understood that he was talking to them about John the Baptist.

Jesus Heals a Demon-Possessed Boy

14When they came to the crowd, a man approached Jesus and knelt before him. 15"Lord, have mercy on my son," he said. "He has seizures and is suffering greatly. He often falls into the fire or into the water. 16I brought him to your disciples, but they could not heal him."

17"You unbelieving and perverse generation," Jesus replied, "how long shall I stay with you? How long shall I put up with you? Bring the boy here to me." 18Jesus rebuked the demon, and it came out of the boy, and he was healed at that moment.

19Then the disciples came to Jesus in private and asked, "Why couldn't we drive it out?"

20He replied, "Because you have so little faith. Truly I tell you, if you have faith as small as a mustard seed, you can say to this mountain, 'Move from here to there,' and it will move. Nothing will be impossible for you." [21]*b*

---

a 25 The Greek word means either *life* or *soul*; also in verse 26.   *b* 21 Some manuscripts include here words similar to Mark 9:29.

Jesus Predicts His Death a Second Time

22When they came together in Galilee, he said to them, "The Son of Man is going to be delivered into the hands of men. 23They will kill him, and on the third day he will be raised to life." And the disciples were filled with grief.

The Temple Tax

24After Jesus and his disciples arrived in Capernaum, the collectors of the two-drachma temple tax came to Peter and asked, "Doesn't your teacher pay the temple tax?"

25"Yes, he does," he replied.

When Peter came into the house, Jesus was the first to speak. "What do you think, Simon?" he asked. "From whom do the kings of the earth collect duty and taxes — from their own children or from others?"

26"From others," Peter answered.

"Then the children are exempt," Jesus said to him. 27"But so that we may not cause offense, go to the lake and throw out your line. Take the first fish you catch; open its mouth and you will find a four-drachma coin. Take it and give it to them for my tax and yours."

The Greatest in the Kingdom of Heaven

18

At that time the disciples came to Jesus and asked, "Who, then, is the greatest in the kingdom of heaven?"

2He called a little child to him, and placed the child among them. 3And he said: "Truly I tell you, unless you change and become like little children, you will never enter the kingdom of heaven. 4Therefore, whoever takes the lowly position of this child is the greatest in the kingdom of heaven. 5And whoever welcomes one such child in my name welcomes me.

Causing to Stumble

6"If anyone causes one of these little ones — those who believe in me — to stumble, it would be better for them to have a large millstone hung around their neck and to be drowned in the depths of the sea. 7Woe to the world because of the things that cause people to stumble! Such things must come, but woe to the person through whom they come! 8If your hand or your foot causes you to stumble, cut it off and throw it away. It is better for you to enter life maimed or crippled than to have two hands or two feet and be thrown into eternal fire. 9And if your eye causes you to stumble, gouge it out and throw it away. It is better for you to enter life with one eye than to have two eyes and be thrown into the fire of hell.

The Parable of the Wandering Sheep

10"See that you do not despise one of these little ones. For I tell you that their angels in heaven always see the face of my Father in heaven. [11]a

12"What do you think? If a man owns a hundred sheep, and one of them wanders away, will he not leave the ninety-nine on the hills and go to look for the one that wandered off? 13And if he finds it, truly I tell you, he is happier about that one sheep than about the ninety-nine that did not wander off. 14In the same way your Father in heaven is not willing that any of these little ones should perish.

Dealing With Sin in the Church

15"If your brother or sisterb sins,c go and point out their fault, just between the two of you. If they listen to you, you have won them over. 16But if they will not listen, take one or two others along, so that 'every matter may be established by the testimony of two or three witnesses.'d 17If they still refuse to listen, tell it to the church; and if they refuse to listen even to the church, treat them as you would a pagan or a tax collector.

---

a 11 Some manuscripts include here the words of Luke 19:10.   b 15 The Greek word for brother or sister (adelphos) refers here to a fellow disciple, whether man or woman; also in verses 21 and 35.   c 15 Some manuscripts sins against you   d 16 Deut. 19:15

¹⁸"Truly I tell you, whatever you bind on earth will be*ᵃ* bound in heaven, and whatever you loose on earth will be*ᵃ* loosed in heaven.

¹⁹"Again, truly I tell you that if two of you on earth agree about anything they ask for, it will be done for them by my Father in heaven. ²⁰For where two or three gather in my name, there am I with them."

The Parable of the Unmerciful Servant

²¹Then Peter came to Jesus and asked, "Lord, how many times shall I forgive my brother or sister who sins against me? Up to seven times?"

²²Jesus answered, "I tell you, not seven times, but seventy-seven times.*ᵇ*

²³"Therefore, the kingdom of heaven is like a king who wanted to settle accounts with his servants. ²⁴As he began the settlement, a man who owed him ten thousand bags of gold*ᶜ* was brought to him. ²⁵Since he was not able to pay, the master ordered that he and his wife and his children and all that he had be sold to repay the debt.

²⁶"At this the servant fell on his knees before him. 'Be patient with me,' he begged, 'and I will pay back everything.' ²⁷The servant's master took pity on him, canceled the debt and let him go.

²⁸"But when that servant went out, he found one of his fellow servants who owed him a hundred silver coins.*ᵈ* He grabbed him and began to choke him. 'Pay back what you owe me!' he demanded.

²⁹"His fellow servant fell to his knees and begged him, 'Be patient with me, and I will pay it back.'

³⁰"But he refused. Instead, he went off and had the man thrown into prison until he could pay the debt. ³¹When the other servants saw what had happened, they were outraged and went and told their master everything that had happened.

³²"Then the master called the servant in.

'You wicked servant,' he said, 'I canceled all that debt of yours because you begged me to. ³³Shouldn't you have had mercy on your fellow servant just as I had on you?' ³⁴In anger his master handed him over to the jailers to be tortured, until he should pay back all he owed.

³⁵"This is how my heavenly Father will treat each of you unless you forgive your brother or sister from your heart."

Divorce

19 When Jesus had finished saying these things, he left Galilee and went into the region of Judea to the other side of the Jordan. ²Large crowds followed him, and he healed them there.

³Some Pharisees came to him to test him. They asked, "Is it lawful for a man to divorce his wife for any and every reason?"

⁴"Haven't you read," he replied, "that at the beginning the Creator 'made them male and female,'*ᵉ* ⁵and said, 'For this reason a man will leave his father and mother and be united to his wife, and the two will become one flesh'*ᶠ*? ⁶So they are no longer two, but one flesh. Therefore what God has joined together, let no one separate."

⁷"Why then," they asked, "did Moses command that a man give his wife a certificate of divorce and send her away?"

⁸Jesus replied, "Moses permitted you to divorce your wives because your hearts were hard. But it was not this way from the beginning. ⁹I tell you that anyone who divorces his wife, except for sexual immorality, and marries another woman commits adultery."

¹⁰The disciples said to him, "If this is the situation between a husband and wife, it is better not to marry."

¹¹Jesus replied, "Not everyone can accept this word, but only those to whom it has been given. ¹²For there are eunuchs who were born that way, and there are

---

ᵃ 18 Or *will have been*   *ᵇ 22* Or *seventy times seven*   *ᶜ 24* Greek *ten thousand talents*; a talent was worth about 20 years of a day laborer's wages.   *ᵈ 28* Greek *a hundred denarii*; a denarius was the usual daily wage of a day laborer (see 20:2).   *ᵉ 4* Gen. 1:27   *ᶠ 5* Gen. 2:24

eunuchs who have been made eunuchs by others — and there are those who choose to live like eunuchs for the sake of the kingdom of heaven. The one who can accept this should accept it."

The Little Children and Jesus

13Then people brought little children to Jesus for him to place his hands on them and pray for them. But the disciples rebuked them.

14Jesus said, "Let the little children come to me, and do not hinder them, for the kingdom of heaven belongs to such as these." 15When he had placed his hands on them, he went on from there.

The Rich and the Kingdom of God

16Just then a man came up to Jesus and asked, "Teacher, what good thing must I do to get eternal life?"

17"Why do you ask me about what is good?" Jesus replied. "There is only One who is good. If you want to enter life, keep the commandments."

18"Which ones?" he inquired.

Jesus replied, "'You shall not murder, you shall not commit adultery, you shall not steal, you shall not give false testimony, 19honor your father and mother,'a and 'love your neighbor as yourself.'b"

20"All these I have kept," the young man said. "What do I still lack?"

21Jesus answered, "If you want to be perfect, go, sell your possessions and give to the poor, and you will have treasure in heaven. Then come, follow me."

22When the young man heard this, he went away sad, because he had great wealth.

23Then Jesus said to his disciples, "Truly I tell you, it is hard for someone who is rich to enter the kingdom of heaven. 24Again I tell you, it is easier for a camel to go through the eye of a needle than for someone who is rich to enter the kingdom of God."

25When the disciples heard this, they were greatly astonished and asked, "Who then can be saved?"

26Jesus looked at them and said, "With man this is impossible, but with God all things are possible."

27Peter answered him, "We have left everything to follow you! What then will there be for us?"

28Jesus said to them, "Truly I tell you, at the renewal of all things, when the Son of Man sits on his glorious throne, you who have followed me will also sit on twelve thrones, judging the twelve tribes of Israel. 29And everyone who has left houses or brothers or sisters or father or mother or wifec or children or fields for my sake will receive a hundred times as much and will inherit eternal life. 30But many who are first will be last, and many who are last will be first.

The Parable of the Workers in the Vineyard

20 "For the kingdom of heaven is like a landowner who went out early in the morning to hire workers for his vineyard. 2He agreed to pay them a denariusd for the day and sent them into his vineyard.

3"About nine in the morning he went out and saw others standing in the marketplace doing nothing. 4He told them, 'You also go and work in my vineyard, and I will pay you whatever is right.' 5So they went.

"He went out again about noon and about three in the afternoon and did the same thing. 6About five in the afternoon he went out and found still others standing around. He asked them, 'Why have you been standing here all day long doing nothing?'

7"'Because no one has hired us,' they answered.

"He said to them, 'You also go and work in my vineyard.'

8"When evening came, the owner of

---

a 19 Exodus 20:12-16; Deut. 5:16-20   b 19 Lev. 19:18   c 29 Some manuscripts do not have or wife.
d 2 A denarius was the usual daily wage of a day laborer.

MY NAME IS
THE RICH YOUNG MAN

MATTHEW 19:16–26

This young man is a source for understanding some of the lies that keep us from beginning recovery. The same lies will knock us off the recovery road. The first lie is "I can do it on my own." This young man asked, "Teacher, what good thing must I do to get eternal life?" (Matthew 19:16). He assumed that he had at his disposal the power to do whatever was necessary and wanted to know what he should strive next to achieve. Many of us can relate to this approach. We've piled one accomplishment on top of another for years. We may have seen this tactic as a way to gain love — to block out our inner message of insecurity. Jesus pointed out first to this young seeker that only God is good. Then he spoke to him in terms of the Mosaic Law: "If you want to enter life, keep the commandments" (v. 17). In other words, only God is good, so do what God demands as an expression of your faith.

Jesus wasn't promoting legalism as a path to salvation. He was revealing that this confident young man couldn't accomplish the one good thing necessary for eternal life: finding faith in Jesus Christ. If we really have faith, we'll follow his commands. Jesus in effect set up a test of this seeker's faith: "If you want to be perfect, go, sell your possessions and give to the poor, and you will have treasure in heaven. Then come, follow me" (v. 21). This frustrated seeker went away sad, unable to part with his extensive wealth (see v. 22). This reveals a second lie that endangers our recovery: "I can withhold some areas of my life from the control of Jesus."

Recovery isn't a program we fit neatly into some available niche in our old life. Recovery is all about living an entirely new life. Recovery doesn't allow us — because Jesus doesn't allow us — to stop short of genuine life change. The principles of recovery aren't props we arrange on the stage of our life. Instead, they make us a screen upon which God projects his own glory — the truth about himself and his power to transform lives. Representing God accurately is the goal of recovery, and that requires uncompromising obedience. Let's not fool ourselves; partial or delayed obedience is simply disobedience.

Real recovery may seem impossible right now. But Jesus wants to remind us of the truth that alone makes recovery possible: "With man this is impossible, but with God all things are possible" (v. 26). Principle Three calls each of us to consciously choose to commit *all* our life and will to Christ's care and control. Stop short of this, and we too will walk away sad. Hebrews 12:1 urges us to "throw off everything that hinders and the sin that so easily entangles . . . run with perseverance the race marked out for us." The operative word here is "everything."

the vineyard said to his foreman, 'Call the workers and pay them their wages, beginning with the last ones hired and going on to the first.'

9"The workers who were hired about five in the afternoon came and each received a denarius. 10So when those came who were hired first, they expected to receive more. But each one of them also received a denarius. 11When they received it, they began to grumble against the landowner. 12'These who were hired last worked only one hour,' they said, 'and you have made them equal to us who have borne the burden of the work and the heat of the day.'

13"But he answered one of them, 'I am not being unfair to you, friend. Didn't you agree to work for a denarius? 14Take your pay and go. I want to give the one who was hired last the same as I gave you. 15Don't I have the right to do what I want with my own money? Or are you envious because I am generous?'

16"So the last will be first, and the first will be last."

Jesus Predicts His Death a Third Time

17Now Jesus was going up to Jerusalem. On the way, he took the Twelve aside and said to them, 18"We are going up to Jerusalem, and the Son of Man will be delivered over to the chief priests and the teachers of the law. They will condemn him to death 19and will hand him over to the Gentiles to be mocked and flogged and crucified. On the third day he will be raised to life!"

A Mother's Request

20Then the mother of Zebedee's sons came to Jesus with her sons and, kneeling down, asked a favor of him.

21"What is it you want?" he asked.

She said, "Grant that one of these two sons of mine may sit at your right and the other at your left in your kingdom."

22"You don't know what you are asking," Jesus said to them. "Can you drink the cup I am going to drink?"

"We can," they answered.

23Jesus said to them, "You will indeed drink from my cup, but to sit at my right or left is not for me to grant. These places belong to those for whom they have been prepared by my Father."

24When the ten heard about this, they were indignant with the two brothers. 25Jesus called them together and said, "You know that the rulers of the Gentiles lord it over them, and their high officials exercise authority over them. 26Not so with you. Instead, whoever wants to become great among you must be your servant, 27and whoever wants to be first must be your slave — 28just as the Son of Man did not come to be served, but to serve, and to give his life as a ransom for many."

Two Blind Men Receive Sight

29As Jesus and his disciples were leaving Jericho, a large crowd followed him. 30Two blind men were sitting by the roadside, and when they heard that Jesus was going by, they shouted, "Lord, Son of David, have mercy on us!"

31The crowd rebuked them and told them to be quiet, but they shouted all the louder, "Lord, Son of David, have mercy on us!"

32Jesus stopped and called them. "What do you want me to do for you?" he asked.

33"Lord," they answered, "we want our sight."

34Jesus had compassion on them and touched their eyes. Immediately they received their sight and followed him.

Jesus Comes to Jerusalem as King

21 As they approached Jerusalem and came to Bethphage on the Mount of Olives, Jesus sent two disciples, 2saying to them, "Go to the village ahead of you, and at once you will find a donkey tied there, with her colt by her. Untie them and bring them to me. 3If anyone says anything to you, say that the Lord needs them, and he will send them right away."

4This took place to fulfill what was spoken through the prophet:

5 "Say to Daughter Zion,
   'See, your king comes to you,
gentle and riding on a donkey,
   and on a colt, the foal of a
      donkey.' "*a*

6The disciples went and did as Jesus had instructed them. 7They brought the donkey and the colt and placed their cloaks on them for Jesus to sit on. 8A very large crowd spread their cloaks on the road, while others cut branches from the trees and spread them on the road. 9The crowds that went ahead of him and those that followed shouted,

"Hosanna*b* to the Son of David!"

"Blessed is he who comes in the name
   of the Lord!"*c*

"Hosanna*b* in the highest heaven!"

10When Jesus entered Jerusalem, the whole city was stirred and asked, "Who is this?"

11The crowds answered, "This is Jesus, the prophet from Nazareth in Galilee."

Jesus at the Temple

12Jesus entered the temple courts and drove out all who were buying and selling there. He overturned the tables of the money changers and the benches of those selling doves. 13"It is written," he said to them, " 'My house will be called a house of prayer,'*d* but you are making it 'a den of robbers.'*e*"

14The blind and the lame came to him at the temple, and he healed them. 15But when the chief priests and the teachers of the law saw the wonderful things he did and the children shouting in the temple courts, "Hosanna to the Son of David," they were indignant.

16"Do you hear what these children are saying?" they asked him.

"Yes," replied Jesus, "have you never read,

" 'From the lips of children and infants
   you, Lord, have called forth your
      praise'*f*?"

17And he left them and went out of the city to Bethany, where he spent the night.

Jesus Curses a Fig Tree

18Early in the morning, as Jesus was on his way back to the city, he was hungry. 19Seeing a fig tree by the road, he went up to it but found nothing on it except leaves. Then he said to it, "May you never bear fruit again!" Immediately the tree withered.

20When the disciples saw this, they were amazed. "How did the fig tree wither so quickly?" they asked.

21Jesus replied, "Truly I tell you, if you have faith and do not doubt, not only can you do what was done to the fig tree, but also you can say to this mountain, 'Go, throw yourself into the sea,' and it will be done. 22If you believe, you will receive whatever you ask for in prayer."

The Authority of Jesus Questioned

23Jesus entered the temple courts, and, while he was teaching, the chief priests and the elders of the people came to him. "By what authority are you doing these things?" they asked. "And who gave you this authority?"

24Jesus replied, "I will also ask you one question. If you answer me, I will tell you by what authority I am doing these things. 25John's baptism — where did it come from? Was it from heaven, or of human origin?"

They discussed it among themselves and said, "If we say, 'From heaven,' he will ask, 'Then why didn't you believe him?' 26But if we say, 'Of human origin' — we are afraid of the people, for they all hold that John was a prophet."

27So they answered Jesus, "We don't know."

Then he said, "Neither will I tell you by what authority I am doing these things.

---

a 5 Zech. 9:9   *b* 9 A Hebrew expression meaning "Save!" which became an exclamation of praise; also in verse 15
c 9 Psalm 118:25,26   *d* 13 Isaiah 56:7   *e* 13 Jer. 7:11   *f* 16 Psalm 8:2 (see Septuagint)

My Name Is Paul

I'M A BELIEVER WHO STRUGGLES WITH FINANCES AND WORKAHOLISM

Please read the story of the encounter between Jesus and the rich young man in Matthew 19:16 – 26.

When I was about eight years old, I became increasingly aware that my dad wasn't around much; he worked hard, and his hours were long. My mom was raising five children with very little physical help from Dad; his role was that of breadwinner, of self-employed, sole provider. We moved around the country as job opportunities dictated. Each time we moved, he put in even longer hours, and his company continued to do better and better. He was achieving remarkable success and doing it single-handedly.

At a youth retreat when I was 15 years old, I accepted Jesus Christ as my Savior and Lord. I wasn't connected to a church, though, so when I returned home, I had no one to nurture or mentor me in the things of the Lord. I internalized my newfound faith and went about life as before.

My first job after graduating from college with a business degree was in the restaurant business. I worked five or six days a week, 12 to 14 hours per day, and was promoted quickly. Like my dad, and like the rich young man of Mark 10, I was relying on myself. As I progressed in my career, I ended up working with my dad in the family construction business.

Business was booming, and I continued working long hours and weekends. The overtime checks were great and the year-end bonuses were unbelievable. *I* was the rich young man. By the world's standards our family was living the American dream — but not in God's economy.

Then the housing bubble burst, and construction crawled to a virtual standstill. The bonuses ended, the overtime evaporated and my salary was cut by 75 percent. My wife and I got further and further behind on our payments. Our credit cards were maxed out, our house payment was substantial, and the cost of keeping up with the neighbors was staggering. My answer was to ignore these negative signs. I assured myself that this was only an economic slowdown, not a recession.

I had always believed I could handle my finances on my own. I looked into a second job, but this would have been like bailing out the Titanic with a teacup. We were forced to sell our house before the lender could begin foreclosure proceedings. Having lost the privilege of owning a home, we began renting. I was angry, hurt, frightened, depressed and deflated.

I had been holding back on God in terms of relinquishing control over this one area of my life. When at long last I made the decision to do so, God in return gave me a verse about tithing (donating 10 percent of our money). Malachi 3:10 counsels us to " 'bring the whole tithe into the storehouse, that there may be food in my house. Test me in this,' says the LORD Almighty, 'and see if I will not throw open the floodgates of heaven and pour out so much blessing that there will not be room enough to store it.' "

This was *not* what I wanted to hear, and I reacted to God in frustration: "*How* can I give you 10 percent when we can't even meet our monthly expenses? You're asking the impossible." All the while, though, I recognized with a sinking heart that if I really had faith I would follow his commands. I needed to humble myself before the Lord in order to give him the opportunity to lift me up. I needed to internalize the truth: "With man such tithing is impossible, but not with God; all things are possible with God" (Matthew 19:26, author's paraphrase).

It wasn't until I began attending Celebrate Recovery that I stopped denying and running from my financial situation. And when I turned over my life and will to the care of God, I began to heal. The apostle Paul entreats us in Romans 12:1: "I urge you, brothers and sisters, in view of God's mercy, to offer your bodies as a living sacrifice, holy and pleasing to God — this is your true and proper worship." Once I did that, God changed my focus in life from success (a worldly value) to significance (a godly value).

I did as God asked and started tithing. That first check was tough because my wife and I did it on pure faith that God is precisely who he says he is. But God began working miracles in our lives, and over the next three years our debt load gradually disappeared.

Today I still work hard at the family business. But my motivation is different. I have come to realize that God wants more for me than success at work. I find significance in serving him at Celebrate Recovery: as a small group leader, a sponsor and a caring friend reaching out to the newcomer.

On a daily basis I consciously embrace Hebrews 12:1: "Therefore, since we are surrounded by such a great cloud of witnesses, let us throw off everything that hinders and the sin that so easily entangles. And let us run with perseverance the race marked out for us."

Paul

The Parable of the Two Sons

28"What do you think? There was a man who had two sons. He went to the first and said, 'Son, go and work today in the vineyard.'

29"'I will not,' he answered, but later he changed his mind and went.

30"Then the father went to the other son and said the same thing. He answered, 'I will, sir,' but he did not go.

31"Which of the two did what his father wanted?"

"The first," they answered.

Jesus said to them, "Truly I tell you, the tax collectors and the prostitutes are entering the kingdom of God ahead of you. 32For John came to you to show you the way of righteousness, and you did not believe him, but the tax collectors and the prostitutes did. And even after you saw this, you did not repent and believe him.

The Parable of the Tenants

33"Listen to another parable: There was a landowner who planted a vineyard. He put a wall around it, dug a winepress in it and built a watchtower. Then he rented the vineyard to some farmers and moved to another place. 34When the harvest time approached, he sent his servants to the tenants to collect his fruit.

35"The tenants seized his servants; they beat one, killed another, and stoned a third. 36Then he sent other servants to them, more than the first time, and the tenants treated them the same way. 37Last of all, he sent his son to them. 'They will respect my son,' he said.

38"But when the tenants saw the son, they said to each other, 'This is the heir. Come, let's kill him and take his inheritance.' 39So they took him and threw him out of the vineyard and killed him.

40"Therefore, when the owner of the vineyard comes, what will he do to those tenants?"

41"He will bring those wretches to a wretched end," they replied, "and he will rent the vineyard to other tenants, who will give him his share of the crop at harvest time."

42Jesus said to them, "Have you never read in the Scriptures:

"'The stone the builders rejected
   has become the cornerstone;
the Lord has done this,
   and it is marvelous in our eyes'[a]?

43"Therefore I tell you that the kingdom of God will be taken away from you and given to a people who will produce its fruit. 44Anyone who falls on this stone will be broken to pieces; anyone on whom it falls will be crushed."[b]

45When the chief priests and the Pharisees heard Jesus' parables, they knew he was talking about them. 46They looked for a way to arrest him, but they were afraid of the crowd because the people held that he was a prophet.

The Parable of the Wedding Banquet

22 Jesus spoke to them again in parables, saying: 2"The kingdom of heaven is like a king who prepared a wedding banquet for his son. 3He sent his servants to those who had been invited to the banquet to tell them to come, but they refused to come.

4"Then he sent some more servants and said, 'Tell those who have been invited that I have prepared my dinner: My oxen and fattened cattle have been butchered, and everything is ready. Come to the wedding banquet.'

5"But they paid no attention and went off—one to his field, another to his business. 6The rest seized his servants, mistreated them and killed them. 7The king was enraged. He sent his army and destroyed those murderers and burned their city.

8"Then he said to his servants, 'The wedding banquet is ready, but those I invited

---

a 42 Psalm 118:22,23   *b 44* Some manuscripts do not have verse 44.

did not deserve to come. ⁹So go to the street corners and invite to the banquet anyone you find.' ¹⁰So the servants went out into the streets and gathered all the people they could find, the bad as well as the good, and the wedding hall was filled with guests.

¹¹"But when the king came in to see the guests, he noticed a man there who was not wearing wedding clothes. ¹²He asked, 'How did you get in here without wedding clothes, friend?' The man was speechless.

¹³"Then the king told the attendants, 'Tie him hand and foot, and throw him outside, into the darkness, where there will be weeping and gnashing of teeth.'

¹⁴"For many are invited, but few are chosen."

Paying the Imperial Tax to Caesar

¹⁵Then the Pharisees went out and laid plans to trap him in his words. ¹⁶They sent their disciples to him along with the Herodians. "Teacher," they said, "we know that you are a man of integrity and that you teach the way of God in accordance with the truth. You aren't swayed by others, because you pay no attention to who they are. ¹⁷Tell us then, what is your opinion? Is it right to pay the imperial tax[a] to Caesar or not?"

¹⁸But Jesus, knowing their evil intent, said, "You hypocrites, why are you trying to trap me? ¹⁹Show me the coin used for paying the tax." They brought him a denarius, ²⁰and he asked them, "Whose image is this? And whose inscription?"

²¹"Caesar's," they replied.

Then he said to them, "So give back to Caesar what is Caesar's, and to God what is God's."

²²When they heard this, they were amazed. So they left him and went away.

Marriage at the Resurrection

²³That same day the Sadducees, who say there is no resurrection, came to him with a question. ²⁴"Teacher," they said, "Moses told us that if a man dies without having children, his brother must marry the widow and raise up offspring for him. ²⁵Now there were seven brothers among us. The first one married and died, and since he had no children, he left his wife to his brother. ²⁶The same thing happened to the second and third brother, right on down to the seventh. ²⁷Finally, the woman died. ²⁸Now then, at the resurrection, whose wife will she be of the seven, since all of them were married to her?"

²⁹Jesus replied, "You are in error because you do not know the Scriptures or the power of God. ³⁰At the resurrection people will neither marry nor be given in marriage; they will be like the angels in heaven. ³¹But about the resurrection of the dead—have you not read what God said to you, ³²'I am the God of Abraham, the God of Isaac, and the God of Jacob'[b]? He is not the God of the dead but of the living."

³³When the crowds heard this, they were astonished at his teaching.

The Greatest Commandment

³⁴Hearing that Jesus had silenced the Sadducees, the Pharisees got together. ³⁵One of them, an expert in the law, tested him with this question: ³⁶"Teacher, which is the greatest commandment in the Law?"

³⁷Jesus replied: "'Love the Lord your God with all your heart and with all your soul and with all your mind.'[c] ³⁸This is the first and greatest commandment. ³⁹And the second is like it: 'Love your neighbor as yourself.'[d] ⁴⁰All the Law and the Prophets hang on these two commandments."

Whose Son Is the Messiah?

⁴¹While the Pharisees were gathered together, Jesus asked them, ⁴²"What do you think about the Messiah? Whose son is he?"

"The son of David," they replied.

⁴³He said to them, "How is it then that

---

a 17 A special tax levied on subject peoples, not on Roman citizens   *b 32* Exodus 3:6   *c 37* Deut. 6:5   *d 39* Lev. 19:18

David, speaking by the Spirit, calls him 'Lord'? For he says,

44 " 'The Lord said to my Lord:
    "Sit at my right hand
    until I put your enemies
    under your feet." '[a]

45 If then David calls him 'Lord,' how can he be his son?" 46 No one could say a word in reply, and from that day on no one dared to ask him any more questions.

[a] 44 Psalm 110:1

A Warning Against Hypocrisy

23 Then Jesus said to the crowds and to his disciples: 2 "The teachers of the law and the Pharisees sit in Moses' seat. 3 So you must be careful to do everything they tell you. But do not do what they do, for they do not practice what they preach. 4 They tie up heavy, cumbersome loads and put them on other people's shoulders, but they themselves are not willing to lift a finger to move them.

SPIRITUAL INVENTORY LESSON [*Principle Seven*]

This is the first and only page of the DAILY INVENTORY lesson.

For a discussion of Principles One through Eight and a listing of their related lessons,
go to pages xvii – xliv.

*Jesus replied: " 'Love the Lord your God with all your heart
and with all your soul and with all your mind.'
This is the first and greatest commandment. And the second is like it:
'Love your neighbor as yourself.' All the Law and the Prophets
hang on these two commandments."*

MATTHEW 22:37–40

In Principle Seven we reserve a daily quiet time with God for self-examination, Bible reading and prayer in order to get to know God and his will for our lives and to gain the power to follow his will. As we work this principle, we begin the journey of applying and living what we've discovered in the first six principles. We live daily in humility — as well as in reality, not in denial. We've done our best to amend our past. Through God's guidance we can now make choices about the emotions that will affect our ongoing thinking and actions. We can start to take *action* — positive action — instead of operating in a mode of continual *reaction*.

In Principle Seven we desire to grow daily in our new relationships with Jesus Christ and others. Instead of attempting to be in control of every situation and every person with whom we come into contact, or instead of spinning out of control ourselves, we're starting to exhibit self-control, living the way God wants us to. Remember that "self under control" is what we're initially seeking but that self under God's control is what we're ultimately striving for.

Jesus has provided us with a daily checklist for our new lifestyle. It's called the Great Commandment, and we can find it in Matthew 22:37–40. When we do our daily personal inventory, we need to ask ourselves, "Today, did my actions reflect what the second greatest commandment requires? Did I truly love my neighbor [others] as much as I love myself?"

⁵"Everything they do is done for people to see: They make their phylacteries*ᵃ* wide and the tassels on their garments long; ⁶they love the place of honor at banquets and the most important seats in the synagogues; ⁷they love to be greeted with respect in the marketplaces and to be called 'Rabbi' by others.

⁸"But you are not to be called 'Rabbi,' for you have one Teacher, and you are all brothers. ⁹And do not call anyone on earth 'father,' for you have one Father, and he is in heaven. ¹⁰Nor are you to be called instructors, for you have one Instructor, the Messiah. ¹¹The greatest among you will be your servant. ¹²For those who exalt themselves will be humbled, and those who humble themselves will be exalted.

Seven Woes on the Teachers of the Law and the Pharisees

¹³"Woe to you, teachers of the law and Pharisees, you hypocrites! You shut the

---

ᵃ 5 That is, boxes containing Scripture verses, worn on forehead and arm

As we live out these two commandments by putting the principles and steps into action in our lives, we become more and more like Christ. We become active doers of God's Word, not just passive listeners. James 1:22 states this need clearly: "Do not merely listen to the word, and so deceive yourselves. Do what it says."

In Principle Seven we actually do three different inventories:

1. *An ongoing inventory.* We can maintain an ongoing inventory throughout the day. The best time to admit we're wrong is at the exact moment we're made aware of it. Why wait?

2. *A daily inventory.* At the end of each day we can look back over our daily activities, both the good and the bad, paying special attention to points at which we might have harmed someone else or reacted out of anger or fear. But once again, we need to remember to keep our daily inventory balanced. We should be sure to include the things we did right throughout the day, no matter how easy they may be to overlook or discount.

3. *A periodic inventory.* We should take a periodic inventory every 90 days or so. We may even want to get away on a mini retreat. We should bring our daily journals with us and pray as we read through the entries for the last 90 days. We should ask God to show us areas in our lives in which we can improve during the next 90 days. But we should also remember to identify and celebrate the victories we've experienced.

Principle Seven is so important. It also includes Step Eleven of the Christ-centered 12 steps.

Step Eleven: We've sought through prayer and meditation to improve our conscious contact with God, praying for knowledge of his will for us, as well as for the power to carry out that will.

We should remember to summarize the events of our day in our journals. By diligently maintaining ongoing, daily and periodic journal entries, we can work the first part of Principle Seven to the best of our abilities. With God's help we can keep our side of the street clean.

The DAILY INVENTORY lesson is complete on this page.

door of the kingdom of heaven in people's faces. You yourselves do not enter, nor will you let those enter who are trying to. [14]*a*

15 "Woe to you, teachers of the law and Pharisees, you hypocrites! You travel over land and sea to win a single convert, and when you have succeeded, you make them twice as much a child of hell as you are.

16 "Woe to you, blind guides! You say, 'If anyone swears by the temple, it means nothing; but anyone who swears by the gold of the temple is bound by that oath.' 17 You blind fools! Which is greater: the gold, or the temple that makes the gold sacred? 18 You also say, 'If anyone swears by the altar, it means nothing; but anyone who swears by the gift on the altar is bound by that oath.' 19 You blind men! Which is greater: the gift, or the altar that makes the gift sacred? 20 Therefore, anyone who swears by the altar swears by it and by everything on it. 21 And anyone who swears by the temple swears by it and by the one who dwells in it. 22 And anyone who swears by heaven swears by God's throne and by the one who sits on it.

23 "Woe to you, teachers of the law and Pharisees, you hypocrites! You give a tenth of your spices — mint, dill and cumin. But you have neglected the more important matters of the law — justice, mercy and faithfulness. You should have practiced the latter, without neglecting the former. 24 You blind guides! You strain out a gnat but swallow a camel.

25 "Woe to you, teachers of the law and Pharisees, you hypocrites! You clean the outside of the cup and dish, but inside they are full of greed and self-indulgence. 26 Blind Pharisee! First clean the inside of the cup and dish, and then the outside also will be clean.

27 "Woe to you, teachers of the law and Pharisees, you hypocrites! You are like whitewashed tombs, which look beautiful on the outside but on the inside are full of the bones of the dead and everything un-

clean. 28 In the same way, on the outside you appear to people as righteous but on the inside you are full of hypocrisy and wickedness.

29 "Woe to you, teachers of the law and Pharisees, you hypocrites! You build tombs for the prophets and decorate the graves of the righteous. 30 And you say, 'If we had lived in the days of our ancestors, we would not have taken part with them in shedding the blood of the prophets.' 31 So you testify against yourselves that you are the descendants of those who murdered the prophets. 32 Go ahead, then, and complete what your ancestors started!

33 "You snakes! You brood of vipers! How will you escape being condemned to hell? 34 Therefore I am sending you prophets and sages and teachers. Some of them you will kill and crucify; others you will flog in your synagogues and pursue from town to town. 35 And so upon you will come all the righteous blood that has been shed on earth, from the blood of righteous Abel to the blood of Zechariah son of Berekiah, whom you murdered between the temple and the altar. 36 Truly I tell you, all this will come on this generation.

37 "Jerusalem, Jerusalem, you who kill the prophets and stone those sent to you, how often I have longed to gather your children together, as a hen gathers her chicks under her wings, and you were not willing. 38 Look, your house is left to you desolate. 39 For I tell you, you will not see me again until you say, 'Blessed is he who comes in the name of the Lord.'*b*"

The Destruction of the Temple and Signs of the End Times

24 Jesus left the temple and was walking away when his disciples came up to him to call his attention to its buildings. 2 "Do you see all these things?" he asked. "Truly I tell you, not one stone here will be left on another; every one will be thrown down."

---

a 14 Some manuscripts include here words similar to Mark 12:40 and Luke 20:47.   *b* 39 Psalm 118:26

³As Jesus was sitting on the Mount of Olives, the disciples came to him privately. "Tell us," they said, "when will this happen, and what will be the sign of your coming and of the end of the age?"

⁴Jesus answered: "Watch out that no one deceives you. ⁵For many will come in my name, claiming, 'I am the Messiah,' and will deceive many. ⁶You will hear of wars and rumors of wars, but see to it that you are not alarmed. Such things must happen, but the end is still to come. ⁷Nation will rise against nation, and kingdom against kingdom. There will be famines and earthquakes in various places. ⁸All these are the beginning of birth pains.

⁹"Then you will be handed over to be persecuted and put to death, and you will be hated by all nations because of me. ¹⁰At that time many will turn away from the faith and will betray and hate each other, ¹¹and many false prophets will appear and deceive many people. ¹²Because of the increase of wickedness, the love of most will grow cold, ¹³but the one who stands firm to the end will be saved. ¹⁴And this gospel of the kingdom will be preached in the whole world as a testimony to all nations, and then the end will come.

¹⁵"So when you see standing in the holy place 'the abomination that causes desolation,'ᵃ spoken of through the prophet Daniel—let the reader understand— ¹⁶then let those who are in Judea flee to the mountains. ¹⁷Let no one on the housetop go down to take anything out of the house. ¹⁸Let no one in the field go back to get their cloak. ¹⁹How dreadful it will be in those days for pregnant women and nursing mothers! ²⁰Pray that your flight will not take place in winter or on the Sabbath. ²¹For then there will be great distress, unequaled from the beginning of the world until now—and never to be equaled again. ²²"If those days had not been cut short, no one would survive, but for the sake of the elect those days will be shortened. ²³At that time if anyone says to you, 'Look, here is the Messiah!' or, 'There he is!' do not believe it. ²⁴For false messiahs and false prophets will appear and perform great signs and wonders to deceive, if possible, even the elect. ²⁵See, I have told you ahead of time.

²⁶"So if anyone tells you, 'There he is, out in the wilderness,' do not go out; or, 'Here he is, in the inner rooms,' do not believe it. ²⁷For as lightning that comes from the east is visible even in the west, so will be the coming of the Son of Man. ²⁸Wherever there is a carcass, there the vultures will gather.

²⁹"Immediately after the distress of those days

"'the sun will be darkened,
    and the moon will not give its light;
the stars will fall from the sky,
    and the heavenly bodies will be
        shaken.'ᵇ

³⁰"Then will appear the sign of the Son of Man in heaven. And then all the peoples of the earthᶜ will mourn when they see the Son of Man coming on the clouds of heaven, with power and great glory.ᵈ ³¹And he will send his angels with a loud trumpet call, and they will gather his elect from the four winds, from one end of the heavens to the other.

³²"Now learn this lesson from the fig tree: As soon as its twigs get tender and its leaves come out, you know that summer is near. ³³Even so, when you see all these things, you know that itᵉ is near, right at the door. ³⁴Truly I tell you, this generation will certainly not pass away until all these things have happened. ³⁵Heaven and earth will pass away, but my words will never pass away.

The Day and Hour Unknown

³⁶"But about that day or hour no one knows, not even the angels in heaven, nor

---

ᵃ 15 Daniel 9:27; 11:31; 12:11   ᵇ 29 Isaiah 13:10; 34:4   ᶜ 30 Or *the tribes of the land*   ᵈ 30 See Daniel 7:13-14.
ᵉ 33 Or *he*

the Son,[a] but only the Father. [37]As it was in the days of Noah, so it will be at the coming of the Son of Man. [38]For in the days before the flood, people were eating and drinking, marrying and giving in marriage, up to the day Noah entered the ark; [39]and they knew nothing about what would happen until the flood came and took them all away. That is how it will be at the coming of the Son of Man. [40]Two men will be in the field; one will be taken and the other left. [41]Two women will be grinding with a hand mill; one will be taken and the other left.

[42]"Therefore keep watch, because you do not know on what day your Lord will come. [43]But understand this: If the owner of the house had known at what time of night the thief was coming, he would have kept watch and would not have let his house be broken into. [44]So you also must be ready, because the Son of Man will come at an hour when you do not expect him.

[45]"Who then is the faithful and wise servant, whom the master has put in charge of the servants in his household to give them their food at the proper time? [46]It will be good for that servant whose master finds him doing so when he returns. [47]Truly I tell you, he will put him in charge of all his possessions. [48]But suppose that servant is wicked and says to himself, 'My master is staying away a long time,' [49]and he then begins to beat his fellow servants and to eat and drink with drunkards. [50]The master of that servant will come on a day when he does not expect him and at an hour he is not aware of. [51]He will cut him to pieces and assign him a place with the hypocrites, where there will be weeping and gnashing of teeth.

The Parable of the Ten Virgins

25 "At that time the kingdom of heaven will be like ten virgins who took their lamps and went out to meet the bridegroom. [2]Five of them were foolish and five were wise. [3]The foolish ones took their lamps but did not take any oil with them. [4]The wise ones, however, took oil in jars along with their lamps. [5]The bridegroom was a long time in coming, and they all became drowsy and fell asleep.

[6]"At midnight the cry rang out: 'Here's the bridegroom! Come out to meet him!'

[7]"Then all the virgins woke up and trimmed their lamps. [8]The foolish ones said to the wise, 'Give us some of your oil; our lamps are going out.'

[9]"'No,' they replied, 'there may not be enough for both us and you. Instead, go to those who sell oil and buy some for yourselves.'

[10]"But while they were on their way to buy the oil, the bridegroom arrived. The virgins who were ready went in with him to the wedding banquet. And the door was shut.

[11]"Later the others also came. 'Lord, Lord,' they said, 'open the door for us!'

[12]"But he replied, 'Truly I tell you, I don't know you.'

[13]"Therefore keep watch, because you do not know the day or the hour.

The Parable of the Bags of Gold

[14]"Again, it will be like a man going on a journey, who called his servants and entrusted his wealth to them. [15]To one he gave five bags of gold, to another two bags, and to another one bag,[b] each according to his ability. Then he went on his journey. [16]The man who had received five bags of gold went at once and put his money to work and gained five bags more. [17]So also, the one with two bags of gold gained two more. [18]But the man who had received one bag went off, dug a hole in the ground and hid his master's money.

[19]"After a long time the master of those servants returned and settled accounts with them. [20]The man who had received five bags of gold brought the other five.

---

[a] 36 Some manuscripts do not have *nor the Son*.   [b] 15 Greek *five talents . . . two talents . . . one talent*; also throughout this parable; a talent was worth about 20 years of a day laborer's wage.

'Master,' he said, 'you entrusted me with five bags of gold. See, I have gained five more.'

21"His master replied, 'Well done, good and faithful servant! You have been faithful with a few things; I will put you in charge of many things. Come and share your master's happiness!'

22"The man with two bags of gold also came. 'Master,' he said, 'you entrusted me with two bags of gold; see, I have gained two more.'

23"His master replied, 'Well done, good and faithful servant! You have been faithful with a few things; I will put you in charge of many things. Come and share your master's happiness!'

24"Then the man who had received one bag of gold came. 'Master,' he said, 'I knew that you are a hard man, harvesting where you have not sown and gathering where you have not scattered seed. 25So I was afraid and went out and hid your gold in the ground. See, here is what belongs to you.'

26"His master replied, 'You wicked, lazy servant! So you knew that I harvest where I have not sown and gather where I have not scattered seed? 27Well then, you should have put my money on deposit with the bankers, so that when I returned I would have received it back with interest.

28"'So take the bag of gold from him and give it to the one who has ten bags. 29For whoever has will be given more, and they will have an abundance. Whoever does not have, even what they have will be taken from them. 30And throw that worthless servant outside, into the darkness, where there will be weeping and gnashing of teeth.'

The Sheep and the Goats

31"When the Son of Man comes in his glory, and all the angels with him, he will sit on his glorious throne. 32All the nations will be gathered before him, and he will separate the people one from another as a shepherd separates the sheep from the goats. 33He will put the sheep on his right and the goats on his left.

34"Then the King will say to those on his right, 'Come, you who are blessed by my Father; take your inheritance, the kingdom prepared for you since the creation of the world. 35For I was hungry and you gave me something to eat, I was thirsty and you gave me something to drink, I was a stranger and you invited me in, 36I needed clothes and you clothed me, I was sick and you looked after me, I was in prison and you came to visit me.'

37"Then the righteous will answer him, 'Lord, when did we see you hungry and feed you, or thirsty and give you something to drink? 38When did we see you a stranger and invite you in, or needing clothes and clothe you? 39When did we see you sick or in prison and go to visit you?'

40"The King will reply, 'Truly I tell you, whatever you did for one of the least of these brothers and sisters of mine, you did for me.'

41"Then he will say to those on his left, 'Depart from me, you who are cursed, into the eternal fire prepared for the devil and his angels. 42For I was hungry and you gave me nothing to eat, I was thirsty and you gave me nothing to drink, 43I was a stranger and you did not invite me in, I needed clothes and you did not clothe me, I was sick and in prison and you did not look after me.'

44"They also will answer, 'Lord, when did we see you hungry or thirsty or a stranger or needing clothes or sick or in prison, and did not help you?'

45"He will reply, 'Truly I tell you, whatever you did not do for one of the least of these, you did not do for me.'

46"Then they will go away to eternal punishment, but the righteous to eternal life."

The Plot Against Jesus

26 When Jesus had finished saying all these things, he said to his disciples, 2"As you know, the Passover is two days away — and the Son of Man will be handed over to be crucified."

3Then the chief priests and the elders of the people assembled in the palace of the high priest, whose name was Caiaphas, 4and they schemed to arrest Jesus secretly and kill him. 5"But not during the festival," they said, "or there may be a riot among the people."

Jesus Anointed at Bethany

6While Jesus was in Bethany in the home of Simon the Leper, 7a woman came to him with an alabaster jar of very expensive perfume, which she poured on his head as he was reclining at the table.

8When the disciples saw this, they were indignant. "Why this waste?" they asked. 9"This perfume could have been sold at a high price and the money given to the poor."

10Aware of this, Jesus said to them, "Why are you bothering this woman? She has done a beautiful thing to me. 11The poor you will always have with you,*a* but you will not always have me. 12When she poured this perfume on my body, she did it to prepare me for burial. 13Truly I tell you, wherever this gospel is preached throughout the world, what she has done will also be told, in memory of her."

Judas Agrees to Betray Jesus

14Then one of the Twelve — the one called Judas Iscariot — went to the chief priests 15and asked, "What are you willing to give me if I deliver him over to you?" So they counted out for him thirty pieces of silver. 16From then on Judas watched for an opportunity to hand him over.

The Last Supper

17On the first day of the Festival of Unleavened Bread, the disciples came to Jesus and asked, "Where do you want us to make preparations for you to eat the Passover?"

18He replied, "Go into the city to a certain man and tell him, 'The Teacher says: My appointed time is near. I am going to celebrate the Passover with my disciples at your house.'" 19So the disciples did as Jesus had directed them and prepared the Passover.

20When evening came, Jesus was reclining at the table with the Twelve. 21And while they were eating, he said, "Truly I tell you, one of you will betray me."

22They were very sad and began to say to him one after the other, "Surely you don't mean me, Lord?"

23Jesus replied, "The one who has dipped his hand into the bowl with me will betray me. 24The Son of Man will go just as it is written about him. But woe to that man who betrays the Son of Man! It would be better for him if he had not been born."

25Then Judas, the one who would betray him, said, "Surely you don't mean me, Rabbi?"

Jesus answered, "You have said so."

26While they were eating, Jesus took bread, and when he had given thanks, he broke it and gave it to his disciples, saying, "Take and eat; this is my body."

27Then he took a cup, and when he had given thanks, he gave it to them, saying, "Drink from it, all of you. 28This is my blood of the*b* covenant, which is poured out for many for the forgiveness of sins. 29I tell you, I will not drink from this fruit of the vine from now on until that day when I drink it new with you in my Father's kingdom."

30When they had sung a hymn, they went out to the Mount of Olives.

Jesus Predicts Peter's Denial

31Then Jesus told them, "This very night you will all fall away on account of me, for it is written:

"'I will strike the shepherd,
    and the sheep of the flock will be
        scattered.'*c*

32But after I have risen, I will go ahead of you into Galilee."

---

a 11 See Deut. 15:11.   *b 28* Some manuscripts *the new*   *c 31* Zech. 13:7

33Peter replied, "Even if all fall away on account of you, I never will."

34"Truly I tell you," Jesus answered, "this very night, before the rooster crows, you will disown me three times."

35But Peter declared, "Even if I have to die with you, I will never disown you." And all the other disciples said the same.

Gethsemane

36Then Jesus went with his disciples to a place called Gethsemane, and he said to them, "Sit here while I go over there and pray." 37He took Peter and the two sons of Zebedee along with him, and he began to be sorrowful and troubled. 38Then he said to them, "My soul is overwhelmed with sorrow to the point of death. Stay here and keep watch with me."

39Going a little farther, he fell with his face to the ground and prayed, "My Father, if it is possible, may this cup be taken from me. Yet not as I will, but as you will."

40Then he returned to his disciples and found them sleeping. "Couldn't you men keep watch with me for one hour?" he asked Peter. 41"Watch and pray so that you will not fall into temptation. The spirit is willing, but the flesh is weak."

42He went away a second time and prayed, "My Father, if it is not possible for this cup to be taken away unless I drink it, may your will be done."

43When he came back, he again found them sleeping, because their eyes were heavy. 44So he left them and went away once more and prayed the third time, saying the same thing.

45Then he returned to the disciples and said to them, "Are you still sleeping and resting? Look, the hour has come, and the Son of Man is delivered into the hands of sinners. 46Rise! Let us go! Here comes my betrayer!"

Jesus Arrested

47While he was still speaking, Judas, one of the Twelve, arrived. With him was a large crowd armed with swords and clubs, sent from the chief priests and the elders of the people. 48Now the betrayer had arranged a signal with them: "The one I kiss is the man; arrest him." 49Going at once to Jesus, Judas said, "Greetings, Rabbi!" and kissed him.

50Jesus replied, "Do what you came for, friend."*a*

Then the men stepped forward, seized Jesus and arrested him. 51With that, one of Jesus' companions reached for his sword, drew it out and struck the servant of the high priest, cutting off his ear.

52"Put your sword back in its place," Jesus said to him, "for all who draw the sword will die by the sword. 53Do you think I cannot call on my Father, and he will at once put at my disposal more than twelve legions of angels? 54But how then would the Scriptures be fulfilled that say it must happen in this way?"

55In that hour Jesus said to the crowd, "Am I leading a rebellion, that you have come out with swords and clubs to capture me? Every day I sat in the temple courts teaching, and you did not arrest me. 56But this has all taken place that the writings of the prophets might be fulfilled." Then all the disciples deserted him and fled.

Jesus Before the Sanhedrin

57Those who had arrested Jesus took him to Caiaphas the high priest, where the teachers of the law and the elders had assembled. 58But Peter followed him at a distance, right up to the courtyard of the high priest. He entered and sat down with the guards to see the outcome.

59The chief priests and the whole Sanhedrin were looking for false evidence against Jesus so that they could put him to death. 60But they did not find any, though many false witnesses came forward.

Finally two came forward 61and declared, "This fellow said, 'I am able to destroy the temple of God and rebuild it in three days.'"

---

a 50 Or *"Why have you come, friend?"*

⁶²Then the high priest stood up and said to Jesus, "Are you not going to answer? What is this testimony that these men are bringing against you?" ⁶³But Jesus remained silent.

The high priest said to him, "I charge you under oath by the living God: Tell us if you are the Messiah, the Son of God."

⁶⁴"You have said so," Jesus replied. "But I say to all of you: From now on you will see the Son of Man sitting at the right hand of the Mighty One and coming on the clouds of heaven."ᵃ

⁶⁵Then the high priest tore his clothes and said, "He has spoken blasphemy! Why do we need any more witnesses? Look, now you have heard the blasphemy. ⁶⁶What do you think?"

"He is worthy of death," they answered.

⁶⁷Then they spit in his face and struck him with their fists. Others slapped him ⁶⁸and said, "Prophesy to us, Messiah. Who hit you?"

Peter Disowns Jesus

⁶⁹Now Peter was sitting out in the courtyard, and a servant girl came to him. "You also were with Jesus of Galilee," she said.

⁷⁰But he denied it before them all. "I don't know what you're talking about," he said.

⁷¹Then he went out to the gateway, where another servant girl saw him and said to the people there, "This fellow was with Jesus of Nazareth."

⁷²He denied it again, with an oath: "I don't know the man!"

⁷³After a little while, those standing there went up to Peter and said, "Surely you are one of them; your accent gives you away."

⁷⁴Then he began to call down curses, and he swore to them, "I don't know the man!"

Immediately a rooster crowed. ⁷⁵Then Peter remembered the word Jesus had spoken: "Before the rooster crows, you will disown me three times." And he went outside and wept bitterly.

Judas Hangs Himself

27 Early in the morning, all the chief priests and the elders of the people made their plans how to have Jesus executed. ²So they bound him, led him away and handed him over to Pilate the governor.

³When Judas, who had betrayed him, saw that Jesus was condemned, he was seized with remorse and returned the thirty pieces of silver to the chief priests and the elders. ⁴"I have sinned," he said, "for I have betrayed innocent blood."

"What is that to us?" they replied. "That's your responsibility."

⁵So Judas threw the money into the temple and left. Then he went away and hanged himself.

⁶The chief priests picked up the coins and said, "It is against the law to put this into the treasury, since it is blood money." ⁷So they decided to use the money to buy the potter's field as a burial place for foreigners. ⁸That is why it has been called the Field of Blood to this day. ⁹Then what was spoken by Jeremiah the prophet was fulfilled: "They took the thirty pieces of silver, the price set on him by the people of Israel, ¹⁰and they used them to buy the potter's field, as the Lord commanded me."ᵇ

Jesus Before Pilate

¹¹Meanwhile Jesus stood before the governor, and the governor asked him, "Are you the king of the Jews?"

"You have said so," Jesus replied.

¹²When he was accused by the chief priests and the elders, he gave no answer. ¹³Then Pilate asked him, "Don't you hear the testimony they are bringing against you?" ¹⁴But Jesus made no reply, not even to a single charge — to the great amazement of the governor.

¹⁵Now it was the governor's custom at

ᵃ 64 See Psalm 110:1; Daniel 7:13.   ᵇ 10 See Zech. 11:12,13; Jer. 19:1-13; 32:6-9.

the festival to release a prisoner chosen by the crowd. [16]At that time they had a well-known prisoner whose name was Jesus[a] Barabbas. [17]So when the crowd had gathered, Pilate asked them, "Which one do you want me to release to you: Jesus Barabbas, or Jesus who is called the Messiah?" [18]For he knew it was out of self-interest that they had handed Jesus over to him.

[19]While Pilate was sitting on the judge's seat, his wife sent him this message: "Don't have anything to do with that innocent man, for I have suffered a great deal today in a dream because of him."

[20]But the chief priests and the elders persuaded the crowd to ask for Barabbas and to have Jesus executed.

[21]"Which of the two do you want me to release to you?" asked the governor.

"Barabbas," they answered.

[22]"What shall I do, then, with Jesus who is called the Messiah?" Pilate asked.

They all answered, "Crucify him!"

[23]"Why? What crime has he committed?" asked Pilate.

But they shouted all the louder, "Crucify him!"

[24]When Pilate saw that he was getting nowhere, but that instead an uproar was starting, he took water and washed his hands in front of the crowd. "I am innocent of this man's blood," he said. "It is your responsibility!"

[25]All the people answered, "His blood is on us and on our children!"

[26]Then he released Barabbas to them. But he had Jesus flogged, and handed him over to be crucified.

The Soldiers Mock Jesus

[27]Then the governor's soldiers took Jesus into the Praetorium and gathered the whole company of soldiers around him. [28]They stripped him and put a scarlet robe on him, [29]and then twisted together a crown of thorns and set it on his head. They put a staff in his right hand. Then they knelt in front of him and mocked him. "Hail, king of the Jews!" they said. [30]They spit on him, and took the staff and struck him on the head again and again. [31]After they had mocked him, they took off the robe and put his own clothes on him. Then they led him away to crucify him.

The Crucifixion of Jesus

[32]As they were going out, they met a man from Cyrene, named Simon, and they forced him to carry the cross. [33]They came to a place called Golgotha (which means "the place of the skull"). [34]There they offered Jesus wine to drink, mixed with gall; but after tasting it, he refused to drink it. [35]When they had crucified him, they divided up his clothes by casting lots. [36]And sitting down, they kept watch over him there. [37]Above his head they placed the written charge against him: THIS IS JESUS, THE KING OF THE JEWS.

[38]Two rebels were crucified with him, one on his right and one on his left. [39]Those who passed by hurled insults at him, shaking their heads [40]and saying, "You who are going to destroy the temple and build it in three days, save yourself! Come down from the cross, if you are the Son of God!" [41]In the same way the chief priests, the teachers of the law and the elders mocked him. [42]"He saved others," they said, "but he can't save himself! He's the king of Israel! Let him come down now from the cross, and we will believe in him. [43]He trusts in God. Let God rescue him now if he wants him, for he said, 'I am the Son of God.'" [44]In the same way the rebels who were crucified with him also heaped insults on him.

The Death of Jesus

[45]From noon until three in the afternoon darkness came over all the land. [46]About three in the afternoon Jesus cried out in a loud voice, "Eli, Eli,[b] lema sabachthani?" (which means "My God, my God, why have you forsaken me?").[c]

---

⁴⁷When some of those standing there heard this, they said, "He's calling Elijah." ⁴⁸Immediately one of them ran and got a sponge. He filled it with wine vinegar, put it on a staff, and offered it to Jesus to drink. ⁴⁹The rest said, "Now leave him alone. Let's see if Elijah comes to save him."

⁵⁰And when Jesus had cried out again in a loud voice, he gave up his spirit.

⁵¹At that moment the curtain of the temple was torn in two from top to bottom. The earth shook, the rocks split ⁵²and the tombs broke open. The bodies of many holy people who had died were raised to life. ⁵³They came out of the tombs after Jesus' resurrection and*ᵃ* went into the holy city and appeared to many people.

⁵⁴When the centurion and those with him who were guarding Jesus saw the earthquake and all that had happened, they were terrified, and exclaimed, "Surely he was the Son of God!"

⁵⁵Many women were there, watching from a distance. They had followed Jesus from Galilee to care for his needs. ⁵⁶Among them were Mary Magdalene, Mary the mother of James and Joseph,*ᵇ* and the mother of Zebedee's sons.

The Burial of Jesus

⁵⁷As evening approached, there came a rich man from Arimathea, named Joseph, who had himself become a disciple of Jesus. ⁵⁸Going to Pilate, he asked for Jesus' body, and Pilate ordered that it be given to him. ⁵⁹Joseph took the body, wrapped it in a clean linen cloth, ⁶⁰and placed it in his own new tomb that he had cut out of the rock. He rolled a big stone in front of the entrance to the tomb and went away. ⁶¹Mary Magdalene and the other Mary were sitting there opposite the tomb.

The Guard at the Tomb

⁶²The next day, the one after Preparation Day, the chief priests and the Pharisees went to Pilate. ⁶³"Sir," they said, "we remember that while he was still alive that deceiver said, 'After three days I will rise again.' ⁶⁴So give the order for the tomb to be made secure until the third day. Otherwise, his disciples may come and steal the body and tell the people that he has been raised from the dead. This last deception will be worse than the first."

⁶⁵"Take a guard," Pilate answered. "Go, make the tomb as secure as you know how." ⁶⁶So they went and made the tomb secure by putting a seal on the stone and posting the guard.

Jesus Has Risen

28 After the Sabbath, at dawn on the first day of the week, Mary Magdalene and the other Mary went to look at the tomb.

²There was a violent earthquake, for an angel of the Lord came down from heaven and, going to the tomb, rolled back the stone and sat on it. ³His appearance was like lightning, and his clothes were white as snow. ⁴The guards were so afraid of him that they shook and became like dead men.

⁵The angel said to the women, "Do not be afraid, for I know that you are looking for Jesus, who was crucified. ⁶He is not here; he has risen, just as he said. Come and see the place where he lay. ⁷Then go quickly and tell his disciples: 'He has risen from the dead and is going ahead of you into Galilee. There you will see him.' Now I have told you."

⁸So the women hurried away from the tomb, afraid yet filled with joy, and ran to tell his disciples. ⁹Suddenly Jesus met them. "Greetings," he said. They came to him, clasped his feet and worshiped him. ¹⁰Then Jesus said to them, "Do not be afraid. Go and tell my brothers to go to Galilee; there they will see me."

The Guards' Report

¹¹While the women were on their way, some of the guards went into the city and

---

ᵃ 53 Or *tombs, and after Jesus' resurrection they*   *ᵇ 56* Greek *Joses,* a variant of *Joseph* reported to the chief priests everything that had happened. 12When the chief priests had met with the elders and devised a plan, they gave the soldiers a large sum of money, 13telling them, "You are to say, 'His disciples came during the night and stole him away while we were asleep.' 14If this report gets to the governor, we will satisfy him and keep you out of trouble." 15So the soldiers took the money and did as they were instructed. And this story has been widely circulated among the Jews to this very day.

The Great Commission

16Then the eleven disciples went to Galilee, to the mountain where Jesus had told them to go. 17When they saw him, they worshiped him; but some doubted. 18Then Jesus came to them and said, "All authority in heaven and on earth has been given to me. 19Therefore go and make disciples of all nations, baptizing them in the name of the Father and of the Son and of the Holy Spirit, 20and teaching them to obey everything I have commanded you. And surely I am with you always, to the very end of the age."

Mark

THEME: Jesus is the Savior of all who will receive him by faith.

AUTHOR: The earliest testimony connects this Gospel to Mark, also known as John Mark (see character study on page 1510).

DATE OF WRITING: Mark was probably written between AD 50 and 70.

ENCOURAGEMENT FROM MARK: "Jesus said . . . 'It is not the healthy who need a doctor, but the sick. I have not come to call the righteous, but sinners' " (Mark 2:17).

CHALLENGE FROM MARK: "When you stand praying, if you hold anything against anyone, forgive him, so that your Father in heaven may forgive you your sins" (Mark 11:25).

REFLECTION FROM MARK: "As Jesus was getting into the boat, the man who had been demon-possessed begged to go with him. Jesus did not let him, but said, 'Go home to your own people and tell them how much the Lord has done for you, and how he has had mercy on you' " (Mark 5:18–19).

The Gospel of Mark gives us an insider's view of the life of Christ. One of the most amazing things about Jesus is that he chose regular, normal people to be his followers. He didn't call the religious, the educated or the wealthy. Rather, he called rugged fishermen and despised tax collectors. He called men who were ready to drop everything and follow him with absolute trust.

It's not uncommon for those of us in recovery to feel as though we aren't good enough for Jesus. We think we need to get our act together before we can have a relationship with him. The Gospel of Mark shows us just how wrong we are. Jesus loves us right where, and how, we are. He wants us to walk with him and be changed on the basis of that relationship, not before we enter into it.

The Gospel of Mark makes clear that finding healing for our hurts, hang-ups and habits requires action on our part as well. From the man with leprosy who asked Jesus for healing (see Mark 1:40) to the paralyzed man whose friends lowered him through the roof to get to Jesus (see 2:3–4) to the bleeding woman who took the risk to reach out and touch him (see 5:25), we see that Jesus is willing to heal us if only we're willing to seek him out.

John the Baptist Prepares the Way

1 The beginning of the good news about Jesus the Messiah,[a] the Son of God,[b] [2]as it is written in Isaiah the prophet:

"I will send my messenger ahead of you,
who will prepare your way"[c] —
[3]"a voice of one calling in the wilderness,
'Prepare the way for the Lord,
make straight paths for him.' "[d]

[4]And so John the Baptist appeared in the wilderness, preaching a baptism of repentance for the forgiveness of sins. [5]The whole Judean countryside and all the people of Jerusalem went out to him. Confessing their sins, they were baptized by him in the Jordan River. [6]John wore clothing made of camel's hair, with a leather belt around his waist, and he ate locusts and wild honey. [7]And this was his message: "After me comes the one more powerful than I, the straps of whose sandals I am not worthy to stoop down and untie. [8]I baptize you with[e] water, but he will baptize you with[e] the Holy Spirit."

The Baptism and Testing of Jesus

[9]At that time Jesus came from Nazareth in Galilee and was baptized by John in the Jordan. [10]Just as Jesus was coming up out of the water, he saw heaven being torn open and the Spirit descending on him like a dove. [11]And a voice came from heaven: "You are my Son, whom I love; with you I am well pleased."

[12]At once the Spirit sent him out into the wilderness, [13]and he was in the wilderness forty days, being tempted[f] by Satan. He was with the wild animals, and angels attended him.

Jesus Announces the Good News

[14]After John was put in prison, Jesus went into Galilee, proclaiming the good news of God. [15]"The time has come," he said. "The kingdom of God has come near. Repent and believe the good news!"

Jesus Calls His First Disciples

[16]As Jesus walked beside the Sea of Galilee, he saw Simon and his brother Andrew casting a net into the lake, for they were fishermen. [17]"Come, follow me," Jesus said, "and I will send you out to fish for people." [18]At once they left their nets and followed him.

[19]When he had gone a little farther, he saw James son of Zebedee and his brother John in a boat, preparing their nets. [20]Without delay he called them, and they left their father Zebedee in the boat with the hired men and followed him.

Jesus Drives Out an Impure Spirit

[21]They went to Capernaum, and when the Sabbath came, Jesus went into the synagogue and began to teach. [22]The people were amazed at his teaching, because he taught them as one who had authority, not as the teachers of the law. [23]Just then a man in their synagogue who was possessed by an impure spirit cried out, [24]"What do you want with us, Jesus of Nazareth? Have you come to destroy us? I know who you are — the Holy One of God!"

[25]"Be quiet!" said Jesus sternly. "Come out of him!" [26]The impure spirit shook the man violently and came out of him with a shriek.

[27]The people were all so amazed that they asked each other, "What is this? A new teaching — and with authority! He even gives orders to impure spirits and they obey him." [28]News about him spread quickly over the whole region of Galilee.

Jesus Heals Many

[29]As soon as they left the synagogue, they went with James and John to the home of Simon and Andrew. [30]Simon's mother-in-law was in bed with a fever, and they

---

a 1 Or *Jesus Christ. Messiah* (Hebrew) and *Christ* (Greek) both mean *Anointed One.*   *b 1* Some manuscripts do not have *the Son of God.*   *c 2* Mal. 3:1   *d 3* Isaiah 40:3   *e 8* Or *in*   *f 13* The Greek for *tempted* can also mean *tested.*

MY NAME IS
A MAN WITH LEPROSY

MARK 1:40–45

In Celebrate Recovery our identity isn't tied to our past failures. We're what we've become solely by God's grace. The recipient of grace in this story is described simply as "a man with leprosy" (Mark 1:40), but Christ's healing touch would transform this individual's anonymous suffering into a powerful testimony (see Matthew 8:2). Labeling his problem was simple, and obtaining cleansing from Christ was, in his case, immediate (see Mark 1:42). For some, sobriety comes quickly, instantaneously, as soon as they surrender to Jesus. But for others it is a process.

This one-time leper was cured of his disease by the touch of Jesus. But Jesus wasn't through with him. There were still some steps to take. Our Lord instructed the man to

- keep silent about the miracle,

- show himself to the priest, and

- offer the gift (sacrifice) required by the Mosaic Law.

All of these steps tie directly in to that law. Jesus was careful to do everything according to the law under which he had been born and now lived. The new covenant, which depended on Jesus' death and resurrection, was still in the future. Under the law, neither the cured man nor Jesus had the authority to publicly declare a leper cleansed. That was work assigned by God to the priests (see Leviticus 14:2–32). Jesus wouldn't consider breaking the law, and keeping that particular law would make this man a "testimony to them" (Matthew 8:4) — that is, to the priests who would carry out the required rituals.

Jesus wants to transform us, too, into testimonies as we practice the principles that Christ presented (see 5:1–10) during his Sermon on the Mount in Matthew 5–7. This man's healing took place as Jesus "came down from the mountainside" (8:1) after delivering the great sermon that encapsulates the principles of recovery. These principles, combined with God's power, change our identity. Rather than being an alcoholic, an addict or an abuse victim, each of us becomes a testimony to God's grace.

immediately told Jesus about her. [31]So he went to her, took her hand and helped her up. The fever left her and she began to wait on them.

[32]That evening after sunset the people brought to Jesus all the sick and demon-possessed. [33]The whole town gathered at the door, [34]and Jesus healed many who had various diseases. He also drove out many demons, but he would not let the demons speak because they knew who he was.

Jesus Prays in a Solitary Place

[35]Very early in the morning, while it was still dark, Jesus got up, left the house and went off to a solitary place, where he prayed. [36]Simon and his companions went to look for him, [37]and when they found him, they exclaimed: "Everyone is looking for you!"

[38]Jesus replied, "Let us go somewhere else — to the nearby villages — so I can preach there also. That is why I have come." [39]So he traveled throughout Galilee, preaching in their synagogues and driving out demons.

Jesus Heals a Man With Leprosy

[40]A man with leprosy[a] came to him and begged him on his knees, "If you are willing, you can make me clean."

[41]Jesus was indignant.[b] He reached out his hand and touched the man. "I am willing," he said. "Be clean!" [42]Immediately the leprosy left him and he was cleansed.

[43]Jesus sent him away at once with a strong warning: [44]"See that you don't tell this to anyone. But go, show yourself to the priest and offer the sacrifices that Moses commanded for your cleansing, as a testimony to them." [45]Instead he went out and began to talk freely, spreading the news. As a result, Jesus could no longer enter a town openly but stayed outside in lonely places. Yet the people still came to him from everywhere.

Jesus Forgives and Heals a Paralyzed Man

2 A few days later, when Jesus again entered Capernaum, the people heard that he had come home. [2]They gathered in such large numbers that there was no room left, not even outside the door, and he preached the word to them. [3]Some men came, bringing to him a paralyzed man, carried by four of them. [4]Since they could not get him to Jesus because of the crowd, they made an opening in the roof above Jesus by digging through it and then lowered the mat the man was lying on. [5]When Jesus saw their faith, he said to the paralyzed man, "Son, your sins are forgiven."

[6]Now some teachers of the law were sitting there, thinking to themselves, [7]"Why does this fellow talk like that? He's blaspheming! Who can forgive sins but God alone?"

[8]Immediately Jesus knew in his spirit that this was what they were thinking in their hearts, and he said to them, "Why are you thinking these things? [9]Which is easier: to say to this paralyzed man, 'Your sins are forgiven,' or to say, 'Get up, take your mat and walk'? [10]But I want you to know that the Son of Man has authority on earth to forgive sins." So he said to the man, [11]"I tell you, get up, take your mat and go home." [12]He got up, took his mat and walked out in full view of them all. This amazed everyone and they praised God, saying, "We have never seen anything like this!"

Jesus Calls Levi and Eats With Sinners

[13]Once again Jesus went out beside the lake. A large crowd came to him, and he began to teach them. [14]As he walked along, he saw Levi son of Alphaeus sitting at the tax collector's booth. "Follow me," Jesus told him, and Levi got up and followed him.

---

[a] 40 The Greek word traditionally translated leprosy was used for various diseases affecting the skin.   [b] 41 Many manuscripts Jesus was filled with compassion

My Name Is Kimberley

I'M A BELIEVER WHO STRUGGLES WITH CHEMICAL ADDICTION

Please read the story of the healed leper in Mark 1:40–45.

From the outside it would appear as though I came from a normal family. But from the inside looking out, the view was much different. My mother was a raging alcoholic, and my father was emotionally unavailable. Their love for us was manifested through the lavish provision of material things, but whippings were a regular part of life.

The only time God entered our lives was on Sunday mornings, when we'd get dressed up to look good for church. Afterward we'd either go to our ranch, ride our horses and watch Mom get drunk or go home and watch her get drunk. Either way the day invariably ended in a major altercation between my parents.

Still, when they divorced my world fell apart. This propelled me into a new reality of addiction, and I soon discovered the formula for fitting in with the "cool" kids: cigarettes, alcohol, drugs and boys. My addictions tainted every aspect of my life. I started failing classes and ditching school, ultimately dropping out after my freshman year. I couldn't imagine anyone ever loving me, especially God, who, after all, had taken my dad from me. I had committed so many sins. I was, in my own words, a terrible, dishonest, lying, cheating person.

In 1990 I married and shortly afterward gave birth to a son. (Following the agony of two abortions, I had vowed I would never stoop to that level again.) During my pregnancy I managed to stay sober, although after C.J.'s birth I did resume some of my earlier behavior, limiting myself to social, weekend drinking. I wanted to be a good parent and tried to get my husband to attend church services with me, to little avail.

When I look back at my marriage I see how much it lacked. We had no communication or intimacy and had even stopped being friends. Eventually my infidelity penetrated our marriage, though, and we were divorced following my husband's departure with another woman in 1995, after the birth of our second son, Zachary, in 1994.

Once again my world fell apart. "How could he do this to me?" I thought. (Quite the double standard, right?) I immediately resumed my earlier habits of drinking, using drugs and sexually acting out. As a matter of fact, I had no trouble picking up right where I had left off. I moved in with a friend who had a huge house — ideal for throwing lavish parties. One night

I was out barhopping with friends when one of the guys decided to put me on his shoulders. I awoke lying flat on my back with a fractured spine. Through this experience I discovered Vicodin, to which I quickly became addicted. To my credit, when I realized I still wanted the pills after the pain was gone, I asked my doctor not to write any more prescriptions.

In December of 1998 I realized I was powerless to control my addictions. I fell to the floor and cried out to God. My no-frills plea was as basic as I could blurt out: "Please help me!" In light of my experiences with my mom while growing up, I was terribly afraid of becoming an alcoholic. God answered my prayer immediately; the very next day I embarked on my new life in Christ. His healing touch transformed me instantaneously, turning my life into a living testimony. As was the case with the leper cured by the touch of Jesus, the Savior wasn't finished with me yet. The leper's temple sacrifices were intended by Jesus as evidence to the priests and the people that the cure was the real thing. The healing was also a testimony to Jesus' divine power (see 2 Kings 5:1 – 14). My involvement in Celebrate Recovery demonstrated the same realities in my life.

I jumped into recovery with both feet, never looking back. I attended my first Celebrate Recovery meeting on Christmas Day and knew right away I was home. I found a wonderful Christian woman to be my sponsor, and she guided me through the principles and steps with love, kindness and patience. Through recovery I'm learning to be a functional, honest, principled woman.

I started serving as soon as I could, and still today I share my testimony whenever an opportunity arises. After working through my own Step Study, I joined the Celebrate Recovery leadership team, and I have since that time led countless Step Studies and have taken the program to the Orange County Rescue Mission. In addition, I'm sponsoring other women who struggle with addictions. Most importantly, I have the privilege of teaching my 11- and 7-year-old sons, the two greatest blessings in my life, how to meet life's challenges head-on. I've even experienced my lifelong dream of graduating from high school. My experiences with Celebrate Recovery have been incredible. I was so afraid when I entered the program, but Christ took me by the hand and guided me all the way.

All of my life I had struggled with insecurities, never feeling that I was good enough or pretty enough or smart enough. Through God and Celebrate Recovery, I've finally come to realize that I am, in fact, God's perfect masterpiece.

Kimberley

15While Jesus was having dinner at Levi's house, many tax collectors and sinners were eating with him and his disciples, for there were many who followed him. 16When the teachers of the law who were Pharisees saw him eating with the sinners and tax collectors, they asked his disciples: "Why does he eat with tax collectors and sinners?"

17On hearing this, Jesus said to them, "It is not the healthy who need a doctor, but the sick. I have not come to call the righteous, but sinners."

Jesus Questioned About Fasting

18Now John's disciples and the Pharisees were fasting. Some people came and asked Jesus, "How is it that John's disciples and the disciples of the Pharisees are fasting, but yours are not?"

19Jesus answered, "How can the guests of the bridegroom fast while he is with them? They cannot, so long as they have him with them. 20But the time will come when the bridegroom will be taken from them, and on that day they will fast.

21"No one sews a patch of unshrunk cloth on an old garment. Otherwise, the new piece will pull away from the old, making the tear worse. 22And no one pours new wine into old wineskins. Otherwise, the wine will burst the skins, and both the wine and the wineskins will be ruined. No, they pour new wine into new wineskins."

Jesus Is Lord of the Sabbath

23One Sabbath Jesus was going through the grainfields, and as his disciples walked along, they began to pick some heads of grain. 24The Pharisees said to him, "Look, why are they doing what is unlawful on the Sabbath?"

25He answered, "Have you never read what David did when he and his companions were hungry and in need? 26In the days of Abiathar the high priest, he entered the house of God and ate the consecrated bread, which is lawful only for priests to eat. And he also gave some to his companions."

27Then he said to them, "The Sabbath was made for man, not man for the Sabbath. 28So the Son of Man is Lord even of the Sabbath."

Jesus Heals on the Sabbath

3 Another time Jesus went into the synagogue, and a man with a shriveled hand was there. 2Some of them were looking for a reason to accuse Jesus, so they watched him closely to see if he would heal him on the Sabbath. 3Jesus said to the man with the shriveled hand, "Stand up in front of everyone."

4Then Jesus asked them, "Which is lawful on the Sabbath: to do good or to do evil, to save life or to kill?" But they remained silent.

5He looked around at them in anger and, deeply distressed at their stubborn hearts, said to the man, "Stretch out your hand." He stretched it out, and his hand was completely restored. 6Then the Pharisees went out and began to plot with the Herodians how they might kill Jesus.

Crowds Follow Jesus

7Jesus withdrew with his disciples to the lake, and a large crowd from Galilee followed. 8When they heard about all he was doing, many people came to him from Judea, Jerusalem, Idumea, and the regions across the Jordan and around Tyre and Sidon. 9Because of the crowd he told his disciples to have a small boat ready for him, to keep the people from crowding him. 10For he had healed many, so that those with diseases were pushing forward to touch him. 11Whenever the impure spirits saw him, they fell down before him and cried out, "You are the Son of God." 12But he gave them strict orders not to tell others about him.

Jesus Appoints the Twelve

13Jesus went up on a mountainside and called to him those he wanted, and they came to him. ¹⁴He appointed twelve*ᵃ* that they might be with him and that he might send them out to preach ¹⁵and to have authority to drive out demons. ¹⁶These are the twelve he appointed: Simon (to whom he gave the name Peter), ¹⁷James son of Zebedee and his brother John (to them he gave the name Boanerges, which means "sons of thunder"), ¹⁸Andrew, Philip, Bartholomew, Matthew, Thomas, James son of Alphaeus, Thaddaeus, Simon the Zealot ¹⁹and Judas Iscariot, who betrayed him.

Jesus Accused by His Family and by Teachers of the Law

²⁰Then Jesus entered a house, and again a crowd gathered, so that he and his disciples were not even able to eat. ²¹When his family*ᵇ* heard about this, they went to take charge of him, for they said, "He is out of his mind."

²²And the teachers of the law who came down from Jerusalem said, "He is possessed by Beelzebul! By the prince of demons he is driving out demons."

²³So Jesus called them over to him and began to speak to them in parables: "How can Satan drive out Satan? ²⁴If a kingdom is divided against itself, that kingdom cannot stand. ²⁵If a house is divided against itself, that house cannot stand. ²⁶And if Satan opposes himself and is divided, he cannot stand; his end has come. ²⁷In fact, no one can enter a strong man's house without first tying him up. Then he can plunder the strong man's house. ²⁸Truly I tell you, people can be forgiven all their sins and every slander they utter, ²⁹but whoever blasphemes against the Holy Spirit will never be forgiven; they are guilty of an eternal sin."

³⁰He said this because they were saying, "He has an impure spirit."

³¹Then Jesus' mother and brothers arrived. Standing outside, they sent someone in to call him. ³²A crowd was sitting around him, and they told him, "Your mother and brothers are outside looking for you."

³³"Who are my mother and my brothers?" he asked.

³⁴Then he looked at those seated in a circle around him and said, "Here are my mother and my brothers! ³⁵Whoever does God's will is my brother and sister and mother."

The Parable of the Sower

4 Again Jesus began to teach by the lake. The crowd that gathered around him was so large that he got into a boat and sat in it out on the lake, while all the people were along the shore at the water's edge. ²He taught them many things by parables, and in his teaching said: ³"Listen! A farmer went out to sow his seed. ⁴As he was scattering the seed, some fell along the path, and the birds came and ate it up. ⁵Some fell on rocky places, where it did not have much soil. It sprang up quickly, because the soil was shallow. ⁶But when the sun came up, the plants were scorched, and they withered because they had no root. ⁷Other seed fell among thorns, which grew up and choked the plants, so that they did not bear grain. ⁸Still other seed fell on good soil. It came up, grew and produced a crop, some multiplying thirty, some sixty, some a hundred times."

⁹Then Jesus said, "Whoever has ears to hear, let them hear."

¹⁰When he was alone, the Twelve and the others around him asked him about the parables. ¹¹He told them, "The secret of the kingdom of God has been given to you. But to those on the outside everything is said in parables ¹²so that,

"'they may be ever seeing but never
        perceiving,
    and ever hearing but never
        understanding;
otherwise they might turn and be
        forgiven!'*ᶜ*"

¹³Then Jesus said to them, "Don't you understand this parable? How then will you understand any parable? ¹⁴The farmer sows

---

ᵃ 14 Some manuscripts twelve — designating them apostles —   *ᵇ* 21 Or his associates   *ᶜ* 12 Isaiah 6:9,10 the word. ¹⁵Some people are like seed along the path, where the word is sown. As soon as they hear it, Satan comes and takes away the word that was sown in them. ¹⁶Others, like seed sown on rocky places, hear the word and at once receive it with joy. ¹⁷But since they have no root, they last only a short time. When trouble or persecution comes because of the word, they quickly fall away. ¹⁸Still others, like seed sown among thorns, hear the word; ¹⁹but the worries of this life, the deceitfulness of wealth and the desires for other things come in and choke the word, making it unfruitful. ²⁰Others, like seed sown on good soil, hear the word, accept it, and produce a crop—some thirty, some sixty, some a hundred times what was sown."

A Lamp on a Stand

²¹He said to them, "Do you bring in a lamp to put it under a bowl or a bed? Instead, don't you put it on its stand? ²²For whatever is hidden is meant to be disclosed, and whatever is concealed is meant to be brought out into the open. ²³If anyone has ears to hear, let them hear."

²⁴"Consider carefully what you hear," he continued. "With the measure you use, it will be measured to you—and even more. ²⁵Whoever has will be given more; whoever does not have, even what they have will be taken from them."

The Parable of the Growing Seed

²⁶He also said, "This is what the kingdom of God is like. A man scatters seed on the ground. ²⁷Night and day, whether he sleeps or gets up, the seed sprouts and grows, though he does not know how. ²⁸All by itself the soil produces grain—first the stalk, then the head, then the full kernel in the head. ²⁹As soon as the grain is ripe, he puts the sickle to it, because the harvest has come."

The Parable of the Mustard Seed

³⁰Again he said, "What shall we say the kingdom of God is like, or what parable shall we use to describe it? ³¹It is like a mustard seed, which is the smallest of all seeds on earth. ³²Yet when planted, it grows and becomes the largest of all garden plants, with such big branches that the birds can perch in its shade."

³³With many similar parables Jesus spoke the word to them, as much as they could understand. ³⁴He did not say anything to them without using a parable. But when he was alone with his own disciples, he explained everything.

Jesus Calms the Storm

³⁵That day when evening came, he said to his disciples, "Let us go over to the other side." ³⁶Leaving the crowd behind, they took him along, just as he was, in the boat. There were also other boats with him. ³⁷A furious squall came up, and the waves broke over the boat, so that it was nearly swamped. ³⁸Jesus was in the stern, sleeping on a cushion. The disciples woke him and said to him, "Teacher, don't you care if we drown?"

³⁹He got up, rebuked the wind and said to the waves, "Quiet! Be still!" Then the wind died down and it was completely calm.

⁴⁰He said to his disciples, "Why are you so afraid? Do you still have no faith?"

⁴¹They were terrified and asked each other, "Who is this? Even the wind and the waves obey him!"

Jesus Restores a Demon-Possessed Man

5 They went across the lake to the region of the Gerasenes.ᵃ ²When Jesus got out of the boat, a man with an impure spirit came from the tombs to meet him. ³This man lived in the tombs, and no one could bind him anymore, not even with a chain. ⁴For he had often been chained hand and foot, but he tore the chains apart and broke the irons on his feet. No one was strong enough to subdue him. ⁵Night and day among the tombs and in the hills he would cry out and cut himself with stones.

ᵃ 1 Some manuscripts *Gadarenes*; other manuscripts *Gergesenes*

⁶When he saw Jesus from a distance, he ran and fell on his knees in front of him. ⁷He shouted at the top of his voice, "What do you want with me, Jesus, Son of the Most High God? In God's name don't torture me!" ⁸For Jesus had said to him, "Come out of this man, you impure spirit!"

⁹Then Jesus asked him, "What is your name?"

"My name is Legion," he replied, "for we are many." ¹⁰And he begged Jesus again and again not to send them out of the area.

¹¹A large herd of pigs was feeding on the nearby hillside. ¹²The demons begged Jesus, "Send us among the pigs; allow us to go into them." ¹³He gave them permission, and the impure spirits came out and went into the pigs. The herd, about two thousand in number, rushed down the steep bank into the lake and were drowned.

¹⁴Those tending the pigs ran off and reported this in the town and countryside, and the people went out to see what had happened. ¹⁵When they came to Jesus, they saw the man who had been possessed by the legion of demons, sitting there, dressed and in his right mind; and they were afraid. ¹⁶Those who had seen it told the people what had happened to the demon-possessed man — and told about the pigs as well. ¹⁷Then the people began to plead with Jesus to leave their region.

¹⁸As Jesus was getting into the boat, the man who had been demon-possessed begged to go with him. ¹⁹Jesus did not let him, but said, "Go home to your own people and tell them how much the Lord has done for you, and how he has had mercy on you." ²⁰So the man went away and began to tell in the Decapolis*ᵃ* how much Jesus had done for him. And all the people were amazed.

Jesus Raises a Dead Girl and Heals a Sick Woman

²¹When Jesus had again crossed over by boat to the other side of the lake, a large crowd gathered around him while he was by the lake. ²²Then one of the synagogue leaders, named Jairus, came, and when he saw Jesus, he fell at his feet. ²³He pleaded earnestly with him, "My little daughter is dying. Please come and put your hands on her so that she will be healed and live." ²⁴So Jesus went with him.

A large crowd followed and pressed around him. ²⁵And a woman was there who had been subject to bleeding for twelve years. ²⁶She had suffered a great deal under the care of many doctors and had spent all she had, yet instead of getting better she grew worse. ²⁷When she heard about Jesus, she came up behind him in the crowd and touched his cloak, ²⁸because she thought, "If I just touch his clothes, I will be healed." ²⁹Immediately her bleeding stopped and she felt in her body that she was freed from her suffering.

³⁰At once Jesus realized that power had gone out from him. He turned around in the crowd and asked, "Who touched my clothes?"

³¹"You see the people crowding against you," his disciples answered, "and yet you can ask, 'Who touched me?'"

³²But Jesus kept looking around to see who had done it. ³³Then the woman, knowing what had happened to her, came and fell at his feet and, trembling with fear, told him the whole truth. ³⁴He said to her, "Daughter, your faith has healed you. Go in peace and be freed from your suffering."

³⁵While Jesus was still speaking, some people came from the house of Jairus, the synagogue leader. "Your daughter is dead," they said. "Why bother the teacher anymore?"

³⁶Overhearing*ᵇ* what they said, Jesus told him, "Don't be afraid; just believe."

³⁷He did not let anyone follow him except Peter, James and John the brother of James. ³⁸When they came to the home of the synagogue leader, Jesus saw a commotion, with people crying and wailing loudly.

MY NAME IS
THE GERASENE DEMONIAC

MARK 5:1–20

Strangely, it's possible to be both a strong individual and powerless in relation to our own problems. The demoniac suffering in the land of the Gerasenes had enormous physical strength, so much so that he could obstruct every human attempt to control his behavior (see Mark 5:4). Inside that powerful body, though, were forces dedicated to his destruction (see v. 5). There was a label for his very real problem: demon possession. But naming and curing a condition are two different propositions. Only Jesus is our cure. Our bondage isn't forged by others, like iron chains; instead, it's a force that enslaves and cripples us from within our own hearts. The good news is that our Savior seeks us out when our lives are totally out of control. And he has the power to look deep within us to identify and confront the roots of our strangulating, ever-more-destructive bonds.

When Jesus entered into a face-off with this man's demons, they recognized him immediately as the "Son of the Most High God" and realized that they were at his mercy (see v. 7). At their request Jesus cast them out of the man and into a herd of pigs. As soon as they took possession of the pigs, the demonic horde rushed off a cliff and into the lake, drowning its hosts (see v. 13). The demons, addictions, memories, destructive habits or resentments that torment us will similarly destroy us apart from the free exercise of Jesus' authority in our lives.

The demon-possessed man is a crucial reminder to each of us that recovery is ultimately about a person, not a process. Without Christ we inflict damage on ourselves and endanger others. If we're to be truly free, we must submit to every change God wants to make in our lives (Principle Five).

How do we relate this intervention by Jesus to our own working of our recovery program? After all, the demoniac didn't do anything to facilitate his deliverance — and, ultimately, neither do we. Life-changing principles are gifts of God to hurting humans. In the case of the demoniac, these truths came special delivery from Jesus himself. Most of the time, though, Jesus used his disciples to convey his liberating truths to those in bondage. Often these truths reach our hearts via those who love us enough to confront us about realities we've refused to face for many years.

Whatever the method of delivery, this truth is the product of God's grace, a grace that enables us to carry out our purpose on this earth (see Ephesians 2:8–10). The demon-possessed man moved all the way to Principle Eight, sharing the message of Christ's healing with everyone he encountered. We need to be willing to tell our story, and, like those who heard the former demoniac, our audience will hear and be "amazed" at "how much Jesus [has] done" (Mark 5:20).

³⁹He went in and said to them, "Why all this commotion and wailing? The child is not dead but asleep." ⁴⁰But they laughed at him.

After he put them all out, he took the child's father and mother and the disciples who were with him, and went in where the child was. ⁴¹He took her by the hand and said to her, *"Talitha koum!"* (which means "Little girl, I say to you, get up!"). ⁴²Immediately the girl stood up and began to walk around (she was twelve years old). At this they were completely astonished. ⁴³He gave strict orders not to let anyone know about this, and told them to give her something to eat.

A Prophet Without Honor

6 Jesus left there and went to his hometown, accompanied by his disciples. ²When the Sabbath came, he began to teach in the synagogue, and many who heard him were amazed.

"Where did this man get these things?" they asked. "What's this wisdom that has been given him? What are these remarkable miracles he is performing? ³Isn't this the carpenter? Isn't this Mary's son and the brother of James, Joseph,ᵃ Judas and Simon? Aren't his sisters here with us?" And they took offense at him.

⁴Jesus said to them, "A prophet is not without honor except in his own town, among his relatives and in his own home." ⁵He could not do any miracles there, except lay his hands on a few sick people and heal them. ⁶He was amazed at their lack of faith.

Jesus Sends Out the Twelve

Then Jesus went around teaching from village to village. ⁷Calling the Twelve to him, he began to send them out two by two and gave them authority over impure spirits.

⁸These were his instructions: "Take nothing for the journey except a staff—

no bread, no bag, no money in your belts. ⁹Wear sandals but not an extra shirt. ¹⁰Whenever you enter a house, stay there until you leave that town. ¹¹And if any place will not welcome you or listen to you, leave that place and shake the dust off your feet as a testimony against them."

¹²They went out and preached that people should repent. ¹³They drove out many demons and anointed many sick people with oil and healed them.

John the Baptist Beheaded

¹⁴King Herod heard about this, for Jesus' name had become well known. Some were saying,ᵇ "John the Baptist has been raised from the dead, and that is why miraculous powers are at work in him."

¹⁵Others said, "He is Elijah."

And still others claimed, "He is a prophet, like one of the prophets of long ago."

¹⁶But when Herod heard this, he said, "John, whom I beheaded, has been raised from the dead!"

¹⁷For Herod himself had given orders to have John arrested, and he had him bound and put in prison. He did this because of Herodias, his brother Philip's wife, whom he had married. ¹⁸For John had been saying to Herod, "It is not lawful for you to have your brother's wife." ¹⁹So Herodias nursed a grudge against John and wanted to kill him. But she was not able to, ²⁰because Herod feared John and protected him, knowing him to be a righteous and holy man. When Herod heard John, he was greatly puzzledᶜ; yet he liked to listen to him.

²¹Finally the opportune time came. On his birthday Herod gave a banquet for his high officials and military commanders and the leading men of Galilee. ²²When the daughter ofᵈ Herodias came in and danced, she pleased Herod and his dinner guests.

The king said to the girl, "Ask me for

ᵃ 3 Greek *Joses*, a variant of *Joseph*   ᵇ 14 Some early manuscripts *He was saying*   ᶜ 20 Some early manuscripts *he did many things*   ᵈ 22 Some early manuscripts *When his daughter*

My Name Is Gary

I'M A BELIEVER WHO STRUGGLES WITH SEXUAL ABUSE, SEXUAL ADDICTION, DRUG ADDICTION AND FEAR

Please read the story of the Gerasene demoniac in Mark 5:1–20.

Before I was two years old my parents divorced. Mom abandoned us, and Dad couldn't care for us, so he left us with my grandma until he remarried. My stepmother was emotionally abusive and physically violent. She and my dad would have terrible fights in the middle of the night; my dreams would be punctuated by screaming and flying objects. These clashes were rarely resolved during the night, and the next morning, after Dad had left for work, I would become the target. All too often I was secluded from public view because of my bruises. By the time I was seven years old, the truth had started to emerge. I was placed repeatedly in temporary foster care, where I was sexually abused. And each time I returned home, the abuse escalated.

At the age of 12, I was confirmed in my church, and I promised to serve God. But the abuse worsened, and I grew angry with God for not helping me. I began to immerse myself in Greek mythology, escaping into the stories. I started praying to the Greek goddess Athena, inviting her to be my god. Part of my false worship of Athena involved fantasies of intercourse with temple prostitutes. Sex became an obsession.

When I was 16, I ran away for good. But I was in for a rude awakening. Heading for Los Angeles on a bus, I was molested by a stranger. Once I reached El Paso, another man approached me. He seemed genuinely concerned and asked whether I had a place to stay. He took me to a backstreet, dumpy hotel in Mexico and kept me there for three days before bringing me back to the United States. There he made arrangements for another man to pick up where he had left off.

Shortly afterward I met a lesbian who introduced me to gay bars. I decided that I was bisexual. This gave me an identity; and it also helped me to justify my behavior with the pedophiles. I cursed God and praised Satan. Gay bars, adult theaters and sexually-oriented clubs became the daily realities of my life. All of this required money, which I hustled or stole.

At the age of 18, I was arrested for armed robbery and faced prison. In my loneliness and fear I agreed to talk with a Teen Challenge volunteer. He spent a lot of time with me and, in the process, led me to Christ. I received ten years probation and was back on the streets again, soon forgetting Jesus and my newfound faith. I moved to Tulsa, where I later met my wife.

After six years of marriage, my drug use peaked. I had been using cocaine heavily and had suddenly run out. As the pain of my whole life came crashing in, I panicked, recognizing for the first time that I was absolutely out of control and in need of help. I had finally hit bottom, and I wanted to die. I jotted a suicide note to my wife and headed down to the storm cellar. Suddenly, though, I felt the same presence I had experienced in church at my confirmation, and I heard the most comforting voice. It wasn't audible, but neither was it imaginary. I heard the words clearly: "Gary, I love you. I have always loved you and always will love you." Recognizing the voice of God, I emerged from the cellar.

I found the closest church and started attending. The next year our son was born. But I knew I didn't have control over my addictions and realized how vulnerable I was to losing everything. One day I prayed the most important prayer of my life: "God, I surrender. Do whatever it takes to change me." I started attending a secular sexual addiction group and worked the 12 steps. An ability to trust God started to develop in my heart. Like the Gerasene demoniac in Mark 5, my body was inhabited by forces dedicated to my destruction (see Mark 5:5). But simply identifying the problem wouldn't affect my cure. I needed God to employ his X-ray vision to look beyond the bricks that were walling up my heart — bricks of mistrust, guilt and shame, anger and resentment, and failure to trust anyone.

After spending a year in the program, God laid something on my heart. In my secular program it was difficult for me to express my feelings about Christ. I shared this with my counselor at church, who handed me a brochure about an upcoming Celebrate Recovery conference. I recognized instantly that this was what God had been showing me. I decided to join the Celebrate Recovery program at my own church.

In the life of the demoniac, the Truth came in the person of Jesus himself. In my case, the people in Celebrate Recovery are the instruments God uses to continually confront me about the realities I've refused to face for so many years. Like the demon-possessed man (see Mark 5:20), I desire to share the message of Christ's liberating work with everyone around me. I know from my own experience that God both can and does change lives.

anything you want, and I'll give it to you." ²³And he promised her with an oath, "Whatever you ask I will give you, up to half my kingdom."

²⁴She went out and said to her mother, "What shall I ask for?"

"The head of John the Baptist," she answered.

²⁵At once the girl hurried in to the king with the request: "I want you to give me right now the head of John the Baptist on a platter."

²⁶The king was greatly distressed, but because of his oaths and his dinner guests, he did not want to refuse her. ²⁷So he immediately sent an executioner with orders to bring John's head. The man went, beheaded John in the prison, ²⁸and brought back his head on a platter. He presented it to the girl, and she gave it to her mother. ²⁹On hearing of this, John's disciples came and took his body and laid it in a tomb.

Jesus Feeds the Five Thousand

³⁰The apostles gathered around Jesus and reported to him all they had done and taught. ³¹Then, because so many people were coming and going that they did not even have a chance to eat, he said to them, "Come with me by yourselves to a quiet place and get some rest."

³²So they went away by themselves in a boat to a solitary place. ³³But many who saw them leaving recognized them and ran on foot from all the towns and got there ahead of them. ³⁴When Jesus landed and saw a large crowd, he had compassion on them, because they were like sheep without a shepherd. So he began teaching them many things.

³⁵By this time it was late in the day, so his disciples came to him. "This is a remote place," they said, "and it's already very late. ³⁶Send the people away so that they can go to the surrounding countryside and villages and buy themselves something to eat."

³⁷But he answered, "You give them something to eat."

They said to him, "That would take more than half a year's wages*a*! Are we to go and spend that much on bread and give it to them to eat?"

³⁸"How many loaves do you have?" he asked. "Go and see."

When they found out, they said, "Five — and two fish."

³⁹Then Jesus directed them to have all the people sit down in groups on the green grass. ⁴⁰So they sat down in groups of hundreds and fifties. ⁴¹Taking the five loaves and the two fish and looking up to heaven, he gave thanks and broke the loaves. Then he gave them to his disciples to distribute to the people. He also divided the two fish among them all. ⁴²They all ate and were satisfied, ⁴³and the disciples picked up twelve basketfuls of broken pieces of bread and fish. ⁴⁴The number of the men who had eaten was five thousand.

Jesus Walks on the Water

⁴⁵Immediately Jesus made his disciples get into the boat and go on ahead of him to Bethsaida, while he dismissed the crowd. ⁴⁶After leaving them, he went up on a mountainside to pray.

⁴⁷Later that night, the boat was in the middle of the lake, and he was alone on land. ⁴⁸He saw the disciples straining at the oars, because the wind was against them. Shortly before dawn he went out to them, walking on the lake. He was about to pass by them, ⁴⁹but when they saw him walking on the lake, they thought he was a ghost. They cried out, ⁵⁰because they all saw him and were terrified.

Immediately he spoke to them and said, "Take courage! It is I. Don't be afraid." ⁵¹Then he climbed into the boat with them, and the wind died down. They were completely amazed, ⁵²for they had not understood about the loaves; their hearts were hardened.

---

a 37 Greek *take two hundred denarii*

⁵³When they had crossed over, they landed at Gennesaret and anchored there. ⁵⁴As soon as they got out of the boat, people recognized Jesus. ⁵⁵They ran throughout that whole region and carried the sick on mats to wherever they heard he was. ⁵⁶And wherever he went — into villages, towns or countryside — they placed the sick in the marketplaces. They begged him to let them touch even the edge of his cloak, and all who touched it were healed.

That Which Defiles

7 The Pharisees and some of the teachers of the law who had come from Jerusalem gathered around Jesus ²and saw some of his disciples eating food with hands that were defiled, that is, unwashed. ³(The Pharisees and all the Jews do not eat unless they give their hands a ceremonial washing, holding to the tradition of the elders. ⁴When they come from the marketplace they do not eat unless they wash. And they observe many other traditions, such as the washing of cups, pitchers and kettles.ᵃ)

⁵So the Pharisees and teachers of the law asked Jesus, "Why don't your disciples live according to the tradition of the elders instead of eating their food with defiled hands?"

⁶He replied, "Isaiah was right when he prophesied about you hypocrites; as it is written:

" 'These people honor me with their lips,
    but their hearts are far from me.
⁷They worship me in vain;
    their teachings are merely human rules.'ᵇ

⁸You have let go of the commands of God and are holding on to human traditions."

⁹And he continued, "You have a fine way of setting aside the commands of God in order to observeᶜ your own traditions! ¹⁰For Moses said, 'Honor your father and mother,'ᵈ and, 'Anyone who curses their father or mother is to be put to death.'ᵉ ¹¹But you say that if anyone declares that what might have been used to help their father or mother is Corban (that is, devoted to God) — ¹²then you no longer let them do anything for their father or mother. ¹³Thus you nullify the word of God by your tradition that you have handed down. And you do many things like that."

¹⁴Again Jesus called the crowd to him and said, "Listen to me, everyone, and understand this. ¹⁵Nothing outside a person can defile them by going into them. Rather, it is what comes out of a person that defiles them." [16]ᶠ

¹⁷After he had left the crowd and entered the house, his disciples asked him about this parable. ¹⁸"Are you so dull?" he asked. "Don't you see that nothing that enters a person from the outside can defile them? ¹⁹For it doesn't go into their heart but into their stomach, and then out of the body." (In saying this, Jesus declared all foods clean.)

²⁰He went on: "What comes out of a person is what defiles them. ²¹For it is from within, out of a person's heart, that evil thoughts come — sexual immorality, theft, murder, ²²adultery, greed, malice, deceit, lewdness, envy, slander, arrogance and folly. ²³All these evils come from inside and defile a person."

Jesus Honors a Syrophoenician Woman's Faith

²⁴Jesus left that place and went to the vicinity of Tyre.ᵍ He entered a house and did not want anyone to know it; yet he could not keep his presence secret. ²⁵In fact, as soon as she heard about him, a woman whose little daughter was possessed by an impure spirit came and fell at his feet.

ᵃ 4 Some early manuscripts *pitchers, kettles and dining couches*   ᵇ 6,7 Isaiah 29:13   ᶜ 9 Some manuscripts *set up*   ᵈ 10 Exodus 20:12; Deut. 5:16   ᵉ 10 Exodus 21:17; Lev. 20:9   ᶠ 16 Some manuscripts include here the words of 4:23.   ᵍ 24 Many early manuscripts *Tyre and Sidon*

MY NAME IS THE SYROPHOENICIAN WOMAN

MARK 7:24–30

This woman was a Gentile mother with a demon-possessed daughter. Jesus had tried to slip quietly into the area of Tyre. Our Lord was probably on a retreat from Galilee with his disciples. Both his popularity and his opposition were growing. It was time for him to focus on training his disciples before his return to his Father by way of the cross and the resurrection and ascension.

Word of Jesus' presence leaked out, though, and this determined mother approached and fell to her knees before him. There at his feet, "she begged Jesus to drive the demon out of her daughter" (Mark 7:26). The Master's response strikes us as harsh. He pointed out that his first responsibility as Messiah was to the children of Israel. They had to be fed before his saving work could be extended to the Gentiles (see v. 27). Yet this undaunted mother answered Jesus with determination, wisdom and faith (see v. 28). Jesus granted her petition, and she returned home to find her daughter delivered from the demon (see vv. 29–30).

If our children are afflicted, perhaps addicted to drugs, we can relate to this woman's pain. Her encounter with Jesus includes lessons for the family of an addict. It's easy to become codependent. We can allow our lives to center on our child's problems instead of on our own walk with Christ. The truth is, though, that even as parents we can't ultimately control our sons or daughters. The reality is that only God can change our children, and they will have to personally invite him to make that change.

What can we do? We can focus on Jesus. We can allow him to transform and guide us as we travel the road to recovery. Our children's only hope is Jesus, and the best way to help our son or daughter is to allow Jesus to assist us. He'll help us to change, to handle the hurts and disappointments we encounter. And we can find the support of other parents who share our painful experiences. Our healthy responses to our children's behavior will become a witness to Christ's transforming power. We need to do what the Syrophoenician woman did: Concentrate on Jesus. Put our faith in him and what he alone can do. Fall at his feet and voice our petitions. Let him increase our faith and heal our hearts. We must live before our children as a model of the hope they must embrace to take those first steps toward recovery.

26The woman was a Greek, born in Syrian Phoenicia. She begged Jesus to drive the demon out of her daughter.

27"First let the children eat all they want," he told her, "for it is not right to take the children's bread and toss it to the dogs."

28"Lord," she replied, "even the dogs under the table eat the children's crumbs."

29Then he told her, "For such a reply, you may go; the demon has left your daughter."

30She went home and found her child lying on the bed, and the demon gone.

Jesus Heals a Deaf and Mute Man

31Then Jesus left the vicinity of Tyre and went through Sidon, down to the Sea of Galilee and into the region of the Decapolis.*a* 32There some people brought to him a man who was deaf and could hardly talk, and they begged Jesus to place his hand on him.

33After he took him aside, away from the crowd, Jesus put his fingers into the man's ears. Then he spit and touched the man's tongue. 34He looked up to heaven and with a deep sigh said to him, *"Ephphatha!"* (which means "Be opened!"). 35At this, the man's ears were opened, his tongue was loosened and he began to speak plainly.

36Jesus commanded them not to tell anyone. But the more he did so, the more they kept talking about it. 37People were overwhelmed with amazement. "He has done everything well," they said. "He even makes the deaf hear and the mute speak."

Jesus Feeds the Four Thousand

8 During those days another large crowd gathered. Since they had nothing to eat, Jesus called his disciples to him and said, 2"I have compassion for these people; they have already been with me three days and have nothing to eat. 3If I send them home hungry, they will collapse on the way, because some of them have come a long distance."

4His disciples answered, "But where in this remote place can anyone get enough bread to feed them?"

5"How many loaves do you have?" Jesus asked.

"Seven," they replied.

6He told the crowd to sit down on the ground. When he had taken the seven loaves and given thanks, he broke them and gave them to his disciples to distribute to the people, and they did so. 7They had a few small fish as well; he gave thanks for them also and told the disciples to distribute them. 8The people ate and were satisfied. Afterward the disciples picked up seven basketfuls of broken pieces that were left over. 9About four thousand were present. After he had sent them away, 10he got into the boat with his disciples and went to the region of Dalmanutha.

11The Pharisees came and began to question Jesus. To test him, they asked him for a sign from heaven. 12He sighed deeply and said, "Why does this generation ask for a sign? Truly I tell you, no sign will be given to it." 13Then he left them, got back into the boat and crossed to the other side.

The Yeast of the Pharisees and Herod

14The disciples had forgotten to bring bread, except for one loaf they had with them in the boat. 15"Be careful," Jesus warned them. "Watch out for the yeast of the Pharisees and that of Herod."

16They discussed this with one another and said, "It is because we have no bread."

17Aware of their discussion, Jesus asked them: "Why are you talking about having no bread? Do you still not see or understand? Are your hearts hardened? 18Do you have eyes but fail to see, and ears but fail to hear? And don't you remember? 19When I broke the five loaves for the five thousand, how many basketfuls of pieces did you pick up?"

"Twelve," they replied.

20"And when I broke the seven loaves for the four thousand, how many basketfuls of pieces did you pick up?"

---

a 31 That is, the Ten Cities

My Name Is Libby

I'M A BELIEVER WHO STRUGGLES WITH CODEPENDENCY

Please read the story of the woman from Syrian Phoenicia in Mark 7:24–30.

Growing up, I didn't know what codependency was and certainly had no idea I was living in that world. But now, looking back, I can see it very clearly. I grew up in the "ideal Christian family." Our family life, in fact, revolved around the church. But when my father unexpectedly died from a massive brain aneurysm, my life changed forever. He had been my security and my best friend. I had lived to make my dad happy. I hungered for other people to like me and tried valiantly to win their approval.

After graduate school I met my future husband, a career army man. Sadly, my fantasy of marriage and its reality were worlds apart. After nearly 20 years of marriage and three sons, our home life became completely tumultuous. My husband's career kept him away for long periods of time, resulting in extramarital affairs. He became emotionally and verbally abusive, and I suffered from feelings of rejection. Still, I struggled to balance our home life for the sake of my sons. My husband eventually moved out of state to start a new job. He actually chose to begin a whole new life without us. I was finally forced to accept the fact that my marriage was over.

I had a very close relationship with my boys and tried to provide them with whatever I thought they needed, even though I couldn't afford those things. Guilt and shame haunted me day and night because of the way life had changed for my boys: no father, very little money, the death of their dreams and of my own. I tried desperately to discourage their rebellion, their hanging with the wrong crowd and their use of alcohol, tobacco and drugs. After several years of trying to keep the family together, though, we fell apart. One son ended up in rehab for alcohol and drug addiction and attempted suicide; another decided to live part of the time away from home; and the youngest quit school in his junior year, left home and chose to live under a bridge with some other homeless people. Feeling like a complete and total failure, I blamed both myself and their father.

I had absolutely no control over my children. If I kicked them out and changed the locks, they knew how to crawl in through a bedroom window. I was threatened and lied to. It was not uncommon, in the middle of the night, to receive a "collect call from an inmate at the County Detention Center." I bailed my kids out of jail with borrowed money and with lies.

I paid to retrieve cars from the impound lot and covered lawyers' fees, court costs, tickets and probation fees. I warned them not to call me if they ended up in jail again. But the cycle didn't stop. And over and over again I found myself going back to get them out of trouble. I didn't know why I was doing this, except that I felt so guilty that they had been cheated out of having a father. Like the Syrophoenician woman, I was anguished by my sons' pain. But instead of going straight to Jesus for healing for my family, I tried — and failed miserably — on my own (see Mark 7:26).

But God's caring was persistent, and he caught my attention through the hopelessness of my circumstances and the three friends who counseled me to go to Celebrate Recovery. I decided to step way out of my comfort zone and attend a meeting. It didn't take me long, though, to realize that God had me right where he wanted me. I had allowed my life to center on my children, and it was time to work on me.

Over time I began to understand how I was enabling my boys. I was preventing them from having to take responsibility for their own actions and experience the necessary consequences. Even beyond my behavior, I began to recognize the source of deep feelings that had been causing me to react on the basis of a sense of guilt and shame. I was trying desperately to be needed, attempting frantically to control every situation.

It's amazing how my boys have grown and healed as I've given them to God and focused on my own journey (see Mark 7:29 – 30). I relate to my sons differently now, and our relationship has become healthy. This healing in my family would never have happened had I not accepted my own need for recovery and taken the steps I did. The Syrophoenician woman petitioned God with her requests and allowed her faith in him to heal her family. The best gift I could ever have given my boys was to allow Jesus to help me. I wanted to prevent them from drinking and using drugs — to take their life journeys for them. Now their walks are their own. Just like my own recovery, theirs will depend on how badly they want it and the effort they are willing to put into it.

They answered, "Seven."

²¹He said to them, "Do you still not understand?"

Jesus Heals a Blind Man at Bethsaida

²²They came to Bethsaida, and some people brought a blind man and begged Jesus to touch him. ²³He took the blind man by the hand and led him outside the village. When he had spit on the man's eyes and put his hands on him, Jesus asked, "Do you see anything?"

²⁴He looked up and said, "I see people; they look like trees walking around."

²⁵Once more Jesus put his hands on the man's eyes. Then his eyes were opened, his sight was restored, and he saw everything clearly. ²⁶Jesus sent him home, saying, "Don't even go into*a* the village."

Peter Declares That Jesus Is the Messiah

²⁷Jesus and his disciples went on to the villages around Caesarea Philippi. On the way he asked them, "Who do people say I am?"

²⁸They replied, "Some say John the Baptist; others say Elijah; and still others, one of the prophets."

²⁹"But what about you?" he asked. "Who do you say I am?"

Peter answered, "You are the Messiah."

³⁰Jesus warned them not to tell anyone about him.

Jesus Predicts His Death

³¹He then began to teach them that the Son of Man must suffer many things and be rejected by the elders, the chief priests and the teachers of the law, and that he must be killed and after three days rise again. ³²He spoke plainly about this, and Peter took him aside and began to rebuke him.

³³But when Jesus turned and looked at his disciples, he rebuked Peter. "Get behind me, Satan!" he said. "You do not have in mind the concerns of God, but merely human concerns."

The Way of the Cross

³⁴Then he called the crowd to him along with his disciples and said: "Whoever wants to be my disciple must deny themselves and take up their cross and follow me. ³⁵For whoever wants to save their life*b* will lose it, but whoever loses their life for me and for the gospel will save it. ³⁶What good is it for someone to gain the whole world, yet forfeit their soul? ³⁷Or what can anyone give in exchange for their soul? ³⁸If anyone is ashamed of me and my words in this adulterous and sinful generation, the Son of Man will be ashamed of them when he comes in his Father's glory with the holy angels."

9 And he said to them, "Truly I tell you, some who are standing here will not taste death before they see that the kingdom of God has come with power."

The Transfiguration

²After six days Jesus took Peter, James and John with him and led them up a high mountain, where they were all alone. There he was transfigured before them. ³His clothes became dazzling white, whiter than anyone in the world could bleach them. ⁴And there appeared before them Elijah and Moses, who were talking with Jesus.

⁵Peter said to Jesus, "Rabbi, it is good for us to be here. Let us put up three shelters—one for you, one for Moses and one for Elijah." ⁶(He did not know what to say, they were so frightened.)

⁷Then a cloud appeared and covered them, and a voice came from the cloud: "This is my Son, whom I love. Listen to him!"

⁸Suddenly, when they looked around, they no longer saw anyone with them except Jesus.

⁹As they were coming down the mountain, Jesus gave them orders not to tell anyone what they had seen until the Son of Man had risen from the dead. ¹⁰They kept

---

a 26 Some manuscripts *go and tell anyone in* and 37.   *b 35* The Greek word means either *life* or *soul*; also in verses 36 the matter to themselves, discussing what "rising from the dead" meant.

[11]And they asked him, "Why do the teachers of the law say that Elijah must come first?"

[12]Jesus replied, "To be sure, Elijah does come first, and restores all things. Why then is it written that the Son of Man must suffer much and be rejected? [13]But I tell you, Elijah has come, and they have done to him everything they wished, just as it is written about him."

Jesus Heals a Boy Possessed by an Impure Spirit

[14]When they came to the other disciples, they saw a large crowd around them and the teachers of the law arguing with them. [15]As soon as all the people saw Jesus, they were overwhelmed with wonder and ran to greet him.

[16]"What are you arguing with them about?" he asked.

[17]A man in the crowd answered, "Teacher, I brought you my son, who is possessed by a spirit that has robbed him of speech. [18]Whenever it seizes him, it throws him to the ground. He foams at the mouth, gnashes his teeth and becomes rigid. I asked your disciples to drive out the spirit, but they could not."

[19]"You unbelieving generation," Jesus replied, "how long shall I stay with you? How long shall I put up with you? Bring the boy to me."

[20]So they brought him. When the spirit saw Jesus, it immediately threw the boy into a convulsion. He fell to the ground and rolled around, foaming at the mouth.

[21]Jesus asked the boy's father, "How long has he been like this?"

"From childhood," he answered. [22]"It has often thrown him into fire or water to kill him. But if you can do anything, take pity on us and help us."

[23]" 'If you can'?" said Jesus. "Everything is possible for one who believes."

[24]Immediately the boy's father exclaimed, "I do believe; help me overcome my unbelief!"

[25]When Jesus saw that a crowd was running to the scene, he rebuked the impure spirit. "You deaf and mute spirit," he said, "I command you, come out of him and never enter him again."

[26]The spirit shrieked, convulsed him violently and came out. The boy looked so much like a corpse that many said, "He's dead." [27]But Jesus took him by the hand and lifted him to his feet, and he stood up.

[28]After Jesus had gone indoors, his disciples asked him privately, "Why couldn't we drive it out?"

[29]He replied, "This kind can come out only by prayer.[a]"

Jesus Predicts His Death a Second Time

[30]They left that place and passed through Galilee. Jesus did not want anyone to know where they were, [31]because he was teaching his disciples. He said to them, "The Son of Man is going to be delivered into the hands of men. They will kill him, and after three days he will rise." [32]But they did not understand what he meant and were afraid to ask him about it.

[33]They came to Capernaum. When he was in the house, he asked them, "What were you arguing about on the road?" [34]But they kept quiet because on the way they had argued about who was the greatest.

[35]Sitting down, Jesus called the Twelve and said, "Anyone who wants to be first must be the very last, and the servant of all."

[36]He took a little child whom he placed among them. Taking the child in his arms, he said to them, [37]"Whoever welcomes one of these little children in my name welcomes me; and whoever welcomes me does not welcome me but the one who sent me."

Whoever Is Not Against Us Is for Us

[38]"Teacher," said John, "we saw someone driving out demons in your name and we

---

a 29 Some manuscripts *prayer and fasting*

told him to stop, because he was not one of us."

39"Do not stop him," Jesus said. "For no one who does a miracle in my name can in the next moment say anything bad about me, 40for whoever is not against us is for us. 41Truly I tell you, anyone who gives you a cup of water in my name because you belong to the Messiah will certainly not lose their reward.

Causing to Stumble

42"If anyone causes one of these little ones — those who believe in me — to stumble, it would be better for them if a large millstone were hung around their neck and they were thrown into the sea. 43If your hand causes you to stumble, cut it off. It is better for you to enter life maimed than with two hands to go into hell, where the fire never goes out. [44]a 45And if your foot causes you to stumble, cut it off. It is better for you to enter life crippled than to have two feet and be thrown into hell. [46]a 47And if your eye causes you to stumble, pluck it out. It is better for you to enter the kingdom of God with one eye than to have two eyes and be thrown into hell, 48where

> "'the worms that eat them do not die,
> and the fire is not quenched.'b

49Everyone will be salted with fire.

50"Salt is good, but if it loses its saltiness, how can you make it salty again? Have salt among yourselves, and be at peace with each other."

Divorce

10 Jesus then left that place and went into the region of Judea and across the Jordan. Again crowds of people came to him, and as was his custom, he taught them.

2Some Pharisees came and tested him by asking, "Is it lawful for a man to divorce his wife?"

3"What did Moses command you?" he replied.

4They said, "Moses permitted a man to write a certificate of divorce and send her away."

5"It was because your hearts were hard that Moses wrote you this law," Jesus replied. 6"But at the beginning of creation God 'made them male and female.'c 7'For this reason a man will leave his father and mother and be united to his wife,d 8and the two will become one flesh.'e So they are no longer two, but one flesh. 9Therefore what God has joined together, let no one separate."

10When they were in the house again, the disciples asked Jesus about this. 11He answered, "Anyone who divorces his wife and marries another woman commits adultery against her. 12And if she divorces her husband and marries another man, she commits adultery."

The Little Children and Jesus

13People were bringing little children to Jesus for him to place his hands on them, but the disciples rebuked them. 14When Jesus saw this, he was indignant. He said to them, "Let the little children come to me, and do not hinder them, for the kingdom of God belongs to such as these. 15Truly I tell you, anyone who will not receive the kingdom of God like a little child will never enter it." 16And he took the children in his arms, placed his hands on them and blessed them.

The Rich and the Kingdom of God

17As Jesus started on his way, a man ran up to him and fell on his knees before him. "Good teacher," he asked, "what must I do to inherit eternal life?"

18"Why do you call me good?" Jesus answered. "No one is good — except God alone. 19You know the commandments: 'You shall not murder, you shall not com-

---

a 44,46 Some manuscripts include here the words of verse 48. b 48 Isaiah 66:24 c 6 Gen. 1:27 d 7 Some early manuscripts do not have and be united to his wife. e 8 Gen. 2:24

mit adultery, you shall not steal, you shall not give false testimony, you shall not defraud, honor your father and mother.'*a*"

²⁰"Teacher," he declared, "all these I have kept since I was a boy."

²¹Jesus looked at him and loved him. "One thing you lack," he said. "Go, sell everything you have and give to the poor, and you will have treasure in heaven. Then come, follow me."

²²At this the man's face fell. He went away sad, because he had great wealth.

²³Jesus looked around and said to his disciples, "How hard it is for the rich to enter the kingdom of God!"

²⁴The disciples were amazed at his words. But Jesus said again, "Children, how hard it is*b* to enter the kingdom of God! ²⁵It is easier for a camel to go through the eye of a needle than for someone who is rich to enter the kingdom of God."

²⁶The disciples were even more amazed, and said to each other, "Who then can be saved?"

²⁷Jesus looked at them and said, "With man this is impossible, but not with God; all things are possible with God."

²⁸Then Peter spoke up, "We have left everything to follow you!"

²⁹"Truly I tell you," Jesus replied, "no one who has left home or brothers or sisters or mother or father or children or fields for me and the gospel ³⁰will fail to receive a hundred times as much in this present age: homes, brothers, sisters, mothers, children and fields — along with persecutions — and in the age to come eternal life. ³¹But many who are first will be last, and the last first."

Jesus Predicts His Death a Third Time

³²They were on their way up to Jerusalem, with Jesus leading the way, and the disciples were astonished, while those who followed were afraid. Again he took the Twelve aside and told them what was going to happen to him. ³³"We are going up to Jerusalem," he said, "and the Son of Man will be delivered over to the chief priests and the teachers of the law. They will condemn him to death and will hand him over to the Gentiles, ³⁴who will mock him and spit on him, flog him and kill him. Three days later he will rise."

The Request of James and John

³⁵Then James and John, the sons of Zebedee, came to him. "Teacher," they said, "we want you to do for us whatever we ask."

³⁶"What do you want me to do for you?" he asked.

³⁷They replied, "Let one of us sit at your right and the other at your left in your glory."

³⁸"You don't know what you are asking," Jesus said. "Can you drink the cup I drink or be baptized with the baptism I am baptized with?"

³⁹"We can," they answered.

Jesus said to them, "You will drink the cup I drink and be baptized with the baptism I am baptized with, ⁴⁰but to sit at my right or left is not for me to grant. These places belong to those for whom they have been prepared."

⁴¹When the ten heard about this, they became indignant with James and John. ⁴²Jesus called them together and said, "You know that those who are regarded as rulers of the Gentiles lord it over them, and their high officials exercise authority over them. ⁴³Not so with you. Instead, whoever wants to become great among you must be your servant, ⁴⁴and whoever wants to be first must be slave of all. ⁴⁵For even the Son of Man did not come to be served, but to serve, and to give his life as a ransom for many."

Blind Bartimaeus Receives His Sight

⁴⁶Then they came to Jericho. As Jesus and his disciples, together with a large crowd, were leaving the city, a blind man, Bartimaeus (which means "son of Timaeus"), was sitting by the roadside begging. ⁴⁷When he

---

a 19 Exodus 20:12-16; Deut. 5:16-20   *b 24* Some manuscripts *is for those who trust in riches*

MY NAME IS BARTIMAEUS

MARK 10:46–52

Blindness for Bartimaeus was a physical disability. Although physical blindness was commonplace in Jesus' day, the type of blindness most prevalent in Scripture is spiritual. In both Testaments, God's people are often referred to with this designation or revealed to be spiritually sightless by their action or lack of it. The reality is that spiritual blindness is the natural condition of every human being. Too often we can't see — and when we do see, we fail to understand — spiritual things. Spiritual sight comes to us along with our spiritual rebirth and the indwelling of the Holy Spirit (see 1 Corinthians 2:14–16).

Denial, a manifestation of spiritual blindness, stays with us until we become desperate for help. Bartimaeus, a blind man in Jericho whom we meet "sitting by the roadside begging" (Mark 10:46), was desperate. He had gained enough information about Jesus to understand his true identity, and so he shouted to him when the opportunity arose, addressing him as "Son of David" (Mark 10:47). In that day this was a clear confession that Jesus was the promised Messiah. Isaiah had long ago predicted that in the day Messiah reigns, "the eyes of the blind will see" (Isaiah 29:18).

Many in the crowd tried to shush Bartimaeus. But instead the suffering man, no doubt swallowing his own pride, "shouted all the more" (Mark 10:48). Jesus stopped in his tracks and instructed the reluctant crowd to call the blind man. They did so, in as belittling a tone as possible: "Cheer up! On your feet! He's calling you" (v. 49). Bartimaeus threw aside his cloak (probably his most valuable possession) in his haste to reach Jesus (see 7:50).

As he so often did, Jesus asked the man to articulate his obvious need. Part of recovery is identifying precisely what Jesus needs to remove from our lives. Stepping out of denial requires recognition of the hurts, hang-ups and habits that are dominating our lives. Real change in life necessitates getting specific about the harmful behaviors and character defects we need to allow God to change. Bartimaeus wanted one thing: to see. And Jesus granted him healing in response to his faith. Once he regained his sight, Bartimaeus "followed Jesus along the road" (see 7:52). Recovery is a road we travel with Jesus.

Sadly, the throng around Jesus lacked his compassion. Our old crowd may try to pull us back into our addiction. Or we may encounter a church group uncomfortable with honest, desperate cries for help. Bartimaeus ignored the crowd and sought the Christ, and we in our recovery must do the same. Like Bartimaeus we need to leave behind anything that might slow us down in our race to recovery: "Let us throw off everything that hinders and the sin that so easily entangles. And let us run with perseverance the race marked out for us" (Hebrews 12:1).

heard that it was Jesus of Nazareth, he began to shout, "Jesus, Son of David, have mercy on me!"

48Many rebuked him and told him to be quiet, but he shouted all the more, "Son of David, have mercy on me!"

49Jesus stopped and said, "Call him."

So they called to the blind man, "Cheer up! On your feet! He's calling you." 50Throwing his cloak aside, he jumped to his feet and came to Jesus.

51"What do you want me to do for you?" Jesus asked him.

The blind man said, "Rabbi, I want to see."

52"Go," said Jesus, "your faith has healed you." Immediately he received his sight and followed Jesus along the road.

Jesus Comes to Jerusalem as King

11 As they approached Jerusalem and came to Bethphage and Bethany at the Mount of Olives, Jesus sent two of his disciples, 2saying to them, "Go to the village ahead of you, and just as you enter it, you will find a colt tied there, which no one has ever ridden. Untie it and bring it here. 3If anyone asks you, 'Why are you doing this?' say, 'The Lord needs it and will send it back here shortly.'"

4They went and found a colt outside in the street, tied at a doorway. As they untied it, 5some people standing there asked, "What are you doing, untying that colt?" 6They answered as Jesus had told them to, and the people let them go. 7When they brought the colt to Jesus and threw their cloaks over it, he sat on it. 8Many people spread their cloaks on the road, while others spread branches they had cut in the fields. 9Those who went ahead and those who followed shouted,

"Hosanna!*a*"

"Blessed is he who comes in the name of the Lord!"*b*

10"Blessed is the coming kingdom of our father David!"

"Hosanna in the highest heaven!"

11Jesus entered Jerusalem and went into the temple courts. He looked around at everything, but since it was already late, he went out to Bethany with the Twelve.

Jesus Curses a Fig Tree and Clears the Temple Courts

12The next day as they were leaving Bethany, Jesus was hungry. 13Seeing in the distance a fig tree in leaf, he went to find out if it had any fruit. When he reached it, he found nothing but leaves, because it was not the season for figs. 14Then he said to the tree, "May no one ever eat fruit from you again." And his disciples heard him say it.

15On reaching Jerusalem, Jesus entered the temple courts and began driving out those who were buying and selling there. He overturned the tables of the money changers and the benches of those selling doves, 16and would not allow anyone to carry merchandise through the temple courts. 17And as he taught them, he said, "Is it not written: 'My house will be called a house of prayer for all nations'*c*? But you have made it 'a den of robbers.'*d*"

18The chief priests and the teachers of the law heard this and began looking for a way to kill him, for they feared him, because the whole crowd was amazed at his teaching.

19When evening came, Jesus and his disciples*e* went out of the city.

20In the morning, as they went along, they saw the fig tree withered from the roots. 21Peter remembered and said to Jesus, "Rabbi, look! The fig tree you cursed has withered!"

22"Have faith in God," Jesus answered. 23"Truly*f* I tell you, if anyone says to this mountain, 'Go, throw yourself into the sea,' and does not doubt in their heart but

---

a 9 A Hebrew expression meaning "Save!" which became an exclamation of praise; also in verse 10   *b 9* Psalm 118:25,26   *c 17* Isaiah 56:7   *d 17* Jer. 7:11   *e 19* Some early manuscripts *came, Jesus*   *f 22,23* Some early manuscripts *"If you have faith in God," Jesus answered, 23"truly*

My Name Is Brandon

I'M A BELIEVER WHO STRUGGLES WITH DRUG ADDICTION, ANGER AND SEXUAL ABUSE

Please read the story in Mark 10:46 – 52 of Jesus' restoration of sight to blind Bartimaeus.

I was raised in the church by loving parents. Every summer during grade school I would spend two weeks at my aunt's house. The summer before third grade I was sexually abused there by my cousin. I pleaded with my parents to let me come home, unable to tell them the truth because my abuser had threatened me. Mom and Dad empathized with my "home-sickness" but counseled me to "tough it out." From that point on I never felt I could depend on anyone.

My parents ended up divorcing, and I believed, as many kids do, that this was my fault. I became involved in criminal activities, convincing myself that I was doing these things for the "right reasons." On January 4, 1991, my chosen lifestyle came to a screeching halt. I was 16 and on Christmas break when I was arrested. I was certified as an adult and sentenced to 15 years in prison.

I learned a number of things while serving my time. On the positive side, I received my GED, high school diploma and an associate's degree. The negatives were the things I learned outside the classroom: how to live without a conscience, how to use my talents and gifts to manipulate other people and the ins and outs of drug usage. I turned my back on God completely, began studying the occult and delighted in persecuting others. Thankfully, this changed in the fall of 1994, when I had the privilege of working in the prison school with a sincere Christian man. I began joining him at church services and Bible studies, and that October I accepted the Lord.

I was released on parole, certain that good things lay ahead. But the next four months were devastating. My girlfriend became pregnant, had an abortion and dumped me. I also lost my job. It was shortly thereafter that a buddy shared drugs with me. The next seven years of my life were consumed with whatever it took to make sure I had a steady supply of drugs. There were practically no limits to what I would do to stay high. Drugs became my best friend, my lover and my god. During this time I went through multiple cars, jobs and relationships — destroying or discarding any and all of them thoughtlessly. I slept in vacant houses, cars and under a bridge.

In the winter of 1998, during a brief stint of clean time, I met a young lady whom I began dating. I relapsed a short time later, though. I was living a double life, and I managed to hide my addiction from her until I was again arrested. This time I was sentenced to five years in prison and served a year and a half. During that time I went through an intensive drug and alcohol treatment program but continued both using and dealing drugs. I fooled myself into thinking I would be able to leave this addiction behind upon my release.

After I was released, my girlfriend and a good job were both waiting for me. Less than two months later, though, I relapsed again. During another halfhearted attempt to get clean, I heard about a Christ-centered recovery ministry called Celebrate Recovery. I attended the program off and on for a few months but never really connected. My life and my addiction continued to spiral out of control. I felt as though I was on the verge of losing everything once again, and the truth was that I really didn't care. I had finally hit bottom.

Like Bartimaeus, who had no doubt lived his life in desolate anguish as he sat by the roadside begging (see Mark 10:46), I was overwhelmed by desperation, and I returned to Celebrate Recovery. During a worship session I, too, cried out to Jesus (see v. 47): "I'm through! I can't fight any longer!" I knew I needed the help that only Jesus could provide. I realized that night that I needed him to reveal himself to me in an intimate and personal way. God did exactly that. I was so overcome by an awesome sense of peace and love that I allowed the tears to flow. I recognized at last that I was completely helpless on my own. In response to my "can't," Jesus' simple response was, "I can."

Although I've been in recovery for three years, it hasn't been an easy time for me. I still struggle with my hurts, hang-ups and habits. In fact, I relapsed a few months before I got married. But I learned through that experience that a mistake doesn't have to escalate into a failure. I contacted my sponsor immediately and told him I needed help. After developing an action plan together, I informed my fiancée, my accountability partners and the leadership team with whom I served. These people all helped me in my journey from relapse to restoration; each of them loved me through my guilt and shame. I pray that I'll never again have to experience relapse. I've learned that on my own I can all too easily become blind to the truth. I know and believe that with God all things are possible, and I look forward to the future.

Brandon

believes that what they say will happen, it will be done for them. 24Therefore I tell you, whatever you ask for in prayer, believe that you have received it, and it will be yours. 25And when you stand praying, if you hold anything against anyone, forgive them, so that your Father in heaven may forgive you your sins." [26]ᵃ

The Authority of Jesus Questioned

27They arrived again in Jerusalem, and while Jesus was walking in the temple courts, the chief priests, the teachers of the law and the elders came to him. 28"By what authority are you doing these things?" they asked. "And who gave you authority to do this?"

29Jesus replied, "I will ask you one question. Answer me, and I will tell you by what authority I am doing these things. 30John's baptism — was it from heaven, or of human origin? Tell me!"

31They discussed it among themselves and said, "If we say, 'From heaven,' he will ask, 'Then why didn't you believe him?' 32But if we say, 'Of human origin' . . ." (They feared the people, for everyone held that John really was a prophet.)

33So they answered Jesus, "We don't know."

Jesus said, "Neither will I tell you by what authority I am doing these things."

The Parable of the Tenants

12 Jesus then began to speak to them in parables: "A man planted a vineyard. He put a wall around it, dug a pit for the winepress and built a watchtower. Then he rented the vineyard to some farmers and moved to another place. 2At harvest time he sent a servant to the tenants to collect from them some of the fruit of the vineyard. 3But they seized him, beat him and sent him away empty-handed. 4Then he sent another servant to them; they struck this man on the head and treated him shamefully. 5He sent still another, and that one they killed. He sent many others; some of them they beat, others they killed.

6"He had one left to send, a son, whom he loved. He sent him last of all, saying, 'They will respect my son.'

7"But the tenants said to one another, 'This is the heir. Come, let's kill him, and the inheritance will be ours.' 8So they took him and killed him, and threw him out of the vineyard.

9"What then will the owner of the vineyard do? He will come and kill those tenants and give the vineyard to others. 10Haven't you read this passage of Scripture:

" 'The stone the builders rejected
   has become the cornerstone;
11the Lord has done this,
   and it is marvelous in our eyes'ᵇ?"

12Then the chief priests, the teachers of the law and the elders looked for a way to arrest him because they knew he had spoken the parable against them. But they were afraid of the crowd; so they left him and went away.

Paying the Imperial Tax to Caesar

13Later they sent some of the Pharisees and Herodians to Jesus to catch him in his words. 14They came to him and said, "Teacher, we know that you are a man of integrity. You aren't swayed by others, because you pay no attention to who they are; but you teach the way of God in accordance with the truth. Is it right to pay the imperial taxᶜ to Caesar or not? 15Should we pay or shouldn't we?"

But Jesus knew their hypocrisy. "Why are you trying to trap me?" he asked. "Bring me a denarius and let me look at it." 16They brought the coin, and he asked them, "Whose image is this? And whose inscription?"

ᵃ 26 Some manuscripts include here words similar to Matt. 6:15.   ᵇ 11 Psalm 118:22,23   ᶜ 14 A special tax levied on subject peoples, not on Roman citizens

"Caesar's," they replied.

¹⁷Then Jesus said to them, "Give back to Caesar what is Caesar's and to God what is God's."

And they were amazed at him.

Marriage at the Resurrection

¹⁸Then the Sadducees, who say there is no resurrection, came to him with a question. ¹⁹"Teacher," they said, "Moses wrote for us that if a man's brother dies and leaves a wife but no children, the man must marry the widow and raise up offspring for his brother. ²⁰Now there were seven brothers. The first one married and died without leaving any children. ²¹The second one married the widow, but he also died, leaving no child. It was the same with the third. ²²In fact, none of the seven left any children. Last of all, the woman died too. ²³At the resurrection*ᵃ* whose wife will she be, since the seven were married to her?"

²⁴Jesus replied, "Are you not in error because you do not know the Scriptures or the power of God? ²⁵When the dead rise, they will neither marry nor be given in marriage; they will be like the angels in heaven. ²⁶Now about the dead rising — have you not read in the Book of Moses, in the account of the burning bush, how God said to him, 'I am the God of Abraham, the God of Isaac, and the God of Jacob'*ᵇ*? ²⁷He is not the God of the dead, but of the living. You are badly mistaken!"

The Greatest Commandment

²⁸One of the teachers of the law came and heard them debating. Noticing that Jesus had given them a good answer, he asked him, "Of all the commandments, which is the most important?"

²⁹"The most important one," answered Jesus, "is this: 'Hear, O Israel: The Lord our God, the Lord is one.*ᶜ* ³⁰Love the Lord your God with all your heart and with all your soul and with all your mind and with all your strength.'*ᵈ* ³¹The second is this: 'Love your neighbor as yourself.'*ᵉ* There is no commandment greater than these."

³²"Well said, teacher," the man replied. "You are right in saying that God is one and there is no other but him. ³³To love him with all your heart, with all your understanding and with all your strength, and to love your neighbor as yourself is more important than all burnt offerings and sacrifices."

³⁴When Jesus saw that he had answered wisely, he said to him, "You are not far from the kingdom of God." And from then on no one dared ask him any more questions.

Whose Son Is the Messiah?

³⁵While Jesus was teaching in the temple courts, he asked, "Why do the teachers of the law say that the Messiah is the son of David? ³⁶David himself, speaking by the Holy Spirit, declared:

> "'The Lord said to my Lord:
>   "Sit at my right hand
> until I put your enemies
>   under your feet."'*ᶠ*

³⁷David himself calls him 'Lord.' How then can he be his son?"

The large crowd listened to him with delight.

Warning Against the Teachers of the Law

³⁸As he taught, Jesus said, "Watch out for the teachers of the law. They like to walk around in flowing robes and be greeted with respect in the marketplaces, ³⁹and have the most important seats in the synagogues and the places of honor at banquets. ⁴⁰They devour widows' houses and for a show make lengthy prayers. These men will be punished most severely."

The Widow's Offering

⁴¹Jesus sat down opposite the place where the offerings were put and watched

---

ᵃ 23 Some manuscripts *resurrection, when people rise from the dead,*   *ᵇ 26* Exodus 3:6   *ᶜ 29* Or *The Lord our God is one Lord*   *ᵈ 30* Deut. 6:4,5   *ᵉ 31* Lev. 19:18   *ᶠ 36* Psalm 110:1

MY NAME IS
THE POOR WIDOW

MARK 12:41–44

Ultimately, our life decisions are investment decisions. Whether the subject is time, talent or treasure, we're continuously making decisions about what we'll invest in. In this simple account, "rich people" made large investments designed to impress others. The poor widow, in contrast, donated a small amount of money. Given her circumstances, it was actually a gigantic investment: It was all the money she had. She wasn't trying to impress anybody — not people, not God. She simply placed a priority on investing in God's work. She was willing to give all in an act of worship and sacrifice from a pure motive of love for her God.

This is especially striking since she was a victim of difficult circumstances. Widows in that day and culture often faced privation. She could have resented her circumstances, fixing her thoughts on what she had lost. Instead she chose to focus on God and the privilege of worshiping him. She gave out of gratitude for what she had instead of grieving over what she had lost. This made her heroic in Jesus' estimation, so exemplary that her humble act of faith would be recalled throughout the history of Christianity.

Recovery requires extensive, wise investment. It also takes a lot of time, humility and absolute surrender to Jesus Christ. As our recovery continues, our motives must mature. Ultimately we need to come to a point where what was once our cry for help from God is replaced by our grateful service to him. In seeking sobriety we find the Savior. And once we know him, we desire to please him. Like the widow, we can offer no more than what we have. But, again like the widow, we can give all we have to God. Time, talent and treasure, in whatever degree we enjoy them, are God's gifts to us. He asks us only to invest what he has already freely given us. We need to stop talking and start giving out of gratitude to God for his grace in our lives.

Are you stuck? Has your recovery slowed down? Perhaps it's time to check your motives, to examine your kingdom portfolio. Where are you investing? Whose glory do you seek? Are you faithfully seeking to share with others the Good News you've discovered? Give *all* you have: time, treasure and talent. If you're not getting what you expected out of your recovery experience, stop taking and start giving. Give out of gratitude to God for his grace in your life.

the crowd putting their money into the temple treasury. Many rich people threw in large amounts. 42But a poor widow came and put in two very small copper coins, worth only a few cents.

43Calling his disciples to him, Jesus said, "Truly I tell you, this poor widow has put more into the treasury than all the others. 44They all gave out of their wealth; but she, out of her poverty, put in everything—all she had to live on."

The Destruction of the Temple and Signs of the End Times

13 As Jesus was leaving the temple, one of his disciples said to him, "Look, Teacher! What massive stones! What magnificent buildings!"

2"Do you see all these great buildings?" replied Jesus. "Not one stone here will be left on another; every one will be thrown down."

3As Jesus was sitting on the Mount of Olives opposite the temple, Peter, James, John and Andrew asked him privately, 4"Tell us, when will these things happen? And what will be the sign that they are all about to be fulfilled?"

5Jesus said to them: "Watch out that no one deceives you. 6Many will come in my name, claiming, 'I am he,' and will deceive many. 7When you hear of wars and rumors of wars, do not be alarmed. Such things must happen, but the end is still to come. 8Nation will rise against nation, and kingdom against kingdom. There will be earthquakes in various places, and famines. These are the beginning of birth pains.

9"You must be on your guard. You will be handed over to the local councils and flogged in the synagogues. On account of me you will stand before governors and kings as witnesses to them. 10And the gospel must first be preached to all nations. 11Whenever you are arrested and brought to trial, do not worry beforehand about what to say. Just say whatever is given you

at the time, for it is not you speaking, but the Holy Spirit.

12"Brother will betray brother to death, and a father his child. Children will rebel against their parents and have them put to death. 13Everyone will hate you because of me, but the one who stands firm to the end will be saved.

14"When you see 'the abomination that causes desolation'[a] standing where it[b] does not belong—let the reader understand—then let those who are in Judea flee to the mountains. 15Let no one on the housetop go down or enter the house to take anything out. 16Let no one in the field go back to get their cloak. 17How dreadful it will be in those days for pregnant women and nursing mothers! 18Pray that this will not take place in winter, 19because those will be days of distress unequaled from the beginning, when God created the world, until now—and never to be equaled again.

20"If the Lord had not cut short those days, no one would survive. But for the sake of the elect, whom he has chosen, he has shortened them. 21At that time if anyone says to you, 'Look, here is the Messiah!' or, 'Look, there he is!' do not believe it. 22For false messiahs and false prophets will appear and perform signs and wonders to deceive, if possible, even the elect. 23So be on your guard; I have told you everything ahead of time.

24"But in those days, following that distress,

"'the sun will be darkened,
    and the moon will not give its light;
25the stars will fall from the sky,
    and the heavenly bodies will be
        shaken.'[c]

26"At that time people will see the Son of Man coming in clouds with great power and glory. 27And he will send his angels and gather his elect from the four winds, from the ends of the earth to the ends of the heavens.

---

a 14 Daniel 9:27; 11:31; 12:11   *b* 14 Or *he*   *c* 25 Isaiah 13:10; 34:4

My Name Is Terri

I'M A BELIEVER WHO STRUGGLES WITH CODEPENDENCY AND FINANCES

Please read the story of the poor widow's generous offering in Mark 12:41 – 44.

I was raised in a "normal" family. My parents worked hard to make ends meet, providing a safe, comfortable home for my brother and me. But we were never quite up to the standard of the neighborhood we lived in. If there had been railroad tracks dividing our town, we would have been living just over the line on the "wrong" side. I never could keep up with the kids from those families who had "made it." I attended church and knew that God loved me, but I never realized I could develop a day-to-day relationship with Christ.

I met the love of my life in high school, and we were married a few years later. He was on the fast track in his career, spending most of his time at work and moving quickly up the corporate ladder. We were regularly moving into bigger homes in better neighborhoods. Three children and several relocations later, we found ourselves moving into the big house on the hill. This to me was the ultimate. We had the view, the pool, the basketball court, the horse property, a great income and a wonderful family. Life was good.

While I was busy enjoying a lavish lifestyle, though, and spending every penny on whatever impulse purchase I wanted, my husband's business began to slow, almost to the point of closing. His income suddenly dropped to next to nothing. He worked harder than ever, though, and was rarely at home during waking hours. The credit cards were maxed out, bills kept pouring in and our savings was quickly depleted. I was accustomed to frequent phone calls offering new products, travel destinations or easy credit terms for purchasing the next, best "thing." But now the calls were increasingly from creditors who not so politely requested the next payment. No longer able to keep up with the neighbors, we were quickly left behind socially.

We lost the house on the hill and moved into a rental unit. From the depths of despair at losing all of the material extras and lifestyle privileges I thought were so important, I cried out to God for help.

A woman at work befriended me and invited me to church. I began attending, and hearing God's Word brought me a glimmer of hope. I began to focus on his Word and what I had to be grateful for, taking with a grain of salt what my creditors and the world were telling me. This was a major step for me because the message I thought I was getting from "the world" was to run away from my creditors and my marriage. I chose God's way instead, opting to concentrate on my wonderful family; my health; my church family; and my vital, growing relationship with my Lord and Savior, Jesus Christ.

Like the poor widow in Luke 21, I had nothing to give by the world's standards, but I stepped out in faith and offered myself to God. When I didn't have enough money to pay the bills, I was obedient and offered the first 10 percent to God. It was the least I could do. He was there for me when everything else was falling apart, offering me the peace and security I hadn't found even when I'd been rich in material possessions.

I began to volunteer at church, wanting God to be the top priority in my calendar too. A few hours of service each week brought new friendships and helped me focus on doing God's work. This volunteer involvement also brought me to Celebrate Recovery. At first I didn't think I needed recovery; after all, I was struggling with finances only as a result of a turn in the economy. But I kept attending and soon came to realize that I'd been using money, and what it could buy, to fill a void in my heart, a craving only God could truly satisfy. I'd been trying to buy significance and value to cover up my low self-esteem. Money, and the lifestyle it offered, had proved to be false and fleeting. It had let me down and left me crying and alone. Through Celebrate Recovery I came to see myself as a child of God, someone truly significant in his eyes.

I continue to give of my time, talents and treasure, and I find myself blessed beyond my wildest dreams. God has completely turned my life around. Instead of trying to measure up to the world's standards, I'm content with what I have and anxious to be about God's work. We now own a lovely home. It's not on the hilltop. In fact, it's by the railroad tracks, but it's warm and safe and full of love. My kids have grown to know and love Christ and have been shaped in positive ways by our mutual experiences. I have a wonderful job in ministry that uses my talents and skills and allows me to give back to God in gratitude for all that Christ has done for me. I recognize that everything I have is first of all a gift from God, and I strive to be a good steward of all that I've been given.

28"Now learn this lesson from the fig tree: As soon as its twigs get tender and its leaves come out, you know that summer is near. 29Even so, when you see these things happening, you know that it*a* is near, right at the door. 30Truly I tell you, this generation will certainly not pass away until all these things have happened. 31Heaven and earth will pass away, but my words will never pass away.

The Day and Hour Unknown

32"But about that day or hour no one knows, not even the angels in heaven, nor the Son, but only the Father. 33Be on guard! Be alert*b*! You do not know when that time will come. 34It's like a man going away: He leaves his house and puts his servants in charge, each with their assigned task, and tells the one at the door to keep watch.

35"Therefore keep watch because you do not know when the owner of the house will come back — whether in the evening, or at midnight, or when the rooster crows, or at dawn. 36If he comes suddenly, do not let him find you sleeping. 37What I say to you, I say to everyone: 'Watch!'"

Jesus Anointed at Bethany

14 Now the Passover and the Festival of Unleavened Bread were only two days away, and the chief priests and the teachers of the law were scheming to arrest Jesus secretly and kill him. 2"But not during the festival," they said, "or the people may riot."

3While he was in Bethany, reclining at the table in the home of Simon the Leper, a woman came with an alabaster jar of very expensive perfume, made of pure nard. She broke the jar and poured the perfume on his head.

4Some of those present were saying indignantly to one another, "Why this waste of perfume? 5It could have been sold for more than a year's wages*c* and the money given to the poor." And they rebuked her harshly.

6"Leave her alone," said Jesus. "Why are you bothering her? She has done a beautiful thing to me. 7The poor you will always have with you,*d* and you can help them any time you want. But you will not always have me. 8She did what she could. She poured perfume on my body beforehand to prepare for my burial. 9Truly I tell you, wherever the gospel is preached throughout the world, what she has done will also be told, in memory of her."

10Then Judas Iscariot, one of the Twelve, went to the chief priests to betray Jesus to them. 11They were delighted to hear this and promised to give him money. So he watched for an opportunity to hand him over.

The Last Supper

12On the first day of the Festival of Unleavened Bread, when it was customary to sacrifice the Passover lamb, Jesus' disciples asked him, "Where do you want us to go and make preparations for you to eat the Passover?"

13So he sent two of his disciples, telling them, "Go into the city, and a man carrying a jar of water will meet you. Follow him. 14Say to the owner of the house he enters, 'The Teacher asks: Where is my guest room, where I may eat the Passover with my disciples?' 15He will show you a large room upstairs, furnished and ready. Make preparations for us there."

16The disciples left, went into the city and found things just as Jesus had told them. So they prepared the Passover.

17When evening came, Jesus arrived with the Twelve. 18While they were reclining at the table eating, he said, "Truly I tell you, one of you will betray me — one who is eating with me."

19They were saddened, and one by one they said to him, "Surely you don't mean me?"

20"It is one of the Twelve," he replied, "one who dips bread into the bowl with me.

---

a 29 Or *he*   *b 33* Some manuscripts *alert and pray*   *c 5* Greek *than three hundred denarii*   *d 7* See Deut. 15:11.

21The Son of Man will go just as it is written about him. But woe to that man who betrays the Son of Man! It would be better for him if he had not been born."

22While they were eating, Jesus took bread, and when he had given thanks, he broke it and gave it to his disciples, saying, "Take it; this is my body."

23Then he took a cup, and when he had given thanks, he gave it to them, and they all drank from it.

24"This is my blood of thea covenant, which is poured out for many," he said to them. 25"Truly I tell you, I will not drink again from the fruit of the vine until that day when I drink it new in the kingdom of God."

26When they had sung a hymn, they went out to the Mount of Olives.

Jesus Predicts Peter's Denial

27"You will all fall away," Jesus told them, "for it is written:

> " 'I will strike the shepherd,
>   and the sheep will be scattered.'b

28But after I have risen, I will go ahead of you into Galilee."

29Peter declared, "Even if all fall away, I will not."

30"Truly I tell you," Jesus answered, "today — yes, tonight — before the rooster crows twicec you yourself will disown me three times."

31But Peter insisted emphatically, "Even if I have to die with you, I will never disown you." And all the others said the same.

Gethsemane

32They went to a place called Gethsemane, and Jesus said to his disciples, "Sit here while I pray." 33He took Peter, James and John along with him, and he began to be deeply distressed and troubled. 34"My soul is overwhelmed with sorrow to the point of death," he said to them. "Stay here and keep watch."

35Going a little farther, he fell to the ground and prayed that if possible the hour might pass from him. 36"Abba,d Father," he said, "everything is possible for you. Take this cup from me. Yet not what I will, but what you will."

37Then he returned to his disciples and found them sleeping. "Simon," he said to Peter, "are you asleep? Couldn't you keep watch for one hour? 38Watch and pray so that you will not fall into temptation. The spirit is willing, but the flesh is weak."

39Once more he went away and prayed the same thing. 40When he came back, he again found them sleeping, because their eyes were heavy. They did not know what to say to him.

41Returning the third time, he said to them, "Are you still sleeping and resting? Enough! The hour has come. Look, the Son of Man is delivered into the hands of sinners. 42Rise! Let us go! Here comes my betrayer!"

Jesus Arrested

43Just as he was speaking, Judas, one of the Twelve, appeared. With him was a crowd armed with swords and clubs, sent from the chief priests, the teachers of the law, and the elders. 44Now the betrayer had arranged a signal with them: "The one I kiss is the man; arrest him and lead him away under guard." 45Going at once to Jesus, Judas said, "Rabbi!" and kissed him. 46The men seized Jesus and arrested him. 47Then one of those standing near drew his sword and struck the servant of the high priest, cutting off his ear.

48"Am I leading a rebellion," said Jesus, "that you have come out with swords and clubs to capture me? 49Every day I was with you, teaching in the temple courts, and you did not arrest me. But the Scriptures must be fulfilled." 50Then everyone deserted him and fled.

---

a 24 Some manuscripts *the new*   b 27 Zech. 13:7   c 30 Some early manuscripts do not have *twice*.
d 36 Aramaic for *father*

This is the first page of the RELAPSE lesson.

For a discussion of Principles One through Eight and a listing of their related lessons,
go to pages xvii – xliv.

> *Watch and pray so that you will not fall into temptation.*
> *The spirit is willing, but the flesh is weak.*

MARK 14:38

In Principle Seven we reserve a daily quiet time with God for self-examination, Bible reading and prayer in order to get to know God and his will for our lives and to gain the power to follow his will. As we work this principle, we begin the journey of applying and living what we've discovered in the first six principles. We live daily in humility — as well as in reality, not in denial. We've done our best to amend our past. Through God's guidance we can now make choices about the emotions that will affect our ongoing thinking and actions. We can start to take *action* — positive action — instead of operating in a mode of continual *reaction*.

The second part of this principle — the call to reserve a daily quiet time with God for Bible reading and prayer in order to get to know God and his will for our lives and to gain the power to follow his will — also relates to Step Eleven of the Christ-centered 12 Steps.

Step Eleven: We've sought through prayer and meditation to improve our conscious contact with God, praying for knowledge of his will for us, as well as for the power to carry out that will.

This is the best relapse prevention plan we can have. If we're not daily working this principle, we can easily slip back into our old hurts, hang-ups and habits. The alcoholic goes back to drinking, the overeater gains back the lost weight, the gambler returns to his bookie, the workaholic fills up his schedule, the codependent immerses herself in an unhealthy relationship and ... the list goes on and on.

The *R* in RELAPSE stands for RESERVE A DAILY QUIET TIME. The first step in preventing a relapse is to admit that we'll be tempted — in essence, that we're not above temptation (see Mark 14:38).

Jesus wasn't unaffected by temptation, so why should we be? We can find the account of Jesus' temptation in Matthew 4:1 – 11. Jesus was indeed tempted, but through it all he never sinned. Being tempted isn't in itself a sin. It's falling into the harmful action underlying the temptation that gets us into trouble. Spending time alone with our Creator gives us the strength to avoid temptations.

We've established that temptation isn't a sin. In fact, on the positive side, it's a call to battle. When we're tempted to fall back into our old hurts, hang-ups and habits, we need to command the devil, as Jesus did in Matthew 4:10, "Away from me, Satan! For it is written: 'Worship the Lord your God, and serve him only.'"

The next letter in RELAPSE is *E*. Go to Romans 12: 3,9 – 10,12,16 – 17 (page 1411).

51A young man, wearing nothing but a linen garment, was following Jesus. When they seized him, 52he fled naked, leaving his garment behind.

Jesus Before the Sanhedrin

53They took Jesus to the high priest, and all the chief priests, the elders and the teachers of the law came together. 54Peter followed him at a distance, right into the courtyard of the high priest. There he sat with the guards and warmed himself at the fire.

55The chief priests and the whole Sanhedrin were looking for evidence against Jesus so that they could put him to death, but they did not find any. 56Many testified falsely against him, but their statements did not agree.

57Then some stood up and gave this false testimony against him: 58"We heard him say, 'I will destroy this temple made with human hands and in three days will build another, not made with hands.'" 59Yet even then their testimony did not agree.

60Then the high priest stood up before them and asked Jesus, "Are you not going to answer? What is this testimony that these men are bringing against you?" 61But Jesus remained silent and gave no answer.

Again the high priest asked him, "Are you the Messiah, the Son of the Blessed One?"

62"I am," said Jesus. "And you will see the Son of Man sitting at the right hand of the Mighty One and coming on the clouds of heaven."

63The high priest tore his clothes. "Why do we need any more witnesses?" he asked. 64"You have heard the blasphemy. What do you think?"

They all condemned him as worthy of death. 65Then some began to spit at him; they blindfolded him, struck him with their fists, and said, "Prophesy!" And the guards took him and beat him.

Peter Disowns Jesus

66While Peter was below in the courtyard, one of the servant girls of the high priest came by. 67When she saw Peter warming himself, she looked closely at him.

"You also were with that Nazarene, Jesus," she said.

68But he denied it. "I don't know or understand what you're talking about," he said, and went out into the entryway.[a]

69When the servant girl saw him there, she said again to those standing around, "This fellow is one of them." 70Again he denied it.

After a little while, those standing near said to Peter, "Surely you are one of them, for you are a Galilean."

71He began to call down curses, and he swore to them, "I don't know this man you're talking about."

72Immediately the rooster crowed the second time.[b] Then Peter remembered the word Jesus had spoken to him: "Before the rooster crows twice[c] you will disown me three times." And he broke down and wept.

Jesus Before Pilate

15 Very early in the morning, the chief priests, with the elders, the teachers of the law and the whole Sanhedrin, made their plans. So they bound Jesus, led him away and handed him over to Pilate.

2"Are you the king of the Jews?" asked Pilate.

"You have said so," Jesus replied.

3The chief priests accused him of many things. 4So again Pilate asked him, "Aren't you going to answer? See how many things they are accusing you of."

5But Jesus still made no reply, and Pilate was amazed.

6Now it was the custom at the festival to release a prisoner whom the people requested. 7A man called Barabbas was in

---

a 68 Some early manuscripts *entryway and the rooster crowed*   *b 72* Some early manuscripts do not have *the*
second time.   *c 72* Some early manuscripts do not have *twice.*

prison with the insurrectionists who had committed murder in the uprising. 8The crowd came up and asked Pilate to do for them what he usually did.

9"Do you want me to release to you the king of the Jews?" asked Pilate, 10knowing it was out of self-interest that the chief priests had handed Jesus over to him. 11But the chief priests stirred up the crowd to have Pilate release Barabbas instead.

12"What shall I do, then, with the one you call the king of the Jews?" Pilate asked them.

13"Crucify him!" they shouted.

14"Why? What crime has he committed?" asked Pilate.

But they shouted all the louder, "Crucify him!"

15Wanting to satisfy the crowd, Pilate released Barabbas to them. He had Jesus flogged, and handed him over to be crucified.

The Soldiers Mock Jesus

16The soldiers led Jesus away into the palace (that is, the Praetorium) and called together the whole company of soldiers. 17They put a purple robe on him, then twisted together a crown of thorns and set it on him. 18And they began to call out to him, "Hail, king of the Jews!" 19Again and again they struck him on the head with a staff and spit on him. Falling on their knees, they paid homage to him. 20And when they had mocked him, they took off the purple robe and put his own clothes on him. Then they led him out to crucify him.

The Crucifixion of Jesus

21A certain man from Cyrene, Simon, the father of Alexander and Rufus, was passing by on his way in from the country, and they forced him to carry the cross. 22They brought Jesus to the place called Golgotha (which means "the place of the skull"). 23Then they offered him wine

mixed with myrrh, but he did not take it. 24And they crucified him. Dividing up his clothes, they cast lots to see what each would get.

25It was nine in the morning when they crucified him. 26The written notice of the charge against him read: THE KING OF THE JEWS.

27They crucified two rebels with him, one on his right and one on his left. [28] a 29Those who passed by hurled insults at him, shaking their heads and saying, "So! You who are going to destroy the temple and build it in three days, 30come down from the cross and save yourself!" 31In the same way the chief priests and the teachers of the law mocked him among themselves. "He saved others," they said, "but he can't save himself! 32Let this Messiah, this king of Israel, come down now from the cross, that we may see and believe." Those crucified with him also heaped insults on him.

The Death of Jesus

33At noon, darkness came over the whole land until three in the afternoon. 34And at three in the afternoon Jesus cried out in a loud voice, *"Eloi, Eloi, lema sabachthani?"* (which means "My God, my God, why have you forsaken me?").b

35When some of those standing near heard this, they said, "Listen, he's calling Elijah."

36Someone ran, filled a sponge with wine vinegar, put it on a staff, and offered it to Jesus to drink. "Now leave him alone. Let's see if Elijah comes to take him down," he said.

37With a loud cry, Jesus breathed his last.

38The curtain of the temple was torn in two from top to bottom. 39And when the centurion, who stood there in front of Jesus, saw how he died,c he said, "Surely this man was the Son of God!"

40Some women were watching from a distance. Among them were Mary Magda-

---

a 28 Some manuscripts include here words similar to Luke 22:37.   b 34 Psalm 22:1   c 39 Some manuscripts saw that he died with such a cry lene, Mary the mother of James the younger and of Joseph,[a] and Salome. ⁴¹In Galilee these women had followed him and cared for his needs. Many other women who had come up with him to Jerusalem were also there.

The Burial of Jesus

⁴²It was Preparation Day (that is, the day before the Sabbath). So as evening approached, ⁴³Joseph of Arimathea, a prominent member of the Council, who was himself waiting for the kingdom of God, went boldly to Pilate and asked for Jesus' body. ⁴⁴Pilate was surprised to hear that he was already dead. Summoning the centurion, he asked him if Jesus had already died. ⁴⁵When he learned from the centurion that it was so, he gave the body to Joseph. ⁴⁶So Joseph bought some linen cloth, took down the body, wrapped it in the linen, and placed it in a tomb cut out of rock. Then he rolled a stone against the entrance of the tomb. ⁴⁷Mary Magdalene and Mary the mother of Joseph saw where he was laid.

Jesus Has Risen

16 When the Sabbath was over, Mary Magdalene, Mary the mother of James, and Salome bought spices so that they might go to anoint Jesus' body. ²Very early on the first day of the week, just after sunrise, they were on their way to the tomb ³and they asked each other, "Who will roll the stone away from the entrance of the tomb?"

⁴But when they looked up, they saw that the stone, which was very large, had been rolled away. ⁵As they entered the tomb, they saw a young man dressed in a white robe sitting on the right side, and they were alarmed.

⁶"Don't be alarmed," he said. "You are looking for Jesus the Nazarene, who was crucified. He has risen! He is not here. See the place where they laid him. ⁷But go, tell his disciples and Peter, 'He is going ahead of you into Galilee. There you will see him, just as he told you.'"

⁸Trembling and bewildered, the women went out and fled from the tomb. They said nothing to anyone, because they were afraid.[b]

[The earliest manuscripts and some other ancient witnesses do not have verses 9–20.]

⁹*When Jesus rose early on the first day of the week, he appeared first to Mary Magdalene, out of whom he had driven seven demons. ¹⁰She went and told those who had been with him and who were mourning and weeping. ¹¹When they heard that Jesus was alive and that she had seen him, they did not believe it.*

¹²*Afterward Jesus appeared in a different form to two of them while they were walking in the country. ¹³These returned and reported it to the rest; but they did not believe them either.*

¹⁴*Later Jesus appeared to the Eleven as they were eating; he rebuked them for their lack of faith and their stubborn refusal to believe those who had seen him after he had risen.*

¹⁵*He said to them, "Go into all the world and preach the gospel to all creation. ¹⁶Whoever believes and is baptized will be saved, but whoever does not believe will be condemned. ¹⁷And these signs will accompany those who believe: In my name they will drive out demons; they will speak in new tongues; ¹⁸they will pick up snakes with their hands; and when they drink deadly poison, it will not hurt them at all; they will place their hands on sick people, and they will get well."*

¹⁹*After the Lord Jesus had spoken to them, he was taken up into heaven and he sat at the right hand of God. ²⁰Then the disciples went out and preached everywhere, and the Lord worked with them and confirmed his word by the signs that accompanied it.*

---

[a] 40 Greek *Joses*, a variant of *Joseph*; also in verse 47   [b] 8 Some manuscripts have the following ending between verses 8 and 9, and one manuscript has it after verse 8 (omitting verses 9-20): *Then they quickly reported all these instructions to those around Peter. After this, Jesus himself also sent out through them from east to west the sacred and imperishable proclamation of eternal salvation. Amen.*

Luke

THEME: The vocabulary of repentance is prominent in Luke. Repentance requires a fundamental reorientation toward God, which then leads to reconciliation of human relationships.

AUTHOR: The third Gospel doesn't identify its author, but tradition has identified him as Luke, the beloved physician. Luke wrote as a historian, not as a firsthand observer of the events he recorded.

DATE OF WRITING: Luke was probably written between AD 59 and 63.

ENCOURAGEMENT FROM LUKE: "There will be more rejoicing in heaven over one sinner who repents than over ninety-nine righteous persons who do not need to repent" (Luke 15:7).

CHALLENGE FROM LUKE: "Love your enemies, do good to those who hate you, bless those who curse you, pray for those who mistreat you" (Luke 6:27–28).

REFLECTION FROM LUKE: "Whoever has been forgiven little loves little" (Luke 7:47).

At a Glance

Recovery Themes in Luke

The religious "authorities" often got it wrong when it came to understanding and responding to Jesus. They wanted him to conform to the way of life they had established through their rigid commitment to tradition. Jesus had no desire to make them feel comfortable. He wanted to draw the lost, the outsiders and the marginalized to himself. He reached out to those who had been left behind. And he's still reaching out today.

The Gospel of Luke shows Jesus loving the brokenhearted and rejoicing when someone who has been lost is found. Luke's account of Jesus' life is full of stories the Teacher himself tells to illustrate his desire to see people find healing from their hurts, hang-ups and habits. Jesus cares about our sorrows. He cares deeply when we're lost, and he actively seeks us out and rejoices when we're found.

Introduction

1 Many have undertaken to draw up an account of the things that have been fulfilled[a] among us, ²just as they were handed down to us by those who from the first were eyewitnesses and servants of the word. ³With this in mind, since I myself have carefully investigated everything from the beginning, I too decided to write an orderly account for you, most excellent Theophilus, ⁴so that you may know the certainty of the things you have been taught.

The Birth of John the Baptist Foretold

⁵In the time of Herod king of Judea there was a priest named Zechariah, who belonged to the priestly division of Abijah; his

---

a 1 Or been surely believed

wife Elizabeth was also a descendant of Aaron. ⁶Both of them were righteous in the sight of God, observing all the Lord's commands and decrees blamelessly. ⁷But they were childless because Elizabeth was not able to conceive, and they were both very old.

⁸Once when Zechariah's division was on duty and he was serving as priest before God, ⁹he was chosen by lot, according to the custom of the priesthood, to go into the temple of the Lord and burn incense. ¹⁰And when the time for the burning of incense came, all the assembled worshipers were praying outside.

¹¹Then an angel of the Lord appeared to him, standing at the right side of the altar of incense. ¹²When Zechariah saw him, he was startled and was gripped with fear. ¹³But the angel said to him: "Do not be afraid, Zechariah; your prayer has been heard. Your wife Elizabeth will bear you a son, and you are to call him John. ¹⁴He will be a joy and delight to you, and many will rejoice because of his birth, ¹⁵for he will be great in the sight of the Lord. He is never to take wine or other fermented drink, and he will be filled with the Holy Spirit even before he is born. ¹⁶He will bring back many of the people of Israel to the Lord their God. ¹⁷And he will go on before the Lord, in the spirit and power of Elijah, to turn the hearts of the parents to their children and the disobedient to the wisdom of the righteous—to make ready a people prepared for the Lord."

¹⁸Zechariah asked the angel, "How can I be sure of this? I am an old man and my wife is well along in years."

¹⁹The angel said to him, "I am Gabriel. I stand in the presence of God, and I have been sent to speak to you and to tell you this good news. ²⁰And now you will be silent and not able to speak until the day this happens, because you did not believe my words, which will come true at their appointed time."

²¹Meanwhile, the people were waiting for Zechariah and wondering why he stayed so long in the temple. ²²When he came out, he could not speak to them. They realized he had seen a vision in the temple, for he kept making signs to them but remained unable to speak.

²³When his time of service was completed, he returned home. ²⁴After this his wife Elizabeth became pregnant and for five months remained in seclusion. ²⁵"The Lord has done this for me," she said. "In these days he has shown his favor and taken away my disgrace among the people."

The Birth of Jesus Foretold

²⁶In the sixth month of Elizabeth's pregnancy, God sent the angel Gabriel to Nazareth, a town in Galilee, ²⁷to a virgin pledged to be married to a man named Joseph, a descendant of David. The virgin's name was Mary. ²⁸The angel went to her and said, "Greetings, you who are highly favored! The Lord is with you."

²⁹Mary was greatly troubled at his words and wondered what kind of greeting this might be. ³⁰But the angel said to her, "Do not be afraid, Mary; you have found favor with God. ³¹You will conceive and give birth to a son, and you are to call him Jesus. ³²He will be great and will be called the Son of the Most High. The Lord God will give him the throne of his father David, ³³and he will reign over Jacob's descendants forever; his kingdom will never end."

³⁴"How will this be," Mary asked the angel, "since I am a virgin?"

³⁵The angel answered, "The Holy Spirit will come on you, and the power of the Most High will overshadow you. So the holy one to be born will be called[a] the Son of God. ³⁶Even Elizabeth your relative is going to have a child in her old age, and she who was said to be unable to conceive is in her sixth month. ³⁷For no word from God will ever fail."

³⁸"I am the Lord's servant," Mary answered. "May your word to me be fulfilled." Then the angel left her.

---

a 35 Or *So the child to be born will be called holy,*

MY NAME IS ZECHARIAH

LUKE 1 : 5 – 2 5 , 5 7 – 8 0

Zechariah seems an unlikely illustration of recovery. He and his wife, Elizabeth, after all, "were righteous in the sight of God, observing all the Lord's commands . . . blamelessly" (Luke 1: 6). Could people like this stumble seriously? Zechariah did. His faith faltered. As a priest, Zechariah received an angelic revelation at an appropriate place and time: while he was in the temple offering incense. The incense offering always drew a large crowd of people who had come to pray (see v. 10). Most petitioned God for deliverance from Roman oppression through the coming of the Messiah. Just outside the Most Holy Place, Zechariah came face-to-face with the angel Gabriel (see vv. 11,19), who instructed the terrified priest not to fear. Many of the Jews believed that if a priest were to make a mistake in the ritual, an angel would strike him dead. Yet Gabriel came not in judgment but with a message: Elizabeth, though aged and barren, would have a son. He was to be named John, and his function would be to introduce the Messiah. Fantastic news! But Zechariah responded with doubt, not faith (see v. 18).

Gabriel went on to announce the consequences of the priest's disbelief: Zechariah would be unable to speak until after John's birth. Gabriel's decree included a principle important in maintaining our own faith: God's promises "will come true at their appointed time" (v. 20). The impact of practicing God's principles may not be immediately evident, but it's vital that we apply the principles patiently, trusting God to change us.

John was born as promised, and this couple's joy was shared by neighbors and relatives (see vv. 57–58). At the baby's circumcision, though, the onlookers were shocked to hear his mother announce that the child would not be named, according to tradition, after his father. The skeptical well-wishers appealed to Zechariah by making signs (apparently he had become deaf as well as mute). Zechariah wrote out his response: The baby would be named John. Then the priest, his tongue at last loosed, took on a prophetic role and sang a song of praise to God, also making predictions concerning John and the soon-to-be-born Messiah (see vv. 67–79).

God's handling of Zechariah's moment of doubt may seem severe. Many of us measure sin on a sliding scale, comparing one person's faults to another's. But Scripture establishes a different standard: Every action that doesn't proceed from faith is sin (see Romans 14:23). God commands us to trust him exclusively and entirely. The apostle Paul voices this principle as he explains matters of conscience, not of revealed law. Even acts not expressly prohibited in Scripture are sin if we do what we believe to be sinful. Only faith will allow us to take the next step in our recovery, and every individual sin and sinful pattern in our life reveals a failure of faith.

Why is it so difficult to write a completely honest inventory? We may lack faith. We may find it hard to call a sin a sin. When it comes right down to it, though, isn't it because we doubt God's love and his promise to forgive? We fail to face our sins because we're afraid to face God. His promise seems too fantastic for us to believe. That was Zechariah's sin. Honesty with God and others requires faith in God's seemingly too-good-to-be-true promise to pardon us. We're called to believe in a love that our life experience has made inconceivable. We've learned to rationalize — but not to repent. Repentance requires a reversal of the false beliefs that brought us into bondage.

We begin by embracing God's unconditional love rather than trying to earn his love. That reversal will plant us squarely on the road to recovery. Continuing the journey will necessitate repentance based on an honest inventory: "If we confess our sins, he is faithful and just and will forgive us our sins and purify us from all unrighteousness" (1 John 1:9). We don't want to fall into the trap Zechariah did. Through Jesus Christ, we can believe what seems impossible.

Mary Visits Elizabeth

³⁹At that time Mary got ready and hurried to a town in the hill country of Judea, ⁴⁰where she entered Zechariah's home and greeted Elizabeth. ⁴¹When Elizabeth heard Mary's greeting, the baby leaped in her womb, and Elizabeth was filled with the Holy Spirit. ⁴²In a loud voice she exclaimed: "Blessed are you among women, and blessed is the child you will bear! ⁴³But why am I so favored, that the mother of my Lord should come to me? ⁴⁴As soon as the sound of your greeting reached my ears, the baby in my womb leaped for joy. ⁴⁵Blessed is she who has believed that the Lord would fulfill his promises to her!"

Mary's Song

⁴⁶And Mary said:

"My soul glorifies the Lord
⁴⁷   and my spirit rejoices in God my
        Savior,
⁴⁸for he has been mindful
        of the humble state of his servant.
    From now on all generations will call
        me blessed,
⁴⁹   for the Mighty One has done great
            things for me —
    holy is his name.
⁵⁰His mercy extends to those who fear him,
        from generation to generation.
⁵¹He has performed mighty deeds with
        his arm;
    he has scattered those who are proud
        in their inmost thoughts.
⁵²He has brought down rulers from their
        thrones
    but has lifted up the humble.
⁵³He has filled the hungry with good
        things
    but has sent the rich away empty.
⁵⁴He has helped his servant Israel,
    remembering to be merciful
⁵⁵to Abraham and his descendants
        forever,
    just as he promised our ancestors."

⁵⁶Mary stayed with Elizabeth for about three months and then returned home.

The Birth of John the Baptist

⁵⁷When it was time for Elizabeth to have her baby, she gave birth to a son. ⁵⁸Her neighbors and relatives heard that the Lord had shown her great mercy, and they shared her joy.

⁵⁹On the eighth day they came to circumcise the child, and they were going to name him after his father Zechariah, ⁶⁰but his mother spoke up and said, "No! He is to be called John."

⁶¹They said to her, "There is no one among your relatives who has that name."

⁶²Then they made signs to his father, to find out what he would like to name the child. ⁶³He asked for a writing tablet, and to everyone's astonishment he wrote, "His name is John." ⁶⁴Immediately his mouth was opened and his tongue set free, and he began to speak, praising God. ⁶⁵All the neighbors were filled with awe, and throughout the hill country of Judea people were talking about all these things. ⁶⁶Everyone who heard this wondered about it, asking, "What then is this child going to be?" For the Lord's hand was with him.

Zechariah's Song

⁶⁷His father Zechariah was filled with the Holy Spirit and prophesied:

⁶⁸"Praise be to the Lord, the God of Israel,
        because he has come to his people
            and redeemed them.
⁶⁹He has raised up a horn*ᵃ* of salvation
        for us
    in the house of his servant David
⁷⁰(as he said through his holy prophets of
        long ago),
⁷¹salvation from our enemies
        and from the hand of all who hate
            us —
⁷²to show mercy to our ancestors
    and to remember his holy covenant,

ᵃ *69* Horn here symbolizes a strong king.

My Name Is Jim

I'M A BELIEVER WHO STRUGGLES WITH ALCOHOLISM AND LUST

Please read the account of the angel Gabriel's revelation to Zechariah as recorded in Luke 1:1–25. The story continues in verses 57 through 80.

Over six years ago, more than three years after I began leading the Celebrate Recovery ministry of my church, I was confronted with the reality that I was serving on a church staff, leading Celebrate Recovery — and living a lie. Like Zechariah, I experienced a serious failure of faith (see Luke 1:18–20).

While engaged in ministry as a member of the pastoral staff and leading a successful Celebrate Recovery program, I was harboring a secret and selfish plan within my heart. While allowing my eyes and thoughts to wander, I began to formulate a plan to leave my wife. I was deceived into thinking that I could find happiness elsewhere, far removed from God's plan. (That's always a dangerous sign.)

God pointed out, though, that while I was quick to apply the principles of recovery to the issue of alcohol, I wasn't being totally honest with him, my wife or my fellow staff members on this other critical issue. I wasn't allowing God unrestricted access to all areas of my life. I was content advising others on how to apply Celebrate Recovery principles to their lives while carefully compartmentalizing my own. My battle with God didn't last long; I anxiously composed a plan to confess to my wife that my life had become unmanageable and that I was in need of healing and restoration in terms of our marriage. "What's the worst that can happen?" I wondered. I was overcome with anxiety, fearful that I would confess my plan to her and be dismissed to follow my selfish ambition. Still, I knew I had to trust God exclusively and entirely.

I'm happy to report that through confession, tears, repentance and a massive dose of God's mercy, our marriage has been healed and our love restored. My wife is once again my heart's desire as a marriage partner, and I've found that living a life of honesty before God, my wife and others has truly produced a harvest of joy. I'm glad to report that I'm well on the way to experiencing the life God planned for me — a life of full and honest relationships.

I'm painfully aware, though, that had I been foolish enough to carry out my plan, the consequences would have been quite different for my marriage, for my ministry opportunities and for the hurting individuals who trust me in their own journeys through Celebrate Recovery. Through my work in pastoral care and in Celebrate Recovery, I've learned firsthand the truth of the Biblical statement that the Lord will "bring to light what is hidden in darkness and will expose the motives of the heart" (1 Corinthians 4:5). It isn't a matter of if but of when.

Does Celebrate Recovery work? My answer is a resounding yes. I've found that as a ministry leader I've been able to apply God's Word to all the issues of my life, and, as a direct consequence, my life is never going to be the same. A key to my own recovery is encapsulated in Psalm 51:17: "My sacrifice, O God, is a broken spirit; a broken and contrite heart you, God, will not despise." This verse serves as a reminder to me that I need to remain clean and obedient before God in thought, word and deed. To grow in my Christian walk as a husband, father and ministry leader, I must remain pure in my motives and the manner in which I share with others. I've found that when I'm "right" and honest before God, it follows naturally that I'm right with my wife, my children and my friends.

My guiding principle is Principle Eight, the one that allows me to put all the other principles to work by loving and serving others. After more than 12 years of working with the ministry at my church, I truly consider it a privilege and an opportunity to introduce others to the road to recovery. My daily work is truly a labor of love.

The Celebrate Recovery principles have made a huge difference in my life, my marriage and my ministry. The fact that it took three years of involvement with the program for my eyes to be opened to *all* the promises of God, though, serves as a testimony to the statement participants in the program so often hear: "Don't quit before the miracle happens!" It's definitely vital to apply the principles patiently, trusting that God will help us to change in his own good time.

My faith faltered, just as Zechariah's did. But God came to my rescue, not in judgment but in love, gently pointing out to me, in Jesus' own words, that "what you have said in the dark will be heard in the daylight, and what you have whispered in the ear in the inner rooms will be proclaimed from the roofs" (Luke 12:3). In order for me to live "righteous in the sight of God" (Luke 1:6), I had to come clean and "confess my sins to myself, to God and to someone else I trust" (Principle Four).

73 the oath he swore to our father
Abraham:
74 to rescue us from the hand of our enemies,
and to enable us to serve him without
fear
75 in holiness and righteousness before
him all our days.

76 And you, my child, will be called a
prophet of the Most High;
for you will go on before the Lord to
prepare the way for him,
77 to give his people the knowledge of
salvation
through the forgiveness of their sins,
78 because of the tender mercy of our God,
by which the rising sun will come to
us from heaven
79 to shine on those living in darkness
and in the shadow of death,
to guide our feet into the path of peace."

80 And the child grew and became strong
in spirit*a*; and he lived in the wilderness
until he appeared publicly to Israel.

The Birth of Jesus

2 In those days Caesar Augustus issued
a decree that a census should be tak-
en of the entire Roman world. 2(This
was the first census that took place while*b*
Quirinius was governor of Syria.) 3And everyone went to their own town to register.

4 So Joseph also went up from the town of
Nazareth in Galilee to Judea, to Bethlehem
the town of David, because he belonged to
the house and line of David. 5He went there
to register with Mary, who was pledged to be
married to him and was expecting a child.
6 While they were there, the time came for
the baby to be born, 7and she gave birth to
her firstborn, a son. She wrapped him in
cloths and placed him in a manger, because
there was no guest room available for them.

8 And there were shepherds living out in
the fields nearby, keeping watch over their
flocks at night. 9An angel of the Lord appeared to them, and the glory of the Lord
shone around them, and they were terrified. 10But the angel said to them, "Do not
be afraid. I bring you good news that will
cause great joy for all the people. 11Today in
the town of David a Savior has been born
to you; he is the Messiah, the Lord. 12This
will be a sign to you: You will find a baby
wrapped in cloths and lying in a manger."

13 Suddenly a great company of the heavenly host appeared with the angel, praising
God and saying,

14 "Glory to God in the highest heaven,
and on earth peace to those on whom
his favor rests."

15 When the angels had left them and
gone into heaven, the shepherds said to
one another, "Let's go to Bethlehem and
see this thing that has happened, which the
Lord has told us about."

16 So they hurried off and found Mary
and Joseph, and the baby, who was lying
in the manger. 17When they had seen him,
they spread the word concerning what had
been told them about this child, 18and all
who heard it were amazed at what the shepherds said to them. 19But Mary treasured
up all these things and pondered them in
her heart. 20The shepherds returned, glo-
rifying and praising God for all the things
they had heard and seen, which were just as
they had been told.

21 On the eighth day, when it was time to
circumcise the child, he was named Jesus,
the name the angel had given him before he
was conceived.

Jesus Presented in the Temple

22 When the time came for the purification rites required by the Law of Moses, Joseph and Mary took him to Jerusalem to
present him to the Lord 23(as it is written in
the Law of the Lord, "Every firstborn male
is to be consecrated to the Lord"*c*), 24and to
offer a sacrifice in keeping with what is said
in the Law of the Lord: "a pair of doves or
two young pigeons."*d*

---

a 80 Or *in the Spirit*   *b* 2 Or *This census took place before*   *c* 23 Exodus 13:2,12   *d* 24 Lev. 12:8

25Now there was a man in Jerusalem called Simeon, who was righteous and devout. He was waiting for the consolation of Israel, and the Holy Spirit was on him. 26It had been revealed to him by the Holy Spirit that he would not die before he had seen the Lord's Messiah. 27Moved by the Spirit, he went into the temple courts. When the parents brought in the child Jesus to do for him what the custom of the Law required, 28Simeon took him in his arms and praised God, saying:

29"Sovereign Lord, as you have promised,*a*
    you may now dismiss*a* your servant
    in peace.
30For my eyes have seen your salvation,
31   which you have prepared in the sight
    of all nations:
32a light for revelation to the Gentiles,
    and the glory of your people Israel."

33The child's father and mother marveled at what was said about him. 34Then Simeon blessed them and said to Mary, his mother: "This child is destined to cause the falling and rising of many in Israel, and to be a sign that will be spoken against, 35so that the thoughts of many hearts will be revealed. And a sword will pierce your own soul too."

36There was also a prophet, Anna, the daughter of Penuel, of the tribe of Asher. She was very old; she had lived with her husband seven years after her marriage, 37and then was a widow until she was eighty-four.*b* She never left the temple but worshiped night and day, fasting and praying. 38Coming up to them at that very moment, she gave thanks to God and spoke about the child to all who were looking forward to the redemption of Jerusalem.

39When Joseph and Mary had done everything required by the Law of the Lord, they returned to Galilee to their own town of Nazareth. 40And the child grew and became strong; he was filled with wisdom, and the grace of God was on him.

The Boy Jesus at the Temple

41Every year Jesus' parents went to Jerusalem for the Festival of the Passover. 42When he was twelve years old, they went up to the festival, according to the custom. 43After the festival was over, while his parents were returning home, the boy Jesus stayed behind in Jerusalem, but they were unaware of it. 44Thinking he was in their company, they traveled on for a day. Then they began looking for him among their relatives and friends. 45When they did not find him, they went back to Jerusalem to look for him. 46After three days they found him in the temple courts, sitting among the teachers, listening to them and asking them questions. 47Everyone who heard him was amazed at his understanding and his answers. 48When his parents saw him, they were astonished. His mother said to him, "Son, why have you treated us like this? Your father and I have been anxiously searching for you."

49"Why were you searching for me?" he asked. "Didn't you know I had to be in my Father's house?"*c* 50But they did not understand what he was saying to them.

51Then he went down to Nazareth with them and was obedient to them. But his mother treasured all these things in her heart. 52And Jesus grew in wisdom and stature, and in favor with God and man.

John the Baptist Prepares the Way

3 In the fifteenth year of the reign of Tiberius Caesar—when Pontius Pilate was governor of Judea, Herod tetrarch of Galilee, his brother Philip tetrarch of Iturea and Traconitis, and Lysanias tetrarch of Abilene—2during the high-priesthood of Annas and Caiaphas, the word of God came to John son of Zechariah in the wilderness. 3He went into all the country around the Jordan, preaching a baptism of repentance for the forgiveness of sins. 4As it is written in the book of the words of Isaiah the prophet:

---

a 29 Or *promised, / now dismiss*   *b 37* Or *then had been a widow for eighty-four years.*   *c 49* Or *be about my Father's business*

MY NAME IS ANNA

LUKE 2:36–38

Married only seven years before becoming a widow, Anna could have waved a white flag of defeat over her life. She could have labeled herself a helpless victim, robbed of her protector and provider at an early age. Anger at God could have brewed the poison of bitterness in her soul.

But Anna didn't let despondency over the loss of her husband turn into depression and isolation. She refused to let her circumstances rob her life of its joy and purpose. Instead, Anna allowed God to fill the void left by her loss. Luke tells us that every single day she got up, got dressed, got out and joined God's people in worship at the temple.

This elderly woman's selfless service in the temple paved the way for an incredible honor. She became the first to proclaim the Good News "to all who were looking forward to the redemption of Jerusalem" (Luke 2:38) that the nation's longed-for Redeemer had arrived in the form of this helpless baby. To Anna's ministry of worship was added a mission — to proclaim hope and the promise of redemption to those in need of a Savior.

Some of us find ourselves in Anna's earlier situation. The circumstances of our lives lead to loss and heartache. At times life's pains, including our own shame, bitterness and addictions, drive many of us into isolation, which can lead to depression. Avoiding or overcoming depression when deep hurt comes our way requires that we say no to seclusion by following in Anna's footsteps and participating in community with others who empathize with our struggles. We need to connect with individuals within a community of people who understand our hurts, hang-ups and habits and can guide us on the path to healing. When we add worship to that community aspect, the circle of fellowship is complete.

Anna is a beautiful example of a humble servant of God whose life revolved around worship. The Bible's account shows us that worship of God oozed out of her day and night. That kind of worship has the power to transform a life.

We know that for us today, real life change requires worship; in fact, worship is one of the seven keys for building a strong Celebrate Recovery ministry. And consistent personal devotion to God will inevitably move us toward the next phase of our recovery — into ministry to others. Anna's continuous contact with God was the best possible preparation for her own ministry as a prophet (see 2:36).

Fellowship with God's people, worship, fasting, prayer and ministry are all important steps we must take in the process of overcoming our hurts. As crucial as the application of right principles can be, their real importance lies in the fact that they place us in a position to encounter Jesus — the true Higher Power.

"A voice of one calling in the
    wilderness,
'Prepare the way for the Lord,
    make straight paths for him.
5 Every valley shall be filled in,
    every mountain and hill made low.
The crooked roads shall become
    straight,
    the rough ways smooth.
6 And all people will see God's
    salvation.'"[a]

7 John said to the crowds coming out to be baptized by him, "You brood of vipers! Who warned you to flee from the coming wrath? 8 Produce fruit in keeping with repentance. And do not begin to say to yourselves, 'We have Abraham as our father.' For I tell you that out of these stones God can raise up children for Abraham. 9 The ax is already at the root of the trees, and every tree that does not produce good fruit will be cut down and thrown into the fire."

10 "What should we do then?" the crowd asked.

11 John answered, "Anyone who has two shirts should share with the one who has none, and anyone who has food should do the same."

12 Even tax collectors came to be baptized. "Teacher," they asked, "what should we do?"

13 "Don't collect any more than you are required to," he told them.

14 Then some soldiers asked him, "And what should we do?"

He replied, "Don't extort money and don't accuse people falsely — be content with your pay."

15 The people were waiting expectantly and were all wondering in their hearts if John might possibly be the Messiah. 16 John answered them all, "I baptize you with[b] water. But one who is more powerful than I will come, the straps of whose sandals I am not worthy to untie. He will baptize you with[b] the Holy Spirit and fire. 17 His winnowing fork is in his hand to clear his threshing floor and to gather the wheat into his barn, but he will burn up the chaff with unquenchable fire." 18 And with many other words John exhorted the people and proclaimed the good news to them.

19 But when John rebuked Herod the tetrarch because of his marriage to Herodias, his brother's wife, and all the other evil things he had done, 20 Herod added this to them all: He locked John up in prison.

The Baptism and Genealogy of Jesus

21 When all the people were being baptized, Jesus was baptized too. And as he was praying, heaven was opened 22 and the Holy Spirit descended on him in bodily form like a dove. And a voice came from heaven: "You are my Son, whom I love; with you I am well pleased."

23 Now Jesus himself was about thirty years old when he began his ministry. He was the son, so it was thought, of Joseph,

the son of Heli, 24 the son of Matthat,
    the son of Levi, the son of Melki,
    the son of Jannai, the son of Joseph,
25 the son of Mattathias, the son of
    Amos,
    the son of Nahum, the son of Esli,
    the son of Naggai, 26 the son of Maath,
    the son of Mattathias, the son of
    Semein,
    the son of Josek, the son of Joda,
27 the son of Joanan, the son of Rhesa,
    the son of Zerubbabel, the son of
    Shealtiel,
    the son of Neri, 28 the son of Melki,
    the son of Addi, the son of Cosam,
    the son of Elmadam, the son of Er,
29 the son of Joshua, the son of Eliezer,
    the son of Jorim, the son of Matthat,
    the son of Levi, 30 the son of Simeon,
    the son of Judah, the son of Joseph,
    the son of Jonam, the son of Eliakim,
31 the son of Melea, the son of Menna,
    the son of Mattatha, the son of Nathan,

---

[a] 6 Isaiah 40:3-5   [b] 16 Or in

My Name Is Kathy

I'M A BELIEVER WHO STRUGGLES WITH FOOD ADDICTION AND CODEPENDENCY

Please read the story of the elderly Anna's prophecy about the infant Jesus in Luke 2:36 – 38.

"What happens in this house stays in this house." These words may sound familiar to those in recovery. In my case, living in an alcoholic household created an atmosphere governed by three cardinal rules: Don't talk, don't feel and don't trust. My dad was a "functioning alcoholic" who was filled with rage, and my mom fancied herself a "nighttime alcoholic." Her drinking was done after hours for what she deemed "medicinal purposes" to help her sleep. I learned many life lessons from my childhood, among them that verbal and physical abuse perpetrated against me were to be followed by *me* apologizing to my father, and that eating sweets was a good way for me to keep my emotions in check. I mastered these early lessons on how to be a good codependent and a compulsive overeater.

Our family was divided along religious lines, even though neither of my parents was particularly religious. Still, there was a battle to be waged anew each time a child was born into the home. I was Catholic, like my mom, while my sister (Dad's favorite) was Protestant, like my dad. My sister learned to do all the "boy" things that made Dad happy, thereby managing to escape his wrath. She was "tiny," my mom pointed out, and might break. New lesson learned: Being thin meant being treated well. Along with my unhealthy relationship with food came skewed body- and self-images.

Education wasn't a priority in our family. Girls didn't need to attend college; it was a waste of money. After all, they just get married and have babies. My self-esteem — or what was left of it — plummeted. When I was 19 my dad hit me one last time, and I left home with my boyfriend. I was now labeled "fast and loose." In order to be a "good girl," I needed to get married, which we dutifully did. That lasted two years — two years filled with lies, cheating, drinking and violence. My addiction to food now became obsessive.

I remarried at 23 and, after five years on the infertility roller coaster, we began the adoption process, which resulted in the addition to our family of a son and a daughter. Wayne had a good job, and we had two kids, two cars and a nice house, but it was never enough.

To the outside world I seemed to have it all. Then why was I dying inside? My anger was out of control, a condition that was fueled by my sugar habit. I was irate with everyone, including myself, resulting in outbursts of rage. My emotional state led me to physically and emotionally abuse my own kids, especially my son. I had become a carbon copy of my father, only without the alcohol. I wanted to wave a white flag of defeat over my life. Then, after 27 years of marriage, my husband died.

Ironically, I hit bottom in 2004, after having become a Christian in 2003. I was at the time dating Bill, a wonderful man who is now my husband and who was very instrumental in my coming to know the Lord. Yet, like the Biblical Anna, I refused to allow my defeat and depression to isolate me, an attitude that carried over into my involvement in Celebrate Recovery. I deliberately joined with God's "people in worship" and as a result found an understanding community.

Before becoming a Christian and joining Celebrate Recovery, I caved in to whatever demands others made of me, just so they would like me. But through my involvement in the program, I have learned to identify my addictions as compulsive overeating and codependency. I still pray that my children may find healing from the pain I inflicted on them — and find it within themselves to forgive me. My recovery has been up and down, and I need to pay attention to the boomerang effect of my addictions: When one is down, the other tends to be up.

On days when I've wanted to quit, the women of Celebrate Recovery have rallied around me and pulled me along. When I've celebrated successes, they've cheered me on. My husband, Bill, has stood by me without judgment and continues to encourage me every day. I'm so blessed to have him in my life.

It never ceases to amaze me how cunning, baffling and powerful addictions and compulsive behaviors can be. Without God's help and that of the special people he has placed in my life, I would have been so susceptible to falling back into the cycle that can only lead to shame and remorse. But applying the principles and steps of Celebrate Recovery has placed me in a position to regularly encounter God — my true Higher Power. As a result I desire to worship him "night and day" (Luke 2:37), just as Anna did. I've finally come to realize and accept that only God can fill that void deep inside me.

Kathy

the son of David, 32the son of Jesse,
the son of Obed, the son of Boaz,
the son of Salmon,*a* the son of Nahshon,
33the son of Amminadab, the son of Ram,*b*
the son of Hezron, the son of Perez,
the son of Judah, 34the son of Jacob,
the son of Isaac, the son of Abraham,
the son of Terah, the son of Nahor,
35the son of Serug, the son of Reu,
the son of Peleg, the son of Eber,
the son of Shelah, 36the son of Cainan,
the son of Arphaxad, the son of Shem,
the son of Noah, the son of Lamech,
37the son of Methuselah, the son of Enoch,
the son of Jared, the son of Mahalalel,
the son of Kenan, 38the son of Enosh,
the son of Seth, the son of Adam,
the son of God.

Jesus Is Tested in the Wilderness

4 Jesus, full of the Holy Spirit, left the Jordan and was led by the Spirit into the wilderness, 2where for forty days he was tempted*c* by the devil. He ate nothing during those days, and at the end of them he was hungry.

3The devil said to him, "If you are the Son of God, tell this stone to become bread."

4Jesus answered, "It is written: 'Man shall not live on bread alone.'*d*"

5The devil led him up to a high place and showed him in an instant all the kingdoms of the world. 6And he said to him, "I will give you all their authority and splendor; it has been given to me, and I can give it to anyone I want to. 7If you worship me, it will all be yours."

8Jesus answered, "It is written: 'Worship the Lord your God and serve him only.'*e*"

9The devil led him to Jerusalem and had him stand on the highest point of the temple. "If you are the Son of God," he said, "throw yourself down from here. 10For it is written:

"'He will command his angels
    concerning you
    to guard you carefully;
11they will lift you up in their hands,
    so that you will not strike your foot
        against a stone.'*f*"

12Jesus answered, "It is said: 'Do not put the Lord your God to the test.'*g*"

13When the devil had finished all this tempting, he left him until an opportune time.

Jesus Rejected at Nazareth

14Jesus returned to Galilee in the power of the Spirit, and news about him spread through the whole countryside. 15He was teaching in their synagogues, and everyone praised him.

16He went to Nazareth, where he had been brought up, and on the Sabbath day he went into the synagogue, as was his custom. He stood up to read, 17and the scroll of the prophet Isaiah was handed to him. Unrolling it, he found the place where it is written:

18"The Spirit of the Lord is on me,
    because he has anointed me
    to proclaim good news to the poor.
He has sent me to proclaim freedom for
    the prisoners
    and recovery of sight for the blind,
to set the oppressed free,
19   to proclaim the year of the Lord's
        favor."*h*

20Then he rolled up the scroll, gave it back to the attendant and sat down. The eyes of everyone in the synagogue were fastened on him. 21He began by saying to them, "Today this scripture is fulfilled in your hearing."

---

a 32 Some early manuscripts *Sala*   *b 33* Some manuscripts *Amminadab, the son of Admin, the son of Arni*; other manuscripts vary widely.   *c 2* The Greek for *tempted* can also mean *tested*.   *d 4* Deut. 8:3   *e 8* Deut. 6:13
f 11 Psalm 91:11,12   *g 12* Deut. 6:16   *h 19* Isaiah 61:1,2 (see Septuagint); Isaiah 58:6

[22]All spoke well of him and were amazed at the gracious words that came from his lips. "Isn't this Joseph's son?" they asked.

[23]Jesus said to them, "Surely you will quote this proverb to me: 'Physician, heal yourself!' And you will tell me, 'Do here in your hometown what we have heard that you did in Capernaum.'"

[24]"Truly I tell you," he continued, "no prophet is accepted in his hometown. [25]I assure you that there were many widows in Israel in Elijah's time, when the sky was shut for three and a half years and there was a severe famine throughout the land. [26]Yet Elijah was not sent to any of them, but to a widow in Zarephath in the region of Sidon. [27]And there were many in Israel with leprosy[a] in the time of Elisha the prophet, yet not one of them was cleansed — only Naaman the Syrian."

[28]All the people in the synagogue were furious when they heard this. [29]They got up, drove him out of the town, and took him to the brow of the hill on which the town was built, in order to throw him off the cliff. [30]But he walked right through the crowd and went on his way.

Jesus Drives Out an Impure Spirit

[31]Then he went down to Capernaum, a town in Galilee, and on the Sabbath he taught the people. [32]They were amazed at his teaching, because his words had authority.

[33]In the synagogue there was a man possessed by a demon, an impure spirit. He cried out at the top of his voice, [34]"Go away! What do you want with us, Jesus of Nazareth? Have you come to destroy us? I know who you are — the Holy One of God!"

[35]"Be quiet!" Jesus said sternly. "Come out of him!" Then the demon threw the man down before them all and came out without injuring him.

[36]All the people were amazed and said to each other, "What words these are! With authority and power he gives orders to impure spirits and they come out!" [37]And the news about him spread throughout the surrounding area.

Jesus Heals Many

[38]Jesus left the synagogue and went to the home of Simon. Now Simon's mother-in-law was suffering from a high fever, and they asked Jesus to help her. [39]So he bent over her and rebuked the fever, and it left her. She got up at once and began to wait on them.

[40]At sunset, the people brought to Jesus all who had various kinds of sickness, and laying his hands on each one, he healed them. [41]Moreover, demons came out of many people, shouting, "You are the Son of God!" But he rebuked them and would not allow them to speak, because they knew he was the Messiah.

[42]At daybreak, Jesus went out to a solitary place. The people were looking for him and when they came to where he was, they tried to keep him from leaving them. [43]But he said, "I must proclaim the good news of the kingdom of God to the other towns also, because that is why I was sent." [44]And he kept on preaching in the synagogues of Judea.

Jesus Calls His First Disciples

5 One day as Jesus was standing by the Lake of Gennesaret,[b] the people were crowding around him and listening to the word of God. [2]He saw at the water's edge two boats, left there by the fishermen, who were washing their nets. [3]He got into one of the boats, the one belonging to Simon, and asked him to put out a little from shore. Then he sat down and taught the people from the boat.

[4]When he had finished speaking, he said to Simon, "Put out into deep water, and let down the nets for a catch."

[5]Simon answered, "Master, we've worked

---

[a] 27 The Greek word traditionally translated leprosy was used for various diseases affecting the skin.   [b] 1 That is, the Sea of Galilee

My Name Is The Paralytic

Luke 5:17–26

Sometimes recovery begins with the intervention of friends. The paralytic (a person who is paraplegic or quadriplegic, in today's terminology) was the epitome of powerlessness. He had to be carried to Jesus by devoted friends, who faced an unforeseen obstacle when they came to the house where Jesus was teaching and healing. The curious bystanders were crowding out those who were coming for healing. But the paralytic had some loyal and determined friends. They broke through the roof and lowered their friend to the feet of Jesus.

Jesus, moved by their determined faith, declared to the paralyzed man, "Friend, your sins are forgiven" (Luke 5:20). It surprises us that Jesus didn't immediately heal the man's paralysis, as the crowd of that day would also have expected. The balance of this story makes the reason clear. Jesus had a lesson for his critics, the "Pharisees and teachers of the law" (v. 17). They were probably there from Jerusalem in force because of the miracle recorded in verses 12–15. Hearing Jesus' unexpected declaration of forgiveness, they immediately jumped at the opportunity to label him a blasphemer (see v. 21). Jesus, knowing their thoughts, asked them, "Which is easier: to say, 'Your sins are forgiven' or to say, 'Get up and walk'?" (v. 23). Obviously, it would have been easier for Jesus to claim that the sick man's sins were forgiven, since that statement carried no visible evidence. But in order to demonstrate his authority to forgive sins, Jesus did command the paralytic to get up and walk. The man stood up, picked up his mat and "went home praising God" (v. 25). The impact of this miracle among the local onlookers was amazement and praise to God.

If we've been freed from a hurt, hang-up or habit, we appropriately recognize this as a miracle of God. Yet the greater miracle is that we've been forgiven of our sins. Our forgiveness required more than a word or touch from Jesus. It required the death of God the Son and his resurrection from the dead (see Romans 4:25).

We may relate to the intervention of friends in this story. Perhaps our denial was so great that it called for a loving confrontation by friends and/or family. But even if we didn't profit from such intervention, our introduction to Christ included the faithful transmission of the gospel message by generations of Christians. Sometimes we find a recovery program and discover friends we never realized we had.

If we fall into thinking "My problem's not that bad" or "I can handle it," we may need to listen to our friends and allow them to introduce us to Jesus. We too can be declared forgiven. Then we can stand up, praise the Lord and carry the message to others.

hard all night and haven't caught anything. But because you say so, I will let down the nets."

6When they had done so, they caught such a large number of fish that their nets began to break. 7So they signaled their partners in the other boat to come and help them, and they came and filled both boats so full that they began to sink.

8When Simon Peter saw this, he fell at Jesus' knees and said, "Go away from me, Lord; I am a sinful man!" 9For he and all his companions were astonished at the catch of fish they had taken, 10and so were James and John, the sons of Zebedee, Simon's partners.

Then Jesus said to Simon, "Don't be afraid; from now on you will fish for people." 11So they pulled their boats up on shore, left everything and followed him.

Jesus Heals a Man With Leprosy

12While Jesus was in one of the towns, a man came along who was covered with leprosy.*a* When he saw Jesus, he fell with his face to the ground and begged him, "Lord, if you are willing, you can make me clean."

13Jesus reached out his hand and touched the man. "I am willing," he said. "Be clean!" And immediately the leprosy left him.

14Then Jesus ordered him, "Don't tell anyone, but go, show yourself to the priest and offer the sacrifices that Moses commanded for your cleansing, as a testimony to them."

15Yet the news about him spread all the more, so that crowds of people came to hear him and to be healed of their sicknesses. 16But Jesus often withdrew to lonely places and prayed.

Jesus Forgives and Heals a Paralyzed Man

17One day Jesus was teaching, and Pharisees and teachers of the law were sitting there. They had come from every village of Galilee and from Judea and Jerusalem. And the power of the Lord was with Jesus to heal the sick. 18Some men came carrying a paralyzed man on a mat and tried to take him into the house to lay him before Jesus. 19When they could not find a way to do this because of the crowd, they went up on the roof and lowered him on his mat through the tiles into the middle of the crowd, right in front of Jesus.

20When Jesus saw their faith, he said, "Friend, your sins are forgiven."

21The Pharisees and the teachers of the law began thinking to themselves, "Who is this fellow who speaks blasphemy? Who can forgive sins but God alone?"

22Jesus knew what they were thinking and asked, "Why are you thinking these things in your hearts? 23Which is easier: to say, 'Your sins are forgiven,' or to say, 'Get up and walk'? 24But I want you to know that the Son of Man has authority on earth to forgive sins." So he said to the paralyzed man, "I tell you, get up, take your mat and go home." 25Immediately he stood up in front of them, took what he had been lying on and went home praising God. 26Everyone was amazed and gave praise to God. They were filled with awe and said, "We have seen remarkable things today."

Jesus Calls Levi and Eats With Sinners

27After this, Jesus went out and saw a tax collector by the name of Levi sitting at his tax booth. "Follow me," Jesus said to him, 28and Levi got up, left everything and followed him.

29Then Levi held a great banquet for Jesus at his house, and a large crowd of tax collectors and others were eating with them. 30But the Pharisees and the teachers of the law who belonged to their sect complained to his disciples, "Why do you eat and drink with tax collectors and sinners?"

31Jesus answered them, "It is not the healthy who need a doctor, but the sick. 32I have not come to call the righteous, but sinners to repentance."

---

a 12 The Greek word traditionally translated *leprosy* was used for various diseases affecting the skin.

My Name Is CJ

I'M A BELIEVER WHO STRUGGLES WITH ALCOHOLISM

Please read of Jesus' healing of the paralyzed man in Luke 5:17 – 26.

I grew up on a farm in the "dust bowl." A strict German father who didn't express his feelings shaped my childhood experiences. We never talked about God, sorrow or relationships and certainly never discussed words like *love* or *intimacy*. This dysfunctional background set the stage for a life of repressed emotion.

I left home at 18, moved to California at 20, was drafted into the service during the Korean conflict and married my wife, Linda. Our three children were born during the next seven years. I was ill-equipped for marriage and even less prepared for fatherhood. Unable to communicate effectively about family issues and conflict, I began to numb my feelings with alcohol.

My wife and I became active in our church, but I never allowed God to be a daily part of my life. Having grown up in a legalistic religious setting, I was continuously trying to please an unloving God. In fact, I was baptized twice, thinking that maybe the second time would "take." This thinking drove my addiction into all other aspects of my life. In fact, alcohol became my priority. I began to disrespect my family, my marriage vows and, inevitably, myself. My heart became hardened, and I completely turned away from the God I'd grown up fearing. I was a full-blown alcoholic, a practicing liar who, as time passed, came to believe my own deceptions.

My relationship with my wife became almost nonexistent. We lived in stony silence for days at a time. She seldom smiled, and I always felt guilty around her. Our communication was fueled by anger and resentment.

Those who cared about me finally decided it was time for a confrontation. Like the paralytic's friends, I felt as though my family and friends literally picked me up and carried me to Jesus. Soon after this intervention I committed to attending Celebrate Recovery at Saddleback Church. Jesus addressed me with the beautiful words, "Friend, your sins are forgiven" (Luke 5:20), and I learned that there is a God who loves me in spite of what I've done or what I am. Best of all, I entered a personal relationship with my Higher Power, Jesus Christ.

"Get up and walk" (Luke 5:23), he directed me. I jumped to my feet, picked up my mat and went home praising God (see v. 25).

I know that only walking in God's will can prevent a relapse. For me that means service. One thing I love about Celebrate Recovery is that I don't have to maintain a perfect walk or have it all together to be involved in service. About four months into my recovery, I was asked to help with the BBQ team and was even designated "Head Onion Slicer." As my faith grew, so did my ministry involvement. It was by asking me to serve in this small way that God made me accountable. As I peeled, sliced and diced those onions, I began to see through the "tears" how God was using me to serve others. After all the years of pain, lies and disrespect, it became apparent that God was changing me.

He began to turn my bad habits into good—or at least better—traits. My wife noticed the difference and soon began to walk next to me—taking my hand. I can't begin to express how much love has opened up between us in our marriage because of Jesus Christ.

As Pastor John Baker has stated, "Courage is when you move ahead in spite of fear." By placing my fears and my doubts in God's hands and by taking the necessary risks to serve in ministry, God has slowly removed the lie that "God could never use me." After my humble start, God brought further opportunities my way. I've had the privilege of leading recovery small groups and encouraging other men who, like me, thought they could never be used by God.

God has also given my wife and me opportunities to share our testimonies in other churches. It seems as though the testimony of a changed life is a far better witness of God's grace than a lecture could ever be. When hurting people see how God has brought us through our challenges to a place of growth and contentment, they want to know what God can do for them. With the help of my wife and many others from Celebrate Recovery, I've been blessed to bring the ministry to men's and women's shelters, to Recovery homes and to numerous churches in South Central Los Angeles.

If someone would have asked me a few years ago whether I could imagine God using me like this, I would have responded emphatically, "No way!" But once I put my total faith in Jesus Christ and followed this program, he began to stretch me. I know that when we let go of our fear and doubt that God will take us on a great adventure. Those around us will exclaim in awe, "We have seen remarkable things today" (v. 26).

Jesus Questioned About Fasting

³³They said to him, "John's disciples often fast and pray, and so do the disciples of the Pharisees, but yours go on eating and drinking."

³⁴Jesus answered, "Can you make the friends of the bridegroom fast while he is with them? ³⁵But the time will come when the bridegroom will be taken from them; in those days they will fast."

³⁶He told them this parable: "No one tears a piece out of a new garment to patch an old one. Otherwise, they will have torn the new garment, and the patch from the new will not match the old. ³⁷And no one pours new wine into old wineskins. Otherwise, the new wine will burst the skins; the wine will run out and the wineskins will be ruined. ³⁸No, new wine must be poured into new wineskins. ³⁹And no one after drinking old wine wants the new, for they say, 'The old is better.'"

Jesus Is Lord of the Sabbath

6 One Sabbath Jesus was going through the grainfields, and his disciples began to pick some heads of grain, rub them in their hands and eat the kernels. ²Some of the Pharisees asked, "Why are you doing what is unlawful on the Sabbath?"

³Jesus answered them, "Have you never read what David did when he and his companions were hungry? ⁴He entered the house of God, and taking the consecrated bread, he ate what is lawful only for priests to eat. And he also gave some to his companions." ⁵Then Jesus said to them, "The Son of Man is Lord of the Sabbath."

⁶On another Sabbath he went into the synagogue and was teaching, and a man was there whose right hand was shriveled. ⁷The Pharisees and the teachers of the law were looking for a reason to accuse Jesus, so they watched him closely to see if he would heal on the Sabbath. ⁸But Jesus knew what they were thinking and said to the man with the shriveled hand, "Get up

and stand in front of everyone." So he got up and stood there.

⁹Then Jesus said to them, "I ask you, which is lawful on the Sabbath: to do good or to do evil, to save life or to destroy it?"

¹⁰He looked around at them all, and then said to the man, "Stretch out your hand." He did so, and his hand was completely restored. ¹¹But the Pharisees and the teachers of the law were furious and began to discuss with one another what they might do to Jesus.

The Twelve Apostles

¹²One of those days Jesus went out to a mountainside to pray, and spent the night praying to God. ¹³When morning came, he called his disciples to him and chose twelve of them, whom he also designated apostles: ¹⁴Simon (whom he named Peter), his brother Andrew, James, John, Philip, Bartholomew, ¹⁵Matthew, Thomas, James son of Alphaeus, Simon who was called the Zealot, ¹⁶Judas son of James, and Judas Iscariot, who became a traitor.

Blessings and Woes

¹⁷He went down with them and stood on a level place. A large crowd of his disciples was there and a great number of people from all over Judea, from Jerusalem, and from the coastal region around Tyre and Sidon, ¹⁸who had come to hear him and to be healed of their diseases. Those troubled by impure spirits were cured, ¹⁹and the people all tried to touch him, because power was coming from him and healing them all.

²⁰Looking at his disciples, he said:

"Blessed are you who are poor,
    for yours is the kingdom of God.
²¹Blessed are you who hunger now,
    for you will be satisfied.
Blessed are you who weep now,
    for you will laugh.
²²Blessed are you when people hate you,
    when they exclude you and insult
        you

and reject your name as evil,
    because of the Son of Man.

23 "Rejoice in that day and leap for joy, because great is your reward in heaven. For that is how their ancestors treated the prophets.

24 "But woe to you who are rich,
    for you have already received your
        comfort.
25 Woe to you who are well fed now,
    for you will go hungry.
  Woe to you who laugh now,
    for you will mourn and weep.
26 Woe to you when everyone speaks well
    of you,
    for that is how their ancestors treated
        the false prophets.

Love for Enemies

27 "But to you who are listening I say: Love your enemies, do good to those who hate you, 28 bless those who curse you, pray for those who mistreat you. 29 If someone slaps you on one cheek, turn to them the other also. If someone takes your coat, do not withhold your shirt from them. 30 Give to everyone who asks you, and if anyone takes what belongs to you, do not demand it back. 31 Do to others as you would have them do to you.

32 "If you love those who love you, what credit is that to you? Even sinners love those who love them. 33 And if you do good to those who are good to you, what credit is that to you? Even sinners do that. 34 And if you lend to those from whom you expect repayment, what credit is that to you? Even sinners lend to sinners, expecting to be repaid in full. 35 But love your enemies, do good to them, and lend to them without expecting to get anything back. Then your reward will be great, and you will be children of the Most High, because he is kind to the ungrateful and wicked. 36 Be merciful, just as your Father is merciful.

AMENDS LESSON [*Principle Six*]

For the previous entry in the AMENDS lesson, go to Luke 6:37 (page 1241).

For a discussion of Principles One through Eight and a listing of their related lessons, go to pages xvii – xliv.

Do to others as you would have them do to you.

Luke 6:31

Principle Six calls for us to evaluate all our relationships and to offer forgiveness to those who have hurt us and make amends for harm we've done to others, except when doing so would injure them or others. We need to be willing to admit our part in our relationships that have been broken or damaged. We begin by making AMENDS for the harm we've caused others.

The *M* in AMENDS stands for MAKE A LIST. When we make our amends list, we shouldn't worry about the how-tos of making our amends. It's important at this stage not to ask ourselves questions like "How could I ever ask my dad for forgiveness?" or "How could my brother ever forgive me for what I did?" We need to go ahead and put the person on our list anyway. In this part of Principle Six all we're looking for is the willingness to make amends and offer forgiveness. Luke 6:31 reminds us to treat others the way we want to be treated.

The next letter in AMENDS is *E*. Go to Hebrews 10:24 (page 1531).

Judging Others

37"Do not judge, and you will not be judged. Do not condemn, and you will not be condemned. Forgive, and you will be forgiven. 38Give, and it will be given to you. A good measure, pressed down, shaken together and running over, will be poured into your lap. For with the measure you use, it will be measured to you."

39He also told them this parable: "Can the blind lead the blind? Will they not both fall into a pit? 40The student is not above the teacher, but everyone who is fully trained will be like their teacher.

41"Why do you look at the speck of sawdust in your brother's eye and pay no attention to the plank in your own eye? 42How can you say to your brother, 'Brother, let me take the speck out of your eye,' when you yourself fail to see the plank in your own eye? You hypocrite, first take the plank out of your eye, and then you will see clearly to remove the speck from your brother's eye.

A Tree and Its Fruit

43"No good tree bears bad fruit, nor does a bad tree bear good fruit. 44Each tree is recognized by its own fruit. People do not pick figs from thornbushes, or grapes from briers. 45A good man brings good things out of the good stored up in his heart, and an evil man brings evil things out of the evil stored up in his heart. For the mouth speaks what the heart is full of.

The Wise and Foolish Builders

46"Why do you call me, 'Lord, Lord,' and do not do what I say? 47As for everyone who comes to me and hears my words and puts

AMENDS LESSON [*Principle Six*]

For the previous entry in the AMENDS lesson, go to Hebrews 10:24 (page 1531).

For a discussion of Principles One through Eight and a listing of their related lessons, go to pages xvii – xliv.

Love your enemies, do good to them, and lend to them without expecting to get anything back. Then your reward will be great, and you will be children of the Most High, because he is kind to the ungrateful and wicked.

LUKE 6:35

Principle Six calls for us to evaluate all our relationships and to offer forgiveness to those who have hurt us and make amends for harm we've done to others, except when doing so would injure them or others. We need to be willing to admit our part in our relationships that have been broken or damaged. We begin by making AMENDS for the harm we've caused others.

The *N* in AMENDS stands for NOT JUST FOR THEM, which is an important aspect of our reason for making amends. We need to approach those to whom we're offering amends or forgiveness with the right attitude: honestly, sincerely and willingly. It's important that we not offer excuses or attempt to justify our past actions. We need to focus only on our part of the situation. In five words, the secret to making successful amends is: Do not expect anything back. That's what Jesus is telling us in Luke 6:35. We're to offer amends, not for a reward or expected positive payback, but to achieve freedom from our hurts, hang-ups and habits.

The next letter in AMENDS is *D*. Go to Ecclesiastes 3:1 (page 784).

them into practice, I will show you what they are like. 48They are like a man building a house, who dug down deep and laid the foundation on rock. When a flood came, the torrent struck that house but could not shake it, because it was well built. 49But the one who hears my words and does not put them into practice is like a man who built a house on the ground without a foundation. The moment the torrent struck that house, it collapsed and its destruction was complete."

The Faith of the Centurion

7 When Jesus had finished saying all this to the people who were listening, he entered Capernaum. 2There a centurion's servant, whom his master valued highly, was sick and about to die. 3The centurion heard of Jesus and sent some elders of the Jews to him, asking him to come and heal his servant. 4When they came to Jesus, they pleaded earnestly with him, "This man deserves to have you do this, 5because he loves our nation and has built our synagogue." 6So Jesus went with them.

He was not far from the house when the centurion sent friends to say to him: "Lord, don't trouble yourself, for I do not deserve to have you come under my roof. 7That is why I did not even consider myself worthy to come to you. But say the word, and my servant will be healed. 8For I myself am a man under authority, with soldiers under me. I tell this one, 'Go,' and he goes; and that one, 'Come,' and he comes. I say to my servant, 'Do this,' and he does it."

9When Jesus heard this, he was amazed at him, and turning to the crowd following him, he said, "I tell you, I have not found such great faith even in Israel." 10Then the men who had been sent returned to the house and found the servant well.

AMENDS LESSON [*Principle Six*]

This is the first page of the AMENDS lesson.

For a discussion of Principles One through Eight and a listing of their related lessons, go to pages xvii – xliv.

Do not judge, and you will not be judged. Do not condemn, and you will not be condemned. Forgive, and you will be forgiven.

LUKE 6:37

Principle Six calls for us to evaluate all our relationships and to offer forgiveness to those who have hurt us and make amends for harm we've done to others, except when doing so would injure them or others. We need to be willing to admit our part in our relationships that have been broken or damaged. We begin by making AMENDS for the harm we've caused others.

The *A* in AMENDS calls for us to ADMIT THE HURT AND THE HARM we've caused others. Principle Four showed us how important it is to open up to God and to others. Our feelings have been bottled up for far too long, and this has interfered with all our important relationships. In this principle we need to once again face our hurts and resentments and the wrongs that others have done to us or that we've done to others. Holding on to resentments blocks not only our recovery but also God's forgiveness in our lives. That's what Jesus is telling us in Luke 6:37.

The next letter in AMENDS is *M*. Go to Luke 6:31 (page 1239).

MY NAME IS
THE CENTURION

LUKE 7:1–10

A Roman centurion would ordinarily have been a hated outsider in a Jewish city like Capernaum. But this man had won the hearts of the Jewish elders; he had a love for Israel and had paid from his own pocket to build the local Jewish synagogue. When the centurion's highly valued servant became sick, some of the elders approached Jesus and pleaded with him to come and heal the servant. They claimed that this Roman deserved Jesus' attention (see Luke 7:4). Jesus went with them.

As they neared the centurion's house, the delegation was met by his friends, whom he had sent to cut off their approach. In contrast to his fans among the elders, the centurion had a more sobering estimation of his own worth (vv. 6–7):

- "I do not deserve to have you come under my roof."

- "I did not even consider myself worthy to come to you."

- "But say the word, and my servant will be healed."

Jesus declared this Gentile's faith to be greater than any he had encountered among his own people. This man trusted in Jesus as one who spoke and acted with God's own authority. His was a faith based on true humility. When the centurion's friends returned to the house, they did indeed find the servant healed.

This is the kind of faith we need to have as we seek recovery. Humility before God is essential. What he longs to give us is forgiveness, power over sinful habits, a place of service in his kingdom and an eternity in his presence. After conversion, it's easy for us to become casual in our approach to God. But the reality is that we have free access to him only because Jesus has justified us by his blood and has lifted us up into God's throne room (see Ephesians 2:1–10). We're unworthy to enter God's presence apart from the work of Jesus.

The centurion gained what he sought because he understood Jesus' authority. Jesus doesn't have to be physically present to bring healing to our life. He need only speak the word, and it's done (see Luke 7:7–8). Our core issue in life will always be "Who has authority over me?" Running our own life didn't work before beginning our recovery. So let's not slip back into self-management. We can't do as we wish with "our life" because as children of God "our" life isn't really our own. Our life in Christ isn't a matter of bargaining with God, as the elders in this story sought to do. It's God's free and gracious gift of love. Jesus is anxious to bless us when we come to him with humility and faith. We must recognize his authority every moment of every day and set apart a time each day to seek him for the direction and power we need to continue our recovery.

Jesus Raises a Widow's Son

¹¹Soon afterward, Jesus went to a town called Nain, and his disciples and a large crowd went along with him. ¹²As he approached the town gate, a dead person was being carried out — the only son of his mother, and she was a widow. And a large crowd from the town was with her. ¹³When the Lord saw her, his heart went out to her and he said, "Don't cry."

¹⁴Then he went up and touched the bier they were carrying him on, and the bearers stood still. He said, "Young man, I say to you, get up!" ¹⁵The dead man sat up and began to talk, and Jesus gave him back to his mother.

¹⁶They were all filled with awe and praised God. "A great prophet has appeared among us," they said. "God has come to help his people." ¹⁷This news about Jesus spread throughout Judea and the surrounding country.

Jesus and John the Baptist

¹⁸John's disciples told him about all these things. Calling two of them, ¹⁹he sent them to the Lord to ask, "Are you the one who is to come, or should we expect someone else?"

²⁰When the men came to Jesus, they said, "John the Baptist sent us to you to ask, 'Are you the one who is to come, or should we expect someone else?'"

²¹At that very time Jesus cured many who had diseases, sicknesses and evil spirits, and gave sight to many who were blind. ²²So he replied to the messengers, "Go back and report to John what you have seen and heard: The blind receive sight, the lame walk, those who have leprosy^a are cleansed, the deaf hear, the dead are raised, and the good news is proclaimed to the poor. ²³Blessed is anyone who does not stumble on account of me."

²⁴After John's messengers left, Jesus began to speak to the crowd about John: "What did you go out into the wilderness to see? A reed swayed by the wind? ²⁵If not, what did you go out to see? A man dressed in fine clothes? No, those who wear expensive clothes and indulge in luxury are in palaces. ²⁶But what did you go out to see? A prophet? Yes, I tell you, and more than a prophet. ²⁷This is the one about whom it is written:

"'I will send my messenger ahead of you,
who will prepare your way before
you.'^{b}

²⁸I tell you, among those born of women there is no one greater than John; yet the one who is least in the kingdom of God is greater than he."

²⁹(All the people, even the tax collectors, when they heard Jesus' words, acknowledged that God's way was right, because they had been baptized by John. ³⁰But the Pharisees and the experts in the law rejected God's purpose for themselves, because they had not been baptized by John.)

³¹Jesus went on to say, "To what, then, can I compare the people of this generation? What are they like? ³²They are like children sitting in the marketplace and calling out to each other:

"'We played the pipe for you,
and you did not dance;
we sang a dirge,
and you did not cry.'

³³For John the Baptist came neither eating bread nor drinking wine, and you say, 'He has a demon.' ³⁴The Son of Man came eating and drinking, and you say, 'Here is a glutton and a drunkard, a friend of tax collectors and sinners.' ³⁵But wisdom is proved right by all her children."

Jesus Anointed by a Sinful Woman

³⁶When one of the Pharisees invited Jesus to have dinner with him, he went to the Pharisee's house and reclined at the table. ³⁷A woman in that town who lived a sinful life learned that Jesus was eating at the Pharisee's house, so she came there

My Name Is Richard

I'M A BELIEVER WHO STRUGGLES WITH CHEMICAL DEPENDENCY

Please read the story in Luke 7:1 – 10 of the amazing faith of the centurion and Jesus' "long-distance" healing of his servant.

There I was, sitting once again in the backseat of a police cruiser, cuffed, run-down and defeated. "What will this term be like?" I wondered briefly, only to quickly retract the question. "After all," I reasoned ruefully, "I've spent half my life in prison. What's going to be different this time?" At that moment my whole life flashed before me. What had I become? I couldn't even cry out to God because I had cut off my relationship with him long ago at a prison gate.

I had been an arrogant and selfish kid. At 15 I left home and learned from the streets that I didn't need anyone. I began my "run," fueled by the gradual transition from pot to coke and speed. I gained a wide variety of survival skills. One day an "old-timer" pulled me aside and advised me that I could make real money. He handed me 15 balloons, each filled with heroin. At 18 I entered the prison system for the first time, with a five-year sentence for peddling drugs. I did my time, in the process learning more of the ropes and even educating myself through the study of law books. This started the revolving-door process for me. The prison's welcome mat had my name emblazoned on it. I spent the next 22 years in and out of the prison system. In some strange way prison had become my second home, my comfort zone. I came to believe that I couldn't survive outside those walls.

I had become a product of my environment, erecting a wall so high around me that no one could have broken it down. I had mastered the elementary skill of "trusting *no one*." My defining moment came, though, while I was spending time in Corcoran State Prison. I was sitting in a cell labeled "the hole," a consequence of my recent involvement in a prison riot. At long last I questioned myself about whether or not I wanted to continue this process for the rest of my life. Through the Spirit's intervention, I "found" the courage to cry out to God to take me out of this facility alive. I invited him to change my life and my ways. I asked God to eliminate the load of fear I'd been carrying around all these years. I wanted to feel again, to care for others again, to become humble.

God spared me, both physically and spiritually. I deserved his wrath; instead he gave me undeserved forgiveness, power over sinful habits, a place of service in his kingdom and an eternity in his presence — all made available to me through my introduction to Celebrate Recovery after my release from prison. Initially, I wasn't ready to accept what Celebrate Recovery people were "pushing," but I was met with the love of Jesus Christ and wanted more. I knew God had me there "for such a time as this" (Esther 4:14).

For years I had been under the authority of the prison system. Now, through Celebrate Recovery, I'm under the authority of Jesus Christ. I realize today that trying to rule my own life simply doesn't work. My life, after all, isn't even my own. It's God's. Like the centurion in Luke 7, I gained what I was seeking because I finally understood the reality of Jesus' authority. After years of sobriety, I now have inner peace, confidence and a purpose for living. That purpose is to serve men who are currently incarcerated. My goal is to accomplish this by leading a group of them through Celebrate Recovery — Inside.

I realize today that I'm just a cracked pot but that God still can and wants to use all of me, all of the time, for his glory. Today I have hope: hope for a future (see Jeremiah 29:11), hope for continued sobriety, hope for the remainder of my lifetime spent in freedom, hope to continue trusting — and hope to share with others. I'm continually reminded of this verse from Galatians 5:13: "You, my brothers and sisters, were called to be free. But do not use your freedom to indulge the flesh; rather, serve one another humbly in love."

with an alabaster jar of perfume. [38]As she stood behind him at his feet weeping, she began to wet his feet with her tears. Then she wiped them with her hair, kissed them and poured perfume on them.

[39]When the Pharisee who had invited him saw this, he said to himself, "If this man were a prophet, he would know who is touching him and what kind of woman she is — that she is a sinner."

[40]Jesus answered him, "Simon, I have something to tell you."

"Tell me, teacher," he said.

[41]"Two people owed money to a certain moneylender. One owed him five hundred denarii,[a] and the other fifty. [42]Neither of them had the money to pay him back, so he forgave the debts of both. Now which of them will love him more?"

[43]Simon replied, "I suppose the one who had the bigger debt forgiven."

"You have judged correctly," Jesus said.

[44]Then he turned toward the woman and said to Simon, "Do you see this woman? I came into your house. You did not give me any water for my feet, but she wet my feet with her tears and wiped them with her hair. [45]You did not give me a kiss, but this woman, from the time I entered, has not stopped kissing my feet. [46]You did not put oil on my head, but she has poured perfume on my feet. [47]Therefore, I tell you, her many sins have been forgiven — as her great love has shown. But whoever has been forgiven little loves little."

[48]Then Jesus said to her, "Your sins are forgiven."

[49]The other guests began to say among themselves, "Who is this who even forgives sins?"

[50]Jesus said to the woman, "Your faith has saved you; go in peace."

The Parable of the Sower

8 After this, Jesus traveled about from one town and village to another, proclaiming the good news of the kingdom of God. The Twelve were with him, [2]and also some women who had been cured of evil spirits and diseases: Mary (called Magdalene) from whom seven demons had come out; [3]Joanna the wife of Chuza, the manager of Herod's household; Susanna; and many others. These women were helping to support them out of their own means.

[4]While a large crowd was gathering and people were coming to Jesus from town after town, he told this parable: [5]"A farmer went out to sow his seed. As he was scattering the seed, some fell along the path; it was trampled on, and the birds ate it up. [6]Some fell on rocky ground, and when it came up, the plants withered because they had no moisture. [7]Other seed fell among thorns, which grew up with it and choked the plants. [8]Still other seed fell on good soil. It came up and yielded a crop, a hundred times more than was sown."

When he said this, he called out, "Whoever has ears to hear, let them hear."

[9]His disciples asked him what this parable meant. [10]He said, "The knowledge of the secrets of the kingdom of God has been given to you, but to others I speak in parables, so that,

"'though seeing, they may not see;
though hearing, they may not understand.'[b]

[11]"This is the meaning of the parable: The seed is the word of God. [12]Those along the path are the ones who hear, and then the devil comes and takes away the word from their hearts, so that they may not believe and be saved. [13]Those on the rocky ground are the ones who receive the word with joy when they hear it, but they have no root. They believe for a while, but in the time of testing they fall away. [14]The seed that fell among thorns stands for those who hear, but as they go on their way they are choked by life's worries, riches and pleasures, and they do not mature. [15]But the seed on good soil stands for those with a noble and good

---

a 41 A denarius was the usual daily wage of a day laborer (see Matt. 20:2).   *b 10* Isaiah 6:9

MY NAME IS
THE SINFUL WOMAN

LUKE 7:36–50

One evening Jesus came to dine in the home of a Pharisee named Simon. Pharisees were self-appointed guardians of the law. To protect the Mosaic Law they had built a "hedge" of tradition around it. Jesus rejected this approach, pointing out that their tradition often caused them to "break the command of God" and "nullify the word of God" (Matthew 15:3,6). Simon's purpose in inviting Jesus into his home isn't stated. But God's plan is evident. God had prepared a stage and invited a captive audience for the testimony of a sinner and a lesson from the Lord. Both are essential ingredients in recovery.

While host and guests reclined at the table, a woman entered, washed Jesus' feet with her tears and anointed them with perfume. As a Pharisee, Simon considered himself both a defender and teacher of the law. That also made him, in his own mind, an expert on sin. He knew enough about this woman to label her "a sinner" (Luke 7:39). In his mind, Jesus, if he were "a prophet" (v. 39), would have recognized her as such and avoided her touch. In effect, he was classifying his invited guest as a phony.

Jesus wasn't into labels, but he was into lessons. He didn't deny that this woman was a sinner; instead he went out of his way to confirm that she had "many sins" (v. 47). The occasion for the lesson was the testimony delivered by her loving service and genuine humility. Testimonies always provoke a response. To any Pharisees in the crowd that response would likely have been rejection. Simon had a lot to learn about sin and forgiveness. The sinful woman, in contrast, had a first-hand, in-depth knowledge of both. Having experienced both, she recognized and loved the Savior to such a degree that she felt compelled to express it.

She could never have matched the eloquence or religious knowledge of Simon the Pharisee. Instead, her testimony was silent. But it was powerful. Its potency came from her motive. She didn't come to impress an audience but to serve her Lord from a motivation of pure love. Jesus made the most of her simple but touching example. Emerging from denial, recognizing our helplessness, surrendering to Jesus' control and openly confessing our sins produce loving service to Jesus.

Simon, as Jesus' host, should have provided water to wash his guest's feet — an obligation of hospitality in that culture. But Simon thought little of Jesus because he thought little of his own sins. Simon was long on labels but short on love and service. Failing to see the enormity of our sins will blind us to the magnitude of God's grace. Apparently the other guests shared Simon's spiritual blindness, inquiring "among themselves, 'Who is this who even forgives sins?' " (v. 49).

When we face our painful past, it's a starting place, not a destination. We can take our past to Jesus and leave it at his feet. To really recognize our Savior we have to clearly see our sins. Once we do, we'll hear him mouth these blessed words: "Your sins are forgiven" (v. 48), and "Your faith has saved you; go in peace" (v. 50).

My Name Is Reneé

I'M A BELIEVER WHO STRUGGLES WITH ALCOHOLISM

Please read the story in Luke 7:36 – 50 of the sinful woman who anointed Jesus' feet with her tears and with perfume.

My obsessive-compulsive behaviors and perfectionism started when, at the age of 8, I was convinced that my brother's death was my fault. Then at age 15 I found myself virtually raising my sister and brother and, eight months later, my infant twin sisters. As a high school student, I was for all intents and purposes a full-time mother, maid, cook and student. This pressure, fueled by resentment, anger, pain and disappointment, led to a nervous breakdown when I was 17. As soon as I turned 18, I found an "out" through marriage.

Soon enough I "woke up" to find myself married to an alcoholic from an extremely dysfunctional family. At that point I discovered a new source of freedom, a means of forgetting the pain of the present and releasing the anger from a robbed childhood: alcohol. During my first two years of marriage I had two miscarriages, a daughter . . . and several affairs. I was soon left with a new baby, a divorce and a new emotion: guilt. But I gave in to denial and quickly remarried. My new husband, Brad, had one suitcase of possessions to his name, smoked pot and never held down a job for long. As an "I can fix that" kind of person, I assured myself that my love would change him. Boy, was I insane! The next five years were characterized by marijuana growing in our bedroom closet, financial nightmares, heavy drinking, drug abuse, the abortion of my second child and the pervasive fear that we'd be raided by the police and I'd lose my daughter. I spiraled downward, finally asking my husband to leave.

Five days later, at his parents' home, he asked God to lead his life. When he told me, I was furious. I had fought for five agonizing years to make him change, but nothing had worked; now all he had to do was mouth a prayer and stop doing drugs? I felt as though I'd wasted five years of my life. But God began to work the first of many miracles in my life: I began to see a changed man. My husband and I were reunited, I started attending church with him, and I stopped drinking, cold turkey. I kept beer in the house "just in case," as a test for God. After a while I conceded that he'd passed the test and proceeded to pour it down the drain. I no longer needed alcohol to ease the pain. God was able and willing to take over in that department.

By this point I was alcohol free, drug free, attending church and living for and serving Christ. I had an awesome marriage, a wonderful family, a good job and even a new house. Everything, I assured myself, was clicking perfectly. The reality, though, is that I had gone from being an alcoholic to becoming a familyaholic, churchaholic and workaholic. I hadn't taken the time to deal with my deep-seated emotions, and, as a result, I twice relapsed with my drinking. I loved Jesus and thanked him for my restoration, but as soon as I took my eyes off him, the old desires started creeping back into my life. I had learned just enough about God to make me dangerous to myself, but I hadn't established a personal relationship with him. I had on my church mask, and I wore it well.

I had also missed the message that Christ would come to me wherever I happened to be if only I would ask, and that he would completely forgive me even though I had let him down so shamefully. I realized with a start that, though I had been asking for help with my drinking, I had neglected to repent and ask for forgiveness, not just for relapsing but also for turning my back on God. Like the sinful woman in the Gospel of Luke, I found my way to Jesus' feet and wept. For the first time I truly turned over my life and will to Christ's care and control. I felt my Savior putting his loving arms around me, comforting my soul and gently lifting the heavy burdens from my aching shoulders.

God has led me to Celebrate Recovery, and I have now, with his guidance, resolved the entire list of negative emotions that had been feeding my addictions. My new list of guiding principles consists of love, peace, patience, kindness, goodness, faithfulness, gentleness and self-control. God, through Celebrate Recovery, has given me the desire to discover who I am — and who he wants Reneé to be.

Over these many years I have grieved over my sins and found forgiveness in Jesus. I have also learned to forgive myself and to love God without reservation. I realize that this is a process, but God has truly transformed my life, and I can now share that hope with others.

heart, who hear the word, retain it, and by persevering produce a crop.

A Lamp on a Stand

16 "No one lights a lamp and hides it in a clay jar or puts it under a bed. Instead, they put it on a stand, so that those who come in can see the light. 17 For there is nothing hidden that will not be disclosed, and nothing concealed that will not be known or brought out into the open. 18 Therefore consider carefully how you listen. Whoever has will be given more; whoever does not have, even what they think they have will be taken from them."

Jesus' Mother and Brothers

19 Now Jesus' mother and brothers came to see him, but they were not able to get near him because of the crowd. 20 Someone told him, "Your mother and brothers are standing outside, wanting to see you."

21 He replied, "My mother and brothers are those who hear God's word and put it into practice."

Jesus Calms the Storm

22 One day Jesus said to his disciples, "Let us go over to the other side of the lake." So they got into a boat and set out. 23 As they sailed, he fell asleep. A squall came down on the lake, so that the boat was being swamped, and they were in great danger.

24 The disciples went and woke him, saying, "Master, Master, we're going to drown!"

He got up and rebuked the wind and the raging waters; the storm subsided, and all was calm. 25 "Where is your faith?" he asked his disciples.

In fear and amazement they asked one another, "Who is this? He commands even the winds and the water, and they obey him."

Jesus Restores a Demon-Possessed Man

26 They sailed to the region of the Gerasenes,[a] which is across the lake from Galilee. 27 When Jesus stepped ashore, he was met by a demon-possessed man from the town. For a long time this man had not worn clothes or lived in a house, but had lived in the tombs. 28 When he saw Jesus, he cried out and fell at his feet, shouting at the top of his voice, "What do you want with me, Jesus, Son of the Most High God? I beg you, don't torture me!" 29 For Jesus had commanded the impure spirit to come out of the man. Many times it had seized him, and though he was chained hand and foot and kept under guard, he had broken his chains and had been driven by the demon into solitary places.

30 Jesus asked him, "What is your name?"

"Legion," he replied, because many demons had gone into him. 31 And they begged Jesus repeatedly not to order them to go into the Abyss.

32 A large herd of pigs was feeding there on the hillside. The demons begged Jesus to let them go into the pigs, and he gave them permission. 33 When the demons came out of the man, they went into the pigs, and the herd rushed down the steep bank into the lake and was drowned.

34 When those tending the pigs saw what had happened, they ran off and reported this in the town and countryside, 35 and the people went out to see what had happened. When they came to Jesus, they found the man from whom the demons had gone out, sitting at Jesus' feet, dressed and in his right mind; and they were afraid. 36 Those who had seen it told the people how the demon-possessed man had been cured. 37 Then all the people of the region of the Gerasenes asked Jesus to leave them, because they were overcome with fear. So he got into the boat and left.

38 The man from whom the demons had gone out begged to go with him, but Jesus sent him away, saying, 39 "Return home and tell how much God has done for you." So the man went away and told all over town how much Jesus had done for him.

---

a 26 Some manuscripts *Gadarenes*; other manuscripts *Gergesenes*; also in verse 37

Jesus Raises a Dead Girl and Heals a Sick Woman

40Now when Jesus returned, a crowd welcomed him, for they were all expecting him. 41Then a man named Jairus, a synagogue leader, came and fell at Jesus' feet, pleading with him to come to his house 42because his only daughter, a girl of about twelve, was dying.

As Jesus was on his way, the crowds almost crushed him. 43And a woman was there who had been subject to bleeding for twelve years,*a* but no one could heal her. 44She came up behind him and touched the edge of his cloak, and immediately her bleeding stopped.

45"Who touched me?" Jesus asked.

When they all denied it, Peter said, "Master, the people are crowding and pressing against you."

46But Jesus said, "Someone touched me; I know that power has gone out from me."

47Then the woman, seeing that she could not go unnoticed, came trembling and fell at his feet. In the presence of all the people, she told why she had touched him and how she had been instantly healed. 48Then he said to her, "Daughter, your faith has healed you. Go in peace."

49While Jesus was still speaking, someone came from the house of Jairus, the synagogue leader. "Your daughter is dead," he said. "Don't bother the teacher anymore."

50Hearing this, Jesus said to Jairus, "Don't be afraid; just believe, and she will be healed."

51When he arrived at the house of Jairus, he did not let anyone go in with him except Peter, John and James, and the child's father and mother. 52Meanwhile, all the people were wailing and mourning for her. "Stop wailing," Jesus said. "She is not dead but asleep."

53They laughed at him, knowing that she was dead. 54But he took her by the hand and said, "My child, get up!" 55Her spirit returned, and at once she stood up. Then Jesus told them to give her something to eat. 56Her parents were astonished, but he ordered them not to tell anyone what had happened.

Jesus Sends Out the Twelve

9 When Jesus had called the Twelve together, he gave them power and authority to drive out all demons and to cure diseases, 2and he sent them out to proclaim the kingdom of God and to heal the sick. 3He told them: "Take nothing for the journey—no staff, no bag, no bread, no money, no extra shirt. 4Whatever house you enter, stay there until you leave that town. 5If people do not welcome you, leave their town and shake the dust off your feet as a testimony against them." 6So they set out and went from village to village, proclaiming the good news and healing people everywhere.

7Now Herod the tetrarch heard about all that was going on. And he was perplexed because some were saying that John had been raised from the dead, 8others that Elijah had appeared, and still others that one of the prophets of long ago had come back to life. 9But Herod said, "I beheaded John. Who, then, is this I hear such things about?" And he tried to see him.

Jesus Feeds the Five Thousand

10When the apostles returned, they reported to Jesus what they had done. Then he took them with him and they withdrew by themselves to a town called Bethsaida, 11but the crowds learned about it and followed him. He welcomed them and spoke to them about the kingdom of God, and healed those who needed healing.

12Late in the afternoon the Twelve came to him and said, "Send the crowd away so they can go to the surrounding villages and countryside and find food and lodging, because we are in a remote place here."

13He replied, "You give them something to eat."

---

a 43 Many manuscripts *years, and she had spent all she had on doctors*

MY NAME IS SHAME

LUKE 8:40–48

Her name may not have been Shame, but that's the emotion the woman felt most strongly. For 12 years her illness had made her mere touch something that defiled others. So when she furtively approached Jesus, her only hope, she fleetingly stroked the "edge" (Luke 8:44) of Jesus' cloak. Her fingers brushed against the tassel of Jesus' outer garment, one of four such tassels every Jewish man was to wear as a reminder to obey the commands and keep himself holy (see Numbers 15:37–41).

Even a command from God can be perverted in the name of religion. Jesus said that the Pharisees, in their religious pride, went beyond the law because, "everything they do is done for people to see: They make ... the tassels on their garments long" (Matthew 23:5). Had this woman touched the tassel of a Pharisee, he would have recoiled in horror, considering himself corrupted. But the touch of Jesus brings cleansing and restoration. Somehow this woman summoned up just enough faith to reach out, believing that if she only touched his cloak, she would be healed. By faith she tapped into his healing power (see Luke 8:46,48).

The Gospel accounts give no indication that the woman was responsible for her own illness. Nevertheless, her shame had isolated her from others for many years. There is no indication, as a matter of fact, of any sin as the source of her condition. She was simply a victim of circumstances beyond her control. But her shame — even after her secretive "confrontation" with Jesus — caused her to try to slip away unnoticed, trembling in fear of a negative response from Jesus to her tentative touch (see v. 47). Victims of abuse know this kind of shame. The perpetrator is responsible for their terrible physical and psychological wounds. But shame still makes it hard for them to face Jesus, hard to share the truth of their past with others.

But from this woman's reaching out to Jesus we learn that Jesus is sensitive, even when the crowd is callous (see vv. 42–46). Jesus meets us at the point of our desperation (see v. 43). It's the object, not the intensity, of our faith that brings about our healing (see v. 44). We need only enough faith to fall at Jesus' feet (see v. 47). Overcoming shame requires rejecting human ideas and accepting God's words.

Jesus sought out the woman in public, referring to her as "Daughter" and declaring her to be "healed" (v. 48). When he directed her to "go in peace" (v. 48), he would have used the Hebrew word *shalom* — a term that encompasses wholeness, restoration and blessing. It was vitally important that both she and those who had shunned her hear his declaration of healing and restoration.

They answered, "We have only five loaves of bread and two fish — unless we go and buy food for all this crowd." [14](About five thousand men were there.)

But he said to his disciples, "Have them sit down in groups of about fifty each." [15]The disciples did so, and everyone sat down. [16]Taking the five loaves and the two fish and looking up to heaven, he gave thanks and broke them. Then he gave them to the disciples to distribute to the people. [17]They all ate and were satisfied, and the disciples picked up twelve basketfuls of broken pieces that were left over.

Peter Declares That Jesus Is the Messiah

[18]Once when Jesus was praying in private and his disciples were with him, he asked them, "Who do the crowds say I am?"

[19]They replied, "Some say John the Baptist; others say Elijah; and still others, that one of the prophets of long ago has come back to life."

[20]"But what about you?" he asked. "Who do you say I am?"

Peter answered, "God's Messiah."

Jesus Predicts His Death

[21]Jesus strictly warned them not to tell this to anyone. [22]And he said, "The Son of Man must suffer many things and be rejected by the elders, the chief priests and the teachers of the law, and he must be killed and on the third day be raised to life."

[23]Then he said to them all: "Whoever wants to be my disciple must deny themselves and take up their cross daily and follow me. [24]For whoever wants to save their life will lose it, but whoever loses their life for me will save it. [25]What good is it for someone to gain the whole world, and yet lose or forfeit their very self? [26]Whoever is ashamed of me and my words, the Son of Man will be ashamed of them when he comes in his glory and in the glory of the Father and of the holy angels.

[27]"Truly I tell you, some who are standing here will not taste death before they see the kingdom of God."

The Transfiguration

[28]About eight days after Jesus said this, he took Peter, John and James with him and went up onto a mountain to pray. [29]As he was praying, the appearance of his face changed, and his clothes became as bright as a flash of lightning. [30]Two men, Moses and Elijah, appeared in glorious splendor, talking with Jesus. [31]They spoke about his departure,[a] which he was about to bring to fulfillment at Jerusalem. [32]Peter and his companions were very sleepy, but when they became fully awake, they saw his glory and the two men standing with him. [33]As the men were leaving Jesus, Peter said to him, "Master, it is good for us to be here. Let us put up three shelters — one for you, one for Moses and one for Elijah." (He did not know what he was saying.)

[34]While he was speaking, a cloud appeared and covered them, and they were afraid as they entered the cloud. [35]A voice came from the cloud, saying, "This is my Son, whom I have chosen; listen to him." [36]When the voice had spoken, they found that Jesus was alone. The disciples kept this to themselves and did not tell anyone at that time what they had seen.

Jesus Heals a Demon-Possessed Boy

[37]The next day, when they came down from the mountain, a large crowd met him. [38]A man in the crowd called out, "Teacher, I beg you to look at my son, for he is my only child. [39]A spirit seizes him and he suddenly screams; it throws him into convulsions so that he foams at the mouth. It scarcely ever leaves him and is destroying him. [40]I begged your disciples to drive it out, but they could not."

[41]"You unbelieving and perverse generation," Jesus replied, "how long shall I stay with you and put up with you? Bring your son here."

---

[a] 31 Greek *exodos*

My Name Is Regina

I'M A BELIEVER WHO STRUGGLES WITH SEXUAL, PHYSICAL
AND EMOTIONAL ABUSE

Please read the story of the woman who touched Jesus' robe in
Luke 8:40 – 48.

My earliest childhood memories are of fighting, yelling and hitting. Most of my father's angry outbursts were aimed at my mother, but I too became a target of his aggression. I loved my dad and liked being with him, but his favorite means of control was to terrify me, so I learned to fear him too. My father was also sexually abusive. I was expected to do whatever made "Daddy" happy and was far too scared to resist his promptings. My mother's protests on my behalf were met with severe beatings. His anger finally brought him to murder my mother. I was never able to say goodbye to her. This started my practice of never allowing anyone in.

While I was living with my gram, my 17-year-old uncle started molesting me. Again, I was too afraid to resist. Social Services was made aware of the situation, and my sister and I entered the foster care system. Loss and confusion continued to follow me as I was introduced to my new family. My gram slipped out of the picture, never to return. Once again I was unable to say goodbye and too afraid to cry. All I could feel was shame.

In my new home I was met with hugs and safety. When I was ten, my new family adopted both my sister and me. This should have been the start of a new life, but the only real change was my last name. My fears continued to consume me. The sexual abuse was never addressed, and I found I had no good reference point to govern my future behavior. When I was raped at the age of 12 or 13 by older teens, I felt out of control. I decided that day that no other man would ever take away my power. I decided to build a wall and become my own protector.

Throughout high school I was quite feministic. I dated, but once I was sure a guy liked me, I would do whatever I could to drive him away. I became really tough and rarely smiled. I sported a crew cut and made huge efforts to detract from my appearance. I became more and more caustic in my responses to others.

I knew who God was and even had a relationship with him. I knew he had to be different from the molesters from my past, but my shame caused me to view him with fear and trembling, wondering how he would really respond if I were to approach him (see Luke 8:47). But God in his love pursued me. During a drama about the crucifixion, I reached out to him like the woman who reached out for Jesus' cloak, and I held on tight. That was the turning point in my life. I began serving God with full abandon.

During this time God began working in my heart. Through his tenderness and mercy, he began revealing himself to me, and I started to turn my pain over to him. Several years later I met my husband, Don. My old fears started to resurface, and I lived in constant fear. The wall of isolation I had built when I was younger was being reinforced.

But God didn't give up on me. He wouldn't let me slip away unnoticed. Instead he led me to Celebrate Recovery at my church. He met me at the point of my desperation (see v. 43). When I first heard about Celebrate Recovery, I knew I had to be there, but the thought of being so open and exposed terrified me. I reached out with all the faith I had, believing that if God were really there, he would heal me (see Matthew 9:21). When I attended my first meeting, I was surprised with how open I was and how safe and supported I felt. God was truly there. As I continued to work the principles and the steps of Celebrate Recovery, changes began to happen in my life. It was a painful process at times, especially when I began to feel the pain from my past that I had been numb to for so long.

Overcoming my shame required me to learn new beliefs about myself and my past. I had to learn to believe in God's Word over my own ideas and those of others. I had to sort through what was and wasn't my responsibility. This journey has been freeing. The touch of Jesus has brought cleansing and restoration to my life. I now know that the abuse wasn't my fault and that the shame is not from God. I've also learned that there's great healing in offering forgiveness to those who've wronged me, even when they don't acknowledge it. My healing and recovery are for me, not them.

When I read that the woman who touched Jesus' cloak was healed by her faith and told to "go in peace" (Luke 8:48), I know that I too have been made whole, that I've been fully restored and blessed by God.

Regina

⁴²Even while the boy was coming, the demon threw him to the ground in a convulsion. But Jesus rebuked the impure spirit, healed the boy and gave him back to his father. ⁴³And they were all amazed at the greatness of God.

Jesus Predicts His Death a Second Time

While everyone was marveling at all that Jesus did, he said to his disciples, ⁴⁴"Listen carefully to what I am about to tell you: The Son of Man is going to be delivered into the hands of men." ⁴⁵But they did not understand what this meant. It was hidden from them, so that they did not grasp it, and they were afraid to ask him about it.

⁴⁶An argument started among the disciples as to which of them would be the greatest. ⁴⁷Jesus, knowing their thoughts, took a little child and had him stand beside him. ⁴⁸Then he said to them, "Whoever welcomes this little child in my name welcomes me; and whoever welcomes me welcomes the one who sent me. For it is the one who is least among you all who is the greatest."

⁴⁹"Master," said John, "we saw someone driving out demons in your name and we tried to stop him, because he is not one of us."

⁵⁰"Do not stop him," Jesus said, "for whoever is not against you is for you."

Samaritan Opposition

⁵¹As the time approached for him to be taken up to heaven, Jesus resolutely set out for Jerusalem. ⁵²And he sent messengers on ahead, who went into a Samaritan village to get things ready for him; ⁵³but the people there did not welcome him, because he was heading for Jerusalem. ⁵⁴When the disciples James and John saw this, they asked, "Lord, do you want us to call fire down from heaven to destroy them*a*?" ⁵⁵But Jesus turned and rebuked them. ⁵⁶Then he and his disciples went to another village.

The Cost of Following Jesus

⁵⁷As they were walking along the road, a man said to him, "I will follow you wherever you go."

⁵⁸Jesus replied, "Foxes have dens and birds have nests, but the Son of Man has no place to lay his head."

⁵⁹He said to another man, "Follow me."

But he replied, "Lord, first let me go and bury my father."

⁶⁰Jesus said to him, "Let the dead bury their own dead, but you go and proclaim the kingdom of God."

⁶¹Still another said, "I will follow you, Lord; but first let me go back and say goodbye to my family."

⁶²Jesus replied, "No one who puts a hand to the plow and looks back is fit for service in the kingdom of God."

Jesus Sends Out the Seventy-Two

10 After this the Lord appointed seventy-two*b* others and sent them two by two ahead of him to every town and place where he was about to go. ²He told them, "The harvest is plentiful, but the workers are few. Ask the Lord of the harvest, therefore, to send out workers into his harvest field. ³Go! I am sending you out like lambs among wolves. ⁴Do not take a purse or bag or sandals; and do not greet anyone on the road.

⁵"When you enter a house, first say, 'Peace to this house.' ⁶If someone who promotes peace is there, your peace will rest on them; if not, it will return to you. ⁷Stay there, eating and drinking whatever they give you, for the worker deserves his wages. Do not move around from house to house.

⁸"When you enter a town and are welcomed, eat what is offered to you. ⁹Heal the sick who are there and tell them, 'The kingdom of God has come near to you.' ¹⁰But when you enter a town and are not welcomed, go into its streets and say, ¹¹'Even the dust of your town we wipe

---

from our feet as a warning to you. Yet be sure of this: The kingdom of God has come near.' ¹²I tell you, it will be more bearable on that day for Sodom than for that town.

¹³"Woe to you, Chorazin! Woe to you, Bethsaida! For if the miracles that were performed in you had been performed in Tyre and Sidon, they would have repented long ago, sitting in sackcloth and ashes. ¹⁴But it will be more bearable for Tyre and Sidon at the judgment than for you. ¹⁵And you, Capernaum, will you be lifted to the heavens? No, you will go down to Hades.*ᵃ*

¹⁶"Whoever listens to you listens to me; whoever rejects you rejects me; but whoever rejects me rejects him who sent me."

¹⁷The seventy-two returned with joy and said, "Lord, even the demons submit to us in your name."

¹⁸He replied, "I saw Satan fall like lightning from heaven. ¹⁹I have given you authority to trample on snakes and scorpions and to overcome all the power of the enemy; nothing will harm you. ²⁰However, do not rejoice that the spirits submit to you, but rejoice that your names are written in heaven."

²¹At that time Jesus, full of joy through the Holy Spirit, said, "I praise you, Father, Lord of heaven and earth, because you have hidden these things from the wise and learned, and revealed them to little children. Yes, Father, for this is what you were pleased to do.

²²"All things have been committed to me by my Father. No one knows who the Son is except the Father, and no one knows who the Father is except the Son and those to whom the Son chooses to reveal him."

²³Then he turned to his disciples and said privately, "Blessed are the eyes that see what you see. ²⁴For I tell you that many prophets and kings wanted to see what you see but did not see it, and to hear what you hear but did not hear it."

The Parable of the Good Samaritan

²⁵On one occasion an expert in the law stood up to test Jesus. "Teacher," he asked, "what must I do to inherit eternal life?"

²⁶"What is written in the Law?" he replied. "How do you read it?"

²⁷He answered, "'Love the Lord your God with all your heart and with all your soul and with all your strength and with all your mind'ᵇ; and, 'Love your neighbor as yourself.'ᶜ"

²⁸"You have answered correctly," Jesus replied. "Do this and you will live."

²⁹But he wanted to justify himself, so he asked Jesus, "And who is my neighbor?"

³⁰In reply Jesus said: "A man was going down from Jerusalem to Jericho, when he was attacked by robbers. They stripped him of his clothes, beat him and went away, leaving him half dead. ³¹A priest happened to be going down the same road, and when he saw the man, he passed by on the other side. ³²So too, a Levite, when he came to the place and saw him, passed by on the other side. ³³But a Samaritan, as he traveled, came where the man was; and when he saw him, he took pity on him. ³⁴He went to him and bandaged his wounds, pouring on oil and wine. Then he put the man on his own donkey, brought him to an inn and took care of him. ³⁵The next day he took out two denariiᵈ and gave them to the innkeeper. 'Look after him,' he said, 'and when I return, I will reimburse you for any extra expense you may have.'

³⁶"Which of these three do you think was a neighbor to the man who fell into the hands of robbers?"

³⁷The expert in the law replied, "The one who had mercy on him."

Jesus told him, "Go and do likewise."

At the Home of Martha and Mary

³⁸As Jesus and his disciples were on their way, he came to a village where a woman named Martha opened her home to him.

ᵃ 15 That is, the realm of the dead   *ᵇ 27* Deut. 6:5   *ᶜ 27* Lev. 19:18   *ᵈ 35* A denarius was the usual daily wage of a day laborer (see Matt. 20:2).

MY NAME IS MARTHA

LUKE 10:38–42

Like so many today, Martha was busy in the Lord's service but still spiritually barren. She worked hard at caring for others. She was hospitable, welcoming Jesus and his band into her home. Jesus took the opportunity to offer spiritual food as Martha toiled in the kitchen, her sights fixed on the perfect meal. Her first recorded words accuse Jesus of not caring about her or about her sister's laziness. Hostility had replaced hospitality. She called Jesus "Lord" and in the very next breath insulted him (see Luke 10:40). Martha's apparent hospitality was rooted in codependency. She was a people-pleaser. Her self-identity revolved around entertaining—and perhaps impressing—those who entered her household. Her performance had become more significant to her than her personal relationship with, or even her respect for, her Lord. Addictions, compulsions and pain can blind us to the "crazy" contradictions between our beliefs and our behavior.

Mary wasn't lazy; she was tuned in to Jesus, and the Lord pointed this out to Martha. Martha's compulsions (see v. 41) were keeping her from the worship Mary was enjoying at the Master's feet (see vv. 39,42). For Martha, the good had crowded out the best. Martha was worried about temporal, passing things, while Mary was locked into the eternal. Jesus is forever. Our relationship with him is forever. His Word is forever (see 1 Peter 1:23–25).

Recovery requires the same shift in focus—off circumstances and addictions, off our painful past and onto Jesus. We're not asked to ignore our pain. Instead, we're called to face it and to allow Christ to remove it. Jesus helped Martha confront her weaknesses. She was "worried and upset about many things" (Luke 10:41). That describes many people today—maybe even a majority of people in our culture. Jesus knew that Martha had desires. But what we *want* isn't worth getting upset about. What matters is what we *need*: an intimate relationship with Jesus. We need to find our place at his feet, taking directions from him. That's a life, a peace, that "will not be taken away" (v. 42).

Jesus confronted Martha's nonproductive habits and emotions. He pointed her in a new direction. Did Martha experience recovery? There's evidence that she did in John 11, the account of Jesus' raising of Lazarus from the dead. Lazarus was in the tomb, and Mary was in the house with the mourners. But as soon as "Martha heard that Jesus was coming, she went out to meet him" (John 11:20). It's likely that the "old Martha" would have run into the kitchen and started cooking. But the "new Martha" took the opportunity to have a dynamic dialogue with her Savior. She had grown in her knowledge of Jesus. In fact, Martha was one of the very few who confessed, prior to his resurrection, Jesus as "the Son of God" (v. 27).

Martha changed. She discovered the one true Higher Power. Martha could continue to serve (see 12:1–2), but no longer out of worry. She was free from the pressure to perform for the purpose of pleasing others. Recovery isn't drudgery. It's a way to celebrate our love for Jesus and others. We can be busy, tuned in to Jesus and fruitful rather than barren.

³⁹She had a sister called Mary, who sat at the Lord's feet listening to what he said. ⁴⁰But Martha was distracted by all the preparations that had to be made. She came to him and asked, "Lord, don't you care that my sister has left me to do the work by myself? Tell her to help me!"

⁴¹"Martha, Martha," the Lord answered, "you are worried and upset about many things, ⁴²but few things are needed — or indeed only one.ᵃ Mary has chosen what is better, and it will not be taken away from her."

Jesus' Teaching on Prayer

11 One day Jesus was praying in a certain place. When he finished, one of his disciples said to him, "Lord, teach us to pray, just as John taught his disciples."

²He said to them, "When you pray, say:

" 'Father,ᵇ
hallowed be your name,
your kingdom come.ᶜ
³Give us each day our daily bread.
⁴Forgive us our sins,
for we also forgive everyone who sins
against us.ᵈ
And lead us not into temptation.ᵉ' "

⁵Then Jesus said to them, "Suppose you have a friend, and you go to him at midnight and say, 'Friend, lend me three loaves of bread; ⁶a friend of mine on a journey has come to me, and I have no food to offer him.' ⁷And suppose the one inside answers, 'Don't bother me. The door is already locked, and my children and I are in bed. I can't get up and give you anything.' ⁸I tell you, even though he will not get up and give you the bread because of friendship, yet because of your shameless audacityᶠ he will surely get up and give you as much as you need.

⁹"So I say to you: Ask and it will be given

to you; seek and you will find; knock and the door will be opened to you. ¹⁰For everyone who asks receives; the one who seeks finds; and to the one who knocks, the door will be opened.

¹¹"Which of you fathers, if your son asks forᵍ a fish, will give him a snake instead? ¹²Or if he asks for an egg, will give him a scorpion? ¹³If you then, though you are evil, know how to give good gifts to your children, how much more will your Father in heaven give the Holy Spirit to those who ask him!"

Jesus and Beelzebul

¹⁴Jesus was driving out a demon that was mute. When the demon left, the man who had been mute spoke, and the crowd was amazed. ¹⁵But some of them said, "By Beelzebul, the prince of demons, he is driving out demons." ¹⁶Others tested him by asking for a sign from heaven.

¹⁷Jesus knew their thoughts and said to them: "Any kingdom divided against itself will be ruined, and a house divided against itself will fall. ¹⁸If Satan is divided against himself, how can his kingdom stand? I say this because you claim that I drive out demons by Beelzebul. ¹⁹Now if I drive out demons by Beelzebul, by whom do your followers drive them out? So then, they will be your judges. ²⁰But if I drive out demons by the finger of God, then the kingdom of God has come upon you.

²¹"When a strong man, fully armed, guards his own house, his possessions are safe. ²²But when someone stronger attacks and overpowers him, he takes away the armor in which the man trusted and divides up his plunder.

²³"Whoever is not with me is against me, and whoever does not gather with me scatters.

²⁴"When an impure spirit comes out of a person, it goes through arid places seeking

---

ᵃ 42 Some manuscripts *but only one thing is needed*   ᵇ 2 Some manuscripts *Our Father in heaven*   ᶜ 2 Some manuscripts *come. May your will be done on earth as it is in heaven.*   ᵈ 4 Greek *everyone who is indebted to us*   ᵉ 4 Some manuscripts *temptation, but deliver us from the evil one*   ᶠ 8 Or *yet to preserve his good name*   ᵍ 11 Some manuscripts *for bread, will give him a stone? Or if he asks for*

My Name Is Janet

I'M A BELIEVER WHO STRUGGLES WITH CODEPENDENCY

Please read in Luke 10:38–42 the story of Martha's compulsion to help others while ignoring her own needs.

While I was growing up, I had a wonderful relationship with my mother. She was warm, patient and loving. My dad, though, was a perfectionist who had unrealistically high expectations for me. I worked hard to win his favor and tried to avoid failure at all costs. I felt as though I was never good enough to please him — and that, to me, translated into "He doesn't love me." I decided that I didn't need my dad and went about seeking love and affirmation in other places. I shut out the rest of my family as well and began a cycle of self-reliance and cover-ups. Like Martha, I tried to please everyone. My friends would come to me looking for advice and support, but I could never admit that I needed others just as much as they needed me.

I met my future husband, Joe, when I was 18 years old. He convinced me that we were going to be rich and successful and never have a care in the world. The first 15 years of our marriage were filled with hurt feelings, disappointments and an endless pattern of arguments followed by reconciliation. We moved our family to Idaho so that Joe could accomplish the one dream we thought would solve everything: owning our own business. Those were tough years. I lived with a continual need to manage our lives so that nothing bad would happen. I was in bondage to the "if only's": If only we had more money. If only the business would take off so Joe wouldn't have to work so many hours. If only Joe would deal better with his anger, etc. It seemed as though there was always one more external change that needed to happen in order for us to be happy. I was so caught up in my feelings of discontent that I failed to realize that the only way we could be happy was through an internal change — a change that could come from only one source: Jesus Christ.

Several years later, our business seemed to be doing well, but, much to my dismay, money hadn't solved our problems. Our marriage was in serious trouble, and our children were becoming rebellious.

We found a church called The Vineyard. I learned in this church that it's okay to be "real." I knew that I needed to deal with my codependency struggles. I cried buckets of tears as

I begged God to rescue me, the one who had been everyone else's rescuer. I could no longer fake it; I needed help. I was exhausted and ready to admit that I had failed miserably in trying to control things on my own. In fact, I no longer wanted to be in control.

When I started attending Celebrate Recovery, I was like an infant learning to walk for the first time. By taking what seemed like "baby steps," I learned about forgiveness — about how to receive it and how to give it. I've learned that I'm safe as long as I remain in the arms of my heavenly Father. For the first time in my life, I have a Father who has proven himself faithful and trustworthy. I regularly run to him for comfort, direction and correction. Perfection used to be something I would strive for in order to earn love and acceptance. Now I serve the Lord with gladness and joy because I know that I'm loved — completely and unconditionally. My relationships are stronger because, for the first time, I can express feelings of love without the high expectations that once accompanied them.

By working the tools of the program, I'm learning to be honest about my inadequacies. God has performed such a miraculous healing in my life and marriage. I'm blessed and grateful for the privilege of serving in this ministry and of watching as other lives are transformed by the love and power of Jesus Christ.

My codependent behaviors had led me down the same path Martha walked 2,000 years ago. Only Jesus could point me in a new direction. If I hadn't heeded the guidance of the Holy Spirit, I too would still be blind to the crazy contradictions between my beliefs and my behaviors.

rest and does not find it. Then it says, 'I will return to the house I left.' 25When it arrives, it finds the house swept clean and put in order. 26Then it goes and takes seven other spirits more wicked than itself, and they go in and live there. And the final condition of that person is worse than the first."

27As Jesus was saying these things, a woman in the crowd called out, "Blessed is the mother who gave you birth and nursed you."

28He replied, "Blessed rather are those who hear the word of God and obey it."

The Sign of Jonah

29As the crowds increased, Jesus said, "This is a wicked generation. It asks for a sign, but none will be given it except the sign of Jonah. 30For as Jonah was a sign to the Ninevites, so also will the Son of Man be to this generation. 31The Queen of the South will rise at the judgment with the people of this generation and condemn them, for she came from the ends of the earth to listen to Solomon's wisdom; and now something greater than Solomon is here. 32The men of Nineveh will stand up at the judgment with this generation and condemn it, for they repented at the preaching of Jonah; and now something greater than Jonah is here.

The Lamp of the Body

33"No one lights a lamp and puts it in a place where it will be hidden, or under a bowl. Instead they put it on its stand, so that those who come in may see the light. 34Your eye is the lamp of your body. When your eyes are healthy,ᵃ your whole body also is full of light. But when they are unhealthy,ᵇ your body also is full of darkness. 35See to it, then, that the light within you is not darkness. 36Therefore, if your whole body is full of light, and no part of it dark, it will be just as full of light as when a lamp shines its light on you."

Woes on the Pharisees and the Experts in the Law

37When Jesus had finished speaking, a Pharisee invited him to eat with him; so he went in and reclined at the table. 38But the Pharisee was surprised when he noticed that Jesus did not first wash before the meal.

39Then the Lord said to him, "Now then, you Pharisees clean the outside of the cup and dish, but inside you are full of greed and wickedness. 40You foolish people! Did not the one who made the outside make the inside also? 41But now as for what is inside you — be generous to the poor, and everything will be clean for you.

42"Woe to you Pharisees, because you give God a tenth of your mint, rue and all other kinds of garden herbs, but you neglect justice and the love of God. You should have practiced the latter without leaving the former undone.

43"Woe to you Pharisees, because you love the most important seats in the synagogues and respectful greetings in the marketplaces.

44"Woe to you, because you are like unmarked graves, which people walk over without knowing it."

45One of the experts in the law answered him, "Teacher, when you say these things, you insult us also."

46Jesus replied, "And you experts in the law, woe to you, because you load people down with burdens they can hardly carry, and you yourselves will not lift one finger to help them.

47"Woe to you, because you build tombs for the prophets, and it was your ancestors who killed them. 48So you testify that you approve of what your ancestors did; they killed the prophets, and you build their tombs. 49Because of this, God in his wisdom said, 'I will send them prophets and apostles, some of whom they will kill and others they will persecute.' 50Therefore this generation will be held responsible for the

---

ᵃ 34 The Greek for *healthy* here implies *generous*.   ᵇ 34 The Greek for *unhealthy* here implies *stingy*.

blood of all the prophets that has been shed since the beginning of the world, 51from the blood of Abel to the blood of Zechariah, who was killed between the altar and the sanctuary. Yes, I tell you, this generation will be held responsible for it all.

52"Woe to you experts in the law, because you have taken away the key to knowledge. You yourselves have not entered, and you have hindered those who were entering."

53When Jesus went outside, the Pharisees and the teachers of the law began to oppose him fiercely and to besiege him with questions, 54waiting to catch him in something he might say.

Warnings and Encouragements

12 Meanwhile, when a crowd of many thousands had gathered, so that they were trampling on one another, Jesus began to speak first to his disciples, saying: "Be*a* on your guard against the yeast of the Pharisees, which is hypocrisy. 2There is nothing concealed that will not be disclosed, or hidden that will not be made known. 3What you have said in the dark will be heard in the daylight, and what you have whispered in the ear in the inner rooms will be proclaimed from the roofs.

4"I tell you, my friends, do not be afraid of those who kill the body and after that can do no more. 5But I will show you whom you should fear: Fear him who, after your body has been killed, has authority to throw you into hell. Yes, I tell you, fear him. 6Are not five sparrows sold for two pennies? Yet not one of them is forgotten by God. 7Indeed, the very hairs of your head are all numbered. Don't be afraid; you are worth more than many sparrows.

8"I tell you, whoever publicly acknowledges me before others, the Son of Man will also acknowledge before the angels of God. 9But whoever disowns me before others will be disowned before the angels of God. 10And everyone who speaks a word against the Son of Man will be forgiven, but anyone who blasphemes against the Holy Spirit will not be forgiven.

11"When you are brought before synagogues, rulers and authorities, do not worry about how you will defend yourselves or what you will say, 12for the Holy Spirit will teach you at that time what you should say."

The Parable of the Rich Fool

13Someone in the crowd said to him, "Teacher, tell my brother to divide the inheritance with me."

14Jesus replied, "Man, who appointed me a judge or an arbiter between you?" 15Then he said to them, "Watch out! Be on your guard against all kinds of greed; life does not consist in an abundance of possessions."

16And he told them this parable: "The ground of a certain rich man yielded an abundant harvest. 17He thought to himself, 'What shall I do? I have no place to store my crops.'

18"Then he said, 'This is what I'll do. I will tear down my barns and build bigger ones, and there I will store my surplus grain. 19And I'll say to myself, "You have plenty of grain laid up for many years. Take life easy; eat, drink and be merry."'

20"But God said to him, 'You fool! This very night your life will be demanded from you. Then who will get what you have prepared for yourself?'

21"This is how it will be with whoever stores up things for themselves but is not rich toward God."

Do Not Worry

22Then Jesus said to his disciples: "Therefore I tell you, do not worry about your life, what you will eat; or about your body, what you will wear. 23For life is more than food, and the body more than clothes. 24Consider the ravens: They do not sow or reap, they have no storeroom or barn; yet God feeds them. And how much more valuable you

---

a 1 Or *speak to his disciples, saying: "First of all, be* are than birds! ²⁵Who of you by worrying can add a single hour to your life*ª*? ²⁶Since you cannot do this very little thing, why do you worry about the rest?

²⁷"Consider how the wild flowers grow. They do not labor or spin. Yet I tell you, not even Solomon in all his splendor was dressed like one of these. ²⁸If that is how God clothes the grass of the field, which is here today, and tomorrow is thrown into the fire, how much more will he clothe you—you of little faith! ²⁹And do not set your heart on what you will eat or drink; do not worry about it. ³⁰For the pagan world runs after all such things, and your Father knows that you need them. ³¹But seek his kingdom, and these things will be given to you as well.

³²"Do not be afraid, little flock, for your Father has been pleased to give you the kingdom. ³³Sell your possessions and give to the poor. Provide purses for yourselves that will not wear out, a treasure in heaven that will never fail, where no thief comes

---

ª 25 Or *single cubit to your height*

POWERLESS LESSON [*Principle One*]

For the previous entry in the POWERLESS lesson, go to Proverbs 29:23 (page 777).

For a discussion of Principles One through Eight and a listing of their related lessons, go to pages xvii–xliv.

There is nothing concealed that will not be disclosed, or hidden that will not be made known. What you have said in the dark will be heard in the daylight, and what you have whispered in the ear in the inner rooms will be proclaimed from the roofs.

Luke 12:2–3

The power to change comes only through God's grace. Principle One states: "Realize I'm not God. I admit that I'm powerless to control my tendency to do the wrong thing and that my life has become unmanageable." If we admit that we're powerless, we recognize our need for a power greater than ourselves to restore us. That power is our Higher Power, the one and only true Higher Power, Jesus Christ.

In Principle One we discover that we're POWERLESS to control our own lives and that our lives have become unmanageable. The next letter in POWERLESS is *O*, which stands for those pesky ONLY IFS.

Have you ever had a case of the "only if's" (or the "if only's")?

- "If only they hadn't walked out."
- "If only I had stopped drinking."
- If only this. If only that.

How reluctantly the mind consents to reality. But when we admit that we're powerless, we start walking in the truth rather than living in the fantasy land of rationalization.

The next letter in POWERLESS is *W*. Go to Matthew 6:34 (page 1135).

near and no moth destroys. 34For where your treasure is, there your heart will be also.

Watchfulness

35"Be dressed ready for service and keep your lamps burning, 36like servants waiting for their master to return from a wedding banquet, so that when he comes and knocks they can immediately open the door for him. 37It will be good for those servants whose master finds them watching when he comes. Truly I tell you, he will dress himself to serve, will have them recline at the table and will come and wait on them. 38It will be good for those servants whose master finds them ready, even if he comes in the middle of the night or toward daybreak. 39But understand this: If the owner of the house had known at what hour the thief was coming, he would not have let his house be broken into. 40You also must be ready, because the Son of Man will come at an hour when you do not expect him."

41Peter asked, "Lord, are you telling this parable to us, or to everyone?"

42The Lord answered, "Who then is the faithful and wise manager, whom the master puts in charge of his servants to give them their food allowance at the proper time? 43It will be good for that servant whom the master finds doing so when he returns. 44Truly I tell you, he will put him in charge of all his possessions. 45But suppose the servant says to himself, 'My master is taking a long time in coming,' and he then begins to beat the other servants, both men and women, and to eat and drink and get drunk. 46The master of that servant will come on a day when he does not expect him and at an hour he is not aware of. He will cut him to pieces and assign him a place with the unbelievers.

47"The servant who knows the master's will and does not get ready or does not do what the master wants will be beaten with many blows. 48But the one who does not know and does things deserving punishment will be beaten with few blows. From everyone who has been given much, much will be demanded; and from the one who has been entrusted with much, much more will be asked.

Not Peace but Division

49"I have come to bring fire on the earth, and how I wish it were already kindled! 50But I have a baptism to undergo, and what constraint I am under until it is completed! 51Do you think I came to bring peace on earth? No, I tell you, but division. 52From now on there will be five in one family divided against each other, three against two and two against three. 53They will be divided, father against son and son against father, mother against daughter and daughter against mother, mother-in-law against daughter-in-law and daughter-in-law against mother-in-law."

Interpreting the Times

54He said to the crowd: "When you see a cloud rising in the west, immediately you say, 'It's going to rain,' and it does. 55And when the south wind blows, you say, 'It's going to be hot,' and it is. 56Hypocrites! You know how to interpret the appearance of the earth and the sky. How is it that you don't know how to interpret this present time?

57"Why don't you judge for yourselves what is right? 58As you are going with your adversary to the magistrate, try hard to be reconciled on the way, or your adversary may drag you off to the judge, and the judge turn you over to the officer, and the officer throw you into prison. 59I tell you, you will not get out until you have paid the last penny."

Repent or Perish

13 Now there were some present at that time who told Jesus about the Galileans whose blood Pilate had mixed with their sacrifices. 2Jesus answered, "Do you think that these Galileans were worse sinners than all the other

Galileans because they suffered this way? ³I tell you, no! But unless you repent, you too will all perish. ⁴Or those eighteen who died when the tower in Siloam fell on them — do you think they were more guilty than all the others living in Jerusalem? ⁵I tell you, no! But unless you repent, you too will all perish."

⁶Then he told this parable: "A man had a fig tree growing in his vineyard, and he went to look for fruit on it but did not find any. ⁷So he said to the man who took care of the vineyard, 'For three years now I've been coming to look for fruit on this fig tree and haven't found any. Cut it down! Why should it use up the soil?'

⁸"'Sir,' the man replied, 'leave it alone for one more year, and I'll dig around it and fertilize it. ⁹If it bears fruit next year, fine! If not, then cut it down.'"

Jesus Heals a Crippled Woman on the Sabbath

¹⁰On a Sabbath Jesus was teaching in one of the synagogues, ¹¹and a woman was there who had been crippled by a spirit for eighteen years. She was bent over and could not straighten up at all. ¹²When Jesus saw her, he called her forward and said to her, "Woman, you are set free from your infirmity." ¹³Then he put his hands on her, and immediately she straightened up and praised God.

¹⁴Indignant because Jesus had healed on the Sabbath, the synagogue leader said to the people, "There are six days for work. So come and be healed on those days, not on the Sabbath."

¹⁵The Lord answered him, "You hypocrites! Doesn't each of you on the Sabbath untie your ox or donkey from the stall and lead it out to give it water? ¹⁶Then should not this woman, a daughter of Abraham, whom Satan has kept bound for eighteen long years, be set free on the Sabbath day from what bound her?"

¹⁷When he said this, all his opponents were humiliated, but the people were delighted with all the wonderful things he was doing.

The Parables of the Mustard Seed and the Yeast

¹⁸Then Jesus asked, "What is the kingdom of God like? What shall I compare it to? ¹⁹It is like a mustard seed, which a man took and planted in his garden. It grew and became a tree, and the birds perched in its branches."

²⁰Again he asked, "What shall I compare the kingdom of God to? ²¹It is like yeast that a woman took and mixed into about sixty pounds[a] of flour until it worked all through the dough."

The Narrow Door

²²Then Jesus went through the towns and villages, teaching as he made his way to Jerusalem. ²³Someone asked him, "Lord, are only a few people going to be saved?"

He said to them, ²⁴"Make every effort to enter through the narrow door, because many, I tell you, will try to enter and will not be able to. ²⁵Once the owner of the house gets up and closes the door, you will stand outside knocking and pleading, 'Sir, open the door for us.'

"But he will answer, 'I don't know you or where you come from.'

²⁶"Then you will say, 'We ate and drank with you, and you taught in our streets.'

²⁷"But he will reply, 'I don't know you or where you come from. Away from me, all you evildoers!'

²⁸"There will be weeping there, and gnashing of teeth, when you see Abraham, Isaac and Jacob and all the prophets in the kingdom of God, but you yourselves thrown out. ²⁹People will come from east and west and north and south, and will take their places at the feast in the kingdom of God. ³⁰Indeed there are those who are last who will be first, and first who will be last."

---

a 21 Or about 27 kilograms

Jesus' Sorrow for Jerusalem

31 At that time some Pharisees came to Jesus and said to him, "Leave this place and go somewhere else. Herod wants to kill you."

32 He replied, "Go tell that fox, 'I will keep on driving out demons and healing people today and tomorrow, and on the third day I will reach my goal.' 33 In any case, I must press on today and tomorrow and the next day — for surely no prophet can die outside Jerusalem!

34 "Jerusalem, Jerusalem, you who kill the prophets and stone those sent to you, how often I have longed to gather your children together, as a hen gathers her chicks under her wings, and you were not willing. 35 Look, your house is left to you desolate. I tell you, you will not see me again until you say, 'Blessed is he who comes in the name of the Lord.'*a*

Jesus at a Pharisee's House

14 One Sabbath, when Jesus went to eat in the house of a prominent Pharisee, he was being carefully watched. 2 There in front of him was a man suffering from abnormal swelling of his body. 3 Jesus asked the Pharisees and experts in the law, "Is it lawful to heal on the Sabbath or not?" 4 But they remained silent. So taking hold of the man, he healed him and sent him on his way.

5 Then he asked them, "If one of you has a child*b* or an ox that falls into a well on the Sabbath day, will you not immediately pull it out?" 6 And they had nothing to say.

7 When he noticed how the guests picked the places of honor at the table, he told them this parable: 8 "When someone invites you to a wedding feast, do not take the place of honor, for a person more distinguished than you may have been invited. 9 If so, the host who invited both of you will come and say to you, 'Give this person your seat.' Then, humiliated, you will have to take the least important place. 10 But when you are

invited, take the lowest place, so that when your host comes, he will say to you, 'Friend, move up to a better place.' Then you will be honored in the presence of all the other guests. 11 For all those who exalt themselves will be humbled, and those who humble themselves will be exalted."

12 Then Jesus said to his host, "When you give a luncheon or dinner, do not invite your friends, your brothers or sisters, your relatives, or your rich neighbors; if you do, they may invite you back and so you will be repaid. 13 But when you give a banquet, invite the poor, the crippled, the lame, the blind, 14 and you will be blessed. Although they cannot repay you, you will be repaid at the resurrection of the righteous."

The Parable of the Great Banquet

15 When one of those at the table with him heard this, he said to Jesus, "Blessed is the one who will eat at the feast in the kingdom of God."

16 Jesus replied: "A certain man was preparing a great banquet and invited many guests. 17 At the time of the banquet he sent his servant to tell those who had been invited, 'Come, for everything is now ready.'

18 "But they all alike began to make excuses. The first said, 'I have just bought a field, and I must go and see it. Please excuse me.'

19 "Another said, 'I have just bought five yoke of oxen, and I'm on my way to try them out. Please excuse me.'

20 "Still another said, 'I just got married, so I can't come.'

21 "The servant came back and reported this to his master. Then the owner of the house became angry and ordered his servant, 'Go out quickly into the streets and alleys of the town and bring in the poor, the crippled, the blind and the lame.'

22 "'Sir,' the servant said, 'what you ordered has been done, but there is still room.'

23 "Then the master told his servant, 'Go out to the roads and country lanes and

---

a 35 Psalm 118:26   *b 5* Some manuscripts *donkey*

compel them to come in, so that my house will be full. ²⁴I tell you, not one of those who were invited will get a taste of my banquet.'"

The Cost of Being a Disciple

²⁵Large crowds were traveling with Jesus, and turning to them he said: ²⁶"If anyone comes to me and does not hate father and mother, wife and children, brothers and sisters — yes, even their own life — such a person cannot be my disciple. ²⁷And whoever does not carry their cross and follow me cannot be my disciple.

²⁸"Suppose one of you wants to build a tower. Won't you first sit down and estimate the cost to see if you have enough money to complete it? ²⁹For if you lay the foundation and are not able to finish it, everyone who sees it will ridicule you, ³⁰saying, 'This person began to build and wasn't able to finish.'

³¹"Or suppose a king is about to go to war against another king. Won't he first sit down and consider whether he is able with ten thousand men to oppose the one coming against him with twenty thousand? ³²If he is not able, he will send a delegation while the other is still a long way off and will ask for terms of peace. ³³In the same way, those of you who do not give up everything you have cannot be my disciples.

³⁴"Salt is good, but if it loses its saltiness, how can it be made salty again? ³⁵It is fit neither for the soil nor for the manure pile; it is thrown out.

"Whoever has ears to hear, let them hear."

The Parable of the Lost Sheep

15 Now the tax collectors and sinners were all gathering around to hear Jesus. ²But the Pharisees and the teachers of the law muttered, "This man welcomes sinners and eats with them."

³Then Jesus told them this parable: ⁴"Suppose one of you has a hundred sheep and loses one of them. Doesn't he leave the ninety-nine in the open country and go after the lost sheep until he finds it? ⁵And when he finds it, he joyfully puts it on his shoulders ⁶and goes home. Then he calls his friends and neighbors together and says, 'Rejoice with me; I have found my lost sheep.' ⁷I tell you that in the same way there will be more rejoicing in heaven over one sinner who repents than over ninety-nine righteous persons who do not need to repent.

The Parable of the Lost Coin

⁸"Or suppose a woman has ten silver coinsᵃ and loses one. Doesn't she light a lamp, sweep the house and search carefully until she finds it? ⁹And when she finds it, she calls her friends and neighbors together and says, 'Rejoice with me; I have found my lost coin.' ¹⁰In the same way, I tell you, there is rejoicing in the presence of the angels of God over one sinner who repents."

The Parable of the Lost Son

¹¹Jesus continued: "There was a man who had two sons. ¹²The younger one said to his father, 'Father, give me my share of the estate.' So he divided his property between them.

¹³"Not long after that, the younger son got together all he had, set off for a distant country and there squandered his wealth in wild living. ¹⁴After he had spent everything, there was a severe famine in that whole country, and he began to be in need. ¹⁵So he went and hired himself out to a citizen of that country, who sent him to his fields to feed pigs. ¹⁶He longed to fill his stomach with the pods that the pigs were eating, but no one gave him anything.

¹⁷"When he came to his senses, he said, 'How many of my father's hired servants have food to spare, and here I am starving to death! ¹⁸I will set out and go back to my father and say to him: Father, I have sinned against heaven and against you. ¹⁹I am no

---

ᵃ 8 Greek *ten drachmas,* each worth about a day's wages

longer worthy to be called your son; make me like one of your hired servants.' ²⁰So he got up and went to his father.

"But while he was still a long way off, his father saw him and was filled with compassion for him; he ran to his son, threw his arms around him and kissed him.

²¹"The son said to him, 'Father, I have sinned against heaven and against you. I am no longer worthy to be called your son.'

²²"But the father said to his servants, 'Quick! Bring the best robe and put it on him. Put a ring on his finger and sandals on his feet. ²³Bring the fattened calf and kill it. Let's have a feast and celebrate. ²⁴For this son of mine was dead and is alive again; he was lost and is found.' So they began to celebrate.

²⁵"Meanwhile, the older son was in the field. When he came near the house, he heard music and dancing. ²⁶So he called one of the servants and asked him what was going on. ²⁷'Your brother has come,' he replied, 'and your father has killed the fattened calf because he has him back safe and sound.'

²⁸"The older brother became angry and refused to go in. So his father went out and pleaded with him. ²⁹But he answered his father, 'Look! All these years I've been slaving for you and never disobeyed your orders. Yet you never gave me even a young goat so I could celebrate with my friends. ³⁰But when this son of yours who has squandered your property with prostitutes comes home, you kill the fattened calf for him!'

³¹"'My son,' the father said, 'you are always with me, and everything I have is yours. ³²But we had to celebrate and be glad, because this brother of yours was dead and is alive again; he was lost and is found.'"

The Parable of the Shrewd Manager

16 Jesus told his disciples: "There was a rich man whose manager was accused of wasting his pos-

sessions. ²So he called him in and asked him, 'What is this I hear about you? Give an account of your management, because you cannot be manager any longer.'

³"The manager said to himself, 'What shall I do now? My master is taking away my job. I'm not strong enough to dig, and I'm ashamed to beg— ⁴I know what I'll do so that, when I lose my job here, people will welcome me into their houses.'

⁵"So he called in each one of his master's debtors. He asked the first, 'How much do you owe my master?'

⁶"'Nine hundred gallonsᵃ of olive oil,' he replied.

"The manager told him, 'Take your bill, sit down quickly, and make it four hundred and fifty.'

⁷"Then he asked the second, 'And how much do you owe?'

"'A thousand bushelsᵇ of wheat,' he replied.

"He told him, 'Take your bill and make it eight hundred.'

⁸"The master commended the dishonest manager because he had acted shrewdly. For the people of this world are more shrewd in dealing with their own kind than are the people of the light. ⁹I tell you, use worldly wealth to gain friends for yourselves, so that when it is gone, you will be welcomed into eternal dwellings.

¹⁰"Whoever can be trusted with very little can also be trusted with much, and whoever is dishonest with very little will also be dishonest with much. ¹¹So if you have not been trustworthy in handling worldly wealth, who will trust you with true riches? ¹²And if you have not been trustworthy with someone else's property, who will give you property of your own?

¹³"No one can serve two masters. Either you will hate the one and love the other, or you will be devoted to the one and despise the other. You cannot serve both God and money."

¹⁴The Pharisees, who loved money,

ᵃ 6 Or about 3,000 liters   ᵇ 7 Or about 30 tons

MY NAME IS
THE LOST SON

LUKE 15:11–32

The younger son in this story squandered the inheritance he had received from his father, buying into a materialistic, hedonistic view of life. Perhaps he hoped that adding the buffer of some distance would serve to keep his sin a secret. But God's Word warns us that what is done in the darkness eventually comes to light (see 1 Corinthians 4:5). All too soon the place where the lost son had found pleasure became a source of pain and hunger (see Luke 15:14–16). Physical pleasures can never meet our deep personal needs. In fact, the only source of real and lasting satisfaction is Jesus Christ.

The lost son hit rock bottom, wallowing in a pig trough far from home. To Jesus' audience the idea of a Jewish boy touching an "unclean" pig was appalling. Falling so far as to become a nursemaid to hogs would have been evidence of absolute failure. In verse 20 the defeated young man shuffled back to his father. In Jewish thought, the notion of return was inseparable from that of repentance. Ultimately, ancient Israel looked for a day when all Jews would return in penitence to a restored Israel, ruled by the Messiah.

Tradition has named Jesus' story the "Parable of the Prodigal (or Lost) Son." But a more accurate title might be the "Parable of the Compassionate Father and His Two Confused Sons." Both sons had total misconceptions about their father's nature. Each believed that his father's love and favor were contingent on his performance. The younger son assumed that he'd lost his father's love on the basis of his wasteful, immoral living (see vv. 18–19,21), while his brother was convinced that he should already have earned his father's appreciation and favor (see vv. 28–30).

Recovery is precisely that: a return based on repentance. Until we surrender our life completely to God's care, we're moving further and further away from him with every step. This is a journey Isaiah 53:6 describes as going our "own way," like a lost sheep. Recovery begins when, face down in our own personal pig trough, we realize that apart from God our life is a disaster. Repentance is the beginning of our journey back to the arms of our loving Father.

The lost son was smart enough to realize in the end that he couldn't handle his life apart from his father's provision, love and grace. Likewise, none of us can recover without the care of our loving Father. The lost son's father ran to take him in his arms, embracing him just because he was his son. There's nothing more important to our recovery than a clear understanding and acceptance of our heavenly Father's love. That love for sinners is so great that the apostle Peter explained the delay in Christ's return in relation to God's love: "The Lord is not slow in keeping his promise . . . he is patient with you, not wanting anyone to perish, but everyone to come to repentance" (2 Peter 3:9).

Like the lost son, our recovery can't begin until we realize how desperately we need our Father's love and provision, which are available to us in Jesus Christ. It's possible that we've repeatedly been sober for a season but that we've once again relapsed. Wherever we are right now, it's time to come home. Once we turn around to take those first steps, God's Son, Jesus, will run in our direction, thrilled at the opportunity to join us on our return journey.

heard all this and were sneering at Jesus. [15]He said to them, "You are the ones who justify yourselves in the eyes of others, but God knows your hearts. What people value highly is detestable in God's sight.

Additional Teachings

[16]"The Law and the Prophets were proclaimed until John. Since that time, the good news of the kingdom of God is being preached, and everyone is forcing their way into it. [17]It is easier for heaven and earth to disappear than for the least stroke of a pen to drop out of the Law.

[18]"Anyone who divorces his wife and marries another woman commits adultery, and the man who marries a divorced woman commits adultery.

The Rich Man and Lazarus

[19]"There was a rich man who was dressed in purple and fine linen and lived in luxury every day. [20]At his gate was laid a beggar named Lazarus, covered with sores [21]and longing to eat what fell from the rich man's table. Even the dogs came and licked his sores.

[22]"The time came when the beggar died and the angels carried him to Abraham's side. The rich man also died and was buried. [23]In Hades, where he was in torment, he looked up and saw Abraham far away, with Lazarus by his side. [24]So he called to him, 'Father Abraham, have pity on me and send Lazarus to dip the tip of his finger in water and cool my tongue, because I am in agony in this fire.'

[25]"But Abraham replied, 'Son, remember that in your lifetime you received your good things, while Lazarus received bad things, but now he is comforted here and you are in agony. [26]And besides all this, between us and you a great chasm has been set in place, so that those who want to go from here to you cannot, nor can anyone cross over from there to us.'

[27]"He answered, 'Then I beg you, father, send Lazarus to my family, [28]for I have five brothers. Let him warn them, so that they will not also come to this place of torment.'

[29]"Abraham replied, 'They have Moses and the Prophets; let them listen to them.'

[30]"'No, father Abraham,' he said, 'but if someone from the dead goes to them, they will repent.'

[31]"He said to him, 'If they do not listen to Moses and the Prophets, they will not be convinced even if someone rises from the dead.'"

Sin, Faith, Duty

17 Jesus said to his disciples: "Things that cause people to stumble are bound to come, but woe to anyone through whom they come. [2]It would be better for them to be thrown into the sea with a millstone tied around their neck than to cause one of these little ones to stumble. [3]So watch yourselves.

"If your brother or sister[a] sins against you, rebuke them; and if they repent, forgive them. [4]Even if they sin against you seven times in a day and seven times come back to you saying 'I repent,' you must forgive them."

[5]The apostles said to the Lord, "Increase our faith!"

[6]He replied, "If you have faith as small as a mustard seed, you can say to this mulberry tree, 'Be uprooted and planted in the sea,' and it will obey you.

[7]"Suppose one of you has a servant plowing or looking after the sheep. Will he say to the servant when he comes in from the field, 'Come along now and sit down to eat'? [8]Won't he rather say, 'Prepare my supper, get yourself ready and wait on me while I eat and drink; after that you may eat and drink'? [9]Will he thank the servant because he did what he was told to do? [10]So you also, when you have done everything you were told to do, should say, 'We are unworthy servants; we have only done our duty.'"

---

[a] 3 The Greek word for *brother or sister* (*adelphos*) refers here to a fellow disciple, whether man or woman.

My Name Is Johnny

I'm a believer who struggles with alcoholism

Please read Jesus' parable of the lost son (often called the "prodigal son") in Luke 15:11 – 32.

As long as I can remember I've had a relationship with God. As a preschooler I heard stories about Jesus and how much he loved me. As I grew older I participated in youth group activities, but I had a compulsion within me to go against the grain.

When I was 14 my parents separated due to my dad's alcoholism. I found in this the perfect excuse to act out. I tried pot for the first time and began having sex with my girlfriend. Fortunately, after 13 months, my parents reconciled, and our family began attending Saddleback Church.

My parents founded Celebrate Recovery, and I was one of the first participants. I began leading the teen group and became deeply involved with the youth group at Saddleback. A short time later I went through a Step Study as a codependent. At 16 I was determined never to struggle with alcohol.

When I was 21, though, I found myself on my own for the first time. Like the lost son of Jesus' parable, I felt as though I was in my own "distant country" (Luke 15:13). Until that time I hadn't been much of a drinker. All too soon, though, I was frequenting bars several nights each week, sometimes alone. Before long my habit escalated into a nightly activity. I convinced myself that I was 21 and just having fun.

There was one small problem, though: I was still volunteering every weekend at church. Deeply ashamed of the total hypocrisy this represented, I tried many times to stop drinking on my own. Around this time I met Jeni, who wasn't at all interested in a "drinking" Johnny. I knew I would have to keep the extent of my drinking a secret.

In December of 1999, I went to my friend's house to celebrate my birthday. At 3:30 a.m. I left for home. There was a problem: At this hour three days before Christmas I was the only car on the road that wasn't a police cruiser. I was pulled over and failed my field sobriety test. I remember rationalizing to myself, "I don't have a problem with alcohol. I just need to be smarter about driving after I drink."

Jeni and I got married in May of 2000. At first we rarely had alcohol in the house. I would sometimes convince her that we could enjoy margaritas or that we needed some kind of cooking alcohol. One night after she was asleep, I went into the kitchen and had a few drinks before returning to bed. This was the first time I drank behind her back, but it wasn't the last.

I worked nights as a waiter and had trouble sleeping after a busy shift. I began drinking as a way to fall asleep, and I came up with clever ways to disguise this activity. But I finally became aware that my drinking might be a problem when Jeni got pregnant with our first daughter. I decided to stop drinking and finally accepted that I was an alcoholic. When my daughter was born it had been eight months since my last drink, but I wasn't going to meetings or working the program. Thankfully, I was able to apply the recovery principles I'd learned as a teen, but I didn't have an accountability partner or a sponsor. When my daughter wouldn't sleep or cried a lot, I fantasized about having a drink. I knew at that point that it was time for me to get involved in Celebrate Recovery.

When I finally faced my addiction, I knew right where to go. Like the lost son in Luke, I returned to my father to ask for help. My parents never judged me. Instead, they loved me and helped me begin my true recovery.

I'm doing my best to work the program every day. I've found a sponsor and remind myself daily that Christ is in control and that it is only through him that I can remain sober. My sobriety has lasted now for over four years. There are still days when I feel overwhelmed, but I no longer think of drinking as a coping mechanism.

Friday nights have become a highlight of my week. I love the opportunity to worship and to *celebrate* my recovery. I openly share with my group without fear of judgment. I'm just me, banged up and imperfect, but because of Jesus' work I've been forgiven and am getting better each day. I now try to live by 2 Peter 1:5 – 7: "Make every effort to add to your faith goodness; and to goodness, knowledge; and to knowledge, self-control; and to self-control, perseverance; and to perseverance, godliness; and to godliness, mutual affection; and to mutual affection, love."

Jeni and I have been blessed with a second daughter, and I love knowing that as long as I keep working this program, she and her big sister will never have to watch me drink. Because I'm an adult child of an alcoholic who also chose to become an alcoholic, I'm determined to do my part to break this cycle of dysfunction in my family.

Jesus Heals Ten Men With Leprosy

11Now on his way to Jerusalem, Jesus traveled along the border between Samaria and Galilee. 12As he was going into a village, ten men who had leprosy*a* met him. They stood at a distance 13and called out in a loud voice, "Jesus, Master, have pity on us!"

14When he saw them, he said, "Go, show yourselves to the priests." And as they went, they were cleansed.

15One of them, when he saw he was healed, came back, praising God in a loud voice. 16He threw himself at Jesus' feet and thanked him—and he was a Samaritan.

17Jesus asked, "Were not all ten cleansed? Where are the other nine? 18Has no one returned to give praise to God except this foreigner?" 19Then he said to him, "Rise and go; your faith has made you well."

The Coming of the Kingdom of God

20Once, on being asked by the Pharisees when the kingdom of God would come, Jesus replied, "The coming of the kingdom of God is not something that can be observed, 21nor will people say, 'Here it is,' or 'There it is,' because the kingdom of God is in your midst."*b*

22Then he said to his disciples, "The time is coming when you will long to see one of the days of the Son of Man, but you will not see it. 23People will tell you, 'There he is!' or 'Here he is!' Do not go running off after them. 24For the Son of Man in his day*c* will be like the lightning, which flashes and lights up the sky from one end to the other. 25But first he must suffer many things and be rejected by this generation.

26"Just as it was in the days of Noah, so also will it be in the days of the Son of Man. 27People were eating, drinking, marrying and being given in marriage up to the day Noah entered the ark. Then the flood came and destroyed them all.

28"It was the same in the days of Lot. People were eating and drinking, buying and selling, planting and building. 29But the day Lot left Sodom, fire and sulfur rained down from heaven and destroyed them all.

30"It will be just like this on the day the Son of Man is revealed. 31On that day no one who is on the housetop, with possessions inside, should go down to get them. Likewise, no one in the field should go back for anything. 32Remember Lot's wife! 33Whoever tries to keep their life will lose it, and whoever loses their life will preserve it. 34I tell you, on that night two people will be in one bed; one will be taken and the other left. 35Two women will be grinding grain together; one will be taken and the other left." [36]*d*

37"Where, Lord?" they asked.

He replied, "Where there is a dead body, there the vultures will gather."

The Parable of the Persistent Widow

18 Then Jesus told his disciples a parable to show them that they should always pray and not give up. 2He said: "In a certain town there was a judge who neither feared God nor cared what people thought. 3And there was a widow in that town who kept coming to him with the plea, 'Grant me justice against my adversary.'

4"For some time he refused. But finally he said to himself, 'Even though I don't fear God or care what people think, 5yet because this widow keeps bothering me, I will see that she gets justice, so that she won't eventually come and attack me!'"

6And the Lord said, "Listen to what the unjust judge says. 7And will not God bring about justice for his chosen ones, who cry out to him day and night? Will he keep putting them off? 8I tell you, he will see that they get justice, and quickly. However,

---

a 12 The Greek word traditionally translated *leprosy* was used for various diseases affecting the skin.   *b 21* Or *is within you*   *c 24* Some manuscripts do not have *in his day.*   *d 36* Some manuscripts include here words similar to Matt. 24:40.

when the Son of Man comes, will he find faith on the earth?"

The Parable of the Pharisee and the Tax Collector

9To some who were confident of their own righteousness and looked down on everyone else, Jesus told this parable: 10"Two men went up to the temple to pray, one a Pharisee and the other a tax collector. 11The Pharisee stood by himself and prayed: 'God, I thank you that I am not like other people — robbers, evildoers, adulterers — or even like this tax collector. 12I fast twice a week and give a tenth of all I get.'

13"But the tax collector stood at a distance. He would not even look up to heaven, but beat his breast and said, 'God, have mercy on me, a sinner.'

14"I tell you that this man, rather than the other, went home justified before God. For all those who exalt themselves will be humbled, and those who humble themselves will be exalted."

The Little Children and Jesus

15People were also bringing babies to Jesus for him to place his hands on them. When the disciples saw this, they rebuked them. 16But Jesus called the children to him and said, "Let the little children come to me, and do not hinder them, for the kingdom of God belongs to such as these. 17Truly I tell you, anyone who will not receive the kingdom of God like a little child will never enter it."

The Rich and the Kingdom of God

18A certain ruler asked him, "Good teacher, what must I do to inherit eternal life?"

POWERLESS LESSON [Principle One]

For the previous entry in the POWERLESS lesson, go to John 10:10 (page 1311).

For a discussion of Principles One through Eight and a listing of their related lessons, go to pages xvii – xliv.

Whoever tries to keep their life will lose it,
and whoever loses their life will preserve it.

LUKE 17:33

The power to change comes only through God's grace. Principle One states: "Realize I'm not God. I admit that I'm powerless to control my tendency to do the wrong thing and that my life has become unmanageable." If we admit that we're powerless, we recognize our need for a power greater than ourselves to restore us. That power is our Higher Power, the one and only true Higher Power, Jesus Christ.

In Principle One we discover that we're POWERLESS to control our own lives and that our lives have become unmanageable. The first S in POWERLESS stands for SELFISHNESS. Simply put, selfishness is at the heart of most problems between people. Individuals have come into recovery thinking that the Lord's Prayer goes something like this: "Our Father who art in heaven,... Gimme ... gimme ... gimme." As we continue along on our road to recovery, we'll discover that we're becoming less self-centered.

For the last letter in POWERLESS, the second S, go to Romans 8:38 – 39 (page 1403).

[19]"Why do you call me good?" Jesus answered. "No one is good — except God alone. [20]You know the commandments: 'You shall not commit adultery, you shall not murder, you shall not steal, you shall not give false testimony, honor your father and mother.'[a]"

[21]"All these I have kept since I was a boy," he said.

[22]When Jesus heard this, he said to him, "You still lack one thing. Sell everything you have and give to the poor, and you will have treasure in heaven. Then come, follow me."

[23]When he heard this, he became very sad, because he was very wealthy. [24]Jesus looked at him and said, "How hard it is for the rich to enter the kingdom of God! [25]Indeed, it is easier for a camel to go through the eye of a needle than for someone who is rich to enter the kingdom of God."

[26]Those who heard this asked, "Who then can be saved?"

[27]Jesus replied, "What is impossible with man is possible with God."

[28]Peter said to him, "We have left all we had to follow you!"

[29]"Truly I tell you," Jesus said to them, "no one who has left home or wife or brothers or sisters or parents or children for the sake of the kingdom of God [30]will fail to receive many times as much in this age, and in the age to come eternal life."

Jesus Predicts His Death a Third Time

[31]Jesus took the Twelve aside and told them, "We are going up to Jerusalem, and everything that is written by the prophets about the Son of Man will be fulfilled. [32]He will be delivered over to the Gentiles. They will mock him, insult him and spit on him; [33]they will flog him and kill him. On the third day he will rise again."

[34]The disciples did not understand any of this. Its meaning was hidden from them, and they did not know what he was talking about.

A Blind Beggar Receives His Sight

[35]As Jesus approached Jericho, a blind man was sitting by the roadside begging. [36]When he heard the crowd going by, he asked what was happening. [37]They told him, "Jesus of Nazareth is passing by."

[38]He called out, "Jesus, Son of David, have mercy on me!"

[39]Those who led the way rebuked him and told him to be quiet, but he shouted all the more, "Son of David, have mercy on me!"

[40]Jesus stopped and ordered the man to be brought to him. When he came near, Jesus asked him, [41]"What do you want me to do for you?"

"Lord, I want to see," he replied.

[42]Jesus said to him, "Receive your sight; your faith has healed you." [43]Immediately he received his sight and followed Jesus, praising God. When all the people saw it, they also praised God.

Zacchaeus the Tax Collector

19 Jesus entered Jericho and was passing through. [2]A man was there by the name of Zacchaeus; he was a chief tax collector and was wealthy. [3]He wanted to see who Jesus was, but because he was short he could not see over the crowd. [4]So he ran ahead and climbed a sycamore-fig tree to see him, since Jesus was coming that way.

[5]When Jesus reached the spot, he looked up and said to him, "Zacchaeus, come down immediately. I must stay at your house today." [6]So he came down at once and welcomed him gladly.

[7]All the people saw this and began to mutter, "He has gone to be the guest of a sinner."

[8]But Zacchaeus stood up and said to the Lord, "Look, Lord! Here and now I give half of my possessions to the poor, and if I have cheated anybody out of anything, I will pay back four times the amount."

[9]Jesus said to him, "Today salvation has

---

[a] 20 Exodus 20:12-16; Deut. 5:16-20

come to this house, because this man, too, is a son of Abraham. ¹⁰For the Son of Man came to seek and to save the lost."

The Parable of the Ten Minas

¹¹While they were listening to this, he went on to tell them a parable, because he was near Jerusalem and the people thought that the kingdom of God was going to appear at once. ¹²He said: "A man of noble birth went to a distant country to have himself appointed king and then to return. ¹³So he called ten of his servants and gave them ten minas.ᵃ 'Put this money to work,' he said, 'until I come back.'

¹⁴"But his subjects hated him and sent a delegation after him to say, 'We don't want this man to be our king.'

¹⁵"He was made king, however, and returned home. Then he sent for the servants to whom he had given the money, in order to find out what they had gained with it.

¹⁶"The first one came and said, 'Sir, your mina has earned ten more.'

¹⁷"'Well done, my good servant!' his master replied. 'Because you have been trustworthy in a very small matter, take charge of ten cities.'

¹⁸"The second came and said, 'Sir, your mina has earned five more.'

¹⁹"His master answered, 'You take charge of five cities.'

²⁰"Then another servant came and said, 'Sir, here is your mina; I have kept it laid away in a piece of cloth. ²¹I was afraid of you, because you are a hard man. You take out what you did not put in and reap what you did not sow.'

²²"His master replied, 'I will judge you by your own words, you wicked servant! You knew, did you, that I am a hard man, taking out what I did not put in, and reaping what I did not sow? ²³Why then didn't you put my money on deposit, so that when I came back, I could have collected it with interest?'

²⁴"Then he said to those standing by, 'Take his mina away from him and give it to the one who has ten minas.'

²⁵"'Sir,' they said, 'he already has ten!'

²⁶"He replied, 'I tell you that to everyone who has, more will be given, but as for the one who has nothing, even what they have will be taken away. ²⁷But those enemies of mine who did not want me to be king over them—bring them here and kill them in front of me.'"

Jesus Comes to Jerusalem as King

²⁸After Jesus had said this, he went on ahead, going up to Jerusalem. ²⁹As he approached Bethphage and Bethany at the hill called the Mount of Olives, he sent two of his disciples, saying to them, ³⁰"Go to the village ahead of you, and as you enter it, you will find a colt tied there, which no one has ever ridden. Untie it and bring it here. ³¹If anyone asks you, 'Why are you untying it?' say, 'The Lord needs it.'"

³²Those who were sent ahead went and found it just as he had told them. ³³As they were untying the colt, its owners asked them, "Why are you untying the colt?"

³⁴They replied, "The Lord needs it."

³⁵They brought it to Jesus, threw their cloaks on the colt and put Jesus on it. ³⁶As he went along, people spread their cloaks on the road.

³⁷When he came near the place where the road goes down the Mount of Olives, the whole crowd of disciples began joyfully to praise God in loud voices for all the miracles they had seen:

³⁸"Blessed is the king who comes in the name of the Lord!"ᵇ

"Peace in heaven and glory in the highest!"

³⁹Some of the Pharisees in the crowd said to Jesus, "Teacher, rebuke your disciples!"

⁴⁰"I tell you," he replied, "if they keep quiet, the stones will cry out."

⁴¹As he approached Jerusalem and saw

ᵃ 13 A mina was about three months' wages.   ᵇ 38 Psalm 118:26

the city, he wept over it ⁴²and said, "If you, even you, had only known on this day what would bring you peace — but now it is hidden from your eyes. ⁴³The days will come upon you when your enemies will build an embankment against you and encircle you and hem you in on every side. ⁴⁴They will dash you to the ground, you and the children within your walls. They will not leave one stone on another, because you did not recognize the time of God's coming to you."

Jesus at the Temple

⁴⁵When Jesus entered the temple courts, he began to drive out those who were selling. ⁴⁶"It is written," he said to them, " 'My house will be a house of prayer'ᵃ; but you have made it 'a den of robbers.'ᵇ"

⁴⁷Every day he was teaching at the temple. But the chief priests, the teachers of the law and the leaders among the people were trying to kill him. ⁴⁸Yet they could not find any way to do it, because all the people hung on his words.

The Authority of Jesus Questioned

20 One day as Jesus was teaching the people in the temple courts and proclaiming the good news, the chief priests and the teachers of the law, together with the elders, came up to him. ²"Tell us by what authority you are doing these things," they said. "Who gave you this authority?"

³He replied, "I will also ask you a question. Tell me: ⁴John's baptism — was it from heaven, or of human origin?"

⁵They discussed it among themselves and said, "If we say, 'From heaven,' he will ask, 'Why didn't you believe him?' ⁶But if we say, 'Of human origin,' all the people will stone us, because they are persuaded that John was a prophet."

⁷So they answered, "We don't know where it was from."

⁸Jesus said, "Neither will I tell you by what authority I am doing these things."

The Parable of the Tenants

⁹He went on to tell the people this parable: "A man planted a vineyard, rented it to some farmers and went away for a long time. ¹⁰At harvest time he sent a servant to the tenants so they would give him some of the fruit of the vineyard. But the tenants beat him and sent him away empty-handed. ¹¹He sent another servant, but that one also they beat and treated shamefully and sent away empty-handed. ¹²He sent still a third, and they wounded him and threw him out.

¹³"Then the owner of the vineyard said, 'What shall I do? I will send my son, whom I love; perhaps they will respect him.'

¹⁴"But when the tenants saw him, they talked the matter over. 'This is the heir,' they said. 'Let's kill him, and the inheritance will be ours.' ¹⁵So they threw him out of the vineyard and killed him.

"What then will the owner of the vineyard do to them? ¹⁶He will come and kill those tenants and give the vineyard to others."

When the people heard this, they said, "God forbid!"

¹⁷Jesus looked directly at them and asked, "Then what is the meaning of that which is written:

" 'The stone the builders rejected
    has become the cornerstone'ᶜ?

¹⁸Everyone who falls on that stone will be broken to pieces; anyone on whom it falls will be crushed."

¹⁹The teachers of the law and the chief priests looked for a way to arrest him immediately, because they knew he had spoken this parable against them. But they were afraid of the people.

Paying Taxes to Caesar

²⁰Keeping a close watch on him, they sent spies, who pretended to be sincere. They hoped to catch Jesus in something he said, so that they might hand him over to

---

ᵃ 46 Isaiah 56:7   ᵇ 46 Jer. 7:11   ᶜ 17 Psalm 118:22

the power and authority of the governor. ²¹So the spies questioned him: "Teacher, we know that you speak and teach what is right, and that you do not show partiality but teach the way of God in accordance with the truth. ²²Is it right for us to pay taxes to Caesar or not?"

²³He saw through their duplicity and said to them, ²⁴"Show me a denarius. Whose image and inscription are on it?"

"Caesar's," they replied.

²⁵He said to them, "Then give back to Caesar what is Caesar's, and to God what is God's."

²⁶They were unable to trap him in what he had said there in public. And astonished by his answer, they became silent.

The Resurrection and Marriage

²⁷Some of the Sadducees, who say there is no resurrection, came to Jesus with a question. ²⁸"Teacher," they said, "Moses wrote for us that if a man's brother dies and leaves a wife but no children, the man must marry the widow and raise up offspring for his brother. ²⁹Now there were seven brothers. The first one married a woman and died childless. ³⁰The second ³¹and then the third married her, and in the same way the seven died, leaving no children. ³²Finally, the woman died too. ³³Now then, at the resurrection whose wife will she be, since the seven were married to her?"

³⁴Jesus replied, "The people of this age marry and are given in marriage. ³⁵But those who are considered worthy of taking part in the age to come and in the resurrection from the dead will neither marry nor be given in marriage, ³⁶and they can no longer die; for they are like the angels. They are God's children, since they are children of the resurrection. ³⁷But in the account of the burning bush, even Moses showed that the dead rise, for he calls the Lord 'the God of Abraham, and the God of Isaac, and the God of Jacob.'ᵃ ³⁸He is not the God of the dead, but of the living, for to him all are alive."

³⁹Some of the teachers of the law responded, "Well said, teacher!" ⁴⁰And no one dared to ask him any more questions.

Whose Son Is the Messiah?

⁴¹Then Jesus said to them, "Why is it said that the Messiah is the son of David? ⁴²David himself declares in the Book of Psalms:

"'The Lord said to my Lord:
    "Sit at my right hand
⁴³until I make your enemies
    a footstool for your feet."'ᵇ

⁴⁴David calls him 'Lord.' How then can he be his son?"

Warning Against the Teachers of the Law

⁴⁵While all the people were listening, Jesus said to his disciples, ⁴⁶"Beware of the teachers of the law. They like to walk around in flowing robes and love to be greeted with respect in the marketplaces and have the most important seats in the synagogues and the places of honor at banquets. ⁴⁷They devour widows' houses and for a show make lengthy prayers. These men will be punished most severely."

The Widow's Offering

21 As Jesus looked up, he saw the rich putting their gifts into the temple treasury. ²He also saw a poor widow put in two very small copper coins. ³"Truly I tell you," he said, "this poor widow has put in more than all the others. ⁴All these people gave their gifts out of their wealth; but she out of her poverty put in all she had to live on."

The Destruction of the Temple and Signs of the End Times

⁵Some of his disciples were remarking about how the temple was adorned with beautiful stones and with gifts dedicated to God. But Jesus said, ⁶"As for what you

---

ᵃ 37 Exodus 3:6   ᵇ 43 Psalm 110:1

see here, the time will come when not one stone will be left on another; every one of them will be thrown down."

7"Teacher," they asked, "when will these things happen? And what will be the sign that they are about to take place?"

8He replied: "Watch out that you are not deceived. For many will come in my name, claiming, 'I am he,' and, 'The time is near.' Do not follow them. 9When you hear of wars and uprisings, do not be frightened. These things must happen first, but the end will not come right away."

10Then he said to them: "Nation will rise against nation, and kingdom against kingdom. 11There will be great earthquakes, famines and pestilences in various places, and fearful events and great signs from heaven.

12"But before all this, they will seize you and persecute you. They will hand you over to synagogues and put you in prison, and you will be brought before kings and governors, and all on account of my name. 13And so you will bear testimony to me. 14But make up your mind not to worry beforehand how you will defend yourselves. 15For I will give you words and wisdom that none of your adversaries will be able to resist or contradict. 16You will be betrayed even by parents, brothers and sisters, relatives and friends, and they will put some of you to death. 17Everyone will hate you because of me. 18But not a hair of your head will perish. 19Stand firm, and you will win life.

20"When you see Jerusalem being surrounded by armies, you will know that its desolation is near. 21Then let those who are in Judea flee to the mountains, let those in the city get out, and let those in the country not enter the city. 22For this is the time of punishment in fulfillment of all that has been written. 23How dreadful it will be in those days for pregnant women and nursing mothers! There will be great distress in the land and wrath against this people. 24They will fall by the sword and will be taken as prisoners to all the nations. Jeru-

salem will be trampled on by the Gentiles until the times of the Gentiles are fulfilled.

25"There will be signs in the sun, moon and stars. On the earth, nations will be in anguish and perplexity at the roaring and tossing of the sea. 26People will faint from terror, apprehensive of what is coming on the world, for the heavenly bodies will be shaken. 27At that time they will see the Son of Man coming in a cloud with power and great glory. 28When these things begin to take place, stand up and lift up your heads, because your redemption is drawing near."

29He told them this parable: "Look at the fig tree and all the trees. 30When they sprout leaves, you can see for yourselves and know that summer is near. 31Even so, when you see these things happening, you know that the kingdom of God is near.

32"Truly I tell you, this generation will certainly not pass away until all these things have happened. 33Heaven and earth will pass away, but my words will never pass away.

34"Be careful, or your hearts will be weighed down with carousing, drunkenness and the anxieties of life, and that day will close on you suddenly like a trap. 35For it will come on all those who live on the face of the whole earth. 36Be always on the watch, and pray that you may be able to escape all that is about to happen, and that you may be able to stand before the Son of Man."

37Each day Jesus was teaching at the temple, and each evening he went out to spend the night on the hill called the Mount of Olives, 38and all the people came early in the morning to hear him at the temple.

Judas Agrees to Betray Jesus

22 Now the Festival of Unleavened Bread, called the Passover, was approaching, 2and the chief priests and the teachers of the law were looking for some way to get rid of Jesus, for they were afraid of the people. 3Then Satan entered Judas, called Iscariot, one of the Twelve. 4And Judas went to the chief priests and the officers of the temple guard and discussed with them how he might betray Jesus. [5]They were delighted and agreed to give him money. [6]He consented, and watched for an opportunity to hand Jesus over to them when no crowd was present.

The Last Supper

[7]Then came the day of Unleavened Bread on which the Passover lamb had to be sacrificed. [8]Jesus sent Peter and John, saying, "Go and make preparations for us to eat the Passover."

[9]"Where do you want us to prepare for it?" they asked.

[10]He replied, "As you enter the city, a man carrying a jar of water will meet you. Follow him to the house that he enters, [11]and say to the owner of the house, 'The Teacher asks: Where is the guest room, where I may eat the Passover with my disciples?' [12]He will show you a large room upstairs, all furnished. Make preparations there."

[13]They left and found things just as Jesus had told them. So they prepared the Passover.

[14]When the hour came, Jesus and his apostles reclined at the table. [15]And he said to them, "I have eagerly desired to eat this Passover with you before I suffer. [16]For I tell you, I will not eat it again until it finds fulfillment in the kingdom of God."

[17]After taking the cup, he gave thanks and said, "Take this and divide it among you. [18]For I tell you I will not drink again from the fruit of the vine until the kingdom of God comes."

[19]And he took bread, gave thanks and broke it, and gave it to them, saying, "This is my body given for you; do this in remembrance of me."

[20]In the same way, after the supper he took the cup, saying, "This cup is the new covenant in my blood, which is poured out for you.[a] [21]But the hand of him who is going to betray me is with mine on the table.

[22]The Son of Man will go as it has been decreed. But woe to that man who betrays him!" [23]They began to question among themselves which of them it might be who would do this.

[24]A dispute also arose among them as to which of them was considered to be greatest. [25]Jesus said to them, "The kings of the Gentiles lord it over them; and those who exercise authority over them call themselves Benefactors. [26]But you are not to be like that. Instead, the greatest among you should be like the youngest, and the one who rules like the one who serves. [27]For who is greater, the one who is at the table or the one who serves? Is it not the one who is at the table? But I am among you as one who serves. [28]You are those who have stood by me in my trials. [29]And I confer on you a kingdom, just as my Father conferred one on me, [30]so that you may eat and drink at my table in my kingdom and sit on thrones, judging the twelve tribes of Israel.

[31]"Simon, Simon, Satan has asked to sift all of you as wheat. [32]But I have prayed for you, Simon, that your faith may not fail. And when you have turned back, strengthen your brothers."

[33]But he replied, "Lord, I am ready to go with you to prison and to death."

[34]Jesus answered, "I tell you, Peter, before the rooster crows today, you will deny three times that you know me."

[35]Then Jesus asked them, "When I sent you without purse, bag or sandals, did you lack anything?"

"Nothing," they answered.

[36]He said to them, "But now if you have a purse, take it, and also a bag; and if you don't have a sword, sell your cloak and buy one. [37]It is written: 'And he was numbered with the transgressors'[b]; and I tell you that this must be fulfilled in me. Yes, what is written about me is reaching its fulfillment."

[38]The disciples said, "See, Lord, here are two swords."

"That's enough!" he replied.

---

a 19,20 Some manuscripts do not have *given for you . . . poured out for you.*   *b 37* Isaiah 53:12

Jesus Prays on the Mount of Olives

³⁹Jesus went out as usual to the Mount of Olives, and his disciples followed him. ⁴⁰On reaching the place, he said to them, "Pray that you will not fall into temptation." ⁴¹He withdrew about a stone's throw beyond them, knelt down and prayed, ⁴²"Father, if you are willing, take this cup from me; yet not my will, but yours be done." ⁴³An angel from heaven appeared to him and strengthened him. ⁴⁴And being in anguish, he prayed more earnestly, and his sweat was like drops of blood falling to the ground.ᵃ

⁴⁵When he rose from prayer and went back to the disciples, he found them asleep, exhausted from sorrow. ⁴⁶"Why are you sleeping?" he asked them. "Get up and pray so that you will not fall into temptation."

Jesus Arrested

⁴⁷While he was still speaking a crowd came up, and the man who was called Judas, one of the Twelve, was leading them. He approached Jesus to kiss him, ⁴⁸but Jesus asked him, "Judas, are you betraying the Son of Man with a kiss?"

⁴⁹When Jesus' followers saw what was going to happen, they said, "Lord, should we strike with our swords?" ⁵⁰And one of them struck the servant of the high priest, cutting off his right ear.

⁵¹But Jesus answered, "No more of this!" And he touched the man's ear and healed him.

⁵²Then Jesus said to the chief priests, the officers of the temple guard, and the elders, who had come for him, "Am I leading a rebellion, that you have come with swords and clubs? ⁵³Every day I was with you in the temple courts, and you did not lay a hand on me. But this is your hour — when darkness reigns."

Peter Disowns Jesus

⁵⁴Then seizing him, they led him away and took him into the house of the high priest. Peter followed at a distance. ⁵⁵And when some there had kindled a fire in the middle of the courtyard and had sat down together, Peter sat down with them. ⁵⁶A servant girl saw him seated there in the firelight. She looked closely at him and said, "This man was with him."

⁵⁷But he denied it. "Woman, I don't know him," he said.

⁵⁸A little later someone else saw him and said, "You also are one of them."

"Man, I am not!" Peter replied.

⁵⁹About an hour later another asserted, "Certainly this fellow was with him, for he is a Galilean."

⁶⁰Peter replied, "Man, I don't know what you're talking about!" Just as he was speaking, the rooster crowed. ⁶¹The Lord turned and looked straight at Peter. Then Peter remembered the word the Lord had spoken to him: "Before the rooster crows today, you will disown me three times." ⁶²And he went outside and wept bitterly.

The Guards Mock Jesus

⁶³The men who were guarding Jesus began mocking and beating him. ⁶⁴They blindfolded him and demanded, "Prophesy! Who hit you?" ⁶⁵And they said many other insulting things to him.

Jesus Before Pilate and Herod

⁶⁶At daybreak the council of the elders of the people, both the chief priests and the teachers of the law, met together, and Jesus was led before them. ⁶⁷"If you are the Messiah," they said, "tell us."

Jesus answered, "If I tell you, you will not believe me, ⁶⁸and if I asked you, you would not answer. ⁶⁹But from now on, the Son of Man will be seated at the right hand of the mighty God."

⁷⁰They all asked, "Are you then the Son of God?"

He replied, "You say that I am."

⁷¹Then they said, "Why do we need any more testimony? We have heard it from his own lips."

ᵃ 43,44 Many early manuscripts do not have verses 43 and 44.

23

Then the whole assembly rose and led him off to Pilate. ²And they began to accuse him, saying, "We have found this man subverting our nation. He opposes payment of taxes to Caesar and claims to be Messiah, a king."

³So Pilate asked Jesus, "Are you the king of the Jews?"

"You have said so," Jesus replied.

⁴Then Pilate announced to the chief priests and the crowd, "I find no basis for a charge against this man."

⁵But they insisted, "He stirs up the people all over Judea by his teaching. He started in Galilee and has come all the way here."

⁶On hearing this, Pilate asked if the man was a Galilean. ⁷When he learned that Jesus was under Herod's jurisdiction, he sent him to Herod, who was also in Jerusalem at that time.

⁸When Herod saw Jesus, he was greatly pleased, because for a long time he had been wanting to see him. From what he had heard about him, he hoped to see him perform a sign of some sort. ⁹He plied him with many questions, but Jesus gave him no answer. ¹⁰The chief priests and the teachers of the law were standing there, vehemently accusing him. ¹¹Then Herod and his soldiers ridiculed and mocked him. Dressing him in an elegant robe, they sent him back to Pilate. ¹²That day Herod and Pilate became friends — before this they had been enemies.

¹³Pilate called together the chief priests, the rulers and the people, ¹⁴and said to them, "You brought me this man as one who was inciting the people to rebellion. I have examined him in your presence and have found no basis for your charges against him. ¹⁵Neither has Herod, for he sent him back to us; as you can see, he has done nothing to deserve death. ¹⁶Therefore, I will punish him and then release him." [17] *a*

¹⁸But the whole crowd shouted, "Away with this man! Release Barabbas to us!" ¹⁹(Barabbas had been thrown into prison for an insurrection in the city, and for murder.)

²⁰Wanting to release Jesus, Pilate appealed to them again. ²¹But they kept shouting, "Crucify him! Crucify him!"

²²For the third time he spoke to them: "Why? What crime has this man committed? I have found in him no grounds for the death penalty. Therefore I will have him punished and then release him."

²³But with loud shouts they insistently demanded that he be crucified, and their shouts prevailed. ²⁴So Pilate decided to grant their demand. ²⁵He released the man who had been thrown into prison for insurrection and murder, the one they asked for, and surrendered Jesus to their will.

The Crucifixion of Jesus

²⁶As the soldiers led him away, they seized Simon from Cyrene, who was on his way in from the country, and put the cross on him and made him carry it behind Jesus. ²⁷A large number of people followed him, including women who mourned and wailed for him. ²⁸Jesus turned and said to them, "Daughters of Jerusalem, do not weep for me; weep for yourselves and for your children. ²⁹For the time will come when you will say, 'Blessed are the childless women, the wombs that never bore and the breasts that never nursed!' ³⁰Then

""'they will say to the mountains, "Fall
    on us!"
and to the hills, "Cover us!" ' *b*

³¹For if people do these things when the tree is green, what will happen when it is dry?"

³²Two other men, both criminals, were also led out with him to be executed. ³³When they came to the place called the Skull, they crucified him there, along with the criminals — one on his right, the other

---

a 17 Some manuscripts include here words similar to Matt. 27:15 and Mark 15:6.   *b 30* Hosea 10:8

on his left. 34Jesus said, "Father, forgive them, for they do not know what they are doing."*a* And they divided up his clothes by casting lots.

35The people stood watching, and the rulers even sneered at him. They said, "He saved others; let him save himself if he is God's Messiah, the Chosen One."

36The soldiers also came up and mocked him. They offered him wine vinegar 37and said, "If you are the king of the Jews, save yourself."

38There was a written notice above him, which read: THIS IS THE KING OF THE JEWS.

39One of the criminals who hung there hurled insults at him: "Aren't you the Messiah? Save yourself and us!"

40But the other criminal rebuked him. "Don't you fear God," he said, "since you are under the same sentence? 41We are punished justly, for we are getting what our deeds deserve. But this man has done nothing wrong."

42Then he said, "Jesus, remember me when you come into your kingdom.*b*"

43Jesus answered him, "Truly I tell you, today you will be with me in paradise."

The Death of Jesus

44It was now about noon, and darkness came over the whole land until three in the afternoon, 45for the sun stopped shining. And the curtain of the temple was torn in two. 46Jesus called out with a loud voice, "Father, into your hands I commit my spirit."*c* When he had said this, he breathed his last.

47The centurion, seeing what had happened, praised God and said, "Surely this was a righteous man." 48When all the people who had gathered to witness this sight saw what took place, they beat their breasts and went away. 49But all those who knew him, including the women who had followed him from Galilee, stood at a distance, watching these things.

The Burial of Jesus

50Now there was a man named Joseph, a member of the Council, a good and upright man, 51who had not consented to their decision and action. He came from the Judean town of Arimathea, and he himself was waiting for the kingdom of God. 52Going to Pilate, he asked for Jesus' body. 53Then he took it down, wrapped it in linen cloth and placed it in a tomb cut in the rock, one in which no one had yet been laid. 54It was Preparation Day, and the Sabbath was about to begin.

55The women who had come with Jesus from Galilee followed Joseph and saw the tomb and how his body was laid in it. 56Then they went home and prepared spices and perfumes. But they rested on the Sabbath in obedience to the commandment.

Jesus Has Risen

24 On the first day of the week, very early in the morning, the women took the spices they had prepared and went to the tomb. 2They found the stone rolled away from the tomb, 3but when they entered, they did not find the body of the Lord Jesus. 4While they were wondering about this, suddenly two men in clothes that gleamed like lightning stood beside them. 5In their fright the women bowed down with their faces to the ground, but the men said to them, "Why do you look for the living among the dead? 6He is not here; he has risen! Remember how he told you, while he was still with you in Galilee: 7'The Son of Man must be delivered over to the hands of sinners, be crucified and on the third day be raised again.'" 8Then they remembered his words.

9When they came back from the tomb, they told all these things to the Eleven and to all the others. 10It was Mary Magdalene, Joanna, Mary the mother of James, and the others with them who told this to the apos-

---

a 34 Some early manuscripts do not have this sentence.   *b 42* Some manuscripts *come with your kingly power*
c 46 Psalm 31:5

tles. [11]But they did not believe the women, because their words seemed to them like nonsense. [12]Peter, however, got up and ran to the tomb. Bending over, he saw the strips of linen lying by themselves, and he went away, wondering to himself what had happened.

On the Road to Emmaus

[13]Now that same day two of them were going to a village called Emmaus, about seven miles[a] from Jerusalem. [14]They were talking with each other about everything that had happened. [15]As they talked and discussed these things with each other, Jesus himself came up and walked along with them; [16]but they were kept from recognizing him.

[17]He asked them, "What are you discussing together as you walk along?"

They stood still, their faces downcast. [18]One of them, named Cleopas, asked him, "Are you the only one visiting Jerusalem who does not know the things that have happened there in these days?"

[19]"What things?" he asked.

"About Jesus of Nazareth," they replied. "He was a prophet, powerful in word and deed before God and all the people. [20]The chief priests and our rulers handed him over to be sentenced to death, and they crucified him; [21]but we had hoped that he was the one who was going to redeem Israel. And what is more, it is the third day since all this took place. [22]In addition, some of our women amazed us. They went to the tomb early this morning [23]but didn't find his body. They came and told us that they had seen a vision of angels, who said he was alive. [24]Then some of our companions went to the tomb and found it just as the women had said, but they did not see Jesus."

[25]He said to them, "How foolish you are, and how slow to believe all that the prophets have spoken! [26]Did not the Messiah have to suffer these things and then enter his glory?" [27]And beginning with Moses and all the Prophets, he explained to them what was said in all the Scriptures concerning himself.

[28]As they approached the village to which they were going, Jesus continued on as if he were going farther. [29]But they urged him strongly, "Stay with us, for it is nearly evening; the day is almost over." So he went in to stay with them.

[30]When he was at the table with them, he took bread, gave thanks, broke it and began to give it to them. [31]Then their eyes were opened and they recognized him, and he disappeared from their sight. [32]They asked each other, "Were not our hearts burning within us while he talked with us on the road and opened the Scriptures to us?"

[33]They got up and returned at once to Jerusalem. There they found the Eleven and those with them, assembled together [34]and saying, "It is true! The Lord has risen and has appeared to Simon." [35]Then the two told what had happened on the way, and how Jesus was recognized by them when he broke the bread.

Jesus Appears to the Disciples

[36]While they were still talking about this, Jesus himself stood among them and said to them, "Peace be with you."

[37]They were startled and frightened, thinking they saw a ghost. [38]He said to them, "Why are you troubled, and why do doubts rise in your minds? [39]Look at my hands and my feet. It is I myself! Touch me and see; a ghost does not have flesh and bones, as you see I have."

[40]When he had said this, he showed them his hands and feet. [41]And while they still did not believe it because of joy and amazement, he asked them, "Do you have anything here to eat?" [42]They gave him a piece of broiled fish, [43]and he took it and ate it in their presence.

[44]He said to them, "This is what I told you while I was still with you: Everything

---

[a] 13 Or about 11 kilometers

must be fulfilled that is written about me in the Law of Moses, the Prophets and the Psalms."

⁴⁵Then he opened their minds so they could understand the Scriptures. ⁴⁶He told them, "This is what is written: The Messiah will suffer and rise from the dead on the third day, ⁴⁷and repentance for the forgiveness of sins will be preached in his name to all nations, beginning at Jerusalem. ⁴⁸You are witnesses of these things. ⁴⁹I am going to send you what my Father has promised; but stay in the city until you have been clothed with power from on high."

The Ascension of Jesus

⁵⁰When he had led them out to the vicinity of Bethany, he lifted up his hands and blessed them. ⁵¹While he was blessing them, he left them and was taken up into heaven. ⁵²Then they worshiped him and returned to Jerusalem with great joy. ⁵³And they stayed continually at the temple, praising God.

John

THEME: Jesus' miracles fostered belief in some but only hardened unbelief and opposition in others. We say, "Seeing is believing," but in John believing is seeing.

AUTHOR: Scholars and early church tradition have long held that this Gospel was written by the apostle John, Jesus' disciple and a firsthand witness to the events recorded.

DATE OF WRITING: John was probably written between AD 89 and 95.

ENCOURAGEMENT FROM JOHN: "My sheep listen to my voice; I know them, and they follow me. I give them eternal life, and they shall never perish; no one will snatch them out of my hand" (John 10:27 – 28).

CHALLENGE FROM JOHN: "A new command I give you: Love one another. As I have loved you, so you must love one another. By this everyone will know that you are my disciples, if you love one another" (John 13:34 – 35).

REFLECTION FROM JOHN: "God did not send his Son into the world to condemn the world, but to save the world through him" (John 3:17).

The Gospel of John declares that Jesus is the Word of God. He was with God in the beginning, and through him the world was created. In fact, Jesus is not only with God, he is God.

Nothing in this universe was made without Jesus. In fact, it's only because of Jesus that we're able to take our next breath. And it's because of Jesus that we've been able to find healing for our past, hope for our present and assurance of a future, eternal home with him. Because of Jesus' light we're able to move through the steps of recovery and find true and lasting healing.

As we witness more of Jesus' miracles in this Gospel, we clearly see that he cares personally about our well-being. He loves us and wants us to be whole. In the Gospel of John, Jesus identifies himself as the good shepherd—the one who laid down his life for us, his sheep, so that we may be with him and the Father forever. Jesus has paid the full price for our sins and gladly welcomes us into his family.

The Word Became Flesh

1 In the beginning was the Word, and the Word was with God, and the Word was God. ²He was with God in the beginning. ³Through him all things were made; without him nothing was made that has been made. ⁴In him was life, and that life was the light of all mankind. ⁵The light shines in the darkness, and the darkness has not overcome*ᵃ* it.

⁶There was a man sent from God whose name was John. ⁷He came as a witness to testify concerning that light, so that through him all might believe. ⁸He himself

ᵃ 5 Or *understood*

was not the light; he came only as a witness to the light.

⁹The true light that gives light to everyone was coming into the world. ¹⁰He was in the world, and though the world was made through him, the world did not recognize him. ¹¹He came to that which was his own, but his own did not receive him. ¹²Yet to all who did receive him, to those who believed in his name, he gave the right to become children of God— ¹³children born not of natural descent, nor of human decision or a husband's will, but born of God.

¹⁴The Word became flesh and made his dwelling among us. We have seen his glory, the glory of the one and only Son, who came from the Father, full of grace and truth.

¹⁵(John testified concerning him. He cried out, saying, "This is the one I spoke about when I said, 'He who comes after me has surpassed me because he was before me.'") ¹⁶Out of his fullness we have all received grace in place of grace already given. ¹⁷For the law was given through Moses; grace and truth came through Jesus Christ. ¹⁸No one has ever seen God, but the one and only Son, who is himself God and*ᵃ* is in closest relationship with the Father, has made him known.

John the Baptist Denies Being the Messiah

¹⁹Now this was John's testimony when the Jewish leadersᵇ in Jerusalem sent priests and Levites to ask him who he was. ²⁰He did not fail to confess, but confessed freely, "I am not the Messiah."

²¹They asked him, "Then who are you? Are you Elijah?"

He said, "I am not."

"Are you the Prophet?"

He answered, "No."

²²Finally they said, "Who are you? Give us an answer to take back to those who sent us. What do you say about yourself?"

²³John replied in the words of Isaiah the prophet, "I am the voice of one calling in the wilderness, 'Make straight the way for the Lord.'"ᶜ

²⁴Now the Pharisees who had been sent ²⁵questioned him, "Why then do you baptize if you are not the Messiah, nor Elijah, nor the Prophet?"

²⁶"I baptize withᵈ water," John replied, "but among you stands one you do not know. ²⁷He is the one who comes after me, the straps of whose sandals I am not worthy to untie."

²⁸This all happened at Bethany on the other side of the Jordan, where John was baptizing.

John Testifies About Jesus

²⁹The next day John saw Jesus coming toward him and said, "Look, the Lamb of God, who takes away the sin of the world! ³⁰This is the one I meant when I said, 'A man who comes after me has surpassed me because he was before me.' ³¹I myself did not know him, but the reason I came baptizing with water was that he might be revealed to Israel."

³²Then John gave this testimony: "I saw the Spirit come down from heaven as a dove and remain on him. ³³And I myself did not know him, but the one who sent me to baptize with water told me, 'The man on whom you see the Spirit come down and remain is the one who will baptize with the Holy Spirit.' ³⁴I have seen and I testify that this is God's Chosen One."ᵉ

John's Disciples Follow Jesus

³⁵The next day John was there again with two of his disciples. ³⁶When he saw Jesus passing by, he said, "Look, the Lamb of God!"

³⁷When the two disciples heard him say this, they followed Jesus. ³⁸Turning around, Jesus saw them following and asked, "What do you want?"

ᵃ 18 Some manuscripts *but the only Son, who*   ᵇ 19 The Greek term traditionally translated *the Jews* (*hoi Ioudaioi*) refers here and elsewhere in John's Gospel to those Jewish leaders who opposed Jesus; also in 5:10, 15, 16; 7:1, 11, 13; 9:22; 18:14, 28, 36; 19:7, 12, 31, 38; 20:19.   ᶜ 23 Isaiah 40:3   ᵈ 26 Or *in*; also in verses 31 and 33 (twice) ᵉ 34 See Isaiah 42:1; many manuscripts *is the Son of God.*

They said, "Rabbi" (which means "Teacher"), "where are you staying?"

[39]"Come," he replied, "and you will see."

So they went and saw where he was staying, and they spent that day with him. It was about four in the afternoon.

[40]Andrew, Simon Peter's brother, was one of the two who heard what John had said and who had followed Jesus. [41]The first thing Andrew did was to find his brother Simon and tell him, "We have found the Messiah" (that is, the Christ). [42]And he brought him to Jesus.

Jesus looked at him and said, "You are Simon son of John. You will be called Cephas" (which, when translated, is Peter[a]).

Jesus Calls Philip and Nathanael

[43]The next day Jesus decided to leave for Galilee. Finding Philip, he said to him, "Follow me."

[44]Philip, like Andrew and Peter, was from the town of Bethsaida. [45]Philip found Nathanael and told him, "We have found the one Moses wrote about in the Law, and about whom the prophets also wrote — Jesus of Nazareth, the son of Joseph."

[46]"Nazareth! Can anything good come from there?" Nathanael asked.

"Come and see," said Philip.

[47]When Jesus saw Nathanael approaching, he said of him, "Here truly is an Israelite in whom there is no deceit."

[48]"How do you know me?" Nathanael asked.

Jesus answered, "I saw you while you were still under the fig tree before Philip called you."

[49]Then Nathanael declared, "Rabbi, you are the Son of God; you are the king of Israel."

[50]Jesus said, "You believe[b] because I told you I saw you under the fig tree. You will see greater things than that." [51]He then added, "Very truly I tell you,[c] you[c] will see 'heaven open, and the angels of God ascending and descending on'[d] the Son of Man."

Jesus Changes Water Into Wine

2 On the third day a wedding took place at Cana in Galilee. Jesus' mother was there, [2]and Jesus and his disciples had also been invited to the wedding. [3]When the wine was gone, Jesus' mother said to him, "They have no more wine."

[4]"Woman,[e] why do you involve me?" Jesus replied. "My hour has not yet come."

[5]His mother said to the servants, "Do whatever he tells you."

[6]Nearby stood six stone water jars, the kind used by the Jews for ceremonial washing, each holding from twenty to thirty gallons.[f]

[7]Jesus said to the servants, "Fill the jars with water"; so they filled them to the brim.

[8]Then he told them, "Now draw some out and take it to the master of the banquet."

They did so, [9]and the master of the banquet tasted the water that had been turned into wine. He did not realize where it had come from, though the servants who had drawn the water knew. Then he called the bridegroom aside [10]and said, "Everyone brings out the choice wine first and then the cheaper wine after the guests have had too much to drink; but you have saved the best till now."

[11]What Jesus did here in Cana of Galilee was the first of the signs through which he revealed his glory; and his disciples believed in him.

[12]After this he went down to Capernaum with his mother and brothers and his disciples. There they stayed for a few days.

Jesus Clears the Temple Courts

[13]When it was almost time for the Jewish Passover, Jesus went up to Jerusalem. [14]In

---

[a] 42 *Cephas* (Aramaic) and *Peter* (Greek) both mean *rock*.   [b] 50 Or *Do you believe...?*   [c] 51 The Greek is plural.   [d] 51 Gen. 28:12   [e] 4 The Greek for *Woman* does not denote any disrespect.   [f] 6 Or from about 75 to about 115 liters

Character Study

My Name Is Nathanael

JOHN 1:45–51

Nathanael seems to have been an honest seeker, a man who sought truth in the Scriptures and who refused to live behind a mask. Philip found Nathanael and informed him, no doubt with unveiled excitement, "We have found the one Moses wrote about in the Law, and about whom the prophets also wrote" (John 1:45). Nathanael made a skeptical, and possibly even cynical, response, but to his credit he did get up and follow Philip.

Jesus greeted Nathanael with the words: "Here truly is an Israelite in whom there is no deceit" (v. 47). Jesus informed Nathanael that he had seen him earlier "under the fig tree" (v. 48), a phrase that in Jesus' culture described the place where a rabbi might instruct his disciples. Such a shady spot might also have been a cool retreat for study and prayer. After Nathanael's response (amazingly, after so brief an introduction, he acknowledged Jesus as "Rabbi," "the Son of God" and "the king of Israel"—v. 49), Jesus alluded to the story of Jacob's ladder, one that he expected Nathanael to understand (see v. 51; see also Genesis 28:12).

Nathanael's diligent habit of Scripture study seems to have prepared him to meet Jesus. But knowledge alone is no substitute for a personal encounter with the Lord. That meeting occurred because of the invitation of a believer, and it resulted in Nathanael making his own decision to trust Jesus. To be convinced, Nathanael himself had to see, hear and converse with Jesus. Philip couldn't have done that for him.

Nathanael was a seeker after God. In recovery, it's often the pain of our own behavior that turns us into seekers. Like this young man, we may search the Scriptures, and we can certainly be introduced to Jesus through God's powerful Word, but often God uses a Philip, someone who is willing to take the time to share with us his or her own experience of the Lord. Such an individual can bring us, in a spiritual sense, face-to-face with Jesus.

However, each of us must make our own decision. When we do, we need to verbalize it, to share it in turn with others. Celebrate Recovery provides that opportunity. Testimonies from others in recovery, sharing in an Open Share Group, joining a Step Study, linking up with a sponsor and becoming a child of God in whom the Holy Spirit is at work—all these steps make honesty possible.

Nathanael declared his newfound faith in no uncertain terms (see John 1:49). He had already at that point begun his recovery. He was ready. As we experience God's transforming power in our own recovery, we'll want to share our experience with others who need to trust in Jesus. As we do, we must remember that not everyone will be ready to respond. Our responsibility is to maintain our own recovery and to willingly share the Good News about the one true Higher Power, Jesus Christ.

the temple courts he found people selling cattle, sheep and doves, and others sitting at tables exchanging money. 15So he made a whip out of cords, and drove all from the temple courts, both sheep and cattle; he scattered the coins of the money changers and overturned their tables. 16To those who sold doves he said, "Get these out of here! Stop turning my Father's house into a market!" 17His disciples remembered that it is written: "Zeal for your house will consume me."a

18The Jews then responded to him, "What sign can you show us to prove your authority to do all this?"

19Jesus answered them, "Destroy this temple, and I will raise it again in three days."

20They replied, "It has taken forty-six years to build this temple, and you are going to raise it in three days?" 21But the temple he had spoken of was his body. 22After he was raised from the dead, his disciples recalled what he had said. Then they believed the scripture and the words that Jesus had spoken.

23Now while he was in Jerusalem at the Passover Festival, many people saw the signs he was performing and believed in his name.b 24But Jesus would not entrust himself to them, for he knew all people. 25He did not need any testimony about mankind, for he knew what was in each person.

Jesus Teaches Nicodemus

3 Now there was a Pharisee, a man named Nicodemus who was a member of the Jewish ruling council. 2He came to Jesus at night and said, "Rabbi, we know that you are a teacher who has come from God. For no one could perform the signs you are doing if God were not with him."

3Jesus replied, "Very truly I tell you, no one can see the kingdom of God unless they are born again.c"

4"How can someone be born when they are old?" Nicodemus asked. "Surely they cannot enter a second time into their mother's womb to be born!"

5Jesus answered, "Very truly I tell you, no one can enter the kingdom of God unless they are born of water and the Spirit. 6Flesh gives birth to flesh, but the Spiritd gives birth to spirit. 7You should not be surprised at my saying, 'Youe must be born again.' 8The wind blows wherever it pleases. You hear its sound, but you cannot tell where it comes from or where it is going. So it is with everyone born of the Spirit."f

9"How can this be?" Nicodemus asked.

10"You are Israel's teacher," said Jesus, "and do you not understand these things? 11Very truly I tell you, we speak of what we know, and we testify to what we have seen, but still you people do not accept our testimony. 12I have spoken to you of earthly things and you do not believe; how then will you believe if I speak of heavenly things? 13No one has ever gone into heaven except the one who came from heaven—the Son of Man.g 14Just as Moses lifted up the snake in the wilderness, so the Son of Man must be lifted up,h 15that everyone who believes may have eternal life in him."i

16For God so loved the world that he gave his one and only Son, that whoever believes in him shall not perish but have eternal life. 17For God did not send his Son into the world to condemn the world, but to save the world through him. 18Whoever believes in him is not condemned, but whoever does not believe stands condemned already because they have not believed in the name of God's one and only Son. 19This is the verdict: Light has come into the world, but people loved darkness instead of light because their deeds were evil. 20Everyone who does evil hates the light, and will not

a 17 Psalm 69:9   b 23 Or in him   c 3 The Greek for again also means from above; also in verse 7.   d 6 Or but spirit   e 7 The Greek is plural.   f 8 The Greek for Spirit is the same as that for wind.   g 13 Some manuscripts Man, who is in heaven   h 14 The Greek for lifted up also means exalted.   i 15 Some interpreters end the quotation with verse 21.

My Name Is Joe

I'M A BELIEVER WHO STRUGGLES WITH ALCOHOLISM

Please read in John 1:43 – 51 the story of Nathanael's transformation from sarcasm to heartfelt acceptance of Jesus Christ.

I remember my first drink quite well. I was 13 years old, trying with my limited knowledge to understand why my parents had decided to get a divorce. I wondered for a long time, *Was it me? Was it something I did?* Drinking became my comfort — a newfound way of dealing with my pain.

This difficult passage in my young life took me on a journey of adolescent misbehavior. Through the course of my high school years I partied, drank daily and either skipped classes or ditched school altogether. This was my season of fake IDs and cocaine, my drug of choice at the time.

As I carried addiction into my adult life (my poison was now primarily alcohol), I found myself avoiding all financial responsibilities, wanting only to support my habit, a choice that led me into financial ruin. Over the span of two years I received two DUIs, the second of which landed me in jail for 30 days. That wasn't enough to capture my attention, but my next arrest definitely did. It became my moment of clarity. Ironically, the strangest feeling of relief settled over me; I knew right then that this would be the end to the insanity I'd been living with for so many years. Even as I'd continued to indulge my habit, I'd also continued to experience an unexplainable, chronic ache of loneliness that wouldn't leave me alone no matter how heavily I drank. For so long alcohol had merely camouflaged those feelings, had buried them temporarily just beneath the surface. In the conflict between God and alcohol, alcohol had always won out — until now.

This time I served 126 days in jail. I was hurting, but without alcohol to fall back on, I resorted to prayer. I prayed over and over again, crying out to a mysterious God I neither knew nor understood. I was overwhelmed by shame, embarrassment, guilt and loneliness. During my incarceration I heard about a program called Celebrate Recovery at Saddleback Church. I received a Bible that became my lifeline to God, and I became more and more thirsty to learn all I could about him. I read that Bible from cover to cover and began working the steps of recovery right then and there. I started attending counseling sessions with one of the jail psychologists, who helped me work through Step One through Step Four.

After my release from jail, I started attending Celebrate Recovery weekly and finished working both the principles and the 12 steps. I remember feeling as though I was finally home. The sense of belonging and the warmth of the people there were amazing. I had finally found Jesus Christ, my Savior and Lord.

My own story reminds me of the short Scriptural account of Nathanael's skepticism when it came to recognizing and accepting the long-awaited Messiah. When confronted with Philip's testimony that the Messiah had indeed come and that he was even then in their midst, Nathanael responded with derision: "Nazareth! Can anything good come from there?" (John 1:46). We can just hear the sarcasm dripping from his lips. But like Nathanael, I at long last found myself able to connect the head knowledge I'd obtained about Christ with my heart.

It was at that point that I distinctly heard God promise, "Never will I leave you; never will I forsake you" (Hebrews 13:5). The gaping hole in my heart had finally been filled. I asked God to remove my obsession to drink, and he has stripped it of its power over me for ten years now. I was once told that we can't keep our sobriety unless we're willing to give it away, so I've happily shared my experiences, victories and hopes with others. I joyfully give back to this program that has given me so much. We as believers are called upon to spread the light. So I focus on the miracles with which God has blessed me, as well as on the impact on my own heart of this wonderful, God-inspired, Christ-centered recovery program that has literally saved my life.

Today I know what true happiness is, and for this reason I wouldn't change a thing in my past. Although I wish I hadn't inflicted so much pain on my family, I now understand how necessary it was for me to go through what I did in order to come to grips with the underlying issues that were motivating my behavior. God has firmly gripped my shoulders and gently turned me around 180 degrees, and he has used this program to do it. Today I'm quick to admit when I'm wrong and willing to make amends promptly. I no longer leave behind me a wake of destruction, but instead help others to reconstruct their own shattered and battered lives. I try not to think primarily in terms of what will benefit me but try to focus instead on what I can do for the well-being of others. I appreciate the daily opportunity to grow in Christ and to dedicate myself to this ministry, serving side by side with my best friend on Earth — my wife.

Joe

come into the light for fear that their deeds will be exposed. 21But whoever lives by the truth comes into the light, so that it may be seen plainly that what they have done has been done in the sight of God.

John Testifies Again About Jesus

22After this, Jesus and his disciples went out into the Judean countryside, where he spent some time with them, and baptized. 23Now John also was baptizing at Aenon near Salim, because there was plenty of water, and people were coming and being baptized. 24(This was before John was put in prison.) 25An argument developed between some of John's disciples and a certain Jew over the matter of ceremonial washing. 26They came to John and said to him, "Rabbi, that man who was with you on the other side of the Jordan — the one you testified about — look, he is baptizing, and everyone is going to him."

27To this John replied, "A person can receive only what is given them from heaven. 28You yourselves can testify that I said, 'I am not the Messiah but am sent ahead of him.' 29The bride belongs to the bridegroom. The friend who attends the bridegroom waits and listens for him, and is full of joy when he hears the bridegroom's voice. That joy is mine, and it is now complete. 30He must become greater; I must become less."a

31The one who comes from above is above all; the one who is from the earth belongs to the earth, and speaks as one from the earth. The one who comes from heaven is above all. 32He testifies to what he has seen and heard, but no one accepts his testimony. 33Whoever has accepted it has certified that God is truthful. 34For the one whom God has sent speaks the words of God, for Godb gives the Spirit without limit. 35The Father loves the Son and has placed everything in his hands. 36Whoever believes in the Son has eternal life, but whoever rejects the Son will not see life, for God's wrath remains on them.

Jesus Talks With a Samaritan Woman

4 Now Jesus learned that the Pharisees had heard that he was gaining and baptizing more disciples than John — 2although in fact it was not Jesus who baptized, but his disciples. 3So he left Judea and went back once more to Galilee.

4Now he had to go through Samaria. 5So he came to a town in Samaria called Sychar, near the plot of ground Jacob had given to his son Joseph. 6Jacob's well was there, and Jesus, tired as he was from the journey, sat down by the well. It was about noon.

7When a Samaritan woman came to draw water, Jesus said to her, "Will you give me a drink?" 8(His disciples had gone into the town to buy food.)

9The Samaritan woman said to him, "You are a Jew and I am a Samaritan woman. How can you ask me for a drink?" (For Jews do not associate with Samaritans.c)

10Jesus answered her, "If you knew the gift of God and who it is that asks you for a drink, you would have asked him and he would have given you living water."

11"Sir," the woman said, "you have nothing to draw with and the well is deep. Where can you get this living water? 12Are you greater than our father Jacob, who gave us the well and drank from it himself, as did also his sons and his livestock?"

13Jesus answered, "Everyone who drinks this water will be thirsty again, 14but whoever drinks the water I give them will never thirst. Indeed, the water I give them will become in them a spring of water welling up to eternal life."

15The woman said to him, "Sir, give me this water so that I won't get thirsty and have to keep coming here to draw water."

16He told her, "Go, call your husband and come back."

17"I have no husband," she replied.

---

a 30 Some interpreters end the quotation with verse 36.   b 34 Greek he   c 9 Or do not use dishes Samaritans have used

Jesus said to her, "You are right when you say you have no husband. ¹⁸The fact is, you have had five husbands, and the man you now have is not your husband. What you have just said is quite true."

¹⁹"Sir," the woman said, "I can see that you are a prophet. ²⁰Our ancestors worshiped on this mountain, but you Jews claim that the place where we must worship is in Jerusalem."

²¹"Woman," Jesus replied, "believe me, a time is coming when you will worship the Father neither on this mountain nor in Jerusalem. ²²You Samaritans worship what you do not know; we worship what we do know, for salvation is from the Jews. ²³Yet a time is coming and has now come when the true worshipers will worship the Father in the Spirit and in truth, for they are the kind of worshipers the Father seeks. ²⁴God is spirit, and his worshipers must worship in the Spirit and in truth."

²⁵The woman said, "I know that Messiah" (called Christ) "is coming. When he comes, he will explain everything to us."

²⁶Then Jesus declared, "I, the one speaking to you — I am he."

The Disciples Rejoin Jesus

²⁷Just then his disciples returned and were surprised to find him talking with a woman. But no one asked, "What do you want?" or "Why are you talking with her?"

²⁸Then, leaving her water jar, the woman went back to the town and said to the people, ²⁹"Come, see a man who told me everything I ever did. Could this be the Messiah?" ³⁰They came out of the town and made their way toward him.

³¹Meanwhile his disciples urged him, "Rabbi, eat something."

³²But he said to them, "I have food to eat that you know nothing about."

³³Then his disciples said to each other, "Could someone have brought him food?"

³⁴"My food," said Jesus, "is to do the will of him who sent me and to finish his work. ³⁵Don't you have a saying, 'It's still four months until harvest'? I tell you, open your eyes and look at the fields! They are ripe for harvest. ³⁶Even now the one who reaps draws a wage and harvests a crop for eternal life, so that the sower and the reaper may be glad together. ³⁷Thus the saying 'One sows and another reaps' is true. ³⁸I sent you to reap what you have not worked for. Others have done the hard work, and you have reaped the benefits of their labor."

Many Samaritans Believe

³⁹Many of the Samaritans from that town believed in him because of the woman's testimony, "He told me everything I ever did." ⁴⁰So when the Samaritans came to him, they urged him to stay with them, and he stayed two days. ⁴¹And because of his words many more became believers.

⁴²They said to the woman, "We no longer believe just because of what you said; now we have heard for ourselves, and we know that this man really is the Savior of the world."

Jesus Heals an Official's Son

⁴³After the two days he left for Galilee. ⁴⁴(Now Jesus himself had pointed out that a prophet has no honor in his own country.) ⁴⁵When he arrived in Galilee, the Galileans welcomed him. They had seen all that he had done in Jerusalem at the Passover Festival, for they also had been there.

⁴⁶Once more he visited Cana in Galilee, where he had turned the water into wine. And there was a certain royal official whose son lay sick at Capernaum. ⁴⁷When this man heard that Jesus had arrived in Galilee from Judea, he went to him and begged him to come and heal his son, who was close to death.

⁴⁸"Unless you people see signs and wonders," Jesus told him, "you will never believe."

⁴⁹The royal official said, "Sir, come down before my child dies."

⁵⁰"Go," Jesus replied, "your son will live."

The man took Jesus at his word and departed. ⁵¹While he was still on the way, his servants met him with the news that his

MY NAME IS
THE WOMAN AT THE WELL

JOHN 4:1-26,39-42

When the Jewish man asked her for a drink, she was wary. Every earlier experience in her life excluded the possibility that she could trust a man. Her instinctive caution was intensified by the fact that she was a Samaritan, an unclean person in the eyes of most Jews. Her suspicions provoked an immediate question: "You are a Jew and I am a Samaritan woman. How can you ask me for a drink?" (John 4:9). Jesus' reply included an offer of "living water" (v. 10). The suspicious woman had no idea what that might mean, but she knew that men lived to take, not to give. Still, her curiosity overcame her disgust; she did want to know how this strange man thought he could give her water when he had no jar or rope. So she engaged him in conversation, and his responses confused her even more.

The mysterious stranger claimed that he could give her water that would forever quench her thirst, water that would give her eternal life. That sounded too good to be true. She admitted to him that she was ready to end her exhausting trips to the well. But that response didn't seem to satisfy the man. Impossibly, he revealed his knowledge of her secret shame (see vv. 16–18). Her life so far had been bound up in giving men her body in the hope of satisfying her own thirst, her desperate need to be desired—no, to be loved. She had bounced from one destructive relationship to another, a pattern she seemed helpless to change.

This wounded woman was determined to conceal her hurts. Initially, she ignored the truth about her own life and tried to change the painful path this conversation was taking. Clearly the man was a prophet. So it should be easy enough to shift the focus from herself onto the religious rift between Samaritans and Jews. But he wouldn't enter into a debate, choosing instead to inform her simply that an hour was coming when truth would triumph and real worship would be a matter of spiritual condition and truth, not mountaintops or temples (see vv. 21–24).

His simple words fired the embers of hope, hidden somewhere deep within an otherwise frozen and aloof heart. He was speaking of the Messiah who would solve all problems, end all conflicts and answer all questions. Then he threw in the clincher, declaring that *he* was that Messiah, her Savior (see v. 26).

Why did this Samaritan woman find it so hard to understand the Master? So hard to focus on the reality of her own need? Sin and shame harden our hearts and pervert our perceptions. We become blind to reality and oblivious to the deliverance available to us in Jesus Christ.

Jesus cared enough for this woman to confront her with her sins and to fan into flame the embers of her hope in a coming Messiah. He was offering her real love, real life. Once she recognized the greatness of the gift, she felt compelled to share it with her fellow villagers (see vv. 28–30).

boy was living. ⁵²When he inquired as to the time when his son got better, they said to him, "Yesterday, at one in the afternoon, the fever left him."

⁵³Then the father realized that this was the exact time at which Jesus had said to him, "Your son will live." So he and his whole household believed.

⁵⁴This was the second sign Jesus performed after coming from Judea to Galilee.

The Healing at the Pool

5 Some time later, Jesus went up to Jerusalem for one of the Jewish festivals. ²Now there is in Jerusalem near the Sheep Gate a pool, which in Aramaic is called Bethesda*ᵃ* and which is surrounded by five covered colonnades. ³Here a great number of disabled people used to lie — the blind, the lame, the paralyzed. [4] *ᵇ* ⁵One who was there had been an invalid for thirty-eight years. ⁶When Jesus saw him lying there and learned that he had been in this condition for a long time, he asked him, "Do you want to get well?"

⁷"Sir," the invalid replied, "I have no one to help me into the pool when the water is stirred. While I am trying to get in, someone else goes down ahead of me."

⁸Then Jesus said to him, "Get up! Pick up your mat and walk." ⁹At once the man was cured; he picked up his mat and walked.

The day on which this took place was a Sabbath, ¹⁰and so the Jewish leaders said to the man who had been healed, "It is the Sabbath; the law forbids you to carry your mat."

¹¹But he replied, "The man who made me well said to me, 'Pick up your mat and walk.'"

¹²So they asked him, "Who is this fellow who told you to pick it up and walk?"

¹³The man who was healed had no idea who it was, for Jesus had slipped away into the crowd that was there.

¹⁴Later Jesus found him at the temple and said to him, "See, you are well again. Stop sinning or something worse may happen to you." ¹⁵The man went away and told the Jewish leaders that it was Jesus who had made him well.

The Authority of the Son

¹⁶So, because Jesus was doing these things on the Sabbath, the Jewish leaders began to persecute him. ¹⁷In his defense Jesus said to them, "My Father is always at his work to this very day, and I too am working." ¹⁸For this reason they tried all the more to kill him; not only was he breaking the Sabbath, but he was even calling God his own Father, making himself equal with God.

¹⁹Jesus gave them this answer: "Very truly I tell you, the Son can do nothing by himself; he can do only what he sees his Father doing, because whatever the Father does the Son also does. ²⁰For the Father loves the Son and shows him all he does. Yes, and he will show him even greater works than these, so that you will be amazed. ²¹For just as the Father raises the dead and gives them life, even so the Son gives life to whom he is pleased to give it. ²²Moreover, the Father judges no one, but has entrusted all judgment to the Son, ²³that all may honor the Son just as they honor the Father. Whoever does not honor the Son does not honor the Father, who sent him.

²⁴"Very truly I tell you, whoever hears my word and believes him who sent me has eternal life and will not be judged but has crossed over from death to life. ²⁵Very truly I tell you, a time is coming and has now come when the dead will hear the voice of the Son of God and those who hear will live. ²⁶For as the Father has life in himself, so he has granted the Son also to have life in himself. ²⁷And he has given him authority to judge because he is the Son of Man.

ᵃ 2 Some manuscripts *Bethzatha*; other manuscripts *Bethsaida*   *ᵇ 3,4* Some manuscripts include here, wholly or in part, *paralyzed — and they waited for the moving of the waters. ⁴From time to time an angel of the Lord would come down and stir up the waters. The first one into the pool after each such disturbance would be cured of whatever disease they had.*

My Name Is Tina

I'M A BELIEVER WHO STRUGGLES WITH SEXUAL ADDICTION

Please read the story of Jesus' encounter with the woman at the well in John 4:1 – 42.

I grew up in a love-hate family relationship with constant chaos. The methods of communication during conflict were yelling, name-calling and door slamming. There was no resolution, no forgiveness. The central battleground for my parents' arguments was the table at dinnertime. When they fought about finances, I felt like a burden. When they fought about parenting, I felt unwanted. When they fought about sex, I felt dirty.

One afternoon I found a box of pornographic magazines. I became visually obsessed; when the magazines disappeared, I sought out illicit books. This started me down a dark path, creating a thought life that took me in and out of reality. In high school my mind was consumed with sexual thoughts about my teachers and classmates. The only fulfillment I found was in attending parties. When I came home late, my mom would knock me to the ground and call me a whore. I raged inside but knew I couldn't say a word or shed a tear. My father was willing to communicate with me, but my heart was too hard. In my rebellion, I gave away my virginity at the age of 14. I continued being sexually active with my boyfriends. Eventually, at 17, I became pregnant and aborted my child.

One afternoon I overheard my father tell my mother that there was blood in his urine. It turned out his kidney was filled with cancer. Over the next six months I watched him deteriorate and then die in a hospital bed. I became a lost soul, a hazard to myself. My life revolved around bars and men; my steady relationships always ended up broken due to my constant unfaithfulness to the men who cared most about me.

I took a job in "corporate America" and changed my appearance. But this new environment only brought greater temptations. Over the next two years I engaged in illicit relationships, mostly with men I knew: married coworkers, someone else's boyfriend, a friend's husband. My roommate asked me how I did it. My answer: "I just keep it separate."

The night I met my husband-to-be I was convinced he could save me from myself. Shortly thereafter I became pregnant. Unable to justify another abortion, I agreed to get married, only to abort the baby three months later. Following the procedure I told everyone I'd experienced a miscarriage. I buried this lie deep inside me.

Eventually we married and moved into a new house. My surroundings changed, but I didn't. By the third year of our marriage I was allowing myself thoughts of other men. Then one day I crossed the line with a coworker. This triggered a resurgence of my old behavior, only this time it was worse. After each affair I swore I'd never do it again. Unable to focus, I was eventually fired from my job.

One night I was invited to an evangelical crusade. The pastor spoke about Jesus and the woman at the well and all the men in her life (see John 4:18). The Holy Spirit began pulling on my heart, but I fought him; no way could this Christ love or want me. I shared the sentiment of the woman at the well, asking, "How is it that you would ask me for a drink since I am an adulterer?" (v. 9, author's paraphrase). I ran from the stadium, but something inside me had changed.

Weeks later I went alone to Saddleback Church and asked Jesus into my life. Slowly God began revealing his knowledge of my secret shame. I told my husband the truth about the abortion and the affairs, including the one I'd pursued with our neighbor, his best friend. He admitted that he'd had suspicions but had never wanted to face the truth. As he walked out of my life, I felt paralyzed.

I couldn't understand why I habitually risked everything for sex. I tried to keep the secrets in my life separate, this time from my relationship with the Creator of the universe. But God was too big for me, and I finally started attending Celebrate Recovery. Pastor John was teaching on Principle One: "Realize I'm not God. I admit that I'm powerless to control my tendency to do the wrong thing and that my life has become unmanageable." As I worked the Biblical principles, I began to feel whole.

Today I don't hide behind my addictions as an excuse for my past behavior. I recognize them as sin in my life. I've come to realize that female sexual addiction isn't something new; it's misunderstood. I wasn't looking for love; I was running from love, fearing commitment and true intimacy. I've learned that it was never about sex but about acting out my deep wounds, my inadequacies, rage, self-hatred and need to be in control. I've learned that my self-worth comes from my identity in Christ. I've accepted Jesus' living water (see vv. 13–14) — and have never thirsted again.

God led me to pioneer a Celebrate Recovery women's group for sexual addiction. I have now been serving with Celebrate Recovery since 1996. I've had opportunities to lead seven Step Study groups and have sponsored dozens of women. I'm serving full time on Saddleback Church's staff with Celebrate Recovery.

28"Do not be amazed at this, for a time is coming when all who are in their graves will hear his voice 29and come out — those who have done what is good will rise to live, and those who have done what is evil will rise to be condemned. 30By myself I can do nothing; I judge only as I hear, and my judgment is just, for I seek not to please myself but him who sent me.

Testimonies About Jesus

31"If I testify about myself, my testimony is not true. 32There is another who testifies in my favor, and I know that his testimony about me is true.

33"You have sent to John and he has testified to the truth. 34Not that I accept human testimony; but I mention it that you may be saved. 35John was a lamp that burned and gave light, and you chose for a time to enjoy his light.

36"I have testimony weightier than that of John. For the works that the Father has given me to finish — the very works that I am doing — testify that the Father has sent me. 37And the Father who sent me has himself testified concerning me. You have never heard his voice nor seen his form, 38nor does his word dwell in you, for you do not believe the one he sent. 39You study*a* the Scriptures diligently because you think that in them you have eternal life. These are the very Scriptures that testify about me, 40yet you refuse to come to me to have life.

41"I do not accept glory from human beings, 42but I know you. I know that you do not have the love of God in your hearts. 43I have come in my Father's name, and you do not accept me; but if someone else comes in his own name, you will accept him. 44How can you believe since you accept glory from one another but do not seek the glory that comes from the only God*b*?

45"But do not think I will accuse you before the Father. Your accuser is Moses, on whom your hopes are set. 46If you believed Moses, you would believe me, for he wrote about me. 47But since you do not believe what he wrote, how are you going to believe what I say?"

Jesus Feeds the Five Thousand

6 Some time after this, Jesus crossed to the far shore of the Sea of Galilee (that is, the Sea of Tiberias), 2and a great crowd of people followed him because they saw the signs he had performed by healing the sick. 3Then Jesus went up on a mountainside and sat down with his disciples. 4The Jewish Passover Festival was near.

5When Jesus looked up and saw a great crowd coming toward him, he said to Philip, "Where shall we buy bread for these people to eat?" 6He asked this only to test him, for he already had in mind what he was going to do.

7Philip answered him, "It would take more than half a year's wages*c* to buy enough bread for each one to have a bite!"

8Another of his disciples, Andrew, Simon Peter's brother, spoke up, 9"Here is a boy with five small barley loaves and two small fish, but how far will they go among so many?"

10Jesus said, "Have the people sit down." There was plenty of grass in that place, and they sat down (about five thousand men were there). 11Jesus then took the loaves, gave thanks, and distributed to those who were seated as much as they wanted. He did the same with the fish.

12When they had all had enough to eat, he said to his disciples, "Gather the pieces that are left over. Let nothing be wasted." 13So they gathered them and filled twelve baskets with the pieces of the five barley loaves left over by those who had eaten.

14After the people saw the sign Jesus performed, they began to say, "Surely this is the Prophet who is to come into the world." 15Jesus, knowing that they intended to come and make him king by force, withdrew again to a mountain by himself.

---

a 39 Or 39*Study*   *b* 44 Some early manuscripts *the Only One*   *c* 7 Greek *take two hundred denarii*

Jesus Walks on the Water

16When evening came, his disciples went down to the lake, 17where they got into a boat and set off across the lake for Capernaum. By now it was dark, and Jesus had not yet joined them. 18A strong wind was blowing and the waters grew rough. 19When they had rowed about three or four miles,ᵃ they saw Jesus approaching the boat, walking on the water; and they were frightened. 20But he said to them, "It is I; don't be afraid." 21Then they were willing to take him into the boat, and immediately the boat reached the shore where they were heading.

22The next day the crowd that had stayed on the opposite shore of the lake realized that only one boat had been there, and that Jesus had not entered it with his disciples, but that they had gone away alone. 23Then some boats from Tiberias landed near the place where the people had eaten the bread after the Lord had given thanks. 24Once the crowd realized that neither Jesus nor his disciples were there, they got into the boats and went to Capernaum in search of Jesus.

Jesus the Bread of Life

25When they found him on the other side of the lake, they asked him, "Rabbi, when did you get here?"

26Jesus answered, "Very truly I tell you, you are looking for me, not because you saw the signs I performed but because you ate the loaves and had your fill. 27Do not work for food that spoils, but for food that endures to eternal life, which the Son of Man will give you. For on him God the Father has placed his seal of approval."

28Then they asked him, "What must we do to do the works God requires?"

29Jesus answered, "The work of God is this: to believe in the one he has sent."

30So they asked him, "What sign then will you give that we may see it and believe you? What will you do? 31Our ancestors ate the manna in the wilderness; as it is writ-

ten: 'He gave them bread from heaven to eat.'ᵇ"

32Jesus said to them, "Very truly I tell you, it is not Moses who has given you the bread from heaven, but it is my Father who gives you the true bread from heaven. 33For the bread of God is the bread that comes down from heaven and gives life to the world."

34"Sir," they said, "always give us this bread."

35Then Jesus declared, "I am the bread of life. Whoever comes to me will never go hungry, and whoever believes in me will never be thirsty. 36But as I told you, you have seen me and still you do not believe. 37All those the Father gives me will come to me, and whoever comes to me I will never drive away. 38For I have come down from heaven not to do my will but to do the will of him who sent me. 39And this is the will of him who sent me, that I shall lose none of all those he has given me, but raise them up at the last day. 40For my Father's will is that everyone who looks to the Son and believes in him shall have eternal life, and I will raise them up at the last day."

41At this the Jews there began to grumble about him because he said, "I am the bread that came down from heaven." 42They said, "Is this not Jesus, the son of Joseph, whose father and mother we know? How can he now say, 'I came down from heaven'?"

43"Stop grumbling among yourselves," Jesus answered. 44"No one can come to me unless the Father who sent me draws them, and I will raise them up at the last day. 45It is written in the Prophets: 'They will all be taught by God.'ᶜ Everyone who has heard the Father and learned from him comes to me. 46No one has seen the Father except the one who is from God; only he has seen the Father. 47Very truly I tell you, the one who believes has eternal life. 48I am the bread of life. 49Your ancestors ate the manna in the wilderness, yet they died. 50But here is the bread that comes down from heaven,

---

ᵃ 19 Or about 5 or 6 kilometers   ᵇ 31 Exodus 16:4; Neh. 9:15; Psalm 78:24,25   ᶜ 45 Isaiah 54:13

which anyone may eat and not die. 51I am the living bread that came down from heaven. Whoever eats this bread will live forever. This bread is my flesh, which I will give for the life of the world."

52Then the Jews began to argue sharply among themselves, "How can this man give us his flesh to eat?"

53Jesus said to them, "Very truly I tell you, unless you eat the flesh of the Son of Man and drink his blood, you have no life in you. 54Whoever eats my flesh and drinks my blood has eternal life, and I will raise them up at the last day. 55For my flesh is real food and my blood is real drink. 56Whoever eats my flesh and drinks my blood remains in me, and I in them. 57Just as the living Father sent me and I live because of the Father, so the one who feeds on me will live because of me. 58This is the bread that came down from heaven. Your ancestors ate manna and died, but whoever feeds on this bread will live forever." 59He said this while teaching in the synagogue in Capernaum.

Many Disciples Desert Jesus

60On hearing it, many of his disciples said, "This is a hard teaching. Who can accept it?"

61Aware that his disciples were grumbling about this, Jesus said to them, "Does this offend you? 62Then what if you see the Son of Man ascend to where he was before! 63The Spirit gives life; the flesh counts for nothing. The words I have spoken to you—they are full of the Spirit*a* and life. 64Yet there are some of you who do not believe." For Jesus had known from the beginning which of them did not believe and who would betray him. 65He went on to say, "This is why I told you that no one can come to me unless the Father has enabled them."

66From this time many of his disciples turned back and no longer followed him.

67"You do not want to leave too, do you?" Jesus asked the Twelve.

68Simon Peter answered him, "Lord, to whom shall we go? You have the words of eternal life. 69We have come to believe and to know that you are the Holy One of God."

70Then Jesus replied, "Have I not chosen you, the Twelve? Yet one of you is a devil!" 71(He meant Judas, the son of Simon Iscariot, who, though one of the Twelve, was later to betray him.)

Jesus Goes to the Festival of Tabernacles

7 After this, Jesus went around in Galilee. He did not want*b* to go about in Judea because the Jewish leaders there were looking for a way to kill him. 2But when the Jewish Festival of Tabernacles was near, 3Jesus' brothers said to him, "Leave Galilee and go to Judea, so that your disciples there may see the works you do. 4No one who wants to become a public figure acts in secret. Since you are doing these things, show yourself to the world." 5For even his own brothers did not believe in him.

6Therefore Jesus told them, "My time is not yet here; for you any time will do. 7The world cannot hate you, but it hates me because I testify that its works are evil. 8You go to the festival. I am not*c* going up to this festival, because my time has not yet fully come." 9After he had said this, he stayed in Galilee.

10However, after his brothers had left for the festival, he went also, not publicly, but in secret. 11Now at the festival the Jewish leaders were watching for Jesus and asking, "Where is he?"

12Among the crowds there was widespread whispering about him. Some said, "He is a good man."

Others replied, "No, he deceives the people." 13But no one would say anything publicly about him for fear of the leaders.

Jesus Teaches at the Festival

14Not until halfway through the festival did Jesus go up to the temple courts and begin to teach. 15The Jews there were amazed

---

a 63 Or *are Spirit*; or *are spirit*   *b* 1 Some manuscripts *not have authority*   *c* 8 Some manuscripts *not yet* and asked, "How did this man get such learning without having been taught?"

16 Jesus answered, "My teaching is not my own. It comes from the one who sent me. 17 Anyone who chooses to do the will of God will find out whether my teaching comes from God or whether I speak on my own. 18 Whoever speaks on their own does so to gain personal glory, but he who seeks the glory of the one who sent him is a man of truth; there is nothing false about him. 19 Has not Moses given you the law? Yet not one of you keeps the law. Why are you trying to kill me?"

20 "You are demon-possessed," the crowd answered. "Who is trying to kill you?"

21 Jesus said to them, "I did one miracle, and you are all amazed. 22 Yet, because Moses gave you circumcision (though actually it did not come from Moses, but from the patriarchs), you circumcise a boy on the Sabbath. 23 Now if a boy can be circumcised on the Sabbath so that the law of Moses may not be broken, why are you angry with me for healing a man's whole body on the Sabbath? 24 Stop judging by mere appearances, but instead judge correctly."

Division Over Who Jesus Is

25 At that point some of the people of Jerusalem began to ask, "Isn't this the man they are trying to kill? 26 Here he is, speaking publicly, and they are not saying a word to him. Have the authorities really concluded that he is the Messiah? 27 But we know where this man is from; when the Messiah comes, no one will know where he is from."

28 Then Jesus, still teaching in the temple courts, cried out, "Yes, you know me, and you know where I am from. I am not here on my own authority, but he who sent me is true. You do not know him, 29 but I know him because I am from him and he sent me."

30 At this they tried to seize him, but no one laid a hand on him, because his hour had not yet come. 31 Still, many in the crowd believed in him. They said, "When the Messiah comes, will he perform more signs than this man?"

32 The Pharisees heard the crowd whispering such things about him. Then the chief priests and the Pharisees sent temple guards to arrest him.

33 Jesus said, "I am with you for only a short time, and then I am going to the one who sent me. 34 You will look for me, but you will not find me; and where I am, you cannot come."

35 The Jews said to one another, "Where does this man intend to go that we cannot find him? Will he go where our people live scattered among the Greeks, and teach the Greeks? 36 What did he mean when he said, 'You will look for me, but you will not find me,' and 'Where I am, you cannot come'?"

37 On the last and greatest day of the festival, Jesus stood and said in a loud voice, "Let anyone who is thirsty come to me and drink. 38 Whoever believes in me, as Scripture has said, rivers of living water will flow from within them." *a* 39 By this he meant the Spirit, whom those who believed in him were later to receive. Up to that time the Spirit had not been given, since Jesus had not yet been glorified.

40 On hearing his words, some of the people said, "Surely this man is the Prophet."

41 Others said, "He is the Messiah."

Still others asked, "How can the Messiah come from Galilee? 42 Does not Scripture say that the Messiah will come from David's descendants and from Bethlehem, the town where David lived?" 43 Thus the people were divided because of Jesus. 44 Some wanted to seize him, but no one laid a hand on him.

Unbelief of the Jewish Leaders

45 Finally the temple guards went back to the chief priests and the Pharisees, who asked them, "Why didn't you bring him in?"

---

a 37,38 Or me. And let anyone drink 38 who believes in me." As Scripture has said, "Out of him (or them) will flow rivers of living water."

⁴⁶"No one ever spoke the way this man does," the guards replied.

⁴⁷"You mean he has deceived you also?" the Pharisees retorted. ⁴⁸"Have any of the rulers or of the Pharisees believed in him? ⁴⁹No! But this mob that knows nothing of the law — there is a curse on them."

⁵⁰Nicodemus, who had gone to Jesus earlier and who was one of their own number, asked, ⁵¹"Does our law condemn a man without first hearing him to find out what he has been doing?"

⁵²They replied, "Are you from Galilee, too? Look into it, and you will find that a prophet does not come out of Galilee."

[The earliest manuscripts and many other ancient witnesses do not have John 7:53 — 8:11. A few manuscripts include these verses, wholly or in part, after John 7:36, John 21:25, Luke 21:38 or Luke 24:53.]

8 ⁵³*Then they all went home, ¹but Jesus went to the Mount of Olives.*

²At dawn he appeared again in the temple courts, where all the people gathered around him, and he sat down to teach them. ³The teachers of the law and the Pharisees brought in a woman caught in adultery. They made her stand before the group ⁴and said to Jesus, "Teacher, this woman was caught in the act of adultery. ⁵In the Law Moses commanded us to stone such women. Now what do you say?" ⁶They were using this question as a trap, in order to have a basis for accusing him.

But Jesus bent down and started to write on the ground with his finger. ⁷When they kept on questioning him, he straightened up and said to them, "Let any one of you who is without sin be the first to throw a stone at her." ⁸Again he stooped down and wrote on the ground.

⁹At this, those who heard began to go away one at a time, the older ones first, until only Jesus was left, with the woman still standing there. ¹⁰Jesus straightened up and asked her, "Woman, where are they? Has no one condemned you?"

¹¹"No one, sir," she said.

"Then neither do I condemn you," Jesus declared. "Go now and leave your life of sin."

Dispute Over Jesus' Testimony

¹²When Jesus spoke again to the people, he said, "I am the light of the world. Whoever follows me will never walk in darkness, but will have the light of life."

¹³The Pharisees challenged him, "Here you are, appearing as your own witness; your testimony is not valid."

¹⁴Jesus answered, "Even if I testify on my own behalf, my testimony is valid, for I know where I came from and where I am going. But you have no idea where I come from or where I am going. ¹⁵You judge by human standards; I pass judgment on no one. ¹⁶But if I do judge, my decisions are true, because I am not alone. I stand with the Father, who sent me. ¹⁷In your own Law it is written that the testimony of two witnesses is true. ¹⁸I am one who testifies for myself; my other witness is the Father, who sent me."

¹⁹Then they asked him, "Where is your father?"

"You do not know me or my Father," Jesus replied. "If you knew me, you would know my Father also." ²⁰He spoke these words while teaching in the temple courts near the place where the offerings were put. Yet no one seized him, because his hour had not yet come.

Dispute Over Who Jesus Is

²¹Once more Jesus said to them, "I am going away, and you will look for me, and you will die in your sin. Where I go, you cannot come."

²²This made the Jews ask, "Will he kill himself? Is that why he says, 'Where I go, you cannot come'?"

²³But he continued, "You are from below; I am from above. You are of this world; I am not of this world. ²⁴I told you that you would die in your sins; if you do not believe that I am he, you will indeed die in your sins."

²⁵"Who are you?" they asked.

"Just what I have been telling you from the beginning," Jesus replied. ²⁶"I have much to say in judgment of you. But he who sent me is trustworthy, and what I have heard from him I tell the world."

²⁷They did not understand that he was telling them about his Father. ²⁸So Jesus said, "When you have lifted up*a* the Son of Man, then you will know that I am he and that I do nothing on my own but speak just what the Father has taught me. ²⁹The one who sent me is with me; he has not left me alone, for I always do what pleases him." ³⁰Even as he spoke, many believed in him.

Dispute Over Whose Children Jesus' Opponents Are

³¹To the Jews who had believed him, Jesus said, "If you hold to my teaching, you are really my disciples. ³²Then you will know the truth, and the truth will set you free."

³³They answered him, "We are Abra-ham's descendants and have never been slaves of anyone. How can you say that we shall be set free?"

³⁴Jesus replied, "Very truly I tell you, everyone who sins is a slave to sin. ³⁵Now a slave has no permanent place in the family, but a son belongs to it forever. ³⁶So if the Son sets you free, you will be free indeed. ³⁷I know that you are Abraham's descendants. Yet you are looking for a way to kill me, because you have no room for my word. ³⁸I am telling you what I have seen in the Father's presence, and you are doing what you have heard from your fa-ther.*b*"

³⁹"Abraham is our father," they an-swered.

"If you were Abraham's children," said Jesus, "then you would*c* do what Abraham did. ⁴⁰As it is, you are looking for a way to kill me, a man who has told you the truth that I heard from God. Abraham did not

---

a 28 The Greek for *lifted up* also means *exalted.*   *b 38* Or *presence. Therefore do what you have heard from the Father.*   *c 39* Some early manuscripts *"If you are Abraham's children," said Jesus, "then*

CONFESS LESSON [*Principle Four*]

For the previous entry in the CONFESS lesson, go to Romans 8:1 (page 1400).

For a discussion of Principles One through Eight and a listing of their related lessons, go to pages xvii – xliv.

[Jesus] said, "I am the light of the world. Whoever follows me will never walk in darkness, but will have the light of life."

JOHN 8:12

Principle Four begins the process of "coming clean." In the second part of Principle Four, we confess our faults to ourselves, to God and to someone else we trust.

The *F* in CONFESS reminds us to FACE THE TRUTH. After we "fess up," we'll have four positive changes in our lives. The first is that we'll be able from that point on to FACE the truth. It has been said that "man occasionally stumbles over the truth, but most of the time he'll pick himself up and continue on." Recovery doesn't work like that. Recovery requires honesty — honesty that will keep us from returning to the darkness of our hurts, hang-ups and habits.

The next letter in CONFESS is *E*. Go to Psalm 32:3 – 5 (page 652).

do such things. ⁴¹You are doing the works of your own father."

"We are not illegitimate children," they protested. "The only Father we have is God himself."

⁴²Jesus said to them, "If God were your Father, you would love me, for I have come here from God. I have not come on my own; God sent me. ⁴³Why is my language not clear to you? Because you are unable to hear what I say. ⁴⁴You belong to your father, the devil, and you want to carry out your father's desires. He was a murderer from the beginning, not holding to the truth, for there is no truth in him. When he lies, he speaks his native language, for he is a liar and the father of lies. ⁴⁵Yet because I tell the truth, you do not believe me! ⁴⁶Can any of you prove me guilty of sin? If I am telling the truth, why don't you believe me? ⁴⁷Whoever belongs to God hears what God says. The reason you do not hear is that you do not belong to God."

Jesus' Claims About Himself

⁴⁸The Jews answered him, "Aren't we right in saying that you are a Samaritan and demon-possessed?"

⁴⁹"I am not possessed by a demon," said Jesus, "but I honor my Father and you dishonor me. ⁵⁰I am not seeking glory for myself; but there is one who seeks it, and he is the judge. ⁵¹Very truly I tell you, whoever obeys my word will never see death."

⁵²At this they exclaimed, "Now we know that you are demon-possessed! Abraham died and so did the prophets, yet you say that whoever obeys your word will never taste death. ⁵³Are you greater than our father Abraham? He died, and so did the prophets. Who do you think you are?"

⁵⁴Jesus replied, "If I glorify myself, my glory means nothing. My Father, whom you claim as your God, is the one who glorifies me. ⁵⁵Though you do not know him, I know him. If I said I did not, I would be a liar like you, but I do know him and obey his word. ⁵⁶Your father Abraham rejoiced at the thought of seeing my day; he saw it and was glad."

⁵⁷"You are not yet fifty years old," they said to him, "and you have seen Abraham!"

⁵⁸"Very truly I tell you," Jesus answered, "before Abraham was born, I am!" ⁵⁹At this, they picked up stones to stone him, but Jesus hid himself, slipping away from the temple grounds.

Jesus Heals a Man Born Blind

9 As he went along, he saw a man blind from birth. ²His disciples asked him, "Rabbi, who sinned, this man or his parents, that he was born blind?"

³"Neither this man nor his parents sinned," said Jesus, "but this happened so that the works of God might be displayed in him. ⁴As long as it is day, we must do the works of him who sent me. Night is coming, when no one can work. ⁵While I am in the world, I am the light of the world."

⁶After saying this, he spit on the ground, made some mud with the saliva, and put it on the man's eyes. ⁷"Go," he told him, "wash in the Pool of Siloam" (this word means "Sent"). So the man went and washed, and came home seeing.

⁸His neighbors and those who had formerly seen him begging asked, "Isn't this the same man who used to sit and beg?" ⁹Some claimed that he was.

Others said, "No, he only looks like him."

But he himself insisted, "I am the man."

¹⁰"How then were your eyes opened?" they asked.

¹¹He replied, "The man they call Jesus made some mud and put it on my eyes. He told me to go to Siloam and wash. So I went and washed, and then I could see."

¹²"Where is this man?" they asked him.

"I don't know," he said.

The Pharisees Investigate the Healing

¹³They brought to the Pharisees the man who had been blind. ¹⁴Now the day on which Jesus had made the mud and opened

MY NAME IS
THE MAN BORN BLIND

JOHN 9

This man, who was blind from birth, is the lead actor in this dramatic comedy. It's dramatic because it showcases the tragic blindness of the religious leaders in Jerusalem. It's a comedy because it's ironic: The man born blind can truly see, while those who think they see are truly blind.

Nobody in that culture occupied a lower rung on the social ladder than a lifelong beggar unfortunate enough to have been born blind. Most people assumed that he deserved his condition on the basis of his own or his parents' specific sins (see John 9:2). The common "wisdom" of that culture diagnosed the man's condition as hopeless. But the sightless man found hope in an encounter with Jesus.

When Jesus approached this beggar, he did something that seemed strange: He smeared mud on the man's eyes, then he instructed him to go and wash it off in the Pool of Siloam. With little knowledge (he knew only that the One who heals was called Jesus — see v. 11) but a simple faith, the blind man obeyed Jesus and took the steps of faith that brought healing.

The blind man's healing created a stir among those who knew him, and they asked the Pharisees to investigate. The Jewish leaders tried to discredit the man's story and even threatened him and his parents. They insulted him and challenged every detail of his account. Then they called Jesus a sinner. But the formerly blind man had a secret weapon: his testimony. He made fools of the Pharisees every time they came at him with another verbal attack. How? He simply stayed with his story. Reality can't be argued away. Defeated, the Pharisees cast the man out of the synagogue.

The Pharisees had long taught that only the Messiah could heal a person born blind. This once-blind beggar corroborated their teaching as he neatly summed up his own recovery: "Nobody has ever heard of opening the eyes of a man born blind. If this man were not from God, he could do nothing" (vv. 32 – 33).

This story confirms the power of our own recovery testimony: As a once-despised beggar sticks to his story, the controlling Pharisees are defeated. In the same way, each time we faithfully share our own story of recovery we grow stronger in our faith and more dedicated to worship.

This blind man recovered because Jesus worked a miracle. And Jesus alone is the power that moves us along our own path to recovery.

As he approached that blind man so many years ago, so also Jesus approaches us now, no matter how far we've fallen. He comes to us with the power and the willingness to heal us, to turn our lives into a living testimony to his grace. With very little understanding and a little faith fixed entirely upon Jesus, we can follow his instructions and become his servants. He'll give us a testimony of his power that will confound the proud but attract the humble. When we obey what we know today, he'll reveal more and more of himself to us (see 14:21).

My Name Is Mike

I'M A BELIEVER WHO STRUGGLES WITH SEXUAL AND CHEMICAL ADDICTION

Please read the account of Jesus' healing of the man born blind in John 9.

Growing up in my household was tough. My parents divorced when I was seven years old, and in those days divorce was considered socially unacceptable. Because of my mom and dad's intense hatred for each other, I often felt as though I was in an emotional tug-of-war, and I blamed myself. Although I was never physically abused, I was both mentally and emotionally abused by my mother. I can remember her saying things to me like, "You're a bad person," "You're no good" or "Someday you're going to end up in prison." I believed her.

I wasn't the smartest kid in school or the best in athletics, and I felt as though the only place I fit in was with the kids who were doing drugs. I also stumbled into pornography. In my father's attic were hundreds of pornographic magazines, and this led me to believe that pornography was acceptable. The problem was that, because of my low self-esteem and discomfort when talking to girls, I began fantasizing about them. I felt like a total outcast.

In 1985 I joined the U.S. Navy. My life themes became sex, drugs and alcohol. My addictions, and particularly my sexual addiction, really began to take off. I lost all sense of morality. You name it, I probably did it. I rationalized my behavior, assuring myself that I was young and having fun. I had no respect for myself or anyone else; I wanted only to get drunker, get higher and be "satisfied." In 1988 I was offered an "early out" of the service, which I accepted, fully aware that sooner or later the Navy would have clashed with my lifestyle. In 1990 I received my third DWI, at which time I was ordered to get a drug and alcohol evaluation. I lied, describing myself as a social drinker. Imagine my surprise when the testers identified me as an alcoholic. I reluctantly went into treatment, only to be kicked out of the program for noncompliance.

I was now getting my sexual thrills in any way I could. I even began to steal money from my brother. Then one day I found a note he'd left me: "Only scumbags steal from their own family." That hit me hard, and I experienced an awful moment of clarity. My life wasn't even close to what I'd imagined it would be as a kid. I was 25 and still living at home with my mother because I drank my money away. At that point I called my original counselor, conceding that I might have a problem after all. I admitted myself into an outpatient clinic for drug and alcohol abuse treatment.

I believed at that point that my situation was hopeless. My alcohol supply dried up, but I continued to feed my addiction with pornography. My overwhelming feelings of guilt led me back into drinking, which in turn pushed me back into drugs. I felt like the blind man in the Gospel of John — a despised beggar desperately needing God to intervene. The only thing I knew for sure was that only God could heal me (see John 9:11). I screamed out in desperation, "God, if you want me to stop, you have to help me because I can't do it by myself!" I took my last drink on February 21, 1991. Through working the steps in traditional programs I had already discovered the "hole" I'd had since I was a kid, and I knew that if I didn't fill it with something good, I would soon choose the alternative. So I began to seek God. I went to church and several weeks later accepted Christ as my Savior. I'm sure that many of the people who knew me still saw me as "hopeless," but, like the blind man, I found hope in a personal encounter with Jesus.

I began to read my Bible every day and, incredibly, I heard God's voice distinctly calling me to full-time ministry. Nobody occupied a lower rung on the social ladder than a lifelong beggar born blind — except for maybe me. So why would God call me? The reality is that Jesus saw in me a screen upon which to project God's glory (see v. 3). In his wisdom he has given me a testimony of his power and grace that will confound the proud but attract the humble (see 1 Corinthians 1:26–31).

I now sought a ministry for my own church that would do the same — and I found Celebrate Recovery. I still struggle at times, but my accountability partners and support group in Celebrate Recovery help me when doubts and temptations occur. I recognize that the key to my recovery is staying active in this process. I can't afford to think for even a minute that I have everything under control.

I encourage everyone to faithfully share their own recovery story and to share with others the miracle of God in their life. The blind man aptly summed up his own recovery: "Nobody has ever heard of opening the eyes of a man born blind. If this man were not from God, he could do nothing" (John 9:32–33).

the man's eyes was a Sabbath. ¹⁵Therefore the Pharisees also asked him how he had received his sight. "He put mud on my eyes," the man replied, "and I washed, and now I see."

¹⁶Some of the Pharisees said, "This man is not from God, for he does not keep the Sabbath."

But others asked, "How can a sinner perform such signs?" So they were divided.

¹⁷Then they turned again to the blind man, "What have you to say about him? It was your eyes he opened."

The man replied, "He is a prophet."

¹⁸They still did not believe that he had been blind and had received his sight until they sent for the man's parents. ¹⁹"Is this your son?" they asked. "Is this the one you say was born blind? How is it that now he can see?"

²⁰"We know he is our son," the parents answered, "and we know he was born blind. ²¹But how he can see now, or who opened his eyes, we don't know. Ask him. He is of age; he will speak for himself." ²²His parents said this because they were afraid of the Jewish leaders, who already had decided that anyone who acknowledged that Jesus was the Messiah would be put out of the synagogue. ²³That was why his parents said, "He is of age; ask him."

²⁴A second time they summoned the man who had been blind. "Give glory to God by telling the truth," they said. "We know this man is a sinner."

²⁵He replied, "Whether he is a sinner or not, I don't know. One thing I do know. I was blind but now I see!"

²⁶Then they asked him, "What did he do to you? How did he open your eyes?"

²⁷He answered, "I have told you already and you did not listen. Why do you want to hear it again? Do you want to become his disciples too?"

²⁸Then they hurled insults at him and said, "You are this fellow's disciple! We are disciples of Moses! ²⁹We know that God

spoke to Moses, but as for this fellow, we don't even know where he comes from."

³⁰The man answered, "Now that is remarkable! You don't know where he comes from, yet he opened my eyes. ³¹We know that God does not listen to sinners. He listens to the godly person who does his will. ³²Nobody has ever heard of opening the eyes of a man born blind. ³³If this man were not from God, he could do nothing."

³⁴To this they replied, "You were steeped in sin at birth; how dare you lecture us!" And they threw him out.

Spiritual Blindness

³⁵Jesus heard that they had thrown him out, and when he found him, he said, "Do you believe in the Son of Man?"

³⁶"Who is he, sir?" the man asked. "Tell me so that I may believe in him."

³⁷Jesus said, "You have now seen him; in fact, he is the one speaking with you."

³⁸Then the man said, "Lord, I believe," and he worshiped him.

³⁹Jesus said,ᵃ "For judgment I have come into this world, so that the blind will see and those who see will become blind."

⁴⁰Some Pharisees who were with him heard him say this and asked, "What? Are we blind too?"

⁴¹Jesus said, "If you were blind, you would not be guilty of sin; but now that you claim you can see, your guilt remains.

The Good Shepherd and His Sheep

10 "Very truly I tell you Pharisees, anyone who does not enter the sheep pen by the gate, but climbs in by some other way, is a thief and a robber. ²The one who enters by the gate is the shepherd of the sheep. ³The gatekeeper opens the gate for him, and the sheep listen to his voice. He calls his own sheep by name and leads them out. ⁴When he has brought out all his own, he goes on ahead of them, and his sheep follow him because they know his voice. ⁵But they will never

---

ᵃ 38,39 Some early manuscripts do not have *Then the man said . . . ³⁹Jesus said.*

follow a stranger; in fact, they will run away from him because they do not recognize a stranger's voice." ⁶Jesus used this figure of speech, but the Pharisees did not understand what he was telling them.

⁷Therefore Jesus said again, "Very truly I tell you, I am the gate for the sheep. ⁸All who have come before me are thieves and robbers, but the sheep have not listened to them. ⁹I am the gate; whoever enters through me will be saved.ᵃ They will come in and go out, and find pasture. ¹⁰The thief comes only to steal and kill and destroy; I have come that they may have life, and have it to the full.

¹¹"I am the good shepherd. The good shepherd lays down his life for the sheep. ¹²The hired hand is not the shepherd and does not own the sheep. So when he sees the wolf coming, he abandons the sheep and runs away. Then the wolf attacks the flock and scatters it. ¹³The man runs away because he is a hired hand and cares nothing for the sheep.

¹⁴"I am the good shepherd; I know my sheep and my sheep know me— ¹⁵just as the Father knows me and I know the Father—and I lay down my life for the sheep. ¹⁶I have other sheep that are not of this sheep pen. I must bring them also. They too will listen to my voice, and there shall be one flock and one shepherd. ¹⁷The reason my Father loves me is that I lay down my life—only to take it up again. ¹⁸No one takes it from me, but I lay it down of my own accord. I have authority to lay it down

ᵃ 9 Or *kept safe*

POWERLESS LESSON [*Principle One*]

For the previous entry in the POWERLESS lesson, go to Hebrews 13:1 – 2 (page 1536).

For a discussion of Principles One through Eight and a listing of their related lessons, go to pages xvii – xliv.

The thief comes only to steal and kill and destroy;
I have come that they may have life, and have it to the full.

JOHN 10:10

The power to change comes only through God's grace. Principle One states: "Realize I'm not God. I admit that I'm powerless to control my tendency to do the wrong thing and that my life has become unmanageable." If we admit that we're powerless, we recognize our need for a power greater than ourselves to restore us. That power is our Higher Power, the one and only true Higher Power, Jesus Christ.

In Principle One we discover that we're POWERLESS to control our own lives and that our lives have become unmanageable.

The *E* in POWERLESS stands for EMPTINESS. When we finally admit that we're truly powerless by ourselves, that empty feeling deep inside—that cold wind that blows right through us—goes away.

Let Jesus fill up the hollow void inside you. Tell him how empty you feel, and he'll be faithful to his promise.

The next letter in POWERLESS is S. Go to Luke 17:33 (page 1275).

and authority to take it up again. This command I received from my Father."

19 The Jews who heard these words were again divided. 20 Many of them said, "He is demon-possessed and raving mad. Why listen to him?"

21 But others said, "These are not the sayings of a man possessed by a demon. Can a demon open the eyes of the blind?"

Further Conflict Over Jesus' Claims

22 Then came the Festival of Dedication*a* at Jerusalem. It was winter, 23 and Jesus was in the temple courts walking in Solomon's Colonnade. 24 The Jews who were there gathered around him, saying, "How long will you keep us in suspense? If you are the Messiah, tell us plainly."

25 Jesus answered, "I did tell you, but you do not believe. The works I do in my Father's name testify about me, 26 but you do not believe because you are not my sheep. 27 My sheep listen to my voice; I know them, and they follow me. 28 I give them eternal life, and they shall never perish; no one will snatch them out of my hand. 29 My Father, who has given them to me, is greater than all*b*; no one can snatch them out of my Father's hand. 30 I and the Father are one."

31 Again his Jewish opponents picked up stones to stone him, 32 but Jesus said to them, "I have shown you many good works from the Father. For which of these do you stone me?"

33 "We are not stoning you for any good work," they replied, "but for blasphemy, because you, a mere man, claim to be God."

34 Jesus answered them, "Is it not written in your Law, 'I have said you are "gods"'*c*? 35 If he called them 'gods,' to whom the word of God came — and Scripture cannot be set aside — 36 what about the one whom the Father set apart as his very own and sent into the world? Why then do you accuse me of blasphemy because I said, 'I am God's Son'? 37 Do not believe me unless I do the works of my Father. 38 But if I do them, even though you do not believe me, believe the works, that you may know and understand that the Father is in me, and I in the Father." 39 Again they tried to seize him, but he escaped their grasp.

40 Then Jesus went back across the Jordan to the place where John had been baptizing in the early days. There he stayed, 41 and many people came to him. They said, "Though John never performed a sign, all that John said about this man was true." 42 And in that place many believed in Jesus.

The Death of Lazarus

11 Now a man named Lazarus was sick. He was from Bethany, the village of Mary and her sister Martha. 2 (This Mary, whose brother Lazarus now lay sick, was the same one who poured perfume on the Lord and wiped his feet with her hair.) 3 So the sisters sent word to Jesus, "Lord, the one you love is sick."

4 When he heard this, Jesus said, "This sickness will not end in death. No, it is for God's glory so that God's Son may be glorified through it." 5 Now Jesus loved Martha and her sister and Lazarus. 6 So when he heard that Lazarus was sick, he stayed where he was two more days, 7 and then he said to his disciples, "Let us go back to Judea."

8 "But Rabbi," they said, "a short while ago the Jews there tried to stone you, and yet you are going back?"

9 Jesus answered, "Are there not twelve hours of daylight? Anyone who walks in the daytime will not stumble, for they see by this world's light. 10 It is when a person walks at night that they stumble, for they have no light."

11 After he had said this, he went on to tell them, "Our friend Lazarus has fallen asleep; but I am going there to wake him up."

12 His disciples replied, "Lord, if he

---

a 22 That is, Hanukkah   *b 29* Many early manuscripts *What my Father has given me is greater than all*
c 34 Psalm 82:6

sleeps, he will get better." ¹³Jesus had been speaking of his death, but his disciples thought he meant natural sleep.

¹⁴So then he told them plainly, "Lazarus is dead, ¹⁵and for your sake I am glad I was not there, so that you may believe. But let us go to him."

¹⁶Then Thomas (also known as Didymus*ᵃ*) said to the rest of the disciples, "Let us also go, that we may die with him."

Jesus Comforts the Sisters of Lazarus

¹⁷On his arrival, Jesus found that Lazarus had already been in the tomb for four days. ¹⁸Now Bethany was less than two miles*ᵇ* from Jerusalem, ¹⁹and many Jews had come to Martha and Mary to comfort them in the loss of their brother. ²⁰When Martha heard that Jesus was coming, she went out to meet him, but Mary stayed at home.

²¹"Lord," Martha said to Jesus, "if you had been here, my brother would not have died. ²²But I know that even now God will give you whatever you ask."

²³Jesus said to her, "Your brother will rise again."

²⁴Martha answered, "I know he will rise again in the resurrection at the last day."

²⁵Jesus said to her, "I am the resurrection and the life. The one who believes in me will live, even though they die; ²⁶and whoever lives by believing in me will never die. Do you believe this?"

²⁷"Yes, Lord," she replied, "I believe that you are the Messiah, the Son of God, who is to come into the world."

²⁸After she had said this, she went back and called her sister Mary aside. "The Teacher is here," she said, "and is asking for you." ²⁹When Mary heard this, she got up quickly and went to him. ³⁰Now Jesus had not yet entered the village, but was still at the place where Martha had met him. ³¹When the Jews who had been with Mary in the house, comforting her, noticed how quickly she got up and went out, they fol-

lowed her, supposing she was going to the tomb to mourn there.

³²When Mary reached the place where Jesus was and saw him, she fell at his feet and said, "Lord, if you had been here, my brother would not have died."

³³When Jesus saw her weeping, and the Jews who had come along with her also weeping, he was deeply moved in spirit and troubled. ³⁴"Where have you laid him?" he asked.

"Come and see, Lord," they replied.

³⁵Jesus wept.

³⁶Then the Jews said, "See how he loved him!"

³⁷But some of them said, "Could not he who opened the eyes of the blind man have kept this man from dying?"

Jesus Raises Lazarus From the Dead

³⁸Jesus, once more deeply moved, came to the tomb. It was a cave with a stone laid across the entrance. ³⁹"Take away the stone," he said.

"But, Lord," said Martha, the sister of the dead man, "by this time there is a bad odor, for he has been there four days."

⁴⁰Then Jesus said, "Did I not tell you that if you believe, you will see the glory of God?"

⁴¹So they took away the stone. Then Jesus looked up and said, "Father, I thank you that you have heard me. ⁴²I knew that you always hear me, but I said this for the benefit of the people standing here, that they may believe that you sent me."

⁴³When he had said this, Jesus called in a loud voice, "Lazarus, come out!" ⁴⁴The dead man came out, his hands and feet wrapped with strips of linen, and a cloth around his face.

Jesus said to them, "Take off the grave clothes and let him go."

The Plot to Kill Jesus

⁴⁵Therefore many of the Jews who had come to visit Mary, and had seen what

---

ᵃ 16 Thomas (Aramaic) and Didymus (Greek) both mean twin.   *ᵇ 18* Or about 3 kilometers

MY NAME IS LAZARUS

JOHN 11:1—12:19

Lazarus, a close friend of Jesus, became seriously ill. Word was sent to Jesus from the sick man's sisters, Mary and Martha. When Jesus received the news, he unaccountably stayed put for two more days before heading back to Judea. He made it clear, in fact, that he had delayed until he knew Lazarus was dead, even adding that he was glad he hadn't gone sooner (see John 11:1 – 15). In hindsight, we can be glad as well because Lazarus's story is undeniable proof of Jesus' power to deliver those who are powerless over their hurts, hang-ups and habits.

When Jesus neared Bethany, he found that Lazarus had already been in the tomb for four days. After speaking individually with both Martha and Mary, the Lord wept at the sight of so much grief (see vv. 17 – 35). Then, amazingly, Jesus called Lazarus back to life. Lazarus emerged from the tomb, still in his burial wrappings. Jesus commanded those present to remove the grave clothes from his friend. Many believed in Jesus as a result of this miracle. But some who were present, far from being happy about this unexpected turn of events, hurried to Jerusalem (two miles down the side of the Mount of Olives) to report this disturbing news to the Jewish ruling council, the Sanhedrin (see vv. 45 – 47).

There is no evidence that these naysayers denied the reality of the miracle. In fact, they had to confess that Jesus was "performing many signs" (v. 47). In spite of this admission, the Jewish council, guided by the high priest, Caiaphas, made plans to arrest and execute Jesus (see vv. 49 – 57). A man who could raise the dead had to be killed. Why? Because a man who can raise the dead is a threat to those who want to hold on to power (see v. 48).

What about Lazarus? He had experienced one of the most amazing miracles recorded in the Bible. How would he now be accepted? True, this undeniable account of new life brought many to faith in Jesus (see 12:9,11). But Lazarus wasn't accepted by the Sanhedrin, who plotted to kill the man who had only so recently been restored to life. Again, why? Because resurrected people are dangerous to those who want to believe in their own power. Still, the story of Lazarus continued to spread like wildfire through the masses gathered in Jerusalem for Passover (see vv. 7 – 19).

When we first place our faith in Jesus, he moves us from a condition of spiritual death into one of life (see Ephesians 2:1 – 10). Lazarus was physically powerless to change his condition of physical deadness — and each of us is spiritually powerless over the addictions, hurts and hang-ups that have taken over our lives. As he did with Lazarus, Jesus calls us to life out of death. His life and power in us can set us free. The reality of this new life becomes apparent as we, working through recovery, begin to cast off our own "grave clothes." Our new life gives hope to others as our story spreads through the community around us. Opposition will come, but the demonstration of new life within irresistibly attracts others to Jesus.

Jesus did, believed in him. ⁴⁶But some of them went to the Pharisees and told them what Jesus had done. ⁴⁷Then the chief priests and the Pharisees called a meeting of the Sanhedrin.

"What are we accomplishing?" they asked. "Here is this man performing many signs. ⁴⁸If we let him go on like this, everyone will believe in him, and then the Romans will come and take away both our temple and our nation."

⁴⁹Then one of them, named Caiaphas, who was high priest that year, spoke up, "You know nothing at all! ⁵⁰You do not realize that it is better for you that one man die for the people than that the whole nation perish."

⁵¹He did not say this on his own, but as high priest that year he prophesied that Jesus would die for the Jewish nation, ⁵²and not only for that nation but also for the scattered children of God, to bring them together and make them one. ⁵³So from that day on they plotted to take his life.

⁵⁴Therefore Jesus no longer moved about publicly among the people of Judea. Instead he withdrew to a region near the wilderness, to a village called Ephraim, where he stayed with his disciples.

⁵⁵When it was almost time for the Jewish Passover, many went up from the country to Jerusalem for their ceremonial cleansing before the Passover. ⁵⁶They kept looking for Jesus, and as they stood in the temple courts they asked one another, "What do you think? Isn't he coming to the festival at all?" ⁵⁷But the chief priests and the Pharisees had given orders that anyone who found out where Jesus was should report it so that they might arrest him.

Jesus Anointed at Bethany

12 Six days before the Passover, Jesus came to Bethany, where Lazarus lived, whom Jesus had raised from the dead. ²Here a dinner was given in Jesus' honor. Martha served, while Lazarus was among those reclining at the table with him. ³Then Mary took about a pint*ᵃ* of pure nard, an expensive perfume; she poured it on Jesus' feet and wiped his feet with her hair. And the house was filled with the fragrance of the perfume.

⁴But one of his disciples, Judas Iscariot, who was later to betray him, objected, ⁵"Why wasn't this perfume sold and the money given to the poor? It was worth a year's wages.*ᵇ*" ⁶He did not say this because he cared about the poor but because he was a thief; as keeper of the money bag, he used to help himself to what was put into it.

⁷"Leave her alone," Jesus replied. "It was intended that she should save this perfume for the day of my burial. ⁸You will always have the poor among you,*ᶜ* but you will not always have me."

⁹Meanwhile a large crowd of Jews found out that Jesus was there and came, not only because of him but also to see Lazarus, whom he had raised from the dead. ¹⁰So the chief priests made plans to kill Lazarus as well, ¹¹for on account of him many of the Jews were going over to Jesus and believing in him.

Jesus Comes to Jerusalem as King

¹²The next day the great crowd that had come for the festival heard that Jesus was on his way to Jerusalem. ¹³They took palm branches and went out to meet him, shouting,

"Hosanna!*ᵈ*"

"Blessed is he who comes in the name
      of the Lord!"*ᵉ*

"Blessed is the king of Israel!"

¹⁴Jesus found a young donkey and sat on it, as it is written:

¹⁵"Do not be afraid, Daughter Zion;
      see, your king is coming,
         seated on a donkey's colt."*ᶠ*

ᵃ 3 Or about 0.5 liter   *ᵇ 5* Greek *three hundred denarii* meaning "Save!" which became an exclamation of praise   *ᶜ 8* See Deut. 15:11.   *ᵈ 13* A Hebrew expression   *ᵉ 13* Psalm 118:25,26   *ᶠ 15* Zech. 9:9

My Name Is Jacki

I'M A BELIEVER WHO STRUGGLES WITH SEXUAL ADDICTION

Please read the story of Lazarus's resurrection in John 11:1 — 12:19.

I came to know the Lord while attending a Christian high school. When I graduated, I felt that my foundation in him was strong enough to withstand the challenges that often come with young adulthood. I quickly found out, though, that I was wrong. A few years after my graduation, my mom was diagnosed with a neurological disease. As a child, I had been taught to mask my emotions with laughter. Watching the progression of Mom's illness left me feeling helpless. I turned to alcohol in an attempt to eradicate the pain.

I had experienced my first encounter with pornography when I was only seven years old. I could never have foreseen how that one event would follow me into my adult life. It started out as curiosity, but before long I was spending four to five hours per night visiting porno-graphic websites, online dating services and adult chat rooms, as well as utilizing the tele-phone to act out with people all over the country. I was a bartender at a local restaurant, and after a while I began dating some of my customers. In the beginning I told myself I'd just go out for the casual dinner. But before long I was regularly taking customers home with me.

I continued keeping up the variety of appearances that had sustained me through the years. At work I was the professional. To my family I was strong and responsible. To my church I was a devoted Christian who never missed a Sunday. I had everyone fooled, including myself. I honestly believed that I could stop acting out anytime I wanted. I crossed every boundary I had set for myself, though, and eventually entered a whole new realm of acting out: I began having sexual relations with other women. The addiction in my life had taken me on a journey I would never have thought possible. I had become so disconnected from reality that it didn't matter who the people were, where they came from, whether there was a spouse involved or even whether the person was healthy. The guilt of this lifestyle was becoming unbearable, and I made the decision to walk away from the church and my relationship with the Lord. It was clear that my sin had not only interrupted my fellowship with God but had distorted my vision of him as well. I was spiritually dead, in need of a resurrection like Lazarus's.

When I started attending Celebrate Recovery, I couldn't even pray, couldn't bear the thought of admitting my failures to God. I'd been with many different people and spent thousands of dollars supporting my addiction to various pornographic behaviors. For years I had filled my head with all these images, and now that was all my eyes could see. It was as though I was being mentally tortured by my thought life. These very thoughts kept me from experiencing healing during the first stage of my recovery.

Then I encountered Principle Three: "Consciously choose to commit all of my life and will to Christ's care and control." At this point I knew I had to make a choice: life or death. I chose life. I made the decision to turn my life and will over to God's care and finally accepted that he loves me. He met me where I was and offered abundant forgiveness and grace. "He saved us, not because of righteous things we had done, but because of his mercy. He saved us through the washing of rebirth and renewal by the Holy Spirit" (Titus 3:5).

I'm amazed at how the Lord has used such incredible dysfunction to bring me into a Christ-centered recovery program that has reinstated in my heart and mind the all-important truths of Scripture. Celebrate Recovery has brought me to a place where the longing to be pure and right with the Lord has become much bigger than my weak and selfish desires. Had I never experienced the pain of failure, I don't believe I would have come to a place where I was secure enough to trust the Lord for my physical and spiritual health and for my future.

I was physically and spiritually powerless over the addictions, hurts and hang-ups that had overtaken my life. Jesus called Lazarus out of the tomb after four days, instructing the bystanders to remove the grave clothes from his friend. My sponsor and accountability partners have done just that; they took me in with open arms and, with the Lord's help, removed the grave clothes that had kept me bound for so long.

For the last three-and-a-half years I've driven 180 miles round-trip to Saddleback's Celebrate Recovery program. Now God has led me to start a Celebrate Recovery ministry at my home church. I want to be used by God to create a safe environment where people from my community can experience genuine recovery for themselves.

"I can't believe this is what my life has come to," I vividly recall saying when I first visited the Women's Sexual Addiction Group at Saddleback Church. Now, after three years of sobriety, I say those same words for a different reason. Like Lazarus, I've been miraculously raised from death to life. I can't begin to express how grateful I am to be in this place.

Jacki

16At first his disciples did not understand all this. Only after Jesus was glorified did they realize that these things had been written about him and that these things had been done to him.

17Now the crowd that was with him when he called Lazarus from the tomb and raised him from the dead continued to spread the word. 18Many people, because they had heard that he had performed this sign, went out to meet him. 19So the Pharisees said to one another, "See, this is getting us nowhere. Look how the whole world has gone after him!"

Jesus Predicts His Death

20Now there were some Greeks among those who went up to worship at the festival. 21They came to Philip, who was from Bethsaida in Galilee, with a request. "Sir," they said, "we would like to see Jesus." 22Philip went to tell Andrew; Andrew and Philip in turn told Jesus.

23Jesus replied, "The hour has come for the Son of Man to be glorified. 24Very truly I tell you, unless a kernel of wheat falls to the ground and dies, it remains only a single seed. But if it dies, it produces many seeds. 25Anyone who loves their life will lose it, while anyone who hates their life in this world will keep it for eternal life. 26Whoever serves me must follow me; and where I am, my servant also will be. My Father will honor the one who serves me.

27"Now my soul is troubled, and what shall I say? 'Father, save me from this hour'? No, it was for this very reason I came to this hour. 28Father, glorify your name!"

Then a voice came from heaven, "I have glorified it, and will glorify it again." 29The crowd that was there and heard it said it had thundered; others said an angel had spoken to him.

30Jesus said, "This voice was for your benefit, not mine. 31Now is the time for judgment on this world; now the prince of this world will be driven out. 32And I, when I am lifted up*a* from the earth, will draw all people to myself." 33He said this to show the kind of death he was going to die.

34The crowd spoke up, "We have heard from the Law that the Messiah will remain forever, so how can you say, 'The Son of Man must be lifted up'? Who is this 'Son of Man'?"

35Then Jesus told them, "You are going to have the light just a little while longer. Walk while you have the light, before darkness overtakes you. Whoever walks in the dark does not know where they are going. 36Believe in the light while you have the light, so that you may become children of light." When he had finished speaking, Jesus left and hid himself from them.

Belief and Unbelief Among the Jews

37Even after Jesus had performed so many signs in their presence, they still would not believe in him. 38This was to fulfill the word of Isaiah the prophet:

> "Lord, who has believed our message
>   and to whom has the arm of the Lord
>   been revealed?"*b*

39For this reason they could not believe, because, as Isaiah says elsewhere:

> 40"He has blinded their eyes
>   and hardened their hearts,
> so they can neither see with their eyes,
>   nor understand with their hearts,
>   nor turn — and I would heal them."*c*

41Isaiah said this because he saw Jesus' glory and spoke about him.

42Yet at the same time many even among the leaders believed in him. But because of the Pharisees they would not openly acknowledge their faith for fear they would be put out of the synagogue; 43for they loved human praise more than praise from God.

44Then Jesus cried out, "Whoever believes in me does not believe in me only, but in the one who sent me. 45The one who looks at me is seeing the one who sent me.

---

a 32 The Greek for *lifted up* also means *exalted.*   *b 38* Isaiah 53:1   *c 40* Isaiah 6:10

MY NAME IS
MARY OF BETHANY

JOHN 12:1–8

Mary is the character in the Gospels most often found at Jesus' feet—evidently her favorite place (see Luke 10:39). Overcome by grief, she had recently fallen at his feet in worship (see John 11:32). She also anointed Jesus' feet and wiped them with her hair (see 12:3). Judas Iscariot criticized her extravagant worship as wasteful (see vv. 4–5). Judas's problem was one of unbelief and greed. He lacked the capacity to understand Mary's intense love for Jesus. Jesus in turn rebuked Judas. In doing so he revealed a meaning to Mary's actions that she most likely didn't realize herself: She was honoring the Lord in anticipation of his sacrificial death (see vv. 7–8).

Mary's devotion in this story flowed naturally from her earlier experiences with Jesus. She had been at his feet to learn from and about him (see Luke 10:38–42). She had fallen at his feet, acknowledging him as Master over sickness and death (see John 11:32). Finally, she now anointed his feet in wordless worship of him as the Savior, soon to become the sacrifice (see 12:3,7–8).

In defending Mary's actions, Jesus reminded his disciples that his physical presence among them would end (see 12:8). His days with them were numbered. Soon Jesus would die on the cross and then spend a few more precious days with his friends following his resurrection. After that, his mission accomplished, Jesus would return to his Father. The same is true for each of us as a disciple in recovery. Our time on this earth will end sooner than we might expect. When our mission is complete, we'll go home to our heavenly Father, to a place prepared for us by Jesus (see 14:1–4).

One measure of our progress in recovery is a growing gratitude for all God has done in our lives. This is one reason our inventory (Principle Four) and continuing self-examination (Principle Six) are so important. These actions are essential in putting down and refusing to pick back up the destructive baggage we've accumulated. But our inventory and daily evaluation are also vivid reminders of the greatness of God's grace.

Our proper place, the only place in which to continue our recovery, is at Jesus' feet. Mary understood her place in relation to Jesus. And we're to follow her example until, like her, our work on Earth is done. Like Mary, we need to find our way to the feet of Jesus, to sit there and learn from him, to fall at his feet in our times of despair. Our worship should be extravagant as we praise our Savior for all he's done for us.

My Name Is Michelle

I'M A BELIEVER WHO STRUGGLES WITH SEXUAL ABUSE AND CODEPENDENCY

Please read about Mary of Bethany's devotion to Jesus in Luke 10:38–42.

When I was two years old my parents divorced, and Mom and Dad both remarried. At Dad's house, structure and routine made me feel safe; we went to church and prayed regularly. At Mom's house, the situation was the opposite: no religious observance and no predictability. I looked forward anxiously to Dad's Sunday evening phone calls.

When I was around ten years old, my stepdad informed us kids that he and Mom were divorcing. We moved in with my uncle, his family, and another unmarried uncle with whom my cousin and I started to hang out. One day he gave us wine and began to sexually molest us — a pattern that continued for some time. I recall only a few incidents, but I remember my feelings of shame. I started acting out sexually as a way of coping, but this only made me feel worse.

Dad's weekly calls faded into monthly calls. Mom found us a place to live, but my uncle came along to watch us while she worked. One night I awoke to find him standing over my bed. I asked my older sister whether I could sleep in her room, never suspecting he would shift his attention to my little sister.

Mom again remarried but soon began confiding in me about her marital and financial problems. I felt responsible for her. By now Dad's contact had dwindled to holiday and birthday visits and calls.

In high school I met an older girl. She claimed to believe in God and was beautiful and confident — two qualities I coveted. When we were together, though, we drank, shoplifted and hung around with some guys. I was uncomfortable but didn't protest. Around that time I started my first job. I never spent the money, saving it in case my mom should need it.

Another girl asked me whether I wanted to hang out. She inquired about whether I believed in God, and I told her I had accepted Jesus. I slowly began to live two different lifestyles, one with each friend. I realized I couldn't continue this double life, though, and felt I was losing my identity altogether. One night I prayed, inviting God to take control of my life. Like Mary of Bethany, I sat at Jesus' feet and worshiped him. I terminated my relationship with my older friend and strengthened the bond with my new friend.

I opened up to her about my past abuse, and she insisted I tell Mom. So when Mom picked me up from school, I told her how her brother had abused me. She informed me that my little sister had made similar allegations, and she promised we would talk that evening. Mom gave us a difficult ultimatum: Keep quiet or tell someone — but if we told someone, they would surely take us girls away from her. We decided to keep the past a secret.

My older sister married, leaving me to "save" Mom's marriage. It wasn't long before I started to formulate any excuse to be away from home. On the weekends I isolated myself by sleeping all day and working at night. I didn't like myself and was convinced nobody else liked me either.

It had been two years since I'd committed to following Christ, but I knelt again at Jesus' feet, this time seeking intimacy with him. I had to face my fear of rejection and continue trusting in his love, protection, grace and healing. My friend and I spent every Sunday together, reading the Bible, fasting and praying.

One night after church I noticed the Celebrate Recovery table. I asked whether there was a group for children of divorce and was invited to a codependency group, which I started attending every Friday evening. After a few weeks I was introduced to Karrie. We shared our stories, and she told me about a women's 12-step group she was leading, which I joined. At first I thought I needed to hide my pain, save my family and deny my shame. I was unprepared, though, for the freedom and relief I gained by acknowledging my powerlessness and admitting that my life had become unmanageable.

On November 5, 2003, I jotted down three goals: to lead a group, continue working the principles and remain connected to at least one other person in the program. I've been privileged to lead the junior high Life Hurts, God Heals group twice and have met weekly with my accountability group, which consists of myself and two other women. I've made amends with Dad, my sister and my best friend, and I look forward to the day when God will present the opportunity for me to do so with Mom.

I now enjoy intimacy with Christ, just as Mary of Bethany did. I know how much he loves me and recognize my God-given gifts and talents. Before Celebrate Recovery I had simply settled for whatever circumstances life dealt me. Now I feel confident and ready to fulfill God's purpose for my life: " 'For I know the plans I have for you,' declares the LORD, 'plans to prosper you and not to harm you, plans to give you hope and a future' " (Jeremiah 29:11).

Michelle

⁴⁶I have come into the world as a light, so that no one who believes in me should stay in darkness.

⁴⁷"If anyone hears my words but does not keep them, I do not judge that person. For I did not come to judge the world, but to save the world. ⁴⁸There is a judge for the one who rejects me and does not accept my words; the very words I have spoken will condemn them at the last day. ⁴⁹For I did not speak on my own, but the Father who sent me commanded me to say all that I have spoken. ⁵⁰I know that his command leads to eternal life. So whatever I say is just what the Father has told me to say."

Jesus Washes His Disciples' Feet

13 It was just before the Passover Festival. Jesus knew that the hour had come for him to leave this world and go to the Father. Having loved his own who were in the world, he loved them to the end.

²The evening meal was in progress, and the devil had already prompted Judas, the son of Simon Iscariot, to betray Jesus. ³Jesus knew that the Father had put all things under his power, and that he had come from God and was returning to God; ⁴so he got up from the meal, took off his outer clothing, and wrapped a towel around his waist. ⁵After that, he poured water into a basin and began to wash his disciples' feet, drying them with the towel that was wrapped around him.

⁶He came to Simon Peter, who said to him, "Lord, are you going to wash my feet?"

⁷Jesus replied, "You do not realize now what I am doing, but later you will understand."

⁸"No," said Peter, "you shall never wash my feet."

Jesus answered, "Unless I wash you, you have no part with me."

⁹"Then, Lord," Simon Peter replied, "not just my feet but my hands and my head as well!"

¹⁰Jesus answered, "Those who have had a bath need only to wash their feet; their whole body is clean. And you are clean, though not every one of you." ¹¹For he knew who was going to betray him, and that was why he said not every one was clean.

¹²When he had finished washing their feet, he put on his clothes and returned to his place. "Do you understand what I have done for you?" he asked them. ¹³"You call me 'Teacher' and 'Lord,' and rightly so, for that is what I am. ¹⁴Now that I, your Lord and Teacher, have washed your feet, you also should wash one another's feet. ¹⁵I have set you an example that you should do as I have done for you. ¹⁶Very truly I tell you, no servant is greater than his master, nor is a messenger greater than the one who sent him. ¹⁷Now that you know these things, you will be blessed if you do them.

Jesus Predicts His Betrayal

¹⁸"I am not referring to all of you; I know those I have chosen. But this is to fulfill this passage of Scripture: 'He who shared my bread has turned*ᵃ* against me.'*ᵇ*

¹⁹"I am telling you now before it happens, so that when it does happen you will believe that I am who I am. ²⁰Very truly I tell you, whoever accepts anyone I send accepts me; and whoever accepts me accepts the one who sent me."

²¹After he had said this, Jesus was troubled in spirit and testified, "Very truly I tell you, one of you is going to betray me."

²²His disciples stared at one another, at a loss to know which of them he meant. ²³One of them, the disciple whom Jesus loved, was reclining next to him. ²⁴Simon Peter motioned to this disciple and said, "Ask him which one he means."

²⁵Leaning back against Jesus, he asked him, "Lord, who is it?"

²⁶Jesus answered, "It is the one to whom I will give this piece of bread when I have dipped it in the dish." Then, dipping the piece of bread, he gave it to Judas, the son

---

ᵃ 18 Greek *has lifted up his heel*   *ᵇ 18* Psalm 41:9

YES LESSON [*Principle Eight*]

For the previous entry in the YES lesson, go to 1 Timothy 1:5 (page 1502).

For a discussion of Principles One through Eight and a listing of their related lessons,
go to pages xvii – xliv.

*Now that I, your Lord and Teacher, have washed your feet,
you also should wash one another's feet. I have set you an example
that you should do as I have done for you.*

JOHN 13:14–15

Principle Eight calls for us to yield ourselves to God to be used by him to bring this good news to others, both through our example and through our words. This principle recycles our pain by allowing God's fire and light to shine on it, to melt down our old hurts, hang-ups and habits so we can be used again in a positive way. Our lives can be recycled to show others how we've worked the principles and steps, with Jesus' healing, and how we've come through the darkness of our pain into Christ's glorious freedom and light.

Society tells us that pain is useless. In fact, some people believe that *people* in pain are useless. At Celebrate Recovery, we know that pain has great value, as do the people who experience it. So, while the world says no, Principle Eight shouts a resounding YES.

The last letter in YES is *S*, which stands for SERVE OTHERS AS JESUS CHRIST DID. When we've reached Principle Eight, we're ready to pick up our Lord's towel, the one with which he washed his disciples' feet in the upper room the night before he was crucified. In John 13:14 – 15 Jesus calls on us to follow his example in serving others.

All service ranks the same with God. We can say YES to Principle Eight in many different and creative ways. These are just a few examples:

1. Be an accountability partner.

2. Be a sponsor.

3. Become a greeter.

4. Help with the fellowship events.

5. Give your testimony.

6. Invite someone to Celebrate Recovery or to church.

7. Be a small group leader.

There are so many other areas in which to serve. Make suggestions. Get involved. Bear in mind that the world is populated with two kinds of people — givers and takers. The takers eat well, but the givers sleep well. Be a giver.

Principle Eight comes down to this: Do what you can with what you have, where you are. Make your life a mission, not an intermission. The Lord spreads his message through the eight principles and the Christ-centered 12 steps. We're the instruments for delivering the good news. The way we live will demonstrate to others our commitment to our Lord, to our program and to them.

This is the final page of the YES lesson.

of Simon Iscariot. 27As soon as Judas took the bread, Satan entered into him.

So Jesus told him, "What you are about to do, do quickly." 28But no one at the meal understood why Jesus said this to him. 29Since Judas had charge of the money, some thought Jesus was telling him to buy what was needed for the festival, or to give something to the poor. 30As soon as Judas had taken the bread, he went out. And it was night.

Jesus Predicts Peter's Denial

31When he was gone, Jesus said, "Now the Son of Man is glorified and God is glorified in him. 32If God is glorified in him,*a* God will glorify the Son in himself, and will glorify him at once.

33"My children, I will be with you only a little longer. You will look for me, and just as I told the Jews, so I tell you now: Where I am going, you cannot come.

34"A new command I give you: Love one another. As I have loved you, so you must love one another. 35By this everyone will know that you are my disciples, if you love one another."

36Simon Peter asked him, "Lord, where are you going?"

Jesus replied, "Where I am going, you cannot follow now, but you will follow later."

37Peter asked, "Lord, why can't I follow you now? I will lay down my life for you."

38Then Jesus answered, "Will you really lay down your life for me? Very truly I tell you, before the rooster crows, you will disown me three times!

Jesus Comforts His Disciples

14 "Do not let your hearts be troubled. You believe in God*b*; believe also in me. 2My Father's house has many rooms; if that were not so, would I have told you that I am going there to prepare a place for you? 3And if I go and prepare a place for you, I will come back and take you to be with me that you also may be where I am. 4You know the way to the place where I am going."

Jesus the Way to the Father

5Thomas said to him, "Lord, we don't know where you are going, so how can we know the way?"

6Jesus answered, "I am the way and the truth and the life. No one comes to the Father except through me. 7If you really know me, you will know*c* my Father as well. From now on, you do know him and have seen him."

8Philip said, "Lord, show us the Father and that will be enough for us."

9Jesus answered: "Don't you know me, Philip, even after I have been among you such a long time? Anyone who has seen me has seen the Father. How can you say, 'Show us the Father'? 10Don't you believe that I am in the Father, and that the Father is in me? The words I say to you I do not speak on my own authority. Rather, it is the Father, living in me, who is doing his work. 11Believe me when I say that I am in the Father and the Father is in me; or at least believe on the evidence of the works themselves. 12Very truly I tell you, whoever believes in me will do the works I have been doing, and they will do even greater things than these, because I am going to the Father. 13And I will do whatever you ask in my name, so that the Father may be glorified in the Son. 14You may ask me for anything in my name, and I will do it.

Jesus Promises the Holy Spirit

15"If you love me, keep my commands. 16And I will ask the Father, and he will give you another advocate to help you and be with you forever— 17the Spirit of truth. The world cannot accept him, because it neither sees him nor knows him. But you know him, for he lives with you and will be*d* in you. 18I will not leave you as or-

---

a 32 Many early manuscripts do not have *If God is glorified in him.*   *b 1* Or *Believe in God*   *c 7* Some manuscripts *If you really knew me, you would know*   *d 17* Some early manuscripts *and is* phans; I will come to you. ¹⁹Before long, the world will not see me anymore, but you will see me. Because I live, you also will live. ²⁰On that day you will realize that I am in my Father, and you are in me, and I am in you. ²¹Whoever has my commands and keeps them is the one who loves me. The one who loves me will be loved by my Father, and I too will love them and show myself to them."

²²Then Judas (not Judas Iscariot) said, "But, Lord, why do you intend to show yourself to us and not to the world?"

²³Jesus replied, "Anyone who loves me will obey my teaching. My Father will love them, and we will come to them and make our home with them. ²⁴Anyone who does not love me will not obey my teaching. These words you hear are not my own; they belong to the Father who sent me.

²⁵"All this I have spoken while still with you. ²⁶But the Advocate, the Holy Spirit, whom the Father will send in my name, will teach you all things and will remind you of everything I have said to you. ²⁷Peace I leave with you; my peace I give you. I do not give to you as the world gives. Do not let your hearts be troubled and do not be afraid.

²⁸"You heard me say, 'I am going away and I am coming back to you.' If you loved me, you would be glad that I am going to the Father, for the Father is greater than I. ²⁹I have told you now before it happens, so that when it does happen you will believe. ³⁰I will not say much more to you, for the prince of this world is coming. He has no hold over me, ³¹but he comes so that the world may learn that I love the Father and do exactly what my Father has commanded me.

"Come now; let us leave.

The Vine and the Branches

15 "I am the true vine, and my Father is the gardener. ²He cuts off every branch in me that bears no fruit, while every branch that does bear fruit he prunes*ᵃ* so that it will be even more fruitful. ³You are already clean because of the word I have spoken to you. ⁴Remain in me, as I also remain in you. No branch can bear fruit by itself; it must remain in the vine. Neither can you bear fruit unless you remain in me.

⁵"I am the vine; you are the branches. If you remain in me and I in you, you will bear much fruit; apart from me you can do nothing. ⁶If you do not remain in me, you are like a branch that is thrown away and withers; such branches are picked up, thrown into the fire and burned. ⁷If you remain in me and my words remain in you, ask whatever you wish, and it will be done for you. ⁸This is to my Father's glory, that you bear much fruit, showing yourselves to be my disciples.

⁹"As the Father has loved me, so have I loved you. Now remain in my love. ¹⁰If you keep my commands, you will remain in my love, just as I have kept my Father's commands and remain in his love. ¹¹I have told you this so that my joy may be in you and that your joy may be complete. ¹²My command is this: Love each other as I have loved you. ¹³Greater love has no one than this: to lay down one's life for one's friends. ¹⁴You are my friends if you do what I command. ¹⁵I no longer call you servants, because a servant does not know his master's business. Instead, I have called you friends, for everything that I learned from my Father I have made known to you. ¹⁶You did not choose me, but I chose you and appointed you so that you might go and bear fruit — fruit that will last — and so that whatever you ask in my name the Father will give you. ¹⁷This is my command: Love each other.

The World Hates the Disciples

¹⁸"If the world hates you, keep in mind that it hated me first. ¹⁹If you belonged to the world, it would love you as its own. As it is, you do not belong to the world, but I

ᵃ 2 The Greek for *he prunes* also means *he cleans.*

have chosen you out of the world. That is why the world hates you. ²⁰Remember what I told you: 'A servant is not greater than his master.'ᵃ If they persecuted me, they will persecute you also. If they obeyed my teaching, they will obey yours also. ²¹They will treat you this way because of my name, for they do not know the one who sent me. ²²If I had not come and spoken to them, they would not be guilty of sin; but now they have no excuse for their sin. ²³Whoever hates me hates my Father as well. ²⁴If I had not done among them the works no one else did, they would not be guilty of sin. As it is, they have seen, and yet they have hated both me and my Father. ²⁵But this is to fulfill what is written in their Law: 'They hated me without reason.'ᵇ

The Work of the Holy Spirit

²⁶"When the Advocate comes, whom I will send to you from the Father — the Spirit of truth who goes out from the Father — he will testify about me. ²⁷And you also must testify, for you have been with me from the beginning.

16 "All this I have told you so that you will not fall away. ²They will put you out of the synagogue; in fact, the time is coming when anyone who kills you will think they are offering a service to God. ³They will do such things because they have not known the Father or me. ⁴I have told you this, so that when their time comes you will remember that I warned you about them. I did not tell you this from the beginning because I was with you, ⁵but now I am going to him who sent me. None of you asks me, 'Where are you going?' ⁶Rather, you are filled with grief because I have said these things. ⁷But very truly I tell you, it is for your good that I am going away. Unless I go away, the Advocate will not come to you; but if I go, I will send him to you. ⁸When he comes, he will prove the world to be in the wrong about sin and righteousness and judgment:

⁹about sin, because people do not believe in me; ¹⁰about righteousness, because I am going to the Father, where you can see me no longer; ¹¹and about judgment, because the prince of this world now stands condemned.

¹²"I have much more to say to you, more than you can now bear. ¹³But when he, the Spirit of truth, comes, he will guide you into all the truth. He will not speak on his own; he will speak only what he hears, and he will tell you what is yet to come. ¹⁴He will glorify me because it is from me that he will receive what he will make known to you. ¹⁵All that belongs to the Father is mine. That is why I said the Spirit will receive from me what he will make known to you."

The Disciples' Grief Will Turn to Joy

¹⁶Jesus went on to say, "In a little while you will see me no more, and then after a little while you will see me."

¹⁷At this, some of his disciples said to one another, "What does he mean by saying, 'In a little while you will see me no more, and then after a little while you will see me,' and 'Because I am going to the Father'?" ¹⁸They kept asking, "What does he mean by 'a little while'? We don't understand what he is saying."

¹⁹Jesus saw that they wanted to ask him about this, so he said to them, "Are you asking one another what I meant when I said, 'In a little while you will see me no more, and then after a little while you will see me'? ²⁰Very truly I tell you, you will weep and mourn while the world rejoices. You will grieve, but your grief will turn to joy. ²¹A woman giving birth to a child has pain because her time has come; but when her baby is born she forgets the anguish because of her joy that a child is born into the world. ²²So with you: Now is your time of grief, but I will see you again and you will rejoice, and no one will take away your joy. ²³In that day you will no longer

---

ᵃ 20 John 13:16   ᵇ 25 Psalms 35:19; 69:4

ask me anything. Very truly I tell you, my Father will give you whatever you ask in my name. ²⁴Until now you have not asked for anything in my name. Ask and you will receive, and your joy will be complete.

²⁵"Though I have been speaking figuratively, a time is coming when I will no longer use this kind of language but will tell you plainly about my Father. ²⁶In that day you will ask in my name. I am not saying that I will ask the Father on your behalf. ²⁷No, the Father himself loves you because you have loved me and have believed that I came from God. ²⁸I came from the Father and entered the world; now I am leaving the world and going back to the Father."

²⁹Then Jesus' disciples said, "Now you are speaking clearly and without figures of speech. ³⁰Now we can see that you know all things and that you do not even need to have anyone ask you questions. This makes us believe that you came from God."

³¹"Do you now believe?" Jesus replied. ³²"A time is coming and in fact has come when you will be scattered, each to your own home. You will leave me all alone. Yet I am not alone, for my Father is with me.

³³"I have told you these things, so that in me you may have peace. In this world you will have trouble. But take heart! I have overcome the world."

Jesus Prays to Be Glorified

17 After Jesus said this, he looked toward heaven and prayed:

"Father, the hour has come. Glorify your Son, that your Son may glorify you. ²For you granted him authority over all people that he might give eternal life to all those you have given him. ³Now this is eternal life: that they know you, the only true God, and Jesus Christ, whom you have sent. ⁴I have brought you glory on earth by finishing the work you gave me to do. ⁵And now, Father, glorify me in your presence with the glory I had with you before the world began.

Jesus Prays for His Disciples

⁶"I have revealed you[a] to those whom you gave me out of the world. They were yours; you gave them to me and they have obeyed your word. ⁷Now they know that everything you have given me comes from you. ⁸For I gave them the words you gave me and they accepted them. They knew with certainty that I came from you, and they believed that you sent me. ⁹I pray for them. I am not praying for the world, but for those you have given me, for they are yours. ¹⁰All I have is yours, and all you have is mine. And glory has come to me through them. ¹¹I will remain in the world no longer, but they are still in the world, and I am coming to you. Holy Father, protect them by the power of[b] your name, the name you gave me, so that they may be one as we are one. ¹²While I was with them, I protected them and kept them safe by[c] that name you gave me. None has been lost except the one doomed to destruction so that Scripture would be fulfilled.

¹³"I am coming to you now, but I say these things while I am still in the world, so that they may have the full measure of my joy within them. ¹⁴I have given them your word and the world has hated them, for they are not of the world any more than I am of the world. ¹⁵My prayer is not that you take them out of the world but that you protect them from the evil one. ¹⁶They are not of the world, even as I am not of it. ¹⁷Sanctify them by[d] the truth; your word is truth. ¹⁸As you sent me into the world, I have

sent them into the world. ¹⁹For them I sanctify myself, that they too may be truly sanctified.

Jesus Prays for All Believers

²⁰"My prayer is not for them alone. I pray also for those who will believe in me through their message, ²¹that all of them may be one, Father, just as you are in me and I am in you. May they also be in us so that the world may believe that you have sent me. ²²I have given them the glory that you gave me, that they may be one as we are one — ²³I in them and you in me — so that they may be brought to complete unity. Then the world will know that you sent me and have loved them even as you have loved me.

²⁴"Father, I want those you have given me to be with me where I am, and to see my glory, the glory you have given me because you loved me before the creation of the world.

²⁵"Righteous Father, though the world does not know you, I know you, and they know that you have sent me. ²⁶I have made you*ᵃ* known to them, and will continue to make you known in order that the love you have for me may be in them and that I myself may be in them."

Jesus Arrested

18 When he had finished praying, Jesus left with his disciples and crossed the Kidron Valley. On the other side there was a garden, and he and his disciples went into it.

²Now Judas, who betrayed him, knew the place, because Jesus had often met there with his disciples. ³So Judas came to the garden, guiding a detachment of soldiers and some officials from the chief priests and the Pharisees. They were carrying torches, lanterns and weapons.

⁴Jesus, knowing all that was going to happen to him, went out and asked them, "Who is it you want?"

⁵"Jesus of Nazareth," they replied.

"I am he," Jesus said. (And Judas the traitor was standing there with them.) ⁶When Jesus said, "I am he," they drew back and fell to the ground.

⁷Again he asked them, "Who is it you want?"

"Jesus of Nazareth," they said.

⁸Jesus answered, "I told you that I am he. If you are looking for me, then let these men go." ⁹This happened so that the words he had spoken would be fulfilled: "I have not lost one of those you gave me."*ᵇ*

¹⁰Then Simon Peter, who had a sword, drew it and struck the high priest's servant, cutting off his right ear. (The servant's name was Malchus.)

¹¹Jesus commanded Peter, "Put your sword away! Shall I not drink the cup the Father has given me?"

¹²Then the detachment of soldiers with its commander and the Jewish officials arrested Jesus. They bound him ¹³and brought him first to Annas, who was the father-in-law of Caiaphas, the high priest that year. ¹⁴Caiaphas was the one who had advised the Jewish leaders that it would be good if one man died for the people.

Peter's First Denial

¹⁵Simon Peter and another disciple were following Jesus. Because this disciple was known to the high priest, he went with Jesus into the high priest's courtyard, ¹⁶but Peter had to wait outside at the door. The other disciple, who was known to the high priest, came back, spoke to the servant girl on duty there and brought Peter in.

¹⁷"You aren't one of this man's disciples too, are you?" she asked Peter.

He replied, "I am not."

¹⁸It was cold, and the servants and officials stood around a fire they had made to keep warm. Peter also was standing with them, warming himself.

ᵃ 26 Greek *your name*   *ᵇ 9* John 6:39

The High Priest Questions Jesus

¹⁹Meanwhile, the high priest questioned Jesus about his disciples and his teaching.

²⁰"I have spoken openly to the world," Jesus replied. "I always taught in synagogues or at the temple, where all the Jews come together. I said nothing in secret. ²¹Why question me? Ask those who heard me. Surely they know what I said."

²²When Jesus said this, one of the officials nearby slapped him in the face. "Is this the way you answer the high priest?" he demanded.

²³"If I said something wrong," Jesus replied, "testify as to what is wrong. But if I spoke the truth, why did you strike me?" ²⁴Then Annas sent him bound to Caiaphas the high priest.

Peter's Second and Third Denials

²⁵Meanwhile, Simon Peter was still standing there warming himself. So they asked him, "You aren't one of his disciples too, are you?"

He denied it, saying, "I am not."

²⁶One of the high priest's servants, a relative of the man whose ear Peter had cut off, challenged him, "Didn't I see you with him in the garden?" ²⁷Again Peter denied it, and at that moment a rooster began to crow.

Jesus Before Pilate

²⁸Then the Jewish leaders took Jesus from Caiaphas to the palace of the Roman governor. By now it was early morning, and to avoid ceremonial uncleanness they did not enter the palace, because they wanted to be able to eat the Passover. ²⁹So Pilate came out to them and asked, "What charges are you bringing against this man?"

³⁰"If he were not a criminal," they replied, "we would not have handed him over to you."

³¹Pilate said, "Take him yourselves and judge him by your own law."

"But we have no right to execute anyone," they objected. ³²This took place to fulfill what Jesus had said about the kind of death he was going to die.

³³Pilate then went back inside the palace, summoned Jesus and asked him, "Are you the king of the Jews?"

³⁴"Is that your own idea," Jesus asked, "or did others talk to you about me?"

³⁵"Am I a Jew?" Pilate replied. "Your own people and chief priests handed you over to me. What is it you have done?"

³⁶Jesus said, "My kingdom is not of this world. If it were, my servants would fight to prevent my arrest by the Jewish leaders. But now my kingdom is from another place."

³⁷"You are a king, then!" said Pilate.

Jesus answered, "You say that I am a king. In fact, the reason I was born and came into the world is to testify to the truth. Everyone on the side of truth listens to me."

³⁸"What is truth?" retorted Pilate. With this he went out again to the Jews gathered there and said, "I find no basis for a charge against him. ³⁹But it is your custom for me to release to you one prisoner at the time of the Passover. Do you want me to release 'the king of the Jews'?"

⁴⁰They shouted back, "No, not him! Give us Barabbas!" Now Barabbas had taken part in an uprising.

Jesus Sentenced to Be Crucified

19 Then Pilate took Jesus and had him flogged. ²The soldiers twisted together a crown of thorns and put it on his head. They clothed him in a purple robe ³and went up to him again and again, saying, "Hail, king of the Jews!" And they slapped him in the face.

⁴Once more Pilate came out and said to the Jews gathered there, "Look, I am bringing him out to you to let you know that I find no basis for a charge against him." ⁵When Jesus came out wearing the crown of thorns and the purple robe, Pilate said to them, "Here is the man!"

⁶As soon as the chief priests and their officials saw him, they shouted, "Crucify! Crucify!"

But Pilate answered, "You take him and crucify him. As for me, I find no basis for a charge against him."

7The Jewish leaders insisted, "We have a law, and according to that law he must die, because he claimed to be the Son of God."

8When Pilate heard this, he was even more afraid, 9and he went back inside the palace. "Where do you come from?" he asked Jesus, but Jesus gave him no answer. 10"Do you refuse to speak to me?" Pilate said. "Don't you realize I have power either to free you or to crucify you?"

11Jesus answered, "You would have no power over me if it were not given to you from above. Therefore the one who handed me over to you is guilty of a greater sin."

12From then on, Pilate tried to set Jesus free, but the Jewish leaders kept shouting, "If you let this man go, you are no friend of Caesar. Anyone who claims to be a king opposes Caesar."

13When Pilate heard this, he brought Jesus out and sat down on the judge's seat at a place known as the Stone Pavement (which in Aramaic is Gabbatha). 14It was the day of Preparation of the Passover; it was about noon.

"Here is your king," Pilate said to the Jews.

15But they shouted, "Take him away! Take him away! Crucify him!"

"Shall I crucify your king?" Pilate asked.

"We have no king but Caesar," the chief priests answered.

16Finally Pilate handed him over to them to be crucified.

The Crucifixion of Jesus

So the soldiers took charge of Jesus. 17Carrying his own cross, he went out to the place of the Skull (which in Aramaic is called Golgotha). 18There they crucified him, and with him two others — one on each side and Jesus in the middle.

19Pilate had a notice prepared and fastened to the cross. It read: JESUS OF NAZARETH, THE KING OF THE JEWS. 20Many of the Jews read this sign, for the place where Jesus was crucified was near the city, and the sign was written in Aramaic, Latin and Greek. 21The chief priests of the Jews protested to Pilate, "Do not write 'The King of the Jews,' but that this man claimed to be king of the Jews."

22Pilate answered, "What I have written, I have written."

23When the soldiers crucified Jesus, they took his clothes, dividing them into four shares, one for each of them, with the undergarment remaining. This garment was seamless, woven in one piece from top to bottom.

24"Let's not tear it," they said to one another. "Let's decide by lot who will get it."

This happened that the scripture might be fulfilled that said,

"They divided my clothes among them
  and cast lots for my garment."[a]

So this is what the soldiers did.

25Near the cross of Jesus stood his mother, his mother's sister, Mary the wife of Clopas, and Mary Magdalene. 26When Jesus saw his mother there, and the disciple whom he loved standing nearby, he said to her, "Woman,[b] here is your son," 27and to the disciple, "Here is your mother." From that time on, this disciple took her into his home.

The Death of Jesus

28Later, knowing that everything had now been finished, and so that Scripture would be fulfilled, Jesus said, "I am thirsty." 29A jar of wine vinegar was there, so they soaked a sponge in it, put the sponge on a stalk of the hyssop plant, and lifted it to Jesus' lips. 30When he had received the drink, Jesus said, "It is finished." With that, he bowed his head and gave up his spirit.

31Now it was the day of Preparation, and the next day was to be a special Sabbath. Because the Jewish leaders did not want the bodies left on the crosses during the Sabbath, they asked Pilate to have the legs broken and the bodies taken down. 32The soldiers there-

---

a 24 Psalm 22:18   *b 26* The Greek for *Woman* does not denote any disrespect.

fore came and broke the legs of the first man who had been crucified with Jesus, and then those of the other. ³³But when they came to Jesus and found that he was already dead, they did not break his legs. ³⁴Instead, one of the soldiers pierced Jesus' side with a spear, bringing a sudden flow of blood and water. ³⁵The man who saw it has given testimony, and his testimony is true. He knows that he tells the truth, and he testifies so that you also may believe. ³⁶These things happened so that the scripture would be fulfilled: "Not one of his bones will be broken,"ᵃ ³⁷and, as another scripture says, "They will look on the one they have pierced."ᵇ

The Burial of Jesus

³⁸Later, Joseph of Arimathea asked Pilate for the body of Jesus. Now Joseph was a disciple of Jesus, but secretly because he feared the Jewish leaders. With Pilate's permission, he came and took the body away. ³⁹He was accompanied by Nicodemus, the man who earlier had visited Jesus at night. Nicodemus brought a mixture of myrrh and aloes, about seventy-five pounds.ᶜ ⁴⁰Taking Jesus' body, the two of them wrapped it, with the spices, in strips of linen. This was in accordance with Jewish burial customs. ⁴¹At the place where Jesus was crucified, there was a garden, and in the garden a new tomb, in which no one had ever been laid. ⁴²Because it was the Jewish day of Preparation and since the tomb was nearby, they laid Jesus there.

The Empty Tomb

20 Early on the first day of the week, while it was still dark, Mary Magdalene went to the tomb and saw that the stone had been removed from the entrance. ²So she came running to Simon Peter and the other disciple, the one Jesus loved, and said, "They have taken the Lord out of the tomb, and we don't know where they have put him!"

³So Peter and the other disciple started for the tomb. ⁴Both were running, but the other disciple outran Peter and reached the tomb first. ⁵He bent over and looked in at the strips of linen lying there but did not go in. ⁶Then Simon Peter came along behind him and went straight into the tomb. He saw the strips of linen lying there, ⁷as well as the cloth that had been wrapped around Jesus' head. The cloth was still lying in its place, separate from the linen. ⁸Finally the other disciple, who had reached the tomb first, also went inside. He saw and believed. ⁹(They still did not understand from Scripture that Jesus had to rise from the dead.) ¹⁰Then the disciples went back to where they were staying.

Jesus Appears to Mary Magdalene

¹¹Now Mary stood outside the tomb crying. As she wept, she bent over to look into the tomb ¹²and saw two angels in white, seated where Jesus' body had been, one at the head and the other at the foot.

¹³They asked her, "Woman, why are you crying?"

"They have taken my Lord away," she said, "and I don't know where they have put him." ¹⁴At this, she turned around and saw Jesus standing there, but she did not realize that it was Jesus.

¹⁵He asked her, "Woman, why are you crying? Who is it you are looking for?"

Thinking he was the gardener, she said, "Sir, if you have carried him away, tell me where you have put him, and I will get him."

¹⁶Jesus said to her, "Mary."

She turned toward him and cried out in Aramaic, "Rabboni!" (which means "Teacher").

¹⁷Jesus said, "Do not hold on to me, for I have not yet ascended to the Father. Go instead to my brothers and tell them, 'I am ascending to my Father and your Father, to my God and your God.'"

¹⁸Mary Magdalene went to the disciples with the news: "I have seen the Lord!" And she told them that he had said these things to her.

ᵃ 36 Exodus 12:46; Num. 9:12; Psalm 34:20   ᵇ 37 Zech. 12:10   ᶜ 39 Or about 34 kilograms

My Name Is Brenda

I'M A BELIEVER IN RECOVERY FROM PHYSICAL, EMOTIONAL AND SEXUAL ABUSE AND ALCOHOLISM

Please read in John 20:1 – 18 the brief story of Mary Magdalene.

As I was growing up, my family attended church every Sunday. The truth was, though, that we got dressed up once a week so that everyone in town could see how religious we were, only to return home to drunken rages and abusive lives.

My father was an alcoholic, and as his drinking worsened, so did his abuse. At first it was strictly verbal, but around the time I turned nine it turned physical. My mother and I were the primary targets. I remember one horrible night watching my dad attempt to strangle my mom. I tried to stop him, but he threw me across the room and kicked me several times in disgust.

The abuse in my life wasn't all perpetrated by my father. I also suffered sexual impropriety at the hands of other family members. Three of my grandparents were also practicing and abusive alcoholics.

Despite the chaos, I excelled in school. Tragically, though, at the age of eleven I too discovered alcohol. Suddenly I felt comfortable in my own skin. I began to drink more often, always to the point of passing out. At age 14, I acquired a fake ID so I could buy liquor. I wore heavy makeup, acted out sexually and tried drugs. As my alcohol and drug use increased, so did my promiscuity. I relied on relationships with men to feel loved and to soothe the pain of my childhood. I was sexually active with multiple partners from the ages of 14 to 25, during which time I had two abortions.

I continued to believe I was in control of my life, but this was not the case. I was fired from my job, which had entailed traveling across the country for a large corporation. I never traveled without a supply of illicit drugs, and I'd drink to the point of blackouts and sleep with strangers in every city. My boss caught me in a lie that put the company's reputation at risk, and he rightly questioned my integrity. My shame was compounded when I received a DUI that same year and realized that my live-in boyfriend was dealing drugs from our home.

Spiritually bankrupt, I sank to the lowest point in my life, crying out for God but truly expecting nothing. I was in bondage to alcohol, drugs, sex and the aftereffects of my childhood abuse. I was at this point willing to do *anything* to obliterate the pain. After a failed suicide attempt, I entered treatment for drug and alcohol addiction. There I was introduced to the secular 12 steps but steered clear of the God I'd known as a child—the one who had deserted me in my suffering.

Although I managed to stay clean and sober for eight years, other addictions filled the void. I became a workaholic who would turn around and spend my hard-earned money on other temporary fixes. I dined at the finest restaurants and began struggling with my weight, all the while continuing on the path of destructive sexual relationships.

Just when I began to wonder whether that was all there was to life, I received a job offer that promised to relocate me to the other side of the country. Far away from family, friends and accountability, I slipped away from reality almost to the point of relapse. At that point God intervened and saved my life. Several of my new business associates were bold enough to talk about their church: Saddleback Church in Lake Forest. I had never before witnessed young, successful adults talking about a church with such enthusiasm. For the first time in my life, I began hearing the true message of hope. Pastor Rick spoke about a ministry called Celebrate Recovery, and I wondered whether God could truly love me in spite of my sin and shame.

In the summer of 1997 I first attended Celebrate Recovery. I fell in love with Jesus Christ and made him my Higher Power, and through the experience I was also reunited with a man I had once hurt but who is now my loving husband. We serve God together at Celebrate Recovery and live to offer our experiences, victories and hope to other hurting people. Like Mary Magdalene, my bondage to the "demons" in my life was broken by Jesus.

I have more love in my life than I'd ever before imagined, more friends than I can count, a devoted husband, a darling baby daughter and a God who has delivered me from bondage. My purpose in life has been clarified: I'll follow God's leading with all my heart and help others find their way out of darkness. I've also discovered my life's verse here at Celebrate Recovery: " 'Not by might nor by power, but by my Spirit,' says the LORD Almighty" (Zechariah 4:6).

MY NAME IS
MARY MAGDALENE

JOHN 20:1–18

In some traditions Mary Magdalene is identified as a former prostitute; however, she's mentioned 14 times in the Gospels, and not one reference identifies her in this way. Luke notes that she had been delivered from seven demons (see Luke 8:2). Mary's bondage to multiple demons is paralleled in the experience of many who have suffered abuse and sought escape in multiple addictions. Out of gratitude for her deliverance by Jesus, she joined a band of women who supported Jesus' ministry (see vv. 1–3). Mary was present at the cross with Jesus' mother and aunt (see 24:10). Every other time Mary is mentioned along with other women, hers is the first name listed. This suggests that Mary was a leader among the women who served and supported Jesus. Five times Mary is mentioned alone, all five with reference to Jesus' resurrection.

Mary was the first witness to the empty tomb and the first to share this incredible news with the disciples. Peter and John ran to the tomb in response to her message (see John 20:2–4). They saw evidence of the resurrection but couldn't explain what had happened (see vv. 5–9). They returned home (see v. 10), but Mary remained behind and wept, believing that Jesus' body had been stolen. This led to a conversation with angels (see vv. 10–13) and to a personal encounter with Jesus himself (see vv. 14–17).

In the Passion narratives and resurrection accounts, no other disciple of Jesus matches Mary's courage and devotion. She struggled to understand the resurrection, but unlike Peter and John, she stayed near the tomb. Her encounter with Jesus made her the first messenger of the gospel (see v. 18). This honor didn't place her above Christ's appointed apostles, but it did give her a unique ministry. Her deliverance from bondage to Satan had left her with a depth of devotion to Jesus the other disciples lacked.

There's a sharp contrast in this story between Mary Magdalene and the male disciples. Her gratitude for recovery had made her a permanent, faithful servant of Christ. Although each of the disciples had received a special call and commission, they lacked Mary's history of bondage. Only John among the Eleven witnessed Jesus on the cross. Mary Magdalene was there, supporting Jesus and his mother and aunt. And Mary Magdalene and another Mary followed Joseph of Arimathea and Nicodemus to see the location of the tomb (see Mark 15:42–47; see also John 19:38–42). After the Sabbath, Mary Magdalene led other women to the tomb to anoint the body of her Savior (see Mark 16:1).

If Jesus could deliver Mary from the power of seven demons, he can set us free from multiple compulsions. Many who suffer chemical and sexual addictions are trying to escape the pain of childhood abuse. Many are themselves the children of alcoholics or addicts. The deeper our bondage, the greater will be our gratitude for God's grace. This equips us, like Mary, with a story and dedication to Jesus that many other disciples lack. The pain of Mary's past kept her close to Jesus even when others deserted him.

God never wastes pain. He used the pain of Mary's past to shape her into his messenger. Jesus wants us to tell our stories in recovery meetings, in church services and out in the world. His command to us echoes his directive to Mary: Tell others there's nothing more to fear; after all, you've seen the Lord (see John 20:18). We can tell our story to those who languish behind locked doors and look for opportunities to share it with the fearful, the imprisoned, the hurting.

Jesus Appears to His Disciples

¹⁹On the evening of that first day of the week, when the disciples were together, with the doors locked for fear of the Jewish leaders, Jesus came and stood among them and said, "Peace be with you!" ²⁰After he said this, he showed them his hands and side. The disciples were overjoyed when they saw the Lord.

²¹Again Jesus said, "Peace be with you! As the Father has sent me, I am sending you." ²²And with that he breathed on them and said, "Receive the Holy Spirit. ²³If you forgive anyone's sins, their sins are forgiven; if you do not forgive them, they are not forgiven."

Jesus Appears to Thomas

²⁴Now Thomas (also known as Didymus*a*), one of the Twelve, was not with the disciples when Jesus came. ²⁵So the other disciples told him, "We have seen the Lord!"

But he said to them, "Unless I see the nail marks in his hands and put my finger where the nails were, and put my hand into his side, I will not believe."

²⁶A week later his disciples were in the house again, and Thomas was with them. Though the doors were locked, Jesus came and stood among them and said, "Peace be with you!" ²⁷Then he said to Thomas, "Put your finger here; see my hands. Reach out your hand and put it into my side. Stop doubting and believe."

²⁸Thomas said to him, "My Lord and my God!"

²⁹Then Jesus told him, "Because you have seen me, you have believed; blessed are those who have not seen and yet have believed."

The Purpose of John's Gospel

³⁰Jesus performed many other signs in the presence of his disciples, which are not recorded in this book. ³¹But these are written that you may believe*b* that Jesus is the Messiah, the Son of God, and that by believing you may have life in his name.

Jesus and the Miraculous Catch of Fish

21 Afterward Jesus appeared again to his disciples, by the Sea of Galilee.*c* It happened this way: ²Simon Peter, Thomas (also known as Didymus*a*), Nathanael from Cana in Galilee, the sons of Zebedee, and two other disciples were together. ³"I'm going out to fish," Simon Peter told them, and they said, "We'll go with you." So they went out and got into the boat, but that night they caught nothing.

⁴Early in the morning, Jesus stood on the shore, but the disciples did not realize that it was Jesus.

⁵He called out to them, "Friends, haven't you any fish?"

"No," they answered.

⁶He said, "Throw your net on the right side of the boat and you will find some." When they did, they were unable to haul the net in because of the large number of fish.

⁷Then the disciple whom Jesus loved said to Peter, "It is the Lord!" As soon as Simon Peter heard him say, "It is the Lord," he wrapped his outer garment around him (for he had taken it off) and jumped into the water. ⁸The other disciples followed in the boat, towing the net full of fish, for they were not far from shore, about a hundred yards.*d* ⁹When they landed, they saw a fire of burning coals there with fish on it, and some bread.

¹⁰Jesus said to them, "Bring some of the fish you have just caught." ¹¹So Simon Peter climbed back into the boat and dragged the net ashore. It was full of large fish, 153, but even with so many the net was not torn. ¹²Jesus said to them, "Come and have breakfast." None of the disciples dared ask him, "Who are you?" They knew it was the Lord. ¹³Jesus came, took the bread and gave it to them, and did the same with the fish.

---

a 24,2 Thomas (Aramaic) and Didymus (Greek) both mean twin.   *b* 31 Or may continue to believe   *c* 1 Greek Tiberias   *d* 8 Or about 90 meters

My Name Is Gary

I'M A BELIEVER WHO STRUGGLES WITH CODEPENDENCY, ALCOHOLISM AND DRUG ADDICTION

Please read in John 21:15 – 25 about Jesus' reinstatement of Peter after Peter's threefold denial of his Lord.

Many of us believe that addictions invariably stem from a rough childhood. In my case, though, I enjoyed a nearly ideal childhood. Both of my parents worked and had good jobs. I lived in a nice neighborhood, went to private schools and regularly attended services at the Catholic Church. Yet in the sixth grade I started drinking and then getting drunk. The alcohol worked on me like liquid courage. By the ninth grade, while enrolled in a Catholic high school, I started smoking marijuana to fit in with the cool kids. One night I talked my friend into getting slobbering drunk. He got really sick. I took him home, put him in bed and left. His mom came home, found him and called my mom to inform her that we'd been drinking. My friend decided that he'd rather die than disappoint his dad. His solution: He took a .357 magnum and shot himself in the head. That was the day my entire world changed. Grief and guilt overpowered me.

Shortly afterward I went backpacking with my youth group. While perched at a vantage point high in the Rocky Mountains, I felt so close to God. Suddenly it all made sense. Jesus would be my Savior, and all my problems would be resolved. I asked God into my heart that very night and couldn't wait to get home to tell my mom. To my utter amazement, she responded in anger: She wouldn't hear of my leaving the Catholic Church. Shocked and deflated, I ran outside and started to cry. I couldn't believe the Almighty God would sit back and do nothing. At that moment I turned the blame for my friend's suicide from myself to God. He had turned my own mom against me; now I would turn my back on him. My addiction continued, and the drugs became progressively harder.

Still living my life as though I were in control, I fed the deep-seated hole within my spirit with anything I thought might fill the void. I married my first wife under the assumption that I could "fix" her. We had two incredible sons whom I thought would change everything and give me purpose. However, I soon started frequenting strip clubs and seeking meaningless relationships, which led to my divorce. I married two more times, still thinking I could ride up on my white horse, swoop down and rescue these women in distress. But none of these actions cured my pain, depression and emptiness.

The apostle Peter had denied his Lord, his teacher and his best friend. He needed to get on the road to recovery, and so did I. My wife threatened to leave me unless we talked to a pastor at our church. We followed through, and the pastor with whom we met "happened" to be the Celebrate Recovery pastor. My wife joined the ministry, and I supported her because I could see that she needed it. She started to change, which, ironically, made me uncomfortable, probably because I couldn't help but compare my own lack of progress to her transformation.

Finally I relented and joined Celebrate Recovery. In John 21 we read about Jesus taking Peter aside and helping him face his pain and shame (see John 21:15 – 22). God did just that for me, and my life truly changed! I felt peace I'd never known existed. I had to face a fear that had haunted me for some time: Was this God stuff real? What about his love for me, and mine for him? By God's grace my marriage was saved, not only on the basis of hard work on both our parts, but also because God helped me to stop thinking primarily about myself and to think more of others. I knew then that the mutual love between God and me was the genuine article.

Before recovery could work for me, I had to acknowledge my absolute brokenness and surrender unconditionally to him. He opened my eyes to the damage I'd done in my relationships, due in large part to my codependent and self-destructive behaviors. He showed me that he has a purpose for my life — one that doesn't include "fixing" anything or anyone else. He helped me to be completely honest, which was demonstrated by my faithful attendance at meetings, my perseverance in staying connected with him and with my sponsor on a daily basis, and my service to others.

I find myself most blessed when I'm given the opportunity to share the changes in my life with other hurting people. I had always thought that the only way God could use me was as an example of what *not* to do. It's so liberating to be able to serve others without the need to manipulate or control them. I've come to recognize that serenity never comes from rescuing and changing others. It comes from following Jesus and inviting others to join in the journey. To Christ belongs all the glory, because without him I'm absolutely powerless. I know, because I tried life on my own for over 30 years.

MY NAME IS PETER

JOHN 21

All of us, without exception, need a sponsor and/or accountability partner — someone who can confront us with truth and love without placing shame and guilt. A sponsor must demonstrate compassion, care and hope — but not pity.

In John 21 we see an ideal sponsor working to help Peter in his recovery. Peter had publicly denied ever knowing Jesus — the man who was his Lord, his teacher and his best friend. He needed to get back on the road to recovery, to undergo some authentic character changes. To Peter's credit, note that, even in the pain of his failure, he stayed with his group (see vv. 1–3).

Jesus himself filled the role of the sponsor/accountability partner for his fallen disciple. He sought Peter out, fed him (see vv. 4–14) and showed him compassion before he moved to confrontation. Then Jesus took Peter aside to help him face his pain and shame (see vv. 15–22). Jesus' words to Peter included a call to evaluate his love for Jesus and to minister to others (see vv. 15–17). How would this disciple take the first step? The Lord gave him a simple instruction: "Follow me!" (21:19)

In recovery, we are called to honestly examine the past and to face our pain and shame so that our love for Jesus can continue to grow. We are able to do this by making attendance at our recovery meetings a priority, maintaining an honest view of ourselves, staying connected to a group, getting involved in service, and maintaining spiritual contact with Jesus through prayer and study.

How do we know our love for Jesus is growing? How do we know when we are following him? We know we love the Lord when we think less about ourselves and more about the needs of others.

14This was now the third time Jesus appeared to his disciples after he was raised from the dead.

Jesus Reinstates Peter

15When they had finished eating, Jesus said to Simon Peter, "Simon son of John, do you love me more than these?"

"Yes, Lord," he said, "you know that I love you."

Jesus said, "Feed my lambs."

16Again Jesus said, "Simon son of John, do you love me?"

He answered, "Yes, Lord, you know that I love you."

Jesus said, "Take care of my sheep."

17The third time he said to him, "Simon son of John, do you love me?"

Peter was hurt because Jesus asked him the third time, "Do you love me?" He said, "Lord, you know all things; you know that I love you."

Jesus said, "Feed my sheep. 18Very truly I tell you, when you were younger you dressed yourself and went where you wanted; but when you are old you will stretch out your hands, and someone else will dress you and lead you where you do not want to go." 19Jesus said this to indicate the kind of death by which Peter would glorify God. Then he said to him, "Follow me!"

20Peter turned and saw that the disciple whom Jesus loved was following them. (This was the one who had leaned back against Jesus at the supper and had said, "Lord, who is going to betray you?") 21When Peter saw him, he asked, "Lord, what about him?"

22Jesus answered, "If I want him to remain alive until I return, what is that to you? You must follow me." 23Because of this, the rumor spread among the believers that this disciple would not die. But Jesus did not say that he would not die; he only said, "If I want him to remain alive until I return, what is that to you?"

24This is the disciple who testifies to these things and who wrote them down. We know that his testimony is true.

25Jesus did many other things as well. If every one of them were written down, I suppose that even the whole world would not have room for the books that would be written.

THEME: Believers today aren't eyewitnesses to Christ in the flesh, but we're empowered by the Spirit to experience Christ in our hearts. This impels us to share him with others.

AUTHOR: Acts nowhere identifies its author, but tradition from as early as the second century has held that the book was written by Luke as a sequel to his Gospel.

DATE OF WRITING: Acts was probably written between AD 63 and 70.

ENCOURAGEMENT FROM ACTS: "Leave these men alone! Let them go! For if their purpose or activity is of human origin, it will fail. But if it is from God, you will not be able to stop these men; you will only find yourselves fighting against God" (Acts 5:38 – 39).

CHALLENGE FROM ACTS: "Repent . . . and turn to God, so that your sins may be wiped out, that times of refreshing may come from the Lord" (Acts 3:19).

REFLECTION FROM ACTS: "While they were stoning him, Stephen prayed, 'Lord Jesus, receive my spirit.' Then he fell on his knees and cried out, 'Lord, do not hold this sin against them' " (Acts 7:59 – 60).

The book of Acts is proof that the Good News of Jesus is for everyone. Up to this point nearly all of the Messianic promises have been offered exclusively to the nation of Israel. The gospel message and invitation were for God's chosen people. That all changes in the book of Acts.

In the greatest news flash in all of human history, salvation has been made available to all people. Simply believe in Christ Jesus and our sins will be forgiven, our lives will be made meaningful, and everlasting life will be ours, beginning right now and culminating in an eternity in God's presence. This gift isn't just for a select group of people; the offer is inclusive — available with no fine print to every one of us.

When we're in recovery, we can often feel like outsiders — like broken sinners who just don't fit in. The book of Acts makes clear, though, that our background doesn't matter. It doesn't matter where we live, what we look like or what we've done. If we put our trust in Jesus, he offers us his forgiveness and healing.

Jesus Taken Up Into Heaven

1 In my former book, Theophilus, I wrote about all that Jesus began to do and to teach [2]until the day he was taken up to heaven, after giving instructions through the Holy Spirit to the apostles he had chosen. [3]After his suffering, he presented himself to them and gave many convincing proofs that he was alive. He appeared to them over a period of forty days and spoke about the kingdom of God. [4]On one occasion, while he was eating with them, he gave them this command: "Do not leave Jerusalem, but wait for the gift my Father promised, which you have heard me speak about. ⁵For John baptized with*ᵃ* water, but in a few days you will be baptized with*ᵃ* the Holy Spirit."

⁶Then they gathered around him and asked him, "Lord, are you at this time going to restore the kingdom to Israel?"

⁷He said to them: "It is not for you to know the times or dates the Father has set by his own authority. ⁸But you will receive power when the Holy Spirit comes on you; and you will be my witnesses in Jerusalem, and in all Judea and Samaria, and to the ends of the earth."

⁹After he said this, he was taken up before their very eyes, and a cloud hid him from their sight.

¹⁰They were looking intently up into the sky as he was going, when suddenly two men dressed in white stood beside them. ¹¹"Men of Galilee," they said, "why do you stand here looking into the sky? This same Jesus, who has been taken from you into heaven, will come back in the same way you have seen him go into heaven."

Matthias Chosen to Replace Judas

¹²Then the apostles returned to Jerusalem from the hill called the Mount of Olives, a Sabbath day's walk*ᵇ* from the city. ¹³When they arrived, they went upstairs to the room where they were staying. Those present were Peter, John, James and Andrew; Philip and Thomas, Bartholomew and Matthew; James son of Alphaeus and Simon the Zealot, and Judas son of James. ¹⁴They all joined together constantly in prayer, along with the women and Mary the mother of Jesus, and with his brothers.

¹⁵In those days Peter stood up among the believers (a group numbering about a hundred and twenty) ¹⁶and said, "Brothers and sisters,*ᶜ* the Scripture had to be fulfilled in which the Holy Spirit spoke long ago through David concerning Judas, who served as guide for those who arrested Jesus. ¹⁷He was one of our number and shared in our ministry."

¹⁸(With the payment he received for his wickedness, Judas bought a field; there he fell headlong, his body burst open and all his intestines spilled out. ¹⁹Everyone in Jerusalem heard about this, so they called that field in their language Akeldama, that is, Field of Blood.)

²⁰"For," said Peter, "it is written in the Book of Psalms:

> "'May his place be deserted;
> let there be no one to dwell in it,'*ᵈ*

and,

> "'May another take his place of
> leadership.'*ᵉ*

²¹Therefore it is necessary to choose one of the men who have been with us the whole time the Lord Jesus was living among us, ²²beginning from John's baptism to the time when Jesus was taken up from us. For one of these must become a witness with us of his resurrection."

²³So they nominated two men: Joseph called Barsabbas (also known as Justus) and Matthias. ²⁴Then they prayed, "Lord, you know everyone's heart. Show us which of these two you have chosen ²⁵to take over this apostolic ministry, which Judas left to go where he belongs." ²⁶Then they cast lots, and the lot fell to Matthias; so he was added to the eleven apostles.

The Holy Spirit Comes at Pentecost

2 When the day of Pentecost came, they were all together in one place. ²Suddenly a sound like the blowing of a violent wind came from heaven and filled the whole house where they were sitting. ³They saw what seemed to be tongues

---

ᵃ 5 Or *in*   *ᵇ 12* That is, about 5/8 mile or about 1 kilometer   *ᶜ 16* The Greek word for *brothers and sisters* (*adelphoi*) refers here to believers, both men and women, as part of God's family; also in 6:3; 11:29; 12:17; 16:40; 18:18, 27; 21:7, 17; 28:14, 15.   *ᵈ 20* Psalm 69:25   *ᵉ 20* Psalm 109:8

of fire that separated and came to rest on each of them. ⁴All of them were filled with the Holy Spirit and began to speak in other tongues*a* as the Spirit enabled them.

⁵Now there were staying in Jerusalem God-fearing Jews from every nation under heaven. ⁶When they heard this sound, a crowd came together in bewilderment, because each one heard their own language being spoken. ⁷Utterly amazed, they asked: "Aren't all these who are speaking Galileans? ⁸Then how is it that each of us hears them in our native language? ⁹Parthians, Medes and Elamites; residents of Mesopotamia, Judea and Cappadocia, Pontus and Asia,*b* ¹⁰Phrygia and Pamphylia, Egypt and the parts of Libya near Cyrene; visitors from Rome ¹¹(both Jews and converts to Judaism); Cretans and Arabs — we hear them declaring the wonders of God in our own tongues!" ¹²Amazed and perplexed, they asked one another, "What does this mean?"

¹³Some, however, made fun of them and said, "They have had too much wine."

Peter Addresses the Crowd

¹⁴Then Peter stood up with the Eleven, raised his voice and addressed the crowd: "Fellow Jews and all of you who live in Jerusalem, let me explain this to you; listen carefully to what I say. ¹⁵These people are not drunk, as you suppose. It's only nine in the morning! ¹⁶No, this is what was spoken by the prophet Joel:

¹⁷ " 'In the last days, God says,
   I will pour out my Spirit on all
      people.
   Your sons and daughters will prophesy,
      your young men will see visions,
      your old men will dream dreams.
¹⁸ Even on my servants, both men and
      women,
   I will pour out my Spirit in those
      days,
      and they will prophesy.

¹⁹ I will show wonders in the heavens
      above
   and signs on the earth below,
      blood and fire and billows of smoke.
²⁰ The sun will be turned to darkness
      and the moon to blood
   before the coming of the great and
      glorious day of the Lord.
²¹ And everyone who calls
      on the name of the Lord will be
         saved.'*c*

²²"Fellow Israelites, listen to this: Jesus of Nazareth was a man accredited by God to you by miracles, wonders and signs, which God did among you through him, as you yourselves know. ²³This man was handed over to you by God's deliberate plan and foreknowledge; and you, with the help of wicked men,*d* put him to death by nailing him to the cross. ²⁴But God raised him from the dead, freeing him from the agony of death, because it was impossible for death to keep its hold on him. ²⁵David said about him:

" 'I saw the Lord always before me.
      Because he is at my right hand,
      I will not be shaken.
²⁶ Therefore my heart is glad and my
      tongue rejoices;
   my body also will rest in hope,
²⁷ because you will not abandon me to the
      realm of the dead,
   you will not let your holy one see
      decay.
²⁸ You have made known to me the paths
      of life;
   you will fill me with joy in your
      presence.'*e*

²⁹"Fellow Israelites, I can tell you confidently that the patriarch David died and was buried, and his tomb is here to this day. ³⁰But he was a prophet and knew that God had promised him on oath that he would place one of his descendants on his throne. ³¹Seeing what was to come, he

---

a 4 Or *languages*; also in verse 11   *b 9* That is, the Roman province by that name   *c 21* Joel 2:28-32   *d 23* Or *of those not having the law* (that is, Gentiles)   *e 28* Psalm 16:8-11 (see Septuagint) spoke of the resurrection of the Messiah, that he was not abandoned to the realm of the dead, nor did his body see decay. ³²God has raised this Jesus to life, and we are all witnesses of it. ³³Exalted to the right hand of God, he has received from the Father the promised Holy Spirit and has poured out what you now see and hear. ³⁴For David did not ascend to heaven, and yet he said,

"'The Lord said to my Lord:
    "Sit at my right hand
³⁵until I make your enemies
    a footstool for your feet."'ᵃ

³⁶"Therefore let all Israel be assured of this: God has made this Jesus, whom you crucified, both Lord and Messiah."

³⁷When the people heard this, they were cut to the heart and said to Peter and the other apostles, "Brothers, what shall we do?"

³⁸Peter replied, "Repent and be baptized, every one of you, in the name of Jesus Christ for the forgiveness of your sins. And you will receive the gift of the Holy Spirit. ³⁹The promise is for you and your children and for all who are far off—for all whom the Lord our God will call."

⁴⁰With many other words he warned them; and he pleaded with them, "Save yourselves from this corrupt generation." ⁴¹Those who accepted his message were baptized, and about three thousand were added to their number that day.

The Fellowship of the Believers

⁴²They devoted themselves to the apostles' teaching and to fellowship, to the breaking of bread and to prayer. ⁴³Everyone was filled with awe at the many wonders and signs performed by the apostles. ⁴⁴All the believers were together and had everything in common. ⁴⁵They sold property and possessions to give to anyone who had need. ⁴⁶Every day they continued to meet together in the temple courts. They broke bread in their homes and ate together with glad and sincere hearts, ⁴⁷praising God and enjoying the favor of all the people. And the Lord added to their number daily those who were being saved.

Peter Heals a Lame Beggar

3 One day Peter and John were going up to the temple at the time of prayer—at three in the afternoon. ²Now a man who was lame from birth was being carried to the temple gate called Beautiful, where he was put every day to beg from those going into the temple courts. ³When he saw Peter and John about to enter, he asked them for money. ⁴Peter looked straight at him, as did John. Then Peter said, "Look at us!" ⁵So the man gave them his attention, expecting to get something from them.

⁶Then Peter said, "Silver or gold I do not have, but what I do have I give you. In the name of Jesus Christ of Nazareth, walk." ⁷Taking him by the right hand, he helped him up, and instantly the man's feet and ankles became strong. ⁸He jumped to his feet and began to walk. Then he went with them into the temple courts, walking and jumping, and praising God. ⁹When all the people saw him walking and praising God, ¹⁰they recognized him as the same man who used to sit begging at the temple gate called Beautiful, and they were filled with wonder and amazement at what had happened to him.

Peter Speaks to the Onlookers

¹¹While the man held on to Peter and John, all the people were astonished and came running to them in the place called Solomon's Colonnade. ¹²When Peter saw this, he said to them: "Fellow Israelites, why does this surprise you? Why do you stare at us as if by our own power or godliness we had made this man walk? ¹³The God of Abraham, Isaac and Jacob, the God of our fathers, has glorified his servant Jesus. You handed him over to be killed, and you

disowned him before Pilate, though he had decided to let him go. 14You disowned the Holy and Righteous One and asked that a murderer be released to you. 15You killed the author of life, but God raised him from the dead. We are witnesses of this. 16By faith in the name of Jesus, this man whom you see and know was made strong. It is Jesus' name and the faith that comes through him that has completely healed him, as you can all see.

17"Now, fellow Israelites, I know that you acted in ignorance, as did your leaders. 18But this is how God fulfilled what he had foretold through all the prophets, saying that his Messiah would suffer. 19Repent, then, and turn to God, so that your sins may be wiped out, that times of refreshing may come from the Lord, 20and that he may send the Messiah, who has been appointed for you — even Jesus. 21Heaven must receive him until the time comes for God to restore everything, as he promised long ago through his holy prophets. 22For Moses said, 'The Lord your God will raise up for you a prophet like me from among your own people; you must listen to everything he tells you. 23Anyone who does not listen to him will be completely cut off from their people.'a

24"Indeed, beginning with Samuel, all the prophets who have spoken have foretold these days. 25And you are heirs of the prophets and of the covenant God made with your fathers. He said to Abraham, 'Through your offspring all peoples on earth will be blessed.'b 26When God raised up his servant, he sent him first to you to bless you by turning each of you from your wicked ways."

Peter and John Before the Sanhedrin

4 The priests and the captain of the temple guard and the Sadducees came up to Peter and John while they were speaking to the people. 2They were greatly disturbed because the apos-tles were teaching the people, proclaiming in Jesus the resurrection of the dead. 3They seized Peter and John and, because it was evening, they put them in jail until the next day. 4But many who heard the message believed; so the number of men who believed grew to about five thousand.

5The next day the rulers, the elders and the teachers of the law met in Jerusalem. 6Annas the high priest was there, and so were Caiaphas, John, Alexander and others of the high priest's family. 7They had Peter and John brought before them and began to question them: "By what power or what name did you do this?"

8Then Peter, filled with the Holy Spirit, said to them: "Rulers and elders of the people! 9If we are being called to account today for an act of kindness shown to a man who was lame and are being asked how he was healed, 10then know this, you and all the people of Israel: It is by the name of Jesus Christ of Nazareth, whom you crucified but whom God raised from the dead, that this man stands before you healed. 11Jesus is

" 'the stone you builders rejected,
    which has become the cornerstone.'c

12Salvation is found in no one else, for there is no other name under heaven given to mankind by which we must be saved."

13When they saw the courage of Peter and John and realized that they were unschooled, ordinary men, they were astonished and they took note that these men had been with Jesus. 14But since they could see the man who had been healed standing there with them, there was nothing they could say. 15So they ordered them to withdraw from the Sanhedrin and then conferred together. 16"What are we going to do with these men?" they asked. "Everyone living in Jerusalem knows they have performed a notable sign, and we cannot deny it. 17But to stop this thing from spreading any further among the people, we must

---

a 23 Deut. 18:15,18,19   b 25 Gen. 22:18; 26:4   c 11 Psalm 118:22

warn them to speak no longer to anyone in this name."

[18]Then they called them in again and commanded them not to speak or teach at all in the name of Jesus. [19]But Peter and John replied, "Which is right in God's eyes: to listen to you, or to him? You be the judges! [20]As for us, we cannot help speaking about what we have seen and heard."

[21]After further threats they let them go. They could not decide how to punish them, because all the people were praising God for what had happened. [22]For the man who was miraculously healed was over forty years old.

The Believers Pray

[23]On their release, Peter and John went back to their own people and reported all that the chief priests and the elders had said to them. [24]When they heard this, they raised their voices together in prayer to God. "Sovereign Lord," they said, "you made the heavens and the earth and the sea, and everything in them. [25]You spoke by the Holy Spirit through the mouth of your servant, our father David:

"'Why do the nations rage
      and the peoples plot in vain?
[26]The kings of the earth rise up
      and the rulers band together
    against the Lord
      and against his anointed one.'[a][b]

[27]Indeed Herod and Pontius Pilate met together with the Gentiles and the people of Israel in this city to conspire against your holy servant Jesus, whom you anointed. [28]They did what your power and will had decided beforehand should happen. [29]Now, Lord, consider their threats and enable your servants to speak your word with great boldness. [30]Stretch out your hand to heal and perform signs and wonders through the name of your holy servant Jesus."

[31]After they prayed, the place where they were meeting was shaken. And they were all filled with the Holy Spirit and spoke the word of God boldly.

The Believers Share Their Possessions

[32]All the believers were one in heart and mind. No one claimed that any of their possessions was their own, but they shared everything they had. [33]With great power the apostles continued to testify to the resurrection of the Lord Jesus. And God's grace was so powerfully at work in them all [34]that there were no needy persons among them. For from time to time those who owned land or houses sold them, brought the money from the sales [35]and put it at the apostles' feet, and it was distributed to anyone who had need.

[36]Joseph, a Levite from Cyprus, whom the apostles called Barnabas (which means "son of encouragement"), [37]sold a field he owned and brought the money and put it at the apostles' feet.

Ananias and Sapphira

5 Now a man named Ananias, together with his wife Sapphira, also sold a piece of property. [2]With his wife's full knowledge he kept back part of the money for himself, but brought the rest and put it at the apostles' feet.

[3]Then Peter said, "Ananias, how is it that Satan has so filled your heart that you have lied to the Holy Spirit and have kept for yourself some of the money you received for the land? [4]Didn't it belong to you before it was sold? And after it was sold, wasn't the money at your disposal? What made you think of doing such a thing? You have not lied just to human beings but to God."

[5]When Ananias heard this, he fell down and died. And great fear seized all who heard what had happened. [6]Then some young men came forward, wrapped up his body, and carried him out and buried him.

[7]About three hours later his wife came in, not knowing what had happened. [8]Peter

---

[a] 26 That is, Messiah or Christ   [b] 26 Psalm 2:1,2

asked her, "Tell me, is this the price you and Ananias got for the land?"

"Yes," she said, "that is the price."

9Peter said to her, "How could you conspire to test the Spirit of the Lord? Listen! The feet of the men who buried your husband are at the door, and they will carry you out also."

10At that moment she fell down at his feet and died. Then the young men came in and, finding her dead, carried her out and buried her beside her husband. 11Great fear seized the whole church and all who heard about these events.

The Apostles Heal Many

12The apostles performed many signs and wonders among the people. And all the believers used to meet together in Solomon's Colonnade. 13No one else dared join them, even though they were highly regarded by the people. 14Nevertheless, more and more men and women believed in the Lord and were added to their number. 15As a result, people brought the sick into the streets and laid them on beds and mats so that at least Peter's shadow might fall on some of them as he passed by. 16Crowds gathered also from the towns around Jerusalem, bringing their sick and those tormented by impure spirits, and all of them were healed.

The Apostles Persecuted

17Then the high priest and all his associates, who were members of the party of the Sadducees, were filled with jealousy. 18They arrested the apostles and put them in the public jail. 19But during the night an angel of the Lord opened the doors of the jail and brought them out. 20"Go, stand in the temple courts," he said, "and tell the people all about this new life."

21At daybreak they entered the temple courts, as they had been told, and began to teach the people.

When the high priest and his associates arrived, they called together the Sanhedrin — the full assembly of the elders of Israel — and sent to the jail for the apostles. 22But on arriving at the jail, the officers did not find them there. So they went back and reported, 23"We found the jail securely locked, with the guards standing at the doors; but when we opened them, we found no one inside." 24On hearing this report, the captain of the temple guard and the chief priests were at a loss, wondering what this might lead to.

25Then someone came and said, "Look! The men you put in jail are standing in the temple courts teaching the people." 26At that, the captain went with his officers and brought the apostles. They did not use force, because they feared that the people would stone them.

27The apostles were brought in and made to appear before the Sanhedrin to be questioned by the high priest. 28"We gave you strict orders not to teach in this name," he said. "Yet you have filled Jerusalem with your teaching and are determined to make us guilty of this man's blood."

29Peter and the other apostles replied: "We must obey God rather than human beings! 30The God of our ancestors raised Jesus from the dead — whom you killed by hanging him on a cross. 31God exalted him to his own right hand as Prince and Savior that he might bring Israel to repentance and forgive their sins. 32We are witnesses of these things, and so is the Holy Spirit, whom God has given to those who obey him."

33When they heard this, they were furious and wanted to put them to death. 34But a Pharisee named Gamaliel, a teacher of the law, who was honored by all the people, stood up in the Sanhedrin and ordered that the men be put outside for a little while. 35Then he addressed the Sanhedrin: "Men of Israel, consider carefully what you intend to do to these men. 36Some time ago Theudas appeared, claiming to be somebody, and about four hundred men rallied to him. He was killed, all his followers were dispersed, and it all came to nothing. 37After him, Judas the Galilean appeared in the days of the census and led a band of people in revolt. He too was killed, and all his followers were scattered. [38]Therefore, in the present case I advise you: Leave these men alone! Let them go! For if their purpose or activity is of human origin, it will fail. [39]But if it is from God, you will not be able to stop these men; you will only find yourselves fighting against God."

[40]His speech persuaded them. They called the apostles in and had them flogged. Then they ordered them not to speak in the name of Jesus, and let them go.

[41]The apostles left the Sanhedrin, rejoicing because they had been counted worthy of suffering disgrace for the Name. [42]Day after day, in the temple courts and from house to house, they never stopped teaching and proclaiming the good news that Jesus is the Messiah.

The Choosing of the Seven

6 In those days when the number of disciples was increasing, the Hellenistic Jews[a] among them complained against the Hebraic Jews because their widows were being overlooked in the daily distribution of food. [2]So the Twelve gathered all the disciples together and said, "It would not be right for us to neglect the ministry of the word of God in order to wait on tables. [3]Brothers and sisters, choose seven men from among you who are known to be full of the Spirit and wisdom. We will turn this responsibility over to them [4]and will give our attention to prayer and the ministry of the word."

[5]This proposal pleased the whole group. They chose Stephen, a man full of faith and of the Holy Spirit; also Philip, Procorus, Nicanor, Timon, Parmenas, and Nicolas from Antioch, a convert to Judaism. [6]They presented these men to the apostles, who prayed and laid their hands on them.

[7]So the word of God spread. The number of disciples in Jerusalem increased rapidly, and a large number of priests became obedient to the faith.

Stephen Seized

[8]Now Stephen, a man full of God's grace and power, performed great wonders and signs among the people. [9]Opposition arose, however, from members of the Synagogue of the Freedmen (as it was called) — Jews of Cyrene and Alexandria as well as the provinces of Cilicia and Asia — who began to argue with Stephen. [10]But they could not stand up against the wisdom the Spirit gave him as he spoke.

[11]Then they secretly persuaded some men to say, "We have heard Stephen speak blasphemous words against Moses and against God."

[12]So they stirred up the people and the elders and the teachers of the law. They seized Stephen and brought him before the Sanhedrin. [13]They produced false witnesses, who testified, "This fellow never stops speaking against this holy place and against the law. [14]For we have heard him say that this Jesus of Nazareth will destroy this place and change the customs Moses handed down to us."

[15]All who were sitting in the Sanhedrin looked intently at Stephen, and they saw that his face was like the face of an angel.

Stephen's Speech to the Sanhedrin

7 Then the high priest asked Stephen, "Are these charges true?"

[2]To this he replied: "Brothers and fathers, listen to me! The God of glory appeared to our father Abraham while he was still in Mesopotamia, before he lived in Harran. [3]'Leave your country and your people,' God said, 'and go to the land I will show you.'[b]

[4]"So he left the land of the Chaldeans and settled in Harran. After the death of his father, God sent him to this land where you are now living. [5]He gave him no inheritance here, not even enough ground to set his foot on. But God promised him that he and his descendants after him would possess the land, even though at that time

---

[a] 1 That is, Jews who had adopted the Greek language and culture   [b] 3 Gen. 12:1

Abraham had no child. ⁶God spoke to him in this way: 'For four hundred years your descendants will be strangers in a country not their own, and they will be enslaved and mistreated. ⁷But I will punish the nation they serve as slaves,' God said, 'and afterward they will come out of that country and worship me in this place.'ᵃ ⁸Then he gave Abraham the covenant of circumcision. And Abraham became the father of Isaac and circumcised him eight days after his birth. Later Isaac became the father of Jacob, and Jacob became the father of the twelve patriarchs.

⁹"Because the patriarchs were jealous of Joseph, they sold him as a slave into Egypt. But God was with him ¹⁰and rescued him from all his troubles. He gave Joseph wisdom and enabled him to gain the goodwill of Pharaoh king of Egypt. So Pharaoh made him ruler over Egypt and all his palace.

¹¹"Then a famine struck all Egypt and Canaan, bringing great suffering, and our ancestors could not find food. ¹²When Jacob heard that there was grain in Egypt, he sent our forefathers on their first visit. ¹³On their second visit, Joseph told his brothers who he was, and Pharaoh learned about Joseph's family. ¹⁴After this, Joseph sent for his father Jacob and his whole family, seventy-five in all. ¹⁵Then Jacob went down to Egypt, where he and our ancestors died. ¹⁶Their bodies were brought back to Shechem and placed in the tomb that Abraham had bought from the sons of Hamor at Shechem for a certain sum of money.

¹⁷"As the time drew near for God to fulfill his promise to Abraham, the number of our people in Egypt had greatly increased. ¹⁸Then 'a new king, to whom Joseph meant nothing, came to power in Egypt.'ᵇ ¹⁹He dealt treacherously with our people and oppressed our ancestors by forcing them to throw out their newborn babies so that they would die.

²⁰"At that time Moses was born, and he was no ordinary child.ᶜ For three months he was cared for by his family. ²¹When he was placed outside, Pharaoh's daughter took him and brought him up as her own son. ²²Moses was educated in all the wisdom of the Egyptians and was powerful in speech and action.

²³"When Moses was forty years old, he decided to visit his own people, the Israelites. ²⁴He saw one of them being mistreated by an Egyptian, so he went to his defense and avenged him by killing the Egyptian. ²⁵Moses thought that his own people would realize that God was using him to rescue them, but they did not. ²⁶The next day Moses came upon two Israelites who were fighting. He tried to reconcile them by saying, 'Men, you are brothers; why do you want to hurt each other?'

²⁷"But the man who was mistreating the other pushed Moses aside and said, 'Who made you ruler and judge over us? ²⁸Are you thinking of killing me as you killed the Egyptian yesterday?'ᵈ ²⁹When Moses heard this, he fled to Midian, where he settled as a foreigner and had two sons.

³⁰"After forty years had passed, an angel appeared to Moses in the flames of a burning bush in the desert near Mount Sinai. ³¹When he saw this, he was amazed at the sight. As he went over to get a closer look, he heard the Lord say: ³²'I am the God of your fathers, the God of Abraham, Isaac and Jacob.'ᵉ Moses trembled with fear and did not dare to look.

³³"Then the Lord said to him, 'Take off your sandals, for the place where you are standing is holy ground. ³⁴I have indeed seen the oppression of my people in Egypt. I have heard their groaning and have come down to set them free. Now come, I will send you back to Egypt.'ᶠ

³⁵"This is the same Moses they had rejected with the words, 'Who made you ruler and judge?' He was sent to be their ruler and deliverer by God himself, through the

---

ᵃ 7 Gen. 15:13,14   ᵇ 18 Exodus 1:8   ᶜ 20 Or *was fair in the sight of God*   ᵈ 28 Exodus 2:14
ᵉ 32 Exodus 3:6   ᶠ 34 Exodus 3:5,7,8,10

angel who appeared to him in the bush. [36]He led them out of Egypt and performed wonders and signs in Egypt, at the Red Sea and for forty years in the wilderness.

[37]"This is the Moses who told the Israelites, 'God will raise up for you a prophet like me from your own people.'[a] [38]He was in the assembly in the wilderness, with the angel who spoke to him on Mount Sinai, and with our ancestors; and he received living words to pass on to us.

[39]"But our ancestors refused to obey him. Instead, they rejected him and in their hearts turned back to Egypt. [40]They told Aaron, 'Make us gods who will go before us. As for this fellow Moses who led us out of Egypt—we don't know what has happened to him!'[b] [41]That was the time they made an idol in the form of a calf. They brought sacrifices to it and reveled in what their own hands had made. [42]But God turned away from them and gave them over to the worship of the sun, moon and stars. This agrees with what is written in the book of the prophets:

> "'Did you bring me sacrifices and
>   offerings
>   forty years in the wilderness, people
>   of Israel?
> [43]You have taken up the tabernacle of
>   Molek
>   and the star of your god Rephan,
>   the idols you made to worship.
> Therefore I will send you into exile'[c]
>   beyond Babylon.

[44]"Our ancestors had the tabernacle of the covenant law with them in the wilderness. It had been made as God directed Moses, according to the pattern he had seen. [45]After receiving the tabernacle, our ancestors under Joshua brought it with them when they took the land from the nations God drove out before them. It remained in the land until the time of David, [46]who enjoyed God's favor and asked that

he might provide a dwelling place for the God of Jacob.[d] [47]But it was Solomon who built a house for him.

[48]"However, the Most High does not live in houses made by human hands. As the prophet says:

> [49]"'Heaven is my throne,
>   and the earth is my footstool.
> What kind of house will you build for
>   me?
>   says the Lord.
> Or where will my resting place be?
> [50]Has not my hand made all these
>   things?'[e]

[51]"You stiff-necked people! Your hearts and ears are still uncircumcised. You are just like your ancestors: You always resist the Holy Spirit! [52]Was there ever a prophet your ancestors did not persecute? They even killed those who predicted the coming of the Righteous One. And now you have betrayed and murdered him— [53]you who have received the law that was given through angels but have not obeyed it."

The Stoning of Stephen

[54]When the members of the Sanhedrin heard this, they were furious and gnashed their teeth at him. [55]But Stephen, full of the Holy Spirit, looked up to heaven and saw the glory of God, and Jesus standing at the right hand of God. [56]"Look," he said, "I see heaven open and the Son of Man standing at the right hand of God."

[57]At this they covered their ears and, yelling at the top of their voices, they all rushed at him, [58]dragged him out of the city and began to stone him. Meanwhile, the witnesses laid their coats at the feet of a young man named Saul.

[59]While they were stoning him, Stephen prayed, "Lord Jesus, receive my spirit." [60]Then he fell on his knees and cried out, "Lord, do not hold this sin against them." When he had said this, he fell asleep.

---

[a] 37 Deut. 18:15   [b] 40 Exodus 32:1   [c] 43 Amos 5:25-27 (see Septuagint)   [d] 46 Some early manuscripts *the house of Jacob*   [e] 50 Isaiah 66:1,2

8

And Saul approved of their killing him.

The Church Persecuted and Scattered

On that day a great persecution broke out against the church in Jerusalem, and all except the apostles were scattered throughout Judea and Samaria. [2]Godly men buried Stephen and mourned deeply for him. [3]But Saul began to destroy the church. Going from house to house, he dragged off both men and women and put them in prison.

Philip in Samaria

[4]Those who had been scattered preached the word wherever they went. [5]Philip went down to a city in Samaria and proclaimed the Messiah there. [6]When the crowds heard Philip and saw the signs he performed, they all paid close attention to what he said. [7]For with shrieks, impure spirits came out of many, and many who were paralyzed or lame were healed. [8]So there was great joy in that city.

Simon the Sorcerer

[9]Now for some time a man named Simon had practiced sorcery in the city and amazed all the people of Samaria. He boasted that he was someone great, [10]and all the people, both high and low, gave him their attention and exclaimed, "This man is rightly called the Great Power of God." [11]They followed him because he had amazed them for a long time with his sorcery. [12]But when they believed Philip as he proclaimed the good news of the kingdom of God and the name of Jesus Christ, they were baptized, both men and women. [13]Simon himself believed and was baptized. And he followed Philip everywhere, astonished by the great signs and miracles he saw.

[14]When the apostles in Jerusalem heard that Samaria had accepted the word of God, they sent Peter and John to Samaria. [15]When they arrived, they prayed for the new believers there that they might receive the Holy Spirit, [16]because the Holy Spirit had not yet come on any of them; they had simply been baptized in the name of the Lord Jesus. [17]Then Peter and John placed their hands on them, and they received the Holy Spirit.

[18]When Simon saw that the Spirit was given at the laying on of the apostles' hands, he offered them money [19]and said, "Give me also this ability so that everyone on whom I lay my hands may receive the Holy Spirit."

[20]Peter answered: "May your money perish with you, because you thought you could buy the gift of God with money! [21]You have no part or share in this ministry, because your heart is not right before God. [22]Repent of this wickedness and pray to the Lord in the hope that he may forgive you for having such a thought in your heart. [23]For I see that you are full of bitterness and captive to sin."

[24]Then Simon answered, "Pray to the Lord for me so that nothing you have said may happen to me."

[25]After they had further proclaimed the word of the Lord and testified about Jesus, Peter and John returned to Jerusalem, preaching the gospel in many Samaritan villages.

Philip and the Ethiopian

[26]Now an angel of the Lord said to Philip, "Go south to the road — the desert road — that goes down from Jerusalem to Gaza." [27]So he started out, and on his way he met an Ethiopian[a] eunuch, an important official in charge of all the treasury of the Kandake (which means "queen of the Ethiopians"). This man had gone to Jerusalem to worship, [28]and on his way home was sitting in his chariot reading the Book of Isaiah the prophet. [29]The Spirit told Philip, "Go to that chariot and stay near it."

[30]Then Philip ran up to the chariot and heard the man reading Isaiah the proph-

---

a 27 That is, from the southern Nile region

et. "Do you understand what you are reading?" Philip asked.

³¹"How can I," he said, "unless someone explains it to me?" So he invited Philip to come up and sit with him.

³²This is the passage of Scripture the eunuch was reading:

> "He was led like a sheep to the
>   slaughter,
> and as a lamb before its shearer is
>   silent,
> so he did not open his mouth.
> ³³In his humiliation he was deprived of
>   justice.
> Who can speak of his descendants?
> For his life was taken from the
>   earth."ᵃ

³⁴The eunuch asked Philip, "Tell me, please, who is the prophet talking about, himself or someone else?" ³⁵Then Philip began with that very passage of Scripture and told him the good news about Jesus.

³⁶As they traveled along the road, they came to some water and the eunuch said, "Look, here is water. What can stand in the way of my being baptized?" [37]ᵇ ³⁸And he gave orders to stop the chariot. Then both Philip and the eunuch went down into the water and Philip baptized him. ³⁹When they came up out of the water, the Spirit of the Lord suddenly took Philip away, and the eunuch did not see him again, but went on his way rejoicing. ⁴⁰Philip, however, appeared at Azotus and traveled about, preaching the gospel in all the towns until he reached Caesarea.

Saul's Conversion

9 Meanwhile, Saul was still breathing out murderous threats against the Lord's disciples. He went to the high priest ²and asked him for letters to the synagogues in Damascus, so that if he found any there who belonged to the Way, whether men or women, he might take them as prisoners to Jerusalem. ³As he neared Damascus on his journey, suddenly a light from heaven flashed around him. ⁴He fell to the ground and heard a voice say to him, "Saul, Saul, why do you persecute me?"

⁵"Who are you, Lord?" Saul asked.

"I am Jesus, whom you are persecuting," he replied. ⁶"Now get up and go into the city, and you will be told what you must do."

⁷The men traveling with Saul stood there speechless; they heard the sound but did not see anyone. ⁸Saul got up from the ground, but when he opened his eyes he could see nothing. So they led him by the hand into Damascus. ⁹For three days he was blind, and did not eat or drink anything.

¹⁰In Damascus there was a disciple named Ananias. The Lord called to him in a vision, "Ananias!"

"Yes, Lord," he answered.

¹¹The Lord told him, "Go to the house of Judas on Straight Street and ask for a man from Tarsus named Saul, for he is praying. ¹²In a vision he has seen a man named Ananias come and place his hands on him to restore his sight."

¹³"Lord," Ananias answered, "I have heard many reports about this man and all the harm he has done to your holy people in Jerusalem. ¹⁴And he has come here with authority from the chief priests to arrest all who call on your name."

¹⁵But the Lord said to Ananias, "Go! This man is my chosen instrument to proclaim my name to the Gentiles and their kings and to the people of Israel. ¹⁶I will show him how much he must suffer for my name."

¹⁷Then Ananias went to the house and entered it. Placing his hands on Saul, he said, "Brother Saul, the Lord — Jesus, who appeared to you on the road as you were coming here — has sent me so that you may see again and be filled with the Holy Spirit."

ᵃ 33 Isaiah 53:7,8 (see Septuagint)   ᵇ 37 Some manuscripts include here *Philip said, "If you believe with all your heart, you may." The eunuch answered, "I believe that Jesus Christ is the Son of God."*

My Name Is Bob

I'M A BELIEVER WHO STRUGGLES WITH DRUG ADDICTION AND LUST

Please read the story of Paul's conversion in Acts 9:1 – 19.

I'll never forget that first night I drove up the long driveway to my first Celebrate Recovery meeting. I was scared and not really sure why I was there. But when I walked in, I met so many people who had once felt the same way I did. Their warm smiles and friendly hugs made me feel at home.

I had no idea where this step of faith would lead me. Up to this point in my life, I'd been like a tornado swirling through the lives of everyone around me because of drug and lust addictions. Like the apostle Paul before his conversion, I'd been relentless in my pursuit. But I couldn't stop God's plan for my life. Along my own road to Damascus, Jesus got involved by using my family to do an intervention (see Acts 26:13 – 15). Because I was a threat to their safety, they wrote a letter saying how much they loved and cared about me, but they added that they could no longer watch me destroy my life. I was faced with a decision: continue to deny my problem or get help. I chose to get help. For the first time in my life I began attending church on a regular basis. I had a lot of questions about who God was and why he would want to know me — a man who had hurt those closest to him. As I walked down my new road of recovery, I discovered a relationship with Jesus Christ that has completely transformed my life. As he did for Paul, he restored my sight and turned my selfishness and self-centeredness into a sincere desire to serve him with all my heart (see 9:8 – 19).

For my first year and a half of being a new Christian, I attended everything Saddleback Church had to offer. I was young and single and had nothing but time. I went to small groups, midweek services, Celebrate Recovery twice a week, several Bible studies and all the church membership classes. Need I say more? I was like a sponge. I felt like I couldn't get enough of my newfound faith, and dating wasn't on my radar — until the night *she* walked in! It was during my Thursday night Bible study. I thought there was no way a woman this beautiful could be interested in a guy like me. Well, let's just say that God's plans were far greater than anything either of us could have imagined, and the following April Pastor John married us. By this time we were both serving as Celebrate Recovery leaders to help others overcome their own hurts, hang-ups and habits. The ministry that *brought* us together is continuing to *keep* us together.

It was completely humbling to think that God could use me in such extraordinary ways to help change lives for eternity. No matter what I do or where I go, God confirms in my heart his plan for my life. Being able to serve God is the most incredible journey I've ever been on, and being able to serve him with my wife makes it irresistible.

As for my family, God has brought healing to those relationships. Because my life was truly changing, their trust of me began to be restored. Through this transformation God has seen fit to use me to bring members of my family to a saving knowledge of him. My sister, seeing what had happened in my life, gave her life to Christ. She's now an active leader in Celebrate Recovery. My mother, who never gave up on me and faithfully prayed for me for over ten years, went to be with Jesus after battling cancer. She'd been there for me every step of the way, and because of God using Celebrate Recovery, I was able to be there for her during her final days and to see her take her last breath on Earth.

A few years later God gave me the courage to talk to my dad about Christ. This was especially difficult because I didn't talk to him much at this level, but I knew that if I didn't share with him, I would always regret it. God gave me the privilege of leading my dad in a prayer to ask Jesus into his life, and he has now gone home to be with the Lord. God hasn't stopped amazing me along my spiritual journey. After having my eyes opened by him, I've been given a mission by him similar to that of the apostle Paul: to go and "open their eyes and turn them from darkness to light" (Acts 26:18). God has now entrusted me with serving as a Celebrate Recovery pastor. It really is true that "in all things God works for the good of those who love him, who have been called according to his purpose" (Romans 8:28).

God rescued me from the depths of destruction, and the Holy Spirit empowers me to minister to those who are hurting. Like Paul, I'm now a pastor who delivers God's message to the wounded. I'm eternally thankful for that day when God knocked me flat.

MY NAME IS PAUL

ACTS 9

Religion can be as addictive as any drug. Add pride, position and power, and dramatic intervention may be needed. That was the case with Paul — then called Saul. No one could have been more addicted to religion than Paul was. He had every reason to feel smug about his religious heritage, training, position and accomplishments (see Acts 9:4 – 5; see also Philippians 3:4 – 6). Fully convinced that he was doing God's work, Paul did all he could to undermine the infant church (see Acts 26:9 – 11). In fact, after Stephen was executed by the authorities, Paul took upon himself the task of trying to destroy the church. Going from house to house, he dragged off men and women and put them in prison (see 8:3). But even that wasn't enough for Paul, who was locked in the grip of his compulsion. Paul, "still breathing out murderous threats against the Lord's disciples" (9:1), secured from the high priest "letters to the synagogues in Damascus, so that if he found any there who belonged to the Way, whether men or women, he might take them as prisoners to Jerusalem" (9:2). Addiction is devoid of mercy and relentless in its pursuits. Paul the apostle would look back in time and correctly label his earlier religious zeal an obsession (see 26:11).

Paul's schemes, though, couldn't cancel out God's plan. Paul, the most fanatical persecutor of Jesus' followers (see 9:14), was to become the most passionate proclaimer of Jesus (see vv. 19 – 20; see also 1 Corinthians 15:9 – 10). This transformation would include some important ingredients:

- Intervention. Jesus had to confront Paul in the depths of his obsession. He quite literally knocked Paul flat (see Acts 9:4).

- Insight. Paul had to understand his weakness: spiritual blindness. Jesus made this point by first rendering Paul physically blind and then restoring his sight (see vv. 8 – 19).

- Mission. Paul, having had his own eyes opened, was equipped to go to the Gentiles "to open their eyes and turn them from darkness to light" (26:18).

Paul the apostle had been hurt by others — and he himself had injured and even murdered many. He of all people had an intimate knowledge of insane compulsions. Satan uses such devices to keep us in his domain, but truth moves us into the domain of God's kingdom. Entering God's domain we find freedom "from the power of Satan," "forgiveness of sins" and "a place among those who are sanctified by faith in [Christ]" (26:18).

To be sanctified is to be set apart from the world as Christ's servant (see 28:16). That's the radical reality of recovery. We move from bondage to sin to being God's chosen servants. To serve him is to convey the Good News by words and example to those still in darkness. When we experience the joys of serving him, we, like Paul, can thank God for the day he knocked us flat.

¹⁸Immediately, something like scales fell from Saul's eyes, and he could see again. He got up and was baptized, ¹⁹and after taking some food, he regained his strength.

Saul in Damascus and Jerusalem

Saul spent several days with the disciples in Damascus. ²⁰At once he began to preach in the synagogues that Jesus is the Son of God. ²¹All those who heard him were astonished and asked, "Isn't he the man who raised havoc in Jerusalem among those who call on this name? And hasn't he come here to take them as prisoners to the chief priests?" ²²Yet Saul grew more and more powerful and baffled the Jews living in Damascus by proving that Jesus is the Messiah.

²³After many days had gone by, there was a conspiracy among the Jews to kill him, ²⁴but Saul learned of their plan. Day and night they kept close watch on the city gates in order to kill him. ²⁵But his followers took him by night and lowered him in a basket through an opening in the wall.

²⁶When he came to Jerusalem, he tried to join the disciples, but they were all afraid of him, not believing that he really was a disciple. ²⁷But Barnabas took him and brought him to the apostles. He told them how Saul on his journey had seen the Lord and that the Lord had spoken to him, and how in Damascus he had preached fearlessly in the name of Jesus. ²⁸So Saul stayed with them and moved about freely in Jerusalem, speaking boldly in the name of the Lord. ²⁹He talked and debated with the Hellenistic Jews,ᵃ but they tried to kill him. ³⁰When the believers learned of this, they took him down to Caesarea and sent him off to Tarsus.

³¹Then the church throughout Judea, Galilee and Samaria enjoyed a time of peace and was strengthened. Living in the fear of the Lord and encouraged by the Holy Spirit, it increased in numbers.

Aeneas and Dorcas

³²As Peter traveled about the country, he went to visit the Lord's people who lived in Lydda. ³³There he found a man named Aeneas, who was paralyzed and had been bedridden for eight years. ³⁴"Aeneas," Peter said to him, "Jesus Christ heals you. Get up and roll up your mat." Immediately Aeneas got up. ³⁵All those who lived in Lydda and Sharon saw him and turned to the Lord.

³⁶In Joppa there was a disciple named Tabitha (in Greek her name is Dorcas); she was always doing good and helping the poor. ³⁷About that time she became sick and died, and her body was washed and placed in an upstairs room. ³⁸Lydda was near Joppa; so when the disciples heard that Peter was in Lydda, they sent two men to him and urged him, "Please come at once!"

³⁹Peter went with them, and when he arrived he was taken upstairs to the room. All the widows stood around him, crying and showing him the robes and other clothing that Dorcas had made while she was still with them.

⁴⁰Peter sent them all out of the room; then he got down on his knees and prayed. Turning toward the dead woman, he said, "Tabitha, get up." She opened her eyes, and seeing Peter she sat up. ⁴¹He took her by the hand and helped her to her feet. Then he called for the believers, especially the widows, and presented her to them alive. ⁴²This became known all over Joppa, and many people believed in the Lord. ⁴³Peter stayed in Joppa for some time with a tanner named Simon.

Cornelius Calls for Peter

10 At Caesarea there was a man named Cornelius, a centurion in what was known as the Italian Regiment. ²He and all his family were devout and God-fearing; he gave generously to those in need and prayed to God

---

ᵃ 29 That is, Jews who had adopted the Greek language and culture

My Name Is Diane

I'M A BELIEVER WHO STRUGGLES WITH WORKAHOLISM AND CODEPENDENCY

Please read the story of Tabitha's servant attitude in Acts 9:36 – 42.

As an infant I had severe asthma and food allergies. Mom would remind me in later years of how difficult it had been to care for me. We attended church regularly, and if I didn't do as Mom wanted, she would say, "That's a sin." From early on I developed a view of religion based on her perspective: God was all-powerful, all-noticing, unforgiving and punishing.

One Sunday when I was 13, I was helping in the kitchen and moved a pan filled with boiling oil. The handle was loose and the oil spilled, severely burning both my thighs. The pain was excruciating, but I'd learned that tears were futile. My recovery was slow and painful, and I was left with ugly scars. It wasn't easy dealing with people's reactions.

As I attended church school, I was taught to question and interpret the Bible. Through this process it occurred to me that God might not be punishing me. But a case of infidelity involving a church elder caused me to leave the church, and it would be years before I returned.

I decided to go into nursing. The school was highly structured and regimented, but I was taking care of others and loved the pace and discipline. I recall an instructor cautioning me, "You're too confident." I thought, "Good, that's what I want them to think." Looking back, my behavior was viewed as arrogance. After graduation I went to work in an intensive care unit.

While still in school I had met the man I would marry, and in 1972 our daughter was born. I was a '70s mom, working full time and still doing the home stuff. Most of my time with my daughter was spent in the car, as I worked 35 miles from home. In 1977 our son, born prematurely at 31 weeks, was given a 50 – 50 chance of surviving. He was allowed to come home at three weeks old, since I was a nurse. Immature and weak, he required two ounces of milk every two hours, and he had a pattern of turning blue without sound or warning. I began having him sleep across my chest so I could feel his breathing. Around the time of his second birthday I realized he was here to stay.

Years passed, and my world became too busy for me to see the big picture of my life. My husband was retreating to his chair in the evening in the company of his friend, scotch.

I developed a sudden finger infection that entered my bloodstream and caused my hospitalization. A week later my mother had a stroke and my daughter ran away. Little did I know that God was trying to get my attention. I sat in a chair feeling as though I was going to explode with no one to know or care. I did mouth prayers but doubted that the Lord would be there for someone as unworthy as me.

Shortly afterward I sustained a serious back injury. Once again in excruciating pain, I lost my job and retirement benefits after 16 years of employment. I had no social outlets and felt like a ghost in my own home. Feeling as though I had already died, I made plans to end my life. But slowly, from somewhere deep inside me, I began to recall Psalm 23. That day I was restored to life through God's miraculous intervention. Whereas Tabitha's life was restored physically, mine was renewed spiritually. The process was slow, but I started to make positive choices. I prayed the Serenity Prayer and began attending meetings. I had no idea where I was going, and I grieved the losses of career and physical ability, but I made up my mind that, though I might have a physical disability, I was not going to be handicapped.

Eventually my granddaughter was born, and as she grew, my back strengthened. I had to get down on the floor and play with her. Slowly I began to laugh and sing, becoming the kid I'd never allowed myself to be. I started attending Saddleback Church and began to relate to a loving, caring God. I served in the children's ministry and took home more in blessing than I gave.

I began attending Celebrate Recovery and found the Christ-centered Step Study to be an enlightening experience. I had worked the secular 12 steps previously, but this time it was different: I was experiencing God's life-giving power and grace. This program has given me great friendships, as well as a leadership outlet. Anticipating the Friday evening meetings rejuvenates me all week long. I serve coffee and dessert at Celebrate Recovery's Solid Rock Café and am lovingly referred to as the Cake Whacker. I believe that serving God keeps my recovery strong.

I see in retrospect that my good deeds as a workaholic nurse did nothing to deliver me from my difficulties, and I've learned through Tabitha's example to serve God in genuine love and humility. As a believer who struggled with workaholism and codependency, the "me" had gotten lost in becoming what I thought would please others. Today I want to please Jesus.

Diane

MY NAME IS TABITHA

ACTS 9:36–43

One of the "proverbs" of recovery is this: Service keeps us healthy. But in Christ-centered recovery, service does far, far more. Giving of ourselves is central to our ability to enjoy life as Jesus desires and be a blessing to others.

Tabitha had an impressive résumé: She "was always doing good and helping the poor" (Acts 9:36). She wasn't an apostle, a preacher, a professor or a famous evangelist. But she assisted others in need. Good deeds didn't deliver her from difficulties or disease. In fact, she became sick and died. Tabitha, like many others who give of themselves out of genuine love and humility, probably never thought of herself as having any great impact on God's kingdom. But her death revealed just how much she mattered to so many.

Tabitha's hometown was Joppa, an ancient seaport on the Mediterranean. Peter was at the time nearby in the town of Lydda. The impact of Tabitha's illness and death is seen in the disciples' urgent plea that Peter come immediately (see v. 38). When the apostle arrived, he was shown examples of Tabitha's love: "All the widows stood around him, crying and showing him the robes and other clothing that Dorcas [Tabitha] had made while she was still with them" (v. 39). What were the results of Tabitha's service to others? First, she was restored to life by God's miraculous intervention (see v. 40). Then she became an example for all time to come of God's life-giving power and grace (see v. 41). Finally, her story led to the salvation of many (see v. 42).

Like Tabitha, we need to make ourselves available continuously in a helping capacity. Our deeds of love bless others in ways we may never know. Indeed, our service makes us shining examples of God's grace.

This is reality: If you're not yet serving, you're not yet recovering.

regularly. ³One day at about three in the afternoon he had a vision. He distinctly saw an angel of God, who came to him and said, "Cornelius!"

⁴Cornelius stared at him in fear. "What is it, Lord?" he asked.

The angel answered, "Your prayers and gifts to the poor have come up as a memorial offering before God. ⁵Now send men to Joppa to bring back a man named Simon who is called Peter. ⁶He is staying with Simon the tanner, whose house is by the sea."

⁷When the angel who spoke to him had gone, Cornelius called two of his servants and a devout soldier who was one of his attendants. ⁸He told them everything that had happened and sent them to Joppa.

Peter's Vision

⁹About noon the following day as they were on their journey and approaching the city, Peter went up on the roof to pray. ¹⁰He became hungry and wanted something to eat, and while the meal was being prepared, he fell into a trance. ¹¹He saw heaven opened and something like a large sheet being let down to earth by its four corners. ¹²It contained all kinds of four-footed animals, as well as reptiles and birds. ¹³Then a voice told him, "Get up, Peter. Kill and eat."

¹⁴"Surely not, Lord!" Peter replied. "I have never eaten anything impure or unclean."

¹⁵The voice spoke to him a second time, "Do not call anything impure that God has made clean."

¹⁶This happened three times, and immediately the sheet was taken back to heaven.

¹⁷While Peter was wondering about the meaning of the vision, the men sent by Cornelius found out where Simon's house was and stopped at the gate. ¹⁸They called out, asking if Simon who was known as Peter was staying there.

¹⁹While Peter was still thinking about the vision, the Spirit said to him, "Simon, three*ᵃ* men are looking for you. ²⁰So get up and go downstairs. Do not hesitate to go with them, for I have sent them."

²¹Peter went down and said to the men, "I'm the one you're looking for. Why have you come?"

²²The men replied, "We have come from Cornelius the centurion. He is a righteous and God-fearing man, who is respected by all the Jewish people. A holy angel told him to ask you to come to his house so that he could hear what you have to say." ²³Then Peter invited the men into the house to be his guests.

Peter at Cornelius's House

The next day Peter started out with them, and some of the believers from Joppa went along. ²⁴The following day he arrived in Caesarea. Cornelius was expecting them and had called together his relatives and close friends. ²⁵As Peter entered the house, Cornelius met him and fell at his feet in reverence. ²⁶But Peter made him get up. "Stand up," he said, "I am only a man myself."

²⁷While talking with him, Peter went inside and found a large gathering of people. ²⁸He said to them: "You are well aware that it is against our law for a Jew to associate with or visit a Gentile. But God has shown me that I should not call anyone impure or unclean. ²⁹So when I was sent for, I came without raising any objection. May I ask why you sent for me?"

³⁰Cornelius answered: "Three days ago I was in my house praying at this hour, at three in the afternoon. Suddenly a man in shining clothes stood before me ³¹and said, 'Cornelius, God has heard your prayer and remembered your gifts to the poor. ³²Send to Joppa for Simon who is called Peter. He is a guest in the home of Simon the tanner, who lives by the sea.' ³³So I sent for you immediately, and it was good of you to come. Now we are all here in the presence of God

---

ᵃ 19 One early manuscript *two*; other manuscripts do not have the number.

MY NAME IS CORNELIUS

ACTS 10

Despite living as a Gentile in a Roman city, Cornelius had enough contact with Jews to learn about and accept their God. He was devout, God-fearing and generous (see Acts 10:2). Caesarea, on Israel's Mediterranean coast, was a wealthy, decadent city, the seat of Roman rule over Judea. Herod the Great had built this city with a pleasure palace for himself and a temple to Augustus Caesar. Here Herod was able to abandon his hypocritical adherence to Judaism.

Into this city God, ever sensitive to the seeker, sent a messenger, an angel. But Cornelius would actually meet Jesus not through angelic intervention but through the preaching of a devout Jew, the reluctant missionary named Peter.

Cornelius sets a good example for anyone coming out of bondage (see v. 2): First, he included his family in his growing faith. Then he put feet to his faith through his generous gifts to the poor. Finally, he prayed regularly.

The last point is vital. God responded to Cornelius's prayers on one particular day in a spectacular way. But prayer was already an established pattern in this centurion's life. Without daily devotion to prayer we can miss out on miracles. Breakthroughs in recovery often come through devotion to spiritual disciplines. It's easy to see how the faithful, fervent prayers of Cornelius led to an angelic visitation.

God hasn't chosen angels as his missionaries in our lives; instead, he opts to use chosen believers who have actually experienced God's transforming, saving power. The angel in Cornelius's case served in the role of a go-between, instructing Cornelius to send for Peter (see vv. 5–8). While the centurion's servants traveled south along the coast to Joppa, God prepared Peter for the coming encounter through a vision (see vv. 9–16). After experiencing the vision three times, Peter was ready to go when Cornelius's servants arrived.

When Peter arrived at Cornelius's house, he explained how God had delivered him from prejudice and then shared the Good News of Jesus Christ. The crowd included Cornelius's entire family and close friends, a "large gathering" (v. 27). As Peter was speaking, "the Holy Spirit" was "poured out . . . on [the] Gentiles" (v. 45).

Years later, with large numbers of Gentiles entering the church, a crisis loomed. Some Jewish believers insisted that the converted Gentiles be circumcised and required to observe the Mosaic Law. There was extended discussion of this issue at the first church council of apostles and elders. Then Peter stood up and shared the story of Cornelius and the other Gentile believers of Caesarea. Combining this testimony with the stories of Barnabas and Paul, the council refused to make it difficult for "Gentiles who are turning to God" (15:19). The freedom from legalism you enjoy in the church today can be traced back to the wise decision of this council and then back still further to a Gentile Roman centurion who "prayed to God regularly" (10:2). Principle Seven in Celebrate Recovery establishes our time alone with God as the way we gain the power to follow his will.

to listen to everything the Lord has commanded you to tell us."

³⁴Then Peter began to speak: "I now realize how true it is that God does not show favoritism ³⁵but accepts from every nation the one who fears him and does what is right. ³⁶You know the message God sent to the people of Israel, announcing the good news of peace through Jesus Christ, who is Lord of all. ³⁷You know what has happened throughout the province of Judea, beginning in Galilee after the baptism that John preached— ³⁸how God anointed Jesus of Nazareth with the Holy Spirit and power, and how he went around doing good and healing all who were under the power of the devil, because God was with him.

³⁹"We are witnesses of everything he did in the country of the Jews and in Jerusalem. They killed him by hanging him on a cross, ⁴⁰but God raised him from the dead on the third day and caused him to be seen. ⁴¹He was not seen by all the people, but by witnesses whom God had already chosen—by us who ate and drank with him after he rose from the dead. ⁴²He commanded us to preach to the people and to testify that he is the one whom God appointed as judge of the living and the dead. ⁴³All the prophets testify about him that everyone who believes in him receives forgiveness of sins through his name."

⁴⁴While Peter was still speaking these words, the Holy Spirit came on all who heard the message. ⁴⁵The circumcised believers who had come with Peter were astonished that the gift of the Holy Spirit had been poured out even on Gentiles. ⁴⁶For they heard them speaking in tongues*ᵃ* and praising God.

Then Peter said, ⁴⁷"Surely no one can stand in the way of their being baptized with water. They have received the Holy Spirit just as we have." ⁴⁸So he ordered that they be baptized in the name of Jesus Christ. Then they asked Peter to stay with them for a few days.

Peter Explains His Actions

11 The apostles and the believers throughout Judea heard that the Gentiles also had received the word of God. ²So when Peter went up to Jerusalem, the circumcised believers criticized him ³and said, "You went into the house of uncircumcised men and ate with them."

⁴Starting from the beginning, Peter told them the whole story: ⁵"I was in the city of Joppa praying, and in a trance I saw a vision. I saw something like a large sheet being let down from heaven by its four corners, and it came down to where I was. ⁶I looked into it and saw four-footed animals of the earth, wild beasts, reptiles and birds. ⁷Then I heard a voice telling me, 'Get up, Peter. Kill and eat.'

⁸"I replied, 'Surely not, Lord! Nothing impure or unclean has ever entered my mouth.'

⁹"The voice spoke from heaven a second time, 'Do not call anything impure that God has made clean.' ¹⁰This happened three times, and then it was all pulled up to heaven again.

¹¹"Right then three men who had been sent to me from Caesarea stopped at the house where I was staying. ¹²The Spirit told me to have no hesitation about going with them. These six brothers also went with me, and we entered the man's house. ¹³He told us how he had seen an angel appear in his house and say, 'Send to Joppa for Simon who is called Peter. ¹⁴He will bring you a message through which you and all your household will be saved.'

¹⁵"As I began to speak, the Holy Spirit came on them as he had come on us at the beginning. ¹⁶Then I remembered what the Lord had said: 'John baptized with*ᵇ* water, but you will be baptized with*ᵇ* the Holy Spirit.' ¹⁷So if God gave them the same gift he gave us who believed in the Lord Jesus Christ, who was I to think that I could stand in God's way?"

My Name Is Scott

I'M A BELIEVER WHO STRUGGLES WITH SEXUAL ABUSE AND ALCOHOLISM

Please read the story of Cornelius's conversion, as well as his positive influence on his family and friends, in Acts 10.

Born in the 1960s as the youngest of three kids, I grew up in a fairly normal household. I suffered from low self-esteem, though, and would often withdraw to my room to handle pain and disappointment. We attended church and were active in various groups, but I didn't know Christ as my Savior and Lord.

When I was ten years old, I was sexually molested several times by older boys in the neighborhood. I began to develop distorted views concerning sex and tried to seduce a neighbor boy and some of the girls, none of whom would cooperate.

I started drinking at the age of 14 to escape the inadequacy I felt. "Peer pressure" in my case wasn't pressure at all; I went along willingly with everything that was put in front of me. Instead of withdrawing, I could drink, have fun, fit in and feel grown up. At this point I turned completely away from God and progressively developed a cycle of binge drinking.

I met my wife when she was a senior in high school. We were married nine months to the day after we met, just before she started college. I was working for the Bureau of Reclamation, helping to build a large dam north of Phoenix. After my wife's graduation from college, she was hired by a large company and placed on their fast-track executive program.

My mother was diagnosed with breast cancer, and, after undergoing chemotherapy and radiation, she was put into a care facility. The cancer had metastasized into her bones, and she went into a partial coma. For a week I was at her side for 18 hours a day, after which I watched her pass away silently. My only coping mechanism was drinking.

Then my best friend from childhood entered the hospital. He had been hospitalized many times due to asthma, and I told him I'd visit the next day. But the next day never came for him; he died suddenly at the age of 35. Once again, devastated, I turned to alcohol.

When our first daughter was born, I became a stay-at-home dad. Despite my happiness I spent many nights alone in my garage, drinking, building and organizing until the wee hours. I was taking prescription medications for depression and anxiety but began abusing both in an effort to regulate my sleep. By this point I knew I had a problem, but on my own I was helpless to remedy it. I would promise to slow down but couldn't do so for very long. I prayed to God to show me a way out before someone got hurt.

During a weekend visit to my sister's, I sat and drank three cases of beer. I should have been dead. The next day my brother, sister and brother-in law did an intervention, and my wife informed me that if I didn't commit myself to a treatment center, she would file for divorce. I knew at that moment that this was a God thing in my life.

I checked into a treatment center for 28 days and began to work a secular 12-step program with a sponsor. But I felt miserable and empty. Then God placed one of his missionaries in our lives, our realtor, who attended Saddleback Church. My wife and I had been looking for a church, and he suggested we try Saddleback.

A few months later, our realtor was at the house and overheard me complaining about working Step Four. He revealed that he was also in recovery but that his was the Christ-centered program called Celebrate Recovery. He invited me to attend with him. As Peter was to Cornelius, my realtor was to me. Although it took me a few months, I did begin attending. I joined a Step Study group and began working through the participants' guide. Week after week I grew in the Lord.

I gave my life to Christ and was baptized along with my wife, who had recommitted her life. As an addict, I needed structure and guidance. Through God's grace, my wife's support and the influence of Celebrate Recovery, I've been able to grow daily, taking on more and more responsibility in my family and in my own life.

God has blessed us with another daughter. Through the church I've become part of a stay-at-home fathers' group called Home Dads Teaching Values. We meet twice a week — once for playtime and once for support and Bible study. Being a stay-at-home *sober* dad has been one of the most rewarding experiences of my life.

I want to set a good example, as Cornelius did, to those coming out of bondage. For me this involves freely sharing my past struggles with alcoholism, drug abuse and sexual abuse, as well as the insanity that goes along with these addictions. I've been able to share my recovery story with people in Germany, Ireland, England, Costa Rica, Florida, Kansas, Texas — and the list goes on. Like Cornelius, I include my entire family in my growing faith, as we regularly host in our home pastors and others who are attending conferences at Saddleback Church.

Scott

18When they heard this, they had no further objections and praised God, saying, "So then, even to Gentiles God has granted repentance that leads to life."

The Church in Antioch

19Now those who had been scattered by the persecution that broke out when Stephen was killed traveled as far as Phoenicia, Cyprus and Antioch, spreading the word only among Jews. 20Some of them, however, men from Cyprus and Cyrene, went to Antioch and began to speak to Greeks also, telling them the good news about the Lord Jesus. 21The Lord's hand was with them, and a great number of people believed and turned to the Lord.

22News of this reached the church in Jerusalem, and they sent Barnabas to Antioch. 23When he arrived and saw what the grace of God had done, he was glad and encouraged them all to remain true to the Lord with all their hearts. 24He was a good man, full of the Holy Spirit and faith, and a great number of people were brought to the Lord.

25Then Barnabas went to Tarsus to look for Saul, 26and when he found him, he brought him to Antioch. So for a whole year Barnabas and Saul met with the church and taught great numbers of people. The disciples were called Christians first at Antioch.

27During this time some prophets came down from Jerusalem to Antioch. 28One of them, named Agabus, stood up and through the Spirit predicted that a severe famine would spread over the entire Roman world. (This happened during the reign of Claudius.) 29The disciples, as each one was able, decided to provide help for the brothers and sisters living in Judea. 30This they did, sending their gift to the elders by Barnabas and Saul.

Peter's Miraculous Escape From Prison

12 It was about this time that King Herod arrested some who belonged to the church, intending to persecute them. 2He had James,
the brother of John, put to death with the sword. 3When he saw that this met with approval among the Jews, he proceeded to seize Peter also. This happened during the Festival of Unleavened Bread. 4After arresting him, he put him in prison, handing him over to be guarded by four squads of four soldiers each. Herod intended to bring him out for public trial after the Passover.

5So Peter was kept in prison, but the church was earnestly praying to God for him.

6The night before Herod was to bring him to trial, Peter was sleeping between two soldiers, bound with two chains, and sentries stood guard at the entrance. 7Suddenly an angel of the Lord appeared and a light shone in the cell. He struck Peter on the side and woke him up. "Quick, get up!" he said, and the chains fell off Peter's wrists.

8Then the angel said to him, "Put on your clothes and sandals." And Peter did so. "Wrap your cloak around you and follow me," the angel told him. 9Peter followed him out of the prison, but he had no idea that what the angel was doing was really happening; he thought he was seeing a vision. 10They passed the first and second guards and came to the iron gate leading to the city. It opened for them by itself, and they went through it. When they had walked the length of one street, suddenly the angel left him.

11Then Peter came to himself and said, "Now I know without a doubt that the Lord has sent his angel and rescued me from Herod's clutches and from everything the Jewish people were hoping would happen."

12When this had dawned on him, he went to the house of Mary the mother of John, also called Mark, where many people had gathered and were praying. 13Peter knocked at the outer entrance, and a servant named Rhoda came to answer the door. 14When she recognized Peter's voice, she was so overjoyed she ran back without opening it and exclaimed, "Peter is at the door!"

15"You're out of your mind," they told her. When she kept insisting that it was so, they said, "It must be his angel."

16But Peter kept on knocking, and when they opened the door and saw him, they were astonished. 17Peter motioned with his hand for them to be quiet and described how the Lord had brought him out of prison. "Tell James and the other brothers and sisters about this," he said, and then he left for another place.

18In the morning, there was no small commotion among the soldiers as to what had become of Peter. 19After Herod had a thorough search made for him and did not find him, he cross-examined the guards and ordered that they be executed.

Herod's Death

Then Herod went from Judea to Caesarea and stayed there. 20He had been quarreling with the people of Tyre and Sidon; they now joined together and sought an audience with him. After securing the support of Blastus, a trusted personal servant of the king, they asked for peace, because they depended on the king's country for their food supply.

21On the appointed day Herod, wearing his royal robes, sat on his throne and delivered a public address to the people. 22They shouted, "This is the voice of a god, not of a man." 23Immediately, because Herod did not give praise to God, an angel of the Lord struck him down, and he was eaten by worms and died.

24But the word of God continued to spread and flourish.

Barnabas and Saul Sent Off

25When Barnabas and Saul had finished their mission, they returned from*a* Jerusalem, taking with them John, also called

13 Mark. 1Now in the church at Antioch there were prophets and teachers: Barnabas, Simeon called Niger, Lucius of Cyrene, Manaen

(who had been brought up with Herod the tetrarch) and Saul. 2While they were worshiping the Lord and fasting, the Holy Spirit said, "Set apart for me Barnabas and Saul for the work to which I have called them." 3So after they had fasted and prayed, they placed their hands on them and sent them off.

On Cyprus

4The two of them, sent on their way by the Holy Spirit, went down to Seleucia and sailed from there to Cyprus. 5When they arrived at Salamis, they proclaimed the word of God in the Jewish synagogues. John was with them as their helper.

6They traveled through the whole island until they came to Paphos. There they met a Jewish sorcerer and false prophet named Bar-Jesus, 7who was an attendant of the proconsul, Sergius Paulus. The proconsul, an intelligent man, sent for Barnabas and Saul because he wanted to hear the word of God. 8But Elymas the sorcerer (for that is what his name means) opposed them and tried to turn the proconsul from the faith. 9Then Saul, who was also called Paul, filled with the Holy Spirit, looked straight at Elymas and said, 10"You are a child of the devil and an enemy of everything that is right! You are full of all kinds of deceit and trickery. Will you never stop perverting the right ways of the Lord? 11Now the hand of the Lord is against you. You are going to be blind for a time, not even able to see the light of the sun."

Immediately mist and darkness came over him, and he groped about, seeking someone to lead him by the hand. 12When the proconsul saw what had happened, he believed, for he was amazed at the teaching about the Lord.

In Pisidian Antioch

13From Paphos, Paul and his companions sailed to Perga in Pamphylia, where John left them to return to Jerusalem.

14From Perga they went on to Pisidian Antioch. On the Sabbath they entered the synagogue and sat down. 15After the reading from the Law and the Prophets, the leaders of the synagogue sent word to them, saying, "Brothers, if you have a word of exhortation for the people, please speak."

16Standing up, Paul motioned with his hand and said: "Fellow Israelites and you Gentiles who worship God, listen to me! 17The God of the people of Israel chose our ancestors; he made the people prosper during their stay in Egypt; with mighty power he led them out of that country; 18for about forty years he endured their conduct*a* in the wilderness; 19and he overthrew seven nations in Canaan, giving their land to his people as their inheritance. 20All this took about 450 years.

"After this, God gave them judges until the time of Samuel the prophet. 21Then the people asked for a king, and he gave them Saul son of Kish, of the tribe of Benjamin, who ruled forty years. 22After removing Saul, he made David their king. God testified concerning him: 'I have found David son of Jesse, a man after my own heart; he will do everything I want him to do.'

23"From this man's descendants God has brought to Israel the Savior Jesus, as he promised. 24Before the coming of Jesus, John preached repentance and baptism to all the people of Israel. 25As John was completing his work, he said: 'Who do you suppose I am? I am not the one you are looking for. But there is one coming after me whose sandals I am not worthy to untie.'

26"Fellow children of Abraham and you God-fearing Gentiles, it is to us that this message of salvation has been sent. 27The people of Jerusalem and their rulers did not recognize Jesus, yet in condemning him they fulfilled the words of the prophets that are read every Sabbath. 28Though

they found no proper ground for a death sentence, they asked Pilate to have him executed. 29When they had carried out all that was written about him, they took him down from the cross and laid him in a tomb. 30But God raised him from the dead, 31and for many days he was seen by those who had traveled with him from Galilee to Jerusalem. They are now his witnesses to our people.

32"We tell you the good news: What God promised our ancestors 33he has fulfilled for us, their children, by raising up Jesus. As it is written in the second Psalm:

"'You are my son;
    today I have become your father.'*b*

34God raised him from the dead so that he will never be subject to decay. As God has said,

"'I will give you the holy and sure
    blessings promised to David.'*c*

35So it is also stated elsewhere:

"'You will not let your holy one see
    decay.'*d*

36"Now when David had served God's purpose in his own generation, he fell asleep; he was buried with his ancestors and his body decayed. 37But the one whom God raised from the dead did not see decay.

38"Therefore, my friends, I want you to know that through Jesus the forgiveness of sins is proclaimed to you. 39Through him everyone who believes is set free from every sin, a justification you were not able to obtain under the law of Moses. 40Take care that what the prophets have said does not happen to you:

41"'Look, you scoffers,
    wonder and perish,
for I am going to do something in your
    days
that you would never believe,
    even if someone told you.'*e*"

---

a 18 Some manuscripts *he cared for them*   *b 33* Psalm 2:7   *c 34* Isaiah 55:3   *d 35* Psalm 16:10 (see Septuagint)   *e 41* Hab. 1:5

⁴²As Paul and Barnabas were leaving the synagogue, the people invited them to speak further about these things on the next Sabbath. ⁴³When the congregation was dismissed, many of the Jews and devout converts to Judaism followed Paul and Barnabas, who talked with them and urged them to continue in the grace of God.

⁴⁴On the next Sabbath almost the whole city gathered to hear the word of the Lord. ⁴⁵When the Jews saw the crowds, they were filled with jealousy. They began to contradict what Paul was saying and heaped abuse on him.

⁴⁶Then Paul and Barnabas answered them boldly: "We had to speak the word of God to you first. Since you reject it and do not consider yourselves worthy of eternal life, we now turn to the Gentiles. ⁴⁷For this is what the Lord has commanded us:

> "'I have made you^a a light for the
>   Gentiles,
>   that you^a may bring salvation to the
>   ends of the earth.'^b"

⁴⁸When the Gentiles heard this, they were glad and honored the word of the Lord; and all who were appointed for eternal life believed.

⁴⁹The word of the Lord spread through the whole region. ⁵⁰But the Jewish leaders incited the God-fearing women of high standing and the leading men of the city. They stirred up persecution against Paul and Barnabas, and expelled them from their region. ⁵¹So they shook the dust off their feet as a warning to them and went to Iconium. ⁵²And the disciples were filled with joy and with the Holy Spirit.

In Iconium

14 At Iconium Paul and Barnabas went as usual into the Jewish synagogue. There they spoke so effectively that a great number of Jews and Greeks believed. ²But the Jews who refused to believe stirred up the other Gentiles and poisoned their minds against the brothers. ³So Paul and Barnabas spent considerable time there, speaking boldly for the Lord, who confirmed the message of his grace by enabling them to perform signs and wonders. ⁴The people of the city were divided; some sided with the Jews, others with the apostles. ⁵There was a plot afoot among both Gentiles and Jews, together with their leaders, to mistreat them and stone them. ⁶But they found out about it and fled to the Lycaonian cities of Lystra and Derbe and to the surrounding country, ⁷where they continued to preach the gospel.

In Lystra and Derbe

⁸In Lystra there sat a man who was lame. He had been that way from birth and had never walked. ⁹He listened to Paul as he was speaking. Paul looked directly at him, saw that he had faith to be healed ¹⁰and called out, "Stand up on your feet!" At that, the man jumped up and began to walk.

¹¹When the crowd saw what Paul had done, they shouted in the Lycaonian language, "The gods have come down to us in human form!" ¹²Barnabas they called Zeus, and Paul they called Hermes because he was the chief speaker. ¹³The priest of Zeus, whose temple was just outside the city, brought bulls and wreaths to the city gates because he and the crowd wanted to offer sacrifices to them.

¹⁴But when the apostles Barnabas and Paul heard of this, they tore their clothes and rushed out into the crowd, shouting: ¹⁵"Friends, why are you doing this? We too are only human, like you. We are bringing you good news, telling you to turn from these worthless things to the living God, who made the heavens and the earth and the sea and everything in them. ¹⁶In the past, he let all nations go their own way. ¹⁷Yet he has not left himself without testimony: He has shown kindness by giving you rain from heaven and crops in their seasons; he provides you with plenty of

---

^a 47 The Greek is singular.   ^b 47 Isaiah 49:6

food and fills your hearts with joy." [18]Even with these words, they had difficulty keeping the crowd from sacrificing to them.

[19]Then some Jews came from Antioch and Iconium and won the crowd over. They stoned Paul and dragged him outside the city, thinking he was dead. [20]But after the disciples had gathered around him, he got up and went back into the city. The next day he and Barnabas left for Derbe.

The Return to Antioch in Syria

[21]They preached the gospel in that city and won a large number of disciples. Then they returned to Lystra, Iconium and Antioch, [22]strengthening the disciples and encouraging them to remain true to the faith. "We must go through many hardships to enter the kingdom of God," they said. [23]Paul and Barnabas appointed elders[a] for them in each church and, with prayer and fasting, committed them to the Lord, in whom they had put their trust. [24]After going through Pisidia, they came into Pamphylia, [25]and when they had preached the word in Perga, they went down to Attalia.

[26]From Attalia they sailed back to Antioch, where they had been committed to the grace of God for the work they had now completed. [27]On arriving there, they gathered the church together and reported all that God had done through them and how he had opened a door of faith to the Gentiles. [28]And they stayed there a long time with the disciples.

The Council at Jerusalem

15 Certain people came down from Judea to Antioch and were teaching the believers: "Unless you are circumcised, according to the custom taught by Moses, you cannot be saved." [2]This brought Paul and Barnabas into sharp dispute and debate with them. So Paul and Barnabas were appointed, along with some other believers, to go up to Jerusalem to see the apostles and elders about this question. [3]The church sent them on their way, and as they traveled through Phoenicia and Samaria, they told how the Gentiles had been converted. This news made all the believers very glad. [4]When they came to Jerusalem, they were welcomed by the church and the apostles and elders, to whom they reported everything God had done through them.

[5]Then some of the believers who belonged to the party of the Pharisees stood up and said, "The Gentiles must be circumcised and required to keep the law of Moses."

[6]The apostles and elders met to consider this question. [7]After much discussion, Peter got up and addressed them: "Brothers, you know that some time ago God made a choice among you that the Gentiles might hear from my lips the message of the gospel and believe. [8]God, who knows the heart, showed that he accepted them by giving the Holy Spirit to them, just as he did to us. [9]He did not discriminate between us and them, for he purified their hearts by faith. [10]Now then, why do you try to test God by putting on the necks of Gentiles a yoke that neither we nor our ancestors have been able to bear? [11]No! We believe it is through the grace of our Lord Jesus that we are saved, just as they are."

[12]The whole assembly became silent as they listened to Barnabas and Paul telling about the signs and wonders God had done among the Gentiles through them. [13]When they finished, James spoke up. "Brothers," he said, "listen to me. [14]Simon[b] has described to us how God first intervened to choose a people for his name from the Gentiles. [15]The words of the prophets are in agreement with this, as it is written:

[16]" 'After this I will return
    and rebuild David's fallen tent.
Its ruins I will rebuild,
    and I will restore it,

---

a 23 Or *Barnabas ordained elders*; or *Barnabas had elders elected*   *b 14* Greek *Simeon*, a variant of *Simon*; that is, Peter

17that the rest of mankind may seek the
  Lord,
    even all the Gentiles who bear my
      name,
  says the Lord, who does these
    things'a—
18   things known from long ago.b

19"It is my judgment, therefore, that we
should not make it difficult for the Gentiles who are turning to God. 20Instead
we should write to them, telling them to
abstain from food polluted by idols, from
sexual immorality, from the meat of strangled animals and from blood. 21For the law
of Moses has been preached in every city
from the earliest times and is read in the
synagogues on every Sabbath."

The Council's Letter to Gentile Believers

22Then the apostles and elders, with the
whole church, decided to choose some of
their own men and send them to Antioch
with Paul and Barnabas. They chose Judas
(called Barsabbas) and Silas, men who were
leaders among the believers. 23With them
they sent the following letter:

The apostles and elders, your brothers,

To the Gentile believers in Antioch,
Syria and Cilicia:

Greetings.

24We have heard that some went
out from us without our authorization
and disturbed you, troubling your
minds by what they said. 25So we all
agreed to choose some men and send
them to you with our dear friends
Barnabas and Paul— 26men who have
risked their lives for the name of our
Lord Jesus Christ. 27Therefore we are
sending Judas and Silas to confirm by
word of mouth what we are writing.
28It seemed good to the Holy Spirit

and to us not to burden you with anything beyond the following requirements: 29You are to abstain from food
sacrificed to idols, from blood, from
the meat of strangled animals and
from sexual immorality. You will do
well to avoid these things.

Farewell.

30So the men were sent off and went down
to Antioch, where they gathered the church
together and delivered the letter. 31The people read it and were glad for its encouraging
message. 32Judas and Silas, who themselves
were prophets, said much to encourage and
strengthen the believers. 33After spending
some time there, they were sent off by the
believers with the blessing of peace to return to those who had sent them. [34]c 35But
Paul and Barnabas remained in Antioch,
where they and many others taught and
preached the word of the Lord.

Disagreement Between Paul and Barnabas

36Some time later Paul said to Barnabas,
"Let us go back and visit the believers in
all the towns where we preached the word
of the Lord and see how they are doing."
37Barnabas wanted to take John, also called
Mark, with them, 38but Paul did not think
it wise to take him, because he had deserted
them in Pamphylia and had not continued
with them in the work. 39They had such a
sharp disagreement that they parted company. Barnabas took Mark and sailed for
Cyprus, 40but Paul chose Silas and left,
commended by the believers to the grace
of the Lord. 41He went through Syria and
Cilicia, strengthening the churches.

Timothy Joins Paul and Silas

16 Paul came to Derbe and then to
Lystra, where a disciple named
Timothy lived, whose mother
was Jewish and a believer but whose father

---

a 17 Amos 9:11,12 (see Septuagint)   b 17,18 Some manuscripts things'— / 18the Lord's work is known to him from
long ago   c 34 Some manuscripts include here But Silas decided to remain there.

was a Greek. ²The believers at Lystra and Iconium spoke well of him. ³Paul wanted to take him along on the journey, so he circumcised him because of the Jews who lived in that area, for they all knew that his father was a Greek. ⁴As they traveled from town to town, they delivered the decisions reached by the apostles and elders in Jerusalem for the people to obey. ⁵So the churches were strengthened in the faith and grew daily in numbers.

Paul's Vision of the Man of Macedonia

⁶Paul and his companions traveled throughout the region of Phrygia and Galatia, having been kept by the Holy Spirit from preaching the word in the province of Asia. ⁷When they came to the border of Mysia, they tried to enter Bithynia, but the Spirit of Jesus would not allow them to. ⁸So they passed by Mysia and went down to Troas. ⁹During the night Paul had a vision of a man of Macedonia standing and begging him, "Come over to Macedonia and help us." ¹⁰After Paul had seen the vision, we got ready at once to leave for Macedonia, concluding that God had called us to preach the gospel to them.

Lydia's Conversion in Philippi

¹¹From Troas we put out to sea and sailed straight for Samothrace, and the next day we went on to Neapolis. ¹²From there we traveled to Philippi, a Roman colony and the leading city of that district*a* of Macedonia. And we stayed there several days.

¹³On the Sabbath we went outside the city gate to the river, where we expected to find a place of prayer. We sat down and began to speak to the women who had gathered there. ¹⁴One of those listening was a woman from the city of Thyatira named Lydia, a dealer in purple cloth. She was a worshiper of God. The Lord opened her heart to respond to Paul's message. ¹⁵When she and the members of her household were baptized, she invited us to her home.

"If you consider me a believer in the Lord," she said, "come and stay at my house." And she persuaded us.

Paul and Silas in Prison

¹⁶Once when we were going to the place of prayer, we were met by a female slave who had a spirit by which she predicted the future. She earned a great deal of money for her owners by fortune-telling. ¹⁷She followed Paul and the rest of us, shouting, "These men are servants of the Most High God, who are telling you the way to be saved." ¹⁸She kept this up for many days. Finally Paul became so annoyed that he turned around and said to the spirit, "In the name of Jesus Christ I command you to come out of her!" At that moment the spirit left her.

¹⁹When her owners realized that their hope of making money was gone, they seized Paul and Silas and dragged them into the marketplace to face the authorities. ²⁰They brought them before the magistrates and said, "These men are Jews, and are throwing our city into an uproar ²¹by advocating customs unlawful for us Romans to accept or practice."

²²The crowd joined in the attack against Paul and Silas, and the magistrates ordered them to be stripped and beaten with rods. ²³After they had been severely flogged, they were thrown into prison, and the jailer was commanded to guard them carefully. ²⁴When he received these orders, he put them in the inner cell and fastened their feet in the stocks.

²⁵About midnight Paul and Silas were praying and singing hymns to God, and the other prisoners were listening to them. ²⁶Suddenly there was such a violent earthquake that the foundations of the prison were shaken. At once all the prison doors flew open, and everyone's chains came loose. ²⁷The jailer woke up, and when he saw the prison doors open, he drew his sword and was about to kill himself be-

---

a 12 The text and meaning of the Greek for *the leading city of that district* are uncertain.

cause he thought the prisoners had escaped. [28]But Paul shouted, "Don't harm yourself! We are all here!"

[29]The jailer called for lights, rushed in and fell trembling before Paul and Silas. [30]He then brought them out and asked, "Sirs, what must I do to be saved?"

[31]They replied, "Believe in the Lord Jesus, and you will be saved — you and your household." [32]Then they spoke the word of the Lord to him and to all the others in his house. [33]At that hour of the night the jailer took them and washed their wounds; then immediately he and all his household were baptized. [34]The jailer brought them into his house and set a meal before them; he was filled with joy because he had come to believe in God — he and his whole household.

[35]When it was daylight, the magistrates sent their officers to the jailer with the order: "Release those men." [36]The jailer told Paul, "The magistrates have ordered that you and Silas be released. Now you can leave. Go in peace."

[37]But Paul said to the officers: "They beat us publicly without a trial, even though we are Roman citizens, and threw us into prison. And now do they want to get rid of us quietly? No! Let them come themselves and escort us out."

[38]The officers reported this to the magistrates, and when they heard that Paul and Silas were Roman citizens, they were alarmed. [39]They came to appease them and escorted them from the prison, requesting them to leave the city. [40]After Paul and Silas came out of the prison, they went to Lydia's house, where they met with the brothers and sisters and encouraged them. Then they left.

In Thessalonica

17

When Paul and his companions had passed through Amphipolis and Apollonia, they came to Thessalonica, where there was a Jewish synagogue. [2]As was his custom, Paul went into the synagogue, and on three Sabbath days he reasoned with them from the Scriptures, [3]explaining and proving that the Messiah had to suffer and rise from the dead. "This Jesus I am proclaiming to you is the Messiah," he said. [4]Some of the Jews were persuaded and joined Paul and Silas, as did a large number of God-fearing Greeks and quite a few prominent women.

[5]But other Jews were jealous; so they rounded up some bad characters from the marketplace, formed a mob and started a riot in the city. They rushed to Jason's house in search of Paul and Silas in order to bring them out to the crowd.[a] [6]But when they did not find them, they dragged Jason and some other believers before the city officials, shouting: "These men who have caused trouble all over the world have now come here, [7]and Jason has welcomed them into his house. They are all defying Caesar's decrees, saying that there is another king, one called Jesus." [8]When they heard this, the crowd and the city officials were thrown into turmoil. [9]Then they made Jason and the others post bond and let them go.

In Berea

[10]As soon as it was night, the believers sent Paul and Silas away to Berea. On arriving there, they went to the Jewish synagogue. [11]Now the Berean Jews were of more noble character than those in Thessalonica, for they received the message with great eagerness and examined the Scriptures every day to see if what Paul said was true. [12]As a result, many of them believed, as did also a number of prominent Greek women and many Greek men.

[13]But when the Jews in Thessalonica learned that Paul was preaching the word of God at Berea, some of them went there too, agitating the crowds and stirring them up. [14]The believers immediately sent Paul to the coast, but Silas and Timothy stayed at

---

[a] 5 Or *the assembly of the people*

Berea. [15]Those who escorted Paul brought him to Athens and then left with instructions for Silas and Timothy to join him as soon as possible.

In Athens

[16]While Paul was waiting for them in Athens, he was greatly distressed to see that the city was full of idols. [17]So he reasoned in the synagogue with both Jews and God-fearing Greeks, as well as in the marketplace day by day with those who happened to be there. [18]A group of Epicurean and Stoic philosophers began to debate with him. Some of them asked, "What is this babbler trying to say?" Others remarked, "He seems to be advocating foreign gods." They said this because Paul was preaching the good news about Jesus and the resurrection. [19]Then they took him and brought him to a meeting of the Areopagus, where they said to him, "May we know what this new teaching is that you are presenting? [20]You are bringing some strange ideas to our ears, and we would like to know what they mean." [21](All the Athenians and the foreigners who lived there spent their time doing nothing but talking about and listening to the latest ideas.)

[22]Paul then stood up in the meeting of the Areopagus and said: "People of Athens! I see that in every way you are very religious. [23]For as I walked around and looked carefully at your objects of worship, I even found an altar with this inscription: TO AN UNKNOWN GOD. So you are ignorant of the very thing you worship — and this is what I am going to proclaim to you.

[24]"The God who made the world and everything in it is the Lord of heaven and earth and does not live in temples built by human hands. [25]And he is not served by human hands, as if he needed anything. Rather, he himself gives everyone life and breath and everything else. [26]From one man he made all the nations, that they should inhabit the whole earth; and he marked out their appointed times in history and the boundaries of their lands. [27]God did this so that they would seek him and perhaps reach out for him and find him, though he is not far from any one of us. [28]'For in him we live and move and have our being.'[a] As some of your own poets have said, 'We are his offspring.'[b]

[29]"Therefore since we are God's offspring, we should not think that the divine being is like gold or silver or stone — an image made by human design and skill. [30]In the past God overlooked such ignorance, but now he commands all people everywhere to repent. [31]For he has set a day when he will judge the world with justice by the man he has appointed. He has given proof of this to everyone by raising him from the dead."

[32]When they heard about the resurrection of the dead, some of them sneered, but others said, "We want to hear you again on this subject." [33]At that, Paul left the Council. [34]Some of the people became followers of Paul and believed. Among them was Dionysius, a member of the Areopagus, also a woman named Damaris, and a number of others.

In Corinth

18 After this, Paul left Athens and went to Corinth. [2]There he met a Jew named Aquila, a native of Pontus, who had recently come from Italy with his wife Priscilla, because Claudius had ordered all Jews to leave Rome. Paul went to see them, [3]and because he was a tentmaker as they were, he stayed and worked with them. [4]Every Sabbath he reasoned in the synagogue, trying to persuade Jews and Greeks.

[5]When Silas and Timothy came from Macedonia, Paul devoted himself exclusively to preaching, testifying to the Jews that Jesus was the Messiah. [6]But when they opposed Paul and became abusive, he shook out his clothes in protest and said to

---

[a] 28 From the Cretan philosopher Epimenides   [b] 28 From the Cilician Stoic philosopher Aratus

them, "Your blood be on your own heads! I am innocent of it. From now on I will go to the Gentiles."

7Then Paul left the synagogue and went next door to the house of Titius Justus, a worshiper of God. 8Crispus, the synagogue leader, and his entire household believed in the Lord; and many of the Corinthians who heard Paul believed and were baptized.

9One night the Lord spoke to Paul in a vision: "Do not be afraid; keep on speaking, do not be silent. 10For I am with you, and no one is going to attack and harm you, because I have many people in this city." 11So Paul stayed in Corinth for a year and a half, teaching them the word of God.

12While Gallio was proconsul of Achaia, the Jews of Corinth made a united attack on Paul and brought him to the place of judgment. 13"This man," they charged, "is persuading the people to worship God in ways contrary to the law."

14Just as Paul was about to speak, Gallio said to them, "If you Jews were making a complaint about some misdemeanor or serious crime, it would be reasonable for me to listen to you. 15But since it involves questions about words and names and your own law — settle the matter yourselves. I will not be a judge of such things." 16So he drove them off. 17Then the crowd there turned on Sosthenes the synagogue leader and beat him in front of the proconsul; and Gallio showed no concern whatever.

Priscilla, Aquila and Apollos

18Paul stayed on in Corinth for some time. Then he left the brothers and sisters and sailed for Syria, accompanied by Priscilla and Aquila. Before he sailed, he had his hair cut off at Cenchreae because of a vow he had taken. 19They arrived at Ephesus, where Paul left Priscilla and Aquila. He himself went into the synagogue and reasoned with the Jews. 20When they asked him to spend more time with them, he declined. 21But as he left, he promised,

"I will come back if it is God's will." Then he set sail from Ephesus. 22When he landed at Caesarea, he went up to Jerusalem and greeted the church and then went down to Antioch.

23After spending some time in Antioch, Paul set out from there and traveled from place to place throughout the region of Galatia and Phrygia, strengthening all the disciples.

24Meanwhile a Jew named Apollos, a native of Alexandria, came to Ephesus. He was a learned man, with a thorough knowledge of the Scriptures. 25He had been instructed in the way of the Lord, and he spoke with great fervora and taught about Jesus accurately, though he knew only the baptism of John. 26He began to speak boldly in the synagogue. When Priscilla and Aquila heard him, they invited him to their home and explained to him the way of God more adequately.

27When Apollos wanted to go to Achaia, the brothers and sisters encouraged him and wrote to the disciples there to welcome him. When he arrived, he was a great help to those who by grace had believed. 28For he vigorously refuted his Jewish opponents in public debate, proving from the Scriptures that Jesus was the Messiah.

Paul in Ephesus

19 While Apollos was at Corinth, Paul took the road through the interior and arrived at Ephesus. There he found some disciples 2and asked them, "Did you receive the Holy Spirit whenb you believed?"

They answered, "No, we have not even heard that there is a Holy Spirit."

3So Paul asked, "Then what baptism did you receive?"

"John's baptism," they replied.

4Paul said, "John's baptism was a baptism of repentance. He told the people to believe in the one coming after him, that is, in Jesus." 5On hearing this, they were

---

a 25 Or *with fervor in the Spirit*   b 2 Or *after*

baptized in the name of the Lord Jesus. ⁶When Paul placed his hands on them, the Holy Spirit came on them, and they spoke in tongues*a* and prophesied. ⁷There were about twelve men in all.

⁸Paul entered the synagogue and spoke boldly there for three months, arguing persuasively about the kingdom of God. ⁹But some of them became obstinate; they refused to believe and publicly maligned the Way. So Paul left them. He took the disciples with him and had discussions daily in the lecture hall of Tyrannus. ¹⁰This went on for two years, so that all the Jews and Greeks who lived in the province of Asia heard the word of the Lord.

¹¹God did extraordinary miracles through Paul, ¹²so that even handkerchiefs and aprons that had touched him were taken to the sick, and their illnesses were cured and the evil spirits left them.

¹³Some Jews who went around driving out evil spirits tried to invoke the name of the Lord Jesus over those who were demon-possessed. They would say, "In the name of the Jesus whom Paul preaches, I command you to come out." ¹⁴Seven sons of Sceva, a Jewish chief priest, were doing this. ¹⁵One day the evil spirit answered them, "Jesus I know, and Paul I know about, but who are you?" ¹⁶Then the man who had the evil spirit jumped on them and overpowered them all. He gave them such a beating that they ran out of the house naked and bleeding.

¹⁷When this became known to the Jews and Greeks living in Ephesus, they were all seized with fear, and the name of the Lord Jesus was held in high honor. ¹⁸Many of those who believed now came and openly confessed what they had done. ¹⁹A number who had practiced sorcery brought their scrolls together and burned them publicly. When they calculated the value of the scrolls, the total came to fifty thousand drachmas.*b* ²⁰In this way the word of the Lord spread widely and grew in power.

²¹After all this had happened, Paul decided*c* to go to Jerusalem, passing through Macedonia and Achaia. "After I have been there," he said, "I must visit Rome also." ²²He sent two of his helpers, Timothy and Erastus, to Macedonia, while he stayed in the province of Asia a little longer.

The Riot in Ephesus

²³About that time there arose a great disturbance about the Way. ²⁴A silversmith named Demetrius, who made silver shrines of Artemis, brought in a lot of business for the craftsmen there. ²⁵He called them together, along with the workers in related trades, and said: "You know, my friends, that we receive a good income from this business. ²⁶And you see and hear how this fellow Paul has convinced and led astray large numbers of people here in Ephesus and in practically the whole province of Asia. He says that gods made by human hands are no gods at all. ²⁷There is danger not only that our trade will lose its good name, but also that the temple of the great goddess Artemis will be discredited; and the goddess herself, who is worshiped throughout the province of Asia and the world, will be robbed of her divine majesty."

²⁸When they heard this, they were furious and began shouting: "Great is Artemis of the Ephesians!" ²⁹Soon the whole city was in an uproar. The people seized Gaius and Aristarchus, Paul's traveling companions from Macedonia, and all of them rushed into the theater together. ³⁰Paul wanted to appear before the crowd, but the disciples would not let him. ³¹Even some of the officials of the province, friends of Paul, sent him a message begging him not to venture into the theater.

³²The assembly was in confusion: Some were shouting one thing, some another. Most of the people did not even know why they were there. ³³The Jews in the crowd

---

a 6 Or *other languages*   *b 19* A drachma was a silver coin worth about a day's wages.   *c 21* Or *decided in the Spirit* pushed Alexander to the front, and they shouted instructions to him. He motioned for silence in order to make a defense before the people. [34]But when they realized he was a Jew, they all shouted in unison for about two hours: "Great is Artemis of the Ephesians!"

[35]The city clerk quieted the crowd and said: "Fellow Ephesians, doesn't all the world know that the city of Ephesus is the guardian of the temple of the great Artemis and of her image, which fell from heaven? [36]Therefore, since these facts are undeniable, you ought to calm down and not do anything rash. [37]You have brought these men here, though they have neither robbed temples nor blasphemed our goddess. [38]If, then, Demetrius and his fellow craftsmen have a grievance against anybody, the courts are open and there are proconsuls. They can press charges. [39]If there is anything further you want to bring up, it must be settled in a legal assembly. [40]As it is, we are in danger of being charged with rioting because of what happened today. In that case we would not be able to account for this commotion, since there is no reason for it." [41]After he had said this, he dismissed the assembly.

Through Macedonia and Greece

20 When the uproar had ended, Paul sent for the disciples and, after encouraging them, said goodbye and set out for Macedonia. [2]He traveled through that area, speaking many words of encouragement to the people, and finally arrived in Greece, [3]where he stayed three months. Because some Jews had plotted against him just as he was about to sail for Syria, he decided to go back through Macedonia. [4]He was accompanied by Sopater son of Pyrrhus from Berea, Aristarchus and Secundus from Thessalonica, Gaius from Derbe, Timothy also, and Tychicus and Trophimus from the province of Asia. [5]These men went on ahead and waited for us at Troas. [6]But we sailed from Philippi after the Festival of Unleavened Bread, and five days later joined the others at Troas, where we stayed seven days.

Eutychus Raised From the Dead at Troas

[7]On the first day of the week we came together to break bread. Paul spoke to the people and, because he intended to leave the next day, kept on talking until midnight. [8]There were many lamps in the upstairs room where we were meeting. [9]Seated in a window was a young man named Eutychus, who was sinking into a deep sleep as Paul talked on and on. When he was sound asleep, he fell to the ground from the third story and was picked up dead. [10]Paul went down, threw himself on the young man and put his arms around him. "Don't be alarmed," he said. "He's alive!" [11]Then he went upstairs again and broke bread and ate. After talking until daylight, he left. [12]The people took the young man home alive and were greatly comforted.

Paul's Farewell to the Ephesian Elders

[13]We went on ahead to the ship and sailed for Assos, where we were going to take Paul aboard. He had made this arrangement because he was going there on foot. [14]When he met us at Assos, we took him aboard and went on to Mitylene. [15]The next day we set sail from there and arrived off Chios. The day after that we crossed over to Samos, and on the following day arrived at Miletus. [16]Paul had decided to sail past Ephesus to avoid spending time in the province of Asia, for he was in a hurry to reach Jerusalem, if possible, by the day of Pentecost.

[17]From Miletus, Paul sent to Ephesus for the elders of the church. [18]When they arrived, he said to them: "You know how I lived the whole time I was with you, from the first day I came into the province of Asia. [19]I served the Lord with great humility and with tears and in the midst of severe testing by the plots of my Jewish opponents. [20]You know that I have not hesitated to preach anything that would be helpful to you but have taught you publicly and

from house to house. 21I have declared to both Jews and Greeks that they must turn to God in repentance and have faith in our Lord Jesus.

22"And now, compelled by the Spirit, I am going to Jerusalem, not knowing what will happen to me there. 23I only know that in every city the Holy Spirit warns me that prison and hardships are facing me. 24However, I consider my life worth nothing to me; my only aim is to finish the race and complete the task the Lord Jesus has given me — the task of testifying to the good news of God's grace.

25"Now I know that none of you among whom I have gone about preaching the kingdom will ever see me again. 26Therefore, I declare to you today that I am innocent of the blood of any of you. 27For I have not hesitated to proclaim to you the whole will of God. 28Keep watch over yourselves and all the flock of which the Holy Spirit has made you overseers. Be shepherds of the church of God,*a* which he bought with his own blood.*b* 29I know that after I leave, savage wolves will come in among you and will not spare the flock. 30Even from your own number men will arise and distort the truth in order to draw away disciples after them. 31So be on your guard! Remember that for three years I never stopped warning each of you night and day with tears.

32"Now I commit you to God and to the word of his grace, which can build you up and give you an inheritance among all those who are sanctified. 33I have not coveted anyone's silver or gold or clothing. 34You yourselves know that these hands of mine have supplied my own needs and the needs of my companions. 35In everything I did, I showed you that by this kind of hard work we must help the weak, remembering the words the Lord Jesus himself said: 'It is more blessed to give than to receive.'"

36When Paul had finished speaking, he knelt down with all of them and prayed. 37They all wept as they embraced him and kissed him. 38What grieved them most was his statement that they would never see his face again. Then they accompanied him to the ship.

On to Jerusalem

21 After we had torn ourselves away from them, we put out to sea and sailed straight to Kos. The next day we went to Rhodes and from there to Patara. 2We found a ship crossing over to Phoenicia, went on board and set sail. 3After sighting Cyprus and passing to the south of it, we sailed on to Syria. We landed at Tyre, where our ship was to unload its cargo. 4We sought out the disciples there and stayed with them seven days. Through the Spirit they urged Paul not to go on to Jerusalem. 5When it was time to leave, we left and continued on our way. All of them, including wives and children, accompanied us out of the city, and there on the beach we knelt to pray. 6After saying goodbye to each other, we went aboard the ship, and they returned home.

7We continued our voyage from Tyre and landed at Ptolemais, where we greeted the brothers and sisters and stayed with them for a day. 8Leaving the next day, we reached Caesarea and stayed at the house of Philip the evangelist, one of the Seven. 9He had four unmarried daughters who prophesied.

10After we had been there a number of days, a prophet named Agabus came down from Judea. 11Coming over to us, he took Paul's belt, tied his own hands and feet with it and said, "The Holy Spirit says, 'In this way the Jewish leaders in Jerusalem will bind the owner of this belt and will hand him over to the Gentiles.'"

12When we heard this, we and the people there pleaded with Paul not to go up to Jerusalem. 13Then Paul answered, "Why are you weeping and breaking my heart? I

---

a 28 Many manuscripts *of the Lord*   *b 28* Or *with the blood of his own Son.*

am ready not only to be bound, but also to die in Jerusalem for the name of the Lord Jesus." ¹⁴When he would not be dissuaded, we gave up and said, "The Lord's will be done."

¹⁵After this, we started on our way up to Jerusalem. ¹⁶Some of the disciples from Caesarea accompanied us and brought us to the home of Mnason, where we were to stay. He was a man from Cyprus and one of the early disciples.

Paul's Arrival at Jerusalem

¹⁷When we arrived at Jerusalem, the brothers and sisters received us warmly. ¹⁸The next day Paul and the rest of us went to see James, and all the elders were present. ¹⁹Paul greeted them and reported in detail what God had done among the Gentiles through his ministry.

²⁰When they heard this, they praised God. Then they said to Paul: "You see, brother, how many thousands of Jews have believed, and all of them are zealous for the law. ²¹They have been informed that you teach all the Jews who live among the Gentiles to turn away from Moses, telling them not to circumcise their children or live according to our customs. ²²What shall we do? They will certainly hear that you have come, ²³so do what we tell you. There are four men with us who have made a vow. ²⁴Take these men, join in their purification rites and pay their expenses, so that they can have their heads shaved. Then everyone will know there is no truth in these reports about you, but that you yourself are living in obedience to the law. ²⁵As for the Gentile believers, we have written to them our decision that they should abstain from food sacrificed to idols, from blood, from the meat of strangled animals and from sexual immorality."

²⁶The next day Paul took the men and purified himself along with them. Then he went to the temple to give notice of the date when the days of purification would end and the offering would be made for each of them.

Paul Arrested

²⁷When the seven days were nearly over, some Jews from the province of Asia saw Paul at the temple. They stirred up the whole crowd and seized him, ²⁸shouting, "Fellow Israelites, help us! This is the man who teaches everyone everywhere against our people and our law and this place. And besides, he has brought Greeks into the temple and defiled this holy place." ²⁹(They had previously seen Trophimus the Ephesian in the city with Paul and assumed that Paul had brought him into the temple.)

³⁰The whole city was aroused, and the people came running from all directions. Seizing Paul, they dragged him from the temple, and immediately the gates were shut. ³¹While they were trying to kill him, news reached the commander of the Roman troops that the whole city of Jerusalem was in an uproar. ³²He at once took some officers and soldiers and ran down to the crowd. When the rioters saw the commander and his soldiers, they stopped beating Paul.

³³The commander came up and arrested him and ordered him to be bound with two chains. Then he asked who he was and what he had done. ³⁴Some in the crowd shouted one thing and some another, and since the commander could not get at the truth because of the uproar, he ordered that Paul be taken into the barracks. ³⁵When Paul reached the steps, the violence of the mob was so great he had to be carried by the soldiers. ³⁶The crowd that followed kept shouting, "Get rid of him!"

Paul Speaks to the Crowd

³⁷As the soldiers were about to take Paul into the barracks, he asked the commander, "May I say something to you?"

"Do you speak Greek?" he replied. ³⁸"Aren't you the Egyptian who started a revolt and led four thousand terrorists out into the wilderness some time ago?"

³⁹Paul answered, "I am a Jew, from Tarsus in Cilicia, a citizen of no ordinary city. Please let me speak to the people."

40After receiving the commander's permission, Paul stood on the steps and motioned to the crowd. When they were all silent, he said

22

to them in Aramaic*a*: **1**"Brothers and fathers, listen now to my defense."

2When they heard him speak to them in Aramaic, they became very quiet.

Then Paul said: **3**"I am a Jew, born in Tarsus of Cilicia, but brought up in this city. I studied under Gamaliel and was thoroughly trained in the law of our ancestors. I was just as zealous for God as any of you are today. **4**I persecuted the followers of this Way to their death, arresting both men and women and throwing them into prison, **5**as the high priest and all the Council can themselves testify. I even obtained letters from them to their associates in Damascus, and went there to bring these people as prisoners to Jerusalem to be punished.

6"About noon as I came near Damascus, suddenly a bright light from heaven flashed around me. **7**I fell to the ground and heard a voice say to me, 'Saul! Saul! Why do you persecute me?'

8"'Who are you, Lord?' I asked.

"'I am Jesus of Nazareth, whom you are persecuting,' he replied. **9**My companions saw the light, but they did not understand the voice of him who was speaking to me.

10"'What shall I do, Lord?' I asked.

"'Get up,' the Lord said, 'and go into Damascus. There you will be told all that you have been assigned to do.' **11**My companions led me by the hand into Damascus, because the brilliance of the light had blinded me.

12"A man named Ananias came to see me. He was a devout observer of the law and highly respected by all the Jews living there. **13**He stood beside me and said, 'Brother Saul, receive your sight!' And at that very moment I was able to see him.

14"Then he said: 'The God of our ancestors has chosen you to know his will and to

see the Righteous One and to hear words from his mouth. **15**You will be his witness to all people of what you have seen and heard. **16**And now what are you waiting for? Get up, be baptized and wash your sins away, calling on his name.'

17"When I returned to Jerusalem and was praying at the temple, I fell into a trance **18**and saw the Lord speaking to me. 'Quick!' he said. 'Leave Jerusalem immediately, because the people here will not accept your testimony about me.'

19"'Lord,' I replied, 'these people know that I went from one synagogue to another to imprison and beat those who believe in you. **20**And when the blood of your martyr*b* Stephen was shed, I stood there giving my approval and guarding the clothes of those who were killing him.'

21"Then the Lord said to me, 'Go; I will send you far away to the Gentiles.'"

Paul the Roman Citizen

22The crowd listened to Paul until he said this. Then they raised their voices and shouted, "Rid the earth of him! He's not fit to live!"

23As they were shouting and throwing off their cloaks and flinging dust into the air, **24**the commander ordered that Paul be taken into the barracks. He directed that he be flogged and interrogated in order to find out why the people were shouting at him like this. **25**As they stretched him out to flog him, Paul said to the centurion standing there, "Is it legal for you to flog a Roman citizen who hasn't even been found guilty?"

26When the centurion heard this, he went to the commander and reported it. "What are you going to do?" he asked. "This man is a Roman citizen."

27The commander went to Paul and asked, "Tell me, are you a Roman citizen?"

"Yes, I am," he answered.

28Then the commander said, "I had to pay a lot of money for my citizenship."

---

a 40 Or possibly *Hebrew*; also in 22:2   *b 20* Or *witness*

"But I was born a citizen," Paul replied.

²⁹Those who were about to interrogate him withdrew immediately. The commander himself was alarmed when he realized that he had put Paul, a Roman citizen, in chains.

Paul Before the Sanhedrin

³⁰The commander wanted to find out exactly why Paul was being accused by the Jews. So the next day he released him and ordered the chief priests and all the members of the Sanhedrin to assemble. Then he brought Paul and had him stand before them.

23 Paul looked straight at the Sanhedrin and said, "My brothers, I have fulfilled my duty to God in all good conscience to this day." ²At this the high priest Ananias ordered those standing near Paul to strike him on the mouth. ³Then Paul said to him, "God will strike you, you whitewashed wall! You sit there to judge me according to the law, yet you yourself violate the law by commanding that I be struck!"

⁴Those who were standing near Paul said, "How dare you insult God's high priest!"

⁵Paul replied, "Brothers, I did not realize that he was the high priest; for it is written: 'Do not speak evil about the ruler of your people.'ᵃ"

⁶Then Paul, knowing that some of them were Sadducees and the others Pharisees, called out in the Sanhedrin, "My brothers, I am a Pharisee, descended from Pharisees. I stand on trial because of the hope of the resurrection of the dead." ⁷When he said this, a dispute broke out between the Pharisees and the Sadducees, and the assembly was divided. ⁸(The Sadducees say that there is no resurrection, and that there are neither angels nor spirits, but the Pharisees believe all these things.)

⁹There was a great uproar, and some of the teachers of the law who were Pharisees stood up and argued vigorously. "We find nothing wrong with this man," they said. "What if a spirit or an angel has spoken to him?" ¹⁰The dispute became so violent that the commander was afraid Paul would be torn to pieces by them. He ordered the troops to go down and take him away from them by force and bring him into the barracks.

¹¹The following night the Lord stood near Paul and said, "Take courage! As you have testified about me in Jerusalem, so you must also testify in Rome."

The Plot to Kill Paul

¹²The next morning some Jews formed a conspiracy and bound themselves with an oath not to eat or drink until they had killed Paul. ¹³More than forty men were involved in this plot. ¹⁴They went to the chief priests and the elders and said, "We have taken a solemn oath not to eat anything until we have killed Paul. ¹⁵Now then, you and the Sanhedrin petition the commander to bring him before you on the pretext of wanting more accurate information about his case. We are ready to kill him before he gets here."

¹⁶But when the son of Paul's sister heard of this plot, he went into the barracks and told Paul.

¹⁷Then Paul called one of the centurions and said, "Take this young man to the commander; he has something to tell him." ¹⁸So he took him to the commander.

The centurion said, "Paul, the prisoner, sent for me and asked me to bring this young man to you because he has something to tell you."

¹⁹The commander took the young man by the hand, drew him aside and asked, "What is it you want to tell me?"

²⁰He said: "Some Jews have agreed to ask you to bring Paul before the Sanhedrin tomorrow on the pretext of wanting more accurate information about him. ²¹Don't give in to them, because more than forty of

---

them are waiting in ambush for him. They have taken an oath not to eat or drink until they have killed him. They are ready now, waiting for your consent to their request."

22The commander dismissed the young man with this warning: "Don't tell anyone that you have reported this to me."

Paul Transferred to Caesarea

23Then he called two of his centurions and ordered them, "Get ready a detachment of two hundred soldiers, seventy horsemen and two hundred spearmen*a* to go to Caesarea at nine tonight. 24Provide horses for Paul so that he may be taken safely to Governor Felix."

25He wrote a letter as follows:

26Claudius Lysias,

To His Excellency, Governor Felix:

Greetings.

27This man was seized by the Jews and they were about to kill him, but I came with my troops and rescued him, for I had learned that he is a Roman citizen. 28I wanted to know why they were accusing him, so I brought him to their Sanhedrin. 29I found that the accusation had to do with questions about their law, but there was no charge against him that deserved death or imprisonment. 30When I was informed of a plot to be carried out against the man, I sent him to you at once. I also ordered his accusers to present to you their case against him.

31So the soldiers, carrying out their orders, took Paul with them during the night and brought him as far as Antipatris. 32The next day they let the cavalry go on with him, while they returned to the barracks. 33When the cavalry arrived in Caesarea, they delivered the letter to the governor

and handed Paul over to him. 34The governor read the letter and asked what province he was from. Learning that he was from Cilicia, 35he said, "I will hear your case when your accusers get here." Then he ordered that Paul be kept under guard in Herod's palace.

Paul's Trial Before Felix

24 Five days later the high priest Ananias went down to Caesarea with some of the elders and a lawyer named Tertullus, and they brought their charges against Paul before the governor. 2When Paul was called in, Tertullus presented his case before Felix: "We have enjoyed a long period of peace under you, and your foresight has brought about reforms in this nation. 3Everywhere and in every way, most excellent Felix, we acknowledge this with profound gratitude. 4But in order not to weary you further, I would request that you be kind enough to hear us briefly.

5"We have found this man to be a troublemaker, stirring up riots among the Jews all over the world. He is a ringleader of the Nazarene sect 6and even tried to desecrate the temple; so we seized him. [7]*b* 8By examining him yourself you will be able to learn the truth about all these charges we are bringing against him."

9The other Jews joined in the accusation, asserting that these things were true.

10When the governor motioned for him to speak, Paul replied: "I know that for a number of years you have been a judge over this nation; so I gladly make my defense. 11You can easily verify that no more than twelve days ago I went up to Jerusalem to worship. 12My accusers did not find me arguing with anyone at the temple, or stirring up a crowd in the synagogues or anywhere else in the city. 13And they cannot prove to you the charges they are now

---

a 23 The meaning of the Greek for this word is uncertain.   *b 6-8* Some manuscripts include here *him, and we would have judged him in accordance with our law. 7But the commander Lysias came and took him from us with much violence, 8ordering his accusers to come before you.*

making against me. [14]However, I admit that I worship the God of our ancestors as a follower of the Way, which they call a sect. I believe everything that is in accordance with the Law and that is written in the Prophets, [15]and I have the same hope in God as these men themselves have, that there will be a resurrection of both the righteous and the wicked. [16]So I strive always to keep my conscience clear before God and man.

[17]"After an absence of several years, I came to Jerusalem to bring my people gifts for the poor and to present offerings. [18]I was ceremonially clean when they found me in the temple courts doing this. There was no crowd with me, nor was I involved in any disturbance. [19]But there are some Jews from the province of Asia, who ought to be here before you and bring charges if they have anything against me. [20]Or these who are here should state what crime they found in me when I stood before the Sanhedrin— [21]unless it was this one thing I shouted as I stood in their presence: 'It is concerning the resurrection of the dead that I am on trial before you today.'"

[22]Then Felix, who was well acquainted with the Way, adjourned the proceedings. "When Lysias the commander comes," he said, "I will decide your case." [23]He ordered the centurion to keep Paul under guard but to give him some freedom and permit his friends to take care of his needs.

[24]Several days later Felix came with his wife Drusilla, who was Jewish. He sent for Paul and listened to him as he spoke about faith in Christ Jesus. [25]As Paul talked about righteousness, self-control and the judgment to come, Felix was afraid and said, "That's enough for now! You may leave. When I find it convenient, I will send for you." [26]At the same time he was hoping that Paul would offer him a bribe, so he sent for him frequently and talked with him.

[27]When two years had passed, Felix was succeeded by Porcius Festus, but because Felix wanted to grant a favor to the Jews, he left Paul in prison.

Paul's Trial Before Festus

25 Three days after arriving in the province, Festus went up from Caesarea to Jerusalem, [2]where the chief priests and the Jewish leaders appeared before him and presented the charges against Paul. [3]They requested Festus, as a favor to them, to have Paul transferred to Jerusalem, for they were preparing an ambush to kill him along the way. [4]Festus answered, "Paul is being held at Caesarea, and I myself am going there soon. [5]Let some of your leaders come with me, and if the man has done anything wrong, they can press charges against him there."

[6]After spending eight or ten days with them, Festus went down to Caesarea. The next day he convened the court and ordered that Paul be brought before him. [7]When Paul came in, the Jews who had come down from Jerusalem stood around him. They brought many serious charges against him, but they could not prove them.

[8]Then Paul made his defense: "I have done nothing wrong against the Jewish law or against the temple or against Caesar."

[9]Festus, wishing to do the Jews a favor, said to Paul, "Are you willing to go up to Jerusalem and stand trial before me there on these charges?"

[10]Paul answered: "I am now standing before Caesar's court, where I ought to be tried. I have not done any wrong to the Jews, as you yourself know very well. [11]If, however, I am guilty of doing anything deserving death, I do not refuse to die. But if the charges brought against me by these Jews are not true, no one has the right to hand me over to them. I appeal to Caesar!"

[12]After Festus had conferred with his council, he declared: "You have appealed to Caesar. To Caesar you will go!"

Festus Consults King Agrippa

[13]A few days later King Agrippa and Bernice arrived at Caesarea to pay their respects to Festus. [14]Since they were spending

many days there, Festus discussed Paul's case with the king. He said: "There is a man here whom Felix left as a prisoner. ¹⁵When I went to Jerusalem, the chief priests and the elders of the Jews brought charges against him and asked that he be condemned.

¹⁶"I told them that it is not the Roman custom to hand over anyone before they have faced their accusers and have had an opportunity to defend themselves against the charges. ¹⁷When they came here with me, I did not delay the case, but convened the court the next day and ordered the man to be brought in. ¹⁸When his accusers got up to speak, they did not charge him with any of the crimes I had expected. ¹⁹Instead, they had some points of dispute with him about their own religion and about a dead man named Jesus who Paul claimed was alive. ²⁰I was at a loss how to investigate such matters; so I asked if he would be willing to go to Jerusalem and stand trial there on these charges. ²¹But when Paul made his appeal to be held over for the Emperor's decision, I ordered him held until I could send him to Caesar."

²²Then Agrippa said to Festus, "I would like to hear this man myself."

He replied, "Tomorrow you will hear him."

Paul Before Agrippa

²³The next day Agrippa and Bernice came with great pomp and entered the audience room with the high-ranking military officers and the prominent men of the city. At the command of Festus, Paul was brought in. ²⁴Festus said: "King Agrippa, and all who are present with us, you see this man! The whole Jewish community has petitioned me about him in Jerusalem and here in Caesarea, shouting that he ought not to live any longer. ²⁵I found he had done nothing deserving of death, but because he made his appeal to the Emperor I decided to send him to Rome. ²⁶But I have nothing definite to write to His Majesty about him. Therefore I have brought him before all of you, and especially before you, King Agrippa, so that as a result of this in-vestigation I may have something to write. ²⁷For I think it is unreasonable to send a prisoner on to Rome without specifying the charges against him."

26 Then Agrippa said to Paul, "You have permission to speak for yourself."

So Paul motioned with his hand and began his defense: ²"King Agrippa, I consider myself fortunate to stand before you today as I make my defense against all the accusations of the Jews, ³and especially so because you are well acquainted with all the Jewish customs and controversies. Therefore, I beg you to listen to me patiently.

⁴"The Jewish people all know the way I have lived ever since I was a child, from the beginning of my life in my own country, and also in Jerusalem. ⁵They have known me for a long time and can testify, if they are willing, that I conformed to the strictest sect of our religion, living as a Pharisee. ⁶And now it is because of my hope in what God has promised our ancestors that I am on trial today. ⁷This is the promise our twelve tribes are hoping to see fulfilled as they earnestly serve God day and night. King Agrippa, it is because of this hope that these Jews are accusing me. ⁸Why should any of you consider it incredible that God raises the dead?

⁹"I too was convinced that I ought to do all that was possible to oppose the name of Jesus of Nazareth. ¹⁰And that is just what I did in Jerusalem. On the authority of the chief priests I put many of the Lord's people in prison, and when they were put to death, I cast my vote against them. ¹¹Many a time I went from one synagogue to another to have them punished, and I tried to force them to blaspheme. I was so obsessed with persecuting them that I even hunted them down in foreign cities.

¹²"On one of these journeys I was going to Damascus with the authority and commission of the chief priests. ¹³About noon, King Agrippa, as I was on the road, I saw a light from heaven, brighter than the sun, blazing around me and my companions.

14We all fell to the ground, and I heard a voice saying to me in Aramaic,*a* 'Saul, Saul, why do you persecute me? It is hard for you to kick against the goads.'

15"Then I asked, 'Who are you, Lord?'

"'I am Jesus, whom you are persecuting,' the Lord replied. 16'Now get up and stand on your feet. I have appeared to you to appoint you as a servant and as a witness of what you have seen and will see of me. 17I will rescue you from your own people and from the Gentiles. I am sending you to them 18to open their eyes and turn them from darkness to light, and from the power of Satan to God, so that they may receive forgiveness of sins and a place among those who are sanctified by faith in me.'

19"So then, King Agrippa, I was not disobedient to the vision from heaven. 20First to those in Damascus, then to those in Jerusalem and in all Judea, and then to the Gentiles, I preached that they should repent and turn to God and demonstrate their repentance by their deeds. 21That is why some Jews seized me in the temple courts and tried to kill me. 22But God has helped me to this very day; so I stand here and testify to small and great alike. I am saying nothing beyond what the prophets and Moses said would happen— 23that the Messiah would suffer and, as the first to rise from the dead, would bring the message of light to his own people and to the Gentiles."

24At this point Festus interrupted Paul's defense. "You are out of your mind, Paul!" he shouted. "Your great learning is driving you insane."

25"I am not insane, most excellent Festus," Paul replied. "What I am saying is true and reasonable. 26The king is familiar with these things, and I can speak freely to him. I am convinced that none of this has escaped his notice, because it was not done in a corner. 27King Agrippa, do you believe the prophets? I know you do."

28Then Agrippa said to Paul, "Do you think that in such a short time you can persuade me to be a Christian?"

29Paul replied, "Short time or long—I pray to God that not only you but all who are listening to me today may become what I am, except for these chains."

30The king rose, and with him the governor and Bernice and those sitting with them. 31After they left the room, they began saying to one another, "This man is not doing anything that deserves death or imprisonment."

32Agrippa said to Festus, "This man could have been set free if he had not appealed to Caesar."

Paul Sails for Rome

27 When it was decided that we would sail for Italy, Paul and some other prisoners were handed over to a centurion named Julius, who belonged to the Imperial Regiment. 2We boarded a ship from Adramyttium about to sail for ports along the coast of the province of Asia, and we put out to sea. Aristarchus, a Macedonian from Thessalonica, was with us.

3The next day we landed at Sidon; and Julius, in kindness to Paul, allowed him to go to his friends so they might provide for his needs. 4From there we put out to sea again and passed to the lee of Cyprus because the winds were against us. 5When we had sailed across the open sea off the coast of Cilicia and Pamphylia, we landed at Myra in Lycia. 6There the centurion found an Alexandrian ship sailing for Italy and put us on board. 7We made slow headway for many days and had difficulty arriving off Cnidus. When the wind did not allow us to hold our course, we sailed to the lee of Crete, opposite Salmone. 8We moved along the coast with difficulty and came to a place called Fair Havens, near the town of Lasea.

9Much time had been lost, and sailing had already become dangerous because by now it was after the Day of Atonement.*b*

---

a 14 Or *Hebrew*   *b* 9 That is, Yom Kippur

So Paul warned them, [10]"Men, I can see that our voyage is going to be disastrous and bring great loss to ship and cargo, and to our own lives also." [11]But the centurion, instead of listening to what Paul said, followed the advice of the pilot and of the owner of the ship. [12]Since the harbor was unsuitable to winter in, the majority decided that we should sail on, hoping to reach Phoenix and winter there. This was a harbor in Crete, facing both southwest and northwest.

The Storm

[13]When a gentle south wind began to blow, they saw their opportunity; so they weighed anchor and sailed along the shore of Crete. [14]Before very long, a wind of hurricane force, called the Northeaster, swept down from the island. [15]The ship was caught by the storm and could not head into the wind; so we gave way to it and were driven along. [16]As we passed to the lee of a small island called Cauda, we were hardly able to make the lifeboat secure, [17]so the men hoisted it aboard. Then they passed ropes under the ship itself to hold it together. Because they were afraid they would run aground on the sandbars of Syrtis, they lowered the sea anchor[a] and let the ship be driven along. [18]We took such a violent battering from the storm that the next day they began to throw the cargo overboard. [19]On the third day, they threw the ship's tackle overboard with their own hands. [20]When neither sun nor stars appeared for many days and the storm continued raging, we finally gave up all hope of being saved.

[21]After they had gone a long time without food, Paul stood up before them and said: "Men, you should have taken my advice not to sail from Crete; then you would have spared yourselves this damage and loss. [22]But now I urge you to keep up your courage, because not one of you will be lost; only the ship will be destroyed. [23]Last night an angel of the God to whom I belong and whom I serve stood beside me [24]and said, 'Do not be afraid, Paul. You must stand trial before Caesar; and God has graciously given you the lives of all who sail with you.' [25]So keep up your courage, men, for I have faith in God that it will happen just as he told me. [26]Nevertheless, we must run aground on some island."

The Shipwreck

[27]On the fourteenth night we were still being driven across the Adriatic[b] Sea, when about midnight the sailors sensed they were approaching land. [28]They took soundings and found that the water was a hundred and twenty feet[c] deep. A short time later they took soundings again and found it was ninety feet[d] deep. [29]Fearing that we would be dashed against the rocks, they dropped four anchors from the stern and prayed for daylight. [30]In an attempt to escape from the ship, the sailors let the lifeboat down into the sea, pretending they were going to lower some anchors from the bow. [31]Then Paul said to the centurion and the soldiers, "Unless these men stay with the ship, you cannot be saved." [32]So the soldiers cut the ropes that held the lifeboat and let it drift away.

[33]Just before dawn Paul urged them all to eat. "For the last fourteen days," he said, "you have been in constant suspense and have gone without food — you haven't eaten anything. [34]Now I urge you to take some food. You need it to survive. Not one of you will lose a single hair from his head." [35]After he said this, he took some bread and gave thanks to God in front of them all. Then he broke it and began to eat. [36]They were all encouraged and ate some food themselves. [37]Altogether there were 276 of us on board. [38]When they had eaten as much as they wanted, they lightened the ship by throwing the grain into the sea.

[39]When daylight came, they did not rec-

---

[a] 17 Or *the sails*   [b] 27 In ancient times the name referred to an area extending well south of Italy.   [c] 28 Or about 37 meters   [d] 28 Or about 27 meters

ognize the land, but they saw a bay with a sandy beach, where they decided to run the ship aground if they could. 40Cutting loose the anchors, they left them in the sea and at the same time untied the ropes that held the rudders. Then they hoisted the foresail to the wind and made for the beach. 41But the ship struck a sandbar and ran aground. The bow stuck fast and would not move, and the stern was broken to pieces by the pounding of the surf.

42The soldiers planned to kill the prisoners to prevent any of them from swimming away and escaping. 43But the centurion wanted to spare Paul's life and kept them from carrying out their plan. He ordered those who could swim to jump overboard first and get to land. 44The rest were to get there on planks or on other pieces of the ship. In this way everyone reached land safely.

Paul Ashore on Malta

28 Once safely on shore, we found out that the island was called Malta. 2The islanders showed us unusual kindness. They built a fire and welcomed us all because it was raining and cold. 3Paul gathered a pile of brushwood and, as he put it on the fire, a viper, driven out by the heat, fastened itself on his hand. 4When the islanders saw the snake hanging from his hand, they said to each other, "This man must be a murderer; for though he escaped from the sea, the goddess Justice has not allowed him to live." 5But Paul shook the snake off into the fire and suffered no ill effects. 6The people expected him to swell up or suddenly fall dead; but after waiting a long time and seeing nothing unusual happen to him, they changed their minds and said he was a god.

7There was an estate nearby that belonged to Publius, the chief official of the island. He welcomed us to his home and showed us generous hospitality for three days. 8His father was sick in bed, suffering from fever and dysentery. Paul went in to see him and, after prayer, placed his hands

on him and healed him. 9When this had happened, the rest of the sick on the island came and were cured. 10They honored us in many ways; and when we were ready to sail, they furnished us with the supplies we needed.

Paul's Arrival at Rome

11After three months we put out to sea in a ship that had wintered in the island — it was an Alexandrian ship with the figurehead of the twin gods Castor and Pollux. 12We put in at Syracuse and stayed there three days. 13From there we set sail and arrived at Rhegium. The next day the south wind came up, and on the following day we reached Puteoli. 14There we found some brothers and sisters who invited us to spend a week with them. And so we came to Rome. 15The brothers and sisters there had heard that we were coming, and they traveled as far as the Forum of Appius and the Three Taverns to meet us. At the sight of these people Paul thanked God and was encouraged. 16When we got to Rome, Paul was allowed to live by himself, with a soldier to guard him.

Paul Preaches at Rome Under Guard

17Three days later he called together the local Jewish leaders. When they had assembled, Paul said to them: "My brothers, although I have done nothing against our people or against the customs of our ancestors, I was arrested in Jerusalem and handed over to the Romans. 18They examined me and wanted to release me, because I was not guilty of any crime deserving death. 19The Jews objected, so I was compelled to make an appeal to Caesar. I certainly did not intend to bring any charge against my own people. 20For this reason I have asked to see you and talk with you. It is because of the hope of Israel that I am bound with this chain."

21They replied, "We have not received any letters from Judea concerning you, and none of our people who have come from there has reported or said anything bad about you. 22But we want to hear what your views are, for we know that people everywhere are talking against this sect."

23They arranged to meet Paul on a certain day, and came in even larger numbers to the place where he was staying. He witnessed to them from morning till evening, explaining about the kingdom of God, and from the Law of Moses and from the Prophets he tried to persuade them about Jesus. 24Some were convinced by what he said, but others would not believe. 25They disagreed among themselves and began to leave after Paul had made this final statement: "The Holy Spirit spoke the truth to your ancestors when he said through Isaiah the prophet:

26" 'Go to this people and say,
    "You will be ever hearing but never
        understanding;

you will be ever seeing but never
    perceiving."
27For this people's heart has become
        calloused;
    they hardly hear with their ears,
    and they have closed their eyes.
Otherwise they might see with their
        eyes,
    hear with their ears,
    understand with their hearts
and turn, and I would heal them.' a

28"Therefore I want you to know that God's salvation has been sent to the Gentiles, and they will listen!" [29] b

30For two whole years Paul stayed there in his own rented house and welcomed all who came to see him. 31He proclaimed the kingdom of God and taught about the Lord Jesus Christ — with all boldness and without hindrance!

---

a 27 Isaiah 6:9,10 (see Septuagint)   b 29 Some manuscripts include here *After he said this, the Jews left, arguing vigorously among themselves.*

THEME: Through Jesus' death, God credits his own righteousness to all who believe in him and rely on his promise of salvation in Jesus Christ.

AUTHOR: That the apostle Paul is the author of this letter is unquestioned.

DATE OF WRITING: Romans was probably written in AD 57.

ENCOURAGEMENT FROM ROMANS: "I am convinced that neither death nor life, neither angels nor demons, neither the present nor the future, nor any powers, neither height nor depth, nor anything else in all creation, will be able to separate us from the love of God that is in Christ Jesus our Lord" (Romans 8:38 – 39).

CHALLENGE FROM ROMANS: "The night is nearly over; the day is almost here. So let us put aside the deeds of darkness and put on the armor of light. Let us behave decently, as in the daytime, not in carousing and drunkenness, not in sexual immorality and debauchery, not in dissension and jealousy" (Romans 13:12 – 13).

REFLECTION FROM ROMANS: "The Spirit helps us in our weakness. We do not know what we ought to pray for, but the Spirit himself intercedes for us through wordless groans" (Romans 8:26).

At a Glance

On our own, we just don't have the power to get it all together. We know right from wrong, we know what we should and shouldn't do, but we have a hard time doing the right thing. This reality is uncomfortable for believers who are trying to put God's Word into practice. While we know what we should do, on our own we just can't do it.

That's what the book of Romans is all about. As long as we keep trying to do things in our own power, driven by our own self-will, we'll always fail. We need to plug in to Christ's power in order to experience victory over our hurts, hang-ups and habits. As long as we keep trying on our own, we'll encounter nothing but frustration and failure. But when we accept Christ's power, we'll find out that there is truly no condemnation for those who are in Christ Jesus (see Romans 8:1).

Recovery Themes in Romans

1 Paul, a servant of Christ Jesus, called to be an apostle and set apart for the gospel of God — ²the gospel he promised beforehand through his prophets in the Holy Scriptures ³regarding his Son, who as to his earthly life*a* was a descendant of David, ⁴and who through the Spirit of holiness was appointed the Son of God in power*b* by his resurrection from the dead: Jesus Christ our Lord. ⁵Through him we received grace and apostleship to call all the Gentiles to the obedience that comes from*c* faith for his name's sake. ⁶And you also are among those Gentiles who are called to belong to Jesus Christ.

---

a 3 Or *who according to the flesh*   *b 4* Or *was declared with power to be the Son of God*   *c 5* Or *that is*

⁷To all in Rome who are loved by God and called to be his holy people:

Grace and peace to you from God our Father and from the Lord Jesus Christ.

Paul's Longing to Visit Rome

⁸First, I thank my God through Jesus Christ for all of you, because your faith is being reported all over the world. ⁹God, whom I serve in my spirit in preaching the gospel of his Son, is my witness how constantly I remember you ¹⁰in my prayers at all times; and I pray that now at last by God's will the way may be opened for me to come to you.

¹¹I long to see you so that I may impart to you some spiritual gift to make you strong— ¹²that is, that you and I may be mutually encouraged by each other's faith. ¹³I do not want you to be unaware, brothers and sisters,ᵃ that I planned many times to come to you (but have been prevented from doing so until now) in order that I might have a harvest among you, just as I have had among the other Gentiles.

¹⁴I am obligated both to Greeks and non-Greeks, both to the wise and the foolish. ¹⁵That is why I am so eager to preach the gospel also to you who are in Rome.

¹⁶For I am not ashamed of the gospel, because it is the power of God that brings salvation to everyone who believes: first to the Jew, then to the Gentile. ¹⁷For in the gospel the righteousness of God is revealed—a righteousness that is by faith from first to last,ᵇ just as it is written: "The righteous will live by faith."ᶜ

God's Wrath Against Sinful Humanity

¹⁸The wrath of God is being revealed from heaven against all the godlessness and wickedness of people, who suppress the truth by their wickedness, ¹⁹since what may be known about God is plain to them, because God has made it plain to them.

²⁰For since the creation of the world God's invisible qualities—his eternal power and divine nature—have been clearly seen, being understood from what has been made, so that people are without excuse.

²¹For although they knew God, they neither glorified him as God nor gave thanks to him, but their thinking became futile and their foolish hearts were darkened. ²²Although they claimed to be wise, they became fools ²³and exchanged the glory of the immortal God for images made to look like a mortal human being and birds and animals and reptiles.

²⁴Therefore God gave them over in the sinful desires of their hearts to sexual impurity for the degrading of their bodies with one another. ²⁵They exchanged the truth about God for a lie, and worshiped and served created things rather than the Creator—who is forever praised. Amen.

²⁶Because of this, God gave them over to shameful lusts. Even their women exchanged natural sexual relations for unnatural ones. ²⁷In the same way the men also abandoned natural relations with women and were inflamed with lust for one another. Men committed shameful acts with other men, and received in themselves the due penalty for their error.

²⁸Furthermore, just as they did not think it worthwhile to retain the knowledge of God, so God gave them over to a depraved mind, so that they do what ought not to be done. ²⁹They have become filled with every kind of wickedness, evil, greed and depravity. They are full of envy, murder, strife, deceit and malice. They are gossips, ³⁰slanderers, God-haters, insolent, arrogant and boastful; they invent ways of doing evil; they disobey their parents; ³¹they have no understanding, no fidelity, no love, no mercy. ³²Although they know God's righteous decree that those who do such things deserve death, they not only continue to do these very things

---

ᵃ 13 The Greek word for *brothers and sisters* (*adelphoi*) refers here to believers, both men and women, as part of God's family; also in 7:1, 4; 8:12, 29; 10:1; 11:25; 12:1; 15:14, 30; 16:14, 17.   ᵇ 17 Or *is from faith to faith*   ᶜ 17 Hab. 2:4

but also approve of those who practice them.

God's Righteous Judgment

2 You, therefore, have no excuse, you who pass judgment on someone else, for at whatever point you judge another, you are condemning yourself, because you who pass judgment do the same things. [2]Now we know that God's judgment against those who do such things is based on truth. [3]So when you, a mere human being, pass judgment on them and yet do the same things, do you think you will escape God's judgment? [4]Or do you show contempt for the riches of his kindness, forbearance and patience, not realizing that God's kindness is intended to lead you to repentance?

[5]But because of your stubbornness and your unrepentant heart, you are storing up wrath against yourself for the day of God's wrath, when his righteous judgment will be revealed. [6]God "will repay each person according to what they have done."[a] [7]To those who by persistence in doing good seek glory, honor and immortality, he will give eternal life. [8]But for those who are self-seeking and who reject the truth and follow evil, there will be wrath and anger. [9]There will be trouble and distress for every human being who does evil: first for the Jew, then for the Gentile; [10]but glory, honor and peace for everyone who does good: first for the Jew, then for the Gentile. [11]For God does not show favoritism.

[12]All who sin apart from the law will also perish apart from the law, and all who sin under the law will be judged by the law. [13]For it is not those who hear the law who are righteous in God's sight, but it is those who obey the law who will be declared righteous. [14](Indeed, when Gentiles, who do not have the law, do by nature things required by the law, they are a law for themselves, even though they do not have the law. [15]They show that the requirements of the law are written on their hearts, their consciences also bearing witness, and their thoughts sometimes accusing them and at other times even defending them.) [16]This will take place on the day when God judges people's secrets through Jesus Christ, as my gospel declares.

The Jews and the Law

[17]Now you, if you call yourself a Jew; if you rely on the law and boast in God; [18]if you know his will and approve of what is superior because you are instructed by the law; [19]if you are convinced that you are a guide for the blind, a light for those who are in the dark, [20]an instructor of the foolish, a teacher of little children, because you have in the law the embodiment of knowledge and truth — [21]you, then, who teach others, do you not teach yourself? You who preach against stealing, do you steal? [22]You who say that people should not commit adultery, do you commit adultery? You who abhor idols, do you rob temples? [23]You who boast in the law, do you dishonor God by breaking the law? [24]As it is written: "God's name is blasphemed among the Gentiles because of you."[b]

[25]Circumcision has value if you observe the law, but if you break the law, you have become as though you had not been circumcised. [26]So then, if those who are not circumcised keep the law's requirements, will they not be regarded as though they were circumcised? [27]The one who is not circumcised physically and yet obeys the law will condemn you who, even though you have the[c] written code and circumcision, are a lawbreaker.

[28]A person is not a Jew who is one only outwardly, nor is circumcision merely outward and physical. [29]No, a person is a Jew who is one inwardly; and circumcision is circumcision of the heart, by the Spirit, not by the written code. Such a person's praise is not from other people, but from God.

---

[a] 6 Psalm 62:12; Prov. 24:12   [b] 24 Isaiah 52:5 (see Septuagint); Ezek. 36:20,22   [c] 27 Or *who, by means of a*

God's Faithfulness

3 What advantage, then, is there in being a Jew, or what value is there in circumcision? [2] Much in every way! First of all, the Jews have been entrusted with the very words of God.

[3] What if some were unfaithful? Will their unfaithfulness nullify God's faithfulness? [4] Not at all! Let God be true, and every human being a liar. As it is written:

"So that you may be proved right when you speak
and prevail when you judge."[a]

[5] But if our unrighteousness brings out God's righteousness more clearly, what shall we say? That God is unjust in bringing his wrath on us? (I am using a human argument.) [6] Certainly not! If that were so, how could God judge the world? [7] Someone might argue, "If my falsehood enhances God's truthfulness and so increases his glory, why am I still condemned as a sinner?" [8] Why not say—as some slanderously claim that we say—"Let us do evil that good may result"? Their condemnation is just!

No One Is Righteous

[9] What shall we conclude then? Do we have any advantage? Not at all! For we have already made the charge that Jews and Gentiles alike are all under the power of sin. [10] As it is written:

"There is no one righteous, not even one;
[11]   there is no one who understands;
there is no one who seeks God.
[12] All have turned away,
they have together become worthless;
there is no one who does good,
not even one."[b]
[13] "Their throats are open graves;
their tongues practice deceit."[c]

"The poison of vipers is on their lips."[d]
[14]   "Their mouths are full of cursing and bitterness."[e]
[15] "Their feet are swift to shed blood;
[16]   ruin and misery mark their ways,
[17] and the way of peace they do not know."[f]
[18]   "There is no fear of God before their eyes."[g]

[19] Now we know that whatever the law says, it says to those who are under the law, so that every mouth may be silenced and the whole world held accountable to God. [20] Therefore no one will be declared righteous in God's sight by the works of the law; rather, through the law we become conscious of our sin.

Righteousness Through Faith

[21] But now apart from the law the righteousness of God has been made known, to which the Law and the Prophets testify. [22] This righteousness is given through faith in[h] Jesus Christ to all who believe. There is no difference between Jew and Gentile, [23] for all have sinned and fall short of the glory of God, [24] and all are justified freely by his grace through the redemption that came by Christ Jesus. [25] God presented Christ as a sacrifice of atonement,[i] through the shedding of his blood—to be received by faith. He did this to demonstrate his righteousness, because in his forbearance he had left the sins committed beforehand unpunished— [26] he did it to demonstrate his righteousness at the present time, so as to be just and the one who justifies those who have faith in Jesus.

[27] Where, then, is boasting? It is excluded. Because of what law? The law that requires works? No, because of the law that requires faith. [28] For we maintain that a person is justified by faith apart from the works of the law. [29] Or is God the God of Jews only? Is he not the God of Gentiles too? Yes, of

---

a 4 Psalm 51:4   *b 12* Psalms 14:1-3; 53:1-3; Eccles. 7:20   *c 13* Psalm 5:9   *d 13* Psalm 140:3
e 14 Psalm 10:7 (see Septuagint)   *f 17* Isaiah 59:7,8   *g 18* Psalm 36:1   *h 22* Or *through the faithfulness of*
i 25 The Greek for *sacrifice of atonement* refers to the atonement cover on the ark of the covenant (see Lev. 16:15,16).

Gentiles too, ³⁰since there is only one God, who will justify the circumcised by faith and the uncircumcised through that same faith. ³¹Do we, then, nullify the law by this faith? Not at all! Rather, we uphold the law.

Abraham Justified by Faith

4 What then shall we say that Abraham, our forefather according to the flesh, discovered in this matter? ²If, in fact, Abraham was justified by

---

FORGIVENESS LESSON [Principle Six]

This is the first page of the FORGIVENESS lesson.

For a discussion of Principles One through Eight and a listing of their related lessons, go to pages xvii – xliv.

This righteousness is given through faith in Jesus Christ to all who believe.
There is no difference between Jew and Gentile, for all have sinned and fall short
of the glory of God, and all are justified freely by his grace through the redemption
that came by Christ Jesus. God presented Christ as a sacrifice of atonement, through
the shedding of his blood — to be received by faith. He did this to demonstrate his
righteousness, because in his forbearance he had left the sins committed beforehand
unpunished — he did it to demonstrate his righteousness at the present time,
so as to be just and the one who justifies those who have faith in Jesus.

Romans 3:22–26

Principle Six calls for us to evaluate all our relationships and to offer FORGIVENESS to those who have hurt us and make amends for harm we've done to others, except when doing so would injure them or others. We need to be willing to admit our part in our relationships that have been broken or damaged.

In order to be completely free from resentment, anger, fear, guilt and shame, we need to offer and accept forgiveness in all applicable areas of our lives. If we don't, our recovery will be stalled and remain incomplete.

The first and most important kind of forgiveness is extended from God to us. Have you accepted God's forgiveness? Have you accepted Jesus' work on the cross? By his willingness to take our punishment, all our sins were canceled. Our debt was paid in full — a free gift for all those who are willing to put their faith in him as the true and only Higher Power, Savior and Lord. Jesus himself exclaimed from the cross, "It is finished" (John 19:30) — possibly the most significant three words ever uttered. No matter how grievously we may have injured others or ourselves, the grace of God is always sufficient. His forgiveness is always complete, with no strings attached.

Romans 3:22–26 points out not only that all of us have sinned but that because we have asked Christ into our hearts we can receive God's freely offered gift of grace and forgiveness. Remember: If God were unwilling to forgive our sins, none of us could look forward to being in heaven with him.

The second type of forgiveness is the kind we extend from ourselves to others.
Go to Romans 12:17 – 18 (page 1412).

works, he had something to boast about — but not before God. ³What does Scripture say? "Abraham believed God, and it was credited to him as righteousness."ᵃ

⁴Now to the one who works, wages are not credited as a gift but as an obligation. ⁵However, to the one who does not work but trusts God who justifies the ungodly, their faith is credited as righteousness. ⁶David says the same thing when he speaks of the blessedness of the one to whom God credits righteousness apart from works:

⁷"Blessed are those
  whose transgressions are forgiven,
  whose sins are covered.
⁸Blessed is the one
  whose sin the Lord will never count
  against them."ᵇ

⁹Is this blessedness only for the circumcised, or also for the uncircumcised? We

ᵃ 3 Gen. 15:6; also in verse 22   ᵇ 8 Psalm 32:1,2

GRACE LESSON [*Principle Six*]

This is the first page of the GRACE lesson.

For a discussion of Principles One through Eight and a listing of their related lessons,
go to pages xvii – xliv.

*All have sinned and fall short of the glory of God, and all are justified freely
by his grace through the redemption that came by Christ Jesus.*

ROMANS 3:23–24

Principle Six calls for us to evaluate all our relationships and to offer FORGIVENESS to those who have hurt us and make amends for harm we've done to others, except when doing so would injure them or others. We need to be willing to admit our part in our relationships that have been broken or damaged.

As we grow as Christians and move through our recovery process, we want to follow the guidance and directions of Jesus Christ. As we get to know him better, we want to model his teachings and his ways — to become more like him. If we're going to implement Principle Six to the best of our abilities, we need to learn to model God's GRACE.

The *G* in GRACE stands for GOD'S GIFT. Romans 3:24 tells us that grace is a gift, something that can't be bought but that is freely offered by God to us. First Peter 1:13 instructs us: "With minds that are alert and fully sober, set your hope on the grace to be brought to you when Jesus Christ is revealed." When we extend our forgiveness, it's our gift of grace to those who have hurt us. Similarly, when we offer amends without expecting anything in return, it's a gift from us to those we've hurt.

If our relationship with God were dependent upon our being perfect, we would have trouble relating to God most of the time. Thank God that our intimacy with him is built on his grace and love for us. He alone gives us the strength to make the amends and offer the forgiveness Principle Six requires.

The next letter in GRACE is *R*. Go to Ephesians 2:8 – 9 (page 1464).

have been saying that Abraham's faith was credited to him as righteousness. [10]Under what circumstances was it credited? Was it after he was circumcised, or before? It was not after, but before! [11]And he received circumcision as a sign, a seal of the righteousness that he had by faith while he was still uncircumcised. So then, he is the father of all who believe but have not been circumcised, in order that righteousness might be credited to them. [12]And he is then also the father of the circumcised who not only are circumcised but who also follow in the footsteps of the faith that our father Abraham had before he was circumcised.

[13]It was not through the law that Abraham and his offspring received the promise that he would be heir of the world, but through the righteousness that comes by faith. [14]For if those who depend on the law are heirs, faith means nothing and the promise is worthless, [15]because the law brings wrath. And where there is no law there is no transgression.

[16]Therefore, the promise comes by faith, so that it may be by grace and may be guaranteed to all Abraham's offspring—not only to those who are of the law but also to those who have the faith of Abraham. He is the father of us all. [17]As it is written: "I have made you a father of many nations."[a] He is our father in the sight of God, in whom he believed—the God who gives life to the dead and calls into being things that were not.

[18]Against all hope, Abraham in hope believed and so became the father of many nations, just as it had been said to him, "So shall your offspring be."[b] [19]Without weakening in his faith, he faced the fact that his body was as good as dead—since he was about a hundred years old—and that Sarah's womb was also dead. [20]Yet he did not waver through unbelief regarding the promise of God, but was strengthened in his faith and gave glory to God, [21]being fully persuaded that God had power to do what he had promised. [22]This is why

"it was credited to him as righteousness." [23]The words "it was credited to him" were written not for him alone, [24]but also for us, to whom God will credit righteousness—for us who believe in him who raised Jesus our Lord from the dead. [25]He was delivered over to death for our sins and was raised to life for our justification.

Peace and Hope

5 Therefore, since we have been justified through faith, we[c] have peace with God through our Lord Jesus Christ, [2]through whom we have gained access by faith into this grace in which we now stand. And we[d] boast in the hope of the glory of God. [3]Not only so, but we[d] also glory in our sufferings, because we know that suffering produces perseverance; [4]perseverance, character; and character, hope. [5]And hope does not put us to shame, because God's love has been poured out into our hearts through the Holy Spirit, who has been given to us.

[6]You see, at just the right time, when we were still powerless, Christ died for the ungodly. [7]Very rarely will anyone die for a righteous person, though for a good person someone might possibly dare to die. [8]But God demonstrates his own love for us in this: While we were still sinners, Christ died for us.

[9]Since we have now been justified by his blood, how much more shall we be saved from God's wrath through him! [10]For if, while we were God's enemies, we were reconciled to him through the death of his Son, how much more, having been reconciled, shall we be saved through his life! [11]Not only is this so, but we also boast in God through our Lord Jesus Christ, through whom we have now received reconciliation.

Death Through Adam, Life Through Christ

[12]Therefore, just as sin entered the world through one man, and death through sin,

---

a 17 Gen. 17:5   *b 18* Gen. 15:5   *c 1* Many manuscripts *let us*   *d 2* Or *let us*

CHARACTER STUDY

MY NAME IS
THE ENEMY OF GOD

ROMANS 5:1–11

According to Romans 5:1–1, each of us is either God's child or God's enemy. Paul's words offer reassurance to suffering Christians. He wants his readers to know that their misery doesn't signify that God has rejected them. The apostle reasons that, if Jesus died for us when we were still God's enemies, he certainly won't abandon us after we've joined his side (see v. 10).

As God's children we begin to recognize that the path of trials, when traveled with perseverance, improves our character. And God is more interested in our character than in our comfort. Our improved character may be identified as an informed hope and a deepened experience of God's love (see vv. 3–5). That Christ lives in us becomes apparent when our endurance of suffering differs from that of an unbeliever.

As children of God, we don't have to react negatively and powerlessly to changing circumstances. Instead, we can respond positively and proactively to Jesus Christ. This new capacity isn't our creation but God's. Jesus made this attitude possible at the point where we were most incapacitated, at our worst rather than at our best (see v. 6). Understanding that Jesus came to restore relationships, not to establish another religion, is the key to enjoying reconciliation. As we grow in our relationship to him, God removes anything in us that has separated us from him (see vv. 9–11).

Jesus died for our sins once and for all (see Hebrews 7:27). And he did this while we were helpless, ungodly sinners and enemies of God. Therefore, in Principle Seven, we can complete our daily inventory and pray confidently, knowing that God's love for us can't be diminished by any failure on our part. We can pray for direction and power, knowing that, since we have already "been reconciled," there's no doubt that we'll "be saved through his life" (Romans 5:10).

and in this way death came to all people, because all sinned —

13To be sure, sin was in the world before the law was given, but sin is not charged against anyone's account where there is no law. 14Nevertheless, death reigned from the time of Adam to the time of Moses, even over those who did not sin by breaking a command, as did Adam, who is a pattern of the one to come.

15But the gift is not like the trespass. For if the many died by the trespass of the one man, how much more did God's grace and the gift that came by the grace of the one man, Jesus Christ, overflow to the many! 16Nor can the gift of God be compared with the result of one man's sin: The judgment followed one sin and brought condemnation, but the gift followed many trespasses and brought justification. 17For if, by the trespass of the one man, death reigned through that one man, how much more will those who receive God's abundant provision of grace and of the gift of righteousness reign in life through the one man, Jesus Christ!

18Consequently, just as one trespass resulted in condemnation for all people, so also one righteous act resulted in justification and life for all people. 19For just as through the disobedience of the one man the many were made sinners, so also through the obedience of the one man the many will be made righteous.

20The law was brought in so that the trespass might increase. But where sin increased, grace increased all the more, 21so that, just as sin reigned in death, so also grace might reign through righteousness to bring eternal life through Jesus Christ our Lord.

Dead to Sin, Alive in Christ

6 What shall we say, then? Shall we go on sinning so that grace may increase? 2By no means! We are those

---

SANITY LESSON [*Principle Two*]

For the previous entry in the SANITY lesson, go to Proverbs 29:25 (page 778).

For a discussion of Principles One through Eight and a listing of their related lessons, go to pages xvii – xliv.

God demonstrates his own love for us in this:
While we were still sinners, Christ died for us.

ROMANS 5:8

In Principle Two we earnestly believe that God exists, that we matter to him and that he has the power to help us recover. It's in this principle that we find the SANITY to begin to stop making the same poor choices again and again.

The last letter in SANITY is *Y*, which stands for YOUR HIGHER POWER, Jesus Christ. Jesus loves us just the way we are. His unconditional love for us is shown in its fullest in the above verse. No matter what comes our way, we can handle it with the help of our all-powerful God. Recovery is a daily program, and we need a power greater than ourselves — the Higher Power, Jesus Christ — to provide us with the strength, acceptance, new life, integrity and trust that will allow us to make sane decisions based on his truth.

This is the final page of the SANITY lesson.

My Name is Ken

I'M A BELIEVER WHO STRUGGLES WITH ANGER AND ALCOHOLISM

Please read Paul's description of how God responds to people who are still his enemies in Romans 5:1 – 11.

Not long after my 8th birthday, my mom became sick and spent a lot of time in the hospital. The illness that started as breast cancer progressed to bone cancer, and she passed away. I remember that I didn't get a chance to say goodbye. To this day I can't remember the sound of her voice.

My dad remarried, and although the new family pretended to get along, my stepsisters and I fought a lot. We didn't think of the strain this put on our parents' new marriage — as it is with most kids, we only thought of ourselves. Then we started going to my stepmother's church, which was a first for my dad and me. I learned about the Bible there, but I also had my first taste of alcohol during communion. In those days I didn't take to church, and I certainly didn't have a relationship with God.

By my junior year of high school, I was drinking every day. After graduation I married my high school sweetheart and continued my daily drinking. We divorced four years later.

Not long after, my dad died of cancer. Although I couldn't make things right with him for my rebellious years, I did tell him that I loved him before he passed away. Shortly after, I met a young lady at the beach. After a five month courtship we got married. As Tanya and I began our marriage I joined the Air Force and we were relocated to Madrid, Spain.

While we were in Spain, Tanya had surgery as a result of losing a child. I'm ashamed to admit that I was not there for her emotionally during this time. I did not deal with issues well then. I would remain silent and ignore problems hoping they would go away on their own.

We moved back to the states two years later and Tanya gave birth to our son. We changed situations, friends and locations, but I was still the same. I was still living as if God did not exist. I was living as if I was in control. Things really came to a head one morning when I woke up on the kitchen floor of our apartment. I realized that I was in the house all by myself. Tanya had left me.

As the fog in my mind lifted, I remembered that the night before I had been drinking. During a fight, I had hit her. At that moment, sitting on the kitchen floor all alone, I realized and silently admitted that I had a drinking problem. I was powerless to control my compulsion to drink.

Tanya eventually came back to me. We moved several more times in the next few years, but no matter how many times I moved or tried to start over, I continued to return to my old hurts, hang-ups, and habits. Like 2 Peter 2:22 says, "the proverbs are true: 'A dog returns to its vomit,' and 'A sow that is washed returns to her wallowing in the mud.' " That was me. I kept returning to my old ways. I had not made a decision that I needed God to help me, and my problems came with me everywhere I moved.

After one move, our situation seemed to be improving. Some neighbors invited us to attend a local church. The pastor there took me through the Scriptures and led me to accept Christ as my Lord and Savior. I was finally on God's side. I had moved from being an enemy of God to becoming a child of God. I started learning that as a child of God, I didn't have to react to changing circumstances. Instead, I could rely on Jesus to direct me to the correct response.

Tanya was approached to begin a Celebrate Recovery ministry at our new church. As they say in the program, "God never wastes a hurt." Because of what she had gone through, she was uniquely prepared to take on this task.

Then our world was rocked again. Two days before we were set to begin the program I was laid off from what I considered would be my career job — the best job I'd ever had. Although I didn't understand why God would let us go through this hardship, I had amazing accountability, both from Tanya and from men in my groups. They helped me see that I had not fully given the situation over to Christ's care.

By going through this tough job loss, this time in line with God's will, I realized that I needed to accept hardship as a pathway to peace. I needed to demonstrate the obedience that God requires of us all. I knew then that only Jesus could make this change in attitude possible. At the point where I was most powerless, when I was at my worst not my best, he worked in me to change my perspective.

I'm now able to give back with service. I'm able to reach out to others to show them that they're not alone, that there's hope for them as well. I'm no longer an enemy of God. Now, I'm reaching out to others and I'm able to draw on God's power. I would never have believed that I would be able to serve God like I am today. But God knew it long ago; God knew it before I even knew him.

Ken

who have died to sin; how can we live in it any longer? ³Or don't you know that all of us who were baptized into Christ Jesus were baptized into his death? ⁴We were therefore buried with him through baptism into death in order that, just as Christ was raised from the dead through the glory of the Father, we too may live a new life.

⁵For if we have been united with him in a death like his, we will certainly also be united with him in a resurrection like his. ⁶For we know that our old self was crucified with him so that the body ruled by sin might be done away with,ᵃ that we should no longer be slaves to sin— ⁷because anyone who has died has been set free from sin.

⁸Now if we died with Christ, we believe that we will also live with him. ⁹For we know that since Christ was raised from the dead, he cannot die again; death no longer has mastery over him. ¹⁰The death he died, he died to sin once for all; but the life he lives, he lives to God.

¹¹In the same way, count yourselves dead to sin but alive to God in Christ Jesus. ¹²Therefore do not let sin reign in your mortal body so that you obey its evil desires. ¹³Do not offer any part of yourself to sin as an instrument of wickedness, but rather offer yourselves to God as those who have been brought from death to life; and offer every part of yourself to him as an instrument of righteousness. ¹⁴For sin shall no longer be your master, because you are not under the law, but under grace.

Slaves to Righteousness

¹⁵What then? Shall we sin because we are not under the law but under grace? By no means! ¹⁶Don't you know that when you offer yourselves to someone as obedient slaves, you are slaves of the one you obey— whether you are slaves to sin, which leads to death, or to obedience, which leads to righteousness? ¹⁷But thanks be to God that, though you used to be slaves to sin, you have come to obey from your heart the pattern of teaching that has now claimed your allegiance. ¹⁸You have been set free from sin and have become slaves to righteousness.

¹⁹I am using an example from everyday life because of your human limitations. Just as you used to offer yourselves as slaves to impurity and to ever-increasing wickedness, so now offer yourselves as slaves to righteousness leading to holiness. ²⁰When you were slaves to sin, you were free from the control of righteousness. ²¹What benefit did you reap at that time from the things you are now ashamed of? Those things result in death! ²²But now that you have been set free from sin and have become slaves of God, the benefit you reap leads to holiness, and the result is eternal life. ²³For the wages of sin is death, but the gift of God is eternal life inᵇ Christ Jesus our Lord.

Released From the Law, Bound to Christ

7 Do you not know, brothers and sisters— for I am speaking to those who know the law— that the law has authority over someone only as long as that person lives? ²For example, by law a married woman is bound to her husband as long as he is alive, but if her husband dies, she is released from the law that binds her to him. ³So then, if she has sexual relations with another man while her husband is still alive, she is called an adulteress. But if her husband dies, she is released from that law and is not an adulteress if she marries another man.

⁴So, my brothers and sisters, you also died to the law through the body of Christ, that you might belong to another, to him who was raised from the dead, in order that we might bear fruit for God. ⁵For when we were in the realm of the flesh,ᶜ the sinful passions aroused by the law were at work in us, so that we bore fruit for death. ⁶But now, by dying to what once bound us, we have been released from the law so that we

---

ᵃ 6 Or *be rendered powerless*   ᵇ 23 Or *through*   ᶜ 5 In contexts like this, the Greek word for *flesh* (*sarx*) refers to the sinful state of human beings, often presented as a power in opposition to the Spirit.

serve in the new way of the Spirit, and not in the old way of the written code.

The Law and Sin

[7]What shall we say, then? Is the law sinful? Certainly not! Nevertheless, I would not have known what sin was had it not been for the law. For I would not have known what coveting really was if the law had not said, "You shall not covet."[a] [8]But sin, seizing the opportunity afforded by the commandment, produced in me every kind of coveting. For apart from the law, sin was dead. [9]Once I was alive apart from the law; but when the commandment came, sin sprang to life and I died. [10]I found that the very commandment that was intended to bring life actually brought death. [11]For sin, seizing the opportunity afforded by the commandment, deceived me, and through the commandment put me to death. [12]So then, the law is holy, and the commandment is holy, righteous and good.

[13]Did that which is good, then, become death to me? By no means! Nevertheless, in order that sin might be recognized as sin, it used what is good to bring about my death, so that through the commandment sin might become utterly sinful.

[14]We know that the law is spiritual; but I am unspiritual, sold as a slave to sin. [15]I do not understand what I do. For what I want to do I do not do, but what I hate I do. [16]And if I do what I do not want to do, I agree that the law is good. [17]As it is, it is no longer I myself who do it, but it is sin living in me. [18]For I know that good itself does not dwell in me, that is, in my sinful nature.[b] For I have the desire to do what is good, but I cannot carry it out. [19]For I do not do the good I want to do, but the evil I do not want to do—this I keep on doing. [20]Now if I do what I do not want to do, it is no longer I who do it, but it is sin living in me that does it.

[21]So I find this law at work: Although I want to do good, evil is right there with me. [22]For in my inner being I delight in God's law; [23]but I see another law at work in me, waging war against the law of my mind and making me a prisoner of the law of sin at work within me. [24]What a wretched man I am! Who will rescue me from this body that is subject to death? [25]Thanks be to God, who delivers me through Jesus Christ our Lord!

So then, I myself in my mind am a slave to God's law, but in my sinful nature[c] a slave to the law of sin.

Life Through the Spirit

8 Therefore, there is now no condemnation for those who are in Christ Jesus, [2]because through Christ Jesus the law of the Spirit who gives life has set you[d] free from the law of sin and death. [3]For what the law was powerless to do because it was weakened by the flesh,[e] God did by sending his own Son in the likeness of sinful flesh to be a sin offering.[f] And so he condemned sin in the flesh, [4]in order that the righteous requirement of the law might be fully met in us, who do not live according to the flesh but according to the Spirit.

[5]Those who live according to the flesh have their minds set on what the flesh desires; but those who live in accordance with the Spirit have their minds set on what the Spirit desires. [6]The mind governed by the flesh is death, but the mind governed by the Spirit is life and peace. [7]The mind governed by the flesh is hostile to God; it does not submit to God's law, nor can it do so. [8]Those who are in the realm of the flesh cannot please God.

[9]You, however, are not in the realm of the flesh but are in the realm of the Spirit, if indeed the Spirit of God lives in you. And if anyone does not have the Spirit of Christ, they do not belong to Christ. [10]But if Christ is in you, then even though your body is subject

---

a 7 Exodus 20:17; Deut. 5:21   *b* 18 Or *my flesh*   *c* 25 Or *in the flesh*   *d* 2 The Greek is singular; some manuscripts *me*   *e* 3 In contexts like this, the Greek word for *flesh* (*sarx*) refers to the sinful state of human beings, often presented as a power in opposition to the Spirit; also in verses 4-13.   *f* 3 Or *flesh, for sin* to death because of sin, the Spirit gives life[a] because of righteousness. [11]And if the Spirit of him who raised Jesus from the dead is living in you, he who raised Christ from the dead will also give life to your mortal bodies because of[b] his Spirit who lives in you.

[12]Therefore, brothers and sisters, we have an obligation — but it is not to the flesh, to live according to it. [13]For if you live according to the flesh, you will die; but if by the Spirit you put to death the misdeeds of the body, you will live.

[14]For those who are led by the Spirit of God are the children of God. [15]The Spirit you received does not make you slaves, so that you live in fear again; rather, the Spirit you received brought about your adoption to sonship.[c] And by him we cry, "Abba,[d] Father." [16]The Spirit himself testifies with our spirit that we are God's children. [17]Now if we are children, then we are heirs — heirs of God and co-heirs with Christ, if indeed we share in his sufferings in order that we may also share in his glory.

Present Suffering and Future Glory

[18]I consider that our present sufferings are not worth comparing with the glory that will be revealed in us. [19]For the creation waits in eager expectation for the children of God to be revealed. [20]For the creation was subjected to frustration, not by its own choice, but by the will of the one who subjected it, in hope [21]that[e] the creation itself will be liberated from its bondage to decay and brought into the freedom and glory of the children of God.

[22]We know that the whole creation has been groaning as in the pains of childbirth right up to the present time. [23]Not only so, but we ourselves, who have the firstfruits of the Spirit, groan inwardly as we wait ea-

---

[a] 10 Or you, your body is dead because of sin, yet your spirit is alive   [b] 11 Some manuscripts bodies through
[c] 15 The Greek word for adoption to sonship is a term referring to the full legal standing of an adopted male heir in Roman culture; also in verse 23.   [d] 15 Aramaic for father   [e] 20,21 Or subjected it in hope. 21For

---

CONFESS LESSON [Principle Four]

For the previous entry in the CONFESS lesson, go to Romans 14:11 – 12 (page 1414).

For a discussion of Principles One through Eight and a listing of their related lessons, go to pages xvii – xliv.

There is now no condemnation for those who are in Christ Jesus.

ROMANS 8:1

Principle Four begins the process of "coming clean." In the second part of Principle Four, we confess our faults to ourselves, to God and to someone else we trust.

The *N* in CONFESS stands for NO MORE GUILT. This principle can restore our confidence and repair our relationships. It allows us to move on from our "rearview mirror" way of living that has kept us looking back and second-guessing both ourselves and others. The verdict is in: "All have sinned and fall short of the glory of God, and all are justified freely by his grace through the redemption that came by Christ Jesus" (Romans 3:23 – 24).

So that's the C-O-N of CONFESS. The point is that the "con" is over! We've followed God's directions on how to confess our wrongs. All the secrets we've been hiding are finally out in the open.

The next letter in CONFESS is *F*. Go to John 8:12 (page 1305).

gerly for our adoption to sonship, the redemption of our bodies. [24]For in this hope we were saved. But hope that is seen is no hope at all. Who hopes for what they already have? [25]But if we hope for what we do not yet have, we wait for it patiently.

[26]In the same way, the Spirit helps us in our weakness. We do not know what we ought to pray for, but the Spirit himself intercedes for us through wordless groans. [27]And he who searches our hearts knows the mind of the Spirit, because the Spirit intercedes for God's people in accordance with the will of God.

[28]And we know that in all things God works for the good of those who love him, who[a] have been called according to his purpose. [29]For those God foreknew he also predestined to be conformed to the image of his Son, that he might be the firstborn among many brothers and sisters. [30]And those he predestined, he also called; those he called, he also justified; those he justified, he also glorified.

More Than Conquerors

[31]What, then, shall we say in response to these things? If God is for us, who can be against us? [32]He who did not spare his own Son, but gave him up for us all—how will he not also, along with him, graciously give us all things? [33]Who will bring any charge against those whom God has chosen? It is God who justifies. [34]Who then is the one who condemns? No one. Christ Jesus who died—more than that, who was raised to life—is at the right hand of God and is also interceding for us. [35]Who shall separate us from the love of Christ? Shall trouble or hardship or persecution or famine or nakedness or danger or sword? [36]As it is written:

"For your sake we face death all day long;
    we are considered as sheep to be
        slaughtered."[b]

[37]No, in all these things we are more than conquerors through him who loved us. [38]For I am convinced that neither death nor life, neither angels nor demons,[c] neither the present nor the future, nor any powers, [39]neither height nor depth, nor anything else in all creation, will be able to separate us from the love of God that is in Christ Jesus our Lord.

Paul's Anguish Over Israel

9 I speak the truth in Christ—I am not lying, my conscience confirms it through the Holy Spirit— [2]I have great sorrow and unceasing anguish in my heart. [3]For I could wish that I myself were cursed and cut off from Christ for the sake of my people, those of my own race, [4]the people of Israel. Theirs is the adoption to sonship; theirs the divine glory, the covenants, the receiving of the law, the temple worship and the promises. [5]Theirs are the patriarchs, and from them is traced the human ancestry of the Messiah, who is God over all, forever praised![d] Amen.

God's Sovereign Choice

[6]It is not as though God's word had failed. For not all who are descended from Israel are Israel. [7]Nor because they are his descendants are they all Abraham's children. On the contrary, "It is through Isaac that your offspring will be reckoned."[e] [8]In other words, it is not the children by physical descent who are God's children, but it is the children of the promise who are regarded as Abraham's offspring. [9]For this was how the promise was stated: "At the appointed time I will return, and Sarah will have a son."[f]

[10]Not only that, but Rebekah's children were conceived at the same time by our father Isaac. [11]Yet, before the twins were born or had done anything good or bad— in order that God's purpose in election

---

a 28 Or *that all things work together for good to those who love God, who;* or *that in all things God works together with those who love him to bring about what is good—with those who*   *b 36* Psalm 44:22   *c 38* Or *nor heavenly rulers*
d 5 Or *Messiah, who is over all. God be forever praised! Or Messiah. God who is over all be forever praised!*
e 7 Gen. 21:12   *f 9* Gen. 18:10,14

might stand: ¹²not by works but by him who calls—she was told, "The older will serve the younger."*ᵃ ¹³Just as it is written: "Jacob I loved, but Esau I hated."ᵇ

¹⁴What then shall we say? Is God unjust? Not at all! ¹⁵For he says to Moses,

> "I will have mercy on whom I have mercy,
> and I will have compassion on whom
> I have compassion."ᶜ

¹⁶It does not, therefore, depend on human desire or effort, but on God's mercy. ¹⁷For Scripture says to Pharaoh: "I raised you up for this very purpose, that I might display my power in you and that my name might be proclaimed in all the earth."ᵈ ¹⁸Therefore God has mercy on whom he wants to have mercy, and he hardens whom he wants to harden.

¹⁹One of you will say to me: "Then why does God still blame us? For who is able to resist his will?" ²⁰But who are you, a human being, to talk back to God? "Shall what is formed say to the one who formed it, 'Why

---

ᵃ 12 Gen. 25:23   ᵇ 13 Mal. 1:2,3   ᶜ 15 Exodus 33:19   ᵈ 17 Exodus 9:16

GIVE LESSON [*Principle Eight*]

This is the first page of the GIVE lesson.

For a discussion of Principles One through Eight and a listing of their related lessons, go to pages xvii–xliv.

He who did not spare his own Son, but gave him up for us all—
how will he not also, along with him, graciously give us all things?

ROMANS 8:32

Major, miraculous progress and growth have occurred in our lives since we started our recovery program, way back when we began working Principle One. We've stepped out of our denial into God's grace. We've taken an honest, spiritual inventory. We've worked on getting right with God, ourselves and others, and we've grown in our relationship with Christ. We've discovered a new way to live life, and we're finding the serenity we've always been seeking. But the most exciting part is yet to come—Principle Eight: "Yield myself to God to be used by him to bring this good news to others, both through my example and through my words."

Principle Eight is the "giving back" principle. Matthew 10:8 offers a reminder and an instruction: "Freely you have received: freely give." The *G* in GIVE stands for GOD, THE FIRST GIVER. When we place God first in our lives, we realize that everything we are and have is a gift from him. We recognize that our recovery isn't dependent on or based on material things; it's built on our faith and our desire to follow Jesus' directions.

Romans 8:32 reminds us that God loves us so much that he allowed his only Son to go to the cross, taking our punishment so we could be with him forever. If he was willing to make this ultimate sacrifice, doesn't it stand to reason that he'll supply all our other needs too?

We're never more like God than when we give—not just our money or our things, but our very selves. That's exactly what Jesus did for us. He freely offered us the greatest gift of all: himself.

The next letter in GIVE is *I*. Go to Ecclesiastes 4:9–12 (page 787).

did you make me like this?'"*a* ²¹Does not the potter have the right to make out of the same lump of clay some pottery for special purposes and some for common use?

²²What if God, although choosing to show his wrath and make his power known, bore with great patience the objects of his wrath—prepared for destruction? ²³What if he did this to make the riches of his glory known to the objects of his mercy, whom he prepared in advance for glory—²⁴even us, whom he also called, not only from the Jews but also from the Gentiles? ²⁵As he says in Hosea:

"I will call them 'my people' who are
not my people;

and I will call her 'my loved one' who
is not my loved one,"*b*

²⁶and,

"In the very place where it was said to
them,
'You are not my people,'
there they will be called 'children of
the living God.'"*c*

²⁷Isaiah cries out concerning Israel:

"Though the number of the Israelites be
like the sand by the sea,
only the remnant will be saved.
²⁸For the Lord will carry out
his sentence on earth with speed and
finality."*d*

---

a 20 Isaiah 29:16; 45:9   *b 25* Hosea 2:23   *c 26* Hosea 1:10   *d 28* Isaiah 10:22,23 (see Septuagint)

POWERLESS LESSON [*Principle One*]

For the previous entry in the POWERLESS lesson, go to Luke 17:33 (page 1275).

For a discussion of Principles One through Eight and a listing of their related lessons, go to pages xvii–xliv.

I am convinced that neither death nor life, neither angels nor demons, neither the present nor the future, nor any powers, neither height nor depth, nor anything else in all creation, will be able to separate us from the love of God that is in Christ Jesus our Lord.

ROMANS 8:38–39

The power to change comes only through God's grace. Principle One states: "Realize I'm not God. I admit that I'm powerless to control my tendency to do the wrong thing and that my life has become unmanageable." If we admit that we're powerless, we recognize our need for a power greater than ourselves to restore us. That power is our Higher Power, the one and only true Higher Power, Jesus Christ.

In Principle One we discover that we're POWERLESS to control our own lives and that our lives have become unmanageable. The last S in POWERLESS stands for SEPARATION. Some people talk about "finding" God—as though he could ever be lost. Separation from God can feel real, but it's never permanent. Remember, Christ seeks the lost. When we can't find God, we need to ask ourselves, "Who got lost?" We can rest assured that the answer is the same every time: It wasn't God!

This is the final page of the POWERLESS lesson.

²⁹It is just as Isaiah said previously:

> "Unless the Lord Almighty
>   had left us descendants,
> we would have become like Sodom,
>   we would have been like
>   Gomorrah."ᵃ

Israel's Unbelief

³⁰What then shall we say? That the Gentiles, who did not pursue righteousness, have obtained it, a righteousness that is by faith; ³¹but the people of Israel, who pursued the law as the way of righteousness, have not attained their goal. ³²Why not? Because they pursued it not by faith but as if it were by works. They stumbled over the stumbling stone. ³³As it is written:

> "See, I lay in Zion a stone that causes
>   people to stumble
> and a rock that makes them fall,
>   and the one who believes in him will
>   never be put to shame."ᵇ

10 Brothers and sisters, my heart's desire and prayer to God for the Israelites is that they may be saved. ²For I can testify about them that they are zealous for God, but their zeal is not based on knowledge. ³Since they did not know the righteousness of God and sought to establish their own, they did not

---

ᵃ 29 Isaiah 1:9   ᵇ 33 Isaiah 8:14; 28:16

TURN LESSON [*Principle Three*]

This is the first page of the TURN lesson.

For a discussion of Principles One through Eight and a listing of their related lessons,
go to pages xvii – xliv.

*If you declare with your mouth, "Jesus is Lord," and believe in your heart
that God raised him from the dead, you will be saved.*

ROMANS 10:9

In Principle Three we consciously choose to commit all our lives and will to Christ's care and control. We make the decision to TURN over every aspect of our lives and will to our Higher Power, Jesus Christ. This principle ends with our having new lives, but first we need to trust, understand and repent.

The first letter in TURN is *T*, which stands for TRUST. We trust our lives to complete strangers every day. We trust, for example, that oncoming traffic will stop at red lights at intersections. We trust that the burgers we eat at fast-food restaurants won't make us sick. Why, then, is it so hard for us to trust our lives to the care of God, whose eye is always on us? In Matthew 10:29 we reflect on the reality that not even a lowly sparrow can "fall to the ground" without God's knowledge.

In Principle Three we make the one-time, yet permanent, decision to turn our lives over to God's care. Our choice, not chance, determines our destiny. And that decision requires trust — putting our faith into action.

But what is faith? Faith isn't a sense, and it isn't sight or reason. Faith is simply taking God at his word. And God's Word spells out for us how to ask Christ into our lives (see Romans 10:9).

The next letter in TURN is *U*. Go to Proverbs 3:5 – 6 (page 743).

submit to God's righteousness. ⁴Christ is the culmination of the law so that there may be righteousness for everyone who believes.

⁵Moses writes this about the righteousness that is by the law: "The person who does these things will live by them."ᵃ ⁶But the righteousness that is by faith says: "Do not say in your heart, 'Who will ascend into heaven?'"ᵇ (that is, to bring Christ down) ⁷"or 'Who will descend into the deep?'"ᶜ (that is, to bring Christ up from the dead). ⁸But what does it say? "The word is near you; it is in your mouth and in your heart,"ᵈ that is, the message concerning faith that we proclaim: ⁹If you declare with your mouth, "Jesus is Lord," and believe in your heart that God raised him from the dead, you will be saved. ¹⁰For it is with your heart that you believe and are justified, and it is with your mouth that you profess your faith and are saved. ¹¹As Scripture says, "Anyone who believes in him will never be put to shame."ᵉ ¹²For there is no difference between Jew and Gentile—the same Lord is Lord of all and richly blesses all who call on him, ¹³for, "Everyone who calls on the name of the Lord will be saved."ᶠ

¹⁴How, then, can they call on the one they have not believed in? And how can they believe in the one of whom they have not heard? And how can they hear without someone preaching to them? ¹⁵And how can anyone preach unless they are sent? As it is written: "How beautiful are the feet of those who bring good news!"ᵍ

¹⁶But not all the Israelites accepted the

ᵃ5 Lev. 18:5   ᵇ6 Deut. 30:12   ᶜ7 Deut. 30:13   ᵈ8 Deut. 30:14   ᵉ11 Isaiah 28:16 (see Septuagint)
ᶠ13 Joel 2:32   ᵍ15 Isaiah 52:7

ACTION LESSON [*Principle Three*]

This is the first page of the ACTION lesson.

For a discussion of Principles One through Eight and a listing of their related lessons, go to pages xvii – xliv.

If you declare with your mouth, "Jesus is Lord," and believe in your heart that God raised him from the dead, you will be saved.

ROMANS 10:9

In Principle Three we consciously choose to commit all our lives and will to Christ's care and control. We make the decision to TURN our lives and will over to our Higher Power, Jesus Christ. In order to turn over our lives to Christ's care and control, we need to take ACTION.

The first letter in ACTION, *A*, stands for ACCEPT. We need to accept Jesus Christ as our Higher Power and Savior. We make the one-time, yet permanent, choice to ask Jesus into our hearts—the most important decision we'll ever make. In making that decision we establish a personal, permanent relationship with our Higher Power. If you haven't already done so, God is pleading with you to do so today. Satan, on the other hand, urges you to put it off till tomorrow.

In Romans 10:9 God's Word tells us how to ask Christ into our lives. It's only after we've made this decision that we can begin to COMMIT, to start asking for and following his will for our lives.

The next letter in ACTION is *C*. Go to Psalm 143:10 (page 731).

good news. For Isaiah says, "Lord, who has believed our message?"[a] [17]Consequently, faith comes from hearing the message, and the message is heard through the word about Christ. [18]But I ask: Did they not hear? Of course they did:

> "Their voice has gone out into all the
>   earth,
>   their words to the ends of the world."[b]

[19]Again I ask: Did Israel not understand? First, Moses says,

> "I will make you envious by those who
>   are not a nation;
>   I will make you angry by a nation
>   that has no understanding."[c]

[20]And Isaiah boldly says,

> "I was found by those who did not seek
>   me;
>   I revealed myself to those who did
>   not ask for me."[d]

[21]But concerning Israel he says,

> "All day long I have held out my hands
>   to a disobedient and obstinate
>   people."[e]

The Remnant of Israel

11 I ask then: Did God reject his people? By no means! I am an Israelite myself, a descendant of Abraham, from the tribe of Benjamin. [2]God did not reject his people, whom he foreknew. Don't you know what Scripture says in the passage about Elijah—how he appealed to God against Israel: [3]"Lord, they have killed your prophets and torn down your altars; I am the only one left, and they are trying to kill me"[f]? [4]And what was God's answer to him? "I have reserved for myself seven thousand who have not bowed the knee to Baal."[g] [5]So too, at the present time there is a remnant chosen by grace. [6]And if by grace, then it cannot be based on works; if it were, grace would no longer be grace.

[7]What then? What the people of Israel sought so earnestly they did not obtain. The elect among them did, but the others were hardened, [8]as it is written:

> "God gave them a spirit of stupor,
>   eyes that could not see
>   and ears that could not hear,
>   to this very day."[h]

[9]And David says:

> "May their table become a snare and a
>   trap,
>   a stumbling block and a retribution
>   for them.
> [10]May their eyes be darkened so they
>   cannot see,
>   and their backs be bent forever."[i]

Ingrafted Branches

[11]Again I ask: Did they stumble so as to fall beyond recovery? Not at all! Rather, because of their transgression, salvation has come to the Gentiles to make Israel envious. [12]But if their transgression means riches for the world, and their loss means riches for the Gentiles, how much greater riches will their full inclusion bring!

[13]I am talking to you Gentiles. Inasmuch as I am the apostle to the Gentiles, I take pride in my ministry [14]in the hope that I may somehow arouse my own people to envy and save some of them. [15]For if their rejection brought reconciliation to the world, what will their acceptance be but life from the dead? [16]If the part of the dough offered as firstfruits is holy, then the whole batch is holy; if the root is holy, so are the branches.

[17]If some of the branches have been broken off, and you, though a wild olive shoot, have been grafted in among the others and now share in the nourishing sap from the olive root, [18]do not consider yourself to be superior to those other branches. If you do, consider this: You do not support the root, but the root supports you. [19]You will say

---

[a] 16 Isaiah 53:1   [b] 18 Psalm 19:4   [c] 19 Deut. 32:21   [d] 20 Isaiah 65:1   [e] 21 Isaiah 65:2
[f] 3 1 Kings 19:10,14   [g] 4 1 Kings 19:18   [h] 8 Deut. 29:4; Isaiah 29:10   [i] 10 Psalm 69:22,23

then, "Branches were broken off so that I could be grafted in." [20]Granted. But they were broken off because of unbelief, and you stand by faith. Do not be arrogant, but tremble. [21]For if God did not spare the natural branches, he will not spare you either.

[22]Consider therefore the kindness and sternness of God: sternness to those who fell, but kindness to you, provided that you continue in his kindness. Otherwise, you also will be cut off. [23]And if they do not persist in unbelief, they will be grafted in, for God is able to graft them in again. [24]After all, if you were cut out of an olive tree that is wild by nature, and contrary to nature were grafted into a cultivated olive tree, how much more readily will these, the natural branches, be grafted into their own olive tree!

All Israel Will Be Saved

[25]I do not want you to be ignorant of this mystery, brothers and sisters, so that

---

HOPE LESSON [*Principle Two*]

This is the first page of the HOPE lesson.

For a discussion of Principles One through Eight and a listing of their related lessons,
go to pages xvii – xliv.

From him and through him and for him are all things.
To him be the glory forever! Amen.

ROMANS 11:36

In Principle Two we earnestly believe that God exists, that we matter to him and that he has the power to help us recover. It's in this principle that we find the HOPE we need to start our recovery journey.

The *H* in hope stands for HIGHER POWER. Our Higher Power is the one and only true Higher Power — and he has a name: Jesus Christ. In the past we may have believed in Jesus' existence and even attended church. But it's quite possible that we've never had a personal relationship with Christ. In this principle we'll see that Jesus desires a hands-on, day-to-day, moment-by-moment intimacy with us. We'll begin to understand that he can do for us what we've never been able to do for ourselves. That's what Romans 11:36 is telling us.

We can't complete anything unless we start. Jesus informs us in Matthew 17:20 just how much faith we need in order to get going: "Truly I tell you, if you have faith as small as a mustard seed, you can say to this mountain, 'Move from here to there' and it will move. Nothing will be impossible for you."

It's reassuring to know that we don't need a heaping helping of faith to begin the recovery process. We need only a smidgen — "faith as small as a mustard seed" — for God to get busy effecting change, change that will begin to move our mountains of hurts, hang-ups and habits. That's right, to complete Principle Two, all we need is a *little* faith. If we're only willing to utilize whatever faith we can muster in Jesus, our lives will be changed. We'll find the courage to reach out and take hold of Christ's hand, so that we can face the present with confidence and the future with realistic expectancy.

The next letter in HOPE is O. Go to Ephesians 4:22 – 23 (page 1466).

you may not be conceited: Israel has experienced a hardening in part until the full number of the Gentiles has come in, ²⁶and in this way*a* all Israel will be saved. As it is written:

> "The deliverer will come from Zion;
>   he will turn godlessness away from Jacob.
> ²⁷And this is*b* my covenant with them
>   when I take away their sins."*c*

²⁸As far as the gospel is concerned, they are enemies for your sake; but as far as election is concerned, they are loved on account of the patriarchs, ²⁹for God's gifts and his call are irrevocable. ³⁰Just as you who were at one time disobedient to God have now received mercy as a result of their disobedience, ³¹so they too have now become disobedient in order that they too may now*d* receive mercy as a result of God's mercy to you. ³²For God has bound everyone over to disobedience so that he may have mercy on them all.

Doxology

> ³³Oh, the depth of the riches of the
>   wisdom and*e* knowledge of God!
> How unsearchable his judgments,
>   and his paths beyond tracing out!
> ³⁴"Who has known the mind of the
>   Lord?
> Or who has been his counselor?"*f*
> ³⁵"Who has ever given to God,
>   that God should repay them?"*g*
> ³⁶For from him and through him and for
>   him are all things.
> To him be the glory forever! Amen.

A Living Sacrifice

12 Therefore, I urge you, brothers and sisters, in view of God's mercy, to offer your bodies as a living sacrifice, holy and pleasing to God — this is your true and proper worship.

²Do not conform to the pattern of this world, but be transformed by the renewing of your mind. Then you will be able to test and approve what God's will is — his good, pleasing and perfect will.

Humble Service in the Body of Christ

³For by the grace given me I say to every one of you: Do not think of yourself more highly than you ought, but rather think of yourself with sober judgment, in accordance with the faith God has distributed to each of you. ⁴For just as each of us has one body with many members, and these members do not all have the same function, ⁵so in Christ we, though many, form one body, and each member belongs to all the others. ⁶We have different gifts, according to the grace given to each of us. If your gift is prophesying, then prophesy in accordance with your*h* faith; ⁷if it is serving, then serve; if it is teaching, then teach; ⁸if it is to encourage, then give encouragement; if it is giving, then give generously; if it is to lead,*i* do it diligently; if it is to show mercy, do it cheerfully.

Love in Action

⁹Love must be sincere. Hate what is evil; cling to what is good. ¹⁰Be devoted to one another in love. Honor one another above yourselves. ¹¹Never be lacking in zeal, but keep your spiritual fervor, serving the Lord. ¹²Be joyful in hope, patient in affliction, faithful in prayer. ¹³Share with the Lord's people who are in need. Practice hospitality.

¹⁴Bless those who persecute you; bless and do not curse. ¹⁵Rejoice with those who rejoice; mourn with those who mourn. ¹⁶Live in harmony with one another. Do not be proud, but be willing to associate with people of low position.*j* Do not be conceited.

¹⁷Do not repay anyone evil for evil. Be

---

a 26 Or *and so*   *b 27* Or *will be*   *c 27* Isaiah 59:20,21; 27:9 (see Septuagint); Jer. 31:33,34   *d 31* Some manuscripts do not have *now.*   *e 33* Or *riches and the wisdom and the*   *f 34* Isaiah 40:13   *g 35* Job 41:11   *h 6* Or *the*   *i 8* Or *to provide for others*   *j 16* Or *willing to do menial work* careful to do what is right in the eyes of everyone. ¹⁸If it is possible, as far as it depends on you, live at peace with everyone. ¹⁹Do not take revenge, my dear friends, but leave room for God's wrath, for it is written: "It is mine to avenge; I will repay,"ᵃ says the Lord. ²⁰On the contrary:

"If your enemy is hungry, feed him;
    if he is thirsty, give him something to drink.
In doing this, you will heap burning coals on his head."ᵇ

²¹Do not be overcome by evil, but overcome evil with good.

ᵃ 19 Deut. 32:35   ᵇ 20 Prov. 25:21,22

VICTORY LESSON [*Principle Five*]

This is the first page of the VICTORY lesson.

For a discussion of Principles One through Eight and a listing of their related lessons, go to pages xvii–xliv.

I urge you, brothers and sisters, in view of God's mercy, to offer your bodies as a living sacrifice, holy and pleasing to God—this is your true and proper worship. Do not conform to the pattern of this world, but be transformed by the renewing of your mind. Then you will be able to test and approve what God's will is—his good, pleasing and perfect will.

ROMANS 12:1–2

In Principle Five, as we voluntarily submit to every change God wants to make in our lives and humbly ask him to remove our character defects, we'll find VICTORY in our recovery.

The *V* in VICTORY reminds us to VOLUNTARILY SUBMIT to following Romans 12:1–2.

When we completed Principle Three, we made the most important decision of our lives by choosing to turn our lives over to God's will. That decision got us right with God; we accepted and committed to following his Son, Jesus Christ, as our Savior and Lord. Then we began to work on us. We made fearless, moral inventories of ourselves. The first step in any victory is recognizing the enemy. Our inventories showed us that in a lot of cases we were our own worst enemy. We came clean by admitting and confessing our sins to ourselves, to God and to someone else we trust. For perhaps the first time in our lives, we were able to take off the muddy glasses of denial and look at reality with a clear and clean focus.

Now, in Principle Five, we've come to a place in our recovery where we say, "We don't want to live this way anymore." We want to get rid of our hurts, hang-ups and habits. But how do we do this?

The good news is that we don't do it. Notice that Principle Five doesn't read, "Voluntarily submit to every change God wants to make in my life and humbly ask *myself* to remove my character defects." No, we're instructed to humbly ask God to remove those defects. So how do we begin the process of having God make positive changes in our lives, those changes that both he and we so deeply desire? That process begins with the next letter in VICTORY.

The next letter in VICTORY is I. Go to Proverbs 16:9 (page 758).

Submission to Governing Authorities

13 Let everyone be subject to the governing authorities, for there is no authority except that which God has established. The authorities that exist have been established by God. ²Consequently, whoever rebels against the authority is rebelling against what God has instituted, and those who do so will bring judgment on themselves. ³For rulers hold no terror for those who do right, but for those who do wrong. Do you want to be free from fear of the one in authority? Then do what is right and you will be commended. ⁴For the one in authority is God's servant for your good. But if you do wrong, be afraid, for rulers do not bear the sword for no reason. They are God's servants, agents of wrath to bring punishment on the wrongdoer.

SPIRITUAL INVENTORY LESSON [Principle Four]

For the previous entry in the SPIRITUAL INVENTORY lesson, go to Colossians 3:9 (page 1487).

For a discussion of Principles One through Eight and a listing of their related lessons, go to pages xvii – xliv.

Do not conform to the pattern of this world, but be transformed by the renewing of your mind. Then you will be able to test and approve what God's will is — his good, pleasing and perfect will.

ROMANS 12:2

Principle Four begins the process of "coming clean." It's here that we openly examine and confess our faults to ourselves, to God and to someone else we trust. In the first part of Principle Four we openly examine our lives.

As part of completing Principle Four, we do a SPIRITUAL INVENTORY. We look at eight critical areas of our lives. The fifth area is OUR MINDS. The most difficult thing to open is a closed mind. Romans 12:2 gives us clear direction regarding our minds. The reality is that two competing thoughts can't occupy our minds at the same time. It's our choice whether our thoughts will be constructive or destructive, positive or negative.

We need to ask ourselves the following questions regarding our minds:

- How have we guarded our minds in the past? What thought patterns have we consciously denied entry into our minds?

- Have we filled our minds with hurtful and unhealthy movies, Internet sites, television programs, magazines or books?

- Have we failed to concentrate on the positive truths of the Bible?

Three of the more prevalent sins today are indifference to, neglect of and disrespect for the Word of God. We need to set aside a daily quiet time to get into God's instruction manual for our lives. Why? Because our ears and eyes are doors and windows to our soul, as in "Truth in = Truth out." As Proverbs 15:14 reminds us, "The discerning heart seeks knowledge, but the mouth of a fool feeds on folly."

The sixth area of our Spiritual Inventory is OUR BODIES. Go to 1 Corinthians 6:19 – 20 (page 1425).

RELAPSE LESSON [*Principle Seven*]

For the previous entry in the RELAPSE lesson, go to Mark 14:38 (page 1216).

For a discussion of Principles One through Eight and a listing of their related lessons,
go to pages xvii – xliv.

*By the grace given me I say to every one of you: Do not think of yourself
more highly than you ought, but rather think of yourself with sober judgment,
in accordance with the faith God has distributed to each of you … Hate what is evil;
cling to what is good. Be devoted to one another in love. Honor one another
above yourselves … Be joyful in hope, patient in affliction, faithful in prayer …
Live in harmony with one another. Do not be proud, but be willing to associate with
people of low position. Do not be conceited. Do not repay anyone evil for evil.
Be careful to do what is right in the eyes of everyone.*

ROMANS 12:3,9 – 10,12,16 – 17

In Principle Seven we reserve a daily quiet time with God for self-examination, Bible reading and prayer in order to get to know God and his will for our lives and to gain the power to follow his will. As we work this principle, we begin the journey of applying and living what we've discovered in the first six principles. We live daily in humility — as well as in reality, not in denial. We've done our best to amend our past. Through God's guidance we can now make choices about the emotions that will affect our ongoing thinking and actions. We can start to take *action* — positive action — instead of operating in a mode of continual *reaction*.

The second part of this principle — the call to reserve a daily quiet time with God for Bible reading and prayer in order to get to know God and his will for our lives and to gain the power to follow his will — also relates to Step Eleven of the Christ-centered 12 steps.

**Step Eleven: We've sought through prayer and meditation
to improve our conscious contact with God, praying for knowledge
of his will for us, as well as for the power to carry out that will.**

The *E* in RELAPSE stands for EVALUATE. Our evaluation needs to include our physical, emotional, relational and spiritual health.

Do a daily H-E-A-R-T check. We need to ask ourselves daily whether we are:

Hurting

Exhausted

Angry

Resentful

Tense

If we answer yes to any of the above, we should use the tools we've learned in recovery to help us get back on track. We find specific instructions in Romans 12 (see the verses above). Daily practice of Principle Seven maintains our honesty and humility.

The next letter in RELAPSE is *L*. Go to 1 Thessalonians 5:21 (page 1495).

5Therefore, it is necessary to submit to the authorities, not only because of possible punishment but also as a matter of conscience.

6This is also why you pay taxes, for the authorities are God's servants, who give their full time to governing. 7Give to everyone what you owe them: If you owe taxes, pay taxes; if revenue, then revenue; if respect, then respect; if honor, then honor.

Love Fulfills the Law

8Let no debt remain outstanding, except the continuing debt to love one another, for whoever loves others has fulfilled the law. 9The commandments, "You shall not commit adultery," "You shall not murder," "You shall not steal," "You shall not covet,"*a* and whatever other command there may be, are summed up in this one command: "Love your neighbor as yourself."*b* 10Love does no

---

a 9 Exodus 20:13-15,17; Deut. 5:17-19,21   *b* 9 Lev. 19:18

FORGIVENESS LESSON [*Principle Six*]

For the previous entry in the FORGIVENESS lesson, go to Romans 3:22 – 26 (page 1391).

For a discussion of Principles One through Eight and a listing of their related lessons, go to pages xvii – xliv.

Do not repay anyone evil for evil. Be careful to do what is right in the eyes of everyone. If it is possible, as far as it depends on you, live at peace with everyone.

ROMANS 12:17–18

Principle Six calls for us to evaluate all our relationships and to offer forgiveness to those who have hurt us and make amends for harm we've done to others, except when doing so would injure them or others. We need to be willing to admit our part in our relationships that have been broken or damaged.

In order to be completely free from resentment, anger, fear, guilt and shame, we need to offer and accept forgiveness in all applicable areas of our lives. If we don't, our recovery will be stalled and remain incomplete.

The second type of forgiveness is the kind we extend from ourselves to others. This type of forgiveness is a process. We first need to be willing to forgive. But in order to become truly free, we have to let go of the pain of the past harm and abuse caused by others.

Forgiveness is all about letting go. Remember playing tug-of-war as a child? As long as the people on each end of the rope are tugging, we have a war. We let go of our end of the rope when we forgive others. No matter how hard they may tug on their end, if we've released ours, the war is over. But until we release that rope, we're prisoners of war.

If we follow Romans 12:17 – 18, our forgiveness of others will free us of our anger and enable us to move forward positively in terms of doing whatever is in our power to salvage or repair our damaged relationships.

Bear in mind that causing an injury puts us *below* our enemy. Revenging an injury makes us even with our opponent. But forgiving him *sets us free*.

harm to a neighbor. Therefore love is the fulfillment of the law.

The Day Is Near

11 And do this, understanding the present time: The hour has already come for you to wake up from your slumber, because our salvation is nearer now than when we first believed. 12 The night is nearly over; the day is almost here. So let us put aside the deeds of darkness and put on the armor of light. 13 Let us behave decently, as in the daytime, not in carousing and drunkenness, not in sexual immorality and debauchery, not in dissension and jealousy. 14 Rather, clothe yourselves with the Lord Jesus Christ, and do not think about how to gratify the desires of the flesh.*a*

a 14 In contexts like this, the Greek word for *flesh* (*sarx*) refers to the sinful state of human beings, often presented as a power in opposition to the Spirit.

It's possible that we may be mad at God. In fact, we may have been blaming him for the harm others have done to us. Remember, though, that God doesn't — and, in fact, can't — sin. His very nature is marked by perfect holiness that is reflected in his every attribute and action. God is perfect in love, mercy and grace. But he loved us so much that he gave each of us a free will. He didn't want us to be his puppets. He wanted us to freely choose to love him. We need to understand and believe that the harm others have done to us was an acting out of their own free will. It was *their* choice, not God's, and it was *not* God's will. Once we understand the concept of free will, we realize that our anger against God has been misdirected. First Peter 5:10 contains a beautiful promise: "The God of all grace, who called you to his eternal glory in Christ, after you have suffered a little while, will himself restore you and make you strong, firm and steadfast."

NOTE: If you've been the victim of sexual abuse, physical abuse or childhood emotional abuse or neglect, you won't find complete peace and freedom from your perpetrators until you're able to forgive them. Forgiving them in no way excuses them for the harm they've caused you, but it does release you from the power they've had over you. In Celebrate Recovery, Steps Eight and Nine have been rewritten for those recovering from physical or sexual abuse.

Step Eight: Make a list of all the persons who've harmed you and become willing to seek God's help in forgiving your perpetrators, as well as in forgiving yourself. Realize that you've also harmed others and become willing to make amends to them.

Step Nine: Extend forgiveness to yourself and to others who've perpetrated against you, realizing that this has everything to do with the attitude of your heart, whether or not it involves a physical confrontation. Make direct amends, asking forgiveness from those people you've harmed, except when doing so would injure them or others.

The third, and often the most difficult, type of forgiveness has to do with extending forgiveness to ourselves.

Go to Isaiah 1:18 – 19 (page 806).

The Weak and the Strong

14 Accept the one whose faith is weak, without quarreling over disputable matters. ²One person's faith allows them to eat anything, but another, whose faith is weak, eats only vegetables. ³The one who eats everything must not treat with contempt the one who does not, and the one who does not eat everything must not judge the one who does, for God has accepted them. ⁴Who are you to judge someone else's servant? To their own master, servants stand or fall. And they will stand, for the Lord is able to make them stand.

⁵One person considers one day more sacred than another; another considers every day alike. Each of them should be fully convinced in their own mind. ⁶Whoever regards one day as special does so to the Lord. Whoever eats meat does so to the Lord, for they give thanks to God; and whoever abstains does so to the Lord and gives thanks to God. ⁷For none of us lives for ourselves alone, and none of us dies for ourselves alone. ⁸If we live, we live for the Lord; and if we die, we die for the Lord. So, whether we live or die, we belong to the Lord. ⁹For this very reason, Christ died and returned to life so that he might be the Lord of both the dead and the living.

¹⁰You, then, why do you judge your brother or sister*a*? Or why do you treat them with contempt? For we will all stand before God's judgment seat. ¹¹It is written:

> "'As surely as I live,' says the Lord,
> 'every knee will bow before me;
>   every tongue will acknowledge God.'"*b*

¹²So then, each of us will give an account of ourselves to God.

---

a 10 The Greek word for *brother or sister* (*adelphos*) refers here to a believer, whether man or woman, as part of God's family; also in verses 13, 15 and 21.   *b 11* Isaiah 45:23

CONFESS LESSON [*Principle Four*]

For the previous entry in the CONFESS lesson, go to Proverbs 28:13 (page 775).

For a discussion of Principles One through Eight and a listing of their related lessons, go to pages xvii – xliv.

It is written: "As surely as I live," says the Lord, "every knee will bow before me; every tongue will acknowledge God." So then, each of us will give an account of ourselves to God.

ROMANS 14:11–12

Principle Four begins the process of "coming clean." In the second part of Principle Four, we confess our faults to ourselves, to God and to someone else we trust.

The *O* in CONFESS stands for OBEY GOD'S DIRECTION. Principle Four sums up how we obey God's direction in confessing our sins. First, we confess (admit) our faults to ourselves and to God. We do that so we can be forgiven. Then we do as we're instructed in James 5:16: "Confess your sins to each other and pray for each other so that you may be healed. The prayer of a righteous person is powerful and effective." We do this so we can start the healing process with ourselves and others.

The next letter in CONFESS is N. Go to Romans 8:1 (page 1400).

¹³Therefore let us stop passing judgment on one another. Instead, make up your mind not to put any stumbling block or obstacle in the way of a brother or sister. ¹⁴I am convinced, being fully persuaded in the Lord Jesus, that nothing is unclean in itself. But if anyone regards something as unclean, then for that person it is unclean. ¹⁵If your brother or sister is distressed because of what you eat, you are no longer acting in love. Do not by your eating destroy someone for whom Christ died. ¹⁶Therefore do not let what you know is good be spoken of as evil. ¹⁷For the kingdom of God is not a matter of eating and drinking, but of righteousness, peace and joy in the Holy Spirit, ¹⁸because anyone who serves Christ in this way is pleasing to God and receives human approval.

¹⁹Let us therefore make every effort to do what leads to peace and to mutual edification. ²⁰Do not destroy the work of God for the sake of food. All food is clean, but it is wrong for a person to eat anything that causes someone else to stumble. ²¹It is better not to eat meat or drink wine or to do anything else that will cause your brother or sister to fall.

²²So whatever you believe about these things keep between yourself and God. Blessed is the one who does not condemn himself by what he approves. ²³But whoever has doubts is condemned if they eat, because their eating is not from faith; and everything that does not come from faith is sin.[a]

15 We who are strong ought to bear with the failings of the weak and not to please ourselves. ²Each of us should please our neighbors for their good, to build them up. ³For even Christ did not please himself but, as it is written: "The insults of those who insult you have fallen on me."[b] ⁴For everything that was written in the past was written to teach us, so that through the endurance

taught in the Scriptures and the encouragement they provide we might have hope.

⁵May the God who gives endurance and encouragement give you the same attitude of mind toward each other that Christ Jesus had, ⁶so that with one mind and one voice you may glorify the God and Father of our Lord Jesus Christ.

⁷Accept one another, then, just as Christ accepted you, in order to bring praise to God. ⁸For I tell you that Christ has become a servant of the Jews[c] on behalf of God's truth, so that the promises made to the patriarchs might be confirmed ⁹and, moreover, that the Gentiles might glorify God for his mercy. As it is written:

> "Therefore I will praise you among the
>   Gentiles;
>   I will sing the praises of your name."[d]

¹⁰Again, it says,

> "Rejoice, you Gentiles, with his
>   people."[e]

¹¹And again,

> "Praise the Lord, all you Gentiles;
>   let all the peoples extol him."[f]

¹²And again, Isaiah says,

> "The Root of Jesse will spring up,
>   one who will arise to rule over the
>   nations;
>   in him the Gentiles will hope."[g]

¹³May the God of hope fill you with all joy and peace as you trust in him, so that you may overflow with hope by the power of the Holy Spirit.

Paul the Minister to the Gentiles

¹⁴I myself am convinced, my brothers and sisters, that you yourselves are full of goodness, filled with knowledge and competent to instruct one another. ¹⁵Yet I have written you quite boldly on some points to remind you of them again, because of

---

a 23 Some manuscripts place 16:25-27 here; others after 15:33.   *b 3* Psalm 69:9   *c 8* Greek *circumcision*
d 9 2 Samuel 22:50; Psalm 18:49   *e 10* Deut. 32:43   *f 11* Psalm 117:1   *g 12* Isaiah 11:10 (see Septuagint)

the grace God gave me ¹⁶to be a minister of Christ Jesus to the Gentiles. He gave me the priestly duty of proclaiming the gospel of God, so that the Gentiles might become an offering acceptable to God, sanctified by the Holy Spirit.

¹⁷Therefore I glory in Christ Jesus in my service to God. ¹⁸I will not venture to speak of anything except what Christ has accomplished through me in leading the Gentiles to obey God by what I have said and done— ¹⁹by the power of signs and wonders, through the power of the Spirit of God. So from Jerusalem all the way around to Illyricum, I have fully proclaimed the gospel of Christ. ²⁰It has always been my ambition to preach the gospel where Christ was not known, so that I would not be building on someone else's foundation. ²¹Rather, as it is written:

"Those who were not told about him
     will see,
   and those who have not heard will
     understand."ᵃ

²²This is why I have often been hindered from coming to you.

Paul's Plan to Visit Rome

²³But now that there is no more place for me to work in these regions, and since I have been longing for many years to visit you, ²⁴I plan to do so when I go to Spain. I hope to see you while passing through and

---

ᵃ 21 Isaiah 52:15 (see Septuagint)

SANITY LESSON [Principle Two]

For the previous entry in the SANITY lesson, go to Psalm 46:1 (page 664).

For a discussion of Principles One through Eight and a listing of their related lessons,
go to pages xvii – xliv.

Accept one another, then, just as Christ accepted you,
in order to bring praise to God.

ROMANS 15:7

In Principle Two we earnestly believe that God exists, that we matter to him and that he has the power to help us recover. It's in this principle that we find the SANITY to begin to stop making the same poor choices again and again.

The next letter in SANITY, *A*, stands for ACCEPTANCE. As we complete this principle, we'll learn to have realistic expectations of ourselves and others. We'll learn not to relate to others in the same old ways; we'll stop expecting a different response or result from those that have already been given us time and time again. We begin to find the sanity for which we've been searching. And we remember, as expressed in the Serenity Prayer, to ask God for the courage to change the things we can change and to accept what's beyond our control.

As our faith grows and we become better acquainted with our Higher Power, it becomes easier for us to accept others as they really are, not as we'd like them to be. With acceptance, however, comes responsibility. We begin to stop placing all the blame on others for our own past actions and hurts.

The next letter in SANITY is *N*. Go to 2 Corinthians 1:8 – 9 (page 1439).

to have you assist me on my journey there, after I have enjoyed your company for a while. 25Now, however, I am on my way to Jerusalem in the service of the Lord's people there. 26For Macedonia and Achaia were pleased to make a contribution for the poor among the Lord's people in Jerusalem. 27They were pleased to do it, and indeed they owe it to them. For if the Gentiles have shared in the Jews' spiritual blessings, they owe it to the Jews to share with them their material blessings. 28So after I have completed this task and have made sure that they have received this contribution, I will go to Spain and visit you on the way. 29I know that when I come to you, I will come in the full measure of the blessing of Christ.

30I urge you, brothers and sisters, by our Lord Jesus Christ and by the love of the Spirit, to join me in my struggle by praying to God for me. 31Pray that I may be kept safe from the unbelievers in Judea and that the contribution I take to Jerusalem may be favorably received by the Lord's people there, 32so that I may come to you with joy, by God's will, and in your company be refreshed. 33The God of peace be with you all. Amen.

Personal Greetings

16 I commend to you our sister Phoebe, a deacon*a,b* of the church in Cenchreae. 2I ask you to receive her in the Lord in a way worthy of his people and to give her any help she may need from you, for she has been the benefactor of many people, including me.

3Greet Priscilla*c* and Aquila, my co-workers in Christ Jesus. 4They risked their lives for me. Not only I but all the churches of the Gentiles are grateful to them.
5Greet also the church that meets at their house.
Greet my dear friend Epenetus, who was the first convert to Christ in the province of Asia.
6Greet Mary, who worked very hard for you.
7Greet Andronicus and Junia, my fellow Jews who have been in prison with me. They are outstanding among*d* the apostles, and they were in Christ before I was.
8Greet Ampliatus, my dear friend in the Lord.
9Greet Urbanus, our co-worker in Christ, and my dear friend Stachys.
10Greet Apelles, whose fidelity to Christ has stood the test.
Greet those who belong to the household of Aristobulus.
11Greet Herodion, my fellow Jew.
Greet those in the household of Narcissus who are in the Lord.
12Greet Tryphena and Tryphosa, those women who work hard in the Lord.
Greet my dear friend Persis, another woman who has worked very hard in the Lord.
13Greet Rufus, chosen in the Lord, and his mother, who has been a mother to me, too.
14Greet Asyncritus, Phlegon, Hermes, Patrobas, Hermas and the other brothers and sisters with them.
15Greet Philologus, Julia, Nereus and his sister, and Olympas and all the Lord's people who are with them.
16Greet one another with a holy kiss.
All the churches of Christ send greetings.

17I urge you, brothers and sisters, to watch out for those who cause divisions and put obstacles in your way that are contrary to the teaching you have learned. Keep away from them. 18For such people are not serving our Lord Christ, but their own appetites. By smooth talk and flattery they deceive the minds of naive people.

---

a 1 Or *servant*   *b 1* The word *deacon* refers here to a Christian designated to serve with the overseers/elders of the church in a variety of ways; similarly in Phil. 1:1 and 1 Tim. 3:8,12.   *c 3* Greek *Prisca*, a variant of *Priscilla*
d 7 Or *are esteemed by*

19Everyone has heard about your obedience, so I rejoice because of you; but I want you to be wise about what is good, and innocent about what is evil.

20The God of peace will soon crush Satan under your feet.

The grace of our Lord Jesus be with you.

21Timothy, my co-worker, sends his greetings to you, as do Lucius, Jason and Sosipater, my fellow Jews.

22I, Tertius, who wrote down this letter, greet you in the Lord.

23Gaius, whose hospitality I and the whole church here enjoy, sends you his greetings.

Erastus, who is the city's director of public works, and our brother Quartus send you their greetings. [24]a

25Now to him who is able to establish you in accordance with my gospel, the message I proclaim about Jesus Christ, in keeping with the revelation of the mystery hidden for long ages past, 26but now revealed and made known through the prophetic writings by the command of the eternal God, so that all the Gentiles might come to the obedience that comes fromb faith — 27to the only wise God be glory forever through Jesus Christ! Amen.

---

a 24 Some manuscripts include here *May the grace of our Lord Jesus Christ be with all of you. Amen.*   b 26 Or *that is*

1 Corinthians

THEME: Correct living (our Christian conduct) is rooted in correct thinking.

AUTHOR: Early church fathers, as well as the letter itself, acknowledge Paul as the author of 1 Corinthians.

DATE OF WRITING: First Corinthians was probably written in AD 54 or 55.

ENCOURAGEMENT FROM 1 CORINTHIANS: "No temptation has overtaken you except what is common to mankind. And God is faithful; he will not let you be tempted beyond what you can bear. But when you are tempted, he will also provide a way out so that you can endure it" (1 Corinthians 10:13).

CHALLENGE FROM 1 CORINTHIANS: "Do you not know that your bodies are temples of the Holy Spirit, who is in you, whom you have received from God? You are not your own; you were bought at a price. Therefore honor God with your bodies" (1 Corinthians 6:19 – 20).

REFLECTION FROM 1 CORINTHIANS: "God chose the foolish things of the world to shame the wise; God chose the weak things of the world to shame the strong. God chose the lowly things of this world and the despised things — and the things that are not — to nullify the things that are, so that no one may boast before him" (1 Corinthians 1:27 – 29).

Direction. Guidance. Reproach. Encouragement. However you look at 1 Corinthians, it's clear that Paul wasn't happy with the church at Corinth. This group of people had a reputation for hard living. They had hurts, hang-ups and habits just as we do. Once they were saved, they didn't become perfect — again, just like us. They continued to struggle with their old lives and, on occasion, acted as though they hadn't been changed.

In 1 Corinthians Paul is hard on this group. He takes them to task for dragging each other into court, not calling out sin, living in discord with each other and abusing the Lord's Supper. The lesson for us is clear: In order to live out our changed lives we must live together in unity — a unity that becomes possible only when we make Christ the center of our lives.

By putting the needs of others above our own, we're modeling Christ's example. In Celebrate Recovery this falls under Principle Six ("Evaluate all my relationships. Offer forgiveness to those who have hurt me and make amends for harm I've done to other people, except when doing so would injure them or others."). If we would all make it a point to live out this principle, we'd experience the kind of unity Paul is calling for.

1

Paul, called to be an apostle of Christ Jesus by the will of God, and our brother Sosthenes,

2To the church of God in Corinth, to those sanctified in Christ Jesus and called to be his holy people, together with all those everywhere who call on the name of our Lord Jesus Christ—their Lord and ours:

3Grace and peace to you from God our Father and the Lord Jesus Christ.

Thanksgiving

4I always thank my God for you because of his grace given you in Christ Jesus. 5For in him you have been enriched in every way—with all kinds of speech and with all knowledge— 6God thus confirming our testimony about Christ among you. 7Therefore you do not lack any spiritual gift as you eagerly wait for our Lord Jesus Christ to be revealed. 8He will also keep you firm to the end, so that you will be blameless on the day of our Lord Jesus Christ. 9God is faithful, who has called you into fellowship with his Son, Jesus Christ our Lord.

A Church Divided Over Leaders

10I appeal to you, brothers and sisters,a in the name of our Lord Jesus Christ, that all of you agree with one another in what you say and that there be no divisions among you, but that you be perfectly united in mind and thought. 11My brothers and sisters, some from Chloe's household have informed me that there are quarrels among you. 12What I mean is this: One of you says, "I follow Paul"; another, "I follow Apollos"; another, "I follow Cephasb"; still another, "I follow Christ."

13Is Christ divided? Was Paul crucified for you? Were you baptized in the name of Paul? 14I thank God that I did not baptize any of you except Crispus and Gaius, 15so

no one can say that you were baptized in my name. 16(Yes, I also baptized the household of Stephanas; beyond that, I don't remember if I baptized anyone else.) 17For Christ did not send me to baptize, but to preach the gospel—not with wisdom and eloquence, lest the cross of Christ be emptied of its power.

Christ Crucified Is God's Power and Wisdom

18For the message of the cross is foolishness to those who are perishing, but to us who are being saved it is the power of God. 19For it is written:

> "I will destroy the wisdom of the wise;
>   the intelligence of the intelligent I
>   will frustrate."c

20Where is the wise person? Where is the teacher of the law? Where is the philosopher of this age? Has not God made foolish the wisdom of the world? 21For since in the wisdom of God the world through its wisdom did not know him, God was pleased through the foolishness of what was preached to save those who believe. 22Jews demand signs and Greeks look for wisdom, 23but we preach Christ crucified: a stumbling block to Jews and foolishness to Gentiles, 24but to those whom God has called, both Jews and Greeks, Christ the power of God and the wisdom of God. 25For the foolishness of God is wiser than human wisdom, and the weakness of God is stronger than human strength.

26Brothers and sisters, think of what you were when you were called. Not many of you were wise by human standards; not many were influential; not many were of noble birth. 27But God chose the foolish things of the world to shame the wise; God chose the weak things of the world to shame the strong. 28God chose the lowly things of this world and the despised things—and the things that are not—to

---

a 10 The Greek word for *brothers and sisters* (*adelphoi*) refers here to believers, both men and women, as part of God's family; also in verses 11 and 26; and in 2:1; 3:1; 4:6; 6:8; 7:24, 29; 10:1; 11:33; 12:1; 14:6, 20, 26, 39; 15:1, 6, 50, 58; 16:15, 20.   b 12 That is, Peter   c 19 Isaiah 29:14

nullify the things that are, [29]so that no one may boast before him. [30]It is because of him that you are in Christ Jesus, who has become for us wisdom from God — that is, our righteousness, holiness and redemption. [31]Therefore, as it is written: "Let the one who boasts boast in the Lord."[a]

2 And so it was with me, brothers and sisters. When I came to you, I did not come with eloquence or human wisdom as I proclaimed to you the testimony about God.[b] [2]For I resolved to know nothing while I was with you except Jesus Christ and him crucified. [3]I came to you in weakness with great fear and trembling. [4]My message and my preaching were not with wise and persuasive words, but with a demonstration of the Spirit's power, [5]so that your faith might not rest on human wisdom, but on God's power.

God's Wisdom Revealed by the Spirit

[6]We do, however, speak a message of wisdom among the mature, but not the wisdom of this age or of the rulers of this age, who are coming to nothing. [7]No, we declare God's wisdom, a mystery that has been hidden and that God destined for our glory before time began. [8]None of the rulers of this age understood it, for if they had, they would not have crucified the Lord of glory. [9]However, as it is written:

"What no eye has seen,
what no ear has heard,
and what no human mind has
conceived"[c] —
the things God has prepared for
those who love him —

[10]these are the things God has revealed to us by his Spirit.

The Spirit searches all things, even the deep things of God. [11]For who knows a person's thoughts except their own spirit within them? In the same way no one knows the thoughts of God except the Spirit of God.

[12]What we have received is not the spirit of the world, but the Spirit who is from God, so that we may understand what God has freely given us. [13]This is what we speak, not in words taught us by human wisdom but in words taught by the Spirit, explaining spiritual realities with Spirit-taught words.[d] [14]The person without the Spirit does not accept the things that come from the Spirit of God but considers them foolishness, and cannot understand them because they are discerned only through the Spirit. [15]The person with the Spirit makes judgments about all things, but such a person is not subject to merely human judgments, [16]for,

"Who has known the mind of the Lord
so as to instruct him?"[e]

But we have the mind of Christ.

The Church and Its Leaders

3 Brothers and sisters, I could not address you as people who live by the Spirit but as people who are still worldly — mere infants in Christ. [2]I gave you milk, not solid food, for you were not yet ready for it. Indeed, you are still not ready. [3]You are still worldly. For since there is jealousy and quarreling among you, are you not worldly? Are you not acting like mere humans? [4]For when one says, "I follow Paul," and another, "I follow Apollos," are you not mere human beings?

[5]What, after all, is Apollos? And what is Paul? Only servants, through whom you came to believe — as the Lord has assigned to each his task. [6]I planted the seed, Apollos watered it, but God has been making it grow. [7]So neither the one who plants nor the one who waters is anything, but only God, who makes things grow. [8]The one who plants and the one who waters have one purpose, and they will each be rewarded according to their own labor. [9]For we are co-workers in God's service; you are God's field, God's building.

---

a 31 Jer. 9:24   *b 1* Some manuscripts *proclaimed to you God's mystery*   *c 9* Isaiah 64:4   *d 13* Or *Spirit, interpreting spiritual truths to those who are spiritual*   *e 16* Isaiah 40:13

10By the grace God has given me, I laid a foundation as a wise builder, and someone else is building on it. But each one should build with care. 11For no one can lay any foundation other than the one already laid, which is Jesus Christ. 12If anyone builds on this foundation using gold, silver, costly stones, wood, hay or straw, 13their work will be shown for what it is, because the Day will bring it to light. It will be revealed with fire, and the fire will test the quality of each person's work. 14If what has been built survives, the builder will receive a reward. 15If it is burned up, the builder will suffer loss but yet will be saved — even though only as one escaping through the flames.

16Don't you know that you yourselves are God's temple and that God's Spirit dwells in your midst? 17If anyone destroys God's temple, God will destroy that person; for God's temple is sacred, and you together are that temple.

18Do not deceive yourselves. If any of you think you are wise by the standards of this age, you should become "fools" so that you may become wise. 19For the wisdom of this world is foolishness in God's sight. As it is written: "He catches the wise in their craftiness"*a*; 20and again, "The Lord knows that the thoughts of the wise are futile."*b* 21So then, no more boasting about human leaders! All things are yours, 22whether Paul or Apollos or Cephas*c* or the world or life or death or the present or the future — all are yours, 23and you are of Christ, and Christ is of God.

The Nature of True Apostleship

4 This, then, is how you ought to regard us: as servants of Christ and as those entrusted with the mysteries God has revealed. 2Now it is required that those who have been given a trust must prove faithful. 3I care very little if I am judged by you or by any human court; indeed, I do not even judge myself. 4My conscience is clear, but that does not make me innocent. It is the Lord who judges me. 5Therefore judge nothing before the appointed time; wait until the Lord comes. He will bring to light what is hidden in darkness and will expose the motives of the heart. At that time each will receive their praise from God.

6Now, brothers and sisters, I have applied these things to myself and Apollos for your benefit, so that you may learn from us the meaning of the saying, "Do not go beyond what is written." Then you will not be puffed up in being a follower of one of us over against the other. 7For who makes you different from anyone else? What do you have that you did not receive? And if you did receive it, why do you boast as though you did not?

8Already you have all you want! Already you have become rich! You have begun to reign — and that without us! How I wish that you really had begun to reign so that we also might reign with you! 9For it seems to me that God has put us apostles on display at the end of the procession, like those condemned to die in the arena. We have been made a spectacle to the whole universe, to angels as well as to human beings. 10We are fools for Christ, but you are so wise in Christ! We are weak, but you are strong! You are honored, we are dishonored! 11To this very hour we go hungry and thirsty, we are in rags, we are brutally treated, we are homeless. 12We work hard with our own hands. When we are cursed, we bless; when we are persecuted, we endure it; 13when we are slandered, we answer kindly. We have become the scum of the earth, the garbage of the world — right up to this moment.

Paul's Appeal and Warning

14I am writing this not to shame you but to warn you as my dear children. 15Even if you had ten thousand guardians in Christ, you do not have many fathers, for in Christ Jesus I became your father through the gospel. 16Therefore I urge you to imitate me.

---

a 19 Job 5:13   *b 20* Psalm 94:11   *c 22* That is, Peter

¹⁷For this reason I have sent to you Timothy, my son whom I love, who is faithful in the Lord. He will remind you of my way of life in Christ Jesus, which agrees with what I teach everywhere in every church.

¹⁸Some of you have become arrogant, as if I were not coming to you. ¹⁹But I will come to you very soon, if the Lord is willing, and then I will find out not only how these arrogant people are talking, but what power they have. ²⁰For the kingdom of God is not a matter of talk but of power. ²¹What do you prefer? Shall I come to you with a rod of discipline, or shall I come in love and with a gentle spirit?

Dealing With a Case of Incest

5 It is actually reported that there is sexual immorality among you, and of a kind that even pagans do not tolerate: A man is sleeping with his father's wife. ²And you are proud! Shouldn't you rather have gone into mourning and have put out of your fellowship the man who has been doing this? ³For my part, even though I am not physically present, I am with you in spirit. As one who is present with you in this way, I have already passed judgment in the name of our Lord Jesus on the one who has been doing this. ⁴So when you are assembled and I am with you in spirit, and the power of our Lord Jesus is present, ⁵hand this man over to Satan for the destruction of the flesh,ᵃ,ᵇ so that his spirit may be saved on the day of the Lord.

⁶Your boasting is not good. Don't you know that a little yeast leavens the whole batch of dough? ⁷Get rid of the old yeast, so that you may be a new unleavened batch — as you really are. For Christ, our Passover lamb, has been sacrificed. ⁸Therefore let us keep the Festival, not with the old bread leavened with malice and wickedness, but with the unleavened bread of sincerity and truth.

⁹I wrote to you in my letter not to associate with sexually immoral people — ¹⁰not at all meaning the people of this world who are immoral, or the greedy and swindlers, or idolaters. In that case you would have to leave this world. ¹¹But now I am writing to you that you must not associate with anyone who claims to be a brother or sisterᶜ but is sexually immoral or greedy, an idolater or slanderer, a drunkard or swindler. Do not even eat with such people.

¹²What business is it of mine to judge those outside the church? Are you not to judge those inside? ¹³God will judge those outside. "Expel the wicked person from among you."ᵈ

Lawsuits Among Believers

6 If any of you has a dispute with another, do you dare to take it before the ungodly for judgment instead of before the Lord's people? ²Or do you not know that the Lord's people will judge the world? And if you are to judge the world, are you not competent to judge trivial cases? ³Do you not know that we will judge angels? How much more the things of this life! ⁴Therefore, if you have disputes about such matters, do you ask for a ruling from those whose way of life is scorned in the church? ⁵I say this to shame you. Is it possible that there is nobody among you wise enough to judge a dispute between believers? ⁶But instead, one brother takes another to court — and this in front of unbelievers!

⁷The very fact that you have lawsuits among you means you have been completely defeated already. Why not rather be wronged? Why not rather be cheated? ⁸Instead, you yourselves cheat and do wrong, and you do this to your brothers and sisters. ⁹Or do you not know that wrongdoers will not inherit the kingdom of God? Do not be deceived: Neither the sexually immoral nor idolaters nor adulterers nor men

---

ᵃ 5 In contexts like this, the Greek word for *flesh* (*sarx*) refers to the sinful state of human beings, often presented as a power in opposition to the Spirit.   ᵇ 5 Or *of his body*   ᶜ 11 The Greek word for *brother or sister* (*adelphos*) refers here to a believer, whether man or woman, as part of God's family; also in 8:11, 13.   ᵈ 13 Deut. 13:5; 17:7; 19:19; 21:21; 22:21,24; 24:7

who have sex with men*a* *10*nor thieves nor the greedy nor drunkards nor slanderers nor swindlers will inherit the kingdom of God. *11*And that is what some of you were. But you were washed, you were sanctified, you were justified in the name of the Lord Jesus Christ and by the Spirit of our God.

Sexual Immorality

12"I have the right to do anything," you say — but not everything is beneficial. "I have the right to do anything" — but I will not be mastered by anything. *13*You say, "Food for the stomach and the stomach for food, and God will destroy them both." The body, however, is not meant for sexual immorality but for the Lord, and the Lord for the body. *14*By his power God raised the Lord from the dead, and he will raise us also. *15*Do you not know that your bodies are members of Christ himself? Shall I then take the members of Christ and unite them with a prostitute? Never! *16*Do you not know that he who unites himself with a prostitute is one with her in body? For it is said, "The two will become one flesh."*b* *17*But whoever is united with the Lord is one with him in spirit.*c*

*18*Flee from sexual immorality. All other sins a person commits are outside the body, but whoever sins sexually, sins against their own body. *19*Do you not know that your bodies are temples of the Holy Spirit, who is in you, whom you have received from God? You are not your own; *20*you were bought at a price. Therefore honor God with your bodies.

Concerning Married Life

7 Now for the matters you wrote about: "It is good for a man not to have sexual relations with a woman." *2*But since sexual immorality is occurring, each man should have sexual relations with his own wife, and each woman with her own husband. *3*The husband should fulfill his marital duty to his wife, and likewise the wife to her husband. *4*The wife does not have authority over her own body but yields it to her husband. In the same way, the husband does not have authority over his own body but yields it to his wife. *5*Do not deprive each other except perhaps by mutual consent and for a time, so that you may devote yourselves to prayer. Then come together again so that Satan will not tempt you because of your lack of self-control. *6*I say this as a concession, not as a command. *7*I wish that all of you were as I am. But each of you has your own gift from God; one has this gift, another has that.

*8*Now to the unmarried*d* and the widows I say: It is good for them to stay unmarried, as I do. *9*But if they cannot control themselves, they should marry, for it is better to marry than to burn with passion.

*10*To the married I give this command (not I, but the Lord): A wife must not separate from her husband. *11*But if she does, she must remain unmarried or else be reconciled to her husband. And a husband must not divorce his wife.

*12*To the rest I say this (I, not the Lord): If any brother has a wife who is not a believer and she is willing to live with him, he must not divorce her. *13*And if a woman has a husband who is not a believer and he is willing to live with her, she must not divorce him. *14*For the unbelieving husband has been sanctified through his wife, and the unbelieving wife has been sanctified through her believing husband. Otherwise your children would be unclean, but as it is, they are holy.

*15*But if the unbeliever leaves, let it be so. The brother or the sister is not bound in such circumstances; God has called us to live in peace. *16*How do you know, wife, whether you will save your husband? Or, how do you know, husband, whether you will save your wife?

---

a 9 The words *men who have sex with men* translate two Greek words that refer to the passive and active participants in homosexual acts.   *b 16* Gen. 2:24   *c 17* Or *in the Spirit*   *d 8* Or *widowers*

Concerning Change of Status

17Nevertheless, each person should live as a believer in whatever situation the Lord has assigned to them, just as God has called them. This is the rule I lay down in all the churches. 18Was a man already circumcised when he was called? He should not become uncircumcised. Was a man uncircumcised when he was called? He should not be cir- cumcised. 19Circumcision is nothing and uncircumcision is nothing. Keeping God's commands is what counts. 20Each person should remain in the situation they were in when God called them.

21Were you a slave when you were called? Don't let it trouble you — although if you can gain your freedom, do so. 22For the one who was a slave when called to faith in the

---

SPIRITUAL INVENTORY LESSON [Principle Four]

For the previous entry in the SPIRITUAL INVENTORY lesson, go to Romans 12:2 (page 1410).

For a discussion of Principles One through Eight and a listing of their related lessons, go to pages xvii–xliv.

Do you not know that your bodies are temples of the Holy Spirit, who is in you, whom you have received from God? You are not your own; you were bought at a price. Therefore honor God with your bodies.

1 Corinthians 6:19–20

Principle Four begins the process of "coming clean." It's here that we openly examine and confess our faults to ourselves, to God and to someone else we trust. In the first part of Principle Four we openly examine our lives.

As part of completing Principle Four, we do a SPIRITUAL INVENTORY. We look at eight critical areas of our lives. The sixth area is OUR BODY. It's through our body or flesh that Satan works, but thank God that a believer's body has been set apart by God as a temple of the Holy Spirit. God freely gives us the grace of his Spirit. He values us so highly, in fact, that he chose to place his Spirit within us. We need to have as much respect for ourselves as our Creator has for us. First Corinthians 6:19–20 directs us to use our bodies in such a way as to give glory to God.

We need to ask ourselves the following questions regarding our bodies:

- In what ways have we mistreated our bodies?

- What activities or habits have caused harm to our physical health?

Remember that the God of creation made us. Psalm 139:13–14, 16 reminds us: "You created my inmost being; you knit me together in my mother's womb. I praise you because I am fearfully and wonderfully made; your works are wonderful, I know that full well ... Your eyes saw my unformed body; all the days ordained for me were written in your book before one of them came to be."

Today many people insist that they have the right to do whatever they want to their own bodies. Although they think this is freedom, they end up becoming enslaved to their own desires, which ultimately causes them great pain and harm.

The seventh area of our Spiritual Inventory is OUR FAMILY. Go to Joshua 24:15 (page 274).

Lord is the Lord's freed person; similarly, the one who was free when called is Christ's slave. [23]You were bought at a price; do not become slaves of human beings. [24]Brothers and sisters, each person, as responsible to God, should remain in the situation they were in when God called them.

Concerning the Unmarried

[25]Now about virgins: I have no command from the Lord, but I give a judgment as one who by the Lord's mercy is trustworthy. [26]Because of the present crisis, I think that it is good for a man to remain as he is. [27]Are you pledged to a woman? Do not seek to be released. Are you free from such a commitment? Do not look for a wife. [28]But if you do marry, you have not sinned; and if a virgin marries, she has not sinned. But those who marry will face many troubles in this life, and I want to spare you this.

[29]What I mean, brothers and sisters, is that the time is short. From now on those who have wives should live as if they do not; [30]those who mourn, as if they did not; those who are happy, as if they were not; those who buy something, as if it were not theirs to keep; [31]those who use the things of the world, as if not engrossed in them. For this world in its present form is passing away.

[32]I would like you to be free from concern. An unmarried man is concerned about the Lord's affairs — how he can please the Lord. [33]But a married man is concerned about the affairs of this world — how he can please his wife — [34]and his interests are divided. An unmarried woman or virgin is concerned about the Lord's affairs: Her aim is to be devoted to the Lord in both body and spirit. But a married woman is concerned about the affairs of this world — how she can please her husband. [35]I am saying this for your own good, not to restrict you, but that you may live in a right way in undivided devotion to the Lord.

[36]If anyone is worried that he might not be acting honorably toward the virgin he is engaged to, and if his passions are too strong[a] and he feels he ought to marry, he should do as he wants. He is not sinning. They should get married. [37]But the man who has settled the matter in his own mind, who is under no compulsion but has control over his own will, and who has made up his mind not to marry the virgin — this man also does the right thing. [38]So then, he who marries the virgin does right, but he who does not marry her does better.[b]

[39]A woman is bound to her husband as long as he lives. But if her husband dies, she is free to marry anyone she wishes, but he must belong to the Lord. [40]In my judgment, she is happier if she stays as she is — and I think that I too have the Spirit of God.

Concerning Food Sacrificed to Idols

8 Now about food sacrificed to idols: We know that "We all possess knowledge." But knowledge puffs up while love builds up. [2]Those who think they know something do not yet know as they ought to know. [3]But whoever loves God is known by God.[c]

[4]So then, about eating food sacrificed to idols: We know that "An idol is nothing at all in the world" and that "There is no God but one." [5]For even if there are so-called gods, whether in heaven or on earth (as indeed there are many "gods" and many "lords"), [6]yet for us there is but one God, the Father, from whom all things came and for whom we live; and there is

---

[a] 36 Or *if she is getting beyond the usual age for marriage*   [b] 36-38 Or [36]*If anyone thinks he is not treating his*
daughter properly, and if she is getting along in years (or if her passions are too strong), and he feels she ought to marry,
he should do as he wants. He is not sinning. He should let her get married. [37]*But the man who has settled the matter in*
his own mind, who is under no compulsion but has control over his own will, and who has made up his mind to keep the
virgin unmarried — this man also does the right thing. [38]*So then, he who gives his virgin in marriage does right, but he*
who does not give her in marriage does better.   [c] 2,3 An early manuscript and another ancient witness *think they*
have knowledge do not yet know as they ought to know. [3]*But whoever loves truly knows.*

but one Lord, Jesus Christ, through whom all things came and through whom we live.

7But not everyone possesses this knowledge. Some people are still so accustomed to idols that when they eat sacrificial food they think of it as having been sacrificed to a god, and since their conscience is weak, it is defiled. 8But food does not bring us near to God; we are no worse if we do not eat, and no better if we do.

9Be careful, however, that the exercise of your rights does not become a stumbling block to the weak. 10For if someone with a weak conscience sees you, with all your knowledge, eating in an idol's temple, won't that person be emboldened to eat what is sacrificed to idols? 11So this weak brother or sister, for whom Christ died, is destroyed by your knowledge. 12When you sin against them in this way and wound their weak conscience, you sin against Christ. 13Therefore, if what I eat causes my brother or sister to fall into sin, I will never eat meat again, so that I will not cause them to fall.

Paul's Rights as an Apostle

9 Am I not free? Am I not an apostle? Have I not seen Jesus our Lord? Are you not the result of my work in the Lord? 2Even though I may not be an apostle to others, surely I am to you! For you are the seal of my apostleship in the Lord.

3This is my defense to those who sit in judgment on me. 4Don't we have the right to food and drink? 5Don't we have the right to take a believing wife along with us, as do the other apostles and the Lord's brothers and Cephas*a*? 6Or is it only I and Barnabas who lack the right to not work for a living?

7Who serves as a soldier at his own expense? Who plants a vineyard and does not eat its grapes? Who tends a flock and does not drink the milk? 8Do I say this merely on human authority? Doesn't the Law say the same thing? 9For it is written in the Law of Moses: "Do not muzzle an

ox while it is treading out the grain."*b* Is it about oxen that God is concerned? 10Surely he says this for us, doesn't he? Yes, this was written for us, because whoever plows and threshes should be able to do so in the hope of sharing in the harvest. 11If we have sown spiritual seed among you, is it too much if we reap a material harvest from you? 12If others have this right of support from you, shouldn't we have it all the more?

But we did not use this right. On the contrary, we put up with anything rather than hinder the gospel of Christ.

13Don't you know that those who serve in the temple get their food from the temple, and that those who serve at the altar share in what is offered on the altar? 14In the same way, the Lord has commanded that those who preach the gospel should receive their living from the gospel.

15But I have not used any of these rights. And I am not writing this in the hope that you will do such things for me, for I would rather die than allow anyone to deprive me of this boast. 16For when I preach the gospel, I cannot boast, since I am compelled to preach. Woe to me if I do not preach the gospel! 17If I preach voluntarily, I have a reward; if not voluntarily, I am simply discharging the trust committed to me. 18What then is my reward? Just this: that in preaching the gospel I may offer it free of charge, and so not make full use of my rights as a preacher of the gospel.

Paul's Use of His Freedom

19Though I am free and belong to no one, I have made myself a slave to everyone, to win as many as possible. 20To the Jews I became like a Jew, to win the Jews. To those under the law I became like one under the law (though I myself am not under the law), so as to win those under the law. 21To those not having the law I became like one not having the law (though I am not free from God's law but am under Christ's law), so as to win those not having the law. 22To the

---

a 5 That is, Peter   *b 9* Deut. 25:4

weak I became weak, to win the weak. I have become all things to all people so that by all possible means I might save some. ²³I do all this for the sake of the gospel, that I may share in its blessings.

The Need for Self-Discipline

²⁴Do you not know that in a race all the runners run, but only one gets the prize? Run in such a way as to get the prize. ²⁵Everyone who competes in the games goes into strict training. They do it to get a crown that will not last, but we do it to get a crown that will last forever. ²⁶Therefore I do not run like someone running aimlessly; I do not fight like a boxer beating the air. ²⁷No, I strike a blow to my body and make it my slave so that after I have preached to others, I myself will not be disqualified for the prize.

Warnings From Israel's History

10 For I do not want you to be ignorant of the fact, brothers and sisters, that our ancestors were all under the cloud and that they all passed through the sea. ²They were all baptized into Moses in the cloud and in the sea. ³They all ate the same spiritual food ⁴and drank the same spiritual drink; for they drank from the spiritual rock that accompanied them, and that rock was Christ. ⁵Nevertheless, God was not pleased with most of them; their bodies were scattered in the wilderness.

⁶Now these things occurred as examples to keep us from setting our hearts on evil things as they did. ⁷Do not be idolaters, as some of them were; as it is written: "The people sat down to eat and drink and got up to indulge in revelry."ᵃ ⁸We should not commit sexual immorality, as some of them did — and in one day twenty-three thousand of them died. ⁹We should not test Christ,ᵇ as some of them did — and were killed by snakes. ¹⁰And do not grumble, as

some of them did — and were killed by the destroying angel.

¹¹These things happened to them as examples and were written down as warnings for us, on whom the culmination of the ages has come. ¹²So, if you think you are standing firm, be careful that you don't fall! ¹³No temptationᶜ has overtaken you except what is common to mankind. And God is faithful; he will not let you be temptedᶜ beyond what you can bear. But when you are tempted,ᶜ he will also provide a way out so that you can endure it.

Idol Feasts and the Lord's Supper

¹⁴Therefore, my dear friends, flee from idolatry. ¹⁵I speak to sensible people; judge for yourselves what I say. ¹⁶Is not the cup of thanksgiving for which we give thanks a participation in the blood of Christ? And is not the bread that we break a participation in the body of Christ? ¹⁷Because there is one loaf, we, who are many, are one body, for we all share the one loaf.

¹⁸Consider the people of Israel: Do not those who eat the sacrifices participate in the altar? ¹⁹Do I mean then that food sacrificed to an idol is anything, or that an idol is anything? ²⁰No, but the sacrifices of pagans are offered to demons, not to God, and I do not want you to be participants with demons. ²¹You cannot drink the cup of the Lord and the cup of demons too; you cannot have a part in both the Lord's table and the table of demons. ²²Are we trying to arouse the Lord's jealousy? Are we stronger than he?

The Believer's Freedom

²³"I have the right to do anything," you say — but not everything is beneficial. "I have the right to do anything" — but not everything is constructive. ²⁴No one should seek their own good, but the good of others.

²⁵Eat anything sold in the meat market

ᵃ 7 Exodus 32:6   ᵇ 9 Some manuscripts *test the Lord testing* and *tested.*   ᶜ 13 The Greek for *temptation* and *tempted* can also mean without raising questions of conscience, [26]for, "The earth is the Lord's, and everything in it."[a]

[27]If an unbeliever invites you to a meal and you want to go, eat whatever is put before you without raising questions of conscience. [28]But if someone says to you, "This has been offered in sacrifice," then do not eat it, both for the sake of the one who told you and for the sake of conscience. [29]I am referring to the other person's conscience, not yours. For why is my freedom being judged by another's conscience? [30]If I take part in the meal with thankfulness, why am I denounced because of something I thank God for?

[31]So whether you eat or drink or whatever you do, do it all for the glory of God. [32]Do not cause anyone to stumble, whether Jews, Greeks or the church of God — [33]even as I try to please everyone in every way. For I am not seeking my own good but the good of many, so that they may be saved. [1]Follow my example, as I follow the example of Christ.

On Covering the Head in Worship

[2]I praise you for remembering me in everything and for holding to the traditions just as I passed them on to you. [3]But I want you to realize that the head of every man is Christ, and the head of the woman is man,[b] and the head of Christ is God. [4]Every man who prays or prophesies with his head covered dishonors his head. [5]But every woman who prays or prophesies with her head uncovered dishonors her head — it is the same as having her head shaved. [6]For if a woman does not cover her head, she might as well have her hair cut off; but if it is a disgrace for a woman to have her hair cut off or her head shaved, then she should cover her head.

[7]A man ought not to cover his head,[c]

since he is the image and glory of God; but woman is the glory of man. [8]For man did not come from woman, but woman from man; [9]neither was man created for woman, but woman for man. [10]It is for this reason that a woman ought to have authority over her own[d] head, because of the angels. [11]Nevertheless, in the Lord woman is not independent of man, nor is man independent of woman. [12]For as woman came from man, so also man is born of woman. But everything comes from God.

[13]Judge for yourselves: Is it proper for a woman to pray to God with her head uncovered? [14]Does not the very nature of things teach you that if a man has long hair, it is a disgrace to him, [15]but that if a woman has long hair, it is her glory? For long hair is given to her as a covering. [16]If anyone wants to be contentious about this, we have no other practice — nor do the churches of God.

Correcting an Abuse of the Lord's Supper

[17]In the following directives I have no praise for you, for your meetings do more harm than good. [18]In the first place, I hear that when you come together as a church, there are divisions among you, and to some extent I believe it. [19]No doubt there have to be differences among you to show which of you have God's approval. [20]So then, when you come together, it is not the Lord's Supper you eat, [21]for when you are eating, some of you go ahead with your own private suppers. As a result, one person remains hungry and another gets drunk. [22]Don't you have homes to eat and drink in? Or do you despise the church of God by humiliating those who have nothing? What shall I say to you? Shall I praise you? Certainly not in this matter!

[23]For I received from the Lord what I also passed on to you: The Lord Jesus, on

---

[a] 26 Psalm 24:1   [b] 3 Or of the wife is her husband   [c] 4-7 Or [4]Every man who prays or prophesies with long hair dishonors his head. [5]But every woman who prays or prophesies with no covering of hair dishonors her head — she is just like one of the "shorn women." [6]If a woman has no covering, let her be for now with short hair; but since it is a disgrace for a woman to have her hair shorn or shaved, she should grow it again. [7]A man ought not to have long hair   [d] 10 Or have a sign of authority on her

the night he was betrayed, took bread, ²⁴and when he had given thanks, he broke it and said, "This is my body, which is for you; do this in remembrance of me." ²⁵In the same way, after supper he took the cup, saying, "This cup is the new covenant in my blood; do this, whenever you drink it, in remembrance of me." ²⁶For whenever you eat this bread and drink this cup, you proclaim the Lord's death until he comes.

²⁷So then, whoever eats the bread or drinks the cup of the Lord in an unworthy manner will be guilty of sinning against the body and blood of the Lord. ²⁸Everyone ought to examine themselves before they eat of the bread and drink from the cup. ²⁹For those who eat and drink without discerning the body of Christ eat and drink judgment on themselves. ³⁰That is why many among you are weak and sick, and a number of you have fallen asleep. ³¹But if we were more discerning with regard to ourselves, we would not come under such judgment. ³²Nevertheless, when we are judged in this way by the Lord, we are being disciplined so that we will not be finally condemned with the world.

³³So then, my brothers and sisters, when you gather to eat, you should all eat together. ³⁴Anyone who is hungry should eat something at home, so that when you meet together it may not result in judgment.

And when I come I will give further directions.

Concerning Spiritual Gifts

12 Now about the gifts of the Spirit, brothers and sisters, I do not want you to be uninformed. ²You know that when you were pagans, somehow or other you were influenced and led astray to mute idols. ³Therefore I want you to know that no one who is speaking by the Spirit of God says, "Jesus be cursed," and no one can say, "Jesus is Lord," except by the Holy Spirit.

⁴There are different kinds of gifts, but the same Spirit distributes them. ⁵There are different kinds of service, but the same Lord. ⁶There are different kinds of working, but in all of them and in everyone it is the same God at work.

⁷Now to each one the manifestation of the Spirit is given for the common good. ⁸To one there is given through the Spirit a message of wisdom, to another a message of knowledge by means of the same Spirit, ⁹to another faith by the same Spirit, to another gifts of healing by that one Spirit, ¹⁰to another miraculous powers, to another prophecy, to another distinguishing between spirits, to another speaking in different kinds of tongues,^a and to still another the interpretation of tongues.^a ¹¹All these are the work of one and the same Spirit, and he distributes them to each one, just as he determines.

Unity and Diversity in the Body

¹²Just as a body, though one, has many parts, but all its many parts form one body, so it is with Christ. ¹³For we were all baptized by^b one Spirit so as to form one body — whether Jews or Gentiles, slave or free — and we were all given the one Spirit to drink. ¹⁴Even so the body is not made up of one part but of many.

¹⁵Now if the foot should say, "Because I am not a hand, I do not belong to the body," it would not for that reason stop being part of the body. ¹⁶And if the ear should say, "Because I am not an eye, I do not belong to the body," it would not for that reason stop being part of the body. ¹⁷If the whole body were an eye, where would the sense of hearing be? If the whole body were an ear, where would the sense of smell be? ¹⁸But in fact God has placed the parts in the body, every one of them, just as he wanted them to be. ¹⁹If they were all one part, where would the body be? ²⁰As it is, there are many parts, but one body.

²¹The eye cannot say to the hand, "I don't need you!" And the head cannot say

---

^a 10 Or languages; also in verse 28   ^b 13 Or with; or in

to the feet, "I don't need you!" 22On the contrary, those parts of the body that seem to be weaker are indispensable, 23and the parts that we think are less honorable we treat with special honor. And the parts that are unpresentable are treated with special modesty, 24while our presentable parts need no special treatment. But God has put the body together, giving greater honor to the parts that lacked it, 25so that there should be no division in the body, but that its parts should have equal concern for each other. 26If one part suffers, every part suffers with it; if one part is honored, every part rejoices with it.

27Now you are the body of Christ, and each one of you is a part of it. 28And God has placed in the church first of all apostles, second prophets, third teachers, then miracles, then gifts of healing, of helping, of guidance, and of different kinds of tongues. 29Are all apostles? Are all prophets? Are all teachers? Do all work miracles? 30Do all have gifts of healing? Do all speak in tongues*a*? Do all interpret? 31Now eagerly desire the greater gifts.

Love Is Indispensable

And yet I will show you the most excellent way.

13 If I speak in the tongues*b* of men or of angels, but do not have love, I am only a resounding gong or a clanging cymbal. 2If I have the gift of prophecy and can fathom all mysteries and all knowledge, and if I have a faith that can move mountains, but do not have love, I am nothing. 3If I give all I possess to the poor and give over my body to hardship that I may boast,*c* but do not have love, I gain nothing.

4Love is patient, love is kind. It does not envy, it does not boast, it is not proud. 5It does not dishonor others, it is not self-seeking, it is not easily angered, it keeps no record of wrongs. 6Love does not delight in

evil but rejoices with the truth. 7It always protects, always trusts, always hopes, always perseveres.

8Love never fails. But where there are prophecies, they will cease; where there are tongues, they will be stilled; where there is knowledge, it will pass away. 9For we know in part and we prophesy in part, 10but when completeness comes, what is in part disappears. 11When I was a child, I talked like a child, I thought like a child, I reasoned like a child. When I became a man, I put the ways of childhood behind me. 12For now we see only a reflection as in a mirror; then we shall see face to face. Now I know in part; then I shall know fully, even as I am fully known.

13And now these three remain: faith, hope and love. But the greatest of these is love.

Intelligibility in Worship

14 Follow the way of love and eagerly desire gifts of the Spirit, especially prophecy. 2For anyone who speaks in a tongue*d* does not speak to people but to God. Indeed, no one understands them; they utter mysteries by the Spirit. 3But the one who prophesies speaks to people for their strengthening, encouraging and comfort. 4Anyone who speaks in a tongue edifies themselves, but the one who prophesies edifies the church. 5I would like every one of you to speak in tongues,*e* but I would rather have you prophesy. The one who prophesies is greater than the one who speaks in tongues,*e* unless someone interprets, so that the church may be edified.

6Now, brothers and sisters, if I come to you and speak in tongues, what good will I be to you, unless I bring you some revelation or knowledge or prophecy or word of instruction? 7Even in the case of lifeless things that make sounds, such as the pipe or harp, how will anyone know what tune is being played unless there is a distinction

---

a 30 Or *other languages*   *b 1* Or *languages*   *c 3* Some manuscripts *body to the flames*   *d 2* Or *in another language*; also in verses 4, 13, 14, 19, 26 and 27   *e 5* Or *in other languages*; also in verses 6, 18, 22, 23 and 39 in the notes? [8]Again, if the trumpet does not sound a clear call, who will get ready for battle? [9]So it is with you. Unless you speak intelligible words with your tongue, how will anyone know what you are saying? You will just be speaking into the air. [10]Undoubtedly there are all sorts of languages in the world, yet none of them is without meaning. [11]If then I do not grasp the meaning of what someone is saying, I am a foreigner to the speaker, and the speaker is a foreigner to me. [12]So it is with you. Since you are eager for gifts of the Spirit, try to excel in those that build up the church.

[13]For this reason the one who speaks in a tongue should pray that they may interpret what they say. [14]For if I pray in a tongue, my spirit prays, but my mind is unfruitful. [15]So what shall I do? I will pray with my spirit, but I will also pray with my understanding; I will sing with my spirit, but I will also sing with my understanding. [16]Otherwise when you are praising God in the Spirit, how can someone else, who is now put in the position of an inquirer,[a] say "Amen" to your thanksgiving, since they do not know what you are saying? [17]You are giving thanks well enough, but no one else is edified.

[18]I thank God that I speak in tongues more than all of you. [19]But in the church I would rather speak five intelligible words to instruct others than ten thousand words in a tongue.

[20]Brothers and sisters, stop thinking like children. In regard to evil be infants, but in your thinking be adults. [21]In the Law it is written:

"With other tongues
and through the lips of foreigners
I will speak to this people,
but even then they will not listen to me,
says the Lord."[b]

[22]Tongues, then, are a sign, not for believers but for unbelievers; prophecy, however, is not for unbelievers but for believers. [23]So if the whole church comes together and everyone speaks in tongues, and inquirers or unbelievers come in, will they not say that you are out of your mind? [24]But if an unbeliever or an inquirer comes in while everyone is prophesying, they are convicted of sin and are brought under judgment by all, [25]as the secrets of their hearts are laid bare. So they will fall down and worship God, exclaiming, "God is really among you!"

Good Order in Worship

[26]What then shall we say, brothers and sisters? When you come together, each of you has a hymn, or a word of instruction, a revelation, a tongue or an interpretation. Everything must be done so that the church may be built up. [27]If anyone speaks in a tongue, two — or at the most three — should speak, one at a time, and someone must interpret. [28]If there is no interpreter, the speaker should keep quiet in the church and speak to himself and to God.

[29]Two or three prophets should speak, and the others should weigh carefully what is said. [30]And if a revelation comes to someone who is sitting down, the first speaker should stop. [31]For you can all prophesy in turn so that everyone may be instructed and encouraged. [32]The spirits of prophets are subject to the control of prophets. [33]For God is not a God of disorder but of peace — as in all the congregations of the Lord's people.

[34]Women[c] should remain silent in the churches. They are not allowed to speak, but must be in submission, as the law says. [35]If they want to inquire about something, they should ask their own husbands at home; for it is disgraceful for a woman to speak in the church.[d]

[36]Or did the word of God originate with you? Or are you the only people it has reached? [37]If anyone thinks they are a

---

[a] 16 The Greek word for *inquirer* is a technical term for someone not fully initiated into a religion; also in verses 23 and 24.   [b] 21 Isaiah 28:11,12   [c] 33,34 Or *peace. As in all the congregations of the Lord's people,* [34]*women*   [d] 34,35 In a few manuscripts these verses come after verse 40.

prophet or otherwise gifted by the Spirit, let them acknowledge that what I am writing to you is the Lord's command. 38But if anyone ignores this, they will themselves be ignored.*a*

39Therefore, my brothers and sisters, be eager to prophesy, and do not forbid speaking in tongues. 40But everything should be done in a fitting and orderly way.

The Resurrection of Christ

15 Now, brothers and sisters, I want to remind you of the gospel I preached to you, which you received and on which you have taken your stand. 2By this gospel you are saved, if you hold firmly to the word I preached to you. Otherwise, you have believed in vain.

3For what I received I passed on to you as of first importance*b*: that Christ died for our sins according to the Scriptures, 4that he was buried, that he was raised on the third day according to the Scriptures, 5and that he appeared to Cephas,*c* and then to the Twelve. 6After that, he appeared to more than five hundred of the brothers and sisters at the same time, most of whom are still living, though some have fallen asleep. 7Then he appeared to James, then to all the apostles, 8and last of all he appeared to me also, as to one abnormally born.

9For I am the least of the apostles and do not even deserve to be called an apostle, because I persecuted the church of God. 10But by the grace of God I am what I am, and his grace to me was not without effect. No, I worked harder than all of them — yet not I, but the grace of God that was with me. 11Whether, then, it is I or they, this is what we preach, and this is what you believed.

The Resurrection of the Dead

12But if it is preached that Christ has been raised from the dead, how can some of you say that there is no resurrection of the dead? 13If there is no resurrection of the dead,

then not even Christ has been raised. 14And if Christ has not been raised, our preaching is useless and so is your faith. 15More than that, we are then found to be false witnesses about God, for we have testified about God that he raised Christ from the dead. But he did not raise him if in fact the dead are not raised. 16For if the dead are not raised, then Christ has not been raised either. 17And if Christ has not been raised, your faith is futile; you are still in your sins. 18Then those also who have fallen asleep in Christ are lost. 19If only for this life we have hope in Christ, we are of all people most to be pitied.

20But Christ has indeed been raised from the dead, the firstfruits of those who have fallen asleep. 21For since death came through a man, the resurrection of the dead comes also through a man. 22For as in Adam all die, so in Christ all will be made alive. 23But each in turn: Christ, the firstfruits; then, when he comes, those who belong to him. 24Then the end will come, when he hands over the kingdom to God the Father after he has destroyed all dominion, authority and power. 25For he must reign until he has put all his enemies under his feet. 26The last enemy to be destroyed is death. 27For he "has put everything under his feet."*d* Now when it says that "everything" has been put under him, it is clear that this does not include God himself, who put everything under Christ. 28When he has done this, then the Son himself will be made subject to him who put everything under him, so that God may be all in all.

29Now if there is no resurrection, what will those do who are baptized for the dead? If the dead are not raised at all, why are people baptized for them? 30And as for us, why do we endanger ourselves every hour? 31I face death every day — yes, just as surely as I boast about you in Christ Jesus our Lord. 32If I fought wild beasts in Ephesus with no more than human hopes, what have I gained? If the dead are not raised,

---

a 38 Some manuscripts *But anyone who is ignorant of this will be ignorant*   *b 3* Or *you at the first*   *c 5* That is, Peter   *d 27* Psalm 8:6

"Let us eat and drink,
for tomorrow we die."*a*

4
5
33Do not be misled: "Bad company corrupts good character."*b* 34Come back to your senses as you ought, and stop sinning; for there are some who are ignorant of God — I say this to your shame.

The Resurrection Body

35But someone will ask, "How are the dead raised? With what kind of body will they come?" 36How foolish! What you sow does not come to life unless it dies. 37When you sow, you do not plant the body that will be, but just a seed, perhaps of wheat or of something else. 38But God gives it a body as he has determined, and to each kind of seed he gives its own body. 39Not all flesh is the same: People have one kind of flesh, animals have another, birds another and fish another. 40There are also heavenly bodies and there are earthly bodies; but the splendor of the heavenly bodies is one kind, and the splendor of the earthly bodies is another. 41The sun has one kind of splendor, the moon another and the stars another; and star differs from star in splendor.

42So will it be with the resurrection of the dead. The body that is sown is perishable, it is raised imperishable; 43it is sown in dishonor, it is raised in glory; it is sown in weakness, it is raised in power; 44it is sown a natural body, it is raised a spiritual body.

If there is a natural body, there is also a spiritual body. 45So it is written: "The first man Adam became a living being"*c*; the last Adam, a life-giving spirit. 46The spiritual did not come first, but the natural, and after that the spiritual. 47The first man was of the dust of the earth; the second man is of heaven. 48As was the earthly man, so are those who are of the earth; and as is the heavenly man, so also are those who are of heaven. 49And just as we have borne the image of the earthly man, so shall we*d* bear the image of the heavenly man.

50I declare to you, brothers and sisters, that flesh and blood cannot inherit the kingdom of God, nor does the perishable inherit the imperishable. 51Listen, I tell you a mystery: We will not all sleep, but we will all be changed — 52in a flash, in the twinkling of an eye, at the last trumpet. For the trumpet will sound, the dead will be raised imperishable, and we will be changed. 53For the perishable must clothe itself with the imperishable, and the mortal with immortality. 54When the perishable has been clothed with the imperishable, and the mortal with immortality, then the saying that is written will come true: "Death has been swallowed up in victory."*e*

55"Where, O death, is your victory?
Where, O death, is your sting?"*f*

56The sting of death is sin, and the power of sin is the law. 57But thanks be to God! He gives us the victory through our Lord Jesus Christ.

58Therefore, my dear brothers and sisters, stand firm. Let nothing move you. Always give yourselves fully to the work of the Lord, because you know that your labor in the Lord is not in vain.

The Collection for the Lord's People

16 Now about the collection for the Lord's people: Do what I told the Galatian churches to do. 2On the first day of every week, each one of you should set aside a sum of money in keeping with your income, saving it up, so that when I come no collections will have to be made. 3Then, when I arrive, I will give letters of introduction to the men you approve and send them with your gift to Jerusalem. 4If it seems advisable for me to go also, they will accompany me.

Personal Requests

5After I go through Macedonia, I will come to you — for I will be going through

---

a 32 Isaiah 22:13   *b* 33 From the Greek poet Menander   *c* 45 Gen. 2:7   *d* 49 Some early manuscripts *so let us*
e 54 Isaiah 25:8   *f* 55 Hosea 13:14

Macedonia. 6Perhaps I will stay with you for a while, or even spend the winter, so that you can help me on my journey, wherever I go. 7For I do not want to see you now and make only a passing visit; I hope to spend some time with you, if the Lord permits. 8But I will stay on at Ephesus until Pentecost, 9because a great door for effective work has opened to me, and there are many who oppose me.

ACTION LESSON [*Principle Three*]

For the previous entry in the ACTION lesson, go to Matthew 6:34 (page 1136).

For a discussion of Principles One through Eight and a listing of their related lessons, go to pages xvii – xliv.

By this gospel you are saved, if you hold firmly to the word I preached to you. Otherwise, you have believed in vain. For what I received I passed on to you as of first importance: that Christ died for our sins according to the Scriptures, that he was buried, [and] that he was raised on the third day according to the Scriptures.

1 CORINTHIANS 15:2–4

In Principle Three we consciously choose to commit all our lives and will to Christ's care and control. We make the decision to TURN every aspect of our lives and will over to our Higher Power, Jesus Christ. In order to turn our lives over to Christ's care and control, we need to take ACTION.

The last letter in ACTION is *N*. It stands for NEXT STEP. The next step is to ask Jesus into our lives to be our Higher Power. How? It's really very simple. Pastor Rick Warren has developed a way for us to establish a "spiritual B.A.S.E." for our lives. Simply answer the following four questions, and if you answer yes to all of them, pray the prayer that follows. That's it. That's all you have to do.

1. Do I **B**elieve that Jesus Christ died on the cross for me and showed he was God by coming back to life (see 1 Corinthians 15:2 – 4)?

2. Do I **A**ccept God's free forgiveness of my sins (see Romans 3:22 – 24)?

3. Do I want to **S**witch to God's plan for my life see (see Mark 1:15; Romans 12:2)?

4. Do I want to **E**xpress my desire for Christ to be the director of my life (see Romans 10:9)?

If you answered yes to all four questions, you're ready to move on. Just pray the following prayer. If you've already taken this step, use this prayer to recommit, to promise that you'll continue to seek and follow God's will and purpose for your life.

Dear God, I believe you sent your Son, Jesus, to die for my sins so I can be forgiven. I'm sorry for my sins, and I want to live the rest of my life the way you want me to. Please implant your Spirit in my life to direct me. Amen.

If you made the decision to invite Christ into your life, let someone know. And welcome to Christ's family!

This is the final page of the ACTION lesson.

[10]When Timothy comes, see to it that he has nothing to fear while he is with you, for he is carrying on the work of the Lord, just as I am. [11]No one, then, should treat him with contempt. Send him on his way in peace so that he may return to me. I am expecting him along with the brothers.

[12]Now about our brother Apollos: I strongly urged him to go to you with the brothers. He was quite unwilling to go now, but he will go when he has the opportunity.

[13]Be on your guard; stand firm in the faith; be courageous; be strong. [14]Do everything in love.

[15]You know that the household of Stephanas were the first converts in Achaia, and they have devoted themselves to the service of the Lord's people. I urge you, brothers and sisters, [16]to submit to such people and to everyone who joins in the work and labors at it. [17]I was glad when Stephanas, Fortunatus and Achaicus arrived, because they have supplied what was lacking from you. [18]For they refreshed my spirit and yours also. Such men deserve recognition.

Final Greetings

[19]The churches in the province of Asia send you greetings. Aquila and Priscilla[a] greet you warmly in the Lord, and so does the church that meets at their house. [20]All the brothers and sisters here send you greetings. Greet one another with a holy kiss.

[21]I, Paul, write this greeting in my own hand.

[22]If anyone does not love the Lord, let that person be cursed! Come, Lord[b]!

[23]The grace of the Lord Jesus be with you.

[24]My love to all of you in Christ Jesus. Amen.[c]

---

[a] 19 Greek *Prisca*, a variant of *Priscilla* (*Marana tha*) used by early Christians.   [b] 22 The Greek for *Come, Lord* reproduces an Aramaic expression   [c] 24 Some manuscripts do not have *Amen*.

2 Corinthians

THEME: Paul's "ministry of reconciliation" (2 Corinthians 5:18) is the ministry of every believer. Believers, as "Christ's ambassadors" (2 Corinthians 5:20), are to implore sinners to be reconciled to God through Jesus Christ.

AUTHOR: Because of this letter's internal evidence, writing style and autobiographical information, Paul's authorship has never been disputed.

DATE OF WRITING: Second Corinthians was probably written in AD 55.

ENCOURAGEMENT FROM 2 CORINTHIANS: "I will boast all the more gladly about my weaknesses, so that Christ's power may rest on me. That is why, for Christ's sake, I delight in weaknesses, in insults, in hardships, in persecutions, in difficulties. For when I am weak, then I am strong" (2 Corinthians 12:9 – 10).

CHALLENGE FROM 2 CORINTHIANS: "Since we have these promises, dear friends, let us purify ourselves from everything that contaminates body and spirit, perfecting holiness out of reverence for God" (2 Corinthians 7:1).

REFLECTION FROM 2 CORINTHIANS: "We have renounced secret and shameful ways; we do not use deception, nor do we distort the word of God" (2 Corinthians 4:2).

Paul's second letter to the church in Corinth incorporates two of the central messages of recovery. First, we're made new creations when we put our trust in Christ. Our old self is gone. We've been made new in Christ. We all know people who continue to beat themselves up over their pasts. But the truth is that we don't need to do that any longer. True, we must deal with our pasts head-on by taking an honest moral inventory in order to experience Christ's healing power. But we don't need to dredge up that past over and over again. We're no longer slaves to our old hurts, hang-ups and habits. We can rightfully claim that our old ways hold no power over us.

The second central recovery message found in 2 Corinthians is that God's grace is enough for us. All we need to be made whole is found in Christ. We don't have to be ashamed of our weaknesses. In fact, Paul points out, we can *brag* about them (see 2 Corinthians 12:9 – 10, above). Why? Because Christ's power is best seen through weaknesses. That's why there's no shame in identifying with whatever has brought us to Celebrate Recovery. In that weakness, in that brokenness, Jesus' life-transforming power is shown to the world.

1 Paul, an apostle of Christ Jesus by the will of God, and Timothy our brother,

To the church of God in Corinth, together with all his holy people throughout Achaia:

²Grace and peace to you from God our Father and the Lord Jesus Christ.

Praise to the God of All Comfort

³Praise be to the God and Father of our Lord Jesus Christ, the Father of compassion

and the God of all comfort, ⁴who comforts us in all our troubles, so that we can comfort those in any trouble with the comfort we ourselves receive from God. ⁵For just as we share abundantly in the sufferings of Christ, so also our comfort abounds through Christ. ⁶If we are distressed, it is for your comfort and salvation; if we are comforted, it is for your comfort, which produces in you patient endurance of the same sufferings we suffer. ⁷And our hope for you is firm, because we know that just as you share in our sufferings, so also you share in our comfort.

⁸We do not want you to be uninformed, brothers and sisters,ᵃ about the troubles we experienced in the province of Asia. We were under great pressure, far beyond our ability to endure, so that we despaired of life itself. ⁹Indeed, we felt we had received the sentence of death. But this happened that we might not rely on ourselves but on God, who raises the dead. ¹⁰He has delivered us from such a deadly peril, and he will deliver us again. On him we have set our hope that he will continue to deliver us, ¹¹as you help us by your prayers. Then

ᵃ 8 The Greek word for *brothers and sisters* (*adelphoi*) refers here to believers, both men and women, as part of God's family; also in 8:1; 13:11.

GIVE LESSON [*Principle Eight*]

For the previous entry in the GIVE lesson, go to Ecclesiastes 4:9 – 12 (page 787).

For a discussion of Principles One through Eight and a listing of their related lessons, go to pages xvii – xliv.

Praise be to the God and Father of our Lord Jesus Christ, the Father of compassion and the God of all comfort, who comforts us in all our troubles, so that we can comfort those in any trouble with the comfort we ourselves receive from God.

2 CORINTHIANS 1:3 – 4

Major, miraculous progress and growth have occurred in our lives since we started our recovery program, way back when we began working Principle One. We've stepped out of our denial into God's grace. We've taken an honest, spiritual inventory. We've worked on getting right with God, ourselves and others, and we've grown in our relationship with Christ. We've discovered a new way to live life, and we're finding the serenity we've always been seeking. But the most exciting part is yet to come — Principle Eight: "Yield myself to God to be used by him to bring this good news to others, both through my example and through my words."

Principle Eight is the "giving back" principle. Matthew 10:8 offers a reminder and an instruction: "Freely you have received, freely give." The *V* in GIVE stands for VICTORIES SHARED. God never wastes a hurt. He can take our pain and use it to help others. Principle Eight gives us the opportunity to share our experiences, victories and hopes with one another.

We start off by saying, "This is how it was for me; this is my personal experience with my addiction. This is how I gained the victory in my recovery — and there's hope for you as well." Second Corinthians 1:3 – 4 is one of Celebrate Recovery's key verses. God helps us overcome our hurts, hang-ups and habits so we in turn can help others gain the victory over theirs.

The last letter in GIVE is *E*. Go to 1 John 3:18 (page 1561).

many will give thanks on our behalf for the gracious favor granted us in answer to the prayers of many.

Paul's Change of Plans

12Now this is our boast: Our conscience testifies that we have conducted ourselves in the world, and especially in our relations with you, with integrity*a* and godly sincerity. We have done so, relying not on worldly wisdom but on God's grace. 13For we do not write you anything you cannot read or understand. And I hope that, 14as you have understood us in part, you will come to understand fully that you can boast of us just as we will boast of you in the day of the Lord Jesus.

15Because I was confident of this, I wanted to visit you first so that you might benefit twice. 16I wanted to visit you on my way to Macedonia and to come back to you from Macedonia, and then to have you send me on my way to Judea. 17Was I fickle when I intended to do this? Or do I make my plans in a worldly manner so that in the same breath I say both "Yes, yes" and "No, no"?

18But as surely as God is faithful, our message to you is not "Yes" and "No." 19For the Son of God, Jesus Christ, who was preached among you by us — by me and Silas*b* and Timothy — was not "Yes" and "No," but in him it has always been "Yes." 20For no matter how many promises God has made, they are "Yes" in Christ. And so through him the "Amen" is spoken by us to the glory of God. 21Now it is God who makes both us and you stand firm in Christ. He anointed us,

---

a 12 Many manuscripts *holiness*   *b 19* Greek *Silvanus*, a variant of *Silas*

SANITY LESSON [*Principle Two*]

For the previous entry in the SANITY lesson, go to Romans 15:7 (page 1416).

For a discussion of Principles One through Eight and a listing of their related lessons, go to pages xvii – xliv.

We do not want you to be uninformed, brothers and sisters, about the troubles we experienced in the province of Asia. We were under great pressure, far beyond our ability to endure, so that we despaired of life itself. Indeed, we felt we had received the sentence of death. But this happened that we might not rely on ourselves but on God, who raises the dead.

2 CORINTHIANS 1:8 – 9

In Principle Two we earnestly believe that God exists, that we matter to him and that he has the power to help us recover. It's in this principle that we find the SANITY to begin to stop making the same poor choices again and again.

The next letter in SANITY is *N*, which stands for NEW LIFE. Down in the pit of our hurts, hang-ups and habits we've reached rock bottom. We know the feelings of despair expressed in 2 Corinthians 1:8 – 9. But the penalty for our sins was paid in full by Jesus on the cross. The hope of new life allows us to wait in expectation for freedom from our bondage. As the apostle Paul enthuses in 2 Corinthians 5:17, "If anyone is in Christ, the new creation has come: The old has gone, the new is here!"

The next letter in SANITY is *I*. Go to 3 John 4 (page 1565).

22set his seal of ownership on us, and put his Spirit in our hearts as a deposit, guaranteeing what is to come.

23I call God as my witness — and I stake my life on it — that it was in order to spare you that I did not return to Corinth. 24Not that we lord it over your faith, but we work with you for your joy, because it is by faith you stand firm. 1So I made up my mind that I would not make another painful visit to you. 2For if I grieve you, who is left to make me glad but you whom I have grieved? 3I wrote as I did, so that when I came I would not be distressed by those who should have made me rejoice. I had confidence in all of you, that you would all share my joy. 4For I wrote you out of great distress and anguish of heart and with many tears, not to grieve you but to let you know the depth of my love for you.

Forgiveness for the Offender

5If anyone has caused grief, he has not so much grieved me as he has grieved all of you to some extent — not to put it too severely. 6The punishment inflicted on him by the majority is sufficient. 7Now instead, you ought to forgive and comfort him, so that he will not be overwhelmed by excessive sorrow. 8I urge you, therefore, to reaffirm your love for him. 9Another reason I wrote you was to see if you would stand the test and be obedient in everything. 10Anyone you forgive, I also forgive. And what I have forgiven — if there was anything to forgive — I have forgiven in the sight of Christ for your sake, 11in order that Satan might not outwit us. For we are not unaware of his schemes.

Ministers of the New Covenant

12Now when I went to Troas to preach the gospel of Christ and found that the Lord had opened a door for me, 13I still had no peace of mind, because I did not find my brother Titus there. So I said goodbye to them and went on to Macedonia.

14But thanks be to God, who always leads us as captives in Christ's triumphal procession and uses us to spread the aroma of the knowledge of him everywhere. 15For we are to God the pleasing aroma of Christ among those who are being saved and those who are perishing. 16To the one we are an aroma that brings death; to the other, an aroma that brings life. And who is equal to such a task? 17Unlike so many, we do not peddle the word of God for profit. On the contrary, in Christ we speak before God with sincerity, as those sent from God.

3Are we beginning to commend ourselves again? Or do we need, like some people, letters of recommendation to you or from you? 2You yourselves are our letter, written on our hearts, known and read by everyone. 3You show that you are a letter from Christ, the result of our ministry, written not with ink but with the Spirit of the living God, not on tablets of stone but on tablets of human hearts.

4Such confidence we have through Christ before God. 5Not that we are competent in ourselves to claim anything for ourselves, but our competence comes from God. 6He has made us competent as ministers of a new covenant — not of the letter but of the Spirit; for the letter kills, but the Spirit gives life.

The Greater Glory of the New Covenant

7Now if the ministry that brought death, which was engraved in letters on stone, came with glory, so that the Israelites could not look steadily at the face of Moses because of its glory, transitory though it was, 8will not the ministry of the Spirit be even more glorious? 9If the ministry that brought condemnation was glorious, how much more glorious is the ministry that brings righteousness! 10For what was glorious has no glory now in comparison with the surpassing glory. 11And if what was transitory came with glory, how much greater is the glory of that which lasts!

12Therefore, since we have such a hope, we are very bold. 13We are not like Moses, who would put a veil over his face to prevent the Israelites from seeing the end of what was passing away. 14But their minds were made dull, for to this day the same veil remains when the old covenant is read. It has not been removed, because only in Christ is it taken away. 15Even to this day when Moses is read, a veil covers their hearts. 16But whenever anyone turns to the Lord, the veil is taken away. 17Now the Lord is the Spirit, and where the Spirit of the Lord is, there is freedom. 18And we all, who with unveiled faces contemplate*a* the Lord's glory, are being transformed into his image with ever-increasing glory, which comes from the Lord, who is the Spirit.

Present Weakness and Resurrection Life

4 Therefore, since through God's mercy we have this ministry, we do not lose heart. 2Rather, we have renounced secret and shameful ways; we do not use deception, nor do we distort the word of God. On the contrary, by setting forth the truth plainly we commend ourselves to everyone's conscience in the sight of God. 3And even if our gospel is veiled, it is veiled to those who are perishing. 4The god of this age has blinded the minds of unbelievers, so that they cannot see the light of the gospel that displays the glory of Christ, who is the image of God. 5For what we preach is not ourselves, but Jesus Christ as Lord, and ourselves as your servants for Jesus' sake. 6For God, who said, "Let light shine out of darkness,"*b* made his light shine in our hearts to give us the light of the knowledge of God's glory displayed in the face of Christ.

7But we have this treasure in jars of clay to show that this all-surpassing power is from God and not from us. 8We are hard pressed on every side, but not crushed; perplexed, but not in despair; 9persecuted, but not abandoned; struck down, but not destroyed. 10We always carry around in our body the death of Jesus, so that the life of Jesus may also be revealed in our body. 11For we who are alive are always being given over to death for Jesus' sake, so that his life may also be re-

vealed in our mortal body. 12So then, death is at work in us, but life is at work in you.

13It is written: "I believed; therefore I have spoken."*c* Since we have that same spirit of*d* faith, we also believe and therefore speak, 14because we know that the one who raised the Lord Jesus from the dead will also raise us with Jesus and present us with you to himself. 15All this is for your benefit, so that the grace that is reaching more and more people may cause thanksgiving to overflow to the glory of God.

16Therefore we do not lose heart. Though outwardly we are wasting away, yet inwardly we are being renewed day by day. 17For our light and momentary troubles are achieving for us an eternal glory that far outweighs them all. 18So we fix our eyes not on what is seen, but on what is unseen, since what is seen is temporary, but what is unseen is eternal.

Awaiting the New Body

5 For we know that if the earthly tent we live in is destroyed, we have a building from God, an eternal house in heaven, not built by human hands. 2Meanwhile we groan, longing to be clothed instead with our heavenly dwelling, 3because when we are clothed, we will not be found naked. 4For while we are in this tent, we groan and are burdened, because we do not wish to be unclothed but to be clothed instead with our heavenly dwelling, so that what is mortal may be swallowed up by life. 5Now the one who has fashioned us for this very purpose is God, who has given us the Spirit as a deposit, guaranteeing what is to come.

6Therefore we are always confident and know that as long as we are at home in the body we are away from the Lord. 7For we live by faith, not by sight. 8We are confident, I say, and would prefer to be away from the body and at home with the Lord. 9So we make it our goal to please him, whether we are at home in the body or away from it. 10For we must all appear before the judgment seat

---

of Christ, so that each of us may receive what is due us for the things done while in the body, whether good or bad.

The Ministry of Reconciliation

11Since, then, we know what it is to fear the Lord, we try to persuade others. What we are is plain to God, and I hope it is also plain to your conscience. 12We are not trying to commend ourselves to you again, but are giving you an opportunity to take pride in us, so that you can answer those who take pride in what is seen rather than in what is in the heart. 13If we are "out of our mind," as some say, it is for God; if we are in our right mind, it is for you. 14For Christ's love compels us, because we are convinced that one died for all, and therefore all died. 15And he died for all, that those who live should no longer live for themselves but for him who died for them and was raised again.

16So from now on we regard no one from a worldly point of view. Though we once regarded Christ in this way, we do so no longer. 17Therefore, if anyone is in Christ, the new creation has come:a The old has gone,

a 17 Or Christ, that person is a new creation.

TURN LESSON [Principle Three]

For the previous entry in the TURN lesson, go to Ezekiel 18:30–32 (page 986).

For a discussion of Principles One through Eight and a listing of their related lessons, go to pages xvii–xliv.

If anyone is in Christ, the new creation has come:
The old has gone, the new is here!

2 CORINTHIANS 5:17

In Principle Three we consciously choose to commit all our lives and will to Christ's care and control. We make the decision to TURN over every aspect of our lives and will to our Higher Power, Jesus Christ.

The last letter in TURN is N, which stands for NEW LIFE. Our new lives in Christ will come about once we've taken three actions: trusting, understanding and repenting.

We've heard some pretty grim definitions of life. These are just a sampling:

- "Life is a hereditary disease."
- "Life is a sentence we have to serve for being born."
- "Life is a predicament that precedes death."
- "Life's a tough proposition, and the first hundred years are the hardest."

Those are depressing words to which we can probably relate if our lives don't include Jesus Christ. After we ask Jesus into our hearts, we'll experience new and different lives. We'll no longer be bound to our old, sinful natures but will receive new, loving natures from Christ. Each of us will truly be a "new creation." In John 10:10 Jesus tells us, "I have come that they may have life, and have it to the full."

This is the final page of the TURN lesson.

the new is here! ¹⁸All this is from God, who reconciled us to himself through Christ and gave us the ministry of reconciliation: ¹⁹that God was reconciling the world to himself in Christ, not counting people's sins against them. And he has committed to us the message of reconciliation. ²⁰We are therefore Christ's ambassadors, as though God were making his appeal through us. We implore you on Christ's behalf: Be reconciled to God. ²¹God made him who had no sin to be sin*a* for us, so that in him we might become the righteousness of God.

6 As God's co-workers we urge you not to receive God's grace in vain. ²For he says,

"In the time of my favor I heard you,

and in the day of salvation I helped you."*b*

I tell you, now is the time of God's favor, now is the day of salvation.

Paul's Hardships

³We put no stumbling block in anyone's path, so that our ministry will not be discredited. ⁴Rather, as servants of God we commend ourselves in every way: in great endurance; in troubles, hardships and distresses; ⁵in beatings, imprisonments and riots; in hard work, sleepless nights and hunger; ⁶in purity, understanding, patience and kindness; in the Holy Spirit and in sincere love; ⁷in truthful speech and in the power of God; with weapons of righteousness in the right hand and in the left; ⁸through

---

a 21 Or *be a sin offering*   *b 2* Isaiah 49:8

VICTORY LESSON [*Principle Five*]

For the previous entry in the VICTORY lesson, go to Proverbs 16:9 (page 758).

For a discussion of Principles One through Eight and a listing of their related lessons, go to pages xvii – xliv.

If anyone is in Christ, the new creation has come:
The old has gone, the new is here!

2 CORINTHIANS 5:17

In Principle Five, as we voluntarily submit to every change God wants to make in our lives and humbly ask him to remove our character defects, we'll find VICTORY in our recovery.

The next letter in VICTORY is *C*, which stands for CHANGE OUR MINDS. Second Corinthians 5:17 tells us that when we ask Christ into our hearts, we become brand new people on the inside. Our old natures are gone. The changes that are going to take place will be the result of a team effort. Our responsibility is to take the action of following God's direction for change. We have to allow God to transform (change) us by renewing our minds (see Romans 12:2).

To transform something means to change its condition, nature, function and identity. God wants to change more than just our behaviors. He wants to change the way we think. He wants us to stop believing lies and start living in his truth. Simply changing behaviors is like trimming the weeds in a garden instead of removing them. Weeds always grow back unless they're pulled up by their roots. We need to let God transform our minds and uproot our character defects.

The next letter in VICTORY is *T*. Go to James 4:10 (page 1542).

MY NAME IS
NEW CREATION

2 CORINTHIANS 5:11–21

Recovery is the work of Jesus in our lives. Paul's most common description of a child of God is a person who is "in Christ." In 2 Corinthians 5:17 we discover that if we are "in Christ," we're in fact a "new creation." We have infinitely more than just a new start or a second or third chance: We have a new life.

In Celebrate Recovery we understand that healing occurs in a community, and that we need to support each other in recovery. Consistently meeting together in Large Group, Open-Share/Issue groups and Step Studies is essential. In yielding our life entirely to the control of Jesus Christ, we experience a new birth. In our new life we find a new, healthy compulsion, a new motivation: "Christ's love compels us" (v. 14). Our self-centered existence ends. Instead of living for ourselves as slaves to our old habits, we now live for the One who died for us and then rose victorious from death (see vv. 14 – 15). This yields an entirely new outlook on life (see vv. 16 – 17).

As a new creation, each of us has both a new ministry, "the ministry of reconciliation" (v. 18), and a new message, "the message of reconciliation" (v. 19). To carry out our ministry and share our message, we've also been given a new office: Each one of us is an ambassador of Christ (see v. 20). We belong to God's kingdom but remain in this world as his representatives. We can enjoy our access to God and invite others into his kingdom.

Love of Jesus, expressed in loving service to others, is the new activity of the new creature. It isn't really accurate to say, "I'm just a sinner saved by grace." No, we're much more than that: We are children of God, new creations.

As children of God, we need to continue our spiritual growth. A newborn baby is complete but not mature. Growth occurs within the context of a caring community, the church. We need to grow, but at the same time we've already been freed from our past. Whatever we've done, the truth is that "the old has gone, the new is here!" (v. 17). In Celebrate Recovery, our identity is no longer tied to our addiction, hurt or compulsion. Our identity is defined by our relationship to Jesus. Each of us has a new name: New Creation.

glory and dishonor, bad report and good report; genuine, yet regarded as impostors; [9]known, yet regarded as unknown; dying, and yet we live on; beaten, and yet not killed; [10]sorrowful, yet always rejoicing; poor, yet making many rich; having nothing, and yet possessing everything.

[11]We have spoken freely to you, Corinthians, and opened wide our hearts to you. [12]We are not withholding our affection from us, but you are withholding yours from us. [13]As a fair exchange — I speak as to my children — open wide your hearts also.

Warning Against Idolatry

[14]Do not be yoked together with unbelievers. For what do righteousness and wickedness have in common? Or what fellowship can light have with darkness? [15]What harmony is there between Christ and Belial[a]? Or what does a believer have in common with an unbeliever? [16]What agreement is there between the temple of God and idols? For we are the temple of the living God. As God has said:

> "I will live with them
>   and walk among them,
> and I will be their God,
>   and they will be my people."[b]

[17]Therefore,

> "Come out from them
>   and be separate,
>   says the Lord.
> Touch no unclean thing,
>   and I will receive you."[c]

---

[a] 15 Greek *Beliar*, a variant of *Belial*   [b] 16 Lev. 26:12; Jer. 32:38; Ezek. 37:27   [c] 17 Isaiah 52:11; Ezek. 20:34,41

CONFESS LESSON [*Principle Four*]

For the previous entry in the CONFESS lesson, go to Matthew 7:3 (page 1138).

For a discussion of Principles One through Eight and a listing of their related lessons, go to pages xvii – xliv.

God was reconciling the world to himself in Christ, not counting people's sins against them. And he has committed to us the message of reconciliation.

2 CORINTHIANS 5:19

Principle Four begins the process of "coming clean." In the second part of Principle Four, we confess our faults to ourselves, to God and to someone else we trust.

The final S in CONFESS stands for START ACCEPTING GOD'S FORGIVENESS. That's the fourth positive change we receive when we confess. Once we accept God's forgiveness, we're able to look others in the eye. We see ourselves and our actions in a new light. We're ready to find the humility to exchange our shortcomings in Principle Five.

A one-sentence summary of the benefits of working Principle Four goes like this: In confession we open our lives to the healing, reconciling, restoring, uplifting grace of Jesus Christ, who loves us in spite of ourselves.

First John 1:9 reminds us, "If we confess our sins, he is faithful and just and will forgive us our sins and purify us from all unrighteousness."

This is the final page of the CONFESS lesson.

My Name Is Tim

I'M A BELIEVER WHO STRUGGLES WITH CODEPENDENCY, SEXUAL ABUSE, SEXUAL ADDICTION AND ANGER

Please read Paul's glowing words in 2 Corinthians 5:16–21 about every believer's identity as a new creation in Christ.

My dad was an automotive service manager whose passion was racing stock cars. When I was four years old, I went to see him race and watched in horror and disbelief as his car exploded, resulting in his death. Over the years I comforted myself with food, and the kids at school were cruel about my weight. When I was nine years old, I was playing in the woods with my friend. His older brother, who was lying in wait for me, raped me, warning me that if I told anyone, he would kill both my mother and me.

My mom found escape from her own pain over my dad's death in alcohol. When I was ten years old, she died of cirrhosis of the liver, leaving me an orphan. I felt abandoned and afraid. I was passed around among my relatives, and one of my cousins threatened me with a knife and sexually abused me. Eventually, when I was 12, an aunt and uncle adopted me. I was an angry, untrusting, selfish fat kid who started to get into trouble on a regular basis.

I left home when I was 19, and my behavior turned increasingly dark: I engaged in drug and alcohol abuse and had multiple sexual encounters. I married but was unfaithful; in less than two years we were divorced. During the next 21 years I remarried, fathered three children, earned degrees, became an ordained pastor, planted a church and ran a prison ministry. My sexual behaviors continued, though, as I fantasized about women I knew and acted out in secret. I was physically faithful to my wife while having numerous mental affairs. A pastor is expected to be perfect. Who could I talk to?

After we had been married for 15 years, my wife had an affair and sought my forgiveness. But I was crushed by the pain of once again feeling abandoned, and we divorced, with me accepting sole responsibility for another failed marriage. I got involved in therapy, and God prepared me for his next step. A friend suggested that I become involved in Celebrate Recovery, but I thought he was mistaken in considering me "one of those people."

One day in a coffee shop I was reading my Bible when a man walked in wearing his Celebrate Recovery cap. He invited me to join the program, and I agreed to attend on the following Friday. I fully intended to go to the Men's Anger group, but God directed me instead to the Men's Codependency group, where I've remained ever since. I also immediately joined a men's Step Study group. God's Spirit prompted me to share my darkest secrets, and for the first time in 40 years I felt unconditionally loved.

Principle Six literally changed my life. In my heart I had always hated the individuals who had sexually abused me. But God moved me to include them on the list of those I needed to forgive. I wrote both of those men letters I knew I couldn't send, letters describing the years of wreckage and pain that had resulted from the acts they'd perpetrated against me. I explained that I was extending forgiveness to them as part of my recovery. It wasn't about them; it was all about God and me. Then, suddenly, God changed my heart. I no longer wanted these men to suffer God's wrath for what they had done to me. I had indeed become a new creation. My anger simply melted away, leaving only compassion. I began to pray, asking God to forgive them for their sins against me, and in an instant he changed my heart toward those two individuals I had hated for over 35 years.

During my first year of recovery, I experienced more pain and shed more tears than ever before. I revisited and reopened wounds I had hoped only to bury, but in the process I began to find healing. The men in my Step Study became my lifeline. To this day we continue to hold one another accountable.

Although I thought I could never open my heart to another woman, without my knowledge a friend set up a date for me. I was incredulous. As it turned out, though, Lori is the most wonderful woman I've ever known. Our friendship grew into a dating relationship, we fell in love, and in March of 2003 she became my wife. Through Lori God has taught me more about his grace and love than I've ever known before.

I no longer regret my past because God has used it to bring me to where I am today. Although I revel in being a new creation in Christ, the Lord in his infinite wisdom has used and continues to use the vestiges of my brokenness to give others strength and hope. By his grace I now have the privilege of giving back by co-leading the Men's Codependency group and a men's Step Study group, as well as serving as a counselor and chaplain of recovery in a drug and alcohol treatment center. I was wrong: I truly am "one of those people." And I thank God for that fact every day.

Tim

18And,

"I will be a Father to you,
    and you will be my sons and
        daughters,
            says the Lord Almighty."a

7 Therefore, since we have these promises, dear friends, let us purify ourselves from everything that contaminates body and spirit, perfecting holiness out of reverence for God.

Paul's Joy Over the Church's Repentance

2Make room for us in your hearts. We have wronged no one, we have corrupted no one, we have exploited no one. 3I do not say this to condemn you; I have said before that you have such a place in our hearts that we would live or die with you. 4I have spoken to you with great frankness; I take great pride in you. I am greatly encouraged; in all our troubles my joy knows no bounds.

5For when we came into Macedonia, we had no rest, but we were harassed at every turn—conflicts on the outside, fears within. 6But God, who comforts the downcast, comforted us by the coming of Titus, 7and not only by his coming but also by the comfort you had given him. He told us about your longing for me, your deep sorrow, your ardent concern for me, so that my joy was greater than ever.

8Even if I caused you sorrow by my letter, I do not regret it. Though I did regret it—I see that my letter hurt you, but only for a little while— 9yet now I am happy, not because you were made sorry, but because your sorrow led you to repentance. For you became sorrowful as God intended and so were not harmed in any way by us. 10Godly sorrow brings repentance that leads to salvation and leaves no regret, but worldly sorrow brings death. 11See what this godly sorrow has produced in you: what earnestness, what eagerness to clear yourselves, what indignation, what alarm, what longing, what concern, what readiness to see justice done. At every point you have proved yourselves to be innocent in this matter. 12So even though I wrote to you, it was neither on account of the one who did the wrong nor on account of the injured party, but rather that before God you could see for yourselves how devoted to us you are. 13By all this we are encouraged.

In addition to our own encouragement, we were especially delighted to see how happy Titus was, because his spirit has been refreshed by all of you. 14I had boasted to him about you, and you have not embarrassed me. But just as everything we said to you was true, so our boasting about you to Titus has proved to be true as well. 15And his affection for you is all the greater when he remembers that you were all obedient, receiving him with fear and trembling. 16I am glad I can have complete confidence in you.

The Collection for the Lord's People

8 And now, brothers and sisters, we want you to know about the grace that God has given the Macedonian churches. 2In the midst of a very severe trial, their overflowing joy and their extreme poverty welled up in rich generosity. 3For I testify that they gave as much as they were able, and even beyond their ability. Entirely on their own, 4they urgently pleaded with us for the privilege of sharing in this service to the Lord's people. 5And they exceeded our expectations: They gave themselves first of all to the Lord, and then by the will of God also to us. 6So we urged Titus, just as he had earlier made a beginning, to bring also to completion this act of grace on your part. 7But since you excel in everything—in faith, in speech, in knowledge, in complete earnestness and in the love we have kindled in youb—see that you also excel in this grace of giving.

8I am not commanding you, but I want

---

a 18 2 Samuel 7:14; 7:8   b 7 Some manuscripts and in your love for us to test the sincerity of your love by comparing it with the earnestness of others. 9For you know the grace of our Lord Jesus Christ, that though he was rich, yet for your sake he became poor, so that you through his poverty might become rich.

10And here is my judgment about what is best for you in this matter. Last year you were the first not only to give but also to have the desire to do so. 11Now finish the work, so that your eager willingness to do it may be matched by your completion of it, according to your means. 12For if the willingness is there, the gift is acceptable according to what one has, not according to what one does not have.

13Our desire is not that others might be relieved while you are hard pressed, but that there might be equality. 14At the present time your plenty will supply what they need, so that in turn their plenty will supply what you need. The goal is equality, 15as it is written: "The one who gathered much did not have too much, and the one who gathered little did not have too little."a

Titus Sent to Receive the Collection

16Thanks be to God, who put into the heart of Titus the same concern I have for you. 17For Titus not only welcomed our appeal, but he is coming to you with much enthusiasm and on his own initiative. 18And we are sending along with him the brother who is praised by all the churches for his service to the gospel. 19What is more, he was chosen by the churches to accompany us as we carry the offering, which we administer in order to honor the Lord himself and to show our eagerness to help. 20We want to avoid any criticism of the way we administer this liberal gift. 21For we are taking pains to do what is right, not only in the eyes of the Lord but also in the eyes of man.

22In addition, we are sending with them our brother who has often proved to us in many ways that he is zealous, and now even

more so because of his great confidence in you. 23As for Titus, he is my partner and co-worker among you; as for our brothers, they are representatives of the churches and an honor to Christ. 24Therefore show these men the proof of your love and the reason for our pride in you, so that the churches can see it.

9 There is no need for me to write to you about this service to the Lord's people. 2For I know your eagerness to help, and I have been boasting about it to the Macedonians, telling them that since last year you in Achaia were ready to give; and your enthusiasm has stirred most of them to action. 3But I am sending the brothers in order that our boasting about you in this matter should not prove hollow, but that you may be ready, as I said you would be. 4For if any Macedonians come with me and find you unprepared, we — not to say anything about you — would be ashamed of having been so confident. 5So I thought it necessary to urge the brothers to visit you in advance and finish the arrangements for the generous gift you had promised. Then it will be ready as a generous gift, not as one grudgingly given.

Generosity Encouraged

6Remember this: Whoever sows sparingly will also reap sparingly, and whoever sows generously will also reap generously. 7Each of you should give what you have decided in your heart to give, not reluctantly or under compulsion, for God loves a cheerful giver. 8And God is able to bless you abundantly, so that in all things at all times, having all that you need, you will abound in every good work. 9As it is written:

"They have freely scattered their gifts to the poor;
their righteousness endures forever."b

10Now he who supplies seed to the sower and bread for food will also supply and

---

a 15 Exodus 16:18   b 9 Psalm 112:9

increase your store of seed and will enlarge the harvest of your righteousness. ¹¹You will be enriched in every way so that you can be generous on every occasion, and through us your generosity will result in thanksgiving to God.

¹²This service that you perform is not only supplying the needs of the Lord's people but is also overflowing in many expressions of thanks to God. ¹³Because of the service by which you have proved yourselves, others will praise God for the obedience that accompanies your confession of the gospel of Christ, and for your generosity in sharing with them and with everyone else. ¹⁴And in their prayers for you their hearts will go out to you, because of the surpassing grace God has given you. ¹⁵Thanks be to God for his indescribable gift!

Paul's Defense of His Ministry

10 By the humility and gentleness of Christ, I appeal to you — I, Paul, who am "timid" when face to face with you, but "bold" toward you when away! ²I beg you that when I come I may not have to be as bold as I expect to be toward some people who think that we live by the standards of this world. ³For though we live in the world, we do not wage war as the world does. ⁴The weapons we fight with are not the weapons of the world. On the contrary, they have divine power to demolish strongholds. ⁵We demolish arguments and every pretension that sets itself up against the knowledge of God, and we take captive every thought to make it obedient to Christ. ⁶And we will be ready to punish every act of disobedience, once your obedience is complete.

⁷You are judging by appearances.ᵃ If anyone is confident that they belong to Christ, they should consider again that we belong to Christ just as much as they do. ⁸So even if I boast somewhat freely about the authority the Lord gave us for building

you up rather than tearing you down, I will not be ashamed of it. ⁹I do not want to seem to be trying to frighten you with my letters. ¹⁰For some say, "His letters are weighty and forceful, but in person he is unimpressive and his speaking amounts to nothing." ¹¹Such people should realize that what we are in our letters when we are absent, we will be in our actions when we are present.

¹²We do not dare to classify or compare ourselves with some who commend themselves. When they measure themselves by themselves and compare themselves with themselves, they are not wise. ¹³We, however, will not boast beyond proper limits, but will confine our boasting to the sphere of service God himself has assigned to us, a sphere that also includes you. ¹⁴We are not going too far in our boasting, as would be the case if we had not come to you, for we did get as far as you with the gospel of Christ. ¹⁵Neither do we go beyond our limits by boasting of work done by others. Our hope is that, as your faith continues to grow, our sphere of activity among you will greatly expand, ¹⁶so that we can preach the gospel in the regions beyond you. For we do not want to boast about work already done in someone else's territory. ¹⁷But, "Let the one who boasts boast in the Lord."ᵇ ¹⁸For it is not the one who commends himself who is approved, but the one whom the Lord commends.

Paul and the False Apostles

11 I hope you will put up with me in a little foolishness. Yes, please put up with me! ²I am jealous for you with a godly jealousy. I promised you to one husband, to Christ, so that I might present you as a pure virgin to him. ³But I am afraid that just as Eve was deceived by the serpent's cunning, your minds may somehow be led astray from your sincere and pure devotion to Christ. ⁴For if someone comes to you and preaches a Jesus other than the Jesus we preached, or if you re-

---

ᵃ 7 Or *Look at the obvious facts*   ᵇ 17 Jer. 9:24

ceive a different spirit from the Spirit you received, or a different gospel from the one you accepted, you put up with it easily enough.

⁵I do not think I am in the least inferior to those "super-apostles."*ᵃ ⁶I may indeed be untrained as a speaker, but I do have knowledge. We have made this perfectly clear to you in every way. ⁷Was it a sin for me to lower myself in order to elevate you by preaching the gospel of God to you free of charge? ⁸I robbed other churches by receiving support from them so as to serve you. ⁹And when I was with you and needed something, I was not a burden to anyone, for the brothers who came from Macedonia supplied what I needed. I have kept myself from being a burden to you in any way, and will continue to do so. ¹⁰As surely as the truth of Christ is in me, nobody in the regions of Achaia will stop this boasting of mine. ¹¹Why? Because I do not love you? God knows I do!

¹²And I will keep on doing what I am doing in order to cut the ground from under those who want an opportunity to be considered equal with us in the things they boast about. ¹³For such people are false apostles, deceitful workers, masquerading as apostles of Christ. ¹⁴And no wonder, for Satan himself masquerades as an angel of light. ¹⁵It is not surprising, then, if his servants also masquerade as servants of righteousness. Their end will be what their actions deserve.

Paul Boasts About His Sufferings

¹⁶I repeat: Let no one take me for a fool. But if you do, then tolerate me just as you would a fool, so that I may do a little boasting. ¹⁷In this self-confident boasting I am not talking as the Lord would, but as a fool. ¹⁸Since many are boasting in the way the world does, I too will boast. ¹⁹You gladly put up with fools since you are so wise! ²⁰In fact, you even put up with anyone who enslaves you or exploits you or takes advan-

tage of you or puts on airs or slaps you in the face. ²¹To my shame I admit that we were too weak for that!

Whatever anyone else dares to boast about—I am speaking as a fool—I also dare to boast about. ²²Are they Hebrews? So am I. Are they Israelites? So am I. Are they Abraham's descendants? So am I. ²³Are they servants of Christ? (I am out of my mind to talk like this.) I am more. I have worked much harder, been in prison more frequently, been flogged more severely, and been exposed to death again and again. ²⁴Five times I received from the Jews the forty lashes minus one. ²⁵Three times I was beaten with rods, once I was pelted with stones, three times I was shipwrecked, I spent a night and a day in the open sea, ²⁶I have been constantly on the move. I have been in danger from rivers, in danger from bandits, in danger from my fellow Jews, in danger from Gentiles; in danger in the city, in danger in the country, in danger at sea; and in danger from false believers. ²⁷I have labored and toiled and have often gone without sleep; I have known hunger and thirst and have often gone without food; I have been cold and naked. ²⁸Besides everything else, I face daily the pressure of my concern for all the churches. ²⁹Who is weak, and I do not feel weak? Who is led into sin, and I do not inwardly burn?

³⁰If I must boast, I will boast of the things that show my weakness. ³¹The God and Father of the Lord Jesus, who is to be praised forever, knows that I am not lying. ³²In Damascus the governor under King Aretas had the city of the Damascenes guarded in order to arrest me. ³³But I was lowered in a basket from a window in the wall and slipped through his hands.

Paul's Vision and His Thorn

12 I must go on boasting. Although there is nothing to be gained, I will go on to visions and revelations from the Lord. ²I know a

---

ᵃ 5 Or to the most eminent apostles

man in Christ who fourteen years ago was caught up to the third heaven. Whether it was in the body or out of the body I do not know — God knows. ³And I know that this man — whether in the body or apart from the body I do not know, but God knows — ⁴was caught up to paradise and heard inexpressible things, things that no one is permitted to tell. ⁵I will boast about a man like that, but I will not boast about myself, except about my weaknesses. ⁶Even if I should choose to boast, I would not be a fool, because I would be speaking the truth. But I refrain, so no one will think more of me than is warranted by what I do or say, ⁷or because of these surpassingly great revelations. Therefore, in order to keep me from becoming conceited, I was given a thorn in my flesh, a messenger of Satan, to torment me. ⁸Three times I pleaded with the Lord to take it away from me. ⁹But he said to me, "My grace is sufficient for you, for my power is made perfect in weakness." Therefore I will boast all the more gladly about my weaknesses, so that Christ's power may rest on me. ¹⁰That is why, for Christ's sake, I delight in weaknesses, in insults, in hardships, in persecutions, in difficulties. For when I am weak, then I am strong.

Paul's Concern for the Corinthians

¹¹I have made a fool of myself, but you drove me to it. I ought to have been commended by you, for I am not in the least inferior to the "super-apostles,"ᵃ even though I am nothing. ¹²I persevered in demonstrating among you the marks of a true apostle, including signs, wonders and miracles. ¹³How were you inferior to the other churches, except that I was never a burden to you? Forgive me this wrong!

¹⁴Now I am ready to visit you for the third time, and I will not be a burden to you, because what I want is not your possessions but you. After all, children should not have to save up for their parents, but parents for their children. ¹⁵So I will very gladly spend for you everything I have and expend myself as well. If I love you more, will you love me less? ¹⁶Be that as it may, I have not been a burden to you. Yet, crafty fellow that I am, I caught you by trickery! ¹⁷Did I exploit you through any of the men I sent to you? ¹⁸I urged Titus to go to you and I sent our brother with him. Titus did not exploit you, did he? Did we not walk in the same footsteps by the same Spirit?

¹⁹Have you been thinking all along that we have been defending ourselves to you? We have been speaking in the sight of God as those in Christ; and everything we do, dear friends, is for your strengthening. ²⁰For I am afraid that when I come I may not find you as I want you to be, and you may not find me as you want me to be. I fear that there may be discord, jealousy, fits of rage, selfish ambition, slander, gossip, arrogance and disorder. ²¹I am afraid that when I come again my God will humble me before you, and I will be grieved over many who have sinned earlier and have not repented of the impurity, sexual sin and debauchery in which they have indulged.

Final Warnings

13 This will be my third visit to you. "Every matter must be established by the testimony of two or three witnesses."ᵇ ²I already gave you a warning when I was with you the second time. I now repeat it while absent: On my return I will not spare those who sinned earlier or any of the others, ³since you are demanding proof that Christ is speaking through me. He is not weak in dealing with you, but is powerful among you. ⁴For to be sure, he was crucified in weakness, yet he lives by God's power. Likewise, we are weak in him, yet by God's power we will live with him in our dealing with you.

⁵Examine yourselves to see whether you are in the faith; test yourselves. Do you not realize that Christ Jesus is in you — unless,

---

ᵃ 11 Or *the most eminent apostles*   ᵇ 1 Deut. 19:15

of course, you fail the test? 6And I trust that you will discover that we have not failed the test. 7Now we pray to God that you will not do anything wrong — not so that people will see that we have stood the test but so that you will do what is right even though we may seem to have failed. 8For we cannot do anything against the truth, but only for the truth. 9We are glad whenever we are weak but you are strong; and our prayer is that you may be fully restored. 10This is why I write these things when I am absent, that when I come I may not have to be harsh in my use of authority — the authority the Lord gave me for building you up, not for tearing you down.

Final Greetings

11Finally, brothers and sisters, rejoice! Strive for full restoration, encourage one another, be of one mind, live in peace. And the God of love and peace will be with you.

12Greet one another with a holy kiss. 13All God's people here send their greetings.

14May the grace of the Lord Jesus Christ, and the love of God, and the fellowship of the Holy Spirit be with you all.

Galatians

THEME: Justification by faith, a doctrine central to this letter, creates harmonious community. We're all joined to Christ as equals.

AUTHOR: The apostle Paul wrote Galatians. His authorship has never been seriously disputed.

DATE OF WRITING: Galatians was probably written between AD 48 and 53.

ENCOURAGEMENT FROM GALATIANS: "I have been crucified with Christ and I no longer live, but Christ lives in me. The life I live in the body, I live by faith in the Son of God, who loved me and gave himself for me" (Galatians 2:20).

CHALLENGE FROM GALATIANS: "You, my brothers and sisters, were called to be free. But do not use your freedom to indulge the flesh; rather, serve one another humbly in love" (Galatians 5:13).

REFLECTION FROM GALATIANS: "The fruit of the Spirit is love, joy, peace, forbearance, kindness, goodness, faithfulness, gentleness and self-control. Against such things there is no law. Those who belong to Christ Jesus have crucified the flesh with its passions and desires" (Galatians 5:22 – 24).

In the book of Galatians Paul offers a warning to us as Christians. First, the apostle reminds us that we were made right with Christ through faith. The Christians to whom Paul was writing were trying to live by the old law code in order to earn God's approval. Like them, we can so easily forget that we've been made new in Christ simply on the basis of our accepting him as our Lord and Savior through faith alone. Adding on extra hoops to jump through doesn't add a thing to our salvation.

Christ's sacrifice on the cross has set us free from a life of hurts, hang-ups and habits. We've been forever set free, not because of anything we've done but because Jesus paid the price for us. We've been made right with God; in fact, we've become his very own children. To go back to our old ways would be to turn our backs on God and say that his loving sacrifice just wasn't enough for us.

As we work out our recoveries and apply the eight principles, it's important to bear in mind that these steps don't save us from sin. They're merely guideposts that help us to apply the Biblical principles. We've tried to live on our own power for long enough, and, like the experience of the Christians in Galatia, this has brought us only pain. The eight recovery principles will help us learn to apply and draw on Christ's power. In the book of Galatians, Paul points us to the one and only Higher Power, the only one capable of saving us from a life of sin and separation from God: his Son, Jesus Christ.

1 Paul, an apostle — sent not from men nor by a man, but by Jesus Christ and God the Father, who raised him from the dead — [2]and all the brothers and sisters[a] with me,

To the churches in Galatia:

[3]Grace and peace to you from God our Father and the Lord Jesus Christ, [4]who gave himself for our sins to rescue us from the present evil age, according to the will of our God and Father, [5]to whom be glory for ever and ever. Amen.

No Other Gospel

[6]I am astonished that you are so quickly deserting the one who called you to live in the grace of Christ and are turning to a different gospel — [7]which is really no gospel at all. Evidently some people are throwing you into confusion and are trying to pervert the gospel of Christ. [8]But even if we or an angel from heaven should preach a gospel other than the one we preached to you, let them be under God's curse! [9]As we have already said, so now I say again: If anybody is preaching to you a gospel other than what you accepted, let them be under God's curse!

[10]Am I now trying to win the approval of human beings, or of God? Or am I trying to please people? If I were still trying to please people, I would not be a servant of Christ.

Paul Called by God

[11]I want you to know, brothers and sisters, that the gospel I preached is not of human origin. [12]I did not receive it from any man, nor was I taught it; rather, I received it by revelation from Jesus Christ. [13]For you have heard of my previous way of life in Judaism, how intensely I persecuted the church of God and tried to destroy it. [14]I was advancing in Judaism beyond many of my own age among my people and was extremely zealous for the traditions of my

fathers. [15]But when God, who set me apart from my mother's womb and called me by his grace, was pleased [16]to reveal his Son in me so that I might preach him among the Gentiles, my immediate response was not to consult any human being. [17]I did not go up to Jerusalem to see those who were apostles before I was, but I went into Arabia. Later I returned to Damascus.

[18]Then after three years, I went up to Jerusalem to get acquainted with Cephas[b] and stayed with him fifteen days. [19]I saw none of the other apostles — only James, the Lord's brother. [20]I assure you before God that what I am writing you is no lie.

[21]Then I went to Syria and Cilicia. [22]I was personally unknown to the churches of Judea that are in Christ. [23]They only heard the report: "The man who formerly persecuted us is now preaching the faith he once tried to destroy." [24]And they praised God because of me.

Paul Accepted by the Apostles

2 Then after fourteen years, I went up again to Jerusalem, this time with Barnabas. I took Titus along also. [2]I went in response to a revelation and, meeting privately with those esteemed as leaders, I presented to them the gospel that I preach among the Gentiles. I wanted to be sure I was not running and had not been running my race in vain. [3]Yet not even Titus, who was with me, was compelled to be circumcised, even though he was a Greek. [4]This matter arose because some false believers had infiltrated our ranks to spy on the freedom we have in Christ Jesus and to make us slaves. [5]We did not give in to them for a moment, so that the truth of the gospel might be preserved for you.

[6]As for those who were held in high esteem — whatever they were makes no difference to me; God does not show favoritism — they added nothing to my message. [7]On the contrary, they recognized that I

---

a 2 The Greek word for *brothers and sisters* (*adelphoi*) refers here to believers, both men and women, as part of God's family; also in verse 11; and in 3:15; 4:12, 28, 31; 5:11, 13; 6:1, 18.   *b 18* That is, Peter had been entrusted with the task of preaching the gospel to the uncircumcised,*a* just as Peter had been to the circumcised.*b* 8For God, who was at work in Peter as an apostle to the circumcised, was also at work in me as an apostle to the Gentiles. 9James, Cephas*c* and John, those esteemed as pillars, gave me and Barnabas the right hand of fellowship when they recognized the grace given to me. They agreed that we should go to the Gentiles, and they to the circumcised. 10All they asked was that we should continue to remember the poor, the very thing I had been eager to do all along.

Paul Opposes Cephas

11When Cephas came to Antioch, I opposed him to his face, because he stood condemned. 12For before certain men came from James, he used to eat with the Gentiles. But when they arrived, he began to draw back and separate himself from the Gentiles because he was afraid of those who belonged to the circumcision group. 13The other Jews joined him in his hypocrisy, so that by their hypocrisy even Barnabas was led astray.

14When I saw that they were not acting in line with the truth of the gospel, I said to Cephas in front of them all, "You are a Jew, yet you live like a Gentile and not like a Jew. How is it, then, that you force Gentiles to follow Jewish customs?

15"We who are Jews by birth and not sinful Gentiles 16know that a person is not justified by the works of the law, but by faith in Jesus Christ. So we, too, have put our faith in Christ Jesus that we may be justified by faith in*d* Christ and not by the works of the law, because by the works of the law no one will be justified.

17"But if, in seeking to be justified in Christ, we Jews find ourselves also among the sinners, doesn't that mean that Christ promotes sin? Absolutely not! 18If I rebuild

what I destroyed, then I really would be a lawbreaker.

19"For through the law I died to the law so that I might live for God. 20I have been crucified with Christ and I no longer live, but Christ lives in me. The life I now live in the body, I live by faith in the Son of God, who loved me and gave himself for me. 21I do not set aside the grace of God, for if righteousness could be gained through the law, Christ died for nothing!"*e*

Faith or Works of the Law

3 You foolish Galatians! Who has bewitched you? Before your very eyes Jesus Christ was clearly portrayed as crucified. 2I would like to learn just one thing from you: Did you receive the Spirit by the works of the law, or by believing what you heard? 3Are you so foolish? After beginning by means of the Spirit, are you now trying to finish by means of the flesh?*f* 4Have you experienced*g* so much in vain — if it really was in vain? 5So again I ask, does God give you his Spirit and work miracles among you by the works of the law, or by your believing what you heard? 6So also Abraham "believed God, and it was credited to him as righteousness."*h*

7Understand, then, that those who have faith are children of Abraham. 8Scripture foresaw that God would justify the Gentiles by faith, and announced the gospel in advance to Abraham: "All nations will be blessed through you."*i* 9So those who rely on faith are blessed along with Abraham, the man of faith.

10For all who rely on the works of the law are under a curse, as it is written: "Cursed is everyone who does not continue to do everything written in the Book of the Law."*j* 11Clearly no one who relies on the law is justified before God, because "the righteous will live by faith."*k* 12The law is

---

a 7 That is, Gentiles   *b 7* That is, Jews; also in verses 8 and 9   *c 9* That is, Peter; also in verses 11 and 14   *d 16* Or *but through the faithfulness of . . . justified on the basis of the faithfulness of*   *e 21* Some interpreters end the quotation after verse 14.   *f 3* In contexts like this, the Greek word for *flesh (sarx)* refers to the sinful state of human beings, often presented as a power in opposition to the Spirit.   *g 4* Or *suffered*   *h 6* Gen. 15:6   *i 8* Gen. 12:3; 18:18; 22:18   *j 10* Deut. 27:26   *k 11* Hab. 2:4

not based on faith; on the contrary, it says, "The person who does these things will live by them."[a] [13]Christ redeemed us from the curse of the law by becoming a curse for us, for it is written: "Cursed is everyone who is hung on a pole."[b] [14]He redeemed us in order that the blessing given to Abraham might come to the Gentiles through Christ Jesus, so that by faith we might receive the promise of the Spirit.

The Law and the Promise

[15]Brothers and sisters, let me take an example from everyday life. Just as no one can set aside or add to a human covenant that has been duly established, so it is in this case. [16]The promises were spoken to Abraham and to his seed. Scripture does not say "and to seeds," meaning many people, but "and to your seed,"[c] meaning one person, who is Christ. [17]What I mean is this: The law, introduced 430 years later, does not set aside the covenant previously established by God and thus do away with the promise. [18]For if the inheritance depends on the law, then it no longer depends on the promise; but God in his grace gave it to Abraham through a promise.

[19]Why, then, was the law given at all? It was added because of transgressions until the Seed to whom the promise referred had come. The law was given through angels and entrusted to a mediator. [20]A mediator, however, implies more than one party; but God is one.

[21]Is the law, therefore, opposed to the promises of God? Absolutely not! For if a law had been given that could impart life, then righteousness would certainly have come by the law. [22]But Scripture has locked up everything under the control of sin, so that what was promised, being given through faith in Jesus Christ, might be given to those who believe.

Children of God

[23]Before the coming of this faith,[d] we were held in custody under the law, locked up until the faith that was to come would be revealed. [24]So the law was our guardian until Christ came that we might be justified by faith. [25]Now that this faith has come, we are no longer under a guardian.

[26]So in Christ Jesus you are all children of God through faith, [27]for all of you who were baptized into Christ have clothed yourselves with Christ. [28]There is neither Jew nor Gentile, neither slave nor free, nor is there male and female, for you are all one in Christ Jesus. [29]If you belong to Christ, then you are Abraham's seed, and heirs according to the promise.

4 What I am saying is that as long as an heir is underage, he is no different from a slave, although he owns the whole estate. [2]The heir is subject to guardians and trustees until the time set by his father. [3]So also, when we were underage, we were in slavery under the elemental spiritual forces[e] of the world. [4]But when the set time had fully come, God sent his Son, born of a woman, born under the law, [5]to redeem those under the law, that we might receive adoption to sonship.[f] [6]Because you are his sons, God sent the Spirit of his Son into our hearts, the Spirit who calls out, "Abba,[g] Father." [7]So you are no longer a slave, but God's child; and since you are his child, God has made you also an heir.

Paul's Concern for the Galatians

[8]Formerly, when you did not know God, you were slaves to those who by nature are not gods. [9]But now that you know God — or rather are known by God — how is it that you are turning back to those weak and miserable forces[h]? Do you wish to be enslaved by them all over again? [10]You are observing special days and months and

---

[a] 12 Lev. 18:5   [b] 13 Deut. 21:23   [c] 16 Gen. 12:7; 13:15; 24:7   [d] 22,23 Or through the faithfulness of Jesus... [23]Before faith came   [e] 3 Or under the basic principles   [f] 5 The Greek word for adoption to sonship is a legal term referring to the full legal standing of an adopted male heir in Roman culture.   [g] 6 Aramaic for Father   [h] 9 Or principles

seasons and years! ¹¹I fear for you, that somehow I have wasted my efforts on you.

¹²I plead with you, brothers and sisters, become like me, for I became like you. You did me no wrong. ¹³As you know, it was because of an illness that I first preached the gospel to you, ¹⁴and even though my illness was a trial to you, you did not treat me with contempt or scorn. Instead, you welcomed me as if I were an angel of God, as if I were Christ Jesus himself. ¹⁵Where, then, is your blessing of me now? I can testify that, if you could have done so, you would have torn out your eyes and given them to me. ¹⁶Have I now become your enemy by telling you the truth?

¹⁷Those people are zealous to win you over, but for no good. What they want is to alienate you from us, so that you may have zeal for them. ¹⁸It is fine to be zealous, provided the purpose is good, and to be so always, not just when I am with you. ¹⁹My dear children, for whom I am again in the pains of childbirth until Christ is formed in you, ²⁰how I wish I could be with you now and change my tone, because I am perplexed about you!

Hagar and Sarah

²¹Tell me, you who want to be under the law, are you not aware of what the law says? ²²For it is written that Abraham had two sons, one by the slave woman and the other by the free woman. ²³His son by the slave woman was born according to the flesh, but his son by the free woman was born as the result of a divine promise.

²⁴These things are being taken figuratively: The women represent two covenants. One covenant is from Mount Sinai and bears children who are to be slaves: This is Hagar. ²⁵Now Hagar stands for Mount Sinai in Arabia and corresponds to the present city of Jerusalem, because she is in slavery with her children. ²⁶But the Jerusalem that is above is free, and she is our mother. ²⁷For it is written:

"Be glad, barren woman,
    you who never bore a child;
shout for joy and cry aloud,
    you who were never in labor;
because more are the children of the
        desolate woman
    than of her who has a husband."ᵃ

²⁸Now you, brothers and sisters, like Isaac, are children of promise. ²⁹At that time the son born according to the flesh persecuted the son born by the power of the Spirit. It is the same now. ³⁰But what does Scripture say? "Get rid of the slave woman and her son, for the slave woman's son will never share in the inheritance with the free woman's son."ᵇ ³¹Therefore, brothers and sisters, we are not children of the slave woman, but of the free woman.

Freedom in Christ

5 It is for freedom that Christ has set us free. Stand firm, then, and do not let yourselves be burdened again by a yoke of slavery.

²Mark my words! I, Paul, tell you that if you let yourselves be circumcised, Christ will be of no value to you at all. ³Again I declare to every man who lets himself be circumcised that he is obligated to obey the whole law. ⁴You who are trying to be justified by the law have been alienated from Christ; you have fallen away from grace. ⁵For through the Spirit we eagerly await by faith the righteousness for which we hope. ⁶For in Christ Jesus neither circumcision nor uncircumcision has any value. The only thing that counts is faith expressing itself through love.

⁷You were running a good race. Who cut in on you to keep you from obeying the truth? ⁸That kind of persuasion does not come from the one who calls you. ⁹"A little yeast works through the whole batch of dough." ¹⁰I am confident in the Lord that you will take no other view. The one who is throwing you into confusion, whoever that may be, will have to pay the penalty.

ᵃ 27 Isaiah 54:1   ᵇ 30 Gen. 21:10

¹¹Brothers and sisters, if I am still preaching circumcision, why am I still being persecuted? In that case the offense of the cross has been abolished. ¹²As for those agitators, I wish they would go the whole way and emasculate themselves!

Life by the Spirit

¹³You, my brothers and sisters, were called to be free. But do not use your freedom to indulge the flesh*ᵃ*; rather, serve one another humbly in love. ¹⁴For the entire law is fulfilled in keeping this one command: "Love your neighbor as yourself."*ᵇ* ¹⁵If you bite and devour each other, watch out or you will be destroyed by each other.

¹⁶So I say, walk by the Spirit, and you will not gratify the desires of the flesh. ¹⁷For the flesh desires what is contrary to the Spirit, and the Spirit what is contrary to the flesh. They are in conflict with each other, so that you are not to do whatever*ᶜ* you want. ¹⁸But if you are led by the Spirit, you are not under the law.

ᵃ 13 In contexts like this, the Greek word for *flesh* (*sarx*) refers to the sinful state of human beings, often presented as a power in opposition to the Spirit; also in verses 16, 17, 19 and 24; and in 6:8.   *ᵇ 14* Lev. 19:18   *ᶜ 17* Or *you do not do what*

YES LESSON [*Principle Eight*]

This is the first page of the YES lesson.

For a discussion of Principles One through Eight and a listing of their related lessons, go to pages xvii – xliv.

Brothers and sisters, if someone is caught in a sin, you who live by the Spirit should restore that person gently. But watch yourselves, or you also may be tempted. Carry each other's burdens, and in this way you will fulfill the law of Christ.

GALATIANS 6:1–2

Principle Eight calls for us to yield ourselves to God to be used by him to bring this good news to others, both through our example and through our words. This principle recycles our pain by allowing God's fire and light to shine on it, to melt down our old hurts, hang-ups and habits so we can be used again in a positive way. Our lives can be recycled to show others how we've worked the principles and steps, with Jesus' healing, and how we've come through the darkness of our pain into Christ's glorious freedom and light.

Society tells us that pain is useless. In fact, some people believe that people in pain are useless. At Celebrate Recovery, we know that pain has great value, as do the people who experience it. So, while the world says no, Principle Eight shouts a resounding YES.

The *Y* in YES is Principle Eight itself: YIELD MYSELF TO GOD. To truly practice this principle, we have to give God the latitude he needs to use us as he sees fit. We do that by presenting everything we have — our time, talents and treasures — to him. We hold loosely everything we call our own, recognizing that all of it comes from his hand. When we've yielded ourselves to him, God can use us as his instruments to carry the message to others. Only then can we put Galatians 6:1–2 into practice.

The next letter in YES is *E*. Go to 1 Timothy 1:5 (page 1502).

¹⁹The acts of the flesh are obvious: sexual immorality, impurity and debauchery; ²⁰idolatry and witchcraft; hatred, discord, jealousy, fits of rage, selfish ambition, dissensions, factions ²¹and envy; drunkenness, orgies, and the like. I warn you, as I did before, that those who live like this will not inherit the kingdom of God.

²²But the fruit of the Spirit is love, joy, peace, forbearance, kindness, goodness, faithfulness, ²³gentleness and self-control. Against such things there is no law. ²⁴Those who belong to Christ Jesus have crucified the flesh with its passions and desires. ²⁵Since we live by the Spirit, let us keep in step with the Spirit. ²⁶Let us not become conceited, provoking and envying each other.

Doing Good to All

6 Brothers and sisters, if someone is caught in a sin, you who live by the Spirit should restore that person gently. But watch yourselves, or you also may be tempted. ²Carry each other's burdens, and in this way you will fulfill the law of Christ. ³If anyone thinks they are something when they are not, they deceive themselves. ⁴Each one should test their own actions. Then they can take pride in themselves alone, without comparing themselves to someone else, ⁵for each one should carry their own load. ⁶Nevertheless, the one who receives instruction in the word should share all good things with their instructor.

⁷Do not be deceived: God cannot be mocked. A man reaps what he sows. ⁸Whoever sows to please their flesh, from the flesh will reap destruction; whoever sows to please the Spirit, from the Spirit will reap eternal life. ⁹Let us not become weary in doing good, for at the proper time we will reap a harvest if we do not give up. ¹⁰Therefore, as we have opportunity, let us do good to all people, especially to those who belong to the family of believers.

Not Circumcision but the New Creation

¹¹See what large letters I use as I write to you with my own hand!

¹²Those who want to impress people by means of the flesh are trying to compel you to be circumcised. The only reason they do this is to avoid being persecuted for the cross of Christ. ¹³Not even those who are circumcised keep the law, yet they want you to be circumcised that they may boast about your circumcision in the flesh. ¹⁴May I never boast except in the cross of our Lord Jesus Christ, through which[a] the world has been crucified to me, and I to the world. ¹⁵Neither circumcision nor uncircumcision means anything; what counts is the new creation. ¹⁶Peace and mercy to all who follow this rule—to[b] the Israel of God.

¹⁷From now on, let no one cause me trouble, for I bear on my body the marks of Jesus.

¹⁸The grace of our Lord Jesus Christ be with your spirit, brothers and sisters. Amen.

---

a 14 Or *whom*   *b 16* Or *rule and to*

Ephesians

THEME: Paul sought to explain that the church, as the people of God, is both the goal and the instrument of achieving God's purpose of bringing "unity to all things in heaven and on earth under Christ" (Ephesians 1:10).

AUTHOR: Ephesians was written by the apostle Paul.

DATE OF WRITING: The letter was probably written between AD 60 and 62, during Paul's imprisonment in Rome.

ENCOURAGEMENT FROM EPHESIANS: "Because of his great love for us, God, who is rich in mercy, made us alive with Christ even when we were dead in transgressions — it is by grace you have been saved" (Ephesians 2:4 – 5).

CHALLENGE FROM EPHESIANS: "You were once darkness, but now you are light in the Lord. Live as children of light . . . and find out what pleases the Lord. Have nothing to do with the fruitless deeds of darkness, but rather expose them. It is shameful even to mention what the disobedient do in secret" (Ephesians 5:8,10 – 12).

REFLECTION FROM EPHESIANS: "Our struggle is not against flesh and blood, but against the rulers, against the authorities, against the powers of this dark world and against the spiritual forces of evil in the heavenly realms" (Ephesians 6:12).

At a Glance

Once we've been set free from our hurts, hang-ups and habits by accepting Jesus' gift of grace, how are we to live? Now that we've established some distance between ourselves and our old ways, can we experiment with them again and this time control them? Not according to the book of Ephesians.

In this letter Paul warns the Christians in Ephesus: Now that you've seen the light, be careful to avoid participating in the darkness. We've been made new in Christ, freed because of Jesus' sacrifice. Now it's time to act like it. We need to be different from the rest of the world; our old ways need to go.

The book of Ephesians is a gentle reminder, a redirection from a trusted friend. Like a sponsor or an accountability partner pointing out areas of our lives that need attention and activities that don't fit with our new life of freedom, Paul shows that our walk needs to match our talk.

Recovery Themes in Ephesians

1 Paul, an apostle of Christ Jesus by the will of God,

To God's holy people in Ephesus,[a] the faithful in Christ Jesus:

²Grace and peace to you from God our Father and the Lord Jesus Christ.

Praise for Spiritual Blessings in Christ

³Praise be to the God and Father of our

---

a 1 Some early manuscripts do not have *in Ephesus.*

Lord Jesus Christ, who has blessed us in the heavenly realms with every spiritual blessing in Christ. 4For he chose us in him before the creation of the world to be holy and blameless in his sight. In love 5he*a* predestined us for adoption to sonship*b* through Jesus Christ, in accordance with his pleasure and will — 6to the praise of his glorious grace, which he has freely given us in the One he loves. 7In him we have redemption through his blood, the forgiveness of sins, in accordance with the riches of God's grace 8that he lavished on us. With all wisdom and understanding, 9he*c* made known to us the mystery of his will according to his good pleasure, which he purposed in Christ, 10to be put into effect when the times reach their fulfillment — to bring unity to all things in heaven and on earth under Christ.

11In him we were also chosen,*d* having been predestined according to the plan of

---

a 4,5 Or *sight in love. 5He*   *b* 5 The Greek word for *adoption to sonship* is a legal term referring to the full legal standing of an adopted male heir in Roman culture.   *c* 8,9 Or *us with all wisdom and understanding. 9And he*
d 11 Or *were made heirs*

GRACE LESSON [*Principle Six*]

For the previous entry in the GRACE lesson, go to Colossians 3:13 (page 1488).

For a discussion of Principles One through Eight and a listing of their related lessons, go to pages xvii – xliv.

In him we have redemption through his blood, the forgiveness of sins, in accordance with the riches of God's grace.

EPHESIANS 1:7

Principle Six calls for us to evaluate all our relationships and to offer FORGIVENESS to those who have hurt us and make amends for harm we've done to others, except when doing so would injure them or others. We need to be willing to admit our part in our relationships that have been broken or damaged.

As we grow as Christians and move through our recovery process, we want to follow the guidance and direction of Jesus Christ. As we get to know him better, we want to model his teachings and his ways — to become more like him. If we're going to implement Principle Six to the best of our abilities, we need to learn to model God's GRACE.

The *C* in GRACE stands for Christ PAID THE PRICE. Ephesians 1:7 informs us that Jesus died on the cross, bearing the punishment we deserve, so that we can find forgiveness for all our sins. This verse doesn't say that Christ died for "some" of our sins or for "just the big ones." No, Christ died for all of our sins! He paid the debt that was due to a just God, sacrificing himself for us so that we might be with him forever.

When we accept Christ's finished work on the cross, we're remade; we become, in a spiritual sense, a new creation. We can then rely on God's strength and power to enable us to forgive those who have hurt us. We can set aside our selfishness and speak the truth in love. We can focus only on our part in making amends.

The last letter in GRACE is *E*. Go to 2 Thessalonians 2:16 – 17 (page 1499).

him who works out everything in conformity with the purpose of his will, ¹²in order that we, who were the first to put our hope in Christ, might be for the praise of his glory. ¹³And you also were included in Christ when you heard the message of truth, the gospel of your salvation. When you believed, you were marked in him with a seal, the promised Holy Spirit, ¹⁴who is a deposit guaranteeing our inheritance until the redemption of those who are God's possession — to the praise of his glory.

Thanksgiving and Prayer

¹⁵For this reason, ever since I heard about your faith in the Lord Jesus and your love for all God's people, ¹⁶I have not stopped giving thanks for you, remembering you in my prayers. ¹⁷I keep asking that the God of our Lord Jesus Christ, the glorious Father, may give you the Spirit^a of wisdom and revelation, so that you may know him better. ¹⁸I pray that the eyes of your heart may be enlightened in order that you may know the hope to which he has called you, the riches of his glorious inheritance in his holy people, ¹⁹and his incomparably great power for us who believe. That power is the same as the mighty strength ²⁰he exerted when he raised Christ from the dead and seated him at his right hand in the heavenly realms, ²¹far above all rule and authority, power and dominion, and every name that is invoked, not only in the present age but also in the one to come. ²²And God placed all things under his feet and appointed him to be head over everything for the church, ²³which is his body, the fullness of him who fills everything in every way.

Made Alive in Christ

2 As for you, you were dead in your transgressions and sins, ²in which you used to live when you followed the ways of this world and of the ruler of the kingdom of the air, the spirit who is now at work in those who are disobedient. ³All of us also lived among them at one time, gratifying the cravings of our flesh^b and following its desires and thoughts. Like the rest, we were by nature deserving of wrath. ⁴But because of his great love for us, God, who is rich in mercy, ⁵made us alive with Christ even when we were dead in transgressions — it is by grace you have been saved. ⁶And God raised us up with Christ and seated us with him in the heavenly realms in Christ Jesus, ⁷in order that in the coming ages he might show the incomparable riches of his grace, expressed in his kindness to us in Christ Jesus. ⁸For it is by grace you have been saved, through faith — and this is not from yourselves, it is the gift of God — ⁹not by works, so that no one can boast. ¹⁰For we are God's handiwork, created in Christ Jesus to do good works, which God prepared in advance for us to do.

Jew and Gentile Reconciled Through Christ

¹¹Therefore, remember that formerly you who are Gentiles by birth and called "uncircumcised" by those who call themselves "the circumcision" (which is done in the body by human hands) — ¹²remember that at that time you were separate from Christ, excluded from citizenship in Israel and foreigners to the covenants of the promise, without hope and without God in the world. ¹³But now in Christ Jesus you who once were far away have been brought near by the blood of Christ.

¹⁴For he himself is our peace, who has made the two groups one and has destroyed the barrier, the dividing wall of hostility, ¹⁵by setting aside in his flesh the law with its commands and regulations. His purpose was to create in himself one new humanity out of the two, thus making peace, ¹⁶and in one body to reconcile both of them to God through the cross, by

---

^{a} 17 Or *a spirit* ^{b} 3 In contexts like this, the Greek word for *flesh* (*sarx*) refers to the sinful state of human beings, often presented as a power in opposition to the Spirit.

which he put to death their hostility. ¹⁷He came and preached peace to you who were far away and peace to those who were near. ¹⁸For through him we both have access to the Father by one Spirit.

¹⁹Consequently, you are no longer foreigners and strangers, but fellow citizens with God's people and also members of his household, ²⁰built on the foundation of the apostles and prophets, with Christ Jesus himself as the chief cornerstone. ²¹In him the whole building is joined together and rises to become a holy temple in the Lord.

²²And in him you too are being built together to become a dwelling in which God lives by his Spirit.

God's Marvelous Plan for the Gentiles

3 For this reason I, Paul, the prisoner of Christ Jesus for the sake of you Gentiles —

²Surely you have heard about the administration of God's grace that was given to me for you, ³that is, the mystery made known to me by revelation, as I have already written briefly. ⁴In reading this,

---

GRACE LESSON [*Principle Six*]

For the previous entry in the GRACE lesson, go to Romans 3:23 – 24 (page 1392).

For a discussion of Principles One through Eight and a listing of their related lessons, go to pages xvii – xliv.

It is by grace you have been saved, through faith — and this not from yourselves, it is the gift of God — not by works, so that no one can boast.

EPHESIANS 2:8–9

Principle Six calls for us to evaluate all our relationships and to offer FORGIVENESS to those who have hurt us and make amends for harm we've done to others, except when doing so would injure them or others. We need to be willing to admit our part in our relationships that have been broken or damaged.

As we grow as Christians and move through our recovery process, we want to follow the guidance and direction of Jesus Christ. As we get to know him better, we want to model his teachings and his ways — to become more like him. If we're going to implement Principle Six to the best of our abilities, we need to learn to model God's GRACE.

How do we receive God's gift of grace? The *R* in GRACE stands for RECEIVED BY OUR FAITH. Ephesians 2:8 – 9 makes it clear that no matter how hard we may work, we can't earn our way into heaven. Only by professing our faith in Jesus Christ as our Savior and Lord can we experience his grace and inherit eternal life.

We tend to focus on what we *do*, but God is more interested in who we *are*. Romans 5:1 – 2 assures us that "since we have been justified through faith, we have peace with God through our Lord Jesus Christ, through whom we have gained access by faith into this grace in which we now stand. And we boast in the hope of the glory of God." Our beliefs and values are discerned by others through our actions. And it's through our faith in Christ that we can find the strength and courage we need to take the action Principle Six requires: making amends and offering forgiveness.

The next letter in GRACE is *A*. Go to Colossians 3:13 (page 1488).

then, you will be able to understand my insight into the mystery of Christ, 5which was not made known to people in other generations as it has now been revealed by the Spirit to God's holy apostles and prophets. 6This mystery is that through the gospel the Gentiles are heirs together with Israel, members together of one body, and sharers together in the promise in Christ Jesus.

7I became a servant of this gospel by the gift of God's grace given me through the working of his power. 8Although I am less than the least of all the Lord's people, this grace was given me: to preach to the Gentiles the boundless riches of Christ, 9and to make plain to everyone the administration of this mystery, which for ages past was kept hidden in God, who created all things. 10His intent was that now, through the church, the manifold wisdom of God should be made known to the rulers and authorities in the heavenly realms, 11according to his eternal purpose that he accomplished in Christ Jesus our Lord. 12In him and through faith in him we may approach God with freedom and confidence. 13I ask you, therefore, not to be discouraged because of my sufferings for you, which are your glory.

A Prayer for the Ephesians

14For this reason I kneel before the Father, 15from whom every family*a* in heaven and on earth derives its name. 16I pray that out of his glorious riches he may strengthen you with power through his Spirit in your inner being, 17so that Christ may dwell in your hearts through faith. And I pray that you, being rooted and established in love, 18may have power, together with all the Lord's holy people, to grasp how wide and long and high and deep is the love of Christ, 19and to know this love that surpasses knowledge — that you may be filled to the measure of all the fullness of God.

20Now to him who is able to do immeasurably more than all we ask or imagine, according to his power that is at work within us, 21to him be glory in the church and in Christ Jesus throughout all generations, for ever and ever! Amen.

Unity and Maturity in the Body of Christ

4 As a prisoner for the Lord, then, I urge you to live a life worthy of the calling you have received. 2Be completely humble and gentle; be patient, bearing with one another in love. 3Make every effort to keep the unity of the Spirit through the bond of peace. 4There is one body and one Spirit, just as you were called to one hope when you were called; 5one Lord, one faith, one baptism; 6one God and Father of all, who is over all and through all and in all.

7But to each one of us grace has been given as Christ apportioned it. 8This is why it*b* says:

> "When he ascended on high,
>   he took many captives
>   and gave gifts to his people."*c*

9(What does "he ascended" mean except that he also descended to the lower, earthly regions*d*? 10He who descended is the very one who ascended higher than all the heavens, in order to fill the whole universe.) 11So Christ himself gave the apostles, the prophets, the evangelists, the pastors and teachers, 12to equip his people for works of service, so that the body of Christ may be built up 13until we all reach unity in the faith and in the knowledge of the Son of God and become mature, attaining to the whole measure of the fullness of Christ.

14Then we will no longer be infants, tossed back and forth by the waves, and blown here and there by every wind of teaching and by the cunning and craftiness of people in their deceitful scheming.

---

a 15 The Greek for *family* (*patria*) is derived from the Greek for *father* (*pater*).   *b 8* Or *God*   *c 8* Psalm 68:18
d 9 Or *the depths of the earth*

15Instead, speaking the truth in love, we will grow to become in every respect the mature body of him who is the head, that is, Christ. 16From him the whole body, joined and held together by every supporting ligament, grows and builds itself up in love, as each part does its work.

Instructions for Christian Living

17So I tell you this, and insist on it in the Lord, that you must no longer live as the Gentiles do, in the futility of their thinking. 18They are darkened in their understanding and separated from the life of God because of the ignorance that is in them due to the hardening of their hearts. 19Having lost all sensitivity, they have given themselves over to sensuality so as to indulge in every kind of impurity, and they are full of greed.

20That, however, is not the way of life you learned 21when you heard about Christ and were taught in him in accordance with the truth that is in Jesus. 22You were taught, with regard to your former way of life, to put off your old self, which is being corrupted by its deceitful desires; 23to be made new in the attitude of your minds; 24and to put on the new self, created to be like God in true righteousness and holiness.

25Therefore each of you must put off falsehood and speak truthfully to your neighbor, for we are all members of one

HOPE LESSON [Principle Two]

For the previous entry in the HOPE lesson, go to Romans 11:36 (page 1407).

For a discussion of Principles One through Eight and a listing of their related lessons, go to pages xvii – xliv.

You were taught, with regard to your former way of life,
to put off your old self, which is being corrupted by its deceitful desires;
to be made new in the attitude of your minds.

Ephesians 4:22–23

In Principle Two we earnestly believe that God exists, that we matter to him and that he has the power to help us recover. It's in this principle that we find the HOPE we need to start our recovery journey.

The next letter in HOPE is *O*, which stands for OPENNESS TO CHANGE. Sometimes we're afraid to change, even if our past was painful. We may resist change because of our fear of the unknown. Or, in our despair, we may think we don't deserve anything better than what we're currently experiencing.

Here's the good news: Hope opens the doors despair has slammed shut. Hope discovers what can be done instead of grumbling about what "can't." Throughout our lives we'll continue to encounter hurts and trials that we're powerless by ourselves to change, but with God's help we can be open enough to allow those very circumstances and situations to change us — to make us better, not bitter. Our attitudes can and must always be changing for the better, and hope allows us to do just that.

The next letter in HOPE is *P*. Go to Psalm 25:5 (page 648).

body. 26"In your anger do not sin"*a*: Do not let the sun go down while you are still angry, 27and do not give the devil a foothold. 28Anyone who has been stealing must steal no longer, but must work, doing something useful with their own hands, that they may have something to share with those in need.

29Do not let any unwholesome talk come out of your mouths, but only what is helpful for building others up according to their needs, that it may benefit those who listen. 30And do not grieve the Holy Spirit of God, with whom you were sealed for the day of redemption. 31Get rid of all bitterness, rage and anger, brawling and slander, along with every form of malice. 32Be kind and compassionate to one another, forgiving each other, just as in Christ God forgave you.

5 1Follow God's example, therefore, as dearly loved children 2and walk in the way of love, just as Christ loved us and gave himself up for us as a fragrant offering and sacrifice to God.

3But among you there must not be even a hint of sexual immorality, or of any kind of impurity, or of greed, because these are improper for God's holy people. 4Nor should there be obscenity, foolish talk or coarse joking, which are out of place, but rather thanksgiving. 5For of this you can be sure: No immoral, impure or greedy

---

a 26 Psalm 4:4 (see Septuagint)

DENIAL LESSON [*Principle One*]

For the previous entry in the DENIAL lesson, go to Genesis 3:7–8 (page 5).

For a discussion of Principles One through Eight and a listing of their related lessons, go to pages xvii–xliv.

Each of you must put off falsehood and speak truthfully to your neighbor, for we are all members of one body.

EPHESIANS 4:25

The power to change comes only through God's grace. Principle One states: "Realize I'm not God. I admit that I'm powerless to control my tendency to do the wrong thing and that my life has become unmanageable." If we admit that we're powerless, we recognize our need for a power greater than ourselves to restore us. That power is our Higher Power, the one and only true Higher Power, Jesus Christ.

In Principle One we discover that we've been in DENIAL of our hurts, hang-ups and habits. The next letter in DENIAL is *A*. Our denial not only isolates us from God but ALIENATES US FROM other human RELATIONSHIPS. Denial tells us that we're getting away with our secrets. We think that no one knows — but they do. While denial may shield us from the full force of the hurt, it also prevents us from helping ourselves or the people we love the most. We don't dare to reveal our true self to others for fear of what they'll think or say if they catch a glimpse of the real us. We're convinced that we have to protect ourselves — and our secrets — at any cost. So we isolate ourselves to minimize the risk of exposure and possible rejection by others. But at what price? The eventual loss of all our important relationships.

The last letter in DENIAL is *L*. Go to Jeremiah 30:17 (page 924).

person — such a person is an idolater — has any inheritance in the kingdom of Christ and of God.*a* 6Let no one deceive you with empty words, for because of such things God's wrath comes on those who are disobedient. 7Therefore do not be partners with them.

8For you were once darkness, but now you are light in the Lord. Live as children of light 9(for the fruit of the light consists in all goodness, righteousness and truth) 10and find out what pleases the Lord. 11Have nothing to do with the fruitless deeds of darkness, but rather expose them. 12It is shameful even to mention what the disobedient do in secret. 13But everything exposed by the light becomes visible — and everything that is illuminated becomes a light. 14This is why it is said:

> "Wake up, sleeper,
>   rise from the dead,
>   and Christ will shine on you."

15Be very careful, then, how you live — not as unwise but as wise, 16making the most of every opportunity, because the days are evil. 17Therefore do not be foolish, but understand what the Lord's will is. 18Do not get drunk on wine, which leads to debauchery. Instead, be filled with the Spirit, 19speaking to one another with psalms, hymns, and songs from the Spirit. Sing and make music from your heart to the Lord, 20always giving thanks to God

a 5 Or kingdom of the Messiah and God

POWERLESS LESSON [*Principle One*]

For the previous entry in the POWERLESS lesson, go to Ephesians 5:13 – 14 (page 1474).

For a discussion of Principles One through Eight and a listing of their related lessons, go to pages xvii – xliv.

"In your anger do not sin": Do not let the sun go down while you are still angry, and do not give the devil a foothold.

EPHESIANS 4:26–27

The power to change comes only through God's grace. Principle One states: "Realize I'm not God. I admit that I'm powerless to control my tendency to do the wrong thing and that my life has become unmanageable." If we admit that we're powerless, we recognize our need for a power greater than ourselves to restore us. That power is our Higher Power, the one and only true Higher Power, Jesus Christ.

In Principle One we discover that we're POWERLESS to control our own lives and that our lives have become unmanageable. The *R* in POWERLESS stands for RESENTMENT. If our resentment is suppressed and allowed to fester, it can spread like emotional gangrene. Paul tells us in Ephesians 4:26 – 27 how to properly handle our anger and resentment.

As we continue to work the principles, we'll come to understand that in letting go of our resentment by offering our forgiveness to those who have hurt us, we're not just freeing the person who has harmed us; we're freeing ourselves!

The next letter in POWERLESS is *L*. Go to Hebrews 13:1 – 2 (page 1536).

the Father for everything, in the name of our Lord Jesus Christ.

Instructions for Christian Households

21 Submit to one another out of reverence for Christ.

22 Wives, submit yourselves to your own husbands as you do to the Lord. 23 For the husband is the head of the wife as Christ is the head of the church, his body, of which he is the Savior. 24 Now as the church submits to Christ, so also wives should submit to their husbands in everything.

25 Husbands, love your wives, just as Christ loved the church and gave himself up for her 26 to make her holy, cleansing[a] her by the washing with water through the word, 27 and to present her to himself as a radiant church, without stain or wrinkle or any other blemish, but holy and blameless. 28 In this same way, husbands ought to love their wives as their own bodies. He who loves his wife loves himself. 29 After all, no one ever hated their own body, but they feed and care for their body, just as Christ does the church — 30 for we are members of his body. 31 "For this reason a man will leave his father and mother and be united to his wife, and the two will become one flesh."[b] 32 This is a profound mystery — but I am talking about Christ and the church. 33 However, each one of you also must love his wife as he loves himself, and the wife must respect her husband.

---

[a] 26 Or *having cleansed*   [b] 31 Gen. 2:24

INVENTORY LESSON [*Principle Four*]

This is the first page of the INVENTORY lesson.

For a discussion of Principles One through Eight and a listing of their related lessons, go to pages xvii – xliv.

Get rid of all bitterness, rage and anger, brawling and slander,
along with every form of malice.

EPHESIANS 4:31

Principle Four begins the process of "coming clean." It's here that we openly examine and confess our faults to ourselves, to God and to someone else we trust. In the first part of Principle Four we openly examine our lives. As we get ready to write out our inventories in Principle Four, we divide them into five specific sections.

The first area we write about is labeled THE PERSON. We begin by listing the persons or objects we resent or fear. We go as far back as we can recall. Remember that resentment is mostly unexpressed anger and fear. The good news is that as we work our way completely through Principle Four, we'll see that our feelings of resentment fade as the light of our faith in Jesus Christ is allowed to shine on them.

It is important to list all the people and things we're holding resentment against. Our goal is to accomplish what Ephesians 4:31 instructs us to do. The sins we discover are from our old self. We need to list them in our inventory so we can eventually release them and break the hold they've had on us.

In the second section we address THE CAUSE. Go to Isaiah 41:10 (page 852).

6 Children, obey your parents in the Lord, for this is right. [2]"Honor your father and mother" — which is the first commandment with a promise — [3]"so that it may go well with you and that you may enjoy long life on the earth."[a]

[4]Fathers,[b] do not exasperate your children; instead, bring them up in the training and instruction of the Lord.

[5]Slaves, obey your earthly masters with respect and fear, and with sincerity of heart, just as you would obey Christ. [6]Obey them not only to win their favor when their eye is on you, but as slaves of Christ, doing

---

[a] 3 Deut. 5:16   [b] 4 Or *Parents*

SPIRITUAL INVENTORY LESSON [*Principle Four*]

For the previous entry in the SPIRITUAL INVENTORY lesson, go to Matthew 6:33 (page 1134).

For a discussion of Principles One through Eight and a listing of their related lessons, go to pages xvii – xliv.

Get rid of all bitterness, rage and anger, brawling and slander, along with every form of malice.

EPHESIANS 4:31

Principle Four begins the process of "coming clean." It's here that we openly examine and confess our faults to ourselves, to God and to someone else we trust. In the first part of Principle Four we openly examine our lives.

As part of completing Principle Four, we do a SPIRITUAL INVENTORY. We look at eight critical areas of our lives. The third area is OUR ATTITUDE. A reality for which we can all be grateful is pointed out in 1 Corinthians 15:57: "Thanks be to God! He gives us the victory through our Lord Jesus Christ."

We need to ask the following questions regarding our attitude:

1. Do we try to have an "attitude of gratitude," or do we find ourselves frequently complaining about our circumstances?

2. In what areas of our lives are we ungrateful?

3. Have we gotten angry and blown up at other people?

4. Have we been sarcastic?

5. What in our past is still causing us fear or anxiety?

The last of these questions is a big one. Our fears can prevent us from completing our spiritual inventory and can stall our recovery. Our fear imprisons us, but our faith liberates us. Fear paralyzes, while faith empowers. Fear disheartens; faith encourages. Fear sickens; faith heals. Faith in Jesus Christ will allow us to face our past fears, and with that faith we can be freed of fear's chains. First John 4:18 points out that "there is no fear in love. But perfect love drives out fear, because fear has to do with punishment. The one who fears is not made perfect in love."

The fourth area of our Spiritual Inventory is OUR INTEGRITY. Go to Colossians 3:9 (page 1487).

MY NAME IS
CHILD OF LIGHT

EPHESIANS 4:17 — 5:20

There are numerous secular recovery programs that help many people to reform their lives. But only Jesus Christ gives us an entirely new life. That new life is one of total transformation from darkness into "light in the Lord" (Ephesians 5:8). We must make sure we don't stop short of this goal.

When is a thief no longer a thief? When he stops stealing? Society, the world and our culture might settle for that response. But Paul provides a higher standard. A thief is no longer a thief when he not only has stopped stealing but also is seeking hard work as a means of sharing with those in need (see 4:28).

Paul offers many similar contrasts in this passage. Most of us can probably find our "former way of life" and our "old self" (4:22) in his writings. However, running down the road to recovery while looking over our shoulder results in a lot of unnecessary bruises. So as we advance down the road of recovery, it's crucial that we also identify our "new self."

Celebrate Recovery is forward-looking. We entered recovery in the first place because we've experienced the damaging dangers of the darkness (see 4:17–19). Every single child of the light was, after all, like ourselves, "once darkness" (5:8). We're discovering as we work the principles that we can "put off [our] old self . . . to be made new . . . created to be like God in true righteousness and holiness" (4:22–24). Celebrate Recovery guides us through the process of becoming an accurate reflection of God. Our goal is to "live as children of light . . . and find out what pleases the Lord" (5:8,10).

My Name Is Leigh

I'M A BELIEVER WHO STRUGGLES WITH SEXUAL ABUSE AND SEXUAL ADDICTION

Please read Paul's memorable words about being a child of light in
Ephesians 4:17 — 5:20.

I was the only child of an emotionally distant father and a codependent mother. My father was a compulsive workaholic and a functional alcoholic. Although he was an excellent provider, his lack of nurturing left me vulnerable to unhealthful influences.

I learned to use food as a means of comfort. But as I started to mature, I changed from a chubby adolescent to a willowy teen nicknamed "bones." I firmly believed that I had finally arrived. I would now be noticed, valued and loved by my father. Not surprisingly, this was not to be the case.

When I was 14, I met "Coach," a charismatic, attractive older man who took a special interest in me. Craving the attention, love and acceptance of a father figure, I was drawn to him. He would stay after basketball practice and arrange private meetings with me behind closed doors to discuss my potential. The sexual abuse, as I now understand it, seemed so exciting and natural. For the first time in my life, I felt worthy of love. Eventually I learned that this wasn't the first such "episode" in Coach's career. I was completely devastated. The hole inside my heart seemed beyond repair. Shortly after Coach's exodus from my life, I had random sexual encounters with several older men, accompanied by liberal amounts of alcohol to make the sex more palatable.

At 21, following a failed marriage, I found myself unemployed and in need of money for rent, food — and drugs. A friend suggested I try exotic dancing. If marijuana is a gateway drug, for me exotic dancing was a gateway behavior leading to prostitution. Feeling that I had no value, I yielded control of my life to a pimp named "KJ" on the streets of Los Angeles. I was branded with a tattoo on my shoulder, marked as his personal property. I was dropped off on the street at 8:00 a.m. and not allowed to return until 3:00 or 4:00 the following morning — and then only if I'd made him enough money.

I was arrested several times, regularly beaten by KJ, raped on numerous occasions and at one point I was abducted and raped by four males who held a gun and a knife to my head.

After the abduction I knew I had to escape, even though I knew that KJ would try to kill both me and my family if I were to succeed. One morning, after receiving yet another blow to my face, I knew the day had come. The Lord provided an "angel" in the form of an undercover police officer who led me to safety in exchange for information about KJ. The abuse left ugly scars, both visible and invisible. I lived in a continual state of terror, perpetually looking over my shoulder.

Trapped in a vicious cycle of bingeing, purging and drug abuse, I turned to the lesbian community for a sense of belonging and acceptance, but I still felt empty. I rotated back and forth between homosexuality and heterosexuality for years, finally remarrying in the belief that marriage would solve my problems. But divorce was the outcome. Denouncing Christianity, I reluctantly embraced atheism as the only logical option open to me. How, after all, could I continue in the lifestyle I was living and still believe in God?

At this point I determined that there was only one way out: suicide. I had a plan. But God had a different one. Someone gave me a book titled *The Purpose Driven Life*. I have no idea why I decided to open it; perhaps there was a glimmer of hope left. While reading, I asked Jesus Christ into my heart as my Savior and Lord. I was finally able to admit my powerlessness and recognize that my life had become unmanageable. My mother's best friend told me about Celebrate Recovery.

Through my involvement in the program my life has been completely transformed. I've truly learned what it means to live as a child of light and to walk in the light (see 1 John 1:7). The shame and guilt I used to feel about my past have been replaced with a positive self-image that is based on the true love I've been consistently receiving from others. God has shown me both how to forgive and how to be forgiven. I'm no longer willing to function in constant apprehension; instead, I live in the courage of Christ. God has also taken away my compulsive need for approval, as well as my fascination with the "forbidden." As an incredible bonus, he has given me a new husband who is truly my soul mate. I'm walking proof of God's restorative power. In the words of the apostle Peter, "You are a chosen people, a royal priesthood, a holy nation, God's special possession, that you may declare the praises of him who called you out of darkness into his wonderful light" (1 Peter 2:9). And the apostle John echoes those words, saying, "If we walk in the light, as he is in the light, we have fellowship with one another, and the blood of Jesus, his Son, purifies us from all sin" (1 John 1:7).

Leigh

the will of God from your heart. ⁷Serve wholeheartedly, as if you were serving the Lord, not people, ⁸because you know that the Lord will reward each one for whatever good they do, whether they are slave or free.

⁹And masters, treat your slaves in the same way. Do not threaten them, since you know that he who is both their Master and yours is in heaven, and there is no favoritism with him.

The Armor of God

¹⁰Finally, be strong in the Lord and in his mighty power. ¹¹Put on the full armor of God, so that you can take your stand against the devil's schemes. ¹²For our struggle is not against flesh and blood, but against the rulers, against the authorities, against the powers of this dark world and against the spiritual forces of evil in the heavenly realms. ¹³Therefore put on the full armor of God, so that when the day of evil comes, you may be able to stand your ground, and after you have done everything, to stand. ¹⁴Stand firm then, with the belt of truth buckled around your waist, with the breastplate of righteousness in place, ¹⁵and with your feet fitted with the readiness that comes from the gospel of peace. ¹⁶In addition to all this, take up the shield of faith, with which you can extinguish all the flaming arrows of the evil one. ¹⁷Take the helmet of salvation and

POWERLESS LESSON [*Principle One*]

For the previous entry in the POWERLESS lesson, go to Matthew 6:34 (page 1135).

For a discussion of Principles One through Eight and a listing of their related lessons, go to pages xvii–xliv.

Everything exposed by the light becomes visible — and everything that is illuminated becomes a light. This is why it is said: "Wake up, sleeper, rise from the dead, and Christ will shine on you."

Ephesians 5:13–14

The power to change comes only through God's grace. Principle One states: "Realize I'm not God. I admit that I'm powerless to control my tendency to do the wrong thing and that my life has become unmanageable." If we admit that we're powerless, we recognize our need for a power greater than ourselves to restore us. That power is our Higher Power, the one and only true Higher Power, Jesus Christ.

In Principle One we discover that we're POWERLESS to control our own lives and that our lives have become unmanageable. The *E* in POWERLESS stands for ESCAPE. Before we admitted we were powerless, we tried to hide from our hurts, hang-ups and habits by getting involved in unhealthy relationships; by abusing drugs, such as alcohol; or possibly by eating unhealthily or refusing to eat.

Trying to escape from pain drains away our precious energy. When we take this first step, however, God opens up to us *true* escape routes, legitimate "ways out" of our predicaments through access to his power and grace.

The next letter in POWERLESS is *R*. Go to Ephesians 4:26–27 (page 1468).

the sword of the Spirit, which is the word of God.

18And pray in the Spirit on all occasions with all kinds of prayers and requests. With this in mind, be alert and always keep on praying for all the Lord's people. 19Pray also for me, that whenever I speak, words may be given me so that I will fearlessly make known the mystery of the gospel, 20for which I am an ambassador in chains. Pray that I may declare it fearlessly, as I should.

Final Greetings

21Tychicus, the dear brother and faithful servant in the Lord, will tell you everything, so that you also may know how I am and what I am doing. 22I am sending him to you for this very purpose, that you may know how we are, and that he may encourage you.

23Peace to the brothers and sisters,a and love with faith from God the Father and the Lord Jesus Christ. 24Grace to all who love our Lord Jesus Christ with an undying love.b

---

a 23 The Greek word for brothers and sisters (adelphoi) refers here to believers, both men and women, as part of God's family.   b 24 Or Grace and immortality to all who love our Lord Jesus Christ.

Philippians

THEME: Paul modeled joy in the midst of suffering and guided the Philippians in their situation of persecution.

AUTHOR: Paul identified himself as the author of this letter, and the early church unanimously attributed it to him.

DATE OF WRITING: The letter to the Philippians was probably written between AD 60 and 62, during Paul's imprisonment in Rome.

ENCOURAGEMENT FROM PHILIPPIANS: "He who began a good work in you will carry it on to completion until the day of Christ Jesus" (Philippians 1:6).

CHALLENGE FROM PHILIPPIANS: "Do everything without grumbling or arguing, so that you may become blameless and pure, 'children of God without fault in a warped and crooked generation.' Then you will shine among them like stars in the sky as you hold firmly to the word of life" (Philippians 2:14 – 16).

REFLECTION FROM PHILIPPIANS: "One thing I do: Forgetting what is behind and straining toward what is ahead, I press on toward the goal to win the prize for which God has called me heavenward in Christ Jesus" (Philippians 3:13 – 14).

Paul writes to the church at Philippi to remind its members that they aren't on their own. Not only does he think of them and pray for them often, but he points out that Christ himself has never left them. God is working within them to accomplish his divine purpose.

Paul also lets them know that, although he is getting closer to attaining his own goal, he hasn't yet arrived. Recovery can be difficult and frustrating. Often in our recovery it's easy to feel that since we've been at this a while, we ought to have it all together. Our relationships should be repaired and our hurts, hang-ups and habits left behind us; we should be perfect, free from sin. In Philippians, Paul promises that though this will happen, it won't be until Christ has completed his transforming work in us.

---

1 Paul and Timothy, servants of Christ Jesus,

To all God's holy people in Christ Jesus at Philippi, together with the overseers and deacons[a]:

²Grace and peace to you from God our Father and the Lord Jesus Christ.

Thanksgiving and Prayer

³I thank my God every time I remember you. ⁴In all my prayers for all of you, I always

---

[a] 1 The word *deacons* refers here to Christians designated to serve with the overseers/elders of the church in a variety of ways; similarly in Romans 16:1 and 1 Tim. 3:8,12.

pray with joy ⁵because of your partnership in the gospel from the first day until now, ⁶being confident of this, that he who began a good work in you will carry it on to completion until the day of Christ Jesus.

⁷It is right for me to feel this way about all of you, since I have you in my heart and, whether I am in chains or defending and confirming the gospel, all of you share in God's grace with me. ⁸God can testify how I long for all of you with the affection of Christ Jesus.

⁹And this is my prayer: that your love may abound more and more in knowledge and depth of insight, ¹⁰so that you may be able to discern what is best and may be pure and blameless for the day of Christ, ¹¹filled with the fruit of righteousness that comes through Jesus Christ — to the glory and praise of God.

Paul's Chains Advance the Gospel

¹²Now I want you to know, brothers and sisters,^a that what has happened to me has actually served to advance the gospel. ¹³As a result, it has become clear throughout the

---

^a 12 The Greek word for *brothers and sisters* (*adelphoi*) refers here to believers, both men and women, as part of God's family; also in verse 14; and in 3:1, 13, 17; 4:1, 8, 21.

HOPE LESSON [*Principle Two*]

For the previous entry in the HOPE lesson, go to Psalm 25:5 (page 648).

For a discussion of Principles One through Eight and a listing of their related lessons, go to pages xvii–xliv.

He who began a good work in you will carry it on to completion until the day of Christ Jesus.

PHILIPPIANS 1:6

In Principle Two we earnestly believe that God exists, that we matter to him and that he has the power to help us recover. It's in this principle that we find the HOPE we need to start our recovery journey.

The last letter in HOPE is *E*, which stands for EXPECTATION TO CHANGE. Remember that we're only at the second principle. Don't quit before the miracle happens. With God's help the changes we've longed for are just steps away. That's what's so reassuring about Philippians 1:6. Jesus is going to be with us, walking at our sides, each step along our road to recovery. It's important to keep the following in the forefront of our minds as we proceed: Life without Christ is a hopeless end, but with him it's an endless hope.

Yes, my soul, find rest in God; my hope comes from him.

PSALM 62:5

In Principle Two we discover that the hope for which we've been searching is found in God alone. We finally dare to start hoping that, relying on God's power and grace, we can begin our recovery from our hurts, hang-ups and habits.

This is the final page of the HOPE lesson.

whole palace guard[a] and to everyone else that I am in chains for Christ. 14And because of my chains, most of the brothers and sisters have become confident in the Lord and dare all the more to proclaim the gospel without fear.

15It is true that some preach Christ out of envy and rivalry, but others out of goodwill. 16The latter do so out of love, knowing that I am put here for the defense of the gospel. 17The former preach Christ out of selfish ambition, not sincerely, supposing that they can stir up trouble for me while I am in chains. 18But what does it matter? The important thing is that in every way, whether from false motives or true, Christ is preached. And because of this I rejoice.

Yes, and I will continue to rejoice, 19for I know that through your prayers and God's provision of the Spirit of Jesus Christ what has happened to me will turn out for my deliverance.[b] 20I eagerly expect and hope that I will in no way be ashamed, but will have sufficient courage so that now as always Christ will be exalted in my body, whether by life or by death. 21For to me, to live is Christ and to die is gain. 22If I am to go on living in the body, this will mean fruitful labor for me. Yet what shall I choose? I do not know! 23I am torn between the two: I desire to depart and be with Christ, which is better by far; 24but it is more necessary for you that I remain in the body. 25Convinced of this, I know that I will remain, and I will continue with all of you for your progress and joy in the faith, 26so that through my being with you again your boasting in Christ Jesus will abound on account of me.

---

a 13 Or *whole palace*   *b 19* Or *vindication;* or *salvation*

ACTION LESSON [*Principle Three*]

For the previous entry in the ACTION lesson, go to Proverbs 3:6 (page 744).

For a discussion of Principles One through Eight and a listing of their related lessons, go to pages xvii – xliv.

He who began a good work in you will carry it on to completion until the day of Christ Jesus.

PHILIPPIANS 1:6

In Principle Three we consciously choose to commit all our lives and will to Christ's care and control. We make the decision to TURN every aspect of our lives and will over to our Higher Power, Jesus Christ. In order to turn our lives over to Christ's care and control, we need to take ACTION.

The next letter in ACTION is *I*, reminding us that IT'S ONLY THE BEGINNING. In the third principle we make the decision to accept Christ as our personal Savior. Only then can we make the commitment to seek and follow God's will. The new life that begins with this decision is followed by a lifelong process of growing as a Christian. Philippians 1:6 assures us that Christ will keep on helping us grow.

Recovery isn't a three-principle program. Principle Three is only the exciting beginning of a new life — a life we'll live in a whole new way: one day at a time.

The next letter in ACTION is *O*. Go to Matthew 6:34 (page 1136).

Life Worthy of the Gospel

27Whatever happens, conduct yourselves in a manner worthy of the gospel of Christ. Then, whether I come and see you or only hear about you in my absence, I will know that you stand firm in the one Spirit,*a* striving together as one for the faith of the gospel 28without being frightened in any way by those who oppose you. This is a sign to them that they will be destroyed, but that you will be saved — and that by God. 29For it has been granted to you on behalf of Christ not only to believe in him, but also to suffer for him, 30since you are going through the same struggle you saw I had, and now hear that I still have.

Imitating Christ's Humility

2 Therefore if you have any encouragement from being united with Christ, if any comfort from his love, if any common sharing in the Spirit, if any tenderness and compassion, 2then make my joy complete by being like-minded, having the same love, being one in spirit and of one mind. 3Do nothing out of selfish ambition or vain conceit. Rather, in humility value others above yourselves, 4not looking to your own interests but each of you to the interests of the others.

5In your relationships with one another, have the same mindset as Christ Jesus:

6Who, being in very nature*b* God,
   did not consider equality with God
      something to be used to his own
         advantage;
7rather, he made himself nothing
   by taking the very nature*c* of a servant,
   being made in human likeness.
8And being found in appearance as a man,
   he humbled himself
   by becoming obedient to death —
      even death on a cross!

---

a 27 Or *in one spirit*   *b* 6 Or *in the form of*   *c* 7 Or *the form*

VICTORY LESSON [*Principle Five*]

For the previous entry in the VICTORY lesson, go to Matthew 6:34 (page 1137).

For a discussion of Principles One through Eight and a listing of their related lessons,
go to pages xvii – xliv.

*He who began a good work in you will carry it on
to completion until the day of Christ Jesus.*

PHILIPPIANS 1:6

In Principle Five, as we voluntarily submit to every change God wants to make in our lives and humbly ask him to remove our character defects, we'll find VICTORY in our recovery.

The next letter in VICTORY is *R*, which stands for RECOVERY IS A PROCESS — one day at a time followed by another single day at a time. Once we ask God to remove our character defects, we begin a journey that will lead us to new freedom from our past. Principle Five calls us to rejoice in steady progress and improvement rather than to look for instantaneous perfection. God will keep on helping us grow in our recovery — right up to the end of our lives or the day when Christ returns.

The last letter in VICTORY is *Y*. Go to James 4:6 – 8 (page 1541).

⁹Therefore God exalted him to the
　　highest place
　and gave him the name that is above
　　every name,
¹⁰that at the name of Jesus every knee
　　should bow,
　in heaven and on earth and under
　　the earth,
¹¹and every tongue acknowledge that
　　Jesus Christ is Lord,
　to the glory of God the Father.

Do Everything Without Grumbling

¹²Therefore, my dear friends, as you have always obeyed — not only in my presence, but now much more in my absence — continue to work out your salvation with fear and trembling, ¹³for it is God who works in you to will and to act in order to fulfill his good purpose.

¹⁴Do everything without grumbling or arguing, ¹⁵so that you may become blameless and pure, "children of God without fault in a warped and crooked generation."ᵃ Then you will shine among them like stars in the sky ¹⁶as you hold firmly to the word of life. And then I will be able to boast on the day of Christ that I did not run or labor in vain. ¹⁷But even if I am being poured out like a drink offering on the sacrifice and service coming from your faith, I am glad and rejoice with all of you. ¹⁸So you too should be glad and rejoice with me.

Timothy and Epaphroditus

¹⁹I hope in the Lord Jesus to send Timothy to you soon, that I also may be cheered when I receive news about you. ²⁰I have no one else like him, who will show genuine concern for your welfare. ²¹For everyone looks out for their own interests, not those of Jesus Christ. ²²But you know that Timothy has proved himself, because as a son with his father he has served with me in the work of the gospel. ²³I hope, therefore, to send him as soon as I see how things go

with me. ²⁴And I am confident in the Lord that I myself will come soon.

²⁵But I think it is necessary to send back to you Epaphroditus, my brother, co-worker and fellow soldier, who is also your messenger, whom you sent to take care of my needs. ²⁶For he longs for all of you and is distressed because you heard he was ill. ²⁷Indeed he was ill, and almost died. But God had mercy on him, and not on him only but also on me, to spare me sorrow upon sorrow. ²⁸Therefore I am all the more eager to send him, so that when you see him again you may be glad and I may have less anxiety. ²⁹So then, welcome him in the Lord with great joy, and honor people like him, ³⁰because he almost died for the work of Christ. He risked his life to make up for the help you yourselves could not give me.

No Confidence in the Flesh

3 Further, my brothers and sisters, rejoice in the Lord! It is no trouble for me to write the same things to you again, and it is a safeguard for you. ²Watch out for those dogs, those evildoers, those mutilators of the flesh. ³For it is we who are the circumcision, we who serve God by his Spirit, who boast in Christ Jesus, and who put no confidence in the flesh — ⁴though I myself have reasons for such confidence.

If someone else thinks they have reasons to put confidence in the flesh, I have more: ⁵circumcised on the eighth day, of the people of Israel, of the tribe of Benjamin, a Hebrew of Hebrews; in regard to the law, a Pharisee; ⁶as for zeal, persecuting the church; as for righteousness based on the law, faultless.

⁷But whatever were gains to me I now consider loss for the sake of Christ. ⁸What is more, I consider everything a loss because of the surpassing worth of knowing Christ Jesus my Lord, for whose sake I have lost all things. I consider them garbage, that I may gain Christ ⁹and be found in him, not having a righteousness of my own that comes from the law, but that which is through

---

ᵃ 15 Deut. 32:5

faith in[a] Christ — the righteousness that comes from God on the basis of faith. [10]I want to know Christ — yes, to know the power of his resurrection and participation in his sufferings, becoming like him in his death, [11]and so, somehow, attaining to the resurrection from the dead.

[12]Not that I have already obtained all this, or have already arrived at my goal, but I press on to take hold of that for which Christ Jesus took hold of me. [13]Brothers and sisters, I do not consider myself yet to have taken hold of it. But one thing I do: Forgetting what is behind and straining toward what is ahead, [14]I press on toward the goal to win the prize for which God has called me heavenward in Christ Jesus.

Following Paul's Example

[15]All of us, then, who are mature should take such a view of things. And if on some point you think differently, that too God will make clear to you. [16]Only let us live up to what we have already attained.

[17]Join together in following my example, brothers and sisters, and just as you have us as a model, keep your eyes on those who live as we do. [18]For, as I have often told you before and now tell you again even with tears, many live as enemies of the cross of Christ. [19]Their destiny is destruction, their god is their stomach, and their glory is in their shame. Their mind is set on earthly things. [20]But our citizenship is in heaven. And we eagerly await a Savior from there, the Lord Jesus Christ, [21]who, by the power that enables him to bring everything under his control, will transform our lowly bodies so that they will be like his glorious body.

Closing Appeal for Steadfastness and Unity

4 Therefore, my brothers and sisters, you whom I love and long for, my joy and crown, stand firm in the Lord in this way, dear friends!

[2]I plead with Euodia and I plead with Syntyche to be of the same mind in the Lord.

[3]Yes, and I ask you, my true companion, help these women since they have contended at my side in the cause of the gospel, along with Clement and the rest of my co-workers, whose names are in the book of life.

Final Exhortations

[4]Rejoice in the Lord always. I will say it again: Rejoice! [5]Let your gentleness be evident to all. The Lord is near. [6]Do not be anxious about anything, but in every situation, by prayer and petition, with thanksgiving, present your requests to God. [7]And the peace of God, which transcends all understanding, will guard your hearts and your minds in Christ Jesus.

[8]Finally, brothers and sisters, whatever is true, whatever is noble, whatever is right, whatever is pure, whatever is lovely, whatever is admirable — if anything is excellent or praiseworthy — think about such things. [9]Whatever you have learned or received or heard from me, or seen in me — put it into practice. And the God of peace will be with you.

Thanks for Their Gifts

[10]I rejoiced greatly in the Lord that at last you renewed your concern for me. Indeed, you were concerned, but you had no opportunity to show it. [11]I am not saying this because I am in need, for I have learned to be content whatever the circumstances. [12]I know what it is to be in need, and I know what it is to have plenty. I have learned the secret of being content in any and every situation, whether well fed or hungry, whether living in plenty or in want. [13]I can do all this through him who gives me strength.

[14]Yet it was good of you to share in my troubles. [15]Moreover, as you Philippians know, in the early days of your acquaintance with the gospel, when I set out from Macedonia, not one church shared with me in the matter of giving and receiving, except you only; [16]for even when I was in Thessalonica, you sent me aid more than

---

[a] 9 Or through the faithfulness of

once when I was in need. ¹⁷Not that I desire your gifts; what I desire is that more be credited to your account. ¹⁸I have received full payment and have more than enough. I am amply supplied, now that I have received from Epaphroditus the gifts you sent. They are a fragrant offering, an acceptable sacrifice, pleasing to God. ¹⁹And my God will meet all your needs according to the riches of his glory in Christ Jesus.

²⁰To our God and Father be glory for ever and ever. Amen.

RELAPSE LESSON [*Principle Seven*]

For the previous entry in the RELAPSE lesson, go to Psalm 46:10 (page 666).

For a discussion of Principles One through Eight and a listing of their related lessons, go to pages xvii–xliv.

Do not be anxious about anything, but in every situation, by prayer and petition, with thanksgiving, present your requests to God.

PHILIPPIANS 4:6

In Principle Seven we reserve a daily quiet time with God for self-examination, Bible reading and prayer in order to get to know God and his will for our lives and to gain the power to follow his will. As we work this principle, we begin the journey of applying and living what we've discovered in the first six principles. We live daily in humility — as well as in reality, not in denial. We've done our best to amend our past. Through God's guidance we can now make choices about the emotions that will affect our ongoing thinking and actions. We can start to take *action* — positive action — instead of operating in a mode of continual *reaction*.

The second part of this principle — the call to reserve a daily quiet time with God for Bible reading and prayer in order to get to know God and his will for our lives and to gain the power to follow his will — also relates to Step Eleven of the Christ-centered 12 steps.

Step Eleven: We've sought through prayer and meditation to improve our conscious contact with God, praying for knowledge of his will for us, as well as for the power to carry out that will.

The next letter in our RELAPSE prevention plan is *P*, which stands for PLUG IN TO GOD'S POWER through prayer. Sometimes we may wonder, Why did God allow that to happen to me? At such moments we need to stop and think. Did we pray and seek his will and guidance before we made the decision to get married, change jobs, etc.? If we don't make a practice of daily seeking his will for our lives, how can we blame him when things go wrong?

Some people assign themselves the job of giving God instructions. They have things backward. Our job is to daily seek his will for our lives. God's guidance and direction can start only after our own demands have stopped. We need to quit demanding things from God and start requesting things of him. Specific prayer requests are another way to plug in to God's power. In Philippians 4:6 Paul instructs us to pray about everything, asking for God to reveal his perfect will for all our decisions.

The next letter in RELAPSE is S. Go to Philippians 4:7 (page 1483).

Final Greetings

21Greet all God's people in Christ Jesus. The brothers and sisters who are with me send greetings. 22All God's people here send you greetings, especially those who belong to Caesar's household.

23The grace of the Lord Jesus Christ be with your spirit. Amen.*a*

---

a 23 Some manuscripts do not have *Amen.*

RELAPSE LESSON [*Principle Seven*]

For the previous entry in the RELAPSE lesson, go to Philippians 4:6 (page 1482).

For a discussion of Principles One through Eight and a listing of their related lessons, go to pages xvii – xliv.

The peace of God, which transcends all understanding, will guard your hearts and your minds in Christ Jesus.

PHILIPPIANS 4:7

In Principle Seven we reserve a daily quiet time with God for self-examination, Bible reading and prayer in order to get to know God and his will for our lives and to gain the power to follow his will. As we work this principle, we begin the journey of applying and living what we've discovered in the first six principles. We live daily in humility — as well as in reality, not in denial. We've done our best to amend our past. Through God's guidance we can now make choices about the emotions that will affect our ongoing thinking and actions. We can start to take *action* — positive action — instead of operating in a mode of continual *reaction.*

The second part of this principle — the call to reserve a daily quiet time with God for Bible reading and prayer in order to get to know God and his will for our lives and to gain the power to follow his will — also relates to Step Eleven of the Christ-centered 12 steps.

Step Eleven: We've sought through prayer and meditation to improve our conscious contact with God, praying for knowledge of his will for us, as well as for the power to carry out that will.

The next letter in our RELAPSE prevention plan is *S*, which cautions us to SLOW DOWN long enough to hear God's answers. After we've spent time praying to God, we need to shift into a waiting, listening mode long enough to allow ourselves to hear his answers and take in his directions. It's so easy to become impatient, demanding that God answer us now. But we need to remember that our timing can be flawed, while God's is always perfect. After we pray and ask, then, we need to listen. God instructed Job, " 'Then listen to me; be silent, and I will teach you wisdom' " (Job 33:33).

In Philippians 4:7 Paul tells us that if we present our prayer requests to God, we'll experience his peace as never before — a peace so irresistible and overwhelming that we can never begin to understand it.

The last letter in RELAPSE is another *E*. Go to 1 Thessalonians 5:16 – 18 (page 1494).

Colossians

THEME: Paul, insisting that the believer's union with Christ results in holy living, outlined clear standards regarding the attitudes that are to govern relationships within family and church: submission, love, service, obedience, conscientious work and fairness.

AUTHOR: The letter identifies its author as the apostle Paul.

DATE OF WRITING: Colossians was probably written between AD 60 and 62.

ENCOURAGEMENT FROM COLOSSIANS: "[The Father] has rescued us from the dominion of darkness and brought us into the kingdom of the Son he loves, in whom we have redemption, the forgiveness of sins" (Colossians 1:13 – 14).

CHALLENGE FROM COLOSSIANS: "Put to death . . . whatever belongs to your earthly nature: sexual immorality, impurity, lust, evil desires and greed, which is idolatry . . . You used to walk in these ways, in the life you once lived" (Colossians 3:5,7).

REFLECTION FROM COLOSSIANS: "Once you were alienated from God and were enemies in your minds because of your evil behavior. But now he has reconciled you by Christ's physical body through death to present you holy in his sight, without blemish and free from accusation — if you continue in your faith" (Colossians 1:21 – 23).

At a Glance

Recovery Themes in Colossians

In his letter to the Colossians, Paul continues his guidance on how we as Christians are called to live. He reminds us again that we don't have to be concerned about impressing God — that Christ died for us, paying the ultimate price to make us right with the Father. Christ holds the world together, and he holds our individual lives together as well.

Paul tells us to keep our minds on godly things and to put our old ways behind us. Why return to empty lives full of pain when we can experience full life in Christ? Why focus on the past when Jesus has given us an amazing future? The book of Colossians gives us insight into how we should live now that we've been set free, now that we've been raised up together with Christ. This book assures us that our past is behind us; it's time, then, to move beyond our old ways as well, to focus on the things that concern Christ.

---

1 Paul, an apostle of Christ Jesus by the will of God, and Timothy our brother,

²To God's holy people in Colossae, the faithful brothers and sisters*a* in Christ:

Grace and peace to you from God our Father.*b*

Thanksgiving and Prayer

³We always thank God, the Father of our

---

a 2 The Greek word for *brothers and sisters* (*adelphoi*) refers here to believers, both men and women, as part of God's family; also in 4:15.   *b 2* Some manuscripts *Father and the Lord Jesus Christ*

Lord Jesus Christ, when we pray for you, [4]because we have heard of your faith in Christ Jesus and of the love you have for all God's people — [5]the faith and love that spring from the hope stored up for you in heaven and about which you have already heard in the true message of the gospel [6]that has come to you. In the same way, the gospel is bearing fruit and growing throughout the whole world — just as it has been doing among you since the day you heard it and truly understood God's grace. [7]You learned it from Epaphras, our dear fellow servant,[a] who is a faithful minister of Christ on our[b] behalf, [8]and who also told us of your love in the Spirit.

[9]For this reason, since the day we heard about you, we have not stopped praying for you. We continually ask God to fill you with the knowledge of his will through all the wisdom and understanding that the Spirit gives,[c] [10]so that you may live a life worthy of the Lord and please him in every way: bearing fruit in every good work, growing in the knowledge of God, [11]being strengthened with all power according to his glorious might so that you may have great endurance and patience, [12]and giving joyful thanks to the Father, who has qualified you[d] to share in the inheritance of his holy people in the kingdom of light. [13]For he has rescued us from the dominion of darkness and brought us into the kingdom of the Son he loves, [14]in whom we have redemption, the forgiveness of sins.

The Supremacy of the Son of God

[15]The Son is the image of the invisible God, the firstborn over all creation. [16]For in him all things were created: things in heaven and on earth, visible and invisible, whether thrones or powers or rulers or authorities; all things have been created through him and for him. [17]He is before all things, and in him all things hold together. [18]And he is the head of the body, the church;

he is the beginning and the firstborn from among the dead, so that in everything he might have the supremacy. [19]For God was pleased to have all his fullness dwell in him, [20]and through him to reconcile to himself all things, whether things on earth or things in heaven, by making peace through his blood, shed on the cross.

[21]Once you were alienated from God and were enemies in your minds because of[e] your evil behavior. [22]But now he has reconciled you by Christ's physical body through death to present you holy in his sight, without blemish and free from accusation — [23]if you continue in your faith, established and firm, and do not move from the hope held out in the gospel. This is the gospel that you heard and that has been proclaimed to every creature under heaven, and of which I, Paul, have become a servant.

Paul's Labor for the Church

[24]Now I rejoice in what I am suffering for you, and I fill up in my flesh what is still lacking in regard to Christ's afflictions, for the sake of his body, which is the church. [25]I have become its servant by the commission God gave me to present to you the word of God in its fullness — [26]the mystery that has been kept hidden for ages and generations, but is now disclosed to the Lord's people. [27]To them God has chosen to make known among the Gentiles the glorious riches of this mystery, which is Christ in you, the hope of glory.

[28]He is the one we proclaim, admonishing and teaching everyone with all wisdom, so that we may present everyone fully mature in Christ. [29]To this end I strenuously contend with all the energy Christ so powerfully works in me.

2 I want you to know how hard I am contending for you and for those at Laodicea, and for all who have not met me personally. [2]My goal is that they

---

[a] 7 Or *slave*   [b] 7 Some manuscripts *your*   [c] 9 Or *all spiritual wisdom and understanding*   [d] 12 Some manuscripts *us*   [e] 21 Or *minds, as shown by*

may be encouraged in heart and united in love, so that they may have the full riches of complete understanding, in order that they may know the mystery of God, namely, Christ, 3in whom are hidden all the treasures of wisdom and knowledge. 4I tell you this so that no one may deceive you by fine-sounding arguments. 5For though I am absent from you in body, I am present with you in spirit and delight to see how disciplined you are and how firm your faith in Christ is.

Spiritual Fullness in Christ

6So then, just as you received Christ Jesus as Lord, continue to live your lives in him, 7rooted and built up in him, strengthened in the faith as you were taught, and overflowing with thankfulness.

8See to it that no one takes you captive through hollow and deceptive philosophy, which depends on human tradition and the elemental spiritual forces*a* of this world rather than on Christ.

9For in Christ all the fullness of the Deity lives in bodily form, 10and in Christ you have been brought to fullness. He is the head over every power and authority. 11In him you were also circumcised with a circumcision not performed by human hands. Your whole self ruled by the flesh*b* was put off when you were circumcised by*c* Christ, 12having been buried with him in baptism, in which you were also raised with him through your faith in the working of God, who raised him from the dead.

13When you were dead in your sins and in the uncircumcision of your flesh, God made you*d* alive with Christ. He forgave us all our sins, 14having canceled the charge of our legal indebtedness, which stood against us and condemned us; he has taken it away, nailing it to the cross. 15And having disarmed the powers and authorities, he

made a public spectacle of them, triumphing over them by the cross.*e*

Freedom From Human Rules

16Therefore do not let anyone judge you by what you eat or drink, or with regard to a religious festival, a New Moon celebration or a Sabbath day. 17These are a shadow of the things that were to come; the reality, however, is found in Christ. 18Do not let anyone who delights in false humility and the worship of angels disqualify you. Such a person also goes into great detail about what they have seen; they are puffed up with idle notions by their unspiritual mind. 19They have lost connection with the head, from whom the whole body, supported and held together by its ligaments and sinews, grows as God causes it to grow.

20Since you died with Christ to the elemental spiritual forces of this world, why, as though you still belonged to the world, do you submit to its rules: 21"Do not handle! Do not taste! Do not touch!"? 22These rules, which have to do with things that are all destined to perish with use, are based on merely human commands and teachings. 23Such regulations indeed have an appearance of wisdom, with their self-imposed worship, their false humility and their harsh treatment of the body, but they lack any value in restraining sensual indulgence.

Living as Those Made Alive in Christ

3 Since, then, you have been raised with Christ, set your hearts on things above, where Christ is, seated at the right hand of God. 2Set your minds on things above, not on earthly things. 3For you died, and your life is now hidden with Christ in God. 4When Christ, who is your*f* life, appears, then you also will appear with him in glory.

---

a 8 Or *the basic principles*; also in verse 20   *b* 11 In contexts like this, the Greek word for *flesh* (*sarx*) refers to the sinful state of human beings, often presented as a power in opposition to the Spirit; also in verse 13.   *c* 11 Or *put off in the circumcision of*   *d* 13 Some manuscripts *us*   *e* 15 Or *them in him*   *f* 4 Some manuscripts *our*

⁵Put to death, therefore, whatever belongs to your earthly nature: sexual immorality, impurity, lust, evil desires and greed, which is idolatry. ⁶Because of these, the wrath of God is coming.*ᵃ* ⁷You used to walk in these ways, in the life you once lived. ⁸But now you must also rid yourselves of all such things as these: anger, rage, malice, slander, and filthy language from your lips. ⁹Do not lie to each other, since you have taken off your old self with its practices ¹⁰and have put on the new self, which is being renewed in knowledge in the image of its Creator. ¹¹Here there is no Gentile or Jew, circumcised or uncircumcised, barbarian, Scythian, slave or free, but Christ is all, and is in all.

¹²Therefore, as God's chosen people, holy and dearly loved, clothe yourselves with compassion, kindness, humility,

---

ᵃ 6 Some early manuscripts coming on those who are disobedient

SPIRITUAL INVENTORY LESSON [*Principle Four*]

For the previous entry in the SPIRITUAL INVENTORY lesson, go to Ephesians 4:31 (page 1470).

For a discussion of Principles One through Eight and a listing of their related lessons, go to pages xvii – xliv.

Do not lie to each other, since you have taken off your old self with its practices.

COLOSSIANS 3:9

Principle Four begins the process of "coming clean." It's here that we openly examine and confess our faults to ourselves, to God and to someone else we trust. In the first part of Principle Four we openly examine our lives.

As part of completing Principle Four, we do a SPIRITUAL INVENTORY. We look at eight critical areas of our lives. The fourth area is OUR INTEGRITY. Did you know that there are no degrees of honesty? Either we're truthful or we aren't. An honest man alters his ideas to fit the truth; a dishonest man alters the truth to fit his ideas. We're called to follow the pattern of Colossians 3:9.

We need to ask the following questions regarding our integrity:

1. In what past dealings have we been dishonest?

2. Have we stolen things?

3. Have we exaggerated our strengths or abilities to make ourselves look better?

4. In what areas of our past have we practiced false humility?

5. Have we pretended to live one way in front of our Christian friends and behaved another way at home or at work?

At this halfway point in our Spiritual Inventory we need to remind ourselves to keep our inventory balanced. We should list our positive new relationships, the areas of our lives we've been able to turn over to God, ways in which our attitude has improved since we've been in recovery, and areas in which we've been able to step out of our denial into God's grace.

The fifth area of our Spiritual Inventory is OUR MIND. Go to Romans 12:2 (page 1410).

gentleness and patience. ¹³Bear with each other and forgive one another if any of you has a grievance against someone. Forgive as the Lord forgave you. ¹⁴And over all these virtues put on love, which binds them all together in perfect unity.

¹⁵Let the peace of Christ rule in your hearts, since as members of one body you were called to peace. And be thankful. ¹⁶Let the message of Christ dwell among you richly as you teach and admonish one another with all wisdom through psalms, hymns, and songs from the Spirit, sing-ing to God with gratitude in your hearts. ¹⁷And whatever you do, whether in word or deed, do it all in the name of the Lord Jesus, giving thanks to God the Father through him.

Instructions for Christian Households

¹⁸Wives, submit yourselves to your husbands, as is fitting in the Lord.

¹⁹Husbands, love your wives and do not be harsh with them.

²⁰Children, obey your parents in everything, for this pleases the Lord.

GRACE LESSON [Principle Six]

For the previous entry in the GRACE lesson, go to Ephesians 2:8–9 (page 1464).

For a discussion of Principles One through Eight and a listing of their related lessons, go to pages xvii–xliv.

Bear with each other and forgive one another if any of you has a grievance against someone. Forgive as the Lord forgave you.

COLOSSIANS 3:13

Principle Six calls for us to evaluate all our relationships and to offer forgiveness to those who have hurt us and make amends for harm we've done to others, except when doing so would injure them or others. We need to be willing to admit our part in our relationships that have been broken or damaged.

As we grow as Christians and move through our recovery process, we want to follow the guidance and directions of Jesus Christ. As we get to know him better, we want to model his teachings and his ways — to become more like him. If we're going to implement Principle Six to the best of our ability, we need to learn to model God's GRACE.

The next letter in GRACE is A, which stands for ACCEPTED BY GOD'S LOVE. The wonder is that God already loved us while we were out there living in sin. Romans 5:8 spells it out for us: "God demonstrates his own love for us in this: While we were still sinners [still living in blatant sin or controlled by sin], Christ died for us." We can love others because God first loved us. We can also forgive others because God took the initiative to forgive us first. Colossians 3:13 points out that forgiveness is more than simply one of many good options available to us.

The good news is that we don't have to make amends or offer forgiveness in our own power. Hebrews 4:16 invites us to "approach God's throne of grace with confidence, so that we may receive mercy and find grace to help us in our time of need."

The next letter in GRACE is C. Go to Ephesians 1:7 (page 1462).

²¹Fathers,ᵃ do not embitter your children, or they will become discouraged.

²²Slaves, obey your earthly masters in everything; and do it, not only when their eye is on you and to curry their favor, but with sincerity of heart and reverence for the Lord. ²³Whatever you do, work at it with all your heart, as working for the Lord, not for human masters, ²⁴since you know that you will receive an inheritance from the Lord as a reward. It is the Lord Christ you are serving. ²⁵Anyone who does wrong will be repaid for their wrongs, and there is no favoritism.

4 Masters, provide your slaves with what is right and fair, because you know that you also have a Master in heaven.

Further Instructions

²Devote yourselves to prayer, being watchful and thankful. ³And pray for us,

ᵃ 21 Or *Parents*

GRATITUDE LESSON [*Principle Seven*]

For the previous entry in the GRATITUDE lesson, go to Psalm 107:15 (page 710).

For a discussion of Principles One through Eight and a listing of their related lessons, go to pages xvii–xliv.

Let the peace of Christ rule in your hearts, since as members of one body you were called to peace. And be thankful. Let the message of Christ dwell among you richly as you teach and admonish one another with all wisdom through psalms, hymns, and songs from the Spirit, singing to God with gratitude in your hearts.

COLOSSIANS 3:15–16

In Principle Seven we reserve a daily quiet time with God for self-examination, Bible reading and prayer in order to get to know God and his will for our lives and to gain the power to follow his will. Once we've been working this principle for a while, we'll understand that we have much for which to be thankful: We're growing closer to our Higher Power, the one and only true Higher Power, Jesus Christ. Our relationships are being restored. We're experiencing peace and freedom from our hurts, hang-ups and habits. We've found a new purpose for our lives. It's important for us to maintain an "attitude of GRATITUDE" for all the positive changes that have occurred and are still occurring in our lives.

The second area for which we can be thankful has to do with those individuals God has placed in our lives to walk alongside us on our road of recovery. We need to be thankful for others, to remember not to take those special people for granted, to recognize that we're not alone, even from the purely human perspective. We have others who either have gone before us or are now striding alongside us to support and guide us as we grow in Christ and in our recovery. In Colossians 3:15–16 we're called upon to teach and counsel one another. Who are the individuals who have helped us on our road to recovery? Are we truly thankful for their support?

The next area in our lives for which we can be thankful is OUR RECOVERY.
Go to Hebrews 12:1 (page 1534).

too, that God may open a door for our message, so that we may proclaim the mystery of Christ, for which I am in chains. 4Pray that I may proclaim it clearly, as I should. 5Be wise in the way you act toward outsiders; make the most of every opportunity. 6Let your conversation be always full of grace, seasoned with salt, so that you may know how to answer everyone.

Final Greetings

7Tychicus will tell you all the news about me. He is a dear brother, a faithful minister and fellow servant*a* in the Lord. 8I am sending him to you for the express purpose that you may know about our*b* circumstances and that he may encourage your hearts. 9He is coming with Onesimus, our faithful and dear brother, who is one of you. They will tell you everything that is happening here.

10My fellow prisoner Aristarchus sends you his greetings, as does Mark, the cousin of Barnabas. (You have received instructions about him; if he comes to you, welcome him.) 11Jesus, who is called Justus, also sends greetings. These are the only Jews*c* among my co-workers for the kingdom of God, and they have proved a comfort to me. 12Epaphras, who is one of you and a servant of Christ Jesus, sends greetings. He is always wrestling in prayer for you, that you may stand firm in all the will of God, mature and fully assured. 13I vouch for him that he is working hard for you and for those at Laodicea and Hierapolis. 14Our dear friend Luke, the doctor, and Demas send greetings. 15Give my greetings to the brothers and sisters at Laodicea, and to Nympha and the church in her house.

16After this letter has been read to you, see that it is also read in the church of the Laodiceans and that you in turn read the letter from Laodicea.

17Tell Archippus: "See to it that you complete the ministry you have received in the Lord."

18I, Paul, write this greeting in my own hand. Remember my chains. Grace be with you.

---

a 7 Or *slave*; also in verse 12   *b* 8 Some manuscripts *that he may know about your*   *c* 11 Greek *only ones of the circumcision group*

1 Thessalonians

THEME: While a moral life isn't a precondition for acceptance by God, an immoral lifestyle is irreconcilable with being a Christian.

AUTHOR: The apostle Paul wrote this letter.

DATE OF WRITING: Paul probably wrote this letter between AD 50 and 51.

ENCOURAGEMENT FROM 1 THESSALONIANS: "You know that we dealt with each of you as a father deals with his own children, encouraging, comforting and urging you to live lives worthy of God, who calls you into his kingdom and glory" (1 Thessalonians 2:11 – 12).

CHALLENGE FROM 1 THESSALONIANS: "It is God's will that you should be sanctified: that you should avoid sexual immorality; that each of you should learn to control his own body in a way that is holy and honorable" (1 Thessalonians 4:3 – 4).

REFLECTION FROM 1 THESSALONIANS: "May God himself . . . sanctify you through and through . . . The one who calls you is faithful, and he will do it" (1 Thessalonians 5:23 – 24).

Sometimes the Bible gets a bad reputation. People feel as though it's nothing more than a guilt-inducing collection of dos and don'ts. But, to counter this impression, 1 and 2 Thessalonians are books of encouragement. The new church in Thessalonica was off to a great start, and Paul wanted that to continue.

As we work out our recoveries, we can experience discouragement. Does anyone even notice the change in us? Is all our hard work really making a difference? If Jesus truly is our Higher Power, the answer is a resounding "yes!" Christ is hard at work in each of us for our healing. He doesn't want us to keep this good news to ourselves; he wants us to share it with others. In 1 Thessalonians Paul encourages us to keep at it — to continue walking the path of recovery, of changed life in Christ. If we do, we'll undoubtedly bring others alongside us to faith in Jesus Christ.

1

Paul, Silas[a] and Timothy,

To the church of the Thessalonians in God the Father and the Lord Jesus Christ:

Grace and peace to you.

Thanksgiving for the Thessalonians' Faith

2 We always thank God for all of you and continually mention you in our prayers. 3 We remember before our God and Father your work produced by faith, your labor

---

[a] 1 Greek *Silvanus*, a variant of *Silas*

prompted by love, and your endurance inspired by hope in our Lord Jesus Christ.

[4] For we know, brothers and sisters[a] loved by God, that he has chosen you, [5] because our gospel came to you not simply with words but also with power, with the Holy Spirit and deep conviction. You know how we lived among you for your sake. [6] You became imitators of us and of the Lord, for you welcomed the message in the midst of severe suffering with the joy given by the Holy Spirit. [7] And so you became a model to all the believers in Macedonia and Achaia. [8] The Lord's message rang out from you not only in Macedonia and Achaia — your faith in God has become known everywhere. Therefore we do not need to say anything about it, [9] for they themselves report what kind of reception you gave us. They tell how you turned to God from idols to serve the living and true God, [10] and to wait for his Son from heaven, whom he raised from the dead — Jesus, who rescues us from the coming wrath.

Paul's Ministry in Thessalonica

2 You know, brothers and sisters, that our visit to you was not without results. [2] We had previously suffered and been treated outrageously in Philippi, as you know, but with the help of our God we dared to tell you his gospel in the face of strong opposition. [3] For the appeal we make does not spring from error or impure motives, nor are we trying to trick you. [4] On the contrary, we speak as those approved by God to be entrusted with the gospel. We are not trying to please people but God, who tests our hearts. [5] You know we never used flattery, nor did we put on a mask to cover up greed — God is our witness. [6] We were not looking for praise from people, not from you or anyone else, even though as apostles of Christ we could have asserted our authority. [7] Instead, we were like young children[b] among you.

Just as a nursing mother cares for her children, [8] so we cared for you. Because we loved you so much, we were delighted to share with you not only the gospel of God but our lives as well. [9] Surely you remember, brothers and sisters, our toil and hardship; we worked night and day in order not to be a burden to anyone while we preached the gospel of God to you. [10] You are witnesses, and so is God, of how holy, righteous and blameless we were among you who believed. [11] For you know that we dealt with each of you as a father deals with his own children, [12] encouraging, comforting and urging you to live lives worthy of God, who calls you into his kingdom and glory.

[13] And we also thank God continually because, when you received the word of God, which you heard from us, you accepted it not as a human word, but as it actually is, the word of God, which is indeed at work in you who believe. [14] For you, brothers and sisters, became imitators of God's churches in Judea, which are in Christ Jesus: You suffered from your own people the same things those churches suffered from the Jews [15] who killed the Lord Jesus and the prophets and also drove us out. They displease God and are hostile to everyone [16] in their effort to keep us from speaking to the Gentiles so that they may be saved. In this way they always heap up their sins to the limit. The wrath of God has come upon them at last.[c]

Paul's Longing to See the Thessalonians

[17] But, brothers and sisters, when we were orphaned by being separated from you for a short time (in person, not in thought), out of our intense longing we made every effort to see you. [18] For we wanted to come to you — certainly I, Paul, did, again and again — but Satan blocked our way. [19] For what is our hope, our joy, or the crown in which we will glory in the presence of our Lord Jesus when he comes? Is it not you? [20] Indeed, you are our glory and joy.

---

[a] 4 The Greek word for *brothers and sisters* (*adelphoi*) refers here to believers, both men and women, as part of God's family; also in 2:1, 9, 14, 17; 3:7; 4:1, 10, 13; 5:1, 4, 12, 14, 25, 27.   [b] 7 Some manuscripts *were gentle*   [c] 16 Or *them fully*

3 So when we could stand it no longer, we thought it best to be left by ourselves in Athens. ²We sent Timothy, who is our brother and co-worker in God's service in spreading the gospel of Christ, to strengthen and encourage you in your faith, ³so that no one would be unsettled by these trials. For you know quite well that we are destined for them. ⁴In fact, when we were with you, we kept telling you that we would be persecuted. And it turned out that way, as you well know. ⁵For this reason, when I could stand it no longer, I sent to find out about your faith. I was afraid that in some way the tempter had tempted you and that our labors might have been in vain.

Timothy's Encouraging Report

⁶But Timothy has just now come to us from you and has brought good news about your faith and love. He has told us that you always have pleasant memories of us and that you long to see us, just as we also long to see you. ⁷Therefore, brothers and sisters, in all our distress and persecution we were encouraged about you because of your faith. ⁸For now we really live, since you are standing firm in the Lord. ⁹How can we thank God enough for you in return for all the joy we have in the presence of our God because of you? ¹⁰Night and day we pray most earnestly that we may see you again and supply what is lacking in your faith.

¹¹Now may our God and Father himself and our Lord Jesus clear the way for us to come to you. ¹²May the Lord make your love increase and overflow for each other and for everyone else, just as ours does for you. ¹³May he strengthen your hearts so that you will be blameless and holy in the presence of our God and Father when our Lord Jesus comes with all his holy ones.

Living to Please God

4 As for other matters, brothers and sisters, we instructed you how to live in order to please God, as in fact you are living. Now we ask you and urge you in the Lord Jesus to do this more and more. ²For you know what instructions we gave you by the authority of the Lord Jesus.

³It is God's will that you should be sanctified: that you should avoid sexual immorality; ⁴that each of you should learn to control your own body*ᵃ* in a way that is holy and honorable, ⁵not in passionate lust like the pagans, who do not know God; ⁶and that in this matter no one should wrong or take advantage of a brother or sister.*ᵇ* The Lord will punish all those who commit such sins, as we told you and warned you before. ⁷For God did not call us to be impure, but to live a holy life. ⁸Therefore, anyone who rejects this instruction does not reject a human being but God, the very God who gives you his Holy Spirit.

⁹Now about your love for one another we do not need to write to you, for you yourselves have been taught by God to love each other. ¹⁰And in fact, you do love all of God's family throughout Macedonia. Yet we urge you, brothers and sisters, to do so more and more, ¹¹and to make it your ambition to lead a quiet life: You should mind your own business and work with your hands, just as we told you, ¹²so that your daily life may win the respect of outsiders and so that you will not be dependent on anybody.

Believers Who Have Died

¹³Brothers and sisters, we do not want you to be uninformed about those who sleep in death, so that you do not grieve like the rest of mankind, who have no hope. ¹⁴For we believe that Jesus died and rose again, and so we believe that God will bring with Jesus those who have fallen asleep in him. ¹⁵According to the Lord's word, we tell you that we who are still alive, who are left until the coming of the Lord, will certainly not precede those who have fallen asleep. ¹⁶For the Lord himself will come down from heaven, with a loud command, with the voice of the archangel

---

ᵃ 4 Or *learn to live with your own wife;* or *learn to acquire a wife*   *ᵇ 6* The Greek word for *brother or sister* (*adelphos*) refers here to a believer, whether man or woman, as part of God's family.

and with the trumpet call of God, and the dead in Christ will rise first. ¹⁷After that, we who are still alive and are left will be caught up together with them in the clouds to meet the Lord in the air. And so we will be with the Lord forever. ¹⁸Therefore encourage one another with these words.

The Day of the Lord

5 Now, brothers and sisters, about times and dates we do not need to write to you, ²for you know very well that the day of the Lord will come like a thief in the night. ³While people are saying, "Peace and safety," destruction will come on them suddenly, as labor pains on a pregnant woman, and they will not escape.

⁴But you, brothers and sisters, are not in darkness so that this day should surprise you like a thief. ⁵You are all children of the light and children of the day. We do not belong to the night or to the darkness. ⁶So then, let us not be like others, who are asleep, but let us be awake and sober. ⁷For those who sleep, sleep at night, and those who get drunk, get drunk at night. ⁸But since we belong to

RELAPSE LESSON [*Principle Seven*]

For the previous entry in the RELAPSE lesson, go to Philippians 4:7 (page 1483).

For a discussion of Principles One through Eight and a listing of their related lessons, go to pages xvii – xliv.

Rejoice always, pray continually, give thanks in all circumstances;
for this is God's will for you in Christ Jesus.

1 THESSALONIANS 5:16 – 18

In Principle Seven we reserve a daily quiet time with God for self-examination, Bible reading and prayer in order to get to know God and his will for our lives and to gain the power to follow his will. As we work this principle, we begin the journey of applying and living what we've discovered in the first six principles. We live daily in humility — as well as in reality, not in denial. We've done our best to amend our past. Through God's guidance we can now make choices about the emotions that will affect our ongoing thinking and actions. We can start to take *action* — positive action — instead of operating in a mode of continual *reaction*.

The second part of this principle — the call to reserve a daily quiet time with God for Bible reading and prayer in order to get to know God and his will for our lives and to gain the power to follow his will — also relates to Step Eleven of the Christ-centered 12 steps.

Step Eleven: We've sought through prayer and meditation to improve our conscious contact with God, praying for knowledge of his will for us, as well as for the power to carry out that will.

The last letter in our RELAPSE prevention plan is the second *E*, which stands for ENJOY YOUR GROWTH. We need to take pleasure in our victories, to "Celebrate our Recovery" — and that includes the individual mile markers, those small successes along our road to recovery. First Thessalonians 5:16 – 18 tells us that we can get and keep that joy through prayer and thankfulness. When we share our victories, no matter how minor, our growth will give others hope.

This is the final page of the RELAPSE lesson.

the day, let us be sober, putting on faith and love as a breastplate, and the hope of salvation as a helmet. 9For God did not appoint us to suffer wrath but to receive salvation through our Lord Jesus Christ. 10He died for us so that, whether we are awake or asleep, we may live together with him. 11Therefore encourage one another and build each other up, just as in fact you are doing.

Final Instructions

12Now we ask you, brothers and sisters, to acknowledge those who work hard among you, who care for you in the Lord and who admonish you. 13Hold them in the highest regard in love because of their work. Live in peace with each other. 14And we urge you, brothers and sisters, warn those who are idle and disruptive, encourage the disheartened, help the weak, be patient with everyone. 15Make sure that nobody pays back wrong for wrong, but always strive to do what is good for each other and for everyone else.

16Rejoice always, 17pray continually, 18give thanks in all circumstances; for this is God's will for you in Christ Jesus.

19Do not quench the Spirit. 20Do not treat prophecies with contempt 21but test them all; hold on to what is good, 22reject every kind of evil.

RELAPSE LESSON [*Principle Seven*]

For the previous entry in the RELAPSE lesson, go to Romans 12:3,9–10,12,16–17 (page 1411).

For a discussion of Principles One through Eight and a listing of their related lessons, go to pages xvii–xliv.

Test them all; hold on to what is good.

1 THESSALONIANS 5:21

In Principle Seven we reserve a daily quiet time with God for self-examination, Bible reading and prayer in order to get to know God and his will for our lives and to gain the power to follow his will. As we work this principle, we begin the journey of applying and living what we've discovered in the first six principles. We live daily in humility — as well as in reality, not in denial. We've done our best to amend our past. Through God's guidance we can now make choices about the emotions that will affect our ongoing thinking and actions. We can start to take *action* — positive action — instead of operating in a mode of continual *reaction*.

The second part of this principle — the call to reserve a daily quiet time with God for Bible reading and prayer in order to get to know God and his will for our lives and to gain the power to follow his will — also relates to Step Eleven of the Christ-centered 12 steps.

Step Eleven: We've sought through prayer and meditation to improve our conscious contact with God, praying for knowledge of his will for us, as well as for the power to carry out that will.

The *L* in RELAPSE stands for LISTEN TO JESUS. We need to take a time-out from the world's rat race long enough to listen to our body, our mind and our soul. We need to slow down enough to hear the Lord's directions. Jesus is our "litmus test" — the Truth against which 1 Thessalonians 5:21 is calling us to measure our actions.

The next letter in RELAPSE is *A*. Go to Psalm 46:10 (page 666).

23May God himself, the God of peace, sanctify you through and through. May your whole spirit, soul and body be kept blameless at the coming of our Lord Jesus Christ. 24The one who calls you is faithful, and he will do it.

25Brothers and sisters, pray for us. 26Greet all God's people with a holy kiss. 27I charge you before the Lord to have this letter read to all the brothers and sisters.

28The grace of our Lord Jesus Christ be with you.

2 Thessalonians

THEME: Paul reminded these believers that they had been chosen for salvation through sanctification by God and that they must stand firm to the end. Since God will inflict vengeance on those who afflict the faithful, Christians are to wait patiently and faithfully for Christ's return.

AUTHOR: The apostle Paul is the letter's stated author.

DATE OF WRITING: Second Thessalonians was probably written in AD 51 or 52, shortly after 1 Thessalonians.

ENCOURAGEMENT FROM 2 THESSALONIANS: "May our Lord Jesus Christ himself and God our Father, who loved us and by his grace gave us eternal encouragement and good hope, encourage your hearts and strengthen you in every good deed and word" (2 Thessalonians 2:16 – 17).

CHALLENGE FROM 2 THESSALONIANS: "We hear that some among you are idle and disruptive. They are not busy; they are busybodies. Such people we command and urge in the Lord Jesus Christ to settle down and earn the food they eat. And as for you, brothers and sisters, never tire of doing what is good" (2 Thessalonians 3:11 – 13).

REFLECTION FROM 2 THESSALONIANS: "May the Lord direct your hearts into God's love and Christ's perseverance" (2 Thessalonians 3:5).

See the introduction to 1 Thessalonians.

1

Paul, Silas[a] and Timothy,

To the church of the Thessalonians in God our Father and the Lord Jesus Christ:

[2] Grace and peace to you from God the Father and the Lord Jesus Christ.

Thanksgiving and Prayer

[3] We ought always to thank God for you, brothers and sisters,[b] and rightly so, because your faith is growing more and more, and the love all of you have for one another is increasing. [4] Therefore, among God's churches we boast about your perseverance and faith in all the persecutions and trials you are enduring.

[5] All this is evidence that God's judgment is right, and as a result you will be counted worthy of the kingdom of God, for which you are suffering. [6] God is just: He will pay back trouble to those who trouble you [7] and give relief to you who are troubled, and to us as well. This will happen when the Lord Jesus is revealed from heaven in blazing fire with his powerful angels. [8] He will

---

a 1 Greek *Silvanus*, a variant of *Silas*   *b 3* The Greek word for *brothers and sisters* (*adelphoi*) refers here to believers, both men and women, as part of God's family; also in 2:1, 13, 15; 3:1, 6, 13.

punish those who do not know God and do not obey the gospel of our Lord Jesus. ⁹They will be punished with everlasting destruction and shut out from the presence of the Lord and from the glory of his might ¹⁰on the day he comes to be glorified in his holy people and to be marveled at among all those who have believed. This includes you, because you believed our testimony to you.

¹¹With this in mind, we constantly pray for you, that our God may make you worthy of his calling, and that by his power he may bring to fruition your every desire for goodness and your every deed prompted by faith. ¹²We pray this so that the name of our Lord Jesus may be glorified in you, and you in him, according to the grace of our God and the Lord Jesus Christ.ᵃ

The Man of Lawlessness

2 Concerning the coming of our Lord Jesus Christ and our being gathered to him, we ask you, brothers and sisters, ²not to become easily unsettled or alarmed by the teaching allegedly from us — whether by a prophecy or by word of mouth or by letter — asserting that the day of the Lord has already come. ³Don't let anyone deceive you in any way, for that day will not come until the rebellion occurs and the man of lawlessnessᵇ is revealed, the man doomed to destruction. ⁴He will oppose and will exalt himself over everything that is called God or is worshiped, so that he sets himself up in God's temple, proclaiming himself to be God.

⁵Don't you remember that when I was with you I used to tell you these things? ⁶And now you know what is holding him back, so that he may be revealed at the proper time. ⁷For the secret power of lawlessness is already at work; but the one who now holds it back will continue to do so till he is taken out of the way. ⁸And then the lawless one will be revealed, whom the Lord Jesus will overthrow with the breath of his mouth and destroy by the splendor of his coming. ⁹The coming of the lawless one will be in accordance with how Satan works. He will use all sorts of displays of power through signs and wonders that serve the lie, ¹⁰and all the ways that wickedness deceives those who are perishing. They perish because they refused to love the truth and so be saved. ¹¹For this reason God sends them a powerful delusion so that they will believe the lie ¹²and so that all will be condemned who have not believed the truth but have delighted in wickedness.

Stand Firm

¹³But we ought always to thank God for you, brothers and sisters loved by the Lord, because God chose you as firstfruitsᶜ to be saved through the sanctifying work of the Spirit and through belief in the truth. ¹⁴He called you to this through our gospel, that you might share in the glory of our Lord Jesus Christ.

¹⁵So then, brothers and sisters, stand firm and hold fast to the teachingsᵈ we passed on to you, whether by word of mouth or by letter.

¹⁶May our Lord Jesus Christ himself and God our Father, who loved us and by his grace gave us eternal encouragement and good hope, ¹⁷encourage your hearts and strengthen you in every good deed and word.

Request for Prayer

3 As for other matters, brothers and sisters, pray for us that the message of the Lord may spread rapidly and be honored, just as it was with you. ²And pray that we may be delivered from wicked and evil people, for not everyone has faith. ³But the Lord is faithful, and he will strengthen you and protect you from the evil one. ⁴We have confidence in the Lord that you are doing and will contin-

---

ᵃ 12 Or God and Lord, Jesus Christ   ᵇ 3 Some manuscripts sin   ᶜ 13 Some manuscripts because from the beginning God chose you   ᵈ 15 Or traditions

⑦
⑧

ue to do the things we command. ⁵May the Lord direct your hearts into God's love and Christ's perseverance.

Warning Against Idleness

⑦
⑧

⁶In the name of the Lord Jesus Christ, we command you, brothers and sisters, to keep away from every believer who is idle and disruptive and does not live according to the teaching*a* you received from us. ⁷For you yourselves know how you ought to follow our example. We were not idle when we were with you, ⁸nor did we eat anyone's

food without paying for it. On the contrary, we worked night and day, laboring and toiling so that we would not be a burden to any of you. ⁹We did this, not because we do not have the right to such help, but in order to offer ourselves as a model for you to imitate. ¹⁰For even when we were with you, we gave you this rule: "The one who is unwilling to work shall not eat."

¹¹We hear that some among you are idle and disruptive. They are not busy; they are busybodies. ¹²Such people we command and urge in the Lord Jesus Christ to settle

⑦
⑧

a 6 Or tradition

GRACE LESSON [*Principle Six*]

For the previous entry in the GRACE lesson, go to Ephesians 1:7 (page 1462).

For a discussion of Principles One through Eight and a listing of their related lessons, go to pages xvii – xliv.

May our Lord Jesus Christ himself and God our Father, who loved us and by his grace gave us eternal encouragement and good hope, encourage your hearts and strengthen you in every good deed and word.

2 Thessalonians 2:16 – 17

Principle Six calls for us to evaluate all our relationships and to offer FORGIVENESS to those who have hurt us and make amends for harm we've done to others, except when doing so would injure them or others. We need to be willing to admit our part in our relationships that have been broken or damaged.

As we grow as Christians and move forward in our recovery process, we want to follow the guidance and directions of Jesus Christ. As we get to know him better, we want to model his teachings and his ways — to become more like him. If we're going to implement Principle Six to the best of our ability, we need to learn to model God's GRACE.

The last letter in GRACE is *E*: God's grace is an EVERLASTING GIFT. Once we've accepted Jesus Christ as our Savior and Lord, God's gift of grace is eternal and irreversible. Second Thessalonians 2:16 tells us that God loves us so much that his gift of grace will last forever. And Philippians 1:6 promises us that "he who began a good work in you will carry it on to completion until the day of Christ Jesus."

All of us who have asked Christ into our lives are a product of God's grace. As we model that grace, we'll be able to complete the freeing work Principle Six asks of us.

This is the final page of the GRACE lesson.

down and earn the food they eat. 13And as for you, brothers and sisters, never tire of doing what is good.

14Take special note of anyone who does not obey our instruction in this letter. Do not associate with them, in order that they may feel ashamed. 15Yet do not regard them as an enemy, but warn them as you would a fellow believer.

Final Greetings

16Now may the Lord of peace himself give you peace at all times and in every way. The Lord be with all of you.

17I, Paul, write this greeting in my own hand, which is the distinguishing mark in all my letters. This is how I write.

18The grace of our Lord Jesus Christ be with you all.

1 Timothy

THEME: The conduct of Christians must be above reproach because it has a direct effect on the success of their evangelism.

AUTHOR: This letter identifies its author as the apostle Paul.

DATE OF WRITING: Paul probably wrote this letter between AD 63 and 65.

ENCOURAGEMENT FROM 1 TIMOTHY: "Even though I was once a blasphemer and a persecutor and a violent man, I was shown mercy because I acted in ignorance and unbelief. The grace of our Lord was poured out on me abundantly, along with the faith and love that are in Christ Jesus" (1 Timothy 1:13 – 14).

CHALLENGE FROM 1 TIMOTHY: "I want the men everywhere to pray, lifting up holy hands without anger or disputing" (1 Timothy 2:8).

REFLECTION FROM 1 TIMOTHY: "Here is a trustworthy saying that deserves full acceptance: Christ Jesus came into the world to save sinners — of whom I am the worst" (1 Timothy 1:15).

Advice from a friend or from someone else we look up to can be so valuable. In this book Paul lays out specific written guidance to his young protégé Timothy. It's a letter full of instruction and encouragement. We can only imagine that Timothy must have been eager to keep going strong after reading this letter from his trusted friend and spiritual mentor.

It's so important in recovery to have a sponsor. We all need someone who has had more experience, who benefits from the perspective of looking back on more time spent working out his or her own recovery. We all need someone who can guide us when we need help, someone who can correct us when we're wrong, encourage us when we're frustrated and say, "Well done!" when we've achieved victory over a hurt, hang-up or habit. Paul illustrates this kind of guidance here in his first letter to Timothy.

1

Paul, an apostle of Christ Jesus by the command of God our Savior and of Christ Jesus our hope,

2 To Timothy my true son in the faith:

Grace, mercy and peace from God the Father and Christ Jesus our Lord.

Timothy Charged to Oppose False Teachers

3 As I urged you when I went into Macedonia, stay there in Ephesus so that you may command certain people not to teach false doctrines any longer 4 or to devote themselves to myths and endless genealogies. Such things promote controversial speculations rather than advancing God's work — which is by faith. 5 The goal of this command is love, which comes from a pure heart and a good conscience and a sincere faith. 6 Some have departed from these and have turned to meaningless talk. 7 They want to be teachers of the law, but they do not know what they are talking about or what they so confidently affirm.

⁸We know that the law is good if one uses it properly. ⁹We also know that the law is made not for the righteous but for lawbreakers and rebels, the ungodly and sinful, the unholy and irreligious, for those who kill their fathers or mothers, for murderers, ¹⁰for the sexually immoral, for those practicing homosexuality, for slave traders and liars and perjurers—and for whatever else is contrary to the sound doctrine ¹¹that conforms to the gospel concerning the glory of the blessed God, which he entrusted to me.

The Lord's Grace to Paul

¹²I thank Christ Jesus our Lord, who has given me strength, that he considered me

YES LESSON [*Principle Eight*]

For the previous entry in the YES lesson, go to Galatians 6:1–2 (page 1459).

For a discussion of Principles One through Eight and a listing of their related lessons, go to pages xvii–xliv.

The goal of this command is love, which comes from a pure heart and a good conscience and a sincere faith.

1 TIMOTHY 1:5

Principle Eight calls for us to yield ourselves to God to be used by him to bring this good news to others, both through our example and through our words. This principle recycles our pain by allowing God's fire and light to shine on it, to melt down our old hurts, hang-ups and habits so we can be used again in a positive way. Our lives can be recycled to show others how we've worked the principles and steps, with Jesus' healing, and how we've come through the darkness of our pain into Christ's glorious freedom and light.

Society tells us that pain is useless. In fact, some people believe that *people* in pain are useless. At Celebrate Recovery, we know that pain has great value, as do the people who experience it. So, while the world says no, Principle Eight shouts a resounding YES.

People take our example far more seriously than they take our advice. That leads us to the *E* in YES: EXAMPLE IS IMPORTANT.

Our walk needs to match our talk. If we want someone else to see what Christ will do for them, we need to clue them in on what he's done for us. In this principle we need to ask ourselves, "Does my lifestyle reflect what I believe?" In other words, does it imitate the patterns of the world—selfishness, pride and lust—or does it reflect the love, humility and service of Jesus Christ? We want our lifestyle to be in line with 1 Timothy 1:5.

Testimonies are a key component of Celebrate Recovery. Individuals who have given their testimonies believe in Principle Eight—enough to share not only in the safety of their small groups but also within the context of the larger recovery family. They believe in Jesus Christ enough to share their life with others, to discuss both their weaknesses and their strengths with other individuals who are suffering from similar hurts, hang-ups and habits. They give others a piece of their heart—not a piece of their mind. If you haven't given your testimony yet, do so. The rewards are many, and you'll be a living example of saying YES.

The last letter in YES is *S*. Go to John 13:14–15 (page 1323).

trustworthy, appointing me to his service. 13Even though I was once a blasphemer and a persecutor and a violent man, I was shown mercy because I acted in ignorance and unbelief. 14The grace of our Lord was poured out on me abundantly, along with the faith and love that are in Christ Jesus.

15Here is a trustworthy saying that deserves full acceptance: Christ Jesus came into the world to save sinners — of whom I am the worst. 16But for that very reason I was shown mercy so that in me, the worst of sinners, Christ Jesus might display his immense patience as an example for those who would believe in him and receive eternal life. 17Now to the King eternal, immortal, invisible, the only God, be honor and glory for ever and ever. Amen.

The Charge to Timothy Renewed

18Timothy, my son, I am giving you this command in keeping with the prophecies once made about you, so that by recalling them you may fight the battle well, 19holding on to faith and a good conscience, which some have rejected and so have suffered shipwreck with regard to the faith. 20Among them are Hymenaeus and Alexander, whom I have handed over to Satan to be taught not to blaspheme.

Instructions on Worship

2 I urge, then, first of all, that petitions, prayers, intercession and thanksgiving be made for all people — 2for kings and all those in authority, that we may live peaceful and quiet lives in all godliness and holiness. 3This is good, and pleases God our Savior, 4who wants all people to be saved and to come to a knowledge of the truth. 5For there is one God and one mediator between God and mankind, the man Christ Jesus, 6who gave himself as a ransom for all people. This has now been witnessed to at the proper time. 7And for this purpose I was appointed a herald and

an apostle — I am telling the truth, I am not lying — and a true and faithful teacher of the Gentiles.

8Therefore I want the men everywhere to pray, lifting up holy hands without anger or disputing. 9I also want the women to dress modestly, with decency and propriety, adorning themselves, not with elaborate hairstyles or gold or pearls or expensive clothes, 10but with good deeds, appropriate for women who profess to worship God.

11A woman*a* should learn in quietness and full submission. 12I do not permit a woman to teach or to assume authority over a man;*b* she must be quiet. 13For Adam was formed first, then Eve. 14And Adam was not the one deceived; it was the woman who was deceived and became a sinner. 15But women*c* will be saved through childbearing — if they continue in faith, love and holiness with propriety.

Qualifications for Overseers and Deacons

3 Here is a trustworthy saying: Whoever aspires to be an overseer desires a noble task. 2Now the overseer is to be above reproach, faithful to his wife, temperate, self-controlled, respectable, hospitable, able to teach, 3not given to drunkenness, not violent but gentle, not quarrelsome, not a lover of money. 4He must manage his own family well and see that his children obey him, and he must do so in a manner worthy of full*d* respect. 5(If anyone does not know how to manage his own family, how can he take care of God's church?) 6He must not be a recent convert, or he may become conceited and fall under the same judgment as the devil. 7He must also have a good reputation with outsiders, so that he will not fall into disgrace and into the devil's trap.

8In the same way, deacons*e* are to be worthy of respect, sincere, not indulging in much wine, and not pursuing dishonest

---

a 11 Or *wife*; also in verse 12   *b 12* Or *over her husband*   *c 15* Greek *she*   *d 4* Or *him with proper*   *e 8* The word *deacons* refers here to Christians designated to serve with the overseers/elders of the church in a variety of ways; similarly in verse 12; and in Romans 16:1 and Phil. 1:1.

gain. [9]They must keep hold of the deep truths of the faith with a clear conscience. [10]They must first be tested; and then if there is nothing against them, let them serve as deacons.

[11]In the same way, the women[a] are to be worthy of respect, not malicious talkers but temperate and trustworthy in everything.

[12]A deacon must be faithful to his wife and must manage his children and his household well. [13]Those who have served well gain an excellent standing and great assurance in their faith in Christ Jesus.

Reasons for Paul's Instructions

[14]Although I hope to come to you soon, I am writing you these instructions so that, [15]if I am delayed, you will know how people ought to conduct themselves in God's household, which is the church of the living God, the pillar and foundation of the truth. [16]Beyond all question, the mystery from which true godliness springs is great:

He appeared in the flesh,
    was vindicated by the Spirit,[b]
was seen by angels,
    was preached among the nations,
was believed on in the world,
    was taken up in glory.

[4] The Spirit clearly says that in later times some will abandon the faith and follow deceiving spirits and things taught by demons. [2]Such teachings come through hypocritical liars, whose consciences have been seared as with a hot iron. [3]They forbid people to marry and order them to abstain from certain foods, which God created to be received with thanksgiving by those who believe and who know the truth. [4]For everything God created is good, and nothing is to be rejected if it is received with thanksgiving, [5]because it is consecrated by the word of God and prayer.

[6]If you point these things out to the brothers and sisters,[c] you will be a good minister of Christ Jesus, nourished on the truths of the faith and of the good teaching that you have followed. [7]Have nothing to do with godless myths and old wives' tales; rather, train yourself to be godly. [8]For physical training is of some value, but godliness has value for all things, holding promise for both the present life and the life to come. [9]This is a trustworthy saying that deserves full acceptance. [10]That is why we labor and strive, because we have put our hope in the living God, who is the Savior of all people, and especially of those who believe.

[11]Command and teach these things. [12]Don't let anyone look down on you because you are young, but set an example for the believers in speech, in conduct, in love, in faith and in purity. [13]Until I come, devote yourself to the public reading of Scripture, to preaching and to teaching. [14]Do not neglect your gift, which was given you through prophecy when the body of elders laid their hands on you.

[15]Be diligent in these matters; give yourself wholly to them, so that everyone may see your progress. [16]Watch your life and doctrine closely. Persevere in them, because if you do, you will save both yourself and your hearers.

Widows, Elders and Slaves

[5] Do not rebuke an older man harshly, but exhort him as if he were your father. Treat younger men as brothers, [2]older women as mothers, and younger women as sisters, with absolute purity.

[3]Give proper recognition to those widows who are really in need. [4]But if a widow has children or grandchildren, these should learn first of all to put their religion into practice by caring for their own family and so repaying their parents and grandparents, for this is pleasing to God. [5]The widow who is really in need and left all

---

[a] 11 Possibly deacons' wives or women who are deacons   [b] 16 Or *vindicated in spirit*   [c] 6 The Greek word for *brothers and sisters* (*adelphoi*) refers here to believers, both men and women, as part of God's family.

alone puts her hope in God and continues night and day to pray and to ask God for help. 6But the widow who lives for pleasure is dead even while she lives. 7Give the people these instructions, so that no one may be open to blame. 8Anyone who does not provide for their relatives, and especially for their own household, has denied the faith and is worse than an unbeliever.

9No widow may be put on the list of widows unless she is over sixty, has been faithful to her husband, 10and is well known for her good deeds, such as bringing up children, showing hospitality, washing the feet of the Lord's people, helping those in trouble and devoting herself to all kinds of good deeds.

11As for younger widows, do not put them on such a list. For when their sensual desires overcome their dedication to Christ, they want to marry. 12Thus they bring judgment on themselves, because they have broken their first pledge. 13Besides, they get into the habit of being idle and going about from house to house. And not only do they become idlers, but also busybodies who talk nonsense, saying things they ought not to. 14So I counsel younger widows to marry, to have children, to manage their homes and to give the enemy no opportunity for slander. 15Some have in fact already turned away to follow Satan.

16If any woman who is a believer has widows in her care, she should continue to help them and not let the church be burdened with them, so that the church can help those widows who are really in need.

17The elders who direct the affairs of the church well are worthy of double honor, especially those whose work is preaching and teaching. 18For Scripture says, "Do not muzzle an ox while it is treading out the grain,"a and "The worker deserves his wages."b 19Do not entertain an accusation against an elder unless it is brought by two or three witnesses. 20But those elders who

are sinning you are to reprove before everyone, so that the others may take warning. 21I charge you, in the sight of God and Christ Jesus and the elect angels, to keep these instructions without partiality, and to do nothing out of favoritism.

22Do not be hasty in the laying on of hands, and do not share in the sins of others. Keep yourself pure.

23Stop drinking only water, and use a little wine because of your stomach and your frequent illnesses.

24The sins of some are obvious, reaching the place of judgment ahead of them; the sins of others trail behind them. 25In the same way, good deeds are obvious, and even those that are not obvious cannot remain hidden forever.

6 All who are under the yoke of slavery should consider their masters worthy of full respect, so that God's name and our teaching may not be slandered. 2Those who have believing masters should not show them disrespect just because they are fellow believers. Instead, they should serve them even better because their masters are dear to them as fellow believers and are devoted to the welfarec of their slaves.

False Teachers and the Love of Money

These are the things you are to teach and insist on. 3If anyone teaches otherwise and does not agree to the sound instruction of our Lord Jesus Christ and to godly teaching, 4they are conceited and understand nothing. They have an unhealthy interest in controversies and quarrels about words that result in envy, strife, malicious talk, evil suspicions 5and constant friction between people of corrupt mind, who have been robbed of the truth and who think that godliness is a means to financial gain.

6But godliness with contentment is great gain. 7For we brought nothing into the world, and we can take nothing out of it. 8But if we have food and clothing, we will

---

a 18 Deut. 25:4   b 18 Luke 10:7   c 2 Or and benefit from the service be content with that. ⁹Those who want to get rich fall into temptation and a trap and into many foolish and harmful desires that plunge people into ruin and destruction. ¹⁰For the love of money is a root of all kinds of evil. Some people, eager for money, have wandered from the faith and pierced themselves with many griefs.

Final Charge to Timothy

¹¹But you, man of God, flee from all this, and pursue righteousness, godliness, faith, love, endurance and gentleness. ¹²Fight the good fight of the faith. Take hold of the eternal life to which you were called when you made your good confession in the presence of many witnesses. ¹³In the sight of God, who gives life to everything, and of Christ Jesus, who while testifying before Pontius Pilate made the good confession, I charge you ¹⁴to keep this command without spot or blame until the appearing of our Lord Jesus Christ, ¹⁵which God will bring about in his own time — God, the blessed and only Ruler, the King of kings and Lord of lords, ¹⁶who alone is immortal and who lives in unapproachable light, whom no one has seen or can see. To him be honor and might forever. Amen.

¹⁷Command those who are rich in this present world not to be arrogant nor to put their hope in wealth, which is so uncertain, but to put their hope in God, who richly provides us with everything for our enjoyment. ¹⁸Command them to do good, to be rich in good deeds, and to be generous and willing to share. ¹⁹In this way they will lay up treasure for themselves as a firm foundation for the coming age, so that they may take hold of the life that is truly life.

²⁰Timothy, guard what has been entrusted to your care. Turn away from godless chatter and the opposing ideas of what is falsely called knowledge, ²¹which some have professed and in so doing have departed from the faith.

Grace be with you all.

2 Timothy

THEME: God's faithfulness and the promise of a righteous reward enable believers to endure mistreatment.

AUTHOR: The apostle Paul is the letter's stated author.

DATE OF WRITING: Second Timothy was probably written in AD 66 or 67.

ENCOURAGEMENT FROM 2 TIMOTHY: "What you heard from me, keep as the pattern of sound teaching, with faith and love in Christ Jesus. Guard the good deposit that was entrusted to you — guard it with the help of the Holy Spirit who lives in us" (2 Timothy 1:13 – 14).

CHALLENGE FROM 2 TIMOTHY: "Do your best to present yourself to God as one approved, a worker who does not need to be ashamed and who correctly handles the word of truth . . . 'Everyone who confesses the name of the Lord must turn away from wickedness' " (2 Timothy 2:15,19).

REFLECTION FROM 2 TIMOTHY: "For the Spirit God gave us does not make us timid, but gives us power, love and self-discipline" (2 Timothy 1:7).

See the introduction to 1 Timothy.

1 Paul, an apostle of Christ Jesus by the will of God, in keeping with the promise of life that is in Christ Jesus,

²To Timothy, my dear son:

Grace, mercy and peace from God the Father and Christ Jesus our Lord.

Thanksgiving

³I thank God, whom I serve, as my ancestors did, with a clear conscience, as night and day I constantly remember you in my prayers. ⁴Recalling your tears, I long to see you, so that I may be filled with joy. ⁵I am reminded of your sincere faith, which first lived in your grandmother Lois and in your mother Eunice and, I am persuaded, now lives in you also.

Appeal for Loyalty to Paul and the Gospel

⁶For this reason I remind you to fan into flame the gift of God, which is in you through the laying on of my hands. ⁷For the Spirit God gave us does not make us timid, but gives us power, love and self-discipline. ⁸So do not be ashamed of the testimony about our Lord or of me his prisoner. Rather, join with me in suffering for the gospel, by the power of God. ⁹He has saved us and called us to a holy life — not because of anything we have done but because of his own purpose and grace. This grace was given us in Christ Jesus before the beginning of time, ¹⁰but it has now been revealed through the appearing of our Savior, Christ Jesus, who has destroyed death and has brought life and immortality to light through the gospel. ¹¹And of this gospel I

was appointed a herald and an apostle and a teacher. ¹²That is why I am suffering as I am. Yet this is no cause for shame, because I know whom I have believed, and am convinced that he is able to guard what I have entrusted to him until that day.

¹³What you heard from me, keep as the pattern of sound teaching, with faith and love in Christ Jesus. ¹⁴Guard the good deposit that was entrusted to you — guard it with the help of the Holy Spirit who lives in us.

Examples of Disloyalty and Loyalty

¹⁵You know that everyone in the province of Asia has deserted me, including Phygelus and Hermogenes.

¹⁶May the Lord show mercy to the household of Onesiphorus, because he often refreshed me and was not ashamed of my chains. ¹⁷On the contrary, when he was in Rome, he searched hard for me until he found me. ¹⁸May the Lord grant that he will find mercy from the Lord on that day! You know very well in how many ways he helped me in Ephesus.

The Appeal Renewed

2 You then, my son, be strong in the grace that is in Christ Jesus. ²And the things you have heard me say in the presence of many witnesses entrust to reliable people who will also be qualified to teach others. ³Join with me in suffering, like a good soldier of Christ Jesus. ⁴No one serving as a soldier gets entangled in civilian affairs, but rather tries to please his commanding officer. ⁵Similarly, anyone who competes as an athlete does not receive the victor's crown except by competing according to the rules. ⁶The hardworking farmer should be the first to receive a share of the crops. ⁷Reflect on what I am saying, for the Lord will give you insight into all this.

⁸Remember Jesus Christ, raised from the dead, descended from David. This is my gospel, ⁹for which I am suffering even to the point of being chained like a criminal. But God's word is not chained. ¹⁰Therefore I endure everything for the sake of the elect, that they too may obtain the salvation that is in Christ Jesus, with eternal glory.

¹¹Here is a trustworthy saying:

If we died with him,
    we will also live with him;
¹²if we endure,
    we will also reign with him.
If we disown him,
    he will also disown us;
¹³if we are faithless,
    he remains faithful,
    for he cannot disown himself.

Dealing With False Teachers

¹⁴Keep reminding God's people of these things. Warn them before God against quarreling about words; it is of no value, and only ruins those who listen. ¹⁵Do your best to present yourself to God as one approved, a worker who does not need to be ashamed and who correctly handles the word of truth. ¹⁶Avoid godless chatter, because those who indulge in it will become more and more ungodly. ¹⁷Their teaching will spread like gangrene. Among them are Hymenaeus and Philetus, ¹⁸who have departed from the truth. They say that the resurrection has already taken place, and they destroy the faith of some. ¹⁹Nevertheless, God's solid foundation stands firm, sealed with this inscription: "The Lord knows those who are his," and, "Everyone who confesses the name of the Lord must turn away from wickedness."

²⁰In a large house there are articles not only of gold and silver, but also of wood and clay; some are for special purposes and some for common use. ²¹Those who cleanse themselves from the latter will be instruments for special purposes, made holy, useful to the Master and prepared to do any good work.

²²Flee the evil desires of youth and pursue righteousness, faith, love and peace, along with those who call on the Lord out

of a pure heart. ²³Don't have anything to do with foolish and stupid arguments, because you know they produce quarrels. ²⁴And the Lord's servant must not be quarrelsome but must be kind to everyone, able to teach, not resentful. ²⁵Opponents must be gently instructed, in the hope that God will grant them repentance leading them to a knowledge of the truth, ²⁶and that they will come to their senses and escape from the trap of the devil, who has taken them captive to do his will.

3 But mark this: There will be terrible times in the last days. ²People will be lovers of themselves, lovers of money, boastful, proud, abusive, disobedient to their parents, ungrateful, unholy, ³without love, unforgiving, slanderous, without self-control, brutal, not lovers of the good, ⁴treacherous, rash, conceited, lovers of pleasure rather than lovers of God— ⁵having a form of godliness but denying its power. Have nothing to do with such people.

⁶They are the kind who worm their way into homes and gain control over gullible women, who are loaded down with sins and are swayed by all kinds of evil desires, ⁷always learning but never able to come to a knowledge of the truth. ⁸Just as Jannes and Jambres opposed Moses, so also these teachers oppose the truth. They are men of depraved minds, who, as far as the faith is concerned, are rejected. ⁹But they will not get very far because, as in the case of those men, their folly will be clear to everyone.

A Final Charge to Timothy

¹⁰You, however, know all about my teaching, my way of life, my purpose, faith, patience, love, endurance, ¹¹persecutions, sufferings—what kinds of things happened to me in Antioch, Iconium and Lystra, the persecutions I endured. Yet the Lord rescued me from all of them. ¹²In fact, everyone who wants to live a godly life in Christ Jesus will be persecuted, ¹³while

evildoers and impostors will go from bad to worse, deceiving and being deceived. ¹⁴But as for you, continue in what you have learned and have become convinced of, because you know those from whom you learned it, ¹⁵and how from infancy you have known the Holy Scriptures, which are able to make you wise for salvation through faith in Christ Jesus. ¹⁶All Scripture is God-breathed and is useful for teaching, rebuking, correcting and training in righteousness, ¹⁷so that the servant of God[a] may be thoroughly equipped for every good work.

4 In the presence of God and of Christ Jesus, who will judge the living and the dead, and in view of his appearing and his kingdom, I give you this charge: ²Preach the word; be prepared in season and out of season; correct, rebuke and encourage—with great patience and careful instruction. ³For the time will come when people will not put up with sound doctrine. Instead, to suit their own desires, they will gather around them a great number of teachers to say what their itching ears want to hear. ⁴They will turn their ears away from the truth and turn aside to myths. ⁵But you, keep your head in all situations, endure hardship, do the work of an evangelist, discharge all the duties of your ministry.

⁶For I am already being poured out like a drink offering, and the time for my departure is near. ⁷I have fought the good fight, I have finished the race, I have kept the faith. ⁸Now there is in store for me the crown of righteousness, which the Lord, the righteous Judge, will award to me on that day—and not only to me, but also to all who have longed for his appearing.

Personal Remarks

⁹Do your best to come to me quickly, ¹⁰for Demas, because he loved this world, has deserted me and has gone to Thessalonica. Crescens has gone to Galatia, and

---

a 17 Or that you, a man of God,

MY NAME IS JOHN MARK

2 TIMOTHY 4:11

John Mark (or Mark) was a cousin of Barnabas, Paul's partner on his first missionary journey. Here in 2 Timothy the aged Paul urged Timothy to bring Mark to him because "he is helpful to me in my ministry" (2 Timothy 4:11). That wasn't always the case. Mark had known failure in the ministry. John Mark, then a young man, had accompanied Paul and Barnabas as they began their first missionary journey (see Acts 13:5). For some reason, though, Mark had deserted the team at Pamphylia (see 13:13), before the group had traveled beyond the Taurus Mountains of Asia Minor. Because Mark had let them down once, Paul refused to take him along on his and Barnabas's planned second journey. Barnabas, who had stood with Paul when he was needed (see 9:26–27), evidently saw potential in his maturing cousin, so he and Mark embarked instead on a separate journey to Cyprus, while Paul picked Silas as his new partner (see 15:36–41).

Paul's rejection and Mark's own role in splitting a great team of missionaries must have been heavy burdens for this young man to bear. The details of Mark's recovery aren't supplied in Scripture, apart from the fact that he continued in service in the company of Barnabas, the great encourager (see Acts 4:36–37). Wherever we are in our recovery, it's crucial that we find the right companions — accountability partner, pastor or spiritual mentor, sponsor or Step Study group — if we're to succeed. Barnabas — "a good man, full of the Holy Spirit and faith" (11:24) — was the man to whom the Jerusalem church turned when it needed someone in Antioch (see 11:19–24). Mark found the right "sponsor" in his recovery. And he did recover.

Paul, who had once rejected the company of this young man, later recommended John Mark to others (see Colossians 4:10). Paul included Mark's name in his designation of a group of his "co-workers for the kingdom of God" who had "proved a comfort to [him]" (Colossians 4:11). Don't miss the fact that Paul's commendation of these men was based on their record. We must realize during the course of our own recovery that, as we aspire to become leaders, we too need to prove ourselves faithful. Paul as an apostle had a responsibility to be certain that he placed only proven men in positions of authority and ministry.

Mark became a companion to Paul during Paul's imprisonment (see Philemon 24). Paul now knew that he could count on Mark to be a comfort to him instead of a disappointment. No wonder, as Paul neared the end of his life, he instructed Timothy to "get Mark and bring him with you" (2 Timothy 4:11).

One of the deepest pains any of us can experience is being labeled a disappointment. For some of us, this pattern began in childhood. Others of us simply blew it later in life. Now, facing reality, beginning our recovery, we feel the deep shame of knowing that we've disappointed those who loved and depended on us. Perhaps you've recently suffered a relapse. Mark knew that pain. But he persevered in his recovery. He kept on serving. He stuck close to a sponsor who had proven to be a spiritual man.

Mark and Paul were reconciled, to the point that John Mark became someone Paul wanted with him as he faced execution. We can follow these same steps. In fact, past failure and pain can become our credentials for service in Celebrate Recovery. TURN: Trust — Understand — Repent — New life. Find the right sponsor. Why? "As iron sharpens iron, so one person sharpens another" (Proverbs 27:17). Find a Barnabas. Don't attempt recovery alone.

Titus to Dalmatia. [11]Only Luke is with me. Get Mark and bring him with you, because he is helpful to me in my ministry. [12]I sent Tychicus to Ephesus. [13]When you come, bring the cloak that I left with Carpus at Troas, and my scrolls, especially the parchments.

[14]Alexander the metalworker did me a great deal of harm. The Lord will repay him for what he has done. [15]You too should be on your guard against him, because he strongly opposed our message.

[16]At my first defense, no one came to my support, but everyone deserted me. May it not be held against them. [17]But the Lord stood at my side and gave me strength, so that through me the message might be fully proclaimed and all the Gentiles might hear it. And I was delivered from the lion's mouth. [18]The Lord will rescue me from every evil attack and will bring me safely to his heavenly kingdom. To him be glory for ever and ever. Amen.

Final Greetings

[19]Greet Priscilla[a] and Aquila and the household of Onesiphorus. [20]Erastus stayed in Corinth, and I left Trophimus sick in Miletus. [21]Do your best to get here before winter. Eubulus greets you, and so do Pudens, Linus, Claudia and all the brothers and sisters.[b]

[22]The Lord be with your spirit. Grace be with you all.

---

[a] 19 Greek *Prisca*, a variant of *Priscilla*   [b] 21 The Greek word for *brothers and sisters* (*adelphoi*) refers here to believers, both men and women, as part of God's family.

My Name Is Jim

I'M A BELIEVER WHO STRUGGLES WITH SEXUAL ADDICTION, ALCOHOLISM AND WORKAHOLISM

Please read 2 Timothy 4:11, and also read in Acts 15:36 – 41 the aftermath of John Mark's desertion of his ministry team, which is related in Acts 13:13.

Before coming to Celebrate Recovery, I managed to maintain the persona of having it all together; I was a successful corporate attorney with a fancy car and a nice home. On the inside, though, I believed myself to be a complete failure. I was terribly isolated, desperately concealing my fears and anguish.

By the age of 35 I was caught in a vicious cycle, using a combination of sex, alcohol and my career in an attempt to fill a God-shaped vacuum deep within my soul. The professional recognition I received made me feel temporarily better, but later I would act out sexually by indulging in pornography, frequenting strip clubs, engaging in one-night stands and even having sex with prostitutes. This insanity served only to isolate me further and to fill me with added layers of shame.

Acts 13:13 doesn't record the reason why John Mark (Mark) deserted his ministry team, but I definitely know that my addictions were what led me to desert two marriages before I reached the age of 40. My sexual addiction, alcoholism and workaholism, which had at one point served as "cures" to the problems in my life, were no longer working. In fact, they had together become a new and more menacing problem. My life was out of control, and I had emotionally reached bottom. I finally gave up on trying to fix myself, and that's precisely when I found God. At the suggestion of a counselor, I started attending Celebrate Recovery.

In Celebrate Recovery I heard the very message I needed: I can't change myself, but God can, and he will — if I let him. At first I couldn't accept that God would actually want to help me. Sure, I believed he existed; I just couldn't bring myself to believe I mattered to him. And if I didn't matter, why would he help me? God used Celebrate Recovery to shatter my mistaken belief. I heard the testimonies of those who had gone through the program before me and witnessed the changes God was making in their lives. By identifying with their stories, victories and struggles, I became willing to believe that God really did care about me and that Jesus really wanted a personal relationship with me.

I saw for the first time the pattern of destruction in which I'd been engaging for over a decade. I recognized how performance driven I was in my relationships and realized that my self-esteem was entirely dependent on everyone else's good opinion of me. I also saw how the emotional abuse I'd inflicted, the adultery I'd committed and the lies I'd told had devastated the women in my life. I even had to accept that I shared responsibility for keeping the prostitutes and strippers I had encountered trapped in their own cycles of abuse. Through my involvement in Celebrate Recovery I could finally accept God's pardon.

I have sought to pick up the debris from my past and to make amends. I've acknowledged to both of my former wives my responsibility for my behavior. They deserved to hear from me that it wasn't their fault, and I am committed to honoring their pain by living a changed life.

Today, many years later, I'm no longer a slave to my old way of life. God snapped my chains. I don't need to make money, succeed in my career, commit adultery, go to strip clubs or drink to feel better about myself. There are days when I feel temptation. It tends to start when I doubt myself, throw myself into my work or want to be in control. When this happens I look to see where God is in the struggle I'm facing that day, reminding myself that God is God — and I'm not him.

Because I've faced reality, I've felt the deep shame of knowing I disappointed those who loved me and depended on me, much as John Mark did. But now God sees me as faithful, and he has used me as a bridge to other men who are struggling with sexual addiction. He has also found me to be trustworthy. I had given up on my dreams to ever have a family, but after I surrendered that dream to him, he sent me my wife, Leigh. Today I'm making amends by living a changed life, honoring those I've hurt in my wake of abuse.

Several years into my recovery, my Celebrate Recovery pastor, Pastor Bob (who has become my best friend), was able to look beyond the failures of my past and view me, as Paul later viewed John Mark: as one of his "co-workers for the kingdom of God" who had "proved a comfort to [him]" (Colossians 4:10–11; see also 2 Timothy 4:11). He has called me to join him and others to carry the message of hope throughout America and to many countries in Asia, including Mongolia. I want to be a faithful and trustworthy man because of what God has done in my life. As was the case with John Mark, my past failure and pain have become my credentials for service, and for that I will always be grateful.

Titus

THEME: The gospel has a civilizing effect on all aspects of a Christian's life, including relationships within the home.

AUTHOR: The apostle Paul is the letter's stated author.

DATE OF WRITING: This letter was probably written between AD 63 and 65.

ENCOURAGEMENT FROM TITUS: "At one time we . . . were foolish, disobedient, deceived and enslaved by all kinds of passions and pleasures. We lived in malice and envy, being hated and hating one another. But when the kindness and love of God our Savior appeared, he saved us, not because of righteous things we had done, but because of his mercy" (Titus 3:3 – 5).

CHALLENGE FROM TITUS: "Since an overseer manages God's household, he must be blameless — not overbearing, not quick-tempered, not given to drunkenness, not violent, not pursuing dishonest gain" (Titus 1:7).

REFLECTION FROM TITUS: "The grace of God has appeared that offers salvation to all people. It teaches us to say 'No' to ungodliness and worldly passions, and to live self-controlled, upright and godly lives in this present age" (Titus 2:11 – 12).

At a Glance

Recovery Themes in Titus

The book of Titus allows us to again appreciate Paul's words of guidance and counsel to one of his followers. As he has done with Timothy, Paul guides Titus in his ministry efforts, encouraging him to put into practice the things he has seen and been taught. The best way to teach these life values is to live them.

The same goes for us. When we learn to apply the principles of recovery in our lives, when we've accepted Jesus Christ as our Savior and Lord, we're to tell others about it. They won't otherwise understand how and why we've abandoned our past behavior. But those around us will notice the change Christ has made in us when they witness our positive actions. In the book of Titus, Paul quite simply instructs us to put our faith into action.

---

1 Paul, a servant of God and an apostle of Jesus Christ to further the faith of God's elect and their knowledge of the truth that leads to godliness — ²in the hope of eternal life, which God, who does not lie, promised before the beginning of time, ³and which now at his appointed season he has brought to light through the preaching entrusted to me by the command of God our Savior,

⁴To Titus, my true son in our common faith:

Grace and peace from God the Father and Christ Jesus our Savior.

Appointing Elders Who Love What Is Good

⁵The reason I left you in Crete was that you might put in order what was left unfin-

ished and appoint[a] elders in every town, as I directed you. 6An elder must be blameless, faithful to his wife, a man whose children believe[b] and are not open to the charge of being wild and disobedient. 7Since an overseer manages God's household, he must be blameless — not overbearing, not quick-tempered, not given to drunkenness, not violent, not pursuing dishonest gain. 8Rather, he must be hospitable, one who loves what is good, who is self-controlled, upright, holy and disciplined. 9He must hold firmly to the trustworthy message as it has been taught, so that he can encourage others by sound doctrine and refute those who oppose it.

Rebuking Those Who Fail to Do Good

10For there are many rebellious people, full of meaningless talk and deception, especially those of the circumcision group. 11They must be silenced, because they are disrupting whole households by teaching things they ought not to teach — and that for the sake of dishonest gain. 12One of Crete's own prophets has said it: "Cretans are always liars, evil brutes, lazy gluttons."[c] 13This saying is true. Therefore rebuke them sharply, so that they will be sound in the faith 14and will pay no attention to Jewish myths or to the merely human commands of those who reject the truth. 15To the pure, all things are pure, but to those who are corrupted and do not believe, nothing is pure. In fact, both their minds and consciences are corrupted. 16They claim to know God, but by their actions they deny him. They are detestable, disobedient and unfit for doing anything good.

Doing Good for the Sake of the Gospel

2 You, however, must teach what is appropriate to sound doctrine. 2Teach the older men to be temperate, worthy of respect, self-controlled, and sound in faith, in love and in endurance. 3Likewise, teach the older women to

be reverent in the way they live, not to be slanderers or addicted to much wine, but to teach what is good. 4Then they can urge the younger women to love their husbands and children, 5to be self-controlled and pure, to be busy at home, to be kind, and to be subject to their husbands, so that no one will malign the word of God.

6Similarly, encourage the young men to be self-controlled. 7In everything set them an example by doing what is good. In your teaching show integrity, seriousness 8and soundness of speech that cannot be condemned, so that those who oppose you may be ashamed because they have nothing bad to say about us.

9Teach slaves to be subject to their masters in everything, to try to please them, not to talk back to them, 10and not to steal from them, but to show that they can be fully trusted, so that in every way they will make the teaching about God our Savior attractive.

11For the grace of God has appeared that offers salvation to all people. 12It teaches us to say "No" to ungodliness and worldly passions, and to live self-controlled, upright and godly lives in this present age, 13while we wait for the blessed hope — the appearing of the glory of our great God and Savior, Jesus Christ, 14who gave himself for us to redeem us from all wickedness and to purify for himself a people that are his very own, eager to do what is good.

15These, then, are the things you should teach. Encourage and rebuke with all authority. Do not let anyone despise you.

Saved in Order to Do Good

3 Remind the people to be subject to rulers and authorities, to be obedient, to be ready to do whatever is good, 2to slander no one, to be peaceable and considerate, and always to be gentle toward everyone.

3At one time we too were foolish, disobedient, deceived and enslaved by all kinds

---

a 5 Or ordain   *b 6 Or children are trustworthy*   *c 12 From the Cretan philosopher Epimenides* of passions and pleasures. We lived in malice and envy, being hated and hating one another. 4But when the kindness and love of God our Savior appeared, 5he saved us, not because of righteous things we had done, but because of his mercy. He saved us through the washing of rebirth and renewal by the Holy Spirit, 6whom he poured out on us generously through Jesus Christ our Savior, 7so that, having been justified by his grace, we might become heirs having the hope of eternal life. 8This is a trustworthy saying. And I want you to stress these things, so that those who have trusted in God may be careful to devote themselves to doing what is good. These things are excellent and profitable for everyone.

9But avoid foolish controversies and genealogies and arguments and quarrels about the law, because these are unprofitable and useless. 10Warn a divisive person once, and then warn them a second time. After that, have nothing to do with them. 11You may be sure that such people are warped and sinful; they are self-condemned.

Final Remarks

12As soon as I send Artemas or Tychicus to you, do your best to come to me at Nicopolis, because I have decided to winter there. 13Do everything you can to help Zenas the lawyer and Apollos on their way and see that they have everything they need. 14Our people must learn to devote themselves to doing what is good, in order to provide for urgent needs and not live unproductive lives.

15Everyone with me sends you greetings. Greet those who love us in the faith.

Grace be with you all.

Philemon

THEME: Regardless of how they might have been wronged, genuine disciples are to relate to fellow believers with grace, forgiveness and encouragement.

AUTHOR: The letter identifies its author as the apostle Paul.

DATE OF WRITING: This letter was probably written between AD 60 and 62, during Paul's imprisonment in Rome, at about the same time Ephesians and Colossians were written.

CHALLENGE FROM PHILEMON: "I pray that your partnership with us in the faith may be effective in deepening your understanding of every good thing we share for the sake of Christ" (Philemon 6).

ENCOURAGEMENT FROM PHILEMON: "Your love has given me great joy and encouragement, because you . . . have refreshed the hearts of the Lord's people" (Philemon 7).

REFLECTION FROM PHILEMON: "If you consider me a partner, welcome [Onesimus, your runaway slave] as you would welcome me. If he has done you any wrong or owes you anything, charge it to me" (Philemon 17–18).

Paul's letter to Philemon is short and to the point. There isn't a good deal of instruction. There isn't much in the way of how to live a changed life. What there is, though, is news of a changed life. Not only do we change in God's eyes when we accept the gift of Christ's salvation, but we also bring change in the lives of those around us.

In this short letter Paul tells Philemon that his rebellious, once "useless" (Philemon 11) runaway slave has become his brother — and all because of Jesus Christ. When we accept Christ, our old self truly disappears. The nature and quality of our relationships change. Accepting Christ and working out our recovery not only changes us personally, but also has the power to alter our relationships in amazing ways.

¹Paul, a prisoner of Christ Jesus, and Timothy our brother,

To Philemon our dear friend and fellow worker — ²also to Apphia our sister and Archippus our fellow soldier — and to the church that meets in your home:

³Grace and peace to you*a* from God our Father and the Lord Jesus Christ.

Thanksgiving and Prayer

⁴I always thank my God as I remember you in my prayers, ⁵because I hear about your love for all his holy people and your faith in the Lord Jesus. ⁶I pray that your partnership with us in the faith may be effective in deepening your understanding of every good thing we share for the sake of Christ. ⁷Your love has given me great joy

---

a 3 The Greek is plural; also in verses 22 and 25; elsewhere in this letter "you" is singular.

MY NAME IS ONESIMUS

PHILEMON 10

The name Onesimus is mentioned only twice in Scripture, in Philemon 10 and in Colossians 4:9. But his character receives repeated high praise from Paul in this short letter to Philemon. Onesimus was a slave who may have stolen from his master (see Philemon 18) before fleeing. The prescribed penalty for this crime was death. But Paul urged Philemon to receive back Onesimus with mercy, no longer as a slave but "as a dear brother" (v. 16). Paul was probably suggesting that Philemon, far from having his runaway slave executed, grant him his freedom.

Onesimus's name means "useful," which made it a common name for slaves. Paul made a wordplay on this name, noting that earlier Onesimus had been "useless to you, but now he has become useful both to you and to me" (v. 11). The difference came in Onesimus's conversion and mentoring by Paul. Paul wanted to keep Onesimus with him but knew that he had to respect the laws of the day. Related as this is to the issue of slavery, it's a hard concept for us to swallow today. Christianity would become the force that would abolish slavery in the Western world in later centuries, but, at this point in history, Paul was obligated to respect the commonly accepted laws that were in force.

You might be tempted to think, "That was easy enough for Paul, but what about Onesimus?" Don't miss the fact that Paul never doubted that Onesimus would return as instructed. Paul's confidence came from the fact that this one-time slave had found true freedom. Onesimus had the same freedom in Christ that we all possess as children of God—the freedom to become what God created us to be. We too are free to become "useful" to God's people. Each of us has been freed to fulfill God's purpose for our lives.

But there's another lesson in Paul's plans for Onesimus. Paul wanted Onesimus to do what this former rebel no doubt least wanted to do: return to Philemon and make amends. That's part of recovery. Completing an inventory and being open and honest with God and another person can be hard tasks to face. Confronting someone we've wronged may be the last thing we want to do. But the road to recovery doesn't allow for detours—and it demands determination.

and encouragement, because you, brother, have refreshed the hearts of the Lord's people.

Paul's Plea for Onesimus

8Therefore, although in Christ I could be bold and order you to do what you ought to do, 9yet I prefer to appeal to you on the basis of love. It is as none other than Paul — an old man and now also a prisoner of Christ Jesus — 10that I appeal to you for my son Onesimus,*a* who became my son while I was in chains. 11Formerly he was useless to you, but now he has become useful both to you and to me.

12I am sending him — who is my very heart — back to you. 13I would have liked to keep him with me so that he could take your place in helping me while I am in chains for the gospel. 14But I did not want to do anything without your consent, so that any favor you do would not seem forced but would be voluntary. 15Perhaps the reason he was separated from you for a little while was that you might have him back forever — 16no longer as a slave, but better than a slave, as a dear brother. He is very dear to me but even dearer to you, both as a fellow man and as a brother in the Lord.

17So if you consider me a partner, welcome him as you would welcome me. 18If he has done you any wrong or owes you anything, charge it to me. 19I, Paul, am writing this with my own hand. I will pay it back — not to mention that you owe me your very self. 20I do wish, brother, that I may have some benefit from you in the Lord; refresh my heart in Christ. 21Confident of your obedience, I write to you, knowing that you will do even more than I ask.

22And one thing more: Prepare a guest room for me, because I hope to be restored to you in answer to your prayers.

23Epaphras, my fellow prisoner in Christ Jesus, sends you greetings. 24And so do Mark, Aristarchus, Demas and Luke, my fellow workers.

25The grace of the Lord Jesus Christ be with your spirit.

---

a 10 Onesimus means *useful.*

My Name Is Tony

I'M A BELIEVER WHO STRUGGLES WITH DRUG ADDICTION

Please read the whole of Paul's short letter to Philemon, which asks him to accept back his runaway slave, Onesimus, in a spirit of Christian love.

I'll never forget the day that changed my life. I was at my station in the barber shop where I worked, and sitting in my chair was the chief of the state police. My wife walked into the barber shop and challenged me, asking, "Does everyone in here know you smoke crack?" The night before she had caught me doing drugs at home. I managed to convince the police chief in my chair that everything was fine. The assumption that I was getting away with something only served to bolster my denial. But three days later the owner of the barber shop asked me to call my wife to see whether she could join us for lunch.

When we sat down, everyone around the table told me how much they loved me — but that if I wanted to continue working at the shop, and being a husband and father, I needed to get help.

Allow me to rewind a little. I had a pretty good childhood, except that my dad was an alcoholic. I never thought much about the drinking; family events were always based around the ice chest. That was just a part of life.

I continually sought my father's approval, whether in academics or in sports. I remember on various occasions trying to talk to him, but he was unapproachable. Even when drinking he remained a frustrating arm's length away. I realized in my teens that I didn't want to be an alcoholic like my dad, so I opted for pot instead.

At 21 I decided to go to barber school. The following week I learned that my girlfriend — later my wife — was pregnant. Within a week after my finishing school we moved in together, our son was born and I started my career. Around this time I tried prescription pain medications. Most opiates make people sick or tired, but they had just the opposite effect on me. I began to go to any lengths to stay high: doctor shopping, trading pills for haircuts and even raiding people's medicine cabinets. This insanity went on for six years.

Eventually the pills were no longer effective, and a neighbor introduced me to crack. This new habit consumed my life; over the course of the first three weeks it cost me almost

$4,000 and 40 pounds. I was spinning out of control and had become a threat to my family and coworkers. Like Onesimus, I had become a slave — but my masters were drugs and alcohol.

The day after the intervention with my wife and coworkers, my close friend and mentor brought a pastor from my church into the barbershop. He shared with me the story of his own struggle with drugs and his eventual triumph over his habit. I told him I was done with drugs, only to have him introduce me to the reality of denial. I had to deal with my issues, and Celebrate Recovery was a safe place to do just that.

Later that night I walked up the steps to my first Celebrate Recovery experience. To my surprise, I wasn't alone. I met people with all kinds of hurts, hang-ups and habits. I was afraid to surrender control of my life, realizing that once I let go and let God, there would be no turning back. Still, I made the decision to trust God, to let go of something that wasn't mine in the first place (my life) and give it back to him. Now, with my new identity in Christ intact, I had to repair the most important relationships in my life. In Philemon, Paul called upon Onesimus to do what he least wanted to do: make amends. I too had to face those I'd wronged.

I asked God for the courage to say the right words to my wife. Holding her face, I told her, "I'm sorry I caused so much pain in our marriage. None of it was your fault. It was all me, and I want to thank you for stepping in and saving my life and for sticking around with me through all the bad years. You mean so much to me, and I love you." This was one of the best moments in my recovery.

About four months ago God gave me the opportunity to make amends to my six-year-old son, Riley. One night he looked up at me and said, "Dad, I'm so glad you don't do bad stuff anymore." "Do you remember the bad stuff I did?" I asked — and he broke down crying. I apologized over and over, assuring him that it wasn't his or his mom's fault. Now when I lose my patience at home, Riley tells me, "Dad, you need to go to one of your talk-talk meetings and get you some patience." Every time I attend Celebrate Recovery I come back a better husband and father.

Like Onesimus, I've found the freedom to become what God created me to be, to be "useful" (Philemon 11) to God's people and to fulfill God's purpose for me. My new life in Christ has been like a country song played backward: I got back my life, my family, my job and even a new home.

Hebrews

THEME: "Today" is the time of decision, because God's call always requires a response and carries a time limit.

AUTHOR: The author of Hebrews is unknown. This individual was well schooled in the Old Testament, acquainted with his audience, capable of writing excellent Greek and a friend of Timothy.

DATE OF WRITING: Hebrews was probably written between AD 60 and 70.

ENCOURAGEMENT FROM HEBREWS: "We do not have a high priest who is unable to empathize with our weaknesses, but we have one who has been tempted in every way, just as we are — yet he did not sin. Let us then approach God's throne of grace with confidence, so that we may receive mercy and find grace to help us in our time of need" (Hebrews 4:15 – 16).

CHALLENGE FROM HEBREWS: "Let us hold unswervingly to the hope we profess, for he who promised is faithful. And let us consider how we may spur one another on toward love and good deeds" (Hebrews 10:23 – 24).

REFLECTION FROM HEBREWS: "Nothing in all creation is hidden from God's sight. Everything is uncovered and laid bare before the eyes of him to whom we must give account" (Hebrews 4:13).

Recovery Themes in Hebrews

How we approach God has everything to do with how we perceive him. Do we picture him as far off, aloof, disinterested? As wanting to help but unable? Or do we see him as he truly is, personally, intimately and powerfully involved in our lives?

The author of Hebrews asks these questions and answers that we're able to come to God through Jesus on the basis of our faith. We don't need to walk an intricate maze to find the Savior; we just need to accept that we need and want him. Hebrews points out that our sins are already obvious to us as human beings. By trying to get rid of them on our own merit, or by any other way besides trust in Christ, we only heighten our awareness of our sin. Only by faith in the sacrifice of Jesus are we made whole. Once we recognize that we're powerless and out of control, once we believe that God exists and can help us recover, we need only to come to Christ. We need to make the choice to commit our lives and wills to his care and control.

God's Final Word: His Son

1 In the past God spoke to our ancestors through the prophets at many times and in various ways, 2but in these last days he has spoken to us by his Son, whom he appointed heir of all things, and through whom also he made the universe. 3The Son is the radiance of God's glory and the exact representation of his being, sustaining all things by his powerful word. After he had provided purification for sins, he sat down at the right hand

of the Majesty in heaven. ⁴So he became as much superior to the angels as the name he has inherited is superior to theirs.

The Son Superior to Angels

⁵For to which of the angels did God ever say,

"You are my Son;
today I have become your Father"ᵃ?

Or again,

"I will be his Father,
and he will be my Son"ᵇ?

⁶And again, when God brings his firstborn into the world, he says,

"Let all God's angels worship him."ᶜ

⁷In speaking of the angels he says,

"He makes his angels spirits,
and his servants flames of fire."ᵈ

⁸But about the Son he says,

"Your throne, O God, will last for ever
and ever;
a scepter of justice will be the scepter
of your kingdom.
⁹You have loved righteousness and hated
wickedness;
therefore God, your God, has set you
above your companions
by anointing you with the oil of joy."ᵉ

¹⁰He also says,

"In the beginning, Lord, you laid the
foundations of the earth,
and the heavens are the work of your
hands.
¹¹They will perish, but you remain;
they will all wear out like a garment.
¹²You will roll them up like a robe;
like a garment they will be changed.
But you remain the same,
and your years will never end."ᶠ

¹³To which of the angels did God ever say,

"Sit at my right hand
until I make your enemies
a footstool for your feet"ᵍ?

¹⁴Are not all angels ministering spirits sent to serve those who will inherit salvation?

Warning to Pay Attention

2 We must pay the most careful attention, therefore, to what we have heard, so that we do not drift away. ²For since the message spoken through angels was binding, and every violation and disobedience received its just punishment, ³how shall we escape if we ignore so great a salvation? This salvation, which was first announced by the Lord, was confirmed to us by those who heard him. ⁴God also testified to it by signs, wonders and various miracles, and by gifts of the Holy Spirit distributed according to his will.

Jesus Made Fully Human

⁵It is not to angels that he has subjected the world to come, about which we are speaking. ⁶But there is a place where someone has testified:

"What is mankind that you are mindful
of them,
a son of man that you care for him?
⁷You made them a littleʰ lower than the
angels;
you crowned them with glory and
honor
⁸   and put everything under their
feet."ⁱ·ʲ

In putting everything under them,ᵏ God left nothing that is not subject to them.ᵏ Yet at present we do not see everything subject to them.ᵏ ⁹But we do see Jesus, who was made lower than the angels for a little while, now crowned with glory and honor because he suffered death, so that by the

---

ᵃ 5 Psalm 2:7   ᵇ 5 2 Samuel 7:14; 1 Chron. 17:13   ᶜ 6 Deut. 32:43 (see Dead Sea Scrolls and Septuagint)
ᵈ 7 Psalm 104:4   ᵉ 9 Psalm 45:6,7   ᶠ 12 Psalm 102:25-27   ᵍ 13 Psalm 110:1   ʰ 7 Or them for a little while
ⁱ 6-8 Psalm 8:4-6   ʲ 7,8 Or *You made him a little lower than the angels;/ you crowned him with glory and honor/
⁸and put everything under his feet.*   ᵏ 8 Or him

grace of God he might taste death for everyone.

[10]In bringing many sons and daughters to glory, it was fitting that God, for whom and through whom everything exists, should make the pioneer of their salvation perfect through what he suffered. [11]Both the one who makes people holy and those who are made holy are of the same family. So Jesus is not ashamed to call them brothers and sisters.[a] [12]He says,

"I will declare your name to my
brothers and sisters;
in the assembly I will sing your
praises."[b]

[13]And again,

"I will put my trust in him."[c]

And again he says,

"Here am I, and the children God has
given me."[d]

[14]Since the children have flesh and blood, he too shared in their humanity so that by his death he might break the power of him who holds the power of death — that is, the devil — [15]and free those who all their lives were held in slavery by their fear of death. [16]For surely it is not angels he helps, but Abraham's descendants. [17]For this reason he had to be made like them,[e] fully human in every way, in order that he might become a merciful and faithful high priest in service to God, and that he might make atonement for the sins of the people. [18]Because he himself suffered when he was tempted, he is able to help those who are being tempted.

Jesus Greater Than Moses

3 Therefore, holy brothers and sisters, who share in the heavenly calling, fix your thoughts on Jesus, whom we acknowledge as our apostle and high priest. [2]He was faithful to the one who appointed him, just as Moses was faithful in all God's house. [3]Jesus has been found worthy of greater honor than Moses, just as the builder of a house has greater honor than the house itself. [4]For every house is built by someone, but God is the builder of everything. [5]"Moses was faithful as a servant in all God's house,"[f] bearing witness to what would be spoken by God in the future. [6]But Christ is faithful as the Son over God's house. And we are his house, if indeed we hold firmly to our confidence and the hope in which we glory.

Warning Against Unbelief

[7]So, as the Holy Spirit says:

"Today, if you hear his voice,
[8]   do not harden your hearts
as you did in the rebellion,
    during the time of testing in the
        wilderness,
[9]where your ancestors tested and tried
    me,
    though for forty years they saw what
        I did.
[10]That is why I was angry with that
        generation;
    I said, 'Their hearts are always going
        astray,
    and they have not known my ways.'
[11]So I declared on oath in my anger,
    'They shall never enter my rest.' "[g]

[12]See to it, brothers and sisters, that none of you has a sinful, unbelieving heart that turns away from the living God. [13]But encourage one another daily, as long as it is called "Today," so that none of you may be hardened by sin's deceitfulness. [14]We have come to share in Christ, if indeed we hold our original conviction firmly to the very end. [15]As has just been said:

"Today, if you hear his voice,
    do not harden your hearts
    as you did in the rebellion."[h]

---

[a] 11 The Greek word for *brothers and sisters* (*adelphoi*) refers here to believers, both men and women, as part of God's family; also in verse 12; and in 3:1, 12; 10:19; 13:22.   [b] 12 Psalm 22:22   [c] 13 Isaiah 8:17   [d] 13 Isaiah 8:18   [e] 17 Or *like his brothers*   [f] 5 Num. 12:7   [g] 11 Psalm 95:7-11   [h] 15 Psalm 95:7,8

16Who were they who heard and rebelled? Were they not all those Moses led out of Egypt? 17And with whom was he angry for forty years? Was it not with those who sinned, whose bodies perished in the wilderness? 18And to whom did God swear that they would never enter his rest if not to those who disobeyed? 19So we see that they were not able to enter, because of their unbelief.

A Sabbath-Rest for the People of God

4 Therefore, since the promise of entering his rest still stands, let us be careful that none of you be found to have fallen short of it. 2For we also have had the good news proclaimed to us, just as they did; but the message they heard was of no value to them, because they did not share the faith of those who obeyed.a 3Now we who have believed enter that rest, just as God has said,

"So I declared on oath in my anger,
  'They shall never enter my rest.'"b

And yet his works have been finished since the creation of the world. 4For somewhere he has spoken about the seventh day in these words: "On the seventh day God rested from all his works."c 5And again in the passage above he says, "They shall never enter my rest."

6Therefore since it still remains for some to enter that rest, and since those who formerly had the good news proclaimed to them did not go in because of their disobedience, 7God again set a certain day, calling it "Today." This he did when a long time later he spoke through David, as in the passage already quoted:

"Today, if you hear his voice,
  do not harden your hearts."d

8For if Joshua had given them rest, God would not have spoken later about another day. 9There remains, then, a Sabbath-rest

for the people of God; 10for anyone who enters God's rest also rests from their works,e just as God did from his. 11Let us, therefore, make every effort to enter that rest, so that no one will perish by following their example of disobedience.

12For the word of God is alive and active. Sharper than any double-edged sword, it penetrates even to dividing soul and spirit, joints and marrow; it judges the thoughts and attitudes of the heart. 13Nothing in all creation is hidden from God's sight. Everything is uncovered and laid bare before the eyes of him to whom we must give account.

Jesus the Great High Priest

14Therefore, since we have a great high priest who has ascended into heaven,f Jesus the Son of God, let us hold firmly to the faith we profess. 15For we do not have a high priest who is unable to empathize with our weaknesses, but we have one who has been tempted in every way, just as we are — yet he did not sin. 16Let us then approach God's throne of grace with confidence, so that we may receive mercy and find grace to help us in our time of need.

5 Every high priest is selected from among the people and is appointed to represent the people in matters related to God, to offer gifts and sacrifices for sins. 2He is able to deal gently with those who are ignorant and are going astray, since he himself is subject to weakness. 3This is why he has to offer sacrifices for his own sins, as well as for the sins of the people. 4And no one takes this honor on himself, but he receives it when called by God, just as Aaron was.

5In the same way, Christ did not take on himself the glory of becoming a high priest. But God said to him,

"You are my Son;
  today I have become your Father."g

6And he says in another place,

---

a 2 Some manuscripts because those who heard did not combine it with faith   b 3 Psalm 95:11; also in verse 5
c 4 Gen. 2:2   d 7 Psalm 95:7,8   e 10 Or labor   f 14 Greek has gone through the heavens   g 5 Psalm 2:7

"You are a priest forever,
in the order of Melchizedek."*a*

7During the days of Jesus' life on earth, he offered up prayers and petitions with fervent cries and tears to the one who could save him from death, and he was heard because of his reverent submission. 8Son though he was, he learned obedience from what he suffered 9and, once made perfect, he became the source of eternal salvation for all who obey him 10and was designated by God to be high priest in the order of Melchizedek.

Warning Against Falling Away

11We have much to say about this, but it is hard to make it clear to you because you no longer try to understand. 12In fact, though by this time you ought to be teachers, you need someone to teach you the elementary truths of God's word all over again. You need milk, not solid food! 13Anyone who lives on milk, being still an infant, is not acquainted with the teaching about righteousness. 14But solid food is for the mature, who by constant use have trained themselves to distinguish good from evil.

6 Therefore let us move beyond the elementary teachings about Christ and be taken forward to maturity, not laying again the foundation of repentance from acts that lead to death,*b* and of faith in God, 2instruction about cleansing rites,*c* the laying on of hands, the resurrection of the dead, and eternal judgment. 3And God permitting, we will do so.

4It is impossible for those who have once been enlightened, who have tasted the heavenly gift, who have shared in the Holy Spirit, 5who have tasted the goodness of the word of God and the powers of the coming age 6and who have fallen*d* away, to be brought back to repentance. To their loss they are crucifying the Son of God all over again and subjecting him to public dis-

grace. 7Land that drinks in the rain often falling on it and that produces a crop useful to those for whom it is farmed receives the blessing of God. 8But land that produces thorns and thistles is worthless and is in danger of being cursed. In the end it will be burned.

9Even though we speak like this, dear friends, we are convinced of better things in your case — the things that have to do with salvation. 10God is not unjust; he will not forget your work and the love you have shown him as you have helped his people and continue to help them. 11We want each of you to show this same diligence to the very end, so that what you hope for may be fully realized. 12We do not want you to become lazy, but to imitate those who through faith and patience inherit what has been promised.

The Certainty of God's Promise

13When God made his promise to Abraham, since there was no one greater for him to swear by, he swore by himself, 14saying, "I will surely bless you and give you many descendants."*e* 15And so after waiting patiently, Abraham received what was promised.

16People swear by someone greater than themselves, and the oath confirms what is said and puts an end to all argument. 17Because God wanted to make the unchanging nature of his purpose very clear to the heirs of what was promised, he confirmed it with an oath. 18God did this so that, by two unchangeable things in which it is impossible for God to lie, we who have fled to take hold of the hope set before us may be greatly encouraged. 19We have this hope as an anchor for the soul, firm and secure. It enters the inner sanctuary behind the curtain, 20where our forerunner, Jesus, has entered on our behalf. He has become a high priest forever, in the order of Melchizedek.

---

a 6 Psalm 110:4   *b 1* Or *from useless rituals*   *c 2* Or *about baptisms*   *d 6* Or *age,* 6*if they fall*
e 14 Gen. 22:17

Melchizedek the Priest

7 This Melchizedek was king of Salem and priest of God Most High. He met Abraham returning from the defeat of the kings and blessed him, ²and Abraham gave him a tenth of everything. First, the name Melchizedek means "king of righteousness"; then also, "king of Salem" means "king of peace." ³Without father or mother, without genealogy, without beginning of days or end of life, resembling the Son of God, he remains a priest forever.

⁴Just think how great he was: Even the patriarch Abraham gave him a tenth of the plunder! ⁵Now the law requires the descendants of Levi who become priests to collect a tenth from the people — that is, from their fellow Israelites — even though they also are descended from Abraham. ⁶This man, however, did not trace his descent from Levi, yet he collected a tenth from Abraham and blessed him who had the promises. ⁷And without doubt the lesser is blessed by the greater. ⁸In the one case, the tenth is collected by people who die; but in the other case, by him who is declared to be living. ⁹One might even say that Levi, who collects the tenth, paid the tenth through Abraham, ¹⁰because when Melchizedek met Abraham, Levi was still in the body of his ancestor.

Jesus Like Melchizedek

¹¹If perfection could have been attained through the Levitical priesthood — and indeed the law given to the people established that priesthood — why was there still need for another priest to come, one in the order of Melchizedek, not in the order of Aaron? ¹²For when the priesthood is changed, the law must be changed also. ¹³He of whom these things are said belonged to a different tribe, and no one from that tribe has ever served at the altar. ¹⁴For it is clear that our Lord descended from Judah, and in regard to that tribe Moses said nothing about priests. ¹⁵And what we have said is even more clear if another priest like Melchizedek appears, ¹⁶one who has become a priest not on the basis of a regulation as to his ancestry but on the basis of the power of an indestructible life. ¹⁷For it is declared:

"You are a priest forever,
  in the order of Melchizedek."*a*

¹⁸The former regulation is set aside because it was weak and useless ¹⁹(for the law made nothing perfect), and a better hope is introduced, by which we draw near to God.

²⁰And it was not without an oath! Others became priests without any oath, ²¹but he became a priest with an oath when God said to him:

"The Lord has sworn
  and will not change his mind:
  'You are a priest forever.'"*a*

²²Because of this oath, Jesus has become the guarantor of a better covenant.

²³Now there have been many of those priests, since death prevented them from continuing in office; ²⁴but because Jesus lives forever, he has a permanent priesthood. ²⁵Therefore he is able to save completely*b* those who come to God through him, because he always lives to intercede for them.

²⁶Such a high priest truly meets our need — one who is holy, blameless, pure, set apart from sinners, exalted above the heavens. ²⁷Unlike the other high priests, he does not need to offer sacrifices day after day, first for his own sins, and then for the sins of the people. He sacrificed for their sins once for all when he offered himself. ²⁸For the law appoints as high priests men in all their weakness; but the oath, which came after the law, appointed the Son, who has been made perfect forever.

The High Priest of a New Covenant

8 Now the main point of what we are saying is this: We do have such a high priest, who sat down at the right hand of the throne of the Majesty in

---

a 17,21 Psalm 110:4   *b 25* Or *forever*

heaven, [2]and who serves in the sanctuary, the true tabernacle set up by the Lord, not by a mere human being.

[3]Every high priest is appointed to offer both gifts and sacrifices, and so it was necessary for this one also to have something to offer. [4]If he were on earth, he would not be a priest, for there are already priests who offer the gifts prescribed by the law. [5]They serve at a sanctuary that is a copy and shadow of what is in heaven. This is why Moses was warned when he was about to build the tabernacle: "See to it that you make everything according to the pattern shown you on the mountain."[a] [6]But in fact the ministry Jesus has received is as superior to theirs as the covenant of which he is mediator is superior to the old one, since the new covenant is established on better promises.

[7]For if there had been nothing wrong with that first covenant, no place would have been sought for another. [8]But God found fault with the people and said[b]:

"The days are coming, declares the Lord,
    when I will make a new covenant
with the people of Israel
    and with the people of Judah.
[9]It will not be like the covenant
    I made with their ancestors
when I took them by the hand
    to lead them out of Egypt,
because they did not remain faithful to
        my covenant,
    and I turned away from them,
        declares the Lord.
[10]This is the covenant I will establish
    with the people of Israel
after that time, declares the Lord.
I will put my laws in their minds
    and write them on their hearts.
I will be their God,
    and they will be my people.
[11]No longer will they teach their
        neighbor,

or say to one another, 'Know the
        Lord,'
because they will all know me,
    from the least of them to the greatest.
[12]For I will forgive their wickedness
    and will remember their sins no
        more."[c]

[13]By calling this covenant "new," he has made the first one obsolete; and what is obsolete and outdated will soon disappear.

Worship in the Earthly Tabernacle

9 Now the first covenant had regulations for worship and also an earthly sanctuary. [2]A tabernacle was set up. In its first room were the lampstand and the table with its consecrated bread; this was called the Holy Place. [3]Behind the second curtain was a room called the Most Holy Place, [4]which had the golden altar of incense and the gold-covered ark of the covenant. This ark contained the gold jar of manna, Aaron's staff that had budded, and the stone tablets of the covenant. [5]Above the ark were the cherubim of the Glory, overshadowing the atonement cover. But we cannot discuss these things in detail now.

[6]When everything had been arranged like this, the priests entered regularly into the outer room to carry on their ministry. [7]But only the high priest entered the inner room, and that only once a year, and never without blood, which he offered for himself and for the sins the people had committed in ignorance. [8]The Holy Spirit was showing by this that the way into the Most Holy Place had not yet been disclosed as long as the first tabernacle was still functioning. [9]This is an illustration for the present time, indicating that the gifts and sacrifices being offered were not able to clear the conscience of the worshiper. [10]They are only a matter of food and drink and various ceremonial washings — external regulations applying until the time of the new order.

---

[a] 5 Exodus 25:40   [b] 8 Some manuscripts may be translated *fault and said to the people.*   [c] 12 Jer. 31:31-34

The Blood of Christ

¹¹But when Christ came as high priest of the good things that are now already here,ᵃ he went through the greater and more perfect tabernacle that is not made with human hands, that is to say, is not a part of this creation. ¹²He did not enter by means of the blood of goats and calves; but he entered the Most Holy Place once for all by his own blood, thus obtainingᵇ eternal redemption. ¹³The blood of goats and bulls and the ashes of a heifer sprinkled on those who are ceremonially unclean sanctify them so that they are outwardly clean. ¹⁴How much more, then, will the blood of Christ, who through the eternal Spirit offered himself unblemished to God, cleanse our consciences from acts that lead to death,ᶜ so that we may serve the living God!

¹⁵For this reason Christ is the mediator of a new covenant, that those who are called may receive the promised eternal inheritance—now that he has died as a ransom to set them free from the sins committed under the first covenant.

¹⁶In the case of a will,ᵈ it is necessary to prove the death of the one who made it, ¹⁷because a will is in force only when somebody has died; it never takes effect while the one who made it is living. ¹⁸This is why even the first covenant was not put into effect without blood. ¹⁹When Moses had proclaimed every command of the law to all the people, he took the blood of calves, together with water, scarlet wool and branches of hyssop, and sprinkled the scroll and all the people. ²⁰He said, "This is the blood of the covenant, which God has commanded you to keep."ᵉ ²¹In the same way, he sprinkled with the blood both the tabernacle and everything used in its ceremonies. ²²In fact, the law requires that nearly everything be cleansed with blood, and without the shedding of blood there is no forgiveness.

²³It was necessary, then, for the copies of the heavenly things to be purified with these sacrifices, but the heavenly things themselves with better sacrifices than these. ²⁴For Christ did not enter a sanctuary made with human hands that was only a copy of the true one; he entered heaven itself, now to appear for us in God's presence. ²⁵Nor did he enter heaven to offer himself again and again, the way the high priest enters the Most Holy Place every year with blood that is not his own. ²⁶Otherwise Christ would have had to suffer many times since the creation of the world. But he has appeared once for all at the culmination of the ages to do away with sin by the sacrifice of himself. ²⁷Just as people are destined to die once, and after that to face judgment, ²⁸so Christ was sacrificed once to take away the sins of many; and he will appear a second time, not to bear sin, but to bring salvation to those who are waiting for him.

Christ's Sacrifice Once for All

10 The law is only a shadow of the good things that are coming—not the realities themselves. For this reason it can never, by the same sacrifices repeated endlessly year after year, make perfect those who draw near to worship. ²Otherwise, would they not have stopped being offered? For the worshipers would have been cleansed once for all, and would no longer have felt guilty for their sins. ³But those sacrifices are an annual reminder of sins. ⁴It is impossible for the blood of bulls and goats to take away sins.

⁵Therefore, when Christ came into the world, he said:

"Sacrifice and offering you did not
    desire,
  but a body you prepared for me;
⁶with burnt offerings and sin offerings
    you were not pleased.

ᵃ 11 Some early manuscripts *are to come*   ᵇ 12 Or *blood, having obtained*   ᶜ 14 Or *from useless rituals*
ᵈ 16 Same Greek word as *covenant*; also in verse 17   ᵉ 20 Exodus 24:8

⁷Then I said, 'Here I am—it is written
    about me in the scroll—
I have come to do your will, my
    God.'"ᵃ

⁸First he said, "Sacrifices and offerings, burnt offerings and sin offerings you did not desire, nor were you pleased with them"—though they were offered in accordance with the law. ⁹Then he said, "Here I am, I have come to do your will." He sets aside the first to establish the second. ¹⁰And by that will, we have been made holy through the sacrifice of the body of Jesus Christ once for all.

¹¹Day after day every priest stands and performs his religious duties; again and again he offers the same sacrifices, which can never take away sins. ¹²But when this priest had offered for all time one sacrifice for sins, he sat down at the right hand of God, ¹³and since that time he waits for his enemies to be made his footstool. ¹⁴For by one sacrifice he has made perfect forever those who are being made holy.

¹⁵The Holy Spirit also testifies to us about this. First he says:

¹⁶"This is the covenant I will make with
    them
    after that time, says the Lord.
I will put my laws in their hearts,
    and I will write them on their minds."ᵇ

¹⁷Then he adds:

"Their sins and lawless acts
    I will remember no more."ᶜ

¹⁸And where these have been forgiven, sacrifice for sin is no longer necessary.

A Call to Persevere in Faith

¹⁹Therefore, brothers and sisters, since we have confidence to enter the Most Holy Place by the blood of Jesus, ²⁰by a new and living way opened for us through the curtain, that is, his body, ²¹and since we have a great priest over the house of God, ²²let us draw near to God with a sincere heart and with the full assurance that faith brings, having our hearts sprinkled to cleanse us from a guilty conscience and having our bodies washed with pure water. ²³Let us hold unswervingly to the hope we profess, for he who promised is faithful. ²⁴And let us consider how we may spur one another on toward love and good deeds, ²⁵not giving up meeting together, as some are in the habit of doing, but encouraging one another—and all the more as you see the Day approaching.

²⁶If we deliberately keep on sinning after we have received the knowledge of the truth, no sacrifice for sins is left, ²⁷but only a fearful expectation of judgment and of raging fire that will consume the enemies of God. ²⁸Anyone who rejected the law of Moses died without mercy on the testimony of two or three witnesses. ²⁹How much more severely do you think someone deserves to be punished who has trampled the Son of God underfoot, who has treated as an unholy thing the blood of the covenant that sanctified them, and who has insulted the Spirit of grace? ³⁰For we know him who said, "It is mine to avenge; I will repay,"ᵈ and again, "The Lord will judge his people."ᵉ ³¹It is a dreadful thing to fall into the hands of the living God.

³²Remember those earlier days after you had received the light, when you endured in a great conflict full of suffering. ³³Sometimes you were publicly exposed to insult and persecution; at other times you stood side by side with those who were so treated. ³⁴You suffered along with those in prison and joyfully accepted the confiscation of your property, because you knew that you yourselves had better and lasting possessions. ³⁵So do not throw away your confidence; it will be richly rewarded.

³⁶You need to persevere so that when you have done the will of God, you will receive what he has promised. ³⁷For,

---

ᵃ 7 Psalm 40:6-8 (see Septuagint)   ᵇ 16 Jer. 31:33   ᶜ 17 Jer. 31:34   ᵈ 30 Deut. 32:35   ᵉ 30 Deut. 32:36; Psalm 135:14

"In just a little while,
   he who is coming will come
   and will not delay."*a*

38And,

"But my righteous*b* one will live by
      faith.
   And I take no pleasure
   in the one who shrinks back."*c*

39But we do not belong to those who shrink back and are destroyed, but to those who have faith and are saved.

Faith in Action

11 Now faith is confidence in what we hope for and assurance about what we do not see. 2This is what the ancients were commended for.

3By faith we understand that the universe was formed at God's command, so that what is seen was not made out of what was visible.

4By faith Abel brought God a better offering than Cain did. By faith he was commended as righteous, when God spoke well of his offerings. And by faith Abel still speaks, even though he is dead.

5By faith Enoch was taken from this life, so that he did not experience death: "He could not be found, because God had taken him away."*d* For before he was taken, he was commended as one who pleased God. 6And without faith it is impossible to please God, because anyone who comes to him must believe that he exists and that he rewards those who earnestly seek him.

---

a 37 Isaiah 26:20; Hab. 2:3   *b 38* Some early manuscripts *But the righteous*   *c 38* Hab. 2:4 (see Septuagint)
d 5 Gen. 5:24

AMENDS LESSON [*Principle Six*]

For the previous entry in the AMENDS lesson, go to Luke 6:31 (page 1239).

For a discussion of Principles One through Eight and a listing of their related lessons,
go to pages xvii – xliv.

Let us consider how we may spur one another on toward love and good deeds.

HEBREWS 10:24

Principle Six calls for us to evaluate all our relationships and to offer forgiveness to those who have hurt us and make amends for harm we've done to others, except when doing so would injure them or others. We need to be willing to admit our part in our relationships that have been broken or damaged. We begin by making AMENDS for the harm we've caused others.

The *E* in AMENDS calls on us to ENCOURAGE ONE ANOTHER. It has been said that encouragement is oxygen for the soul. Before we move ahead with making amends or offering forgiveness to others, we need to meet with our accountability partner or sponsor. We need someone to encourage us and to function for us as a sounding board. That person's objective opinion is valuable to ensure that we make amends and/or offer forgiveness from the right motives. That's what we're told in Hebrews 10:24. When we're asked to serve as an encourager, accountability partner or sponsor for someone else, we're being honored. Remember that no one can hold a torch to light another's path without brightening their own.

The next letter in AMENDS is *N*. Go to Luke 6:35 (page 1240).

⁷By faith Noah, when warned about things not yet seen, in holy fear built an ark to save his family. By his faith he condemned the world and became heir of the righteousness that is in keeping with faith.

⁸By faith Abraham, when called to go to a place he would later receive as his inheritance, obeyed and went, even though he did not know where he was going. ⁹By faith he made his home in the promised land like a stranger in a foreign country; he lived in tents, as did Isaac and Jacob, who were heirs with him of the same promise. ¹⁰For he was looking forward to the city with foundations, whose architect and builder is God. ¹¹And by faith even Sarah, who was past childbearing age, was enabled to bear children because she*a* considered him faithful who had made the promise. ¹²And so from this one man, and he as good as dead, came descendants as numerous as the stars in the sky and as countless as the sand on the seashore.

¹³All these people were still living by

---

a 11 Or *By faith Abraham, even though he was too old to have children — and Sarah herself was not able to conceive — was enabled to become a father because he*

SPIRITUAL INVENTORY LESSON [*Principle Four*]

For the previous entry in the SPIRITUAL INVENTORY lesson, go to Joshua 24:15 (page 274).

For a discussion of Principles One through Eight and a listing of their related lessons, go to pages xvii – xliv.

[Let us] not [give] up meeting together, as some are in the habit of doing, but [let us encourage] one another — and all the more as you see the Day approaching.

HEBREWS 10:25

Principle Four begins the process of "coming clean." It's here that we openly examine and confess our faults to ourselves, to God and to someone else we trust. In the first part of Principle Four we openly examine our lives.

As part of completing Principle Four, we do a SPIRITUAL INVENTORY. We look at eight critical areas of our lives. The eighth and final area is OUR CHURCH. Our church is like a bank: The more we put into it, the more interest we gain from it. If we don't like something in our church, we should get involved so we can help change it or at least understand it better. We should turn our grumbling into service.

We need to ask the following questions with regard to our church:

1. Have we been faithful to our church in the past?

2. Have we been critical instead of active or supportive?

3. Have we discouraged our family's support of their/our church?

Before we start our inventory, there is one vital step we need to take: If we're not already attending Celebrate Recovery, we should find a participating church near us, get into the Word daily and find an accountability partner and/or a sponsor.

This is the final page of the SPIRITUAL INVENTORY lesson.

faith when they died. They did not receive the things promised; they only saw them and welcomed them from a distance, admitting that they were foreigners and strangers on earth. [14]People who say such things show that they are looking for a country of their own. [15]If they had been thinking of the country they had left, they would have had opportunity to return. [16]Instead, they were longing for a better country—a heavenly one. Therefore God is not ashamed to be called their God, for he has prepared a city for them.

[17]By faith Abraham, when God tested him, offered Isaac as a sacrifice. He who had embraced the promises was about to sacrifice his one and only son, [18]even though God had said to him, "It is through Isaac that your offspring will be reckoned."[a] [19]Abraham reasoned that God could even raise the dead, and so in a manner of speaking he did receive Isaac back from death.

[20]By faith Isaac blessed Jacob and Esau in regard to their future.

[21]By faith Jacob, when he was dying, blessed each of Joseph's sons, and worshiped as he leaned on the top of his staff.

[22]By faith Joseph, when his end was near, spoke about the exodus of the Israelites from Egypt and gave instructions concerning the burial of his bones.

[23]By faith Moses' parents hid him for three months after he was born, because they saw he was no ordinary child, and they were not afraid of the king's edict.

[24]By faith Moses, when he had grown up, refused to be known as the son of Pharaoh's daughter. [25]He chose to be mistreated along with the people of God rather than to enjoy the fleeting pleasures of sin. [26]He regarded disgrace for the sake of Christ as of greater value than the treasures of Egypt, because he was looking ahead to his reward. [27]By faith he left Egypt, not fearing the king's anger; he persevered because he saw him who is invisible. [28]By faith he kept

the Passover and the application of blood, so that the destroyer of the firstborn would not touch the firstborn of Israel.

[29]By faith the people passed through the Red Sea as on dry land; but when the Egyptians tried to do so, they were drowned.

[30]By faith the walls of Jericho fell, after the army had marched around them for seven days.

[31]By faith the prostitute Rahab, because she welcomed the spies, was not killed with those who were disobedient.[b]

[32]And what more shall I say? I do not have time to tell about Gideon, Barak, Samson and Jephthah, about David and Samuel and the prophets, [33]who through faith conquered kingdoms, administered justice, and gained what was promised; who shut the mouths of lions, [34]quenched the fury of the flames, and escaped the edge of the sword; whose weakness was turned to strength; and who became powerful in battle and routed foreign armies. [35]Women received back their dead, raised to life again. There were others who were tortured, refusing to be released so that they might gain an even better resurrection. [36]Some faced jeers and flogging, and even chains and imprisonment. [37]They were put to death by stoning;[c] they were sawed in two; they were killed by the sword. They went about in sheepskins and goatskins, destitute, persecuted and mistreated— [38]the world was not worthy of them. They wandered in deserts and mountains, living in caves and in holes in the ground.

[39]These were all commended for their faith, yet none of them received what had been promised, [40]since God had planned something better for us so that only together with us would they be made perfect.

12

Therefore, since we are surrounded by such a great cloud of witnesses, let us throw off everything that hinders and the sin that so easily entangles. And let us run with perseverance the race marked out for us, [2]fixing

---

[a] 18 Gen. 21:12   [b] 31 Or *unbelieving*   [c] 37 Some early manuscripts *stoning; they were put to the test;*

our eyes on Jesus, the pioneer and perfecter of faith. For the joy set before him he endured the cross, scorning its shame, and sat down at the right hand of the throne of God. ³Consider him who endured such opposition from sinners, so that you will not grow weary and lose heart.

God Disciplines His Children

⁴In your struggle against sin, you have not yet resisted to the point of shedding your blood. ⁵And have you completely forgotten this word of encouragement that addresses you as a father addresses his son? It says,

"My son, do not make light of the
	Lord's discipline,
	and do not lose heart when he
		rebukes you,
⁶because the Lord disciplines the one he
		loves,
	and he chastens everyone he accepts
		as his son."ᵃ

⁷Endure hardship as discipline; God is treating you as his children. For what children are not disciplined by their father? ⁸If you are not disciplined — and everyone undergoes discipline — then you are not legitimate, not true sons and daughters at

ᵃ 5,6 Prov. 3:11,12 (see Septuagint)

GRATITUDE LESSON [*Principle Seven*]

For the previous entry in the GRATITUDE lesson, go to Colossians 3:15 – 16 (page 1489).

For a discussion of Principles One through Eight and a listing of their related lessons, go to pages xvii – xliv.

Since we are surrounded by such a great cloud of witnesses,
let us throw off everything that hinders and the sin that so easily entangles,
and let us run with perseverance the race marked out for us.

HEBREWS 12:1

In Principle Seven we reserve a daily quiet time with God for self-examination, Bible reading and prayer in order to get to know God and his will for our lives and to gain the power to follow his will. Once we've been working this principle for a while, we'll understand that we have much for which to be thankful: We're growing closer to our Higher Power, the one and only true Higher Power, Jesus Christ. Our relationships are being restored. We're experiencing peace and freedom from our hurts, hang-ups and habits. We've found a new purpose for our lives. It's important for us to maintain an "attitude of GRATITUDE" for all the positive changes that have occurred and are still occurring in our lives.

We can all be thankful for at least four key areas of our lives. The third area that we can be grateful for is our recovery. We need to thank God for leading us to our recovery program and then thank the other people who have offered us a hug and a hand. We're also called to be grateful for the progress we've made as we've worked the principles and steps, thankful that we've been able to this point to run the race that lies before us — and that we're still on our feet, moving forward (see Hebrews 12:1).

The last focal point for our gratitude is OUR CHURCH. Go to Psalm 100:4 (page 701).

all. [9]Moreover, we have all had human fathers who disciplined us and we respected them for it. How much more should we submit to the Father of spirits and live! [10]They disciplined us for a little while as they thought best; but God disciplines us for our good, in order that we may share in his holiness. [11]No discipline seems pleasant at the time, but painful. Later on, however, it produces a harvest of righteousness and peace for those who have been trained by it.

[12]Therefore, strengthen your feeble arms and weak knees. [13]"Make level paths for your feet,"[a] so that the lame may not be disabled, but rather healed.

Warning and Encouragement

[14]Make every effort to live in peace with everyone and to be holy; without holiness no one will see the Lord. [15]See to it that no one falls short of the grace of God and that no bitter root grows up to cause trouble and defile many. [16]See that no one is sexually immoral, or is godless like Esau, who for a single meal sold his inheritance rights as the oldest son. [17]Afterward, as you know, when he wanted to inherit this blessing, he was rejected. Even though he sought the blessing with tears, he could not change what he had done.

The Mountain of Fear and the Mountain of Joy

[18]You have not come to a mountain that can be touched and that is burning with fire; to darkness, gloom and storm; [19]to a trumpet blast or to such a voice speaking words that those who heard it begged that no further word be spoken to them, [20]because they could not bear what was commanded: "If even an animal touches the mountain, it must be stoned to death."[b] [21]The sight was so terrifying that Moses said, "I am trembling with fear."[c]

[22]But you have come to Mount Zion, to the city of the living God, the heavenly Jerusalem. You have come to thousands upon thousands of angels in joyful assembly, [23]to the church of the firstborn, whose names are written in heaven. You have come to God, the Judge of all, to the spirits of the righteous made perfect, [24]to Jesus the mediator of a new covenant, and to the sprinkled blood that speaks a better word than the blood of Abel.

[25]See to it that you do not refuse him who speaks. If they did not escape when they refused him who warned them on earth, how much less will we, if we turn away from him who warns us from heaven? [26]At that time his voice shook the earth, but now he has promised, "Once more I will shake not only the earth but also the heavens."[d] [27]The words "once more" indicate the removing of what can be shaken—that is, created things—so that what cannot be shaken may remain.

[28]Therefore, since we are receiving a kingdom that cannot be shaken, let us be thankful, and so worship God acceptably with reverence and awe, [29]for our "God is a consuming fire."[e]

Concluding Exhortations

13

Keep on loving one another as brothers and sisters. [2]Do not forget to show hospitality to strangers, for by so doing some people have shown hospitality to angels without knowing it. [3]Continue to remember those in prison as if you were together with them in prison, and those who are mistreated as if you yourselves were suffering.

[4]Marriage should be honored by all, and the marriage bed kept pure, for God will judge the adulterer and all the sexually immoral. [5]Keep your lives free from the love of money and be content with what you have, because God has said,

"Never will I leave you;
  never will I forsake you."[f]

---

[a] 13 Prov. 4:26   [b] 20 Exodus 19:12,13   [c] 21 See Deut. 9:19.   [d] 26 Haggai 2:6   [e] 29 Deut. 4:24
[f] 5 Deut. 31:6

⁶So we say with confidence,

"The Lord is my helper; I will not be
    afraid.
    What can mere mortals do to
        me?"ᵃ

⁷Remember your leaders, who spoke the word of God to you. Consider the outcome of their way of life and imitate their faith. ⁸Jesus Christ is the same yesterday and today and forever.

⁹Do not be carried away by all kinds of strange teachings. It is good for our hearts to be strengthened by grace, not by eating ceremonial foods, which is of no benefit to those who do so. ¹⁰We have an altar from which those who minister at the tabernacle have no right to eat.

¹¹The high priest carries the blood of animals into the Most Holy Place as a sin offering, but the bodies are burned outside the camp. ¹²And so Jesus also suffered outside the city gate to make the people holy through his own blood. ¹³Let us, then, go to him outside the camp, bearing the disgrace he bore. ¹⁴For here we do not have an enduring city, but we are looking for the city that is to come.

¹⁵Through Jesus, therefore, let us continually offer to God a sacrifice of praise — the fruit of lips that openly profess his name. ¹⁶And do not forget to do good and to share

---

ᵃ 6 Psalm 118:6,7

POWERLESS LESSON [*Principle One*]

For the previous entry in the POWERLESS lesson, go to Ephesians 4:26–27 (page 1468).

For a discussion of Principles One through Eight and a listing of their related lessons,
go to pages xvii–xliv.

*Keep on loving one another as brothers and sisters. Do not forget
to show hospitality to strangers, for by so doing some people
have shown hospitality to angels without knowing it.*

HEBREWS 13:1–2

The power to change comes only through God's grace. Principle One states: "Realize I'm not God. I admit that I'm powerless to control my tendency to do the wrong thing and that my life has become unmanageable." If we admit that we're powerless, we recognize our need for a power greater than ourselves to restore us. That power is our Higher Power, the one and only true Higher Power, Jesus Christ.

In Principle One we discover that we're POWERLESS to control our own lives and that our lives have become unmanageable. The *L* in POWERLESS stands for LONELINESS. When we try to maintain a false sense of power, we become isolated and cut off. But when we admit that we're powerless and start to face reality, we find that we don't have to face life alone.

Loneliness is a choice. But so is friendship. When we become involved in recovery and accept Christ as our Savior and begin a personal relationship with him, we never have to walk solo again. Did you know that caring for the lonely can cure loneliness? We take the first steps toward intimacy by becoming involved in our church, in Celebrate Recovery and in our community.

The next letter in POWERLESS is *E*. Go to John 10:10 (page 1311).

with others, for with such sacrifices God is pleased.

[17] Have confidence in your leaders and submit to their authority, because they keep watch over you as those who must give an account. Do this so that their work will be a joy, not a burden, for that would be of no benefit to you.

[18] Pray for us. We are sure that we have a clear conscience and desire to live honorably in every way. [19] I particularly urge you to pray so that I may be restored to you soon.

Benediction and Final Greetings

[20] Now may the God of peace, who through the blood of the eternal covenant brought back from the dead our Lord Jesus, that great Shepherd of the sheep, [21] equip you with everything good for doing his will, and may he work in us what is pleasing to him, through Jesus Christ, to whom be glory for ever and ever. Amen.

[22] Brothers and sisters, I urge you to bear with my word of exhortation, for in fact I have written to you quite briefly.

[23] I want you to know that our brother Timothy has been released. If he arrives soon, I will come with him to see you.

[24] Greet all your leaders and all the Lord's people. Those from Italy send you their greetings.

[25] Grace be with you all.

James

At a Glance

THEME: Genuine, saving faith will transform lives and be demonstrated through good deeds.

AUTHOR: James the half-brother of Jesus is the author of this epistle.

DATE OF WRITING: James was probably written between AD 40 and 50.

ENCOURAGEMENT FROM JAMES: "My brothers and sisters, if one of you should wander from the truth and someone should bring that person back, remember this: Whoever turns a sinner from the error of their way will save them from death and cover over a multitude of sins" (James 5:19 – 20).

CHALLENGE FROM JAMES: "Submit yourselves . . . to God. Resist the devil, and he will flee from you. Come near to God and he will come near to you" (James 4:7 – 8).

REFLECTION FROM JAMES: "If any of you lacks wisdom, you should ask God, who gives generously to all without finding fault, and it will be given to you" (James 1:5).

Recovery Themes in James

When we've been at recovery for a while, we can sometimes get complacent. Comfortable. Even overconfident. The things we used to do in gratitude for having our lives turned around start to seem less and less important. We can begin to think we've got it all together, that there's no longer any need for Step Studies and meetings. We're fine and in control.

The book of James holds up a mirror for us when we begin to think this way. More than any other New Testament letter, James's to-the-point epistle instructs us to put our faith into action. We believe that Jesus is Lord, and now it's time to act like it. We say that Jesus is our Higher Power; now is the time to live as those who've experienced authentic life change. The book of James reminds us that we need to stay in fellowship with other believers, that every day we need to turn over our lives and wills to Christ's care.

1

James, a servant of God and of the Lord Jesus Christ,

To the twelve tribes scattered among the nations:

Greetings.

Trials and Temptations

²Consider it pure joy, my brothers and sisters,ᵃ whenever you face trials of many kinds, ³because you know that the testing of your faith produces perseverance. ⁴Let perseverance finish its work so that you may be mature and complete, not lacking anything. ⁵If any of you lacks wisdom, you should ask God, who gives generously to all without finding fault, and it will be given to you. ⁶But when you ask, you must believe

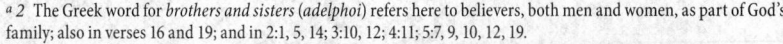
a 2 The Greek word for *brothers and sisters* (*adelphoi*) refers here to believers, both men and women, as part of God's family; also in verses 16 and 19; and in 2:1, 5, 14; 3:10, 12; 4:11; 5:7, 9, 10, 12, 19.

and not doubt, because the one who doubts is like a wave of the sea, blown and tossed by the wind. ⁷That person should not expect to receive anything from the Lord. ⁸Such a person is double-minded and unstable in all they do.

⁹Believers in humble circumstances ought to take pride in their high position. ¹⁰But the rich should take pride in their humiliation — since they will pass away like a wild flower. ¹¹For the sun rises with scorching heat and withers the plant; its blossom falls and its beauty is destroyed. In the same way, the rich will fade away even while they go about their business.

¹²Blessed is the one who perseveres under trial because, having stood the test, that person will receive the crown of life that the Lord has promised to those who love him.

¹³When tempted, no one should say, "God is tempting me." For God cannot be tempted by evil, nor does he tempt anyone; ¹⁴but each person is tempted when they are dragged away by their own evil desire and enticed. ¹⁵Then, after desire has conceived, it gives birth to sin; and sin, when it is full-grown, gives birth to death.

¹⁶Don't be deceived, my dear brothers and sisters. ¹⁷Every good and perfect gift is from above, coming down from the Father of the heavenly lights, who does not change like shifting shadows. ¹⁸He chose to give us birth through the word of truth, that we might be a kind of firstfruits of all he created.

Listening and Doing

¹⁹My dear brothers and sisters, take note of this: Everyone should be quick to listen, slow to speak and slow to become angry, ²⁰because human anger does not produce the righteousness that God desires. ²¹Therefore, get rid of all moral filth and the evil that is so prevalent and humbly accept the word planted in you, which can save you.

²²Do not merely listen to the word, and so deceive yourselves. Do what it says.

²³Anyone who listens to the word but does not do what it says is like someone who looks at his face in a mirror ²⁴and, after looking at himself, goes away and immediately forgets what he looks like. ²⁵But whoever looks intently into the perfect law that gives freedom, and continues in it — not forgetting what they have heard, but doing it — they will be blessed in what they do.

²⁶Those who consider themselves religious and yet do not keep a tight rein on their tongues deceive themselves, and their religion is worthless. ²⁷Religion that God our Father accepts as pure and faultless is this: to look after orphans and widows in their distress and to keep oneself from being polluted by the world.

Favoritism Forbidden

2 My brothers and sisters, believers in our glorious Lord Jesus Christ must not show favoritism. ²Suppose a man comes into your meeting wearing a gold ring and fine clothes, and a poor man in filthy old clothes also comes in. ³If you show special attention to the man wearing fine clothes and say, "Here's a good seat for you," but say to the poor man, "You stand there" or "Sit on the floor by my feet," ⁴have you not discriminated among yourselves and become judges with evil thoughts?

⁵Listen, my dear brothers and sisters: Has not God chosen those who are poor in the eyes of the world to be rich in faith and to inherit the kingdom he promised those who love him? ⁶But you have dishonored the poor. Is it not the rich who are exploiting you? Are they not the ones who are dragging you into court? ⁷Are they not the ones who are blaspheming the noble name of him to whom you belong?

⁸If you really keep the royal law found in Scripture, "Love your neighbor as yourself,"ᵃ you are doing right. ⁹But if you show favoritism, you sin and are convicted by the law as lawbreakers. ¹⁰For whoever keeps the whole law and yet stumbles at just one

ᵃ 8 Lev. 19:18

point is guilty of breaking all of it. 11For he who said, "You shall not commit adultery,"*a* also said, "You shall not murder."*b* If you do not commit adultery but do commit murder, you have become a lawbreaker.

12Speak and act as those who are going to be judged by the law that gives freedom, 13because judgment without mercy will be shown to anyone who has not been merciful. Mercy triumphs over judgment.

Faith and Deeds

14What good is it, my brothers and sisters, if someone claims to have faith but has no deeds? Can such faith save them? 15Suppose a brother or a sister is without clothes and daily food. 16If one of you says to them, "Go in peace; keep warm and well fed," but does nothing about their physical needs, what good is it? 17In the same way, faith by itself, if it is not accompanied by action, is dead.

18But someone will say, "You have faith; I have deeds."

Show me your faith without deeds, and I will show you my faith by my deeds. 19You believe that there is one God. Good! Even the demons believe that—and shudder.

20You foolish person, do you want evidence that faith without deeds is useless*c*? 21Was not our father Abraham considered righteous for what he did when he offered his son Isaac on the altar? 22You see that his faith and his actions were working together, and his faith was made complete by what he did. 23And the scripture was fulfilled that says, "Abraham believed God, and it was credited to him as righteousness,"*d* and he was called God's friend. 24You see that a person is considered righteous by what they do and not by faith alone.

25In the same way, was not even Rahab the prostitute considered righteous for what she did when she gave lodging to the spies and sent them off in a different direction? 26As the body without the spirit is dead, so faith without deeds is dead.

Taming the Tongue

3 Not many of you should become teachers, my fellow believers, because you know that we who teach will be judged more strictly. 2We all stumble in many ways. Anyone who is never at fault in what they say is perfect, able to keep their whole body in check.

3When we put bits into the mouths of horses to make them obey us, we can turn the whole animal. 4Or take ships as an example. Although they are so large and are driven by strong winds, they are steered by a very small rudder wherever the pilot wants to go. 5Likewise, the tongue is a small part of the body, but it makes great boasts. Consider what a great forest is set on fire by a small spark. 6The tongue also is a fire, a world of evil among the parts of the body. It corrupts the whole body, sets the whole course of one's life on fire, and is itself set on fire by hell.

7All kinds of animals, birds, reptiles and sea creatures are being tamed and have been tamed by mankind, 8but no human being can tame the tongue. It is a restless evil, full of deadly poison.

9With the tongue we praise our Lord and Father, and with it we curse human beings, who have been made in God's likeness. 10Out of the same mouth come praise and cursing. My brothers and sisters, this should not be. 11Can both fresh water and salt water flow from the same spring? 12My brothers and sisters, can a fig tree bear olives, or a grapevine bear figs? Neither can a salt spring produce fresh water.

Two Kinds of Wisdom

13Who is wise and understanding among you? Let them show it by their good life, by deeds done in the humility that comes from wisdom. 14But if you harbor bitter envy and selfish ambition in your hearts, do not boast about it or deny the truth. 15Such "wisdom" does not come down from heaven but is earthly, unspiritual, demonic. 16For where you have envy

---

a 11 Exodus 20:14; Deut. 5:18   *b 11* Exodus 20:13; Deut. 5:17   *c 20* Some early manuscripts *dead*   *d 23* Gen. 15:6

and selfish ambition, there you find disorder and every evil practice.

[17]But the wisdom that comes from heaven is first of all pure; then peace-loving, considerate, submissive, full of mercy and good fruit, impartial and sincere. [18]Peacemakers who sow in peace reap a harvest of righteousness.

Submit Yourselves to God

4 What causes fights and quarrels among you? Don't they come from your desires that battle within you? [2]You desire but do not have, so you kill. You covet but you cannot get what you want, so you quarrel and fight. You do not have because you do not ask God. [3]When you ask, you do not receive, because you ask with wrong motives, that you may spend what you get on your pleasures.

[4]You adulterous people,[a] don't you know that friendship with the world means enmity against God? Therefore, anyone who chooses to be a friend of the world becomes an enemy of God. [5]Or do you think Scripture says without reason that he jealously longs for the spirit he has caused to dwell in us[b]? [6]But he gives us more grace. That is why Scripture says:

"God opposes the proud
    but shows favor to the humble."[c]

[7]Submit yourselves, then, to God. Resist the devil, and he will flee from you. [8]Come

---

[a] 4 An allusion to covenant unfaithfulness; see Hosea 3:1.   [b] 5 Or that the spirit he caused to dwell in us envies intensely; or that the Spirit he caused to dwell in us longs jealously   [c] 6 Prov. 3:34

VICTORY LESSON [Principle Five]

For the previous entry in the VICTORY lesson, go to Philippians 1:6 (page 1479).

For a discussion of Principles One through Eight and a listing of their related lessons,
go to pages xvii–xliv.

He gives us more grace. That is why Scripture says: "God opposes the proud but shows favor to the humble." Submit yourselves, then, to God. Resist the devil, and he will flee from you. Come near to God and he will come near to you. Wash your hands, you sinners, and purify your hearts, you double-minded.

JAMES 4:6–8

In Principle Five, as we voluntarily submit to every change God wants to make in our lives and humbly ask him to remove our character defects, we'll find VICTORY in our recovery.

The last letter in VICTORY is Y, which stands for YOU MUST CHOOSE TO CHANGE.

As long as we place self-reliance first, a true reliance on Jesus Christ will be impossible. We need to voluntarily submit to every change God wants us to make in our lives and to humbly ask him to remove our shortcomings. God is waiting to turn our weaknesses into strengths. All he wants us to do is humbly ask.

In Principle Five, when we're ready for change in our lives, we need to be entirely willing to let God be our life-changer. We're not the how-and-when committee. We're the preparation committee. All we have to be is READY. God will give us VICTORY over our defects of character.

This is the final page of the VICTORY lesson.

near to God and he will come near to you. Wash your hands, you sinners, and purify your hearts, you double-minded. ⁹Grieve, mourn and wail. Change your laughter to mourning and your joy to gloom. ¹⁰Humble yourselves before the Lord, and he will lift you up.

¹¹Brothers and sisters, do not slander one another. Anyone who speaks against a brother or sister*a* or judges them speaks against the law and judges it. When you judge the law, you are not keeping it, but sitting in judgment on it. ¹²There is only one Lawgiver and Judge, the one who is able to save and destroy. But you — who are you to judge your neighbor?

Boasting About Tomorrow

¹³Now listen, you who say, "Today or tomorrow we will go to this or that city, spend a year there, carry on business and make money." ¹⁴Why, you do not even know what will happen tomorrow. What is your life? You are a mist that appears for a little while and then vanishes. ¹⁵Instead, you ought to say, "If it is the Lord's will, we will live and do this or that." ¹⁶As it is, you boast in your arrogant schemes. All such boasting is evil. ¹⁷If anyone, then, knows the good they ought to do and doesn't do it, it is sin for them.

Warning to Rich Oppressors

5 Now listen, you rich people, weep and wail because of the misery that is coming on you. ²Your wealth has rotted, and moths have eaten your clothes. ³Your gold and silver are corroded. Their corrosion will testify against you and eat your flesh like fire. You have hoarded wealth in the last days. ⁴Look! The wages you failed to pay the workers who mowed your fields

---

a 11 The Greek word for *brother or sister* (*adelphos*) refers here to a believer, whether man or woman, as part of God's family.

VICTORY LESSON [*Principle Five*]

For the previous entry in the VICTORY lesson, go to 2 Corinthians 5:17 (page 1443).

For a discussion of Principles One through Eight and a listing of their related lessons, go to pages xvii – xliv.

Humble yourselves before the Lord, and he will lift you up.

JAMES 4:10

In Principle Five, as we voluntarily submit to every change God wants to make in our lives and humbly ask him to remove our character defects, we'll find VICTORY in our recovery.

The *T* in VICTORY stands for TURN OVER OUR CHARACTER DEFECTS TO GOD. Relying on our own willpower, our own self-will, has blocked our recovery. Our past efforts to change our hurts, hang-ups and habits on our own, by our own power, were unsuccessful. But if we follow the instruction to humble ourselves given in James 4:10, we'll succeed.

Humility isn't a bad word, and being humble doesn't mean being weak. Humility involves having the right opinion of ourselves or seeing ourselves as God sees us. We can't proceed in our recovery until we turn over our character defects to Jesus. First let go. Then let God.

The next letter in VICTORY is *O*. Go to Matthew 6:34 (page 1137).

ADMIT LESSON [*Principle Four*]

This is the first page of the ADMIT lesson.

For a discussion of Principles One through Eight and a listing of their related lessons, go to pages xvii – xliv.

Confess your sins to each other and pray for each other so that you may be healed. The prayer of a righteous person is powerful and effective.

JAMES 5:16

Principle Four begins the process of "coming clean." In the second part of Principle Four, we confess our faults to ourselves, to God and to someone else we trust.

Why is it necessary for us to ADMIT our faults to someone else? The reason is that many of us have been keeping secrets almost all our lives. Every day those carefully guarded skeletons in our closet take a toll on us. They cause loss of self-respect and energy, as well as bondage to old, codependent habits. Admitting — out loud — those secrets strips them of their power. They lose much of their hold on us when they're shared with someone we can trust.

We may, however. still be reluctant or afraid to reveal our secrets to another person, even someone we trust. We somehow feel as though we have everything to lose and nothing to gain by doing so. The truth is that we really have four things to lose by sharing our Principle Four inventories, as well as our secrets and sins, with another person.

We lose:

1. Our sense of isolation. Our feeling of aloneness, of separation from others, will begin to vanish.

2. Our unwillingness to forgive. When people accept and forgive us, we start to see that we can, in turn, forgive others.

3. Our inflated, false pride. As we realistically see and accept ourselves, we begin to gain true humility, which involves seeing ourselves as we really are and seeing God as he really is.

4. Our sense of denial. Being truthful with another person tears away at our denial. We begin to feel clean and honest.

That's what we have to lose when we admit our wrongs to another. And that's a pretty good deal. We also have three outstanding benefits to gain.

The first benefit is found in James 5:16 (above). We gain the healing that the Bible promises. The key word in this verse is "healed." Notice that the verse doesn't say, "Confess your sins to one another and you'll be forgiven" — although we hope this will be so, at least in terms of the other person's willingness to forgive us. God already forgave us when we confessed our sins to him. Now he promises that we'll begin the healing process when we confess those sins to someone else.

The second and third benefits of sharing our Principle Four inventories with someone we trust are found in Psalm 107:13 – 14 (page 709).

are crying out against you. The cries of the harvesters have reached the ears of the Lord Almighty. ⁵You have lived on earth in luxury and self-indulgence. You have fattened yourselves in the day of slaughter.ᵃ ⁶You have condemned and murdered the innocent one, who was not opposing you.

Patience in Suffering

⁷Be patient, then, brothers and sisters, until the Lord's coming. See how the farmer waits for the land to yield its valuable crop, patiently waiting for the autumn and spring rains. ⁸You too, be patient and stand firm, because the Lord's coming is near. ⁹Don't grumble against one another, brothers and sisters, or you will be judged. The Judge is standing at the door!

¹⁰Brothers and sisters, as an example of patience in the face of suffering, take the prophets who spoke in the name of the Lord. ¹¹As you know, we count as blessed those who have persevered. You have heard of Job's perseverance and have seen what the Lord finally brought about. The Lord is full of compassion and mercy.

¹²Above all, my brothers and sisters, do not swear — not by heaven or by earth or by anything else. All you need to say is a simple "Yes" or "No." Otherwise you will be condemned.

The Prayer of Faith

¹³Is anyone among you in trouble? Let them pray. Is anyone happy? Let them sing songs of praise. ¹⁴Is anyone among you sick? Let them call the elders of the church to pray over them and anoint them with oil in the name of the Lord. ¹⁵And the prayer offered in faith will make the sick person well; the Lord will raise them up. If they have sinned, they will be forgiven. ¹⁶Therefore confess your sins to each other and pray for each other so that you may be healed. The prayer of a righteous person is powerful and effective.

¹⁷Elijah was a human being, even as we are. He prayed earnestly that it would not rain, and it did not rain on the land for three and a half years. ¹⁸Again he prayed, and the heavens gave rain, and the earth produced its crops.

¹⁹My brothers and sisters, if one of you should wander from the truth and someone should bring that person back, ²⁰remember this: Whoever turns a sinner from the error of their way will save them from death and cover over a multitude of sins.

ᵃ 5 Or *yourselves as in a day of feasting*

THEME: Because of the glorious future reserved for them, Christians are to rejoice and be encouraged in the midst of suffering.

AUTHOR: The author of this epistle identified himself as "Peter, an apostle of Jesus Christ" (1 Peter 1:1).

DATE OF WRITING: This letter was probably written in Rome between AD 60 and 64, at a time when persecution was imminent or intensifying.

ENCOURAGEMENT FROM 1 PETER: "You are a chosen people, a royal priesthood, a holy nation, God's special possession, that you may declare the praises of him who called you out of darkness into his wonderful light" (1 Peter 2:9).

CHALLENGE FROM 1 PETER: "Be alert and of sober mind. Your enemy the devil prowls around like a roaring lion looking for someone to devour. Resist him, standing firm in the faith" (1 Peter 5:8–9).

REFLECTION FROM 1 PETER: "If you suffer as a Christian, do not be ashamed, but praise God that you bear that name" (1 Peter 4:16).

Hopefully, no one has ever misled you to believe that being a Christian is easy. Recovery isn't easy either. Once we come to Christ, it isn't as though all our problems are magically whisked away. We still have pain, maybe even more of it because of our relationship with Christ.

The book of 1 Peter instructs us to be joyful in these times of trouble. Relationships may change, old friends may turn their backs, or people may judge us unfairly simply because we're Christians. First Peter provides us with a guidebook on how to handle such difficulties. Peter encourages us to learn from the example of Jesus so we can endure hard times as he did, bringing glory to God in the process.

---

1 Peter, an apostle of Jesus Christ,

To God's elect, exiles scattered throughout the provinces of Pontus, Galatia, Cappadocia, Asia and Bithynia, ²who have been chosen according to the foreknowledge of God the Father, through the sanctifying work of the Spirit, to be obedient to Jesus Christ and sprinkled with his blood:

Grace and peace be yours in abundance.

Praise to God for a Living Hope

³Praise be to the God and Father of our Lord Jesus Christ! In his great mercy he has given us new birth into a living hope through the resurrection of Jesus Christ from the dead, ⁴and into an inheritance that can never perish, spoil or fade. This inheritance is kept in heaven for you, ⁵who through faith are shielded by God's power until the coming of the salvation that is ready to be revealed in the last time.

6In all this you greatly rejoice, though now for a little while you may have had to suffer grief in all kinds of trials. 7These have come so that the proven genuineness of your faith — of greater worth than gold, which perishes even though refined by fire — may result in praise, glory and honor when Jesus Christ is revealed. 8Though you have not seen him, you love him; and even though you do not see him now, you believe in him and are filled with an inexpressible and glorious joy, 9for you are receiving the end result of your faith, the salvation of your souls.

10Concerning this salvation, the prophets, who spoke of the grace that was to come to you, searched intently and with the greatest care, 11trying to find out the time and circumstances to which the Spirit of Christ in them was pointing when he predicted the sufferings of the Messiah and the glories that would follow. 12It was revealed to them that they were not serving themselves but you, when they spoke of the things that have now been told you by those who have preached the gospel to you by the Holy Spirit sent from heaven. Even angels long to look into these things.

Be Holy

13Therefore, with minds that are alert and fully sober, set your hope on the grace to be brought to you when Jesus Christ is revealed at his coming. 14As obedient children, do not conform to the evil desires you had when you lived in ignorance. 15But just as he who called you is holy, so be holy in all you do; 16for it is written: "Be holy, because I am holy."a

17Since you call on a Father who judges each person's work impartially, live out your time as foreigners here in reverent fear. 18For you know that it was not with perishable things such as silver or gold that you were redeemed from the empty way of life handed down to you from your ancestors, 19but with the precious blood of

Christ, a lamb without blemish or defect. 20He was chosen before the creation of the world, but was revealed in these last times for your sake. 21Through him you believe in God, who raised him from the dead and glorified him, and so your faith and hope are in God.

22Now that you have purified yourselves by obeying the truth so that you have sincere love for each other, love one another deeply, from the heart.b 23For you have been born again, not of perishable seed, but of imperishable, through the living and enduring word of God. 24For,

"All people are like grass,
  and all their glory is like the flowers
    of the field;
the grass withers and the flowers fall,
25 but the word of the Lord endures
    forever."c

And this is the word that was preached to you.

2 Therefore, rid yourselves of all malice and all deceit, hypocrisy, envy, and slander of every kind. 2Like newborn babies, crave pure spiritual milk, so that by it you may grow up in your salvation, 3now that you have tasted that the Lord is good.

The Living Stone and a Chosen People

4As you come to him, the living Stone — rejected by humans but chosen by God and precious to him — 5you also, like living stones, are being built into a spiritual housed to be a holy priesthood, offering spiritual sacrifices acceptable to God through Jesus Christ. 6For in Scripture it says:

"See, I lay a stone in Zion,
  a chosen and precious cornerstone,
and the one who trusts in him
  will never be put to shame."e

7Now to you who believe, this stone is precious. But to those who do not believe,

---

a 16 Lev. 11:44,45; 19:2   b 22 Some early manuscripts *from a pure heart*   c 25 Isaiah 40:6-8 (see Septuagint)
d 5 Or *into a temple of the Spirit*   e 6 Isaiah 28:16

"The stone the builders rejected
  has become the cornerstone,"[a]

[8]and,

"A stone that causes people to stumble
  and a rock that makes them fall."[b]

They stumble because they disobey the message — which is also what they were destined for.

[9]But you are a chosen people, a royal priesthood, a holy nation, God's special possession, that you may declare the praises of him who called you out of darkness into his wonderful light. [10]Once you were not a people, but now you are the people of God; once you had not received mercy, but now you have received mercy.

Living Godly Lives in a Pagan Society

[11]Dear friends, I urge you, as foreigners and exiles, to abstain from sinful desires, which wage war against your soul. [12]Live such good lives among the pagans that, though they accuse you of doing wrong, they may see your good deeds and glorify God on the day he visits us.

[13]Submit yourselves for the Lord's sake to every human authority: whether to the emperor, as the supreme authority, [14]or to governors, who are sent by him to punish those who do wrong and to commend those who do right. [15]For it is God's will that by doing good you should silence the ignorant talk of foolish people. [16]Live as free people, but do not use your freedom as a cover-up

[a] 7 Psalm 118:22   [b] 8 Isaiah 8:14

READY LESSON [*Principle Five*]

For the previous entry in the READY lesson, go to Psalm 37:5 – 6 (page 657).

For a discussion of Principles One through Eight and a listing of their related lessons, go to pages xvii – xliv.

Therefore, with minds that are alert and fully sober, set your hope on the grace to be brought to you when Jesus Christ is revealed at his coming. As obedient children, do not conform to the evil desires you had when you lived in ignorance.

1 PETER 1:13–14

In Principle Five we need to be READY to voluntarily submit to every change God wants to make in our lives and humbly ask him to remove our character defects.

The next letter in READY is *A*, which stands for ACCEPT THE CHANGE. Seeing the need for change and allowing that change to occur are two different things, and the space between recognition and willingness can be filled with fear. Fear can trigger our old dependency on self-control. This principle won't work if we're still trapped by our self-will. We need to be ready to accept God's help throughout the transition.

All the principles we've already completed on the road to recovery have helped us build the foundation for the ultimate surrender that's found in Principle Five. James 4:10 includes a directive and a promise: "Humble yourselves before the Lord, and he will lift you up." All we need is the willingness to let God lead us on our road to recovery.

The next letter in READY is *D*. Go to Matthew 12:43 – 45 (page 1151).

for evil; live as God's slaves. ¹⁷Show proper respect to everyone, love the family of believers, fear God, honor the emperor.

¹⁸Slaves, in reverent fear of God submit yourselves to your masters, not only to those who are good and considerate, but also to those who are harsh. ¹⁹For it is commendable if someone bears up under the pain of unjust suffering because they are conscious of God. ²⁰But how is it to your credit if you receive a beating for doing wrong and endure it? But if you suffer for doing good and you endure it, this is commendable before God. ²¹To this you were called, because Christ suffered for you, leaving you an example, that you should follow in his steps.

> ²²"He committed no sin,
>   and no deceit was found in his
>   mouth."[a]

²³When they hurled their insults at him, he did not retaliate; when he suffered, he made no threats. Instead, he entrusted himself to him who judges justly. ²⁴"He himself bore our sins" in his body on the cross, so that we might die to sins and live for righteousness; "by his wounds you have been healed." ²⁵For "you were like sheep going astray,"[b] but now you have returned to the Shepherd and Overseer of your souls.

3 Wives, in the same way submit yourselves to your own husbands so that, if any of them do not believe the word, they may be won over without words by the behavior of their wives, ²when they see the purity and reverence of your lives. ³Your beauty should not come from outward adornment, such as elaborate hairstyles and the wearing of gold jewelry or fine clothes. ⁴Rather, it should be that of your inner self, the unfading beauty of a gentle and quiet spirit, which is of great worth in God's sight. ⁵For this is the way the holy women of the past who put their hope in God used to adorn themselves.

They submitted themselves to their own husbands, ⁶like Sarah, who obeyed Abraham and called him her lord. You are her daughters if you do what is right and do not give way to fear.

⁷Husbands, in the same way be considerate as you live with your wives, and treat them with respect as the weaker partner and as heirs with you of the gracious gift of life, so that nothing will hinder your prayers.

Suffering for Doing Good

⁸Finally, all of you, be like-minded, be sympathetic, love one another, be compassionate and humble. ⁹Do not repay evil with evil or insult with insult. On the contrary, repay evil with blessing, because to this you were called so that you may inherit a blessing. ¹⁰For,

> "Whoever would love life
>   and see good days
> must keep their tongue from evil
>   and their lips from deceitful speech.
> ¹¹They must turn from evil and do good;
>   they must seek peace and pursue it.
> ¹²For the eyes of the Lord are on the
>   righteous
>   and his ears are attentive to their
>   prayer,
> but the face of the Lord is against those
>   who do evil."[c]

¹³Who is going to harm you if you are eager to do good? ¹⁴But even if you should suffer for what is right, you are blessed. "Do not fear their threats[d]; do not be frightened."[e] ¹⁵But in your hearts revere Christ as Lord. Always be prepared to give an answer to everyone who asks you to give the reason for the hope that you have. But do this with gentleness and respect, ¹⁶keeping a clear conscience, so that those who speak maliciously against your good behavior in Christ may be ashamed of their slander. ¹⁷For it is better, if it is God's will, to suf-

---

[a] 22 Isaiah 53:9   [b] 24,25 Isaiah 53:4,5,6 (see Septuagint)   [c] 12 Psalm 34:12-16   [d] 14 Or fear what they fear
[e] 14 Isaiah 8:12

fer for doing good than for doing evil. ¹⁸For Christ also suffered once for sins, the righteous for the unrighteous, to bring you to God. He was put to death in the body but made alive in the Spirit. ¹⁹After being made alive,ᵃ he went and made proclamation to the imprisoned spirits— ²⁰to those who were disobedient long ago when God waited patiently in the days of Noah while the ark was being built. In it only a few people, eight in all, were saved through water, ²¹and this water symbolizes baptism that now saves you also—not the removal of dirt from the body but the pledge of a clear conscience toward God.ᵇ It saves you by the resurrection of Jesus Christ, ²²who has gone into heaven and is at God's right hand—with angels, authorities and powers in submission to him.

Living for God

4 Therefore, since Christ suffered in his body, arm yourselves also with the same attitude, because whoever suffers in the body is done with sin. ²As a result, they do not live the rest of their earthly lives for evil human desires, but rather for the will of God. ³For you have spent enough time in the past doing what pagans choose to do—living in debauchery, lust, drunkenness, orgies, carousing and detestable idolatry. ⁴They are surprised that you do not join them in their reckless, wild living, and they heap abuse on you. ⁵But they will have to give account to him who is ready to judge the living and the dead. ⁶For this is the reason the gospel was preached even to those who are now dead, so that they might be judged according to human standards in regard to the body, but live according to God in regard to the spirit.

⁷The end of all things is near. Therefore be alert and of sober mind so that you may pray. ⁸Above all, love each other deeply, because love covers over a multitude of sins. ⁹Offer hospitality to one another without grumbling. ¹⁰Each of you should use whatever gift you have received to serve others, as faithful stewards of God's grace in its various forms. ¹¹If anyone speaks, they should do so as one who speaks the very words of God. If anyone serves, they should do so with the strength God provides, so that in all things God may be praised through Jesus Christ. To him be the glory and the power for ever and ever. Amen.

Suffering for Being a Christian

¹²Dear friends, do not be surprised at the fiery ordeal that has come on you to test you, as though something strange were happening to you. ¹³But rejoice inasmuch as you participate in the sufferings of Christ, so that you may be overjoyed when his glory is revealed. ¹⁴If you are insulted because of the name of Christ, you are blessed, for the Spirit of glory and of God rests on you. ¹⁵If you suffer, it should not be as a murderer or thief or any other kind of criminal, or even as a meddler. ¹⁶However, if you suffer as a Christian, do not be ashamed, but praise God that you bear that name. ¹⁷For it is time for judgment to begin with God's household; and if it begins with us, what will the outcome be for those who do not obey the gospel of God? ¹⁸And,

"If it is hard for the righteous to be
    saved,
  what will become of the ungodly and
    the sinner?"ᶜ

¹⁹So then, those who suffer according to God's will should commit themselves to their faithful Creator and continue to do good.

To the Elders and the Flock

5 To the elders among you, I appeal as a fellow elder and a witness of Christ's sufferings who also will share in the glory to be revealed: ²Be shepherds of God's flock that is under your

---

ᵃ 18,19 Or but made alive in the spirit, ¹⁹in which also   ᵇ 21 Or but an appeal to God for a clear conscience
ᶜ 18 Prov. 11:31 (see Septuagint)

care, watching over them — not because you must, but because you are willing, as God wants you to be; not pursuing dishonest gain, but eager to serve; ³not lording it over those entrusted to you, but being examples to the flock. ⁴And when the Chief Shepherd appears, you will receive the crown of glory that will never fade away.

⁵In the same way, you who are younger, submit yourselves to your elders. All of you, clothe yourselves with humility toward one another, because,

> "God opposes the proud
>   but shows favor to the humble."ᵃ

⁶Humble yourselves, therefore, under God's mighty hand, that he may lift you up in due time. ⁷Cast all your anxiety on him because he cares for you.

⁸Be alert and of sober mind. Your enemy the devil prowls around like a roaring lion looking for someone to devour. ⁹Resist him, standing firm in the faith, because you know that the family of believers throughout the world is undergoing the same kind of sufferings.

¹⁰And the God of all grace, who called you to his eternal glory in Christ, after you have suffered a little while, will himself restore you and make you strong, firm and steadfast. ¹¹To him be the power for ever and ever. Amen.

Final Greetings

¹²With the help of Silas,ᵇ whom I regard as a faithful brother, I have written to you briefly, encouraging you and testifying that this is the true grace of God. Stand fast in it.

¹³She who is in Babylon, chosen together with you, sends you her greetings, and so does my son Mark. ¹⁴Greet one another with a kiss of love.

Peace to all of you who are in Christ.

ᵃ 5 Prov. 3:34   ᵇ 12 Greek *Silvanus*, a variant of *Silas*

2 Peter

THEME: Believers are to work toward spiritual maturity, adding to their faith godly character in "increasing measure" (2 Peter 1:8). Godly character includes goodness, knowledge, self-control, perseverance, godliness, kindness and love.

AUTHOR: The author identified himself as the apostle Peter.

DATE OF WRITING: This epistle was probably written between AD 64 and 68, near the end of Peter's life.

ENCOURAGEMENT FROM 2 PETER: "The Lord is not slow in keeping his promise . . . He is patient with you, not wanting anyone to perish, but everyone to come to repentance" (2 Peter 3:9).

CHALLENGE FROM 2 PETER: "Make every effort to add to your faith goodness; and to goodness, knowledge; and to knowledge, self-control; and to self-control, perseverance; and to perseverance, godliness; and to godliness, mutual affection; and to mutual affection, love" (2 Peter 1:5 – 7).

REFLECTION FROM 2 PETER: "The Lord knows how to rescue godly from trials" (2 Peter 2:9).

In the book of 2 Peter, the apostle picks up where he left off at the end of his previous letter. In this letter he asserts the authenticity of his claims. He had, after all, lived and walked daily with Jesus throughout his ministry years. Peter wasn't making things up — he was there and knows that what Christ said and did were true.

As we experience recovery, this kind of assurance is a tremendous blessing. We have a Higher Power in Jesus after whom we can model ourselves. He isn't invented. He's real, and he has the power to heal us. In light of this, Peter cautions us not to return to our old ways. We've been changed by Christ and are experiencing the life he's promised us. Let's live that life, doing all we can to avoid reverting back to our old hurts, hang-ups and habits. By living out this changed life, we not only experience salvation but bring glory to Christ. Now that's a life worth living!

1

Simon Peter, a servant and apostle of Jesus Christ,

To those who through the righteousness of our God and Savior Jesus Christ have received a faith as precious as ours:

²Grace and peace be yours in abundance through the knowledge of God and of Jesus our Lord.

Confirming One's Calling and Election

³His divine power has given us everything we need for a godly life through our knowledge of him who called us by his own glory and goodness. ⁴Through these he has given us his very great and precious promises, so that through them you may participate in the divine nature, having escaped the corruption in the world caused by evil desires.

⁵For this very reason, make every effort to add to your faith goodness; and to goodness, knowledge; ⁶and to knowledge, self-control; and to self-control, perseverance; and to perseverance, godliness; ⁷and to godliness, mutual affection; and to mutual affection, love. ⁸For if you possess these qualities in increasing measure, they will keep you from being ineffective and unproductive in your knowledge of our Lord Jesus Christ. ⁹But whoever does not have them is nearsighted and blind, forgetting that they have been cleansed from their past sins.

¹⁰Therefore, my brothers and sisters,ᵃ make every effort to confirm your calling and election. For if you do these things, you will never stumble, ¹¹and you will receive a rich welcome into the eternal kingdom of our Lord and Savior Jesus Christ.

Prophecy of Scripture

¹²So I will always remind you of these things, even though you know them and are firmly established in the truth you now have. ¹³I think it is right to refresh your memory as long as I live in the tent of this body, ¹⁴because I know that I will soon put it aside, as our Lord Jesus Christ has made clear to me. ¹⁵And I will make every effort to see that after my departure you will always be able to remember these things.

¹⁶For we did not follow cleverly devised stories when we told you about the coming of our Lord Jesus Christ in power, but we were eyewitnesses of his majesty. ¹⁷He received honor and glory from God the Father when the voice came to him from the Majestic Glory, saying, "This is my Son, whom I love; with him I am well pleased."ᵇ ¹⁸We ourselves heard this voice that came from heaven when we were with him on the sacred mountain.

¹⁹We also have the prophetic message as something completely reliable, and you will do well to pay attention to it, as to a light shining in a dark place, until the day dawns and the morning star rises in your hearts. ²⁰Above all, you must understand that no prophecy of Scripture came about by the prophet's own interpretation of things. ²¹For prophecy never had its origin in the human will, but prophets, though human, spoke from God as they were carried along by the Holy Spirit.

False Teachers and Their Destruction

2 But there were also false prophets among the people, just as there will be false teachers among you. They will secretly introduce destructive heresies, even denying the sovereign Lord who bought them — bringing swift destruction on themselves. ²Many will follow their depraved conduct and will bring the way of truth into disrepute. ³In their greed these teachers will exploit you with fabricated stories. Their condemnation has long been hanging over them, and their destruction has not been sleeping.

⁴For if God did not spare angels when they sinned, but sent them to hell,ᶜ putting them in chains of darknessᵈ to be held for judgment; ⁵if he did not spare the ancient world when he brought the flood on its ungodly people, but protected Noah, a preacher of righteousness, and seven others; ⁶if he condemned the cities of Sodom and Gomorrah by burning them to ashes, and made them an example of what is going to happen to the ungodly; ⁷and if he rescued Lot, a righteous man, who was distressed by the depraved conduct of the lawless ⁸(for that righteous man, living among them day after day, was tormented in his righteous soul by the lawless deeds he saw and heard) — ⁹if this is so, then the Lord knows how to rescue the godly from trials and to hold the unrighteous for punishment on the day of judgment. ¹⁰This is especially true of those who follow the

---

ᵃ 10 The Greek word for *brothers and sisters* (*adelphoi*) refers here to believers, both men and women, as part of God's family.   ᵇ 17 Matt. 17:5; Mark 9:7; Luke 9:35   ᶜ 4 Greek *Tartarus*   ᵈ 4 Some manuscripts *in gloomy dungeons* corrupt desire of the flesh*a* and despise authority.

Bold and arrogant, they are not afraid to heap abuse on celestial beings; ¹¹yet even angels, although they are stronger and more powerful, do not heap abuse on such beings when bringing judgment on them from*b* the Lord. ¹²But these people blaspheme in matters they do not understand. They are like unreasoning animals, creatures of instinct, born only to be caught and destroyed, and like animals they too will perish.

¹³They will be paid back with harm for the harm they have done. Their idea of pleasure is to carouse in broad daylight. They are blots and blemishes, reveling in their pleasures while they feast with you.*c* ¹⁴With eyes full of adultery, they never stop sinning; they seduce the unstable; they are experts in greed — an accursed brood! ¹⁵They have left the straight way and wandered off to follow the way of Balaam son of Bezer,*d* who loved the wages of wickedness. ¹⁶But he was rebuked for his wrongdoing by a donkey — an animal without speech — who spoke with a human voice and restrained the prophet's madness.

¹⁷These people are springs without water and mists driven by a storm. Blackest darkness is reserved for them. ¹⁸For they mouth empty, boastful words and, by appealing to the lustful desires of the flesh, they entice people who are just escaping from those who live in error. ¹⁹They promise them freedom, while they themselves are slaves of depravity — for "people are slaves to whatever has mastered them." ²⁰If they have escaped the corruption of the world by knowing our Lord and Savior Jesus Christ and are again entangled in it and are overcome, they are worse off at the end than they were at the beginning. ²¹It would have been better for them not to have known the way of righteousness, than

to have known it and then to turn their backs on the sacred command that was passed on to them. ²²Of them the proverbs are true: "A dog returns to its vomit,"*e* and, "A sow that is washed returns to her wallowing in the mud."

The Day of the Lord

3 Dear friends, this is now my second letter to you. I have written both of them as reminders to stimulate you to wholesome thinking. ²I want you to recall the words spoken in the past by the holy prophets and the command given by our Lord and Savior through your apostles.

³Above all, you must understand that in the last days scoffers will come, scoffing and following their own evil desires. ⁴They will say, "Where is this 'coming' he promised? Ever since our ancestors died, everything goes on as it has since the beginning of creation." ⁵But they deliberately forget that long ago by God's word the heavens came into being and the earth was formed out of water and by water. ⁶By these waters also the world of that time was deluged and destroyed. ⁷By the same word the present heavens and earth are reserved for fire, being kept for the day of judgment and destruction of the ungodly.

⁸But do not forget this one thing, dear friends: With the Lord a day is like a thousand years, and a thousand years are like a day. ⁹The Lord is not slow in keeping his promise, as some understand slowness. Instead he is patient with you, not wanting anyone to perish, but everyone to come to repentance.

¹⁰But the day of the Lord will come like a thief. The heavens will disappear with a roar; the elements will be destroyed by fire, and the earth and everything done in it will be laid bare.*f*

¹¹Since everything will be destroyed in

---

a 10 In contexts like this, the Greek word for *flesh* (*sarx*) refers to the sinful state of human beings, often presented as a power in opposition to the Spirit; also in verse 18.   *b 11* Many manuscripts *beings in the presence of*   *c 13* Some manuscripts *in their love feasts*   *d 15* Greek *Bosor*   *e 22* Prov. 26:11   *f 10* Some manuscripts *be burned up* this way, what kind of people ought you to be? You ought to live holy and godly lives ¹²as you look forward to the day of God and speed its coming.ᵃ That day will bring about the destruction of the heavens by fire, and the elements will melt in the heat. ¹³But in keeping with his promise we are looking forward to a new heaven and a new earth, where righteousness dwells.

¹⁴So then, dear friends, since you are looking forward to this, make every effort to be found spotless, blameless and at peace with him. ¹⁵Bear in mind that our Lord's patience means salvation, just as our dear brother Paul also wrote you with the wisdom that God gave him. ¹⁶He writes the same way in all his letters, speaking in them of these matters. His letters contain

---

ᵃ 12 Or *as you wait eagerly for the day of God to come*

DENIAL LESSON [*Principle One*]

This is the first page of the DENIAL lesson.

For a discussion of Principles One through Eight and a listing of their related lessons, go to pages xvii – xliv.

*They promise them freedom, while they themselves are slaves of depravity —
for "people are slaves to whatever has mastered them."*

2 PETER 2:19

The power to change comes only through God's grace. Principle One states: "Realize I'm not God. I admit that I'm powerless to control my tendency to do the wrong thing and that my life has become unmanageable." If we admit that we're powerless, we recognize our need for a power greater than ourselves to restore us. That power is our Higher Power, the one and only true Higher Power, Jesus Christ.

In Principle One we discover that we've been in DENIAL of our hurts, hang-ups and habits. The D in denial stands for DISABLES OUR FEELINGS. Hiding those feelings, stuffing them down, living in denial, freezes our emotions and binds us. Allowing ourselves to feel and then to understand those feelings is where we begin to find freedom.

The basic test of freedom isn't what we're free to do but what we're free not to do. In recovery alcoholics find that they're free not to take that next drink. We find freedom to experience our true feelings when we meet Christ and step out of denial.

Romans 7:18 sums up the situation for all sinful human beings: "I know that good itself does not dwell in me, that is, in my sinful nature. For I have the desire to do what is good, but I cannot carry it out."

We all want desperately to do the right thing. But because of our hurts, hang-ups and habits, no matter how hard we try, in our own power we always fall short. We end up doing precisely what we really don't want to do. In Principle One we finally face the reality that we're not God. We admit that we're powerless to control our tendency to do the wrong thing and that our lives have become unmanageable. Our recovery journey has begun.

The second letter in DENIAL is *E*. Go to Psalm 146:7 – 8 (page 734).

some things that are hard to understand, which ignorant and unstable people distort, as they do the other Scriptures, to their own destruction.

17Therefore, dear friends, since you have been forewarned, be on your guard so that you may not be carried away by the error of the lawless and fall from your secure position. 18But grow in the grace and knowledge of our Lord and Savior Jesus Christ. To him be glory both now and forever! Amen.

1 John

THEME: The key command of this beautiful little book is the call to love. Christians are to follow Christ's example by loving one another and caring for those in need, even to the point of laying down their lives for one another.

AUTHOR: The author of this epistle didn't identify himself, but evidence indicates that he was almost certainly the apostle John.

DATE OF WRITING: This epistle was probably written between AD 85 and 95.

ENCOURAGEMENT FROM 1 JOHN: "If we claim to be without sin, we deceive ourselves and the truth is not in us. If we confess our sins, he is faithful and just and will forgive us our sins and purify us from all unrighteousness" (1 John 1:8–9).

CHALLENGE FROM 1 JOHN: "Dear friends, since God so loved us, we also ought to love one another. No one has ever seen God; but if we love one another, God lives in us and his love is made complete in us" (1 John 4:11–12).

REFLECTION FROM 1 JOHN: "My dear children, I write this to you so that you will not sin. But if anybody does sin, we have an advocate with the Father — Jesus Christ, the Righteous One" (1 John 2:1).

The letters of 1, 2 and 3 John collectively tell us that when we've put our hope in Jesus, when we've handed over the reins of our lives to him, we become children of God. What an amazing claim. Many of us have lived in darkness for years, separated from God because of our sins. We've lived attached to our own hurts, hang-ups and habits and allowed them to become our god. Now that we've come into the light, we can have a relationship with God, a relationship so personal that we can call him our Father.

First, Second and Third John provide us with ways to test our faith to make sure we're staying in Christ. The most foolproof method to tell if we're in Christ is this: Do we show love? Love is the litmus test for our words. It puts our faith into action. Love is what allows us to give back, to yield ourselves to God, so we can be used by him to bring the Good News to others, both through our words and by our examples.

The Incarnation of the Word of Life

1 That which was from the beginning, which we have heard, which we have seen with our eyes, which we have looked at and our hands have touched — this we proclaim concerning the Word of life. ²The life appeared; we have seen it and testify to it, and we proclaim to you the eternal life, which was with the Father and has appeared to us. ³We proclaim to you what we have seen and heard, so that you also may have fellowship with us. And our fellowship is with the Father and with his Son, Jesus Christ. ⁴We write this to make our*ᵃ* joy complete.

ᵃ 4 Some manuscripts *your*

Light and Darkness, Sin and Forgiveness

5This is the message we have heard from him and declare to you: God is light; in him there is no darkness at all. 6If we claim to have fellowship with him and yet walk in the darkness, we lie and do not live out the truth. 7But if we walk in the light, as he is in the light, we have fellowship with one another, and the blood of Jesus, his Son, purifies us from all*a* sin.

8If we claim to be without sin, we deceive ourselves and the truth is not in us. 9If we confess our sins, he is faithful and just and will forgive us our sins and purify us from all unrighteousness. 10If we claim we have

a 7 Or *every*

CROSSROADS LESSON [*Principle Seven*]

For the previous entry in the CROSSROADS lesson, go to Lamentations 3:40 (page 964).

For a discussion of Principles One through Eight and a listing of their related lessons, go to pages xvii–xliv.

If we claim to be without sin, we deceive ourselves and the truth is not in us. If we confess our sins, he is faithful and just and will forgive us our sins and purify us from all unrighteousness. If we claim we have not sinned, we make him out to be a liar and his word is not in us.

1 JOHN 1:8–10

In Principle Seven we reserve a daily quiet time with God for self-examination, Bible reading and prayer in order to get to know God and his will for our lives and to gain the power to follow his will. We're at the CROSSROADS of our recovery. We need to thank God for getting us this far on our road to recovery, to praise him for the many victories we've already experienced over our hurts, hang-ups and habits. But we also need to continue working the last two principles with the same devotion and enthusiasm that got us to this point in our recovery. In the first part of Principle Seven we reserve a daily quiet time with God for self-examination. This relates to Step Ten of the Christ-centered 12 steps.

Step Ten: We continued to take personal inventory and, when we were wrong, promptly admitted it.

This step is made up of three key actions. The second action is represented by the letter *E* of Step TEN: EVALUATE BOTH THE GOOD AND THE BAD. Principle Seven forces us to admit that, on a daily basis, we're going to be wrong and we're bound to make some mistakes. That's what 1 John 1:8–10 makes clear.

A sign hanging in a recovery meeting room asks the question, "Would you rather be right … or well?" In this principle we evaluate our daily behaviors and, when we're wrong, we take the appropriate action. Our goal for each day: to choose to be well.

The last action we need to take is represented by the letter *N* of Step TEN.
Go to Matthew 5:23–24 (page 1131).

not sinned, we make him out to be a liar and his word is not in us.

2 My dear children, I write this to you so that you will not sin. But if anybody does sin, we have an advocate with the Father — Jesus Christ, the Righteous One. [2] He is the atoning sacrifice for our sins, and not only for ours but also for the sins of the whole world.

Love and Hatred for Fellow Believers

[3] We know that we have come to know him if we keep his commands. [4] Whoever says, "I know him," but does not do what he commands is a liar, and the truth is not in that person. [5] But if anyone obeys his word, love for God[a] is truly made complete in them. This is how we know we are in him: [6] Whoever claims to live in him must live as Jesus did.

[7] Dear friends, I am not writing you a new command but an old one, which you have had since the beginning. This old command is the message you have heard. [8] Yet I am writing you a new command; its truth is seen in him and in you, because the darkness is passing and the true light is already shining.

[9] Anyone who claims to be in the light but hates a brother or sister[b] is still in the darkness. [10] Anyone who loves their brother and sister[c] lives in the light, and there is nothing in them to make them stumble. [11] But anyone who hates a brother or sister is in the darkness and walks around in the darkness. They do not know where they are going, because the darkness has blinded them.

Reasons for Writing

[12] I am writing to you, dear children,
    because your sins have been forgiven
        on account of his name.
[13] I am writing to you, fathers,
    because you know him who is from
        the beginning.
I am writing to you, young men,
    because you have overcome the evil one.

[14] I write to you, dear children,
    because you know the Father.
I write to you, fathers,
    because you know him who is from
        the beginning.
I write to you, young men,
    because you are strong,
    and the word of God lives in you,
    and you have overcome the evil one.

On Not Loving the World

[15] Do not love the world or anything in the world. If anyone loves the world, love for the Father[d] is not in them. [16] For everything in the world — the lust of the flesh, the lust of the eyes, and the pride of life — comes not from the Father but from the world. [17] The world and its desires pass away, but whoever does the will of God lives forever.

Warnings Against Denying the Son

[18] Dear children, this is the last hour; and as you have heard that the antichrist is coming, even now many antichrists have come. This is how we know it is the last hour. [19] They went out from us, but they did not really belong to us. For if they had belonged to us, they would have remained with us; but their going showed that none of them belonged to us.

[20] But you have an anointing from the Holy One, and all of you know the truth.[e] [21] I do not write to you because you do not know the truth, but because you do know it and because no lie comes from the truth. [22] Who is the liar? It is whoever denies that Jesus is the Christ. Such a person is the antichrist — denying the Father and the Son. [23] No one who denies the Son has the Father; whoever acknowledges the Son has the Father also.

[24] As for you, see that what you have heard from the beginning remains in you. If it does, you also will remain in the Son and in the Father. [25] And this is what he promised us — eternal life.

---

a 5 Or *word, God's love*   *b 9* The Greek word for *brother or sister* (*adelphos*) refers here to a believer, whether man or woman, as part of God's family; also in verse 11; and in 3:15, 17; 4:20; 5:16.   *c 10* The Greek word for *brother and sister* (*adelphos*) refers here to a believer, whether man or woman, as part of God's family; also in 3:10; 4:20, 21.   *d 15* Or *world, the Father's love*   *e 20* Some manuscripts *and you know all things*

26I am writing these things to you about those who are trying to lead you astray. 27As for you, the anointing you received from him remains in you, and you do not need anyone to teach you. But as his anointing teaches you about all things and as that anointing is real, not counterfeit — just as it has taught you, remain in him.

God's Children and Sin

28And now, dear children, continue in him, so that when he appears we may be confident and unashamed before him at his coming.

29If you know that he is righteous, you know that everyone who does what is right has been born of him.

3 See what great love the Father has lavished on us, that we should be called children of God! And that is what we are! The reason the world does not know us is that it did not know him. 2Dear friends, now we are children of God, and what we will be has not yet been made known. But we know that when Christ appears,a we shall be like him, for we shall see him as he is. 3All who have this hope in him purify themselves, just as he is pure.

4Everyone who sins breaks the law; in fact, sin is lawlessness. 5But you know that he appeared so that he might take away our sins. And in him is no sin. 6No one who lives in him keeps on sinning. No one who continues to sin has either seen him or known him.

7Dear children, do not let anyone lead you astray. The one who does what is right is righteous, just as he is righteous. 8The one who does what is sinful is of the devil, because the devil has been sinning from the beginning. The reason the Son of God appeared was to destroy the devil's work. 9No one who is born of God will continue to sin, because God's seed remains in them; they cannot go on sinning, because they have been born of God. 10This is how

a 2 Or when it is made known

READY LESSON [*Principle Five*]

For the previous entry in the READY lesson, go to Matthew 12:43 – 45 (page 1151).

For a discussion of Principles One through Eight and a listing of their related lessons, go to pages xvii – xliv.

No one who is born of God will continue to sin, because God's seed remains in them; they cannot go on sinning, because they have been born of God.

1 JOHN 3:9

In Principle Five we need to be READY to voluntarily submit to every change God wants to make in our lives and humbly ask him to remove our character defects.

The last letter in READY is *Y*, which stands for Yield TO THE GROWTH. At first our old self-doubts and low self-image may tell us we're not worthy of the growth and progress we're making in the program. We need to consciously turn off those old, negative tapes and then yield, or give in, to the growth. It's the Holy Spirit's work within us. We've been reborn into a new, exciting life, one that allows us to live free and find victory from our old hurts, hang-ups and habits.

This is the final page of the READY lesson.

we know who the children of God are and who the children of the devil are: Anyone who does not do what is right is not God's child, nor is anyone who does not love their brother and sister.

More on Love and Hatred

11For this is the message you heard from the beginning: We should love one another. 12Do not be like Cain, who belonged to the evil one and murdered his brother. And why did he murder him? Because his own actions were evil and his brother's were righteous. 13Do not be surprised, my brothers and sisters,*a* if the world hates you. 14We know that we have passed from death to life, because we love each other. Anyone who does not love remains in death. 15Anyone who hates a brother or sister is a murderer, and you know that no murderer has eternal life residing in him.

16This is how we know what love is: Jesus Christ laid down his life for us. And we ought to lay down our lives for our brothers and sisters. 17If anyone has material possessions and sees a brother or sister in need but has no pity on them, how can the love of God be in that person? 18Dear children, let us not love with words or speech but with actions and in truth.

19This is how we know that we belong to the truth and how we set our hearts at rest in his presence: 20If our hearts condemn us, we know that God is greater than our hearts, and he knows everything. 21Dear friends, if our hearts do not condemn us, we have confidence before God 22and receive from him anything we ask, because we keep his commands and do what pleases him. 23And this is his command: to believe in the name of his Son, Jesus Christ, and to love one another as he commanded us. 24The one who keeps God's commands lives in him, and he in them. And this is how we know that he lives in us: We know it by the Spirit he gave us.

On Denying the Incarnation

4Dear friends, do not believe every spirit, but test the spirits to see whether they are from God, because many false prophets have gone out into the world. 2This is how you can recognize the Spirit of God: Every spirit that acknowledges that Jesus Christ has come in the flesh is from God, 3but every spirit that does not acknowledge Jesus is not from God. This is the spirit of the antichrist, which you have heard is coming and even now is already in the world.

4You, dear children, are from God and have overcome them, because the one who is in you is greater than the one who is in the world. 5They are from the world and therefore speak from the viewpoint of the world, and the world listens to them. 6We are from God, and whoever knows God listens to us; but whoever is not from God does not listen to us. This is how we recognize the Spirit*b* of truth and the spirit of falsehood.

God's Love and Ours

7Dear friends, let us love one another, for love comes from God. Everyone who loves has been born of God and knows God. 8Whoever does not love does not know God, because God is love. 9This is how God showed his love among us: He sent his one and only Son into the world that we might live through him. 10This is love: not that we loved God, but that he loved us and sent his Son as an atoning sacrifice for our sins. 11Dear friends, since God so loved us, we also ought to love one another. 12No one has ever seen God; but if we love one another, God lives in us and his love is made complete in us.

13This is how we know that we live in him and he in us: He has given us of his Spirit. 14And we have seen and testify that the Father has sent his Son to be the Savior of the world. 15If anyone acknowledges that Jesus is the Son of God, God lives in them

---

a 13 The Greek word for *brothers and sisters* (*adelphoi*) refers here to believers, both men and women, as part of God's family; also in verse 16.   *b 6* Or *spirit* and they in God. ¹⁶And so we know and rely on the love God has for us.

God is love. Whoever lives in love lives in God, and God in them. ¹⁷This is how love is made complete among us so that we will have confidence on the day of judgment: In this world we are like Jesus. ¹⁸There is no fear in love. But perfect love drives out fear, because fear has to do with punishment. The one who fears is not made perfect in love.

¹⁹We love because he first loved us. ²⁰Whoever claims to love God yet hates a brother or sister is a liar. For whoever does not love their brother and sister, whom they have seen, cannot love God, whom they have not seen. ²¹And he has given us this command: Anyone who loves God must also love their brother and sister.

Faith in the Incarnate Son of God

5 Everyone who believes that Jesus is the Christ is born of God, and everyone who loves the father loves his child as well. ²This is how we know that we love the children of God: by loving God and carrying out his commands. ³In fact, this is love for God: to keep his commands. And his commands are not burdensome,

---

GIVE LESSON [*Principle Eight*]

For the previous entry in the GIVE lesson, go to 2 Corinthians 1:3–4 (page 1438).

For a discussion of Principles One through Eight and a listing of their related lessons,
go to pages xvii–xliv.

Dear children, let us not love with words or speech but with actions and in truth.

1 JOHN 3:18

Major, miraculous progress and growth have occurred in our lives since we started our recovery program, way back when we began working Principle One. We've stepped out of our denial into God's grace. We've taken an honest, spiritual inventory. We've worked on getting right with God, ourselves and others, and we've grown in our relationship with Christ. We've discovered a new way to live life, and we're finding the serenity we've always been seeking. But the most exciting part is yet to come—Principle Eight: "Yield myself to God to be used by him to bring this good news to others, both through my example and through my words."

Principle Eight is the "giving back" principle. Matthew 10:8 offers a reminder and an instruction: "Freely you have received, freely give." The *E* in GIVE stands for EXAMPLE OF OUR ACTIONS. As the old maxim so accurately points out, our actions speak louder than our words. Good intentions die unless they're carried out. In James 1:22 we're reminded, "Do not merely listen to the word, and so deceive yourselves. Do what it says."

So, if we're going to be of help to another, we need to bring the good news to that person. Our actions, not our words, are proof of our love for God and for that hurting individual. Faith without works is like a new car without gasoline. It may look good, but it's not going anywhere.

First John 3:18 makes that abundantly clear. Giving and serving are the thermometer of our love. We can give without loving—that's what we sometimes do in a codependent relationship—but we can't love without giving.

This is the final page of the GIVE lesson.

⁴for everyone born of God overcomes the world. This is the victory that has overcome the world, even our faith. ⁵Who is it that overcomes the world? Only the one who believes that Jesus is the Son of God.

⁶This is the one who came by water and blood — Jesus Christ. He did not come by water only, but by water and blood. And it is the Spirit who testifies, because the Spirit is the truth. ⁷For there are three that testify: ⁸theᵃ Spirit, the water and the blood; and the three are in agreement. ⁹We accept human testimony, but God's testimony is greater because it is the testimony of God, which he has given about his Son. ¹⁰Whoever believes in the Son of God accepts this testimony. Whoever does not believe God has made him out to be a liar, because they have not believed the testimony God has given about his Son. ¹¹And this is the testimony: God has given us eternal life, and this life is in his Son. ¹²Whoever has the Son has life; whoever does not have the Son of God does not have life.

Concluding Affirmations

¹³I write these things to you who believe in the name of the Son of God so that you may know that you have eternal life. ¹⁴This is the confidence we have in approaching God: that if we ask anything according to his will, he hears us. ¹⁵And if we know that he hears us — whatever we ask — we know that we have what we asked of him.

¹⁶If you see any brother or sister commit a sin that does not lead to death, you should pray and God will give them life. I refer to those whose sin does not lead to death. There is a sin that leads to death. I am not saying that you should pray about that. ¹⁷All wrongdoing is sin, and there is sin that does not lead to death.

¹⁸We know that anyone born of God does not continue to sin; the One who was born of God keeps them safe, and the evil one cannot harm them. ¹⁹We know that we are children of God, and that the whole world is under the control of the evil one. ²⁰We know also that the Son of God has come and has given us understanding, so that we may know him who is true. And we are in him who is true by being in his Son Jesus Christ. He is the true God and eternal life.

²¹Dear children, keep yourselves from idols.

ᵃ 7,8 Late manuscripts of the Vulgate *testify in heaven: the Father, the Word and the Holy Spirit, and these three are one.* ⁸*And there are three that testify on earth: the* (not found in any Greek manuscript before the fourteenth century)

2 John

THEME: Like 1 John, this letter emphasizes the command to love one another. This is the command John's audience had heard from the beginning, and it's the test of a true believer.

AUTHOR: The author of this epistle, who referred to himself only as "the elder" (2 John 1), has traditionally been identified as the apostle John.

DATE OF WRITING: This letter was probably written between AD 85 and 95.

ENCOURAGEMENT FROM 2 JOHN: "Grace, mercy and peace from God the Father and from Jesus Christ, the Father's Son, will be with us in truth and love" (2 John 3).

CHALLENGE FROM 2 JOHN: "Now, dear lady, I am not writing you a new command but one we have had from the beginning. I ask that we love one another. And this is love: that we walk in obedience to his commands" (2 John 5–6).

REFLECTION FROM 2 JOHN: "Watch out that you do not lose what we have worked for, but that you may be rewarded fully" (1 John 8).

See the introduction to 1 John.

---

¹The elder,

To the lady chosen by God and to her children, whom I love in the truth — and not I only, but also all who know the truth — ²because of the truth, which lives in us and will be with us forever:

³Grace, mercy and peace from God the Father and from Jesus Christ, the Father's Son, will be with us in truth and love.

⁴It has given me great joy to find some of your children walking in the truth, just as the Father commanded us. ⁵And now, dear lady, I am not writing you a new command but one we have had from the beginning. I ask that we love one another. ⁶And this is love: that we walk in obedience to his commands. As you have heard from the beginning, his command is that you walk in love.

⁷I say this because many deceivers, who do not acknowledge Jesus Christ as coming in the flesh, have gone out into the world. Any such person is the deceiver and the antichrist. ⁸Watch out that you do not lose what we*a* have worked for, but that you may be rewarded fully. ⁹Anyone who runs ahead and does not continue in the teaching of Christ does not have God; whoever continues in the teaching has both the Father and the Son. ¹⁰If anyone comes to you and does not bring this teaching, do not take them into your house or welcome them. ¹¹Anyone who welcomes them shares in their wicked work.

¹²I have much to write to you, but I do not want to use paper and ink. Instead, I hope to visit you and talk with you face to face, so that our joy may be complete.

¹³The children of your sister, who is chosen by God, send their greetings.

---

a 8 Some manuscripts *you*

3 John

THEME: The hospitality of the early church built up networks between the scattered churches and fostered a sense of solidarity. The local churches saw themselves as belonging to the one church, united around the foundational truth of the gospel.

AUTHOR: The author of this epistle, who referred to himself only as "the elder" (John 1), has traditionally been identified as the apostle John.

DATE OF WRITING: This letter was probably written between AD 85 and 95.

ENCOURAGEMENT FROM 3 JOHN: "It gave me great joy when some believers came and testified about your faithfulness to the truth, telling how you continue to walk in it. I have no greater joy than to hear that my children are walking in the truth" (3 John 3 – 4).

CHALLENGE FROM 3 JOHN: "Do not imitate what is evil but what is good" (3 John 11).

REFLECTION FROM 3 JOHN: "Anyone who does what is good is from God. Anyone who does what is evil has not seen God" (3 John 11).

At a Glance

See the introduction to 1 John.

¹The elder,

To my dear friend Gaius, whom I love in the truth.

²Dear friend, I pray that you may enjoy good health and that all may go well with you, even as your soul is getting along well. ³It gave me great joy when some believers came and testified about your faithfulness to the truth, telling how you continue to walk in it. ⁴I have no greater joy than to hear that my children are walking in the truth.

⁵Dear friend, you are faithful in what you are doing for the brothers and sisters,*a* even though they are strangers to you. ⁶They have told the church about your love. Please send them on their way in a manner that honors God. ⁷It was for the sake of the Name that they went out, receiving no help from the pagans. ⁸We ought therefore to show hospitality to such people so that we may work together for the truth.

⁹I wrote to the church, but Diotrephes, who loves to be first, will not welcome us. ¹⁰So when I come, I will call attention to what he is doing, spreading malicious nonsense about us. Not satisfied with that, he even refuses to welcome other believers. He also stops those who want to do so and puts them out of the church.

¹¹Dear friend, do not imitate what is evil but what is good. Anyone who does what is good is from God. Anyone who does what

---

a 5 The Greek word for *brothers and sisters* (*adelphoi*) refers here to believers, both men and women, as part of God's family.

is evil has not seen God. ¹²Demetrius is well spoken of by everyone—and even by the truth itself. We also speak well of him, and you know that our testimony is true.

¹³I have much to write you, but I do not want to do so with pen and ink. ¹⁴I hope to see you soon, and we will talk face to face.

Peace to you. The friends here send their greetings. Greet the friends there by name.

SANITY LESSON [*Principle Two*]

For the previous entry in the SANITY lesson, go to 2 Corinthians 1:8–9 (page 1439).

For a discussion of Principles One through Eight and a listing of their related lessons, go to pages xvii–xliv.

I have no greater joy than to hear that my children are walking in the truth.

3 JOHN 4

In Principle Two we earnestly believe that God exists, that we matter to him and that he has the power to help us recover. It's in this principle that we find the SANITY to begin to stop making the same poor choices again and again.

The next benefit we receive in completing this principle is represented by the *I* in SANITY, which stands for INTEGRITY. The apostle John placed great value on integrity, which we gain as we begin to follow through on our promises. One result is that others start trusting what we say. Remember that a half-truth is a whole lie—and a lie is the result of weakness and fear. Truth fears nothing—nothing, that is, but concealment. True, the truth often hurts. But it's the lie that leaves a scar.

A man or woman of integrity and courage isn't afraid to tell the truth. And that courage comes from a power greater than ourselves—Jesus Christ, the way, the *truth* and the life.

The next letter in SANITY is *T*. Go to Proverbs 29:25 (page 778).

Jude

THEME: Jude's primary focus was the ethical dangers posed by false teachers who denied Christ's lordship by using Christian freedom and God's grace as a "license for immorality" (Jude 4).

AUTHOR: The writer identified himself as "Jude . . . a brother of James" (Jude 1). Though there are several persons in the New Testament with the name James, it's likely that this James was the half-brother of Jesus, who became a follower of Christ after the resurrection and emerged as a church leader. James and Jude (Greek "Judas") are listed as Jesus' brothers in Matthew 13:55.

DATE OF WRITING: If 2 Peter makes use of Jude, which is a commonly accepted view, then this epistle was probably written around AD 65 or earlier.

ENCOURAGEMENT FROM JUDE: "To him who is able to keep you from stumbling and to present you before his glorious presence without fault and with great joy — to the only God our Savior be glory, majesty, power and authority, through Jesus Christ our Lord, before all ages, now and forevermore!" (Jude 24 – 25).

CHALLENGE FROM JUDE: "Dear friends, by building yourselves up in your most holy faith and praying in the Holy Spirit, keep yourselves in God's love as you wait for the mercy of our Lord Jesus Christ to bring you to eternal life" (Jude 20 – 21).

REFLECTION FROM JUDE: "Contend for the faith that was once for all entrusted to God's holy people" (Jude 3).

Recovery Themes in Jude

The book of Jude is short and to the point. Its premise: There are people out there who say they believe in Jesus, but they're lying. They want to pull us out of our churches and do away with Jesus Christ. There are those who would laugh at us for believing in Christ, those who would argue that we don't need Christ for recovery, that any old "higher power" will do.

But Jude warns us to stay the course, encouraging us to remain rooted in Christ's love, to reach out to the lost, to love the sinner but not the sin. The book of Jude points us to service. We've been saved, most likely because someone loved us enough to tell us about Jesus. Now it's our turn to gently do the same for another person who is hurting. Jude puts it this way: We need to snatch others from the fire and save them (see Jude 23). We do this by giving back in selfless service, by continuously working our recovery so that newcomers may find access to the same healing we've received.

¹Jude, a servant of Jesus Christ and a brother of James,

To those who have been called, who are loved in God the Father and kept for*a* Jesus Christ:

²Mercy, peace and love be yours in abundance.

The Sin and Doom of Ungodly People

³Dear friends, although I was very eager to write to you about the salvation we share, I felt compelled to write and urge you to contend for the faith that was once for all entrusted to God's holy people. ⁴For certain individuals whose condemnation was written about*b* long ago have secretly slipped in among you. They are ungodly people, who pervert the grace of our God into a license for immorality and deny Jesus Christ our only Sovereign and Lord.

⁵Though you already know all this, I want to remind you that the Lord*c* at one time delivered his people out of Egypt, but later destroyed those who did not believe. ⁶And the angels who did not keep their positions of authority but abandoned their proper dwelling — these he has kept in darkness, bound with everlasting chains for judgment on the great Day. ⁷In a similar way, Sodom and Gomorrah and the surrounding towns gave themselves up to sexual immorality and perversion. They serve as an example of those who suffer the punishment of eternal fire.

⁸In the very same way, on the strength of their dreams these ungodly people pollute their own bodies, reject authority and heap abuse on celestial beings. ⁹But even the archangel Michael, when he was disputing with the devil about the body of Moses, did not himself dare to condemn him for slander but said, "The Lord rebuke you!"*d* ¹⁰Yet these people slander whatever they do not understand, and the very things they do understand by instinct — as irrational animals do — will destroy them.

¹¹Woe to them! They have taken the way of Cain; they have rushed for profit into Balaam's error; they have been destroyed in Korah's rebellion.

¹²These people are blemishes at your love feasts, eating with you without the slightest qualm — shepherds who feed only themselves. They are clouds without rain, blown along by the wind; autumn trees, without fruit and uprooted — twice dead. ¹³They are wild waves of the sea, foaming up their shame; wandering stars, for whom blackest darkness has been reserved forever.

¹⁴Enoch, the seventh from Adam, prophesied about them: "See, the Lord is coming with thousands upon thousands of his holy ones ¹⁵to judge everyone, and to convict all of them of all the ungodly acts they have committed in their ungodliness, and of all the defiant words ungodly sinners have spoken against him."*e* ¹⁶These people are grumblers and faultfinders; they follow their own evil desires; they boast about themselves and flatter others for their own advantage.

A Call to Persevere

¹⁷But, dear friends, remember what the apostles of our Lord Jesus Christ foretold. ¹⁸They said to you, "In the last times there will be scoffers who will follow their own ungodly desires." ¹⁹These are the people who divide you, who follow mere natural instincts and do not have the Spirit.

²⁰But you, dear friends, by building yourselves up in your most holy faith and praying in the Holy Spirit, ²¹keep yourselves in God's love as you wait for the mercy of our Lord Jesus Christ to bring you to eternal life.

²²Be merciful to those who doubt; ²³save others by snatching them from the fire; to others show mercy, mixed with fear — hating even the clothing stained by corrupted flesh.*f*

---

a 1 Or *by;* or *in*   *b 4* Or *individuals who were marked out for condemnation*   *c 5* Some early manuscripts *Jesus*   *d 9* Jude is alluding to the Jewish *Testament of Moses* (approximately the first century A.D.).   *e 14,15* From the Jewish *First Book of Enoch* (approximately the first century B.C.)   *f 22,23* The Greek manuscripts of these verses vary at several points.

Doxology

24To him who is able to keep you from stumbling and to present you before his glorious presence without fault and with great joy — 25to the only God our Savior be glory, majesty, power and authority, through Jesus Christ our Lord, before all ages, now and forevermore! Amen.

Revelation

THEME: Humans must decide now whose side they will choose — that of God, who will triumph in the end, or of Satan and his followers, who may prevail momentarily but are destined to eternal destruction.

AUTHOR: The author identified himself as John, and authorship of Revelation has been attributed to the apostle John from as early as the second century. He is believed to have been exiled to Patmos, an island that was used as a Roman penal settlement, on the basis of his testimony about Jesus.

DATE OF WRITING: Revelation was probably written between AD 90 and 96.

ENCOURAGEMENT FROM REVELATION: "To the thirsty I will give water without cost from the spring of the water of life. Those who are victorious will inherit all this, and I will be their God and they will be my children" (Revelation 21:6 – 7).

CHALLENGE FROM REVELATION: "Be faithful, even to the point of death, and I will give you life as your victor's crown" (Revelation 2:10).

REFLECTION FROM REVELATION: "To the one who is victorious, I will give the right to sit with me on my throne, just as I was victorious and sat down with my Father on his throne" (Revelation 3:21).

Just as Genesis is the book of beginnings, Revelation is the book of completion. This is God's final act of redemption: Christ will return to establish his kingdom. At that time, Jesus will oversee the final judgments of Satan, the nations, the angels and all people. It's also then that the new heaven and the new earth will be created, ushering in God's final, perfect, eternal order.

Revelation is full of visions and symbolism, and it contains the Bible's final letters to New Testament churches. In this case, the words come straight from Jesus' mouth to John's pen. Each of these letters follows a similar pattern: The Lord promises rewards to faithful individuals, to those who overcome, to those who triumph over trial and temptation.

In recovery we're already experiencing the reward that comes when we, with the Spirit's help, overcome the hurts, hang-ups and habits that have kept us enslaved to sin for so long. Just imagine that joy multiplied uncountable times throughout eternity! The last book in the Bible shows God's determination to complete his eternal purposes through the history of creation. Revelation shows a Christ-centered recovery of the whole hurting world. God is fully as determined to finish his work in us, in our day, as we walk down our individual roads to recovery. All the future actions of God in Revelation, as in our recovery, flow from the works of Jesus.

Prologue

1 The revelation from Jesus Christ, which God gave him to show his servants what must soon take place. He made it known by sending his angel to his servant John, ²who testifies to everything he saw—that is, the word of God and the testimony of Jesus Christ. ³Blessed is the one who reads aloud the words of this prophecy, and blessed are those who hear it and take to heart what is written in it, because the time is near.

Greetings and Doxology

⁴John,

To the seven churches in the province of Asia:

Grace and peace to you from him who is, and who was, and who is to come, and from the seven spirits*a* before his throne, ⁵and from Jesus Christ, who is the faithful witness, the firstborn from the dead, and the ruler of the kings of the earth.

To him who loves us and has freed us from our sins by his blood, ⁶and has made us to be a kingdom and priests to serve his God and Father—to him be glory and power for ever and ever! Amen.

⁷"Look, he is coming with the clouds,"*b*
and "every eye will see him,
even those who pierced him";
and all peoples on earth "will mourn
because of him."*c*
So shall it be! Amen.

⁸"I am the Alpha and the Omega," says the Lord God, "who is, and who was, and who is to come, the Almighty."

John's Vision of Christ

⁹I, John, your brother and companion in the suffering and kingdom and patient endurance that are ours in Jesus, was on the island of Patmos because of the word of God and the testimony of Jesus. ¹⁰On the Lord's Day I was in the Spirit, and I heard behind me a loud voice like a trumpet, ¹¹which said: "Write on a scroll what you see and send it to the seven churches: to Ephesus, Smyrna, Pergamum, Thyatira, Sardis, Philadelphia and Laodicea."

¹²I turned around to see the voice that was speaking to me. And when I turned I saw seven golden lampstands, ¹³and among the lampstands was someone like a son of man,*d* dressed in a robe reaching down to his feet and with a golden sash around his chest. ¹⁴The hair on his head was white like wool, as white as snow, and his eyes were like blazing fire. ¹⁵His feet were like bronze glowing in a furnace, and his voice was like the sound of rushing waters. ¹⁶In his right hand he held seven stars, and coming out of his mouth was a sharp, double-edged sword. His face was like the sun shining in all its brilliance.

¹⁷When I saw him, I fell at his feet as though dead. Then he placed his right hand on me and said: "Do not be afraid. I am the First and the Last. ¹⁸I am the Living One; I was dead, and now look, I am alive for ever and ever! And I hold the keys of death and Hades.

¹⁹"Write, therefore, what you have seen, what is now and what will take place later. ²⁰The mystery of the seven stars that you saw in my right hand and of the seven golden lampstands is this: The seven stars are the angels*e* of the seven churches, and the seven lampstands are the seven churches.

To the Church in Ephesus

2 "To the angel*f* of the church in Ephesus write:

These are the words of him who holds the seven stars in his right hand and walks among the seven golden lampstands. ²I know your deeds, your hard work and your perseverance. I

---

a 4 That is, the sevenfold Spirit   *b 7* Daniel 7:13   *c 7* Zech. 12:10   *d 13* See Daniel 7:13.   *e 20* Or messengers   *f 1* Or *messenger*; also in verses 8, 12 and 18

MY NAME IS JOHN

REVELATION 1:9–20

John was a dedicated disciple of Jesus. In fact, he refers to himself in his Gospel as "the disciple whom Jesus loved" (John 13:23; 21:7,20; see John 19:26; 20:2). Can you think of a better description of any person? Being in the center of the Lord's affections, though, doesn't insulate any disciple from suffering at the hands of evil people. John knew this. In fact, he had recorded Jesus' warning, along with its accompanying promise, in his Gospel account: "In this world you will have trouble. But take heart! I have overcome the world" (John 16:33). Christ won a decisive victory over sin, death and Satan through his death and resurrection. The final words and works of Jesus recorded by John in Revelation promise a future, visible reign of Christ upon the new earth he will establish. With this will come an end to all suffering and sorrow (see Revelation 21:3–4).

Until that time Christians will continue to experience pain. Many, like John, will endure abuse at the hands of others. The elderly John, a prisoner of Rome, was exiled to the small prison island of Patmos because of his faithful proclamation of the gospel (see Revelation 1:9). He was isolated from the churches in Asia that he had so lovingly nurtured for decades. How easy it would have been for John to assume that his ministry was over. What, after all, can a "voiceless" prisoner do? The answer for the apostle was clear: He could pray, be filled with the Holy Spirit and receive and record a message and commission from Christ (see vv. 10–11).

John's faithfulness in focusing on God in the context of his imprisonment was rewarded by Jesus. This dedicated apostle was given a unique vision of his beloved Lord. Christ appeared to him in all his splendor as the divine head of the church (see vv. 12–16). John's response to this awesome vision was to fall at Jesus' feet "as though dead" (v. 17). John was comforted by Christ and commissioned to record the Lord's final messages to the churches (see vv. 19–20). John's isolation from pastoral duties may in fact have been a major aid to his completion of one of the most complex and fascinating books in the Bible. The product of this prisoner's diligence is a book that promises a blessing to all who read, hear and apply the words of Revelation (see v. 3).

John's experience is evidence that even a prisoner has access to Christ's presence through prayer. A prisoner, an exile, can experience recovery, grow closer to Jesus and serve as his instrument for sharing truth. Our prison might be either literal or emotional—the result of our own sins or the product of abuse by others. But Jesus can penetrate all barriers, and we can experience his touch. We can be reassured, comforted, informed and productive in his kingdom.

know that you cannot tolerate wicked people, that you have tested those who claim to be apostles but are not, and have found them false. ³You have persevered and have endured hardships for my name, and have not grown weary.

⁴Yet I hold this against you: You have forsaken the love you had at first. ⁵Consider how far you have fallen! Repent and do the things you did at first. If you do not repent, I will come to you and remove your lampstand from its place. ⁶But you have this in your favor: You hate the practices of the Nicolaitans, which I also hate.

⁷Whoever has ears, let them hear what the Spirit says to the churches. To the one who is victorious, I will give the right to eat from the tree of life, which is in the paradise of God.

To the Church in Smyrna

⁸"To the angel of the church in Smyrna write:

These are the words of him who is the First and the Last, who died and came to life again. ⁹I know your afflictions and your poverty—yet you are rich! I know about the slander of those who say they are Jews and are not, but are a synagogue of Satan. ¹⁰Do not be afraid of what you are about to suffer. I tell you, the devil will put some of you in prison to test you, and you will suffer persecution for ten days. Be faithful, even to the point of death, and I will give you life as your victor's crown.

¹¹Whoever has ears, let them hear what the Spirit says to the churches. The one who is victorious will not be hurt at all by the second death.

To the Church in Pergamum

¹²"To the angel of the church in Pergamum write:

These are the words of him who has the sharp, double-edged sword. ¹³I

know where you live—where Satan has his throne. Yet you remain true to my name. You did not renounce your faith in me, not even in the days of Antipas, my faithful witness, who was put to death in your city—where Satan lives.

¹⁴Nevertheless, I have a few things against you: There are some among you who hold to the teaching of Balaam, who taught Balak to entice the Israelites to sin so that they ate food sacrificed to idols and committed sexual immorality. ¹⁵Likewise, you also have those who hold to the teaching of the Nicolaitans. ¹⁶Repent therefore! Otherwise, I will soon come to you and will fight against them with the sword of my mouth.

¹⁷Whoever has ears, let them hear what the Spirit says to the churches. To the one who is victorious, I will give some of the hidden manna. I will also give that person a white stone with a new name written on it, known only to the one who receives it.

To the Church in Thyatira

¹⁸"To the angel of the church in Thyatira write:

These are the words of the Son of God, whose eyes are like blazing fire and whose feet are like burnished bronze. ¹⁹I know your deeds, your love and faith, your service and perseverance, and that you are now doing more than you did at first.

²⁰Nevertheless, I have this against you: You tolerate that woman Jezebel, who calls herself a prophet. By her teaching she misleads my servants into sexual immorality and the eating of food sacrificed to idols. ²¹I have given her time to repent of her immorality, but she is unwilling. ²²So I will cast her on a bed of suffering, and I will make those who commit adultery with her suffer intensely, unless they

repent of her ways. ²³I will strike her children dead. Then all the churches will know that I am he who searches hearts and minds, and I will repay each of you according to your deeds.

²⁴Now I say to the rest of you in Thyatira, to you who do not hold to her teaching and have not learned Satan's so-called deep secrets, 'I will not impose any other burden on you, ²⁵except to hold on to what you have until I come.'

²⁶To the one who is victorious and does my will to the end, I will give authority over the nations— ²⁷that one 'will rule them with an iron scepter and will dash them to pieces like pottery'ᵃ—just as I have received authority from my Father. ²⁸I will also give that one the morning star. ²⁹Whoever has ears, let them hear what the Spirit says to the churches.

To the Church in Sardis

3 "To the angelᵇ of the church in Sardis write:

These are the words of him who holds the seven spiritsᶜ of God and the seven stars. I know your deeds; you have a reputation of being alive, but you are dead. ²Wake up! Strengthen what remains and is about to die, for I have found your deeds unfinished in the sight of my God. ³Remember, therefore, what you have received and heard; hold it fast, and repent. But if you do not wake up, I will come like a thief, and you will not know at what time I will come to you.

⁴Yet you have a few people in Sardis who have not soiled their clothes. They will walk with me, dressed in white, for they are worthy. ⁵The one who is victorious will, like them, be dressed in white. I will never blot out the name of that person from the book of life, but will acknowledge that name before my Father and his angels. ⁶Whoever has ears, let them hear what the Spirit says to the churches.

To the Church in Philadelphia

⁷"To the angel of the church in Philadelphia write:

These are the words of him who is holy and true, who holds the key of David. What he opens no one can shut, and what he shuts no one can open. ⁸I know your deeds. See, I have placed before you an open door that no one can shut. I know that you have little strength, yet you have kept my word and have not denied my name. ⁹I will make those who are of the synagogue of Satan, who claim to be Jews though they are not, but are liars—I will make them come and fall down at your feet and acknowledge that I have loved you. ¹⁰Since you have kept my command to endure patiently, I will also keep you from the hour of trial that is going to come on the whole world to test the inhabitants of the earth.

¹¹I am coming soon. Hold on to what you have, so that no one will take your crown. ¹²The one who is victorious I will make a pillar in the temple of my God. Never again will they leave it. I will write on them the name of my God and the name of the city of my God, the new Jerusalem, which is coming down out of heaven from my God; and I will also write on them my new name. ¹³Whoever has ears, let them hear what the Spirit says to the churches.

To the Church in Laodicea

¹⁴"To the angel of the church in Laodicea write:

These are the words of the Amen, the faithful and true witness, the

---

ᵃ 27 Psalm 2:9   ᵇ 1 Or *messenger*; also in verses 7 and 14   ᶜ 1 That is, the sevenfold Spirit

My Name Is Mike

I'M A BELIEVER WHO STRUGGLES WITH ALCOHOLISM AND SEXUAL ADDICTION

Please read in Revelation 1:9 a brief description of the dire condition in which the apostle John found himself at the time the Lord Jesus appeared to him with his remarkable revelation.

"Shut up!" "Quit your crying!" "Shut your mouth! If you make another sound, I'll give you more of what you deserve." "You're going to burn in hell." Domestic violence, both verbal and physical, was a relentless reality in my house. I don't remember my first black eye, bloody lip or beating. These are just a few of the horrific memories I've retained of the things my mother said and did to me as she was "training" me as a child. During my first 12 years of life, my mom tried to destroy me as a boy in a desperate but unacknowledged attempt to make certain I wouldn't become the kind of man my father was. I wondered when she was going to kill me — or when one of my parents would kill the other.

I felt like a prisoner, utterly trapped by the drunken rampages of my father and the unrelenting abuse of my mother. Although I recognize now that domestic violence is a reality for men as well as women, I was afraid to talk about my experiences until I came to Celebrate Recovery. I realize today that the Lord's affections don't insulate any disciple from suffering at the hands of evil people. But where was he during my growing up years? Answer: He was right where he was supposed to be. He didn't, after all, allow either of my parents to kill the other, nor did he permit my mom to kill me. Is God happy, though, that these are the pervasive memories of my childhood? Absolutely not.

Understandably, my thoughts and feelings about God were seriously distorted. I knew him as a punishing God, a God who saw fit to chastise me for being a boy (my mom never abused my sisters). Mom knew the Bible like the back of her hand and could quote "relevant" passages word for word. When she told me I was going to hell — and backed up her dire prediction with irrefutable proof — I had no reason not to believe her.

I've learned in Celebrate Recovery that all of the many methods I employed to deal with my pain were linked to deep, internal wounds. I was afraid of criticism, feeling overwhelming shame and guilt whenever I heard it. I searched continually and desperately for ways to look better, feel better, act better and just be better. Abuse, neglect, self-mutilation, drugs, alcohol, sex, anger, depression, food abuse, isolation, performance addiction, workaholism, power and control issues, sexual identity issues, love-hate relationship issues, codependency, gambling — these were just a few of my struggles. I had to somehow get past the fears of losing my friends, my wife, my kids, my reputation, my success — and my life. Ironically, I have, in fact, lost all of those things, but God has given them back to me, along with so much more. My life is now filled with real friends, real passion, real love and real energy. The experience of the exiled evangelist John in Revelation is proof that even a prisoner retains unimpeded access to Christ's presence. Like the apostle John, this "prisoner" has, despite his pain, grown closer to God and is now serving as his instrument for sharing the truth.

I used to dream of conducting an outreach ministry for abused kids and/or people like myself who just didn't get it, who were afraid to tell anyone the truth about their anguish. But my own suffering has actually been a major aid in my ability to handle what God has actually called me to do: lead a Celebrate Recovery program in my home church. I am now able and anxious to share with others the true and living God who loves them so deeply and who has promised in Revelation that all suffering will one day come to an end (see Revelation 21:3 – 4).

I hope that my willingness to share the abuse and violence of my childhood will encourage and enable others who are still hanging on to the debilitating pain of abuse. I pray that they will step out of their fear of divulging their dark secrets and into a freeing relationship with Christ. I am truly grateful that God has given me this ministry opportunity and hope that you too will be willing to let go of the carefully protected memories that haunt you, that you'll let down your guard and allow him to change your life as he has changed mine.

ruler of God's creation. 15I know your deeds, that you are neither cold nor hot. I wish you were either one or the other! 16So, because you are lukewarm — neither hot nor cold — I am about to spit you out of my mouth. 17You say, 'I am rich; I have acquired wealth and do not need a thing.' But you do not realize that you are wretched, pitiful, poor, blind and naked. 18I counsel you to buy from me gold refined in the fire, so you can become rich; and white clothes to wear, so you can cover your shameful nakedness; and salve to put on your eyes, so you can see.

19Those whom I love I rebuke and discipline. So be earnest and repent. 20Here I am! I stand at the door and knock. If anyone hears my voice and opens the door, I will come in and eat with that person, and they with me.

21To the one who is victorious, I will give the right to sit with me on my throne, just as I was victorious and sat down with my Father on his throne. 22Whoever has ears, let them hear what the Spirit says to the churches."

The Throne in Heaven

4 After this I looked, and there before me was a door standing open in heaven. And the voice I had first heard speaking to me like a trumpet said, "Come up here, and I will show you what must take place after this." 2At once I was in the Spirit, and there before me was a throne in heaven with someone sitting on it. 3And the one who sat there had the appearance of jasper and ruby. A rainbow that shone like an emerald encircled the throne. 4Surrounding the throne were twenty-four other thrones, and seated on them were twenty-four elders. They were dressed in white and had crowns of gold on their heads. 5From the throne came flashes of lightning, rumblings and peals of thunder. In front of the throne, seven lamps were blazing. These are the seven spirits*a* of God. 6Also in front of the throne there was what looked like a sea of glass, clear as crystal.

In the center, around the throne, were four living creatures, and they were covered with eyes, in front and in back. 7The first living creature was like a lion, the second was like an ox, the third had a face like a man, the fourth was like a flying eagle. 8Each of the four living creatures had six wings and was covered with eyes all around, even under its wings. Day and night they never stop saying:

> "'Holy, holy, holy
> is the Lord God Almighty,'*b*
> who was, and is, and is to come."

9Whenever the living creatures give glory, honor and thanks to him who sits on the throne and who lives for ever and ever, 10the twenty-four elders fall down before him who sits on the throne and worship him who lives for ever and ever. They lay their crowns before the throne and say:

> 11"You are worthy, our Lord and God,
> to receive glory and honor and power,
> for you created all things,
> and by your will they were created
> and have their being."

The Scroll and the Lamb

5 Then I saw in the right hand of him who sat on the throne a scroll with writing on both sides and sealed with seven seals. 2And I saw a mighty angel proclaiming in a loud voice, "Who is worthy to break the seals and open the scroll?" 3But no one in heaven or on earth or under the earth could open the scroll or even look inside it. 4I wept and wept because no one was found who was worthy to open the scroll or look inside. 5Then one of the elders said to me, "Do not weep! See, the Lion of the tribe of Judah, the Root of Da-

---

a 5 That is, the sevenfold Spirit   *b* 8 Isaiah 6:3

vid, has triumphed. He is able to open the scroll and its seven seals."

⁶Then I saw a Lamb, looking as if it had been slain, standing at the center of the throne, encircled by the four living creatures and the elders. The Lamb had seven horns and seven eyes, which are the seven spirits*a* of God sent out into all the earth. ⁷He went and took the scroll from the right hand of him who sat on the throne. ⁸And when he had taken it, the four living creatures and the twenty-four elders fell down before the Lamb. Each one had a harp and they were holding golden bowls full of incense, which are the prayers of God's people. ⁹And they sang a new song, saying:

"You are worthy to take the scroll
      and to open its seals,
because you were slain,
      and with your blood you purchased
            for God
      persons from every tribe and
            language and people and nation.
¹⁰You have made them to be a kingdom
      and priests to serve our God,
      and they will reign*b* on the earth."

¹¹Then I looked and heard the voice of many angels, numbering thousands upon thousands, and ten thousand times ten thousand. They encircled the throne and the living creatures and the elders. ¹²In a loud voice they were saying:

"Worthy is the Lamb, who was slain,
      to receive power and wealth and
            wisdom and strength
      and honor and glory and praise!"

¹³Then I heard every creature in heaven and on earth and under the earth and on the sea, and all that is in them, saying:

"To him who sits on the throne and to
      the Lamb
      be praise and honor and glory and
            power,
            for ever and ever!"

¹⁴The four living creatures said, "Amen," and the elders fell down and worshiped.

The Seals

6 I watched as the Lamb opened the first of the seven seals. Then I heard one of the four living creatures say in a voice like thunder, "Come!" ²I looked, and there before me was a white horse! Its rider held a bow, and he was given a crown, and he rode out as a conqueror bent on conquest.

³When the Lamb opened the second seal, I heard the second living creature say, "Come!" ⁴Then another horse came out, a fiery red one. Its rider was given power to take peace from the earth and to make people kill each other. To him was given a large sword.

⁵When the Lamb opened the third seal, I heard the third living creature say, "Come!" I looked, and there before me was a black horse! Its rider was holding a pair of scales in his hand. ⁶Then I heard what sounded like a voice among the four living creatures, saying, "Two pounds*c* of wheat for a day's wages,*d* and six pounds*e* of barley for a day's wages,*d* and do not damage the oil and the wine!"

⁷When the Lamb opened the fourth seal, I heard the voice of the fourth living creature say, "Come!" ⁸I looked, and there before me was a pale horse! Its rider was named Death, and Hades was following close behind him. They were given power over a fourth of the earth to kill by sword, famine and plague, and by the wild beasts of the earth.

⁹When he opened the fifth seal, I saw under the altar the souls of those who had been slain because of the word of God and the testimony they had maintained. ¹⁰They called out in a loud voice, "How long, Sovereign Lord, holy and true, until you judge the inhabitants of the earth and avenge our blood?" ¹¹Then each of them was given a

---

a 6 That is, the sevenfold Spirit   *b 10* Some manuscripts *they reign*   *c 6* Or about 1 kilogram   *d 6* Greek *a denarius*   *e 6* Or about 3 kilograms white robe, and they were told to wait a little longer, until the full number of their fellow servants, their brothers and sisters,[a] were killed just as they had been.

¹²I watched as he opened the sixth seal. There was a great earthquake. The sun turned black like sackcloth made of goat hair, the whole moon turned blood red, ¹³and the stars in the sky fell to earth, as figs drop from a fig tree when shaken by a strong wind. ¹⁴The heavens receded like a scroll being rolled up, and every mountain and island was removed from its place.

¹⁵Then the kings of the earth, the princes, the generals, the rich, the mighty, and everyone else, both slave and free, hid in caves and among the rocks of the mountains. ¹⁶They called to the mountains and the rocks, "Fall on us and hide us[b] from the face of him who sits on the throne and from the wrath of the Lamb! ¹⁷For the great day of their[c] wrath has come, and who can withstand it?"

144,000 Sealed

7 After this I saw four angels standing at the four corners of the earth, holding back the four winds of the earth to prevent any wind from blowing on the land or on the sea or on any tree. ²Then I saw another angel coming up from the east, having the seal of the living God. He called out in a loud voice to the four angels who had been given power to harm the land and the sea: ³"Do not harm the land or the sea or the trees until we put a seal on the foreheads of the servants of our God." ⁴Then I heard the number of those who were sealed: 144,000 from all the tribes of Israel.

⁵From the tribe of Judah 12,000 were
    sealed,
from the tribe of Reuben 12,000,
from the tribe of Gad 12,000,
⁶from the tribe of Asher 12,000,
from the tribe of Naphtali 12,000,

from the tribe of Manasseh 12,000,
⁷from the tribe of Simeon 12,000,
from the tribe of Levi 12,000,
from the tribe of Issachar 12,000,
⁸from the tribe of Zebulun 12,000,
from the tribe of Joseph 12,000,
from the tribe of Benjamin 12,000.

The Great Multitude in White Robes

⁹After this I looked, and there before me was a great multitude that no one could count, from every nation, tribe, people and language, standing before the throne and before the Lamb. They were wearing white robes and were holding palm branches in their hands. ¹⁰And they cried out in a loud voice:

"Salvation belongs to our God,
    who sits on the throne,
    and to the Lamb."

¹¹All the angels were standing around the throne and around the elders and the four living creatures. They fell down on their faces before the throne and worshiped God, ¹²saying:

"Amen!
Praise and glory
and wisdom and thanks and honor
and power and strength
be to our God for ever and ever.
Amen!"

¹³Then one of the elders asked me, "These in white robes—who are they, and where did they come from?"

¹⁴I answered, "Sir, you know."

And he said, "These are they who have come out of the great tribulation; they have washed their robes and made them white in the blood of the Lamb. ¹⁵Therefore,

"they are before the throne of God
    and serve him day and night in his
        temple;
and he who sits on the throne
    will shelter them with his presence.

---

[a] 11 The Greek word for *brothers and sisters* (*adelphoi*) refers here to believers, both men and women, as part of God's family; also in 12:10; 19:10.   [b] 16 See Hosea 10:8.   [c] 17 Some manuscripts *his*

¹⁶'Never again will they hunger;
    never again will they thirst.
The sun will not beat down on them,'ᵃ
    nor any scorching heat.
¹⁷For the Lamb at the center of the throne
    will be their shepherd;
'he will lead them to springs of living
    water.'ᵃ
'And God will wipe away every tear
    from their eyes.'ᵇ"

The Seventh Seal and the Golden Censer

8 When he opened the seventh seal, there was silence in heaven for about half an hour.

²And I saw the seven angels who stand before God, and seven trumpets were given to them.

³Another angel, who had a golden censer, came and stood at the altar. He was given much incense to offer, with the prayers of all God's people, on the golden altar in front of the throne. ⁴The smoke of the incense, together with the prayers of God's people, went up before God from the angel's hand. ⁵Then the angel took the censer, filled it with fire from the altar, and hurled it on the earth; and there came peals of thunder, rumblings, flashes of lightning and an earthquake.

The Trumpets

⁶Then the seven angels who had the seven trumpets prepared to sound them.

⁷The first angel sounded his trumpet, and there came hail and fire mixed with blood, and it was hurled down on the earth. A third of the earth was burned up, a third of the trees were burned up, and all the green grass was burned up.

⁸The second angel sounded his trumpet, and something like a huge mountain, all ablaze, was thrown into the sea. A third of the sea turned into blood, ⁹a third of the living creatures in the sea died, and a third of the ships were destroyed.

¹⁰The third angel sounded his trumpet, and a great star, blazing like a torch, fell from the sky on a third of the rivers and on the springs of water — ¹¹the name of the star is Wormwood.ᶜ A third of the waters turned bitter, and many people died from the waters that had become bitter.

¹²The fourth angel sounded his trumpet, and a third of the sun was struck, a third of the moon, and a third of the stars, so that a third of them turned dark. A third of the day was without light, and also a third of the night.

¹³As I watched, I heard an eagle that was flying in midair call out in a loud voice: "Woe! Woe! Woe to the inhabitants of the earth, because of the trumpet blasts about to be sounded by the other three angels!"

9 The fifth angel sounded his trumpet, and I saw a star that had fallen from the sky to the earth. The star was given the key to the shaft of the Abyss. ²When he opened the Abyss, smoke rose from it like the smoke from a gigantic furnace. The sun and sky were darkened by the smoke from the Abyss. ³And out of the smoke locusts came down on the earth and were given power like that of scorpions of the earth. ⁴They were told not to harm the grass of the earth or any plant or tree, but only those people who did not have the seal of God on their foreheads. ⁵They were not allowed to kill them but only to torture them for five months. And the agony they suffered was like that of the sting of a scorpion when it strikes. ⁶During those days people will seek death but will not find it; they will long to die, but death will elude them.

⁷The locusts looked like horses prepared for battle. On their heads they wore something like crowns of gold, and their faces resembled human faces. ⁸Their hair was like women's hair, and their teeth were like lions' teeth. ⁹They had breastplates like breastplates of iron, and the sound of their wings was like the thundering of many horses and chariots rushing into battle.

ᵃ 16,17 Isaiah 49:10   ᵇ 17 Isaiah 25:8   ᶜ 11 Wormwood is a bitter substance.

10They had tails with stingers, like scorpions, and in their tails they had power to torment people for five months. 11They had as king over them the angel of the Abyss, whose name in Hebrew is Abaddon and in Greek is Apollyon (that is, Destroyer).

12The first woe is past; two other woes are yet to come.

13The sixth angel sounded his trumpet, and I heard a voice coming from the four horns of the golden altar that is before God. 14It said to the sixth angel who had the trumpet, "Release the four angels who are bound at the great river Euphrates." 15And the four angels who had been kept ready for this very hour and day and month and year were released to kill a third of mankind. 16The number of the mounted troops was twice ten thousand times ten thousand. I heard their number.

17The horses and riders I saw in my vision looked like this: Their breastplates were fiery red, dark blue, and yellow as sulfur. The heads of the horses resembled the heads of lions, and out of their mouths came fire, smoke and sulfur. 18A third of mankind was killed by the three plagues of fire, smoke and sulfur that came out of their mouths. 19The power of the horses was in their mouths and in their tails; for their tails were like snakes, having heads with which they inflict injury.

20The rest of mankind who were not killed by these plagues still did not repent of the work of their hands; they did not stop worshiping demons, and idols of gold, silver, bronze, stone and wood — idols that cannot see or hear or walk. 21Nor did they repent of their murders, their magic arts, their sexual immorality or their thefts.

The Angel and the Little Scroll

10 Then I saw another mighty angel coming down from heaven. He was robed in a cloud, with a rainbow above his head; his face was like the sun, and his legs were like fiery pillars. 2He was holding a little scroll, which lay open in his hand. He planted his right foot on the sea and his left foot on the land, 3and he gave a loud shout like the roar of a lion. When he shouted, the voices of the seven thunders spoke. 4And when the seven thunders spoke, I was about to write; but I heard a voice from heaven say, "Seal up what the seven thunders have said and do not write it down."

5Then the angel I had seen standing on the sea and on the land raised his right hand to heaven. 6And he swore by him who lives for ever and ever, who created the heavens and all that is in them, the earth and all that is in it, and the sea and all that is in it, and said, "There will be no more delay! 7But in the days when the seventh angel is about to sound his trumpet, the mystery of God will be accomplished, just as he announced to his servants the prophets."

8Then the voice that I had heard from heaven spoke to me once more: "Go, take the scroll that lies open in the hand of the angel who is standing on the sea and on the land."

9So I went to the angel and asked him to give me the little scroll. He said to me, "Take it and eat it. It will turn your stomach sour, but 'in your mouth it will be as sweet as honey.'ᵃ" 10I took the little scroll from the angel's hand and ate it. It tasted as sweet as honey in my mouth, but when I had eaten it, my stomach turned sour. 11Then I was told, "You must prophesy again about many peoples, nations, languages and kings."

The Two Witnesses

11 I was given a reed like a measuring rod and was told, "Go and measure the temple of God and the altar, with its worshipers. 2But exclude the outer court; do not measure it, because it has been given to the Gentiles. They will trample on the holy city for 42 months. 3And I will appoint my two witnesses, and

---

ᵃ 9 Ezek. 3:3

they will prophesy for 1,260 days, clothed in sackcloth." ⁴They are "the two olive trees" and the two lampstands, and "they stand before the Lord of the earth."ᵃ ⁵If anyone tries to harm them, fire comes from their mouths and devours their enemies. This is how anyone who wants to harm them must die. ⁶They have power to shut up the heavens so that it will not rain during the time they are prophesying; and they have power to turn the waters into blood and to strike the earth with every kind of plague as often as they want.

⁷Now when they have finished their testimony, the beast that comes up from the Abyss will attack them, and overpower and kill them. ⁸Their bodies will lie in the public square of the great city — which is figuratively called Sodom and Egypt — where also their Lord was crucified. ⁹For three and a half days some from every people, tribe, language and nation will gaze on their bodies and refuse them burial. ¹⁰The inhabitants of the earth will gloat over them and will celebrate by sending each other gifts, because these two prophets had tormented those who live on the earth.

¹¹But after the three and a half days the breathᵇ of life from God entered them, and they stood on their feet, and terror struck those who saw them. ¹²Then they heard a loud voice from heaven saying to them, "Come up here." And they went up to heaven in a cloud, while their enemies looked on.

¹³At that very hour there was a severe earthquake and a tenth of the city collapsed. Seven thousand people were killed in the earthquake, and the survivors were terrified and gave glory to the God of heaven.

¹⁴The second woe has passed; the third woe is coming soon.

The Seventh Trumpet

¹⁵The seventh angel sounded his trumpet, and there were loud voices in heaven, which said:

"The kingdom of the world has become
    the kingdom of our Lord and of his
        Messiah,
    and he will reign for ever and ever."

¹⁶And the twenty-four elders, who were seated on their thrones before God, fell on their faces and worshiped God, ¹⁷saying:

"We give thanks to you, Lord God
    Almighty,
    the One who is and who was,
    because you have taken your great
        power
    and have begun to reign.
¹⁸The nations were angry,
    and your wrath has come.
The time has come for judging the dead,
    and for rewarding your servants the
        prophets
and your people who revere your name,
    both great and small —
and for destroying those who destroy
    the earth."

¹⁹Then God's temple in heaven was opened, and within his temple was seen the ark of his covenant. And there came flashes of lightning, rumblings, peals of thunder, an earthquake and a severe hailstorm.

The Woman and the Dragon

12 A great sign appeared in heaven: a woman clothed with the sun, with the moon under her feet and a crown of twelve stars on her head. ²She was pregnant and cried out in pain as she was about to give birth. ³Then another sign appeared in heaven: an enormous red dragon with seven heads and ten horns and seven crowns on its heads. ⁴Its tail swept a third of the stars out of the sky and flung them to the earth. The dragon stood in front of the woman who was about to give birth, so that it might devour her child the moment he was born. ⁵She gave birth to a son, a male child, who "will rule all the nations with an iron scepter."ᶜ And her child was snatched up to God and to

---

ᵃ 4 See Zech. 4:3,11,14.   ᵇ 11 Or *Spirit* (see Ezek. 37:5,14)   ᶜ 5 Psalm 2:9

his throne. 6The woman fled into the wilderness to a place prepared for her by God, where she might be taken care of for 1,260 days.

7Then war broke out in heaven. Michael and his angels fought against the dragon, and the dragon and his angels fought back. 8But he was not strong enough, and they lost their place in heaven. 9The great dragon was hurled down — that ancient serpent called the devil, or Satan, who leads the whole world astray. He was hurled to the earth, and his angels with him.

10Then I heard a loud voice in heaven say:

"Now have come the salvation and the power
　and the kingdom of our God,
　and the authority of his Messiah.
For the accuser of our brothers and sisters,
　who accuses them before our God day and night,
　has been hurled down.
11They triumphed over him
　by the blood of the Lamb
　and by the word of their testimony;
they did not love their lives so much
　as to shrink from death.
12Therefore rejoice, you heavens
　and you who dwell in them!
But woe to the earth and the sea,
　because the devil has gone down to you!
He is filled with fury,
　because he knows that his time is short."

13When the dragon saw that he had been hurled to the earth, he pursued the woman who had given birth to the male child. 14The woman was given the two wings of a great eagle, so that she might fly to the place prepared for her in the wilderness, where she would be taken care of for a time, times and half a time, out of the serpent's reach. 15Then from his mouth the serpent spewed water like a river, to overtake the woman and sweep her away with the torrent. 16But the earth helped the woman by opening its mouth and swallowing the river that the dragon had spewed out of his mouth. 17Then the dragon was enraged at the woman and went off to wage war against the rest of her offspring — those who keep God's commands and hold fast their testimony about Jesus.

The Beast out of the Sea

13 The dragon*a* stood on the shore of the sea. And I saw a beast coming out of the sea. It had ten horns and seven heads, with ten crowns on its horns, and on each head a blasphemous name. 2The beast I saw resembled a leopard, but had feet like those of a bear and a mouth like that of a lion. The dragon gave the beast his power and his throne and great authority. 3One of the heads of the beast seemed to have had a fatal wound, but the fatal wound had been healed. The whole world was filled with wonder and followed the beast. 4People worshiped the dragon because he had given authority to the beast, and they also worshiped the beast and asked, "Who is like the beast? Who can wage war against it?"

5The beast was given a mouth to utter proud words and blasphemies and to exercise its authority for forty-two months. 6It opened its mouth to blaspheme God, and to slander his name and his dwelling place and those who live in heaven. 7It was given power to wage war against God's holy people and to conquer them. And it was given authority over every tribe, people, language and nation. 8All inhabitants of the earth will worship the beast — all whose names have not been written in the Lamb's book of life, the Lamb who was slain from the creation of the world.*b*

---

a 1 Some manuscripts *And I*　*b 8* Or *written from the creation of the world in the book of life belonging to the Lamb who was slain*

⁹Whoever has ears, let them hear.

¹⁰"If anyone is to go into captivity,
   into captivity they will go.
If anyone is to be killed*a* with the sword,
   with the sword they will be killed."*b*

This calls for patient endurance and faithfulness on the part of God's people.

The Beast out of the Earth

¹¹Then I saw a second beast, coming out of the earth. It had two horns like a lamb, but it spoke like a dragon. ¹²It exercised all the authority of the first beast on its behalf, and made the earth and its inhabitants worship the first beast, whose fatal wound had been healed. ¹³And it performed great signs, even causing fire to come down from heaven to the earth in full view of the people. ¹⁴Because of the signs it was given power to perform on behalf of the first beast, it deceived the inhabitants of the earth. It ordered them to set up an image in honor of the beast who was wounded by the sword and yet lived. ¹⁵The second beast was given power to give breath to the image of the first beast, so that the image could speak and cause all who refused to worship the image to be killed. ¹⁶It also forced all people, great and small, rich and poor, free and slave, to receive a mark on their right hands or on their foreheads, ¹⁷so that they could not buy or sell unless they had the mark, which is the name of the beast or the number of its name.

¹⁸This calls for wisdom. Let the person who has insight calculate the number of the beast, for it is the number of a man.*c* That number is 666.

The Lamb and the 144,000

14 Then I looked, and there before me was the Lamb, standing on Mount Zion, and with him 144,000 who had his name and his Father's name written on their foreheads. ²And I heard a sound from heaven like the roar of rushing waters and like a loud peal of thunder. The sound I heard was like that of harpists playing their harps. ³And they sang a new song before the throne and before the four living creatures and the elders. No one could learn the song except the 144,000 who had been redeemed from the earth. ⁴These are those who did not defile themselves with women, for they remained virgins. They follow the Lamb wherever he goes. They were purchased from among mankind and offered as firstfruits to God and the Lamb. ⁵No lie was found in their mouths; they are blameless.

The Three Angels

⁶Then I saw another angel flying in midair, and he had the eternal gospel to proclaim to those who live on the earth — to every nation, tribe, language and people. ⁷He said in a loud voice, "Fear God and give him glory, because the hour of his judgment has come. Worship him who made the heavens, the earth, the sea and the springs of water."

⁸A second angel followed and said, "'Fallen! Fallen is Babylon the Great,'*d* which made all the nations drink the maddening wine of her adulteries."

⁹A third angel followed them and said in a loud voice: "If anyone worships the beast and its image and receives its mark on their forehead or on their hand, ¹⁰they, too, will drink the wine of God's fury, which has been poured full strength into the cup of his wrath. They will be tormented with burning sulfur in the presence of the holy angels and of the Lamb. ¹¹And the smoke of their torment will rise for ever and ever. There will be no rest day or night for those who worship the beast and its image, or for anyone who receives the mark of its name." ¹²This calls for patient endurance on the part of the people of God who keep his commands and remain faithful to Jesus.

¹³Then I heard a voice from heaven say, "Write this: Blessed are the dead who die in the Lord from now on."

---

a 10 Some manuscripts *anyone kills*   *b 10* Jer. 15:2   *c 18* Or *is humanity's number*   *d 8* Isaiah 21:9

"Yes," says the Spirit, "they will rest from their labor, for their deeds will follow them."

Harvesting the Earth and Trampling the Winepress

¹⁴I looked, and there before me was a white cloud, and seated on the cloud was one like a son of man[a] with a crown of gold on his head and a sharp sickle in his hand. ¹⁵Then another angel came out of the temple and called in a loud voice to him who was sitting on the cloud, "Take your sickle and reap, because the time to reap has come, for the harvest of the earth is ripe." ¹⁶So he who was seated on the cloud swung his sickle over the earth, and the earth was harvested.

¹⁷Another angel came out of the temple in heaven, and he too had a sharp sickle. ¹⁸Still another angel, who had charge of the fire, came from the altar and called in a loud voice to him who had the sharp sickle, "Take your sharp sickle and gather the clusters of grapes from the earth's vine, because its grapes are ripe." ¹⁹The angel swung his sickle on the earth, gathered its grapes and threw them into the great winepress of God's wrath. ²⁰They were trampled in the winepress outside the city, and blood flowed out of the press, rising as high as the horses' bridles for a distance of 1,600 stadia.[b]

Seven Angels With Seven Plagues

15 I saw in heaven another great and marvelous sign: seven angels with the seven last plagues—last, because with them God's wrath is completed. ²And I saw what looked like a sea of glass glowing with fire and, standing beside the sea, those who had been victorious over the beast and its image and over the number of its name. They held harps given them by God ³and sang the song of God's servant Moses and of the Lamb:

"Great and marvelous are your deeds,
     Lord God Almighty.

Just and true are your ways,
     King of the nations.[c]
⁴Who will not fear you, Lord,
     and bring glory to your name?
For you alone are holy.
All nations will come
     and worship before you,
for your righteous acts have been
     revealed."[d]

⁵After this I looked, and I saw in heaven the temple—that is, the tabernacle of the covenant law—and it was opened. ⁶Out of the temple came the seven angels with the seven plagues. They were dressed in clean, shining linen and wore golden sashes around their chests. ⁷Then one of the four living creatures gave to the seven angels seven golden bowls filled with the wrath of God, who lives for ever and ever. ⁸And the temple was filled with smoke from the glory of God and from his power, and no one could enter the temple until the seven plagues of the seven angels were completed.

The Seven Bowls of God's Wrath

16 Then I heard a loud voice from the temple saying to the seven angels, "Go, pour out the seven bowls of God's wrath on the earth."

²The first angel went and poured out his bowl on the land, and ugly, festering sores broke out on the people who had the mark of the beast and worshiped its image.

³The second angel poured out his bowl on the sea, and it turned into blood like that of a dead person, and every living thing in the sea died.

⁴The third angel poured out his bowl on the rivers and springs of water, and they became blood. ⁵Then I heard the angel in charge of the waters say:

"You are just in these judgments,
     O Holy One,
you who are and who were;

---

[a] 14 See Daniel 7:13.   [b] 20 That is, about 180 miles or about 300 kilometers   [c] 3 Some manuscripts *ages*
[d] 3,4 Phrases in this song are drawn from Psalm 111:2,3; Deut. 32:4; Jer. 10:7; Psalms 86:9; 98:2.

6for they have shed the blood of your
    holy people and your prophets,
and you have given them blood to
    drink as they deserve."

7And I heard the altar respond:

"Yes, Lord God Almighty,
    true and just are your judgments."

8The fourth angel poured out his bowl on the sun, and the sun was allowed to scorch people with fire. 9They were seared by the intense heat and they cursed the name of God, who had control over these plagues, but they refused to repent and glorify him.

10The fifth angel poured out his bowl on the throne of the beast, and its kingdom was plunged into darkness. People gnawed their tongues in agony 11and cursed the God of heaven because of their pains and their sores, but they refused to repent of what they had done.

12The sixth angel poured out his bowl on the great river Euphrates, and its water was dried up to prepare the way for the kings from the East. 13Then I saw three impure spirits that looked like frogs; they came out of the mouth of the dragon, out of the mouth of the beast and out of the mouth of the false prophet. 14They are demonic spirits that perform signs, and they go out to the kings of the whole world, to gather them for the battle on the great day of God Almighty.

15"Look, I come like a thief! Blessed is the one who stays awake and remains clothed, so as not to go naked and be shamefully exposed."

16Then they gathered the kings together to the place that in Hebrew is called Armageddon.

17The seventh angel poured out his bowl into the air, and out of the temple came a loud voice from the throne, saying, "It is done!" 18Then there came flashes of lightning, rumblings, peals of thunder and a severe earthquake. No earthquake like it has ever occurred since mankind has been on earth, so tremendous was the quake. 19The great city split into three parts, and the cities of the nations collapsed. God remembered Babylon the Great and gave her the cup filled with the wine of the fury of his wrath. 20Every island fled away and the mountains could not be found. 21From the sky huge hailstones, each weighing about a hundred pounds,*a* fell on people. And they cursed God on account of the plague of hail, because the plague was so terrible.

Babylon, the Prostitute on the Beast

17 One of the seven angels who had the seven bowls came and said to me, "Come, I will show you the punishment of the great prostitute, who sits by many waters. 2With her the kings of the earth committed adultery, and the inhabitants of the earth were intoxicated with the wine of her adulteries."

3Then the angel carried me away in the Spirit into a wilderness. There I saw a woman sitting on a scarlet beast that was covered with blasphemous names and had seven heads and ten horns. 4The woman was dressed in purple and scarlet, and was glittering with gold, precious stones and pearls. She held a golden cup in her hand, filled with abominable things and the filth of her adulteries. 5The name written on her forehead was a mystery:

BABYLON THE GREAT
THE MOTHER OF PROSTITUTES
AND OF THE ABOMINATIONS OF THE
EARTH.

6I saw that the woman was drunk with the blood of God's holy people, the blood of those who bore testimony to Jesus.

When I saw her, I was greatly astonished. 7Then the angel said to me: "Why are you astonished? I will explain to you the mystery of the woman and of the beast she rides, which has the seven heads and ten horns. [8]The beast, which you saw, once was, now is not, and yet will come up out of the Abyss and go to its destruction. The inhabitants of the earth whose names have not been written in the book of life from the creation of the world will be astonished when they see the beast, because it once was, now is not, and yet will come.

[9]"This calls for a mind with wisdom. The seven heads are seven hills on which the woman sits. [10]They are also seven kings. Five have fallen, one is, the other has not yet come; but when he does come, he must remain for only a little while. [11]The beast who once was, and now is not, is an eighth king. He belongs to the seven and is going to his destruction.

[12]"The ten horns you saw are ten kings who have not yet received a kingdom, but who for one hour will receive authority as kings along with the beast. [13]They have one purpose and will give their power and authority to the beast. [14]They will wage war against the Lamb, but the Lamb will triumph over them because he is Lord of lords and King of kings — and with him will be his called, chosen and faithful followers."

[15]Then the angel said to me, "The waters you saw, where the prostitute sits, are peoples, multitudes, nations and languages. [16]The beast and the ten horns you saw will hate the prostitute. They will bring her to ruin and leave her naked; they will eat her flesh and burn her with fire. [17]For God has put it into their hearts to accomplish his purpose by agreeing to hand over to the beast their royal authority, until God's words are fulfilled. [18]The woman you saw is the great city that rules over the kings of the earth."

Lament Over Fallen Babylon

18

After this I saw another angel coming down from heaven. He had great authority, and the earth was illuminated by his splendor. [2]With a mighty voice he shouted:

" 'Fallen! Fallen is Babylon the Great!'[a]
  She has become a dwelling for demons
and a haunt for every impure spirit,
  a haunt for every unclean bird,
  a haunt for every unclean and
    detestable animal.
[3]For all the nations have drunk
  the maddening wine of her adulteries.
The kings of the earth committed
    adultery with her,
  and the merchants of the earth
    grew rich from her excessive
    luxuries."

Warning to Escape Babylon's Judgment

[4]Then I heard another voice from heaven say:

" 'Come out of her, my people,'[b]
  so that you will not share in her sins,
  so that you will not receive any of her
    plagues;
[5]for her sins are piled up to heaven,
  and God has remembered her
    crimes.
[6]Give back to her as she has given;
  pay her back double for what she has
    done.
  Pour her a double portion from her
    own cup.
[7]Give her as much torment and grief
  as the glory and luxury she gave
    herself.
In her heart she boasts,
  'I sit enthroned as queen.
I am not a widow;[c]
  I will never mourn.'
[8]Therefore in one day her plagues will
    overtake her:
  death, mourning and famine.
She will be consumed by fire,
  for mighty is the Lord God who
    judges her.

Threefold Woe Over Babylon's Fall

[9]"When the kings of the earth who committed adultery with her and shared her

---

[a] 2 Isaiah 21:9   [b] 4 Jer. 51:45   [c] 7 See Isaiah 47:7,8.

luxury see the smoke of her burning, they will weep and mourn over her. [10]Terrified at her torment, they will stand far off and cry:

> "'Woe! Woe to you, great city,
>   you mighty city of Babylon!
> In one hour your doom has come!'

[11]"The merchants of the earth will weep and mourn over her because no one buys their cargoes anymore — [12]cargoes of gold, silver, precious stones and pearls; fine linen, purple, silk and scarlet cloth; every sort of citron wood, and articles of every kind made of ivory, costly wood, bronze, iron and marble; [13]cargoes of cinnamon and spice, of incense, myrrh and frankincense, of wine and olive oil, of fine flour and wheat; cattle and sheep; horses and carriages; and human beings sold as slaves.

[14]"They will say, 'The fruit you longed for is gone from you. All your luxury and splendor have vanished, never to be recovered.' [15]The merchants who sold these things and gained their wealth from her will stand far off, terrified at her torment. They will weep and mourn [16]and cry out:

> "'Woe! Woe to you, great city,
>   dressed in fine linen, purple and
>   scarlet,
>   and glittering with gold, precious
>   stones and pearls!
> [17]In one hour such great wealth has been
>   brought to ruin!'

"Every sea captain, and all who travel by ship, the sailors, and all who earn their living from the sea, will stand far off. [18]When they see the smoke of her burning, they will exclaim, 'Was there ever a city like this great city?' [19]They will throw dust on their heads, and with weeping and mourning cry out:

> "'Woe! Woe to you, great city,
>   where all who had ships on the sea
>   became rich through her wealth!
> In one hour she has been brought to
>   ruin!'

> [20]"Rejoice over her, you heavens!
>   Rejoice, you people of God!
>   Rejoice, apostles and prophets!
> For God has judged her
>   with the judgment she imposed on
>   you."

The Finality of Babylon's Doom

[21]Then a mighty angel picked up a boulder the size of a large millstone and threw it into the sea, and said:

> "With such violence
>   the great city of Babylon will be
>   thrown down,
>   never to be found again.
> [22]The music of harpists and musicians,
>   pipers and trumpeters,
>   will never be heard in you again.
> No worker of any trade
>   will ever be found in you again.
> The sound of a millstone
>   will never be heard in you again.
> [23]The light of a lamp
>   will never shine in you again.
> The voice of bridegroom and bride
>   will never be heard in you again.
> Your merchants were the world's
>   important people.
> By your magic spell all the nations
>   were led astray.
> [24]In her was found the blood of prophets
>   and of God's holy people,
> of all who have been slaughtered on
>   the earth."

Threefold Hallelujah Over Babylon's Fall

19 After this I heard what sounded like the roar of a great multitude in heaven shouting:

> "Hallelujah!
> Salvation and glory and power belong
>   to our God,
> [2] for true and just are his judgments.
> He has condemned the great prostitute
>   who corrupted the earth by her
>   adulteries.
> He has avenged on her the blood of his
>   servants."

³And again they shouted:

"Hallelujah!
The smoke from her goes up for ever
    and ever."

⁴The twenty-four elders and the four living creatures fell down and worshiped God, who was seated on the throne. And they cried:

"Amen, Hallelujah!"

⁵Then a voice came from the throne, saying:

"Praise our God,
    all you his servants,
you who fear him,
    both great and small!"

⁶Then I heard what sounded like a great multitude, like the roar of rushing waters and like loud peals of thunder, shouting:

"Hallelujah!
    For our Lord God Almighty reigns.
⁷Let us rejoice and be glad
    and give him glory!
For the wedding of the Lamb has come,
    and his bride has made herself ready.
⁸Fine linen, bright and clean,
    was given her to wear."

(Fine linen stands for the righteous acts of God's holy people.)

⁹Then the angel said to me, "Write this: Blessed are those who are invited to the wedding supper of the Lamb!" And he added, "These are the true words of God."

¹⁰At this I fell at his feet to worship him. But he said to me, "Don't do that! I am a fellow servant with you and with your brothers and sisters who hold to the testimony of Jesus. Worship God! For it is the Spirit of prophecy who bears testimony to Jesus."

The Heavenly Warrior Defeats the Beast

¹¹I saw heaven standing open and there before me was a white horse, whose rider is called Faithful and True. With justice he judges and wages war. ¹²His eyes are like blazing fire, and on his head are many crowns. He has a name written on him that no one knows but he himself. ¹³He is dressed in a robe dipped in blood, and his name is the Word of God. ¹⁴The armies of heaven were following him, riding on white horses and dressed in fine linen, white and clean. ¹⁵Coming out of his mouth is a sharp sword with which to strike down the nations. "He will rule them with an iron scepter."ᵃ He treads the winepress of the fury of the wrath of God Almighty. ¹⁶On his robe and on his thigh he has this name written:

KING OF KINGS AND LORD OF LORDS.

¹⁷And I saw an angel standing in the sun, who cried in a loud voice to all the birds flying in midair, "Come, gather together for the great supper of God, ¹⁸so that you may eat the flesh of kings, generals, and the mighty, of horses and their riders, and the flesh of all people, free and slave, great and small."

¹⁹Then I saw the beast and the kings of the earth and their armies gathered together to wage war against the rider on the horse and his army. ²⁰But the beast was captured, and with it the false prophet who had performed the signs on its behalf. With these signs he had deluded those who had received the mark of the beast and worshiped its image. The two of them were thrown alive into the fiery lake of burning sulfur. ²¹The rest were killed with the sword coming out of the mouth of the rider on the horse, and all the birds gorged themselves on their flesh.

The Thousand Years

20 And I saw an angel coming down out of heaven, having the key to the Abyss and holding in his hand a great chain. ²He seized the dragon, that ancient serpent, who is the

---

ᵃ 15 Psalm 2:9

devil, or Satan, and bound him for a thousand years. [3]He threw him into the Abyss, and locked and sealed it over him, to keep him from deceiving the nations anymore until the thousand years were ended. After that, he must be set free for a short time.

[4]I saw thrones on which were seated those who had been given authority to judge. And I saw the souls of those who had been beheaded because of their testimony about Jesus and because of the word of God. They[a] had not worshiped the beast or its image and had not received its mark on their foreheads or their hands. They came to life and reigned with Christ a thousand years. [5](The rest of the dead did not come to life until the thousand years were ended.) This is the first resurrection. [6]Blessed and holy are those who share in the first resurrection. The second death has no power over them, but they will be priests of God and of Christ and will reign with him for a thousand years.

The Judgment of Satan

[7]When the thousand years are over, Satan will be released from his prison [8]and will go out to deceive the nations in the four corners of the earth — Gog and Magog — and to gather them for battle. In number they are like the sand on the seashore. [9]They marched across the breadth of the earth and surrounded the camp of God's people, the city he loves. But fire came down from heaven and devoured them. [10]And the devil, who deceived them, was thrown into the lake of burning sulfur, where the beast and the false prophet had been thrown. They will be tormented day and night for ever and ever.

The Judgment of the Dead

[11]Then I saw a great white throne and him who was seated on it. The earth and the heavens fled from his presence, and there was no place for them. [12]And I saw the dead, great and small, standing before the throne, and books were opened. Another book was opened, which is the book of life. The dead were judged according to what they had done as recorded in the books. [13]The sea gave up the dead that were in it, and death and Hades gave up the dead that were in them, and each person was judged according to what they had done. [14]Then death and Hades were thrown into the lake of fire. The lake of fire is the second death. [15]Anyone whose name was not found written in the book of life was thrown into the lake of fire.

A New Heaven and a New Earth

21 Then I saw "a new heaven and a new earth,"[b] for the first heaven and the first earth had passed away, and there was no longer any sea. [2]I saw the Holy City, the new Jerusalem, coming down out of heaven from God, prepared as a bride beautifully dressed for her husband. [3]And I heard a loud voice from the throne saying, "Look! God's dwelling place is now among the people, and he will dwell with them. They will be his people, and God himself will be with them and be their God. [4]'He will wipe every tear from their eyes. There will be no more death'[c] or mourning or crying or pain, for the old order of things has passed away."

[5]He who was seated on the throne said, "I am making everything new!" Then he said, "Write this down, for these words are trustworthy and true."

[6]He said to me: "It is done. I am the Alpha and the Omega, the Beginning and the End. To the thirsty I will give water without cost from the spring of the water of life. [7]Those who are victorious will inherit all this, and I will be their God and they will be my children. [8]But the cowardly, the unbelieving, the vile, the murderers, the sexually immoral, those who practice magic arts, the idolaters and all liars — they will be consigned to the fiery lake of burning sulfur. This is the second death."

---

[a] 4 Or *God; I also saw those who*   [b] 1 Isaiah 65:17   [c] 4 Isaiah 25:8

The New Jerusalem, the Bride of the Lamb

⁹One of the seven angels who had the seven bowls full of the seven last plagues came and said to me, "Come, I will show you the bride, the wife of the Lamb." ¹⁰And he carried me away in the Spirit to a mountain great and high, and showed me the Holy City, Jerusalem, coming down out of heaven from God. ¹¹It shone with the glory of God, and its brilliance was like that of a very precious jewel, like a jasper, clear as crystal. ¹²It had a great, high wall with twelve gates, and with twelve angels at the gates. On the gates were written the names of the twelve tribes of Israel. ¹³There were three gates on the east, three on the north, three on the south and three on the west. ¹⁴The wall of the city had twelve foundations, and on them were the names of the twelve apostles of the Lamb.

¹⁵The angel who talked with me had a measuring rod of gold to measure the city, its gates and its walls. ¹⁶The city was laid out like a square, as long as it was wide. He measured the city with the rod and found it to be 12,000 stadia*a* in length, and as wide and high as it is long. ¹⁷The angel measured the wall using human measurement, and it was 144 cubits*b* thick.*c* ¹⁸The wall was made of jasper, and the city of pure gold, as pure as glass. ¹⁹The foundations of the city walls were decorated with every kind of precious stone. The first foundation was jasper, the second sapphire, the third agate, the fourth emerald, ²⁰the fifth onyx, the sixth ruby, the seventh chrysolite, the eighth beryl, the ninth topaz, the tenth turquoise, the eleventh jacinth, and the twelfth amethyst.*d* ²¹The twelve gates were twelve pearls, each gate made of a single pearl. The great street of the city was of gold, as pure as transparent glass.

²²I did not see a temple in the city, because the Lord God Almighty and the Lamb are its temple. ²³The city does not need the sun or the moon to shine on it, for the glory of God gives it light, and the Lamb is its lamp. ²⁴The nations will walk by its light, and the kings of the earth will bring their splendor into it. ²⁵On no day will its gates ever be shut, for there will be no night there. ²⁶The glory and honor of the nations will be brought into it. ²⁷Nothing impure will ever enter it, nor will anyone who does what is shameful or deceitful, but only those whose names are written in the Lamb's book of life.

Eden Restored

22 Then the angel showed me the river of the water of life, as clear as crystal, flowing from the throne of God and of the Lamb ²down the middle of the great street of the city. On each side of the river stood the tree of life, bearing twelve crops of fruit, yielding its fruit every month. And the leaves of the tree are for the healing of the nations. ³No longer will there be any curse. The throne of God and of the Lamb will be in the city, and his servants will serve him. ⁴They will see his face, and his name will be on their foreheads. ⁵There will be no more night. They will not need the light of a lamp or the light of the sun, for the Lord God will give them light. And they will reign for ever and ever.

John and the Angel

⁶The angel said to me, "These words are trustworthy and true. The Lord, the God who inspires the prophets, sent his angel to show his servants the things that must soon take place."

⁷"Look, I am coming soon! Blessed is the one who keeps the words of the prophecy written in this scroll."

⁸I, John, am the one who heard and saw these things. And when I had heard and seen them, I fell down to worship at the feet of the angel who had been showing them

---

a 16 That is, about 1,400 miles or about 2,200 kilometers   *b 17* That is, about 200 feet or about 65 meters
c 17 Or *high*   *d 20* The precise identification of some of these precious stones is uncertain.

to me. ⁹But he said to me, "Don't do that! I am a fellow servant with you and with your fellow prophets and with all who keep the words of this scroll. Worship God!"

¹⁰Then he told me, "Do not seal up the words of the prophecy of this scroll, because the time is near. ¹¹Let the one who does wrong continue to do wrong; let the vile person continue to be vile; let the one who does right continue to do right; and let the holy person continue to be holy."

Epilogue: Invitation and Warning

¹²"Look, I am coming soon! My reward is with me, and I will give to each person according to what they have done. ¹³I am the Alpha and the Omega, the First and the Last, the Beginning and the End.

¹⁴"Blessed are those who wash their robes, that they may have the right to the tree of life and may go through the gates into the city. ¹⁵Outside are the dogs, those who practice magic arts, the sexually immoral, the murderers, the idolaters and everyone who loves and practices falsehood.

¹⁶"I, Jesus, have sent my angel to give you*ᵃ* this testimony for the churches. I am the Root and the Offspring of David, and the bright Morning Star."

¹⁷The Spirit and the bride say, "Come!" And let the one who hears say, "Come!" Let the one who is thirsty come; and let the one who wishes take the free gift of the water of life.

¹⁸I warn everyone who hears the words of the prophecy of this scroll: If anyone adds anything to them, God will add to that person the plagues described in this scroll. ¹⁹And if anyone takes words away from this scroll of prophecy, God will take away from that person any share in the tree of life and in the Holy City, which are described in this scroll.

²⁰He who testifies to these things says, "Yes, I am coming soon."

Amen. Come, Lord Jesus.

²¹The grace of the Lord Jesus be with God's people. Amen.

ᵃ 16 The Greek is plural.

TABLE OF
WEIGHTS AND MEASURES

	Biblical Unit	Approximate American Equivalent	Approximate Metric Equivalent
WEIGHTS	talent (60 minas)	75 pounds	34 kilograms
	mina (50 shekels)	1 1/4 pounds	560 grams
	shekel (2 bekas)	2/5 ounce	11.5 grams
	pim (2/3 shekel)	1/4 ounce	7.8 grams
	beka (10 gerahs)	1/5 ounce	5.7 grams
	gerah	1/50 ounce	0.6 gram
	daric	1/3 ounce	8.4 grams
LENGTH	cubit	18 inches	45 centimeters
	span	9 inches	23 centimeters
	handbreadth	3 inches	7.5 centimeters
	stadion (pl. stadia)	600 feet	183 meters
CAPACITY			
Dry Measure	cor [homer] (10 ephahs)	6 bushels	220 liters
	lethek (5 ephahs)	3 bushels	110 liters
	ephah (10 omers)	3/5 bushel	22 liters
	seah (1/3 ephah)	7 quarts	7.5 liters
	omer (1/10 ephah)	2 quarts	2 liters
	cab (1/18 ephah)	1 quart	1 liter
Liquid Measure	bath (1 ephah)	6 gallons	22 liters
	hin (1/6 bath)	1 gallon	3.8 liters
	log (1/72 bath)	1/3 quart	0.3 liter

The figures of the table are calculated on the basis of a shekel equaling 11.5 grams, a cubit equaling 18 inches and an ephah equaling 22 liters. The quart referred to is either a dry quart (slightly larger than a liter) or a liquid quart (slightly smaller than a liter), whichever is applicable. The ton referred to in the footnotes is the American ton of 2,000 pounds. These weights are calculated relative to the particular commodity involved. Accordingly, the same measure of capacity in the text may be converted into different weights in the footnotes.

This table is based upon the best available information, but it is not intended to be mathematically precise; like the measurement equivalents in the footnotes, it merely gives approximate amounts and distances. Weights and measures differed somewhat at various times and places in the ancient world. There is uncertainty particularly about the ephah and the bath; further discoveries may shed more light on these units of capacity.

STUDY HELPS

CHARACTER STUDY INDEX

RECOVERY STORIES INDEX

Features Topical Index

ABOUT THE NIV

The goal of the New International Version (NIV) is to enable English-speaking people from around the world to read and hear God's eternal Word in their own language. Our work as translators is motivated by our conviction that the Bible is God's Word in written form. We believe that the Bible contains the divine answer to the deepest needs of humanity, sheds unique light on our path in a dark world and sets forth the way to our eternal well-being. Out of these deep convictions, we have sought to recreate as far as possible the experience of the original audience — blending transparency to the original text with accessibility for the millions of English speakers around the world. We have prioritized accuracy, clarity and literary quality with the goal of creating a translation suitable for public and private reading, evangelism, teaching, preaching, memorizing and liturgical use. We have also sought to preserve a measure of continuity with the long tradition of translating the Scriptures into English.

The complete NIV Bible was first published in 1978. It was a completely new translation made by over a hundred scholars working directly from the best available Hebrew, Aramaic and Greek texts. The translators came from the United States, Great Britain, Canada, Australia and New Zealand, giving the translation an international scope. They were from many denominations and churches — including Anglican, Assemblies of God, Baptist, Brethren, Christian Reformed, Church of Christ, Evangelical Covenant, Evangelical Free, Lutheran, Mennonite, Methodist, Nazarene, Presbyterian, Wesleyan and others. This breadth of denominational and theological perspective helped to safeguard the translation from sectarian bias. For these reasons, and by the grace of God, the NIV has gained a wide readership in all parts of the English-speaking world.

The work of translating the Bible is never finished. As good as they are, English translations must be regularly updated so that they will continue to communicate accurately the meaning of God's Word. Updates are needed in order to reflect the latest developments in our understanding of the biblical world and its languages and to keep pace with changes in English usage. Recognizing, then, that the NIV would retain its ability to communicate God's Word accurately only if it were regularly updated, the original translators established the Committee on Bible Translation (CBT). The Committee is a self-perpetuating group of biblical scholars charged with keeping abreast of advances in biblical scholarship and changes in English and issuing periodic updates to the NIV. The CBT is an independent, self-governing body and has sole responsibility for the NIV text. The Committee mirrors the original group of translators in its diverse international and denominational makeup and in its unifying commitment to the Bible as God's inspired Word.

In obedience to its mandate, the Committee has issued periodic updates to the NIV. An initial revision was released in 1984. A more thorough revision process was completed in 2005, resulting in the separately published TNIV. The updated NIV you now have in your hands builds on both the original NIV and the TNIV and represents the latest effort of the Committee to articulate God's unchanging Word in the way the original authors might have said it had they been speaking in English to the global English-speaking audience today.

Translation Philosophy

The Committee's translating work has been governed by three widely accepted principles about the way people use words and about the way we understand them.

First, the meaning of words is determined

by the way that users of the language actually use them at any given time. For the biblical languages, therefore, the Committee utilizes the best and most recent scholarship on the way Hebrew, Aramaic and Greek words were being used in biblical times. At the same time, the Committee carefully studies the state of modern English. Good translation is like good communication: one must know the target audience so that the appropriate choices can be made about which English words to use to represent the original words of Scripture. From its inception, the NIV has had as its target the general English-speaking population all over the world, the "International" in its title reflecting this concern. The aim of the Committee is to put the Scriptures into natural English that will communicate effectively with the broadest possible audience of English speakers.

Modern technology has enhanced the Committee's ability to choose the right English words to convey the meaning of the original text. The field of computational linguistics harnesses the power of computers to provide broadly applicable and current data about the state of the language. Translators can now access huge databases of modern English to better understand the current meaning and usage of key words. The Committee utilized this resource in preparing the 2011 edition of the NIV. An area of especially rapid and significant change in English is the way certain nouns and pronouns are used to refer to human beings. The Committee therefore requested experts in computational linguistics at Collins Dictionaries to pose some key questions about this usage to its database of English — the largest in the world, with over 4.4 billion words, gathered from several English-speaking countries and including both spoken and written English. (The Collins Study, called "The Development and Use of Gender Language in Contemporary English," can be accessed at *http://www.thenivbible. com/about-the-niv/about-the-2011-edition/*.) The study revealed that the most popular words to describe the human race in modern U.S. English were "humanity," "man"

and "mankind." The Committee then used this data in the updated NIV, choosing from among these three words (and occasionally others also) depending on the context.

A related issue creates a larger problem for modern translations: the move away from using the third-person masculine singular pronouns — "he/him/his" — to refer to men and women equally. This usage does persist in some forms of English, and this revision therefore occasionally uses these pronouns in a generic sense. But the tendency, recognized in day-to-day usage and confirmed by the Collins study, is away from the generic use of "he," "him" and "his." In recognition of this shift in language and in an effort to translate into the natural English that people are actually using, this revision of the NIV generally uses other constructions when the biblical text is plainly addressed to men and women equally. The reader will encounter especially frequently a "they," "their" or "them" to express a generic singular idea. Thus, for instance, Mark 8:36 reads: "What good is it for someone to gain the whole world, yet forfeit their soul?" This generic use of the "distributive" or "singular" "they/them/their" has been used for many centuries by respected writers of English and has now become established as standard English, spoken and written, all over the world.

A second linguistic principle that feeds into the Committee's translation work is that meaning is found not in individual words, as vital as they are, but in larger clusters: phrases, clauses, sentences, discourses. Translation is not, as many people think, a matter of word substitution: English word *x* in place of Hebrew word *y*. Translators must first determine the meaning of the words of the biblical languages in the context of the passage and then select English words that accurately communicate that meaning to modern listeners and readers. This means that accurate translation will not always reflect the exact structure of the original language. To be sure, there is debate over the degree to which translators should try to preserve the "form" of the original text in English. From the beginning, the NIV has taken a mediating position on this issue. The manual produced when the translation that became the NIV was first being planned states: "If the Greek or Hebrew syntax has a good parallel in modern English, it should be used. But if there is no good parallel, the English syntax appropriate to the meaning of the original is to be chosen." It is fine, in other words, to carry over the form of the biblical languages into English — but not at the expense of natural expression. The principle that meaning resides in larger clusters of words means that the Committee has not insisted on a "word-for-word" approach to translation. We certainly believe that every word of Scripture is inspired by God and therefore to be carefully studied to determine what God is saying to us. It is for this reason that the Committee labors over every single word of the original texts, working hard to determine how each of those words contributes to what the text is saying. Ultimately, however, it is how these individual words function in combination with other words that determines meaning.

A third linguistic principle guiding the Committee in its translation work is the recognition that words have a spectrum of meaning. It is popular to define a word by using another word, or "gloss," to substitute for it. This substitute word is then sometimes called the "literal" meaning of a word. In fact, however, words have a range of possible meanings. Those meanings will vary depending on the context, and words in one language will usually not occupy the same semantic range as words in another language. The Committee therefore studies each original word of Scripture in its context to identify its meaning in a particular verse and then chooses an appropriate English word (or phrase) to represent it. It is impossible, then, to translate any given Hebrew, Aramaic or Greek word with the same English word all the time. The Committee does try to translate related occurrences of a word in the original languages with the same English word in order to preserve the

connection for the English reader. But the Committee generally privileges clear natural meaning over a concern with consistency in rendering particular words.

Textual Basis

For the Old Testament the standard Hebrew text, the Masoretic Text as published in the latest edition of *Biblia Hebraica*, has been used throughout. The Masoretic Text tradition contains marginal notations that offer variant readings. These have sometimes been followed instead of the text itself. Because such instances involve variants within the Masoretic tradition, they have not been indicated in the textual notes. In a few cases, words in the basic consonantal text have been divided differently than in the Masoretic Text. Such cases are usually indicated in the textual footnotes. The Dead Sea Scrolls contain biblical texts that represent an earlier stage of the transmission of the Hebrew text. They have been consulted, as have been the Samaritan Pentateuch and the ancient scribal traditions concerning deliberate textual changes. The translators also consulted the more important early versions. Readings from these versions, the Dead Sea Scrolls and the scribal traditions were occasionally followed where the Masoretic Text seemed doubtful and where accepted principles of textual criticism showed that one or more of these textual witnesses appeared to provide the correct reading. In rare cases, the translators have emended the Hebrew text where it appears to have become corrupted at an even earlier stage of its transmission. These departures from the Masoretic Text are also indicated in the textual footnotes. Sometimes the vowel indicators (which are later additions to the basic consonantal text) found in the Masoretic Text did not, in the judgment of the translators, represent the correct vowels for the original text. Accordingly, some words have been read with a different set of vowels. These instances are usually not indicated in the footnotes.

The Greek text used in translating the New Testament has been an eclectic one, based on the latest editions of the Nestle-Aland/United Bible Societies' Greek New Testament. The translators have made their choices among the variant readings in accordance with widely accepted principles of New Testament textual criticism. Footnotes call attention to places where uncertainty remains.

The New Testament authors, writing in Greek, often quote the Old Testament from its ancient Greek version, the Septuagint. This is one reason why some of the Old Testament quotations in the NIV New Testament are not identical to the corresponding passages in the NIV Old Testament. Such quotations in the New Testament are indicated with the footnote "(see Septuagint)."

Footnotes and Formatting

Footnotes in this version are of several kinds, most of which need no explanation. Those giving alternative translations begin with "Or" and generally introduce the alternative with the last word preceding it in the text, except when it is a single-word alternative. When poetry is quoted in a footnote a slash mark indicates a line division.

It should be noted that references to diseases, minerals, flora and fauna, architectural details, clothing, jewelry, musical instruments and other articles cannot always be identified with precision. Also, linear measurements and measures of capacity can only be approximated (see the Table of Weights and Measures). Although *Selah*, used mainly in the Psalms, is probably a musical term, its meaning is uncertain. Since it may interrupt reading and distract the reader, this word has not been kept in the English text, but every occurrence has been signaled by a footnote.

As an aid to the reader, sectional headings have been inserted. They are not to be regarded as part of the biblical text and are not intended for oral reading. It is the Committee's hope that these headings may prove more helpful to the reader than the traditional chapter divisions, which were introduced long after the Bible was written.

Sometimes the chapter and/or verse numbering in English translations of the Old Testament differs from that found in published Hebrew texts. This is particularly the case in the Psalms, where the traditional titles are included in the Hebrew verse numbering. Such differences are indicated in the footnotes at the bottom of the page. In the New Testament, verse numbers that marked off portions of the traditional English text not supported by the best Greek manuscripts now appear in brackets, with a footnote indicating the text that has been omitted (see, for example, Matthew 17:[21]).

Mark 16:9 – 20 and John 7:53 — 8:11, although long accorded virtually equal status with the rest of the Gospels in which they stand, have a questionable standing in the textual history of the New Testament, as noted in the bracketed annotations with which they are set off. A different typeface has been chosen for these passages to indicate their uncertain status.

Basic formatting of the text, such as lining the poetry, paragraphing (both prose and poetry), setting up of (administrative-like) lists, indenting letters and lengthy prayers within narratives and the insertion of sectional headings, has been the work of the Committee. However, the choice between single-column and double-column formats has been left to the publishers. Also the issuing of "red-letter" editions is a publisher's choice — one that the Committee does not endorse.

The Committee has again been reminded that every human effort is flawed — including this revision of the NIV. We trust, however, that many will find in it an improved representation of the Word of God, through which they hear his call to faith in our Lord Jesus Christ and to service in his kingdom. We offer this version of the Bible to him in whose name and for whose glory it has been made.

The Committee on Bible Translation

SUBJECT INDEX

The Subject Index will lead you to key texts on a variety of subjects covered in the *NIV Celebrate Recovery Study Bible*. Many of these key texts also have helpful study notes on these subjects.

A

Aaron Ex 4:10 — 12:50; 28 – 29; 32; Nu 17; 20:23 – 29

Abandonment Ezr 10:3

Abuse (physical) Ge 16:9; Ex 20:4 – 5; Isa 50:4 – 6

Abraham Ge 11:26 — 12:20; 14:18 – 24; 15:18; 16; 18:16 – 33; 22; 25:1 – 11; Ro 4; Gal 3:6 – 29; Jas 2:20 – 24

Adam Ge 1:26 — 5:5; Lk 3:23 – 38; Ro 5:12 – 21; 1Co 15:21 – 22,42 – 57

Addiction Pr 5:22 – 23; Jer 13:23; Mk 9:43 – 47

Adoption Ge 15:2; 41:51 – 52; 48:5; 50:23; Ex 2:10; Dt 21:17; Eph 1:5

Adultery Ge 35:22; Nu 5:31; Pr 2:22; 5:3 – 10; 5:22 – 23; 23:27; 31:3; Eze 23:25; Mt 19:1 – 9; Mk 10:1 – 12

Advice 1Ch 21:3 – 4; Pr 15:22; Da 6:2

Alcohol use Ge 9:22 – 25; Lev 10:9; Est 1:8; Ps 104:14 – 15; 116:13; Pr 20:1; 23:29 – 35; Hos 4:11; Joel 1:5; Mt 26:17 – 30; Lk 1:15; Jn 2:1 – 11; 1Ti 5:23

Altars Ge 12:7 – 8; 33:20; Jos 8:31; 2Ki 16:10; Am 3:14; Rev 6:9; 16:7

Ambition Ge 11:4; Nu 16:3; Jdg 18:20; Jer 45:5; Mt 20:20 – 21; 1Co 7:17,20,26

Angel of the Lord Jdg 2:1,4; 6:11,14; Ps 34:7; Isa 31:8 – 9; Eze 40:3; Zec 12:8

Angels Ex 23:20 – 23; 2Ch 32:21; Job 33:23 – 24; Ps 29:1; Da 8:16; 10:12; Lk 1:19; Ac 6:15; 1Co 6:2 – 3; Heb 1:7; 2Pe 2:4; Jude 6

> **Guardian** Ps 91:11; Eze 9:1 – 2; Mt 18:8; Ac 12:15

Anger 1Ch 13:11; Job 15:13; 32:2 – 5; 32:19; Pr 14:29; Da 2:5; Ac 15:39; Eph 4:26; Jas 1:19 – 20

Anointing Ge 28:18; Ex 29:1,7; 40:9; Lev 8:12; Ru 3:3; 1Sa 10:1; 12:3; 16:1,13; 26:9; 1Ki 19:16; 2Ch 6:42; Ps 2:2; 104:15; 105:15; Isa 61:1; Da 9:25; Mt 3:16; Lk 10:34; Jn 1:32; 2:20,27; 2Co 1:21; Jas 5:14

Antichrist 2Th 2:3 – 12; 1Jn 2:18

Anxiety Mt 6:25 – 34; Lk 12:22 – 34; Php 4:4 – 9

Apostles Lk 6:13; Ac 1:26; 8:1; 15:19 – 21; 1Co 9:15; 12:28; 15:8; 2Co 12:12; Gal 1:1

Arguments Job 18:2; Ac 15:39

Ark of the covenant Ex 16:34; 25:10 – 22; Nu 4:5; 7:89; Jos 6:9; 1Sa 4:5,7,10; 2Sa 6:7; 1Ki 8:1 – 6; 8:9; 1Ch 13:10,14; 13:9 – 10; 15:2; 2Ch 35:3

Armageddon Jos 12:21; 17:11; Jdg 1:27; 5:19; 1Ki 9:15; 2Ki 9:27; 23:29; Zec 12:3; Rev 16:14 – 16; 19:19

Ascension Ps 27; Lk 24:36 – 53; Ac 1:1 – 11; Jn 16:5 – 16; Eph 4:7 – 13

Assurance of salvation Ps 37; Ro 8; 2Ti 1:8 – 12; 1Jn 2:28 – 3:24; 5:9 – 13

Atonement Isa 27:8 – 9; 53:5; Eze 16:63; Jn 1:29; Ro 3:25

Attitude Ge 4:5 – 7; Ps 73:3 – 5; 77:12; 81:11; 86:11; Ecc 11:10; Isa 1:11 – 14; Jer 17:10; Joel 2:13; Php 4:8; Col 3:2

B

Baptism Mt 3:11; 3:6; Mk 1:4; 1:8; Lk 12:50; Jn 3:23 – 25; Ac 8:14 – 17; 19:5; Ro 6:3 – 5; 1Co 10:2; Heb 10:22; 1Pe 3:21

> **Of the Holy Spirit** Mt 3:11; 3:16; Lk 3:16; Jn 1:32 – 33; 3:5; Ac 1:5; 2:1 – 4; 2:38 – 39; 8:12,14 – 17; 9:17 – 18; 10:44 – 48; 19:1 – 6; 1Co 12:13; Titus 3:5

Belonging Ne 10:36

Bethlehem Ge 35:19 – 20; Jdg 12:8 – 10; Ru 1:1,19 – 22; 4:11 – 13; 1Sa 16:4 – 13; 2Sa 23:14 – 17; 2Ch 11:5 – 6; Mic 5:2; Mt 2:16 – 18; Lk 2:1 – 7; 2:4,11

Betrayal Ps 41:9; 109:1 – 3; Jer 40:16; 41:6; Ob 7; Mt 26:14 – 16; 26:49; 26:75; Mk 14:10 – 11; 14:45; 14:72; Lk 22:47 – 48; 22:61 – 62

Bitterness Ru 1:13,20 – 21; Job 15:13; 38:2; Ps 140:10

Blame
> **God** Ge 42:28; Ex 16:3; Ru 1:13,20 – 21; 2Ki 3:10; Job 35:12 – 13; Ps 88:6; Pr 19:3; Ecc 5:19 – 20; Jer 2:29; 4:10

> **Others** Ge 16:5; Jdg 19:25; 20:6; 1Ki 17:18,20; Hos 4:4

Blameless 2Sa 22:24; Ps 26:1; 84:11; 101:2; Pr 20:7; Titus 1:6

Blasphemy Ex 20:7; Lev 24:13 – 23; Mt 9:1 – 8; 26:57 – 67; Mk 3:20 – 30

Blessed Ps 32:1; Mt 5:3 – 10; Eph 1:3

Blessings Dt 7:12 – 16; Ps 32; 67; Eze 34:26 – 30; Jn 1:14 – 17; Eph 1:3 – 14; Mt 5:1 – 11; Lk 6:20 – 22

Blood Ge 9:4; Ex 24:6,8; 29:11 – 21; Lev 17:11; Heb 9:14; 9:22

Born again Jn 3:1 – 21; Titus 3:4 – 8

Demon possession Mt 8:28–34; Mk 1:23; 5:1–10; Lk 4:33; Ac 16:16–19; 1Ti 4:1–10

Denial Ps 32:3; Eze 33:32; Mk 16:7

Depending on God Jos 24:19; Ps 62:3–6; 86:1; 104:16–30; Pr 27:1; Zec 10:1; Mt 10:9–10; Mk 6:8; Lk 6:24–26; Jn 15:4; 2Co 9:11; 1Ti 6:6–8; 1Jn 2:24

Depression Job 17:15; Ps 61:2; 69:1–3; Pr 25:20; Ecc 4:1–3

Despair 1Ki 11:10–12; Job 7:8–10; 7:15–16; 9:22–24; Ps 10:1; 142:6; Ecc 1:15; Isa 33:7–9; Jer 8:20; Eze 37:11; Hab 3:17–18

Disabilities Ex 4:10; 4:11; Lev 21:17–23; Dt 27:18; 2Sa 19:24; Ps 6:2–7; Lk 13:11

Discipleship Mt 4:20; 8:20; 16:24; 28:19; Mk 1:16–17; 8:34; 10:21; Lk 6:13; 9:23; 9:57–62; 14:25–34; Jn 1:40–42; 8:51; 15:1–17; 21:15–19; Ro 12:1; Php 3:10

Discipline Ps 6:1; 66:10; 94:12–13; 141:5; Pr 3:11–12; 19:18; 29:19; Jer 16:15; 30:11; 1Co 9:27; 1Th 4:6; Heb 12:5

Discouragement 1Ki 19:3; Ne 4:10; Hag 1–2; 2Ti 4:9–11

Discrimination Ge 43:32; 1Ch 1:5; Gal 3:28; Col 3:11; Phm 16; Jas 2:1–7

Disobedience

    God's response Ge 2:17; Lev 10:1; Nu 14:40–41; 20:12; Dt 1:37; 28:46; 1Ki 20:36; 2Ch 18:28; Ps 81:11; Pr 28:14; Jer 42:20; Eze 7:27

    Leaders' response 2Sa 18:14

Disrespect 2Ki 2:23–24

Divorce Dt 21:14; 24:1; 1Ch 8:8; Ezr 10:17; Isa 50:1; Mal 2:14; Mt 1:19; 19:1–9; Mk 10:1–12; Jn 4:18; 1Co 7:15

Doubts 1Ki 17:24; Job 40:2; Ps 69:1–3; 73:3–5; Ecc 9:4–6; Jer 15:18; Mal 3:14–15; Lk 7:19–23; Jn 21:15–17; Jas 1:6–8

Dreams (visions) Ge 28:12–15; 31:11; Jdg 7:14; 7:15; 1Ki 3:15; 1Ch 17:2; Job 42:5; Isa 1:1; 6:1; Eze 1:1; 3:14; Zec 1:8; Rev 1:19–20; 4:2

E

Education Jdg 5:1; 2Ch 17:7; Pr 19:18

    Religious Jdg 2:10; 2Ki 22:2; 2Ch 29:3; 32:7–8; Ne 8:7; Job 3:3; Ps 22:9–10; 103:17–18

Elder Ac 5:17–42; 14:21–25; 20:13–38; Titus 1:5–9; 1Ti 3:1–7

Elderly Ps 92:14–15; Pr 16:31; Ecc 12:3–5

Election Ge 12:1–9; Ex 19:1–6; Dt 10:12–22; Isa 41:8–16; Jn 15:9–17; Ro 9:6–13; Eph 1:3–14; 1Pe 2:1–10; 2Pe 1:3–10

Elijah 1Ki 17–19,21; 2Ki 2; Lk 9:28–36

Elisha 1Ki 19:16–21; 2Ki 2—13

Emotions (expressing) Ps 13:1–5; 88:5; 140:1–11; Pr 14:29; La 1:12

Encouragement 1Sa 23:16; Job 4:1; Pr 25:20; Isa 12:1–6

Enemies Ps 27:2; 31:6; 35:11–16; Pr 25:21–22; Lk 6:27–36; Ro 12:19–21

Envy Ge 37; Mk 7:20–23; Jas 3:13—4:10

Eternal life Mt 19:16–30; Jn 3:1–21; Jn 6:46,57; Ro 2:7; Ro 6:15–23; 1Jn 5:1–13; Rev 21:22–27

Eternity Job 20:5–9; Ps 21:4; 30:9; Ecc 3:11

Eve Ge 1:26—5:2; 1Co 11:2–16; 1Ti 2:8–15

Evil

    Destroyed Mal 4:1; 1Co 15:24; Col 2:15

    Fighting Ps 94:16; Mt 5:39; 18:10; Lk 6:29–30; Jas 4:7; 1Jn 5:4; Rev 16:16

    Source Ge 2:9; Ex 11:3; Dt 31:16–21; Jdg 9:23; 1Ch 21:1; Job 19:8–12; Ps 71:20; Ecc 7:13–14; La 3:38; Am 9:4; Jn 9:2

    Spirits 1Sa 16:14; 18:10; Mt 8:31–32; Mk 1:23; 5:13; 9:18; Lk 4:33; 9:39; 11:19; Ac 16:17–18; 19:13; 1Jn 4:1; Rev 16:13

    Used by God 1Ki 22:20–22; Am 9:4; Hab 1:6,13; Jn 14:30; Ac 2:23

Example Jn 13:1–17; 1Co 10:1–13; Php 2:1–11; 2:14–15; 1Th 1; Heb 11:4–40; Jas 5:10–11; 5:16–18; 1Pe 2:11–12

Exile Isa 5:13; 2Ki 17,25; 2Ch 36

Exodus

    God's deliverance Ex 4:1–9; 5:1–5; 7:10—10:29; 11:1—12:39; 14:5–29

    God's motive Ge 15:13–16; Dt 7:8–9; Hos 11:1

F

Failures Jdg 14:4; Ps 106:7–43; Mt 26:75; Mk 14:72; Lk 22:61–62

Faith

    Abraham's Ge 15:6; Ro 4:1–3

    Asking for proof Mt 12:39; Lk 11:29

    Beginning Jos 9:9,25; 2Ki 5:17; Mt 17:20; Lk 17:6

    Childlike Ps 22:9–10; Mt 19:14; Mk 10:14–15

    Cost of Mt 10:35–37; Lk 12:51–53; 2Ti 3:12

    Defending Jude 3

    Defined Heb 11:1

    During crisis Ps 116:10; Isa 10:24; Jer 12:5–6; La 3:21–24; Hab 2:3; Zep 3:15; Mt 11:3; 1Pe 1:7

    In action Jos 2:4–5; Mt 25:35–36; Lk 17:6; Ac 3:6; 2Ti 2:15; Heb 11:7; Jas 2:14–24

    Power of Jn 14:12

    Results of 1Ch 11:11; 2Ch 27:6; Ps 106:31; Mk 11:22–24

    Rewarded Job 22:21–25; Jer 39:18; Mt 5:19; 9:22; Mk 5:34–36; Lk 8:48; 2Co 5:10; Eph 1:3; 2Jn 8

    Signs of Mt 3:6; Lk 3:3

    Ups and downs Ge 26:7; Nu 21:5–6; 1Ki 9:20–21; 2Ki 13:18–19; 2Ch 16:12; 24:18; Ps 13:1–5; Isa 54:1–17; Mt 8:10; Mk 6:51–52; Lk 8:13; 17:5

Jesus Christ

Divinity Jn 5:18; 6:46,57; 8:58 – 59; 10:33; 14:9 – 28; Ac 1:9; Ro 1:4; 1Co 15:28; Col 1:19; Heb 1:3

Enemies Lk 5:17; Heb 10:13

Glory Mt 17:2; Mk 9:2 – 3; Jn 17:1,5,24; 2Co 4:17

Humanity Mt 4:3 – 11; 26:38 – 39; Mk 13:32; 14:33 – 35; Lk 4:3 – 13; 22:42 – 44; Ro 8:29; Heb 2:6 – 8; 4:15; 1Jn 5:6; 2Jn 7

Humility Php 2:6 – 7

Power Mt 14:25; Mk 3:22; 5:11 – 13,25 – 29; 6:48; Lk 5:17; 8:46; Jn 6:19; 1Co 15:28; Rev 9:17 – 19

Prayers Mt 14:23; Mk 6:46; Heb 8:2

Purpose Lk 13:32; Heb 5:5,10

Reign Zec 14:9; Eph 1:10,20; 4:10; Php 2:10; Rev 5:11 – 14

Second coming Isa 35:1 – 2; Jer 23:5 – 8; Hos 14:5 – 7; Mt 24:29; Mk 13:24; Lk 17:22 – 37; Ac 1:11; Ro 13:11 – 12; 1Th 4:15; 2Th 2:3 – 12; 2Pe 3:12; Rev 22:6,10

Jobs (attitude toward) Pr 18:9; 24:30 – 34; 28:19; 2Th 3:10

Joy Ps 100:2; Isa 12; 35; Mt 5:1 – 12; Lk 15; Jn 13:1 – 17; Gal 5:16 – 26; Php 4:4 – 9; Col 1:24; Jas 1:2 – 18; 1Pe 1:1 – 9; 4:12 – 19

Judah Dt 33:7; Nu 1:27; 26:22; Jos 15; Jdg 1:1 – 20; 2Sa 2:1 – 4; 1Ki 12:21 – 22; 14:21 – 22; 2Ki 24:1 – 16; 1Ch 28:2 – 4; Ezr 1:1 – 5; Eze 48:7; Mt 1:2 – 6; Rev 7:5

Judging others Lk 13:3 – 5; Jn 5:22; 8:7; Ac 10:4; Ro 14:1; 1Co 4:3; Jas 2:13

Judgment

Attitude about Mt 7:1 – 5; 19:28; Lk 22:30; Ro 14:1 – 4,13; 1Co 4:5; 10:29; Gal 6:1 – 4; Jas 4:11 – 12

God's Ge 18:26; Dt 32:4; Job 34:10; Ps 94:2; Jn 5:22; Ac 10:42; 2Th 1:5; 2Ti 4:1

Judgment day Isa 13:10; Joel 2:30 – 32; Ro 14:10; Heb 10:25

Justice Lev 24:20; 2Ch 19:4 – 5; Job 24:18; Ps 122:5; Eze 38:22 – 23

Delayed Job 27:1 – 2; 34:19; 36:6,9 – 11; Isa 11:4 – 5

God's Nu 14:20 – 35; Dt 28:58 – 59,63; Job 1:13 – 19; Ps 78:34; Ecc 3:17; Jer 12:1; Eze 14:22 – 23; Na 2:13; Zep 3:5

Justification Lk 18:13 – 14; Ac 13:39; Ro 3:22 – 28; 5:1 – 21; 9:31 – 32; 1Co 1:30; Gal 2:21; 3:11; Jas 2:14 – 26; 1Pe 2:22

K

Kindness Ge 32:10; 39:21; Ru 2:20; 1Ki 3:6; Ezr 9:9; Job 10:12; Isa 54:8; Gal 5:16 – 26; Hos 11:4; Ac 14:17; Titus 3:4

King 1Sa 8; 12; Ps 47; 99; Lk 1:26 – 38; Eph 1:15 – 34; 1Ti 1:15 – 17; Heb 1:1 – 12

Kingdom of God 1Ch 17:9; Jer 3:14 – 16; Mt 4:17; 5:3 – 10; 13:24; Lk 3:4 – 6; 16:16; 17:20 – 21

Kings Dt 17:15; 1Sa 8:5 – 9; 10:24; 1Ki 12:16; 2Ki 11:12; 23:34; 25:30; 2Ch 25:2; Eze 28:2; Da 3:13 – 14

L

Last days Isa 2:2; 24:18 – 20; Joel 2:30 – 32; Mic 4:1; Ac 2:19 – 20; 1Co 7:29; 2Th 2:2; 2Ti 3:1; Heb 9:26; 1Pe 4:7

Lazarus Jn 11:1 – 44; Lk 16:19 – 31

Laziness Pr 6:6 – 11; 2Th 3:6 – 13

Leaders

Ability Jdg 6:25; 12:8,11,13; 13:25; 14:6; 1Sa 10:9 – 11; 11:6; 2Ki 2:9; Isa 45:1

Choosing Ge 49:10 – 12; Ex 6:14 – 27; Dt 16:18; 31:3; Jdg 11:4 – 6; 1Ch 5:2; 12:2; Isa 3:6; Hos 8:4; 1Ti 3:2 – 7; 5:24 – 25

Preparation Ex 17:9; Dt 34:9; 1Ki 3:7; 19:19; Pr 30:21 – 23

Responsibility Jer 23:1; Eze 44:20 – 23; Mal 2:3; Jas 3:1

Spiritual Nu 27:18; 2Ki 4:13; 6:21; 13:14; 16:15 – 16; 2Ch 24:16; Ne 12:1; 13:28; Isa 29:9 – 10; 32:5 – 6; 56:10; Jer 29:21 – 23; Hos 6:9; Zep 3:4; Mal 2:3; Mt 20:26 – 28; 23:33; Lk 11:44; Jn 21:15 – 17; 1Co 4:16

Wicked Job 34:29 – 30; Eze 11:3

Life

After death (Old Testament) Nu 20:24; 1Sa 28:19; 2Sa 12:23; Ps 6:5; 17:15; 30:9; 49:15; Pr 2:18; Ecc 9:10; 12:7

Principles Pr 3:1 – 4

Source Ge 2:7; Job 27:3; Ps 104:30; Ecc 12:7

Unfair Ge 18:25; 2Sa 21:6,9,14; Job 1:13 – 19; 34:19; Ps 73:3 – 5; Ecc 2:26; 4:13 – 16

Value of 2Ki 11:1 – 2; Job 3:10 – 16; Ecc 12:6

Without God Ecc 1:2; 6:12

Light Ge 1:14 – 16; Ps 13:3; 112:4; 119:105; Isa 42:6; 58:8,10; 60:3; 1Jn 1:5

Loneliness Ps 42:3 – 4; 102:6 – 7,16 – 18

Lord's Supper Mt 6:29; 26:26,28; Lk 22:17 – 20; Jn 6:51 – 56; 21:13; Ac 1:4; 2:42,46 – 47; 20:7,11; 1Co 10:16 – 17; 11:20 – 26; 24:30,35,41 – 43

Love

For God Nu 30:2; Ps 37:4; 69:9; 112:2 – 8; 130:5 – 6; Lk 14:26; Jn 21:15 – 17; Ro 13:10; Heb 10:6,8; Rev 2:4

For others Mt 5:48; Jn 13:34 – 35; 15:12 – 14,17; Ro 12:18,20; 13:10; 1Co 1:7; 3:2; 13:1 – 3; 1Jn 4:16

Loyalty 1Ki 11:17 – 19; 2Ch 11:13 – 14,16; Ps 16:4; 84:11; Pr 17:17

Lying Ex 1:19 – 20; 1Sa 21:2; 27:8 – 10; 2Ki 8:10; 10:19; 2Ch 18:22; Ps 62:4; Jer 38:27; Ac 5:5,10

M

Magic, witchcraft and sorcery Ex 22:18;
Lev 19:26,31; 20:6,27; Dt 18:10 – 12,20 – 21;
Isa 2:6; 47:10 – 14; Jer 27:9; Mic 5:12; Mal 3:5;
Ac 8:9 – 24; 13:6 – 12; 16:16 – 18; 19:13 – 19;
Gal 5:20

Marriage
Choosing a spouse Ru 3:10; 2Ch 21:6; Pr 21:9
Customs Ge 24:50 – 51; 24:67; 29:18,23 – 25,27;
31:15; 34:4; Ru 3:7 – 8,13 – 14; 1Ch 2:21;
2:34 – 35
Interfaith Ge 38:2; Dt 7:3 – 4; Jdg 12:9; 1Ki 7:8;
11:1 – 4; 16:31; 2Ch 8:11; 21:6; Ne 13:26; 13:28;
1Co 7:14
Interracial Lev 24:10; Ru 1:4; Jer 31:8
Political Ge 20:2; 41:45; 1Ki 3:1; 2Ch 18:1
Relationship Ge 2:24; 3:16; Pr 31:23; Jer 16:2;
Mk 10:8
Remarriage Dt 24:4; Mt 19:9

Martyrs 1Ki 18:4,13; 2Ki 21:16; Ps 37:3 – 25;
Isa 57:1 – 2; Da 6:22 – 23; Lk 21:18; Php 3:10;
1Pe 1:6; Rev 6:9; 11:7; 20:4 – 5

Materialism Mt 5:3 – 12; Lk 6:20 – 22 1Co 3:3;
Eph 4:13

Meaning of life Ps 73:13; 90:17; 102:9 – 10;
Pr 1:7; Ecc 1:2; 2:3 – 11,13 – 16; 8:16 – 17; 11:8;
2Co 5:10

Mercy Ps 7:11; 25:11; 39:13; 51:1; 78:39; 139:19;
143:1 – 2; Isa 30:18; Jer 3:1; 22:2 – 5; 24:7; Eze 3:7;
39:25; Hos 11:8; Na 2:13; Jas 2:13

Messiah Ps 110:4; Isa 16:5; 32:3; Jer 33:16;
Na 1:15; Zec 11:7; Mt 16:20; 17:2; 20:30; Mk 8:30;
10:47; 11:8; Lk 2:32; 18:34; 20:41 – 44; Jn 1:46
Other names for Ps 2:2; 110:1; Zec 3:8; 10:4;
Lk 2:25; Jn 10:1 – 15; Rev 5:5 – 6
Prophecy about Isa 7:14 – 16; 9:4 – 6; 32:1;
53:2; Eze 34:11; Da 9:24 – 27; Zec 6:13; 12:10;
Lk 3:4 – 6
Son of David Ps 72:5; 132:12; Isa 11:1;
Eze 17:22 – 24; 34:23 – 24; Hag 2:23;
Mk 12:35 – 37; Lk 18:38

Miracles Ex 4:1 – 9; 14:21; 16:31; Jos 3:16;
10:13 – 14; 2Ki 20:11; Jnh 1:17; Mk 8:12; Lk 11:29

Moderation Pr 25:16; Ecc 10:16 – 17

Money Dt 8; Ps 24; 62:10; Mt 6:19 – 34;
1Ti 6:3 – 19 Jas 5:1 – 5

Moses Ex 2 – 40; Nu 1 – 36; Dt 1 – 34; Mt 17:1 – 13;
Heb 11:24 – 28

Murder Ge 9:6; Ex 2:12; Nu 35:24 – 25; Dt 19:13;
21:1 – 9; 2Sa 20:10; 2Ki 11:1 – 2; 2Ch 22:10

Mystery 1Co 15:50 – 58; Eph 3; Col 1:24 — 2:5;
1Ti 3:16

N

Natural disasters Ge 7:11; 19:24; Isa 24:1 – 6;
Jer 27:8 – 15; 36:3; Am 4:6 – 11
God's control Ge 9:13; Dt 3:22; 4:26; Jos 10:11;
2Ki 3:20; 20:11; Ps 148:1 – 10; Isa 38:7 – 8;
Jnh 1:10; Zec 10:1; Lk 4:39; 24:31
Lessons from Ps 29:10; Pr 30:24 – 28

Needs (spiritual) Ps 40:17; 63:1; 70:5; 86:1;
Mt 5:20

Neighbor Lev 19:18; Mt 22:37 – 40; Lk 10:25 – 37;
Ro 13:8 – 10

O

Obedience
To God Ex 4:13; Nu 15:3; Dt 6:3; Jdg 2:22;
1Sa 15:22; 1Ki 17:3; Pr 1:7; 10:27; Jer 36:8 – 9;
Mic 6:8; Hag 1 – 2; Jn 13:34 – 35; Heb 5:8
To the law Dt 30:11; Mk 2:27; Ac 16:21;
Titus 3:1 – 2
To leaders 2Ki 4:2 – 7; Jer 38:2 – 3; Da 3:13 – 14;
Ac 4:19; Titus 3:1 – 2; 1Pe 2:13 – 17
To parents Ge 22:9; Jer 35:8 – 16; Eph 6:1
Rewards of Ge 22:2; Ex 33:12; Lev 26:3 – 39;
Jos 6:3; 1Ki 11:4 – 8; 2Ki 24:4; 2Ch 25:2;
Mt 6:10

Occult 1Sa 28:12; Job 31:24 – 28; Da 5:11;
Mic 5:12; Mt 2:2; Ac 16:17 – 18; 19:18 – 19
Astrology 2Ki 17:16; Isa 47:9,12 – 13;
Jer 10:1 – 2; Mt 2:1
Black magic Ge 41:8; Ex 7:11 – 12,22; 8:7;
Eze 13:18; Rev 9:21
Fortune telling (divination) Ge 30:27;
44:5,15; Nu 22:7; Dt 18:14 – 15; 2Ki 16:15;
Eze 13:17; 21:21
Sorcery Ex 22:18; 2Ki 9:22; Job 3:8; Isa 8:19;
Ac 8:9 – 11; 19:13

Offerings Ex 23:15; 35:21; Lev 1:14; 3:3 – 5;
3:16; Dt 26:2; 1Ch 21:26; Ezr 1:4 – 6; Ps 96:8;
Pr 3:9 – 10; Eze 45:13 – 25; Mal 1:10; Mt 26:10;
2Co 8:1,7

Oil Lev 8:10; Dt 33:24; 1Ki 1:39; Ps 45:7; 133:2;
Isa 21:5; Mk 6:13; Jas 5:14

Ordination Lev 8:22; 1Ki 19:19; 2Ti 1:6

P

Pain Job 16:6; 33:19; Jer 15:15 – 21; Hab 1 – 3;
Ro 5:1 – 5; 8:28 – 39; Rev 21:1 – 4

Parables 2Sa 14:2 – 3; 1Ki 22:19 – 20;
2Ch 18:18 – 21; 25:18 – 19; Mt 13:11 – 13;
Mk 4:10 – 12,21 – 25; Lk 8:4 – 10

Parenting Jdg 13:8; 2Sa 18:33; Pr 19:18; 22:6; 31:1;
Lk 2:44; Eph 6:4

Passover Mt 26:26 – 29; Mk 14:22 – 24;
Lk 22:19 – 20

Patience Ge 40:23; 1Sa 13:11; Ps 27:14; Pr 14:29;
21:12; Jas 5:7 – 11

Paul Ac 9:1 – 31; 13:1 — 14:28; 15:36 — 19:41;
27:1 — 28:31; Ro 1

Peace Ps 85:10 – 11; 147:14; Ecc 11:10; Isa 11:6 – 9;
Na 1:15; Ro 12:18

Persecution Ps 118:6; Da 11:35; Mt 5:11 – 12;
Lk 6:29 – 30; 10:3; Ac 7:51 – 53; 14:22; 28:22;
Php 3:10; 2Th 1:4 – 5; 1Pe 1:6; Rev 7:14; 13:17
Forms of Ps 119:86; Lk 21:18; Gal 6:17;
Php 1:29; 2Ti 3:12

Examples of 1Ch 12:18; 25:1,6 – 7; 2Ch 18:9;
Isa 12:1 – 6; Jer 13:1 – 11; 28:10; 29:26; Hos 1:2;
Mic 1:8

Fulfilled Isa 49:22; Jer 31:8,15; Eze 17:22 – 24;
Da 2:31 – 45; 11:2 – 45; Ob 18 – 20; Mt 1:1;
Lk 3:4 – 6; 19:41 – 44

Future 2Ch 7:14; Isa 41:18; Jer 7:30 – 34;
Eze 3:25; 4:3 – 6; 38:2 – 6; Da 7:24

Purpose today Isa 15:1 – 9; 21:1; Da 12:9 – 10;
Hos 1:11; Am 9:11; Zec 1:8; Ac 11:27 – 30;
1Co 14:1

Understanding Jer 23:5 – 8; Da 7:1; 8:27;
Zep 1:2; Zec 6:6; Mt 24:15; Mk 13:5 – 25;
Lk 18:34; 24:45; Rev 1:19 – 20; 17:9 – 14

Warning Jer 25:15 – 17; Jnh 3:4; Ac 21:4,11 – 12

Prophets 1Sa 10:5; 1Co 12:28

Mistreated Jer 11:21; 20:1 – 2; 26:20 – 23; 32:3;
36:5; 37:16; Hos 9:7

Reliable Dt 18:21; 2Ch 18:5 – 6

Role 2Sa 12:1; 1Ki 1:9 – 10; 12:24; 2Ki 4:13;
Jer 1:10; Jn 1:6

Test 1Ki 12:24; 22:6 – 7; Jer 23:18; 26:8 – 9;
28:8 – 9,15 – 16; Da 1:17; Mt 7:15 – 16;
1Th 5:20 – 21

Prostitutes Ge 19:4 – 5; 38:15,21; 1Ki 14:24;
2Ki 23:7; Pr 7:4 – 5; 23:28; Jas 2:25

Providence of God Ps 104; Mt 10:29 – 30;
Ac 14:14 – 17

Punishment Ge 20:16; Ex 34:6 – 7; Nu 14:20 – 35;
Mt 12:31 – 32; Ac 13:46; Ro 11:8; 2Th 1:8

Delayed Nu 33:52 – 53; 2Ki 23:24 – 26;
2Ch 34:27 – 28; Ps 140:12

Limits Dt 25:3; Zec 1:15; 9:1 – 6

Physical Pr 26:3

Substitute Isa 53:5,10; Ro 9:3; Gal 3:13

Purity Lev 6:10; Jos 5:15; Mal 3:2; 1Jn 3:3

Q

Quiet time Ps 1:2; 16:7; 77:12; 119:11,15; Mt 6:23

R

Racism Ex 1:9 – 10; Est 2:10; Am 1:13

Rape Ge 19:8; 34:26; Dt 22:19,29; Jdg 19:24;
2Sa 13:13

Rebellion (against God) Nu 15:30; Ps 85:4;
107:11; Isa 1:24; 57:17; Hos 4:4; Na 3:1 – 4;
Ac 26:14; Rev 16:6; 17:3

Reconciliation Mt 5:23 – 26; Php 4:2 – 3;
2Co 5:11 – 6:2; Eph 2:11 – 22; Col 1:15 – 23

Redemption Ex 12:29; Nu 35:19; Ru 2:20; 3:12;
4:3 – 6; Job 19:25; Ps 54:7; 90:11 – 14; 130:7 – 8;
Isa 35:10; Jer 17:9; Hos 13:14; Col 1:17

Rejection Ps 88:14; Jn 9:22

Relationship (to God) Ps 5:5; 50:16;
Ecc 12:13 – 14; Eze 43:10; Ac 17:30; Ro 5:1

National Isa 43:3; 59:18; Jer 18:7 – 10

Personal Ps 32:9; 107:33 – 43; Isa 37:14; 64:8;
Jer 22:16; Hag 1:8; Lk 18:22 – 30; Mt 19:21

Repentance Lev 26:41; 1Ki 21:27; 2Ki 6:30;
2Ch 33:1 – 2; Ps 79:8; Joel 2:12 – 14

National Jdg 3:15; 1Sa 7:6; Ne 8:9 – 11; La 5:21;
Da 9:3; Hos 6:1 – 3

Personal Ps 38:4; 39:13; 143:1 – 2; Eze 11:19;
Zec 1:3; Mt 3:11; Lk 7:29 – 30; Jn 1:6; Phm 12;
Rev 22:11

Respect

Elderly Job 33:2 – 7

God Ex 3:5; 30:20 – 21; Lev 16:2; 1Ch 13:9 – 10;
15:29; 2Ch 27:2; Job 9:9; 28:28; Ps 103:11;
Ecc 5:1; Isa 6:1 – 8; 54:5; Zec 2:13; Mal 2:17;
Jn 12:3; 2Co 7:1

Leaders 1Sa 26:9; 2Sa 1:6 – 10; 2Ch 24:15 – 16;
Ecc 10:20; Ro 13:4; 1Th 5:12

Parents Ex 21:17; Pr 13:1; Jer 9:13 – 16; Mt 8:22;
12:46 – 50; Mk 3:31 – 35; Jn 2:4; Eph 6:1

Responsibility 2Ki 21:9; 1Ti 4:14

Accepting 2Ki 6:5; Ps 104:14 – 15; 139:16;
Isa 4:4; 2Th 3:6 – 13

Resurrection Eze 37:10; Da 12:2,13; Mt 28:17;
Lk 24:5 – 6,31,37 – 39; Ac 10:41; 23:9; Ro 1:4;
1Co 15:2

Last days Isa 26:19; Jn 20:17; 1Co 15:35 – 57;
Heb 11:35; Rev 20:4 – 5

Revelation Ps 19:1 – 6; Jn 1:1 – 18; Ac 14:14 – 1;
Ro 1:18 – 23; Heb 1; 2Ti 3:14 – 17; 2Pe 1:19 – 21

Revenge Ex 21:23 – 25; Lev 24:20; 2Sa 19:22;
1Ki 2:6; Ps 58:6 – 8; 94:1 – 3; 149:6 – 9; Jer 46:10;
Eze 25:3 – 7; Mt 5:39; 2Ti 4:14

Revival 2Ki 23:24 – 26; 2Ch 15:12; 19:4 – 5; Ne 1:6;
Ps 19:7; 80:18; Isa 19:19 – 25; Eze 37:10

The rich and the poor Ex 35:4 – 9; Dt 8:18;
1Ch 29:3,12; Ps 62:10; 82:3 – 4; Hos 2:8;
Mal 3:8 – 10; Mt 6:19 – 25; 19:16 – 21; Eph 4:28;
5:3; Col 3:5; 1Ti 6:17 – 18; 1Pe 5:2

Righteousness Ps 7; Jer 23:1 – 6; Mt 6:25 – 34;
Ro 4:6 – 8; Gal 2:15 – 21; Php 3:7 – 11;
1Ti 6:11 – 16; 1Pe 2:24 – 25

Role models Est 4:16; Job 15:4; 2Co 8:8; Eph 5:1;
Php 4:9; Heb 12:1

S

Sacrifices Ex 20:24; 29:11 – 21; Lev 1:1; 17:11;
Nu 7:41 – 80; Ps 40:6; 50:5,8 – 15,23; 51:19;
1Pe 2:5

Sadducees Mt 16:1 – 12; Mk 12:18 – 23;
Ac 4:1 – 22; 5:17 – 42; 23:1 – 11

Salvation

Belief in Christ Jn 3:16 – 18; 6:29; 8:37,40,51;
13:8; 17:2,6,9; Ac 13:48; 2Co 13:5; 2Ti 2:19

By faith Ge 15:6; Ps 106:31; 127:1 – 2; Isa 26:2;
Eze 33:13; Mt 5:20; 25:35 – 36; Lk 19:9;
Ac 15:20; Ro 10:3 – 7; Heb 4:11; Jas 2:14 – 24

For all people Ge 35:11; Dt 4:33; Ru 4:22;
2Ch 6:33; Est 8:1 – 3; Ps 22:27; 86:9; Isa 42:6;
Jer 31:31; 48:47; Am 9:12; Jnh 2:7 – 9;
Zep 2:11; Zec 9:7; Mt 2:2; 15:23 – 26; Lk 2:32;
Jn 10:16; Ac 10:45; 1Ti 2:4

God's promise to Abraham Ge 12:3;
Dt 26:18; 1Ki 8:43; Ps 47:9; Isa 19:19 – 25;
Eph 3:3 – 4,6,9

Losing Ro 11:21 – 22; 1Co 9:27; Heb 6:6;
2Pe 2:20 – 22

Understanding Ps 67:2; 87:4; 98:2 – 3; Pr 10:16;
Isa 52:15; Jer 22:16; Mt 10:5; 19:17; Ac 4:12;
Ro 1:16; Php 2:12 – 13

Sanctify Jn 17:17,19; 1Co 1:2; Php 1:6;
1Th 4:3 – 12

Satan

Limited by God Job 1:12; 19:8 – 12; Lk 10:18;
Ro 16:20; Col 2:15; 1Jn 5:18

Names for 2Sa 24:1; 2Ki 1:2; Job 31:35; Zec 3:1;
Mt 4:1,3 – 4; 10:25; Mk 1:12 – 13; 8:33; Lk 4:3;
Jn 12:31; Col 1:13; Jas 4:7; Rev 12:11

Power of Job 1:13 – 19; Mt 4:8 – 9; 7:22 – 23;
Lk 4:6; 22:3; Jn 13:27; Ac 19:19; 2Co 2:11;
Eph 2:2; 6:12; 1Th 2:18; 1Pe 5:8; 1Jn 1:8;
Rev 6:1 – 17

Scapegoat Lev 16:20 – 22; 2Ki 6:32 – 33; 1Pe 1:6

Second chances La 5:22

Second coming Mt 24 – 25; Jn 14:1 – 4; Ac 1:6 – 8;
1Co 15:12 – 28; 1Th 4:13 – 5:11; 2Th 2; 2Pe 3;
Rev 19 — 20

Self

Confidence 1Sa 10:22; Ps 22:6 – 7; Pr 12:9;
Ro 12:3; 1Co 2:3; Gal 6:4

Control Pr 6:6 – 11; 25:28; Titus 2:2

Defense Ex 22:3; 2Sa 20:10

Denial Mt 7:13 – 14

Esteem Ex 30:15; 1Ch 4:9 – 10; Ezr 2:2 – 61;
Job 25:6; Ps 8:5; 103:14; 139:13 – 16; Pr 22:2;
Isa 41:14; 1Pe 2:18 – 21

Reliance 2Ch 12:14; Isa 2:7 – 8; 26:18; 50:10 – 11

Will Jdg 16:17

Servant Isa 49:1 – 6; 50:4 – 9; 52:13 — 53:12;
Mk 10:35 – 45; Jn 13:1 – 17; 1Co 9:19 – 23;
Gal 5:13 – 26; Php 2:6 – 11; 1Pe 2:18 – 25

Service (to God and others) Nu 35:2;
1Ch 23:7 – 23; Mt 25:26 – 27; Jn 13:14 – 15;
1Ti 3:13

Sex

Homosexuality Ge 13:13; 19:4 – 5; Lev 18:22;
Jdg 19:24; 2Ki 23:7; Ro 1:26 – 27

In marriage 1Co 6:20

Pleasure Pr 5:18 – 19

Religious rituals Nu 25:1; Jos 22:17; 1Ki 14:24;
16:32; Hos 4:12; 4:14

Rules about Ex 19:15; 2Sa 11:11

Temptation 2Sa 11:2 – 3; Pr 5:3 – 10; 9:17;
23:28; 1Co 6:18

Shame Ezr 9:6 – 15; Ps 25; 34:1 – 7; Ro 1:16 – 17;
2Ti 1:8 – 14

Sin

Acceptance Lev 26:41; Ps 38:4; Jn 9:41

Communal Jos 7:11; 2Sa 24:15; Ezr 9:6;
Isa 59:12; Eze 21:4; Da 9:3; 9:5; Mal 4:6

Defeating Ro 6:2 – 14; 7:14 – 25

Development 2Ki 18:4

Hated by God Ps 5:5

Individual Lev 20:9; Nu 14:18; Dt 5:9; 23:2;
Eze 18:2

Punished 1Ch 21:14; 1Th 4:6

Secret 2Ki 17:9; Ps 90:8

Unforgivable Mt 12:31 – 32; Mk 3:29

Unintentional Ps 19:12; Ac 3:14 – 15,17;
Jas 4:17

Sin's effects Ge 12:17; 1Sa 2:31 – 33;
2Sa 12:9 – 10; 21:6,9,14; 1Ch 21:14; Job 5:7;
15:20; Ps 7:13,16; 51:4; 103:10; Jer 17:9; Eze 7:27;
18:24; Mt 5:29 – 30; Ro 1:24,26,28; 5:13 – 14; 6:1;
2Co 7:9

Church 1Co 5:7; 8:12

Creation Ge 9:2; Ps 107:33 – 34; Jer 7:20; Jn 9:2;
9:3; Ro 8:20 – 21; Rev 8:7 – 11

Families Ps 79:8; Jer 2:9; 31:29; 32:18;
La 2:11 – 12; Eze 18:19 – 20; Hos 2:4 – 5

God Job 35:6; Jer 12:7 – 8; Eze 33:11; Jn 11:35

Health Ge 3:16; Jn 5:14

Nations Ne 1:6; Ps 51:18; Jer 9:3 – 8; 18:7 – 10;
29:21 – 23; La 2:11 – 12; Eze 21:4; 22:30; Da 9:5

Removed Rev 22:2

Slander Ps 12:5; Pr 10:18 – 21; Jas 4:11

Slavery Ex 10:27 – 28; Lev 22:6,11; 25:44 – 46;
Jos 16:10; Jdg 1:28; 1Ki 12:18; 1Ch 5:21;
Mt 20:26 – 28; Mk 10:43 – 45; 1Co 7:21 – 24;
1Pe 2:18 – 21

Son of God Mt 16:18; Lk 22:70 – 71; Jn 1:18;
Heb 7:11

Son of man Ps 80:17; Eze 2:1; Da 7:13; 8:17;
Mk 2:10; Heb 2:6 – 8; Rev 1:13; 14:14

Sorrow Ex 3:1 – 9; Mt 26:36 – 46

Soul Dt 6:1 – 5; 30:6; Ps 25:1; 42; 103; 130;
Ecc 12:7; 1Th 5:23; Heb 4:12; Rev 6:9 – 10

Spirit of God Ge 6:3; Ex 24:2; 31:3; Jdg 13:25;
1Sa 11:6; 16:14; 2Sa 23:2; 1Ch 12:18; 28:12,19;
2Ch 20:14; Ps 104:30; Pr 20:27; Joel 2:28;
Zec 4:6; Mk 1:10

Stealing Ex 20:15; 22:1 – 15; Lev 19:11 – 13;
Mal 3:8 – 10; Eph 4:28

Stewardship Mt 25:14 – 30; Lk 12:35 – 48;
16:10 – 12; Eph 5:15 – 16

Stubbornness Pr 29:1

Submission

In marriage Eph 5:24 – 33; 1Pe 3:5 – 6

To authority Col 3:18 — 4:1; 1Pe 2:13 – 17

To God Isa 18:7; 19:18; Jer 27:8 – 15; 29:7

To others Eph 5:21

Success Dt 28:2 – 6; 2Ch 26:5; Job 22:21 – 25;
Ps 1:3 – 4; 90:17; Pr 6:6 – 11

Suffering Job 5:7; 6:24; 11:16; 34:37; Ps 88:3;
Mk 8:34; 15:23; Ac 5:41; Rev 13:10

Alone Job 19:13 – 20; Ps 10:1; 12:1; 22:1; 88:6;
102:3 – 5; La 3:3; Mt 26:41; 27:46; Mk 14:38;
14:51 – 52; 15:34; Lk 22:40; 2Ti 1:15

God's role 2Sa 12:14 – 15; 2Ki 5:1; Ps 34:17; 71:20; 97:10; Rev 13:8

Purpose of Job 32:14; 33:19; Ps 22:30 – 31; 102:9 – 10; Pr 22:4; Isa 45:7; 48:10; La 3:38; Eze 24:16 – 18; Jn 9:3; 1Th 3:3

Results Job 3:10 – 16; 23:10; Ps 119:67 – 75; Pr 17:3; Ecc 11:8; La 3:38; Jn 11:4; Ro 5:3; 2Co 4:12; Rev 9:20 – 21

Understanding Job 5:27; 9:22 – 24; 17:7 – 8; 23:10; 42:8; Isa 13:16; 53:9; Ro 8:17; 2Co 1:5; 1Pe 4:1

Suicide 1Sa 31:5; 2Sa 17:23; Isa 57:1 – 2; Ac 1:18 – 19; 16:22 – 36

T

Talents 1Ch 22:8; Mt 25:26 – 27; 1Ti 4:14

Talking (with God) Ge 12:1; 18:10; Nu 1:1; 7:89; Jos 1:1; 1Sa 3:21; 30:6; Job 38:1; Ps 95:7; Hab 2:1; Mal 2:17

Temple 2Ch 3:1,3 – 17; Mt 24:2 – 3

Employees 1Ch 23:26,28 – 32; 2Ch 4:6 – 16; 23:8; Ne 12:29; Ps 134:1; Eze 44:16

Finances Lev 27:2,13; Nu 5:10; 18:31; Jos 13:33; 2Ki 12:6 – 8; 2Ch 24:5; 31:4; Ezr 6:4

Temptation Dt 13:3; 1Ch 21:1; Job 29:2; 31:1; Ps 81:7; Mt 4:1,3 – 4; Mk 1:12 – 13; Lk 4:3; 1Co 10:13; Eph 6:14 – 17; Heb 4:15; Jas 1:13; 1Jn 5:4

Ten Commandments Ex 3:1; 20:1 – 17; 31:18; Lev 16:13; Dt 5:1; 9:10; Jos 8:32; Mk 2:27; Ro 10:4

Terrorism 2Ki 25:7 – 9; Jer 39:7

Testing

By God Dt 8:2; 13:3; 1Ch 29:17; 2Ch 32:31; Job 1:8; 7:18; 16:9; 23:10; Ps 66:10; 81:7; Mt 4:1; 15:23 – 26; Mk 7:26 – 27; Ro 16:10; 1Th 3:3; Jas 1:13; 1Pe 1:7

Of God Ps 78:18

Thanksgiving Ex 23:15; 1Sa 31:12; Ps 116:13; 116:17; Eph 5:20

Time Ecc 3:1 – 8; Eph 5:15; Col 4:5

Tithes Ge 14:20; 28:22; Lev 27:30; Dt 12:17; 26:12; 1Ch 6:54; 2Ch 31:5; Pr 3:9 – 10; Mal 3:9 – 10; 2Co 9:7

Tongues Ac 2:1 – 13; 10:44 – 48; 19:1 – 7; 1Co 12 — 14

Trinity Ge 1:26; 11:7; Dt 6:4; Mt 28:16 – 20; Jn 14:9 – 28; 2Co 13:14; Titus 3:3 – 8; Jude 20 — 21

Trust Dt 28:65; Ps 77:2; Ecc 11:10; Mt 6:25; Lk 12:22

In God Ge 22:2; Ex 30:12; Jos 11:6; Jdg 7:5 – 6; 2Ki 4:2 – 7; 18:14; 1Ch 18:4; 2Ch 28:5; Ne 6:13; Job 2:10; 12:15 – 16,22 – 23; 19:25; 23:14 – 15; Ps 11:1; 91:16; 112:6 – 7; 116:10; 142:6; Isa 30:18; Mic 7:7; Hab 3:17; Jas 1:2; 1:7 – 8

In idols 2Ch 25:14; Isa 27:10 – 11

In military power Jos 11:6; 1Sa 12:12; 2Sa 24:3,10; 1Ch 21:1,6 – 7; Isa 20:5 – 6; 22:8 – 11; 30:1 – 2; 31:1; 34:1 – 3; Jer 2:36; Eze 16:26 – 29; 29:6 – 7; Hos 7:11; Hab 1:16

In money Job 36:19; Ps 12:8; 97:7; Isa 2:7 – 8; 39:1 – 2

In people Ps 146:3 – 4

Learning to Ex 16:4; Ps 78:5 – 7; Isa 43:2

Truth Pr 22:17; 23:23; Isa 45:23; Jer 22:5; 38:2 – 3; Mt 5:34 – 37; Ac 16:18; 2Ti 3:7; Jas 5:12; 2Jn 1; Rev 1:19 – 20

U

Unbelief Nu 20:12; Dt 1:34; Ps 78:32; 95:11; 115:2; Isa 29:9 – 10; Mt 12:39; Mk 6:5 – 6; Lk 11:29; Jn 6:29; 10:26

Understanding God Ge 14:18; 41:37 – 39; Ex 5:1 – 3; Dt 10:17; 29:4; 1Ki 5:7; 10:1; 2Ch 32:16 – 19; Ezr 6:10; Job 10:2; 41:11; Ps 65:8; 97:2 – 5; Pr 25:2; 30:2 – 3; Ecc 11:5; Eze 20:9; Jnh 2:7 – 9; Lk 15:25 – 32; Jn 6:46,57

Unity Ps 133; Jn 17; Ac 2:42 – 47; 1Co 1 – 4; 10:16 – 17; 11:17 – 34; Gal 3:26 – 28; Eph 4:1 – 16

Unity of believers Ps 133:1; Jn 17:21 – 23; Ac 15:20; Ro 15:5 – 7; Eph 4:13; 5:21; Php 2:2 – 5

V

Values (spiritual) Mt 5:3 – 10; 5:19

Virgin birth Mt 1:23

W

Wait (for God) Isa 64:4; Am 5:13; Hab 2:1

Warning (others) Eze 3:17; 33:6 – 9

Wars Ge 49:24; Jos 11:23; Jdg 20:8 – 43

Atrocities Jos 10:24 – 26; 1Sa 27:9; 2Ki 15:16; Ps 137:8 – 9; Isa 21:3 – 4

Destruction 2Ki 3:25

Spiritual Job 1:13 – 19; Ps 70:2; 83:2,6 – 8; Isa 24:21 – 22; Da 10:12; Mt 11:12; 2Co 10:4; Eph 6:14 – 17; 6:12; 2Ti 2:3

Water Jn 4:10 – 14; 7:37 – 38; Rev 22:1 – 2

Wealth Nu 7:26 – 80; Ps 12:8; Pr 8:10 – 11; 11:25 – 28; 19:10; 22:2; Ecc 5:11; 10:19; Am 3:12; Lk 6:24 – 26; 16:19 – 31; 18:25; 1Ti 6:9 – 11; Jas 5:1 – 6

Widows Dt 25:5 – 9; Isa 4:1; 54:1 – 6; Mic 2:9; 1Ti 5:9

Will of God Mt 26:36 – 46; Jn 4:34; 6:38; Ro 12:1 – 8; Eph 1:3 – 14; Php 2:5 – 11; 1Th 4:1 – 8; Jas 4:13 – 15 1Pe 4:12 – 19

Wisdom Nu 27:18; Pr 1:2; 8:10 – 11; 21:5; 24:27; Ecc 1:18; Jas 4:13 – 15

God's 1Ki 4:29 – 34; Job 2:10; 28:1 – 23; 1Co 2:13; 4:6; Jas 1:5

Using 1Ki 11:4 – 8; Pr 21:22

Worldly 1Ki 4:29 – 34

Witchcraft Lev 20:6 – 7; Dt 18:10 – 12; 1Sa 28; Isa 8:19 – 22; 47:10 – 14; Ac 8:9 – 24; 13:6 – 12; 19:13 – 19; Gal 5:19 – 21

Women

As property Ge 19:8; 30:3; 31:15; 38:14; Ex 21:7 – 11; Dt 20:14; Jdg 19:24; 2Sa 3:7; 20:3; 1Ki 2:22 – 23; Isa 13:16

DENIAL

Hebrews 12:1 offers a challenge none of us can afford to ignore:

Therefore, since we are surrounded by such a great cloud of witnesses,
let us throw off everything that hinders and the sin that so easily entangles.
And let us run with perseverance the race marked out for us.

For many of us, though, past hurts, hang-ups and habits are holding us back and tripping us up. We may be stuck in a mode of bitterness over what someone else has done to us, continuing to hold on to the pain and refusing to forgive those who are responsible. In all fairness, some of us have been hurt very deeply. Perhaps we were abused as a child, or maybe our spouse has committed adultery. But it's important for us to understand that holding on to that hurt and being unwilling to forgive the person who has injured us in the past only allows them to continue hurting us today. By starting to work our recovery program, we can, with God's power, begin to find the courage and strength to forgive the guilty party.

Others of us are bound by guilt. We keep beating ourselves up over some past failure. We're trapped, stuck fast in self-reproach and shame. We reason that no one else anywhere could be as bad as we are, that no one could love the *real* us or forgive us for the terrible things we've done. But we're wrong: For starters, God can. Jesus went to the cross for all our sins. He knows everything we've ever done or experienced. The apostle Paul harbored a lot of regret about his past. He'd even participated in Stephen's murder. Yet in Philippians 3:13 – 14 he inspires us with these words: "Brothers and sisters, I do not consider myself yet to have taken hold of it. But one thing I do: Forgetting what is behind and straining toward what is ahead, I press on toward the goal to win the prize for which God has called me heavenward in Christ Jesus."

If we want to be free from our hurts, hang-ups and habits, we need to deal with our past bitterness and guilt once and for all. In the words of Isaiah 43:18, "Forget the former things; do not dwell on the past." That doesn't mean we're to ignore the past. Instead, we need to learn from our past, offer forgiveness and make amends; in doing so, we break its hold on us.

Some of us, on the other hand, are trapped in fear of the future. We may worry about what's coming next and be afraid to change. We're naturally apprehensive about things over which we have no control. The truth is, though, that we can "say with confidence, 'The Lord is my helper; I will not be afraid. What can mere mortals do to me?'" (Hebrews 13:6).

Some of us have been entangled in our hurts, hang-ups or habits for so long that they've become intertwined with our identity. We're so accustomed to them and comfortable with them that we confuse what we've *done* with who we *are*. We may be thinking, "What will happen if I really give recovery a chance? Will I change? If I give up my old hurts, hang-ups and habits, what will I become? Who will I be? What will be left of me?"

We may have been abusing alcohol, prescription drugs or food. We're afraid of what we'll do without our substance of choice. We may have been enabling someone else in a dysfunctional relationship for years. We wonder, "What if I change and my alcoholic husband gets mad at me?" But God doesn't want us to stay frozen in an unhealthy relationship or a bad habit. He wants us to do our part in helping the relationship or habit become healthy.

Even if our past has been extremely painful, we may still resist change and the freedom that can be found in really working our program. Because of our fear of the unknown or our feelings of despair, we choose to close our minds, reasoning that we don't deserve any better than what we have right now.

Principle One states: "Realize I'm not God; I admit that I am powerless to control my tendency to do the wrong thing and that my life is unmanageable." As we begin working this principle, we need to remember 1 John 4:18: "There is no fear in love. But perfect love drives out fear."

Because of Christ's unconditional love, power, grace and complete forgiveness, we don't have to let our past failures or future fears stop us from completing Principle One. Remember that we've all stumbled over a hurt, hang-up or habit. But the race isn't over yet. God isn't nearly as interested in how we start the race as he is in how we finish it.

Take a Look:

- What past hurts are you holding on to?

- What past or present actions make you feel guilty?

- What are you afraid to change in your life? Why?

- What are your fears about the future? Why?

POWERLESS

The routine of our daily lives often reminds us of our lack of control. We stand in a slow line at the grocery store waiting for a cashier-in-training. Our car breaks down on the way to work. We wait over a weekend to learn the results of a medical test. Our coworker gets promoted, while we continue to wait for recognition.

In our attempts to deal with our lack of control, we worry about the details in our lives, pretend that it just doesn't matter, or we become angry and resentful. We may isolate ourselves from other people to keep the pain at a distance. Many of us try in one way or another to control our circumstances and the people around us.

Some of us are too proud to admit that certain areas of our lives have become unmanageable. This pride can undermine our faith, cut us off from God and prevent us from recognizing our own powerlessness. In this mode we refuse to allow ourselves to reach out for help. Stories we encounter in the news distress us. We hear about a man who left his three-year-old son in a car when it was 35 degrees outside, The man was visiting a strip club! Outraged, we ask ourselves, "Why doesn't this father get help for his struggle with sexual addiction?" Meanwhile, we're attempting to escape our own pain through the repeated cycle of overeating and dieting. Like the father visiting the strip club, we refuse to admit our own struggle or reach out for help.

By facing our powerlessness and admitting our weaknesses, we invite God to step in to change our lives. After hearing a testimony at a Celebrate Recovery conference, a pastor approached the speakers, saying, "I want to tell you some bad news and some good news. The bad news is that I've been struggling with my pride. Your testimony made it clear to me that I'm a codependent who is powerless over my issues and that I need recovery. The good news is that I'm going back to my church to start a Celebrate Recovery program. My prayer is that our church can reach out and help people deal with their hurts, hang-ups and habits."

We need to take four actions in order to complete Principle One:

1. Stop denying the pain. Psalm 6:2–3 describes a time in David's life when he came to the end of his emotional and physical resources: "Have mercy on me, LORD, for I am faint; heal me, LORD, for my bones are in agony. My soul is in deep anguish. How long, LORD, how long?" When David's pain finally surpassed

his fear, he was able to face his denial and feel the reality of his agony. In the same way, if we want to be rid of our pain, we need to face it and work our way through it.

2. Stop playing God. The simple truth is that we're either going to serve God or ourselves. We can't do both. In the words of Matthew 6:24, "No one can serve two masters. Either you will hate the one and love the other, or you will be devoted to the one and despise the other. You cannot serve both God and money." When our "self" is out of control, all our attempts at control—of ourselves or others—will fail. We need to admit that we're not God and that we're powerless without him. Then, when we've finally emptied ourselves, God will have room to come in and begin his healing work.

3. Start admitting our powerlessness. Our lust for power isn't rooted in our strengths but in our weaknesses. We need to recognize our human limitations and quit trying to resolve the issues by ourselves. We need to admit that we're powerless and be willing to turn over our lives to God. Jesus knew how difficult this would be for us to do. Matthew 19:26 sums up the situation for us, recording Jesus' own words: "With man this is impossible, but with God all things are possible."

4. Start admitting that our lives have become unmanageable. With this admission we finally acknowledge that we're out of control and powerless to change on our own. David shared his feelings in Psalm 40:12: "Troubles without number surround me; my sins have overtaken me, and I cannot see. They are more than the hairs of my head, and my heart fails within me."

Take a Look:

- Of what are you still in denial, or what are you still trying to control in your own power?

- Are there any other "masters" besides God in your life that you're still trying to serve?

- What are some of the things you keep doing that you really don't want to do?

- Can you relate to Psalms 40:12? How?

HOPE

After years of participating in Celebrate Recovery, we may be surprised to find that some of our good friends are former drug addicts, sex addicts, alcoholics or controlling codependents. We've learned that we're more alike than we are different. We all struggle and we all make mistakes. Some of us hurt ourselves and others without breaking the law. Some of us break the law and scrape by without getting caught. And some of us break the law, get caught and spend time in jail or prison

Men and women are being incarcerated at an alarming rate. Eighty percent of prisoners are addicts, and fifty percent of them committed their crimes while they were high. More than seventy percent of female prisoners are victims of sexual or physical abuse.

While in prison, a person's feelings of powerlessness can be overwhelming. Prisoners don't get to choose whom to live with, what to eat, what to wear, when to go outside or stay inside or what time to get up in the morning or go to bed at night. One young woman explained that incarceration provides an environment without choices, decisions . . . or hope.

However, more and more prisoners are beginning to find the hope to change their lives through their Higher Power, Jesus Christ. By facing their denial and powerlessness, they can begin their recovery. Prisoners are studying the Bible, working the steps and forming accountability teams to help them learn different behaviors that will enable them to cope with life both inside and outside the prison walls.

Many of us are trapped inside our own walls. Sometimes we're afraid to hope for a life free of hurt or pain. We don't want to be disappointed again. We may think we don't deserve a better life. Or we may assume that our faith is too small to get us through the process of change. But we can break the chains of our past by putting our faith, no matter how weak or strong, in our Savior and Lord, Jesus Christ.

In the first recovery principle, we admitted that we were powerless. It's through this admission that we're able to both *believe* and *receive* God's power to help us recover. However, we do need to resist the temptation to cover the bottomless pit of our hurts, hang-ups and habits with layers of denial or just to try some quick fix. Instead, we need to keep those hurts exposed to the light so that through God's power they can truly heal.

In the second principle we come to believe that God exists and that we're important to him. And in this principle we find access to the one true Higher Power, Jesus Christ. Hebrews 11:6 informs us that "without faith it is impossible to please God, because anyone who comes to him must believe that he exists and that he rewards those who earnestly seek him." Psalm 62:5 points us to the source of our hope: "Yes, my soul, find rest in God; my hope comes from him."

In working this principle we come to understand that God wants to fill our lives with his love, joy and presence. One of the much-loved parables of Jesus is found in Luke 15, the story of the lost son. On the surface the account is about a father's love for his drifting son, but its deeper message is of the unconditional love of God the Father for us. God's love is looking for us, no matter how lost we may feel. And God's searching love can find us, no matter how many times we may have fallen into sin. God's hands of mercy are reaching out to pick us up and to love and forgive us.

It's in Jesus Christ that we find hope, and that's why Principle Two is called the "hope principle." We find that eternal life doesn't begin with death; it begins with faith. Hebrews 11:1 defines faith for us: "Faith is confidence in what we hope for and assurance about what we do not see." We can't find salvation through intellectual understanding, monetary gifts, good works or church attendance. No! The only way to salvation is described in Romans 10:9: "If you declare with your mouth, 'Jesus is Lord,' and believe in your heart that God raised him from the dead, you will be saved."

All we need is a little faith to begin the journey of freedom from our hurts, hang-ups and habits. Faith — even faith the size of a tiny mustard seed (see Matthew 17:20) — is the only avenue to salvation and freedom. When we put whatever degree of faith we have in Jesus, he promises that our lives will be changed. We'll find the hope for which we've been searching in the only Higher Power, Jesus Christ. His Spirit will come with supernatural power and move into our hearts.

Simply put, life without Christ is a hopeless end; with him it is an endless hope.

Take a Look:

- What hurt, hang-up or habit in your life has been keeping you a prisoner? How has it affected your life?

- Is Hebrews 11:1 meaningful to you? How has the description of faith in this verse helped you put things in perspective?

- How has the "new hope" you've found in Christ changed your life?

- What has the statement "life without Christ is a hopeless end; with him it is an endless hope" meant in your life?

SANITY

At first our coping mechanisms may affect our lives only in small ways. However, over time we can develop hurts, hang-ups and habits that have devastating consequences. In the beginning, for example, the need to control all of life's circumstances may only cause arguments in a family. However, these control issues may eventually result in the separation of a husband and wife and the destruction of a family. A mother's occasional loss of temper may escalate into daily beatings and the removal of the child from the home. Trying to lose weight quickly by skipping meals may result in anorexia and lengthy hospital confinements. A drink at the end of each day for relaxation could develop into alcoholism and lead to time spent in jail for drunk driving.

Our hurts, hang-ups and habits can impact our lives by pushing us into dangerous situations. After her third divorce, a busy career woman began using the Internet to connect with other people. She soon became fascinated with her exchanges with some of the men and began to fantasize about meeting them. She began by arranging meetings in public restaurants or coffee houses. However, without considering the consequences, she soon began meeting total strangers in their cars or apartments. After managing to escape from a car in a deserted area of the city, she finally realized that she could have been kidnapped or killed. The insanity of her choices had become a matter of life or death.

We often continue in our extreme behaviors because we don't know how to change — or even where to start. However, in Principle One we finally faced our denial, and we admitted that we're powerless to control our tendency to do the wrong thing and that our lives have become unmanageable.

How and where do we access the needed control? The answer is that we need to practice the second principle on our journey of recovery: "Earnestly believe that God exists, that I matter to him and that he has the power to help me recover." We can begin to change by allowing Jesus Christ to restore sanity, order and meaning to our lives. He'll give us the strength to change and to set realistic expectations, as well as the ability to trust others as he continues to walk with us through the principles of recovery.

Step Two of the Christ-centered 12 steps states, "We came to believe that a power greater than ourselves could restore us to sanity." Step Two doesn't imply that we're crazy or insane. It's important for us to understand what the word *sanity* means in this step. *Insanity* in this context is "doing the same thing over and over again, expecting a different result each time." *Sanity*, on the other hand, may be defined as "wholeness of mind; making decisions based on the truth."

Jesus is the only Higher Power who offers the truth, the way, the life and the power.

As a result of admitting our powerlessness in Principle One, we can move from chaos to hope in Principle Two. Hope enters the picture when we come to believe that a power greater than ourselves, our Higher Power, Jesus Christ, can and will restore us. Christ alone can provide the needed power over our addictions and compulsive behaviors. He alone can restore order and meaning to our lives. He alone can restore us to sanity.

In this context we finally begin to understand Philippians 2:13:

> *It is God who works in you to will and to act*
> *according to his good purpose.*

Take a Look:

- Identify some of the negative effects of your attempts to control someone or something in your life.

- How and when have you been disappointed after thinking that "this time" the individual or circumstance would change?

- How and when have you been disappointed after assuming that you would change? (Remember, "insanity" is doing the same thing over and over again, expecting a different result each time.)

- After you came to believe that a power greater than yourself — your Higher Power, Jesus Christ — could and would restore you to sanity, how did your life and decision-making change?

TURN

Every day we surrender our lives to people we don't even know. We rely on the fast-food server to wash his hands before handing us our hamburger. We're confident that our dentist has the necessary education and skill to correctly fill our cavity. When we stop at the gas station to ask for directions, we believe that the attendant is more familiar with the area than we are. As we board the airplane to cross the United States, we depend on the skill of the pilot to reach our destination safely.

Some of us have driven behind a slow-moving semi laboring up a mountain grade on a winding, two-lane road. The trucker would periodically motion for a string of cars to go around him. By merely waving us on, a complete stranger was taking responsibility for our physical safety and that of our families. We passed the truck safely and, glancing into our rearview mirror, observed a line of cars whose drivers had also put their blind trust and faith in a stranger as they, too, passed the 18-wheeler.

It's so hard for us to surrender our own will and control, to trust our lives unreservedly to God's care. Yet the reality is that this one-time decision determines our destiny. We put our faith into action by simply taking God at his word. In Romans 10:9 the apostle Paul assures us that "if you declare with your mouth, 'Jesus is Lord,' and believe in your heart that God raised him from the dead, you will be saved."

Turning over our lives to our Higher Power, Jesus Christ, just seems too simple for some of us. "What's the catch?" we wonder. At that point it's important for us to accept the fact that we don't need to understand all the implications of our decision.

First Corinthians 13:12 explains the situation this way:

> Now we see only a reflection as in a mirror;
> then we shall see face to face.
> Now I know in part; then I shall know fully,
> even as I am fully known.

We can learn so much about uncomplicated faith from children. The parent of a preschooler shared with the teacher an episode pertaining to her daughter's recent visit to the pediatrician. When the doctor got out the stethoscope to listen to the little girl's chest, she requested solemnly, "Please don't push too hard with that thing. I don't want you to hurt Jesus. He lives in my heart."

Principle Three calls on each of us to "consciously choose to commit all my life and will to Christ's care and control." This principle includes three vitally important actions that we must take as we turn over our lives to Christ: trusting, understanding and repenting.

The good news is that when we choose to turn over our lives to Christ, it's a once-in-a-lifetime decision. Once we accept Christ into our lives as our Savior and Lord, it's a done deal. Ephesians 1:13 assures each of us that "you also were included in Christ when you heard the message of truth, the gospel of your salvation. When you believed, you were marked in him with a seal, the promised Holy Spirit."

The rest of this principle deals with turning over our will to God. This part of the decision requires a daily choice to seek and follow God's will (his purpose for our lives). We can begin by going to the Bible regularly, opening it prayerfully, reading it expectantly and living it joyfully.

If you haven't asked Jesus Christ to be your Higher Power, the Savior and Lord of your life, what are you waiting for? If you're ready to take this step right now, just pray this prayer:

Dear God, I've tried to do it all by myself by my own power, and I've failed. Today I want to turn over my life to you. I ask you to be my Savior and Lord. You are the one and only Higher Power. I ask you to help me think less about myself and my will. Daily I want to turn over my will to you, to seek your direction and wisdom for my life. Please continue to help me overcome my hurts, hang-ups and habits. I recognize, Lord, that victory over them may also help others as they see your power at work in changing my life. Help me to do your will always. In Jesus' name I pray, Amen.

Take a Look:

- What are some everyday situations in which you put your trust entirely in the hands of complete strangers?

- Have you consciously chosen to commit all of your life and will to Christ's care and control? If you have, how has your life changed? If you haven't, what's holding you back from making this decision?

- What does Ephesians 1:13 mean to you, not just in terms of your understanding but in terms of your experience?

- In what ways do you continue to turn over your will to Christ's care every day?

ACTION

Sometimes we fail to take action in our lives because we're caught in a comfortable cycle. How often, for example, do we follow the crowd because it's just easier than doing the right thing? We procrastinate because we've convinced ourselves that we'll feel stronger and be better equipped to deal with life "tomorrow." We don't take action because we feel overwhelmed, unable or unwilling to choose from the variety of options available to us.

Every August the pastor of a small, rural church in Texas is confronted with a decision regarding the church budget. One option is to use the money designated for conferences to purchase airline tickets for the Celebrate Recovery summit in California. However, with the limited resources available, choosing this option means only two people can attend the meetings. With this option comes a resulting second choice: The pastor must choose two people from the six Celebrate Recovery leaders, all of whom are anxious to make the trip. The second option is to take the church van and make the 14-hour drive so that all six leaders can attend together.

After facing the same decision for years, the pastor no longer spends time weighing the options. His annual plan of action is to drive the church van. The long drive hasn't always been uneventful. One year the van broke down, and the group had to spend hours in a diner waiting for repairs to be made, finally arriving at the three-day summit only minutes before it began. Another year, after driving halfway to California, the van had to return to Texas because of a family emergency. After dropping off the one passenger, the group got back on the road. Within a couple of hours another passenger became carsick and had to lie down in the back seat, forcing the others to squeeze into the remaining seats.

Each year, though, in spite of—or perhaps because of—the hardships encountered, the trek strengthens the bond of the leaders and unifies the church group from the small Texas town. Now the pastor doesn't even consider the easier option of traveling by airplane.

When it comes to choosing Jesus Christ as our Higher Power, there are only two options: He either is or isn't our Savior and Lord. We need to be willing to take action and make our choice. Putting off the decision to accept Jesus Christ as our Higher Power, Savior and Lord is, in effect, deciding *not* to accept him. *Today* is the day to accept Jesus Christ as our Higher Power. Only then can we make the initial commitment to seek and follow God's will for our life.

Working Principle Three — "Consciously choose to commit all my life and will to Christ's care and control" — is like opening the door. All we need is the willingness to make the decision. Christ will do the rest. He invites us: "Here I am! I stand at the door and knock. If anyone hears my voice and opens the door, I will come in and eat with that person, and they with me" (Revelation 3:20).

Pastor Rick Warren has developed a simple way for each of us to establish a "Spiritual B.A.S.E." for our life. Ask yourself the following four questions. If you answer yes to all of them, pray the prayer that follows. That's it. That's all you have to do.

Start each question with "Do I . . .":

- Believe that Jesus Christ died on the cross for me and showed that he was God by coming back to life (see 1 Corinthians 15:2 – 4)?
- Accept God's free forgiveness for my sins (see Romans 3:22 – 24)?
- Switch to God's plan for my life (see Mark 1:16 – 18; Romans 12:2)?
- Express my desire for Christ to be the director of my life (see Romans 10:9)?

Then take action and pray the most important prayer of your life:

> Dear God, I believe that you sent your Son, Jesus, to die
> for my sins so I can be forgiven. I'm sorry for my sins, and
> I want to live the rest of my life the way you want me to.
> Please put your Spirit in my life to direct me. Amen.

Congratulations, and welcome to God's family!

If you've already taken this step, use this prayer to recommit to seeking and following God's perfect will for your life and recovery.

Take a Look:

- In what areas of your life are you just "following the crowd" or procrastinating?
- In what areas of your life and recovery do you need to take action to move ahead?
- Do you need to invite Christ into your life as your Savior and Lord?
- What areas of your life do you need to recommit to Christ's care and control?

MORAL

The events of our past, both the good and the bad, have affected us and those we love. Our hurts, choices, resentments and fears can often be traced back to childhood memories. It takes courage to dig into our past to discover the source of our hurts, hang-ups and habits.

A young mother who had been working on her two preschoolers' scrapbooks during their nap times finally decided that the project was complete. Now she felt ready to tackle a task that had been nagging at her for some time. She wanted to search through her parents' photographs and begin to document her family history for her children. As she sifted through the photo albums, though, she began to experience some confusing emotions.

She quickly noticed that the photographs taken during the early years of her and her brothers' childhoods were creatively arranged in the albums. But when she realized that there were years not represented by any photographs, she felt sad. There were, for instance, no snapshots representing the two years of her parents' separation. Then she discovered albums in which the photographs were once again carefully arranged, showcasing the happier remaining years after the reconciliation of the marriage. She began smiling over these pictures, reminding herself that the happier years were of longer duration than the unhappy ones.

Someone in a family typically chronicles its history by lovingly arranging photographs in an album. However, if a family begins to fall apart, the visual record often stops. This isn't a conscious decision; it's just that no one wants to document the demise of something they love. It may be years before regular photos begin again to recount the life of the family. Photographs fill every page of the album, so the gap is hardly noticeable as a blurred seam marks the "before" and "after" of some unfortunate rift in a family's story.

Many of us have gaps in our photo albums that represent dark periods in our personal histories. Or maybe we don't have an album at all. Now is the time to look at our past, both the good and the bad times, and to start our Celebrate Recovery inventory. It's time for us to invite others in the program to walk with us through this important part of our journey.

Principle Four states: "Openly examine and confess my faults to myself, to God and to someone I trust." In this principle we complete our "moral inventory." The word moral scares some people, but the term here simply means "honest."

As we prepare to work this principle, we're ready to begin the growth process of recovery. Principle Four may carry with it some growing pains. It's natural for us to wish we could escape altogether the pain of our past by skirting it or jumping over it. But the only way to truly rid ourselves of that pain is to work through it — while avoiding the temptation to get stuck in it. It has been said that "we need to use our past as a springboard, not a sofa — a guidepost, not a hitching post."

Some people spend their lives rationalizing the past, complaining about the present and fearing the future. They, of course, aren't moving forward on the road to recovery. By working Principle Four we've chosen to continue on a forward course by beginning the process of coming clean. We're going after the years of "truth decay." We begin to chip away at and clean out the "plaque" that has built up over the years and has kept us from really seeing the truth about our past and present situations.

As you begin to fill in the missing pictures from your life, be sure to keep your moral inventory balanced by listing both the good and the bad aspects of your life.

Throughout the process, hold on to the promise of Joshua 1:9:

> Be strong and courageous. Do not be afraid; do not be discouraged,
> for the LORD your God will be with you wherever you go.

Take a Look:

- Are there years missing in the scrapbook of your life? What was going on during that time?

- What are your fears about doing a moral inventory?

- Do you have a support team to guide and encourage you as you complete your moral inventory? Who are these individuals?

- What does Joshua 1:9 mean to you as you begin to complete your inventory?

SPONSOR

Most of us will admit that we like to have people we care about walking alongside us through the bad times as well as the good times in life. With others there to encourage us, obstacles don't seem nearly as large. On the other side of the coin, it isn't much fun to celebrate by ourselves. All of us enjoy commemorating the turning points of our lives with our families and friends.

In California one thousand people took part in an eight-week, countywide "weight meltdown." Restaurants planned special menus and local gyms offered free or discounted memberships. After the eight weeks, the participants learned that they had together lost a total of 7,500 pounds. They attributed their success to countywide support and to the division of participants into teams of five whose members stayed in touch with one another throughout the week.

Recent scientific evidence has found that a woman with breast cancer improves her survival rate by 60 percent if she has six or more friends. As a woman undergoes the traumatic recuperation process from this form of cancer, her friends — not her doctors, the hospital personnel or chemotherapy — are often the most significant factor in her survival.

Similarly, as we walk through our recovery journey, the people in our lives — our friends, sponsor and accountability partners — can be the most significant factor in our ability to successfully complete the program. These important people remind us to continue attending meetings and to keep journaling and working the principles. Sponsors and accountability partners help us to keep our inventory balanced, honest and complete. They can join us as we serve others. And, most importantly, they remind us that we're not alone.

Identifying a sponsor and/or accountability partners is especially important before you begin Principles Four through Six — principles in which you work on getting right with God, yourself and others. Having a sponsor and/or accountability partners is vital before you attempt to begin your moral inventory. It has been said that attempting an inventory by yourself can be as futile as peeling an onion to find the core. When you're finished, there's nothing left but the peelings and the tears.

Principle Four — "Openly examine and confess my faults to myself, to God and to someone I trust" — is all about getting rid of our "truth decay." It's about coming clean. Proverbs 15:14 points out that "the discerning heart seeks knowledge, but the mouth of a fool feeds on folly."

Are you ready to feed on the truth about your life? Well then, it's time to take out the trash. That garbage can get pretty heavy at times, and you don't need to handle it alone. You need someone who has gone before you on the road to recovery to help you bear the burden.

The following are four ways in which your sponsor and/or accountability partners can assist you:

1. They can be there to discuss in detail issues that are too personal or would take up too much time in a meeting. This is especially needed while working Principle Four. These individuals model Christ's grace and forgiveness and give you a sense of perspective.

2. They're available in times of crisis or potential relapse. Ecclesiastes 4:12 states: "Though one may be overpowered, two can defend themselves. A cord of three strands is not quickly broken."

3. They serve as a sounding board by providing an objective point of view based on their own experiences, victories and hope. This is especially valuable while working Principle Six. When you're dealing with the sensitive area of making amends and offering forgiveness, you need a reliable sounding board.

4. They're there to encourage you to work the principles at your own speed. It's not their job to work the principles for you, but they can coach your progress, confront you when you're stuck and slow you down when you're working through the program too fast.

Proverbs 27:17 says, "As iron sharpens iron, so one person sharpens another." While we're on the subject, you may be surprised to learn that a form of the phrase "one another" is used in the New Testament more than 118 times. Having a sponsor and an accountability team are essential to your recovery. It's important to start forming your accountability team as soon as you embark on your recovery journey.

Take a Look:

- Do you have someone involved in your recovery to whom you can go for advice? If not, why not?

- If you don't have an accountability team established, who are you going to turn to during times of struggle and temptation?

- How are each of the four services a sponsor or accountability partner can provide important to your recovery?

- If you've completed working the eight principles, have you made yourself available to be a sponsor for someone else? If not, why not?

SPIRITUAL INVENTORY, PART 1

When we began our recovery journey, we were anxious to complete the process as quickly as possible. Over time, we realized that our hurts, hang-ups and habits hadn't developed overnight, and they weren't going to be instantly removed either. The eight principles provide an action plan that allows us to continue to work on our recoveries.

A married couple had been separated for five months before getting into recovery together. Six months later they renewed their marriage vows. In order to celebrate their twenty-fifth wedding anniversary, the couple decided to schedule a trip to Europe. However, there were so many details to consider that they began to feel overwhelmed. They decided to form a plan of action that involved breaking the arrangements into smaller, bite-size pieces. They chose the destination, made reservations for air travel and hotel accommodations, collected maps, researched the weather, and selected and packed their clothing. They also had to learn about the differences in currency, cultural mannerisms and driving rules (for example, driving on the "wrong side of the road"). Planning the trip took a good deal of time, persistence and patience, but they ended up having a wonderful adventure to commemorate their years together.

The goals of our spiritual inventory are (1) to form a closer relationship with our Higher Power, Jesus Christ, (2) to forgive ourselves and others for our past, and (3) to become spiritually healed. To be successful with each of these objectives, a course of action is required. When completing the participant's guides, we need a private place and a scheduled time to work on our answers. It's critical that we stay connected with our accountability partners and sponsors, so that we don't feel alone. We need to learn how to keep our answers balanced with regard to our weaknesses and our strengths. Although this will require time, persistence and patience, we'll ultimately be able to celebrate the adventure with a changed life.

Most of us don't like to look within ourselves for the same reason we don't like to open a letter that we know contains bad news. But remember that we need to keep our evaluation—our inventory—balanced. It's critical that it take into account both the good and the bad qualities that make us who we are. As you begin to work on your spiritual inventory in Principle Four, you need to look at several areas of your life. Before launching into this endeavor, pray this prayer: "Search me, God, and know my heart; test me and know my anxious thoughts" (Psalm 139:23).

The first area we need to evaluate is that of our relationships with others. In Matthew 6:12 – 14 Jesus instructs us to pray, "Forgive us our debts, as we also have forgiven our debtors. And lead us not into temptation, but deliver us from the evil one. For if you forgive other people when they sin against you, your heavenly Father will also forgive you." In this area of our spiritual inventory we explore our resentments and grudges, and we determine whether we're jealous of someone else. Take the time to evaluate whether you've been blaming others for your own ill-advised choices, and be sure to list those people you've hurt, been critical of or gossiped about.

The second area to explore is that of our priorities in life. We naturally do what's important to us. Others identify our priorities by our actions, not by our words. Matthew 6:33 tells us what will happen if we make God our number-one focus: "Seek first his kingdom and his righteousness, and all these things will be given to you as well." In this section, seek to identify those areas of your life in which you're still not putting God first. Notice whether or not your priorities have been self-centered or self-serving. Examine the possibility that misplaced priorities may have had a negative effect on those close to you.

The next area of our spiritual inventory involves examining our attitudes. Ephesians 4:31 counsels us to "get rid of all bitterness, rage and anger, brawling and slander, along with every form of malice." Look for areas of your life for which you're ungrateful. Reflect upon whether you've been easily angered by or sarcastic toward someone else. Explore why you're still fearful of certain people and situations.

The fourth area to look at in this part of our spiritual inventory is that of our integrity. In Colossians 3:9 – 10 we're instructed, "Do not lie to each other, since you have taken off your old self with its practices and have put on the new self, which is being renewed in knowledge in the image of its Creator." Look for areas in your life in which you've been dishonest; areas in which you may have exaggerated your own good qualities or achievements to make yourself look good. Examine whether or not you live one way in front of your Christian friends and another way at home or at work.

Take a Look:

- What do you see as the major reasons some of your relationships have been lost or are less than they could be?

- What are some of the positive priorities in your life? Which priorities do you need to change?

- How do you go about maintaining an "attitude of gratitude"?

- How would you rate your integrity? Do others trust you to follow through on your promises?

SPIRITUAL INVENTORY, PART 2

The cycle of unhealthful choices continues as our parents repeat to us some of the old-fashioned maxims their parents quoted to them: "You just have to pull yourself up by your bootstraps and go on." "It's our secret; nobody else needs to know." "God helps those who help themselves." "Let sleeping dogs lie." These pat answers can keep us from reaching out to get the help we need, while our hurts, hang-ups and habits only continue to escalate.

A man bears scars from his childhood due to years of physical abuse from his father. While growing up, a woman was subjected to her mother's rage. A family loses its home and cars because the father can't refrain from daily gambling. Through Internet contacts, a woman reunites with her high school sweetheart and becomes unfaithful to her husband.

Of course, no child ever deserves to be abused in any way. A young woman never willingly subjects herself to longwinded tirades from her mother. The family never expects to lose its home due to betting on horse races. And a husband never foresees his marital relationship being torn apart through the use of a computer.

Things have happened to each of us that we never wanted to happen. We didn't ask for physical abuse, rage, financial pitfalls or the loss of our possessions or relationships. But if we continue to keep our secrets, the cycle of unhealthful choices will continue into the next generation.

Our spiritual inventory can offer us freedom, perhaps for the first time in our lives. We have the unprecedented opportunity to share our secrets with safe people and can finally exempt ourselves from the unmerited guilt and shame we've carried for so long. In some instances we find ourselves able to acknowledge, particularly when we see the details in writing, that we carry no part of the blame for what has happened to us, that we had no responsibility for others' actions. With the obstacle of undeserved guilt and shame set aside, we're free to focus on other areas of our inventory. We can, for instance, concentrate on aspects of our lives in which we've blown it by making poor choices.

In Part 1 of our spiritual inventory we looked at our relationships with others, our priorities, our attitudes and our integrity. We evaluated ways in which our past actions in each of these areas had either a negative or a positive effect on our lives and the lives of others.

To complete our spiritual inventory, we need to examine shortcomings or sins that may be preventing God from working effectively in our lives and recoveries.

The fifth area we need to evaluate is that of our mind. Did you know that the most difficult thing to open is a closed mind? Romans 12:2 gives us clear direction regarding our minds: "Do not conform to the pattern of this world, but be transformed by the renewing of your mind. Then you will be able to test and approve what God's will is—his good, pleasing and perfect will." We need to acknowledge and examine ways in which our coping skills—our denial—may have protected us from pain and hurt in the past. Our denial may have afforded us protection, but it did so by preventing us from living in and dealing with reality. Have you filled your mind with hurtful and unhealthful movies, Internet sites, television programs, magazines or books? If so, it's possible that you've failed to concentrate on the positive truths of the Bible.

The next area to examine is our body. Satan works through our bodies, our flesh, but thank God that the believer's body is the temple of the Holy Spirit. God freely gives us the grace of his Spirit. He values us so highly, in fact, that he chose to place his Spirit within each of us. We owe it to our Creator to have as much respect for ourselves as he has for us. First Corinthians 6:19–20 asks, "Do you not know that your bodies are temples of the Holy Spirit, who is in you, whom you have received from God? You are not your own; you were bought at a price. Therefore honor God with your bodies."

The seventh area we need to examine is that of our family. Joshua, one of Israel's Old Testament leaders, made a bold statement regarding his household: "If serving the Lord seems undesirable to you, then choose for yourselves this day whom you will serve . . . But as for me and my household, we will serve the Lord" (Joshua 24:15). Perhaps you have physically or emotionally mistreated your family. Emotional abuse doesn't have to take the form of raging, yelling or screaming. Tearing down a child's or spouse's self-esteem and being emotionally unavailable to them are both ways in which you may have harmed your loved ones. God designed the family to be a safety net from life's storms. As much as it depends on us, we need to provide a haven for our family. If that isn't possible and you don't feel safe there, let Celebrate Recovery be your family.

The final area to explore in our spiritual inventory is that of our church. Hebrews 10:24–25 motivates us with these words: "Let us consider how we may spur one another on toward love and good deeds, not giving up meeting together, as some are in the habit of doing, but encouraging one another—and all the more as you see the Day approaching." Analyze whether or not you've been faithful to your church in the past. Your church is like a bank: The more you put into it, the more interest you gain. Determine whether you've been supportive or critical of your church. If you don't like something about it, get involved so you can help change it or at least understand it better. Replace your grumbling with service.

These are the eight different areas that will help you begin and complete your inventory. As you start to work on your spiritual inventory, remember two things. First, in Isaiah 1:18 God invites us: "Come now, let us settle the matter . . . Though your sins are like scarlet, they shall be as white as snow; though they are red as crimson, they shall be like wool." Second, keep your inventory balanced by listing not only the negatives but also the positives in your life. List your positive new relationships, the areas of your life you've been able to turn over to God, the improvement in your attitude since you've been in recovery and the ways in which you've been able to step out of your denial into God's truth.

Take a Look:

- In what ways do you try to fill your mind with the truth and with other positive thoughts?

- How have you mistreated your body in the past? How are you treating it today?

- How would you rate your relationship with your family? How can you improve it?

- Do you have a church home? Do you actively support it with your time, talents and treasures?

Once again, listen to Isaiah 1:18. Memorize it. God assures you that no matter how deep the stain of your sin he can remove it and make you as clean as freshly fallen snow.

A couple of reminders:

- Keep your inventory balanced. List your strengths along with your weaknesses.

- Find an accountability partner and/or a sponsor. The road to recovery isn't a journey to be made alone.

- God bless you as you courageously face and own your past. He *will* see you through!

CONFESS

As children, most of us kept secrets from our parents. If a neighbor's window was shattered by a baseball, we didn't tattle on our buddy. Although we knew we were failing a subject at school, we didn't come home and ask for more homework time. We didn't tell our parents we were dating the "bad boy" at school. And we conveniently never mentioned that there would be alcohol at the party.

Of course, one way or another, our parents usually found out. Punishment, guilt and shame followed—a cycle repeated throughout our childhood. Sometimes our parents already knew what we were up to but deliberately waited for us to come forward and tell them. We weren't really fooling them in the first place.

Some of us quickly learned that the punishment would be less severe if we confessed our misbehavior before our parents learned of it from some other source. Not only were the consequences less harsh, but we discovered that the guilt and shame were more manageable.

As we start to confess the mistakes and poor choices of our past, we begin to find a new freedom in our present. Taking responsibility for our behavior relieves the guilt and shame, and we become open to healing, reconciliation and restoration. We weren't really fooling God in the first place; he knows about our past, present and future and has been waiting for us to come forward and confess to him. Now we can begin to experience his unconditional love and forgiveness on a deeper level. Second Corinthians 5:19 tells us that "God was reconciling the world to himself in Christ, not counting people's sins against them. And he has committed to us the message of reconciliation."

After we've completed our inventories, we've finished the first part of Principle Four ("Openly examine . . ."). The second aspect of this principle takes us to our next step: to "confess my faults to myself, to God and to someone I trust." Confession means that we agree with God regarding our sins, and this consensus restores our fellowship. Principle Four sums up how we're to obey God's direction in confessing our sins. First, we own up to our sins before God so we can be forgiven. In 1 John 1:9 we're assured that "if we confess our sins, he is faithful and just and will forgive us our sins and purify us from all unrighteousness."

Then we confess our sins to someone else whom we trust so that we can begin the healing process. James 5:16 says, "Therefore confess your sins to each other and pray for each other so that you may be healed."

We may be afraid to share our inventory, the good and bad aspects of our past and present. But when we do, we find the peace and freedom for which we've been searching, perhaps for our entire life. We need to acknowledge our short-comings, resentments and sins. God wants us to come clean, to admit that wrong is wrong and that we're "guilty as charged." We need to own up, to confess the sins we've pinpointed in our inventory. We've been given incredible news in Romans 8:1: "Therefore, there is now no condemnation for those who are in Christ Jesus."

It has been said that "we are only as sick as our secrets." When we share our deepest secrets, we begin to divide the pain and the shame. A healthy sense of self-worth develops, a self-esteem that's no longer based on the world's standards but on the truth of Jesus Christ.

Pain is inevitable for all of us, but misery is optional. In fact, when we confess, the misery goes away. In Psalm 32:3 – 5 David recalls, "When I kept silent, my bones wasted away through my groaning all day long. For day and night your hand was heavy on me; my strength was sapped as in the heat of summer. Then I acknowledged my sin to you and did not cover up my iniquity. I said, 'I will confess my transgressions to the LORD.' And you forgave the guilt of my sin."

Take a Look:

- What secret are you holding on to that needs to be brought out into the light?

- What is holding you back from sharing your secrets and sins?

- Describe the feelings you experienced after you confessed a sin to God and to someone else.

- What does James 5:16 mean to you?

ADMIT

During a Celebrate Recovery seminar, a man approached a leader to express his frustration. He stated quite adamantly that he didn't need recovery. His pastor had paid for him to make the trip to "check out this Christian recovery thing," and he just didn't understand why he had been selected. The leader responded by explaining that everyone has a hurt, hang-up or habit and can find healing by working through the principles. The man angrily stomped away, convinced that he was wasting his day.

Weeks later, the man sent a message to the leader that began with three little words: "You were right." He went on to explain that the seminar had opened his eyes to the fact that he did have hurts, hang-ups and habits that he needed to face. He admitted that he had a problem with trying to control everyone in his family, his neighborhood, his workplace and his church. He took the first step to freedom by admitting his problems to another person. This took tremendous courage. As a result, this man worked through the principles and started a Celebrate Recovery program at his own church so that others could begin the healing process by admitting their secrets.

This courageous step of admitting our past, and especially our secrets, to another person as we complete our spiritual inventory will be the turning point in our recovery. As we complete Principle Four — "Openly examine and confess my faults to myself, to God and to someone I trust" — we'll begin to feel freedom from a past that has held us in bondage to our guilt and shame, and we'll look forward to completing the four remaining principles.

Like the man who attended the Celebrate Recovery seminar, many of us have been keeping secrets most of our lives. Every day those secrets take a toll on us: loss of self-respect and energy, as well as bondage to old, codependent habits. Admitting — out loud — those secrets strips them of their power. They lose much of their hold on us when they're verbalized.

Still, some of us are afraid to reveal our secrets to another person, even to someone we trust. We somehow feel as though we have everything to lose and nothing to gain by doing so. Are you aware, though, of what you really have to lose by telling your secrets and sins to another person?

1. Your sense of aloneness will begin to vanish. The isolation you've felt from God and others will start to disappear.

2. As you learn to forgive, the stranglehold you've felt from the people who have hurt you will begin to loosen. When people accept and forgive you, you'll start to see that you also can forgive others.

3. You'll lose your false pride. As you see and accept who you truly are, you'll begin to gain true humility, a byproduct of which is seeing God as he really is.

4. Being truthful with another person will tear away at your denial. You'll begin to feel clean and honest.

Now that you know what you have to lose by admitting your wrongs to another, note the following three benefits you stand to gain:

1. You'll gain the healing the Bible promises. James 5:16 instructs each of us to "confess your sins to each other and pray for each other so that you may be healed." The key word here is "healed." Notice that the verse doesn't say, "Confess your sins to one another and you will be forgiven." God forgave you already when you confessed your sins to him. Now he tells you that you'll begin the healing process when you confess your sins to someone else.

2. You'll gain freedom. Your secrets have kept you in chains — bound, frozen, unable to move forward in your relationships with God and others. Admitting your sins snaps the chains so that God's healing power can take effect. "Openness is to wholeness as secrets are to sickness." Psalm 107:13 recounts: "Then they cried to the LORD in their trouble, and he saved them from their distress." God snapped their chains and he can snap yours too.

3. You'll gain real friends and support. When you share your inventory with another person, you invite their support. They can help you stay focused and provide feedback. When your old friend "denial" surfaces and you hear Satan's list of excuses — "It's really not that bad"; "They deserved it"; "It really wasn't your fault" — your support team can be there to challenge you with the truth. But most of all, you need another person simply to listen and hear what you have to say.

Considering what you have to lose and to gain by sharing your inventory with God and another person, you can see that there's really nothing to fear.

Take a Look:

- What's holding you back from sharing your Principle Four inventory?
- How do the above lists — the four things you have to lose and the three things you have to gain by sharing your inventory — help you want to complete Principle Four?
- If you've already shared your inventory, what are some negative things you've lost?
- If you've already shared your inventory, what are some positive things you've gained?

READY

Families often celebrate special days and holidays with traditions that have been passed down from generation to generation. Attempting to keep prior traditions consistent for both families, a young couple traveled to the home of each of their parents for the holidays. However, the situation was particularly complicated at Christmas. Each set of parents went to church on Christmas Eve and opened presents on Christmas morning. The young couple couldn't be at two different places at the same time. Hurt feelings always seemed to be the result of their good intentions to honor their families' traditions.

In order to help this young couple, one of the families expressed a willingness to change some of their time-honored customs. After some experimentation, they discovered that some of their traditions were important enough to keep the same, while others could be changed or dropped altogether. They even added some new activities to their holiday celebrations.

By allowing God into every area of our lives, we demonstrate our willingness to change, allowing him free rein to remove our character defects. This readiness requires our ultimate surrender and involves some pain and resistance. Some of our old habits can stay the same, other coping mechanisms can be changed and still other behaviors must be dropped completely. Such nonproductive, habitual behaviors can be replaced with new and better activities. For example, instead of devoting time to our old hang-ups, compulsions and obsessions, we can attend recovery meetings and church activities and volunteer for service.

This is what Principle Five is all about: "Voluntarily submit to every change God wants to make in my life and humbly ask him to remove my character defects." When you're ready to start working the fifth principle, congratulations are definitely in order. You've already made some major progress on your road to recovery. You admitted that you had a problem that you were powerless to change; you came to believe that God could and would help you; you sought him and turned your life and will over to his care and direction; and you wrote a spiritual inventory and shared it both with God and with another person. You've been busy. That's a lot of work — hard work.

Maybe you're thinking it's about time to take a breather and relax for a while. Think again. In some secular recovery material, Step Six (which relates to

Principle Five) has been referred to as the step "that separates the men from the boys." One of the reasons Step Six is so powerful is its assertion that "we were entirely *ready* to have God remove all these defects of character" (emphasis added). This process takes time, but God is true to his word, and he has promised, "Commit your way to the LORD; trust in him and he will do this" (Psalm 37:5).

Most, if not all, of us would be more than willing to leave behind certain character defects. The sooner the better. But let's face it: Some defects are hard to give up. An alcoholic may hit bottom and be ready to stop drinking. But is she ready to stop lying? To stop being greedy? To let go of resentments? These defects of character have been with us for a long time. Like weeds in a garden, they've developed roots. We've formed our defects of character, our hang-ups and habits over periods of ten, twenty, thirty or more years. In this principle you and God—together—are going after these defects. All of them.

We need to remember that sin is the *symptom* of a character defect. That sin is like a weed in a garden: It will keep reappearing unless it's pulled out by the roots—the actual character defect that *caused* the particular sin or allowed it to happen. A sex addict's major sin may have been cheating on his wife. That was the act. The defect of character was his lack of a positive self-image. When he worked Principle Five, he went after the defect that caused him to sin by having affairs.

God is amazingly patient. Recall that, as explained in Principle Three, he didn't impose his will on us but waited for us to invite him in. Now, in Principle Five, we need to be "entirely ready"; we need to be willing to let God into every area of our life. He won't come in and clean up an area unless we invite him in.

It has been said that "willingness is the key that goes into the lock and opens the door that allows God to begin to remove your character defects." Psalm 143:10 invites, "Teach me to do your will, for you are my God; may your good Spirit lead me on level ground."

Take a Look:

- What are some character defects you're more than ready to give up?
- What are some character defects that will be harder for you to let go of?
- Can you explain the difference, specifically, between your character defects and your sins?
- In Psalm 143:10, what does "level ground" mean to you?

VICTORY

The world bombards us with the message that accomplishments are more noteworthy if they've been achieved quickly. The preadolescent athlete is heralded for her performance because we're amazed at what she has managed to accomplish in such a short time. The piano prodigy is applauded because he is so young to have perfected his craft. However quickly an accomplishment might appear to have come, though, we do realize that those kinds of successes were the result of hours and weeks and months and years of practice and dedication.

A frail, thin young woman hesitatingly slipped into the back of the Celebrate Recovery meeting. Her arms wrapped tightly around her, she began crying as soon as the music started. With eyes downcast, she walked quickly to the door as soon as the large group meeting ended. An older woman gently approached her, walked with her to the Newcomers' group, and invited her to join her during the fellowship coffee time after the group ended.

Three years later, with her head held high and a beautiful smile on her face, that same young woman gave her testimony of child abuse and a struggle with anorexia in front of three thousand people at a Celebrate Recovery summit. She shared the victory of her changed life — a changed life that had begun by simply attending that first meeting. She looked affectionately at the older woman who had become her sponsor. Her testimony included the long and difficult process of working through the principles, being willing to humble herself so she could ask for help, and surrounding herself with others who could share her pain. Her hurts, hang-ups and habits hadn't developed overnight, and she shared that they weren't instantly removed. But the victory of a changed life was worth the three years' journey of recovery.

Principle Five calls upon each of us to "voluntarily submit to every change God wants to make in my life and humbly ask him to remove my character defects." It's not a quick fix. It takes time, humility, prayer and a whole lot of effort. You're at the place in your recovery where you say, "I don't want to live this way anymore. I want to get rid of my hurts, hang-ups and habits. But how do I do it?" The good news is that you don't have to do it.

Notice that Principle Five doesn't read, "Voluntarily submit to every change I want to make in my life." No, it says, "Voluntarily submit to every change God wants to make in my life." You're asking *God* to make every change in you that he wants to make.

God doesn't just want you to admit your wrongs; he wants to make you right. He wants to give you a hope and a future. God doesn't just want to forgive you; he wants to change you. He wants to give you victory over your defects of character.

So how do you begin the process of having God make the positive changes in your life that you and he both desire? First, ask God to remove those character defects that are causing you the most pain. Be specific. "In their hearts humans plan their course," a wise man once noted, "but the LORD establishes their steps" (Proverbs 16:9).

When you start to regret the past or fear the future, look to Exodus 3:14, where God identifies himself as "I AM." When you live in the past with its mistakes and regrets, life is hard. You can invite God to go back there to heal you and forgive your sins. But God doesn't say, "My name is 'I was.'" He says, "My name is 'I AM.'"

When you try to live in the future, with its unknown problems and fears, life is hard. Take comfort in knowing that God will be with you when that day comes. But God doesn't say, "My name is 'I will be.'" He says, "My name is 'I AM.'"

When you live in the present, in this single moment in time, one day at a time, life isn't so hard. Jesus promised us in Matthew 11:28–30, "Come to me, all you who are weary and burdened, and I will give you rest. Take my yoke upon you and learn from me, for I am gentle and humble in heart, and you will find rest for your souls. For my yoke is easy and my burden is light."

Once you ask God to remove your character defects, you begin a journey that will lead you to new freedom from your past. Don't look for perfection; instead, rejoice in steady progress. Seek patient improvement. Hear these words of encouragement from God's Word: "Being confident of this, that he who began a good work in you will carry it on to completion until the day of Christ Jesus" (Philippians 1:6). Now that's victory.

Take a Look:

- Are you ready to submit to all the changes God wants to make in you?
- How can your accountability partners support and encourage you to achieve victory over your defects of character?
- How does understanding Exodus 3:14 help you to work Principle Five?
- Why is it important to seek steady progress and patient improvement while working this principle?

AMENDS

Three of the hardest words in the English language are "I am sorry." We usually know well enough who deserves to hear those words from us and when we should say them, but finding the courage and the willingness to verbalize them can take us hours, weeks or even years. On the other hand, we often self-righteously expect someone else to make their amends immediately after we've been made to feel hurt or betrayed.

After 40 years of a turbulent life together, an older couple began attending Celebrate Recovery in one last attempt to save their marriage. Hopeless that anything could improve their relationship, they nonetheless each committed to a step study and to working through the participant's guides. While sitting in the backyard one evening, the wife began working on an especially difficult question in her workbook. As she thought of an errand she needed to run the next day, she groped about for a scrap of paper to write herself a reminder. Noticing a notebook on the patio table, she opened it to begin writing, only to find the words seeming to jump off the paper. Without forethought, she found herself reading through her husband's commentary on the fourth step—his spiritual inventory.

When her husband returned that evening, she immediately confessed to having read his journal. Although she knew she had invaded his privacy, she was so hurt by the entries she had read that she wasn't willing or able to ask for forgiveness. The husband was worried that the secrets he'd recorded would only further alienate his wife. However, he was also furious and unwilling to apologize for his past actions.

Although the couple wasn't able to ask for or offer forgiveness immediately, they both contacted their sponsors and accountability partners to ask for prayer for the mending of their relationship. Within the next few months both the wife and the husband did make their amends and offer their forgiveness to one another.

They worked Principle Six: "Evaluate all my relationships. Offer forgiveness to those who have hurt me and make amends for harm I've done to others, except when to do so would harm them or others." Principle Six is all about making amends. "Forgive me as I learn to forgive" sums it up pretty well.

We started doing repair work on the personal side of our life earlier in our recovery by admitting our powerlessness, turning our life and will over to God's care, doing our moral inventory, sharing our sins or wrongs with another, admitting our shortcomings and asking God to remove them. Now we begin to do repair work on the relational side of our life. Making our amends is the beginning of the end of our isolation from God and others.

Yet some of us balk at making our amends, reasoning, If God has forgiven me, isn't that enough? Why should I drag up the past? The answer to that objection is simple: Making amends isn't about our past so much as it is about our future. Before we can have the healthy relationships we desire, we need to clean out the guilt, shame and pain that have caused many of our past relationships to fail. In Luke 6:31 our Lord instructs us to "do to others as you would have them do to you." That verse reminds us to treat others the way we'd like to be treated. For some of us that may be extremely difficult. We've been badly hurt or abused and may have had no responsibility for the wrong committed against us. The first part of Principle Six — "Evaluate all my relationships" — deals with our willingness to consider forgiveness. The second part of Principle Six calls us to action as we make our amends and offer our forgiveness. Going back to the garden metaphor, we need to pull out all the dead weeds in our past broken relationships so that we can clear a place where our new relationships can be successfully planted and our old relationships restored. That's why Principle Six is so important.

Remember Christ's instruction from Matthew 5:23–24:

> *If you are offering your gift at the altar and there remember that*
> *your brother or sister has something against you,*
> *leave your gift there in front of the altar. First go and be reconciled*
> *to them; then come and offer your gift.*

Jesus Christ will help us say both "I'm sorry" and "I forgive you."

Take a Look:

- How and why have you had trouble saying "I'm sorry" or "I forgive you" in the past?

- How has holding back from making your amends and offering your forgiveness affected your important relationships (past and present)?

- How can you become more willing to make your amends and offer your forgiveness?

- What does Matthew 5:23–24 mean to you?

FORGIVENESS

Appearances can be deceiving. Many of us have spent a lifetime creating the mask that we wear out in public. We want people to respond to us in a certain way based on the mask we wear. For example, if we project a loving mother to the world, we hope to be treated tenderly. If our mask is one of a ruthless corporate executive, we expect others' response to be fear. But the real purpose of our masks is to safeguard our hurts, hang-ups and habits so that people can't get to know the "real us."

A large, unsmiling man sat in the back row of a Celebrate Recovery conference. He was covered with tattoos, sported a variety of earrings in each ear and wore a black leather vest and boots and a red bandana around his head and neck. Throughout the day the man sat with his back erect and his arms folded across his massive chest, never once participating in the discussion. He just stared at the speakers with a piercing expression in his eyes.

At the end of the day, one of the speakers hesitatingly approached him to ask whether he had any questions and to learn about any objections he might have. With tears streaming down his face, the man responded simply, "I love everything you said about this program, and I think it could change my life and the members of our congregation. But I just don't think God would use me, with all the sins of my past, to begin this program at our church."

This man needed to accept forgiveness by acknowledging what Jesus did on the cross for him (Jesus exclaimed from the cross, "It is finished"; John 19:30). No matter how grievously this individual may have injured others or himself, he needed to hear and accept that God's grace is always sufficient and his forgiveness is always complete. Romans 3:22 – 24 says, "This righteousness is given through faith in Jesus Christ to all who believe. There is no difference between Jew and Gentile, for all have sinned and fall short of the glory of God, and all are justified freely by his grace through the redemption that came by Christ Jesus."

In recovery, we can put aside our masks once and for all and allow people to get to know the "real us." We do that by completing Principle Six: "Evaluate all my relationships. Offer forgiveness to those who have hurt me and make amends for harm I've done to others, except when to do so would harm them or others."

Forgiveness is clearly God's prescription for the broken. No matter how dreadful the offense or abuse, along the path to healing lies forgiveness.

We all need to learn to ask for and accept God's forgiveness. In addition, we all need to model his forgiveness with respect to ourselves before we can begin to truly forgive others and experience God's love. Self-forgiveness isn't a matter of assigning the blame to someone else and letting ourselves off the hook. Nor is it a license for irresponsibility. It's simply an acknowledgment that we're human, just like everybody else, and that we've reached the stage in our recovery where we're able to give ourselves greater respect.

This breaks the cycle. It doesn't settle all the questions about blame, justice or fairness, but it does allow relationships to heal and possibly even start afresh. This is the essence of God's invitation in Isaiah 1:18: " 'Come now, let us settle the matter,' says the LORD. 'Though your sins are like scarlet, they shall be as white as snow; though they are red as crimson, they shall be like wool.' "

As we take the necessary steps of forgiveness, we'll discover that we're letting go of the guilt and shame. We'll be able to acknowledge, "I'm not perfect, but Christ is. God and I are still working on me. I still fall down, but with my Savior's help, I can get up, brush myself off and try again."

By offering our forgiveness we can't change our past — but we most definitely can brighten our future.

Take a Look:

- Is there something you did in the past that's still making you feel unlovable today? Have you turned it over to God and done what Principle Six asks you to do?

- Can you recall specific examples of the freedom you felt when you forgave someone else for hurting you?

- How does Romans 3:22 – 24 help you to accept God's forgiveness in your life?

- How will offering your forgiveness to others change your future?

GRACE

Sitting in church while dealing with a hurt, hang-up or habit can be a lonely experience. We look around at the neatly dressed couples with their immaculate children and feel as though we're the only ones experiencing struggles in life. Even though we've read the Bible over and over again looking for the answers and have attended all of the classes offered by the church, our lives are far from perfect.

The pastor of a large church spent eight weeks preaching about the principles of recovery. Each week the message concluded with a testimony from a member of Celebrate Recovery. Week after week, as the testimonies were shared, the congregation responded by crying in empathy, groaning in grief or sitting in stunned silence. Understanding that the testimonies had begun to change the congregation, the pastor wanted to conclude the sermon series with communion served by participants in Celebrate Recovery.

The men and women from the recovery leadership team served the communion elements with tears streaming down their faces. As they passed one another in the aisles, they patted each other on the back or clasped hands. Each of them had experienced the loneliness of a hurt, hang-up or habit, and now they were serving communion in a church that had become a safe place for people willing to own up to their less-than-perfect lives. Later that day each of the participants expressed profound gratitude for being able to serve in a church that modeled forgiveness.

People who become committed to Celebrate Recovery have often been away from church for a long time, if they've ever attended at all. Many are discovering Jesus Christ for the first time in their lives. They know they need a safe place to heal from the wounds of their past, a safe context in which to work on forgiving themselves and, most important, a safe setting in which to experience the grace and forgiveness of Christ.

The key verses of Celebrate Recovery are 2 Corinthians 12:9 – 10:

He said to me, "My grace is sufficient for you, for my power is made perfect
in weakness." Therefore I will boast all the more gladly about my weaknesses,
so that Christ's power may rest on me. That is why, for Christ's sake,
I delight in weaknesses, in insults, in hardships, in persecutions,
in difficulties. For when I am weak, then I am strong.

As we grow, both as Christians and in our recovery, we want to follow the guidance and direction of Jesus Christ. As we get to know him better, we're anxious to model his teachings and his ways. We want to become more like him. Principle Six says: "Evaluate all my relationships. Offer forgiveness to those who have hurt me and make amends for harm I've done to others, except when to do so would harm them or others." To implement this principle to the best of our ability, we need to learn to model God's grace.

Celebrate Recovery is built on and centered in Christ's grace and love for each of us. Grace is a gift. It can't be bought but is freely given by God to us. When we offer (give) our amends and expect nothing back, we are giving a gift to those whom we've hurt.

First Peter 1:13 directs us, "Therefore, with minds that are alert and fully sober, set your hope on the grace to be brought to you when Jesus Christ is revealed." If our relationship with God were dependent on our being perfect, we would have trouble relating to God most — no, actually, *all* — of the time. Thank God that our relationship with him is built instead on his grace and love for us. He alone gives us the strength to make our amends and to offer the forgiveness that Principle Six requires.

We can love others only because God first loved us. It follows that we can also forgive others because God first forgave us. Colossians 3:13 instructs us to "bear with each other and forgive one another if any of you has a grievance against someone. Forgive as the Lord forgave you."

Each of us who has invited Jesus Christ into our lives is a product of God's grace. As we model this grace, we'll be able to do the work Principle Six requires.

Take a Look:

- Where have you found a safe place to experience the grace and forgiveness of Christ?

- Describe the feeling of liberation you experience when you offer your forgiveness to another person.

- In what ways are you modeling God's grace to others?

- What does being a product of God's grace mean to you?

CROSSROADS

Being punctual is really a struggle for some of us. One young woman regularly leaves her house precisely at the time when she is supposed to arrive at a given function. As a result, she is habitually late for work, school—even dates. This pattern is a source of frustration to all those who are close to her. If there's an important occasion, her family solves the problem by telling her that the event is to take place an hour prior to the actual starting time.

This young woman has been in Celebrate Recovery working through other pressing issues. She has faced her denial, surrendered her life to Jesus Christ and completed an honest inventory by listing, confessing and sharing all of her wrongdoings as well as the wrongs that have been done to her. After she became willing to make amends and offer forgiveness, God made major changes in her life. In fact, she has come such a long way on her recovery journey that she probably doesn't feel that her tendency toward tardiness is any big deal.

By this time in our journey, many of us haven't had a drink in years, no longer surf the Internet for porn sites, haven't lost our temper in months, or have been diligently following our budget. We've turned over our lives to Jesus Christ and find that they've truly been changed.

But we're human beings. We're going to have some great days, and we're going to have some not-so-great—okay, even awful—days. Our inventories aren't a closed book. We need to keep journaling. It's important to keep track of the things we're doing well, and it's equally necessary for us to evaluate the areas in our lives that still need improvement. By journaling, we can look for troublesome patterns—like this young woman's lack of punctuality—that call for additional work.

Even an issue as minor as being late for a luncheon appointment can cause someone else a hurt that deserves our amends. Promptly. Not tomorrow. Today. Maybe right now.

When we get to Principle Seven—"Reserve a daily time with God for self-examination, Bible reading and prayer in order to know God and his will for my life and to gain the power to follow his will"—we've come to an important junction on our road to recovery. We're at the crossroads of our journey.

This isn't a place to stop and rest on our past accomplishments. We need to thank God for getting us this far on our road to recovery, to praise him for the many victories we've experienced over our hurts, hang-ups and habits while we were working the first six principles. But we also need to continue working Principles Seven and Eight with the same devotion and enthusiasm that got us to this point in our recoveries.

First Corinthians 10:12 puts it this way: "If you think you are standing firm, be careful that you don't fall!" Most recovery material refers to Steps Ten through Twelve (Principles Seven and Eight) as the "maintenance steps." But Principles Seven and Eight are much more than mere maintenance. They involve much more than just preserving the progress we've already made in our recoveries. It's in implementing these principles that your recovery, your new way of living, really takes off, bearing the fruit of all the changes God and you have been working on together. It's in Principles Seven and Eight that you'll live out your recovery for the remainder of your time here on this earth — one day at a time!

The first part of Principle Seven — "Reserve a daily time with God for self-examination" — relates to Step Ten of the Christ-centered 12 Steps: "We continued to take personal inventory and, when we were wrong, promptly admitted it." In order to successfully work the first part of Principle Seven, we need to do the following on a daily basis:

- Take the time to do a daily inventory.
- Evaluate the good and the bad choices we've made that day.
- Admit our wrongs promptly.

John 3:21 states that "whoever lives by the truth comes into the light." Principle Seven brings us, on a daily basis, into that light. Once we've seen the light, we have only two choices: We can either ignore it or act upon it.

Take a Look:

- What are some of the poor choices you're continuing to make that are negatively affecting yourself and/or others?
- What are some new, positive choices you've made today?
- Do you have difficulty admitting your wrongs promptly? Why or why not?
- Express in your own words what John 3:21 means to you.

DAILY INVENTORY

How easily we justify our rudeness toward others. We're too busy to say "thank you" to the clerk in the mall. Our waitress took too long to refill our drinks, so we brusquely order without a "please." Loving our neighbor as ourselves simply doesn't apply to the man next door with the incessantly barking dogs.

In the middle of the night, a pastor was whisked away to the emergency room and promptly admitted into the hospital. His nervous wife, adult children and a long line of friends followed the pastor and the admitting nurse into the examining room. The nurse turned to the group and announced sternly, "Patient only; everyone else must go to the waiting room." As the friends left the room, the shaken family informed the nurse in no uncertain terms that no one was going to make them leave, saying, "We'll go to management if you try to make us leave our dad," and "We want to make sure somebody takes care of him."

As the nurse was asking the patient about his medical history, she questioned him about his occupation. The pastor lovingly glanced toward his wife and children and proudly announced that he had changed careers and was currently serving in ministry at a large, local church. The tension dissipated as the questionnaire was completed.

The nurse left the room to finish her duties, and the pastor's wife quickly followed. She sincerely apologized for the family's impulsive rudeness. The nurse, in turn, expressed regret for her severity and explained that she had never intended for the family to leave. She had simply felt it to be in the interest of the pastor to ask the many anxious friends to wait elsewhere. Through this brief interchange, a strong bond of mutual respect was formed between the two women. Throughout the pastor's hospital stay, the nurse regularly updated the family about the tests, insisted that the wife and children rest, brought them coffee and, even when assigned to a different ward, spent her breaks checking in on the pastor and his family.

As you complete each day, you can get into the habit of asking your Higher Power, Jesus Christ, whether or not your actions throughout the course of the day displayed love for your neighbors. Principle Seven will dramatically change both you and your relationships.

As you work Principle Seven — "Reserve a daily time with God for self-examination, Bible reading and prayer in order to know God and his will for my life and to gain the power to follow his will" — you'll begin the journey of applying what you've discovered in the first six principles. You'll live each day humbly — in reality, not in denial. You've done your best to amend your past. With God's guidance, you can now make choices about the emotions that will affect your thinking and behavior. You start to take *action* — positive action — instead of being stuck in a cycle of constant *reaction*.

In Principle Seven we desire to grow daily in our new relationship with Jesus Christ and in our relationships with others. Instead of attempting to be in control of every situation and every person with whom we come into contact, or spinning out of control ourselves, we're starting to exhibit self-control — to act and respond in the way God wants us to. Remember that "self under control" is our immediate aim but that our ultimate goal is self under *God's* control.

Jesus has provided us with a daily checklist for our new lifestyle. It's called the "Great Commandment," and it's found in Matthew 22:37 – 39: " 'Love the Lord your God with all your heart and with all your soul and with all your mind.' This is the first and greatest commandment. And the second is like it: 'Love your neighbor as yourself.' "

As you daily live out these two commandments by putting Principle Seven into action in your life, you'll become more and more like Christ. You'll become a doer of God's Word, not just a passive hearer. James 1:22 instructs us: "Do not merely listen to the word, and so deceive yourselves. Do what it says." Your actions need to be consistent with your talk. *You,* after all, may be the only "Bible" someone else ever sees or hears. How does it feel to view yourself as a real-life "Living Bible"? That's how the apostle Paul lived. As he expressed in 1 Thessalonians 1:5, "Our gospel came to you not simply with words, but also with power, with the Holy Spirit and with deep conviction. You know how we lived among you for your sake." Others need to see God's truth reflected in your life.

That can happen only if you spend time daily:

- with God completing your inventory;
- reading the Bible;
- praying in order to know God and his will for your life.

Take a Look:

- When did you last go out of your way to thank someone else? Do others see God's truth reflected in your life?

- When has the practice of taking your daily inventory helped you in terms of your relationships?

- Do you build into your daily schedule a "quiet time" to read your Bible, pray and spend moments alone with God? What has God taught you in the past week?

- What does James 1:22 mean to you? How are you functioning as a "doer" of God's Word?

RELAPSE

After years of eating the wrong foods and failing to exercise, it's not unusual for someone to be rushed to the hospital for heart bypass surgery. After the surgery, pain and fear are foremost in the patient's mind. The family begins to relax, though, as the patient "turns over a new leaf," establishing new priorities of eating nutritious foods, exercising and getting proper rest.

Unfortunately, it's not unusual for loved ones to watch helplessly as the heart attack patient gradually returns to his former lifestyle. Time restraints make it difficult, he insists, to keep up the daily walking regimen, and unhealthy foods begin to slip back into his diet. A second heart attack and surgery may be the result of giving up the components of a healthier lifestyle. Those of us on the sidelines find it difficult to understand why someone would be so careless about the health of their own body.

We can often effectively break the cycle of our dysfunctions or compulsions by working our recovery programs for months or even years. But gradually, we may become complacent about the practices and safeguards that have helped us achieve our success. Meetings get skipped, we stop writing in our journal, and we lose touch with our accountability partners and sponsors. Much to our surprise, after years of success, we relapse back into our old hurts, hang-ups and habits.

Working Principle Seven — "Reserve a daily quiet time with God for self-examination, Bible reading and prayer in order to know God and his will for my life and to gain the power to follow his will" — is our best defense against a relapse.

The first step in preventing a relapse is to admit to ourselves that we will be tempted, that we're not above temptation. Jesus wasn't, so why should we be? Take the time to read the full account of Jesus' temptation in Matthew 4:1–11.

The end of the story: When the test was over, the devil left. Jesus had been tempted, but he hadn't succumbed. Throughout his entire earthly life, God's Son never once sinned, though the temptation he endured was as real as any we've struggled through. Mark 14:38 directs each of us to "watch and pray so that you will not fall into temptation. The spirit is willing, but the flesh is weak." Keep in mind that being tempted isn't a sin. It's falling into the action the temptation invites that gets us into trouble. No, temptation isn't a sin; it's a call to battle. When we're tempted to fall back into our old hurts, hang-ups and habits, we need to confront Satan as emphatically as Jesus did in Matthew 4:10: "Away from me, Satan! For it is written: 'Worship the Lord your God, and serve him only.'"

When you find yourself being tempted, stop and do a HEART check, asking yourself, Am I:

> **H**urting?
>
> **E**xhausted?
>
> **A**ngry?
>
> **R**esentful?
>
> **T**ense?

If you answer yes to any of the above, use the tools you've learned in recovery to help get yourself back on track. Call your sponsor or accountability partners immediately and work Principle Seven.

Take a Look:

- When was the last time you remember being tempted? If you were able to resist, how did you do it?

- How can working Principle Seven help prevent a relapse in your recovery?

- What does Mark 14:38 mean to you?

- Take a moment right now to do a HEART check. Are you **H**urting, **E**xhausted, **A**ngry, **R**esentful or **T**ense? How does it help to know when you're vulnerable to temptation?

GRATITUDE

It's so easy to fall into the trap of wanting what others have. That old adage about "keeping up with the Joneses" still holds true. We want our neighbor's new car, we envy our best friend's beauty, a larger house would make us happier, and things would be so much better if our spouse were just more attentive. We can go for a long time without taking an account of the things in our lives for which we're grateful.

A newlywed couple spent some of their hard-earned money on annual passes to a local amusement park. The new husband frequently asked friends to join them on these visits to distract his wife with shopping while he left for a short time with his buddies to have a few beers. A couple of hours later, hoping she hadn't missed him, he would join his wife to ride the attractions.

Five years later, the young couple decided to purchase annual passes to the same amusement park as anniversary gifts to one another. The young man had spent the last two years in Celebrate Recovery, and the visit to the amusement park brought back memories of drinking with his friends. As he rode the rides with his two young daughters and visited the shops with his wife, he found himself mouthing prayers of gratitude. He was so thankful to his Higher Power, Jesus Christ, that his children would never have to see him drink.

The recovery journey isn't always easy, and we're wise to make it a point to celebrate our successes along our road to recovery. Developing a "gratitude list" is a good way to remind ourselves that we've made progress in our recovery, that God has changed our lives and that Jesus Christ is always with us.

Our prayers of gratitude can focus on four specific areas of our life: God, others, our recovery and our church. Write them down and keep your "gratitude list" in your journal or leave it in some conspicuous location, such as on your refrigerator door. Keep the ever-changing list in a place where you'll regularly see it and can easily add your new victories to it.

First, for what are you thankful to God? Offer prayers of gratitude to your Creator. In Philippians 4:6 we're directed, "Do not be anxious about anything, but in every situation, by prayer and petition, with thanksgiving, present your requests to God." Psalm 107:15 encourages us to "give thanks to the LORD for his unfailing love and his wonderful deeds for mankind." And, truly, what wonderful deeds they are! Identify at least two areas of your life in which you can see God's hand at work in your recovery. You can reflect on the past year or on what God has done for you this week or even as recently as today. Then take a moment to jot down just a few of the special things for which you're thankful to your Higher Power.

Second, list the individuals God has placed in your life to walk alongside you on your road of recovery. In Colossians 3:15 – 16 the apostle Paul calls us as Christians to "let the peace of Christ rule in your hearts, since as members of one body you were called to peace. And be thankful. Let the message of Christ dwell among you richly as you teach and admonish one another with all wisdom through psalms, hymns, and songs from the Spirit, singing to God with gratitude in your hearts." Who are you thankful for? How have these special people helped you? Take a moment to acknowledge them by jotting down their names.

Third, be thankful for your recovery. "Therefore," said the author of Hebrews, "since we are surrounded by such a great cloud of witnesses, let us throw off everything that hinders and the sin that so easily entangles. And let us run with perseverance the race marked out for us" (Hebrews 12:1). List two recent areas of growth in your recovery for which you're thankful.

Fourth, express gratitude for your church. "Enter his gates with thanksgiving and his courts with praise; give thanks to him and praise his name" (Psalm 100:4). For what two things about your church are you particularly grateful?

Gratitude is a major component of Principle Seven: "Reserve a daily time with God for self-examination, Bible reading and prayer in order to know God and his will for my life and to gain the power to follow his will." If you start off each day by expressing your thanks, more often than not you'll have a pretty good day — a reasonably happy day. This is the best way to choose to live your life "one day at a time."

Take a Look:

- Why is maintaining an "attitude of gratitude" important to your recovery?
- What is holding you back from developing your gratitude list?
- How does your "attitude of gratitude" affect your relationships?
- How does a reasonably happy day look and feel to you?

GIVE

Our time is precious to us. When our children's teachers ask for help, we're quick to send supplies rather than volunteer our time in the classroom. If a distant relative moves into a nursing home, it's easier to send cards than to visit. We know we need to give to our church, but it's much easier throwing money into the offering basket than devoting our time and energy to teaching church school.

For ten years, a Celebrate Recovery volunteer has faithfully worked behind the scenes for the Barbeque Fellowship time and the coffee shop. Without much advance notice, he has repeatedly purchased hot dogs, chicken, beans, salads and desserts. When asked how many hot dogs he thinks he has supplied over the years, he laughs and replies, "Too many thousands to count." In addition to purchasing the supplies, he hauls them to the storage area and completes a weekly inventory to help maintain the shopping list. He arranges his work schedule and vacations so that he doesn't miss a week. And as if that weren't enough, for the annual Celebrate Recovery conferences, he has purchased enough supplies to feed 3,000 attendees at one time.

Grocery shopping hardly brings a standing ovation from participants of Celebrate Recovery, and this particular volunteer likes it that way. He doesn't want anyone to single him out as an exceptional servant. He knows that it takes a team of dedicated servants to plan the program, answer questions at the information table, greet newcomers, set up and clean up. By serving in his quiet manner, he clearly demonstrates his love for Christ by giving back to others.

This man is a living example of what Principle Eight is all about: "Yield myself to God to be used to bring this good news to others, both by my example and by my words." In God's ledger all services rank the same. In fact, Jesus tells us in Matthew 10:42, "If anyone gives even a cup of cold water to one of these little ones who is my disciple, truly I tell you, that person will certainly not lose their reward."

Principle Eight doesn't tell you to give in unhealthy ways, in ways that would hurt you or cause you to relapse into your old, codependent behaviors. No, Principle Eight is talking about healthy, non-codependent giving of oneself without expecting to receive anything in return. Remember that no person has ever been honored for what he or she has received. Honor has always been a reward for what a person has given.

Matthew 10:8 neatly sums up Principle Eight: "Freely you have received, freely give." God never, ever wastes a hurt! In fact, he can take your hurts and use them to help others. Principle Eight gives you the opportunity to share your experiences, victories and hopes with others. Remember what you've learned about the Lord through your personal experiences with him. You can start off by saying, "This is how it was for me; this is the *experience* I went through. This is how I gained the *strength* to begin my recovery, and there's definitely *hope* for you."

Second Corinthians 1:3–4 encourages us to praise "the God and Father of our Lord Jesus Christ, the Father of compassion and the God of all comfort, who comforts us in all our troubles, so that we can comfort those in any trouble with the comfort we ourselves receive from God."

All the pain the years of your hurts, hang-ups and habits have caused, all the destruction you may have brought upon yourself and those you love — it all finally makes sense when you begin to live out Principle Eight. You finally come to understand Romans 8:28: "We know that in all things God works for the good of those who love him, who have been called according to his purpose."

The Lord spreads his message through the eight principles and the Christ-centered twelve steps. We're the instruments he uses for delivering the good news. The way we live will demonstrate to others our commitment to our Lord, to our recovery program and to them.

Luke 8:16 points out that "no one lights a lamp and hides it in a clay jar or puts it under a bed. Instead, they put it on a stand, so that those who come in can see the light."

Principle Eight calls us to joyfully share the good news.

Take a Look:

- Express in your own words what 2 Corinthians 1:3–4 means to you.
- In what way(s) are you setting aside some of your precious time to serve and reach out to others?
- In living out Principle Eight, does your example match your words?
- In what ways are you allowing God to use you to spread the good news to others?

YES

How many times have we learned and relearned the lesson that we have to be careful how we respond when we're asked to do something? If we say yes too quickly, we find that we must somehow set aside the precious time needed to complete the requested task or disappoint someone else by failing to get the job done. The husband of a codependent wife asked her to attach a sticker with the word *no* to every telephone in the house. When someone called to ask for help, he wanted her to read the note on the phone and at least consider turning the caller down.

A Celebrate Recovery group in a small church in a rural town has a unique way of helping one another with their testimonies. Many members of the church have had little schooling and can't express themselves well in writing. The first step in the writing process is for two of the more educated women to interview the person who is ready to give a testimony. These two women spend a great deal of time asking questions about the individual's family history; the specifics of her hurt, habit or hang-up; the consequences of her addiction or compulsion; and the success of her recovery journey.

At that point the answers to the interview questions are sent to a third woman, who functions as the official "writer." After this phase is completed, the writer meets with the individual to make certain that the written testimony "feels right," that the facts are correct and that the person's genuine personality is reflected.

As a final follow-up, the individual is provided with several opportunities to practice the testimony in front of an additional group of volunteers.

In total, volunteers donate a minimum of 20 hours for every testimony given. Most of these testimonies simply wouldn't happen without a group of volunteers willing to say yes to one another. These willing servants are demonstrating their commitment both to their own recoveries and to their Higher Power, Jesus Christ, by giving their time and gifts to the recording of these personal stories.

Principle Eight — "Yield myself to God to be used to bring this good news to others, both by my example and by my words" — is all about saying yes. One of the feelings that prevents a lot of people in recovery from saying yes to serving others is that they don't feel that they're good enough. Some participants believe that they have nothing to offer anyone else. The reality is that nothing could be further from the truth.

Principle Eight has been referred to as the recycling principle. You allow God to recycle your pain by allowing his fire and light to shine on it, to melt down your old hurts, hang-ups and habits so they can be used again in a positive way. They can be recycled to show others how you've worked the principles and steps, with Jesus' healing, to a solution and how you've come through the darkness of your pain into Christ's glorious freedom and light.

Society tells us that pain is useless. In fact, too many people have come to believe that people in pain are useless. At Celebrate Recovery, we know that pain has value, as do the people who experience it. So while the world says no, Principle Eight calls us to say yes to serving others.

To truly practice this principle, we must give God the latitude he needs to use us as he sees fit. We do that by presenting everything we have — our time, talents and treasures — to him. We hold on loosely to all that we call our own, recognizing that all of it comes from his hand. When we're yielded to him, God can use us as his instruments to carry the message to others through our words and actions.

Galatians 6:1 – 2 directs us, "Brothers and sisters, if someone is caught in a sin, you who live by the Spirit should restore that person gently. But watch yourselves, or you also may be tempted. Carry each other's burdens, and in this way you will fulfill the law of Christ."

We need to share each other's troubles and problems. Principle Eight comes down to this: Do what you can with what you have, where you are. Make your life a mission, not an intermission. The road to recovery leads to service. When you reach Principle Eight, the road splits. Some will choose to serve within the context of Celebrate Recovery; others will elect to serve in other areas of the church. Both areas are in need of your service.

As a leader, sponsor or accountability partner, you can share your experiences, victories and hopes with newcomers at recovery meetings. Outside Celebrate Recovery, you can share with others and encourage them to get into recovery when they're ready to work on their hurts, hang-ups and habits.

Every morning before you get out of bed, pray this Principle Eight prayer: "Dear Jesus, as it would please you, bring me someone today whom I can serve. Amen."

Take a Look:

- If you could do one thing for God, knowing that you couldn't fail, what would that one thing be?

- What is stopping you from saying yes to service?

- Describe in your own words what Galatians 6:1 – 2 means to you.

- What avenue of service has brought you the most joy?

STUCK

We've caused problems in our own lives and in the lives of those we love because we continue to make the same choices we've always made. We get stuck in our individual patterns of coping. After hurting someone we love, perhaps we rush to buy them a gift as a way of apologizing. Unable to express our feelings adequately, we may stuff ourselves with junk food. Feeling rejected by our spouse, we may turn to Internet porn sites.

A petite young woman was driving to work one day when her rear tire exploded. She pulled over to the side of the road and considered her options. She could continue to drive several miles until she reached a gas station, she could change the tire herself, or she could call for help. This would have been an easy decision for most of us, but the young lady actually took several minutes before choosing her course of action.

She considered the following: If she continued to drive on the tire rim, her car might sustain further damage and possibly cause injury to herself or others. Even if she did successfully change the tire, she would probably ruin her clothes and be very late for work. If she called a tow truck, she could avoid these difficulties. Finally, the young lady chose to call the tow truck to change the tire. By calling a tow truck, she moved past her rely-only-on-yourself mentality and reached out to someone else for help. She also called one of her accountability partners to share her dilemma with and to laugh with her about her hesitation to reach out for help.

Sometimes we continue to rely on ourselves instead of relying on our Higher Power, Jesus Christ. During our recovery journey, we may get stuck when we hesitate to reach out and ask for help. We need to be able to share with others, to develop an accountability team, to consider new choices and behaviors, and to understand that we are not alone. Our Higher Power, Jesus Christ, will help us whenever we reach out to him.

It has been said that our choices control our circumstances and our decisions determine our destiny. In recovery we are learning to make good choices, healthy choices, for perhaps the first time in our lives. But if we neglect our quiet time, meetings, service to others, or our support team, we can easily fall back into — and get stuck in — our old, dysfunctional decision-making patterns. Then we slowly begin to take back our will and try to run our lives on our own power. When this happens we need to go back to Principle One: "Realize I'm not God. I admit that I'm powerless to control my tendency to do the wrong thing and that my life has become unmanageable."

The Bible can help us get "unstuck." Romans 7:18 says, "I know that good itself does not dwell in me, that is, in my sinful nature. For I have the desire to do what is good, but I cannot carry it out." When we keep doing things we don't want to do and when we fail to do the things we have decided we need to do, we begin to see that we do not, in fact, have the power to change on our own.

Proverbs 29:23 says, "Pride brings a person low, but the lowly in spirit gain honor." Our false pride can begin to creep back into our life. It undermines our faith and cuts us off from God and others. When God's presence is welcome, there is no room for pride because he makes us aware of our true self.

Proverbs 3:5–6 says,

Trust in the LORD with all your heart and lean not on your own understanding; in all your ways submit to him, and he will make your paths straight.

In addition to going back to Principle One, we can also review Principle Three: "Consciously choose to commit all of my life and will to Christ's care and control." There are two parts to Principle Three: The first is to ask Jesus Christ into our heart as our Higher Power, our Lord and Savior. The second is to seek to follow his will for our life in all our decisions. Perhaps we are trusting Jesus with the "big" things but still think we can handle the "small" things.

Matthew 19:26 says, "Jesus looked at them and said, 'With man this is impossible, but with God all things are possible.'" The good news is that with Jesus and the support of other people that he provides for us, we can get back on track. We can get unstuck and start working a healthy and fruitful recovery program once again.

Take a Look:

- Are you doing things that you really don't want to do? Things that you know are harmful to your recovery?

- Has your pride returned? In what ways has it shown up in your life?

- Is there a part of your life you are still holding on to? Is there an area of your life you are withholding from God? What are you not trusting him with?

- What is your action plan for getting "unstuck"? Share it with your accountability team.

STUCK ON FORGIVENESS

"I will never forgive you." Those words strike fear and pain in our hearts. And although we may not say the words out loud, we may also be thinking, "I will never forgive myself. My sins are too terrible for forgiveness."

Recalling her early experiences at Celebrate Recovery, a woman recounted that her first challenge was to make the long, lonely walk from the parking lot to the large group meeting. She began her journey by physically taking one step at a time from her car, calling upon every ounce of courage to respond to the greeters, and sitting down for worship time — all the while resisting the powerful urge to leave.

Years later, after attending the women's chemical addiction group, serving at the information table and becoming a leader in the program, she recognized her need to address her sexual addiction. It was at this point that she faced her next great challenge. Though she was able to forgive those who had hurt her in her past, she wasn't sure that she could forgive herself for her past choices and behaviors. She had hurt other women by having affairs with their husbands, she had hurt men by refusing to emotionally connect with them, and she had hurt herself because she continued the same cycle for years. How could she be forgiven for so many terrible sins?

The sexual addiction group for men was several years old, but there was no sexual addiction group for women. This added to her shame and strengthened her fear that she would never be forgiven. Uncertain if she was the only woman struggling with this issue, she decided to start a sexual addiction group for women. For six months, she sat in the room by herself. But, one by one, the women began to come, and by working through the principles, they have found healing and their lives have been changed.

This courageous woman has finally forgiven herself. In her testimony, she often encourages others by saying, "If my present belongs to God, and my future belongs to God, then I've made the conscious decision that my past belongs to God."

There are several places along our recovery journey where we can get stuck. Sometimes we are unable to forgive ourselves. When this happens, we need to go back to Principle Six: "Evaluate all my relationships. Offer forgiveness to those who have hurt me and make amends for harm I've done to others, except when to do so would harm them or others." God's Word tells us that he will cleanse us from every wrong, every sin! First John 1:9 says, "If we confess our sins, he is faithful and just and will forgive us our sins and purify us from all unrighteousness." Not just some of our wrongs, but all of them!

Ephesians 1:7 says, "In him we have redemption through his blood, the forgiveness of sins, in accordance with the riches of God's grace." Our sin isn't "special" or "different." It is covered by what Christ did on the cross for each of us.

Isaiah 1:18 says, " 'Come now, let us settle the matter,' says the LORD. 'Though your sins are like scarlet, they shall be as white as snow; though they are red as crimson, they shall be like wool.' " This is what God wants us to do with the darkness of our past so we can truly accept his forgiveness and forgive ourselves.

Romans 8:1 says, "Therefore, there is now no condemnation for those who are in Christ Jesus." When we finally forgive ourselves, make our amends and offer restitution, our recovery will again flourish.

Take a Look:

- Do you still feel shame and guilt over what you did in the past? Why do you think you still carry it with you?

- Have you completely forgiven yourself for the pain and hurt you caused yourself and others?

- When you were finally able to forgive yourself, describe the freedom that you felt.

- What do the freeing words found in Romans 8:1 mean to you?

FEAR OF CHANGE

Fear of change can keep us from confronting problems in our lives and get us stuck in our recoveries. Deep down inside, we know that change is inevitable. However, because we already have to adjust to so many changes that we have no control over — growing older, loss of employment, floods, fires, car accidents, medical crises — we delude ourselves into believing that things will be all right if they just stay the same.

Due to the success of bestselling self-help books on any number of topics, it would seem that there are many of us who really do want to change our patterns of behavior. But after reading the books, we often question ourselves. How will our relationships be altered if we change? Will we be comfortable with our new identity?

A team of church volunteers was hosting a meeting with several other churches in their city. Because the meeting included a breakfast buffet, some of the furniture in the small room had to be rearranged. When the senior pastor of the church saw the new set-up, he called together the volunteers and stated that the room needed to return to its original arrangement immediately. He frantically pointed to the indentations in the carpet and instructed that the tables and chairs be put back into those exact same spots. The pastor could not accept the change in the room. For him, everything in the room needed to stay precisely the same. Noting their pastor's discomfort, the team began to discuss a new plan for the breakfast buffet while moving the furniture back. The pastor dropped to his hands and knees to supervise the move, issuing instructions to ensure the placement of the furniture legs into the critical carpet indentations.

Most of us fear change, and we can sometimes allow that fear to get us stuck in our recovery journey. When we begin to fear change, we need to go back to Principle Five: "Voluntarily submit to every change God wants to make in my life and humbly ask him to remove my character defects." It helps to understand that there are three main reasons we resist change.

1. We may be paralyzed by the fear of failure. But falling down doesn't make us a failure; staying down does. This is where our faith and trust in Jesus Christ come into play.

Philippians 4:19 assures us:

> And my God will meet all your needs according
> to the riches of his glory in Christ Jesus.

2. We may fear intimacy because of the fear of rejection or of being hurt again. This is why it is so important to move slowly in a new relationship, taking time to seek God's will, to develop realistic expectations and to establish proper boundaries. We hold tightly to Psalm 118:6: "The LORD is with me; I will not be afraid. What can mere mortals do to me?"

3. We may resist change (growth) because of the fear of the unknown. We may think, "My life is a mess, my relationships are a mess, but at least I know what to expect—a mess!" The unknown can be scary if we are trying to face it alone. That is why we need to rely on Christ and our accountability team. God tells us in Isaiah 41:10, "So do not fear, for I am with you; do not be dismayed, for I am your God. I will strengthen you and help you; I will uphold you with my righteous right hand."

If we find ourselves "stuck" in our recovery, it may be that we are resisting a change that God wants us to make. It is only through change that growth can occur. It is only through change that our recovery can happen. It is only through change that we can become free from our hurts, hang-ups and habits.

Take a Look:

- Are you paralyzed by your fear of failure? In what specific area are you afraid of failing?

- Are you fearful of intimacy because of your fear of rejection or of being hurt again? What "old baggage" from a prior unhealthy relationship are you still carrying with you?

- Is your fear of the unknown stopping you from making the changes that are necessary for your continued growth? What are they?

- What do the words found in Isaiah 41:10 mean to you?

OWNING RESPONSIBILITY

While growing up, we've all made excuses for our inappropriate behaviors and choices. But as mature adults, some of us continue to blame other people or circumstances as a way to avoid accepting responsibility and moving forward with our recoveries.

"It's not my fault." "Billy made me do it." "It's not fair." When a teenager's mother discovered marijuana in his jacket, he immediately used those excuses in an attempt to avoid the punishment he thought was coming. His parents contacted their church to get information about a Christ-centered recovery program for teenagers called "Life Hurts, God Heals." The teenager didn't want to go; it wasn't "cool," he would feel "alone," and "no one would understand." At his parents' insistence, he reluctantly attended his first meeting. He was surprised to find that some of the adults leading the program had smoked marijuana in their youth, while others had struggled with alcohol. Some of the other young people had experimented with marijuana and other drugs, starved themselves, cut themselves or struck out at loved ones in anger. He realized he was not alone. Others understood. A few months later, the young man began to encourage some of his friends to join him in order to deal with their hurts, hang-ups and habits.

There are many things, however, that happen to us that we are not responsible for. We are not responsible for an alcoholic parent, the divorce of our parents or the sexual or physical abuse we may have endured. We are, however, responsible for our reactions to the traumatic events in our lives. We still need to seek help and be accountable to others for our behaviors.

We can get stuck in our recoveries when we can't stop placing the blame on others who have hurt us. That is why it is so important to work Principle Six: "Evaluate all my relationships. Offer forgiveness to those who have hurt me and make amends for harm I've done to others, except when to do so would harm them or others." Doing so frees us from the hold that someone's hurtful behavior has had on our lives.

If we keep going back to the "blame" or "excuse" game, we need to go back and do some more work on Principle Six. A good way to see if we are still blaming others for our own poor choices is found in Psalm 139:23 – 24: "Search me, God, and know my heart; test me and know my anxious thoughts. See if there is any offensive way in me, and lead me in the way everlasting." After we ask God to search our hearts, we need to allow time to hear his response.

We need to practice living Psalm 46:10: "Be still, and know that I am God." Then we can hear God's response. That verse tells us first to "be still." We cannot hear God if we are busy, distracted or talking back to him. We hear God when we are quiet. Then we can hear his response to the request we asked of him in Psalm 139:23 – 24. He will show us if we are trying to always fix the blame on others for our actions or if we are accepting responsibility for them.

If we find that we are not accepting responsibility for our actions, that we are still blaming others for the way we misbehave today, we can rely on the second part of Psalm 46:10 for help: " . . . and know that I am God." God can and will help us take responsibility for our actions. He will give us the strength to face our part in a failing relationship. He will give us the courage to make things right with others we may have hurt. We will finally be able to break free from living in yesterday. We will be able to enjoy the blessings found in today.

Take a Look:

- Have you blamed those who have hurt you for the poor choices that you are making today?
- How have you learned to stop blaming others for your actions?
- What do the words found in Psalm 139:23 – 24 mean to you?
- How have you been able to do what Psalm 46:10 asks of you?

SURRENDERING LIFE AND WILL

The desire for instant gratification happens even in recovery. Newcomers attending Celebrate Recovery often ask the same question, "How long will recovery take?" Even though hurts, hang-ups and habits do not develop overnight, we hope that we can get through the process of breaking them with as little pain and in as little time as possible. It takes faith, work, patience and humility to change our lives.

A gentleman has been going to his local Celebrate Recovery since it began. He knows how to recite the principles and steps from memory, attends every fellowship event and humorously recounts stories of his escapades with alcohol. He has managed to remain sober but has been in and out of numerous relationships, has declared bankruptcy and has had to depend on friends for a place to stay. He has not completely surrendered his life and will over to Jesus Christ, has not stayed accountable to a group or a sponsor, is not willing to change his character defects, and has not volunteered to serve in the program or at church. He has failed to connect all his head knowledge about recovery to his heart.

We must work through the recovery principles completely, not just commit them to memory. In Principle Three, we learned that we must "consciously choose to commit all my life and will to Christ's care and control." By completely surrendering our life to Christ, we soon learn that we must seek his will for the small decisions as well as the big ones. One of the best ways to see if we are following God's will for our lives is to keep a daily journal.

As we write down both the good and bad decisions of our day, we will begin to see patterns of our growth in black and white. We will also be able to see any negative patterns that are developing that may get us stuck in our recovery.

Journaling may be new to you. You may have trouble getting started. The following are three hints that will help you start putting the ink on the paper:

1. Start out by writing down one thing you are thankful for from your experiences from the day. Just that one thing will get you started, and it will also help you sleep better that night.

2. Ask your accountability partner/sponsor to hold you accountable for writing in your journal every night.

3. Memorize Galatians 5:22 – 23: "The fruit of the Spirit is love, joy, peace, forbearance, kindness, goodness, faithfulness, gentleness and self-control."

Daily ask yourself any of these questions to prompt your writing, starting each question with the word "today":

- How did I show *love* to others? Did I act in an unloving way toward anyone?

- Did others see in me the *joy* of having a personal relationship with the Lord? If not, why not?

- How was my level of serenity, my *peace*? Did anything happen that caused me to lose it? What was my part in it?

- Was I *patient*? What caused me to lose my patience? Do I owe anyone amends?

- Would anyone say that I was *kind/good*? In what ways was I unkind?

- How was my level of *faithfulness*? Did I keep my word to everyone?

- How was my level of *gentleness* and *self-control*? Did I lose my temper or speak a harsh or unkind word to someone?

We want to humbly live each day — in reality, not denial, turning our lives and our wills over to our Higher Power, Jesus Christ. Through his guidance, we can learn to make choices about the emotions that affect our thinking and actions. We start to take action — positive action — instead of constantly reacting. Self under God's control is what we are striving for. Journaling will help us stay on track.

We need to remember to keep our daily inventory and our journaling balanced. We need to be sure to include not only the things we did wrong throughout the day, but also the things we did right. It's important to write down even the smallest victories.

Take a Look:

- What has been keeping you from starting your daily journal?

- What are some of the benefits you could receive from journaling?

- Why is it important to focus on Galatians 5:22 – 23 as you journal?

- Why is it important to keep your daily journal entries balanced?

CELEBRATE: PART 1

Why do we call our program "Celebrate Recovery"? Because we do truly "celebrate" what God has done for each of us along our road to recovery. We celebrate the victories and freedom he is giving us over our hurts, hang-ups and habits.

Celebrate Recovery works when our program contains each of the following nine positive actions:

Celebrate Everything

Embrace Change

Love God and Others

Encourage Others

Be Involved in Service

Read the Bible Daily

Attend Your Meetings Regularly

Take Time to Reflect

Enjoy Sharing the Good News

Celebrate Everything

In New England, there is a restaurant that daily celebrates the setting of the sun by playing Tchaikovsky's 1812 Overture and ringing a bell. Now, most of us don't usually celebrate the sunrise or sunset each day, but we do celebrate the milestones of our lives: anniversaries, birthdays, school graduations, promotions at work, etc. Just the fact that we are attempting to make changes in our lives is worthy of celebrating!

We need to celebrate our victories over our struggles. Philippians 4:4 tells us to "rejoice in the Lord always. I will say it again: Rejoice!" We need to rejoice and thank God for the victories he has given us — no matter how small. And we need to also thank him for getting us through our tough times, knowing that he is with us each step of the way.

Embrace Change

Principle Five states: "Voluntarily submit to every change God wants to make in my life." Sometimes change is hard. Sometimes it's painful. But we know that on the other side of change is healing. We need to embrace it. As part of the Serenity Prayer we pray:

> God, grant me the serenity
> To accept the things I cannot change,
> The courage to change the things I can,
> And the wisdom to know the difference.

We need to hold on to Philippians 4:7: "And the peace of God, which transcends all understanding, will guard your hearts and your minds in Christ Jesus."

Love God and Others

In Matthew 22:37 – 40 Jesus tells us, " 'Love the Lord your God with all your heart and with all your soul and with all your mind.' This is the first and greatest commandment. And the second is like it: 'Love your neighbor as yourself.' All the Law and the Prophets hang on these two commandments."

The most important relationship in our lives is a loving, personal relationship with our Lord and Savior Jesus Christ. But, we also need to have loving relationships with the other people that God places along our road to recovery. As we grow in Christ and in our recovery, we will learn to love the unlovable.

Encourage Others

We need a genuine mentor or, in recovery terms, a sponsor and/or accountability partner to walk alongside us on our road to recovery. We need them to provide feedback to keep us on track. A sponsor and/or accountability partner can see our old, dysfunctional, self-defeating patterns beginning to surface, quickly point them out to us, and confront us with truth and love without placing shame or guilt.

In the same way, we need to encourage others by stepping up and being sponsors and accountability partners for them. We need to model 2 Corinthians 1:3 – 4: "Praise be to the God and Father of our Lord Jesus Christ, the Father of compassion and the God of all comfort, who comforts us in all our troubles, so that we can comfort those in any trouble with the comfort we ourselves receive from God."

We will continue with the last five actions — **B**e Involved in Service, **R**ead the Bible Daily, **A**ttend Your Meetings Regularly, **T**ake Time to Reflect, and **E**njoy Sharing the Good News — in the next devotion.

Take a Look:

- How do you celebrate your victories over your hurts, hang-ups and habits?
- How do the first four lines of the Serenity Prayer help you deal with change?
- What has been your experience in learning to love the unlovable?
- List some of the ways you encourage others.

CELEBRATE: PART 2

In Celebrate Recovery, we truly "celebrate" what God has done for each of us along our road to recovery. We celebrate the victories and freedom he is giving us over our hurts, hang-ups and habits.

If you want to guarantee that Celebrate Recovery will work for you, be sure your program contains each of the following nine positive actions:

Celebrate Everything

Embrace Change

Love God and Others

Encourage Others

Be Involved in Service

Read the Bible Daily

Attend Your Meetings Regularly

Take Time to Reflect

Enjoy Sharing the Good News

In the previous devotion, we covered **C**elebrate Everything, **E**mbrace Change, **L**ove God and Others, and **E**ncourage Others. The last five positive actions are discussed below.

Be Involved in Service

Service is nothing more than love in work clothes, and there are plenty of opportunities to "suit up" for service at Celebrate Recovery. Our actions, not words, are proof of our love for God and other people. Giving and serving is a thermometer of our love. We can give without loving—which is what we sometimes do in a codependent relationship or what we do because we feel we have to—but we can't love without giving and serving.

Jesus tells us in John 13:14–15 that we are to follow his example: "Now that I, your Lord and Teacher, have washed your feet, you also should wash one another's feet. I have set you an example that you should do as I have done for you."

Read the Bible Daily

Principle Seven states: "Reserve a daily time with God for self-examination, Bible reading and prayer in order to know God and his will for my life and to gain the power to follow his will." In order to keep our recovery growing, we need to have a daily "quiet time" with God. Even Jesus spent time alone with his Father; we need to do the same. We should set a daily appointment time to be alone with God, for a time of Bible reading and prayer. We are told in Romans 15:4, "For everything that was written in the past was written to teach us, so that through the endurance taught in the Scriptures and the encouragement they provide we might have hope."

Attend Meetings Regularly

It is essential to make recovery meetings a priority in life. It is there that we connect with "safe people" who understand what we are going through. It is there that we find unconditional love. It is tempting to skip meetings when things are going well. But it is important to remember that attending meetings regularly was a key part of what helped turn our lives around. Also, we need to be there to share with newcomers how God has helped us with our hurts, hang-ups and habits.

Hebrews 10:24–25 tells us, "Let us consider how we may spur one another on toward love and good deeds, not giving up meeting together, as some are in the habit of doing, but encouraging one another—and all the more as you see the Day approaching."

Take Time to Reflect

Lamentations 3:40 says, "Let us examine our ways and test them, and let us return to the LORD." We need to do an "ongoing inventory" throughout the day. The best time to admit we are wrong is the exact time that we are made aware of it. Why wait? If we do an ongoing inventory during the day, we can keep our list of amends very short!

At the end of the day we can look over our "daily inventory," reviewing our daily activities—the good and the bad. We need to review situations in which we might have harmed someone or in which we acted out of anger or fear. The best way to do this is to journal.

We need to take a "periodic inventory" about every three months. A mini-retreat is a good time to take our journal to a quiet place and to pray as we read through the last 90 days' worth of journal entries. Then we can not only ask God to show us areas in our lives that we can improve on in the next 90 days, but we can also celebrate the victories that we have made.

Enjoy Sharing the Good News

Principle Eight states: "Yield myself to God to be used to bring this good news to others, both by my example and by my words." Luke 8:16 tells us, "No one lights a lamp and hides it in a clay jar or puts it under a bed. Instead, they put it on a stand, so that those who come in can see the light."

If we want someone to see what Christ will do for them, we need to let them see what Christ has done for us. A great way to do this is by sharing our testimony. We can share our weaknesses and victories with others who are suffering from similar hurts, hang-ups and habits. We can give others a piece of our heart — not a piece of our mind.

It is also important to share the "Good News" with others outside of our recovery family. We always need to be ready to share what Christ has done for us and what he will also do for them — with our family, coworkers and neighbors. We can share the "Good News" with joy!

That's how we "celebrate recovery."

Take a Look:

- In what ways are you "giving back" by serving others?
- What are some of the recent things God has shown you during your quiet time?
- How has your decision to make attending recovery meetings a priority helped you?
- How has keeping a journal helped your recovery journey?
- How do you feel each time you have an opportunity to share your testimony?